HOLY BIBLE

Containing the
Old and New Testaments

HCSB

HOLMAN
BIBLE PUBLISHERS

Nashville, Tennessee

Holman Christian Standard Bible®
Copyright © 1999, 2000, 2002, 2003, 2009
by Holman Bible Publishers.

The text of the Holman Christian Standard Bible may be quoted in any form (written, visual, electronic, or audio) up to and inclusive of one-thousand (1,000) verses without the written permission of the publisher, provided that the verses quoted do not account for more than 50 percent of the work in which they are quoted, and provided that a complete book of the Bible is not quoted. Requests for permission are to be directed to and approved in writing by Holman Bible Publishers, One LifeWay Plaza, Nashville, Tennessee 37234.

When the Holman Christian Standard Bible is quoted, one of the following credit lines must appear on the copyright page or title page of the work:

> Scripture quotations marked HCSB have been taken from the Holman Christian Standard Bible®, Copyright © 1999, 2000, 2002, 2003, 2009 by Holman Bible Publishers. Used by permission. Holman Christian Standard Bible®, Holman CSB®, and HCSB® are federally registered trademarks of Holman Bible Publishers.

> Unless otherwise noted, all Scripture quotations are taken from the Holman Christian Standard Bible®, Copyright © 1999, 2000, 2002, 2003, 2009 by Holman Bible Publishers. Used by permission. Holman Christian Standard Bible®, Holman CSB®, and HCSB® are federally registered trademarks of Holman Bible Publishers.

ISBN: 978-1-43361-436-1

Printed in the United States

1 2 3 4 5 6 – 16 15 14

DP

CONTENTS

The Old Testament

The New Testament

Additional Material

God's Plan for Salvation

"How can I find meaning and purpose in life?" is a common question and worth considering. So what is life all about—and how does this relate to God, me, and eternity?

It's about how we got here.

People on this planet didn't get here by some cosmic accident. At creation, God said "Let Us make man in Our image" (Genesis 1:26). God created men and women and placed us here on the earth.

It's about why God put us here.

God loved what He created and created us to truly know and enjoy Him. He loved us and wanted to live in fellowship with us. In the beginning, we lived in harmony and happiness with God and one another (Genesis 1:31).

It's about how we responded.

In our early history the first humans turned away from God and went their own way—and fellowship with God was broken. Now, all people are born with a sinful nature, and without exception all of us have sinned (Romans 3:23). The consequence of this is that we are separated from God and deserve punishment for our sins.

It's about how God rescues us.

Out of His deep love for us, God sent His only Son, Jesus Christ, into the world to rescue us from our dilemma by dying on the cross (John 3:16). By sacrificing His life on behalf of sinners He took the punishment we deserve in order to provide salvation. Then God raised Jesus from the dead, confirming the work of Jesus on the cross and establishing His power over death.

It's about our response.

Jesus has sufficiently paid the debt for all of our wrong-doing, and we are called to turn from our sin, rebellion, and isolation and trust what Jesus has done on our behalf.

God makes very clear the conditions by which the salvation Jesus offers can be ours. In Mark 1:15 Jesus said, "Repent and believe in the good news!"

First, God says we must repent. The word "repent" means a change of direction. This means when we turn to God, we are turning away from sin and giving up on the attempt to make ourselves right before God.

Second, God says we must believe. The word "believe" as it is used in the Bible means trust. The object of our trust is the One who paid the price for our wrong-doing. We must trust Jesus to remove our guilt and the penalty of all the wrongs we have done. The Bible says when we put our faith in Jesus, God takes our sins away and gives us the gift of eternal life.

How will you respond?

The Bible says that "everyone who calls on the name of the Lord" will be rescued (Romans 10:13). If you've not trusted in Christ as Lord and Savior, why not stop right now, turn from your sin, and believe in Him who alone can save you and give you new and eternal life?

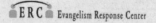

ERC Evangelism Response Center

If you would like to talk to someone about Jesus,
call toll free anytime 888-537-8720

Introduction to the
Holman Christian Standard Bible®

The Bible is God's revelation to man. It is the only book that gives us accurate information about God, man's need, and God's provision for that need. It provides us with guidance for life and tells us how to receive eternal life. The Bible can do these things because it is God's inspired Word, inerrant in the original manuscripts.

The Bible describes God's dealings with the ancient Jewish people and the early Christian church. It tells us about the great gift of God's Son, Jesus Christ, who fulfilled Jewish prophecies of the Messiah. It tells us about the salvation He accomplished through His death on the cross, His triumph over death in the resurrection, and His promised return to earth. It is the only book that gives us reliable information about the future, about what will happen to us when we die, and about where history is headed.

Bible translation is both a science and an art. It is a bridge that brings God's Word from the ancient world to the world today. In dependence on God to accomplish this sacred task, Holman Bible Publishers presents the *Holman Christian Standard Bible* [HCSB], a new English translation of God's Word.

Textual base of the HCSB®

The textual base for the HCSB New Testament [NT] is the Nestle-Aland *Novum Testamentum Graece*, 27th edition, and the United Bible Societies' *Greek New Testament*, 4th corrected edition. The text for the HCSB Old Testament [OT] is the *Biblia Hebraica Stuttgartensia*, 5th edition. At times, however, the translators have followed an alternative manuscript tradition, disagreeing with the editors of these texts about the original reading.

In a few places in the NT, square brackets indicate texts that the HCSB translation team and most biblical scholars today believe were not part of the original text. However, these texts have been retained in brackets in the HCSB because of their undeniable antiquity and their value for tradition and the history of NT interpretation in the church. The HCSB uses traditional verse divisions found in most Protestant Bibles.

Goals of this translation

The goals of this translation are:

- to provide English-speaking people across the world with an accurate, readable Bible in contemporary English;
- to equip serious Bible students with an accurate translation for personal study, private devotions, and memorization;
- to give those who love God's Word a text that has numerous reader helps, is visually attractive on the page, and is appealing when heard;
- to affirm the authority of Scripture as God's Word and to champion its absolute truth against social or cultural agendas that would compromise its accuracy.

The name, *Holman Christian Standard Bible*, captures these goals: *Holman* Bible Publishers presents a new *Bible* translation, for *Christian* and English-speaking communities, which will be a *standard* in Bible translations for years to come.

Why is there a need for another English translation of the Bible?

There are several good reasons why Holman Bible publishers invested its resources in a modern language translation of the Bible:

1. *Each generation needs a fresh translation of the Bible in its own language.*

The Bible is the world's most important book, confronting each individual and each culture with issues that affect life, both now and forever. Since each new generation must be introduced to God's Word in its own language, there will always be a need for new translations such as the *Holman Christian Standard Bible*. The majority of Bible translations on the market today are revisions of translations from previous generations. The HCSB is a new translation for today's generation.

2. *English, one of the world's greatest languages, is rapidly changing, and Bible translations must keep in step with those changes.*

English is the first truly global language in history. It is the language of education, business, medicine, travel, research, and the Internet. More than 1.3 billion people around the world speak or read English as a primary or secondary language. The HCSB seeks to serve many of those people with a translation they can easily use and understand.

English is also the world's most rapidly changing language. The HCSB seeks to reflect recent changes in English by using modern punctuation, formatting, and vocabulary, while avoiding slang, regionalisms, or changes made specifically for the sake of political or social agendas. Modern linguistic and semantic advances have been incorporated into the HCSB, including modern grammar.

3. *Rapid advances in biblical research provide new data for Bible translators.*

This has been called the "information age," a term that accurately describes the field of biblical research. Never before in history has there been as much information about the Bible as there is today—from archaeological discoveries to analysis of ancient manuscripts to years of study and statistical research on individual Bible books. Translations made as recently as 10 or 20 years ago do not reflect many of these advances in biblical research. The translators of the HCSB have taken into consideration as much of this new data as possible.

4. *Advances in computer technology have opened a new door for Bible translation.*

The HCSB has used computer technology and telecommunications in its creation perhaps more than any Bible translation in history. Electronic mail was used daily and sometimes hourly for communication and transmission of manuscripts. An advanced Bible software program, Accordance®, was used to create and revise the translation at each step in its production. A developmental copy of the HCSB itself was used within Accordance to facilitate crosschecking during the translation process—something never done before with a Bible translation.

History of the HCSB

After several years of preliminary development, Holman Bible Publishers, the oldest Bible publisher in America, assembled an international, interdenominational team of 100 scholars, editors, stylists, and proofreaders, all of whom were committed to biblical inerrancy. Outside consultants and reviewers contributed valuable suggestions from their areas of expertise. An executive team then edited, polished, and reviewed the final manuscripts.

Features found in the HCSB

In keeping with a long line of Bible publications, the *Holman Christian Standard Bible* has retained a number of features found in traditional Bibles:

1. Traditional theological vocabulary (such as *justification, sanctification, redemption*, etc.) has been retained in the HCSB, since such terms have no translation equivalent that adequately communicates their exact meaning.
2. OT passages quoted in the NT are set in boldface type. OT quotes consisting of two or more lines are block indented.
3. Traditional spellings of names and places found in most Bibles have been used to make the HCSB compatible with most Bible study tools.
4. Some editions of the HCSB will print the words of Christ in red letters to help readers easily locate the spoken words of the Lord Jesus Christ.
5. Nouns and personal pronouns that clearly refer to any person of the Trinity are capitalized.
6. Certain foreign, geographical, cultural, or ancient words are preceded by a superscripted bullet (*Abba) at their first occurrence in each chapter. These words are listed in alphabetical order at the back of the Bible under the heading **HCSB Bullet Notes**.

Commonly Used Abbreviations

A.D.	in the year of our Lord	Lat	Latin	sg	singular
alt	alternate	Lit	Literally	Sym	Symmachus
a.m.	from midnight until noon	LXX	Septuagint—an ancient translation of the Old Testament into Greek	syn.	synonym
Aram	Aramaic			Syr	Syriac
B.C.	before Christ	MT	Masoretic Text	Tg	Targum
ca	circa	NT	New Testament	Theod	Theodotian
chap.	chapter	ms(s)	manuscript(s)	v., vv.	verse, verses
DSS	Dead Sea Scrolls	OT	Old Testament	Vg	Vulgate —an ancient translation of the Bible into Latin
Eng	English	p.m.	from noon until midnight		
Gk	Greek			vol(s).	volume(s)
Hb	Hebrew	pl	plural		
Jer	Latin translation of Psalms by Jerome	Ps(s)	psalm(s)		
		Sam	Samaritan Pentateuch		

THE
OLD TESTAMENT

GENESIS

1 In the beginning God created the heavens and the earth.

²Now the earth was formless and empty, darkness covered the surface of the watery depths, and the Spirit of God was hovering over the surface of the waters. ³Then God said, "Let there be light," and there was light. ⁴God saw that the light was good, and God separated the light from the darkness. ⁵God called the light "day," and He called the darkness "night." Evening came and then morning: the first day.

⁶Then God said, "Let there be an expanse between the waters, separating water from water." ⁷So God made the expanse and separated the water under the expanse from the water above the expanse. And it was so. ⁸God called the expanse "sky." Evening came and then morning: the second day.

⁹Then God said, "Let the water under the sky be gathered into one place, and let the dry land appear." And it was so. ¹⁰God called the dry land "earth," and He called the gathering of the water "seas." And God saw that it was good. ¹¹Then God said, "Let the earth produce vegetation: seed-bearing plants and fruit trees on the earth bearing fruit with seed in it according to their kinds." And it was so. ¹²The earth produced vegetation: seed-bearing plants according to their kinds and trees bearing fruit with seed in it according to their kinds. And God saw that it was good. ¹³Evening came and then morning: the third day.

¹⁴Then God said, "Let there be lights in the expanse of the sky to separate the day from the night. They will serve as signs for festivals and for days and years. ¹⁵They will be lights in the expanse of the sky to provide light on the earth." And it was so. ¹⁶God made the two great lights—the greater light to have dominion over the day and the lesser light to have dominion over the night—as well as the stars. ¹⁷God placed them in the expanse of the sky to provide light on the earth, ¹⁸to dominate the day and the night, and to separate light from darkness. And God saw that it was good. ¹⁹Evening came and then morning: the fourth day.

²⁰Then God said, "Let the water swarm with living creatures, and let birds fly above the earth across the expanse of the sky." ²¹So God created the large sea-creatures and every living creature that moves and swarms in the water, according to their kinds. He also created every winged bird according to its kind. And God saw that it was good. ²²So God blessed them, "Be fruitful, multiply, and fill the waters of the seas, and let the birds multiply on the earth." ²³Evening came and then morning: the fifth day.

²⁴Then God said, "Let the earth produce living creatures according to their kinds: livestock, creatures that crawl, and the wildlife of the earth according to their kinds." And it was so. ²⁵So God made the wildlife of the earth according to their kinds, the livestock according to their kinds, and creatures that crawl on the ground according to their kinds. And God saw that it was good.

²⁶Then God said, "Let Us make man in Our image, according to Our likeness. They will rule the fish of the sea, the birds of the sky, the livestock, all the earth, and the creatures that crawl on the earth."

²⁷ So God created man in His own image;
He created him in the image of God;
He created them male and female.

²⁸God blessed them, and God said to them, "Be fruitful, multiply, fill the earth, and subdue it. Rule the fish of the sea, the birds of the sky, and every creature that crawls on the earth." ²⁹God also said, "Look, I have given you every seed-bearing plant on the surface of the entire earth and every tree whose fruit contains seed. This food will be for you, ³⁰for all the wildlife of the earth, for every bird of the sky, and for every creature that crawls on the earth—everything having the breath of life in it. I have given every green plant for food." And it was so. ³¹God saw all that He had made, and it was very good. Evening came and then morning: the sixth day.

2 So the heavens and the earth and everything in them were completed. ²By the seventh day God completed His work that He had done, and He rested on the seventh day from all His work that He had done. ³God blessed the seventh day and declared it holy, for on it He rested from His work of creation.

⁴These are the records of the heavens and the earth, concerning their creation at the time that the LORD God made the earth and the heavens. ⁵No shrub of the field had yet grown on the land, and no plant of the field had yet sprouted, for the LORD God had not made it rain on the land, and there was no man to work the ground. ⁶But water would come out of the ground and water the entire surface of the land. ⁷Then the LORD God formed the man out of the dust from the ground and breathed the breath of life into his nostrils, and the man became a living being.

⁸The LORD God planted a garden in Eden, in the east, and there He placed the man He had formed. ⁹The LORD God caused to grow out of the ground every tree pleasing in appearance and good for food, including the tree of life in the middle of the garden, as well as the tree of the knowledge of good and evil.

¹⁰A river went out from Eden to water the garden. From there it divided and became the source of four rivers. ¹¹The name of the first is Pishon, which flows through the entire land of Havilah, where there is gold. ¹²Gold from that land is pure; bdellium and onyx are also there. ¹³The name of the second river is Gihon, which flows through the entire land of 'Cush. ¹⁴The name of the third river is the Tigris, which runs east of Assyria. And the fourth river is the Euphrates.

¹⁵The LORD God took the man and placed him in the garden of Eden to work it and watch over it. ¹⁶And the LORD God commanded the man, "You are free to eat from any tree of the garden, ¹⁷but you must not eat from the tree of the knowledge of good and evil, for on the day you eat from it, you will certainly die." ¹⁸Then the LORD God said, "It is not good for the man to be alone. I will make a helper as his complement." ¹⁹So the LORD God formed out of the ground every wild animal and every bird of the sky, and brought each to the man to see what he would call it. And whatever the man called a living creature, that was its name. ²⁰The man gave names to all the livestock, to the birds of the sky, and to every wild animal; but for the man no helper was found as his complement. ²¹So the LORD God caused a deep sleep to come over the man, and he slept. God took one of his ribs and closed the flesh at that place. ²²Then the LORD God made the rib He had

taken from the man into a woman and brought her to the man. ²³And the man said:

This one, at last, is bone of my bone
and flesh of my flesh;
this one will be called "woman,"
for she was taken from man.

²⁴This is why a man leaves his father and mother and bonds with his wife, and they become one flesh. ²⁵Both the man and his wife were naked, yet felt no shame.

3 Now the serpent was the most cunning of all the wild animals that the Lord God had made. He said to the woman, "Did God really say, 'You can't eat from any tree in the garden'?"

²The woman said to the serpent, "We may eat the fruit from the trees in the garden. ³But about the fruit of the tree in the middle of the garden, God said, 'You must not eat it or touch it, or you will die.'"

⁴"No! You will not die," the serpent said to the woman. ⁵"In fact, God knows that when you eat it your eyes will be opened and you will be like God, knowing good and evil." ⁶Then the woman saw that the tree was good for food and delightful to look at, and that it was desirable for obtaining wisdom. So she took some of its fruit and ate it; she also gave some to her husband, who was with her, and he ate it. ⁷Then the eyes of both of them were opened, and they knew they were naked; so they sewed fig leaves together and made loincloths for themselves.

⁸Then the man and his wife heard the sound of the Lord God walking in the garden at the time of the evening breeze, and they hid themselves from the Lord God among the trees of the garden. ⁹So the Lord God called out to the man and said to him, "Where are you?"

¹⁰And he said, "I heard You in the garden and I was afraid because I was naked, so I hid."

¹¹Then He asked, "Who told you that you were naked? Did you eat from the tree that I commanded you not to eat from?"

¹²Then the man replied, "The woman You gave to be with me—she gave me some fruit from the tree, and I ate."

¹³So the Lord God asked the woman, "What is this you have done?"

And the woman said, "It was the serpent. He deceived me, and I ate."

¹⁴Then the Lord God said to the serpent:

Because you have done this,
you are cursed more than any livestock
and more than any wild animal.
You will move on your belly
and eat dust all the days of your life.
¹⁵ I will put hostility between you
   and the woman,
and between your *seed and her seed.
He will strike your head,
and you will strike his heel.

¹⁶He said to the woman:

I will intensify your labor pains;
you will bear children in anguish.
Your desire will be for your husband,
yet he will rule over you.

¹⁷And He said to Adam, "Because you listened to your wife's voice and ate from the tree about which I commanded you, 'Do not eat from it':

The ground is cursed because of you.

You will eat from it by means of painful labor
all the days of your life.
¹⁸ It will produce thorns and thistles for you,
   and you will eat the plants of the field.
¹⁹ You will eat bread by the sweat of your brow
until you return to the ground,
since you were taken from it.
For you are dust,
and you will return to dust."

²⁰Adam named his wife Eve because she was the mother of all the living. ²¹The Lord God made clothing out of skins for Adam and his wife, and He clothed them. ²²The Lord God said, "Since man has become like one of Us, knowing good and evil, he must not reach out, take from the tree of life, eat, and live forever." ²³So the Lord God sent him away from the garden of Eden to work the ground from which he was taken. ²⁴He drove man out and stationed the *cherubim and the flaming, whirling sword east of the garden of Eden to guard the way to the tree of life.

4 Adam was intimate with his wife Eve, and she conceived and gave birth to Cain. She said, "I have had a male child with the Lord's help." ²Then she also gave birth to his brother Abel. Now Abel became a shepherd of flocks, but Cain worked the ground. ³In the course of time Cain presented some of the land's produce as an offering to the Lord. ⁴And Abel also presented an offering—some of the firstborn of his flock and their fat portions. The Lord had regard for Abel and his offering, ⁵but He did not have regard for Cain and his offering. Cain was furious, and he looked despondent.

⁶Then the Lord said to Cain, "Why are you furious? And why do you look despondent? ⁷If you do what is right, won't you be accepted? But if you do not do what is right, sin is crouching at the door. Its desire is for you, but you must rule over it."

⁸Cain said to his brother Abel, "Let's go out to the field." And while they were in the field, Cain attacked his brother Abel and killed him.

⁹Then the Lord said to Cain, "Where is your brother Abel?"

"I don't know," he replied. "Am I my brother's guardian?"

¹⁰Then He said, "What have you done? Your brother's blood cries out to Me from the ground! ¹¹So now you are cursed, alienated, from the ground that opened its mouth to receive your brother's blood you have shed. ¹²If you work the ground, it will never again give you its yield. You will be a restless wanderer on the earth."

¹³But Cain answered the Lord, "My punishment is too great to bear! ¹⁴Since You are banishing me today from the soil, and I must hide myself from Your presence and become a restless wanderer on the earth, whoever finds me will kill me."

¹⁵Then the Lord replied to him, "In that case, whoever kills Cain will suffer vengeance seven times over." And He placed a mark on Cain so that whoever found him would not kill him. ¹⁶Then Cain went out from the Lord's presence and lived in the land of Nod, east of Eden.

¹⁷Cain was intimate with his wife, and she conceived and gave birth to Enoch. Then Cain became the builder of a city, and he named the city Enoch after his son. ¹⁸Irad was born to Enoch, Irad fathered Mehujael, Mehujael fathered Methushael, and Methushael fathered

Lamech. ¹⁹Lamech took two wives for himself, one named Adah and the other named Zillah. ²⁰Adah bore Jabal; he was the father of the nomadic herdsmen. ²¹His brother was named Jubal; he was the father of all who play the lyre and the flute. ²²Zillah bore Tubal-cain, who made all kinds of bronze and iron tools. Tubal-cain's sister was Naamah.

²³Lamech said to his wives:

Adah and Zillah, hear my voice;
wives of Lamech, pay attention to my words.
For I killed a man for wounding me,
a young man for striking me.
²⁴ If Cain is to be avenged seven times over,
then for Lamech it will be
seventy-seven times!

²⁵Adam was intimate with his wife again, and she gave birth to a son and named him Seth, for she said, "God has given me another child in place of Abel, since Cain killed him." ²⁶A son was born to Seth also, and he named him Enosh. At that time people began to call on the name of ˙Yahweh.

5 These are the family records of the descendants of Adam. On the day that God created man, He made him in the likeness of God; ²He created them male and female. When they were created, He blessed them and called them man.

³Adam was 130 years old when he fathered a son in his likeness, according to his image, and named him Seth. ⁴Adam lived 800 years after the birth of Seth, and he fathered other sons and daughters. ⁵So Adam's life lasted 930 years; then he died.

⁶Seth was 105 years old when he fathered Enosh. ⁷Seth lived 807 years after the birth of Enosh, and he fathered other sons and daughters. ⁸So Seth's life lasted 912 years; then he died.

⁹Enosh was 90 years old when he fathered Kenan. ¹⁰Enosh lived 815 years after the birth of Kenan, and he fathered other sons and daughters. ¹¹So Enosh's life lasted 905 years; then he died.

¹²Kenan was 70 years old when he fathered Mahalalel. ¹³Kenan lived 840 years after the birth of Mahalalel, and he fathered other sons and daughters. ¹⁴So Kenan's life lasted 910 years; then he died.

¹⁵Mahalalel was 65 years old when he fathered Jared. ¹⁶Mahalalel lived 830 years after the birth of Jared, and he fathered other sons and daughters. ¹⁷So Mahalalel's life lasted 895 years; then he died.

¹⁸Jared was 162 years old when he fathered Enoch. ¹⁹Jared lived 800 years after the birth of Enoch, and he fathered other sons and daughters. ²⁰So Jared's life lasted 962 years; then he died.

²¹Enoch was 65 years old when he fathered Methuselah. ²²And after the birth of Methuselah, Enoch walked with God 300 years and fathered other sons and daughters. ²³So Enoch's life lasted 365 years. ²⁴Enoch walked with God; then he was not there because God took him.

²⁵Methuselah was 187 years old when he fathered Lamech. ²⁶Methuselah lived 782 years after the birth of Lamech, and he fathered other sons and daughters. ²⁷So Methuselah's life lasted 969 years; then he died.

²⁸Lamech was 182 years old when he fathered a son. ²⁹And he named him Noah, saying, "This one will bring us relief from the agonizing labor of our hands, caused by the ground the LORD has cursed." ³⁰Lamech lived 595 years after Noah's birth, and he fathered oth-er sons and daughters. ³¹So Lamech's life lasted 777 years; then he died.

³²Noah was 500 years old, and he fathered Shem, Ham, and Japheth.

6 When mankind began to multiply on the earth and daughters were born to them, ²the sons of God saw that the daughters of mankind were beautiful, and they took any they chose as wives for themselves. ³And the LORD said, "My Spirit will not remain with mankind forever, because they are corrupt. Their days will be 120 years." ⁴The Nephilim were on the earth both in those days and afterward, when the sons of God came to the daughters of mankind, who bore children to them. They were the powerful men of old, the famous men.

⁵When the LORD saw that man's wickedness was widespread on the earth and that every scheme his mind thought of was nothing but evil all the time, ⁶the LORD regretted that He had made man on the earth, and He was grieved in His heart. ⁷Then the LORD said, "I will wipe off from the face of the earth mankind, whom I created, together with the animals, creatures that crawl, and birds of the sky—for I regret that I made them." ⁸Noah, however, found favor in the sight of the LORD.

⁹These are the family records of Noah. Noah was a righteous man, blameless among his contemporaries; Noah walked with God. ¹⁰And Noah fathered three sons: Shem, Ham, and Japheth.

¹¹Now the earth was corrupt in God's sight, and the earth was filled with wickedness. ¹²God saw how corrupt the earth was, for every creature had corrupted its way on the earth. ¹³Then God said to Noah, "I have decided to put an end to every creature, for the earth is filled with wickedness because of them; therefore I am going to destroy them along with the earth.

¹⁴"Make yourself an ark of gopher wood. Make rooms in the ark, and cover it with pitch inside and outside. ¹⁵This is how you are to make it: The ark will be 450 feet long, 75 feet wide, and 45 feet high. ¹⁶You are to make a roof, finishing the sides of the ark to within 18 inches of the roof. You are to put a door in the side of the ark. Make it with lower, middle, and upper decks.

¹⁷"Understand that I am bringing a flood—floodwaters on the earth to destroy every creature under heaven with the breath of life in it. Everything on earth will die. ¹⁸But I will establish My covenant with you, and you will enter the ark with your sons, your wife, and your sons' wives. ¹⁹You are also to bring into the ark two of all the living creatures, male and female, to keep them alive with you. ²⁰Two of everything—from the birds according to their kinds, from the livestock according to their kinds, and from the animals that crawl on the ground according to their kinds—will come to you so that you can keep them alive. ²¹Take with you every kind of food that is eaten; gather it as food for you and for them." ²²And Noah did this. He did everything that God had commanded him.

7 Then the LORD said to Noah, "Enter the ark, you and all your household, for I have seen that you alone are righteous before Me in this generation. ²You are to take with you seven pairs, a male and its female, of all the ˙clean animals, and two of the animals that are not clean, a male and its female, ³and seven pairs, male and female, of the birds of the sky—in order to keep ˙offspring alive on the face of the whole earth.

⁴Seven days from now I will make it rain on the earth 40 days and 40 nights, and I will wipe off from the face of the earth every living thing I have made." ⁵And Noah did everything that the Lᴏʀᴅ commanded him.

⁶Noah was 600 years old when the flood came and water covered the earth. ⁷So Noah, his sons, his wife, and his sons' wives entered the ark because of the waters of the flood. ⁸From the clean animals, ˙unclean animals, birds, and every creature that crawls on the ground, ⁹two of each, male and female, entered the ark with Noah, just as God had commanded him. ¹⁰Seven days later the waters of the flood came on the earth.

¹¹In the six hundredth year of Noah's life, in the second month, on the seventeenth day of the month, on that day all the sources of the watery depths burst open, the floodgates of the sky were opened, ¹²and the rain fell on the earth 40 days and 40 nights. ¹³On that same day Noah along with his sons Shem, Ham, and Japheth, Noah's wife, and his three sons' wives entered the ark with him. ¹⁴They entered it with all the wildlife according to their kinds, all livestock according to their kinds, the creatures that crawl on the earth according to their kinds, all birds, every fowl, and everything with wings according to their kinds. ¹⁵Two of all flesh that has the breath of life in it entered the ark with Noah. ¹⁶Those that entered, male and female of all flesh, entered just as God had commanded him. Then the Lᴏʀᴅ shut him in.

¹⁷The flood continued for 40 days on the earth; the waters increased and lifted up the ark so that it rose above the earth. ¹⁸The waters surged and increased greatly on the earth, and the ark floated on the surface of the water. ¹⁹Then the waters surged even higher on the earth, and all the high mountains under the whole sky were covered. ²⁰The mountains were covered as the waters surged above them more than 20 feet. ²¹Every creature perished—those that crawl on the earth, birds, livestock, wildlife, and those that swarm on the earth, as well as all mankind. ²²Everything with the breath of the spirit of life in its nostrils—everything on dry land died. ²³He wiped out every living thing that was on the surface of the ground, from mankind to livestock, to creatures that crawl, to the birds of the sky, and they were wiped off the earth. Only Noah was left, and those that were with him in the ark. ²⁴And the waters surged on the earth 150 days.

8 God remembered Noah, as well as all the wildlife and all the livestock that were with him in the ark. God caused a wind to pass over the earth, and the water began to subside. ²The sources of the watery depths and the floodgates of the sky were closed, and the rain from the sky stopped. ³The water steadily receded from the earth, and by the end of 150 days the waters had decreased significantly. ⁴The ark came to rest in the seventh month, on the seventeenth day of the month, on the mountains of Ararat.

⁵The waters continued to recede until the tenth month; in the tenth month, on the first day of the month, the tops of the mountains were visible. ⁶After 40 days Noah opened the window of the ark that he had made, ⁷and he sent out a raven. It went back and forth until the waters had dried up from the earth. ⁸Then he sent out a dove to see whether the water on the earth's surface had gone down, ⁹but the dove found no resting place for her foot. She returned to him in the ark because water covered the surface of the whole earth. He reached out and brought her into the ark to himself.

¹⁰So Noah waited seven more days and sent out the dove from the ark again. ¹¹When the dove came to him at evening, there was a plucked olive leaf in her beak. So Noah knew that the water on the earth's surface had gone down. ¹²After he had waited another seven days, he sent out the dove, but she did not return to him again. ¹³In the six hundred and first year, in the first month, on the first day of the month, the water that had covered the earth was dried up. Then Noah removed the ark's cover and saw that the surface of the ground was drying. ¹⁴By the twenty-seventh day of the second month, the earth was dry.

¹⁵Then God spoke to Noah, ¹⁶"Come out of the ark, you, your wife, your sons, and your sons' wives with you. ¹⁷Bring out all the living creatures that are with you—birds, livestock, those that crawl on the ground—and they will spread over the earth and be fruitful and multiply on the earth." ¹⁸So Noah, along with his sons, his wife, and his sons' wives, came out. ¹⁹All wildlife, all livestock, every bird, and every creature that crawls on the earth came out of the ark by their groups.

²⁰Then Noah built an altar to the Lᴏʀᴅ. He took some of every kind of ˙clean animal and every kind of clean bird and offered ˙burnt offerings on the altar. ²¹When the Lᴏʀᴅ smelled the pleasing aroma, He said to Himself, "I will never again curse the ground because of man, even though man's inclination is evil from his youth. And I will never again strike down every living thing as I have done.

²²   As long as the earth endures,
    seedtime and harvest, cold and heat,
    summer and winter, and day and night
    will not cease."

9 God blessed Noah and his sons and said to them, "Be fruitful and multiply and fill the earth. ²The fear and terror of you will be in every living creature on the earth, every bird of the sky, every creature that crawls on the ground, and all the fish of the sea. They are placed under your authority. ³Every living creature will be food for you; as I gave the green plants, I have given you everything. ⁴However, you must not eat meat with its lifeblood in it. ⁵I will require the life of every animal and every man for your life and your blood. I will require the life of each man's brother for a man's life.

⁶   Whoever sheds man's blood,
    his blood will be shed by man,
    for God made man in His image.

⁷But you, be fruitful and multiply; spread out over the earth and multiply on it."

⁸Then God said to Noah and his sons with him, ⁹"Understand that I am confirming My covenant with you and your descendants after you, ¹⁰and with every living creature that is with you—birds, livestock, and all wildlife of the earth that are with you—all the animals of the earth that came out of the ark. ¹¹I confirm My covenant with you that never again will every creature be wiped out by the waters of a flood; there will never again be a flood to destroy the earth."

¹²And God said, "This is the sign of the covenant I am making between Me and you and every living creature with you, a covenant for all future generations: ¹³I have placed My bow in the clouds, and it will be a sign of the covenant between Me and the earth. ¹⁴Whenever I form clouds over the earth and the bow appears in the clouds, ¹⁵I will remember My covenant between

Me and you and all the living creatures: water will never again become a flood to destroy every creature. ¹⁶The bow will be in the clouds, and I will look at it and remember the everlasting covenant between God and all the living creatures on earth." ¹⁷God said to Noah, "This is the sign of the covenant that I have confirmed between Me and every creature on earth."

¹⁸Noah's sons who came out of the ark were Shem, Ham, and Japheth. Ham was the father of Canaan. ¹⁹These three were Noah's sons, and from them the whole earth was populated.

²⁰Noah, a man of the soil, was the first to plant a vineyard. ²¹He drank some of the wine, became drunk, and uncovered himself inside his tent. ²²Ham, the father of Canaan, saw his father naked and told his two brothers outside. ²³Then Shem and Japheth took a cloak and placed it over both their shoulders, and walking backward, they covered their father's nakedness. Their faces were turned away, and they did not see their father naked.

²⁴When Noah awoke from his drinking and learned what his youngest son had done to him, ²⁵he said:

Canaan will be cursed.
He will be the lowest of slaves to his brothers.

²⁶He also said:

Praise the Lᴏʀᴅ, the God of Shem;
Canaan will be his slave.
²⁷   God will extend Japheth;
he will dwell in the tents of Shem;
Canaan will be his slave.

²⁸Now Noah lived 350 years after the flood. ²⁹So Noah's life lasted 950 years; then he died.

10 These are the family records of Noah's sons, Shem, Ham, and Japheth. They also had sons after the flood.

²Japheth's sons: Gomer, Magog, Madai, Javan, Tubal, Meshech, and Tiras. ³Gomer's sons: Ashkenaz, Riphath, and Togarmah. ⁴And Javan's sons: Elishah, Tarshish, Kittim, and Dodanim. ⁵The coastland peoples spread out into their lands. These are Japheth's sons by their clans, in their nations. Each group had its own language.

⁶Ham's sons: Cush, Egypt, Put, and Canaan. ⁷Cush's sons: Seba, Havilah, Sabtah, Raamah, and Sabteca. And Raamah's sons: Sheba and Dedan.

⁸Cush fathered Nimrod, who was the first powerful man on earth. ⁹He was a powerful hunter in the sight of the Lᴏʀᴅ. That is why it is said, "Like Nimrod, a powerful hunter in the sight of the Lᴏʀᴅ." ¹⁰His kingdom started with Babylon, Erech, Accad, and Calneh, in the land of ˙Shinar. ¹¹From that land he went to Assyria and built Nineveh, Rehoboth-ir, Calah, ¹²and Resen, between Nineveh and the great city Calah.

¹³Mizraim fathered Ludim, Anamim, Lehabim, Naphtuhim, ¹⁴Pathrusim, Casluhim (the Philistines came from them), and Caphtorim.

¹⁵Canaan fathered Sidon his firstborn, then Heth, ¹⁶the Jebusites, the Amorites, the Girgashites, ¹⁷the Hivites, the Arkites, the Sinites, ¹⁸the Arvadites, the Zemarites, and the Hamathites. Afterward the Canaanite clans scattered. ¹⁹The Canaanite border went from Sidon going toward Gerar as far as Gaza, and going toward Sodom, Gomorrah, Admah, and Zeboiim as far as Lasha.

²⁰These are Ham's sons, by their clans, according to their languages, in their own lands and their nations. ²¹And Shem, Japheth's older brother, also had sons.

Shem was the father of all the sons of Eber. ²²Shem's sons were Elam, Asshur, Arpachshad, Lud, and Aram. ²³Aram's sons: Uz, Hul, Gether, and Mash. ²⁴Arpachshad fathered Shelah, and Shelah fathered Eber. ²⁵Eber had two sons. One was named Peleg, for during his days the earth was divided; his brother was named Joktan. ²⁶And Joktan fathered Almodad, Sheleph, Hazarmaveth, Jerah, ²⁷Hadoram, Uzal, Diklah, ²⁸Obal, Abimael, Sheba, ²⁹Ophir, Havilah, and Jobab. All these were Joktan's sons. ³⁰Their settlements extended from Mesha to Sephar, the eastern hill country. ³¹These are Shem's sons by their clans, according to their languages, in their lands and their nations.

³²These are the clans of Noah's sons, according to their family records, in their nations. The nations on earth spread out from these after the flood.

11 At one time the whole earth had the same language and vocabulary. ²As people migrated from the east, they found a valley in the land of ˙Shinar and settled there. ³They said to each other, "Come, let us make oven-fired bricks." They used brick for stone and asphalt for mortar. ⁴And they said, "Come, let us build ourselves a city and a tower with its top in the sky. Let us make a name for ourselves; otherwise, we will be scattered over the face of the whole earth."

⁵Then the Lᴏʀᴅ came down to look over the city and the tower that the ˙men were building. ⁶The Lᴏʀᴅ said, "If they have begun to do this as one people all having the same language, then nothing they plan to do will be impossible for them. ⁷Come, let Us go down there and confuse their language so that they will not understand one another's speech." ⁸So from there the Lᴏʀᴅ scattered them over the face of the whole earth, and they stopped building the city. ⁹Therefore its name is called Babylon, for there the Lᴏʀᴅ confused the language of the whole earth, and from there the Lᴏʀᴅ scattered them over the face of the whole earth.

¹⁰These are the family records of Shem. Shem lived 100 years and fathered Arpachshad two years after the flood. ¹¹After he fathered Arpachshad, Shem lived 500 years and fathered other sons and daughters. ¹²Arpachshad lived 35 years and fathered Shelah. ¹³After he fathered Shelah, Arpachshad lived 403 years and fathered other sons and daughters. ¹⁴Shelah lived 30 years and fathered Eber. ¹⁵After he fathered Eber, Shelah lived 403 years and fathered other sons and daughters. ¹⁶Eber lived 34 years and fathered Peleg. ¹⁷After he fathered Peleg, Eber lived 430 years and fathered other sons and daughters. ¹⁸Peleg lived 30 years and fathered Reu. ¹⁹After he fathered Reu, Peleg lived 209 years and fathered other sons and daughters. ²⁰Reu lived 32 years and fathered Serug. ²¹After he fathered Serug, Reu lived 207 years and fathered other sons and daughters. ²²Serug lived 30 years and fathered Nahor. ²³After he fathered Nahor, Serug lived 200 years and fathered other sons and daughters. ²⁴Nahor lived 29 years and fathered Terah. ²⁵After he fathered Terah, Nahor lived 119 years and fathered other sons and daughters. ²⁶Terah lived 70 years and fathered Abram, Nahor, and Haran.

²⁷These are the family records of Terah. Terah fathered Abram, Nahor, and Haran, and Haran fathered Lot. ²⁸Haran died in his native land, in Ur of the Chaldeans, during his father Terah's lifetime. ²⁹Abram and Nahor took wives: Abram's wife was named Sarai, and Nahor's wife was named Milcah. She was the daughter

of Haran, the father of both Milcah and Iscah. ³⁰Sarai was unable to conceive; she did not have a child.

³¹Terah took his son Abram, his grandson Lot (Haran's son), and his daughter-in-law Sarai, his son Abram's wife, and they set out together from Ur of the Chaldeans to go to the land of Canaan. But when they came to Haran, they settled there. ³²Terah lived 205 years and died in Haran.

12 The Lord said to Abram:
Go out from your land,
　your relatives,
　and your father's house
　to the land that I will show you.
²　I will make you into a great nation,
　I will bless you,
　I will make your name great,
　and you will be a blessing.
³　I will bless those who bless you,
　I will curse those who treat you
　　with contempt,
　and all the peoples on earth
　will be blessed through you.

⁴So Abram went, as the Lord had told him, and Lot went with him. Abram was 75 years old when he left Haran. ⁵He took his wife Sarai, his nephew Lot, all the possessions they had accumulated, and the people he had acquired in Haran, and they set out for the land of Canaan. When they came to the land of Canaan, ⁶Abram passed through the land to the site of Shechem, at the oak of Moreh. At that time the Canaanites were in the land. ⁷Then the Lord appeared to Abram and said, "I will give this land to your •offspring." So he built an altar there to the Lord who had appeared to him. ⁸From there he moved on to the hill country east of Bethel and pitched his tent, with Bethel on the west and Ai on the east. He built an altar to •Yahweh there, and he called on the name of •Yahweh. ⁹Then Abram journeyed by stages to the •Negev.

¹⁰There was a famine in the land, so Abram went down to Egypt to live there for a while because the famine in the land was severe. ¹¹When he was about to enter Egypt, he said to his wife Sarai, "Look, I know what a beautiful woman you are. ¹²When the Egyptians see you, they will say, 'This is his wife.' They will kill me but let you live. ¹³Please say you're my sister so it will go well for me because of you, and my life will be spared on your account." ¹⁴When Abram entered Egypt, the Egyptians saw that the woman was very beautiful. ¹⁵Pharaoh's officials saw her and praised her to Pharaoh, so the woman was taken to Pharaoh's household. ¹⁶He treated Abram well because of her, and Abram acquired flocks and herds, male and female donkeys, male and female slaves, and camels.

¹⁷But the Lord struck Pharaoh and his household with severe plagues because of Abram's wife Sarai. ¹⁸So Pharaoh sent for Abram and said, "What have you done to me? Why didn't you tell me she was your wife? ¹⁹Why did you say, 'She's my sister,' so that I took her as my wife? Now, here is your wife. Take her and go!" ²⁰Then Pharaoh gave his men orders about him, and they sent him away with his wife and all he had.

13 Then Abram went up from Egypt to the •Negev—he, his wife, and all he had, and Lot with him. ²Abram was very rich in livestock, silver, and gold. ³He went by stages from the Negev to Bethel, to the place between Bethel and Ai where his tent had

formerly been, ⁴to the site where he had built the altar. And Abram called on the name of •Yahweh there.

⁵Now Lot, who was traveling with Abram, also had flocks, herds, and tents. ⁶But the land was unable to support them as long as they stayed together, for they had so many possessions that they could not stay together, ⁷and there was quarreling between the herdsmen of Abram's livestock and the herdsmen of Lot's livestock. At that time the Canaanites and the Perizzites were living in the land.

⁸Then Abram said to Lot, "Please, let's not have quarreling between you and me, or between your herdsmen and my herdsmen, since we are relatives. ⁹Isn't the whole land before you? Separate from me: if you go to the left, I will go to the right; if you go to the right, I will go to the left."

¹⁰Lot looked out and saw that the entire Jordan Valley as far as Zoar was well watered everywhere like the Lord's garden and the land of Egypt. This was before the Lord destroyed Sodom and Gomorrah. ¹¹So Lot chose the entire Jordan Valley for himself. Then Lot journeyed eastward, and they separated from each other. ¹²Abram lived in the land of Canaan, but Lot lived in the cities of the valley and set up his tent near Sodom. ¹³Now the men of Sodom were evil, sinning greatly against the Lord.

¹⁴After Lot had separated from him, the Lord said to Abram, "Look from the place where you are. Look north and south, east and west, ¹⁵for I will give you and your •offspring forever all the land that you see. ¹⁶I will make your offspring like the dust of the earth, so that if anyone could count the dust of the earth, then your offspring could be counted. ¹⁷Get up and walk around the land, through its length and width, for I will give it to you."

¹⁸So Abram moved his tent and went to live near the oaks of Mamre at Hebron, where he built an altar to the Lord.

14 In those days Amraphel king of •Shinar, Arioch king of Ellasar, Chedorlaomer king of Elam, and Tidal king of Goiim ²waged war against Bera king of Sodom, Birsha king of Gomorrah, Shinab king of Admah, and Shemeber king of Zeboiim, as well as the king of Bela (that is, Zoar). ³All of these came as allies to the Valley of Siddim (that is, the Dead Sea). ⁴They were subject to Chedorlaomer for 12 years, but in the thirteenth year they rebelled. ⁵In the fourteenth year Chedorlaomer and the kings who were with him came and defeated the Rephaim in Ashteroth-karnaim, the Zuzim in Ham, the Emim in Shaveh-kiriathaim, ⁶and the Horites in the mountains of Seir, as far as El-paran by the wilderness. ⁷Then they came back to invade Enmishpat (that is, Kadesh), and they defeated all the territory of the Amalekites, as well as the Amorites who lived in Hazazon-tamar.

⁸Then the king of Sodom, the king of Gomorrah, the king of Admah, the king of Zeboiim, and the king of Bela (that is, Zoar) went out and lined up for battle in the Valley of Siddim ⁹against Chedorlaomer king of Elam, Tidal king of Goiim, Amraphel king of Shinar, and Arioch king of Ellasar—four kings against five. ¹⁰Now the Valley of Siddim contained many asphalt pits, and as the kings of Sodom and Gomorrah fled, some fell into them, but the rest fled to the mountains. ¹¹The four kings took all the goods of Sodom and Gomorrah and all their food and went on. ¹²They also

took Abram's nephew Lot and his possessions, for he was living in Sodom, and they went on.

¹³One of the survivors came and told Abram the Hebrew, who lived near the oaks belonging to Mamre the Amorite, the brother of Eshcol and the brother of Aner. They were bound by a treaty with Abram. ¹⁴When Abram heard that his relative had been taken prisoner, he assembled his 318 trained men, born in his household, and they went in pursuit as far as Dan. ¹⁵And he and his servants deployed against them by night, attacked them, and pursued them as far as Hobah to the north of Damascus. ¹⁶He brought back all the goods and also his relative Lot and his goods, as well as the women and the other people.

¹⁷After Abram returned from defeating Chedorlaomer and the kings who were with him, the king of Sodom went out to meet him in the Valley of Shaveh (that is, the King's Valley). ¹⁸Then Melchizedek, king of Salem, brought out bread and wine; he was a priest to God •Most High. ¹⁹He blessed him and said:

Abram is blessed by God Most High,
Creator of heaven and earth,
²⁰   and I give praise to God Most High
who has handed over your enemies to you.

And Abram gave him a tenth of everything.

²¹Then the king of Sodom said to Abram, "Give me the people, but take the possessions for yourself."

²²But Abram said to the king of Sodom, "I have raised my hand in an oath to •Yahweh, God Most High, Creator of heaven and earth, ²³that I will not take a thread or sandal strap or anything that belongs to you, so you can never say, 'I made Abram rich.' ²⁴I will take nothing except what the servants have eaten. But as for the share of the men who came with me—Aner, Eshcol, and Mamre—they can take their share."

15 After these events, the word of the Lord came to Abram in a vision:

Do not be afraid, Abram.
I am your shield;
your reward will be very great.

²But Abram said, "Lord God, what can You give me, since I am childless and the heir of my house is Eliezer of Damascus?" ³Abram continued, "Look, You have given me no •offspring, so a slave born in my house will be my heir." ⁴Now the word of the Lord came to him: "This one will not be your heir; instead, one who comes from your own body will be your heir." ⁵He took him outside and said, "Look at the sky and count the stars, if you are able to count them." Then He said to him, "Your offspring will be that numerous."

⁶Abram believed the Lord, and He credited it to him as righteousness.

⁷He also said to him, "I am •Yahweh who brought you from Ur of the Chaldeans to give you this land to possess."

⁸But he said, "Lord God, how can I know that I will possess it?"

⁹He said to him, "Bring Me a three-year-old cow, a three-year-old female goat, a three-year-old ram, a turtledove, and a young pigeon." ¹⁰So he brought all these to Him, split them down the middle, and laid the pieces opposite each other, but he did not cut up the birds. ¹¹Birds of prey came down on the carcasses, but Abram drove them away. ¹²As the sun was setting, a deep sleep fell on Abram, and suddenly great terror and darkness descended on him.

¹³Then the Lord said to Abram, "Know this for certain: Your offspring will be foreigners in a land that does not belong to them; they will be enslaved and oppressed 400 years. ¹⁴However, I will judge the nation they serve, and afterward they will go out with many possessions. ¹⁵But you will go to your fathers in peace and be buried at a ripe old age. ¹⁶In the fourth generation they will return here, for the iniquity of the Amorites has not yet reached its full measure."

¹⁷When the sun had set and it was dark, a smoking fire pot and a flaming torch appeared and passed between the divided animals. ¹⁸On that day the Lord made a covenant with Abram, saying, "I give this land to your offspring, from the brook of Egypt to the Euphrates River: ¹⁹the land of the Kenites, Kenizzites, Kadmonites, ²⁰Hittites, Perizzites, Rephaim, ²¹Amorites, Canaanites, Girgashites, and Jebusites."

16 Abram's wife Sarai had not borne any children for him, but she owned an Egyptian slave named Hagar. ²Sarai said to Abram, "Since the Lord has prevented me from bearing children, go to my slave; perhaps through her I can build a family." And Abram agreed to what Sarai said. ³So Abram's wife Sarai took Hagar, her Egyptian slave, and gave her to her husband Abram as a wife for him. This happened after Abram had lived in the land of Canaan 10 years. ⁴He slept with Hagar, and she became pregnant. When she realized that she was pregnant, she treated her mistress with contempt. ⁵Then Sarai said to Abram, "You are responsible for my suffering! I put my slave in your arms, and ever since she saw that she was pregnant, she has treated me with contempt. May the Lord judge between me and you."

⁶Abram replied to Sarai, "Here, your slave is in your hands; do whatever you want with her." Then Sarai mistreated her so much that she ran away from her.

⁷The Angel of the Lord found her by a spring of water in the wilderness, the spring on the way to Shur. ⁸He said, "Hagar, slave of Sarai, where have you come from and where are you going?"

She replied, "I'm running away from my mistress Sarai."

⁹Then the Angel of the Lord said to her, "You must go back to your mistress and submit to her mistreatment." ¹⁰The Angel of the Lord also said to her, "I will greatly multiply your •offspring, and they will be too many to count."

¹¹Then the Angel of the Lord said to her:

You have conceived and will have a son.
You will name him Ishmael,
for the Lord has heard your cry of affliction.
¹²   This man will be like a wild donkey.
His hand will be against everyone,
and everyone's hand will be against him;
he will live at odds with all his brothers.

¹³So she called the Lord who spoke to her: The God Who Sees, for she said, "In this place, have I actually seen the One who sees me?" ¹⁴That is why she named the spring, "A Well of the Living One Who Sees Me." It is located between Kadesh and Bered.

¹⁵So Hagar gave birth to Abram's son, and Abram gave the name Ishmael to the son Hagar had. ¹⁶Abram was 86 years old when Hagar bore Ishmael to him.

17 When Abram was 99 years old, the Lord appeared to him, saying, "I am •God Almighty. Live in My presence and be blameless. ²I will establish

My covenant between Me and you, and I will multiply you greatly."

[3] Then Abram fell facedown and God spoke with him: [4] "As for Me, My covenant is with you: you will become the father of many nations. [5] Your name will no longer be Abram, but your name will be Abraham, for I will make you the father of many nations. [6] I will make you extremely fruitful and will make nations and kings come from you. [7] I will keep My covenant between Me and you, and your future ·offspring throughout their generations, as an everlasting covenant to be your God and the God of your offspring after you. [8] And to you and your future offspring I will give the land where you are residing—all the land of Canaan—as an eternal possession, and I will be their God."

[9] God also said to Abraham, "As for you, you and your offspring after you throughout their generations are to keep My covenant. [10] This is My covenant, which you are to keep, between Me and you and your offspring after you: Every one of your males must be circumcised. [11] You must circumcise the flesh of your foreskin to serve as a sign of the covenant between Me and you. [12] Throughout your generations, every male among you at eight days old is to be circumcised. This includes a slave born in your house and one purchased with money from any foreigner. The one who is not your offspring, [13] a slave born in your house, as well as one purchased with money, must be circumcised. My covenant will be marked in your flesh as an everlasting covenant. [14] If any male is not circumcised in the flesh of his foreskin, that man will be cut off from his people; he has broken My covenant."

[15] God said to Abraham, "As for your wife Sarai, do not call her Sarai, for Sarah will be her name. [16] I will bless her; indeed, I will give you a son by her. I will bless her, and she will produce nations; kings of peoples will come from her."

[17] Abraham fell facedown. Then he laughed and said to himself, "Can a child be born to a hundred-year-old man? Can Sarah, a ninety-year-old woman, give birth?" [18] So Abraham said to God, "If only Ishmael were acceptable to You!"

[19] But God said, "No. Your wife Sarah will bear you a son, and you will name him Isaac. I will confirm My covenant with him as an everlasting covenant for his future offspring. [20] As for Ishmael, I have heard you. I will certainly bless him; I will make him fruitful and will multiply him greatly. He will father 12 tribal leaders, and I will make him into a great nation. [21] But I will confirm My covenant with Isaac, whom Sarah will bear to you at this time next year." [22] When He finished talking with him, God withdrew from Abraham.

[23] Then Abraham took his son Ishmael and all the slaves born in his house or purchased with his money—every male among the members of Abraham's household—and he circumcised the flesh of their foreskin on that very day, just as God had said to him. [24] Abraham was 99 years old when the flesh of his foreskin was circumcised, [25] and his son Ishmael was 13 years old when the flesh of his foreskin was circumcised. [26] On that same day Abraham and his son Ishmael were circumcised. [27] And all the men of his household—both slaves born in his house and those purchased with money from a foreigner—were circumcised with him.

18 Then the LORD appeared to Abraham at the oaks of Mamre while he was sitting in the entrance of his tent during the heat of the day. [2] He looked up, and he saw three men standing near him. When he saw them, he ran from the entrance of the tent to meet them and bowed to the ground. [3] Then he said, "My. lord, if I have found favor in your sight, please do not go on past your servant. [4] Let a little water be brought, that you may wash your feet and rest yourselves under the tree. [5] I will bring a bit of bread so that you may strengthen yourselves. This is why you have passed your servant's way. Later, you can continue on."

"Yes," they replied, "do as you have said."

[6] So Abraham hurried into the tent and said to Sarah, "Quick! Knead three measures of fine flour and make bread." [7] Meanwhile, Abraham ran to the herd and got a tender, choice calf. He gave it to a young man, who hurried to prepare it. [8] Then Abraham took curds and milk, and the calf that he had prepared, and set them before the men. He served them as they ate under the tree.

[9] "Where is your wife Sarah?" they asked him.

"There, in the tent," he answered.

[10] The LORD said, "I will certainly come back to you in about a year's time, and your wife Sarah will have a son!" Now Sarah was listening at the entrance of the tent behind him.

[11] Abraham and Sarah were old and getting on in years. Sarah had passed the age of childbearing. [12] So she laughed to herself: "After I have become shriveled up and my lord is old, will I have delight?"

[13] But the LORD asked Abraham, "Why did Sarah laugh, saying, 'Can I really have a baby when I'm old?' [14] Is anything impossible for the LORD? At the appointed time I will come back to you, and in about a year she will have a son."

[15] Sarah denied it. "I did not laugh," she said, because she was afraid.

But He replied, "No, you did laugh."

[16] The men got up from there and looked out over Sodom, and Abraham was walking with them to see them off. [17] Then the LORD said, "Should I hide what I am about to do from Abraham? [18] Abraham is to become a great and powerful nation, and all the nations of the earth will be blessed through him. [19] For I have chosen him so that he will command his children and his house after him to keep the way of the LORD by doing what is right and just. This is how the LORD will fulfill to Abraham what He promised him." [20] Then the LORD said, "The outcry against Sodom and Gomorrah is immense, and their sin is extremely serious. [21] I will go down to see if what they have done justifies the cry that has come up to Me. If not, I will find out."

[22] The men turned from there and went toward Sodom while Abraham remained standing before the LORD. [23] Abraham stepped forward and said, "Will You really sweep away the righteous with the wicked? [24] What if there are 50 righteous people in the city? Will You really sweep it away instead of sparing the place for the sake of the 50 righteous people who are in it? [25] You could not possibly do such a thing: to kill the righteous with the wicked, treating the righteous and the wicked alike. You could not possibly do that! Won't the Judge of all the earth do what is just?"

[26] The LORD said, "If I find 50 righteous people in the city of Sodom, I will spare the whole place for their sake."

²⁷Then Abraham answered, "Since I have ventured to speak to the Lord—even though I am dust and ashes— ²⁸suppose the 50 righteous lack five. Will you destroy the whole city for lack of five?"

He replied, "I will not destroy it if I find 45 there."

²⁹Then he spoke to Him again, "Suppose 40 are found there?"

He answered, "I will not do it on account of 40."

³⁰Then he said, "Let the Lord not be angry, and I will speak further. Suppose 30 are found there?"

He answered, "I will not do it if I find 30 there."

³¹Then he said, "Since I have ventured to speak to the Lord, suppose 20 are found there?"

He replied, "I will not destroy it on account of 20."

³²Then he said, "Let the Lord not be angry, and I will speak one more time. Suppose 10 are found there?"

He answered, "I will not destroy it on account of 10." ³³When the Lord had finished speaking with Abraham, He departed, and Abraham returned to his place.

19 The two angels entered Sodom in the evening as Lot was sitting at Sodom's °gate. When Lot saw them, he got up to meet them. He bowed with his face to the ground ²and said, "My lords, turn aside to your servant's house, wash your feet, and spend the night. Then you can get up early and go on your way."

"No," they said. "We would rather spend the night in the square." ³But he urged them so strongly that they followed him and went into his house. He prepared a feast and baked unleavened bread for them, and they ate.

⁴Before they went to bed, the men of the city of Sodom, both young and old, the whole population, surrounded the house. ⁵They called out to Lot and said, "Where are the men who came to you tonight? Send them out to us so we can have sex with them!"

⁶Lot went out to them at the entrance and shut the door behind him. ⁷He said, "Don't do this evil, my brothers. ⁸Look, I've got two daughters who haven't had sexual relations with a man. I'll bring them out to you, and you can do whatever you want to them. However, don't do anything to these men, because they have come under the protection of my roof."

⁹"Get out of the way!" they said, adding, "This one came here as a foreigner, but he's acting like a judge! Now we'll do more harm to you than to them." They put pressure on Lot and came up to break down the door. ¹⁰But the angels reached out, brought Lot into the house with them, and shut the door. ¹¹They struck the men who were at the entrance of the house, both young and old, with a blinding light so that they were unable to find the entrance.

¹²Then the angels said to Lot, "Do you have anyone else here: a son-in-law, your sons and daughters, or anyone else in the city who belongs to you? Get them out of this place, ¹³for we are about to destroy this place because the outcry against its people is so great before the Lord, that the Lord has sent us to destroy it."

¹⁴So Lot went out and spoke to his sons-in-law, who were going to marry his daughters. "Get up," he said. "Get out of this place, for the Lord is about to destroy the city!" But his sons-in-law thought he was joking.

¹⁵At daybreak the angels urged Lot on: "Get up! Take your wife and your two daughters who are here, or you will be swept away in the punishment of the city." ¹⁶But he hesitated. Because of the Lord's compassion for him, the men grabbed his hand, his wife's hand, and the hands of his two daughters. Then they brought him out and left him outside the city.

¹⁷As soon as the angels got them outside, one of them said, "Run for your lives! Don't look back and don't stop anywhere on the plain! Run to the mountains, or you will be swept away!"

¹⁸But Lot said to them, "No, my lords—please. ¹⁹Your servant has indeed found favor in your sight, and you have shown me great kindness by saving my life. But I can't run to the mountains; the disaster will overtake me, and I will die. ²⁰Look, this town is close enough for me to run to. It is a small place. Please let me go there—it's only a small place, isn't it?—so that I can survive."

²¹And he said to him, "All right, I'll grant your request about this matter too and will not demolish the town you mentioned. ²²Hurry up! Run there, for I cannot do anything until you get there." Therefore the name of the city is Zoar.

²³The sun had risen over the land when Lot reached Zoar. ²⁴Then out of the sky the Lord rained burning sulfur on Sodom and Gomorrah from the Lord. ²⁵He demolished these cities, the entire plain, all the inhabitants of the cities, and whatever grew on the ground. ²⁶But his wife looked back and became a pillar of salt.

²⁷Early in the morning Abraham went to the place where he had stood before the Lord. ²⁸He looked down toward Sodom and Gomorrah and all the land of the plain, and he saw that smoke was going up from the land like the smoke of a furnace. ²⁹So it was, when God destroyed the cities of the plain, He remembered Abraham and brought Lot out of the middle of the upheaval when He demolished the cities where Lot had lived.

³⁰Lot departed from Zoar and lived in the mountains along with his two daughters, because he was afraid to live in Zoar. Instead, he and his two daughters lived in a cave. ³¹Then the firstborn said to the younger, "Our father is old, and there is no man in the land to sleep with us as is the custom of all the land. ³²Come, let's get our father to drink wine so that we can sleep with him and preserve our father's line." ³³So they got their father to drink wine that night, and the firstborn came and slept with her father; he did not know when she lay down or when she got up.

³⁴The next day the firstborn said to the younger, "Look, I slept with my father last night. Let's get him to drink wine again tonight so you can go sleep with him and we can preserve our father's line." ³⁵That night they again got their father to drink wine, and the younger went and slept with him; he did not know when she lay down or when she got up.

³⁶So both of Lot's daughters became pregnant by their father. ³⁷The firstborn gave birth to a son and named him Moab. He is the father of the Moabites of today. ³⁸The younger also gave birth to a son, and she named him Ben-ammi. He is the father of the Ammonites of today.

20 From there Abraham traveled to the region of the °Negev and settled between Kadesh and Shur. While he lived in Gerar, ²Abraham said about his wife Sarah, "She is my sister." So Abimelech king of Gerar had Sarah brought to him.

³But God came to Abimelech in a dream by night and said to him, "You are about to die because of the woman you have taken, for she is a married woman."

⁴Now Abimelech had not approached her, so he said,

"Lord, would You destroy a nation even though it is innocent? ⁵Didn't he himself say to me, 'She is my sister'? And she herself said, 'He is my brother.' I did this with a clear conscience and ˙clean hands."

⁶Then God said to him in the dream, "Yes, I know that you did this with a clear conscience. I have also kept you from sinning against Me. Therefore I have not let you touch her. ⁷Now return the man's wife, for he is a prophet, and he will pray for you and you will live. But if you do not return her, know that you will certainly die, you and all who are yours."

⁸Early in the morning Abimelech got up, called all his servants together, and personally told them all these things, and the men were terrified.

⁹Then Abimelech called Abraham in and said to him, "What have you done to us? How did I sin against you that you have brought such enormous ˙guilt on me and on my kingdom? You have done things to me that should never be done." ¹⁰Abimelech also said to Abraham, "What did you intend when you did this thing?"

¹¹Abraham replied, "I thought, 'There is absolutely no ˙fear of God in this place. They will kill me because of my wife.' ¹²Besides, she really is my sister, the daughter of my father though not the daughter of my mother, and she became my wife. ¹³So when God had me wander from my father's house, I said to her: Show your loyalty to me wherever we go and say about me: 'He's my brother.'"

¹⁴Then Abimelech took sheep and cattle and male and female slaves, gave them to Abraham, and returned his wife Sarah to him. ¹⁵Abimelech said, "Look, my land is before you. Settle wherever you want." ¹⁶And he said to Sarah, "Look, I am giving your brother 1,000 pieces of silver. It is a verification of your honor to all who are with you. You are fully vindicated."

¹⁷Then Abraham prayed to God, and God healed Abimelech, his wife, and his female slaves so that they could bear children, ¹⁸for the Lᴏʀᴅ had completely closed all the wombs in Abimelech's household on account of Sarah, Abraham's wife.

21 The Lᴏʀᴅ came to Sarah as He had said, and the Lᴏʀᴅ did for Sarah what He had promised. ²Sarah became pregnant and bore a son to Abraham in his old age, at the appointed time God had told him. ³Abraham named his son who was born to him—the one Sarah bore to him—Isaac. ⁴When his son Isaac was eight days old, Abraham circumcised him, as God had commanded him. ⁵Abraham was 100 years old when his son Isaac was born to him.

⁶Sarah said, "God has made me laugh, and everyone who hears will laugh with me." ⁷She also said, "Who would have told Abraham that Sarah would nurse children? Yet I have borne a son for him in his old age."

⁸The child grew and was weaned, and Abraham held a great feast on the day Isaac was weaned. ⁹But Sarah saw the son mocking—the one Hagar the Egyptian had borne to Abraham. ¹⁰So she said to Abraham, "Drive out this slave with her son, for the son of this slave will not be a coheir with my son Isaac!"

¹¹Now this was a very difficult thing for Abraham because of his son. ¹²But God said to Abraham, "Do not be concerned about the boy and your slave. Whatever Sarah says to you, listen to her, because your ˙offspring will be traced through Isaac. ¹³But I will also make a nation of the slave's son because he is your offspring."

¹⁴Early in the morning Abraham got up, took bread and a waterskin, put them on Hagar's shoulders, and sent her and the boy away. She left and wandered in the Wilderness of Beer-sheba. ¹⁵When the water in the skin was gone, she left the boy under one of the bushes. ¹⁶Then she went and sat down nearby, about a bowshot away, for she said, "I can't bear to watch the boy die!" So as she sat nearby, she wept loudly.

¹⁷God heard the voice of the boy, and the angel of God called to Hagar from heaven and said to her, "What's wrong, Hagar? Don't be afraid, for God has heard the voice of the boy from the place where he is. ¹⁸Get up, help the boy up, and support him, for I will make him a great nation." ¹⁹Then God opened her eyes, and she saw a well of water. So she went and filled the waterskin and gave the boy a drink. ²⁰God was with the boy, and he grew; he settled in the wilderness and became an archer. ²¹He settled in the Wilderness of Paran, and his mother got a wife for him from the land of Egypt.

²²At that time Abimelech, accompanied by Phicol the commander of his army, said to Abraham, "God is with you in everything you do. ²³Swear to me by God here and now, that you will not break an agreement with me or with my children and descendants. As I have been loyal to you, so you will be loyal to me and to the country where you are a foreign resident."

²⁴And Abraham said, "I swear it." ²⁵But Abraham complained to Abimelech because of the water well that Abimelech's servants had seized.

²⁶Abimelech replied, "I don't know who did this thing. You didn't report anything to me, so I hadn't heard about it until today."

²⁷Abraham took sheep and cattle and gave them to Abimelech, and the two of them made a covenant. ²⁸Abraham separated seven ewe lambs from the flock. ²⁹And Abimelech said to Abraham, "Why have you separated these seven ewe lambs?"

³⁰He replied, "You are to accept the seven ewe lambs from my hand so that this act will serve as my witness that I dug this well." ³¹Therefore that place was called Beer-sheba because it was there that the two of them swore an oath. ³²After they had made a covenant at Beer-sheba, Abimelech and Phicol, the commander of his army, left and returned to the land of the Philistines.

³³Abraham planted a tamarisk tree in Beer-sheba, and there he called on the name of ˙Yahweh, the Everlasting God. ³⁴And Abraham lived as a foreigner in the land of the Philistines for many days.

22 After these things God tested Abraham and said to him, "Abraham!"

"Here I am," he answered.

²"Take your son," He said, "your only son Isaac, whom you love, go to the land of Moriah, and offer him there as a ˙burnt offering on one of the mountains I will tell you about."

³So Abraham got up early in the morning, saddled his donkey, and took with him two of his young men and his son Isaac. He split wood for a burnt offering and set out to go to the place God had told him about. ⁴On the third day Abraham looked up and saw the place in the distance. ⁵Then Abraham said to his young men, "Stay here with the donkey. The boy and I will go over there to worship; then we'll come back to you." ⁶Abraham took the wood for the burnt offering and laid it on his son Isaac. In his hand he took the fire and the sacrificial knife, and the two of them walked on together.

⁷Then Isaac spoke to his father Abraham and said, "My father."

And he replied, "Here I am, my son."

Isaac said, "The fire and the wood are here, but where is the lamb for the burnt offering?"

⁸Abraham answered, "God Himself will provide the lamb for the burnt offering, my son." Then the two of them walked on together.

⁹When they arrived at the place that God had told him about, Abraham built the altar there and arranged the wood. He bound his son Isaac and placed him on the altar on top of the wood. ¹⁰Then Abraham reached out and took the knife to slaughter his son.

¹¹But the Angel of the LORD called to him from heaven and said, "Abraham, Abraham!"

He replied, "Here I am."

¹²Then He said, "Do not lay a hand on the boy or do anything to him. For now I know that you •fear God, since you have not withheld your only son from Me."

¹³Abraham looked up and saw a ram caught in the thicket by its horns. So Abraham went and took the ram and offered it as a burnt offering in place of his son. ¹⁴And Abraham named that place The LORD Will Provide, so today it is said: "It will be provided on the LORD's mountain."

¹⁵Then the Angel of the LORD called to Abraham a second time from heaven ¹⁶and said, "By Myself I have sworn," this is the LORD's declaration: "Because you have done this thing and have not withheld your only son, ¹⁷I will indeed bless you and make your •offspring as numerous as the stars of the sky and the sand on the seashore. Your offspring will possess the gates of their enemies. ¹⁸And all the nations of the earth will be blessed by your offspring because you have obeyed My command."

¹⁹Abraham went back to his young men, and they got up and went together to Beer-sheba. And Abraham settled in Beer-sheba.

²⁰Now after these things Abraham was told, "Milcah also has borne sons to your brother Nahor: ²¹Uz his firstborn, his brother Buz, Kemuel the father of Aram, ²²Chesed, Hazo, Pildash, Jidlaph, and Bethuel." ²³And Bethuel fathered Rebekah. Milcah bore these eight to Nahor, Abraham's brother. ²⁴His concubine, whose name was Reumah, also bore Tebah, Gaham, Tahash, and Maacah.

23 Now Sarah lived 127 years; these were all the years of her life. ²Sarah died in Kiriath-arba (that is, Hebron) in the land of Canaan, and Abraham went to mourn for Sarah and to weep for her.

³Then Abraham got up from beside his dead wife and spoke to the Hittites: ⁴"I am a foreign resident among you. Give me a burial site among you so that I can bury my dead."

⁵The Hittites replied to Abraham, ⁶"Listen to us, lord. You are God's chosen one among us. Bury your dead in our finest burial place. None of us will withhold from you his burial place for burying your dead."

⁷Then Abraham rose and bowed down to the Hittites, the people of the land. ⁸He said to them, "If you are willing for me to bury my dead, listen to me and ask Ephron son of Zohar on my behalf ⁹to give me the cave of Machpelah that belongs to him; it is at the end of his field. Let him give it to me in your presence, for the full price, as a burial place."

¹⁰Ephron was sitting among the Hittites. So in the presence of all the Hittites who came to the •gate of his city, Ephron the Hittite answered Abraham: ¹¹"No, my lord. Listen to me. I give you the field, and I give you the cave that is in it. I give it to you in the presence of my people. Bury your dead."

¹²Abraham bowed down to the people of the land ¹³and said to Ephron in the presence of the people of the land, "Please listen to me. Let me pay the price of the field. Accept it from me, and let me bury my dead there."

¹⁴Ephron answered Abraham and said to him, ¹⁵"My lord, listen to me. Land worth 400 •shekels of silver—what is that between you and me? Bury your dead." ¹⁶Abraham agreed with Ephron, and Abraham weighed out to Ephron the silver that he had agreed to in the presence of the Hittites: 400 shekels of silver at the current commercial rate. ¹⁷So Ephron's field at Machpelah near Mamre—the field with its cave and all the trees anywhere within the boundaries of the field—became ¹⁸Abraham's possession in the presence of all the Hittites who came to the gate of his city. ¹⁹After this, Abraham buried his wife Sarah in the cave of the field at Machpelah near Mamre (that is, Hebron) in the land of Canaan. ²⁰The field with its cave passed from the Hittites to Abraham as a burial place.

24 Abraham was now old, getting on in years, and the LORD had blessed him in everything. ²Abraham said to his servant, the elder of his household who managed all he owned, "Place your hand under my thigh, ³and I will have you swear by the LORD, God of heaven and God of earth, that you will not take a wife for my son from the daughters of the Canaanites among whom I live, ⁴but will go to my land and my family to take a wife for my son Isaac."

⁵The servant said to him, "Suppose the woman is unwilling to follow me to this land? Should I have your son go back to the land you came from?"

⁶Abraham answered him, "Make sure that you don't take my son back there. ⁷The LORD, the God of heaven, who took me from my father's house and from my native land, who spoke to me and swore to me, 'I will give this land to your •offspring'—He will send His angel before you, and you can take a wife for my son from there. ⁸If the woman is unwilling to follow you, then you are free from this oath to me, but don't let my son go back there." ⁹So the servant placed his hand under his master Abraham's thigh and swore an oath to him concerning this matter.

¹⁰The servant took 10 of his master's camels and departed with all kinds of his master's goods in hand. Then he set out for Nahor's town Aram-naharaim. ¹¹He made the camels kneel beside a well of water outside the town at evening. This was the time when the women went out to draw water.

¹²"LORD, God of my master Abraham," he prayed, "give me success today, and show kindness to my master Abraham. ¹³I am standing here at the spring where the daughters of the men of the town are coming out to draw water. ¹⁴Let the girl to whom I say, 'Please lower your water jug so that I may drink,' and who responds, 'Drink, and I'll water your camels also'—let her be the one You have appointed for Your servant Isaac. By this I will know that You have shown kindness to my master."

¹⁵Before he had finished speaking, there was Rebekah—daughter of Bethuel son of Milcah, the wife of Abraham's brother Nahor—coming with a jug on her shoulder. ¹⁶Now the girl was very beautiful, a young

woman who had not known a man intimately. She went down to the spring, filled her jug, and came up. [17]Then the servant ran to meet her and said, "Please let me have a little water from your jug."

[18]She replied, "Drink, my lord." She quickly lowered her jug to her hand and gave him a drink. [19]When she had finished giving him a drink, she said, "I'll also draw water for your camels until they have had enough to drink." [20]She quickly emptied her jug into the trough and hurried to the well again to draw water. She drew water for all his camels [21]while the man silently watched her to see whether or not the LORD had made his journey a success.

[22]After the camels had finished drinking, the man took a gold ring weighing half a ·shekel, and for her wrists two bracelets weighing 10 shekels of gold. [23]"Whose daughter are you?" he asked. "Please tell me, is there room in your father's house for us to spend the night?"

[24]She answered him, "I am the daughter of Bethuel son of Milcah, whom she bore to Nahor." [25]She also said to him, "We have plenty of straw and feed and a place to spend the night."

[26]Then the man bowed down, worshiped the LORD, [27]and said, "Praise the LORD, the God of my master Abraham, who has not withheld His kindness and faithfulness from my master. As for me, the LORD has led me on the journey to the house of my master's relatives."

[28]The girl ran and told her mother's household about these things. [29]Now Rebekah had a brother named Laban, and Laban ran out to the man at the spring. [30]As soon as he had seen the ring and the bracelets on his sister's wrists, and when he had heard his sister Rebekah's words—"The man said this to me!"—he went to the man. He was standing there by the camels at the spring.

[31]Laban said, "Come, you who are blessed by the LORD. Why are you standing out here? I have prepared the house and a place for the camels." [32]So the man came to the house, and the camels were unloaded. Straw and feed were given to the camels, and water was brought to wash his feet and the feet of the men with him.

[33]A meal was set before him, but he said, "I will not eat until I have said what I have to say."

So Laban said, "Please speak."

[34]"I am Abraham's servant," he said. [35]"The LORD has greatly blessed my master, and he has become rich. He has given him sheep and cattle, silver and gold, male and female slaves, and camels and donkeys. [36]Sarah, my master's wife, bore a son to my master in her old age, and he has given him everything he owns. [37]My master put me under this oath: 'You will not take a wife for my son from the daughters of the Canaanites in whose land I live [38]but will go to my father's household and to my family to take a wife for my son.' [39]But I said to my master, 'Suppose the woman will not come back with me?' [40]He said to me, 'The LORD, before whom I have walked will send His angel with you and make your journey a success, and you will take a wife for my son from my family and from my father's household. [41]Then you will be free from my oath if you go to my family and they do not give her to you—you will be free from my oath.'

[42]"Today when I came to the spring, I prayed: LORD, God of my master Abraham, if only You will make my journey successful! [43]I am standing here at a spring. Let the virgin who comes out to draw water, and I say to her: Please let me drink a little water from your jug, [44]and who responds to me, 'Drink, and I'll draw water for your camels also'—let her be the woman the LORD has appointed for my master's son.'

[45]"Before I had finished praying silently, there was Rebekah coming with her jug on her shoulder, and she went down to the spring and drew water. So I said to her: Please let me have a drink. [46]She quickly lowered her jug from her shoulder and said, 'Drink, and I'll water your camels also.' So I drank, and she also watered the camels. [47]Then I asked her: Whose daughter are you? She responded, 'The daughter of Bethuel son of Nahor, whom Milcah bore to him.' So I put the ring on her nose and the bracelets on her wrists. [48]Then I bowed down, worshiped the LORD, and praised the LORD, the God of my master Abraham, who guided me on the right way to take the granddaughter of my master's brother for his son. [49]Now, if you are going to show kindness and faithfulness to my master, tell me; if not, tell me, and I will go elsewhere."

[50]Laban and Bethuel answered, "This is from the LORD; we have no choice in the matter. [51]Rebekah is here in front of you. Take her and go, and let her be a wife for your master's son, just as the LORD has spoken."

[52]When Abraham's servant heard their words, he bowed to the ground before the LORD. [53]Then he brought out objects of silver and gold, and garments, and gave them to Rebekah. He also gave precious gifts to her brother and her mother. [54]Then he and the men with him ate and drank and spent the night.

When they got up in the morning, he said, "Send me to my master."

[55]But her brother and mother said, "Let the girl stay with us for about 10 days. Then she can go."

[56]But he responded to them, "Do not delay me, since the LORD has made my journey a success. Send me away so that I may go to my master."

[57]So they said, "Let's call the girl and ask her opinion."

[58]They called Rebekah and said to her, "Will you go with this man?"

She replied, "I will go." [59]So they sent away their sister Rebekah with the one who had nursed and raised her, and Abraham's servant and his men.

[60]They blessed Rebekah, saying to her:

Our sister, may you become
thousands upon ten thousands.
May your offspring possess
the gates of their enemies.

[61]Then Rebekah and her female servants got up, mounted the camels, and followed the man. So the servant took Rebekah and left.

[62]Now Isaac was returning from Beer-lahai-roi, for he was living in the ·Negev region. [63]In the early evening Isaac went out to walk in the field, and looking up he saw camels coming. [64]Rebekah looked up, and when she saw Isaac, she got down from her camel [65]and asked the servant, "Who is that man in the field coming to meet us?"

The servant answered, "It is my master." So she took her veil and covered herself. [66]Then the servant told Isaac everything he had done.

[67]And Isaac brought her into the tent of his mother

Sarah and took Rebekah to be his wife. Isaac loved her, and he was comforted after his mother's death.

25 Now Abraham had taken another wife, whose name was Keturah, ²and she bore him Zimran, Jokshan, Medan, Midian, Ishbak, and Shuah. ³Jokshan fathered Sheba and Dedan. Dedan's sons were the Asshurim, Letushim, and Leummim. ⁴And Midian's sons were Ephah, Epher, Hanoch, Abida, and Eldaah. All these were sons of Keturah. ⁵Abraham gave everything he owned to Isaac. ⁶And Abraham gave gifts to the sons of his concubines, but while he was still alive he sent them eastward, away from his son Isaac, to the land of the East.

⁷This is the length of Abraham's life: 175 years. ⁸He took his last breath and died at a ripe old age, old and contented, and he was gathered to his people. ⁹His sons Isaac and Ishmael buried him in the cave of Machpelah near Mamre, in the field of Ephron son of Zohar the Hittite. ¹⁰This was the field that Abraham bought from the Hittites. Abraham was buried there with his wife Sarah. ¹¹After Abraham's death, God blessed his son Isaac, who lived near Beer-lahai-roi.

¹²These are the family records of Abraham's son Ishmael, whom Hagar the Egyptian, Sarah's slave, bore to Abraham. ¹³These are the names of Ishmael's sons; their names according to the family records are: Nebaioth, Ishmael's firstborn, then Kedar, Adbeel, Mibsam, ¹⁴Mishma, Dumah, Massa, ¹⁵Hadad, Tema, Jetur, Naphish, and Kedemah. ¹⁶These are Ishmael's sons, and these are their names by their villages and encampments: 12 leaders of their clans. ¹⁷This is the length of Ishmael's life: 137 years. He took his last breath and died, and was gathered to his people. ¹⁸And they settled from Havilah to Shur, which is opposite Egypt as you go toward Asshur. He lived in opposition to all his brothers.

¹⁹These are the family records of Isaac son of Abraham. Abraham fathered Isaac. ²⁰Isaac was 40 years old when he took as his wife Rebekah daughter of Bethuel the Aramean from Paddan-aram and sister of Laban the Aramean. ²¹Isaac prayed to the LORD on behalf of his wife because she was childless. The LORD heard his prayer, and his wife Rebekah conceived. ²²But the children inside her struggled with each other, and she said, "Why is this happening to me?" So she went to inquire of the LORD. ²³And the LORD said to her:

Two nations are in your womb;
two people will come from you
    and be separated.
One people will be stronger than the other,
    and the older will serve the younger.

²⁴When her time came to give birth, there were indeed twins in her womb. ²⁵The first one came out red-looking, covered with hair like a fur coat, and they named him Esau. ²⁶After this, his brother came out grasping Esau's heel with his hand. So he was named Jacob. Isaac was 60 years old when they were born.

²⁷When the boys grew up, Esau became an expert hunter, an outdoorsman, but Jacob was a quiet man who stayed at home. ²⁸Isaac loved Esau because he had a taste for wild game, but Rebekah loved Jacob.

²⁹Once when Jacob was cooking a stew, Esau came in from the field exhausted. ³⁰He said to Jacob, "Let me eat some of that red stuff, because I'm exhausted." That is why he was also named Edom.

³¹Jacob replied, "First sell me your birthright."

³²"Look," said Esau, "I'm about to die, so what good is a birthright to me?"

³³Jacob said, "Swear to me first." So he swore to Jacob and sold his birthright to him. ³⁴Then Jacob gave bread and lentil stew to Esau; he ate, drank, got up, and went away. So Esau despised his birthright.

26 There was another famine in the land in addition to the one that had occurred in Abraham's time. And Isaac went to Abimelech, king of the Philistines, at Gerar. ²The LORD appeared to him and said, "Do not go down to Egypt. Live in the land that I tell you about; ³stay in this land as a foreigner, and I will be with you and bless you. For I will give all these lands to you and your *offspring, and I will confirm the oath that I swore to your father Abraham. ⁴I will make your offspring as numerous as the stars of the sky, I will give your offspring all these lands, and all the nations of the earth will be blessed by your offspring, ⁵because Abraham listened to My voice and kept My mandate, My commands, My statutes, and My instructions." ⁶So Isaac settled in Gerar.

⁷When the men of the place asked about his wife, he said, "She is my sister," for he was afraid to say "my wife," thinking, "The men of the place will kill me on account of Rebekah, for she is a beautiful woman." ⁸When Isaac had been there for some time, Abimelech king of the Philistines looked down from the window and was surprised to see Isaac caressing his wife Rebekah.

⁹Abimelech sent for Isaac and said, "So she is really your wife! How could you say, 'She is my sister'?"

Isaac answered him, "Because I thought I might die on account of her."

¹⁰Then Abimelech said, "What is this you've done to us? One of the people could easily have slept with your wife, and you would have brought *guilt on us." ¹¹So Abimelech warned all the people with these words: "Whoever harms this man or his wife will certainly die."

¹²Isaac sowed seed in that land, and in that year he reaped a hundred times what was sown. The LORD blessed him, ¹³and the man became rich and kept getting richer until he was very wealthy. ¹⁴He had flocks of sheep, herds of cattle, and many slaves, and the Philistines were envious of him. ¹⁵The Philistines stopped up all the wells that his father's slaves had dug in the days of his father Abraham, filling them with dirt. ¹⁶And Abimelech said to Isaac, "Leave us, for you are much too powerful for us."

¹⁷So Isaac left there, camped in the Valley of Gerar, and lived there. ¹⁸Isaac reopened the water wells that had been dug in the days of his father Abraham and that the Philistines had stopped up after Abraham died. He gave them the same names his father had given them. ¹⁹Then Isaac's slaves dug in the valley and found a well of spring water there. ²⁰But the herdsmen of Gerar quarreled with Isaac's herdsmen and said, "The water is ours!" So he named the well Quarrel because they quarreled with him. ²¹Then they dug another well and quarreled over that one also, so he named it Hostility. ²²He moved from there and dug another, and they did not quarrel over it. He named it Open Spaces and said, "For now the LORD has made room for us, and we will be fruitful in the land."

²³From there he went up to Beer-sheba, ²⁴and the LORD appeared to him that night and said, "I am the God of your father Abraham. Do not be afraid, for I am

with you. I will bless you and multiply your offspring because of My servant Abraham."

²⁵So he built an altar there, called on the name of ˙Yahweh, and pitched his tent there. Isaac's slaves also dug a well there.

²⁶Now Abimelech came to him from Gerar with Ahuzzath his adviser and Phicol the commander of his army. ²⁷Isaac said to them, "Why have you come to me? You hated me and sent me away from you."

²⁸They replied, "We have clearly seen how the Lᴏʀᴅ has been with you. We think there should be an oath between two parties—between us and you. Let us make a covenant with you: ²⁹You will not harm us, just as we have not harmed you but have only done what was good to you, sending you away in peace. You are now blessed by the Lᴏʀᴅ."

³⁰So he prepared a banquet for them, and they ate and drank. ³¹They got up early in the morning and swore an oath to each other. Then Isaac sent them on their way, and they left him in peace. ³²On that same day Isaac's slaves came to tell him about the well they had dug, saying to him, "We have found water!" ³³He called it Sheba. Therefore the name of the city is Beersheba to this day.

³⁴When Esau was 40 years old, he took as his wives Judith daughter of Beeri the Hittite, and Basemath daughter of Elon the Hittite. ³⁵They made life bitter for Isaac and Rebekah.

27 When Isaac was old and his eyes were so weak that he could not see, he called his older son Esau and said to him, "My son."

And he answered, "Here I am."

²He said, "Look, I am old and do not know the day of my death. ³Take your hunting gear, your quiver and bow, and go out in the field to hunt some game for me. ⁴Then make me a delicious meal that I love and bring it to me to eat, so that I can bless you before I die."

⁵Now Rebekah was listening to what Isaac said to his son Esau. So while Esau went to the field to hunt some game to bring in, ⁶Rebekah said to her son Jacob, "Listen! I heard your father talking with your brother Esau. He said, ⁷'Bring me the game and make a delicious meal for me to eat so that I can bless you in the Lᴏʀᴅ's presence before I die.' ⁸Now obey every order I give you, my son. ⁹Go to the flock and bring me two choice young goats, and I will make them into a delicious meal for your father—the kind he loves. ¹⁰Then take it to your father to eat so that he may bless you before he dies."

¹¹Jacob answered Rebekah his mother, "Look, my brother Esau is a hairy man, but I am a man with smooth skin. ¹²Suppose my father touches me. Then I will be revealed to him as a deceiver and bring a curse rather than a blessing on myself."

¹³His mother said to him, "Your curse be on me, my son. Just obey me and go get them for me."

¹⁴So he went and got the goats and brought them to his mother, and his mother made the delicious food his father loved. ¹⁵Then Rebekah took the best clothes of her older son Esau, which were in the house, and had her younger son Jacob wear them. ¹⁶She put the skins of the young goats on his hands and the smooth part of his neck. ¹⁷Then she handed the delicious food and the bread she had made to her son Jacob.

¹⁸When he came to his father, he said, "My father."

And he answered, "Here I am. Who are you, my son?"

¹⁹Jacob replied to his father, "I am Esau, your firstborn. I have done as you told me. Please sit up and eat some of my game so that you may bless me."

²⁰But Isaac said to his son, "How did you ever find it so quickly, my son?"

He replied, "Because the Lᴏʀᴅ your God worked it out for me."

²¹Then Isaac said to Jacob, "Please come closer so I can touch you, my son. Are you really my son Esau or not?"

²²So Jacob came closer to his father Isaac. When he touched him, he said, "The voice is the voice of Jacob, but the hands are the hands of Esau." ²³He did not recognize him, because his hands were hairy like those of his brother Esau; so he blessed him. ²⁴Again he asked, "Are you really my son Esau?"

And he replied, "I am."

²⁵Then he said, "Serve me, and let me eat some of my son's game so that I can bless you." Jacob brought it to him, and he ate; he brought him wine, and he drank.

²⁶Then his father Isaac said to him, "Please come closer and kiss me, my son." ²⁷So he came closer and kissed him. When Isaac smelled his clothes, he blessed him and said:

> Ah, the smell of my son
> is like the smell of a field
> that the Lᴏʀᴅ has blessed.
> ²⁸ May God give to you—
> from the dew of the sky
> and from the richness of the land—
> an abundance of grain and new wine.
> ²⁹ May peoples serve you
> and nations bow down to you.
> Be master over your brothers;
> may your mother's sons bow down to you.
> Those who curse you will be cursed,
> and those who bless you will be blessed.

³⁰As soon as Isaac had finished blessing Jacob and Jacob had left the presence of his father Isaac, his brother Esau arrived from the hunt. ³¹He had also made some delicious food and brought it to his father. Then he said to his father, "Let my father get up and eat some of his son's game, so that you may bless me."

³²But his father Isaac said to him, "Who are you?"

He answered, "I am Esau your firstborn son."

³³Isaac began to tremble uncontrollably. "Who was it then," he said, "who hunted game and brought it to me? I ate it all before you came in, and I blessed him. Indeed, he will be blessed!"

³⁴When Esau heard his father's words, he cried out with a loud and bitter cry and said to his father, "Bless me too, my father!"

³⁵But he replied, "Your brother came deceitfully and took your blessing."

³⁶So he said, "Isn't he rightly named Jacob? For he has cheated me twice now. He took my birthright, and look, now he has taken my blessing." Then he asked, "Haven't you saved a blessing for me?"

³⁷But Isaac answered Esau: "Look, I have made him a master over you, have given him all of his relatives as his servants, and have sustained him with grain and new wine. What then can I do for you, my son?"

³⁸Esau said to his father, "Do you only have one blessing, my father? Bless me too, my father!" And Esau wept loudly.

³⁹Then his father Isaac answered him:

Look, your dwelling place will be
away from the richness of the land,
away from the dew of the sky above.
[40] You will live by your sword,
and you will serve your brother.
But when you rebel,
you will break his yoke from your neck.

[41] Esau held a grudge against Jacob because of the blessing his father had given him. And Esau determined in his heart: "The days of mourning for my father are approaching; then I will kill my brother Jacob."

[42] When the words of her older son Esau were reported to Rebekah, she summoned her younger son Jacob and said to him, "Listen, your brother Esau is consoling himself by planning to kill you. [43] So now, my son, listen to me. Flee at once to my brother Laban in Haran, [44] and stay with him for a few days until your brother's anger subsides— [45] until your brother's rage turns away from you and he forgets what you have done to him. Then I will send for you and bring you back from there. Why should I lose you both in one day?"

[46] So Rebekah said to Isaac, "I'm sick of my life because of these Hittite women. If Jacob marries a Hittite woman like one of them, what good is my life?"

28 Isaac summoned Jacob, blessed him, and commanded him: "Don't take a wife from the Canaanite women. [2] Go at once to Paddan-aram, to the house of Bethuel, your mother's father. Marry one of the daughters of Laban, your mother's brother. [3] May ·God Almighty bless you and make you fruitful and multiply you so that you become an assembly of peoples. [4] May God give you and your ·offspring the blessing of Abraham so that you may possess the land where you live as a foreigner, the land God gave to Abraham." [5] So Isaac sent Jacob to Paddan-aram, to Laban son of Bethuel the Aramean, the brother of Rebekah, the mother of Jacob and Esau.

[6] Esau noticed that Isaac blessed Jacob and sent him to Paddan-aram to get a wife there. When he blessed him, Isaac commanded Jacob, "Do not marry a Canaanite woman." [7] And Jacob listened to his father and mother and went to Paddan-aram. [8] Esau realized that his father Isaac disapproved of the Canaanite women, [9] so Esau went to Ishmael and married, in addition to his other wives, Mahalath daughter of Ishmael, Abraham's son. She was the sister of Nebaioth.

[10] Jacob left Beer-sheba and went toward Haran. [11] He reached a certain place and spent the night there because the sun had set. He took one of the stones from the place, put it there at his head, and lay down in that place. [12] And he dreamed: A stairway was set on the ground with its top reaching heaven, and God's angels were going up and down on it. [13] ·Yahweh was standing there beside him, saying, "I am Yahweh, the God of your father Abraham and the God of Isaac. I will give you and your offspring the land that you are now sleeping on. [14] Your offspring will be like the dust of the earth, and you will spread out toward the west, the east, the north, and the south. All the peoples on earth will be blessed through you and your offspring. [15] Look, I am with you and will watch over you wherever you go. I will bring you back to this land, for I will not leave you until I have done what I have promised you."

[16] When Jacob awoke from his sleep, he said, "Surely the LORD is in this place, and I did not know it." [17] He

was afraid and said, "What an awesome place this is! This is none other than the house of God. This is the gate of heaven."

[18] Early in the morning Jacob took the stone that was near his head and set it up as a marker. He poured oil on top of it [19] and named the place Bethel, though previously the city was named Luz. [20] Then Jacob made a vow: "If God will be with me and watch over me on this journey, if He provides me with food to eat and clothing to wear, [21] and if I return safely to my father's house, then the LORD will be my God. [22] This stone that I have set up as a marker will be God's house, and I will give to You a tenth of all that You give me."

29 Jacob resumed his journey and went to the eastern country. [2] He looked and saw a well in a field. Three flocks of sheep were lying there beside it because the sheep were watered from this well. A large stone covered the opening of the well. [3] When all the flocks were gathered there, the shepherds would roll the stone from the opening of the well and water the sheep. The stone was then placed back on the well's opening.

[4] Jacob asked the men at the well, "My brothers! Where are you from?"

"We're from Haran," they answered.

[5] "Do you know Laban grandson of Nahor?" Jacob asked them.

They answered, "We know him."

[6] "Is he well?" Jacob asked.

"Yes," they said, "and here is his daughter Rachel, coming with his sheep."

[7] Then Jacob said, "Look, it is still broad daylight. It's not time for the animals to be gathered. Water the flock, then go out and let them graze."

[8] But they replied, "We can't until all the flocks have been gathered and the stone is rolled from the well's opening. Then we will water the sheep."

[9] While he was still speaking with them, Rachel came with her father's sheep, for she was a shepherdess. [10] As soon as Jacob saw his uncle Laban's daughter Rachel with his sheep, he went up and rolled the stone from the opening and watered his uncle Laban's sheep. [11] Then Jacob kissed Rachel and wept loudly. [12] He told Rachel that he was her father's relative, Rebekah's son. She ran and told her father.

[13] When Laban heard the news about his sister's son Jacob, he ran to meet him, hugged him, and kissed him. Then he took him to his house, and Jacob told him all that had happened.

[14] Laban said to him, "Yes, you are my own flesh and blood."

After Jacob had stayed with him a month, [15] Laban said to him, "Just because you're my relative, should you work for me for nothing? Tell me what your wages should be."

[16] Now Laban had two daughters: the older was named Leah, and the younger was named Rachel. [17] Leah had ordinary eyes, but Rachel was shapely and beautiful. [18] Jacob loved Rachel, so he answered Laban, "I'll work for you seven years for your younger daughter Rachel."

[19] Laban replied, "Better that I give her to you than to some other man. Stay with me." [20] So Jacob worked seven years for Rachel, and they seemed like only a few days to him because of his love for her.

[21] Then Jacob said to Laban, "Give me my wife, for my time is completed. I want to sleep with her." [22] So

Laban invited all the men of the place to a feast. ²³That evening, Laban took his daughter Leah and gave her to Jacob, and he slept with her. ²⁴And Laban gave his slave Zilpah to his daughter Leah as her slave.

²⁵When morning came, there was Leah! So he said to Laban, "What is this you have done to me? Wasn't it for Rachel that I worked for you? Why have you deceived me?"

²⁶Laban answered, "It is not the custom in this place to give the younger daughter in marriage before the firstborn. ²⁷Complete this week of wedding celebration, and we will also give you this younger one in return for working yet another seven years for me."

²⁸And Jacob did just that. He finished the week of celebration, and Laban gave him his daughter Rachel as his wife. ²⁹And Laban gave his slave Bilhah to his daughter Rachel as her slave. ³⁰Jacob slept with Rachel also, and indeed, he loved Rachel more than Leah. And he worked for Laban another seven years.

³¹When the LORD saw that Leah was unloved, He opened her womb; but Rachel was unable to conceive. ³²Leah conceived, gave birth to a son, and named him Reuben, for she said, "The LORD has seen my affliction; surely my husband will love me now."

³³She conceived again, gave birth to a son, and said, "The LORD heard that I am unloved and has given me this son also." So she named him Simeon.

³⁴She conceived again, gave birth to a son, and said, "At last, my husband will become attached to me because I have borne three sons for him." Therefore he was named Levi.

³⁵And she conceived again, gave birth to a son, and said, "This time I will praise the LORD." Therefore she named him Judah. Then Leah stopped having children.

30 When Rachel saw that she was not bearing Jacob any children, she envied her sister. "Give me sons, or I will die!" she said to Jacob.

²Jacob became angry with Rachel and said, "Am I in God's place, who has withheld children from you?"

³Then she said, "Here is my slave Bilhah. Go sleep with her, and she'll bear children for me so that through her I too can build a family." ⁴So Rachel gave her slave Bilhah to Jacob as a wife, and he slept with her. ⁵Bilhah conceived and bore Jacob a son. ⁶Rachel said, "God has vindicated me; yes, He has heard me and given me a son," and she named him Dan.

⁷Rachel's slave Bilhah conceived again and bore Jacob a second son. ⁸Rachel said, "In my wrestlings with God, I have wrestled with my sister and won," and she named him Naphtali.

⁹When Leah saw that she had stopped having children, she took her slave Zilpah and gave her to Jacob as a wife. ¹⁰Leah's slave Zilpah bore Jacob a son. ¹¹Then Leah said, "What good fortune!" and she named him Gad.

¹²When Leah's slave Zilpah bore Jacob a second son, ¹³Leah said, "I am happy that the women call me happy," so she named him Asher.

¹⁴Reuben went out during the wheat harvest and found some mandrakes in the field. When he brought them to his mother Leah, Rachel asked, "Please give me some of your son's mandrakes."

¹⁵But Leah replied to her, "Isn't it enough that you have taken my husband? Now you also want to take my son's mandrakes?"

"Well," Rachel said, "you can sleep with him tonight in exchange for your son's mandrakes."

¹⁶When Jacob came in from the field that evening, Leah went out to meet him and said, "You must come with me, for I have hired you with my son's mandrakes." So Jacob slept with her that night.

¹⁷God listened to Leah, and she conceived and bore Jacob a fifth son. ¹⁸Leah said, "God has rewarded me for giving my slave to my husband," and she named him Issachar.

¹⁹Then Leah conceived again and bore Jacob a sixth son. ²⁰"God has given me a good gift," Leah said. "This time my husband will honor me because I have borne six sons for him," and she named him Zebulun. ²¹Later, Leah bore a daughter and named her Dinah.

²²Then God remembered Rachel. He listened to her and opened her womb. ²³She conceived and bore a son, and said, "God has taken away my shame." ²⁴She named him Joseph: "May the LORD add another son to me."

²⁵After Rachel gave birth to Joseph, Jacob said to Laban, "Send me on my way so that I can return to my homeland. ²⁶Give me my wives and my children that I have worked for, and let me go. You know how hard I have worked for you."

²⁷But Laban said to him, "If I have found favor in your sight, stay. I have learned by ˙divination that the LORD has blessed me because of you." ²⁸Then Laban said, "Name your wages, and I will pay them."

²⁹So Jacob said to him, "You know what I have done for you and your herds. ³⁰For you had very little before I came, but now your wealth has increased. The LORD has blessed you because of me. And now, when will I also do something for my own family?"

³¹Laban asked, "What should I give you?"

And Jacob said, "You don't need to give me anything. If you do this one thing for me, I will continue to shepherd and keep your flock. ³²Let me go through all your sheep today and remove every sheep that is speckled or spotted, every dark-colored sheep among the lambs, and the spotted and speckled among the female goats. Such will be my wages. ³³In the future when you come to check on my wages, my honesty will testify for me. If I have any female goats that are not speckled or spotted, or any lambs that are not black, they will be considered stolen."

³⁴"Good," said Laban. "Let it be as you have said."

³⁵That day Laban removed the streaked and spotted male goats and all the speckled and spotted female goats—every one that had any white on it—and every dark-colored one among the lambs, and he placed his sons in charge of them. ³⁶He put a three-day journey between himself and Jacob. Jacob, meanwhile, was shepherding the rest of Laban's flock.

³⁷Jacob then took branches of fresh poplar, almond, and plane wood, and peeled the bark, exposing white stripes on the branches. ³⁸He set the peeled branches in the troughs in front of the sheep—in the water channels where the sheep came to drink. And the sheep bred when they came to drink. ³⁹The flocks bred in front of the branches and bore streaked, speckled, and spotted young. ⁴⁰Jacob separated the lambs and made the flocks face the streaked and the completely dark sheep in Laban's flocks. Then he set his own stock apart and didn't put them with Laban's sheep.

⁴¹Whenever the stronger of the flock were breeding, Jacob placed the branches in the troughs, in full

view of the flocks, and they would breed in front of the branches. [42] As for the weaklings of the flocks, he did not put out the branches. So it turned out that the weak sheep belonged to Laban and the stronger ones to Jacob. [43] And the man became very rich. He had many flocks, male and female slaves, and camels and donkeys.

31 Now Jacob heard what Laban's sons were saying: "Jacob has taken all that was our father's and has built this wealth from what belonged to our father." [2] And Jacob saw from Laban's face that his attitude toward him was not the same.

[3] Then the LORD said to him, "Go back to the land of your fathers and to your family, and I will be with you."

[4] Jacob had Rachel and Leah called to the field where his flocks were. [5] He said to them, "I can see from your father's face that his attitude toward me is not the same, but the God of my father has been with me. [6] You know that I've worked hard for your father [7] and that he has cheated me and changed my wages 10 times. But God has not let him harm me. [8] If he said, 'The spotted sheep will be your wages,' then all the sheep were born spotted. If he said, 'The streaked sheep will be your wages,' then all the sheep were born streaked. [9] God has taken away your father's herds and given them to me.

[10] "When the flocks were breeding, I saw in a dream that the streaked, spotted, and speckled males were mating with the females. [11] In that dream the Angel of God said to me, 'Jacob!' and I said, 'Here I am.' [12] And He said, 'Look up and see: all the males that are mating with the flocks are streaked, spotted, and speckled, for I have seen all that Laban has been doing to you. [13] I am the God of Bethel, where you poured oil on the stone marker and made a solemn vow to Me. Get up, leave this land, and return to your native land.'"

[14] Then Rachel and Leah answered him, "Do we have any portion or inheritance in our father's household? [15] Are we not regarded by him as outsiders? For he has sold us and has certainly spent our money. [16] In fact, all the wealth that God has taken away from our father belongs to us and to our children. So do whatever God has said to you."

[17] So Jacob got up and put his children and wives on the camels. [18] He took all the livestock and possessions he had acquired in Paddan-aram, and he drove his herds to go to the land of his father Isaac in Canaan. [19] When Laban had gone to shear his sheep, Rachel stole her father's household idols. [20] And Jacob deceived Laban the Aramean, not telling him that he was fleeing. [21] He fled with all his possessions, crossed the Euphrates, and headed for the hill country of Gilead.

[22] On the third day Laban was told that Jacob had fled. [23] So he took his relatives with him, pursued Jacob for seven days, and overtook him at Mount Gilead. [24] But God came to Laban the Aramean in a dream at night. "Watch yourself!" God warned him. "Don't say anything to Jacob, either good or bad."

[25] When Laban overtook Jacob, Jacob had pitched his tent in the hill country, and Laban and his brothers also pitched their tents in the hill country of Gilead. [26] Then Laban said to Jacob, "What have you done? You have deceived me and taken my daughters away like prisoners of war! [27] Why did you secretly flee from me, deceive me, and not tell me? I would have sent you away with joy and singing, with tambourines and lyres, [28] but you didn't even let me kiss my grandchildren and my daughters. You have acted foolishly. [29] I could do you great harm, but last night the God of your father said to me: 'Watch yourself. Don't say anything to Jacob, either good or bad.' [30] Now you have gone off because you long for your father—but why have you stolen my gods?"

[31] Jacob answered, "I was afraid, for I thought you would take your daughters from me by force. [32] If you find your gods with anyone here, he will not live! Before our relatives, point out anything that is yours and take it." Jacob did not know that Rachel had stolen the idols.

[33] So Laban went into Jacob's tent, then Leah's tent, and then the tents of the two female slaves, but he found nothing. Then he left Leah's tent and entered Rachel's. [34] Now Rachel had taken Laban's household idols, put them in the saddlebag of the camel, and sat on them. Laban searched the whole tent but found nothing.

[35] She said to her father, "Sir, don't be angry that I cannot stand up in your presence; I am having my period." So Laban searched, but could not find the household idols.

[36] Then Jacob became incensed and brought charges against Laban. "What is my crime?" he said to Laban. "What is my sin, that you have pursued me? [37] You've searched all my possessions! Have you found anything of yours? Put it here before my relatives and yours, and let them decide between the two of us. [38] I've been with you these 20 years. Your ewes and female goats have not miscarried, and I have not eaten the rams from your flock. [39] I did not bring you any of the flock torn by wild beasts; I myself bore the loss. You demanded payment from me for what was stolen by day or by night. [40] There I was—the heat consumed me by day and the frost by night, and sleep fled from my eyes. [41] For 20 years I have worked in your household—14 years for your two daughters and six years for your flocks—and you have changed my wages 10 times! [42] If the God of my father, the God of Abraham, the Fear of Isaac, had not been with me, certainly now you would have sent me off empty-handed. But God has seen my affliction and my hard work, and He issued His verdict last night."

[43] Then Laban answered Jacob, "The daughters are my daughters; the sons, my sons; and the flocks, my flocks! Everything you see is mine! But what can I do today for these daughters of mine or for the children they have borne? [44] Come now, let's make a covenant, you and I. Let it be a witness between the two of us."

[45] So Jacob picked out a stone and set it up as a marker. [46] Then Jacob said to his relatives, "Gather stones." And they took stones and made a mound, then ate there by the mound. [47] Laban named the mound Jegar-sahadutha, but Jacob named it Galeed.

[48] Then Laban said, "This mound is a witness between you and me today." Therefore the place was called Galeed [49] and also Mizpah, for he said, "May the LORD watch between you and me when we are out of each other's sight. [50] If you mistreat my daughters or take other wives, though no one is with us, understand that God will be a witness between you and me."

[51] Laban also said to Jacob, "Look at this mound and the marker I have set up between you and me. [52] This mound is a witness and the marker is a witness that I will not pass beyond this mound to you, and you will

not pass beyond this mound and this marker to do me harm. ⁵³The God of Abraham, and the gods of Nahor—the gods of their father—will judge between us." And Jacob swore by the Fear of his father Isaac. ⁵⁴Then Jacob offered a sacrifice on the mountain and invited his relatives to eat a meal. So they ate a meal and spent the night on the mountain. ⁵⁵Laban got up early in the morning, kissed his grandchildren and daughters, and blessed them. Then Laban left to return home.

32 Jacob went on his way, and God's angels met him. ²When he saw them, Jacob said, "This is God's camp." So he called that place Mahanaim.

³Jacob sent messengers ahead of him to his brother Esau in the land of Seir, the country of Edom. ⁴He commanded them, "You are to say to my lord Esau, 'This is what your servant Jacob says. I have been staying with Laban and have been delayed until now. ⁵I have oxen, donkeys, flocks, male and female slaves. I have sent this message to inform my lord, in order to seek your favor.'"

⁶When the messengers returned to Jacob, they said, "We went to your brother Esau; he is coming to meet you—and he has 400 men with him." ⁷Jacob was greatly afraid and distressed; he divided the people with him into two camps, along with the flocks, cattle, and camels. ⁸He thought, "If Esau comes to one camp and attacks it, the remaining one can escape."

⁹Then Jacob said, "God of my father Abraham and God of my father Isaac, the LORD who said to me, 'Go back to your land and to your family, and I will cause you to prosper,' ¹⁰I am unworthy of all the kindness and faithfulness You have shown Your servant. Indeed, I crossed over this Jordan with my staff, and now I have become two camps. ¹¹Please rescue me from the hand of my brother Esau, for I am afraid of him; otherwise, he may come and attack me, the mothers, and their children. ¹²You have said, 'I will cause you to prosper, and I will make your *offspring like the sand of the sea, which cannot be counted.'"

¹³He spent the night there and took part of what he had brought with him as a gift for his brother Esau: ¹⁴200 female goats, 20 male goats, 200 ewes, 20 rams, ¹⁵30 milk camels with their young, 40 cows, 10 bulls, 20 female donkeys, and 10 male donkeys. ¹⁶He entrusted them to his slaves as separate herds and said to them, "Go on ahead of me, and leave some distance between the herds."

¹⁷And he told the first one: "When my brother Esau meets you and asks, 'Who do you belong to? Where are you going? And whose animals are these ahead of you?' ¹⁸then tell him, 'They belong to your servant Jacob. They are a gift sent to my lord Esau. And look, he is behind us.'"

¹⁹He also told the second one, the third, and everyone who was walking behind the animals, "Say the same thing to Esau when you find him. ²⁰You are also to say, 'Look, your servant Jacob is right behind us.'" For he thought, "I want to appease Esau with the gift that is going ahead of me. After that, I can face him, and perhaps he will forgive me."

²¹So the gift was sent on ahead of him while he remained in the camp that night. ²²During the night Jacob got up and took his two wives, his two female slaves, and his 11 sons, and crossed the ford of Jabbok. ²³He took them and sent them across the stream, along with all his possessions.

²⁴Jacob was left alone, and a man wrestled with him until daybreak. ²⁵When the man saw that He could not defeat him, He struck Jacob's hip socket as they wrestled and dislocated his hip. ²⁶Then He said to Jacob, "Let Me go, for it is daybreak."

But Jacob said, "I will not let You go unless You bless me."

²⁷"What is your name?" the man asked.

"Jacob," he replied.

²⁸"Your name will no longer be Jacob," He said. "It will be Israel because you have struggled with God and with men and have prevailed."

²⁹Then Jacob asked Him, "Please tell me Your name."

But He answered, "Why do you ask My name?" And He blessed him there.

³⁰Jacob then named the place Peniel, "For I have seen God face to face," he said, "and I have been delivered." ³¹The sun shone on him as he passed by Penuel—limping because of his hip. ³²That is why, to this day, the Israelites don't eat the thigh muscle that is at the hip socket: because He struck Jacob's hip socket at the thigh muscle.

33 Now Jacob looked up and saw Esau coming toward him with 400 men. So he divided the children among Leah, Rachel, and the two female slaves. ²He put the female slaves and their children first, Leah and her children next, and Rachel and Joseph last. ³He himself went on ahead and bowed to the ground seven times until he approached his brother.

⁴But Esau ran to meet him, hugged him, threw his arms around him, and kissed him. Then they wept. ⁵When Esau looked up and saw the women and children, he asked, "Who are these with you?"

He answered, "The children God has graciously given your servant." ⁶Then the female slaves and their children approached him and bowed down. ⁷Leah and her children also approached and bowed down, and then Joseph and Rachel approached and bowed down.

⁸So Esau said, "What do you mean by this whole procession I met?"

"To find favor with you, my lord," he answered.

⁹"I have enough, my brother," Esau replied. "Keep what you have."

¹⁰But Jacob said, "No, please! If I have found favor with you, take this gift from my hand. For indeed, I have seen your face, and it is like seeing God's face, since you have accepted me. ¹¹Please take my present that was brought to you, because God has been gracious to me and I have everything I need." So Jacob urged him until he accepted.

¹²Then Esau said, "Let's move on, and I'll go ahead of you."

¹³Jacob replied, "My lord knows that the children are weak, and I have nursing sheep and cattle. If they are driven hard for one day, the whole herd will die. ¹⁴Let my lord go ahead of his servant. I will continue on slowly, at a pace suited to the livestock and the children, until I come to my lord at Seir."

¹⁵Esau said, "Let me leave some of my people with you."

But he replied, "Why do that? Please indulge me, my lord."

¹⁶That day Esau started on his way back to Seir, ¹⁷but Jacob went on to Succoth. He built a house for himself and stalls for his livestock; that is why the place was called Succoth.

¹⁸After Jacob came from Paddan-aram, he arrived

safely at Shechem in the land of Canaan and camped in front of the city. ¹⁹He purchased a section of the field where he had pitched his tent from the sons of Hamor, Shechem's father, for 100 *qesitahs*. ²⁰And he set up an altar there and called it "God, the God of Israel."

34 Dinah, Leah's daughter whom she bore to Jacob, went out to see some of the young women of the area. ²When Shechem son of Hamor the Hivite, a prince of a region, saw her, he took her and raped her. ³He became infatuated with Dinah, daughter of Jacob. He loved the young girl and spoke tenderly to her. ⁴"Get me this girl as a wife," he told his father Hamor.

⁵Jacob heard that Shechem had defiled his daughter Dinah, but since his sons were with his livestock in the field, he remained silent until they returned. ⁶Meanwhile, Shechem's father Hamor came to speak with Jacob. ⁷Jacob's sons returned from the field when they heard about the incident and were deeply grieved and angry. For Shechem had committed an outrage against Israel by raping Jacob's daughter, and such a thing should not be done.

⁸Hamor said to Jacob's sons, "My son Shechem is strongly attracted to your daughter. Please give her to him as a wife. ⁹Intermarry with us; give your daughters to us, and take our daughters for yourselves. ¹⁰Live with us. The land is before you. Settle here, move about, and acquire property in it."

¹¹Then Shechem said to Dinah's father and brothers, "Grant me this favor, and I'll give you whatever you say. ¹²Demand of me a high compensation and gift; I'll give you whatever you ask me. Just give the girl to me be my wife!"

¹³But Jacob's sons answered Shechem and his father Hamor deceitfully because he had defiled their sister Dinah. ¹⁴"We cannot do this thing," they said to them. "Giving our sister to an uncircumcised man is a disgrace to us. ¹⁵We will agree with you only on this condition: if all your males are circumcised as we are. ¹⁶Then we will give you our daughters, take your daughters for ourselves, live with you, and become one people. ¹⁷But if you will not listen to us and be circumcised, then we will take our daughter and go."

¹⁸Their words seemed good to Hamor and his son Shechem. ¹⁹The young man did not delay doing this, because he was delighted with Jacob's daughter. Now he was the most important in all his father's house. ²⁰So Hamor and his son Shechem went to the ˙gate of their city and spoke to the men there.

²¹"These men are peaceful toward us," they said. "Let them live in our land and move about in it, for indeed, the region is large enough for them. Let us take their daughters as our wives and give our daughters to them. ²²But the men will agree to live with us and be one people only on this condition: if all our men are circumcised as they are. ²³Won't their livestock, their possessions, and all their animals become ours? Only let us agree with them, and they will live with us."

²⁴All the able-bodied men listened to Hamor and his son Shechem, and all the able-bodied men were circumcised. ²⁵On the third day, when they were still in pain, two of Jacob's sons, Simeon and Levi, Dinah's brothers, took their swords, went into the unsuspecting city, and killed every male. ²⁶They killed Hamor and his son Shechem with their swords, took Dinah from Shechem's house, and went away. ²⁷Jacob's other sons came to the slaughter and plundered the city because their sister had been defiled. ²⁸They took their sheep, cattle, donkeys, and whatever was in the city and in the field. ²⁹They captured all their possessions, children, and wives and plundered everything in the houses.

³⁰Then Jacob said to Simeon and Levi, "You have brought trouble on me, making me odious to the inhabitants of the land, the Canaanites and the Perizzites. We are few in number; if they unite against me and attack me, I and my household will be destroyed." ³¹But they answered, "Should he have treated our sister like a prostitute?"

35 God said to Jacob, "Get up! Go to Bethel and settle there. Build an altar there to the God who appeared to you when you fled from your brother Esau."

²So Jacob said to his family and all who were with him, "Get rid of the foreign gods that are among you. Purify yourselves and change your clothes. ³We must get up and go to Bethel. I will build an altar there to the God who answered me in my day of distress. He has been with me everywhere I have gone."

⁴Then they gave Jacob all their foreign gods and their earrings, and Jacob hid them under the oak near Shechem. ⁵When they set out, a terror from God came over the cities around them, and they did not pursue Jacob's sons. ⁶So Jacob and all who were with him came to Luz (that is, Bethel) in the land of Canaan. ⁷Jacob built an altar there and called the place God of Bethel because it was there that God had revealed Himself to him when he was fleeing from his brother.

⁸Deborah, the one who had nursed and raised Rebekah, died and was buried under the oak south of Bethel. So Jacob named it Oak of Weeping.

⁹God appeared to Jacob again after he returned from Paddan-aram, and He blessed him. ¹⁰God said to him:

Your name is Jacob;
you will no longer be named Jacob,
but your name will be Israel.

So He named him Israel. ¹¹God also said to him:

I am ˙God Almighty.
Be fruitful and multiply.
A nation, indeed an assembly of nations,
will come from you,
and kings will descend from you.
¹²   I will give to you the land
that I gave to Abraham and Isaac.
And I will give the land
to your future descendants.

¹³Then God withdrew from him at the place where He had spoken to him.

¹⁴Jacob set up a marker at the place where He had spoken to him—a stone marker. He poured a drink offering on it and anointed it with oil. ¹⁵Jacob named the place where God had spoken with him Bethel.

¹⁶They set out from Bethel. When they were still some distance from Ephrath, Rachel began to give birth, and her labor was difficult. ¹⁷During her difficult labor, the midwife said to her, "Don't be afraid, for you have another son." ¹⁸With her last breath—for she was dying—she named him Ben-oni, but his father called him Benjamin. ¹⁹So Rachel died and was buried on the way to Ephrath (that is, Bethlehem). ²⁰Jacob set up a marker on her grave; it is the marker at Rachel's grave to this day.

²¹Israel set out again and pitched his tent beyond the Tower of Eder. ²²While Israel was living in that

region, Reuben went in and slept with his father's concubine Bilhah, and Israel heard about it.

Jacob had 12 sons:
²³ Leah's sons were Reuben (Jacob's firstborn),
Simeon, Levi, Judah,
Issachar, and Zebulun.
²⁴ Rachel's sons were
Joseph and Benjamin.
²⁵ The sons of Rachel's slave Bilhah
were Dan and Naphtali.
²⁶ The sons of Leah's slave Zilpah
were Gad and Asher.

These are the sons of Jacob, who were born to him in Paddan-aram.

²⁷ Jacob came to his father Isaac at Mamre in Kiriath-arba (that is, Hebron), where Abraham and Isaac had stayed. ²⁸ Isaac lived 180 years. ²⁹ He took his last breath and died, and was gathered to his people, old and full of days. His sons Esau and Jacob buried him.

36 These are the family records of Esau (that is, Edom). ² Esau took his wives from the Canaanite women: Adah daughter of Elon the Hittite, Oholibamah daughter of Anah and granddaughter of Zibeon the Hivite, ³ and Basemath daughter of Ishmael and sister of Nebaioth. ⁴ Adah bore Eliphaz to Esau, Basemath bore Reuel, ⁵ and Oholibamah bore Jeush, Jalam, and Korah. These were Esau's sons, who were born to him in the land of Canaan.

⁶ Esau took his wives, sons, daughters, and all the people of his household, as well as his herds, all his livestock, and all the property he had acquired in Canaan; he went to a land away from his brother Jacob. ⁷ For their possessions were too many for them to live together, and because of their herds, the land where they stayed could not support them. ⁸ So Esau (that is, Edom) lived in the mountains of Seir.

⁹ These are the family records of Esau, father of the Edomites in the mountains of Seir.
¹⁰ These are the names of Esau's sons:
Eliphaz son of Esau's wife Adah,
and Reuel son of Esau's wife Basemath.
¹¹ The sons of Eliphaz were
Teman, Omar, Zepho, Gatam, and Kenaz.
¹² Timna, a concubine of Esau's son Eliphaz,
bore Amalek to Eliphaz.
These were the sons of Esau's wife Adah.
¹³ These are Reuel's sons:
Nahath, Zerah, Shammah, and Mizzah.
These were the sons of Esau's wife Basemath.
¹⁴ These are the sons of Esau's wife Oholibamah
daughter of Anah and granddaughter
of Zibeon:
She bore Jeush, Jalam, and Korah to Edom.
¹⁵ These are the chiefs of Esau's sons:
the sons of Eliphaz, Esau's firstborn:
Chiefs Teman, Omar, Zepho, Kenaz,
¹⁶ Korah, Gatam, and Amalek.
These are the chiefs of Eliphaz
in the land of Edom.
These are the sons of Adah.
¹⁷ These are the sons of Reuel, Esau's son:
Chiefs Nahath, Zerah, Shammah, and Mizzah.
These are the chiefs of Reuel
in the land of Edom.
These are the sons of Esau's wife Basemath.
¹⁸ These are the sons of Esau's wife Oholibamah:
Chiefs Jeush, Jalam, and Korah.

These are the chiefs of Esau's wife
Oholibamah
daughter of Anah.
¹⁹ These are the sons of Esau (that is, Edom),
and these are their chiefs.
²⁰ These are the sons of Seir the Horite,
the inhabitants of the land:
Lotan, Shobal, Zibeon, Anah,
²¹ Dishon, Ezer, and Dishan.
These are the chiefs of the Horites,
the sons of Seir, in the land of Edom.
²² The sons of Lotan were Hori and Heman.
Timna was Lotan's sister.
²³ These are Shobal's sons:
Alvan, Manahath, Ebal, Shepho, and Onam.
²⁴ These was Zibeon's sons: Aiah and Anah.
This was the Anah who found the hot springs
in the wilderness
while he was pasturing the donkeys
of his father Zibeon.
²⁵ These are the children of Anah:
Dishon and Oholibamah daughter of Anah.
²⁶ These are Dishon's sons:
Hemdan, Eshban, Ithran, and Cheran.
²⁷ These are Ezer's sons:
Bilhan, Zaavan, and Akan.
²⁸ These are Dishan's sons: Uz and Aran.
²⁹ These are the chiefs of the Horites:
Chiefs Lotan, Shobal, Zibeon, Anah,
³⁰ Dishon, Ezer, and Dishan.
These are the chiefs of the Horites,
according to their divisions, in the land
of Seir.
³¹ These are the kings who ruled in the land
of Edom
before any king ruled over the Israelites:
³² Bela son of Beor ruled in Edom;
the name of his city was Dinhabah.
³³ When Bela died, Jobab son of Zerah
from Bozrah became king in his place.
³⁴ When Jobab died, Husham from the land
of the Temanites became king in his place.
³⁵ When Husham died, Hadad son of Bedad
became king in his place.
He defeated Midian in the field of Moab;
the name of his city was Avith.
³⁶ When Hadad died, Samlah from Masrekah
became king in his place.
³⁷ When Samlah died, Shaul from Rehoboth
on the Euphrates River became king
in his place.
³⁸ When Shaul died, Baal-hanan son of Achbor
became king in his place.
³⁹ When Baal-hanan son of Achbor died, Hadar
became king in his place.
His city was Pau, and his wife's name
was Mehetabel
daughter of Matred daughter of Me-zahab.
⁴⁰ These are the names of Esau's chiefs,
according to their families and their localities,
by their names:
Chiefs Timna, Alvah, Jetheth,
⁴¹ Oholibamah, Elah, Pinon,
⁴² Kenaz, Teman, Mibzar,
⁴³ Magdiel, and Iram.
These are Edom's chiefs,

according to their settlements in the land
they possessed.
Esau was father of the Edomites.

37 Jacob lived in the land where his father had stayed, the land of Canaan. ²These are the family records of Jacob.

At 17 years of age, Joseph tended sheep with his brothers. The young man was working with the sons of Bilhah and Zilpah, his father's wives, and he brought a bad report about them to their father.

³Now Israel loved Joseph more than his other sons because Joseph was a son born to him in his old age, and he made a robe of many colors for him. ⁴When his brothers saw that their father loved him more than all his brothers, they hated him and could not bring themselves to speak peaceably to him.

⁵Then Joseph had a dream. When he told it to his brothers, they hated him even more. ⁶He said to them, "Listen to this dream I had: ⁷There we were, binding sheaves of grain in the field. Suddenly my sheaf stood up, and your sheaves gathered around it and bowed down to my sheaf."

⁸"Are you really going to reign over us?" his brothers asked him. "Are you really going to rule us?" So they hated him even more because of his dream and what he had said.

⁹Then he had another dream and told it to his brothers. "Look," he said, "I had another dream, and this time the sun, moon, and 11 stars were bowing down to me."

¹⁰He told his father and brothers, but his father rebuked him. "What kind of dream is this that you have had?" he said. "Are your mother and brothers and I going to come and bow down to the ground before you?" ¹¹His brothers were jealous of him, but his father kept the matter in mind.

¹²His brothers had gone to pasture their father's flocks at Shechem. ¹³Israel said to Joseph, "Your brothers, you know, are pasturing the flocks at Shechem. Get ready. I'm sending you to them."

"I'm ready," Joseph replied.

¹⁴Then Israel said to him, "Go and see how your brothers and the flocks are doing, and bring word back to me." So he sent him from the Valley of Hebron, and he went to Shechem.

¹⁵A man found him there, wandering in the field, and asked him, "What are you looking for?"

¹⁶"I'm looking for my brothers," Joseph said. "Can you tell me where they are pasturing their flocks?"

¹⁷"They've moved on from here," the man said. "I heard them say, 'Let's go to Dothan.'" So Joseph set out after his brothers and found them at Dothan.

¹⁸They saw him in the distance, and before he had reached them, they plotted to kill him. ¹⁹They said to one another, "Here comes that dreamer! ²⁰Come on, let's kill him and throw him into one of the pits. We can say that a vicious animal ate him. Then we'll see what becomes of his dreams!"

²¹When Reuben heard this, he tried to save him from them. He said, "Let's not take his life." ²²Reuben also said to them, "Don't shed blood. Throw him into this pit in the wilderness, but don't lay a hand on him"—intending to rescue him from their hands and return him to his father.

²³When Joseph came to his brothers, they stripped off his robe, the robe of many colors that he had on.

²⁴Then they took him and threw him into the pit. The pit was empty; there was no water in it.

²⁵Then they sat down to eat a meal. They looked up, and there was a caravan of Ishmaelites coming from Gilead. Their camels were carrying aromatic gum, balsam, and resin, going down to Egypt.

²⁶Then Judah said to his brothers, "What do we gain if we kill our brother and cover up his blood? ²⁷Come, let's sell him to the Ishmaelites and not lay a hand on him, for he is our brother, our own flesh," and they agreed. ²⁸When Midianite traders passed by, his brothers pulled Joseph out of the pit and sold him for 20 pieces of silver to the Ishmaelites, who took Joseph to Egypt.

²⁹When Reuben returned to the pit and saw that Joseph was not there, he tore his clothes. ³⁰He went back to his brothers and said, "The boy is gone! What am I going to do?" ³¹So they took Joseph's robe, slaughtered a young goat, and dipped the robe in its blood. ³²They sent the robe of many colors to their father and said, "We found this. Examine it. Is it your son's robe or not?"

³³His father recognized it. "It is my son's robe," he said. "A vicious animal has devoured him. Joseph has been torn to pieces!" ³⁴Then Jacob tore his clothes, put •sackcloth around his waist, and mourned for his son many days. ³⁵All his sons and daughters tried to comfort him, but he refused to be comforted. "No," he said. "I will go down to •Sheol to my son, mourning." And his father wept for him.

³⁶Meanwhile, the Midianites sold Joseph in Egypt to Potiphar, an officer of Pharaoh and the captain of the guard.

38 At that time Judah left his brothers and settled near an Adullamite named Hirah. ²There Judah saw the daughter of a Canaanite named Shua; he took her as a wife and slept with her. ³She conceived and gave birth to a son, and he named him Er. ⁴She conceived again, gave birth to a son, and named him Onan. ⁵She gave birth to another son and named him Shelah. It was at Chezib that she gave birth to him.

⁶Judah got a wife for Er, his firstborn, and her name was Tamar. ⁷Now Er, Judah's firstborn, was evil in the LORD's sight, and the LORD put him to death. ⁸Then Judah said to Onan, "Sleep with your brother's wife. Perform your duty as her brother-in-law and produce •offspring for your brother." ⁹But Onan knew that the offspring would not be his, so whenever he slept with his brother's wife, he released his semen on the ground so that he would not produce offspring for his brother. ¹⁰What he did was evil in the LORD's sight, so He put him to death also.

¹¹Then Judah said to his daughter-in-law Tamar, "Remain a widow in your father's house until my son Shelah grows up." For he thought, "He might die too, like his brothers." So Tamar went to live in her father's house.

¹²After a long time Judah's wife, the daughter of Shua, died. When Judah had finished mourning, he and his friend Hirah the Adullamite went up to Timnah to the sheepshearers. ¹³Tamar was told, "Your father-in-law is going up to Timnah to shear his sheep." ¹⁴So she took off her widow's clothes, veiled her face, covered herself, and sat at the entrance to Enaim, which is on the way to Timnah. For she saw that, though Shelah had grown up, she had not been given

to him as a wife. ¹⁵When Judah saw her, he thought she was a prostitute, for she had covered her face.

¹⁶He went over to her and said, "Come, let me sleep with you," for he did not know that she was his daughter-in-law.

She said, "What will you give me for sleeping with me?"

¹⁷"I will send you a young goat from my flock," he replied.

But she said, "Only if you leave something with me until you send it."

¹⁸"What should I give you?" he asked.

She answered, "Your signet ring, your cord, and the staff in your hand." So he gave them to her and slept with her, and she got pregnant by him. ¹⁹She got up and left, then removed her veil and put her widow's clothes back on.

²⁰When Judah sent the young goat by his friend the Adullamite in order to get back the items he had left with the woman, he could not find her. ²¹He asked the men of the place, "Where is the cult prostitute who was beside the road at Enaim?"

"There has been no cult prostitute here," they answered.

²²So the Adullamite returned to Judah, saying, "I couldn't find her, and furthermore, the men of the place said, 'There has been no cult prostitute here.'"

²³Judah replied, "Let her keep the items for herself; otherwise we will become a laughingstock. After all, I did send this young goat, but you couldn't find her."

²⁴About three months later Judah was told, "Your daughter-in-law, Tamar, has been acting like a prostitute, and now she is pregnant."

"Bring her out!" Judah said. "Let her be burned to death!"

²⁵As she was being brought out, she sent her father-in-law this message: "I am pregnant by the man to whom these items belong." And she added, "Examine them. Whose signet ring, cord, and staff are these?"

²⁶Judah recognized them and said, "She is more in the right than I, since I did not give her to my son Shelah." And he did not know her intimately again.

²⁷When the time came for her to give birth, there were twins in her womb. ²⁸As she was giving birth, one of them put out his hand, and the midwife took it and tied a scarlet thread around it, announcing, "This one came out first." ²⁹But then he pulled his hand back, and his brother came out. Then she said, "You have broken out first!" So he was named Perez. ³⁰Then his brother, who had the scarlet thread tied to his hand, came out, and was named Zerah.

39 Now Joseph had been taken to Egypt. An Egyptian named Potiphar, an officer of Pharaoh and the captain of the guard, bought him from the Ishmaelites who had brought him there. ²The Lᴏʀᴅ was with Joseph, and he became a successful man, serving in the household of his Egyptian master. ³When his master saw that the Lᴏʀᴅ was with him and that the Lᴏʀᴅ made everything he did successful, ⁴Joseph found favor in his master's sight and became his personal attendant. Potiphar also put him in charge of his household and placed all that he owned under his authority. ⁵From the time that he put him in charge of his household and of all that he owned, the Lᴏʀᴅ blessed the Egyptian's house because of Joseph. The Lᴏʀᴅ's blessing was on all that he owned, in his house and in his fields. ⁶He left all that he owned under Jo-

seph's authority; he did not concern himself with anything except the food he ate.

Now Joseph was well-built and handsome. ⁷After some time his master's wife looked longingly at Joseph and said, "Sleep with me."

⁸But he refused. "Look," he said to his master's wife, "with me here my master does not concern himself with anything in his house, and he has put all that he owns under my authority. ⁹No one in this house is greater than I am. He has withheld nothing from me except you, because you are his wife. So how could I do such a great evil and sin against God?"

¹⁰Although she spoke to Joseph day after day, he refused to go to bed with her. ¹¹Now one day he went into the house to do his work, and none of the household servants were there. ¹²She grabbed him by his garment and said, "Sleep with me!" But leaving his garment in her hand, he escaped and ran outside. ¹³When she saw that he had left his garment with her and had run outside, ¹⁴she called the household servants. "Look," she said to them, "my husband brought a Hebrew man to make fools of us. He came to me so he could sleep with me, and I screamed as loud as I could. ¹⁵When he heard me screaming for help, he left his garment with me and ran outside."

¹⁶She put Joseph's garment beside her until his master came home. ¹⁷Then she told him the same story: "The Hebrew slave you brought to us came to make a fool of me, ¹⁸but when I screamed for help, he left his garment with me and ran outside."

¹⁹When his master heard the story his wife told him—"These are the things your slave did to me"—he was furious ²⁰and had him thrown into prison, where the king's prisoners were confined. So Joseph was there in prison.

²¹But the Lᴏʀᴅ was with Joseph and extended kindness to him. He granted him favor in the eyes of the prison warden. ²²The warden put all the prisoners who were in the prison under Joseph's authority, and he was responsible for everything that was done there. ²³The warden did not bother with anything under Joseph's authority, because the Lᴏʀᴅ was with him, and the Lᴏʀᴅ made everything that he did successful.

40 After this, the Egyptian king's cupbearer and baker offended their master, the king of Egypt. ²Pharaoh was angry with his two officers, the chief cupbearer and the chief baker, ³and put them in custody in the house of the captain of the guard in the prison where Joseph was confined. ⁴The captain of the guard assigned Joseph to them, and he became their personal attendant. And they were in custody for some time.

⁵The Egyptian king's cupbearer and baker, who were confined in the prison, each had a dream. Both had a dream on the same night, and each dream had its own meaning. ⁶When Joseph came to them in the morning, he saw that they looked distraught. ⁷So he asked Pharaoh's officers who were in custody with him in his master's house, "Why do you look so sad today?"

⁸"We had dreams," they said to him, "but there is no one to interpret them."

Then Joseph said to them, "Don't interpretations belong to God? Tell me your dreams."

⁹So the chief cupbearer told his dream to Joseph: "In my dream there was a vine in front of me. ¹⁰On the vine were three branches. As soon as it budded, its blossoms came out and its clusters ripened into

grapes. [11] Pharaoh's cup was in my hand, and I took the grapes, squeezed them into Pharaoh's cup, and placed the cup in Pharaoh's hand."

[12] "This is its interpretation," Joseph said to him. "The three branches are three days. [13] In just three days Pharaoh will lift up your head and restore you to your position. You will put Pharaoh's cup in his hand the way you used to when you were his cupbearer. [14] But when all goes well for you, remember that I was with you. Please show kindness to me by mentioning me to Pharaoh, and get me out of this prison. [15] For I was kidnapped from the land of the Hebrews, and even here I have done nothing that they should put me in the dungeon."

[16] When the chief baker saw that the interpretation was positive, he said to Joseph, "I also had a dream. Three baskets of white bread were on my head. [17] In the top basket were all sorts of baked goods for Pharaoh, but the birds were eating them out of the basket on my head."

[18] "This is its interpretation," Joseph replied. "The three baskets are three days. [19] In just three days Pharaoh will lift up your head—from off you—and hang you on a tree. Then the birds will eat the flesh from your body."

[20] On the third day, which was Pharaoh's birthday, he gave a feast for all his servants. He lifted up the heads of the chief cupbearer and the chief baker. [21] Pharaoh restored the chief cupbearer to his position as cupbearer, and he placed the cup in Pharaoh's hand. [22] But Pharaoh hanged the chief baker, just as Joseph had explained to them. [23] Yet the chief cupbearer did not remember Joseph; he forgot him.

41 Two years later Pharaoh had a dream: He was standing beside the Nile, [2] when seven healthy-looking, well-fed cows came up from the Nile and began to graze among the reeds. [3] After them, seven other cows, sickly and thin, came up from the Nile and stood beside those cows along the bank of the Nile. [4] The sickly, thin cows ate the healthy, well-fed cows. Then Pharaoh woke up. [5] He fell asleep and dreamed a second time: Seven heads of grain, plump and ripe, came up on one stalk. [6] After them, seven heads of grain, thin and scorched by the east wind, sprouted up. [7] The thin heads of grain swallowed up the seven plump, ripe ones. Then Pharaoh woke up, and it was only a dream.

[8] When morning came, he was troubled, so he summoned all the magicians of Egypt and all its wise men. Pharaoh told them his dreams, but no one could interpret them for him.

[9] Then the chief cupbearer said to Pharaoh, "Today I remember my faults. [10] Pharaoh had been angry with his servants, and he put me and the chief baker in the custody of the captain of the guard. [11] He and I had dreams on the same night; each dream had its own meaning. [12] Now a young Hebrew, a slave of the captain of the guards, was with us there. We told him our dreams, he interpreted our dreams for us, and each had its own interpretation. [13] It turned out just the way he interpreted them to us: I was restored to my position, and the other man was hanged."

[14] Then Pharaoh sent for Joseph, and they quickly brought him from the dungeon. He shaved, changed his clothes, and went to Pharaoh.

[15] Pharaoh said to Joseph, "I have had a dream, and

no one can interpret it. But I have heard it said about you that you can hear a dream and interpret it."

[16] "I am not able to," Joseph answered Pharaoh. "It is God who will give Pharaoh a favorable answer."

[17] So Pharaoh said to Joseph: "In my dream I was standing on the bank of the Nile, [18] when seven well-fed, healthy-looking cows came up from the Nile and began to graze among the reeds. [19] After them, seven other cows—ugly, very sickly, and thin—came up. I've never seen such ugly ones as these in all the land of Egypt. [20] Then the thin, ugly cows ate the first seven well-fed cows. [21] When they had devoured them, you could not tell that they had devoured them; their appearance was as bad as it had been before. Then I woke up. [22] In my dream I had also seen seven heads of grain, plump and ripe, coming up on one stalk. [23] After them, seven heads of grain—withered, thin, and scorched by the east wind—sprouted up. [24] The thin heads of grain swallowed the seven plump ones. I told this to the magicians, but no one can tell me what it means."

[25] Then Joseph said to Pharaoh, "Pharaoh's dreams mean the same thing. God has revealed to Pharaoh what He is about to do. [26] The seven good cows are seven years, and the seven ripe heads are seven years. The dreams mean the same thing. [27] The seven thin, ugly cows that came up after them are seven years, and the seven worthless, scorched heads of grain are seven years of famine.

[28] "It is just as I told Pharaoh: God has shown Pharaoh what He is about to do. [29] Seven years of great abundance are coming throughout the land of Egypt. [30] After them, seven years of famine will take place, and all the abundance in the land of Egypt will be forgotten. The famine will devastate the land. [31] The abundance in the land will not be remembered because of the famine that follows it, for the famine will be very severe. [32] Since the dream was given twice to Pharaoh, it means that the matter has been determined by God, and He will carry it out soon.

[33] "So now, let Pharaoh look for a discerning and wise man and set him over the land of Egypt. [34] Let Pharaoh do this: Let him appoint overseers over the land and take a fifth of the harvest of the land of Egypt during the seven years of abundance. [35] Let them gather all the excess food during these good years that are coming. Under Pharaoh's authority, store the grain in the cities, so they may preserve it as food. [36] The food will be a reserve for the land during the seven years of famine that will take place in the land of Egypt. Then the country will not be wiped out by the famine."

[37] The proposal pleased Pharaoh and all his servants. [38] Then Pharaoh said to his servants, "Can we find anyone like this, a man who has God's spirit in him?" [39] So Pharaoh said to Joseph, "Since God has made all this known to you, there is no one as intelligent and wise as you are. [40] You will be over my house, and all my people will obey your commands. Only with regard to the throne will I be greater than you." [41] Pharaoh also said to Joseph, "See, I am placing you over all the land of Egypt." [42] Pharaoh removed his signet ring from his hand and put it on Joseph's hand, clothed him with fine linen garments, and placed a gold chain around his neck. [43] He had Joseph ride in his second chariot, and servants called out before him, *"Abrek!"* So he placed him over all the land of Egypt. [44] Pharaoh said to Joseph, "I am Pharaoh, but no one will be able to raise his hand or foot in all the land of Egypt without your

permission." ⁴⁵Pharaoh gave Joseph the name Zaphenath-paneah and gave him a wife, Asenath daughter of Potiphera, priest at On. And Joseph went throughout the land of Egypt.

⁴⁶Joseph was 30 years old when he entered the service of Pharaoh king of Egypt. Joseph left Pharaoh's presence and traveled throughout the land of Egypt.

⁴⁷During the seven years of abundance the land produced outstanding harvests. ⁴⁸Joseph gathered all the excess food in the land of Egypt during the seven years and put it in the cities. He put the food in every city from the fields around it. ⁴⁹So Joseph stored up grain in such abundance—like the sand of the sea—that he stopped measuring it because it was beyond measure.

⁵⁰Two sons were born to Joseph before the years of famine arrived. Asenath daughter of Potiphera, priest at On, bore them to him. ⁵¹Joseph named the firstborn Manasseh, meaning, "God has made me forget all my hardship in my father's house." ⁵²And the second son he named Ephraim, meaning, "God has made me fruitful in the land of my affliction."

⁵³Then the seven years of abundance in the land of Egypt came to an end, ⁵⁴and the seven years of famine began, just as Joseph had said. There was famine in every country, but throughout the land of Egypt there was food. ⁵⁵Extreme hunger came to all the land of Egypt, and the people cried out to Pharaoh for food. Pharaoh told all Egypt, "Go to Joseph and do whatever he tells you." ⁵⁶Because the famine had spread across the whole country, Joseph opened up all the storehouses and sold grain to the Egyptians, for the famine was severe in the land of Egypt. ⁵⁷Every nation came to Joseph in Egypt to buy grain, for the famine was severe in every land.

42 When Jacob learned that there was grain in Egypt, he said to his sons, "Why do you keep looking at each other? ²Listen," he went on, "I have heard there is grain in Egypt. Go down there and buy some for us so that we will live and not die." ³So 10 of Joseph's brothers went down to buy grain from Egypt. ⁴But Jacob did not send Joseph's brother Benjamin with his brothers, for he thought, "Something might happen to him."

⁵The sons of Israel were among those who came to buy grain, for the famine was in the land of Canaan. ⁶Joseph was in charge of the country; he sold grain to all its people. His brothers came and bowed down before him with their faces to the ground. ⁷When Joseph saw his brothers, he recognized them, but he treated them like strangers and spoke harshly to them.

"Where do you come from?" he asked.

"From the land of Canaan to buy food," they replied.

⁸Although Joseph recognized his brothers, they did not recognize him. ⁹Joseph remembered his dreams about them and said to them, "You are spies. You have come to see the weakness of the land."

¹⁰"No, my lord. Your servants have come to buy food," they said. ¹¹"We are all sons of one man. We are honest; your servants are not spies."

¹²"No," he said to them. "You have come to see the weakness of the land."

¹³But they replied, "We, your servants, were 12 brothers, the sons of one man in the land of Canaan. The youngest is now with our father, and one is no longer living."

¹⁴Then Joseph said to them, "I have spoken: You are spies!" ¹⁵This is how you will be tested: As surely as Pharaoh lives, you will not leave this place unless your youngest brother comes here. ¹⁶Send one from among you to get your brother. The rest of you will be imprisoned so that your words can be tested to see if they are true. If they are not, then as surely as Pharaoh lives, you are spies!" ¹⁷So Joseph imprisoned them together for three days.

¹⁸On the third day Joseph said to them, "I ·fear God—do this and you will live. ¹⁹If you are honest, let one of you be confined to the guardhouse, while the rest of you go and take grain to relieve the hunger of your households. ²⁰Bring your youngest brother to me so that your words can be confirmed; then you won't die." And they consented to this.

²¹Then they said to each other, "Obviously, we are being punished for what we did to our brother. We saw his deep distress when he pleaded with us, but we would not listen. That is why this trouble has come to us."

²²But Reuben replied: "Didn't I tell you not to harm the boy? But you wouldn't listen. Now we must account for his blood!"

²³They did not realize that Joseph understood them, since there was an interpreter between them. ²⁴He turned away from them and wept. Then he turned back and spoke to them. He took Simeon from them and had him bound before their eyes. ²⁵Joseph then gave orders to fill their containers with grain, return each man's money to his sack, and give them provisions for their journey. This order was carried out. ²⁶They loaded the grain on their donkeys and left there.

²⁷At the place where they lodged for the night, one of them opened his sack to get feed for his donkey, and he saw his money there at the top of the bag. ²⁸He said to his brothers, "My money has been returned! It's here in my bag." Their hearts sank. Trembling, they turned to one another and said, "What is this that God has done to us?"

²⁹When they reached their father Jacob in the land of Canaan, they told him all that had happened to them: ³⁰"The man who is the lord of the country spoke harshly to us and accused us of spying on the country. ³¹But we told him: We are honest and not spies. ³²We were 12 brothers, sons of the same father. One is no longer living, and the youngest is now with our father in the land of Canaan. ³³The man who is the lord of the country said to us, 'This is how I will know if you are honest: Leave one brother with me, take food to relieve the hunger of your households, and go. ³⁴Bring back your youngest brother to me, and I will know that you are not spies but honest men. I will then give your brother back to you, and you can trade in the country.'"

³⁵As they began emptying their sacks, there in each man's sack was his bag of money! When they and their father saw their bags of money, they were afraid.

³⁶Their father Jacob said to them, "You have deprived me of my sons. Joseph is gone and Simeon is gone. Now you want to take Benjamin. Everything happens to me!"

³⁷Then Reuben said to his father, "You can kill my two sons if I don't bring him back to you. Put him in my care, and I will return him to you."

³⁸But Jacob answered, "My son will not go down with you, for his brother is dead and he alone is left. If anything happens to him on your journey, you will bring my gray hairs down to ·Sheol in sorrow."

43 Now the famine in the land was severe. ²When they had used up the grain they had brought back from Egypt, their father said to them, "Go back and buy us some food."

³But Judah said to him, "The man specifically warned us: 'You will not see me again unless your brother is with you.' ⁴If you will send our brother with us, we will go down and buy food for you. ⁵But if you will not send him, we will not go, for the man said to us, 'You will not see me again unless your brother is with you.'"

⁶"Why did you cause me so much trouble?" Israel asked. "Why did you tell the man that you had another brother?"

⁷They answered, "The man kept asking about us and our family: 'Is your father still alive? Do you have another brother?' And we answered him accordingly. How could we know that he would say, 'Bring your brother here'?"

⁸Then Judah said to his father Israel, "Send the boy with me. We will be on our way so that we may live and not die—neither we, nor you, nor our children. ⁹I will be responsible for him. You can hold me personally accountable! If I do not bring him back to you and set him before you, I will be *guilty before you forever. ¹⁰If we had not wasted time, we could have come back twice by now."

¹¹Then their father Israel said to them, "If it must be so, then do this: Put some of the best products of the land in your packs and take them down to the man as a gift—some balsam and some honey, aromatic gum and resin, pistachios and almonds. ¹²Take twice as much money with you. Return the money that was returned to you in the top of your bags. Perhaps it was a mistake. ¹³Take your brother also, and go back at once to the man. ¹⁴May *God Almighty cause the man to be merciful to you so that he will release your other brother and Benjamin to you. As for me, if I am deprived of my sons, then I am deprived."

¹⁵The men took this gift, double the amount of money, and Benjamin. They made their way down to Egypt and stood before Joseph.

¹⁶When Joseph saw Benjamin with them, he said to his steward, "Take the men to my house. Slaughter an animal and prepare it, for they will eat with me at noon." ¹⁷The man did as Joseph had said and brought them to Joseph's house.

¹⁸But the men were afraid because they were taken to Joseph's house. They said, "We have been brought here because of the money that was returned in our bags the first time. They intend to overpower us, seize us, make us slaves, and take our donkeys." ¹⁹So they approached Joseph's steward and spoke to him at the doorway of the house.

²⁰They said, "Sir, we really did come down here the first time only to buy food. ²¹When we came to the place where we lodged for the night and opened our bags of grain, each one's money was at the top of his bag! It was the full amount of our money, and we have brought it back with us. ²²We have brought additional money with us to buy food. We don't know who put our money in the bags."

²³Then the steward said, "May you be well. Don't be afraid. Your God and the God of your father must have put treasure in your bags. I received your money." Then he brought Simeon out to them. ²⁴The steward brought the men into Joseph's house, gave them wa-ter to wash their feet, and got feed for their donkeys. ²⁵Since the men had heard that they were going to eat a meal there, they prepared their gift for Joseph's arrival at noon. ²⁶When Joseph came home, they brought him the gift they had carried into the house, and they bowed to the ground before him.

²⁷He asked if they were well, and he said, "How is your elderly father that you told me about? Is he still alive?"

²⁸They answered, "Your servant our father is well. He is still alive." And they bowed down to honor him.

²⁹When he looked up and saw his brother Benjamin, his mother's son, he asked, "Is this your youngest brother that you told me about?" Then he said, "May God be gracious to you, my son." ³⁰Joseph hurried out because he was overcome with emotion for his brother, and he was about to weep. He went into an inner room to weep. ³¹Then he washed his face and came out. Regaining his composure, he said, "Serve the meal."

³²They served him by himself, his brothers by themselves, and the Egyptians who were eating with him by themselves, because Egyptians could not eat with Hebrews, since that is abhorrent to them. ³³They were seated before him in order by age, from the firstborn to the youngest. The men looked at each other in astonishment. ³⁴Portions were served to them from Joseph's table, and Benjamin's portion was five times larger than any of theirs. They drank, and they got intoxicated with Joseph.

44 Then Joseph commanded his steward: "Fill the men's bags with as much food as they can carry, and put each one's money at the top of his bag. ²Put my cup, the silver one, at the top of the youngest one's bag, along with his grain money." So he did as Joseph told him.

³At morning light, the men were sent off with their donkeys. ⁴They had not gone very far from the city when Joseph said to his steward, "Get up. Pursue the men, and when you overtake them, say to them, 'Why have you repaid evil for good? ⁵Isn't this the cup that my master drinks from and uses for *divination? What you have done is wrong!'"

⁶When he overtook them, he said these words to them. ⁷They said to him, "Why does my lord say these things? Your servants could not possibly do such a thing. ⁸We even brought back to you from the land of Canaan the money we found at the top of our bags. How could we steal gold and silver from your master's house? ⁹If any of us is found to have it, he must die, and we also will become my lord's slaves."

¹⁰The steward replied, "What you have said is right, but only the one who is found to have it will be my slave, and the rest of you will be blameless."

¹¹So each one quickly lowered his sack to the ground and opened it. ¹²The steward searched, beginning with the oldest and ending with the youngest, and the cup was found in Benjamin's sack. ¹³Then they tore their clothes, and each one loaded his donkey and returned to the city.

¹⁴When Judah and his brothers reached Joseph's house, he was still there. They fell to the ground before him. ¹⁵"What is this you have done?" Joseph said to them. "Didn't you know that a man like me could uncover the truth by divination?"

¹⁶"What can we say to my lord?" Judah replied. "How can we plead? How can we justify ourselves?

God has exposed your servants' iniquity. We are now my lord's slaves—both we and the one in whose possession the cup was found."

[17] Then Joseph said, "I swear that I will not do this. The man in whose possession the cup was found will be my slave. The rest of you can go in peace to your father."

[18] But Judah approached him and said, "Sir, please let your servant speak personally to my lord. Do not be angry with your servant, for you are like Pharaoh. [19] My lord asked his servants, 'Do you have a father or a brother?' [20] and we answered my lord, 'We have an elderly father and a younger brother, the child of his old age. The boy's brother is dead. He is the only one of his mother's sons left, and his father loves him.' [21] Then you said to your servants, 'Bring him to me so that I can see him.' [22] But we said to my lord, 'The boy cannot leave his father. If he were to leave, his father would die.' [23] Then you said to your servants, 'If your younger brother does not come down with you, you will not see me again.'

[24] "This is what happened when we went back to your servant my father: We reported your words to him. [25] But our father said, 'Go again, and buy us some food.' [26] We told him, 'We cannot go down unless our younger brother goes with us. So if our younger brother isn't with us, we cannot see the man.' [27] Your servant my father said to us, 'You know that my wife bore me two sons. [28] One left—I said that he must have been torn to pieces—and I have never seen him again. [29] If you also take this one from me and anything happens to him, you will bring my gray hairs down to *Sheol in sorrow.'

[30] "So if I come to your servant my father and the boy is not with us—his life is wrapped up with the boy's life— [31] when he sees that the boy is not with us, he will die. Then your servants will have brought the gray hairs of your servant our father down to Sheol in sorrow. [32] Your servant became accountable to my father for the boy, saying, 'If I do not return him to you, I will always bear the *guilt for sinning against you, my father.' [33] Now please let your servant remain here as my lord's slave, in place of the boy. Let him go back with his brothers. [34] For how can I go back to my father without the boy? I could not bear to see the grief that would overwhelm my father."

45 Joseph could no longer keep his composure in front of all his attendants, so he called out, "Send everyone away from me!" No one was with him when he revealed his identity to his brothers. [2] But he wept so loudly that the Egyptians heard it, and also Pharaoh's household heard it. [3] Joseph said to his brothers, "I am Joseph! Is my father still living?" But they could not answer him because they were terrified in his presence.

[4] Then Joseph said to his brothers, "Please, come near me," and they came near. "I am Joseph, your brother," he said, "the one you sold into Egypt. [5] And now don't be worried or angry with yourselves for selling me here, because God sent me ahead of you to preserve life. [6] For the famine has been in the land these two years, and there will be five more years without plowing or harvesting. [7] God sent me ahead of you to establish you as a remnant within the land and to keep you alive by a great deliverance. [8] Therefore it was not you who sent me here, but God. He has made me a father to Pharaoh, lord of his entire household, and ruler over all the land of Egypt.

[9] "Return quickly to my father and say to him, 'This is what your son Joseph says: "God has made me lord of all Egypt. Come down to me without delay. [10] You can settle in the land of Goshen and be near me—you, your children, and grandchildren, your sheep, cattle, and all you have. [11] There I will sustain you, for there will be five more years of famine. Otherwise, you, your household, and everything you have will become destitute."' [12] Look! Your eyes and my brother Benjamin's eyes can see that it is I, Joseph, who am speaking to you. [13] Tell my father about all my glory in Egypt and about all you have seen. And bring my father here quickly."

[14] Then Joseph threw his arms around Benjamin and wept, and Benjamin wept on his shoulder. [15] Joseph kissed each of his brothers as he wept, and afterward his brothers talked with him.

[16] When the news reached Pharaoh's palace, "Joseph's brothers have come," Pharaoh and his servants were pleased. [17] Pharaoh said to Joseph, "Tell your brothers, 'Do this: Load your animals and go on back to the land of Canaan. [18] Get your father and your families, and come back to me. I will give you the best of the land of Egypt, and you can eat from the richness of the land.' [19] You are also commanded, 'Do this: Take wagons from the land of Egypt for your young children and your wives and bring your father here. [20] Do not be concerned about your belongings, for the best of all the land of Egypt is yours.'"

[21] The sons of Israel did this. Joseph gave them wagons as Pharaoh had commanded, and he gave them provisions for the journey. [22] He gave each of the brothers changes of clothes, but he gave Benjamin 300 pieces of silver and five changes of clothes. [23] He sent his father the following: 10 donkeys carrying the best products of Egypt and 10 female donkeys carrying grain, food, and provisions for his father on the journey. [24] So Joseph sent his brothers on their way, and as they were leaving, he said to them, "Don't argue on the way."

[25] So they went up from Egypt and came to their father Jacob in the land of Canaan. [26] They said, "Joseph is still alive, and he is ruler over all the land of Egypt!" Jacob was stunned, for he did not believe them. [27] But when they told Jacob all that Joseph had said to them, and when he saw the wagons that Joseph had sent to transport him, the spirit of their father Jacob revived. [28] Then Israel said, "Enough! My son Joseph is still alive. I will go to see him before I die."

46 Israel set out with all that he had and came to Beer-sheba, and he offered sacrifices to the God of his father Isaac. [2] That night God spoke to Israel in a vision: "Jacob, Jacob!" He said.

And Jacob replied, "Here I am."

[3] God said, "I am God, the God of your father. Do not be afraid to go down to Egypt, for I will make you into a great nation there. [4] I will go down with you to Egypt, and I will also bring you back. Joseph will put his hands on your eyes."

[5] Jacob left Beer-sheba. The sons of Israel took their father Jacob in the wagons Pharaoh had sent to carry him, along with their children and their wives. [6] They also took their cattle and possessions they had acquired in the land of Canaan. Then Jacob and all his

children went with him to Egypt. ⁷His sons and grandsons, his daughters and granddaughters, indeed all his ˙offspring, he brought with him to Egypt.

⁸These are the names of the Israelites, Jacob and his sons, who went to Egypt:

Jacob's firstborn: Reuben.

⁹ Reuben's sons: Hanoch, Pallu, Hezron, and Carmi.

¹⁰ Simeon's sons: Jemuel, Jamin, Ohad, Jachin, Zohar, and Shaul, the son of a Canaanite woman.

¹¹ Levi's sons: Gershon, Kohath, and Merari.

¹² Judah's sons: Er, Onan, Shelah, Perez, and Zerah; but Er and Onan died in the land of Canaan.

Perez's sons: Hezron and Hamul.

¹³ Issachar's sons: Tola, Puvah, Jashub, and Shimron.

¹⁴ Zebulun's sons: Sered, Elon, and Jahleel.

¹⁵ These were Leah's sons born to Jacob in Paddan-aram, as well as his daughter Dinah. The total number of persons: 33.

¹⁶ Gad's sons: Ziphion, Haggi, Shuni, Ezbon, Eri, Arodi, and Areli.

¹⁷ Asher's sons: Imnah, Ishvah, Ishvi, Beriah, and their sister Serah.

Beriah's sons were Heber and Malchiel.

¹⁸ These were the sons of Zilpah—whom Laban gave to his daughter Leah—that she bore to Jacob: 16 persons.

¹⁹ The sons of Jacob's wife Rachel: Joseph and Benjamin.

²⁰ Manasseh and Ephraim were born to Joseph in the land of Egypt. They were born to him by Asenath daughter of Potiphera, a priest at On.

²¹ Benjamin's sons: Bela, Becher, Ashbel, Gera, Naaman, Ehi, Rosh, Muppim, Huppim, and Ard.

²² These were Rachel's sons who were born to Jacob: 14 persons.

²³ Dan's son: Hushim.

²⁴ Naphtali's sons: Jahzeel, Guni, Jezer, and Shillem.

²⁵ These were the sons of Bilhah, whom Laban gave to his daughter Rachel. She bore to Jacob: seven persons.

²⁶ The total number of persons belonging to Jacob—his direct descendants, not including the wives of Jacob's sons— who came to Egypt: 66.

²⁷ And Joseph's sons who were born to him in Egypt: two persons.

All those of Jacob's household who had come to Egypt: 70 persons.

²⁸Now Jacob had sent Judah ahead of him to Joseph to prepare for his arrival at Goshen. When they came to the land of Goshen, ²⁹Joseph hitched the horses to his chariot and went up to Goshen to meet his father Israel. Joseph presented himself to him, threw his arms around him, and wept for a long time.

³⁰Then Israel said to Joseph, "At last I can die, now that I have seen your face and know you are still alive!"

³¹Joseph said to his brothers and to his father's household, "I will go up and inform Pharaoh, telling him: My brothers and my father's household, who were in the land of Canaan, have come to me. ³²The

men are shepherds; they also raise livestock. They have brought their sheep and cattle and all that they have. ³³When Pharaoh addresses you and asks, 'What is your occupation?' ³⁴you are to say, 'Your servants, both we and our fathers, have raised livestock from our youth until now.' Then you will be allowed to settle in the land of Goshen, since all shepherds are abhorrent to Egyptians."

47 So Joseph went and informed Pharaoh: "My father and my brothers, with their sheep and cattle and all that they own, have come from the land of Canaan and are now in the land of Goshen."

²He took five of his brothers and presented them before Pharaoh. ³Then Pharaoh asked his brothers, "What is your occupation?"

And they said to Pharaoh, "Your servants, both we and our fathers, are shepherds." ⁴Then they said to Pharaoh, "We have come to live in the land for a while because there is no grazing land for your servants' sheep, since the famine in the land of Canaan has been severe. So now, please let your servants settle in the land of Goshen."

⁵Then Pharaoh said to Joseph, "Now that your father and brothers have come to you, ⁶the land of Egypt is open before you; settle your father and brothers in the best part of the land. They can live in the land of Goshen. If you know of any capable men among them, put them in charge of my livestock."

⁷Joseph then brought his father Jacob and presented him before Pharaoh, and Jacob blessed Pharaoh. ⁸Then Pharaoh said to Jacob, "How many years have you lived?"

⁹Jacob said to Pharaoh, "My pilgrimage has lasted 130 years. My years have been few and hard, and they have not surpassed the years of my fathers during their pilgrimages." ¹⁰So Jacob blessed Pharaoh and departed from Pharaoh's presence.

¹¹Then Joseph settled his father and brothers in the land of Egypt and gave them property in the best part of the land, the land of Rameses, as Pharaoh had commanded. ¹²And Joseph provided his father, his brothers, and all his father's household with food for their dependents.

¹³But there was no food in that entire region, for the famine was very severe. The land of Egypt and the land of Canaan were exhausted by the famine. ¹⁴Joseph collected all the money to be found in the land of Egypt and the land of Canaan in exchange for the grain they were purchasing, and he brought the money to Pharaoh's palace. ¹⁵When the money from the land of Egypt and the land of Canaan was gone, all the Egyptians came to Joseph and said, "Give us food. Why should we die here in front of you? The money is gone!"

¹⁶But Joseph said, "Give me your livestock. Since the money is gone, I will give you food in exchange for your livestock." ¹⁷So they brought their livestock to Joseph, and he gave them food in exchange for the horses, the herds of sheep, the herds of cattle, and the donkeys. That year he provided them with food in exchange for all their livestock.

¹⁸When that year was over, they came the next year and said to him, "We cannot hide from our lord that the money is gone and that all our livestock belongs to our lord. There is nothing left for our lord except our bodies and our land. ¹⁹Why should we die here in front of you—both us and our land? Buy us and our land in

exchange for food. Then we with our land will become Pharaoh's slaves. Give us seed so that we can live and not die, and so that the land won't become desolate."

²⁰In this way, Joseph acquired all the land in Egypt for Pharaoh, because every Egyptian sold his field since the famine was so severe for them. The land became Pharaoh's, ²¹and Joseph moved the people to the cities from one end of Egypt to the other. ²²The only land he didn't acquire was the priests' portion, for it was given to them by Pharaoh. They lived off the rations Pharaoh had given them; therefore they did not sell their land.

²³Then Joseph said to the people, "Understand today that I have acquired you and your land for Pharaoh. Here is seed for you. Sow it in the land. ²⁴At harvest, you are to give a fifth of it to Pharaoh, and four-fifths will be yours as seed for the field and as food for yourselves, your households, and your dependents."

²⁵And they said, "You have saved our lives. We have found favor in our lord's eyes and will be Pharaoh's slaves." ²⁶So Joseph made it a law, still in effect today in the land of Egypt, that a fifth of the produce belongs to Pharaoh. Only the priests' land does not belong to Pharaoh.

²⁷Israel settled in the land of Egypt, in the region of Goshen. They acquired property in it and became fruitful and very numerous. ²⁸Now Jacob lived in the land of Egypt 17 years, and his life span was 147 years. ²⁹When the time drew near for him to die, he called his son Joseph and said to him, "If I have found favor in your eyes, put your hand under my thigh and promise me that you will deal with me in kindness and faithfulness. Do not bury me in Egypt. ³⁰When I rest with my fathers, carry me away from Egypt and bury me in their burial place."

Joseph answered, "I will do what you have asked."

³¹And Jacob said, "Swear to me." So Joseph swore to him. Then Israel bowed in thanks at the head of his bed.

48 Some time after this, Joseph was told, "Your father is weaker." So he set out with his two sons, Manasseh and Ephraim. ²When Jacob was told, "Your son Joseph has come to you," Israel summoned his strength and sat up in bed.

³Jacob said to Joseph, "'God Almighty appeared to me at Luz in the land of Canaan and blessed me. ⁴He said to me, 'I will make you fruitful and numerous; I will make many nations come from you, and I will give this land as an eternal possession to your future descendants.' ⁵Your two sons born to you in the land of Egypt before I came to you in Egypt are now mine. Ephraim and Manasseh belong to me just as Reuben and Simeon do. ⁶Children born to you after them will be yours and will be recorded under the names of their brothers with regard to their inheritance. ⁷When I was returning from Paddan, to my sorrow Rachel died along the way, some distance from Ephrath in the land of Canaan. I buried her there along the way to Ephrath," (that is, Bethlehem).

⁸When Israel saw Joseph's sons, he said, "Who are these?"

⁹And Joseph said to his father, "They are my sons God has given me here."

So Jacob said, "Bring them to me and I will bless them." ¹⁰Now his eyesight was poor because of old age; he could hardly see. Joseph brought them to him, and he kissed and embraced them. ¹¹Israel said to Joseph,

"I never expected to see your face again, but now God has even let me see your •offspring." ¹²Then Joseph took them from his father's knees and bowed with his face to the ground.

¹³Then Joseph took them both—with his right hand Ephraim toward Israel's left, and with his left hand Manasseh toward Israel's right—and brought them to Israel. ¹⁴But Israel stretched out his right hand and put it on the head of Ephraim, the younger, and crossing his hands, put his left on Manasseh's head, although Manasseh was the firstborn. ¹⁵Then he blessed Joseph and said:

The God before whom my fathers Abraham
　and Isaac walked,
the God who has been my shepherd all my life
　to this day,
¹⁶　the Angel who has redeemed me
　from all harm—
may He bless these boys.
And may they be called by my name
and the names of my fathers Abraham
　and Isaac,
and may they grow to be numerous
　within the land.

¹⁷When Joseph saw that his father had placed his right hand on Ephraim's head, he thought it was a mistake and took his father's hand to move it from Ephraim's head to Manasseh's. ¹⁸Joseph said to his father, "Not that way, my father! This one is the firstborn. Put your right hand on his head." ¹⁹But his father refused and said, "I know, my son, I know! He too will become a tribe, and he too will be great; nevertheless, his younger brother will be greater than he, and his offspring will become a populous nation." ²⁰So he blessed them that day with these words:

The nation Israel will invoke blessings by
　you, saying,
"May God make you like Ephraim
　and Manasseh,"
putting Ephraim before Manasseh.

²¹Then Israel said to Joseph, "Look, I am about to die, but God will be with you and will bring you back to the land of your fathers. ²²Over and above what I am giving your brothers, I am giving you the one mountain slope that I took from the hand of the Amorites with my sword and bow."

49 Then Jacob called his sons and said, "Gather around, and I will tell you what will happen to you in the days to come.

²　Come together and listen, sons of Jacob;
　listen to your father Israel:
³　Reuben, you are my firstborn,
　my strength and the firstfruits of my virility,
　excelling in prominence, excelling in power.
⁴　Turbulent as water, you will no longer excel,
　because you got into your father's bed
　and you defiled it—he got into my bed.
⁵　Simeon and Levi are brothers;
　their knives are vicious weapons.
⁶　May I never enter their council;
　may I never join their assembly.
　For in their anger they kill men,
　and on a whim they hamstring oxen.
⁷　Their anger is cursed, for it is strong,
　and their fury, for it is cruel!
　I will disperse them throughout Jacob
　and scatter them throughout Israel.

8 Judah, your brothers will praise you.
Your hand will be on the necks
    of your enemies;
your father's sons will bow down to you.
9 Judah is a young lion—
my son, you return from the kill.
He crouches; he lies down like a lion
or a lioness—who dares to rouse him?
10 The scepter will not depart from Judah
or the staff from between his feet
until He whose right it is comes
and the obedience of the peoples belongs
    to Him.
11 He ties his donkey to a vine,
and the colt of his donkey to the choice vine.
He washes his clothes in wine
and his robes in the blood of grapes.
12 His eyes are darker than wine,
and his teeth are whiter than milk.
13 Zebulun will live by the seashore
and will be a harbor for ships,
and his territory will be next to Sidon.
14 Issachar is a strong donkey
lying down between the saddlebags.
15 He saw that his resting place was good
and that the land was pleasant,
so he leaned his shoulder to bear a load
and became a forced laborer.
16 Dan will judge his people
as one of the tribes of Israel.
17 He will be a snake by the road,
a viper beside the path,
that bites the horses' heels
so that its rider falls backward.
18 I wait for Your salvation, LORD.
19 Gad will be attacked by raiders,
but he will attack their heels.
20 Asher's food will be rich,
and he will produce royal delicacies.
21 Naphtali is a doe set free
that bears beautiful fawns.
22 Joseph is a fruitful vine,
a fruitful vine beside a spring;
its branches climb over the wall.
23 The archers attacked him,
shot at him, and were hostile toward him.
24 Yet his bow remained steady,
and his strong arms were made agile
by the hands of the Mighty One of Jacob,
by the name of the Shepherd, the Rock
    of Israel,
25 by the God of your father who helps you,
and by the 'Almighty who blesses you
with blessings of the heavens above,
blessings of the deep that lies below,
and blessings of the breasts and the womb.
26 The blessings of your father excel
the blessings of my ancestors
and the bounty of the eternal hills.
May they rest on the head of Joseph,
on the crown of the prince of his brothers.
27 Benjamin is a wolf; he tears his prey.
In the morning he devours the prey,
and in the evening he divides the plunder."
28 These are the tribes of Israel, 12 in all, and this was
what their father said to them. He blessed them, and
he blessed each one with a suitable blessing.

29 Then he commanded them: "I am about to be
gathered to my people. Bury me with my fathers in
the cave in the field of Ephron the Hittite. 30 The cave
is in the field of Machpelah near Mamre, in the land
of Canaan. This is the field Abraham purchased from
Ephron the Hittite as a burial site. 31 Abraham and his
wife Sarah are buried there, Isaac and his wife Rebekah
are buried there, and I buried Leah there. 32 The field
and the cave in it were purchased from the Hittites."
33 When Jacob had finished instructing his sons, he
drew his feet into the bed and died. He was gathered
to his people.

50 Then Joseph, leaning over his father's face,
wept and kissed him. 2 He commanded his servants who were physicians to embalm his father. So
they embalmed Israel. 3 They took 40 days to complete
this, for embalming takes that long, and the Egyptians
mourned for him 70 days.

4 When the days of mourning were over, Joseph said
to Pharaoh's household, "If I have found favor with
you, please tell Pharaoh 5 my father made me take
an oath, saying, 'I am about to die. You must bury me
there in the tomb that I made for myself in the land
of Canaan.' Now let me go and bury my father. Then
I will return."
6 So Pharaoh said, "Go and bury your father in keeping with your oath."
7 Then Joseph went to bury his father, and all Pharaoh's servants, the elders of his household, and all the
elders of the land of Egypt went with him, 8 along with
all Joseph's household, his brothers, and his father's
household. Only their children, their sheep, and their
cattle were left in the land of Goshen. 9 Horses and
chariots went up with him; it was a very impressive
procession. 10 When they reached the threshing floor
of Atad, which is across the Jordan, they lamented and
wept loudly, and Joseph mourned seven days for his father. 11 When the Canaanite inhabitants of the land saw
the mourning at the threshing floor of Atad, they said,
"This is a solemn mourning on the part of the Egyptians." Therefore the place is named Abel-mizraim. It
is across the Jordan.
12 So Jacob's sons did for him what he had commanded them. 13 They carried him to the land of Canaan and buried him in the cave at Machpelah in the
field near Mamre, which Abraham had purchased as
a burial site from Ephron the Hittite. 14 After Joseph
buried his father, he returned to Egypt with his brothers and all who had gone with him to bury his father.
15 When Joseph's brothers saw that their father was
dead, they said to one another, "If Joseph is holding a
grudge against us, he will certainly repay us for all the
suffering we caused him."
16 So they sent this message to Joseph, "Before he
died your father gave a command: 17 Say this to Joseph: Please forgive your brothers' transgression and
their sin—the suffering they caused you.' Therefore,
please forgive the transgression of the servants of the
God of your father." Joseph wept when their message came to him. 18 Then his brothers also came to
him, bowed down before him, and said, "We are your
slaves!"
19 But Joseph said to them, "Don't be afraid. Am I
in the place of God? 20 You planned evil against me;
God planned it for good to bring about the present
result—the survival of many people. 21 Therefore don't

be afraid. I will take care of you and your little ones." And he comforted them and spoke kindly to them.

²² Joseph and his father's household remained in Egypt. Joseph lived 110 years. ²³ He saw Ephraim's sons to the third generation; the sons of Manasseh's son Machir were recognized by Joseph.

²⁴ Joseph said to his brothers, "I am about to die, but God will certainly come to your aid and bring you up from this land to the land He promised Abraham, Isaac, and Jacob." ²⁵ So Joseph made the sons of Israel take an oath: "When God comes to your aid, you are to carry my bones up from here."

²⁶ Joseph died at the age of 110. They embalmed him and placed him in a coffin in Egypt.

EXODUS

1 These are the names of the sons of Israel who came to Egypt with Jacob; each came with his family:
² Reuben, Simeon, Levi, and Judah;
³ Issachar, Zebulun, and Benjamin;
⁴ Dan and Naphtali; Gad and Asher.
⁵ The total number of Jacob's descendants was 70; Joseph was already in Egypt.

⁶ Then Joseph and all his brothers and all that generation died. ⁷ But the Israelites were fruitful, increased rapidly, multiplied, and became extremely numerous so that the land was filled with them.

⁸ A new king, who had not known Joseph, came to power in Egypt. ⁹ He said to his people, "Look, the Israelite people are more numerous and powerful than we are. ¹⁰ Let us deal shrewdly with them; otherwise they will multiply further, and if war breaks out, they may join our enemies, fight against us, and leave the country." ¹¹ So the Egyptians assigned taskmasters over the Israelites to oppress them with forced labor. They built Pithom and Rameses as supply cities for Pharaoh. ¹² But the more they oppressed them, the more they multiplied and spread so that the Egyptians came to dread the Israelites. ¹³ They worked the Israelites ruthlessly ¹⁴ and made their lives bitter with difficult labor in brick and mortar and in all kinds of fieldwork. They ruthlessly imposed all this work on them.

¹⁵ Then the king of Egypt said to the Hebrew midwives, one of whom was named Shiphrah and the other Puah, ¹⁶ "When you help the Hebrew women give birth, observe them as they deliver. If the child is a son, kill him, but if it's a daughter, she may live." ¹⁷ The Hebrew midwives, however, *feared God and did not do as the king of Egypt had told them; they let the boys live. ¹⁸ So the king of Egypt summoned the midwives and asked them, "Why have you done this and let the boys live?"

¹⁹ The midwives said to Pharaoh, "The Hebrew women are not like the Egyptian women, for they are vigorous and give birth before a midwife can get to them."

²⁰ So God was good to the midwives, and the people multiplied and became very numerous. ²¹ Since the midwives feared God, He gave them families. ²² Pharaoh then commanded all his people: "You must throw every son born to the Hebrews into the Nile, but let every daughter live."

2 Now a man from the family of Levi married a Levite woman. ² The woman became pregnant and gave birth to a son; when she saw that he was beautiful, she hid him for three months. ³ But when she could no longer hide him, she got a papyrus basket for him and coated it with asphalt and pitch. She placed the child in it and set it among the reeds by the bank of the Nile. ⁴ Then his sister stood at a distance in order to see what would happen to him.

⁵ Pharaoh's daughter went down to bathe at the Nile while her servant girls walked along the riverbank. Seeing the basket among the reeds, she sent her slave girl to get it. ⁶ When she opened it, she saw the child— a little boy, crying. She felt sorry for him and said, "This is one of the Hebrew boys."

⁷ Then his sister said to Pharaoh's daughter, "Should I go and call a woman from the Hebrews to nurse the boy for you?"

⁸ "Go," Pharaoh's daughter told her. So the girl went and called the boy's mother. ⁹ Then Pharaoh's daughter said to her, "Take this child and nurse him for me, and I will pay your wages." So the woman took the boy and nursed him. ¹⁰ When the child grew older, she brought him to Pharaoh's daughter, and he became her son. She named him Moses, "Because," she said, "I drew him out of the water."

¹¹ Years later, after Moses had grown up, he went out to his own people and observed their forced labor. He saw an Egyptian beating a Hebrew, one of his people. ¹² Looking all around and seeing no one, he struck the Egyptian dead and hid him in the sand. ¹³ The next day he went out and saw two Hebrews fighting. He asked the one in the wrong, "Why are you attacking your neighbor?"

¹⁴ "Who made you a leader and judge over us?" the man replied. "Are you planning to kill me as you killed the Egyptian?"

Then Moses became afraid and thought: What I did is certainly known. ¹⁵ When Pharaoh heard about this, he tried to kill Moses. But Moses fled from Pharaoh and went to live in the land of Midian, and sat down by a well.

¹⁶ Now the priest of Midian had seven daughters. They came to draw water and filled the troughs to water their father's flock. ¹⁷ Then some shepherds arrived and drove them away, but Moses came to their rescue and watered their flock. ¹⁸ When they returned to their father Reuel he asked, "Why have you come back so quickly today?"

¹⁹ They answered, "An Egyptian rescued us from the shepherds. He even drew water for us and watered the flock."

²⁰ "So where is he?" he asked his daughters. "Why then did you leave the man behind? Invite him to eat dinner."

²¹ Moses agreed to stay with the man, and he gave his daughter Zipporah to Moses in marriage. ²² She gave birth to a son whom he named Gershom, for he said, "I have been a foreigner in a foreign land."

²³ After a long time, the king of Egypt died. The Israelites groaned because of their difficult labor, and they cried out; and their cry for help ascended to God because of the difficult labor. ²⁴ So God heard their groan-

ing, and He remembered His covenant with Abraham, Isaac, and Jacob. ²⁵God saw the Israelites, and He took notice.

3 Meanwhile, Moses was shepherding the flock of his father-in-law Jethro, the priest of Midian. He led the flock to the far side of the wilderness and came to Horeb, the mountain of God. ²Then the Angel of the LORD appeared to him in a flame of fire within a bush. As Moses looked, he saw that the bush was on fire but was not consumed. ³So Moses thought: I must go over and look at this remarkable sight. Why isn't the bush burning up?

⁴When the LORD saw that he had gone over to look, God called out to him from the bush, "Moses, Moses!"

"Here I am," he answered.

⁵"Do not come closer," He said. "Remove the sandals from your feet, for the place where you are standing is holy ground." ⁶Then He continued, "I am the God of your father, the God of Abraham, the God of Isaac, and the God of Jacob." Moses hid his face because he was afraid to look at God.

⁷Then the LORD said, "I have observed the misery of My people in Egypt, and have heard them crying out because of their oppressors, and I know about their sufferings. ⁸I have come down to rescue them from the power of the Egyptians and to bring them from that land to a good and spacious land, a land flowing with milk and honey—the territory of the Canaanites, Hittites, Amorites, Perizzites, Hivites, and Jebusites. ⁹The Israelites' cry for help has come to Me, and I have also seen the way the Egyptians are oppressing them. ¹⁰Therefore, go. I am sending you to Pharaoh so that you may lead My people, the Israelites, out of Egypt."

¹¹But Moses asked God, "Who am I that I should go to Pharaoh and that I should bring the Israelites out of Egypt?"

¹²He answered, "I will certainly be with you, and this will be the sign to you that I have sent you: when you bring the people out of Egypt, you will all worship God at this mountain."

¹³Then Moses asked God, "If I go to the Israelites and say to them: The God of your fathers has sent me to you, and they ask me, 'What is His name?' what should I tell them?"

¹⁴God replied to Moses, "I AM WHO I AM. This is what you are to say to the Israelites: I AM has sent me to you." ¹⁵God also said to Moses, "Say this to the Israelites: ˙Yahweh, the God of your fathers, the God of Abraham, the God of Isaac, and the God of Jacob, has sent me to you. This is My name forever; this is how I am to be remembered in every generation.

¹⁶"Go and assemble the elders of Israel and say to them: Yahweh, the God of your fathers, the God of Abraham, Isaac, and Jacob, has appeared to me and said: I have paid close attention to you and to what has been done to you in Egypt. ¹⁷And I have promised you that I will bring you up from the misery of Egypt to the land of the Canaanites, Hittites, Amorites, Perizzites, Hivites, and Jebusites—a land flowing with milk and honey. ¹⁸They will listen to what you say. Then you, along with the elders of Israel, must go to the king of Egypt and say to him: Yahweh, the God of the Hebrews, has met with us. Now please let us go on a three-day trip into the wilderness so that we may sacrifice to Yahweh our God.

¹⁹"However, I know that the king of Egypt will not allow you to go, unless he is forced by a strong hand.

²⁰I will stretch out My hand and strike Egypt with all My miracles that I will perform in it. After that, he will let you go. ²¹And I will give these people such favor in the sight of the Egyptians that when you go, you will not go empty-handed. ²²Each woman will ask her neighbor and any woman staying in her house for silver and gold jewelry, and clothing, and you will put them on your sons and daughters. So you will plunder the Egyptians."

4 Then Moses answered, "What if they won't believe me and will not obey me but say, 'The LORD did not appear to you'?"

²The LORD asked him, "What is that in your hand?"

"A staff," he replied.

³Then He said, "Throw it on the ground." He threw it on the ground, and it became a snake. Moses ran from it, ⁴but the LORD told him, "Stretch out your hand and grab it by the tail." So he stretched out his hand and caught it, and it became a staff in his hand. ⁵"This will take place," He continued, "so they will believe that ˙Yahweh, the God of their fathers, the God of Abraham, the God of Isaac, and the God of Jacob, has appeared to you."

⁶In addition the LORD said to him, "Put your hand inside your cloak." So he put his hand inside his cloak, and when he took it out, his hand was diseased, white as snow. ⁷Then He said, "Put your hand back inside your cloak." He put his hand back inside his cloak, and when he took it out, it had again become like the rest of his skin. ⁸"If they will not believe you and will not respond to the evidence of the first sign, they may believe the evidence of the second sign. ⁹And if they don't believe even these two signs or listen to what you say, take some water from the Nile and pour it on the dry ground. The water you take from the Nile will become blood on the ground."

¹⁰But Moses replied to the LORD, "Please, Lord, I have never been eloquent—either in the past or recently or since You have been speaking to Your servant—because I am slow and hesitant in speech."

¹¹Yahweh said to him, "Who made the human mouth? Who makes him mute or deaf, seeing or blind? Is it not I, Yahweh? ¹²Now go! I will help you speak and I will teach you what to say."

¹³Moses said, "Please, Lord, send someone else."

¹⁴Then the LORD's anger burned against Moses, and He said, "Isn't Aaron the Levite your brother? I know that he can speak well. And also, he is on his way now to meet you. He will rejoice when he sees you. ¹⁵You will speak with him and tell him what to say. I will help both you and him to speak and will teach you both what to do. ¹⁶He will speak to the people for you. He will be your spokesman, and you will serve as God to him. ¹⁷And take this staff in your hand that you will perform the signs with."

¹⁸Then Moses went back to his father-in-law Jethro and said to him, "Please let me return to my relatives in Egypt and see if they are still living."

Jethro said to Moses, "Go in peace."

¹⁹Now in Midian the LORD told Moses, "Return to Egypt, for all the men who wanted to kill you are dead." ²⁰So Moses took his wife and sons, put them on a donkey, and returned to the land of Egypt. And Moses took God's staff in his hand.

²¹The LORD instructed Moses, "When you go back to Egypt, make sure you do all the wonders before Pharaoh that I have put within your power. But I will

harden his heart so that he won't let the people go. ²² Then you will say to Pharaoh: This is what Yahweh says: Israel is My firstborn son. ²³ I told you: Let My son go so that he may worship Me, but you refused to let him go. Now I will kill your firstborn son!"

²⁴ On the trip, at an overnight campsite, it happened that the Lord confronted him and sought to put him to death. ²⁵ So Zipporah took a flint, cut off her son's foreskin, and threw it at Moses' feet. Then she said, "You are a bridegroom of blood to me!" ²⁶ So He let him alone. At that time she said, "You are a bridegroom of blood," referring to the circumcision.

²⁷ Now the Lord had said to Aaron, "Go and meet Moses in the wilderness." So he went and met him at the mountain of God and kissed him. ²⁸ Moses told Aaron everything the Lord had sent him to say, and about all the signs He had commanded him to do. ²⁹ Then Moses and Aaron went and assembled all the elders of the Israelites. ³⁰ Aaron repeated everything the Lord had said to Moses and performed the signs before the people. ³¹ The people believed, and when they heard that the Lord had paid attention to them and that He had seen their misery, they bowed down and worshiped.

5 Later, Moses and Aaron went in and said to Pharaoh, "This is what *Yahweh, the God of Israel, says: Let My people go, so that they may hold a festival for Me in the wilderness."

² But Pharaoh responded, "Who is Yahweh that I should obey Him by letting Israel go? I do not know anything about Yahweh, and besides, I will not let Israel go."

³ Then they answered, "The God of the Hebrews has met with us. Please let us go on a three-day trip into the wilderness so that we may sacrifice to Yahweh our God, or else He may strike us with plague or sword."

⁴ The king of Egypt said to them, "Moses and Aaron, why are you causing the people to neglect their work? Get to your work!" ⁵ Pharaoh also said, "Look, the people of the land are so numerous, and you would stop them from working."

⁶ That day Pharaoh commanded the overseers of the people as well as their foremen: ⁷ "Don't continue to supply the people with straw for making bricks, as before. They must go and gather straw for themselves. ⁸ But require the same quota of bricks from them as they were making before; do not reduce it. For they are slackers—that is why they are crying out, 'Let us go and sacrifice to our God.' ⁹ Impose heavier work on the men. Then they will be occupied with it and not pay attention to deceptive words."

¹⁰ So the overseers and foremen of the people went out and said to them, "This is what Pharaoh says: 'I am not giving you straw. ¹¹ Go get straw yourselves wherever you can find it, but there will be no reduction at all in your workload.'" ¹² So the people scattered throughout the land of Egypt to gather stubble for straw. ¹³ The overseers insisted, "Finish your assigned work each day, just as you did when straw was provided." ¹⁴ Then the Israelite foremen, whom Pharaoh's slave drivers had set over the people, were beaten and asked, "Why haven't you finished making your prescribed number of bricks yesterday or today, as you did before?"

¹⁵ So the Israelite foremen went in and cried for help to Pharaoh: "Why are you treating your servants this way? ¹⁶ No straw has been given to your servants, yet they say to us, 'Make bricks!' Look, your servants are being beaten, but it is your own people who are at fault."

¹⁷ But he said, "You are slackers. Slackers! That is why you are saying, 'Let us go sacrifice to the Lord.' ¹⁸ Now get to work. No straw will be given to you, but you must produce the same quantity of bricks."

¹⁹ The Israelite foremen saw that they were in trouble when they were told, "You cannot reduce your daily quota of bricks." ²⁰ When they left Pharaoh, they confronted Moses and Aaron, who stood waiting to meet them.

²¹ "May the Lord take note of you and judge," they said to them, "because you have made us reek in front of Pharaoh and his officials—putting a sword in their hand to kill us!"

²² So Moses went back to the Lord and asked, "Lord, why have You caused trouble for this people? And why did You ever send me? ²³ Ever since I went in to Pharaoh to speak in Your name he has caused trouble for this people, and You haven't delivered Your people at all." ¹ But the Lord replied to Moses, "Now you are going to see what I will do to Pharaoh: he will let them go because of My strong hand; he will drive them out of his land because of My strong hand."

² Then God spoke to Moses, telling him, "I am *Yahweh. ³ I appeared to Abraham, Isaac, and Jacob as *God Almighty, but I did not reveal My name Yahweh to them. ⁴ I also established My covenant with them to give them the land of Canaan, the land they lived in as foreigners. ⁵ Furthermore, I have heard the groaning of the Israelites, whom the Egyptians are forcing to work as slaves, and I have remembered My covenant. ⁶ "Therefore tell the Israelites: I am Yahweh, and I will deliver you from the forced labor of the Egyptians and free you from slavery to them. I will redeem you with an outstretched arm and great acts of judgment. ⁷ I will take you as My people, and I will be your God. You will know that I am Yahweh your God, who delivered you from the forced labor of the Egyptians. ⁸ I will bring you to the land that I swore to give to Abraham, Isaac, and Jacob, and I will give it to you as a possession. I am Yahweh." ⁹ Moses told this to the Israelites, but they did not listen to him because of their broken spirit and hard labor.

¹⁰ Then the Lord spoke to Moses, ¹¹ "Go and tell Pharaoh king of Egypt to let the Israelites go from his land."

¹² But Moses said in the Lord's presence: "If the Israelites will not listen to me, then how will Pharaoh listen to me, since I am such a poor speaker?" ¹³ Then the Lord spoke to Moses and Aaron and gave them commands concerning both the Israelites and Pharaoh king of Egypt to bring the Israelites out of the land of Egypt.

¹⁴ These are the heads of their fathers' families:

The sons of Reuben, the firstborn of Israel:
Hanoch and Pallu, Hezron and Carmi.
These are the clans of Reuben.

¹⁵ The sons of Simeon:
Jemuel, Jamin, Ohad, Jachin,
Zohar, and Shaul, the son
of a Canaanite woman.
These are the clans of Simeon.

¹⁶ These are the names of the sons of Levi
according to their genealogy:
Gershon, Kohath, and Merari.

Levi lived 137 years.
¹⁷ The sons of Gershon:
Libni and Shimei, by their clans.
¹⁸ The sons of Kohath:
Amram, Izhar, Hebron, and Uzziel.
Kohath lived 133 years.
¹⁹ The sons of Merari:
Mahli and Mushi.
These are the clans of the Levites
according to their genealogy.
²⁰ Amram married his father's sister Jochebed,
and she bore him Aaron and Moses.
Amram lived 137 years.
²¹ The sons of Izhar:
Korah, Nepheg, and Zichri.
²² The sons of Uzziel:
Mishael, Elzaphan, and Sithri.
²³ Aaron married Elisheba,
daughter of Amminadab and sister
of Nahshon.
She bore him Nadab and Abihu, Eleazar
and Ithamar.
²⁴ The sons of Korah:
Assir, Elkanah, and Abiasaph.
These are the clans of the Korahites.
²⁵ Aaron's son Eleazar married
one of the daughters of Putiel
and she bore him Phinehas.
These are the heads of the Levite families
by their clans.

²⁶ It was this Aaron and Moses whom the Lord told, "Bring the Israelites out of the land of Egypt according to their divisions." ²⁷ Moses and Aaron were the ones who spoke to Pharaoh king of Egypt in order to bring the Israelites out of Egypt.

²⁸ On the day the Lord spoke to Moses in the land of Egypt, ²⁹ He said to him, "I am Yahweh; tell Pharaoh king of Egypt everything I am telling you."

³⁰ But Moses replied in the Lord's presence, "Since I am such a poor speaker, how will Pharaoh listen to me?"

7 The Lord answered Moses, "See, I have made you like God to Pharaoh, and Aaron your brother will be your prophet. ²You must say whatever I command you; then Aaron your brother must declare it to Pharaoh so that he will let the Israelites go from his land. ³But I will harden Pharaoh's heart and multiply My signs and wonders in the land of Egypt. ⁴Pharaoh will not listen to you, but I will put My hand on Egypt and bring the divisions of My people the Israelites out of the land of Egypt by great acts of judgment. ⁵The Egyptians will know that I am ˙Yahweh when I stretch out My hand against Egypt, and bring out the Israelites from among them."

⁶So Moses and Aaron did this; they did just as the Lord commanded them. ⁷Moses was 80 years old and Aaron 83 when they spoke to Pharaoh.

⁸The Lord said to Moses and Aaron, ⁹ "When Pharaoh tells you, 'Perform a miracle,' tell Aaron, 'Take your staff and throw it down before Pharaoh. It will become a serpent.'" ¹⁰So Moses and Aaron went in to Pharaoh and did just as the Lord had commanded. Aaron threw down his staff before Pharaoh and his officials, and it became a serpent. ¹¹But then Pharaoh called the wise men and sorcerers—the magicians of Egypt, and they also did the same thing by their occult practices. ¹²Each one threw down his staff, and

it became a serpent. But Aaron's staff swallowed their staffs. ¹³However, Pharaoh's heart hardened, and he did not listen to them, as the Lord had said.

¹⁴Then the Lord said to Moses, "Pharaoh's heart is hard: he refuses to let the people go. ¹⁵Go to Pharaoh in the morning. When you see him walking out to the water, stand ready to meet him by the bank of the Nile. Take in your hand the staff that turned into a snake. ¹⁶Tell him: Yahweh, the God of the Hebrews, has sent me to tell you: Let My people go, so that they may worship Me in the wilderness, but so far you have not listened. ¹⁷This is what Yahweh says: Here is how you will know that I am Yahweh. Watch. I will strike the water in the Nile with the staff in my hand, and it will turn to blood. ¹⁸The fish in the Nile will die, the river will stink, and the Egyptians will be unable to drink water from it."

¹⁹So the Lord said to Moses, "Tell Aaron: Take your staff and stretch out your hand over the waters of Egypt—over their rivers, canals, ponds, and all their water reservoirs—and they will become blood. There will be blood throughout the land of Egypt, even in wooden and stone containers."

²⁰Moses and Aaron did just as the Lord had commanded; in the sight of Pharaoh and his officials, he raised the staff and struck the water in the Nile, and all the water in the Nile was turned to blood. ²¹The fish in the Nile died, and the river smelled so bad the Egyptians could not drink water from it. There was blood throughout the land of Egypt.

²²But the magicians of Egypt did the same thing by their occult practices. So Pharaoh's heart hardened, and he would not listen to them, as the Lord had said. ²³Pharaoh turned around, went into his palace, and didn't even take this to heart. ²⁴All the Egyptians dug around the Nile for water to drink because they could not drink the water from the river. ²⁵Seven days passed after the Lord struck the Nile.

8 Then the Lord said to Moses, "Go in to Pharaoh and tell him: This is what ˙Yahweh says: Let My people go, so that they may worship Me. ²But if you refuse to let them go, then I will plague all your territory with frogs. ³The Nile will swarm with frogs; they will come up and go into your palace, into your bedroom and on your bed, into the houses of your officials and your people, and into your ovens and kneading bowls. ⁴The frogs will come up on you, your people, and all your officials."

⁵ The Lord then said to Moses, "Tell Aaron: Stretch out your hand with your staff over the rivers, canals, and ponds, and cause the frogs to come up onto the land of Egypt." ⁶When Aaron stretched out his hand over the waters of Egypt, the frogs came up and covered the land of Egypt. ⁷But the magicians did the same thing by their occult practices and brought frogs up onto the land of Egypt.

⁸Pharaoh summoned Moses and Aaron and said, "Ask Yahweh to remove the frogs from me and my people. Then I will let the people go and they can sacrifice to Yahweh."

⁹Moses said to Pharaoh, "You make the choice rather than me. When should I ask on behalf of you, your officials, and your people, that the frogs be taken away from you and your houses, and remain only in the Nile?"

¹⁰ "Tomorrow," he answered.

Moses replied, "As you have said, so you may know

there is no one like Yahweh our God, ¹¹the frogs will go away from you, your houses, your officials, and your people. The frogs will remain only in the Nile." ¹²After Moses and Aaron went out from Pharaoh, Moses cried out to the Lord for help concerning the frogs that He had brought against Pharaoh. ¹³The Lord did as Moses had said: the frogs in the houses, courtyards, and fields died. ¹⁴They piled them in countless heaps, and there was a terrible odor in the land. ¹⁵But when Pharaoh saw there was relief, he hardened his heart and would not listen to them, as the Lord had said.

¹⁶Then the Lord said to Moses, "Tell Aaron: Stretch out your staff and strike the dust of the earth, and it will become gnats throughout the land of Egypt." ¹⁷And they did this. Aaron stretched out his hand with his staff, and when he struck the dust of the earth, gnats were on man and beast. All the dust of the earth became gnats throughout the land of Egypt. ¹⁸The magicians tried to produce gnats using their occult practices, but they could not. The gnats remained on man and beast.

¹⁹"This is the finger of God," the magicians said to Pharaoh. But Pharaoh's heart hardened, and he would not listen to them, as the Lord had said.

²⁰The Lord said to Moses, "Get up early in the morning and present yourself to Pharaoh when you see him going out to the water. Tell him: This is what Yahweh says: Let My people go, so that they may worship Me. ²¹But if you will not let My people go, then I will send swarms of flies against you, your officials, your people, and your houses. The Egyptians' houses will swarm with flies, and so will the land where they live. ²²But on that day I will give special treatment to the land of Goshen, where My people are living; no flies will be there. This way you will know that I, Yahweh, am in the land. ²³I will make a distinction between My people and your people. This sign will take place tomorrow."

²⁴And the Lord did this. Thick swarms of flies went into Pharaoh's palace and his officials' houses. Throughout Egypt the land was ruined because of the swarms of flies. ²⁵Then Pharaoh summoned Moses and Aaron and said, "Go sacrifice to your God within the country."

²⁶But Moses said, "It would not be right to do that, because what we will sacrifice to the Lord our God is detestable to the Egyptians. If we sacrifice what the Egyptians detest in front of them, won't they stone us? ²⁷We must go a distance of three days into the wilderness and sacrifice to the Lord our God as He instructs us."

²⁸Pharaoh responded, "I will let you go and sacrifice to the Lord your God in the wilderness, but don't go very far. Make an appeal for me."

²⁹"As soon as I leave you," Moses said, "I will appeal to the Lord, and tomorrow the swarms of flies will depart from Pharaoh, his officials, and his people. But Pharaoh must not act deceptively again by refusing to let the people go and sacrifice to the Lord." ³⁰Then Moses left Pharaoh's presence and appealed to the Lord. ³¹The Lord did as Moses had said: He removed the swarms of flies from Pharaoh, his officials, and his people; not one was left. ³²But Pharaoh hardened his heart this time also and did not let the people go.

9 Then the Lord said to Moses, "Go in to Pharaoh and say to him: This is what ⋅Yahweh, the God of the Hebrews, says: Let My people go, so that they may worship Me. ²But if you refuse to let them go and keep holding them, ³then the Lord's hand will bring a severe plague against your livestock in the field—the horses, donkeys, camels, herds, and flocks. ⁴But the Lord will make a distinction between the livestock of Israel and the livestock of Egypt, so that nothing of all that the Israelites own will die." ⁵And the Lord set a time, saying, "Tomorrow the Lord will do this thing in the land." ⁶The Lord did this the next day. All the Egyptian livestock died, but none among the Israelite livestock died. ⁷Pharaoh sent messengers who saw that not a single one of the Israelite livestock was dead. But Pharaoh's heart was hardened, and he did not let the people go.

⁸Then the Lord said to Moses and Aaron, "Take handfuls of furnace soot, and Moses is to throw it toward heaven in the sight of Pharaoh. ⁹It will become fine dust over the entire land of Egypt. It will become festering boils on man and beast throughout the land of Egypt." ¹⁰So they took furnace soot and stood before Pharaoh. Moses threw it toward heaven, and it became festering boils on man and beast. ¹¹The magicians could not stand before Moses because of the boils, for the boils were on the magicians as well as on all the Egyptians. ¹²But the Lord hardened Pharaoh's heart and he did not listen to them, as the Lord had told Moses.

¹³Then the Lord said to Moses, "Get up early in the morning and present yourself to Pharaoh. Tell him: This is what Yahweh, the God of the Hebrews says: Let My people go, so that they may worship Me. ¹⁴Otherwise, I am going to send all My plagues against you, your officials, and your people. Then you will know there is no one like Me in all the earth. ¹⁵By now I could have stretched out My hand and struck you and your people with a plague, and you would have been obliterated from the earth. ¹⁶However, I have let you live for this purpose: to show you My power and to make My name known in all the earth. ¹⁷You are still acting arrogantly against My people by not letting them go. ¹⁸Tomorrow at this time I will rain down the worst hail that has ever occurred in Egypt from the day it was founded until now. ¹⁹Therefore give orders to bring your livestock and all that you have in the field into shelters. Every person and animal that is in the field and not brought inside will die when the hail falls on them." ²⁰Those among Pharaoh's officials who ⋅feared the word of the Lord made their servants and livestock flee to shelters, ²¹but those who didn't take the Lord's word seriously left their servants and livestock in the field.

²²Then the Lord said to Moses, "Stretch out your hand toward heaven and let there be hail throughout the land of Egypt—on man and beast and every plant of the field in the land of Egypt." ²³So Moses stretched out his staff toward heaven, and the Lord sent thunder and hail. Lightning struck the earth, and the Lord rained hail on the land of Egypt. ²⁴The hail, with lightning flashing through it, was so severe that nothing like it had occurred in the land of Egypt since it had become a nation. ²⁵Throughout the land of Egypt, the hail struck down everything in the field, both man and beast. The hail beat down every plant of the field and shattered every tree in the field. ²⁶The only place it didn't hail was in the land of Goshen where the Israelites were.

²⁷Pharaoh sent for Moses and Aaron. "I have sinned this time," he said to them. "Yahweh is the Righteous

One, and I and my people are the *guilty ones. ²⁸ Make an appeal to Yahweh. There has been enough of God's thunder and hail. I will let you go; you don't need to stay any longer."

²⁹ Moses said to him, "When I have left the city, I will extend my hands to Yahweh. The thunder will cease, and there will be no more hail, so that you may know the earth belongs to Yahweh. ³⁰ But as for you and your officials, I know that you still do not fear Yahweh our God."

³¹ The flax and the barley were destroyed because the barley was ripe and the flax was budding, ³² but the wheat and the spelt were not destroyed since they are later crops.

³³ Moses went out from Pharaoh and the city, and extended his hands to the LORD. Then the thunder and hail ceased, and rain no longer poured down on the land. ³⁴ When Pharaoh saw that the rain, hail, and thunder had ceased, he sinned again and hardened his heart, he and his officials. ³⁵ So Pharaoh's heart hardened, and he did not let the Israelites go, as the LORD had said through Moses.

10 Then the LORD said to Moses, "Go to Pharaoh, for I have hardened his heart and the hearts of his officials so that I may do these miraculous signs of Mine among them, ² and so that you may tell your son and grandson how severely I dealt with the Egyptians and performed miraculous signs among them, and you will know that I am *Yahweh."

³ So Moses and Aaron went in to Pharaoh and told him, "This is what Yahweh, the God of the Hebrews, says: How long will you refuse to humble yourself before Me? Let My people go, that they may worship Me. ⁴ But if you refuse to let My people go, then tomorrow I will bring locusts into your territory. ⁵ They will cover the surface of the land so that no one will be able to see the land. They will eat the remainder left to you that escaped the hail; they will eat every tree you have growing in the fields. ⁶ They will fill your houses, all your officials' houses, and the houses of all the Egyptians—something your fathers and ancestors never saw since the time they occupied the land until today." Then he turned and left Pharaoh's presence.

⁷ Pharaoh's officials asked him, "How long must this man be a snare to us? Let the men go, so that they may worship Yahweh their God. Don't you realize yet that Egypt is devastated?"

⁸ So Moses and Aaron were brought back to Pharaoh. "Go, worship Yahweh your God," Pharaoh said. "But exactly who will be going?"

⁹ Moses replied, "We will go with our young and our old; we will go with our sons and daughters and with our flocks and herds because we must hold Yahweh's festival."

¹⁰ He said to them, "May Yahweh be with you if I ever let you and your families go! Look out—you are planning evil. ¹¹ No, only the men may go and worship Yahweh, for that is what you have been asking for." And they were driven from Pharaoh's presence.

¹² The LORD then said to Moses, "Stretch out your hand over the land of Egypt and the locusts will come up over it and eat every plant in the land, everything that the hail left." ¹³ So Moses stretched out his staff over the land of Egypt, and the LORD sent an east wind over the land all that day and through the night. By morning the east wind had brought in the locusts. ¹⁴ The locusts went up over the entire land of Egypt

and settled on the whole territory of Egypt. Never before had there been such a large number of locusts, and there never will be again. ¹⁵ They covered the surface of the whole land so that the land was black, and they consumed all the plants on the ground and all the fruit on the trees that the hail had left. Nothing green was left on the trees or the plants in the field throughout the land of Egypt.

¹⁶ Pharaoh urgently sent for Moses and Aaron and said, "I have sinned against Yahweh your God and against you. ¹⁷ Please forgive my sin once more and make an appeal to Yahweh your God, so that He will take this death away from me." ¹⁸ Moses left Pharaoh's presence and appealed to the LORD. ¹⁹ Then the LORD changed the wind to a strong west wind, and it carried off the locusts and blew them into the *Red Sea. Not a single locust was left in all the territory of Egypt. ²⁰ But the LORD hardened Pharaoh's heart, and he did not let the Israelites go.

²¹ Then the LORD said to Moses, "Stretch out your hand toward heaven, and there will be darkness over the land of Egypt, a darkness that can be felt." ²² So Moses stretched out his hand toward heaven, and there was thick darkness throughout the land of Egypt for three days. ²³ One person could not see another, and for three days they did not move from where they were. Yet all the Israelites had light where they lived.

²⁴ Pharaoh summoned Moses and said, "Go, worship Yahweh. Even your families may go with you; only your flocks and herds must stay behind."

²⁵ Moses responded, "You must also let us have sacrifices and *burnt offerings to prepare for Yahweh our God. ²⁶ Even our livestock must go with us; not a hoof will be left behind because we will take some of them to worship Yahweh our God. We will not know what we will use to worship Yahweh until we get there."

²⁷ But the LORD hardened Pharaoh's heart, and he was unwilling to let them go. ²⁸ Pharaoh said to him, "Leave me! Make sure you never see my face again, for on the day you see my face, you will die."

²⁹ "As you have said," Moses replied, "I will never see your face again."

11 The LORD said to Moses, "I will bring one more plague on Pharaoh and on Egypt. After that, he will let you go from here. When he lets you go, he will drive you out of here. ² Now announce to the people that both men and women should ask their neighbors for silver and gold jewelry." ³ The LORD gave the people favor in the sight of the Egyptians. And the man Moses was highly regarded in the land of Egypt by Pharaoh's officials and the people.

⁴ So Moses said, "This is what *Yahweh says: 'About midnight I will go throughout Egypt, ⁵ and every firstborn male in the land of Egypt will die, from the firstborn of Pharaoh who sits on his throne to the firstborn of the servant girl who is behind the millstones, as well as every firstborn of the livestock. ⁶ Then there will be a great cry of anguish through all the land of Egypt such as never was before, or ever will be again. ⁷ But against all the Israelites, whether man or beast, not even a dog will snarl, so that you may know that Yahweh makes a distinction between Egypt and Israel. ⁸ All these officials of yours will come down to me and bow before me, saying: Leave, you and all the people who follow you. After that, I will leave.'" And he left Pharaoh's presence in fierce anger.

⁹ The LORD said to Moses, "Pharaoh will not listen to

you, so that My wonders may be multiplied in the land of Egypt." ¹⁰Moses and Aaron did all these wonders before Pharaoh, but the LORD hardened Pharaoh's heart, and he would not let the Israelites go out of his land.

12 The LORD said to Moses and Aaron in the land of Egypt: ²"This month is to be the beginning of months for you; it is the first month of your year. ³Tell the whole community of Israel that on the tenth day of this month they must each select an animal of the flock according to their fathers' households, one animal per household. ⁴If the household is too small for a whole animal, that person and the neighbor nearest his house are to select one based on the combined number of people; you should apportion the animal according to what each person will eat. ⁵You must have an unblemished animal, a year-old male; you may take it from either the sheep or the goats. ⁶You are to keep it until the fourteenth day of this month; then the whole assembly of the community of Israel will slaughter the animals at twilight. ⁷They must take some of the blood and put it on the two doorposts and the lintel of the houses where they eat them. ⁸They are to eat the meat that night; they should eat it, roasted over the fire along with unleavened bread and bitter herbs. ⁹Do not eat any of it raw or cooked in boiling water, but only roasted over fire—its head as well as its legs and inner organs. ¹⁰Do not let any of it remain until morning; you must burn up any part of it that does remain before morning. ¹¹Here is how you must eat it: you must be dressed for travel, your sandals on your feet, and your staff in your hand. You are to eat it in a hurry; it is the LORD's *Passover.

¹²"I will pass through the land of Egypt on that night and strike every firstborn male in the land of Egypt, both man and beast. I am *Yahweh; I will execute judgments against all the gods of Egypt. ¹³The blood on the houses where you are staying will be a distinguishing mark for you; when I see the blood, I will pass over you. No plague will be among you to destroy you when I strike the land of Egypt.

¹⁴"This day is to be a memorial for you, and you must celebrate it as a festival to the LORD. You are to celebrate it throughout your generations as a permanent statute. ¹⁵You must eat unleavened bread for seven days. On the first day you must remove yeast from your houses. Whoever eats what is leavened from the first day through the seventh day must be cut off from Israel. ¹⁶You are to hold a sacred assembly on the first day and another sacred assembly on the seventh day. No work may be done on those days except for preparing what people need to eat—you may do only that.

¹⁷"You are to observe the Festival of *Unleavened Bread because on this very day I brought your divisions out of the land of Egypt. You must observe this day throughout your generations as a permanent statute. ¹⁸You are to eat unleavened bread in the first month, from the evening of the fourteenth day of the month until the evening of the twenty-first day. ¹⁹Yeast must not be found in your houses for seven days. If anyone eats something leavened, that person, whether a foreign resident or native of the land, must be cut off from the community of Israel. ²⁰Do not eat anything leavened; eat unleavened bread in all your homes."

²¹Then Moses summoned all the elders of Israel and said to them, "Go, select an animal from the flock according to your families, and slaughter the Passover

animal. ²²Take a cluster of hyssop, dip it in the blood that is in the basin, and brush the lintel and the two doorposts with some of the blood in the basin. None of you may go out the door of his house until morning. ²³When the LORD passes through to strike Egypt and sees the blood on the lintel and the two doorposts, He will pass over the door and not let the destroyer enter your houses to strike you.

²⁴"Keep this command permanently as a statute for you and your descendants. ²⁵When you enter the land that the LORD will give you as He promised, you are to observe this ritual. ²⁶When your children ask you, 'What does this ritual mean to you?' ²⁷you are to reply, 'It is the Passover sacrifice to the LORD, for He passed over the houses of the Israelites in Egypt when He struck the Egyptians and spared our homes.'" So the people bowed down and worshiped. ²⁸Then the Israelites went and did this; they did just as the LORD had commanded Moses and Aaron.

²⁹Now at midnight the LORD struck every firstborn male in the land of Egypt, from the firstborn of Pharaoh who sat on his throne to the firstborn of the prisoner who was in the dungeon, and every firstborn of the livestock. ³⁰During the night Pharaoh got up, he along with all his officials and all the Egyptians, and there was a loud wailing throughout Egypt because there wasn't a house without someone dead. ³¹He summoned Moses and Aaron during the night and said, "Get up, leave my people, both you and the Israelites, and go, worship Yahweh as you have asked. ³²Take even your flocks and your herds as you asked and leave, and also bless me."

³³Now the Egyptians pressured the people in order to send them quickly out of the country, for they said, "We're all going to die!" ³⁴So the people took their dough before it was leavened, with their kneading bowls wrapped up in their clothes on their shoulders. ³⁵The Israelites acted on Moses' word and asked the Egyptians for silver and gold jewelry and for clothing. ³⁶And the LORD gave the people such favor in the Egyptians' sight that they gave them what they requested. In this way they plundered the Egyptians.

³⁷The Israelites traveled from Rameses to Succoth, about 600,000 soldiers on foot, besides their families. ³⁸An ethnically diverse crowd also went up with them, along with a huge number of livestock, both flocks and herds. ³⁹The people baked the dough they had brought out of Egypt into unleavened loaves, since it had no yeast; for when they had been driven out of Egypt they could not delay and had not prepared any provisions for themselves.

⁴⁰The time that the Israelites lived in Egypt was 430 years. ⁴¹At the end of 430 years, on that same day, all the LORD's divisions went out from the land of Egypt. ⁴²It was a night of vigil in honor of the LORD, because He would bring them out of the land of Egypt. This same night is in honor of the LORD, a night vigil for all the Israelites throughout their generations.

⁴³The LORD said to Moses and Aaron, "This is the statute of the Passover: no foreigner may eat it. ⁴⁴But any slave a man has purchased may eat it, after you have circumcised him. ⁴⁵A temporary resident or hired hand may not eat the Passover. ⁴⁶It is to be eaten in one house. You may not take any of the meat outside the house, and you may not break any of its bones. ⁴⁷The whole community of Israel must celebrate it. ⁴⁸If a foreigner resides with you and wants to celebrate the

LORD's Passover, every male in his household must be circumcised, and then he may participate; he will become like a native of the land. But no uncircumcised person may eat it. ⁴⁹The same law will apply to both the native and the foreigner who resides among you."

⁵⁰Then all the Israelites did this; they did just as the LORD had commanded Moses and Aaron. ⁵¹On that same day the LORD brought the Israelites out of the land of Egypt according to their divisions.

13 The LORD spoke to Moses: ²"Consecrate every firstborn male to Me, the firstborn from every womb among the Israelites, both man and domestic animal; it is Mine."

³Then Moses said to the people, "Remember this day when you came out of Egypt, out of the place of slavery, for the LORD brought you out of here by the strength of His hand. Nothing leavened may be eaten. ⁴Today, in the month of Abib, you are leaving. ⁵When the LORD brings you into the land of the Canaanites, Hittites, Amorites, Hivites, and Jebusites, which He swore to your fathers that He would give you, a land flowing with milk and honey, you must carry out this ritual in this month. ⁶For seven days you must eat unleavened bread, and on the seventh day there is to be a festival to the LORD. ⁷Unleavened bread is to be eaten for those seven days. Nothing leavened may be found among you, and no yeast may be found among you in all your territory. ⁸On that day explain to your son, 'This is because of what the LORD did for me when I came out of Egypt.' ⁹Let it serve as a sign for you on your hand and as a reminder on your forehead, so that the LORD's instruction may be in your mouth; for the LORD brought you out of Egypt with a strong hand. ¹⁰Keep this statute at its appointed time from year to year.

¹¹"When the LORD brings you into the land of the Canaanites, as He swore to you and your fathers, and gives it to you, ¹²you are to present to the LORD every firstborn male of the womb. All firstborn offspring of the livestock you own that are males will be the LORD's. ¹³You must redeem every firstborn of a donkey with a flock animal, but if you do not redeem it, break its neck. However, you must redeem every firstborn among your sons.

¹⁴"In the future, when your son asks you, 'What does this mean?' say to him, 'By the strength of His hand the LORD brought us out of Egypt, out of the place of slavery. ¹⁵When Pharaoh stubbornly refused to let us go, the LORD killed every firstborn male in the land of Egypt, from the firstborn of man to the firstborn of livestock. That is why I sacrifice to the LORD all the firstborn of the womb that are males, but I redeem all the firstborn of my sons.' ¹⁶So let it be a sign on your hand and a symbol on your forehead, for the LORD brought us out of Egypt by the strength of His hand."

¹⁷When Pharaoh let the people go, God did not lead them along the road to the land of the Philistines, even though it was nearby; for God said, "The people will change their minds and return to Egypt if they face war." ¹⁸So He led the people around toward the •Red Sea along the road of the wilderness. And the Israelites left the land of Egypt in battle formation.

¹⁹Moses took the bones of Joseph with him, because Joseph had made the Israelites swear a solemn oath, saying, "God will certainly come to your aid; then you must take my bones with you from this place."

²⁰They set out from Succoth and camped at Etham on the edge of the wilderness. ²¹The LORD went ahead of them in a pillar of cloud to lead them on their way during the day and in a pillar of fire to give them light at night, so that they could travel day or night. ²²The pillar of cloud by day and the pillar of fire by night never left its place in front of the people.

14 Then the LORD spoke to Moses: ²"Tell the Israelites to turn back and camp in front of Pi-hahiroth, between Migdol and the sea; you must camp in front of Baal-zephon, facing it by the sea. ³Pharaoh will say of the Israelites: They are wandering around the land in confusion; the wilderness has boxed them in. ⁴I will harden Pharaoh's heart so that he will pursue them. Then I will receive glory by means of Pharaoh and all his army, and the Egyptians will know that I am •Yahweh." So the Israelites did this.

⁵When the king of Egypt was told that the people had fled, Pharaoh and his officials changed their minds about the people and said: "What have we done? We have released Israel from serving us." ⁶So he got his chariot ready and took his troops with him; ⁷he took 600 of the best chariots and all the rest of the chariots of Egypt, with officers in each one. ⁸The LORD hardened the heart of Pharaoh king of Egypt, and he pursued the Israelites, who were going out triumphantly. ⁹The Egyptians—all Pharaoh's horses and chariots, his horsemen, and his army—chased after them and caught up with them as they camped by the sea beside Pi-hahiroth, in front of Baal-zephon.

¹⁰As Pharaoh approached, the Israelites looked up and saw the Egyptians coming after them. Then the Israelites were terrified and cried out to the LORD for help. ¹¹They said to Moses: "Is it because there are no graves in Egypt that you took us to die in the wilderness? What have you done to us by bringing us out of Egypt? ¹²Isn't this what we told you in Egypt: Leave us alone so that we may serve the Egyptians? It would have been better for us to serve the Egyptians than to die in the wilderness."

¹³But Moses said to the people, "Don't be afraid. Stand firm and see the LORD's salvation He will provide for you today; for the Egyptians you see today, you will never see again. ¹⁴The LORD will fight for you; you must be quiet."

¹⁵The LORD said to Moses, "Why are you crying out to Me? Tell the Israelites to break camp. ¹⁶As for you, lift up your staff, stretch out your hand over the sea, and divide it so that the Israelites can go through the sea on dry ground. ¹⁷I am going to harden the hearts of the Egyptians so that they will go in after them, and I will receive glory by means of Pharaoh, all his army, and his chariots and horsemen. ¹⁸The Egyptians will know that I am Yahweh when I receive glory through Pharaoh, his chariots, and his horsemen."

¹⁹Then the Angel of God, who was going in front of the Israelite forces, moved and went behind them. The pillar of cloud moved from in front of them and stood behind them. ²⁰It came between the Egyptian and Israelite forces. The cloud was there in the darkness, yet it lit up the night. So neither group came near the other all night long.

²¹Then Moses stretched out his hand over the sea. The LORD drove the sea back with a powerful east wind all that night and turned the sea into dry land. So the waters were divided, ²²and the Israelites went through the sea on dry ground, with the waters like a wall to them on their right and their left.

²³The Egyptians set out in pursuit—all Pharaoh's horses, his chariots, and his horsemen—and went into the sea after them. ²⁴Then during the morning watch, the Lord looked down on the Egyptian forces from the pillar of fire and cloud, and threw them into confusion. ²⁵He caused their chariot wheels to swerve and made them drive with difficulty. "Let's get away from Israel," the Egyptians said, "because Yahweh is fighting for them against Egypt!"

²⁶Then the Lord said to Moses, "Stretch out your hand over the sea so that the waters may come back on the Egyptians, on their chariots and horsemen." ²⁷So Moses stretched out his hand over the sea, and at daybreak the sea returned to its normal depth. While the Egyptians were trying to escape from it, the Lord threw them into the sea. ²⁸The waters came back and covered the chariots and horsemen, the entire army of Pharaoh, that had gone after them into the sea. None of them survived.

²⁹But the Israelites had walked through the sea on dry ground, with the waters like a wall to them on their right and their left. ³⁰That day the Lord saved Israel from the power of the Egyptians, and Israel saw the Egyptians dead on the seashore. ³¹When Israel saw the great power that the Lord used against the Egyptians, the people ˙feared the Lord and believed in Him and in His servant Moses.

15 Then Moses and the Israelites sang this song to the Lord. They said:

> I will sing to the Lord,
> for He is highly exalted;
> He has thrown the horse
> and its rider into the sea.
> ² The Lord is my strength and my song;
> He has become my salvation.
> This is my God, and I will praise Him,
> my father's God, and I will exalt Him.
> ³ The Lord is a warrior;
> ˙Yahweh is His name.
> ⁴ He threw Pharaoh's chariots
> and his army into the sea;
> the elite of his officers
> were drowned in the ˙Red Sea.
> ⁵ The floods covered them;
> they sank to the depths like a stone.
> ⁶ Lord, Your right hand is glorious in power.
> Lord, Your right hand shattered the enemy.
> ⁷ You overthrew Your adversaries
> by Your great majesty.
> You unleashed Your burning wrath;
> it consumed them like stubble.
> ⁸ The waters heaped up at the blast
> of Your nostrils;
> the currents stood firm like a dam.
> The watery depths congealed in the heart
> of the sea.
> ⁹ The enemy said:
> "I will pursue, I will overtake,
> I will divide the spoil.
> My desire will be gratified at their expense.
> I will draw my sword;
> my hand will destroy them."
> ¹⁰ But You blew with Your breath,
> and the sea covered them.
> They sank like lead
> in the mighty waters.
> ¹¹ Lord, who is like You among the gods?

> Who is like You, glorious in holiness,
> revered with praises, performing wonders?
> ¹² You stretched out Your right hand,
> and the earth swallowed them.
> ¹³ You will lead the people
> You have redeemed
> with Your faithful love;
> You will guide them to Your holy dwelling
> with Your strength.
> ¹⁴ When the peoples hear, they will shudder;
> anguish will seize the inhabitants of Philistia.
> ¹⁵ Then the chiefs of Edom will be terrified;
> trembling will seize the leaders of Moab;
> the inhabitants of Canaan will panic;
> ¹⁶ and terror and dread will fall on them.
> They will be as still as a stone
> because of Your powerful arm
> until Your people pass by, Lord,
> until the people whom You purchased pass by.
> ¹⁷ You will bring them in and plant them
> on the mountain of Your possession;
> Lord, You have prepared the place
> for Your dwelling;
> Lord, Your hands have established
> the sanctuary.
> ¹⁸ The Lord will reign forever and ever!

¹⁹When Pharaoh's horses with his chariots and horsemen went into the sea, the Lord brought the waters of the sea back over them. But the Israelites walked through the sea on dry ground. ²⁰Then Miriam the prophetess, Aaron's sister, took a tambourine in her hand, and all the women followed her with their tambourines and danced. ²¹Miriam sang to them:

> Sing to the Lord,
> for He is highly exalted;
> He has thrown the horse
> and its rider into the sea.

²²Then Moses led Israel on from the Red Sea, and they went out to the Wilderness of Shur. They journeyed for three days in the wilderness without finding water. ²³They came to Marah, but they could not drink the water at Marah because it was bitter—that is why it was named Marah. ²⁴The people grumbled to Moses, "What are we going to drink?" ²⁵So he cried out to the Lord, and the Lord showed him a tree. When he threw it into the water, the water became drinkable.

He made a statute and ordinance for them at Marah and He tested them there. ²⁶He said, "If you will carefully obey the Lord your God, do what is right in His eyes, pay attention to His commands, and keep all His statutes, I will not inflict any illnesses on you that I inflicted on the Egyptians. For I am Yahweh who heals you."

²⁷Then they came to Elim, where there were 12 springs of water and 70 date palms, and they camped there by the waters.

16 The entire Israelite community departed from Elim and came to the Wilderness of Sin, which is between Elim and Sinai, on the fifteenth day of the second month after they had left the land of Egypt. ²The entire Israelite community grumbled against Moses and Aaron in the wilderness. ³The Israelites said to them, "If only we had died by the Lord's hand in the land of Egypt, when we sat by pots of meat and ate all the bread we wanted. Instead, you brought us into this wilderness to make this whole assembly die of hunger!"

⁴Then the LORD said to Moses, "I am going to rain bread from heaven for you. The people are to go out each day and gather enough for that day. This way I will test them to see whether or not they will follow My instructions. ⁵On the sixth day, when they prepare what they bring in, it will be twice as much as they gather on other days."

⁶So Moses and Aaron said to all the Israelites: "This evening you will know that it was the LORD who brought you out of the land of Egypt; ⁷in the morning you will see the LORD's glory because He has heard your complaints about Him. For who are we that you complain about us?" ⁸Moses continued, "The LORD will give you meat to eat this evening and more than enough bread in the morning, for He has heard the complaints that you are raising against Him. Who are we? Your complaints are not against us but against the LORD."

⁹Then Moses told Aaron, "Say to the entire Israelite community, 'Come before the LORD, for He has heard your complaints.'" ¹⁰As Aaron was speaking to the entire Israelite community, they turned toward the wilderness, and there in a cloud the LORD's glory appeared.

¹¹The LORD spoke to Moses, ¹²"I have heard the complaints of the Israelites. Tell them: At twilight you will eat meat, and in the morning you will eat bread until you are full. Then you will know that I am ˙Yahweh your God."

¹³So at evening quail came and covered the camp. In the morning there was a layer of dew all around the camp. ¹⁴When the layer of dew evaporated, there were fine flakes on the desert surface, as fine as frost on the ground. ¹⁵When the Israelites saw it, they asked one another, "What is it?" because they didn't know what it was.

Moses told them, "It is the bread the LORD has given you to eat. ¹⁶This is what the LORD has commanded: 'Gather as much of it as each person needs to eat. You may take two quarts per individual, according to the number of people each of you has in his tent.'"

¹⁷So the Israelites did this. Some gathered a lot, some a little. ¹⁸When they measured it by quarts, the person who gathered a lot had no surplus, and the person who gathered a little had no shortage. Each gathered as much as he needed to eat. ¹⁹Moses said to them, "No one is to let any of it remain until morning." ²⁰But they didn't listen to Moses; some people left part of it until morning, and it bred worms and smelled. Therefore Moses was angry with them.

²¹They gathered it every morning. Each gathered as much as he needed to eat, but when the sun grew hot, it melted. ²²On the sixth day they gathered twice as much food, four quarts apiece, and all the leaders of the community came and reported this to Moses. ²³He told them, "This is what the LORD has said: 'Tomorrow is a day of complete rest, a holy Sabbath to the LORD. Bake what you want to bake, and boil what you want to boil, and set aside everything left over to be kept until morning.'"

²⁴So they set it aside until morning as Moses commanded, and it didn't smell or have any maggots in it. ²⁵"Eat it today," Moses said, "because today is a Sabbath to the LORD. Today you won't find any in the field. ²⁶For six days you may gather it, but on the seventh day, the Sabbath, there will be none."

²⁷Yet on the seventh day some of the people went out to gather, but they did not find any. ²⁸Then the LORD said to Moses, "How long will you refuse to keep My commands and instructions? ²⁹Understand that the LORD has given you the Sabbath; therefore on the sixth day He will give you two days' worth of bread. Each of you stay where you are; no one is to leave his place on the seventh day." ³⁰So the people rested on the seventh day.

³¹The house of Israel named the substance manna. It resembled coriander seed, was white, and tasted like wafers made with honey. ³²Moses said, "This is what the LORD has commanded: 'Two quarts of it are to be preserved throughout your generations, so that they may see the bread I fed you in the wilderness when I brought you out of the land of Egypt.'"

³³Moses told Aaron, "Take a container and put two quarts of manna in it. Then place it before the LORD to be preserved throughout your generations." ³⁴As the LORD commanded Moses, Aaron placed it before the ˙testimony to be preserved.

³⁵The Israelites ate manna for 40 years, until they came to an inhabited land. They ate manna until they reached the border of the land of Canaan. ³⁶(Two quarts are a tenth of an ephah.)

17 The entire Israelite community left the Wilderness of Sin, moving from one place to the next according to the LORD's command. They camped at Rephidim, but there was no water for the people to drink. ²So the people complained to Moses, "Give us water to drink."

"Why are you complaining to me?" Moses replied to them. "Why are you testing the LORD?"

³But the people thirsted there for water, and grumbled against Moses. They said, "Why did you ever bring us out of Egypt to kill us and our children and our livestock with thirst?"

⁴Then Moses cried out to the LORD, "What should I do with these people? In a little while they will stone me!"

⁵The LORD answered Moses, "Go on ahead of the people and take some of the elders of Israel with you. Take the staff you struck the Nile with in your hand and go. ⁶I am going to stand there in front of you on the rock at Horeb; when you hit the rock, water will come out of it and the people will drink." Moses did this in the sight of the elders of Israel. ⁷He named the place Massah and Meribah because the Israelites complained, and because they tested the LORD, saying, "Is the LORD among us or not?"

⁸At Rephidim, Amalek came and fought against Israel. Moses said to Joshua, "Select some men for us and go fight against Amalek. Tomorrow I will stand on the hilltop with God's staff in my hand."

¹⁰Joshua did as Moses had told him, and fought against Amalek, while Moses, Aaron, and Hur went up to the top of the hill. ¹¹While Moses held up his hand, Israel prevailed, but whenever he put his hand down, Amalek prevailed. ¹²When Moses' hands grew heavy, they took a stone and put it under him, and he sat down on it. Then Aaron and Hur supported his hands, one on one side and one on the other so that his hands remained steady until the sun went down. ¹³So Joshua defeated Amalek and his army with the sword.

¹⁴The LORD then said to Moses, "Write this down on a scroll as a reminder and recite it to Joshua: I will completely blot out the memory of Amalek under heaven."

[15] And Moses built an altar and named it, "The LORD Is My Banner." [16] He said, "Indeed, my hand is lifted up toward the LORD's throne. The LORD will be at war with Amalek from generation to generation."

18 Moses' father-in-law Jethro, the priest of Midian, heard about everything that God had done for Moses and His people Israel, and how the LORD had brought Israel out of Egypt.

[2] Now Jethro, Moses' father-in-law, had taken in Zipporah, Moses' wife, after he had sent her back, [3] along with her two sons, one of whom was named Gershom (because Moses had said, "I have been a foreigner in a foreign land") [4] and the other Eliezer (because he had said, "The God of my father was my helper and delivered me from Pharaoh's sword").

[5] Moses' father-in-law Jethro, along with Moses' wife and sons, came to him in the wilderness where he was camped at the mountain of God. [6] He sent word to Moses, "I, your father-in-law Jethro, am coming to you with your wife and her two sons."

[7] So Moses went out to meet his father-in-law, bowed down, and then kissed him. They asked each other how they had been and went into the tent. [8] Moses recounted to his father-in-law all that the LORD had done to Pharaoh and the Egyptians for Israel's sake, all the hardships that confronted them on the way, and how the LORD delivered them.

[9] Jethro rejoiced over all the good things the LORD had done for Israel when He rescued them from the power of the Egyptians. [10] "Praise the LORD," Jethro exclaimed, "who rescued you from Pharaoh and the power of the Egyptians and snatched the people from the power of the Egyptians. [11] Now I know that •Yahweh is greater than all gods, because He did wonders when the Egyptians acted arrogantly against Israel."

[12] Then Jethro, Moses' father-in-law, brought a •burnt offering and sacrifices to God, and Aaron came with all the elders of Israel to eat a meal with Moses' father-in-law in God's presence.

[13] The next day Moses sat down to judge the people, and they stood around Moses from morning until evening. [14] When Moses' father-in-law saw everything he was doing for them he asked, "What is this thing you're doing for the people? Why are you alone sitting as judge, while all the people stand around you from morning until evening?"

[15] Moses replied to his father-in-law, "Because the people come to me to inquire of God. [16] Whenever they have a dispute, it comes to me, and I make a decision between one man and another. I teach them God's statutes and laws."

[17] "What you're doing is not good," Moses' father-in-law said to him. [18] "You will certainly wear out both yourself and these people who are with you, because the task is too heavy for you. You can't do it alone. [19] Now listen to me; I will give you some advice, and God be with you. You be the one to represent the people before God and bring their cases to Him. [20] Instruct them about the statutes and laws, and teach them the way to live and what they must do. [21] But you should select from all the people able men, God-fearing, trustworthy, and hating bribes. Place them over the people as commanders of thousands, hundreds, fifties, and tens. [22] They should judge the people at all times. Then they can bring you every important case but judge every minor case themselves. In this way you will lighten your load, and they will bear it with you.

[23] If you do this, and God so directs you, you will be able to endure, and also all these people will be able to go home satisfied."

[24] Moses listened to his father-in-law and did everything he said. [25] So Moses chose able men from all Israel and made them leaders over the people as commanders of thousands, hundreds, fifties, and tens. [26] They judged the people at all times; they would bring the hard cases to Moses, but they would judge every minor case themselves.

[27] Then Moses said good-bye to his father-in-law, and he journeyed to his own land.

19 In the third month, on the same day of the month that the Israelites had left the land of Egypt, they entered the Wilderness of Sinai. [2] After they departed from Rephidim, they entered the Wilderness of Sinai and camped in the wilderness, and Israel camped there in front of the mountain.

[3] Moses went up the mountain to God, and the LORD called to him from the mountain: "This is what you must say to the house of Jacob, and explain to the Israelites: [4] 'You have seen what I did to the Egyptians and how I carried you on eagles' wings and brought you to Me. [5] Now if you will listen to Me and carefully keep My covenant, you will be My own possession out of all the peoples, although all the earth is Mine, [6] and you will be My kingdom of priests and My holy nation.' These are the words that you are to say to the Israelites."

[7] After Moses came back, he summoned the elders of the people and set before them all these words that the LORD had commanded him. [8] Then all the people responded together, "We will do all that the LORD has spoken." So Moses brought the people's words back to the LORD.

[9] The LORD said to Moses, "I am going to come to you in a dense cloud, so that the people will hear when I speak with you and will always believe you." Then Moses reported the people's words to the LORD. [10] And the LORD told Moses, "Go to the people and consecrate them today and tomorrow. They must wash their clothes [11] and be prepared by the third day, for on the third day the LORD will come down on Mount Sinai in the sight of all the people. [12] Put boundaries for the people all around the mountain and say: Be careful that you don't go up on the mountain or touch its base. Anyone who touches the mountain will be put to death. [13] No hand may touch him; instead he will be stoned or shot with arrows. No animal or man will live. When the ram's horn sounds a long blast, they may go up the mountain."

[14] Then Moses came down from the mountain to the people and consecrated them, and they washed their clothes. [15] He said to the people, "Be prepared by the third day. Do not have sexual relations with women."

[16] On the third day, when morning came, there was thunder and lightning, a thick cloud on the mountain, and a loud trumpet sound, so that all the people in the camp shuddered. [17] Then Moses brought the people out of the camp to meet God, and they stood at the foot of the mountain. [18] Mount Sinai was completely enveloped in smoke because the LORD came down on it in fire. Its smoke went up like the smoke of a furnace, and the whole mountain shook violently. [19] As the sound of the trumpet grew louder and louder, Moses spoke and God answered him in the thunder.

[20] The LORD came down on Mount Sinai at the top of the mountain. Then the LORD summoned Moses to

the top of the mountain, and he went up. ²¹The Lord directed Moses, "Go down and warn the people not to break through to see the Lord; otherwise many of them will die. ²²Even the priests who come near the Lord must purify themselves or the Lord will break out in anger against them."

²³But Moses responded to the Lord, "The people cannot come up Mount Sinai, since You warned us: Put a boundary around the mountain and consider it holy." ²⁴And the Lord replied to him, "Go down and come back with Aaron. But the priests and the people must not break through to come up to the Lord, or He will break out in anger against them." ²⁵So Moses went down to the people and told them.

20 Then God spoke all these words:

²¹ I am the Lord your God, who brought you out of the land of Egypt, out of the place of slavery.

³   Do not have other gods besides Me.

⁴   Do not make an idol for yourself, whether in the shape of anything in the heavens above or on the earth below or in the waters under the earth. ⁵You must not bow down to them or worship them; for I, the Lord your God, am a jealous God, punishing the children for the fathers' sin, to the third and fourth generations of those who hate Me, ⁶but showing faithful love to a thousand generations of those who love Me and keep My commands.

⁷   Do not misuse the name of the Lord your God, because the Lord will not leave anyone unpunished who misuses His name.

⁸   Remember the Sabbath day, to keep it holy: ⁹You are to labor six days and do all your work, ¹⁰but the seventh day is a Sabbath to the Lord your God. You must not do any work—you, your son or daughter, your male or female slave, your livestock, or the foreigner who is within your gates. ¹¹For the Lord made the heavens and the earth, the sea, and everything in them in six days; then He rested on the seventh day. Therefore the Lord blessed the Sabbath day and declared it holy.

¹²   Honor your father and your mother so that you may have a long life in the land that the Lord your God is giving you.

¹³   Do not murder.

¹⁴   Do not commit adultery.

¹⁵   Do not steal.

¹⁶   Do not give false testimony against your neighbor.

¹⁷   Do not covet your neighbor's house. Do not covet your neighbor's wife, his male or female slave, his ox or donkey, or anything that belongs to your neighbor.

¹⁸All the people witnessed the thunder and lightning, the sound of the trumpet, and the mountain surrounded by smoke. When the people saw it they trembled and stood at a distance. ¹⁹"You speak to us, and we will listen," they said to Moses, "but don't let God speak to us, or we will die."

²⁰Moses responded to the people, "Don't be afraid, for God has come to test you, so that you will *fear Him and will not sin." ²¹And the people remained standing at a distance as Moses approached the thick darkness where God was.

²²Then the Lord told Moses, "This is what you are to say to the Israelites: You have seen that I have spo-

ken to you from heaven. ²³You must not make gods of silver to rival Me; you must not make gods of gold for yourselves.

²⁴"You must make an earthen altar for Me and sacrifice on it your *burnt offerings and *fellowship offerings, your sheep and goats, as well as your cattle. I will come to you and bless you in every place where I cause My name to be remembered. ²⁵If you make a stone altar for Me, you must not build it out of cut stones. If you use your chisel on it, you will defile it. ²⁶You must not go up to My altar on steps, so that your nakedness is not exposed on it.

21 "These are the ordinances that you must set before them:

²"When you buy a Hebrew slave, he is to serve for six years; then in the seventh he is to leave as a free man without paying anything. ³If he arrives alone, he is to leave alone; if he arrives with a wife, his wife is to leave with him. ⁴If his master gives him a wife and she bears him sons or daughters, the wife and her children belong to her master, and the man must leave alone.

⁵"But if the slave declares: 'I love my master, my wife, and my children; I do not want to leave as a free man,' ⁶his master is to bring him to the judges and then bring him to the door or doorpost. His master must pierce his ear with an awl, and he will serve his master for life.

⁷"When a man sells his daughter as a slave, she is not to leave as the male slaves do. ⁸If she is displeasing to her master, who chose her for himself, then he must let her be redeemed. He has no right to sell her to foreigners because he has acted treacherously toward her. ⁹Or if he chooses her for his son, he must deal with her according to the customary treatment of daughters. ¹⁰If he takes an additional wife, he must not reduce the food, clothing, or marital rights of the first wife. ¹¹And if he does not do these three things for her, she may leave free of charge, without any exchange of money.

¹²"Whoever strikes a person so that he dies must be put to death. ¹³But if he didn't intend any harm, and yet God caused it to happen by his hand, I will appoint a place for you where he may flee. ¹⁴If a person schemes and willfully acts against his neighbor to murder him, you must take him from My altar to be put to death.

¹⁵"Whoever strikes his father or his mother must be put to death.

¹⁶"Whoever kidnaps a person must be put to death, whether he sells him or the person is found in his possession.

¹⁷"Whoever curses his father or his mother must be put to death.

¹⁸"When men quarrel and one strikes the other with a stone or his fist, and the injured man does not die but is confined to bed, ¹⁹if he can later get up and walk around outside leaning on his staff, then the one who struck him will be exempt from punishment. Nevertheless, he must pay for his lost work time and provide for his complete recovery.

²⁰"When a man strikes his male or female slave with a rod, and the slave dies under his abuse, the owner must be punished. ²¹However, if the slave can stand up after a day or two, the owner should not be punished because he is his owner's property.

²²"When men get in a fight and hit a pregnant woman so that her children are born prematurely but there is no injury, the one who hit her must be fined

as the woman's husband demands from him, and he must pay according to judicial assessment. ²³If there is an injury, then you must give life for life, ²⁴eye for eye, tooth for tooth, hand for hand, foot for foot, ²⁵burn for burn, bruise for bruise, wound for wound.

²⁶"When a man strikes the eye of his male or female slave and destroys it, he must let the slave go free in compensation for his eye. ²⁷If he knocks out the tooth of his male or female slave, he must let the slave go free in compensation for his tooth.

²⁸"When an ox gores a man or a woman to death, the ox must be stoned, and its meat may not be eaten, but the ox's owner is innocent. ²⁹However, if the ox was in the habit of goring, and its owner has been warned yet does not restrain it, and it kills a man or a woman, the ox must be stoned, and its owner must also be put to death. ³⁰If instead a ransom is demanded of him, he can pay a redemption price for his life in the full amount demanded from him. ³¹If it gores a son or a daughter, he is to be dealt with according to this same law. ³²If the ox gores a male or female slave, he must give 30 •shekels of silver to the slave's master, and the ox must be stoned.

³³"When a man uncovers a pit or digs a pit, and does not cover it, and an ox or a donkey falls into it, ³⁴the owner of the pit must give compensation; he must pay money to its owner, but the dead animal will become his.

³⁵"When a man's ox injures his neighbor's ox and it dies, they must sell the live ox and divide its proceeds; they must also divide the dead animal. ³⁶If, however, it is known that the ox was in the habit of goring, yet its owner has not restrained it, he must compensate fully, ox for ox; the dead animal will become his.

22 "When a man steals an ox or a sheep and butchers it or sells it, he must repay five cattle for the ox or four sheep for the sheep. ²If a thief is caught in the act of breaking in, and he is beaten to death, no one is •guilty of bloodshed. ³But if this happens after sunrise, there is guilt of bloodshed. A thief must make full restitution. If he is unable, he is to be sold because of his theft. ⁴If what was stolen—whether ox, donkey, or sheep—is actually found alive in his possession, he must repay double.

•⁵"When a man lets a field or vineyard be grazed in, and then allows his animals to go and graze in someone else's field, he must repay with the best of his own field or vineyard.

⁶"When a fire gets out of control, spreads to thornbushes, and consumes stacks of cut grain, standing grain, or a field, the one who started the fire must make full restitution for what was burned.

⁷"When a man gives his neighbor money or goods to keep, but they are stolen from that person's house, the thief, if caught, must repay double. ⁸If the thief is not caught, the owner of the house must present himself to the judges to determine whether or not he has taken his neighbor's property. ⁹In any case of wrongdoing involving an ox, a donkey, a sheep, a garment, or anything else lost, and someone claims, 'That's mine,' the case between the two parties is to come before the judges. The one the judges condemn must repay double to his neighbor.

¹⁰"When a man gives his neighbor a donkey, an ox, a sheep, or any other animal to care for, but it dies, is injured, or is stolen, while no one is watching, ¹¹there must be an oath before the LORD between the two of them to determine whether or not he has taken his neighbor's property. Its owner must accept the oath, and the other man does not have to make restitution. ¹²But if, in fact, the animal was stolen from his custody, he must make restitution to its owner. ¹³If it was actually torn apart by a wild animal, he is to bring it as evidence; he does not have to make restitution for the torn carcass.

¹⁴"When a man borrows an animal from his neighbor, and it is injured or dies while its owner is not there with it, the man must make full restitution. ¹⁵If its owner is there with it, the man does not have to make restitution. If it was rented, the loss is covered by its rental price.

¹⁶"If a man seduces a virgin who is not engaged, and he has sexual relations with her, he must certainly pay the bridal price for her to be his wife. ¹⁷If her father absolutely refuses to give her to him, he must pay an amount in silver equal to the bridal price for virgins.

¹⁸"You must not allow a sorceress to live.

¹⁹"Whoever has sexual intercourse with an animal must be put to death.

²⁰"Whoever sacrifices to any gods, except the LORD alone, is to be •set apart for destruction.

²¹"You must not exploit a foreign resident or oppress him, since you were foreigners in the land of Egypt.

²²"You must not mistreat any widow or fatherless child. ²³If you do mistreat them, they will no doubt cry to Me, and I will certainly hear their cry. ²⁴My anger will burn, and I will kill you with the sword; then your wives will be widows and your children fatherless.

²⁵"If you lend money to My people, to the poor person among you, you must not be like a moneylender to him; you must not charge him interest.

²⁶"If you ever take your neighbor's cloak as collateral, return it to him before sunset. ²⁷For it is his only covering; it is the clothing for his body. What will he sleep in? And if he cries out to Me, I will listen because I am compassionate.

²⁸"You must not blaspheme God or curse a leader among your people.

²⁹"You must not hold back offerings from your harvest or your vats. Give Me the firstborn of your sons. ³⁰Do the same with your cattle and your flock. Let them stay with their mothers for seven days, but on the eighth day you are to give them to Me.

³¹"Be My holy people. You must not eat the meat of a mauled animal found in the field; throw it to the dogs.

23 "You must not spread a false report. Do not join the wicked to be a malicious witness.

²"You must not follow a crowd in wrongdoing. Do not testify in a lawsuit and go along with a crowd to pervert justice. ³Do not show favoritism to a poor person in his lawsuit.

⁴"If you come across your enemy's stray ox or donkey, you must return it to him.

⁵"If you see the donkey of someone who hates you lying helpless under its load, and you want to refrain from helping it, you must help with it.

⁶"You must not deny justice to a poor person among you in his lawsuit. ⁷Stay far away from a false accusation. Do not kill the innocent and the just, because I will not justify the •guilty. ⁸You must not take a bribe, for a bribe blinds the clear-sighted and corrupts the words of the righteous. ⁹You must not oppress a foreign resident; you yourselves know how it feels to be

a foreigner because you were foreigners in the land of Egypt.

[10] "Sow your land for six years and gather its produce. [11] But during the seventh year you are to let it rest and leave it uncultivated, so that the poor among your people may eat from it and the wild animals may consume what they leave. Do the same with your vineyard and your olive grove.

[12] "Do your work for six days but rest on the seventh day so that your ox and your donkey may rest, and the son of your female slave as well as the foreign resident may be refreshed.

[13] "Pay strict attention to everything I have said to you. You must not invoke the names of other gods; they must not be heard on your lips.

[14] "Celebrate a festival in My honor three times a year. [15] Observe the Festival of *Unleavened Bread. As I commanded you, you are to eat unleavened bread for seven days at the appointed time in the month of Abib, because you came out of Egypt in that month. No one is to appear before Me empty-handed. [16] Also observe the Festival of Harvest with the *firstfruits of your produce from what you sow in the field, and observe the Festival of Ingathering at the end of the year, when you gather your produce from the field. [17] Three times a year all your males are to appear before the Lord God.

[18] "You must not offer the blood of My sacrifices with anything leavened. The fat of My festival offering must not remain until morning.

[19] "Bring the best of the firstfruits of your land to the house of the Lord your God.

"You must not boil a young goat in its mother's milk.

[20] "I am going to send an angel before you to protect you on the way and bring you to the place I have prepared. [21] Be attentive to him and listen to his voice. Do not defy him, because he will not forgive your acts of rebellion, for My name is in him. [22] But if you will carefully obey him and do everything I say, then I will be an enemy to your enemies and a foe to your foes. [23] For My angel will go before you and bring you to the land of the Amorites, Hittites, Perizzites, Canaanites, Hivites, and Jebusites, and I will wipe them out. [24] You must not bow down to their gods or worship them. Do not imitate their practices. Instead, demolish them and smash their sacred pillars to pieces. [25] Worship the Lord your God, and He will bless your bread and your water. I will remove illnesses from you. [26] No woman will miscarry or be childless in your land. I will give you the full number of your days.

[27] "I will cause the people ahead of you to feel terror and throw into confusion all the nations you come to. I will make all your enemies turn their backs to you in retreat. [28] I will send the hornet in front of you, and it will drive the Hivites, Canaanites, and Hittites away from you. [29] I will not drive them out ahead of you in a single year; otherwise, the land would become desolate, and wild animals would multiply against you. [30] I will drive them out little by little ahead of you until you have become numerous and take possession of the land. [31] I will set your borders from the *Red Sea to the Mediterranean Sea, and from the wilderness to the Euphrates River. For I will place the inhabitants of the land under your control, and you will drive them out ahead of you. [32] You must not make a covenant with them or their gods. [33] They must not remain in your

land, or else they will make you sin against Me. If you worship their gods, it will be a snare for you."

24 Then He said to Moses, "Go up to the Lord, you and Aaron, Nadab, and Abihu, and 70 of Israel's elders, and bow in worship at a distance. [2] Moses alone is to approach the Lord, but the others are not to approach, and the people are not to go up with him."

[3] Moses came and told the people all the commands of the Lord and all the ordinances. Then all the people responded with a single voice, "We will do everything that the Lord has commanded." [4] And Moses wrote down all the words of the Lord. He rose early the next morning and set up an altar and 12 pillars for the 12 tribes of Israel at the base of the mountain. [5] Then he sent out young Israelite men, and they offered *burnt offerings and sacrificed bulls as *fellowship offerings to the Lord. [6] Moses took half the blood and set it in basins; the other half of the blood he sprinkled on the altar. [7] He then took the covenant scroll and read it aloud to the people. They responded, "We will do and obey everything that the Lord has commanded."

[8] Moses took the blood, sprinkled it on the people, and said, "This is the blood of the covenant that the Lord has made with you concerning all these words."

[9] Then Moses went up with Aaron, Nadab, and Abihu, and 70 of Israel's elders, [10] and they saw the God of Israel. Beneath His feet was something like a pavement made of sapphire stone, as clear as the sky itself. [11] God did not harm the Israelite nobles; they saw Him, and they ate and drank.

[12] The Lord said to Moses, "Come up to Me on the mountain and stay there so that I may give you the stone tablets with the law and commandments I have written for their instruction."

[13] So Moses arose with his assistant Joshua and went up the mountain of God. [14] He told the elders, "Wait here for us until we return to you. Aaron and Hur are here with you. Whoever has a dispute should go to them." [15] When Moses went up the mountain, the cloud covered it. [16] The glory of the Lord settled on Mount Sinai, and the cloud covered it for six days. On the seventh day He called to Moses from the cloud. [17] The appearance of the Lord's glory to the Israelites was like a consuming fire on the mountaintop. [18] Moses entered the cloud as he went up the mountain, and he remained on the mountain 40 days and 40 nights.

25 The Lord spoke to Moses: [2] "Tell the Israelites to take an offering for Me. You are to take My offering from everyone who is willing to give. [3] This is the offering you are to receive from them: gold, silver, and bronze; [4] blue, purple, and scarlet yarn; fine linen and goat hair; [5] ram skins dyed red and manatee skins; acacia wood; [6] oil for the light; spices for the anointing oil and for the fragrant incense; [7] and onyx along with other gemstones for mounting on the *ephod and breastpiece.

[8] "They are to make a sanctuary for Me so that I may dwell among them. [9] You must make it according to all that I show you—the pattern of the tabernacle as well as the pattern of all its furnishings.

[10] "They are to make an ark of acacia wood, 45 inches long, 27 inches wide, and 27 inches high. [11] Overlay it with pure gold; overlay it both inside and out. Also make a gold molding all around it. [12] Cast four gold rings for it and place them on its four feet, two rings on one side and two rings on the other side. [13] Make poles of acacia wood and overlay them with gold. [14] Insert the

poles into the rings on the sides of the ark in order to carry the ark with them. [15] The poles are to remain in the rings of the ark; they must not be removed from it. [16] Put the tablets of the •testimony that I will give you into the ark. [17] Make a •mercy seat of pure gold, 45 inches long and 27 inches wide. [18] Make two •cherubim of gold; make them of hammered work at the two ends of the mercy seat. [19] Make one cherub at one end and one cherub at the other end. At its two ends, make the cherubim of one piece with the mercy seat. [20] The cherubim are to have wings spread out above, covering the mercy seat with their wings, and are to face one another. The faces of the cherubim should be toward the mercy seat. [21] Set the mercy seat on top of the ark and put the testimony that I will give you into the ark. [22] I will meet with you there above the mercy seat, between the two cherubim that are over the ark of the testimony; I will speak with you from there about all that I command you regarding the Israelites.

[23] "You are to construct a table of acacia wood, 36 inches long, 18 inches wide, and 27 inches high. [24] Overlay it with pure gold and make a gold molding all around it. [25] Make a three-inch frame all around it and make a gold molding for it all around its frame. [26] Make four gold rings for it, and attach the rings to the four corners at its four legs. [27] The rings should be next to the frame as holders for the poles to carry the table. [28] Make the poles of acacia wood and overlay them with gold, and the table can be carried by them. [29] You are also to make its plates and cups, as well as its pitchers and bowls for pouring •drink offerings. Make them out of pure gold. [30] Put the •bread of the Presence on the table before Me at all times.

[31] "You are to make a lampstand out of pure, hammered gold. It is to be made of one piece: its base and shaft, its ornamental cups, and its calyxes and petals. [32] Six branches are to extend from its sides, three branches of the lampstand from one side and three branches of the lampstand from the other side. [33] There are to be three cups shaped like almond blossoms, each with a calyx and petals, on the first branch, and three cups shaped like almond blossoms, each with a calyx and petals, on the next branch. It is to be this way for the six branches that extend from the lampstand. [34] There are to be four cups shaped like almond blossoms on the lampstand shaft along with its calyxes and petals. [35] For the six branches that extend from the lampstand, a calyx must be under the first pair of branches from it, a calyx under the second pair of branches from it, and a calyx under the third pair of branches from it. [36] Their calyxes and branches are to be of one piece. All of it is to be a single hammered piece of pure gold.

[37] "Make seven lamps on it. Its lamps are to be set up so they illuminate the area in front of it. [38] Its snuffers and firepans must be of pure gold. [39] The lampstand with all these utensils is to be made from 75 pounds of pure gold. [40] Be careful to make them according to the pattern you have been shown on the mountain.

26
"You are to construct the tabernacle itself with 10 curtains. You must make them of finely spun linen, and blue, purple, and scarlet yarn, with a design of •cherubim worked into them. [2] The length of each curtain should be 42 feet, and the width of each curtain six feet; all the curtains are to have the same measurements. [3] Five of the curtains should be joined together, and the other five curtains joined together.

[4] Make loops of blue yarn on the edge of the last curtain in the first set, and do the same on the edge of the outermost curtain in the second set. [5] Make 50 loops on the one curtain and make 50 loops on the edge of the curtain in the second set, so that the loops line up together. [6] Also make 50 gold clasps and join the curtains together with the clasps, so that the tabernacle may be a single unit.

[7] "You are to make curtains of goat hair for a tent over the tabernacle; make 11 of these curtains. [8] The length of each curtain should be 45 feet and the width of each curtain six feet. All 11 curtains are to have the same measurements. [9] Join five of the curtains by themselves, and the other six curtains by themselves. Then fold the sixth curtain double at the front of the tent. [10] Make 50 loops on the edge of the one curtain, the outermost in the first set, and make 50 loops on the edge of the corresponding curtain of the second set. [11] Make 50 bronze clasps; put the clasps through the loops and join the tent together so that it is a single unit. [12] As for the flap that is left over from the tent curtains, the leftover half curtain is to hang down over the back of the tabernacle. [13] The half yard on one side and the half yard on the other of what is left over along the length of the tent curtains should be hanging down over the sides of the tabernacle on either side to cover it. [14] Make a covering for the tent from ram skins dyed red and a covering of manatee skins on top of that.

[15] "You are to make upright planks of acacia wood for the tabernacle. [16] The length of each plank is to be 15 feet, and the width of each plank 27 inches. [17] Each plank must be connected together with two tenons. Do the same for all the planks of the tabernacle. [18] Make the planks for the tabernacle as follows: 20 planks for the south side, [19] and make 40 silver bases under the 20 planks, two bases under the first plank for its two tenons, and two bases under the next plank for its two tenons; [20] 20 planks for the second side of the tabernacle, the north side, [21] along with their 40 silver bases, two bases under the first plank and two bases under each plank; [22] and make six planks for the west side of the tabernacle. [23] Make two additional planks for the two back corners of the tabernacle. [24] They are to be paired at the bottom, and joined together at the top in a single ring. So it should be for both of them; they will serve as the two corners. [25] There are to be eight planks with their silver bases: 16 bases; two bases under the first plank and two bases under each plank.

[26] "You are to make five crossbars of acacia wood for the planks on one side of the tabernacle, [27] five crossbars for the planks on the other side of the tabernacle, and five crossbars for the planks of the back side of the tabernacle on the west. [28] The central crossbar is to run through the middle of the planks from one end to the other. [29] Then overlay the planks with gold, and make their rings of gold as the holders for the crossbars. Also overlay the crossbars with gold. [30] You are to set up the tabernacle according to the plan for it that you have been shown on the mountain.

[31] "You are to make a veil of blue, purple, and scarlet yarn, and finely spun linen with a design of cherubim worked into it. [32] Hang it on four gold-plated posts of acacia wood that have gold hooks and that stand on four silver bases. [33] Hang the veil under the clasps and bring the ark of the •testimony there behind the veil, so the veil will make a separation for you between the

holy place and the most holy place. ³⁴Put the ‘mercy seat on the ark of the testimony in the most holy place. ³⁵Place the table outside the veil and the lampstand on the south side of the tabernacle, opposite the table; put the table on the north side.

³⁶"For the entrance to the tent you are to make a screen embroidered with blue, purple, and scarlet yarn, and finely spun linen. ³⁷Make five posts of acacia wood for the screen and overlay them with gold; their hooks are to be gold, and you are to cast five bronze bases for them.

27 "You are to construct the altar of acacia wood. The altar must be square, 7¹/₂ feet long, and 7¹/₂ feet wide; it must be 4¹/₂ feet high. ²Make horns for it on its four corners; the horns are to be of one piece. Overlay it with bronze. ³Make its pots for removing ashes, and its shovels, basins, meat forks, and firepans; make all its utensils of bronze. ⁴Construct a grate for it of bronze mesh, and make four bronze rings on the mesh at its four corners. ⁵Set it below, under the altar's ledge, so that the mesh comes halfway up the altar. ⁶Then make poles for the altar, poles of acacia wood, and overlay them with bronze. ⁷The poles are to be inserted into the rings so that the poles are on two sides of the altar when it is carried. ⁸Construct the altar with boards so that it is hollow. They are to make it just as it was shown to you on the mountain.

⁹"You are to make the courtyard for the tabernacle. Make the hangings on the south of the courtyard out of finely spun linen, 150 feet long on that side. ¹⁰There are to be 20 posts and 20 bronze bases. The hooks and bands of the posts must be silver. ¹¹Then make the hangings on the north side 150 feet long. There are to be 20 posts and 20 bronze bases. The hooks and bands of the posts must be silver. ¹²Make the hangings of the courtyard on the west side 75 feet long, including their 10 posts and 10 bases. ¹³Make the hangings of the courtyard on the east side toward the sunrise 75 feet. ¹⁴Make the hangings on one side of the gate 22¹/₂ feet, including their three posts and their three bases. ¹⁵And make the hangings on the other side 22¹/₂ feet, including their three posts and their three bases. ¹⁶The gate of the courtyard is to have a thirty-foot screen embroidered with blue, purple, and scarlet yarn, and finely spun linen. It is to have four posts including their four bases.

¹⁷"All the posts around the courtyard are to be banded with silver and have silver hooks and bronze bases. ¹⁸The length of the courtyard is to be 150 feet, the width 75 feet at each end, and the height 7¹/₂ feet, all of it made of finely spun linen. The bases of the posts must be bronze. ¹⁹All the tools of the tabernacle for every use and all its tent pegs as well as all the tent pegs of the courtyard are to be made of bronze.

²⁰"You are to command the Israelites to bring you pure oil from crushed olives for the light, in order to keep the lamp burning continually. ²¹In the tent of meeting outside the veil that is in front of the ‘testimony, Aaron and his sons are to tend the lamp from evening until morning before the LORD. This is to be a permanent statute for the Israelites throughout their generations.

28 "Have your brother Aaron, with his sons, come to you from the Israelites to serve Me as priest—Aaron, his sons Nadab and Abihu, Eleazar and Ithamar. ²Make holy garments for your brother Aaron, for glory and beauty. ³You are to instruct all the skilled craftsmen, whom I have filled with a spirit of wisdom, to make Aaron's garments for consecrating him to serve Me as priest. ⁴These are the garments that they must make: a breastpiece, an ‘ephod, a robe, a specially woven tunic, a turban, and a sash. They are to make holy garments for your brother Aaron and his sons so that they may serve Me as priests. ⁵They should use gold; blue, purple, and scarlet yarn; and fine linen.

⁶"They are to make the ephod of finely spun linen embroidered with gold, and with blue, purple, and scarlet yarn. ⁷It must have two shoulder pieces attached to its two edges so that it can be joined together. ⁸The artistically woven waistband that is on the ephod must be of one piece, according to the same workmanship of gold, of blue, purple, and scarlet yarn, and of finely spun linen.

⁹"Take two onyx stones and engrave on them the names of Israel's sons: ¹⁰six of their names on the first stone and the remaining six names on the second stone, in the order of their birth. ¹¹Engrave the two stones with the names of Israel's sons as a gem cutter engraves a seal. Mount them, surrounded with gold filigree settings. ¹²Fasten both stones on the shoulder pieces of the ephod as memorial stones for the Israelites. Aaron will carry their names on his two shoulders before the LORD as a reminder. ¹³Fashion gold filigree settings ¹⁴and two chains of pure gold; you will make them of braided cord work, and attach the cord chains to the settings.

¹⁵"You are to make an embroidered breastpiece for making decisions. Make it with the same workmanship as the ephod; make it of gold, of blue, purple, and scarlet yarn, and of finely spun linen. ¹⁶It must be square and folded double, nine inches long and nine inches wide. ¹⁷Place a setting of gemstones on it, four rows of stones:

The first row should be
a row of carnelian, topaz, and emerald;
¹⁸   the second row,
a turquoise, a sapphire, and a diamond;
¹⁹   the third row,
a jacinth, an agate, and an amethyst;
²⁰   and the fourth row,
a beryl, an onyx, and a jasper.

They should be adorned with gold filigree in their settings. ²¹The 12 stones are to correspond to the names of Israel's sons. Each stone must be engraved like a seal, with one of the names of the 12 tribes.

²²"You are to make braided chains of pure gold cord work for the breastpiece. ²³Fashion two gold rings for the breastpiece and attach them to its two corners. ²⁴Then attach the two gold cords to the two gold rings at the corners of the breastpiece. ²⁵Attach the other ends of the two cords to the two filigree settings, and in this way attach them to the ephod's shoulder pieces in the front. ²⁶Make two other gold rings and put them at the two other corners of the breastpiece on the edge that is next to the inner border of the ephod. ²⁷Make two more gold rings and attach them to the bottom of the ephod's two shoulder pieces on its front, close to its seam, and above the ephod's woven waistband. ²⁸The craftsmen are to tie the breastpiece from its rings to the rings of the ephod with a cord of blue yarn, so that the breastpiece is above the ephod's waistband and does not come loose from the ephod.

²⁹"Whenever he enters the sanctuary, Aaron is to carry the names of Israel's sons over his heart on the

breastpiece for decisions, as a continual reminder before the LORD. ³⁰Place the *Urim and Thummim in the breastpiece for decisions, so that they will also be over Aaron's heart whenever he comes before the LORD. Aaron will continually carry the means of decisions for the Israelites over his heart before the LORD.

³¹"You are to make the robe of the ephod entirely of blue yarn. ³²There should be an opening at its top in the center of it. Around the opening, there should be a woven collar with an opening like that of body armor so that it does not tear. ³³Make pomegranates of blue, purple, and scarlet yarn on its lower hem and all around it. Put gold bells between them all the way around, ³⁴so that gold bells and pomegranates alternate around the lower hem of the robe. ³⁵The robe must be worn by Aaron whenever he ministers, and its sound will be heard when he enters the sanctuary before the LORD and when he exits, so that he does not die.

³⁶"You are to make a pure gold medallion and engrave it, like the engraving of a seal:

HOLY TO THE LORD.

³⁷Fasten it to a cord of blue yarn so it can be placed on the turban; the medallion is to be on the front of the turban. ³⁸It will be on Aaron's forehead so that Aaron may bear the *guilt connected with the holy offerings that the Israelites consecrate as all their holy gifts. It is always to be on his forehead, so that they may find acceptance with the LORD.

³⁹"You are to weave the tunic from fine linen, make a turban of fine linen, and make an embroidered sash. ⁴⁰Make tunics, sashes, and headbands for Aaron's sons to give them glory and beauty. ⁴¹Put these on your brother Aaron and his sons; then anoint, ordain, and consecrate them, so that they may serve Me as priests. ⁴²Make them linen undergarments to cover their naked bodies; they must extend from the waist to the thighs. ⁴³These must be worn by Aaron and his sons whenever they enter the tent of meeting or approach the altar to minister in the sanctuary area, so that they do not incur guilt and die. This is to be a permanent statute for Aaron and for his future descendants.

29 "This is what you are to do for them to consecrate them to serve Me as priests. Take a young bull and two unblemished rams, ²with unleavened bread, unleavened cakes mixed with oil, and unleavened wafers coated with oil. Make them out of fine wheat flour, ³put them in a basket, and bring them in the basket, along with the bull and two rams. ⁴Bring Aaron and his sons to the entrance to the tent of meeting and wash them with water. ⁵Then take the garments and clothe Aaron with the tunic, the robe for the *ephod, the ephod itself, and the breastpiece; fasten the ephod on him with its woven waistband. ⁶Put the turban on his head and place the holy diadem on the turban. ⁷Take the anointing oil, pour it on his head, and anoint him. ⁸You must also bring his sons and clothe them with tunics. ⁹Tie the sashes on Aaron and his sons and fasten headbands on them. The priesthood is to be theirs by a permanent statute. This is the way you will ordain Aaron and his sons.

¹⁰"You are to bring the bull to the front of the tent of meeting, and Aaron and his sons must lay their hands on the bull's head. ¹¹Slaughter the bull before the LORD at the entrance to the tent of meeting. ¹²Take some of the bull's blood and apply it to the horns of the altar with your finger; then pour out all the rest of the blood

at the base of the altar. ¹³Take all the fat that covers the entrails, the fatty lobe of the liver, and the two kidneys with the fat on them, and burn them on the altar. ¹⁴But burn up the bull's flesh, its hide, and its dung outside the camp; it is a *sin offering.

¹⁵"Take one ram, and Aaron and his sons are to lay their hands on the ram's head. ¹⁶You are to slaughter the ram, take its blood, and sprinkle it on all sides of the altar. ¹⁷Cut the ram into pieces. Wash its entrails and shanks, and place them with its head and its pieces on the altar. ¹⁸Then burn the whole ram on the altar; it is a *burnt offering to the LORD. It is a pleasing aroma, a fire offering to the LORD.

¹⁹"You are to take the second ram, and Aaron and his sons must lay their hands on the ram's head. ²⁰Slaughter the ram, take some of its blood, and put it on Aaron's right earlobe, on his sons' right earlobes, on the thumbs of their right hands, and on the big toes of their right feet. Sprinkle the remaining blood on all sides of the altar. ²¹Take some of the blood that is on the altar and some of the anointing oil, and sprinkle them on Aaron and his garments, as well as on his sons and their garments. In this way, he and his garments will become holy, as well as his sons and their garments.

²²"Take the fat from the ram, the fat tail, the fat covering the entrails, the fatty lobe of the liver, the two kidneys and the fat on them, and the right thigh (since this is a ram for ordination); ²³take one loaf of bread, one cake of bread made with oil, and one wafer from the basket of unleavened bread that is before the LORD; ²⁴and put all of them in the hands of Aaron and his sons and wave them as a presentation offering before the LORD. ²⁵Take them from their hands and burn them on the altar on top of the burnt offering, as a pleasing aroma before the LORD; it is a fire offering to the LORD.

²⁶"Take the breast from the ram of Aaron's ordination and wave it as a presentation offering before the LORD; it is to be your portion. ²⁷Consecrate for Aaron and his sons the breast of the presentation offering that is waved and the thigh of the contribution that is lifted up from the ram of ordination. ²⁸This will belong to Aaron and his sons as a regular portion from the Israelites, for it is a contribution. It will be the Israelites' contribution from their *fellowship sacrifices, their contribution to the LORD.

²⁹"The holy garments that belong to Aaron are to belong to his sons after him, so that they can be anointed and ordained in them. ³⁰Any priest who is one of his sons and who succeeds him and enters the tent of meeting to minister in the sanctuary must wear them for seven days.

³¹"You are to take the ram of ordination and boil its flesh in a holy place. ³²Aaron and his sons are to eat the meat of the ram and the bread that is in the basket at the entrance to the tent of meeting. ³³They must eat those things by which *atonement was made at the time of their ordination and consecration. An unauthorized person must not eat them, for these things are holy. ³⁴If any of the meat of ordination or any of the bread is left until morning, burn up what is left over. It must not be eaten because it is holy.

³⁵"This is what you are to do for Aaron and his sons based on all I have commanded you. Take seven days to ordain them. ³⁶Sacrifice a bull as a sin offering each day for atonement. Purify the altar when you make

atonement for it, and anoint it in order to consecrate it. [37] For seven days you must make atonement for the altar and consecrate it. The altar will become especially holy; whatever touches the altar will become holy.

[38] "This is what you are to offer regularly on the altar every day: two year-old lambs. [39] In the morning offer one lamb, and at twilight offer the other lamb. [40] With the first lamb offer two quarts of fine flour mixed with one quart of oil from crushed olives, and a •drink offering of one quart of wine. [41] You are to offer the second lamb at twilight. Offer a •grain offering and a drink offering with it, like the one in the morning, as a pleasing aroma, a fire offering to the LORD. [42] This will be a regular burnt offering throughout your generations at the entrance to the tent of meeting before the LORD, where I will meet you to speak with you. [43] I will also meet with the Israelites, and that place will be consecrated by My glory. [44] I will consecrate the tent of meeting and the altar; I will also consecrate Aaron and his sons to serve Me as priests. [45] I will dwell among the Israelites and be their God. [46] And they will know that I am •Yahweh their God, who brought them out of the land of Egypt, so that I might dwell among them. I am Yahweh their God.

30 "You are to make an altar for the burning of incense; make it of acacia wood. [2] It must be square, 18 inches long and 18 inches wide; it must be 36 inches high. Its horns must be of one piece. [3] Overlay its top, all around its sides, and its horns with pure gold; make a gold molding all around it. [4] Make two gold rings for it under the molding on two of its sides; put these on opposite sides of it to be holders for the poles to carry it with. [5] Make the poles of acacia wood and overlay them with gold.

[6] "You are to place the altar in front of the veil by the ark of the •testimony—in front of the •mercy seat that is over the testimony—where I will meet with you. [7] Aaron must burn fragrant incense on it; he must burn it every morning when he tends the lamps. [8] When Aaron sets up the lamps at twilight, he must burn incense. There is to be an incense offering before the LORD throughout your generations. [9] You must not offer unauthorized incense on it, or a •burnt or •grain offering; you are not to pour a •drink offering on it.

[10] "Once a year Aaron is to perform the purification rite on the horns of the altar. Throughout your generations he is to perform the purification rite for it once a year, with the blood of the •sin offering for •atonement. The altar is especially holy to the LORD."

[11] The LORD spoke to Moses: [12] "When you take a census of the Israelites to register them, each of the men must pay a ransom for himself to the LORD as they are registered. Then no plague will come on them as they are registered. [13] Everyone who is registered must pay half a •shekel according to the sanctuary shekel (20 *gerahs* to the shekel). This half shekel is a contribution to the LORD. [14] Each man who is registered, 20 years old or more, must give this contribution to the LORD. [15] The wealthy may not give more and the poor may not give less than half a shekel when giving the contribution to the LORD to atone for your lives. [16] Take the atonement money from the Israelites and use it for the service of the tent of meeting. It will serve as a reminder for the Israelites before the LORD to atone for your lives."

[17] The LORD spoke to Moses: [18] "Make a bronze basin for washing and a bronze stand for it. Set it between the tent of meeting and the altar, and put water in it. [19] Aaron and his sons must wash their hands and feet from the basin. [20] Whenever they enter the tent of meeting or approach the altar to minister by burning up an offering to the LORD, they must wash with water so that they will not die. [21] They must wash their hands and feet so that they will not die; this is to be a permanent statute for them, for Aaron and his descendants throughout their generations."

[22] The LORD spoke to Moses: [23] "Take for yourself the finest spices: 12½ pounds of liquid myrrh, half as much (6¼ pounds) of fragrant cinnamon, 6¼ pounds of fragrant cane, [24] 12½ pounds of cassia (by the sanctuary shekel), and one gallon of olive oil. [25] Prepare from these a holy anointing oil, a scented blend, the work of a perfumer; it will be holy anointing oil.

[26] "With it you are to anoint the tent of meeting, the ark of the testimony, [27] the table with all its utensils, the lampstand with its utensils, the altar of incense, [28] the altar of burnt offering with all its utensils, and the basin with its stand. [29] Consecrate them and they will be especially holy. Whatever touches them will be consecrated. [30] Anoint Aaron and his sons and consecrate them to serve Me as priests.

[31] "Tell the Israelites: This will be My holy anointing oil throughout your generations. [32] It must not be used for ordinary anointing on a person's body, and you must not make anything like it using its formula. It is holy, and it must be holy to you. [33] Anyone who blends something like it or puts some of it on an unauthorized person must be cut off from his people."

[34] The LORD said to Moses: "Take fragrant spices: stacte, onycha, and galbanum; the spices and pure frankincense are to be in equal measures. [35] Prepare expertly blended incense from these; it is to be seasoned with salt, pure and holy. [36] Grind some of it into a fine powder and put some in front of the testimony in the tent of meeting, where I will meet with you. It must be especially holy to you. [37] As for the incense you are making, you must not make any for yourselves using its formula. It is to be regarded by you as sacred to the LORD. [38] Anyone who makes something like it to smell its fragrance must be cut off from his people."

31 The LORD also spoke to Moses: [2] "Look, I have appointed by name Bezalel son of Uri, son of Hur, of the tribe of Judah. [3] I have filled him with God's Spirit, with wisdom, understanding, and ability in every craft [4] to design artistic works in gold, silver, and bronze, [5] to cut gemstones for mounting, and to carve wood for work in every craft. [6] I have also selected Oholiab son of Ahisamach, of the tribe of Dan, to be with him. I have placed wisdom within every skilled craftsman in order to make all that I have commanded you: [7] the tent of meeting, the ark of the •testimony, the •mercy seat that is on top of it, and all the other furnishings of the tent— [8] the table with its utensils, the pure gold lampstand with all its utensils, the altar of incense, [9] the altar of •burnt offering with all its utensils, the basin with its stand— [10] the specially woven garments, both the holy garments for Aaron the priest and the garments for his sons to serve as priests, [11] the anointing oil, and the fragrant incense for the sanctuary. They must make them according to all that I have commanded you."

[12] The LORD said to Moses: [13] "Tell the Israelites: You must observe My Sabbaths, for it is a sign between Me and you throughout your generations, so that you will

know that I am •Yahweh who sets you apart. ¹⁴Observe the Sabbath, for it is holy to you. Whoever profanes it must be put to death. If anyone does work on it, that person must be cut off from his people. ¹⁵Work may be done for six days, but on the seventh day there must be a Sabbath of complete rest, dedicated to the LORD. Anyone who does work on the Sabbath day must be put to death. ¹⁶The Israelites must observe the Sabbath, celebrating it throughout their generations as a perpetual covenant. ¹⁷It is a sign forever between Me and the Israelites, for in six days the LORD made the heavens and the earth, but on the seventh day He rested and was refreshed."

¹⁸When He finished speaking with Moses on Mount Sinai, He gave him the two tablets of the testimony, stone tablets inscribed by the finger of God.

32 When the people saw that Moses delayed in coming down from the mountain, they gathered around Aaron and said to him, "Come, make us a god who will go before us because this Moses, the man who brought us up from the land of Egypt—we don't know what has happened to him!"

²Then Aaron replied to them, "Take off the gold rings that are on the ears of your wives, your sons, and your daughters and bring them to me." ³So all the people took off the gold rings that were on their ears and brought them to Aaron. ⁴He took the gold from their hands, fashioned it with an engraving tool, and made it into an image of a calf.

Then they said, "Israel, this is your God, who brought you up from the land of Egypt!"

⁵When Aaron saw this, he built an altar before it; then he made an announcement: "There will be a festival to the LORD tomorrow." ⁶Early the next morning they arose, offered •burnt offerings, and presented •fellowship offerings. The people sat down to eat and drink, then got up to play.

⁷The LORD spoke to Moses: "Go down at once! For your people you brought up from the land of Egypt have acted corruptly. ⁸They have quickly turned from the way I commanded them; they have made for themselves an image of a calf. They have bowed down to it, sacrificed to it, and said, 'Israel, this is your God, who brought you up from the land of Egypt.'" ⁹The LORD also said to Moses: "I have seen this people, and they are indeed a stiff-necked people. ¹⁰Now leave Me alone, so that My anger can burn against them and I can destroy them. Then I will make you into a great nation."

¹¹But Moses interceded with the LORD his God: "LORD, why does Your anger burn against Your people You brought out of the land of Egypt with great power and a strong hand? ¹²Why should the Egyptians say, 'He brought them out with an evil intent to kill them in the mountains and wipe them off the face of the earth'? Turn from Your great anger and relent concerning this disaster planned for Your people. ¹³Remember Your servants Abraham, Isaac, and Israel—You swore to them by Your very self and declared, 'I will make your •offspring as numerous as the stars of the sky and will give your offspring all this land that I have promised, and they will inherit it forever.'" ¹⁴So the LORD relented concerning the disaster He said He would bring on His people.

¹⁵Then Moses turned and went down the mountain with the two tablets of the •testimony in his hands. They were inscribed on both sides—inscribed front

and back. ¹⁶The tablets were the work of God, and the writing was God's writing, engraved on the tablets.

¹⁷When Joshua heard the sound of the people as they shouted, he said to Moses, "There is a sound of war in the camp."

¹⁸But Moses replied:

It's not the sound of a victory cry
and not the sound of a cry of defeat;
I hear the sound of singing!

¹⁹As he approached the camp and saw the calf and the dancing, Moses became enraged and threw the tablets out of his hands, smashing them at the base of the mountain. ²⁰Then he took the calf they had made, burned it up, and ground it to powder. He scattered the powder over the surface of the water and forced the Israelites to drink the water.

²¹Then Moses asked Aaron, "What did these people do to you that you have led them into such a grave sin?"

²²"Don't be enraged, my lord," Aaron replied. "You yourself know that the people are intent on evil. ²³They said to me, 'Make us a god who will go before us because this Moses, the man who brought us up from the land of Egypt—we don't know what has happened to him!' ²⁴So I said to them, 'Whoever has gold, take it off,' and they gave it to me. When I threw it into the fire, out came this calf!"

²⁵Moses saw that the people were out of control, for Aaron had let them get out of control, resulting in weakness before their enemies. ²⁶And Moses stood at the camp's entrance and said, "Whoever is for the LORD, come to me." And all the Levites gathered around him. ²⁷He told them, "This is what the LORD, the God of Israel, says, 'Every man fasten his sword to his side; go back and forth through the camp from entrance to entrance, and each of you kill his brother, his friend, and his neighbor.'" ²⁸The Levites did as Moses commanded, and about 3,000 men fell dead that day among the people. ²⁹Afterward Moses said, "Today you have been dedicated to the LORD, since each man went against his son and his brother. Therefore you have brought a blessing on yourselves today."

³⁰The following day Moses said to the people, "You have committed a grave sin. Now I will go up to the LORD; perhaps I will be able to atone for your sin."

³¹So Moses returned to the LORD and said, "Oh, these people have committed a grave sin; they have made a god of gold for themselves. ³²Now if You would only forgive their sin. But if not, please erase me from the book You have written."

³³The LORD replied to Moses: "I will erase whoever has sinned against Me from My book. ³⁴Now go, lead the people to the place I told you about; see, My angel will go before you. But on the day I settle accounts, I will hold them accountable for their sin." ³⁵And the LORD inflicted a plague on the people for what they did with the calf Aaron had made.

33 The LORD spoke to Moses: "Go, leave here, you and the people you brought up from the land of Egypt, to the land I promised to Abraham, Isaac, and Jacob, saying: I will give it to your •offspring. ²I will send an angel ahead of you and will drive out the Canaanites, Amorites, Hittites, Perizzites, Hivites, and Jebusites. ³Go up to a land flowing with milk and honey. But I will not go with you because you are a stiff-necked people; otherwise, I might destroy you on the way." ⁴When the people heard this bad news, they mourned and didn't put on their jewelry.

⁵For the LORD said to Moses: "Tell the Israelites: You are a stiff-necked people. If I went with you for a single moment, I would destroy you. Now take off your jewelry, and I will decide what to do with you." ⁶So the Israelites remained stripped of their jewelry from Mount Horeb onward.

⁷Now Moses took a tent and set it up outside the camp, far away from the camp; he called it the tent of meeting. Anyone who wanted to consult the LORD would go to the tent of meeting that was outside the camp. ⁸Whenever Moses went out to the tent, all the people would stand up, each one at the door of his tent, and they would watch Moses until he entered the tent. ⁹When Moses entered the tent, the pillar of cloud would come down and remain at the entrance to the tent, and the LORD would speak with Moses. ¹⁰As all the people saw the pillar of cloud remaining at the entrance to the tent, they would stand up, then bow in worship, each one at the door of his tent. ¹¹The LORD spoke with Moses face to face, just as a man speaks with his friend. Then Moses would return to the camp, but his assistant, the young man Joshua son of Nun, would not leave the inside of the tent.

¹²Moses said to the LORD, "Look, You have told me, 'Lead this people up,' but You have not let me know whom You will send with me. You said, 'I know you by name, and you have also found favor in My sight.' ¹³Now if I have indeed found favor in Your sight, please teach me Your ways, and I will know You and find favor in Your sight. Now consider that this nation is Your people."

¹⁴Then He replied, "My presence will go with you, and I will give you rest."

¹⁵"If Your presence does not go," Moses responded to Him, "don't make us go up from here. ¹⁶How will it be known that I and Your people have found favor in Your sight unless You go with us? I and Your people will be distinguished by this from all the other people on the face of the earth."

¹⁷The LORD answered Moses, "I will do this very thing you have asked, for you have found favor in My sight, and I know you by name."

¹⁸Then Moses said, "Please, let me see Your glory."

¹⁹He said, "I will cause all My goodness to pass in front of you, and I will proclaim the name ˙Yahweh before you. I will be gracious to whom I will be gracious, and I will have compassion on whom I will have compassion." ²⁰But He answered, "You cannot see My face, for no one can see Me and live." ²¹The LORD said, "Here is a place near Me. You are to stand on the rock, ²²and when My glory passes by, I will put you in the crevice of the rock and cover you with My hand until I have passed by. ²³Then I will take My hand away, and you will see My back, but My face will not be seen."

34 The LORD said to Moses, "Cut two stone tablets like the first ones, and I will write on them the words that were on the first tablets, which you broke. ²Be prepared by morning. Come up Mount Sinai in the morning and stand before Me on the mountaintop. ³No one may go up with you; in fact, no one must be seen anywhere on the mountain. Even the flocks and herds are not to graze in front of that mountain."

⁴Moses cut two stone tablets like the first ones. He got up early in the morning, and taking the two stone tablets in his hand, he climbed Mount Sinai, just as the LORD had commanded him.

⁵The LORD came down in a cloud, stood with him there, and proclaimed His name ˙Yahweh. ⁶Then the LORD passed in front of him and proclaimed:

Yahweh—Yahweh is a compassionate and gracious God, slow to anger and rich in faithful love and truth, ⁷ maintaining faithful love to a thousand generations, forgiving wrongdoing, rebellion, and sin. But He will not leave the ˙guilty unpunished, bringing the consequences of the fathers' wrongdoing on the children and grandchildren to the third and fourth generation.

⁸Moses immediately bowed down to the ground and worshiped. ⁹Then he said, "My Lord, if I have indeed found favor in Your sight, my Lord, please go with us. Even though this is a stiff-necked people, forgive our wrongdoing and sin, and accept us as Your own possession."

¹⁰And the LORD responded: "Look, I am making a covenant. I will perform wonders in the presence of all your people that have never been done in all the earth or in any nation. All the people you live among will see the LORD's work, for what I am doing with you is awe-inspiring. ¹¹Observe what I command you today. I am going to drive out before you the Amorites, Canaanites, Hittites, Perizzites, Hivites, and Jebusites. ¹²Be careful not to make a treaty with the inhabitants of the land that you are going to enter; otherwise, they will become a snare among you. ¹³Instead, you must tear down their altars, smash their sacred pillars, and chop down their ˙Asherah poles. ¹⁴You are never to bow down to another god because Yahweh, being jealous by nature, is a jealous God.

¹⁵"Do not make a treaty with the inhabitants of the land, or else when they prostitute themselves with their gods and sacrifice to their gods, they will invite you, and you will eat their sacrifices. ¹⁶Then you will take some of their daughters as brides for your sons. Their daughters will prostitute themselves with their gods and cause your sons to prostitute themselves with their gods.

¹⁷"Do not make cast images of gods for yourselves.

¹⁸"Observe the Festival of ˙Unleavened Bread. You are to eat unleavened bread for seven days at the appointed time in the month of Abib as I commanded you. For you came out of Egypt in the month of Abib.

¹⁹"The firstborn male from every womb belongs to Me, including all your male livestock, the firstborn of cattle or sheep. ²⁰You must redeem the firstborn of a donkey with a sheep, but if you do not redeem it, break its neck. You must redeem all the firstborn of your sons. No one is to appear before Me empty-handed.

²¹"You are to labor six days but you must rest on the seventh day; you must even rest during plowing and harvesting times.

²²"Observe the Festival of Weeks with the ˙firstfruits of the wheat harvest, and the Festival of Ingathering at the turn of the agricultural year. ²³Three times a year all your males are to appear before the Lord GOD, the God of Israel. ²⁴For I will drive out nations before you and enlarge your territory. No one will covet your land when you go up three times a year to appear before the LORD your God.

²⁵"Do not present the blood for My sacrifice with anything leavened. The sacrifice of the ˙Passover Festival must not remain until morning.

²⁶"Bring the best firstfruits of your land to the house of the LORD your God.

"You must not boil a young goat in its mother's milk."

²⁷The LORD also said to Moses, "Write down these words, for I have made a covenant with you and with Israel based on these words."

²⁸Moses was there with the LORD 40 days and 40 nights; he did not eat bread or drink water. He wrote the Ten Commandments, the words of the covenant, on the tablets.

²⁹As Moses descended from Mount Sinai—with the two tablets of the ˚testimony in his hands as he descended the mountain—he did not realize that the skin of his face shone as a result of his speaking with the LORD. ³⁰When Aaron and all the Israelites saw Moses, the skin of his face shone! They were afraid to come near him. ³¹But Moses called out to them, so Aaron and all the leaders of the community returned to him, and Moses spoke to them. ³²Afterward all the Israelites came near, and he commanded them to do everything the LORD had told him on Mount Sinai. ³³When Moses had finished speaking with them, he put a veil over his face. ³⁴But whenever Moses went before the LORD to speak with Him, he would remove the veil until he came out. After he came out, he would tell the Israelites what he had been commanded, ³⁵and the Israelites would see that Moses' face was radiant. Then Moses would put the veil over his face again until he went to speak with the LORD.

35 Moses assembled the entire Israelite community and said to them, "These are the things that the LORD has commanded you to do: ²For six days work is to be done, but on the seventh day you are to have a holy day, a Sabbath of complete rest to the LORD. Anyone who does work on it must be executed. ³Do not light a fire in any of your homes on the Sabbath day."

⁴Then Moses said to the entire Israelite community, "This is what the LORD has commanded: ⁵Take up an offering among you for the LORD. Let everyone whose heart is willing bring this as the LORD's offering: gold, silver, and bronze; ⁶blue, purple, and scarlet yarn; fine linen and goat hair; ⁷ram skins dyed red and manatee skins; acacia wood; ⁸oil for the light; spices for the anointing oil and for the fragrant incense; ⁹and onyx with gemstones to mount on the ˚ephod and breastpiece.

¹⁰"Let all the skilled craftsmen among you come and make everything that the LORD has commanded: ¹¹the tabernacle—its tent and covering, its clasps and planks, its crossbars, its posts and bases; ¹²the ark with its poles, the ˚mercy seat, and the veil for the screen; ¹³the table with its poles, all its utensils, and the ˚bread of the Presence; ¹⁴the lampstand for light with its utensils and lamps as well as the oil for the light; ¹⁵the altar of incense with its poles; the anointing oil and the fragrant incense; the entryway screen for the entrance to the tabernacle; ¹⁶the altar of ˚burnt offering with its bronze grate, its poles, and all its utensils; the basin with its stand; ¹⁷the hangings of the courtyard, its posts and bases, and the screen for the gate of the courtyard; ¹⁸the tent pegs for the tabernacle and the tent pegs for the courtyard, along with their ropes; ¹⁹and the specially woven garments for ministering in the sanctuary—the holy garments for Aaron the priest and the garments for his sons to serve as priests."

²⁰Then the entire Israelite community left Moses'

presence. ²¹Everyone whose heart was moved and whose spirit prompted him came and brought an offering to the LORD for the work on the tent of meeting, for all its services, and for the holy garments. ²²Both men and women came; all who had willing hearts brought brooches, earrings, rings, necklaces, and all kinds of gold jewelry—everyone who waved a presentation offering of gold to the LORD. ²³Everyone who had in his possession blue, purple, or scarlet yarn, fine linen or goat hair, ram skins dyed red or manatee skins, brought them. ²⁴Everyone making an offering of silver or bronze brought it as a contribution to the LORD. Everyone who possessed acacia wood useful for any task in the work brought it. ²⁵Every skilled woman spun yarn with her hands and brought it: blue, purple, and scarlet yarn, and fine linen. ²⁶And all the women whose hearts were moved spun the goat hair by virtue of their skill. ²⁷The leaders brought onyx and gemstones to mount on the ephod and breastpiece, ²⁸as well as the spice and oil for the light, for the anointing oil, and for the fragrant incense. ²⁹So the Israelites brought a freewill offering to the LORD, all the men and women whose hearts prompted them to bring something for all the work that the LORD, through Moses, had commanded to be done.

³⁰Moses then said to the Israelites: "Look, the LORD has appointed by name Bezalel son of Uri, son of Hur, of the tribe of Judah. ³¹He has filled him with God's Spirit, with wisdom, understanding, and ability in every kind of craft ³²to design artistic works in gold, silver, and bronze, ³³to cut gemstones for mounting, and to carve wood for work in every kind of artistic craft. ³⁴He has also given both him and Oholiab son of Ahisamach, of the tribe of Dan, the ability to teach others. ³⁵He has filled them with skill to do all the work of a gem cutter; a designer; an embroiderer in blue, purple, and scarlet yarn and fine linen; and a weaver. They can do every kind of craft

36 and design artistic designs. ¹Bezalel, Oholiab, and all the skilled people are to work based on everything the LORD has commanded. The LORD has given them wisdom and understanding to know how to do all the work of constructing the sanctuary."

²So Moses summoned Bezalel, Oholiab, and every skilled person in whose heart the LORD had placed wisdom, everyone whose heart moved him, to come to the work and do it. ³They took from Moses' presence all the contributions that the Israelites had brought for the task of making the sanctuary. Meanwhile, the people continued to bring freewill offerings morning after morning.

⁴Then all the craftsmen who were doing all the work for the sanctuary came one by one from the work they were doing ⁵and said to Moses, "The people are bringing more than is needed for the construction of the work the LORD commanded to be done."

⁶After Moses gave an order, they sent a proclamation throughout the camp: "Let no man or woman make anything else as an offering for the sanctuary." So the people stopped. ⁷The materials were sufficient for them to do all the work. There was more than enough.

⁸All the skilled craftsmen among those doing the work made the tabernacle with 10 curtains. Bezalel made them of finely spun linen, as well as blue, purple, and scarlet yarn, with a design of ˚cherubim worked into them. ⁹The length of each curtain was 42 feet, and the width of each curtain six feet; all the curtains

had the same measurements. [10] He joined five of the curtains to each other, and the other five curtains he joined to each other. [11] He made loops of blue yarn on the edge of the last curtain in the first set and did the same on the edge of the outermost curtain in the second set. [12] He made 50 loops on the one curtain and 50 loops on the edge of the curtain in the second set, so that the loops lined up with each other. [13] He also made 50 gold clasps and joined the curtains to each other, so that the tabernacle became a single unit.

[14] He made curtains of goat hair for a tent over the tabernacle; he made 11 of them. [15] The length of each curtain was 45 feet, and the width of each curtain six feet. All 11 curtains had the same measurements. [16] He joined five of the curtains together, and the other six together. [17] He made 50 loops on the edge of the outermost curtain in the first set and 50 loops on the edge of the corresponding curtain in the second set. [18] He made 50 bronze clasps to join the tent together as a single unit. [19] He also made a covering for the tent from ram skins dyed red and a covering of manatee skins on top of it.

[20] He made upright planks of acacia wood for the tabernacle. [21] The length of each plank was 15 feet, and the width of each was 27 inches. [22] There were two tenons connected to each other for each plank. He did the same for all the planks of the tabernacle. [23] He made planks for the tabernacle as follows: 20 for the south side, [24] and he made 40 silver bases to put under the 20 planks, two bases under the first plank for its two tenons, and two bases under each of the following planks for their two tenons; [25] for the second side of the tabernacle, the north side, he made 20 planks, [26] with their 40 silver bases, two bases under the first plank and two bases under each of the following ones; [27] and for the west side of the tabernacle he made six planks. [28] He also made two additional planks for the two back corners of the tabernacle. [29] They were paired at the bottom and joined together at the top in a single ring. This is what he did with both of them for the two corners. [30] So there were eight planks with their 16 silver bases, two bases under each one.

[31] He made five crossbars of acacia wood for the planks on one side of the tabernacle, [32] five crossbars for the planks on the other side of the tabernacle, and five crossbars for those at the back of the tabernacle on the west. [33] He made the central crossbar run through the middle of the planks from one end to the other. [34] He overlaid them with gold and made their rings out of gold as holders for the crossbars. He also overlaid the crossbars with gold.

[35] Then he made the veil with blue, purple, and scarlet yarn, and finely spun linen. He made it with a design of cherubim worked into it. [36] He made four posts of acacia wood for it and overlaid them with gold; their hooks were of gold. And he cast four silver bases for the posts.

[37] He made a screen embroidered with blue, purple, and scarlet yarn, and finely spun linen for the entrance to the tent, [38] together with its five posts and their hooks. He overlaid the tops of the posts and their bands with gold, but their five bases were bronze.

37 Bezalel made the ark of acacia wood, 45 inches long, 27 inches wide, and 27 inches high. [2] He overlaid it with pure gold inside and out and made a gold molding all around it. [3] He cast four gold rings for it, for its four feet, two rings on one side and two rings on the other side. [4] He made poles of acacia wood and overlaid them with gold. [5] He inserted the poles into the rings on the sides of the ark for carrying the ark.

[6] He made a *mercy seat of pure gold, 45 inches long and 27 inches wide. [7] He made two *cherubim of gold; he made them of hammered work at the two ends of the mercy seat, [8] one cherub at one end and one cherub at the other end. At each end, he made a cherub of one piece with the mercy seat. [9] They had wings spread out. They faced each other and covered the mercy seat with their wings. The faces of the cherubim were looking toward the mercy seat.

[10] He constructed the table of acacia wood, 36 inches long, 18 inches wide, and 27 inches high. [11] He overlaid it with pure gold and made a gold molding all around it. [12] He made a three-inch frame all around it and made a gold molding all around its frame. [13] He cast four gold rings for it and attached the rings to the four corners at its four legs. [14] The rings were next to the frame as holders for the poles to carry the table. [15] He made the poles for carrying the table from acacia wood and overlaid them with gold. [16] He also made the utensils that would be on the table out of pure gold: its plates and cups, as well as its bowls and pitchers for pouring *drink offerings.

[17] Then he made the lampstand out of pure hammered gold. He made it all of one piece: its base and shaft, its ornamental cups, and its calyxes and petals. [18] Six branches extended from its sides, three branches of the lampstand from one side and three branches of the lampstand from the other side. [19] There were three cups shaped like almond blossoms, each with a calyx and petals, on the first branch, and three cups shaped like almond blossoms, each with a calyx and petals, on the next branch. It was this way for the six branches that extended from the lampstand. [20] On the lampstand shaft there were four cups shaped like almond blossoms with its calyxes and petals. [21] For the six branches that extended from it, a calyx was under the first pair of branches from it, a calyx under the second pair of branches from it, and a calyx under the third pair of branches from it. [22] Their calyxes and branches were of one piece. All of it was a single hammered piece of pure gold. [23] He also made its seven lamps, snuffers, and firepans of pure gold. [24] He made it and all its utensils of 75 pounds of pure gold.

[25] He made the altar of incense out of acacia wood. It was square, 18 inches long and 18 inches wide; it was 36 inches high. Its horns were of one piece. [26] He overlaid it, its top, all around its sides, and its horns with pure gold. Then he made a gold molding all around it. [27] He made two gold rings for it under the molding on two of its sides; he put these on opposite sides of it to be holders for the poles to carry it with. [28] He made the poles of acacia wood and overlaid them with gold.

[29] He also made the holy anointing oil and the pure, fragrant, and expertly blended incense.

38 Bezalel constructed the altar of *burnt offering from acacia wood. It was square, 7½ feet long and 7½ feet wide, and was 4½ feet high. [2] He made horns for it on its four corners; the horns were of one piece. Then he overlaid it with bronze. [3] He made all the altar's utensils: the pots, shovels, basins, meat forks, and firepans; he made all its utensils of bronze. [4] He constructed for the altar a grate of bronze mesh under its ledge, halfway up from the bottom. [5] At the four corners of the bronze grate he cast

four rings as holders for the poles. ⁶ Also, he made the poles of acacia wood and overlaid them with bronze. ⁷ Then he inserted the poles into the rings on the sides of the altar in order to carry it with them. He constructed the altar with boards so that it was hollow.

⁸ He made the bronze basin and its stand from the bronze mirrors of the women who served at the entrance to the tent of meeting.

⁹ Then he made the courtyard. The hangings on the south side of the courtyard were of finely spun linen, 150 feet in length, ¹⁰ including their 20 posts and 20 bronze bases. The hooks and bands of the posts were silver. ¹¹ The hangings on the north side were also 150 feet in length, including their 20 posts and 20 bronze bases. The hooks and bands of the posts were silver. ¹² The hangings on the west side were 75 feet in length, including their 10 posts and 10 bases. The hooks and bands of the posts were silver. ¹³ The hangings on the east toward the sunrise were also 75 feet in length. ¹⁴ The hangings on one side of the gate were 22¹/₂ feet, including their three posts and three bases. ¹⁵ It was the same for the other side. The hangings were 22¹/₂ feet, including their three posts and three bases on both sides of the courtyard gate. ¹⁶ All the hangings around the courtyard were of finely spun linen. ¹⁷ The bases for the posts were bronze; the hooks and bands of the posts were silver; and the plating for the tops of the posts was silver. All the posts of the courtyard were banded with silver.

¹⁸ The screen for the gate of the courtyard was embroidered with blue, purple, and scarlet yarn, and finely spun linen. It was 30 feet long, and like the hangings of the courtyard, 7¹/₂ feet high. ¹⁹ It had four posts, including their four bronze bases. Their hooks were silver, and the bands as well as the plating of their tops were silver. ²⁰ All the tent pegs for the tabernacle and for the surrounding courtyard were bronze.

²¹ This is the inventory for the tabernacle, the tabernacle of the ˙testimony, that was recorded at Moses' command. It was the work of the Levites under the direction of Ithamar son of Aaron the priest. ²² Bezalel son of Uri, son of Hur, of the tribe of Judah, made everything that the Lord commanded Moses. ²³ With him was Oholiab son of Ahisamach, of the tribe of Dan, a gem cutter, a designer, and an embroiderer with blue, purple, and scarlet yarn, and fine linen.

²⁴ All the gold of the presentation offering that was used for the project in all the work on the sanctuary, was 2,193 pounds, according to the sanctuary ˙shekel. ²⁵ The silver from those of the community who were registered was 7,544 pounds, according to the sanctuary shekel— ²⁶²/₅ of an ounce per man, that is, half a shekel according to the sanctuary shekel, from everyone 20 years old or more who had crossed over to the registered group, 603,550 men. ²⁷ There were 7,500 pounds of silver used to cast the bases of the sanctuary and the bases of the veil—100 bases from 7,500 pounds, 75 pounds for each base. ²⁸ With the remaining 44 pounds he made the hooks for the posts, overlaid their tops, and supplied bands for them.

²⁹ The bronze of the presentation offering totaled 5,310 pounds. ³⁰ He made with it the bases for the entrance to the tent of meeting, the bronze altar and its bronze grate, all the utensils for the altar, ³¹ the bases for the surrounding courtyard, the bases for the gate of the courtyard, all the tent pegs for the tabernacle, and all the tent pegs for the surrounding courtyard.

39 They made specially woven garments for ministry in the sanctuary, and the holy garments for Aaron from the blue, purple, and scarlet yarn, just as the Lord had commanded Moses.

² Bezalel made the ˙ephod of gold, of blue, purple, and scarlet yarn, and of finely spun linen. ³ They hammered out thin sheets of gold, and he cut threads from them to interweave with the blue, purple, and scarlet yarn, and the fine linen in a skillful design. ⁴ They made shoulder pieces for attaching it; it was joined together at its two edges. ⁵ The artistically woven waistband that was on the ephod was of one piece with the ephod, according to the same workmanship of gold, of blue, purple, and scarlet yarn, and of finely spun linen, just as the Lord had commanded Moses.

⁶ Then they mounted the onyx stones surrounded with gold filigree settings, engraved with the names of Israel's sons as a gem cutter engraves a seal. ⁷ He fastened them on the shoulder pieces of the ephod as memorial stones for the Israelites, just as the Lord had commanded Moses.

⁸ He also made the embroidered breastpiece with the same workmanship as the ephod of gold, of blue, purple, and scarlet yarn, and of finely spun linen. ⁹ They made the breastpiece square and folded double, nine inches long and nine inches wide. ¹⁰ They mounted four rows of gemstones on it. The first row was a row of carnelian, topaz, and emerald; ¹¹ the second row, a turquoise, a sapphire, and a diamond; ¹² the third row, a jacinth, an agate, and an amethyst; ¹³ and the fourth row, a beryl, an onyx, and a jasper. They were surrounded with gold filigree in their settings.

¹⁴ The 12 stones corresponded to the names of Israel's sons. Each stone was engraved like a seal with one of the names of the 12 tribes.

¹⁵ They made braided chains of pure gold cord for the breastpiece. ¹⁶ They also fashioned two gold filigree settings and two gold rings and attached the two rings to its two corners. ¹⁷ Then they attached the two gold cords to the two gold rings on the corners of the breastpiece. ¹⁸ They attached the other ends of the two cords to the two filigree settings and, in this way, attached them to the ephod's shoulder pieces in front. ¹⁹ They made two other gold rings and put them at the two other corners of the breastpiece on the edge that is next to the inner border of the ephod. ²⁰ They made two more gold rings and attached them to the bottom of the ephod's two shoulder pieces on its front, close to its seam, above the ephod's woven waistband. ²¹ Then they tied the breastpiece from its rings to the rings of the ephod with a cord of blue yarn, so that the breastpiece was above the ephod's waistband and did not come loose from the ephod. They did just as the Lord had commanded Moses.

²² They made the woven robe of the ephod entirely of blue yarn. ²³ There was an opening in the center of the robe like that of body armor with a collar around the opening so that it would not tear. ²⁴ They made pomegranates of finely spun blue, purple, and scarlet yarn on the lower hem of the robe. ²⁵ They made bells of pure gold and attached the bells between the pomegranates, all around the hem of the robe between the pomegranates, ²⁶ a bell and a pomegranate alternating all around the lower hem of the robe to be worn for ministry. They made it just as the Lord had commanded Moses.

²⁷ They made the tunics of fine woven linen for Aaron and his sons. ²⁸ They also made the turban and the

ornate headbands of fine linen, the undergarments, [29] and the sash of finely spun linen of embroidered blue, purple, and scarlet yarn. They did just as the LORD had commanded Moses.

[30] They also made a medallion, the holy diadem, out of pure gold and wrote on it an inscription like the engraving on a seal:

HOLY TO THE LORD.

[31] Then they attached a cord of blue yarn to it in order to mount it on the turban, just as the LORD had commanded Moses.

[32] So all the work for the tabernacle, the tent of meeting, was finished. The Israelites did everything just as the LORD had commanded Moses. [33] Then they brought the tabernacle to Moses: the tent with all its furnishings, its clasps, its planks, its crossbars, and its posts and bases; [34] the covering of ram skins dyed red and the covering of manatee skins; the veil for the screen; [35] the ark of the ˙testimony with its poles and the ˙mercy seat; [36] the table, all its utensils, and the ˙bread of the Presence; [37] the pure gold lampstand, with its lamps arranged and all its utensils, as well as the oil for the light; [38] the gold altar; the anointing oil; the fragrant incense; the screen for the entrance to the tent; [39] the bronze altar with its bronze grate, its poles, and all its utensils; the basin with its stand; [40] the hangings of the courtyard, its posts and bases, the screen for the gate of the courtyard, its ropes and tent pegs, and all the equipment for the service of the tabernacle, the tent of meeting; [41] and the specially woven garments for ministering in the sanctuary, the holy garments for Aaron the priest and the garments for his sons to serve as priests. [42] The Israelites had done all the work according to everything the LORD had commanded Moses. [43] Moses inspected all the work they had accomplished. They had done just as the LORD commanded. Then Moses blessed them.

40 The LORD spoke to Moses: [2] "You are to set up the tabernacle, the tent of meeting, on the first day of the first month. [3] Put the ark of the ˙testimony there and screen off the ark with the veil. [4] Then bring in the table and lay out its arrangement; also bring in the lampstand and set up its lamps. [5] Place the gold altar for incense in front of the ark of the testimony. Put up the screen for the entrance to the tabernacle. [6] Position the altar of ˙burnt offering in front of the entrance to the tabernacle, the tent of meeting. [7] Place the basin between the tent of meeting and the altar, and put water in it. [8] Assemble the surrounding courtyard and hang the screen for the gate of the courtyard.

[9] "Take the anointing oil and anoint the tabernacle and everything in it; consecrate it along with all its furnishings so that it will be holy. [10] Anoint the altar of burnt offering and all its utensils; consecrate the altar so that it will be especially holy. [11] Anoint the basin and its stand and consecrate it.

[12] "Then bring Aaron and his sons to the entrance to the tent of meeting and wash them with water. [13] Clothe Aaron with the holy garments, anoint him, and consecrate him, so that he can serve Me as a priest. [14] Have his sons come forward and clothe them in tunics. [15] Anoint them just as you anointed their father, so that they may also serve Me as priests. Their anointing will serve to inaugurate a permanent priesthood for them throughout their generations."

[16] Moses did everything just as the LORD had commanded him. [17] The tabernacle was set up in the first month of the second year, on the first day of the month. [18] Moses set up the tabernacle: he laid its bases, positioned its planks, inserted its crossbars, and set up its posts. [19] Then he spread the tent over the tabernacle and put the covering of the tent on top of it, just as the LORD had commanded Moses.˙

[20] Moses took the testimony and placed it in the ark, and attached the poles to the ark. He set the ˙mercy seat on top of the ark. [21] He brought the ark into the tabernacle, put up the veil for the screen, and screened off the ark of the testimony, just as the LORD had commanded him.

[22] Moses placed the table in the tent of meeting on the north side of the tabernacle, outside the veil. [23] He arranged the bread on it before the LORD, just as the LORD had commanded him. [24] He also put the lampstand in the tent of meeting opposite the table on the south side of the tabernacle [25] and set up the lamps before the LORD, just as the LORD had commanded him.

[26] Moses also installed the gold altar in the tent of meeting, in front of the veil, [27] and burned fragrant incense on it, just as the LORD had commanded him. [28] He put up the screen at the entrance to the tabernacle. [29] Then he placed the altar of burnt offering at the entrance to the tabernacle, the tent of meeting, and offered the burnt offering and the ˙grain offering on it, just as the LORD had commanded him.

[30] He set the basin between the tent of meeting and the altar and put water in it for washing. [31] Moses, Aaron, and his sons washed their hands and feet from it. [32] They washed whenever they came to the tent of meeting and approached the altar, just as the LORD had commanded Moses.

[33] Next Moses set up the surrounding courtyard for the tabernacle and the altar and hung a screen for the gate of the courtyard. So Moses finished the work.

[34] The cloud covered the tent of meeting, and the glory of the LORD filled the tabernacle. [35] Moses was unable to enter the tent of meeting because the cloud rested on it, and the glory of the LORD filled the tabernacle.

[36] The Israelites set out whenever the cloud was taken up from the tabernacle throughout all the stages of their journey. [37] If the cloud was not taken up, they did not set out until the day it was taken up. [38] For the cloud of the LORD was over the tabernacle by day, and there was a fire inside the cloud by night, visible to the entire house of Israel throughout all the stages of their journey.

LEVITICUS

1 Then the LORD summoned Moses and spoke to him from the tent of meeting: ²"Speak to the Israelites and tell them: When any of you brings an offering to the LORD from the livestock, you may bring your offering from the herd or the flock.

³"If his gift is a *burnt offering from the herd, he is to bring an unblemished male. He must bring it to the entrance to the tent of meeting so that he may be accepted by the LORD. ⁴He is to lay his hand on the head of the burnt offering so it can be accepted on his behalf to make *atonement for him. ⁵He is to slaughter the bull before the LORD; Aaron's sons the priests are to present the blood and sprinkle it on all sides of the altar that is at the entrance to the tent of meeting. ⁶Then he must skin the burnt offering and cut it into pieces. ⁷The sons of Aaron the priest will prepare a fire on the altar and arrange wood on the fire. ⁸Aaron's sons the priests are to arrange the pieces, the head, and the suet on top of the burning wood on the altar. ⁹The offerer must wash its entrails and shanks with water. Then the priest will burn all of it on the altar as a burnt offering, a fire offering of a pleasing aroma to the LORD.

¹⁰"But if his gift for a burnt offering is from the flock, from sheep or goats, he is to present an unblemished male. ¹¹He will slaughter it on the north side of the altar before the LORD. Aaron's sons the priests will sprinkle its blood against the altar on all sides. ¹²He will cut the animal into pieces with its head and its suet, and the priest will arrange them on top of the burning wood on the altar. ¹³But he is to wash the entrails and shanks with water. The priest will then present all of it and burn it on the altar; it is a burnt offering, a fire offering of a pleasing aroma to the LORD.

¹⁴"If his gift to the LORD is a burnt offering of birds, he is to present his offering from the turtledoves or young pigeons. ¹⁵Then the priest must bring it to the altar, and must twist off its head and burn it on the altar; its blood should be drained at the side of the altar. ¹⁶He will remove its digestive tract, cutting off the tail feathers, and throw it on the east side of the altar at the place for ashes. ¹⁷He will tear it open by its wings without dividing the bird. Then the priest is to burn it on the altar on top of the burning wood. It is a burnt offering, a fire offering of a pleasing aroma to the LORD.

2 "When anyone presents a *grain offering as a gift to the LORD, his gift must consist of fine flour. He is to pour olive oil on it, put frankincense on it, ²and bring it to Aaron's sons the priests. The priest will take a handful of fine flour and oil from it, along with all its frankincense, and will burn this memorial portion of it on the altar, a fire offering of a pleasing aroma to the LORD. ³But the rest of the grain offering will belong to Aaron and his sons; it is the holiest part of the fire offerings to the LORD.

⁴"When you present a grain offering baked in an oven, it must be made of fine flour, either unleavened cakes mixed with oil or unleavened wafers coated with oil. ⁵If your gift is a grain offering prepared on a griddle, it must be unleavened bread made of fine flour mixed with oil. ⁶Break it into pieces and pour oil on it; it is a grain offering. ⁷If your gift is a grain offering prepared in a pan, it must be made of fine flour with

oil. ⁸When you bring to the LORD the grain offering made in any of these ways, it is to be presented to the priest, and he will take it to the altar. ⁹The priest will remove the memorial portion from the grain offering and burn it on the altar, a fire offering of a pleasing aroma to the LORD. ¹⁰But the rest of the grain offering will belong to Aaron and his sons; it is the holiest part of the fire offerings to the LORD.

¹¹"No grain offering that you present to the LORD is to be made with yeast, for you are not to burn any yeast or honey as a fire offering to the LORD. ¹²You may present them to the LORD as an offering of *firstfruits, but they are not to be offered on the altar as a pleasing aroma. ¹³You are to season each of your grain offerings with salt; you must not omit from your grain offering the salt of the covenant with your God. You are to present salt with each of your offerings.

¹⁴"If you present a grain offering of firstfruits to the LORD, you must present fresh heads of grain, crushed kernels, roasted on the fire, for your grain offering of firstfruits. ¹⁵You are to put oil and frankincense on it; it is a grain offering. ¹⁶The priest will then burn some of its crushed kernels and oil with all its frankincense as a fire offering to the LORD.

3 "If his offering is a *fellowship sacrifice, and he is presenting an animal from the herd, whether male or female, he must present one without blemish before the LORD. ²He is to lay his hand on the head of his offering and slaughter it at the entrance to the tent of meeting. Then Aaron's sons the priests will sprinkle the blood on all sides of the altar. ³He will present part of the fellowship sacrifice as a fire offering to the LORD: the fat surrounding the entrails, all the fat that is on the entrails, ⁴and the two kidneys with the fat on them at the loins; he will also remove the fatty lobe of the liver with the kidneys. ⁵Aaron's sons will burn it on the altar along with the *burnt offering that is on the burning wood, a fire offering of a pleasing aroma to the LORD.

⁶"If his offering as a fellowship sacrifice to the LORD is from the flock, he must present a male or female without blemish. ⁷If he is presenting a lamb for his offering, he is to present it before the LORD. ⁸He must lay his hand on the head of his offering, then slaughter it before the tent of meeting. Aaron's sons will sprinkle its blood on all sides of the altar. ⁹He will then present part of the fellowship sacrifice as a fire offering to the LORD consisting of its fat and the entire fat tail, which he is to remove close to the backbone. He will also remove the fat surrounding the entrails, all the fat on the entrails, ¹⁰the two kidneys with the fat on them at the loins, and the fatty lobe of the liver above the kidneys. ¹¹Then the priest will burn the food on the altar, as a fire offering to the LORD.

¹²"If his offering is a goat, he is to present it before the LORD. ¹³He must lay his hand on its head and slaughter it before the tent of meeting. Aaron's sons will sprinkle its blood on all sides of the altar. ¹⁴He will present part of his offering as a fire offering to the LORD: the fat surrounding the entrails, all the fat that is on the entrails, ¹⁵and the two kidneys with the fat on them at the loins; he will also remove the fatty lobe of the liver with the kidneys. ¹⁶Then the priest will burn

the food on the altar, as a fire offering for a pleasing aroma.

"All fat belongs to the LORD. [17] This is a permanent statute throughout your generations, wherever you live: you must not eat any fat or any blood."

4 Then the LORD spoke to Moses: [2] "Tell the Israelites: When someone sins unintentionally against any of the LORD's commands and does anything prohibited by them—

[3] "If the anointed priest sins, bringing ˙guilt on the people, he is to present to the LORD a young, unblemished bull as a ˙sin offering for the sin he has committed. [4] He must bring the bull to the entrance to the tent of meeting before the LORD, lay his hand on the bull's head, and slaughter it before the LORD. [5] The anointed priest must then take some of the bull's blood and bring it into the tent of meeting. [6] The priest is to dip his finger in the blood and sprinkle some of it seven times before the LORD in front of the veil of the sanctuary. [7] The priest must apply some of the blood to the horns of the altar of fragrant incense that is before the LORD in the tent of meeting. He must pour out the rest of the bull's blood at the base of the altar of burnt offering that is at the entrance to the tent of meeting. [8] He is to remove all the fat from the bull of the sin offering: the fat surrounding the entrails, all the fat that is on the entrails, [9] and the two kidneys with the fat on them at the loins. He will also remove the fatty lobe of the liver with the kidneys, [10] just as the fat is removed from the ox of the ˙fellowship sacrifice. The priest is to burn them on the altar of burnt offering. [11] But the hide of the bull and all its flesh, with its head and shanks, and its entrails and dung— [12] all the rest of the bull—he must bring to a ceremonially ˙clean place outside the camp to the ash heap, and must burn it on a wood fire. It is to be burned at the ash heap.

[13] "Now if the whole community of Israel errs, and the matter escapes the notice of the assembly, so that they violate any of the LORD's commands and incur guilt by doing what is prohibited, [14] then the assembly must present a young bull as a sin offering. When the sin they have committed in regard to the command becomes known, they are to bring it before the tent of meeting. [15] The elders of the community are to lay their hands on the bull's head before the LORD and it is to be slaughtered before the LORD. [16] The anointed priest will bring some of the bull's blood into the tent of meeting. [17] The priest is to dip his finger in the blood and sprinkle it seven times before the LORD in front of the veil. [18] He is to apply some of the blood to the horns of the altar that is before the LORD in the tent of meeting. He must pour out the rest of the blood at the base of the altar of burnt offering that is at the entrance to the tent of meeting. [19] He is to remove all the fat from it and burn it on the altar. [20] He is to offer this bull just as he did with the bull in the sin offering; he will offer it the same way. So the priest will make ˙atonement on their behalf, and they will be forgiven. [21] Then he will bring the bull outside the camp and burn it just as he burned the first bull. It is the sin offering for the assembly.

[22] "When a leader sins and unintentionally violates any of the commands of the LORD his God by doing what is prohibited, and incurs guilt, [23] or someone informs him about the sin he has committed, he is to bring an unblemished male goat as his offering. [24] He is to lay his hand on the head of the goat and slaughter it at the place where the ˙burnt offering is slaughtered before the LORD. It is a sin offering. [25] Then the priest must take some of the blood from the sin offering with his finger and apply it to the horns of the altar of burnt offering. The rest of its blood he must pour out at the base of the altar of burnt offering. [26] He must burn all its fat on the altar, like the fat of the fellowship sacrifice. In this way the priest will make atonement on his behalf for that person's sin, and he will be forgiven.

[27] "Now if any of the common people sins unintentionally by violating one of the LORD's commands, does what is prohibited, and incurs guilt, [28] or if someone informs him about the sin he has committed, then he is to bring an unblemished female goat as his offering for the sin that he has committed. [29] He is to lay his hand on the head of the sin offering and slaughter it at the place of the burnt offering. [30] Then the priest must take some of its blood with his finger and apply it to the horns of the altar of burnt offering. He must pour out the rest of its blood at the base of the altar. [31] He is to remove all its fat just as the fat is removed from the fellowship sacrifice. The priest is to burn it on the altar as a pleasing aroma to the LORD. In this way the priest will make atonement on his behalf, and he will be forgiven.

[32] "Or if the offering that he brings as a sin offering is a lamb, he is to bring an unblemished female. [33] He is to lay his hand on the head of the sin offering and slaughter it as a sin offering at the place where the burnt offering is slaughtered. [34] Then the priest must take some of the blood of the sin offering with his finger and apply it to the horns of the altar of burnt offering. He must pour out the rest of its blood at the base of the altar. [35] He is to remove all its fat just as the fat of the lamb is removed from the fellowship sacrifice. The priest will burn it on the altar along with the fire offerings to the LORD. In this way the priest will make atonement on his behalf for the sin he has committed, and he will be forgiven.

5 "When someone sins in any of these ways: If he has seen, heard, or known about something he has witnessed, and did not respond to a public call to testify, he is responsible for his sin. [2] Or if someone touches anything ˙unclean—a carcass of an unclean wild animal, or unclean livestock, or an unclean swarming creature—without being aware of it, he is unclean and ˙guilty. [3] Or if he touches human uncleanness—any uncleanness by which one can become defiled—without being aware of it, but later recognizes it, he is guilty. [4] Or if someone swears rashly to do what is good or evil—concerning anything a person may speak rashly in an oath—without being aware of it, but later recognizes it, he incurs guilt in such an instance. [5] If someone incurs guilt in one of these cases, he is to confess he has committed that sin. [6] He must bring his restitution for the sin he has committed to the LORD: a female lamb or goat from the flock as a ˙sin offering. In this way the priest will make ˙atonement on his behalf for his sin.

[7] "But if he cannot afford an animal from the flock, then he may bring to the LORD two turtledoves or two young pigeons as restitution for his sin—one as a sin offering and the other as a ˙burnt offering. [8] He is to

bring them to the priest, who will first present the one for the sin offering. He must twist its head at the back of the neck without severing it. ⁹Then he will sprinkle some of the blood of the sin offering on the side of the altar, while the rest of the blood is to be drained out at the base of the altar; it is a sin offering. ¹⁰He must prepare the second bird as a burnt offering according to the regulation. In this way the priest will make atonement on his behalf for the sin he has committed, and he will be forgiven.

¹¹"But if he cannot afford two turtledoves or two young pigeons, he may bring two quarts of fine flour as an offering for his sin. He must not put olive oil or frankincense on it, for it is a sin offering. ¹²He is to bring it to the priest, who will take a handful from it as its memorial portion and burn it on the altar along with the fire offerings to the LORD; it is a sin offering. ¹³In this way the priest will make atonement on his behalf concerning the sin he has committed in any of these cases, and he will be forgiven. The rest will belong to the priest, like the *grain offering."

¹⁴Then the LORD spoke to Moses: ¹⁵"If someone offends by sinning unintentionally in regard to any of the LORD's holy things, he must bring his *restitution offering to the LORD: an unblemished ram from the flock (based on your assessment of its value in silver *shekels, according to the sanctuary shekel) as a restitution offering. ¹⁶He must make restitution for his sin regarding any holy thing, adding a fifth of its value to it, and give it to the priest. Then the priest will make atonement on his behalf with the ram of the restitution offering, and he will be forgiven.

¹⁷"If someone sins and without knowing it violates any of the LORD's commands concerning anything prohibited, he bears the consequences of his guilt. ¹⁸He must bring an unblemished ram from the flock according to your assessment of its value as a restitution offering to the priest. Then the priest will make atonement on his behalf for the error he has committed unintentionally, and he will be forgiven. ¹⁹It is a restitution offering; he is indeed guilty before the LORD."

6 The LORD spoke to Moses: ²"When someone sins and offends the LORD by deceiving his neighbor in regard to a deposit, a security, or a robbery; or defrauds his neighbor; ³or finds something lost and lies about it; or swears falsely about any of the sinful things a person may do— ⁴once he has sinned and acknowledged his *guilt—he must return what he stole or defrauded, or the deposit entrusted to him, or the lost item he found, ⁵or anything else about which he swore falsely. He must make full restitution for it and add a fifth of its value to it. He is to pay it to its owner on the day he acknowledges his guilt. ⁶Then he must bring his *restitution offering to the LORD: an unblemished ram from the flock according to your assessment of its value as a restitution offering to the priest. ⁷In this way the priest will make *atonement on his behalf before the LORD, and he will be forgiven for anything he may have done to incur guilt."

⁸The LORD spoke to Moses: ⁹"Command Aaron and his sons: This is the law of the *burnt offering; the burnt offering itself must remain on the altar's hearth all night until morning, while the fire of the altar is kept burning on it. ¹⁰The priest is to put on his linen robe and linen undergarments. He is to remove the ashes of the burnt offering the fire has consumed on the altar, and place them beside the altar. ¹¹Then he

must take off his garments, put on other clothes, and bring the ashes outside the camp to a ceremonially *clean place. ¹²The fire on the altar is to be kept burning; it must not go out. Every morning the priest will burn wood on the fire. He is to arrange the burnt offering on the fire and burn the fat portions from the *fellowship offerings on it. ¹³Fire must be kept burning on the altar continually; it must not go out.

¹⁴"Now this is the law of the *grain offering: Aaron's sons will present it before the LORD in front of the altar. ¹⁵The priest is to remove a handful of fine flour and olive oil from the grain offering, with all the frankincense that is on the offering, and burn its memorial portion on the altar as a pleasing aroma to the LORD. ¹⁶Aaron and his sons may eat the rest of it. It is to be eaten in the form of unleavened bread in a holy place; they are to eat it in the courtyard of the tent of meeting. ¹⁷It must not be baked with yeast; I have assigned it as their portion from My fire offerings. It is especially holy, like the *sin offering and the restitution offering. ¹⁸Any male among Aaron's descendants may eat it. It is a permanent portion throughout your generations from the fire offerings to the LORD. Anything that touches the offerings will become holy."

¹⁹The LORD spoke to Moses: ²⁰"This is the offering that Aaron and his sons must present to the LORD on the day that he is anointed: two quarts of fine flour as a regular grain offering, half of it in the morning and half in the evening. ²¹It is to be prepared with oil on a griddle; you are to bring it well-kneaded. You must present it as a grain offering of baked pieces, a pleasing aroma to the LORD. ²²The priest, who is one of Aaron's sons and will be anointed to take his place, is to prepare it. It must be completely burned as a permanent portion for the LORD. ²³Every grain offering for a priest will be a whole burnt offering; it is not to be eaten."

²⁴The LORD spoke to Moses: ²⁵"Tell Aaron and his sons: This is the law of the sin offering. The sin offering is most holy and must be slaughtered before the LORD at the place where the burnt offering is slaughtered. ²⁶The priest who offers it as a sin offering is to eat it. It must be eaten in a holy place, in the courtyard of the tent of meeting. ²⁷Anything that touches its flesh will become holy, and if any of its blood spatters on a garment, then you must wash that garment in a holy place. ²⁸A clay pot in which the sin offering is boiled must be broken; if it is boiled in a bronze vessel, it must be scoured and rinsed with water. ²⁹Any male among the priests may eat it; it is especially holy. ³⁰But no sin offering may be eaten if its blood has been brought into the tent of meeting to make atonement in the holy place; it must be burned up.

7 "Now this is the law of the *restitution offering; it is especially holy. ²The restitution offering must be slaughtered at the place where the *burnt offering is slaughtered, and the priest is to sprinkle its blood on all sides of the altar. ³The offerer must present all the fat from it: the fat tail, the fat surrounding the entrails, ⁴and the two kidneys with the fat on them at the loins; he will also remove the fatty lobe of the liver with the kidneys. ⁵The priest will burn them on the altar as a fire offering to the LORD; it is a restitution offering. ⁶Any male among the priests may eat it. It is to be eaten in a holy place; it is especially holy.

⁷"The restitution offering is like the *sin offering; the law is the same for both. It belongs to the priest who makes *atonement with it. ⁸As for the priest who

presents someone's burnt offering, the hide of the burnt offering he has presented belongs to him; it is the priest's. ⁹Any *grain offering that is baked in an oven or prepared in a pan or on a griddle belongs to the priest who presents it; it is his. ¹⁰But any grain offering, whether dry or mixed with oil, belongs equally to all of Aaron's sons.

¹¹"Now this is the law of the *fellowship sacrifice that someone may present to the LORD: ¹²If he presents it for thanksgiving, in addition to the thanksgiving sacrifice, he is to present unleavened cakes mixed with olive oil, unleavened wafers coated with oil, and well-kneaded cakes of fine flour mixed with oil. ¹³He is to present as his offering cakes of leavened bread with his thanksgiving sacrifice of fellowship. ¹⁴From the cakes he must present one portion of each offering as a contribution to the LORD. It will belong to the priest who sprinkles the blood of the fellowship offering; it is his. ¹⁵The meat of his thanksgiving sacrifice of fellowship must be eaten on the day he offers it; he may not leave any of it until morning.

¹⁶"If the sacrifice he offers is a vow or a freewill offering, it is to be eaten on the day he presents his sacrifice, and what is left over may be eaten on the next day. ¹⁷But what remains of the sacrificial meat by the third day must be burned up. ¹⁸If any of the meat of his fellowship sacrifice is eaten on the third day, it will not be accepted. It will not be credited to the one who presents it; it is repulsive. The person who eats any of it will be responsible for his sin.

¹⁹"Meat that touches anything *unclean must not be eaten; it is to be burned up. Everyone who is *clean may eat any other meat. ²⁰But the one who eats meat from the LORD's fellowship sacrifice while he is unclean, that person must be cut off from his people. ²¹If someone touches anything unclean, whether human uncleanness, an unclean animal, or any unclean, detestable creature, and eats meat from the LORD's fellowship sacrifice, that person must be cut off from his people."

²²The LORD spoke to Moses: ²³"Tell the Israelites: You are not to eat any fat of an ox, a sheep, or a goat. ²⁴The fat of an animal that dies naturally or is mauled by wild beasts may be used for any purpose, but you must not eat it. ²⁵If anyone eats animal fat from a fire offering presented to the LORD, the person who eats it must be cut off from his people. ²⁶Wherever you live, you must not eat the blood of any bird or animal. ²⁷Whoever eats any blood, that person must be cut off from his people."

²⁸The LORD spoke to Moses: ²⁹"Tell the Israelites: The one who presents a fellowship sacrifice to the LORD must bring an offering to the LORD from his sacrifice. ³⁰His own hands will bring the fire offerings to the LORD. He will bring the fat together with the breast. The breast is to be waved as a presentation offering before the LORD. ³¹The priest is to burn the fat on the altar, but the breast belongs to Aaron and his sons. ³²You are to give the right thigh to the priest as a contribution from your fellowship sacrifices. ³³The son of Aaron who presents the blood of the fellowship offering and the fat will have the right thigh as a portion. ³⁴I have taken from the Israelites the breast of the presentation offering and the thigh of the contribution from their fellowship sacrifices, and have assigned them to Aaron the priest and his sons as a permanent portion from the Israelites."

³⁵This is the portion from the fire offerings to the LORD for Aaron and his sons since the day they were presented to serve the LORD as priests. ³⁶The LORD commanded this to be given to them by the Israelites on the day He anointed them. It is a permanent portion throughout their generations.

³⁷This is the law for the burnt offering, the grain offering, the sin offering, the restitution offering, the ordination offering, and the fellowship sacrifice, ³⁸which the LORD commanded Moses on Mount Sinai on the day He commanded the Israelites to present their offerings to the LORD in the Wilderness of Sinai.

8 The LORD spoke to Moses: ²"Take Aaron, his sons with him, the garments, the anointing oil, the bull of the *sin offering, the two rams, and the basket of unleavened bread, ³and assemble the whole community at the entrance to the tent of meeting." ⁴So Moses did as the LORD commanded him, and the community assembled at the entrance to the tent of meeting. ⁵Moses said to them, "This is what the LORD has commanded to be done."

⁶Then Moses presented Aaron and his sons and washed them with water. ⁷He put the tunic on Aaron, wrapped the sash around him, clothed him with the robe, and put the *ephod on him. He put the woven band of the ephod around him and fastened it to him. ⁸Then he put the breastpiece on him and placed the *Urim and Thummim into the breastpiece. ⁹He also put the turban on his head and placed the gold medallion, the holy diadem, on the front of the turban, as the LORD had commanded Moses.

¹⁰Then Moses took the anointing oil and anointed the tabernacle and everything in it to consecrate them. ¹¹He sprinkled some of the oil on the altar seven times, anointing the altar with all its utensils, and the basin with its stand, to consecrate them. ¹²He poured some of the anointing oil on Aaron's head and anointed and consecrated him. ¹³Then Moses presented Aaron's sons, clothed them with tunics, wrapped sashes around them, and fastened headbands on them, as the LORD had commanded Moses.

¹⁴Then he brought the bull near for the sin offering, and Aaron and his sons laid their hands on the head of the bull for the sin offering. ¹⁵Then Moses slaughtered it, took the blood, and applied it with his finger to the horns of the altar on all sides, purifying the altar. He poured out the blood at the base of the altar and consecrated it so that *atonement can be made on it. ¹⁶Moses took all the fat that was on the entrails, the fatty lobe of the liver, and the two kidneys with their fat, and he burned them on the altar. ¹⁷He burned up the bull with its hide, flesh, and dung outside the camp, as the LORD had commanded Moses.

¹⁸Then he presented the ram for the *burnt offering, and Aaron and his sons laid their hands on the head of the ram. ¹⁹Moses slaughtered it and sprinkled the blood on all sides of the altar. ²⁰Moses cut the ram into pieces and burned the head, the pieces, and the suet, ²¹but he washed the entrails and shanks with water. He then burned the entire ram on the altar. It was a burnt offering for a pleasing aroma, a fire offering to the LORD as He had commanded Moses.

²²Next he presented the second ram, the ram of ordination, and Aaron and his sons laid their hands on the head of the ram. ²³Moses slaughtered it, took some of its blood, and put it on Aaron's right earlobe, on the thumb of his right hand, and on the big toe of

his right foot. ²⁴Moses also presented Aaron's sons and put some of the blood on their right earlobes, on the thumbs of their right hands, and on the big toes of their right feet. Then Moses sprinkled the blood on all sides of the altar. ²⁵He took the fat—the fat tail, all the fat that was on the entrails, the fatty lobe of the liver, and the two kidneys with their fat—as well as the right thigh. ²⁶From the basket of unleavened bread that was before the Lord he took one cake of unleavened bread, one cake of bread made with oil, and one wafer, and placed them on the fat portions and the right thigh. ²⁷He put all these in the hands of Aaron and his sons and waved them before the Lord as a presentation offering. ²⁸Then Moses took them from their hands and burned them on the altar with the burnt offering. This was an ordination offering for a pleasing aroma, a fire offering to the Lord. ²⁹He also took the breast and waved it before the Lord as a presentation offering; it was Moses' portion of the ordination ram as the Lord had commanded him.

³⁰Then Moses took some of the anointing oil and some of the blood that was on the altar and sprinkled them on Aaron and his garments, as well as on his sons and their garments. In this way he consecrated Aaron and his garments, as well as his sons and their garments.

³¹Moses said to Aaron and his sons, "Boil the meat at the entrance to the tent of meeting and eat it there with the bread that is in the basket for the ordination offering as I commanded: Aaron and his sons are to eat it. ³²You must burn up what remains of the meat and bread. ³³You must not go outside the entrance to the tent of meeting for seven days, until the time your days of ordination are completed, because it will take seven days to ordain you. ³⁴The Lord commanded what has been done today in order to make atonement for you. ³⁵You must remain at the entrance to the tent of meeting day and night for seven days and keep the Lord's charge so that you will not die, for this is what I was commanded." ³⁶So Aaron and his sons did everything the Lord had commanded through Moses.

9 On the eighth day Moses summoned Aaron, his sons, and the elders of Israel. ²He said to Aaron, "Take a young bull for a ˙sin offering and a ram for a ˙burnt offering, both without blemish, and present them before the Lord. ³And tell the Israelites: Take a male goat for a sin offering; a calf and a lamb, male yearlings without blemish, for a burnt offering; ⁴an ox and a ram for a ˙fellowship offering to sacrifice before the Lord; and a ˙grain offering mixed with oil. For today the Lord is going to appear to you."

⁵They brought what Moses had commanded to the front of the tent of meeting, and the whole community came forward and stood before the Lord. ⁶Moses said, "This is what the Lord commanded you to do, that the glory of the Lord may appear to you." ⁷Then Moses said to Aaron, "Approach the altar and sacrifice your sin offering and your burnt offering; make ˙atonement for yourself and the people. Sacrifice the people's offering and make atonement for them, as the Lord commanded."

⁸So Aaron approached the altar and slaughtered the calf as a sin offering for himself. ⁹Aaron's sons brought the blood to him, and he dipped his finger in the blood and applied it to the horns of the altar. He poured out the blood at the base of the altar. ¹⁰He burned the fat, the kidneys, and the fatty lobe of the liver from the

sin offering on the altar, as the Lord had commanded Moses. ¹¹He burned up the flesh and the hide outside the camp.

¹²Then he slaughtered the burnt offering. Aaron's sons brought him the blood, and he sprinkled it on all sides of the altar. ¹³They brought him the burnt offering piece by piece, along with the head, and he burned them on the altar. ¹⁴He washed the entrails and the shanks and burned them with the burnt offering on the altar.

¹⁵Aaron presented the people's offering. He took the male goat for the people's sin offering, slaughtered it, and made a sin offering with it as he did before. ¹⁶He presented the burnt offering and sacrificed it according to the regulation. ¹⁷Next he presented the grain offering, took a handful of it, and burned it on the altar in addition to the morning burnt offering.

¹⁸Finally, he slaughtered the ox and the ram as the people's fellowship sacrifice. Aaron's sons brought him the blood, and he sprinkled it on all sides of the altar. ¹⁹They also brought the fat portions from the ox and the ram—the fat tail, the fat surrounding the entrails, the kidneys, and the fatty lobe of the liver— ²⁰and placed these on the breasts. Aaron burned the fat portions on the altar, ²¹but he waved the breasts and the right thigh as a presentation offering before the Lord, as Moses had commanded.

²²Aaron lifted up his hands toward the people and blessed them. He came down after sacrificing the sin offering, the burnt offering, and the fellowship offering. ²³Moses and Aaron then entered the tent of meeting. When they came out, they blessed the people, and the glory of the Lord appeared to all the people. ²⁴Fire came from the Lord and consumed the burnt offering and the fat portions on the altar. And when all the people saw it, they shouted and fell facedown on the ground.

10 Aaron's sons Nadab and Abihu each took his own firepan, put fire in it, placed incense on it, and presented unauthorized fire before the Lord, which He had not commanded them to do. ²Then fire came from the Lord and burned them to death before the Lord. ³So Moses said to Aaron, "This is what the Lord meant when He said:

> I will show My holiness
> to those who are near Me,
> and I will reveal My glory
> before all the people."

But Aaron remained silent.

⁴Moses summoned Mishael and Elzaphan, sons of Aaron's uncle Uzziel, and said to them, "Come here and carry your relatives away from the front of the sanctuary to a place outside the camp." ⁵So they came forward and carried them in their tunics outside the camp, as Moses had said.

⁶Then Moses said to Aaron and his sons Eleazar and Ithamar, "Do not let your hair hang loose and do not tear your garments, or else you will die, and the Lord will become angry with the whole community. However, your brothers, the whole house of Israel, may mourn over that tragedy when the Lord sent the fire. ⁷You must not go outside the entrance to the tent of meeting or you will die, for the Lord's anointing oil is on you." So they did as Moses said.

⁸The Lord spoke to Aaron: ⁹"You and your sons are not to drink wine or beer when you enter the tent of meeting, or else you will die; this is a permanent

statute throughout your generations. ¹⁰You must distinguish between the holy and the common, and the *clean and the *unclean, ¹¹and teach the Israelites all the statutes that the Lᴏʀᴅ has given to them through Moses."

¹²Moses spoke to Aaron and his remaining sons, Eleazar and Ithamar: "Take the *grain offering that is left over from the fire offerings to the Lᴏʀᴅ, and eat it prepared without yeast beside the altar, because it is especially holy. ¹³You must eat it in a holy place because it is your portion and your sons' from the fire offerings to the Lᴏʀᴅ, for this is what I was commanded. ¹⁴But you and your sons and your daughters may eat the breast of the presentation offering and the thigh of the contribution in any ceremonially clean place, because these portions have been assigned to you and your children from the Israelites' *fellowship sacrifices. ¹⁵They are to bring the thigh of the contribution and the breast of the presentation offering, together with the offerings of fat portions made by fire, to wave as a presentation offering before the Lᴏʀᴅ. It will belong permanently to you and your children, as the Lᴏʀᴅ commanded."

¹⁶Later, Moses inquired about the male goat of the *sin offering, but it had already been burned up. He was angry with Eleazar and Ithamar, Aaron's surviving sons, and asked, ¹⁷"Why didn't you eat the sin offering in the sanctuary area? For it is especially holy, and He has assigned it to you to take away the *guilt of the community and make *atonement for them before the Lᴏʀᴅ. ¹⁸Since its blood was not brought inside the sanctuary, you should have eaten it in the sanctuary area, as I commanded."

¹⁹But Aaron replied to Moses, "See, today they presented their sin offering and their *burnt offering before the Lᴏʀᴅ. Since these things have happened to me, if I had eaten the sin offering today, would it have been acceptable in the Lᴏʀᴅ's sight?" ²⁰When Moses heard this, it was acceptable to him.

11 The Lᴏʀᴅ spoke to Moses and Aaron: ²"Tell the Israelites: You may eat all these kinds of land animals. ³You may eat any animal with divided hooves and that chews the cud. ⁴But among the ones that chew the cud or have divided hooves you are not to eat these:

> the camel, though it chews the cud,
> does not have divided hooves—it is *unclean for you;
> ⁵ the hyrax, though it chews the cud,
> does not have hooves—it is unclean for you;
> ⁶ the hare, though it chews the cud,
> does not have hooves—it is unclean for you;
> ⁷ the pig, though it has divided hooves,
> does not chew the cud—it is unclean for you.

⁸Do not eat any of their meat or touch their carcasses—they are unclean for you.

⁹"This is what you may eat from all that is in the water: You may eat everything in the water that has fins and scales, whether in the seas or streams. ¹⁰But these are to be detestable to you: everything in the seas or streams that does not have fins and scales among all the swarming things and other living creatures in the water. ¹¹They are to remain detestable to you; you must not eat any of their meat, and you must detest their carcasses. ¹²Everything in the water that does not have fins and scales will be detestable to you.

¹³"You are to detest these birds. They must not be eaten because they are detestable:

> the eagle, the bearded vulture,
> the black vulture, ¹⁴the kite,
> any kind of falcon,
> ¹⁵ every kind of raven, ¹⁶the ostrich,
> the short-eared owl, the gull,
> any kind of hawk,
> ¹⁷ the little owl, the cormorant,
> the long-eared owl,
> ¹⁸ the white owl, the desert owl,
> the osprey, ¹⁹the stork,
> any kind of heron,
> the hoopoe, and the bat.

²⁰"All winged insects that walk on all fours are to be detestable to you. ²¹But you may eat these kinds of all the winged insects that walk on all fours: those that have jointed legs above their feet for hopping on the ground. ²²You may eat these:

> any kind of locust, katydid, cricket,
> and grasshopper.

²³All other winged insects that have four feet are to be detestable to you.

²⁴"These will make you unclean. Whoever touches their carcasses will be unclean until evening, ²⁵and whoever carries any of their carcasses must wash his clothes and will be unclean until evening. ²⁶All animals that have hooves but do not have a divided hoof and do not chew the cud are unclean for you. Whoever touches them becomes unclean. ²⁷All the four-footed animals that walk on their paws are unclean for you. Whoever touches their carcasses will be unclean until evening, ²⁸and anyone who carries their carcasses must wash his clothes and will be unclean until evening. They are unclean for you.

²⁹"These creatures that swarm on the ground are unclean for you:

> the weasel, the mouse,
> any kind of large lizard,
> ³⁰ the gecko, the monitor lizard,
> the common lizard, the skink,
> and the chameleon.

³¹These are unclean for you among all the swarming creatures. Whoever touches them when they are dead will be unclean until evening. ³²When any one of them dies and falls on anything it becomes unclean—any item of wood, clothing, leather, *sackcloth, or any implement used for work. It is to be rinsed with water and will remain unclean until evening; then it will be *clean. ³³If any of them falls into any clay pot, everything in it will become unclean; you must break it. ³⁴Any edible food coming into contact with that unclean water will become unclean, and any drinkable liquid in any container will become unclean. ³⁵Anything one of their carcasses falls on will become unclean. If it is an oven or stove, it must be smashed; it is unclean and will remain unclean for you. ³⁶A spring or cistern containing water will remain clean, but someone who touches a carcass in it will become unclean. ³⁷If one of their carcasses falls on any seed that is to be sown, it is clean; ³⁸but if water has been put on the seed and one of their carcasses falls on it, it is unclean for you.

³⁹"If one of the animals that you use for food dies, anyone who touches its carcass will be unclean until evening. ⁴⁰Anyone who eats some of its carcass must wash his clothes and will be unclean until evening.

Anyone who carries its carcass must wash his clothes and will be unclean until evening. ⁴¹"All the creatures that swarm on the earth are detestable; they must not be eaten. ⁴²Do not eat any of the creatures that swarm on the earth, anything that moves on its belly or walks on all fours or on many feet, for they are detestable. ⁴³Do not become contaminated by any creature that swarms; do not become unclean or defiled by them. ⁴⁴For I am *Yahweh your God, so you must consecrate yourselves and be holy because I am holy. You must not defile yourselves by any swarming creature that crawls on the ground. ⁴⁵For I am Yahweh, who brought you up from the land of Egypt to be your God, so you must be holy because I am holy.

⁴⁶"This is the law concerning animals, birds, all living creatures that move in the water, and all creatures that swarm on the ground, ⁴⁷in order to distinguish between the unclean and the clean, between the animals that may be eaten and those that may not be eaten."

12 The LORD spoke to Moses: ²"Tell the Israelites: When a woman becomes pregnant and gives birth to a male child, she will be *unclean seven days, as she is during the days of her menstrual impurity. ³The flesh of his foreskin must be circumcised on the eighth day. ⁴She will continue in purification from her bleeding for 33 days. She must not touch any holy thing or go into the sanctuary until completing her days of purification. ⁵But if she gives birth to a female child, she will be unclean for two weeks as she is during her menstrual impurity. She will continue in purification from her bleeding for 66 days.

⁶"When her days of purification are complete, whether for a son or daughter, she is to bring to the priest at the entrance to the tent of meeting a year-old male lamb for a *burnt offering, and a young pigeon or a turtledove for a *sin offering. ⁷He will present them before the LORD and make *atonement on her behalf; she will be *clean from her discharge of blood. This is the law for a woman giving birth, whether to a male or female. ⁸But if she doesn't have sufficient means for a sheep, she may take two turtledoves or two young pigeons, one for a burnt offering and the other for a sin offering. Then the priest will make atonement on her behalf, and she will be clean."

13 The LORD spoke to Moses and Aaron: ²"When a person has a swelling, scab, or spot on the skin of his body, and it becomes a disease on the skin of his body, he is to be brought to Aaron the priest or to one of his sons, the priests. ³The priest will examine the infection on the skin of his body. If the hair in the infection has turned white and the infection appears to be deeper than the skin of his body, it is a skin disease. After the priest examines him, he must pronounce him *unclean. ⁴But if the spot on the skin of his body is white and does not appear to be deeper than the skin, and the hair in it has not turned white, the priest must quarantine the infected person for seven days. ⁵The priest will then reexamine him on the seventh day. If he sees that the infection remains unchanged and has not spread on the skin, the priest must quarantine him for another seven days. ⁶The priest will examine him again on the seventh day. If the infection has faded and has not spread on the skin, the priest is to pronounce him *clean; it is a scab. The person is to wash his clothes and will become clean. ⁷But if

the scab spreads further on his skin after he has presented himself to the priest for his cleansing, he must present himself again to the priest. ⁸The priest will examine him, and if the scab has spread on the skin, then the priest must pronounce him unclean; he has a skin disease.

⁹"When a skin disease develops on a person, he is to be brought to the priest. ¹⁰The priest will examine him. If there is a white swelling on the skin that has turned the hair white, and there is a patch of raw flesh in the swelling, ¹¹it is a chronic disease on the skin of his body, and the priest must pronounce him unclean. He need not quarantine him, for he is unclean. ¹²But if the skin disease breaks out all over the skin so that it covers all the skin of the infected person from his head to his feet so far as the priest can see, ¹³the priest will look, and if the skin disease has covered his entire body, he is to pronounce the infected person clean. Since he has turned totally white, he is clean. ¹⁴But whenever raw flesh appears on him, he will be unclean. ¹⁵When the priest examines the raw flesh, he must pronounce him unclean. Raw flesh is unclean; it is a skin disease. ¹⁶But if the raw flesh changes and turns white, he must go to the priest. ¹⁷The priest will examine him, and if the infection has turned white, the priest must pronounce the infected person clean; he is clean.

¹⁸"When a boil appears on the skin of one's body and it heals, ¹⁹and a white swelling or a reddish-white spot develops where the boil was, the person must present himself to the priest. ²⁰The priest will make an examination, and if the spot seems to be beneath the skin and the hair in it has turned white, the priest must pronounce him unclean; it is a skin disease that has broken out in the boil. ²¹But when the priest examines it, if there is no white hair in it, and it is not beneath the skin but is faded, the priest must quarantine him seven days. ²²If it spreads further on the skin, the priest must pronounce him unclean; it is an infection. ²³But if the spot remains where it is and does not spread, it is only the scar from the boil. The priest is to pronounce him clean.

²⁴"When there is a burn on the skin of one's body produced by fire, and the patch made raw by the burn becomes reddish-white or white, ²⁵the priest is to examine it. If the hair in the spot has turned white and the spot appears to be deeper than the skin, it is a skin disease that has broken out in the burn. The priest must pronounce him unclean; it is a skin disease. ²⁶But when the priest examines it, if there is no white hair in the spot and it is not beneath the skin but is faded, the priest must quarantine him seven days. ²⁷The priest will reexamine him on the seventh day. If it has spread further on the skin, the priest must pronounce him unclean; it is a skin disease. ²⁸But if the spot has remained where it was and has not spread on the skin but is faded, it is the swelling from the burn. The priest is to pronounce him clean, for it is only the scar from the burn.

²⁹"When a man or woman has an infection on the head or chin, ³⁰the priest must examine the infection. If it appears to be deeper than the skin, and the hair in it is yellow and sparse, the priest must pronounce the person unclean. It is a scaly outbreak, a skin disease of the head or chin. ³¹When the priest examines the scaly infection, if it does not appear to be deeper than the skin, and there is no black hair in it, the priest

must quarantine the person with the scaly infection for seven days. [32] The priest will reexamine the infection on the seventh day. If the scaly outbreak has not spread and there is no yellow hair in it and it does not appear to be deeper than the skin, [33] the person must shave himself but not shave the scaly area. Then the priest must quarantine the person who has the scaly outbreak for another seven days. [34] The priest will examine the scaly outbreak on the seventh day, and if it has not spread on the skin and does not appear to be deeper than the skin, the priest is to pronounce the person clean. He is to wash his clothes, and he will be clean. [35] But if the scaly outbreak spreads further on the skin after his cleansing, [36] the priest is to examine the person. If the scaly outbreak has spread on the skin, the priest does not need to look for yellow hair; the person is unclean. [37] But if as far as he can see, the scaly outbreak remains unchanged and black hair has grown in it, then it has healed; he is clean. The priest is to pronounce the person clean.

[38] "When a man or a woman has white spots on the skin of the body, [39] the priest is to make an examination. If the spots on the skin of the body are dull white, it is only a rash that has broken out on the skin; the person is clean.

[40] "If a man loses the hair of his head, he is bald, but he is clean. [41] Or if he loses the hair at his hairline, he is bald on his forehead, but he is clean. [42] But if there is a reddish-white infection on the bald head or forehead, it is a skin disease breaking out on his head or forehead. [43] The priest is to examine him, and if the swelling of the infection on his bald head or forehead is reddish-white, like the appearance of a skin disease on his body, [44] the man is afflicted with a skin disease; he is unclean. The priest must pronounce him unclean; the infection is on his head.

[45] "The person afflicted with an infectious skin disease is to have his clothes torn and his hair hanging loose, and he must cover his mouth and cry out, 'Unclean, unclean!' [46] He will remain unclean as long as he has the infection; he is unclean. He must live alone in a place outside the camp.

[47] "If a fabric is contaminated with mildew—in wool or linen fabric, [48] in the warp or woof of linen or wool, or in leather or anything made of leather— [49] and if the contamination is green or red in the fabric, the leather, the warp, the woof, or any leather article, it is a mildew contamination and is to be shown to the priest. [50] The priest is to examine the contamination and quarantine the contaminated fabric for seven days. [51] The priest is to reexamine the contamination on the seventh day. If it has spread in the fabric, the warp, the woof, or the leather, regardless of how it is used, the contamination is harmful mildew; it is unclean. [52] He is to burn the fabric, the warp or woof in wool or linen, or any leather article, which is contaminated. Since it is harmful mildew it must be burned up.

[53] "When the priest examines it, if the contamination has not spread in the fabric, the warp or woof, or any leather article, [54] the priest is to order whatever is contaminated to be washed and quarantined for another seven days. [55] After it has been washed, the priest is to reexamine the contamination. If the appearance of the contaminated article has not changed, it is unclean. Even though the contamination has not spread, you must burn up the fabric. It is a fungus on the front or back of the fabric.

[56] "If the priest examines it, and the contamination has faded after it has been washed, he must cut the contaminated section out of the fabric, the leather, or the warp or woof. [57] But if it reappears in the fabric, the warp or woof, or any leather article, it has broken out again. You must burn up whatever is contaminated. [58] But if the contamination disappears from the fabric, the warp or woof, or any leather article, which have been washed, it is to be washed again, and it will be clean.

[59] "This is the law concerning a mildew contamination in wool or linen fabric, warp or woof, or any leather article, in order to pronounce it clean or unclean."

14 The Lord spoke to Moses: [2] "This is the law concerning the person afflicted with a skin disease on the day of his cleansing. He is to be brought to the priest, [3] who will go outside the camp and examine him. If the skin disease has disappeared from the afflicted person, [4] the priest will order that two live *clean birds, cedar wood, scarlet yarn, and hyssop be brought for the one who is to be cleansed. [5] Then the priest will order that one of the birds be slaughtered over fresh water in a clay pot. [6] He is to take the live bird together with the cedar wood, scarlet yarn, and hyssop, and dip them all into the blood of the bird that was slaughtered over the fresh water. [7] He will then sprinkle the blood seven times on the one who is to be cleansed from the skin disease. He is to pronounce him clean and release the live bird over the open countryside. [8] The one who is to be cleansed must wash his clothes, shave off all his hair, and bathe with water; he is clean. Afterward he may enter the camp, but he must remain outside his tent for seven days. [9] He is to shave off all his hair again on the seventh day: his head, his beard, his eyebrows, and the rest of his hair. He is to wash his clothes and bathe himself with water; he is clean.

[10] "On the eighth day he must take two unblemished male lambs, an unblemished year-old ewe lamb, a *grain offering of three quarts of fine flour mixed with olive oil, and one-third of a quart of olive oil. [11] The priest who performs the cleansing will place the person who is to be cleansed, together with these offerings, before the Lord at the entrance to the tent of meeting. [12] The priest is to take one male lamb and present it as a *restitution offering, along with the one-third quart of olive oil, and he must wave them as a presentation offering before the Lord. [13] He is to slaughter the male lamb at the place in the sanctuary area where the *sin offering and *burnt offering are slaughtered, for like the sin offering, the restitution offering belongs to the priest; it is especially holy. [14] The priest is to take some of the blood from the restitution offering and put it on the lobe of the right ear of the one to be cleansed, on the thumb of his right hand, and on the big toe of his right foot. [15] Then the priest will take some of the one-third quart of olive oil and pour it into his left palm. [16] The priest will dip his right finger into the oil in his left palm and sprinkle some of the oil with his finger seven times before the Lord. [17] From the oil remaining in his palm the priest will put some on the lobe of the right ear of the one to be cleansed, on the thumb of his right hand, and on the big toe of his right foot, on top of the blood of the restitution offering. [18] What is left of the oil in the priest's palm he is to put on the head of the one to be cleansed. In this way the priest will make *atonement for him before the Lord. [19] The priest must sacrifice the sin offering and make atonement for the

one to be cleansed from his uncleanness. Afterward he will slaughter the burnt offering. ²⁰The priest is to offer the burnt offering and the grain offering on the altar. The priest will make atonement for him, and he will be clean.

²¹"But if he is poor and cannot afford these, he is to take one male lamb for a restitution offering to be waved in order to make atonement for him, along with two quarts of fine flour mixed with olive oil for a grain offering, one-third of a quart of olive oil, ²²and two turtledoves or two young pigeons, whatever he can afford, one to be a sin offering and the other a burnt offering. ²³On the eighth day he is to bring these things for his cleansing to the priest at the entrance to the tent of meeting before the Lord. ²⁴The priest will take the male lamb for the restitution offering and the one-third quart of olive oil, and wave them as a presentation offering before the Lord. ²⁵After he slaughters the male lamb for the restitution offering, the priest is to take some of the blood of the restitution offering and put it on the right earlobe of the one to be cleansed, on the thumb of his right hand, and on the big toe of his right foot. ²⁶Then the priest will pour some of the oil into his left palm. ²⁷With his right finger the priest will sprinkle some of the oil in his left palm seven times before the Lord. ²⁸The priest will also put some of the oil in his palm on the right earlobe of the one to be cleansed, on the thumb of his right hand, and on the big toe of his right foot, on the same place as the blood of the restitution offering. ²⁹What is left of the oil in the priest's palm he is to put on the head of the one to be cleansed to make atonement for him before the Lord. ³⁰He must then sacrifice one type of what he can afford, either the turtledoves or young pigeons, ³¹one as a sin offering and the other as a burnt offering, sacrificing what he can afford together with the grain offering. In this way the priest will make atonement before the Lord for the one to be cleansed. ³²This is the law for someone who has a skin disease and cannot afford the cost of his cleansing."

³³The Lord spoke to Moses and Aaron: ³⁴"When you enter the land of Canaan that I am giving you as a possession, and I place a mildew contamination in a house in the land you possess, ³⁵the owner of the house is to come and tell the priest: Something like mildew contamination has appeared in my house. ³⁶The priest must order them to clear the house before he enters to examine the contamination, so that nothing in the house becomes ˙unclean. Afterward the priest will come to examine the house. ³⁷He will examine it, and if the contamination in the walls of the house consists of green or red indentations that appear to be beneath the surface of the wall, ³⁸the priest is to go outside the house to its doorway and quarantine the house for seven days. ³⁹The priest is to return on the seventh day and examine it. If the contamination has spread on the walls of the house, ⁴⁰the priest must order that the stones with the contamination be pulled out and thrown into an unclean place outside the city. ⁴¹He is to have the inside of the house completely scraped, and the plaster that is scraped off must be dumped in an unclean place outside the city. ⁴²Then they must take different stones to replace the former ones and take additional plaster to replaster the house.

⁴³"If the contamination reappears in the house after the stones have been pulled out, and after the house has been scraped and replastered, ⁴⁴the priest must come and examine it. If the contamination has spread in the house, it is harmful mildew; the house is unclean. ⁴⁵It must be torn down with its stones, its beams, and all its plaster, and taken outside the city to an unclean place. ⁴⁶Whoever enters the house during any of the days the priest quarantines it will be unclean until evening. ⁴⁷Whoever lies down in the house is to wash his clothes, and whoever eats in it is to wash his clothes.

⁴⁸"But when the priest comes and examines it, if the contamination has not spread in the house after it was replastered, he is to pronounce the house clean because the contamination has disappeared. ⁴⁹He is to take two birds, cedar wood, scarlet yarn, and hyssop to purify the house, ⁵⁰and he is to slaughter one of the birds over a clay pot containing fresh water. ⁵¹He will take the cedar wood, the hyssop, the scarlet yarn, and the live bird, dip them in the blood of the slaughtered bird and the fresh water, and sprinkle the house seven times. ⁵²He will purify the house with the blood of the bird, the fresh water, the live bird, the cedar wood, the hyssop, and the scarlet yarn. ⁵³Then he is to release the live bird into the open countryside outside the city. In this way he will make atonement for the house, and it will be clean.

⁵⁴"This is the law for any skin disease or mildew, for a scaly outbreak, ⁵⁵for mildew in clothing or on a house, ⁵⁶and for a swelling, scab, or spot, ⁵⁷to determine when something is unclean or clean. This is the law regarding skin disease and mildew."

15 The Lord spoke to Moses and Aaron: ²"Speak to the Israelites and tell them: When any man has a discharge from his body, he is ˙unclean. ³This is uncleanness of his discharge: Whether his body secretes the discharge or retains it, he is unclean. All the days that his body secretes or retains anything because of his discharge, he is unclean. ⁴Any bed the man with the discharge lies on will be unclean, and any furniture he sits on will be unclean. ⁵Anyone who touches his bed is to wash his clothes and bathe with water, and he will remain unclean until evening. ⁶Whoever sits on furniture that the man with the discharge was sitting on is to wash his clothes and bathe with water, and he will remain unclean until evening. ⁷Whoever touches the body of the man with a discharge is to wash his clothes and bathe with water, and he will remain unclean until evening. ⁸If the man with the discharge spits on anyone who is ˙clean, he is to wash his clothes and bathe with water, and he will remain unclean until evening. ⁹Any saddle the man with the discharge rides on will be unclean. ¹⁰Whoever touches anything that was under him will be unclean until evening, and whoever carries such things is to wash his clothes and bathe with water, and he will remain unclean until evening. ¹¹If the man with the discharge touches anyone without first rinsing his hands in water, the person who was touched is to wash his clothes and bathe with water, and he will remain unclean until evening. ¹²Any clay pot that the man with the discharge touches must be broken, while any wooden utensil must be rinsed with water.

¹³"When the man with the discharge has been cured of it, he is to count seven days for his cleansing, wash his clothes, and bathe his body in fresh water; he will be clean. ¹⁴He must take two turtledoves or two young pigeons on the eighth day, come before the Lord at the entrance to the tent of meeting, and give them to the

priest. ¹⁵The priest is to sacrifice them, one as a ˙sin offering and the other as a ˙burnt offering. In this way the priest will make ˙atonement for him before the LORD because of his discharge.

¹⁶"When a man has an emission of semen, he is to bathe himself completely with water, and he will remain unclean until evening. ¹⁷Any clothing or leather on which there is an emission of semen must be washed with water, and it will remain unclean until evening. ¹⁸If a man sleeps with a woman and has an emission of semen, both of them are to bathe with water, and they will remain unclean until evening.

¹⁹"When a woman has a discharge, and it consists of blood from her body, she will be unclean because of her menstruation for seven days. Everyone who touches her will be unclean until evening. ²⁰Anything she lies on during her menstruation will become unclean, and anything she sits on will become unclean. ²¹Everyone who touches her bed is to wash his clothes and bathe with water, and he will remain unclean until evening. ²²Everyone who touches any furniture she was sitting on is to wash his clothes and bathe with water, and he will remain unclean until evening. ²³If discharge is on the bed or the furniture she was sitting on, when he touches it he will be unclean until evening. ²⁴If a man sleeps with her, and blood from her menstruation gets on him, he will be unclean for seven days, and every bed he lies on will become unclean.

²⁵"When a woman has a discharge of her blood for many days, though it is not the time of her menstruation, or if she has a discharge beyond her period, she will be unclean all the days of her unclean discharge, as she is during the days of her menstruation. ²⁶Any bed she lies on during the days of her discharge will be like her bed during menstrual impurity; any furniture she sits on will be unclean as in her menstrual period. ²⁷Everyone who touches them will be unclean; he must wash his clothes and bathe with water, and he will remain unclean until evening. ²⁸When she is cured of her discharge, she is to count seven days, and after that she will be clean. ²⁹On the eighth day she must take two turtledoves or two young pigeons and bring them to the priest at the entrance to the tent of meeting. ³⁰The priest is to sacrifice one as a sin offering and the other as a burnt offering. In this way the priest will make atonement for her before the LORD because of her unclean discharge.

³¹"You must keep the Israelites from their uncleanness, so that they do not die by defiling My tabernacle that is among them. ³²This is the law for someone with a discharge: a man who has an emission of semen, becoming unclean by it; ³³a woman who is in her menstrual period; anyone who has a discharge, whether male or female; and a man who sleeps with an unclean woman."

16 The LORD spoke to Moses after the death of two of Aaron's sons when they approached the presence of the LORD and died. ²The LORD said to Moses: "Tell your brother Aaron that he may not come whenever he wants into the holy place behind the veil in front of the ˙mercy seat on the ark or else he will die, because I appear in the cloud above the mercy seat.

³"Aaron is to enter the most holy place in this way: with a young bull for a ˙sin offering and a ram for a ˙burnt offering. ⁴He is to wear a holy linen tunic, and linen undergarments are to be on his body. He must tie a linen sash around him and wrap his head with a linen turban. These are holy garments; he must bathe his body with water before he wears them. ⁵He is to take from the Israelite community two male goats for a sin offering and one ram for a burnt offering.

⁶"Aaron will present the bull for his sin offering and make ˙atonement for himself and his household. ⁷Next he will take the two goats and place them before the LORD at the entrance to the tent of meeting. ⁸After Aaron casts lots for the two goats, one lot for the LORD and the other for azazel, ⁹he is to present the goat chosen by lot for the LORD and sacrifice it as a sin offering. ¹⁰But the goat chosen by lot for azazel is to be presented alive before the LORD to make purification with it by sending it into the wilderness for azazel.

¹¹"When Aaron presents the bull for his sin offering and makes atonement for himself and his household, he will slaughter the bull for his sin offering. ¹²Then he must take a firepan full of fiery coals from the altar before the LORD and two handfuls of finely ground fragrant incense, and bring them inside the veil. ¹³He is to put the incense on the fire before the LORD, so that the cloud of incense covers the mercy seat that is over the ˙testimony, or else he will die. ¹⁴He is to take some of the bull's blood and sprinkle it with his finger against the east side of the mercy seat; then he will sprinkle some of the blood with his finger before the mercy seat seven times.

¹⁵"When he slaughters the male goat for the people's sin offering and brings its blood inside the veil, he must do the same with its blood as he did with the bull's blood: he is to sprinkle it against the mercy seat and in front of it. ¹⁶He will purify the most holy place in this way for all their sins because of the Israelites' impurities and rebellious acts. He will do the same for the tent of meeting that remains among them, because it is surrounded by their impurities. ¹⁷No one may be in the tent of meeting from the time he enters to make atonement in the most holy place until he leaves after he has made atonement for himself, his household, and the whole assembly of Israel. ¹⁸Then he will go out to the altar that is before the LORD and make atonement for it. He is to take some of the bull's blood and some of the goat's blood and put it on the horns on all sides of the altar. ¹⁹He is to sprinkle some of the blood on it with his finger seven times to cleanse and set it apart from the Israelites' impurities.

²⁰"When he has finished purifying the most holy place, the tent of meeting, and the altar, he is to present the live male goat. ²¹Aaron will lay both his hands on the head of the live goat and confess over it all the Israelites' wrongdoings and rebellious acts—all their sins. He is to put them on the goat's head and send it away into the wilderness by the man appointed for the task. ²²The goat will carry on it all their wrongdoings into a desolate land, and he will release it there.

²³"Then Aaron is to enter the tent of meeting, take off the linen garments he wore when he entered the most holy place, and leave them there. ²⁴He will bathe his body with water in a holy place and put on his clothes. Then he must go out and sacrifice his burnt offering and the people's burnt offering; he will make atonement for himself and for the people. ²⁵He is to burn the fat of the sin offering on the altar. ²⁶The man who released the goat for azazel is to wash his clothes and bathe his body with water; afterward he may reenter the camp. ²⁷The bull for the sin offering and the goat for the sin offering, whose blood was brought

into the most holy place to make atonement, must be brought outside the camp and their hide, flesh, and dung burned up. [28] The one who burns them is to wash his clothes and bathe himself with water; afterward he may reenter the camp.

[29] "This is to be a permanent statute for you: In the seventh month, on the tenth day of the month you are to practice self-denial and do no work, both the native and the foreigner who resides among you. [30] Atonement will be made for you on this day to cleanse you, and you will be •clean from all your sins before the Lord. [31] It is a Sabbath of complete rest for you, and you must practice self-denial; it is a permanent statute. [32] The priest who is anointed and ordained to serve as high priest in place of his father will make atonement. He will put on the linen garments, the holy garments, [33] and purify the most holy place. He will purify the tent of meeting and the altar and will make atonement for the priests and all the people of the assembly. [34] This is to be a permanent statute for you, to make atonement for the Israelites once a year because of all their sins." And all this was done as the Lord commanded Moses.

17 The Lord spoke to Moses: [2] "Speak to Aaron, his sons, and all the Israelites and tell them: This is what the Lord has commanded: [3] Anyone from the house of Israel who slaughters an ox, sheep, or goat in the camp, or slaughters it outside the camp, [4] instead of bringing it to the entrance to the tent of meeting to present it as an offering to the Lord before His tabernacle—that person will be considered •guilty. He has shed blood and must be cut off from his people. [5] This is so the Israelites will bring to the Lord the sacrifices they have been offering in the open country. They are to bring them to the priest at the entrance to the tent of meeting and offer them as •fellowship sacrifices to the Lord. [6] The priest will then sprinkle the blood on the Lord's altar at the entrance to the tent of meeting and burn the fat as a pleasing aroma to the Lord. [7] They must no longer offer their sacrifices to the goat-demons that they have prostituted themselves with. This will be a permanent statute for them throughout their generations.

[8] "Say to them: Anyone from the house of Israel or from the foreigners who live among them who offers a •burnt offering or a sacrifice [9] but does not bring it to the entrance to the tent of meeting to sacrifice it to the Lord, that person must be cut off from his people.

[10] "Anyone from the house of Israel or from the foreigners who live among them who eats any blood, I will turn against that person who eats blood and cut him off from his people. [11] For the life of a creature is in the blood, and I have appointed it to you to make •atonement on the altar for your lives, since it is the lifeblood that makes atonement. [12] Therefore I say to the Israelites: None of you and no foreigner who lives among you may eat blood.

[13] "Any Israelite or foreigner living among them, who hunts down a wild animal or bird that may be eaten must drain its blood and cover it with dirt. [14] Since the life of every creature is its blood, I have told the Israelites: You must not eat the blood of any creature, because the life of every creature is its blood; whoever eats it must be cut off.

[15] "Every person, whether the native or the foreigner, who eats an animal that died a natural death or was mauled by wild beasts is to wash his clothes and

bathe with water, and he will remain •unclean until evening; then he will be •clean. [16] But if he does not wash his clothes and bathe himself, he will bear his punishment."

18 •Yahweh spoke to Moses: [2] "Speak to the Israelites and tell them: I am Yahweh your God. [3] Do not follow the practices of the land of Egypt, where you used to live, or follow the practices of the land of Canaan, where I am bringing you. You must not follow their customs. [4] You are to practice My ordinances and you are to keep My statutes by following them; I am Yahweh your God. [5] Keep My statutes and ordinances; a person will live if he does them. I am Yahweh.

[6] "You are not to come near any close relative for sexual intercourse; I am Yahweh. [7] You are not to shame your father by having sex with your mother. She is your mother; you must not have sexual intercourse with her. [8] You are not to have sex with your father's wife; it will shame your father. [9] You are not to have sexual intercourse with your sister, either your father's daughter or your mother's, whether born at home or born elsewhere. You are not to have sex with her. [10] You are not to have sexual intercourse with your son's daughter or your daughter's daughter, because it will shame your family. [11] You are not to have sexual intercourse with your father's wife's daughter, who is adopted by your father; she is your sister. [12] You are not to have sexual intercourse with your father's sister; she is your father's close relative. [13] You are not to have sexual intercourse with your mother's sister, for she is your mother's close relative. [14] You are not to shame your father's brother by coming near his wife to have sexual intercourse; she is your aunt. [15] You are not to have sexual intercourse with your daughter-in-law. She is your son's wife; you are not to have sex with her. [16] You are not to have sexual intercourse with your brother's wife; it will shame your brother. [17] You are not to have sexual intercourse with a woman and her daughter. You are not to marry her son's daughter or her daughter's daughter and have sex with her. They are close relatives; it is depraved. [18] You are not to marry a woman as a rival to her sister and have sexual intercourse with her during her sister's lifetime.

[19] "You are not to come near a woman during her menstrual impurity to have sexual intercourse with her. [20] You are not to have sexual intercourse with your neighbor's wife, defiling yourself with her.

[21] "You are not to make any of your children pass through the fire to •Molech. Do not profane the name of your God; I am Yahweh. [22] You are not to sleep with a man as with a woman; it is detestable. [23] You are not to have sexual intercourse with any animal, defiling yourself with it; a woman is not to present herself to an animal to mate with it; it is a perversion.

[24] "Do not defile yourselves by any of these practices, for the nations I am driving out before you have defiled themselves by all these things. [25] The land has become defiled, so I am punishing it for its sin, and the land will vomit out its inhabitants. [26] But you are to keep My statutes and ordinances. You must not commit any of these detestable things—not the native or the foreigner who lives among you. [27] For the men who were in the land prior to you have committed all these detestable things, and the land has become defiled. [28] If you defile the land, it will vomit you out as it has vomited out the nations that were before you. [29] Any person who does any of these detestable practices must be cut

off from his people. ³⁰You must keep My instruction to not do any of the detestable customs that were practiced before you, so that you do not defile yourselves by them; I am Yahweh your God."

19 The LORD spoke to Moses: ²"Speak to the entire Israelite community and tell them: Be holy because I, ˙Yahweh your God, am holy.

³"Each of you is to respect his mother and father. You are to keep My Sabbaths; I am Yahweh your God. ⁴Do not turn to idols or make cast images of gods for yourselves; I am Yahweh your God.

⁵"When you offer a ˙fellowship sacrifice to the LORD, sacrifice it so that you may be accepted. ⁶It is to be eaten on the day you sacrifice it or on the next day, but what remains on the third day must be burned up. ⁷If any is eaten on the third day, it is a repulsive thing; it will not be accepted. ⁸Anyone who eats it will bear his punishment, for he has profaned what is holy to the LORD. That person must be cut off from his people.

⁹"When you reap the harvest of your land, you are not to reap to the very edge of your field or gather the gleanings of your harvest. ¹⁰You must not strip your vineyard bare or gather its fallen grapes. Leave them for the poor and the foreign resident; I am Yahweh your God.

¹¹"You must not steal. You must not act deceptively or lie to one another. ¹²You must not swear falsely by My name, profaning the name of your God; I am Yahweh.

¹³"You must not oppress your neighbor or rob him. The wages due a hired hand must not remain with you until morning. ¹⁴You must not curse the deaf or put a stumbling block in front of the blind, but you are to ˙fear your God; I am Yahweh.

¹⁵"You must not act unjustly when deciding a case. Do not be partial to the poor or give preference to the rich; judge your neighbor fairly. ¹⁶You must not go about spreading slander among your people; you must not jeopardize your neighbor's life; I am Yahweh.

¹⁷"You must not harbor hatred against your brother. Rebuke your neighbor directly, and you will not incur ˙guilt because of him. ¹⁸Do not take revenge or bear a grudge against members of your community, but love your neighbor as yourself; I am Yahweh.

¹⁹"You are to keep My statutes. You must not crossbreed two different kinds of your livestock, sow your fields with two kinds of seed, or put on a garment made of two kinds of material.

²⁰"If a man has sexual intercourse with a woman who is a slave designated for another man, but she has not been redeemed or given her freedom, there must be punishment. They are not to be put to death, because she had not been freed. ²¹However, he must bring a ram as his ˙restitution offering to the LORD at the entrance to the tent of meeting. ²²The priest will make ˙atonement on his behalf before the LORD with the ram of the restitution offering for the sin he has committed, and he will be forgiven for the sin he committed.

²³"When you come into the land and plant any kind of tree for food, you are to consider the fruit forbidden. It will be forbidden to you for three years; it is not to be eaten. ²⁴In the fourth year all its fruit must be consecrated as a praise offering to the LORD. ²⁵But in the fifth year you may eat its fruit. In this way its yield will increase for you; I am Yahweh your God.

²⁶"You are not to eat anything with blood in it. You

are not to practice ˙divination or sorcery. ²⁷You are not to cut off the hair at the sides of your head or mar the edge of your beard. ²⁸You are not to make gashes on your bodies for the dead or put tattoo marks on yourselves; I am Yahweh.

²⁹"Do not debase your daughter by making her a prostitute, or the land will be prostituted and filled with depravity. ³⁰You must keep My Sabbaths and revere My sanctuary; I am Yahweh.

³¹"Do not turn to mediums or consult spiritists, or you will be defiled by them; I am Yahweh your God.

³²"You are to rise in the presence of the elderly and honor the old. Fear your God; I am Yahweh.

³³"When a foreigner lives with you in your land, you must not oppress him. ³⁴You must regard the foreigner who lives with you as the native-born among you. You are to love him as yourself, for you were foreigners in the land of Egypt; I am Yahweh your God.

³⁵"You must not be unfair in measurements of length, weight, or volume. ³⁶You are to have honest balances, honest weights, an honest dry measure, and an honest liquid measure; I am Yahweh your God, who brought you out of the land of Egypt. ³⁷You must keep all My statutes and all My ordinances and do them; I am Yahweh."

20 The LORD spoke to Moses: ²"Say to the Israelites: Any Israelite or foreigner living in Israel who gives any of his children to ˙Molech must be put to death; the people of the country are to stone him. ³I will turn against that man and cut him off from his people, because he gave his ˙offspring to Molech, defiling My sanctuary and profaning My holy name. ⁴But if the people of the country look the other way when that man gives any of his children to Molech, and do not put him to death, ⁵then I will turn against that man and his family, and cut off from their people both him and all who follow him in prostituting themselves with Molech.

⁶"Whoever turns to mediums or spiritists and prostitutes himself with them, I will turn against that person and cut him off from his people. ⁷Consecrate yourselves and be holy, for I am ˙Yahweh your God. ⁸Keep My statutes and do them; I am Yahweh who sets you apart.

⁹"If anyone curses his father or mother, he must be put to death. He has cursed his father or mother; his blood is on his own hands.

¹⁰If a man commits adultery with a married woman—if he commits adultery with his neighbor's wife—both the adulterer and the adulteress must be put to death. ¹¹If a man sleeps with his father's wife, he has shamed his father. Both of them must be put to death; their blood is on their own hands. ¹²If a man sleeps with his daughter-in-law, both of them must be put to death. They have acted perversely; their blood is on their own hands. ¹³If a man sleeps with a man as with a woman, they have both committed a detestable thing. They must be put to death; their blood is on their own hands. ¹⁴If a man marries a woman and her mother, it is depraved. Both he and they must be burned with fire, so that there will be no depravity among you. ¹⁵If a man has sexual intercourse with an animal, he must be put to death; you are also to kill the animal. ¹⁶If a woman comes near any animal and mates with it, you are to kill the woman and the animal. They must be put to death; their own blood is on them. ¹⁷If a man marries his sister, whether his father's daughter or his

mother's daughter, and they have sexual relations, it is a disgrace. They must be cut off publicly from their people. He has had sexual intercourse with his sister; he will bear his punishment. ¹⁸ If a man sleeps with a menstruating woman and has sexual intercourse with her, he has exposed the source of her flow, and she has uncovered the source of her blood. Both of them must be cut off from their people. ¹⁹ You must not have sexual intercourse with your mother's sister or your father's sister, for it is exposing one's own blood relative; both people will bear their punishment. ²⁰ If a man sleeps with his aunt, he has shamed his uncle; they will bear their *guilt and die childless. ²¹ If a man marries his brother's wife, it is impurity. He has shamed his brother; they will be childless.

²² "You are to keep all My statutes and all My ordinances, and do them, so that the land where I am bringing you to live will not vomit you out. ²³ You must not follow the statutes of the nations I am driving out before you, for they did all these things, and I abhorred them. ²⁴ And I promised you: You will inherit their land, since I will give it to you to possess, a land flowing with milk and honey. I am Yahweh your God who set you apart from the peoples. ²⁵ Therefore you must distinguish the *clean animal from the *unclean one, and the unclean bird from the clean one. Do not become contaminated by any land animal, bird, or whatever crawls on the ground; I have set these apart as unclean for you. ²⁶ You are to be holy to Me because I, Yahweh, am holy, and I have set you apart from the nations to be Mine.

²⁷ A man or a woman who is a medium or a spiritist must be put to death. They are to be stoned; their blood is on their own hands."

21 The Lord said to Moses: "Speak to Aaron's sons, the priests, and tell them: A priest is not to make himself ceremonially *unclean for a dead person among his relatives, ² except for his immediate family: his mother, father, son, daughter, or brother. ³ He may make himself unclean for his young unmarried sister in his immediate family. ⁴ He is not to make himself unclean for those related to him by marriage and so defile himself.

⁵ "Priests may not make bald spots on their heads, shave the edge of their beards, or make gashes on their bodies. ⁶ They are to be holy to their God and not profane the name of their God. For they present the fire offerings to *Yahweh, the food of their God, and they must be holy. ⁷ They are not to marry a woman defiled by prostitution. They are not to marry one divorced by her husband, for the priest is holy to his God. ⁸ You are to consider him holy since he presents the food of your God. He will be holy to you because I, Yahweh who sets you apart, am holy. ⁹ If a priest's daughter defiles herself by promiscuity, she defiles her father; she must be burned up.

¹⁰ "The priest who is highest among his brothers, who has had the anointing oil poured on his head and has been ordained to wear the garments, must not dishevel his hair or tear his garments. ¹¹ He must not go near any dead person or make himself unclean even for his father or mother. ¹² He must not leave the sanctuary or he will desecrate the sanctuary of his God, for the consecration of the anointing oil of his God is on him; I am Yahweh.

¹³ "He is to marry a woman who is a virgin. ¹⁴ He is not to marry a widow, a divorced woman, or one de-

filed by prostitution. He is to marry a virgin from his own people, ¹⁵ so that he does not corrupt his bloodline among his people, for I am Yahweh who sets him apart."

¹⁶ The Lord spoke to Moses: ¹⁷ "Tell Aaron: None of your descendants throughout your generations who has a physical defect is to come near to present the food of his God. ¹⁸ No man who has any defect is to come near: no man who is blind, lame, facially disfigured, or deformed; ¹⁹ no man who has a broken foot or hand, ²⁰ or who is a hunchback or a dwarf, or who has an eye defect, a festering rash, scabs, or a crushed testicle. ²¹ No descendant of Aaron the priest who has a defect is to come near to present the fire offerings to the Lord. He has a defect and is not to come near to present the food of his God. ²² He may eat the food of his God from what is especially holy as well as from what is holy. ²³ But because he has a defect, he must not go near the curtain or approach the altar. He is not to desecrate My sanctuaries, for I am Yahweh who sets them apart." ²⁴ Moses said this to Aaron and his sons and to all the Israelites.

22 The Lord spoke to Moses: ² "Tell Aaron and his sons to deal respectfully with the holy offerings of the Israelites that they have consecrated to Me, so they do not profane My holy name; I am *Yahweh. ³ Say to them: If any man from any of your descendants throughout your generations is in a state of uncleanness yet approaches the holy offerings that the Israelites consecrate to the Lord, that person will be cut off from My presence; I am Yahweh. ⁴ No man of Aaron's descendants who has a skin disease or a discharge is to eat from the holy offerings until he is *clean. Whoever touches anything made *unclean by a dead person or by a man who has an emission of semen, ⁵ or whoever touches any swarming creature that makes him unclean or any person who makes him unclean—whatever his uncleanness— ⁶ the man who touches any of these will remain unclean until evening and is not to eat from the holy offerings unless he has bathed his body with water. ⁷ When the sun has set, he will become clean, and then he may eat from the holy offerings, for that is his food. ⁸ He must not eat an animal that died naturally or was mauled by wild beasts, making himself unclean by it; I am Yahweh. ⁹ They must keep My instruction, or they will be *guilty and die because they profane it; I am Yahweh who sets them apart.

¹⁰ "No one outside a priest's family is to eat the holy offering. A foreigner staying with a priest or a hired hand is not to eat the holy offering. ¹¹ But if a priest purchases someone with his money, that person may eat it, and those born in his house may eat his food. ¹² If the priest's daughter is married to a man outside a priest's family, she is not to eat from the holy contributions. ¹³ But if the priest's daughter becomes widowed or divorced, has no children, and returns to her father's house as in her youth, she may share her father's food. But no outsider may share it. ¹⁴ If anyone eats a holy offering in error, he must add a fifth to its value and give the holy offering to the priest. ¹⁵ The priests must not profane the holy offerings the Israelites give to the Lord ¹⁶ by letting the people eat their holy offerings and having them bear the penalty of restitution. For I am Yahweh who sets them apart."

¹⁷ The Lord spoke to Moses: ¹⁸ "Speak to Aaron, his sons, and all the Israelites and tell them: Any man of

the house of Israel or of the foreign residents in Israel who presents his offering—whether they present freewill gifts or payment of vows to the Lord as *burnt offerings— ¹⁹must offer an unblemished male from the cattle, sheep, or goats in order for you to be accepted. ²⁰You are not to present anything that has a defect, because it will not be accepted on your behalf.

²¹"When a man presents a *fellowship sacrifice to the Lord to fulfill a vow or as a freewill offering from the herd or flock, it has to be unblemished to be acceptable; there must be no defect in it. ²²You are not to present any animal to the Lord that is blind, injured, maimed, or has a running sore, festering rash, or scabs; you may not put any of them on the altar as a fire offering to the Lord. ²³You may sacrifice as a freewill offering any animal from the herd or flock that has an elongated or stunted limb, but it is not acceptable as a vow offering. ²⁴You are not to present to the Lord anything that has bruised, crushed, torn, or severed testicles; you must not sacrifice them in your land. ²⁵Neither you nor a foreigner are to present food to your God from any of these animals. They will not be accepted for you because they are deformed and have a defect."

²⁶The Lord spoke to Moses: ²⁷"When an ox, sheep, or goat is born, it must remain with its mother for seven days; from the eighth day on, it will be acceptable as a gift, a fire offering to the Lord. ²⁸But you are not to slaughter an animal from the herd or flock on the same day as its young. ²⁹When you sacrifice a thank offering to the Lord, sacrifice it so that you may be accepted. ³⁰It is to be eaten on the same day. Do not let any of it remain until morning; I am Yahweh.

³¹"You are to keep My commands and do them; I am Yahweh. ³²You must not profane My holy name; I must be treated as holy among the Israelites. I am Yahweh who sets you apart, ³³the One who brought you out of the land of Egypt to be your God; I am Yahweh."

23 The Lord spoke to Moses: ²"Speak to the Israelites and tell them: These are My appointed times, the times of the Lord that you will proclaim as sacred assemblies.

³"Work may be done for six days, but on the seventh day there must be a Sabbath of complete rest, a sacred assembly. You are not to do any work; it is a Sabbath to the Lord wherever you live.

⁴"These are the Lord's appointed times, the sacred assemblies you are to proclaim at their appointed times. ⁵The *Passover to the Lord comes in the first month, at twilight on the fourteenth day of the month. ⁶The Festival of *Unleavened Bread to the Lord is on the fifteenth day of the same month. For seven days you must eat unleavened bread. ⁷On the first day you are to hold a sacred assembly; you are not to do any daily work. ⁸You are to present a fire offering to the Lord for seven days. On the seventh day there will be a sacred assembly; you must not do any daily work."

⁹The Lord spoke to Moses: ¹⁰"Speak to the Israelites and tell them: When you enter the land I am giving you and reap its harvest, you are to bring the first sheaf of your harvest to the priest. ¹¹He will wave the sheaf before the Lord so that you may be accepted; the priest is to wave it on the day after the Sabbath. ¹²On the day you wave the sheaf, you are to offer a year-old male lamb without blemish as a *burnt offering to the Lord. ¹³Its *grain offering is to be four quarts of fine flour mixed with oil as a fire offering to the Lord, a pleas-

ing aroma, and its *drink offering will be one quart of wine. ¹⁴You must not eat bread, roasted grain, or any new grain until this very day, and until you have brought the offering to your God. This is to be a permanent statute throughout your generations wherever you live.

¹⁵"You are to count seven complete weeks starting from the day after the Sabbath, the day you brought the sheaf of the presentation offering. ¹⁶You are to count 50 days until the day after the seventh Sabbath and then present an offering of new grain to the Lord. ¹⁷Bring two loaves of bread from your settlements as a presentation offering, each of them made from four quarts of fine flour, baked with yeast, as *firstfruits to the Lord. ¹⁸You are to present with the bread seven unblemished male lambs a year old, one young bull, and two rams. They will be a burnt offering to the Lord, with their grain offerings and drink offerings, a fire offering of a pleasing aroma to the Lord. ¹⁹You are also to prepare one male goat as a *sin offering, and two male lambs a year old as a *fellowship sacrifice. ²⁰The priest will wave the lambs with the bread of firstfruits as a presentation offering before the Lord; the bread and the two lambs will be holy to the Lord for the priest. ²¹On that same day you are to make a proclamation and hold a sacred assembly. You are not to do any daily work. This is to be a permanent statute wherever you live throughout your generations. ²²When you reap the harvest of your land, you are not to reap all the way to the edge of your field or gather the gleanings of your harvest. Leave them for the poor and the foreign resident; I am *Yahweh your God."

²³The Lord spoke to Moses: ²⁴"Tell the Israelites: In the seventh month, on the first day of the month, you are to have a day of complete rest, commemoration, and joyful shouting—a sacred assembly. ²⁵You must not do any daily work, but you must present a fire offering to the Lord."

²⁶The Lord again spoke to Moses: ²⁷"The tenth day of this seventh month is the Day of *Atonement. You are to hold a sacred assembly and practice self-denial; you are to present a fire offering to the Lord. ²⁸On this particular day you are not to do any work, for it is a Day of Atonement to make atonement for yourselves before the Lord your God. ²⁹If any person does not practice self-denial on this particular day, he must be cut off from his people. ³⁰I will destroy among his people anyone who does any work on this same day. ³¹You are not to do any work. This is a permanent statute throughout your generations wherever you live. ³²It will be a Sabbath of complete rest for you, and you must practice self-denial. You are to observe your Sabbath from the evening of the ninth day of the month until the following evening."

³³The Lord spoke to Moses: ³⁴"Tell the Israelites: The Festival of Booths to the Lord begins on the fifteenth day of this seventh month and continues for seven days. ³⁵There is to be a sacred assembly on the first day; you are not to do any daily work. ³⁶You are to present a fire offering to the Lord for seven days. On the eighth day you are to hold a sacred assembly and present a fire offering to the Lord. It is a solemn gathering; you are not to do any daily work.

³⁷"These are the Lord's appointed times that you are to proclaim as sacred assemblies for presenting fire offerings to the Lord, burnt offerings and grain offerings, sacrifices and drink offerings, each on its

designated day. ³⁸These are in addition to the offerings for the Lord's Sabbaths, your gifts, all your vow offerings, and all your freewill offerings that you give to the Lord.

³⁹"You are to celebrate the Lord's festival on the fifteenth day of the seventh month for seven days after you have gathered the produce of the land. There will be complete rest on the first day and complete rest on the eighth day. ⁴⁰On the first day you are to take the product of majestic trees—palm fronds, boughs of leafy trees, and willows of the brook—and rejoice before the Lord your God for seven days. ⁴¹You are to celebrate it as a festival to the Lord seven days each year. This is a permanent statute for you throughout your generations; you must celebrate it in the seventh month. ⁴²You are to live in booths for seven days. All the native-born of Israel must live in booths, ⁴³so that your generations may know that I made the Israelites live in booths when I brought them out of the land of Egypt; I am Yahweh your God." ⁴⁴So Moses declared the Lord's appointed times to the Israelites.

24 The Lord spoke to Moses: ²"Command the Israelites to bring you pure oil from crushed olives for the light, in order to keep the lamp burning continually. ³Aaron is to tend it continually from evening until morning before the Lord outside the veil of the *testimony in the tent of meeting. This is a permanent statute throughout your generations. ⁴He must continually tend the lamps on the pure gold lampstand in the Lord's presence.

⁵"Take fine flour and bake it into 12 loaves; each loaf is to be made with four quarts. ⁶Arrange them in two rows, six to a row, on the pure gold table before the Lord. ⁷Place pure frankincense near each row, so that it may serve as a memorial portion for the bread and a fire offering to the Lord. ⁸The bread is to be set out before the Lord every Sabbath day as a perpetual covenant obligation on the part of the Israelites. ⁹It belongs to Aaron and his sons, who are to eat it in a holy place, for it is the holiest portion for him from the fire offerings to the Lord; this is a permanent rule."

¹⁰Now the son of an Israelite mother and an Egyptian father was among the Israelites. A fight broke out in the camp between the Israelite woman's son and an Israelite man. ¹¹Her son cursed and blasphemed the Name, and they brought him to Moses. (His mother's name was Shelomith, a daughter of Dibri of the tribe of Dan.) ¹²They put him in custody until the Lord's decision could be made clear to them.

¹³Then the Lord spoke to Moses: ¹⁴"Bring the one who has cursed to the outside of the camp and have all who heard him lay their hands on his head; then have the whole community stone him. ¹⁵And tell the Israelites: If anyone curses his God, he will bear the consequences of his sin. ¹⁶Whoever blasphemes the name of *Yahweh is to be put to death; the whole community must stone him. If he blasphemes the Name, he is to be put to death, whether the foreign resident or the native.

¹⁷"If a man kills anyone, he must be put to death. ¹⁸Whoever kills an animal is to make restitution for it, life for life. ¹⁹If any man inflicts a permanent injury on his neighbor, whatever he has done is to be done to him: ²⁰fracture for fracture, eye for eye, tooth for tooth. Whatever injury he inflicted on the person, the same is to be inflicted on him. ²¹Whoever kills an animal is to make restitution for it, but whoever kills a

person is to be put to death. ²²You are to have the same law for the foreign resident and the native, because I am Yahweh your God."

²³After Moses spoke to the Israelites, they brought the one who had cursed to the outside of the camp and stoned him. So the Israelites did as the Lord had commanded Moses.

25 The Lord spoke to Moses on Mount Sinai: ²"Speak to the Israelites and tell them: When you enter the land I am giving you, the land will observe a Sabbath to the Lord. ³You may sow your field for six years, and you may prune your vineyard and gather its produce for six years. ⁴But there will be a Sabbath of complete rest for the land in the seventh year, a Sabbath to the Lord: you are not to sow your field or prune your vineyard. ⁵You are not to reap what grows by itself from your crop, or harvest the grapes of your untended vines. It must be a year of complete rest for the land. ⁶Whatever the land produces during the Sabbath year can be food for you—for yourself, your male or female slave, and the hired hand or foreigner who stays with you. ⁷All of its growth may serve as food for your livestock and the wild animals in your land.

⁸"You are to count seven sabbatical years, seven times seven years, so that the time period of the seven sabbatical years amounts to 49. ⁹Then you are to sound a trumpet loudly in the seventh month, on the tenth day of the month; you will sound it throughout your land on the Day of *Atonement. ¹⁰You are to consecrate the fiftieth year and proclaim freedom in the land for all its inhabitants. It will be your Jubilee, when each of you is to return to his property and each of you to his clan. ¹¹The fiftieth year will be your Jubilee; you are not to sow, reap what grows by itself, or harvest its untended vines. ¹²It is to be holy to you because it is the Jubilee; you may only eat its produce directly from the field.

¹³"In this Year of Jubilee, each of you will return to his property. ¹⁴If you make a sale to your neighbor or a purchase from him, do not cheat one another. ¹⁵You are to make the purchase from your neighbor based on the number of years since the last Jubilee. He is to sell to you based on the number of remaining harvest years. ¹⁶You are to increase its price in proportion to a greater amount of years, and decrease its price in proportion to a lesser amount of years, because what he is selling to you is a number of harvests. ¹⁷You are not to cheat one another, but *fear your God, for I am *Yahweh your God.

¹⁸"You are to keep My statutes and ordinances and carefully observe them, so that you may live securely in the land. ¹⁹Then the land will yield its fruit, so that you can eat, be satisfied, and live securely in the land. ²⁰If you wonder: 'What will we eat in the seventh year if we don't sow or gather our produce?' ²¹I will appoint My blessing for you in the sixth year, so that it will produce a crop sufficient for three years. ²²When you sow in the eighth year, you will be eating from the previous harvest. You will be eating this until the ninth year when its harvest comes in.

²³"The land is not to be permanently sold because it is Mine, and you are only foreigners and temporary residents on My land. ²⁴You are to allow the redemption of any land you occupy. ²⁵If your brother becomes destitute and sells part of his property, his nearest relative may come and redeem what his brother has sold. ²⁶If a man has no *family redeemer, but he prospers

and obtains enough to redeem his land, [27] he may calculate the years since its sale, repay the balance to the man he sold it to, and return to his property. [28] But if he cannot obtain enough to repay him, what he sold will remain in the possession of its purchaser until the Year of Jubilee. It is to be released at the Jubilee, so that he may return to his property.

[29] "If a man sells a residence in a walled city, his right of redemption will last until a year has passed after its sale; his right of redemption will last a year. [30] If it is not redeemed by the end of a full year, then the house in the walled city is permanently transferred to its purchaser throughout his generations. It is not to be released on the Jubilee. [31] But houses in villages that have no walls around them are to be classified as open fields. The right to redeem such houses stays in effect, and they are to be released at the Jubilee.

[32] "Concerning the Levitical cities, the Levites always have the right to redeem houses in the cities they possess. [33] Whatever property one of the Levites can redeem—a house sold in a city they possess—must be released at the Jubilee, because the houses in the Levitical cities are their possession among the Israelites. [34] The open pastureland around their cities may not be sold, for it is their permanent possession.

[35] "If your brother becomes destitute and cannot sustain himself among you, you are to support him as a foreigner or temporary resident, so that he can continue to live among you. [36] Do not profit or take interest from him, but fear your God and let your brother live among you. [37] You are not to lend him your silver with interest or sell him your food for profit. [38] I am Yahweh your God, who brought you out of the land of Egypt to give you the land of Canaan and to be your God.

[39] "If your brother among you becomes destitute and sells himself to you, you must not force him to do slave labor. [40] Let him stay with you as a hired hand or temporary resident; he may work for you until the Year of Jubilee. [41] Then he and his children are to be released from you, and he may return to his clan and his ancestral property. [42] They are not to be sold as slaves, because they are My slaves that I brought out of the land of Egypt. [43] You are not to rule over them harshly but fear your God. [44] Your male and female slaves are to be from the nations around you; you may purchase male and female slaves. [45] You may also purchase them from the foreigners staying with you, or from their families living among you—those born in your land. These may become your property. [46] You may leave them to your sons after you to inherit as property; you can make them slaves for life. But concerning your brothers, the Israelites, you must not rule over one another harshly.

[47] "If a foreigner or temporary resident living among you prospers, but your brother living near him becomes destitute and sells himself to the foreigner living among you, or to a member of the foreigner's clan, [48] he has the right of redemption after he has been sold. One of his brothers may redeem him. [49] His uncle or cousin may redeem him, or any of his close relatives from his clan may redeem him. If he prospers, he may redeem himself. [50] The one who purchased him is to calculate the time from the year he sold himself to him until the Year of Jubilee. The price of his sale will be determined by the number of years. It will be set for him like the daily wages of a hired hand. [51] If many years are still left, he must pay his redemption price in proportion to them based on his purchase price. [52] If only a few years remain until the Year of Jubilee, he will calculate and pay the price of his redemption in proportion to his remaining years. [53] He will stay with him like a man hired year by year. A foreign owner is not to rule over him harshly in your sight. [54] If he is not redeemed in any of these ways, he and his children are to be released at the Year of Jubilee. [55] For the Israelites are My slaves. They are My slaves that I brought out of the land of Egypt; I am Yahweh your God.

26 "Do not make idols for yourselves, set up a carved image or sacred pillar for yourselves, or place a sculpted stone in your land to bow down to it, for I am *Yahweh your God. [2] You must keep My Sabbaths and revere My sanctuary; I am Yahweh.

[3] "If you follow My statutes and faithfully observe My commands, [4] I will give you rain at the right time, and the land will yield its produce, and the trees of the field will bear their fruit. [5] Your threshing will continue until grape harvest, and the grape harvest will continue until sowing time; you will have plenty of food to eat and live securely in your land. [6] I will give peace to the land, and you will lie down with nothing to frighten you. I will remove dangerous animals from the land, and no sword will pass through your land. [7] You will pursue your enemies, and they will fall before you by the sword. [8] Five of you will pursue 100, and 100 of you will pursue 10,000; your enemies will fall before you by the sword.

[9] "I will turn to you, make you fruitful and multiply you, and confirm My covenant with you. [10] You will eat the old grain of the previous year and will clear out the old to make room for the new. [11] I will place My residence among you, and I will not reject you. [12] I will walk among you and be your God, and you will be My people. [13] I am Yahweh your God, who brought you out of the land of Egypt, so that you would no longer be their slaves. I broke the bars of your yoke and enabled you to live in freedom.

[14] "But if you do not obey Me and observe all these commands— [15] if you reject My statutes and despise My ordinances, and do not observe all My commands—and break My covenant, [16] then I will do this to you: I will bring terror on you—wasting disease and fever that will cause your eyes to fail and your life to ebb away. You will sow your seed in vain because your enemies will eat it. [17] I will turn against you, so that you will be defeated by your enemies. Those who hate you will rule over you, and you will flee even though no one is pursuing you.

[18] "But if after these things you will not obey Me, I will proceed to discipline you seven times for your sins. [19] I will break down your strong pride. I will make your sky like iron and your land like bronze, [20] and your strength will be used up for nothing. Your land will not yield its produce, and the trees of the land will not bear their fruit.

[21] "If you act with hostility toward Me and are unwilling to obey Me, I will multiply your plagues seven times for your sins. [22] I will send wild animals against you that will deprive you of your children, ravage your livestock, and reduce your numbers until your roads are deserted.

[23] "If in spite of these things you do not accept My discipline, but act with hostility toward Me, [24] then I will act with hostility toward you; I also will strike

you seven times for your sins. ²⁵I will bring a sword against you to execute the vengeance of the covenant. Though you withdraw into your cities, I will send a pestilence among you, and you will be delivered into enemy hands. ²⁶When I cut off your supply of bread, 10 women will bake your bread in a single oven and ration out your bread by weight, so that you will eat but not be satisfied.

²⁷"And if in spite of this you do not obey Me but act with hostility toward Me, ²⁸I will act with furious hostility toward you; I will also discipline you seven times for your sins. ²⁹You will eat the flesh of your sons; you will eat the flesh of your daughters. ³⁰I will destroy your *high places, cut down your incense altars, and heap your dead bodies on the lifeless bodies of your idols; I will reject you. ³¹I will reduce your cities to ruins and devastate your sanctuaries. I will not smell the pleasing aroma of your sacrifices. ³²I also will devastate the land, so that your enemies who come to live there will be appalled by it. ³³But I will scatter you among the nations, and I will draw a sword to chase after you. So your land will become desolate, and your cities will become ruins.

³⁴"Then the land will make up for its Sabbath years during the time it lies desolate, while you are in the land of your enemies. At that time the land will rest and make up for its Sabbaths. ³⁵As long as it lies desolate, it will have the rest it did not have during your Sabbaths when you lived there.

³⁶"I will put anxiety in the hearts of those of you who survive in the lands of their enemies. The sound of a wind-driven leaf will put them to flight, and they will flee as one flees from a sword, and fall though no one is pursuing them. ³⁷They will stumble over one another as if fleeing from a sword though no one is pursuing them. You will not be able to stand against your enemies. ³⁸You will perish among the nations; the land of your enemies will devour you. ³⁹Those who survive in the lands of your enemies will waste away because of their sin; they will also waste away because of their fathers' sins along with theirs.

⁴⁰"But if they will confess their sin and the sin of their fathers—their unfaithfulness that they practiced against Me, and how they acted with hostility toward Me, ⁴¹and I acted with hostility toward them and brought them into the land of their enemies—and if their uncircumcised hearts will be humbled, and if they will pay the penalty for their sin, ⁴²then I will remember My covenant with Jacob. I will also remember My covenant with Isaac and My covenant with Abraham, and I will remember the land. ⁴³For the land abandoned by them will make up for its Sabbaths by lying desolate without the people, while they pay the penalty for their sin, because they rejected My ordinances and abhorred My statutes. ⁴⁴Yet in spite of this, while they are in the land of their enemies, I will not reject or abhor them so as to destroy them and break My covenant with them, since I am Yahweh their God. ⁴⁵For their sake I will remember the covenant with their fathers, whom I brought out of the land of Egypt in the sight of the nations to be their God; I am Yahweh."

⁴⁶These are the statutes, ordinances, and laws the Lord established between Himself and the Israelites through Moses on Mount Sinai.

27 The Lord spoke to Moses: ²"Speak to the Israelites and tell them: When someone makes a special vow to the Lord that involves the assessment of people, ³if the assessment concerns a male from 20 to 60 years old, your assessment is 50 silver *shekels measured by the standard sanctuary shekel. ⁴If the person is a female, your assessment is 30 shekels. ⁵If the person is from five to 20 years old, your assessment for a male is 20 shekels and for a female 10 shekels. ⁶If the person is from one month to five years old, your assessment for a male is five silver shekels, and for a female your assessment is three shekels of silver. ⁷If the person is 60 years or more, your assessment is 15 shekels for a male and 10 shekels for a female. ⁸But if one is too poor to pay the assessment, he must present the person before the priest and the priest will set a value for him. The priest will set a value for him according to what the one making the vow can afford.

⁹"If the vow involves one of the animals that may be brought as an offering to the Lord, any of these he gives to the Lord will be holy. ¹⁰He may not replace it or make a substitution for it, either good for bad, or bad for good. But if he does substitute one animal for another, both that animal and its substitute will be holy.

¹¹"If the vow involves any of the *unclean animals that may not be brought as an offering to the Lord, the animal must be presented before the priest. ¹²The priest will set its value, whether high or low; the price will be set as the priest makes the assessment for you. ¹³If the one who brought it decides to redeem it, he must add a fifth to the assessed value.

¹⁴"When a man consecrates his house as holy to the Lord, the priest will assess its value, whether high or low. The price will stand just as the priest assesses it. ¹⁵But if the one who consecrated his house redeems it, he must add a fifth to the assessed value, and it will be his.

¹⁶"If a man consecrates to the Lord any part of a field that he possesses, your assessment of value will be proportional to the seed needed to sow it, at the rate of 50 silver shekels for every five bushels of barley seed. ¹⁷If he consecrates his field during the Year of Jubilee, the price will stand according to your assessment. ¹⁸But if he consecrates his field after the Jubilee, the priest will calculate the price for him in proportion to the years left until the next Year of Jubilee, so that your assessment will be reduced. ¹⁹If the one who consecrated the field decides to redeem it, he must add a fifth to the assessed value, and the field will transfer back to him. ²⁰But if he does not redeem the field or if he has sold it to another man, it is no longer redeemable. ²¹When the field is released in the Jubilee, it will be holy to the Lord like a field permanently set apart; it becomes the priest's property.

²²"If a person consecrates to the Lord a field he has purchased that is not part of his inherited landholding, ²³then the priest will calculate for him the amount of the assessment up to the Year of Jubilee, and the person will pay the assessed value on that day as a holy offering to the Lord. ²⁴In the Year of Jubilee the field will return to the one he bought it from, the original owner. ²⁵All your assessed values will be measured by the standard sanctuary shekel, 20 *gerahs* to the shekel.

²⁶"But no one can consecrate a firstborn of the livestock, whether an animal from the herd or flock, to the Lord, because a firstborn already belongs to the

LORD. ²⁷If it is one of the unclean livestock, it must be ransomed according to your assessment by adding a fifth of its value to it. If it is not redeemed, it can be sold according to your assessment. ²⁸"Nothing that a man permanently sets apart to the LORD from all he owns, whether a person, an animal, or his inherited landholding, can be sold or redeemed; everything set apart is especially holy to the LORD. ²⁹No person who has been set apart for destruction is to be ransomed; he must be put to death.

³⁰"Every tenth of the land's produce, grain from the soil or fruit from the trees, belongs to the LORD; it is holy to the LORD. ³¹If a man decides to redeem any part of this tenth, he must add a fifth to its value. ³²Every tenth animal from the herd or flock, which passes under the shepherd's rod, will be holy to the LORD. ³³He is not to inspect whether it is good or bad, and he is not to make a substitution for it. But if he does make a substitution, both the animal and its substitute will be holy; they cannot be redeemed."

³⁴These are the commands the LORD gave Moses for the Israelites on Mount Sinai.

NUMBERS

1 The LORD spoke to Moses in the tent of meeting in the Wilderness of Sinai, on the first day of the second month of the second year after Israel's departure from the land of Egypt: ²"Take a census of the entire Israelite community by their clans and their ancestral houses, counting the names of every male one by one. ³You and Aaron are to register those who are 20 years old or more by their military divisions—everyone who can serve in Israel's army. ⁴A man from each tribe is to be with you, each one the head of his ancestral house. ⁵These are the names of the men who are to assist you:

- Elizur son of Shedeur from Reuben;
⁶ Shelumiel son of Zurishaddai from Simeon;
⁷ Nahshon son of Amminadab from Judah;
⁸ Nethanel son of Zuar from Issachar;
⁹ Eliab son of Helon from Zebulun;
¹⁰ from the sons of Joseph:
  Elishama son of Ammihud from Ephraim,
  Gamaliel son of Pedahzur from Manasseh;
¹¹ Abidan son of Gideoni from Benjamin;
¹² Ahiezer son of Ammishaddai from Dan;
¹³ Pagiel son of Ochran from Asher;
¹⁴ Eliasaph son of Deuel from Gad;
¹⁵ Ahira son of Enan from Naphtali.

¹⁶These are the men called from the community; they are leaders of their ancestral tribes, the heads of Israel's clans."

¹⁷So Moses and Aaron took these men who had been designated by name, ¹⁸and they assembled the whole community on the first day of the second month. They recorded their ancestry by their clans and their ancestral houses, counting one by one the names of those 20 years old or more, ¹⁹just as the LORD commanded Moses. He registered them in the Wilderness of Sinai:

²⁰The descendants of Reuben, the firstborn of Israel: according to their family records by their clans and their ancestral houses, counting one by one the names of every male 20 years old or more, everyone who could serve in the army, ²¹those registered for the tribe of Reuben numbered 46,500.

²²The descendants of Simeon: according to their family records by their clans and their ancestral houses, those registered counting one by one the names of every male 20 years old or more, everyone who could serve in the army, ²³those registered for the tribe of Simeon numbered 59,300.

²⁴The descendants of Gad: according to their family records by their clans and their ancestral houses, counting the names of those 20 years old or more, everyone who could serve in the army, ²⁵those registered for the tribe of Gad numbered 45,650.

²⁶The descendants of Judah: according to their family records by their clans and their ancestral houses, counting the names of those 20 years old or more, everyone who could serve in the army, ²⁷those registered for the tribe of Judah numbered 74,600.

²⁸The descendants of Issachar: according to their family records by their clans and their ancestral houses, counting the names of those 20 years old or more, everyone who could serve in the army, ²⁹those registered for the tribe of Issachar numbered 54,400.

³⁰The descendants of Zebulun: according to their family records by their clans and their ancestral houses, counting the names of those 20 years old or more, everyone who could serve in the army, ³¹those registered for the tribe of Zebulun numbered 57,400.

³²The descendants of Joseph:
The descendants of Ephraim: according to their family records by their clans and their ancestral houses, counting the names of those 20 years old or more, everyone who could serve in the army, ³³those registered for the tribe of Ephraim numbered 40,500.

³⁴The descendants of Manasseh: according to their family records by their clans and their ancestral houses, counting the names of those 20 years old or more, everyone who could serve in the army, ³⁵those registered for the tribe of Manasseh numbered 32,200.

³⁶The descendants of Benjamin: according to their family records by their clans and their ancestral houses, counting the names of those 20 years old or more, everyone who could serve in the army, ³⁷those registered for the tribe of Benjamin numbered 35,400.

³⁸The descendants of Dan: according to their family records by their clans and their ancestral houses, counting the names of those 20 years old or more, everyone who could serve in the army, ³⁹those registered for the tribe of Dan numbered 62,700.

⁴⁰The descendants of Asher: according to their family records by their clans and their ancestral houses, counting the names of those 20 years

old or more, everyone who could serve in the army, ⁴¹ those registered for the tribe of Asher numbered 41,500.

⁴² The descendants of Naphtali: according to their family records by their clans and their ancestral houses, counting the names of those 20 years old or more, everyone who could serve in the army, ⁴³ those registered for the tribe of Naphtali numbered 53,400.

⁴⁴ These are the men Moses and Aaron registered, with the assistance of the 12 leaders of Israel; each represented his ancestral house. ⁴⁵ So all the Israelites 20 years old or more, everyone who could serve in Israel's army, were registered by their ancestral houses. ⁴⁶ All those registered numbered 603,550.

⁴⁷ But the Levites were not registered with them by their ancestral tribe. ⁴⁸ For the LORD had told Moses: ⁴⁹ "Do not register or take a census of the tribe of Levi with the other Israelites. ⁵⁰ Appoint the Levites over the tabernacle of the ˙testimony, all its furnishings, and everything in it. They are to transport the tabernacle and all its articles, take care of it, and camp around it. ⁵¹ Whenever the tabernacle is to move, the Levites are to take it down, and whenever it is to stop at a campsite, the Levites are to set it up. Any unauthorized person who comes near it must be put to death.

⁵² "The Israelites are to camp by their military divisions, each man with his encampment and under his banner. ⁵³ The Levites are to camp around the tabernacle of the testimony and watch over it, so that no wrath will fall on the Israelite community." ⁵⁴ The Israelites did everything just as the LORD had commanded Moses.

2 The LORD spoke to Moses and Aaron: ² "The Israelites are to camp under their respective banners beside the flags of their ancestral houses. They are to camp around the tent of meeting at a distance from it: ³ Judah's military divisions will camp on the east side toward the sunrise under their banner. The leader of the descendants of Judah is Nahshon son of Amminadab. ⁴ His military division numbers 74,600. ⁵ The tribe of Issachar will camp next to it. The leader of the Issacharites is Nethanel son of Zuar. ⁶ His military division numbers 54,400. ⁷ The tribe of Zebulun will be next. The leader of the Zebulunites is Eliab son of Helon. ⁸ His military division numbers 57,400. ⁹ The total number in their military divisions who belong to Judah's encampment is 186,400; they will move out first.

¹⁰ Reuben's military divisions will camp on the south side under their banner. The leader of the Reubenites is Elizur son of Shedeur. ¹¹ His military division numbers 46,500. ¹² The tribe of Simeon will camp next to it. The leader of the Simeonites is Shelumiel son of Zurishaddai. ¹³ His military division numbers 59,300. ¹⁴ The tribe of Gad will be next. The leader of the Gadites is Eliasaph son of Deuel. ¹⁵ His military division numbers 45,650. ¹⁶ The total number in their military divisions who belong to Reuben's encampment is 151,450; they will move out second.

¹⁷ The tent of meeting is to move out with the Levites' camp, which is in the middle of the camps. They are to move out just as they camp, each in his place, with their banners.

¹⁸ Ephraim's military divisions will camp on the west side under their banner. The leader of the Ephraimites is Elishama son of Ammihud. ¹⁹ His military division numbers 40,500. ²⁰ The tribe of Manasseh will be next to it. The leader of the Manassites is Gamaliel son of Pedahzur. ²¹ His military division numbers 32,200. ²² The tribe of Benjamin will be next. The leader of the Benjaminites is Abidan son of Gideoni. ²³ His military division numbers 35,400. ²⁴ The total in their military divisions who belong to Ephraim's encampment number 108,100; they will move out third.

²⁵ Dan's military divisions will camp on the north side under their banner. The leader of the Danites is Ahiezer son of Ammishaddai. ²⁶ His military division numbers 62,700. ²⁷ The tribe of Asher will camp next to it. The leader of the Asherites is Pagiel son of Ochran. ²⁸ His military division numbers 41,500. ²⁹ The tribe of Naphtali will be next. The leader of the Naphtalites is Ahira son of Enan. ³⁰ His military division numbers 53,400. ³¹ The total number who belong to Dan's encampment is 157,600; they are to move out last, with their banners."

³² These are the Israelites registered by their ancestral houses. The total number in the camps by their military divisions is 603,550. ³³ But the Levites were not registered among the Israelites, just as the LORD had commanded Moses.

³⁴ The Israelites did everything the LORD commanded Moses; they camped by their banners in this way and moved out the same way, each man by his clan and by his ancestral house.

3 These are the family records of Aaron and Moses at the time the LORD spoke with Moses on Mount Sinai. ² These are the names of Aaron's sons: Nadab, the firstborn, and Abihu, Eleazar, and Ithamar. ³ These are the names of Aaron's sons, the anointed priests, who were ordained to serve as priests. ⁴ But Nadab and Abihu died in the LORD's presence when they presented unauthorized fire before the LORD in the Wilderness of Sinai, and they had no sons. So Eleazar and Ithamar served as priests under the direction of Aaron their father.

⁵ The LORD spoke to Moses: ⁶ "Bring the tribe of Levi near and present them to Aaron the priest to assist him. ⁷ They are to perform duties for him and the entire community before the tent of meeting by attending to the service of the tabernacle. ⁸ They are to take care of all the furnishings of the tent of meeting and perform duties for the Israelites by attending to the service of the tabernacle. ⁹ Assign the Levites to Aaron and his sons; they have been assigned exclusively to him from the Israelites. ¹⁰ You are to appoint Aaron and his sons to carry out their priestly responsibilities, but any unauthorized person who comes near the sanctuary must be put to death."

¹¹ The LORD spoke to Moses: ¹² "See, I have taken the Levites from the Israelites in place of every firstborn Israelite from the womb. The Levites belong to Me, ¹³ because every firstborn belongs to Me. At the time I struck down every firstborn in the land of Egypt, I consecrated every firstborn in Israel to Myself, both man and animal. They are Mine; I am ˙Yahweh."

¹⁴ The LORD spoke to Moses in the Wilderness of Sinai: ¹⁵ "Register the Levites by their ancestral houses

and their clans. You are to register every male one month old or more." ¹⁶So Moses registered them in obedience to the Lord as he had been commanded:

¹⁷These were Levi's sons by name: Gershon, Kohath, and Merari. ¹⁸These were the names of Gershon's sons by their clans: Libni and Shimei. ¹⁹Kohath's sons by their clans were Amram, Izhar, Hebron, and Uzziel. ²⁰Merari's sons by their clans were Mahli and Mushi. These were the Levite clans by their ancestral houses.

²¹The Libnite clan and the Shimeite clan came from Gershon; these were the Gershonite clans. ²²Those registered, counting every male one month old or more, numbered 7,500. ²³The Gershonite clans camped behind the tabernacle on the west side, ²⁴and the leader of the Gershonite family was Eliasaph son of Lael. ²⁵The Gershonites' duties at the tent of meeting involved the tabernacle, the tent, its covering, the screen for the entrance to the tent of meeting, ²⁶the hangings of the courtyard, the screen for the entrance to the courtyard that surrounds the tabernacle and the altar, and the tent ropes—all the work relating to these.

²⁷The Amramite clan, the Izharite clan, the Hebronite clan, and the Uzzielite clan came from Kohath; these were the Kohathites. ²⁸Counting every male one month old or more, there were 8,600 responsible for the duties of the sanctuary. ²⁹The clans of the Kohathites camped on the south side of the tabernacle, ³⁰and the leader of the family of the Kohathite clans was Elizaphan son of Uzziel. ³¹Their duties involved the ark, the table, the lampstand, the altars, the sanctuary utensils that were used with these, and the screen—and all the work relating to them. ³²The chief of the Levite leaders was Eleazar son of Aaron the priest; he had oversight of those responsible for the duties of the sanctuary.

³³The Mahlite clan and the Mushite clan came from Merari; these were the Merarite clans. ³⁴Those registered, counting every male one month old or more, numbered 6,200. ³⁵The leader of the family of the Merarite clans was Zuriel son of Abihail; they camped on the north side of the tabernacle. ³⁶The assigned duties of Merari's descendants involved the tabernacle's supports, crossbars, posts, bases, all its equipment, and all the work related to these, ³⁷in addition to the posts of the surrounding courtyard with their bases, tent pegs, and ropes. ³⁸Moses, Aaron, and his sons, who performed the duties of the sanctuary as a service on behalf of the Israelites, camped in front of the tabernacle on the east, in front of the tent of meeting toward the sunrise. Any unauthorized person who came near it was to be put to death. ³⁹The total number of all the Levite males one month old or more that Moses and Aaron registered by their clans at the Lord's command was 22,000.

⁴⁰The Lord told Moses: "Register every firstborn male of the Israelites one month old or more, and list their names. ⁴¹You are to take the Levites for Me—I am Yahweh—in place of every firstborn among the Israelites, and the Levites' cattle in place of every firstborn among the Israelites' cattle." ⁴²So Moses registered every firstborn among the Israelites, as the Lord commanded him. ⁴³The total number of the firstborn males one month old or more listed by name was 22,273.

⁴⁴The Lord spoke to Moses again: ⁴⁵"Take the Levites in place of every firstborn among the Israelites, and the Levites' cattle in place of their cattle. The Levites belong to Me; I am Yahweh. ⁴⁶As the redemption price for the 273 firstborn Israelites who outnumber the Levites, ⁴⁷collect five ˙shekels for each person, according to the standard sanctuary shekel—20 *gerahs* to the shekel. ⁴⁸Give the money to Aaron and his sons as the redemption price for those who are in excess among the Israelites."

⁴⁹So Moses collected the redemption money from those in excess of the ones redeemed by the Levites. ⁵⁰He collected the money from the firstborn Israelites: 1,365 shekels measured by the standard sanctuary shekel. ⁵¹He gave the redemption money to Aaron and his sons in obedience to the Lord, just as the Lord commanded Moses.

4 The Lord spoke to Moses and Aaron: ²"Among the Levites, take a census of the Kohathites by their clans and their ancestral houses, ³men from 30 years old to 50 years old—everyone who is qualified to do work at the tent of meeting.

⁴"The service of the Kohathites at the tent of meeting concerns the most holy objects. ⁵Whenever the camp is about to move on, Aaron and his sons are to go in, take down the screening veil, and cover the ark of the ˙testimony with it. ⁶They are to place over this a covering made of manatee skin, spread a solid blue cloth on top, and insert its poles.

⁷"They are to spread a blue cloth over the table of the Presence and place the plates and cups on it, as well as the bowls and pitchers for the ˙drink offering. The regular bread offering is to be on it. ⁸They are to spread a scarlet cloth over them, cover them with a covering made of manatee skin, and insert the poles in the table.

⁹"They are to take a blue cloth and cover the lampstand used for light, with its lamps, snuffers, and firepans, as well as its jars of oil by which they service it. ¹⁰Then they must place it with all its utensils inside a covering made of manatee skin and put them on the carrying frame.

¹¹"They are to spread a blue cloth over the gold altar, cover it with a covering made of manatee skin, and insert its poles. ¹²They are to take all the serving utensils they use in the sanctuary, place them in a blue cloth, cover them with a covering made of manatee skin, and put them on a carrying frame.

¹³"They are to remove the ashes from the bronze altar, spread a purple cloth over it, ¹⁴and place all the equipment on it that they use in serving: the firepans, meat forks, shovels, and basins—all the equipment of the altar. They are to spread a covering made of manatee skin over it and insert its poles.

¹⁵"Aaron and his sons are to finish covering the holy objects and all their equipment whenever the camp is to move on. The Kohathites will come and carry them, but they are not to touch the holy objects or they will die. These are the transportation duties of the Kohathites regarding the tent of meeting.

¹⁶"Eleazar, son of Aaron the priest, has oversight of the lamp oil, the fragrant incense, the daily ˙grain offering, and the anointing oil. He has oversight of the entire tabernacle and everything in it, the holy objects and their utensils."

¹⁷Then the LORD spoke to Moses and Aaron: ¹⁸"Do not allow the Kohathite tribal clans to be wiped out from the Levites. ¹⁹Do this for them so that they may live and not die when they come near the most holy objects: Aaron and his sons are to go in and assign each man his task and transportation duty. ²⁰The Kohathites are not to go in and look at the holy objects, even for a moment, or they will die."

²¹The LORD spoke to Moses: ²²"Take a census of the Gershonites also, by their ancestral houses and their clans. ²³Register men from 30 years old to 50 years old, everyone who is qualified to perform service, to do work at the tent of meeting. ²⁴This is the service of the Gershonite clans regarding work and transportation duties: ²⁵They are to transport the tabernacle curtains, the tent of meeting with its covering and the covering made of manatee skin on top of it, the screen for the entrance to the tent of meeting, ²⁶the hangings of the courtyard, the screen for the entrance at the gate of the courtyard that surrounds the tabernacle and the altar, along with their ropes and all the equipment for their service. They will carry out everything that needs to be done with these items.

²⁷"All the service of the Gershonites, all their transportation duties and all their other work, is to be done at the command of Aaron and his sons; you are to assign to them all that they are responsible to carry. ²⁸This is the service of the Gershonite clans at the tent of meeting, and their duties will be under the direction of Ithamar son of Aaron the priest.

²⁹"As for the Merarites, you are to register them by their clans and their ancestral houses. ³⁰Register men from 30 years old to 50 years old, everyone who is qualified to do the work of the tent of meeting. ³¹This is what they are responsible to carry as the whole of their service at the tent of meeting: the supports of the tabernacle, with its crossbars, posts, and bases, ³²the posts of the surrounding courtyard with their bases, tent pegs, and ropes, including all their equipment and all the work related to them. You are to assign by name the items that they are responsible to carry. ³³This is the service of the Merarite clans regarding all their work at the tent of meeting, under the direction of Ithamar son of Aaron the priest."

³⁴So Moses, Aaron, and the leaders of the community registered the Kohathites by their clans and their ancestral houses, ³⁵men from 30 years old to 50 years old, everyone who was qualified for work at the tent of meeting. ³⁶The men registered by their clans numbered 2,750. ³⁷These were the registered men of the Kohathite clans, everyone who could serve at the tent of meeting. Moses and Aaron registered them at the LORD's command through Moses.

³⁸The Gershonites were registered by their clans and their ancestral houses, ³⁹men from 30 years old to 50 years old, everyone who was qualified for work at the tent of meeting. ⁴⁰The men registered by their clans and their ancestral houses numbered 2,630. ⁴¹These were the registered men of the Gershonite clans. At the LORD's command Moses and Aaron registered everyone who could serve at the tent of meeting.

⁴²The men of the Merarite clans were registered by their clans and their ancestral houses, ⁴³those from 30 years old to 50 years old, everyone who was qualified for work at the tent of meeting. ⁴⁴The men registered by their clans numbered 3,200. ⁴⁵These were the regis-tered men of the Merarite clans; Moses and Aaron reg-istered them at the LORD's command through Moses.

⁴⁶Moses, Aaron, and the leaders of Israel registered all the Levites by their clans and their ancestral hous-es, ⁴⁷from 30 years old to 50 years old, everyone who was qualified to do the work of serving at the tent of meeting and transporting it. ⁴⁸Their registered men numbered 8,580. ⁴⁹At the LORD's command they were registered under the direction of Moses, each one ac-cording to his work and transportation duty, and his assignment was as the LORD commanded Moses.

5 The LORD instructed Moses: ²"Command the Is-raelites to send away anyone from the camp who is afflicted with a skin disease, anyone who has a bodily discharge, or anyone who is defiled because of a corpse. ³You must send away both male or female; send them outside the camp, so that they will not defile their camps where I dwell among them." ⁴The Israelites did this, sending them outside the camp. The Israelites did as the LORD instructed Moses.

⁵The LORD spoke to Moses: ⁶"Tell the Israelites: When a man or woman commits any sin against an-other, that person acts unfaithfully toward the LORD and is *guilty. ⁷The person is to confess the sin he has committed. He is to pay full compensation, add a fifth of its value to it, and give it to the individual he has wronged. ⁸But if that individual has no relative to receive compensation, the compensation goes to the LORD for the priest, along with the *atonement ram by which the priest will make atonement for the guilty person. ⁹Every holy contribution the Israelites present to the priest will be his. ¹⁰Each one's holy contribu-tion is his to give; what each one gives to the priest will be his."

¹¹The LORD spoke to Moses: ¹²"Speak to the Isra-elites and tell them: If any man's wife goes astray, is unfaithful to him, ¹³and sleeps with another, but it is concealed from her husband, and she is undetected, even though she has defiled herself, since there is no witness against her, and she wasn't caught in the act; ¹⁴and if a feeling of jealousy comes over the husband and he becomes jealous because of his wife who has defiled herself—or if a feeling of jealousy comes over him and he becomes jealous of her though she has not defiled herself— ¹⁵then the man is to bring his wife to the priest. He is also to bring an offering for her of two quarts of barley flour. He is not to pour oil over it or put frankincense on it because it is a *grain offering of jealousy, a grain offering for remembrance that brings sin to mind.

¹⁶"The priest is to bring her forward and have her stand before the LORD. ¹⁷Then the priest is to take holy water in a clay bowl, and take some of the dust from the tabernacle floor and put it in the water. ¹⁸After the priest has the woman stand before the LORD, he is to let down her hair and place in her hands the grain of-fering for remembrance, which is the grain offering of jealousy. The priest is to hold the bitter water that brings a curse. ¹⁹The priest will require the woman to take an oath and will say to her, 'If no man has slept with you, if you have not gone astray and become de-filed while under your husband's authority, be unaf-fected by this bitter water that brings a curse. ²⁰But if you have gone astray while under your husband's authority, if you have defiled yourself and a man other than your husband has slept with you'— ²¹at this point the priest must make the woman take the oath with

the sworn curse, and he is to say to her—'May the LORD make you into an object of your people's cursing and swearing when He makes your thigh shrivel and your belly swell. ²²May this water that brings a curse enter your stomach, causing your belly to swell and your thigh to shrivel.'

"And the woman must reply, '"Amen, Amen.'

²³"Then the priest is to write these curses on a scroll and wash them off into the bitter water. ²⁴He will require the woman to drink the bitter water that brings a curse, and it will enter her and cause bitter suffering. ²⁵The priest is to take the grain offering of jealousy from the woman's hand, wave the offering before the LORD, and bring it to the altar. ²⁶The priest is to take a handful of the grain offering as a memorial portion and burn it on the altar. Then he will require the woman to drink the water.

²⁷"When he makes her drink the water, if she has defiled herself and been unfaithful to her husband, the water that brings a curse will enter her and cause bitter suffering; her belly will swell, and her thigh will shrivel. She will become a curse among her people. ²⁸But if the woman has not defiled herself and is pure, she will be unaffected and will be able to conceive children.

²⁹"This is the law regarding jealousy when a wife goes astray and defiles herself while under her husband's authority, ³⁰or when a feeling of jealousy comes over a husband and he becomes jealous of his wife. He is to have the woman stand before the LORD, and the priest will apply this entire ritual to her. ³¹The husband will be free of guilt, but that woman will bear the consequences of her guilt."

6 The LORD instructed Moses: ²"Speak to the Israelites and tell them: When a man or woman makes a special vow, a Nazirite vow, to consecrate himself to the LORD, ³he is to abstain from wine and beer. He must not drink vinegar made from wine or from beer. He must not drink any grape juice or eat fresh grapes or raisins. ⁴He is not to eat anything produced by the grapevine, from seeds to skin, during his vow.

⁵"You must not cut his hair throughout the time of his vow of consecration. He must be holy until the time is completed during which he consecrates himself to the LORD; he is to let the hair of his head grow long. ⁶He must not go near a dead body during the time he consecrates himself to the LORD. ⁷He is not to defile himself for his father or mother, or his brother or sister, when they die, because the hair consecrated to his God is on his head. ⁸He is holy to the LORD during the time of consecration.

⁹"If someone suddenly dies near him, defiling his consecrated head of hair, he must shave his head on the day of his purification; he is to shave it on the seventh day. ¹⁰On the eighth day he is to bring two turtledoves or two young pigeons to the priest at the entrance to the tent of meeting. ¹¹The priest is to offer one as a *sin offering and the other as a *burnt offering to make *atonement on behalf of the Nazirite, since he sinned because of the corpse. On that day he must consecrate his head again. ¹²He is to rededicate his time of consecration to the LORD and to bring a year-old male lamb as a *restitution offering. But do not count the previous period, because his consecrated hair became defiled.

¹³"This is the law of the Nazirite: On the day his time of consecration is completed, he must be brought to the entrance to the tent of meeting. ¹⁴He is to present an offering to the LORD of one unblemished year-old male lamb as a burnt offering, one unblemished year-old female lamb as a sin offering, one unblemished ram as a *fellowship offering, ¹⁵along with their *grain offerings and *drink offerings, and a basket of unleavened cakes made from fine flour mixed with oil, and unleavened wafers coated with oil.

¹⁶"The priest is to present these before the LORD and sacrifice the Nazirite's sin offering and burnt offering. ¹⁷He will also offer the ram as a fellowship sacrifice to the LORD, together with the basket of unleavened bread. Then the priest will offer the accompanying grain offering and drink offering.

¹⁸"The Nazirite is to shave his consecrated head at the entrance to the tent of meeting, take the hair from his head, and put it on the fire under the fellowship sacrifice. ¹⁹The priest is to take the boiled shoulder from the ram, one unleavened cake from the basket, and one unleavened wafer, and put them into the hands of the Nazirite after he has shaved his consecrated head. ²⁰The priest is to wave them as a presentation offering before the LORD. It is a holy portion for the priest, in addition to the breast of the presentation offering and the thigh of the contribution. After that, the Nazirite may drink wine.

²¹"This is the ritual of the Nazirite who vows his offering to the LORD for his consecration, in addition to whatever else he can afford; he must fulfill whatever vow he makes in keeping with the ritual for his consecration."

²²The LORD spoke to Moses: ²³"Tell Aaron and his sons how you are to bless the Israelites. Say to them:

²⁴   May *Yahweh bless you and protect you;
²⁵   may Yahweh make His face shine on you
    and be gracious to you;
²⁶   may Yahweh look with favor on you
    and give you peace.

²⁷In this way they will pronounce My name over the Israelites, and I will bless them."

7 On the day Moses finished setting up the tabernacle, he anointed and consecrated it and all its furnishings, along with the altar and all its utensils. After he anointed and consecrated these things, ²the leaders of Israel, the heads of their ancestral houses, presented an offering. They were the tribal leaders who supervised the registration. ³They brought as their offering before the LORD six covered carts and 12 oxen, a cart from every two leaders and an ox from each one, and presented them in front of the tabernacle.

⁴The LORD said to Moses, ⁵"Accept these from them to be used in the work of the tent of meeting, and give this offering to the Levites, to each division according to their service."

⁶So Moses took the carts and oxen and gave them to the Levites. ⁷He gave the Gershonites two carts and four oxen corresponding to their service, ⁸and gave the Merarites four carts and eight oxen corresponding to their service, under the direction of Ithamar son of Aaron the priest. ⁹But he did not give any to the Kohathites, since their responsibility was service related to the holy objects carried on their shoulders.

¹⁰The leaders also presented the dedication gift for the altar when it was anointed. The leaders presented their offerings in front of the altar. ¹¹The LORD told Moses, "Each day have one leader present his offering for the dedication of the altar."

[12] The one who presented his offering on the first day was Nahshon son of Amminadab from the tribe of Judah. [13] His offering was one silver dish weighing 3¼ pounds and one silver basin weighing 1¾ pounds, measured by the standard sanctuary *shekel, both of them full of fine flour mixed with oil for a *grain offering; [14] one gold bowl weighing four ounces, full of incense; [15] one young bull, one ram, and one male lamb a year old, for a *burnt offering; [16] one male goat for a *sin offering; [17] and two bulls, five rams, five male breeding goats, and five male lambs a year old, for the *fellowship sacrifice. This was the offering of Nahshon son of Amminadab.

[18] On the second day Nethanel son of Zuar, leader of Issachar, presented an offering. [19] As his offering, he presented one silver dish weighing 3¼ pounds and one silver basin weighing 1¾ pounds, measured by the standard sanctuary shekel, both of them full of fine flour mixed with oil for a grain offering; [20] one gold bowl weighing four ounces, full of incense; [21] one young bull, one ram, and one male lamb a year old, for a burnt offering; [22] one male goat for a sin offering; [23] and two bulls, five rams, five male breeding goats, and five male lambs a year old, for the fellowship sacrifice. This was the offering of Nethanel son of Zuar.

[24] On the third day Eliab son of Helon, leader of the Zebulunites, presented an offering. [25] His offering was one silver dish weighing 3¼ pounds and one silver basin weighing 1¾ pounds, measured by the standard sanctuary shekel, both of them full of fine flour mixed with oil for a grain offering; [26] one gold bowl weighing four ounces, full of incense; [27] one young bull, one ram, and one male lamb a year old, for a burnt offering; [28] one male goat for a sin offering; [29] and two bulls, five rams, five male breeding goats, and five male lambs a year old, for the fellowship sacrifice. This was the offering of Eliab son of Helon.

[30] On the fourth day Elizur son of Shedeur, leader of the Reubenites, presented an offering. [31] His offering was one silver dish weighing 3¼ pounds and one silver basin weighing 1¾ pounds, measured by the standard sanctuary shekel, both of them full of fine flour mixed with oil for a grain offering; [32] one gold bowl weighing four ounces, full of incense; [33] one young bull, one ram, and one male lamb a year old, for a burnt offering; [34] one male goat for a sin offering; [35] and two bulls, five rams, five male breeding goats, and five male lambs a year old, for the fellowship sacrifice. This was the offering of Elizur son of Shedeur.

[36] On the fifth day Shelumiel son of Zurishaddai, leader of the Simeonites, presented an offering. [37] His offering was one silver dish weighing 3¼ pounds and one silver basin weighing 1¾ pounds, measured by the standard sanctuary shekel, both of them full of fine flour mixed with oil for a grain offering; [38] one gold bowl weighing four ounces, full of incense; [39] one young bull, one ram, and one male lamb a year old, for a burnt offering; [40] one male goat for a sin offering; [41] and two bulls, five rams, five male breed-

ing goats, and five male lambs a year old, for the fellowship sacrifice. This was the offering of Shelumiel son of Zurishaddai.

[42] On the sixth day Eliasaph son of Deuel, leader of the Gadites, presented an offering. [43] His offering was one silver dish weighing 3¼ pounds and one silver basin weighing 1¾ pounds, measured by the standard sanctuary shekel, both of them full of fine flour mixed with oil for a grain offering; [44] one gold bowl weighing four ounces, full of incense; [45] one young bull, one ram, and one male lamb a year old, for a burnt offering; [46] one male goat for a sin offering; [47] and two bulls, five rams, five male breeding goats, and five male lambs a year old, for the fellowship sacrifice. This was the offering of Eliasaph son of Deuel.

[48] On the seventh day Elishama son of Ammihud, leader of the Ephraimites, presented an offering. [49] His offering was one silver dish weighing 3¼ pounds and one silver basin weighing 1¾ pounds, measured by the standard sanctuary shekel, both of them full of fine flour mixed with oil for a grain offering; [50] one gold bowl weighing four ounces, full of incense; [51] one young bull, one ram, and one male lamb a year old, for a burnt offering; [52] one male goat for a sin offering; [53] and two bulls, five rams, five male breeding goats, and five male lambs a year old, for the fellowship sacrifice. This was the offering of Elishama son of Ammihud.

[54] On the eighth day Gamaliel son of Pedahzur, leader of the Manassites, presented an offering. [55] His offering was one silver dish weighing 3¼ pounds and one silver basin weighing 1¾ pounds, measured by the standard sanctuary shekel, both of them full of fine flour mixed with oil for a grain offering; [56] one gold bowl weighing four ounces, full of incense; [57] one young bull, one ram, and one male lamb a year old, for a burnt offering; [58] one male goat for a sin offering; [59] and two bulls, five rams, five male breeding goats, and five male lambs a year old, for the fellowship sacrifice. This was the offering of Gamaliel son of Pedahzur.

[60] On the ninth day Abidan son of Gideoni, leader of the Benjaminites, presented an offering. [61] His offering was one silver dish weighing 3¼ pounds and one silver basin weighing 1¾ pounds, measured by the standard sanctuary shekel, both of them full of fine flour mixed with oil for a grain offering; [62] one gold bowl weighing four ounces, full of incense; [63] one young bull, one ram, and one male lamb a year old, for a burnt offering; [64] one male goat for a sin offering; [65] and two bulls, five rams, five male breeding goats, and five male lambs a year old, for the fellowship sacrifice. This was the offering of Abidan son of Gideoni.

[66] On the tenth day Ahiezer son of Ammishaddai, leader of the Danites, presented an offering. [67] His offering was one silver dish weighing 3¼ pounds and one silver basin weighing 1¾ pounds, measured by the standard sanctuary shekel, both of them full of fine flour mixed with oil for a grain offering; [68] one gold bowl weighing four ounces, full of incense; [69] one young bull, one ram, and one male lamb a year old, for a

burnt offering; [70] one male goat for a sin offering; [71] and two bulls, five rams, five male breeding goats, and five male lambs a year old, for the fellowship sacrifice. This was the offering of Ahiezer son of Ammishaddai.

[72] On the eleventh day Pagiel son of Ochran, leader of the Asherites, presented an offering. [73] His offering was one silver dish weighing 3 1/4 pounds and one silver basin weighing 1 3/4 pounds, measured by the standard sanctuary shekel, both of them full of fine flour mixed with oil for a grain offering; [74] one gold bowl weighing four ounces, full of incense; [75] one young bull, one ram, and one male lamb a year old, for a burnt offering; [76] one male goat for a sin offering; [77] and two bulls, five rams, five male breeding goats, and five male lambs a year old, for the fellowship sacrifice. This was the offering of Pagiel son of Ochran.

[78] On the twelfth day Ahira son of Enan, leader of the Naphtalites, presented an offering. [79] His offering was one silver dish weighing 3 1/4 pounds and one silver basin weighing 1 3/4 pounds, measured by the standard sanctuary shekel, both of them full of fine flour mixed with oil for a grain offering; [80] one gold bowl weighing four ounces, full of incense; [81] one young bull, one ram, and one male lamb a year old, for a burnt offering; [82] one male goat for a sin offering; [83] and two bulls, five rams, five male breeding goats, and five male lambs a year old, for the fellowship sacrifice. This was the offering of Ahira son of Enan.

[84] This was the dedication gift from the leaders of Israel for the altar when it was anointed: 12 silver dishes, 12 silver basins, and 12 gold bowls. [85] Each silver dish weighed 3 1/4 pounds, and each basin 1 3/4 pounds. The total weight of the silver articles was 60 pounds measured by the standard sanctuary shekel. [86] The 12 gold bowls full of incense each weighed four ounces measured by the standard sanctuary shekel. The total weight of the gold bowls was three pounds. [87] All the livestock for the burnt offering totaled 12 bulls, 12 rams, and 12 male lambs a year old, with their grain offerings, and 12 male goats for the sin offering. [88] All the livestock for the fellowship sacrifice totaled 24 bulls, 60 rams, 60 male breeding goats, and 60 male lambs a year old. This was the dedication gift for the altar after it was anointed.

[89] When Moses entered the tent of meeting to speak with the LORD, he heard the voice speaking to him from above the *mercy seat that was on the ark of the *testimony, from between the two *cherubim. He spoke to him that way.

8 The LORD spoke to Moses: [2] "Speak to Aaron and tell him: When you set up the lamps, the seven lamps are to give light in front of the lampstand." [3] So Aaron did this; he set up its lamps to give light in front of the lampstand just as the LORD had commanded Moses. [4] This is the way the lampstand was made: it was a hammered work of gold, hammered from its base to its flower petals. The lampstand was made according to the pattern the LORD had shown Moses.

[5] The LORD spoke to Moses: [6] "Take the Levites from among the Israelites and ceremonially cleanse them. [7] This is what you must do to them for their purification: Sprinkle them with the purification water. Have

them shave their entire bodies and wash their clothes, and so purify themselves.

[8] "They are to take a young bull and its *grain offering of fine flour mixed with oil, and you are to take a second young bull for a *sin offering. [9] Bring the Levites before the tent of meeting and assemble the entire Israelite community. [10] Then present the Levites before the LORD, and have the Israelites lay their hands on them. [11] Aaron is to present the Levites before the LORD as a presentation offering from the Israelites, so that they may perform the LORD's work. [12] Next the Levites are to lay their hands on the heads of the bulls. Sacrifice one as a sin offering and the other as a *burnt offering to the LORD, to make *atonement for the Levites.

[13] "You are to have the Levites stand before Aaron and his sons, and you are to present them before the LORD as a presentation offering. [14] In this way you are to separate the Levites from the rest of the Israelites so that the Levites will belong to Me. [15] After that the Levites may come to serve at the tent of meeting, once you have ceremonially cleansed them and presented them as a presentation offering. [16] For they have been exclusively assigned to Me from the Israelites. I have taken them for Myself in place of all who come first from the womb, every Israelite firstborn. [17] For every firstborn among the Israelites is Mine, both man and animal. I consecrated them to Myself on the day I struck down every firstborn in the land of Egypt. [18] But I have taken the Levites in place of every firstborn among the Israelites. [19] From the Israelites, I have given the Levites exclusively to Aaron and his sons to perform the work for the Israelites at the tent of meeting and to make atonement on their behalf, so that no plague will come against the Israelites when they approach the sanctuary."

[20] Moses, Aaron, and the entire Israelite community did this to the Levites. The Israelites did everything to them the LORD commanded Moses regarding the Levites. [21] The Levites purified themselves and washed their clothes; then Aaron presented them before the LORD as a presentation offering. Aaron also made atonement for them to ceremonially cleanse them. [22] After that, the Levites came to do their work at the tent of meeting in the presence of Aaron and his sons. So they did to them as the LORD had commanded Moses concerning the Levites.

[23] The LORD spoke to Moses: [24] "In regard to the Levites: From 25 years old or more, a man enters the service in the work at the tent of meeting. [25] But at 50 years old he is to retire from his service in the work and no longer serve. [26] He may assist his brothers to fulfill responsibilities at the tent of meeting, but he must not do the work. This is how you are to deal with the Levites regarding their duties."

9 In the first month of the second year after their departure from the land of Egypt, the LORD told Moses in the Wilderness of Sinai: [2] "The Israelites are to observe the *Passover at its appointed time. [3] You must observe it at its appointed time on the fourteenth day of this month at twilight; you are to observe it according to all its statutes and ordinances." [4] So Moses told the Israelites to observe the Passover, [5] and they observed it in the first month on the fourteenth day at twilight in the Wilderness of Sinai. The Israelites did everything as the LORD had commanded Moses.

[6] But there were some men who were *unclean because of a human corpse, so they could not observe

the Passover on that day. These men came before Moses and Aaron the same day ⁷and said to him, "We are unclean because of a human corpse. Why should we be excluded from presenting the LORD's offering at its appointed time with the other Israelites?"

⁸Moses replied to them, "Wait here until I hear what the LORD commands for you."

⁹Then the LORD spoke to Moses: ¹⁰"Tell the Israelites: When any one of you or your descendants is unclean because of a corpse or is on a distant journey, he may still observe the Passover to the LORD. ¹¹Such people are to observe it in the second month, on the fourteenth day at twilight. They are to eat the animal with unleavened bread and bitter herbs; ¹²they may not leave any of it until morning or break any of its bones. They must observe the Passover according to all its statutes.

¹³"But the man who is ceremonially 'clean, is not on a journey, and yet fails to observe the Passover is to be cut off from his people, because he did not present the LORD's offering at its appointed time. That man will bear the consequences of his sin.

¹⁴"If a foreigner resides with you and wants to observe the Passover to the LORD, he is to do so according to the Passover statute and its ordinances. You are to apply the same statute to both the foreign resident and the native of the land."

¹⁵On the day the tabernacle was set up, the cloud covered the tabernacle, the tent of the 'testimony, and it appeared like fire above the tabernacle from evening until morning. ¹⁶It remained that way continuously: the cloud would cover it, appearing like fire at night. ¹⁷Whenever the cloud was lifted up above the tent, the Israelites would set out; at the place where the cloud stopped, there the Israelites camped. ¹⁸At the LORD's command the Israelites set out, and at the LORD's command they camped. As long as the cloud stayed over the tabernacle, they camped.

¹⁹Even when the cloud stayed over the tabernacle many days, the Israelites carried out the LORD's requirement and did not set out. ²⁰Sometimes the cloud remained over the tabernacle for only a few days. They would camp at the LORD's command and set out at the LORD's command. ²¹Sometimes the cloud remained only from evening until morning; when the cloud lifted in the morning, they set out. Or if it remained a day and a night, they moved out when the cloud lifted. ²²Whether it was two days, a month, or longer, the Israelites camped and did not set out as long as the cloud stayed over the tabernacle. But when it was lifted, they set out. ²³They camped at the LORD's command, and they set out at the LORD's command. They carried out the LORD's requirement according to His command through Moses.

10 The LORD spoke to Moses: ²"Make two trumpets of hammered silver to summon the community and have the camps set out. ³When both are sounded in long blasts, the entire community is to gather before you at the entrance to the tent of meeting. ⁴However, if one is sounded, only the leaders, the heads of Israel's clans, are to gather before you.

⁵"When you sound short blasts, the camps pitched on the east are to set out. ⁶When you sound short blasts a second time, the camps pitched on the south are to set out. Short blasts are to be sounded for them to set out. ⁷When calling the assembly together, you are to sound long blasts, not short ones. ⁸The sons of Aaron, the priests, are to sound the trumpets. Your use of these is a permanent statute throughout your generations.

⁹"When you enter into battle in your land against an adversary who is attacking you, sound short blasts on the trumpets, and you will be remembered before the LORD your God and be delivered from your enemies. ¹⁰You are to sound the trumpets over your 'burnt offerings and your 'fellowship sacrifices and on your joyous occasions, your appointed festivals, and the beginning of each of your months. They will serve as a reminder for you before your God: I am 'Yahweh your God."

¹¹During the second year, in the second month on the twentieth day of the month, the cloud was lifted up above the tabernacle of the 'testimony. ¹²The Israelites traveled on from the Wilderness of Sinai, moving from one place to the next until the cloud stopped in the Wilderness of Paran. ¹³They set out for the first time according to the LORD's command through Moses.

¹⁴The military divisions of the camp of Judah with their banner set out first, and Nahshon son of Amminadab was over Judah's divisions. ¹⁵Nethanel son of Zuar was over the division of the Issachar tribe, ¹⁶and Eliab son of Helon was over the division of the Zebulun tribe. ¹⁷The tabernacle was then taken down, and the Gershonites and the Merarites set out, transporting the tabernacle.

¹⁸The military divisions of the camp of Reuben with their banner set out, and Elizur son of Shedeur was over Reuben's division. ¹⁹Shelumiel son of Zurishaddai was over the division of Simeon's tribe, ²⁰and Eliasaph son of Deuel was over the division of the tribe of Gad. ²¹The Kohathites then set out, transporting the holy objects; the tabernacle was to be set up before their arrival.

²²Next the military divisions of the camp of Ephraim with their banner set out, and Elishama son of Ammihud was over Ephraim's division. ²³Gamaliel son of Pedahzur was over the division of the tribe of Manasseh, ²⁴and Abidan son of Gideoni was over the division of the tribe of Benjamin.

²⁵The military divisions of the camp of Dan with their banner set out, serving as rear guard for all the camps, and Ahiezer son of Ammishaddai was over Dan's division. ²⁶Pagiel son of Ochran was over the division of the tribe of Asher, ²⁷and Ahira son of Enan was over the division of the tribe of Naphtali. ²⁸This was the order of march for the Israelites by their military divisions as they set out.

²⁹Moses said to Hobab, son of Moses' father-in-law Reuel the Midianite: "We're setting out for the place the LORD promised: 'I will give it to you.' Come with us, and we will treat you well, for the LORD has promised good things to Israel."

³⁰But he replied to him, "I don't want to go. Instead, I will go to my own land and my relatives."

³¹"Please don't leave us," Moses said, "since you know where we should camp in the wilderness, and you can serve as our eyes. ³²If you come with us, whatever good the LORD does for us we will do for you."

³³They set out from the mountain of the LORD on a three-day journey with the ark of the LORD's covenant traveling ahead of them for those three days to seek a resting place for them. ³⁴Meanwhile, the cloud of the LORD was over them by day when they set out from the camp.

³⁵Whenever the ark set out, Moses would say:

Arise, LORD!
Let Your enemies be scattered,
and those who hate You flee
from Your presence.
[36] When it came to rest, he would say:
Return, LORD,
to the countless thousands of Israel.

11 Now the people began complaining openly before the LORD about hardship. When the LORD heard, His anger burned, and fire from the LORD blazed among them and consumed the outskirts of the camp. [2] Then the people cried out to Moses, and he prayed to the LORD, and the fire died down. [3] So that place was named Taberah, because the LORD's fire had blazed among them.

[4] Contemptible people among them had a strong craving for other food. The Israelites cried again and said, "Who will feed us meat? [5] We remember the free fish we ate in Egypt, along with the cucumbers, melons, leeks, onions, and garlic. [6] But now our appetite is gone; there's nothing to look at but this manna!"

[7] The manna resembled coriander seed, and its appearance was like that of bdellium. [8] The people walked around and gathered it. They ground it on a pair of grinding stones or crushed it in a mortar, then boiled it in a cooking pot and shaped it into cakes. It tasted like a pastry cooked with the finest oil. [9] When the dew fell on the camp at night, the manna would fall with it.

[10] Moses heard the people, family after family, crying at the entrance of their tents. The LORD was very angry; Moses was also provoked. [11] So Moses asked the LORD, "Why have You brought such trouble on Your servant? Why are You angry with me, and why do You burden me with all these people? [12] Did I conceive all these people? Did I give them birth so You should tell me, 'Carry them at your breast, as a nursing woman carries a baby,' to the land that You swore to give their fathers? [13] Where can I get meat to give all these people? For they are crying to me: 'Give us meat to eat!' [14] I can't carry all these people by myself. They are too much for me. [15] If You are going to treat me like this, please kill me right now. If You are pleased with me, don't let me see my misery anymore."

[16] The LORD answered Moses, "Bring Me 70 men from Israel known to you as elders and officers of the people. Take them to the tent of meeting and have them stand there with you. [17] Then I will come down and speak with you there. I will take some of the Spirit who is on you and put the Spirit on them. They will help you bear the burden of the people, so that you do not have to bear it by yourself.

[18] "Tell the people: Purify yourselves in readiness for tomorrow, and you will eat meat because you cried before the LORD: 'Who will feed us meat? We really had it good in Egypt.' The LORD will give you meat and you will eat. [19] You will eat, not for one day, or two days, or five days, or 10 days, or 20 days, [20] but for a whole month—until it comes out of your nostrils and becomes nauseating to you—because you have rejected the LORD who is among you, and cried to Him: 'Why did we ever leave Egypt?'"

[21] But Moses replied, "I'm in the middle of a people with 600,000 foot soldiers, yet You say, 'I will give them meat, and they will eat for a month.' [22] If flocks and herds were slaughtered for them, would they have enough? Or if all the fish in the sea were caught for them, would they have enough?"

[23] The LORD answered Moses, "Is the LORD's power limited? You will see whether or not what I have promised will happen to you."

[24] Moses went out and told the people the words of the LORD. He brought 70 men from the elders of the people and had them stand around the tent. [25] Then the LORD descended in the cloud and spoke to him. He took some of the Spirit that was on Moses and placed the Spirit on the 70 elders. As the Spirit rested on them, they prophesied, but they never did it again. [26] Two men had remained in the camp, one named Eldad and the other Medad; the Spirit rested on them—they were among those listed, but had not gone out to the tent—and they prophesied in the camp. [27] A young man ran and reported to Moses, "Eldad and Medad are prophesying in the camp."

[28] Joshua son of Nun, assistant to Moses since his youth, responded, "Moses, my lord, stop them!"

[29] But Moses asked him, "Are you jealous on my account? If only all the LORD's people were prophets and the LORD would place His Spirit on them!" [30] Then Moses returned to the camp along with the elders of Israel.

[31] A wind sent by the LORD came up and blew quail in from the sea; it dropped them at the camp all around, three feet off the ground, about a day's journey in every direction. [32] The people were up all that day and night and all the next day gathering the quail—the one who took the least gathered 50 bushels—and they spread them out all around the camp.

[33] While the meat was still between their teeth, before it was chewed, the LORD's anger burned against the people, and the LORD struck them with a very severe plague. [34] So they named that place Kibroth-hattaavah, because there they buried the people who had craved the meat.

[35] From Kibroth-hattaavah the people moved on to Hazeroth and remained there.

12 Miriam and Aaron criticized Moses because of the ʻCushite woman he married (for he had married a Cushite woman). [2] They said, "Does the LORD speak only through Moses? Does He not also speak through us?" And the LORD heard it. [3] Moses was a very humble man, more so than any man on the face of the earth.

[4] Suddenly the LORD said to Moses, Aaron, and Miriam, "You three come out to the tent of meeting." So the three of them went out. [5] Then the LORD descended in a pillar of cloud, stood at the entrance to the tent, and summoned Aaron and Miriam. When the two of them came forward, [6] He said:

"Listen to what I say:
If there is a prophet among you from the LORD,
I make Myself known to him in a vision;
I speak with him in a dream.
[7] Not so with My servant Moses;
he is faithful in all My household.
[8] I speak with him directly,
openly, and not in riddles;
he sees the form of the LORD.

So why were you not afraid to speak against My servant Moses?" [9] The LORD's anger burned against them, and He left.

[10] As the cloud moved away from the tent, Miriam's skin suddenly became diseased, as white as snow. When Aaron turned toward her, he saw that she was diseased [11] and said to Moses, "My lord, please don't

hold against us this sin we have so foolishly committed. ¹²Please don't let her be like a dead baby whose flesh is half eaten away when he comes out of his mother's womb."

¹³Then Moses cried out to the LORD, "God, please heal her!"

¹⁴The LORD answered Moses, "If her father had merely spit in her face, wouldn't she remain in disgrace for seven days? Let her be confined outside the camp for seven days; after that she may be brought back in." ¹⁵So Miriam was confined outside the camp for seven days, and the people did not move on until Miriam was brought back in. ¹⁶After that, the people set out from Hazeroth and camped in the Wilderness of Paran.

13 The LORD spoke to Moses: ²"Send men to scout out the land of Canaan I am giving to the Israelites. Send one man who is a leader among them from each of their ancestral tribes." ³Moses sent them from the Wilderness of Paran at the LORD's command. All the men were leaders in Israel. ⁴These were their names:

Shammua son of Zaccur from the tribe
    of Reuben;
⁵   Shaphat son of Hori from the tribe of Simeon;
⁶   Caleb son of Jephunneh from the tribe
    of Judah;
⁷   Igal son of Joseph from the tribe of Issachar;
⁸   Hoshea son of Nun from the tribe of Ephraim;
⁹   Palti son of Raphu from the tribe of Benjamin;
¹⁰ Gaddiel son of Sodi from the tribe of Zebulun;
¹¹ Gaddi son of Susi from the tribe of Manasseh
    (from the tribe of Joseph);
¹² Ammiel son of Gemalli from the tribe of Dan;
¹³ Sethur son of Michael from the tribe of Asher;
¹⁴ Nahbi son of Vophsi from the tribe
    of Naphtali;
¹⁵ Geuel son of Machi from the tribe of Gad.

¹⁶These were the names of the men Moses sent to scout out the land, and Moses renamed Hoshea son of Nun, Joshua.

¹⁷When Moses sent them to scout out the land of Canaan, he told them, "Go up this way to the ˙Negev, then go up into the hill country. ¹⁸See what the land is like, and whether the people who live there are strong or weak, few or many. ¹⁹Is the land they live in good or bad? Are the cities they live in encampments or fortifications? ²⁰Is the land fertile or unproductive? Are there trees in it or not? Be courageous. Bring back some fruit from the land." It was the season for the first ripe grapes.

²¹So they went up and scouted out the land from the Wilderness of Zin as far as Rehob near the entrance to Hamath. ²²They went up through the Negev and came to Hebron, where Ahiman, Sheshai, and Talmai, the descendants of Anak, were living. Hebron was built seven years before Zoan in Egypt. ²³When they came to the Valley of Eshcol, they cut down a branch with a single cluster of grapes, which was carried on a pole by two men. They also took some pomegranates and figs. ²⁴That place was called the Valley of Eshcol because of the cluster of grapes the Israelites cut there. ²⁵At the end of 40 days they returned from scouting out the land.

²⁶The men went back to Moses, Aaron, and the entire Israelite community in the Wilderness of Paran at Kadesh. They brought back a report for them and the whole community, and they showed them the fruit of the land. ²⁷They reported to Moses: "We went into the land where you sent us. Indeed it is flowing with milk and honey, and here is some of its fruit. ²⁸However, the people living in the land are strong, and the cities are large and fortified. We also saw the descendants of Anak there. ²⁹The Amalekites are living in the land of the Negev; the Hittites, Jebusites, and Amorites live in the hill country; and the Canaanites live by the sea and along the Jordan."

³⁰Then Caleb quieted the people in the presence of Moses and said, "We must go up and take possession of the land because we can certainly conquer it!"

³¹But the men who had gone up with him responded, "We can't go up against the people because they are stronger than we are!" ³²So they gave a negative report to the Israelites about the land they had scouted: "The land we passed through to explore is one that devours its inhabitants, and all the people we saw in it are men of great size. ³³We even saw the Nephilim there—the descendants of Anak come from the Nephilim! To ourselves we seemed like grasshoppers, and we must have seemed the same to them."

14 Then the whole community broke into loud cries, and the people wept that night. ²All the Israelites complained about Moses and Aaron, and the whole community told them, "If only we had died in the land of Egypt, or if only we had died in this wilderness! ³Why is the LORD bringing us into this land to die by the sword? Our wives and little children will become plunder. Wouldn't it be better for us to go back to Egypt?" ⁴So they said to one another, "Let's appoint a leader and go back to Egypt."

⁵Then Moses and Aaron fell down with their faces to the ground in front of the whole assembly of the Israelite community. ⁶Joshua son of Nun and Caleb son of Jephunneh, who were among those who scouted out the land, tore their clothes ⁷and said to the entire Israelite community: "The land we passed through and explored is an extremely good land. ⁸If the LORD is pleased with us, He will bring us into this land, a land flowing with milk and honey, and give it to us. ⁹Only don't rebel against the LORD, and don't be afraid of the people of the land, for we will devour them. Their protection has been removed from them, and the LORD is with us. Don't be afraid of them!"

¹⁰While the whole community threatened to stone them, the glory of the LORD appeared to all the Israelites at the tent of meeting.

¹¹The LORD said to Moses, "How long will these people despise Me? How long will they not trust in Me despite all the signs I have performed among them? ¹²I will strike them with a plague and destroy them. Then I will make you into a greater and mightier nation than they are."

¹³But Moses replied to the LORD, "The Egyptians will hear about it, for by Your strength You brought up this people from them. ¹⁴They will tell it to the inhabitants of this land. They have heard that You, LORD, are among these people, how You, LORD, are seen face to face, how Your cloud stands over them, and how You go before them in a pillar of cloud by day and in a pillar of fire by night. ¹⁵If You kill this people with a single blow, the nations that have heard of Your fame will declare, ¹⁶'Since the LORD wasn't able to bring this people into the land He swore to give them, He has slaughtered them in the wilderness.'

¹⁷"So now, may my Lord's power be magnified just

as You have spoken: ¹⁸The Lᴏʀᴅ is slow to anger and rich in faithful love, forgiving wrongdoing and rebellion. But He will not leave the ˙guilty unpunished, bringing the consequences of the fathers' wrongdoing on the children to the third and fourth generation. ¹⁹Please pardon the wrongdoing of this people, in keeping with the greatness of Your faithful love, just as You have forgiven them from Egypt until now."

²⁰The Lᴏʀᴅ responded, "I have pardoned them as you requested. ²¹Yet as surely as I live and as the whole earth is filled with the Lᴏʀᴅ's glory, ²²none of the men who have seen My glory and the signs I performed in Egypt and in the wilderness, and have tested Me these 10 times and did not obey Me, ²³will ever see the land I swore to give their fathers. None of those who have despised Me will see it. ²⁴But since My servant Caleb has a different spirit and has followed Me completely, I will bring him into the land where he has gone, and his descendants will inherit it. ²⁵Since the Amalekites and Canaanites are living in the lowlands, turn back tomorrow and head for the wilderness in the direction of the ˙Red Sea."

²⁶Then the Lᴏʀᴅ spoke to Moses and Aaron: ²⁷"How long must I endure this evil community that keeps complaining about Me? I have heard the Israelites' complaints that they make against Me. ²⁸Tell them: As surely as I live," this is the Lᴏʀᴅ's declaration, "I will do to you exactly as I heard you say. ²⁹Your corpses will fall in this wilderness—all of you who were registered in the census, the entire number of you 20 years old or more—because you have complained about Me. ³⁰I swear that none of you will enter the land I promised to settle you in, except Caleb son of Jephunneh and Joshua son of Nun. ³¹I will bring your children whom you said would become plunder into the land you rejected, and they will enjoy it. ³²But as for you, your corpses will fall in this wilderness. ³³Your children will be shepherds in the wilderness for 40 years and bear the penalty for your acts of unfaithfulness until all your corpses lie scattered in the wilderness. ³⁴You will bear the consequences of your sins 40 years based on the number of the 40 days that you scouted the land, a year for each day. You will know My displeasure. ³⁵I, ˙Yahweh, have spoken. I swear that I will do this to the entire evil community that has conspired against Me. They will come to an end in the wilderness, and there they will die."

³⁶So the men Moses sent to scout out the land, and who returned and incited the entire community to complain about him by spreading a negative report about the land— ³⁷those men who spread the negative report about the land were struck down by the Lᴏʀᴅ. ³⁸Only Joshua son of Nun and Caleb son of Jephunneh remained alive of those men who went to scout out the land.

³⁹When Moses reported these words to all the Israelites, the people were overcome with grief. ⁴⁰They got up early the next morning and went up the ridge of the hill country, saying, "Let's go to the place the Lᴏʀᴅ promised, for we were wrong."

⁴¹But Moses responded, "Why are you going against the Lᴏʀᴅ's command? It won't succeed. ⁴²Don't go, because the Lᴏʀᴅ is not among you and you will be defeated by your enemies. ⁴³The Amalekites and Canaanites are right in front of you, and you will fall by the sword. The Lᴏʀᴅ won't be with you, since you have turned from following Him."

⁴⁴But they dared to go up the ridge of the hill country, even though the ark of the Lᴏʀᴅ's covenant and Moses did not leave the camp. ⁴⁵Then the Amalekites and Canaanites who lived in that part of the hill country came down, attacked them, and routed them as far as Hormah.

15 The Lᴏʀᴅ instructed Moses: ²"Speak to the Israelites and tell them: When you enter the land I am giving you to settle in, ³and you make a fire offering to the Lᴏʀᴅ from the herd or flock—either a ˙burnt offering or a sacrifice, to fulfill a vow, or as a freewill offering, or at your appointed festivals—to produce a pleasing aroma for the Lᴏʀᴅ, ⁴the one presenting his offering to the Lᴏʀᴅ must also present a ˙grain offering of two quarts of fine flour mixed with a quart of oil. ⁵Prepare a quart of wine as a ˙drink offering with the burnt offering or sacrifice of each lamb.

⁶"If you prepare a grain offering with a ram, it must be four quarts of fine flour mixed with a third of a gallon of oil. ⁷Also present a third of a gallon of wine for a drink offering as a pleasing aroma to the Lᴏʀᴅ.

⁸"If you prepare a young bull as a burnt offering or as a sacrifice, to fulfill a vow, or as a ˙fellowship offering to the Lᴏʀᴅ, ⁹a grain offering of six quarts of fine flour mixed with two quarts of oil must be presented with the bull. ¹⁰Also present two quarts of wine as a drink offering. It is a fire offering of pleasing aroma to the Lᴏʀᴅ. ¹¹This is to be done for each ox, ram, lamb, or goat. ¹²This is how you must prepare each of them, no matter how many.

¹³"Every Israelite is to prepare these things in this way when he presents a fire offering as a pleasing aroma to the Lᴏʀᴅ. ¹⁴When a foreigner resides with you or someone else is among you and wants to prepare a fire offering as a pleasing aroma to the Lᴏʀᴅ, he is to do exactly as you do throughout your generations. ¹⁵The assembly is to have the same statute for both you and the foreign resident as a permanent statute throughout your generations. You and the foreigner will be alike before the Lᴏʀᴅ. ¹⁶The same law and the same ordinance will apply to both you and the foreigner who resides with you."

¹⁷The Lᴏʀᴅ instructed Moses: ¹⁸"Speak to the Israelites and tell them: After you enter the land where I am bringing you, ¹⁹you are to offer a contribution to the Lᴏʀᴅ when you eat from the food of the land. ²⁰You are to offer a loaf from your first batch of dough as a contribution; offer it just like a contribution from the threshing floor. ²¹Throughout your generations, you are to give the Lᴏʀᴅ a contribution from the first batch of your dough.

²²"When you sin unintentionally and do not obey all these commands that the Lᴏʀᴅ spoke to Moses— ²³all that the Lᴏʀᴅ has commanded you through Moses, from the day the Lᴏʀᴅ issued the commands and onward throughout your generations— ²⁴and if it was done unintentionally without the community's awareness, the entire community is to prepare one young bull for a burnt offering as a pleasing aroma to the Lᴏʀᴅ, with its grain offering and drink offering according to the regulation, and one male goat as a ˙sin offering. ²⁵The priest must then make ˙atonement for the entire Israelite community so that they may be forgiven, for the sin was unintentional. They are to bring their offering, one made by fire to the Lᴏʀᴅ, and their sin offering before the Lᴏʀᴅ for their unintentional sin. ²⁶The entire Israelite community and the foreigner

who resides among them will be forgiven, since it happened to all the people unintentionally.

27 "If one person sins unintentionally, he is to present a year-old female goat as a sin offering. 28 The priest must then make atonement before the LORD on behalf of the person who acts in error sinning unintentionally, and when he makes atonement for him, he will be forgiven. 29 You are to have the same law for the person who acts in error, whether he is an Israelite or a foreigner who lives among you.

30 "But the person who acts defiantly, whether native or foreign resident, blasphemes the LORD. That person is to be cut off from his people. 31 He will certainly be cut off, because he has despised the LORD's word and broken His command; his *guilt remains on him."

32 While the Israelites were in the wilderness, they found a man gathering wood on the Sabbath day. 33 Those who found him gathering wood brought him to Moses, Aaron, and the entire community. 34 They placed him in custody because it had not been decided what should be done to him. 35 Then the LORD told Moses, "The man is to be put to death. The entire community is to stone him outside the camp." 36 So the entire community brought him outside the camp and stoned him to death, as the LORD had commanded Moses.

37 The LORD said to Moses, 38 "Speak to the Israelites and tell them that throughout their generations they are to make tassels for the corners of their garments, and put a blue cord on the tassel at each corner. 39 These will serve as tassels for you to look at, so that you may remember all the LORD's commands and obey them and not become unfaithful by following your own heart and your own eyes. 40 This way you will remember and obey all My commands and be holy to your God. 41 I am *Yahweh your God who brought you out of the land of Egypt to be your God; I am Yahweh your God."

16 Now Korah son of Izhar, son of Kohath, son of Levi, with Dathan and Abiram, sons of Eliab, and On son of Peleth, sons of Reuben, took 2 250 prominent Israelite men who were leaders of the community and representatives in the assembly, and they rebelled against Moses. 3 They came together against Moses and Aaron and told them, "You have gone too far! Everyone in the entire community is holy, and the LORD is among them. Why then do you exalt yourselves above the LORD's assembly?"

4 When Moses heard this, he fell facedown. 5 Then he said to Korah and all his followers, "Tomorrow morning the LORD will reveal who belongs to Him, who is set apart, and the one He will let come near Him. He will let the one He chooses come near Him. 6 Korah, you and all your followers are to do this: take firepans, and tomorrow 7 place fire in them and put incense on them before the LORD. Then the man the LORD chooses will be the one who is set apart. It is you Levites who have gone too far!"

8 Moses also told Korah, "Now listen, Levites! 9 Isn't it enough for you that the God of Israel has separated you from the Israelite community to bring you near to Himself, to perform the work at the LORD's tabernacle, and to stand before the community to minister to them? 10 He has brought you near, and all your fellow Levites who are with you, but you are seeking the priesthood as well. 11 Therefore, it is you and all your followers who have conspired against the LORD!

As for Aaron, who is he that you should complain about him?"

12 Moses sent for Dathan and Abiram, the sons of Eliab, but they said, "We will not come! 13 Is it not enough that you brought us up from a land flowing with milk and honey to kill us in the wilderness? Do you also have to appoint yourself as ruler over us? 14 Furthermore, you didn't bring us to a land flowing with milk and honey or give us an inheritance of fields and vineyards. Will you gouge out the eyes of these men? We will not come!"

15 Then Moses became angry and said to the LORD, "Don't respect their offering. I have not taken one donkey from them or mistreated a single one of them." 16 So Moses told Korah, "You and all your followers are to appear before the LORD tomorrow—you, they, and Aaron. 17 Each of you is to take his firepan, place incense on it, and present his firepan before the LORD—250 firepans. You and Aaron are each to present your firepan also."

18 Each man took his firepan, placed fire in it, put incense on it, and stood at the entrance to the tent of meeting along with Moses and Aaron. 19 After Korah assembled the whole community against them at the entrance to the tent of meeting, the glory of the LORD appeared to the whole community. 20 The LORD spoke to Moses and Aaron, 21 "Separate yourselves from this community so I may consume them instantly."

22 But Moses and Aaron fell facedown and said, "God, God of the spirits of all flesh, when one man sins, will You vent Your wrath on the whole community?"

23 The LORD replied to Moses, 24 "Tell the community: Get away from the dwellings of Korah, Dathan, and Abiram."

25 Moses got up and went to Dathan and Abiram, and the elders of Israel followed him. 26 He warned the community, "Get away now from the tents of these wicked men. Don't touch anything that belongs to them, or you will be swept away because of all their sins." 27 So they got away from the dwellings of Korah, Dathan, and Abiram. Meanwhile, Dathan and Abiram came out and stood at the entrance of their tents with their wives, children, and infants.

28 Then Moses said, "This is how you will know that the LORD sent me to do all these things and that it was not of my own will: 29 If these men die naturally as all people would, and suffer the fate of all, then the LORD has not sent me. 30 But if the LORD brings about something unprecedented, and the ground opens its mouth and swallows them along with all that belongs to them so that they go down alive into *Sheol, then you will know that these men have despised the LORD."

31 Just as he finished speaking all these words, the ground beneath them split open. 32 The earth opened its mouth and swallowed them and their households, all Korah's people, and all their possessions. 33 They went down alive into Sheol with all that belonged to them. The earth closed over them, and they vanished from the assembly. 34 At their cries, all the people of Israel who were around them fled because they thought, "The earth may swallow us too!" 35 Fire also came out from the LORD and consumed the 250 men who were presenting the incense.

36 Then the LORD spoke to Moses: 37 "Tell Eleazar son of Aaron the priest to remove the firepans from the burning debris, because they are holy, and scatter the fire far away. 38 As for the firepans of those who sinned

at the cost of their own lives, make them into hammered sheets as plating for the altar, for they presented them before the LORD, and the firepans are holy. They will be a sign to the Israelites."

³⁹ So Eleazar the priest took the bronze firepans that those who were burned had presented, and they were hammered into plating for the altar, ⁴⁰ just as the LORD commanded him through Moses. It was to be a reminder for the Israelites that no unauthorized person outside the lineage of Aaron should approach to offer incense before the LORD and become like Korah and his followers.

⁴¹ The next day the entire Israelite community complained about Moses and Aaron, saying, "You have killed the LORD's people!" ⁴² When the community assembled against them, Moses and Aaron turned toward the tent of meeting, and suddenly the cloud covered it, and the LORD's glory appeared.

⁴³ Moses and Aaron went to the front of the tent of meeting, ⁴⁴ and the LORD said to Moses, ⁴⁵ "Get away from this community so that I may consume them instantly." But they fell facedown.

⁴⁶ Then Moses told Aaron, "Take your firepan, place fire from the altar in it, and add incense. Go quickly to the community and make ˚atonement for them, because wrath has come from the LORD; the plague has begun." ⁴⁷ So Aaron took his firepan as Moses had ordered, ran into the middle of the assembly, and saw that the plague had begun among the people. After he added incense, he made atonement for the people. ⁴⁸ He stood between the dead and the living, and the plague was halted. ⁴⁹ But those who died from the plague numbered 14,700, in addition to those who died because of the Korah incident. ⁵⁰ Aaron then returned to Moses at the entrance to the tent of meeting, since the plague had been halted.

17 The LORD instructed Moses: ² "Speak to the Israelites and take one staff from them for each ancestral house, 12 staffs from all the leaders of their ancestral houses. Write each man's name on his staff. ³ Write Aaron's name on Levi's staff, because there must be one staff for the head of each ancestral house. ⁴ Then place them in the tent of meeting in front of the ˚testimony where I meet with you. ⁵ The staff of the man I choose will sprout, and I will rid Myself of the Israelites' complaints that they have been making about you."

⁶ So Moses spoke to the Israelites, and each of their leaders gave him a staff, one for each of the leaders of their ancestral houses, 12 staffs in all. Aaron's staff was among them. ⁷ Moses placed the staffs before the LORD in the tent of the testimony.

⁸ The next day Moses entered the tent of the testimony and saw that Aaron's staff, representing the house of Levi, had sprouted, formed buds, blossomed, and produced almonds! ⁹ Moses then brought out all the staffs from the LORD's presence to all the Israelites. They saw them, and each man took his own staff. ¹⁰ The LORD told Moses, "Put Aaron's staff back in front of the testimony to be kept as a sign for the rebels, so that you may put an end to their complaints before Me, or else they will die." ¹¹ So Moses did as the LORD commanded him.

¹² Then the Israelites declared to Moses, "Look, we're perishing! We're lost; we're all lost! ¹³ Anyone who comes near the LORD's tabernacle will die. Will we all perish?"

18 The LORD said to Aaron, "You, your sons, and your ancestral house will be responsible for sin against the sanctuary. You and your sons will be responsible for sin involving your priesthood. ² But also bring your relatives with you from the tribe of Levi, your ancestral tribe, so they may join you and assist you and your sons in front of the tent of the ˚testimony. ³ They are to perform duties for you and for the whole tent. They must not come near the sanctuary equipment or the altar; otherwise, both they and you will die. ⁴ They are to join you and guard the tent of meeting, doing all the work at the tent, but no unauthorized person may come near you.

⁵ "You are to guard the sanctuary and the altar so that wrath may not fall on the Israelites again. ⁶ Look, I have selected your fellow Levites from the Israelites as a gift for you, assigned by the LORD to work at the tent of meeting. ⁷ But you and your sons will carry out your priestly responsibilities for everything concerning the altar and for what is inside the veil, and you will do that work. I am giving you the work of the priesthood as a gift, but an unauthorized person who comes near the sanctuary will be put to death."

⁸ Then the LORD spoke to Aaron, "Look, I have put you in charge of the contributions brought to Me. As for all the holy offerings of the Israelites, I have given them to you and your sons as a portion and a permanent statute. ⁹ A portion of the holiest offerings kept from the fire will be yours; every one of their offerings that they give Me, whether the ˚grain offering, ˚sin offering, or ˚restitution offering will be most holy for you and your sons. ¹⁰ You are to eat it as a most holy offering. Every male may eat it; it is to be holy to you.

¹¹ "The contribution of their gifts also belongs to you. I have given all the Israelites' presentation offerings to you and to your sons and daughters as a permanent statute. Every ceremonially ˚clean person in your house may eat it. ¹² I am giving you all the best of the fresh olive oil, new wine, and grain, which the Israelites give to the LORD as their ˚firstfruits. ¹³ The firstfruits of all that is in their land, which they bring to the LORD, belong to you. Every clean person in your house may eat them.

¹⁴ "Everything in Israel that is permanently dedicated to the LORD belongs to you. ¹⁵ The firstborn of every living thing, man or animal, presented to the LORD belongs to you. But you must certainly redeem the firstborn of man, and redeem the firstborn of an ˚unclean animal. ¹⁶ You will pay the redemption price for a month-old male according to your assessment: five ˚shekels of silver by the standard sanctuary shekel, which is 20 *gerahs*.

¹⁷ "However, you must not redeem the firstborn of an ox, a sheep, or a goat; they are holy. You are to sprinkle their blood on the altar and burn their fat as a fire offering for a pleasing aroma to the LORD. ¹⁸ But their meat belongs to you. It belongs to you like the breast of the presentation offering and the right thigh.

¹⁹ "I give to you and to your sons and daughters all the holy contributions that the Israelites present to the LORD as a permanent statute. It is a permanent covenant of salt before the LORD for you as well as your ˚offspring."

²⁰ The LORD told Aaron, "You will not have an inheritance in their land; there will be no portion among

them for you. I am your portion and your inheritance among the Israelites.

²¹"Look, I have given the Levites every tenth in Israel as an inheritance in return for the work they do, the work of the tent of meeting. ²²The Israelites must never again come near the tent of meeting, or they will incur ˙guilt and die. ²³The Levites will do the work of the tent of meeting, and they will bear the consequences of their sin. The Levites will not receive an inheritance among the Israelites; this is a permanent statute throughout your generations. ²⁴For I have given them the tenth that the Israelites present to the Lord as a contribution for their inheritance. That is why I told them that they would not receive an inheritance among the Israelites."

²⁵The Lord instructed Moses, ²⁶"Speak to the Levites and tell them: When you receive from the Israelites the tenth that I have given you as your inheritance, you must present part of it as an offering to the Lord— a tenth of the tenth. ²⁷Your offering will be credited to you as if it were your grain from the threshing floor or the full harvest from the winepress. ²⁸You are to present an offering to the Lord from every tenth you receive from the Israelites. Give some of it to Aaron the priest as an offering to the Lord. ²⁹You must present the entire offering due the Lord from all your gifts. The best part of the tenth is to be consecrated.

³⁰"Tell them further: Once you have presented the best part of the tenth, and it is credited to you Levites as the produce of the threshing floor or the winepress, ³¹then you and your household may eat it anywhere. It is your wage in return for your work at the tent of meeting. ³²You will not incur guilt because of it once you have presented the best part of it, but you must not defile the Israelites' holy offerings, so that you will not die."

19 The Lord spoke to Moses and Aaron, ²"This is the legal statute that the Lord has commanded: Instruct the Israelites to bring you an unblemished red cow that has no defect and has never been yoked. ³Give it to Eleazar the priest, and he will have it brought outside the camp and slaughtered in his presence. ⁴Eleazar the priest is to take some of its blood with his finger and sprinkle it seven times toward the front of the tent of meeting. ⁵The cow must be burned in his sight. Its hide, flesh, and blood, are to be burned along with its dung. ⁶The priest is to take cedar wood, hyssop, and crimson yarn, and throw them onto the fire where the cow is burning. ⁷Then the priest must wash his clothes and bathe his body in water; after that he may enter the camp, but he will remain ceremonially ˙unclean until evening. ⁸The one who burned the cow must also wash his clothes and bathe his body in water, and he will remain unclean until evening.

⁹"A man who is ˙clean is to gather up the cow's ashes and deposit them outside the camp in a ceremonially clean place. The ashes must be kept by the Israelite community for preparing the water to remove impurity; it is a ˙sin offering. ¹⁰Then the one who gathers up the cow's ashes must wash his clothes, and he will remain unclean until evening. This is a permanent statute for the Israelites and for the foreigner who resides among them.

¹¹"The person who touches any human corpse will be unclean for seven days. ¹²He is to purify himself with the water on the third day and the seventh day; then he will be clean. But if he does not purify himself

on the third and seventh days, he will not be clean. ¹³Anyone who touches a body of a person who has died, and does not purify himself, defiles the tabernacle of the Lord. That person will be cut off from Israel. He remains unclean because the water for impurity has not been sprinkled on him, and his uncleanness is still on him.

¹⁴"This is the law when a person dies in a tent: everyone who enters the tent and everyone who is already in the tent will be unclean for seven days, ¹⁵and any open container without a lid tied on it is unclean. ¹⁶Anyone in the open field who touches a person who has been killed by the sword or has died, or who even touches a human bone, or a grave, will be unclean for seven days. ¹⁷For the purification of the unclean person, they are to take some of the ashes of the burnt sin offering, put them in a jar, and add fresh water to them. ¹⁸A person who is clean is to take hyssop, dip it in the water, and sprinkle the tent, all the furnishings, and the people who were there. He is also to sprinkle the one who touched a bone, a grave, a corpse, or a person who had been killed.

¹⁹"The one who is clean is to sprinkle the unclean person on the third day and the seventh day. After he purifies the unclean person on the seventh day, the one being purified must wash his clothes and bathe in water, and he will be clean by evening. ²⁰But a person who is unclean and does not purify himself, that person will be cut off from the assembly because he has defiled the sanctuary of the Lord. The water for impurity has not been sprinkled on him; he is unclean. ²¹This is a permanent statute for them. The person who sprinkles the water for impurity is to wash his clothes, and whoever touches the water for impurity will be unclean until evening. ²²Anything the unclean person touches will become unclean, and anyone who touches it will be unclean until evening."

20 The entire Israelite community entered the Wilderness of Zin in the first month, and they settled in Kadesh. Miriam died and was buried there.

²There was no water for the community, so they assembled against Moses and Aaron. ³The people quarreled with Moses and said, "If only we had perished when our brothers perished before the Lord. ⁴Why have you brought the Lord's assembly into this wilderness for us and our livestock to die here? ⁵Why have you led us up from Egypt to bring us to this evil place? It's not a place of grain, figs, vines, and pomegranates, and there is no water to drink!"

⁶Then Moses and Aaron went from the presence of the assembly to the doorway of the tent of meeting. They fell down with their faces to the ground, and the glory of the Lord appeared to them. ⁷The Lord spoke to Moses, ⁸"Take the staff and assemble the community. You and your brother Aaron are to speak to the rock while they watch, and it will yield its water. You will bring out water for them from the rock and provide drink for the community and their livestock."

⁹So Moses took the staff from the Lord's presence just as He had commanded him. ¹⁰Moses and Aaron summoned the assembly in front of the rock, and Moses said to them, "Listen, you rebels! Must we bring water out of this rock for you?" ¹¹Then Moses raised his hand and struck the rock twice with his staff, so that a great amount of water gushed out, and the community and their livestock drank.

¹²But the Lord said to Moses and Aaron, "Because

you did not trust Me to show My holiness in the sight of the Israelites, you will not bring this assembly into the land I have given them." [13] These are the waters of Meribah, where the Israelites quarreled with the LORD, and He showed His holiness to them.

[14] Moses sent messengers from Kadesh to the king of Edom, "This is what your brother Israel says, 'You know all the hardships that have overtaken us. [15] Our fathers went down to Egypt, and we lived in Egypt many years, but the Egyptians treated us and our fathers badly. [16] When we cried out to the LORD, He heard our voice, sent an angel, and brought us out of Egypt. Now look, we are in Kadesh, a city on the border of your territory. [17] Please let us travel through your land. We won't travel through any field or vineyard, or drink any well water. We will travel the King's Highway; we won't turn to the right or the left until we have traveled through your territory.'"

[18] But Edom answered him, "You must not travel through our land, or we will come out and confront you with the sword."

[19] "We will go on the main road," the Israelites replied to them, "and if we or our herds drink your water, we will pay its price. There will be no problem; only let us travel through on foot."

[20] Yet Edom insisted, "You must not travel through." And they came out to confront them with a large force of heavily-armed people. [21] Edom refused to allow Israel to travel through their territory, and Israel turned away from them.

[22] After they set out from Kadesh, the entire Israelite community came to Mount Hor. [23] The LORD said to Moses and Aaron at Mount Hor on the border of the land of Edom, [24] "Aaron will be gathered to his people; he will not enter the land I have given the Israelites, because you both rebelled against My command at the waters of Meribah. [25] Take Aaron and his son Eleazar and bring them up Mount Hor. [26] Remove Aaron's garments and put them on his son Eleazar. Aaron will be gathered to his people and die there."

[27] So Moses did as the LORD commanded, and they climbed Mount Hor in the sight of the whole community. [28] After Moses removed Aaron's garments and put them on his son Eleazar, Aaron died there on top of the mountain. Then Moses and Eleazar came down from the mountain. [29] When the whole community saw that Aaron had passed away, the entire house of Israel mourned for him 30 days.

21 When the Canaanite king of Arad, who lived in the ·Negev, heard that Israel was coming on the Atharim road, he fought against Israel and captured some prisoners. [2] Then Israel made a vow to the LORD, "If You will deliver this people into our hands, we will ·completely destroy their cities." [3] The LORD listened to Israel's request, the Canaanites were defeated, and Israel completely destroyed them and their cities. So they named the place Hormah.

[4] Then they set out from Mount Hor by way of the ·Red Sea to bypass the land of Edom, but the people became impatient because of the journey. [5] The people spoke against God and Moses: "Why have you led us up from Egypt to die in the wilderness? There is no bread or water, and we detest this wretched food!" [6] Then the LORD sent poisonous snakes among the people, and they bit them so that many Israelites died.

[7] The people then came to Moses and said, "We have sinned by speaking against the LORD and against you.

Intercede with the LORD so that He will take the snakes away from us." And Moses interceded for the people.

[8] Then the LORD said to Moses, "Make a snake image and mount it on a pole. When anyone who is bitten looks at it, he will recover." [9] So Moses made a bronze snake and mounted it on a pole. Whenever someone was bitten, and he looked at the bronze snake, he recovered.

[10] The Israelites set out and camped at Oboth. [11] They set out from Oboth and camped at Iye-abarim in the wilderness that borders Moab on the east. [12] From there they went and camped at Zered Valley. [13] They set out from there and camped on the other side of the Arnon River, in the wilderness that extends from the Amorite border, because the Arnon was the Moabite border between Moab and the Amorites. [14] Therefore it is stated in the Book of the LORD's Wars:

> Waheb in Suphah
> and the ravines of the Arnon,
> [15] even the slopes of the ravines
> that extend to the site of Ar
> and lie along the border of Moab.

[16] From there they went to Beer, the well the LORD told Moses about, "Gather the people so I may give them water." [17] Then Israel sang this song:

> Spring up, well—sing to it!
> [18] The princes dug the well;
> the nobles of the people hollowed it out
> with a scepter and with their staffs.

They went from the wilderness to Mattanah, [19] from Mattanah to Nahaliel, from Nahaliel to Bamoth, [20] from Bamoth to the valley in the territory of Moab near the Pisgah highlands that overlook the wasteland.

[21] Israel sent messengers to say to Sihon king of the Amorites: [22] "Let us travel through your land. We won't go into the fields or vineyards. We won't drink any well water. We will travel the King's Highway until we have traveled through your territory." [23] But Sihon would not let Israel travel through his territory. Instead, he gathered his whole army and went out to confront Israel in the wilderness. When he came to Jahaz, he fought against Israel. [24] Israel struck him with the sword and took possession of his land from the Arnon to the Jabbok, but only up to the Ammonite border, because it was fortified.

[25] Israel took all the cities and lived in all these Amorite cities, including Heshbon and all its villages. [26] Heshbon was the city of Sihon king of the Amorites, who had fought against the former king of Moab and had taken control of all his land as far as the Arnon. [27] Therefore the poets say:

> Come to Heshbon, let it be rebuilt;
> let the city of Sihon be restored.
> [28] For fire came out of Heshbon,
> a flame from the city of Sihon.
> It consumed Ar of Moab,
> the lords of Arnon's heights.
> [29] Woe to you, Moab!
> You have been destroyed, people of Chemosh!
> He gave up his sons as refugees,
> and his daughters into captivity
> to Sihon the Amorite king.
> [30] We threw them down;
> Heshbon has been destroyed as far as Dibon.
> We caused desolation as far as Nophah,
> which reaches as far as Medeba.

[31] So Israel lived in the Amorites' land. [32] After Moses

sent spies to Jazer, Israel captured its villages and drove out the Amorites who were there.

³³Then they turned and went up the road to Bashan, and Og king of Bashan came out against them with his whole army to do battle at Edrei. ³⁴But the LORD said to Moses, "Do not fear him, for I have handed him over to you along with his whole army and his land. Do to him as you did to Sihon king of the Amorites, who lived in Heshbon." ³⁵So they struck him, his sons, and his whole army until no one was left, and they took possession of his land.

22 The Israelites traveled on and camped in the plains of Moab near the Jordan across from Jericho. ²Now Balak son of Zippor saw all that Israel had done to the Amorites. ³Moab was terrified of the people because they were numerous, and Moab dreaded the Israelites. ⁴So the Moabites said to the elders of Midian, "This horde will devour everything around us like an ox eats up the green plants in the field."

Since Balak son of Zippor was Moab's king at that time, ⁵he sent messengers to Balaam son of Beor at Pethor, which is by the Euphrates in the land of his people. Balak said to him: "Look, a people has come out of Egypt; they cover the surface of the land and are living right across from me. ⁶Please come and put a curse on these people for me because they are more powerful than I am. I may be able to defeat them and drive them out of the land, for I know that those you bless are blessed and those you curse are cursed."

⁷The elders of Moab and Midian departed with fees for *divination in hand. They came to Balaam and reported Balak's words to him. ⁸He said to them, "Spend the night here, and I will give you the answer the LORD tells me." So the officials of Moab stayed with Balaam.

⁹Then God came to Balaam and asked, "Who are these men with you?"

¹⁰Balaam replied to God, "Balak son of Zippor, king of Moab, sent this message to me: ¹¹'Look, a people has come out of Egypt, and they cover the surface of the land. Now come and put a curse on them for me. I may be able to fight against them and drive them away.'"

¹²Then God said to Balaam, "You are not to go with them. You are not to curse this people, for they are blessed."

¹³So Balaam got up the next morning and said to Balak's officials, "Go back to your land, because the LORD has refused to let me go with you."

¹⁴The officials of Moab arose, returned to Balak, and reported, "Balaam refused to come with us."

¹⁵Balak sent officials again who were more numerous and higher in rank than the others. ¹⁶They came to Balaam and said to him, "This is what Balak son of Zippor says: 'Let nothing keep you from coming to me, ¹⁷for I will greatly honor you and do whatever you ask me. So please come and put a curse on these people for me!'"

¹⁸But Balaam responded to the servants of Balak, "If Balak were to give me his house full of silver and gold, I could not go against the command of the LORD my God to do anything small or great. ¹⁹Please stay here overnight as the others did, so that I may find out what else the LORD has to tell me."

²⁰God came to Balaam at night and said to him, "Since these men have come to summon you, get up and go with them, but you must only do what I tell you." ²¹When he got up in the morning, Balaam saddled his donkey and went with the officials of Moab.

²²But God was incensed that Balaam was going, and the Angel of the LORD took His stand on the path to oppose him. Balaam was riding his donkey, and his two servants were with him. ²³When the donkey saw the Angel of the LORD standing on the path with a drawn sword in His hand, she turned off the path and went into the field. So Balaam hit her to return her to the path. ²⁴Then the Angel of the LORD stood in a narrow passage between the vineyards, with a stone wall on either side. ²⁵The donkey saw the Angel of the LORD and pressed herself against the wall, squeezing Balaam's foot against it. So he hit her once again. ²⁶The Angel of the LORD went ahead and stood in a narrow place where there was no room to turn to the right or the left. ²⁷When the donkey saw the Angel of the LORD, she crouched down under Balaam. So he became furious and beat the donkey with his stick.

²⁸Then the LORD opened the donkey's mouth, and she asked Balaam, "What have I done to you that you have beaten me these three times?"

²⁹Balaam answered the donkey, "You made me look like a fool. If I had a sword in my hand, I'd kill you now!"

³⁰But the donkey said, "Am I not the donkey you've ridden all your life until today? Have I ever treated you this way before?"

"No," he replied.

³¹Then the LORD opened Balaam's eyes, and he saw the Angel of the LORD standing in the path with a drawn sword in His hand. Balaam knelt and bowed with his face to the ground. ³²The Angel of the LORD asked him, "Why have you beaten your donkey these three times? Look, I came out to oppose you, because what you are doing is evil in My sight. ³³The donkey saw Me and turned away from Me these three times. If she had not turned away from Me, I would have killed you by now and let her live."

³⁴Balaam said to the Angel of the LORD, "I have sinned, for I did not know that You were standing in the path to confront me. And now, if it is evil in Your sight, I will go back."

³⁵Then the Angel of the LORD said to Balaam, "Go with the men, but you are to say only what I tell you." So Balaam went with Balak's officials.

³⁶When Balak heard that Balaam was coming, he went out to meet him at the Moabite city on the Arnon border at the edge of his territory. ³⁷Balak asked Balaam, "Did I not send you an urgent summons? Why didn't you come to me? Am I really not able to reward you?"

³⁸Balaam said to him, "Look, I have come to you, but can I say anything I want? I must speak only the message God puts in my mouth." ³⁹So Balaam went with Balak, and they came to Kiriath-huzoth. ⁴⁰Balak sacrificed cattle and sheep, and sent for Balaam and the officials who were with him.

⁴¹In the morning, Balak took Balaam and brought him to Bamoth-baal. From there he saw the outskirts of the people's camp.

23 Then Balaam said to Balak, "Build me seven altars here and prepare seven bulls and seven rams for me." ²So Balak did as Balaam directed, and they offered a bull and a ram on each altar. ³Balaam said to Balak, "Stay here by your *burnt offering while I am gone. Maybe the LORD will meet with me. I will tell you whatever He reveals to me." So he went to a barren hill.

[4] God met with him and Balaam said to Him, "I have arranged seven altars and offered a bull and a ram on each altar." [5] Then the LORD put a message in Balaam's mouth and said, "Return to Balak and say what I tell you."

[6] So he returned to Balak, who was standing there by his burnt offering with all the officials of Moab.

[7] Balaam proclaimed his poem:

> Balak brought me from Aram;
> the king of Moab, from the eastern mountains:
> "Come, put a curse on Jacob for me;
> come, denounce Israel!"
> [8] How can I curse someone God has not cursed?
> How can I denounce someone the LORD
> has not denounced?
> [9] I see them from the top of rocky cliffs,
> and I watch them from the hills.
> There is a people living alone;
> it does not consider itself among the nations.
> [10] Who has counted the dust of Jacob
> or numbered the dust clouds of Israel?
> Let me die the death of the upright;
> let the end of my life be like theirs.

[11] "What have you done to me?" Balak asked Balaam. "I brought you to curse my enemies, but look, you have only blessed them!"

[12] He answered, "Shouldn't I say exactly what the LORD puts in my mouth?"

[13] Then Balak said to him, "Please come with me to another place where you can see them. You will only see the outskirts of their camp; you won't see all of them. From there, put a curse on them for me." [14] So Balak took him to Lookout Field on top of Pisgah, built seven altars, and offered a bull and a ram on each altar.

[15] Balaam said to Balak, "Stay here by your burnt offering while I seek the LORD over there."

[16] The LORD met with Balaam and put a message in his mouth. Then He said, "Return to Balak and say what I tell you."

[17] So he returned to Balak, who was standing there by his burnt offering with the officials of Moab. Balak asked him, "What did the LORD say?"

[18] Balaam proclaimed his poem:

> Balak, get up and listen;
> son of Zippor, pay attention to what I say!
> [19] God is not a man who lies,
> or a son of man who changes His mind.
> Does He speak and not act,
> or promise and not fulfill?
> [20] I have indeed received a command to bless;
> since He has blessed, I cannot change it.
> [21] He considers no disaster for Jacob;
> He sees no trouble for Israel.
> The LORD their God is with them,
> and there is rejoicing over the King
> among them.
> [22] God brought them out of Egypt;
> He is like the horns of a wild ox for them.
> [23] There is no magic curse against Jacob
> and no •divination against Israel.
> It will now be said about Jacob and Israel,
> "What great things God has done!"
> [24] A people rise up like a lioness;
> They rouse themselves like a lion.
> They will not lie down until they devour
> the prey
> and drink the blood of the slain.

[25] Then Balak told Balaam, "Don't curse them and don't bless them!"

[26] But Balaam answered him, "Didn't I tell you: Whatever the LORD says, I must do?"

[27] Again Balak said to Balaam, "Please come. I will take you to another place. Maybe it will be agreeable to God that you can put a curse on them for me there." [28] So Balak took Balaam to the top of Peor, which overlooks the wasteland.

[29] Balaam told Balak, "Build me seven altars here and prepare seven bulls and seven rams for me." [30] So Balak did as Balaam said and offered a bull and a ram on each altar.

24

Since Balaam saw that it pleased the LORD to bless Israel, he did not go to seek omens as on previous occasions, but turned toward the wilderness. [2] When Balaam looked up and saw Israel encamped tribe by tribe, the Spirit of God came on him, [3] and he proclaimed his poem:

> The •oracle of Balaam son of Beor,
> the oracle of the man whose eyes are opened,
> [4] the oracle of one who hears the sayings
> of God,
> who sees a vision from the •Almighty,
> who falls into a trance with his eyes
> uncovered:
> [5] How beautiful are your tents, Jacob,
> your dwellings, Israel.
> [6] They stretch out like river valleys,
> like gardens beside a stream,
> like aloes the LORD has planted,
> like cedars beside the water.
> [7] Water will flow from his buckets,
> and his seed will be by abundant water.
> His king will be greater than Agag,
> and his kingdom will be exalted.
> [8] God brought him out of Egypt;
> He is like the horns of a wild ox for them.
> He will feed on enemy nations
> and gnaw their bones;
> he will strike them with his arrows.
> [9] He crouches, he lies down like a lion
> or a lioness—who dares to rouse him?
> Those who bless you will be blessed,
> and those who curse you will be cursed.

[10] Then Balak became furious with Balaam, struck his hands together, and said to him, "I summoned you to put a curse on my enemies, but instead, you have blessed them these three times. [11] Now go to your home! I said I would reward you richly, but look, the LORD has denied you a reward."

[12] Balaam answered Balak, "Didn't I previously tell the messengers you sent me: [13] If Balak were to give me his house full of silver and gold, I could not go against the LORD's command, to do anything good or bad of my own will? I will say whatever the LORD says. [14] Now I am going back to my people, but first, let me warn you what these people will do to your people in the future."

[15] Then he proclaimed his poem:

> The oracle of Balaam son of Beor,
> the oracle of the man whose eyes are opened;
> [16] the oracle of one who hears the sayings of God
> and has knowledge from the •Most High,
> who sees a vision from the Almighty,
> who falls into a trance with his
> eyes uncovered:
> [17] I see him, but not now;

I perceive him, but not near.
A star will come from Jacob,
and a scepter will arise from Israel.
He will smash the forehead of Moab
and strike down all the Shethites.
¹⁸ Edom will become a possession;
Seir will become a possession of its enemies,
but Israel will be triumphant.
¹⁹ One who comes from Jacob will rule;
he will destroy the city's survivors.
²⁰ Then Balaam saw Amalek and proclaimed his poem:
Amalek was first among the nations,
but his future is destruction.
²¹ Next he saw the Kenites and proclaimed his poem:
Your dwelling place is enduring;
your nest is set in the cliffs.
²² Kain will be destroyed
when Asshur takes you captive.
²³ Once more he proclaimed his poem:
Ah, who can live when God does this?
²⁴ Ships will come from the coast of Kittim;
they will afflict Asshur and Eber,
but they too will come to destruction.
²⁵ Balaam then arose and went back to his homeland, and Balak also went his way.

25 While Israel was staying in the Acacia Grove, the people began to have sexual relations with the women of Moab. ² The women invited them to the sacrifices for their gods, and the people ate and bowed in worship to their gods. ³ So Israel aligned itself with ·Baal of Peor, and the LORD's anger burned against Israel. ⁴ The LORD said to Moses, "Take all the leaders of the people and execute them in broad daylight before the LORD so that His burning anger may turn away from Israel."

⁵ So Moses told Israel's judges, "Kill each of the men who aligned themselves with Baal of Peor."

⁶ An Israelite man came bringing a Midianite woman to his relatives in the sight of Moses and the whole Israelite community while they were weeping at the entrance to the tent of meeting. ⁷ When Phinehas son of Eleazar, son of Aaron the priest, saw this, he got up from the assembly, took a spear in his hand, ⁸ followed the Israelite man into the tent, and drove it through both the Israelite man and the woman—through her belly. Then the plague on the Israelites was stopped, ⁹ but those who died in the plague numbered 24,000.

¹⁰ The LORD spoke to Moses, ¹¹ "Phinehas son of Eleazar, son of Aaron the priest, has turned back My wrath from the Israelites because he was zealous among them with My zeal, so that I did not destroy the Israelites in My zeal. ¹² Therefore declare: I grant him My covenant of peace. ¹³ It will be a covenant of perpetual priesthood for him and his future descendants, because he was zealous for his God and made ·atonement for the Israelites."

¹⁴ The name of the slain Israelite man, who was struck dead with the Midianite woman, was Zimri son of Salu, the leader of a Simeonite ancestral house. ¹⁵ The name of the slain Midianite woman was Cozbi, the daughter of Zur, a tribal head of an ancestral house in Midian.

¹⁶ The LORD told Moses: ¹⁷ "Attack the Midianites and strike them dead. ¹⁸ For they attacked you with the treachery that they used against you in the Peor incident. They did the same in the case involving their sister Cozbi, daughter of the Midianite leader who was killed the day the plague came at Peor."

26 After the plague, the LORD said to Moses and Eleazar son of Aaron the priest, ² "Take a census of the entire Israelite community by their ancestral houses of those 20 years old or more who can serve in Israel's army."

³ So Moses and Eleazar the priest said to them in the plains of Moab by the Jordan across from Jericho, ⁴ "Take a census of those 20 years old or more, as the LORD had commanded Moses and the Israelites who came out of the land of Egypt."

⁵ Reuben was the firstborn of Israel.
Reuben's descendants:
the Hanochite clan from Hanoch;
the Palluite clan from Pallu;
⁶ the Hezronite clan from Hezron;
the Carmite clan from Carmi.
⁷ These were the Reubenite clans,
and their registered men numbered 43,730.
⁸ The son of Pallu was Eliab.
⁹ The sons of Eliab were Nemuel, Dathan, and Abiram.
(It was Dathan and Abiram, chosen by the community, who fought against Moses and Aaron; they and Korah's followers fought against the LORD. ¹⁰ The earth opened its mouth and swallowed them with Korah, when his followers died and the fire consumed 250 men. They serve as a warning sign. ¹¹ The sons of Korah, however, did not die.)
¹² Simeon's descendants by their clans:
the Nemuelite clan from Nemuel;
the Jaminite clan from Jamin;
the Jachinite clan from Jachin;
¹³ the Zerahite clan from Zerah;
the Shaulite clan from Shaul.
¹⁴ These were the Simeonite clans,
numbering 22,200 men.
¹⁵ Gad's descendants by their clans:
the Zephonite clan from Zephon;
the Haggite clan from Haggi;
the Shunite clan from Shuni;
¹⁶ the Oznite clan from Ozni;
the Erite clan from Eri;
¹⁷ the Arodite clan from Arod;
the Arelite clan from Areli.
¹⁸ These were the Gadite clans numbered
by their registered men: 40,500.
¹⁹ Judah's sons included Er and Onan, but they died in the land of Canaan. ²⁰ Judah's descendants by their clans:
the Shelanite clan from Shelah;
the Perezite clan from Perez;
the Zerahite clan from Zerah.
²¹ The descendants of Perez:
the Hezronite clan from Hezron;
the Hamulite clan from Hamul.
²² These were Judah's clans numbered by their registered men: 76,500.
²³ Issachar's descendants by their clans:
the Tolaite clan from Tola;
the Punite clan from Puvah;
²⁴ the Jashubite clan from Jashub;
the Shimronite clan from Shimron.
²⁵ These were Issachar's clans numbered by their registered men: 64,300.

²⁶ Zebulun's descendants by their clans:
the Seredite clan from Sered;
the Elonite clan from Elon;
the Jahleelite clan from Jahleel.
²⁷ These were the Zebulunite clans numbered
by their registered men: 60,500.
²⁸ Joseph's descendants by their clans
from Manasseh and Ephraim:
²⁹ Manasseh's descendants:
the Machirite clan from Machir.
Machir fathered Gilead;
the Gileadite clan from Gilead.
³⁰ These were Gilead's descendants:
the Iezerite clan from Iezer;
the Helekite clan from Helek;
³¹ the Asrielite clan from Asriel;
the Shechemite clan from Shechem;
³² the Shemidaite clan from Shemida;
the Hepherite clan from Hepher;
³³ Zelophehad son of Hepher had no sons—only
daughters. The names of Zelophehad's
daughters were Mahlah, Noah, Hoglah,
Milcah, and Tirzah.
³⁴ These were Manasseh's clans, numbered
by their registered men: 52,700.
³⁵ These were Ephraim's descendants
by their clans:
the Shuthelahite clan from Shuthelah;
the Becherite clan from Becher;
the Tahanite clan from Tahan.
³⁶ These were Shuthelah's descendants:
the Eranite clan from Eran.
³⁷ These were the Ephraimite clans numbered
by their registered men: 32,500.
These were Joseph's descendants
by their clans.
³⁸ Benjamin's descendants by their clans:
the Belaite clan from Bela;
the Ashbelite clan from Ashbel;
the Ahiramite clan from Ahiram;
³⁹ the Shuphamite clan from Shupham;
the Huphamite clan from Hupham.
⁴⁰ Bela's descendants from Ard and Naaman:
the Ardite clan from Ard;
the Naamite clan from Naaman.
⁴¹ These were the Benjaminite clans numbered
by their registered men: 45,600.
⁴² These were Dan's descendants by their clans:
the Shuhamite clan from Shuham.
These were the clans of Dan by their clans.
⁴³ All the Shuhamite clans numbered by their
registered men: 64,400.
⁴⁴ Asher's descendants by their clans:
the Imnite clan from Imnah;
the Ishvite clan from Ishvi;
the Beriite clan from Beriah;
⁴⁵ From Beriah's descendants:
the Heberite clan from Heber;
the Malchielite clan from Malchiel.
⁴⁶ And the name of Asher's daughter was Serah.
⁴⁷ These were the Asherite clans numbered
by their registered men: 53,400.
⁴⁸ Naphtali's descendants by their clans:
the Jahzeelite clan from Jahzeel;
the Gunite clan from Guni;
⁴⁹ the Jezerite clan from Jezer;
the Shillemite clan from Shillem.

⁵⁰ These were the Naphtali clans numbered
by their registered men: 45,400.
⁵¹ These registered Israelite men
numbered 601,730.
⁵² The LORD spoke to Moses, ⁵³ "The land is to be divided among them as an inheritance based on the number of names. ⁵⁴ Increase the inheritance for a large tribe and decrease it for a small one. Each is to be given its inheritance according to those who were registered in it. ⁵⁵ The land must be divided by lot; they will receive an inheritance according to the names of their ancestral tribes. ⁵⁶ Each inheritance will be divided by lot among the larger and smaller tribes."
⁵⁷ These were the Levites registered
by their clans:
the Gershonite clan from Gershon;
the Kohathite clan from Kohath;
the Merarite clan from Merari.
⁵⁸ These were the Levite family groups:
the Libnite clan,
the Hebronite clan,
the Mahlite clan,
the Mushite clan,
and the Korahite clan.
Kohath was the ancestor of Amram. ⁵⁹ The name of Amram's wife was Jochebed, a descendant of Levi, born to Levi in Egypt. She bore to Amram: Aaron, Moses, and their sister Miriam. ⁶⁰ Nadab, Abihu, Eleazar, and Ithamar were born to Aaron, ⁶¹ but Nadab and Abihu died when they presented unauthorized fire before the LORD. ⁶² Those registered were 23,000, every male one month old or more; they were not registered among the other Israelites, because no inheritance was given to them among the Israelites.

⁶³ These were the ones registered by Moses and Eleazar the priest when they registered the Israelites on the plains of Moab by the Jordan across from Jericho. ⁶⁴ But among them there was not one of those who had been registered by Moses and Aaron the priest when they registered the Israelites in the Wilderness of Sinai. ⁶⁵ For the LORD had said to them that they would all die in the wilderness. None of them was left except Caleb son of Jephunneh and Joshua son of Nun.

27 The daughters of Zelophehad approached; Zelophehad was the son of Hepher, son of Gilead, son of Machir, son of Manasseh from the clans of Manasseh, the son of Joseph. These were the names of his daughters: Mahlah, Noah, Hoglah, Milcah, and Tirzah. ² They stood before Moses, Eleazar the priest, the leaders, and the entire community at the entrance to the tent of meeting and said, ³ "Our father died in the wilderness, but he was not among Korah's followers, who gathered together against the LORD. Instead, he died because of his own sin, and he had no sons. ⁴ Why should the name of our father be taken away from his clan? Since he had no son, give us property among our father's brothers."

⁵ Moses brought their case before the LORD, ⁶ and the LORD answered him, ⁷ "What Zelophehad's daughters say is correct. You are to give them hereditary property among their father's brothers and transfer their father's inheritance to them. ⁸ Tell the Israelites: When a man dies without having a son, transfer his inheritance to his daughter. ⁹ If he has no daughter, give his inheritance to his brothers. ¹⁰ If he has no brothers, give his inheritance to his father's brothers. ¹¹ If

his father has no brothers, give his inheritance to the nearest relative of his clan, and he will take possession of it. This is to be a statutory ordinance for the Israelites as the LORD commanded Moses."

¹²Then the LORD said to Moses, "Go up this mountain of the Abarim range and see the land that I have given the Israelites. ¹³After you have seen it, you will also be gathered to your people, as Aaron your brother was. ¹⁴When the community quarreled in the Wilderness of Zin, both of you rebelled against My command to show My holiness in their sight at the waters." Those were the waters of Meribah of Kadesh in the Wilderness of Zin.

¹⁵So Moses appealed to the LORD, ¹⁶"May the LORD, the God of the spirits of all flesh, appoint a man over the community ¹⁷who will go out before them and come back in before them, and who will bring them out and bring them in, so that the LORD's community won't be like sheep without a shepherd."

¹⁸The LORD replied to Moses, "Take Joshua son of Nun, a man who has the Spirit in him, and lay your hands on him. ¹⁹Have him stand before Eleazar the priest and the whole community, and commission him in their sight. ²⁰Confer some of your authority on him so that the entire Israelite community will obey him. ²¹He will stand before Eleazar who will consult the LORD for him with the decision of the *Urim. He and all the Israelites with him, even the entire community, will go out and come back in at his command."

²²Moses did as the LORD commanded him. He took Joshua, had him stand before Eleazar the priest and the entire community, ²³laid his hands on him, and commissioned him, as the LORD had spoken through Moses.

28 The LORD spoke to Moses, ²"Command the Israelites and say to them: Be sure to present to Me at its appointed time My offering and My food as My fire offering, a pleasing aroma to Me. ³And say to them: This is the fire offering you are to present to the LORD:

"Each day present two unblemished year-old male lambs as a regular *burnt offering. ⁴Offer one lamb in the morning and the other lamb at twilight, ⁵along with two quarts of fine flour for a *grain offering mixed with a quart of olive oil from crushed olives. ⁶It is a regular burnt offering established at Mount Sinai for a pleasing aroma, a fire offering to the LORD. ⁷The *drink offering is to be a quart with each lamb. Pour out the offering of beer to the LORD in the sanctuary area. ⁸Offer the second lamb at twilight, along with the same kind of grain offering and drink offering as in the morning. It is a fire offering, a pleasing aroma to the LORD.

⁹"On the Sabbath day present two unblemished year-old male lambs, four quarts of fine flour mixed with oil as a grain offering, and its drink offering. ¹⁰It is the burnt offering for every Sabbath, in addition to the regular burnt offering and its drink offering.

¹¹"At the beginning of each of your months present a burnt offering to the LORD: two young bulls, one ram, seven male lambs a year old—all unblemished— ¹²with six quarts of fine flour mixed with oil as a grain offering for each bull, four quarts of fine flour mixed with oil as a grain offering for the ram, ¹³and two quarts of fine flour mixed with oil as a grain offering for each lamb. It is a burnt offering, a pleasing aroma, a fire offering to the LORD. ¹⁴Their drink offerings are to be two quarts of wine with each bull, one

and a third quarts with the ram, and one quart with each male lamb. This is the monthly burnt offering for all the months of the year. ¹⁵And one male goat is to be offered as a *sin offering to the LORD, in addition to the regular burnt offering with its drink offering.

¹⁶"The *Passover to the LORD comes in the first month, on the fourteenth day of the month. ¹⁷On the fifteenth day of this month there will be a festival; unleavened bread is to be eaten for seven days. ¹⁸On the first day there is to be a sacred assembly; you are not to do any daily work. ¹⁹Present a fire offering, a burnt offering to the LORD: two young bulls, one ram, and seven male lambs a year old. Your animals are to be unblemished. ²⁰The grain offering with them is to be of fine flour mixed with oil; offer six quarts with each bull and four quarts with the ram. ²¹Offer two quarts with each of the seven lambs ²²and one male goat for a sin offering to make *atonement for yourselves. ²³Offer these with the morning burnt offering that is part of the regular burnt offering. ²⁴You are to offer the same food each day for seven days as a fire offering, a pleasing aroma to the LORD. It is to be offered with its drink offering and the regular burnt offering. ²⁵On the seventh day you are to hold a sacred assembly; you are not to do any daily work.

²⁶"On the day of *firstfruits, you are to hold a sacred assembly when you present an offering of new grain to the LORD at your Festival of Weeks; you are not to do any daily work. ²⁷Present a burnt offering for a pleasing aroma to the LORD: two young bulls, one ram, and seven male lambs a year old, ²⁸with their grain offering of fine flour mixed with oil, six quarts with each bull, four quarts with the ram, ²⁹and two quarts with each of the seven lambs, ³⁰and one male goat to make atonement for yourselves. ³¹Offer them with their drink offerings in addition to the regular burnt offering and its grain offering. Your animals are to be unblemished.

29 "You are to hold a sacred assembly in the seventh month, on the first day of the month, and you are not to do any daily work. This will be a day of joyful shouting for you. ²Offer a *burnt offering as a pleasing aroma to the LORD: one young bull, one ram, seven male lambs a year old—all unblemished— ³with their *grain offering of fine flour mixed with oil, six quarts with the bull, four quarts with the ram, ⁴and two quarts with each of the seven male lambs. ⁵Also offer one male goat as a *sin offering to make *atonement for yourselves. ⁶These are in addition to the monthly and regular burnt offerings with their prescribed grain offerings and *drink offerings. They are a pleasing aroma, a fire offering to the LORD.

⁷"You are to hold a sacred assembly on the tenth day of this seventh month and practice self-denial; you must not do any work. ⁸Present a burnt offering to the LORD, a pleasing aroma: one young bull, one ram, and seven male lambs a year old. All your animals are to be unblemished. ⁹Their grain offering is to be of fine flour mixed with oil, six quarts with the bull, four quarts with the ram, ¹⁰and two quarts with each of the seven lambs. ¹¹Offer one male goat for a sin offering. The regular burnt offering with its grain offering and drink offerings are in addition to the sin offering of atonement.

¹²"You are to hold a sacred assembly on the fifteenth day of the seventh month; you must not do any daily work. You are to celebrate a seven-day festival for the

Lord. [13] Present a burnt offering, a fire offering as a pleasing aroma to the Lord: 13 young bulls, two rams, and 14 male lambs a year old. They are to be unblemished. [14] Their grain offering is to be of fine flour mixed with oil, six quarts with each of the 13 bulls, four quarts with each of the two rams, [15] and two quarts with each of the 14 lambs. [16] Also offer one male goat as a sin offering. These are in addition to the regular burnt offering with its grain and drink offerings.

[17] "On the second day present 12 young bulls, two rams, and 14 male lambs a year old—all unblemished— [18] with their grain and drink offerings for the bulls, rams, and lambs, in proportion to their number. [19] Also offer one male goat as a sin offering. These are in addition to the regular burnt offering with its grain and drink offerings.

[20] "On the third day present 11 bulls, two rams, 14 male lambs a year old—all unblemished— [21] with their grain and drink offerings for the bulls, rams, and lambs, in proportion to their number. [22] Also offer one male goat as a sin offering. These are in addition to the regular burnt offering with its grain and drink offerings.

[23] "On the fourth day present 10 bulls, two rams, 14 male lambs a year old—all unblemished— [24] with their grain and drink offerings for the bulls, rams, and lambs, in proportion to their number. [25] Also offer one male goat as a sin offering. These are in addition to the regular burnt offering with its grain and drink offerings.

[26] "On the fifth day present nine bulls, two rams, 14 male lambs a year old—all unblemished— [27] with their grain and drink offerings for the bulls, rams, and lambs, in proportion to their number. [28] Also offer one male goat as a sin offering. These are in addition to the regular burnt offering with its grain and drink offerings.

[29] "On the sixth day present eight bulls, two rams, 14 male lambs a year old—all unblemished— [30] with their grain and drink offerings for the bulls, rams, and lambs, in proportion to their number. [31] Also offer one male goat as a sin offering. These are in addition to the regular burnt offering with its grain and drink offerings.

[32] "On the seventh day present seven bulls, two rams, and 14 male lambs a year old—all unblemished— [33] with their grain and drink offerings for the bulls, rams, and lambs, in proportion to their number. [34] Also offer one male goat as a sin offering. These are in addition to the regular burnt offering with its grain and drink offerings.

[35] "On the eighth day you are to hold a solemn assembly; you are not to do any daily work. [36] Present a burnt offering, a fire offering as a pleasing aroma to the Lord: one bull, one ram, seven male lambs a year old—all unblemished— [37] with their grain and drink offerings for the bulls, rams, and lambs, in proportion to their number. [38] Also offer one male goat as a sin offering. These are in addition to the regular burnt offering with its grain and drink offerings.

[39] "You must offer these to the Lord at your appointed times in addition to your vow and freewill offerings, whether burnt, grain, drink, or 'fellowship offerings." [40] So Moses told the Israelites everything the Lord had commanded him.

30 Moses told the leaders of the Israelite tribes, "This is what the Lord has commanded: [2] When a man makes a vow to the Lord or swears an oath to put himself under an obligation, he must not break his word; he must do whatever he has promised.

[3] "When a woman in her father's house during her youth makes a vow to the Lord or puts herself under an obligation, [4] and her father hears about her vow or the obligation she put herself under, and he says nothing to her, all her vows and every obligation she put herself under are binding. [5] But if her father prohibits her on the day he hears about it, none of her vows and none of the obligations she put herself under are binding. The Lord will absolve her because her father has prohibited her.

[6] "If a woman marries while her vows or the rash commitment she herself made are binding, [7] and her husband hears about it and says nothing to her when he finds out, her vows are binding, and the obligations she put herself under are binding. [8] But if her husband prohibits her when he hears about it, he will cancel her vow that is binding or the rash commitment she herself made, and the Lord will forgive her.

[9] "Every vow a widow or divorced woman puts herself under is binding on her.

[10] "If a woman in her husband's house has made a vow or put herself under an obligation with an oath, [11] and her husband hears about it, says nothing to her, and does not prohibit her, all her vows are binding, and every obligation she put herself under is binding. [12] But if her husband cancels them on the day he hears about it, nothing that came from her lips, whether her vows or her obligation, is binding. Her husband has canceled them, and the Lord will absolve her. [13] Her husband may confirm or cancel any vow or any sworn obligation to deny herself. [14] If her husband says nothing at all to her from day to day, he confirms all her vows and obligations, which are binding. He has confirmed them because he said nothing to her when he heard about them. [15] But if he cancels them after he hears about them, he will be responsible for her commitment."

[16] These are the statutes that the Lord commanded Moses concerning the relationship between a man and his wife, or between a father and his daughter in his house during her youth.

31 The Lord spoke to Moses, [2] "Execute vengeance for the Israelites against the Midianites. After that, you will be gathered to your people."

[3] So Moses spoke to the people, "Equip some of your men for war. They will go against Midian to inflict the Lord's vengeance on them. [4] Send 1,000 men to war from each Israelite tribe." [5] So 1,000 were recruited from each Israelite tribe out of the thousands in Israel—12,000 equipped for war. [6] Moses sent 1,000 from each tribe to war. They went with Phinehas son of Eleazar the priest, in whose care were the holy objects and signal trumpets.

[7] They waged war against Midian, as the Lord had commanded Moses, and killed every male. [8] Along with the others slain by them, they killed the Midianite kings—Evi, Rekem, Zur, Hur, and Reba, the five kings of Midian. They also killed Balaam son of Beor with the sword. [9] The Israelites took the Midianite women and their children captive, and they plundered all their cattle, flocks, and property. [10] Then they burned all the cities where the Midianites lived, as well as all their

encampments, [11] and took away all the spoils of war and the captives, both man and beast. [12] They brought the prisoners, animals, and spoils of war to Moses, Eleazar the priest, and the Israelite community at the camp on the plains of Moab by the Jordan across from Jericho.

[13] Moses, Eleazar the priest, and all the leaders of the community went to meet them outside the camp. [14] But Moses became furious with the officers, the commanders of thousands and commanders of hundreds, who were returning from the military campaign. [15] "Have you let every female live?" he asked them. [16] "Yet they are the ones who, at Balaam's advice, incited the Israelites to unfaithfulness against the Lord in the Peor incident, so that the plague came against the Lord's community. [17] So now, kill all the male children and kill every woman who has had sexual relations with a man, [18] but keep alive for yourselves all the young females who have not had sexual relations.

[19] "You are to remain outside the camp for seven days. All of you and your prisoners who have killed a person or touched the dead are to purify yourselves on the third day and the seventh day. [20] Also purify everything: garments, leather goods, things made of goat hair, and every article of wood."

[21] Then Eleazar the priest said to the soldiers who had gone to battle, "This is the legal statute the Lord commanded Moses: [22] Only the gold, silver, bronze, iron, tin, and lead— [23] everything that can withstand fire—you are to pass through fire, and it will be ·clean. It must still be purified with the purification water. Anything that cannot withstand fire, pass through the water. [24] On the seventh day wash your clothes, and you will be clean. After that you may enter the camp."

[25] The Lord told Moses, [26] "You, Eleazar the priest, and the family leaders of the community are to take a count of what was captured, man and beast. [27] Then divide the captives between the troops who went out to war and the entire community. [28] Set aside a tribute for the Lord from what belongs to the fighting men who went out to war: one out of every 500 humans, cattle, donkeys, sheep, and goats. [29] Take the tribute from their half and give it to Eleazar the priest as a contribution to the Lord. [30] From the Israelites' half, take one out of every 50 from the people, cattle, donkeys, sheep, and goats, all the livestock, and give them to the Levites who perform the duties of the Lord's tabernacle."

[31] So Moses and Eleazar the priest did as the Lord commanded Moses. [32] The captives remaining from the plunder the army had taken totaled:

675,000 sheep and goats,
[33] 72,000 cattle,
[34] 61,000 donkeys,
[35] and 32,000 people, all the females
    who had not had sexual relations
    with a man.

[36] The half portion for those who went out to war numbered:

337,500 sheep and goats,
[37] and the tribute to the Lord was 675
    from the sheep and goats;
[38] from the 36,000 cattle,
    the tribute to the Lord was 72;
[39] from the 30,500 donkeys,
    the tribute to the Lord was 61;
[40] and from the 16,000 people,
    the tribute to the Lord was 32 people.

[41] Moses gave the tribute to Eleazar the priest as a contribution for the Lord, as the Lord had commanded Moses.

[42] From the Israelites' half, which Moses separated from the men who fought, [43] the community's half was:

337,500 sheep and goats,
[44] 36,000 cattle,
[45] 30,500 donkeys,
[46] and 16,000 people.

[47] Moses took one out of every 50, selected from the people and the livestock of the Israelites' half. He gave them to the Levites who perform the duties of the Lord's tabernacle, as the Lord had commanded him.

[48] The officers who were over the thousands of the army, the commanders of thousands and of hundreds, approached Moses [49] and told him, "Your servants have taken a census of the fighting men under our command, and not one of us is missing. [50] So we have presented to the Lord an offering of the gold articles each man found—armlets, bracelets, rings, earrings, and necklaces—to make ·atonement for ourselves before the Lord."

[51] Moses and Eleazar the priest received from them all the articles made out of gold. [52] All the gold of the contribution they offered to the Lord, from the commanders of thousands and of hundreds, was 420 pounds. [53] Each of the soldiers had taken plunder for himself. [54] Moses and Eleazar the priest received the gold from the commanders of thousands and of hundreds and brought it into the tent of meeting as a memorial for the Israelites before the Lord.

32 The Reubenites and Gadites had a very large number of livestock. When they surveyed the lands of Jazer and Gilead, they saw that the region was a good one for livestock. [2] So the Gadites and Reubenites came to Moses, Eleazar the priest, and the leaders of the community and said: [3] "The territory of Ataroth, Dibon, Jazer, Nimrah, Heshbon, Elealeh, Sebam, Nebo, and Beon, [4] which the Lord struck down before the community of Israel, is good land for livestock, and your servants own livestock." [5] They said, "If we have found favor in your sight, let this land be given to your servants as a possession. Don't make us cross the Jordan."

[6] But Moses asked the Gadites and Reubenites, "Should your brothers go to war while you stay here? [7] Why are you discouraging the Israelites from crossing into the land the Lord has given them? [8] That's what your fathers did when I sent them from Kadesh-barnea to see the land. [9] After they went up as far as Eshcol Valley and saw the land, they discouraged the Israelites from entering the land the Lord had given them. [10] So the Lord's anger burned that day, and He swore an oath: [11] 'Because they did not follow Me completely, none of the men 20 years old or more who came up from Egypt will see the land I swore to give Abraham, Isaac, and Jacob— [12] none except Caleb son of Jephunneh the Kenizzite and Joshua son of Nun, because they did follow the Lord completely.' [13] The Lord's anger burned against Israel, and He made them wander in the wilderness 40 years until the whole generation that had done what was evil in the Lord's sight was gone. [14] And here you, a brood of sinners, stand in your fathers' place adding even more to the Lord's burning anger against Israel. [15] If you turn back from following Him, He will once again leave this people in the wilderness, and you will destroy all of them."

[16] Then they approached him and said, "We want

to build sheepfolds here for our livestock and cities for our dependents. ¹⁷But we will arm ourselves and be ready to go ahead of the Israelites until we have brought them into their place. Meanwhile, our dependents will remain in the fortified cities because of the inhabitants of the land. ¹⁸We will not return to our homes until each of the Israelites has taken possession of his inheritance. ¹⁹Yet we will not have an inheritance with them across the Jordan and beyond, because our inheritance will be across the Jordan to the east."

²⁰Moses replied to them, "If you do this—if you arm yourselves for battle before the Lord, ²¹and every one of your armed men crosses the Jordan before the Lord until He has driven His enemies from His presence, ²²and the land is subdued before the Lord—afterward you may return and be free from obligation to the Lord and to Israel. And this land will belong to you as a possession before the Lord. ²³But if you don't do this, you will certainly sin against the Lord; be sure your sin will catch up with you. ²⁴Build cities for your dependents and folds for your flocks, but do what you have promised."

²⁵The Gadites and Reubenites answered Moses, "Your servants will do just as my lord commands. ²⁶Our little children, wives, livestock, and all our animals will remain here in the cities of Gilead, ²⁷but your servants are equipped for war before the Lord and will go across to the battle as my lord orders."

²⁸So Moses gave orders about them to Eleazar the priest, Joshua son of Nun, and the family leaders of the Israelite tribes. ²⁹Moses told them, "If the Gadites and Reubenites cross the Jordan with you, every man in battle formation before the Lord, and the land is subdued before you, you are to give them the land of Gilead as a possession. ³⁰But if they don't go across with you in battle formation, they must accept land in Canaan with you."

³¹The Gadites and Reubenites replied, "What the Lord has spoken to your servants is what we will do. ³²We will cross over in battle formation before the Lord into the land of Canaan, but we will keep our hereditary possession across the Jordan."

³³So Moses gave them—the Gadites, Reubenites, and half the tribe of Manasseh son of Joseph—the kingdom of Sihon king of the Amorites and the kingdom of Og king of Bashan, the land including its cities with the territories surrounding them. ³⁴The Gadites rebuilt Dibon, Ataroth, Aroer, ³⁵Atroth-shophan, Jazer, Jogbehah, ³⁶Beth-nimrah, and Beth-haran as fortified cities, and built sheepfolds. ³⁷The Reubenites rebuilt Heshbon, Elealeh, Kiriathaim, ³⁸as well as Nebo and Baal-meon (whose names were changed), and Sibmah. They gave names to the cities they rebuilt.

³⁹The descendants of Machir son of Manasseh went to Gilead, captured it, and drove out the Amorites who were there. ⁴⁰So Moses gave Gilead to the clan of Machir son of Manasseh, and they settled in it. ⁴¹Jair, a descendant of Manasseh, went and captured their villages, which he renamed Jair's Villages. ⁴²Nobah went and captured Kenath with its villages and called it Nobah after his own name.

33 These were the stages of the Israelites' journey when they went out of the land of Egypt by their military divisions under the leadership of Moses and Aaron. ²At the Lord's command, Moses wrote down the starting points for the stages of their journey; these are the stages listed by their starting points:

³They departed from Rameses in the first month, on the fifteenth day of the month. On the day after the *Passover the Israelites went out triumphantly in the sight of all the Egyptians. ⁴Meanwhile, the Egyptians were burying every firstborn male the Lord had struck down among them, for the Lord had executed judgment against their gods. ⁵The Israelites departed from Rameses and camped at Succoth.

⁶They departed from Succoth and camped at Etham, which is on the edge of the wilderness. ⁷They departed from Etham and turned back to Pi-hahiroth, which faces Baal-zephon, and they camped before Migdol.

⁸They departed from Pi-hahiroth and crossed through the middle of the sea into the wilderness. They took a three-day journey into the Wilderness of Etham and camped at Marah.

⁹They departed from Marah and came to Elim. There were 12 springs of water and 70 date palms at Elim, so they camped there.

¹⁰They departed from Elim and camped by the *Red Sea.

¹¹They departed from the Red Sea and camped in the Wilderness of Sin.

¹²They departed from the Wilderness of Sin and camped in Dophkah.

¹³They departed from Dophkah and camped at Alush.

¹⁴They departed from Alush and camped at Rephidim, where there was no water for the people to drink.

¹⁵They departed from Rephidim and camped in the Wilderness of Sinai.

¹⁶They departed from the Wilderness of Sinai and camped at Kibroth-hattaavah.

¹⁷They departed from Kibroth-hattaavah and camped at Hazeroth.

¹⁸They departed from Hazeroth and camped at Rithmah.

¹⁹They departed from Rithmah and camped at Rimmon-perez.

²⁰They departed from Rimmon-perez and camped at Libnah.

²¹They departed from Libnah and camped at Rissah.

²²They departed from Rissah and camped at Kehelathah.

²³They departed from Kehelathah and camped at Mount Shepher.

²⁴They departed from Mount Shepher and camped at Haradah.

²⁵They departed from Haradah and camped at Makheloth.

²⁶They departed from Makheloth and camped at Tahath.

²⁷They departed from Tahath and camped at Terah.

²⁸They departed from Terah and camped at Mithkah.

²⁹They departed from Mithkah and camped at Hashmonah.

³⁰They departed from Hashmonah and camped at Moseroth.
³¹They departed from Moseroth and camped at Bene-jaakan.
³²They departed from Bene-jaakan and camped at Hor-haggidgad.
³³They departed from Hor-haggidgad and camped at Jotbathah.
³⁴They departed from Jotbathah and camped at Abronah.
³⁵They departed from Abronah and camped at Ezion-geber.
³⁶They departed from Ezion-geber and camped in the Wilderness of Zin (that is, Kadesh).
³⁷They departed from Kadesh and camped at Mount Hor on the edge of the land of Edom.
³⁸At the Lord's command, Aaron the priest climbed Mount Hor and died there on the first day of the fifth month in the fortieth year after the Israelites went out of the land of Egypt.
³⁹Aaron was 123 years old when he died on Mount Hor. ⁴⁰At that time the Canaanite king of Arad, who lived in the *Negev in the land of Canaan, heard the Israelites were coming.
⁴¹They departed from Mount Hor and camped at Zalmonah.
⁴²They departed from Zalmonah and camped at Punon.
⁴³They departed from Punon and camped at Oboth.
⁴⁴They departed from Oboth and camped at Iye-abarim on the border of Moab.
⁴⁵They departed from Iyim and camped at Dibon-gad.
⁴⁶They departed from Dibon-gad and camped at Almon-diblathaim.
⁴⁷They departed from Almon-diblathaim and camped in the Abarim range facing Nebo.
⁴⁸They departed from the Abarim range and camped on the plains of Moab by the Jordan across from Jericho. ⁴⁹They camped by the Jordan from Beth-jeshimoth to the Acacia Meadow on the plains of Moab.

⁵⁰The Lord spoke to Moses in the plains of Moab by the Jordan across from Jericho, ⁵¹"Tell the Israelites: When you cross the Jordan into the land of Canaan, ⁵²you must drive out all the inhabitants of the land before you, destroy all their stone images and cast images, and demolish all their *high places. ⁵³You are to take possession of the land and settle in it because I have given you the land to possess. ⁵⁴You are to receive the land as an inheritance by lot according to your clans. Increase the inheritance for a large clan and decrease it for a small one. Whatever place the lot indicates for someone will be his. You will receive an inheritance according to your ancestral tribes. ⁵⁵But if you don't drive out the inhabitants of the land before you, those you allow to remain will become thorns in your eyes and in your sides; they will harass you in the land where you will live. ⁵⁶And what I had planned to do to them, I will do to you."

34 The Lord spoke to Moses, ²"Command the Israelites and say to them: When you enter the land of Canaan, it will be allotted to you as an inheritance with these borders:
³Your southern side will be from the Wilderness

of Zin along the boundary of Edom. Your southern border on the east will begin at the east end of the Dead Sea. ⁴Your border will turn south of the Ascent of Akrabbim, proceed to Zin, and end south of Kadesh-barnea. It will go to Hazar-addar and proceed to Azmon. ⁵The border will turn from Azmon to the Brook of Egypt, where it will end at the Mediterranean Sea.
⁶Your western border will be the coastline of the Mediterranean Sea; this will be your western border.
⁷This will be your northern border: From the Mediterranean Sea draw a line to Mount Hor; ⁸from Mount Hor draw a line to the entrance of Hamath, and the border will reach Zedad. ⁹Then the border will go to Ziphron and end at Hazar-enan. This will be your northern border.
¹⁰For your eastern border, draw a line from Hazar-enan to Shepham. ¹¹The border will go down from Shepham to Riblah east of Ain. It will continue down and reach the eastern slope of the Sea of Chinnereth. ¹²Then the border will go down to the Jordan and end at the Dead Sea. This will be your land defined by its borders on all sides."

¹³So Moses commanded the Israelites, "This is the land you are to receive by lot as an inheritance, which the Lord commanded to be given to the nine and a half tribes. ¹⁴For the tribe of the Reubenites and the tribe of the Gadites have received their inheritance according to their ancestral houses, and half the tribe of Manasseh has received its inheritance. ¹⁵The two and a half tribes have received their inheritance across the Jordan from Jericho, eastward toward the sunrise."

¹⁶The Lord spoke to Moses, ¹⁷"These are the names of the men who are to distribute the land as an inheritance for you: Eleazar the priest and Joshua son of Nun. ¹⁸Take one leader from each tribe to distribute the land. ¹⁹These are the names of the men:
Caleb son of Jephunneh from the tribe of Judah;
²⁰Shemuel son of Ammihud from the tribe of Simeon;
²¹Elidad son of Chislon from the tribe of Benjamin;
²²Bukki son of Jogli, a leader from the tribe of Dan;
²³from the sons of Joseph:
Hanniel son of Ephod, a leader from the tribe of Manasseh,
²⁴Kemuel son of Shiphtan, a leader from the tribe of Ephraim;
²⁵Eli-zaphan son of Parnach, a leader from the tribe of Zebulun;
²⁶Paltiel son of Azzan, a leader from the tribe of Issachar;
²⁷Ahihud son of Shelomi, a leader from the tribe of Asher;
²⁸Pedahel son of Ammihud, a leader from the tribe of Naphtali."
²⁹These are the ones the Lord commanded to distribute the inheritance to the Israelites in the land of Canaan.

35 The Lord again spoke to Moses in the plains of Moab by the Jordan across from Jericho: ²"Command the Israelites to give cities out of their hereditary property for the Levites to live in and pas-

tureland around the cities. ³The cities will be for them to live in, and their pasturelands will be for their herds, flocks, and all their other animals. ⁴The pasturelands of the cities you are to give the Levites will extend from the city wall 500 yards on every side. ⁵Measure 1,000 yards outside the city for the east side, 1,000 yards for the south side, 1,000 yards for the west side, and 1,000 yards for the north side, with the city in the center. This will belong to them as pasturelands for the cities.

⁶"The cities you give the Levites will include six cities of refuge, which you must provide so that the one who kills someone may flee there; in addition to these, give 42 other cities. ⁷The total number of cities you give the Levites will be 48, along with their pasturelands. ⁸Of the cities that you give from the Israelites' territory, you should take more from a larger tribe and less from a smaller one. Each tribe is to give some of its cities to the Levites in proportion to the inheritance it receives."

⁹The Lᴏʀᴅ said to Moses, ¹⁰"Speak to the Israelites and tell them: When you cross the Jordan into the land of Canaan, ¹¹designate cities to serve as cities of refuge for you, so that a person who kills someone unintentionally may flee there. ¹²You will have the cities as a refuge from the avenger, so that the one who kills someone will not die until he stands trial before the assembly. ¹³The cities you select will be your six cities of refuge. ¹⁴Select three cities across the Jordan and three cities in the land of Canaan to be cities of refuge. ¹⁵These six cities will serve as a refuge for the Israelites and for the foreigner or temporary resident among them, so that anyone who kills a person unintentionally may flee there.

¹⁶"If anyone strikes a person with an iron object and death results, he is a murderer; the murderer must be put to death. ¹⁷If a man has in his hand a stone capable of causing death and strikes another person and he dies, the murderer must be put to death. ¹⁸If a man has in his hand a wooden object capable of causing death and strikes another person and he dies, the murderer must be put to death. ¹⁹The avenger of blood himself is to kill the murderer; when he finds him, he is to kill him. ²⁰Likewise, if anyone in hatred pushes a person or throws an object at him with malicious intent and he dies, ²¹or if in hostility he strikes him with his hand and he dies, the one who struck him must be put to death; he is a murderer. The avenger of blood is to kill the murderer when he finds him.

²²"But if anyone suddenly pushes a person without hostility or throws any object at him without malicious intent ²³or without looking drops a stone that could kill a person and he dies, but he was not his enemy and wasn't trying to harm him, ²⁴the assembly is to judge between the slayer and the avenger of blood according to these ordinances. ²⁵The assembly is to protect the one who kills someone from the hand of the avenger of blood. Then the assembly will return him to the city of refuge he fled to, and he must live there until the death of the high priest who was anointed with the holy oil.

²⁶"If the one who kills someone ever goes outside the border of the city of refuge he fled to, ²⁷and the avenger of blood finds him outside the border of his city of refuge and kills him, the avenger will not be

*guilty of bloodshed, ²⁸for the one who killed a person was supposed to live in his city of refuge until the death of the high priest. Only after the death of the high priest may the one who has killed a person return to the land he possesses. ²⁹These instructions will be a statutory ordinance for you throughout your generations wherever you live.

³⁰"If anyone kills a person, the murderer is to be put to death based on the word of witnesses. But no one is to be put to death based on the testimony of one witness. ³¹You are not to accept a ransom for the life of a murderer who is guilty of killing someone; he must be put to death. ³²Neither should you accept a ransom for the person who flees to his city of refuge, allowing him to return and live in the land before the death of the high priest.

³³"Do not defile the land where you are, for bloodshed defiles the land, and there can be no *atonement for the land because of the blood that is shed on it, except by the blood of the person who shed it. ³⁴Do not make the land *unclean where you live and where I reside; for I, *Yahweh, reside among the Israelites."

36 The family leaders from the clan of the descendants of Gilead—the son of Machir, son of Manasseh—who were from the clans of the sons of Joseph, approached and addressed Moses and the leaders who were over the Israelite families. ²They said, "*Yahweh commanded my lord to give the land as an inheritance by lot to the Israelites. My lord was further commanded by Yahweh to give our brother Zelophehad's inheritance to his daughters. ³If they marry any of the men from the other Israelite tribes, their inheritance will be taken away from our fathers' inheritance and added to that of the tribe into which they marry. Therefore, part of our allotted inheritance would be taken away. ⁴When the Jubilee comes for the Israelites, their inheritance will be added to that of the tribe into which they marry, and their inheritance will be taken away from the inheritance of our ancestral tribe."

⁵So Moses commanded the Israelites at the word of the Lᴏʀᴅ, "What the tribe of Joseph's descendants says is right. ⁶This is what the Lᴏʀᴅ has commanded concerning Zelophehad's daughters: They may marry anyone they like provided they marry within a clan of their ancestral tribe. ⁷An inheritance belonging to the Israelites must not transfer from tribe to tribe, because each of the Israelites is to retain the inheritance of his ancestral tribe. ⁸Any daughter who possesses an inheritance from an Israelite tribe must marry someone from the clan of her ancestral tribe, so that each of the Israelites will possess the inheritance of his fathers. ⁹No inheritance is to transfer from one tribe to another, because each of the Israelite tribes is to retain its inheritance."

¹⁰The daughters of Zelophehad did as the Lᴏʀᴅ commanded Moses. ¹¹Mahlah, Tirzah, Hoglah, Milcah, and Noah, the daughters of Zelophehad, married cousins on their father's side. ¹²They married men from the clans of the descendants of Manasseh son of Joseph, and their inheritance remained within the tribe of their father's clan.

¹³These are the commands and ordinances the Lᴏʀᴅ commanded the Israelites through Moses in the plains of Moab by the Jordan across from Jericho.

DEUTERONOMY

1 These are the words Moses spoke to all Israel across the Jordan in the wilderness, in the *Arabah opposite Suph, between Paran and Tophel, Laban, Hazeroth, and Di-zahab. [2] It is an eleven-day journey from Horeb to Kadesh-barnea by way of Mount Seir. [3] In the fortieth year, in the eleventh month, on the first of the month, Moses told the Israelites everything the LORD had commanded him to say to them. [4] This was after he had defeated Sihon king of the Amorites, who lived in Heshbon, and Og king of Bashan, who lived in Ashtaroth, at Edrei. [5] Across the Jordan in the land of Moab, Moses began to explain this law, saying:

[6] "The LORD our God spoke to us at Horeb: 'You have stayed at this mountain long enough. [7] Resume your journey and go to the hill country of the Amorites and their neighbors in the Arabah, the hill country, the Judean foothills, the *Negev and the sea coast—to the land of the Canaanites and to Lebanon as far as the Euphrates River. [8] See, I have set the land before you. Enter and take possession of the land the LORD swore to give to your fathers Abraham, Isaac, and Jacob and their future descendants.'

[9] "I said to you at that time: I can't bear the responsibility for you on my own. [10] The LORD your God has so multiplied you that today you are as numerous as the stars of the sky. [11] May *Yahweh, the God of your fathers, increase you a thousand times more, and bless you as He promised you. [12] But how can I bear your troubles, burdens, and disputes by myself? [13] Appoint for yourselves wise, understanding, and respected men from each of your tribes, and I will make them your leaders.

[14] "You replied to me, 'What you propose to do is good.'

[15] "So I took the leaders of your tribes, wise and respected men, and set them over you as leaders: officials for thousands, hundreds, fifties, and tens, and officers for your tribes. [16] I commanded your judges at that time: Hear the cases between your brothers, and judge rightly between a man and his brother or a foreign resident. [17] Do not show partiality when deciding a case; listen to small and great alike. Do not be intimidated by anyone, for judgment belongs to God. Bring me any case too difficult for you, and I will hear it. [18] At that time I commanded you about all the things you were to do.

[19] "We then set out from Horeb and went across all the great and terrible wilderness you saw on the way to the hill country of the Amorites, just as the LORD our God had commanded us. When we reached Kadesh-barnea, [20] I said to you: You have reached the hill country of the Amorites, which the LORD our God is giving us. [21] See, the LORD your God has set the land before you. Go up and take possession of it as Yahweh, the God of your fathers, has told you. Do not be afraid or discouraged.

[22] "Then all of you approached me and said, 'Let's send men ahead of us, so that they may explore the land for us and bring us back a report about the route we should go up and the cities we will come to.' [23] The plan seemed good to me, so I selected 12 men from among you, one man for each tribe. [24] They left and went up into the hill country and came to the Valley of Eshcol, scouting the land. [25] They took some of the fruit from the land in their hands, carried it down to us, and brought us back a report: 'The land the LORD our God is giving us is good.'

[26] "But you were not willing to go up, rebelling against the command of the LORD your God. [27] You grumbled in your tents and said, 'The LORD brought us out of the land of Egypt to deliver us into the hands of the Amorites so they would destroy us, because He hated us. [28] Where can we go? Our brothers have discouraged us, saying: The people are larger and taller than we are; the cities are large, fortified to the heavens. We also saw the descendants of the Anakim there.'

[29] "So I said to you: Don't be terrified or afraid of them! [30] The LORD your God who goes before you will fight for you, just as you saw Him do for you in Egypt. [31] And you saw in the wilderness how the LORD your God carried you as a man carries his son all along the way you traveled until you reached this place. [32] But in spite of this you did not trust the LORD your God, [33] who went before you on the journey to seek out a place for you to camp. He went in the fire by night and in the cloud by day to guide you on the road you were to travel.

[34] "When the LORD heard your words, He grew angry and swore an oath: [35] 'None of these men in this evil generation will see the good land I swore to give your fathers, [36] except Caleb the son of Jephunneh. He will see it, and I will give him and his descendants the land on which he has set foot, because he followed the LORD completely.'

[37] "The LORD was angry with me also because of you and said: 'You will not enter there either. [38] Joshua son of Nun, who attends you, will enter it. Encourage him, for he will enable Israel to inherit it. [39] Your little children, whom you said would be plunder, your sons who don't know good from evil, will enter there. I will give them the land, and they will take possession of it. [40] But you are to turn back and head for the wilderness by way of the *Red Sea.'

[41] "You answered me, 'We have sinned against the LORD. We will go up and fight just as the LORD our God commanded us.' Then each of you put on his weapons of war and thought it would be easy to go up into the hill country.

[42] "But the LORD said to me, 'Tell them: Don't go up and fight, for I am not with you to keep you from being defeated by your enemies.' [43] So I spoke to you, but you didn't listen. You rebelled against the LORD's command and defiantly went up into the hill country. [44] Then the Amorites who lived there came out against you and chased you like a swarm of bees. They routed you from Seir as far as Hormah. [45] When you returned, you wept before the LORD, but He didn't listen to your requests or pay attention to you. [46] For this reason you stayed in Kadesh as long as you did.

2 "Then we turned back and headed for the wilderness by way of the *Red Sea, as the LORD had told me, and we traveled around the hill country of Seir for many days. [2] The LORD then said to me, [3] 'You've been traveling around this hill country long enough; turn north. [4] Command the people: You are about to travel through the territory of your brothers, the descendants of Esau, who live in Seir. They will be afraid of you, so you must be very careful. [5] Don't fight with

them, for I will not give you any of their land, not even an inch of it, because I have given Esau the hill country of Seir as his possession. ⁶You may purchase food from them with silver, so that you may eat, and buy water from them to drink. ⁷For the LORD your God has blessed you in all the work of your hands. He has watched over your journey through this immense wilderness. The LORD your God has been with you this past 40 years, and you have lacked nothing.'

⁸"So we bypassed our brothers, the descendants of Esau, who live in Seir. We turned away from the ˙Arabah road and from Elath and Ezion-geber. We traveled along the road to the Wilderness of Moab. ⁹The LORD said to me, 'Show no hostility toward Moab, and do not provoke them to battle, for I will not give you any of their land as a possession, since I have given Ar as a possession to the descendants of Lot.'"

¹⁰The Emim, a great and numerous people as tall as the Anakim, had previously lived there. ¹¹They were also regarded as Rephaim, like the Anakim, though the Moabites called them Emim. ¹²The Horites had previously lived in Seir, but the descendants of Esau drove them out, destroying them completely and settling in their place, just as Israel did in the land of its possession the LORD gave them.

¹³"The LORD said, 'Now get up and cross the Zered Valley.' So we crossed the Zered Valley. ¹⁴The time we spent traveling from Kadesh-barnea until we crossed the Zered Valley was 38 years until the entire generation of fighting men had perished from the camp, as the LORD had sworn to them. ¹⁵Indeed, the LORD's hand was against them, to eliminate them from the camp until they had all perished.

¹⁶"When all the fighting men had died among the people, ¹⁷the LORD spoke to me, ¹⁸'Today you are going to cross the border of Moab at Ar. ¹⁹When you get close to the Ammonites, don't show any hostility to them or fight with them, for I will not give you any of the Ammonites' land as a possession; I have given it as a possession to the descendants of Lot.'"

²⁰This too used to be regarded as the land of the Rephaim. The Rephaim lived there previously, though the Ammonites called them Zamzummim, ²¹a great and numerous people, tall as the Anakim. The LORD destroyed the Rephaim at the advance of the Ammonites, so that they drove them out and settled in their place. ²²This was just as He had done for the descendants of Esau who lived in Seir, when He destroyed the Horites before them; they drove them out and have lived in their place until now. ²³The Caphtorim, who came from Caphtor, destroyed the Avvim, who lived in villages as far as Gaza, and settled in their place.

²⁴"The LORD also said, 'Get up, move out, and cross the Arnon Valley. See, I have handed Sihon the Amorite, king of Heshbon, and his land over to you. Begin to take possession of it; engage him in battle. ²⁵Today I will begin to put the fear and dread of you on the peoples everywhere under heaven. They will hear the report about you, tremble, and be in anguish because of you.'

²⁶"So I sent messengers with an offer of peace to Sihon king of Heshbon from the Wilderness of Kedemoth, saying, ²⁷'Let us travel through your land; we will keep strictly to the highway. We will not turn to the right or the left. ²⁸You can sell us food in exchange for silver so we may eat, and give us water for silver so we may drink. Only let us travel through on foot, ²⁹just

as the descendants of Esau who live in Seir did for us, and the Moabites who live in Ar, until we cross the Jordan into the land the LORD our God is giving us.' ³⁰But Sihon king of Heshbon would not let us travel through his land, for the LORD your God had made his spirit stubborn and his heart obstinate in order to hand him over to you, as has now taken place.

³¹"Then the LORD said to me, 'See, I have begun to give Sihon and his land to you. Begin to take possession of it.' ³²So Sihon and his whole army came out against us for battle at Jahaz. ³³The LORD our God handed him over to us, and we defeated him, his sons, and his whole army. ³⁴At that time we captured all his cities and ˙completely destroyed the people of every city, including the women and children. We left no survivors. ³⁵We took only the livestock and the spoil from the cities we captured as plunder for ourselves. ³⁶There was no city that was inaccessible to us, from Aroer on the rim of the Arnon Valley, along with the city in the valley, even as far as Gilead. The LORD our God gave everything to us. ³⁷But you did not go near the Ammonites' land, all along the bank of the Jabbok River, the cities of the hill country, or any place that the LORD our God had forbidden.

3 "Then we turned and went up the road to Bashan, and Og king of Bashan came out against us with his whole army to do battle at Edrei. ²But the LORD said to me, 'Do not fear him, for I have handed him over to you along with his whole army and his land. Do to him as you did to Sihon king of the Amorites, who lived in Heshbon.' ³So the LORD our God also handed over Og king of Bashan and his whole army to us. We struck him until there was no survivor left. ⁴We captured all his cities at that time. There wasn't a city that we didn't take from them: 60 cities, the entire region of Argob, the kingdom of Og in Bashan. ⁵All these were fortified with high walls, gates, and bars, besides a large number of rural villages. ⁶We ˙completely destroyed them, as we had done to Sihon king of Heshbon, destroying the men, women, and children of every city. ⁷But we took all the livestock and the spoil from the cities as plunder for ourselves.

⁸"At that time we took the land from the two Amorite kings across the Jordan, from the Arnon Valley as far as Mount Hermon, ⁹which the Sidonians call Sirion, but the Amorites call Senir, ¹⁰all the cities of the plateau, Gilead, and Bashan as far as Salecah and Edrei, cities of Og's kingdom in Bashan. ¹¹(Only Og king of Bashan was left of the remnant of the Rephaim. His bed was made of iron. Isn't it in Rabbah of the Ammonites? It is 13 feet six inches long and six feet wide by a standard measure.)

¹²"At that time we took possession of this land. I gave to the Reubenites and Gadites the area extending from Aroer by the Arnon Valley, and half the hill country of Gilead along with its cities. ¹³I gave to half the tribe of Manasseh the rest of Gilead and all Bashan, the kingdom of Og. The entire region of Argob, the whole territory of Bashan, used to be called the land of the Rephaim. ¹⁴Jair, a descendant of Manasseh, took over the entire region of Argob as far as the border of the Geshurites and Maacathites. He called Bashan by his own name, Jair's Villages, as it is today. ¹⁵I gave Gilead to Machir, ¹⁶and I gave to the Reubenites and Gadites the area extending from Gilead to the Arnon Valley (the middle of the valley was the border) and up to the Jabbok River, the border of the Ammonites.

¹⁷The *Arabah and Jordan are also borders from Chinnereth as far as the Sea of the Arabah, the Dead Sea, under the slopes of Pisgah on the east.

¹⁸"I commanded you at that time: The LORD your God has given you this land to possess. All your fighting men will cross over in battle formation ahead of your brothers the Israelites. ¹⁹But your wives, young children, and livestock—I know that you have a lot of livestock—will remain in the cities I have given you ²⁰until the LORD gives rest to your brothers as He has to you, and they also take possession of the land the LORD your God is giving them across the Jordan. Then each of you may return to his possession that I have given you.

²¹"I commanded Joshua at that time: Your own eyes have seen everything the LORD your God has done to these two kings. The LORD will do the same to all the kingdoms you are about to enter. ²²Don't be afraid of them, for the LORD your God fights for you.

²³"At that time I begged the LORD: ²⁴Lord GOD, You have begun to show Your greatness and power to Your servant, for what god is there in heaven or on earth who can perform deeds and mighty acts like Yours? ²⁵Please let me cross over and see the beautiful land on the other side of the Jordan, that good hill country and Lebanon.

²⁶"But the LORD was angry with me on account of you and would not listen to me. The LORD said to me, 'That's enough! Do not speak to Me again about this matter. ²⁷Go to the top of Pisgah and look to the west, north, south, and east, and see it with your own eyes, for you will not cross this Jordan. ²⁸But commission Joshua and encourage and strengthen him, for he will cross over ahead of the people and enable them to inherit this land that you will see.' ²⁹So we stayed in the valley facing Beth-peor.

4 "Now, Israel, listen to the statutes and ordinances I am teaching you to follow, so that you may live, enter, and take possession of the land *Yahweh, the God of your fathers, is giving you. ²You must not add anything to what I command you or take anything away from it, so that you may keep the commands of the LORD your God I am giving you. ³Your eyes have seen what the LORD did at Baal-peor, for the LORD your God destroyed every one of you who followed *Baal of Peor. ⁴But you who have remained faithful to the LORD your God are all alive today. ⁵Look, I have taught you statutes and ordinances as the LORD my God has commanded me, so that you may follow them in the land you are entering to possess. ⁶Carefully follow them, for this will show your wisdom and understanding in the eyes of the peoples. When they hear about all these statutes, they will say, 'This great nation is indeed a wise and understanding people.' ⁷For what great nation is there that has a god near to it as the LORD our God is to us whenever we call to Him? ⁸And what great nation has righteous statutes and ordinances like this entire law I set before you today?

⁹"Only be on your guard and diligently watch yourselves, so that you don't forget the things your eyes have seen and so that they don't slip from your mind as long as you live. Teach them to your children and your grandchildren. ¹⁰The day you stood before the LORD your God at Horeb, the LORD said to me, 'Assemble the people before Me, and I will let them hear My words, so that they may learn to *fear Me all the days they live on the earth and may instruct their chil-

dren.' ¹¹You came near and stood at the base of the mountain, a mountain blazing with fire into the heavens and enveloped in a dense, black cloud. ¹²Then the LORD spoke to you from the fire. You kept hearing the sound of the words, but didn't see a form; there was only a voice. ¹³He declared His covenant to you. He commanded you to follow the Ten Commandments, which He wrote on two stone tablets. ¹⁴At that time the LORD commanded me to teach you statutes and ordinances for you to follow in the land you are about to cross into and possess.

¹⁵"For your own good, be extremely careful—because you did not see any form on the day the LORD spoke to you out of the fire at Horeb— ¹⁶not to act corruptly and make an idol for yourselves in the shape of any figure: a male or female form, ¹⁷or the form of any beast on the earth, any winged creature that flies in the sky, ¹⁸any creature that crawls on the ground, or any fish in the waters under the earth. ¹⁹When you look to the heavens and see the sun, moon, and stars—all the array of heaven—do not be led astray to bow down and worship them. The LORD your God has provided them for all people everywhere under heaven. ²⁰But the LORD selected you and brought you out of Egypt's iron furnace to be a people for His inheritance, as you are today.

²¹"The LORD was angry with me on your account. He swore that I would not cross the Jordan and enter the good land the LORD your God is giving you as an inheritance. ²²I won't be crossing the Jordan because I am going to die in this land. But you are about to cross over and take possession of this good land. ²³Be careful not to forget the covenant of the LORD your God that He made with you, and make an idol for yourselves in the shape of anything He has forbidden you. ²⁴For the LORD your God is a consuming fire, a jealous God.

²⁵"When you have children and grandchildren and have been in the land a long time, and if you act corruptly, make an idol in the form of anything, and do what is evil in the sight of the LORD your God, provoking Him to anger, ²⁶I call heaven and earth as witnesses against you today that you will quickly perish from the land you are about to cross the Jordan to possess. You will not live long there, but you will certainly be destroyed. ²⁷The LORD will scatter you among the peoples, and you will be reduced to a few survivors among the nations where the LORD your God will drive you. ²⁸There you will worship man-made gods of wood and stone, which cannot see, hear, eat, or smell. ²⁹But from there, you will search for the LORD your God, and you will find Him when you seek Him with all your heart and all your soul. ³⁰When you are in distress and all these things have happened to you, you will return to the LORD your God in later days and obey Him. ³¹He will not leave you, destroy you, or forget the covenant with your fathers that He swore to them by oath, because the LORD your God is a compassionate God.

³²"Indeed, ask about the earlier days that preceded you, from the day God created man on the earth and from one end of the heavens to the other: Has anything like this great event ever happened, or has anything like it been heard of? ³³Has a people heard God's voice speaking from the fire as you have, and lived? ³⁴Or has a god attempted to go and take a nation as his own out of another nation, by trials, signs, wonders, and war, by a strong hand and an outstretched arm, by great terrors, as the LORD your God did for you

in Egypt before your eyes? ³⁵ You were shown these things so that you would know that the LORD is God; there is no other besides Him. ³⁶ He let you hear His voice from heaven to instruct you. He showed you His great fire on earth, and you heard His words from the fire. ³⁷ Because He loved your fathers, He chose their descendants after them and brought you out of Egypt by His presence and great power, ³⁸ to drive out before you nations greater and stronger than you and to bring you in and give you their land as an inheritance, as is now taking place. ³⁹ Today, recognize and keep in mind that the LORD is God in heaven above and on earth below; there is no other. ⁴⁰ Keep His statutes and commands, which I am giving you today, so that you and your children after you may prosper and so that you may live long in the land the LORD your God is giving you for all time."

⁴¹ Then Moses set apart three cities across the Jordan to the east. ⁴² Someone could flee there who committed manslaughter, killing his neighbor accidentally without previously hating him. He could flee to one of these cities and stay alive: ⁴³ Bezer in the wilderness on the plateau land, belonging to the Reubenites; Ramoth in Gilead, belonging to the Gadites; or Golan in Bashan, belonging to the Manassites.

⁴⁴ This is the law Moses gave the Israelites. ⁴⁵ These are the decrees, statutes, and ordinances Moses proclaimed to them after they came out of Egypt, ⁴⁶ across the Jordan in the valley facing Beth-peor in the land of Sihon king of the Amorites. He lived in Heshbon, and Moses and the Israelites defeated him after they came out of Egypt. ⁴⁷ They took possession of his land and the land of Og king of Bashan, the two Amorite kings who were across the Jordan to the east, ⁴⁸ from Aroer on the rim of the Arnon Valley as far as Mount Sion (that is, Hermon) ⁴⁹ and all the ˚Arabah on the east side of the Jordan as far as the Dead Sea below the slopes of Pisgah.

5 Moses summoned all Israel and said to them, "Israel, listen to the statutes and ordinances I am proclaiming as you hear them today. Learn and follow them carefully. ² The LORD our God made a covenant with us at Horeb. ³ He did not make this covenant with our fathers, but with all of us who are alive here today. ⁴ The LORD spoke to you face to face from the fire on the mountain. ⁵ At that time I was standing between the LORD and you to report the word of the LORD to you, because you were afraid of the fire and did not go up the mountain. And He said:

⁶ I am the LORD your God, who brought you out of the land of Egypt, out of the place of slavery.

⁷ Do not have other gods besides Me.

⁸ Do not make an idol for yourself in the shape of anything in the heavens above or on the earth below or in the waters under the earth. ⁹ You must not bow down to them or worship them, because I, the LORD your God, am a jealous God, punishing the children for the fathers' sin to the third and fourth generations of those who hate Me, ¹⁰ but showing faithful love to a thousand generations of those who love Me and keep My commands.

¹¹ Do not misuse the name of the LORD your God, because the LORD will not leave anyone unpunished who misuses His name.

¹² Be careful to remember the Sabbath day, to keep it holy as the LORD your God has commanded you. ¹³ You are to labor six days and do all your work, ¹⁴ but the seventh day is a Sabbath to the LORD your God. You must not do any work—you, your son or daughter, your male or female slave, your ox or donkey, any of your livestock, or the foreigner who lives within your gates, so that your male and female slaves may rest as you do. ¹⁵ Remember that you were a slave in the land of Egypt, and the LORD your God brought you out of there with a strong hand and an outstretched arm. That is why the LORD your God has commanded you to keep the Sabbath day.

¹⁶ Honor your father and your mother, as the LORD your God has commanded you, so that you may live long and so that you may prosper in the land the LORD your God is giving you.

¹⁷ Do not murder.

¹⁸ Do not commit adultery.

¹⁹ Do not steal.

²⁰ Do not give dishonest testimony against your neighbor.

²¹ Do not covet your neighbor's wife or desire your neighbor's house, his field, his male or female slave, his ox or donkey, or anything that belongs to your neighbor.

²² "The LORD spoke these commands in a loud voice to your entire assembly from the fire, cloud, and thick darkness on the mountain; He added nothing more. He wrote them on two stone tablets and gave them to me. ²³ All of you approached me with your tribal leaders and elders when you heard the voice from the darkness and while the mountain was blazing with fire. ²⁴ You said, 'Look, the LORD our God has shown us His glory and greatness, and we have heard His voice from the fire. Today we have seen that God speaks with a person, yet he still lives. ²⁵ But now, why should we die? This great fire will consume us and we will die if we hear the voice of the LORD our God any longer. ²⁶ For who out of all mankind has heard the voice of the living God speaking from the fire, as we have, and lived? ²⁷ Go near and listen to everything the LORD our God says. Then you can tell us everything the LORD our God tells you; we will listen and obey.'

²⁸ "The LORD heard your words when you spoke to me. He said to me, 'I have heard the words that these people have spoken to you. Everything they have said is right. ²⁹ If only they had such a heart to ˚fear Me and keep all My commands always, so that they and their children will prosper forever. ³⁰ Go and tell them: Return to your tents. ³¹ But you stand here with Me, and I will tell you every command—the statutes and ordinances—you are to teach them, so that they may follow them in the land I am giving them to possess.'

³² "Be careful to do as the LORD your God has commanded you; you are not to turn aside to the right or the left. ³³ Follow the whole instruction the LORD your God has commanded you, so that you may live, prosper, and have a long life in the land you will possess.

6 "This is the command—the statutes and ordinances—the LORD your God has instructed me to teach you, so that you may follow them in the land you are about to enter and possess. ² Do this so that you may ˚fear the LORD your God all the days of your life by keeping all His statutes and commands I am giving you, your son, and your grandson, and so that

you may have a long life. ³Listen, Israel, and be careful to follow them, so that you may prosper and multiply greatly, because ˚Yahweh, the God of your fathers, has promised you a land flowing with milk and honey.

⁴"Listen, Israel: The Lord our God, the Lord is One. ⁵Love the Lord your God with all your heart, with all your soul, and with all your strength. ⁶These words that I am giving you today are to be in your heart. ⁷Repeat them to your children. Talk about them when you sit in your house and when you walk along the road, when you lie down and when you get up. ⁸Bind them as a sign on your hand and let them be a symbol on your forehead. ⁹Write them on the doorposts of your house and on your gates.

¹⁰"When the Lord your God brings you into the land He swore to your fathers Abraham, Isaac, and Jacob that He would give you—a land with large and beautiful cities that you did not build, ¹¹houses full of every good thing that you did not fill them with, wells dug that you did not dig, and vineyards and olive groves that you did not plant—and when you eat and are satisfied, ¹²be careful not to forget the Lord who brought you out of the land of Egypt, out of the place of slavery. ¹³Fear Yahweh your God, worship Him, and take your oaths in His name. ¹⁴Do not follow other gods, the gods of the peoples around you, ¹⁵for the Lord your God, who is among you, is a jealous God. Otherwise, the Lord your God will become angry with you and wipe you off the face of the earth. ¹⁶Do not test the Lord your God as you tested Him at Massah. ¹⁷Carefully observe the commands of the Lord your God, the decrees and statutes He has commanded you. ¹⁸Do what is right and good in the Lord's sight, so that you may prosper and so that you may enter and possess the good land the Lord your God swore to give your fathers, ¹⁹by driving out all your enemies before you, as the Lord has said.

²⁰"When your son asks you in the future, 'What is the meaning of the decrees, statutes, and ordinances, which the Lord our God has commanded you?' ²¹tell him, 'We were slaves of Pharaoh in Egypt, but the Lord brought us out of Egypt with a strong hand. ²²Before our eyes the Lord inflicted great and devastating signs and wonders on Egypt, on Pharaoh, and on all his household, ²³but He brought us from there in order to lead us in and give us the land that He swore to our fathers. ²⁴The Lord commanded us to follow all these statutes and to fear the Lord our God for our prosperity always and for our preservation, as it is today. ²⁵Righteousness will be ours if we are careful to follow every one of these commands before the Lord our God, as He has commanded us.'

7 "When the Lord your God brings you into the land you are entering to possess, and He drives out many nations before you—the Hittites, Girgashites, Amorites, Canaanites, Perizzites, Hivites and Jebusites, seven nations more numerous and powerful than you— ²and when the Lord your God delivers them over to you and you defeat them, you must ˚completely destroy them. Make no treaty with them and show them no mercy. ³Do not intermarry with them. Do not give your daughters to their sons or take their daughters for your sons, ⁴because they will turn your sons away from Me to worship other gods. Then the Lord's anger will burn against you, and He will swiftly destroy you. ⁵Instead, this is what you are to do to them: tear down their altars, smash their sacred pil-

lars, cut down their ˚Asherah poles, and burn up their carved images. ⁶For you are a holy people belonging to the Lord your God. The Lord your God has chosen you to be His own possession out of all the peoples on the face of the earth.

⁷"The Lord was devoted to you and chose you, not because you were more numerous than all peoples, for you were the fewest of all peoples. ⁸But because the Lord loved you and kept the oath He swore to your fathers, He brought you out with a strong hand and redeemed you from the place of slavery, from the power of Pharaoh king of Egypt. ⁹Know that ˚Yahweh your God is God, the faithful God who keeps His gracious covenant loyalty for a thousand generations with those who love Him and keep His commands. ¹⁰But He directly pays back and destroys those who hate Him. He will not hesitate to directly pay back the one who hates Him. ¹¹So keep the command—the statutes and ordinances—that I am giving you to follow today.

¹²"If you listen to and are careful to keep these ordinances, the Lord your God will keep His covenant loyalty with you, as He swore to your fathers. ¹³He will love you, bless you, and multiply you. He will bless your descendants, and the produce of your land—your grain, new wine, and oil—the young of your herds, and the newborn of your flocks, in the land He swore to your fathers that He would give you. ¹⁴You will be blessed above all peoples; there will be no infertile male or female among you or your livestock. ¹⁵The Lord will remove all sickness from you; He will not put on you all the terrible diseases of Egypt that you know about, but He will inflict them on all who hate you. ¹⁶You must destroy all the peoples the Lord your God is delivering over to you and not look on them with pity. Do not worship their gods, for that will be a snare to you.

¹⁷"If you say to yourself, 'These nations are greater than I; how can I drive them out?' ¹⁸do not be afraid of them. Be sure to remember what the Lord your God did to Pharaoh and all Egypt: ¹⁹the great trials that you saw, the signs and wonders, the strong hand and outstretched arm, by which the Lord your God brought you out. The Lord your God will do the same to all the peoples you fear. ²⁰The Lord your God will also send the hornet against them until all the survivors and those hiding from you perish. ²¹Don't be terrified of them, for the Lord your God, a great and awesome God, is among you. ²²The Lord your God will drive out these nations before you little by little. You will not be able to destroy them all at once; otherwise, the wild animals will become too numerous for you. ²³The Lord your God will give them over to you and throw them into great confusion until they are destroyed. ²⁴He will hand their kings over to you, and you will wipe out their names under heaven. No one will be able to stand against you; you will annihilate them. ²⁵You must burn up the carved images of their gods. Don't covet the silver and gold on the images and take it for yourself, or else you will be ensnared by it, for it is abhorrent to the Lord your God. ²⁶You must not bring any abhorrent thing into your house, or you will be ˚set apart for destruction like it. You are to utterly detest and abhor it, because it is set apart for destruction.

8 "You must carefully follow every command I am giving you today, so that you may live and increase, and may enter and take possession of the land the Lord swore to your fathers. ²Remember that the

LORD your God led you on the entire journey these 40 years in the wilderness, so that He might humble you and test you to know what was in your heart, whether or not you would keep His commands. ³He humbled you by letting you go hungry; then He gave you manna to eat, which you and your fathers had not known, so that you might learn that man does not live on bread alone but on every word that comes from the mouth of the LORD. ⁴Your clothing did not wear out, and your feet did not swell these 40 years. ⁵Keep in mind that the LORD your God has been disciplining you just as a man disciplines his son. ⁶So keep the commands of the LORD your God by walking in His ways and *fearing Him. ⁷For the LORD your God is bringing you into a good land, a land with streams of water, springs, and deep water sources, flowing in both valleys and hills; ⁸a land of wheat, barley, vines, figs, and pomegranates; a land of olive oil and honey; ⁹a land where you will eat food without shortage, where you will lack nothing; a land whose rocks are iron and from whose hills you will mine copper. ¹⁰When you eat and are full, you will praise the LORD your God for the good land He has given you.

¹¹"Be careful that you don't forget the LORD your God by failing to keep His command—the ordinances and statutes—I am giving you today. ¹²When you eat and are full, and build beautiful houses to live in, ¹³and your herds and flocks grow large, and your silver and gold multiply, and everything else you have increases, ¹⁴be careful that your heart doesn't become proud and you forget the LORD your God who brought you out of the land of Egypt, out of the place of slavery. ¹⁵He led you through the great and terrible wilderness with its poisonous snakes and scorpions, a thirsty land where there was no water. He brought water out of the flint-like rock for you. ¹⁶He fed you in the wilderness with manna that your fathers had not known, in order to humble and test you, so that in the end He might cause you to prosper. ¹⁷You may say to yourself, 'My power and my own ability have gained this wealth for me,' ¹⁸but remember that the LORD your God gives you the power to gain wealth, in order to confirm His covenant He swore to your fathers, as it is today. ¹⁹If you ever forget the LORD your God and go after other gods to worship and bow down to them, I testify against you today that you will perish. ²⁰Like the nations the LORD is about to destroy before you, you will perish if you do not obey the LORD your God.

9 "Listen, Israel: Today you are about to cross the Jordan to go and drive out nations greater and stronger than you, with large cities fortified to the heavens. ²The people are strong and tall, the descendants of the Anakim. You know about them and you have heard it said about them, 'Who can stand up to the sons of Anak?' ³But understand that today the LORD your God will cross over ahead of you as a consuming fire; He will devastate and subdue them before you. You will drive them out and destroy them swiftly, as the LORD has told you. ⁴When the LORD your God drives them out before you, do not say to yourself, 'The LORD brought me in to take possession of this land because of my righteousness.' Instead, the LORD will drive out these nations before you because of their wickedness. ⁵You are not going to take possession of their land because of your righteousness or your integrity. Instead, the LORD your God will drive out these nations before you because of their wickedness, in order to keep the promise He swore to your fathers, Abraham, Isaac, and Jacob. ⁶Understand that the LORD your God is not giving you this good land to possess because of your righteousness, for you are a stiff-necked people.

⁷"Remember and do not forget how you provoked the LORD your God in the wilderness. You have been rebelling against the LORD from the day you left the land of Egypt until you reached this place. ⁸You provoked the LORD at Horeb, and He was angry enough with you to destroy you. ⁹When I went up the mountain to receive the stone tablets, the tablets of the covenant the LORD made with you, I stayed on the mountain 40 days and 40 nights. I did not eat bread or drink water. ¹⁰On the day of the assembly the LORD gave me the two stone tablets, inscribed by God's finger. The exact words were on them, which the LORD spoke to you from the fire on the mountain. ¹¹The LORD gave me the two stone tablets, the tablets of the covenant, at the end of the 40 days and 40 nights.

¹²"The LORD said to me, 'Get up and go down immediately from here. For your people whom you brought out of Egypt have acted corruptly. They have quickly turned from the way that I commanded them; they have made a cast image for themselves.' ¹³The LORD also said to me, 'I have seen this people, and indeed, they are a stiff-necked people. ¹⁴Leave Me alone, and I will destroy them and blot out their name under heaven. Then I will make you into a nation stronger and more numerous than they.'

¹⁵"So I went back down the mountain, while it was blazing with fire, and the two tablets of the covenant were in my hands. ¹⁶I saw how you had sinned against the LORD your God; you had made a calf image for yourselves. You had quickly turned from the way the LORD had commanded for you. ¹⁷So I took hold of the two tablets and threw them from my hands, shattering them before your eyes. ¹⁸Then I fell down like the first time in the presence of the LORD for 40 days and 40 nights; I did not eat bread or drink water because of all the sin you committed, doing what was evil in the LORD's sight and provoking Him to anger. ¹⁹I was afraid of the fierce anger the LORD had directed against you, because He was about to destroy you. But again the LORD listened to me on that occasion. ²⁰The LORD was angry enough with Aaron to destroy him. But I prayed for Aaron at that time also. ²¹I took the sinful calf you had made, burned it up, and crushed it, thoroughly grinding it to powder as fine as dust. Then I threw it into the stream that came down from the mountain.

²²"You continued to provoke the LORD at Taberah, Massah, and Kibroth-hattaavah. ²³When the LORD sent you from Kadesh-barnea, He said, 'Go up and possess the land I have given you'; you rebelled against the command of the LORD your God. You did not believe or obey Him. ²⁴You have been rebelling against the LORD ever since I have known you.

²⁵"I fell down in the presence of the LORD 40 days and 40 nights because the LORD had threatened to destroy you. ²⁶I prayed to the LORD:

Lord GOD, do not annihilate Your people, Your inheritance, whom You redeemed through Your greatness and brought out of Egypt with a strong hand. ²⁷Remember Your servants Abraham, Isaac, and Jacob. Disregard this people's stubbornness, and their wickedness and sin. ²⁸Otherwise, those in the land you brought us from will say, 'Because the LORD wasn't able to bring them into the land He had promised them, and because He hated them, He brought them out to kill them in the wilderness.' ²⁹But they are Your people, Your inheritance, whom You brought out by Your great power and out-stretched arm.

10 "The LORD said to me at that time, 'Cut two stone tablets like the first ones and come to Me on the mountain and make a wooden ark. ²I will write on the tablets the words that were on the first tablets you broke, and you are to place them in the ark.' ³So I made an ark of acacia wood, cut two stone tablets like the first ones, and climbed the mountain with the two tablets in my hand. ⁴Then on the day of the assembly, the LORD wrote on the tablets what had been written previously, the Ten Commandments that He had spoken to you on the mountain from the fire. The LORD gave them to me, ⁵and I went back down the mountain and placed the tablets in the ark I had made. And they have remained there, as the LORD commanded me."

⁶The Israelites traveled from Beeroth Bene-jaakan to Moserah. Aaron died and was buried there, and Eleazar his son became priest in his place. ⁷They traveled from there to Gudgodah, and from Gudgodah to Jotbathah, a land with streams of water.

⁸"At that time the LORD set apart the tribe of Levi to carry the ark of the LORD's covenant, to stand before ˙Yahweh to serve Him, and to pronounce blessings in His name, as it is today. ⁹For this reason, Levi does not have a portion or inheritance like his brothers; the LORD is his inheritance, as the LORD your God told him.

¹⁰"I stayed on the mountain 40 days and 40 nights like the first time. The LORD also listened to me on this occasion; He agreed not to annihilate you. ¹¹Then the LORD said to me, 'Get up. Continue your journey ahead of the people, so that they may enter and possess the land I swore to give their fathers.'

¹²"And now, Israel, what does the LORD your God ask of you except to ˙fear the LORD your God by walking in all His ways, to love Him, and to worship the LORD your God with all your heart and all your soul? ¹³Keep the LORD's commands and statutes I am giving you today, for your own good. ¹⁴The heavens, indeed the highest heavens, belong to the LORD your God, as does the earth and everything in it. ¹⁵Yet the LORD was devoted to your fathers and loved them. He chose their descendants after them—He chose you out of all the peoples, as it is today. ¹⁶Therefore, circumcise your hearts and don't be stiff-necked any longer. ¹⁷For the LORD your God is the God of gods and Lord of lords, the great, mighty, and awesome God, showing no partiality and taking no bribe. ¹⁸He executes justice for the fatherless and the widow, and loves the foreigner, giving him food and clothing. ¹⁹You also must love the foreigner, since you were foreigners in the land of Egypt. ²⁰You are to fear Yahweh your God and worship Him. Remain faithful to Him and take oaths in His name. ²¹He is your praise and He is your God, who has done for you these great and awesome works your eyes have seen. ²²Your fathers went down to Egypt, 70 people in all, and now the LORD your God has made you as numerous as the stars of the sky.

11 "Therefore, love the LORD your God and always keep His mandate and His statutes, ordinances, and commands. ²You must understand today that it is

not your children who experienced or saw the discipline of the LORD your God:

His greatness, strong hand, and outstretched arm; ³His signs and the works He did in Egypt to Pharaoh king of Egypt and all his land; ⁴what He did to Egypt's army, its horses and chariots, when He made the waters of the ˙Red Sea flow over them as they pursued you, and He destroyed them completely; ⁵what He did to you in the wilderness until you reached this place; ⁶and what He did to Dathan and Abiram, the sons of Eliab the Reubenite, when in the middle of the whole Israelite camp the earth opened its mouth and swallowed them, their households, their tents, and every living thing with them. ⁷Your own eyes have seen every great work the LORD has done.

⁸"Keep every command I am giving you today, so that you may have the strength to cross into and possess the land you are to inherit, ⁹and so that you may live long in the land the LORD swore to your fathers to give them and their descendants, a land flowing with milk and honey. ¹⁰For the land you are entering to possess is not like the land of Egypt, from which you have come, where you sowed your seed and irrigated by hand as in a vegetable garden. ¹¹But the land you are entering to possess is a land of mountains and valleys, watered by rain from the sky. ¹²It is a land the LORD your God cares for. He is always watching over it from the beginning to the end of the year.

¹³"If you carefully obey my commands I am giving you today, to love the LORD your God and worship Him with all your heart and all your soul, ¹⁴I will provide rain for your land in the proper time, the autumn and spring rains, and you will harvest your grain, new wine, and oil. ¹⁵I will provide grass in your fields for your livestock. You will eat and be satisfied. ¹⁶Be careful that you are not enticed to turn aside, worship, and bow down to other gods. ¹⁷Then the LORD's anger will burn against you. He will close the sky, and there will be no rain; the land will not yield its produce, and you will perish quickly from the good land the LORD is giving you.

¹⁸"Imprint these words of mine on your hearts and minds, bind them as a sign on your hands, and let them be a symbol on your foreheads. ¹⁹Teach them to your children, talking about them when you sit in your house and when you walk along the road, when you lie down and when you get up. ²⁰Write them on the doorposts of your house and on your gates, ²¹so that as long as the heavens are above the earth, your days and those of your children may be many in the land the LORD swore to give your fathers. ²²For if you carefully observe every one of these commands I am giving you to follow—to love the LORD your God, walk in all His ways, and remain faithful to Him— ²³the LORD will drive out all these nations before you, and you will drive out nations greater and stronger than you are. ²⁴Every place the sole of your foot treads will be yours. Your territory will extend from the wilderness to Lebanon and from the Euphrates River to the Mediterranean Sea. ²⁵No one will be able to stand against you; the LORD your God will put fear and dread of you in all the land where you set foot, as He has promised you.

²⁶"Look, today I set before you a blessing and a curse: ²⁷there will be a blessing, if you obey the com-

mands of the LORD your God I am giving you today, [28] and a curse, if you do not obey the commands of the LORD your God and you turn aside from the path I command you today by following other gods you have not known. [29] When the LORD your God brings you into the land you are entering to possess, you are to proclaim the blessing at Mount Gerizim and the curse at Mount Ebal. [30] Aren't these mountains across the Jordan, beyond the western road in the land of the Canaanites, who live in the *Arabah, opposite Gilgal, near the oaks of Moreh? [31] For you are about to cross the Jordan to enter and take possession of the land the LORD your God is giving you. When you possess it and settle in it, [32] be careful to follow all the statutes and ordinances I set before you today.

12 "Be careful to follow these statutes and ordinances in the land that *Yahweh, the God of your fathers, has given you to possess all the days you live on the earth. [2] Destroy completely all the places where the nations that you are driving out worship their gods—on the high mountains, on the hills, and under every green tree. [3] Tear down their altars, smash their sacred pillars, burn up their *Asherah poles, cut down the carved images of their gods, and wipe out their names from every place. [4] Don't worship the LORD your God this way. [5] Instead, you must turn to the place Yahweh your God chooses from all your tribes to put His name for His dwelling and go there. [6] You are to bring there your *burnt offerings and sacrifices, your tenths and personal contributions, your vow offerings and freewill offerings, and the firstborn of your herds and flocks. [7] You will eat there in the presence of the LORD your God and rejoice with your household in everything you do, because the LORD your God has blessed you.

[8] "You are not to do as we are doing here today; everyone is doing whatever seems right in his own eyes. [9] Indeed, you have not yet come into the resting place and the inheritance the LORD your God is giving you. [10] When you cross the Jordan and live in the land the LORD your God is giving you to inherit, and He gives you rest from all the enemies around you and you live in security, [11] then Yahweh your God will choose the place to have His name dwell. Bring there everything I command you: your burnt offerings, sacrifices, offerings of the tenth, personal contributions, and all your choice offerings you vow to the LORD. [12] You will rejoice before the LORD your God—you, your sons and daughters, your male and female slaves, and the Levite who is within your gates, since he has no portion or inheritance among you. [13] Be careful not to offer your burnt offerings in all the sacred places you see. [14] You must offer your burnt offerings only in the place the LORD chooses in one of your tribes, and there you must do everything I command you.

[15] "But whenever you want, you may slaughter and eat meat within any of your gates, according to the blessing the LORD your God has given you. Those who are *clean or *unclean may eat it, as they would a gazelle or deer, [16] but you must not eat the blood; pour it on the ground like water. [17] Within your gates you may not eat: the tenth of your grain, new wine, or oil; the firstborn of your herd or flock; any of your vow offerings that you pledge; your freewill offerings; or your personal contributions. [18] You must eat them in the presence of the LORD your God at the place the LORD your God chooses—you, your son and daughter, your

male and female slave, and the Levite who is within your gates. Rejoice before the LORD your God in everything you do, [19] and be careful not to neglect the Levite, as long as you live in your land.

[20] "When the LORD your God enlarges your territory as He has promised you, and you say, 'I want to eat meat' because you have a strong desire to eat meat, you may eat it whenever you want. [21] If the place where Yahweh your God chooses to put His name is too far from you, you may slaughter any of your herd or flock He has given you, as I have commanded you, and you may eat it within your gates whenever you want. [22] Indeed, you may eat it as the gazelle and deer are eaten; both the clean and the unclean may eat it. [23] But don't eat the blood, since the blood is the life, and you must not eat the life with the meat. [24] Do not eat blood; pour it on the ground like water. [25] Do not eat it, so that you and your children after you will prosper, because you will be doing what is right in the LORD's sight.

[26] "But you are to take the holy offerings you have and your vow offerings and go to the place the LORD chooses. [27] Present the meat and blood of your burnt offerings on the altar of the LORD your God. The blood of your other sacrifices is to be poured out beside the altar of the LORD your God, but you may eat the meat. [28] Be careful to obey all these things I command you, so that you and your children after you may prosper forever, because you will be doing what is good and right in the sight of the LORD your God.

[29] "When the LORD your God annihilates the nations before you, which you are entering to take possession of, and you drive them out and live in their land, [30] be careful not to be ensnared by their ways after they have been destroyed before you. Do not inquire about their gods, asking, 'How did these nations worship their gods? I'll also do the same.' [31] You must not do the same to the LORD your God, because they practice every detestable thing, which the LORD hates, for their gods. They even burn their sons and daughters in the fire to their gods. [32] You must be careful to do everything I command you; do not add anything to it or take anything away from it.

13 "If a prophet or someone who has dreams arises among you and proclaims a sign or wonder to you, [2] and that sign or wonder he has promised you comes about, but he says, 'Let us follow other gods,' which you have not known, 'and let us worship them,' [3] do not listen to that prophet's words or to that dreamer. For the LORD your God is testing you to know whether you love the LORD your God with all your heart and all your soul. [4] You must follow the LORD your God and *fear Him. You must keep His commands and listen to His voice; you must worship Him and remain faithful to Him. [5] That prophet or dreamer must be put to death, because he has urged rebellion against the LORD your God who brought you out of the land of Egypt and redeemed you from the place of slavery, to turn you from the way the LORD your God has commanded you to walk. You must purge the evil from you.

[6] "If your brother, the son of your mother, or your son or daughter, or the wife you embrace, or your closest friend secretly entices you, saying, 'Let us go and worship other gods'—which neither you nor your fathers have known, [7] any of the gods of the peoples around you, near you or far from you, from one end of the earth to the other— [8] you must not yield to him or

listen to him. Show him no pity, and do not spare him or shield him. ⁹Instead, you must kill him. Your hand is to be the first against him to put him to death, and then the hands of all the people. ¹⁰Stone him to death for trying to turn you away from the LORD your God who brought you out of the land of Egypt, out of the place of slavery. ¹¹All Israel will hear and be afraid, and they will no longer do anything evil like this among you.

¹²"If you hear it said about one of your cities the LORD your God is giving you to live in, ¹³that ˙wicked men have sprung up among you, led the inhabitants of their city astray, and said, 'Let us go and worship other gods,' which you have not known, ¹⁴you are to inquire, investigate, and interrogate thoroughly. If the report turns out to be true that this detestable thing has happened among you, ¹⁵you must strike down the inhabitants of that city with the sword. ˙Completely destroy everyone in it as well as its livestock with the sword. ¹⁶You are to gather all its spoil in the middle of the city square and completely burn up the city and all its spoil for the LORD your God. The city must remain a mound of ruins forever; it is not to be rebuilt. ¹⁷Nothing ˙set apart for destruction is to remain in your hand, so that the LORD will turn from His burning anger and grant you mercy, show you compassion, and multiply you as He swore to your fathers. ¹⁸This will occur if you obey the LORD your God, keeping all His commands I am giving you today, doing what is right in the sight of the LORD your God.

14 "You are sons of the LORD your God; do not cut yourselves or make a bald spot on your head on behalf of the dead, ²for you are a holy people belonging to the LORD your God. The LORD has chosen you to be His own possession out of all the peoples on the face of the earth.

³"You must not eat any detestable thing. ⁴These are the animals you may eat:
the ox, the sheep, the goat,
⁵   the deer, the gazelle, the roe deer,
the wild goat, the ibex, the antelope,
and the mountain sheep.

⁶You may eat any animal that has hooves divided in two and chews the cud. ⁷But among the ones that chew the cud or have divided hooves, you are not to eat these:
the camel, the hare, and the hyrax,
though they chew the cud, they do not
have hooves—
they are ˙unclean for you;
⁸   and the pig, though it has hooves, it does not
chew the cud—
it is unclean for you.
You must not eat their meat or touch their carcasses.

⁹"You may eat everything from the water that has fins and scales, ¹⁰but you may not eat anything that does not have fins and scales—it is unclean for you. ¹¹"You may eat every ˙clean bird, ¹²but these are the ones you may not eat:
the eagle, the bearded vulture,
the black vulture, ¹³the kite,
any kind of falcon,
¹⁴   every kind of raven, ¹⁵the ostrich,
the short-eared owl, the gull,
any kind of hawk,
¹⁶   the little owl, the long-eared owl,
the white owl, ¹⁷the desert owl,

the osprey, the cormorant, ¹⁸the stork,
any kind of heron,
the hoopoe, and the bat.
¹⁹All winged insects are unclean for you; they may not be eaten. ²⁰But you may eat every clean flying creature.

²¹"You are not to eat any carcass; you may give it to a temporary resident living within your gates, and he may eat it, or you may sell it to a foreigner. For you are a holy people belonging to the LORD your God. You must not boil a young goat in its mother's milk.

²²"Each year you are to set aside a tenth of all the produce grown in your fields. ²³You are to eat a tenth of your grain, new wine, and oil, and the firstborn of your herd and flock, in the presence of ˙Yahweh your God at the place where He chooses to have His name dwell, so that you will always learn to ˙fear the LORD your God. ²⁴But if the distance is too great for you to carry it, since the place where Yahweh your God chooses to put His name is too far away from you and since the LORD your God has blessed you, ²⁵then exchange it for money, take the money in your hand, and go to the place the LORD your God chooses. ²⁶You may spend the money on anything you want: cattle, sheep, wine, beer, or anything you desire. You are to feast there in the presence of the LORD your God and rejoice with your family. ²⁷Do not neglect the Levite within your gates, since he has no portion or inheritance among you.

²⁸"At the end of every three years, bring a tenth of all your produce for that year and store it within your gates. ²⁹Then the Levite, who has no portion or inheritance among you, the foreigner, the fatherless, and the widow within your gates may come, eat, and be satisfied. And the LORD your God will bless you in all the work of your hands that you do.

15 "At the end of every seven years you must cancel debts. ²This is how to cancel debt: Every creditor is to cancel what he has lent his neighbor. He is not to collect anything from his neighbor or brother, because the LORD's release of debts has been proclaimed. ³You may collect something from a foreigner, but you must forgive whatever your brother owes you.

⁴"There will be no poor among you, however, because the LORD is certain to bless you in the land the LORD your God is giving you to possess as an inheritance— ⁵if only you obey the LORD your God and are careful to follow every one of these commands I am giving you today. ⁶When the LORD your God blesses you as He has promised you, you will lend to many nations but not borrow; you will rule over many nations, but they will not rule over you.

⁷"If there is a poor person among you, one of your brothers within any of your gates in the land the LORD your God is giving you, you must not be hardhearted or tightfisted toward your poor brother. ⁸Instead, you are to open your hand to him and freely loan him enough for whatever need he has. ⁹Be careful that there isn't this wicked thought in your heart, 'The seventh year, the year of canceling debts, is near,' and you are stingy toward your poor brother and give him nothing. He will cry out to the LORD against you, and you will be ˙guilty. ¹⁰Give to him, and don't have a stingy heart when you give, and because of this the LORD your God will bless you in all your work and in everything you do. ¹¹For there will never cease to be poor people in the land; that is why I am command-

ing you, 'You must willingly open your hand to your afflicted and poor brother in your land.'

[12] "If your fellow Hebrew, a man or woman, is sold to you and serves you six years, you must set him free in the seventh year. [13] When you set him free, do not send him away empty-handed. [14] Give generously to him from your flock, your threshing floor, and your winepress. You are to give him whatever the Lord your God has blessed you with. [15] Remember that you were a slave in the land of Egypt and the Lord your God redeemed you; that is why I am giving you this command today. [16] But if your slave says to you, 'I don't want to leave you,' because he loves you and your family, and is well off with you, [17] take an awl and pierce through his ear into the door, and he will become your slave for life. Also treat your female slave the same way. [18] Do not regard it as a hardship when you set him free, because he worked for you six years—worth twice the wages of a hired hand. Then the Lord your God will bless you in everything you do.

[19] "You must consecrate to the Lord your God every firstborn male produced by your herd and flock. You are not to put the firstborn of your oxen to work or shear the firstborn of your flock. [20] Each year you and your family are to eat it before the Lord your God in the place the Lord chooses. [21] But if there is a defect in the animal, if it is lame or blind or has any serious defect, you must not sacrifice it to the Lord your God. [22] Eat it within your gates; both the *unclean person and the *clean may eat it, as though it were a gazelle or deer. [23] But you must not eat its blood; pour it on the ground like water.

16 "Observe the month of Abib and celebrate the *Passover to the Lord your God, because the Lord your God brought you out of Egypt by night in the month of Abib. [2] Sacrifice to *Yahweh your God a Passover animal from the herd or flock in the place where the Lord chooses to have His name dwell. [3] You must not eat leavened bread with it. For seven days you are to eat unleavened bread with it, the bread of hardship—because you left the land of Egypt in a hurry—so that you may remember for the rest of your life the day you left the land of Egypt. [4] No yeast is to be found anywhere in your territory for seven days, and none of the meat you sacrifice in the evening of the first day is to remain until morning. [5] You are not to sacrifice the Passover animal in any of the towns the Lord your God is giving you. [6] You must only sacrifice the Passover animal at the place where Yahweh your God chooses to have His name dwell. Do this in the evening as the sun sets at the same time of day you departed from Egypt. [7] You are to cook and eat it in the place the Lord your God chooses, and you are to return to your tents in the morning. [8] You must eat unleavened bread for six days. On the seventh day there is to be a solemn assembly to the Lord your God, and you must not do any work.

[9] "You are to count seven weeks, counting the weeks from the time the sickle is first put to the standing grain. [10] You are to celebrate the Festival of Weeks to the Lord your God with a freewill offering that you give in proportion to how the Lord your God has blessed you. [11] Rejoice before Yahweh your God in the place where He chooses to have His name dwell—you, your son and daughter, your male and female slave, the Levite within your gates, as well as the foreigner, the fatherless, and the widow among you. [12] Remember

that you were slaves in Egypt; carefully follow these statutes.

[13] "You are to celebrate the Festival of Booths for seven days when you have gathered in everything from your threshing floor and winepress. [14] Rejoice during your festival—you, your son and daughter, your male and female slave, as well as the Levite, the foreigner, the fatherless, and the widow within your gates. [15] You are to hold a seven-day festival for the Lord your God in the place He chooses, because the Lord your God will bless you in all your produce and in all the work of your hands, and you will have abundant joy.

[16] "All your males are to appear three times a year before the Lord your God in the place He chooses: at the Festival of *Unleavened Bread, the Festival of Weeks, and the Festival of Booths. No one is to appear before the Lord empty-handed. [17] Everyone must appear with a gift suited to his means, according to the blessing the Lord your God has given you.

[18] "Appoint judges and officials for your tribes in all your towns the Lord your God is giving you. They are to judge the people with righteous judgment. [19] Do not deny justice or show partiality to anyone. Do not accept a bribe, for it blinds the eyes of the wise and twists the words of the righteous. [20] Pursue justice and justice alone, so that you will live and possess the land the Lord your God is giving you.

[21] "Do not set up an *Asherah of any kind of wood next to the altar you will build for the Lord your God, [22] and do not set up a sacred pillar; the Lord your God hates them.

17 "You must not sacrifice to the Lord your God an ox or sheep with a defect or any serious flaw, for that is detestable to the Lord your God.

[2] "If a man or woman among you in one of your towns that the Lord your God will give you is discovered doing evil in the sight of the Lord your God and violating His covenant [3] and has gone to worship other gods by bowing down to the sun, moon, or all the stars in the sky—which I have forbidden— [4] and if you are told or hear about it, you must investigate it thoroughly. If the report turns out to be true that this detestable thing has happened in Israel, [5] you must bring out to your *gates that man or woman who has done this evil thing and stone them to death. [6] The one condemned to die is to be executed on the testimony of two or three witnesses. No one is to be executed on the testimony of a single witness. [7] The witnesses' hands are to be the first in putting him to death, and after that, the hands of all the people. You must purge the evil from you.

[8] "If a case is too difficult for you—concerning bloodshed, lawsuits, or assaults—cases disputed at your gates, you must go up to the place the Lord your God chooses. [9] You are to go to the Levitical priests and to the judge who presides at that time. Ask, and they will give you a verdict in the case. [10] You must abide by the verdict they give you at the place the Lord chooses. Be careful to do exactly as they instruct you. [11] You must abide by the instruction they give you and the verdict they announce to you. Do not turn to the right or the left from the decision they declare to you. [12] The person who acts arrogantly, refusing to listen either to the priest who stands there serving the Lord your God or to the judge, must die. You must purge the evil from Israel. [13] Then all the people will hear about it, be afraid, and no longer behave arrogantly.

¹⁴"When you enter the land the Lᴏʀᴅ your God is giving you, take possession of it, live in it, and say, 'I will set a king over me like all the nations around me,' ¹⁵you are to appoint over you the king the Lᴏʀᴅ your God chooses. Appoint a king from your brothers. You are not to set a foreigner over you, or one who is not of your people. ¹⁶However, he must not acquire many horses for himself or send the people back to Egypt to acquire many horses, for the Lᴏʀᴅ has told you, 'You are never to go back that way again.' ¹⁷He must not acquire many wives for himself so that his heart won't go astray. He must not acquire very large amounts of silver and gold for himself. ¹⁸When he is seated on his royal throne, he is to write a copy of this instruction for himself on a scroll in the presence of the Levitical priests. ¹⁹It is to remain with him, and he is to read from it all the days of his life, so that he may learn to ˙fear the Lᴏʀᴅ his God, to observe all the words of this instruction, and to do these statutes. ²⁰Then his heart will not be exalted above his countrymen, he will not turn from this command to the right or the left, and he and his sons will continue ruling many years over Israel.

18 "The Levitical priests, the whole tribe of Levi, will have no portion or inheritance with Israel. They will eat the Lᴏʀᴅ's fire offerings; that is their inheritance. ²Although Levi has no inheritance among his brothers, the Lᴏʀᴅ is his inheritance, as He promised him. ³This is the priests' share from the people who offer a sacrifice, whether it is an ox, a sheep, or a goat; the priests are to be given the shoulder, jaws, and stomach. ⁴You are to give him the ˙firstfruits of your grain, new wine, and oil, and the first sheared wool of your flock. ⁵For ˙Yahweh your God has chosen him and his sons from all your tribes to stand and minister in His name from now on. ⁶When a Levite leaves one of your towns where he lives in Israel and wants to go to the place the Lᴏʀᴅ chooses, ⁷he may serve in the name of Yahweh his God like all his fellow Levites who minister there in the presence of the Lᴏʀᴅ. ⁸They will eat equal portions besides what he has received from the sale of the family estate.

⁹"When you enter the land the Lᴏʀᴅ your God is giving you, do not imitate the detestable customs of those nations. ¹⁰No one among you is to make his son or daughter pass through the fire, practice ˙divination, tell fortunes, interpret omens, practice sorcery, ¹¹cast spells, consult a medium or a familiar spirit, or inquire of the dead. ¹²Everyone who does these things is detestable to the Lᴏʀᴅ, and the Lᴏʀᴅ your God is driving out the nations before you because of these detestable things. ¹³You must be blameless before the Lᴏʀᴅ your God. ¹⁴Though these nations you are about to drive out listen to fortune-tellers and diviners, the Lᴏʀᴅ your God has not permitted you to do this.

¹⁵"The Lᴏʀᴅ your God will raise up for you a prophet like me from among your own brothers. You must listen to him. ¹⁶This is what you requested from the Lᴏʀᴅ your God at Horeb on the day of the assembly when you said, 'Let us not continue to hear the voice of the Lᴏʀᴅ our God or see this great fire any longer, so that we will not die!' ¹⁷Then the Lᴏʀᴅ said to me, 'They have spoken well. ¹⁸I will raise up for them a prophet like you from among their brothers. I will put My words in his mouth, and he will tell them everything I command him. ¹⁹I will hold accountable whoever does not listen to My words that he speaks in My name. ²⁰But the prophet who dares to speak a message in My name that I have not commanded him to speak, or who speaks in the name of other gods—that prophet must die.' ²¹You may say to yourself, 'How can we recognize a message the Lᴏʀᴅ has not spoken?' ²²When a prophet speaks in the Lᴏʀᴅ's name, and the message does not come true or is not fulfilled, that is a message the Lᴏʀᴅ has not spoken. The prophet has spoken it presumptuously. Do not be afraid of him.

19 "When the Lᴏʀᴅ your God annihilates the nations whose land He is giving you, so that you drive them out and live in their cities and houses, ²you are to set apart three cities for yourselves within the land the Lᴏʀᴅ your God is giving you to possess. ³You are to determine the distances and divide the land the Lᴏʀᴅ your God is granting you as an inheritance into three regions, so that anyone who commits manslaughter can flee to these cities.

⁴"Here is the law concerning a case of someone who kills a person and flees there to save his life, having killed his neighbor accidentally without previously hating him: ⁵If he goes into the forest with his neighbor to cut timber, and his hand swings the ax to chop down a tree, but the blade flies off the handle and strikes his neighbor so that he dies, that person may flee to one of these cities and live. ⁶Otherwise, the avenger of blood in the heat of his anger might pursue the one who committed manslaughter, overtake him because the distance is great, and strike him dead. Yet he did not deserve to die, since he did not previously hate his neighbor. ⁷This is why I am commanding you to set apart three cities for yourselves. ⁸If the Lᴏʀᴅ your God enlarges your territory as He swore to your fathers, and gives you all the land He promised to give them— ⁹provided you keep every one of these commands I am giving you today and follow them, loving the Lᴏʀᴅ your God and walking in His ways at all times—you are to add three more cities to these three. ¹⁰In this way, innocent blood will not be shed, and you will not become ˙guilty of bloodshed in the land the Lᴏʀᴅ your God is giving you as an inheritance. ¹¹But if someone hates his neighbor, lies in ambush for him, attacks him, and strikes him fatally, and flees to one of these cities, ¹²the elders of his city must send for him, take him from there, and hand him over to the avenger of blood and he will die. ¹³You must not look on him with pity but purge from Israel the guilt of shedding innocent blood, and you will prosper.

¹⁴"You must not move your neighbor's boundary marker, established at the start in the inheritance you will receive in the land the Lᴏʀᴅ your God is giving you to possess.

¹⁵"One witness cannot establish any wrongdoing or sin against a person, whatever that person has done. A fact must be established by the testimony of two or three witnesses.

¹⁶"If a malicious witness testifies against someone accusing him of a crime, ¹⁷the two people in the dispute must stand in the presence of the Lᴏʀᴅ before the priests and judges in authority at that time. ¹⁸The judges are to make a careful investigation, and if the witness turns out to be a liar who has falsely accused his brother, ¹⁹you must do to him as he intended to do to his brother. You must purge the evil from you. ²⁰Then everyone else will hear and be afraid, and they will never again do anything evil like this among you.

²¹ You must not show pity: life for life, eye for eye, tooth for tooth, hand for hand, and foot for foot.

20 "When you go out to war against your enemies and see horses, chariots, and an army larger than yours, do not be afraid of them, for the Lᴏʀᴅ your God, who brought you out of the land of Egypt, is with you. ² When you are about to engage in battle, the priest is to come forward and address the army. ³ He is to say to them: 'Listen, Israel: Today you are about to engage in battle with your enemies. Do not be cowardly. Do not be afraid, alarmed, or terrified because of them. ⁴ For the Lᴏʀᴅ your God is the One who goes with you to fight for you against your enemies to give you victory.'

⁵ "The officers are to address the army, 'Has any man built a new house and not dedicated it? Let him leave and return home. Otherwise, he may die in battle and another man dedicate it. ⁶ Has any man planted a vineyard and not begun to enjoy its fruit? Let him leave and return home. Otherwise he may die in battle and another man enjoy its fruit. ⁷ Has any man become *engaged to a woman and not married her? Let him leave and return home. Otherwise he may die in battle and another man marry her.' ⁸ The officers will continue to address the army and say, 'Is there any man who is afraid or cowardly? Let him leave and return home, so that his brothers' hearts won't melt like his own.' ⁹ When the officers have finished addressing the army, they will appoint military commanders to lead it.

¹⁰ "When you approach a city to fight against it, you must make an offer of peace. ¹¹ If it accepts your offer of peace and opens its gates to you, all the people found in it will become forced laborers for you and serve you. ¹² However, if it does not make peace with you but wages war against you, lay siege to it. ¹³ When the Lᴏʀᴅ your God hands it over to you, you must strike down all its males with the sword. ¹⁴ But you may take the women, children, animals, and whatever else is in the city—all its spoil—as plunder. You may enjoy the spoil of your enemies that the Lᴏʀᴅ your God has given you. ¹⁵ This is how you are to treat all the cities that are far away from you and are not among the cities of these nations. ¹⁶ However, you must not let any living thing survive among the cities of these people the Lᴏʀᴅ your God is giving you as an inheritance. ¹⁷ You must *completely destroy them—the Hittite, Amorite, Canaanite, Perizzite, Hivite, and Jebusite—as the Lᴏʀᴅ your God has commanded you, ¹⁸ so that they won't teach you to do all the detestable things they do for their gods, and you sin against the Lᴏʀᴅ your God.

¹⁹ "When you lay siege to a city for a long time, fighting against it in order to capture it, you must not destroy its trees by putting an ax to them, because you can get food from them. You must not cut them down. Are trees of the field human, to come under siege by you? ²⁰ But you may destroy the trees that you know do not produce food. You may cut them down to build siege works against the city that is waging war against you, until it falls.

21 "If a murder victim is found lying in a field in the land the Lᴏʀᴅ your God is giving you to possess, and it is not known who killed him, ² your elders and judges must come out and measure the distance from the victim to the nearby cities. ³ The elders of the city nearest to the victim are to get a young cow that has not been yoked or used for work. ⁴ The elders of that city will bring the cow down to a continually flowing stream, to a place not tilled or sown, and they will break its neck there by the stream. ⁵ Then the priests, the sons of Levi, will come forward, for *Yahweh your God has chosen them to serve Him and pronounce blessings in His name, and they are to give a ruling in every dispute and case of assault. ⁶ All the elders of the city nearest to the victim will wash their hands by the stream over the young cow whose neck has been broken. ⁷ They will declare, 'Our hands did not shed this blood; our eyes did not see it. ⁸ Lᴏʀᴅ, forgive Your people Israel You redeemed, and do not hold the shedding of innocent blood against them.' Then they will be absolved of responsibility for bloodshed. ⁹ You must purge from yourselves the *guilt of shedding innocent blood, for you will be doing what is right in the Lᴏʀᴅ's sight.

¹⁰ "When you go to war against your enemies and the Lᴏʀᴅ your God hands them over to you and you take some of them prisoner, and ¹¹ if you see a beautiful woman among the captives, desire her, and want to take her as your wife, ¹² you are to bring her into your house. She must shave her head, trim her nails, ¹³ remove the clothes she was wearing when she was taken prisoner, live in your house, and mourn for her father and mother a full month. After that, you may have sexual relations with her and be her husband, and she will be your wife. ¹⁴ Then if you are not satisfied with her, you are to let her go where she wants, but you must not sell her for money or treat her as merchandise, because you have humiliated her.

¹⁵ "If a man has two wives, one loved and the other unloved, and both the loved and the unloved bear him sons, and if the unloved wife has the firstborn son, ¹⁶ when that man gives what he has to his sons as an inheritance, he is not to show favoritism to the son of the loved wife as his firstborn over the firstborn of the unloved wife. ¹⁷ He must acknowledge the firstborn, the son of the unloved wife, by giving him two shares of his estate, for he is the firstfruits of his virility; he has the rights of the firstborn.

¹⁸ "If a man has a stubborn and rebellious son who does not obey his father or mother and doesn't listen to them even after they discipline him, ¹⁹ his father and mother must take hold of him and bring him to the elders of his city, to the *gate of his hometown. ²⁰ They will say to the elders of his city, 'This son of ours is stubborn and rebellious; he doesn't obey us. He's a glutton and a drunkard.' ²¹ Then all the men of his city will stone him to death. You must purge the evil from you, and all Israel will hear and be afraid.

²² "If anyone is found guilty of an offense deserving the death penalty and is executed, and you hang his body on a tree, ²³ you are not to leave his corpse on the tree overnight but are to bury him that day, for anyone hung on a tree is under God's curse. You must not defile the land the Lᴏʀᴅ your God is giving you as an inheritance.

22 "If you see your brother's ox or sheep straying, you must not ignore it; make sure you return it to your brother. ² If your brother does not live near you or you don't know him, you are to bring the animal to your home to remain with you until your brother comes looking for it; then you can return it to him. ³ Do the same for his donkey, his garment, or anything your brother has lost and you have found. You must not ignore it. ⁴ If you see your brother's donkey or ox

fallen down on the road, you must not ignore it; you must help him lift it up.

⁵ "A woman is not to wear male clothing, and a man is not to put on a woman's garment, for everyone who does these things is detestable to the Lord your God.

⁶ "If you come across a bird's nest with chicks or eggs, either in a tree or on the ground along the road, and the mother is sitting on the chicks or eggs, you must not take the mother along with the young. ⁷ You may take the young for yourself, but be sure to let the mother go free, so that you may prosper and live long. ⁸ If you build a new house, make a railing around your roof, so that you don't bring bloodguilt on your house if someone falls from it. ⁹ Do not plant your vineyard with two types of seed; otherwise, the entire harvest, both the crop you plant and the produce of the vineyard, will be defiled. ¹⁰ Do not plow with an ox and a donkey together. ¹¹ Do not wear clothes made of both wool and linen. ¹² Make tassels on the four corners of the outer garment you wear.

¹³ "If a man marries a woman, has sexual relations with her, and comes to hate her, ¹⁴ and accuses her of shameful conduct, and gives her a bad name, saying, 'I married this woman and was intimate with her, but I didn't find any evidence of her virginity,' ¹⁵ the young woman's father and mother will take the evidence of her virginity and bring it to the city elders at the ˚gate. ¹⁶ The young woman's father will say to the elders, 'I gave my daughter to this man as a wife, but he hates her. ¹⁷ He has accused her of shameful conduct, saying: "I didn't find any evidence of your daughter's virginity," but here is the evidence of my daughter's virginity.' They will spread out the cloth before the city elders. ¹⁸ Then the elders of that city will take the man and punish him. ¹⁹ They will also fine him 100 silver shekels and give them to the young woman's father, because that man gave an Israelite virgin a bad name. She will remain his wife; he cannot divorce her as long as he lives. ²⁰ But if this accusation is true and no evidence of the young woman's virginity is found, ²¹ they will bring the woman to the door of her father's house, and the men of her city will stone her to death. For she has committed an outrage in Israel by being promiscuous in her father's house. You must purge the evil from you.

²² "If a man is discovered having sexual relations with another man's wife, both the man who had sex with the woman and the woman must die. You must purge the evil from Israel. ²³ If there is a young woman who is a virgin ˚engaged to a man, and another man encounters her in the city and has sex with her, ²⁴ you must take the two of them out to the gate of that city and stone them to death—the young woman because she did not cry out in the city and the man because he has violated his neighbor's fiancée. You must purge the evil from you. ²⁵ But if the man encounters an engaged woman in the open country, and he seizes and rapes her, only the man who raped her must die. ²⁶ Do nothing to the young woman, because she is not ˚guilty of an offense deserving death. This case is just like one in which a man attacks his neighbor and murders him. ²⁷ When he found her in the field, the engaged woman cried out, but there was no one to rescue her. ²⁸ If a man encounters a young woman, a virgin who is not engaged, takes hold of her and rapes her, and they are discovered, ²⁹ the man who raped her must give the young woman's father 50 silver shekels,

and she must become his wife because he violated her. He cannot divorce her as long as he lives.

³⁰ "A man is not to marry his father's wife; he must not violate his father's marriage bed.

23 "No man whose testicles have been crushed or whose penis has been cut off may enter the Lord's assembly. ² No one of illegitimate birth may enter the Lord's assembly; none of his descendants, even to the tenth generation, may enter the Lord's assembly. ³ No Ammonite or Moabite may enter the Lord's assembly; none of their descendants, even to the tenth generation, may ever enter the Lord's assembly. ⁴ This is because they did not meet you with food and water on the journey after you came out of Egypt, and because Balaam son of Beor from Pethor in Aram-naharaim was hired to curse you. ⁵ Yet the Lord your God would not listen to Balaam, but He turned the curse into a blessing for you because the Lord your God loves you. ⁶ Never seek their peace or prosperity as long as you live. ⁷ Do not despise an Edomite, because he is your brother. Do not despise an Egyptian, because you were a foreign resident in his land. ⁸ The children born to them in the third generation may enter the Lord's assembly.

⁹ "When you are encamped against your enemies, be careful to avoid anything offensive. ¹⁰ If there is a man among you who is ˚unclean because of a bodily emission during the night, he must go outside the camp; he may not come anywhere inside the camp. ¹¹ When evening approaches, he must wash with water, and when the sun sets he may come inside the camp. ¹² You must have a place outside the camp and go there to relieve yourself. ¹³ You must have a digging tool in your equipment; when you relieve yourself, dig a hole with it and cover up your excrement. ¹⁴ For the Lord your God walks throughout your camp to protect you and deliver your enemies to you; so your encampments must be holy. He must not see anything improper among you or He will turn away from you.

¹⁵ "Do not return a slave to his master when he has escaped from his master to you. ¹⁶ Let him live among you wherever he wants within your gates. Do not mistreat him.

¹⁷ "No Israelite woman is to be a cult prostitute, and no Israelite man is to be a cult prostitute. ¹⁸ Do not bring a female prostitute's wages or a male prostitute's earnings into the house of the Lord your God to fulfill any vow, because both are detestable to the Lord your God.

¹⁹ "Do not charge your brother interest on money, food, or anything that can earn interest. ²⁰ You may charge a foreigner interest, but you must not charge your brother interest, so that the Lord your God may bless you in everything you do in the land you are entering to possess.

²¹ "If you make a vow to the Lord your God, do not be slow to keep it, because He will require it of you, and it will be counted against you as sin. ²² But if you refrain from making a vow, it will not be counted against you as sin. ²³ Be careful to do whatever comes from your lips, because you have freely vowed what you promised to the Lord your God.

²⁴ "When you enter your neighbor's vineyard, you may eat as many grapes as you want until you are full, but you must not put any in your container. ²⁵ When you enter your neighbor's standing grain, you may

pluck heads of grain with your hand, but you must not put a sickle to your neighbor's grain.

24 "If a man marries a woman, but she becomes displeasing to him because he finds something improper about her, he may write her a divorce certificate, hand it to her, and send her away from his house. ²If after leaving his house she goes and becomes another man's wife, ³and the second man hates her, writes her a divorce certificate, hands it to her, and sends her away from his house or if he dies, ⁴the first husband who sent her away may not marry her again after she has been defiled, because that would be detestable to the LORD. You must not bring ˚guilt on the land the LORD your God is giving you as an inheritance.

⁵"When a man takes a bride, he must not go out with the army or be liable for any duty. He is free to stay at home for one year, so that he can bring joy to the wife he has married.

⁶"Do not take a pair of millstones or an upper millstone as security for a debt, because that is like taking a life as security.

⁷"If a man is discovered kidnapping one of his Israelite brothers, whether he treats him as a slave or sells him, the kidnapper must die. You must purge the evil from you.

⁸"Be careful in a case of infectious skin disease, following carefully everything the Levitical priests instruct you to do. Be careful to do as I have commanded them. ⁹Remember what the LORD your God did to Miriam on the journey after you left Egypt.

¹⁰"When you make a loan of any kind to your neighbor, do not enter his house to collect what he offers as security. ¹¹You must stand outside while the man you are making the loan to brings the security out to you. ¹²If he is a poor man, you must not sleep in the garment he has given as security. ¹³Be sure to return it to him at sunset. Then he will sleep in it and bless you, and this will be counted as righteousness to you before the LORD your God.

¹⁴"Do not oppress a hired hand who is poor and needy, whether one of your brothers or one of the foreigners residing within a town in your land. ¹⁵You are to pay him his wages each day before the sun sets, because he is poor and depends on them. Otherwise he will cry out to the LORD against you, and you will be held guilty.

¹⁶"Fathers are not to be put to death for their children or children for their fathers; each person will be put to death for his own sin. ¹⁷Do not deny justice to a foreigner or fatherless child, and do not take a widow's garment as security. ¹⁸Remember that you were a slave in Egypt, and the LORD your God redeemed you from there. Therefore I am commanding you to do this.

¹⁹"When you reap the harvest in your field, and you forget a sheaf in the field, do not go back to get it. It is to be left for the foreigner, the fatherless, and the widow, so that the LORD your God may bless you in all the work of your hands. ²⁰When you knock down the fruit from your olive tree, you must not go over the branches again. What remains will be for the foreigner, the fatherless, and the widow. ²¹When you gather the grapes of your vineyard, you must not glean what is left. What remains will be for the foreigner, the fatherless, and the widow. ²²Remember that you were a slave in the land of Egypt. Therefore I am commanding you to do this.

25 "If there is a dispute between men, they are to go to court, and the judges will hear their case. They will clear the innocent and condemn the ˚guilty. ²If the guilty party deserves to be flogged, the judge will make him lie down and be flogged in his presence with the number of lashes appropriate for his crime. ³He may be flogged with 40 lashes, but no more. Otherwise, if he is flogged with more lashes than these, your brother will be degraded in your sight.

⁴"Do not muzzle an ox while it treads out grain.

⁵"When brothers live on the same property and one of them dies without a son, the wife of the dead man may not marry a stranger outside the family. Her brother-in-law is to take her as his wife, have sexual relations with her, and perform the duty of a brother-in-law for her. ⁶The first son she bears will carry on the name of the dead brother, so his name will not be blotted out from Israel. ⁷But if the man doesn't want to marry his sister-in-law, she must go to the elders at the city ˚gate and say, 'My brother-in-law refuses to preserve his brother's name in Israel. He isn't willing to perform the duty of a brother-in-law for me.' ⁸The elders of his city will summon him and speak with him. If he persists and says, 'I don't want to marry her,' ⁹then his sister-in-law will go up to him in the sight of the elders, remove his sandal from his foot, and spit in his face. Then she will declare, 'This is what is done to a man who will not build up his brother's house.' ¹⁰And his family name in Israel will be called 'The house of the man whose sandal was removed.'

¹¹"If two men are fighting with each other, and the wife of one steps in to rescue her husband from the one striking him, and she puts out her hand and grabs his genitals, ¹²you are to cut off her hand. You must not show pity.

¹³"You must not have two different weights in your bag, one heavy and one light. ¹⁴You must not have two differing dry measures in your house, a larger and a smaller. ¹⁵You must have a full and honest weight, a full and honest dry measure, so that you may live long in the land the LORD your God is giving you. ¹⁶For everyone who does such things and acts unfairly is detestable to the LORD your God.

¹⁷"Remember what the Amalekites did to you on the journey after you left Egypt. ¹⁸They met you along the way and attacked all your stragglers from behind when you were tired and weary. They did not ˚fear God. ¹⁹When the LORD your God gives you rest from all the enemies around you in the land the LORD your God is giving you to possess as an inheritance, blot out the memory of Amalek under heaven. Do not forget.

26 "When you enter the land the LORD your God is giving you as an inheritance, and you take possession of it and live in it, ²you must take some of the first of all the land's produce that you harvest from the land ˚Yahweh your God is giving you and put it in a container. Then go to the place where the LORD your God chooses to have His name dwell. ³When you come before the priest who is serving at that time, you must say to him, 'Today I acknowledge to the LORD your God that I have entered the land the LORD swore to our fathers to give us.'

⁴"Then the priest will take the container from your hand and place it before the altar of the LORD your God. ⁵You are to respond by saying in the presence of the LORD your God:

My father was a wandering Aramean. He went

down to Egypt with a few people and lived there. There he became a great, powerful, and populous nation. ⁶ But the Egyptians mistreated and afflicted us, and forced us to do hard labor. ⁷ So we called out to Yahweh, the God of our fathers, and the Lᴏʀᴅ heard our cry and saw our misery, hardship, and oppression. ⁸ Then the Lᴏʀᴅ brought us out of Egypt with a strong hand and an outstretched arm, with terrifying power, and with signs and wonders. ⁹ He led us to this place and gave us this land, a land flowing with milk and honey. ¹⁰ I have now brought the first of the land's produce that You, Lᴏʀᴅ, have given me.

You will then place the container before the Lᴏʀᴅ your God and bow down to Him. ¹¹ You, the Levite, and the foreign resident among you will rejoice in all the good things the Lᴏʀᴅ your God has given you and your household.

¹² "When you have finished paying all the tenth of your produce in the third year, the year of the tenth, you are to give it to the Levite, the foreigner, the fatherless, and the widow, so that they may eat in your towns and be satisfied. ¹³ Then you will say in the presence of the Lᴏʀᴅ your God:

I have taken the consecrated portion out of my house; I have also given it to the Levite, the foreigner, the fatherless, and the widow, according to all the commands You gave me. I have not violated or forgotten Your commands. ¹⁴ I have not eaten any of it while in mourning, or removed any of it while ˙unclean, or offered any of it for the dead. I have obeyed the Lᴏʀᴅ my God; I have done all You commanded me. ¹⁵ Look down from Your holy dwelling, from heaven, and bless Your people Israel and the land You have given us as You swore to our fathers, a land flowing with milk and honey.

¹⁶ "The Lᴏʀᴅ your God is commanding you this day to follow these statutes and ordinances. You must be careful to follow them with all your heart and all your soul. ¹⁷ Today you have affirmed that the Lᴏʀᴅ is your God and that you will walk in His ways, keep His statutes, commands, and ordinances, and obey Him. ¹⁸ And today the Lᴏʀᴅ has affirmed that you are His special people as He promised you, that you are to keep all His commands, ¹⁹ that He will elevate you to praise, fame, and glory above all the nations He has made, and that you will be a holy people to the Lᴏʀᴅ your God as He promised."

27 Moses and the elders of Israel commanded the people, "Keep every command I am giving you today. ² At the time you cross the Jordan into the land the Lᴏʀᴅ your God is giving you, you must set up large stones and cover them with plaster. ³ Write all the words of this law on the stones after you cross to enter the land the Lᴏʀᴅ your God is giving you, a land flowing with milk and honey, as ˙Yahweh, the God of your fathers, has promised you. ⁴ When you have crossed the Jordan, you are to set up these stones on Mount Ebal, as I am commanding you today, and you are to cover them with plaster. ⁵ Build an altar of stones there to the Lᴏʀᴅ your God—you must not use any iron tool on them. ⁶ Use uncut stones to build the altar of the Lᴏʀᴅ your God and offer ˙burnt offerings to the Lᴏʀᴅ your God on it. ⁷ There you are to sacrifice ˙fellowship offerings, eat, and rejoice in the presence of the Lᴏʀᴅ

your God. ⁸ Write clearly all the words of this law on the plastered stones."

⁹ Moses and the Levitical priests spoke to all Israel, "Be silent, Israel, and listen! This day you have become the people of the Lᴏʀᴅ your God. ¹⁰ Obey the Lᴏʀᴅ your God and follow His commands and statutes I am giving you today."

¹¹ On that day Moses commanded the people, ¹² "When you have crossed the Jordan, these tribes will stand on Mount Gerizim to bless the people: Simeon, Levi, Judah, Issachar, Joseph, and Benjamin. ¹³ And these tribes will stand on Mount Ebal to deliver the curse: Reuben, Gad, Asher, Zebulun, Dan, and Naphtali. ¹⁴ The Levites will proclaim in a loud voice to every Israelite:

¹⁵ 'The person who makes a carved idol or cast image, which is detestable to the Lᴏʀᴅ, the work of a craftsman, and sets it up in secret is cursed.'
And all the people will reply, "Amen!'
¹⁶ 'The one who dishonors his father or mother is cursed.'
And all the people will say, 'Amen!'
¹⁷ 'The one who moves his neighbor's boundary marker is cursed.'
And all the people will say, 'Amen!'
¹⁸ 'The one who leads a blind person astray on the road is cursed.'
And all the people will say, 'Amen!'
¹⁹ 'The one who denies justice to a foreigner, a fatherless child, or a widow is cursed.'
And all the people will say, 'Amen!'
²⁰ 'The one who sleeps with his father's wife is cursed, for he has violated his father's marriage bed.'
And all the people will say, 'Amen!'
²¹ 'The one who has sexual intercourse with any animal is cursed.'
And all the people will say, 'Amen!'
²² 'The one who sleeps with his sister, whether his father's daughter or his mother's daughter is cursed.'
And all the people will say, 'Amen!'
²³ 'The one who sleeps with his mother-in-law is cursed.'
And all the people will say, 'Amen!'
²⁴ 'The one who secretly kills his neighbor is cursed.'
And all the people will say, 'Amen!'
²⁵ 'The one who accepts a bribe to kill an innocent person is cursed.'
And all the people will say, 'Amen!'
²⁶ 'Anyone who does not put the words of this law into practice is cursed.'
And all the people will say, 'Amen!'

28 "Now if you faithfully obey the Lᴏʀᴅ your God and are careful to follow all His commands I am giving you today, the Lᴏʀᴅ your God will put you far above all the nations of the earth. ² All these blessings will come and overtake you, because you obey the Lᴏʀᴅ your God:

³ 　You will be blessed in the city
　　and blessed in the country.
⁴ 　Your descendants will be blessed,
　　and your land's produce,
　　and the offspring of your livestock,
　　including the young of your herds
　　and the newborn of your flocks.

⁵   Your basket and kneading bowl will be blessed.
⁶   You will be blessed when you come in
     and blessed when you go out.

⁷ "The Lᴏʀᴅ will cause the enemies who rise up against you to be defeated before you. They will march out against you from one direction but flee from you in seven directions. ⁸ The Lᴏʀᴅ will grant you a blessing on your storehouses and on everything you do; He will bless you in the land your God is giving you. ⁹ The Lᴏʀᴅ will establish you as His holy people, as He swore to you, if you obey the commands of the Lᴏʀᴅ your God and walk in His ways. ¹⁰ Then all the peoples of the earth will see that you are called by ˙Yahweh's name, and they will stand in awe of you. ¹¹ The Lᴏʀᴅ will make you prosper abundantly with children, the offspring of your livestock, and your land's produce in the land the Lᴏʀᴅ swore to your fathers to give you. ¹² The Lᴏʀᴅ will open for you His abundant storehouse, the sky, to give your land rain in its season and to bless all the work of your hands. You will lend to many nations, but you will not borrow. ¹³ The Lᴏʀᴅ will make you the head and not the tail; you will only move upward and never downward if you listen to the Lᴏʀᴅ your God's commands I am giving you today and are careful to follow them. ¹⁴ Do not turn aside to the right or the left from all the things I am commanding you today, and do not go after other gods to worship them.

¹⁵ "But if you do not obey the Lᴏʀᴅ your God by carefully following all His commands and statutes I am giving you today, all these curses will come and overtake you:
¹⁶   You will be cursed in the city
       and cursed in the country.
¹⁷   Your basket and kneading bowl will be cursed.
¹⁸   Your descendants will be cursed,
       and your land's produce,
       the young of your herds,
       and the newborn of your flocks.
¹⁹   You will be cursed when you come in
       and cursed when you go out.

²⁰ The Lᴏʀᴅ will send against you curses, confusion, and rebuke in everything you do until you are destroyed and quickly perish, because of the wickedness of your actions in abandoning Me. ²¹ The Lᴏʀᴅ will make pestilence cling to you until He has exterminated you from the land you are entering to possess. ²² The Lᴏʀᴅ will afflict you with wasting disease, fever, inflammation, burning heat, drought, blight, and mildew; these will pursue you until you perish. ²³ The sky above you will be bronze, and the earth beneath you iron. ²⁴ The Lᴏʀᴅ will turn the rain of your land into falling dust; it will descend on you from the sky until you are destroyed. ²⁵ The Lᴏʀᴅ will cause you to be defeated before your enemies. You will march out against them from one direction but flee from them in seven directions. You will be an object of horror to all the kingdoms of the earth. ²⁶ Your corpses will be food for all the birds of the sky and the wild animals of the land, with no one to scare them away.

²⁷ "The Lᴏʀᴅ will afflict you with the boils of Egypt, tumors, a festering rash, and scabies, from which you cannot be cured. ²⁸ The Lᴏʀᴅ will afflict you with madness, blindness, and mental confusion, ²⁹ so that at noon you will grope as a blind man gropes in the dark. You will not be successful in anything you do. You will only be oppressed and robbed continually, and no one will help you. ³⁰ You will become ˙engaged to a woman, but another man will rape her. You will build a house but not live in it. You will plant a vineyard but not enjoy its fruit. ³¹ Your ox will be slaughtered before your eyes, but you will not eat any of it. Your donkey will be taken away from you and not returned to you. Your flock will be given to your enemies, and no one will help you. ³² Your sons and daughters will be given to another people, while your eyes grow weary looking for them every day. But you will be powerless to do anything. ³³ A people you don't know will eat your land's produce and everything you have labored for. You will only be oppressed and crushed continually. ³⁴ You will be driven mad by what you see. ³⁵ The Lᴏʀᴅ will afflict you with painful and incurable boils on your knees and thighs—from the sole of your foot to the top of your head.

³⁶ "The Lᴏʀᴅ will bring you and your king that you have appointed to a nation neither you nor your fathers have known, and there you will worship other gods, of wood and stone. ³⁷ You will become an object of horror, scorn, and ridicule among all the peoples where the Lᴏʀᴅ will drive you.

³⁸ "You will sow much seed in the field but harvest little, because locusts will devour it. ³⁹ You will plant and cultivate vineyards but not drink the wine or gather the grapes, because worms will eat them. ⁴⁰ You will have olive trees throughout your territory but not anoint yourself with oil, because your olives will drop off. ⁴¹ You will father sons and daughters, but they will not remain yours, because they will be taken prisoner. ⁴² Whirring insects will take possession of all your trees and your land's produce. ⁴³ The foreign resident among you will rise higher and higher above you, while you sink lower and lower. ⁴⁴ He will lend to you, but you won't lend to him. He will be the head, and you will be the tail.

⁴⁵ "All these curses will come, pursue, and overtake you until you are destroyed, since you did not obey the Lᴏʀᴅ your God and keep the commands and statutes He gave you. ⁴⁶ These curses will be a sign and a wonder against you and your descendants forever. ⁴⁷ Because you didn't serve the Lᴏʀᴅ your God with joy and a cheerful heart, even though you had an abundance of everything, ⁴⁸ you will serve your enemies the Lᴏʀᴅ will send against you, in famine, thirst, nakedness, and a lack of everything. He will place an iron yoke on your neck until He has destroyed you. ⁴⁹ The Lᴏʀᴅ will bring a nation from far away, from the ends of the earth, to swoop down on you like an eagle, a nation whose language you don't understand, ⁵⁰ a ruthless nation, showing no respect for the old and not sparing the young. ⁵¹ They will eat the offspring of your livestock and your land's produce until you are destroyed. They will leave you no grain, new wine, oil, young of your herds, or newborn of your flocks until they cause you to perish. ⁵² They will besiege you within all your gates until your high and fortified walls, that you trust in, come down throughout your land. They will besiege you within all your gates throughout the land the Lᴏʀᴅ your God has given you.

⁵³ "You will eat your children, the flesh of your sons and daughters the Lᴏʀᴅ your God has given you during the siege and hardship your enemy imposes on you. ⁵⁴ The most sensitive and refined man among you will look grudgingly at his brother, the wife he embraces, and the rest of his children, ⁵⁵ refusing to share with

any of them his children's flesh that he will eat because he has nothing left during the siege and hardship your enemy imposes on you in all your towns. [56] The most sensitive and refined woman among you, who would not venture to set the sole of her foot on the ground because of her refinement and sensitivity, will begrudge the husband she embraces, her son, and her daughter, [57] the afterbirth that comes out from between her legs and the children she bears, because she will secretly eat them for lack of anything else during the siege and hardship your enemy imposes on you within your gates.

[58] "If you are not careful to obey all the words of this law, which are written in this scroll, by *fearing this glorious and awesome name—Yahweh, your God— [59] He will bring extraordinary plagues on you and your descendants, severe and lasting plagues, and terrible and chronic sicknesses. [60] He will afflict you again with all the diseases of Egypt, which you dreaded, and they will cling to you. [61] The Lord will also afflict you with every sickness and plague not recorded in the book of this law, until you are destroyed. [62] Though you were as numerous as the stars of the sky, you will be left with only a few people, because you did not obey the Lord your God. [63] Just as the Lord was glad to cause you to prosper and to multiply you, so He will also be glad to cause you to perish and to destroy you. You will be deported from the land you are entering to possess. [64] Then the Lord will scatter you among all peoples from one end of the earth to the other, and there you will worship other gods, of wood and stone, which neither you nor your fathers have known. [65] You will find no peace among those nations, and there will be no resting place for the sole of your foot. There the Lord will give you a trembling heart, failing eyes, and a despondent spirit. [66] Your life will hang in doubt before you. You will be in dread night and day, never certain of survival. [67] In the morning you will say, 'If only it were evening!' and in the evening you will say, 'If only it were morning!'—because of the dread you will have in your heart and because of what you will see. [68] The Lord will take you back in ships to Egypt by a route that I said you would never see again. There you will sell yourselves to your enemies as male and female slaves, but no one will buy you."

29 These are the words of the covenant the Lord commanded Moses to make with the Israelites in the land of Moab, in addition to the covenant He had made with them at Horeb. [2] Moses summoned all Israel and said to them, "You have seen with your own eyes everything the Lord did in Egypt to Pharaoh, to all his officials, and to his entire land. [3] You saw with your own eyes the great trials and those great signs and wonders. [4] Yet to this day the Lord has not given you a mind to understand, eyes to see, or ears to hear. [5] I led you 40 years in the wilderness; your clothes and the sandals on your feet did not wear out; [6] you did not eat bread or drink wine or beer—so that you might know that I am *Yahweh your God. [7] When you reached this place, Sihon king of Heshbon and Og king of Bashan came out against us in battle, but we defeated them. [8] We took their land and gave it as an inheritance to the Reubenites, the Gadites, and half the tribe of Manasseh. [9] Therefore, observe the words of this covenant and follow them, so that you will succeed in everything you do.

[10] "All of you are standing today before the Lord your God—your leaders, tribes, elders, officials, all the men of Israel, [11] your children, your wives, and the foreigners in your camps who cut your wood and draw your water— [12] so that you may enter into the covenant of the Lord your God, which He is making with you today, so that you may enter into His oath [13] and so that He may establish you today as His people and He may be your God as He promised you and as He swore to your fathers Abraham, Isaac, and Jacob. [14] I am making this covenant and this oath not only with you, [15] but also with those who are standing here with us today in the presence of the Lord our God and with those who are not here today.

[16] "Indeed, you know how we lived in the land of Egypt and passed through the nations where you traveled. [17] You saw their detestable images and idols made of wood, stone, silver, and gold, which were among them. [18] Be sure there is no man, woman, clan, or tribe among you today whose heart turns away from the Lord our God to go and worship the gods of those nations. Be sure there is no root among you bearing poisonous and bitter fruit. [19] When someone hears the words of this oath, he may consider himself exempt, thinking, 'I will have peace even though I follow my own stubborn heart.' This will lead to the destruction of the well-watered land as well as the dry land. [20] The Lord will not be willing to forgive him. Instead, His anger and jealousy will burn against that person, and every curse written in this scroll will descend on him. The Lord will blot out his name under heaven, [21] and single him out for harm from all the tribes of Israel, according to all the curses of the covenant written in this book of the law.

[22] "Future generations of your children who follow you and the foreigner who comes from a distant country will see the plagues of the land and the sicknesses the Lord has inflicted on it. [23] All its soil will be a burning waste of sulfur and salt, unsown, producing nothing, with no plant growing on it, just like the fall of Sodom and Gomorrah, Admah and Zeboiim, which the Lord demolished in His fierce anger. [24] All the nations will ask, 'Why has the Lord done this to this land? Why this great outburst of anger?' [25] Then people will answer, 'It is because they abandoned the covenant of Yahweh, the God of their fathers, which He had made with them when He brought them out of the land of Egypt. [26] They began to worship other gods, bowing down to gods they had not known—gods that the Lord had not permitted them to worship. [27] Therefore the Lord's anger burned against this land, and He brought every curse written in this book on it. [28] The Lord uprooted them from their land in His anger, rage, and great wrath, and threw them into another land where they are today.' [29] The hidden things belong to the Lord our God, but the revealed things belong to us and our children forever, so that we may follow all the words of this law.

30 "When all these things happen to you—the blessings and curses I have set before you— and you come to your senses while you are in all the nations where the Lord your God has driven you, [2] and you and your children return to the Lord your God and obey Him with all your heart and all your soul by doing everything I am giving you today, [3] then He will restore your fortunes, have compassion on you, and gather you again from all the peoples where the Lord your God has scattered you. [4] Even if your exiles are

at the ends of the earth, He will gather you and bring you back from there. ⁵The LORD your God will bring you into the land your fathers possessed, and you will take possession of it. He will cause you to prosper and multiply you more than He did your fathers. ⁶The LORD your God will circumcise your heart and the hearts of your descendants, and you will love Him with all your heart and all your soul so that you will live. ⁷The LORD your God will put all these curses on your enemies who hate and persecute you. ⁸Then you will again obey Him and follow all His commands I am giving you today. ⁹The LORD your God will make you prosper abundantly in all the work of your hands with children, the offspring of your livestock, and your land's produce. Indeed, the LORD will again delight in your prosperity, as He delighted in that of your fathers, ¹⁰when you obey the LORD your God by keeping His commands and statutes that are written in this book of the law and return to Him with all your heart and all your soul.

¹¹"This command that I give you today is certainly not too difficult or beyond your reach. ¹²It is not in heaven so that you have to ask, 'Who will go up to heaven, get it for us, and proclaim it to us so that we may follow it?' ¹³And it is not across the sea so that you have to ask, 'Who will cross the sea, get it for us, and proclaim it to us so that we may follow it?' ¹⁴But the message is very near you, in your mouth and in your heart, so that you may follow it. ¹⁵See, today I have set before you life and prosperity, death and adversity. ¹⁶For I am commanding you today to love the LORD your God, to walk in His ways, and to keep His commands, statutes, and ordinances, so that you may live and multiply, and the LORD your God may bless you in the land you are entering to possess. ¹⁷But if your heart turns away and you do not listen and you are led astray to bow down to other gods and worship them, ¹⁸I tell you today that you will certainly perish and will not live long in the land you are entering to possess across the Jordan. ¹⁹I call heaven and earth as witnesses against you today that I have set before you life and death, blessing and curse. Choose life so that you and your descendants may live, ²⁰love the LORD your God, obey Him, and remain faithful to Him. For He is your life, and He will prolong your life in the land the LORD swore to give to your fathers Abraham, Isaac, and Jacob.

31 Then Moses continued to speak these words to all Israel, ²saying, "I am now 120 years old; I can no longer act as your leader. The LORD has told me, 'You will not cross this Jordan.' ³The LORD your God is the One who will cross ahead of you. He will destroy these nations before you, and you will drive them out. Joshua is the one who will cross ahead of you, as the LORD has said. ⁴The LORD will deal with them as He did Sihon and Og, the kings of the Amorites, and their land when He destroyed them. ⁵The LORD will deliver them over to you, and you must do to them exactly as I have commanded you. ⁶Be strong and courageous; don't be terrified or afraid of them. For it is the LORD your God who goes with you; He will not leave you or forsake you."

⁷Moses then summoned Joshua and said to him in the sight of all Israel, "Be strong and courageous, for you will go with this people into the land the LORD swore to give to their fathers. You will enable them to take possession of it. ⁸The LORD is the One who will go before you. He will be with you; He will not leave you or forsake you. Do not be afraid or discouraged."

⁹Moses wrote down this law and gave it to the priests, the sons of Levi, who carried the ark of the LORD's covenant, and to all the elders of Israel. ¹⁰Moses commanded them, "At the end of every seven years, at the appointed time in the year of debt cancellation, during the Festival of Booths, ¹¹when all Israel assembles in the presence of the LORD your God at the place He chooses, you are to read this law aloud before all Israel. ¹²Gather the people—men, women, children, and foreigners living within your gates—so that they may listen and learn to *fear the LORD your God and be careful to follow all the words of this law. ¹³Then their children who do not know the law will listen and learn to fear the LORD your God as long as you live in the land you are crossing the Jordan to possess."

¹⁴The LORD said to Moses, "The time of your death is now approaching. Call Joshua and present yourselves at the tent of meeting so that I may commission him." When Moses and Joshua went and presented themselves at the tent of meeting, ¹⁵the LORD appeared at the tent in a pillar of cloud, and the cloud stood at the entrance to the tent.

¹⁶The LORD said to Moses, "You are about to rest with your fathers, and these people will soon commit adultery with the foreign gods of the land they are entering. They will abandon Me and break the covenant I have made with them. ¹⁷My anger will burn against them on that day; I will abandon them and hide My face from them so that they will become easy prey. Many troubles and afflictions will come to them. On that day they will say, 'Haven't these troubles come to us because our God is no longer with us?' ¹⁸I will certainly hide My face on that day because of all the evil they have done by turning to other gods. ¹⁹Therefore write down this song for yourselves and teach it to the Israelites; have them recite it, so that this song may be a witness for Me against the Israelites. ²⁰When I bring them into the land I swore to give their fathers, a land flowing with milk and honey, they will eat their fill and prosper. They will turn to other gods and worship them, despising Me and breaking My covenant. ²¹And when many troubles and afflictions come to them, this song will testify against them, because their descendants will not have forgotten it. For I know what they are prone to do, even before I bring them into the land I swore to give them." ²²So Moses wrote down this song on that day and taught it to the Israelites.

²³The LORD commissioned Joshua son of Nun, "Be strong and courageous, for you will bring the Israelites into the land I swore to them, and I will be with you."

²⁴When Moses had finished writing down on a scroll every single word of this law, ²⁵he commanded the Levites who carried the ark of the LORD's covenant, ²⁶"Take this book of the law and place it beside the ark of the covenant of the LORD your God so that it may remain there as a witness against you. ²⁷For I know how rebellious and stiff-necked you are. If you are rebelling against the LORD now, while I am still alive, how much more will you rebel after I am dead! ²⁸Assemble all your tribal elders and officers before me so that I may speak these words directly to them and call heaven and earth as witnesses against them. ²⁹For I know that after my death you will become completely corrupt and turn from the path I have commanded you. Disaster will come to you in the future, because

you will do what is evil in the LORD's sight, infuriating Him with what your hands have made." ³⁰ Then Moses recited aloud every single word of this song to the entire assembly of Israel:

32

Pay attention, heavens, and I will speak;
listen, earth, to the words of my mouth.

² Let my teaching fall like rain
and my word settle like dew,
like gentle rain on new grass
and showers on tender plants.

³ For I will proclaim *Yahweh's name.
Declare the greatness of our God!

⁴ The Rock—His work is perfect;
all His ways are entirely just.
A faithful God, without prejudice,
He is righteous and true.

⁵ His people have acted corruptly toward Him;
this is their defect—they are not His children
but a devious and crooked generation.

⁶ Is this how you repay the LORD,
you foolish and senseless people?
Isn't He your Father and Creator?
Didn't He make you and sustain you?

⁷ Remember the days of old;
consider the years long past.
Ask your father, and he will tell you,
your elders, and they will teach you.

⁸ When the *Most High gave the nations
their inheritance
and divided the *human race,
He set the boundaries of the peoples
according to the number of the people
of Israel.

⁹ But the LORD's portion is His people,
Jacob, His own inheritance.

¹⁰ He found him in a desolate land,
in a barren, howling wilderness;
He surrounded him, cared for him,
and protected him as the pupil of His eye.

¹¹ He watches over His nest like an eagle
and hovers over His young;
He spreads His wings, catches him,
and lifts him up on His pinions.

¹² The LORD alone led him,
with no help from a foreign god.

¹³ He made him ride on the heights of the land
and eat the produce of the field.
He nourished him with honey from the rock
and oil from flint-like rock,

¹⁴ cream from the herd and milk from the flock,
with the fat of lambs,
rams from Bashan, and goats,
with the choicest grains of wheat;
you drank wine from the finest grapes.

¹⁵ Then Jeshurun became fat and rebelled—
you became fat, bloated, and gorged.
He abandoned the God who made him
and scorned the Rock of his salvation.

¹⁶ They provoked His jealousy with foreign gods;
they enraged Him with detestable practices.

¹⁷ They sacrificed to demons, not God,
to gods they had not known,
new gods that had just arrived,
which your fathers did not fear.

¹⁸ You ignored the Rock who gave you birth;
you forgot the God who gave birth to you.

¹⁹ When the LORD saw this, He despised them,
provoked to anger by His sons and daughters.

²⁰ He said: "I will hide My face from them;
I will see what will become of them,
for they are a perverse generation—
unfaithful children.

²¹ They have provoked My jealousy
with their so-called gods;
they have enraged Me with their worthless
idols.
So I will provoke their jealousy
with an inferior people;
I will enrage them with a foolish nation.

²² For fire has been kindled because of My anger
and burns to the depths of *Sheol;
it devours the land and its produce,
and scorches the foundations
of the mountains.

²³ "I will pile disasters on them;
I will use up My arrows against them.

²⁴ They will be weak from hunger,
ravaged by pestilence and bitter plague;
I will unleash on them wild beasts with fangs,
as well as venomous snakes that slither
in the dust.

²⁵ Outside, the sword will take their children,
and inside, there will be terror;
the young man and the young woman
will be killed,
the infant and the gray-haired man.

²⁶ I would have said: I will cut them to pieces
and blot out the memory of them
from mankind,

²⁷ if I had not feared insult from the enemy,
or feared that these foes might misunderstand
and say: 'Our own hand has prevailed;
it wasn't the LORD who did all this.'"

²⁸ Israel is a nation lacking sense
with no understanding at all.

²⁹ If only they were wise,
they would figure it out;
they would understand their fate.

³⁰ How could one man pursue a thousand,
or two put ten thousand to flight,
unless their Rock had sold them,
unless the LORD had given them up?

³¹ But their "rock" is not like our Rock;
even our enemies concede.

³² For their vine is from the vine of Sodom
and from the fields of Gomorrah.
Their grapes are poisonous;
their clusters are bitter.

³³ Their wine is serpents' venom,
the deadly poison of cobras.

³⁴ "Is it not stored up with Me,
sealed up in My vaults?

³⁵ Vengeance belongs to Me; I will repay.
In time their foot will slip,
for their day of disaster is near,
and their doom is coming quickly."

³⁶ The LORD will indeed vindicate His people
and have compassion on His servants
when He sees that their strength is gone
and no one is left—slave or free.

³⁷ He will say: "Where are their gods,
the 'rock' they found refuge in?

³⁸ Who ate the fat of their sacrifices
and drank the wine of their *drink offerings?

Let them rise up and help you;
    let it be a shelter for you.
39 See now that I alone am He;
    there is no God but Me.
I bring death and I give life;
I wound and I heal.
No one can rescue anyone from My hand.
40 I raise My hand to heaven and declare:
    As surely as I live forever,
41 when I sharpen My flashing sword,
and my hand takes hold of judgment,
I will take vengeance on My adversaries
and repay those who hate Me.
42 I will make My arrows drunk with blood
while My sword devours flesh—
    the blood of the slain and the captives,
    the heads of the enemy leaders."
43 Rejoice, you nations, concerning
    His people,
for He will avenge the blood of His servants.
He will take vengeance on His adversaries;
He will purify His land and His people.

44 Moses came with Joshua son of Nun and recited all the words of this song in the presence of the people. 45 After Moses finished reciting all these words to all Israel, 46 he said to them, "Take to heart all these words I am giving as a warning to you today, so that you may command your children to carefully follow all the words of this law. 47 For they are not meaningless words to you but they are your life, and by them you will live long in the land you are crossing the Jordan to possess."

48 On that same day the LORD spoke to Moses, 49 "Go up Mount Nebo in the Abarim range in the land of Moab, across from Jericho, and view the land of Canaan I am giving the Israelites as a possession. 50 Then you will die on the mountain that you go up, and you will be gathered to your people, just as your brother Aaron died on Mount Hor and was gathered to his people. 51 For both of you broke faith with Me among the Israelites at the waters of Meribath-kadesh in the Wilderness of Zin by failing to treat Me as holy in their presence. 52 Although from a distance you will view the land that I am giving the Israelites, you will not go there."

33 This is the blessing that Moses, the man of God, gave the Israelites before his death. 2 He said:
The LORD came from Sinai
    and appeared to them from Seir;
He shone on them from Mount Paran
and came with ten thousand holy ones,
with lightning from His right hand for them.
3 Indeed He loves the people.
All Your holy ones are in Your hand,
and they assemble at Your feet.
Each receives Your words.
4 Moses gave us instruction,
    a possession for the assembly of Jacob.
5 So He became King in Jeshurun
when the leaders of the people gathered
with the tribes of Israel.
6 Let Reuben live and not die
though his people become few.
7 He said this about Judah:
    LORD, hear Judah's cry and bring him
        to his people.
He fights for his cause with his own hands,
but may You be a help against his foes.

8 He said about Levi:
    Your *Thummim and Urim belong to
        Your faithful one;
You tested him at Massah
and contended with him at the waters
    of Meribah.
9 He said about his father and mother,
    "I do not regard them."
He disregarded his brothers
and didn't acknowledge his sons,
for they kept Your word
and maintained Your covenant.
10 They will teach Your ordinances to Jacob
and Your instruction to Israel;
they will set incense before You
and whole *burnt offerings on Your altar.
11 LORD, bless his possessions,
and accept the work of his hands.
Smash the loins of his adversaries
    and enemies,
so that they cannot rise again.
12 He said about Benjamin:
    The LORD's beloved rests securely
        on Him.
He shields him all day long,
and he rests on His shoulders.
13 He said about Joseph:
    May his land be blessed by the LORD
    with the dew of heaven's bounty
    and the watery depths that lie beneath;
14 with the bountiful harvest from the sun
and the abundant yield of the seasons;
15 with the best products
    of the ancient mountains
and the bounty of the eternal hills;
16 with the choice gifts of the land
and everything in it;
and with the favor of Him
who appeared in the burning bush.
May these rest on the head of Joseph,
on the crown of the prince
    of his brothers.
17 His firstborn bull has splendor,
and horns like those of a wild ox;
he gores all the peoples with them
to the ends of the earth.
Such are the ten thousands of Ephraim,
and such are the thousands of Manasseh.
18 He said about Zebulun:
    Rejoice, Zebulun, in your journeys,
    and Issachar, in your tents.
19 They summon the peoples to a mountain;
there they offer acceptable sacrifices.
For they draw from the wealth of the seas
and the hidden treasures of the sand.
20 He said about Gad:
    The one who enlarges Gad's territory
    will be blessed.
He lies down like a lion
and tears off an arm or even a head.
21 He chose the best part for himself,
because a ruler's portion was assigned there
    for him.
He came with the leaders
    of the people;
he carried out the LORD's justice
and His ordinances for Israel.

²²He said about Dan:
>Dan is a young lion,
>leaping out of Bashan.
²³He said about Naphtali:
>Naphtali, enjoying approval,
>full of the LORD's blessing,
>take possession to the west and the south.
²⁴He said about Asher:
>May Asher be the most blessed
>of the sons;
>may he be the most favored
>among his brothers
>and dip his foot in olive oil.
²⁵ May the bolts of your gate be iron and bronze,
>and your strength last as long as you live.
²⁶ There is none like the God of Jeshurun,
>who rides the heavens to your aid,
>the clouds in His majesty.
²⁷ The God of old is your dwelling place,
>and underneath are the everlasting arms.
>He drives out the enemy before you
>and commands, "Destroy!"
²⁸ So Israel dwells securely;
>Jacob lives untroubled
>in a land of grain and new wine;
>even his skies drip with dew.
²⁹ How happy you are, Israel!
>Who is like you,
>a people saved by the LORD?
>He is the shield that protects you,
>the sword you boast in.

>Your enemies will cringe before you,
>and you will tread on their backs.

34 Then Moses went up from the plains of Moab to Mount Nebo, to the top of Pisgah, which faces Jericho, and the LORD showed him all the land: Gilead as far as Dan, ²all of Naphtali, the land of Ephraim and Manasseh, all the land of Judah as far as the Mediterranean Sea; ³the *Negev, and the region from the Valley of Jericho, the City of Palms, as far as Zoar. ⁴The LORD then said to him, "This is the land I promised Abraham, Isaac, and Jacob, 'I will give it to your descendants.' I have let you see it with your own eyes, but you will not cross into it."

⁵So Moses the servant of the LORD died there in the land of Moab, as the LORD had said. ⁶He buried him in the valley in the land of Moab facing Beth-peor, and no one to this day knows where his grave is. ⁷Moses was 120 years old when he died; his eyes were not weak, and his vitality had not left him. ⁸The Israelites wept for Moses in the plains of Moab 30 days. Then the days of weeping and mourning for Moses came to an end.

⁹Joshua son of Nun was filled with the spirit of wisdom because Moses had laid his hands on him. So the Israelites obeyed him and did as the LORD had commanded Moses. ¹⁰No prophet has arisen again in Israel like Moses, whom the LORD knew face to face. ¹¹He was unparalleled for all the signs and wonders the LORD sent him to do against the land of Egypt—to Pharaoh, to all his officials, and to all his land, ¹²and for all the mighty acts of power and terrifying deeds that Moses performed in the sight of all Israel.

JOSHUA

1 After the death of Moses the LORD's servant, the LORD spoke to Joshua son of Nun, who had served Moses: ²"Moses My servant is dead. Now you and all the people prepare to cross over the Jordan to the land I am giving the Israelites. ³I have given you every place where the sole of your foot treads, just as I promised Moses. ⁴Your territory will be from the wilderness and Lebanon to the great Euphrates River—all the land of the Hittites—and west to the Mediterranean Sea. ⁵No one will be able to stand against you as long as you live. I will be with you, just as I was with Moses. I will not leave you or forsake you.

⁶"Be strong and courageous, for you will distribute the land I swore to their fathers to give them as an inheritance. ⁷Above all, be strong and very courageous to carefully observe the whole instruction My servant Moses commanded you. Do not turn from it to the right or the left, so that you will have success wherever you go. ⁸This book of instruction must not depart from your mouth; you are to recite it day and night so that you may carefully observe everything written in it. For then you will prosper and succeed in whatever you do. ⁹Haven't I commanded you: be strong and courageous? Do not be afraid or discouraged, for the LORD your God is with you wherever you go."

¹⁰Then Joshua commanded the officers of the people: ¹¹"Go through the camp and tell the people, 'Get provisions ready for yourselves, for within three days you will be crossing the Jordan to go in and take possession of the land the LORD your God is giving you to inherit.'"

¹²Joshua said to the Reubenites, the Gadites, and half the tribe of Manasseh: ¹³"Remember what Moses the LORD's servant commanded you when he said, 'The LORD your God will give you rest, and He will give you this land.' ¹⁴Your wives, young children, and livestock may remain in the land Moses gave you on this side of the Jordan. But your fighting men must cross over in battle formation ahead of your brothers and help them ¹⁵until the LORD gives your brothers rest, as He has given you, and they too possess the land the LORD your God is giving them. You may then return to the land of your inheritance and take possession of what Moses the LORD's servant gave you on the east side of the Jordan."

¹⁶They answered Joshua, "Everything you have commanded us we will do, and everywhere you send us we will go. ¹⁷We will obey you, just as we obeyed Moses in everything. And may the LORD your God be with you, as He was with Moses. ¹⁸Anyone who rebels against your order and does not obey your words in all that you command him, will be put to death. Above all, be strong and courageous!"

2 Joshua son of Nun secretly sent two men as spies from the Acacia Grove, saying, "Go and scout the land, especially Jericho." So they left, and they came to the house of a woman, a prostitute named Rahab, and stayed there.

²The king of Jericho was told, "Look, some of the

Israelite men have come here tonight to investigate the land." ³Then the king of Jericho sent word to Rahab and said, "Bring out the men who came to you and entered your house, for they came to investigate the entire land."

⁴But the woman had taken the two men and hidden them. So she said, "Yes, the men did come to me, but I didn't know where they were from. ⁵At nightfall, when the gate was about to close, the men went out, and I don't know where they were going. Chase after them quickly, and you can catch up with them!" ⁶But she had taken them up to the roof and hidden them among the stalks of flax that she had arranged on the roof. ⁷The men pursued them along the road to the fords of the Jordan, and as soon as they left to pursue them, the gate was shut.

⁸Before the men fell asleep, she went up on the roof ⁹and said to them, "I know that the LORD has given you this land and that the terror of you has fallen on us, and everyone who lives in the land is panicking because of you. ¹⁰For we have heard how the LORD dried up the waters of the ·Red Sea before you when you came out of Egypt, and what you did to Sihon and Og, the two Amorite kings you ·completely destroyed across the Jordan. ¹¹When we heard this, we lost heart, and everyone's courage failed because of you, for the LORD your God is God in heaven above and on earth below. ¹²Now please swear to me by the LORD that you will also show kindness to my family, because I showed kindness to you. Give me a sure sign ¹³that you will spare the lives of my father, mother, brothers, sisters, and all who belong to them, and save us from death."

¹⁴The men answered her, "We will give our lives for yours. If you don't report our mission, we will show kindness and faithfulness to you when the LORD gives us the land."

¹⁵Then she let them down by a rope through the window, since she lived in a house that was built into the wall of the city. ¹⁶"Go to the hill country so that the men pursuing you won't find you," she said to them. "Hide yourselves there for three days until they return; afterward, go on your way."

¹⁷The men said to her, "We will be free from this oath you made us swear, ¹⁸unless, when we enter the land, you tie this scarlet cord to the window through which you let us down. Bring your father, mother, brothers, and all your father's family into your house. ¹⁹If anyone goes out the doors of your house, his blood will be on his own head, and we will be innocent. But if anyone with you in the house should be harmed, his blood will be on our heads. ²⁰And if you report our mission, we are free from the oath you made us swear."

²¹"Let it be as you say," she replied, and she sent them away. After they had gone, she tied the scarlet cord to the window.

²²So the two men went into the hill country and stayed there three days until the pursuers had returned. They searched all along the way, but did not find them. ²³Then the men returned, came down from the hill country, and crossed the Jordan. They went to Joshua son of Nun and reported everything that had happened to them. ²⁴They told Joshua, "The LORD has handed over the entire land to us. Everyone who lives in the land is also panicking because of us."

3 Joshua started early the next morning and left Acacia Grove with all the Israelites. They went as far as the Jordan and stayed there before crossing. ²After three days the officers went through the camp ³and commanded the people: "When you see the ark of the covenant of the LORD your God carried by the Levitical priests, you must break camp and follow it. ⁴But keep a distance of about 1,000 yards between yourselves and the ark. Don't go near it, so that you can see the way to go, for you haven't traveled this way before."

⁵Joshua told the people, "Consecrate yourselves, because the LORD will do wonders among you tomorrow." ⁶Then he said to the priests, "Take the ark of the covenant and go on ahead of the people." So they carried the ark of the covenant and went ahead of them.

⁷The LORD spoke to Joshua: "Today I will begin to exalt you in the sight of all Israel, so they will know that I will be with you just as I was with Moses. ⁸Command the priests carrying the ark of the covenant: When you reach the edge of the waters, stand in the Jordan."

⁹Then Joshua told the Israelites, "Come closer and listen to the words of the LORD your God." ¹⁰He said: "You will know that the living God is among you and that He will certainly dispossess before you the Canaanites, Hittites, Hivites, Perizzites, Girgashites, Amorites, and Jebusites ¹¹when the ark of the covenant of the Lord of all the earth goes ahead of you into the Jordan. ¹²Now choose 12 men from the tribes of Israel, one man for each tribe. ¹³When the feet of the priests who carry the ark of the LORD, the Lord of all the earth, come to rest in the Jordan's waters, its waters will be cut off. The water flowing downstream will stand up in a mass."

¹⁴When the people broke camp to cross the Jordan, the priests carried the ark of the covenant ahead of the people. ¹⁵Now the Jordan overflows its banks throughout the harvest season. But as soon as the priests carrying the ark reached the Jordan, their feet touched the water at its edge ¹⁶and the water flowing downstream stood still, rising up in a mass that extended as far as Adam, a city next to Zarethan. The water flowing downstream into the Sea of the ·Arabah (the Dead Sea) was completely cut off, and the people crossed opposite Jericho. ¹⁷The priests carrying the ark of the LORD's covenant stood firmly on dry ground in the middle of the Jordan, while all Israel crossed on dry ground until the entire nation had finished crossing the Jordan.

4 After the entire nation had finished crossing the Jordan, the LORD spoke to Joshua: ²"Choose 12 men from the people, one man for each tribe, ³and command them: Take 12 stones from this place in the middle of the Jordan where the priests are standing, carry them with you, and set them down at the place where you spend the night."

⁴So Joshua summoned the 12 men he had selected from the Israelites, one man for each tribe, ⁵and said to them, "Go across to the ark of the LORD your God in the middle of the Jordan. Each of you lift a stone onto his shoulder, one for each of the Israelite tribes, ⁶so that this will be a sign among you. In the future, when your children ask you, 'What do these stones mean to you?' ⁷you should tell them, 'The waters of the Jordan were cut off in front of the ark of the LORD's covenant. When it crossed the Jordan, the Jordan's waters were cut off.' Therefore these stones will always be a memorial for the Israelites."

⁸The Israelites did just as Joshua had commanded them. The 12 men took stones from the middle of the Jordan, one for each of the Israelite tribes, just as the LORD had told Joshua. They carried them to the camp

and set them down there. ⁹Joshua also set up 12 stones in the middle of the Jordan where the priests who carried the ark of the covenant were standing. The stones are there to this day.

¹⁰The priests carrying the ark continued standing in the middle of the Jordan until everything was completed that the Lᴏʀᴅ had commanded Joshua to tell the people, in keeping with all that Moses had commanded Joshua. The people hurried across, ¹¹and after everyone had finished crossing, the priests with the ark of the Lᴏʀᴅ crossed in the sight of the people. ¹²The Reubenites, Gadites, and half the tribe of Manasseh went in battle formation in front of the Israelites, as Moses had instructed them. ¹³About 40,000 equipped for war crossed to the plains of Jericho in the Lᴏʀᴅ's presence.

¹⁴On that day the Lᴏʀᴅ exalted Joshua in the sight of all Israel, and they revered him throughout his life, as they had revered Moses. ¹⁵The Lᴏʀᴅ told Joshua, ¹⁶"Command the priests who carry the ark of the ˙testimony to come up from the Jordan."

¹⁷So Joshua commanded the priests, "Come up from the Jordan." ¹⁸When the priests carrying the ark of the Lᴏʀᴅ's covenant came up from the middle of the Jordan, and their feet stepped out on solid ground, the waters of the Jordan resumed their course, flowing over all the banks as before.

¹⁹The people came up from the Jordan on the tenth day of the first month, and camped at Gilgal on the eastern limits of Jericho. ²⁰Then Joshua set up in Gilgal the 12 stones they had taken from the Jordan, ²¹and he said to the Israelites, "In the future, when your children ask their fathers, 'What is the meaning of these stones?' ²²you should tell your children, 'Israel crossed the Jordan on dry ground.' ²³For the Lᴏʀᴅ your God dried up the waters of the Jordan before you until you had crossed over, just as the Lᴏʀᴅ your God did to the ˙Red Sea, which He dried up before us until we had crossed over. ²⁴This is so that all the people of the earth may know that the Lᴏʀᴅ's hand is mighty, and so that you may always ˙fear the Lᴏʀᴅ your God."

5 When all the Amorite kings across the Jordan to the west and all the Canaanite kings near the sea heard how the Lᴏʀᴅ had dried up the waters of the Jordan before the Israelites until they had crossed over, they lost heart and their courage failed because of the Israelites.

²At that time the Lᴏʀᴅ said to Joshua, "Make flint knives and circumcise the Israelite men again." ³So Joshua made flint knives and circumcised the Israelite men at Gibeath-haaraloth. ⁴This is the reason Joshua circumcised them: All the people who came out of Egypt who were males—all the men of war—had died in the wilderness along the way after they had come out of Egypt. ⁵Though all the people who came out were circumcised, none of the people born in the wilderness along the way were circumcised after they had come out of Egypt. ⁶For the Israelites wandered in the wilderness 40 years until all the nation's men of war who came out of Egypt had died off because they did not obey the Lᴏʀᴅ. So the Lᴏʀᴅ vowed never to let them see the land He had sworn to their fathers to give us, a land flowing with milk and honey. ⁷Joshua raised up their sons in their place; it was these he circumcised. They were still uncircumcised, since they had not been circumcised along the way. ⁸After the entire nation had been circumcised, they stayed where they were in the camp until they recovered. ⁹The Lᴏʀᴅ then

said to Joshua, "Today I have rolled away the disgrace of Egypt from you." Therefore, that place is called Gilgal to this day.

¹⁰While the Israelites camped at Gilgal on the plains of Jericho, they kept the ˙Passover on the evening of the fourteenth day of the month. ¹¹The day after Passover they ate unleavened bread and roasted grain from the produce of the land. ¹²And the day after they ate from the produce of the land, the manna ceased. Since there was no more manna for the Israelites, they ate from the crops of the land of Canaan that year.

¹³When Joshua was near Jericho, he looked up and saw a man standing in front of him with a drawn sword in His hand. Joshua approached Him and asked, "Are You for us or for our enemies?"

¹⁴"Neither," He replied. "I have now come as commander of the Lᴏʀᴅ's army."

Then Joshua bowed with his face to the ground in worship and asked Him, "What does my Lord want to say to His servant?"

¹⁵The commander of the Lᴏʀᴅ's army said to Joshua, "Remove the sandals from your feet, for the place where you are standing is holy." And Joshua did so.

6 Now Jericho was strongly fortified because of the Israelites—no one leaving or entering. ²The Lᴏʀᴅ said to Joshua, "Look, I have handed Jericho, its king, and its fighting men over to you. ³March around the city with all the men of war, circling the city one time. Do this for six days. ⁴Have seven priests carry seven ram's-horn trumpets in front of the ark. But on the seventh day, march around the city seven times, while the priests blow the trumpets. ⁵When there is a prolonged blast of the horn and you hear its sound, have all the people give a mighty shout. Then the city wall will collapse, and the people will advance, each man straight ahead."

⁶So Joshua son of Nun summoned the priests and said to them, "Take up the ark of the covenant and have seven priests carry seven trumpets in front of the ark of the Lᴏʀᴅ." ⁷He said to the people, "Move forward, march around the city, and have the armed troops go ahead of the ark of the Lᴏʀᴅ."

⁸After Joshua had spoken to the people, seven priests carrying seven trumpets before the Lᴏʀᴅ moved forward and blew the trumpets; the ark of the Lᴏʀᴅ's covenant followed them. ⁹While the trumpets were blowing, the armed troops went in front of the priests who blew the trumpets, and the rear guard went behind the ark. ¹⁰But Joshua had commanded the people: "Do not shout or let your voice be heard. Don't let one word come out of your mouth until the time I say, 'Shout!' Then you are to shout." ¹¹So the ark of the Lᴏʀᴅ was carried around the city, circling it once. They returned to the camp and spent the night there.

¹²Joshua got up early the next morning. The priests took the ark of the Lᴏʀᴅ, ¹³and the seven priests carrying seven trumpets marched in front of the ark of the Lᴏʀᴅ. While the trumpets were blowing, the armed troops went in front of them, and the rear guard went behind the ark of the Lᴏʀᴅ. ¹⁴On the second day they marched around the city once and returned to the camp. They did this for six days.

¹⁵Early on the seventh day, they started at dawn and marched around the city seven times in the same way. That was the only day they marched around the city seven times. ¹⁶After the seventh time, the priests blew the trumpets, and Joshua said to the people, "Shout!

For the Lord has given you the city. [17] But the city and everything in it are *set apart to the Lord for destruction. Only Rahab the prostitute and everyone with her in the house will live, because she hid the men we sent. [18] But keep yourselves from the things set apart, or you will be set apart for destruction. If you take any of those things, you will set apart the camp of Israel for destruction and bring disaster on it. [19] For all the silver and gold, and the articles of bronze and iron, are dedicated to the Lord and must go into the Lord's treasury."

[20] So the people shouted, and the trumpets sounded. When they heard the blast of the trumpet, the people gave a great shout, and the wall collapsed. The people advanced into the city, each man straight ahead, and they captured the city. [21] They *completely destroyed everything in the city with the sword—every man and woman, both young and old, and every ox, sheep, and donkey.

[22] Joshua said to the two men who had scouted the land, "Go to the prostitute's house and bring the woman out of there, and all who are with her, just as you promised her." [23] So the young men who had scouted went in and brought out Rahab and her father, mother, brothers, and all who belonged to her. They brought out her whole family and settled them outside the camp of Israel.

[24] They burned up the city and everything in it, but they put the silver and gold and the articles of bronze and iron into the treasury of the Lord's house. [25] However, Joshua spared Rahab the prostitute, her father's household, and all who belonged to her, because she hid the men Joshua had sent to spy on Jericho, and she lives in Israel to this day.

[26] At that time Joshua imposed this curse:

The man who undertakes
the rebuilding of this city, Jericho,
is cursed before the Lord.
He will lay its foundation
at the cost of his firstborn;
he will set up its gates
at the cost of his youngest.

[27] And the Lord was with Joshua, and his fame spread throughout the land.

7 The Israelites, however, were unfaithful regarding the things *set apart for destruction. Achan son of Carmi, son of Zabdi, son of Zerah, of the tribe of Judah, took some of what was set apart, and the Lord's anger burned against the Israelites.

[2] Joshua sent men from Jericho to Ai, which is near Beth-aven, east of Bethel, and told them, "Go up and scout the land." So the men went up and scouted Ai.

[3] After returning to Joshua they reported to him, "Don't send all the people, but send about 2,000 or 3,000 men to attack Ai. Since the people of Ai are so few, don't wear out all our people there." [4] So about 3,000 men went up there, but they fled from the men of Ai. [5] The men of Ai struck down about 36 of them and chased them from outside the gate to the quarries, striking them down on the descent. As a result, the people's hearts melted and became like water.

[6] Then Joshua tore his clothes and fell before the ark of the Lord with his face to the ground until evening, as did the elders of Israel; they all put dust on their heads. [7] "Oh, Lord God," Joshua said, "why did You ever bring these people across the Jordan to hand us over to the Amorites for our destruction? If only we had been content to remain on the other side of the Jordan! [8] What can I say, Lord, now that Israel has turned its back and run from its enemies? [9] When the Canaanites and all who live in the land hear about this, they will surround us and wipe out our name from the earth. Then what will You do about Your great name?"

[10] The Lord then said to Joshua, "Stand up! Why are you on the ground? [11] Israel has sinned. They have violated My covenant that I appointed for them. They have taken some of what was set apart. They have stolen, deceived, and put the things with their own belongings. [12] This is why the Israelites cannot stand against their enemies. They will turn their backs and run from their enemies, because they have been set apart for destruction. I will no longer be with you unless you remove from you what is set apart.

[13] "Go and consecrate the people. Tell them to consecrate themselves for tomorrow, for this is what the Lord, the God of Israel, says: There are things that are set apart among you, Israel. You will not be able to stand against your enemies until you remove what is set apart. [14] In the morning you must present yourselves tribe by tribe. The tribe the Lord selects is to come forward clan by clan. The clan the Lord selects is to come forward family by family. The family the Lord selects is to come forward man by man. [15] The one who is caught with the things set apart must be burned, along with everything he has, because he has violated the Lord's covenant and committed an outrage in Israel."

[16] Joshua got up early the next morning. He had Israel come forward tribe by tribe, and the tribe of Judah was selected. [17] He had the clans of Judah come forward, and the Zerahite clan was selected. He had the Zerahite clan come forward by heads of families, and Zabdi was selected. [18] He then had Zabdi's family come forward man by man, and Achan son of Carmi, son of Zabdi, son of Zerah, of the tribe of Judah, was selected.

[19] So Joshua said to Achan, "My son, give glory to the Lord, the God of Israel, and make a confession to Him. I urge you, tell me what you have done. Don't hide anything from me."

[20] Achan replied to Joshua, "It is true. I have sinned against the Lord, the God of Israel. This is what I did: [21] When I saw among the spoils a beautiful cloak from Babylon, 200 silver *shekels, and a bar of gold weighing 50 shekels, I coveted them and took them. You can see for yourself. They are concealed in the ground inside my tent, with the money under the cloak." [22] So Joshua sent messengers who ran to the tent, and there was the cloak, concealed in his tent, with the money underneath. [23] They took the things from inside the tent, brought them to Joshua and all the Israelites, and spread them out in the Lord's presence.

[24] Then Joshua and all Israel with him took Achan son of Zerah, the silver, the cloak, and the bar of gold, his sons and daughters, his ox, donkey, and sheep, his tent, and all that he had, and brought them up to the Valley of Achor. [25] Joshua said, "Why have you troubled us? Today the Lord will trouble you!" So all Israel stoned them to death. They burned their bodies, threw stones on them, [26] and raised over him a large pile of rocks that remains to this day. Then the Lord turned from His burning anger. Therefore that place is called the Valley of Achor to this day.

8 The LORD said to Joshua, "Do not be afraid or dis-couraged. Take the whole military force with you and go attack Ai. Look, I have handed over to you the king of Ai, his people, city, and land. [2] Treat Ai and its king as you did Jericho and its king; you may plunder its spoil and livestock for yourselves. Set an ambush behind the city."

[3] So Joshua and the whole military force set out to attack Ai. Joshua selected 30,000 fighting men and sent them out at night. [4] He commanded them: "Pay attention. Lie in ambush behind the city, not too far from it, and all of you be ready. [5] Then I and all the peo-ple who are with me will approach the city. When they come out against us as they did the first time, we will flee from them. [6] They will come after us until we have drawn them away from the city, for they will say, 'They are fleeing from us as before.' While we are fleeing from them,[7] you are to come out of your ambush and seize the city, for the LORD your God has handed it over to you. [8] After taking the city, set it on fire. Follow the LORD's command—see that you do as I have ordered you." [9] So Joshua sent them out, and they went to the ambush site and waited between Bethel and Ai, to the west of Ai. But he spent that night with the troops.

[10] Joshua started early the next morning and mobi-lized them. Then he and the elders of Israel led the troops up to Ai. [11] All those who were with him went up and approached the city, arriving opposite Ai, and camped to the north of it, with a valley between them and the city. [12] Now Joshua had taken about 5,000 men and set them in ambush between Bethel and Ai, to the west of the city. [13] The military force was stationed in this way: the main camp to the north of the city and its rear guard to the west of the city. And that night Joshua went into the valley.

[14] When the king of Ai saw the Israelites, the men of the city hurried and went out early in the morning so that he and all his people could engage Israel in battle at a suitable place facing the *Arabah. But he did not know there was an ambush waiting for him behind the city. [15] Joshua and all Israel pretended to be beaten back by them and fled toward the wilderness. [16] Then all the troops of Ai were summoned to pursue them, and they pursued Joshua and were drawn away from the city. [17] Not a man was left in Ai or Bethel who did not go out after Israel, leaving the city exposed while they pursued Israel.

[18] Then the LORD said to Joshua, "Hold out the sword in your hand toward Ai, for I will hand the city over to you." So Joshua held out his sword toward it. [19] When he held out his hand, the men in ambush rose quickly from their position. They ran, entered the city, cap-tured it, and immediately set it on fire. [20] The men of Ai turned and looked back, and smoke from the city was rising to the sky! They could not escape in any direction, and the troops who had fled to the wilderness now became the pursuers. [21] When Joshua and all Israel saw that the men in ambush had captured the city and that smoke was rising from it, they turned back and struck down the men of Ai. [22] Then men in ambush came out of the city against them, and the men of Ai were trapped between the Is-raelite forces, some on one side and some on the other. They struck them down until no survivor or fugitive remained, [23] but they captured the king of Ai alive and brought him to Joshua. [24] When Israel had finished killing everyone living in

Ai who had pursued them into the open country, and when every last one of them had fallen by the sword, all Israel returned to Ai and struck it down with the sword. [25] The total of those who fell that day, both men and women, was 12,000—all the people of Ai. [26] Joshua did not draw back his hand that was holding the sword until all the inhabitants of Ai were *completely de-stroyed. [27] Israel plundered only the cattle and spoil of that city for themselves, according to the LORD's com-mand that He had given Joshua.

[28] Joshua burned Ai and left it a permanent ruin, desolate to this day. [29] He hung the body of the king of Ai on a tree until evening, and at sunset Joshua com-manded that they take his body down from the tree. They threw it down at the entrance of the city gate and put a large pile of rocks over it, which remains to this day.

[30] At that time Joshua built an altar on Mount Ebal to the LORD, the God of Israel, [31] just as Moses the LORD's servant had commanded the Israelites. He built it according to what is written in the book of the law of Moses: an altar of uncut stones on which no iron tool has been used. Then they offered *burnt offerings to the LORD and sacrificed *fellowship offerings on it. [32] There on the stones, Joshua copied the law of Moses, which he had written in the presence of the Israelites. [33] All Israel, foreigner and citizen alike, with their el-ders, officers, and judges, stood on either side of the ark of the LORD's covenant facing the Levitical priests who carried it. As Moses the LORD's servant had com-manded earlier, half of them were in front of Mount Gerizim and half in front of Mount Ebal, to bless the people of Israel. [34] Afterward, Joshua read aloud all the words of the law—the blessings as well as the curses—according to all that is written in the book of the law. [35] There was not a word of all that Moses had commanded that Joshua did not read before the entire assembly of Israel, including the women, the little children, and the foreigners who were with them.

9 When all the kings heard about Jericho and Ai, those who were west of the Jordan in the hill country, in the Judean foothills, and all along the coast of the Mediterranean Sea toward Lebanon—the Hittites, Amorites, Canaanites, Perizzites, Hivites, and Jebusites— [2] they formed a unified alliance to fight against Joshua and Israel.

[3] When the inhabitants of Gibeon heard what Joshua had done to Jericho and Ai, [4] they acted deceptively. They gathered provisions and took worn-out sacks on their donkeys and old wineskins, cracked and mended. [5] They wore old, patched sandals on their feet and threadbare clothing on their bodies. Their entire provision of bread was dry and crumbly. [6] They went to Joshua in the camp at Gilgal and said to him and the men of Israel, "We have come from a distant land. Please make a treaty with us."

[7] The men of Israel replied to the Hivites, "Perhaps you live among us. How can we make a treaty with you?"

[8] They said to Joshua, "We are your servants."

Then Joshua asked them, "Who are you and where do you come from?"

[9] They replied to him, "Your servants have come from a far away land because of the reputation of the LORD your God. For we have heard of His fame, and all that He did in Egypt, [10] and all that He did to the two Amorite kings beyond the Jordan—Sihon king of

Heshbon and Og king of Bashan, who was in Ashtaroth. ¹¹So our elders and all the inhabitants of our land told us, 'Take provisions with you for the journey; go and meet them and say, "We are your servants. Please make a treaty with us."' ¹²This bread of ours was warm when we took it from our houses as food on the day we left to come to you. But take a look, it is now dry and crumbly. ¹³These wineskins were new when we filled them, but look, they are cracked. And these clothes and sandals of ours are worn out from the extremely long journey." ¹⁴Then the men of Israel took some of their provisions, but did not seek the LORD's counsel. ¹⁵So Joshua established peace with them and made a treaty to let them live, and the leaders of the community swore an oath to them.

¹⁶Three days after making the treaty with them, they heard that the Gibeonites were their neighbors, living among them. ¹⁷So the Israelites set out and reached the Gibeonite cities on the third day. Now their cities were Gibeon, Chephirah, Beeroth, and Kiriath-jearim. ¹⁸But the Israelites did not attack them, because the leaders of the community had sworn an oath to them by the LORD, the God of Israel. Then the whole community grumbled against the leaders.

¹⁹All the leaders answered them, "We have sworn an oath to them by the LORD, the God of Israel, and now we cannot touch them. ²⁰This is how we will treat them: we will let them live, so that no wrath will fall on us because of the oath we swore to them." ²¹They also said, "Let them live." So the Gibeonites became wood-cutters and water carriers for the whole community, as the leaders had promised them.

²²Joshua summoned the Gibeonites and said to them, "Why did you deceive us by telling us you live far away from us, when in fact you live among us? ²³Therefore you are cursed and will always be slaves—woodcutters and water carriers for the house of my God."

²⁴The Gibeonites answered him, "It was clearly communicated to your servants that the LORD your God had commanded His servant Moses to give you all the land and to destroy all the inhabitants of the land before you. We greatly feared for our lives because of you, and that is why we did this. ²⁵Now we are in your hands. Do to us whatever you think is right." ²⁶This is what Joshua did to them: he delivered them from the hands of the Israelites, and they did not kill them. ²⁷On that day he made them woodcutters and water carriers—as they are today—for the community and for the LORD's altar at the place He would choose.

10 Now Adoni-zedek king of Jerusalem heard that Joshua had captured Ai and *completely destroyed it, treating Ai and its king as he had Jericho and its king, and that the inhabitants of Gibeon had made peace with Israel and were living among them. ²So Adoni-zedek and his people were greatly alarmed because Gibeon was a large city like one of the royal cities; it was larger than Ai, and all its men were warriors. ³Therefore Adoni-zedek king of Jerusalem sent word to Hoham king of Hebron, Piram king of Jarmuth, Japhia king of Lachish, and Debir king of Eglon, saying, ⁴"Come up and help me. We will attack Gibeon, because they have made peace with Joshua and the Israelites." ⁵So the five Amorite kings—the kings of Jerusalem, Hebron, Jarmuth, Lachish, and Eglon—joined forces, advanced with all their armies, besieged Gibeon, and fought against it.

⁶Then the men of Gibeon sent word to Joshua in the camp at Gilgal: "Don't abandon your servants. Come quickly and save us! Help us, for all the Amorite kings living in the hill country have joined forces against us." ⁷So Joshua and his whole military force, including all the fighting men, came from Gilgal.

⁸The LORD said to Joshua, "Do not be afraid of them, for I have handed them over to you. Not one of them will be able to stand against you."

⁹So Joshua caught them by surprise, after marching all night from Gilgal. ¹⁰The LORD threw them into confusion before Israel. He defeated them in a great slaughter at Gibeon, chased them through the ascent of Beth-horon, and struck them down as far as Azekah and Makkedah. ¹¹As they fled before Israel, the LORD threw large hailstones on them from the sky along the descent of Beth-horon all the way to Azekah, and they died. More of them died from the hail than the Israelites killed with the sword.

¹²On the day the LORD gave the Amorites over to the Israelites, Joshua spoke to the LORD in the presence of Israel:

"Sun, stand still over Gibeon,
and moon, over the Valley of Aijalon."

¹³ And the sun stood still
and the moon stopped
until the nation took vengeance
on its enemies.

Isn't this written in the Book of Jashar?
So the sun stopped
in the middle of the sky
and delayed its setting
almost a full day.

¹⁴There has been no day like it before or since, when the LORD listened to the voice of a man, because the LORD fought for Israel. ¹⁵Then Joshua and all Israel with him returned to the camp at Gilgal.

¹⁶Now the five defeated kings had fled and hidden themselves in the cave at Makkedah. ¹⁷It was reported to Joshua: "The five kings have been found; they are hiding in the cave at Makkedah."

¹⁸Joshua said, "Roll large stones against the mouth of the cave, and station men by it to guard the kings. ¹⁹But as for the rest of you, don't stay there. Pursue your enemies and attack them from behind. Don't let them enter their cities, for the LORD your God has handed them over to you." ²⁰So Joshua and the Israelites finished inflicting a terrible slaughter on them until they were destroyed, although a few survivors ran away to the fortified cities. ²¹The people returned safely to Joshua in the camp at Makkedah. And no one dared to threaten the Israelites.

²²Then Joshua said, "Open the mouth of the cave, and bring those five kings to me out of there." ²³That is what they did. They brought the five kings of Jerusalem, Hebron, Jarmuth, Lachish, and Eglon out of the cave. ²⁴When they had brought the kings to him, Joshua summoned all the men of Israel and said to the military commanders who had accompanied him, "Come here and put your feet on the necks of these kings." So the commanders came forward and put their feet on their necks. ²⁵Joshua said to them, "Do not be afraid or discouraged. Be strong and courageous, for the LORD will do this to all the enemies you fight."

²⁶After this, Joshua struck them down and executed them. He hung their bodies on five trees and they were

there until evening. ²⁷At sunset Joshua commanded that they be taken down from the trees and thrown into the cave where they had hidden. Then large stones were placed against the mouth of the cave, and the stones are there to this day.

²⁸On that day Joshua captured Makkedah and struck it down with the sword, including its king. He completely destroyed it and everyone in it, leaving no survivors. So he treated the king of Makkedah as he had the king of Jericho.

²⁹Joshua and all Israel with him crossed from Makkedah to Libnah and fought against Libnah. ³⁰The Lord also handed it and its king over to Israel. He struck it down, putting everyone in it to the sword, and left no survivors in it. He treated Libnah's king as he had the king of Jericho.

³¹From Libnah, Joshua and all Israel with him crossed to Lachish. They laid siege to it and attacked it. ³²The Lord handed Lachish over to Israel, and Joshua captured it on the second day. He struck it down, putting everyone in it to the sword, just as he had done to Libnah. ³³At that time Horam king of Gezer went to help Lachish, but Joshua struck him down along with his people, leaving no survivors in it.

³⁴Then Joshua crossed from Lachish to Eglon and all Israel with him. They laid siege to it and attacked it. ³⁵On that day they captured it and struck it down, putting everyone in it to the sword. He completely destroyed it that day, just as he had done to Lachish.

³⁶Next, Joshua and all Israel with him went up from Eglon to Hebron and attacked it. ³⁷They captured it and struck down its king, all its villages, and everyone in it with the sword. He left no survivors, just as he had done at Eglon. He completely destroyed Hebron and everyone in it.

³⁸Finally, Joshua turned toward Debir and attacked it. And all Israel was with him. ³⁹He captured it—its king and all its villages. They struck them down with the sword and completely destroyed everyone in it, leaving no survivors. He treated Debir and its king as he had treated Hebron and as he had treated Libnah and its king.

⁴⁰So Joshua conquered the whole region—the hill country, the ˙Negev, the Judean foothills, and the slopes—with all their kings, leaving no survivors. He completely destroyed every living being, as the Lord, the God of Israel, had commanded. ⁴¹Joshua conquered everyone from Kadesh-barnea to Gaza, and all the land of Goshen as far as Gibeon. ⁴²Joshua captured all these kings and their land in one campaign, because the Lord, the God of Israel, fought for Israel. ⁴³Then Joshua returned with all Israel to the camp at Gilgal.

11 When Jabin king of Hazor heard this news, he sent a message to:
    Jobab king of Madon,
    the kings of Shimron and Achshaph,
    ² and the kings of the north in the hill country,
    the ˙Arabah south of Chinnereth,
    the Judean foothills,
    and the Slopes of Dor to the west,
    ³ the Canaanites in the east and west,
    the Amorites, Hittites, Perizzites,
    and Jebusites in the hill country,
    and the Hivites at the foot of Hermon
    in the land of Mizpah.
⁴They went out with all their armies—a multitude as

numerous as the sand on the seashore—along with a vast number of horses and chariots. ⁵All these kings joined forces; they came together and camped at the waters of Merom to attack Israel.

⁶The Lord said to Joshua, "Do not be afraid of them, for at this time tomorrow I will cause all of them to be killed before Israel. You are to hamstring their horses and burn up their chariots." ⁷So Joshua and his whole military force surprised them at the waters of Merom and attacked them. ⁸The Lord handed them over to Israel, and they struck them down, pursuing them as far as Great Sidon and Misrephoth-maim, and to the east as far as the Valley of Mizpeh. They struck them down, leaving no survivors. ⁹Joshua treated them as the Lord had told him; he hamstrung their horses and burned up their chariots.

¹⁰At that time Joshua turned back, captured Hazor, and struck down its king with the sword, because Hazor had formerly been the leader of all these kingdoms. ¹¹They struck down everyone in it with the sword, ˙completely destroying them; he left no one alive. Then he burned down Hazor.

¹²Joshua captured all these kings and their cities and struck them down with the sword. He completely destroyed them, as Moses the Lord's servant had commanded. ¹³However, Israel did not burn any of the cities that stood on their mounds except Hazor, which Joshua burned. ¹⁴The Israelites plundered all the spoils and cattle of these cities for themselves. But they struck down every person with the sword until they had annihilated them, leaving no one alive. ¹⁵Just as the Lord had commanded His servant Moses, Moses commanded Joshua. That is what Joshua did, leaving nothing undone of all that the Lord had commanded Moses.

¹⁶So Joshua took all this land—the hill country, all the ˙Negev, all the land of Goshen, the foothills, the Arabah, and the hill country of Israel with its foothills— ¹⁷from Mount Halak, which ascends to Seir, as far as Baal-gad in the Valley of Lebanon at the foot of Mount Hermon. He captured all their kings and struck them down, putting them to death. ¹⁸Joshua waged war with all these kings for a long time. ¹⁹No city made peace with the Israelites except the Hivites who inhabited Gibeon; all of them were taken in battle. ²⁰For it was the Lord's intention to harden their hearts, so that they would engage Israel in battle, be completely destroyed without mercy, and be annihilated, just as the Lord had commanded Moses.

²¹At that time Joshua proceeded to exterminate the Anakim from the hill country—Hebron, Debir, Anab—all the hill country of Judah and of Israel. Joshua completely destroyed them with their cities. ²²No Anakim were left in the land of the Israelites, except for some remaining in Gaza, Gath, and Ashdod.

²³So Joshua took the entire land, in keeping with all that the Lord had told Moses. Joshua then gave it as an inheritance to Israel according to their tribal allotments. After this, the land had rest from war.

12 The Israelites struck down the following kings of the land and took possession of their land beyond the Jordan to the east and from the Arnon Valley to Mount Hermon, including all the ˙Arabah eastward: ²Sihon king of the Amorites lived in Heshbon. He ruled over the territory from Aroer on the rim of the Arnon Valley, along the middle of the valley, and half of Gilead up to the Jabbok River

(the border of the Ammonites), ³the Arabah east of the Sea of Chinnereth to the Sea of the Arabah (that is, the Dead Sea), eastward through Beth-jeshimoth and southward below the slopes of Pisgah.

⁴Og king of Bashan, of the remnant of the Rephaim, lived in Ashtaroth and Edrei. ⁵He ruled over Mount Hermon, Salecah, all Bashan up to the Geshurite and Maacathite border, and half of Gilead to the border of Sihon, king of Heshbon.

⁶Moses the LORD's servant and the Israelites struck them down. And Moses the LORD's servant gave their land as an inheritance to the Reubenites, Gadites, and half the tribe of Manasseh.

⁷Joshua and the Israelites struck down the following kings of the land beyond the Jordan to the west, from Baal-gad in the Valley of Lebanon to Mount Halak, which ascends toward Seir (Joshua gave their land as an inheritance to the tribes of Israel according to their allotments: ⁸the hill country, the Judean foothills, the Arabah, the slopes, the desert, and the ˙Negev of the Hittites, Amorites, Canaanites, Perizzites, Hivites, and Jebusites):

⁹	the king of Jericho	one
	the king of Ai, which is next to Bethel	one
¹⁰	the king of Jerusalem	one
	the king of Hebron	one
¹¹	the king of Jarmuth	one
	the king of Lachish	one
¹²	the king of Eglon	one
	the king of Gezer	one
¹³	the king of Debir	one
	the king of Geder	one
¹⁴	the king of Hormah	one
	the king of Arad	one
¹⁵	the king of Libnah	one
	the king of Adullam	one
¹⁶	the king of Makkedah	one
	the king of Bethel	one
¹⁷	the king of Tappuah	one
	the king of Hepher	one
¹⁸	the king of Aphek	one
	the king of Lasharon	one
¹⁹	the king of Madon	one
	the king of Hazor	one
²⁰	the king of Shimron-meron	one
	the king of Achshaph	one
²¹	the king of Taanach	one
	the king of Megiddo	one
²²	the king of Kedesh	one
	the king of Jokneam in Carmel	one
²³	the king of Dor in Naphath-dor	one
	the king of Goiim in Gilgal	one
²⁴	the king of Tirzah	one
	the total number of all kings:	31.

13 Joshua was now old, getting on in years, and the LORD said to him, "You have become old, getting on in years, but a great deal of the land remains to be possessed. ²This is the land that remains:

All the districts of the Philistines and the Geshurites: ³from the Shihor east of Egypt to the border of Ekron on the north (considered to be Canaanite territory)—the five Philistine rulers of Gaza, Ashdod, Ashkelon, Gath, and Ekron, as well as the Avvites ⁴in the south; all the land of the Canaanites: from Arah of the Sidonians to Aphek and as far as the border of the Amorites; ⁵the land of the Gebalites; and all Lebanon east from Baal-gad below Mount Hermon to the entrance of Hamath— ⁶all the inhabitants of the hill country from Lebanon to Misrephoth-maim, all the Sidonians.

I will drive them out before the Israelites, only distribute the land as an inheritance for Israel, as I have commanded you. ⁷Therefore, divide this land as an inheritance to the nine tribes and half the tribe of Manasseh."

⁸With the other half of the tribe, the Reubenites and Gadites had received the inheritance Moses gave them beyond the Jordan to the east, just as Moses the LORD's servant had given them:

⁹From Aroer on the rim of the Arnon Valley, along with the city in the middle of the valley, all the Medeba plateau as far as Dibon, ¹⁰and all the cities of Sihon king of the Amorites, who reigned in Heshbon, to the border of the Ammonites; ¹¹also Gilead and the territory of the Geshurites and Maacathites, all Mount Hermon, and all Bashan to Salecah— ¹²the whole kingdom of Og in Bashan, who reigned in Ashtaroth and Edrei; he was one of the remaining Rephaim.

Moses struck them down and drove them out, ¹³but the Israelites did not drive out the Geshurites and Maacathites. So Geshur and Maacath live in Israel to this day.

¹⁴He did not give any inheritance to the tribe of Levi. This was its inheritance, just as He had promised: the offerings made by fire to the LORD, the God of Israel.

¹⁵To the tribe of the Reubenites by their clans, Moses gave ¹⁶this as their territory:

From Aroer on the rim of the Arnon Valley, along with the city in the middle of the valley, to the whole plateau as far as Medeba, ¹⁷with Heshbon and all its cities on the plateau—Dibon, Bamoth-baal, Beth-baal-meon, ¹⁸Jahaz, Kedemoth, Mephaath, ¹⁹Kiriathaim, Sibmah, Zereth-shahar on the hill in the valley, ²⁰Beth-peor, the slopes of Pisgah, and Beth-jeshimoth— ²¹all the cities of the plateau, and all the kingdom of Sihon king of the Amorites, who reigned in Heshbon. Moses had killed him and the chiefs of Midian—Evi, Rekem, Zur, Hur, and Reba—the princes of Sihon who lived in the land. ²²Along with those the Israelites put to death, they also killed the diviner, Balaam son of Beor, with the sword.

²³The border of the Reubenites was the Jordan and its plain. This was the inheritance of the Reubenites by their clans, with the cities and their villages.

²⁴To the tribe of the Gadites by their clans, Moses gave ²⁵this as their territory:

Jazer and all the cities of Gilead, and half the land of the Ammonites to Aroer, near Rabbah; ²⁶from Heshbon to Ramath-mizpeh and Betonim, and from Mahanaim to the border of Debir; ²⁷in the valley: Beth-haram, Beth-nimrah, Succoth, and Zaphon—the rest of the kingdom of Sihon king of Heshbon. Their land also included the Jordan and its territory as far as the edge of the Sea of Chinnereth on the east side of the Jordan.

²⁸This was the inheritance of the Gadites by their clans, with the cities and their villages.

²⁹And to half the tribe of Manasseh, that is, to half the tribe of Manasseh's descendants by their clans, Moses gave ³⁰this as their territory:

From Mahanaim through all Bashan—all the kingdom of Og king of Bashan, including all of Jair's Villages that are in Bashan—60 cities. ³¹But half of Gilead, and Og's royal cities in Bashan—Ashtaroth and Edrei—are for the descendants of Machir son of Manasseh, that is, half the descendants of Machir by their clans.

³²These were the portions Moses gave them on the plains of Moab beyond the Jordan east of Jericho. ³³But Moses did not give a portion to the tribe of Levi. The Lord, the God of Israel, was their inheritance, just as He had promised them.

14 The Israelites received these portions that Eleazar the priest, Joshua son of Nun, and the heads of the families of the Israelite tribes gave them in the land of Canaan. ²Their inheritance was by lot as the Lord commanded through Moses for the nine and a half tribes, ³because Moses had given the inheritance to the two and a half tribes beyond the Jordan. But he gave no inheritance among them to the Levites. ⁴The descendants of Joseph became two tribes, Manasseh and Ephraim. No portion of the land was given to the Levites except cities to live in, along with pasturelands for their cattle and livestock. ⁵So the Israelites did as the Lord commanded Moses, and they divided the land.

⁶The descendants of Judah approached Joshua at Gilgal, and Caleb son of Jephunneh the Kenizzite said to him, "You know what the Lord promised Moses the man of God at Kadesh-barnea about you and me. ⁷I was 40 years old when Moses the Lord's servant sent me from Kadesh-barnea to scout the land, and I brought back an honest report. ⁸My brothers who went with me caused the people's hearts to melt with fear, but I remained loyal to the Lord my God. ⁹On that day Moses promised me: 'The land where you have set foot will be an inheritance for you and your descendants forever, because you have remained loyal to the Lord my God.'

¹⁰"As you see, the Lord has kept me alive these 45 years as He promised, since the Lord spoke this word to Moses while Israel was journeying in the wilderness. Here I am today, 85 years old. ¹¹I am still as strong today as I was the day Moses sent me out. My strength for battle and for daily tasks is now as it was then. ¹²Now give me this hill country the Lord promised me on that day, because you heard then that the Anakim are there, as well as large fortified cities. Perhaps the Lord will be with me and I will drive them out as the Lord promised."

¹³Then Joshua blessed Caleb son of Jephunneh and gave him Hebron as an inheritance. ¹⁴Therefore, Hebron belongs to Caleb son of Jephunneh the Kenizzite as an inheritance to this day, because he remained loyal to the Lord, the God of Israel. ¹⁵Hebron's name used to be Kiriath-arba; Arba was the greatest man among the Anakim. After this, the land had rest from war.

15 Now the allotment for the tribe of the descendants of Judah by their clans was in the southernmost region, south to the Wilderness of Zin and over to the border of Edom.

²Their southern border began at the tip of the Dead Sea on the south bay ³and went south of the Ascent of Akrabbim, proceeded to Zin, as-

cended to the south of Kadesh-barnea, passed Hezron, ascended to Addar, and turned to Karka. ⁴It proceeded to Azmon and to the Brook of Egypt and so the border ended at the Mediterranean Sea. This is your southern border.

⁵Now the eastern border was along the Dead Sea to the mouth of the Jordan.

The border on the north side was from the bay of the sea at the mouth of the Jordan. ⁶It ascended to Beth-hoglah, proceeded north of Beth-arabah, and ascended to the Stone of Bohan son of Reuben. ⁷Then the border ascended to Debir from the Valley of Achor, turning north to the Gilgal that is opposite the Ascent of Adummim, which is south of the ravine. The border proceeded to the waters of En-shemesh and ended at En-rogel. ⁸From there the border ascended the Valley of Hinnom to the southern Jebusite slope (that is, Jerusalem) and ascended to the top of the hill that faces the Valley of Hinnom on the west, at the northern end of the Valley of Rephaim. ⁹From the top of the hill the border curved to the spring of the Waters of Nephtoah, went to the cities of Mount Ephron, and then curved to Baalah (that is, Kiriath-jearim). ¹⁰The border turned westward from Baalah to Mount Seir, went to the northern slope of Mount Jearim (that is, Chesalon), descended to Beth-shemesh, and proceeded to Timnah. ¹¹Then the border reached to the slope north of Ekron, curved to Shikkeron, proceeded to Mount Baalah, went to Jabneel, and ended at the Mediterranean Sea.

¹²Now the western border was the coastline of the Mediterranean Sea.

This was the boundary of the descendants of Judah around their clans.

¹³He gave Caleb son of Jephunneh the following portion among the descendants of Judah based on the Lord's instruction to Joshua: Kiriath-arba (that is, Hebron; Arba was the father of Anak). ¹⁴Caleb drove out from there the three sons of Anak: Sheshai, Ahiman, and Talmai, descendants of Anak. ¹⁵From there he marched against the inhabitants of Debir whose name used to be Kiriath-sepher. ¹⁶and Caleb said, "I will give my daughter Achsah as a wife to the one who strikes down and captures Kiriath-sepher." ¹⁷So Othniel son of Caleb's brother, Kenaz, captured it, and Caleb gave his daughter Achsah to him as a wife. ¹⁸When she arrived, she persuaded Othniel to ask her father for a field. As she got off her donkey, Caleb asked her, "What do you want?" ¹⁹She replied, "Give me a blessing. Since you have given me land in the *Negev, give me the springs of water also." So he gave her the upper and lower springs.

²⁰This was the inheritance of the tribe of the descendants of Judah by their clans.

²¹These were the outermost cities of the tribe of the descendants of Judah toward the border of Edom in the Negev: Kabzeel, Eder, Jagur, ²²Kinah, Dimonah, Adadah, ²³Kedesh, Hazor, Ithnan, ²⁴Ziph, Telem, Bealoth, ²⁵Hazor-hadattah, Kerioth-hezron (that is, Hazor), ²⁶Amam, Shema, Moladah, ²⁷Hazar-gaddah, Heshmon, Bethpelet, ²⁸Hazar-shual, Beer-sheba, Biziothiah, ²⁹Baalah, Iim, Ezem, ³⁰Eltolad, Chesil, Hormah, ³¹Ziklag, Madmannah, Sansannah, ³²Lebaoth,

Shilhim, Ain, and Rimmon—29 cities in all, with their villages.
³³In the Judean foothills: Eshtaol, Zorah, Ashnah, ³⁴Zanoah, En-gannim, Tappuah, Enam, ³⁵Jarmuth, Adullam, Socoh, Azekah, ³⁶Shaaraim, Adithaim, Gederah, and Gederothaim—14 cities, with their villages; ³⁷Zenan, Hadashah, Migdal-gad, ³⁸Dilan, Mizpeh, Jokthe-el, ³⁹Lachish, Bozkath, Eglon, ⁴⁰Cabbon, Lahmam, Chitlish, ⁴¹Gederoth, Beth-dagon, Naamah, and Makkedah—16 cities, with their villages; ⁴²Libnah, Ether, Ashan, ⁴³Iphtah, Ashnah, Nezib, ⁴⁴Keilah, Achzib, and Mareshah—nine cities, with their villages; ⁴⁵Ekron, with its towns and villages; ⁴⁶from Ekron to the sea, all the cities near Ashdod, with their villages; ⁴⁷Ashdod, with its towns and villages; Gaza, with its towns and villages, to the Brook of Egypt and the coastline of the Mediterranean Sea.

⁴⁸In the hill country: Shamir, Jattir, Socoh, ⁴⁹Dannah, Kiriath-sannah (that is, Debir), ⁵⁰Anab, Eshtemoh, Anim, ⁵¹Goshen, Holon, and Giloh—11 cities, with their villages; ⁵²Arab, Dumah, Eshan, ⁵³Janim, Beth-tappuah, Aphekah, ⁵⁴Humtah, Kiriath-arba (that is, Hebron), and Zior—nine cities, with their villages; ⁵⁵Maon, Carmel, Ziph, Juttah, ⁵⁶Jezreel, Jokdeam, Zanoah, ⁵⁷Kain, Gibeah, and Timnah—10 cities, with their villages; ⁵⁸Halhul, Beth-zur, Gedor, ⁵⁹Maarath, Beth-anoth, and Eltekon—six cities, with their villages; ⁶⁰Kiriath-baal (that is, Kiriath-jearim), and Rabbah—two cities, with their villages.

⁶¹In the wilderness: Beth-arabah, Middin, Secacah, ⁶²Nibshan, the City of Salt, and En-gedi—six cities, with their villages.
⁶³But the descendants of Judah could not drive out the Jebusites who lived in Jerusalem. So the Jebusites live in Jerusalem among the descendants of Judah to this day.

16 The allotment for the descendants of Joseph went from the Jordan at Jericho to the waters of Jericho on the east, through the wilderness ascending from Jericho into the hill country of Bethel. ²From Bethel it went to Luz and proceeded to the border of the Archites by Ataroth. ³It then descended westward to the border of the Japhletites as far as the border of lower Beth-horon, then to Gezer, and ended at the Mediterranean Sea. ⁴So Ephraim and Manasseh, the sons of Joseph, received their inheritance.

⁵This was the territory of the descendants of Ephraim by their clans:
The border of their inheritance went from Ataroth-addar on the east of Upper Beth-horon. ⁶In the north the border went westward from Michmethath; it turned eastward from Taanath-shiloh and passed it east of Janoah. ⁷From Janoah it descended to Ataroth and Naarah, and then reached Jericho and went to the Jordan. ⁸From Tappuah the border went westward along the Brook of Kanah and ended at the Mediterranean Sea.

This was the inheritance of the tribe of the descendants of Ephraim by their clans, together with ⁹the cities set apart for the descendants of Ephraim within the inheritance of the descendants of Manasseh—all these cities with their villages. ¹⁰But, they did not drive out the Canaanites who lived in Gezer. So the Canaanites live in Ephraim to this day, but they are forced laborers.

17 This was the allotment for the tribe of Manasseh as Joseph's firstborn. Gilead and Bashan came to Machir, the firstborn of Manasseh and the father of Gilead, who was a man of war. ²So the allotment was for the rest of Manasseh's descendants by their clans, for the sons of Abiezer, Helek, Asriel, Shechem, Hepher, and Shemida. These are the male descendants of Manasseh son of Joseph, by their clans.

³Now Zelophehad son of Hepher, son of Gilead, son of Machir, son of Manasseh, had no sons, only daughters. These are the names of his daughters: Mahlah, Noah, Hoglah, Milcah, and Tirzah. ⁴They came before Eleazar the priest, Joshua son of Nun, and the leaders, saying, "The LORD commanded Moses to give us an inheritance among our male relatives." So they gave them an inheritance among their father's brothers, in keeping with the LORD's instruction. ⁵As a result, 10 tracts fell to Manasseh, besides the land of Gilead and Bashan, which are beyond the Jordan, ⁶because Manasseh's daughters received an inheritance among his sons. The land of Gilead belonged to the rest of Manasseh's sons.

⁷The border of Manasseh went from Asher to Michmethath near Shechem. It then went southward toward the inhabitants of En-tappuah. ⁸The region of Tappuah belonged to Manasseh, but Tappuah itself on Manasseh's border belonged to the descendants of Ephraim. ⁹From there the border descended to the Brook of Kanah; south of the brook, cities belonged to Ephraim among Manasseh's cities. Manasseh's border was on the north side of the brook and ended at the Mediterranean Sea. ¹⁰Ephraim's territory was to the south and Manasseh's to the north, with the Sea as its border. They reached Asher on the north and Issachar on the east. ¹¹Within Issachar and Asher, Manasseh had Beth-shean with its towns, Ibleam with its towns, and the inhabitants of Dor with its towns; the inhabitants of En-dor with its towns, the inhabitants of Taanach with its towns, and the inhabitants of Megiddo with its towns—the three cities of Naphath.

¹²The descendants of Manasseh could not possess these cities, because the Canaanites were determined to stay in this land. ¹³However, when the Israelites grew stronger, they imposed forced labor on the Canaanites but did not drive them out completely.

¹⁴Joseph's descendants said to Joshua, "Why did you give us only one tribal allotment as an inheritance? We have many people, because the LORD has been blessing us greatly."

¹⁵"If you have so many people," Joshua replied to them, "go to the forest and clear an area for yourselves there in the land of the Perizzites and the Rephaim, because Ephraim's hill country is too small for you."

¹⁶But the descendants of Joseph said, "The hill country is not enough for us, and all the Canaanites who inhabit the valley area have iron chariots, both at Beth-shean with its towns and in the Jezreel Valley."

¹⁷So Joshua replied to Joseph's family (that is, Ephraim and Manasseh), "You have many people and great strength. You will not have just one allotment,

[18] because the hill country will be yours also. It is a forest; clear it and its outlying areas will be yours. You can also drive out the Canaanites, even though they have iron chariots and are strong."

18 The entire Israelite community assembled at Shiloh where it set up the tent of meeting there; the land had been subdued by them. [2] Seven tribes among the Israelites were left who had not divided up their inheritance. [3] So Joshua said to the Israelites, "How long will you delay going out to take possession of the land that the LORD, the God of your fathers, gave you? [4] Appoint for yourselves three men from each tribe, and I will send them out. They are to go and survey the land, write a description of it for the purpose of their inheritance, and return to me. [5] Then they are to divide it into seven portions. Judah is to remain in its territory in the south and Joseph's family in their territory in the north. [6] When you have written a description of the seven portions of land and brought it to me, I will cast lots for you here in the presence of the LORD our God. [7] But the Levites among you do not get a portion, because their inheritance is the priesthood of the LORD. Gad, Reuben, and half the tribe of Manasseh have taken their inheritance beyond the Jordan to the east, which Moses the LORD's servant gave them."

[8] As the men prepared to go, Joshua commanded them to write down a description of the land, saying, "Go and survey the land, write a description of it, and return to me. I will then cast lots for you here in Shiloh in the presence of the LORD." [9] So the men left, went through the land, and described it by towns in a document of seven sections. They returned to Joshua at the camp in Shiloh. [10] Joshua cast lots for them at Shiloh in the presence of the LORD where he distributed the land to the Israelites according to their divisions.

[11] The lot came up for the tribe of Benjamin's descendants by their clans, and their allotted territory lay between Judah's descendants and Joseph's descendants. [12] Their border on the north side began at the Jordan, ascended to the slope of Jericho on the north, through the hill country westward, and ended at the wilderness of Beth-aven. [13] From there the border went toward Luz, to the southern slope of Luz (that is, Bethel); it then went down by Ataroth-addar, over the hill south of Lower Beth-horon. [14] On the west side, from the hill facing Beth-horon on the south, the border curved, turning southward, and ended at Kiriath-baal (that is, Kiriath-jearim), a city of the descendants of Judah. This was the west side of their border. [15] The south side began at the edge of Kiriath-jearim, and the border extended westward; it went to the spring at the Waters of Nephtoah. [16] The border descended to the foot of the hill that faces the Valley of Hinnom at the northern end of the Valley of Rephaim. It ran down the Valley of Hinnom toward the south Jebusite slope and downward to En-rogel. [17] It curved northward and went to En-shemesh and on to Geliloth, which is opposite the Ascent of Adummim, and continued down to the Stone of Bohan son of Reuben. [18] Then it went north to the slope opposite the Jordan Valley and proceeded

into the valley. [19] The border continued to the north slope of Beth-hoglah and ended at the northern bay of the Dead Sea, at the southern end of the Jordan. This was the southern border. [20] The Jordan formed the border on the east side. This was the inheritance of Benjamin's descendants, by their clans, according to its surrounding borders.

[21] These were the cities of the tribe of Benjamin's descendants by their clans:

Jericho, Beth-hoglah, Emek-keziz, [22] Beth-arabah, Zemaraim, Bethel, [23] Avvim, Parah, Ophrah, [24] Chephar-ammoni, Ophni, and Geba—12 cities, with their villages; [25] Gibeon, Ramah, Beeroth, [26] Mizpeh, Chephirah, Mozah, [27] Rekem, Irpeel, Taralah, [28] Zela, Haeleph, Jebus (that is, Jerusalem), Gibeah, and Kiriath—14 cities, with their villages.

This was the inheritance for Benjamin's descendants by their clans.

19 The second lot came out for Simeon, for the tribe of his descendants by their clans, but their inheritance was within the portion of Judah's descendants. [2] Their inheritance included:

Beer-sheba (or Sheba), Moladah, [3] Hazar-shual, Balah, Ezem, [4] Eltolad, Bethul, Hormah, [5] Ziklag, Beth-marcaboth, Hazar-susah, [6] Bethlebaoth, and Sharuhen—13 cities, with their villages; [7] Ain, Rimmon, Ether, and Ashan—four cities, with their villages; [8] and all the villages surrounding these cities as far as Baalath-beer (Ramah of the south).

This was the inheritance of the tribe of Simeon's descendants by their clans. [9] The inheritance of Simeon's descendants was within the territory of Judah's descendants, because the share for Judah's descendants was too large for them. So Simeon's descendants received an inheritance within Judah's portion.

[10] The third lot came up for Zebulun's descendants by their clans.

The territory of their inheritance stretched as far as Sarid; [11] their border went up westward to Maralah, reached Dabbesheth, and met the brook east of Jokneam. [12] From Sarid, it turned east toward the sunrise along the border of Chisloth-tabor, went to Daberath, and went up to Japhia. [13] From there, it went east toward the sunrise to Gath-hepher and to Eth-kazin; it extended to Rimmon, curving around to Neah. [14] The border then circled around Neah on the north to Hannathon and ended at the Valley of Iphtah-el, [15] along with Kattath, Nahalal, Shimron, Idalah, and Bethlehem—12 cities, with their villages.

[16] This was the inheritance of Zebulun's descendants by their clans, these cities, with their villages.

[17] The fourth lot came out for the tribe of Issachar's descendants by their clans.

[18] Their territory went to Jezreel, and included Chesulloth, Shunem, [19] Hapharaim, Shion, Anaharath, [20] Rabbith, Kishion, Ebez, [21] Remeth, En-gannim, En-haddah, Beth-pazzez. [22] The border reached Tabor, Shahazumah, and Beth-shemesh, and ended at the Jordan—16 cities, with their villages.

[23] This was the inheritance of the tribe of Issachar's descendants by their clans, the cities, with their villages.

²⁴The fifth lot came out for the tribe of Asher's descendants by their clans.

²⁵Their boundary included Helkath, Hali, Beten, Achshaph, ²⁶Allammelech, Amad, and Mishal and reached westward to Carmel and Shihor-libnath. ²⁷It turned eastward to Beth-dagon, passed Zebulun and the Valley of Iphtah-el, north toward Beth-emek and Neiel, and went north to Cabul, ²⁸Ebron, Rehob, Hammon, and Kanah, as far as Great Sidon. ²⁹The boundary then turned to Ramah as far as the fortified city of Tyre; it turned back to Hosah and ended at the sea, including Mahalab, Achzib, ³⁰Ummah, Aphek, and Rehob—22 cities, with their villages.

³¹This was the inheritance of the tribe of Asher's descendants by their clans, these cities with their villages.

³²The sixth lot came out for Naphtali's descendants by their clans.

³³Their boundary went from Heleph and from the oak in Zaanannim, including Adami-nekeb and Jabneel, as far as Lakkum, and ended at the Jordan. ³⁴To the west, the boundary turned to Aznoth-tabor and went from there to Hukkok, reaching Zebulun on the south, Asher on the west, and Judah at the Jordan on the east. ³⁵The fortified cities were Ziddim, Zer, Hammath, Rakkath, Chinnereth, ³⁶Adamah, Ramah, Hazor, ³⁷Kedesh, Edrei, En-hazor, ³⁸Iron, Migdal-el, Horem, Beth-anath, and Beth-shemesh—19 cities, with their villages.

³⁹This was the inheritance of the tribe of Naphtali's descendants by their clans, the cities with their villages.

⁴⁰The seventh lot came out for the Danite tribe by its clans.

⁴¹The territory of their inheritance included Zorah, Eshtaol, Ir-shemesh, ⁴²Shaalabbin, Aijalon, Ithlah, ⁴³Elon, Timnah, Ekron, ⁴⁴Eltekeh, Gibbethon, Baalath, ⁴⁵Jehud, Bene-berak, Gath-rimmon, ⁴⁶Me-jarkon, and Rakkon, with the territory facing Joppa.

⁴⁷When the territory of the Danites slipped out of their control, they went up and fought against Leshem, captured it, and struck it down with the sword. So they took possession of it, lived there, and renamed Leshem after their ancestor Dan. ⁴⁸This was the inheritance of the Danite tribe by its clans, these cities with their villages.

⁴⁹When they had finished distributing the land into its territories, the Israelites gave Joshua son of Nun an inheritance among them. ⁵⁰By the LORD's command, they gave him the city Timnath-serah in the hill country of Ephraim, which he requested. He rebuilt the city and lived in it.

⁵¹These were the portions that Eleazar the priest, Joshua son of Nun, and the heads of the families distributed to the Israelite tribes by lot at Shiloh in the LORD's presence at the entrance to the tent of meeting. So they finished dividing up the land.

20 Then the LORD spoke to Joshua, ²"Tell the Israelites: Select your cities of refuge, as I instructed you through Moses, ³so that a person who kills someone unintentionally or accidentally may flee there. These will be your refuge from the avenger of blood. ⁴When someone flees to one of these cities, stands at the entrance of the city ·gate, and states his case before the elders of that city, they are to bring him into the city and give him a place to live among them. ⁵And if the avenger of blood pursues him, they must not hand the one who committed manslaughter over to him, for he killed his neighbor accidentally and did not hate him beforehand. ⁶He is to stay in that city until he stands trial before the assembly and until the death of the high priest serving at that time. Then the one who committed manslaughter may return home to his own city from which he fled."

⁷So they designated Kedesh in the hill country of Naphtali in Galilee, Shechem in the hill country of Ephraim, and Kiriath-arba (that is, Hebron) in the hill country of Judah. ⁸Across the Jordan east of Jericho, they selected Bezer on the wilderness plateau from Reuben's tribe, Ramoth in Gilead from Gad's tribe, and Golan in Bashan from Manasseh's tribe.

⁹These are the cities appointed for all the Israelites and foreigners among them, so that anyone who kills a person unintentionally may flee there and not die at the hand of the avenger of blood until he stands before the assembly.

21 The heads of the Levite families approached Eleazar the priest, Joshua son of Nun, and the heads of the families of the Israelite tribes. ²At Shiloh, in the land of Canaan, they told them, "The LORD commanded through Moses that we be given cities to live in, with their pasturelands for our livestock." ³So the Israelites, by the LORD's command, gave the Levites these cities with their pasturelands from their inheritance.

⁴The lot came out for the Kohathite clans: The Levites who were the descendants of Aaron the priest received 13 cities by lot from the tribes of Judah, Simeon, and Benjamin. ⁵The remaining descendants of Kohath received 10 cities by lot from the clans of the tribes of Ephraim, Dan, and half the tribe of Manasseh.

⁶Gershon's descendants received 13 cities by lot from the clans of the tribes of Issachar, Asher, Naphtali, and half the tribe of Manasseh in Bashan.

⁷Merari's descendants received 12 cities for their clans from the tribes of Reuben, Gad, and Zebulun.

⁸The Israelites gave these cities with their pasturelands around them to the Levites by lot, as the LORD had commanded through Moses.

⁹The Israelites gave these cities by name from the tribes of the descendants of Judah and Simeon ¹⁰to the descendants of Aaron from the Kohathite clans of the Levites, because they received the first lot. ¹¹They gave them Kiriath-arba (that is, Hebron) with its surrounding pasturelands in the hill country of Judah. Arba was the father of Anak. ¹²But they gave the fields and villages of the city to Caleb son of Jephunneh as his possession.

¹³They gave to the descendants of Aaron the priest: Hebron, the city of refuge for the one who commits manslaughter, with its pasturelands, Libnah with its pasturelands, ¹⁴Jattir with its pasturelands, Eshtemoa with its pasturelands, ¹⁵Holon with its pasturelands, Debir with its pasturelands, ¹⁶Ain with its pasturelands, Juttah with its pasturelands, and Beth-shemesh with its pasturelands—nine cities from these two tribes.

¹⁷From the tribe of Benjamin they gave:

Gibeon with its pasturelands, Geba with its pasturelands, [18]Anathoth with its pasturelands, and Almon with its pasturelands—four cities. [19]All 13 cities with their pasturelands were for the priests, the descendants of Aaron.

[20]The allotted cities to the remaining clans of Kohath's descendants, who were Levites, came from the tribe of Ephraim. [21]The Israelites gave them: Shechem, the city of refuge for the one who commits manslaughter, with its pasturelands in the hill country of Ephraim, Gezer with its pasturelands, [22]Kibzaim with its pasturelands, and Beth-horon with its pasturelands—four cities. [23]From the tribe of Dan they gave: Elteke with its pasturelands, Gibbethon with its pasturelands, [24]Aijalon with its pasturelands, and Gath-rimmon with its pasturelands—four cities. [25]From half the tribe of Manasseh they gave: Taanach with its pasturelands and Gath-rimmon with its pasturelands—two cities. [26]All 10 cities with their pasturelands were for the clans of Kohath's other descendants.

[27]From half the tribe of Manasseh, they gave to the descendants of Gershon, who were one of the Levite clans: Golan, the city of refuge for the one who commits manslaughter, with its pasturelands in Bashan, and Beeshterah with its pasturelands—two cities. [28]From the tribe of Issachar they gave: Kishion with its pasturelands, Daberath with its pasturelands, [29]Jarmuth with its pasturelands, and En-gannim with its pasturelands—four cities. [30]From the tribe of Asher they gave: Mishal with its pasturelands, Abdon with its pasturelands, [31]Helkath with its pasturelands, and Rehob with its pasturelands—four cities. [32]From the tribe of Naphtali they gave: Kedesh in Galilee, the city of refuge for the one who commits manslaughter, with its pasturelands, Hammoth-dor with its pasturelands, and Kartan with its pasturelands—three cities. [33]All 13 cities with their pasturelands were for the Gershonites by their clans.

[34]From the tribe of Zebulun, they gave to the clans of the descendants of Merari, who were the remaining Levites: Jokneam with its pasturelands, Kartah with its pasturelands, [35]Dimnah with its pasturelands, and Nahalal with its pasturelands—four cities. [36]From the tribe of Reuben they gave: Bezer with its pasturelands, Jahzah with its pasturelands, [37]Kedemoth with its pasturelands, and Mephaath with its pasturelands—four cities. [38]From the tribe of Gad they gave: Ramoth in Gilead, the city of refuge for the one who commits manslaughter, with its pasturelands, Mahanaim with its pasturelands, [39]Heshbon with its pasturelands, and Jazer with its pasturelands—four cities in all. [40]All 12 cities were allotted to the clans of Merari's descendants, the remaining Levite clans.

[41]Within the Israelite possession there were 48 cities in all with their pasturelands for the Levites. [42]Each of these cities had its own surrounding pasturelands; this was true for all the cities.

[43]So the LORD gave Israel all the land He had sworn to give their fathers, and they took possession of it and settled there. [44]The LORD gave them rest on every side according to all He had sworn to their fathers. None of their enemies were able to stand against them, for the LORD handed over all their enemies to them. [45]None of the good promises the LORD had made to the house of Israel failed. Everything was fulfilled.

22 Joshua summoned the Reubenites, Gadites, and half the tribe of Manasseh [2]and told them, "You have done everything Moses the LORD's servant commanded you and have obeyed me in everything I commanded you. [3]You have not deserted your brothers even once this whole time but have carried out the requirement of the command of the LORD your God. [4]Now that He has given your brothers rest, just as He promised them, return to your homes in your own land that Moses the LORD's servant gave you across the Jordan. [5]Only carefully obey the command and instruction that Moses the LORD's servant gave you: to love the LORD your God, walk in all His ways, keep His commands, remain faithful to Him, and serve Him with all your heart and all your soul."

[6]Joshua blessed them and sent them on their way, and they went to their homes. [7]Moses had given territory to half the tribe of Manasseh in Bashan, but Joshua had given territory to the other half, with their brothers, on the west side of the Jordan. When Joshua sent them to their homes and blessed them, [8]he said, "Return to your homes with great wealth: a huge number of cattle, and silver, gold, bronze, iron, and a large quantity of clothing. Share the spoil of your enemies with your brothers."

[9]The Reubenites, Gadites, and half the tribe of Manasseh left the Israelites at Shiloh in the land of Canaan to return to their own land of Gilead, which they took possession of according to the LORD's command through Moses. [10]When they came to the region of the Jordan in the land of Canaan, the Reubenites, Gadites, and half the tribe of Manasseh built a large, impressive altar there by the Jordan.

[11]Then the Israelites heard it said, "Look, the Reubenites, Gadites, and half the tribe of Manasseh have built an altar on the frontier of the land of Canaan at the region of the Jordan, on the Israelite side." [12]When the Israelites heard this, the entire Israelite community assembled at Shiloh to go to war against them.

[13]The Israelites sent Phinehas son of Eleazar the priest to the Reubenites, Gadites, and half the tribe of Manasseh, in the land of Gilead. [14]He sent 10 leaders with him—one family leader for each tribe of Israel. All of them were heads of their families among the clans of Israel. [15]They went to the Reubenites, Gadites, and half the tribe of Manasseh, in the land of Gilead, and told them, [16]"This is what the LORD's entire community says: 'What is this treachery you have committed today against the God of Israel by turning away from the LORD and building an altar for yourselves, so that you are in rebellion against the LORD today? [17]Wasn't the sin of Peor, which brought a plague on the LORD's community, enough for us, so that we have not cleansed ourselves from it even to this day, [18]and now, you would turn away from the LORD? If you rebel against the LORD today, tomorrow He will be angry with the entire community of Israel. [19]But if the land

you possess is defiled, cross over to the land the LORD possesses where the LORD's tabernacle stands, and take possession of it among us. But don't rebel against the LORD or against us by building for yourselves an altar other than the altar of the LORD our God. ²⁰Wasn't Achan son of Zerah unfaithful regarding what was *set apart for destruction, bringing wrath on the entire community of Israel? He was not the only one who perished because of his sin.'"

²¹The Reubenites, Gadites, and half the tribe of Manasseh answered the leaders of the Israelite clans, ²²"'Yahweh is the God of gods! Yahweh is the God of gods! He knows, and may Israel also know. Do not spare us today, if it was in rebellion or treachery against the LORD ²³that we have built for ourselves an altar to turn away from Him. May the LORD Himself hold us accountable if we intended to offer *burnt offerings and *grain offerings on it, or to sacrifice *fellowship offerings on it. ²⁴We actually did this from a specific concern that in the future your descendants might say to our descendants, 'What relationship do you have with the LORD, the God of Israel? ²⁵For the LORD has made the Jordan a border between us and you descendants of Reuben and Gad. You have no share in the LORD!' So your descendants may cause our descendants to stop fearing the LORD.

²⁶"Therefore we said: Let us take action and build an altar for ourselves, but not for burnt offering or sacrifice. ²⁷Instead, it is to be a witness between us and you, and between the generations after us, so that we may carry out the worship of the LORD in His presence with our burnt offerings, sacrifices, and fellowship offerings. Then in the future, your descendants will not be able to say to our descendants, 'You have no share in the LORD!' ²⁸We thought that if they said this to us or to our generations in the future, we would reply: Look at the replica of the LORD's altar that our fathers made, not for burnt offering or sacrifice, but as a witness between us and you. ²⁹We would never rebel against the LORD or turn away from Him today by building an altar for burnt offering, grain offering, or sacrifice, other than the altar of the LORD our God, which is in front of His tabernacle."

³⁰When Phinehas the priest and the community leaders, the heads of Israel's clans who were with him, heard what the descendants of Reuben, Gad, and Manasseh had to say, they were pleased. ³¹Phinehas son of Eleazar the priest said to the descendants of Reuben, Gad, and Manasseh, "Today we know that the LORD is among us, because you have not committed this treachery against Him. As a result, you have delivered the Israelites from the LORD's power."

³²Then Phinehas son of Eleazar the priest and the leaders returned from the Reubenites and Gadites in the land of Gilead to the Israelites in the land of Canaan and brought back a report to them. ³³The Israelites were pleased with the report, and they praised God. They spoke no more about going to war against them to ravage the land where the Reubenites and Gadites lived. ³⁴So the Reubenites and Gadites named the altar: It is a witness between us that the LORD is God.

23 A long time after the LORD had given Israel rest from all the enemies around them, Joshua was old, getting on in years. ²So Joshua summoned all Israel, including its elders, leaders, judges, and officers, and said to them, "I am old, getting on in years, ³and

you have seen for yourselves everything the LORD your God did to all these nations on your account, because it was the LORD your God who was fighting for you. ⁴See, I have allotted these remaining nations to you as an inheritance for your tribes, including all the nations I have destroyed, from the Jordan westward to the Mediterranean Sea. ⁵The LORD your God will force them back on your account and drive them out before you so that you can take possession of their land, as the LORD your God promised you.

⁶"Be very strong and continue obeying all that is written in the book of the law of Moses, so that you do not turn from it to the right or left ⁷and so that you do not associate with these nations remaining among you. Do not call on the names of their gods or make an oath to them; do not worship them or bow down to them. ⁸Instead, remain faithful to the LORD your God, as you have done to this day.

⁹"The LORD has driven out great and powerful nations before you, and no one is able to stand against you to this day. ¹⁰One of you routed a thousand because the LORD your God was fighting for you, as He promised. ¹¹So be very diligent to love the LORD your God for your own well-being. ¹²For if you turn away and cling to the rest of these nations remaining among you, and if you intermarry or associate with them and they with you, ¹³know for certain that the LORD your God will not continue to drive these nations out before you. They will become a snare and a trap for you, a scourge for your sides and thorns in your eyes, until you disappear from this good land the LORD your God has given you.

¹⁴"I am now going the way of all the earth, and you know with all your heart and all your soul that none of the good promises the LORD your God made to you has failed. Everything was fulfilled for you; not one promise has failed. ¹⁵Since every good thing the LORD your God promised you has come about, so He will bring on you every bad thing until He has annihilated you from this good land the LORD your God has given you. ¹⁶If you break the covenant of the LORD your God, which He commanded you, and go and worship other gods, and bow down to them, the LORD's anger will burn against you, and you will quickly disappear from this good land He has given you."

24 Joshua assembled all the tribes of Israel at Shechem and summoned Israel's elders, leaders, judges, and officers, and they presented themselves before God. ²Joshua said to all the people, "This is what the LORD, the God of Israel, says: 'Long ago your ancestors, including Terah, the father of Abraham and Nahor, lived beyond the Euphrates River and worshiped other gods. ³But I took your father Abraham from the region beyond the Euphrates River, led him throughout the land of Canaan, and multiplied his descendants. I gave him Isaac, ⁴and to Isaac I gave Jacob and Esau. I gave the hill country of Seir to Esau as a possession, but Jacob and his sons went down to Egypt.

⁵"'Then I sent Moses and Aaron; I plagued Egypt by what I did there and afterward I brought you out. ⁶When I brought your fathers out of Egypt and you reached the *Red Sea, the Egyptians pursued your fathers with chariots and horsemen as far as the sea. ⁷Your fathers cried out to the LORD, so He put darkness between you and the Egyptians, and brought the sea over them, engulfing them. Your own eyes saw what

I did to Egypt. After that, you lived in the wilderness a long time.

8 "'Later, I brought you to the land of the Amorites who lived beyond the Jordan. They fought against you, but I handed them over to you. You possessed their land, and I annihilated them before you. 9 Balak son of Zippor, king of Moab, set out to fight against Israel. He sent for Balaam son of Beor to curse you, 10 but I would not listen to Balaam. Instead, he repeatedly blessed you, and I delivered you from his hand.

11 "'You then crossed the Jordan and came to Jericho. The people of Jericho—as well as the Amorites, Perizzites, Canaanites, Hittites, Girgashites, Hivites, and Jebusites—fought against you, but I handed them over to you. 12 I sent the hornet ahead of you, and it drove out the two Amorite kings before you. It was not by your sword or bow. 13 I gave you a land you did not labor for, and cities you did not build, though you live in them; you are eating from vineyards and olive groves you did not plant.'

14 "Therefore, ˙fear the LORD and worship Him in sincerity and truth. Get rid of the gods your fathers worshiped beyond the Euphrates River and in Egypt, and worship ˙Yahweh. 15 But if it doesn't please you to worship Yahweh, choose for yourselves today the one you will worship: the gods your fathers worshiped beyond the Euphrates River or the gods of the Amorites in whose land you are living. As for me and my family, we will worship Yahweh."

16 The people replied, "We will certainly not abandon the LORD to worship other gods! 17 For the LORD our God brought us and our fathers out of the land of Egypt, out of the place of slavery, and performed these great signs before our eyes. He also protected us all along the way we went and among all the peoples whose lands we traveled through. 18 The LORD drove out before us all the peoples, including the Amorites who lived in the land. We too will worship the LORD, because He is our God."

19 But Joshua told the people, "You will not be able to worship Yahweh, because He is a holy God. He is a jealous God; He will not remove your transgressions and sins. 20 If you abandon the LORD and worship foreign gods, He will turn against you, harm you, and completely destroy you, after He has been good to you."

21 "No!" the people answered Joshua. "We will worship the LORD."

22 Joshua then told the people, "You are witnesses against yourselves that you yourselves have chosen to worship Yahweh."

"We are witnesses," they said.

23 "Then get rid of the foreign gods that are among you and offer your hearts to the LORD, the God of Israel."

24 So the people said to Joshua, "We will worship the LORD our God and obey Him."

25 On that day Joshua made a covenant for the people at Shechem and established a statute and ordinance for them. 26 Joshua recorded these things in the book of the law of God; he also took a large stone and set it up there under the oak next to the sanctuary of the LORD. 27 And Joshua said to all the people, "You see this stone—it will be a witness against us, for it has heard all the words the LORD said to us, and it will be a witness against you, so that you will not deny your God." 28 Then Joshua sent the people away, each to his own inheritance.

29 After these things, the LORD's servant, Joshua son of Nun, died at the age of 110. 30 They buried him in his allotted territory at Timnath-serah, in the hill country of Ephraim north of Mount Gaash. 31 Israel worshiped Yahweh throughout Joshua's lifetime and during the lifetimes of the elders who outlived Joshua and who had experienced all the works Yahweh had done for Israel.

32 Joseph's bones, which the Israelites had brought up from Egypt, were buried at Shechem in the parcel of land Jacob had purchased from the sons of Hamor, Shechem's father, for 100 *qesitahs*. It was an inheritance for Joseph's descendants.

33 And Eleazar son of Aaron died, and they buried him at Gibeah, which had been given to his son Phinehas in the hill country of Ephraim.

JUDGES

1 After the death of Joshua, the Israelites inquired of the LORD, "Who will be the first to fight for us against the Canaanites?"

2 The LORD answered, "Judah is to go. I have handed the land over to him."

3 Judah said to his brother Simeon, "Come with me to my territory, and let us fight against the Canaanites. I will also go with you to your territory." So Simeon went with him.

4 When Judah attacked, the LORD handed the Canaanites and Perizzites over to them. They struck down 10,000 men in Bezek. 5 They found Adoni-bezek in Bezek, fought against him, and struck down the Canaanites and Perizzites.

6 When Adoni-bezek fled, they pursued him, seized him, and cut off his thumbs and big toes. 7 Adoni-bezek said, "Seventy kings with their thumbs and big toes cut off used to pick up scraps under my table. God has repaid me for what I have done." They brought him to Jerusalem, and he died there.

8 The men of Judah fought against Jerusalem and captured it. They put the city to the sword and set it on fire. 9 Afterward, the men of Judah marched down to fight against the Canaanites who were living in the hill country, the ˙Negev, and the Judean foothills. 10 Judah also marched against the Canaanites who were living in Hebron (Hebron was formerly named Kirath-arba). They struck down Sheshai, Ahiman, and Talmai. 11 From there they marched against the residents of Debir (Debir was formerly named Kiriath-sepher).

12 Caleb said, "Whoever strikes down and captures Kiriath-sepher, I will give my daughter Achsah to him as a wife." 13 So Othniel son of Kenaz, Caleb's youngest brother, captured it, and Caleb gave his daughter Achsah to him as his wife.

14 When she arrived, she persuaded Othniel to ask her father for a field. As she got off her donkey, Caleb

asked her, "What do you want?" ¹⁵She answered him, "Give me a blessing. Since you have given me land in the Negev, give me springs of water also." So Caleb gave her both the upper and lower springs.

¹⁶The descendants of the Kenite, Moses' father-in-law, had gone up with the men of Judah from the City of Palms to the Wilderness of Judah, which was in the Negev of Arad. They went to live among the people.

¹⁷Judah went with his brother Simeon, struck the Canaanites who were living in Zephath, and *completely destroyed the town. So they named the town Hormah. ¹⁸Judah captured Gaza and its territory, Ashkelon and its territory, and Ekron and its territory. ¹⁹The Lord was with Judah and enabled them to take possession of the hill country, but they could not drive out the people who were living in the valley because those people had iron chariots.

²⁰Judah gave Hebron to Caleb, just as Moses had promised. Then Caleb drove out the three sons of Anak who lived there.

²¹At the same time the Benjaminites did not drive out the Jebusites who were living in Jerusalem. The Jebusites have lived among the Benjaminites in Jerusalem to this day.

²²The house of Joseph also attacked Bethel, and the Lord was with them. ²³They sent spies to Bethel (the town was formerly named Luz). ²⁴The spies saw a man coming out of the town and said to him, "Please show us how to get into town, and we will treat you well." ²⁵When he showed them the way into the town, they put the town to the sword but released the man and his entire family. ²⁶Then the man went to the land of the Hittites, built a town, and named it Luz. That is its name to this day.

²⁷At that time Manasseh failed to take possession of Beth-shean and its villages, or Taanach and its villages, or the residents of Dor and its villages, or the residents of Ibleam and its villages, or the residents of Megiddo and its villages; the Canaanites refused to leave this land. ²⁸When Israel became stronger, they made the Canaanites serve as forced labor but never drove them out completely.

²⁹At that time Ephraim failed to drive out the Canaanites who were living in Gezer, so the Canaanites have lived among them in Gezer.

³⁰Zebulun failed to drive out the residents of Kitron or the residents of Nahalol, so the Canaanites lived among them and served as forced labor.

³¹Asher failed to drive out the residents of Acco or of Sidon, or Ahlab, Achzib, Helbah, Aphik, or Rehob. ³²The Asherites lived among the Canaanites who were living in the land, because they failed to drive them out.

³³Naphtali did not drive out the residents of Beth-shemesh or the residents of Beth-anath. They lived among the Canaanites who were living in the land, but the residents of Beth-shemesh and Beth-anath served as their forced labor.

³⁴The Amorites forced the Danites into the hill country and did not allow them to go down into the valley. ³⁵The Amorites refused to leave Har-heres, Aijalon, and Shaalbim. When the house of Joseph got the upper hand, the Amorites were made to serve as forced labor. ³⁶The territory of the Amorites extended from the Ascent of Akrabbim, that is from Sela upward.

2 The Angel of the Lord went up from Gilgal to Bochim and said, "I brought you out of Egypt and led you into the land I had promised to your fathers. I also said: I will never break My covenant with you. ²You are not to make a covenant with the people who are living in this land, and you are to tear down their altars. But you have not obeyed Me. What is this you have done? ³Therefore, I now say: I will not drive out these people before you. They will be thorns in your sides, and their gods will be a trap for you." ⁴When the Angel of the Lord had spoken these words to all the Israelites, the people wept loudly. ⁵So they named that place Bochim and offered sacrifices there to the Lord.

⁶Joshua sent the people away, and the Israelites went to take possession of the land, each to his own inheritance. ⁷The people worshiped the Lord throughout Joshua's lifetime and during the lifetimes of the elders who outlived Joshua. They had seen all the Lord's great works He had done for Israel.

⁸Joshua son of Nun, the servant of the Lord, died at the age of 110. ⁹They buried him in the territory of his inheritance, in Timnath-heres, in the hill country of Ephraim, north of Mount Gaash. ¹⁰That whole generation was also gathered to their ancestors. After them another generation rose up who did not know the Lord or the works He had done for Israel.

¹¹The Israelites did what was evil in the Lord's sight. They worshiped the *Baals ¹²and abandoned the Lord, the God of their fathers, who had brought them out of Egypt. They went after other gods from the surrounding peoples and bowed down to them. They infuriated the Lord, ¹³for they abandoned Him and worshiped Baal and the *Ashtoreths.

¹⁴The Lord's anger burned against Israel, and He handed them over to marauders who raided them. He sold them to the enemies around them, and they could no longer resist their enemies. ¹⁵Whenever the Israelites went out, the Lord was against them and brought disaster on them, just as He had promised and sworn to them. So they suffered greatly.

¹⁶The Lord raised up judges, who saved them from the power of their marauders, ¹⁷but they did not listen to their judges. Instead, they prostituted themselves with other gods, bowing down to them. They quickly turned from the way of their fathers, who had walked in obedience to the Lord's commands. They did not do as their fathers did. ¹⁸Whenever the Lord raised up a judge for the Israelites, the Lord was with him and saved the people from the power of their enemies while the judge was still alive. The Lord was moved to pity whenever they groaned because of those who were oppressing and afflicting them. ¹⁹Whenever the judge died, the Israelites would act even more corruptly than their fathers, going after other gods to worship and bow down to them. They did not turn from their evil practices or their obstinate ways.

²⁰The Lord's anger burned against Israel, and He declared, "Because this nation has violated My covenant that I made with their fathers and disobeyed Me, ²¹I will no longer drive out before them any of the nations Joshua left when he died. ²²I did this to test Israel and to see whether they would keep the Lord's way by walking in it, as their fathers had." ²³The Lord left these nations and did not drive them out immediately. He did not hand them over to Joshua.

3 These are the nations the LORD left in order to test Israel, since the Israelites had fought none of these in any of the wars with Canaan. ²This was to teach the future generations of the Israelites how to fight in battle, especially those who had not fought before. ³These nations included: the five rulers of the Philistines and all of the Canaanites, the Sidonians, and the Hivites who lived in the Lebanese mountains from Mount Baal-hermon as far as the entrance to Hamath. ⁴The LORD left them to test Israel, to determine if they would keep the LORD's commands He had given their fathers through Moses. ⁵But they settled among the Canaanites, Hittites, Amorites, Perizzites, Hivites, and Jebusites. ⁶The Israelites took their daughters as wives for themselves, gave their own daughters to their sons, and worshiped their gods.

⁷The Israelites did what was evil in the LORD's sight; they forgot the LORD their God and worshiped the *Baals and the *Asherahs. ⁸The LORD's anger burned against Israel, and He sold them to Cushan-rishathaim king of Aram-naharaim, and the Israelites served him eight years.

⁹The Israelites cried out to the LORD. So the LORD raised up Othniel son of Kenaz, Caleb's youngest brother, as a deliverer to save the Israelites. ¹⁰The Spirit of the LORD came on him, and he judged Israel. Othniel went out to battle, and the LORD handed over Cushan-rishathaim king of Aram to him, so that Othniel overpowered him. ¹¹Then the land was peaceful 40 years, and Othniel son of Kenaz died.

¹²The Israelites again did what was evil in the LORD's sight. He gave Eglon king of Moab power over Israel, because they had done what was evil in the LORD's sight. ¹³After Eglon convinced the Ammonites and the Amalekites to join forces with him, he attacked and defeated Israel and took possession of the City of Palms. ¹⁴The Israelites served Eglon king of Moab 18 years.

¹⁵Then the Israelites cried out to the LORD, and He raised up Ehud son of Gera, a left-handed Benjaminite, as a deliverer for them. The Israelites sent him to Eglon king of Moab with tribute money.

¹⁶Ehud made himself a double-edged sword 18 inches long. He strapped it to his right thigh under his clothes ¹⁷and brought the tribute to Eglon king of Moab, who was an extremely fat man. ¹⁸When Ehud had finished presenting the tribute, he dismissed the people who had carried it. ¹⁹At the carved images near Gilgal he returned and said, "King Eglon, I have a secret message for you." The king called for silence, and all his attendants left him. ²⁰Then Ehud approached him while he was sitting alone in his room upstairs where it was cool. Ehud said, "I have a word from God for you," and the king stood up from his throne. ²¹Ehud reached with his left hand, took the sword from his right thigh, and plunged it into Eglon's belly. ²²Even the handle went in after the blade, and Eglon's fat closed in over it, so that Ehud did not withdraw the sword from his belly. And Eglon's insides came out. ²³Ehud escaped by way of the porch, closing and locking the doors of the upstairs room behind him.

²⁴Ehud was gone when Eglon's servants came in. They looked and found the doors of the upstairs room locked and thought he was relieving himself in the cool room. ²⁵The servants waited until they became worried and saw that he had still not opened the doors of the upstairs room. So they took the key and opened the doors—and there was their lord lying dead on the floor!

²⁶Ehud escaped while the servants waited. He crossed over the Jordan near the carved images and reached Seirah. ²⁷After he arrived, he sounded the ram's horn throughout the hill country of Ephraim. The Israelites came down with him from the hill country, and he became their leader. ²⁸He told them, "Follow me, because the LORD has handed over your enemies, the Moabites, to you." So they followed him, captured the fords of the Jordan leading to Moab, and did not allow anyone to cross over. ²⁹At that time they struck down about 10,000 Moabites, all strong and able-bodied men. Not one of them escaped. ³⁰Moab became subject to Israel that day, and the land was peaceful 80 years.

³¹After Ehud, Shamgar son of Anath became judge. He delivered Israel by striking down 600 Philistines with an oxgoad.

4 The Israelites again did what was evil in the sight of the LORD after Ehud had died. ²So the LORD sold them into the hand of Jabin king of Canaan, who reigned in Hazor. The commander of his forces was Sisera who lived in Harosheth of the Nations. ³Then the Israelites cried out to the LORD, because Jabin had 900 iron chariots and he harshly oppressed them 20 years.

⁴Deborah, a woman who was a prophetess and the wife of Lappidoth, was judging Israel at that time. ⁵It was her custom to sit under the palm tree of Deborah between Ramah and Bethel in the hill country of Ephraim, and the Israelites went up to her for judgment.

⁶She summoned Barak son of Abinoam from Kedesh in Naphtali and said to him, "Hasn't the LORD, the God of Israel, commanded you: 'Go, deploy the troops on Mount Tabor, and take with you 10,000 men from the Naphtalites and Zebulunites? ⁷Then I will lure Sisera commander of Jabin's forces, his chariots, and his army at the *Wadi Kishon to fight against you, and I will hand him over to you.'"

⁸Barak said to her, "If you will go with me, I will go. But if you will not go with me, I will not go."

⁹"I will go with you," she said, "but you will receive no honor on the road you are about to take, because the LORD will sell Sisera into a woman's hand." So Deborah got up and went with Barak to Kedesh. ¹⁰Barak summoned Zebulun and Naphtali to Kedesh; 10,000 men followed him, and Deborah also went with him.

¹¹Now Heber the Kenite had moved away from the Kenites, the sons of Hobab, Moses' father-in-law, and pitched his tent beside the oak tree of Zaanannim, which was near Kedesh.

¹²It was reported to Sisera that Barak son of Abinoam had gone up Mount Tabor. ¹³Sisera summoned all his 900 iron chariots and all the people who were with him from Harosheth of the Nations to the Wadi Kishon. ¹⁴Then Deborah said to Barak, "Move on, for this is the day the LORD has handed Sisera over to you. Hasn't the LORD gone before you?" So Barak came down from Mount Tabor with 10,000 men following him.

¹⁵The LORD threw Sisera, all his charioteers, and all his army into confusion with the sword before Barak. Sisera left his chariot and fled on foot. ¹⁶Barak pursued the chariots and the army as far as Harosheth of

the Nations, and the whole army of Sisera fell by the sword; not a single man was left. ·

¹⁷ Meanwhile, Sisera had fled on foot to the tent of Jael, the wife of Heber the Kenite, because there was peace between Jabin king of Hazor and the family of Heber the Kenite. ¹⁸ Jael went out to greet Sisera and said to him, "Come in, my lord. Come in with me. Don't be afraid." So he went into her tent, and she covered him with a rug. ¹⁹ He said to her, "Please give me a little water to drink for I am thirsty." She opened a container of milk, gave him a drink, and covered him again. ²⁰ Then he said to her, "Stand at the entrance to the tent. If a man comes and asks you, 'Is there a man here?' say, 'No.'" ²¹ While he was sleeping from exhaustion, Heber's wife Jael took a tent peg, grabbed a hammer, and went silently to Sisera. She hammered the peg into his temple and drove it into the ground, and he died.

²² When Barak arrived in pursuit of Sisera, Jael went out to greet him and said to him, "Come and I will show you the man you are looking for." So he went in with her, and there was Sisera lying dead with a tent peg through his temple!

²³ That day God subdued Jabin king of Canaan before the Israelites. ²⁴ The power of the Israelites continued to increase against Jabin king of Canaan until they destroyed him.

5 On that day Deborah and Barak son of Abinoam sang:
² When the leaders lead in Israel,
  when the people volunteer,
  praise the Lord.
³ Listen, kings! Pay attention, princes!
  I will sing to the Lord;
  I will sing praise to the Lord God of Israel.
⁴ Lord, when You came from Seir,
  when You marched from the fields of Edom,
  the earth trembled,
  the heavens poured rain,
  and the clouds poured water.
⁵ The mountains melted before the Lord,
  even Sinai before the Lord, the God
    of Israel.
⁶ In the days of Shamgar son of Anath,
  in the days of Jael,
  the main ways were deserted
  because travelers kept to the side roads.
⁷ Villages were deserted,
  they were deserted in Israel,
  until I, Deborah, arose,
  a mother in Israel.
⁸ Israel chose new gods,
  then war was in the gates.
  Not a shield or spear was seen
  among 40,000 in Israel.
⁹ My heart is with the leaders of Israel,
  with the volunteers of the people.
  Praise the Lord!
¹⁰ You who ride on white donkeys,
  who sit on saddle blankets,
  and who travel on the road, give praise!
¹¹ Let them tell the righteous acts of the Lord,
  the righteous deeds of His warriors in Israel,
  with the voices of the singers
    at the watering places.
  Then the Lord's people went down
    to the gates.

¹² "Awake! Awake, Deborah!
  Awake! Awake, sing a song!
  Arise, Barak,
  and take hold of your captives,
  son of Abinoam!"
¹³ The survivors came down to the nobles;
  the Lord's people came down to me
    with the warriors.
¹⁴ Those with their roots in Amalek came
    from Ephraim;
  Benjamin came with your people after you.
  The leaders came down from Machir,
  and those who carry a marshal's staff came
    from Zebulun.
¹⁵ The princes of Issachar were with Deborah;
  Issachar was with Barak.
  They set out at his heels in the valley.
  There was great searching of heart
  among the clans of Reuben.
¹⁶ Why did you sit among the sheepfolds
  listening to the playing of pipes for the flocks?
  There was great searching of heart
  among the clans of Reuben.
¹⁷ Gilead remained beyond the Jordan.
  Dan, why did you linger at the ships?
  Asher remained at the seashore
  and stayed in his harbors.
¹⁸ Zebulun was a people risking their lives,
  Naphtali also, on the heights of the battlefield.
¹⁹ Kings came and fought.
  Then the kings of Canaan fought
  at Taanach by the waters of Megiddo,
  but they took no spoil of silver.
²⁰ The stars fought from the heavens;
  the stars fought with Sisera
    from their courses.
²¹ The river Kishon swept them away,
  the ancient river, the river Kishon.
  March on, my soul, in strength!
²² The horses' hooves then hammered—
  the galloping, galloping of his stallions.
²³ "Curse Meroz," says the Angel of the Lord,
  "Bitterly curse her inhabitants,
  for they did not come to help the Lord,
  to help the Lord against the mighty warriors."
²⁴ Jael is most blessed of women,
  the wife of Heber the Kenite; ·
  she is most blessed among
    tent-dwelling women.
²⁵ He asked for water; she gave him milk.
  She brought him curdled milk
    in a majestic bowl.
²⁶ She reached for a tent peg,
  her right hand, for a workman's mallet.
  Then she hammered Sisera—
  she crushed his head;
  she shattered and pierced his temple.
²⁷ He collapsed, he fell, he lay down at her feet;
  he collapsed, he fell at her feet;
  where he collapsed, there he fell—dead.
²⁸ Sisera's mother looked through the window;
  she peered through the lattice, crying out:
  "Why is his chariot so long in coming?
  Why don't I hear the hoofbeats of his horses?"
²⁹ Her wisest princesses answer her;
  she even answers herself:
³⁰ "Are they not finding and dividing the spoil—

a girl or two for each warrior,
the spoil of colored garments for Sisera,
the spoil of an embroidered garment or two
    for my neck?"
³¹ Lord, may all your enemies perish
    as Sisera did.
But may those who love Him
    be like the rising of the sun in its strength.
And the land was peaceful 40 years.

6 The Israelites did what was evil in the sight of the Lord. So the Lord handed them over to Midian seven years, ²and they oppressed Israel. Because of Midian, the Israelites made hiding places for themselves in the mountains, caves, and strongholds. ³Whenever the Israelites planted crops, the Midianites, Amalekites, and the Qedemites came and attacked them. ⁴They encamped against them and destroyed the produce of the land, even as far as Gaza. They left nothing for Israel to eat, as well as no sheep, ox or donkey. ⁵For the Midianites came with their cattle and their tents like a great swarm of locusts. They and their camels were without number, and they entered the land to waste it. ⁶So Israel became poverty-stricken because of Midian, and the Israelites cried out to the Lord.

⁷When the Israelites cried out to Him because of Midian, ⁸the Lord sent a prophet to them. He said to them, "This is what the Lord God of Israel says: 'I brought you out of Egypt and out of the place of slavery. ⁹I delivered you from the power of Egypt and the power of all who oppressed you. I drove them out before you and gave you their land. ¹⁰I said to you: I am ˙Yahweh your God. Do not fear the gods of the Amorites whose land you live in. But you did not obey Me.'"

¹¹The Angel of the Lord came, and He sat under the oak that was in Ophrah, which belonged to Joash, the Abiezrite. His son Gideon was threshing wheat in the wine vat in order to hide it from the Midianites. ¹²Then the Angel of the Lord appeared to him and said: "The Lord is with you, mighty warrior."

¹³Gideon said to Him, "Please Sir, if the Lord is with us, why has all this happened? And where are all His wonders that our fathers told us about? They said, 'Hasn't the Lord brought us out of Egypt?' But now the Lord has abandoned us and handed us over to Midian."

¹⁴The Lord turned to him and said, "Go in the strength you have and deliver Israel from the power of Midian. Am I not sending you?"

¹⁵He said to Him, "Please, Lord, how can I deliver Israel? Look, my family is the weakest in Manasseh, and I am the youngest in my father's house."

¹⁶"But I will be with you," the Lord said to him. "You will strike Midian down as if it were one man."

¹⁷Then he said to Him, "If I have found favor in Your sight, give me a sign that You are speaking with me. ¹⁸Please do not leave this place until I return to You. Let me bring my gift and set it before You."

And He said, "I will stay until you return."

¹⁹So Gideon went and prepared a young goat and unleavened bread from a half bushel of flour. He placed the meat in a basket and the broth in a pot. He brought them out and offered them to Him under the oak.

²⁰The Angel of God said to him, "Take the meat with the unleavened bread, put it on this stone, and pour the broth on it." And he did so.

²¹The Angel of the Lord extended the tip of the staff that was in His hand and touched the meat and the unleavened bread. Fire came up from the rock and

consumed the meat and the unleavened bread. Then the Angel of the Lord vanished from his sight.

²²When Gideon realized that He was the Angel of the Lord, he said, "Oh no, Lord God! I have seen the Angel of the Lord face to face!"

²³But the Lord said to him, "Peace to you. Don't be afraid, for you will not die." ²⁴So Gideon built an altar to the Lord there and called it Yahweh Shalom. It is in Ophrah of the Abiezrites until today.

²⁵On that very night the Lord said to him, "Take your father's young bull and a second bull seven years old. Then tear down the altar of ˙Baal that belongs to your father and cut down the ˙Asherah pole beside it. ²⁶Build a well-constructed altar to the Lord your God on the top of this rock. Take the second bull and offer it as a ˙burnt offering with the wood of the Asherah pole you cut down." ²⁷So Gideon took 10 of his male servants and did as the Lord had told him. But because he was too afraid of his father's household and the men of the city to do it in the daytime, he did it at night.

²⁸When the men of the city got up in the morning, they found Baal's altar torn down, the Asherah pole beside it cut down, and the second bull offered up on the altar that had been built. ²⁹They said to each other, "Who did this?" After they made a thorough investigation, they said, "Gideon son of Joash did it."

³⁰Then the men of the city said to Joash, "Bring out your son. He must die, because he tore down Baal's altar and cut down the Asherah pole beside it."

³¹But Joash said to all who stood against him, "Would you plead Baal's case for him? Would you save him? Whoever pleads his case will be put to death by morning! If he is a god, let him plead his own case because someone tore down his altar." ³²That day, Gideon's father called him Jerubbaal, saying, "Let Baal plead his case with him," because he tore down his altar.

³³All the Midianites, Amalekites, and Qedemites gathered together, crossed over the Jordan, and camped in the Valley of Jezreel. ³⁴The Spirit of the Lord took control of Gideon, and he blew the ram's horn and the Abiezrites rallied behind him. ³⁵He sent messengers throughout all of Manasseh, who rallied behind him. He also sent messengers throughout Asher, Zebulun, and Naphtali, who also came to meet him.

³⁶Then Gideon said to God, "If You will deliver Israel by my hand, as You said, ³⁷I will put a fleece of wool here on the threshing floor. If dew is only on the fleece, and all the ground is dry, I will know that You will deliver Israel by my strength, as You said." ³⁸And that is what happened. When he got up early in the morning, he squeezed the fleece and wrung dew out of it, filling a bowl with water.

³⁹Gideon then said to God, "Don't be angry with me; let me speak one more time. Please allow me to make one more test with the fleece. Let it remain dry, and the dew be all over the ground." ⁴⁰That night God did as Gideon requested: only the fleece was dry, and dew was all over the ground.

7 Jerubbaal (that is, Gideon) and everyone who was with him, got up early and camped beside the spring of Harod. The camp of Midian was north of them, below the hill of Moreh, in the valley. ²The Lord said to Gideon, "You have too many people for Me to hand the Midianites over to you, or else Israel might brag: 'I did it myself.' ³Now announce in the presence

of the people: 'Whoever is fearful and trembling may turn back and leave Mount Gilead.'" So 22,000 of the people turned back, but 10,000 remained.

⁴Then the LORD said to Gideon, "There are still too many people. Take them down to the water, and I will test them for you there. If I say to you, 'This one can go with you,' he can go. But if I say about anyone, 'This one cannot go with you,' he cannot go." ⁵So he brought the people down to the water, and the LORD said to Gideon, "Separate everyone who laps water with his tongue like a dog. Do the same with everyone who kneels to drink." ⁶The number of those who lapped with their hands to their mouths was 300 men, and all the rest of the people knelt to drink water. ⁷The LORD said to Gideon, "I will deliver you with the 300 men who lapped and hand the Midianites over to you. But everyone else is to go home." ⁸So Gideon sent all the Israelites to their tents but kept the 300, who took the people's provisions and their trumpets. The camp of Midian was below him in the valley.

⁹That night the LORD said to him, "Get up and go into the camp, for I have given it into your hand. ¹⁰But if you are afraid to go to the camp, go with Purah your servant. ¹¹Listen to what they say, and then you will be strengthened to go to the camp." So he went with Purah his servant to the outpost of the troops who were in the camp.

¹²Now the Midianites, Amalekites, and all the Qedemites had settled down in the valley like a swarm of locusts, and their camels were as innumerable as the sand on the seashore. ¹³When Gideon arrived, there was a man telling his friend about a dream. He said, "Listen, I had a dream: a loaf of barley bread came tumbling into the Midianite camp, struck a tent, and it fell. The loaf turned the tent upside down so that it collapsed."

¹⁴His friend answered: "This is nothing less than the sword of Gideon son of Joash, the Israelite. God has handed the entire Midianite camp over to him."

¹⁵When Gideon heard the account of the dream and its interpretation, he bowed in worship. He returned to Israel's camp and said, "Get up, for the LORD has handed the Midianite camp over to you." ¹⁶Then he divided the 300 men into three companies and gave each of the men a trumpet in one hand and an empty pitcher with a torch inside it in the other.

¹⁷"Watch me," he said, "and do the same. When I come to the outpost of the camp, do as I do. ¹⁸When I and everyone with me blow our trumpets, you are also to blow your trumpets all around the camp. Then you will say, 'For *Yahweh and for Gideon!'"

¹⁹Gideon and the 100 men who were with him went to the outpost of the camp at the beginning of the middle watch after the sentries had been stationed. They blew their trumpets and broke the pitchers that were in their hands. ²⁰The three companies blew their trumpets and shattered their pitchers. They held their torches in their left hands, their trumpets in their right hands, and shouted, "A sword for Yahweh and for Gideon!" ²¹Each Israelite took his position around the camp, and the entire Midianite army fled, and cried out as they ran. ²²When Gideon's men blew their 300 trumpets, the LORD set the swords of each man in the army against each other. They fled to Beth-shittah in the direction of Zererah as far as the border of Abel-meholah near Tabbath. ²³Then the men of Israel were

called from Naphtali, Asher, and Manasseh, and they pursued the Midianites.

²⁴Gideon sent messengers throughout the hill country of Ephraim with this message: "Come down to intercept the Midianites and take control of the watercourses ahead of them as far as Beth-barah and the Jordan." So all the men of Ephraim were called out, and they took control of the watercourses as far as Beth-barah and the Jordan. ²⁵They captured Oreb and Zeeb, the two princes of Midian; they killed Oreb at the rock of Oreb and Zeeb at the winepress of Zeeb, while they were pursuing the Midianites. They brought the heads of Oreb and Zeeb to Gideon across the Jordan.

8 The men of Ephraim said to him, "Why have you done this to us, not calling us when you went to fight against the Midianites?" And they argued with him violently.

²So he said to them, "What have I done now compared to you? Is not the gleaning of Ephraim better than the vintage of Abiezer? ³God handed over to you Oreb and Zeeb, the two princes of Midian. What was I able to do compared to you?" When he said this, their anger against him subsided.

⁴Gideon and the 300 men came to the Jordan and crossed it. They were exhausted but still in pursuit. ⁵He said to the men of Succoth, "Please give some loaves of bread to the people who are following me, because they are exhausted, for I am pursuing Zebah and Zalmunna, the kings of Midian."

⁶But the princes of Succoth asked, "Are Zebah and Zalmunna now in your hands that we should give bread to your army?"

⁷Gideon replied, "Very well, when the LORD has handed Zebah and Zalmunna over to me, I will trample your flesh on thorns and briers from the wilderness!" ⁸He went from there to Penuel and asked the same thing from them. The men of Penuel answered just as the men of Succoth had answered. ⁹He also told the men of Penuel, "When I return in peace, I will tear down this tower!"

¹⁰Now Zebah and Zalmunna were in Karkor, and with them was their army of about 15,000 men, who were all those left of the entire army of the Qedemites. Those who had been killed were 120,000 warriors. ¹¹Gideon traveled on the caravan route east of Nobah and Jogbehah and attacked their army while the army was unsuspecting. ¹²Zebah and Zalmunna fled, and he pursued them. He captured these two kings of Midian and routed the entire army.

¹³Gideon son of Joash returned from the battle by the Ascent of Heres. ¹⁴He captured a youth from the men of Succoth and interrogated him. The youth wrote down for him the names of the 77 princes and elders of Succoth. ¹⁵Then he went to the men of Succoth and said, "Here are Zebah and Zalmunna. You taunted me about them, saying, 'Are Zebah and Zalmunna now in your power that we should give bread to your exhausted men?'" ¹⁶So he took the elders of the city, and he took some thorns and briers from the wilderness, and he disciplined the men of Succoth with them. ¹⁷He also tore down the tower of Penuel and killed the men of the city.

¹⁸He asked Zebah and Zalmunna, "What kind of men did you kill at Tabor?"

"They were like you," they said. "Each resembled the son of a king."

¹⁹So he said, "They were my brothers, the sons of

my mother! As the LORD lives, if you had let them live, I would not kill you." ²⁰Then he said to Jether, his firstborn, "Get up and kill them." The youth did not draw his sword, for he was afraid because he was still a youth.

²¹Zebah and Zalmunna said, "Get up and kill us yourself, for a man is judged by his strength." So Gideon got up, killed Zebah and Zalmunna, and took the crescent ornaments that were on the necks of their camels.

²²Then the Israelites said to Gideon, "Rule over us, you as well as your sons and your grandsons, for you delivered us from the power of Midian."

²³But Gideon said to them, "I will not rule over you, and my son will not rule over you; the LORD will rule over you." ²⁴Then he said to them, "Let me make a request of you: Everyone give me an earring from his plunder." Now the enemy had gold earrings because they were Ishmaelites.

²⁵They said, "We agree to give them." So they spread out a mantle, and everyone threw an earring from his plunder on it. ²⁶The weight of the gold earrings he requested was about 43 pounds of gold, in addition to the crescent ornaments and ear pendants, the purple garments on the kings of Midian, and the chains on the necks of their camels. ²⁷Gideon made an ephod from all this and put it in Ophrah, his hometown. Then all Israel prostituted themselves with it there, and it became a snare to Gideon and his household.

²⁸So Midian was subdued before the Israelites, and they were no longer a threat. The land was peaceful 40 years during the days of Gideon. ²⁹Jerubbaal (that is, Gideon) son of Joash went back to live at his house. ³⁰Gideon had 70 sons, his own offspring, since he had many wives. ³¹His concubine who was in Shechem also bore him a son, and he named him Abimelech. ³²Then Gideon son of Joash died at a ripe old age and was buried in the tomb of his father Joash in Ophrah of the Abiezrites.

³³When Gideon died, the Israelites turned and prostituted themselves with the *Baals and made Baal-berith their god. ³⁴The Israelites did not remember the LORD their God who had delivered them from the power of the enemies around them. ³⁵They did not show kindness to the house of Jerubbaal (that is, Gideon) for all the good he had done for Israel.

9 Abimelech son of Jerubbaal went to his mother's brothers at Shechem and spoke to them and to all his maternal grandfather's clan, saying, ²"Please speak in the presence of all the lords of Shechem, 'Is it better for you that 70 men, all the sons of Jerubbaal, rule over you or that one man rule over you?' Remember that I am your own flesh and blood."

³His mother's relatives spoke all these words about him in the presence of all the lords of Shechem, and they were favorable to Abimelech, for they said, "He is our brother." ⁴So they gave him 70 pieces of silver from the temple of Baal-berith. Abimelech hired worthless and reckless men with this money, and they followed him. ⁵He went to his father's house in Ophrah and killed his 70 brothers, the sons of Jerubbaal, on top of a large stone. But Jotham, the youngest son of Jerubbaal, survived, because he hid himself. ⁶Then all the lords of Shechem and of Beth-millo gathered together and proceeded to make Abimelech king at the oak of the pillar in Shechem.

⁷When they told Jotham, he climbed to the top of Mount Gerizim, raised his voice, and called to them:

Listen to me, lords of Shechem,
and may God listen to you:
⁸ The trees set out
to anoint a king over themselves.
They said to the olive tree, "Reign over us."
⁹ But the olive tree said to them,
"Should I stop giving my oil
that honors both God and man,
and rule over the trees?"
¹⁰ Then the trees said to the fig tree,
"Come and reign over us."
¹¹ But the fig tree said to them,
"Should I stop giving
my sweetness and my good fruit,
and rule over trees?"
¹² Later, the trees said to the grapevine,
"Come and reign over us."
¹³ But the grapevine said to them,
"Should I stop giving my wine
that cheers both God and man,
and rule over trees?"
¹⁴ Finally, all the trees said to the bramble,
"Come and reign over us."
¹⁵ The bramble said to the trees,
"If you really are anointing me
as king over you,
come and find refuge in my shade.
But if not,
may fire come out from the bramble
and consume the cedars of Lebanon."

¹⁶"Now if you have acted faithfully and honestly in making Abimelech king, if you have done well by Jerubbaal and his family, and if you have rewarded him appropriately for what he did— ¹⁷for my father fought for you, risked his life, and delivered you from the hand of Midian, ¹⁸and now you have attacked my father's house today, killed his 70 sons on top of a large stone, and made Abimelech, the son of his slave, king over the lords of Shechem 'because he is your brother'— ¹⁹if then you have acted faithfully and honestly with Jerubbaal and his house this day, rejoice in Abimelech and may he also rejoice in you. ²⁰But if not, may fire come from Abimelech and consume the lords of Shechem and Beth-millo, and may fire come from the lords of Shechem and Beth-millo and consume Abimelech." ²¹Then Jotham fled, escaping to Beer, and lived there because of his brother Abimelech.

²²When Abimelech had ruled over Israel three years, ²³God sent an evil spirit between Abimelech and the lords of Shechem. They treated Abimelech deceitfully, ²⁴so that the crime against the 70 sons of Jerubbaal might come to justice and their blood would be avenged on their brother Abimelech, who killed them, and on the lords of Shechem, who had helped him kill his brothers. ²⁵The lords of Shechem rebelled against him by putting people on the tops of the mountains to ambush and rob everyone who passed by them on the road. So this was reported to Abimelech.

²⁶Gaal son of Ebed came with his brothers and crossed into Shechem, and the lords of Shechem trusted him. ²⁷So they went out to the countryside and harvested grapes from their vineyards. They trampled the grapes and held a celebration. Then they went to the house of their god, and as they ate and drank, they cursed Abimelech. ²⁸Gaal son of Ebed said, "Who is

Abimelech and who is Shechem that we should serve him? Isn't he the son of Jerubbaal, and isn't Zebul his officer? You are to serve the men of Hamor, the father of Shechem. Why should we serve Abimelech? ²⁹ If only these people were in my power, I would remove Abimelech." So he said to Abimelech, "Gather your army and come out."

³⁰ When Zebul, the ruler of the city, heard the words of Gaal son of Ebed, he was angry. ³¹ So he sent messengers secretly to Abimelech, saying, "Look, Gaal son of Ebed, with his brothers, have come to Shechem and are turning the city against you. ³² Now tonight, you and the people with you are to come wait in ambush in the countryside. ³³ Then get up early, and at sunrise charge the city. When he and the people who are with him come out against you, do to him whatever you can." ³⁴ So Abimelech and all the people with him got up at night and waited in ambush for Shechem in four units.

³⁵ Gaal son of Ebed went out and stood at the entrance of the city gate. Then Abimelech and the people who were with him got up from their ambush. ³⁶ When Gaal saw the people, he said to Zebul, "Look, people are coming down from the mountaintops!" But Zebul said to him, "The shadows of the mountains look like men to you."

³⁷ Then Gaal spoke again, "Look, people are coming down from the central part of the land, and one unit is coming from the direction of the Diviners' Oak." ³⁸ Zebul replied, "Where is your mouthing off now? You said, 'Who is Abimelech that we should serve him?' Aren't these the people you despised? Now go and fight them!"

³⁹ So Gaal went out leading the lords of Shechem and fought against Abimelech, ⁴⁰ but Abimelech pursued him, and Gaal fled before him. Many wounded died as far as the entrance of the gate. ⁴¹ Abimelech stayed in Arumah, and Zebul drove Gaal and his brothers from Shechem.

⁴² The next day when the people went into the countryside, this was reported to Abimelech. ⁴³ He took the people, divided them into three companies, and waited in ambush in the countryside. He looked, and the people were coming out of the city, so he arose against them and struck them down. ⁴⁴ Then Abimelech and the units that were with him rushed forward and took their stand at the entrance of the city gate. The other two units rushed against all who were in the countryside and struck them down. ⁴⁵ So Abimelech fought against the city that entire day, captured it, and killed the people who were in it. Then he tore down the city and sowed it with salt.

⁴⁶ When all the lords of the Tower of Shechem heard, they entered the inner chamber of the temple of El-berith. ⁴⁷ Then it was reported to Abimelech that all the lords of the Tower of Shechem had gathered together. ⁴⁸ So Abimelech and all the people who were with him went up to Mount Zalmon. Abimelech took his ax in his hand and cut a branch from the trees. He picked up the branch, put it on his shoulder, and said to the people who were with him, "Hurry and do what you have seen me do." ⁴⁹ Each person also cut his own branch and followed Abimelech. They put the branches against the inner chamber and set it on fire around the people, and all the people in the Tower of Shechem died—about 1,000 men and women.

⁵⁰ Abimelech went to Thebez, camped against it,

and captured it. ⁵¹ There was a strong tower inside the city, and all the men, women, and lords of the city fled there. They locked themselves in and went up to the roof of the tower. ⁵² When Abimelech came to attack the tower, he approached its entrance to set it on fire. ⁵³ But a woman threw the upper portion of a millstone on Abimelech's head and fractured his skull. ⁵⁴ He quickly called his armor-bearer and said to him, "Draw your sword and kill me, or they'll say about me, 'A woman killed him.'" So his armor-bearer thrust him through, and he died. ⁵⁵ When the Israelites saw that Abimelech was dead, they all went home.

⁵⁶ In this way, God turned back on Abimelech the evil that he had done against his father, by killing his 70 brothers. ⁵⁷ And God also returned all the evil of the men of Shechem on their heads. So the curse of Jotham son of Jerubbaal came on them.

10 After Abimelech, Tola son of Puah, son of Dodo became judge and began to deliver Israel. He was from Issachar and lived in Shamir, in the hill country of Ephraim. ² Tola judged Israel 23 years and when he died, was buried in Shamir.

³ After him came Jair the Gileadite, who judged Israel 22 years. ⁴ He had 30 sons who rode on 30 donkeys. They had 30 towns in Gilead, which are called Jair's Villages to this day. ⁵ When Jair died, he was buried in Kamon.

⁶ Then the Israelites again did what was evil in the sight of the LORD. They worshiped the *Baals and the *Ashtoreths, the gods of Aram, Sidon, and Moab, and the gods of the Ammonites and the Philistines. They abandoned *Yahweh and did not worship Him. ⁷ So the LORD's anger burned against Israel, and He sold them to the Philistines and the Ammonites. ⁸ They shattered and crushed the Israelites that year, and for 18 years they did the same to all the Israelites who were on the other side of the Jordan in the land of the Amorites in Gilead. ⁹ The Ammonites also crossed the Jordan to fight against Judah, Benjamin, and the house of Ephraim. Israel was greatly oppressed, ¹⁰ so they cried out to the LORD, saying, "We have sinned against You. We have abandoned our God and worshiped the Baals."

¹¹ The LORD said to the Israelites, "When the Egyptians, Amorites, Ammonites, Philistines, ¹² Sidonians, Amalekites, and Maonites oppressed you, and you cried out to Me, did I not deliver you from their power? ¹³ But you have abandoned Me and worshiped other gods. Therefore, I will not deliver you again. ¹⁴ Go and cry out to the gods you have chosen. Let them deliver you in the time of your oppression."

¹⁵ But the Israelites said, "We have sinned. Deal with us as You see fit; only deliver us today!" ¹⁶ So they got rid of the foreign gods among them and worshiped the LORD, and He became weary of Israel's misery.

¹⁷ The Ammonites were called together, and they camped in Gilead. So the Israelites assembled and camped at Mizpah. ¹⁸ The rulers of Gilead said to one another, "Which man will lead the fight against the Ammonites? He will be the leader of all the inhabitants of Gilead."

11 Jephthah the Gileadite was a great warrior, but he was the son of a prostitute, and Gilead was his father. ² Gilead's wife bore him sons, and when they grew up, they drove Jephthah out and said to him, "You will have no inheritance in our father's house, because you are the son of another woman." ³ So Jephthah fled from his brothers and lived in the land of

Tob. Then some lawless men joined Jephthah and traveled with him.

⁴ Some time later, the Ammonites fought against Israel. ⁵ When the Ammonites made war with Israel, the elders of Gilead went to get Jephthah from the land of Tob. ⁶ They said to him, "Come, be our commander, and let's fight against the Ammonites."

⁷ Jephthah replied to the elders of Gilead, "Didn't you hate me and drive me from my father's house? Why then have you come to me now when you're in trouble?"

⁸ They answered Jephthah, "Since that's true, we now turn to you. Come with us, fight the Ammonites, and you will become leader of all the inhabitants of Gilead."

⁹ So Jephthah said to them, "If you are bringing me back to fight the Ammonites and the Lord gives them to me, I will be your leader."

¹⁰ The elders of Gilead said to Jephthah, "The Lord is our witness if we don't do as you say." ¹¹ So Jephthah went with the elders of Gilead. The people put him over themselves as leader and commander, and Jephthah repeated all his terms in the presence of the Lord at Mizpah.

¹² Jephthah sent messengers to the king of the Ammonites, saying, "What do you have against me that you have come to fight against me in my land?"

¹³ The king of the Ammonites said to Jephthah's messengers, "When Israel came from Egypt, they seized my land from the Arnon to the Jabbok and the Jordan. Now restore it peaceably."

¹⁴ Jephthah again sent messengers to the king of the Ammonites ¹⁵ to tell him, "This is what Jephthah says: Israel did not take away the land of Moab or the land of the Ammonites. ¹⁶ But when they came from Egypt, Israel traveled through the wilderness to the ˙Red Sea and came to Kadesh. ¹⁷ Israel sent messengers to the king of Edom, saying, 'Please let us travel through your land,' but the king of Edom would not listen. They also sent messengers to the king of Moab, but he refused. So Israel stayed in Kadesh.

¹⁸ "Then they traveled through the wilderness and around the lands of Edom and Moab. They came to the east side of the land of Moab and camped on the other side of the Arnon but did not enter into the territory of Moab, for the Arnon was the boundary of Moab.

¹⁹ "Then Israel sent messengers to Sihon king of the Amorites, king of Heshbon. Israel said to him, 'Please let us travel through your land to our country,' ²⁰ but Sihon would not trust Israel to pass through his territory. Instead, Sihon gathered all his people, camped at Jahaz, and fought with Israel. ²¹ Then the Lord God of Israel handed over Sihon and all his people to Israel, and they defeated them. So Israel took possession of the entire land of the Amorites who lived in that country. ²² They took possession of all the territory of the Amorites from the Arnon to the Jabbok and from the wilderness to the Jordan.

²³ "The Lord God of Israel has now driven out the Amorites before His people Israel, and will you now force us out? ²⁴ Isn't it true that you may possess whatever your god Chemosh drives out for you, and we may possess everything the Lord our God drives out before us? ²⁵ Now are you any better than Balak son of Zippor, king of Moab? Did he ever contend with Israel or fight against them? ²⁶ While Israel lived 300 years in Heshbon and its villages, in Aroer and its villages, and in all the cities that are on the banks of the Arnon, why didn't you take them back at that time? ²⁷ I have not sinned against you, but you have wronged me by fighting against me. Let the Lord who is the Judge decide today between the Israelites and the Ammonites."

²⁸ But the king of the Ammonites would not listen to Jephthah's message that he sent him.

²⁹ The Spirit of the Lord came on Jephthah, who traveled through Gilead and Manasseh, and then through Mizpah of Gilead. He crossed over to the Ammonites from Mizpah of Gilead. ³⁰ Jephthah made this vow to the Lord: "If You will hand over the Ammonites to me, ³¹ whatever comes out of the doors of my house to greet me when I return in peace from the Ammonites will belong to the Lord, and I will offer it as a ˙burnt offering."

³² Jephthah crossed over to the Ammonites to fight against them, and the Lord handed them over to him. ³³ He defeated 20 of their cities with a great slaughter from Aroer all the way to the entrance of Minnith and to Abel-keramim. So the Ammonites were subdued before the Israelites.

³⁴ When Jephthah went to his home in Mizpah, there was his daughter, coming out to meet him with tambourines and dancing! She was his only child; he had no other son or daughter besides her. ³⁵ When he saw her, he tore his clothes and said, "No! Not my daughter! You have devastated me! You have brought great misery on me. I have given my word to the Lord and cannot take it back."

³⁶ Then she said to him, "My father, you have given your word to the Lord. Do to me as you have said, for the Lord brought vengeance on your enemies, the Ammonites." ³⁷ She also said to her father, "Let me do this one thing: Let me wander two months through the mountains with my friends and mourn my virginity."

³⁸ "Go," he said. And he sent her away two months. So she left with her friends and mourned her virginity as she wandered through the mountains. ³⁹ At the end of two months, she returned to her father, and he kept the vow he had made about her. And she had never been intimate with a man. Now it became a custom in Israel ⁴⁰ that four days each year the young women of Israel would commemorate the daughter of Jephthah the Gileadite.

12 The men of Ephraim were called together and crossed the Jordan to Zaphon. They said to Jephthah, "Why have you crossed over to fight against the Ammonites but didn't call us to go with you? We will burn your house down with you in it!"

² Then Jephthah said to them, "My people and I had a serious conflict with the Ammonites. So I called for you, but you didn't deliver me from their power. ³ When I saw that you weren't going to deliver me, I took my life in my own hands and crossed over to the Ammonites, and the Lord handed them over to me. Why then have you come today to fight against me?"

⁴ Then Jephthah gathered all of the men of Gilead. They fought and defeated Ephraim, because Ephraim had said, "You Gileadites are Ephraimite fugitives in the territories of Ephraim and Manasseh." ⁵ The Gileadites captured the fords of the Jordan leading to Ephraim. Whenever a fugitive from Ephraim said, "Let me cross over," the Gileadites asked him, "Are you an Ephraimite?" If he answered, "No," ⁶ they told him, "Please say Shibboleth." If he said, "Sibboleth," because he could not pronounce it correctly, they seized

him and killed him at the fords of the Jordan. At that time 42,000 from Ephraim died.

[7] Jephthah judged Israel six years, and when he died, he was buried in one of the cities of Gilead.

[8] Ibzan, who was from Bethlehem, judged Israel after Jephthah [9] and had 30 sons. He gave his 30 daughters in marriage to men outside the tribe and brought back 30 wives for his sons from outside the tribe. Ibzan judged Israel seven years, [10] and when he died, he was buried in Bethlehem.

[11] Elon, who was from Zebulun, judged Israel after Ibzan. He judged Israel 10 years, [12] and when he died, he was buried in Aijalon in the land of Zebulun.

[13] After Elon, Abdon son of Hillel, who was from Pirathon, judged Israel. [14] He had 40 sons and 30 grandsons, who rode on 70 donkeys. Abdon judged Israel eight years, [15] and when he died, he was buried in Pirathon in the land of Ephraim, in the hill country of the Amalekites.

13 The Israelites again did what was evil in the LORD's sight, so the LORD handed them over to the Philistines 40 years. [2] There was a certain man from Zorah, from the family of Dan, whose name was Manoah; his wife was unable to conceive and had no children. [3] The Angel of the LORD appeared to the woman and said to her, "It is true that you are unable to conceive and have no children, but you will conceive and give birth to a son. [4] Now please be careful not to drink wine or beer, or to eat anything *unclean; [5] for indeed, you will conceive and give birth to a son. You must never cut his hair, because the boy will be a Nazirite to God from birth, and he will begin to save Israel from the power of the Philistines."

[6] Then the woman went and told her husband, "A man of God came to me. He looked like the awe-inspiring Angel of God. I didn't ask Him where He came from, and He didn't tell me His name. [7] He said to me, 'You will conceive and give birth to a son. Therefore, do not drink wine or beer, and do not eat anything unclean, because the boy will be a Nazirite to God from birth until the day of his death.'"

[8] Manoah prayed to the LORD and said, "Please Lord, let the man of God you sent come again to us and teach us what we should do for the boy who will be born."

[9] God listened to Manoah, and the Angel of God came again to the woman. She was sitting in the field, and her husband Manoah was not with her. [10] The woman ran quickly to her husband and told him, "The man who came to me today has just come back!"

[11] So Manoah got up and followed his wife. When he came to the man, he asked, "Are You the man who spoke to my wife?"

"I am," He said.

[12] Then Manoah asked, "When Your words come true, what will the boy's responsibilities and mission be?"

[13] The Angel of the LORD answered Manoah, "Your wife needs to do everything I told her. [14] She must not eat anything that comes from the grapevine or drink wine or beer. And she must not eat anything unclean. Your wife must do everything I have commanded her."

[15] "Please stay here," Manoah told Him, "and we will prepare a young goat for You."

[16] The Angel of the LORD said to him, "If I stay, I won't eat your food. But if you want to prepare a *burnt offering, offer it to the LORD." For Manoah did not know He was the Angel of the LORD.

[17] Then Manoah said to Him, "What is Your name, so that we may honor You when Your words come true?"

[18] "Why do you ask My name," the Angel of the LORD asked him, "since it is wonderful."

[19] Manoah took a young goat and a *grain offering and offered them on a rock to the LORD, and He did a wonderful thing while Manoah and his wife were watching. [20] When the flame went up from the altar to the sky, the Angel of the LORD went up in its flame. When Manoah and his wife saw this, they fell facedown on the ground. [21] The Angel of the LORD did not appear again to Manoah and his wife. Then Manoah realized that it was the Angel of the LORD.

[22] "We're going to die," he said to his wife, "because we have seen God!"

[23] But his wife said to him, "If the LORD had intended to kill us, He wouldn't have accepted the burnt offering and the grain offering from us, and He would not have shown us all these things or spoken to us now like this."

[24] So the woman gave birth to a son and named him Samson. The boy grew, and the LORD blessed him. [25] Then the Spirit of the LORD began to direct him in the Camp of Dan, between Zorah and Eshtaol.

14 Samson went down to Timnah and saw a young Philistine woman there. [2] He went back and told his father and his mother: "I have seen a young Philistine woman in Timnah. Now get her for me as a wife."

[3] But his father and mother said to him, "Can't you find a young woman among your relatives or among any of our people? Must you go to the uncircumcised Philistines for a wife?"

But Samson told his father, "Get her for me, because I want her." [4] Now his father and mother did not know this was from the LORD, who was seeking an occasion against the Philistines. At that time, the Philistines were ruling over Israel.

[5] Samson went down to Timnah with his father and mother and came to the vineyards of Timnah. Suddenly a young lion came roaring at him, [6] the Spirit of the LORD took control of him, and he tore the lion apart with his bare hands as he might have torn a young goat. But he did not tell his father or mother what he had done. [7] Then he went and spoke to the woman, because Samson wanted her.

[8] After some time, when he returned to get her, he left the road to see the lion's carcass, and there was a swarm of bees with honey in the carcass. [9] He scooped some honey into his hands and ate it as he went along. When he returned to his father and mother, he gave some to them and they ate it. But he did not tell them that he had scooped the honey from the lion's carcass.

[10] His father went to visit the woman, and Samson prepared a feast there, as young men were accustomed to do. [11] When the Philistines saw him, they brought 30 men to accompany him.

[12] "Let me tell you a riddle," Samson said to them. "If you can explain it to me during the seven days of the feast and figure it out, I will give you 30 linen garments and 30 changes of clothes. [13] But if you can't explain it to me, you must give me 30 linen garments and 30 changes of clothes."

"Tell us your riddle," they replied. "Let's hear it."

[14] So he said to them:

Out of the eater came something to eat,
and out of the strong came something sweet.

After three days, they were unable to explain the riddle. [15] On the fourth day they said to Samson's wife, "Persuade your husband to explain the riddle to us, or we will burn you and your father's household to death. Did you invite us here to rob us?"

[16] So Samson's wife came to him, weeping, and said, "You hate me and don't love me! You told my people the riddle, but haven't explained it to me."

"Look," he said, "I haven't even explained it to my father or mother, so why should I explain it to you?"

[17] She wept the whole seven days of the feast, and at last, on the seventh day, he explained it to her, because she had nagged him so much. Then she explained it to her people. [18] On the seventh day, before sunset, the men of the city said to him:

What is sweeter than honey?
What is stronger than a lion?

So he said to them:

If you hadn't plowed with my young cow,
you wouldn't know my riddle now!

[19] The Spirit of the LORD took control of him, and he went down to Ashkelon and killed 30 of their men. He stripped them and gave their clothes to those who had explained the riddle. In a rage, Samson returned to his father's house, [20] and his wife was given to one of the men who had accompanied him.

15 Later on, during the wheat harvest, Samson took a young goat as a gift and visited his wife. "I want to go to my wife in her room," he said. But her father would not let him enter.

[2] "I was sure you hated her," her father said, "so I gave her to one of the men who accompanied you. Isn't her younger sister more beautiful than she is? Why not take her instead?"

[3] Samson said to them, "This time I won't be responsible when I harm the Philistines." [4] So he went out and caught 300 foxes. He took torches, turned the foxes tail-to-tail, and put a torch between each pair of tails. [5] Then he ignited the torches and released the foxes into the standing grain of the Philistines. He burned up the piles of grain and the standing grain as well as the vineyards and olive groves.

[6] Then the Philistines asked, "Who did this?"

They were told, "It was Samson, the Timnite's son-in-law, because he has taken Samson's wife and given her to another man." So the Philistines went to her and her father and burned them to death.

[7] Then Samson told them, "Because you did this, I swear that I won't rest until I have taken vengeance on you." [8] He tore them limb from limb with a great slaughter, and he went down and stayed in the cave at the rock of Etam.

[9] The Philistines went up, camped in Judah, and raided Lehi. [10] So the men of Judah said, "Why have you attacked us?"

They replied, "We have come to arrest Samson and pay him back for what he did to us."

[11] Then 3,000 men of Judah went to the cave at the rock of Etam, and they asked Samson, "Don't you realize that the Philistines rule over us? What have you done to us?"

"I have done to them what they did to me," he answered.

[12] They said to him, "We've come to arrest you and hand you over to the Philistines."

Then Samson told them, "Swear to me that you yourselves won't kill me."

[13] "No," they said, "we won't kill you, but we will tie you up securely and hand you over to them." So they tied him up with two new ropes and led him away from the rock.

[14] When he came to Lehi, the Philistines came to meet him shouting. The Spirit of the LORD took control of him, and the ropes that were on his arms became like burnt flax and his bonds fell off his wrists. [15] He found a fresh jawbone of a donkey, reached out his hand, took it, and killed 1,000 men with it. [16] Then Samson said:

With the jawbone of a donkey
I have piled them in a heap.
With the jawbone of a donkey
I have killed 1,000 men.

[17] When he finished speaking, he threw away the jawbone and named that place Ramath-lehi. [18] He became very thirsty and called out to the LORD: "You have accomplished this great victory through Your servant. Must I now die of thirst and fall into the hands of the uncircumcised?" [19] So God split a hollow place in the ground at Lehi, and water came out of it. After Samson drank, his strength returned, and he revived. That is why he named it En-hakkore, which is in Lehi to this day. [20] And he judged Israel 20 years in the days of the Philistines.

16 Samson went to Gaza, where he saw a prostitute and went to bed with her. [2] When the Gazites heard that Samson was there, they surrounded the place and waited in ambush for him all that night at the city gate. While they were waiting quietly, they said, "Let us wait until dawn; then we will kill him." [3] But Samson stayed in bed until midnight when he got up, took hold of the doors of the city gate along with the two gateposts, and pulled them out, bar and all. He put them on his shoulders and took them to the top of the mountain overlooking Hebron.

[4] Some time later, he fell in love with a woman named Delilah, who lived in the Sorek Valley. [5] The Philistine leaders went to her and said, "Persuade him to tell you where his great strength comes from, so we can overpower him, tie him up, and make him helpless. Each of us will then give you 1,100 pieces of silver."

[6] So Delilah said to Samson, "Please tell me, where does your great strength come from? How could someone tie you up and make you helpless?"

[7] Samson told her, "If they tie me up with seven fresh bowstrings that have not been dried, I will become weak and be like any other man."

[8] The Philistine leaders brought her seven fresh bowstrings that had not been dried, and she tied him up with them. [9] While the men in ambush were waiting in her room, she called out to him, "Samson, the Philistines are here!" But he snapped the bowstrings as a strand of yarn snaps when it touches fire. The secret of his strength remained unknown.

[10] Then Delilah said to Samson, "You have mocked me and told me lies! Won't you please tell me how you can be tied up?"

[11] He told her, "If they tie me up with new ropes that have never been used, I will become weak and be like any other man."

[12] Delilah took new ropes, tied him up with them, and shouted, "Samson, the Philistines are here!" But

while the men in ambush were waiting in her room, he snapped the ropes off his arms like a thread.

¹³ Then Delilah said to Samson, "You have mocked me all along and told me lies! Tell me how you can be tied up."

He told her, "If you weave the seven braids on my head with the web of a loom—"

¹⁴ She fastened the braids with a pin and called to him, "Samson, the Philistines are here!" He awoke from his sleep and pulled out the pin, with the loom and the web.

¹⁵ "How can you say, 'I love you,'" she told him, "when your heart is not with me? This is the third time you have mocked me and not told me what makes your strength so great!"

¹⁶ Because she nagged him day after day and pleaded with him until she wore him out, ¹⁷ he told her the whole truth and said to her, "My hair has never been cut, because I am a Nazirite to God from birth. If I am shaved, my strength will leave me, and I will become weak and be like any other man."

¹⁸ When Delilah realized that he had told her the whole truth, she sent this message to the Philistine leaders: "Come one more time, for he has told me the whole truth." The Philistine leaders came to her and brought the money with them.

¹⁹ Then she let him fall asleep on her lap and called a man to shave off the seven braids on his head. In this way, she made him helpless, and his strength left him.

²⁰ Then she cried, "Samson, the Philistines are here!" When he awoke from his sleep, he said, "I will escape as I did before and shake myself free." But he did not know that the Lord had left him.

²¹ The Philistines seized him and gouged out his eyes. They brought him down to Gaza and bound him with bronze shackles, and he was forced to grind grain in the prison. ²² But his hair began to grow back after it had been shaved.

²³ Now the Philistine leaders gathered together to offer a great sacrifice to their god Dagon. They rejoiced and said:

> Our god has handed over
> our enemy Samson to us.

²⁴ When the people saw him, they praised their god and said:

> Our god has handed over to us
> our enemy who destroyed our land
> and who multiplied our dead.

²⁵ When they were drunk, they said, "Bring Samson here to entertain us." So they brought Samson from prison, and he entertained them. They had him stand between the pillars.

²⁶ Samson said to the young man who was leading him by the hand, "Lead me where I can feel the pillars supporting the temple, so I can lean against them." ²⁷ The temple was full of men and women; all the leaders of the Philistines were there, and about 3,000 men and women were on the roof watching Samson entertain them. ²⁸ He called out to the Lord: "Lord God, please remember me. Strengthen me, God, just once more. With one act of vengeance, let me pay back the Philistines for my two eyes." ²⁹ Samson took hold of the two middle pillars supporting the temple and leaned against them, one on his right hand and the other on his left. ³⁰ Samson said, "Let me die with the Philistines." He pushed with all his might, and the temple fell on the leaders and all the people in it. And

the dead he killed at his death were more than those he had killed in his life.

³¹ Then his brothers and his father's family came down, carried him back, and buried him between Zorah and Eshtaol in the tomb of his father Manoah. So he judged Israel 20 years.

17 There was a man from the hill country of Ephraim named Micah. ² He said to his mother, "The 1,100 pieces of silver taken from you, and that I heard you utter a curse about—here, I have the silver with me. I took it. So now I return it to you."

Then his mother said, "My son, you are blessed by the Lord!"

³ He returned the 1,100 pieces of silver to his mother, and his mother said, "I personally consecrate the silver to the Lord for my son's benefit to make a carved image overlaid with silver." ⁴ So he returned the silver to his mother, and she took five pounds of silver and gave it to a silversmith. He made it into a carved image overlaid with silver, and it was in Micah's house.

⁵ This man Micah had a shrine, and he made an ⁎ephod and household idols, and installed one of his sons to be his priest. ⁶ In those days there was no king in Israel; everyone did whatever he wanted.

⁷ There was a young man, a Levite from Bethlehem in Judah, who resided within the clan of Judah. ⁸ The man left the town of Bethlehem in Judah to settle wherever he could find a place. On his way he came to Micah's home in the hill country of Ephraim.

⁹ "Where do you come from?" Micah asked him.

He answered him, "I am a Levite from Bethlehem in Judah, and I'm going to settle wherever I can find a place."

¹⁰ Micah replied, "Stay with me and be my father and priest, and I will give you four ounces of silver a year, along with your clothing and provisions." So the Levite went in ¹¹ and agreed to stay with the man, and the young man became like one of his sons. ¹² Micah consecrated the Levite, and the young man became his priest and lived in Micah's house. ¹³ Then Micah said, "Now I know that the Lord will be good to me, because a Levite has become my priest."

18 In those days, there was no king in Israel, and the Danite tribe was looking for territory to occupy. Up to that time no territory had been captured by them among the tribes of Israel. ² So the Danites sent out five brave men from all their clans, from Zorah and Eshtaol, to scout out the land and explore it. They told them, "Go and explore the land."

They came to the hill country of Ephraim as far as the home of Micah and spent the night there. ³ While they were near Micah's home, they recognized the speech of the young Levite. So they went over to him and asked, "Who brought you here? What are you doing in this place? What is keeping you here?" ⁴ He told them what Micah had done for him and that he had hired him as his priest.

⁵ Then they said to him, "Please inquire of God so we will know if we will have a successful journey."

⁶ The priest told them, "Go in peace. The Lord is watching over the journey you are going on."

⁷ The five men left and came to Laish. They saw that the people who were there were living securely, in the same way as the Sidonians, quiet and unsuspecting. There was nothing lacking in the land and no oppressive ruler. They were far from the Sidonians, having no alliance with anyone.

⁸When the men went back to their clans at Zorah and Eshtaol, their people asked them, "What did you find out?"

⁹They answered, "Come on, let's go up against them, for we have seen the land, and it is very good. Why wait? Don't hesitate to go and invade and take possession of the land! ¹⁰When you get there, you will come to an unsuspecting people and a spacious land, for God has handed it over to you. It is a place where nothing on earth is lacking." ¹¹Six hundred Danites departed from Zorah and Eshtaol armed with weapons of war. ¹²They went up and camped at Kiriath-jearim in Judah. This is why the place is called the Camp of Dan to this day; it is west of Kiriath-jearim. ¹³From there they traveled to the hill country of Ephraim and arrived at Micah's house.

¹⁴The five men who had gone to scout out the land of Laish told their brothers, "Did you know that there are an *ephod, household gods, and a carved image overlaid with silver in these houses? Now think about what you should do." ¹⁵So they detoured there and went to the house of the young Levite at the home of Micah and greeted him. ¹⁶The 600 Danite men were standing by the entrance of the gate, armed with their weapons of war. ¹⁷Then the five men who had gone to scout out the land went in and took the carved image overlaid with silver, the ephod, and the household idols, while the priest was standing by the entrance of the gate with the 600 men armed with weapons of war.

¹⁸When they entered Micah's house and took the carved image overlaid with silver, the ephod, and the household idols, the priest said to them, "What are you doing?"

¹⁹They told him, "Be quiet. Keep your mouth shut. Come with us and be a father and a priest to us. Is it better for you to be a priest for the house of one person or for you to be a priest for a tribe and family in Israel?" ²⁰So the priest was pleased and took his ephod, household idols, and carved image, and went with the people. ²¹They prepared to leave, putting their small children, livestock, and possessions in front of them.

²²After they were some distance from Micah's house, the men who were in the houses near it mobilized and caught up with the Danites. ²³They called to the Danites, who turned to face them, and said to Micah, "What's the matter with you that you mobilized the men?"

²⁴He said, "You took the gods I had made and the priest, and went away. What do I have left? How can you say to me, 'What's the matter with you?'"

²⁵The Danites said to him, "Don't raise your voice against us, or angry men will attack you, and you and your family will lose your lives." ²⁶The Danites went on their way, and Micah turned to go back home, because he saw that they were stronger than he was.

²⁷After they had taken the gods Micah had made and the priest that belonged to him, they went to Laish, to a quiet and unsuspecting people. They killed them with their swords and burned down the city. ²⁸There was no one to rescue them because it was far from Sidon and they had no alliance with anyone. It was in a valley that belonged to Beth-rehob. They rebuilt the city and lived in it. ²⁹They named the city Dan, after the name of their ancestor Dan, who was born to Israel. The city was formerly named Laish.

³⁰The Danites set up the carved image for themselves. Jonathan son of Gershom, son of Moses, and his sons were priests for the Danite tribe until the time of the exile from the land. ³¹So they set up for themselves Micah's carved image that he had made, and it was there as long as the house of God was in Shiloh.

19 In those days, when there was no king in Israel, a Levite living in a remote part of the hill country of Ephraim acquired a woman from Bethlehem in Judah as his concubine. ²But she was unfaithful to him and left him for her father's house in Bethlehem in Judah. She was there for a period of four months. ³Then her husband got up and went after her to speak kindly to her and bring her back. He had his servant with him and a pair of donkeys. So she brought him to her father's house, and when the girl's father saw him, he gladly welcomed him. ⁴His father-in-law, the girl's father, detained him, and he stayed with him for three days. They ate, drank, and spent the nights there.

⁵On the fourth day, they got up early in the morning and prepared to go, but the girl's father said to his son-in-law, "Have something to eat to keep up your strength and then you can go." ⁶So they sat down and the two of them ate and drank together. Then the girl's father said to the man, "Please agree to stay overnight and enjoy yourself." ⁷The man got up to go, but his father-in-law persuaded him, so he stayed and spent the night there again. ⁸He got up early in the morning of the fifth day to leave, but the girl's father said to him, "Please keep up your strength." So they waited until late afternoon and the two of them ate. ⁹The man got up to go with his concubine and his servant, when his father-in-law, the girl's father, said to him, "Look, night is coming. Please spend the night. See, the day is almost over. Spend the night here, enjoy yourself, then you can get up early tomorrow for your journey and go home."

¹⁰But the man was unwilling to spend the night. He got up, departed, and arrived opposite Jebus (that is, Jerusalem). The man had his two saddled donkeys and his concubine with him. ¹¹When they were near Jebus and the day was almost gone, the servant said to his master, "Please, why not let us stop at this Jebusite city and spend the night here?"

¹²But his master replied to him, "We will not stop at a foreign city where there are no Israelites. Let's move on to Gibeah." ¹³"Come on," he said, "let's try to reach one of these places and spend the night in Gibeah or Ramah." ¹⁴So they continued on their journey, and the sun set as they neared Gibeah in Benjamin. ¹⁵They stopped to go in and spend the night in Gibeah. The Levite went in and sat down in the city square, but no one took them into their home to spend the night.

¹⁶In the evening, an old man came in from his work in the field. He was from the hill country of Ephraim but was residing in Gibeah, and the men of that place were Benjaminites. ¹⁷When he looked up and saw the traveler in the city square, the old man asked, "Where are you going, and where do you come from?"

¹⁸He answered him, "We're traveling from Bethlehem in Judah to the remote hill country of Ephraim, where I am from. I went to Bethlehem in Judah, and now I'm going to the house of the LORD. No one has taken me into his home, ¹⁹although we have both straw and feed for our donkeys, and bread and wine for me, your female servant, and the young man with your servant. There is nothing we lack."

²⁰"Peace to you," said the old man. "I'll take care of everything you need. Only don't spend the night in

the square." ²¹So he brought him to his house and fed the donkeys. Then they washed their feet and ate and drank. ²²While they were enjoying themselves, all of a sudden, •perverted men of the city surrounded the house and beat on the door. They said to the old man who came to your house so we can have sex with him!"

²³The owner of the house went out and said to them, "No, don't do this evil, my brothers. After all, this man has come into my house. Don't do this horrible thing. ²⁴Here, let me bring out my virgin daughter and the man's concubine now. Use them and do whatever you want to them. But don't do this horrible thing to this man."

²⁵But the men would not listen to him, so the man seized his concubine and took her outside to them. They raped her and abused her all night until morning. At daybreak they let her go. ²⁶Early that morning, the woman made her way back, and as it was getting light, she collapsed at the doorway of the man's house where her master was.

²⁷When her master got up in the morning, opened the doors of the house, and went out to leave on his journey, there was the woman, his concubine, collapsed near the doorway of the house with her hands on the threshold. ²⁸"Get up," he told her. "Let's go." But there was no response. So the man put her on his donkey and set out for home.

²⁹When he entered his house, he picked up a knife, took hold of his concubine, cut her into 12 pieces, limb by limb, and then sent her throughout the territory of Israel. ³⁰Everyone who saw it said, "Nothing like this has ever happened or has been seen since the day the Israelites came out of the land of Egypt to this day. Think it over, discuss it, and speak up!"

20 All the Israelites from Dan to Beer-sheba and from the land of Gilead came out, and the community assembled as one body before the Lᴏʀᴅ at Mizpah. ²The leaders of all the people and of all the tribes of Israel presented themselves in the assembly of God's people: 400,000 armed foot soldiers. ³The Benjaminites heard that the Israelites had gone up to Mizpah.

The Israelites asked, "Tell us, how did this outrage occur?"

⁴The Levite, the husband of the murdered woman, answered: "I went to Gibeah in Benjamin with my concubine to spend the night. ⁵Citizens of Gibeah ganged up on me and surrounded the house at night. They intended to kill me, but they raped my concubine, and she died. ⁶Then I took my concubine and cut her in pieces, and sent her throughout Israel's territory, because they committed a horrible shame in Israel. ⁷Look, all of you are Israelites. Give your judgment and verdict here and now."

⁸Then all the people stood united and said, "None of us will go to his tent or return to his house. ⁹Now this is what we will do to Gibeah: we will go against it by lot. ¹⁰We will take 10 men out of every 100 from all the tribes of Israel, and 100 out of every 1,000, and 1,000 out of every 10,000 to get provisions for the people when they go to Gibeah in Benjamin to punish them for all the horror they did in Israel."

¹¹So all the men of Israel gathered united against the city. ¹²Then the tribes of Israel sent men throughout the tribe of Benjamin, saying, "What is this outrage that has occurred among you? ¹³Hand over the •perverted men in Gibeah so we can put them to death

and eradicate evil from Israel." But the Benjaminites would not obey their fellow Israelites. ¹⁴Instead, the Benjaminites gathered together from their cities to Gibeah to go out and fight against the Israelites. ¹⁵On that day the Benjaminites rallied 26,000 armed men from their cities, besides 700 choice men rallied by the inhabitants of Gibeah. ¹⁶There were 700 choice men who were left-handed among all these people; all could sling a stone at a hair and not miss.

¹⁷The Israelites, apart from Benjamin, rallied 400,000 armed men, every one an experienced warrior. ¹⁸They set out, went to Bethel, and inquired of God. The Israelites asked, "Who is to go first to fight for us against the Benjaminites?"

And the Lᴏʀᴅ answered: "Judah will be first."

¹⁹In the morning, the Israelites set out and camped near Gibeah. ²⁰The men of Israel went out to fight against Benjamin and took their battle positions against Gibeah. ²¹The Benjaminites came out of Gibeah and slaughtered 22,000 men of Israel on the field that day. ²²But the Israelite army rallied and again took their battle positions in the same place where they positioned themselves on the first day. ²³They went up, wept before the Lᴏʀᴅ until evening, and inquired of Him: "Should we again fight against our brothers the Benjaminites?"

And the Lᴏʀᴅ answered: "Fight against them."

²⁴On the second day the Israelites advanced against the Benjaminites. ²⁵That same day the Benjaminites came out from Gibeah to meet them and slaughtered an additional 18,000 Israelites on the field; all were armed men.

²⁶The whole Israelite army went to Bethel where they wept and sat before the Lᴏʀᴅ. They fasted that day until evening and offered •burnt offerings and •fellowship offerings to the Lᴏʀᴅ. ²⁷Then the Israelites inquired of the Lᴏʀᴅ. In those days, the ark of the covenant of God was there, ²⁸and Phinehas son of Eleazar, son of Aaron, was serving before it. The Israelites asked: "Should we again fight against our brothers the Benjaminites or should we stop?"

The Lᴏʀᴅ answered: "Fight, because I will hand them over to you tomorrow." ²⁹So Israel set up an ambush around Gibeah. ³⁰On the third day the Israelites fought against the Benjaminites and took their battle positions against Gibeah as before. ³¹Then the Benjaminites came out against the people and were drawn away from the city. They began to attack the people as before, killing about 30 men of Israel on the highways, one of which goes up to Bethel and the other to Gibeah through the open country. ³²The Benjaminites said, "We are defeating them as before."

But the Israelites said, "Let's flee and draw them away from the city to the highways." ³³So all the men of Israel got up from their places and took their battle positions at Baal-tamar, while the Israelites in ambush charged out of their places west of Geba. ³⁴Then 10,000 choice men from all Israel made a frontal assault against Gibeah, and the battle was fierce, but the Benjaminites did not know that disaster was about to strike them. ³⁵The Lᴏʀᴅ defeated Benjamin in the presence of Israel, and on that day the Israelites slaughtered 25,100 men of Benjamin; all were armed men. ³⁶Then the Benjaminites realized they had been defeated.

The men of Israel had retreated before Benjamin, because they were confident in the ambush they had set against Gibeah. ³⁷ The men in ambush had rushed quickly against Gibeah; they advanced and put the whole city to the sword. ³⁸ The men of Israel had a prearranged signal with the men in ambush: when they sent up a great cloud of smoke from the city, ³⁹ the men of Israel would return to the battle. When Benjamin had begun to strike them down, killing about 30 men of Israel, they said, "They're defeated before us, just as they were in the first battle." ⁴⁰ But when the column of smoke began to go up from the city, Benjamin looked behind them, and the whole city was going up in smoke. ⁴¹ Then the men of Israel returned, and the men of Benjamin were terrified when they realized that disaster had struck them. ⁴² They retreated before the men of Israel toward the wilderness, but the battle overtook them, and those who came out of the cities slaughtered those between them. ⁴³ They surrounded the Benjaminites, pursued them, and easily overtook them near Gibeah toward the east. ⁴⁴ There were 18,000 men who died from Benjamin; all were warriors. ⁴⁵ Then Benjamin turned and fled toward the wilderness to the rock of Rimmon, and Israel killed 5,000 men on the highways. They overtook them at Gidom and struck 2,000 more dead.

⁴⁶ All the Benjaminites who died that day were 25,000 armed men; all were warriors. ⁴⁷ But 600 men escaped into the wilderness to the rock of Rimmon and stayed there four months. ⁴⁸ The men of Israel turned back against the other Benjaminites and killed them with their swords—the entire city, the animals, and everything that remained. They also burned down all the cities that remained.

21 The men of Israel had sworn an oath at Mizpah: "None of us will give his daughter to a Benjaminite in marriage." ² So the people went to Bethel and sat there before God until evening. They wept loudly and bitterly, ³ and cried out, "Why, Lord God of Israel, has it occurred that one tribe is missing in Israel today?" ⁴ The next day the people got up early, built an altar there, and offered *burnt offerings and *fellowship offerings. ⁵ The Israelites asked, "Who of all the tribes of Israel didn't come to the Lord with the assembly?" For a great oath had been taken that anyone who had not come to the Lord at Mizpah would certainly be put to death.

⁶ But the Israelites had compassion on their brothers, the Benjaminites, and said, "Today a tribe has been cut off from Israel. ⁷ What should we do about wives for the survivors? We've sworn to the Lord not to give them any of our daughters as wives." ⁸ They asked,

"Which city among the tribes of Israel didn't come to the Lord at Mizpah?" It turned out that no one from Jabesh-gilead had come to the camp and the assembly. ⁹ For when the people were counted, no one was there from the inhabitants of Jabesh-gilead.

¹⁰ The congregation sent 12,000 brave warriors there and commanded them: "Go and kill the inhabitants of Jabesh-gilead with the sword, including women and children. ¹¹ This is what you should do: *Completely destroy every male, as well as every female who has slept with a man." ¹² They found among the inhabitants of Jabesh-gilead 400 young women, who had not had sexual relations with a man, and they brought them to the camp at Shiloh in the land of Canaan.

¹³ The whole congregation sent a message of peace to the Benjaminites who were at the rock of Rimmon. ¹⁴ Benjamin returned at that time, and Israel gave them the women they had kept alive from Jabesh-gilead. But there were not enough for them.

¹⁵ The people had compassion on Benjamin, because the Lord had made this gap in the tribes of Israel. ¹⁶ The elders of the congregation said, "What should we do about wives for those who are left, since the women of Benjamin have been destroyed?" ¹⁷ They said, "There must be heirs for the survivors of Benjamin, so that a tribe of Israel will not be wiped out. ¹⁸ But we can't give them our daughters as wives." For the Israelites had sworn, "Anyone who gives a wife to a Benjaminite is cursed." ¹⁹ They also said, "Look, there's an annual festival to the Lord in Shiloh, which is north of Bethel, east of the highway that goes up from Bethel to Shechem, and south of Lebonah."

²⁰ Then they commanded the Benjaminites: "Go and hide in the vineyards. ²¹ Watch, and when you see the young women of Shiloh come out to perform the dances, each of you leave the vineyards and catch a wife for yourself from the young women of Shiloh, and go to the land of Benjamin. ²² When their fathers or brothers come to us and protest, we will tell them, 'Show favor to them, since we did not get enough wives for each of them in the battle. You didn't actually give the women to them, so you are not *guilty of breaking your oath.'"

²³ The Benjaminites did this and took the number of women they needed from the dancers they caught. They went back to their own inheritance, rebuilt their cities, and lived in them. ²⁴ At that time, each of the Israelites returned from there to his own tribe and family. Each returned from there to his own inheritance.

²⁵ In those days there was no king in Israel; everyone did whatever he wanted.

RUTH

1 During the time of the judges, there was a famine in the land. A man left Bethlehem in Judah with his wife and two sons to live in the land of Moab for a while. ² The man's name was Elimelech, and his wife's name was Naomi. The names of his two sons were Mahlon and Chilion. They were Ephrathites from Bethlehem in Judah. They entered the land of Moab and settled there. ³ Naomi's husband Elimelech died, and she was left with her two sons. ⁴ Her sons took

Moabite women as their wives: one was named Orpah and the second was named Ruth. After they lived in Moab about 10 years, ⁵ both Mahlon and Chilion also died, and Naomi was left without her two children and without her husband.

⁶ She and her daughters-in-law prepared to leave the land of Moab, because she had heard in Moab that the Lord had paid attention to His people's need by providing them food. ⁷ She left the place where she had

been living, accompanied by her two daughters-in-law, and traveled along the road leading back to the land of Judah.

[8] She said to them, "Each of you go back to your mother's home. May the LORD show faithful love to you as you have shown to the dead and to me. [9] May the LORD enable each of you to find security in the house of your new husband." She kissed them, and they wept loudly.

[10] "No," they said to her. "We will go with you to your people."

[11] But Naomi replied, "Return home, my daughters. Why do you want to go with me? Am I able to have any more sons who could become your husbands? [12] Return home, my daughters. Go on, for I am too old to have another husband. Even if I thought there was still hope for me to have a husband tonight and to bear sons, [13] would you be willing to wait for them to grow up? Would you restrain yourselves from remarrying? No, my daughters, my life is much too bitter for you to share, because the LORD's hand has turned against me." [14] Again they wept loudly, and Orpah kissed her mother-in-law, but Ruth clung to her. [15] Naomi said, "Look, your sister-in-law has gone back to her people and to her god. Follow your sister-in-law."

[16] But Ruth replied:

Do not persuade me to leave you
or go back and not follow you.
For wherever you go, I will go,
and wherever you live, I will live;
your people will be my people,
and your God will be my God.
[17] Where you die, I will die,
and there I will be buried.
May •Yahweh punish me,
and do so severely,
if anything but death separates you and me.

[18] When Naomi saw that Ruth was determined to go with her, she stopped trying to persuade her.

[19] The two of them traveled until they came to Bethlehem. When they entered Bethlehem, the whole town was excited about their arrival and the local women exclaimed, "Can this be Naomi?"

[20] "Don't call me Naomi. Call me Mara," she answered, "for the •Almighty has made me very bitter. [21] I went away full, but the LORD has brought me back empty. Why do you call me Naomi, since the LORD has pronounced judgment on me, and the Almighty has afflicted me?"

[22] So Naomi came back from the land of Moab with her daughter-in-law Ruth the Moabitess. They arrived in Bethlehem at the beginning of the barley harvest.

2 Now Naomi had a relative on her husband's side named Boaz. He was a prominent man of noble character from Elimelech's family.

[2] Ruth the Moabitess asked Naomi, "Will you let me go into the fields and gather fallen grain behind someone who allows me to?"

Naomi answered her, "Go ahead, my daughter." [3] So Ruth left and entered the field to gather grain behind the harvesters. She happened to be in the portion of land belonging to Boaz, who was from Elimelech's family.

[4] Later, when Boaz arrived from Bethlehem, he said to the harvesters, "The LORD be with you."

"The LORD bless you," they replied.

[5] Boaz asked his servant who was in charge of the harvesters, "Whose young woman is this?"

[6] The servant answered, "She is the young Moabite woman who returned with Naomi from the land of Moab. [7] She asked, 'Will you let me gather fallen grain among the bundles behind the harvesters?' She came and has remained from early morning until now, except that she rested a little in the shelter."

[8] Then Boaz said to Ruth, "Listen, my daughter. Don't go and gather grain in another field, and don't leave this one, but stay here close to my female servants. [9] See which field they are harvesting, and follow them. Haven't I ordered the young men not to touch you? When you are thirsty, go and drink from the jars the young men have filled."

[10] She bowed with her face to the ground and said to him, "Why are you so kind to notice me, although I am a foreigner?"

[11] Boaz answered her, "Everything you have done for your mother-in-law since your husband's death has been fully reported to me: how you left your father and mother and the land of your birth, and how you came to a people you didn't previously know. [12] May the LORD reward you for what you have done, and may you receive a full reward from the LORD God of Israel, under whose wings you have come for refuge."

[13] "My lord," she said, "you have been so kind to me, for you have comforted and encouraged your slave, although I am not like one of your female servants."

[14] At mealtime Boaz told her, "Come over here and have some bread and dip it in the vinegar sauce." So she sat beside the harvesters, and he offered her roasted grain. She ate and was satisfied and had some left over.

[15] When she got up to gather grain, Boaz ordered his young men, "Let her even gather grain among the bundles, and don't humiliate her. [16] Pull out some stalks from the bundles for her and leave them for her to gather. Don't rebuke her." [17] So Ruth gathered grain in the field until evening. She beat out what she had gathered, and it was about 26 quarts of barley. [18] She picked up the grain and went into the town, where her mother-in-law saw what she had gleaned. Then she brought out what she had left over from her meal and gave it to her.

[19] Then her mother-in-law said to her, "Where did you gather barley today, and where did you work? May the LORD bless the man who noticed you."

Ruth told her mother-in-law about the men she had worked with and said, "The name of the man I worked with today is Boaz."

[20] Then Naomi said to her daughter-in-law, "May he be blessed by the LORD, who has not forsaken his kindness to the living or the dead." Naomi continued, "The man is a close relative. He is one of our •family redeemers."

[21] Ruth the Moabitess said, "He also told me, 'Stay with my young men until they have finished all of my harvest.'"

[22] So Naomi said to her daughter-in-law Ruth, "My daughter, it is good for you to work with his female servants, so that nothing will happen to you in another field." [23] Ruth stayed close to Boaz's female servants and gathered grain until the barley and the wheat harvests were finished. And she lived with her mother-in-law.

3 Ruth's mother-in-law Naomi said to her, "My daughter, shouldn't I find security for you, so that you will be taken care of? ²Now isn't Boaz our relative? Haven't you been working with his female servants? This evening he will be winnowing barley on the threshing floor. ³Wash, put on perfumed oil, and wear your best clothes. Go down to the threshing floor, but don't let the man know you are there until he has finished eating and drinking. ⁴When he lies down, notice the place where he's lying, go in and uncover his feet, and lie down. Then he will explain to you what you should do."

⁵So Ruth said to her, "I will do everything you say." ⁶She went down to the threshing floor and did everything her mother-in-law had instructed her. ⁷After Boaz ate, drank, and was in good spirits, he went to lie down at the end of the pile of barley. Then she went in secretly, uncovered his feet, and lay down.

⁸At midnight, Boaz was startled, turned over, and there lying at his feet was a woman! ⁹So he asked, "Who are you?"

"I am Ruth, your slave," she replied. "Spread your cloak over me, for you are a *family redeemer."

¹⁰Then he said, "May the Lord bless you, my daughter. You have shown more kindness now than before, because you have not pursued younger men, whether rich or poor. ¹¹Now don't be afraid, my daughter. I will do for you whatever you say, since all the people in my town know that you are a woman of noble character. ¹²Yes, it is true that I am a family redeemer, but there is a redeemer closer than I am. ¹³Stay here tonight, and in the morning, if he wants to redeem you, that's good. Let him redeem you. But if he doesn't want to redeem you, as the Lord lives, I will. Now lie down until morning."

¹⁴So she lay down at his feet until morning but got up while it was still dark. Then Boaz said, "Don't let it be known that a woman came to the threshing floor." ¹⁵And he told Ruth, "Bring the shawl you're wearing and hold it out." When she held it out, he shoveled six measures of barley into her shawl, and she went into the town.

¹⁶She went to her mother-in-law, Naomi, who asked her, "How did it go, my daughter?"

Then Ruth told her everything the man had done for her. ¹⁷She said, "He gave me these six measures of barley, because he said, 'Don't go back to your mother-in-law empty-handed.'"

¹⁸Naomi said, "My daughter, wait until you find out how things go, for he won't rest unless he resolves this today."

4 Boaz went to the *gate of the town and sat down there. Soon the *family redeemer Boaz had spoken about came by. Boaz called him by name and said, "Come over here and sit down." So he went over and sat down. ²Then Boaz took 10 men of the town's elders and said, "Sit here." And they sat down. ³He said to the redeemer, "Naomi, who has returned from the land of Moab, is selling a piece of land that belonged to our brother Elimelech. ⁴I thought I should inform you: Buy it back in the presence of those seated here and in the presence of the elders of my people. If you want to redeem it, do so. But if you do not want to redeem it, tell me so that I will know, because there isn't anyone other than you to redeem it, and I am next after you."

"I want to redeem it," he answered.

⁵Then Boaz said, "On the day you buy the land from Naomi, you will also acquire Ruth the Moabitess, the wife of the deceased man, to perpetuate the man's name on his property."

⁶The redeemer replied, "I can't redeem it myself, or I will ruin my own inheritance. Take my right of redemption, because I can't redeem it."

⁷At an earlier period in Israel, a man removed his sandal and gave it to the other party in order to make any matter legally binding concerning the right of redemption or the exchange of property. This was the method of legally binding a transaction in Israel.

⁸So the redeemer removed his sandal and said to Boaz, "Buy back the property yourself."

⁹Boaz said to the elders and all the people, "You are witnesses today that I am buying from Naomi everything that belonged to Elimelech, Chilion, and Mahlon. ¹⁰I will also acquire Ruth the Moabitess, Mahlon's widow, as my wife, to perpetuate the deceased man's name on his property, so that his name will not disappear among his relatives or from the gate of his home. You are witnesses today."

¹¹The elders and all the people who were at the gate said, "We are witnesses. May the Lord make the woman who is entering your house like Rachel and Leah, who together built the house of Israel. May you be powerful in Ephrathah and famous in Bethlehem. ¹²May your house become like the house of Perez, the son Tamar bore to Judah, because of the offspring the Lord will give you by this young woman."

¹³Boaz took Ruth and she became his wife. When he was intimate with her, the Lord enabled her to conceive, and she gave birth to a son. ¹⁴Then the women said to Naomi, "Praise the Lord, who has not left you without a family redeemer today. May his name become well known in Israel. ¹⁵He will renew your life and sustain you in your old age. Indeed, your daughter-in-law, who loves you and is better to you than seven sons, has given birth to him." ¹⁶Naomi took the child, placed him on her lap, and took care of him. ¹⁷The neighbor women said, "A son has been born to Naomi," and they named him Obed. He was the father of Jesse, the father of David.

¹⁸Now this is the genealogy of Perez:
Perez fathered Hezron.
¹⁹ Hezron fathered Ram,
who fathered Amminadab.
²⁰ Amminadab fathered Nahshon,
who fathered Salmon.
²¹ Salmon fathered Boaz,
who fathered Obed.
²² And Obed fathered Jesse,
who fathered David.

1 Samuel

1 There was a man from Ramathaim-zophim in the hill country of Ephraim. His name was Elkanah son of Jeroham, son of Elihu, son of Tohu, son of Zuph, an Ephraimite. ²He had two wives, the first named Hannah and the second Peninnah. Peninnah had children, but Hannah was childless. ³This man would go up from his town every year to worship and to sacrifice to the LORD of •Hosts at Shiloh, where Eli's two sons, Hophni and Phinehas, were the LORD's priests.

⁴Whenever Elkanah offered a sacrifice, he always gave portions of the meat to his wife Peninnah and to each of her sons and daughters. ⁵But he gave a double portion to Hannah, for he loved her even though the LORD had kept her from conceiving. ⁶Her rival would taunt her severely just to provoke her, because the LORD had kept Hannah from conceiving. ⁷Whenever she went up to the LORD's house, her rival taunted her in this way every year. Hannah wept and would not eat. ⁸"Hannah, why are you crying?" her husband Elkanah asked. "Why won't you eat? Why are you troubled? Am I not better to you than 10 sons?"

⁹Hannah got up after they ate and drank at Shiloh. Eli the priest was sitting on a chair by the doorpost of the LORD's tabernacle. ¹⁰Deeply hurt, Hannah prayed to the LORD and wept with many tears. ¹¹Making a vow, she pleaded, "LORD of Hosts, if You will take notice of Your servant's affliction, remember and not forget me, and give Your servant a son, I will give him to the LORD all the days of his life, and his hair will never be cut."

¹²While she continued praying in the LORD's presence, Eli watched her lips. ¹³Hannah was praying silently, and though her lips were moving, her voice could not be heard. Eli thought she was drunk ¹⁴and scolded her, "How long are you going to be drunk? Get rid of your wine!"

¹⁵"No, my lord," Hannah replied. "I am a woman with a broken heart. I haven't had any wine or beer; I've been pouring out my heart before the LORD. ¹⁶Don't think of me as a wicked woman; I've been praying from the depth of my anguish and resentment."

¹⁷Eli responded, "Go in peace, and may the God of Israel grant the petition you've requested from Him."

¹⁸"May your servant find favor with you," she replied. Then Hannah went on her way; she ate and no longer looked despondent.

¹⁹The next morning Elkanah and Hannah got up early to bow in worship before the LORD. Afterward, they returned home to Ramah. Then Elkanah was intimate with his wife Hannah, and the LORD remembered her. ²⁰After some time, Hannah conceived and gave birth to a son. She named him Samuel, because she said, "I requested him from the LORD."

²¹When Elkanah and all his household went up to make the annual sacrifice and his vow offering to the LORD, ²²Hannah did not go and explained to her husband, "After the child is weaned, I'll take him to appear in the LORD's presence and to stay there permanently."

²³Her husband Elkanah replied, "Do what you think is best, and stay here until you've weaned him. May the LORD confirm your word." So Hannah stayed there and nursed her son until she weaned him. ²⁴When she had weaned him, she took him with her to Shiloh, as well as a three-year-old bull, half a bushel of flour, and a jar of wine. Though the boy was still young, she took him to the LORD's house at Shiloh. ²⁵Then they slaughtered the bull and brought the boy to Eli.

²⁶"Please, my lord," she said, "as sure as you live, my lord, I am the woman who stood here beside you praying to the LORD. ²⁷I prayed for this boy, and since the LORD gave me what I asked Him for, ²⁸I now give the boy to the LORD. For as long as he lives, he is given to the LORD." Then he bowed in worship to the LORD there.

2 Hannah prayed:

My heart rejoices in the LORD;
    my •horn is lifted up by the LORD.
My mouth boasts over my enemies,
    because I rejoice in Your salvation.
²   There is no one holy like the LORD.
    There is no one besides You!
    And there is no rock like our God.
³   Do not boast so proudly,
    or let arrogant words come out of
        your mouth,
    for the LORD is a God of knowledge,
    and actions are weighed by Him.
⁴   The bows of the warriors are broken,
    but the feeble are clothed with strength.
⁵   Those who are full hire themselves out
        for food,
    but those who are starving hunger no more.
    The woman who is childless gives birth
        to seven,
    but the woman with many sons
        pines away.
⁶   The LORD brings death and gives life;
    He sends some to •Sheol, and He raises
        others up.
⁷   The LORD brings poverty and gives wealth;
    He humbles and He exalts.
⁸   He raises the poor from the dust
    and lifts the needy from the garbage pile.
    He seats them with noblemen
    and gives them a throne of honor.
    For the foundations of the earth
        are the LORD's;
    He has set the world on them.
⁹   He guards the steps of His faithful ones,
    but the wicked perish in darkness,
    for a man does not prevail by his own
        strength.
¹⁰ Those who oppose the LORD will be shattered;
    He will thunder in the heavens against them.
    The LORD will judge the ends of the earth.
    He will give power to His king;
    He will lift up the horn of His anointed.

¹¹Elkanah went home to Ramah, but the boy served the LORD in the presence of Eli the priest.

¹²Eli's sons were •wicked men; they had no regard for the LORD ¹³or for the priests' share of the sacrifices from the people. When any man offered a sacrifice, the priest's servant would come with a three-pronged meat fork while the meat was boiling ¹⁴and plunge it into the container or kettle or cauldron or cooking pot. The priest would claim for himself whatever the meat fork brought up. This is the way they treated all the Israelites who came there to Shiloh. ¹⁵Even

before the fat was burned, the priest's servant would come and say to the man who was sacrificing, "Give the priest some meat to roast, because he won't accept boiled meat from you—only raw." [16] If that man said to him, "The fat must be burned first; then you can take whatever you want for yourself," the servant would reply, "No, I insist that you hand it over right now. If you don't, I'll take it by force!" [17] So the servants' sin was very severe in the presence of the LORD, because they treated the LORD's offering with contempt.

[18] The boy Samuel served in the LORD's presence and wore a linen ephod. [19] Each year his mother made him a little robe and took it to him when she went with her husband to offer the annual sacrifice. [20] Eli would bless Elkanah and his wife: "May the LORD give you children by this woman in place of the one she has given to the LORD." Then they would go home.

[21] The LORD paid attention to Hannah's need, and she conceived and gave birth to three sons and two daughters. Meanwhile, the boy Samuel grew up in the presence of the LORD.

[22] Now Eli was very old. He heard about everything his sons were doing to all Israel and how they were sleeping with the women who served at the tent of meeting. [23] He said to them, "Why are you doing these things? I have heard about your evil actions from all these people. [24] No, my sons, the report I hear from the LORD's people is not good. [25] If a man sins against another man, God can intercede for him, but if a man sins against the LORD, who can intercede for him?" But they would not listen to their father, since the LORD intended to kill them. [26] By contrast, the boy Samuel grew in stature and in favor with the LORD and with men.

[27] A man of God came to Eli and said to him, "This is what the LORD says: 'Didn't I reveal Myself to your ancestral house when it was in Egypt and belonged to Pharaoh's palace? [28] Out of all the tribes of Israel, I selected your house to be priests, to offer sacrifices on My altar, to burn incense, and to wear an *ephod in My presence. I also gave your house all the Israelite fire offerings. [29] Why, then, do all of you despise My sacrifices and offerings that I require at the place of worship? You have honored your sons more than Me, by making yourselves fat with the best part of all of the offerings of My people Israel.'

[30] "Therefore, this is the declaration of the LORD, the God of Israel:

'Although I said
your family and your ancestral house
would walk before Me forever,
the LORD now says, "No longer!"
I will honor those who honor Me,
but those who despise Me will be disgraced.

[31] "'Look, the days are coming when I will cut off your strength and the strength of your ancestral family, so that none in your family will reach old age. [32] You will see distress in the place of worship, in spite of all that is good in Israel, and no one in your family will ever again reach old age. [33] Any man from your family I do not cut off from My altar will bring grief and sadness to you. All your descendants will die violently. [34] This will be the sign that will come to you concerning your two sons Hophni and Phinehas: both of them will die on the same day.

[35] "'Then I will raise up a faithful priest for Myself. He will do whatever is in My heart and mind. I will establish a lasting dynasty for him, and he will walk before My anointed one for all time. [36] Anyone who is left in your family will come and bow down to him for a piece of silver or a loaf of bread. He will say: Please appoint me to some priestly office so I can have a piece of bread to eat.'"

3 The boy Samuel served the LORD in Eli's presence. In those days the word of the LORD was rare and prophetic visions were not widespread.

[2] One day Eli, whose eyesight was failing, was lying in his room. [3] Before the lamp of God had gone out, Samuel was lying down in the tabernacle of the LORD, where the ark of God was located.

[4] Then the LORD called Samuel, and he answered, "Here I am." [5] He ran to Eli and said, "Here I am; you called me."

"I didn't call," Eli replied. "Go back and lie down." So he went and lay down.

[6] Once again the LORD called, "Samuel!"

Samuel got up, went to Eli, and said, "Here I am; you called me."

"I didn't call, my son," he replied. "Go back and lie down."

[7] Now Samuel had not yet experienced the LORD, because the word of the LORD had not yet been revealed to him. [8] Once again, for the third time, the LORD called Samuel. He got up, went to Eli, and said, "Here I am; you called me."

Then Eli understood that the LORD was calling the boy. [9] He told Samuel, "Go and lie down. If He calls you, say, 'Speak, LORD, for Your servant is listening.'" So Samuel went and lay down in his place.

[10] The LORD came, stood there, and called as before, "Samuel, Samuel!"

Samuel responded, "Speak, for Your servant is listening."

[11] The LORD said to Samuel, "I am about to do something in Israel that everyone who hears about it will shudder. [12] On that day I will carry out against Eli everything I said about his family, from beginning to end. [13] I told him that I am going to judge his family forever because of the iniquity he knows about: his sons are defiling the sanctuary, and he has not stopped them. [14] Therefore, I have sworn to Eli's family: The iniquity of Eli's family will never be wiped out by either sacrifice or offering."

[15] Samuel lay down until the morning; then he opened the doors of the LORD's house. He was afraid to tell Eli the vision, [16] but Eli called him and said, "Samuel, my son."

"Here I am," answered Samuel.

[17] "What was the message He gave you?" Eli asked. "Don't hide it from me. May God punish you and do so severely if you hide anything from me that He told you." [18] So Samuel told him everything and did not hide anything from him. Eli responded, "He is the LORD. He will do what He thinks is good."

[19] Samuel grew, and the LORD was with him, and He fulfilled everything Samuel prophesied. [20] All Israel from Dan to Beer-sheba knew that Samuel was a confirmed prophet of the LORD. [21] The LORD continued to appear in Shiloh, because there He revealed Himself to Samuel by His word. [1] And Samuel's 4 words came to all Israel.

Israel went out to meet the Philistines in battle and camped at Ebenezer while the Philistines camped at Aphek. [2] The Philistines lined up in battle formation against Israel, and as the battle intensified, Israel was defeated by the Philistines, who struck down about 4,000 men on the battlefield.

³When the troops returned to the camp, the elders of Israel asked, "Why did the Lord let us be defeated today by the Philistines? Let's bring the ark of the Lord's covenant from Shiloh. Then it will go with us and save us from the hand of our enemies." ⁴So the people sent men to Shiloh to bring back the ark of the covenant of the Lord of ˙Hosts, who dwells between the ˙cherubim. Eli's two sons, Hophni and Phinehas, were there with the ark of the covenant of God. ⁵When the ark of the covenant of the Lord entered the camp, all the Israelites raised such a loud shout that the ground shook.

⁶The Philistines heard the sound of the war cry and asked, "What's this loud shout in the Hebrews' camp?" When the Philistines discovered that the ark of the Lord had entered the camp, ⁷they panicked. "The gods have entered their camp!" they said. "Woe to us, nothing like this has happened before. ⁸Woe to us, who will rescue us from the hand of these magnificent gods? These are the gods that slaughtered the Egyptians with all kinds of plagues in the wilderness. ⁹Show some courage and be men, Philistines! Otherwise, you'll serve the Hebrews just as they served you. Now be men and fight!"

¹⁰So the Philistines fought, and Israel was defeated, and each man fled to his tent. The slaughter was severe—30,000 of the Israelite foot soldiers fell. ¹¹The ark of God was captured, and Eli's two sons, Hophni and Phinehas, died.

¹²That same day, a Benjaminite man ran from the battle and came to Shiloh. His clothes were torn, and there was dirt on his head. ¹³When he arrived, there was Eli sitting on his chair beside the road watching, because he was anxious about the ark of God. When the man entered the city to give a report, the entire city cried out.

¹⁴Eli heard the outcry and asked, "Why this commotion?" The man quickly came and reported to Eli. ¹⁵At that time Eli was 98 years old, and his gaze was fixed because he couldn't see.

¹⁶The man said to Eli, "I'm the one who came from the battle. I fled from there today."

"What happened, my son?" Eli asked.

¹⁷The messenger answered, "Israel has fled from the Philistines, and also there was a great slaughter among the people. Your two sons, Hophni and Phinehas, are both dead, and the ark of God has been captured." ¹⁸When he mentioned the ark of God, Eli fell backward off the chair by the city gate, and since he was old and heavy, his neck broke and he died. Eli had judged Israel 40 years.

¹⁹Eli's daughter-in-law, the wife of Phinehas, was pregnant and about to give birth. When she heard the news about the capture of God's ark and the deaths of her father-in-law and her husband, she collapsed and gave birth because her labor pains came on her. ²⁰As she was dying, the women taking care of her said, "Don't be afraid. You've given birth to a son!" But she did not respond or pay attention. ²¹She named the boy Ichabod, saying, "The glory has departed from Israel," referring to the capture of the ark of God and to the deaths of her father-in-law and her husband. ²²"The glory has departed from Israel," she said, "because the ark of God has been captured."

5 After the Philistines had captured the ark of God, they took it from Ebenezer to Ashdod, ²brought it into the temple of Dagon and placed it next to his statue. ³When the people of Ashdod got up early the next morning, there was Dagon, fallen with his face to the ground before the ark of the Lord. So they took Dagon and returned him to his place. ⁴But when they got up early the next morning, there was Dagon, fallen with his face to the ground before the ark of the Lord. This time, both Dagon's head and the palms of his hands were broken off and lying on the threshold. Only Dagon's torso remained. ⁵That is why, to this day, the priests of Dagon and everyone who enters the temple of Dagon in Ashdod do not step on Dagon's threshold.

⁶The Lord's hand was heavy on the people of Ashdod, terrorizing and afflicting the people of Ashdod and its territory with tumors. ⁷When the men of Ashdod saw what was happening, they said, "The ark of Israel's God must not stay here with us, because His hand is strongly against us and our god Dagon." ⁸So they called all the Philistine rulers together and asked, "What should we do with the ark of Israel's God?"

"The ark of Israel's God should be moved to Gath," they replied. So the men of Ashdod moved the ark. ⁹After they had moved it, the Lord's hand was against the city of Gath, causing a great panic. He afflicted the men of the city, from the youngest to the oldest, with an outbreak of tumors.

¹⁰The Gittites then sent the ark of God to Ekron, but when it got there, the Ekronites cried out, "They've moved the ark of Israel's God to us to kill us and our people!"

¹¹The Ekronites called all the Philistine rulers together. They said, "Send the ark of Israel's God away. It must return to its place so it won't kill us and our people!" For the fear of death pervaded the city; God's hand was oppressing them. ¹²The men who did not die were afflicted with tumors, and the outcry of the city went up to heaven.

6 When the ark of the Lord had been in the land of the Philistines for seven months, ²the Philistines summoned the priests and the diviners and pleaded, "What should we do with the ark of the Lord? Tell us how we can send it back to its place."

³They replied, "If you send the ark of Israel's God away, you must not send it without an offering. You must send back a restitution offering to Him, and you will be healed. Then the reason His hand hasn't been removed from you will be revealed."

⁴They asked, "What restitution offering should we send back to Him?"

And they answered, "Five gold tumors and five gold mice corresponding to the number of Philistine rulers, since there was one plague for both you and your rulers. ⁵Make images of your tumors and of your mice that are destroying the land. Give glory to Israel's God, and perhaps He will stop oppressing you, your gods, and your land. ⁶Why harden your hearts as the Egyptians and Pharaoh hardened theirs? When He afflicted them, didn't they send Israel away, and Israel left?

⁷"Now then, prepare one new cart and two milk cows that have never been yoked. Hitch the cows to the cart, but take their calves away and pen them up. ⁸Take the ark of the Lord, place it on the cart, and put the gold objects that you're sending Him as a restitution offering in a box beside the ark. Send it off and let it go its way. ⁹Then watch: If it goes up the road

to its homeland toward Beth-shemesh, it is the LORD who has made this terrible trouble for us. However, if it doesn't, we will know that it was not His hand that punished us—it was just something that happened to us by chance."

¹⁰The men did this: They took two milk cows, hitched them to the cart, and confined their calves in the pen. ¹¹Then they put the ark of the LORD on the cart, along with the box containing the gold mice and the images of their tumors. ¹²The cows went straight up the road to Beth-shemesh. They stayed on that one highway, lowing as they went; they never strayed to the right or to the left. The Philistine rulers were walking behind them to the territory of Beth-shemesh.

¹³The people of Beth-shemesh were harvesting wheat in the valley, and when they looked up and saw the ark, they were overjoyed to see it. ¹⁴The cart came to the field of Joshua of Beth-shemesh and stopped there near a large rock. The people of the city chopped up the cart and offered the cows as a *burnt offering to the LORD. ¹⁵The Levites removed the ark of the LORD, along with the box containing the gold objects, and placed them on the large rock. That day the men of Beth-shemesh offered burnt offerings and made sacrifices to the LORD. ¹⁶When the five Philistine rulers observed this, they returned to Ekron that same day.

¹⁷As a restitution offering to the LORD, the Philistines had sent back one gold tumor for each city: Ashdod, Gaza, Ashkelon, Gath, and Ekron. ¹⁸The number of gold mice also corresponded to the number of Philistine cities of the five rulers, the fortified cities and the outlying villages. The large rock on which the ark of the LORD was placed is in the field of Joshua of Beth-shemesh to this day.

¹⁹God struck down the men of Beth-shemesh because they looked inside the ark of the LORD. He struck down 70 men out of 50,000 men. The people mourned because the LORD struck them with a great slaughter. ²⁰The men of Beth-shemesh asked, "Who is able to stand in the presence of this holy LORD God? Who should the ark go to from here?"

²¹They sent messengers to the residents of Kiriath-jearim, saying, "The Philistines have returned the ark of the LORD. Come down and get it."

7 So the men of Kiriath-jearim came for the ark of the LORD and took it to Abinadab's house on the hill. They consecrated his son Eleazar to take care of it. ²Time went by until 20 years had passed since the ark had been taken to Kiriath-jearim. Then the whole house of Israel began to seek the LORD. ³Samuel told them, "If you are returning to the LORD with all your heart, get rid of the foreign gods and the *Ashtoreths that are among you, dedicate yourselves to the LORD, and worship only Him. Then He will rescue you from the hand of the Philistines." ⁴So the Israelites removed the *Baals and the Ashtoreths and only worshiped the LORD.

⁵Samuel said, "Gather all Israel at Mizpah, and I will pray to the LORD on your behalf." ⁶When they gathered at Mizpah, they drew water and poured it out in the LORD's presence. They fasted that day, and there they confessed, "We have sinned against the LORD." And Samuel judged the Israelites at Mizpah.

⁷When the Philistines heard that the Israelites had gathered at Mizpah, their rulers marched up toward Israel. When the Israelites heard about it, they were afraid because of the Philistines. ⁸The Israelites said to Samuel, "Don't stop crying out to the LORD our God for us, so that He will save us from the hand of the Philistines."

⁹Then Samuel took a young lamb and offered it as a whole *burnt offering to the LORD. He cried out to the LORD on behalf of Israel, and the LORD answered him. ¹⁰Samuel was offering the burnt offering as the Philistines drew near to fight against Israel. The LORD thundered loudly against the Philistines that day and threw them into such confusion that they fled before Israel. ¹¹Then the men of Israel charged out of Mizpah and pursued the Philistines striking them down all the way to a place below Beth-car.

¹²Afterward, Samuel took a stone and set it upright between Mizpah and Shen. He named it Ebenezer, explaining, "The LORD has helped us to this point." ¹³So the Philistines were subdued and did not invade Israel's territory again. The LORD's hand was against the Philistines all of Samuel's life. ¹⁴The cities from Ekron to Gath, which they had taken from Israel, were restored; Israel even rescued their surrounding territories from Philistine control. There was also peace between Israel and the Amorites.

¹⁵Samuel judged Israel throughout his life. ¹⁶Every year he would go on a circuit to Bethel, Gilgal, and Mizpah and would judge Israel at all these locations. ¹⁷Then he would return to Ramah because his home was there, he judged Israel there, and he built an altar to the LORD there.

8 When Samuel grew old, he appointed his sons as judges over Israel. ²His firstborn son's name was Joel and his second was Abijah. They were judges in Beer-sheba. ³However, his sons did not walk in his ways—they turned toward dishonest gain, took bribes, and perverted justice.

⁴So all the elders of Israel gathered together and went to Samuel at Ramah. ⁵They said to him, "Look, you are old, and your sons do not follow your example. Therefore, appoint a king to judge us the same as all the other nations have."

⁶When they said, "Give us a king to judge us," Samuel considered their demand sinful, so he prayed to the LORD. ⁷But the LORD told him, "Listen to the people and everything they say to you. They have not rejected you; they have rejected Me as their king. ⁸They are doing the same thing to you that they have done to Me, since the day I brought them out of Egypt until this day, abandoning Me and worshiping other gods. ⁹Listen to them, but you must solemnly warn them and tell them about the rights of the king who will rule over them."

¹⁰Samuel told all the LORD's words to the people who were asking him for a king. ¹¹He said, "These are the rights of the king who will rule over you: He will take your sons and put them to his use in his chariots, on his horses, or running in front of his chariots. ¹²He can appoint them for his use as commanders of thousands or commanders of fifties, to plow his ground or reap his harvest, or to make his weapons of war or the equipment for his chariots. ¹³He can take your daughters to become perfumers, cooks, and bakers. ¹⁴He can take your best fields, vineyards, and olive orchards and give them to his servants. ¹⁵He can take a tenth of your grain and your vineyards and give them to his officials and servants. ¹⁶He can take your male servants, your female servants, your best young men, and your donkeys and use them for his work. ¹⁷He can take a tenth

of your flocks, and you yourselves can become his servants. [18] When that day comes, you will cry out because of the king you've chosen for yourselves, but the LORD won't answer you on that day."

[19] The people refused to listen to Samuel. "No!" they said. "We must have a king over us. [20] Then we'll be like all the other nations: our king will judge us, go out before us, and fight our battles."

[21] Samuel listened to all the people's words and then repeated them to the LORD. [22] "Listen to them," the LORD told Samuel. "Appoint a king for them."

Then Samuel told the men of Israel, "Each of you, go back to your city."

9 There was an influential man of Benjamin named Kish son of Abiel, son of Zeror, son of Becorath, son of Aphiah, son of a Benjaminite. [2] He had a son named Saul, an impressive young man. There was no one more impressive among the Israelites than he. He stood a head taller than anyone else.

[3] One day the donkeys of Saul's father Kish wandered off. Kish said to his son Saul, "Take one of the attendants with you and go look for the donkeys." [4] Saul and his attendant went through the hill country of Ephraim and then through the region of Shalishah, but they didn't find them. They went through the region of Shaalim—nothing. Then they went through the Benjaminite region but still didn't find them.

[5] When they came to the land of Zuph, Saul said to the attendant who was with him, "Come on, let's go back, or my father will stop worrying about the donkeys and start worrying about us."

[6] "Look," the attendant said, "there's a man of God in this city who is highly respected; everything he says is sure to come true. Let's go there now. Maybe he'll tell us which way we should go."

[7] "Suppose we do go," Saul said to his attendant, "what do we take the man? The food from our packs is gone, and there's no gift to take to the man of God. What do we have?"

[8] The attendant answered Saul: "Here, I have a piece of silver. I'll give it to the man of God, and he will tell us our way."

[9] Formerly in Israel, a man who was going to inquire of God would say, "Come, let's go to the seer," for the prophet of today was formerly called the seer.

[10] "Good," Saul replied to his attendant. "Come on, let's go." So they went to the city where the man of God was. [11] As they were climbing the hill to the city, they found some young women coming out to draw water and asked, "Is the seer here?"

[12] The women answered, "Yes, he is ahead of you. Hurry, he just now came to the city, because there's a sacrifice for the people at the •high place today. [13] If you go quickly, you can catch up with him before he goes to the high place to eat. The people won't eat until he comes because he must bless the sacrifice; after that, the guests can eat. Go up immediately—you can find him now." [14] So they went up toward the city.

Saul and his attendant were entering the city when they saw Samuel coming toward them on his way to the high place. [15] Now the day before Saul's arrival, the LORD had informed Samuel, [16] "At this time tomorrow I will send you a man from the land of Benjamin. Anoint him ruler over My people Israel. He will save them from the hand of the Philistines because I have seen the affliction of My people, for their cry has come to Me." [17] When Samuel saw Saul, the LORD told him,

"Here is the man I told you about; he will rule over My people."

[18] Saul approached Samuel in the gate area and asked, "Would you please tell me where the seer's house is?"

[19] "I am the seer," Samuel answered. "Go up ahead of me to the high place and eat with me today. When I send you off in the morning, I'll tell you everything that's in your heart. [20] As for the donkeys that wandered away from you three days ago, don't worry about them because they've been found. And who does all Israel desire but you and all your father's family?"

[21] Saul responded, "Am I not a Benjaminite from the smallest of Israel's tribes and isn't my clan the least important of all the clans of the Benjaminite tribe? So why have you said something like this to me?"

[22] Samuel took Saul and his attendant, brought them to the banquet hall, and gave them a place at the head of the 30 or so men who had been invited. [23] Then Samuel said to the cook, "Get the portion of meat that I gave you and told you to set aside."

[24] The cook picked up the thigh and what was attached to it and set it before Saul. Then Samuel said, "Notice that the reserved piece is set before you. Eat it because it was saved for you for this solemn event at the time I said, 'I've invited the people.'" So Saul ate with Samuel that day. [25] Afterward, they went down from the high place to the city, and Samuel spoke with Saul on the roof.

[26] They got up early, and just before dawn, Samuel called to Saul on the roof, "Get up, and I'll send you on your way!" Saul got up, and both he and Samuel went outside. [27] As they were going down to the edge of the city, Samuel said to Saul, "Tell the attendant to go on ahead of us, but you stay for a while, and I'll reveal the word of God to you." So the attendant went on.

10 Samuel took the flask of oil, poured it out on Saul's head, kissed him, and said, "Hasn't the LORD anointed you ruler over His inheritance? [2] Today when you leave me, you'll find two men at Rachel's Grave at Zelzah in the land of Benjamin. They will say to you, 'The donkeys you went looking for have been found, and now your father has stopped being concerned about the donkeys and is worried about you, asking: What should I do about my son?'

[3] "You will proceed from there until you come to the oak of Tabor. Three men going up to God at Bethel will meet you there, one bringing three goats, one bringing three loaves of bread, and one bringing a skin of wine. [4] They will ask how you are and give you two loaves of bread, which you will accept from them.

[5] "After that you will come to the Hill of God where there are Philistine garrisons. When you arrive at the city, you will meet a group of prophets coming down from the •high place prophesying. They will be preceded by harps, tambourines, flutes, and lyres. [6] The Spirit of the LORD will control you, you will prophesy with them, and you will be transformed into a different person. [7] When these signs have happened to you, do whatever your circumstances require because God is with you. [8] Afterward, go ahead of me to Gilgal. I will come to you to offer •burnt offerings and to sacrifice •fellowship offerings. Wait seven days until I come to you and show you what to do."

[9] When Saul turned around to leave Samuel, God changed his heart, and all the signs came about that day. [10] When Saul and his attendant arrived at Gibeah,

a group of prophets met him. Then the Spirit of God took control of him, and he prophesied along with them.

¹¹Everyone who knew him previously and saw him prophesy with the prophets asked each other, "What has happened to the son of Kish? Is Saul also among the prophets?"

¹²Then a man who was from there asked, "And who is their father?"

As a result, "Is Saul also among the prophets?" became a popular saying. ¹³Then Saul finished prophesying and went to the high place.

¹⁴Saul's uncle asked him and his attendant, "Where did you go?"

"To look for the donkeys," Saul answered. "When we saw they weren't there, we went to Samuel."

¹⁵"Tell me," Saul's uncle asked, "what did Samuel say to you?"

¹⁶Saul told him, "He assured us the donkeys had been found." However, Saul did not tell him what Samuel had said about the matter of kingship.

¹⁷Samuel summoned the people to the Lord at Mizpah ¹⁸and said to the Israelites, "This is what the Lord, the God of Israel, says: 'I brought Israel out of Egypt, and I rescued you from the power of the Egyptians and all the kingdoms that were oppressing you.' ¹⁹But today you have rejected your God, who saves you from all your troubles and afflictions. You said to Him, 'You must set a king over us.' Now therefore present yourselves before the Lord by your tribes and clans."

²⁰Samuel had all the tribes of Israel come forward, and the tribe of Benjamin was selected. ²¹He had the tribe of Benjamin come forward by its clans, and the Matrite clan was selected. Finally, Saul son of Kish was selected. But when they searched for him, they could not find him. ²²They again inquired of the Lord, "Has the man come here yet?"

The Lord replied, "There he is, hidden among the supplies."

²³They ran and got him from there. When he stood among the people, he stood a head taller than anyone else. ²⁴Samuel said to all the people, "Do you see the one the Lord has chosen? There is no one like him among the entire population."

And all the people shouted, "Long live the king!"

²⁵Samuel proclaimed to the people the rights of kingship. He wrote them on a scroll, which he placed in the presence of the Lord. Then Samuel sent all the people away, each to his home.

²⁶Saul also went to his home in Gibeah, and brave men whose hearts God had touched went with him. ²⁷But some *wicked men said, "How can this guy save us?" They despised him and did not bring him a gift, but Saul said nothing.

11 Nahash the Ammonite came up and laid siege to Jabesh-gilead. All the men of Jabesh said to him, "Make a treaty with us, and we will serve you."

²Nahash the Ammonite replied, "I'll make one with you on this condition: that I gouge out everyone's right eye and humiliate all Israel."

³"Don't do anything to us for seven days," the elders of Jabesh said to him, "and let us send messengers throughout the territory of Israel. If no one saves us, we will surrender to you."

⁴When the messengers came to Gibeah, Saul's hometown, and told the terms to the people, all wept aloud. ⁵Just then Saul was coming in from the field behind his oxen. "What's the matter with the people? Why are they weeping?" Saul inquired, and they repeated to him the words of the men from Jabesh.

⁶When Saul heard these words, the Spirit of God suddenly took control of him, and his anger burned furiously. ⁷He took a team of oxen, cut them in pieces, and sent them throughout the land of Israel by messengers who said, "This is what will be done to the ox of anyone who doesn't march behind Saul and Samuel." As a result, the terror of the Lord fell on the people, and they went out united.

⁸Saul counted them at Bezek. There were 300,000 Israelites and 30,000 men from Judah. ⁹He told the messengers who had come, "Tell this to the men of Jabesh-gilead: 'Deliverance will be yours tomorrow by the time the sun is hot.'" So the messengers told the men of Jabesh, and they rejoiced.

¹⁰Then the men of Jabesh said to Nahash, "Tomorrow we will come out, and you can do whatever you want to us."

¹¹The next day Saul organized the troops into three divisions. During the morning watch, they invaded the Ammonite camp and slaughtered them until the heat of the day. There were survivors, but they were so scattered that no two of them were left together.

¹²Afterward, the people said to Samuel, "Who said that Saul should not reign over us? Give us those men so we can kill them!"

¹³But Saul ordered, "No one will be executed this day, for today the Lord has provided deliverance in Israel."

¹⁴Then Samuel said to the people, "Come, let's go to Gilgal, so we can renew the kingship there." ¹⁵So all the people went to Gilgal, and there in the Lord's presence they made Saul king. There they sacrificed *fellowship offerings in the Lord's presence, and Saul and all the men of Israel greatly rejoiced.

12 Then Samuel said to all Israel, "I have carefully listened to everything you said to me and placed a king over you. ²Now you can see that the king is leading you. As for me, I'm old and gray, and my sons are here with you. I have led you from my youth until today. ³Here I am. Bring charges against me before the Lord and His anointed: Whose ox or donkey have I taken? Whom have I wronged or mistreated? From whose hand have I taken a bribe to overlook something? I will return it to you."

⁴"You haven't wronged us, you haven't mistreated us, and you haven't taken anything from anyone's hand," they responded.

⁵He said to them, "The Lord is a witness against you, and His anointed is a witness today that you haven't found anything in my hand."

"He is a witness," they said.

⁶Then Samuel said to the people, "The Lord, who appointed Moses and Aaron and who brought your ancestors up from the land of Egypt, is a witness. ⁷Now present yourselves, so I may confront you before the Lord about all the righteous acts He has done for you and your ancestors.

⁸"When Jacob went to Egypt, your ancestors cried out to the Lord, and He sent them Moses and Aaron, who led your ancestors out of Egypt and settled them in this place. ⁹But they forgot the Lord their God, so He handed them over to Sisera commander of the army of Hazor, to the Philistines, and to the king of Moab. These enemies fought against them. ¹⁰Then

they cried out to the LORD and said, 'We have sinned, for we abandoned the LORD and worshiped the *Baals and the *Ashtoreths. Now deliver us from the power of our enemies, and we will serve You.' ¹¹So the LORD sent Jerubbaal, Barak, Jephthah, and Samuel. He rescued you from the power of the enemies around you, and you lived securely. ¹²But when you saw that Nahash king of the Ammonites was coming against you, you said to me, 'No, we must have a king rule over us'— even though the LORD your God is your king.

¹³"Now here is the king you've chosen, the one you requested. Look, this is the king the LORD has placed over you. ¹⁴If you *fear the LORD, worship and obey Him, and if you don't rebel against the LORD's command, then both you and the king who rules over you will follow the LORD your God. ¹⁵However, if you disobey the LORD and rebel against His command, the LORD's hand will be against you and against your ancestors.

¹⁶"Now, therefore, present yourselves and see this great thing that the LORD will do before your eyes. ¹⁷Isn't the wheat harvest today? I will call on the LORD and He will send thunder and rain, so that you will know and see what a great evil you committed in the LORD's sight by requesting a king for yourselves." ¹⁸Samuel called on the LORD, and on that day the LORD sent thunder and rain. As a result, all the people greatly feared the LORD and Samuel.

¹⁹They pleaded with Samuel, "Pray to the LORD your God for your servants, so we won't die! For we have added to all our sins the evil of requesting a king for ourselves."

²⁰Samuel replied, "Don't be afraid. Even though you have committed all this evil, don't turn away from following the LORD. Instead, worship the LORD with all your heart. ²¹Don't turn away to follow worthless things that can't profit or deliver you; they are worthless. ²²The LORD will not abandon His people, because of His great name and because He has determined to make you His own people.

²³"As for me, I vow that I will not sin against the LORD by ceasing to pray for you. I will teach you the good and right way. ²⁴Above all, fear the LORD and worship Him faithfully with all your heart; consider the great things He has done for you. ²⁵However, if you continue to do what is evil, both you and your king will be swept away."

13 Saul was 30 years old when he became king, and he reigned 42 years over Israel. ²He chose 3,000 men from Israel for himself: 2,000 were with Saul at Michmash and in Bethel's hill country, and 1,000 were with Jonathan in Gibeah of Benjamin. He sent the rest of the troops away, each to his own tent.

³Jonathan attacked the Philistine garrison that was in Geba, and the Philistines heard about it. So Saul blew the ram's horn throughout the land saying, "Let the Hebrews hear!" ⁴And all Israel heard the news, "Saul has attacked the Philistine garrison, and Israel is now repulsive to the Philistines." Then the troops were summoned to join Saul at Gilgal.

⁵The Philistines also gathered to fight against Israel: 3,000 chariots, 6,000 horsemen, and troops as numerous as the sand on the seashore. They went up and camped at Michmash, east of Beth-aven.

⁶The men of Israel saw that they were in trouble because the troops were in a difficult situation. They hid in caves, thickets, among rocks, and in holes and cisterns. ⁷Some Hebrews even crossed the Jordan to the land of Gad and Gilead.

Saul, however, was still at Gilgal, and all his troops were gripped with fear. ⁸He waited seven days for the appointed time that Samuel had set, but Samuel didn't come to Gilgal, and the troops were deserting him. ⁹So Saul said, "Bring me the *burnt offering and the *fellowship offerings." Then he offered the burnt offering. ¹⁰Just as he finished offering the burnt offering, Samuel arrived. So Saul went out to greet him, ¹¹and Samuel asked, "What have you done?"

Saul answered, "When I saw that the troops were deserting me and you didn't come within the appointed days and the Philistines were gathering at Michmash, ¹²I thought: The Philistines will now descend on me at Gilgal, and I haven't sought the LORD's favor. So I forced myself to offer the burnt offering."

¹³Samuel said to Saul, "You have been foolish. You have not kept the command which the LORD your God gave you. It was at this time that the LORD would have permanently established your reign over Israel, ¹⁴but now your reign will not endure. The LORD has found a man loyal to Him, and the LORD has appointed him as ruler over His people, because you have not done what the LORD commanded." ¹⁵Then Samuel went from Gilgal to Gibeah in Benjamin. Saul registered the troops who were with him, about 600 men.

¹⁶Saul, his son Jonathan, and the troops who were with them were staying in Geba of Benjamin, and the Philistines were camped at Michmash. ¹⁷Raiding parties went out from the Philistine camp in three divisions. One division headed toward the Ophrah road leading to the land of Shual. ¹⁸The next division headed toward the Beth-horon road, and the last division headed down the border road that looks out over the Valley of Zeboim toward the wilderness.

¹⁹No blacksmith could be found in all the land of Israel, because the Philistines had said, "Otherwise, the Hebrews will make swords or spears." ²⁰So all the Israelites went to the Philistines to sharpen their plows, mattocks, axes, and sickles. ²¹The price was two-thirds of a *shekel for plows and mattocks, and one-third of a shekel for pitchforks and axes, and for putting a point on an oxgoad. ²²So on the day of battle not a sword or spear could be found in the hand of any of the troops who were with Saul and Jonathan; only Saul and his son Jonathan had weapons.

²³Now a Philistine garrison took control of the pass at Michmash. 14 ¹That same day Saul's son Jonathan said to the attendant who carried his weapons, "Come on, let's cross over to the Philistine garrison on the other side." However, he did not tell his father.

²Saul was staying under the pomegranate tree in Migron on the outskirts of Gibeah. The troops with him numbered about 600. ³Ahijah, who was wearing an *ephod, was also there. He was the son of Ahitub, the brother of Ichabod son of Phinehas, son of Eli the LORD's priest at Shiloh. But the troops did not know that Jonathan had left.

⁴There were sharp columns of rock on both sides of the pass that Jonathan intended to cross to reach the Philistine garrison. One was named Bozez and the other Seneh; ⁵one stood to the north in front of Michmash and the other to the south in front of Geba. ⁶Jonathan said to the attendant who carried his weapons, "Come on, let's cross over to the garrison of these

uncircumcised men. Perhaps the LORD will help us. Nothing can keep the LORD from saving, whether by many or by few."

[7] His armor-bearer responded, "Do what is in your heart. You choose. I'm right here with you whatever you decide."

[8] "All right," Jonathan replied, "we'll cross over to the men and then let them see us. [9] If they say, 'Wait until we reach you,' then we will stay where we are and not go up to them. [10] But if they say, 'Come on up,' then we'll go up, because the LORD has handed them over to us—that will be our sign."

[11] They let themselves be seen by the Philistine garrison, and the Philistines said, "Look, the Hebrews are coming out of the holes where they've been hiding!" [12] The men of the garrison called to Jonathan and his armor-bearer. "Come on up, and we'll teach you a lesson!" they said.

"Follow me," Jonathan told his armor-bearer, "for the LORD has handed them over to Israel." [13] Jonathan climbed up using his hands and feet, with his armor-bearer behind him. Jonathan cut them down, and his armor-bearer followed and finished them off. [14] In that first assault Jonathan and his armor-bearer struck down about 20 men in a half-acre field.

[15] Terror spread through the Philistine camp and the open fields to all the troops. Even the garrison and the raiding parties were terrified. The earth shook, and terror spread from God. [16] When Saul's watchmen in Gibeah of Benjamin looked, they saw the panicking troops scattering in every direction. [17] So Saul said to the troops with him, "Call the roll and determine who has left us." They called the roll and saw that Jonathan and his armor-bearer were gone.

[18] Saul told Ahijah, "Bring the ark of God," for it was with the Israelites at that time. [19] While Saul spoke to the priest, the panic in the Philistine camp increased in intensity. So Saul said to the priest, "Stop what you're doing."

[20] Saul and all the troops with him assembled and marched to the battle, and there, the Philistines were fighting against each other in great confusion! [21] There were Hebrews from the area who had gone earlier into the camp to join the Philistines, but even they joined the Israelites who were with Saul and Jonathan. [22] When all the Israelite men who had been hiding in the hill country of Ephraim heard that the Philistines were fleeing, they also joined Saul and Jonathan in the battle. [23] So the LORD saved Israel that day.

The battle extended beyond Beth-aven, [24] and the men of Israel were worn out that day, for Saul had placed the troops under an oath: "The man who eats food before evening, before I have taken vengeance on my enemies is cursed." So none of the troops tasted any food.

[25] Everyone went into the forest, and there was honey on the ground. [26] When the troops entered the forest, they saw the flow of honey, but none of them ate any of it because they feared the oath. [27] However, Jonathan had not heard his father make the troops swear the oath. He reached out with the end of the staff he was carrying and dipped it into the honeycomb. When he ate the honey, he had renewed energy. [28] Then, one of the troops said, "Your father made the troops solemnly swear, 'The man who eats food today is cursed,' and the troops are exhausted."

[29] Jonathan replied, "My father has brought trouble to the land. Just look at how I have renewed energy because I tasted a little honey. [30] How much better if the troops had eaten freely today from the plunder they took from their enemies! Then the slaughter of the Philistines would have been much greater."

[31] The Israelites struck down the Philistines that day from Michmash all the way to Aijalon. Since the Israelites were completely exhausted, [32] they rushed to the plunder, took sheep, cattle, and calves, slaughtered them on the ground, and ate meat with the blood still in it. [33] Some reported to Saul: "Look, the troops are sinning against the LORD by eating meat with the blood still in it."

Saul said, "You have been unfaithful. Roll a large stone over here at once." [34] He then said, "Go among the troops and say to them, 'Each man must bring me his ox or his sheep. Do the slaughtering here and then you can eat. Don't sin against the LORD by eating meat with the blood in it.'" So every one of the troops brought his ox that night and slaughtered it there. [35] Then Saul built an altar to the LORD; it was the first time he had built an altar to the LORD.

[36] Saul said, "Let's go down after the Philistines tonight and plunder them until morning. Don't let even one remain!"

"Do whatever you want," the troops replied.

But the priest said, "We must consult God here."

[37] So Saul inquired of God, "Should I go after the Philistines? Will You hand them over to Israel?" But God did not answer him that day.

[38] Saul said, "All you leaders of the troops, come here. Let us investigate how this sin has occurred today. [39] As surely as the LORD lives who saves Israel, even if it is because of my son Jonathan, he must die!" Not one of the troops answered him.

[40] So he said to all Israel, "You will be on one side, and I and my son Jonathan will be on the other side."

And the troops replied, "Do whatever you want."

[41] So Saul said to the LORD, "God of Israel, give us the right decision." Jonathan and Saul were selected, and the troops were cleared of the charge.

[42] Then Saul said, "Cast the lot between me and my son Jonathan," and Jonathan was selected. [43] Saul commanded him, "Tell me what you did."

Jonathan told him, "I tasted a little honey with the end of the staff I was carrying. I am ready to die!"

[44] Saul declared to him, "May God punish me and do so severely if you do not die, Jonathan!"

[45] But the people said to Saul, "Must Jonathan die, who accomplished such a great deliverance for Israel? No, as the LORD lives, not a hair of his head will fall to the ground, for he worked with God's help today." So the people redeemed Jonathan, and he did not die.

[46] Then Saul gave up the pursuit of the Philistines, and the Philistines returned to their own territory.

[47] When Saul assumed the kingship over Israel, he fought against all his enemies in every direction: against Moab, the Ammonites, Edom, the kings of Zobah, and the Philistines. Wherever he turned, he caused havoc. [48] He fought bravely, defeated the Amalekites, and delivered Israel from the hand of those who plundered them.

[49] Saul's sons were Jonathan, Ishvi, and Malchishua. The names of his two daughters were: Merab, his firstborn, and Michal, the younger. [50] The name of Saul's wife was Ahinoam daughter of Ahimaaz. The name of the commander of his army was Abner son of Saul's

uncle Ner. [51] Saul's father was Kish. Abner's father was Ner son of Abiel.

[52] The conflict with the Philistines was fierce all of Saul's days, so whenever Saul noticed any strong or brave man, he enlisted him.

15 Samuel told Saul, "The LORD sent me to anoint you as king over His people Israel. Now, listen to the words of the LORD. [2] This is what the LORD of 'Hosts says: 'I witnessed what the Amalekites did to the Israelites when they opposed them along the way as they were coming out of Egypt. [3] Now go and attack the Amalekites and 'completely destroy everything they have. Do not spare them. Kill men and women, children and infants, oxen and sheep, camels and donkeys.'"

[4] Then Saul summoned the troops and counted them at Telaim: 200,000 foot soldiers and 10,000 men from Judah. [5] Saul came to the city of Amalek and set up an ambush in the 'wadi. [6] He warned the Kenites, "Since you showed kindness to all the Israelites when they came out of Egypt, go on and leave! Get away from the Amalekites, or I'll sweep you away with them." So the Kenites withdrew from the Amalekites.

[7] Then Saul struck down the Amalekites from Havilah all the way to Shur, which is next to Egypt. [8] He captured Agag king of Amalek alive, but he completely destroyed all the rest of the people with the sword. [9] Saul and the troops spared Agag, and the best of the sheep, cattle, and choice animals, as well as the young rams and the best of everything else. They were not willing to destroy them, but they did destroy all the worthless and unwanted things.

[10] Then the word of the LORD came to Samuel, [11] "I regret that I made Saul king, for he has turned away from following Me and has not carried out My instructions." So Samuel became angry and cried out to the LORD all night.

[12] Early in the morning Samuel got up to confront Saul, but it was reported to Samuel, "Saul went to Carmel where he set up a monument for himself. Then he turned around and went down to Gilgal." [13] When Samuel came to him, Saul said, "May the LORD bless you. I have carried out the LORD's instructions."

[14] Samuel replied, "Then what is this sound of sheep and cattle I hear?"

[15] Saul answered, "The troops brought them from the Amalekites and spared the best sheep and cattle in order to offer a sacrifice to the LORD your God, but the rest we destroyed."

[16] "Stop!" exclaimed Samuel. "Let me tell you what the LORD said to me last night."

"Tell me," he replied.

[17] Samuel continued, "Although you once considered yourself unimportant, have you not become the leader of the tribes of Israel? The LORD anointed you king over Israel [18] and then sent you on a mission and said: 'Go and completely destroy the sinful Amalekites. Fight against them until you have annihilated them.' [19] So why didn't you obey the LORD? Why did you rush on the plunder and do what was evil in the LORD's sight?"

[20] "But I did obey the LORD!" Saul answered. "I went on the mission the LORD gave me: I brought back Agag, king of Amalek, and I completely destroyed the Amalekites. [21] The troops took sheep and cattle from the plunder—the best of what was 'set apart for destruction—to sacrifice to the LORD your God at Gilgal."

[22] Then Samuel said:

Does the LORD take pleasure
  in 'burnt offerings and sacrifices
as much as in obeying the LORD?
Look: to obey is better than sacrifice,
  to pay attention is better than the fat of rams.
[23] For rebellion is like the sin of 'divination,
  and defiance is like wickedness and idolatry.
Because you have rejected the word
  of the LORD,
He has rejected you as king.

[24] Saul answered Samuel, "I have sinned. I have transgressed the LORD's command and your words. Because I was afraid of the people, I obeyed them. [25] Now therefore, please forgive my sin and return with me so I can worship the LORD."

[26] Samuel replied to Saul, "I will not return with you. Because you rejected the word of the LORD, the LORD has rejected you from being king over Israel." [27] When Samuel turned to go, Saul grabbed the hem of his robe, and it tore. [28] Samuel said to him, "The LORD has torn the kingship of Israel away from you today and has given it to your neighbor who is better than you. [29] Furthermore, the Eternal One of Israel does not lie or change His mind, for He is not man who changes his mind."

[30] Saul said, "I have sinned. Please honor me now before the elders of my people and before Israel. Come back with me so I can bow in worship to the LORD your God." [31] Then Samuel went back, following Saul, and Saul bowed down to the LORD.

[32] Samuel said, "Bring me Agag king of Amalek."

Agag came to him trembling, for he thought, "Certainly the bitterness of death has come."

[33] Samuel declared:

As your sword has made women childless,
  so your mother will be childless
    among women.

Then he hacked Agag to pieces before the LORD at Gilgal.

[34] Samuel went to Ramah, and Saul went up to his home in Gibeah of Saul. [35] Even to the day of his death, Samuel never again visited Saul. Samuel mourned for Saul, and the LORD regretted He had made Saul king over Israel.

16 The LORD said to Samuel, "How long are you going to mourn for Saul, since I have rejected him as king over Israel? Fill your horn with oil and go. I am sending you to Jesse of Bethlehem because I have selected a king from his sons."

[2] Samuel asked, "How can I go? Saul will hear about it and kill me!"

The LORD answered, "Take a young cow with you and say, 'I have come to sacrifice to the LORD.' [3] Then invite Jesse to the sacrifice, and I will let you know what you are to do. You are to anoint for Me the one I indicate to you."

[4] Samuel did what the LORD directed and went to Bethlehem. When the elders of the town met him, they trembled and asked, "Do you come in peace?"

[5] "In peace," he replied. "I've come to sacrifice to the LORD. Consecrate yourselves and come with me to the sacrifice." Then he consecrated Jesse and his sons and invited them to the sacrifice. [6] When they arrived, Samuel saw Eliab and said, "Certainly the LORD's anointed one is here before Him."

[7] But the LORD said to Samuel, "Do not look at his

appearance or his stature, because I have rejected him. Man does not see what the LORD sees, for man sees what is visible, but the LORD sees the heart."

⁸ Jesse called Abinadab and presented him to Samuel. "The LORD hasn't chosen this one either," Samuel said. ⁹ Then Jesse presented Shammah, but Samuel said, "The LORD hasn't chosen this one either." ¹⁰ After Jesse presented seven of his sons to him, Samuel told Jesse, "The LORD hasn't chosen any of these." ¹¹ Samuel asked him, "Are these all the sons you have?"

"There is still the youngest," he answered, "but right now he's tending the sheep." Samuel told Jesse, "Send for him. We won't sit down to eat until he gets here." ¹² So Jesse sent for him. He had beautiful eyes and a healthy, handsome appearance.

Then the LORD said, "Anoint him, for he is the one." ¹³ So Samuel took the horn of oil, anointed him in the presence of his brothers, and the Spirit of the LORD took control of David from that day forward. Then Samuel set out and went to Ramah.

¹⁴ Now the Spirit of the LORD had left Saul, and an evil spirit sent from the LORD began to torment him, ¹⁵ so Saul's servants said to him, "You see that an evil spirit from God is tormenting you. ¹⁶ Let our lord command your servants here in your presence to look for someone who knows how to play the lyre. Whenever the evil spirit from God troubles you, that person can play the lyre, and you will feel better."

¹⁷ Then Saul commanded his servants, "Find me someone who plays well and bring him to me."

¹⁸ One of the young men answered, "I have seen a son of Jesse of Bethlehem who knows how to play the lyre. He is also a valiant man, a warrior, eloquent, handsome, and the LORD is with him."

¹⁹ Then Saul dispatched messengers to Jesse and said, "Send me your son David, who is with the sheep." ²⁰ So Jesse took a donkey loaded with bread, a skin of wine, and one young goat and sent them by his son David to Saul. ²¹ When David came to Saul and entered his service, Saul admired him greatly, and David became his armor-bearer. ²² Then Saul sent word to Jesse: "Let David remain in my service, for I am pleased with him." ²³ Whenever the spirit from God troubled Saul, David would pick up his lyre and play, and Saul would then be relieved, feel better, and the evil spirit would leave him.

17 The Philistines gathered their forces for war at Socoh in Judah and camped between Socoh and Azekah in Ephes-dammim. ² Saul and the men of Israel gathered and camped in the Valley of Elah; then they lined up in battle formation to face the Philistines.

³ The Philistines were standing on one hill, and the Israelites were standing on another hill with a ravine between them. ⁴ Then a champion named Goliath, from Gath, came out from the Philistine camp. He was nine feet, nine inches tall ⁵ and wore a bronze helmet and bronze scale armor that weighed 125 pounds. ⁶ There was bronze armor on his shins, and a bronze sword was slung between his shoulders. ⁷ His spear shaft was like a weaver's beam, and the iron point of his spear weighed 15 pounds. In addition, a shield-bearer was walking in front of him.

⁸ He stood and shouted to the Israelite battle formations: "Why do you come out to line up in battle formation?" He asked them, "Am I not a Philistine and are you not servants of Saul? Choose one of your men and have him come down against me. ⁹ If he wins in a

fight against me and kills me, we will be your servants. But if I win against him and kill him, then you will be our servants and serve us." ¹⁰ Then the Philistine said, "I defy the ranks of Israel today. Send me a man so we can fight each other!" ¹¹ When Saul and all Israel heard these words from the Philistine, they lost their courage and were terrified.

¹² Now David was the son of the Ephrathite from Bethlehem of Judah named Jesse. Jesse had eight sons and during Saul's reign was already an old man. ¹³ Jesse's three oldest sons had followed Saul to the war, and their names were Eliab, the firstborn, Abinadab, the next, and Shammah, the third, ¹⁴ and David was the youngest. The three oldest had followed Saul, ¹⁵ but David kept going back and forth from Saul to tend his father's flock in Bethlehem.

¹⁶ Every morning and evening for 40 days the Philistine came forward and took his stand. ¹⁷ One day Jesse had told his son David: "Take this half-bushel of roasted grain along with these 10 loaves of bread for your brothers and hurry to their camp. ¹⁸ Also take these 10 portions of cheese to the field commander. Check on the welfare of your brothers and bring a confirmation from them. ¹⁹ They are with Saul and all the men of Israel in the Valley of Elah fighting with the Philistines."

²⁰ So David got up early in the morning, left the flock with someone to keep it, loaded up, and set out as Jesse had instructed him.

He arrived at the perimeter of the camp as the army was marching out to its battle formation shouting their battle cry. ²¹ Israel and the Philistines lined up in battle formation facing each other. ²² David left his supplies in the care of the quartermaster and ran to the battle line. When he arrived, he asked his brothers how they were. ²³ While he was speaking with them, suddenly the champion named Goliath, the Philistine from Gath, came forward from the Philistine battle line and shouted his usual words, which David heard. ²⁴ When all the Israelite men saw Goliath, they retreated from him terrified.

²⁵ Previously, an Israelite man had declared: "Do you see this man who keeps coming out? He comes to defy Israel. The king will make the man who kills him very rich and will give him his daughter. The king will also make the household of that man's father exempt from paying taxes in Israel."

²⁶ David spoke to the men who were standing with him: "What will be done for the man who kills this Philistine and removes this disgrace from Israel? Just who is this uncircumcised Philistine that he should defy the armies of the living God?"

²⁷ The people told him about the offer, concluding, "That is what will be done for the man who kills him."

²⁸ David's oldest brother Eliab listened as he spoke to the men, and became angry with him. "Why did you come down here?" he asked. "Who did you leave those few sheep with in the wilderness? I know your arrogance and your evil heart—you came down to see the battle!"

²⁹ "What have I done now?" protested David. "It was just a question." ³⁰ Then he turned from those beside him to others in front of him and asked about the offer. The people gave him the same answer as before.

³¹ What David said was overheard and reported to Saul, so he had David brought to him. ³² David said to Saul, "Don't let anyone be discouraged by him; your servant will go and fight this Philistine!"

³³But Saul replied, "You can't go fight this Philistine. You're just a youth, and he's been a warrior since he was young."

³⁴David answered Saul: "Your servant has been tending his father's sheep. Whenever a lion or a bear came and carried off a lamb from the flock, ³⁵I went after it, struck it down, and rescued the lamb from its mouth. If it reared up against me, I would grab it by its fur, strike it down, and kill it. ³⁶Your servant has killed lions and bears; this uncircumcised Philistine will be like one of them, for he has defied the armies of the living God." ³⁷Then David said, "The LORD who rescued me from the paw of the lion and the paw of the bear will rescue me from the hand of this Philistine."

Saul said to David, "Go, and may the LORD be with you."

³⁸Then Saul had his own military clothes put on David. He put a bronze helmet on David's head and had him put on armor. ³⁹David strapped his sword on over the military clothes and tried to walk, but he was not used to them. "I can't walk in these," David said to Saul, "I'm not used to them." So David took them off. ⁴⁰Instead, he took his staff in his hand and chose five smooth stones from the ˙wadi and put them in the pouch, in his shepherd's bag. Then, with his sling in his hand, he approached the Philistine.

⁴¹The Philistine came closer and closer to David, with the shield-bearer in front of him. ⁴²When the Philistine looked and saw David, he despised him because he was just a youth, healthy and handsome. ⁴³He said to David, "Am I a dog that you come against me with sticks?" Then he cursed David by his gods. ⁴⁴"Come here," the Philistine called to David, "and I'll give your flesh to the birds of the sky and the wild beasts!"

⁴⁵David said to the Philistine: "You come against me with a dagger, spear, and sword, but I come against you in the name of ˙Yahweh of ˙Hosts, the God of Israel's armies—you have defied Him. ⁴⁶Today, the LORD will hand you over to me. Today, I'll strike you down, cut your head off, and give the corpses of the Philistine camp to the birds of the sky and the creatures of the earth. Then all the world will know that Israel has a God, ⁴⁷and this whole assembly will know that it is not by sword or by spear that the LORD saves, for the battle is the LORD's. He will hand you over to us."

⁴⁸When the Philistine started forward to attack him, David ran quickly to the battle line to meet the Philistine. ⁴⁹David put his hand in the bag, took out a stone, slung it, and hit the Philistine on his forehead. The stone sank into his forehead, and he fell on his face to the ground. ⁵⁰David defeated the Philistine with a sling and a stone. Even though David had no sword, he struck down the Philistine and killed him. ⁵¹David ran and stood over him. He grabbed the Philistine's sword, pulled it from its sheath, and used it to kill him. Then he cut off his head. When the Philistines saw that their hero was dead, they ran. ⁵²The men of Israel and Judah rallied, shouting their battle cry, and chased the Philistines to the entrance of the valley and to the gates of Ekron. Philistine bodies were strewn all along the Shaaraim road to Gath and Ekron.

⁵³When the Israelites returned from the pursuit of the Philistines, they plundered their camps. ⁵⁴David took Goliath's head and brought it to Jerusalem, but he put Goliath's weapons in his own tent.

⁵⁵When Saul had seen David going out to confront the Philistine, he asked Abner the commander of the army, "Whose son is this youth, Abner?"

"My king, as surely as you live, I don't know," Abner replied.

⁵⁶The king said, "Find out whose son this young man is!"

⁵⁷When David returned from killing the Philistine, Abner took him and brought him before Saul with the Philistine's head still in his hand. ⁵⁸Saul said to him, "Whose son are you, young man?"

"The son of your servant Jesse of Bethlehem," David answered.

18 When David had finished speaking with Saul, Jonathan committed himself to David, and loved him as much as he loved himself. ²Saul kept David with him from that day on and did not let him return to his father's house.

³Jonathan made a covenant with David because he loved him as much as himself. ⁴Then Jonathan removed the robe he was wearing and gave it to David, along with his military tunic, his sword, his bow, and his belt.

⁵David marched out with the army and was successful in everything Saul sent him to do. Saul put him in command of the soldiers, which pleased all the people and Saul's servants as well.

⁶As the troops were coming back, when David was returning from killing the Philistine, the women came out from all the cities of Israel to meet King Saul, singing and dancing with tambourines, with shouts of joy, and with three-stringed instruments. ⁷As they celebrated, the women sang:

Saul has killed his thousands,
but David his tens of thousands.

⁸Saul was furious and resented this song. "They credited tens of thousands to David," he complained, "but they only credited me with thousands. What more can he have but the kingdom?" ⁹So Saul watched David jealously from that day forward.

¹⁰The next day an evil spirit sent from God took control of Saul, and he began to rave inside the palace. David was playing the lyre as usual, but Saul was holding a spear, ¹¹and he threw it, thinking, "I'll pin David to the wall." But David got away from him twice.

¹²Saul was afraid of David, because the LORD was with David but had left Saul. ¹³Therefore, Saul reassigned David and made him commander over 1,000 men. David led the troops ¹⁴and continued to be successful in all his activities because the LORD was with him. ¹⁵When Saul observed that David was very successful, he dreaded him. ¹⁶But all Israel and Judah loved David because he was leading their troops. ¹⁷Saul told David, "Here is my oldest daughter Merab. I'll give her to you as a wife, if you will be a warrior for me and fight the LORD's battles." But Saul was thinking, "My hand doesn't need to be against him; let the hand of the Philistines be against him."

¹⁸Then David responded, "Who am I, and what is my family or my father's clan in Israel that I should become the king's son-in-law?" ¹⁹When it was time to give Saul's daughter Merab to David, she was given to Adriel the Meholathite as a wife.

²⁰Now Saul's daughter Michal loved David, and when it was reported to Saul, it pleased him. ²¹"I'll give her to him," Saul thought. "She'll be a trap for him, and the hand of the Philistines will be against him."

So Saul said to David a second time, "You can now be my son-in-law."

²²Saul then ordered his servants, "Speak to David in private and tell him, 'Look, the king is pleased with you, and all his servants love you. Therefore, you should become the king's son-in-law.'"

²³Saul's servants reported these words directly to David, but he replied, "Is it trivial in your sight to become the king's son-in-law? I am a poor man who is common."

²⁴The servants reported back to Saul, "These are the words David spoke."

²⁵Then Saul replied, "Say this to David: 'The king desires no other bride-price except 100 Philistine foreskins, to take revenge on his enemies.'" Actually, Saul intended to cause David's death at the hands of the Philistines.

²⁶When the servants reported these terms to David, he was pleased to become the king's son-in-law. Before the wedding day arrived, ²⁷David and his men went out and killed 200 Philistines. He brought their foreskins and presented them as full payment to the king to become his son-in-law. Then Saul gave his daughter Michal to David as his wife. ²⁸Saul realized that the LORD was with David and that his daughter Michal loved him, ²⁹and he became even more afraid of David. As a result, Saul was David's enemy from then on.

³⁰Every time the Philistine commanders came out to fight, David was more successful than all of Saul's officers. So his name became well known.

19 Saul ordered his son Jonathan and all his servants to kill David. But Saul's son Jonathan liked David very much, ²so he told him: "My father Saul intends to kill you. Be on your guard in the morning and hide in a secret place and stay there. ³I'll go out and stand beside my father in the field where you are and talk to him about you. When I see what he says, I'll tell you."

⁴Jonathan spoke well of David to his father Saul. He said to him: "The king should not sin against his servant David. He hasn't sinned against you; in fact, his actions have been a great advantage to you. ⁵He took his life in his hands when he struck down the Philistine, and the LORD brought about a great victory for all Israel. You saw it and rejoiced, so why would you sin against innocent blood by killing David for no reason?"

⁶Saul listened to Jonathan's advice and swore an oath: "As surely as the LORD lives, David will not be killed." ⁷So Jonathan summoned David and told him all these words. Then Jonathan brought David to Saul, and he served him as he did before.

⁸When war broke out again, David went out and fought against the Philistines. He defeated them with such a great force that they fled from him.

⁹Now an evil spirit sent from the LORD came on Saul as he was sitting in his palace holding a spear. David was playing the lyre, ¹⁰and Saul tried to pin David to the wall with the spear. As the spear struck the wall, David eluded Saul, ran away, and escaped that night. ¹¹Saul sent agents to David's house to watch for him and kill him in the morning. But his wife Michal warned David, "If you don't escape tonight, you will be dead tomorrow!" ¹²So she lowered David from the window, and he fled and escaped. ¹³Then Michal took the household idol and put it on the bed, placed some goat hair on its head, and covered it with a garment.

¹⁴When Saul sent agents to seize David, Michal said, "He's sick."

¹⁵Saul sent the agents back to see David and said, "Bring him on his bed so I can kill him." ¹⁶When the messengers arrived, to their surprise, the household idol was on the bed with some goat hair on its head.

¹⁷Saul asked Michal, "Why did you deceive me like this? You sent my enemy away, and he has escaped!"

She answered him, "He said to me, 'Let me go! Why should I kill you?'"

¹⁸So David fled and escaped and went to Samuel at Ramah and told him everything Saul had done to him. Then he and Samuel left and stayed at Naioth.

¹⁹When it was reported to Saul that David was at Naioth in Ramah, ²⁰he sent agents to seize David. However, when they saw the group of prophets prophesying with Samuel leading them, the Spirit of God came on Saul's agents, and they also started prophesying. ²¹When they reported to Saul, he sent other agents, and they also began prophesying. So Saul tried again and sent a third group of agents, and even they began prophesying. ²²Then Saul himself went to Ramah. He came to the large cistern at Secu, looked around, and asked, "Where are Samuel and David?"

"At Naioth in Ramah," someone said.

²³So he went to Naioth in Ramah. The Spirit of God also came on him, and as he walked along, he prophesied until he entered Naioth in Ramah. ²⁴Saul then removed his clothes and also prophesied before Samuel; he collapsed and lay naked all that day and all that night. That is why they say, "Is Saul also among the prophets?"

20 David fled from Naioth in Ramah and came to Jonathan and asked, "What have I done? What did I do wrong? How have I sinned against your father so that he wants to take my life?"

²Jonathan said to him, "No, you won't die. Listen, my father doesn't do anything, great or small, without telling me. So why would he hide this matter from me? This can't be true."

³But David said, "Your father certainly knows that you have come to look favorably on me. He has said, 'Jonathan must not know of this, or else he will be grieved.'" David also swore, "As surely as the LORD lives and as you yourself live, there is but a step between me and death."

⁴Jonathan said to David, "Whatever you say, I will do for you."

⁵So David told him, "Look, tomorrow is the New Moon, and I'm supposed to sit down and eat with the king. Instead, let me go, and I'll hide in the field until the third night. ⁶If your father misses me at all, say, 'David urgently requested my permission to quickly go to his town Bethlehem for an annual sacrifice there involving the whole clan.' ⁷If he says, 'Good,' then your servant is safe, but if he becomes angry, you will know he has evil intentions. ⁸Deal faithfully with your servant, for you have brought me into a covenant with you before the LORD. If I have done anything wrong, then kill me yourself; why take me to your father?"

⁹"No!" Jonathan responded. "If I ever find out my father has evil intentions against you, wouldn't I tell you about it?"

¹⁰So David asked Jonathan, "Who will tell me if your father answers you harshly?"

¹¹He answered David, "Come on, let's go out to the field." So both of them went out to the field. ¹²"By the

LORD, the God of Israel, I will sound out my father by this time tomorrow or the next day. If I find out that he is favorable toward you, will I not send for you and tell you? [13] If my father intends to bring evil on you, may God punish Jonathan and do so severely if I do not tell you and send you away so you may go in peace. May the LORD be with you, just as He was with my father. [14] If I continue to live, treat me with the LORD's faithful love, but if I die, [15] don't ever withdraw your faithful love from my household—not even when the LORD cuts off every one of David's enemies from the face of the earth." [16] Then Jonathan made a covenant with the house of David, saying, "May the LORD hold David's enemies accountable." [17] Jonathan once again swore to David in his love for him, because he loved him as he loved himself.

[18] Then Jonathan said to him, "Tomorrow is the New Moon; you'll be missed because your seat will be empty. [19] The following day hurry down and go to the place where you hid on the day this incident began and stay beside the rock Ezel. [20] I will shoot three arrows beside it as if I'm aiming at a target. [21] Then I will send the young man and say, 'Go and find the arrows!' Now, if I expressly say to the young man, 'Look, the arrows are on this side of you—get them,' then come, because as the LORD lives, it is safe for you and there is no problem. [22] But if I say this to the youth: 'Look, the arrows are beyond you!' then go, for the LORD is sending you away. [23] As for the matter you and I have spoken about, the LORD will be a witness between you and me forever." [24] So David hid in the field.

At the New Moon, the king sat down to eat the meal. [25] He sat at his usual place on the seat by the wall. Jonathan sat facing him and Abner took his place beside Saul, but David's place was empty. [26] Saul did not say anything that day because he thought, "Something unexpected has happened; he must be ceremonially ·unclean—yes, that's it, he is unclean."

[27] However, the day after the New Moon, the second day, David's place was still empty, and Saul asked his son Jonathan, "Why didn't Jesse's son come to the meal either yesterday or today?"

[28] Jonathan answered, "David asked for my permission to go to Bethlehem. [29] He said, 'Please let me go because our clan is holding a sacrifice in the town, and my brother has told me to be there. So now, if you are pleased with me, let me go so I can see my brothers.' That's why he didn't come to the king's table."

[30] Then Saul became angry with Jonathan and shouted, "You son of a perverse and rebellious woman! Don't I know that you are siding with Jesse's son to your own shame and to the disgrace of your mother? [31] Every day Jesse's son lives on earth you and your kingship are not secure. Now send for him and bring him to me—he deserves to die."

[32] Jonathan answered his father back: "Why is he to be killed? What has he done?"

[33] Then Saul threw his spear at Jonathan to kill him, so he knew that his father was determined to kill David. [34] He got up from the table in fierce anger and did not eat any food that second day of the New Moon, for he was grieved because of his father's shameful behavior toward David.

[35] In the morning Jonathan went out to the field for the appointed meeting with David. A small young man was with him. [36] He said to the young man, "Run and find the arrows I'm shooting." As the young man ran,

Jonathan shot an arrow beyond him. [37] He came to the location of the arrow that Jonathan had shot, but Jonathan called to him and said, "The arrow is beyond you, isn't it?" [38] Then Jonathan called to him, "Hurry up and don't stop!" Jonathan's young man picked up the arrow and returned to his master. [39] He did not know anything; only Jonathan and David knew the arrangement. [40] Then Jonathan gave his equipment to the young man who was with him and said, "Go, take it back to the city."

[41] When the young man had gone, David got up from the south side of the stone Ezel, fell with his face to the ground, and bowed three times. Then he and Jonathan kissed each other and wept with each other, though David wept more.

[42] Jonathan then said to David, "Go in the assurance the two of us pledged in the name of the LORD when we said: The LORD will be a witness between you and me and between my offspring and your offspring forever." Then David left, and Jonathan went into the city.

21 David went to Ahimelech the priest at Nob. Ahimelech was afraid to meet David, so he said to him, "Why are you alone and no one is with you?"

[2] David answered Ahimelech the priest, "The king gave me a mission, but he told me, 'Don't let anyone know anything about the mission I'm sending you on or what I have ordered you to do.' I have stationed my young men at a certain place. [3] Now what do you have on hand? Give me five loaves of bread or whatever can be found."

[4] The priest told him, "There is no ordinary bread on hand. However, there is consecrated bread, but the young men may eat it only if they have kept themselves from women."

[5] David answered him, "I swear that women are being kept from us, as always when I go out to battle. The young men's bodies are consecrated even on an ordinary mission, so of course their bodies are consecrated today." [6] So the priest gave him the consecrated bread, for there was no bread there except the ·bread of the Presence that had been removed from the presence of the LORD. When the bread was removed, it had been replaced with warm bread.

[7] One of Saul's servants, detained before the LORD, was there that day. His name was Doeg the Edomite, chief of Saul's shepherds.

[8] David said to Ahimelech, "Do you have a spear or sword on hand? I didn't even bring my sword or my weapons since the king's mission was urgent."

[9] The priest replied, "The sword of Goliath the Philistine, whom you killed in the Valley of Elah, is here, wrapped in a cloth behind the ·ephod. If you want to take it for yourself, then take it, for there isn't another one here."

"There's none like it!" David said. "Give it to me."

[10] David fled that day from Saul's presence and went to King Achish of Gath. [11] But Achish's servants said to him, "Isn't this David, the king of the land? Don't they sing about him during their dances:

Saul has killed his thousands,
but David his tens of thousands?"

[12] David took this to heart and became very afraid of King Achish of Gath, [13] so he pretended to be insane in their presence. He acted like a madman around them, scribbling on the doors of the gate and letting saliva run down his beard.

[14] "Look! You can see the man is crazy," Achish said

to his servants. "Why did you bring him to me? [15] Do I have such a shortage of crazy people that you brought this one to act crazy around me? Is this one going to come into my house?"

22 So David left Gath and took refuge in the cave of Adullam. When David's brothers and his father's whole family heard, they went down and joined him there. [2] In addition, every man who was desperate, in debt, or discontented rallied around him, and he became their leader. About 400 men were with him.

[3] From there David went to Mizpeh of Moab where he said to the king of Moab, "Please let my father and mother stay with you until I know what God will do for me." [4] So he left them in the care of the king of Moab, and they stayed with him the whole time David was in the stronghold.

[5] Then the prophet Gad said to David, "Don't stay in the stronghold. Leave and return to the land of Judah." So David left and went to the forest of Hereth.

[6] Saul heard that David and his men had been discovered. At that time Saul was in Gibeah, sitting under the tamarisk tree at the *high place. His spear was in his hand, and all his servants were standing around him. [7] Saul said to his servants, "Listen, men of Benjamin: Is Jesse's son going to give all of you fields and vineyards? Do you think he'll make all of you commanders of thousands and commanders of hundreds? [8] That's why all of you have conspired against me! Nobody tells me when my own son makes a covenant with Jesse's son. None of you cares about me or tells me that my son has stirred up my own servant to wait in ambush for me, as is the case today."

[9] Then Doeg the Edomite, who was in charge of Saul's servants, answered: "I saw Jesse's son come to Ahimelech son of Ahitub at Nob. [10] Ahimelech inquired of the LORD for him and gave him provisions. He also gave him the sword of Goliath the Philistine."

[11] The king sent messengers to summon Ahimelech the priest, son of Ahitub, and his father's whole family, who were priests in Nob. All of them came to the king. [12] Then Saul said, "Listen, son of Ahitub!"

"I'm at your service, my lord," he said.

[13] Saul asked him, "Why did you and Jesse's son conspire against me? You gave him bread and a sword and inquired of God for him, so he could rise up against me and wait in ambush, as is the case today."

[14] Ahimelech replied to the king: "Who among all your servants is as faithful as David? He is the king's son-in-law, captain of your bodyguard, and honored in your house. [15] Was today the first time I inquired of God for him? Of course not! Please don't let the king make an accusation against your servant or any of my father's household, for your servant didn't have any idea about all this."

[16] But the king said, "You will die, Ahimelech—you and your father's whole family!"

[17] Then the king ordered the guards standing by him, "Turn and kill the priests of the LORD because they sided with David. For they knew he was fleeing, but they didn't tell me." But the king's servants would not lift a hand to execute the priests of the LORD.

[18] So the king said to Doeg, "Go and execute the priests!" So Doeg the Edomite went and executed the priests himself. On that day, he killed 85 men who wore linen *ephods. [19] He also struck down Nob, the city of the priests, with the sword—both men and women, children and infants, oxen, donkeys, and sheep.

[20] However, one of the sons of Ahimelech son of Ahitub escaped. His name was Abiathar, and he fled to David. [21] Abiathar told David that Saul had killed the priests of the LORD. [22] Then David said to Abiathar, "I knew that Doeg the Edomite was there that day and that he was sure to report to Saul. I myself am responsible for the lives of everyone in your father's family. [23] Stay with me. Don't be afraid, for the one who wants to take my life wants to take your life. You will be safe with me."

23 It was reported to David: "Look, the Philistines are fighting against Keilah and raiding the threshing floors."

[2] So David inquired of the LORD: "Should I launch an attack against these Philistines?"

The LORD answered David, "Launch an attack against the Philistines and rescue Keilah."

[3] But David's men said to him, "Look, we're afraid here in Judah; how much more if we go to Keilah against the Philistine forces!"

[4] Once again, David inquired of the LORD, and the LORD answered him: "Go at once to Keilah, for I will hand the Philistines over to you." [5] Then David and his men went to Keilah, fought against the Philistines, drove their livestock away, and inflicted heavy losses on them. So David rescued the inhabitants of Keilah. [6] Abiathar son of Ahimelech fled to David at Keilah, and he brought an *ephod with him.

[7] When it was reported to Saul that David had gone to Keilah, he said, "God has handed him over to me, for he has trapped himself by entering a town with barred gates." [8] Then Saul summoned all the troops to go to war at Keilah and besiege David and his men.

[9] When David learned that Saul was plotting evil against him, he said to Abiathar the priest, "Bring the ephod." [10] Then David said, "LORD God of Israel, Your servant has heard that Saul intends to come to Keilah and destroy the town because of me. [11] Will the citizens of Keilah hand me over to him? Will Saul come down as Your servant has heard? LORD God of Israel, please tell Your servant."

The LORD answered, "He will come down."

[12] Then David asked, "Will the citizens of Keilah hand me and my men over to Saul?"

"They will," the LORD responded.

[13] So David and his men, numbering about 600, left Keilah at once and moved from place to place. When it was reported to Saul that David had escaped from Keilah, he called off the expedition. [14] David then stayed in the wilderness strongholds and in the hill country of the Wilderness of Ziph. Saul searched for him every day, but God did not hand David over to him.

[15] David was in the Wilderness of Ziph in Horesh when he saw that Saul had come out to take his life. [16] Then Saul's son Jonathan came to David in Horesh and encouraged him in his faith in God, [17] saying, "Don't be afraid, for my father Saul will never lay a hand on you. You yourself will be king over Israel, and I'll be your second-in-command. Even my father Saul knows it is true." [18] Then the two of them made a covenant in the LORD's presence. Afterward, David remained in Horesh, while Jonathan went home.

[19] Some Ziphites came up to Saul at Gibeah and said, "David is hiding among us in the strongholds in Horesh on the hill of Hachilah south of Jeshimon.

20 Now, whenever the king wants to come down, let him come down. Our part will be to hand him over to the king."

21 "May you be blessed by the LORD," replied Saul, "for you have taken pity on me. 22 Go and check again. Investigate and watch carefully where he goes and who has seen him there; they tell me he is extremely cunning. 23 Look and find out all the places where he hides. Then come back to me with accurate information, and I'll go with you. If it turns out he really is in the region, I'll search for him among all the clans of Judah." 24 So they went to Ziph ahead of Saul.

Now David and his men were in the wilderness near Maon in the ʿArabah south of Jeshimon, 25 and Saul and his men went to look for him. When David was told about it, he went down to the rock and stayed in the Wilderness of Maon. Saul heard of this and pursued David there.

26 Saul went along one side of the mountain and David and his men went along the other side. Even though David was hurrying to get away from Saul, Saul and his men were closing in on David and his men to capture them. 27 Then a messenger came to Saul saying, "Come quickly, because the Philistines have raided the land!" 28 So Saul broke off his pursuit of David and went to engage the Philistines. Therefore, that place was named the Rock of Separation. 29 From there David went up and stayed in the strongholds of En-gedi.

24 When Saul returned from pursuing the Philistines, he was told, "David is in the wilderness near En-gedi." 2 So Saul took 3,000 of Israel's choice men and went to look for David and his men in front of the Rocks of the Wild Goats. 3 When Saul came to the sheep pens along the road, a cave was there, and he went in to relieve himself. David and his men were staying in the back of the cave, 4 so they said to him, "Look, this is the day the LORD told you about: 'I will hand your enemy over to you so you can do to him whatever you desire.'" Then David got up and secretly cut off the corner of Saul's robe.

5 Afterward, David's conscience bothered him because he had cut off the corner of Saul's robe. 6 He said to his men, "I swear before the LORD: I would never do such a thing to my lord, the LORD's anointed. I will never lift my hand against him, since he is the LORD's anointed." 7 With these words David persuaded his men, and he did not let them rise up against Saul.

Then Saul left the cave and went on his way. 8 After that, David got up, went out of the cave, and called to Saul, "My lord the king!" When Saul looked behind him, David bowed to the ground in homage. 9 David said to Saul, "Why do you listen to the words of people who say, 'Look, David intends to harm you'? 10 You can see with your own eyes that the LORD handed you over to me today in the cave. Someone advised me to kill you, but I took pity on you and said: I won't lift my hand against my lord, since he is the LORD's anointed. 11 See, my father! Look at the corner of your robe in my hand, for I cut it off, but I didn't kill you. Look and recognize that there is no evil or rebellion in me. I haven't sinned against you even though you are hunting me down to take my life.

12 "May the LORD judge between you and me, and may the LORD take vengeance on you for me, but my hand will never be against you. 13 As the old proverb says, 'Wickedness comes from wicked people.' My

hand will never be against you. 14 Who has the king of Israel come after? What are you chasing after? A dead dog? A flea? 15 May the LORD be judge and decide between you and me. May He take notice and plead my case and deliver me from you."

16 When David finished saying these things to him, Saul replied, "Is that your voice, David my son?" Then Saul wept aloud 17 and said to David, "You are more righteous than I, for you have done what is good to me though I have done what is evil to you. 18 You yourself have told me today what good you did for me: when the LORD handed me over to you, you didn't kill me. 19 When a man finds his enemy, does he let him go unharmed? May the LORD repay you with good for what you've done for me today.

20 "Now I know for certain you will be king, and the kingdom of Israel will be established in your hand. 21 Therefore swear to me by the LORD that you will not cut off my descendants or wipe out my name from my father's family." 22 So David swore to Saul. Then Saul went back home, and David and his men went up to the stronghold.

25 Samuel died, and all Israel assembled to mourn for him, and they buried him by his home in Ramah. David then went down to the Wilderness of Paran.

2 A man in Maon had a business in Carmel; he was a very rich man with 3,000 sheep and 1,000 goats and was shearing his sheep in Carmel. 3 The man's name was Nabal, and his wife's name, Abigail. The woman was intelligent and beautiful, but the man, a Calebite, was harsh and evil in his dealings.

4 While David was in the wilderness, he heard that Nabal was shearing sheep, 5 so David sent 10 young men instructing them, "Go up to Carmel, and when you come to Nabal, greet him in my name. 6 Then say this: 'Long life to you, and peace to you, to your family, and to all that is yours. 7 I hear that you are shearing. When your shepherds were with us, we did not harass them, and nothing of theirs was missing the whole time they were in Carmel. 8 Ask your young men, and they will tell you. So let my young men find favor with you, for we have come on a feast day. Please give whatever you can afford to your servants and to your son David.'"

9 David's young men went and said all these things to Nabal on David's behalf, and they waited. 10 Nabal asked them, "Who is David? Who is Jesse's son? Many slaves these days are running away from their masters. 11 Am I supposed to take my bread, my water, and my meat that I butchered for my shearers and give them to these men? I don't know where they are from."

12 David's men retraced their steps. When they returned to him, they reported all these words. 13 He said to his men, "All of you, put on your swords!" So David and all his men put on their swords. About 400 men followed David while 200 stayed with the supplies.

14 One of Nabal's young men informed Abigail, Nabal's wife: "Look, David sent messengers from the wilderness to greet our master, but he yelled at them. 15 The men treated us well. When we were in the field, we weren't harassed and nothing of ours was missing the whole time we were living among them. 16 They were a wall around us, both day and night, the entire time we were herding the sheep. 17 Now consider carefully what you must do, because there is certain to be

trouble for our master and his entire family. He is such a worthless fool nobody can talk to him!"

¹⁸Abigail hurried, taking 200 loaves of bread, two skins of wine, five butchered sheep, a bushel of roasted grain, 100 clusters of raisins, and 200 cakes of pressed figs, and loaded them on donkeys. ¹⁹Then she said to her male servants, "Go ahead of me. I will be right behind you." But she did not tell her husband Nabal.

²⁰As she rode the donkey down a mountain pass hidden from view, she saw David and his men coming toward her and met them. ²¹David had just said, "I guarded everything that belonged to this man in the wilderness for nothing. He was not missing anything, yet he paid me back evil for good. ²²May God punish me and do so severely if I let any of his men survive until morning."

²³When Abigail saw David, she quickly got off the donkey and fell with her face to the ground in front of David. ²⁴She fell at his feet and said, "The ˙guilt is mine, my lord, but please let your servant speak to you directly. Listen to the words of your servant. ²⁵My lord should pay no attention to this worthless man Nabal, for he lives up to his name: His name is Nabal, and stupidity is all he knows. I, your servant, didn't see my lord's young men whom you sent. ²⁶Now my lord, as surely as the Lord lives and as you yourself live, it is the Lord who kept you from participating in bloodshed and avenging yourself by your own hand. May your enemies and those who want trouble for my lord be like Nabal. ²⁷Accept this gift your servant has brought to my lord, and let it be given to the young men who follow my lord. ²⁸Please forgive your servant's offense, for the Lord is certain to make a lasting dynasty for my lord because he fights the Lord's battles. Throughout your life, may evil not be found in you.

²⁹"When someone pursues you and attempts to take your life, my lord's life will be tucked safely in the place where the Lord your God protects the living. However, He will fling away your enemies' lives like stones from a sling. ³⁰When the Lord does for my lord all the good He promised and appoints you ruler over Israel, ³¹there will not be remorse or a troubled conscience for my lord because of needless bloodshed or my lord's revenge. And when the Lord does good things for my lord, may you remember me your servant."

³²Then David said to Abigail, "Praise to the Lord God of Israel, who sent you to meet me today! ³³Your discernment is blessed, and you are blessed. Today you kept me from participating in bloodshed and avenging myself by my own hand. ³⁴Otherwise, as surely as the Lord God of Israel lives, who prevented me from harming you, if you had not come quickly to meet me, Nabal wouldn't have had any men left by morning light." ³⁵Then David accepted what she had brought him and said, "Go home in peace. See, I have heard what you said and have granted your request."

³⁶Then Abigail went to Nabal, and there he was in his house, holding a feast fit for a king. Nabal was in a good mood and very drunk, so she didn't say anything to him until morning light.

³⁷In the morning when Nabal sobered up, his wife told him about these events. Then he had a seizure and became paralyzed. ³⁸About 10 days later, the Lord struck Nabal dead.

³⁹When David heard that Nabal was dead, he said, "Praise the Lord who championed my cause against Nabal's insults and restrained His servant from doing evil. The Lord brought Nabal's evil deeds back on his own head."

Then David sent messengers to speak to Abigail about marrying him. ⁴⁰When David's servants came to Abigail at Carmel, they said to her, "David sent us to bring you to him as a wife."

⁴¹She stood up, then bowed her face to the ground and said, "Here I am, your servant, to wash the feet of my lord's servants." ⁴²Then Abigail got up quickly, and with her five female servants accompanying her, rode on the donkey following David's messengers. And so she became his wife.

⁴³David also married Ahinoam of Jezreel, and the two of them became his wives. ⁴⁴But Saul gave his daughter Michal, David's wife, to Palti son of Laish, who was from Gallim.

26 Then the Ziphites came to Saul at Gibeah saying, "David is hiding on the hill of Hachilah opposite Jeshimon." ²So Saul, accompanied by 3,000 of the choice men of Israel, went to the Wilderness of Ziph to search for David there. ³Saul camped beside the road at the hill of Hachilah opposite Jeshimon. David was living in the wilderness and discovered Saul had come there after him. ⁴So David sent out spies and knew for certain that Saul had come. ⁵Immediately, David went to the place where Saul had camped. He saw the place where Saul and Abner son of Ner, the general of his army, were lying down. Saul was lying inside the inner circle of the camp with the troops camped around him. ⁶Then David asked Ahimelech the Hittite and Joab's brother Abishai son of Zeruiah, "Who will go with me into the camp to Saul?"

"I'll go with you," answered Abishai.

⁷That night, David and Abishai came to the troops, and Saul was lying there asleep in the inner circle of the camp with his spear stuck in the ground by his head. Abner and the troops were lying around him. ⁸Then Abishai said to David, "Today God has handed your enemy over to you. Let me thrust the spear through him into the ground just once. I won't have to strike him twice!"

⁹But David said to Abishai, "Don't destroy him, for who can lift a hand against the Lord's anointed and be blameless?" ¹⁰David added, "As the Lord lives, the Lord will certainly strike him down: either his day will come and he will die, or he will go into battle and perish. ¹¹However, because of the Lord, I will never lift my hand against the Lord's anointed. Instead, take the spear and the water jug by his head, and let's go."

¹²So David took the spear and the water jug by Saul's head, and they went their way. No one saw them, no one knew, and no one woke up; they all remained asleep because a deep sleep from the Lord came over them. ¹³David crossed to the other side and stood on top of the mountain at a distance; there was a considerable space between them. ¹⁴Then David shouted to the troops and to Abner son of Ner: "Aren't you going to answer, Abner?"

"Who are you who calls to the king?" Abner asked.

¹⁵David called to Abner, "You're a man, aren't you? Who in Israel is your equal? So why didn't you protect your lord the king when one of the people came to destroy him? ¹⁶What you have done is not good. As the Lord lives, all of you deserve to die since you didn't protect your lord, the Lord's anointed. Now look around; where are the king's spear and water jug that were by his head?"

¹⁷Saul recognized David's voice and asked, "Is that your voice, my son David?"

"It is my voice, my lord and king," David said. ¹⁸Then he continued, "Why is my lord pursuing his servant? What have I done? What evil is in my hand? ¹⁹Now, may my lord the king please hear the words of his servant: If it is the LORD who has incited you against me, then may He accept an offering. But if it is people, may they be cursed in the presence of the LORD, for today they have driven me away from sharing in the inheritance of the LORD saying, 'Go and worship other gods.' ²⁰So don't let my blood fall to the ground far from the LORD's presence, for the king of Israel has come out to search for a flea, like one who pursues a partridge in the mountains."

²¹Saul responded, "I have sinned. Come back, my son David, I will never harm you again because today you considered my life precious. I have been a fool! I've committed a grave error."

²²David answered, "Here is the king's spear; have one of the young men come over and get it. ²³May the LORD repay every man for his righteousness and his loyalty. I wasn't willing to lift my hand against the LORD's anointed, even though the LORD handed you over to me today. ²⁴Just as I considered your life valuable today, so may the LORD consider my life valuable and rescue me from all trouble."

²⁵Saul said to him, "You are blessed, my son David. You will certainly do great things and will also prevail." Then David went on his way, and Saul returned home.

27 David said to himself, "One of these days I'll be swept away by Saul. There is nothing better for me than to escape immediately to the land of the Philistines. Then Saul will stop searching for me everywhere in Israel, and I'll escape from him." ²So David set out with his 600 men and went to Achish son of Maoch, the king of Gath. ³David and his men stayed with Achish in Gath. Each man had his family with him, and David had his two wives: Ahinoam of Jezreel and Abigail of Carmel, Nabal's widow. ⁴When it was reported to Saul that David had fled to Gath, he no longer searched for him.

⁵Now David said to Achish, "If I have found favor with you, let me be given a place in one of the outlying towns, so I can live there. Why should your servant live in the royal city with you?" ⁶That day Achish gave Ziklag to him, and it still belongs to the kings of Judah today. ⁷The time that David stayed in the Philistine territory amounted to a year and four months.

⁸David and his men went up and raided the Geshurites, the Girzites, and the Amalekites. From ancient times they had been the inhabitants of the region through Shur as far as the land of Egypt. ⁹Whenever David attacked the land, he did not leave a single person alive, either man or woman, but he took flocks, herds, donkeys, camels, and clothing. Then he came back to Achish, ¹⁰who inquired, "Where did you raid today?"

David replied, "The south country of Judah," "The south country of the Jerahmeelites," or "Against the south country of the Kenites."

¹¹David did not let a man or woman live to be brought to Gath, for he said, "Or they will inform on us and say, 'This is what David did.'" This was David's custom during the whole time he stayed in the Philistine territory. ¹²So Achish trusted David, thinking,

"Since he has made himself detestable to his people Israel, he will be my servant forever."

28 At that time, the Philistines brought their military units together into one army to fight against Israel. So Achish said to David, "You know, of course, that you and your men must march out in the army with me."

²David replied to Achish, "Good, you will find out what your servant can do."

So Achish said to David, "Very well, I will appoint you as my permanent bodyguard."

³By this time Samuel had died, and all Israel had mourned for him and buried him in Ramah, his city, and Saul had removed the mediums and spiritists from the land. ⁴The Philistines came together and camped at Shunem. So Saul gathered all Israel, and they camped at Gilboa. ⁵When Saul saw the Philistine camp, he was afraid and trembled violently. ⁶He inquired of the LORD, but the LORD did not answer him in dreams or by the ʾUrim or by the prophets. ⁷Saul then said to his servants, "Find me a woman who is a medium, so I can go and consult her."

His servants replied, "There is a woman at En-dor who is a medium."

⁸Saul disguised himself by putting on different clothes and set out with two of his men. They came to the woman at night, and Saul said, "Consult a spirit for me. Bring up for me the one I tell you."

⁹But the woman said to him, "You surely know what Saul has done, how he has killed the mediums and spiritists in the land. Why are you setting a trap for me to get me killed?"

¹⁰Then Saul swore to her by the LORD: "As surely as the LORD lives, nothing bad will happen to you because of this."

¹¹"Who is it that you want me to bring up for you?" the woman asked.

"Bring up Samuel for me," he answered.

¹²When the woman saw Samuel, she screamed, and then she asked Saul, "Why did you deceive me? You are Saul!"

¹³But the king said to her, "Don't be afraid. What do you see?"

"I see a spirit form coming up out of the earth," the woman answered.

¹⁴Then Saul asked her, "What does he look like?"

"An old man is coming up," she replied. "He's wearing a robe." Then Saul knew that it was Samuel, and he bowed his face to the ground and paid homage.

¹⁵"Why have you disturbed me by bringing me up?" Samuel asked Saul.

"I'm in serious trouble," replied Saul. "The Philistines are fighting against me and God has turned away from me. He doesn't answer me anymore, either through the prophets or in dreams. So I've called on you to tell me what I should do."

¹⁶Samuel answered, "Since the LORD has turned away from you and has become your enemy, why are you asking me? ¹⁷The LORD has done exactly what He said through me: The LORD has torn the kingship out of your hand and given it to your neighbor David. ¹⁸You did not obey the LORD and did not carry out His burning anger against Amalek; therefore the LORD has done this to you today. ¹⁹The LORD will also hand Israel over to the Philistines along with you. Tomorrow you and your sons will be with me, and the LORD will hand Israel's army over to the Philistines."

²⁰Immediately, Saul fell flat on the ground. He was terrified by Samuel's words and was also weak because he hadn't had any food all day and all night. ²¹The woman came over to Saul, and she saw that he was terrified and said to him, "Look, your servant has obeyed you. I took my life in my hands and did what you told me to do. ²²Now please listen to your servant. Let me set some food in front of you. Eat and it will give you strength so you can go on your way."

²³He refused, saying, "I won't eat," but when his servants and the woman urged him, he listened to them. He got up off the ground and sat on the bed.

²⁴The woman had a fattened calf at her house, and she quickly slaughtered it. She also took flour, kneaded it, and baked unleavened bread. ²⁵She served it to Saul and his servants, and they ate. Afterward, they got up and left that night.

29 The Philistines brought all their military units together at Aphek while Israel was camped by the spring in Jezreel. ²As the Philistine leaders were passing in review with their units of hundreds and thousands, David and his men were passing in review behind them with Achish. ³Then the Philistine commanders asked, "What are these Hebrews doing here?"

Achish answered the Philistine commanders, "That is David, servant of King Saul of Israel. He has been with me a considerable period of time. From the day he defected until today, I've found no fault with him."

⁴The Philistine commanders, however, were enraged with Achish and told him, "Send that man back and let him return to the place you assigned him. He must not go down with us into battle only to become our adversary during the battle. What better way could he regain his master's favor than with the heads of our men? ⁵Isn't this the David they sing about during their dances:

Saul has killed his thousands,
but David his tens of thousands?"

⁶So Achish summoned David and told him, "As the Lord lives, you are an honorable man. I think it is good to have you working with me in the camp, because I have found no fault in you from the day you came to me until today. But the leaders don't think you are reliable. ⁷Now go back quietly and you won't be doing anything the Philistine leaders think is wrong."

⁸"But what have I done?" David replied to Achish. "From the first day I was with you until today, what have you found against your servant to keep me from going along to fight against the enemies of my lord the king?"

⁹Achish answered David, "I'm convinced that you are as reliable as the Angel of God. But the Philistine commanders have said, 'He must not go into battle with us.' ¹⁰So get up early in the morning, you and your masters' servants who came with you. When you've all gotten up early, go as soon as it's light." ¹¹So David and his men got up early in the morning to return to the land of the Philistines. And the Philistines went up to Jezreel.

30 David and his men arrived in Ziklag on the third day. The Amalekites had raided the •Negev and attacked and burned down Ziklag. ²They also had kidnapped the women and everyone in it from the youngest to the oldest. They had killed no one but had carried them off as they went on their way.

³When David and his men arrived at the town, they found it burned down. Their wives, sons, and daughters had been kidnapped. ⁴David and the troops with him wept loudly until they had no strength left to weep. ⁵David's two wives, Ahinoam the Jezreelite and Abigail the widow of Nabal the Carmelite, had also been kidnapped. ⁶David was in a difficult position because the troops talked about stoning him, for they were all very bitter over the loss of their sons and daughters. But David found strength in the Lord his God.

⁷David said to Abiathar the priest, son of Ahimelech, "Bring me the •ephod." So Abiathar brought it to him, ⁸and David asked the Lord: "Should I pursue these raiders? Will I overtake them?"

The Lord replied to him, "Pursue them, for you will certainly overtake them and rescue the people."

⁹David and the 600 men with him went as far as the •Wadi Besor, where 200 men who were to remain behind would stop. ¹⁰They stopped because they were too exhausted to cross the Wadi Besor. David and 400 of the men continued in pursuit.

¹¹They found an Egyptian in the open country and brought him to David. They gave him some bread to eat and water to drink. ¹²Then they gave him some pressed figs and two clusters of raisins. After he ate he revived, for he hadn't eaten food or drunk water for three days and three nights.

¹³Then David said to him, "Who do you belong to? Where are you from?"

"I'm an Egyptian, the slave of an Amalekite man," he said. "My master abandoned me when I got sick three days ago. ¹⁴We raided the south country of the Cherethites, the territory of Judah, and the south country of Caleb, and we burned down Ziklag."

¹⁵David then asked him, "Will you lead me to these raiders?"

He said, "Swear to me by God that you won't kill me or turn me over to my master, and I will lead you to them."

¹⁶So he led him, and there were the Amalekites, spread out over the entire area, eating, drinking, and celebrating because of the great amount of plunder they had taken from the land of the Philistines and the land of Judah. ¹⁷David slaughtered them from twilight until the evening of the next day. None of them escaped, except 400 young men who got on camels and fled.

¹⁸David recovered everything the Amalekites had taken; he also rescued his two wives. ¹⁹Nothing of theirs was missing from the youngest to the oldest, including the sons and daughters, of all the plunder the Amalekites had taken. David got everything back. ²⁰He took all the sheep and cattle, which were driven ahead of the other livestock, and the people shouted, "This is David's plunder!"

²¹When David came to the 200 men who had been too exhausted to go with him and had been left at the Wadi Besor, they came out to meet him and to meet the troops with him. When David approached the men, he greeted them, ²²but all the corrupt and •worthless men among those who had gone with David argued, "Because they didn't go with us, we will not give any of the plunder we recovered to them except for each man's wife and children. They may take them and go."

²³But David said, "My brothers, you must not do this with what the Lord has given us. He protected us and handed over to us the raiders who came against us. ²⁴Who can agree to your proposal? The share of

the one who goes into battle is to be the same as the share of the one who remains with the supplies. They will share equally." ²⁵ And it has been so from that day forward. David established this policy as a law and an ordinance for Israel and it continues to this very day.

²⁶ When David came to Ziklag, he sent some of the plunder to his friends, the elders of Judah, saying, "Here is a gift for you from the plunder of the Lᴏʀᴅ's enemies." ²⁷ He sent gifts to those in Bethel, in Ramoth of the Negev, and in Jattir; ²⁸ to those in Aroer, in Siphmoth, and in Eshtemoa; ²⁹ to those in Racal, in the towns of the Jerahmeelites, and in the towns of the Kenites; ³⁰ to those in Hormah, in Bor-ashan, and in Athach; ³¹ to those in Hebron, and to those in all the places where David and his men had roamed.

31 The Philistines fought against Israel, and Israel's men fled from them. Many were killed on Mount Gilboa. ² The Philistines overtook Saul and his sons and killed his sons, Jonathan, Abinadab, and Malchishua. ³ When the battle intensified against Saul, the archers caught up with him and severely wounded him. ⁴ Then Saul said to his armor-bearer, "Draw your sword and run me through with it, or these uncircumcised men will come and run me through and torture me." But his armor-bearer would not do it because he

was terrified. Then Saul took his sword and fell on it. ⁵ When his armor-bearer saw that Saul was dead, he also fell on his own sword and died with him. ⁶ So on that day, Saul died together with his three sons, his armor-bearer, and all his men.

⁷ When the men of Israel on the other side of the valley and on the other side of the Jordan saw that Israel's men had run away and that Saul and his sons were dead, they abandoned the cities and fled. So the Philistines came and settled in them.

⁸ The next day when the Philistines came to strip the dead, they found Saul and his three sons dead on Mount Gilboa. ⁹ They cut off Saul's head, stripped off his armor, and sent messengers throughout the land of the Philistines to spread the good news in the temples of their idols and among the people. ¹⁰ Then they put his armor in the temple of the ˙Ashtoreths and hung his body on the wall of Beth-shan.

¹¹ When the residents of Jabesh-gilead heard what the Philistines had done to Saul, ¹² all their brave men set out, journeyed all night, and retrieved the body of Saul and the bodies of his sons from the wall of Beth-shan. When they arrived at Jabesh, they burned the bodies there. ¹³ Afterward, they took their bones and buried them under the tamarisk tree in Jabesh and fasted seven days.

2 Samuel

1 After the death of Saul, David returned from defeating the Amalekites and stayed at Ziklag two days. ² On the third day a man with torn clothes and dust on his head came from Saul's camp. When he came to David, he fell to the ground and paid homage. ³ David asked him, "Where have you come from?"

He replied to him, "I've escaped from the Israelite camp."

⁴ "What was the outcome? Tell me," David asked him.

"The troops fled from the battle," he answered. "Many of the troops have fallen and are dead. Also, Saul and his son Jonathan are dead."

⁵ David asked the young man who had brought him the report, "How do you know Saul and his son Jonathan are dead?"

⁶ "I happened to be on Mount Gilboa," he replied, "and there was Saul, leaning on his spear. At that very moment the chariots and the cavalry were closing in on him. ⁷ When he turned around and saw me, he called out to me, so I answered: I'm at your service. ⁸ He asked me, 'Who are you?' I told him: I'm an Amalekite. ⁹ Then he begged me, 'Stand over me and kill me, for I'm mortally wounded, but my life still lingers.' ¹⁰ So I stood over him and killed him because I knew that after he had fallen he couldn't survive. I took the crown that was on his head and the armband that was on his arm, and I've brought them here to my lord."

¹¹ Then David took hold of his clothes and tore them, and all the men with him did the same. ¹² They mourned, wept, and fasted until the evening for those who died by the sword—for Saul, his son Jonathan, the Lᴏʀᴅ's people, and the house of Israel.

¹³ David inquired of the young man who had brought him the report, "Where are you from?"

"I'm the son of a foreigner," he said. "I'm an Amalekite."

¹⁴ David questioned him, "How is it that you were not afraid to lift your hand to destroy the Lᴏʀᴅ's anointed?" ¹⁵ Then David summoned one of his servants and said, "Come here and kill him!" The servant struck him, and he died. ¹⁶ For David had said to the Amalekite, "Your blood is on your own head because your own mouth testified against you by saying, 'I killed the Lᴏʀᴅ's anointed.'"

¹⁷ David sang the following lament for Saul and his son Jonathan, ¹⁸ and he ordered that the Judahites be taught The Song of the Bow. It is written in the Book of Jashar:

¹⁹   The splendor of Israel lies slain
          on your heights.
      How the mighty have fallen!
²⁰   Do not tell it in Gath,
          don't announce it in the marketplaces
          of Ashkelon,
      or the daughters of the Philistines will rejoice,
      and the daughters of the uncircumcised
          will gloat.
²¹   Mountains of Gilboa,
      let no dew or rain be on you,
      or fields of offerings,
      for there the shield of the mighty
          was defiled—
      the shield of Saul, no longer anointed with oil.
²²   Jonathan's bow never retreated,
      Saul's sword never returned unstained,
      from the blood of the slain,
      from the bodies of the mighty.
²³   Saul and Jonathan,
      loved and delightful,

they were not parted in life or in death.
They were swifter than eagles,
   stronger than lions.
24 Daughters of Israel, weep for Saul,
   who clothed you in scarlet,
     with luxurious things,
   who decked your garments
     with gold ornaments.
25 How the mighty have fallen in the thick
     of battle!
Jonathan lies slain on your heights.
26 I grieve for you, Jonathan, my brother.
You were such a friend to me.
Your love for me was more wonderful
   than the love of women.
27 How the mighty have fallen
   and the weapons of war have perished!

2 Some time later, David inquired of the LORD: "Should I go to one of the towns of Judah?"

The LORD answered him, "Go."

Then David asked, "Where should I go?"

"To Hebron," the LORD replied.

2 So David went there with his two wives, Ahinoam the Jezreelite and Abigail, the widow of Nabal the Carmelite. 3 In addition, David brought the men who were with him, each one with his household, and they settled in the towns near Hebron. 4 Then the men of Judah came, and there they anointed David king over the house of Judah. They told David: "It was the men of Jabesh-gilead who buried Saul."

5 David sent messengers to the men of Jabesh-gilead and said to them, "The LORD bless you, because you have shown this kindness to Saul your lord when you buried him. 6 Now, may the LORD show kindness and faithfulness to you, and I will also show the same goodness to you because you have done this deed. 7 Therefore, be strong and courageous, for though Saul your lord is dead, the house of Judah has anointed me king over them."

8 Abner son of Ner, commander of Saul's army, took Saul's son Ish-bosheth and moved him to Mahanaim. 9 He made him king over Gilead, Asher, Jezreel, Ephraim, Benjamin—over all Israel. 10 Saul's son Ish-bosheth was 40 years old when he began his reign over Israel; he ruled for two years. The house of Judah, however, followed David. 11 The length of time that David was king in Hebron over the house of Judah was seven years and six months.

12 Abner son of Ner and soldiers of Ish-bosheth son of Saul marched out from Mahanaim to Gibeon. 13 So Joab son of Zeruiah and David's soldiers marched out and met them by the pool of Gibeon. The two groups took up positions on opposite sides of the pool.

14 Then Abner said to Joab, "Let's have the young men get up and compete in front of us."

"Let them get up," Joab replied.

15 So they got up and were counted off—12 for Benjamin and Ish-bosheth son of Saul, and 12 from David's soldiers. 16 Then each man grabbed his opponent by the head and thrust his sword into his opponent's side so that they all died together. So this place, which is in Gibeon, is named Field of Blades.

17 The battle that day was extremely fierce, and Abner and the men of Israel were defeated by David's soldiers. 18 The three sons of Zeruiah were there: Joab, Abishai, and Asahel. Asahel was a fast runner, like one of the wild gazelles. 19 He chased Abner and did not turn to the right or the left in his pursuit of him. 20 Abner glanced back and said, "Is that you, Asahel?"

"Yes it is," Asahel replied.

21 Abner said to him, "Turn to your right or left, seize one of the young soldiers, and take whatever you can get from him." But Asahel would not stop chasing him. 22 Once again, Abner warned Asahel, "Stop chasing me. Why should I strike you to the ground? How could I ever look your brother Joab in the face?"

23 But Asahel refused to turn away, so Abner hit him in the stomach with the end of his spear. The spear went through his body, and he fell and died right there. When all who came to the place where Asahel had fallen and died, they stopped, 24 but Joab and Abishai pursued Abner. By sunset, they had gone as far as the hill of Ammah, which is opposite Giah on the way to the wilderness of Gibeon.

25 The Benjaminites rallied to Abner; they formed a single unit and took their stand on top of a hill. 26 Then Abner called out to Joab: "Must the sword devour forever? Don't you realize this will only end in bitterness? How long before you tell the troops to stop pursuing their brothers?"

27 "As God lives," Joab replied, "if you had not spoken up, the troops wouldn't have stopped pursuing their brothers until morning." 28 Then Joab blew the ram's horn, and all the troops stopped; they no longer pursued Israel or continued to fight. 29 So Abner and his men marched through the *Arabah all that night. They crossed the Jordan, marched all morning, and arrived at Mahanaim.

30 When Joab had turned back from pursuing Abner, he gathered all the troops. In addition to Asahel, 19 of David's soldiers were missing, 31 but they had killed 360 of the Benjaminites and Abner's men. 32 Afterward, they carried Asahel to his father's tomb in Bethlehem and buried him. Then Joab and his men marched all night and reached Hebron at dawn.

3 The war between the house of Saul and the house of David was long and drawn out, with David growing stronger and the house of Saul becoming weaker.

2 Sons were born to David in Hebron:
   his firstborn was Amnon,
     by Ahinoam the Jezreelite;
3 his second was Chileab,
     by Abigail, the widow of Nabal the Carmelite;
   the third was Absalom,
     son of Maacah the daughter of King Talmai
      of Geshur;
4 the fourth was Adonijah,
     son of Haggith;
   the fifth was Shephatiah,
     son of Abital;
5 the sixth was Ithream,
     by David's wife Eglah.
These were born to David in Hebron.

6 During the war between the house of Saul and the house of David, Abner kept acquiring more power in the house of Saul. 7 Now Saul had a concubine whose name was Rizpah daughter of Aiah, and Ish-bosheth questioned Abner, "Why did you sleep with my father's concubine?"

8 Abner was very angry about Ish-bosheth's accusation. "Am I a dog's head who belongs to Judah?" he asked. "All this time I've been loyal to the house of your father Saul, to his brothers, and to his friends and haven't handed you over to David, but now you

accuse me of wrongdoing with this woman! ⁹May God punish Abner and do so severely if I don't do for David what the Lᴏʀᴅ swore to him: ¹⁰to transfer the kingdom from the house of Saul and establish the throne of David over Israel and Judah from Dan to Beer-sheba." ¹¹Ish-bosheth could not answer Abner because he was afraid of him.

¹²Abner sent messengers as his representatives to say to David, "Whose land is it? Make your covenant with me, and you can be certain I am on your side to hand all Israel over to you."

¹³David replied, "Good, I will make a covenant with you. However, there's one thing I require of you: Do not appear before me unless you bring Saul's daughter Michal here when you come to see me."

¹⁴Then David sent messengers to say to Ish-bosheth son of Saul, "Give me back my wife, Michal. I was •engaged to her for the price of 100 Philistine foreskins."

¹⁵So Ish-bosheth sent someone to take her away from her husband, Paltiel son of Laish. ¹⁶Her husband followed her, weeping all the way to Bahurim. Abner said to him, "Go back." So he went back.

¹⁷Abner conferred with the elders of Israel: "In the past you wanted David to be king over you. ¹⁸Now take action, because the Lᴏʀᴅ has spoken concerning David: 'Through My servant David I will save My people Israel from the power of the Philistines and the power of all Israel's enemies.'"

¹⁹Abner also informed the Benjaminites and went to Hebron to inform David about all that was agreed on by Israel and the whole house of Benjamin. ²⁰When Abner and 20 men came to David at Hebron, David held a banquet for him and his men.

²¹Abner said to David, "Let me now go and I will gather all Israel to the king. They will make a covenant with you, and you will rule over all you desire." So David dismissed Abner, and he went in peace.

²²Just then David's soldiers and Joab returned from a raid and brought a large amount of plundered goods with them. Abner was not with David in Hebron because David had dismissed him, and he had gone in peace. ²³When Joab and all his army arrived, Joab was informed, "Abner son of Ner came to see the king, the king dismissed him, and he went in peace."

²⁴Joab went to the king and said, "What have you done? Look here, Abner came to you. Why did you dismiss him? Now he's getting away. ²⁵You know that Abner son of Ner came to deceive you and to find out about your activities and everything you're doing."

²⁶Then Joab left David and sent messengers after Abner. They brought him back from the well of Sirah, but David was unaware of it. ²⁷When Abner returned to Hebron, Joab pulled him aside to the middle of the gateway, as if to speak to him privately, and there Joab stabbed him in the stomach. So Abner died in revenge for the death of Asahel, Joab's brother.

²⁸David heard about it later and said: "I and my kingdom are forever innocent before the Lᴏʀᴅ concerning the blood of Abner son of Ner. ²⁹May it hang over Joab's head and his father's whole house, and may the house of Joab never be without someone who has a discharge or a skin disease, or a man who can only work a spindle, or someone who falls by the sword or starves." ³⁰Joab and his brother Abishai killed Abner because he had put their brother Asahel to death in the battle at Gibeon.

³¹David then ordered Joab and all the people who were with him, "Tear your clothes, put on •sackcloth, and mourn over Abner." And King David walked behind the funeral procession.

³²When they buried Abner in Hebron, the king wept aloud at Abner's tomb. All the people wept, ³³and the king sang a lament for Abner:

> Should Abner die as a fool dies?
> ³⁴ Your hands were not bound,
> your feet not placed in bronze shackles.
> You fell like one who falls victim to criminals.

And all the people wept over him even more.

³⁵Then they came to urge David to eat bread while it was still day, but David took an oath: "May God punish me and do so severely if I taste bread or anything else before sunset!" ³⁶All the people took note of this, and it pleased them. In fact, everything the king did pleased them. ³⁷On that day all the troops and all Israel were convinced that the king had no part in the killing of Abner son of Ner.

³⁸Then the king said to his soldiers, "You must know that a great leader has fallen in Israel today. ³⁹As for me, even though I am the anointed king, I have little power today. These men, the sons of Zeruiah, are too fierce for me. May the Lᴏʀᴅ repay the evildoer according to his evil!"

4 When Saul's son Ish-bosheth heard that Abner had died in Hebron, his courage failed, and all Israel was dismayed. ²Saul's son had two men who were leaders of raiding parties: one named Baanah and the other Rechab, sons of Rimmon the Beerothite of the Benjaminites. Beeroth is also considered part of Benjamin, ³and the Beerothites fled to Gittaim and still live there as foreigners to this very day.

⁴Saul's son Jonathan had a son whose feet were crippled. He was five years old when the report about Saul and Jonathan came from Jezreel. The one who had nursed him picked him up and fled, but as she was hurrying to flee, he fell and became lame. His name was Mephibosheth.

⁵Rechab and Baanah, the sons of Rimmon the Beerothite, set out and arrived at Ish-bosheth's house during the heat of the day while the king was taking his midday nap. ⁶They entered the interior of the house as if to get wheat and stabbed him in the stomach. Then Rechab and his brother Baanah escaped. ⁷They had entered the house while Ish-bosheth was lying on his bed in his bedroom and stabbed and killed him. Then they beheaded him, took his head, and traveled by way of the •Arabah all night. ⁸They brought Ish-bosheth's head to David at Hebron and said to the king, "Here's the head of Ish-bosheth son of Saul, your enemy who intended to take your life. Today the Lᴏʀᴅ has granted vengeance to my lord the king against Saul and his offspring."

⁹But David answered Rechab and his brother Baanah, sons of Rimmon the Beerothite, "As the Lᴏʀᴅ lives, the One who has redeemed my life from every distress, ¹⁰when the person told me, 'Look, Saul is dead,' he thought he was a bearer of good news, but I seized him and put him to death at Ziklag. That was my reward to him for his news! ¹¹How much more when wicked men kill a righteous man in his own house on his own bed! So now, should I not require his blood from your hands and wipe you off the earth?"

¹²So David gave orders to the young men, and they killed Rechab and Baanah. They cut off their hands and feet and hung their bodies by the pool in Hebron,

but they took Ish-bosheth's head and buried it in Ab-ner's tomb in Hebron.

5 All the tribes of Israel came to David at Hebron and said, "Here we are, your own flesh and blood. ²Even while Saul was king over us, you were the one who led us out to battle and brought us back. The LORD also said to you, 'You will shepherd My people Israel and be ruler over Israel.'"

³So all the elders of Israel came to the king at Hebron. King David made a covenant with them at Hebron in the LORD's presence, and they anointed David king over Israel.

⁴David was 30 years old when he began his reign; he reigned 40 years. ⁵In Hebron he reigned over Judah seven years and six months, and in Jerusalem he reigned 33 years over all Israel and Judah.

⁶The king and his men marched to Jerusalem against the Jebusites who inhabited the land. The Jebusites had said to David: "You will never get in here. Even the blind and lame can repel you"; thinking, "David can't get in here."

⁷Yet David did capture the stronghold of *Zion, that is, the city of David. ⁸He said that day, "Whoever attacks the Jebusites must go through the water shaft to reach the lame and the blind who are despised by David." For this reason it is said, "The blind and the lame will never enter the house."

⁹David took up residence in the stronghold, which he named the city of David. He built it up all the way around from the supporting terraces inward. ¹⁰David became more and more powerful, and the LORD God of *Hosts was with him. ¹¹King Hiram of Tyre sent envoys to David; he also sent cedar logs, carpenters, and stonemasons, and they built a palace for David. ¹²Then David knew that the LORD had established him as king over Israel and had exalted his kingdom for the sake of His people Israel.

¹³After he arrived from Hebron, David took more concubines and wives from Jerusalem, and more sons and daughters were born to him. ¹⁴These are the names of those born to him in Jerusalem: Shammua, Shobab, Nathan, Solomon, ¹⁵Ibhar, Elishua, Nepheg, Japhia, ¹⁶Elishama, Eliada, and Eliphelet.

¹⁷When the Philistines heard that David had been anointed king over Israel, they all went in search of David, but he heard about it and went down to the stronghold. ¹⁸So the Philistines came and spread out in the Valley of Rephaim.

¹⁹Then David inquired of the LORD: "Should I go to war against the Philistines? Will you hand them over to me?"

The LORD replied to David, "Go, for I will certainly hand the Philistines over to you."

²⁰So David went to Baal-perazim and defeated them there and said, "Like a bursting flood, the LORD has burst out against my enemies before me." Therefore, he named that place the Lord Bursts Out. ²¹The Philistines abandoned their idols there, and David and his men carried them off.

²²The Philistines came up again and spread out in the Valley of Rephaim. ²³So David inquired of the LORD, and He answered, "Do not make a frontal assault. Circle around behind them and attack them opposite the balsam trees. ²⁴When you hear the sound of marching in the tops of the balsam trees, act decisively, for then the LORD will have marched out ahead of you to attack the camp of the Philistines." ²⁵So David did exactly as

the LORD commanded him, and he struck down the Philistines all the way from Geba to Gezer.

6 David again assembled all the choice men in Israel, 30,000. ²He and all his troops set out to bring the ark of God from Baale-judah. The ark is called by the Name, the name of *Yahweh of *Hosts who dwells between the *cherubim. ³They set the ark of God on a new cart and transported it from Abinadab's house, which was on the hill. Uzzah and Ahio, sons of Abinadab, were guiding the cart ⁴and brought it with the ark of God from Abinadab's house on the hill. Ahio walked in front of the ark. ⁵David and the whole house of Israel were celebrating before the LORD with all kinds of fir wood instruments, lyres, harps, tambourines, sistrums, and cymbals.

⁶When they came to Nacon's threshing floor, Uzzah reached out to the ark of God and took hold of it because the oxen had stumbled. ⁷Then the LORD's anger burned against Uzzah, and God struck him dead on the spot for his irreverence, and he died there next to the ark of God. ⁸David was angry because of the LORD's outburst against Uzzah, so he named that place an Outburst Against Uzzah, as it is today. ⁹David feared the LORD that day and said, "How can the ark of the LORD ever come to me?" ¹⁰So he was not willing to move the ark of the LORD to the city of David; instead, he took it to the house of Obed-edom the Gittite. ¹¹The ark of the LORD remained in his house three months, and the LORD blessed Obed-edom and his whole family.

¹²It was reported to King David: "The LORD has blessed Obed-edom's family and all that belongs to him because of the ark of God." So David went and had the ark of God brought up from Obed-edom's house to the city of David with rejoicing. ¹³When those carrying the ark of the LORD advanced six steps, he sacrificed an ox and a fattened calf. ¹⁴David was dancing with all his might before the LORD wearing a linen *ephod. ¹⁵He and the whole house of Israel were bringing up the ark of the LORD with shouts and the sound of the ram's horn. ¹⁶As the ark of the LORD was entering the city of David, Saul's daughter Michal looked down from the window and saw King David leaping and dancing before the LORD, and she despised him in her heart.

¹⁷They brought the ark of the LORD and set it in its place inside the tent David had set up for it. Then David offered *burnt offerings and *fellowship offerings in the LORD's presence. ¹⁸When David had finished offering the burnt offering and the fellowship offerings, he blessed the people in the name of Yahweh of Hosts. ¹⁹Then he distributed a loaf of bread, a date cake, and a raisin cake to each one in the entire Israelite community, both men and women. Then all the people left, each to his own home.

²⁰When David returned home to bless his household, Saul's daughter Michal came out to meet him. "How the king of Israel honored himself today!" she said. "He exposed himself today in the sight of the slave girls of his subjects like a vulgar person would expose himself."

²¹David replied to Michal, "I was dancing before the LORD who chose me over your father and his whole family to appoint me ruler over the LORD's people Israel. I will celebrate before the LORD, ²²and I will humble myself even more and humiliate myself. I will be honored by the slave girls you spoke about." ²³And Saul's daughter Michal had no child to the day of her death.

7 When the king had settled into his palace and the Lord had given him rest on every side from all his enemies, ²the king said to Nathan the prophet, "Look, I am living in a cedar house while the ark of God sits inside tent curtains."

³So Nathan told the king, "Go and do all that is on your heart, for the Lord is with you."

⁴But that night the word of the Lord came to Nathan: ⁵"Go to My servant David and say, 'This is what the Lord says: Are you to build a house for Me to live in? ⁶From the time I brought the Israelites out of Egypt until today I have not lived in a house; instead, I have been moving around with a tent as My dwelling. ⁷In all My journeys with all the Israelites, have I ever asked anyone among the tribes of Israel, whom I commanded to shepherd My people Israel: Why haven't you built Me a house of cedar?'

⁸"Now this is what you are to say to My servant David: 'This is what the Lord of 'Hosts says: I took you from the pasture and from following the sheep to be ruler over My people Israel. ⁹I have been with you wherever you have gone, and I have destroyed all your enemies before you. I will make a name for you like that of the greatest in the land. ¹⁰I will establish a place for My people Israel and plant them, so that they may live there and not be disturbed again. Evildoers will not afflict them as they have done ¹¹ever since the day I ordered judges to be over My people Israel. I will give you rest from all your enemies.

"'The Lord declares to you: The Lord Himself will make a house for you. ¹²When your time comes and you rest with your fathers, I will raise up after you your descendant, who will come from your body, and I'will establish his kingdom. ¹³He will build a house for My name, and I will establish the throne of his kingdom forever. ¹⁴I will be a father to him, and he will be a son to Me. When he does wrong, I will discipline him with a human rod and with blows from others. ¹⁵But My faithful love will never leave him as I removed it from Saul; I removed him from your way. ¹⁶Your house and kingdom will endure before Me forever, and your throne will be established forever.'"

¹⁷Nathan spoke all these words and this entire vision to David.

¹⁸Then King David went in, sat in the Lord's presence, and said,

Who am I, Lord God, and what is my house that You have brought me this far? ¹⁹What You have done so far was a little thing to You, Lord God, for You have also spoken about Your servant's house in the distant future. And this is a revelation for mankind, Lord God. ²⁰What more can David say to You? You know Your servant, Lord God. ²¹Because of Your word and according to Your will, You have revealed all these great things to Your servant.

²²This is why You are great, Lord God. There is no one like You, and there is no God besides You, as all we have heard confirms. ²³And who is like Your people Israel? God came to one nation on earth in order to redeem a people for Himself, to make a name for Himself, and to perform for them great and awesome acts, driving out nations and their gods before Your people You redeemed for Yourself from Egypt. ²⁴You established Your people Israel to be Your own people forever, and You, Lord, have become their God.

²⁵Now, Lord God, fulfill the promise forever that You have made to Your servant and his house. Do as You have promised, ²⁶so that Your name will be exalted forever, when it is said, "The Lord of Hosts is God over Israel." The house of Your servant David will be established before You ²⁷since You, Lord of Hosts, God of Israel, have revealed this to Your servant when You said, "I will build a house for you." Therefore, Your servant has found the courage to pray this prayer to You. ²⁸Lord God, You are God; Your words are true, and You have promised this grace to Your servant. ²⁹Now, please bless Your servant's house so that it will continue before You forever. For You, Lord God, have spoken, and with Your blessing Your servant's house will be blessed forever.

8 After this, David defeated the Philistines, subdued them, and took Metheg-ammah from Philistine control. ²He also defeated the Moabites, and after making them lie down on the ground, he measured them off with a cord. He measured every two cord lengths of those to be put to death and one length of those to be kept alive. So the Moabites became David's subjects and brought tribute.

³David also defeated Hadadezer son of Rehob, king of Zobah, who went to restore his control at the Euphrates River. ⁴David captured 1,700 horsemen and 20,000 foot soldiers from him, and he hamstrung all the horses and kept 100 chariots.

⁵When the Arameans of Damascus came to assist King Hadadezer of Zobah, David struck down 22,000 Aramean men. ⁶Then he placed garrisons in Aram of Damascus, and the Arameans became David's subjects and brought tribute. The Lord made David victorious wherever he went.

⁷David took the gold shields of Hadadezer's officers and brought them to Jerusalem. ⁸King David also took huge quantities of bronze from Betah and Berothai, Hadadezer's cities.

⁹When King Toi of Hamath heard that David had defeated the entire army of Hadadezer, ¹⁰he sent his son Joram to King David to greet him and to congratulate him because David had fought against Hadadezer and defeated him, for Toi and Hadadezer had fought many wars. Joram had items of silver, gold, and bronze with him. ¹¹King David also dedicated these to the Lord, along with the silver and gold he had dedicated from all the nations he had subdued— ¹²from Edom, Moab, the Ammonites, the Philistines, the Amalekites, and the spoil of Hadadezer son of Rehob, king of Zobah.

¹³David made a reputation for himself when he returned from striking down 18,000 Edomites in the Valley of Salt. ¹⁴He placed garrisons throughout Edom, and all the Edomites were subject to David. The Lord made David victorious wherever he went.

¹⁵So David reigned over all Israel, administering justice and righteousness for all his people.

¹⁶ Joab son of Zeruiah was over the army;
Jehoshaphat son of Ahilud was
   court historian;

¹⁷ Zadok son of Ahitub
and Ahimelech son of Abiathar were priests;
Seraiah was court secretary;

¹⁸ Benaiah son of Jehoiada was over
the Cherethites and the Pelethites;
and David's sons were chief officials.

9 David asked, "Is there anyone remaining from Saul's family I can show kindness to because of Jonathan?" ²There was a servant of Saul's family named Ziba. They summoned him to David, and the king said to him, "Are you Ziba?"

"I am your servant," he replied.

³So the king asked, "Is there anyone left of Saul's family that I can show the kindness of God to?"

Ziba said to the king, "There is still Jonathan's son who was injured in both feet."

⁴The king asked him, "Where is he?"

Ziba answered the king, "You'll find him in Lo-debar at the house of Machir son of Ammiel." ⁵So King David had him brought from the house of Machir son of Ammiel in Lo-debar.

⁶Mephibosheth son of Jonathan son of Saul came to David, bowed down to the ground and paid homage. David said, "Mephibosheth!"

"I am your servant," he replied.

⁷"Don't be afraid," David said to him, "since I intend to show you kindness because of your father Jonathan. I will restore to you all your grandfather Saul's fields, and you will always eat meals at my table."

⁸Mephibosheth bowed down and said, "What is your servant that you take an interest in a dead dog like me?"

⁹Then the king summoned Saul's attendant Ziba and said to him, "I have given to your master's grandson all that belonged to Saul and his family. ¹⁰You, your sons, and your servants are to work the ground for him, and you are to bring in the crops so your master's grandson will have food to eat. But Mephibosheth, your master's grandson, is always to eat at my table." Now Ziba had 15 sons and 20 servants.

¹¹Ziba said to the king, "Your servant will do all my lord the king commands."

So Mephibosheth ate at David's table just like one of the king's sons. ¹²Mephibosheth had a young son whose name was Mica. All those living in Ziba's house were Mephibosheth's servants. ¹³However, Mephibosheth lived in Jerusalem because he always ate at the king's table. His feet had been injured.

10 Some time later the king of the Ammonites died, and his son Hanun became king in his place. ²Then David said, "I'll show kindness to Hanun son of Nahash, just as his father showed kindness to me."

So David sent his emissaries to console Hanun concerning his father. However, when they arrived in the land of the Ammonites, ³the Ammonite leaders said to Hanun their lord, "Just because David has sent men with condolences for you, do you really believe he's showing respect for your father? Instead, hasn't David sent his emissaries in order to scout out the city, spy on it, and demolish it?" ⁴So Hanun took David's emissaries, shaved off half their beards, cut their clothes in half at the hips, and sent them away.

⁵When this was reported to David, he sent someone to meet them, since they were deeply humiliated. The king said, "Stay in Jericho until your beards grow back; then return."

⁶When the Ammonites realized they had become repulsive to David, they hired 20,000 foot soldiers from the Arameans of Beth-rehob and Zobah, 1,000 men from the king of Maacah, and 12,000 men from Tob.

⁷David heard about it and sent Joab and all the fighting men. ⁸The Ammonites marched out and lined up in battle formation at the entrance to the city gate while the Arameans of Zobah and Rehob and the men of Tob and Maacah were in the field by themselves. ⁹When Joab saw that there was a battle line in front of him and another behind him, he chose some men out of all the elite troops of Israel and lined up in battle formation to engage the Arameans. ¹⁰He placed the rest of the forces under the command of his brother Abishai who lined up in battle formation to engage the Ammonites.

¹¹"If the Arameans are too strong for me," Joab said, "then you will be my help. However, if the Ammonites are too strong for you, I'll come to help you. ¹²Be strong! We must prove ourselves strong for our people and for the cities of our God. May the LORD's will be done."

¹³Joab and his troops advanced to fight against the Arameans, and they fled before him. ¹⁴When the Ammonites saw that the Arameans had fled, they too fled before Abishai and entered the city. So Joab withdrew from the attack against the Ammonites and went to Jerusalem.

¹⁵When the Arameans saw that they had been defeated by Israel, they regrouped. ¹⁶Hadadezer sent messengers to bring the Arameans who were across the Euphrates River, and they came to Helam with Shobach, commander of Hadadezer's army, leading them.

¹⁷When this was reported to David, he gathered all Israel, crossed the Jordan, and went to Helam. Then the Arameans lined up in formation to engage David in battle and fought against him. ¹⁸But the Arameans fled before Israel, and David killed 700 of their charioteers and 40,000 foot soldiers. He also struck down Shobach commander of their army, who died there. ¹⁹When all the kings who were Hadadezer's subjects saw that they had been defeated by Israel, they made peace with Israel and became their subjects. After this, the Arameans were afraid to ever help the Ammonites again.

11 In the spring when kings march out to war, David sent Joab with his officers and all Israel. They destroyed the Ammonites and besieged Rabbah, but David remained in Jerusalem.

²One evening David got up from his bed and strolled around on the roof of the palace. From the roof he saw a woman bathing—a very beautiful woman. ³So David sent someone to inquire about her, and he reported, "This is Bathsheba, daughter of Eliam and wife of Uriah the Hittite."

⁴David sent messengers to get her, and when she came to him, he slept with her. Now she had just been purifying herself from her uncleanness. Afterward, she returned home. ⁵The woman conceived and sent word to inform David: "I am pregnant."

⁶David sent orders to Joab: "Send me Uriah the Hittite." So Joab sent Uriah to David. ⁷When Uriah came to him, David asked how Joab and the troops were doing and how the war was going. ⁸Then he said to Uriah, "Go down to your house and wash your feet." So Uriah left the palace, and a gift from the king followed him. ⁹But Uriah slept at the door of the palace with all his master's servants; he did not go down to his house.

¹⁰When it was reported to David, "Uriah didn't go home," David questioned Uriah, "Haven't you just come from a journey? Why didn't you go home?"

¹¹Uriah answered David, "The ark, Israel, and Judah are dwelling in tents, and my master Joab and his sol-

diers are camping in the open field. How can I enter my house to eat and drink and sleep with my wife? As surely as you live and by your life, I will not do this!"

[12]"Stay here today also," David said to Uriah, "and tomorrow I will send you back." So Uriah stayed in Jerusalem that day and the next. [13]Then David invited Uriah to eat and drink with him, and David got him drunk. He went out in the evening to lie down on his cot with his master's servants, but he did not go home.

[14]The next morning David wrote a letter to Joab and sent it with Uriah. [15]In the letter he wrote:

Put Uriah at the front of the fiercest fighting, then withdraw from him so that he is struck down and dies.

[16]When Joab was besieging the city, he put Uriah in the place where he knew the best enemy soldiers were. [17]Then the men of the city came out and attacked Joab, and some of the men from David's soldiers fell in battle; Uriah the Hittite also died.

[18]Joab sent someone to report to David all the details of the battle. [19]He commanded the messenger, "When you've finished telling the king all the details of the battle— [20]if the king's anger gets stirred up and he asks you, 'Why did you get so close to the city to fight? Didn't you realize they would shoot from the top of the wall? [21]At Thebez, who struck Abimelech son of Jerubbesheth? Didn't a woman drop an upper millstone on him from the top of the wall so that he died? Why did you get so close to the wall?'—then say, 'Your servant Uriah the Hittite is dead also.'" [22]Then the messenger left.

When he arrived, he reported to David all that Joab had sent him to tell. [23]The messenger reported to David, "The men gained the advantage over us and came out against us in the field, but we counterattacked right up to the entrance of the gate. [24]However, the archers shot down on your soldiers from the top of the wall, and some of the king's soldiers died. Your servant Uriah the Hittite is also dead."

[25]David told the messenger, "Say this to Joab: 'Don't let this matter upset you because the sword devours all alike. Intensify your fight against the city and demolish it.' Encourage him."

[26]When Uriah's wife heard that her husband Uriah had died, she mourned for him. [27]When the time of mourning ended, David had her brought to his house. She became his wife and bore him a son. However, the LORD considered what David had done to be evil.

[12] So the LORD sent Nathan to David. When he arrived, he said to him:

There were two men in a certain city, one rich and the other poor. [2]The rich man had a large number of sheep and cattle, [3]but the poor man had nothing except one small ewe lamb that he had bought. He raised it, and it grew up, living with him and his children. It shared his meager food and drank from his cup; it slept in his arms, and it was like a daughter to him. [4]Now a traveler came to the rich man, but the rich man could not bring himself to take one of his own sheep or cattle to prepare for the traveler who had come to him. Instead, he took the poor man's lamb and prepared it for his guest.

[5]David was infuriated with the man and said to Nathan: "As the LORD lives, the man who did this deserves to die! [6]Because he has done this thing and shown no pity, he must pay four lambs for that lamb."

[7]Nathan replied to David, "You are the man! This is what the LORD God of Israel says: 'I anointed you king over Israel, and I delivered you from the hand of Saul. [8]I gave your master's house to you and your master's wives into your arms, and I gave you the house of Israel and Judah, and if that was not enough, I would have given you even more. [9]Why then have you despised the command of the LORD by doing what I consider evil? You struck down Uriah the Hittite with the sword and took his wife as your own wife—you murdered him with the Ammonite's sword. [10]Now therefore, the sword will never leave your house because you despised Me and took the wife of Uriah the Hittite to be your own wife.'

[11]"This is what the LORD says, 'I am going to bring disaster on you from your own family: I will take your wives and give them to another before your very eyes, and he will sleep with them publicly. [12]You acted in secret, but I will do this before all Israel and in broad daylight.'"

[13]David responded to Nathan, "I have sinned against the LORD."

Then Nathan replied to David, "The LORD has taken away your sin; you will not die. [14]However, because you treated the LORD with such contempt in this matter, the son born to you will die." [15]Then Nathan went home.

The LORD struck the baby that Uriah's wife had borne to David, and he became ill. [16]David pleaded with God for the boy. He fasted, went home, and spent the night lying on the ground. [17]The elders of his house stood beside him to get him up from the ground, but he was unwilling and would not eat anything with them.

[18]On the seventh day the baby died. But David's servants were afraid to tell him the baby was dead. They said, "Look, while the baby was alive, we spoke to him, and he wouldn't listen to us. So how can we tell him the baby is dead? He may do something desperate."

[19]When David saw that his servants were whispering to each other, he guessed that the baby was dead. So he asked his servants, "Is the baby dead?"

"He is dead," they replied.

[20]Then David got up from the ground. He washed, anointed himself, changed his clothes, went to the LORD's house, and worshiped. Then he went home and requested something to eat. So they served him food, and he ate.

[21]His servants asked him, "What did you just do? While the baby was alive, you fasted and wept, but when he died, you got up and ate food."

[22]He answered, "While the baby was alive, I fasted and wept because I thought, 'Who knows? The LORD may be gracious to me and let him live.' [23]But now that he is dead, why should I fast? Can I bring him back again? I'll go to him, but he will never return to me."

[24]Then David comforted his wife Bathsheba; he went and slept with her. She gave birth to a son and named him Solomon. The LORD loved him, [25]and He sent a message through Nathan the prophet, who named him Jedidiah, because of the LORD.

[26]Joab fought against Rabbah of the Ammonites and captured the royal fortress. [27]Then Joab sent messengers to David to say, "I have fought against Rabbah and have also captured the water supply. [28]Now therefore, assemble the rest of the troops, lay siege to the city, and capture it. Otherwise I will be the one to capture

the city, and it will be named after me." ²⁹So David assembled all the troops and went to Rabbah; he fought against it and captured it. ³⁰He took the crown from the head of their king, and it was placed on David's head. The crown weighed 75 pounds of gold, and it had a precious stone in it. In addition, David took away a large quantity of plunder from the city. ³¹He removed the people who were in the city and put them to work with saws, iron picks, and iron axes, and to labor at brickmaking. He did the same to all the Ammonite cities. Then he and all his troops returned to Jerusalem.

13 Some time passed. David's son Absalom had a beautiful sister named Tamar, and David's son Amnon was infatuated with her. ²Amnon was frustrated to the point of making himself sick over his sister Tamar because she was a virgin, but it seemed impossible to do anything to her. ³Amnon had a friend named Jonadab, a son of David's brother Shimeah. Jonadab was a very shrewd man, ⁴and he asked Amnon, "Why are you, the king's son, so miserable every morning? Won't you tell me?"

Amnon replied, "I'm in love with Tamar, my brother Absalom's sister."

⁵Jonadab said to him, "Lie down on your bed and pretend you're sick. When your father comes to see you, say to him, 'Please let my sister Tamar come and give me something to eat. Let her prepare food in my presence so I can watch and eat from her hand.'"

⁶So Amnon lay down and pretended to be sick. When the king came to see him, Amnon said to him, "Please let my sister Tamar come and make a couple of cakes in my presence so I can eat from her hand."

⁷David sent word to Tamar at the palace: "Please go to your brother Amnon's house and prepare a meal for him."

⁸Then Tamar went to his house while Amnon was lying down. She took dough, kneaded it, made cakes in his presence, and baked them. ⁹She brought the pan and set it down in front of him, but he refused to eat. Amnon said, "Everyone leave me!" And everyone left him. ¹⁰"Bring the meal to the bedroom," Amnon told Tamar, "so I can eat from your hand." Tamar took the cakes she had made and went to her brother Amnon's bedroom. ¹¹When she brought them to him to eat, he grabbed her and said, "Come sleep with me, my sister!"

¹²"Don't, my brother!" she cried. "Don't humiliate me, for such a thing should never be done in Israel. Don't do this horrible thing! ¹³Where could I ever go with my disgrace? And you—you would be like one of the immoral men in Israel! Please, speak to the king, for he won't keep me from you." ¹⁴But he refused to listen to her, and because he was stronger than she was, he raped her.

¹⁵After this, Amnon hated Tamar with such intensity that the hatred he hated her with was greater than the love he had loved her with. "Get out of here!" he said.

¹⁶"No," she cried, "sending me away is much worse than the great wrong you've already done to me!" But he refused to listen to her. ¹⁷Instead, he called to the servant who waited on him: "Throw this woman out and bolt the door behind her!" ¹⁸Amnon's servant threw her out and bolted the door behind her. Now Tamar was wearing a long-sleeved garment, because this is what the king's virgin daughters wore. ¹⁹Tamar put ashes on her head and tore the long-sleeved garment she was wearing. She put her hand on her head and went away crying out.

²⁰Her brother Absalom said to her: "Has your brother Amnon been with you? Be quiet for now, my sister. He is your brother. Don't take this thing to heart." So Tamar lived as a desolate woman in the house of her brother Absalom.

²¹When King David heard about all these things, he was furious. ²²Absalom didn't say anything to Amnon, either good or bad, because he hated Amnon since he disgraced his sister Tamar.

²³Two years later, Absalom's sheepshearers were at Baal-hazor near Ephraim, and Absalom invited all the king's sons. ²⁴Then he went to the king and said, "Your servant has just hired sheepshearers. Will the king and his servants please come with your servant?"

²⁵The king replied to Absalom, "No, my son, we should not all go, or we would be a burden to you." Although Absalom urged him, he wasn't willing to go, though he did bless him.

²⁶"If not," Absalom said, "please let my brother Amnon go with us."

The king asked him, "Why should he go with you?" ²⁷But Absalom urged him, so he sent Amnon and all the king's sons.

²⁸Now Absalom commanded his young men, "Watch Amnon until he is in a good mood from the wine. When I order you to strike Amnon, then kill him. Don't be afraid. Am I not the one who has commanded you? Be strong and courageous!" ²⁹So Absalom's young men did to Amnon just as Absalom had commanded. Then all the rest of the king's sons got up, and each fled on his mule.

³⁰While they were on the way, a report reached David: "Absalom struck down all the king's sons; not even one of them survived!" ³¹In response the king stood up, tore his clothes, and lay down on the ground, and all his servants stood by with their clothes torn.

³²But Jonadab, son of David's brother Shimeah, spoke up: "My lord must not think they have killed all the young men, the king's sons, because only Amnon is dead. In fact, Absalom has planned this ever since the day Amnon disgraced his sister Tamar. ³³So now, my lord the king, don't take seriously the report that says all the king's sons are dead. Only Amnon is dead."

³⁴Meanwhile, Absalom had fled. When the young man who was standing watch looked up, there were many people coming from the road west of him from the side of the mountain. ³⁵Jonadab said to the king, "Look, the king's sons have come! It's exactly like your servant said." ³⁶Just as he finished speaking, the king's sons entered and wept loudly. Then the king and all his servants also wept bitterly.

³⁷Now Absalom fled and went to Talmai son of Ammihud, king of Geshur. And David mourned for his son every day. ³⁸Absalom had fled and gone to Geshur where he stayed three years. ³⁹Then King David longed to go to Absalom, for David had finished grieving over Amnon's death.

14 Joab son of Zeruiah observed that the king's mind was on Absalom. ²So Joab sent someone to Tekoa to bring a clever woman from there. He told her, "Pretend to be in mourning: dress in mourning clothes and don't put on any oil. Act like a woman who has been mourning for the dead for a long time. ³Go to the king and speak these words to him." Then Joab told her exactly what to say.

⁴When the woman from Tekoa came to the king, she

fell with her face to the ground in homage and said, "Help me, my king!"

⁵"What's the matter?" the king asked her.

"To tell the truth, I am a widow; my husband died," she said. ⁶"Your servant had two sons. They were fighting in the field with no one to separate them, and one struck the other and killed him. ⁷Now the whole clan has risen up against your servant and said, 'Hand over the one who killed his brother so we may put him to death for the life of the brother he murdered. We will destroy the heir!' They would extinguish my one remaining ember by not preserving my husband's name or posterity on earth."

⁸The king told the woman, "Go home. I will issue a command on your behalf."

⁹Then the woman of Tekoa said to the king, "My lord the king, may any blame be on me and my father's house, and may the king and his throne be innocent."

¹⁰"Whoever speaks to you," the king said, "bring him to me. He will not trouble you again!"

¹¹She replied, "Please, may the king invoke the LORD your God, so that the avenger of blood will not increase the loss, and they will not eliminate my son!"

"As the LORD lives," he vowed, "not a hair of your son will fall to the ground."

¹²Then the woman said, "Please, may your servant speak a word to my lord the king?"

"Speak," he replied.

¹³The woman asked, "Why have you devised something similar against the people of God? When the king spoke as he did about this matter, he has pronounced his own *guilt. The king has not brought back his own banished one. ¹⁴We will certainly die and be like water poured out on the ground, which can't be recovered. But God would not take away a life; He would devise plans so that the one banished from Him does not remain banished.

¹⁵"Now therefore, I've come to present this matter to my lord the king because the people have made me afraid. Your servant thought: I must speak to the king. Perhaps the king will grant his servant's request. ¹⁶The king will surely listen in order to rescue his servant from the hand of this man who would eliminate both me and my son from God's inheritance. ¹⁷Your servant thought: May the word of my lord the king bring relief, for my lord the king is able to discern the good and the bad like the Angel of God. May the LORD your God be with you."

¹⁸Then the king answered the woman, "I'm going to ask you something; don't conceal it from me!"

"Let my lord the king speak," the woman replied.

¹⁹The king asked, "Did Joab put you up to all this?"

The woman answered. "As you live, my lord the king, no one can turn to the right or left from all my lord the king says. Yes, your servant Joab is the one who gave orders to me; he told your servant exactly what to say. ²⁰Joab your servant has done this to address the issue indirectly, but my lord has wisdom like the wisdom of the Angel of God, knowing everything on earth."

²¹Then the king said to Joab, "I hereby grant this request. Go, bring back the young man Absalom."

²²Joab fell with his face to the ground in homage and praised the king. "Today," Joab said, "your servant knows I have found favor with you, my lord the king, because the king has granted the request of your servant."

²³So Joab got up, went to Geshur, and brought Absalom to Jerusalem. ²⁴However, the king added, "He may return to his house, but he may not see my face." So Absalom returned to his house, but he did not see the king.

²⁵No man in all Israel was as handsome and highly praised as Absalom. From the sole of his foot to the top of his head, he did not have a single flaw. ²⁶When he shaved his head—he shaved it every year because his hair got so heavy for him that he had to shave it off—he would weigh the hair from his head and it would be five pounds according to the royal standard.

²⁷Three sons were born to Absalom, and a daughter named Tamar, who was a beautiful woman. ²⁸Absalom resided in Jerusalem two years but never saw the king. ²⁹Then Absalom sent for Joab in order to send him to the king, but Joab was unwilling to come. So he sent again, a second time, but he still wouldn't come. ³⁰Then Absalom said to his servants, "See, Joab has a field right next to mine, and he has barley there. Go and set fire to it!" So Absalom's servants set the field on fire.

³¹Then Joab came to Absalom's house and demanded, "Why did your servants set my field on fire?"

³²"Look," Absalom explained to Joab, "I sent for you and said, 'Come here. I want to send you to the king to ask: Why have I come back from Geshur? I'd be better off if I were still there.' So now, let me see the king. If I am guilty, let him kill me."

³³Joab went to the king and told him. So David summoned Absalom, who came to the king and bowed down with his face to the ground before him. Then the king kissed Absalom.

15 After this, Absalom got himself a chariot, horses, and 50 men to run before him. ²He would get up early and stand beside the road leading to the *city gate. Whenever anyone had a grievance to bring before the king for settlement, Absalom called out to him and asked, "What city are you from?" If he replied, "Your servant is from one of the tribes of Israel," ³Absalom said to him, "Look, your claims are good and right, but the king does not have anyone to listen to you." ⁴He added, "If only someone would appoint me judge in the land. Then anyone who had a grievance or dispute could come to me, and I would make sure he received justice." ⁵When a person approached to bow down to him, Absalom reached out his hand, took hold of him, and kissed him. ⁶Absalom did this to all the Israelites who came to the king for a settlement. So Absalom stole the hearts of the men of Israel.

⁷When four years had passed, Absalom said to the king, "Please let me go to Hebron to fulfill a vow I made to the LORD. ⁸For your servant made a vow when I lived in Geshur of Aram, saying: If the LORD really brings me back to Jerusalem, I will worship the LORD in Hebron."

⁹"Go in peace," the king said to him. So he went to Hebron.

¹⁰Then Absalom sent messengers throughout the tribes of Israel with this message: "When you hear the sound of the ram's horn, you are to say, 'Absalom has become king in Hebron!'"

¹¹Two hundred men from Jerusalem went with Absalom. They had been invited and were going innocently, for they knew nothing about the whole matter. ¹²While he was offering the sacrifices, Absalom sent for David's adviser Ahithophel the Gilonite, from his

city of Giloh. So the conspiracy grew strong, and the people supporting Absalom continued to increase.

¹³ Then an informer came to David and reported, "The hearts of the men of Israel are with Absalom."

¹⁴ David said to all the servants with him in Jerusalem, "Get up. We have to flee, or we will not escape from Absalom! Leave quickly, or he will soon overtake us, heap disaster on us, and strike the city with the edge of the sword."

¹⁵ The king's servants said to him, "Whatever my lord the king decides, we are your servants." ¹⁶ Then the king set out, and his entire household followed him. But he left behind 10 concubines to take care of the palace. ¹⁷ So the king set out, and all the people followed him. They stopped at the last house ¹⁸ while all his servants marched past him. Then all the Cherethites, the Pelethites, and the Gittites—600 men who came with him from Gath—marched past the king.

¹⁹ The king said to Ittai the Gittite, "Why are you also going with us? Go back and stay with the new king since you're both a foreigner and an exile from your homeland. ²⁰ Besides, you only arrived yesterday; should I make you wander around with us today while I go wherever I can? Go back and take your brothers with you. May the LORD show you kindness and faithfulness."

²¹ But in response, Ittai vowed to the king, "As the LORD lives and as my lord the king lives, wherever my lord the king is, whether it means life or death, your servant will be there!"

²² "March on," David replied to Ittai. So Ittai the Gittite marched past with all his men and the children who were with him. ²³ Everyone in the countryside was weeping loudly while all the people were marching past. As the king was crossing the Kidron Valley, all the people were marching past on the road that leads to the desert.

²⁴ Zadok was also there, and all the Levites with him were carrying the ark of the covenant of God. They set the ark of God down, and Abiathar offered sacrifices until the people had finished marching past. ²⁵ Then the king instructed Zadok, "Return the ark of God to the city. If I find favor in the LORD's eyes, He will bring me back and allow me to see both it and its dwelling place. ²⁶ However, if He should say, 'I do not delight in you,' then here I am—He can do with me whatever pleases Him."

²⁷ The king also said to Zadok the priest, "Look, return to the city in peace and your two sons with you: your son Ahimaaz and Abiathar's son Jonathan. ²⁸ Remember, I'll wait at the fords of the wilderness until word comes from you to inform me." ²⁹ So Zadok and Abiathar returned the ark of God to Jerusalem and stayed there.

³⁰ David was climbing the slope of the Mount of Olives, weeping as he ascended. His head was covered, and he was walking barefoot. Each of the people with him covered their heads and went up, weeping as they ascended.

³¹ Then someone reported to David: "Ahithophel is among the conspirators with Absalom."

"LORD," David pleaded, "please turn the counsel of Ahithophel into foolishness!"

³² When David came to the summit where he used to worship God, Hushai the Archite was there to meet him with his robe torn and dust on his head. ³³ David said to him, "If you go away with me, you'll be a burden to me, ³⁴ but if you return to the city and tell Absalom, 'I will be your servant, my king! Previously, I was your father's servant, but now I will be your servant,' then you can counteract Ahithophel's counsel for me. ³⁵ Won't Zadok and Abiathar the priests be there with you? Report everything you hear from the king's palace to Zadok and Abiathar the priests. ³⁶ Take note: their two sons, Zadok's son Ahimaaz and Abiathar's son Jonathan, are there with them. Send me everything you hear through them." ³⁷ So Hushai, David's personal adviser, entered Jerusalem just as Absalom was entering the city.

16 When David had gone a little beyond the summit, Ziba, Mephibosheth's servant, was right there to meet him. He had a pair of saddled donkeys loaded with 200 loaves of bread, 100 clusters of raisins, 100 bunches of summer fruit, and a skin of wine. ² The king said to Ziba, "Why do you have these?"

Ziba answered, "The donkeys are for the king's household to ride, the bread and summer fruit are for the young men to eat, and the wine is for those to drink who become exhausted in the desert."

³ "Where is your master's grandson?" the king asked.

"Why, he's staying in Jerusalem," Ziba replied to the king, "for he said, 'Today, the house of Israel will restore my grandfather's kingdom to me.'"

⁴ The king said to Ziba, "All that belongs to Mephibosheth is now yours!"

"I bow before you," Ziba said. "May you look favorably on me, my lord the king!"

⁵ When King David got to Bahurim, a man belonging to the family of the house of Saul was just coming out. His name was Shimei son of Gera, and he was yelling curses as he approached. ⁶ He threw stones at David and at all the royal servants, the people and the warriors on David's right and left. ⁷ Shimei said as he cursed: "Get out, get out, you worthless murderer! ⁸ The LORD has paid you back for all the blood of the house of Saul in whose place you became king, and the LORD has handed the kingdom over to your son Absalom. Look, you are in trouble because you're a murderer!"

⁹ Then Abishai son of Zeruiah said to the king, "Why should this dead dog curse my lord the king? Let me go over and cut his head off!"

¹⁰ The king replied, "Sons of Zeruiah, do we agree on anything? He curses me this way because the LORD told him, 'Curse David!' Therefore, who can say, 'Why did you do that?'" ¹¹ Then David said to Abishai and all his servants, "Look, my own son, my own flesh and blood, intends to take my life—how much more now this Benjaminite! Leave him alone and let him curse me; the LORD has told him to. ¹² Perhaps the LORD will see my affliction and restore goodness to me instead of Shimei's curses today." ¹³ So David and his men proceeded along the road as Shimei was going along the ridge of the hill opposite him. As Shimei went, he cursed David, and threw stones and dirt at him. ¹⁴ Finally, the king and all the people with him arrived exhausted, so they rested there.

¹⁵ Now Absalom and all the Israelites came to Jerusalem. Ahithophel was also with him. ¹⁶ When David's friend Hushai the Archite came to Absalom, Hushai said to Absalom, "Long live the king! Long live the king!"

¹⁷ "Is this your loyalty to your friend?" Absalom asked Hushai. "Why didn't you go with your friend?"

¹⁸ "Not at all," Hushai answered Absalom. "I am on

the side of the one that the LORD, the people, and all the men of Israel have chosen. I will stay with him. [19] Furthermore, whom will I serve if not his son? As I served in your father's presence, I will also serve in yours."

[20] Then Absalom said to Ahithophel, "Give me your advice. What should we do?"

[21] Ahithophel replied to Absalom, "Sleep with your father's concubines he left to take care of the palace. When all Israel hears that you have become repulsive to your father, everyone with you will be encouraged." [22] So they pitched a tent for Absalom on the roof, and he slept with his father's concubines in the sight of all Israel.

[23] Now the advice Ahithophel gave in those days was like someone asking about a word from God— such was the regard that both David and Absalom had for Ahithophel's advice. [1] Ahithophel said to Absalom, "Let me choose 12,000 men, and I will set out in pursuit of David tonight. [2] I will attack him while he is weak and weary, throw him into a panic, and all the people with him will scatter. I will strike down only the king [3] and bring all the people back to you. When everyone returns except the man you're seeking, all the people will be at peace." [4] This proposal seemed good to Absalom and all the elders of Israel.

[5] Then Absalom said, "Summon Hushai the Archite also. Let's hear what he has to say as well."

[6] So Hushai came to Absalom, and Absalom told him: "Ahithophel offered this proposal. Should we carry out his proposal? If not, what do you say?"

[7] Hushai replied to Absalom, "The advice Ahithophel has given this time is not good." [8] Hushai continued, "You know your father and his men. They are warriors and are desperate like a wild bear robbed of her cubs. Your father is an experienced soldier who won't spend the night with the people. [9] He's probably already hiding in one of the caves or some other place. If some of our troops fall first, someone is sure to hear and say, 'There's been a slaughter among the people who follow Absalom.' [10] Then, even a brave man with the heart of a lion will melt because all Israel knows that your father and the valiant men with him are warriors. [11] Instead, I advise that all Israel from Dan to Beer-sheba—as numerous as the sand by the sea—be gathered to you and that you personally go into battle. [12] Then we will attack David wherever we find him, and we will descend on him like dew on the ground. Not even one will be left of all the men with him. [13] If he retreats to some city, all Israel will bring ropes to that city, and we will drag its stones into the valley until not even a pebble can be found there." [14] Since the LORD had decreed that Ahithophel's good advice be undermined in order to bring about Absalom's ruin, Absalom and all the men of Israel said, "The advice of Hushai the Archite is better than Ahithophel's advice."

[15] Hushai then told the priests Zadok and Abiathar, "This is what Ahithophel advised Absalom and the elders of Israel, and this is what I advised. [16] Now send someone quickly and tell David, 'Don't spend the night at the wilderness ford of the Jordan, but be sure to cross over, or the king and all the people with him will be destroyed.'"

[17] Jonathan and Ahimaaz were staying at En-rogel, where a servant girl would come and pass along information to them. They in turn would go and inform King David, because they dared not be seen entering the city. [18] However, a young man did see them and

informed Absalom. So the two left quickly and came to the house of a man in Bahurim. He had a well in his courtyard, and they climbed down into it. [19] Then his wife took the cover, placed it over the mouth of the well, and scattered grain on it so nobody would know anything.

[20] Absalom's servants came to the woman at the house and asked, "Where are Ahimaaz and Jonathan?"

"They passed by toward the water," the woman replied to them. The men searched but did not find them, so they returned to Jerusalem.

[21] After they had gone, Ahimaaz and Jonathan climbed out of the well and went and informed King David. They told him, "Get up and immediately ford the river, for Ahithophel has given this advice against you." [22] So David and all the people with him got up and crossed the Jordan. By daybreak, there was no one who had not crossed the Jordan. [23] When Ahithophel realized that his advice had not been followed, he saddled his donkey and set out for his house in his hometown. He set his affairs in order and hanged himself. So he died and was buried in his father's tomb.

[24] David had arrived at Mahanaim by the time Absalom crossed the Jordan with all the men of Israel. [25] Now Absalom had appointed Amasa over the army in Joab's place. Amasa was the son of a man named Ithra the Israelite; Ithra had married Abigail daughter of Nahash. Abigail was a sister to Zeruiah, Joab's mother. [26] And Israel and Absalom camped in the land of Gilead. [27] When David came to Mahanaim, Shobi son of Nahash from Rabbah of the Ammonites, Machir son of Ammiel from Lo-debar, and Barzillai the Gileadite from Rogelim [28] brought beds, basins, and pottery items. They also brought wheat, barley, flour, roasted grain, beans, lentils, [29] honey, curds, sheep, and cheese from the herd for David and the people with him to eat. They had reasoned, "The people must be hungry, exhausted, and thirsty in the desert."

18 David reviewed his troops and appointed commanders of hundreds and of thousands over them. [2] He then sent out the troops, a third under Joab, a third under Joab's brother Abishai son of Zeruiah, and a third under Ittai the Gittite. The king said to the troops, "I will also march out with you."

[3] "You must not go!" the people pleaded. "If we have to flee, they will not pay any attention to us. Even if half of us die, they will not pay any attention to us because you are worth 10,000 of us. Therefore, it is better if you support us from the city."

[4] "I will do whatever you think is best," the king replied to them. So he stood beside the gate while all the troops marched out by hundreds and thousands. [5] The king commanded Joab, Abishai, and Ittai, "Treat the young man Absalom gently for my sake." All the people heard the king's orders to all the commanders about Absalom.

[6] Then David's forces marched into the field to engage Israel in battle, which took place in the forest of Ephraim. [7] The people of Israel were defeated by David's soldiers, and the slaughter there was vast that day—20,000 casualties. [8] The battle spread over the entire region, and that day the forest claimed more people than the sword.

[9] Absalom was riding on his mule when he happened to meet David's soldiers. When the mule went under the tangled branches of a large oak tree, Absalom's head was caught fast in the tree. The mule under him

kept going, so he was suspended in midair. [10]One of the men saw him and informed Joab. He said, "I just saw Absalom hanging in an oak tree!"

[11]"You just saw him!" Joab exclaimed. "Why didn't you strike him to the ground right there? I would have given you 10 silver pieces and a belt!"

[12]The man replied to Joab, "Even if I had the weight of 1,000 pieces of silver in my hand, I would not raise my hand against the king's son. For we heard the king command you, Abishai, and Ittai, 'Protect the young man Absalom for me.' [13]If I had jeopardized my own life—and nothing is hidden from the king—you would have abandoned me."

[14]Joab said, "I'm not going to waste time with you!" He then took three spears in his hand and thrust them into Absalom's heart while he was still alive in the oak tree, [15]and 10 young men who were Joab's armor-bearers surrounded Absalom, struck him, and killed him.

[16]Afterward, Joab blew the ram's horn, and the troops broke off their pursuit of Israel because Joab restrained them. [17]They took Absalom, threw him into a large pit in the forest, and piled a huge mound of stones over him. And all Israel fled, each to his tent.

[18]When he was alive, Absalom had set up a pillar for himself in the King's Valley, for he had said, "I have no son to preserve the memory of my name." So he gave the pillar his name. It is still called Absalom's Monument today.

[19]Ahimaaz son of Zadok said, "Please let me run and tell the king the good news that the LORD has delivered him from his enemies."

[20]Joab replied to him, "You are not the man to take good news today. You may do it another day, but today you aren't taking good news, because the king's son is dead." [21]Joab then said to the *Cushite, "Go tell the king what you have seen." The Cushite bowed to Joab and took off running.

[22]However, Ahimaaz son of Zadok persisted and said to Joab, "No matter what, please let me also run behind the Cushite!"

Joab replied, "My son, why do you want to run since you won't get a reward?"

[23]"No matter what, I want to run!"

"Then run!" Joab said to him. So Ahimaaz ran by way of the plain and outran the Cushite.

[24]David was sitting between the two gates when the watchman went up to the roof of the gate and over to the wall. The watchman looked out and saw a man running alone. [25]He called out and told the king.

The king said, "If he's alone, he bears good news."

As the first runner came closer, [26]the watchman saw another man running. He called out to the gatekeeper, "Look! Another man is running alone!"

"This one is also bringing good news," said the king.

[27]The watchman said, "The way the first man runs looks to me like the way Ahimaaz son of Zadok runs."

"This is a good man; he comes with good news," the king commented.

[28]Ahimaaz called out to the king, "All is well," and then bowed down to the king with his face to the ground. He continued, "May the LORD your God be praised! He delivered up the men who rebelled against my lord the king."

[29]The king asked, "Is the young man Absalom all right?"

Ahimaaz replied, "When Joab sent the king's servant and your servant, I saw a big disturbance, but I don't know what it was."

[30]The king said, "Move aside and stand here." So he stood to one side.

[31]Just then the Cushite came and said, "May my lord the king hear the good news: today the LORD has delivered you from all those rising up against you!"

[32]The king asked the Cushite, "Is the young man Absalom all right?"

The Cushite replied, "May what has become of the young man happen to the enemies of my lord the king and to all who rise up against you with evil intent."

[33]The king was deeply moved and went up to the gate chamber and wept. As he walked, he cried, "My son Absalom! My son, my son Absalom! If only I had died instead of you, Absalom, my son, my son!"

19 It was reported to Joab, "The king is weeping. He's mourning over Absalom." [2]That day's victory was turned into mourning for all the troops because on that day the troops heard, "The king is grieving over his son." [3]So they returned to the city quietly that day like people come in when they are humiliated after fleeing in battle. [4]But the king hid his face and cried out at the top of his voice, "My son Absalom! Absalom, my son, my son!"

[5]Then Joab went into the house to the king and said, "Today you have shamed all your soldiers—those who rescued your life and the lives of your sons and daughters, your wives, and your concubines. [6]You love your enemies and hate those who love you! Today you have made it clear that the commanders and soldiers mean nothing to you. In fact, today I know that if Absalom were alive and all of us were dead, it would be fine with you! [7]Now get up! Go out and encourage your soldiers, for I swear by the LORD that if you don't go out, not a man will remain with you tonight. This will be worse for you than all the trouble that has come to you from your youth until now!"

[8]So the king got up and sat in the *gate, and all the people were told: "Look, the king is sitting in the gate." Then they all came into the king's presence.

Meanwhile, each Israelite had fled to his tent. [9]All the people among all the tribes of Israel were arguing: "The king delivered us from the grasp of our enemies, and he rescued us from the grasp of the Philistines, but now he has fled from the land because of Absalom. [10]But Absalom, the man we anointed over us, has died in battle. So why do you say nothing about restoring the king?"

[11]King David sent word to the priests, Zadok and Abiathar: "Say to the elders of Judah, 'Why should you be the last to restore the king to his palace? The talk of all Israel has reached the king at his house. [12]You are my brothers, my flesh and blood. So why should you be the last to restore the king?' [13]And tell Amasa, 'Aren't you my flesh and blood? May God punish me and do so severely if you don't become commander of the army from now on instead of Joab!'"

[14]So he won over all the men of Judah, and they sent word to the king: "Come back, you and all your servants." [15]Then the king returned. When he arrived at the Jordan, Judah came to Gilgal to meet the king and escort him across the Jordan.

[16]Shimei son of Gera, a Benjaminite from Bahurim, hurried down with the men of Judah to meet King David. [17]There were 1,000 men from Benjamin with

him. Ziba, an attendant from the house of Saul, with his 15 sons and 20 servants also rushed down to the Jordan ahead of the king. [18] They forded the Jordan to bring the king's household across and do whatever the king desired.

When Shimei son of Gera crossed the Jordan, he fell down before the king [19] and said to him, "My lord, don't hold me *guilty, and don't remember your servant's wrongdoing on the day my lord the king left Jerusalem. May the king not take it to heart. [20] For your servant knows that I have sinned. But look! Today I am the first one of the entire house of Joseph to come down to meet my lord the king."

[21] Abishai son of Zeruiah asked, "Shouldn't Shimei be put to death for this, because he cursed the LORD's anointed?"

[22] David answered, "Sons of Zeruiah, do we agree on anything? Have you become my adversary today? Should any man be killed in Israel today? Am I not aware that today I'm king over Israel?" [23] So the king said to Shimei, "You will not die." Then the king gave him his oath.

[24] Mephibosheth, Saul's grandson, also went down to meet the king. He had not taken care of his feet, trimmed his mustache, or washed his clothes from the day the king left until the day he returned safely. [25] When he came from Jerusalem to meet the king, the king asked him, "Mephibosheth, why didn't you come with me?"

[26] "My lord the king," he replied, "my servant Ziba betrayed me. Actually your servant said: 'I'll saddle the donkey for myself so that I may ride it and go with the king'—for your servant is lame. [27] Ziba slandered your servant to my lord the king. But my lord the king is like the Angel of God, so do whatever you think best. [28] For my grandfather's entire family deserves death from my lord the king, but you set your servant among those who eat at your table. So what further right do I have to keep on making appeals to the king?"

[29] The king said to him, "Why keep on speaking about these matters of yours? I hereby declare: you and Ziba are to divide the land."

[30] Mephibosheth said to the king, "Instead, since my lord the king has come to his palace safely, let Ziba take it all!"

[31] Barzillai the Gileadite had come down from Rogelim and accompanied the king to the Jordan River to see him off at the Jordan. [32] Barzillai was a very old man—80 years old—and since he was a very wealthy man, he had provided for the needs of the king while he stayed in Mahanaim.

[33] The king said to Barzillai, "Cross over with me, and I'll provide for you at my side in Jerusalem."

[34] Barzillai replied to the king, "How many years of my life are left that I should go up to Jerusalem with the king? [35] I'm now 80 years old. Can I discern what is pleasant and what is not? Can your servant taste what he eats or drinks? Can I still hear the voice of male and female singers? Why should your servant be an added burden to my lord the king? [36] Since your servant is only going with the king a little way across the Jordan, why should the king repay me with such a reward? [37] Please let your servant return so that I may die in my own city near the tomb of my father and mother. But here is your servant Chimham: let him cross over with my lord the king. Do for him what seems good to you."

[38] The king replied, "Chimham will cross over with me, and I will do for him what seems good to you, and whatever you desire from me I will do for you." [39] So all the people crossed the Jordan, and then the king crossed. The king kissed Barzillai and blessed him, and Barzillai returned to his home.

[40] The king went on to Gilgal, and Chimham went with him. All the troops of Judah and half of Israel's escorted the king. [41] Suddenly, all the men of Israel came to the king. They asked him, "Why did our brothers, the men of Judah, take you away secretly and transport the king and his household across the Jordan, along with all of David's men?"

[42] All the men of Judah responded to the men of Israel, "Because the king is our relative. Why does this make you angry? Have we ever eaten anything of the king's or been honored at all?"

[43] The men of Israel answered the men of Judah: "We have 10 shares in the king, so we have a greater claim to David than you. Why then do you despise us? Weren't we the first to speak of restoring our king?" But the words of the men of Judah were harsher than those of the men of Israel.

20 Now a *wicked man, a Benjaminite named Sheba son of Bichri, happened to be there. He blew the ram's horn and shouted:

We have no portion in David,
no inheritance in Jesse's son.
Each man to his tent, Israel!

[2] So all the men of Israel deserted David and followed Sheba son of Bichri, but the men of Judah from the Jordan all the way to Jerusalem remained loyal to their king.

[3] When David came to his palace in Jerusalem, he took the 10 concubines he had left to take care of the palace and placed them under guard. He provided for them, but he was not intimate with them. They were confined until the day of their death, living as widows.

[4] The king said to Amasa, "Summon the men of Judah to me within three days and be here yourself." [5] Amasa went to summon Judah, but he took longer than the time allotted him. [6] So David said to Abishai, "Sheba son of Bichri will do more harm to us than Absalom. Take your lord's soldiers and pursue him, or he will find fortified cities and elude us."

[7] So Joab's men, the Cherethites, the Pelethites, and all the warriors marched out under Abishai's command; they left Jerusalem to pursue Sheba son of Bichri. [8] They were at the great stone in Gibeon when Amasa joined them. Joab was wearing his uniform and over it was a belt around his waist with a sword in its sheath. As he approached, the sword fell out. [9] Joab asked Amasa, "Are you well, my brother?" Then with his right hand Joab grabbed Amasa by the beard to kiss him. [10] Amasa was not on guard against the sword in Joab's hand, and Joab stabbed him in the stomach with it and spilled his intestines out on the ground. Joab did not stab him again for Amasa was dead. Joab and his brother Abishai pursued Sheba son of Bichri.

[11] One of Joab's young men had stood over Amasa saying, "Whoever favors Joab and whoever is for David, follow Joab!" [12] Now Amasa was writhing in his blood in the middle of the highway, and the man had seen that all the people stopped. So he moved Amasa from the highway to the field and threw a garment over him because he realized that all those who encountered Amasa were stopping. [13] When he was removed from

the highway, all the men passed by and followed Joab to pursue Sheba son of Bichri.

¹⁴ Sheba passed through all the tribes of Israel to Abel of Beth-maacah. All the Berites came together and followed him. ¹⁵ Joab's troops came and besieged Sheba in Abel of Beth-maacah. They built an assault ramp against the outer wall of the city. While all the troops with Joab were battering the wall to make it collapse, ¹⁶ a wise woman called out from the city, "Listen! Listen! Please tell Joab to come here and let me speak with him."

¹⁷ When he had come near her, the woman asked, "Are you Joab?"

"I am," he replied.

"Listen to the words of your servant," she said to him.

He answered, "I'm listening."

¹⁸ She said, "In the past they used to say, 'Seek counsel in Abel,' and that's how they settled disputes. ¹⁹ I am a peaceful person, one of the faithful in Israel, but you're trying to destroy a city that is like a mother in Israel. Why would you devour the LORD's inheritance?"

²⁰ Joab protested: "Never! I do not want to destroy! ²¹ That is not my intention. There is a man named Sheba son of Bichri, from the hill country of Ephraim, who has rebelled against King David. Deliver this one man, and I will withdraw from the city."

The woman replied to Joab, "All right. His head will be thrown over the wall to you." ²² The woman went to all the people with her wise counsel, and they cut off the head of Sheba son of Bichri and threw it to Joab. So he blew the ram's horn, and they dispersed from the city, each to his own tent. Joab returned to the king in Jerusalem.

²³ Joab commanded the whole army of Israel; Benaiah son of Jehoiada was over the Cherethites and Pelethites; ²⁴ Adoram was in charge of forced labor; Jehoshaphat son of Ahilud was court historian; ²⁵ Sheva was court secretary; Zadok and Abiathar were priests; ²⁶ and in addition, Ira the Jairite was David's priest.

21 During David's reign there was a famine for three successive years, so David inquired of the LORD. The LORD answered, "It is because of the blood shed by Saul and his family when he killed the Gibeonites."

² The Gibeonites were not Israelites but rather a remnant of the Amorites. The Israelites had taken an oath concerning them, but Saul had tried to kill them in his zeal for the Israelites and Judah. So David summoned the Gibeonites and spoke to them. ³ He asked the Gibeonites, "What should I do for you? How can I make atonement so that you will bring a blessing on the LORD's inheritance?"

⁴ The Gibeonites said to him, "We are not asking for money from Saul or his family, and we cannot put anyone to death in Israel."

"Whatever you say, I will do for you," he said.

⁵ They replied to the king, "As for the man who annihilated us and plotted to destroy us so we would not exist within the whole territory of Israel, ⁶ let seven of his male descendants be handed over to us so we may hang them in the presence of the LORD at Gibeah of Saul, the LORD's chosen."

The king answered, "I will hand them over."

⁷ David spared Mephibosheth, the son of Saul's son Jonathan, because of the oath of the LORD that was between David and Jonathan, Saul's son. ⁸ But the king took Armoni and Mephibosheth, who were the two sons whom Rizpah daughter of Aiah had borne to Saul, and the five sons whom Merab daughter of Saul had borne to Adriel son of Barzillai the Meholathite ⁹ and handed them over to the Gibeonites. They hanged them on the hill in the presence of the LORD; the seven of them died together. They were executed in the first days of the harvest at the beginning of the barley harvest.

¹⁰ Rizpah, Aiah's daughter, took *sackcloth and spread it out for herself on the rock from the beginning of the harvest until the rain poured down from heaven on the bodies. She kept the birds of the sky from them by day and the wild animals by night.

¹¹ When it was reported to David what Saul's concubine Rizpah, daughter of Aiah, had done, ¹² he went and got the bones of Saul and his son Jonathan from the leaders of Jabesh-gilead. They had stolen them from the public square of Beth-shan where the Philistines had hung the bodies the day the Philistines killed Saul at Gilboa. ¹³ David had the bones brought from there. They gathered up the bones of Saul's family who had been hung ¹⁴ and buried the bones of Saul and his son Jonathan at Zela in the land of Benjamin in the tomb of Saul's father Kish. They did everything the king commanded. After this, God answered prayer for the land.

¹⁵ The Philistines again waged war against Israel. David went down with his soldiers, and they fought the Philistines, but David became exhausted. ¹⁶ Then Ishbi-benob, one of the descendants of the giant, whose bronze spear weighed about eight pounds and who wore new armor, intended to kill David. ¹⁷ But Abishai son of Zeruiah came to his aid, struck the Philistine, and killed him. Then David's men swore to him: "You must never again go out with us to battle. You must not extinguish the lamp of Israel."

¹⁸ After this, there was another battle with the Philistines at Gob. At that time Sibbecai the Hushathite killed Saph, who was one of the descendants of the giant.

¹⁹ Once again there was a battle with the Philistines at Gob, and Elhanan son of Jaare-oregim the Bethlehemite killed Goliath the Gittite. The shaft of his spear was like a weaver's beam.

²⁰ At Gath there was still another battle. A huge man was there with six fingers on each hand and six toes on each foot—24 in all. He, too, was descended from the giant. ²¹ When he taunted Israel, Jonathan, son of David's brother Shimei, killed him.

²² These four were descended from the giant in Gath and were killed by David and his soldiers.

22 David spoke the words of this song to the LORD on the day the LORD rescued him from the hand of all his enemies and from the hand of Saul. ² He said:

The LORD is my rock, my fortress,
    and my deliverer,
³   my God, my mountain where I seek refuge.
My shield, the *horn of my salvation,
    my stronghold, my refuge,
and my Savior, You save me from violence.
⁴   I called to the LORD, who is worthy of praise,
and I was saved from my enemies.
⁵   For the waves of death engulfed me;
the torrents of destruction terrified me.
⁶   The ropes of *Sheol entangled me;
the snares of death confronted me.

7 I called to the LORD in my distress;
I called to my God.
From His temple He heard my voice,
and my cry for help reached His ears.

8 Then the earth shook and quaked;
the foundations of the heavens trembled;
they shook because He burned with anger.

9 Smoke rose from His nostrils,
and consuming fire came from His mouth;
coals were set ablaze by it.

10 He parted the heavens and came down,
a dark cloud beneath His feet.

11 He rode on a cherub and flew,
soaring on the wings of the wind.

12 He made darkness a canopy around Him,
a gathering of water and thick clouds.

13 From the radiance of His presence,
flaming coals were ignited.

14 The LORD thundered from heaven;
the *Most High projected His voice.

15 He shot arrows and scattered them;
He hurled lightning bolts and routed them.

16 The depths of the sea became visible,
the foundations of the world were exposed
at the rebuke of the LORD,
at the blast of the breath of His nostrils.

17 He reached down from heaven
and took hold of me;
He pulled me out of deep waters.

18 He rescued me from my powerful enemy
and from those who hated me,
for they were too strong for me.

19 They confronted me in the day of my distress,
but the LORD was my support.

20 He brought me out to a spacious place;
He rescued me because He delighted in me.

21 The LORD rewarded me
according to my righteousness;
He repaid me
according to the cleanness of my hands.

22 For I have kept the ways of the LORD
and have not turned from my God
to wickedness.

23 Indeed, I have kept all His ordinances in mind
and have not disregarded His statutes.

24 I was blameless before Him
and kept myself from sinning.

25 So the LORD repaid me
according to my righteousness,
according to my cleanness in His sight.

26 With the faithful
You prove Yourself faithful;
with the blameless man
You prove Yourself blameless;

27 with the pure
You prove Yourself pure,
but with the crooked
You prove Yourself shrewd.

28 You rescue an afflicted people,
but Your eyes are set against the proud—
You humble them.

29 LORD, You are my lamp;
the LORD illuminates my darkness.

30 With You I can attack a barrier,
and with my God I can leap over a wall.

31 God—His way is perfect;
the word of the LORD is pure.

He is a shield to all who take refuge in Him.

32 For who is God besides the LORD?
And who is a rock? Only our God.

33 God is my strong refuge;
He makes my way perfect.

34 He makes my feet like the feet of a deer
and sets me securely on the heights.

35 He trains my hands for war;
my arms can bend a bow of bronze.

36 You have given me the shield
of Your salvation;
Your help exalts me.

37 You widen a place beneath me for my steps,
and my ankles do not give way.

38 I pursue my enemies and destroy them;
I do not turn back until they are wiped out.

39 I wipe them out and crush them,
and they do not rise;
they fall beneath my feet.

40 You have clothed me with strength for battle;
You subdue my adversaries beneath me.

41 You have made my enemies retreat before me;
I annihilate those who hate me.

42 They look, but there is no one to save them—
they look to the LORD, but He does not
answer them.

43 I pulverize them like dust of the earth;
I crush them and trample them like mud
in the streets.

44 You have freed me from the feuds
among my people;
You have appointed me the head of nations;
a people I had not known serve me.

45 Foreigners submit to me grudgingly;
as soon as they hear, they obey me.

46 Foreigners lose heart
and come trembling from their fortifications.

47 The LORD lives—may my rock be praised!
God, the rock of my salvation, is exalted.

48 God—He gives me vengeance
and casts down peoples under me.

49 He frees me from my enemies.
You exalt me above my adversaries;
You rescue me from violent men.

50 Therefore I will praise You, LORD,
among the nations;
I will sing about Your name.

51 He is a tower of salvation for His king;
He shows loyalty to His anointed,
to David and his descendants forever.

23 These are the last words of David:
The declaration of David son of Jesse,
the declaration of the man raised on high,
the one anointed by the God of Jacob,
the favorite singer of Israel:

2 The Spirit of the LORD spoke through me,
His word was on my tongue.

3 The God of Israel spoke;
the Rock of Israel said to me,
"The one who rules the people
with justice,
who rules in the *fear of God,

4 is like the morning light when the sun rises
on a cloudless morning,
the glisten of rain on sprouting grass."

5 Is it not true my house is with God?

For He has established
　an everlasting covenant with me,
　ordered and secured in every detail.
Will He not bring about
　my whole salvation and my every desire?
6 But all the wicked are like thorns raked aside;
　they can never be picked up by hand.
7 The man who touches them
　must be armed with iron and the shaft
　　of a spear.
They will be completely burned up
　on the spot.

8 These are the names of David's warriors:
Josheb-basshebeth the Tahchemonite was chief of the officers. He wielded his spear against 800 men that he killed at one time.

9 After him, Eleazar son of Dodo son of an Ahohite was among the three warriors with David when they defied the Philistines. The men of Israel retreated in the place they had gathered for battle, 10 but Eleazar stood his ground and attacked the Philistines until his hand was tired and stuck to his sword. The LORD brought about a great victory that day. Then the troops came back to him, but only to plunder the dead.

11 After him was Shammah son of Agee the Hararite. The Philistines had assembled in formation where there was a field full of lentils. The troops fled from the Philistines, 12 but Shammah took his stand in the middle of the field, defended it, and struck down the Philistines. So the LORD brought about a great victory.

13 Three of the 30 leading warriors went down at harvest time and came to David at the cave of Adullam, while a company of Philistines was camping in the Valley of Rephaim. 14 At that time David was in the stronghold, and a Philistine garrison was at Bethlehem. 15 David was extremely thirsty and said, "If only someone would bring me water to drink from the well at the city gate of Bethlehem!" 16 So three of the warriors broke through the Philistine camp and drew water from the well at the gate of Bethlehem. They brought it back to David, but he refused to drink it. Instead, he poured it out to the LORD. 17 David said, "LORD, I would never do such a thing! Is this not the blood of men who risked their lives?" So he refused to drink it. Such were the exploits of the three warriors.

18 Abishai, Joab's brother and son of Zeruiah, was leader of the Three. He raised his spear against 300 men and killed them, gaining a reputation among the Three. 19 Was he not more honored than the Three? He became their commander even though he did not become one of the Three.

20 Benaiah son of Jehoiada was the son of a brave man from Kabzeel, a man of many exploits. Benaiah killed two sons of Ariel of Moab, and he went down into a pit on a snowy day and killed a lion. 21 He also killed an Egyptian, a huge man. Even though the Egyptian had a spear in his hand, Benaiah went down to him with a club, snatched the spear out of the Egyptian's hand, and then killed him with his own spear. 22 These were the exploits of Benaiah son of Jehoiada, who had a reputation among the three warriors. 23 He was the most honored of the Thirty, but he did not become one of the Three. David put him in charge of his bodyguard.

24 Among the Thirty were:
　Joab's brother Asahel,
　Elhanan son of Dodo of Bethlehem,
25 Shammah the Harodite,
　Elika the Harodite,
26 Helez the Paltite,
　Ira son of Ikkesh the Tekoite,
27 Abiezer the Anathothite,
　Mebunnai the Hushathite,
28 Zalmon the Ahohite,
　Maharai the Netophathite,
29 Heleb son of Baanah the Netophahite,
　Ittai son of Ribai from Gibeah
　　of the Benjaminites,
30 Benaiah the Pirathonite,
　Hiddai from the *wadis of Gaash,
31 Abi-albon the Arbathite,
　Azmaveth the Barhumite,
32 Eliahba the Shaalbonite,
　the sons of Jashen,
　Jonathan son of 33 Shammah the Hararite,
　Ahiam son of Sharar the Hararite,
34 Eliphelet son of Ahasbai son of the Maacathite,
　Eliam son of Ahithophel the Gilonite,
35 Hezro the Carmelite,
　Paarai the Arbite,
36 Igal son of Nathan from Zobah,
　Bani the Gadite,
37 Zelek the Ammonite,
　Naharai the Beerothite, the armor-bearer
　　for Joab son of Zeruiah,
38 Ira the Ithrite,
　Gareb the Ithrite,
39 and Uriah the Hittite.
There were 37 in all.

24 The LORD's anger burned against Israel again, and He stirred up David against them to say: "Go, count the people of Israel and Judah."

2 So the king said to Joab, the commander of his army, "Go through all the tribes of Israel from Dan to Beer-sheba and register the troops so I can know their number."

3 Joab replied to the king, "May the LORD your God multiply the troops 100 times more than they are—while my lord the king looks on! But why does my lord the king want to do this?"

4 Yet the king's order prevailed over Joab and the commanders of the army. So Joab and the commanders of the army left the king's presence to register the troops of Israel.

5 They crossed the Jordan and camped in Aroer, south of the town in the middle of the valley, and then proceeded toward Gad and Jazer. 6 They went to Gilead and to the land of the Hittites and continued on to Dan-jaan and around to Sidon. 7 They went to the fortress of Tyre and all the cities of the Hivites and Canaanites. Afterward, they went to the *Negev of Judah at Beer-sheba.

8 When they had gone through the whole land, they returned to Jerusalem at the end of nine months and 20 days. 9 Joab gave the king the total of the registration of the troops. There were 800,000 fighting men from Israel and 500,000 men from Judah.

10 David's conscience troubled him after he had taken a census of the troops. He said to the LORD, "I have sinned greatly in what I've done. Now, LORD, because I've been very foolish, please take away Your servant's *guilt."

11 When David got up in the morning, a revelation from the LORD had come to the prophet Gad, David's

seer: [12] "Go and say to David, 'This is what the LORD says: I am offering you three choices. Choose one of them, and I will do it to you.'"

[13] So Gad went to David, told him the choices, and asked him, "Do you want three years of famine to come on your land, to flee from your foes three months while they pursue you, or to have a plague in your land three days? Now, think it over and decide what answer I should take back to the One who sent me."

[14] David answered Gad, "I have great anxiety. Please, let us fall into the LORD's hands because His mercies are great, but don't let me fall into human hands."

[15] So the LORD sent a plague on Israel from that morning until the appointed time, and from Dan to Beer-sheba 70,000 men died. [16] Then the angel extended his hand toward Jerusalem to destroy it, but the LORD relented concerning the destruction and said to the angel who was destroying the people, "Enough, withdraw your hand now!" The angel of the LORD was then at the threshing floor of Araunah the Jebusite.

[17] When David saw the angel striking the people, he said to the LORD, "Look, I am the one who has sinned; I am the one who has done wrong. But these sheep, what have they done? Please, let Your hand be against me and my father's family."

[18] Gad came to David that day and said to him, "Go up and set up an altar to the LORD on the threshing floor of Araunah the Jebusite." [19] David went up in obedience to Gad's command, just as the LORD had commanded. [20] Araunah looked down and saw the king and his servants coming toward him, so he went out and bowed to the king with his face to the ground.

[21] Araunah said, "Why has my lord the king come to his servant?"

David replied, "To buy the threshing floor from you in order to build an altar to the LORD, so the plague on the people may be halted."

[22] Araunah said to David, "My lord the king may take whatever he wants and offer it. Here are the oxen for a *burnt offering and the threshing sledges and ox yokes for the wood. [23] My king, Araunah gives everything here to the king." Then he said to the king, "May the LORD your God accept you."

[24] The king answered Araunah, "No, I insist on buying it from you for a price, for I will not offer to the LORD my God burnt offerings that cost me nothing." David bought the threshing floor and the oxen for 20 ounces of silver. [25] He built an altar to the LORD there and offered burnt offerings and *fellowship offerings. Then the LORD answered prayer on behalf of the land, and the plague on Israel ended.

1 KINGS

1 Now King David was old and getting on in years. Although they covered him with bedclothes, he could not get warm. [2] So his servants said to him: "Let us search for a young virgin for my lord the king. She is to attend the king and be his caregiver. She is to lie by your side so that my lord the king will get warm." [3] They searched for a beautiful girl throughout the territory of Israel; they found Abishag the Shunammite and brought her to the king. [4] The girl was of unsurpassed beauty, and she became the king's caregiver. She served him, but he was not intimate with her.

[5] Adonijah son of Haggith kept exalting himself, saying, "I will be king!" He prepared chariots, cavalry, and 50 men to run ahead of him. [6] But his father had never once reprimanded him by saying, "Why do you act this way?" In addition, he was quite handsome and was born after Absalom. [7] He conspired with Joab son of Zeruiah and with Abiathar the priest. They supported Adonijah, [8] but Zadok the priest, Benaiah son of Jehoiada, Nathan the prophet, Shimei, Rei, and David's warriors did not side with Adonijah.

[9] Adonijah sacrificed sheep, oxen, and fattened cattle near the stone of Zoheleth, which is next to En-rogel. He invited all his royal brothers and all the men of Judah, the servants of the king, [10] but he did not invite Nathan the prophet, Benaiah, the warriors, or his brother Solomon.

[11] Then Nathan said to Bathsheba, Solomon's mother, "Have you not heard that Adonijah son of Haggith has become king and our lord David does not know it? [12] Now please come and let me advise you. Save your life and the life of your son Solomon. [13] Go, approach King David and say to him, 'My lord the king, did you not swear to your servant: Your son Solomon is to become king after me, and he is the one who is to sit

on my throne? So why has Adonijah become king?' [14] At that moment, while you are still there speaking with the king, I'll come in after you and confirm your words."

[15] So Bathsheba went to the king in his bedroom. Since the king was very old, Abishag the Shunammite was serving him. [16] Bathsheba bowed down and paid homage to the king, and he asked, "What do you want?"

[17] She replied, "My lord, you swore to your servant by the LORD your God, 'Your son Solomon is to become king after me, and he is the one who is to sit on my throne.' [18] Now look, Adonijah has become king. And, my lord the king, you didn't know it. [19] He has lavishly sacrificed oxen, fattened cattle, and sheep. He invited all the king's sons, Abiathar the priest, and Joab the commander of the army, but he did not invite your servant Solomon. [20] Now, my lord the king, the eyes of all Israel are on you to tell them who will sit on the throne of my lord the king after him. [21] Otherwise, when my lord the king rests with his fathers, I and my son Solomon will be regarded as criminals."

[22] At that moment, while she was still speaking with the king, Nathan the prophet arrived, [23] and it was announced to the king, "Nathan the prophet is here." He came into the king's presence and bowed to him with his face to the ground.

[24] "My lord the king," Nathan said, "did you say, 'Adonijah is to become king after me, and he is the one who is to sit on my throne'? [25] For today he went down and lavishly sacrificed oxen, fattened cattle, and sheep. He invited all the sons of the king, the commanders of the army, and Abiathar the priest. And look! They're eating and drinking in his presence, and they're saying, 'Long live King Adonijah!' [26] But he did

not invite me—me, your servant—or Zadok the priest or Benaiah son of Jehoiada or your servant Solomon. ²⁷I'm certain my lord the king would not have let this happen without letting your servant know who will sit on my lord the king's throne after him."

²⁸King David responded by saying, "Call in Bathsheba for me." So she came into the king's presence and stood before him. ²⁹The king swore an oath and said, "As the LORD lives, who has redeemed my life from every difficulty, ³⁰just as I swore to you by the LORD God of Israel: Your son Solomon is to become king after me, and he is the one who is to sit on my throne in my place, that is exactly what I will do this very day."

³¹Bathsheba bowed with her face to the ground, paying homage to the king, and said, "May my lord King David live forever!"

³²King David then said, "Call in Zadok the priest, Nathan the prophet, and Benaiah son of Jehoiada for me." So they came into the king's presence. ³³The king said to them, "Take my servants with you, have my son Solomon ride on my own mule, and take him down to Gihon. ³⁴There, Zadok the priest and Nathan the prophet are to anoint him as king over Israel. You are to blow the ram's horn and say, 'Long live King Solomon!' ³⁵You are to come up after him, and he is to come in and sit on my throne. He is the one who is to become king in my place; he is the one I have commanded to be ruler over Israel and Judah."

³⁶"Amen," Benaiah son of Jehoiada replied to the king. "May the LORD, the God of my lord the king, so affirm it. ³⁷Just as the LORD was with my lord the king, so may He be with Solomon and make his throne greater than the throne of my lord King David."

³⁸Then Zadok the priest, Nathan the prophet, Benaiah son of Jehoiada, the Cherethites, and the Pelethites went down, had Solomon ride on King David's mule, and took him to Gihon. ³⁹Zadok the priest took the horn of oil from the tabernacle and anointed Solomon. Then they blew the ram's horn, and all the people proclaimed, "Long live King Solomon!" ⁴⁰All the people followed him, playing flutes and rejoicing with such a great joy that the earth split open from the sound.

⁴¹Adonijah and all the invited guests who were with him heard the noise as they finished eating. Joab heard the sound of the ram's horn and said, "Why is the town in such an uproar?" ⁴²He was still speaking when Jonathan son of Abiathar the priest, suddenly arrived. Adonijah said, "Come in, for you are an excellent man, and you must be bringing good news."

⁴³"Unfortunately not," Jonathan answered him. "Our lord King David has made Solomon king. ⁴⁴And with Solomon, the king has sent Zadok the priest, Nathan the prophet, Benaiah son of Jehoiada, the Cherethites, and the Pelethites, and they have had him ride on the king's mule. ⁴⁵Zadok the priest and Nathan the prophet have anointed him king in Gihon. They have gone from there rejoicing. The town has been in an uproar; that's the noise you heard. ⁴⁶Solomon has even taken his seat on the royal throne.

⁴⁷"The king's servants have also gone to congratulate our lord King David, saying, 'May your God make the name of Solomon more well known than your name, and may He make his throne greater than your throne.' Then the king bowed in worship on his bed. ⁴⁸And the king went on to say this: 'May the LORD God of Israel be praised! Today He has provided one to sit on my throne, and I am a witness.'"

⁴⁹Then all of Adonijah's guests got up trembling and went their separate ways. ⁵⁰Adonijah was afraid of Solomon, so he got up and went to take hold of the horns of the altar.

⁵¹It was reported to Solomon: "Look, Adonijah fears King Solomon, and he has taken hold of the horns of the altar, saying, 'Let King Solomon first swear to me that he will not kill his servant with the sword.'"

⁵²Then Solomon said, "If he is a man of character, not a single hair of his will fall to the ground, but if evil is found in him, he dies." ⁵³So King Solomon sent for him, and they took him down from the altar. He came and paid homage to King Solomon, and Solomon said to him, "Go to your home."

2 As the time approached for David to die, he instructed his son Solomon, ²"As for me, I am going the way of all of the earth. Be strong and be courageous like a man, ³and keep your obligation to the LORD your God to walk in His ways and to keep His statutes, commands, ordinances, and decrees. This is written in the law of Moses, so that you will have success in everything you do and wherever you turn, ⁴and so that the LORD will carry out His promise that He made to me: 'If your sons are careful to walk faithfully before Me with their whole mind and heart, you will never fail to have a man on the throne of Israel.'

⁵"You also know what Joab son of Zeruiah did to me and what he did to the two commanders of Israel's army, Abner son of Ner and Amasa son of Jether. He murdered them in a time of peace to avenge blood shed in war. He spilled that blood on his own waistband and on the sandals of his feet. ⁶Act according to your wisdom, and do not let his gray head descend to •Sheol in peace.

⁷"Show loyalty to the sons of Barzillai the Gileadite and let them be among those who eat at your table because they supported me when I fled from your brother Absalom.

⁸"Keep an eye on Shimei son of Gera, the Benjaminite from Bahurim who is with you. He uttered malicious curses against me the day I went to Mahanaim. But he came down to meet me at the Jordan River, and I swore to him by the LORD: 'I will never kill you with the sword.' ⁹So don't let him go unpunished, for you are a wise man. You know how to deal with him to bring his gray head down to Sheol with blood."

¹⁰Then David rested with his fathers and was buried in the city of David. ¹¹The length of time David reigned over Israel was 40 years: he reigned seven years in Hebron and 33 years in Jerusalem. ¹²Solomon sat on the throne of his father David, and his kingship was firmly established.

¹³Now Adonijah son of Haggith came to Bathsheba, Solomon's mother. She asked, "Do you come peacefully?"

"Peacefully," he replied, ¹⁴and then asked, "May I talk with you?"

"Go ahead," she answered.

¹⁵"You know the kingship was mine," he said. "All Israel expected me to be king, but then the kingship was turned over to my brother, for the LORD gave it to him. ¹⁶So now I have just one request of you; don't turn me down."

She said to him, "Go on."

¹⁷He replied, "Please speak to King Solomon since he won't turn you down. Let him give me Abishag the Shunammite as a wife."

¹⁸"Very well," Bathsheba replied. "I will speak to the king for you."

¹⁹So Bathsheba went to King Solomon to speak to him about Adonijah. The king stood up to greet her, bowed to her, sat down on his throne, and had a throne placed for the king's mother. So she sat down at his right hand.

²⁰Then she said, "I have just one small request of you. Don't turn me down."

"Go ahead and ask, mother," the king replied, "for I won't turn you down."

²¹So she said, "Let Abishag the Shunammite be given to your brother Adonijah as a wife."

²²King Solomon answered his mother, "Why are you requesting Abishag the Shunammite for Adonijah? Since he is my elder brother, you might as well ask the kingship for him, for Abiathar the priest, and for Joab son of Zeruiah." ²³Then Solomon took an oath by the LORD: "May God punish me and do so severely if Adonijah has not made this request at the cost of his life. ²⁴And now, as the LORD lives, the One who established me, seated me on the throne of my father David, and made me a dynasty as He promised—I swear Adonijah will be put to death today!" ²⁵Then King Solomon gave the order to Benaiah son of Jehoiada, who struck down Adonijah, and he died.

²⁶The king said to Abiathar the priest, "Go to your fields in Anathoth. Even though you deserve to die, I will not put you to death today, since you carried the ark of the Lord GOD in the presence of my father David and you suffered through all that my father suffered." ²⁷So Solomon banished Abiathar from being the LORD's priest, and it fulfilled the LORD's prophecy He had spoken at Shiloh against Eli's family.

²⁸The news reached Joab. Since he had supported Adonijah but not Absalom, Joab fled to the LORD's tabernacle and took hold of the horns of the altar. ²⁹It was reported to King Solomon: "Joab has fled to the LORD's tabernacle and is now beside the altar." Then Solomon sent Benaiah son of Jehoiada and told him, "Go and strike him down!"

³⁰So Benaiah went to the tabernacle and said to Joab, "This is what the king says: 'Come out!'"

But Joab said, "No, for I will die here."

So Benaiah took a message back to the king, "This is what Joab said, and this is how he answered me."

³¹The king said to him, "Do just as he says. Strike him down and bury him in order to remove from me and from my father's house the blood that Joab shed without just cause. ³²The LORD will bring back his own blood on his head because he struck down two men more righteous and better than he, without my father David's knowledge. With his sword, Joab murdered Abner son of Ner, commander of Israel's army, and Amasa son of Jether, commander of Judah's army. ³³Their blood will come back on Joab's head and on the head of his descendants forever, but for David, his descendants, his dynasty, and his throne, there will be peace from the LORD forever."

³⁴Benaiah son of Jehoiada went up, struck down Joab, and put him to death. He was buried at his house in the wilderness. ³⁵Then the king appointed Benaiah son of Jehoiada in Joab's place over the army, and he appointed Zadok the priest in Abiathar's place.

³⁶Then the king summoned Shimei and said to him, "Build a house for yourself in Jerusalem and live there, but don't leave there and go anywhere else. ³⁷On the day you do leave and cross the Kidron Valley, know for sure that you will certainly die. Your blood will be on your own head."

³⁸Shimei said to the king, "The sentence is fair; your servant will do as my lord the king has spoken." And Shimei lived in Jerusalem for a long time.

³⁹But then, at the end of three years, two of Shimei's slaves ran away to Achish son of Maacah, king of Gath. Shimei was informed, "Look, your slaves are in Gath." ⁴⁰So Shimei saddled his donkey and set out to Achish at Gath to search for his slaves. He went and brought them back from Gath.

⁴¹It was reported to Solomon that Shimei had gone from Jerusalem to Gath and had returned. ⁴²So the king summoned Shimei and said to him, "Didn't I make you swear by the LORD and warn you, saying, 'On the day you leave and go anywhere else, know for sure that you will certainly die'? And you said to me, 'The sentence is fair; I will obey.' ⁴³So why have you not kept the LORD's oath and the command that I gave you?" ⁴⁴The king also said, "You yourself know all the evil that you did to my father David. Therefore, the LORD has brought back your evil on your head, ⁴⁵but King Solomon will be blessed, and David's throne will remain established before the LORD forever."

⁴⁶Then the king commanded Benaiah son of Jehoiada, and he went out and struck Shimei down, and he died. So the kingdom was established in Solomon's hand.

3 Solomon made an alliance with Pharaoh king of Egypt by marrying Pharaoh's daughter. Solomon brought her to live in the city of David until he finished building his palace, the LORD's temple, and the wall surrounding Jerusalem. ²However, the people were sacrificing on the *high places, because until that time a temple for the LORD's name had not been built. ³Solomon loved the LORD by walking in the statutes of his father David, but he also sacrificed and burned incense on the high places.

⁴The king went to Gibeon to sacrifice there because it was the most famous high place. He offered 1,000 *burnt offerings on that altar. ⁵At Gibeon the LORD appeared to Solomon in a dream at night. God said, "Ask. What should I give you?"

⁶And Solomon replied, "You have shown great and faithful love to Your servant, my father David, because he walked before You in faithfulness, righteousness, and integrity. You have continued this great and faithful love for him by giving him a son to sit on his throne, as it is today.

⁷"LORD my God, You have now made Your servant king in my father David's place. Yet I am just a youth with no experience in leadership. ⁸Your servant is among Your people You have chosen, a people too numerous to be numbered or counted. ⁹So give Your servant an obedient heart to judge Your people and to discern between good and evil. For who is able to judge this great people of Yours?"

¹⁰Now it pleased the Lord that Solomon had requested this. ¹¹So God said to him, "Because you have requested this and did not ask for long life or riches for yourself, or the death of your enemies, but you asked discernment for yourself to understand justice, ¹²I will therefore do what you have asked. I will give you a wise and understanding heart, so that there has never been anyone like you before and never will be again. ¹³In addition, I will give you what you did not ask for: both

riches and honor, so that no man in any kingdom will be your equal during your entire life. ¹⁴If you walk in My ways and keep My statutes and commands just as your father David did, I will give you a long life."

¹⁵Then Solomon woke up and realized it had been a dream. He went to Jerusalem, stood before the ark of the Lord's covenant, and offered burnt offerings and •fellowship offerings. Then he held a feast for all his servants.

¹⁶Then two women who were prostitutes came to the king and stood before him. ¹⁷One woman said, "Please my lord, this woman and I live in the same house, and I had a baby while she was in the house. ¹⁸On the third day after I gave birth, she also had a baby and we were alone. No one else was with us in the house; just the two of us were there. ¹⁹During the night this woman's son died because she lay on him. ²⁰She got up in the middle of the night and took my son from my side while your servant was asleep. She laid him at her breast, and she put her dead son in my arms. ²¹When I got up in the morning to nurse my son, I discovered he was dead. That morning, when I looked closely at him I realized that he was not the son I gave birth to."

²²"No," the other woman said. "My son is the living one; your son is the dead one."

The first woman said, "No, your son is the dead one; my son is the living one." So they argued before the king.

²³The king replied, "This woman says, 'This is my son who is alive, and your son is dead,' but that woman says, 'No, your son is dead, and my son is alive.'" ²⁴The king continued, "Bring me a sword." So they brought the sword to the king. ²⁵Solomon said, "Cut the living boy in two and give half to one and half to the other."

²⁶The woman whose son was alive spoke to the king because she felt great compassion for her son. "My lord, give her the living baby," she said, "but please don't have him killed!"

But the other one said, "He will not be mine or yours. Cut him in two!"

²⁷The king responded, "Give the living baby to the first woman, and don't kill him. She is his mother." ²⁸All Israel heard about the judgment the king had given, and they stood in awe of the king because they saw that God's wisdom was in him to carry out justice.

4 King Solomon ruled over Israel, ²and these were his officials:

Azariah son of Zadok, priest;
³Elihoreph and Ahijah the sons of Shisha, secretaries;
Jehoshaphat son of Ahilud, court historian;
⁴Benaiah son of Jehoiada, in charge of the army;
Zadok and Abiathar, priests;
⁵Azariah son of Nathan, in charge of the deputies;
Zabud son of Nathan, a priest and adviser to the king;
⁶Ahishar, in charge of the palace;
and Adoniram son of Abda, in charge of forced labor.

⁷Solomon had 12 deputies for all Israel. They provided food for the king and his household; each one made provision for one month out of the year. ⁸These were their names:

Ben-hur, in the hill country of Ephraim;
⁹Ben-deker, in Makaz, Shaalbim, Beth-shemesh, and Elon-beth-hanan;
¹⁰Ben-hesed, in Arubboth (he had Socoh and the whole land of Hepher);
¹¹Ben-abinadab, in all Naphath-dor (Taphath daughter of Solomon was his wife);
¹²Baana son of Ahilud, in Taanach, Megiddo, and all Beth-shean which is beside Zarethan below Jezreel, from Beth-shean to Abel-meholah, as far as the other side of Jokmeam;
¹³Ben-geber, in Ramoth-gilead (he had the villages of Jair son of Manasseh, which are in Gilead, and he had the region of Argob, which is in Bashan, 60 great cities with walls and bronze bars);
¹⁴Ahinadab son of Iddo, in Mahanaim;
¹⁵Ahimaaz, in Naphtali (he also had married a daughter of Solomon—Basemath);
¹⁶Baana son of Hushai, in Asher and Bealoth;
¹⁷Jehoshaphat son of Paruah, in Issachar;
¹⁸Shimei son of Ela, in Benjamin;
¹⁹Geber son of Uri, in the land of Gilead, the country of Sihon king of the Amorites and of Og king of Bashan.

There was one deputy in the land of Judah.

²⁰Judah and Israel were as numerous as the sand by the sea; they were eating, drinking, and rejoicing. ²¹Solomon ruled over all the kingdoms from the Euphrates River to the land of the Philistines and as far as the border of Egypt. They offered tribute and served Solomon all the days of his life.

²²Solomon's provisions for one day were 150 bushels of fine flour and 300 bushels of meal, ²³10 fattened oxen, 20 range oxen, and 100 sheep, besides deer, gazelles, roebucks, and pen-fed poultry, ²⁴for he had dominion over everything west of the Euphrates from Tiphsah to Gaza and over all the kings west of the Euphrates. He had peace on all his surrounding borders. ²⁵Throughout Solomon's reign, Judah and Israel lived in safety from Dan to Beer-sheba, each man under his own vine and his own fig tree. ²⁶Solomon had 40,000 stalls of horses for his chariots, and 12,000 horsemen. ²⁷Each of those deputies for a month in turn provided food for King Solomon and for everyone who came to King Solomon's table. They neglected nothing. ²⁸Each man brought the barley and the straw for the chariot teams and the other horses to the required place according to his assignment.

²⁹God gave Solomon wisdom, very great insight, and understanding as vast as the sand on the seashore. ³⁰Solomon's wisdom was greater than the wisdom of all the people of the East, greater than all the wisdom of Egypt. ³¹He was wiser than anyone—wiser than Ethan the Ezrahite, and Heman, Calcol, and Darda, sons of Mahol. His reputation extended to all the surrounding nations.

³²Solomon composed 3,000 proverbs, and his songs numbered 1,005. ³³He described trees, from the cedar in Lebanon to the hyssop growing out of the wall. He also taught about animals, birds, reptiles, and fish. ³⁴People came from everywhere, sent by every king on earth who had heard of his wisdom, to listen to Solomon's wisdom.

5 Hiram king of Tyre sent his servants to Solomon when he heard that he had been anointed king in his father's place, for Hiram had always been friends with David.

²Solomon sent this message to Hiram: ³"You know my father David was not able to build a temple for the name of ˙Yahweh his God. This was because of the warfare all around him until the LORD put his enemies under his feet. ⁴The LORD my God has now given me rest all around; there is no enemy or crisis. ⁵So I plan to build a temple for the name of Yahweh my God, according to what the LORD promised my father David: 'I will put your son on your throne in your place, and he will build the temple for My name.'

⁶"Therefore, command that cedars from Lebanon be cut down for me. My servants will be with your servants, and I will pay your servants' wages according to whatever you say, for you know that not a man among us knows how to cut timber like the Sidonians."

⁷When Hiram heard Solomon's words, he greatly rejoiced and said, "May the LORD be praised today! He has given David a wise son to be over this great people!" ⁸Then Hiram sent a reply to Solomon, saying, "I have heard your message; I will do everything you want regarding the cedar and cypress timber. ⁹My servants will bring the logs down from Lebanon to the sea, and I will make them into rafts to go by sea to the place you indicate. I will break them apart there, and you can take them away. You then can meet my needs by providing my household with food."

¹⁰So Hiram provided Solomon with all the cedar and cypress timber he wanted, ¹¹and Solomon provided Hiram with 100,000 bushels of wheat as food for his household and 110,000 gallons of oil from crushed olives. Solomon did this for Hiram year after year. •

¹²The LORD gave Solomon wisdom, as He had promised him. There was peace between Hiram and Solomon, and the two of them made a treaty.

¹³Then King Solomon drafted forced laborers from all Israel; the labor force numbered 30,000 men. ¹⁴He sent 10,000 to Lebanon each month in shifts; one month they were in Lebanon, two months they were at home. Adoniram was in charge of the forced labor. ¹⁵Solomon had 70,000 porters and 80,000 stonecutters in the mountains, ¹⁶not including his 3,300 deputies in charge of the work. They ruled over the people doing the work. ¹⁷The king commanded them to quarry large, costly stones to lay the foundation of the temple with dressed stones. ¹⁸So Solomon's builders and Hiram's builders, along with the Gebalites, quarried the stone and prepared the timber and stone for the temple's construction.

6 Solomon began to build the temple for the LORD in the four hundred eightieth year after the Israelites came out of the land of Egypt, in the fourth year of his reign over Israel, in the second month, in the month of Ziv. ²The temple that King Solomon built for the LORD was 90 feet long, 30 feet wide, and 45 feet high. ³The portico in front of the temple sanctuary was 30 feet long extending across the temple's width, and 15 feet deep in front of the temple. ⁴He also made windows with beveled frames for the temple.

⁵He then built a chambered structure along the temple wall, encircling the walls of the temple, that is, the sanctuary and the inner sanctuary. And he made side chambers all around. ⁶The lowest chamber was 7½ feet wide, the middle was nine feet wide, and the third was 10½ feet wide. He also provided offset ledges for the temple all around the outside so that nothing would be inserted into the temple walls. ⁷The temple's construction used finished stones cut at the quarry so that no hammer, chisel, or any iron tool was heard in the temple while it was being built.

⁸The door for the lowest side chamber was on the right side of the temple. They went up a stairway to the middle chamber, and from the middle to the third. ⁹When he finished building the temple, he paneled it with boards and planks of cedar. ¹⁰He built the chambers along the entire temple, joined to the temple with cedar beams; each story was 7½ feet high.

¹¹The word of the LORD came to Solomon: ¹²"As for this temple you are building—if you walk in My statutes, observe My ordinances, and keep all My commands by walking in them, I will fulfill My promise to you, which I made to your father David. ¹³I will live among the Israelites and not abandon My people Israel."

¹⁴When Solomon finished building the temple, ¹⁵he paneled the interior temple walls with cedar boards; from the temple floor to the surface of the ceiling he overlaid the interior with wood. He also overlaid the floor with cypress boards. ¹⁶Then he lined 30 feet of the rear of the temple with cedar boards from the floor to the surface of the ceiling, and he built the interior as an inner sanctuary, the most holy place. ¹⁷The temple, that is, the sanctuary in front of the most holy place, was 60 feet long. ¹⁸The cedar paneling inside the temple was carved with ornamental gourds and flower blossoms. Everything was cedar; not a stone could be seen.

¹⁹He prepared the inner sanctuary inside the temple to put the ark of the LORD's covenant there. ²⁰The interior of the sanctuary was 30 feet long, 30 feet wide, and 30 feet high; he overlaid it with pure gold. He also overlaid the cedar altar. ²¹Next, Solomon overlaid the interior of the temple with pure gold, and he hung gold chains across the front of the inner sanctuary and overlaid it with gold. ²²So he added the gold overlay to the entire temple until everything was completely finished, including the entire altar that belongs to the inner sanctuary.

²³In the inner sanctuary he made two ˙cherubim 15 feet high out of olive wood. ²⁴One wing of the first cherub was 7½ feet long, and the other wing was 7½ feet long. The wingspan was 15 feet from tip to tip. ²⁵The second cherub also was 15 feet; both cherubim had the same size and shape. ²⁶The first cherub's height was 15 feet and so was the second cherub's. ²⁷Then he put the cherubim inside the inner temple. Since their wings were spread out, the first one's wing touched one wall while the second cherub's wing touched the other wall, and in the middle of the temple their wings were touching wing to wing. ²⁸He also overlaid the cherubim with gold.

²⁹He carved all the surrounding temple walls with carved engravings—cherubim, palm trees and flower blossoms—in both the inner and outer sanctuaries. ³⁰He overlaid the temple floor with gold in both the inner and outer sanctuaries.

³¹For the entrance of the inner sanctuary, he made olive wood doors. The pillars of the doorposts were five-sided. ³²The two doors were made of olive wood. He carved cherubim, palm trees, and flower blossoms on them and overlaid them with gold, hammering

gold over the cherubim and palm trees. ³³In the same way, he made four-sided olive wood doorposts for the sanctuary entrance. ³⁴The two doors were made of cypress wood; the first door had two folding sides, and the second door had two folding panels. ³⁵He carved cherubim, palm trees, and flower blossoms on them and overlaid them with gold applied evenly over the carving. ³⁶He built the inner courtyard with three rows of dressed stone and a row of trimmed cedar beams.

³⁷The foundation of the LORD's temple was laid in Solomon's fourth year in the month of Ziv. ³⁸In his eleventh year in the eighth month, in the month of Bul, the temple was completed in every detail and according to every specification. So he built it in seven years.

7 Solomon completed his entire palace complex after 13 years of construction. ²He built the House of the Forest of Lebanon. It was 150 feet long, 75 feet wide, and 45 feet high on four rows of cedar pillars, with cedar beams on top of the pillars. ³It was paneled above with cedar at the top of the chambers that rested on 45 pillars, 15 per row. ⁴There were three rows of window frames, facing each other in three tiers. ⁵All the doors and doorposts had rectangular frames, the openings facing each other in three tiers. ⁶He made the hall of pillars 75 feet long and 45 feet wide. A portico was in front of the pillars, and a canopy with pillars was in front of them. ⁷He made the Hall of the Throne where he would judge—the Hall of Judgment. It was paneled with cedar from the floor to the rafters. ⁸Solomon's own palace where he would live, in the other courtyard behind the hall, was of similar construction. And he made a house like this hall for Pharaoh's daughter, his wife.

⁹All of these buildings were of costly stones, cut to size and sawed with saws on the inner and outer surfaces, from foundation to coping and from the outside to the great courtyard. ¹⁰The foundation was made of large, costly stones 12 and 15 feet long. ¹¹Above were also costly stones, cut to size, as well as cedar wood. ¹²Around the great courtyard, as well as the inner courtyard of the LORD's temple and the portico of the temple, were three rows of dressed stone and a row of trimmed cedar beams.

¹³King Solomon had Hiram brought from Tyre. ¹⁴He was a widow's son from the tribe of Naphtali, and his father was a man of Tyre, a bronze craftsman. Hiram had great skill, understanding, and knowledge to do every kind of bronze work. So he came to King Solomon and carried out all his work.

¹⁵He cast two hollow bronze pillars: each 27 feet high and 18 feet in circumference. ¹⁶He also made two capitals of cast bronze to set on top of the pillars; 7¹/₂ feet was the height of the first capital, and 7¹/₂ feet was also the height of the second capital. ¹⁷The capitals on top of the pillars had gratings of latticework, wreaths made of chainwork—seven for the first capital and seven for the second.

¹⁸He made the pillars with two encircling rows of pomegranates on the one grating to cover the capital on top; he did the same for the second capital. ¹⁹And the capitals on top of the pillars in the portico were shaped like lilies, six feet high. ²⁰The capitals on the two pillars were also immediately above the rounded surface next to the grating, and 200 pomegranates were in rows encircling each capital. ²¹He set up the pillars at the portico of the sanctuary: he set up the right pillar and named it Jachin; then he set up the left pillar and named it Boaz. ²²The tops of the pillars were shaped like lilies. Then the work of the pillars was completed.

²³He made the cast metal reservoir, 15 feet from brim to brim, perfectly round. It was 7¹/₂ feet high and 45 feet in circumference. ²⁴Ornamental gourds encircled it below the brim, 10 every half yard, completely encircling the reservoir. The gourds were cast in two rows when the reservoir was cast. ²⁵It stood on 12 oxen, three facing north, three facing west, three facing south, and three facing east. The reservoir was on top of them and all their hindquarters were toward the center. ²⁶The reservoir was three inches thick, and its rim was fashioned like the brim of a cup or of a lily blossom. It held 11,000 gallons.

²⁷Then he made 10 bronze water carts. Each water cart was six feet long, six feet wide, and 4¹/₂ feet high. ²⁸This was the design of the carts: They had frames; the frames were between the cross-pieces, ²⁹and on the frames between the cross-pieces were lions, oxen, and ⸱cherubim. On the cross-pieces there was a pedestal above, and below the lions and oxen were wreaths of hanging work. ³⁰Each cart had four bronze wheels with bronze axles. Underneath the four corners of the basin were cast supports, each next to a wreath. ³¹And the water cart's opening inside the crown on top was 18 inches wide. The opening was round, made as a pedestal 27 inches wide. On it were carvings, but their frames were square, not round. ³²There were four wheels under the frames, and the wheel axles were part of the water cart; each wheel was 27 inches tall. ³³The wheels' design was similar to that of chariot wheels: their axles, rims, spokes, and hubs were all of cast metal. ³⁴Four supports were at the four corners of each water cart; each support was one piece with the water cart. ³⁵At the top of the cart was a band nine inches high encircling it; also, at the top of the cart, its braces and its frames were one piece with it. ³⁶He engraved cherubim, lions, and palm trees on the plates of its braces and on its frames, wherever each had space, with encircling wreaths. ³⁷In this way he made the 10 water carts using the same casting, dimensions, and shape for all of them.

³⁸Then he made 10 bronze basins—each basin holding 220 gallons and each was six feet wide—one basin for each of the 10 water carts. ³⁹He set five water carts on the right side of the temple and five on the left side. He put the reservoir near the right side of the temple toward the southeast. ⁴⁰Then Hiram made the basins, the shovels, and the sprinkling basins.

So Hiram finished all the work that he was doing for King Solomon on the LORD's temple: ⁴¹two pillars; bowls for the capitals that were on top of the two pillars; the two gratings for covering both bowls of the capitals that were on top of the pillars; ⁴²the 400 pomegranates for the two gratings (two rows of pomegranates for each grating covering both capitals' bowls on top of the pillars); ⁴³the 10 water carts; the 10 basins on the water carts; ⁴⁴the reservoir; the 12 oxen underneath the reservoir; ⁴⁵and the pots, shovels, and sprinkling basins. All the utensils that Hiram made for King Solomon at the LORD's temple were made of burnished bronze. ⁴⁶The king had them cast in clay molds in the Jordan Valley between Succoth and Zarethan. ⁴⁷Solomon left all the utensils unweighed because there were so many; the weight of the bronze was not determined.

⁴⁸ Solomon also made all the equipment in the LORD's temple: the gold altar; the gold table that the *bread of the Presence was placed on; ⁴⁹ the pure gold lampstands in front of the inner sanctuary, five on the right and five on the left; the gold flowers, lamps, and tongs; ⁵⁰ the pure gold ceremonial bowls, wick trimmers, sprinkling basins, ladles, and firepans; and the gold hinges for the doors of the inner temple (that is, the most holy place) and for the doors of the temple sanctuary.

⁵¹ So all the work King Solomon did in the LORD's temple was completed. Then Solomon brought in the consecrated things of his father David—the silver, the gold, and the utensils—and put them in the treasuries of the LORD's temple.

8 At that time Solomon assembled the elders of Israel, all the tribal heads and the ancestral leaders of the Israelites before him at Jerusalem in order to bring the ark of the LORD's covenant from the city of David, that is *Zion. ² So all the men of Israel were assembled in the presence of King Solomon in the seventh month, the month of Ethanim, at the festival.

³ All the elders of Israel came, and the priests picked up the ark. ⁴ The priests and the Levites brought the ark of the LORD, the tent of meeting, and the holy utensils that were in the tent. ⁵ King Solomon and the entire congregation of Israel, who had gathered around him and were with him in front of the ark, were sacrificing sheep and cattle that could not be counted or numbered, because there were so many. ⁶ The priests brought the ark of the LORD's covenant to its place, into the inner sanctuary of the temple, to the most holy place beneath the wings of the *cherubim. ⁷ For the cherubim were spreading their wings over the place of the ark, so that the cherubim covered the ark and its poles from above. ⁸ The poles were so long that their ends were seen from the holy place in front of the inner sanctuary, but they were not seen from outside the sanctuary; they are there to this day. ⁹ Nothing was in the ark except the two stone tablets that Moses had put there at Horeb, where the LORD made a covenant with the Israelites when they came out of the land of Egypt.

¹⁰ When the priests came out of the holy place, the cloud filled the LORD's temple, ¹¹ and because of the cloud, the priests were not able to continue ministering, for the glory of the LORD filled the temple.

¹² Then Solomon said:

The LORD said that He would dwell
  in thick darkness.
¹³ I have indeed built an exalted temple for You,
  a place for Your dwelling forever.

¹⁴ The king turned around and blessed the entire congregation of Israel while they were standing. ¹⁵ He said:

May the LORD God of Israel be praised!
He spoke directly to my father David,
and He has fulfilled the promise by His power.
He said,
¹⁶ "Since the day I brought My people Israel
    out of Egypt,
I have not chosen a city to build a temple in
  among any of the tribes of Israel,
so that My name would be there.
But I have chosen David to rule
  My people Israel."

¹⁷ It was in the desire of my father David

to build a temple for the name of *Yahweh, the
  God of Israel.
¹⁸ But the LORD said to my father David,
"Since it was your desire to build a temple
  for My name,
you have done well to have this desire.
¹⁹ Yet you are not the one to build it;
instead, your son, your own offspring,
will build it for My name."
²⁰ The LORD has fulfilled what He promised.
I have taken the place of my father David,
and I sit on the throne of Israel,
  as the LORD promised.
I have built the temple for the name
  of Yahweh, the God of Israel.
²¹ I have provided a place there for the ark,
where the LORD's covenant is
that He made with our ancestors
when He brought them out of the land
  of Egypt.

²² Then Solomon stood before the altar of the LORD in front of the entire congregation of Israel and spread out his hands toward heaven. ²³ He said:

LORD God of Israel,
there is no God like You
in heaven above or on earth below,
keeping the gracious covenant
with Your servants who walk before You
with their whole heart.
²⁴ You have kept what You promised
to Your servant, my father David.
You spoke directly to him
and You fulfilled Your promise by Your power
as it is today.
²⁵ Therefore, LORD God of Israel,
keep what You promised
to Your servant, my father David:
You will never fail to have a man
to sit before Me on the throne of Israel,
if only your sons guard their walk before Me
as you have walked before Me.
²⁶ Now LORD God of Israel,
please confirm what You promised
to Your servant, my father David.
²⁷ But will God indeed live on earth?
Even heaven, the highest heaven,
  cannot contain You,
much less this temple I have built.
²⁸ Listen to Your servant's prayer
  and his petition,
LORD my God,
so that You may hear the cry and the prayer
that Your servant prays before You today,
²⁹ so that Your eyes may watch over this temple
  night and day,
toward the place where You said:
My name will be there,
and so that You may hear the prayer
that Your servant prays toward this place.
³⁰ Hear the petition of Your servant
and Your people Israel,
which they pray toward this place.
May You hear in Your dwelling place
  in heaven.
May You hear and forgive.
³¹ When a man sins against his neighbor
and is forced to take an oath,

and he comes to take an oath
before Your altar in this temple,
³² may You hear in heaven and act.
May You judge Your servants,
condemning the wicked man by bringing
what he has done on his own head
and providing justice for the righteous
by rewarding him according to
his righteousness.
³³ When Your people Israel are defeated
before an enemy,
because they have sinned against You,
and they return to You and praise Your name,
and they pray and plead with You
for mercy in this temple,
³⁴ may You hear in heaven
and forgive the sin of Your people Israel.
May You restore them to the land
You gave their ancestors.
³⁵ When the skies are shut and there is no rain,
because they have sinned against You,
and they pray toward this place
and praise Your name,
and they turn from their sins
because You are afflicting them,
³⁶ may You hear in heaven
and forgive the sin of Your servants
and Your people Israel,
so that You may teach them the good way
they should walk in.
May You send rain on Your land
that You gave Your people for an inheritance.
³⁷ When there is famine on the earth,
when there is pestilence,
when there is blight, mildew, locust,
or grasshopper,
when their enemy besieges them
in the region of their fortified cities,
when there is any plague or illness,
³⁸ whatever prayer or petition
anyone from Your people Israel might have—
each man knowing his own afflictions
and spreading out his hands
toward this temple—
³⁹ may You hear in heaven, Your dwelling place,
and may You forgive, act, and repay the man,
according to all his ways, since You know
his heart,
for You alone know every human heart,
⁴⁰ so that they may ·fear You
all the days they live on the land
You gave our ancestors.
⁴¹ Even for the foreigner who is not
of Your people Israel
but has come from a distant land
because of Your name—
⁴² for they will hear of Your great name,
mighty hand, and outstretched arm,
and will come and pray toward this temple—
⁴³ may You hear in heaven, Your dwelling place,
and do according to all the foreigner
asks You for.
Then all the people on earth will know
Your name,
to fear You as Your people Israel do
and know that this temple I have built
is called by Your name.

⁴⁴ When Your people go out to fight
against their enemies,
wherever You send them,
and they pray to Yahweh
in the direction of the city You have chosen
and the temple I have built for Your name,
⁴⁵ may You hear their prayer and petition
in heaven
and uphold their cause.
⁴⁶ When they sin against You—
for there is no one who does not sin—
and You are angry with them
and hand them over to the enemy,
and their captors deport them
to the enemy's country—
whether distant or nearby—
⁴⁷ and when they come to their senses
in the land where they were deported
and repent and petition You
in their captors' land:
"We have sinned and done wrong;
we have been wicked,"
⁴⁸ and when they return to You
with their whole mind and heart
in the land of their enemies
who took them captive,
and when they pray to You in the direction
of their land
that You gave their ancestors,
the city You have chosen,
and the temple I have built for Your name,
⁴⁹ may You hear in heaven, Your dwelling place,
their prayer and petition and uphold
their cause.
⁵⁰ May You forgive Your people
who sinned against You
and all their rebellions against You,
and may You give them compassion
in the eyes of their captors,
so that they may be compassionate to them.
⁵¹ For they are Your people
and Your inheritance;
You brought them out of Egypt,
out of the middle of an iron furnace.
⁵² May Your eyes be open
to Your servant's petition
and to the petition of Your people Israel,
listening to them whenever they call to You.
⁵³ For You, Lord GOD, have set them apart
as Your inheritance
from all the people on earth,
as You spoke through Your servant Moses
when You brought their ancestors
out of Egypt.

⁵⁴ When Solomon finished praying this entire prayer
and petition to the LORD, he got up from kneeling before the altar of the LORD, with his hands spread out
toward heaven, ⁵⁵ and he stood and blessed the whole
congregation of Israel with a loud voice: ⁵⁶ "May the
LORD be praised! He has given rest to His people Israel
according to all He has said. Not one of all the good
promises He made through His servant Moses has
failed. ⁵⁷ May the LORD our God be with us as He was
with our ancestors. May He not abandon us or leave us
⁵⁸ so that He causes us to be devoted to Him, to walk
in all His ways, and to keep His commands, statutes,
and ordinances, which He commanded our ancestors.

⁵⁹ May my words I have made my petition with before the Lord be near the Lord our God day and night, so that He may uphold His servant's cause and the cause of His people Israel, as each day requires, ⁶⁰ and so that all the peoples of the earth may know that Yahweh is God. There is no other! ⁶¹ Let your heart be completely devoted to the Lord our God to walk in His statutes and to keep His commands, as it is today."

⁶² The king and all Israel with him were offering sacrifices in the Lord's presence. ⁶³ Solomon offered a sacrifice of ˚fellowship offerings to the Lord: 22,000 cattle and 120,000 sheep. In this manner the king and all the Israelites dedicated the Lord's temple.

⁶⁴ On the same day, the king consecrated the middle of the courtyard that was in front of the Lord's temple because that was where he offered the ˚burnt offering, the ˚grain offering, and the fat of the fellowship offerings since the bronze altar before the Lord was too small to accommodate the burnt offerings, the grain offerings, and the fat of the fellowship offerings.

⁶⁵ Solomon and all Israel with him—a great assembly, from the entrance of Hamath to the Brook of Egypt—observed the festival at that time in the presence of the Lord our God, seven days, and seven more days—14 days. ⁶⁶ On the fifteenth day he sent the people away. So they blessed the king and went home to their tents rejoicing and with joyful hearts for all the goodness that the Lord had done for His servant David and for His people Israel.

9 When Solomon finished building the temple of the Lord, the royal palace, and all that Solomon desired to do, ² the Lord appeared to Solomon a second time just as He had appeared to him at Gibeon. ³ The Lord said to him:

I have heard your prayer and petition you have made before Me. I have consecrated this temple you have built, to put My name there forever; My eyes and My heart will be there at all times. ⁴ As for you, if you walk before Me as your father David walked, with a heart of integrity and in what is right, doing everything I have commanded you, and if you keep My statutes and ordinances, ⁵ I will establish your royal throne over Israel forever, as I promised your father David: You will never fail to have a man on the throne of Israel.

⁶ If you or your sons turn away from following Me and do not keep My commands—My statutes that I have set before you—and if you go and serve other gods and worship them, ⁷ I will cut off Israel from the land I gave them, and I will reject the temple I have sanctified for My name. Israel will become an object of scorn and ridicule among all the peoples. ⁸ Though this temple is now exalted, everyone who passes by will be appalled and will mock. They will say: Why did the Lord do this to this land and this temple? ⁹ Then they will say: Because they abandoned the Lord their God who brought their ancestors out of the land of Egypt. They clung to other gods and worshiped and served them. Because of this, the Lord brought all this ruin on them.

¹⁰ At the end of 20 years during which Solomon had built the two houses, the Lord's temple and the royal palace— ¹¹ Hiram king of Tyre having supplied him with cedar and cypress logs and gold for his every wish—King Solomon gave Hiram 20 towns in the land

of Galilee. ¹² So Hiram went out from Tyre to look over the towns that Solomon had given him, but he was not pleased with them. ¹³ So he said, "What are these towns you've given me, my brother?" So he called them the Land of Cabul, as they are still called today. ¹⁴ Now Hiram had sent the king 9,000 pounds of gold.

¹⁵ This is the account of the forced labor that King Solomon had imposed to build the Lord's temple, his own palace, the supporting terraces, the wall of Jerusalem, and Hazor, Megiddo, and Gezer. ¹⁶ Pharaoh king of Egypt had attacked and captured Gezer. He then burned it down, killed the Canaanites who lived in the city, and gave it as a dowry to his daughter, Solomon's wife. ¹⁷ Then Solomon rebuilt Gezer, Lower Beth-horon, ¹⁸ Baalath, Tamar in the Wilderness of Judah, ¹⁹ all the storage cities that belonged to Solomon, the chariot cities, the cavalry cities, and whatever Solomon desired to build in Jerusalem, Lebanon, or anywhere else in the land of his dominion.

²⁰ As for all the peoples who remained of the Amorites, Hittites, Perizzites, Hivites, and Jebusites, who were not Israelites— ²¹ their descendants who remained in the land after them, those whom the Israelites were unable to ˚completely destroy—Solomon imposed forced labor on them; it is this way until today. ²² But Solomon did not consign the Israelites to slavery; they were soldiers, his servants, his commanders, his captains, and commanders of his chariots and his cavalry. ²³ These were the deputies who were over Solomon's work: 550 who ruled over the people doing the work.

²⁴ Pharaoh's daughter moved from the city of David to the house that Solomon had built for her; he then built the terraces.

²⁵ Three times a year Solomon offered ˚burnt offerings and ˚fellowship offerings on the altar he had built for the Lord, and he burned incense with them in the Lord's presence. So he completed the temple.

²⁶ King Solomon put together a fleet of ships at Ezion-geber, which is near Eloth on the shore of the ˚Red Sea in the land of Edom. ²⁷ With the fleet, Hiram sent his servants, experienced seamen, along with Solomon's servants. ²⁸ They went to Ophir and acquired gold there—16 tons—and delivered it to Solomon.

10 The queen of Sheba heard about Solomon's fame connected with the name of ˚Yahweh and came to test him with difficult questions. ² She came to Jerusalem with a very large entourage, with camels bearing spices, gold in great abundance, and precious stones. She came to Solomon and spoke to him about everything that was on her mind. ³ So Solomon answered all her questions; nothing was too difficult for the king to explain to her. ⁴ When the queen of Sheba observed all of Solomon's wisdom, the palace he had built, ⁵ the food at his table, his servants' residence, his attendants' service and their attire, his cupbearers, and the ˚burnt offerings he offered at the Lord's temple, it took her breath away.

⁶ She said to the king, "The report I heard in my own country about your words and about your wisdom is true. ⁷ But I didn't believe the reports until I came and saw with my own eyes. Indeed, I was not even told half. Your wisdom and prosperity far exceed the report I heard. ⁸ How happy are your men. How happy are these servants of yours, who always stand in your presence hearing your wisdom. ⁹ May Yahweh your God be praised! He delighted in you and put you

on the throne of Israel, because of the LORD's eternal love for Israel. He has made you king to carry out justice and righteousness."

¹⁰Then she gave the king four and a half tons of gold, a great quantity of spices, and precious stones. Never again did such a quantity of spices arrive as those the queen of Sheba gave to King Solomon.

¹¹In addition, Hiram's fleet that carried gold from Ophir brought from Ophir a large quantity of almug wood and precious stones. ¹²The king made the almug wood into steps for the LORD's temple and the king's palace and into lyres and harps for the singers. Never before had such almug wood come, and the like has not been seen again even to this very day.

¹³King Solomon gave the queen of Sheba her every desire—whatever she asked—besides what he had given her out of his royal bounty. Then she, along with her servants, returned to her own country.

¹⁴The weight of gold that came to Solomon annually was 25 tons, ¹⁵besides what came from merchants, traders' merchandise, and all the Arabian kings and governors of the land.

¹⁶King Solomon made 200 large shields of hammered gold; 15 pounds of gold went into each shield. ¹⁷He made 300 small shields of hammered gold; about four pounds of gold went into each shield. The king put them in the House of the Forest of Lebanon.

¹⁸The king also made a large ivory throne and overlaid it with fine gold. ¹⁹The throne had six steps; there was a rounded top at the back of the throne, armrests on either side of the seat, and two lions standing beside the armrests. ²⁰Twelve lions were standing there on the six steps, one at each end. Nothing like it had ever been made in any other kingdom.

²¹All of King Solomon's drinking cups were gold, and all the utensils of the House of the Forest of Lebanon were pure gold. There was no silver, since it was considered as nothing in Solomon's time, ²²for the king had ships of Tarshish at sea with Hiram's fleet, and once every three years the ships of Tarshish would arrive bearing gold, silver, ivory, apes, and peacocks.

²³King Solomon surpassed all the kings of the world in riches and in wisdom. ²⁴The whole world wanted an audience with Solomon to hear the wisdom that God had put in his heart. ²⁵Every man would bring his annual tribute: items of silver and gold, clothing, weapons, spices, and horses and mules.

²⁶Solomon accumulated 1,400 chariots and 12,000 horsemen and stationed them in the chariot cities and with the king in Jerusalem. ²⁷The king made silver as common in Jerusalem as stones, and he made cedar as abundant as sycamore in the Judean foothills. ²⁸Solomon's horses were imported from Egypt and Kue. The king's traders bought them from Kue at the going price. ²⁹A chariot was imported from Egypt for 15 pounds of silver, and a horse for about four pounds. In the same way, they exported them to all the kings of the Hittites and to the kings of Aram through their agents.

11 King Solomon loved many foreign women in addition to Pharaoh's daughter: Moabite, Ammonite, Edomite, Sidonian, and Hittite women ²from the nations that the LORD had told the Israelites about, "Do not intermarry with them, and they must not intermarry with you, because they will turn you away from Me to their gods." Solomon was deeply attached to these women and loved them. ³He had 700 wives who were princesses and 300 concubines, and they turned his heart away from the LORD.

⁴When Solomon was old, his wives seduced him to follow other gods. He was not completely devoted to ˙Yahweh his God, as his father David had been. ⁵Solomon followed ˙Ashtoreth, the goddess of the Sidonians, and ˙Milcom, the detestable idol of the Ammonites. ⁶Solomon did what was evil in the LORD's sight, and unlike his father David, he did not completely follow Yahweh.

⁷At that time, Solomon built a ˙high place for Chemosh, the detestable idol of Moab, and for Milcom, the detestable idol of the Ammonites, on the hill across from Jerusalem. ⁸He did the same for all his foreign wives, who were burning incense and offering sacrifices to their gods.

⁹The LORD was angry with Solomon, because his heart had turned away from Yahweh, the God of Israel, who had appeared to him twice. ¹⁰He had commanded him about this, so that he would not follow other gods, but Solomon did not do what the LORD had commanded.

¹¹Then the LORD said to Solomon, "Since you have done this and did not keep My covenant and My statutes, which I commanded you, I will tear the kingdom away from you and give it to your servant. ¹²However, I will not do it during your lifetime because of your father David; I will tear it out of your son's hand. ¹³Yet I will not tear the entire kingdom away from him. I will give one tribe to your son because of my servant David and because of Jerusalem that I chose."

¹⁴So the LORD raised up Hadad the Edomite as an enemy against Solomon. He was of the royal family in Edom. ¹⁵Earlier, when David was in Edom, Joab, the commander of the army, had gone to bury the dead and had struck down every male in Edom. ¹⁶For Joab and all Israel had remained there six months, until he had killed every male in Edom. ¹⁷Hadad fled to Egypt, along with some Edomites from his father's servants. At the time Hadad was a small boy. ¹⁸Hadad and his men set out from Midian and went to Paran. They took men with them from Paran and went to Egypt, to Pharaoh king of Egypt, who gave Hadad a house, ordered that he be given food, and gave him land. ¹⁹Pharaoh liked Hadad so much that he gave him a wife, the sister of his own wife, Queen Tahpenes. ²⁰Tahpenes' sister gave birth to Hadad's son Genubath. Tahpenes herself weaned him in Pharaoh's palace, and Genubath lived there along with Pharaoh's sons.

²¹When Hadad heard in Egypt that David rested with his fathers and that Joab, the commander of the army, was dead, Hadad said to Pharaoh, "Let me leave, so I can go to my own country."

²²But Pharaoh asked him, "What do you lack here with me for you to want to go back to your own country?"

"Nothing," he replied, "but please let me leave."

²³God raised up Rezon son of Eliada as an enemy against Solomon. Rezon had fled from his master Hadadezer king of Zobah ²⁴and gathered men to himself. He became captain of a raiding party when David killed the Zobaites. He went to Damascus, lived there, and became king in Damascus. ²⁵Rezon was Israel's enemy throughout Solomon's reign, adding to the trouble Hadad had caused. He ruled over Aram, but he loathed Israel.

²⁶Now Solomon's servant, Jeroboam son of Ne-

bat, was an Ephraimite from Zeredah. His widowed mother's name was Zeruah. Jeroboam rebelled against Solomon, ²⁷ and this is the reason he rebelled against the king: Solomon had built the supporting terraces and repaired the opening in the wall of the city of his father David. ²⁸ Now the man Jeroboam was capable, and Solomon noticed the young man because he was getting things done. So he appointed him over the entire labor force of the house of Joseph.

²⁹ During that time, the prophet Ahijah the Shilonite met Jeroboam on the road as Jeroboam came out of Jerusalem. Now Ahijah had wrapped himself with a new cloak, and the two of them were alone in the open field. ³⁰ Then Ahijah took hold of the new cloak he had on, tore it into 12 pieces, ³¹ and said to Jeroboam, "Take 10 pieces for yourself, for this is what the LORD God of Israel says: 'I am about to tear the kingdom out of Solomon's hand. I will give you 10 tribes, ³² but one tribe will remain his because of my servant David and because of Jerusalem, the city I chose out of all the tribes of Israel. ³³ For they have abandoned Me; they have bowed the knee to Ashtoreth, the goddess of the Sidonians, to Chemosh, the god of Moab, and to Milcom, the god of the Ammonites. They have not walked in My ways to do what is right in My eyes and to carry out My statutes and My judgments as his father David did.

³⁴ "'However, I will not take the whole kingdom from his hand but will let him be ruler all the days of his life because of My servant David, whom I chose and who kept My commands and My statutes. ³⁵ I will take 10 tribes of the kingdom from his son's hand and give them to you. ³⁶ I will give one tribe to his son, so that My servant David will always have a lamp before Me in Jerusalem, the city I chose for Myself to put My name there. ³⁷ I will appoint you, and you will reign as king over all you want, and you will be king over Israel.

³⁸ "'After that, if you obey all I command you, walk in My ways, and do what is right in My sight in order to keep My statutes and My commands as My servant David did, I will be with you. I will build you a lasting dynasty just as I built for David, and I will give you Israel. ³⁹ I will humble David's descendants, because of their unfaithfulness, but not forever.'"

⁴⁰ Therefore, Solomon tried to kill Jeroboam, but he fled to Egypt, to Shishak king of Egypt, where he remained until Solomon's death.

⁴¹ The rest of the events of Solomon's reign, along with all his accomplishments and his wisdom, are written in the Book of Solomon's Events. ⁴² The length of Solomon's reign in Jerusalem over all Israel totaled 40 years. ⁴³ Solomon rested with his fathers and was buried in the city of his father David. His son Rehoboam became king in his place.

12 Then Rehoboam went to Shechem, for all Israel had gone to Shechem to make him king. ² When Jeroboam son of Nebat heard about it, for he was still in Egypt where he had fled from King Solomon's presence, Jeroboam stayed in Egypt. ³ They summoned him, and Jeroboam and the whole assembly of Israel came and spoke to Rehoboam: ⁴ "Your father made our yoke difficult. You, therefore, lighten your father's harsh service and the heavy yoke he put on us, and we will serve you."

⁵ Rehoboam replied, "Go home for three days and then return to me." So the people left. ⁶ Then King Rehoboam consulted with the elders who had served his father Solomon when he was alive, asking, "How do you advise me to respond to these people?"

⁷ They replied, "Today if you will be a servant to these people and serve them, and if you respond to them by speaking kind words to them, they will be your servants forever."

⁸ But he rejected the advice of the elders who had advised him and consulted with the young men who had grown up with him and served him. ⁹ He asked them, "What message do you advise that we send back to these people who said to me, 'Lighten the yoke your father put on us'?"

¹⁰ Then the young men who had grown up with him told him, "This is what you should say to these people who said to you, 'Your father made our yoke heavy, but you, make it lighter on us!' This is what you should tell them: 'My little finger is thicker than my father's loins! ¹¹ Although my father burdened you with a heavy yoke, I will add to your yoke; my father disciplined you with whips, but I will discipline you with barbed whips.'"

¹² So Jeroboam and all the people came to Rehoboam on the third day, as the king had ordered: "Return to me on the third day." ¹³ Then the king answered the people harshly. He rejected the advice the elders had given him ¹⁴ and spoke to them according to the young men's advice: "My father made your yoke heavy, but I will add to your yoke; my father disciplined you with whips, but I will discipline you with barbed whips."

¹⁵ The king did not listen to the people, because this turn of events came from the LORD to carry out His word, which the LORD had spoken through Ahijah the Shilonite to Jeroboam son of Nebat. ¹⁶ When all Israel saw that the king had not listened to them, the people answered him:

> What portion do we have in David?
> We have no inheritance in the son of Jesse.
> Israel, return to your tents;
> David, now look after your own house!

So Israel went to their tents, ¹⁷ but Rehoboam reigned over the Israelites living in the cities of Judah.

¹⁸ Then King Rehoboam sent Adoram, who was in charge of forced labor, but all Israel stoned him to death. King Rehoboam managed to get into the chariot and flee to Jerusalem. ¹⁹ Israel is in rebellion against the house of David until today.

²⁰ When all Israel heard that Jeroboam had come back, they summoned him to the assembly and made him king over all Israel. No one followed the house of David except the tribe of Judah alone. ²¹ When Rehoboam arrived in Jerusalem, he mobilized 180,000 choice warriors from the entire house of Judah and the tribe of Benjamin to fight against the house of Israel to restore the kingdom to Rehoboam son of Solomon. ²² But a revelation from God came to Shemaiah, the man of God: ²³ "Say to Rehoboam son of Solomon, king of Judah, to the whole house of Judah and Benjamin, and to the rest of the people, ²⁴ 'This is what the LORD says: You are not to march up and fight against your brothers, the Israelites. Each of you must return home, for I have done this.'"

So they listened to what the LORD said and went back as He had told them.

²⁵ Jeroboam built Shechem in the hill country of Ephraim and lived there. From there he went out and built Penuel. ²⁶ Jeroboam said to himself, "The way things are going now, the kingdom might return

to the house of David. ²⁷If these people regularly go to offer sacrifices in the LORD's temple in Jerusalem, the heart of these people will return to their lord, Rehoboam king of Judah. They will murder me and go back to the king of Judah." ²⁸So the king sought advice.

Then he made two golden calves, and he said to the people, "Going to Jerusalem is too difficult for you. Israel, here is your God who brought you out of the land of Egypt." ²⁹He set up one in Bethel, and put the other in Dan. ³⁰This led to sin; the people walked in procession before one of the calves all the way to Dan.

³¹Jeroboam also built shrines on the ·high places and set up priests from every class of people who were not Levites. ³²Jeroboam made a festival in the eighth month on the fifteenth day of the month, like the festival in Judah. He offered sacrifices on the altar; he made this offering in Bethel to sacrifice to the calves he had set up. He also stationed the priests in Bethel for the high places he had set up. ³³He offered sacrifices on the altar he had set up in Bethel on the fifteenth day of the eighth month. He chose this month on his own. He made a festival for the Israelites, offered sacrifices on the altar, and burned incense.

13 A man of God came from Judah to Bethel by a revelation from the LORD while Jeroboam was standing beside the altar to burn incense. ²The man of God cried out against the altar by a revelation from the LORD: "Altar, altar, this is what the LORD says, 'A son will be born to the house of David, named Josiah, and he will sacrifice on you the priests of the ·high places who are burning incense on you. Human bones will be burned on you.'" ³He gave a sign that day. He said, "This is the sign that the LORD has spoken: 'The altar will now be ripped apart, and the ashes that are on it will be poured out.'"

⁴When the king heard the word that the man of God had cried out against the altar at Bethel, Jeroboam stretched out his hand from the altar and said, "Arrest him!" But the hand he stretched out against him withered, and he could not pull it back to himself. ⁵The altar was ripped apart, and the ashes poured from the altar, according to the sign that the man of God had given by the word of the LORD.

⁶Then the king responded to the man of God, "Plead for the favor of the LORD your God and pray for me so that my hand may be restored to me." So the man of God pleaded for the favor of the LORD, and the king's hand was restored to him and became as it had been at first.

⁷Then the king declared to the man of God, "Come home with me, refresh yourself, and I'll give you a reward."

⁸But the man of God replied, "If you were to give me half your house, I still wouldn't go with you, and I wouldn't eat bread or drink water in this place, ⁹for this is what I was commanded by the word of the LORD: 'You must not eat bread or drink water or go back the way you came.'" ¹⁰So he went another way; he did not go back by the way he had come to Bethel.

¹¹Now a certain old prophet was living in Bethel. His son came and told him all the deeds that the man of God had done that day in Bethel. His sons also told their father the words that he had spoken to the king. ¹²Then their father said to them, "Which way did he go?" His sons had seen the way taken by the man of God who had come from Judah. ¹³Then he said to his

sons, "Saddle the donkey for me." So they saddled the donkey for him, and he got on it. ¹⁴He followed the man of God and found him sitting under an oak tree. He asked him, "Are you the man of God who came from Judah?"

"I am," he said.

¹⁵Then he said to him, "Come home with me and eat bread."

¹⁶But he answered, "I cannot go back with you, eat bread, or drink water with you in this place, ¹⁷for a message came to me by the word of the LORD: 'You must not eat bread or drink water there or go back by the way you came.'"

¹⁸He said to him, "I am also a prophet like you. An angel spoke to me by the word of the LORD: 'Bring him back with you to your house so that he may eat bread and drink water.'" The old prophet deceived him, ¹⁹and the man of God went back with him, ate bread in his house, and drank water.

²⁰While they were sitting at the table, the word of the LORD came to the prophet who had brought him back, ²¹and the prophet cried out to the man of God who had come from Judah, "This is what the LORD says: 'Because you rebelled against the command of the LORD and did not keep the command that the LORD your God commanded you— ²²but you went back and ate bread and drank water in the place that He said to you, "Do not eat bread and do not drink water"— your corpse will never reach the grave of your fathers.'"

²³So after he had eaten bread and after he had drunk, the old prophet saddled the donkey for the prophet he had brought back. ²⁴When he left, a lion attacked him along the way and killed him. His corpse was thrown on the road, and the donkey was standing beside it; the lion was standing beside the corpse too.

²⁵There were men passing by who saw the corpse thrown on the road and the lion standing beside it, and they went and spoke about it in the city where the old prophet lived. ²⁶When the prophet who had brought him back from his way heard about it, he said, "He is the man of God who disobeyed the command of the LORD. The LORD has given him to the lion, and it has mauled and killed him, according to the word of the LORD that He spoke to him."

²⁷Then the old prophet instructed his sons, "Saddle the donkey for me." They saddled it, ²⁸and he went and found the corpse of the man of God thrown on the road with the donkey and the lion standing beside the corpse. The lion had not eaten the corpse or mauled the donkey. ²⁹So the prophet lifted the corpse of the man of God and laid it on the donkey and brought it back. The old prophet came into the city to mourn and bury him. ³⁰Then he laid the corpse in his own grave, and they mourned over him: "Oh, my brother!"

³¹After he had buried him, he said to his sons, "When I die, you must bury me in the grave where the man of God is buried; lay my bones beside his bones, ³²for the word that he cried out by a revelation from the LORD against the altar in Bethel and against all the shrines of the high places in the cities of Samaria is certain to happen."

³³After all this Jeroboam did not repent of his evil way but again set up priests for the high places from every class of people. He ordained whoever so desired it, and they became priests of the high places. ³⁴This was the sin that caused the house of Jeroboam to be wiped out and annihilated from the face of the earth.

14 At that time Abijah son of Jeroboam became sick. ²Jeroboam said to his wife, "Go disguise yourself, so they won't know that you're Jeroboam's wife, and go to Shiloh. Ahijah the prophet is there; it was he who told about me becoming king over this people. ³Take with you 10 loaves of bread, some cakes, and a jar of honey, and go to him. He will tell you what will happen to the boy."

⁴Jeroboam's wife did that: she went to Shiloh and arrived at Ahijah's house. Ahijah could not see; his gaze was fixed due to his age. ⁵But the Lord had said to Ahijah, "Jeroboam's wife is coming soon to ask you about her son, for he is sick. You are to say such and such to her. When she arrives, she will be disguised."

⁶When Ahijah heard the sound of her feet entering the door, he said, "Come in, wife of Jeroboam! Why are you disguised? I have bad news for you. ⁷Go tell Jeroboam, 'This is what the Lord God of Israel says: I raised you up from among the people, appointed you ruler over My people Israel, ⁸tore the kingdom away from the house of David, and gave it to you. But you were not like My servant David, who kept My commands and followed Me with all of his heart, doing only what is right in My eyes. ⁹You behaved more wickedly than all who were before you. In order to provoke Me, you have proceeded to make for yourself other gods and cast images, but you have flung Me behind your back. ¹⁰Because of all this, I am about to bring disaster on the house of Jeroboam:

I will eliminate all of Jeroboam's males,
both slave and free, in Israel;
I will sweep away the house of Jeroboam
as one sweeps away dung until it is all gone!
¹¹ Anyone who belongs to Jeroboam and dies
in the city,
the dogs will eat,
and anyone who dies in the field,
the birds of the sky will eat,
for the Lord has said it!'

¹²"As for you, get up and go to your house. When your feet enter the city, the boy will die. ¹³All Israel will mourn for him and bury him. He alone out of Jeroboam's house will be put in the family tomb, because out of the house of Jeroboam the Lord God of Israel found something good only in him. ¹⁴The Lord will raise up for Himself a king over Israel, who will eliminate the house of Jeroboam. This is the day, yes, even today! ¹⁵For the Lord will strike Israel and the people will shake as a reed shakes in water. He will uproot Israel from this good soil that He gave to their ancestors. He will scatter them beyond the Euphrates because they made their *Asherah poles, provoking the Lord. ¹⁶He will give up Israel because of Jeroboam's sins that he committed and caused Israel to commit."

¹⁷Then Jeroboam's wife got up and left and went to Tirzah. As she was crossing the threshold of the house, the boy died. ¹⁸He was buried, and all Israel mourned for him, according to the word of the Lord He had spoken through His servant Ahijah the prophet.

¹⁹As for the rest of the events of Jeroboam's reign, how he waged war and how he reigned, note that they are written in the Historical Record of Israel's Kings. ²⁰The length of Jeroboam's reign was 22 years. He rested with his fathers, and his son Nadab became king in his place.

²¹Now Rehoboam, Solomon's son, reigned in Judah. Rehoboam was 41 years old when he became king; he reigned 17 years in Jerusalem, the city where *Yahweh had chosen from all the tribes of Israel to put His name. Rehoboam's mother's name was Naamah the Ammonite.

²²Judah did what was evil in the Lord's eyes. They provoked Him to jealous anger more than all that their ancestors had done with the sins they committed. ²³They also built for themselves *high places, sacred pillars, and Asherah poles on every high hill and under every green tree; ²⁴there were even male cult prostitutes in the land. They imitated all the detestable practices of the nations the Lord had dispossessed before the Israelites.

²⁵In the fifth year of King Rehoboam, Shishak king of Egypt went to war against Jerusalem. ²⁶He seized the treasuries of the Lord's temple and the treasuries of the royal palace. He took everything. He took all the gold shields that Solomon had made. ²⁷King Rehoboam made bronze shields in their place and committed them into the care of the captains of the royal escorts who guarded the entrance to the king's palace. ²⁸Whenever the king entered the Lord's temple, the royal escorts would carry the shields, then they would take them back to the royal escorts' armory.

²⁹The rest of the events of Rehoboam's reign, along with all his accomplishments, are written about in the Historical Record of Judah's Kings. ³⁰There was war between Rehoboam and Jeroboam throughout their reigns. ³¹Rehoboam rested with his fathers and was buried with his fathers in the city of David. His mother's name was Naamah the Ammonite. His son Abijam became king in his place.

15 In the eighteenth year of Israel's King Jeroboam son of Nebat, Abijam became king over Judah ²and reigned three years in Jerusalem. His mother's name was Maacah daughter of Abishalom.

³Abijam walked in all the sins his father before him had committed, and he was not completely devoted to the Lord his God as his ancestor David had been. ⁴But because of David, the Lord his God gave him a lamp in Jerusalem to raise up his son after him and to establish Jerusalem. ⁵For David did what was right in the Lord's eyes, and he did not turn aside from anything He had commanded him all the days of his life, except in the matter of Uriah the Hittite.

⁶There had been war between Rehoboam and Jeroboam all the days of Rehoboam's life. ⁷The rest of the events of Abijam's reign, along with all his accomplishments, are written in the Historical Record of Judah's Kings. There was also war between Abijam and Jeroboam. ⁸Abijam rested with his fathers and was buried in the city of David. His son Asa became king in his place.

⁹In the twentieth year of Israel's King Jeroboam, Asa became king of Judah ¹⁰and reigned 41 years in Jerusalem. His grandmother's name was Maacah daughter of Abishalom.

¹¹Asa did what was right in the Lord's eyes, as his ancestor David had done. ¹²He banished the male cult prostitutes from the land and removed all of the idols that his fathers had made. ¹³He also removed his grandmother Maacah from being queen mother because she had made an obscene image of *Asherah. Asa chopped down her obscene image and burned it in the Kidron Valley. ¹⁴The *high places were not taken away; but Asa's heart was completely devoted to the Lord his entire life. ¹⁵He brought his father's consecrated gifts

and his own consecrated gifts into the LORD's temple: silver, gold, and utensils.

[16] There was war between Asa and Baasha king of Israel throughout their reigns. [17] Israel's King Baasha went to war against Judah. He built Ramah in order to deny anyone access to Judah's King Asa. [18] So Asa withdrew all the silver and gold that remained in the treasuries of the LORD's temple and the treasuries of the royal palace and put it into the hands of his servants. Then King Asa sent them to Ben-hadad son of Tabrimmon son of Hezion king of Aram who lived in Damascus, saying, [19] "There is a treaty between me and you, between my father and your father. Look, I have sent you a gift of silver and gold. Go and break your treaty with Baasha king of Israel so that he will withdraw from me."

[20] Ben-hadad listened to King Asa and sent the commanders of his armies against the cities of Israel. He attacked Ijon, Dan, Abel-beth-maacah, all Chinnereth, and the whole land of Naphtali. [21] When Baasha heard about it, he quit building Ramah and stayed in Tirzah. [22] Then King Asa gave a command to everyone without exception in Judah, and they carried away the stones of Ramah and the timbers Baasha had built it with. Then King Asa built Geba of Benjamin and Mizpah with them.

[23] The rest of all the events of Asa's reign, along with all his might, all his accomplishments, and the cities he built, are written in the Historical Record of Judah's Kings. But in his old age he developed a disease in his feet. [24] Then Asa rested with his fathers and was buried in the city of his ancestor David. His son Jehoshaphat became king in his place.

[25] Nadab son of Jeroboam became king over Israel in the second year of Judah's King Asa; he reigned over Israel two years. [26] Nadab did what was evil in the LORD's sight and followed the example of his father and the sin he had caused Israel to commit.

[27] Then Baasha son of Ahijah of the house of Issachar conspired against Nadab, and Baasha struck him down at Gibbethon of the Philistines while Nadab and all Israel were besieging Gibbethon. [28] In the third year of Judah's King Asa, Baasha killed Nadab and reigned in his place.

[29] When Baasha became king, he struck down the entire house of Jeroboam. He did not leave Jeroboam any survivors but destroyed his family according to the word of the LORD He had spoken through His servant Ahijah the Shilonite. [30] This was because Jeroboam had provoked the LORD God of Israel by the sins he had committed and had caused Israel to commit.

[31] The rest of the events of Nadab's reign, along with all his accomplishments, are written in the Historical Record of Israel's Kings. [32] There was war between Asa and Baasha king of Israel throughout their reigns.

[33] In the third year of Judah's King Asa, Baasha son of Ahijah became king over all Israel and reigned in Tirzah 24 years. [34] He did what was evil in the LORD's sight and followed the example of Jeroboam and the sin he had caused Israel to commit.

16 Now the word of the LORD came to Jehu son of Hanani against Baasha: [2] "Because I raised you up from the dust and made you ruler over My people Israel, but you have walked in the way of Jeroboam and have caused My people Israel to sin, provoking Me with their sins, [3] take note: I will sweep away Baasha and his house, and I will make your house like the house of Jeroboam son of Nebat:

[4]   Anyone who belongs to Baasha and dies
       in the city,
      the dogs will eat,
      and anyone who is his and dies in the field,
      the birds of the sky will eat."

[5] The rest of the events of Baasha's reign, along with all his accomplishments and might, are written in the Historical Record of Israel's Kings. [6] Baasha rested with his fathers and was buried in Tirzah. His son Elah became king in his place. [7] Through the prophet Jehu son of Hanani the word of the LORD also came against Baasha and against his house because of all the evil he had done in the LORD's sight, provoking Him with the work of his hands and being like the house of Jeroboam, and because Baasha had struck down the house of Jeroboam.

[8] In the twenty-sixth year of Judah's King Asa, Elah son of Baasha became king over Israel and reigned in Tirzah two years.

[9] His servant Zimri, commander of half his chariots, conspired against him while Elah was in Tirzah getting drunk in the house of Arza, who was in charge of the household at Tirzah. [10] In the twenty-seventh year of Judah's King Asa, Zimri went in, struck Elah down, killing him. Then Zimri became king in his place.

[11] When he became king, as soon as he was seated on his throne, Zimri struck down the entire house of Baasha. He did not leave a single male, including his kinsmen and his friends. [12] So Zimri destroyed the entire house of Baasha, according to the word of the LORD He had spoken against Baasha through Jehu the prophet. [13] This happened because of all the sins of Baasha and those of his son Elah, which they committed and caused Israel to commit, provoking the LORD God of Israel with their worthless idols.

[14] The rest of the events of Elah's reign, along with all his accomplishments, are written in the Historical Record of Israel's Kings.

[15] In the twenty-seventh year of Judah's King Asa, Zimri became king for seven days in Tirzah. Now the troops were encamped against Gibbethon of the Philistines. [16] When these troops heard that Zimri had not only conspired but had also struck down the king, then all Israel made Omri, the army commander, king over Israel that very day in the camp. [17] Omri along with all Israel marched up from Gibbethon and besieged Tirzah. [18] When Zimri saw that the city was captured, he entered the citadel of the royal palace and burned it down over himself. He died [19] because of the sin he committed by doing what was evil in the LORD's sight and by following the example of Jeroboam and the sin he caused Israel to commit.

[20] The rest of the events of Zimri's reign, along with the conspiracy that he instigated, are written in the Historical Record of Israel's Kings. [21] At that time the people of Israel were divided: half the people followed Tibni son of Ginath, to make him king, and half followed Omri. [22] However, the people who followed Omri proved stronger than those who followed Tibni son of Ginath. So Tibni died and Omri became king.

[23] In the thirty-first year of Judah's King Asa, Omri became king over Israel and reigned 12 years. He reigned six years in Tirzah, [24] then he bought the hill of Samaria from Shemer for 150 pounds of silver, and he

built up the hill. He named the city he built Samaria based on the name Shemer, the owner of the hill.

²⁵Omri did what was evil in the Lᴏʀᴅ's sight; he did more evil than all who were before him. ²⁶He followed the example of Jeroboam son of Nebat and in his sins that he caused Israel to commit, provoking the Lᴏʀᴅ God of Israel with their worthless idols. ²⁷The rest of the events of Omri's reign, along with his accomplishments and the might he exercised, are written in the Historical Record of Israel's Kings. ²⁸Omri rested with his fathers and was buried in Samaria. His son Ahab became king in his place.

²⁹Ahab son of Omri became king over Israel in the thirty-eighth year of Judah's King Asa; Ahab son of Omri reigned over Israel in Samaria 22 years. ³⁰But Ahab son of Omri did what was evil in the Lᴏʀᴅ's sight more than all who were before him. ³¹Then, as if following the sin of Jeroboam son of Nebat were a trivial matter, he married Jezebel, the daughter of Ethbaal king of the Sidonians, and then proceeded to serve *Baal and worship him. ³²He set up an altar for Baal in the temple of Baal that he had built in Samaria. ³³Ahab also made an *Asherah pole. Ahab did more to provoke the Lᴏʀᴅ God of Israel than all the kings of Israel who were before him.

³⁴During his reign, Hiel the Bethelite built Jericho. At the cost of Abiram his firstborn, he laid its foundation, and at the cost of Segub his youngest, he set up its gates, according to the word of the Lᴏʀᴅ He had spoken through Joshua son of Nun.

17 Now Elijah the Tishbite, from the Gilead settlers, said to Ahab, "As the Lᴏʀᴅ God of Israel lives, I stand before Him, and there will be no dew or rain during these years except by my command!"

²Then a revelation from the Lᴏʀᴅ came to him: ³"Leave here, turn eastward, and hide yourself at the *Wadi Cherith where it enters the Jordan. ⁴You are to drink from the wadi. I have commanded the ravens to provide for you there."

⁵So he did what the Lᴏʀᴅ commanded. Elijah left and lived by the Wadi Cherith where it enters the Jordan. ⁶The ravens kept bringing him bread and meat in the morning and in the evening, and he drank from the wadi. ⁷After a while, the wadi dried up because there had been no rain in the land.

⁸Then the word of the Lᴏʀᴅ came to him: ⁹"Get up, go to Zarephath that belongs to Sidon and stay there. Look, I have commanded a woman who is a widow to provide for you there." ¹⁰So Elijah got up and went to Zarephath. When he arrived at the city gate, there was a widow woman gathering wood. Elijah called to her and said, "Please bring me a little water in a cup and let me drink." ¹¹As she went to get it, he called to her and said, "Please bring me a piece of bread in your hand."

¹²But she said, "As the Lᴏʀᴅ your God lives, I don't have anything baked—only a handful of flour in the jar and a bit of oil in the jug. Just now, I am gathering a couple of sticks in order to go prepare it for myself and my son so we can eat it and die."

¹³Then Elijah said to her, "Don't be afraid; go and do as you have said. But first make me a small loaf from it and bring it out to me. Afterward, you may make some for yourself and your son, ¹⁴for this is what the Lᴏʀᴅ God of Israel says, 'The flour jar will not become empty and the oil jug will not run dry until the day the Lᴏʀᴅ sends rain on the surface of the land.'"

¹⁵So she proceeded to do according to the word of Elijah. Then the woman, Elijah, and her household ate for many days. ¹⁶The flour jar did not become empty, and the oil jug did not run dry, according to the word of the Lᴏʀᴅ He had spoken through Elijah.

¹⁷After this, the son of the woman who owned the house became ill. His illness became very severe until no breath remained in him. ¹⁸She said to Elijah, "Man of God, what do we have in common? Have you come to remind me of my *guilt and to kill my son?"

¹⁹But Elijah said to her, "Give me your son." So he took him from her arms, brought him up to the upper room where he was staying, and laid him on his own bed. ²⁰Then he cried out to the Lᴏʀᴅ and said, "My Lᴏʀᴅ God, have You also brought tragedy on the widow I am staying with by killing her son?" ²¹Then he stretched himself out over the boy three times. He cried out to the Lᴏʀᴅ and said, "My Lᴏʀᴅ God, please let this boy's life return to him!"

²²So the Lᴏʀᴅ listened to Elijah's voice, and the boy's life returned to him, and he lived. ²³Then Elijah took the boy, brought him down from the upper room into the house, and gave him to his mother. Elijah said, "Look, your son is alive."

²⁴Then the woman said to Elijah, "Now I know you are a man of God and the Lᴏʀᴅ's word from your mouth is true."

18 After a long time, the word of the Lᴏʀᴅ came to Elijah in the third year: "Go and present yourself to Ahab. I will send rain on the surface of the land." ²So Elijah went to present himself to Ahab.

The famine was severe in Samaria. ³Ahab called for Obadiah, who was in charge of the palace. Obadiah was a man who greatly *feared the Lᴏʀᴅ ⁴and took 100 prophets and hid them, 50 men to a cave, and provided them with food and water when Jezebel slaughtered the Lᴏʀᴅ's prophets. ⁵Ahab said to Obadiah, "Go throughout the land to every spring of water and to every *wadi. Perhaps we'll find grass so we can keep the horses and mules alive and not have to destroy any cattle." ⁶They divided the land between them in order to cover it. Ahab went one way by himself, and Obadiah went the other way by himself.

⁷While Obadiah was walking along the road, Elijah suddenly met him. When Obadiah recognized him, he fell with his face to the ground and said, "Is it you, my lord Elijah?"

⁸"It is I," he replied. "Go tell your lord, 'Elijah is here!'"

⁹But Obadiah said, "What sin have I committed, that you are handing your servant over to Ahab to put me to death? ¹⁰As the Lᴏʀᴅ your God lives, there is no nation or kingdom where my lord has not sent someone to search for you. When they said, 'He is not here,' he made that kingdom or nation swear they had not found you.

¹¹"Now you say, 'Go tell your lord, "Elijah is here!"' ¹²But when I leave you, the Spirit of the Lᴏʀᴅ may carry you off to some place I don't know. Then when I go report to Ahab and he doesn't find you, he will kill me. But I, your servant, have feared the Lᴏʀᴅ from my youth. ¹³Wasn't it reported to my lord what I did when Jezebel slaughtered the Lᴏʀᴅ's prophets? I hid 100 of the prophets of the Lᴏʀᴅ, 50 men to a cave, and I provided them with food and water. ¹⁴Now you say, 'Go tell your lord, "Elijah is here!"' He will kill me!"

¹⁵Then Elijah said, "As the Lᴏʀᴅ of *Hosts lives, before whom I stand, today I will present myself to Ahab."

16 Obadiah went to meet Ahab and told him. Then Ahab went to meet Elijah. 17 When Ahab saw Elijah, Ahab said to him, "Is that you, you destroyer of Israel?" 18 He replied, "I have not destroyed Israel, but you and your father's house have, because you have abandoned the LORD's commands and followed the •Baals. 19 Now summon all Israel to meet me at Mount Carmel, along with the 450 prophets of Baal and the 400 prophets of •Asherah who eat at Jezebel's table."

20 So Ahab summoned all the Israelites and gathered the prophets at Mount Carmel. 21 Then Elijah approached all the people and said, "How long will you hesitate between two opinions? If •Yahweh is God, follow Him. But if Baal, follow him." But the people didn't answer him a word.

22 Then Elijah said to the people, "I am the only remaining prophet of the LORD, but Baal's prophets are 450 men. 23 Let two bulls be given to us. They are to choose one bull for themselves, cut it in pieces, and place it on the wood but not light the fire. I will prepare the other bull and place it on the wood but not light the fire. 24 Then you call on the name of your god, and I will call on the name of Yahweh. The God who answers with fire, He is God."

All the people answered, "That sounds good."

25 Then Elijah said to the prophets of Baal, "Since you are so numerous, choose for yourselves one bull and prepare it first. Then call on the name of your god but don't light the fire."

26 So they took the bull that he gave them, prepared it, and called on the name of Baal from morning until noon, saying, "Baal, answer us!" But there was no sound; no one answered. Then they danced, hobbling around the altar they had made.

27 At noon Elijah mocked them. He said, "Shout loudly, for he's a god! Maybe he's thinking it over; maybe he has wandered away; or maybe he's on the road. Perhaps he's sleeping and will wake up!" 28 They shouted loudly, and cut themselves with knives and spears, according to their custom, until blood gushed over them. 29 All afternoon they kept on raving until the offering of the evening sacrifice, but there was no sound; no one answered, no one paid attention.

30 Then Elijah said to all the people, "Come near me." So all the people approached him. Then he repaired the LORD's altar that had been torn down: 31 Elijah took 12 stones—according to the number of the tribes of the sons of Jacob, to whom the word of the LORD had come, saying, "Israel will be your name"— 32 and he built an altar with the stones in the name of Yahweh. Then he made a trench around the altar large enough to hold about four gallons. 33 Next, he arranged the wood, cut up the bull, and placed it on the wood. He said, "Fill four water pots with water and pour it on the offering to be burned and on the wood." 34 Then he said, "A second time!" and they did it a second time. And then he said, "A third time!" and they did it a third time. 35 So the water ran all around the altar; he even filled the trench with water.

36 At the time for offering the evening sacrifice, Elijah the prophet approached the altar and said, "Yahweh, God of Abraham, Isaac, and Israel, today let it be known that You are God in Israel and I am Your servant, and that at Your word I have done all these things. 37 Answer me, LORD! Answer me so that this people will know that You, Yahweh, are God and that You have turned their hearts back."

38 Then Yahweh's fire fell and consumed the •burnt offering, the wood, the stones, and the dust, and it licked up the water that was in the trench. 39 When all the people saw it, they fell facedown and said, "Yahweh, He is God! Yahweh, He is God!"

40 Then Elijah ordered them, "Seize the prophets of Baal! Do not let even one of them escape." So they seized them, and Elijah brought them down to the Wadi Kishon and slaughtered them there. 41 Elijah said to Ahab, "Go up, eat and drink, for there is the sound of a rainstorm."

42 So Ahab went to eat and drink, but Elijah went up to the summit of Carmel. He bowed down on the ground and put his face between his knees. 43 Then he said to his servant, "Go up and look toward the sea."

So he went up, looked, and said, "There's nothing."

Seven times Elijah said, "Go back."

44 On the seventh time, he reported, "There's a cloud as small as a man's hand coming from the sea."

Then Elijah said, "Go and tell Ahab, 'Get your chariot ready and go down so the rain doesn't stop you.'"

45 In a little while, the sky grew dark with clouds and wind, and there was a downpour. So Ahab got in his chariot and went to Jezreel. 46 The power of the LORD was on Elijah, and he tucked his mantle under his belt and ran ahead of Ahab to the entrance of Jezreel.

19 Ahab told Jezebel everything that Elijah had done and how he had killed all the prophets with the sword. 2 So Jezebel sent a messenger to Elijah, saying, "May the gods punish me and do so severely if I don't make your life like the life of one of them by this time tomorrow!"

3 Then Elijah became afraid and immediately ran for his life. When he came to Beer-sheba that belonged to Judah, he left his servant there, 4 but he went on a day's journey into the wilderness. He sat down under a broom tree and prayed that he might die. He said, "I have had enough! LORD, take my life, for I'm no better than my fathers." 5 Then he lay down and slept under the broom tree.

Suddenly, an angel touched him. The angel told him, "Get up and eat." 6 Then he looked, and there at his head was a loaf of bread baked over hot stones, and a jug of water. So he ate and drank and lay down again. 7 Then the angel of the LORD returned for a second time and touched him. He said, "Get up and eat, or the journey will be too much for you." 8 So he got up, ate, and drank. Then on the strength from that food, he walked 40 days and 40 nights to Horeb, the mountain of God. 9 He entered a cave there and spent the night.

Then the word of the LORD came to him, and He said to him, "What are you doing here, Elijah?"

10 He replied, "I have been very zealous for the LORD God of •Hosts, but the Israelites have abandoned Your covenant, torn down Your altars, and killed Your prophets with the sword. I alone am left, and they are looking for me to take my life."

11 Then He said, "Go out and stand on the mountain in the LORD's presence."

At that moment, the LORD passed by. A great and mighty wind was tearing at the mountains and was shattering cliffs before the LORD, but the LORD was not in the wind. After the wind there was an earthquake, but the LORD was not in the earthquake. 12 After the earthquake there was a fire, but the LORD was not in the fire. And after the fire there was a voice, a soft whisper. 13 When Elijah heard it, he wrapped his face in his mantle and went out and stood at the entrance of the cave.

Suddenly, a voice came to him and said, "What are you doing here, Elijah?"

[14] "I have been very zealous for the LORD God of Hosts," he replied, "but the Israelites have abandoned Your covenant, torn down Your altars, and killed Your prophets with the sword. I alone am left, and they're looking for me to take my life."

[15] Then the LORD said to him, "Go and return by the way you came to the Wilderness of Damascus. When you arrive, you are to anoint Hazael as king over Aram. [16] You are to anoint Jehu son of Nimshi as king over Israel and Elisha son of Shaphat from Abel-meholah as prophet in your place. [17] Then Jehu will put to death whoever escapes the sword of Hazael, and Elisha will put to death whoever escapes the sword of Jehu. [18] But I will leave 7,000 in Israel—every knee that has not bowed to ·Baal and every mouth that has not kissed him."

[19] Elijah left there and found Elisha son of Shaphat as he was plowing. Twelve teams of oxen were in front of him, and he was with the twelfth team. Elijah walked by him and threw his mantle over him. [20] Elisha left the oxen, ran to follow Elijah, and said, "Please let me kiss my father and mother, and then I will follow you."

"Go on back," he replied, "for what have I done to you?"

[21] So he turned back from following him, took the team of oxen, and slaughtered them. With the oxen's wooden yoke and plow, he cooked the meat and gave it to the people, and they ate. Then he left, followed Elijah, and served him.

20 Now Ben-hadad king of Aram assembled his entire army. Thirty-two kings, along with horses and chariots, were with him. He marched up, besieged Samaria, and fought against it. [2] He sent messengers into the city to Ahab king of Israel and said to him, "This is what Ben-hadad says: [3] 'Your silver and your gold are mine! And your best wives and children are mine as well!'"

[4] Then the king of Israel answered, "Just as you say, my lord the king: I am yours, along with all that I have."

[5] The messengers then returned and said, "This is what Ben-hadad says: 'I have sent messengers to you, saying: You are to give me your silver, your gold, your wives, and your children. [6] But at this time tomorrow I will send my servants to you, and they will search your palace and your servants' houses. They will lay their hands on and take away whatever is precious to you.'"

[7] Then the king of Israel called for all the elders of the land and said, "Think it over and you will see that this one is only looking for trouble, for he demanded my wives, my children, my silver, and my gold, and I didn't turn him down."

[8] All the elders and all the people said to him, "Don't listen or agree."

[9] So he said to Ben-hadad's messengers, "Say to my lord the king, 'Everything you demanded of your servant the first time, I will do, but this thing I cannot do.'" So the messengers left and took word back to him.

[10] Then Ben-hadad sent messengers to him and said, "May the gods punish me and do so severely if Samaria's dust amounts to a handful for each of the people who follow me."

[11] The king of Israel answered, "Say this: 'Don't let the one who puts on his armor boast like the one who takes it off.'"

[12] When Ben-hadad heard this response, while he and the kings were drinking in the tents, he said to his servants, "Take your positions." So they took their positions against the city.

[13] A prophet came to Ahab king of Israel and said, "This is what the LORD says: 'Do you see this entire great army? Watch, I am handing it over to you today so that you may know that I am ·Yahweh.'"

[14] Ahab asked, "By whom?"

And the prophet said, "This is what the LORD says: 'By the young men of the provincial leaders.'"

Then he asked, "Who is to start the battle?"

He said, "You."

[15] So Ahab counted the young men of the provincial leaders, and there were 232. After them he counted all the Israelite troops: 7,000. [16] They marched out at noon while Ben-hadad and the 32 kings who were helping him were getting drunk in the tents. [17] The young men of the provincial leaders marched out first. Then Ben-hadad sent out scouts, and they reported to him, saying, "Men are marching out of Samaria."

[18] So he said, "If they have marched out in peace, take them alive, and if they have marched out for battle, take them alive."

[19] The young men of the provincial leaders and the army behind them marched out from the city, [20] and each one struck down his opponent. So the Arameans fled and Israel pursued them, but Ben-hadad king of Aram escaped on a horse with the cavalry. [21] Then the king of Israel marched out and attacked the cavalry and the chariots. He inflicted a great slaughter on Aram.

[22] The prophet approached the king of Israel and said to him, "Go and strengthen yourself, then consider what you should do, for in the spring the king of Aram will march against you."

[23] Now the king of Aram's servants said to him, "Their gods are gods of the hill country. That's why they were stronger than we were. Instead, we should fight with them on the plain; then we will certainly be stronger than they will be. [24] Also do this: remove each king from his position and appoint captains in their place. [25] Raise another army for yourself like the army you lost—horse for horse, chariot for chariot—and let's fight with them on the plain; and we will certainly be stronger than they will be." The king listened to them and did so.

[26] In the spring, Ben-hadad mobilized the Arameans and went up to Aphek to battle Israel. [27] The Israelites mobilized, gathered supplies, and went to fight them. The Israelites camped in front of them like two little flocks of goats, while the Arameans filled the landscape.

[28] Then the man of God approached and said to the king of Israel, "This is what the LORD says: 'Because the Arameans have said: Yahweh is a god of the mountains and not a god of the valleys, I will hand over all this great army to you. Then you will know that I am the LORD.'"

[29] They camped opposite each other for seven days. On the seventh day, the battle took place, and the Israelites struck down the Arameans—100,000 foot

soldiers in one day. ³⁰The ones who remained fled into the city of Aphek, and the wall fell on those 27,000 remaining men.

Ben-hadad also fled and went into an inner room in the city. ³¹His servants said to him, "Consider this: we have heard that the kings of the house of Israel are merciful kings. So let's put *sackcloth around our waists and ropes around our heads, and let's go out to the king of Israel. Perhaps he will spare your life."

³²So they dressed with sackcloth around their waists and ropes around their heads, went to the king of Israel, and said, "Your servant Ben-hadad says, 'Please spare my life.'"

So he said, "Is he still alive? He is my brother."

³³Now the men were looking for a sign of hope, so they quickly picked up on this and responded, "Yes, it is your brother Ben-hadad."

Then he said, "Go and bring him."

So Ben-hadad came out to him, and Ahab had him come up into the chariot. ³⁴Then Ben-hadad said to him, "I restore to you the cities that my father took from your father, and you may set up marketplaces for yourself in Damascus, like my father set up in Samaria." •

Ahab responded, "On the basis of this treaty, I release you." So he made a treaty with him and released him.

³⁵One of the sons of the prophets said to his fellow prophet by the word of the LORD, "Strike me!" But the man refused to strike him.

³⁶He told him, "Because you did not listen to the voice of the LORD, mark my words: When you leave me, a lion will kill you." When he left him, a lion attacked and killed him.

³⁷The prophet found another man and said to him, "Strike me!" So the man struck him, inflicting a wound. ³⁸Then the prophet went and waited for the king on the road. He disguised himself with a bandage over his eyes. ³⁹As the king was passing by, he cried out to the king and said, "Your servant marched out into the middle of the battle. Suddenly, a man turned aside and brought someone to me and said, 'Guard this man! If he is ever missing, it will be your life in place of his life, or you will weigh out 75 pounds of silver.' ⁴⁰But while your servant was busy here and there, he disappeared."

The king of Israel said to him, "That will be your sentence; you yourself have decided it."

⁴¹He quickly removed the bandage from his eyes. The king of Israel recognized that he was one of the prophets. ⁴²The prophet said to him, "This is what the LORD says: 'Because you released from your hand the man I had *set apart for destruction, it will be your life in place of his life and your people in place of his people.'" ⁴³The king of Israel left for home resentful and angry, and he entered Samaria.

21 Some time passed after these events. Naboth the Jezreelite had a vineyard; it was in Jezreel next to the palace of Ahab king of Samaria. ²So Ahab spoke to Naboth, saying, "Give me your vineyard so I can have it for a vegetable garden, since it is right next to my palace. I will give you a better vineyard in its place, or if you prefer, I will give you its value in silver."

³But Naboth said to Ahab, "I will never give my fathers' inheritance to you."

⁴So Ahab went to his palace resentful and angry because of what Naboth the Jezreelite had told him.

He had said, "I will not give you my fathers' inheritance." He lay down on his bed, turned his face away, and didn't eat any food.

⁵Then his wife Jezebel came to him and said to him, "Why are you so upset that you refuse to eat?"

⁶"Because I spoke to Naboth the Jezreelite," he replied. "I told him: Give me your vineyard for silver, or if you wish, I will give you a vineyard in its place. But he said, 'I won't give you my vineyard!'"

⁷Then his wife Jezebel said to him, "Now, exercise your royal power over Israel. Get up, eat some food, and be happy. For I will give you the vineyard of Naboth the Jezreelite." ⁸So she wrote letters in Ahab's name and sealed them with his seal. She sent the letters to the elders and nobles who lived with Naboth in his city. ⁹In the letters, she wrote:

Proclaim a fast and seat Naboth at the head of the people. ¹⁰Then seat two *wicked men opposite him and have them testify against him, saying, "You have cursed God and the king!" Then take him out and stone him to death.

¹¹The men of his city, the elders and nobles who lived in his city, did as Jezebel had commanded them, as was written in the letters she had sent them. ¹²They proclaimed a fast and seated Naboth at the head of the people. ¹³The two wicked men came in and sat opposite him. Then the wicked men testified against Naboth in the presence of the people, saying, "Naboth has cursed God and the king!" So they took him outside the city and stoned him to death with stones. ¹⁴Then they sent word to Jezebel, "Naboth has been stoned to death."

¹⁵When Jezebel heard that Naboth had been stoned to death, she said to Ahab, "Get up and take possession of the vineyard of Naboth the Jezreelite who refused to give it to you for silver, since Naboth isn't alive, but dead." ¹⁶When Ahab heard that Naboth was dead, he got up to go down to the vineyard of Naboth the Jezreelite to take possession of it.

¹⁷Then the word of the LORD came to Elijah the Tishbite: ¹⁸"Get up and go to meet Ahab king of Israel, who is in Samaria. You'll find him in Naboth's vineyard, where he has gone to take possession of it. ¹⁹Tell him, 'This is what the LORD says: Have you murdered and also taken possession?' Then tell him, 'This is what the LORD says: In the place where the dogs licked Naboth's blood, the dogs will also lick your blood!'"

²⁰Ahab said to Elijah, "So, you have caught me, my enemy."

He replied, "I have caught you because you devoted yourself to do what is evil in the LORD's sight. ²¹This is what the LORD says: 'I am about to bring disaster on you and will sweep away your descendants:

I will eliminate all of Ahab's males,
both slave and free, in Israel;

²²I will make your house like the house of Jeroboam son of Nebat and like the house of Baasha son of Ahijah, because you have provoked My anger and caused Israel to sin. ²³The LORD also speaks of Jezebel: The dogs will eat Jezebel in the plot of land at Jezreel:

²⁴   He who belongs to Ahab and dies in the city,
          the dogs will eat,
       and he who dies in the field, the birds
          of the sky will eat.'"

²⁵Still, there was no one like Ahab, who devoted himself to do what was evil in the LORD's sight, because his wife Jezebel incited him. ²⁶He committed the most detestable acts by going after idols as the Amorites

had, whom the Lord had dispossessed before the Israelites.

²⁷When Ahab heard these words, he tore his clothes, put ˙sackcloth over his body, and fasted. He lay down in sackcloth and walked around subdued. ²⁸Then the word of the Lord came to Elijah the Tishbite: ²⁹"Have you seen how Ahab has humbled himself before Me? I will not bring the disaster during his lifetime, because he has humbled himself before Me. I will bring the disaster on his house during his son's lifetime."

22 There was a lull of three years without war between Aram and Israel. ²However, in the third year, Jehoshaphat king of Judah went to visit the king of Israel. ³The king of Israel had said to his servants, "Don't you know that Ramoth-gilead is ours, but we have failed to take it from the hand of the king of Aram?" ⁴So he asked Jehoshaphat, "Will you go with me to fight Ramoth-gilead?"

Jehoshaphat replied to the king of Israel, "I am as you are, my people as your people, my horses as your horses." ⁵But Jehoshaphat said to the king of Israel, "First, please ask what the Lord's will is."

⁶So the king of Israel gathered the prophets, about 400 men, and asked them, "Should I go against Ramoth-gilead for war or should I refrain?"

They replied, "March up, and the Lord will hand it over to the king."

⁷But Jehoshaphat asked, "Isn't there a prophet of ˙Yahweh here anymore? Let's ask him."

⁸The king of Israel said to Jehoshaphat, "There is still one man who can ask Yahweh, but I hate him because he never prophesies good about me, but only disaster. He is Micaiah son of Imlah."

"The king shouldn't say that!" Jehoshaphat replied.

⁹So the king of Israel called an officer and said, "Hurry and get Micaiah son of Imlah!"

¹⁰Now the king of Israel and Jehoshaphat king of Judah, clothed in royal attire, were each sitting on his own throne. They were on the threshing floor at the entrance to Samaria's ˙gate, and all the prophets were prophesying in front of them. ¹¹Then Zedekiah son of Chenaanah made iron horns and said, "This is what the Lord says: 'You will gore the Arameans with these until they are finished off.'" ¹²And all the prophets were prophesying the same: "March up to Ramoth-gilead and succeed, for the Lord will hand it over to the king."

¹³The messenger who went to call Micaiah instructed him, "Look, the words of the prophets are unanimously favorable for the king. So let your words be like theirs, and speak favorably."

¹⁴But Micaiah said, "As the Lord lives, I will say whatever the Lord says to me."

¹⁵So he went to the king, and the king asked him, "Micaiah, should we go to Ramoth-gilead for war, or should we refrain?"

Micaiah told him, "March up and succeed. Yahweh will hand it over to the king."

¹⁶But the king said to him, "How many times must I make you swear not to tell me anything but the truth in the name of Yahweh?"

¹⁷So Micaiah said:

I saw all Israel scattered on the hills
like sheep without a shepherd.
And the Lord said,
"They have no master;
let everyone return home in peace."

¹⁸So the king of Israel said to Jehoshaphat, "Didn't I tell you he never prophesies good about me, but only disaster?"

¹⁹Then Micaiah said, "Therefore, hear the word of the Lord: I saw the Lord sitting on His throne, and the whole heavenly ˙host was standing by Him at His right hand and at His left hand. ²⁰And the Lord said, 'Who will entice Ahab to march up and fall at Ramoth-gilead?' So one was saying this and another was saying that.

²¹"Then a spirit came forward, stood before the Lord, and said, 'I will entice him.'

²²"The Lord asked him, 'How?'

"He said, 'I will go and become a lying spirit in the mouth of all his prophets.'

"Then He said, 'You will certainly entice him and prevail. Go and do that.'

²³"You see, the Lord has put a lying spirit into the mouth of all these prophets of yours, and the Lord has pronounced disaster against you."

²⁴Then Zedekiah son of Chenaanah came up, hit Micaiah in the face, and demanded, "Did the Spirit of the Lord leave me to speak to you?"

²⁵Micaiah replied, "You will soon see when you go to hide yourself in an inner chamber on that day."

²⁶Then the king of Israel ordered, "Take Micaiah and return him to Amon, the governor of the city, and to Joash, the king's son, ²⁷and say, 'This is what the king says: Put this guy in prison and feed him only bread and water until I come back safely.'"

²⁸But Micaiah said, "If you ever return safely, the Lord has not spoken through me." Then he said, "Listen, all you people!"

²⁹Then the king of Israel and Judah's King Jehoshaphat went up to Ramoth-gilead. ³⁰But the king of Israel said to Jehoshaphat, "I will disguise myself and go into battle, but you wear your royal attire." So the king of Israel disguised himself and went into battle.

³¹Now the king of Aram had ordered his 32 chariot commanders, "Do not fight with anyone at all except the king of Israel."

³²When the chariot commanders saw Jehoshaphat, they shouted, "He must be the king of Israel!" So they turned to fight against him, but Jehoshaphat cried out. ³³When the chariot commanders saw that he was not the king of Israel, they turned back from pursuing him.

³⁴But a man drew his bow without taking special aim and struck the king of Israel through the joints of his armor. So he said to his charioteer, "Turn around and take me out of the battle, for I am badly wounded!" ³⁵The battle raged throughout that day, and the king was propped up in his chariot facing the Arameans. He died that evening, and blood from his wound flowed into the bottom of the chariot. ³⁶Then the cry rang out in the army as the sun set, declaring:

Each man to his own city,
and each man to his own land!

³⁷So the king died and was brought to Samaria. They buried the king in Samaria. ³⁸Then someone washed the chariot at the pool of Samaria. The dogs licked up his blood, and the prostitutes bathed in it, according to the word of the Lord that He had spoken.

³⁹The rest of the events of Ahab's reign, along with all his accomplishments, including the ivory palace he built, and all the cities he built, are written in the Historical Record of Israel's Kings. ⁴⁰Ahab rested with

his fathers, and his son Ahaziah became king in his place.

⁴¹ Jehoshaphat son of Asa became king over Judah in the fourth year of Israel's King Ahab. ⁴² Jehoshaphat was 35 years old when he became king; he reigned 25 years in Jerusalem. His mother's name was Azubah daughter of Shilhi. ⁴³ He walked in all the ways of his father Asa; he did not turn away from them but did what was right in the LORD's sight. However, the *high places were not taken away; the people still sacrificed and burned incense on the high places. ⁴⁴ Jehoshaphat also made peace with the king of Israel.

⁴⁵ The rest of the events of Jehoshaphat's reign, along with the might he exercised and how he waged war, are written in the Historical Record of Judah's Kings. ⁴⁶ He removed from the land the rest of the male cult prostitutes who were left from the days of his father Asa.

⁴⁷ There was no king in Edom; a deputy served as king. ⁴⁸ Jehoshaphat made ships of Tarshish to go to Ophir for gold, but they did not go because the ships were wrecked at Ezion-geber. ⁴⁹ At that time, Ahaziah son of Ahab said to Jehoshaphat, "Let my servants go with your servants in the ships," but Jehoshaphat was not willing. ⁵⁰ Jehoshaphat rested with his fathers and was buried with them in the city of his ancestor David. His son Jehoram became king in his place.

⁵¹ Ahaziah son of Ahab became king over Israel in Samaria in the seventeenth year of Judah's King Jehoshaphat and reigned over Israel two years. ⁵² He did what was evil in the LORD's sight. He walked in the way of his father, in the way of his mother, and in the way of Jeroboam son of Nebat, who had caused Israel to sin. ⁵³ He served *Baal and worshiped him. He provoked the LORD God of Israel just as his father had done.

2 KINGS

1 After the death of Ahab, Moab rebelled against Israel. ² Ahaziah had fallen through the latticed window of his upper room in Samaria and was injured. So he sent messengers instructing them: "Go inquire of Baal-zebub, the god of Ekron, if I will recover from this injury."

³ But the angel of the LORD said to Elijah the Tishbite, "Go and meet the messengers of the king of Samaria and ask them, 'Is it because there is no God in Israel that you are going to inquire of Baal-zebub, the god of Ekron?' ⁴ Therefore, this is what the LORD says: 'You will not get up from your sickbed—you will certainly die.'" Then Elijah left.

⁵ The messengers returned to the king, who asked them, "Why have you come back?"

⁶ They replied, "A man came to meet us and said, 'Go back to the king who sent you and declare to him: This is what the LORD says: Is it because there is no God in Israel that you're sending these men to inquire of Baal-zebub, the god of Ekron? Therefore, you will not get up from your sickbed—you will certainly die.'"

⁷ The king asked them, "What sort of man came up to meet you and spoke those words to you?"

⁸ They replied, "A hairy man with a leather belt around his waist."

He said, "It's Elijah the Tishbite."

⁹ So King Ahaziah sent a captain of 50 with his 50 men to Elijah. When the captain went up to him, he was sitting on top of the hill. He announced, "Man of God, the king declares, 'Come down!'"

¹⁰ Elijah responded to the captain of the 50, "If I am a man of God, may fire come down from heaven and consume you and your 50 men." Then fire came down from heaven and consumed him and his 50 men.

¹¹ So the king sent another captain of 50 with his 50 men to Elijah. He took in the situation and announced, "Man of God, this is what the king says: 'Come down immediately!'"

¹² Elijah responded, "If I am a man of God, may fire come down from heaven and consume you and your 50 men." So a divine fire came down from heaven and consumed him and his 50 men.

¹³ Then the king sent a third captain of 50 with his 50 men. The third captain of 50 went up and fell on his knees in front of Elijah and begged him, "Man of God, please let my life and the lives of these 50 servants of yours be precious in your sight. ¹⁴ Already fire has come down from heaven and consumed the first two captains of 50 with their fifties, but this time let my life be precious in your sight."

¹⁵ The angel of the LORD said to Elijah, "Go down with him. Don't be afraid of him." So he got up and went down with him to the king.

¹⁶ Then Elijah said to King Ahaziah, "This is what the LORD says: 'Because you have sent messengers to inquire of Baal-zebub, the god of Ekron—is it because there is no God in Israel for you to inquire of His will?—you will not get up from your sickbed; you will certainly die.'"

¹⁷ Ahaziah died according to the word of the LORD that Elijah had spoken. Since he had no son, Joram became king in his place. This happened in the second year of Judah's King Jehoram son of Jehoshaphat. ¹⁸ The rest of the events of Ahaziah's reign, along with his accomplishments, are written in the Historical Record of Israel's Kings.

2 The time had come for the LORD to take Elijah up to heaven in a whirlwind. Elijah and Elisha were traveling from Gilgal, ² and Elijah said to Elisha, "Stay here; the LORD is sending me on to Bethel."

But Elisha replied, "As the LORD lives and as you yourself live, I will not leave you." So they went down to Bethel.

³ Then the sons of the prophets who were at Bethel came out to Elisha and said, "Do you know that the LORD will take your master away from you today?"

He said, "Yes, I know. Be quiet."

⁴ Elijah said to him, "Elisha, stay here; the LORD is sending me to Jericho."

But Elisha said, "As the LORD lives and as you yourself live, I will not leave you." So they went to Jericho.

⁵ Then the sons of the prophets who were in Jericho came up to Elisha and said, "Do you know that the LORD will take your master away from you today?"

He said, "Yes, I know. Be quiet."

⁶ Elijah said to him, "Stay here; the LORD is sending me to the Jordan."

But Elisha said, "As the LORD lives and as you yourself live, I will not leave you." So the two of them went on.

⁷Fifty men from the sons of the prophets came and stood facing them from a distance while the two of them stood by the Jordan. ⁸Elijah took his mantle, rolled it up, and struck the waters, which parted to the right and left. Then the two of them crossed over on dry ground. ⁹After they had crossed over, Elijah said to Elisha, "Tell me what I can do for you before I am taken from you."

So Elisha answered, "Please, let me inherit two shares of your spirit."

¹⁰Elijah replied, "You have asked for something difficult. If you see me being taken from you, you will have it. If not, you won't."

¹¹As they continued walking and talking, a chariot of fire suddenly appeared and separated the two of them. Then Elijah went up into heaven in the whirlwind. ¹²As Elisha watched, he kept crying out, "My father, my father, the chariots and horsemen of Israel!" Then he never saw Elijah again. He took hold of his own clothes and tore them into two pieces.

¹³Elisha picked up the mantle that had fallen off Elijah and went back and stood on the bank of the Jordan. ¹⁴Then he took the mantle Elijah had dropped and struck the waters. "Where is the Lord God of Elijah?" he asked. He struck the waters himself, and they parted to the right and the left, and Elisha crossed over.

¹⁵When the sons of the prophets from Jericho who were facing him saw him, they said, "The spirit of Elijah rests on Elisha." They came to meet him and bowed down to the ground in front of him.

¹⁶Then the sons of the prophets said to Elisha, "Since there are 50 strong men here with your servants, please let them go and search for your master. Maybe the Spirit of the Lord has carried him away and put him on one of the mountains or into one of the valleys."

He answered, "Don't send them."

¹⁷However, they urged him to the point of embarrassment, so he said, "Send them." They sent 50 men, who looked for three days but did not find him. ¹⁸When they returned to him in Jericho where he was staying, he said to them, "Didn't I tell you not to go?"

¹⁹Then the men of the city said to Elisha, "Even though our lord can see that the city's location is good, the water is bad and the land unfruitful."

²⁰He replied, "Bring me a new bowl and put salt in it."

After they had brought him one, ²¹Elisha went out to the spring of water, threw salt in it, and said, "This is what the Lord says: 'I have healed this water. No longer will death or unfruitfulness result from it.'" ²²Therefore, the water remains healthy to this very day according to the word that Elisha spoke.

²³From there Elisha went up to Bethel. As he was walking up the path, some small boys came out of the city and harassed him, chanting, "Go up, baldy! Go up, baldy!" ²⁴He turned around, looked at them, and cursed them in the name of the Lord. Then two female bears came out of the woods and mauled 42 of the children. ²⁵From there Elisha went to Mount Carmel, and then he returned to Samaria.

3 Joram son of Ahab became king over Israel in Samaria during the eighteenth year of Judah's King Jehoshaphat and reigned 12 years. ²He did what was

evil in the Lord's sight, but not like his father and mother, for he removed the sacred pillar of *Baal his father had made. ³Nevertheless, Joram clung to the sins that Jeroboam son of Nebat had caused Israel to commit. He did not turn away from them.

⁴King Mesha of Moab was a sheep breeder. He used to pay the king of Israel 100,000 lambs and the wool of 100,000 rams, ⁵but when Ahab died, the king of Moab rebelled against the king of Israel. ⁶So King Joram marched out from Samaria at that time and mobilized all Israel. ⁷Then he sent a message to King Jehoshaphat of Judah: "The king of Moab has rebelled against me. Will you go with me to fight against Moab?"

Jehoshaphat said, "I will go. I am as you are, my people as your people, my horses as your horses." ⁸Then he asked, "Which route should we take?"

Joram replied, "The route of the Wilderness of Edom."

⁹So the king of Israel, the king of Judah, and the king of Edom set out. After they had traveled their indirect route for seven days, they had no water for the army or their animals.

¹⁰Then the king of Israel said, "Oh no, the Lord has summoned three kings, only to hand them over to Moab."

¹¹But Jehoshaphat said, "Isn't there a prophet of the Lord here? Let's inquire of *Yahweh through him."

One of the servants of the king of Israel answered, "Elisha son of Shaphat, who used to pour water on Elijah's hands, is here."

¹²Jehoshaphat affirmed, "The Lord's words are with him." So the king of Israel and Jehoshaphat and the king of Edom went to him.

¹³However, Elisha said to King Joram of Israel, "We have nothing in common. Go to the prophets of your father and your mother!"

But the king of Israel replied, "No, because it is the Lord who has summoned these three kings to hand them over to Moab."

¹⁴Elisha responded, "As the Lord of *Hosts lives, I stand before Him. If I did not have respect for King Jehoshaphat of Judah, I would not look at you; I wouldn't take notice of you. ¹⁵Now, bring me a musician."

While the musician played, the Lord's hand came on Elisha. ¹⁶Then he said, "This is what the Lord says: 'Dig ditch after ditch in this *wadi.' ¹⁷For the Lord says, 'You will not see wind or rain, but the wadi will be filled with water, and you will drink—you and your cattle and your animals.' ¹⁸This is easy in the Lord's sight. He will also hand Moab over to you. ¹⁹Then you must attack every fortified city and every choice city. You must cut down every good tree and stop up every spring of water. You must ruin every good piece of land with stones."

²⁰About the time for the *grain offering the next morning, water suddenly came from the direction of Edom and filled the land.

²¹All Moab had heard that the kings had come up to fight against them. So all who could bear arms, from the youngest to the oldest, were summoned and took their stand at the border. ²²When they got up early in the morning, the sun was shining on the water, and the Moabites saw that the water across from them was red like blood. ²³"This is blood!" they exclaimed. "The kings have clashed swords and killed each other. So, to the spoil, Moab!"

²⁴However, when the Moabites came to Israel's

camp, the Israelites attacked them, and they fled from them. So Israel went into the land and struck down the Moabites. ²⁵They destroyed the cities, and each of them threw stones to cover every good piece of land. They stopped up every spring of water and cut down every good tree. In the end, only the buildings of Kirhareseth were left. Then men with slings surrounded the city and attacked it.

²⁶When the king of Moab saw that the battle was too fierce for him, he took 700 swordsmen with him to try to break through to the king of Edom, but they could not do it. ²⁷So he took his firstborn son, who was to become king in his place, and offered him as a ˙burnt offering on the city wall. Great wrath was on the Israelites, and they withdrew from him and returned to their land.

4 One of the wives of the sons of the prophets cried out to Elisha, "Your servant, my husband, has died. You know that your servant ˙feared the Lᴏʀᴅ. Now the creditor is coming to take my two children as his slaves."

²Elisha asked her, "What can I do for you? Tell me, what do you have in the house?"

She said, "Your servant has nothing in the house except a jar of oil."

³Then he said, "Go and borrow empty containers from everyone—from all your neighbors. Do not get just a few. ⁴Then go in and shut the door behind you and your sons, and pour oil into all these containers. Set the full ones to one side." ⁵So she left.

After she had shut the door behind her and her sons, they kept bringing her containers, and she kept pouring. ⁶When they were full, she said to her son, "Bring me another container."

But he replied, "There aren't any more." Then the oil stopped.

⁷She went and told the man of God, and he said, "Go sell the oil and pay your debt; you and your sons can live on the rest."

⁸One day Elisha went to Shunem. A prominent woman who lived there persuaded him to eat some food. So whenever he passed by, he stopped there to eat. ⁹Then she said to her husband, "I know that the one who often passes by here is a holy man of God, ¹⁰so let's make a small room upstairs and put a bed, a table, a chair, and a lamp there for him. Whenever he comes, he can stay there."

¹¹One day he came there and stopped and went to the room upstairs to lie down. ¹²He ordered his attendant Gehazi, "Call this Shunammite woman." So he called her and she stood before him.

¹³Then he said to Gehazi, "Say to her, 'Look, you've gone to all this trouble for us. What can we do for you? Can we speak on your behalf to the king or to the commander of the army?'"

She answered, "I am living among my own people."

¹⁴So he asked, "Then what should be done for her?"

Gehazi answered, "Well, she has no son, and her husband is old."

¹⁵"Call her," Elisha said. So Gehazi called her, and she stood in the doorway. ¹⁶Elisha said, "At this time next year you will have a son in your arms."

Then she said, "No, my lord. Man of God, do not deceive your servant."

¹⁷The woman conceived and gave birth to a son at the same time the following year, as Elisha had promised her.

¹⁸The child grew and one day went out to his father and the harvesters. ¹⁹Suddenly he complained to his father, "My head! My head!"

His father told his servant, "Carry him to his mother." ²⁰So he picked him up and took him to his mother. The child sat on her lap until noon and then died. ²¹Then she went up and laid him on the bed of the man of God, shut him in, and left.

²²She summoned her husband and said, "Please send me one of the servants and one of the donkeys, so I can hurry to the man of God and then come back."

²³But he said, "Why go to him today? It's not a New Moon or a Sabbath."

She replied, "Everything is all right."

²⁴Then she saddled the donkey and said to her servant, "Hurry, don't slow the pace for me unless I tell you." ²⁵So she set out and went to the man of God at Mount Carmel.

When the man of God saw her at a distance, he said to his attendant Gehazi, "Look, there's the Shunammite woman. ²⁶Run out to meet her and ask, 'Are you all right? Is your husband all right? Is your son all right?'"

And she answered, "Everything's all right."

²⁷When she came up to the man of God at the mountain, she clung to his feet. Gehazi came to push her away, but the man of God said, "Leave her alone—she is in severe anguish, and the Lᴏʀᴅ has hidden it from me. He hasn't told me."

²⁸Then she said, "Did I ask my lord for a son? Didn't I say, 'Do not deceive me?'"

²⁹So Elisha said to Gehazi, "Tuck your mantle under your belt, take my staff with you, and go. If you meet anyone, don't stop to greet him, and if a man greets you, don't answer him. Then place my staff on the boy's face."

³⁰The boy's mother said to Elisha, "As the Lᴏʀᴅ lives and as you yourself live, I will not leave you." So he got up and followed her.

³¹Gehazi went ahead of them and placed the staff on the boy's face, but there was no sound or sign of life, so he went back to meet Elisha and told him, "The boy didn't wake up."

³²When Elisha got to the house, he discovered the boy lying dead on his bed. ³³So he went in, closed the door behind the two of them, and prayed to the Lᴏʀᴅ. ³⁴Then he went up and lay on the boy: he put mouth to mouth, eye to eye, hand to hand. While he bent down over him, the boy's flesh became warm. ³⁵Elisha got up, went into the house, and paced back and forth. Then he went up and bent down over him again. The boy sneezed seven times and opened his eyes.

³⁶Elisha called Gehazi and said, "Call the Shunammite woman." He called her and she came. Then Elisha said, "Pick up your son." ³⁷She came, fell at his feet, and bowed to the ground; she picked up her son and left.

³⁸When Elisha returned to Gilgal, there was a famine in the land. The sons of the prophets were sitting at his feet. He said to his attendant, "Put on the large pot and make stew for the sons of the prophets."

³⁹One went out to the field to gather herbs and found a wild vine from which he gathered as many wild gourds as his garment would hold. Then he came back and cut them up into the pot of stew, but they were unaware of what they were.

⁴⁰They served some for the men to eat, but when

they ate the stew they cried out, "There's death in the pot, man of God!" And they were unable to eat it. ⁴¹Then Elisha said, "Get some meal." He threw it into the pot and said, "Serve it for the people to eat." And there was nothing bad in the pot.

⁴²A man from Baal-shalishah came to the man of God with his sack full of 20 loaves of barley bread from the first bread of the harvest. Elisha said, "Give it to the people to eat."

⁴³But Elisha's attendant asked, "What? Am I to set 20 loaves before 100 men?"

"Give it to the people to eat," Elisha said, "for this is what the LORD says: 'They will eat, and they will have some left over.'" ⁴⁴So he gave it to them, and as the LORD had promised, they ate and had some left over.

5 Naaman, commander of the army for the king of Aram, was a great man in his master's sight and highly regarded because through him, the LORD had given victory to Aram. The man was a brave warrior, but he had a skin disease. ²Aram had gone on raids and brought back from the land of Israel a young girl who served Naaman's wife. ³She said to her mistress, "If only my master would go to the prophet who is in Samaria, he would cure him of his skin disease."

⁴So Naaman went and told his master what the girl from the land of Israel had said. ⁵Therefore, the king of Aram said, "Go and I will send a letter with you to the king of Israel."

So he went and took with him 750 pounds of silver, 150 pounds of gold, and 10 changes of clothes. ⁶He brought the letter to the king of Israel, and it read:

When this letter comes to you, note that I have sent you my servant Naaman for you to cure him of his skin disease.

⁷When the king of Israel read the letter, he tore his clothes and asked, "Am I God, killing and giving life that this man expects me to cure a man of his skin disease? Think it over and you will see that he is only picking a fight with me."

⁸When Elisha the man of God heard that the king of Israel tore his clothes, he sent a message to the king, "Why have you torn your clothes? Have him come to me, and he will know there is a prophet in Israel." ⁹So Naaman came with his horses and chariots and stood at the door of Elisha's house.

¹⁰Then Elisha sent him a messenger, who said, "Go wash seven times in the Jordan and your flesh will be restored and you will be •clean."

¹¹But Naaman got angry and left, saying, "I was telling myself: He will surely come out, stand and call on the name of •Yahweh his God, and will wave his hand over the spot and cure the skin disease. ¹²Aren't Abana and Pharpar, the rivers of Damascus, better than all the waters of Israel? Could I not wash in them and be clean?" So he turned and left in a rage.

¹³But his servants approached and said to him, "My father, if the prophet had told you to do some great thing, would you not have done it? How much more should you do it when he tells you, 'Wash and be clean'?" ¹⁴So Naaman went down and dipped himself in the Jordan seven times, according to the command of the man of God. Then his skin was restored and became like the skin of a small boy, and he was clean.

¹⁵Then Naaman and his whole company went back to the man of God, stood before him, and declared, "I know there's no God in the whole world except in Israel. Therefore, please accept a gift from your servant."

¹⁶But Elisha said, "As the LORD lives, I stand before Him. I will not accept it." Naaman urged him to accept it, but he refused.

¹⁷Naaman responded, "If not, please let your servant be given as much soil as a pair of mules can carry, for your servant will no longer offer a •burnt offering or a sacrifice to any other god but Yahweh. ¹⁸However, in a particular matter may the LORD pardon your servant: When my master, the king of Aram, goes into the temple of Rimmon to worship and I, as his right-hand man, bow in the temple of Rimmon—when I bow in the temple of Rimmon, may the LORD pardon your servant in this matter."

¹⁹So he said to him, "Go in peace."

After Naaman had traveled a short distance from Elisha, ²⁰Gehazi, the attendant of Elisha the man of God, thought: My master has let this Aramean Naaman off lightly by not accepting from him what he brought. As the LORD lives, I will run after him and get something from him.

²¹So Gehazi pursued Naaman. When Naaman saw someone running after him, he got down from the chariot to meet him and asked, "Is everything all right?"

²²Gehazi said, "It's all right. My master has sent me to say, 'I have just now discovered that two young men from the sons of the prophets have come to me from the hill country of Ephraim. Please give them 75 pounds of silver and two changes of clothes.'"

²³But Naaman insisted, "Please, accept 150 pounds." He urged Gehazi and then packed 150 pounds of silver in two bags with two changes of clothes. Naaman gave them to two of his young men who carried them ahead of Gehazi. ²⁴When Gehazi came to the hill, he took the gifts from them and stored them in the house. Then he dismissed the men, and they left.

²⁵Gehazi came and stood by his master. "Where did you go, Gehazi?" Elisha asked him.

"Your servant didn't go anywhere," he replied.

²⁶But Elisha questioned him, "Wasn't my spirit there when the man got down from his chariot to meet you? Is it a time to accept money and clothes, olive orchards and vineyards, sheep and oxen, and male and female slaves? ²⁷Therefore, Naaman's skin disease will cling to you and your descendants forever." So Gehazi went out from his presence diseased—white as snow.

6 The sons of the prophets said to Elisha, "Please notice that the place where we live under your supervision is too small for us. ²Please let us go to the Jordan where we can each get a log and can build ourselves a place to live there."

"Go," he said.

³Then one said, "Please come with your servants."

"I'll come," he answered.

⁴So he went with them, and when they came to the Jordan, they cut down trees. ⁵As one of them was cutting down a tree, the iron ax head fell into the water, and he cried out, "Oh, my master, it was borrowed!"

⁶Then the man of God asked, "Where did it fall?"

When he showed him the place, the man of God cut a stick, threw it there, and made the iron float. ⁷Then he said, "Pick it up." So he reached out and took it.

⁸When the king of Aram was waging war against Israel, he conferred with his servants, "My camp will be at such and such a place."

⁹But the man of God sent word to the king of Israel: "Be careful passing by this place, for the Arameans are going down there." ¹⁰Consequently, the king of Israel sent word to the place the man of God had told him about. The man of God repeatedly warned the king, so the king would be on his guard.

¹¹The king of Aram was enraged because of this matter, and he called his servants and demanded of them, "Tell me, which one of us is for the king of Israel?"

¹²One of his servants said, "No one, my lord the king. Elisha, the prophet in Israel, tells the king of Israel even the words you speak in your bedroom."

¹³So the king said, "Go and see where he is, so I can send men to capture him."

When he was told, "Elisha is in Dothan," ¹⁴he sent horses, chariots, and a massive army there. They went by night and surrounded the city.

¹⁵When the servant of the man of God got up early and went out, he discovered an army with horses and chariots surrounding the city. So he asked Elisha, "Oh, my master, what are we to do?"

¹⁶Elisha said, "Don't be afraid, for those who are with us outnumber those who are with them."

¹⁷Then Elisha prayed, "Lᴏʀᴅ, please open his eyes and let him see." So the Lᴏʀᴅ opened the servant's eyes. He looked and saw that the mountain was covered with horses and chariots of fire all around Elisha.

¹⁸When the Arameans came against him, Elisha prayed to the Lᴏʀᴅ, "Please strike this nation with blindness." So He struck them with blindness, according to Elisha's word. ¹⁹Then Elisha said to them, "This is not the way, and this is not the city. Follow me, and I will take you to the man you're looking for." And he led them to Samaria. ²⁰When they entered Samaria, Elisha said, "Lᴏʀᴅ, open these men's eyes and let them see." So the Lᴏʀᴅ opened their eyes. They looked and discovered they were in Samaria.

²¹When the king of Israel saw them, he said to Elisha, "My father, should I kill them? I will kill them."

²²Elisha replied, "Don't kill them. Do you kill those you have captured with your sword or your bow? Set food and water in front of them so they can eat and drink and go to their master."

²³So he prepared a great feast for them. When they had eaten and drunk, he sent them away, and they went to their master. The Aramean raiders did not come into Israel's land again.

²⁴Some time later, King Ben-hadad of Aram brought all his military units together and marched up to besiege Samaria. ²⁵So there was a great famine in Samaria, and they continued the siege against it until a donkey's head sold for 80 silver *shekels, and a cup of dove's dung sold for five silver shekels.

²⁶As the king of Israel was passing by on the wall, a woman cried out to him, "My lord the king, help!"

²⁷He answered, "If the Lᴏʀᴅ doesn't help you, where can I get help for you? From the threshing floor or the winepress?" ²⁸Then the king asked her, "What's the matter?"

She said, "This woman said to me, 'Give up your son, and we will eat him today. Then we will eat my son tomorrow.' ²⁹So we boiled my son and ate him, and I said to her the next day, 'Give up your son, and we will eat him,' but she has hidden her son."

³⁰When the king heard the woman's words, he tore his clothes. Then, as he was passing by on the wall, the people saw that there was *sackcloth under his clothes next to his skin. ³¹He announced, "May God punish me and do so severely if the head of Elisha son of Shaphat remains on his shoulders today."

³²Elisha was sitting in his house, and the elders were sitting with him. The king sent a man ahead of him, but before the messenger got to him, Elisha said to the elders, "Do you see how this murderer has sent someone to cut off my head? Look, when the messenger comes, shut the door to keep him out. Isn't the sound of his master's feet behind him?"

³³While Elisha was still speaking with them, the messenger came down to him. Then he said, "This disaster is from the Lᴏʀᴅ. Why should I wait for the Lᴏʀᴅ any longer?"

7 Elisha replied, "Hear the word of the Lᴏʀᴅ! This is what the Lᴏʀᴅ says: 'About this time tomorrow at the gate of Samaria, six quarts of fine meal will sell for a *shekel and 12 quarts of barley will sell for a shekel.'"

²Then the captain, the king's right-hand man, responded to the man of God, "Look, even if the Lᴏʀᴅ were to make windows in heaven, could this really happen?"

Elisha announced, "You will in fact see it with your own eyes, but you won't eat any of it."

³Four men with a skin disease were at the entrance to the gate. They said to each other, "Why just sit here until we die? ⁴If we say, 'Let's go into the city,' we will die there because the famine is in the city, but if we sit here, we will also die. So now, come on. Let's go to the Arameans' camp. If they let us live, we will live; if they kill us, we will die."

⁵So the diseased men got up at twilight to go to the Arameans' camp. When they came to the camp's edge, they discovered that there was not a single man there, ⁶for the Lord had caused the Aramean camp to hear the sound of chariots, horses, and a great army. The Arameans had said to each other, "The king of Israel must have hired the kings of the Hittites and the kings of Egypt to attack us." ⁷So they had gotten up and fled at twilight, abandoning their tents, horses, and donkeys. The camp was intact, and they had fled for their lives.

⁸When these men came to the edge of the camp, they went into a tent to eat and drink. Then they picked up the silver, gold, and clothing and went off and hid them. They came back and entered another tent, picked things up, and hid them. ⁹Then they said to each other, "We're not doing what is right. Today is a day of good news. If we are silent and wait until morning light, our sin will catch up with us. Let's go tell the king's household."

¹⁰The diseased men went and called to the city's gatekeepers and told them, "We went to the Aramean camp and no one was there—no human sounds. There was nothing but tethered horses and donkeys, and the tents were intact." ¹¹The gatekeepers called out, and the news was reported to the king's household.

¹²So the king got up in the night and said to his servants, "Let me tell you what the Arameans have done to us. They know we are starving, so they have left the camp to hide in the open country, thinking, 'When they come out of the city, we will take them alive and go into the city.'"

¹³But one of his servants responded, "Please, let messengers take five of the horses that are left in the city. Their fate is like the entire Israelite community who will die, so let's send them and see."

¹⁴The messengers took two chariots with horses, and the king sent them after the Aramean army, saying, "Go and see." ¹⁵So they followed them as far as the Jordan. They saw that the whole way was littered with clothes and equipment the Arameans had thrown off in their haste. The messengers returned and told the king. ¹⁶Then the people went out and plundered the Aramean camp.

It was then that six quarts of fine meal sold for a shekel and 12 quarts of barley sold for a shekel, according to the word of the Lord. ¹⁷The king had appointed the captain, his right-hand man, to be in charge of the gate, but the people trampled him in the gateway. He died, just as the man of God had predicted when the king came to him. ¹⁸When the man of God had said to the king, "About this time tomorrow 12 quarts of barley will sell for a shekel and six quarts of fine meal will sell for a shekel at the gate of Samaria," ¹⁹this captain had answered the man of God, "Look, even if the Lord were to make windows in heaven, could this really happen?" Elisha had said, "You will in fact see it with your own eyes, but you won't eat any of it." ²⁰This is what happened to him: the people trampled him in the gateway, and he died.

8 Elisha said to the woman whose son he had restored to life, "Get ready, you and your household, and go and live as a foreigner wherever you can. For the Lord has announced a seven-year famine, and it has already come to the land." ²So the woman got ready and did what the man of God said. She and her household lived as foreigners in the land of the Philistines for seven years. ³When the woman returned from the land of the Philistines at the end of seven years, she went to appeal to the king for her house and field.

⁴The king had been speaking to Gehazi, the attendant of the man of God, saying, "Tell me all the great things Elisha has done." ⁵While he was telling the king how Elisha restored the dead son to life, the woman whose son he had restored to life came to appeal to the king for her house and field. So Gehazi said, "My lord the king, this is the woman and this is the son Elisha restored to life." ⁶When the king asked the woman, she told him the story. So the king appointed a court official for her, saying, "Restore all that was hers, along with all the income from the field from the day she left the country until now."

⁷Elisha came to Damascus while Ben-hadad king of Aram was sick, and the king was told, "The man of God has come here." ⁸So the king said to Hazael, "Take a gift with you and go meet the man of God. Inquire of the Lord through him, 'Will I recover from this sickness?'"

⁹Hazael went to meet Elisha, taking with him a gift: 40 camel-loads of all kinds of goods from Damascus. When he came and stood before him, he said, "Your son, Ben-hadad king of Aram, has sent me to ask you, 'Will I recover from this sickness?'"

¹⁰Elisha told him, "Go say to him, 'You are sure to recover.' But the Lord has shown me that he is sure to die." ¹¹Then Elisha stared steadily at him until Hazael was ashamed.

The man of God wept, ¹²and Hazael asked, "Why is my lord weeping?"

He replied, "Because I know the evil you will do to the people of Israel. You will set their fortresses on fire.

You will kill their young men with the sword. You will dash their little ones to pieces. You will rip open their pregnant women."

¹³Hazael said, "How could your servant, a mere dog, do this monstrous thing?"

Elisha answered, "The Lord has shown me that you will be king over Aram."

¹⁴Hazael left Elisha and went to his master, who asked him, "What did Elisha say to you?"

He responded, "He told me you are sure to recover." ¹⁵The next day Hazael took a heavy cloth, dipped it in water, and spread it over the king's face. Ben-hadad died, and Hazael reigned instead of him.

¹⁶In the fifth year of Israel's King Joram son of Ahab, Jehoram son of Jehoshaphat became king of Judah, replacing his father. ¹⁷He was 32 years old when he became king and reigned eight years in Jerusalem. ¹⁸He walked in the way of the kings of Israel, as the house of Ahab had done, for Ahab's daughter was his wife. He did what was evil in the Lord's sight. ¹⁹The Lord was unwilling to destroy Judah because of His servant David, since He had promised to give a lamp to David and his sons forever.

²⁰During Jehoram's reign, Edom rebelled against Judah's control and appointed their own king. ²¹So Jehoram crossed over to Zair with all his chariots. Then at night he set out to attack the Edomites who had surrounded him and the chariot commanders, but his troops fled to their tents. ²²So Edom is still in rebellion against Judah's control today. Libnah also rebelled at that time.

²³The rest of the events of Jehoram's reign, along with all his accomplishments, are written in the Historical Record of Judah's Kings. ²⁴Jehoram rested with his fathers and was buried with his fathers in the city of David, and his son Ahaziah became king in his place.

²⁵In the twelfth year of Israel's King Joram son of Ahab, Ahaziah son of Jehoram became king of Judah. ²⁶Ahaziah was 22 years old when he became king and reigned one year in Jerusalem. His mother's name was Athaliah, granddaughter of Israel's King Omri. ²⁷He walked in the way of the house of Ahab and did what was evil in the Lord's sight like the house of Ahab, for he was a son-in-law to Ahab's family.

²⁸Ahaziah went with Joram son of Ahab to fight against Hazael king of Aram in Ramoth-gilead, and the Arameans wounded Joram. ²⁹So King Joram returned to Jezreel to recover from the wounds that the Arameans had inflicted on him in Ramoth-gilead when he fought against Aram's King Hazael. Then Judah's King Ahaziah son of Jehoram went down to Jezreel to visit Joram son of Ahab since Joram was ill.

9 The prophet Elisha called one of the sons of the prophets and said, "Tuck your mantle under your belt, take this flask of oil with you, and go to Ramoth-gilead. ²When you get there, look for Jehu son of Jehoshaphat, son of Nimshi. Go in, get him away from his colleagues, and take him to an inner room. ³Then, take the flask of oil, pour it on his head, and say, 'This is what the Lord says: "I anoint you king over Israel."' Open the door and escape. Don't wait." ⁴So the young prophet went to Ramoth-gilead.

⁵When he arrived, the army commanders were sitting there, so he said, "I have a message for you, commander."

Jehu asked, "For which one of us?"

He answered, "For you, commander."

⁶So Jehu got up and went into the house. The young prophet poured the oil on his head and said, "This is what the LORD God of Israel says: 'I anoint you king over the LORD's people, Israel. ⁷You are to strike down the house of your master Ahab so that I may avenge the blood shed by the hand of Jezebel—the blood of My servants the prophets and of all the servants of the LORD. ⁸The whole house of Ahab will perish, and I will eliminate all of Ahab's males, both slave and free, in Israel. ⁹I will make the house of Ahab like the house of Jeroboam son of Nebat and like the house of Baasha son of Ahijah. ¹⁰The dogs will eat Jezebel in the plot of land at Jezreel—no one will bury her.'" Then the young prophet opened the door and escaped.

¹¹When Jehu came out to his master's servants, they asked, "Is everything all right? Why did this crazy person come to you?"

Then he said to them, "You know the sort and their ranting."

¹²But they replied, "That's a lie! Tell us!"

So Jehu said, "He talked to me about this and that and said, 'This is what the LORD says: I anoint you king over Israel.'"

¹³Each man quickly took his garment and put it under Jehu on the bare steps. They blew the ram's horn and proclaimed, "Jehu is king!"

¹⁴Then Jehu son of Jehoshaphat, son of Nimshi, conspired against Joram. Joram and all Israel had been at Ramoth-gilead on guard against Hazael king of Aram. ¹⁵But King Joram had returned to Jezreel to recover from the wounds that the Arameans had inflicted on him when he fought against Aram's King Hazael. Jehu said, "If you commanders wish to make me king, then don't let anyone escape from the city to go tell about it in Jezreel."

¹⁶Jehu got into his chariot and went to Jezreel since Joram was laid up there and Ahaziah king of Judah had gone down to visit Joram. ¹⁷Now the watchman was standing on the tower in Jezreel. He saw Jehu's troops approaching and shouted, "I see troops!"

Joram responded, "Choose a rider and send him to meet them and have him ask, 'Do you come in peace?'"

¹⁸So a horseman went to meet Jehu and said, "This is what the king asks: 'Do you come in peace?'"

Jehu replied, "What do you have to do with peace? Fall in behind me."

The watchman reported, "The messenger reached them but hasn't started back."

¹⁹So he sent out a second horseman, who went to them and said, "This is what the king asks: 'Do you come in peace?'"

Jehu answered, "What do you have to do with peace? Fall in behind me."

²⁰Again the watchman reported, "He reached them but hasn't started back. Also, the driving is like that of Jehu son of Nimshi—he drives like a madman."

²¹"Harness!" Joram shouted, and they harnessed his chariot. Then Joram king of Israel and Ahaziah king of Judah set out, each in his own chariot, and met Jehu at the plot of land of Naboth the Jezreelite. ²²When Joram saw Jehu he asked, "Do you come in peace, Jehu?"

He answered, "What peace can there be as long as there is so much prostitution and witchcraft from your mother Jezebel?"

²³Joram turned around and fled, shouting to Ahaziah, "It's treachery, Ahaziah!"

²⁴Then Jehu drew his bow and shot Joram between the shoulders. The arrow went through his heart, and he slumped down in his chariot. ²⁵Jehu said to Bidkar his aide, "Pick him up and throw him on the plot of ground belonging to Naboth the Jezreelite. For remember when you and I were riding side by side behind his father Ahab, and the LORD uttered this •oracle against him: ²⁶'As surely as I saw the blood of Naboth and the blood of his sons yesterday'—this is the LORD's declaration—'so will I repay you on this plot of land'—this is the LORD's declaration. So now, according to the word of the LORD, pick him up and throw him on the plot of land."

²⁷When King Ahaziah of Judah saw what was happening, he fled up the road toward Beth-haggan. Jehu pursued him, shouting, "Shoot him too!" So they shot him in his chariot at Gur Pass near Ibleam, but he fled to Megiddo and died there. ²⁸Then his servants carried him to Jerusalem in a chariot and buried him in his fathers' tomb in the city of David. ²⁹It was in the eleventh year of Joram son of Ahab that Ahaziah had become king over Judah.

³⁰When Jehu came to Jezreel, Jezebel heard about it, so she painted her eyes, adorned her head, and looked down from the window. ³¹As Jehu entered the gate, she said, "Do you come in peace, Zimri, killer of your master?"

³²He looked up toward the window and said, "Who is on my side? Who?" Two or three eunuchs looked down at him, ³³and he said, "Throw her down!" So they threw her down, and some of her blood splattered on the wall and on the horses, and Jehu rode over her. ³⁴Then he went in, ate and drank, and said, "Take care of this cursed woman and bury her, since she's a king's daughter." ³⁵But when they went out to bury her, they did not find anything but her skull, her feet, and the palms of her hands. ³⁶So they went back and told him, and he said, "This fulfills the LORD's word that He spoke through His servant Elijah the Tishbite: 'In the plot of land at Jezreel, the dogs will eat Jezebel's flesh. ³⁷Jezebel's corpse will be like manure on the surface of the field in the plot of land at Jezreel so that no one will be able to say: This is Jezebel.'"

10 Since Ahab had 70 sons in Samaria, Jehu wrote letters and sent them to Samaria to the rulers of Jezreel, to the elders, and to the guardians of Ahab's sons, saying:

²When this letter arrives, since your master's sons are with you and you have chariots, horses, a fortified city, and weaponry, ³select the most qualified of your master's sons, set him on his father's throne, and fight for your master's house.

⁴However, they were terrified and reasoned, "Look, two kings couldn't stand against him; how can we?"

⁵So the overseer of the palace, the overseer of the city, the elders, and the guardians sent a message to Jehu: "We are your servants, and we will do whatever you tell us. We will not make anyone king. Do whatever you think is right."

⁶Then Jehu wrote them a second letter, saying:

If you are on my side, and if you will obey me, bring me the heads of your master's sons at this time tomorrow at Jezreel.

All 70 of the king's sons were being cared for by the city's prominent men. ⁷When the letter came to them, they took the king's sons and slaughtered all 70, put their heads in baskets, and sent them to Jehu at Jezreel. ⁸When the messenger came and told him, "They have brought the heads of the king's sons," the king said, "Pile them in two heaps at the entrance of the gate until morning."

⁹The next morning when he went out and stood at the gate, he said to all the people, "You are innocent. It was I who conspired against my master and killed him. But who struck down all these? ¹⁰Know, then, that not a word the LORD spoke against the house of Ahab will fail, for the LORD has done what He promised through His servant Elijah." ¹¹So Jehu killed all who remained of the house of Ahab in Jezreel—all his great men, close friends, and priests—leaving him no survivors.

¹²Then he set out and went on his way to Samaria. On the way, while he was at Beth-eked of the Shepherds, ¹³Jehu met the relatives of Ahaziah king of Judah and asked, "Who are you?"

They answered, "We're Ahaziah's relatives. We've come down to greet the king's sons and the queen mother's sons."

¹⁴Then Jehu ordered, "Take them alive." So they took them alive and then slaughtered them at the pit of Beth-eked—42 men. He didn't spare any of them.

¹⁵When he left there, he found Jehonadab son of Rechab coming to meet him. He greeted him and then asked, "Is your heart one with mine?"

"It is," Jehonadab replied.

Jehu said, "If it is, give me your hand."

So he gave him his hand, and Jehu pulled him up into the chariot with him. ¹⁶Then he said, "Come with me and see my zeal for the LORD!" So he let him ride with him in his chariot. ¹⁷When Jehu came to Samaria, he struck down all who remained from the house of Ahab in Samaria until he had annihilated his house, according to the word of the LORD spoken to Elijah.

¹⁸Then Jehu brought all the people together and said to them, "Ahab served ˙Baal a little, but Jehu will serve him a lot. ¹⁹Now, therefore, summon to me all the prophets of Baal, all his servants, and all his priests. None must be missing, for I have a great sacrifice for Baal. Whoever is missing will not live." However, Jehu was acting deceptively in order to destroy the servants of Baal. ²⁰Jehu commanded, "Consecrate a solemn assembly for Baal." So they called one.

²¹Then Jehu sent messengers throughout all Israel, and all the servants of Baal came; there was not a man left who did not come. They entered the temple of Baal, and it was filled from one end to the other. ²²Then he said to the custodian of the wardrobe, "Bring out the garments for all the servants of Baal." So he brought out their garments.

²³Then Jehu and Jehonadab son of Rechab entered the temple of Baal, and Jehu said to the servants of Baal, "Look carefully to see that there are no servants of the LORD here among you—only servants of Baal." ²⁴Then they went in to offer sacrifices and ˙burnt offerings.

Now Jehu had stationed 80 men outside, and he warned them, "Whoever allows any of the men I am delivering into your hands to escape will forfeit his life for theirs." ²⁵When he finished offering the burnt offering, Jehu said to the guards and officers, "Go in and kill them. Don't let anyone out." So they struck them down with the sword. Then the guards and officers threw the bodies out and went into the inner room of the temple of Baal. ²⁶They brought out the pillars of the temple of Baal and burned them ²⁷and tore down

the pillar of Baal. Then they tore down the temple of Baal and made it a latrine—which it is to this day.

²⁸Jehu eliminated Baal worship from Israel, ²⁹but he did not turn away from the sins that Jeroboam son of Nebat had caused Israel to commit—worshiping the gold calves that were in Bethel and Dan. ³⁰Nevertheless, the LORD said to Jehu, "Because you have done well in carrying out what is right in My sight and have done to the house of Ahab all that was in My heart, four generations of your sons will sit on the throne of Israel."

³¹Yet Jehu was not careful to follow the instruction of the LORD God of Israel with all his heart. He did not turn from the sins that Jeroboam had caused Israel to commit.

³²In those days the LORD began to reduce the size of Israel. Hazael defeated the Israelites throughout their territory: ³³from the Jordan eastward, all the land of Gilead—the Gadites, the Reubenites, and the Manassites—from Aroer which is by the Arnon Valley through Gilead to Bashan.

³⁴Now the rest of the events of Jehu's reign, along with all his accomplishments and all his might, are written in the Historical Record of Israel's Kings. ³⁵Jehu rested with his fathers and was buried in Samaria. His son Jehoahaz became king in his place. ³⁶The length of Jehu's reign over Israel in Samaria was 28 years.

11 When Athaliah, Ahaziah's mother, saw that her son was dead, she proceeded to annihilate all the royal heirs. ²Jehosheba, who was King Jehoram's daughter and Ahaziah's sister, secretly rescued Joash son of Ahaziah from the king's sons who were being killed and put him and the one who nursed him in a bedroom. So he was hidden from Athaliah and was not killed. ³Joash was in hiding with Jehosheba in the LORD's temple six years while Athaliah ruled over the land.

⁴Then in the seventh year, Jehoiada sent messengers and brought in the commanders of hundreds, the Carites, and the guards. He had them come to him in the LORD's temple, where he made a covenant with them and put them under oath. He showed them the king's son ⁵and commanded them, "This is what you are to do: a third of you who come on duty on the Sabbath are to provide protection for the king's palace. ⁶A third are to be at the Sur gate and a third at the gate behind the guards. You are to take turns providing protection for the palace.

⁷"Your two divisions that go off duty on the Sabbath are to provide protection for the LORD's temple. ⁸You must completely surround the king with weapons in hand. Anyone who approaches the ranks is to be put to death. You must be with the king in all his daily tasks."

⁹So the commanders of hundreds did everything Jehoiada the priest commanded. They each brought their men—those coming on duty on the Sabbath and those going off duty—and went to Jehoiada the priest. ¹⁰The priest gave to the commanders of hundreds King David's spears and shields that were in the LORD's temple. ¹¹Then the guards stood with their weapons in hand surrounding the king—from the right side of the temple to the left side, by the altar and by the temple.

¹²He brought out the king's son, put the crown on him, gave him the ˙testimony, and made him king. They anointed him and clapped their hands and cried, "Long live the king!"

¹³When Athaliah heard the noise from the guard and the crowd, she went out to the people at the Lord's temple. ¹⁴As she looked, there was the king standing by the pillar according to the custom. The commanders and the trumpeters were by the king, and all the people of the land were rejoicing and blowing trumpets. Athaliah tore her clothes and screamed "Treason! Treason!"

¹⁵Then Jehoiada the priest ordered the commanders of hundreds in charge of the army, "Take her out between the ranks, and put to death by the sword anyone who follows her," for the priest had said, "She is not to be put to death in the Lord's temple." ¹⁶So they arrested her, and she went through the horse entrance to the king's palace, where she was put to death.

¹⁷Then Jehoiada made a covenant between the Lord, the king, and the people that they would be the Lord's people and another covenant between the king and the people. ¹⁸So all the people of the land went to the temple of *Baal and tore it down. They broke its altars and images into pieces, and they killed Mattan, the priest of Baal, at the altars.

Then Jehoiada the priest appointed guards for the Lord's temple. ¹⁹He took the commanders of hundreds, the Carites, the guards, and all the people of the land, and they brought the king from the Lord's temple. They entered the king's palace by way of the guards' gate. Then Joash sat on the throne of the kings. ²⁰All the people of the land rejoiced, and the city was quiet, for they had put Athaliah to death by the sword in the king's palace.

12 ²¹Joash was seven years old when he became king. ¹In the seventh year of Jehu, Joash became king and reigned 40 years in Jerusalem. His mother's name was Zibiah, who was from Beer-sheba. ²Throughout the time Jehoiada the priest instructed him, Joash did what was right in the Lord's sight. ³Yet the *high places were not taken away; the people continued sacrificing and burning incense on the high places.

⁴Then Joash said to the priests, "All the dedicated money brought to the Lord's temple, census money, money from vows, and all money voluntarily given for the Lord's temple, ⁵each priest is to take from his assessor and repair whatever damage to the temple is found."

⁶But by the twenty-third year of the reign of King Joash, the priests had not repaired the damage to the temple. ⁷So King Joash called Jehoiada the priest and the other priests and said, "Why haven't you repaired the temple's damage? Since you haven't, don't take any money from your assessors; instead, hand it over for the repair of the temple." ⁸So the priests agreed they would not take money from the people and they would not repair the temple's damage.

⁹Then Jehoiada the priest took a chest, bored a hole in its lid, and set it beside the altar on the right side as one enters the Lord's temple; in it the priests who guarded the threshold put all the money brought into the Lord's temple. ¹⁰Whenever they saw there was a large amount of money in the chest, the king's secretary and the high priest would go to the Lord's temple and count the money found there and tie it up in bags. ¹¹Then they would put the counted money into the hands of those doing the work—those who oversaw the Lord's temple. They in turn would pay it out to those working on the Lord's temple—the carpenters, the builders, ¹²the masons, and the stonecutters—and would use it to buy timber and quarried stone to repair the damage to the Lord's temple and for all spending for temple repairs.

¹³However, no silver bowls, wick trimmers, sprinkling basins, trumpets, or any articles of gold or silver were made for the Lord's temple from the money brought into the temple. ¹⁴Instead, it was given to those doing the work, and they repaired the Lord's temple with it. ¹⁵No accounting was required from the men who received the money to pay those doing the work, since they worked with integrity. ¹⁶The money from the *restitution offering and the *sin offering was not brought to the Lord's temple since it belonged to the priests.

¹⁷At that time Hazael king of Aram marched up and fought against Gath and captured it. Then he planned to attack Jerusalem. ¹⁸So King Joash of Judah took all the consecrated items that his ancestors—Judah's kings Jehoshaphat, Jehoram, and Ahaziah—had consecrated, along with his own consecrated items and all the gold found in the treasuries of the Lord's temple and in the king's palace, and he sent them to Hazael king of Aram. Then Hazael withdrew from Jerusalem.

¹⁹The rest of the events of Joash's reign, along with all his accomplishments, are written in the Historical Record of Judah's Kings. ²⁰Joash's servants conspired against him and killed him at Beth-millo on the road that goes down to Silla. ²¹His servants Jozabad son of Shimeath and Jehozabad son of Shomer struck him down, and he died. Then they buried him with his fathers in the city of David, and his son Amaziah became king in his place.

13 In the twenty-third year of Judah's King Joash son of Ahaziah, Jehoahaz son of Jehu became king over Israel in Samaria and reigned 17 years. ²He did what was evil in the Lord's sight and followed the sins that Jeroboam son of Nebat had caused Israel to commit; he did not turn away from them. ³So the Lord's anger burned against Israel, and He surrendered them to the power of Hazael king of Aram and his son Ben-hadad during their reigns.

⁴Then Jehoahaz sought the Lord's favor, and the Lord heard him, for He saw the oppression the king of Aram inflicted on Israel. ⁵Therefore, the Lord gave Israel a deliverer, and they escaped from the power of the Arameans. Then the people of Israel dwelt in their tents as before, ⁶but they didn't turn away from the sins that the house of Jeroboam had caused Israel to commit. Jehoahaz walked in them, and the *Asherah pole also remained standing in Samaria. ⁷Jehoahaz did not have an army left, except for 50 horsemen, 10 chariots, and 10,000 foot soldiers, because the king of Aram had destroyed them, making them like dust at threshing.

⁸The rest of the events of Jehoahaz's reign, along with all his accomplishments and his might, are written in the Historical Record of Israel's Kings. ⁹Jehoahaz rested with his fathers, and he was buried in Samaria. His son Jehoash became king in his place.

¹⁰In the thirty-seventh year of Judah's King Joash, Jehoash son of Jehoahaz became king over Israel in Samaria and reigned 16 years. ¹¹He did what was evil in the Lord's sight. He did not turn away from all the sins that Jeroboam son of Nebat had caused Israel to commit, but he walked in them.

¹²The rest of the events of Jehoash's reign, along

with all his accomplishments and the power he had to wage war against Judah's King Amaziah, are written in the Historical Record of Israel's Kings. [13]Jehoash rested with his fathers, and Jeroboam sat on his throne. Jehoash was buried in Samaria with the kings of Israel.

[14]When Elisha became sick with the illness that he died from, Jehoash king of Israel went down and wept over him and said, "My father, my father, the chariots and horsemen of Israel!"

[15]Elisha responded, "Take a bow and arrows." So he got a bow and arrows. [16]Then Elisha said to the king of Israel, "Put your hand on the bow." So the king put his hand on it, and Elisha put his hands on the king's hands. [17]Elisha said, "Open the east window." So he opened it. Elisha said, "Shoot!" So he shot. Then Elisha said, "The LORD's arrow of victory, yes, the arrow of victory over Aram. You are to strike down the Arameans in Aphek until you have put an end to them."

[18]Then Elisha said, "Take the arrows!" So he took them. Then Elisha said to the king of Israel, "Strike the ground!" So he struck the ground three times and stopped. [19]The man of God was angry with him and said, "You should have struck the ground five or six times. Then you would have struck down Aram until you had put an end to them, but now you will only strike down Aram three times." [20]Then Elisha died and was buried.

Now Moabite raiders used to come into the land in the spring of the year. [21]Once, as the Israelites were burying a man, suddenly they saw a raiding party, so they threw the man into Elisha's tomb. When he touched Elisha's bones, the man revived and stood up!

[22]Hazael king of Aram oppressed Israel throughout the reign of Jehoahaz, [23]but the LORD was gracious to them, had compassion on them, and turned toward them because of His covenant with Abraham, Isaac, and Jacob. He was not willing to destroy them. Even now He has not banished them from His presence.

[24]King Hazael of Aram died, and his son Ben-hadad became king in his place. [25]Then Jehoash son of Jehoahaz took back from Ben-hadad son of Hazael the cities that Hazael had taken in war from Jehoash's father Jehoahaz. Jehoash defeated Ben-hadad three times and recovered the cities of Israel.

14 In the second year of Israel's King Jehoash son of Jehoahaz, Amaziah son of Joash became king of Judah. [2]He was 25 years old when he became king and reigned 29 years in Jerusalem. His mother's name was Jehoaddan and was from Jerusalem. [3]He did what was right in the LORD's sight, but not like his ancestor David. He did everything his father Joash had done. [4]Yet the ‧high places were not taken away, and the people continued sacrificing and burning incense on the high places.

[5]As soon as the kingdom was firmly in his grasp, Amaziah killed his servants who had murdered his father the king. [6]However, he did not put the children of the murderers to death, as it is written in the book of the law of Moses where the LORD commanded, "Fathers must not be put to death because of children, and children must not be put to death because of fathers; instead, each one will be put to death for his own sin."

[7]Amaziah killed 10,000 Edomites in the Valley of Salt. He took Sela in battle and called it Joktheel, which is its name to this very day. [8]Amaziah then sent messengers to Jehoash son of Jehoahaz, son of Jehu, king of Israel, saying, "Come, let us meet face to face."

[9]King Jehoash of Israel sent word to Amaziah king of Judah, saying, "The thistle that was in Lebanon once sent a message to the cedar that was in Lebanon, saying, 'Give your daughter to my son as a wife.' Then a wild animal that was in Lebanon passed by and trampled the thistle. [10]You have indeed defeated Edom, and you have become overconfident. Enjoy your glory and stay at home. Why should you stir up such trouble that you fall—you and Judah with you?"

[11]But Amaziah would not listen, so King Jehoash of Israel advanced. He and King Amaziah of Judah faced off at Beth-shemesh that belongs to Judah. [12]Judah was routed before Israel, and everyone fled to his own tent. [13]King Jehoash of Israel captured Judah's King Amaziah son of Joash, son of Ahaziah, at Beth-shemesh. Then Jehoash went to Jerusalem and broke down 200 yards of Jerusalem's wall from the Ephraim Gate to the Corner Gate. [14]He took all the gold and silver, all the articles found in the LORD's temple and in the treasuries of the king's palace, and some hostages. Then he returned to Samaria.

[15]The rest of the events of Jehoash's reign, along with his accomplishments, his might, and how he waged war against Amaziah king of Judah, are written in the Historical Record of Israel's Kings. [16]Jehoash rested with his fathers, and he was buried in Samaria with the kings of Israel. His son Jeroboam became king in his place.

[17]Judah's King Amaziah son of Joash lived 15 years after the death of Israel's King Jehoash son of Jehoahaz. [18]The rest of the events of Amaziah's reign are written in the Historical Record of Judah's Kings. [19]A conspiracy was formed against him in Jerusalem, and he fled to Lachish. However, men were sent after him to Lachish, and they put him to death there. [20]They carried him back on horses, and he was buried in Jerusalem with his fathers in the city of David.

[21]Then all the people of Judah took Azariah, who was 16 years old, and made him king in place of his father Amaziah. [22]He rebuilt Elath and restored it to Judah after Amaziah the king rested with his fathers.

[23]In the fifteenth year of Judah's King Amaziah son of Joash, Jeroboam son of Jehoash became king of Israel in Samaria and reigned 41 years. [24]He did what was evil in the LORD's sight. He did not turn away from all the sins Jeroboam son of Nebat had caused Israel to commit.

[25]He restored Israel's border from Lebo-hamath as far as the Sea of the ‧Arabah, according to the word the LORD, the God of Israel, had spoken through His servant, the prophet Jonah son of Amittai from Gathhepher. [26]For the LORD saw that the affliction of Israel was very bitter. There was no one to help Israel, neither bond nor free. [27]However, the LORD had not said He would blot out the name of Israel under heaven, so He delivered them by the hand of Jeroboam son of Jehoash.

[28]The rest of the events of Jeroboam's reign—along with all his accomplishments, the power he had to wage war, and how he recovered for Israel Damascus and Hamath, which had belonged to Judah—are written in the Historical Record of Israel's Kings. [29]Jeroboam rested with his fathers, the kings of Israel. His son Zechariah became king in his place.

15 In the twenty-seventh year of Israel's King Jeroboam, Azariah son of Amaziah became king of Judah. [2] He was 16 years old when he became king and reigned 52 years in Jerusalem. His mother's name was Jecoliah, who was from Jerusalem. [3] Azariah did what was right in the Lord's sight just as his father Amaziah had done. [4] Yet the *high places were not taken away; the people continued sacrificing and burning incense on the high places.

[5] The Lord afflicted the king, and he had a serious skin disease until the day of his death. He lived in a separate house, while Jotham, the king's son, was over the household governing the people of the land.

[6] The rest of the events of Azariah's reign, along with all his accomplishments, are written in the Historical Record of Judah's Kings. [7] Azariah rested with his fathers and was buried with his fathers in the city of David. His son Jotham became king in his place.

[8] In the thirty-eighth year of Judah's King Azariah, Zechariah son of Jeroboam became king over Israel in Samaria for six months. [9] He did what was evil in the Lord's sight as his fathers had done. He did not turn away from the sins Jeroboam son of Nebat had caused Israel to commit.

[10] Shallum son of Jabesh conspired against Zechariah. He struck him down publicly, killed him, and became king in his place. [11] As for the rest of the events of Zechariah's reign, they are written in the Historical Record of Israel's Kings. [12] The word of the Lord that He spoke to Jehu was, "Four generations of your sons will sit on the throne of Israel," and it was so.

[13] In the thirty-ninth year of Judah's King Uzziah, Shallum son of Jabesh became king; he reigned in Samaria a full month. [14] Then Menahem son of Gadi came up from Tirzah to Samaria and struck down Shallum son of Jabesh there. He killed him and became king in his place. [15] As for the rest of the events of Shallum's reign, along with the conspiracy that he formed, they are written in the Historical Record of Israel's Kings.

[16] At that time, starting from Tirzah, Menahem attacked Tiphsah, all who were in it, and its territory. Because they wouldn't surrender, he attacked it and ripped open all the pregnant women.

[17] In the thirty-ninth year of Judah's King Azariah, Menahem son of Gadi became king over Israel and reigned 10 years in Samaria. [18] He did what was evil in the Lord's sight. Throughout his reign, he did not turn away from the sins Jeroboam son of Nebat had caused Israel to commit.

[19] Pul king of Assyria invaded the land, so Menahem gave Pul 75,000 pounds of silver so that Pul would support him to strengthen his grip on the kingdom. [20] Then Menahem exacted 20 ounces of silver from each of the wealthy men of Israel to give to the king of Assyria. So the king of Assyria withdrew and did not stay there in the land.

[21] The rest of the events of Menahem's reign, along with all his accomplishments, are written in the Historical Record of Israel's Kings. [22] Menahem rested with his fathers, and his son Pekahiah became king in his place.

[23] In the fiftieth year of Judah's King Azariah, Pekahiah son of Menahem became king over Israel in Samaria and reigned two years. [24] He did what was evil in the Lord's sight and did not turn away from the sins Jeroboam son of Nebat had caused Israel to commit.

[25] Then his officer, Pekah son of Remaliah, conspired against him and struck him down in Samaria at the citadel of the king's palace—as well as Argob and Arieh. There were 50 Gileadite men with Pekah. He killed Pekahiah and became king in his place.

[26] As for the rest of the events of Pekahiah's reign, along with all his accomplishments, they are written in the Historical Record of Israel's Kings.

[27] In the fifty-second year of Judah's King Azariah, Pekah son of Remaliah became king over Israel in Samaria and reigned 20 years. [28] He did what was evil in the Lord's sight. He did not turn away from the sins Jeroboam son of Nebat had caused Israel to commit.

[29] In the days of Pekah king of Israel, Tiglath-pileser king of Assyria came and captured Ijon, Abel-beth-maacah, Janoah, Kedesh, Hazor, Gilead, and Galilee—all the land of Naphtali—and deported the people to Assyria.

[30] Then Hoshea son of Elah organized a conspiracy against Pekah son of Remaliah. He attacked him, killed him, and became king in his place in the twentieth year of Jotham son of Uzziah.

[31] As for the rest of the events of Pekah's reign, along with all his accomplishments, they are written in the Historical Record of Israel's Kings.

[32] In the second year of Israel's King Pekah son of Remaliah, Jotham son of Uzziah became king of Judah. [33] He was 25 years old when he became king and reigned 16 years in Jerusalem. His mother's name was Jerusha daughter of Zadok. [34] He did what was right in the Lord's sight just as his father Uzziah had done. [35] Yet the high places were not taken away; the people continued sacrificing and burning incense on the high places.

Jotham built the Upper Gate of the Lord's temple. [36] The rest of the events of Jotham's reign, along with all his accomplishments, they are written in the Historical Record of Judah's Kings. [37] In those days the Lord began sending Rezin king of Aram and Pekah son of Remaliah against Judah. [38] Jotham rested with his fathers and was buried with his fathers in the city of his ancestor David. His son Ahaz became king in his place.

16 In the seventeenth year of Pekah son of Remaliah, Ahaz son of Jotham became king of Judah. [2] Ahaz was 20 years old when he became king and reigned 16 years in Jerusalem. He did not do what was right in the sight of the Lord his God like his ancestor David [3] but walked in the way of the kings of Israel. He even made his son pass through the fire, imitating the detestable practices of the nations the Lord had dispossessed before the Israelites. [4] He sacrificed and burned incense on the *high places, on the hills, and under every green tree.

[5] Then Aram's King Rezin and Israel's King Pekah son of Remaliah came to wage war against Jerusalem. They besieged Ahaz but were not able to conquer him. [6] At that time Rezin king of Aram recovered Elath for Aram and expelled the Judahites from Elath. Then the Arameans came to Elath, and they live there until today.

[7] So Ahaz sent messengers to Tiglath-pileser king of Assyria, saying, "I am your servant and your son. March up and save me from the power of the king of Aram and of the king of Israel, who are rising up against me." [8] Ahaz also took the silver and gold found in the Lord's temple and in the treasuries of the king's

palace and sent them to the king of Assyria as a gift. [9] So the king of Assyria listened to him and marched up to Damascus and captured it. He deported its people to Kir but put Rezin to death.

[10] King Ahaz went to Damascus to meet Tiglath-pileser king of Assyria. When he saw the altar that was in Damascus, King Ahaz sent a model of the altar and complete plans for its construction to Uriah the priest. [11] Uriah built the altar according to all the instructions King Ahaz sent from Damascus. Therefore, by the time King Ahaz came back from Damascus, Uriah the priest had completed it. [12] When the king came back from Damascus, he saw the altar. Then he approached the altar and ascended it. [13] He offered his ˚burnt offering and his ˚grain offering, poured out his drink offering, and sprinkled the blood of his ˚fellowship offerings on the altar. [14] He took the bronze altar that was before the LORD in front of the temple between his altar and the LORD's temple, and put it on the north side of his altar.

[15] Then King Ahaz commanded Uriah the priest, "Offer on the great altar the morning burnt offering, the evening grain offering, and the king's burnt offering and his grain offering. Also offer the burnt offering of all the people of the land, their grain offering, and their drink offerings. Sprinkle on the altar all the blood of the burnt offering and all the blood of sacrifice. The bronze altar will be for me to seek guidance." [16] Uriah the priest did everything King Ahaz commanded.

[17] Then King Ahaz cut off the frames of the water carts and removed the bronze basin from each of them. He took the reservoir from the bronze oxen that were under it and put it on a stone pavement. [18] To satisfy the king of Assyria, he removed from the LORD's temple the Sabbath canopy they had built in the palace, and he closed the outer entrance for the king.

[19] The rest of the events of Ahaz's reign, along with his accomplishments, are written in the Historical Record of Judah's Kings. [20] Ahaz rested with his fathers and was buried with his fathers in the city of David, and his son Hezekiah became king in his place.

17 In the twelfth year of Judah's King Ahaz, Hoshea son of Elah became king over Israel in Samaria and reigned nine years. [2] He did what was evil in the LORD's sight, but not like the kings of Israel who preceded him.

[3] Shalmaneser king of Assyria attacked him, and Hoshea became his vassal and paid him tribute money. [4] But the king of Assyria discovered Hoshea's conspiracy. He had sent envoys to So king of Egypt and had not paid tribute money to the king of Assyria as in previous years. Therefore the king of Assyria arrested him and put him in prison. [5] Then the king of Assyria invaded the whole land, marched up to Samaria, and besieged it for three years.

[6] In the ninth year of Hoshea, the king of Assyria captured Samaria. He deported the Israelites to Assyria and settled them in Halah and by the Habor, Gozan's river, and in the cities of the Medes.

[7] This disaster happened because the people of Israel had sinned against the LORD their God who had brought them out of the land of Egypt from the power of Pharaoh king of Egypt and because they had worshiped other gods. [8] They had lived according to the customs of the nations that the LORD had dispossessed before the Israelites and the customs the kings of Israel had introduced. [9] The Israelites secretly did what was not right against the LORD their God. They built ˚high places in all their towns from watchtower to fortified city. [10] They set up for themselves sacred pillars and ˚Asherah poles on every high hill and under every green tree. [11] They burned incense on all the high places just like those nations that the LORD had driven out before them. They did evil things, provoking the LORD. [12] They served idols, although the LORD had told them, "You must not do this." [13] Still, the LORD warned Israel and Judah through every prophet and every seer, saying, "Turn from your evil ways and keep My commands and statutes according to all the law I commanded your ancestors and sent to you through My servants the prophets."

[14] But they would not listen. Instead they became obstinate like their ancestors who did not believe the LORD their God. [15] They rejected His statutes and His covenant He had made with their ancestors and the decrees He had given them. They pursued worthless idols and became worthless themselves, following the surrounding nations the LORD had commanded them not to imitate.

[16] They abandoned all the commands of the LORD their God. They made cast images for themselves, two calves, and an Asherah pole. They worshiped the whole heavenly ˚host and served ˚Baal. [17] They made their sons and daughters pass through the fire and practiced ˚divination and interpreted omens. They devoted themselves to do what was evil in the LORD's sight and provoked Him.

[18] Therefore, the LORD was very angry with Israel, and He removed them from His presence. Only the tribe of Judah remained. [19] Even Judah did not keep the commands of the LORD their God but lived according to the customs Israel had introduced. [20] So the LORD rejected all the descendants of Israel, afflicted them, and handed them over to plunderers until He had banished them from His presence.

[21] When the LORD tore Israel from the house of David, Israel made Jeroboam son of Nebat king. Then Jeroboam led Israel away from following the LORD and caused them to commit great sin. [22] The Israelites persisted in all the sins that Jeroboam committed and did not turn away from them. [23] Finally, the LORD removed Israel from His presence just as He had declared through all His servants the prophets. So Israel has been exiled to Assyria from their homeland until today.

[24] Then the king of Assyria brought people from Babylon, Cuthah, Avva, Hamath, and Sepharvaim and settled them in place of the Israelites in the cities of Samaria. The settlers took possession of Samaria and lived in its cities. [25] When they first lived there, they did not ˚fear ˚Yahweh. So the LORD sent lions among them, which killed some of them. [26] The settlers spoke to the king of Assyria, saying, "The nations that you have deported and placed in the cities of Samaria do not know the requirements of the God of the land. Therefore He has sent lions among them that are killing them because the people don't know the requirements of the God of the land."

[27] Then the king of Assyria issued a command: "Send back one of the priests you deported. Have him go and live there so he can teach them the requirements of the God of the land." [28] So one of the priests they had deported came and lived in Bethel, and he began to teach them how they should fear Yahweh.

[29] But the people of each nation were still making their own gods in the cities where they lived and

putting them in the shrines of the high places that the people of Samaria had made. ³⁰The men of Babylon made Succoth-benoth, the men of Cuth made Nergal, the men of Hamath made Ashima, ³¹the Avvites made Nibhaz and Tartak, and the Sepharvites burned their children in the fire to Adrammelech and Anammelech, the gods of the Sepharvaim. ³²They feared the Lord, but they also appointed from their number priests to serve them in the shrines of the high places. ³³They feared the Lord, but they also worshiped their own gods according to the custom of the nations where they had been deported from.

³⁴They are still practicing the former customs to this day. None of them fear the Lord or observe their statutes and ordinances, the law and commandments the Lord commanded the descendants of Jacob. He had renamed him Israel. ³⁵The Lord made a covenant with them and commanded them, "Do not fear other gods; do not bow down to them; do not serve them; do not sacrifice to them. ³⁶Instead fear the Lord, who brought you from the land of Egypt with great power and an outstretched arm. You are to bow down to Him, and you are to sacrifice to Him. ³⁷You are to be careful always to observe the statutes, the ordinances, the law, and the commandments He wrote for you; do not fear other gods. ³⁸Do not forget the covenant that I have made with you. Do not fear other gods, ³⁹but fear the Lord your God, and He will deliver you from the hand of all your enemies."

⁴⁰However, they would not listen but continued practicing their former customs. ⁴¹These nations feared the Lord but also served their idols. Their children and grandchildren continue doing as their fathers did until today.

18 In the third year of Israel's King Hoshea son of Elah, Hezekiah son of Ahaz became king of Judah. ²He was 25 years old when he became king and reigned 29 years in Jerusalem. His mother's name was Abi daughter of Zechariah. ³He did what was right in the Lord's sight just as his ancestor David had done. ⁴He removed the *high places, shattered the sacred pillars, and cut down the *Asherah poles. He broke into pieces the bronze snake that Moses made, for the Israelites burned incense to it up to that time. He called it Nehushtan.

⁵Hezekiah trusted in the Lord God of Israel; not one of the kings of Judah was like him, either before him or after him. ⁶He remained faithful to *Yahweh and did not turn from following Him but kept the commands the Lord had commanded Moses.

⁷The Lord was with him, and wherever he went he prospered. He rebelled against the king of Assyria and did not serve him. ⁸He defeated the Philistines as far as Gaza and its borders, from watchtower to fortified city.

⁹In the fourth year of King Hezekiah, which was the seventh year of Israel's King Hoshea son of Elah, Shalmaneser king of Assyria marched against Samaria and besieged it. ¹⁰The Assyrians captured it at the end of three years. In the sixth year of Hezekiah, which was the ninth year of Israel's King Hoshea, Samaria was captured. ¹¹The king of Assyria deported the Israelites to Assyria and put them in Halah and by the Habor, Gozan's river, and in the cities of the Medes, ¹²because they did not listen to the voice of the Lord their God but violated His covenant—all He had commanded Moses the servant of the Lord. They did not listen, and they did not obey.

¹³In the fourteenth year of King Hezekiah, Sennacherib king of Assyria attacked all the fortified cities of Judah and captured them. ¹⁴So Hezekiah king of Judah sent word to the king of Assyria at Lachish, saying, "I have done wrong; withdraw from me. Whatever you demand from me, I will pay." The king of Assyria demanded 11 tons of silver and one ton of gold from King Hezekiah of Judah. ¹⁵So Hezekiah gave him all the silver found in the Lord's temple and in the treasuries of the king's palace.

¹⁶At that time Hezekiah stripped the gold from the doors of the Lord's sanctuary and from the doorposts he had overlaid and gave it to the king of Assyria.

¹⁷Then the king of Assyria sent the Tartan, the Rabsaris, and the *Rabshakeh, along with a massive army, from Lachish to King Hezekiah at Jerusalem. They advanced and came to Jerusalem, and they took their position by the aqueduct of the upper pool, which is by the highway to the Fuller's Field. ¹⁸Then they called for the king, but Eliakim son of Hilkiah, who was in charge of the palace, Shebnah the court secretary, and Joah son of Asaph, the court historian, came out to them.

¹⁹Then the Rabshakeh said to them, "Tell Hezekiah this is what the great king, the king of Assyria, says: 'What are you relying on? ²⁰You think mere words are strategy and strength for war. What are you now relying on so that you have rebelled against me? ²¹Look, you are now trusting in Egypt, that splintered reed of a staff that will enter and pierce the hand of anyone who leans on it. This is how Pharaoh king of Egypt is to all who trust in him. ²²Suppose you say to me: We trust in the Lord our God. Isn't He the One whose high places and altars Hezekiah has removed, saying to Judah and to Jerusalem: You must worship at this altar in Jerusalem?'

²³"So now make a bargain with my master the king of Assyria. I'll give you 2,000 horses if you're able to supply riders for them! ²⁴How then can you drive back a single officer among the least of my master's servants and trust in Egypt for chariots and for horsemen? ²⁵Have I attacked this place to destroy it without the Lord's approval? The Lord said to me, 'Attack this land and destroy it.'"

²⁶Then Eliakim son of Hilkiah, Shebnah, and Joah said to the Rabshakeh, "Please speak to your servants in Aramaic, since we understand it. Don't speak with us in Hebrew within earshot of the people on the wall."

²⁷But the Rabshakeh said to them, "Has my master sent me only to your master and to you to speak these words? Hasn't he also sent me to the men who sit on the wall, destined with you to eat their own excrement and drink their own urine?"

²⁸The Rabshakeh stood and called out loudly in Hebrew. Then he spoke: "Hear the word of the great king, the king of Assyria. ²⁹This is what the king says: 'Don't let Hezekiah deceive you; he can't deliver you from my hand. ³⁰Don't let Hezekiah persuade you to trust in the Lord by saying: Certainly the Lord will deliver us! This city will not be handed over to the king of Assyria.'

³¹"Don't listen to Hezekiah, for this is what the king of Assyria says: 'Make peace with me and surrender to me. Then every one of you may eat from his own vine and his own fig tree, and every one may drink water from his own cistern ³²until I come and take you away to a land like your own land—a land of grain and new wine, a land of bread and vineyards, a land of olive

trees and honey—so that you may live and not die. But don't listen to Hezekiah when he misleads you, saying: The LORD will deliver us. ³³Has any of the gods of the nations ever delivered his land from the power of the king of Assyria? ³⁴Where are the gods of Hamath and Arpad? Where are the gods of Sepharvaim, Hena, and Ivvah? Have they delivered Samaria from my hand? ³⁵Who among all the gods of the lands has delivered his land from my power? So will the LORD deliver Jerusalem?'"

³⁶But the people kept silent; they didn't say anything, for the king's command was, "Don't answer him." ³⁷Then Eliakim son of Hilkiah, who was in charge of the palace, Shebna the court secretary, and Joah son of Asaph, the court historian, came to Hezekiah with their clothes torn and reported to him the words of the Rabshakeh.

19 When King Hezekiah heard their report, he tore his clothes, covered himself with *sackcloth, and went into the LORD's temple. ²Then he sent Eliakim, who was in charge of the palace, Shebna the court secretary, and the leading priests, who were wearing sackcloth, to the prophet Isaiah son of Amoz. ³They said to him, "This is what Hezekiah says: 'Today is a day of distress, rebuke, and disgrace, for children have come to the point of birth, but there is no strength to deliver them. ⁴Perhaps *Yahweh your God will hear all the words of the *Rabshakeh, whom his master the king of Assyria sent to mock the living God, and will rebuke him for the words that Yahweh your God has heard. Therefore, offer a prayer for the surviving remnant.'"

⁵So the servants of King Hezekiah went to Isaiah, ⁶who said to them, "Tell your master this, 'The LORD says: Don't be afraid because of the words you have heard, that the king of Assyria's attendants have blasphemed Me with. ⁷I am about to put a spirit in him, and he will hear a rumor and return to his own land where I will cause him to fall by the sword.'"

⁸When the Rabshakeh heard that the king of Assyria had left Lachish, he returned and found him fighting against Libnah. ⁹The king had heard this about Tirhakah king of *Cush: "Look, he has set out to fight against you." So he again sent messengers to Hezekiah, saying, ¹⁰"Say this to Hezekiah king of Judah: 'Don't let your God, whom you trust, deceive you by promising that Jerusalem will not be handed over to the king of Assyria. ¹¹Look, you have heard what the kings of Assyria have done to all the countries: they *completely destroyed them. Will you be rescued? ¹²Did the gods of the nations that my predecessors destroyed rescue them—nations such as Gozan, Haran, Rezeph, and the Edenites in Telassar? ¹³Where is the king of Hamath, the king of Arpad, the king of the city of Sepharvaim, Hena, or Ivvah?'"

¹⁴Hezekiah took the letter from the hand of the messengers, read it, then went up to the LORD's temple, and spread it out before the LORD. ¹⁵Then Hezekiah prayed before the LORD:

LORD God of Israel who is enthroned above the *cherubim, You are God—You alone—of all the kingdoms of the earth. You made the heavens and the earth. ¹⁶Listen closely, LORD, and hear; open Your eyes, LORD, and see. Hear the words that Sennacherib has sent to mock the living God. ¹⁷LORD, it is true that the kings of Assyria have devastated the nations and their lands. ¹⁸They have thrown their gods into the fire, for

they were not gods but made by human hands—wood and stone. So they have destroyed them. ¹⁹Now, LORD our God, please save us from his hand so that all the kingdoms of the earth may know that You are the LORD God—You alone.

²⁰Then Isaiah son of Amoz sent a message to Hezekiah: "The LORD, the God of Israel says: 'I have heard your prayer to Me about Sennacherib king of Assyria.' ²¹This is the word the LORD has spoken against him:

Virgin Daughter *Zion
despises you and scorns you:
Daughter Jerusalem
shakes her head behind your back.
²² Who is it you mocked and blasphemed?
Against whom have you raised your voice
and lifted your eyes in pride?
Against the Holy One of Israel!
²³ You have mocked the Lord through
your messengers.
You have said:
With my many chariots
I have gone up to the heights
of the mountains,
to the far recesses of Lebanon.
I cut down its tallest cedars,
its choice cypress trees.
I came to its farthest outpost,
its densest forest.
²⁴ I dug wells,
and I drank foreign waters.
I dried up all the streams of Egypt
with the soles of my feet.
²⁵ Have you not heard?
I designed it long ago;
I planned it in days gone by.
I have now brought it to pass,
and you have crushed fortified cities
into piles of rubble.
²⁶ Their inhabitants have become powerless,
dismayed, and ashamed.
They are plants of the field,
tender grass,
grass on the rooftops,
blasted by the east wind.
²⁷ But I know your sitting down,
your going out and your coming in,
and your raging against Me.
²⁸ Because your raging against Me
and your arrogance have reached My ears,
I will put My hook in your nose
and My bit in your mouth;
I will make you go back
the way you came.

²⁹"This will be the sign for you: This year you will eat what grows on its own, and in the second year what grows from that. But in the third year sow and reap, plant vineyards and eat their fruit. ³⁰The surviving remnant of the house of Israel will again take root downward and bear fruit upward. ³¹For a remnant will go out from Jerusalem and survivors, from Mount Zion. The zeal of the LORD of *Hosts will accomplish this.

³² Therefore, this is what the LORD says
about the king of Assyria:
He will not enter this city
or shoot an arrow there
or come before it with a shield

or build up an assault ramp against it.
³³ He will go back
    on the road that he came
and he will not enter this city.
        This is the LORD's declaration.
³⁴ I will defend this city and rescue it
    for My sake and for the sake of My
        servant David."

³⁵ That night the angel of the LORD went out and struck down 185,000 in the camp of the Assyrians. When the people got up the next morning—there were all the dead bodies! ³⁶ So Sennacherib king of Assyria broke camp and left. He returned home and lived in Nineveh.

³⁷ One day, while he was worshiping in the temple of his god Nisroch, his sons Adrammelech and Sharezer struck him down with the sword and escaped to the land of Ararat. Then his son Esar-haddon became king in his place.

20 In those days Hezekiah became terminally ill. The prophet Isaiah son of Amoz came and said to him, "This is what the LORD says: 'Put your affairs in order, for you are about to die; you will not recover.'"

² Then Hezekiah turned his face to the wall and prayed to the LORD, ³ "Please LORD, remember how I have walked before You faithfully and wholeheartedly and have done what pleases You." And Hezekiah wept bitterly.

⁴ Isaiah had not yet gone out of the inner courtyard when the word of the LORD came to him: ⁵ "Go back and tell Hezekiah, the leader of My people, 'This is what the LORD God of your ancestor David says: I have heard your prayer; I have seen your tears. Look, I will heal you. On the third day from now you will go up to the LORD's temple. ⁶ I will add 15 years to your life. I will deliver you and this city from the hand of the king of Assyria. I will defend this city for My sake and for the sake of My servant David.'"

⁷ Then Isaiah said, "Bring a lump of pressed figs." So they brought it and applied it to his infected skin, and he recovered.

⁸ Hezekiah had asked Isaiah, "What is the sign that the LORD will heal me and that I will go up to the LORD's temple on the third day?"

⁹ Isaiah said, "This is the sign to you from the LORD that He will do what He has promised: Should the shadow go ahead 10 steps or go back 10 steps?"

¹⁰ Then Hezekiah answered, "It's easy for the shadow to lengthen 10 steps. No, let the shadow go back 10 steps." ¹¹ So Isaiah the prophet called out to the LORD, and He brought the shadow back the 10 steps it had descended on Ahaz's stairway.

¹² At that time Merodach-baladan son of Baladan, king of Babylon, sent letters and a gift to Hezekiah since he heard that he had been sick. ¹³ Hezekiah gave them a hearing and showed them his whole treasure house—the silver, the gold, the spices, and the precious oil—and his armory, and everything that was found in his treasuries. There was nothing in his palace and in all his realm that Hezekiah did not show them.

¹⁴ Then the prophet Isaiah came to King Hezekiah and asked him, "Where did these men come from and what did they say to you?"

Hezekiah replied, "They came from a distant country, from Babylon."

¹⁵ Isaiah asked, "What have they seen in your palace?"

Hezekiah answered, "They have seen everything in my palace. There isn't anything in my treasuries that I didn't show them."

¹⁶ Then Isaiah said to Hezekiah, "Hear the word of the LORD: ¹⁷ 'The time will certainly come when everything in your palace and all that your fathers have stored up until this day will be carried off to Babylon; nothing will be left,' says the LORD. ¹⁸ 'Some of your descendants who come from you will be taken away, and they will become eunuchs in the palace of the king of Babylon.'"

¹⁹ Then Hezekiah said to Isaiah, "The word of the LORD that you have spoken is good," for he thought: Why not, if there will be peace and security during my lifetime?

²⁰ The rest of the events of Hezekiah's reign, along with all his might and how he made the pool and the tunnel and brought water into the city, are written in the Historical Record of Judah's Kings. ²¹ Hezekiah rested with his fathers, and his son Manasseh became king in his place.

21 Manasseh was 12 years old when he became king and reigned 55 years in Jerusalem. His mother's name was Hephzibah. ² He did what was evil in the LORD's sight, imitating the detestable practices of the nations that the LORD had dispossessed before the Israelites. ³ He rebuilt the •high places that his father Hezekiah had destroyed and reestablished the altars for •Baal. He made an •Asherah, as King Ahab of Israel had done; he also worshiped the whole heavenly •host and served them. ⁴ He built altars in the LORD's temple, where the LORD had said, "Jerusalem is where I will put My name." ⁵ He built altars to the whole heavenly host in both courtyards of the LORD's temple. ⁶ He made his son pass through the fire, practiced witchcraft and •divination, and consulted mediums and spiritists. He did a great amount of evil in the LORD's sight, provoking Him.

⁷ Manasseh set up the carved image of Asherah, which he made, in the temple that the LORD had spoken about to David and his son Solomon, "I will establish My name forever in this temple and in Jerusalem, which I have chosen out of all the tribes of Israel. ⁸ I will never again cause the feet of the Israelites to wander from the land I gave to their ancestors if only they will be careful to do all I have commanded them—the whole law that My servant Moses commanded them." ⁹ But they did not listen; Manasseh caused them to stray so that they did greater evil than the nations the LORD had destroyed before the Israelites.

¹⁰ The LORD spoke through His servants the prophets, saying, ¹¹ "Since Manasseh king of Judah has committed all these detestable things—greater evil than the Amorites who preceded him had done—and by means of his idols has also caused Judah to sin, ¹² this is what the LORD God of Israel says: 'I am about to bring such disaster on Jerusalem and Judah that everyone who hears about it will shudder. ¹³ I will stretch over Jerusalem the measuring line used on Samaria and the mason's level used on the house of Ahab, and I will wipe Jerusalem •clean as one wipes a bowl—wiping it and turning it upside down. ¹⁴ I will abandon the remnant of My inheritance and hand them over to their enemies. They will become plunder and spoil to all their enemies, ¹⁵ because they have done what is evil

in My sight and have provoked Me from the day their ancestors came out of Egypt until today.'"

¹⁶Manasseh also shed so much innocent blood that he filled Jerusalem with it from one end to another. This was in addition to his sin that he caused Judah to commit. Consequently, they did what was evil in the Lord's sight.

¹⁷The rest of the events of Manasseh's reign, along with all his accomplishments and the sin that he committed, are written in the Historical Record of Judah's Kings. ¹⁸Manasseh rested with his fathers and was buried in the garden of his own house, the garden of Uzza. His son Amon became king in his place.

¹⁹Amon was 22 years old when he became king and reigned two years in Jerusalem. His mother's name was Meshullemeth daughter of Haruz; she was from Jotbah. ²⁰He did what was evil in the Lord's sight as his father Manasseh had done. ²¹He walked in all the ways his father had walked; he served the idols his father had served, and he worshiped them. ²²He abandoned the Lord God of his ancestors and did not walk in the way of the Lord.

²³Amon's servants conspired against the king and killed him in his own house. ²⁴Then the common people executed all those who had conspired against King Amon and made his son Josiah king in his place.

²⁵The rest of the events of Amon's reign, along with his accomplishments, are written in the Historical Record of Judah's Kings. ²⁶He was buried in his tomb in the garden of Uzza, and his son Josiah became king in his place.

22 Josiah was eight years old when he became king and reigned 31 years in Jerusalem. His mother's name was Jedidah the daughter of Adaiah; she was from Bozkath. ²He did what was right in the Lord's sight and walked in all the ways of his ancestor David; he did not turn to the right or the left.

³In the eighteenth year of King Josiah, the king sent the court secretary Shaphan son of Azaliah, son of Meshullam, to the Lord's temple, saying, ⁴"Go up to Hilkiah the high priest so that he may total up the money brought into the Lord's temple—the money the doorkeepers have collected from the people. ⁵It is to be put into the hands of those doing the work—those who oversee the Lord's temple. They in turn are to give it to the workmen in the Lord's temple to repair the damage. ⁶They are to give it to the carpenters, builders, and masons to buy timber and quarried stone to repair the temple. ⁷But no accounting is to be required from them for the money put into their hands since they work with integrity."

⁸Hilkiah the high priest told Shaphan the court secretary, "I have found the book of the law in the Lord's temple," and he gave the book to Shaphan, who read it.

⁹Then Shaphan the court secretary went to the king and reported, "Your servants have emptied out the money that was found in the temple and have put it into the hand of those doing the work—those who oversee the Lord's temple." ¹⁰Then Shaphan the court secretary told the king, "Hilkiah the priest has given me a book," and Shaphan read it in the presence of the king.

¹¹When the king heard the words of the book of the law, he tore his clothes. ¹²Then he commanded Hilkiah the priest, Ahikam son of Shaphan, Achbor son of Micaiah, Shaphan the court secretary, and the king's servant Asaiah: ¹³"Go and inquire of the Lord for me, the people, and all Judah about the instruction in this book that has been found. For great is the Lord's wrath that is kindled against us because our ancestors have not obeyed the words of this book in order to do everything written about us."

¹⁴So Hilkiah the priest, Ahikam, Achbor, Shaphan, and Asaiah went to the prophetess Huldah, wife of Shallum son of Tikvah, son of Harhas, keeper of the wardrobe. She lived in Jerusalem in the Second District. They spoke with her.

¹⁵She said to them, "This is what the Lord God of Israel says, 'Say to the man who sent you to Me: ¹⁶This is what the Lord says: I am about to bring disaster on this place and on its inhabitants, fulfilling all the words of the book that the king of Judah has read, ¹⁷because they have abandoned Me and burned incense to other gods in order to provoke Me with all the work of their hands. My wrath will be kindled against this place, and it will not be quenched. ¹⁸Say this to the king of Judah who sent you to inquire of the Lord: This is what the Lord God of Israel says: As for the words that you heard, ¹⁹because your heart was tender and you humbled yourself before the Lord when you heard what I spoke against this place and against its inhabitants, that they would become a desolation and a curse, and because you have torn your clothes and wept before Me, I Myself have heard you—this is the Lord's declaration— ²⁰therefore, I will indeed gather you to your fathers, and you will be gathered to your grave in peace. Your eyes will not see all the disaster that I am bringing on this place.'"

Then they reported to the king.

23 So the king sent messengers, and they gathered all the elders of Jerusalem and Judah to him. ²Then the king went to the Lord's temple with all the men of Judah and all the inhabitants of Jerusalem, as well as the priests and the prophets—all the people from the youngest to the oldest. As they listened, he read all the words of the book of the covenant that had been found in the Lord's temple. ³Next, the king stood by the pillar and made a covenant in the presence of the Lord to follow the Lord and to keep His commands, His decrees, and His statutes with all his mind and with all his heart, and to carry out the words of this covenant that were written in this book; all the people agreed to the covenant.

⁴Then the king commanded Hilkiah the high priest and the priests of the second rank and the doorkeepers to bring out of the Lord's temple all the articles made for ˙Baal, ˙Asherah, and the whole heavenly ˙host. He burned them outside Jerusalem in the fields of the Kidron and carried their ashes to Bethel. ⁵Then he did away with the idolatrous priests the kings of Judah had appointed to burn incense at the ˙high places in the cities of Judah and in the areas surrounding Jerusalem. They had burned incense to Baal, and to the sun, moon, constellations, and the whole heavenly host. ⁶He brought out the Asherah pole from the Lord's temple to the Kidron Valley outside Jerusalem. He burned it at the Kidron Valley, beat it to dust, and threw its dust on the graves of the common people. ⁷He also tore down the houses of the male cult prostitutes that were in the Lord's temple, in which the women were weaving tapestries for Asherah.

⁸Then Josiah brought all the priests from the cities of Judah, and he defiled the high places from Geba to

Beer-sheba, where the priests had burned incense. He tore down the high places of the gates at the entrance of the *gate of Joshua the governor of the city (on the left at the city gate). ⁹The priests of the high places, however, did not come up to the altar of the LORD in Jerusalem; instead, they ate unleavened bread with their fellow priests.

¹⁰He defiled *Topheth, which is in the Valley of Hinnom, so that no one could make his son or daughter pass through the fire to *Molech. ¹¹He did away with the horses that the kings of Judah had dedicated to the sun. They had been at the entrance of the LORD's temple in the precincts by the chamber of Nathan-melech the court official, and he burned up the chariots of the sun.

¹²The king tore down the altars that were on the roof—Ahaz's upper chamber that the kings of Judah had made—and the altars that Manasseh had made in the two courtyards of the LORD's temple. Then he smashed them there and threw their dust into the Kidron Valley. ¹³The king also defiled the high places that were across from Jerusalem, to the south of the Mount of Destruction, which King Solomon of Israel had built for *Ashtoreth, the detestable idol of the Sidonians; for Chemosh, the detestable idol of Moab; and for *Milcom, the abomination of the Ammonites. ¹⁴He broke the sacred pillars into pieces, cut down the Asherah poles, then filled their places with human bones.

¹⁵He even tore down the altar at Bethel and the high place that Jeroboam son of Nebat, who caused Israel to sin, had made. Then he burned the high place, crushed it to dust, and burned the Asherah. ¹⁶As Josiah turned, he saw the tombs there on the mountain. He sent someone to take the bones out of the tombs, and he burned them on the altar. He defiled it according to the word of the LORD proclaimed by the man of God who proclaimed these things. ¹⁷Then he said, "What is this monument I see?"

The men of the city told him, "It is the tomb of the man of God who came from Judah and proclaimed these things that you have done to the altar at Bethel."

¹⁸So he said, "Let him rest. Don't let anyone disturb his bones." So they left his bones undisturbed with the bones of the prophet who came from Samaria.

¹⁹Josiah also removed all the shrines of the high places that were in the cities of Samaria, which the kings of Israel had made to provoke the LORD. Josiah did the same things to them that he had done at Bethel. ²⁰He slaughtered on the altars all the priests of the high places who were there, and he burned human bones on the altars. Then he returned to Jerusalem.

²¹The king commanded all the people, "Keep the *Passover of the LORD your God as written in the book of the covenant." ²²No such Passover had ever been kept from the time of the judges who judged Israel through the entire time of the kings of Israel and Judah. ²³But in the eighteenth year of King Josiah, this Passover was observed to the LORD in Jerusalem.

²⁴In addition, Josiah removed the mediums, the spiritists, household idols, images, and all the detestable things that were seen in the land of Judah and in Jerusalem. He did this in order to carry out the words of the law that were written in the book that Hilkiah the priest found in the LORD's temple. ²⁵Before him there was no king like him who turned to the LORD with all his mind and with all his heart and with all his

strength according to all the law of Moses, and no one like him arose after him.

²⁶In spite of all that, the LORD did not turn from the fury of His great burning anger, which burned against Judah because of all that Manasseh had provoked Him with. ²⁷For the LORD had said, "I will also remove Judah from My sight just as I have removed Israel. I will reject this city Jerusalem, that I have chosen, and the temple about which I said, 'My name will be there.'"

²⁸The rest of the events of Josiah's reign, along with all his accomplishments, are written in the Historical Record of Judah's Kings. ²⁹During his reign, Pharaoh Neco king of Egypt marched up to help the king of Assyria at the Euphrates River. King Josiah went to confront him, and at Megiddo when Neco saw him he killed him. ³⁰From Megiddo his servants carried his dead body in a chariot, brought him into Jerusalem, and buried him in his own tomb. Then the common people took Jehoahaz son of Josiah, anointed him, and made him king in place of his father.

³¹Jehoahaz was 23 years old when he became king and reigned three months in Jerusalem. His mother's name was Hamutal daughter of Jeremiah, from Libnah. ³²He did what was evil in the LORD's sight just as his ancestors had done. ³³Pharaoh Neco imprisoned him at Riblah in the land of Hamath to keep him from reigning in Jerusalem, and he imposed on the land a fine of 7,500 pounds of silver and 75 pounds of gold.

³⁴Then Pharaoh Neco made Eliakim son of Josiah king in place of his father Josiah and changed Eliakim's name to Jehoiakim. But Neco took Jehoahaz and went to Egypt, and he died there. ³⁵So Jehoiakim gave the silver and the gold to Pharaoh, but at Pharaoh's command he taxed the land to give the money. He exacted the silver and the gold from the common people, each man according to his assessment, to give it to Pharaoh Neco.

³⁶Jehoiakim was 25 years old when he became king and reigned 11 years in Jerusalem. His mother's name was Zebidah daughter of Pedaiah, from Rumah. ³⁷He did what was evil in the LORD's sight just as his ancestors had done.

24 During Jehoiakim's reign, Nebuchadnezzar king of Babylon attacked. Jehoiakim became his vassal for three years, and then he turned and rebelled against him. ²The LORD sent Chaldean, Aramean, Moabite, and Ammonite raiders against Jehoiakim. He sent them against Judah to destroy it, according to the word of the LORD He had spoken through His servants the prophets. ³Indeed, this happened to Judah at the LORD's command to remove them from His sight. It was because of the sins of Manasseh, according to all he had done, ⁴and also because of all the innocent blood he had shed. He had filled Jerusalem with innocent blood, and the LORD would not forgive.

⁵The rest of the events of Jehoiakim's reign, along with all his accomplishments, are written in the Historical Record of Judah's Kings. ⁶Jehoiakim rested with his fathers, and his son Jehoiachin became king in his place.

⁷Now the king of Egypt did not march out of his land again, for the king of Babylon took everything that belonged to the king of Egypt, from the Brook of Egypt to the Euphrates River.

⁸Jehoiachin was 18 years old when he became king and reigned three months in Jerusalem. His mother's name was Nehushta daughter of Elnathan, from Jeru-

salem. ⁹He did what was evil in the Lord's sight as his father had done.

¹⁰At that time the servants of Nebuchadnezzar king of Babylon marched up to Jerusalem, and the city came under siege. ¹¹Then King Nebuchadnezzar of Babylon came to the city while his servants were besieging it. ¹²Jehoiachin king of Judah, along with his mother, his servants, his commanders, and his officials, surrendered to the king of Babylon.

So the king of Babylon took him captive in the eighth year of his reign. ¹³He also carried off from there all the treasures of the Lord's temple and the treasures of the king's palace, and he cut into pieces all the gold articles that Solomon king of Israel had made for the Lord's sanctuary, just as God had predicted. ¹⁴Then he deported all Jerusalem and all the commanders and all the fighting men, 10,000 captives, and all the craftsmen and metalsmiths. Except for the poorest people of the land, no one remained.

¹⁵Nebuchadnezzar deported Jehoiachin to Babylon. Also, he took the king's mother, the king's wives, his officials, and the leading men of the land into exile from Jerusalem to Babylon. ¹⁶The king of Babylon also brought captive into Babylon all 7,000 fighting men and 1,000 craftsmen and metalsmiths—all strong and fit for war. ¹⁷Then the king of Babylon made Mattaniah, Jehoiachin's uncle, king in his place and changed his name to Zedekiah.

¹⁸Zedekiah was 21 years old when he became king and reigned 11 years in Jerusalem. His mother's name was Hamutal daughter of Jeremiah, from Libnah. ¹⁹Zedekiah did what was evil in the Lord's sight just as Jehoiakim had done. ²⁰Because of the Lord's anger, it came to the point in Jerusalem and Judah that He finally banished them from His presence. Then, Zedekiah rebelled against the king of Babylon.

25 In the ninth year of Zedekiah's reign, on the tenth day of the tenth month, King Nebuchadnezzar of Babylon advanced against Jerusalem with his entire army. They laid siege to the city and built a siege wall against it all around. ²The city was under siege until King Zedekiah's eleventh year.

³By the ninth day of the fourth month the famine was so severe in the city that the people of the land had no food. ⁴Then the city was broken into, and all the warriors fled by night by way of the gate between the two walls near the king's garden, even though the Chaldeans surrounded the city. As the king made his way along the route to the ˙Arabah, ⁵the Chaldean army pursued him and overtook him in the plains of Jericho. Zedekiah's entire army was scattered from him. ⁶The Chaldeans seized the king and brought him up to the king of Babylon at Riblah, and they passed sentence on him. ⁷They slaughtered Zedekiah's sons before his eyes. Finally, the king of Babylon blinded Zedekiah, bound him in bronze chains, and took him to Babylon.

⁸On the seventh day of the fifth month, which was the nineteenth year of Nebuchadnezzar king of Babylon, Nebuzaradan, the commander of the guards, a servant of the king of Babylon, entered Jerusalem. ⁹He burned the Lord's temple, the king's palace, and all the houses of Jerusalem; he burned down all the great houses. ¹⁰The whole Chaldean army with the commander of the guards tore down the walls surrounding Jerusalem. ¹¹Nebuzaradan, the commander of the

guards, deported the rest of the people who were left in the city, the deserters who had defected to the king of Babylon, and the rest of the population. ¹²But the commander of the guards left some of the poorest of the land to be vinedressers and farmers.

¹³Now the Chaldeans broke into pieces the bronze pillars of the Lord's temple, the water carts, and the bronze reservoir, which were in the Lord's temple, and carried the bronze to Babylon. ¹⁴They also took the pots, the shovels, the wick trimmers, the dishes, and all the bronze articles used in temple service. ¹⁵The commander of the guards took away the firepans and the sprinkling basins—whatever was gold or silver.

¹⁶As for the two pillars, the one reservoir, and the water carts that Solomon had made for the Lord's temple, the weight of the bronze of all these articles was beyond measure. ¹⁷One pillar was 27 feet tall and had a bronze capital on top of it. The capital, encircled by a grating and pomegranates of bronze, stood five feet high. The second pillar was the same, with its own grating.

¹⁸The commander of the guards also took away Seraiah the chief priest, Zephaniah the priest of the second rank, and the three doorkeepers. ¹⁹He took a court official who had been appointed over the warriors from the city; five trusted royal aides found in the city; the secretary of the commander of the army, who enlisted the people of the land for military duty; and 60 men from the common people who were found within the city. ²⁰Nebuzaradan, the commander of the guards, took them and brought them to the king of Babylon at Riblah. ²¹The king of Babylon put them to death at Riblah in the land of Hamath. So Judah went into exile from its land.

²²Nebuchadnezzar king of Babylon appointed Gedaliah son of Ahikam, son of Shaphan, over the rest of the people he left in the land of Judah. ²³When all the commanders of the armies—they and their men— heard that the king of Babylon had appointed Gedaliah, they came to Gedaliah at Mizpah. The commanders included Ishmael son of Nethaniah, Johanan son of Kareah, Seraiah son of Tanhumeth the Netophathite, and Jaazaniah son of the Maacathite—they and their men. ²⁴Gedaliah swore an oath to them and their men, assuring them, "Don't be afraid of the servants of the Chaldeans. Live in the land and serve the king of Babylon, and it will go well for you."

²⁵In the seventh month, however, Ishmael son of Nethaniah, son of Elishama, of the royal family, came with 10 men and struck down Gedaliah, and he died. Also, they killed the Judeans and the Chaldeans who were with him at Mizpah. ²⁶Then all the people, from the youngest to the oldest, and the commanders of the army, left and went to Egypt, for they were afraid of the Chaldeans.

²⁷On the twenty-seventh day of the twelfth month of the thirty-seventh year of the exile of Judah's King Jehoiachin, in the year Evil-merodach became king of Babylon, he pardoned King Jehoiachin of Judah and released him from prison. ²⁸He spoke kindly to him and set his throne over the thrones of the kings who were with him in Babylon. ²⁹So Jehoiachin changed his prison clothes, and he dined regularly in the presence of the king of Babylon for the rest of his life. ³⁰As for his allowance, a regular allowance was given to him by the king, a portion for each day, for the rest of his life.

1 CHRONICLES

1 Adam, Seth, Enosh,
2 Kenan, Mahalalel, Jared,
3 Enoch, Methuselah, Lamech,
4 Noah, Noah's sons:
Shem, Ham, and Japheth.
5 Japheth's sons: Gomer, Magog, Madai, Javan, Tubal, Meshech, and Tiras.
6 Gomer's sons: Ashkenaz, Riphath, and Togarmah.
7 Javan's sons: Elishah, Tarshish, Kittim, and Rodanim.
8 Ham's sons: Cush, Mizraim, Put, and Canaan.
9 Cush's sons: Seba, Havilah, Sabta, Raama, and Sabteca.
Raama's sons: Sheba and Dedan.
10 Cush fathered Nimrod, who was the first to become a great warrior on earth.
11 Mizraim fathered Ludim, Anamim, Lehabim, Naphtuhim, 12 Pathrusim, Casluhim (the Philistines came from them), and Caphtorim.
13 Canaan fathered Sidon as his firstborn, then Heth, 14 the Jebusites, Amorites, Girgashites, 15 Hivites, Arkites, Sinites, 16 Arvadites, Zemarites, and Hamathites.
17 Shem's sons: Elam, Asshur, Arpachshad, Lud, Aram, Uz, Hul, Gether, and Meshech.
18 Arpachshad fathered Shelah, and Shelah fathered Eber. 19 Two sons were born to Eber. One of them was named Peleg because the earth was divided during his lifetime, and the name of his brother was Joktan. 20 Joktan fathered Almodad, Sheleph, Hazarmaveth, Jerah, 21 Hadoram, Uzal, Diklah, 22 Ebal, Abimael, Sheba, 23 Ophir, Havilah, and Jobab. All of these were Joktan's sons.
24 Shem, Arpachshad, Shelah,
25 Eber, Peleg, Reu,
26 Serug, Nahor, Terah,
27 and Abram (that is, Abraham).
28 Abraham's sons: Isaac and Ishmael.
29 These are their family records: Nebaioth, Ishmael's firstborn, Kedar, Adbeel, Mibsam, 30 Mishma, Dumah, Massa, Hadad, Tema, 31 Jetur, Naphish, and Kedemah. These were Ishmael's sons.
32 The sons born to Keturah, Abraham's concubine: Zimran, Jokshan, Medan, Midian, Ishbak, and Shuah.
Jokshan's sons: Sheba and Dedan.
33 Midian's sons: Ephah, Epher, Hanoch, Abida, and Eldaah.
All of these were Keturah's sons.
34 Abraham fathered Isaac.
Isaac's sons: Esau and Israel.
35 Esau's sons: Eliphaz, Reuel, Jeush, Jalam, and Korah.
36 Eliphaz's sons: Teman, Omar, Zephi, Gatam, and Kenaz; and by Timna, Amalek.
37 Reuel's sons: Nahath, Zerah, Shammah, and Mizzah.
38 Seir's sons: Lotan, Shobal, Zibeon, Anah, Dishon, Ezer, and Dishan.
39 Lotan's sons: Hori and Homam. Timna was Lotan's sister.
40 Shobal's sons: Alian, Manahath, Ebal, Shephi, and Onam.
Zibeon's sons: Aiah and Anah.
41 Anah's son: Dishon.
Dishon's sons: Hamran, Eshban, Ithran, and Cheran.
42 Ezer's sons: Bilhan, Zaavan, and Jaakan.
Dishan's sons: Uz and Aran.
43 These were the kings who ruled in the land of Edom before any king ruled over the Israelites: Bela son of Beor. Bela's town was named Dinhabah. 44 When Bela died, Jobab son of Zerah from Bozrah ruled in his place. 45 When Jobab died, Husham from the land of the Temanites ruled in his place. 46 When Husham died, Hadad son of Bedad, who defeated Midian in the country of Moab, ruled in his place. Hadad's town was named Avith. 47 When Hadad died, Samlah from Masrekah ruled in his place. 48 When Samlah died, Shaul from Rehoboth on the Euphrates River ruled in his place. 49 When Shaul died, Baal-hanan son of Achbor ruled in his place. 50 When Baal-hanan died, Hadad ruled in his place. Hadad's city was named Pai, and his wife's name was Mehetabel daughter of Matred, daughter of Me-zahab. 51 Then Hadad died.
Edom's chiefs: Timna, Alvah, Jetheth,
52 Oholibamah, Elah, Pinon, 53 Kenaz, Teman, Mibzar, 54 Magdiel, and Iram.
These were Edom's chiefs.

2 These were Israel's sons:
Reuben, Simeon, Levi,
Judah, Issachar, Zebulun,
2 Dan, Joseph, Benjamin,
Naphtali, Gad, and Asher.
3 Judah's sons: Er, Onan, and Shelah. These three were born to him by Bath-shua the Canaanite woman. Er, Judah's firstborn, was evil in the LORD's sight, so He put him to death.
4 Judah's daughter-in-law Tamar bore Perez and Zerah to him. Judah had five sons in all.
5 Perez's sons: Hezron and Hamul.
6 Zerah's sons: Zimri, Ethan, Heman, Calcol, and Dara—five in all.
7 Carmi's son: Achar, who brought trouble on Israel when he was unfaithful by taking the things *set apart for destruction.
8 Ethan's son: Azariah.
9 Hezron's sons, who were born to him:
Jerahmeel, Ram, and Chelubai.
10 Ram fathered Amminadab, and Amminadab fathered Nahshon, a leader of Judah's descendants.
11 Nahshon fathered Salma, and Salma fathered Boaz.
12 Boaz fathered Obed, and Obed fathered Jesse.
13 Jesse fathered Eliab, his firstborn; Abinadab was born second, Shimea third, 14 Nethanel fourth, Raddai fifth, 15 Ozem sixth, and David seventh. 16 Their sisters were Zeruiah and Abigail. Zeruiah's three sons: Abishai, Joab,

and Asahel. [17]Amasa's mother was Abigail, and his father was Jether the Ishmaelite.

[18]Caleb son of Hezron had children by his wife Azubah and by Jerioth. These were Azubah's sons: Jesher, Shobab, and Ardon. [19]When Azubah died, Caleb married Ephrath, and she bore Hur to him. [20]Hur fathered Uri, and Uri fathered Bezalel. [21]After this, Hezron slept with the daughter of Machir the father of Gilead. Hezron had married her when he was 60 years old, and she bore Segub to him. [22]Segub fathered Jair, who possessed 23 towns in the land of Gilead. [23]But Geshur and Aram captured Jair's Villages along with Kenath and its villages—60 towns. All these were the sons of Machir father of Gilead. [24]After Hezron's death in Caleb-ephrathah, his wife Abijah bore Ashhur to him. He was the father of Tekoa.

[25]The sons of Jerahmeel, Hezron's firstborn: Ram, his firstborn, Bunah, Oren, Ozem, and Ahijah. [26]Jerahmeel had another wife named Atarah, who was the mother of Onam. [27]The sons of Ram, Jerahmeel's firstborn: Maaz, Jamin, and Eker.

[28]Onam's sons: Shammai and Jada. Shammai's sons: Nadab and Abishur. [29]Abishur's wife was named Abihail, who bore Ahban and Molid to him.

[30]Nadab's sons: Seled and Appaim. Seled died without children. [31]Appaim's son: Ishi. Ishi's son: Sheshan. Sheshan's descendant: Ahlai.

[32]The sons of Jada, brother of Shammai: Jether and Jonathan. Jether died without children. [33]Jonathan's sons: Peleth and Zaza. These were the descendants of Jerahmeel.

[34]Sheshan had no sons, only daughters, but he did have an Egyptian servant whose name was Jarha. [35]Sheshan gave his daughter in marriage to his servant Jarha, and she bore Attai to him.

[36]Attai fathered Nathan, and Nathan fathered Zabad. [37]Zabad fathered Ephlal, and Ephlal fathered Obed. [38]Obed fathered Jehu, and Jehu fathered Azariah. [39]Azariah fathered Helez, and Helez fathered Elasah. [40]Elasah fathered Sismai, and Sismai fathered Shallum. [41]Shallum fathered Jekamiah, and Jekamiah fathered Elishama.

[42]The sons of Caleb brother of Jerahmeel: Mesha, his firstborn, fathered Ziph, and Mareshah, his second son, fathered Hebron. [43]Hebron's sons: Korah, Tappuah, Rekem, and Shema. [44]Shema fathered Raham, who fathered Jorkeam, and Rekem fathered Shammai. [45]Shammai's son was Maon, and Maon fathered Beth-zur. [46]Caleb's concubine Ephah was the mother of Haran, Moza, and Gazez. Haran fathered Gazez.

[47]Jahdai's sons: Regem, Jotham, Geshan, Pelet, Ephah, and Shaaph.

[48]Caleb's concubine Maacah was the mother of Sheber and Tirhanah. [49]She was also the mother of Shaaph, Madmannah's father, and of Sheva, the father of Machbenah and Gibea. Caleb's daughter was Achsah.

[50]These were Caleb's descendants. The sons of Hur, Ephrathah's firstborn: Shobal fathered Kiriath-jearim; [51]Salma fathered Bethlehem, and Hareph fathered Beth-gader.

[52]These were the descendants of Shobal the father of Kiriath-jearim: Haroeh, half of the Manahathites, [53]and the families of Kiriath-jearim—the Ithrites, Puthites, Shumathites, and Mishraites. The Zorathites and Eshtaolites descended from these.

[54]Salma's sons: Bethlehem, the Netophathites, Atroth-beth-joab, and half of the Manahathites, the Zorites, [55]and the families of scribes who lived in Jabez—the Tirathites, Shimeathites, and Sucathites. These are the Kenites who came from Hammath, the father of Rechab's family.

3 These were David's sons who were born to him in Hebron:

Amnon was the firstborn, by Ahinoam of Jezreel;
Daniel was born second, by Abigail of Carmel;
[2]Absalom son of Maacah, daughter of King Talmai of Geshur, was third;
Adonijah son of Haggith was fourth;
[3]Shephatiah, by Abital, was fifth;
and Ithream, by David's wife Eglah, was sixth. [4]Six sons were born to David in Hebron, where he ruled seven years and six months, and he ruled in Jerusalem 33 years. [5]These sons were born to him in Jerusalem: Shimea, Shobab, Nathan, and Solomon. These four were born to him by Bath-shua daughter of Ammiel. [6]David's other sons: Ibhar, Elishua, Eliphelet, [7]Nogah, Nepheg, Japhia, [8]Elishama, Eliada, and Eliphelet—nine sons. [9]These were all David's sons, with their sister Tamar, in addition to the sons by his concubines.

[10] Solomon's son was Rehoboam;
his son was Abijah, his son Asa,
his son Jehoshaphat, [11]his son Jehoram,
his son Ahaziah, his son Joash,
[12] his son Amaziah, his son Azariah,
his son Jotham, [13]his son Ahaz,
his son Hezekiah, his son Manasseh,
[14] his son Amon, and his son Josiah.
[15] Josiah's sons:
Johanan was the firstborn, Jehoiakim second, Zedekiah third, and Shallum fourth.
[16] Jehoiakim's sons:
his sons Jeconiah and Zedekiah.
[17]The sons of Jeconiah the captive: his sons Shealtiel, [18]Malchiram, Pedaiah, Shenazzar, Jekamiah, Hoshama, and Nedabiah.
[19]Pedaiah's sons: Zerubbabel and Shimei.

Zerubbabel's sons: Meshullam and Hananiah, with their sister Shelomith; [20]and five others—Hashubah, Ohel, Berechiah, Hasadiah, and Jushab-hesed.
[21]Hananiah's descendants: Pelatiah, Jeshaiah, and the sons of Rephaiah, Arnan, Obadiah, and Shecaniah.
[22]The son of Shecaniah: Shemaiah. Shemaiah's sons: Hattush, Igal, Bariah, Neariah, and Shaphat—six.
[23]Neariah's sons: Elioenai, Hizkiah, and Azrikam—three.
[24]Elioenai's sons: Hodaviah, Eliashib, Pelaiah, Akkub, Johanan, Delaiah, and Anani—seven.

4 Judah's sons: Perez, Hezron, Carmi, Hur, and Shobal.
[2]Reaiah son of Shobal fathered Jahath, and Jahath fathered Ahumai and Lahad. These were the families of the Zorathites.
[3]These were Etam's sons: Jezreel, Ishma, and Idbash, and their sister was named Hazzelelponi.
[4]Penuel fathered Gedor, and Ezer fathered Hushah. These were the sons of Hur, Ephrathah's firstborn and the father of Bethlehem:
[5]Ashhur fathered Tekoa and had two wives, Helah and Naarah.
[6]Naarah bore Ahuzzam, Hepher, Temeni, and Haahashtari to him. These were Naarah's sons.
[7]Helah's sons: Zereth, Zohar, and Ethnan.
[8] Koz fathered Anub, Zobebah, and the families of Aharhel son of Harum.
[9]Jabez was more honorable than his brothers. His mother named him Jabez and said, "I gave birth to him in pain."
[10] Jabez called out to the God of Israel: "If only You would bless me, extend my border, let Your hand be with me, and keep me from harm, so that I will not cause any pain." And God granted his request.
[11]Chelub brother of Shuhah fathered Mehir, who was the father of Eshton. [12]Eshton fathered Beth-rapha, Paseah, and Tehinnah the father of Irnahash. These were the men of Recah.
[13]Kenaz's sons: Othniel and Seraiah. Othniel's sons: Hathath and Meonothai.
[14]Meonothai fathered Ophrah, and Seraiah fathered Joab, the ancestor of those in the Valley of Craftsmen, for they were craftsmen.
[15]The sons of Caleb son of Jephunneh: Iru, Elah, and Naam. Elah's son: Kenaz.
[16]Jehallelel's sons: Ziph, Ziphah, Tiria, and Asarel.
[17]Ezrah's sons: Jether, Mered, Epher, and Jalon. Mered's wife Bithiah gave birth to Miriam, Shammai, and Ishbah the father of Eshtemoa. [18]These were the sons of Pharaoh's daughter Bithiah; Mered had married her. His Judean wife gave birth to Jered the father of Gedor, Heber the father of Soco, and Jekuthiel the father of Zanoah. [19]The sons of Hodiah's wife, the sister of Naham: the father of Keilah

the Garmite and the father of Eshtemoa the Maacathite.
[20]Shimon's sons: Amnon, Rinnah, Ben-hanan, and Tilon. Ishi's sons: Zoheth and Ben-zoheth.
[21]The sons of Shelah son of Judah: Er the father of Lecah, Laadah the father of Mareshah, the families of the guild of linen workers at Beth-ashbea, [22]Jokim, the men of Cozeba; and Joash and Saraph, who married Moabites and returned to Lehem. These names are from ancient records. [23]They were the potters and residents of Netaim and Gederah. They lived there in the service of the king.
[24]Simeon's sons: Nemuel, Jamin, Jarib, Zerah, and Shaul;
[25]Shaul's sons: his son Shallum, his son Mibsam, and his son Mishma.
[26]Mishma's sons: his son Hammuel, his son Zaccur, and his son Shimei.
[27]Shimei had 16 sons and six daughters, but his brothers did not have many children, so their whole family did not become as numerous as the Judeans. [28]They lived in Beer-sheba, Moladah, Hazar-shual, [29]Bilhah, Ezem, Tolad, [30]Bethuel, Hormah, Ziklag, [31]Beth-marcaboth, Hazar-susim, Beth-biri, and Shaaraim. These were their cities until David became king. [32]Their villages were Etam, Ain, Rimmon, Tochen, and Ashan—five cities, [33]and all their surrounding villages as far as Baal. These were their settlements, and they kept a genealogical record for themselves.
[34]Meshobab, Jamlech, Joshah son of Amaziah, [35]Joel, Jehu son of Joshibiah, son of Seraiah, son of Asiel, [36]Elioenai, Jaakobah, Jeshohaiah, Asaiah, Adiel, Jesimiel, Benaiah, [37]and Ziza son of Shiphi, son of Allon, son of Jedaiah, son of Shimri, son of Shemaiah— [38]these mentioned by name were leaders in their families. Their ancestral houses increased greatly. [39]They went to the entrance of Gedor, to the east side of the valley to seek pasture for their flocks. [40]They found rich, good pasture, and the land was broad, peaceful, and quiet, for some Hamites had lived there previously.
[41]These who were recorded by name came in the days of King Hezekiah of Judah, attacked the Hamites' tents and the Meunites who were found there, and set them apart for destruction, as they are today. Then they settled in their place because there was pasture for their flocks. [42]Now 500 men from these sons of Simeon went with Pelatiah, Neariah, Rephaiah, and Uzziel, the sons of Ishi, as their leaders to Mount Seir. [43]They struck down the remnant of the Amalekites who had escaped, and they still live there today.

5 These were the sons of Reuben the firstborn of Israel. He was the firstborn, but his birthright was given to the sons of Joseph son of Israel, because Reuben defiled his father's bed. He is not listed in the genealogy according to birthright. [2]Although Judah became strong among his brothers and a ruler came from him, the birthright was given to Joseph.
[3]   The sons of Reuben, Israel's firstborn: Hanoch, Pallu, Hezron, and Carmi.

⁴ Joel's sons: his son Shemaiah,
his son Gog, his son Shimei,
⁵ his son Micah, his son Reaiah,
his son Baal, ⁶and his son Beerah.

Beerah was a leader of the Reubenites, and Tiglath-pileser king of Assyria took him into exile. ⁷His relatives by their families as they are recorded in their genealogy:

Jeiel the chief, Zechariah,
⁸and Bela son of Azaz,
son of Shema, son of Joel.

They settled in Aroer as far as Nebo and Baal-meon. ⁹They also settled in the east as far as the edge of the desert that extends to the Euphrates River, because their herds had increased in the land of Gilead. ¹⁰During Saul's reign they waged war against the Hagrites, who were defeated by their power. And they lived in their tents throughout the region east of Gilead.

¹¹The sons of Gad lived next to them in the land of Bashan as far as Salecah:

¹²Joel the chief, Shapham the second in command, Janai, and Shaphat in Bashan.
¹³Their relatives according to their ancestral houses: Michael, Meshullam, Sheba, Jorai, Jacan, Zia, and Eber—seven.
¹⁴These were the sons of Abihail son of Huri,
son of Jaroah, son of Gilead,
son of Michael, son of Jeshishai,
son of Jahdo, son of Buz.
¹⁵Ahi son of Abdiel, son of Guni, was head of their ancestral houses. ¹⁶They lived in Gilead, in Bashan and its towns, and throughout the pasturelands of Sharon. ¹⁷All of them were registered in the genealogies during the reigns of Judah's King Jotham and Israel's King Jeroboam.

¹⁸The sons of Reuben and Gad and half the tribe of Manasseh had 44,760 warriors who could serve in the army—men who carried shield and sword, drew the bow, and were trained for war. ¹⁹They waged war against the Hagrites, Jetur, Naphish, and Nodab. ²⁰They received help against these enemies because they cried out to God in battle, and the Hagrites and all their allies were handed over to them. He granted their request because they trusted in Him. ²¹They captured the Hagrites' livestock—50,000 of their camels, 250,000 sheep, and 2,000 donkeys—as well as 100,000 people. ²²Many of the Hagrites were killed because it was God's battle. And they lived there in the Hagrites' place until the exile.

²³The sons of half the tribe of Manasseh settled in the land from Bashan to Baal-hermon (that is, Senir or Mount Hermon); they were numerous. ²⁴These were the heads of their ancestral houses: Epher, Ishi, Eliel, Azriel, Jeremiah, Hodaviah, and Jahdiel. They were brave warriors, famous men, and heads of their ancestral houses. ²⁵But they were unfaithful to the God of their ancestors. They prostituted themselves with the gods of the nations God had destroyed before them. ²⁶So the God of Israel put it into the mind of Pul (that is, Tiglath-pileser) king of Assyria to take the Reubenites, Gadites, and half the tribe of Manasseh into exile. He took them to Halah, Habor, Hara, and Gozan's river, where they are until today.

6 ² Levi's sons: Gershom, Kohath, and Merari.
Kohath's sons: Amram, Izhar, Hebron, and Uzziel.
³ Amram's children: Aaron, Moses, and Miriam.
Aaron's sons: Nadab, Abihu, Eleazar, and Ithamar.
⁴ Eleazar fathered Phinehas;
Phinehas fathered Abishua;
⁵ Abishua fathered Bukki;
Bukki fathered Uzzi;
⁶ Uzzi fathered Zerahiah;
Zerahiah fathered Meraioth;
⁷ Meraioth fathered Amariah;
Amariah fathered Ahitub;
⁸ Ahitub fathered Zadok;
Zadok fathered Ahimaaz;
⁹ Ahimaaz fathered Azariah;
Azariah fathered Johanan;
¹⁰ Johanan fathered Azariah, who served as priest in the temple that Solomon built in Jerusalem;
¹¹ Azariah fathered Amariah;
Amariah fathered Ahitub;
¹² Ahitub fathered Zadok;
Zadok fathered Shallum;
¹³ Shallum fathered Hilkiah;
Hilkiah fathered Azariah;
¹⁴ Azariah fathered Seraiah;
and Seraiah fathered Jehozadak.
¹⁵ Jehozadak went into exile when the LORD sent Judah and Jerusalem into exile at the hands of Nebuchadnezzar.
¹⁶ Levi's sons: Gershom, Kohath, and Merari.
¹⁷ These are the names of Gershom's sons: Libni and Shimei.
¹⁸ Kohath's sons: Amram, Izhar, Hebron and Uzziel.
¹⁹ Merari's sons: Mahli and Mushi.
These are the Levites' families according to their fathers:
²⁰ Of Gershom: his son Libni,
his son Jahath, his son Zimmah,
²¹ his son Joah, his son Iddo,
his son Zerah, and his son Jeatherai.
²² Kohath's sons: his son Amminadab,
his son Korah, his son Assir,
²³ his son Elkanah, his son Ebiasaph,
his son Assir, ²⁴his son Tahath,
his son Uriel, his son Uzziah,
and his son Shaul.
²⁵ Elkanah's sons: Amasai and Ahimoth,
²⁶ his son Elkanah, his son Zophai,
his son Nahath, ²⁷his son Eliab,
his son Jeroham, and his son Elkanah.
²⁸ Samuel's sons: his firstborn Joel,
and his second son Abijah.
²⁹ Merari's sons: Mahli, his son Libni,
his son Shimei, his son Uzzah,
³⁰ his son Shimea, his son Haggiah,
and his son Asaiah.

³¹These are the men David put in charge of the music in the LORD's temple after the ark came to rest there. ³²They ministered with song in front of the tabernacle, the tent of meeting, until Solomon built the LORD's temple in Jerusalem, and they performed their task according to the regulations given to them. ³³These are the men who served with their sons.

From the Kohathites: Heman the singer,
son of Joel, son of Samuel,
34 son of Elkanah, son of Jeroham,
son of Eliel, son of Toah,
35 son of Zuph, son of Elkanah,
son of Mahath, son of Amasai,
36 son of Elkanah, son of Joel,
son of Azariah, son of Zephaniah,
37 son of Tahath, son of Assir,
son of Ebiasaph, son of Korah,
38 son of Izhar, son of Kohath,
son of Levi, son of Israel.
39 Heman's relative was ·Asaph, who stood
at his right hand:
Asaph son of Berechiah, son of Shimea,
40 son of Michael, son of Baaseiah,
son of Malchijah, 41 son of Ethni,
son of Zerah, son of Adaiah,
42 son of Ethan, son of Zimmah,
son of Shimei, 43 son of Jahath,
son of Gershom, son of Levi.
44 On the left, their relatives were Merari's sons:
Ethan son of Kishi, son of Abdi,
son of Malluch, 45 son of Hashabiah,
son of Amaziah, son of Hilkiah,
46 son of Amzi, son of Bani,
son of Shemer, 47 son of Mahli,
son of Mushi, son of Merari,
son of Levi.

48 Their relatives, the Levites, were assigned to all the service of the tabernacle, God's temple. 49 But Aaron and his sons did all the work of the most holy place. They presented the offerings on the altar of ·burnt offerings and on the altar of incense to make atonement for Israel according to all that Moses the servant of God had commanded.

50 These are Aaron's sons: his son Eleazar,
his son Phinehas, his son Abishua,
51 his son Bukki, his son Uzzi,
his son Zerahiah, 52 his son Meraioth,
his son Amariah, his son Ahitub,
53 his son Zadok, and his son Ahimaaz.

54 These were the places assigned to Aaron's sons from the Kohathite family for their settlements in their territory, because the first lot was for them. 55 They were given Hebron in the land of Judah and its surrounding pasturelands, 56 but the fields and villages around the city were given to Caleb son of Jephunneh. 57 Aaron's sons were given:

Hebron (a city of refuge), Libnah and its pasturelands, Jattir, Eshtemoa and its pasturelands, 58 Hilen and its pasturelands, Debir and its pasturelands, 59 Ashan and its pasturelands, and Beth-shemesh and its pasturelands. 60 From the tribe of Benjamin they were given Geba and its pasturelands, Alemeth and its pasturelands, and Anathoth and its pasturelands. They had 13 towns in all among their families.

61 To the rest of the Kohathites, 10 towns from half the tribe of Manasseh were assigned by lot.

62 The Gershomites were assigned 13 towns from the tribes of Issachar, Asher, Naphtali, and Manasseh in Bashan according to their families.

63 The Merarites were assigned by lot 12 towns from the tribes of Reuben, Gad, and Zebulun according to their families. 64 So the Israelites gave these towns and their pasturelands to the Levites. 65 They assigned by lot the towns named above from the tribes of the Judahites, Simeonites, and Benjaminites.

66 Some of the families of the Kohathites were given towns from the tribe of Ephraim for their territory: 67 Shechem (a city of refuge) with its pasturelands in the hill country of Ephraim, Gezer and its pasturelands, 68 Jokmeam and its pasturelands, Beth-horon and its pasturelands, 69 Aijalon and its pasturelands, and Gath-rimmon and its pasturelands. 70 From half the tribe of Manasseh, Aner and its pasturelands, and Bileam and its pasturelands were given to the rest of the families of the Kohathites.

71 The Gershomites received:
Golan in Bashan and its pasturelands, and Ashtaroth and its pasturelands from the families of half the tribe of Manasseh. 72 From the tribe of Issachar they received Kedesh and its pasturelands, Daberath and its pasturelands, 73 Ramoth and its pasturelands, and Anem and its pasturelands. 74 From the tribe of Asher they received Mashal and its pasturelands, Abdon and its pasturelands, 75 Hukok and its pasturelands, and Rehob and its pasturelands. 76 From the tribe of Naphtali they received Kedesh in Galilee and its pasturelands, Hammon and its pasturelands, and Kiriathaim and its pasturelands.

77 The rest of the Merarites received:
From the tribe of Zebulun they received Rimmono and its pasturelands and Tabor and its pasturelands. 78 From the tribe of Reuben across the Jordan at Jericho, to the east of the Jordan, they received Bezer in the desert and its pasturelands, Jahzah and its pasturelands, 79 Kedemoth and its pasturelands, and Mephaath and its pasturelands. 80 From the tribe of Gad they received Ramoth in Gilead and its pasturelands, Mahanaim and its pasturelands, 81 Heshbon and its pasturelands, and Jazer and its pasturelands.

7 Issachar's sons: Tola, Puah, Jashub, and Shimron—four.
2 Tola's sons: Uzzi, Rephaiah, Jeriel, Jahmai, Ibsam, and Shemuel, the heads of their ancestral houses. During David's reign, 22,600 descendants of Tola were recorded as warriors in their genealogies.
3 Uzzi's son: Izrahiah.
Izrahiah's sons: Michael, Obadiah, Joel, Isshiah. All five of them were chiefs. 4 Along with them, they had 36,000 troops for battle according to the genealogical records of their ancestral houses, for they had many wives and children. 5 Their tribesmen who were warriors belonging to all the families of Issachar totaled 87,000 in their genealogies.
6 Three of Benjamin's sons: Bela, Becher, and Jediael.
7 Bela's sons: Ezbon, Uzzi, Uzziel, Jerimoth, and Iri—five. They were warriors and heads of their ancestral houses; 22,034 were listed in their genealogies.
8 Becher's sons: Zemirah, Joash, Eliezer, Elioenai, Omri, Jeremoth, Abijah, Anathoth, and Alemeth; all these were Becher's sons. 9 Their genealogies were recorded according to the heads of their ancestral houses—20,200 warriors.

[10] Jediael's son: Bilhan.
Bilhan's sons: Jeush, Benjamin, Ehud,
Chenaanah, Zethan, Tarshish, and Ahishahar.
[11] All these sons of Jediael listed by heads of
families were warriors; there were 17,200
who could serve in the army. [12] Shuppim and
Huppim were sons of Ir, and the Hushim were
the sons of Aher.
[13] Naphtali's sons: Jahziel, Guni, Jezer, and
Shallum—Bilhah's sons.
[14] Manasseh's sons through his Aramean
concubine: Asriel and Machir the father of
Gilead. [15] Machir took wives from Huppim and
Shuppim. The name of his sister was Maacah.
Another descendant was named Zelophehad,
but he had only daughters.
[16] Machir's wife Maacah gave birth to a son,
and she named him Peresh. His brother was
named Sheresh, and his sons were Ulam and
Rekem.
[17] Ulam's son: Bedan. These were the sons of
Gilead son of Machir, son of Manasseh. [18] His
sister Hammolecheth gave birth to Ishhod,
Abiezer, and Mahlah.
[19] Shemida's sons: Ahian, Shechem, Likhi, and
Aniam.
[20] Ephraim's sons: Shuthelah, and his son Bered,
his son Tahath, his son Eleadah,
his son Tahath, [21] his son Zabad,
his son Shuthelah, also Ezer, and Elead.
The men of Gath, born in the land, killed
them because they went down to raid their
cattle. [22] Their father Ephraim mourned a long
time, and his relatives came to comfort him.
[23] He slept with his wife, and she conceived
and gave birth to a son. So he named him
Beriah, because there had been misfortune
in his home. [24] His daughter was Sheerah,
who built Lower and Upper Beth-horon and
Uzzen-sheerah,
[25] his son Rephah, his son Resheph,
his son Telah, his son Tahan,
[26] his son Ladan, his son Ammihud,
his son Elishama, [27] his son Nun,
and his son Joshua.
[28] Their holdings and settlements were Bethel
and its villages; Naaran to the east, Gezer and
its villages to the west, and Shechem and its villages as far as Ayyah and its villages, [29] and along
the borders of the sons of Manasseh, Beth-shean
and its villages, Taanach and its villages, Megiddo and its villages, and Dor and its villages. The
sons of Joseph son of Israel lived in these towns.
[30] Asher's sons: Imnah, Ishvah, Ishvi, and
Beriah, with their sister Serah.
[31] Beriah's sons: Heber, and Malchiel, who
fathered Birzaith.
[32] Heber fathered Japhlet, Shomer, and
Hotham, with their sister Shua.
[33] Japhlet's sons: Pasach, Bimhal, and Ashvath.
These were Japhlet's sons.
[34] Shemer's sons: Ahi, Rohgah, Hubbah, and
Aram.
[35] His brother Helem's sons: Zophah, Imna,
Shelesh, and Amal.
[36] Zophah's sons: Suah, Harnepher, Shual,

Beri, Imrah, [37] Bezer, Hod, Shamma, Shilshah,
Ithran, and Beera.
[38] Jether's sons: Jephunneh, Pispa, and Ara.
[39] Ulla's sons: Arah, Hanniel, and Rizia.
[40] All these were Asher's sons. They were the
heads of their ancestral houses, chosen men,
warriors, and chiefs among the leaders. The
number of men listed in their genealogies for
military service was 26,000.

8 Benjamin fathered Bela, his firstborn; Ashbel
was born second, Aharah third,
[2] Nohah fourth, and Rapha fifth.
[3] Bela's sons: Addar, Gera, Abihud, [4] Abishua,
Naaman, Ahoah, [5] Gera, Shephuphan, and
Huram.
[6] These were Ehud's sons, who were the heads
of the families living in Geba and who were
deported to Manahath: [7] Naaman, Ahijah, and
Gera. Gera deported them and was the father
of Uzza and Ahihud.
[8] Shaharaim had sons in the country of Moab
after he had divorced his wives Hushim
and Baara. [9] His sons by his wife Hodesh:
Jobab, Zibia, Mesha, Malcam, [10] Jeuz, Sachia,
and Mirmah. These were his sons, heads
of families. [11] He also had sons by Hushim:
Abitub and Elpaal.
[12] Elpaal's sons: Eber, Misham, and Shemed
who built Ono and Lod and its villages,
[13] Beriah and Shema, who were the heads of
families of Aijalon's residents and who drove
out the residents of Gath, [14] Ahio, Shashak,
and Jeremoth.
[15] Zebadiah, Arad, Eder, [16] Michael, Ishpah, and
Joha were Beriah's sons.
[17] Zebadiah, Meshullam, Hizki, Heber,
[18] Ishmerai, Izliah, and Jobab were Elpaal's
sons.
[19] Jakim, Zichri, Zabdi, [20] Elienai, Zillethai,
Eliel, [21] Adaiah, Beraiah, and Shimrath were
Shimei's sons.
[22] Ishpan, Eber, Eliel, [23] Abdon, Zichri, Hanan,
[24] Hananiah, Elam, Anthothijah, [25] Iphdeiah,
and Penuel were Shashak's sons.
[26] Shamsherai, Shehariah, Athaliah,
[27] Jaareshiah, Elijah, and Zichri were
Jeroham's sons.
[28] These were heads of families, chiefs
according to their genealogies, and lived in
Jerusalem.
[29] Jeiel fathered Gibeon and lived in Gibeon.
His wife's name was Maacah. [30] Abdon was his
firstborn son, then Zur, Kish, Baal, Nadab,
[31] Gedor, Ahio, Zecher, [32] and Mikloth who
fathered Shimeah. These also lived opposite
their relatives in Jerusalem, with their other
relatives.
[33] Ner fathered Kish, Kish fathered Saul,
and Saul fathered Jonathan, Malchishua,
Abinadab, and Esh-baal.
[34] Jonathan's son was Merib-baal, and Merib-
baal fathered Micah.
[35] Micah's sons: Pithon, Melech, Tarea, and
Ahaz.
[36] Ahaz fathered Jehoaddah, Jehoaddah
fathered Alemeth, Azmaveth, and Zimri, and
Zimri fathered Moza.

37 Moza fathered Binea. His son was Raphah, his son Elasah, and his son Azel. 38 Azel had six sons, and these were their names: Azrikam, Bocheru, Ishmael, Sheariah, Obadiah, and Hanan. All these were Azel's sons. 39 His brother Eshek's sons: Ulam was his firstborn, Jeush second, and Eliphelet third. 40 Ulam's sons were warriors and archers. They had many sons and grandsons—150 of them. All these were among Benjamin's sons.

9 All Israel was registered in the genealogies that are written in the Book of the Kings of Israel. But Judah was exiled to Babylon because of their unfaithfulness. 2 The first to live in their towns on their own property again were Israelites, priests, Levites, and temple servants.

3 These people from the descendants of Judah, Benjamin, Ephraim, and Manasseh settled in Jerusalem:

4 Uthai son of Ammihud, son of Omri, son of Imri, son of Bani, a descendant of Perez son of Judah;

5 from the Shilonites:
Asaiah the firstborn and his sons;

6 and from the sons of Zerah:
Jeuel and 690 of their relatives.

7 The Benjaminites: Sallu son of Meshullam, son of Hodaviah, son of Hassenuah;

8 Ibneiah son of Jeroham;
Elah son of Uzzi, son of Michri;
Meshullam son of Shephatiah, son of Reuel, son of Ibnijah;

9 and 956 of their relatives according to their genealogical records. All these men were heads of their ancestral houses.

10 The priests: Jedaiah; Jehoiarib; Jachin; 11 Azariah son of Hilkiah, son of Meshullam, son of Zadok, son of Meraioth, son of Ahitub, the chief official of God's temple;

12 Adaiah son of Jeroham, son of Pashhur, son of Malchijah;
Maasai son of Adiel, son of Jahzerah, son of Meshullam, son of Meshillemith, son of Immer;

13 and 1,760 of their relatives, the heads of households. They were capable men employed in the ministry of God's temple.

14 The Levites: Shemaiah son of Hasshub, son of Azrikam, son of Hashabiah of the Merarites; 15 Bakbakkar, Heresh, Galal, and Mattaniah, son of Mica, son of Zichri, son of *Asaph; 16 Obadiah son of Shemaiah, son of Galal, son of Jeduthun;
and Berechiah son of Asa, son of Elkanah who lived in the villages of the Netophathites.

17 The gatekeepers: Shallum, Akkub, Talmon, Ahiman, and their relatives.
Shallum was their chief; 18 he was previously stationed at the King's Gate on the east side. These were the gatekeepers from the camp of the Levites.

19 Shallum son of Kore, son of Ebiasaph, son of Korah and his relatives from his ancestral household, the Korahites, were assigned to guard the thresholds of the tent. Their ancestors had been assigned to the Lord's camp as guardians of the entrance. 20 In earlier times Phinehas son of Eleazar had been their leader, and the Lord was with him. 21 Zechariah son of Meshelemiah was the gatekeeper at the entrance to the tent of meeting.

22 The total number of those chosen to be gatekeepers at the thresholds was 212. They were registered by genealogy in their villages. David and Samuel the seer had appointed them to their trusted positions. 23 So they and their sons were assigned to the gates of the Lord's temple, which had been the tent-temple. 24 The gatekeepers were on the four sides: east, west, north, and south. 25 Their relatives came from their villages at fixed times to be with them seven days, 26 but the four chief gatekeepers, who were Levites, were entrusted with the rooms and the treasuries of God's temple. 27 They spent the night in the vicinity of God's temple, because they had guard duty and were in charge of opening it every morning.

28 Some of them were in charge of the utensils used in worship. They would count them when they brought them in and when they took them out. 29 Others were put in charge of the furnishings and all the utensils of the sanctuary, as well as the fine flour, wine, oil, incense, and spices. 30 Some of the priests' sons mixed the spices. 31 A Levite called Mattithiah, the firstborn of Shallum the Korahite, was entrusted with baking the bread. 32 Some of the Kohathites' relatives were responsible for preparing the rows of the *bread of the Presence every Sabbath.

33 The singers, the heads of the Levite families, stayed in the temple chambers and were exempt from other tasks because they were on duty day and night. 34 These were the heads of the Levite families, chiefs according to their genealogies, and lived in Jerusalem.

35 Jeiel fathered Gibeon and lived in Gibeon. His wife's name was Maacah. 36 Abdon was his firstborn son, then Zur, Kish, Baal, Ner, Nadab, 37 Gedor, Ahio, Zechariah, and Mikloth. 38 Mikloth fathered Shimeam. These also lived opposite their relatives in Jerusalem with their other relatives.

39 Ner fathered Kish, Kish fathered Saul, and Saul fathered Jonathan, Malchishua, Abinadab, and Esh-baal.

40 Jonathan's son was Merib-baal, and Merib-baal fathered Micah.

41 Micah's sons: Pithon, Melech, Tahrea, and Ahaz.

42 Ahaz fathered Jarah;
Jarah fathered Alemeth, Azmaveth, and Zimri; Zimri fathered Moza.

43 Moza fathered Binea.
His son was Rephaiah, his son Elasah, and his son Azel.

44 Azel had six sons, and these were their names: Azrikam, Bocheru, Ishmael, Sheariah, Obadiah, and Hanan. These were Azel's sons.

10 The Philistines fought against Israel, and Israel's men fled from them and were killed on Mount Gilboa. 2 The Philistines pursued Saul and his sons and killed Saul's sons Jonathan, Abinadab, and Malchishua. 3 When the battle intensified against Saul, the archers found him and severely wounded him. 4 Then Saul said to his armor-bearer, "Draw your sword and run me through with it, or these uncircumcised

men will come and torture me!" But his armor-bearer wouldn't do it because he was terrified. Then Saul took his sword and fell on it. [5]When his armor-bearer saw that Saul was dead, he also fell on his own sword and died. [6]So Saul and his three sons died—his whole house died together.

[7]When all the men of Israel in the valley saw that the army had fled and that Saul and his sons were dead, they abandoned their cities and fled. So the Philistines came and settled in them.

[8]The next day when the Philistines came to strip the slain, they found Saul and his sons dead on Mount Gilboa. [9]They stripped Saul, cut off his head, took his armor, and sent messengers throughout the land of the Philistines to spread the good news to their idols and their people. [10]Then they put his armor in the temple of their gods and hung his skull in the temple of Dagon.

[11]When all Jabesh-gilead heard of everything the Philistines had done to Saul, [12]all their brave men set out and retrieved the body of Saul and the bodies of his sons and brought them to Jabesh. They buried their bones under the oak in Jabesh and fasted seven days.

[13]Saul died for his unfaithfulness to the LORD because he did not keep the LORD's word. He even consulted a medium for guidance, [14]but he did not inquire of the LORD. So the LORD put him to death and turned the kingdom over to David son of Jesse.

11 All Israel came together to David at Hebron and said, "Here we are, your own flesh and blood. [2]Even when Saul was king, you led us out to battle and brought us back. The LORD your God also said to you, 'You will shepherd My people Israel and be ruler over My people Israel.'"

[3]So all the elders of Israel came to the king at Hebron. David made a covenant with them at Hebron in the LORD's presence, and they anointed David king over Israel, in keeping with the LORD's word through Samuel.

[4]David and all Israel marched to Jerusalem (that is, Jebus); the Jebusites who inhabited the land were there. [5]The inhabitants of Jebus said to David, "You will never get in here." Yet David did capture the stronghold of *Zion, that is, the city of David.

[6]David said, "Whoever is the first to kill a Jebusite will become chief commander." Joab son of Zeruiah went up first, so he became the chief.

[7]Then David took up residence in the stronghold; therefore, it was called the city of David. [8]He built up the city all the way around, from the supporting terraces to the surrounding parts, and Joab restored the rest of the city. [9]David steadily grew more powerful, and the LORD of *Hosts was with him.

[10]The following were the chiefs of David's warriors who, together with all Israel, strongly supported him in his reign to make him king according to the LORD's word about Israel. [11]This is the list of David's warriors:

Jashobeam son of Hachmoni was chief of the Thirty; he wielded his spear against 300 and killed them at one time.

[12]After him, Eleazar son of Dodo the Ahohite was one of the three warriors. [13]He was with David at Pasdammim when the Philistines had gathered there for battle. There was a portion of a field full of barley, where the troops had fled from the Philistines. [14]But Eleazar and David took their stand in the middle of the field and defended it. They killed the Philistines, and the LORD gave them a great victory.

[15]Three of the 30 chief men went down to David, to the rock at the cave of Adullam, while the Philistine army was encamped in the Valley of Rephaim. [16]At that time David was in the stronghold, and a Philistine garrison was at Bethlehem. [17]David was extremely thirsty and said, "If only someone would bring me water to drink from the well at the city gate of Bethlehem!" [18]So the Three broke through the Philistine camp and drew water from the well at the gate of Bethlehem. They brought it back to David, but he refused to drink it. Instead, he poured it out to the LORD. [19]David said, "I would never do such a thing in the presence of God! How can I drink the blood of these men who risked their lives?" For they brought it at the risk of their lives. So he would not drink it. Such were the exploits of the three warriors.

[20]Abishai, Joab's brother, was the leader of the Three. He raised his spear against 300 men and killed them, gaining a reputation among the Three. [21]He was more honored than the Three and became their commander even though he did not become one of the Three.

[22]Benaiah son of Jehoiada was the son of a brave man from Kabzeel, a man of many exploits. Benaiah killed two sons of Ariel of Moab, and he went down into a pit on a snowy day and killed a lion. [23]He also killed an Egyptian who was seven and a half feet tall. Even though the Egyptian had a spear in his hand like a weaver's beam, Benaiah went down to him with a club, snatched the spear out of the Egyptian's hand, and then killed him with his own spear. [24]These were the exploits of Benaiah son of Jehoiada, who had a reputation among the three warriors. [25]He was the most honored of the Thirty, but he did not become one of the Three. David put him in charge of his bodyguard.

[26]The fighting men were:

Joab's brother Asahel,
Elhanan son of Dodo of Bethlehem,
[27] Shammoth the Harorite,
Helez the Pelonite,
[28] Ira son of Ikkesh the Tekoite,
Abiezer the Anathothite,
[29] Sibbecai the Hushathite,
Ilai the Ahohite,
[30] Maharai the Netophathite,
Heled son of Baanah the Netophathite,
[31] Ithai son of Ribai from Gibeah
of the Benjaminites,
Benaiah the Pirathonite,
[32] Hurai from the *wadis of Gaash,
Abiel the Arbathite,
[33] Azmaveth the Baharumite,
Eliahba the Shaalbonite,
[34] the sons of Hashem the Gizonite,
Jonathan son of Shagee the Hararite,
[35] Ahiam son of Sachar the Hararite,
Eliphal son of Ur,
[36] Hepher the Mecherathite,
Ahijah the Pelonite,
[37] Hezro the Carmelite,
Naarai son of Ezbai,
[38] Joel the brother of Nathan,
Mibhar son of Hagri,
[39] Zelek the Ammonite,
Naharai the Beerothite, the armor-bearer
for Joab son of Zeruiah,

40 Ira the Ithrite,
    Gareb the Ithrite,
41 Uriah the Hittite,
    Zabad son of Ahlai,
42 Adina son of Shiza the Reubenite, chief
    of the Reubenites, and 30 with him,
43 Hanan son of Maacah,
    Joshaphat the Mithnite,
44 Uzzia the Ashterathite,
    Shama and Jeiel the sons of Hotham
    the Aroerite,
45 Jediael son of Shimri and his brother Joha
    the Tizite,
46 Eliel the Mahavite,
    Jeribai and Joshaviah, the sons of Elnaam,
    Ithmah the Moabite,
47 Eliel, Obed, and Jaasiel the Mezobaite.

12 The following were the men who came to David at Ziklag while he was still banned from the presence of Saul son of Kish. They were among the warriors who helped him in battle. ²They were archers who could use either the right or left hand, both to sling stones and shoot arrows from a bow. They were Saul's relatives from Benjamin:

³Their chief was Ahiezer son of Shemaah the Gibeathite.
    Then there was his brother Joash;
    Jeziel and Pelet sons of Azmaveth;
    Beracah, Jehu the Anathothite;
⁴Ishmaiah the Gibeonite, a warrior among the Thirty and a leader over the Thirty;
    Jeremiah, Jahaziel, Johanan, Jozabad the Gederathite;
⁵Eluzai, Jerimoth, Bealiah, Shemariah, Shephatiah the Haruphite;
⁶Elkanah, Isshiah, Azarel, Joezer, and Jashobeam, the Korahites;
⁷and Joelah and Zebadiah, the sons of Jeroham from Gedor.

⁸Some Gadites defected to David at his stronghold in the desert. They were fighting men, trained for battle, expert with shield and spear. Their faces were like the faces of lions, and they were as swift as gazelles on the mountains.

⁹ Ezer was the chief, Obadiah second,
    Eliab third,
10 Mishmannah fourth, Jeremiah fifth,
11 Attai sixth, Eliel seventh,
12 Johanan eighth, Elzabad ninth,
13 Jeremiah tenth, and Machbannai eleventh.

¹⁴These Gadites were army commanders; the least of them was a match for a hundred, and the greatest of them for a thousand. ¹⁵These are the men who crossed the Jordan in the first month when it was overflowing all its banks, and put to flight all those in the valleys to the east and to the west.

¹⁶Other Benjaminites and men from Judah also went to David at the stronghold. ¹⁷David went out to meet them and said to them, "If you have come in peace to help me, my heart will be united with you, but if you have come to betray me to my enemies even though my hands have done no wrong, may the God of our ancestors look on it and judge."

¹⁸Then the Spirit took control of Amasai, chief of the Thirty, and he said:

We are yours, David,
    we are with you, son of Jesse!
    Peace, peace to you,
    and peace to him who helps you,
    for your God helps you.

So David received them and made them leaders of his troops.

¹⁹Some Manassites defected to David when he went with the Philistines to fight against Saul. However, they did not help the Philistines because the Philistine rulers sent David away after a discussion. They said, "It will be our heads if he defects to his master Saul." ²⁰When David went to Ziklag, some men from Manasseh defected to him: Adnah, Jozabad, Jediael, Michael, Jozabad, Elihu, and Zillethai, chiefs of thousands in Manasseh. ²¹They helped David against the raiders, for they were all brave warriors and commanders in the army. ²²At that time, men came day after day to help David until there was a great army, like an army of God.

²³The numbers of the armed troops who came to David at Hebron to turn Saul's kingdom over to him, according to the Lord's word, were as follows:

24 From the Judahites: 6,800 armed troops
    bearing shields and spears.
25 From the Simeonites: 7,100 brave warriors
    ready for war.
26 From the Levites: 4,600 ²⁷in addition to
    Jehoiada, leader of the house of Aaron, with
    3,700 men; ²⁸and Zadok, a young brave
    warrior, with 22 commanders from his own
    ancestral house.
29 From the Benjaminites, the relatives of Saul:
    3,000 (up to that time the majority of the
    Benjaminites maintained their allegiance to
    the house of Saul).
30 From the Ephraimites: 20,800 brave
    warriors who were famous men in their
    ancestral houses.
31 From half the tribe of Manasseh: 18,000
    designated by name to come and make
    David king.
32 From the Issacharites, who understood
    the times and knew what Israel should
    do: 200 chiefs with all their relatives
    under their command.
33 From Zebulun: 50,000 who could serve in
    the army, trained for battle with all kinds
    of weapons of war, with one purpose
    to help David.
34 From Naphtali: 1,000 commanders
    accompanied by 37,000 men with
    shield and spear.
35 From the Danites: 28,600 trained for battle.
36 From Asher: 40,000 who could serve in the
    army, trained for battle.
37 From across the Jordan—from the
    Reubenites, Gadites, and half the tribe of
    Manasseh: 120,000 men equipped with all
    the military weapons of war.

³⁸All these warriors, lined up in battle formation, came to Hebron fully determined to make David king over all Israel. All the rest of Israel was also of one mind to make David king. ³⁹They spent three days there eating and drinking with David, for their relatives had provided for them. ⁴⁰In addition, their neighbors from as far away as Issachar, Zebulun, and Naphtali came and brought food on donkeys, camels, mules, and oxen—abundant provisions of flour, fig

cakes, raisins, wine and oil, oxen, and sheep. Indeed, there was joy in Israel.

13 David consulted with all his leaders, the commanders of hundreds and of thousands. [2]Then he said to the whole assembly of Israel, "If it seems good to you, and if this is from the Lord our God, let us spread out and send the message to the rest of our relatives in all the districts of Israel, including the priests and Levites in their cities with pasturelands, that they should gather together with us. [3]Then let us bring back the ark of our God, for we did not inquire of Him in Saul's days." [4]Since the proposal seemed right to all the people, the whole assembly agreed to do it.

[5]So David assembled all Israel, from the Shihor of Egypt to the entrance of Hamath, to bring the ark of God from Kiriath-jearim. [6]David and all Israel went to Baalah (that is, Kiriath-jearim that belongs to Judah) to take the ark of God from there, which is called by the name of the Lord who dwells between the ˙cherubim. [7]At Abinadab's house they set the ark of God on a new cart. Uzzah and Ahio were guiding the cart.

[8]David and all Israel were celebrating with all their might before God with songs and with lyres, harps, tambourines, cymbals, and trumpets. [9]When they came to Chidon's threshing floor, Uzzah reached out to hold the ark because the oxen had stumbled. [10]Then the Lord's anger burned against Uzzah, and He struck him dead because he had reached out to the ark. So he died there in the presence of God.

[11]David was angry because of the Lord's outburst against Uzzah, so he named that place Outburst Against Uzzah, as it is still named today. [12]David feared God that day and said, "How can I ever bring the ark of God to me?" [13]So David did not move the ark of God home to the city of David; instead, he took it to the house of Obed-edom the Gittite. [14]The ark of God remained with Obed-edom's family in his house for three months, and the Lord blessed his family and all that he had.

14 King Hiram of Tyre sent envoys to David, along with cedar logs, stonemasons, and carpenters to build a palace for him. [2]Then David knew that the Lord had established him as king over Israel and that his kingdom had been exalted for the sake of His people Israel.

[3]David took more wives in Jerusalem, and he became the father of more sons and daughters. [4]These are the names of the children born to him in Jerusalem: Shammua, Shobab, Nathan, Solomon, [5]Ibhar, Elishua, Elpelet, [6]Nogah, Nepheg, Japhia, [7]Elishama, Beeliada, and Eliphelet.

[8]When the Philistines heard that David had been anointed king over all Israel, they all went in search of David; when David heard of this, he went out to face them. [9]Now the Philistines had come and raided in the Valley of Rephaim, [10]so David inquired of God, "Should I go to war against the Philistines? Will You hand them over to me?"

The Lord replied, "Go, and I will hand them over to you."

[11]So the Israelites went up to Baal-perazim, and David defeated the Philistines there. Then David said, "Like a bursting flood, God has used me to burst out against my enemies." Therefore, they named that place the Lord Bursts Out. [12]The Philistines abandoned their idols there, and David ordered that they be burned in the fire.

[13]Once again the Philistines raided in the valley. [14]So David again inquired of God, and God answered him, "Do not pursue them directly. Circle around them and attack them opposite the balsam trees. [15]When you hear the sound of marching in the tops of the balsam trees, then march out to battle, for God will have marched out ahead of you to attack the camp of the Philistines." [16]So David did exactly as God commanded him, and they struck down the Philistine army from Gibeon to Gezer. [17]Then David's fame spread throughout the lands, and the Lord caused all the nations to be terrified of him.

15 David built houses for himself in the city of David, and he prepared a place for the ark of God and pitched a tent for it. [2]Then David said, "No one but the Levites may carry the ark of God, because the Lord has chosen them to carry the ark of the Lord and to minister before Him forever."

[3]David assembled all Israel at Jerusalem to bring the ark of the Lord to the place he had prepared for it. [4]Then he gathered together the descendants of Aaron and the Levites:

[5]From the Kohathites, Uriel the leader and 120 of his relatives; [6]from the Merarites, Asaiah the leader and 220 of his relatives; [7]from the Gershomites, Joel the leader and 130 of his relatives; [8]from the Elizaphanites, Shemaiah the leader and 200 of his relatives; [9]from the Hebronites, Eliel the leader and 80 of his relatives; [10]from the Uzzielites, Amminadab the leader and 112 of his relatives.

[11]David summoned the priests Zadok and Abiathar and the Levites Uriel, Asaiah, Joel, Shemaiah, Eliel, and Amminadab. [12]He said to them, "You are the heads of the Levite families. You and your relatives must consecrate yourselves so that you may bring the ark of the Lord God of Israel to the place I have prepared for it. [13]For the Lord our God burst out in anger against us because you Levites were not with us the first time, for we didn't inquire of Him about the proper procedures." [14]So the priests and the Levites consecrated themselves to bring up the ark of the Lord God of Israel. [15]Then the Levites carried the ark of God the way Moses had commanded according to the word of the Lord: on their shoulders with the poles.

[16]Then David told the leaders of the Levites to appoint their relatives as singers and to have them raise their voices with joy accompanied by musical instruments—harps, lyres, and cymbals. [17]So the Levites appointed Heman son of Joel; from his relatives, Asaph son of Berechiah; and from their relatives the Merarites, Ethan son of Kushaiah. [18]With them were their relatives second in rank: Zechariah, Jaaziel, Shemiramoth, Jehiel, Unni, Eliab, Benaiah, Maaseiah, Mattithiah, Eliphelehu, Mikneiah, and the gatekeepers Obed-edom and Jeiel. [19]The singers Heman, Asaph, and Ethan were to sound the bronze cymbals; [20]Zechariah, Aziel, Shemiramoth, Jehiel, Unni, Eliab, Maaseiah, and Benaiah were to play harps according to *Alamoth*; [21]and Mattithiah, Eliphelehu, Mikneiah, Obed-edom, Jeiel, and Azaziah were to lead the music with lyres according to the ˙*Sheminith*. [22]Chenaniah, the leader of the Levites in music, was to direct the music because he was skillful. [23]Berechiah and Elkanah were to be gatekeepers for the ark. [24]The priests, Shebaniah, Joshaphat, Nethanel, Amasai, Zechariah, Benaiah, and Eliezer, were to blow trumpets before

the ark of God. Obed-edom and Jehiah were also to be gatekeepers for the ark.

²⁵ David, the elders of Israel, and the commanders of thousands went with rejoicing to bring the ark of the covenant of the Lᴏʀᴅ from the house of Obed-edom. ²⁶ While the Levites were carrying the ark of the covenant of the Lᴏʀᴅ, with God's help, they sacrificed seven bulls and seven rams.

²⁷ Now David was dressed in a robe of fine linen, as were all the Levites who were carrying the ark, as well as the singers and Chenaniah, the music leader of the singers. David also wore a linen *ephod. ²⁸ So all Israel brought up the ark of the covenant of the Lᴏʀᴅ with shouts, the sound of the ram's horn, trumpets, and cymbals, and the playing of harps and lyres. ²⁹ As the ark of the covenant of the Lᴏʀᴅ was entering the city of David, Saul's daughter Michal looked down from the window and saw King David dancing and celebrating, and she despised him in her heart.

16 They brought the ark of God and placed it inside the tent David had pitched for it. Then they offered *burnt offerings and *fellowship offerings in God's presence. ² When David had finished offering the burnt offerings and the fellowship offerings, he blessed the people in the name of *Yahweh. ³ Then he distributed to each and every Israelite, both men and women, a loaf of bread, a date cake, and a raisin cake.

⁴ David appointed some of the Levites to be ministers before the ark of the Lᴏʀᴅ, to celebrate the Lᴏʀᴅ God of Israel, and to give thanks and praise to Him. ⁵ *Asaph was the chief and Zechariah was second to him. Jeiel, Shemiramoth, Jehiel, Mattithiah, Eliab, Benaiah, Obed-edom, and Jeiel played the harps and lyres, while Asaph sounded the cymbals ⁶ and the priests Benaiah and Jahaziel blew the trumpets regularly before the ark of the covenant of God.

⁷ On that day David decreed for the first time that thanks be given to the Lᴏʀᴅ by Asaph and his relatives:

⁸   Give thanks to Yahweh; call on His name;
    proclaim His deeds among the peoples.
⁹   Sing to Him; sing praise to Him;
    tell about all His wonderful works!
¹⁰ Honor His holy name;
    let the hearts of those who seek Yahweh rejoice.
¹¹ Search for the Lᴏʀᴅ and for His strength;
    seek His face always.
¹² Remember the wonderful works He has done,
    His wonders, and the judgments
    He has pronounced,
¹³ you offspring of Israel His servant,
    Jacob's descendants—His chosen ones.
¹⁴ He is the Lᴏʀᴅ our God;
    His judgments govern the whole earth.
¹⁵ Remember His covenant forever—
    the promise He ordained for a thousand
    generations,
¹⁶ the covenant He made with Abraham,
    swore to Isaac,
¹⁷ and confirmed to Jacob as a decree,
    and to Israel as an everlasting covenant:
¹⁸ "I will give the land of Canaan to you
    as your inherited portion."
¹⁹ When they were few in number,
    very few indeed, and temporary residents
    in Canaan
²⁰ wandering from nation to nation
    and from one kingdom to another,

²¹ He allowed no one to oppress them;
    He rebuked kings on their behalf:
²² "Do not touch My anointed ones
    or harm My prophets."
²³ Sing to the Lᴏʀᴅ, all the earth.
    Proclaim His salvation from day to day.
²⁴ Declare His glory among the nations,
    His wonderful works among all peoples.
²⁵ For the Lᴏʀᴅ is great and highly praised;
    He is feared above all gods.
²⁶ For all the gods of the peoples are idols,
    but the Lᴏʀᴅ made the heavens.
²⁷ Splendor and majesty are before Him;
    strength and joy are in His place.
²⁸ Ascribe to the Lᴏʀᴅ, families of the peoples,
    ascribe to the Lᴏʀᴅ glory and strength.
²⁹ Ascribe to Yahweh the glory of His name;
    bring an offering and come before Him.
    Worship the Lᴏʀᴅ
    in the splendor of His holiness;
³⁰ tremble before Him, all the earth.
    The world is firmly established;
    it cannot be shaken.
³¹ Let the heavens be glad and the earth rejoice,
    and let them say among the nations,
    "The Lᴏʀᴅ is King!"
³² Let the sea and everything in it resound;
    let the fields and all that is in them exult.
³³ Then the trees of the forest will shout for joy
    before the Lᴏʀᴅ,
    for He is coming to judge the earth.
³⁴ Give thanks to the Lᴏʀᴅ, for He is good;
    His faithful love endures forever.
³⁵ And say: "Save us, God of our salvation;
    gather us and rescue us from the nations
    so that we may give thanks to
    Your holy name
    and rejoice in Your praise.
³⁶ May Yahweh, the God of Israel, be praised
    from everlasting to everlasting."

Then all the people said, "*Amen" and "Praise the Lᴏʀᴅ."

³⁷ So David left Asaph and his relatives there before the ark of the Lᴏʀᴅ's covenant to minister regularly before the ark according to the daily requirements. ³⁸ He assigned Obed-edom and his 68 relatives. Obed-edom son of Jeduthun and Hosah were to be gatekeepers. ³⁹ David left Zadok the priest and his fellow priests before the tabernacle of the Lᴏʀᴅ at the *high place in Gibeon ⁴⁰ to offer burnt offerings regularly, morning and evening, to the Lᴏʀᴅ on the altar of burnt offerings and to do everything that was written in the law of the Lᴏʀᴅ, which He had commanded Israel to keep. ⁴¹ With them were Heman, Jeduthun, and the rest who were chosen and designated by name to give thanks to the Lᴏʀᴅ—for His faithful love endures forever. ⁴² Heman and Jeduthun had with them trumpets and cymbals to play and musical instruments of God. Jeduthun's sons were at the gate.

⁴³ Then all the people left for their homes, and David returned home to bless his household.

17 When David had settled into his palace, he said to Nathan the prophet, "Look! I am living in a cedar house while the ark of the Lᴏʀᴅ's covenant is under tent curtains."

² So Nathan told David, "Do all that is on your heart, for God is with you."

³ But that night the word of God came to Nathan:

⁴"Go to David My servant and say, 'This is what the Lord says: You are not the one to build Me a house to dwell in. ⁵From the time I brought Israel out of Egypt until today I have not lived in a house; instead, I have moved from tent to tent and from tabernacle to tabernacle. ⁶In all My travels throughout Israel, have I ever spoken a word to even one of the judges of Israel, whom I commanded to shepherd My people, asking: Why haven't you built Me a house of cedar?'

⁷"Now this is what you will say to My servant David: 'This is what the Lord of 'Hosts says: I took you from the pasture and from following the sheep to be ruler over My people Israel. ⁸I have been with you wherever you have gone, and I have destroyed all your enemies before you. I will make a name for you like that of the greatest in the land. ⁹I will establish a place for My people Israel and plant them, so that they may live there and not be disturbed again. Evildoers will not continue to oppress them as they formerly have ¹⁰ever since the day I ordered judges to be over My people Israel. I will also subdue all your enemies.

"'Furthermore, I declare to you that the Lord Himself will build a house for you. ¹¹When your time comes to be with your fathers, I will raise up after you your descendant, who is one of your own sons, and I will establish his kingdom. ¹²He will build a house for Me, and I will establish his throne forever. ¹³I will be a father to him, and he will be a son to Me. I will not take away My faithful love from him as I took it from the one who was before you. ¹⁴I will appoint him over My house and My kingdom forever, and his throne will be established forever.'"

¹⁵Nathan reported all these words and this entire vision to David.

¹⁶Then King David went in, sat in the Lord's presence, and said,

Who am I, Lord God, and what is my house that You have brought me this far? ¹⁷This was a little thing to You, God, for You have spoken about Your servant's house in the distant future. You regard me as a man of distinction, Lord God. ¹⁸What more can David say to You for honoring Your servant? You know Your servant. ¹⁹Lord, You have done all this greatness, making known all these great promises because of Your servant and according to Your will. ²⁰Lord, there is no one like You, and there is no God besides You, as all we have heard confirms. ²¹And who is like Your people Israel? God, You came to one nation on earth to redeem a people for Yourself, to make a name for Yourself through great and awesome works by driving out nations before Your people You redeemed from Egypt. ²²You made Your people Israel Your own people forever, and You, Lord, have become their God. ²³Now, Lord, let the word that You have spoken concerning Your servant and his house be confirmed forever, and do as You have promised. ²⁴Let Your name be confirmed and magnified forever in the saying, "'Yahweh of Hosts, the God of Israel, is God over Israel." May the house of Your servant David be established before You. ²⁵Since You, my God, have revealed to Your servant that You will build him a house, Your servant has found courage to pray in Your presence. ²⁶Yahweh, You indeed are God, and You have promised this good thing to Your servant.

²⁷So now, You have been pleased to bless Your servant's house that it may continue before You forever. For You, Lord, have blessed it, and it is blessed forever.

18 After this, David defeated the Philistines, subdued them, and took Gath and its villages from Philistine control. ²He also defeated the Moabites, and they became David's subjects and brought tribute.

³David also defeated King Hadadezer of Zobah at Hamath when he went to establish his control at the Euphrates River. ⁴David captured 1,000 chariots, 7,000 horsemen, and 20,000 foot soldiers from him, hamstrung all the horses, and kept 100 chariots.

⁵When the Arameans of Damascus came to assist King Hadadezer of Zobah, David struck down 22,000 Aramean men. ⁶Then he placed garrisons in Aram of Damascus, and the Arameans became David's subjects and brought tribute. The Lord made David victorious wherever he went.

⁷David took the gold shields carried by Hadadezer's officers and brought them to Jerusalem. ⁸From Tibhath and Cun, Hadadezer's cities, David also took huge quantities of bronze, from which Solomon made the bronze reservoir, the pillars, and the bronze articles.

⁹When King Tou of Hamath heard that David had defeated the entire army of King Hadadezer of Zobah, ¹⁰he sent his son Hadoram to King David to greet him and to congratulate him because David had fought against Hadadezer and defeated him, for Tou and Hadadezer had fought many wars. Hadoram brought all kinds of gold, silver, and bronze items. ¹¹King David also dedicated these to the Lord, along with the silver and gold he had carried off from all the nations—from Edom, Moab, the Ammonites, the Philistines, and the Amalekites.

¹²Abishai son of Zeruiah struck down 18,000 Edomites in the Valley of Salt. ¹³He put garrisons in Edom, and all the Edomites were subject to David. The Lord made David victorious wherever he went.

¹⁴So David reigned over all Israel, administering justice and righteousness for all his people.

15 Joab son of Zeruiah was over the army;
Jehoshaphat son of Ahilud was
court historian;

16 Zadok son of Ahitub
and Ahimelech son of Abiathar were priests;
Shavsha was court secretary;

17 Benaiah son of Jehoiada was over
the Cherethites and the Pelethites;
and David's sons were the chief officials
at the king's side.

19 Some time later, King Nahash of the Ammonites died, and his son became king in his place. ²Then David said, "I'll show kindness to Hanun son of Nahash, because his father showed kindness to me."

So David sent messengers to console him concerning his father. However, when David's emissaries arrived in the land of the Ammonites to console him, ³the Ammonite leaders said to Hanun, "Just because David has sent men with condolences for you, do you really believe he's showing respect for your father? Instead, hasn't David sent his emissaries in order to scout out, overthrow, and spy on the land?" ⁴So Hanun took David's emissaries, shaved them, cut their clothes in half at the hips, and sent them away.

⁵It was reported to David about his men, so he sent messengers to meet them, since the men were deeply

humiliated. The king said, "Stay in Jericho until your beards grow back; then return."

⁶When the Ammonites realized they had made themselves repulsive to David, Hanun and the Ammonites sent 38 tons of silver to hire chariots and horsemen from Aram-naharaim, Aram-maacah, and Zobah. ⁷They hired 32,000 chariots and the king of Maacah with his army, who came and camped near Medeba. The Ammonites also came together from their cities for the battle.

⁸David heard about this and sent Joab and the entire army of warriors. ⁹The Ammonites marched out and lined up in battle formation at the entrance of the city while the kings who had come were in the field by themselves. ¹⁰When Joab saw that there was a battle line in front of him and another behind him, he chose some men out of all the elite troops of Israel and lined up in battle formation to engage the Arameans. ¹¹He placed the rest of the forces under the command of his brother Abishai, and they lined up in battle formation to engage the Ammonites.

¹²"If the Arameans are too strong for me," Joab said, "then you'll be my help. However, if the Ammonites are too strong for you, I'll help you. ¹³Be strong! We must prove ourselves strong for our people and for the cities of our God. May the LORD's will be done."

¹⁴Joab and the people with him approached the Arameans for battle, and they fled before him. ¹⁵When the Ammonites saw that the Arameans had fled, they likewise fled before Joab's brother Abishai and entered the city. Then Joab went to Jerusalem.

¹⁶When the Arameans realized that they had been defeated by Israel, they sent messengers to summon the Arameans who were across the Euphrates. They were led by Shophach, the commander of Hadadezer's army.

¹⁷When this was reported to David, he gathered all Israel and crossed the Jordan. He came up to the Arameans and lined up in battle formation against them. When David lined up to engage them in battle, they fought against him. ¹⁸But the Arameans fled before Israel, and David killed 7,000 of their charioteers and 40,000 foot soldiers. He also killed Shophach, commander of the army. ¹⁹When Hadadezer's subjects saw that they had been defeated by Israel, they made peace with David and became his subjects. After this, the Arameans were never willing to help the Ammonites again.

20 In the spring when kings march out to war, Joab led the army and destroyed the Ammonites' land. He came to Rabbah and besieged it, but David remained in Jerusalem. Joab attacked Rabbah and demolished it. ²Then David took the crown from the head of their king, and it was placed on David's head. He found that the crown weighed 75 pounds of gold, and there was a precious stone in it. In addition, David took away a large quantity of plunder from the city. ³He brought out the people who were in it and put them to work with saws, iron picks, and axes. David did the same to all the Ammonite cities. Then he and all his troops returned to Jerusalem.

⁴After this, a war broke out with the Philistines at Gezer. At that time Sibbecai the Hushathite killed Sippai, a descendant of the giants, and the Philistines were subdued.

⁵Once again there was a battle with the Philistines, and Elhanan son of Jair killed Lahmi the brother of Goliath the Gittite. The shaft of his spear was like a weaver's beam.

⁶There was still another battle at Gath where there was a man of extraordinary stature with six fingers on each hand and six toes on each foot—24 in all. He, too, was descended from the giant. ⁷When he taunted Israel, Jonathan son of David's brother Shimei killed him. ⁸These were the descendants of the giant in Gath killed by David and his soldiers.

21 Satan stood up against Israel and incited David to count the people of Israel. ²So David said to Joab and the commanders of the troops, "Go and count Israel from Beer-sheba to Dan and bring a report to me so I can know their number."

³Joab replied, "May the LORD multiply the number of His people a hundred times over! My lord the king, aren't they all my lord's servants? Why does my lord want to do this? Why should he bring *guilt on Israel?"

⁴Yet the king's order prevailed over Joab. So Joab left and traveled throughout Israel and then returned to Jerusalem. ⁵Joab gave the total troop registration to David. In all Israel there were 1,100,000 swordsmen and in Judah itself 470,000 swordsmen. ⁶But he did not include Levi and Benjamin in the count because the king's command was detestable to him. ⁷This command was also evil in God's sight, so He afflicted Israel.

⁸David said to God, "I have sinned greatly because I have done this thing. Now, please take away Your servant's guilt, for I've been very foolish."

⁹Then the LORD instructed Gad, David's seer, ¹⁰"Go and say to David, 'This is what the LORD says: I am offering you three choices. Choose one of them for yourself, and I will do it to you.'"

¹¹So Gad went to David and said to him, "This is what the LORD says: 'Take your choice: ¹²three years of famine, or three months of devastation by your foes with the sword of your enemy overtaking you, or three days of the sword of the LORD—a plague on the land, the angel of the LORD bringing destruction to the whole territory of Israel.' Now decide what answer I should take back to the One who sent me."

¹³David answered Gad, "I'm in anguish. Please, let me fall into the LORD's hands because His mercies are very great, but don't let me fall into human hands."

¹⁴So the LORD sent a plague on Israel, and 70,000 Israelite men died. ¹⁵Then God sent an angel to Jerusalem to destroy it, but when the angel was about to destroy the city, the LORD looked, relented concerning the destruction, and said to the angel who was destroying the people, "Enough, withdraw your hand now!" The angel of the LORD was then standing at the threshing floor of Ornan the Jebusite.

¹⁶When David looked up and saw the angel of the LORD standing between earth and heaven, with his drawn sword in his hand stretched out over Jerusalem, David and the elders, clothed in *sackcloth, fell down with their faces to the ground. ¹⁷David said to God, "Wasn't I the one who gave the order to count the people? I am the one who has sinned and acted very wickedly. But these sheep, what have they done? My LORD God, please let Your hand be against me and against my father's family, but don't let the plague be against Your people."

¹⁸So the angel of the LORD ordered Gad to tell David to go and set up an altar to the LORD on the threshing floor of Ornan the Jebusite. ¹⁹David went up at Gad's command spoken in the name of the LORD.

²⁰Ornan was threshing wheat when he turned and saw the angel. His four sons, who were with him, hid themselves. ²¹David came to Ornan, and when Ornan looked and saw David, he left the threshing floor and bowed to David with his face to the ground.

²²Then David said to Ornan, "Give me this threshing-floor plot so that I may build an altar to the LORD on it. Give it to me for the full price, so the plague on the people may be stopped."

²³Ornan said to David, "Take it! My lord the king may do whatever he wants. See, I give the oxen for the ˙burnt offerings, the threshing sledges for the wood, and the wheat for the ˙grain offering—I give it all."

²⁴King David answered Ornan, "No, I insist on paying the full price, for I will not take for the LORD what belongs to you or offer burnt offerings that cost me nothing."

²⁵So David gave Ornan 15 pounds of gold for the plot. ²⁶He built an altar to the LORD there and offered burnt offerings and ˙fellowship offerings. He called on the LORD, and He answered him with fire from heaven on the altar of burnt offering.

²⁷Then the LORD spoke to the angel, and he put his sword back into its sheath. ²⁸At that time, David offered sacrifices there when he saw that the LORD answered him at the threshing floor of Ornan the Jebusite. ²⁹The tabernacle of the LORD, which Moses made in the desert, and the altar of burnt offering were at the ˙high place in Gibeon, ³⁰but David could not go before it to inquire of God, because he was terrified of the sword of the LORD's angel. ¹Then David said, "This is the house of the LORD God, and this is the altar of ˙burnt offering for Israel."

²So David gave orders to gather the foreigners that were in the land of Israel, and he appointed stonecutters to cut finished stones for building God's house. ³David supplied a great deal of iron to make the nails for the doors of the gateways and for the fittings, together with an immeasurable quantity of bronze, ⁴and innumerable cedar logs because the Sidonians and Tyrians had brought a large quantity of cedar logs to David. ⁵David said, "My son Solomon is young and inexperienced, and the house that is to be built for the LORD must be exceedingly great and famous and glorious in all the lands. Therefore, I must make provision for it." So David made lavish preparations for it before his death.

⁶Then he summoned his son Solomon and instructed him to build a house for the LORD God of Israel. ⁷"My son," David said to Solomon, "It was in my heart to build a house for the name of ˙Yahweh my God, ⁸but the word of the LORD came to me: 'You have shed much blood and waged great wars. You are not to build a house for My name because you have shed so much blood on the ground before Me. ⁹But a son will be born to you; he will be a man of rest. I will give him rest from all his surrounding enemies, for his name will be Solomon, and I will give peace and quiet to Israel during his reign. ¹⁰He is the one who will build a house for My name. He will be My son, and I will be his father. I will establish the throne of his kingdom over Israel forever.'

¹¹"Now, my son, may the LORD be with you, and may you succeed in building the house of the LORD your God, as He said about you. ¹²Above all, may the LORD give you insight and understanding when He puts you in charge of Israel so that you may keep the law of the LORD your God. ¹³Then you will succeed if you carefully follow the statutes and ordinances the LORD commanded Moses for Israel. Be strong and courageous. Don't be afraid or discouraged.

¹⁴"Notice I have taken great pains to provide for the house of the LORD—3,775 tons of gold, 37,750 tons of silver, and bronze and iron that can't be weighed because there is so much of it. I have also provided timber and stone, but you will need to add more to them. ¹⁵You also have many workers: stonecutters, masons, carpenters, and people skilled in every kind of work ¹⁶in gold, silver, bronze, and iron—beyond number. Now begin the work, and may the LORD be with you."

¹⁷Then David ordered all the leaders of Israel to help his son Solomon: ¹⁸"The LORD your God is with you, isn't He? And hasn't He given you rest on every side? For He has handed the land's inhabitants over to me, and the land has been subdued before the LORD and His people. ¹⁹Now determine in your mind and heart to seek the LORD your God. Get started building the LORD God's sanctuary so that you may bring the ark of the LORD's covenant and the holy articles of God to the temple that is to be built for the name of Yahweh."

23 When David was old and full of days, he installed his son Solomon as king over Israel. ²Then he gathered all the leaders of Israel, the priests, and the Levites. ³The Levites 30 years old or more were counted; the total number of men was 38,000 by headcount. ⁴"Of these," David said, "24,000 are to be in charge of the work on the LORD's temple, 6,000 are to be officers and judges, ⁵4,000 are to be gatekeepers, and 4,000 are to praise the LORD with the instruments that I have made for worship."

⁶Then David divided them into divisions according to Levi's sons: Gershom, Kohath, and Merari.

⁷The Gershonites: Ladan and Shimei.

⁸Ladan's sons: Jehiel was the first, then Zetham, and Joel—three.

⁹Shimei's sons: Shelomoth, Haziel, and Haran—three. Those were the heads of the families of Ladan.

¹⁰Shimei's sons: Jahath, Zizah, Jeush, and Beriah. Those were Shimei's sons—four.

¹¹ Jahath was the first and Zizah was the second; however, Jeush and Beriah did not have many sons, so they became an ancestral house and received a single assignment.

¹²Kohath's sons: Amram, Izhar, Hebron, and Uzziel—four.

¹³Amram's sons: Aaron and Moses.

Aaron, along with his descendants, was set apart forever to consecrate the most holy things, to burn incense in the presence of ˙Yahweh, to minister to Him, and to pronounce blessings in His name forever. ¹⁴As for Moses the man of God, his sons were named among the tribe of Levi.

¹⁵Moses' sons: Gershom and Eliezer.

¹⁶Gershom's sons: Shebuel was first.

¹⁷Eliezer's sons were Rehabiah, first; Eliezer did not have any other sons, but Rehabiah's sons were very numerous.

¹⁸Izhar's sons: Shelomith was first.

¹⁹Hebron's sons: Jeriah was first, Amariah second, Jahaziel third, and Jekameam fourth.

²⁰Uzziel's sons: Micah was first, and Isshiah second.

²¹Merari's sons: Mahli and Mushi.

Mahli's sons: Eleazar and Kish.
²² Eleazar died having no sons, only daughters. Their cousins, the sons of Kish, married them. ²³ Mushi's sons: Mahli, Eder, and Jeremoth— three.

²⁴ These were the sons of Levi by their ancestral houses—the heads of families, according to their registration by name in the headcount—20 years old or more, who worked in the service of the Lord's temple. ²⁵ For David said, "The Lord God of Israel has given rest to His people, and He has come to stay in Jerusalem forever. ²⁶ Also, the Levites no longer need to carry the tabernacle or any of the equipment for its service"— ²⁷ for according to the last words of David, the Levites 20 years old or more were to be counted— ²⁸ "but their duty will be to assist the sons of Aaron with the service of the Lord's temple, being responsible for the courts and the chambers, the purification of all the holy things, and the work of the service of God's temple— ²⁹ as well as the rows of the *bread of the Presence, the fine flour for the *grain offering, the wafers of unleavened bread, the baking, the mixing, and all measurements of volume and length. ³⁰ They are also to stand every morning to give thanks and praise to the Lord, and likewise in the evening. ³¹ Whenever *burnt offerings are offered to the Lord on the Sabbaths, New Moons, and appointed festivals, they are to do so regularly in the Lord's presence according to the number prescribed for them. ³² They are to carry out their responsibilities for the tent of meeting, for the holy place, and for their relatives, the sons of Aaron, in the service of the Lord's temple."

24 The divisions of the descendants of Aaron were as follows: Aaron's sons were Nadab, Abihu, Eleazar, and Ithamar. ² But Nadab and Abihu died before their father, and they had no sons, so Eleazar and Ithamar served as priests. ³ Together with Zadok from the sons of Eleazar and Ahimelech from the sons of Ithamar, David divided them according to the assigned duties of their service. ⁴ Since more leaders were found among Eleazar's descendants than Ithamar's, they were divided accordingly: 16 heads of ancestral houses were from Eleazar's descendants, and eight heads of ancestral houses were from Ithamar's. ⁵ They were assigned by lot, for there were officers of the sanctuary and officers of God among both Eleazar's and Ithamar's descendants.

⁶ The secretary, Shemaiah son of Nethanel, a Levite, recorded them in the presence of the king and the officers, Zadok the priest, Ahimelech son of Abiathar, and the heads of families of the priests and the Levites. One ancestral house was taken for Eleazar, and then one for Ithamar.

⁷ The first lot fell to Jehoiarib, the second
    to Jedaiah,
⁸ the third to Harim, the fourth to Seorim,
⁹ the fifth to Malchijah, the sixth to Mijamin,
¹⁰ the seventh to Hakkoz, the eighth to Abijah,
¹¹ the ninth to Jeshua, the tenth to Shecaniah,
¹² the eleventh to Eliashib, the twelfth to Jakim,
¹³ the thirteenth to Huppah, the fourteenth
    to Jeshebeab,
¹⁴ the fifteenth to Bilgah, the sixteenth
    to Immer,
¹⁵ the seventeenth to Hezir, the eighteenth
    to Happizzez,

¹⁶ the nineteenth to Pethahiah, the twentieth
    to Jehezkel,
¹⁷ the twenty-first to Jachin, the twenty-second
    to Gamul,
¹⁸ the twenty-third to Delaiah,
    and the twenty-fourth to Maaziah.
¹⁹ These had their assigned duties for service when they entered the Lord's temple, according to their regulations, which they received from their ancestor Aaron, as the Lord God of Israel had commanded him.
²⁰ As for the rest of Levi's sons:
    from Amram's sons: Shubael;
    from Shubael's sons: Jehdeiah.
²¹ From Rehabiah:
    from Rehabiah's sons: Isshiah was the first.
²² From the Izharites: Shelomoth;
    from Shelomoth's sons: Jahath.
²³ Hebron's sons:
    Jeriah the first, Amariah the second,
    Jahaziel the third, and Jekameam the fourth.
²⁴ From Uzziel's sons: Micah;
    from Micah's sons: Shamir.
²⁵ Micah's brother: Isshiah;
    from Isshiah's sons: Zechariah.
²⁶ Merari's sons: Mahli and Mushi,
    and from his sons, Jaaziah his son.
²⁷ Merari's sons, by his son Jaaziah:
    Shoham, Zaccur, and Ibri.
²⁸ From Mahli: Eleazar, who had no sons.
²⁹ From Kish, from Kish's sons: Jerahmeel.
³⁰ Mushi's sons: Mahli, Eder, and Jerimoth.
Those were the sons of the Levites according to their ancestral houses. ³¹ They also cast lots the same way as their relatives the sons of Aaron did in the presence of King David, Zadok, Ahimelech, and the heads of the families of the priests and Levites—the family heads and their younger brothers alike.

25 David and the officers of the army also set apart some of the sons of *Asaph, Heman, and Jeduthun, who were to prophesy accompanied by lyres, harps, and cymbals. This is the list of the men who performed their service:

² From Asaph's sons:
    Zaccur, Joseph, Nethaniah, and Asarelah,
    sons of Asaph, under Asaph's authority, who
    prophesied under the authority of the king.
³ From Jeduthun: Jeduthun's sons:
    Gedaliah, Zeri, Jeshaiah, Shimei, Hashabiah,
    and Mattithiah—six—under the authority
    of their father Jeduthun, prophesying to the
    accompaniment of lyres, giving thanks and
    praise to the Lord.
⁴ From Heman: Heman's sons:
    Bukkiah, Mattaniah, Uzziel, Shebuel,
    Jerimoth, Hananiah, Hanani, Eliathah,
    Giddalti, Romamti-ezer, Joshbekashah,
    Mallothi, Hothir, and Mahazioth. ⁵ All these
    sons of Heman, the king's seer, were given
    by the promises of God to exalt him, for God
    had given Heman fourteen sons and three
    daughters.

⁶ All these men were under their own fathers' authority for the music in the Lord's temple, with cymbals, harps, and lyres for the service of God's temple. Asaph, Jeduthun, and Heman were under the king's authority. ⁷ They numbered 288 together with their relatives who were all trained and skillful in music for

the LORD. [8]They cast lots for their duties, young and old alike, teacher as well as pupil.

[9] The first lot for Asaph fell to Joseph, his sons, and his brothers— 12

to Gedaliah the second: him, his brothers, and his sons— 12

[10] the third to Zaccur, his sons, and his brothers— 12

[11] the fourth to Izri, his sons, and his brothers— 12

[12] the fifth to Nethaniah, his sons, and his brothers— 12

[13] the sixth to Bukkiah, his sons, and his brothers— 12

[14] the seventh to Jesarelah, his sons, and his brothers— 12

[15] the eighth to Jeshaiah, his sons, and his brothers— 12

[16] the ninth to Mattaniah, his sons, and his brothers— 12

[17] the tenth to Shimei, his sons, and his brothers— 12

[18] the eleventh to Azarel, his sons, and his brothers— 12

[19] the twelfth to Hashabiah, his sons, and his brothers— 12

[20] the thirteenth to Shubael, his sons, and his brothers— 12

[21] the fourteenth to Mattithiah, his sons, and his brothers— 12

[22] the fifteenth to Jeremoth, his sons, and his brothers— 12

[23] the sixteenth to Hananiah, his sons, and his brothers— 12

[24] the seventeenth to Joshbekashah, his sons, and his brothers— 12

[25] the eighteenth to Hanani, his sons, and his brothers— 12

[26] the nineteenth to Mallothi, his sons, and his brothers— 12

[27] the twentieth to Eliathah, his sons, and his brothers— 12

[28] the twenty-first to Hothir, his sons, and his brothers— 12

[29] the twenty-second to Giddalti, his sons, and his brothers— 12

[30] the twenty-third to Mahazioth, his sons, and his brothers— 12

[31] and the twenty-fourth to Romamti-ezer, his sons, and his brothers— 12.

26 The following were the divisions of the gatekeepers:

From the Korahites: Meshelemiah son of Kore, one of the sons of *Asaph. [2]Meshelemiah had sons:

Zechariah the firstborn, Jediael the second, Zebadiah the third, Jathniel the fourth, [3]Elam the fifth, Jehohanan the sixth, and Eliehoenai the seventh.

[4]Obed-edom also had sons: Shemaiah the firstborn, Jehozabad the second, Joah the third, Sachar the fourth, Nethanel the fifth, [5]Ammiel the sixth, Issachar the seventh, and Peullethai the eighth,

for God blessed him.

[6]Also, to his son Shemaiah were born sons who ruled over their ancestral houses because they were strong, capable men. [7]Shemaiah's sons: Othni, Rephael, Obed, and Elzabad; his brothers Elihu and Semachiah were also capable men. [8]All of these were among the sons of Obed-edom with their sons and brothers; they were capable men with strength for the work—62 from Obed-edom. [9]Meshelemiah also had sons and brothers who were capable men—18.

[10]Hosah, from the Merarites, also had sons: Shimri the first (although he was not the firstborn, his father had appointed him as the first), [11]Hilkiah the second, Tebaliah the third, and Zechariah the fourth. The sons and brothers of Hosah were 13 in all.

[12]These divisions of the gatekeepers, under their leading men, had duties for ministering in the LORD's temple, just as their brothers did. [13]They cast lots for each gate according to their ancestral houses, young and old alike.

[14]The lot for the east gate fell to Shelemiah. They also cast lots for his son Zechariah, an insightful counselor, and his lot came out for the north gate. [15]Obed-edom's was the south gate, and his sons' lot was for the storehouses; [16]it was the west gate and the gate of Shallecheth on the ascending highway for Shuppim and Hosah.

There were guards stationed at every watch. [17]There were six Levites each day on the east, four each day on the north, four each day on the south, and two pair at the storehouses. [18]As for the court on the west, there were four at the highway and two at the court. [19]Those were the divisions of the gatekeepers from the sons of the Korahites and Merarites.

[20]From the Levites, Ahijah was in charge of the treasuries of God's temple and the treasuries of what had been dedicated. [21]From the sons of Ladan, who were the sons of the Gershonites through Ladan and were the heads of families belonging to Ladan the Gershonite: Jehieli. [22]The sons of Jehieli, Zetham and his brother Joel, were in charge of the treasuries of the LORD's temple.

[23]From the Amramites, the Izharites, the Hebronites, and the Uzzielites: [24]Shebuel, a descendant of Moses' son Gershom, was the officer in charge of the treasuries. [25]His relative through Eliezer: his son Rehabiah, his son Jeshaiah, his son Joram, his son Zichri, and his son Shelomith. [26]This Shelomith and his brothers were in charge of all the treasuries of what had been dedicated by King David, by the heads of families who were the commanders of thousands and of hundreds, and by the army commanders. [27]They dedicated part of the plunder from their battles for the repair of the LORD's temple. [28]All that Samuel the seer, Saul son of Kish, Abner son of Ner, and Joab son of Zeruiah had dedicated, along with everything else that had been dedicated, were in the care of Shelomith and his brothers.

[29]From the Izrahites: Chenaniah and his sons had the outside duties as officers and judges over Israel. [30]From the Hebronites: Hashabiah and his relatives, 1,700 capable men, had assigned duties in Israel west of the Jordan for all the work of the LORD and for the service of the king. [31]From the Hebronites: Jerijah was the head of the Hebronites, according to the

genealogical records of his ancestors. A search was made in the fortieth year of David's reign and strong, capable men were found among them at Jazer in Gilead. ³²There were among Jerijah's relatives, 2,700 capable men who were heads of families. King David appointed them over the Reubenites, the Gadites, and half the tribe of Manasseh as overseers in every matter relating to God and the king.

27 This is the list of the Israelites, the heads of families, the commanders of thousands and the commanders of hundreds, and their officers who served the king in every matter to do with the divisions that were on rotated military duty each month throughout the year. There were 24,000 in each division:

²Jashobeam son of Zabdiel was in charge of the first division, for the first month; 24,000 were in his division. ³He was a descendant of Perez and chief of all the army commanders for the first month.

⁴Dodai the Ahohite was in charge of the division for the second month, and Mikloth was the leader; 24,000 were in his division. ⁵The third army commander, as chief for the third month, was Benaiah son of Jehoiada the priest; 24,000 were in his division. ⁶This Benaiah was a mighty man among the Thirty and over the Thirty, and his son Ammizabad was in charge of his division.

⁷The fourth commander, for the fourth month, was Joab's brother Asahel, and his son Zebadiah was commander after him; 24,000 were in his division.

⁸The fifth, for the fifth month, was the commander Shamhuth the Izrahite; 24,000 were in his division.

⁹The sixth, for the sixth month, was Ira son of Ikkesh the Tekoite; 24,000 were in his division.

¹⁰The seventh, for the seventh month, was Helez the Pelonite from the sons of Ephraim; 24,000 were in his division.

¹¹The eighth, for the eighth month, was Sibbecai the Hushathite, a Zerahite; 24,000 were in his division.

¹²The ninth, for the ninth month, was Abiezer the Anathothite, a Benjaminite; 24,000 were in his division.

¹³The tenth, for the tenth month, was Maharai the Netophathite, a Zerahite; 24,000 were in his division.

¹⁴The eleventh, for the eleventh month, was Benaiah the Pirathonite from the sons of Ephraim; 24,000 were in his division.

¹⁵The twelfth, for the twelfth month, was Heldai the Netophathite, of Othniel's family; 24,000 were in his division.

¹⁶The following were in charge of the tribes of Israel:

For the Reubenites, Eliezer son of Zichri was the chief official;

for the Simeonites, Shephatiah son of Maacah;

¹⁷for the Levites, Hashabiah son of Kemuel; for Aaron, Zadok;

¹⁸for Judah, Elihu, one of David's brothers; for Issachar, Omri son of Michael;

¹⁹for Zebulun, Ishmaiah son of Obadiah;

for Naphtali, Jerimoth son of Azriel;

²⁰for the Ephraimites, Hoshea son of Azaziah;

for half the tribe of Manasseh, Joel son of Pedaiah;

²¹for half the tribe of Manasseh in Gilead, Iddo son of Zechariah;

for Benjamin, Jaasiel son of Abner;

²²for Dan, Azarel son of Jeroham.

Those were the leaders of the tribes of Israel.

²³David didn't count the men aged 20 or under, for the LORD had said He would make Israel as numerous as the stars of heaven. ²⁴Joab son of Zeruiah began to count them, but he didn't complete it. There was wrath against Israel because of this census, and the number was not entered in the Historical Record of King David.

²⁵Azmaveth son of Adiel was in charge of the king's storehouses.

Jonathan son of Uzziah was in charge of the storehouses in the country, in the cities, in the villages, and in the fortresses.

²⁶Ezri son of Chelub was in charge of those who worked in the fields tilling the soil.

²⁷Shimei the Ramathite was in charge of the vineyards.

Zabdi the Shiphmite was in charge of the produce of the vineyards for the wine cellars.

²⁸Baal-hanan the Gederite was in charge of the olive and sycamore trees in the Judean foothills.

Joash was in charge of the stores of olive oil.

²⁹Shitrai the Sharonite was in charge of the herds that grazed in Sharon, while Shaphat son of Adlai was in charge of the herds in the valleys.

³⁰Obil the Ishmaelite was in charge of the camels.

Jehdeiah the Meronothite was in charge of the donkeys.

³¹Jaziz the Hagrite was in charge of the flocks.

All these were officials in charge of King David's property.

³²David's uncle Jonathan was a counselor; he was a man of understanding and a scribe. Jehiel son of Hachmoni attended the king's sons. ³³Ahithophel was the king's counselor. Hushai the Archite was the king's friend. ³⁴After Ahithophel came Jehoiada son of Benaiah, then Abiathar. Joab was the commander of the king's army.

28 David assembled all the leaders of Israel in Jerusalem: the leaders of the tribes, the leaders of the divisions in the king's service, the commanders of thousands and the commanders of hundreds, and the officials in charge of all the property and cattle of the king and his sons, along with the court officials, the fighting men, and all the brave warriors. ²Then King David rose to his feet and said, "Listen to me, my brothers and my people. It was in my heart to build a house as a resting place for the ark of the LORD's covenant and as a footstool for our God. I had made preparations to build, ³but God said to me, 'You are not to build a house for My name because you are a man of war and have shed blood.'

⁴"Yet the LORD God of Israel chose me out of all my father's household to be king over Israel forever. For He chose Judah as leader, and from the house of Ju-

dah, my father's household, and from my father's sons, He was pleased to make me king over all Israel. [5]And out of all my sons—for the LORD has given me many sons—He has chosen my son Solomon to sit on the throne of the LORD's kingdom over Israel. [6]He said to me, 'Your son Solomon is the one who is to build My house and My courts, for I have chosen him to be My son, and I will be his father. [7]I will establish his kingdom forever if he perseveres in keeping My commands and My ordinances as he is today.'

[8]"So now in the sight of all Israel, the assembly of the LORD, and in the hearing of our God, observe and follow all the commands of the LORD your God so that you may possess this good land and leave it as an inheritance to your descendants forever.

[9]"As for you, Solomon my son, know the God of your father, and serve Him with a whole heart and a willing mind, for the LORD searches every heart and understands the intention of every thought. If you seek Him, He will be found by you, but if you forsake Him, He will reject you forever. [10]Realize now that the LORD has chosen you to build a house for the sanctuary. Be strong, and do it."

[11]Then David gave his son Solomon the plans for the portico of the temple and its buildings, treasuries, upper rooms, inner rooms, and a room for the *mercy seat. [12]The plans contained everything he had in mind for the courts of the LORD's house, all the surrounding chambers, the treasuries of God's house, and the treasuries for what is dedicated. [13]Also included were plans for the divisions of the priests and the Levites; all the work of service in the LORD's house; all the articles of service of the LORD's house; [14]the weight of gold for all the articles for every kind of service; the weight of all the silver articles for every kind of service; [15]the weight of the gold lampstands and their gold lamps, including the weight of each lampstand and its lamps; the weight of each silver lampstand and its lamps, according to the service of each lampstand; [16]the weight of gold for each table for the rows of the *bread of the Presence and the silver for the silver tables; [17]the pure gold for the forks, sprinkling basins, and pitchers; the weight of each gold dish; the weight of each silver bowl; [18]the weight of refined gold for the altar of incense; and the plans for the chariot of the gold *cherubim that spread out their wings and cover the ark of the LORD's covenant.

[19]David concluded, "By the LORD's hand on me, He enabled me to understand everything in writing, all the details of the plan."

[20]Then David said to his son Solomon, "Be strong and courageous, and do the work. Don't be afraid or discouraged, for the LORD God, my God, is with you. He won't leave you or forsake you until all the work for the service of the LORD's house is finished. [21]Here are the divisions of the priests and the Levites for all the service of God's house. Every willing man of any skill will be at your disposal for the work, and the leaders and all the people are at your every command."

29 Then King David said to all the assembly, "My son Solomon—God has chosen him alone—is young and inexperienced. The task is great because the temple will not be for man but for the LORD God. [2]So to the best of my ability I've made provision for the house of my God: gold for the gold articles, silver for the silver, bronze for the bronze, iron for the iron, and wood for the wood, as well as onyx, stones for mounting, an-

timony, stones of various colors, all kinds of precious stones, and a great quantity of marble. [3]Moreover, because of my delight in the house of my God, I now give my personal treasures of gold and silver for the house of my God over and above all that I've provided for the holy house: [4]100 tons of gold (gold of Ophir) and 250 tons of refined silver for overlaying the walls of the buildings, [5]the gold for the gold work and the silver for the silver, for all the work to be done by the craftsmen. Now who will volunteer to consecrate himself to the LORD today?"

[6]Then the leaders of the households, the leaders of the tribes of Israel, the commanders of thousands and of hundreds, and the officials in charge of the king's work gave willingly. [7]For the service of God's house they gave 185 tons of gold and 10,000 gold coins, 375 tons of silver, 675 tons of bronze, and 4,000 tons of iron. [8]Whoever had precious stones gave them to the treasury of the LORD's house under the care of Jehiel the Gershonite. [9]Then the people rejoiced because of their leaders' willingness to give, for they had given to the LORD with a whole heart. King David also rejoiced greatly.

[10]Then David praised the LORD in the sight of all the assembly. David said,

May You be praised, LORD God of our father Israel, from eternity to eternity. [11]Yours, LORD, is the greatness and the power and the glory and the splendor and the majesty, for everything in the heavens and on earth belongs to You. Yours, LORD, is the kingdom, and You are exalted as head over all. [12]Riches and honor come from You, and You are the ruler of everything. Power and might are in Your hand, and it is in Your hand to make great and to give strength to all. [13]Now therefore, our God, we give You thanks and praise Your glorious name.

[14]But who am I, and who are my people, that we should be able to give as generously as this? For everything comes from You, and we have given You only what comes from Your own hand. [15]For we live before You as foreigners and temporary residents in Your presence as were all our ancestors. Our days on earth are like a shadow, without hope. [16]*Yahweh our God, all this wealth that we've provided for building You a house for Your holy name comes from Your hand; everything belongs to You. [17]I know, my God, that You test the heart and that You are pleased with what is right. I have willingly given all these things with an upright heart, and now I have seen Your people who are present here giving joyfully and willingly to You. [18]LORD God of Abraham, Isaac, and Israel, our ancestors, keep this desire forever in the thoughts of the hearts of Your people, and confirm their hearts toward You. [19]Give my son Solomon a whole heart to keep and to carry out all Your commands, Your decrees, and Your statutes, and to build the temple for which I have made provision.

[20]Then David said to the whole assembly, "Praise the LORD your God." So the whole assembly praised the LORD God of their ancestors. They bowed down and paid homage to the LORD and the king.

[21]The following day they offered sacrifices to the LORD and *burnt offerings to the LORD: 1,000 bulls, 1,000 rams, and 1,000 lambs, along with their *drink offerings, and

sacrifices in abundance for all Israel. ²²They ate and drank with great joy in the Lord's presence that day.

Then, for a second time, they made David's son Solomon king; they anointed him as the Lord's ruler, and Zadok as the priest. ²³Solomon sat on the Lord's throne as king in place of his father David. He prospered, and all Israel obeyed him. ²⁴All the leaders and the mighty men, and all of King David's sons as well, pledged their allegiance to King Solomon. ²⁵The Lord highly exalted Solomon in the sight of all Israel and bestowed on him such royal majesty as had not been bestowed on any king over Israel before him.

²⁶David son of Jesse was king over all Israel. ²⁷The length of his reign over Israel was 40 years; he reigned in Hebron for seven years and in Jerusalem for 33. ²⁸He died at a ripe old age, full of days, riches, and honor, and his son Solomon became king in his place. ²⁹As for the events of King David's reign, from beginning to end, note that they are written in the Events of Samuel the Seer, the Events of Nathan the Prophet, and the Events of Gad the Seer, ³⁰along with all his reign, his might, and the incidents that affected him and Israel and all the kingdoms of the surrounding lands.

2 CHRONICLES

1 Solomon son of David strengthened his hold on his kingdom. The Lord his God was with him and highly exalted him. ²Then Solomon spoke to all Israel, to the commanders of thousands and of hundreds, to the judges, and to every leader in all Israel—the heads of the families. ³Solomon and the whole assembly with him went to the ˚high place that was in Gibeon because God's tent of meeting, which the Lord's servant Moses had made in the wilderness, was there. ⁴Now David had brought the ark of God from Kiriath-jearim to the place he had set up for it, because he had pitched a tent for it in Jerusalem, ⁵but he put the bronze altar, which Bezalel son of Uri, son of Hur, had made, in front of the Lord's tabernacle. Solomon and the assembly inquired of Him there. ⁶Solomon offered sacrifices there in the Lord's presence on the bronze altar at the tent of meeting; he offered 1,000 ˚burnt offerings on it.

⁷That night God appeared to Solomon and said to him: "Ask. What should I give you?"

⁸And Solomon said to God: "You have shown great and faithful love to my father David, and You have made me king in his place. ⁹Lord God, let Your promise to my father David now come true. For You have made me king over a people as numerous as the dust of the earth. ¹⁰Now grant me wisdom and knowledge so that I may lead these people, for who can judge this great people of Yours?"

¹¹God said to Solomon, "Since this was in your heart, and you have not requested riches, wealth, or glory, or for the life of those who hate you, and you have not even requested long life, but you have requested for yourself wisdom and knowledge that you may judge My people over whom I have made you king, ¹²wisdom and knowledge are given to you. I will also give you riches, wealth, and ˚glory, unlike what was given to the kings who were before you, or will be given to those after you." ¹³So Solomon went to Jerusalem from the high place that was in Gibeon in front of the tent of meeting, and he reigned over Israel.

¹⁴Solomon accumulated 1,400 chariots and 12,000 horsemen, which he stationed in the chariot cities and with the king in Jerusalem. ¹⁵The king made silver and gold as common in Jerusalem as stones, and he made cedar as abundant as sycamore in the Judean foothills. ¹⁶Solomon's horses came from Egypt and Kue. The king's traders would get them from Kue at the going price. ¹⁷A chariot could be imported from Egypt for 15 pounds of silver and a horse for about four pounds. In the same way, they exported them to all the kings of the Hittites and to the kings of Aram through their agents.

2 Solomon decided to build a temple for the name of ˚Yahweh and a royal palace for himself, ²so he assigned 70,000 men as porters, 80,000 men as stonecutters in the mountains, and 3,600 as supervisors over them.

³Then Solomon sent word to King Hiram of Tyre: Do for me what you did for my father David. You sent him cedars to build him a house to live in. ⁴Now I am building a temple for the name of Yahweh my God in order to dedicate it to Him for burning fragrant incense before Him, for displaying the rows of the ˚bread of the Presence continuously, and for sacrificing ˚burnt offerings for the morning and the evening, the Sabbaths and the New Moons, and the appointed festivals of the Lord our God. This is ordained for Israel forever. ⁵The temple that I am building will be great, for our God is greater than any of the gods. ⁶But who is able to build a temple for Him, since even heaven and the highest heaven cannot contain Him? Who am I then that I should build a temple for Him except as a place to burn incense before Him? ⁷Therefore, send me a craftsman who is skilled in engraving to work with gold, silver, bronze, and iron, and with purple, crimson, and blue yarn. He will work with the craftsmen who are with me in Judah and Jerusalem, appointed by my father David. ⁸Also, send me cedar, cypress, and algum logs from Lebanon, for I know that your servants know how to cut the trees of Lebanon. Note that my servants will be with your servants ⁹to prepare logs for me in abundance because the temple I am building will be great and wonderful. ¹⁰I will give your servants, the woodcutters who cut the trees, 100,000 bushels of wheat flour, 100,000 bushels of barley, 110,000 gallons of wine, and 110,000 gallons of oil.

¹¹Then King Hiram of Tyre wrote a letter and sent it to Solomon:
Because the Lord loves His people, He set you over them as king.

¹²Hiram also said:
May the Lord God of Israel, who made the heavens and the earth, be praised! He gave King David a wise son with insight and understanding, who will build a temple for the Lord and a royal

palace for himself. [13]I have now sent Huram-abi, a skillful man who has understanding. [14]He is the son of a woman from the daughters of Dan. His father is a man of Tyre. He knows how to work with gold, silver, bronze, iron, stone, and wood, with purple, blue, crimson yarn, and fine linen. He knows how to do all kinds of engraving and to execute any design that may be given him. I have sent him to be with your craftsmen and the craftsmen of my lord, your father David. [15]Now, let my lord send the wheat, barley, oil, and wine to his servants as promised. [16]We will cut logs from Lebanon, as many as you need, and bring them to you as rafts by sea to Joppa. You can then take them up to Jerusalem.

[17]Solomon took a census of all the foreign men in the land of Israel, after the census that his father David had conducted, and the total was 153,600. [18]Solomon made 70,000 of them porters, 80,000 stonecutters in the mountains, and 3,600 supervisors to make the people work.

3 Then Solomon began to build the LORD's temple in Jerusalem on Mount Moriah where the LORD had appeared to his father David, at the site David had prepared on the threshing floor of Ornan the Jebusite. [2]He began to build on the second day of the second month in the fourth year of his reign. [3]These are Solomon's foundations for building God's temple: the length was 90 feet, and the width 30 feet. [4]The portico, which was across the front extending across the width of the temple, was 30 feet wide; its height was 30 feet; he overlaid its inner surface with pure gold. [5]The larger room he paneled with cypress wood, overlaid with fine gold, and decorated with palm trees and chains. [6]He adorned the temple with precious stones for beauty, and the gold was the gold of Parvaim. [7]He overlaid the temple—the beams, the thresholds, its walls and doors—with gold, and he carved *cherubim on the walls.

[8]Then he made the most holy place; its length corresponded to the width of the temple, 30 feet, and its width was 30 feet. He overlaid it with 45,000 pounds of fine gold. [9]The weight of the nails was 20 ounces of gold, and he overlaid the ceiling with gold.

[10]He made two cherubim of sculptured work, for the most holy place, and he overlaid them with gold. [11]The overall length of the wings of the cherubim was 30 feet: the wing of one was 7$\frac{1}{2}$ feet, touching the wall of the room; its other wing was 7$\frac{1}{2}$ feet, touching the wing of the other cherub. [12]The wing of the other cherub was 7$\frac{1}{2}$ feet, touching the wall of the room; its other wing was 7$\frac{1}{2}$ feet, reaching the wing of the other cherub. [13]The wingspan of these cherubim was 30 feet. They stood on their feet and faced the larger room.

[14]He made the veil of blue, purple, and crimson yarn and fine linen, and he wove cherubim into it.

[15]In front of the temple he made two pillars, each 27 feet high. The capital on top of each was 7$\frac{1}{2}$ feet high. [16]He had made chainwork in the inner sanctuary and also put it on top of the pillars. He made 100 pomegranates and fastened them into the chainwork. [17]Then he set up the pillars in front of the sanctuary, one on the right and one on the left. He named the one on the right Jachin and the one on the left Boaz.

4 He made a bronze altar 30 feet long, 30 feet wide, and 15 feet high.

[2]Then he made the cast metal reservoir, 15 feet from brim to brim, perfectly round. It was 7$\frac{1}{2}$ feet high and 45 feet in circumference. [3]The likeness of oxen was below it, completely encircling it, 10 every half yard, completely surrounding the reservoir. The oxen were cast in two rows when the reservoir was cast. [4]It stood on 12 oxen, three facing north, three facing west, three facing south, and three facing east. The reservoir was on top of them and all their hindquarters were toward the center. [5]The reservoir was three inches thick, and its rim was fashioned like the brim of a cup or a lily blossom. It could hold 11,000 gallons.

[6]He made 10 basins for washing and he put five on the right and five on the left. The parts of the *burnt offering were rinsed in them, but the reservoir was used by the priests for washing.

[7]He made the 10 gold lampstands according to their specifications and put them in the sanctuary, five on the right and five on the left. [8]He made 10 tables and placed them in the sanctuary, five on the right and five on the left. He also made 100 gold bowls.

[9]He made the courtyard of the priests and the large court, and doors for the court. He overlaid the doors with bronze. [10]He put the reservoir on the right side, toward the southeast. [11]Then Huram made the pots, the shovels, and the bowls.

So Huram finished doing the work that he was doing for King Solomon in God's temple: [12]two pillars; the bowls and the capitals on top of the two pillars; the two gratings for covering both bowls of the capitals that were on top of the pillars; [13]the 400 pomegranates for the two gratings (two rows of pomegranates for each grating covering both capitals' bowls on top of the pillars). [14]He also made the water carts and the basins on the water carts. [15]The one reservoir and the 12 oxen underneath it, [16]the pots, the shovels, the forks, and all their utensils—Huram-abi made them for King Solomon for the LORD's temple. All these were made of polished bronze. [17]The king had them cast in clay molds in the Jordan Valley between Succoth and Zeredah. [18]Solomon made all these utensils in such great abundance that the weight of the bronze was not determined.

[19]Solomon also made all the equipment in God's temple: the gold altar; the tables on which to put the *bread of the Presence; [20]the lampstands and their lamps of pure gold to burn in front of the inner sanctuary according to specifications; [21]the flowers, lamps, and gold tongs—of purest gold; [22]the wick trimmers, sprinkling basins, ladles, and firepans—of purest gold; and the entryway to the temple, its inner doors to the most holy place, and the doors of the temple sanctuary—of gold.

5 So all the work Solomon did for the LORD's temple was completed. Then Solomon brought the consecrated things of his father David—the silver, the gold, and all the utensils—and put them in the treasuries of God's temple.

[2]At that time Solomon assembled at Jerusalem the elders of Israel—all the tribal heads, the ancestral chiefs of the Israelites—in order to bring the ark of the covenant of the LORD up from the city of David, that is, *Zion. [3]So all the men of Israel were assembled in the king's presence at the festival; this was in the seventh month.

[4]All the elders of Israel came, and the Levites picked up the ark. [5]They brought up the ark, the tent of meeting, and the holy utensils that were in the tent. The

priests and the Levites brought them up. ⁶King Solomon and the entire congregation of Israel who had gathered around him were in front of the ark sacrificing sheep and cattle that could not be counted or numbered because there were so many. ⁷The priests brought the ark of the LORD's covenant to its place, into the inner sanctuary of the temple, to the most holy place, beneath the wings of the •cherubim. ⁸And the cherubim spread their wings over the place of the ark so that the cherubim formed a cover above the ark and its poles. ⁹The poles were so long that their ends were seen from the holy place in front of the inner sanctuary, but they were not seen from outside; they are there to this very day. ¹⁰Nothing was in the ark except the two tablets that Moses had put in it at Horeb, where the LORD had made a covenant with the Israelites when they came out of Egypt.

¹¹Now all the priests who were present had consecrated themselves regardless of their divisions. When the priests came out of the holy place, ¹²the Levitical singers dressed in fine linen and carrying cymbals, harps, and lyres were standing east of the altar, and with them were 120 priests blowing trumpets. The Levitical singers were descendants of •Asaph, Heman, and Jeduthun and their sons and relatives. ¹³The trumpeters and singers joined together to praise and thank the LORD with one voice. They raised their voices, accompanied by trumpets, cymbals, and musical instruments, in praise to the LORD:

For He is good;
His faithful love endures forever.

The temple, the LORD's temple, was filled with a cloud. ¹⁴And because of the cloud, the priests were not able to continue ministering, for the glory of the LORD filled God's temple.

6 Then Solomon said:
The LORD said He would dwell
  in thick darkness,
² but I have built an exalted temple for You,
  a place for Your residence forever.

³Then the king turned and blessed the entire congregation of Israel while they were standing. ⁴He said:

May the LORD God of Israel be praised!
He spoke directly to my father David,
and He has fulfilled the promise
by His power.
He said,
⁵ "Since the day I brought My people Israel
out of the land of Egypt,
I have not chosen a city to build
  a temple in
among any of the tribes of Israel,
so that My name would be there,
and I have not chosen a man
to be ruler over My people Israel.
⁶ But I have chosen Jerusalem
so that My name will be there,
and I have chosen David
to be over My people Israel."
⁷ Now it was in the heart of my father David
to build a temple for the name of •Yahweh,
  the God of Israel.
⁸ However, Yahweh said to my father David,
"Since it was your desire to build a temple
  for My name,
you have done well to have this desire.
⁹ Yet, you are not the one to build the temple,

but your son, your own offspring,
will build the temple for My name."
¹⁰ So Yahweh has fulfilled what He promised.
I have taken the place of my father David
and I sit on the throne of Israel,
  as Yahweh promised.
I have built the temple for the name
  of Yahweh, the God of Israel.
¹¹ I have put the ark there,
where Yahweh's covenant is
that He made with the Israelites.

¹²Then Solomon stood before the altar of the LORD in front of the entire congregation of Israel and spread out his hands. ¹³For Solomon had made a bronze platform 7¹/₂ feet long, 7¹/₂ feet wide, and 4¹/₂ feet high and put it in the court. He stood on it, knelt down in front of the entire congregation of Israel, and spread out his hands toward heaven. ¹⁴He said:

LORD God of Israel,
there is no God like You
in heaven or on earth,
keeping His gracious covenant
with Your servants who walk before You
with their whole heart.
¹⁵ You have kept what You promised
to Your servant, my father David.
You spoke directly to him,
and You fulfilled Your promise by Your power,
as it is today.
¹⁶ Therefore, LORD God of Israel,
keep what You promised
to Your servant, my father David:
"You will never fail to have a man
to sit before Me on the throne of Israel,
if only your sons guard their way to walk
  in My Law
as you have walked before Me."
¹⁷ Now, LORD God of Israel, please confirm
what You promised to Your servant David.
¹⁸ But will God indeed live on earth with man?
Even heaven, the highest heaven,
  cannot contain You,
much less this temple I have built.
¹⁹ Listen to Your servant's prayer and his petition,
LORD my God,
so that You may hear the cry and the prayer
that Your servant prays before You,
²⁰ so that Your eyes watch over this temple
day and night,
toward the place where You said
You would put Your name;
and so that You may hear the prayer
Your servant prays toward this place.
²¹ Hear the petitions of Your servant
and Your people Israel,
which they pray toward this place.
May You hear in Your dwelling place
  in heaven.
May You hear and forgive.
²² If a man sins against his neighbor
and is forced to take an oath
and he comes to take an oath
before Your altar in this temple,
²³ may You hear in heaven and act.
May You judge Your servants,
condemning the wicked man by bringing
what he has done on his own head

and providing justice for the righteous
by rewarding him according to
   his righteousness.
²⁴ If Your people Israel are defeated
   before an enemy,
because they have sinned against You,
and they return to You and praise Your name,
and they pray and plead for mercy
before You in this temple,
²⁵ may You hear in heaven
and forgive the sin of Your people Israel.
May You restore them to the land
You gave them and their ancestors.
²⁶ When the skies are shut and there is no rain
because they have sinned against You,
and they pray toward this place
and praise Your name,
and they turn from their sins
because You are afflicting them,
²⁷ may You hear in heaven
and forgive the sin of Your servants
and Your people Israel,
so that You may teach them the good way
they should walk in.
May You send rain on Your land
that You gave Your people for an inheritance.
²⁸ When there is famine on the earth,
when there is pestilence,
when there is blight, mildew, locust,
   or grasshopper,
when their enemies besiege them
in the region of their fortified cities,
when there is any plague or illness,
²⁹ whatever prayer or petition
anyone from your people Israel might have—
each man knowing his own affliction
   and suffering,
and spreading out his hands
   toward this temple—
³⁰ may You hear in heaven, Your dwelling place,
and may You forgive and repay the man
according to all his ways, since You know
   his heart,
for You alone know the human heart,
³¹ so that they may 'fear You
and walk in Your ways
all the days they live on the land
You gave our ancestors.
³² Even for the foreigner who is not of
   Your people Israel
but has come from a distant land
because of Your great name
and Your mighty hand and outstretched arm:
when he comes and prays toward this temple,
³³ may You hear in heaven in Your
   dwelling place,
and do all the foreigner asks You.
Then all the peoples of the earth will know
   Your name,
to fear You as Your people Israel do
and know that this temple I have built
is called by Your name.
³⁴ When Your people go out to fight against
   their enemies,
wherever You send them,
and they pray to You
in the direction of this city You have chosen

and the temple that I have built
   for Your name,
³⁵ may You hear their prayer and petition
   in heaven
and uphold their cause.
³⁶ When they sin against You—
for there is no one who does not sin—
and You are angry with them
and hand them over to the enemy,
and their captors deport them
to a distant or nearby country,
³⁷ and when they come to their senses
in the land where they were deported
and repent and petition You
   in their captors' land,
saying: "We have sinned and done wrong;
we have been wicked,"
³⁸ and when they return to You
   with their whole mind and heart
in the land of their captivity
   where they were taken captive,
and when they pray in the direction
   of their land
that You gave their ancestors,
and the city You have chosen,
and toward the temple I have built
   for Your name,
³⁹ may You hear their prayer and petitions
   in heaven,
Your dwelling place,
and uphold their cause.
May You forgive Your people
who sinned against You.
⁴⁰ Now, my God,
please let Your eyes be open
and Your ears attentive
to the prayer of this place.
⁴¹ Now therefore:
Arise, LORD God, come to Your resting place,
You and Your powerful ark.
May Your priests, LORD God, be clothed
   with salvation,
and may Your godly people rejoice
   in goodness.
⁴² LORD God, do not reject Your anointed one;
remember the loyalty of Your servant David.

7 When Solomon finished praying, fire descended from heaven and consumed the *burnt offering and the sacrifices, and the glory of the LORD filled the temple. ²The priests were not able to enter the LORD's temple because the glory of the LORD filled the temple of the LORD. ³All the Israelites were watching when the fire descended and the glory of the LORD came on the temple. They bowed down on the pavement with their faces to the ground. They worshiped and praised the LORD:

For He is good,
   for His faithful love endures forever.

⁴The king and all the people were offering sacrifices in the LORD's presence. ⁵King Solomon offered a sacrifice of 22,000 cattle and 120,000 sheep. In this manner the king and all the people dedicated God's temple. ⁶The priests and the Levites were standing at their stations. The Levites had the musical instruments of the LORD, which King David had made to praise the LORD—"for His faithful love endures forever"—when he offered praise with them. Across from the Levites,

the priests were blowing trumpets, and all the people were standing. [7]Since the bronze altar that Solomon had made could not accommodate the burnt offering, the 'grain offering, and the fat of the 'fellowship offerings, Solomon first consecrated the middle of the courtyard that was in front of the LORD's temple and then offered the burnt offerings and the fat of the fellowship offerings there.

[8]So Solomon and all Israel with him—a very great assembly, from the entrance to Hamath to the Brook of Egypt—observed the festival at that time for seven days. [9]On the eighth day they held a sacred assembly, for the dedication of the altar lasted seven days and the festival seven days. [10]On the twenty-third day of the seventh month he sent the people away to their tents, rejoicing and with happy hearts for the goodness the LORD had done for David, for Solomon, and for His people Israel.

[11]So Solomon finished the LORD's temple and the royal palace. Everything that had entered Solomon's heart to do for the LORD's temple and for his own palace succeeded.

[12]Then the LORD appeared to Solomon at night and said to him:

I have heard your prayer and have chosen this place for Myself as a temple of sacrifice. [13]If I close the sky so there is no rain, or if I command the grasshopper to consume the land, or if I send pestilence on My people, [14]and My people who are called by My name humble themselves, pray and seek My face, and turn from their evil ways, then I will hear from heaven, forgive their sin, and heal their land. [15]My eyes will now be open and My ears attentive to prayer from this place. [16]And I have now chosen and consecrated this temple so that My name may be there forever; My eyes and My heart will be there at all times. [17]As for you, if you walk before Me as your father David walked, doing everything I have commanded you, and if you keep My statutes and ordinances, [18]I will establish your royal throne, as I promised your father David: You will never fail to have a man ruling in Israel. [19]However, if you turn away and abandon My statutes and My commands that I have set before you and if you go and serve other gods and worship them, [20]then I will uproot Israel from the soil that I gave them, and this temple that I have sanctified for My name I will banish from My presence; I will make it an object of scorn and ridicule among all the peoples. [21]As for this temple, which was exalted, everyone who passes by will be appalled and will say: Why did the LORD do this to this land and this temple? [22]Then they will say: Because they abandoned the LORD God of their ancestors who brought them out of the land of Egypt. They clung to other gods and worshiped and served them. Because of this, He brought all this ruin on them.

8 At the end of 20 years during which Solomon had built the LORD's temple and his own palace— [2]Solomon had rebuilt the cities Hiram gave him and settled Israelites there— [3]Solomon went to Hamath-zobah and seized it. [4]He built Tadmor in the wilderness along with all the storage cities that he built in Hamath. [5]He built Upper Beth-horon and Lower

Beth-horon—fortified cities with walls, gates, and bars— [6]Baalath, all the storage cities that belonged to Solomon, all the chariot cities, the cavalry cities, and everything Solomon desired to build in Jerusalem, Lebanon, or anywhere else in the land of his dominion.

[7]As for all the peoples who remained of the Hittites, Amorites, Perizzites, Hivites, and Jebusites, who were not from Israel— [8]their descendants who remained in the land after them, those the Israelites had not completely destroyed—Solomon imposed forced labor on them; it is this way today. [9]But Solomon did not consign the Israelites to be slaves for his work; they were soldiers, commanders of his captains, and commanders of his chariots and his cavalry. [10]These were King Solomon's deputies: 250 who ruled over the people.

[11]Solomon brought the daughter of Pharaoh from the city of David to the house he had built for her, for he said, "My wife must not live in the house of David king of Israel because the places the ark of the LORD has come into are holy."

[12]At that time Solomon offered 'burnt offerings to the LORD on the LORD's altar he had made in front of the portico. [13]He followed the daily requirement for offerings according to the commandment of Moses for Sabbaths, New Moons, and the three annual appointed festivals: the Festival of Unleavened Bread, the Festival of Weeks, and the Festival of Booths. [14]According to the ordinances of his father David, he appointed the divisions of the priests over their service, of the Levites over their responsibilities to offer praise and to minister before the priests following the daily requirement, and of the gatekeepers by their divisions with respect to each gate, for this had been the command of David, the man of God. [15]They did not turn aside from the king's command regarding the priests and the Levites concerning any matter or concerning the treasuries. [16]All of Solomon's work was carried out from the day the foundation was laid for the LORD's temple until it was finished. So the LORD's temple was completed.

[17]At that time Solomon went to Ezion-geber and to Eloth on the seashore in the land of Edom. [18]So Hiram sent ships to him by his servants along with crews of experienced seamen. They went with Solomon's servants to Ophir, took from there 17 tons of gold, and delivered it to King Solomon.

9 The queen of Sheba heard of Solomon's fame, so she came to test Solomon with difficult questions at Jerusalem with a very large entourage, with camels bearing spices, gold in abundance, and precious stones. She came to Solomon and spoke with him about everything that was on her mind. [2]So Solomon answered all her questions; nothing was too difficult for Solomon to explain to her. [3]When the queen of Sheba observed Solomon's wisdom, the palace he had built, [4]the food at his table, his servants' residence, his attendants' service and their attire, his cupbearers and their attire, and the 'burnt offerings he offered at the LORD's temple, it took her breath away.

[5]She said to the king, "The report I heard in my own country about your words and about your wisdom is true. [6]But I didn't believe their reports until I came and saw with my own eyes. Indeed, I was not even told half of your great wisdom! You far exceed the report I heard. [7]How happy are your men. How happy are these servants of yours, who always stand in your presence hearing your wisdom. [8]May the LORD your God be praised! He delighted in you and put you on His

throne as king for the LORD your God. Because Your God loved Israel enough to establish them forever, He has set you over them as king to carry out justice and righteousness."

⁹Then she gave the king four and a half tons of gold, a great quantity of spices, and precious stones. There never were such spices as those the queen of Sheba gave to King Solomon. ¹⁰In addition, Hiram's servants and Solomon's servants who brought gold from Ophir also brought algum wood and precious stones. ¹¹The king made the algum wood into walkways for the LORD's temple and for the king's palace and into lyres and harps for the singers. Never before had anything like them been seen in the land of Judah.

¹²King Solomon gave the queen of Sheba her every desire, whatever she asked—far more than she had brought the king. Then she, along with her servants, returned to her own country.

¹³The weight of gold that came to Solomon annually was 25 tons, ¹⁴besides what was brought by the merchants and traders. All the Arabian kings and governors of the land also brought gold and silver to Solomon.

¹⁵King Solomon made 200 large shields of hammered gold; 15 pounds of hammered gold went into each shield. ¹⁶He made 300 small shields of hammered gold; about eight pounds of gold went into each shield. The king put them in the House of the Forest of Lebanon.

¹⁷The king also made a large ivory throne and overlaid it with pure gold. ¹⁸The throne had six steps; there was a footstool covered in gold for the throne, armrests on either side of the seat, and two lions standing beside the armrests. ¹⁹Twelve lions were standing there on the six steps, one at each end. Nothing like it had ever been made in any other kingdom.

²⁰All of King Solomon's drinking cups were gold, and all the utensils of the House of the Forest of Lebanon were pure gold. There was no silver, since it was considered as nothing in Solomon's time, ²¹for the king's ships kept going to Tarshish with Hiram's servants, and once every three years the ships of Tarshish would arrive bearing gold, silver, ivory, apes, and peacocks.

²²King Solomon surpassed all the kings of the world in riches and wisdom. ²³All the kings of the world wanted an audience with Solomon to hear the wisdom God had put in his heart. ²⁴Each of them would bring his own gift—items of silver and gold, clothing, weapons, spices, and horses and mules—as an annual tribute.

²⁵Solomon had 4,000 stalls for horses and chariots, and 12,000 horsemen. He stationed them in the chariot cities and with the king in Jerusalem. ²⁶He ruled over all the kings from the Euphrates River to the land of the Philistines and as far as the border of Egypt. ²⁷The king made silver as common in Jerusalem as stones, and he made cedar as abundant as sycamore in the Judean foothills. ²⁸They were bringing horses for Solomon from Egypt and from all the countries.

²⁹The remaining events of Solomon's reign, from beginning to end, are written in the Events of Nathan the Prophet, the Prophecy of Ahijah the Shilonite, and the Visions of Iddo the Seer concerning Jeroboam son of Nebat. ³⁰Solomon reigned in Jerusalem over all Israel for 40 years. ³¹Solomon rested with his fathers

and was buried in the city of his father David. His son Rehoboam became king in his place.

10 Then Rehoboam went to Shechem, for all Israel had gone to Shechem to make him king. ²When Jeroboam son of Nebat heard about it—for he was in Egypt where he had fled from King Solomon's presence—Jeroboam returned from Egypt. ³So they summoned him. Then Jeroboam and all Israel came and spoke to Rehoboam: ⁴"Your father made our yoke difficult. Therefore, lighten your father's harsh service and the heavy yoke he put on us, and we will serve you."

⁵Rehoboam replied, "Return to me in three days." So the people left.

⁶Then King Rehoboam consulted with the elders who had served his father Solomon when he was alive, asking, "How do you advise me to respond to these people?"

⁷They replied, "If you will be kind to these people and please them by speaking kind words to them, they will be your servants forever."

⁸But he rejected the advice of the elders who had advised him, and he consulted with the young men who had grown up with him, the ones serving him. ⁹He asked them, "What message do you advise we send back to these people who said to me, 'Lighten the yoke your father put on us'?"

¹⁰Then the young men who had grown up with him told him, "This is what you should say to the people who said to you, 'Your father made our yoke heavy, but you, make it lighter on us!' This is what you should say to them: 'My little finger is thicker than my father's loins. ¹¹Now therefore, my father burdened you with a heavy yoke, but I will add to your yoke; my father disciplined you with whips, but I, with barbed whips.'"

¹²So Jeroboam and all the people came to Rehoboam on the third day, just as the king had ordered, saying, "Return to me on the third day." ¹³Then the king answered them harshly. King Rehoboam rejected the elders' advice ¹⁴and spoke to them according to the young men's advice, saying, "My father made your yoke heavy, but I will add to it; my father disciplined you with whips, but I, with barbed whips." ¹⁵The king did not listen to the people because the turn of events came from God, in order that the LORD might carry out His word that He had spoken through Ahijah the Shilonite to Jeroboam son of Nebat.

¹⁶When all Israel saw that the king had not listened to them, the people answered the king:

What portion do we have in David?
We have no inheritance in the son of Jesse.
Israel, each man to your tent;
David, look after your own house now!

So all Israel went to their tents. ¹⁷But as for the Israelites living in the cities of Judah, Rehoboam reigned over them.

¹⁸Then King Rehoboam sent Hadoram, who was in charge of the forced labor, but the Israelites stoned him to death. However, King Rehoboam managed to get into his chariot to flee to Jerusalem. ¹⁹Israel is in rebellion against the house of David until today.

11 When Rehoboam arrived in Jerusalem, he mobilized the house of Judah and Benjamin—180,000 choice warriors—to fight against Israel to restore the reign to Rehoboam. ²But the word of the LORD came to Shemaiah, the man of God: ³"Say to Rehoboam son of Solomon, king of Judah, to all Israel in Judah and Benjamin, and to the rest of the people: ⁴"This is what the LORD says: You are not to march up and fight against your brothers. Each of you must return home, for this incident has come from Me.'"

So they listened to what the LORD said and turned back from going against Jeroboam.

⁵Rehoboam stayed in Jerusalem, and he fortified cities in Judah. ⁶He built up Bethlehem, Etam, Tekoa, ⁷Beth-zur, Soco, Adullam, ⁸Gath, Mareshah, Ziph, ⁹Adoraim, Lachish, Azekah, ¹⁰Zorah, Aijalon, and Hebron, which are fortified cities in Judah and in Benjamin. ¹¹He strengthened their fortifications and put leaders in them with supplies of food, oil, and wine. ¹²He also put large shields and spears in each and every city to make them very strong. So Judah and Benjamin were his.

¹³The priests and Levites from all their regions throughout Israel took their stand with Rehoboam, ¹⁴for the Levites left their pasturelands and their possessions and went to Judah and Jerusalem, because Jeroboam and his sons refused to let them serve as priests of ˙Yahweh. ¹⁵Jeroboam appointed his own priests for the ˙high places, the goat-demons, and the golden calves he had made. ¹⁶Those from every tribe of Israel who had determined in their hearts to seek Yahweh their God followed the Levites to Jerusalem to sacrifice to Yahweh, the God of their ancestors. ¹⁷So they strengthened the kingdom of Judah and supported Rehoboam son of Solomon for three years, because they walked in the way of David and Solomon for three years.

¹⁸Rehoboam married Mahalath, daughter of David's son Jerimoth and of Abihail daughter of Jesse's son Eliab. ¹⁹She bore sons to him: Jeush, Shemariah, and Zaham. ²⁰After her, he married Maacah daughter of Absalom. She bore Abijah, Attai, Ziza, and Shelomith to him. ²¹Rehoboam loved Maacah daughter of Absalom more than all his wives and concubines. He acquired 18 wives and 60 concubines and was the father of 28 sons and 60 daughters.

²²Rehoboam appointed Abijah son of Maacah as chief, leader among his brothers, intending to make him king. ²³Rehoboam also showed discernment by dispersing some of his sons to all the regions of Judah and Benjamin and to all the fortified cities. He gave them plenty of provisions and sought many wives for them.

12 When Rehoboam had established his sovereignty and royal power, he abandoned the law of the LORD—he and all Israel with him. ²Because they were unfaithful to the LORD, in the fifth year of King Rehoboam, Shishak king of Egypt went to war against Jerusalem ³with 1,200 chariots, 60,000 cavalrymen, and countless people who came with him from Egypt—Libyans, Sukkiim, and Cushites. ⁴He captured the fortified cities of Judah and came as far as Jerusalem.

⁵Then Shemaiah the prophet went to Rehoboam and the leaders of Judah who were gathered at Jerusalem because of Shishak. He said to them: "This is what the LORD says: ˙You have abandoned Me; therefore, I have abandoned you into the hand of Shishak.'"

⁶So the leaders of Israel and the king humbled themselves and said, "˙Yahweh is righteous."

⁷When the LORD saw that they had humbled themselves, the LORD's message came to Shemaiah: "They have humbled themselves; I will not destroy them but

will grant them a little deliverance. My wrath will not be poured out on Jerusalem through Shishak. ⁸However, they will become his servants so that they may recognize the difference between serving Me and serving the kingdoms of other lands."

⁹So King Shishak of Egypt went to war against Jerusalem. He seized the treasuries of the LORD's temple and the treasuries of the royal palace. He took everything. He took the gold shields that Solomon had made. ¹⁰King Rehoboam made bronze shields in their place and committed them into the care of the captains of the royal escorts who guarded the entrance to the king's palace. ¹¹Whenever the king entered the LORD's temple, the royal escorts would carry the shields and take them back to the royal escorts' armory. ¹²When Rehoboam humbled himself, the LORD's anger turned away from him, and He did not destroy him completely. Besides that, conditions were good in Judah.

¹³King Rehoboam established his royal power in Jerusalem. Rehoboam was 41 years old when he became king and reigned 17 years in Jerusalem, the city the LORD had chosen from all the tribes of Israel to put His name. Rehoboam's mother's name was Naamah the Ammonite. ¹⁴Rehoboam did what was evil, because he did not determine in his heart to seek the LORD.

¹⁵The events of Rehoboam's reign, from beginning to end, are written in the Events of Shemaiah the Prophet and of Iddo the Seer concerning genealogies. There was war between Rehoboam and Jeroboam throughout their reigns. ¹⁶Rehoboam rested with his fathers and was buried in the city of David. His son Abijah became king in his place.

13 In the eighteenth year of Israel's King Jeroboam, Abijah became king over Judah ²and reigned three years in Jerusalem. His mother's name was Micaiah daughter of Uriel; she was from Gibeah.

There was war between Abijah and Jeroboam. ³Abijah set his army of warriors in order with 400,000 choice men. Jeroboam arranged his mighty army of 800,000 choice men in battle formation against him. ⁴Then Abijah stood on Mount Zemaraim, which is in the hill country of Ephraim, and said, "Jeroboam and all Israel, hear me. ⁵Don't you know that the LORD God of Israel gave the kingship over Israel to David and his descendants forever by a covenant of salt? ⁶But Jeroboam son of Nebat, a servant of Solomon son of David, rose up and rebelled against his lord. ⁷Then worthless and ˙wicked men gathered around him to resist Rehoboam son of Solomon when Rehoboam was young, inexperienced, and unable to assert himself against them.

⁸"And now you are saying you can assert yourselves against the LORD's kingdom, which is in the hand of one of David's sons. You are a vast number and have with you the golden calves that Jeroboam made for you as gods. ⁹Didn't you banish the priests of ˙Yahweh, the descendants of Aaron and the Levites, and make your own priests like the peoples of other lands do? Whoever comes to ordain himself with a young bull and seven rams may become a priest of what are not gods.

¹⁰"But as for us, Yahweh is our God. We have not abandoned Him; the priests ministering to the LORD are descendants of Aaron, and the Levites serve at their tasks. ¹¹They offer a ˙burnt offering and fragrant incense to the LORD every morning and every evening,

and they set the rows of the *bread of the Presence on the ceremonially *clean table. They light the lamps of the gold lampstand every evening. We are carrying out the requirements of Yahweh our God, while you have abandoned Him. [12] Look, God and His priests are with us at our head. The trumpets are ready to sound the charge against you. Israelites, don't fight against the LORD God of your ancestors, for you will not succeed."

[13] Now Jeroboam had sent an ambush around to advance from behind them. So they were in front of Judah, and the ambush was behind them. [14] Judah turned and discovered that the battle was in front of them and behind them, so they cried out to the LORD. Then the priests blew the trumpets, [15] and the men of Judah raised the battle cry. When the men of Judah raised the battle cry, God routed Jeroboam and all Israel before Abijah and Judah. [16] So the Israelites fled before Judah, and God handed them over to them. [17] Then Abijah and his people struck them with a mighty blow, and 500,000 choice men of Israel were killed. [18] The Israelites were subdued at that time. The Judahites succeeded because they depended on the LORD, the God of their ancestors.

[19] Abijah pursued Jeroboam and captured some cities from him: Bethel and its villages, Jeshanah and its villages, and Ephron and its villages. [20] Jeroboam no longer retained his power during Abijah's reign; ultimately, the LORD struck him and he died.

[21] However, Abijah grew strong, acquired 14 wives, and fathered 22 sons and 16 daughters. [22] The rest of the events of Abijah's reign, along with his ways and his sayings, are written in the Writing of the Prophet Iddo. [14:1] Abijah rested with his fathers and was buried in the city of David. His son Asa became king in his place. During his reign the land experienced peace for 10 years.

[2] Asa did what was good and right in the sight of the LORD his God. [3] He removed the pagan altars and the *high places. He shattered their sacred pillars and chopped down their *Asherah poles. [4] He told the people of Judah to seek the LORD God of their ancestors and to carry out the instruction and the commands. [5] He also removed the high places and the incense altars from all the cities of Judah, and the kingdom experienced peace under him.

[6] Because the land experienced peace, Asa built fortified cities in Judah. No one made war with him in those days because the LORD gave him rest. [7] So he said to the people of Judah, "Let's build these cities and surround them with walls and towers, with doors and bars. The land is still ours because we sought the LORD our God. We sought Him and He gave us rest on every side." So they built and succeeded.

[8] Asa had an army of 300,000 from Judah bearing large shields and spears, and 280,000 from Benjamin bearing regular shields and drawing the bow. All these were brave warriors. [9] Then Zerah the *Cushite came against them with an army of one million men and 300 chariots. They came as far as Mareshah. [10] So Asa marched out against him and lined up in battle formation in the Valley of Zephathah at Mareshah.

[11] Then Asa cried out to the LORD his God: "LORD, there is no one besides You to help the mighty and those without strength. Help us, LORD our God, for we depend on You, and in Your name we have come against this large army. *Yahweh, You are our God. Do not let a mere mortal hinder You."

[12] So the LORD routed the Cushites before Asa and before Judah, and the Cushites fled. [13] Then Asa and the people who were with him pursued them as far as Gerar. The Cushites fell until they had no survivors, for they were crushed before Yahweh and His army. So the people of Judah carried off a great supply of loot. [14] Then they attacked all the cities around Gerar because the terror of the LORD was on them. They also plundered all the cities, since there was a great deal of plunder in them. [15] They also attacked the tents of the herdsmen and captured many sheep and camels. Then they returned to Jerusalem.

[15] The Spirit of God came on Azariah son of Oded. [2] So he went out to meet Asa and said to him, "Asa and all Judah and Benjamin, hear me. The LORD is with you when you are with Him. If you seek Him, He will be found by you, but if you abandon Him, He will abandon you. [3] For many years Israel has been without the true God, without a teaching priest, and without instruction, [4] but when they turned to the LORD God of Israel in their distress and sought Him, He was found by them. [5] In those times there was no peace for those who went about their daily activities because the residents of the lands had many conflicts. [6] Nation was crushed by nation and city by city, for God troubled them with every possible distress. [7] But as for you, be strong; don't be discouraged, for your work has a reward."

[8] When Asa heard these words and the prophecy of Azariah son of Oded the prophet, he took courage and removed the detestable idols from the whole land of Judah and Benjamin and from the cities he had captured in the hill country of Ephraim. He renovated the altar of the LORD that was in front of the portico of the LORD's temple. [9] Then he gathered all Judah and Benjamin, as well as those from the tribes of Ephraim, Manasseh, and Simeon who had settled among them, for they had defected to him from Israel in great numbers when they saw that *Yahweh his God was with him.

[10] They were gathered in Jerusalem in the third month of the fifteenth year of Asa's reign. [11] At that time they sacrificed to the LORD 700 cattle and 7,000 sheep from all the plunder they had brought. [12] Then they entered into a covenant to seek the LORD God of their ancestors with all their mind and all their heart. [13] Whoever would not seek the LORD God of Israel would be put to death, young or old, man or woman. [14] They took an oath to the LORD in a loud voice, with shouting, with trumpets, and with rams' horns. [15] All Judah rejoiced over the oath, for they had sworn it with all their mind. They had sought Him with all their heart, and He was found by them. So the LORD gave them rest on every side.

[16] King Asa also removed Maacah, his grandmother, from being queen mother because she had made an obscene image of *Asherah. Asa chopped down her obscene image, then crushed it and burned it in the Kidron Valley. [17] The *high places were not taken away from Israel; nevertheless, Asa was wholehearted his entire life. [18] He brought his father's consecrated gifts and his own consecrated gifts into God's temple: silver, gold, and utensils.

[19] There was no war until the thirty-fifth year of Asa's reign.

16 In the thirty-sixth year of Asa, Israel's King Baasha went to war against Judah. He built Ramah in order to deny access to anyone—going or coming—to Judah's King Asa. ²So Asa brought out the silver and gold from the treasuries of the LORD's temple and the royal palace and sent it to Aram's King Ben-hadad, who lived in Damascus, saying, ³"There's a treaty between me and you, between my father and your father. Look, I have sent you silver and gold. Go break your treaty with Israel's King Baasha so that he will withdraw from me."

⁴Ben-hadad listened to King Asa and sent the commanders of his armies to the cities of Israel. They attacked Ijon, Dan, Abel-maim, and all the storage cities of Naphtali. ⁵When Baasha heard about it, he quit building Ramah and stopped his work. ⁶Then King Asa brought all Judah, and they carried away the stones of Ramah and the timbers Baasha had built it with. Then he built Geba and Mizpah with them.

⁷At that time, Hanani the seer came to King Asa of Judah and said to him, "Because you depended on the king of Aram and have not depended on the LORD your God, the army of the king of Aram has escaped from your hand. ⁸Were not the *Cushites and Libyans a vast army with many chariots and horsemen? When you depended on *Yahweh, He handed them over to you. ⁹For the eyes of Yahweh roam throughout the earth to show Himself strong for those whose hearts are completely His. You have been foolish in this matter. Therefore, you will have wars from now on." ¹⁰Asa was angry with the seer and put him in prison because of his anger over this. And Asa mistreated some of the people at that time.

¹¹Note that the events of Asa's reign, from beginning to end, are written in the Book of the Kings of Judah and Israel. ¹²In the thirty-ninth year of his reign, Asa developed a disease in his feet, and his disease became increasingly severe. Yet even in his disease he didn't seek the LORD but only the physicians. ¹³Asa died in the forty-first year of his reign and rested with his fathers. ¹⁴He was buried in his own tomb that he had made for himself in the city of David. They laid him out in a coffin that was full of spices and various mixtures of prepared ointments; then they made a great fire in his honor.

17 His son Jehoshaphat became king in his place and strengthened himself against Israel. ²He stationed troops in every fortified city of Judah and set garrisons in the land of Judah and in the cities of Ephraim that his father Asa had captured.

³Now the LORD was with Jehoshaphat because he walked in the former ways of his father David. He did not seek the *Baals ⁴but sought the God of his father and walked by His commands, not according to the practices of Israel. ⁵So the LORD established the kingdom in his hand. Then all Judah brought him tribute, and he had riches and honor in abundance. ⁶His mind rejoiced in the LORD's ways, and he again removed the *high places and *Asherah poles from Judah.

⁷In the third year of his reign, Jehoshaphat sent his officials—Ben-hail, Obadiah, Zechariah, Nethanel, and Micaiah—to teach in the cities of Judah. ⁸The Levites with them were Shemaiah, Nethaniah, Zebadiah, Asahel, Shemiramoth, Jehonathan, Adonijah, Tobijah, and Tob-adonijah; the priests, Elishama and Jehoram, were with these Levites. ⁹They taught throughout Judah, having the book of the LORD's instruction with

them. They went throughout the towns of Judah and taught the people.

¹⁰The terror of the LORD was on all the kingdoms of the lands that surrounded Judah, so they didn't fight against Jehoshaphat. ¹¹Some of the Philistines also brought gifts and silver as tribute to Jehoshaphat, and the Arabs brought him flocks: 7,700 rams and 7,700 male goats.

¹²Jehoshaphat grew stronger and stronger. He built fortresses and storage cities in Judah ¹³and carried out great works in the towns of Judah. He had fighting men, brave warriors, in Jerusalem. ¹⁴These are their numbers according to their ancestral families. For Judah, the commanders of thousands:

Adnah the commander and 300,000 brave warriors with him;
¹⁵next to him, Jehohanan the commander and 280,000 with him;
¹⁶next to him, Amasiah son of Zichri, the volunteer of the LORD, and 200,000 brave warriors with him;
¹⁷from Benjamin, Eliada, a brave warrior, and 200,000 with him armed with bow and shield;
¹⁸next to him, Jehozabad and 180,000 with him equipped for war.

¹⁹These were the ones who served the king, besides those he stationed in the fortified cities throughout all Judah.

18 Now Jehoshaphat had riches and honor in abundance, and he made an alliance with Ahab through marriage. ²Then after some years, he went down to visit Ahab in Samaria. Ahab sacrificed many sheep and cattle for him and for the people who were with him. Then he persuaded him to march up to Ramoth-gilead, ³for Israel's King Ahab asked Judah's King Jehoshaphat, "Will you go with me to Ramoth-gilead?"

He replied to him, "I am as you are, my people as your people; we will be with you in the battle." ⁴But Jehoshaphat said to the king of Israel, "First, please ask what the LORD's will is."

⁵So the king of Israel gathered the prophets, 400 men, and asked them, "Should we go to Ramoth-gilead for war or should I refrain?"

They replied, "March up, and God will hand it over to the king."

⁶But Jehoshaphat asked, "Isn't there a prophet of *Yahweh here anymore? Let's ask him."

⁷The king of Israel said to Jehoshaphat, "There is still one man who can ask Yahweh, but I hate him because he never prophesies good about me, but only disaster. He is Micaiah son of Imlah."

"The king shouldn't say that," Jehoshaphat replied.

⁸So the king of Israel called an officer and said, "Hurry and get Micaiah son of Imlah!"

⁹Now the king of Israel and King Jehoshaphat of Judah, clothed in royal attire, were each sitting on his own throne. They were sitting on the threshing floor at the entrance to Samaria's *gate, and all the prophets were prophesying in front of them. ¹⁰Then Zedekiah son of Chenaanah made iron horns and said, "This is what the LORD says: 'You will gore the Arameans with these until they are finished off.'" ¹¹And all the prophets were prophesying the same, saying, "March up to Ramoth-gilead and succeed, for the LORD will hand it over to the king."

¹²The messenger who went to call Micaiah instruct-

ed him, "Look, the words of the prophets are unanimously favorable for the king. So let your words be like theirs, and speak favorably."

¹³But Micaiah said, "As the LORD lives, I will say whatever my God says."

¹⁴So he went to the king, and the king asked him, "Micaiah, should we go to Ramoth-gilead for war, or should I refrain?"

Micaiah said, "March up and succeed, for they will be handed over to you."

¹⁵But the king said to him, "How many times must I make you swear not to tell me anything but the truth in the name of Yahweh?"

¹⁶So Micaiah said:

I saw all Israel scattered on the hills
like sheep without a shepherd.
And the LORD said,
"They have no master;
let each return home in peace."

¹⁷So the king of Israel said to Jehoshaphat, "Didn't I tell you he never prophesies good about me, but only disaster?"

¹⁸Then Micaiah said, "Therefore, hear the word of the LORD. I saw the LORD sitting on His throne, and the whole heavenly *host was standing at His right hand and at His left hand. ¹⁹And the LORD said, 'Who will entice Ahab king of Israel to march up and fall at Ramoth-gilead?' So one was saying this and another was saying that.

²⁰"Then a spirit came forward, stood before the LORD, and said, 'I will entice him.'

"The LORD asked him, 'How?'

²¹"So he said, 'I will go and become a lying spirit in the mouth of all his prophets.'

"Then He said, 'You will entice him and also prevail. Go and do that.'

²²"Now, you see, the LORD has put a lying spirit into the mouth of these prophets of yours, and the LORD has pronounced disaster against you."

²³Then Zedekiah son of Chenaanah came up, hit Micaiah in the face, and demanded, "Which way did the spirit from the LORD leave me to speak to you?"

²⁴Micaiah replied, "You will soon see when you go to hide yourself in an inner chamber on that day."

²⁵Then the king of Israel ordered, "Take Micaiah and return him to Amon, the governor of the city, and to Joash, the king's son, ²⁶and say, 'This is what the king says: Put this guy in prison and feed him only bread and water until I come back safely.'"

²⁷But Micaiah said, "If you ever return safely, the LORD has not spoken through me." Then he said, "Listen, all you people!"

²⁸Then the king of Israel and Judah's King Jehoshaphat went up to Ramoth-gilead. ²⁹But the king of Israel said to Jehoshaphat, "I will disguise myself and go into battle, but you wear your royal attire." So the king of Israel disguised himself, and they went into battle.

³⁰Now the king of Aram had ordered his chariot commanders, "Do not fight with anyone, small or great, except the king of Israel."

³¹When the chariot commanders saw Jehoshaphat, they shouted, "He must be the king of Israel!" So they turned to attack him, but Jehoshaphat cried out and the LORD helped him. God drew them away from him. ³²When the chariot commanders saw that he was not the king of Israel, they turned back from pursuing him.

³³But a man drew his bow without taking special aim and struck the king of Israel through the joints of his armor. So he said to the charioteer, "Turn around and take me out of the battle, for I am badly wounded!" ³⁴The battle raged throughout that day, and the king of Israel propped himself up in his chariot facing the Arameans until evening. Then he died at sunset.

19 Jehoshaphat king of Judah returned to his home in Jerusalem in peace. ²Then Jehu son of Hanani the seer went out to confront him and said to King Jehoshaphat, "Do you help the wicked and love those who hate the LORD? Because of this, the LORD's wrath is on you. ³However, some good is found in you, for you have removed the *Asherah poles from the land and have decided to seek God.

⁴Jehoshaphat lived in Jerusalem, and once again he went out among the people from Beer-sheba to the hill country of Ephraim and brought them back to *Yahweh, the God of their ancestors. ⁵He appointed judges in all the fortified cities of the land of Judah, city by city. ⁶Then he said to the judges, "Consider what you are doing, for you do not judge for man, but for the LORD, who is with you in the matter of judgment. ⁷And now, may the terror of the LORD be on you. Watch what you do, for there is no injustice or partiality or taking bribes with the LORD our God."

⁸Jehoshaphat also appointed in Jerusalem some of the Levites and priests and some of the heads of the Israelite families for deciding the LORD's will and for settling disputes of the residents of Jerusalem. ⁹He commanded them, saying, "In the *fear of the LORD, with integrity, and with a whole heart, you are to do the following: ¹⁰for every dispute that comes to you from your brothers who dwell in their cities—whether it regards differences of bloodguilt, law, commandment, statutes, or judgments—you are to warn them, so they will not incur *guilt before the LORD and wrath will not come on you and your brothers. Do this, and you will not incur guilt.

¹¹"Note that Amariah, the chief priest, is over you in all matters related to the LORD, and Zebadiah son of Ishmael, the ruler of the house of Judah, in all matters related to the king, and the Levites are officers in your presence. Be strong; may the LORD be with those who do what is good."

20 After this, the Moabites and Ammonites, together with some of the Meunites, came to fight against Jehoshaphat. ²People came and told Jehoshaphat, "A vast number from beyond the Dead Sea and from Edom has come to fight against you; they are already in Hazazon-tamar" (that is, En-gedi). ³Jehoshaphat was afraid, and he resolved to seek the LORD. Then he proclaimed a fast for all Judah, ⁴who gathered to seek the LORD. They even came from all the cities of Judah to seek Him.

⁵Then Jehoshaphat stood in the assembly of Judah and Jerusalem in the LORD's temple before the new courtyard. ⁶He said:

*Yahweh, the God of our ancestors, are You not the God who is in heaven, and do You not rule over all the kingdoms of the nations? Power and might are in Your hand, and no one can stand against You. ⁷Are You not our God who drove out the inhabitants of this land before Your people Israel and who gave it forever to the descendants of Abraham Your friend? ⁸They have lived in the land and have built You a sanctuary in it for Your name and have said, ⁹"If disaster comes on us—sword or judgment, pestilence or famine—we will stand before this temple and before You, for Your name is in this temple. We will cry out to You because of our distress, and You will hear and deliver."

¹⁰Now here are the Ammonites, Moabites, and the inhabitants of Mount Seir. You did not let Israel invade them when Israel came out of the land of Egypt, but Israel turned away from them and did not destroy them. ¹¹Look how they repay us by coming to drive us out of Your possession that You gave us as an inheritance. ¹²Our God, will You not judge them? For we are powerless before this vast number that comes to fight against us. We do not know what to do, but we look to You.

¹³All Judah was standing before the LORD with their infants, their wives, and their children. ¹⁴In the middle of the congregation, the Spirit of the LORD came on Jahaziel (son of Zechariah, son of Benaiah, son of Jeiel, son of Mattaniah, a Levite from *Asaph's descendants), ¹⁵and he said, "Listen carefully, all Judah and you inhabitants of Jerusalem, and King Jehoshaphat. This is what the LORD says: 'Do not be afraid or discouraged because of this vast number, for the battle is not yours, but God's. ¹⁶Tomorrow, go down against them. You will see them coming up the Ascent of Ziz, and you will find them at the end of the valley facing the Wilderness of Jeruel. ¹⁷You do not have to fight this battle. Position yourselves, stand still, and see the salvation of the LORD. He is with you, Judah and Jerusalem. Do not be afraid or discouraged. Tomorrow, go out to face them, for Yahweh is with you.'"

¹⁸Then Jehoshaphat bowed with his face to the ground, and all Judah and the inhabitants of Jerusalem fell down before the LORD to worship Him. ¹⁹Then the Levites from the sons of the Kohathites and the Korahites stood up to praise the LORD God of Israel shouting with a loud voice.

²⁰In the morning they got up early and went out to the wilderness of Tekoa. As they were about to go out, Jehoshaphat stood and said, "Hear me, Judah and you inhabitants of Jerusalem. Believe in Yahweh your God, and you will be established; believe in His prophets, and you will succeed." ²¹Then he consulted with the people and appointed some to sing for the LORD and some to praise the splendor of His holiness. When they went out in front of the armed forces, they kept singing:

Give thanks to the LORD,
    for His faithful love endures forever.

²²The moment they began their shouts and praises, the LORD set an ambush against the Ammonites, Moabites, and the inhabitants of Mount Seir who came to fight against Judah, and they were defeated. ²³The Ammonites and Moabites turned against the inhabitants of Mount Seir and *completely annihilated them. When they had finished with the inhabitants of Seir, they helped destroy each other.

²⁴When Judah came to a place overlooking the wilderness, they looked for the large army, but there were only corpses lying on the ground; nobody had escaped. ²⁵Then Jehoshaphat and his people went to gather the plunder. They found among them an abundance of goods on the bodies and valuable items. So they stripped them until nobody could carry any more.

They were gathering the plunder for three days because there was so much. ²⁶They assembled in the Valley of Beracah on the fourth day, for there they praised the LORD. Therefore, that place is still called the Valley of Beracah today.

²⁷Then all the men of Judah and Jerusalem turned back with Jehoshaphat their leader, returning joyfully to Jerusalem, for the LORD enabled them to rejoice over their enemies. ²⁸So they came into Jerusalem to the LORD's temple with harps, lyres, and trumpets.

²⁹The terror of God was on all the kingdoms of the lands when they heard that Yahweh had fought against the enemies of Israel. ³⁰Then Jehoshaphat's kingdom was quiet, for his God gave him rest on every side.

³¹Jehoshaphat became king over Judah. He was 35 years old when he became king and reigned 25 years in Jerusalem. His mother's name was Azubah daughter of Shilhi. ³²He walked in the way of Asa his father; he did not turn away from it but did what was right in the LORD's sight. ³³However, the *high places were not taken away; the people had not yet set their hearts on the God of their ancestors.

³⁴The rest of the events of Jehoshaphat's reign from beginning to end are written in the Events of Jehu son of Hanani, which is recorded in the Book of Israel's Kings.

³⁵After this, Judah's King Jehoshaphat made an alliance with Israel's King Ahaziah, who was *guilty of wrongdoing. ³⁶Jehoshaphat formed an alliance with him to make ships to go to Tarshish, and they made the ships in Ezion-geber. ³⁷Then Eliezer son of Dodavahu of Mareshah prophesied against Jehoshaphat, saying, "Because you formed an alliance with Ahaziah, the LORD has broken up what you have made." So the ships were wrecked and were not able to go to Tarshish.

21 Jehoshaphat rested with his fathers and was buried with his fathers in the city of David. His son Jehoram became king in his place. ²He had brothers, sons of Jehoshaphat: Azariah, Jehiel, Zechariah, Azariah, Michael, and Shephatiah; all these were the sons of Jehoshaphat, king of Judah. ³Their father had given them many gifts of silver, gold, and valuable things, along with fortified cities in Judah, but he gave the kingdom to Jehoram because he was the firstborn. ⁴When Jehoram had established himself over his father's kingdom, he strengthened his position by killing with the sword all his brothers as well as some of the princes of Israel.

⁵Jehoram was 32 years old when he became king and reigned eight years in Jerusalem. ⁶He walked in the way of the kings of Israel, as the house of Ahab had done, for Ahab's daughter was his wife. He did what was evil in the LORD's sight, ⁷but because of the covenant the LORD had made with David, He was unwilling to destroy the house of David since the LORD had promised to give a lamp to David and to his sons forever.

⁸During Jehoram's reign, Edom rebelled against Judah's domination and appointed their own king. ⁹So Jehoram crossed into Edom with his commanders and all his chariots. Then at night he set out to attack the Edomites who had surrounded him and the chariot commanders. ¹⁰And now Edom is still in rebellion against Judah's domination today. Libnah also rebelled at that time against his domination because he had abandoned *Yahweh, the God of his ancestors. ¹¹Jehoram also built *high places in the hills of Judah,

and he caused the inhabitants of Jerusalem to prostitute themselves, and he led Judah astray.

¹²Then a letter came to Jehoram from Elijah the prophet, saying:

This is what Yahweh, the God of your ancestor David says: "Because you have not walked in the ways of your father Jehoshaphat or in the ways of Asa king of Judah ¹³but have walked in the way of the kings of Israel, have caused Judah and the inhabitants of Jerusalem to prostitute themselves like the house of Ahab prostituted itself, and also have killed your brothers, your father's family, who were better than you, ¹⁴Yahweh is now about to strike your people, your sons, your wives, and all your possessions with a horrible affliction. ¹⁵You yourself will be struck with many illnesses, including a disease of the intestines, until your intestines come out day after day because of the disease."

¹⁶The Lord put it into the mind of the Philistines and the Arabs who live near the *Cushites to attack Jehoram. ¹⁷So they went to war against Judah and invaded it. They carried off all the possessions found in the king's palace and also his sons and wives; not a son was left to him except Jehoahaz, his youngest son.

¹⁸After all these things, the Lord afflicted him in his intestines with an incurable disease. ¹⁹This continued day after day until two full years passed. Then his intestines came out because of his disease, and he died from severe illnesses. But his people did not hold a fire in his honor like the fire in honor of his fathers.

²⁰Jehoram was 32 years old when he became king; he reigned eight years in Jerusalem. He died to no one's regret and was buried in the city of David but not in the tombs of the kings.

22 Then the inhabitants of Jerusalem made Ahaziah, his youngest son, king in his place, because the troops that had come with the Arabs to the camp had killed all the older sons. So Ahaziah son of Jehoram became king of Judah. ²Ahaziah was 22 years old when he became king and reigned one year in Jerusalem. His mother's name was Athaliah, granddaughter of Omri.

³He walked in the ways of the house of Ahab, for his mother gave him evil advice. ⁴So he did what was evil in the Lord's sight like the house of Ahab, for they were his advisers after the death of his father, to his destruction. ⁵He also followed their advice and went with Joram son of Israel's King Ahab to fight against Hazael, king of Aram, in Ramoth-gilead. The Arameans wounded Joram, ⁶so he returned to Jezreel to recover from the wounds they inflicted on him in Ramoth-gilead when he fought against Aram's King Hazael. Then Judah's King Ahaziah son of Jehoram went down to Jezreel to visit Joram son of Ahab since Joram was ill.

⁷Ahaziah's downfall came from God when he went to Joram. When Ahaziah arrived, he went out with Joram to meet Jehu son of Nimshi, whom the Lord had anointed to destroy the house of Ahab. ⁸So when Jehu executed judgment on the house of Ahab, he found the rulers of Judah and the sons of Ahaziah's brothers who were serving Ahaziah, and he killed them. ⁹Then Jehu looked for Ahaziah, and Jehu's soldiers captured him (he was hiding in Samaria). So they brought Ahaziah to Jehu, and they killed him. The soldiers buried him, for they said, "He is the grandson of Jehoshaphat

who sought the Lord with all his heart." So no one from the house of Ahaziah had the strength to rule the kingdom.

¹⁰When Athaliah, Ahaziah's mother, saw that her son was dead, she proceeded to annihilate all the royal heirs of the house of Judah. ¹¹Jehoshabeath, the king's daughter, rescued Joash son of Ahaziah from the king's sons who were being killed and put him and the one who nursed him in a bedroom. Now Jehoshabeath was the daughter of King Jehoram and the wife of Jehoiada the priest. Since she was Ahaziah's sister, she hid Joash from Athaliah so that she did not kill him. ¹²While Athaliah ruled over the land, he was hiding with them in God's temple six years.

23 Then, in the seventh year, Jehoiada summoned his courage and took the commanders of hundreds into a covenant with him: Azariah son of Jeroham, Ishmael son of Jehohanan, Azariah son of Obed, Maaseiah son of Adaiah, and Elishaphat son of Zichri. ²They made a circuit throughout Judah. They gathered the Levites from all the cities of Judah and the heads of the families of Israel, and they came to Jerusalem.

³Then the whole assembly made a covenant with the king in God's temple. Jehoiada said to them, "Here is the king's son! He must reign, just as the Lord promised concerning David's sons. ⁴This is what you are to do: a third of you, priests and Levites who are coming on duty on the Sabbath, are to be gatekeepers. ⁵A third are to be at the king's palace, and a third are to be at the Foundation Gate, and all the troops will be in the courtyards of the Lord's temple. ⁶No one is to enter the Lord's temple but the priests and those Levites who serve; they may enter because they are holy, but all the people are to obey the requirement of the Lord. ⁷You must completely surround the king with weapons in hand. Anyone who enters the temple is to be put to death. You must be with the king in all his daily tasks."

⁸So the commanders of hundreds did everything Jehoiada the priest commanded. They each brought their men—those coming on duty on the Sabbath and those going off duty on the Sabbath—for Jehoiada the priest did not release the divisions. ⁹Jehoiada the priest gave to the commanders of hundreds King David's spears, shields, and quivers that were in God's temple. ¹⁰Then he stationed all the troops with their weapons in hand surrounding the king—from the right side of the temple to the left side, by the altar and by the temple.

¹¹They brought out the king's son, put the crown on him, gave him the *testimony, and made him king. Jehoiada and his sons anointed him and cried, "Long live the king!"

¹²When Athaliah heard the noise from the troops, the guards, and those praising the king, she went to the troops in the Lord's temple. ¹³As she looked, there was the king standing by his pillar at the entrance. The commanders and the trumpeters were by the king, and all the people of the land were rejoicing and blowing trumpets while the singers with musical instruments were leading the praise. Athaliah tore her clothes and screamed, "Treason, treason!"

¹⁴Then Jehoiada the priest sent out the commanders of hundreds, those in charge of the army, saying, "Take her out between the ranks, and put anyone who follows her to death by the sword," for the priest had said, "Don't put her to death in the Lord's temple."

¹⁵ So they arrested her, and she went by the entrance of the Horses' Gate to the king's palace, where they put her to death.

¹⁶ Then Jehoiada made a covenant between himself, the king, and the people that they would be the LORD's people. ¹⁷ So all the people went to the temple of *Baal and tore it down. They broke its altars and images into pieces and killed Mattan, the priest of Baal, at the altars.

¹⁸ Then Jehoiada put the oversight of the LORD's temple into the hands of the Levitical priests, whom David had appointed over the LORD's temple, to offer *burnt offerings to the LORD as it is written in the law of Moses, with rejoicing and song ordained by David. ¹⁹ He stationed gatekeepers at the gates of the LORD's temple so that nothing *unclean could enter for any reason. ²⁰ Then he took with him the commanders of hundreds, the nobles, the governors of the people, and all the people of the land and brought the king down from the LORD's temple. They entered the king's palace through the Upper Gate and seated the king on the throne of the kingdom. ²¹ All the people of the land rejoiced, and the city was quiet, for they had put Athaliah to death by the sword.

24 Joash was seven years old when he became king and reigned 40 years in Jerusalem. His mother's name was Zibiah; she was from Beer-sheba. ² Throughout the time of Jehoiada the priest, Joash did what was right in the LORD's sight. ³ Jehoiada acquired two wives for him, and he was the father of sons and daughters.

⁴ Afterward, Joash took it to heart to renovate the LORD's temple. ⁵ So he gathered the priests and Levites and said, "Go out to the cities of Judah and collect money from all Israel to repair the temple of your God as needed year by year, and do it quickly."

However, the Levites did not hurry. ⁶ So the king called Jehoiada the high priest and said, "Why haven't you required the Levites to bring from Judah and Jerusalem the tax imposed by the LORD's servant Moses and the assembly of Israel for the tent of the testimony? ⁷ For the sons of that wicked Athaliah broke into the LORD's temple and even used the sacred things of the LORD's temple for the *Baals."

⁸ At the king's command a chest was made and placed outside the gate of the LORD's temple. ⁹ Then a proclamation was issued in Judah and Jerusalem that the tax God's servant Moses imposed on Israel in the wilderness be brought to the LORD. ¹⁰ All the leaders and all the people rejoiced, brought the tax, and put it in the chest until it was full. ¹¹ Whenever the chest was brought by the Levites to the king's overseers, and when they saw that there was a large amount of money, the king's secretary and the high priest's deputy came and emptied the chest, picked it up, and returned it to its place. They did this daily and gathered the money in abundance. ¹² Then the king and Jehoiada gave it to those in charge of the labor on the LORD's temple, who were hiring stonecutters and carpenters to renovate the LORD's temple, also blacksmiths and coppersmiths to repair the LORD's temple.

¹³ The workmen did their work, and through them the repairs progressed. They restored God's temple to its specifications and reinforced it. ¹⁴ When they finished, they presented the rest of the money to the king and Jehoiada, who made articles for the LORD's temple with it—articles for ministry and for making *burnt

offerings, and ladles and articles of gold and silver. They regularly offered burnt offerings in the LORD's temple throughout Jehoiada's life.

¹⁵ Jehoiada died when he was old and full of days; he was 130 years old at his death. ¹⁶ He was buried in the city of David with the kings because he had done what was good in Israel with respect to God and His temple.

¹⁷ However, after Jehoiada died, the rulers of Judah came and paid homage to the king. Then the king listened to them, ¹⁸ and they abandoned the temple of *Yahweh, the God of their ancestors and served the *Asherah poles and the idols. So there was wrath against Judah and Jerusalem for this *guilt of theirs. ¹⁹ Nevertheless, He sent them prophets to bring them back to the LORD; they admonished them, but the people would not listen.

²⁰ The Spirit of God took control of Zechariah son of Jehoiada the priest. He stood above the people and said to them, "This is what God says, 'Why are you transgressing the LORD's commands and you do not prosper? Because you have abandoned the LORD, He has abandoned you.'" ²¹ But they conspired against him and stoned him at the king's command in the courtyard of the LORD's temple. ²² King Joash didn't remember the kindness that Zechariah's father Jehoiada had extended to him, but killed his son. While he was dying, he said, "May the LORD see and demand an account."

²³ At the turn of the year, an Aramean army went to war against Joash. They entered Judah and Jerusalem and destroyed all the leaders of the people among them and sent all the plunder to the king of Damascus. ²⁴ Although the Aramean army came with only a few men, the LORD handed over a vast army to them because the people of Judah had abandoned Yahweh, the God of their ancestors. So they executed judgment on Joash.

²⁵ When the Arameans saw that Joash had many wounds, they left him. His servants conspired against him, and killed him on his bed, because he had shed the blood of the sons of Jehoiada the priest. So he died, and they buried him in the city of David, but they did not bury him in the tombs of the kings.

²⁶ Those who conspired against him were Zabad, son of the Ammonite woman Shimeath, and Jehozabad, son of the Moabite woman Shimrith. ²⁷ Concerning his sons, the many *oracles about him, and the restoration of the LORD's temple, they are recorded in the Writing of the Book of the Kings. His son Amaziah became king in his place.

25 Amaziah became king when he was 25 years old and reigned 29 years in Jerusalem. His mother's name was Jehoaddan; she was from Jerusalem. ² He did what was right in the LORD's sight but not wholeheartedly.

³ As soon as the kingdom was firmly in his grasp, he executed his servants who had murdered his father the king. ⁴ However, he did not put their children to death, because—as it is written in the Law, in the book of Moses, where the LORD commanded—"Fathers must not die because of children, and children must not die because of fathers, but each one will die for his own sin."

⁵ Then Amaziah gathered Judah and assembled them according to ancestral house, according to commanders of thousands, and according to commanders of hundreds. He numbered those 20 years old or more for all Judah and Benjamin. He found there to

be 300,000 choice men who could serve in the army, bearing spear and shield. ⁶Then for 7,500 pounds of silver he hired 100,000 brave warriors from Israel.

⁷However, a man of God came to him and said, "King, do not let Israel's army go with you, for the LORD is not with Israel—all the Ephraimites. ⁸But if you go with them, do it! Be strong for battle! But God will make you stumble before the enemy, for God has the power to help or to make one stumble."

⁹Then Amaziah said to the man of God, "What should I do about the 7,500 pounds of silver I gave to Israel's division?"

The man of God replied, "The LORD is able to give you much more than this."

¹⁰So Amaziah released the division that came to him from Ephraim to go home. But they got very angry with Judah and returned home in a fierce rage.

¹¹Amaziah strengthened his position and led his people to the Valley of Salt. He struck down 10,000 Seirites, ¹²and the Judahites captured 10,000 alive. They took them to the top of a cliff where they threw them off, and all of them were dashed to pieces.

¹³As for the men of the division that Amaziah sent back so they would not go with him into battle, they raided the cities of Judah from Samaria to Beth-horon, struck down 3,000 of their people, and took a great deal of plunder.

¹⁴After Amaziah came from the attack on the Edomites, he brought the gods of the Seirites and set them up as his gods. He worshiped before them and burned incense to them. ¹⁵So the LORD's anger was against Amaziah, and He sent a prophet to him, who said, "Why have you sought a people's gods that could not deliver their own people from your hand?"

¹⁶While he was still speaking to him, the king asked, "Have we made you the king's counselor? Stop, why should you lose your life?"

So the prophet stopped, but he said, "I know that God intends to destroy you, because you have done this and have not listened to my advice."

¹⁷King Amaziah of Judah took counsel and sent word to Jehoash son of Jehoahaz, son of Jehu, king of Israel, saying, "Come, let us meet face to face."

¹⁸King Jehoash of Israel sent word to King Amaziah of Judah, saying, "The thistle that was in Lebanon sent a message to the cedar that was in Lebanon, saying, 'Give your daughter to my son as a wife.' Then a wild animal that was in Lebanon passed by and trampled the thistle. ¹⁹You have said, 'Look, I have defeated Edom,' and you have become overconfident that you will get glory. Now stay at home. Why stir up such trouble so that you fall and Judah with you?"

²⁰But Amaziah would not listen, for this turn of events was from God in order to hand them over to their enemies because they went after the gods of Edom. ²¹So King Jehoash of Israel advanced. He and King Amaziah of Judah faced off at Beth-shemesh in Judah. ²²Judah was routed before Israel, and each fled to his own tent. ²³King Jehoash of Israel captured Judah's King Amaziah son of Joash, son of Jehoahaz, at Beth-shemesh. Then Jehoash took him to Jerusalem and broke down 200 yards of Jerusalem's wall from the Ephraim Gate to the Corner Gate. ²⁴He took all the gold, silver, all the utensils that were found with Obed-edom in God's temple, the treasures of the king's palace, and the hostages. Then he returned to Samaria.

²⁵Judah's King Amaziah son of Joash lived 15 years after the death of Israel's King Jehoash son of Jehoahaz. ²⁶The rest of the events of Amaziah's reign, from beginning to end, are written in the Book of the Kings of Judah and Israel.

²⁷From the time Amaziah turned from following the LORD, a conspiracy was formed against him in Jerusalem, and he fled to Lachish. However, men were sent after him to Lachish, and they put him to death there. ²⁸They carried him back on horses and buried him with his fathers in the city of Judah.

26 All the people of Judah took Uzziah, who was 16 years old, and made him king in place of his father Amaziah. ²He rebuilt Eloth and restored it to Judah after Amaziah the king rested with his fathers.

³Uzziah was 16 years old when he became king and reigned 52 years in Jerusalem. His mother's name was Jecoliah from Jerusalem. ⁴He did what was right in the LORD's sight as his father Amaziah had done. ⁵He sought God throughout the lifetime of Zechariah, the teacher of the ·fear of God. During the time that he sought the LORD, God gave him success.

⁶Uzziah went out to wage war against the Philistines, and he tore down the wall of Gath, the wall of Jabneh, and the wall of Ashdod. Then he built cities in the vicinity of Ashdod and among the Philistines. ⁷God helped him against the Philistines, the Arabs that live in Gur-baal, and the Meunites. ⁸The Ammonites gave Uzziah tribute money, and his fame spread as far as the entrance of Egypt, for God made him very powerful. ⁹Uzziah built towers in Jerusalem at the Corner Gate, the Valley Gate, and the corner buttress, and he fortified them. ¹⁰Since he had many cattle both in the Judean foothills and the plain, he built towers in the desert and dug many wells. And since he was a lover of the soil, he had farmers and vinedressers in the hills and in the fertile lands.

¹¹Uzziah had an army equipped for combat that went out to war by division according to their assignments, as recorded by Jeiel the court secretary and Maaseiah the officer under the authority of Hananiah, one of the king's commanders. ¹²The total number of heads of families was 2,600 brave warriors. ¹³Under their authority was an army of 307,500 equipped for combat, a powerful force to help the king against the enemy. ¹⁴Uzziah provided the entire army with shields, spears, helmets, armor, bows and slingstones. ¹⁵He made skillfully designed devices in Jerusalem to shoot arrows and catapult large stones for use on the towers and on the corners. So his fame spread even to distant places, for he was marvelously helped until he became strong.

¹⁶But when he became strong, he grew arrogant and it led to his own destruction. He acted unfaithfully against the LORD his God by going into the LORD's sanctuary to burn incense on the incense altar. ¹⁷Azariah the priest, along with 80 brave priests of the LORD, went in after him. ¹⁸They took their stand against King Uzziah and said, "Uzziah, you have no right to offer incense to the LORD—only the consecrated priests, the descendants of Aaron, have the right to offer incense. Leave the sanctuary, for you have acted unfaithfully! You will not receive honor from the LORD God."

¹⁹Uzziah, with a firepan in his hand to offer incense, was enraged. But when he became enraged with the priests, in the presence of the priests in the LORD's temple beside the altar of incense, a skin disease broke out on his forehead. ²⁰Then Azariah the chief priest

and all the priests turned to him and saw that he was diseased on his forehead. They rushed him out of there. He himself also hurried to get out because the Lord had afflicted him. ²¹So King Uzziah was diseased to the time of his death. He lived in quarantine with a serious skin disease and was excluded from access to the Lord's temple, while his son Jotham was over the king's household governing the people of the land.

²²Now the prophet Isaiah son of Amoz wrote about the rest of the events of Uzziah's reign, from beginning to end. ²³Uzziah rested with his fathers, and he was buried with his fathers in the burial ground of the kings' cemetery, for they said, "He has a skin disease." His son Jotham became king in his place.

27 Jotham was 25 years old when he became king and reigned 16 years in Jerusalem. His mother's name was Jerushah daughter of Zadok. ²He did what was right in the Lord's sight as his father Uzziah had done. In addition, he didn't enter the Lord's sanctuary, but the people still behaved corruptly.

³Jotham built the Upper Gate of the Lord's temple, and he built extensively on the wall of Ophel. ⁴He also built cities in the hill country of Judah and fortresses and towers in the forests. ⁵He waged war against the king of the Ammonites. He overpowered the Ammonites, and that year they gave him 7,500 pounds of silver, 50,000 bushels of wheat, and 50,000 bushels of barley. They paid him the same in the second and third years. ⁶So Jotham strengthened himself because he did not waver in obeying the Lord his God.

⁷As for the rest of the events of Jotham's reign, along with all his wars and his ways, note that they are written in the Book of the Kings of Israel and Judah. ⁸He was 25 years old when he became king and reigned 16 years in Jerusalem. ⁹Jotham rested with his fathers and was buried in the city of David. His son Ahaz became king in his place.

28 Ahaz was 20 years old when he became king and reigned 16 years in Jerusalem. He did not do what was right in the Lord's sight like his ancestor David, ²for he walked in the ways of the kings of Israel and made cast images of the *Baals. ³He burned incense in the Valley of Hinnom and burned his children in the fire, imitating the detestable practices of the nations the Lord had dispossessed before the Israelites. ⁴He sacrificed and burned incense on the *high places, on the hills, and under every green tree.

⁵So the Lord his God handed Ahaz over to the king of Aram. He attacked him and took many captives to Damascus.

Ahaz was also handed over to the king of Israel, who struck him with great force: ⁶Pekah son of Remaliah killed 120,000 in Judah in one day—all brave men—because they had abandoned the Lord God of their ancestors. ⁷An Ephraimite warrior named Zichri killed the king's son Maaseiah, Azrikam governor of the palace, and Elkanah who was second to the king. ⁸Then the Israelites took 200,000 captives from their brothers—women, sons, and daughters. They also took a great deal of plunder from them and brought it to Samaria.

⁹A prophet of the Lord named Oded was there. He went out to meet the army that came to Samaria and said to them, "Look, the Lord God of your ancestors handed them over to you because of His wrath against Judah, but you slaughtered them in a rage that has reached heaven. ¹⁰Now you plan to reduce the people of Judah and Jerusalem, male and female, to slavery. Are you not also *guilty before *Yahweh your God? ¹¹Listen to me and return the captives you took from your brothers, for the Lord's burning anger is on you."

¹²So some men who were leaders of the Ephraimites—Azariah son of Jehohanan, Berechiah son of Meshillemoth, Jehizkiah son of Shallum, and Amasa son of Hadlai—stood in opposition to those coming from the war. ¹³They said to them, "You must not bring the captives here, for you plan to bring guilt on us from the Lord to add to our sins and our guilt. For we have much guilt, and burning anger is on Israel."

¹⁴The army left the captives and the plunder in the presence of the officers and the congregation. ¹⁵Then the men who were designated by name took charge of the captives and provided clothes for their naked ones from the plunder. They clothed them, gave them sandals, food and drink, dressed their wounds, and provided donkeys for all the feeble. The Israelites brought them to Jericho, the City of Palms, among their brothers. Then they returned to Samaria.

¹⁶At that time King Ahaz asked the king of Assyria for help. ¹⁷The Edomites came again, attacked Judah, and took captives. ¹⁸The Philistines also raided the cities of the Judean foothills and the *Negev of Judah and captured Beth-shemesh, Aijalon, Gederoth, Soco and its villages, Timnah and its villages, Gimzo and its villages, and they lived there. ¹⁹For the Lord humbled Judah because of King Ahaz of Judah, who threw off restraint in Judah and was unfaithful to the Lord. ²⁰Then Tiglath-pileser king of Assyria came against Ahaz; he oppressed him and did not give him support. ²¹Although Ahaz plundered the Lord's temple and the palace of the king and of the rulers and gave the plunder to the king of Assyria, it did not help him.

²²At the time of his distress, King Ahaz himself became more unfaithful to the Lord. ²³He sacrificed to the gods of Damascus which had defeated him; he said, "Since the gods of the kings of Aram are helping them, I will sacrifice to them so that they will help me." But they were the downfall of him and of all Israel. ²⁴Then Ahaz gathered up the utensils of God's temple, cut them into pieces, shut the doors of the Lord's temple, and made himself altars on every street corner in Jerusalem. ²⁵He made high places in every city of Judah to offer incense to other gods, and he provoked the Lord, the God of his ancestors.

²⁶As for the rest of his deeds and all his ways, from beginning to end, they are written in the Book of the Kings of Judah and Israel. ²⁷Ahaz rested with his fathers and was buried in the city, in Jerusalem, but they did not bring him into the tombs of the kings of Israel. His son Hezekiah became king in his place.

29 Hezekiah was 25 years old when he became king and reigned 29 years in Jerusalem. His mother's name was Abijah daughter of Zechariah. ²He did what was right in the Lord's sight just as his ancestor David had done.

³In the first year of his reign, in the first month, he opened the doors of the Lord's temple and repaired them. ⁴Then he brought in the priests and Levites and gathered them in the eastern public square. ⁵He said to them, "Hear me, Levites. Consecrate yourselves now and consecrate the temple of *Yahweh, the God of your ancestors. Remove everything impure from the holy place. ⁶For our fathers were unfaithful and did what is evil in the sight of the Lord our God. They abandoned

Him, turned their faces away from the LORD's tabernacle, and turned their backs on Him. ⁷They also closed the doors of the portico, extinguished the lamps, did not burn incense, and did not offer *burnt offerings in the holy place of the God of Israel. ⁸Therefore, the wrath of the LORD was on Judah and Jerusalem, and He made them an object of terror, horror, and mockery, as you see with your own eyes. ⁹Our fathers fell by the sword, and our sons, our daughters, and our wives are in captivity because of this. ¹⁰It is in my heart now to make a covenant with Yahweh, the God of Israel so that His burning anger may turn away from us. ¹¹My sons, don't be negligent now, for the LORD has chosen you to stand in His presence, to serve Him, and to be His ministers and burners of incense."

¹²Then the Levites stood up:

Mahath son of Amasai and Joel son of Azariah from the Kohathites;

Kish son of Abdi and Azariah son of Jehallelel from the Merarites;

Joah son of Zimmah and Eden son of Joah from the Gershonites;

¹³Shimri and Jeuel from the Elizaphanites;

Zechariah and Mattaniah from the Asaphites;

¹⁴Jehiel and Shimei from the Hemanites;

Shemaiah and Uzziel from the Jeduthunites.

¹⁵They gathered their brothers together, consecrated themselves, and went according to the king's command by the words of the LORD to cleanse the LORD's temple.

¹⁶The priests went to the entrance of the LORD's temple to cleanse it. They took all the unclean things they found in the LORD's sanctuary to the courtyard of the LORD's temple. Then the Levites received them and took them outside to the Kidron Valley. ¹⁷They began the consecration on the first day of the first month, and on the eighth day of the month they came to the portico of the LORD's temple. They consecrated the LORD's temple for eight days, and on the sixteenth day of the first month they finished.

¹⁸Then they went inside to King Hezekiah and said, "We have cleansed the whole temple of the LORD, the altar of burnt offering and all its utensils, and the table for the rows of the *bread of the Presence and all its utensils. ¹⁹We have set up and consecrated all the utensils that King Ahaz rejected during his reign when he became unfaithful. They are in front of the altar of the LORD."

²⁰King Hezekiah got up early, gathered the city officials, and went to the LORD's temple. ²¹They brought seven bulls, seven rams, seven lambs, and seven male goats as a *sin offering for the kingdom, for the sanctuary, and for Judah. Then he told the descendants of Aaron, the priests, to offer them on the altar of the LORD. ²²So they slaughtered the bulls, and the priests received the blood and sprinkled it on the altar. They slaughtered the rams and sprinkled the blood on the altar. They slaughtered the lambs and sprinkled the blood on the altar. ²³Then they brought the goats for the sin offering right into the presence of the king and the congregation, who laid their hands on them. ²⁴The priests slaughtered the goats and put their blood on the altar for a sin offering, to make *atonement for all Israel, for the king said that the burnt offering and sin offering were for all Israel.

²⁵Hezekiah stationed the Levites in the LORD's temple with cymbals, harps, and lyres according to the command of David, Gad the king's seer, and Nathan the prophet. For the command was from the LORD through His prophets. ²⁶The Levites stood with the instruments of David, and the priests with the trumpets.

²⁷Then Hezekiah ordered that the burnt offering be offered on the altar. When the burnt offerings began, the song of the LORD and the trumpets began, accompanied by the instruments of David king of Israel. ²⁸The whole assembly was worshiping, singing the song, and blowing the trumpets—all of this continued until the burnt offering was completed. ²⁹When the burnt offerings were completed, the king and all those present with him bowed down and worshiped. ³⁰Then King Hezekiah and the officials told the Levites to sing praise to the LORD in the words of David and of *Asaph the seer. So they sang praises with rejoicing and bowed down and worshiped.

³¹Hezekiah concluded, "Now you are consecrated to the LORD. Come near and bring sacrifices and thank offerings to the LORD's temple." So the congregation brought sacrifices and thank offerings, and all those with willing hearts brought burnt offerings. ³²The number of burnt offerings the congregation brought was 70 bulls, 100 rams, and 200 lambs; all these were for a burnt offering to the LORD. ³³Six hundred bulls and 3,000 sheep were consecrated.

³⁴However, since there were not enough priests, they weren't able to skin all the burnt offerings, so their Levite brothers helped them until the work was finished and until the priests consecrated themselves. For the Levites were more conscientious to consecrate themselves than the priests were. ³⁵Furthermore, the burnt offerings were abundant, along with the fat of the *fellowship offerings and with the *drink offerings for the burnt offering.

So the service of the LORD's temple was established. ³⁶Then Hezekiah and all the people rejoiced over how God had prepared the people, for it had come about suddenly.

30 Then Hezekiah sent word throughout all Israel and Judah, and he also wrote letters to Ephraim and Manasseh to come to the LORD's temple in Jerusalem to observe the *Passover of *Yahweh, the God of Israel. ²For the king and his officials and the entire congregation in Jerusalem decided to observe the Passover of the LORD in the second month, ³because they were not able to observe it at the appropriate time. Not enough of the priests had consecrated themselves and the people hadn't been gathered together in Jerusalem. ⁴The proposal pleased the king and the congregation, ⁵so they affirmed the proposal and spread the message throughout all Israel, from Beer-sheba to Dan, to come to observe the Passover of Yahweh, the God of Israel in Jerusalem, for they hadn't observed it often, as prescribed.

⁶So the couriers went throughout Israel and Judah with letters from the hand of the king and his officials, and according to the king's command, saying, "Israelites, return to Yahweh, the God of Abraham, Isaac, and Israel so that He may return to those of you who remain, who have escaped from the grasp of the kings of Assyria. ⁷Don't be like your fathers and your brothers who were unfaithful to Yahweh, the God of their ancestors so that He made them an object of horror as you yourselves see. ⁸Don't become obstinate now like your fathers did. Give your allegiance to Yahweh, and come to His sanctuary that He has consecrated

forever. Serve the LORD your God so that He may turn His burning anger away from you, ⁹for when you return to Yahweh, your brothers and your sons will receive mercy in the presence of their captors and will return to this land. For Yahweh your God is gracious and merciful; He will not turn His face away from you if you return to Him."

¹⁰The couriers traveled from city to city in the land of Ephraim and Manasseh as far as Zebulun, but the inhabitants laughed at them and mocked them. ¹¹But some from Asher, Manasseh, and Zebulun humbled themselves and came to Jerusalem. ¹²Also, the power of God was at work in Judah to unite them to carry out the command of the king and his officials by the word of the LORD.

¹³A very large assembly of people was gathered in Jerusalem to observe the Festival of Unleavened Bread in the second month. ¹⁴They proceeded to take away the altars that were in Jerusalem, and they took away the incense altars and threw them into the Kidron Valley. ¹⁵They slaughtered the Passover lamb on the fourteenth day of the second month. The priests and Levites were ashamed, and they consecrated themselves and brought ·burnt offerings to the LORD's temple. ¹⁶They stood at their prescribed posts, according to the law of Moses, the man of God. The priests sprinkled the blood received from the hand of the Levites, ¹⁷for there were many in the assembly who had not consecrated themselves, and so the Levites were in charge of slaughtering the Passover lambs for every ·unclean person to consecrate the lambs to the LORD. ¹⁸A large number of the people—many from Ephraim, Manasseh, Issachar, and Zebulun—were ritually unclean, yet they had eaten the Passover contrary to what was written. But Hezekiah had interceded for them, saying, "May the good LORD provide ·atonement on behalf of ¹⁹whoever sets his whole heart on seeking God, Yahweh, the God of his ancestors, even though not according to the purification rules of the sanctuary." ²⁰So the LORD heard Hezekiah and healed the people. ²¹The Israelites who were present in Jerusalem observed the Festival of Unleavened Bread seven days with great joy, and the Levites and the priests praised the LORD day after day with loud instruments. ²²Then Hezekiah encouraged all the Levites who performed skillfully before the LORD. They ate at the appointed festival for seven days, sacrificing ·fellowship offerings and giving thanks to Yahweh, the God of their ancestors.

²³The whole congregation decided to observe seven more days, so they observed seven days with joy, ²⁴for Hezekiah king of Judah contributed 1,000 bulls and 7,000 sheep for the congregation. Also, the officials contributed 1,000 bulls and 10,000 sheep for the congregation, and many priests consecrated themselves. ²⁵Then the whole assembly of Judah with the priests and Levites, the whole assembly that came from Israel, the foreigners who came from the land of Israel, and those who were living in Judah, rejoiced. ²⁶There was great rejoicing in Jerusalem, for nothing like this was known since the days of Solomon son of David, the king of Israel.

²⁷Then the priests and the Levites stood to bless the people, and God heard their voice, and their prayer came into His holy dwelling place in heaven.

31 When all this was completed, all Israel who had attended went out to the cities of Judah and broke up the sacred pillars, chopped down the ·Asherah poles, and tore down the ·high places and altars throughout Judah and Benjamin, as well as in Ephraim and Manasseh, to the last one. Then all the Israelites returned to their cities, each to his own possession.

²Hezekiah reestablished the divisions of the priests and Levites for the ·burnt offerings and ·fellowship offerings, for ministry, for giving thanks, and for praise in the gates of the camp of the LORD, each division corresponding to his service among the priests and Levites. ³The king contributed from his own possessions for the regular morning and evening burnt offerings, the burnt offerings of the Sabbaths, of the New Moons, and of the appointed feasts, as written in the law of the LORD. ⁴He told the people who lived in Jerusalem to give a contribution for the priests and Levites so that they could devote their energy to the law of the LORD. ⁵When the word spread, the Israelites gave liberally of the best of the grain, new wine, oil, honey, and of all the produce of the field, and they brought in an abundance, a tenth of everything. ⁶As for the Israelites and Judahites who lived in the cities of Judah, they also brought a tenth of the cattle and sheep, and a tenth of the dedicated things that were consecrated to the LORD their God. They gathered them into large piles. ⁷In the third month they began building up the piles, and they finished in the seventh month. ⁸When Hezekiah and his officials came and viewed the piles, they praised the LORD and His people Israel.

⁹Hezekiah asked the priests and Levites about the piles. ¹⁰Azariah, the chief priest of the household of Zadok, answered him, "Since they began bringing the offering to the LORD's temple, we eat and are satisfied and there is plenty left over because the LORD has blessed His people; this abundance is what is left over."

¹¹Hezekiah told them to prepare chambers in the LORD's temple, and they prepared them. ¹²The offering, the tenth, and the dedicated things were brought faithfully. Conaniah the Levite was the officer in charge of them, and his brother Shimei was second. ¹³Jehiel, Azaziah, Nahath, Asahel, Jerimoth, Jozabad, Eliel, Ismachiah, Mahath, and Benaiah were deputies under the authority of Conaniah and his brother Shimei by appointment of King Hezekiah and of Azariah the chief official of God's temple.

¹⁴Kore son of Imnah the Levite, the keeper of the East Gate, was over the freewill offerings to God to distribute the contribution to the LORD and the consecrated things. ¹⁵Eden, Miniamin, Jeshua, Shemaiah, Amariah, and Shecaniah in the cities of the priests were to faithfully distribute it under his authority to their brothers by divisions, whether large or small. ¹⁶In addition, they distributed it to males registered by genealogy three years old and above; to all who would enter the LORD's temple for their daily duty, for their service in their responsibilities according to their divisions. ¹⁷They distributed also to those recorded by genealogy of the priests by their ancestral families and the Levites 20 years old and above, by their responsibilities in their divisions; ¹⁸to those registered by genealogy—with all their infants, wives, sons, and daughters—of the whole assembly (for they had faithfully consecrated themselves as holy); ¹⁹and to the descendants of Aaron, the priests, in the common fields of their cities, in each and every city. There were men who were registered by name to distribute a portion

to every male among the priests and to every Levite recorded by genealogy.

[20] Hezekiah did this throughout all Judah. He did what was good and upright and true before the LORD his God. [21] He was diligent in every deed that he began in the service of God's temple, in the instruction and the commands, in order to seek his God, and he prospered.

32 After these faithful deeds, Sennacherib king of Assyria came and entered Judah. He laid siege to the fortified cities and intended to break into them. [2] Hezekiah saw that Sennacherib had come and that he planned war on Jerusalem, [3] so he consulted with his officials and his warriors about stopping up the waters of the springs that were outside the city, and they helped him. [4] Many people gathered and stopped up all the springs and the stream that flowed through the land; they said, "Why should the kings of Assyria come and find plenty of water?" [5] Then Hezekiah strengthened his position by rebuilding the entire brokendown wall and heightening the towers and the other outside wall. He repaired the supporting terraces of the city of David, and made an abundance of weapons and shields.

[6] He set military commanders over the people and gathered the people in the square of the city gate. Then he encouraged them, saying, [7] "Be strong and courageous! Don't be afraid or discouraged before the king of Assyria or before the large army that is with him, for there are more with us than with him. [8] He has only human strength, but we have •Yahweh our God to help us and to fight our battles." So the people relied on the words of King Hezekiah of Judah.

[9] After this, while Sennacherib king of Assyria with all his armed forces besieged Lachish, he sent his servants to Jerusalem against King Hezekiah of Judah and against all those of Judah who were in Jerusalem, saying, [10] "This is what King Sennacherib of Assyria says: 'What are you relying on that you remain in Jerusalem under siege? [11] Isn't Hezekiah misleading you to give you over to death by famine and thirst when he says, "Yahweh our God will deliver us from the power of the king of Assyria"? [12] Didn't Hezekiah himself remove His •high places and His altars and say to Judah and Jerusalem, "You must worship before one altar, and you must burn incense on it"?

[13] "Don't you know what I and my fathers have done to all the peoples of the lands? Have any of the national gods of the lands been able to deliver their land from my power? [14] Who among all the gods of these nations that my predecessors •completely destroyed was able to deliver his people from my power, that your God should be able to do the same for you? [15] So now, don't let Hezekiah deceive you, and don't let him mislead you like this. Don't believe him, for no god of any nation or kingdom has been able to deliver his people from my power or the power of my fathers. How much less will your God deliver you from my power!'"

[16] His servants said more against the LORD God and against His servant Hezekiah. [17] He also wrote letters to mock Yahweh, the God of Israel, saying against Him:

Just like the national gods of the lands that did not deliver their people from my power, so Hezekiah's God will not deliver His people from my power.

[18] Then they called out loudly in Hebrew to the people of Jerusalem, who were on the wall, to frighten and discourage them in order that he might capture the city. [19] They spoke against the God of Jerusalem like they had spoken against the gods of the peoples of the earth, which were made by human hands.

[20] King Hezekiah and the prophet Isaiah son of Amoz prayed about this and cried out to heaven, [21] and the LORD sent an angel who annihilated every brave warrior, leader, and commander in the camp of the king of Assyria. So the king of Assyria returned in disgrace to his land. He went to the temple of his god, and there some of his own children struck him down with the sword.

[22] So the LORD saved Hezekiah and the inhabitants of Jerusalem from the power of King Sennacherib of Assyria and from the power of all others. He gave them rest on every side. [23] Many were bringing an offering to the LORD to Jerusalem and valuable gifts to King Hezekiah of Judah, and he was exalted in the eyes of all the nations after that.

[24] In those days Hezekiah became sick to the point of death, so he prayed to the LORD, and He spoke to him and gave him a miraculous sign. [25] However, because his heart was proud, Hezekiah didn't respond according to the benefit that had come to him. So there was wrath on him, Judah, and Jerusalem. [26] Then Hezekiah humbled himself for the pride of his heart—he and the inhabitants of Jerusalem—so the LORD's wrath didn't come on them during Hezekiah's lifetime.

[27] Hezekiah had abundant riches and glory, and he made himself treasuries for silver, gold, precious stones, spices, shields, and every desirable item. [28] He made warehouses for the harvest of grain, new wine, and oil, and stalls for all kinds of cattle, and pens for flocks. [29] He made cities for himself, and he acquired herds of sheep and cattle in abundance, for God gave him abundant possessions.

[30] This same Hezekiah blocked the outlet of the water of the Upper Gihon and channeled it smoothly downward and westward to the city of David. Hezekiah succeeded in everything he did. [31] When the ambassadors of Babylon's rulers were sent to him to inquire about the miraculous sign that happened in the land, God left him to test him and discover what was in his heart.

[32] As for the rest of the events of Hezekiah's reign and his deeds of faithful love, note that they are written in the Visions of the Prophet Isaiah son of Amoz, and in the Book of the Kings of Judah and Israel. [33] Hezekiah rested with his fathers and was buried on the ascent to the tombs of David's descendants. All Judah and the inhabitants of Jerusalem paid him honor at his death. His son Manasseh became king in his place.

33 Manasseh was 12 years old when he became king and reigned 55 years in Jerusalem. [2] He did what was evil in the LORD's sight, imitating the detestable practices of the nations that the LORD had dispossessed before the Israelites. [3] He rebuilt the •high places that his father Hezekiah had torn down and reestablished the altars for the •Baals. He made •Asherah poles, and he worshiped the whole heavenly •host and served them. [4] He built altars in the LORD's temple, where •Yahweh had said, "Jerusalem is where My name will remain forever." [5] He built altars to the whole heavenly host in both courtyards of the LORD's temple. [6] He passed his sons through the fire in the Valley of Hinnom. He practiced witchcraft, •divination, and sorcery,

and consulted mediums and spiritists. He did a great deal of evil in the LORD's sight, provoking Him.

⁷Manasseh set up a carved image of the idol he had made, in God's temple, about which God had said to David and his son Solomon, "I will establish My name forever in this temple and in Jerusalem, which I have chosen out of all the tribes of Israel. ⁸I will never again remove the feet of the Israelites from the land where I stationed your ancestors, if only they will be careful to do all that I have commanded them through Moses— all the law, statutes, and judgments." ⁹So Manasseh caused Judah and the inhabitants of Jerusalem to stray so that they did worse evil than the nations the LORD had destroyed before the Israelites.

¹⁰The LORD spoke to Manasseh and his people, but they didn't listen. ¹¹So He brought against them the military commanders of the king of Assyria. They captured Manasseh with hooks, bound him with bronze shackles, and took him to Babylon. ¹²When he was in distress, he sought the favor of Yahweh his God and earnestly humbled himself before the God of his ancestors. ¹³He prayed to Him, so He heard his petition and granted his request, and brought him back to Jerusalem, to his kingdom. So Manasseh came to know that Yahweh is God.

¹⁴After this, he built the outer wall of the city of David from west of Gihon in the valley to the entrance of the Fish Gate; he brought it around the Ophel, and he heightened it considerably. He also placed military commanders in all the fortified cities of Judah.

¹⁵He removed the foreign gods and the idol from the LORD's temple, along with all the altars that he had built on the mountain of the LORD's temple and in Jerusalem, and he threw them outside the city. ¹⁶He built the altar of the LORD and offered ˚fellowship and thank offerings on it. Then he told Judah to serve Yahweh, the God of Israel. ¹⁷However, the people still sacrificed at the high places, but only to Yahweh their God.

¹⁸The rest of the events of Manasseh's reign, along with his prayer to his God and the words of the seers who spoke to him in the name of Yahweh, the God of Israel, are written in the Records of Israel's Kings. ¹⁹His prayer and how God granted his request, and all his sin and unfaithfulness and the sites where he built high places and set up Asherah poles and carved images before he humbled himself, they are written in the Records of Hozai. ²⁰Manasseh rested with his fathers, and he was buried in his own house. His son Amon became king in his place.

²¹Amon was 22 years old when he became king and reigned two years in Jerusalem. ²²He did what was evil in the LORD's sight just as his father Manasseh had done. Amon sacrificed to all the carved images that his father Manasseh had made, and he served them. ²³But he did not humble himself before the LORD like his father Manasseh humbled himself; instead, Amon increased his ˚guilt.

²⁴So his servants conspired against him and put him to death in his own house. ²⁵Then the common people executed all those who conspired against King Amon and made his son Josiah king in his place.

34 Josiah was eight years old when he became king and reigned 31 years in Jerusalem. ²He did what was right in the LORD's sight and walked in the ways of his ancestor David; he did not turn aside to the right or the left.

³In the eighth year of his reign, while he was still a youth, Josiah began to seek the God of his ancestor David, and in the twelfth year he began to cleanse Judah and Jerusalem of the ˚high places, the ˚Asherah poles, the carved images, and the cast images. ⁴Then in his presence the altars of the ˚Baals were torn down, and he chopped down the incense altars that were above them. He shattered the Asherah poles, the carved images, and the cast images, crushed them to dust, and scattered them over the graves of those who had sacrificed to them. ⁵He burned the bones of the priests on their altars. So he cleansed Judah and Jerusalem. ⁶He did the same in the cities of Manasseh, Ephraim, and Simeon, and as far as Naphtali and on their surrounding mountain shrines. ⁷He tore down the altars, and he smashed the Asherah poles and the carved images to powder. He chopped down all the incense altars throughout the land of Israel and returned to Jerusalem.

⁸In the eighteenth year of his reign, in order to cleanse the land and the temple, Josiah sent Shaphan son of Azaliah, along with Maaseiah the governor of the city and the court historian Joah son of Joahaz, to repair the temple of the LORD his God.

⁹So they went to Hilkiah the high priest, and gave him the money brought into God's temple. The Levites and the doorkeepers had collected money from Manasseh, Ephraim, and from the entire remnant of Israel, and from all Judah, Benjamin, and the inhabitants of Jerusalem. ¹⁰They put it into the hands of those doing the work—those who oversaw the LORD's temple. They gave it to the workmen who were working in the LORD's temple, to repair and restore the temple; ¹¹they gave it to the carpenters and builders and also used it to buy quarried stone and timbers— for joining and making beams—for the buildings that Judah's kings had destroyed.

¹²The men were doing the work with integrity. Their overseers were Jahath and Obadiah, Levites from the Merarites, and Zechariah and Meshullam from the Kohathites as supervisors. The Levites were all skilled with musical instruments. ¹³They were also over the porters and were supervising all those doing the work task by task. Some of the Levites were secretaries, officers, and gatekeepers.

¹⁴When they brought out the money that had been deposited in the LORD's temple, Hilkiah the priest found the book of the law of the LORD written by the hand of Moses. ¹⁵Consequently, Hilkiah told Shaphan the court secretary, "I have found the book of the law in the LORD's temple," and he gave the book to Shaphan.

¹⁶Shaphan took the book to the king, and also reported, "Your servants are doing all that was placed in their hands. ¹⁷They have emptied out the money that was found in the LORD's temple and have put it into the hand of the overseers and the hand of those doing the work." ¹⁸Then Shaphan the court secretary told the king, "Hilkiah the priest gave me a book," and Shaphan read from it in the presence of the king.

¹⁹When the king heard the words of the law, he tore his clothes. ²⁰Then he commanded Hilkiah, Ahikam son of Shaphan, Abdon son of Micah, Shaphan the court secretary, and the king's servant Asaiah, ²¹"Go. Ask ˚Yahweh for me and for those remaining in Israel and Judah, concerning the words of the book that was found. For great is the LORD's wrath that is poured

out on us because our fathers have not kept the word of the LORD in order to do everything written in this book."

²²So Hilkiah and those the king had designated went to the prophetess Huldah, the wife of Shallum son of Tokhath, son of Hasrah, keeper of the wardrobe. She lived in Jerusalem in the Second District. They spoke with her about this.

²³She said to them, "This is what Yahweh, the God of Israel says: Say to the man who sent you to Me, ²⁴'This is what Yahweh says: I am about to bring disaster on this place and on its inhabitants, fulfilling all the curses written in the book that they read in the presence of the king of Judah, ²⁵because they have abandoned Me and burned incense to other gods in order to provoke Me with all the works of their hands. My wrath will be poured out on this place, and it will not be quenched.' ²⁶Say this to the king of Judah who sent you to ask Yahweh, 'This is what Yahweh, the God of Israel says: As for the words that you heard, ²⁷because your heart was tender and you humbled yourself before God when you heard His words against this place and against its inhabitants, and because you humbled yourself before Me, and you tore your clothes and wept before Me, I Myself have heard'—this is the LORD's declaration. ²⁸'I will indeed gather you to your fathers, and you will be gathered to your grave in peace. Your eyes will not see all the disaster that I am bringing on this place and on its inhabitants.'"

Then they reported to the king.

²⁹So the king sent messengers and gathered all the elders of Judah and Jerusalem. ³⁰The king went up to the LORD's temple with all the men of Judah and the inhabitants of Jerusalem, as well as the priests and the Levites—all the people from great to small. He read in their hearing all the words of the book of the covenant that had been found in the LORD's temple. ³¹Then the king stood at his post and made a covenant in the LORD's presence to follow the LORD and to keep His commands, His decrees, and His statutes with all his heart and with all his soul in order to carry out the words of the covenant written in this book.

³²He had all those present in Jerusalem and Benjamin agree to it. So all the inhabitants of Jerusalem carried out the covenant of God, the God of their ancestors.

³³So Josiah removed everything that was detestable from all the lands belonging to the Israelites, and he required all who were present in Israel to serve the LORD their God. Throughout his reign they did not turn aside from following Yahweh, the God of their ancestors.

35 Josiah observed the LORD's ⁕Passover and slaughtered the Passover lambs on the fourteenth day of the first month. ²He appointed the priests to their responsibilities and encouraged them to serve in the LORD's temple. ³He said to the Levites who taught all Israel the holy things of the LORD, "Put the holy ark in the temple built by Solomon son of David king of Israel. Since you do not have to carry it on your shoulders, now serve ⁕Yahweh your God and His people Israel.

⁴"Organize your ancestral houses by your divisions according to the written instruction of David king of Israel and that of his son Solomon. ⁵Serve in the holy place by the divisions of the ancestral houses for your brothers, the lay people, and the distribution of the tribal household of the Levites. ⁶Slaughter the Pass-

over lambs, consecrate yourselves, and make preparations for your brothers to carry out the word of the LORD through Moses."

⁷Then Josiah donated 30,000 sheep, lambs, and young goats, plus 3,000 bulls from his own possessions, for the Passover sacrifices for all the lay people who were present. ⁸His officials also donated willingly for the people, the priests, and the Levites. Hilkiah, Zechariah, and Jehiel, chief officials of God's temple, gave 2,600 Passover sacrifices and 300 bulls for the priests. ⁹Conaniah and his brothers Shemaiah and Nethanel, and Hashabiah, Jeiel, and Jozabad, officers of the Levites, donated 5,000 Passover sacrifices for the Levites, plus 500 bulls.

¹⁰So the service was established; the priests stood at their posts and the Levites in their divisions according to the king's command. ¹¹Then they slaughtered the Passover lambs, and while the Levites were skinning the animals, the priests sprinkled the blood they had been given. ¹²They removed the ⁕burnt offerings so that they might be given to the divisions of the ancestral houses of the lay people to offer to the LORD, according to what is written in the book of Moses; they did the same with the bulls. ¹³They roasted the Passover lambs with fire according to regulation. They boiled the holy sacrifices in pots, kettles, and bowls; and they quickly brought them to the lay people. ¹⁴Afterward, they made preparations for themselves and for the priests, since the priests, the descendants of Aaron, were busy offering up burnt offerings and fat until night. So the Levites made preparations for themselves and for the priests, the descendants of Aaron.

¹⁵The singers, the descendants of ⁕Asaph, were at their stations according to the command of David, Asaph, Heman, and Jeduthun the king's seer. Also, the gatekeepers were at each gate. None of them left their tasks because their Levite brothers had made preparations for them.

¹⁶So all the service of the LORD was established that day for observing the Passover and for offering burnt offerings on the altar of the LORD, according to the command of King Josiah. ¹⁷The Israelites who were present in Judah also observed the Passover at that time and the Festival of Unleavened Bread for seven days. ¹⁸No Passover had been observed like it in Israel since the days of Samuel the prophet. None of the kings of Israel ever observed a Passover like the one that Josiah observed with the priests, the Levites, all Judah, the Israelites who were present in Judah, and the inhabitants of Jerusalem. ¹⁹In the eighteenth year of Josiah's reign, this Passover was observed.

²⁰After all this that Josiah had prepared for the temple, Neco king of Egypt marched up to fight at Carchemish by the Euphrates, and Josiah went out to confront him. ²¹But Neco sent messengers to him, saying, "What is the issue between you and me, king of Judah? I have not come against you today but I am fighting another dynasty. God told me to hurry. Stop opposing God who is with me; don't make Him destroy you!"

²²But Josiah did not turn away from him; instead, in order to fight with him he disguised himself. He did not listen to Neco's words from the mouth of God, but went to the Valley of Megiddo to fight. ²³The archers shot King Josiah, and he said to his servants, "Take me away, for I am severely wounded!" ²⁴So his servants

took him out of the war chariot, carried him in his second chariot, and brought him to Jerusalem. Then he died, and they buried him in the tomb of his fathers. All Judah and Jerusalem mourned for Josiah. ²⁵ Jeremiah chanted a dirge over Josiah, and all the singing men and singing women still speak of Josiah in their dirges to this very day. They established them as a statute for Israel, and indeed they are written in the Dirges.

²⁶ The rest of the events of Josiah's reign, along with his deeds of faithful love according to what is written in the law of the LORD, ²⁷ and his words, from beginning to end, are written in the Book of the Kings of Israel and Judah.

36 Then the common people took Jehoahaz son of Josiah and made him king in Jerusalem in place of his father.

² Jehoahaz was 23 years old when he became king and reigned three months in Jerusalem. ³ The king of Egypt deposed him in Jerusalem and fined the land 7,500 pounds of silver and 75 pounds of gold. ⁴ Then Neco king of Egypt made Jehoahaz's brother Eliakim king over Judah and Jerusalem and changed Eliakim's name to Jehoiakim. But Neco took his brother Jehoahaz and brought him to Egypt.

⁵ Jehoiakim was 25 years old when he became king and reigned 11 years in Jerusalem. He did what was evil in the sight of the LORD his God. ⁶ Now Nebuchadnezzar king of Babylon attacked him and bound him in bronze shackles to take him to Babylon. ⁷ Also Nebuchadnezzar took some of the utensils of the LORD's temple to Babylon and put them in his temple in Babylon.

⁸ The rest of the deeds of Jehoiakim, the detestable things he did, and what was found against him, are written in the Book of Israel's Kings. His son Jehoiachin became king in his place.

⁹ Jehoiachin was 18 years old when he became king and reigned three months and 10 days in Jerusalem. He did what was evil in the LORD's sight. ¹⁰ In the spring Nebuchadnezzar sent for him and brought him to Babylon along with the valuable utensils of the LORD's temple. Then he made Jehoiachin's brother Zedekiah king over Judah and Jerusalem.

¹¹ Zedekiah was 21 years old when he became king and reigned 11 years in Jerusalem. ¹² He did what was evil in the sight of the LORD his God and did not humble himself before Jeremiah the prophet at the LORD's command. ¹³ He also rebelled against King Nebuchadnezzar who had made him swear allegiance by God. He became obstinate and hardened his heart against returning to •Yahweh, the God of Israel. ¹⁴ All the leaders of the priests and the people multiplied their unfaithful deeds, imitating all the detestable practices of the nations, and they defiled the LORD's temple that He had consecrated in Jerusalem.

¹⁵ But Yahweh, the God of their ancestors sent word against them by the hand of His messengers, sending them time and time again, for He had compassion on His people and on His dwelling place. ¹⁶ But they kept ridiculing God's messengers, despising His words, and scoffing at His prophets, until the LORD's wrath was so stirred up against His people that there was no remedy. ¹⁷ So He brought up against them the king of the Chaldeans, who killed their choice young men with the sword in the house of their sanctuary. He had no pity on young men or young women, elderly or aged; He handed them all over to him. ¹⁸ He took everything to Babylon—all the articles of God's temple, large and small, the treasures of the LORD's temple, and the treasures of the king and his officials. ¹⁹ Then the Chaldeans burned God's temple. They tore down Jerusalem's wall, burned down all its palaces, and destroyed all its valuable articles.

²⁰ He deported those who escaped from the sword to Babylon, and they became servants to him and his sons until the rise of the Persian kingdom. ²¹ This fulfilled the word of the LORD through Jeremiah and the land enjoyed its Sabbath rest all the days of the desolation until 70 years were fulfilled.

²² In the first year of Cyrus king of Persia, the word of the LORD spoken through Jeremiah was fulfilled. The LORD put it into the mind of King Cyrus of Persia to issue a proclamation throughout his entire kingdom and also to put it in writing:

²³ This is what King Cyrus of Persia says: The LORD, the God of heaven, has given me all the kingdoms of the earth and has appointed me to build Him a temple at Jerusalem in Judah. Whoever among you of His people may go up, and may the LORD his God be with him.

EZRA

1 In the first year of Cyrus king of Persia, the word of the LORD spoken through Jeremiah was fulfilled. The LORD put it into the mind of King Cyrus to issue a proclamation throughout his entire kingdom and to put it in writing:

² This is what King Cyrus of Persia says: "The LORD, the God of heaven, has given me all the kingdoms of the earth and has appointed me to build Him a house at Jerusalem in Judah. ³ Whoever is among His people, may his God be with him, and may he go to Jerusalem in Judah and build the house of the LORD, the God of Israel, the God who is in Jerusalem. ⁴ Let every survivor, wherever he lives, be assisted by the men of that region with silver, gold, goods, and livestock, along with a freewill offering for the house of God in Jerusalem."

⁵ So the family leaders of Judah and Benjamin, along with the priests and Levites—everyone God had motivated—prepared to go up and rebuild the LORD's house in Jerusalem. ⁶ All their neighbors supported them with silver articles, gold, goods, livestock, and valuables, in addition to all that was given as a freewill offering. ⁷ King Cyrus also brought out the articles of the LORD's house that Nebuchadnezzar had taken from Jerusalem and had placed in the house of his gods. ⁸ King Cyrus of Persia had them brought out under the supervision of Mithredath the treasurer, who counted them out to Sheshbazzar the prince of Judah. ⁹ This was the inventory:

30 gold basins, 1,000 silver basins,

29 silver knives, [10]30 gold bowls,
410 various silver bowls,
and 1,000 other articles.
[11]The gold and silver articles totaled 5,400. Sheshbazzar brought all of them when the exiles went up from Babylon to Jerusalem.

2 These now are the people of the province who came from those captive exiles King Nebuchadnezzar of Babylon had deported to Babylon. They returned to Jerusalem and Judah, each to his own town. [2]They came with Zerubbabel, Jeshua, Nehemiah, Seraiah, Reelaiah, Mordecai, Bilshan, Mispar, Bigvai, Rehum, and Baanah.

The number of the Israelite men included:

[3]	Parosh's descendants	2,172
[4]	Shephatiah's descendants	372
[5]	Arah's descendants	775
[6]	Pahath-moab's descendants:	
	Jeshua's and Joab's descendants	2,812
[7]	Elam's descendants	1,254
[8]	Zattu's descendants	945
[9]	Zaccai's descendants	760
[10]	Bani's descendants	642
[11]	Bebai's descendants	623
[12]	Azgad's descendants	1,222
[13]	Adonikam's descendants	666
[14]	Bigvai's descendants	2,056
[15]	Adin's descendants	454
[16]	Ater's descendants: of Hezekiah	98
[17]	Bezai's descendants	323
[18]	Jorah's descendants	112
[19]	Hashum's descendants	223
[20]	Gibbar's descendants	95
[21]	Bethlehem's people	123
[22]	Netophah's men	56
[23]	Anathoth's men	128
[24]	Azmaveth's people	42
[25]	Kiriatharim's, Chephirah's,	
	and Beeroth's people	743
[26]	Ramah's and Geba's people	621
[27]	Michmas's men	122
[28]	Bethel's and Ai's men	223
[29]	Nebo's people	52
[30]	Magbish's people	156
[31]	the other Elam's people	1,254
[32]	Harim's people	320
[33]	Lod's, Hadid's, and Ono's people	725
[34]	Jericho's people	345
[35]	Senaah's people	3,630

[36]The priests included:

Jedaiah's descendants of the house of Jeshua	973
[37] Immer's descendants	1,052
[38] Pashhur's descendants	1,247
[39] and Harim's descendants	1,017

[40]The Levites included:

Jeshua's and Kadmiel's descendants from Hodaviah's descendants	74

[41]The singers included:

*Asaph's descendants	128

[42]The gatekeepers' descendants included:
Shallum's descendants, Ater's descendants, Talmon's descendants, Akkub's descendants, Hatita's descendants,

Shobai's descendants, in all	139

[43]The temple servants included:
Ziha's descendants, Hasupha's descendants, Tabbaoth's descendants,
[44]Keros's descendants,
Siaha's descendants, Padon's descendants,
[45] Lebanah's descendants,
Hagabah's descendants,
Akkub's descendants, [46]Hagab's descendants,
Shalmai's descendants, Hanan's descendants,
[47] Giddel's descendants, Gahar's descendants,
Reaiah's descendants, [48]Rezin's descendants,
Nekoda's descendants, Gazzam's descendants,
[49] Uzza's descendants, Paseah's descendants,
Besai's descendants, [50]Asnah's descendants,
Meunim's descendants,
Nephusim's descendants,
[51] Bakbuk's descendants,
Hakupha's descendants,
Harhur's descendants,
[52]Bazluth's descendants,
Mehida's descendants,
Harsha's descendants,
[53] Barkos's descendants, Sisera's descendants,
Temah's descendants, [54]Neziah's descendants,
and Hatipha's descendants.

[55] The descendants of Solomon's servants included:
Sotai's descendants,
Hassophereth's descendants,
Peruda's descendants, [56]Jaalah's descendants,
Darkon's descendants, Giddel's descendants,
[57] Shephatiah's descendants,
Hattil's descendants,
Pochereth-hazzebaim's descendants,
and Ami's descendants.

[58] All the temple servants and the descendants of Solomon's servants	392.

[59]The following are those who came from Telmelah, Tel-harsha, Cherub, Addan, and Immer but were unable to prove that their families and ancestry were Israelite:

[60] Delaiah's descendants,	
Tobiah's descendants,	
Nekoda's descendants	652

[61]and from the descendants of the priests: the descendants of Hobaiah, the descendants of Hakkoz, the descendants of Barzillai—who had taken a wife from the daughters of Barzillai the Gileadite and was called by their name. [62]These searched for their entries in the genealogical records, but they could not be found, so they were disqualified from the priesthood. [63]The governor ordered them not to eat the most holy things until there was a priest who could consult the *Urim and Thummim.

[64] The whole combined assembly numbered	42,360

[65] not including their 7,337 male
and female slaves,
and their 200 male and female singers.
[66] They had 736 horses, 245 mules,
[67] 435 camels, and 6,720 donkeys.

[68]After they arrived at the Lord's house in Jerusalem, some of the family leaders gave freewill offerings for the house of God in order to have it rebuilt on its original site. [69]Based on what they could give, they gave 61,000 gold coins, 6,250 pounds of silver, and 100 priestly garments to the treasury for the project. [70]The priests, Levites, singers, gatekeepers, temple servants,

and some of the people settled in their towns, and the rest of Israel settled in their towns.

3 By the seventh month, the Israelites had settled in their towns, and the people gathered together in Jerusalem. ²Jeshua son of Jozadak and his brothers the priests along with Zerubbabel son of Shealtiel and his brothers began to build the altar of Israel's God in order to offer ˙burnt offerings on it, as it is written in the law of Moses, the man of God. ³They set up the altar on its foundation and offered burnt offerings for the morning and evening on it to the LORD even though they feared the surrounding peoples. ⁴They celebrated the Festival of Booths as prescribed, and offered burnt offerings each day, based on the number specified by ordinance for each festival day. ⁵After that, they offered the regular burnt offering and the offerings for the beginning of each month and for all the LORD's appointed holy occasions, as well as the freewill offerings brought to the LORD.

⁶On the first day of the seventh month they began to offer burnt offerings to the LORD, even though the foundation of the LORD's temple had not yet been laid. ⁷They gave money to the stonecutters and artisans, and gave food, drink, and oil to the people of Sidon and Tyre, so they could bring cedar wood from Lebanon to Joppa by sea, according to the authorization given them by King Cyrus of Persia.

⁸In the second month of the second year after they arrived at God's house in Jerusalem, Zerubbabel son of Shealtiel, Jeshua son of Jozadak, and the rest of their brothers, including the priests, the Levites, and all who had returned to Jerusalem from the captivity, began to build. They appointed the Levites who were 20 years old or more to supervise the work on the LORD's house. ⁹Jeshua with his sons and brothers, Kadmiel with his sons, and the sons of Judah and of Henadad, with their sons and brothers, the Levites, joined together to supervise those working on the house of God.

¹⁰When the builders had laid the foundation of the LORD's temple, the priests, dressed in their robes and holding trumpets, and the Levites descended from ˙Asaph, holding cymbals, took their positions to praise the LORD, as King David of Israel had instructed. ¹¹They sang with praise and thanksgiving to the LORD: "For He is good; His faithful love to Israel endures forever." Then all the people gave a great shout of praise to the LORD because the foundation of the LORD's house had been laid.

¹²But many of the older priests, Levites, and family leaders, who had seen the first temple, wept loudly when they saw the foundation of this house, but many others shouted joyfully. ¹³The people could not distinguish the sound of the joyful shouting from that of the weeping, because the people were shouting so loudly. And the sound was heard far away.

4 When the enemies of Judah and Benjamin heard that the returned exiles were building a temple for ˙Yahweh, the God of Israel, ²they approached Zerubbabel and the leaders of the families and said to them, "Let us build with you, for we also worship your God and have been sacrificing to Him since the time King Esar-haddon of Assyria brought us here."

³But Zerubbabel, Jeshua, and the other leaders of Israel's families answered them, "You may have no part with us in building a house for our God, since we alone must build it for Yahweh, the God of Israel, as King Cyrus, the king of Persia has commanded us." ⁴Then

the people who were already in the land discouraged the people of Judah and made them afraid to build. ⁵They also bribed officials to act against them to frustrate their plans throughout the reign of King Cyrus of Persia and until the reign of King Darius of Persia.

⁶At the beginning of the reign of Ahasuerus, the people who were already in the land wrote an accusation against the residents of Judah and Jerusalem. ⁷During the time of King Artaxerxes of Persia, Bishlam, Mithredath, Tabeel and the rest of his colleagues wrote to King Artaxerxes. The letter was written in Aramaic and translated.

⁸Rehum the chief deputy and Shimshai the scribe wrote a letter to King Artaxerxes concerning Jerusalem as follows:

⁹From Rehum the chief deputy, Shimshai the scribe, and the rest of their colleagues—the judges and magistrates from Tripolis, Persia, Erech, Babylon, Susa (that is, the people of Elam), ¹⁰and the rest of the peoples whom the great and illustrious Ashurbanipal deported and settled in the cities of Samaria and the region west of the Euphrates River.

¹¹This is the text of the letter they sent to him:

To King Artaxerxes from your servants, the men from the region west of the Euphrates River:

¹²Let it be known to the king that the Jews who came from you have returned to us at Jerusalem. They are rebuilding that rebellious and evil city, finishing its walls, and repairing its foundations. ¹³Let it now be known to the king that if that city is rebuilt and its walls are finished, they will not pay tribute, duty, or land tax, and the royal revenue will suffer. ¹⁴Since we have taken an oath of loyalty to the king, and it is not right for us to witness his dishonor, we have sent to inform the king ¹⁵that a search should be made in your fathers' record books. In these record books you will discover and verify that the city is a rebellious city, harmful to kings and provinces. There have been revolts in it since ancient times. That is why this city was destroyed. ¹⁶We advise the king that if this city is rebuilt and its walls are finished, you will not have any possession west of the Euphrates.

¹⁷The king sent a reply to his chief deputy Rehum, Shimshai the scribe, and the rest of their colleagues living in Samaria and elsewhere in the region west of the Euphrates River:

Greetings.

¹⁸The letter you sent us has been translated and read in my presence. ¹⁹I issued a decree and a search was conducted. It was discovered that this city has had uprisings against kings since ancient times, and there have been rebellions and revolts in it. ²⁰Powerful kings have also ruled over Jerusalem and exercised authority over the whole region, and tribute, duty, and land tax were paid to them. ²¹Therefore, issue an order for these men to stop, so that this city will not be rebuilt until a further decree has been pronounced by me. ²²See that you not neglect this matter. Otherwise, the damage will increase and the royal interests will suffer.

²³As soon as the text of King Artaxerxes' letter was read to Rehum, Shimshai the scribe, and their col-

leagues, they immediately went to the Jews in Jerusalem and forcibly stopped them.

²⁴Now the construction of God's house in Jerusalem had stopped and remained at a standstill until the second year of the reign of King Darius of Persia. 5 ¹But when the prophets Haggai and Zechariah son of Iddo prophesied to the Jews who were in Judah and Jerusalem, in the name of the God of Israel who was over them, ²Zerubbabel son of Shealtiel and Jeshua son of Jozadak began to rebuild God's house in Jerusalem. The prophets of God were with them, helping them.

³At that time Tattenai the governor of the region west of the Euphrates River, Shethar-bozenai, and their colleagues came to the Jews and asked, "Who gave you the order to rebuild this temple and finish this structure?" ⁴They also asked them, "What are the names of the workers who are constructing this building?" ⁵But God was watching over the Jewish elders. These men wouldn't stop them until a report was sent to Darius, so that they could receive written instructions about this matter.

⁶This is the text of the letter that Tattenai the governor of the region west of the Euphrates River, Shethar-bozenai, and their colleagues, the officials in the region, sent to King Darius. ⁷They sent him a report, written as follows:

To King Darius:
All greetings.
⁸Let it be known to the king that we went to the house of the great God in the province of Judah. It is being built with cut stones, and its beams are being set in the walls. This work is being done diligently and succeeding through the people's efforts. ⁹So we questioned the elders and asked, "Who gave you the order to rebuild this temple and finish this structure?" ¹⁰We also asked them for their names, so that we could write down the names of their leaders for your information.

¹¹This is the reply they gave us:
We are the servants of the God of heaven and earth and are rebuilding the temple that was built many years ago, which a great king of Israel built and finished. ¹²But since our fathers angered the God of heaven, He handed them over to King Nebuchadnezzar of Babylon, the Chaldean, who destroyed this temple and deported the people to Babylon. ¹³However, in the first year of Cyrus king of Babylon, he issued a decree to rebuild the house of God. ¹⁴He also took from the temple in Babylon the gold and silver articles of God's house that Nebuchadnezzar had taken from the temple in Jerusalem and carried them to the temple in Babylon. He released them from the temple in Babylon to a man named Sheshbazzar, the governor by the appointment of King Cyrus. ¹⁵Cyrus told him, "Take these articles, put them in the temple in Jerusalem, and let the house of God be rebuilt on its original site." ¹⁶Then this same Sheshbazzar came and laid the foundation of God's house in Jerusalem. It has been under construction from that time until now, yet it has not been completed.

¹⁷So if it pleases the king, let a search of the royal archives in Babylon be conducted to see if it is true that a decree was issued by King Cyrus to rebuild the house of God in Jerusalem. Let the king's decision regarding this matter be sent to us.

6 King Darius gave the order, and they searched in the library of Babylon in the archives. ²But it was in the fortress of Ecbatana in the province of Media that a scroll was found with this record written on it: ³In the first year of King Cyrus, he issued a decree concerning the house of God in Jerusalem: Let the house be rebuilt as a place for offering sacrifices, and let its original foundations be retained. Its height is to be 90 feet and its width 90 feet, ⁴with three layers of cut stones and one of timber. The cost is to be paid from the royal treasury. ⁵The gold and silver articles of God's house that Nebuchadnezzar took from the temple in Jerusalem and carried to Babylon must also be returned. They are to be brought to the temple in Jerusalem where they belong and put into the house of God.

⁶Therefore, you must stay away from that place, Tattenai governor of the region west of the Euphrates River, Shethar-bozenai, and your colleagues, the officials in the region. ⁷Leave the construction of the house of God alone. Let the governor and elders of the Jews rebuild this house of God on its original site.

⁸I hereby issue a decree concerning what you must do, so that the elders of the Jews can rebuild the house of God:
The cost is to be paid in full to these men out of the royal revenues from the taxes of the region west of the Euphrates River, so that the work will not stop. ⁹Whatever is needed—young bulls, rams, and lambs for ·burnt offerings to the God of heaven, or wheat, salt, wine, and oil, as requested by the priests in Jerusalem—let it be given to them every day without fail, ¹⁰so that they can offer sacrifices of pleasing aroma to the God of heaven and pray for the life of the king and his sons.

¹¹I also issue a decree concerning any man who interferes with this directive:
Let a beam be torn from his house and raised up; he will be impaled on it, and his house will be made into a garbage dump because of this offense. ¹²May the God who caused His name to dwell there overthrow any king or people who dares to harm or interfere with this house of God in Jerusalem. I, Darius, have issued the decree. Let it be carried out diligently.

¹³Then Tattenai governor of the region west of the Euphrates River, Shethar-bozenai, and their colleagues diligently carried out what King Darius had decreed. ¹⁴So the Jewish elders continued successfully with the building under the prophesying of Haggai the prophet and Zechariah son of Iddo. They finished the building according to the command of the God of Israel and the decrees of Cyrus, Darius, and King Artaxerxes of Persia. ¹⁵This house was completed on the third day of the month of Adar in the sixth year of the reign of King Darius.

¹⁶Then the Israelites, including the priests, the Levites, and the rest of the exiles, celebrated the dedication of the house of God with joy. ¹⁷For the dedication of God's house they offered 100 bulls, 200 rams, and

400 lambs, as well as 12 male goats as a *sin offering for all Israel—one for each Israelite tribe. ¹⁸They also appointed the priests by their divisions and the Levites by their groups to the service of God in Jerusalem, according to what is written in the book of Moses.

¹⁹The exiles observed the *Passover on the fourteenth day of the first month. ²⁰All of the priests and Levites were ceremonially *clean, because they had purified themselves. They killed the Passover lamb for themselves, their priestly brothers, and all the exiles. ²¹The Israelites who had returned from exile ate it, together with all who had separated themselves from the uncleanness of the Gentiles of the land in order to worship *Yahweh, the God of Israel. ²²They observed the Festival of *Unleavened Bread for seven days with joy, because the LORD had made them joyful, having changed the Assyrian king's attitude toward them, so that he supported them in the work on the house of the God of Israel.

7 After these events, during the reign of King Artaxerxes of Persia, Ezra—
Seraiah's son, Azariah's son,
Hilkiah's son, ²Shallum's son,
Zadok's son, Ahitub's son,
³   Amariah's son, Azariah's son,
Meraioth's son, ⁴Zerahiah's son,
Uzzi's son, Bukki's son,
⁵   Abishua's son, Phinehas's son,
Eleazar's son, Aaron the chief priest's son
⁶—came up from Babylon. He was a scribe skilled in the law of Moses, which *Yahweh, the God of Israel, had given. The king had granted him everything he requested because the hand of Yahweh his God was on him. ⁷Some of the Israelites, priests, Levites, singers, gatekeepers, and temple servants accompanied him to Jerusalem in the seventh year of King Artaxerxes.

⁸Ezra came to Jerusalem in the fifth month, during the seventh year of the king. ⁹He began the journey from Babylon on the first day of the first month and arrived in Jerusalem on the first day of the fifth month since the gracious hand of his God was on him. ¹⁰Now Ezra had determined in his heart to study the law of the LORD, obey it, and teach its statutes and ordinances in Israel.

¹¹This is the text of the letter King Artaxerxes gave to Ezra the priest and scribe, an expert in matters of the LORD's commands and statutes for Israel:

¹²Artaxerxes, king of kings, to Ezra the priest, an expert in the law of the God of heaven:
Greetings.

¹³I issue a decree that any of the Israelites in my kingdom, including their priests and Levites, who want to go to Jerusalem, may go with you. ¹⁴You are sent by the king and his seven counselors to evaluate Judah and Jerusalem according to the law of your God, which is in your possession. ¹⁵You are also to bring the silver and gold the king and his counselors have willingly given to the God of Israel, whose dwelling is in Jerusalem, ¹⁶and all the silver and gold you receive throughout the province of Babylon, together with the freewill offerings given by the people and the priests to the house of their God in Jerusalem. ¹⁷Then you are to buy with this money as many bulls, rams, and lambs as needed, along with their *grain and *drink offerings, and offer them on the altar at the house of your

God in Jerusalem. ¹⁸You may do whatever seems best to you and your brothers with the rest of the silver and gold, according to the will of your God. ¹⁹You must deliver to the God of Jerusalem all the articles given to you for the service of the house of your God. ²⁰You may use the royal treasury to pay for anything else needed for the house of your God.

²¹I, King Artaxerxes, issue a decree to all the treasurers in the region west of the Euphrates River:
Whatever Ezra the priest, an expert in the law of the God of heaven, asks of you must be provided promptly, ²²up to 7,500 pounds of silver, 500 bushels of wheat, 550 gallons of wine, 550 gallons of oil, and salt without limit. ²³Whatever is commanded by the God of heaven must be done diligently for the house of the God of heaven, so that wrath will not fall on the realm of the king and his sons. ²⁴Be advised that tribute, duty, and land tax must not be imposed on any priests, Levites, singers, doorkeepers, temple servants, or other servants of this house of God.

²⁵And you, Ezra, according to God's wisdom that you possess, appoint magistrates and judges to judge all the people in the region west of the Euphrates who know the laws of your God and to teach anyone who does not know them. ²⁶Anyone who does not keep the law of your God and the law of the king, let a fair judgment be executed against him, whether death, banishment, confiscation of property, or imprisonment.

²⁷Praise Yahweh the God of our fathers, who has put it into the king's mind to glorify the house of the LORD in Jerusalem, ²⁸and who has shown favor to me before the king, his counselors, and all his powerful officers. So I took courage because I was strengthened by Yahweh my God, and I gathered Israelite leaders to return with me.

8 These are the family leaders and the genealogical records of those who returned with me from Babylon during the reign of King Artaxerxes:
²   Gershom, from Phinehas's descendants;
Daniel, from Ithamar's descendants;
Hattush, from David's descendants,
³   who was of Shecaniah's descendants;
Zechariah, from Parosh's descendants,
and 150 men with him who were registered
by genealogy;
⁴   Eliehoenai son of Zerahiah
from Pahath-moab's descendants,
and 200 men with him;
⁵   Shecaniah son of Jahaziel
from Zattu's descendants,
and 300 men with him;
⁶   Ebed son of Jonathan
from Adin's descendants,
and 50 men with him;
⁷   Jeshaiah son of Athaliah
from Elam's descendants,
and 70 men with him;
⁸   Zebadiah son of Michael
from Shephatiah's descendants,
and 80 men with him;
⁹   Obadiah son of Jehiel
from Joab's descendants,
and 218 men with him;

¹⁰ Shelomith son of Josiphiah
from Bani's descendants,
and 160 men with him;
¹¹ Zechariah son of Bebai
from Bebai's descendants,
and 28 men with him;
¹² Johanan son of Hakkatan
from Azgad's descendants,
and 110 men with him;
¹³ these are the last ones,
from Adonikam's descendants,
and their names are:
Eliphelet, Jeuel, and Shemaiah,
and 60 men with them;
¹⁴ Uthai and Zaccur
from Bigvai's descendants,
and 70 men with them.

¹⁵ I gathered them at the river that flows to Ahava, and we camped there for three days. I searched among the people and priests, but found no Levites there. ¹⁶ Then I summoned the leaders: Eliezer, Ariel, Shemaiah, Elnathan, Jarib, Elnathan, Nathan, Zechariah, and Meshullam, as well as the teachers Joiarib and Elnathan. ¹⁷ I sent them to Iddo, the leader at Casiphia, with a message for him and his brothers, the temple servants at Casiphia, that they should bring us ministers for the house of our God. ¹⁸ Since the gracious hand of our God was on us, they brought us Sherebiah—a man of insight from the descendants of Mahli, a descendant of Levi son of Israel—along with his sons and brothers, 18 men, ¹⁹ plus Hashabiah, along with Jeshaiah, from the descendants of Merari, and his brothers and their sons, 20 men. ²⁰ There were also 220 of the temple servants, who had been appointed by David and the leaders for the work of the Levites. All were identified by name.

²¹ I proclaimed a fast by the Ahava River, so that we might humble ourselves before our God and ask Him for a safe journey for us, our children, and all our possessions. ²² I did this because I was ashamed to ask the king for infantry and cavalry to protect us from enemies during the journey, since we had told him, "The hand of our God is gracious to all who seek Him, but His great anger is against all who abandon Him." ²³ So we fasted and pleaded with our God about this, and He granted our request.

²⁴ I selected 12 of the leading priests, along with Sherebiah, Hashabiah, and 10 of their brothers. ²⁵ I weighed out to them the silver, the gold, and the articles—the contribution for the house of our God that the king, his counselors, his leaders, and all the Israelites who were present had offered. ²⁶ I weighed out to them 24 tons of silver, silver articles weighing 7,500 pounds, 7,500 pounds of gold, ²⁷ 20 gold bowls worth 1,000 gold coins, and two articles of fine gleaming bronze, as valuable as gold. ²⁸ Then I said to them, "You are holy to the Lord, and the articles are holy. The silver and gold are a freewill offering to the Lord God of your fathers. ²⁹ Guard them carefully until you weigh them out in the chambers of the Lord's house before the leading priests, Levites, and heads of the Israelite families in Jerusalem." ³⁰ So the priests and Levites took charge of the silver, the gold, and the articles that had been weighed out, to bring them to the house of our God in Jerusalem.

³¹ We set out from the Ahava River on the twelfth day of the first month to go to Jerusalem. We were strengthened by our God, and He protected us from the power of the enemy and from ambush along the way. ³² So we arrived at Jerusalem and rested there for three days. ³³ On the fourth day the silver, the gold, and the articles were weighed out in the house of our God into the care of Meremoth the priest, son of Uriah. Eleazar son of Phinehas was with him. The Levites Jozabad son of Jeshua and Noadiah son of Binnui were also with them. ³⁴ Everything was verified by number and weight, and the total weight was recorded at that time.

³⁵ The exiles who had returned from the captivity offered *burnt offerings to the God of Israel: 12 bulls for all Israel, 96 rams, and 77 lambs, along with 12 male goats as a *sin offering. All this was a burnt offering for the Lord. ³⁶ They also delivered the king's edicts to the royal satraps and governors of the region west of the Euphrates, so that they would support the people and the house of God.

9 After these things had been done, the leaders approached me and said: "The people of Israel, the priests, and the Levites have not separated themselves from the surrounding peoples whose detestable practices are like those of the Canaanites, Hittites, Perizzites, Jebusites, Ammonites, Moabites, Egyptians, and Amorites. ² Indeed, the Israelite men have taken some of their daughters as wives for themselves and their sons, so that the holy *seed has become mixed with the surrounding peoples. The leaders and officials have taken the lead in this unfaithfulness!" ³ When I heard this report, I tore my tunic and robe, pulled out some of the hair from my head and beard, and sat down devastated.

⁴ Everyone who trembled at the words of the God of Israel gathered around me, because of the unfaithfulness of the exiles, while I sat devastated until the evening offering. ⁵ At the evening offering, I got up from my humiliation, with my tunic and robe torn. Then I fell on my knees and spread out my hands to *Yahweh my God. ⁶ And I said:

My God, I am ashamed and embarrassed to lift my face toward You, my God, because our iniquities are higher than our heads and our *guilt is as high as the heavens. ⁷ Our guilt has been terrible from the days of our fathers until the present. Because of our iniquities we have been handed over, along with our kings and priests, to the surrounding kings, and to the sword, captivity, plundering, and open shame, as it is today. ⁸ But now, for a brief moment, grace has come from Yahweh our God to preserve a remnant for us and give us a stake in His holy place. Even in our slavery, God has given us new life and light to our eyes. ⁹ Though we are slaves, our God has not abandoned us in our slavery. He has extended grace to us in the presence of the Persian kings, giving us new life, so that we can rebuild the house of our God and repair its ruins, to give us a wall in Judah and Jerusalem.

¹⁰ Now, our God, what can we say in light of this? For we have abandoned the commands ¹¹ You gave through Your servants the prophets, saying: "The land you are entering to possess is an impure land. The surrounding peoples have filled it from end to end with their uncleanness by their impurity and detestable practices. ¹² So do not give your daughters to their sons in

marriage or take their daughters for your sons. Never seek their peace or prosperity, so that you will be strong, eat the good things of the land, and leave it as an inheritance to your sons forever." [13] After all that has happened to us because of our evil deeds and terrible guilt—though You, our God, have punished us less than our sins deserve and have allowed us to survive— [14] should we break Your commands again and intermarry with the peoples who commit these detestable practices? Wouldn't You become so angry with us that You would destroy us, leaving no survivors? [15] LORD God of Israel, You are righteous, for we survive as a remnant today. Here we are before You with our guilt, though no one can stand in Your presence because of this.

10 While Ezra prayed and confessed, weeping and falling facedown before the house of God, an extremely large assembly of Israelite men, women, and children gathered around him. The people also wept bitterly. [2] Then Shecaniah son of Jehiel, an Elamite, responded to Ezra: "We have been unfaithful to our God by marrying foreign women from the surrounding peoples, but there is still hope for Israel in spite of this. [3] Let us therefore make a covenant before our God to send away all the foreign wives and their children, according to the counsel of my lord and of those who tremble at the command of our God. Let it be done according to the law. [4] Get up, for this matter is your responsibility, and we support you. Be strong and take action!"

[5] Then Ezra got up and made the leading priests, Levites, and all Israel take an oath to do what had been said; so they took the oath. [6] Ezra then went from the house of God and walked to the chamber of Jehohanan son of Eliashib, where he spent the night. He did not eat food or drink water, because he was mourning over the unfaithfulness of the exiles.

[7] They circulated a proclamation throughout Judah and Jerusalem that all the exiles should gather at Jerusalem. [8] Whoever did not come within three days would forfeit all his possessions, according to the decision of the leaders and elders, and would be excluded from the assembly of the exiles.

[9] So all the men of Judah and Benjamin gathered in Jerusalem within the three days. On the twentieth day of the ninth month, all the people sat in the square at the house of God, trembling because of this matter and because of the heavy rain. [10] Then Ezra the priest stood up and said to them, "You have been unfaithful by marrying foreign women, adding to Israel's *guilt. [11] Therefore, make a confession to *Yahweh the God of your fathers and do His will. Separate yourselves from the surrounding peoples and your foreign wives."

[12] Then all the assembly responded with a loud voice: "Yes, we will do as you say! [13] But there are many people, and it is the rainy season. We don't have the stamina to stay out in the open. This isn't something that can be done in a day or two, for we have rebelled terribly in this matter. [14] Let our leaders represent the entire assembly. Then let all those in our towns who have married foreign women come at appointed times, together with the elders and judges of each town, in

order to avert the fierce anger of our God concerning this matter." [15] Only Jonathan son of Asahel and Jahzeiah son of Tikvah opposed this, with Meshullam and Shabbethai the Levite supporting them.

[16] The exiles did what had been proposed. Ezra the priest selected men who were family leaders, all identified by name, to represent their ancestral houses. They convened on the first day of the tenth month to investigate the matter, [17] and by the first day of the first month they had dealt with all the men who had married foreign women.

[18] The following were found to have married foreign women from the descendants of the priests:

from the descendants of Jeshua son of Jozadak and his brothers: Maaseiah, Eliezer, Jarib, and Gedaliah. [19] They pledged to send their wives away, and being guilty, they offered a ram from the flock for their guilt;

[20] Hanani and Zebadiah from Immer's descendants;

[21] Maaseiah, Elijah, Shemaiah, Jehiel, and Uzziah from Harim's descendants;

[22] Elioenai, Maaseiah, Ishmael, Nethanel, Jozabad, and Elasah from Pashhur's descendants.

[23] The Levites:

Jozabad, Shimei, Kelaiah (that is Kelita), Pethahiah, Judah, and Eliezer.

[24] The singers:

Eliashib.

The gatekeepers:

Shallum, Telem, and Uri.

[25] The Israelites:

Parosh's descendants: Ramiah, Izziah, Malchijah, Mijamin, Eleazar, Malchijah, and Benaiah;

[26] Elam's descendants: Mattaniah, Zechariah, Jehiel, Abdi, Jeremoth, and Elijah;

[27] Zattu's descendants: Elioenai, Eliashib, Mattaniah, Jeremoth, Zabad, and Aziza;

[28] Bebai's descendants: Jehohanan, Hananiah, Zabbai, and Athlai;

[29] Bani's descendants: Meshullam, Malluch, Adaiah, Jashub, Sheal, and Jeremoth;

[30] Pahath-moab's descendants: Adna, Chelal, Benaiah, Maaseiah, Mattaniah, Bezalel, Binnui, and Manasseh;

[31] Harim's descendants: Eliezer, Isshijah, Malchijah, Shemaiah, Shimeon, [32] Benjamin, Malluch, and Shemariah;

[33] Hashum's descendants: Mattenai, Mattattah, Zabad, Eliphelet, Jeremai, Manasseh, and Shimei;

[34] Bani's descendants: Maadai, Amram, Uel, [35] Benaiah, Bedeiah, Cheluhi, [36] Vaniah, Meremoth, Eliashib, [37] Mattaniah, Mattenai, Jaasu, [38] Bani, Binnui, Shimei, [39] Shelemiah, Nathan, Adaiah, [40] Machnadebai, Shashai, Sharai, [41] Azarel, Shelemiah, Shemariah, [42] Shallum, Amariah, and Joseph;

[43] Nebo's descendants: Jeiel, Mattithiah, Zabad, Zebina, Jaddai, Joel, and Benaiah.

[44] All of these had married foreign women, and some of the wives had given birth to children.

NEHEMIAH

1 The words of Nehemiah son of Hacaliah:

During the month of Chislev in the twentieth year, when I was in the fortress city of Susa, ²Hanani, one of my brothers, arrived with men from Judah, and I questioned them about Jerusalem and the Jewish remnant that had survived the exile. ³They said to me, "The remnant in the province, who survived the exile, are in great trouble and disgrace. Jerusalem's wall has been broken down, and its gates have been burned down."

⁴When I heard these words, I sat down and wept. I mourned for a number of days, fasting and praying before the God of heaven. ⁵I said,

"Yahweh, the God of heaven, the great and awe-inspiring God who keeps His gracious covenant with those who love Him and keep His commands, ⁶let Your eyes be open and Your ears be attentive to hear Your servant's prayer that I now pray to You day and night for Your servants, the Israelites. I confess the sins we have committed against You. Both I and my father's house have sinned. ⁷We have acted corruptly toward You and have not kept the commands, statutes, and ordinances You gave Your servant Moses. ⁸Please remember what You commanded Your servant Moses: "If you are unfaithful, I will scatter you among the peoples. ⁹But if you return to Me and carefully observe My commands, even though your exiles were banished to the ends of the earth, I will gather them from there and bring them to the place where I chose to have My name dwell." ¹⁰They are Your servants and Your people. You redeemed them by Your great power and strong hand. ¹¹Please, Lord, let Your ear be attentive to the prayer of Your servant and to that of Your servants who delight to revere Your name. Give Your servant success today, and have compassion on him in the presence of this man."

At the time, I was the king's cupbearer.

2 During the month of Nisan in the twentieth year of King Artaxerxes, when wine was set before him, I took the wine and gave it to the king. I had never been sad in his presence, ²so the king said to me, "Why are you sad, when you aren't sick? This is nothing but depression."

I was overwhelmed with fear ³and replied to the king, "May the king live forever! Why should I not be sad when the city where my ancestors are buried lies in ruins and its gates have been destroyed by fire?"

⁴Then the king asked me, "What is your request?"

So I prayed to the God of heaven ⁵and answered the king, "If it pleases the king, and if your servant has found favor with you, send me to Judah and to the city where my ancestors are buried, so that I may rebuild it."

⁶The king, with the queen seated beside him, asked me, "How long will your journey take, and when will you return?" So I gave him a definite time, and it pleased the king to send me.

⁷I also said to the king: "If it pleases the king, let me have letters written to the governors of the region west of the Euphrates River, so that they will grant me safe passage until I reach Judah. ⁸And let me have a letter written to Asaph, keeper of the king's forest, so that he will give me timber to rebuild the gates of the temple's fortress, the city wall, and the home where I will live." The king granted my requests, for I was graciously strengthened by my God.

⁹I went to the governors of the region west of the Euphrates and gave them the king's letters. The king had also sent officers of the infantry and cavalry with me. ¹⁰When Sanballat the Horonite and Tobiah the Ammonite official heard that someone had come to seek the well-being of the Israelites, they were greatly displeased.

¹¹After I arrived in Jerusalem and had been there three days, ¹²I got up at night and took a few men with me. I didn't tell anyone what my God had laid on my heart to do for Jerusalem. The only animal I took was the one I was riding. ¹³I went out at night through the Valley Gate toward the Serpent's Well and the Dung Gate, and I inspected the walls of Jerusalem that had been broken down and its gates that had been destroyed by fire. ¹⁴I went on to the Fountain Gate and the King's Pool, but farther down it became too narrow for my animal to go through. ¹⁵So I went up at night by way of the valley and inspected the wall. Then heading back, I entered through the Valley Gate and returned. ¹⁶The officials did not know where I had gone or what I was doing, for I had not yet told the Jews, priests, nobles, officials, or the rest of those who would be doing the work. ¹⁷So I said to them, "You see the trouble we are in. Jerusalem lies in ruins and its gates have been burned down. Come, let's rebuild Jerusalem's wall, so that we will no longer be a disgrace." ¹⁸I told them how the gracious hand of my God had been on me, and what the king had said to me.

They said, "Let's start rebuilding," and they were encouraged to do this good work.

¹⁹When Sanballat the Horonite, Tobiah the Ammonite official, and Geshem the Arab heard about this, they mocked and despised us, and said, "What is this you're doing? Are you rebelling against the king?"

²⁰I gave them this reply, "The God of heaven is the One who will grant us success. We, His servants, will start building, but you have no share, right, or historic claim in Jerusalem."

3 Eliashib the high priest and his fellow priests began rebuilding the Sheep Gate. They dedicated it and installed its doors. After building the wall to the Tower of the Hundred and the Tower of Hananel, they dedicated it. ²The men of Jericho built next to Eliashib, and next to them Zaccur son of Imri built.

³The sons of Hassenaah built the Fish Gate. They built it with beams and installed its doors, bolts, and bars. ⁴Next to them Meremoth son of Uriah, son of Hakkoz, made repairs. Beside them Meshullam son of Berechiah, son of Meshezabel, made repairs. Next to them Zadok son of Baana made repairs. ⁵Beside them the Tekoites made repairs, but their nobles did not lift a finger to help their supervisors.

⁶Joiada son of Paseah and Meshullam son of Besodeiah repaired the Old Gate. They built it with beams and installed its doors, bolts, and bars. ⁷Next to them the repairs were done by Melatiah the Gibeonite, Jadon

the Meronothite, and the men of Gibeon and Mizpah, who were under the authority of the governor of the region west of the Euphrates River. [8] After him Uzziel son of Harhaiah, the goldsmith, made repairs, and next to him Hananiah son of the perfumer made repairs. They restored Jerusalem as far as the Broad Wall.

[9] Next to them Rephaiah son of Hur, ruler over half the district of Jerusalem, made repairs. [10] After them Jedaiah son of Harumaph made repairs across from his house. Next to him Hattush the son of Hashabneiah made repairs. [11] Malchijah son of Harim and Hasshub son of Pahath-moab made repairs to another section, as well as to the Tower of the Ovens. [12] Beside him Shallum son of Hallohesh, ruler over half the district of Jerusalem, made repairs—he and his daughters.

[13] Hanun and the inhabitants of Zanoah repaired the Valley Gate. They rebuilt it and installed its doors, bolts, and bars, and repaired 500 yards of the wall to the Dung Gate. [14] Malchijah son of Rechab, ruler over the district of Beth-haccherem, repaired the Dung Gate. He rebuilt it and installed its doors, bolts, and bars.

[15] Shallun son of Col-hozeh, ruler over the district of Mizpah, repaired the Fountain Gate. He rebuilt it and roofed it. Then he installed its doors, bolts, and bars. He also made repairs to the wall of the Pool of Shelah near the king's garden, as far as the stairs that descend from the city of David.

[16] After him Nehemiah son of Azbuk, ruler over half the district of Beth-zur, made repairs up to a point opposite the tombs of David, as far as the artificial pool and the House of the Warriors. [17] Next to him the Levites made repairs under Rehum son of Bani. Beside him Hashabiah, ruler over half the district of Keilah, made repairs for his district. [18] After him their fellow Levites made repairs under Binnui son of Henadad, ruler over half the district of Keilah. [19] Next to him Ezer son of Jeshua, ruler over Mizpah, made repairs to another section opposite the ascent to the armory at the Angle.

[20] After him Baruch son of Zabbai diligently repaired another section, from the Angle to the door of the house of Eliashib the high priest. [21] Beside him Meremoth son of Uriah, son of Hakkoz, made repairs to another section, from the door of Eliashib's house to the end of his house. [22] And next to him the priests from the surrounding area made repairs.

[23] After them Benjamin and Hasshub made repairs opposite their house. Beside them Azariah son of Maaseiah, son of Ananiah, made repairs beside his house. [24] After him Binnui son of Henadad made repairs to another section, from the house of Azariah to the Angle and the corner. [25] Palal son of Uzai made repairs opposite the Angle and tower that juts out from the upper palace of the king, by the courtyard of the guard. Beside him Pedaiah son of Parosh, [26] and the temple servants living on Ophel made repairs opposite the Water Gate toward the east and the tower that juts out. [27] Next to him the Tekoites made repairs to another section from a point opposite the great tower that juts out, as far as the wall of Ophel.

[28] Each of the priests made repairs above the Horse Gate, each opposite his own house. [29] After them Zadok son of Immer made repairs opposite his house. And beside him Shemaiah son of Shecaniah, guard of the East Gate, made repairs. [30] Next to him Hananiah son

of Shelemiah and Hanun the sixth son of Zalaph made repairs to another section.

After them Meshullam son of Berechiah made repairs opposite his room. [31] Next to him Malchijah, one of the goldsmiths, made repairs to the house of the temple servants and the merchants, opposite the Inspection Gate, and as far as the upper room of the corner. [32] The goldsmiths and merchants made repairs between the upper room of the corner and the Sheep Gate.

4 When Sanballat heard that we were rebuilding the wall, he became furious. He mocked the Jews [2] before his colleagues and the powerful men of Samaria, and said, "What are these pathetic Jews doing? Can they restore it by themselves? Will they offer sacrifices? Will they ever finish it? Can they bring these burnt stones back to life from the mounds of rubble?" [3] Then Tobiah the Ammonite, who was beside him, said, "Indeed, even if a fox climbed up what they are building, he would break down their stone wall!"

[4] Listen, our God, for we are despised. Make their insults return on their own heads and let them be taken as plunder to a land of captivity. [5] Do not cover their *guilt or let their sin be erased from Your sight, because they have provoked the builders.

[6] So we rebuilt the wall until the entire wall was joined together up to half its height, for the people had the will to keep working.

[7] When Sanballat, Tobiah, and the Arabs, Ammonites, and Ashdodites heard that the repair to the walls of Jerusalem was progressing and that the gaps were being closed, they became furious. [8] They all plotted together to come and fight against Jerusalem and throw it into confusion. [9] So we prayed to our God and stationed a guard because of them day and night.

[10] In Judah, it was said:

The strength of the laborer fails,
since there is so much rubble.
We will never be able
to rebuild the wall.

[11] And our enemies said, "They won't know or see anything until we're among them and can kill them and stop the work." [12] When the Jews who lived nearby arrived, they said to us time and again, "Everywhere you turn, they attack us." [13] So I stationed people behind the lowest sections of the wall, at the vulnerable areas. I stationed them by families with their swords, spears, and bows. [14] After I made an inspection, I stood up and said to the nobles, the officials, and the rest of the people, "Don't be afraid of them. Remember the great and awe-inspiring Lord, and fight for your countrymen, your sons and daughters, your wives and homes."

[15] When our enemies heard that we knew their scheme and that God had frustrated it, every one of us returned to his own work on the wall. [16] From that day on, half of my men did the work while the other half held spears, shields, bows, and armor. The officers supported all the people of Judah, [17] who were rebuilding the wall. The laborers who carried the loads worked with one hand and held a weapon with the other. [18] Each of the builders had his sword strapped around his waist while he was building, and the trumpeter was beside me. [19] Then I said to the nobles, the officials, and the rest of the people: "The work is enormous and spread out, and we are separated far from one another along the wall. [20] Wherever you hear the

trumpet sound, rally to us there. Our God will fight for us!" ²¹ So we continued the work, while half of the men were holding spears from daybreak until the stars came out. ²² At that time, I also said to the people, "Let everyone and his servant spend the night inside Jerusalem, so that they can stand guard by night and work by day." ²³ And I, my brothers, my men, and the guards with me never took off our clothes. Each carried his weapon, even when washing.

5 There was a widespread outcry from the people and their wives against their Jewish countrymen. ² Some were saying, "We, our sons, and our daughters are numerous. Let us get grain so that we can eat and live." ³ Others were saying, "We are mortgaging our fields, vineyards, and homes to get grain during the famine." ⁴ Still others were saying, "We have borrowed money to pay the king's tax on our fields and vineyards. ⁵ We and our children are just like our countrymen and their children, yet we are subjecting our sons and daughters to slavery. Some of our daughters are already enslaved, but we are powerless because our fields and vineyards belong to others."

⁶ I became extremely angry when I heard their outcry and these complaints. ⁷ After seriously considering the matter, I accused the nobles and officials, saying to them, "Each of you is charging his countrymen interest." So I called a large assembly against them ⁸ and said, "We have done our best to buy back our Jewish countrymen who were sold to foreigners, but now you sell your own countrymen, and we have to buy them back." They remained silent and could not say a word. ⁹ Then I said, "What you are doing isn't right. Shouldn't you walk in the 'fear of our God and not invite the reproach of our foreign enemies? ¹⁰ Even I, as well as my brothers and my servants, have been lending them money and grain. Please, let us stop charging this interest. ¹¹ Return their fields, vineyards, olive groves, and houses to them immediately, along with the percentage of the money, grain, new wine, and olive oil that you have been assessing them."

¹² They responded: "We will return these things and require nothing more from them. We will do as you say."

So I summoned the priests and made everyone take an oath to do this. ¹³ I also shook the folds of my robe and said, "May God likewise shake from his house and property everyone who doesn't keep this promise. May he be shaken out and have nothing!"

The whole assembly said, "'Amen," and they praised the LORD. Then the people did as they had promised.

¹⁴ Furthermore, from the day King Artaxerxes appointed me to be their governor in the land of Judah— from the twentieth year until his thirty-second year, 12 years—I and my associates never ate from the food allotted to the governor. ¹⁵ The governors who preceded me had heavily burdened the people, taking food and wine from them, as well as a pound of silver. Their subordinates also oppressed the people, but I didn't do this, because of the fear of God. ¹⁶ Instead, I devoted myself to the construction of the wall, and all my subordinates were gathered there for the work. We didn't buy any land.

¹⁷ There were 150 Jews and officials, as well as guests from the surrounding nations at my table. ¹⁸ Each day, one ox, six choice sheep, and some fowl were prepared for me. An abundance of all kinds of wine was provided every 10 days. But I didn't demand the food allotted to

the governor, because the burden on the people was so heavy.

¹⁹ Remember me favorably, my God, for all that I have done for this people.

6 When Sanballat, Tobiah, Geshem the Arab, and the rest of our enemies heard that I had rebuilt the wall and that no gap was left in it—though at that time I had not installed the doors in the gates— ² Sanballat and Geshem sent me a message: "Come, let's meet together in the villages of the Ono Valley." But they were planning to harm me.

³ So I sent messengers to them, saying, "I am doing a great work and cannot come down. Why should the work cease while I leave it and go down to you?" ⁴ Four times they sent me the same proposal, and I gave them the same reply.

⁵ Sanballat sent me this same message a fifth time by his aide, who had an open letter in his hand. ⁶ In it was written:

It is reported among the nations—and Geshem agrees—that you and the Jews plan to rebel. This is the reason you are building the wall. According to these reports, you are to become their king ⁷ and have even set up the prophets in Jerusalem to proclaim on your behalf: "There is a king in Judah." These rumors will be heard by the king. So come, let's confer together.

⁸ Then I replied to him, "There is nothing to these rumors you are spreading; you are inventing them in your own mind." ⁹ For they were all trying to intimidate us, saying, "They will become discouraged in the work, and it will never be finished."

But now, my God, strengthen me.

¹⁰ I went to the house of Shemaiah son of Delaiah, son of Mehetabel, who was restricted to his house. He said:

Let us meet at the house of God
inside the temple.
Let us shut the temple doors
because they are coming to kill you.
They are coming to kill you tonight!

¹¹ But I said, "Should a man like me run away? How can I enter the temple and live? I will not go." ¹² I realized that God had not sent him, because of the prophecy he spoke against me. Tobiah and Sanballat had hired him. ¹³ He was hired, so that I would be intimidated, do as he suggested, sin, and get a bad reputation, in order that they could discredit me.

¹⁴ My God, remember Tobiah and Sanballat for what they have done, and also Noadiah the prophetess and the other prophets who wanted to intimidate me.

¹⁵ The wall was completed in 52 days, on the twenty-fifth day of the month Elul. ¹⁶ When all our enemies heard this, all the surrounding nations were intimidated and lost their confidence, for they realized that this task had been accomplished by our God.

¹⁷ During those days, the nobles of Judah sent many letters to Tobiah, and Tobiah's letters came to them. ¹⁸ For many in Judah were bound by oath to him, since he was a son-in-law of Shecaniah son of Arah, and his son Jehohanan had married the daughter of Meshullam son of Berechiah. ¹⁹ These nobles kept mentioning Tobiah's good deeds to me, and they reported my words to him. And Tobiah sent letters to intimidate me.

7 When the wall had been rebuilt and I had the doors installed, the gatekeepers, singers, and Levites were appointed. ²Then I put my brother Hanani in charge of Jerusalem, along with Hananiah, commander of the fortress, because he was a faithful man who ˙feared God more than most. ³I said to them, "Do not open the gates of Jerusalem until the sun is hot, and let the doors be shut and securely fastened while the guards are on duty. Station the citizens of Jerusalem as guards, some at their posts and some at their homes."

⁴The city was large and spacious, but there were few people in it, and no houses had been built yet. ⁵Then my God put it into my mind to assemble the nobles, the officials, and the people to be registered by genealogy. I found the genealogical record of those who came back first, and I found the following written in it:

⁶These are the people of the province who went up among the captive exiles deported by King Nebuchadnezzar of Babylon. Each of them returned to Jerusalem and Judah, to his own town. ⁷They came with Zerubbabel, Jeshua, Nehemiah, Azariah, Raamiah, Nahamani, Mordecai, Bilshan, Mispereth, Bigvai, Nehum, and Baanah.

The number of the Israelite men included:

⁸	Parosh's descendants	2,172
⁹	Shephatiah's descendants	372
¹⁰	Arah's descendants	652
¹¹	Pahath-moab's descendants:	
	Jeshua's and Joab's descendants	2,818
¹²	Elam's descendants	1,254
¹³	Zattu's descendants	845
¹⁴	Zaccai's descendants	760
¹⁵	Binnui's descendants	648
¹⁶	Bebai's descendants	628
¹⁷	Azgad's descendants	2,322
¹⁸	Adonikam's descendants	667
¹⁹	Bigvai's descendants	2,067
²⁰	Adin's descendants	655
²¹	Ater's descendants: of Hezekiah	98
²²	Hashum's descendants	328
²³	Bezai's descendants	324
²⁴	Hariph's descendants	112
²⁵	Gibeon's descendants	95
²⁶	Bethlehem's and Netophah's men	188
²⁷	Anathoth's men	128
²⁸	Beth-azmaveth's men	42
²⁹	Kiriath-jearim's, Chephirah's, and Beeroth's men	743
³⁰	Ramah's and Geba's men	621
³¹	Michmas's men	122
³²	Bethel's and Ai's men	123
³³	the other Nebo's men	52
³⁴	the other Elam's people	1,254
³⁵	Harim's people	320
³⁶	Jericho's people	345
³⁷	Lod's, Hadid's, and Ono's people	721
³⁸	Senaah's people	3,930.

³⁹The priests included:

	Jedaiah's descendants of the house of Jeshua	973
⁴⁰	Immer's descendants	1,052
⁴¹	Pashhur's descendants	1,247
⁴²	Harim's descendants	1,017.

⁴³The Levites included:

	Jeshua's descendants: of Kadmiel Hodevah's descendants	74.

⁴⁴The singers included:

˙Asaph's descendants	148.

⁴⁵The gatekeepers included:

Shallum's descendants, Ater's descendants, Talmon's descendants, Akkub's descendants, Hatita's descendants,

Shobai's descendants	138.

⁴⁶The temple servants included:

Ziha's descendants, Hasupha's descendants, Tabbaoth's descendants, ⁴⁷Keros's descendants, Sia's descendants, Padon's descendants, ⁴⁸ Lebanah's descendants, Hagabah's descendants, Shalmai's descendants, ⁴⁹Hanan's descendants, Giddel's descendants, Gahar's descendants, ⁵⁰ Reaiah's descendants, Rezin's descendants, Nekoda's descendants, ⁵¹Gazzam's descendants, Uzza's descendants, Paseah's descendants, ⁵² Besai's descendants, Meunim's descendants, Nephishesim's descendants, ⁵³Bakbuk's descendants, Hakupha's descendants, Harhur's descendants, ⁵⁴ Bazlith's descendants, Mehida's descendants, Harsha's descendants, ⁵⁵Barkos's descendants, Sisera's descendants, Temah's descendants, ⁵⁶ Neziah's descendants, Hatipha's descendants.

⁵⁷The descendants of Solomon's servants included:

Sotai's descendants, Sophereth's descendants, Perida's descendants, ⁵⁸Jaala's descendants, Darkon's descendants, Giddel's descendants, ⁵⁹ Shephatiah's descendants, Hattil's descendants, Pochereth-hazzebaim's descendants, Amon's descendants.

⁶⁰ All the temple servants and the descendants of Solomon's servants	392.

⁶¹The following are those who came from Telmelah, Tel-harsha, Cherub, Addon, and Immer, but were unable to prove that their families and ancestors were Israelite:

⁶² Delaiah's descendants, Tobiah's descendants, and Nekoda's descendants	642

⁶³and from the priests: the descendants of Hobaiah, the descendants of Hakkoz, and the descendants of Barzillai—who had taken a wife from the daughters of Barzillai the Gileadite and was called by their name. ⁶⁴These searched for their entries in the genealogical records, but they could not be found, so they were disqualified from the priesthood. ⁶⁵The governor ordered them not to eat the most holy things until there was a priest who could consult the ˙Urim and Thummim.

⁶⁶ The whole combined assembly numbered	42,360

⁶⁷ not including their 7,337 male and female slaves, as well as their 245 male and female singers. ⁶⁸ They had 736 horses, 245 mules, ⁶⁹ 435 camels, and 6,720 donkeys. ⁷⁰Some of the family leaders gave to the project. The governor gave 1,000 gold coins, 50 bowls, and 530 priestly garments to the treasury. ⁷¹Some of the family leaders gave 20,000 gold coins and 2,200 silver minas to the treasury for the project. ⁷²The rest of the

people gave 20,000 gold coins, 2,000 silver minas, and 67 priestly garments. ⁷³So the priests, Levites, gate-keepers, temple singers, some of the people, temple servants, and all Israel settled in their towns.

When the seventh month came and the Israelites had settled in their towns, ¹all the people gathered 8 together at the square in front of the Water Gate. They asked Ezra the scribe to bring the book of the law of Moses that the Lord had given Israel. ²On the first day of the seventh month, Ezra the priest brought the law before the assembly of men, women, and all who could listen with understanding. ³While he was facing the square in front of the Water Gate, he read out of it from daybreak until noon before the men, the women, and those who could understand. All the people listened attentively to the book of the law. ⁴Ezra the scribe stood on a high wooden platform made for this purpose. Mattithiah, Shema, Anaiah, Uriah, Hilki-ah, and Maaseiah stood beside him on his right; to his left were Pedaiah, Mishael, Malchijah, Hashum, Hash-baddanah, Zechariah, and Meshullam. ⁵Ezra opened the book in full view of all the people, since he was elevated above everyone. As he opened it, all the people stood up. ⁶Ezra praised the Lord, the great God, and with their hands uplifted all the people said, "'Amen, Amen!" Then they bowed down and worshiped the Lord with their faces to the ground.

⁷Jeshua, Bani, Sherebiah, Jamin, Akkub, Shab-bethai, Hodiah, Maaseiah, Kelita, Azariah, Jozabad, Hanan, and Pelaiah, who were Levites, explained the law to the people as they stood in their places. ⁸They read out of the book of the law of God, translating and giving the meaning so that the people could under-stand what was read. ⁹Nehemiah the governor, Ezra the priest and scribe, and the Levites who were in-structing the people said to all of them, "This day is holy to the Lord your God. Do not mourn or weep." For all the people were weeping as they heard the words of the law. ¹⁰Then he said to them, "Go and eat what is rich, drink what is sweet, and send portions to those who have nothing prepared, since today is holy to our Lord. Do not grieve, because the joy of the Lord is your stronghold." ¹¹And the Levites quieted all the people, saying, "Be still, since today is holy. Do not grieve." ¹²Then all the people began to eat and drink, send portions, and have a great celebration, because they had understood the words that were explained to them.

¹³On the second day, the family leaders of all the people, along with the priests and Levites, assembled before Ezra the scribe to study the words of the law. ¹⁴They found written in the law how the Lord had commanded through Moses that the Israelites should dwell in booths during the festival of the seventh month. ¹⁵So they proclaimed and spread this news throughout their towns and in Jerusalem, saying, "Go out to the hill country and bring back branches of ol-ive, wild olive, myrtle, palm, and other leafy trees to make booths, just as it is written." ¹⁶The people went out, brought back branches, and made booths for themselves on each of their rooftops, and courtyards, the court of the house of God, the square by the Water Gate, and the square by the Gate of Ephraim. ¹⁷The whole community that had returned from exile made booths and lived in them. They had not celebrated like this from the days of Joshua son of Nun until that day. And there was tremendous joy. ¹⁸Ezra read out of the

book of the law of God every day, from the first day to the last. The Israelites celebrated the festival for seven days, and on the eighth day there was an assembly, ac-cording to the ordinance.

On the twenty-fourth day of this month the Is-9 raelites assembled; they were fasting, wearing ˙sackcloth, and had put dust on their heads. ²Those of Israelite descent separated themselves from all for-eigners, and they stood and confessed their sins and the ˙guilt of their fathers. ³While they stood in their places, they read from the book of the law of the Lord their God for a fourth of the day and spent another fourth of the day in confession and worship of the Lord their God. ⁴Jeshua, Bani, Kadmiel, Shebaniah, Bunni, Sherebiah, Bani, and Chenani stood on the raised plat-form built for the Levites and cried out loudly to the Lord their God. ⁵Then the Levites—Jeshua, Kadmiel, Bani, Hashabneiah, Sherebiah, Hodiah, Shebaniah, and Pethahiah—said, "Stand up. Praise ˙Yahweh your God from everlasting to everlasting."

Praise Your glorious name,
    and may it be exalted above all blessing
        and praise.
⁶ You alone are Yahweh.
   You created the heavens,
        the highest heavens with all their host,
        the earth and all that is on it,
        the seas and all that is in them.
   You give life to all of them,
        and the heavenly host worships You.
⁷ You are Yahweh,
        the God who chose Abram
   and brought him out of Ur of the Chaldeans,
        and changed his name to Abraham.
⁸ You found his heart faithful in Your sight,
        and made a covenant with him
   to give the land of the Canaanites,
   Hittites, Amorites, Perizzites,
   Jebusites, and Girgashites—
        to give it to his descendants.
   You have kept Your promise,
        for You are righteous.
⁹ You saw the oppression of our ancestors
        in Egypt
   and heard their cry at the ˙Red Sea.
¹⁰ You performed signs and wonders
        against Pharaoh,
   all his officials, and all the people of his land,
   for You knew how arrogantly they treated
        our ancestors.
   You made a name for Yourself
        that endures to this day.
¹¹ You divided the sea before them,
        and they crossed through it on dry ground.
   You hurled their pursuers into the depths
        like a stone into churning waters.
¹² You led them with a pillar of cloud by day,
        and with a pillar of fire by night,
        to illuminate the way they should go.
¹³ You came down on Mount Sinai,
        and spoke to them from heaven.
   You gave them impartial ordinances,
        reliable instructions,
        and good statutes and commands.
¹⁴ You revealed Your holy Sabbath to them,
        and gave them commands, statutes,
        and instruction

through Your servant Moses.
15 You provided bread from heaven
 for their hunger;
You brought them water from the rock
 for their thirst.
You told them to go in and possess the land
You had sworn to give them.
16 But our ancestors acted arrogantly;
they became stiff-necked and did not listen
 to Your commands.
17 They refused to listen
and did not remember Your wonders
You performed among them.
They became stiff-necked and appointed
 a leader
to return to their slavery in Egypt.
But You are a forgiving God,
gracious and compassionate,
slow to anger and rich in faithful love,
and You did not abandon them.
18 Even after they had cast an image of a calf
for themselves and said,
"This is your God who brought you
 out of Egypt,"
and they had committed terrible blasphemies,
19 You did not abandon them in the wilderness
because of Your great compassion.
During the day the pillar of cloud
never turned away from them,
guiding them on their journey.
And during the night the pillar of fire
illuminated the way they should go.
20 You sent Your good Spirit to instruct them.
You did not withhold Your manna
 from their mouths,
and You gave them water for their thirst.
21 You provided for them in the wilderness
 40 years
and they lacked nothing.
Their clothes did not wear out,
and their feet did not swell.
22 You gave them kingdoms and peoples
and assigned them to be a boundary.
They took possession
of the land of Sihon king of Heshbon
and of the land of Og king of Bashan.
23 You multiplied their descendants
like the stars of heaven
and brought them to the land
You told their ancestors to go in
 and take possession of it.
24 So their descendants went in and possessed
 the land:
You subdued the Canaanites who inhabited
 the land before them
and handed their kings and the surrounding
 peoples over to them,
to do as they pleased with them.
25 They captured fortified cities and fertile land
and took possession of well-supplied houses,
cisterns cut out of rock, vineyards,
olive groves, and fruit trees in abundance.
They ate, were filled,
became prosperous, and delighted
 in Your great goodness.
26 But they were disobedient and rebelled
 against You.

They flung Your law behind their backs
and killed Your prophets
who warned them
in order to turn them back to You.
They committed terrible blasphemies.
27 So You handed them over to their enemies,
who oppressed them.
In their time of distress, they cried out to You,
and You heard from heaven.
In Your abundant compassion
You gave them deliverers, who rescued them
from the power of their enemies.
28 But as soon as they had relief,
they again did what was evil in Your sight.
So You abandoned them to the power
 of their enemies,
who dominated them.
When they cried out to You again,
You heard from heaven and rescued them
many times in Your compassion.
29 You warned them to turn back to Your law,
but they acted arrogantly
and would not obey Your commands.
They sinned against Your ordinances,
which a person will live by if he does them.
They stubbornly resisted,
stiffened their necks, and would not obey.
30 You were patient with them for many years,
and Your Spirit warned them
 through Your prophets,
but they would not listen.
Therefore, You handed them over
 to the surrounding peoples.
31 However, in Your abundant compassion,
You did not destroy them or abandon them,
for You are a gracious and compassionate God.
32 So now, our God—the great, mighty,
and awe-inspiring God who keeps
 His gracious covenant—
do not view lightly all the hardships
 that have afflicted us,
our kings and leaders,
our priests and prophets,
our ancestors and all Your people,
from the days of the Assyrian kings
 until today.
33 You are righteous concerning all
 that has come on us,
because You have acted faithfully,
while we have acted wickedly.
34 Our kings, leaders, priests, and ancestors
did not obey Your law
or listen to Your commands
and warnings You gave them.
35 When they were in their kingdom,
with Your abundant goodness that
 You gave them,
and in the spacious and fertile land You set
 before them,
they would not serve You or turn
 from their wicked ways.
36 Here we are today,
slaves in the land You gave our ancestors
so that they could enjoy its fruit
 and its goodness.
Here we are—slaves in it!
37 Its abundant harvest goes to the kings

You have set over us,
because of our sins.
They rule over our bodies
and our livestock as they please.
We are in great distress.

[38] In view of all this, we are making a binding agreement in writing on a sealed document containing the names of our leaders, Levites, and priests.

10 Those whose seals were on the document were: Nehemiah the governor, son of Hacaliah, and Zedekiah,

[2] Seraiah, Azariah, Jeremiah,
[3] Pashhur, Amariah, Malchijah,
[4] Hattush, Shebaniah, Malluch,
[5] Harim, Meremoth, Obadiah,
[6] Daniel, Ginnethon, Baruch,
[7] Meshullam, Abijah, Mijamin,
[8] Maaziah, Bilgai, and Shemaiah.
These were the priests.
[9] The Levites were:
Jeshua son of Azaniah,
Binnui of the sons of Henadad, Kadmiel,
[10] and their brothers
Shebaniah, Hodiah, Kelita, Pelaiah, Hanan,
[11] Mica, Rehob, Hashabiah,
[12] Zaccur, Sherebiah, Shebaniah,
[13] Hodiah, Bani, and Beninu.
[14] The leaders of the people were:
Parosh, Pahath-moab, Elam, Zattu, Bani,
[15] Bunni, Azgad, Bebai,
[16] Adonijah, Bigvai, Adin,
[17] Ater, Hezekiah, Azzur,
[18] Hodiah, Hashum, Bezai,
[19] Hariph, Anathoth, Nebai,
[20] Magpiash, Meshullam, Hezir,
[21] Meshezabel, Zadok, Jaddua,
[22] Pelatiah, Hanan, Anaiah,
[23] Hoshea, Hananiah, Hasshub,
[24] Hallohesh, Pilha, Shobek,
[25] Rehum, Hashabnah, Maaseiah,
[26] Ahijah, Hanan, Anan,
[27] Malluch, Harim, Baanah.

[28] The rest of the people—the priests, Levites, gatekeepers, singers, and temple servants, along with their wives, sons, and daughters, everyone who is able to understand and who has separated themselves from the surrounding peoples to obey the law of God— [29] join with their noble brothers and commit themselves with a sworn oath to follow the law of God given through God's servant Moses and to carefully obey all the commands, ordinances, and statutes of •Yahweh our Lord.

[30] We will not give our daughters in marriage to the surrounding peoples and will not take their daughters as wives for our sons.

[31] When the surrounding peoples bring merchandise or any kind of grain to sell on the Sabbath day, we will not buy from them on the Sabbath or a holy day. We will also leave the land uncultivated in the seventh year and will cancel every debt.

[32] We will impose the following commands on ourselves:

To give an eighth of an ounce of silver yearly for the service of the house of our God: [33] the bread displayed before the LORD, the daily •grain offering, the regular •burnt offering, the Sabbath and New Moon offerings, the appointed festivals, the holy things, the •sin offerings to •atone for Israel, and for all the work of the house of our God.

[34] We have cast lots among the priests, Levites, and people for the donation of wood by our ancestral houses at the appointed times each year. They are to bring the wood to our God's house to burn on the altar of the LORD our God, as it is written in the law.

[35] We will bring the •firstfruits of our land and of every fruit tree to the LORD's house year by year.

[36] We will also bring the firstborn of our sons and our livestock, as prescribed by the law, and will bring the firstborn of our herds and flocks to the house of our God, to the priests who serve in our God's house. [37] We will bring a loaf from our first batch of dough to the priests at the storerooms of the house of our God. We will also bring the firstfruits of our grain offerings, of every fruit tree, and of the new wine and oil. A tenth of our land's produce belongs to the Levites, for the Levites are to collect the one-tenth offering in all our agricultural towns. [38] A priest of Aaronic descent must accompany the Levites when they collect the tenth, and the Levites must take a tenth of this offering to the storerooms of the treasury in the house of our God. [39] For the Israelites and the Levites are to bring the contributions of grain, new wine, and oil to the storerooms where the articles of the sanctuary are kept and where the priests who minister are, along with the gatekeepers and singers. We will not neglect the house of our God.

11 Now the leaders of the people stayed in Jerusalem, and the rest of the people cast lots for one out of ten to come and live in Jerusalem, the holy city, while the other nine-tenths remained in their towns. [2] The people praised all the men who volunteered to live in Jerusalem.

[3] These are the heads of the province who stayed in Jerusalem (but in the villages of Judah each lived on his own property in their towns—the Israelites, priests, Levites, temple servants, and descendants of Solomon's servants— [4] while some of the descendants of Judah and Benjamin settled in Jerusalem):

Judah's descendants:
Athaiah son of Uzziah, son of Zechariah, son of Amariah, son of Shephatiah, son of Mahalalel, of Perez's descendants; [5] and Maaseiah son of Baruch, son of Col-hozeh, son of Hazaiah, son of Adaiah, son of Joiarib, son of Zechariah, a descendant of the Shilonite. [6] The total number of Perez's descendants, who settled in Jerusalem, was 468 capable men.

[7] These were Benjamin's descendants:
Sallu son of Meshullam, son of Joed, son of Pedaiah, son of Kolaiah, son of Maaseiah, son of Ithiel, son of Jeshaiah, [8] and after him Gabbai and Sallai: 928. [9] Joel son of Zichri was the officer over them, and Judah son of Hassenuah was second in command over the city.

[10] The priests:
Jedaiah son of Joiarib, Jachin, and [11] Seraiah son of Hilkiah, son of Meshullam, son of Zadok, son of Meraioth, son of Ahitub, the chief official of God's temple, [12] and their relatives who did the work at the temple: 822. Adaiah son of Jeroham, son of Pelaliah, son of Amzi, son of Zechariah,

son of Pashhur, son of Malchijah ¹³and his relatives, the leaders of families: 242. Amashsai son of Azarel, son of Ahzai, son of Meshillemoth, son of Immer, ¹⁴and their relatives, capable men: 128. Zabdiel son of Haggedolim, was their chief. ¹⁵The Levites: Shemaiah son of Hasshub, son of Azrikam, son of Hashabiah, son of Bunni; ¹⁶and Shabbethai and Jozabad, from the leaders of the Levites, who supervised the work outside the house of God; ¹⁷Mattaniah son of Mica, son of Zabdi, son of 'Asaph, the leader who began the thanksgiving in prayer; Bakbukiah, second among his relatives; and Abda son of Shammua, son of Galal, son of Jeduthun. ¹⁸All the Levites in the holy city: 284.

¹⁹The gatekeepers: Akkub, Talmon, and their relatives, who guarded the gates: 172.

²⁰The rest of Israel, the priests, and the Levites were in all the villages of Judah, each on his own inherited property. ²¹The temple servants lived on Ophel; Ziha and Gishpa supervised the temple servants.

²²The leader of the Levites in Jerusalem was Uzzi son of Bani, son of Hashabiah, son of Mattaniah, son of Mica, of the descendants of Asaph, who were singers for the service of God's house. ²³There was, in fact, a command of the king regarding them, and an ordinance regulating the singers' daily tasks. ²⁴Pethahiah son of Meshezabel, of the descendants of Zerah son of Judah, was the king's agent in every matter concerning the people.

²⁵As for the farming settlements with their fields:
Some of Judah's descendants lived
    in Kiriath-arba and its villages,
Dibon and its villages, and Jekabzeel
    and its villages;
²⁶ in Jeshua, Moladah, Beth-pelet,
²⁷ Hazar-shual, and Beer-sheba and its villages;
²⁸ in Ziklag and Meconah and its villages;
²⁹ in En-rimmon, Zorah, Jarmuth, and
³⁰ Zanoah and Adullam with their villages;
    in Lachish with its fields and Azekah
    and its villages.
So they settled from Beer-sheba to the Valley
    of Hinnom.
³¹ Benjamin's descendants:
    from Geba, Michmash, Aija,
    and Bethel—and its villages,
³² Anathoth, Nob, Ananiah,
³³ Hazor, Ramah, Gittaim,
³⁴ Hadid, Zeboim, Neballat,
³⁵ Lod, and Ono, the Valley of Craftsmen.
³⁶ Some of the Judean divisions of Levites
    were in Benjamin.

12 These are the priests and Levites who went up with Zerubbabel son of Shealtiel and with Jeshua:
Seraiah, Jeremiah, Ezra,
²   Amariah, Malluch, Hattush,
³   Shecaniah, Rehum, Meremoth,
⁴   Iddo, Ginnethoi, Abijah,
⁵   Mijamin, Maadiah, Bilgah,
⁶   Shemaiah, Joiarib, Jedaiah,
⁷   Sallu, Amok, Hilkiah, Jedaiah.
These were the leaders of the priests and their relatives in the days of Jeshua.

⁸The Levites:
Jeshua, Binnui, Kadmiel,
Sherebiah, Judah, and Mattaniah—
he and his relatives were in charge
    of the praise songs.
⁹ Bakbukiah, Unni, and their relatives stood
    opposite them in the services.
¹⁰ Jeshua fathered Joiakim,
    Joiakim fathered Eliashib,
    Eliashib fathered Joiada,
¹¹ Joiada fathered Jonathan,
    and Jonathan fathered Jaddua.

¹²In the days of Joiakim, the leaders of the priestly families were:

	Meraiah	of Seraiah,
	Hananiah	of Jeremiah,
¹³	Meshullam	of Ezra,
	Jehohanan	of Amariah,
¹⁴	Jonathan	of Malluchi,
	Joseph	of Shebaniah,
¹⁵	Adna	of Harim,
	Helkai	of Meraioth,
¹⁶	Zechariah	of Iddo,
	Meshullam	of Ginnethon,
¹⁷	Zichri	of Abijah,
	Piltai	of Moadiah, of Miniamin,
¹⁸	Shammua	of Bilgah,
	Jehonathan	of Shemaiah,
¹⁹	Mattenai	of Joiarib,
	Uzzi	of Jedaiah,
²⁰	Kallai	of Sallai,
	Eber	of Amok,
²¹	Hashabiah	of Hilkiah,
	and Nethanel	of Jedaiah.

²²In the days of Eliashib, Joiada, Johanan, and Jaddua, the leaders of the families of the Levites and priests were recorded while Darius the Persian ruled. ²³Levi's descendants, the leaders of families, were recorded in the Book of the Historical Records during the days of Johanan son of Eliashib. ²⁴The leaders of the Levites—Hashabiah, Sherebiah, and Jeshua son of Kadmiel, along with their relatives opposite them—gave praise and thanks, division by division, as David the man of God had prescribed. ²⁵This included Mattaniah, Bakbukiah, and Obadiah. Meshullam, Talmon, and Akkub were gatekeepers who guarded the storerooms at the gates. ²⁶These served in the days of Joiakim son of Jeshua, son of Jozadak, and in the days of Nehemiah the governor and Ezra the priest and scribe.

²⁷At the dedication of the wall of Jerusalem, they sent for the Levites wherever they lived and brought them to Jerusalem to celebrate the joyous dedication with thanksgiving and singing accompanied by cymbals, harps, and lyres. ²⁸The singers gathered from the region around Jerusalem, from the villages of the Netophathites, ²⁹from Beth-gilgal, and from the fields of Geba and Azmaveth, for they had built villages for themselves around Jerusalem. ³⁰After the priests and Levites had purified themselves, they purified the people, the gates, and the wall.

³¹Then I brought the leaders of Judah up on top of the wall, and I appointed two large processions that gave thanks. One went to the right on the wall, toward the Dung Gate. ³²Hoshaiah and half the leaders of Judah followed, ³³along with Azariah, Ezra, Meshullam, ³⁴Judah, Benjamin, Shemaiah, Jeremiah, ³⁵and some

of the priests' sons with trumpets, and Zechariah son of Jonathan, son of Shemaiah, son of Mattaniah, son of Micaiah, son of Zaccur, son of *Asaph followed ³⁶as well as his relatives—Shemaiah, Azarel, Milalai, Gilalai, Maai, Nethanel, Judah, and Hanani, with the musical instruments of David, the man of God. Ezra the scribe went in front of them. ³⁷At the Fountain Gate they climbed the steps of the city of David on the ascent of the wall and went above the house of David to the Water Gate on the east.

³⁸The second thanksgiving procession went to the left, and I followed it with half the people along the top of the wall, past the Tower of the Ovens to the Broad Wall, ³⁹above the Gate of Ephraim, and by the Old Gate, the Fish Gate, the Tower of Hananel, and the Tower of the Hundred, to the Sheep Gate. They stopped at the Gate of the Guard. ⁴⁰The two thanksgiving processions stood in the house of God. So did I and half of the officials accompanying me, ⁴¹as well as the priests:

Eliakim, Maaseiah, Miniamin,
Micaiah, Elioenai, Zechariah,
and Hananiah, with trumpets;
⁴² and Maaseiah, Shemaiah, Eleazar,
Uzzi, Jehohanan, Malchijah, Elam, and Ezer.

Then the singers sang, with Jezrahiah as the leader. ⁴³On that day they offered great sacrifices and rejoiced because God had given them great joy. The women and children also celebrated, and Jerusalem's rejoicing was heard far away.

⁴⁴On that same day men were placed in charge of the rooms that housed the supplies, contributions, *firstfruits, and tenths. The legally required portions for the priests and Levites were gathered from the village fields, because Judah was grateful to the priests and Levites who were serving. ⁴⁵They performed the service of their God and the service of purification, along with the singers and gatekeepers, as David and his son Solomon had prescribed. ⁴⁶For long ago, in the days of David and Asaph, there were leaders of the singers and songs of praise and thanksgiving to God. ⁴⁷So in the days of Zerubbabel and Nehemiah, all Israel contributed the daily portions for the singers and gatekeepers. They also set aside daily portions for the Levites, and the Levites set aside daily portions for the descendants of Aaron.

13 At that time the book of Moses was read publicly to the people. The command was found written in it that no Ammonite or Moabite should ever enter the assembly of God, ²because they did not meet the Israelites with food and water. Instead, they hired Balaam against them to curse them, but our God turned the curse into a blessing. ³When they heard the law, they separated all those of mixed descent from Israel.

⁴Now before this, Eliashib the priest had been put in charge of the storerooms of the house of our God. He was a relative of Tobiah ⁵and had prepared a large room for him where they had previously stored the *grain offerings, the frankincense, the articles, and the tenths of grain, new wine, and oil prescribed for the Levites, singers, and gatekeepers, along with the contributions for the priests.

⁶While all this was happening, I was not in Jerusalem, because I had returned to King Artaxerxes of Babylon in the thirty-second year of his reign. It was only later that I asked the king for a leave of absence

⁷so I could return to Jerusalem. Then I discovered the evil that Eliashib had done on behalf of Tobiah by providing him a room in the courts of God's house. ⁸I was greatly displeased and threw all of Tobiah's household possessions out of the room. ⁹I ordered that the rooms be purified, and I had the articles of the house of God restored there, along with the grain offering and frankincense. ¹⁰I also found out that because the portions for the Levites had not been given, each of the Levites and the singers performing the service had gone back to his own field. ¹¹Therefore, I rebuked the officials, saying, "Why has the house of God been neglected?" I gathered the Levites and singers together and stationed them at their posts. ¹²Then all Judah brought a tenth of the grain, new wine, and oil into the storehouses. ¹³I appointed as treasurers over the storehouses Shelemiah the priest, Zadok the scribe, and Pedaiah of the Levites, with Hanan son of Zaccur, son of Mattaniah to assist them, because they were considered trustworthy. They were responsible for the distribution to their colleagues.

¹⁴Remember me for this, my God, and don't erase the deeds of faithful love I have done for the house of my God and for its services.

¹⁵At that time I saw people in Judah treading wine presses on the Sabbath. They were also bringing in stores of grain and loading them on donkeys, along with wine, grapes, and figs. All kinds of goods were being brought to Jerusalem on the Sabbath day. So I warned them against selling food on that day. ¹⁶The Tyrians living there were importing fish and all kinds of merchandise and selling them on the Sabbath to the people of Judah in Jerusalem.

¹⁷I rebuked the nobles of Judah and said to them: "What is this evil you are doing—profaning the Sabbath day? ¹⁸Didn't your ancestors do the same, so that our God brought all this disaster on us and on this city? And now you are rekindling His anger against Israel by profaning the Sabbath!"

¹⁹When shadows began to fall on the gates of Jerusalem just before the Sabbath, I gave orders that the gates be closed and not opened until after the Sabbath. I posted some of my men at the gates, so that no goods could enter during the Sabbath day. ²⁰Once or twice the merchants and those who sell all kinds of goods camped outside Jerusalem, ²¹but I warned them, "Why are you camping in front of the wall? If you do it again, I'll use force against you." After that they did not come again on the Sabbath. ²²Then I instructed the Levites to purify themselves and guard the gates in order to keep the Sabbath day holy.

Remember me for this also, my God, and look on me with compassion in keeping with Your abundant, faithful love.

²³In those days I also saw Jews who had married women from Ashdod, Ammon, and Moab. ²⁴Half of their children spoke the language of Ashdod or the language of one of the other peoples but could not speak Hebrew. ²⁵I rebuked them, cursed them, beat some of their men, and pulled out their hair. I forced them to take an oath before God and said: "You must not give your daughters in marriage to their sons or take their daughters as wives for your sons or yourselves! ²⁶Didn't King Solomon of Israel sin in matters like this? There was not a king like him among many nations. He was loved by his God and God made him king over all Israel, yet foreign women drew him into

sin. ²⁷Why then should we hear about you doing all this terrible evil and acting unfaithfully against our God by marrying foreign women?"

²⁸Even one of the sons of Jehoiada, son of Eliashib the high priest, had become a son-in-law to Sanballat the Horonite. So I drove him away from me.

²⁹Remember them, my God, for defiling the priest-hood as well as the covenant of the priesthood and the Levites.

³⁰So I purified them from everything foreign and assigned specific duties to each of the priests and Levites. ³¹I also arranged for the donation of wood at the appointed times and for the *firstfruits.

Remember me, my God, with favor.

ESTHER

1 These events took place during the days of Ahasuerus, who ruled 127 provinces from India to *Cush. ²In those days King Ahasuerus reigned from his royal throne in the fortress at Susa. ³He held a feast in the third year of his reign for all his officials and staff, the army of Persia and Media, the nobles, and the officials from the provinces. ⁴He displayed the glorious wealth of his kingdom and the magnificent splendor of his greatness for a total of 180 days.

⁵At the end of this time, the king held a week-long banquet in the garden courtyard of the royal palace for all the people, from the greatest to the least, who were present in the fortress of Susa. ⁶White and violet linen hangings were fastened with fine white and purple linen cords to silver rods on marble columns. Gold and silver couches were arranged on a mosaic pavement of red feldspar, marble, mother-of-pearl, and precious stones.

⁷Beverages were served in an array of gold goblets, each with a different design. Royal wine flowed freely, according to the king's bounty ⁸and no restraint was placed on the drinking. The king had ordered every wine steward in his household to serve as much as each person wanted. ⁹Queen Vashti also gave a feast for the women of King Ahasuerus's palace.

¹⁰On the seventh day, when the king was feeling good from the wine, Ahasuerus commanded Mehuman, Biztha, Harbona, Bigtha, Abagtha, Zethar, and Carkas, the seven eunuchs who personally served him, ¹¹to bring Queen Vashti before him with her royal crown. He wanted to show off her beauty to the people and the officials, because she was very beautiful. ¹²But Queen Vashti refused to come at the king's command that was delivered by his eunuchs. The king became furious and his anger burned within him.

¹³The king consulted the wise men who understood the times, for it was his normal procedure to confer with experts in law and justice. ¹⁴The most trusted ones were Carshena, Shethar, Admatha, Tarshish, Meres, Marsena, and Memucan. They were the seven officials of Persia and Media who had personal access to the king and occupied the highest positions in the kingdom. ¹⁵The king asked, "According to the law, what should be done with Queen Vashti, since she refused to obey King Ahasuerus's command that was delivered by the eunuchs?"

¹⁶Memucan said in the presence of the king and his officials, "Queen Vashti has wronged not only the king, but all the officials and the peoples who are in every one of King Ahasuerus's provinces. ¹⁷For the queen's action will become public knowledge to all the women and cause them to despise their husbands and say, 'King Ahasuerus ordered Queen Vashti brought before him, but she did not come.' ¹⁸Before this day is over,

the noble women of Persia and Media who hear about the queen's act will say the same thing to all the king's officials, resulting in more contempt and fury.

¹⁹"If it meets the king's approval, he should personally issue a royal decree. Let it be recorded in the laws of Persia and Media, so that it cannot be revoked: Vashti is not to enter King Ahasuerus's presence, and her royal position is to be given to another woman who is more worthy than she. ²⁰The decree the king issues will be heard throughout his vast kingdom, so all women will honor their husbands, from the least to the greatest."

²¹The king and his counselors approved the proposal, and he followed Memucan's advice. ²²He sent letters to all the royal provinces, to each province in its own script and to each ethnic group in its own language, that every man should be master of his own house and speak in the language of his own people.

2 Some time later, when King Ahasuerus's rage had cooled down, he remembered Vashti, what she had done, and what was decided against her. ²The king's personal attendants suggested, "Let a search be made for beautiful young women for the king. ³Let the king appoint commissioners in each province of his kingdom, so that they may assemble all the beautiful young women to the harem at the fortress of Susa. Put them under the care of Hegai, the king's eunuch, who is in charge of the women, and give them the required beauty treatments. ⁴Then the young woman who pleases the king will become queen instead of Vashti." This suggestion pleased the king, and he did accordingly.

⁵In the fortress of Susa, there was a Jewish man named Mordecai son of Jair, son of Shimei, son of Kish, a Benjaminite. ⁶He had been taken into exile from Jerusalem with the other captives when King Nebuchadnezzar of Babylon took King Jeconiah of Judah into exile. ⁷Mordecai was the legal guardian of his cousin Hadassah (that is, Esther), because she didn't have a father or mother. The young woman had a beautiful figure and was extremely good-looking. When her father and mother died, Mordecai had adopted her as his own daughter.

⁸When the king's command and edict became public knowledge, many young women gathered at the fortress of Susa under Hegai's care. Esther was also taken to the palace and placed under the care of Hegai, who was in charge of the women. ⁹The young woman pleased him and gained his favor so that he accelerated the process of the beauty treatments and the special diet that she received. He assigned seven hand-picked female servants to her from the palace and transferred her and her servants to the harem's best quarters.

¹⁰Esther did not reveal her ethnic background or

her birthplace, because Mordecai had ordered her not to. [11]Every day Mordecai took a walk in front of the harem's courtyard to learn how Esther was doing and to see what was happening to her.

[12]During the year before each young woman's turn to go to King Ahasuerus, the harem regulation required her to receive beauty treatments with oil of myrrh for six months and then with perfumes and cosmetics for another six months. [13]When the young woman would go to the king, she was given whatever she requested to take with her from the harem to the palace. [14]She would go in the evening, and in the morning she would return to a second harem under the supervision of Shaashgaz, the king's eunuch in charge of the concubines. She never went to the king again, unless he desired her and summoned her by name.

[15]Esther was the daughter of Abihail, the uncle of Mordecai who had adopted her as his own daughter. When her turn came to go to the king, she did not ask for anything except what Hegai, the king's trusted official in charge of the harem, suggested. Esther won approval in the sight of everyone who saw her.

[16]She was taken to King Ahasuerus in the royal palace in the tenth month, the month Tebeth, in the seventh year of his reign. [17]The king loved Esther more than all the other women. She won more favor and approval from him than did any of the other young women. He placed the royal crown on her head and made her queen in place of Vashti. [18]The king held a great banquet for all his officials and staff. It was Esther's banquet. He freed his provinces from tax payments and gave gifts worthy of the king's bounty.

[19]When the young women were assembled together for a second time, Mordecai was sitting at the King's Gate. [20]Esther still had not revealed her birthplace or her ethnic background, as Mordecai had directed. She obeyed Mordecai's orders, as she always had while he raised her.

[21]During those days while Mordecai was sitting at the King's Gate, Bigthan and Teresh, two eunuchs who guarded the king's entrance, became infuriated and planned to assassinate King Ahasuerus. [22]When Mordecai learned of the plot, he reported it to Queen Esther, and she told the king on Mordecai's behalf. [23]When the report was investigated and verified, both men were hanged on the gallows. This event was recorded in the Historical Record in the king's presence.

3 After all this took place, King Ahasuerus honored Haman, son of Hammedatha the Agagite. He promoted him in rank and gave him a higher position than all the other officials. [2]The entire royal staff at the King's Gate bowed down and paid homage to Haman, because the king had commanded this to be done for him. But Mordecai would not bow down or pay homage. [3]The members of the royal staff at the King's Gate asked Mordecai, "Why are you disobeying the king's command?" [4]When they had warned him day after day and he still would not listen to them, they told Haman to see if Mordecai's actions would be tolerated, since he had told them he was a Jew.

[5]When Haman saw that Mordecai was not bowing down or paying him homage, he was filled with rage. [6]And when he learned of Mordecai's ethnic identity, Haman decided not to do away with Mordecai alone. He planned to destroy all of Mordecai's people, the Jews, throughout Ahasuerus's kingdom.

[7]In the first month, the month of Nisan, in King Ahasuerus's twelfth year, Pur (that is, the lot) was cast before Haman for each day in each month, and it fell on the twelfth month, the month Adar. [8]Then Haman informed King Ahasuerus, "There is one ethnic group, scattered throughout the peoples in every province of your kingdom, yet living in isolation. Their laws are different from everyone else's and they do not obey the king's laws. It is not in the king's best interest to tolerate them. [9]If the king approves, let an order be drawn up authorizing their destruction, and I will pay 375 tons of silver to the accountants for deposit in the royal treasury."

[10]The king removed his signet ring from his finger and gave it to Haman son of Hammedatha the Agagite, the enemy of the Jewish people. [11]Then the king told Haman, "The money and people are given to you to do with as you see fit."

[12]The royal scribes were summoned on the thirteenth day of the first month, and the order was written exactly as Haman commanded. It was intended for the royal satraps, the governors of each of the provinces, and the officials of each ethnic group and written for each province in its own script and to each ethnic group in its own language. It was written in the name of King Ahasuerus and sealed with the royal signet ring. [13]Letters were sent by couriers to each of the royal provinces telling the officials to destroy, kill, and annihilate all the Jewish people—young and old, women and children—and plunder their possessions on a single day, the thirteenth day of Adar, the twelfth month.

[14]A copy of the text, issued as law throughout every province, was distributed to all the peoples so that they might get ready for that day. [15]The couriers left, spurred on by royal command, and the law was issued in the fortress of Susa. The king and Haman sat down to drink, while the city of Susa was in confusion.

4 When Mordecai learned all that had occurred, he tore his clothes, put on *sackcloth and ashes, went into the middle of the city, and cried loudly and bitterly. [2]He only went as far as the King's Gate, since the law prohibited anyone wearing sackcloth from entering the King's Gate. [3]There was great mourning among the Jewish people in every province where the king's command and edict came. They fasted, wept, and lamented, and many lay on sackcloth and ashes.

[4]Esther's female servants and her eunuchs came and reported the news to her, and the queen was overcome with fear. She sent clothes for Mordecai to wear so he could take off his sackcloth, but he did not accept them. [5]Esther summoned Hathach, one of the king's eunuchs assigned to her, and dispatched him to Mordecai to learn what he was doing and why. [6]So Hathach went out to Mordecai in the city square in front of the King's Gate. [7]Mordecai told him everything that had happened as well as the exact amount of money Haman had promised to pay the royal treasury for the slaughter of the Jews.

[8]Mordecai also gave him a copy of the written decree issued in Susa ordering their destruction, so that Hathach might show it to Esther, explain it to her, and command her to approach the king, implore his favor, and plead with him personally for her people. [9]Hathach came and repeated Mordecai's response to Esther.

[10]Esther spoke to Hathach and commanded him to

tell Mordecai, ¹¹ "All the royal officials and the people of the royal provinces know that one law applies to every man or woman who approaches the king in the inner courtyard and who has not been summoned—the death penalty. Only if the king extends the gold scepter will that person live. I have not been summoned to appear before the king for the last 30 days." ¹² Esther's response was reported to Mordecai.

¹³ Mordecai told the messenger to reply to Esther, "Don't think that you will escape the fate of all the Jews because you are in the king's palace. ¹⁴ If you keep silent at this time, liberation and deliverance will come to the Jewish people from another place, but you and your father's house will be destroyed. Who knows, perhaps you have come to your royal position for such a time as this."

¹⁵ Esther sent this reply to Mordecai: ¹⁶ "Go and assemble all the Jews who can be found in Susa and fast for me. Don't eat or drink for three days, day or night. I and my female servants will also fast in the same way. After that, I will go to the king even if it is against the law. If I perish, I perish." ¹⁷ So Mordecai went and did everything Esther had ordered him.

5 On the third day, Esther dressed up in her royal clothing and stood in the inner courtyard of the palace facing it. The king was sitting on his royal throne in the royal courtroom, facing its entrance. ² As soon as the king saw Queen Esther standing in the courtyard, she won his approval. The king extended the gold scepter in his hand toward Esther, and she approached and touched the tip of the scepter.

³ "What is it, Queen Esther?" the king asked her. "Whatever you want, even to half the kingdom, will be given to you."

⁴ "If it pleases the king," Esther replied, "may the king and Haman come today to the banquet I have prepared for them."

⁵ The king commanded, "Hurry, and get Haman so we can do as Esther has requested." So the king and Haman went to the banquet Esther had prepared.

⁶ While drinking the wine, the king asked Esther, "Whatever you ask will be given to you. Whatever you want, even to half the kingdom, will be done."

⁷ Esther answered, "This is my petition and my request: ⁸ If the king approves of me and if it pleases the king to grant my petition and perform my request, may the king and Haman come to the banquet I will prepare for them. Tomorrow I will do what the king has asked."

⁹ That day Haman left full of joy and in good spirits. But when Haman saw Mordecai at the King's Gate, and Mordecai didn't rise or tremble in fear at his presence, Haman was filled with rage toward Mordecai. ¹⁰ Yet Haman controlled himself and went home. He sent for his friends and his wife Zeresh to join him. ¹¹ Then Haman described for them his glorious wealth and his many sons. He told them all how the king had honored him and promoted him in rank over the other officials and the royal staff. ¹² "What's more," Haman added, "Queen Esther invited no one but me to join the king at the banquet she had prepared. I am invited again tomorrow to join her with the king. ¹³ Still, none of this satisfies me since I see Mordecai the Jew sitting at the King's Gate all the time."

¹⁴ His wife Zeresh and all his friends told him, "Have them build a gallows 75 feet high. Ask the king in the morning to hang Mordecai on it. Then go to the banquet with the king and enjoy yourself." The advice pleased Haman, so he had the gallows constructed.

6 That night sleep escaped the king, so he ordered the book recording daily events to be brought and read to the king. ² They found the written report of how Mordecai had informed on Bigthana and Teresh, two eunuchs who guarded the king's entrance, when they planned to assassinate King Ahasuerus. ³ The king inquired, "What honor and special recognition have been given to Mordecai for this act?"

The king's personal attendants replied, "Nothing has been done for him."

⁴ The king asked, "Who is in the court?" Now Haman was just entering the outer court of the palace to ask the king to hang Mordecai on the gallows he had prepared for him.

⁵ The king's attendants answered him, "Haman is there, standing in the court."

"Have him enter," the king ordered.

⁶ Haman entered, and the king asked him, "What should be done for the man the king wants to honor?"

Haman thought to himself, "Who is it the king would want to honor more than me?" ⁷ Haman told the king, "For the man the king wants to honor: ⁸ Have them bring a royal garment that the king himself has worn and a horse the king himself has ridden, which has a royal diadem on its head. ⁹ Put the garment and the horse under the charge of one of the king's most noble officials. Have them clothe the man the king wants to honor, parade him on the horse through the city square, and proclaim before him, 'This is what is done for the man the king wants to honor.'"

¹⁰ The king told Haman, "Hurry, and do just as you proposed. Take a garment and a horse for Mordecai the Jew, who is sitting at the King's Gate. Do not leave out anything you have suggested." ¹¹ So Haman took the garment and the horse. He clothed Mordecai and paraded him through the city square, crying out before him, "This is what is done for the man the king wants to honor."

¹² Then Mordecai returned to the King's Gate, but Haman, overwhelmed, hurried off for home with his head covered. ¹³ Haman told his wife Zeresh and all his friends everything that had happened. His advisers and his wife Zeresh said to him, "Since Mordecai is Jewish, and you have begun to fall before him, you won't overcome him, because your downfall is certain." ¹⁴ While they were still speaking with him, the eunuchs of the king arrived and rushed Haman to the banquet Esther had prepared.

7 The king and Haman came to feast with Esther the queen. ² Once again, on the second day while drinking wine, the king asked Esther, "Queen Esther, whatever you ask will be given to you. Whatever you seek, even to half the kingdom, will be done."

³ Queen Esther answered, "If I have obtained your approval, my king, and if the king is pleased, spare my life—this is my request; and spare my people—this is my desire. ⁴ For my people and I have been sold out to destruction, death, and extermination. If we had merely been sold as male and female slaves, I would have kept silent. Indeed, the trouble wouldn't be worth burdening the king."

⁵ King Ahasuerus spoke up and asked Queen Esther, "Who is this, and where is the one who would devise such a scheme?"

⁶Esther answered, "The adversary and enemy is this evil Haman."

Haman stood terrified before the king and queen. ⁷Angered by this, the king arose from where they were drinking wine and went to the palace garden. Haman remained to beg Queen Esther for his life because he realized the king was planning something terrible for him. ⁸Just as the king returned from the palace garden to the house of wine drinking, Haman was falling on the couch where Esther was reclining. The king exclaimed, "Would he actually violate the queen while I am in the palace?" As soon as the statement left the king's mouth, Haman's face was covered.

⁹Harbona, one of the royal eunuchs, said: "There is a gallows 75 feet tall at Haman's house that he made for Mordecai, who gave the report that saved the king."

The king commanded, "Hang him on it."

¹⁰They hanged Haman on the gallows he had prepared for Mordecai. Then the king's anger subsided.

8 That same day King Ahasuerus awarded Queen Esther the estate of Haman, the enemy of the Jews. Mordecai entered the king's presence because Esther had revealed her relationship to Mordecai. ²The king removed his signet ring he had recovered from Haman and gave it to Mordecai, and Esther put him in charge of Haman's estate.

³Then Esther addressed the king again. She fell at his feet, wept, and begged him to revoke the evil of Haman the Agagite, and his plot he had devised against the Jews. ⁴The king extended the gold scepter toward Esther, so she got up and stood before the king.

⁵She said, "If it pleases the king, and I have found approval before him, if the matter seems right to the king and I am pleasing in his sight, let a royal edict be written. Let it revoke the documents the scheming Haman son of Hammedatha the Agagite, wrote to destroy the Jews who are in all the king's provinces. ⁶For how could I bear to see the disaster that would come on my people? How could I bear to see the destruction of my relatives?"

⁷King Ahasuerus said to Esther the Queen and to Mordecai the Jew, "Look, I have given Haman's estate to Esther, and he was hanged on the gallows because he attacked the Jews. ⁸You may write in the king's name whatever pleases you concerning the Jews, and seal it with the royal signet ring. A document written in the king's name and sealed with the royal signet ring cannot be revoked."

⁹On the twenty-third day of the third month (that is, the month Sivan), the royal scribes were summoned. Everything was written exactly as Mordecai ordered for the Jews, to the satraps, the governors, and the officials of the 127 provinces from India to ˙Cush. The edict was written for each province in its own script, for each ethnic group in its own language, and to the Jews in their own script and language.

¹⁰Mordecai wrote in King Ahasuerus's name and sealed the edicts with the royal signet ring. He sent the documents by mounted couriers, who rode fast horses bred from the royal racing mares.

¹¹The king's edict gave the Jews in each and every city the right to assemble and defend themselves, to destroy, kill, and annihilate every ethnic and provincial army hostile to them, including women and children, and to take their possessions as spoils of war. ¹²This would take place on a single day throughout all the provinces of King Ahasuerus, on the thirteenth day of the twelfth month, the month Adar.

¹³A copy of the text, issued as law throughout every province, was distributed to all the peoples so the Jews could be ready to avenge themselves against their enemies on that day. ¹⁴The couriers rode out in haste on their royal horses at the king's urgent command. The law was also issued in the fortress of Susa.

¹⁵Mordecai went from the king's presence clothed in royal purple and white, with a great gold crown and a purple robe of fine linen. The city of Susa shouted and rejoiced, ¹⁶and the Jews celebrated with gladness, joy, and honor. ¹⁷In every province and every city, wherever the king's command and his law reached, joy and rejoicing took place among the Jews. There was a celebration and a holiday. And many of the ethnic groups of the land professed themselves to be Jews because fear of the Jews had overcome them.

9 The king's command and law went into effect on the thirteenth day of the twelfth month, the month Adar. On the day when the Jews' enemies had hoped to overpower them, just the opposite happened. The Jews overpowered those who hated them. ²In each of King Ahasuerus's provinces the Jews assembled in their cities to attack those who intended to harm them. Not a single person could withstand them; terror of them fell on every nationality. ³All the officials of the provinces, the satraps, the governors, and the royal civil administrators aided the Jews because they were afraid of Mordecai. ⁴For Mordecai exercised great power in the palace, and his fame spread throughout the provinces as he became more and more powerful.

⁵The Jews put all their enemies to the sword, killing and destroying them. They did what they pleased to those who hated them. ⁶In the fortress of Susa the Jews killed and destroyed 500 men, ⁷including Parshandatha, Dalphon, Aspatha, ⁸Poratha, Adalia, Aridatha, ⁹Parmashta, Arisai, Aridai, and Vaizatha. ¹⁰They killed these 10 sons of Haman son of Hammedatha, the enemy of the Jews. However, they did not seize any plunder.

¹¹On that day the number of people killed in the fortress of Susa was reported to the king. ¹²The king said to Queen Esther, "In the fortress of Susa the Jews have killed and destroyed 500 men, including Haman's 10 sons. What have they done in the rest of the royal provinces? Whatever you ask will be given to you. Whatever you seek will also be done."

¹³Esther answered, "If it pleases the king, may the Jews who are in Susa also have tomorrow to carry out today's law, and may the bodies of Haman's 10 sons be hung on the gallows." ¹⁴The king gave the orders for this to be done, so a law was announced in Susa, and they hung the bodies of Haman's 10 sons. ¹⁵The Jews in Susa assembled again on the fourteenth day of the month of Adar and killed 300 men in Susa, but they did not seize any plunder.

¹⁶The rest of the Jews in the royal provinces assembled, defended themselves, and got rid of their enemies. They killed 75,000 of those who hated them, but they did not seize any plunder. ¹⁷They fought on the thirteenth day of the month of Adar and rested on the fourteenth, and it became a day of feasting and rejoicing.

¹⁸But the Jews in Susa had assembled on the thirteenth and the fourteenth days of the month. They

rested on the fifteenth day of the month, and it became a day of feasting and rejoicing. ¹⁹This explains why the rural Jews who live in villages observe the fourteenth day of the month of Adar as a time of rejoicing and feasting. It is a holiday when they send gifts to one another.

²⁰Mordecai recorded these events and sent letters to all the Jews in all of King Ahasuerus's provinces, both near and far. ²¹He ordered them to celebrate the fourteenth and fifteenth days of the month Adar every year ²²because during those days the Jews got rid of their enemies. That was the month when their sorrow was turned into rejoicing and their mourning into a holiday. They were to be days of feasting, rejoicing, and of sending gifts to one another and the poor.

²³So the Jews agreed to continue the practice they had begun, as Mordecai had written them to do. ²⁴For Haman son of Hammedatha the Agagite, the enemy of all the Jews, had plotted against the Jews to destroy them. He cast the Pur (that is, the lot) to crush and destroy them. ²⁵But when the matter was brought before the king, he commanded by letter that the evil plan Haman had devised against the Jews return on his own head and that he should be hanged with his sons on the gallows. ²⁶For this reason these days are called Purim, from the word Pur.

Because of all the instructions in this letter as well as what they had witnessed and what had happened to them, ²⁷the Jews bound themselves, their descendants, and all who joined with them to a commitment that they would not fail to celebrate these two days each and every year according to the written instructions and according to the time appointed. ²⁸These days are remembered and celebrated by every generation, family, province, and city, so that these days of Purim will not lose their significance in Jewish life and their memory will not fade from their descendants.

²⁹Queen Esther daughter of Abihail, along with Mordecai the Jew, wrote this second letter with full authority to confirm the letter about Purim. ³⁰He sent letters with messages of peace and faithfulness to all the Jews who were in the 127 provinces of the kingdom of Ahasuerus, ³¹in order to confirm these days of Purim at their proper time just as Mordecai the Jew and Queen Esther had established them and just as they had committed themselves and their descendants to the practices of fasting and lamentation. ³²So Esther's command confirmed these customs of Purim, which were then written into the record.

10 King Ahasuerus imposed a tax throughout the land even to the farthest shores. ²All of his powerful and magnificent accomplishments and the detailed account of Mordecai's great rank to which the king had honored him, have they not been written in the Historical Records of the Kings of Media and Persia? ³Mordecai the Jew was second only to King Ahasuerus, famous among the Jews, and highly popular with many of his relatives. He continued to seek good for his people and to speak for the welfare of all his descendants.

JOB

1 There was a man in the country of Uz named Job. He was a man of perfect integrity, who *feared God and turned away from evil. ²He had seven sons and three daughters. ³His estate included 7,000 sheep, 3,000 camels, 500 yoke of oxen, 500 female donkeys, and a very large number of servants. Job was the greatest man among all the people of the east.

⁴His sons used to take turns having banquets at their homes. They would send an invitation to their three sisters to eat and drink with them. ⁵Whenever a round of banqueting was over, Job would send for his children and purify them, rising early in the morning to offer burnt offerings for all of them. For Job thought: Perhaps my children have sinned, having cursed God in their hearts. This was Job's regular practice.

⁶One day the sons of God came to present themselves before the Lord, and Satan also came with them. ⁷The Lord asked Satan, "Where have you come from?"

"From roaming through the earth," Satan answered Him, "and walking around on it."

⁸Then the Lord said to Satan, "Have you considered My servant Job? No one else on earth is like him, a man of perfect integrity, who fears God and turns away from evil."

⁹Satan answered the Lord, "Does Job fear God for nothing? ¹⁰Haven't You placed a hedge around him, his household, and everything he owns? You have blessed the work of his hands, and his possessions have increased in the land. ¹¹But stretch out Your hand and strike everything he owns, and he will surely curse You to Your face."

¹²"Very well," the Lord told Satan, "everything he owns is in your power. However, you must not lay a hand on Job himself." So Satan left the Lord's presence.

¹³One day when Job's sons and daughters were eating and drinking wine in their oldest brother's house, ¹⁴a messenger came to Job and reported: "While the oxen were plowing and the donkeys grazing nearby, ¹⁵the Sabeans swooped down and took them away. They struck down the servants with the sword, and I alone have escaped to tell you!"

¹⁶He was still speaking when another messenger came and reported: "A lightning storm struck from heaven. It burned up the sheep and the servants and devoured them, and I alone have escaped to tell you!"

¹⁷That messenger was still speaking when yet another came and reported: "The Chaldeans formed three bands, made a raid on the camels, and took them away. They struck down the servants with the sword, and I alone have escaped to tell you!"

¹⁸He was still speaking when another messenger came and reported: "Your sons and daughters were eating and drinking wine in their oldest brother's house. ¹⁹Suddenly a powerful wind swept in from the desert and struck the four corners of the house. It collapsed on the young people so that they died, and I alone have escaped to tell you!"

²⁰Then Job stood up, tore his robe, and shaved his head. He fell to the ground and worshiped, ²¹saying:

Naked I came from my mother's womb,
and naked I will leave this life.
The Lord gives, and the Lord takes away.
Praise the name of *Yahweh.
²² Throughout all this Job did not sin or blame God for anything.

2 One day the sons of God came again to present themselves before the Lord, and Satan also came with them to present himself before the Lord. ²The Lord asked Satan, "Where have you come from?"

"From roaming through the earth," Satan answered Him, "and walking around on it."

³ Then the Lord said to Satan, "Have you considered My servant Job? No one else on earth is like him, a man of perfect integrity, who *fears God and turns away from evil. He still retains his integrity, even though you incited Me against him, to destroy him without just cause."

⁴ "Skin for skin!" Satan answered the Lord. "A man will give up everything he owns in exchange for his life. ⁵ But stretch out Your hand and strike his flesh and bones, and he will surely curse You to Your face."

⁶ "Very well," the Lord told Satan, "he is in your power; only spare his life." ⁷ So Satan left the Lord's presence and infected Job with terrible boils from the sole of his foot to the top of his head. ⁸ Then Job took a piece of broken pottery to scrape himself while he sat among the ashes.

⁹ His wife said to him, "Do you still retain your integrity? Curse God and die!"

¹⁰ "You speak as a foolish woman speaks," he told her. "Should we accept only good from God and not adversity?" Throughout all this Job did not sin in what he said.

¹¹ Now when Job's three friends—Eliphaz the Temanite, Bildad the Shuhite, and Zophar the Naamathite—heard about all this adversity that had happened to him, each of them came from his home. They met together to go and sympathize with him and comfort him. ¹² When they looked from a distance, they could barely recognize him. They wept aloud, and each man tore his robe and threw dust into the air and on his head. ¹³ Then they sat on the ground with him seven days and nights, but no one spoke a word to him because they saw that his suffering was very intense.

3 After this, Job began to speak and cursed the day he was born. ²He said:
³ May the day I was born perish,
and the night when they said,
"A boy is conceived."
⁴ If only that day had turned to darkness!
May God above not care about it,
or light shine on it.
⁵ May darkness and gloom reclaim it,
and a cloud settle over it.
May an eclipse of the sun terrify it.
⁶ If only darkness had taken that night away!
May it not appear among the days of the year
or be listed in the calendar.
⁷ Yes, may that night be barren;
may no joyful shout be heard in it.
⁸ Let those who curse certain days
cast a spell on it,
those who are skilled in rousing *Leviathan.
⁹ May its morning stars grow dark.
May it wait for daylight but have none;
may it not see the breaking of dawn.

¹⁰ For that night did not shut
the doors of my mother's womb,
and hide sorrow from my eyes.
¹¹ Why was I not stillborn;
why didn't I die as I came from the womb?
¹² Why did the knees receive me,
and why were there breasts for me to nurse?
¹³ Now I would certainly be lying down in peace;
I would be asleep.
Then I would be at rest
¹⁴ with the kings and counselors of the earth,
who rebuilt ruined cities for themselves,
¹⁵ or with princes who had gold,
who filled their houses with silver.
¹⁶ Or why was I not hidden
like a miscarried child,
like infants who never see daylight?
¹⁷ There the wicked cease to make trouble,
and there the weary find rest.
¹⁸ The captives are completely at ease;
they do not hear the voice of their oppressor.
¹⁹ Both small and great are there,
and the slave is set free from his master.
²⁰ Why is light given to one burdened with grief,
and life to those whose existence is bitter,
²¹ who wait for death, but it does not come,
and search for it more than
for hidden treasure,
²² who are filled with much joy
and are glad when they reach the grave?
²³ Why is life given to a man whose path
is hidden,
whom God has hedged in?
²⁴ I sigh when food is put before me,
and my groans pour out like water.
²⁵ For the thing I feared has overtaken me,
and what I dreaded has happened to me.
²⁶ I cannot relax or be still;
I have no rest, for trouble comes.

4 Then Eliphaz the Temanite replied:
² Should anyone try to speak with you
when you are exhausted?
Yet who can keep from speaking?
³ Indeed, you have instructed many
and have strengthened weak hands.
⁴ Your words have steadied the one
who was stumbling
and braced the knees that were buckling.
⁵ But now that this has happened to you,
you have become exhausted.
It strikes you, and you are dismayed.
⁶ Isn't your piety your confidence,
and the integrity of your life your hope?
⁷ Consider: who has perished when he
was innocent?
Where have the honest been destroyed?
⁸ In my experience, those who plow injustice
and those who sow trouble reap the same.
⁹ They perish at a single blast from God
and come to an end by the breath
of His nostrils.
¹⁰ The lion may roar and the fierce lion growl,
but the fangs of young lions are broken.
¹¹ The strong lion dies if it catches no prey,
and the cubs of the lioness are scattered.
¹² A word was brought to me in secret;
my ears caught a whisper of it.

13 Among unsettling thoughts from visions
   in the night,
   when deep sleep descends on men,
14 fear and trembling came over me
   and made all my bones shake.
15 A wind passed by me,
   and I shuddered with fear.
16 A figure stood there,
   but I could not recognize its appearance;
   a form loomed before my eyes.
   I heard a quiet voice:
17 "Can a person be more righteous than God,
   or a man more pure than his Maker?"
18 If God puts no trust in His servants
   and He charges His angels with foolishness,
19 how much more those who dwell
   in clay houses,
   whose foundation is in the dust,
   who are crushed like a moth!
20 They are smashed to pieces from dawn
   to dusk;
   they perish forever while no one notices.
21 Are their tent cords not pulled up?
   They die without wisdom.

5 Call out if you please. Will anyone
   answer you?
   Which of the holy ones will you turn to?
2 For anger kills a fool,
   and jealousy slays the gullible.
3 I have seen a fool taking root,
   but I immediately pronounced a curse
   on his home.
4 His children are far from safety.
   They are crushed at the city *gate,
   with no one to rescue them.
5 The hungry consume his harvest,
   even taking it out of the thorns.
   The thirsty pant for his children's wealth.
6 For distress does not grow out of the soil,
   and trouble does not sprout from the ground.
7 But mankind is born for trouble
   as surely as sparks fly upward.
8 However, if I were you, I would appeal to God
   and would present my case to Him.
9 He does great and unsearchable things,
   wonders without number.
10 He gives rain to the earth
   and sends water to the fields.
11 He sets the lowly on high,
   and mourners are lifted to safety.
12 He frustrates the schemes of the crafty
   so that they achieve no success.
13 He traps the wise in their craftiness
   so that the plans of the deceptive
   are quickly brought to an end.
14 They encounter darkness by day,
   and they grope at noon
   as if it were night.
15 He saves the needy from their sharp words
   and from the clutches of the powerful.
16 So the poor have hope,
   and injustice shuts its mouth.
17 See how happy the man is God corrects;
   so do not reject the discipline of the *Almighty.
18 For He crushes but also binds up;
   He strikes, but His hands also heal.
19 He will rescue you from six calamities;

20 no harm will touch you in seven.
20 In famine He will redeem you from death,
   and in battle, from the power of the sword.
21 You will be safe from slander
   and not fear destruction when it comes.
22 You will laugh at destruction and hunger
   and not fear the animals of the earth.
23 For you will have a covenant with the stones
   of the field,
   and the wild animals will be at peace with you.
24 You will know that your tent is secure,
   and nothing will be missing when you inspect
   your home.
25 You will also know that your offspring
   will be many
   and your descendants like the grass
   of the earth.
26 You will approach the grave in full vigor,
   as a stack of sheaves is gathered in its season.
27 We have investigated this, and it is true!
   Hear it and understand it for yourself.

6 Then Job answered:
2 If only my grief could be weighed
   and my devastation placed with it
   in the scales.
3 For then it would outweigh the sand
   of the seas!
   That is why my words are rash.
4 Surely the arrows of the *Almighty
   have pierced me;
   my spirit drinks their poison.
   God's terrors are arrayed against me.
5 Does a wild donkey bray over fresh grass
   or an ox low over its fodder?
6 Is bland food eaten without salt?
   Is there flavor in an egg white?
7 I refuse to touch them;
   they are like contaminated food.
8 If only my request would be granted
   and God would provide what I hope for:
9 that He would decide to crush me,
   to unleash His power and cut me off!
10 It would still bring me comfort,
   and I would leap for joy in unrelenting pain
   that I have not denied the words
   of the Holy One.
11 What strength do I have that I should
   continue to hope?
   What is my future, that I should be patient?
12 Is my strength that of stone,
   or my flesh made of bronze?
13 Since I cannot help myself,
   the hope for success has been banished
   from me.
14 A despairing man should receive loyalty
   from his friends,
   even if he abandons the *fear of the Almighty.
15 My brothers are as treacherous as a *wadi,
   as seasonal streams that overflow
16 and become darkened because of ice,
   and the snow melts into them.
17 The wadis evaporate in warm weather;
   they disappear from their channels
   in hot weather.
18 Caravans turn away from their routes,
   go up into the desert, and perish.
19 The caravans of Tema look for these streams.

The traveling merchants of Sheba hope
　for them.
20 They are ashamed because they
　　had been confident of finding water.
　When they arrive there, they are frustrated.
21 So this is what you have now become to me.
　When you see something dreadful,
　　you are afraid.
22 Have I ever said: "Give me something"
　or "Pay a bribe for me from your wealth"
23 or "Deliver me from the enemy's power"
　or "Redeem me from the grasp
　　of the ruthless"?
24 Teach me, and I will be silent.
　Help me understand what I did wrong.
25 How painful honest words can be!
　But what does your rebuke prove?
26 Do you think that you can disprove my words
　or that a despairing man's words are
　　mere wind?
27 No doubt you would cast lots
　　for a fatherless child
　and negotiate a price to sell your friend.
28 But now, please look at me;
　would I lie to your face?
29 Reconsider; don't be unjust.
　Reconsider; my righteousness is still the issue.
30 Is there injustice on my tongue
　or can my palate not taste disaster?

7 Isn't mankind consigned to forced labor
　　on earth?
　Are not his days like those of a hired hand?
2 Like a slave he longs for shade;
　like a hired man he waits for his pay.
3 So I have been made to inherit months
　　of futility,
　and troubled nights have been assigned to me.
4 When I lie down I think:
　When will I get up?
　But the evening drags on endlessly,
　and I toss and turn until dawn.
5 My flesh is clothed with maggots
　　and encrusted with dirt.
　My skin forms scabs and then oozes.
6 My days pass more swiftly
　　than a weaver's shuttle;
　they come to an end without hope.
7 Remember that my life is but a breath.
　My eye will never again see anything good.
8 The eye of anyone who looks on me
　will no longer see me.
　Your eyes will look for me, but I will be gone.
9 As a cloud fades away and vanishes,
　so the one who goes down to *Sheol will never
　　rise again.
10 He will never return to his house;
　his hometown will no longer remember him.
11 Therefore I will not restrain my mouth.
　I will speak in the anguish of my spirit;
　I will complain in the bitterness of my soul.
12 Am I the sea or a sea monster,
　that You keep me under guard?
13 When I say: My bed will comfort me,
　and my couch will ease my complaint,
14 then You frighten me with dreams,
　and terrify me with visions,
15 so that I prefer strangling—

death rather than life in this body.
16 I give up! I will not live forever.
　Leave me alone, for my days are a breath.
17 What is man, that You think so highly of him
　and pay so much attention to him?
18 You inspect him every morning,
　and put him to the test every moment.
19 Will You ever look away from me,
　or leave me alone long enough to swallow?
20 If I have sinned, what have I done to You,
　Watcher of mankind?
　Why have You made me Your target,
　so that I have become a burden to You?
21 Why not forgive my sin
　and pardon my transgression?
　For soon I will lie down in the grave.
　You will eagerly seek me, but I will be gone.

8 Then Bildad the Shuhite replied:
2 How long will you go on saying these things?
　Your words are a blast of wind.
3 Does God pervert justice?
　Does the •Almighty pervert what is right?
4 Since your children sinned against Him,
　He gave them over to their rebellion.
5 But if you earnestly seek God
　and ask the Almighty for mercy,
6 if you are pure and upright,
　then He will move even now on your behalf
　and restore the home where
　　your righteousness dwells.
7 Then, even if your beginnings were modest,
　your final days will be full of prosperity.
8 For ask the previous generation,
　and pay attention to what
　　their fathers discovered,
9 since we were born only yesterday and know
　　nothing.
　Our days on earth are but a shadow.
10 Will they not teach you and tell you
　and speak from their understanding?
11 Does papyrus grow where there is no marsh?
　Do reeds flourish without water?
12 While still uncut shoots,
　they would dry up quicker than any other plant.
13 Such is the destiny of all who forget God;
　the hope of the godless will perish.
14 His source of confidence is fragile;
　what he trusts in is a spider's web.
15 He leans on his web, but it doesn't stand firm.
　He grabs it, but it does not hold up.
16 He is a well-watered plant in the sunshine;
　his shoots spread out over his garden.
17 His roots are intertwined around a pile
　　of rocks.
　He looks for a home among the stones.
18 If he is uprooted from his place,
　it will deny knowing him, saying,
　　"I never saw you."
19 Surely this is the joy of his way of life;
　yet others will sprout from the dust.
20 Look, God does not reject a person
　　of integrity,
　and He will not support evildoers.
21 He will yet fill your mouth with laughter
　and your lips with a shout of joy.
22 Your enemies will be clothed with shame;
　the tent of the wicked will exist no longer.

9 Then Job answered:
² Yes, I know what you've said is true,
but how can a person be justified before God?
³ If one wanted to take Him to court,
he could not answer God once
in a thousand times.
⁴ God is wise and all-powerful.
Who has opposed Him
and come out unharmed?
⁵ He removes mountains
without their knowledge,
overturning them in His anger.
⁶ He shakes the earth from its place
so that its pillars tremble.
⁷ He commands the sun not to shine
and seals off the stars.
⁸ He alone stretches out the heavens
and treads on the waves of the sea.
⁹ He makes the stars: the Bear, Orion,
the Pleiades, and the constellations
of the southern sky.
¹⁰ He does great and unsearchable things,
wonders without number.
¹¹ If He passes by me, I wouldn't see Him;
if He goes right by, I wouldn't recognize Him.
¹² If He snatches something, who can stop Him?
Who can ask Him, "What are You doing?"
¹³ God does not hold back His anger;
*Rahab's assistants cringe in fear beneath Him!
¹⁴ How then can I answer Him
or choose my arguments against Him?
¹⁵ Even if I were in the right, I could not answer.
I could only beg my Judge for mercy.
¹⁶ If I summoned Him and He answered me,
I do not believe He would pay attention to
what I said.
¹⁷ He batters me with a whirlwind
and multiplies my wounds without cause.
¹⁸ He doesn't let me catch my breath
but soaks me with bitter experiences.
¹⁹ If it is a matter of strength, look, He is
the Mighty One!
If it is a matter of justice, who can
summon Him?
²⁰ Even if I were in the right, my own mouth
would condemn me;
if I were blameless, my mouth would
declare me *guilty.
²¹ Though I am blameless,
I no longer care about myself;
I renounce my life.
²² It is all the same. Therefore I say,
"He destroys both the blameless
and the wicked."
²³ When disaster brings sudden death,
He mocks the despair of the innocent.
²⁴ The earth is handed over to the wicked;
He blindfolds its judges.
If it isn't He, then who is it?
²⁵ My days fly by faster than a runner;
they flee without seeing any good.
²⁶ They sweep by like boats made of papyrus,
like an eagle swooping down on its prey.
²⁷ If I said, "I will forget my complaint,
change my expression, and smile,"
²⁸ I would still live in terror of all my pains.
I know You will not acquit me.

²⁹ Since I will be found guilty,
why should I labor in vain?
³⁰ If I wash myself with snow,
and cleanse my hands with lye,
³¹ then You dip me in a pit of mud,
and my own clothes despise me!
³² For He is not a man like me, that I can
answer Him,
that we can take each other to court.
³³ There is no one to judge between us,
to lay his hand on both of us.
³⁴ Let Him take His rod away from me
so His terror will no longer frighten me.
³⁵ Then I would speak and not fear Him.
But that is not the case; I am on my own.

10 I am disgusted with my life.
I will express my complaint
and speak in the bitterness of my soul.
² I will say to God:
"Do not declare me *guilty!
Let me know why You prosecute me.
³ Is it good for You to oppress,
to reject the work of Your hands,
and favor the plans of the wicked?
⁴ Do You have eyes of flesh,
or do You see as a human sees?
⁵ Are Your days like those of a human,
or Your years like those of a man,
⁶ that You look for my wrongdoing
and search for my sin,
⁷ even though You know that I am not wicked
and that there is no one who can deliver
from Your hand?
⁸ Your hands shaped me and formed me.
Will You now turn and destroy me?
⁹ Please remember that You formed me
like clay.
Will You now return me to dust?
¹⁰ Did You not pour me out like milk
and curdle me like cheese?
¹¹ You clothed me with skin and flesh,
and wove me together with bones
and tendons.
¹² You gave me life and faithful love,
and Your care has guarded my life.
¹³ Yet You concealed these thoughts
in Your heart;
I know that this was Your hidden plan:
¹⁴ if I sin, You would notice,
and would not acquit me of my wrongdoing.
¹⁵ If I am wicked, woe to me!
And even if I am righteous, I cannot lift up
my head.
I am filled with shame
and aware of my affliction.
¹⁶ If I am proud, You hunt me like a lion
and again display Your miraculous power
against me.
¹⁷ You produce new witnesses against me
and multiply Your anger toward me.
Hardships assault me, wave after wave.
¹⁸ Why did You bring me out of the womb?
I should have died and never been seen.
¹⁹ I wish I had never existed
but had been carried from the womb
to the grave.
²⁰ Are my days not few? Stop it!

Leave me alone, so that I can smile a little
21 before I go to a land of darkness and gloom,
never to return.
22 It is a land of blackness
like the deepest darkness,
gloomy and chaotic,
where even the light is like the darkness."

11
Then Zophar the Naamathite replied:
2 Should this stream of words go unanswered
and such a talker be acquitted?
3 Should your babbling put others to silence,
so that you can keep on ridiculing
with no one to humiliate you?
4 You have said, "My teaching is sound,
and I am pure in Your sight."
5 But if only God would speak
and declare His case against you,
6 He would show you the secrets of wisdom,
for true wisdom has two sides.
Know then that God has chosen to overlook
some of your sin.
7 Can you fathom the depths of God
or discover the limits of the *Almighty?
8 They are higher than the heavens—what can
you do?
They are deeper than *Sheol—what can
you know?
9 Their measure is longer than the earth
and wider than the sea.
10 If He passes by and throws someone in prison
or convenes a court, who can stop Him?
11 Surely He knows which people are worthless.
If He sees iniquity, will He not take note of it?
12 But a stupid man will gain understanding
as soon as a wild donkey is born a man!
13 As for you, if you redirect your heart
and lift up your hands to Him in prayer—
14 if there is iniquity in your hand, remove it,
and don't allow injustice to dwell
in your tents—
15 then you will hold your head high,
free from fault.
You will be firmly established and unafraid.
16 For you will forget your suffering,
recalling it only as waters that have flowed by.
17 Your life will be brighter than noonday;
its darkness will be like the morning.
18 You will be confident, because
there is hope.
You will look carefully about and lie down
in safety.
19 You will lie down without fear,
and many will seek your favor.
20 But the sight of the wicked will fail.
Their way of escape will be cut off,
and their only hope is their last breath.

12
Then Job answered:
2 No doubt you are the people,
and wisdom will die with you!
3 But I also have a mind;
I am not inferior to you.
Who doesn't know the things you are
talking about?
4 I am a laughingstock to my friends,
by calling on God, who answers me.
The righteous and upright man is
a laughingstock.

5 The one who is at ease holds calamity
in contempt
and thinks it is prepared for those whose feet
are slipping.
6 The tents of robbers are safe,
and those who provoke God are secure;
God's power provides this.
7 But ask the animals, and they will
instruct you;
ask the birds of the sky, and they will tell you.
8 Or speak to the earth, and it will instruct you;
let the fish of the sea inform you.
9 Which of all these does not know
that the hand of the LORD has done this?
10 The life of every living thing is in His hand,
as well as the breath of all mankind.
11 Doesn't the ear test words
as the palate tastes food?
12 Wisdom is found with the elderly,
and understanding comes with long life.
13 Wisdom and strength belong to God;
counsel and understanding are His.
14 Whatever He tears down cannot be rebuilt;
whoever He imprisons cannot be released.
15 When He withholds the waters, everything
dries up,
and when He releases them, they destroy
the land.
16 True wisdom and power belong to Him.
The deceived and the deceiver are His.
17 He leads counselors away barefoot
and makes judges go mad.
18 He releases the bonds put on by kings
and fastens a belt around their waists.
19 He leads priests away barefoot
and overthrows established leaders.
20 He deprives trusted advisers of speech
and takes away the elders' good judgment.
21 He pours out contempt on nobles
and disarms the strong.
22 He reveals mysteries from the darkness
and brings the deepest darkness into the light.
23 He makes nations great, then destroys them;
He enlarges nations, then leads them away.
24 He deprives the world's leaders of reason,
and makes them wander
in a trackless wasteland.
25 They grope around in darkness without light;
He makes them stagger like drunken men.

13
Look, my eyes have seen all this;
my ears have heard and understood it.
2 Everything you know, I also know;
I am not inferior to you.
3 Yet I prefer to speak to the *Almighty
and argue my case before God.
4 But you coat the truth with lies;
you are all worthless doctors.
5 If only you would shut up
and let that be your wisdom!
6 Hear now my argument,
and listen to my defense.
7 Would you testify unjustly on God's behalf
or speak deceitfully for Him?
8 Would you show partiality to Him
or argue the case in His defense?
9 Would it go well if He examined you?

Could you deceive Him as you would deceive
a man?

10 Surely He would rebuke you
if you secretly showed partiality.

11 Would God's majesty not terrify you?
Would His dread not fall on you?

12 Your memorable sayings are proverbs of ash;
your defenses are made of clay.

13 Be quiet, and I will speak.
Let whatever comes happen to me.

14 Why do I put myself at risk
and take my life in my own hands?

15 Even if He kills me, I will hope in Him.
I will still defend my ways before Him.

16 Yes, this will result in my deliverance,
for no godless person can appear before Him.

17 Pay close attention to my words;
let my declaration ring in your ears.

18 Now then, I have prepared my case;
I know that I am right.

19 Can anyone indict me?
If so, I will be silent and die.

20 Only grant these two things to me, God,
so that I will not have to hide
from Your presence:

21 remove Your hand from me,
and do not let Your terror frighten me.

22 Then call, and I will answer,
or I will speak, and You can respond to me.

23 How many iniquities and sins
have I committed?
Reveal to me my transgression and sin.

24 Why do You hide Your face
and consider me Your enemy?

25 Will You frighten a wind-driven leaf?
Will You chase after dry straw?

26 For You record bitter accusations against me
and make me inherit the iniquities
of my youth.

27 You put my feet in the stocks
and stand watch over all my paths,
setting a limit for the soles of my feet.

28 Man wears out like something rotten,
like a moth-eaten garment.

14 Man born of woman
is short of days and full of trouble.

2 He blossoms like a flower, then withers;
he flees like a shadow and does not last.

3 Do You really take notice of one like this?
Will You bring me into judgment against You?

4 Who can produce something pure from what
is impure?
No one!

5 Since man's days are determined
and the number of his months depends
on You,
and since You have set limits he cannot pass,

6 look away from him and let him rest
so that he can enjoy his day like a hired hand.

7 There is hope for a tree:
If it is cut down, it will sprout again,
and its shoots will not die.

8 If its roots grow old in the ground
and its stump starts to die in the soil,

9 the smell of water makes it thrive
and produce twigs like a sapling.

10 But a man dies and fades away;

he breathes his last—where is he?

11 As water disappears from the sea
and a river becomes parched and dry,

12 so man lies down never to rise again.
They will not wake up until the heavens are
no more;
they will not stir from their sleep.

13 If only You would hide me in *Sheol
and conceal me until Your anger passes.
If only You would appoint a time for me
and then remember me.

14 When a man dies, will he come back to life?
If so, I would wait all the days of my struggle
until my relief comes.

15 You would call, and I would answer You.
You would long for the work of Your hands.

16 For then You would count my steps
but would not take note of my sin.

17 My rebellion would be sealed up in a bag,
and You would cover over my iniquity.

18 But as a mountain collapses and crumbles
and a rock is dislodged from its place,

19 as water wears away stones
and torrents wash away the soil from the land,
so You destroy a man's hope.

20 You completely overpower him, and he
passes on;
You change his appearance
and send him away.

21 If his sons receive honor, he does not know it;
if they become insignificant, he is unaware
of it.

22 He feels only the pain of his own body
and mourns only for himself.

15 Then Eliphaz the Temanite replied:

2 Does a wise man answer with empty counsel
or fill himself with the hot east wind?

3 Should he argue with useless talk
or with words that serve no good purpose?

4 But you even undermine the *fear of God
and hinder meditation before Him.

5 Your iniquity teaches you what to say,
and you choose the language of the crafty.

6 Your own mouth condemns you, not I;
your own lips testify against you.

7 Were you the first person ever born,
or were you brought forth before the hills?

8 Do you listen in on the council of God,
or have a monopoly on wisdom?

9 What do you know that we don't?
What do you understand that is not clear
to us?

10 Both the gray-haired and the elderly are
with us,
men older than your father.

11 Are God's consolations not enough for you,
even the words that deal gently with you?

12 Why has your heart misled you,
and why do your eyes flash

13 as you turn your anger against God
and allow such words to leave your mouth?

14 What is man, that he should be pure,
or one born of woman, that he
should be righteous?

15 If God puts no trust in His holy ones
and the heavens are not pure in His sight,

16 how much less one who is revolting
and corrupt,
who drinks injustice like water?
17 Listen to me and I will inform you.
I will describe what I have seen,
18 what was declared by wise men
and was not suppressed by their ancestors,
19 the land was given to them alone
when no foreigner passed among them.
20 A wicked man writhes in pain all his days;
only a few years are reserved for the ruthless.
21 Dreadful sounds fill his ears;
when he is at peace, a robber attacks him.
22 He doesn't believe he will return
from darkness;
he is destined for the sword.
23 He wanders about for food, saying,
"Where is it?"
He knows the day of darkness is at hand.
24 Trouble and distress terrify him,
overwhelming him like a king prepared
for battle.
25 For he has stretched out his hand against God
and has arrogantly opposed the *Almighty.
26 He rushes headlong at Him
with his thick, studded shields.
27 Though his face is covered with fat
and his waistline bulges with it,
28 he will dwell in ruined cities,
in abandoned houses destined to become piles
of rubble.
29 He will no longer be rich; his wealth
will not endure.
His possessions will not increase in the land.
30 He will not escape from the darkness;
flames will wither his shoots,
and by the breath of God's mouth,
he will depart.
31 Let him not put trust in worthless things,
being led astray,
for what he gets in exchange
will prove worthless.
32 It will be accomplished before his time,
and his branch will not flourish.
33 He will be like a vine that drops
its unripe grapes
and like an olive tree that sheds its blossoms.
34 For the company of the godless
will have no children,
and fire will consume the tents of those
who offer bribes.
35 They conceive trouble and give birth to evil;
their womb prepares deception.

16 Then Job answered:
2 I have heard many things like these.
You are all miserable comforters.
3 Is there no end to your empty words?
What provokes you that you
continue testifying?
4 If you were in my place I could also talk
like you.
I could string words together against you
and shake my head at you.
5 Instead, I would encourage you
with my mouth,
and the consolation from my lips
would bring relief.

6 Even if I speak, my suffering is not relieved,
and if I hold back, what have I lost?
7 Surely He has now exhausted me.
You have devastated my entire family.
8 You have shriveled me up—it has become
a witness;
My frailty rises up against me and testifies
to my face.
9 His anger tears at me, and He harasses me.
He gnashes His teeth at me.
My enemy pierces me with His eyes.
10 They open their mouths against me
and strike my cheeks with contempt;
they join themselves together against me.
11 God hands me over to unjust men;
He throws me into the hands of the wicked.
12 I was at ease, but He shattered me;
He seized me by the scruff of the neck
and smashed me to pieces.
He set me up as His target;
13 His archers surround me.
He pierces my kidneys without mercy
and pours my bile on the ground.
14 He breaks through my defenses again
and again;
He charges at me like a warrior.
15 I have sewn *sackcloth over my skin;
I have buried my strength in the dust.
16 My face has grown red with weeping,
and darkness covers my eyes,
17 although my hands are free from violence
and my prayer is pure.
18 Earth, do not cover my blood;
may my cry for help find no resting place.
19 Even now my witness is in heaven,
and my advocate is in the heights!
20 My friends scoff at me
as I weep before God.
21 I wish that someone might arbitrate
between a man and God
just as a *man pleads for his friend.
22 For only a few years will pass
before I go the way of no return.

17 My spirit is broken.
My days are extinguished.
A graveyard awaits me.
2 Surely mockers surround me
and my eyes must gaze at their rebellion.
3 Make arrangements! Put up security for me.
Who else will be my sponsor?
4 You have closed their minds to understanding,
therefore You will not honor them.
5 If a man informs on his friends for a price,
the eyes of his children will fail.
6 He has made me an object of scorn
to the people;
I have become a man people spit at.
7 My eyes have grown dim from grief,
and my whole body has become but a shadow.
8 The upright are appalled at this,
and the innocent are roused
against the godless.
9 Yet the righteous person will hold to his way,
and the one whose hands are *clean
will grow stronger.
10 But come back and try again, all of you.
I will not find a wise man among you.

11 My days have slipped by;
my plans have been ruined,
even the things dear to my heart.
12 They turned night into day
and made light seem near in the face
of darkness.
13 If I await *Sheol as my home,
spread out my bed in darkness,
14 and say to corruption: You are my father,
and to the maggot: My mother or my sister,
15 where then is my hope?
Who can see any hope for me?
16 Will it go down to the gates of Sheol,
or will we descend together to the dust?

18 Then Bildad the Shuhite replied:
2 How long until you stop talking?
Show some sense, and then we can talk.
3 Why are we regarded as cattle,
as stupid in your sight?
4 You who tear yourself in anger—
should the earth be abandoned
on your account,
or a rock be removed from its place?
5 Yes, the light of the wicked is extinguished;
the flame of his fire does not glow.
6 The light in his tent grows dark,
and the lamp beside him is put out.
7 His powerful stride is shortened,
and his own schemes trip him up.
8 For his own feet lead him into a net,
and he strays into its mesh.
9 A trap catches him by the heel;
a noose seizes him.
10 A rope lies hidden for him on the ground,
and a snare waits for him along the path.
11 Terrors frighten him on every side
and harass him at every step.
12 His strength is depleted;
disaster lies ready for him to stumble.
13 Parts of his skin are eaten away;
death's firstborn consumes his limbs.
14 He is ripped from the security of his tent
and marched away to the king of terrors.
15 Nothing he owned remains in his tent.
Burning sulfur is scattered over his home.
16 His roots below dry up,
and his branches above wither away.
17 All memory of him perishes from the earth;
he has no name anywhere.
18 He is driven from light to darkness
and chased from the inhabited world.
19 He has no children or descendants
among his people,
no survivor where he used to live.
20 Those in the west are appalled at his fate,
while those in the east tremble in horror.
21 Indeed, such is the dwelling of the
unjust man,
and this is the place of the one who does not
know God.

19 Then Job answered:
2 How long will you torment me
and crush me with words?
3 You have humiliated me ten times now,
and you mistreat me without shame.
4 Even if it is true that I have sinned,
my mistake concerns only me.

5 If you really want to appear superior to me
and would use my disgrace as evidence
against me,
6 then understand that it is God
who has wronged me
and caught me in His net.
7 I cry out: "Violence!" but get no response;
I call for help, but there is no justice.
8 He has blocked my way so that I cannot
pass through;
He has veiled my paths with darkness.
9 He has stripped me of my honor
and removed the crown from my head.
10 He tears me down on every side so that
I am ruined.
He uproots my hope like a tree.
11 His anger burns against me,
and He regards me as one of His enemies.
12 His troops advance together;
they construct a ramp against me
and camp around my tent.
13 He has removed my brothers from me;
my acquaintances have abandoned me.
14 My relatives stop coming by,
and my close friends have forgotten me.
15 My house guests and female servants
regard me as a stranger;
I am a foreigner in their sight.
16 I call for my servant, but he does not answer,
even if I beg him with my own mouth.
17 My breath is offensive to my wife,
and my own family finds me repulsive.
18 Even young boys scorn me.
When I stand up, they mock me.
19 All of my best friends despise me,
and those I love have turned against me.
20 My skin and my flesh cling to my bones;
I have escaped by the skin of my teeth.
21 Have mercy on me, my friends, have mercy,
for God's hand has struck me.
22 Why do you persecute me as God does?
Will you never get enough of my flesh?
23 I wish that my words were written down,
that they were recorded on a scroll
24 or were inscribed in stone forever
by an iron stylus and lead!
25 But I know my living Redeemer,
and He will stand on the dust at last.
26 Even after my skin has been destroyed,
yet I will see God in my flesh.
27 I will see Him myself;
my eyes will look at Him, and not
as a stranger.
My heart longs within me.
28 If you say, "How will we pursue him,
since the root of the problem lies with him?"
29 then be afraid of the sword,
because wrath brings punishment
by the sword,
so that you may know there is a judgment.

20 Then Zophar the Naamathite replied:
2 This is why my unsettling thoughts
compel me to answer,
because I am upset!
3 I have heard a rebuke that insults me,
and my understanding makes me reply.
4 Don't you know that ever since antiquity,

from the time man was placed on earth,

5 the joy of the wicked has been brief
and the happiness of the godless has lasted
only a moment?

6 Though his arrogance reaches heaven,
and his head touches the clouds,

7 he will vanish forever like his own dung.
Those who know him will ask, "Where is he?"

8 He will fly away like a dream and never
be found;
he will be chased away like a vision
in the night.

9 The eye that saw him will see him no more,
and his household will no longer see him.

10 His children will beg from the poor,
for his own hands must give back his wealth.

11 His bones may be full of youthful vigor,
but will lie down with him in the grave.

12 Though evil tastes sweet in his mouth
and he conceals it under his tongue,

13 though he cherishes it and will not let it go
but keeps it in his mouth,

14 yet the food in his stomach turns
into cobras' venom inside him.

15 He swallows wealth but must vomit it up;
God will force it from his stomach.

16 He will suck the poison of cobras;
a viper's fangs will kill him.

17 He will not enjoy the streams,
the rivers flowing with honey and cream.

18 He must return the fruit of his labor
without consuming it;
he doesn't enjoy the profits from his trading.

19 For he oppressed and abandoned the poor;
he seized a house he did not build.

20 Because his appetite is never satisfied,
he does not let anything he desires escape.

21 Nothing is left for him to consume;
therefore, his prosperity will not last.

22 At the height of his success distress will come
to him;
the full weight of misery will crush him.

23 When he fills his stomach,
God will send His burning anger against him,
raining it down on him while he is eating.

24 If he flees from an iron weapon,
an arrow from a bronze bow will pierce him.

25 He pulls it out of his back,
the flashing tip out of his liver.
Terrors come over him.

26 Total darkness is reserved for his treasures.
A fire unfanned by human hands
will consume him;
it will feed on what is left in his tent.

27 The heavens will expose his iniquity,
and the earth will rise up against him.

28 The possessions in his house will be removed,
flowing away on the day of God's anger.

29 This is the wicked man's lot from God,
the inheritance God ordained for him.

21 Then Job answered:
2 Pay close attention to my words;
let this be the consolation you offer.

3 Bear with me while I speak;
then after I have spoken, you may
continue mocking.

4 As for me, is my complaint against a man?

Then why shouldn't I be impatient?

5 Look at me and shudder;
put your hand over your mouth.

6 When I think about it, I am terrified
and my body trembles in horror.

7 Why do the wicked continue to live,
growing old and becoming powerful?

8 Their children are established while they are
still alive,
and their descendants, before their eyes.

9 Their homes are secure and free of fear;
no rod from God strikes them.

10 Their bulls breed without fail;
their cows calve and do not miscarry.

11 They let their little ones run
around like lambs;
their children skip about,

12 singing to the tambourine and lyre
and rejoicing at the sound of the flute.

13 They spend their days in prosperity
and go down to *Sheol in peace.

14 Yet they say to God: "Leave us alone!
We don't want to know Your ways.

15 Who is the *Almighty, that we
should serve Him,
and what will we gain by pleading with Him?"

16 But their prosperity is not of their own doing.
The counsel of the wicked is far from me!

17 How often is the lamp of the wicked put out?
Does disaster come on them?
Does He apportion destruction in His anger?

18 Are they like straw before the wind,
like chaff a storm sweeps away?

19 God reserves a person's punishment
for his children.
Let God repay the person himself, so that
he may know it.

20 Let his own eyes see his demise;
let him drink from the Almighty's wrath!

21 For what does he care about his family once
he is dead,
when the number of his months has run out?

22 Can anyone teach God knowledge,
since He judges the exalted ones?

23 One person dies in excellent health,
completely secure and at ease.

24 His body is well fed,
and his bones are full of marrow.

25 Yet another person dies with a bitter soul,
having never tasted prosperity.

26 But they both lie in the dust,
and worms cover them.

27 I know your thoughts very well,
the schemes you would wrong me with.

28 For you say, "Where now is
the nobleman's house?"
and "Where are the tents the wicked lived in?"

29 Have you never consulted those who travel
the roads?
Don't you accept their reports?

30 Indeed, the evil man is spared from the day
of disaster,
rescued from the day of wrath.

31 Who would denounce his behavior to his face?
Who would repay him for what he has done?

32 He is carried to the grave,
and someone keeps watch over his tomb.

33 The dirt on his grave is sweet to him.
Everyone follows behind him,
and those who go before him are
without number.

34 So how can you offer me such futile comfort?
Your answers are deceptive.

22 Then Eliphaz the Temanite replied:
2 Can a man be of any use to God?
Can even a wise man be of use to Him?

3 Does it delight the *Almighty if you
are righteous?
Does He profit if you perfect your behavior?

4 Does He correct you and take you to court
because of your piety?

5 Isn't your wickedness abundant
and aren't your iniquities endless?

6 For you took collateral from your brothers
without cause,
stripping off their clothes
and leaving them naked.

7 You gave no water to the thirsty
and withheld food from the famished,

8 while the land belonged to a powerful man
and an influential man lived on it.

9 You sent widows away empty-handed,
and the strength of the fatherless was crushed.

10 Therefore snares surround you,
and sudden dread terrifies you,

11 or darkness, so you cannot see,
and a flood of water covers you.

12 Isn't God as high as the heavens?
And look at the highest stars—how lofty
they are!

13 Yet you say: "What does God know?
Can He judge through thick darkness?

14 Clouds veil Him so that He cannot see,
as He walks on the circle of the sky."

15 Will you continue on the ancient path
that wicked men have walked?

16 They were snatched away before their time,
and their foundations were washed away
by a river.

17 They were the ones who said to God,
"Leave us alone!"
and "What can the Almighty do to us?"

18 But it was He who filled their houses
with good things.
The counsel of the wicked is far from me!

19 The righteous see this and rejoice;
the innocent mock them, saying,

20 "Surely our opponents are destroyed,
and fire has consumed what they left behind."

21 Come to terms with God and be at peace;
in this way good will come to you.

22 Receive instruction from His mouth,
and place His sayings in your heart.

23 If you return to the Almighty, you will
be renewed.
If you banish injustice from your tent

24 and consign your gold to the dust,
the gold of Ophir to the stones in the *wadis,

25 the Almighty will be your gold
and your finest silver.

26 Then you will delight in the Almighty
and lift up your face to God.

27 You will pray to Him, and He will hear you,
and you will fulfill your vows.

28 When you make a decision, it will be
carried out,
and light will shine on your ways.

29 When others are humiliated and you say,
"Lift them up,"
God will save the humble.

30 He will even rescue the *guilty one,
who will be rescued by the purity
of your hands.

23 Then Job answered:
2 Today also my complaint is bitter.
His hand is heavy despite my groaning.

3 If only I knew how to find Him,
so that I could go to His throne.

4 I would plead my case before Him
and fill my mouth with arguments.

5 I would learn how He would answer me;
and understand what He would say to me.

6 Would He prosecute me forcefully?
No, He will certainly pay attention to me.

7 Then an upright man could reason with Him,
and I would escape from my Judge forever.

8 If I go east, He is not there,
and if I go west, I cannot perceive Him.

9 When He is at work to the north, I cannot
see Him;
when He turns south, I cannot find Him.

10 Yet He knows the way I have taken;
when He has tested me, I will emerge
as pure gold.

11 My feet have followed in His tracks;
I have kept to His way and not turned aside.

12 I have not departed from the commands
of His lips;
I have treasured the words of His mouth
more than my daily food.

13 But He is unchangeable; who can
oppose Him?
He does what He desires.

14 He will certainly accomplish
what He has decreed for me,
and He has many more things like these
in mind.

15 Therefore I am terrified in His presence;
when I consider this, I am afraid of Him.

16 God has made my heart faint;
the *Almighty has terrified me.

17 Yet I am not destroyed by the darkness,
by the thick darkness that covers my face.

24 Why does the *Almighty not reserve times
for judgment?
Why do those who know Him never see
His days?

2 The wicked displace boundary markers.
They steal a flock and provide pasture for it.

3 They drive away the donkeys owned
by the fatherless
and take the widow's ox as collateral.

4 They push the needy off the road;
the poor of the land are forced into hiding.

5 Like wild donkeys in the desert,
the poor go out to their task of foraging
for food;
the wilderness provides nourishment
for their children.

6 They gather their fodder in the field
and glean the vineyards of the wicked.

7 Without clothing, they spend the night naked,
having no covering against the cold.
8 Drenched by mountain rains,
they huddle against the rocks, shelterless.
9 The fatherless infant is snatched
from the breast;
the nursing child of the poor is seized
as collateral.
10 Without clothing, they wander about naked.
They carry sheaves but go hungry.
11 They crush olives in their presses;
they tread the winepresses, but go thirsty.
12 From the city, men groan;
the mortally wounded cry for help,
yet God pays no attention to this crime.
13 The wicked are those who rebel
against the light.
They do not recognize its ways
or stay on its paths.
14 The murderer rises at dawn
to kill the poor and needy,
and by night he becomes a thief.
15 The adulterer's eye watches for twilight,
thinking: No eye will see me;
he covers his face.
16 In the dark they break into houses;
by day they lock themselves in,
never experiencing the light.
17 For the morning is like darkness to them.
Surely they are familiar with the terrors
of darkness!
18 They float on the surface of the water.
Their section of the land is cursed,
so that they never go to their vineyards.
19 As dry ground and heat snatch away
the melted snow,
so •Sheol steals those who have sinned.
20 The womb forgets them;
worms feed on them;
they are remembered no more.
So injustice is broken like a tree.
21 They prey on the childless woman
who is unable to conceive,
and do not deal kindly with the widow.
22 Yet God drags away the mighty by His power;
when He rises up, they have no assurance
of life.
23 He gives them a sense of security, so they
can rely on it,
but His eyes watch over their ways.
24 They are exalted for a moment, then they
are gone;
they are brought low and shrivel up
like everything else.
They wither like heads of grain.
25 If this is not true, then who can prove me
a liar
and show that my speech is worthless?

25

Then Bildad the Shuhite replied:
2 Dominion and dread belong to Him,
the One who establishes harmony
in the heavens.
3 Can His troops be numbered?
Does His light not shine on everyone?
4 How can a person be justified before God?
How can one born of woman be pure?
5 If even the moon does not shine

and the stars are not pure in His sight,
6 how much less man, who is a maggot,
and the son of man, who is a worm!

26

Then Job answered:
2 How you have helped the powerless
and delivered the arm that is weak!
3 How you have counseled the unwise
and thoroughly explained the path to success!
4 Who did you speak these words to?
Whose breath came out of your mouth?
5 The departed spirits tremble
beneath the waters and all that inhabit them.
6 •Sheol is naked before God,
and •Abaddon has no covering.
7 He stretches the northern skies
over empty space;
He hangs the earth on nothing.
8 He wraps up the waters in His clouds,
yet the clouds do not burst
beneath their weight.
9 He obscures the view of His throne,
spreading His cloud over it.
10 He laid out the horizon on the surface
of the waters
at the boundary between light and darkness.
11 The pillars that hold up the sky tremble,
astounded at His rebuke.
12 By His power He stirred the sea,
and by His understanding He crushed •Rahab.
13 By His breath the heavens gained their beauty;
His hand pierced the fleeing serpent.
14 These are but the fringes of His ways;
how faint is the word we hear of Him!
Who can understand His mighty thunder?

27

Job continued his discourse, saying:
2 As God lives, who has deprived me
of justice,
and the •Almighty who has made me bitter,
3 as long as my breath is still in me
and the breath from God remains
in my nostrils,
4 my lips will not speak unjustly,
and my tongue will not utter deceit.
5 I will never affirm that you are right.
I will maintain my integrity until I die.
6 I will cling to my righteousness and never
let it go.
My conscience will not accuse me
as long as I live!
7 May my enemy be like the wicked
and my opponent like the unjust.
8 For what hope does the godless man have
when he is cut off,
when God takes away his life?
9 Will God hear his cry
when distress comes on him?
10 Will he delight in the Almighty?
Will he call on God at all times?
11 I will teach you about God's power.
I will not conceal what the Almighty
has planned.
12 All of you have seen this for yourselves,
why do you keep up this empty talk?
13 This is a wicked man's lot from God,
the inheritance the ruthless receive
from the Almighty.

¹⁴ Even if his children increase, they are destined
    for the sword;
    his descendants will never have enough food.
¹⁵ Those who survive him will be buried
    by the plague,
    yet their widows will not weep for them.
¹⁶ Though he piles up silver like dust
    and heaps up a wardrobe like clay—
¹⁷ he may heap it up, but the righteous
    will wear it,
    and the innocent will divide up his silver.
¹⁸ The house he built is like a moth's cocoon
    or a booth set up by a watchman.
¹⁹ He lies down wealthy, but will do so no more;
    when he opens his eyes, it is gone.
²⁰ Terrors overtake him like a flood;
    a storm wind sweeps him away at night.
²¹ An east wind picks him up, and he is gone;
    it carries him away from his place.
²² It blasts at him without mercy,
    while he flees desperately from its grasp.
²³ It claps its hands at him
    and scorns him from its place.

28 Surely there is a mine for silver
    and a place where gold is refined.
² Iron is taken from the ground,
    and copper is smelted from ore.
³ A miner puts an end to the darkness;
    he probes the deepest recesses
    for ore in the gloomy darkness.
⁴ He cuts a shaft far from human habitation,
    in places unknown to those who walk
    above ground.
    Suspended far away from people,
    the miners swing back and forth.
⁵ Food may come from the earth,
    but below the surface the earth is transformed
    as by fire.
⁶ Its rocks are a source of sapphire,
    containing flecks of gold.
⁷ No bird of prey knows that path;
    no falcon's eye has seen it.
⁸ Proud beasts have never walked on it;
    no lion has ever prowled over it.
⁹ The miner strikes the flint
    and transforms the mountains
    at their foundations.
¹⁰ He cuts out channels in the rocks,
    and his eyes spot every treasure.
¹¹ He dams up the streams from flowing
    so that he may bring to light what is hidden.
¹² But where can wisdom be found,
    and where is understanding located?
¹³ No man can know its value,
    since it cannot be found in the land
    of the living.
¹⁴ The ocean depths say, "It's not in me,"
    while the sea declares, "I don't have it."
¹⁵ Gold cannot be exchanged for it,
    and silver cannot be weighed out for its price.
¹⁶ Wisdom cannot be valued in the gold of Ophir,
    in precious onyx or sapphire.
¹⁷ Gold and glass do not compare with it,
    and articles of fine gold cannot be exchanged
    for it.
¹⁸ Coral and quartz are not worth mentioning.
    The price of wisdom is beyond pearls.

¹⁹ Topaz from •Cush cannot compare with it,
    and it cannot be valued in pure gold.
²⁰ Where then does wisdom come from,
    and where is understanding located?
²¹ It is hidden from the eyes of every living thing
    and concealed from the birds of the sky.
²² •Abaddon and Death say,
    "We have heard news of it with our ears."
²³ But God understands the way to wisdom,
    and He knows its location.
²⁴ For He looks to the ends of the earth
    and sees everything under the heavens.
²⁵ When God fixed the weight of the wind
    and limited the water by measure,
²⁶ when He established a limit for the rain
    and a path for the lightning,
²⁷ He considered wisdom and evaluated it;
    He established it and examined it.
²⁸ He said to mankind,
    "The •fear of the Lord is this: wisdom.
    And to turn from evil is understanding."

29 Job continued his discourse, saying:
² If only I could be as in months gone by,
    in the days when God watched over me,
³ when His lamp shone above my head,
    and I walked through darkness by His light!
⁴ I would be as I was in the days of my youth
    when God's friendship rested on my tent,
⁵ when the •Almighty was still with me
    and my children were around me,
⁶ when my feet were bathed in cream
    and the rock poured out streams of oil for me!
⁷ When I went out to the city •gate
    and took my seat in the town square,
⁸ the young men saw me and withdrew,
    while older men stood to their feet.
⁹ City officials stopped talking
    and covered their mouths with their hands.
¹⁰ The noblemen's voices were hushed,
    and their tongues stuck to the roof
    of their mouths.
¹¹ When they heard me, they blessed me,
    and when they saw me, they spoke well of me.
¹² For I rescued the poor man who cried out
    for help,
    and the fatherless child who had no one
    to support him.
¹³ The dying man blessed me,
    and I made the widow's heart rejoice.
¹⁴ I clothed myself in righteousness,
    and it enveloped me;
    my just decisions were like a robe
    and a turban.
¹⁵ I was eyes to the blind
    and feet to the lame.
¹⁶ I was a father to the needy,
    and I examined the case of the stranger.
¹⁷ I shattered the fangs of the unjust
    and snatched the prey from his teeth.
¹⁸ So I thought: I will die in my own nest
    and multiply my days as the sand.
¹⁹ My roots will have access to water,
    and the dew will rest on my branches
    all night.
²⁰ My strength will be refreshed within me,
    and my bow will be renewed in my hand.
²¹ Men listened to me with expectation,

waiting silently for my advice.

²² After a word from me they did not
speak again;
my speech settled on them like dew.

²³ They waited for me as for the rain
and opened their mouths as for
spring showers.

²⁴ If I smiled at them, they couldn't believe it;
they were thrilled at the light
of my countenance.

²⁵ I directed their course and presided as chief.
I lived as a king among his troops,
like one who comforts those who mourn.

30 But now they mock me,
men younger than I am,
whose fathers I would have refused to put
with my sheep dogs.

² What use to me was the strength
of their hands?
Their vigor had left them.

³ Emaciated from poverty and hunger,
they gnawed the dry land,
the desolate wasteland by night.

⁴ They plucked mallow among the shrubs,
and the roots of the broom tree were
their food.

⁵ They were expelled from human society;
people shouted at them as if they were thieves.

⁶ They are living on the slopes of the ˙wadis,
among the rocks and in holes in the ground.

⁷ They bray among the shrubs;
they huddle beneath the thistles.

⁸ Foolish men, without even a name.
They were forced to leave the land.

⁹ Now I am mocked by their songs;
I have become an object of scorn to them.

¹⁰ They despise me and keep their distance
from me;
they do not hesitate to spit in my face.

¹¹ Because God has loosened my bowstring
and oppressed me,
they have cast off restraint in my presence.

¹² The rabble rise up at my right;
they trap my feet
and construct their siege ramp against me.

¹³ They tear up my path;
they contribute to my destruction,
without anyone to help them.

¹⁴ They advance as through a gaping breach;
they keep rolling in through the ruins.

¹⁵ Terrors are turned loose against me;
they chase my dignity away like the wind,
and my prosperity has passed by like a cloud.

¹⁶ Now my life is poured out before my eyes,
and days of suffering have seized me.

¹⁷ Night pierces my bones,
but my gnawing pains never rest.

¹⁸ My clothing is distorted with great force;
He chokes me by the neck of my garment.

¹⁹ He throws me into the mud,
and I have become like dust and ashes.

²⁰ I cry out to You for help, but You do not
answer me;
when I stand up, You merely look at me.

²¹ You have turned against me with cruelty;
You harass me with Your strong hand.

²² You lift me up on the wind and make me
ride it;
You scatter me in the storm.

²³ Yes, I know that You will lead me to death—
the place appointed for all who live.

²⁴ Yet no one would stretch out his hand
against a ruined man
when he cries out to him for help
because of his distress.

²⁵ Have I not wept for those who have fallen
on hard times?
Has my soul not grieved for the needy?

²⁶ But when I hoped for good, evil came;
when I looked for light, darkness came.

²⁷ I am churning within and cannot rest;
days of suffering confront me.

²⁸ I walk about blackened, but not by the sun.
I stood in the assembly and cried out for help.

²⁹ I have become a brother to jackals
and a companion of ostriches.

³⁰ My skin blackens and flakes off,
and my bones burn with fever.

³¹ My lyre is used for mourning
and my flute for the sound of weeping.

31 I have made a covenant with my eyes.
How then could I look at a young woman?

² For what portion would I have
from God above,
or what inheritance from the ˙Almighty
on high?

³ Doesn't disaster come to the unjust
and misfortune to evildoers?

⁴ Does He not see my ways
and number all my steps?

⁵ If I have walked in falsehood
or my foot has rushed to deceit,

⁶ let God weigh me in accurate scales,
and He will recognize my integrity.

⁷ If my step has turned from the way,
my heart has followed my eyes,
or impurity has stained my hands,

⁸ let someone else eat what I have sown,
and let my crops be uprooted.

⁹ If my heart has been seduced by
my neighbor's wife
or I have lurked at his door,

¹⁰ let my own wife grind grain for another man,
and let other men sleep with her.

¹¹ For that would be a disgrace;
it would be a crime deserving punishment.

¹² For it is a fire that consumes down
to ˙Abaddon;
it would destroy my entire harvest.

¹³ If I have dismissed the case of my male
or female servants
when they made a complaint against me,

¹⁴ what could I do when God stands up to judge?
How should I answer Him when He calls me
to account?

¹⁵ Did not the One who made me in the womb
also make them?
Did not the same God form us both
in the womb?

¹⁶ If I have refused the wishes of the poor
or let the widow's eyes go blind,

¹⁷ if I have eaten my few crumbs alone
without letting the fatherless eat any of it—

18 for from my youth, I raised him as his father,
and since the day I was born I guided
the widow—
19 if I have seen anyone dying for lack of clothing
or a needy person without a cloak,
20 if he did not bless me
while warming himself with the fleece
from my sheep,
21 if I ever cast my vote against a fatherless child
when I saw that I had support in the city ˙gate,
22 then let my shoulder blade fall from my back,
and my arm be pulled from its socket.
23 For disaster from God terrifies me,
and because of His majesty I could not do
these things.
24 If I placed my confidence in gold
or called fine gold my trust,
25 if I have rejoiced because my wealth is great
or because my own hand has acquired
so much,
26 if I have gazed at the sun when it was shining
or at the moon moving in splendor,
27 so that my heart was secretly enticed
and I threw them a kiss,
28 this would also be a crime
deserving punishment,
for I would have denied God above.
29 Have I rejoiced over my enemy's distress,
or become excited when trouble came
his way?
30 I have not allowed my mouth to sin
by asking for his life with a curse.
31 Haven't the members of my household said,
"Who is there who has not had enough to eat
at Job's table?"
32 No stranger had to spend the night
on the street,
for I opened my door to the traveler.
33 Have I covered my transgressions as others do
by hiding my ˙guilt in my heart,
34 because I greatly feared the crowds,
and the contempt of the clans terrified me,
so I grew silent and would not go outside?
35 If only I had someone to hear my case!
Here is my signature; let the Almighty
answer me.
Let my Opponent compose His indictment.
36 I would surely carry it on my shoulder
and wear it like a crown.
37 I would give Him an account of all my steps;
I would approach Him like a prince.
38 If my land cries out against me
and its furrows join in weeping,
39 if I have consumed its produce
without payment
or shown contempt for its tenants,
40 then let thorns grow instead of wheat
and stinkweed instead of barley.
The words of Job are concluded.

32 So these three men quit answering Job, because he was righteous in his own eyes. ²Then Elihu son of Barachel the Buzite from the family of Ram became angry. He was angry at Job because he had justified himself rather than God. ³He was also angry at Job's three friends because they had failed to refute him and yet had condemned him.

⁴Now Elihu had waited to speak to Job because they were all older than he. ⁵But when he saw that the three men could not answer Job, he became angry.

⁶So Elihu son of Barachel the Buzite replied:
I am young in years,
while you are old;
therefore I was timid and afraid
to tell you what I know.
7 I thought that age should speak
and maturity should teach wisdom.
8 But it is a spirit in man
and the breath of the ˙Almighty
that give him understanding.
9 It is not only the old who are wise
or the elderly who understand how to judge.
10 Therefore I say, "Listen to me.
I too will declare what I know."
11 Look, I waited for your conclusions;
I listened to your insights
as you sought for words.
12 I paid close attention to you.
Yet no one proved Job wrong;
not one of you refuted his arguments.
13 So do not claim, "We have found wisdom;
let God deal with him, not man."
14 But Job has not directed his argument to me,
and I will not respond to him
with your arguments.
15 Job's friends are dismayed and can
no longer answer;
words have left them.
16 Should I continue to wait now that
they are silent,
now that they stand there
and no longer answer?
17 I too will answer;
yes, I will tell what I know.
18 For I am full of words,
and my spirit compels me to speak.
19 My heart is like unvented wine;
it is about to burst like new wineskins.
20 I must speak so that I can find relief;
I must open my lips and respond.
21 I will be partial to no one,
and I will not give anyone an undeserved title.
22 For I do not know how to give such titles;
otherwise, my Maker would remove me
in an instant.

33 But now, Job, pay attention to my speech,
and listen to all my words.
2 I am going to open my mouth;
my tongue will form words on my palate.
3 My words come from my upright heart,
and my lips speak with sincerity
what they know.
4 The Spirit of God has made me,
and the breath of the ˙Almighty gives me life.
5 Refute me if you can.
Prepare your case against me; take your stand.
6 I am just like you before God;
I was also pinched off from a piece of clay.
7 Fear of me should not terrify you;
the pressure I exert against you will be light.
8 Surely you have spoken in my hearing,
and I have heard these very words:
9 "I am pure, without transgression;
I am ˙clean and have no ˙guilt.
10 But He finds reasons to oppose me;

He regards me as His enemy.
11 He puts my feet in the stocks;
He stands watch over all my paths."
12 But I tell you that you are wrong
in this matter,
since God is greater than man.
13 Why do you take Him to court
for not answering anything a person asks?
14 For God speaks time and again,
but a person may not notice it.
15 In a dream, a vision in the night,
when deep sleep falls on people
as they slumber on their beds,
16 He uncovers their ears at that time
and terrifies them with warnings,
17 in order to turn a person from his actions
and suppress his pride.
18 God spares his soul from the *Pit,
his life from crossing the river of death.
19 A person may be disciplined on his bed
with pain
and constant distress in his bones,
20 so that he detests bread,
and his soul despises his favorite food.
21 His flesh wastes away to nothing,
and his unseen bones stick out.
22 He draws near to the Pit,
and his life to the executioners.
23 If there is an angel on his side,
one mediator out of a thousand,
to tell a person what is right for him
24 and to be gracious to him and say,
"Spare him from going down to the Pit;
I have found a ransom,"
25 then his flesh will be healthier than
in his youth,
and he will return to the days
of his youthful vigor.
26 He will pray to God, and God will delight
in him.
That man will see His face with a shout of joy,
and God will restore his righteousness to him.
27 He will look at men and say,
"I have sinned and perverted what was right;
yet I did not get what I deserved.
28 He redeemed my soul from going down
to the Pit,
and I will continue to see the light."
29 God certainly does all these things
two or three times to a man
30 in order to turn him back from the Pit,
so he may shine with the light of life.
31 Pay attention, Job, and listen to me.
Be quiet, and I will speak.
32 But if you have something to say, answer me;
speak, for I would like to justify you.
33 If not, then listen to me;
be quiet, and I will teach you wisdom.

34 Then Elihu continued, saying:
2 "Hear my words, you wise men,
and listen to me, you knowledgeable ones.
3 Doesn't the ear test words
as the palate tastes food?
4 Let us judge for ourselves what is right;
let us decide together what is good.
5 For Job has declared, "I am righteous,
yet God has deprived me of justice.

6 Would I lie about my case?
My wound is incurable,
though I am without transgression."
7 What man is like Job?
He drinks derision like water.
8 He keeps company with evildoers
and walks with wicked men.
9 For he has said, "A man gains nothing
when he becomes God's friend."
10 Therefore listen to me, you men
of understanding.
It is impossible for God to do wrong,
and for the *Almighty to act unjustly.
11 For He repays a person according to his deeds,
and He brings his ways on him.
12 Indeed, it is true that God does not
act wickedly
and the Almighty does not pervert justice.
13 Who gave Him authority over the earth?
Who put Him in charge of the entire world?
14 If He put His mind to it
and withdrew the spirit and breath He gave,
15 every living thing would perish together
and mankind would return to the dust.
16 If you have understanding, hear this;
listen to what I have to say.
17 Could one who hates justice govern the world?
Will you condemn the mighty Righteous One,
18 who says to a king, "Worthless man!"
and to nobles, "Wicked men!"?
19 God is not partial to princes
and does not favor the rich over the poor,
for they are all the work of His hands.
20 They die suddenly in the middle of the night;
people shudder, then pass away.
Even the mighty are removed without effort.
21 For His eyes watch over a man's ways,
and He observes all his steps.
22 There is no darkness, no deep darkness,
where evildoers can hide themselves.
23 God does not need to examine
a person further,
that one should approach Him in court.
24 He shatters the mighty
without an investigation
and sets others in their place.
25 Therefore, He recognizes their deeds
and overthrows them by night, and they
are crushed.
26 In full view of the public,
He strikes them for their wickedness,
27 because they turned aside from following Him
and did not understand any of His ways
28 but caused the poor to cry out to Him,
and He heard the outcry of the afflicted.
29 But when God is silent, who can declare
Him *guilty?
When He hides His face, who can see Him?
Yet He watches over both individuals
and nations,
30 so that godless men should not rule
or ensnare the people.
31 Suppose someone says to God,
"I have endured my punishment;
I will no longer act wickedly.
32 Teach me what I cannot see;
if I have done wrong, I won't do it again."

³³ Should God repay you on your terms
   when you have rejected His?
   You must choose, not I!
   So declare what you know.
³⁴ Reasonable men will say to me,
   along with the wise men who hear me,
³⁵ "Job speaks without knowledge;
   his words are without insight."
³⁶ If only Job were tested to the limit,
   because his answers are like those
      of wicked men.
³⁷ For he adds rebellion to his sin;
   he scornfully claps in our presence,
   while multiplying his words against God.

35 Then Elihu continued, saying:
²Do you think it is just when you say,
   "I am righteous before God"?
³ For you ask, "What does it profit You,
   and what benefit comes to me, if I do not sin?"
⁴ I will answer you
   and your friends with you.
⁵ Look at the heavens and see;
   gaze at the clouds high above you.
⁶ If you sin, how does it affect God?
   If you multiply your transgressions, what does
      it do to Him?
⁷ If you are righteous, what do you give Him,
   or what does He receive from your hand?
⁸ Your wickedness affects a person like yourself,
   and your righteousness another human being.
⁹ People cry out because of severe oppression;
   they shout for help because of the arm
      of the mighty.
¹⁰ But no one asks, "Where is God my Maker,
   who provides us with songs in the night,
¹¹ who gives us more understanding
      than the animals of the earth
   and makes us wiser than the birds of the sky?"
¹² There they cry out, but He does not answer,
   because of the pride of evil men.
¹³ Indeed, God does not listen to empty cries,
   and the ˚Almighty does not take note of it—
¹⁴ how much less when you complain
   that you do not see Him,
   that your case is before Him
   and you are waiting for Him.
¹⁵ But now, because God's anger does not punish
   and He does not pay attention
      to transgression,
¹⁶ Job opens his mouth in vain
   and multiplies words without knowledge.

36 Then Elihu continued, saying:
²Be patient with me a little longer, and I will
      inform you,
   for there is still more to be said
      on God's behalf.
³ I will get my knowledge from a distant place
   and ascribe justice to my Maker.
⁴ For my arguments are without flaw;
   one who has perfect knowledge is with you.
⁵ Yes, God is mighty, but He despises no one;
   He understands all things.
⁶ He does not keep the wicked alive,
   but He gives justice to the afflicted.
⁷ He does not remove His gaze
      from the righteous,

but He seats them forever
   with enthroned kings,
and they are exalted.
⁸ If people are bound with chains
   and trapped by the cords of affliction,
⁹ God tells them what they have done
   and how arrogantly they have transgressed.
¹⁰ He opens their ears to correction
   and insists they repent from iniquity.
¹¹ If they serve Him obediently,
   they will end their days in prosperity
   and their years in happiness.
¹² But if they do not obey,
   they will cross the river of death
   and die without knowledge.
¹³ Those who have a godless heart harbor anger;
   even when God binds them, they do not cry
      for help.
¹⁴ They die in their youth;
   their life ends among male cult prostitutes.
¹⁵ God rescues the afflicted by their affliction;
   He instructs them by their torment.
¹⁶ Indeed, He lured you from the jaws of distress
   to a spacious and unconfined place.
   Your table was spread with choice food.
¹⁷ Yet now you are obsessed with the judgment
      due the wicked;
   judgment and justice have seized you.
¹⁸ Be careful that no one lures you with riches;
   do not let a large ransom lead you astray.
¹⁹ Can your wealth or all your physical exertion
   keep you from distress?
²⁰ Do not long for the night
   when nations will disappear from their places.
²¹ Be careful that you do not turn to iniquity,
   for that is why you have been tested
      by affliction.
²² Look, God shows Himself exalted
      by His power.
   Who is a teacher like Him?
²³ Who has appointed His way for Him,
   and who has declared,
      "You have done wrong"?
²⁴ Remember that you should praise His work,
   which people have sung about.
²⁵ All mankind has seen it;
   people have looked at it from a distance.
²⁶ Yes, God is exalted beyond our knowledge;
   the number of His years cannot be counted.
²⁷ For He makes waterdrops evaporate;
   they distill the rain into its mist,
²⁸ which the clouds pour out
   and shower abundantly on mankind.
²⁹ Can anyone understand how the clouds
      spread out
   or how the thunder roars from God's pavilion?
³⁰ See how He spreads His lightning around Him
   and covers the depths of the sea.
³¹ For He judges the nations with these;
   He gives food in abundance.
³² He covers His hands with lightning
   and commands it to hit its mark.
³³ The thunder declares His presence;
   the cattle also, the approaching storm.

37 My heart pounds at this
   and leaps from my chest.
² Just listen to His thunderous voice

and the rumbling that comes from His mouth.
3 He lets it loose beneath the entire sky;
His lightning to the ends of the earth.
4 Then there comes a roaring sound;
God thunders with His majestic voice.
He does not restrain the lightning
when His rumbling voice is heard.
5 God thunders marvelously with His voice;
He does great things that
we cannot comprehend.
6 For He says to the snow, "Fall to the earth,"
and the torrential rains,
His mighty torrential rains,
7 serve as His sign to all mankind,
so that all men may know His work.
8 The wild animals enter their lairs
and stay in their dens.
9 The windstorm comes from its chamber,
and the cold from the driving north winds.
10 Ice is formed by the breath of God,
and watery expanses are frozen.
11 He saturates clouds with moisture;
He scatters His lightning through them.
12 They swirl about,
turning round and round at His direction,
accomplishing everything
He commands them
over the surface of the inhabited world.
13 He causes this to happen for punishment,
for His land, or for His faithful love.
14 Listen to this, Job.
Stop and consider God's wonders.
15 Do you know how God directs His clouds
or makes their lightning flash?
16 Do you understand how the clouds float,
those wonderful works of Him who has
perfect knowledge?
17 You whose clothes get hot
when the south wind brings calm to the land,
18 can you help God spread out the skies
as hard as a cast metal mirror?
19 Teach us what we should say to Him;
we cannot prepare our case because of
our darkness.
20 Should He be told that I want to speak?
Can a man speak when he is confused?
21 Now men cannot even look at the sun
when it is in the skies,
after a wind has swept through and cleared
them away.
22 Yet out of the north He comes, shrouded
in a golden glow;
awesome majesty surrounds Him.
23 The *Almighty—we cannot reach Him—
He is exalted in power!
He will not oppress justice and
abundant righteousness,
24 Therefore, men *fear Him.
He does not look favorably on any
who are wise in heart.

38 Then the Lord answered Job from the whirlwind. He said:
2 Who is this who obscures My counsel
with ignorant words?
3 Get ready to answer Me like a man;
when I question you, you will inform Me.
4 Where were you when I established the earth?

Tell Me, if you have understanding.
5 Who fixed its dimensions?
Certainly you know!
Who stretched a measuring line across it?
6 What supports its foundations?
Or who laid its cornerstone
7 while the morning stars sang together
and all the sons of God shouted for joy?
8 Who enclosed the sea behind doors
when it burst from the womb,
9 when I made the clouds its garment
and thick darkness its blanket,
10 when I determined its boundaries
and put its bars and doors in place,
11 when I declared: "You may come this far,
but no farther;
your proud waves stop here"?
12 Have you ever in your life commanded
the morning
or assigned the dawn its place,
13 so it may seize the edges of the earth
and shake the wicked out of it?
14 The earth is changed as clay is by a seal;
its hills stand out like the folds of a garment.
15 Light is withheld from the wicked,
and the arm raised in violence is broken.
16 Have you traveled to the sources of the sea
or walked in the depths of the oceans?
17 Have the gates of death been revealed to you?
Have you seen the gates of deep darkness?
18 Have you comprehended the extent
of the earth?
Tell Me, if you know all this.
19 Where is the road to the home of light?
Do you know where darkness lives,
20 so you can lead it back to its border?
Are you familiar with the paths to its home?
21 Don't you know? You were already born;
you have lived so long!
22 Have you entered the place where the snow
is stored?
Or have you seen the storehouses of hail,
23 which I hold in reserve for times of trouble,
for the day of warfare and battle?
24 What road leads to the place where light
is dispersed?
Where is the source of the east wind
that spreads across the earth?
25 Who cuts a channel for the flooding rain
or clears the way for lightning,
26 to bring rain on an uninhabited land,
on a desert with no human life,
27 to satisfy the parched wasteland
and cause the grass to sprout?
28 Does the rain have a father?
Who fathered the drops of dew?
29 Whose womb did the ice come from?
Who gave birth to the frost of heaven
30 when water becomes as hard as stone,
and the surface of the watery depths is frozen?
31 Can you fasten the chains of the Pleiades
or loosen the belt of Orion?
32 Can you bring out the constellations
in their season
and lead the Bear and her cubs?
33 Do you know the laws of heaven?
Can you impose its authority on earth?

³⁴ Can you command the clouds
so that a flood of water covers you?
³⁵ Can you send out lightning bolts, and they go?
Do they report to you: "Here we are"?
³⁶ Who put wisdom in the heart
or gave the mind understanding?
³⁷ Who has the wisdom to number the clouds?
Or who can tilt the water jars of heaven
³⁸ when the dust hardens like cast metal
and the clods of dirt stick together?
³⁹ Can you hunt prey for a lioness
or satisfy the appetite of young lions
⁴⁰ when they crouch in their dens
and lie in wait within their lairs?
⁴¹ Who provides the raven's food
when its young cry out to God
and wander about for lack of food?

39 Do you know when mountain goats
give birth?
Have you watched the deer in labor?
² Can you count the months they are pregnant
so you can know the time they give birth?
³ They crouch down to give birth
to their young;
they deliver their newborn.
⁴ Their offspring are healthy and grow up
in the open field.
They leave and do not return.
⁵ Who set the wild donkey free?
Who released the swift donkey
from its harness?
⁶ I made the wilderness its home,
and the salty wasteland its dwelling.
⁷ It scoffs at the noise of the village
and never hears the shouts of a driver.
⁸ It roams the mountains for its pastureland,
searching for anything green.
⁹ Would the wild ox be willing to serve you?
Would it spend the night
by your feeding trough?
¹⁰ Can you hold the wild ox to a furrow
by its harness?
Will it plow the valleys behind you?
¹¹ Can you depend on it because its strength
is great?
Would you leave it to do your hard work?
¹² Can you trust the wild ox to harvest
your grain
and bring it to your threshing floor?
¹³ The wings of the ostrich flap joyfully,
but are her feathers and plumage
like the stork's?
¹⁴ She abandons her eggs on the ground
and lets them be warmed in the sand.
¹⁵ She forgets that a foot may crush them
or that some wild animal may trample them.
¹⁶ She treats her young harshly, as if
they were not her own,
with no fear that her labor may have been
in vain.
¹⁷ For God has deprived her of wisdom;
He has not endowed her with understanding.
¹⁸ When she proudly spreads her wings,
she laughs at the horse and its rider.
¹⁹ Do you give strength to the horse?
Do you adorn his neck with a mane?
²⁰ Do you make him leap like a locust?

His proud snorting fills one with terror.
²¹ He paws in the valley and rejoices
in his strength;
He charges into battle.
²² He laughs at fear, since he is afraid of nothing;
he does not run from the sword.
²³ A quiver rattles at his side,
along with a flashing spear and a lance.
²⁴ He charges ahead with trembling rage;
he cannot stand still at the trumpet's sound.
²⁵ When the trumpet blasts, he snorts defiantly.
He smells the battle from a distance;
he hears the officers' shouts and the battle cry.
²⁶ Does the hawk take flight
by your understanding
and spread its wings to the south?
²⁷ Does the eagle soar at your command
and make its nest on high?
²⁸ It lives on a cliff where it spends the night;
its stronghold is on a rocky crag.
²⁹ From there it searches for prey;
its eyes penetrate the distance.
³⁰ Its brood gulps down blood,
and where the slain are, it is there.

40 The Lord answered Job:
²Will the one who contends
with the *Almighty correct Him?
Let him who argues with God give an answer.
³ Then Job answered the Lord:
⁴ I am so insignificant. How can I answer You?
I place my hand over my mouth.
⁵ I have spoken once, and I will not reply;
twice, but now I can add nothing.
⁶ Then the Lord answered Job from the whirlwind:
⁷ Get ready to answer Me like a man;
When I question you, you will inform Me.
⁸ Would you really challenge My justice?
Would you declare Me *guilty
to justify yourself?
⁹ Do you have an arm like God's?
Can you thunder with a voice like His?
¹⁰ Adorn yourself with majesty and splendor,
and clothe yourself with honor and glory.
¹¹ Unleash your raging anger;
look on every proud person
and humiliate him.
¹² Look on every proud person and humble him;
trample the wicked where they stand.
¹³ Hide them together in the dust;
imprison them in the grave.
¹⁴ Then I will confess to you
that your own right hand can deliver you.
¹⁵ Look at Behemoth,
which I made along with you.
He eats grass like an ox.
¹⁶ Look at the strength of his loins
and the power in the muscles of his belly.
¹⁷ He stiffens his tail like a cedar tree;
the tendons of his thighs are woven
firmly together.
¹⁸ His bones are bronze tubes;
his limbs are like iron rods.
¹⁹ He is the foremost of God's works;
only his Maker can draw the sword
against him.
²⁰ The hills yield food for him,
while all sorts of wild animals play there.

21 He lies under the lotus plants,
    hiding in the protection of marshy reeds.
22 Lotus plants cover him with their shade;
    the willows by the brook surround him.
23 Though the river rages, Behemoth is unafraid;
    he remains confident, even if
        the Jordan surges up to his mouth.
24 Can anyone capture him while he looks on,
    or pierce his nose with snares?

41 Can you pull in *Leviathan with a hook
    or tie his tongue down with a rope?
2 Can you put a cord through his nose
    or pierce his jaw with a hook?
3 Will he beg you for mercy
    or speak softly to you?
4 Will he make a covenant with you
    so that you can take him as a slave forever?
5 Can you play with him like a bird
    or put him on a leash for your girls?
6 Will traders bargain for him
    or divide him among the merchants?
7 Can you fill his hide with harpoons
    or his head with fishing spears?
8 Lay a hand on him.
    You will remember the battle
    and never repeat it!
9 Any hope of capturing him proves false.
    Does a person not collapse at the very sight
        of him?
10 No one is ferocious enough
        to rouse Leviathan;
    who then can stand against Me?
11 Who confronted Me, that I should repay him?
    Everything under heaven belongs to Me.
12 I cannot be silent about his limbs,
    his power, and his graceful proportions.
13 Who can strip off his outer covering?
    Who can penetrate his double layer of armor?
14 Who can open his jaws,
    surrounded by those terrifying teeth?
15 His pride is in his rows of scales,
    closely sealed together.
16 One scale is so close to another
    that no air can pass between them.
17 They are joined to one another,
    so closely connected they cannot be separated.
18 His snorting flashes with light,
    while his eyes are like the rays of dawn.
19 Flaming torches shoot from his mouth;
    fiery sparks fly out!
20 Smoke billows from his nostrils
    as from a boiling pot or burning reeds.
21 His breath sets coals ablaze,
    and flames pour out of his mouth.
22 Strength resides in his neck,
    and dismay dances before him.
23 The folds of his flesh are joined together,
    solid as metal and immovable.
24 His heart is as hard as a rock,
    as hard as a lower millstone!
25 When Leviathan rises, the mighty
        are terrified;
    they withdraw because of his thrashing.
26 The sword that reaches him will have
        no effect,

    nor will a spear, dart, or arrow.
27 He regards iron as straw,
    and bronze as rotten wood.
28 No arrow can make him flee;
    slingstones become like stubble to him.
29 A club is regarded as stubble,
    and he laughs at the sound of a javelin.
30 His undersides are jagged potsherds,
    spreading the mud like a threshing sledge.
31 He makes the depths seethe like a cauldron;
    he makes the sea like an ointment jar.
32 He leaves a shining wake behind him;
    one would think the deep had gray hair!
33 He has no equal on earth—
    a creature devoid of fear!
34 He surveys everything that is haughty;
    he is king over all the proud beasts.

42 Then Job replied to the Lord:
2 I know that You can do anything
    and no plan of Yours can be thwarted.
3 You asked, "Who is this who conceals
        My counsel with ignorance?"
    Surely I spoke about things
        I did not understand,
    things too wonderful for me to know.
4 You said, "Listen now, and I will speak.
    When I question you, you will
        inform Me."
5 I had heard rumors about You,
    but now my eyes have seen You.
6 Therefore I take back my words
    and repent in dust and ashes.

7 After the Lord had finished speaking to Job, He said to Eliphaz the Temanite: "I am angry with you and your two friends, for you have not spoken the truth about Me, as My servant Job has. 8 Now take seven bulls and seven rams, go to My servant Job, and offer a burnt offering for yourselves. Then My servant Job will pray for you. I will surely accept his prayer and not deal with you as your folly deserves. For you have not spoken the truth about Me, as My servant Job has." 9 Then Eliphaz the Temanite, Bildad the Shuhite, and Zophar the Naamathite went and did as the Lord had told them, and the Lord accepted Job's prayer.

10 After Job had prayed for his friends, the Lord restored his prosperity and doubled his previous possessions. 11 All his brothers, sisters, and former acquaintances came to his house and dined with him in his house. They sympathized with him and comforted him concerning all the adversity the Lord had brought on him. Each one gave him a *qesitah* and a gold earring.

12 So the Lord blessed the last part of Job's life more than the first. He owned 14,000 sheep, 6,000 camels, 1,000 yoke of oxen, and 1,000 female donkeys. 13 He also had seven sons and three daughters. 14 He named his first daughter Jemimah, his second Keziah, and his third Keren-happuch. 15 No women as beautiful as Job's daughters could be found in all the land, and their father granted them an inheritance with their brothers.

16 Job lived 140 years after this and saw his children and their children to the fourth generation. 17 Then Job died, old and full of days.

PSALMS

BOOK I
(Psalms 1–41)

Psalm 1

1 How happy is the man
who does not follow the advice of the wicked
or take the path of sinners
or join a group of mockers!
2 Instead, his delight is in the LORD's
instruction,
and he meditates on it day and night.
3 He is like a tree planted beside streams
of water
that bears its fruit in season
and whose leaf does not wither.
Whatever he does prospers.
4 The wicked are not like this;
instead, they are like chaff that the wind
blows away.
5 Therefore the wicked will not survive
the judgment,
and sinners will not be in the community
of the righteous.
6 For the LORD watches over the way
of the righteous,
but the way of the wicked leads to ruin.

Psalm 2

1 Why do the nations rebel
and the peoples plot in vain?
2 The kings of the earth take their stand,
and the rulers conspire together
against the LORD and His Anointed One:
3 "Let us tear off their chains
and free ourselves from their restraints."
4 The One enthroned in heaven laughs;
the Lord ridicules them.
5 Then He speaks to them in His anger
and terrifies them in His wrath:
6 "I have consecrated My King
on •Zion, My holy mountain."
7 I will declare the LORD's decree:
He said to Me, "You are My Son;
today I have become Your Father.
8 Ask of Me,
and I will make the nations Your inheritance
and the ends of the earth Your possession.
9 You will break them with a rod of iron;
You will shatter them like pottery."
10 So now, kings, be wise;
receive instruction, you judges of the earth.
11 Serve the LORD with reverential awe
and rejoice with trembling.
12 Pay homage to the Son or He will be angry
and you will perish in your rebellion,
for His anger may ignite at any moment.
All those who take refuge in Him are happy.

Psalm 3

A psalm of David when he fled
from his son Absalom.

1 LORD, how my foes increase!
There are many who attack me.

2 Many say about me,
"There is no help for him in God."   •Selah
3 But You, LORD, are a shield around me,
my glory, and the One who lifts up my head.
4 I cry aloud to the LORD,
and He answers me from His holy mountain.
Selah
5 I lie down and sleep;
I wake again because the LORD sustains me.
6 I am not afraid of the thousands of people
who have taken their stand against me
on every side.
7 Rise up, LORD!
Save me, my God!
You strike all my enemies on the cheek;
You break the teeth of the wicked.
8 Salvation belongs to the LORD;
may Your blessing be on Your people.   Selah

Psalm 4

For the choir director: with stringed instruments.
A Davidic psalm.

1 Answer me when I call,
God, who vindicates me.
You freed me from affliction;
be gracious to me and hear my prayer.
2 How long, exalted men, will my honor
be insulted?
How long will you love what is worthless
and pursue a lie?   •Selah
3 Know that the LORD has set apart
the faithful for Himself;
the LORD will hear when I call to Him.
4 Be angry and do not sin;
on your bed, reflect in your heart and be still.
Selah
5 Offer sacrifices in righteousness
and trust in the LORD.
6 Many are saying, "Who can show us
anything good?"
Look on us with favor, LORD.
7 You have put more joy in my heart
than they have when their grain and new wine
abound.
8 I will both lie down and sleep in peace,
for You alone, LORD, make me live in safety.

Psalm 5

For the choir director: with the flutes.
A Davidic psalm.

1 Listen to my words, LORD;
consider my sighing.
2 Pay attention to the sound of my cry,
my King and my God,
for I pray to You.
3 At daybreak, LORD, You hear my voice;
at daybreak I plead my case to You and watch
expectantly.
4 For You are not a God who delights
in wickedness;
evil cannot dwell with You.
5 The boastful cannot stand in Your presence;

You hate all evildoers.
6 You destroy those who tell lies;
the LORD abhors a man of bloodshed
and treachery.
7 But I enter Your house
by the abundance of Your faithful love;
I bow down toward Your holy temple
in reverential awe of You.
8 LORD, lead me in Your righteousness
because of my adversaries;
make Your way straight before me.
9 For there is nothing reliable in what they say;
destruction is within them;
their throat is an open grave;
they flatter with their tongues.
10 Punish them, God;
let them fall by their own schemes.
Drive them out because of their many crimes,
for they rebel against You.
11 But let all who take refuge in You rejoice;
let them shout for joy forever.
May You shelter them,
and may those who love Your name boast
about You.
12 For You, LORD, bless the righteous one;
You surround him with favor like a shield.

Psalm 6

For the choir director: with stringed instruments,
according to *Sheminith. A Davidic psalm.

1 LORD, do not rebuke me in Your anger;
do not discipline me in Your wrath.
2 Be gracious to me, LORD, for I am weak;
heal me, LORD, for my bones are shaking;
3 my whole being is shaken with terror.
And You, LORD—how long?
4 Turn, LORD! Rescue me;
save me because of Your faithful love.
5 For there is no remembrance of You in death;
who can thank You in *Sheol?
6 I am weary from my groaning;
with my tears I dampen my pillow
and drench my bed every night.
7 My eyes are swollen from grief;
they grow old because of all my enemies.
8 Depart from me, all evildoers,
for the LORD has heard the sound
of my weeping.
9 The LORD has heard my plea for help;
the LORD accepts my prayer.
10 All my enemies will be ashamed and shake
with terror;
they will turn back and suddenly be disgraced.

Psalm 7

A *Shiggaion* of David, which he sang to the LORD
concerning the words of *Cush, a Benjaminite.

1 *Yahweh my God, I seek refuge in You;
save me from all my pursuers and rescue me
2 or they will tear me like a lion,
ripping me apart with no one to rescue me.
3 Yahweh my God, if I have done this,
if there is injustice on my hands,
4 if I have done harm to one at peace with me
or have plundered my adversary
without cause,
5 may an enemy pursue and overtake me;

may he trample me to the ground
and leave my honor in the dust.   *Selah
6 Rise up, LORD, in Your anger;
lift Yourself up against the fury
of my adversaries;
awake for me;
You have ordained a judgment.
7 Let the assembly of peoples gather
around You;
take Your seat on high over it.
8 The LORD judges the peoples;
vindicate me, LORD,
according to my righteousness
and my integrity.
9 Let the evil of the wicked come to an end,
but establish the righteous.
The One who examines the thoughts
and emotions
is a righteous God.
10 My shield is with God,
who saves the upright in heart.
11 God is a righteous judge
and a God who shows His wrath every day.
12 If anyone does not repent,
God will sharpen His sword;
He has strung His bow and made it ready.
13 He has prepared His deadly weapons;
He tips His arrows with fire.
14 See, the wicked one is pregnant with evil,
conceives trouble, and gives birth to deceit.
15 He dug a pit and hollowed it out
but fell into the hole he had made.
16 His trouble comes back on his own head,
and his violence falls on the top of his head.
17 I will thank the LORD for His righteousness;
I will sing about the name of Yahweh
the *Most High.

Psalm 8

For the choir director: on the *Gittith.
A Davidic psalm.

1 *Yahweh, our Lord,
how magnificent is Your name
throughout the earth!
You have covered the heavens
with Your majesty.
2 Because of Your adversaries,
You have established a stronghold
from the mouths of children
and nursing infants
to silence the enemy and the avenger.
3 When I observe Your heavens,
the work of Your fingers,
the moon and the stars,
which You set in place,
4 what is man that You remember him,
the son of man that You look after him?
5 You made him little less than God
and crowned him with glory and honor.
6 You made him lord over the works
of Your hands;
You put everything under his feet:
7 all the sheep and oxen,
as well as the animals in the wild,
8 the birds of the sky,
and the fish of the sea
that pass through the currents of the seas.

9 Yahweh, our Lord,
how magnificent is Your name
  throughout the earth!

Psalm 9

For the choir director: according to
Muth-labben. A Davidic psalm.

1 I will thank •Yahweh with all my heart;
  I will declare all Your wonderful works.
2 I will rejoice and boast about You;
  I will sing about Your name, •Most High.
3 When my enemies retreat,
  they stumble and perish before You.
4 For You have upheld my just cause;
  You are seated on Your throne
    as a righteous judge.
5 You have rebuked the nations:
  You have destroyed the wicked;
  You have erased their name forever and ever.
6 The enemy has come to eternal ruin;
  You have uprooted the cities,
  and the very memory of them has perished.
7 But the LORD sits enthroned forever;
  He has established His throne for judgment.
8 He judges the world with righteousness;
  He executes judgment on the nations
    with fairness.
9 The LORD is a refuge for the oppressed,
  a refuge in times of trouble.
10 Those who know Your name trust in You
  because You have not abandoned
    those who seek You, Yahweh.
11 Sing to the LORD, who dwells in •Zion;
  proclaim His deeds among the nations.
12 For the One who seeks an accounting
    for bloodshed remembers them;
  He does not forget the cry of the afflicted.
13 Be gracious to me, LORD;
  consider my affliction at the hands of those
    who hate me.
  Lift me up from the gates of death,
14 so that I may declare all Your praises.
  I will rejoice in Your salvation
    within the gates of Daughter Zion.
15 The nations have fallen into the pit they made;
  their foot is caught in the net
    they have concealed.
16 The LORD has revealed Himself;
  He has executed justice,
  striking down the wicked
    by the work of their hands.
                        •*Higgaion.* •*Selah*
17 The wicked will return to •Sheol—
  all the nations that forget God.
18 For the oppressed will not always be forgotten;
  the hope of the afflicted will not perish
    forever.
19 Rise up, LORD! Do not let man prevail;
  let the nations be judged in Your presence.
20 Put terror in them, LORD;
  let the nations know they are only men.
                                Selah

Psalm 10

1 LORD, why do You stand so far away?
  Why do You hide in times of trouble?
2 In arrogance the wicked relentlessly pursue
    the afflicted;

let them be caught in the schemes
  they have devised.
3 For the wicked one boasts about
    his own cravings;
  the one who is greedy curses and despises
    the LORD.
4 In all his scheming,
  the wicked arrogantly thinks:
  "There is no accountability,
  since God does not exist."
5 His ways are always secure;
  Your lofty judgments are beyond his sight;
  he scoffs at all his adversaries.
6 He says to himself, "I will never be moved—
  from generation to generation
    without calamity."
7 Cursing, deceit, and violence fill his mouth;
  trouble and malice are under his tongue.
8 He waits in ambush near the villages;
  he kills the innocent in secret places.
  His eyes are on the lookout for the helpless.
9 he lurks in secret like a lion in a thicket.
  He lurks in order to seize the afflicted;
  he seizes the afflicted and drags him
    in his net.
10 So he is oppressed and beaten down;
  the helpless fall because of his strength.
11 He says to himself, "God has forgotten;
  He hides His face and will never see."
12 Rise up, LORD God! Lift up Your hand.
  Do not forget the afflicted.
13 Why has the wicked person despised God?
  He says to himself, "You will not demand
    an account."
14 But You Yourself have seen trouble and grief,
  observing it in order to take the matter
    into Your hands.
  The helpless entrusts himself to You;
  You are a helper of the fatherless.
15 Break the arm of the wicked
    and evil person;
  call his wickedness into account
  until nothing remains of it.
16 The LORD is King forever and ever;
  the nations will perish from His land.
17 LORD, You have heard the desire
    of the humble;
  You will strengthen their hearts.
  You will listen carefully,
18 doing justice for the fatherless
    and the oppressed
  so that men of the earth may terrify them
    no more.

Psalm 11

For the choir director. Davidic.

1 I have taken refuge in the LORD.
  How can you say to me,
  "Escape to the mountain like a bird!
2 For look, the wicked string the bow;
  they put the arrow on the bowstring
  to shoot from the shadows at the upright
    in heart.
3 When the foundations are destroyed,
  what can the righteous do?"
4 The LORD is in His holy temple;
  the LORD's throne is in heaven.

His eyes watch; He examines ˙everyone.
5 The LORD examines the righteous
    and the wicked.
He hates the lover of violence.
6 He will rain burning coals and sulfur
    on the wicked;
a scorching wind will be their portion.
7 For the LORD is righteous; He loves
    righteous deeds.
The upright will see His face.

Psalm 12
For the choir director: according to ˙*Sheminith*.
A Davidic psalm.

1 Help, LORD, for no faithful one remains;
the loyal have disappeared
    from the ˙human race.
2 They lie to one another;
they speak with flattering lips
    and deceptive hearts.
3 May the LORD cut off all flattering lips
and the tongue that speaks boastfully.
4 They say, "Through our tongues
    we have power;
our lips are our own—who can be
    our master?"
5 "Because of the oppression of the afflicted
and the groaning of the poor,
I will now rise up," says the LORD.
"I will put the one who longs for it
    in a safe place."
6 The words of the LORD are pure words,
like silver refined in an earthen furnace,
    purified seven times.
7 You, LORD, will guard us;
You will protect us from this generation
    forever.
8 The wicked wander everywhere,
and what is worthless is exalted
    by the human race.

Psalm 13
For the choir director. A Davidic psalm.

1 LORD, how long will You forget me?
    Forever?
How long will You hide Your face from me?
2 How long will I store up anxious concerns
    within me,
agony in my mind every day?
How long will my enemy dominate me?
3 Consider me and answer, LORD my God.
Restore brightness to my eyes;
otherwise, I will sleep in death.
4 My enemy will say, "I have triumphed
    over him,"
and my foes will rejoice because I am shaken.
5 But I have trusted in Your faithful love;
my heart will rejoice in Your deliverance.
6 I will sing to the LORD
because He has treated me generously.

Psalm 14
For the choir director. Davidic.

1 The fool says in his heart,
    "God does not exist."
They are corrupt; they do vile deeds.
There is no one who does good.

2 The LORD looks down from heaven
    on the ˙human race
to see if there is one who is wise,
one who seeks God.
3 All have turned away;
all alike have become corrupt.
There is no one who does good,
    not even one.
4 Will evildoers never understand?
They consume My people
    as they consume bread;
they do not call on the LORD.
5 Then they will be filled with terror,
for God is with those who are righteous.
6 You sinners frustrate the plans
    of the afflicted,
but the LORD is his refuge.
7 Oh, that Israel's deliverance would come
    from ˙Zion!
When the LORD restores the fortunes
    of His people,
Jacob will rejoice; Israel will be glad.

Psalm 15
A Davidic psalm.

1 LORD, who can dwell in Your tent?
Who can live on Your holy mountain?
2 The one who lives honestly,
    practices righteousness,
and acknowledges the truth in his heart—
3 who does not slander with his tongue,
who does not harm his friend
    or discredit his neighbor,
4 who despises the one rejected by the LORD
but honors those who ˙fear the LORD,
who keeps his word whatever the cost,
5 who does not lend his money at interest
or take a bribe against the innocent—
the one who does these things will never
    be moved.

Psalm 16
A Davidic ˙*Miktam*.

1 Protect me, God, for I take refuge in You.
2 I said to ˙Yahweh, "You are my Lord;
I have nothing good besides You."
3 As for the holy people who are in the land,
they are the noble ones.
All my delight is in them.
4 The sorrows of those who take another god
for themselves will multiply;
I will not pour out their ˙drink offerings
    of blood,
and I will not speak their names with my lips.
5 LORD, You are my portion
and my cup of blessing;
You hold my future.
6 The boundary lines have fallen for me
in pleasant places;
indeed, I have a beautiful inheritance.
7 I will praise the LORD who counsels me—
even at night my conscience instructs me.
8 I keep the LORD in mind always.
Because He is at my right hand,
I will not be shaken.
9 Therefore my heart is glad
and my spirit rejoices;

my body also rests securely.

10 For You will not abandon me to ⁺Sheol;
You will not allow Your Faithful One to see decay.
11 You reveal the path of life to me;
in Your presence is abundant joy;
in Your right hand are eternal pleasures.

Psalm 17
A Davidic prayer.

1 Lord, hear a just cause;
pay attention to my cry;
listen to my prayer—
from lips free of deceit.
2 Let my vindication come from You,
for You see what is right.
3 You have tested my heart;
You have examined me at night.
You have tried me and found nothing evil;
I have determined that my mouth will not sin.
4 Concerning what people do:
by the word of Your lips
I have avoided the ways of the violent.
5 My steps are on Your paths;
my feet have not slipped.
6 I call on You, God,
because You will answer me;
listen closely to me; hear what I say.
7 Display the wonders of Your faithful love,
Savior of all who seek refuge
from those who rebel against Your right hand.
8 Protect me as the pupil of Your eye;
hide me in the shadow of Your wings
9 from the wicked who treat me violently,
my deadly enemies who surround me.
10 They have become hardened;
their mouths speak arrogantly.
11 They advance against me;
now they surround me.
They are determined
to throw me to the ground.
12 They are like a lion eager to tear,
like a young lion lurking in ambush.
13 Rise up, Lord!
Confront him; bring him down.
With Your sword, save me from the wicked.
14 With Your hand, Lord, save me from men,
from men of the world
whose portion is in this life:
You fill their bellies with what You have
in store;
their sons are satisfied,
and they leave their surplus to their children.
15 But I will see Your face in righteousness;
when I awake, I will be satisfied
with Your presence.

Psalm 18
For the choir director. Of the servant of the Lord,
David, who spoke the words of this song to the Lord
on the day the Lord rescued him from the hand of
all his enemies and from the hand of Saul. He said:

1 I love You, Lord, my strength.
2 The Lord is my rock,
my fortress, and my deliverer,
my God, my mountain where I seek refuge,
my shield and the ⁺horn of my salvation,
my stronghold.
3 I called to the Lord, who is worthy of praise,
and I was saved from my enemies.
4 The ropes of death were wrapped around me;
the torrents of destruction terrified me.
5 The ropes of ⁺Sheol entangled me;
the snares of death confronted me.
6 I called to the Lord in my distress,
and I cried to my God for help.
From His temple He heard my voice,
and my cry to Him reached His ears.
7 Then the earth shook and quaked;
the foundations of the mountains trembled;
they shook because He burned with anger.
8 Smoke rose from His nostrils,
and consuming fire came from His mouth;
coals were set ablaze by it.
9 He parted the heavens and came down,
a dark cloud beneath His feet.
10 He rode on a cherub and flew,
soaring on the wings of the wind.
11 He made darkness His hiding place,
dark storm clouds His canopy around Him.
12 From the radiance of His presence,
His clouds swept onward with hail
and blazing coals.
13 The Lord thundered from heaven;
the ⁺Most High projected His voice.
14 He shot His arrows and scattered them;
He hurled lightning bolts and routed them.
15 The depths of the sea became visible,
the foundations of the world were exposed,
at Your rebuke, Lord,
at the blast of the breath of Your nostrils.
16 He reached down from heaven
and took hold of me;
He pulled me out of deep waters.
17 He rescued me from my powerful enemy
and from those who hated me,
for they were too strong for me.
18 They confronted me in the day of my distress,
but the Lord was my support.
19 He brought me out to a spacious place;
He rescued me because He delighted in me.
20 The Lord rewarded me
according to my righteousness;
He repaid me
according to the cleanness of my hands.
21 For I have kept the ways of the Lord
and have not turned from my God
to wickedness.
22 Indeed, I have kept all His ordinances in mind
and have not disregarded His statutes.
23 I was blameless toward Him
and kept myself from sinning.
24 So the Lord repaid me
according to my righteousness,
according to the cleanness of my hands
in His sight.
25 With the faithful
You prove Yourself faithful;
with the blameless man
You prove Yourself blameless;
26 with the pure
You prove Yourself pure,
but with the crooked
You prove Yourself shrewd.
27 For You rescue an afflicted people,

but You humble those with haughty eyes.
28 LORD, You light my lamp;
my God illuminates my darkness.
29 With You I can attack a barrier,
and with my God I can leap over a wall.
30 God—His way is perfect;
the word of the LORD is pure.
He is a shield to all who take refuge in Him.
31 For who is God besides *Yahweh?
And who is a rock? Only our God.
32 God—He clothes me with strength
and makes my way perfect.
33 He makes my feet like the feet of a deer
and sets me securely on the heights.
34 He trains my hands for war;
my arms can bend a bow of bronze.
35 You have given me the shield
of Your salvation;
Your right hand upholds me,
and Your humility exalts me.
36 You widen a place beneath me for my steps,
and my ankles do not give way.
37 I pursue my enemies and overtake them;
I do not turn back until they are wiped out.
38 I crush them, and they cannot get up;
they fall beneath my feet.
39 You have clothed me with strength for battle;
You subdue my adversaries beneath me.
40 You have made my enemies retreat before me;
I annihilate those who hate me.
41 They cry for help, but there is no one
to save them—
they cry to the LORD, but He does not
answer them.
42 I pulverize them like dust before the wind;
I trample them like mud in the streets.
43 You have freed me from the feuds
among the people;
You have appointed me the head of nations;
a people I had not known serve me.
44 Foreigners submit to me grudgingly;
as soon as they hear, they obey me.
45 Foreigners lose heart
and come trembling from their fortifications.
46 The LORD lives—may my rock be praised!
The God of my salvation is exalted.
47 God—He gives me vengeance
and subdues peoples under me.
48 He frees me from my enemies.
You exalt me above my adversaries;
You rescue me from violent men.
49 Therefore I will praise You, Yahweh,
among the nations;
I will sing about Your name.
50 He gives great victories to His king;
He shows loyalty to His anointed,
to David and his descendants forever.

Psalm 19
For the choir director. A Davidic psalm.

1 The heavens declare the glory of God,
and the sky proclaims the work of His hands.
2 Day after day they pour out speech;
night after night
they communicate knowledge.
3 There is no speech; there are no words;
their voice is not heard.

4 Their message has gone out to all the earth,
and their words to the ends of the world.
In the heavens He has pitched a tent
for the sun.
5 It is like a groom coming from
the bridal chamber;
it rejoices like an athlete running a course.
6 It rises from one end of the heavens
and circles to their other end;
nothing is hidden from its heat.
7 The instruction of the LORD is perfect,
renewing one's life;
the *testimony of the LORD is trustworthy,
making the inexperienced wise.
8 The precepts of the LORD are right,
making the heart glad;
the command of the LORD is radiant,
making the eyes light up.
9 The *fear of the LORD is pure,
enduring forever;
the ordinances of the LORD are reliable
and altogether righteous.
10 They are more desirable than gold—
than an abundance of pure gold;
and sweeter than honey,
which comes from the honeycomb.
11 In addition, Your servant is warned by them;
there is great reward in keeping them.
12 Who perceives his unintentional sins?
Cleanse me from my hidden faults.
13 Moreover, keep Your servant from willful sins;
do not let them rule over me.
Then I will be innocent
and cleansed from blatant rebellion.
14 May the words of my mouth
and the meditation of my heart
be acceptable to You,
LORD, my rock and my Redeemer.

Psalm 20
For the choir director. A Davidic psalm.

1 May *Yahweh answer you in a day of trouble;
may the name of Jacob's God protect you.
2 May He send you help from the sanctuary
and sustain you from *Zion.
3 May He remember all your offerings
and accept your *burnt offering.   *Selah
4 May He give you what your heart desires
and fulfill your whole purpose.
5 Let us shout for joy at your victory
and lift the banner in the name of our God.
May Yahweh fulfill all your requests.
6 Now I know that the LORD gives victory
to His anointed;
He will answer him from His holy heaven
with mighty victories from His right hand.
7 Some take pride in chariots, and others
in horses,
but we take pride in the name of Yahweh
our God.
8 They collapse and fall,
but we rise and stand firm.
9 LORD, give victory to the king!
May He answer us on the day that we call.

Psalm 21

For the choir director. A Davidic psalm.

1 Lord, the king finds joy in Your strength.
How greatly he rejoices in Your victory!
2 You have given him his heart's desire
and have not denied the request
of his lips.	•*Selah*
3 For You meet him with rich blessings;
You place a crown of pure gold on his head.
4 He asked You for life, and You gave it
to him—
length of days forever and ever.
5 His glory is great through Your victory;
You confer majesty and splendor on him.
6 You give him blessings forever;
You cheer him with joy in Your presence.
7 For the king relies on the Lord;
through the faithful love of the •Most High
he is not shaken.
8 Your hand will capture all your enemies;
your right hand will seize those who hate you.
9 You will make them burn
like a fiery furnace when you appear;
the Lord will engulf them in His wrath,
and fire will devour them.
10 You will wipe their descendants from the earth
and their offspring from the •human race.
11 Though they intend to harm you
and devise a wicked plan, they will not prevail.
12 Instead, you will put them to flight
when you aim your bow at their faces.
13 Be exalted, Lord, in Your strength;
we will sing and praise Your might.

Psalm 22

For the choir director: according to "The Deer
of the Dawn." A Davidic psalm.

1 My God, my God, why have You forsaken me?
Why are You so far from my deliverance
and from my words of groaning?
2 My God, I cry by day, but You do not answer,
by night, yet I have no rest.
3 But You are holy,
enthroned on the praises of Israel.
4 Our fathers trusted in You;
they trusted, and You rescued them.
5 They cried to You and were set free;
they trusted in You and were not disgraced.
6 But I am a worm and not a man,
scorned by men and despised by people.
7 Everyone who sees me mocks me;
they sneer and shake their heads:
8 "He relies on the Lord;
let Him rescue him;
let the Lord deliver him,
since He takes pleasure in him."
9 You took me from the womb,
making me secure
while at my mother's breast.
10 I was given over to You at birth;
You have been my God
from my mother's womb.
11 Do not be far from me, because distress
is near
and there is no one to help.
12 Many bulls surround me;
strong ones of Bashan encircle me.

13 They open their mouths against me—
lions, mauling and roaring.
14 I am poured out like water,
and all my bones are disjointed;
my heart is like wax,
melting within me.
15 My strength is dried up like baked clay;
my tongue sticks to the roof of my mouth.
You put me into the dust of death.
16 For dogs have surrounded me;
a gang of evildoers has closed in on me;
they pierced my hands and my feet.
17 I can count all my bones;
people look and stare at me.
18 They divided my garments among themselves,
and they cast lots for my clothing.
19 But You, Lord, don't be far away.
My strength, come quickly to help me.
20 Deliver my life from the sword,
my only life from the power of these dogs.
21 Save me from the mouth of the lion!
You have rescued me
from the horns of the wild oxen.
22 I will proclaim Your name to my brothers;
I will praise You in the congregation.
23 You who •fear •Yahweh, praise Him!
All you descendants of Jacob, honor Him!
All you descendants of Israel, revere Him!
24 For He has not despised or detested
the torment of the afflicted.
He did not hide His face from him
but listened when he cried to Him for help.
25 I will give praise in the great congregation
because of You;
I will fulfill my vows
before those who fear You.
26 The humble will eat and be satisfied;
those who seek the Lord will praise Him.
May your hearts live forever!
27 All the ends of the earth will remember
and turn to the Lord.
All the families of the nations
will bow down before You,
28 for kingship belongs to the Lord;
He rules over the nations.
29 All who prosper on earth will eat
and bow down;
all those who go down to the dust
will kneel before Him—
even the one who cannot preserve his life.
30 Their descendants will serve Him;
the next generation will be told
about the Lord.
31 They will come and tell a people yet to be born
about His righteousness—
what He has done.

Psalm 23

A Davidic psalm.

1 The Lord is my shepherd;
there is nothing I lack.
2 He lets me lie down in green pastures;
He leads me beside quiet waters.
3 He renews my life;
He leads me along the right paths
for His name's sake.
4 Even when I go through the darkest valley,

I fear no danger,
for You are with me;
Your rod and Your staff—they comfort me.
5 You prepare a table before me
in the presence of my enemies;
You anoint my head with oil;
my cup overflows.
6 Only goodness and faithful love
will pursue me
all the days of my life,
and I will dwell in the house of the Lord
as long as I live.

Psalm 24
A Davidic psalm.

1 The earth and everything in it,
the world and its inhabitants,
belong to the Lord;
2 for He laid its foundation on the seas
and established it on the rivers.
3 Who may ascend the mountain of the Lord?
Who may stand in His holy place?
4 The one who has •clean hands
and a pure heart,
who has not set his mind on what is false,
and who has not sworn deceitfully.
5 He will receive blessing from the Lord,
and righteousness from the God
of his salvation.
6 Such is the generation of those who seek Him,
who seek the face of the God of Jacob.
•Selah

7 Lift up your heads, you gates!
Rise up, ancient doors!
Then the King of glory will come in.
8 Who is this King of glory?
The Lord, strong and mighty,
the Lord, mighty in battle.
9 Lift up your heads, you gates!
Rise up, ancient doors!
Then the King of glory will come in.
10 Who is He, this King of glory?
The Lord of •Hosts,
He is the King of glory. *Selah*

Psalm 25
Davidic.

1 Lord, I turn to You.
2 My God, I trust in You.
Do not let me be disgraced;
do not let my enemies gloat over me.
3 No one who waits for You
will be disgraced;
those who act treacherously without cause
will be disgraced.
4 Make Your ways known to me, Lord;
teach me Your paths.
5 Guide me in Your truth and teach me,
for You are the God of my salvation;
I wait for You all day long.
6 Remember, Lord, Your compassion
and Your faithful love,
for they have existed from antiquity.
7 Do not remember the sins of my youth
or my acts of rebellion;
in keeping with Your faithful love,
remember me

because of Your goodness, Lord.
8 The Lord is good and upright;
therefore He shows sinners the way.
9 He leads the humble in what is right
and teaches them His way.
10 All the Lord's ways show faithful love
and truth
to those who keep His covenant and decrees.
11 Because of Your name, •Yahweh,
forgive my sin, for it is great.
12 Who is the man who •fears the Lord?
He will show him the way he should choose.
13 He will live a good life,
and his descendants will inherit the land.
14 The secret counsel of the Lord
is for those who fear Him,
and He reveals His covenant to them.
15 My eyes are always on the Lord,
for He will pull my feet out of the net.
16 Turn to me and be gracious to me,
for I am alone and afflicted.
17 The distresses of my heart increase;
bring me out of my sufferings.
18 Consider my affliction and trouble,
and take away all my sins.
19 Consider my enemies; they are numerous,
and they hate me violently.
20 Guard me and deliver me;
do not let me be put to shame,
for I take refuge in You.
21 May integrity and what is right
watch over me,
for I wait for You.
22 God, redeem Israel,
from all its distresses.

Psalm 26
Davidic.

1 Vindicate me, Lord,
because I have lived with integrity
and have trusted in the Lord
without wavering.
2 Test me, Lord, and try me;
examine my heart and mind.
3 For Your faithful love is before my eyes,
and I live by Your truth.
4 I do not sit with the worthless
or associate with hypocrites.
5 I hate a crowd of evildoers,
and I do not sit with the wicked.
6 I wash my hands in innocence
and go around Your altar, Lord,
7 raising my voice in thanksgiving
and telling about Your wonderful works.
8 Lord, I love the house where You dwell,
the place where Your glory resides.
9 Do not destroy me along with sinners,
or my life along with men of bloodshed
10 in whose hands are evil schemes
and whose right hands are filled
with bribes.
11 But I live with integrity;
redeem me and be gracious to me.
12 My foot stands on level ground;
I will praise the Lord in the assemblies.

Psalm 27
Davidic.

1 The Lord is my light and my salvation—
whom should I fear?
The Lord is the stronghold of my life—
of whom should I be afraid?
2 When evildoers came against me to devour
my flesh,
my foes and my enemies stumbled and fell.
3 Though an army deploys against me,
my heart is not afraid;
though a war breaks out against me,
still I am confident.
4 I have asked one thing from the Lord;
it is what I desire:
to dwell in the house of the Lord
all the days of my life,
gazing on the beauty of the Lord
and seeking Him in His temple.
5 For He will conceal me in His shelter
in the day of adversity;
He will hide me under the cover of His tent;
He will set me high on a rock.
6 Then my head will be high
above my enemies around me;
I will offer sacrifices in His tent with shouts
of joy.
I will sing and make music to the Lord.
7 Lord, hear my voice when I call;
be gracious to me and answer me.
8 My heart says this about You,
"You are to seek My face."
Lord, I will seek Your face.
9 Do not hide Your face from me;
do not turn Your servant away in anger.
You have been my helper;
do not leave me or abandon me,
God of my salvation.
10 Even if my father and mother abandon me,
the Lord cares for me.
11 Because of my adversaries,
show me Your way, Lord,
and lead me on a level path.
12 Do not give me over to the will of my foes,
for false witnesses rise up against me,
breathing violence.
13 I am certain that I will see the Lord's goodness
in the land of the living.
14 Wait for the Lord;
be strong and courageous.
Wait for the Lord.

Psalm 28
Davidic.

1 Lord, I call to You;
my rock, do not be deaf to me.
If You remain silent to me,
I will be like those going down to the *Pit.
2 Listen to the sound of my pleading
when I cry to You for help,
when I lift up my hands
toward Your holy sanctuary.
3 Do not drag me away with the wicked,
with the evildoers,
who speak in friendly ways
with their neighbors
while malice is in their hearts.

4 Repay them according to what
they have done—
according to the evil of their deeds.
Repay them according to the work
of their hands;
give them back what they deserve.
5 Because they do not consider
what the Lord has done
or the work of His hands,
He will tear them down and not rebuild them.
6 May the Lord be praised,
for He has heard the sound of my pleading.
7 The Lord is my strength and my shield;
my heart trusts in Him, and I am helped.
Therefore my heart rejoices,
and I praise Him with my song.
8 The Lord is the strength of His people;
He is a stronghold of salvation
for His anointed.
9 Save Your people, bless Your possession,
shepherd them, and carry them forever.

Psalm 29
A Davidic psalm.

1 Ascribe to *Yahweh, you heavenly beings,
ascribe to the Lord glory and strength.
2 Ascribe to Yahweh the glory due His name;
worship Yahweh
in the splendor of His holiness.
3 The voice of the Lord is above the waters.
The God of glory thunders—
the Lord, above vast waters,
4 the voice of the Lord in power,
the voice of the Lord in splendor.
5 The voice of the Lord breaks the cedars;
the Lord shatters the cedars of Lebanon.
6 He makes Lebanon skip like a calf,
and Sirion, like a young wild ox.
7 The voice of the Lord flashes flames of fire.
8 The voice of the Lord shakes the wilderness;
the Lord shakes the wilderness of Kadesh.
9 The voice of the Lord makes the deer
give birth
and strips the woodlands bare.
In His temple all cry, "Glory!"
10 The Lord sat enthroned at the flood;
the Lord sits enthroned, King forever.
11 The Lord gives His people strength;
the Lord blesses His people with peace.

Psalm 30
A psalm; a dedication song for the house. Davidic.

1 I will exalt You, Lord,
because You have lifted me up
and have not allowed my enemies
to triumph over me.
2 Lord my God,
I cried to You for help, and You healed me.
3 Lord, You brought me up from *Sheol;
You spared me from among those
going down to the *Pit.
4 Sing to *Yahweh, you His faithful ones,
and praise His holy name.
5 For His anger lasts only a moment,
but His favor, a lifetime.
Weeping may spend the night,
but there is joy in the morning.

⁶ When I was secure, I said,
"I will never be shaken."
⁷ LORD, when You showed Your favor,
You made me stand like a strong mountain;
when You hid Your face, I was terrified.
⁸ LORD, I called to You;
I sought favor from my Lord:
⁹ "What gain is there in my death,
if I go down to the Pit?
Will the dust praise You?
Will it proclaim Your truth?
¹⁰ LORD, listen and be gracious to me;
LORD, be my helper."
¹¹ You turned my lament into dancing;
You removed my *sackcloth
and clothed me with gladness,
¹² so that I can sing to You and not be silent.
LORD my God, I will praise You forever.

Psalm 31
For the choir director. A Davidic psalm.

¹ LORD, I seek refuge in You;
let me never be disgraced.
Save me by Your righteousness.
² Listen closely to me; rescue me quickly.
Be a rock of refuge for me,
a mountain fortress to save me.
³ For You are my rock and my fortress;
You lead and guide me
because of Your name.
⁴ You will free me from the net
that is secretly set for me,
for You are my refuge.
⁵ Into Your hand I entrust my spirit;
You redeem me, LORD, God of truth.
⁶ I hate those who are devoted
to worthless idols,
but I trust in the LORD.
⁷ I will rejoice and be glad in Your faithful love
because You have seen my affliction.
You have known the troubles of my life
⁸ and have not handed me over to the enemy.
You have set my feet in a spacious place.
⁹ Be gracious to me, LORD,
because I am in distress;
my eyes are worn out from angry sorrow—
my whole being as well.
¹⁰ Indeed, my life is consumed with grief
and my years with groaning;
my strength has failed
because of my sinfulness,
and my bones waste away.
¹¹ I am ridiculed by all my adversaries
and even by my neighbors.
I am dreaded by my acquaintances;
those who see me in the street run from me.
¹² I am forgotten: gone from memory
like a dead person—like broken pottery.
¹³ I have heard the gossip of many;
terror is on every side.
When they conspired against me,
they plotted to take my life.
¹⁴ But I trust in You, LORD;
I say, "You are my God."
¹⁵ The course of my life is in Your power;
deliver me from the power of my enemies
and from my persecutors.

¹⁶ Show Your favor to Your servant;
save me by Your faithful love.
¹⁷ LORD, do not let me be disgraced when I call
on You.
Let the wicked be disgraced;
let them be silent in *Sheol.
¹⁸ Let lying lips be quieted;
they speak arrogantly against the righteous
with pride and contempt.
¹⁹ How great is Your goodness
that You have stored up for those who *fear You
and accomplished in the sight of *everyone
for those who take refuge in You.
²⁰ You hide them in the protection
of Your presence;
You conceal them in a shelter
from the schemes of men,
from quarrelsome tongues.
²¹ May the LORD be praised,
for He has wonderfully shown His faithful love
to me
in a city under siege.
²² In my alarm I had said,
"I am cut off from Your sight."
But You heard the sound of my pleading
when I cried to You for help.
²³ Love the LORD, all His faithful ones.
The LORD protects the loyal,
but fully repays the arrogant.
²⁴ Be strong and courageous,
all you who put your hope in the LORD.

Psalm 32
Davidic. A *Maskil.

¹ How joyful is the one
whose transgression is forgiven,
whose sin is covered!
² How joyful is the man
the LORD does not charge with sin
and in whose spirit is no deceit!
³ When I kept silent, my bones became brittle
from my groaning all day long.
⁴ For day and night Your hand was heavy
on me;
my strength was drained
as in the summer's heat.　　　*Selah
⁵ Then I acknowledged my sin to You
and did not conceal my iniquity.
I said,
"I will confess my transgressions to the LORD,"
and You took away the *guilt of my sin.
　　　　　　　　　　　　　Selah
⁶ Therefore let everyone who is faithful
pray to You
at a time that You may be found.
When great floodwaters come,
they will not reach him.
⁷ You are my hiding place;
You protect me from trouble.
You surround me with joyful shouts
of deliverance.　　　Selah
⁸ I will instruct you and show you the way
to go;
with My eye on you, I will give counsel.
⁹ Do not be like a horse or mule,
without understanding,
that must be controlled with bit and bridle

or else it will not come near you.
10 Many pains come to the wicked,
but the one who trusts in the LORD
will have faithful love surrounding him.
11 Be glad in the LORD and rejoice,
you righteous ones;
shout for joy,
all you upright in heart.

Psalm 33

1 Rejoice in the LORD, you righteous ones;
praise from the upright is beautiful.
2 Praise the LORD with the lyre;
make music to Him with a ten-stringed harp.
3 Sing a new song to Him;
play skillfully on the strings,
with a joyful shout.
4 For the word of the LORD is right,
and all His work is trustworthy.
5 He loves righteousness and justice;
the earth is full of the LORD's unfailing love.
6 The heavens were made by the word
of the LORD,
and all the stars, by the breath of His mouth.
7 He gathers the waters of the sea into a heap;
He puts the depths into storehouses.
8 Let the whole earth tremble before the LORD;
let all the inhabitants of the world
stand in awe of Him.
9 For He spoke, and it came into being;
He commanded, and it came into existence.
10 The LORD frustrates the counsel of the nations;
He thwarts the plans of the peoples.
11 The counsel of the LORD stands forever,
the plans of His heart from generation
to generation.
12 Happy is the nation whose God is *Yahweh—
the people He has chosen to be
His own possession!
13 The LORD looks down from heaven;
He observes everyone.
14 He gazes on all the inhabitants of the earth
from His dwelling place.
15 He alone shapes their hearts;
He considers all their works.
16 A king is not saved by a large army;
a warrior will not be delivered
by great strength.
17 The horse is a false hope for safety;
it provides no escape by its great power.
18 Now the eye of the LORD is on those
who *fear Him—
those who depend on His faithful love
19 to deliver them from death
and to keep them alive in famine.
20 We wait for Yahweh;
He is our help and shield.
21 For our hearts rejoice in Him
because we trust in His holy name.
22 May Your faithful love rest on us, Yahweh,
for we put our hope in You.

Psalm 34

Concerning David, when he pretended to
be insane in the presence of Abimelech,
who drove him out, and he departed.

1 I will praise the LORD at all times;
His praise will always be on my lips.

2 I will boast in the LORD;
the humble will hear and be glad.
3 Proclaim *Yahweh's greatness with me;
let us exalt His name together.
4 I sought the LORD, and He answered me
and delivered me from all my fears.
5 Those who look to Him are radiant with joy;
their faces will never be ashamed.
6 This poor man cried, and the LORD heard him
and saved him from all his troubles.
7 The Angel of the LORD encamps
around those who *fear Him,
and rescues them.
8 Taste and see that the LORD is good.
How happy is the man who takes refuge
in Him!
9 You who are His holy ones, fear Yahweh,
for those who fear Him lack nothing.
10 Young lions lack food and go hungry,
but those who seek the LORD
will not lack any good thing.
11 Come, children, listen to me;
I will teach you the fear of the LORD.
12 Who is the man who delights in life,
loving a long life to enjoy what is good?
13 Keep your tongue from evil
and your lips from deceitful speech.
14 Turn away from evil and do what is good;
seek peace and pursue it.
15 The eyes of the LORD are on the righteous,
and His ears are open to their cry for help.
16 The face of the LORD is set
against those who do what is evil,
to erase all memory of them from the earth.
17 The righteous cry out, and the LORD hears,
and delivers them from all their troubles.
18 The LORD is near the brokenhearted;
He saves those crushed in spirit.
19 Many adversities come to the one
who is righteous,
but the LORD delivers him from them all.
20 He protects all his bones;
not one of them is broken.
21 Evil brings death to the wicked,
and those who hate the righteous
will be punished.
22 The LORD redeems the life of His servants,
and all who take refuge in Him will not
be punished.

Psalm 35

Davidic.

1 Oppose my opponents, LORD;
fight those who fight me.
2 Take Your shields—large and small—
and come to my aid.
3 Draw the spear and javelin
against my pursuers,
and assure me: "I am your deliverance."
4 Let those who seek to kill me
be disgraced and humiliated;
let those who plan to harm me
be turned back and ashamed.
5 Let them be like chaff in the wind,
with the angel of the LORD driving them away.
6 Let their way be dark and slippery,
with the angel of the LORD pursuing them.

7 They hid their net for me without cause;
 they dug a pit for me without cause.
8 Let ruin come on him unexpectedly,
 and let the net that he hid ensnare him;
 let him fall into it—to his ruin.
9 Then I will rejoice in the LORD;
 I will delight in His deliverance.
10 My very bones will say,
 "LORD, who is like You,
 rescuing the poor from one too strong
 for him,
 the poor or the needy from one
 who robs him?"
11 Malicious witnesses come forward;
 they question me about things I do not know.
12 They repay me evil for good,
 making me desolate.
13 Yet when they were sick,
 my clothing was *sackcloth;
 I humbled myself with fasting,
 and my prayer was genuine.
14 I went about grieving as if for my friend
 or brother;
 I was bowed down with grief,
 like one mourning a mother.
15 But when I stumbled, they gathered in glee;
 they gathered against me.
 Assailants I did not know
 tore at me and did not stop.
16 With godless mockery
 they gnashed their teeth at me.
17 Lord, how long will You look on?
 Rescue my life from their ravages,
 my only one from the young lions.
18 I will praise You in the great congregation;
 I will exalt You among many people.
19 Do not let my deceitful enemies rejoice
 over me;
 do not let those who hate me without cause
 look at me maliciously.
20 For they do not speak in friendly ways,
 but contrive deceitful schemes
 against those who live peacefully in the land.
21 They open their mouths wide against me
 and say,
 "Aha, aha! We saw it!"
22 You saw it, LORD; do not be silent.
 Lord, do not be far from me.
23 Wake up and rise to my defense,
 to my cause, my God and my LORD!
24 Vindicate me, LORD my God,
 in keeping with Your righteousness,
 and do not let them rejoice over me.
25 Do not let them say in their hearts,
 "Aha! Just what we wanted."
 Do not let them say,
 "We have swallowed him up!"
26 Let those who rejoice at my misfortune
 be disgraced and humiliated;
 let those who exalt themselves over me
 be clothed with shame and reproach.
27 Let those who want my vindication
 shout for joy and be glad;
 let them continually say,
 "The LORD be exalted.
 He takes pleasure
 in His servant's well-being."

28 And my tongue will proclaim
 Your righteousness,
 Your praise all day long.

Psalm 36
For the choir director. A psalm
of David, the LORD's servant.

1 An *oracle within my heart
 concerning the transgression of the
 wicked person:
 There is no dread of God before his eyes,
2 for in his own eyes he flatters himself
 too much
 to discover and hate his sin.
3 The words of his mouth are malicious
 and deceptive;
 he has stopped acting wisely and doing good.
4 Even on his bed he makes malicious plans.
 He sets himself on a path that is not good
 and does not reject evil.
5 LORD, Your faithful love reaches to heaven,
 Your faithfulness to the clouds.
6 Your righteousness is
 like the highest mountains;
 Your judgments, like the deepest sea.
 LORD, You preserve man and beast.
7 God, Your faithful love is so valuable
 that *people take refuge in the shadow
 of Your wings.
8 They are filled from the abundance
 of Your house;
 You let them drink
 from Your refreshing stream,
9 for with You is life's fountain.
 In Your light we will see light.
10 Spread Your faithful love over those
 who know You,
 and Your righteousness over the upright
 in heart.
11 Do not let the foot of the arrogant man
 come near me
 or the hand of the wicked one drive me away.
12 There the evildoers fall;
 they have been thrown down and cannot rise.

Psalm 37
Davidic.

1 Do not be agitated by evildoers;
 do not envy those who do wrong.
2 For they wither quickly like grass
 and wilt like tender green plants.
3 Trust in the LORD and do what is good;
 dwell in the land and live securely.
4 Take delight in the LORD,
 and He will give you your heart's desires.
5 Commit your way to the LORD;
 trust in Him, and He will act,
6 making your righteousness shine
 like the dawn,
 your justice like the noonday.
7 Be silent before the LORD and wait expectantly
 for Him;
 do not be agitated by one who prospers
 in his way,
 by the man who carries out evil plans.
8 Refrain from anger and give up your rage;
 do not be agitated—it can only bring harm.

9 For evildoers will be destroyed,
but those who put their hope in the Lord
will inherit the land.

10 A little while, and the wicked person will be
no more;
though you look for him, he will not be there.

11 But the humble will inherit the land
and will enjoy abundant prosperity.

12 The wicked person schemes
against the righteous
and gnashes his teeth at him.

13 The Lord laughs at him
because He sees that his day is coming.

14 The wicked have drawn the sword and strung
the bow
to bring down the afflicted and needy
and to slaughter those whose way is upright.

15 Their swords will enter their own hearts,
and their bows will be broken.

16 The little that the righteous man has is better
than the abundance of many wicked people.

17 For the arms of the wicked will be broken,
but the Lord supports the righteous.

18 The Lord watches over the blameless
all their days,
and their inheritance will last forever.

19 They will not be disgraced in times
of adversity;
they will be satisfied in days of hunger.

20 But the wicked will perish;
the Lord's enemies, like the glory
of the pastures,
will fade away—
they will fade away like smoke.

21 The wicked man borrows and does not repay,
but the righteous one is gracious and giving.

22 Those who are blessed by Him will inherit
the land,
but those cursed by Him will be destroyed.

23 A man's steps are established by the Lord,
and He takes pleasure in his way.

24 Though he falls, he will not be overwhelmed,
because the Lord holds his hand.

25 I have been young and now I am old,
yet I have not seen the righteous abandoned
or his children begging for bread.

26 He is always generous, always lending,
and his children are a blessing.

27 Turn away from evil and do what is good,
and dwell there forever.

28 For the Lord loves justice
and will not abandon His faithful ones.
They are kept safe forever,
but the children of the wicked
will be destroyed.

29 The righteous will inherit the land
and dwell in it permanently.

30 The mouth of the righteous utters wisdom;
his tongue speaks what is just.

31 The instruction of his God is in his heart;
his steps do not falter.

32 The wicked one lies in wait for the righteous
and seeks to kill him;

33 the Lord will not leave him
in the power of the wicked one
or allow him to be condemned
when he is judged.

34 Wait for the Lord and keep His way,
and He will exalt you to inherit the land.
You will watch when the wicked are destroyed.

35 I have seen a wicked, violent man
well-rooted like a flourishing native tree.

36 Then I passed by and noticed he was gone;
I searched for him, but he could not be found.

37 Watch the blameless and observe the upright,
for the man of peace will have a future.

38 But transgressors will all be eliminated;
the future of the wicked will be destroyed.

39 The salvation of the righteous is
from the Lord,
their refuge in a time of distress.

40 The Lord helps and delivers them;
He will deliver them from the wicked
and will save them
because they take refuge in Him.

Psalm 38
A Davidic psalm for remembrance.

1 Lord, do not punish me in Your anger
or discipline me in Your wrath.

2 For Your arrows have sunk into me,
and Your hand has pressed down on me.

3 There is no health in my body
because of Your indignation;
there is no strength in my bones
because of my sin.

4 For my sins have flooded over my head;
they are a burden too heavy for me to bear.

5 My wounds are foul and festering
because of my foolishness.

6 I am bent over and brought low;
all day long I go around in mourning.

7 For my loins are full of burning pain,
and there is no health in my body.

8 I am faint and severely crushed;
I groan because of the anguish of my heart.

9 Lord, my every desire is known to You;
my sighing is not hidden from You.

10 My heart races, my strength leaves me,
and even the light of my eyes has faded.

11 My loved ones and friends stand back
from my affliction,
and my relatives stand at a distance.

12 Those who seek my life set traps,
and those who want to harm me threaten
to destroy me;
they plot treachery all day long.

13 I am like a deaf person; I do not hear.
I am like a speechless person
who does not open his mouth.

14 I am like a man who does not hear
and has no arguments in his mouth.

15 I put my hope in You, Lord;
You will answer, Lord my God.

16 For I said, "Don't let them rejoice over me—
those who are arrogant toward me
when I stumble."

17 For I am about to fall,
and my pain is constantly with me.

18 So I confess my *guilt;
I am anxious because of my sin.

19 But my enemies are vigorous and powerful;
many hate me for no reason.

20 Those who repay evil for good

attack me for pursuing good.
21 LORD, do not abandon me;
my God, do not be far from me.
22 Hurry to help me,
Lord, my Savior.

Psalm 39

For the choir director, for Jeduthun.
A Davidic psalm.

1 I said, "I will guard my ways
so that I may not sin with my tongue;
I will guard my mouth with a muzzle
as long as the wicked are in my presence."
2 I was speechless and quiet;
I kept silent, even from speaking good,
and my pain intensified.
3 My heart grew hot within me;
as I mused, a fire burned.
I spoke with my tongue:
4 "LORD, reveal to me the end of my life
and the number of my days.
Let me know how short-lived I am.
5 You, indeed, have made my days short
in length,
and my life span as nothing in Your sight.
Yes, every mortal man is only a vapor.
*Selah

6 Certainly, man walks about
like a mere shadow.
Indeed, they frantically rush around in vain,
gathering possessions
without knowing who will get them.
7 Now, Lord, what do I wait for?
My hope is in You.
8 Deliver me from all my transgressions;
do not make me the taunt of fools.
9 I am speechless; I do not open my mouth
because of what You have done.
10 Remove Your torment from me;
I fade away because of the force of Your hand.
11 You discipline a man with punishment for sin,
consuming like a moth what is precious
to him;
every man is only a vapor.   Selah
12 Hear my prayer, LORD,
and listen to my cry for help;
do not be silent at my tears.
For I am a foreigner residing with You,
a temporary resident like all my fathers.
13 Turn Your angry gaze from me
so that I may be cheered up
before I die and am gone."

Psalm 40

For the choir director. A Davidic psalm.

1 I waited patiently for the LORD,
and He turned to me and heard my cry
for help.
2 He brought me up from a desolate pit,
out of the muddy clay,
and set my feet on a rock,
making my steps secure.
3 He put a new song in my mouth,
a hymn of praise to our God.
Many will see and fear
and put their trust in the LORD.
4 How happy is the man

who has put his trust in the LORD
and has not turned to the proud
or to those who run after lies!
5 LORD my God, You have done many things—
Your wonderful works and Your plans for us;
none can compare with You.
If I were to report and speak of them,
they are more than can be told.
6 You do not delight in sacrifice and offering;
You open my ears to listen.
You do not ask for a whole *burnt offering
or a *sin offering.
7 Then I said, "See, I have come;
it is written about me in the volume
of the scroll.
8 I delight to do Your will, my God;
Your instruction lives within me."
9 I proclaim righteousness
in the great assembly;
see, I do not keep my mouth closed—
as You know, LORD.
10 I did not hide Your righteousness in my heart;
I spoke about Your faithfulness and salvation;
I did not conceal Your constant love and truth
from the great assembly.
11 LORD, do not withhold Your compassion
from me;
Your constant love and truth will always
guard me.
12 For troubles without number
have surrounded me;
my sins have overtaken me; I am unable
to see.
They are more than the hairs of my head,
and my courage leaves me.
13 LORD, be pleased to deliver me;
hurry to help me, LORD.
14 Let those who seek to take my life
be disgraced and confounded.
Let those who wish me harm
be driven back and humiliated.
15 Let those who say to me, "Aha, aha!"
be horrified because of their shame.
16 Let all who seek You rejoice and be glad
in You;
let those who love Your salvation
continually say,
"The LORD is great!"
17 I am afflicted and needy;
the Lord thinks of me.
You are my helper and my deliverer;
my God, do not delay.

Psalm 41

For the choir director. A Davidic psalm.

1 Happy is one who cares for the poor;
the LORD will save him in a day of adversity.
2 The LORD will keep him and preserve him;
he will be blessed in the land.
You will not give him over to the desire
of his enemies.
3 The LORD will sustain him on his sickbed;
You will heal him on the bed where he lies.
4 I said, "LORD, be gracious to me;
heal me, for I have sinned against You."
5 My enemies speak maliciously about me:
"When will he die and be forgotten?"

6 When one of them comes to visit,
   he speaks deceitfully;
he stores up evil in his heart;
he goes out and talks.
7 All who hate me whisper together about me;
   they plan to harm me.
8 "Lethal poison has been poured into him,
   and he won't rise again from where he lies!"
9 Even my friend in whom I trusted,
   one who ate my bread,
   has raised his heel against me.
10 But You, Lord, be gracious to me
    and raise me up;
   then I will repay them.
11 By this I know that You delight in me:
    my enemy does not shout in triumph over me.
12 You supported me because of my integrity
    and set me in Your presence forever.
13 May *Yahweh, the God of Israel, be praised
    from everlasting to everlasting.
    *Amen and amen.

BOOK II
(Psalms 42–72)

Psalm 42
For the choir director. A *Maskil
of the sons of Korah.

1 As a deer longs for streams of water,
   so I long for You, God.
2 I thirst for God, the living God.
   When can I come and appear before God?
3 My tears have been my food day and night,
   while all day long people say to me,
   "Where is your God?"
4 I remember this as I pour out my heart:
   how I walked with many,
   leading the festive procession to the house
      of God,
   with joyful and thankful shouts.
5 Why am I so depressed?
   Why this turmoil within me?
   Put your hope in God, for I will
      still praise Him,
   my Savior and my God.
6 I am deeply depressed;
   therefore I remember You from the land
      of Jordan
   and the peaks of Hermon, from Mount Mizar.
7 Deep calls to deep in the roar
      of Your waterfalls;
   all Your breakers and Your billows have swept
      over me.
8 The Lord will send His faithful love by day;
   His song will be with me in the night—
   a prayer to the God of my life.
9 I will say to God, my rock,
   "Why have You forgotten me?
   Why must I go about in sorrow
   because of the enemy's oppression?"
10 My adversaries taunt me,
    as if crushing my bones,
   while all day long they say to me,
   "Where is your God?"
11 Why am I so depressed?
    Why this turmoil within me?

Put your hope in God, for I will
   still praise Him,
my Savior and my God.

Psalm 43
1 Vindicate me, God, and defend my cause
   against an ungodly nation;
   rescue me from the deceitful and unjust man.
2 For You are the God of my refuge.
   Why have You rejected me?
   Why must I go about in sorrow
   because of the enemy's oppression?
3 Send Your light and Your truth; let them
      lead me.
   Let them bring me to Your holy mountain,
   to Your dwelling place.
4 Then I will come to the altar of God,
   to God, my greatest joy.
   I will praise You with the lyre,
   God, my God.
5 Why am I so depressed?
   Why this turmoil within me?
   Put your hope in God, for I will
      still praise Him,
   my Savior and my God.

Psalm 44
For the choir director. A *Maskil of the sons of Korah.

1 God, we have heard with our ears—
   our ancestors have told us—
   the work You accomplished in their days,
   in days long ago:
2 to plant them,
   You drove out the nations with Your hand;
   to settle them,
   You crushed the peoples.
3 For they did not take the land
      by their sword—
   their arm did not bring them victory—
   but by Your right hand, Your arm,
   and the light of Your face,
   for You were pleased with them.
4 You are my King, my God,
   who ordains victories for Jacob.
5 Through You we drive back our foes;
   through Your name we trample our enemies.
6 For I do not trust in my bow,
   and my sword does not bring me victory.
7 But You give us victory over our foes
   and let those who hate us be disgraced.
8 We boast in God all day long;
   we will praise Your name forever.   *Selah
9 But You have rejected and humiliated us;
   You do not march out with our armies.
10 You make us retreat from the foe,
    and those who hate us
   have taken plunder for themselves.
11 You hand us over to be eaten like sheep
    and scatter us among the nations.
12 You sell Your people for nothing;
    You make no profit from selling them.
13 You make us an object of reproach
       to our neighbors,
    a source of mockery and ridicule to those
       around us.
14 You make us a joke among the nations,
    a laughingstock among the peoples.
15 My disgrace is before me all day long,

and shame has covered my face,
16 because of the voice of the scorner and reviler,
because of the enemy and avenger.
17 All this has happened to us,
but we have not forgotten You
or betrayed Your covenant.
18 Our hearts have not turned back;
our steps have not strayed from Your path.
19 But You have crushed us in a haunt of jackals
and have covered us with deepest darkness.
20 If we had forgotten the name of our God
and spread out our hands to a foreign god,
21 wouldn't God have found this out,
since He knows the secrets of the heart?
22 Because of You we are slain all day long;
we are counted as sheep to be slaughtered.
23 Wake up, LORD! Why are You sleeping?
Get up! Don't reject us forever!
24 Why do You hide Yourself
and forget our affliction and oppression?
25 For we have sunk down to the dust;
our bodies cling to the ground.
26 Rise up! Help us!
Redeem us because of Your faithful love.

Psalm 45
For the choir director: according to "The Lilies."
A *Maskil* of the sons of Korah. A love song.

1 My heart is moved by a noble theme
as I recite my verses to the king;
my tongue is the pen of a skillful writer.
2 You are the most handsome of *men;
grace flows from your lips.
Therefore God has blessed you forever.
3 Mighty warrior, strap your sword at your side.
In your majesty and splendor—
4 in your splendor ride triumphantly
in the cause of truth, humility, and justice.
May your right hand show
your awe-inspiring acts.
5 Your arrows pierce the hearts
of the king's enemies;
the peoples fall under you.
6 Your throne, God, is forever and ever;
the scepter of Your kingdom is a scepter
of justice.
7 You love righteousness and hate wickedness;
therefore God, your God, has anointed you
with the oil of joy
more than your companions.
8 Myrrh, aloes, and cassia perfume
all your garments;
from ivory palaces harps bring you joy.
9 Kings' daughters are
among your honored women;
the queen, adorned with gold from Ophir,
stands at your right hand.
10 Listen, daughter, pay attention and consider:
forget your people and your father's house,
11 and the king will desire your beauty.
Bow down to him, for he is your lord.
12 The daughter of Tyre, the wealthy people,
will seek your favor with gifts.
13 In her chamber, the royal daughter
is all glorious,
her clothing embroidered with gold.
14 In colorful garments she is led to the king;

after her, the virgins, her companions,
are brought to you.
15 They are led in with gladness and rejoicing;
they enter the king's palace.
16 Your sons will succeed your ancestors;
you will make them princes
throughout the land.
17 I will cause your name to be remembered
for all generations;
therefore the peoples will praise you forever
and ever.

Psalm 46
For the choir director. A song of the sons
of Korah. According to *Alamoth*.

1 God is our refuge and strength,
a helper who is always found
in times of trouble.
2 Therefore we will not be afraid,
though the earth trembles
and the mountains topple
into the depths of the seas,
3 though its waters roar and foam
and the mountains quake
with its turmoil.   *Selah
4 There is a river—
its streams delight the city of God,
the holy dwelling place of the *Most High.
5 God is within her; she will not be toppled.
God will help her when the morning dawns.
6 Nations rage, kingdoms topple;
the earth melts when He lifts His voice.
7 The LORD of *Hosts is with us;
the God of Jacob is our stronghold.   *Selah*
8 Come, see the works of the LORD,
who brings devastation on the earth.
9 He makes wars cease throughout the earth.
He shatters bows and cuts spears to pieces;
He burns up the chariots.
10 "Stop your fighting—and know
that I am God,
exalted among the nations,
exalted on the earth."
11 *Yahweh of Hosts is with us;
the God of Jacob is our stronghold.   *Selah*

Psalm 47
For the choir director. A psalm of the sons of Korah.

1 Clap your hands, all you peoples;
shout to God with a jubilant cry.
2 For *Yahweh, the *Most High,
is awe-inspiring,
a great King over all the earth.
3 He subdues peoples under us
and nations under our feet.
4 He chooses for us our inheritance—
the pride of Jacob, whom He loves.   *Selah
5 God ascends among shouts of joy,
the LORD, among the sound of trumpets.
6 Sing praise to God, sing praise;
sing praise to our King, sing praise!
7 Sing a song of wisdom,
for God is King of all the earth.
8 God reigns over the nations;
God is seated on His holy throne.
9 The nobles of the peoples have assembled
with the people of the God of Abraham.

For the leaders of the earth belong to God;
He is greatly exalted.

Psalm 48

A song. A psalm of the sons of Korah.

1 The LORD is great and highly praised
in the city of our God.
His holy mountain, ²rising splendidly,
is the joy of the whole earth.
Mount ˙Zion on the slopes of the north
is the city of the great King.
3 God is known as a stronghold
in its citadels.
4 Look! The kings assembled;
they advanced together.
5 They looked and froze with fear;
they fled in terror.
6 Trembling seized them there,
agony like that of a woman in labor,
7 as You wrecked the ships of Tarshish
with the east wind.
8 Just as we heard, so we have seen
in the city of ˙Yahweh of ˙Hosts,
in the city of our God;
God will establish it forever. ˙Selah
9 God, within Your temple,
we contemplate Your faithful love.
10 Your name, God, like Your praise,
reaches to the ends of the earth;
Your right hand is filled with justice.
11 Mount Zion is glad.
The towns of Judah rejoice
because of Your judgments.
12 Go around Zion, encircle it;
count its towers,
13 note its ramparts; tour its citadels
so that you can tell a future generation:
14 "This God, our God forever and ever—
He will always lead us."

Psalm 49

For the choir director. A psalm of the sons of Korah.

1 Hear this, all you peoples;
listen, all who inhabit the world,
2 both low and high,
rich and poor together.
3 My mouth speaks wisdom;
my heart's meditation brings understanding.
4 I turn my ear to a proverb;
I explain my riddle with a lyre.
5 Why should I fear in times of trouble?
The iniquity of my foes surrounds me.
6 They trust in their wealth
and boast of their abundant riches.
7 Yet these cannot redeem a person
or pay his ransom to God—
8 since the price of redeeming him is too costly,
one should forever stop trying—
9 so that he may live forever
and not see the ˙Pit.
10 For one can see that wise men die;
foolish and stupid men also pass away.
Then they leave their wealth to others.
11 Their graves are their eternal homes,
their homes from generation to generation,
though they have named estates
after themselves.

12 But despite his assets, man will not last;
he is like the animals that perish.
13 This is the way of those who are arrogant,
and of their followers,
who approve of their words. ˙Selah
14 Like sheep they are headed for ˙Sheol;
Death will shepherd them.
The upright will rule over them
in the morning,
and their form will waste away in Sheol,
far from their lofty abode.
15 But God will redeem my life
from the power of Sheol,
for He will take me. *Selah*
16 Do not be afraid when a man gets rich,
when the wealth of his house increases.
17 For when he dies, he will take nothing at all;
his wealth will not follow him down.
18 Though he praises himself
during his lifetime—
and people praise you when you do well
for yourself—
19 he will go to the generation of his fathers;
they will never see the light.
20 A man with valuable possessions
but without understanding
is like the animals that perish.

Psalm 50

A psalm of ˙Asaph.

1 ˙Yahweh, the God of gods speaks;
He summons the earth from east to west.
2 From ˙Zion, the perfection of beauty,
God appears in radiance.
3 Our God is coming; He will not be silent!
Devouring fire precedes Him,
and a storm rages around Him.
4 On high, He summons heaven and earth
in order to judge His people.
5 "Gather My faithful ones to Me,
those who made a covenant with Me
by sacrifice."
6 The heavens proclaim His righteousness,
for God is the Judge. ˙Selah
7 "Listen, My people, and I will speak;
I will testify against you, Israel.
I am God, your God.
8 I do not rebuke you for your sacrifices
or for your ˙burnt offerings,
which are continually before Me.
9 I will not accept a bull from your household
or male goats from your pens,
10 for every animal of the forest is Mine,
the cattle on a thousand hills.
11 I know every bird of the mountains,
and the creatures of the field are Mine.
12 If I were hungry, I would not tell you,
for the world and everything in it is Mine.
13 Do I eat the flesh of bulls
or drink the blood of goats?
14 Sacrifice a thank offering to God,
and pay your vows to the ˙Most High.
15 Call on Me in a day of trouble;
I will rescue you, and you will honor Me."
16 But God says to the wicked:
"What right do you have to recite My statutes
and to take My covenant on your lips?

17 You hate instruction
and turn your back on My words.
18 When you see a thief,
you make friends with him,
and you associate with adulterers.
19 You unleash your mouth for evil
and harness your tongue for deceit.
20 You sit, maligning your brother,
slandering your mother's son.
21 You have done these things, and I kept silent;
you thought I was just like you.
But I will rebuke you
and lay out the case before you.
22 Understand this, you who forget God,
or I will tear you apart,
and there will be no one to rescue you.
23 Whoever sacrifices a thank offering
honors Me,
and whoever orders his conduct,
I will show him the salvation of God."

Psalm 51

For the choir director. A Davidic psalm,
when Nathan the prophet came to him
after he had gone to Bathsheba.

1 Be gracious to me, God,
according to Your faithful love;
according to Your abundant compassion,
blot out my rebellion.
2 Wash away my *guilt
and cleanse me from my sin.
3 For I am conscious of my rebellion,
and my sin is always before me.
4 Against You—You alone—I have sinned
and done this evil in Your sight.
So You are right when You pass sentence;
You are blameless when You judge.
5 Indeed, I was guilty when I was born;
I was sinful when my mother conceived me.
6 Surely You desire integrity in the inner self,
and You teach me wisdom deep within.
7 Purify me with hyssop, and I will be *clean;
wash me, and I will be whiter than snow.
8 Let me hear joy and gladness;
let the bones You have crushed rejoice.
9 Turn Your face away from my sins
and blot out all my guilt.
10 God, create a clean heart for me
and renew a steadfast spirit within me.
11 Do not banish me from Your presence
or take Your Holy Spirit from me.
12 Restore the joy of Your salvation to me,
and give me a willing spirit.
13 Then I will teach the rebellious Your ways,
and sinners will return to You.
14 Save me from the guilt of bloodshed, God,
the God of my salvation,
and my tongue will sing
of Your righteousness.
15 Lord, open my lips,
and my mouth will declare Your praise.
16 You do not want a sacrifice, or I would give it;
You are not pleased with a *burnt offering.
17 The sacrifice pleasing to God is
a broken spirit.
God, You will not despise a broken
and humbled heart.

18 In Your good pleasure, cause *Zion to prosper;
build the walls of Jerusalem.
19 Then You will delight in righteous sacrifices,
whole burnt offerings;
then bulls will be offered on Your altar.

Psalm 52

For the choir director. A Davidic *Maskil. When
Doeg the Edomite went and reported to Saul,
telling him, "David went to Ahimelech's house."

1 Why brag about evil, you hero!
God's faithful love is constant.
2 Like a sharpened razor,
your tongue devises destruction,
working treachery.
3 You love evil instead of good,
lying instead of speaking truthfully.　　*Selah
4 You love any words that destroy,
you treacherous tongue!
5 This is why God will bring you down forever.
He will take you, ripping you out of your tent;
He will uproot you from the land of the living.
　　　　　　　　　　Selah
6 The righteous will look on with awe
and will ridicule him:
7 "Here is the man
who would not make God his refuge,
but trusted in the abundance of his riches,
taking refuge in his destructive behavior."
8 But I am like a flourishing olive tree
in the house of God;
I trust in God's faithful love forever and ever.
9 I will praise You forever for what
You have done.
In the presence of Your faithful people,
I will put my hope in Your name,
for it is good.

Psalm 53

For the choir director: on *Mahalath*. A Davidic *Maskil.

1 The fool says in his heart,
"God does not exist."
They are corrupt, and they do vile deeds.
There is no one who does good.
2 God looks down from heaven
on the *human race
to see if there is one who is wise,
one who seeks God.
3 All have turned away;
all alike have become corrupt.
There is no one who does good,
not even one.
4 Will evildoers never understand?
They consume My people
as they consume bread;
they do not call on God.
5 Then they will be filled with terror—
terror like no other—
because God will scatter
the bones of those who besiege you.
You will put them to shame,
for God has rejected them.
6 Oh, that Israel's deliverance would come
from *Zion!
When God restores the fortunes of His people,
Jacob will rejoice; Israel will be glad.

Psalm 54

For the choir director: with stringed instruments.
A Davidic *Maskil*. When the Ziphites went and
said to Saul, "Is David not hiding among us?"

1   God, save me by Your name,
     and vindicate me by Your might!
2   God, hear my prayer;
     listen to the words of my mouth.
3   For strangers rise up against me,
     and violent men seek my life.
     They have no regard for God.   *Selah
4   God is my helper;
     the Lord is the sustainer of my life.
5   He will repay my adversaries for their evil.
     Because of Your faithfulness, annihilate them.
6   I will sacrifice a freewill offering to You.
     I will praise Your name, *Yahweh,
     because it is good.
7   For He has delivered me from every trouble,
     and my eye has looked down on my enemies.

Psalm 55

For the choir director: with stringed instruments.
A Davidic *Maskil*.

1   God, listen to my prayer
     and do not ignore my plea for help.
2   Pay attention to me and answer me.
     I am restless and in turmoil
         with my complaint,
3   because of the enemy's voice,
     because of the pressure of the wicked.
     For they bring down disaster on me
     and harass me in anger.
4   My heart shudders within me;
     terrors of death sweep over me.
5   Fear and trembling grip me;
     horror has overwhelmed me.
6   I said, "If only I had wings like a dove!
     I would fly away and find rest.
7   How far away I would flee;
     I would stay in the wilderness.   *Selah
8   I would hurry to my shelter
     from the raging wind and the storm."
9   Lord, confuse and confound their speech,
     for I see violence and strife in the city;
10   day and night they make the rounds
         on its walls.
     Crime and trouble are within it;
11   destruction is inside it;
     oppression and deceit never leave
         its marketplace.
12   Now it is not an enemy who insults me—
     otherwise I could bear it;
     it is not a foe who rises up against me—
     otherwise I could hide from him.
13   But it is you, a man who is my peer,
     my companion and good friend!
14   We used to have close fellowship;
     we walked with the crowd into the house
         of God.
15   Let death take them by surprise;
     let them go down to *Sheol alive,
     because evil is in their homes
         and within them.
16   But I call to God,
     and the Lord will save me.

17   I complain and groan morning, noon,
         and night,
     and He hears my voice.
18   Though many are against me,
     He will redeem me from my battle unharmed.
19   God, the One enthroned from long ago,
     will hear and will humiliate them   Selah
     because they do not change
     and do not *fear God.
20   My friend acts violently
     against those at peace with him;
     he violates his covenant.
21   His buttery words are smooth,
     but war is in his heart.
     His words are softer than oil,
     but they are drawn swords.
22   Cast your burden on the Lord,
     and He will sustain you;
     He will never allow the righteous
         to be shaken.
23   God, You will bring them down
     to the *Pit of destruction;
     men of bloodshed and treachery
     will not live out half their days.
     But I will trust in You.

Psalm 56

For the choir director: according to
"A Silent Dove Far Away." A Davidic *Miktam*.
When the Philistines seized him in Gath.

1   Be gracious to me, God, for man tramples me;
     he fights and oppresses me all day long.
2   My adversaries trample me all day,
     for many arrogantly fight against me.
3   When I am afraid,
     I will trust in You.
4   In God, whose word I praise,
     in God I trust; I will not fear.
     What can man do to me?
5   They twist my words all day long;
     all their thoughts against me are evil.
6   They stir up strife, they lurk;
     they watch my steps
     while they wait to take my life.
7   Will they escape in spite of such sin?
     God, bring down the nations in wrath.
8   You Yourself have recorded my wanderings.
     Put my tears in Your bottle.
     Are they not in Your records?
9   Then my enemies will retreat on the day
         when I call.
     This I know: God is for me.
10   In God, whose word I praise,
     in the Lord, whose word I praise,
11   in God I trust; I will not fear.
     What can man do to me?
12   I am obligated by vows to You, God;
     I will make my thank offerings to You.
13   For You delivered me from death,
     even my feet from stumbling,
     to walk before God in the light of life.

Psalm 57

For the choir director: "Do Not Destroy."
A Davidic *Miktam*. When he fled
before Saul into the cave.

1   Be gracious to me, God, be gracious to me,

for I take refuge in You.
I will seek refuge in the shadow of Your wings
until danger passes.
² I call to God *Most High,
to God who fulfills His purpose for me.
³ He reaches down from heaven and saves me,
challenging the one who tramples me.
*Selah

God sends His faithful love and truth.
⁴ I am surrounded by lions;
I lie down with those who devour *men.
Their teeth are spears and arrows;
their tongues are sharp swords.
⁵ God, be exalted above the heavens;
let Your glory be over the whole earth.
⁶ They prepared a net for my steps;
I was despondent.
They dug a pit ahead of me,
but they fell into it!   Selah
⁷ My heart is confident, God, my heart
is confident.
I will sing; I will sing praises.
⁸ Wake up, my soul!
Wake up, harp and lyre!
I will wake up the dawn.
⁹ I will praise You, Lord, among the peoples;
I will sing praises to You among the nations.
¹⁰ For Your faithful love is as high as
the heavens;
Your faithfulness reaches the clouds.
¹¹ God, be exalted above the heavens;
let Your glory be over the whole earth.

Psalm 58
For the choir director: "Do Not Destroy."
A Davidic *Miktam.

¹ Do you really speak righteously,
you mighty ones?
Do you judge *people fairly?
² No, you practice injustice in your hearts;
with your hands you weigh out violence
in the land.
³ The wicked go astray from the womb;
liars err from birth.
⁴ They have venom like the venom of a snake,
like the deaf cobra that stops up its ears,
⁵ that does not listen to the sound
of the charmers
who skillfully weave spells.
⁶ God, knock the teeth out of their mouths;
Lord, tear out the young lions' fangs.
⁷ They will vanish like water that flows by;
they will aim their useless arrows.
⁸ Like a slug that moves along in slime,
like a woman's miscarried child,
they will not see the sun.
⁹ Before your pots can feel the heat of
the thorns—
whether green or burning—
He will sweep them away.
¹⁰ The righteous one will rejoice
when he sees the retribution;
he will wash his feet in the blood
of the wicked.
¹¹ Then people will say,
"Yes, there is a reward for the righteous!
There is a God who judges on earth!"

Psalm 59
For the choir director: "Do Not Destroy."
A Davidic *Miktam. When Saul sent agents
to watch the house and kill him.

¹ Deliver me from my enemies, my God;
protect me from those who rise up
against me.
² Deliver me from those who practice sin,
and save me from men of bloodshed.
³ Lord, look! They set an ambush for me.
Powerful men attack me,
but not because of any sin or rebellion
of mine.
⁴ For no fault of mine,
they run and take up a position.
Awake to help me, and take notice.
⁵ Lord God of *Hosts, You are the God of Israel,
rise up to punish all the nations;
do not show grace
to any wicked traitors.   *Selah
⁶ They return at evening, snarling like dogs
and prowling around the city.
⁷ Look, they spew from their mouths—
sharp words from their lips.
"For who," they say, "will hear?"
⁸ But You laugh at them, Lord;
You ridicule all the nations.
⁹ I will keep watch for You, my strength,
because God is my stronghold.
¹⁰ My faithful God will come to meet me;
God will let me look down on my adversaries.
¹¹ Do not kill them; otherwise, my people
will forget.
By Your power, make them
homeless wanderers
and bring them down,
Lord, our shield.
¹² For the sin of their mouths and the words of
their lips,
let them be caught in their pride.
They utter curses and lies.
¹³ Consume them in rage;
consume them until they are gone.
Then people will know throughout the earth
that God rules over Jacob.   Selah
¹⁴ And they return at evening, snarling like dogs
and prowling around the city.
¹⁵ They scavenge for food;
they growl if they are not satisfied.
¹⁶ But I will sing of Your strength
and will joyfully proclaim
Your faithful love in the morning.
For You have been a stronghold for me,
a refuge in my day of trouble.
¹⁷ To You, my strength, I sing praises,
because God is my stronghold—
my faithful God.

Psalm 60
For the choir director: according to
"The Lily of Testimony." A Davidic *Miktam
for teaching. When he fought with Aram-naharaim
and Aram-zobah, and Joab returned and struck
Edom in the Valley of Salt, killing 12,000.

¹ God, You have rejected us;
You have broken out against us;
You have been angry. Restore us!

2 You have shaken the land and split it open.
Heal its fissures, for it shudders.
3 You have made Your people suffer hardship;
You have given us wine to drink
that made us stagger.
4 You have given a signal flag to those
who *fear You,
so that they can flee
before the archers.   *Selah*
5 Save with Your right hand, and answer me,
so that those You love may be rescued.
6 God has spoken in His sanctuary:
"I will triumph! I will divide up Shechem.
I will apportion the Valley of Succoth.
7 Gilead is Mine, Manasseh is Mine,
and Ephraim is My helmet;
Judah is My scepter.
8 Moab is My washbasin.
I throw My sandal on Edom;
I shout in triumph over Philistia."
9 Who will bring me to the fortified city?
Who will lead me to Edom?
10 God, haven't You rejected us?
God, You do not march out with our armies.
11 Give us aid against the foe,
for human help is worthless.
12 With God we will perform valiantly;
He will trample our foes.

Psalm 61

For the choir director:
on stringed instruments. Davidic.

1 God, hear my cry;
pay attention to my prayer.
2 I call to You from the ends of the earth
when my heart is without strength.
Lead me to a rock that is high above me,
3 for You have been a refuge for me,
a strong tower in the face of the enemy.
4 I will live in Your tent forever
and take refuge under the shelter
of Your wings.   *Selah*
5 God, You have heard my vows;
You have given a heritage
to those who *fear Your name.
6 Add days to the king's life;
may his years span many generations.
7 May he sit enthroned before God forever;
appoint faithful love and truth to guard him.
8 Then I will continually sing Your name,
fulfilling my vows day by day.

Psalm 62

For the choir director: according to Jeduthun.
A Davidic psalm.

1 I am at rest in God alone;
my salvation comes from Him.
2 He alone is my rock and my salvation,
my stronghold; I will never be shaken.
3 How long will you threaten a man?
Will all of you attack
as if he were a leaning wall
or a tottering stone fence?
4 They only plan to bring him down
from his high position.
They take pleasure in lying;
they bless with their mouths,

but they curse inwardly.   *Selah*
5 Rest in God alone, my soul,
for my hope comes from Him.
6 He alone is my rock and my salvation,
my stronghold; I will not be shaken.
7 My salvation and glory depend on God,
my strong rock.
My refuge is in God.
8 Trust in Him at all times, you people;
pour out your hearts before Him.
God is our refuge.   *Selah*
9 *Men are only a vapor;
exalted men, an illusion.
Weighed in the scales, they go up;
together they are less than a vapor.
10 Place no trust in oppression,
or false hope in robbery.
If wealth increases,
pay no attention to it.
11 God has spoken once;
I have heard this twice:
strength belongs to God,
12 and faithful love belongs to You, LORD.
For You repay each according to his works.

Psalm 63

A Davidic psalm. When he was
in the Wilderness of Judah.

1 God, You are my God; I eagerly seek You.
I thirst for You;
my body faints for You
in a land that is dry, desolate,
and without water.
2 So I gaze on You in the sanctuary
to see Your strength and Your glory.
3 My lips will glorify You
because Your faithful love is better than life.
4 So I will praise You as long as I live;
at Your name, I will lift up my hands.
5 You satisfy me as with rich food;
my mouth will praise You with joyful lips.
6 When I think of You as I lie on my bed,
I meditate on You during the night watches
7 because You are my helper;
I will rejoice in the shadow of Your wings.
8 I follow close to You;
Your right hand holds on to me.
9 But those who seek to destroy my life
will go into the depths of the earth.
10 They will be given over to the power
of the sword;
they will become the jackals' prey.
11 But the king will rejoice in God;
all who swear by Him will boast,
for the mouths of liars will be shut.

Psalm 64

For the choir director. A Davidic psalm.

1 God, hear my voice when I complain.
Protect my life from the terror of the enemy.
2 Hide me from the scheming of wicked people,
from the mob of evildoers,
3 who sharpen their tongues like swords
and aim bitter words like arrows,
4 shooting from concealed places
at the innocent.
They shoot at him suddenly and are not afraid.

5 They encourage each other in an evil plan;
    they talk about hiding traps and say,
    "Who will see them?"
6 They devise crimes and say,
    "We have perfected a secret plan."
    The inner man and the heart are mysterious.
7 But God will shoot them with arrows;
    suddenly, they will be wounded.
8 They will be made to stumble;
    their own tongues work against them.
    All who see them will shake their heads.
9 Then everyone will fear
    and will tell about God's work,
    for they will understand what He has done.
10 The righteous one rejoices in the LORD
    and takes refuge in Him;
    all those who are upright in heart
    will offer praise.

Psalm 65

For the choir director. A Davidic psalm. A song.

1 Praise is rightfully Yours,
    God, in *Zion;
    vows to You will be fulfilled.
2 All humanity will come to You,
    the One who hears prayer.
3 Iniquities overwhelm me;
    only You can *atone for our rebellions.
4 How happy is the one You choose
    and bring near to live in Your courts!
    We will be satisfied with the goodness
        of Your house,
    the holiness of Your temple.
5 You answer us in righteousness,
    with awe-inspiring works,
    God of our salvation,
    the hope of all the ends of the earth
    and of the distant seas.
6 You establish the mountains by Your power,
    robed with strength.
7 You silence the roar of the seas,
    the roar of their waves,
    and the tumult of the nations.
8 Those who live far away are awed
        by Your signs;
    You make east and west shout for joy.
9 You visit the earth and water it abundantly,
    enriching it greatly.
    God's stream is filled with water,
    for You prepare the earth in this way,
    providing people with grain.
10 You soften it with showers and bless
        its growth,
    soaking its furrows and leveling its ridges.
11 You crown the year with Your goodness;
    Your ways overflow with plenty.
12 The wilderness pastures overflow,
    and the hills are robed with joy.
13 The pastures are clothed with flocks
    and the valleys covered with grain.
    They shout in triumph; indeed, they sing.

Psalm 66

For the choir director. A song. A psalm.

1 Shout joyfully to God, all the earth!
2 Sing about the glory of His name;
    make His praise glorious.

3 Say to God, "How awe-inspiring
        are Your works!
    Your enemies will cringe before You
    because of Your great strength.
4 All the earth will worship You
    and sing praise to You.
    They will sing praise to Your name."   *Selah
5 Come and see the wonders of God;
    His acts for *humanity are awe-inspiring.
6 He turned the sea into dry land,
    and they crossed the river on foot.
    There we rejoiced in Him.
7 He rules forever by His might;
    He keeps His eye on the nations.
    The rebellious should not
        exalt themselves.   Selah
8 Praise our God, you peoples;
    let the sound of His praise be heard.
9 He keeps us alive
    and does not allow our feet to slip.
10 For You, God, tested us;
    You refined us as silver is refined.
11 You lured us into a trap;
    You placed burdens on our backs.
12 You let men ride over our heads;
    we went through fire and water,
    but You brought us out to abundance.
13 I will enter Your house with *burnt offerings;
    I will pay You my vows
14 that my lips promised
    and my mouth spoke during my distress.
15 I will offer You fattened sheep
        as burnt offerings,
    with the fragrant smoke of rams;
    I will sacrifice oxen with goats.   Selah
16 Come and listen, all who *fear God,
    and I will tell what He has done for me.
17 I cried out to Him with my mouth,
    and praise was on my tongue.
18 If I had been aware of malice in my heart,
    the Lord would not have listened.
19 However, God has listened;
    He has paid attention to the sound
        of my prayer.
20 May God be praised!
    He has not turned away my prayer
    or turned His faithful love from me.

Psalm 67

For the choir director: with stringed instruments.
A psalm. A song.

1 May God be gracious to us and bless us;
    look on us with favor   *Selah
2 so that Your way may be known on earth,
    Your salvation among all nations.
3 Let the peoples praise You, God;
    let all the peoples praise You.
4 Let the nations rejoice and shout for joy,
    for You judge the peoples with fairness
    and lead the nations on earth   Selah
5 Let the peoples praise You, God,
    let all the peoples praise You.
6 The earth has produced its harvest;
    God, our God, blesses us.
7 God will bless us,
    and all the ends of the earth will *fear Him.

Psalm 68

For the choir director. A Davidic psalm. A song.

1 God arises. His enemies scatter,
    and those who hate Him flee
        from His presence.
2 As smoke is blown away,
    so You blow them away.
    As wax melts before the fire,
    so the wicked are destroyed before God.
3 But the righteous are glad;
    they rejoice before God and celebrate with joy.
4 Sing to God! Sing praises to His name.
    Exalt Him who rides on the clouds —
    His name is *Yahweh—and rejoice before Him.
5 God in His holy dwelling is
    a father of the fatherless
    and a champion of widows.
6 God provides homes for those
        who are deserted.
    He leads out the prisoners to prosperity,
    but the rebellious live in a scorched land.
7 God, when You went out before Your people,
    when You marched
        through the desert,　　　　*Selah
8 the earth trembled and the skies
        poured down rain
    before God, the God of Sinai,
    before God, the God of Israel.
9 You, God, showered abundant rain;
    You revived Your inheritance
        when it languished.
10 Your people settled in it;
    God, You provided for the poor
        by Your goodness.
11 The Lord gave the command;
    a great company of women brought
        the good news:
12 "The kings of the armies flee—they flee!"
    She who stays at home divides the spoil.
13 While you lie among the sheepfolds,
    the wings of a dove are covered with silver,
    and its feathers with glistening gold.
14 When the *Almighty scattered kings
        in the land,
    it snowed on Zalmon.
15 Mount Bashan is God's towering mountain;
    Mount Bashan is a mountain of many peaks.
16 Why gaze with envy, you mountain peaks,
    at the mountain God desired for His dwelling?
    The Lord will live there forever!
17 God's chariots are tens of thousands,
    thousands and thousands;
    the Lord is among them in the sanctuary
    as He was at Sinai.
18 You ascended to the heights,
        taking away captives;
    You received gifts from people,
    even from the rebellious,
    so that the Lord God might live there.
19 May the Lord be praised!
    Day after day He bears our burdens;
    God is our salvation.　　　　*Selah*
20 Our God is a God of salvation,
    and escape from death belongs
        to the Lord God.
21 Surely God crushes the heads of His enemies,

the hairy head of one who goes on
    in his *guilty acts.
22 The Lord said, "I will bring them back
        from Bashan;
    I will bring them back from the depths
        of the sea
23 so that your foot may wade in blood
    and your dogs' tongues may have their share
    from the enemies."
24 People have seen Your procession, God,
    the procession of my God,
    my King, in the sanctuary.
25 Singers lead the way,
    with musicians following;
    among them are young women
    playing tambourines.
26 Praise God in the assemblies;
    praise the Lord from the fountain of Israel.
27 There is Benjamin, the youngest,
        leading them,
    the rulers of Judah in their assembly,
    the rulers of Zebulun, the rulers of Naphtali.
28 Your God has decreed your strength.
    Show Your strength, God,
    You who have acted on our behalf.
29 Because of Your temple at Jerusalem,
    kings will bring tribute to You.
30 Rebuke the beast in the reeds,
    the herd of bulls with the calves
        of the peoples.
    Trample underfoot those with bars of silver.
    Scatter the peoples who take pleasure in war.
31 Ambassadors will come from Egypt;
    *Cush will stretch out its hands to God.
32 Sing to God, you kingdoms of the earth;
    sing praise to the Lord,　　　　*Selah*
33 to Him who rides in the ancient,
        highest heavens.
    Look, He thunders with His powerful voice!
34 Ascribe power to God.
    His majesty is over Israel,
    His power among the clouds.
35 God, You are awe-inspiring
        in Your sanctuaries.
    The God of Israel gives power and strength
        to His people.
    May God be praised!

Psalm 69

For the choir director: according to
"The Lilies." Davidic.

1 Save me, God,
    for the water has risen to my neck.
2 I have sunk in deep mud, and there is
        no footing;
    I have come into deep waters,
    and a flood sweeps over me.
3 I am weary from my crying;
    my throat is parched.
    My eyes fail, looking for my God.
4 Those who hate me without cause
    are more numerous than the hairs
        of my head;
    my deceitful enemies, who would destroy me,
    are powerful.
    Though I did not steal, I must repay.
5 God, You know my foolishness,

and my *guilty acts are not hidden from You.

6 Do not let those who put their hope in You
be disgraced because of me,
Lord God of *Hosts;
do not let those who seek You
be humiliated because of me,
God of Israel.

7 For I have endured insults because of You,
and shame has covered my face.

8 I have become a stranger to my brothers
and a foreigner to my mother's sons

9 because zeal for Your house
has consumed me,
and the insults of those who insult You
have fallen on me.

10 I mourned and fasted,
but it brought me insults.

11 I wore *sackcloth as my clothing,
and I was a joke to them.

12 Those who sit at the city *gate talk about me,
and drunkards make up songs about me.

13 But as for me, Lord,
my prayer to You is for a time of favor.
In Your abundant, faithful love, God,
answer me with Your sure salvation.

14 Rescue me from the miry mud;
don't let me sink.
Let me be rescued from those who hate me
and from the deep waters.

15 Don't let the floodwaters sweep over me
or the deep swallow me up;
don't let the *Pit close its mouth over me.

16 Answer me, Lord,
for Your faithful love is good;
in keeping with Your great compassion,
turn to me.

17 Don't hide Your face from Your servant,
for I am in distress.
Answer me quickly!

18 Draw near to me and redeem me;
ransom me because of my enemies.

19 You know the insults I endure—
my shame and disgrace.
You are aware of all my adversaries.

20 Insults have broken my heart,
and I am in despair.
I waited for sympathy,
but there was none;
for comforters, but found no one.

21 Instead, they gave me gall for my food,
and for my thirst
they gave me vinegar to drink.

22 Let their table set before them be a snare,
and let it be a trap for their allies.

23 Let their eyes grow too dim to see,
and let their loins continually shake.

24 Pour out Your rage on them,
and let Your burning anger overtake them.

25 Make their fortification desolate;
may no one live in their tents.

26 For they persecute the one You struck
and talk about the pain of those You wounded.

27 Add guilt to their guilt;
do not let them share in Your righteousness.

28 Let them be erased from the book of life
and not be recorded with the righteous.

29 But as for me—poor and in pain—

let Your salvation protect me, God.

30 I will praise God's name with song
and exalt Him with thanksgiving.

31 That will please *Yahweh more than an ox,
more than a bull with horns and hooves.

32 The humble will see it and rejoice.
You who seek God, take heart!

33 For the Lord listens to the needy
and does not despise
His own who are prisoners.

34 Let heaven and earth praise Him,
the seas and everything that moves in them,

35 for God will save *Zion
and build up the cities of Judah.
They will live there and possess it.

36 The descendants of His servants will inherit it,
and those who love His name will live in it.

Psalm 70

For the choir director. Davidic.
To bring remembrance.

1 God, deliver me.
Hurry to help me, Lord!

2 Let those who seek my life
be disgraced and confounded;
let those who wish me harm
be driven back and humiliated.

3 Let those who say, "Aha, aha!"
retreat because of their shame.

4 Let all who seek You rejoice and be glad
in You;
let those who love Your salvation
continually say, "God is great!"

5 I am afflicted and needy;
hurry to me, God.
You are my help and my deliverer;
Lord, do not delay.

Psalm 71

1 Lord, I seek refuge in You;
let me never be disgraced.

2 In Your justice, rescue and deliver me;
listen closely to me and save me.

3 Be a rock of refuge for me,
where I can always go.
Give the command to save me,
for You are my rock and fortress.

4 Deliver me, my God, from the power
of the wicked,
from the grasp of the unjust and oppressive.

5 For You are my hope, Lord God,
my confidence from my youth.

6 I have leaned on You from birth;
You took me from my mother's womb.
My praise is always about You.

7 I have become an ominous sign to many,
but You are my strong refuge.

8 My mouth is full of praise
and honor to You all day long.

9 Don't discard me in my old age;
as my strength fails, do not abandon me.

10 For my enemies talk about me,
and those who spy on me plot together,

11 saying, "God has abandoned him;
chase him and catch him,
for there is no one to rescue him."

12 God, do not be far from me;
my God, hurry to help me.

13 May my adversaries be disgraced
   and destroyed;
   may those who seek my harm
   be covered with disgrace and humiliation.
14 But I will hope continually
   and will praise You more and more.
15 My mouth will tell about Your righteousness
   and Your salvation all day long,
   though I cannot sum them up.
16 I come because of the mighty acts
   of the Lord God;
   I will proclaim Your righteousness,
   Yours alone.
17 God, You have taught me from my youth,
   and I still proclaim Your wonderful works.
18 Even when I am old and gray,
   God, do not abandon me.
   Then I will proclaim Your power
   to another generation,
   Your strength to all who are to come.
19 Your righteousness reaches heaven, God,
   You who have done great things;
   God, who is like You?
20 You caused me to experience
   many troubles and misfortunes,
   but You will revive me again.
   You will bring me up again,
   even from the depths of the earth.
21 You will increase my honor
   and comfort me once again.
22 Therefore, I will praise You with a harp
   for Your faithfulness, my God;
   I will sing to You with a lyre,
   Holy One of Israel.
23 My lips will shout for joy
   when I sing praise to You
   because You have redeemed me.
24 Therefore, my tongue will proclaim
   Your righteousness all day long,
   for those who seek my harm
   will be disgraced and confounded.

Psalm 72
Solomonic.

1 God, give Your justice to the king
  and Your righteousness to the king's son.
2 He will judge Your people with righteousness
  and Your afflicted ones with justice.
3 May the mountains bring prosperity
  to the people
  and the hills, righteousness.
4 May he vindicate the afflicted
  among the people,
  help the poor,
  and crush the oppressor.
5 May he continue while the sun endures
  and as long as the moon,
  throughout all generations.
6 May he be like rain that falls on the cut grass,
  like spring showers that water the earth.
7 May the righteous flourish in his days
  and prosperity abound
  until the moon is no more.
8 May he rule from sea to sea
  and from the Euphrates
  to the ends of the earth.
9 May desert tribes kneel before him

and his enemies lick the dust.
10 May the kings of Tarshish
   and the coasts and islands bring tribute,
   the kings of Sheba and Seba offer gifts.
11 Let all kings bow down to him,
   all nations serve him.
12 For he will rescue the poor who cry out
   and the afflicted who have no helper.
13 He will have pity on the poor and helpless
   and save the lives of the poor.
14 He will redeem them from oppression
   and violence,
   for their lives are precious in his sight.
15 May he live long!
   May gold from Sheba be given to him.
   May prayer be offered for him continually,
   and may he be blessed all day long.
16 May there be plenty of grain in the land;
   may it wave on the tops of the mountains.
   May its crops be like Lebanon.
   May people flourish in the cities
   like the grass of the field.
17 May his name endure forever;
   as long as the sun shines,
   may his fame increase.
   May all nations be blessed by him
   and call him blessed.
18 May the Lord God, the God of Israel,
   who alone does wonders, be praised.
19 May His glorious name be praised forever;
   the whole earth is filled with His glory.
   ·Amen and amen.
20 The prayers of David son of Jesse
   are concluded.

BOOK III
(Psalms 73-89)

Psalm 73
A psalm of ·Asaph.

1 God is indeed good to Israel,
  to the pure in heart.
2 But as for me, my feet almost slipped;
  my steps nearly went astray.
3 For I envied the arrogant;
  I saw the prosperity of the wicked.
4 They have an easy time until they die,
  and their bodies are well fed.
5 They are not in trouble like others;
  they are not afflicted like most people.
6 Therefore, pride is their necklace,
  and violence covers them like a garment.
7 Their eyes bulge out from fatness;
  the imaginations of their hearts run wild.
8 They mock, and they speak maliciously;
  they arrogantly threaten oppression.
9 They set their mouths against heaven,
  and their tongues strut across the earth.
10 Therefore His people turn to them
   and drink in their overflowing words.
11 The wicked say, "How can God know?
   Does the ·Most High know everything?"
12 Look at them—the wicked!
   They are always at ease,
   and they increase their wealth.
13 Did I purify my heart

and wash my hands in innocence for nothing?

14 For I am afflicted all day long
and punished every morning.

15 If I had decided to say these things aloud,
I would have betrayed Your people.

16 When I tried to understand all this,
it seemed hopeless

17 until I entered God's sanctuary.
Then I understood their destiny.

18 Indeed, You put them in slippery places;
You make them fall into ruin.

19 How suddenly they become a desolation!
They come to an end, swept away by terrors.

20 Like one waking from a dream,
Lord, when arising, You will despise
their image.

21 When I became embittered
and my innermost being was wounded,

22 I was stupid and didn't understand;
I was an unthinking animal toward You.

23 Yet I am always with You;
You hold my right hand.

24 You guide me with Your counsel,
and afterward You will take me up in glory.

25 Who do I have in heaven but You?
And I desire nothing on earth but You.

26 My flesh and my heart may fail,
but God is the strength of my heart,
my portion forever.

27 Those far from You will certainly perish;
You destroy all who are unfaithful to You.

28 But as for me, God's presence is my good.
I have made the Lord GOD my refuge,
so I can tell about all You do.

Psalm 74

A *Maskil* of *Asaph.

1 Why have You rejected us forever, God?
Why does Your anger burn
against the sheep of Your pasture?

2 Remember Your congregation,
which You purchased long ago
and redeemed as the tribe
for Your own possession.
Remember Mount *Zion where You dwell.

3 Make Your way to the everlasting ruins,
to all that the enemy has destroyed
in the sanctuary.

4 Your adversaries roared in the meeting place
where You met with us.
They set up their emblems as signs.

5 It was like men in a thicket of trees,
wielding axes,

6 then smashing all the carvings
with hatchets and picks.

7 They set Your sanctuary on fire;
they utterly desecrated
the dwelling place of Your name.

8 They said in their hearts,
"Let us oppress them relentlessly."
They burned down every place
throughout the land
where God met with us.

9 There are no signs for us to see.
There is no longer a prophet.
And none of us knows how long this will last.

10 God, how long will the enemy mock?

Will the foe insult Your name forever?

11 Why do You hold back Your hand?
Stretch out Your right hand and destroy them!

12 God my King is from ancient times,
performing saving acts on the earth.

13 You divided the sea with Your strength;
You smashed the heads of the sea monsters
in the waters;

14 You crushed the heads of *Leviathan;
You fed him to the creatures of the desert.

15 You opened up springs and streams;
You dried up ever-flowing rivers.

16 The day is Yours, also the night;
You established the moon and the sun.

17 You set all the boundaries of the earth;
You made summer and winter.

18 Remember this: the enemy
has mocked *Yahweh,
and a foolish people has insulted Your name.

19 Do not give the life of Your dove to beasts;
do not forget the lives
of Your poor people forever.

20 Consider the covenant,
for the dark places of the land
are full of violence.

21 Do not let the oppressed turn away in shame;
let the poor and needy praise Your name.

22 Rise up, God, defend Your cause!
Remember the insults
that fools bring against You all day long.

23 Do not forget the clamor of Your adversaries,
the tumult of Your opponents
that goes up constantly.

Psalm 75

For the choir director: "Do Not Destroy."
A psalm of *Asaph. A song.

1 We give thanks to You, God;
we give thanks to You, for Your name is near.
People tell about Your wonderful works.

2 "When I choose a time,
I will judge fairly.

3 When the earth and all its inhabitants shake,
I am the One who steadies its pillars.   *Selah

4 I say to the boastful, 'Do not boast,'
and to the wicked, 'Do not lift up your *horn.

5 Do not lift up your horn against heaven
or speak arrogantly.'"

6 Exaltation does not come
from the east, the west, or the desert,

7 for God is the Judge:
He brings down one and exalts another.

8 For there is a cup in the LORD's hand,
full of wine blended with spices, and He pours
from it.
All the wicked of the earth will drink,
draining it to the dregs.

9 As for me, I will tell about Him forever;
I will sing praise to the God of Jacob.

10 "I will cut off all the horns of the wicked,
but the horns of the righteous will be
lifted up."

Psalm 76

For the choir director: with stringed instruments.
A psalm of *Asaph. A song.

1 God is known in Judah;

His name is great in Israel.
2 His tent is in Salem,
His dwelling place in •Zion.
3 There He shatters the bow's flaming arrows,
the shield, the sword, and the weapons of war.
•*Selah*
4 You are resplendent and majestic
coming down from the mountains of prey.
5 The brave-hearted have been plundered;
they have slipped into their final sleep.
None of the warriors was able to lift a hand.
6 At Your rebuke, God of Jacob,
both chariot and horse lay still.
7 And You—You are to be •feared.
When You are angry,
who can stand before You?
8 From heaven You pronounced judgment.
The earth feared and grew quiet
9 when God rose up to judge
and to save all the lowly of the earth.   *Selah*
10 Even human wrath will praise You;
You will clothe Yourself
with their remaining wrath.
11 Make and keep your vows
to the Lord your God;
let all who are around Him bring tribute
to the awe-inspiring One.
12 He humbles the spirit of leaders;
He is feared by the kings of the earth.

Psalm 77

For the choir director: according to
Jeduthun. Of •Asaph. A psalm.

1 I cry aloud to God,
aloud to God, and He will hear me.
2 I sought the Lord in my day of trouble.
My hands were continually lifted up
all night long;
I refused to be comforted.
3 I think of God; I groan;
I meditate; my spirit becomes weak.   •*Selah*
4 You have kept me from closing my eyes;
I am troubled and cannot speak.
5 I consider days of old,
years long past.
6 At night I remember my music;
I meditate in my heart, and my spirit ponders.
7 "Will the Lord reject forever
and never again show favor?
8 Has His faithful love ceased forever?
Is His promise at an end for all generations?
9 Has God forgotten to be gracious?
Has He in anger
withheld His compassion?"   *Selah*
10 So I say, "I am grieved
that the right hand of the •Most High
has changed."
11 I will remember the Lord's works;
yes, I will remember Your ancient wonders.
12 I will reflect on all You have done
and meditate on Your actions.
13 God, Your way is holy.
What god is great like God?
14 You are the God who works wonders;
You revealed Your strength
among the peoples.
15 With power You redeemed Your people,

the descendants of Jacob and Joseph.   *Selah*
16 The waters saw You, God.
The waters saw You; they trembled.
Even the depths shook.
17 The clouds poured down water.
The storm clouds thundered;
Your arrows flashed back and forth.
18 The sound of Your thunder was
in the whirlwind;
lightning lit up the world.
The earth shook and quaked.
19 Your way went through the sea
and Your path through the great waters,
but Your footprints were unseen.
20 You led Your people like a flock
by the hand of Moses and Aaron.

Psalm 78

A •*Maskil* of •Asaph.

1 My people, hear my instruction;
listen to what I say.
2 I will declare wise sayings;
I will speak mysteries from the past—
3 things we have heard and known
and that our fathers have passed down to us.
4 We must not hide them from their children,
but must tell a future generation
the praises of the Lord,
His might, and the wonderful works
He has performed.
5 He established a •testimony in Jacob
and set up a law in Israel,
which He commanded our fathers
to teach to their children
6 so that a future generation—
children yet to be born—might know.
They were to rise and tell their children
7 so that they might put their confidence
in God
and not forget God's works,
but keep His commands.
8 Then they would not be like their fathers,
a stubborn and rebellious generation,
a generation whose heart was not loyal
and whose spirit was not faithful to God.
9 The Ephraimite archers turned back
on the day of battle.
10 They did not keep God's covenant
and refused to live by His law.
11 They forgot what He had done,
the wonderful works He had shown them.
12 He worked wonders in the sight of
their fathers
in the land of Egypt, the region of Zoan.
13 He split the sea and brought them across;
the water stood firm like a wall.
14 He led them with a cloud by day
and with a fiery light throughout the night.
15 He split rocks in the wilderness
and gave them drink as abundant
as the depths.
16 He brought streams out of the stone
and made water flow down like rivers.
17 But they continued to sin against Him,
rebelling in the desert against the •Most High.
18 They deliberately tested God,
demanding the food they craved.

¹⁹ They spoke against God, saying,
"Is God able to provide food in the wilderness?
²⁰ Look! He struck the rock and water
　gushed out;
torrents overflowed.
But can He also provide bread
or furnish meat for His people?"
²¹ Therefore, the LORD heard and became furious;
then fire broke out against Jacob,
and anger flared up against Israel
²² because they did not believe God
or rely on His salvation.
²³ He gave a command to the clouds above
and opened the doors of heaven.
²⁴ He rained manna for them to eat;
He gave them grain from heaven.
²⁵ People ate the bread of angels.
He sent them an abundant supply of food.
²⁶ He made the east wind blow in the skies
and drove the south wind by His might.
²⁷ He rained meat on them like dust,
and winged birds like the sand of the seas.
²⁸ He made them fall in His camp,
all around His tent.
²⁹ They ate and were completely satisfied,
for He gave them what they craved.
³⁰ Before they had satisfied their desire,
while the food was still in their mouths,
³¹ God's anger flared up against them,
and He killed some of their best men.
He struck down Israel's choice young men.
³² Despite all this, they kept sinning
and did not believe His wonderful works.
³³ He made their days end in futility,
their years in sudden disaster.
³⁴ When He killed some of them,
the rest began to seek Him;
they repented and searched for God.
³⁵ They remembered that God was their rock,
the Most High God, their Redeemer.
³⁶ But they deceived Him with their mouths,
they lied to Him with their tongues,
³⁷ their hearts were insincere toward Him,
and they were unfaithful to His covenant.
³⁸ Yet He was compassionate;
He *atoned for their *guilt
and did not destroy them.
He often turned His anger aside
and did not unleash all His wrath.
³⁹ He remembered that they were only flesh,
a wind that passes and does not return.
⁴⁰ How often they rebelled against Him
in the wilderness
and grieved Him in the desert.
⁴¹ They constantly tested God
and provoked the Holy One of Israel.
⁴² They did not remember His power shown
on the day He redeemed them from the foe,
⁴³ when He performed His miraculous signs
in Egypt
and His wonders in the region of Zoan.
⁴⁴ He turned their rivers into blood,
and they could not drink from their streams.
⁴⁵ He sent among them swarms of flies,
which fed on them,
and frogs, which devastated them.
⁴⁶ He gave their crops to the caterpillar

and the fruit of their labor to the locust.
⁴⁷ He killed their vines with hail
and their sycamore fig trees with a flood.
⁴⁸ He handed over their livestock to hail
and their cattle to lightning bolts.
⁴⁹ He sent His burning anger against them:
fury, indignation, and calamity—
a band of deadly messengers.
⁵⁰ He cleared a path for His anger.
He did not spare them from death
but delivered their lives to the plague.
⁵¹ He struck all the firstborn in Egypt,
the first progeny of the tents of Ham.
⁵² He led His people out like sheep
and guided them like a flock in the wilderness.
⁵³ He led them safely, and they were not afraid;
but the sea covered their enemies.
⁵⁴ He brought them to His holy land,
to the mountain His right hand acquired.
⁵⁵ He drove out nations before them.
He apportioned their inheritance by lot
and settled the tribes of Israel in their tents.
⁵⁶ But they rebelliously tested
the Most High God,
for they did not keep His decrees.
⁵⁷ They treacherously turned away
like their fathers;
they became warped like a faulty bow.
⁵⁸ They enraged Him with their *high places
and provoked His jealousy
with their carved images.
⁵⁹ God heard and became furious;
He completely rejected Israel.
⁶⁰ He abandoned the tabernacle at Shiloh,
the tent where He resided among men.
⁶¹ He gave up His strength to captivity
and His splendor to the hand of a foe.
⁶² He surrendered His people to the sword
because He was enraged with His heritage.
⁶³ Fire consumed His chosen young men,
and His young women had no wedding songs.
⁶⁴ His priests fell by the sword,
but the widows could not lament.
⁶⁵ Then the Lord awoke as if from sleep,
like a warrior from the effects of wine.
⁶⁶ He beat back His foes;
He gave them lasting shame.
⁶⁷ He rejected the tent of Joseph
and did not choose the tribe of Ephraim.
⁶⁸ He chose instead the tribe of Judah,
Mount *Zion, which He loved.
⁶⁹ He built His sanctuary like the heights,
like the earth that He established forever.
⁷⁰ He chose David His servant
and took him from the sheepfolds;
⁷¹ He brought him from tending ewes
to be shepherd over His people Jacob—
over Israel, His inheritance.
⁷² He shepherded them with a pure heart
and guided them with his skillful hands.

Psalm 79
A psalm of *Asaph.

¹ God, the nations have invaded
Your inheritance,
desecrated Your holy temple,
and turned Jerusalem into ruins.

2 They gave the corpses of Your servants
  to the birds of the sky for food,
  the flesh of Your godly ones
  to the beasts of the earth.
3 They poured out their blood
  like water all around Jerusalem,
  and there was no one to bury them.
4 We have become an object of reproach
  to our neighbors,
  a source of mockery and ridicule
  to those around us.
5 How long, •Yahweh? Will You be angry forever?
  Will Your jealousy keep burning
    like fire?
6 Pour out Your wrath on the nations
  that don't acknowledge You,
  on the kingdoms that don't call on
    Your name,
7 for they have devoured Jacob
  and devastated his homeland.
8 Do not hold past sins against us;
  let Your compassion come
    to us quickly,
  for we have become weak.
9 God of our salvation, help us—
  for the glory of Your name.
  Deliver us and •atone for our sins,
  because of Your name.
10 Why should the nations ask,
  "Where is their God?"
  Before our eyes,
  let vengeance for the shed blood
    of Your servants
  be known among the nations.
11 Let the groans of the prisoners reach You;
  according to Your great power,
  preserve those condemned to die.
12 Pay back sevenfold to our neighbors
  the reproach they have hurled at You, Lord.
13 Then we, Your people, the sheep
  of Your pasture,
  will thank You forever;
  we will declare Your praise
  to generation after generation.

Psalm 80

For the choir director: according to "The Lilies."
A testimony of •Asaph. A psalm.

1 Listen, Shepherd of Israel,
  who leads Joseph like a flock;
  You who sit enthroned on the •cherubim,
  rise up
2 before Ephraim,
  Benjamin, and Manasseh.
  Rally Your power and come to save us.
3 Restore us, God;
  look on us with favor,
  and we will be saved.
4 Lord God of •Hosts,
  how long will You be angry
  with Your people's prayers?
5 You fed them the bread of tears
  and gave them a full measure
  of tears to drink.
6 You make us quarrel with our neighbors;
  our enemies make fun of us.
7 Restore us, God of Hosts;

  look on us with favor, and we will be saved.
8 You uprooted a vine from Egypt;
  You drove out the nations and planted it.
9 You cleared a place for it;
  it took root and filled the land.
10 The mountains were covered by its shade,
  and the mighty cedars with its branches.
11 It sent out sprouts toward the Sea
  and shoots toward the River.
12 Why have You broken down its walls
  so that all who pass by pick its fruit?
13 The boar from the forest tears it
  and creatures of the field feed on it.
14 Return, God of Hosts.
  Look down from heaven and see;
  take care of this vine,
15 the root Your right hand has planted,
  the shoot that You made strong for Yourself.
16 It was cut down and burned up;
  they perish at the rebuke
    of Your countenance.
17 Let Your hand be with the man
    at Your right hand,
  with the son of man
  You have made strong for Yourself.
18 Then we will not turn away from You;
  revive us, and we will call on Your name.
19 Restore us, •Yahweh, the God of Hosts;
  look on us with favor, and we will be saved.

Psalm 81

For the choir director: on the •*Gittith.* Of •Asaph.

1 Sing for joy to God our strength;
  shout in triumph to the God of Jacob.
2 Lift up a song—play the tambourine,
  the melodious lyre, and the harp.
3 Blow the horn on the day of our feasts
  during the new moon
  and during the full moon.
4 For this is a statute for Israel,
  a judgment of the God of Jacob.
5 He set it up as an ordinance for Joseph
  when He went throughout the land of Egypt.
  I heard an unfamiliar language:
6 "I relieved his shoulder from the burden;
  his hands were freed from carrying the basket.
7 You called out in distress, and I rescued you;
  I answered you from the thundercloud.
  I tested you at the waters of Meribah.   •*Selah*
8 Listen, My people, and I will admonish you.
  Israel, if you would only listen to Me!
9 There must not be a strange god
    among you;
  you must not bow down to a foreign god.
10 I am •Yahweh your God,
  who brought you up from the land of Egypt.
  Open your mouth wide, and I will fill it.
11 But My people did not listen to Me;
  Israel did not obey Me.
12 So I gave them over to their stubborn hearts
  to follow their own plans.
13 If only My people would listen to Me
  and Israel would follow My ways,
14 I would quickly subdue their enemies
  and turn My hand against their foes."
15 Those who hate the Lord
  would pretend submission to Him;

their doom would last forever.
16 But He would feed Israel with the best wheat.
"I would satisfy you with honey
from the rock."

Psalm 82
A psalm of *Asaph.

1 God has taken His place
in the divine assembly;
He judges among the gods:
2 "How long will you judge unjustly
and show partiality to the wicked?　　*Selah
3 Provide justice for the needy
and the fatherless;
uphold the rights of the oppressed
and the destitute.
4 Rescue the poor and needy;
save them from the power of the wicked."
5 They do not know or understand;
they wander in darkness.
All the foundations of the earth are shaken.
6 I said, "You are gods;
you are all sons of the *Most High.
7 However, you will die like men
and fall like any other ruler."
8 Rise up, God, judge the earth,
for all the nations belong to You.

Psalm 83
A song. A psalm of *Asaph.

1 God, do not keep silent.
Do not be deaf, God; do not be idle.
2 See how Your enemies make an uproar;
those who hate You have acted arrogantly.
3 They devise clever schemes
against Your people;
they conspire against Your treasured ones.
4 They say, "Come, let us wipe them out
as a nation
so that Israel's name will no longer
be remembered."
5 For they have conspired with one mind;
they form an alliance against You—
6 the tents of Edom and the Ishmaelites,
Moab and the Hagrites,
7 Gebal, Ammon, and Amalek,
Philistia with the inhabitants of Tyre.
8 Even Assyria has joined them;
they lend support to the sons of Lot.　　*Selah
9 Deal with them as You did with Midian,
as You did with Sisera
and Jabin at the Kishon River.
10 They were destroyed at En-dor;
they became manure for the ground.
11 Make their nobles like Oreb and Zeeb,
and all their tribal leaders like Zebah
and Zalmunna,
12 who said, "Let us seize God's pastures
for ourselves."
13 Make them like tumbleweed, my God,
like straw before the wind.
14 As fire burns a forest,
as a flame blazes through mountains,
15 so pursue them with Your tempest
and terrify them with Your storm.
16 Cover their faces with shame
so that they will seek Your name *Yahweh.

17 Let them be put to shame
and terrified forever;
let them perish in disgrace.
18 May they know that You alone—
whose name is Yahweh—
are the *Most High over all the earth.

Psalm 84
For the choir director: on the *Gittith.
A psalm of the sons of Korah.

1 How lovely is Your dwelling place,
LORD of *Hosts.
2 I long and yearn
for the courts of the LORD;
my heart and flesh cry out for the living God.
3 Even a sparrow finds a home,
and a swallow, a nest for herself
where she places her young—
near Your altars, LORD of Hosts,
my King and my God.
4 How happy are those who reside
in Your house,
who praise You continually.　　*Selah
5 Happy are the people whose strength is
in You,
whose hearts are set on pilgrimage.
6 As they pass through the Valley of Baca,
they make it a source of springwater;
even the autumn rain will cover it
with blessings.
7 They go from strength to strength;
each appears before God in *Zion.
8 LORD God of Hosts, hear my prayer;
listen, God of Jacob.　　Selah
9 Consider our shield, God;
look on the face of Your anointed one.
10 Better a day in Your courts
than a thousand anywhere else.
I would rather be at the door of the house
of my God
than to live in the tents of wicked people.
11 For the LORD God is a sun and shield.
The LORD gives grace and glory;
He does not withhold the good
from those who live with integrity.
12 Happy is the person who trusts in You,
LORD of Hosts!

Psalm 85
For the choir director. A psalm of the sons of Korah.

1 LORD, You showed favor to Your land;
You restored Jacob's prosperity.
2 You took away Your people's *guilt;
You covered all their sin.　　*Selah
3 You withdrew all Your fury;
You turned from Your burning anger.
4 Return to us, God of our salvation,
and abandon Your displeasure with us.
5 Will You be angry with us forever?
Will You prolong Your anger for all
generations?
6 Will You not revive us again
so that Your people may rejoice in You?
7 Show us Your faithful love, LORD,
and give us Your salvation.
8 I will listen to what God will say;
surely the LORD will declare peace

to His people, His godly ones,
and not let them go back to foolish ways.
⁹ His salvation is very near
   those who ˙fear Him,
so that glory may dwell in our land.
¹⁰ Faithful love and truth will join together;
righteousness and peace will embrace.
¹¹ Truth will spring up from the earth,
and righteousness will look
   down from heaven.
¹² Also, the LORD will provide what is good,
and our land will yield its crops.
¹³ Righteousness will go before Him
to prepare the way for His steps.

Psalm 86
A Davidic prayer.

¹ Listen, LORD, and answer me,
for I am poor and needy.
² Protect my life, for I am faithful.
You are my God; save Your servant who trusts
   in You.
³ Be gracious to me, Lord,
for I call to You all day long.
⁴ Bring joy to Your servant's life,
because I turn to You, Lord.
⁵ For You, Lord, are kind and ready to forgive,
rich in faithful love to all who call on You.
⁶ LORD, hear my prayer;
listen to my plea for mercy.
⁷ I call on You in the day of my distress,
for You will answer me.
⁸ Lord, there is no one like You among the gods,
and there are no works like Yours.
⁹ All the nations You have made
will come and bow down before You, Lord,
and will honor Your name.
¹⁰ For You are great and perform wonders;
You alone are God.
¹¹ Teach me Your way, ˙Yahweh,
and I will live by Your truth.
Give me an undivided mind to ˙fear
   Your name.
¹² I will praise You with all my heart,
   Lord my God,
and will honor Your name forever.
¹³ For Your faithful love for me is great,
and You deliver my life from the depths
   of ˙Sheol.
¹⁴ God, arrogant people have attacked me;
a gang of ruthless men seeks my life.
They have no regard for You.
¹⁵ But You, Lord, are a compassionate
   and gracious God,
slow to anger and rich in faithful love
   and truth.
¹⁶ Turn to me and be gracious to me.
Give Your strength to Your servant;
save the son of Your female servant.
¹⁷ Show me a sign of Your goodness;
my enemies will see and be put to shame
because You, LORD, have helped
   and comforted me.

Psalm 87
A psalm of the sons of Korah. A song.

¹ His foundation is on the holy mountains.

² The LORD loves the gates of ˙Zion
more than all the dwellings of Jacob.
³ Glorious things are said about you,
   city of God.   ˙*Selah*
⁴ "I will mention those who know Me:
˙Rahab, Babylon, Philistia, Tyre, and ˙Cush—
each one was born there."
⁵ And it will be said of Zion,
"This one and that one were born in her."
The ˙Most High Himself will establish her.
⁶ When He registers the peoples,
the LORD will record,
"This one was born there."   *Selah*
⁷ Singers and dancers alike will say,
"My whole source of joy is in you."

Psalm 88
A song. A psalm of the sons of Korah.
For the choir director: according to *Mahalath
Leannoth*. A ˙*Maskil* of Heman the Ezrahite.

¹ LORD, God of my salvation,
I cry out before You day and night.
² May my prayer reach Your presence;
listen to my cry.
³ For I have had enough troubles,
and my life is near ˙Sheol.
⁴ I am counted among those going down
   to the ˙Pit.
I am like a man without strength,
⁵ abandoned among the dead.
I am like the slain lying in the grave,
whom You no longer remember,
and who are cut off from Your care.
⁶ You have put me in the lowest part of the Pit,
in the darkest places, in the depths.
⁷ Your wrath weighs heavily on me;
You have overwhelmed me with all
   Your waves.   ˙*Selah*
⁸ You have distanced my friends from me;
You have made me repulsive to them.
I am shut in and cannot go out.
⁹ My eyes are worn out from crying.
LORD, I cry out to You all day long;
I spread out my hands to You.
¹⁰ Do You work wonders for the dead?
Do departed spirits rise up
   to praise You?   *Selah*
¹¹ Will Your faithful love be declared
   in the grave,
Your faithfulness in ˙Abaddon?
¹² Will Your wonders be known in the darkness
or Your righteousness in the land of oblivion?
¹³ But I call to You for help, LORD;
in the morning my prayer meets You.
¹⁴ LORD, why do You reject me?
Why do You hide Your face from me?
¹⁵ From my youth,
I have been afflicted and near death.
I suffer Your horrors; I am desperate.
¹⁶ Your wrath sweeps over me;
Your terrors destroy me.
¹⁷ They surround me like water all day long;
they close in on me from every side.
¹⁸ You have distanced loved one and neighbor
   from me;
darkness is my only friend.

Psalm 89

A *Maskil of Ethan the Ezrahite.

1 I will sing about the LORD's
     faithful love forever;
  I will proclaim Your faithfulness to all
     generations
  with my mouth.
2 For I will declare,
  "Faithful love is built up forever;
  You establish Your faithfulness
     in the heavens."
3 The LORD said,
  "I have made a covenant with My chosen one;
  I have sworn an oath to David My servant:
4 'I will establish your offspring forever
  and build up your throne for all generations.'"
                                           *Selah
5 LORD, the heavens praise Your wonders—
  Your faithfulness also—
     in the assembly of the holy ones.
6 For who in the skies can compare
     with the LORD?
  Who among the heavenly beings is
     like the LORD?
7 God is greatly *feared in the council
     of the holy ones,
  more awe-inspiring than
     all who surround Him.
8 LORD God of *Hosts,
  who is strong like You, LORD?
  Your faithfulness surrounds You.
9 You rule the raging sea;
  when its waves surge, You still them.
10 You crushed *Rahab like one who is slain;
  You scattered Your enemies
     with Your powerful arm.
11 The heavens are Yours; the earth also is Yours.
  The world and everything in it—
     You founded them.
12 North and south—You created them.
  Tabor and Hermon shout for joy
     at Your name.
13 You have a mighty arm;
  Your hand is powerful;
     Your right hand is lifted high.
14 Righteousness and justice are the foundation
     of Your throne;
  faithful love and truth go before You.
15 Happy are the people who know
     the joyful shout;
  *Yahweh, they walk in the light
     of Your presence.
16 They rejoice in Your name all day long,
  and they are exalted by Your righteousness.
17 For You are their magnificent strength;
  by Your favor our *horn is exalted.
18 Surely our shield belongs to the LORD,
  our king to the Holy One of Israel.
19 You once spoke in a vision to Your loyal ones
  and said: "I have granted help to a warrior;
  I have exalted one chosen from the people.
20 I have found David My servant;
  I have anointed him with My sacred oil.
21 My hand will always be with him,
  and My arm will strengthen him.
22 The enemy will not afflict him;
  no wicked man will oppress him.

23 I will crush his foes before him
  and strike those who hate him.
24 My faithfulness and love will be with him,
  and through My name
  his horn will be exalted.
25 I will extend his power to the sea
  and his right hand to the rivers.
26 He will call to Me, 'You are my Father,
  my God, the rock of my salvation.'
27 I will also make him My firstborn,
  greatest of the kings of the earth.
28 I will always preserve My faithful love for him,
  and My covenant with him will endure.
29 I will establish his line forever,
  his throne as long as heaven lasts.
30 If his sons forsake My instruction
  and do not live by My ordinances,
31 if they dishonor My statutes
  and do not keep My commands,
32 then I will call their rebellion
  to account with the rod,
  their sin with blows.
33 But I will not withdraw
  My faithful love from him
  or betray My faithfulness.
34 I will not violate My covenant
  or change what My lips have said.
35 Once and for all
  I have sworn an oath by My holiness;
  I will not lie to David.
36 His offspring will continue forever,
  his throne like the sun before Me,
37 like the moon, established forever,
  a faithful witness in the sky."   *Selah*
38 But You have spurned and rejected him;
  You have become enraged with Your anointed.
39 You have repudiated the covenant
     with Your servant;
  You have completely dishonored his crown.
40 You have broken down all his walls;
  You have reduced his fortified cities to ruins.
41 All who pass by plunder him;
  he has become an object of ridicule
  to his neighbors.
42 You have lifted high the right hand of his foes;
  You have made all his enemies rejoice.
43 You have also turned back his sharp sword
  and have not let him stand in battle.
44 You have made his splendor cease
  and have overturned his throne.
45 You have shortened the days of his youth;
  You have covered him with shame.   *Selah*
46 How long, LORD? Will You hide
     Yourself forever?
  Will Your anger keep burning like fire?
47 Remember how short my life is.
  Have You created *everyone for nothing?
48 What man can live and never see death?
  Who can save himself from the power
     of *Sheol?   *Selah*
49 Lord, where are the former acts
     of Your faithful love
  that You swore to David in Your faithfulness?
50 Remember, Lord, the ridicule
     against Your servants—
  in my heart I carry abuse from all
     the peoples—

51 how Your enemies have ridiculed, Lord,
how they have ridiculed every step
  of Your anointed.
52 May the Lord be praised forever.
  *Amen and amen.

BOOK IV
(Psalms 90–106)

Psalm 90
A prayer of Moses, the man of God.

1 Lord, You have been our refuge
in every generation.
2 Before the mountains were born,
before You gave birth to the earth
  and the world,
from eternity to eternity, You are God.
3 You return mankind to the dust,
saying, "Return, descendants of Adam."
4 For in Your sight a thousand years
are like yesterday that passes by,
like a few hours of the night.
5 You end their lives; they sleep.
They are like grass that grows
  in the morning—
6 in the morning it sprouts and grows;
by evening it withers and dries up.
7 For we are consumed by Your anger;
we are terrified by Your wrath.
8 You have set our unjust ways before You,
our secret sins in the light of Your presence.
9 For all our days ebb away under Your wrath;
we end our years like a sigh.
10 Our lives last seventy years
or, if we are strong, eighty years.
Even the best of them are struggle
  and sorrow;
indeed, they pass quickly and we fly away.
11 Who understands the power of Your anger?
Your wrath matches the fear that is due You.
12 Teach us to number our days carefully
so that we may develop wisdom in our hearts.
13 Lord—how long?
Turn and have compassion on Your servants.
14 Satisfy us in the morning
  with Your faithful love
so that we may shout with joy and be glad
  all our days.
15 Make us rejoice for as many days
  as You have humbled us,
for as many years as we have seen adversity.
16 Let Your work be seen by Your servants,
and Your splendor by their children.
17 Let the favor of the Lord our God be on us;
establish for us the work of our hands—
establish the work of our hands!

Psalm 91
1 The one who lives under the protection
  of the *Most High
dwells in the shadow of the *Almighty.
2 I will say to the Lord, "My refuge
  and my fortress,
my God, in whom I trust."
3 He Himself will deliver you
  from the hunter's net,
from the destructive plague.

4 He will cover you with His feathers;
you will take refuge under His wings.
His faithfulness will be a protective shield.
5 You will not fear the terror of the night,
the arrow that flies by day,
6 the plague that stalks in darkness,
or the pestilence that ravages at noon.
7 Though a thousand fall at your side
and ten thousand at your right hand,
the pestilence will not reach you.
8 You will only see it with your eyes
and witness the punishment of the wicked.
9 Because you have made the Lord—my refuge,
the Most High—your dwelling place,
10 no harm will come to you;
no plague will come near your tent.
11 For He will give His angels orders
  concerning you,
to protect you in all your ways.
12 They will support you with their hands
so that you will not strike your foot
  against a stone.
13 You will tread on the lion and the cobra;
you will trample the young lion
  and the serpent.
14 Because he is lovingly devoted to Me,
I will deliver him;
I will protect him because he knows My name.
15 When he calls out to Me, I will answer him;
I will be with him in trouble.
I will rescue him and give him honor.
16 I will satisfy him with a long life
and show him My salvation.

Psalm 92
A psalm. A song for the Sabbath day.

1 It is good to praise *Yahweh,
to sing praise to Your name, *Most High,
2 to declare Your faithful love in the morning
and Your faithfulness at night,
3 with a ten-stringed harp
and the music of a lyre.
4 For You have made me rejoice, Lord,
by what You have done;
I will shout for joy
because of the works of Your hands.
5 How magnificent are Your works, Lord,
how profound Your thoughts!
6 A stupid person does not know,
a fool does not understand this:
7 though the wicked sprout like grass
and all evildoers flourish,
they will be eternally destroyed.
8 But You, Lord, are exalted forever.
9 For indeed, Lord, Your enemies—
indeed, Your enemies will perish;
all evildoers will be scattered.
10 You have lifted up my *horn
like that of a wild ox;
I have been anointed with oil.
11 My eyes look down on my enemies;
my ears hear evildoers when they attack me.
12 The righteous thrive like a palm tree
and grow like a cedar tree in Lebanon.
13 Planted in the house of the Lord,
they thrive in the courts of our God.
14 They will still bear fruit in old age,

healthy and green,
15 to declare: "The LORD is just;
He is my rock,
and there is no unrighteousness in Him."

Psalm 93

1 The LORD reigns! He is robed in majesty;
The LORD is robed, enveloped in strength.
The world is firmly established;
it cannot be shaken.
2 Your throne has been established
from the beginning;
You are from eternity.
3 The floods have lifted up, LORD,
the floods have lifted up their voice;
the floods lift up their pounding waves.
4 Greater than the roar of many waters—
the mighty breakers of the sea—
the LORD on high is majestic.
5 LORD, Your testimonies are completely reliable;
holiness is the beauty of Your house
for all the days to come.

Psalm 94

1 LORD, God of vengeance—
God of vengeance, appear.
2 Rise up, Judge of the earth;
repay the proud what they deserve.
3 LORD, how long will the wicked—
how long will the wicked gloat?
4 They pour out arrogant words;
all the evildoers boast.
5 LORD, they crush Your people;
they afflict Your heritage.
6 They kill the widow and the foreigner
and murder the fatherless.
7 They say, "The LORD doesn't see it.
The God of Jacob doesn't pay attention."
8 Pay attention, you stupid people!
Fools, when will you be wise?
9 Can the One who shaped the ear not hear,
the One who formed the eye not see?
10 The One who instructs nations,
the One who teaches man knowledge—
does He not discipline?
11 The LORD knows man's thoughts;
they are meaningless.
12 LORD, happy is the man You discipline
and teach from Your law
13 to give him relief from troubled times
until a pit is dug for the wicked.
14 The LORD will not forsake His people
or abandon His heritage,
15 for justice will again be righteous,
and all the upright in heart will follow it.
16 Who stands up for me against the wicked?
Who takes a stand for me against evildoers?
17 If the LORD had not been my helper,
I would soon rest in the silence of death.
18 If I say, "My foot is slipping,"
Your faithful love will support me, LORD.
19 When I am filled with cares,
Your comfort brings me joy.
20 Can a corrupt throne—
one that creates trouble by law—
become Your ally?
21 They band together against the life
of the righteous

and condemn the innocent to death.
22 But the LORD is my refuge;
my God is the rock of my protection.
23 He will pay them back for their sins
and destroy them for their evil.
The LORD our God will destroy them.

Psalm 95

1 Come, let us shout joyfully to the LORD,
shout triumphantly to the rock
of our salvation!
2 Let us enter His presence with thanksgiving;
let us shout triumphantly to Him in song.
3 For the LORD is a great God,
a great King above all gods.
4 The depths of the earth are in His hand,
and the mountain peaks are His.
5 The sea is His; He made it.
His hands formed the dry land.
6 Come, let us worship and bow down;
let us kneel before the LORD our Maker.
7 For He is our God,
and we are the people of His pasture,
the sheep under His care.
Today, if you hear His voice:
8 Do not harden your hearts as at Meribah,
as on that day at Massah in the wilderness
9 where your fathers tested Me;
they tried Me, though they had seen
what I did.
10 For 40 years I was disgusted
with that generation;
I said, "They are a people whose hearts
go astray;
they do not know My ways."
11 So I swore in My anger,
"They will not enter My rest."

Psalm 96

1 Sing a new song to the LORD;
sing to the LORD, all the earth.
2 Sing to *Yahweh, praise His name;
proclaim His salvation from day to day.
3 Declare His glory among the nations,
His wonderful works among all peoples.
4 For the LORD is great and is highly praised;
He is feared above all gods.
5 For all the gods of the peoples are idols,
but the LORD made the heavens.
6 Splendor and majesty are before Him;
strength and beauty are in His sanctuary.
7 Ascribe to the LORD, you families
of the peoples,
ascribe to the LORD glory and strength.
8 Ascribe to Yahweh the glory of His name;
bring an offering and enter His courts.
9 Worship the LORD in the splendor
of His holiness;
tremble before Him, all the earth.
10 Say among the nations: "The LORD reigns.
The world is firmly established; it cannot
be shaken.
He judges the peoples fairly."
11 Let the heavens be glad and the earth rejoice;
let the sea and all that fills it resound.
12 Let the fields and everything in them exult.
Then all the trees of the forest will shout
for joy

13 before the LORD, for He is coming—
for He is coming to judge the earth.
He will judge the world with righteousness
and the peoples with His faithfulness.

Psalm 97

1 The LORD reigns! Let the earth rejoice;
let the many coasts and islands be glad.
2 Clouds and thick darkness surround Him;
righteousness and justice are the foundation
of His throne.
3 Fire goes before Him
and burns up His foes on every side.
4 His lightning lights up the world;
the earth sees and trembles.
5 The mountains melt like wax
at the presence of the LORD—
at the presence of the Lord of all the earth.
6 The heavens proclaim His righteousness;
all the peoples see His glory.
7 All who serve carved images,
those who boast in idols, will be put to shame.
All the gods must worship Him.
8 *Zion hears and is glad,
and the towns of Judah rejoice
because of Your judgments, LORD.
9 For You, LORD,
are the *Most High over all the earth;
You are exalted above all the gods.
10 You who love the LORD, hate evil!
He protects the lives of His godly ones;
He rescues them from the power
of the wicked.
11 Light dawns for the righteous,
gladness for the upright in heart.
12 Be glad in *Yahweh, you righteous ones,
and praise His holy name.

Psalm 98

A psalm.

1 Sing a new song to the LORD,
for He has performed wonders;
His right hand and holy arm
have won Him victory.
2 The LORD has made His victory known;
He has revealed His righteousness
in the sight of the nations.
3 He has remembered His love
and faithfulness to the house of Israel;
all the ends of the earth
have seen our God's victory.
4 Shout to the LORD, all the earth;
be jubilant, shout for joy, and sing.
5 Sing to the LORD with the lyre,
with the lyre and melodious song.
6 With trumpets and the blast of the ram's horn
shout triumphantly
in the presence of the LORD, our King.
7 Let the sea and all that fills it,
the world and those who live in it, resound.
8 Let the rivers clap their hands;
let the mountains shout together for joy
9 before the LORD,
for He is coming to judge the earth.
He will judge the world righteously
and the peoples fairly.

Psalm 99

1 The LORD reigns! Let the peoples tremble.
He is enthroned above the *cherubim.
Let the earth quake.
2 *Yahweh is great in *Zion;
He is exalted above all the peoples.
3 Let them praise Your great
and awe-inspiring name.
He is holy.
4 The mighty King loves justice.
You have established fairness;
You have administered justice
and righteousness in Jacob.
5 Exalt the LORD our God;
bow in worship at His footstool.
He is holy.
6 Moses and Aaron were among His priests;
Samuel also was among those calling on
His name.
They called to Yahweh and He answered them.
7 He spoke to them in a pillar
of cloud;
they kept His decrees and the statutes
He gave them.
8 LORD our God, You answered them.
You were a forgiving God to them,
an avenger of their sinful actions.
9 Exalt the LORD our God;
bow in worship at His holy mountain,
for the LORD our God is holy.

Psalm 100

A psalm of thanksgiving.

1 Shout triumphantly to the LORD, all the earth.
2 Serve the LORD with gladness;
come before Him with joyful songs.
3 Acknowledge that *Yahweh is God.
He made us, and we are His —
His people, the sheep of His pasture.
4 Enter His gates with thanksgiving
and His courts with praise.
Give thanks to Him and praise His name.
5 For Yahweh is good, and His love is eternal;
His faithfulness endures
through all generations.

Psalm 101

A Davidic psalm.

1 I will sing of faithful love and justice;
I will sing praise to You, LORD.
2 I will pay attention to the way of integrity.
When will You come to me?
I will live with a heart of integrity
in my house.
3 I will not set anything worthless
before my eyes.
I hate the practice of transgression;
it will not cling to me.
4 A devious heart will be far from me;
I will not be involved with evil.
5 I will destroy anyone
who secretly slanders his neighbor;
I cannot tolerate anyone
with haughty eyes or an arrogant heart.
6 My eyes favor the faithful of the land
so that they may sit down with me.
The one who follows the way of integrity

may serve me.
⁷ No one who acts deceitfully
will live in my palace;
no one who tells lies
will remain in my presence.
⁸ Every morning I will destroy
all the wicked of the land,
eliminating all evildoers from the Lᴏʀᴅ's city.

Psalm 102

A prayer of an afflicted person who is weak
and pours out his lament before the Lᴏʀᴅ.

¹ Lᴏʀᴅ, hear my prayer;
let my cry for help come before You.
² Do not hide Your face from me in my day
of trouble.
Listen closely to me;
answer me quickly when I call.
³ For my days vanish like smoke,
and my bones burn like a furnace.
⁴ My heart is afflicted, withered like grass;
I even forget to eat my food.
⁵ Because of the sound of my groaning,
my flesh sticks to my bones.
⁶ I am like a desert owl,
like an owl among the ruins.
⁷ I stay awake;
I am like a solitary bird on a roof.
⁸ My enemies taunt me all day long;
they ridicule and curse me.
⁹ I eat ashes like bread
and mingle my drinks with tears
¹⁰ because of Your indignation and wrath;
for You have picked me up
and thrown me aside.
¹¹ My days are like a lengthening shadow,
and I wither away like grass.
¹² But You, Lᴏʀᴅ, are enthroned forever;
Your fame endures to all generations.
¹³ You will rise up and have compassion on •Zion,
for it is time to show favor to her—
the appointed time has come.
¹⁴ For Your servants take delight in its stones
and favor its dust.
¹⁵ Then the nations will fear the name
of •Yahweh,
and all the kings of the earth Your glory,
¹⁶ for the Lᴏʀᴅ will rebuild Zion;
He will appear in His glory.
¹⁷ He will pay attention to the prayer
of the destitute
and will not despise their prayer.
¹⁸ This will be written for a later generation,
and a newly created people will praise
the Lᴏʀᴅ:
¹⁹ He looked down from His holy heights—
the Lᴏʀᴅ gazed out from heaven to earth—
²⁰ to hear a prisoner's groaning,
to set free those condemned to die,
²¹ so that they might declare
the name of Yahweh in Zion
and His praise in Jerusalem,
²² when peoples and kingdoms are assembled
to serve the Lᴏʀᴅ.
²³ He has broken my strength in midcourse;
He has shortened my days.
²⁴ I say: "My God, do not take me

in the middle of my life!
Your years continue through all generations.
²⁵ Long ago You established the earth,
and the heavens are the work of Your hands.
²⁶ They will perish, but You will endure;
all of them will wear out like clothing.
You will change them like a garment,
and they will pass away.
²⁷ But You are the same,
and Your years will never end.
²⁸ Your servants' children will dwell securely,
and their offspring will be established
before You."

Psalm 103

Davidic.

¹ My soul, praise •Yahweh,
and all that is within me, praise
His holy name.
² My soul, praise the Lᴏʀᴅ,
and do not forget all His benefits.
³ He forgives all your sin;
He heals all your diseases.
⁴ He redeems your life from the •Pit;
He crowns you with faithful love
and compassion.
⁵ He satisfies you with goodness;
your youth is renewed like the eagle.
⁶ The Lᴏʀᴅ executes acts of righteousness
and justice for all the oppressed.
⁷ He revealed His ways to Moses,
His deeds to the people of Israel.
⁸ The Lᴏʀᴅ is compassionate and gracious,
slow to anger and rich in faithful love.
⁹ He will not always accuse us
or be angry forever.
¹⁰ He has not dealt with us as our sins deserve
or repaid us according to our offenses.
¹¹ For as high as the heavens are above
the earth,
so great is His faithful love
toward those who •fear Him.
¹² As far as the east is from the west,
so far has He removed
our transgressions from us.
¹³ As a father has compassion on his children,
so the Lᴏʀᴅ has compassion on those
who fear Him.
¹⁴ For He knows what we are made of,
remembering that we are dust.
¹⁵ As for man, his days are like grass—
he blooms like a flower of the field;
¹⁶ when the wind passes over it, it vanishes,
and its place is no longer known.
¹⁷ But from eternity to eternity
the Lᴏʀᴅ's faithful love is toward
those who fear Him,
and His righteousness
toward the grandchildren
¹⁸ of those who keep His covenant,
who remember to observe His precepts.
¹⁹ The Lᴏʀᴅ has established His throne
in heaven,
and His kingdom rules over all.
²⁰ Praise the Lᴏʀᴅ,
all His angels of great strength,
who do His word,

obedient to His command.
21 Praise the LORD, all His armies,
His servants who do His will.
22 Praise the LORD, all His works
in all the places where He rules.
My soul, praise Yahweh!

Psalm 104

1 My soul, praise *Yahweh!
LORD my God, You are very great;
You are clothed with majesty and splendor.
2 He wraps Himself in light as if it were a robe,
spreading out the sky like a canopy,
3 laying the beams of His palace
on the waters above,
making the clouds His chariot,
walking on the wings of the wind,
4 and making the winds His messengers,
flames of fire His servants.
5 He established the earth on its foundations;
it will never be shaken.
6 You covered it with the deep
as if it were a garment;
the waters stood above the mountains.
7 At Your rebuke the waters fled;
at the sound of Your thunder
they hurried away—
8 mountains rose and valleys sank—
to the place You established for them.
9 You set a boundary they cannot cross;
they will never cover the earth again.
10 He causes the springs to gush into the valleys;
they flow between the mountains.
11 They supply water for every wild beast;
the wild donkeys quench their thirst.
12 The birds of the sky live beside the springs;
they sing among the foliage.
13 He waters the mountains from His palace;
the earth is satisfied by the fruit of Your labor.
14 He causes grass to grow for the livestock
and provides crops for man to cultivate,
producing food from the earth,
15 wine that makes man's heart glad—
making his face shine with oil—
and bread that sustains man's heart.
16 The trees of the LORD flourish,
the cedars of Lebanon that He planted.
17 There the birds make their nests;
the stork makes its home in the pine trees.
18 The high mountains are for the wild goats;
the cliffs are a refuge for hyraxes.
19 He made the moon to mark the festivals;
the sun knows when to set.
20 You bring darkness, and it becomes night,
when all the forest animals stir.
21 The young lions roar for their prey
and seek their food from God.
22 The sun rises; they go back
and lie down in their dens.
23 Man goes out to his work
and to his labor until evening.
24 How countless are Your works, LORD!
In wisdom You have made them all;
the earth is full of Your creatures.
25 Here is the sea, vast and wide,
teeming with creatures beyond number—
living things both large and small.
26 There the ships move about,

and *Leviathan, which You formed
to play there.
27 All of them wait for You
to give them their food at the right time.
28 When You give it to them,
they gather it;
when You open Your hand,
they are satisfied with good things.
29 When You hide Your face,
they are terrified;
when You take away their breath,
they die and return to the dust.
30 When You send Your breath,
they are created,
and You renew the face of the earth.
31 May the glory of the LORD endure forever;
may the LORD rejoice in His works.
32 He looks at the earth, and it trembles;
He touches the mountains,
and they pour out smoke.
33 I will sing to the LORD all my life;
I will sing praise to my God while I live.
34 May my meditation be pleasing to Him;
I will rejoice in the LORD.
35 May sinners vanish from the earth
and wicked people be no more.
My soul, praise Yahweh!
*Hallelujah!

Psalm 105

1 Give thanks to *Yahweh, call on His name;
proclaim His deeds among the peoples.
2 Sing to Him, sing praise to Him;
tell about all His wonderful works!
3 Honor His holy name;
let the hearts of those who seek
Yahweh rejoice.
4 Search for the LORD and for His strength;
seek His face always.
5 Remember the wonderful works He has done,
His wonders,
and the judgments He has pronounced,
6 you offspring of Abraham His servant,
Jacob's descendants—His chosen ones.
7 He is the LORD our God;
His judgments govern the whole earth.
8 He remembers His covenant forever,
the promise He ordained
for a thousand generations—
9 the covenant He made with Abraham,
swore to Isaac,
10 and confirmed to Jacob as a decree
and to Israel as an everlasting covenant:
11 "I will give the land of Canaan to you
as your inherited portion."
12 When they were few in number,
very few indeed,
and temporary residents in Canaan,
13 wandering from nation to nation
and from one kingdom to another,
14 He allowed no one to oppress them;
He rebuked kings on their behalf:
15 "Do not touch My anointed ones,
or harm My prophets."
16 He called down famine against the land
and destroyed the entire food supply.
17 He had sent a man ahead of them—
Joseph, who was sold as a slave.

18 They hurt his feet with shackles;
his neck was put in an iron collar.
19 Until the time his prediction came true,
the word of the LORD tested him.
20 The king sent for him and released him;
the ruler of peoples set him free.
21 He made him master of his household,
ruler over all his possessions—
22 binding his officials at will
and instructing his elders.
23 Then Israel went to Egypt;
Jacob lived as a foreigner in the land of Ham.
24 The LORD made His people very fruitful;
He made them more numerous
than their foes,
25 whose hearts He turned to hate His people
and to deal deceptively with His servants.
26 He sent Moses His servant,
and Aaron, whom He had chosen.
27 They performed His miraculous signs
among them,
and wonders in the land of Ham.
28 He sent darkness, and it became dark—
for did they not defy His commands?
29 He turned their water into blood
and caused their fish to die.
30 Their land was overrun with frogs,
even in their royal chambers.
31 He spoke, and insects came—
gnats throughout their country.
32 He gave them hail for rain,
and lightning throughout their land.
33 He struck their vines and fig trees
and shattered the trees of their territory.
34 He spoke, and locusts came—
young locusts without number.
35 They devoured all the vegetation in their land
and consumed the produce of their land.
36 He struck all the firstborn in their land,
all their first progeny.
37 Then He brought Israel out with silver
and gold,
and no one among His tribes stumbled.
38 Egypt was glad when they left,
for the dread of Israel had fallen on them.
39 He spread a cloud as a covering
and gave a fire to light up the night.
40 They asked, and He brought quail
and satisfied them with bread from heaven.
41 He opened a rock, and water gushed out;
it flowed like a stream in the desert.
42 For He remembered His holy promise
to Abraham His servant.
43 He brought His people out with rejoicing,
His chosen ones with shouts of joy.
44 He gave them the lands of the nations,
and they inherited
what other peoples had worked for.
45 All this happened
so that they might keep His statutes
and obey His instructions.
•Hallelujah!

Psalm 106

1 •Hallelujah!
Give thanks to the LORD, for He is good;
His faithful love endures forever.
2 Who can declare the LORD's mighty acts

or proclaim all the praise due Him?
3 How happy are those who uphold justice,
who practice righteousness at all times.
4 Remember me, LORD,
when You show favor to Your people.
Come to me with Your salvation
5 so that I may enjoy the prosperity
of Your chosen ones,
rejoice in the joy of Your nation,
and boast about Your heritage.
6 Both we and our fathers have sinned;
we have done wrong and have acted wickedly.
7 Our fathers in Egypt did not grasp
the significance of Your wonderful works
or remember Your many acts of faithful love;
instead, they rebelled by the sea—the •Red Sea.
8 Yet He saved them because of His name,
to make His power known.
9 He rebuked the Red Sea, and it dried up;
He led them through the depths as through
a desert.
10 He saved them from the hand of the adversary;
He redeemed them from the hand
of the enemy.
11 Water covered their foes;
not one of them remained.
12 Then they believed His promises
and sang His praise.
13 They soon forgot His works
and would not wait for His counsel.
14 They were seized with craving
in the wilderness
and tested God in the desert.
15 He gave them what they asked for,
but sent a wasting disease among them.
16 In the camp they were envious of Moses
and of Aaron, the LORD's holy one.
17 The earth opened up and swallowed Dathan;
it covered the assembly of Abiram.
18 Fire blazed throughout their assembly;
flames consumed the wicked.
19 At Horeb they made a calf
and worshiped the cast metal image.
20 They exchanged their glory
for the image of a grass-eating ox.
21 They forgot God their Savior,
who did great things in Egypt,
22 wonderful works in the land of Ham,
awe-inspiring acts at the Red Sea.
23 So He said He would have destroyed them—
if Moses His chosen one
had not stood before Him in the breach
to turn His wrath away from destroying them.
24 They despised the pleasant land
and did not believe His promise.
25 They grumbled in their tents
and did not listen to the LORD's voice.
26 So He raised His hand against them
with an oath
that He would make them fall in the desert
27 and would disperse their descendants
among the nations,
scattering them throughout the lands.
28 They aligned themselves with •Baal of Peor
and ate sacrifices offered to lifeless gods.
29 They provoked the LORD with their deeds,
and a plague broke out against them.

30 But Phinehas stood up and intervened,
and the plague was stopped.
31 It was credited to him as righteousness
throughout all generations to come.
32 They angered the LORD at the waters
of Meribah,
and Moses suffered because of them;
33 for they embittered his spirit,
and he spoke rashly with his lips.
34 They did not destroy the peoples
as the LORD had commanded them
35 but mingled with the nations
and adopted their ways.
36 They served their idols,
which became a snare to them.
37 They sacrificed their sons and daughters
to demons.
38 They shed innocent blood—
the blood of their sons and daughters
whom they sacrificed to the idols of Canaan;
so the land became polluted with blood.
39 They defiled themselves by their actions
and prostituted themselves by their deeds.
40 Therefore the LORD's anger burned
against His people,
and He abhorred His own inheritance.
41 He handed them over to the nations;
those who hated them ruled them.
42 Their enemies oppressed them,
and they were subdued under their power.
43 He rescued them many times,
but they continued to rebel deliberately
and were beaten down by their sin.
44 When He heard their cry,
He took note of their distress,
45 remembered His covenant with them,
and relented according to the riches
of His faithful love.
46 He caused them to be pitied
before all their captors.
47 Save us, *Yahweh our God,
and gather us from the nations,
so that we may give thanks to Your holy name
and rejoice in Your praise.
48 May Yahweh, the God of Israel, be praised
from everlasting to everlasting.
Let all the people say, "'Amen!"
Hallelujah!

BOOK V
(Psalms 107–150)

Psalm 107
1 Give thanks to the LORD, for He is good;
His faithful love endures forever.
2 Let the redeemed of the LORD proclaim
that He has redeemed them from the hand
of the foe
3 and has gathered them from the lands—
from the east and the west,
from the north and the south.
4 Some wandered in the desolate wilderness,
finding no way to a city where they could live.
5 They were hungry and thirsty;
their spirits failed within them.
6 Then they cried out to the LORD
in their trouble;

He rescued them from their distress.
7 He led them by the right path
to go to a city where they could live.
8 Let them give thanks to the LORD
for His faithful love
and His wonderful works for all *humanity.
9 For He has satisfied the thirsty
and filled the hungry with good things.
10 Others sat in darkness and gloom—
prisoners in cruel chains—
11 because they rebelled against God's commands
and despised the counsel of the *Most High.
12 He broke their spirits with hard labor;
they stumbled, and there was no one to help.
13 Then they cried out to the LORD
in their trouble;
He saved them from their distress.
14 He brought them out of darkness and gloom
and broke their chains apart.
15 Let them give thanks to the LORD
for His faithful love
and His wonderful works for all humanity.
16 For He has broken down the bronze gates
and cut through the iron bars.
17 Fools suffered affliction
because of their rebellious ways and their sins.
18 They loathed all food
and came near the gates of death.
19 Then they cried out to the LORD
in their trouble;
He saved them from their distress.
20 He sent His word and healed them;
He rescued them from the *Pit.
21 Let them give thanks to the LORD
for His faithful love
and His wonderful works for all humanity.
22 Let them offer sacrifices of thanksgiving
and announce His works with shouts of joy.
23 Others went to sea in ships,
conducting trade on the vast waters.
24 They saw the LORD's works,
His wonderful works in the deep.
25 He spoke and raised a tempest
that stirred up the waves of the sea.
26 Rising up to the sky, sinking down
to the depths,
their courage melting away in anguish,
27 they reeled and staggered like drunken men,
and all their skill was useless.
28 Then they cried out to the LORD
in their trouble,
and He brought them out of their distress.
29 He stilled the storm to a murmur,
and the waves of the sea were hushed.
30 They rejoiced when the waves grew quiet.
Then He guided them to the harbor
they longed for.
31 Let them give thanks to the LORD
for His faithful love
and His wonderful works for all humanity.
32 Let them exalt Him in the assembly
of the people
and praise Him in the council of the elders.
33 He turns rivers into desert,
springs of water into thirsty ground,
34 and fruitful land into salty wasteland,
because of the wickedness of its inhabitants.

³⁵ He turns a desert into a pool of water,
   dry land into springs of water.
³⁶ He causes the hungry to settle there,
   and they establish a city where they can live.
³⁷ They sow fields and plant vineyards
   that yield a fruitful harvest.
³⁸ He blesses them, and they multiply greatly;
   He does not let their livestock decrease.
³⁹ When they are diminished and are humbled
   by cruel oppression and sorrow,
⁴⁰ He pours contempt on nobles
   and makes them wander
      in a trackless wasteland.
⁴¹ But He lifts the needy out of their suffering
   and makes their families multiply like flocks.
⁴² The upright see it and rejoice,
   and all injustice shuts its mouth.
⁴³ Let whoever is wise pay attention
      to these things
   and consider the LORD's acts of faithful love.

Psalm 108
A song. A Davidic psalm.

¹ My heart is confident, God;
   I will sing; I will sing praises
   with the whole of my being.
² Wake up, harp and lyre!
   I will wake up the dawn.
³ I will praise You, LORD, among the peoples;
   I will sing praises to You among the nations.
⁴ For Your faithful love is higher
      than the heavens,
   and Your faithfulness reaches to the clouds.
⁵ God, be exalted above the heavens,
   and let Your glory be over the whole earth.
⁶ Save with Your right hand and answer me
   so that those You love may be rescued.
⁷ God has spoken in His sanctuary:
   "I will triumph!
   I will divide up Shechem.
   I will apportion the Valley of Succoth.
⁸ Gilead is Mine, Manasseh is Mine,
   and Ephraim is My helmet;
   Judah is My scepter.
⁹ Moab is My washbasin;
   I throw My sandal on Edom.
   I shout in triumph over Philistia."
¹⁰ Who will bring me to the fortified city?
   Who will lead me to Edom?
¹¹ God, haven't You rejected us?
   God, You do not march out with our armies.
¹² Give us aid against the foe,
   for human help is worthless.
¹³ With God we will perform valiantly;
   He will trample our foes.

Psalm 109
For the choir director. A Davidic psalm.

¹ God of my praise, do not be silent.
² For wicked and deceitful mouths open
      against me;
   they speak against me with lying tongues.
³ They surround me with hateful words
   and attack me without cause.
⁴ In return for my love they accuse me,
   but I continue to pray.
⁵ They repay me evil for good,

and hatred for my love.
⁶ Set a wicked person over him;
   let an accuser stand at his right hand.
⁷ When he is judged, let him be found ˙guilty,
   and let his prayer be counted as sin.
⁸ Let his days be few;
   let another take over his position.
⁹ Let his children be fatherless
   and his wife a widow.
¹⁰ Let his children wander as beggars,
   searching for food far
      from their demolished homes.
¹¹ Let a creditor seize all he has;
   let strangers plunder what he has worked for.
¹² Let no one show him kindness,
   and let no one be gracious
      to his fatherless children.
¹³ Let the line of his descendants be cut off;
   let their name be blotted out
      in the next generation.
¹⁴ Let his ancestors' guilt
   be remembered before the LORD,
   and do not let his mother's sin be blotted out.
¹⁵ Let their sins always remain before the LORD,
   and let Him erase all memory of them
      from the earth.
¹⁶ For he did not think to show kindness,
   but pursued the afflicted, poor,
      and brokenhearted
   in order to put them to death.
¹⁷ He loved cursing—let it fall on him;
   he took no delight in blessing—let it be far
      from him.
¹⁸ He wore cursing like his coat—
   let it enter his body like water
   and go into his bones like oil.
¹⁹ Let it be like a robe he wraps around himself,
   like a belt he always wears.
²⁰ Let this be the LORD's payment to my accusers,
   to those who speak evil against me.
²¹ But You, ˙Yahweh my Lord,
   deal kindly with me
      because of Your name;
   deliver me because of the goodness
      of Your faithful love.
²² For I am afflicted and needy;
   my heart is wounded within me.
²³ I fade away like a lengthening shadow;
   I am shaken off like a locust.
²⁴ My knees are weak from fasting,
   and my body is emaciated.
²⁵ I have become an object of ridicule
      to my accusers;
   when they see me, they shake their heads
      in scorn.
²⁶ Help me, LORD my God;
   save me according to Your faithful love
²⁷ so they may know that this is Your hand
   and that You, LORD, have done it.
²⁸ Though they curse, You will bless.
   When they rise up, they will be put to shame,
   but Your servant will rejoice.
²⁹ My accusers will be clothed with disgrace;
   they will wear their shame like a cloak.
³⁰ I will fervently thank the LORD
      with my mouth;
   I will praise Him in the presence of many.

31 For He stands at the right hand of the needy
to save him from those who would
condemn him.

Psalm 110
A Davidic psalm.

1 This is the declaration of the LORD
to my Lord:
"Sit at My right hand
until I make Your enemies Your footstool."
2 The LORD will extend Your mighty scepter
from •Zion.
Rule over Your surrounding enemies.
3 Your people will volunteer
on Your day of battle.
In holy splendor, from the womb of the dawn,
the dew of Your youth belongs to You.
4 The LORD has sworn an oath and will not
take it back:
"Forever, You are a priest
like Melchizedek."
5 The Lord is at Your right hand;
He will crush kings on the day of His anger.
6 He will judge the nations, heaping up corpses;
He will crush leaders over the entire world.
7 He will drink from the brook by the road;
therefore, He will lift up His head.

Psalm 111
1 •Hallelujah!
I will praise the LORD with all my heart
in the assembly of the upright
and in the congregation.
2 The LORD's works are great,
studied by all who delight in them.
3 All that He does is splendid and majestic;
His righteousness endures forever.
4 He has caused His wonderful works
to be remembered.
The LORD is gracious and compassionate.
5 He has provided food for those who fear Him;
He remembers His covenant forever.
6 He has shown His people the power
of His works
by giving them the inheritance of the nations.
7 The works of His hands are truth and justice;
all His instructions are trustworthy.
8 They are established forever and ever,
enacted in truth and in what is right.
9 He has sent redemption to His people.
He has ordained His covenant forever.
His name is holy and awe-inspiring.
10 The •fear of the LORD is the beginning
of wisdom;
all who follow His instructions have
good insight.
His praise endures forever.

Psalm 112
1 •Hallelujah!
Happy is the man who •fears the LORD,
taking great delight in His commands.
2 His descendants will be powerful in the land;
the generation of the upright will be blessed.
3 Wealth and riches are in his house,
and his righteousness endures forever.
4 Light shines in the darkness for the upright.
He is gracious, compassionate, and righteous.

5 Good will come to a man
who lends generously
and conducts his business fairly.
6 He will never be shaken.
The righteous man will be
remembered forever.
7 He will not fear bad news;
his heart is confident, trusting in the LORD.
8 His heart is assured; he will not fear.
In the end he will look in triumph on his foes.
9 He distributes freely to the poor;
his righteousness endures forever.
His •horn will be exalted in honor.
10 The wicked man will see it and be angry;
he will gnash his teeth in despair.
The desire of the wicked man will come
to nothing.

Psalm 113
1 •Hallelujah!
Give praise, servants of •Yahweh;
praise the name of Yahweh.
2 Let the name of Yahweh be praised
both now and forever.
3 From the rising of the sun to its setting,
let the name of Yahweh be praised.
4 Yahweh is exalted above all the nations,
His glory above the heavens.
5 Who is like Yahweh our God—
the One enthroned on high,
6 who stoops down to look
on the heavens and the earth?
7 He raises the poor from the dust
and lifts the needy from the garbage pile
8 in order to seat them with nobles—
with the nobles of His people.
9 He gives the childless woman a household,
making her the joyful mother of children.
Hallelujah!

Psalm 114
1 When Israel came out of Egypt—
the house of Jacob from a people
who spoke a foreign language—
2 Judah became His sanctuary,
Israel, His dominion.
3 The sea looked and fled;
the Jordan turned back.
4 The mountains skipped like rams,
the hills, like lambs.
5 Why was it, sea, that you fled?
Jordan, that you turned back?
6 Mountains, that you skipped like rams?
Hills, like lambs?
7 Tremble, earth, at the presence of the Lord,
at the presence of the God of Jacob,
8 who turned the rock into a pool of water,
the flint into a spring of water.

Psalm 115
1 Not to us, •Yahweh, not to us,
but to Your name give glory
because of Your faithful love, because of
Your truth.
2 Why should the nations say,
"Where is their God?"
3 Our God is in heaven
and does whatever He pleases.

⁴ Their idols are silver and gold,
made by human hands.
⁵ They have mouths but cannot speak,
eyes, but cannot see.
⁶ They have ears but cannot hear,
noses, but cannot smell.
⁷ They have hands but cannot feel,
feet, but cannot walk.
They cannot make a sound with their throats.
⁸ Those who make them are just like them,
as are all who trust in them.
⁹ Israel, trust in the LORD!
He is their help and shield.
¹⁰ House of Aaron, trust in the LORD!
He is their help and shield.
¹¹ You who *fear the LORD, trust in the LORD!
He is their help and shield.
¹² The LORD remembers us and will bless us.
He will bless the house of Israel;
He will bless the house of Aaron;
¹³ He will bless those who fear the LORD—
small and great alike.
¹⁴ May the LORD add to your numbers,
both yours and your children's.
¹⁵ May you be blessed by the LORD,
the Maker of heaven and earth.
¹⁶ The heavens are the LORD's,
but the earth He has given to the *human race.
¹⁷ It is not the dead who praise the LORD,
nor any of those descending into the silence
of death.
¹⁸ But we will praise the LORD,
both now and forever.
*Hallelujah!

Psalm 116

¹ I love the LORD because He has heard
my appeal for mercy.
² Because He has turned His ear to me,
I will call out to Him as long as I live.
³ The ropes of death were wrapped around me,
and the torments of *Sheol overcame me;
I encountered trouble and sorrow.
⁴ Then I called on the name of *Yahweh:
"Yahweh, save me!"
⁵ The LORD is gracious and righteous;
our God is compassionate.
⁶ The LORD guards the inexperienced;
I was helpless, and He saved me.
⁷ Return to your rest, my soul,
for the LORD has been good to you.
⁸ For You, LORD, rescued me from death,
my eyes from tears,
my feet from stumbling.
⁹ I will walk before the LORD
in the land of the living.
¹⁰ I believed, even when I said,
"I am severely afflicted."
¹¹ In my alarm I said,
"Everyone is a liar."
¹² How can I repay the LORD
for all the good He has done for me?
¹³ I will take the cup of salvation
and call on the name of Yahweh.
¹⁴ I will fulfill my vows to the LORD
in the presence of all His people.
¹⁵ The death of His faithful ones
is valuable in the LORD's sight.

¹⁶ LORD, I am indeed Your servant;
I am Your servant, the son
of Your female servant.
You have loosened my bonds.
¹⁷ I will offer You a sacrifice of thanksgiving
and call on the name of Yahweh.
¹⁸ I will fulfill my vows to the LORD
in the presence of all His people,
¹⁹ in the courts of the LORD's house—
within you, Jerusalem.
*Hallelujah!

Psalm 117

¹ Praise the LORD, all nations!
Glorify Him, all peoples!
² For His faithful love to us is great;
the LORD's faithfulness endures forever.
*Hallelujah!

Psalm 118

¹ Give thanks to the LORD, for He is good;
His faithful love endures forever.
² Let Israel say,
"His faithful love endures forever."
³ Let the house of Aaron say,
"His faithful love endures forever."
⁴ Let those who fear the LORD say,
"His faithful love endures forever."
⁵ I called to the LORD in distress;
the LORD answered me
and put me in a spacious place.
⁶ The LORD is for me; I will not be afraid.
What can man do to me?
⁷ The LORD is my helper,
Therefore, I will look in triumph on those
who hate me.
⁸ It is better to take refuge in the LORD
than to trust in man.
⁹ It is better to take refuge in the LORD
than to trust in nobles.
¹⁰ All the nations surrounded me;
in the name of *Yahweh I destroyed them.
¹¹ They surrounded me, yes,
they surrounded me;
in the name of Yahweh I destroyed them.
¹² They surrounded me like bees;
they were extinguished like a fire
among thorns;
in the name of Yahweh I destroyed them.
¹³ You pushed me hard to make me fall,
but the LORD helped me.
¹⁴ The LORD is my strength and my song;
He has become my salvation.
¹⁵ There are shouts of joy and victory
in the tents of the righteous:
"The LORD's right hand performs valiantly!
¹⁶ The LORD's right hand is raised.
The LORD's right hand performs valiantly!"
¹⁷ I will not die, but I will live
and proclaim what the LORD has done.
¹⁸ The LORD disciplined me severely
but did not give me over to death.
¹⁹ Open the gates of righteousness for me;
I will enter through them
and give thanks to the LORD.
²⁰ This is the gate of the LORD;
the righteous will enter through it.
²¹ I will give thanks to You

because You have answered me
and have become my salvation.
22 The stone that the builders rejected
has become the cornerstone.
23 This came from the LORD;
it is wonderful in our eyes.
24 This is the day the LORD has made;
let us rejoice and be glad in it.
25 LORD, save us!
LORD, please grant us success!
26 He who comes in the name
of the LORD is blessed.
From the house of the LORD we bless you.
27 The LORD is God and has given us light.
Bind the festival sacrifice with cords
to the horns of the altar.
28 You are my God, and I will give You thanks.
You are my God; I will exalt You.
29 Give thanks to the LORD, for He is good;
His faithful love endures forever.

Psalm 119
א Alef

1 How happy are those whose way is blameless,
who live according to the LORD's instruction!
2 Happy are those who keep His decrees
and seek Him with all their heart.
3 They do nothing wrong;
they follow His ways.
4 You have commanded that Your precepts
be diligently kept.
5 If only my ways were committed
to keeping Your statutes!
6 Then I would not be ashamed
when I think about all Your commands.
7 I will praise You with a sincere heart
when I learn Your righteous judgments.
8 I will keep Your statutes;
never abandon me.

ב Bet

9 How can a young man keep his way pure?
By keeping Your word.
10 I have sought You with all my heart;
don't let me wander from Your commands.
11 I have treasured Your word in my heart
so that I may not sin against You.
12 LORD, may You be praised;
teach me Your statutes.
13 With my lips I proclaim
all the judgments from Your mouth.
14 I rejoice in the way revealed by Your decrees
as much as in all riches.
15 I will meditate on Your precepts
and think about Your ways.
16 I will delight in Your statutes;
I will not forget Your word.

ג Gimel

17 Deal generously with Your servant
so that I might live;
then I will keep Your word.
18 Open my eyes so that I may contemplate
wonderful things from Your instruction.
19 I am a stranger on earth;
do not hide Your commands from me.
20 I am continually overcome
with longing for Your judgments.

21 You rebuke the proud,
the ones under a curse,
who wander from Your commands.
22 Take insult and contempt away from me,
for I have kept Your decrees.
23 Though princes sit together speaking
against me,
Your servant will think about Your statutes;
24 Your decrees are my delight
and my counselors.

ד Dalet

25 My life is down in the dust;
give me life through Your word.
26 I told You about my life,
and You listened to me;
teach me Your statutes.
27 Help me understand
the meaning of Your precepts
so that I can meditate on Your wonders.
28 I am weary from grief;
strengthen me through Your word.
29 Keep me from the way of deceit
and graciously give me Your instruction.
30 I have chosen the way of truth;
I have set Your ordinances before me.
31 I cling to Your decrees;
LORD, do not put me to shame.
32 I pursue the way of Your commands,
for You broaden my understanding.

ה He

33 Teach me, LORD, the meaning of Your statutes,
and I will always keep them.
34 Help me understand Your instruction,
and I will obey it
and follow it with all my heart.
35 Help me stay on the path of Your commands,
for I take pleasure in it.
36 Turn my heart to Your decrees
and not to material gain.
37 Turn my eyes
from looking at what is worthless;
give me life in Your ways.
38 Confirm what You said to Your servant,
for it produces reverence for You.
39 Turn away the disgrace I dread;
indeed, Your judgments are good.
40 How I long for Your precepts!
Give me life through Your righteousness.

ו Vav

41 Let Your faithful love come to me, LORD,
Your salvation, as You promised.
42 Then I can answer the one who taunts me,
for I trust in Your word.
43 Never take the word of truth
from my mouth,
for I hope in Your judgments.
44 I will always obey Your instruction,
forever and ever.
45 I will walk freely in an open place
because I seek Your precepts.
46 I will speak of Your decrees before kings
and not be ashamed.
47 I delight in Your commands,
which I love.
48 I will lift up my hands to Your commands,

which I love,
and will meditate on Your statutes.

ז Zayin

49 Remember Your word to Your servant;
You have given me hope through it.
50 This is my comfort in my affliction:
Your promise has given me life.
51 The arrogant constantly ridicule me,
but I do not turn away from Your instruction.
52 LORD, I remember Your judgments
from long ago
and find comfort.
53 Rage seizes me because of the wicked
who reject Your instruction.
54 Your statutes are the theme of my song
during my earthly life.
55 'Yahweh, I remember Your name in the night,
and I obey Your instruction.
56 This is my practice:
I obey Your precepts.

ח Khet

57 The LORD is my portion;
I have promised to keep Your words.
58 I have sought Your favor with all my heart;
be gracious to me according to Your promise.
59 I thought about my ways
and turned my steps back to Your decrees.
60 I hurried, not hesitating
to keep Your commands.
61 Though the ropes of the wicked
were wrapped around me,
I did not forget Your instruction.
62 I rise at midnight to thank You
for Your righteous judgments.
63 I am a friend to all who 'fear You,
to those who keep Your precepts.
64 LORD, the earth is filled
with Your faithful love;
teach me Your statutes.

ט Tet

65 LORD, You have treated Your servant well,
just as You promised.
66 Teach me good judgment and discernment,
for I rely on Your commands.
67 Before I was afflicted I went astray,
but now I keep Your word.
68 You are good, and You do what is good;
teach me Your statutes.
69 The arrogant have smeared me with lies,
but I obey Your precepts with all my heart.
70 Their hearts are hard and insensitive,
but I delight in Your instruction.
71 It was good for me to be afflicted
so that I could learn Your statutes.
72 Instruction from Your lips is better for me
than thousands of gold and silver pieces.

י Yod

73 Your hands made me and formed me;
give me understanding
so that I can learn Your commands.
74 Those who fear You will see me and rejoice,
for I put my hope in Your word.
75 I know, LORD, that Your judgments are just
and that You have afflicted me fairly.
76 May Your faithful love comfort me

as You promised Your servant.
77 May Your compassion come to me
so that I may live,
for Your instruction is my delight.
78 Let the arrogant be put to shame
for slandering me with lies;
I will meditate on Your precepts.
79 Let those who fear You,
those who know Your decrees, turn to me.
80 May my heart be blameless
regarding Your statutes
so that I will not be put to shame.

כ Kaf

81 I long for Your salvation;
I put my hope in Your word.
82 My eyes grow weary
looking for what You have promised;
I ask, "When will You comfort me?"
83 Though I have become like a wineskin
dried by smoke,
I do not forget Your statutes.
84 How many days must Your servant wait?
When will You execute judgment
on my persecutors?
85 The arrogant have dug pits for me;
they violate Your instruction.
86 All Your commands are true;
people persecute me with lies—help me!
87 They almost ended my life on earth,
but I did not abandon Your precepts.
88 Give me life in accordance with
Your faithful love,
and I will obey the decree You have spoken.

ל Lamed

89 LORD, Your word is forever;
it is firmly fixed in heaven.
90 Your faithfulness is for all generations;
You established the earth, and it stands firm.
91 They stand today in accordance with
Your judgments,
for all things are Your servants.
92 If Your instruction had not been my delight,
I would have died in my affliction.
93 I will never forget Your precepts,
for You have given me life through them.
94 I am Yours; save me,
for I have sought Your precepts.
95 The wicked hope to destroy me,
but I contemplate Your decrees.
96 I have seen a limit to all perfection,
but Your command is without limit.

מ Mem

97 How I love Your instruction!
It is my meditation all day long.
98 Your commands make me wiser
than my enemies,
for they are always with me.
99 I have more insight than all my teachers
because Your decrees are my meditation.
100 I understand more than the elders
because I obey Your precepts.
101 I have kept my feet from every evil path
to follow Your word.
102 I have not turned from Your judgments,
for You Yourself have instructed me.

¹⁰³ How sweet Your word is to my taste—
sweeter than honey in my mouth.
¹⁰⁴ I gain understanding from Your precepts;
therefore I hate every false way.

‫נ‬ Nun

¹⁰⁵ Your word is a lamp for my feet
and a light on my path.
¹⁰⁶ I have solemnly sworn
to keep Your righteous judgments.
¹⁰⁷ I am severely afflicted;
Lord, give me life through Your word.
¹⁰⁸ Lord, please accept my willing offerings
of praise,
and teach me Your judgments.
¹⁰⁹ My life is constantly in danger,
yet I do not forget Your instruction.
¹¹⁰ The wicked have set a trap for me,
but I have not wandered from Your precepts.
¹¹¹ I have Your decrees as a heritage forever;
indeed, they are the joy of my heart.
¹¹² I am resolved to obey Your statutes
to the very end.

‫ס‬ Samek

¹¹³ I hate those who are double-minded,
but I love Your instruction.
¹¹⁴ You are my shelter and my shield;
I put my hope in Your word.
¹¹⁵ Depart from me, you evil ones,
so that I may obey my God's commands.
¹¹⁶ Sustain me as You promised, and I will live;
do not let me be ashamed of my hope.
¹¹⁷ Sustain me so that I can be safe
and always be concerned about Your statutes.
¹¹⁸ You reject all who stray from Your statutes,
for their deceit is a lie.
¹¹⁹ You remove all the wicked on earth
as if they were dross;
therefore, I love Your decrees.
¹²⁰ I tremble in awe of You;
I fear Your judgments.

‫ע‬ Ayin

¹²¹ I have done what is just and right;
do not leave me to my oppressors.
¹²² Guarantee Your servant's well-being;
do not let the arrogant oppress me.
¹²³ My eyes grow weary looking for Your salvation
and for Your righteous promise.
¹²⁴ Deal with Your servant based on
Your faithful love;
teach me Your statutes.
¹²⁵ I am Your servant; give me understanding
so that I may know Your decrees.
¹²⁶ It is time for the Lord to act,
for they have violated Your instruction.
¹²⁷ Since I love Your commands
more than gold, even the purest gold,
¹²⁸ I carefully follow all Your precepts
and hate every false way.

‫פ‬ Pe

¹²⁹ Your decrees are wonderful;
therefore I obey them.
¹³⁰ The revelation of Your words brings light
and gives understanding to the inexperienced.
¹³¹ I open my mouth and pant
because I long for Your commands.

¹³² Turn to me and be gracious to me,
as is Your practice toward those who love
Your name.
¹³³ Make my steps steady through Your promise;
don't let any sin dominate me.
¹³⁴ Redeem me from human oppression,
and I will keep Your precepts.
¹³⁵ Show favor to Your servant,
and teach me Your statutes.
¹³⁶ My eyes pour out streams of tears
because people do not follow Your instruction.

‫צ‬ Tsade

¹³⁷ You are righteous, Lord,
and Your judgments are just.
¹³⁸ The decrees You issue are righteous
and altogether trustworthy.
¹³⁹ My anger overwhelms me
because my foes forget Your words.
¹⁴⁰ Your word is completely pure,
and Your servant loves it.
¹⁴¹ I am insignificant and despised,
but I do not forget Your precepts.
¹⁴² Your righteousness is
an everlasting righteousness,
and Your instruction is true.
¹⁴³ Trouble and distress have overtaken me,
but Your commands are my delight.
¹⁴⁴ Your decrees are righteous forever.
Give me understanding, and I will live.

‫ק‬ Qof

¹⁴⁵ I call with all my heart; answer me, Lord.
I will obey Your statutes.
¹⁴⁶ I call to You; save me,
and I will keep Your decrees.
¹⁴⁷ I rise before dawn and cry out for help;
I put my hope in Your word.
¹⁴⁸ I am awake through each watch of the night
to meditate on Your promise.
¹⁴⁹ In keeping with Your faithful love,
hear my voice.
Lord, give me life in keeping with Your justice.
¹⁵⁰ Those who pursue evil plans come near;
they are far from Your instruction.
¹⁵¹ You are near, Lord,
and all Your commands are true.
¹⁵² Long ago I learned from Your decrees
that You have established them forever.

‫ר‬ Resh

¹⁵³ Consider my affliction and rescue me,
for I have not forgotten Your instruction.
¹⁵⁴ Defend my cause and redeem me;
give me life as You promised.
¹⁵⁵ Salvation is far from the wicked
because they do not seek Your statutes.
¹⁵⁶ Your compassions are many, Lord;
give me life according to Your judgments.
¹⁵⁷ My persecutors and foes are many.
I have not turned from Your decrees.
¹⁵⁸ I have seen the disloyal and feel disgust
because they do not keep Your word.
¹⁵⁹ Consider how I love Your precepts;
Lord, give me life according to
Your faithful love.
¹⁶⁰ The entirety of Your word is truth,

and all Your righteous judgments
　　endure forever.

ש Sin/ ש Shin

161 Princes have persecuted me without cause,
　　but my heart fears only Your word.
162 I rejoice over Your promise
　　like one who finds vast treasure.
163 I hate and abhor falsehood,
　　but I love Your instruction.
164 I praise You seven times a day
　　for Your righteous judgments.
165 Abundant peace belongs to those
　　who love Your instruction;
　　nothing makes them stumble.
166 LORD, I hope for Your salvation
　　and carry out Your commands.
167 I obey Your decrees
　　and love them greatly.
168 I obey Your precepts and decrees,
　　for all my ways are before You.

ת Tav

169 Let my cry reach You, LORD;
　　give me understanding according to
　　　　Your word.
170 Let my plea reach You;
　　rescue me according to Your promise.
171 My lips pour out praise,
　　for You teach me Your statutes.
172 My tongue sings about Your promise,
　　for all Your commands are righteous.
173 May Your hand be ready to help me,
　　for I have chosen Your precepts.
174 I long for Your salvation, LORD,
　　and Your instruction is my delight.
175 Let me live, and I will praise You;
　　may Your judgments help me.
176 I wander like a lost sheep;
　　seek Your servant,
　　for I do not forget Your commands.

Psalm 120
A *song of ascents.

1 In my distress I called to the LORD,
　　and He answered me.
2 "LORD, deliver me from lying lips
　　and a deceitful tongue."
3 What will He give you,
　　and what will He do to you,
　　you deceitful tongue?
4 A warrior's sharp arrows
　　with burning charcoal!
5 What misery that I have stayed in Meshech,
　　that I have lived among the tents of Kedar!
6 I have lived too long
　　with those who hate peace.
7 I am for peace; but when I speak,
　　they are for war.

Psalm 121
A *song of ascents.

1 I lift my eyes toward the mountains.
　　Where will my help come from?
2 My help comes from the LORD,
　　the Maker of heaven and earth.
3 He will not allow your foot to slip;
　　your Protector will not slumber.

4 Indeed, the Protector of Israel
　　does not slumber or sleep.
5 The LORD protects you;
　　the LORD is a shelter right by your side.
6 The sun will not strike you by day
　　or the moon by night.
7 The LORD will protect you from all harm;
　　He will protect your life.
8 The LORD will protect your coming and going
　　both now and forever.

Psalm 122
A Davidic *song of ascents.

1 I rejoiced with those who said to me,
　　"Let us go to the house of the LORD."
2 Our feet are standing
　　within your gates, Jerusalem—
3 Jerusalem, built as a city should be,
　　solidly joined together,
4 where the tribes, *Yahweh's tribes,
　　go up
　　to give thanks to the name of Yahweh.
　　(This is an ordinance for Israel.)
5 There, thrones for judgment are placed,
　　thrones of the house of David.
6 Pray for the peace of Jerusalem:
　　"May those who love you prosper;
7 may there be peace within your walls,
　　prosperity within your fortresses."
8 Because of my brothers and friends,
　　I will say, "Peace be with you."
9 Because of the house of the LORD
　　our God,
　　I will seek your good.

Psalm 123
A *song of ascents.

1 I lift my eyes to You,
　　the One enthroned in heaven.
2 Like a servant's eyes on his master's hand,
　　like a servant girl's eyes
　　　　on her mistress's hand,
　　so our eyes are on the LORD our God
　　until He shows us favor.
3 Show us favor, LORD, show us favor,
　　for we've had more than
　　　　enough contempt.
4 We've had more than enough
　　scorn from the arrogant
　　and contempt from the proud.

Psalm 124
A Davidic *song of ascents.

1 If the LORD had not been on our side—
　　let Israel say—
2 If the LORD had not been on our side
　　when men attacked us,
3 then they would have swallowed us alive
　　in their burning anger against us.
4 Then the waters would have engulfed us;
　　the torrent would have swept over us;
5 the raging waters would have swept
　　over us.
6 Praise the LORD,
　　who has not let us be ripped apart
　　by their teeth.

7 We have escaped like a bird
   from the hunter's net;
the net is torn, and we have escaped.
8 Our help is in the name of •Yahweh,
   the Maker of heaven and earth.

Psalm 125
A •song of ascents.

1 Those who trust in the LORD
   are like Mount •Zion.
It cannot be shaken; it remains forever.
2 Jerusalem—the mountains surround her.
And the LORD surrounds His people,
   both now and forever.
3 The scepter of the wicked will not remain
over the land allotted to the righteous,
so that the righteous will not apply
   their hands to injustice.
4 Do what is good, LORD, to the good,
to those whose hearts are upright.
5 But as for those who turn aside
   to crooked ways,
the LORD will banish them with the evildoers.
Peace be with Israel.

Psalm 126
A •song of ascents.

1 When the LORD restored the fortunes of •Zion,
we were like those who dream.
2 Our mouths were filled with laughter then,
and our tongues with shouts of joy.
Then they said among the nations,
"The LORD has done great things
   for them."
3 The LORD had done great things for us;
we were joyful.
4 Restore our fortunes, LORD,
like watercourses in the •Negev.
5 Those who sow in tears
will reap with shouts of joy.
6 Though one goes along weeping,
carrying the bag of seed,
he will surely come back with shouts
   of joy,
carrying his sheaves.

Psalm 127
A Solomonic •song of ascents.

1 Unless the LORD builds a house,
its builders labor over it in vain;
unless the LORD watches over a city,
the watchman stays alert in vain.
2 In vain you get up early and stay up late,
working hard to have enough food—
yes, He gives sleep to the one He loves.
3 Sons are indeed a heritage from the LORD,
children, a reward.
4 Like arrows in the hand of a warrior
are the sons born in one's youth.
5 Happy is the man who has filled his quiver
   with them.
Such men will never be put to shame
when they speak with their enemies
   at the city •gate.

Psalm 128
A •song of ascents.

1 How happy is everyone who •fears the LORD,
who walks in His ways!
2 You will surely eat
what your hands have worked for.
You will be happy,
and it will go well for you.
3 Your wife will be like a fruitful vine
within your house,
your sons, like young olive trees
around your table.
4 In this very way
the man who fears the LORD
will be blessed.
5 May the LORD bless you from •Zion,
so that you will see the prosperity
   of Jerusalem
all the days of your life
6 and will see your children's children!
Peace be with Israel.

Psalm 129
A •song of ascents.

1 Since my youth they have often attacked me—
let Israel say—
2 Since my youth they have often attacked me,
but they have not prevailed against me.
3 Plowmen plowed over my back;
they made their furrows long.
4 The LORD is righteous;
He has cut the ropes of the wicked.
5 Let all who hate •Zion
be driven back in disgrace.
6 Let them be like grass on the rooftops,
which withers before it grows up
7 and can't even fill the hands of the reaper
or the arms of the one who binds sheaves.
8 Then none who pass by will say,
"May the LORD's blessing be on you."
We bless you in the name of •Yahweh.

Psalm 130
A •song of ascents.

1 Out of the depths I call to You, •Yahweh!
2 Lord, listen to my voice;
let Your ears be attentive
to my cry for help.
3 Yahweh, if You considered sins,
Lord, who could stand?
4 But with You there is forgiveness,
so that You may be revered.
5 I wait for Yahweh; I wait
and put my hope in His word.
6 I wait for the Lord
more than watchmen for the morning—
more than watchmen for the morning.
7 Israel, put your hope in the LORD.
For there is faithful love with the LORD,
and with Him is redemption in abundance.
8 And He will redeem Israel
from all its sins.

Psalm 131
A Davidic •song of ascents.

1 LORD, my heart is not proud;
my eyes are not haughty.

I do not get involved with things
too great or too difficult for me.
2 Instead, I have calmed and quieted myself
like a little weaned child with its mother;
I am like a little child.
3 Israel, put your hope in the LORD,
both now and forever.

Psalm 132
A *song of ascents.

1 LORD, remember David
and all the hardships he endured,
2 and how he swore an oath to the LORD,
making a vow to the Mighty One of Jacob:
3 "I will not enter my house
or get into my bed,
4 I will not allow my eyes to sleep
or my eyelids to slumber
5 until I find a place for the LORD,
a dwelling for the Mighty One of Jacob."
6 We heard of the ark in Ephrathah;
we found it in the fields of Jaar.
7 Let us go to His dwelling place;
let us worship at His footstool.
8 Rise up, LORD, come to Your resting place,
You and Your powerful ark.
9 May Your priests be clothed
with righteousness,
and may Your godly people shout for joy.
10 Because of Your servant David,
do not reject Your anointed one.
11 The LORD swore an oath to David,
a promise He will not abandon:
"I will set one of your descendants
on your throne.
12 If your sons keep My covenant
and My decrees that I will teach them,
their sons will also sit on your throne forever."
13 For the LORD has chosen *Zion;
He has desired it for His home:
14 "This is My resting place forever;
I will make My home here
because I have desired it.
15 I will abundantly bless its food;
I will satisfy its needy with bread.
16 I will clothe its priests with salvation,
and its godly people will shout for joy.
17 There I will make a *horn grow for David;
I have prepared a lamp for My anointed one.
18 I will clothe his enemies with shame,
but the crown he wears will be glorious."

Psalm 133
A Davidic *song of ascents.

1 How good and pleasant it is
when brothers live together in harmony!
2 It is like fine oil on the head,
running down on the beard,
running down Aaron's beard
onto his robes.
3 It is like the dew of Hermon
falling on the mountains of *Zion.
For there the LORD has appointed
the blessing—
life forevermore.

Psalm 134
A *song of ascents.

1 Now praise the LORD,
all you servants of the LORD
who stand in the LORD's house at night!
2 Lift up your hands in the holy place
and praise the LORD!
3 May the LORD,
Maker of heaven and earth,
bless you from *Zion.

Psalm 135

1 *Hallelujah!
Praise the name of *Yahweh.
Give praise, you servants of Yahweh
2 who stand in the house of Yahweh,
in the courts of the house of our God.
3 Praise Yahweh, for Yahweh is good;
sing praise to His name, for it is delightful.
4 For Yahweh has chosen Jacob for Himself,
Israel as His treasured possession.
5 For I know that Yahweh is great;
our Lord is greater than all gods.
6 Yahweh does whatever He pleases
in heaven and on earth,
in the seas and all the depths.
7 He causes the clouds to rise from the ends
of the earth.
He makes lightning for the rain
and brings the wind from His storehouses.
8 He struck down the firstborn of Egypt,
both man and beast.
9 He sent signs and wonders against you, Egypt,
against Pharaoh and all his officials.
10 He struck down many nations
and slaughtered mighty kings:
11 Sihon king of the Amorites,
Og king of Bashan,
and all the kings of Canaan.
12 He gave their land as an inheritance,
an inheritance to His people Israel.
13 Yahweh, Your name endures forever,
Your reputation, Yahweh,
through all generations.
14 For Yahweh will vindicate His people
and have compassion on His servants.
15 The idols of the nations are of silver and gold,
made by human hands.
16 They have mouths but cannot speak,
eyes, but cannot see.
17 They have ears but cannot hear;
indeed, there is no breath in their mouths.
18 Those who make them are just like them,
as are all who trust in them.
19 House of Israel, praise Yahweh!
House of Aaron, praise Yahweh!
20 House of Levi, praise Yahweh!
You who revere the LORD, praise the LORD!
21 May the LORD be praised from *Zion;
He dwells in Jerusalem.
Hallelujah!

Psalm 136

1 Give thanks to the LORD, for He is good.
His love is eternal.
2 Give thanks to the God of gods.
His love is eternal.
3 Give thanks to the Lord of lords.

His love is eternal.
4 He alone does great wonders.
His love is eternal.
5 He made the heavens skillfully.
His love is eternal.
6 He spread the land on the waters.
His love is eternal.
7 He made the great lights:
His love is eternal.
8 the sun to rule by day,
His love is eternal.
9 the moon and stars to rule by night.
His love is eternal.
10 He struck the firstborn of the Egyptians
His love is eternal.
11 and brought Israel out from among them
His love is eternal.
12 with a strong hand and outstretched arm.
His love is eternal.
13 He divided the *Red Sea
His love is eternal.
14 and led Israel through,
His love is eternal.
15 but hurled Pharaoh and his army
into the Red Sea.
His love is eternal.
16 He led His people in the wilderness.
His love is eternal.
17 He struck down great kings
His love is eternal.
18 and slaughtered famous kings—
His love is eternal.
19 Sihon king of the Amorites
His love is eternal.
20 and Og king of Bashan—
His love is eternal.
21 and gave their land as an inheritance,
His love is eternal.
22 an inheritance to Israel His servant.
His love is eternal.
23 He remembered us in our humiliation
His love is eternal.
24 and rescued us from our foes.
His love is eternal.
25 He gives food to every creature.
His love is eternal.
26 Give thanks to the God of heaven!
His love is eternal.

Psalm 137

1 By the rivers of Babylon—
there we sat down and wept
when we remembered *Zion.
2 There we hung up our lyres
on the poplar trees,
3 for our captors there asked us for songs,
and our tormentors, for rejoicing:
"Sing us one of the songs of Zion."
4 How can we sing the LORD's song
on foreign soil?
5 If I forget you, Jerusalem,
may my right hand forget its skill.
6 May my tongue stick to the roof of my mouth
if I do not remember you,
if I do not exalt Jerusalem as my greatest joy!
7 Remember, LORD, what the Edomites said
that day at Jerusalem:
"Destroy it! Destroy it

down to its foundations!"
8 Daughter Babylon, doomed to destruction,
happy is the one who pays you back
what you have done to us.
9 Happy is he who takes your little ones
and dashes them against the rocks.

Psalm 138
Davidic.

1 I will give You thanks with all my heart;
I will sing Your praise
before the heavenly beings.
2 I will bow down toward Your holy temple
and give thanks to Your name
for Your constant love and truth.
You have exalted Your name
and Your promise above everything else.
3 On the day I called, You answered me;
You increased strength within me.
4 All the kings on earth
will give You thanks, LORD,
when they hear what You have promised.
5 They will sing of the LORD's ways,
for the LORD's glory is great.
6 Though the LORD is exalted,
He takes note of the humble;
but He knows the haughty from a distance.
7 If I walk into the thick of danger,
You will preserve my life
from the anger of my enemies.
You will extend Your hand;
Your right hand will save me.
8 The LORD will fulfill His purpose for me.
LORD, Your love is eternal;
do not abandon the work of Your hands.

Psalm 139
For the choir director. A Davidic psalm.

1 LORD, You have searched me and known me.
2 You know when I sit down and when
I stand up;
You understand my thoughts from far away.
3 You observe my travels and my rest;
You are aware of all my ways.
4 Before a word is on my tongue,
You know all about it, LORD.
5 You have encircled me;
You have placed Your hand on me.
6 This extraordinary knowledge is beyond me.
It is lofty; I am unable to reach it.
7 Where can I go to escape Your Spirit?
Where can I flee from Your presence?
8 If I go up to heaven, You are there;
if I make my bed in *Sheol, You are there.
9 If I live at the eastern horizon
or settle at the western limits,
10 even there Your hand will lead me;
Your right hand will hold on to me.
11 If I say, "Surely the darkness will hide me,
and the light around me will be night"—
12 even the darkness is not dark to You.
The night shines like the day;
darkness and light are alike to You.
13 For it was You who created my inward parts;
You knit me together in my mother's womb.
14 I will praise You

because I have been remarkably
and wonderfully made.
Your works are wonderful,
and I know this very well.
15 My bones were not hidden from You
when I was made in secret,
when I was formed in the depths of the earth.
16 Your eyes saw me when I was formless;
all my days were written in Your book
and planned
before a single one of them began.
17 God, how difficult Your thoughts are
for me to comprehend;
how vast their sum is!
18 If I counted them,
they would outnumber the grains of sand;
when I wake up, I am still with You.
19 God, if only You would kill the wicked—
you bloodthirsty men, stay away from me—
20 who invoke You deceitfully.
Your enemies swear by You falsely.
21 Lord, don't I hate those who hate You,
and detest those who rebel against You?
22 I hate them with extreme hatred;
I consider them my enemies.
23 Search me, God, and know my heart;
test me and know my concerns.
24 See if there is any offensive way in me;
lead me in the everlasting way.

Psalm 140
For the choir director. A Davidic psalm.

1 Rescue me, Lord, from evil men.
Keep me safe from violent men
2 who plan evil in their hearts.
They stir up wars all day long.
3 They make their tongues
as sharp as a snake's bite;
viper's venom is under their lips.   *Selah
4 Protect me, Lord,
from the clutches of the wicked.
Keep me safe from violent men
who plan to make me stumble.
5 The proud hide a trap with ropes for me;
they spread a net along the path
and set snares for me.   Selah
6 I say to the Lord, "You are my God."
Listen, Lord, to my cry for help.
7 Lord God, my strong Savior,
You shield my head on the day of battle.
8 Lord, do not grant the desires of the wicked;
do not let them achieve their goals.
Otherwise, they will become proud.   Selah
9 When those who surround me rise up,
may the trouble their lips cause
overwhelm them.
10 Let hot coals fall on them.
Let them be thrown into the fire,
into the *abyss, never again to rise.
11 Do not let a slanderer stay in the land.
Let evil relentlessly hunt down a violent man.
12 I know that the Lord upholds
the just cause of the poor,
justice for the needy.
13 Surely the righteous will praise Your name;
the upright will live in Your presence.

Psalm 141
A Davidic psalm.

1 Lord, I call on You; hurry to help me.
Listen to my voice when I call on You.
2 May my prayer be set before You as incense,
the raising of my hands
as the evening offering.
3 Lord, set up a guard for my mouth;
keep watch at the door of my lips.
4 Do not let my heart turn to any evil thing
or perform wicked acts
with men who commit sin.
Do not let me feast on their delicacies.
5 Let the righteous one strike me—
it is an act of faithful love;
let him rebuke me—
it is oil for my head;
let me not refuse it.
Even now my prayer is against
the evil acts of the wicked.
6 When their rulers will be thrown off
the sides of a cliff,
the people will listen to my words,
for they are pleasing.
7 As when one plows and breaks up the soil,
turning up rocks,
so our bones have been scattered
at the mouth of *Sheol.
8 But my eyes look to You, Lord God.
I seek refuge in You; do not let me die.
9 Protect me from the trap they have set for me,
and from the snares of evildoers.
10 Let the wicked fall into their own nets,
while I pass by safely.

Psalm 142
A Davidic *Maskil. When he was in the cave. A prayer.

1 I cry aloud to the Lord;
I plead aloud to the Lord for mercy.
2 I pour out my complaint before Him;
I reveal my trouble to Him.
3 Although my spirit is weak within me,
You know my way.
Along this path I travel
they have hidden a trap for me.
4 Look to the right and see:
no one stands up for me;
there is no refuge for me;
no one cares about me.
5 I cry to You, Lord;
I say, "You are my shelter,
my portion in the land of the living."
6 Listen to my cry,
for I am very weak.
Rescue me from those who pursue me,
for they are too strong for me.
7 Free me from prison
so that I can praise Your name.
The righteous will gather around me
because You deal generously with me.

Psalm 143
A Davidic psalm.

1 Lord, hear my prayer.
In Your faithfulness listen to my plea,
and in Your righteousness answer me.
2 Do not bring Your servant into judgment,

for no one alive is righteous in Your sight.

3 For the enemy has pursued me,
crushing me to the ground,
making me live in darkness
like those long dead.

4 My spirit is weak within me;
my heart is overcome with dismay.

5 I remember the days of old;
I meditate on all You have done;
I reflect on the work of Your hands.

6 I spread out my hands to You;
I am like parched land before You.   •*Selah*

7 Answer me quickly, LORD;
my spirit fails.
Don't hide Your face from me,
or I will be like those
going down to the •Pit.

8 Let me experience
Your faithful love in the morning,
for I trust in You.
Reveal to me the way I should go
because I long for You.

9 Rescue me from my enemies, LORD;
I come to You for protection.

10 Teach me to do Your will,
for You are my God.
May Your gracious Spirit
lead me on level ground.

11 Because of Your name, •Yahweh,
let me live.
In Your righteousness deliver me from trouble,

12 and in Your faithful love destroy my enemies.
Wipe out all those who attack me,
for I am Your servant.

Psalm 144
Davidic.

1 May the LORD, my rock, be praised,
who trains my hands for battle
and my fingers for warfare.

2 He is my faithful love and my fortress,
my stronghold and my deliverer.
He is my shield, and I take refuge in Him;
He subdues my people under me.

3 LORD, what is man, that You care for him,
the son of man, that You think of him?

4 Man is like a breath;
his days are like a passing shadow.

5 LORD, part Your heavens and come down.
Touch the mountains, and they will smoke.

6 Flash Your lightning and scatter the foe;
shoot Your arrows and rout them.

7 Reach down from heaven;
rescue me from deep water, and set me free
from the grasp of foreigners

8 whose mouths speak lies,
whose right hands are deceptive.

9 God, I will sing a new song to You;
I will play on a ten-stringed harp for You—

10 the One who gives victory to kings,
who frees His servant David
from the deadly sword.

11 Set me free and rescue me
from the grasp of foreigners
whose mouths speak lies,
whose right hands are deceptive.

12 Then our sons will be like plants
nurtured in their youth,
our daughters, like corner pillars
that are carved in the palace style.

13 Our storehouses will be full,
supplying all kinds of produce;
our flocks will increase by thousands
and tens of thousands in our open fields.

14 Our cattle will be well fed.
There will be no breach in the walls,
no going into captivity,
and no cry of lament in our public squares.

15 Happy are the people with such blessings.
Happy are the people whose God is •Yahweh.

Psalm 145
A Davidic hymn.

1 I exalt You, my God the King,
and praise Your name forever and ever.

2 I will praise You every day;
I will honor Your name forever and ever.

3 •Yahweh is great and is highly praised;
His greatness is unsearchable.

4 One generation will declare Your works
to the next
and will proclaim Your mighty acts.

5 I will speak of Your splendor and
glorious majesty
and Your wonderful works.

6 They will proclaim the power
of Your awe-inspiring acts,
and I will declare Your greatness.

7 They will give a testimony
of Your great goodness
and will joyfully sing of Your righteousness.

8 The LORD is gracious and compassionate,
slow to anger and rich in faithful love.

9 The LORD is good to everyone;
His compassion rests on all He has made.

10 All You have made will thank You, LORD;
the godly will praise You.

11 They will speak of the glory
of Your kingdom
and will declare Your might,

12 informing all •people of Your mighty acts
and of the glorious splendor of Your kingdom.

13 Your kingdom is an everlasting kingdom;
Your rule is for all generations.
The LORD is faithful in all His words
and gracious in all His actions.

14 The LORD helps all who fall;
He raises up all who are oppressed.

15 All eyes look to You,
and You give them their food
at the proper time.

16 You open Your hand
and satisfy the desire of every living thing.

17 The LORD is righteous in all His ways
and gracious in all His acts.

18 The LORD is near all who call out to Him,
all who call out to Him with integrity.

19 He fulfills the desires of those who •fear Him;
He hears their cry for help and saves them.

20 The LORD guards all those who love Him,
but He destroys all the wicked.

21 My mouth will declare Yahweh's praise;
let every living thing
praise His holy name forever and ever.

Psalm 146

1 ·Hallelujah!
My soul, praise the LORD.
2 I will praise the LORD all my life;
I will sing to my God as long as I live.
3 Do not trust in nobles,
in man, who cannot save.
4 When his breath leaves him,
he returns to the ground;
on that day his plans die.
5 Happy is the one whose help is the God
of Jacob,
whose hope is in the LORD his God,
6 the Maker of heaven and earth,
the sea and everything in them.
He remains faithful forever,
7 executing justice for the exploited
and giving food to the hungry.
The LORD frees prisoners.
8 The LORD opens the eyes of the blind.
The LORD raises up those who are oppressed.
The LORD loves the righteous.
9 The LORD protects foreigners
and helps the fatherless and the widow,
but He frustrates the ways of the wicked.
10 The LORD reigns forever;
·Zion, your God reigns for all generations.
Hallelujah!

Psalm 147

1 ·Hallelujah!
How good it is to sing to our God,
for praise is pleasant and lovely.
2 The LORD rebuilds Jerusalem;
He gathers Israel's exiled people.
3 He heals the brokenhearted
and binds up their wounds.
4 He counts the number of the stars;
He gives names to all of them.
5 Our Lord is great, vast in power;
His understanding is infinite.
6 The LORD helps the afflicted
but brings the wicked to the ground.
7 Sing to the LORD with thanksgiving;
play the lyre to our God,
8 who covers the sky with clouds,
prepares rain for the earth,
and causes grass to grow on the hills.
9 He provides the animals with their food,
and the young ravens, what they cry for.
10 He is not impressed by the strength of a horse;
He does not value the power of a man.
11 The LORD values those who fear Him,
those who put their hope in His faithful love.
12 Exalt the LORD, Jerusalem;
praise your God, ·Zion!
13 For He strengthens the bars of your gates
and blesses your children within you.
14 He endows your territory with prosperity;
He satisfies you with the finest wheat.
15 He sends His command throughout the earth;
His word runs swiftly.
16 He spreads snow like wool;
He scatters frost like ashes;
17 He throws His hailstones like crumbs.
Who can withstand His cold?
18 He sends His word and melts them;

He unleashes His winds, and the waters flow.
19 He declares His word to Jacob,
His statutes and judgments to Israel.
20 He has not done this for any nation;
they do not know His judgments.
Hallelujah!

Psalm 148

1 ·Hallelujah!
Praise the LORD from the heavens;
praise Him in the heights.
2 Praise Him, all His angels;
praise Him, all His ·hosts.
3 Praise Him, sun and moon;
praise Him, all you shining stars.
4 Praise Him, highest heavens,
and you waters above the heavens.
5 Let them praise the name of ·Yahweh,
for He commanded, and they were created.
6 He set them in position forever and ever;
He gave an order that will never pass away.
7 Praise the LORD from the earth,
all sea monsters and ocean depths,
8 lightning and hail, snow and cloud,
powerful wind that executes His command,
9 mountains and all hills,
fruit trees and all cedars,
10 wild animals and all cattle,
creatures that crawl and flying birds,
11 kings of the earth and all peoples,
princes and all judges of the earth,
12 young men as well as young women,
old and young together.
13 Let them praise the name of Yahweh,
for His name alone is exalted.
His majesty covers heaven and earth.
14 He has raised up a ·horn for His people,
resulting in praise to all His godly ones,
to the Israelites, the people close to Him.
Hallelujah!

Psalm 149

1 ·Hallelujah!
Sing to the LORD a new song,
His praise in the assembly of the godly.
2 Let Israel celebrate its Maker;
let the children of ·Zion rejoice in their King.
3 Let them praise His name with dancing
and make music to Him with tambourine
and lyre.
4 For ·Yahweh takes pleasure in His people;
He adorns the humble with salvation.
5 Let the godly celebrate in triumphal glory;
let them shout for joy on their beds.
6 Let the exaltation of God be in their mouths
and a double-edged sword in their hands,
7 inflicting vengeance on the nations
and punishment on the peoples,
8 binding their kings with chains
and their dignitaries with iron shackles,
9 carrying out the judgment
decreed against them.
This honor is for all His godly people.
Hallelujah!

Psalm 150

1 ·Hallelujah!
Praise God in His sanctuary.

Praise Him in His mighty heavens.
2 Praise Him for His powerful acts;
praise Him for His abundant greatness.
3 Praise Him with trumpet blast;
praise Him with harp and lyre.
4 Praise Him with tambourine and dance;
praise Him with flute and strings.
5 Praise Him with resounding cymbals;
praise Him with clashing cymbals.
6 Let everything that breathes
praise the LORD.
Hallelujah!

PROVERBS

1 The proverbs of Solomon son of David,
king of Israel:
2 For learning what wisdom and discipline are;
for understanding insightful sayings;
3 for receiving wise instruction
in righteousness, justice, and integrity;
4 for teaching shrewdness to the inexperienced,
knowledge and discretion to a young man—
5 a wise man will listen and increase
his learning,
and a discerning man will obtain guidance—
6 for understanding a proverb or a parable,
the words of the wise, and their riddles.
7 The *fear of the LORD
is the beginning of knowledge;
fools despise wisdom and discipline.
8 Listen, my son, to your father's instruction,
and don't reject your mother's teaching,
9 for they will be a garland of grace
on your head
and a gold chain around your neck.
10 My son, if sinners entice you,
don't be persuaded.
11 If they say—"Come with us!
Let's set an ambush and kill someone.
Let's attack some innocent person just for fun!
12 Let's swallow them alive, like *Sheol,
still healthy as they go down to the *Pit.
13 We'll find all kinds of valuable property
and fill our houses with plunder.
14 Throw in your lot with us,
and we'll all share our money"—
15 my son, don't travel that road with them
or set foot on their path,
16 because their feet run toward trouble
and they hurry to commit murder.
17 It is foolish to spread a net
where any bird can see it,
18 but they set an ambush to kill themselves;
they attack their own lives.
19 Such are the paths of all who make
profit dishonestly;
it takes the lives of those who receive it.
20 Wisdom calls out in the street;
she raises her voice in the public squares.
21 She cries out above the commotion;
she speaks at the entrance of the city *gates:
22 "How long, foolish ones, will you
love ignorance?
How long will you mockers enjoy mocking
and you fools hate knowledge?
23 If you respond to my warning,
then I will pour out my spirit on you
and teach you my words.
24 Since I called out and you refused,

extended my hand and no one paid attention,
25 since you neglected all my counsel
and did not accept my correction,
26 I, in turn, will laugh at your calamity.
I will mock when terror strikes you,
27 when terror strikes you like a storm
and your calamity comes like a whirlwind,
when trouble and stress overcome you.
28 Then they will call me, but I won't answer;
they will search for me, but won't find me.
29 Because they hated knowledge,
didn't choose to fear the LORD,
30 were not interested in my counsel,
and rejected all my correction,
31 they will eat the fruit of their way
and be glutted with their own schemes.
32 For the turning away of the inexperienced
will kill them,
and the complacency of fools
will destroy them.
33 But whoever listens to me will live securely
and be free from the fear of danger."

2 My son, if you accept my words
and store up my commands within you,
2 listening closely to wisdom
and directing your heart to understanding;
3 furthermore, if you call out to insight
and lift your voice to understanding,
4 if you seek it like silver
and search for it like hidden treasure,
5 then you will understand the *fear of the LORD
and discover the knowledge of God.
6 For the LORD gives wisdom;
from His mouth come knowledge
and understanding.
7 He stores up success for the upright;
He is a shield for those who live with integrity
8 so that He may guard the paths of justice
and protect the way of His loyal followers.
9 Then you will understand righteousness,
justice,
and integrity—every good path.
10 For wisdom will enter your mind,
and knowledge will delight your heart.
11 Discretion will watch over you,
and understanding will guard you,
12 rescuing you from the way of evil—
from the one who says perverse things,
13 from those who abandon the right paths
to walk in ways of darkness,
14 from those who enjoy doing evil
and celebrate perversion,
15 whose paths are crooked,
and whose ways are devious.
16 It will rescue you from a forbidden woman,

from a stranger with her flattering talk,

17 who abandons the companion of her youth
and forgets the covenant of her God;

18 for her house sinks down to death
and her ways to the land
of the departed spirits.

19 None return who go to her;
none reach the paths of life.

20 So follow the way of good people,
and keep to the paths of the righteous.

21 For the upright will inhabit the land,
and those of integrity will remain in it;

22 but the wicked will be cut off from the land,
and the treacherous uprooted from it.

3 My son, don't forget my teaching,
but let your heart keep my commands;

2 for they will bring you
many days, a full life, and well-being.

3 Never let loyalty and faithfulness leave you.
Tie them around your neck;
write them on the tablet of your heart.

4 Then you will find favor and high regard
in the sight of God and man.

5 Trust in the L<small>ORD</small> with all your heart,
and do not rely on your own understanding;

6 think about Him in all your ways,
and He will guide you on the right paths.

7 Don't consider yourself to be wise;
‘fear the L<small>ORD</small> and turn away from evil.

8 This will be healing for your body
and strengthening for your bones.

9 Honor the L<small>ORD</small> with your possessions
and with the first produce
of your entire harvest;

10 then your barns will be completely filled,
and your vats will overflow with new wine.

11 Do not despise the L<small>ORD</small>'s instruction, my son,
and do not loathe His discipline;

12 for the L<small>ORD</small> disciplines the one He loves,
just as a father, the son he delights in.

13 Happy is a man who finds wisdom
and who acquires understanding,

14 for she is more profitable than silver,
and her revenue is better than gold.

15 She is more precious than jewels;
nothing you desire compares with her.

16 Long life is in her right hand;
in her left, riches and honor.

17 Her ways are pleasant,
and all her paths, peaceful.

18 She is a tree of life to those who embrace her,
and those who hold on to her are happy.

19 The L<small>ORD</small> founded the earth by wisdom
and established the heavens by understanding.

20 By His knowledge the watery depths
broke open,
and the clouds dripped with dew.

21 Maintain your competence and discretion.
My son, don't lose sight of them.

22 They will be life for you
and adornment for your neck.

23 Then you will go safely on your way;
your foot will not stumble.

24 When you lie down, you will not be afraid;
you will lie down, and your sleep
will be pleasant.

25 Don't fear sudden danger

or the ruin of the wicked when it comes,

26 for the L<small>ORD</small> will be your confidence
and will keep your foot from a snare.

27 When it is in your power,
don't withhold good from the one
it belongs to.

28 Don't say to your neighbor, "Go away!
Come back later.
I'll give it tomorrow"—when it is there
with you.

29 Don't plan any harm against your neighbor,
for he trusts you and lives near you.

30 Don't accuse anyone without cause,
when he has done you no harm.

31 Don't envy a violent man
or choose any of his ways;

32 for the devious are detestable to the L<small>ORD</small>,
but He is a friend to the upright.

33 The L<small>ORD</small>'s curse is on the household
of the wicked,
but He blesses the home of the righteous;

34 He mocks those who mock,
but gives grace to the humble.

35 The wise will inherit honor,
but He holds up fools to dishonor.

4 Listen, my sons, to a father's discipline,
and pay attention so that
you may gain understanding,

2 for I am giving you good instruction.
Don't abandon my teaching.

3 When I was a son with my father,
tender and precious to my mother,

4 he taught me and said:
"Your heart must hold on to my words.
Keep my commands and live.

5 Get wisdom, get understanding;
don't forget or turn away from the words
of my mouth.

6 Don't abandon wisdom, and she will
watch over you;
love her, and she will guard you.

7 Wisdom is supreme—so get wisdom.
And whatever else you get, get understanding.

8 Cherish her, and she will exalt you;
if you embrace her, she will honor you.

9 She will place a garland of grace on your head;
she will give you a crown of beauty."

10 Listen, my son. Accept my words,
and you will live many years.

11 I am teaching you the way of wisdom;
I am guiding you on straight paths.

12 When you walk, your steps will not
be hindered;
when you run, you will not stumble.

13 Hold on to instruction; don't let go.
Guard it, for it is your life.

14 Don't set foot on the path of the wicked;
don't proceed in the way of evil ones.

15 Avoid it; don't travel on it.
Turn away from it, and pass it by.

16 For they can't sleep
unless they have done what is evil;
they are robbed of sleep
unless they make someone stumble.

17 They eat the bread of wickedness
and drink the wine of violence.

18 The path of the righteous is like the light
     of dawn,
   shining brighter and brighter until midday.
19 But the way of the wicked is
     like the darkest gloom;
   they don't know what makes them stumble.
20 My son, pay attention to my words;
   listen closely to my sayings.
21 Don't lose sight of them;
   keep them within your heart.
22 For they are life to those who find them,
   and health to one's whole body.
23 Guard your heart above all else,
   for it is the source of life.
24 Don't let your mouth speak dishonestly,
   and don't let your lips talk deviously.
25 Let your eyes look forward;
   fix your gaze straight ahead.
26 Carefully consider the path for your feet,
   and all your ways will be established.
27 Don't turn to the right or to the left;
   keep your feet away from evil.

5 My son, pay attention to my wisdom;
   listen closely to my understanding
2 so that you may maintain discretion
   and your lips safeguard knowledge.
3 Though the lips of the forbidden woman
     drip honey
   and her words are smoother than oil,
4 in the end she's as bitter as *wormwood
   and as sharp as a double-edged sword.
5 Her feet go down to death;
   her steps head straight for *Sheol.
6 She doesn't consider the path of life;
   she doesn't know that her ways are unstable.
7 So now, my sons, listen to me,
   and don't turn away from the words
     of my mouth.
8 Keep your way far from her.
   Don't go near the door of her house.
9 Otherwise, you will give up your vitality
     to others
   and your years to someone cruel;
10 strangers will drain your resources,
   and your earnings will end up
     in a foreigner's house.
11 At the end of your life, you will lament
   when your physical body has been consumed,
12 and you will say, "How I hated discipline,
   and how my heart despised correction.
13 I didn't obey my teachers
   or listen closely to my mentors.
14 I am on the verge of complete ruin
   before the entire community."
15 Drink water from your own cistern,
   water flowing from your own well.
16 Should your springs flow in the streets,
   streams of water in the public squares?
17 They should be for you alone
   and not for you to share with strangers.
18 Let your fountain be blessed,
   and take pleasure in the wife of your youth.
19 A loving doe, a graceful fawn—
   let her breasts always satisfy you;
   be lost in her love forever.
20 Why, my son, would you be infatuated
   with a forbidden woman

or embrace the breast of a stranger?
21 For a man's ways are before the LORD's eyes,
   and He considers all his paths.
22 A wicked man's iniquities entrap him;
   he is entangled in the ropes of his own sin.
23 He will die because there is no discipline,
   and be lost because of his great stupidity.

6 My son, if you have put up security
     for your neighbor
   or entered into an agreement with a stranger,
2 you have been trapped by the words
     of your lips—
   ensnared by the words of your mouth.
3 Do this, then, my son, and free yourself,
   for you have put yourself
     in your neighbor's power:
   Go, humble yourself, and plead
     with your neighbor.
4 Don't give sleep to your eyes
   or slumber to your eyelids.
5 Escape like a gazelle from a hunter,
   like a bird from a fowler's trap.
6 Go to the ant, you slacker!
   Observe its ways and become wise.
7 Without leader, administrator, or ruler,
8 it prepares its provisions in summer;
   it gathers its food during harvest.
9 How long will you stay in bed, you slacker?
   When will you get up from your sleep?
10 A little sleep, a little slumber,
   a little folding of the arms to rest,
11 and your poverty will come like a robber,
   your need, like a bandit.
12 A worthless person, a wicked man
   goes around speaking dishonestly,
13 winking his eyes, signaling with his feet,
   and gesturing with his fingers.
14 He always plots evil with perversity
     in his heart—
   he stirs up trouble.
15 Therefore calamity will strike him suddenly;
   he will be shattered instantly—
     beyond recovery.
16 The LORD hates six things;
   in fact, seven are detestable to Him:
17 arrogant eyes, a lying tongue,
   hands that shed innocent blood,
18 a heart that plots wicked schemes,
   feet eager to run to evil,
19 a lying witness who gives false testimony,
   and one who stirs up trouble among brothers.
20 My son, keep your father's command,
   and don't reject your mother's teaching.
21 Always bind them to your heart;
   tie them around your neck.
22 When you walk here and there, they will
     guide you;
   when you lie down, they will watch over you;
   when you wake up, they will talk to you.
23 For a command is a lamp, teaching is a light,
   and corrective discipline is the way to life.
24 They will protect you from an evil woman,
   from the flattering tongue of a stranger.
25 Don't lust in your heart for her beauty
   or let her captivate you with her eyelashes.
26 For a prostitute's fee is only a loaf of bread,
   but an adulteress goes after a precious life.

27 Can a man embrace fire
and his clothes not be burned?
28 Can a man walk on burning coals
without scorching his feet?
29 So it is with the one who sleeps with
another man's wife;
no one who touches her will go unpunished.
30 People don't despise the thief if he steals
to satisfy himself when he is hungry.
31 Still, if caught, he must pay seven times
as much;
he must give up all the wealth in his house.
32 The one who commits adultery lacks sense;
whoever does so destroys himself.
33 He will get a beating and dishonor,
and his disgrace will never be removed.
34 For jealousy enrages a husband,
and he will show no mercy
when he takes revenge.
35 He will not be appeased by anything
or be persuaded by lavish gifts.

7 My son, obey my words,
and treasure my commands.
2 Keep my commands and live;
protect my teachings
as the pupil of your eye.
3 Tie them to your fingers;
write them on the tablet of your heart.
4 Say to wisdom, "You are my sister,"
and call understanding your relative.
5 She will keep you from a forbidden woman,
a stranger with her flattering talk.
6 At the window of my house
I looked through my lattice.
7 I saw among the inexperienced,
I noticed among the youths,
a young man lacking sense.
8 Crossing the street near her corner,
he strolled down the road to her house
9 at twilight, in the evening,
in the dark of the night.
10 A woman came to meet him
dressed like a prostitute,
having a hidden agenda.
11 She is loud and defiant;
her feet do not stay at home.
12 Now in the street, now in the squares,
she lurks at every corner.
13 She grabs him and kisses him;
she brazenly says to him,
14 "I've made *fellowship offerings;
today I've fulfilled my vows.
15 So I came out to meet you,
to search for you, and I've found you.
16 I've spread coverings on my bed—
richly colored linen from Egypt.
17 I've perfumed my bed
with myrrh, aloes, and cinnamon.
18 Come, let's drink deeply of lovemaking
until morning.
Let's feast on each other's love!
19 My husband isn't home;
he went on a long journey.
20 He took a bag of money with him
and will come home at the time
of the full moon."
21 She seduces him with her persistent pleading;

she lures with her flattering talk.
22 He follows her impulsively
like an ox going to the slaughter,
like a deer bounding toward a trap
23 until an arrow pierces its liver,
like a bird darting into a snare—
he doesn't know it will cost him his life.
24 Now, my sons, listen to me,
and pay attention to the words of my mouth.
25 Don't let your heart turn aside to her ways;
don't stray onto her paths.
26 For she has brought many down to death;
her victims are countless.
27 Her house is the road to *Sheol,
descending to the chambers of death.

8 Doesn't Wisdom call out?
Doesn't Understanding make her voice heard?
2 At the heights overlooking the road,
at the crossroads, she takes her stand.
3 Beside the gates at the entry to the city,
at the main entrance, she cries out:
4 "People, I call out to you;
my cry is to mankind.
5 Learn to be shrewd,
you who are inexperienced;
develop common sense, you who are foolish.
6 Listen, for I speak of noble things,
and what my lips say is right.
7 For my mouth tells the truth,
and wickedness is detestable to my lips.
8 All the words of my mouth are righteous;
none of them are deceptive or perverse.
9 All of them are clear to the perceptive,
and right to those who discover knowledge.
10 Accept my instruction instead of silver,
and knowledge rather than pure gold.
11 For wisdom is better than jewels,
and nothing desirable can compare with it.
12 I, Wisdom, share a home with shrewdness
and have knowledge and discretion.
13 To *fear the LORD is to hate evil.
I hate arrogant pride, evil conduct,
and perverse speech.
14 I possess good advice and competence;
I have understanding and strength.
15 It is by me that kings reign
and rulers enact just law;
16 by me, princes lead,
as do nobles and all righteous judges.
17 I love those who love me,
and those who search for me find me.
18 With me are riches and honor,
lasting wealth and righteousness.
19 My fruit is better than solid gold,
and my harvest than pure silver.
20 I walk in the way of righteousness,
along the paths of justice,
21 giving wealth as an inheritance to those
who love me,
and filling their treasuries.
22 The LORD made me
at the beginning of His creation,
before His works of long ago.
23 I was formed before ancient times,
from the beginning, before the earth began.
24 I was born
when there were no watery depths

and no springs filled with water.
25 I was delivered
before the mountains and hills
were established,
26 before He made the land, the fields,
or the first soil on earth.
27 I was there when He established the heavens,
when He laid out the horizon on the surface
of the ocean,
28 when He placed the skies above,
when the fountains of the ocean gushed out,
29 when He set a limit for the sea
so that the waters would not violate
His command,
when He laid out the foundations of the earth.
30 I was a skilled craftsman beside Him.
I was His delight every day,
always rejoicing before Him.
31 I was rejoicing in His inhabited world,
delighting in the *human race.
32 And now, my sons, listen to me;
those who keep my ways are happy.
33 Listen to instruction and be wise;
don't ignore it.
34 Anyone who listens to me is happy,
watching at my doors every day,
waiting by the posts of my doorway.
35 For the one who finds me finds life
and obtains favor from the LORD,
36 but the one who misses me harms himself;
all who hate me love death."

9 Wisdom has built her house;
she has carved out her seven pillars.
2 She has prepared her meat; she has mixed
her wine;
she has also set her table.
3 She has sent out her female servants;
she calls out from the highest points
of the city:
4 "Whoever is inexperienced, enter here!"
To the one who lacks sense, she says,
5 "Come, eat my bread,
and drink the wine I have mixed.
6 Leave inexperience behind, and you will live;
pursue the way of understanding.
7 The one who corrects a mocker
will bring dishonor on himself;
the one who rebukes a wicked man
will get hurt.
8 Don't rebuke a mocker, or he will hate you;
rebuke a wise man, and he will love you.
9 Instruct a wise man, and he will be wiser still;
teach a righteous man, and he will
learn more.
10 The *fear of the LORD is the beginning
of wisdom,
and the knowledge of the Holy One
is understanding.
11 For by Wisdom your days will be many,
and years will be added to your life.
12 If you are wise, you are wise
for your own benefit;
if you mock, you alone will bear
the consequences."
13 The woman Folly is rowdy;
she is gullible and knows nothing.
14 She sits by the doorway of her house,

on a seat at the highest point of the city,
15 calling to those who pass by,
who go straight ahead on their paths:
16 "Whoever is inexperienced, enter here!"
To the one who lacks sense, she says,
17 "Stolen water is sweet,
and bread eaten secretly is tasty!"
18 But he doesn't know that the departed spirits
are there,
that her guests are in the depths of *Sheol.

10 Solomon's proverbs:
A wise son brings joy to his father,
but a foolish son, heartache to his mother.
2 Ill-gotten gains do not profit anyone,
but righteousness rescues from death.
3 The LORD will not let the righteous go hungry,
but He denies the wicked what they crave.
4 Idle hands make one poor,
but diligent hands bring riches.
5 The son who gathers during summer
is prudent;
the son who sleeps during harvest
is disgraceful.
6 Blessings are on the head of the righteous,
but the mouth of the wicked
conceals violence.
7 The remembrance of the righteous is
a blessing,
but the name of the wicked will rot.
8 A wise heart accepts commands,
but foolish lips will be destroyed.
9 The one who lives with integrity lives securely,
but whoever perverts his ways will be
found out.
10 A sly wink of the eye causes grief,
and foolish lips will be destroyed.
11 The mouth of the righteous is a fountain
of life,
but the mouth of the wicked
conceals violence.
12 Hatred stirs up conflicts,
but love covers all offenses.
13 Wisdom is found on the lips of the discerning,
but a rod is for the back of the one
who lacks sense.
14 The wise store up knowledge,
but the mouth of the fool hastens destruction.
15 A rich man's wealth is his fortified city;
the poverty of the poor is their destruction.
16 The labor of the righteous leads to life;
the activity of the wicked leads to sin.
17 The one who follows instruction is on the path
to life,
but the one who rejects correction goes astray.
18 The one who conceals hatred has lying lips,
and whoever spreads slander is a fool.
19 When there are many words,
sin is unavoidable,
but the one who controls his lips is wise.
20 The tongue of the righteous is pure silver;
the heart of the wicked is of little value.
21 The lips of the righteous feed many,
but fools die for lack of sense.
22 The LORD's blessing enriches,
and struggle adds nothing to it.
23 As shameful conduct is pleasure for a fool,
so wisdom is for a man of understanding.

24 What the wicked dreads will come to him,
but what the righteous desire will be given
to them.

25 When the whirlwind passes,
the wicked are no more,
but the righteous are secure forever.

26 Like vinegar to the teeth and smoke
to the eyes,
so the slacker is to the one who sends him
on an errand.

27 The *fear of the LORD prolongs life,
but the years of the wicked are cut short.

28 The hope of the righteous is joy,
but the expectation of the wicked
comes to nothing.

29 The way of the LORD is a stronghold
for the honorable,
but destruction awaits the malicious.

30 The righteous will never be shaken,
but the wicked will not remain on the earth.

31 The mouth of the righteous produces wisdom,
but a perverse tongue will be cut out.

32 The lips of the righteous know
what is appropriate,
but the mouth of the wicked,
only what is perverse.

11 Dishonest scales are detestable to the LORD,
but an accurate weight is His delight.

2 When pride comes, disgrace follows,
but with humility comes wisdom.

3 The integrity of the upright guides them,
but the perversity of the treacherous
destroys them.

4 Wealth is not profitable on a day of wrath,
but righteousness rescues from death.

5 The righteousness of the blameless
clears his path,
but the wicked person will fall because of
his wickedness.

6 The righteousness of the upright
rescues them,
but the treacherous are trapped
by their own desires.

7 When the wicked man dies,
his expectation comes to nothing,
and hope placed in wealth vanishes.

8 The righteous one is rescued from trouble;
in his place, the wicked one goes in.

9 With his mouth the ungodly
destroys his neighbor,
but through knowledge the righteous
are rescued.

10 When the righteous thrive, a city rejoices,
and when the wicked die, there is
joyful shouting.

11 A city is built up by the blessing
of the upright,
but it is torn down by the mouth
of the wicked.

12 Whoever shows contempt for his neighbor
lacks sense,
but a man with understanding keeps silent.

13 A gossip goes around revealing a secret,
but a trustworthy person keeps a confidence.

14 Without guidance, people fall,
but with many counselors there is deliverance.

15 If someone puts up security for a stranger,
he will suffer for it,
but the one who hates such agreements
is protected.

16 A gracious woman gains honor,
but violent men gain only riches.

17 A kind man benefits himself,
but a cruel man brings disaster on himself.

18 The wicked man earns an empty wage,
but the one who sows righteousness,
a true reward.

19 Genuine righteousness leads to life,
but pursuing evil leads to death.

20 Those with twisted minds are detestable
to the LORD,
but those with blameless conduct are
His delight.

21 Be assured that the wicked
will not go unpunished,
but the offspring of the righteous will escape.

22 A beautiful woman who rejects good sense
is like a gold ring in a pig's snout.

23 The desire of the righteous turns out well,
but the hope of the wicked leads to wrath.

24 One person gives freely,
yet gains more;
another withholds what is right,
only to become poor.

25 A generous person will be enriched,
and the one who gives a drink of water
will receive water.

26 People will curse anyone who hoards grain,
but a blessing will come to the one
who sells it.

27 The one who searches for what is good
finds favor,
but if someone looks for trouble, it will come
to him.

28 Anyone trusting in his riches will fall,
but the righteous will flourish like foliage.

29 The one who brings ruin on his household
will inherit the wind,
and a fool will be a slave
to someone whose heart is wise.

30 The fruit of the righteous is a tree of life,
but violence takes lives.

31 If the righteous will be repaid on earth,
how much more the wicked and sinful.

12 Whoever loves discipline loves knowledge,
but one who hates correction is stupid.

2 The good person obtains favor from the LORD,
but He condemns a man who schemes.

3 Man cannot be made secure by wickedness,
but the root of the righteous is immovable.

4 A capable wife is her husband's crown,
but a wife who causes shame
is like rottenness in his bones.

5 The thoughts of the righteous are just,
but guidance from the wicked leads to deceit.

6 The words of the wicked are a deadly ambush,
but the speech of the upright rescues them.

7 The wicked are overthrown and perish,
but the house of the righteous will stand.

8 A man is praised for his insight,
but a twisted mind is despised.

9 Better to be dishonored, yet have a servant,
than to act important but have no food.

10 A righteous man cares about
    his animal's health,
    but even the merciful acts of the wicked
    are cruel.
11 The one who works his land will have plenty
    of food,
    but whoever chases fantasies lacks sense.
12 The wicked desire what evil men have,
    but the root of the righteous produces fruit.
13 An evil man is trapped
    by his rebellious speech,
    but a righteous one escapes from trouble.
14 A man will be satisfied with good
    by the words of his mouth,
    and the work of a man's hands
    will reward him.
15 A fool's way is right in his own eyes,
    but whoever listens to counsel is wise.
16 A fool's displeasure is known at once,
    but whoever ignores an insult is sensible.
17 Whoever speaks the truth declares
    what is right,
    but a false witness, deceit.
18 There is one who speaks rashly,
    like a piercing sword;
    but the tongue of the wise brings healing.
19 Truthful lips endure forever,
    but a lying tongue, only a moment.
20 Deceit is in the hearts of those who plot evil,
    but those who promote peace have joy.
21 No disaster overcomes the righteous,
    but the wicked are full of misery.
22 Lying lips are detestable to the LORD,
    but faithful people are His delight.
23 A shrewd person conceals knowledge,
    but a foolish heart publicizes stupidity.
24 The diligent hand will rule,
    but laziness will lead to forced labor.
25 Anxiety in a man's heart weighs it down,
    but a good word cheers it up.
26 A righteous man is careful in dealing
    with his neighbor,
    but the ways of the wicked lead them astray.
27 A lazy man doesn't roast his game,
    but to a diligent man, his wealth is precious.
28 There is life in the path of righteousness,
    but another path leads to death.

13 A wise son responds to his father's discipline,
    but a mocker doesn't listen to rebuke.
2 From the words of his mouth,
    a man will enjoy good things,
    but treacherous people have an appetite
    for violence.
3 The one who guards his mouth protects
    his life;
    the one who opens his lips invites
    his own ruin.
4 The slacker craves, yet has nothing,
    but the diligent is fully satisfied.
5 The righteous hate lying,
    but the wicked act disgustingly
    and disgracefully.
6 Righteousness guards people of integrity,
    but wickedness undermines the sinner.
7 One man pretends to be rich but has nothing;
    another pretends to be poor but has
    great wealth.

8 Riches are a ransom for a man's life,
    but a poor man hears no threat.
9 The light of the righteous shines brightly,
    but the lamp of the wicked is put out.
10 Arrogance leads to nothing but strife,
    but wisdom is gained by those who take advice.
11 Wealth obtained by fraud will dwindle,
    but whoever earns it through labor
    will multiply it.
12 Delayed hope makes the heart sick,
    but fulfilled desire is a tree of life.
13 The one who has contempt for instruction
    will pay the penalty,
    but the one who respects a command
    will be rewarded.
14 A wise man's instruction is a fountain of life,
    turning people away from the snares of death.
15 Good sense wins favor,
    but the way of the treacherous never changes.
16 Every sensible person acts knowledgeably,
    but a fool displays his stupidity.
17 A wicked messenger falls into trouble,
    but a trustworthy courier brings healing.
18 Poverty and disgrace come to those
    who ignore discipline,
    but the one who accepts correction
    will be honored.
19 Desire fulfilled is sweet to the taste,
    but to turn from evil
    is an abomination to fools.
20 The one who walks with the wise
    will become wise,
    but a companion of fools will suffer harm.
21 Disaster pursues sinners,
    but good rewards the righteous.
22 A good man leaves an inheritance
    to his grandchildren,
    but the sinner's wealth is stored up
    for the righteous.
23 The uncultivated field of the poor
    yields abundant food,
    but without justice, it is swept away.
24 The one who will not use the rod hates
    his son,
    but the one who loves him disciplines
    him diligently.
25 A righteous man eats until he is satisfied,
    but the stomach of the wicked is empty.

14 Every wise woman builds her house,
    but a foolish one tears it down
    with her own hands.
2 Whoever lives with integrity ⸳fears the LORD,
    but the one who is devious in his ways
    despises Him.
3 The proud speech of a fool brings a rod
    of discipline,
    but the lips of the wise protect them.
4 Where there are no oxen, the feeding trough
    is empty,
    but an abundant harvest comes
    through the strength of an ox.
5 An honest witness does not deceive,
    but a dishonest witness utters lies.
6 A mocker seeks wisdom and doesn't find it,
    but knowledge comes easily to the perceptive.
7 Stay away from a foolish man;
    you will gain no knowledge from his speech.

8 The sensible man's wisdom is to consider
his way,
but the stupidity of fools deceives them.

9 Fools mock at making restitution,
but there is goodwill among the upright.

10 The heart knows its own bitterness,
and no outsider shares in its joy.

11 The house of the wicked will be destroyed,
but the tent of the upright will stand.

12 There is a way that seems right to a man,
but its end is the way to death.

13 Even in laughter a heart may be sad,
and joy may end in grief.

14 The disloyal one will get
what his conduct deserves,
and a good man, what his deeds deserve.

15 The inexperienced one believes anything,
but the sensible one watches his steps.

16 A wise man is cautious and turns from evil,
but a fool is easily angered and is careless.

17 A quick-tempered man acts foolishly,
and a man who schemes is hated.

18 The inexperienced inherit foolishness,
but the sensible are crowned with knowledge.

19 The evil bow before those who are good,
the wicked, at the gates of the righteous.

20 A poor man is hated even by his neighbor,
but there are many who love the rich.

21 The one who despises his neighbor sins,
but whoever shows kindness to the poor
will be happy.

22 Don't those who plan evil go astray?
But those who plan good find loyalty
and faithfulness.

23 There is profit in all hard work,
but endless talk leads only to poverty.

24 The crown of the wise is their wealth,
but the foolishness of fools
produces foolishness.

25 A truthful witness rescues lives,
but one who utters lies is deceitful.

26 In the fear of the LORD one has
strong confidence
and his children have a refuge.

27 The fear of the LORD is a fountain of life,
turning people away from the snares of death.

28 A large population is a king's splendor,
but a shortage of people is
a ruler's devastation.

29 A patient person shows great understanding,
but a quick-tempered one
promotes foolishness.

30 A tranquil heart is life to the body,
but jealousy is rottenness to the bones.

31 The one who oppresses the poor person
insults his Maker,
but one who is kind to the needy honors Him.

32 The wicked one is thrown down
by his own sin,
but the righteous one has a refuge
in his death.

33 Wisdom resides in the heart of the discerning;
she is known even among fools.

34 Righteousness exalts a nation,
but sin is a disgrace to any people.

35 A king favors a wise servant,
but his anger falls on a disgraceful one.

15 A gentle answer turns away anger,
but a harsh word stirs up wrath.

2 The tongue of the wise
makes knowledge attractive,
but the mouth of fools blurts out foolishness.

3 The eyes of the LORD are everywhere,
observing the wicked and the good.

4 The tongue that heals is a tree of life,
but a devious tongue breaks the spirit.

5 A fool despises his father's discipline,
but a person who accepts correction
is sensible.

6 The house of the righteous has great wealth,
but trouble accompanies the income
of the wicked.

7 The lips of the wise broadcast knowledge,
but not so the heart of fools.

8 The sacrifice of the wicked is detestable
to the LORD,
but the prayer of the upright is His delight.

9 The LORD detests the way of the wicked,
but He loves the one
who pursues righteousness.

10 Discipline is harsh for the one who leaves
the path;
the one who hates correction will die.

11 ˙Sheol and ˙Abaddon lie open before the LORD—
how much more, human hearts.

12 A mocker doesn't love one who corrects him;
he will not consult the wise.

13 A joyful heart makes a face cheerful,
but a sad heart produces a broken spirit.

14 A discerning mind seeks knowledge,
but the mouth of fools feeds on foolishness.

15 All the days of the oppressed are miserable,
but a cheerful heart has a continual feast.

16 Better a little with the ˙fear of the LORD
than great treasure with turmoil.

17 Better a meal of vegetables where there is love
than a fattened ox with hatred.

18 A hot-tempered man stirs up conflict,
but a man slow to anger calms strife.

19 A slacker's way is like a thorny hedge,
but the path of the upright is a highway.

20 A wise son brings joy to his father,
but a foolish man despises his mother.

21 Foolishness brings joy to one without sense,
but a man with understanding walks
a straight path.

22 Plans fail when there is no counsel,
but with many advisers they succeed.

23 A man takes joy in giving an answer;
and a timely word—how good that is!

24 For the discerning the path of life
leads upward,
so that he may avoid going down to Sheol.

25 The LORD destroys the house of the proud,
but He protects the widow's territory.

26 The LORD detests the plans of an evil man,
but pleasant words are pure.

27 The one who profits dishonestly troubles
his household,
but the one who hates bribes will live.

28 The mind of the righteous person thinks
before answering,
but the mouth of the wicked blurts out
evil things.

29 The Lord is far from the wicked,
but He hears the prayer of the righteous.

30 Bright eyes cheer the heart;
good news strengthens the bones.

31 One who listens to life-giving rebukes
will be at home among the wise.

32 Anyone who ignores discipline
despises himself,
but whoever listens to correction acquires
good sense.

33 The fear of the Lord is what wisdom teaches,
and humility comes before honor.

16 The reflections of the heart belong to man,
but the answer of the tongue is from the Lord.

2 All a man's ways seem right to him,
but the Lord evaluates the motives.

3 Commit your activities to the Lord,
and your plans will be achieved.

4 The Lord has prepared everything
for His purpose—
even the wicked for the day of disaster.

5 Everyone with a proud heart is detestable
to the Lord;
be assured, he will not go unpunished.

6 Wickedness is *atoned for by loyalty
and faithfulness,
and one turns from evil by the *fear
of the Lord.

7 When a man's ways please the Lord,
He makes even his enemies to be at peace
with him.

8 Better a little with righteousness
than great income with injustice.

9 A man's heart plans his way,
but the Lord determines his steps.

10 God's verdict is on the lips of a king;
his mouth should not give
an unfair judgment.

11 Honest balances and scales are the Lord's;
all the weights in the bag are His concern.

12 Wicked behavior is detestable to kings,
since a throne is established
through righteousness.

13 Righteous lips are a king's delight,
and he loves one who speaks honestly.

14 A king's fury is a messenger of death,
but a wise man appeases it.

15 When a king's face lights up, there is life;
his favor is like a cloud with spring rain.

16 Get wisdom—
how much better it is than gold!
And get understanding—
it is preferable to silver.

17 The highway of the upright avoids evil;
the one who guards his way protects his life.

18 Pride comes before destruction,
and an arrogant spirit before a fall.

19 Better to be lowly of spirit with the humble
than to divide plunder with the proud.

20 The one who understands a matter
finds success,
and the one who trusts in the Lord
will be happy.

21 Anyone with a wise heart is called discerning,
and pleasant speech increases learning.

22 Insight is a fountain of life for its possessor,
but the discipline of fools is folly.

23 A wise heart instructs its mouth
and increases learning with its speech.

24 Pleasant words are a honeycomb:
sweet to the taste and health to the body.

25 There is a way that seems right to a man,
but its end is the way to death.

26 A worker's appetite works for him
because his hunger urges him on.

27 A worthless man digs up evil,
and his speech is like a scorching fire.

28 A contrary man spreads conflict,
and a gossip separates close friends.

29 A violent man lures his neighbor,
leading him in a way that is not good.

30 The one who narrows his eyes
is planning deceptions;
the one who compresses his lips
brings about evil.

31 Gray hair is a glorious crown;
it is found in the way of righteousness.

32 Patience is better than power,
and controlling one's temper, than capturing
a city.

33 The lot is cast into the lap,
but its every decision is from the Lord.

17 Better a dry crust with peace
than a house full of feasting with strife.

2 A wise servant will rule over a disgraceful son
and share an inheritance among brothers.

3 A crucible for silver, and a smelter for gold,
and the Lord is the tester of hearts.

4 A wicked person listens to malicious talk;
a liar pays attention to a destructive tongue.

5 The one who mocks the poor
insults his Maker,
and one who rejoices over calamity
will not go unpunished.

6 Grandchildren are the crown of the elderly,
and the pride of sons is their fathers.

7 Eloquent words are not appropriate
on a fool's lips;
how much worse are lies for a ruler.

8 A bribe seems like a magic stone to its owner;
wherever he turns, he succeeds.

9 Whoever conceals an offense promotes love,
but whoever gossips about it separates friends.

10 A rebuke cuts into a perceptive person
more than a hundred lashes into a fool.

11 An evil man seeks only rebellion;
a cruel messenger will be sent against him.

12 Better for a man to meet a bear robbed
of her cubs
than a fool in his foolishness.

13 If anyone returns evil for good,
evil will never depart from his house.

14 To start a conflict is to release a flood;
stop the dispute before it breaks out.

15 Acquitting the *guilty and condemning
the just—
both are detestable to the Lord.

16 Why does a fool have money in his hand
with no intention of buying wisdom?

17 A friend loves at all times,
and a brother is born for a difficult time.

18 One without sense enters an agreement
and puts up security for his friend.

19 One who loves to offend loves strife;

one who builds a high threshold invites injury.

20 One with a twisted mind will not succeed,
and one with deceitful speech will fall
into ruin.

21 A man fathers a fool to his own sorrow;
the father of a fool has no joy.

22 A joyful heart is good medicine,
but a broken spirit dries up the bones.

23 A wicked man secretly takes a bribe
to subvert the course of justice.

24 Wisdom is the focus of the perceptive,
but a fool's eyes roam to the ends of the earth.

25 A foolish son is grief to his father
and bitterness to the one who bore him.

26 It is certainly not good to fine
an innocent person
or to beat a noble for his honesty.

27 The intelligent person restrains his words,
and one who keeps a cool head
is a man of understanding.

28 Even a fool is considered wise
when he keeps silent,
discerning when he seals his lips.

18

One who isolates himself pursues
selfish desires;
he rebels against all sound judgment.

2 A fool does not delight in understanding,
but only wants to show off his opinions.

3 When a wicked man comes,
contempt also does,
and along with dishonor, disgrace.

4 The words of a man's mouth are deep waters,
a flowing river, a fountain of wisdom.

5 It is not good to show partiality to the *guilty
by perverting the justice due the innocent.

6 A fool's lips lead to strife,
and his mouth provokes a beating.

7 A fool's mouth is his devastation,
and his lips are a trap for his life.

8 A gossip's words are like choice food
that goes down to one's innermost being.

9 The one who is truly lazy in his work
is brother to a vandal.

10 The name of *Yahweh is a strong tower;
the righteous run to it and are protected.

11 A rich man's wealth is his fortified city;
in his imagination it is like a high wall.

12 Before his downfall a man's heart is proud,
but humility comes before honor.

13 The one who gives an answer
before he listens—
this is foolishness and disgrace for him.

14 A man's spirit can endure sickness,
but who can survive a broken spirit?

15 The mind of the discerning
acquires knowledge,
and the ear of the wise seeks it.

16 A gift opens doors for a man
and brings him before the great.

17 The first to state his case seems right
until another comes
and cross-examines him.

18 Casting the lot ends quarrels
and separates powerful opponents.

19 An offended brother is harder to reach
than a fortified city,
and quarrels are like the bars of a fortress.

20 From the fruit of his mouth a man's stomach
is satisfied;
he is filled with the product of his lips.

21 Life and death are in the power of the tongue,
and those who love it will eat its fruit.

22 A man who finds a wife finds a good thing
and obtains favor from the LORD.

23 The poor man pleads,
but the rich one answers roughly.

24 A man with many friends may be harmed,
but there is a friend who stays closer
than a brother.

19

Better a poor man who lives with integrity
than someone who has deceitful lips and is
a fool.

2 Even zeal is not good without knowledge,
and the one who acts hastily sins.

3 A man's own foolishness leads him astray,
yet his heart rages against the LORD.

4 Wealth attracts many friends,
but a poor man is separated from his friend.

5 A false witness will not go unpunished,
and one who utters lies will not escape.

6 Many seek a ruler's favor,
and everyone is a friend of one who gives gifts.

7 All the brothers of a poor man hate him;
how much more do his friends
keep their distance from him!
He may pursue them with words,
but they are not there.

8 The one who acquires good sense
loves himself;
one who safeguards understanding
finds success.

9 A false witness will not go unpunished,
and one who utters lies perishes.

10 Luxury is not appropriate for a fool—
how much less for a slave to rule over princes!

11 A person's insight gives him patience,
and his virtue is to overlook an offense.

12 A king's rage is like the roaring of a lion,
but his favor is like dew on the grass.

13 A foolish son is his father's ruin,
and a wife's nagging is an endless dripping.

14 A house and wealth are inherited from fathers,
but a sensible wife is from the LORD.

15 Laziness induces deep sleep,
and a lazy person will go hungry.

16 The one who keeps commands
preserves himself;
one who disregards his ways will die.

17 Kindness to the poor is a loan to the LORD,
and He will give a reward to the lender.

18 Discipline your son while there is hope;
don't be intent on killing him.

19 A person with great anger bears the penalty;
if you rescue him, you'll have to do it again.

20 Listen to counsel and receive instruction
so that you may be wise later in life.

21 Many plans are in a man's heart,
but the LORD's decree will prevail.

22 What is desirable in a man is his fidelity;
better to be a poor man than a liar.

23 The *fear of the LORD leads to life;
one will sleep at night without danger.

24 The slacker buries his hand in the bowl;
he doesn't even bring it back to his mouth.

25 Strike a mocker, and the inexperienced learn
      a lesson;
  rebuke the discerning,
      and he gains knowledge.
26 The one who assaults his father and evicts
      his mother
  is a disgraceful and shameful son.
27 If you stop listening to correction, my son,
  you will stray from the words of knowledge.
28 A worthless witness mocks justice,
  and a wicked mouth swallows iniquity.
29 Judgments are prepared for mockers,
  and beatings for the backs of fools.

20 Wine is a mocker, beer is a brawler,
  and whoever staggers because of them
      is not wise.
2 A king's terrible wrath is like the roaring
      of a lion;
  anyone who provokes him endangers himself.
3 It is honorable for a man to resolve a dispute,
  but any fool can get himself into a quarrel.
4 The slacker does not plow
      during planting season;
  at harvest time he looks,
      and there is nothing.
5 Counsel in a man's heart is deep water;
  but a man of understanding draws it out.
6 Many a man proclaims his own loyalty,
  but who can find a trustworthy man?
7 The one who lives with integrity is righteous;
  his children who come after him
      will be happy.
8 A king sitting on a throne to judge
  sifts out all evil with his eyes.
9 Who can say, "I have kept my heart pure;
  I am cleansed from my sin"?
10 Differing weights and varying measures—
  both are detestable to the LORD.
11 Even a young man is known by his actions—
  if his behavior is pure and upright.
12 The hearing ear and the seeing eye—
  the LORD made them both.
13 Don't love sleep, or you will become poor;
  open your eyes, and you'll have enough to eat.
14 "It's worthless, it's worthless!" the buyer says,
  but after he is on his way, he gloats.
15 There is gold and a multitude of jewels,
  but knowledgeable lips are a rare treasure.
16 Take his garment,
  for he has put up security for a stranger;
  get collateral if it is for foreigners.
17 Food gained by fraud is sweet to a man,
  but afterward his mouth is full of gravel.
18 Finalize plans with counsel,
  and wage war with sound guidance.
19 The one who reveals secrets is
      a constant gossip;
  avoid someone with a big mouth.
20 Whoever curses his father or mother—
  his lamp will go out in deep darkness.
21 An inheritance gained prematurely
  will not be blessed ultimately.
22 Don't say, "I will avenge this evil!"
  Wait on the LORD, and He will rescue you.
23 Differing weights are detestable to the LORD,
  and dishonest scales are unfair.
24 A man's steps are determined by the LORD,

so how can anyone understand his own way?
25 It is a trap for anyone to dedicate
      something rashly
  and later to reconsider his vows.
26 A wise king separates out the wicked
  and drives the threshing wheel over them.
27 The LORD's lamp sheds light on a person's life,
  searching the innermost parts.
28 Loyalty and faithfulness deliver a king;
  through loyalty he maintains his throne.
29 The glory of young men is their strength,
  and the splendor of old men is gray hair.
30 Lashes and wounds purge away evil,
  and beatings cleanse the innermost parts.

21 A king's heart is like streams of water
      in the LORD's hand:
  He directs it wherever He chooses.
2 All a man's ways seem right to him,
  but the LORD evaluates the motives.
3 Doing what is righteous and just
  is more acceptable to the LORD than sacrifice.
4 The lamp that guides the wicked—
  haughty eyes and an arrogant heart—is sin.
5 The plans of the diligent certainly lead
      to profit,
  but anyone who is reckless
      certainly becomes poor.
6 Making a fortune through a lying tongue
  is a vanishing mist, a pursuit of death.
7 The violence of the wicked sweeps them away
  because they refuse to act justly.
8 A *guilty man's conduct is crooked,
  but the behavior of the innocent is upright.
9 Better to live on the corner of a roof
  than to share a house with a nagging wife.
10 A wicked person desires evil;
  he has no consideration for his neighbor.
11 When a mocker is punished,
  the inexperienced become wiser;
  when one teaches a wise man,
  he acquires knowledge.
12 The Righteous One considers the house
      of the wicked;
  He brings the wicked to ruin.
13 The one who shuts his ears to the cry
      of the poor
  will himself also call out and not be answered.
14 A secret gift soothes anger,
  and a covert bribe, fierce rage.
15 Justice executed is a joy to the righteous
  but a terror to those who practice iniquity.
16 The man who strays from the way of wisdom
  will come to rest
  in the assembly of the departed spirits.
17 The one who loves pleasure will become
      a poor man;
  whoever loves wine and oil will not get rich.
18 The wicked are a ransom for the righteous,
  and the treacherous, for the upright.
19 Better to live in a wilderness
  than with a nagging and hot-tempered wife.
20 Precious treasure and oil are in the dwelling
      of a wise person,
  but a foolish man consumes them.
21 The one who pursues righteousness
      and faithful love
  will find life, righteousness, and honor.

22 A wise person went up against a city
   of warriors
and brought down its secure fortress.
23 The one who guards his mouth and tongue
keeps himself out of trouble.
24 The proud and arrogant person,
   named "Mocker,"
acts with excessive pride.
25 A slacker's craving will kill him
because his hands refuse to work.
26 He is filled with craving all day long,
but the righteous give and don't hold back.
27 The sacrifice of a wicked person
   is detestable—
how much more so
when he brings it with ulterior motives!
28 A lying witness will perish,
but the one who listens will speak successfully.
29 A wicked man puts on a bold face,
but the upright man considers his way.
30 No wisdom, no understanding, and no counsel
will prevail against the LORD.
31 A horse is prepared for the day of battle,
but victory comes from the LORD.

22 A good name is to be chosen
   over great wealth;
favor is better than silver and gold.
2 The rich and the poor have this in common:
the LORD made them both.
3 A sensible person sees danger and takes cover,
but the inexperienced keep going
   and are punished.
4 The result of humility is *fear of the LORD,
along with wealth, honor, and life.
5 There are thorns and snares on the path
   of the crooked;
the one who guards himself stays
   far from them.
6 Teach a youth about the way he should go;
even when he is old he will not depart from it.
7 The rich rule over the poor,
and the borrower is a slave to the lender.
8 The one who sows injustice will reap disaster,
and the rod of his fury will be destroyed.
9 A generous person will be blessed,
for he shares his food with the poor.
10 Drive out a mocker, and conflict goes too;
then quarreling and dishonor will cease.
11 The one who loves a pure heart
and gracious lips—the king is his friend.
12 The LORD's eyes keep watch over knowledge,
but He overthrows the words
   of the treacherous.
13 The slacker says, "There's a lion outside!
I'll be killed in the public square!"
14 The mouth of the forbidden woman is
   a deep pit;
a man cursed by the LORD will fall into it.
15 Foolishness is tangled up in the heart
   of a youth;
the rod of discipline will drive it away
   from him.
16 Oppressing the poor to enrich oneself,
and giving to the rich—both lead
   only to poverty.
17 Listen closely, pay attention to the words
   of the wise,

and apply your mind to my knowledge.
18 For it is pleasing if you keep them within you
and if they are constantly on your lips.
19 I have instructed you today—even you—
so that your confidence may be in the LORD.
20 Haven't I written for you thirty sayings
about counsel and knowledge,
21 in order to teach you true and reliable words,
so that you may give a dependable report
to those who sent you?
22 Don't rob a poor man because he is poor,
and don't crush the oppressed at the *gate,
23 for the LORD will take up their case
and will plunder those who plunder them.
24 Don't make friends with an angry man,
and don't be a companion
   of a hot-tempered man,
25 or you will learn his ways
and entangle yourself in a snare.
26 Don't be one of those who enter agreements,
who put up security for loans.
27 If you have no money to pay,
even your bed will be taken from under you.
28 Don't move an ancient boundary marker
that your fathers set up.
29 Do you see a man skilled in his work?
He will stand in the presence of kings.
He will not stand in the presence
   of unknown men.

23 When you sit down to dine with a ruler,
consider carefully what is before you,
2 and put a knife to your throat
if you have a big appetite;
3 don't desire his choice food,
for that food is deceptive.
4 Don't wear yourself out to get rich;
stop giving your attention to it.
5 As soon as your eyes fly to it, it disappears,
for it makes wings for itself
and flies like an eagle to the sky.
6 Don't eat a stingy person's bread,
and don't desire his choice food,
7 for it's like someone calculating inwardly.
"Eat and drink," he says to you,
but his heart is not with you.
8 You will vomit the little you've eaten
and waste your pleasant words.
9 Don't speak to a fool,
for he will despise the insight of your words.
10 Don't move an ancient boundary marker,
and don't encroach on the fields
   of the fatherless,
11 for their Redeemer is strong,
and He will take up their case against you.
12 Apply yourself to discipline
and listen to words of knowledge.
13 Don't withhold discipline from a youth;
if you beat him with a rod, he will not die.
14 Strike him with a rod,
and you will rescue his life from *Sheol.
15 My son, if your heart is wise,
my heart will indeed rejoice.
16 My innermost being will cheer
when your lips say what is right.
17 Don't let your heart envy sinners;
instead, always *fear the LORD.
18 For then you will have a future,

and your hope will never fade.

19 Listen, my son, and be wise;
keep your mind on the right course.

20 Don't associate with those who drink
too much wine
or with those who gorge themselves on meat.

21 For the drunkard and the glutton
will become poor,
and grogginess will clothe them in rags.

22 Listen to your father who gave you life,
and don't despise your mother
when she is old.

23 Buy—and do not sell—truth,
wisdom, instruction, and understanding.

24 The father of a righteous son
will rejoice greatly,
and one who fathers a wise son will delight
in him.

25 Let your father and mother have joy,
and let her who gave birth to you rejoice.

26 My son, give me your heart,
and let your eyes observe my ways.

27 For a prostitute is a deep pit,
and a stranger is a narrow well;

28 indeed, she sets an ambush like a robber
and increases those among men
who are unfaithful.

29 Who has woe? Who has sorrow?
Who has conflicts? Who has complaints?
Who has wounds for no reason?
Who has red eyes?

30 Those who linger over wine,
those who go looking for mixed wine.

31 Don't gaze at wine because it is red,
when it gleams in the cup
and goes down smoothly.

32 In the end it bites like a snake
and stings like a viper.

33 Your eyes will see strange things,
and you will say absurd things.

34 You'll be like someone sleeping out at sea
or lying down on the top of a ship's mast.

35 "They struck me, but I feel no pain!
They beat me, but I didn't know it!
When will I wake up?
I'll look for another drink."

24 Don't envy evil men
or desire to be with them,

2 for their hearts plan violence,
and their words stir up trouble.

3 A house is built by wisdom,
and it is established by understanding;

4 by knowledge the rooms are filled
with every precious and beautiful treasure.

5 A wise warrior is better than a strong one,
and a man of knowledge than one of strength;

6 for you should wage war
with sound guidance—
victory comes with many counselors.

7 Wisdom is inaccessible to a fool;
he does not open his mouth at the •gate.

8 The one who plots evil
will be called a schemer.

9 A foolish scheme is sin,
and a mocker is detestable to people.

10 If you do nothing in a difficult time,
your strength is limited.

11 Rescue those being taken off to death,
and save those stumbling toward slaughter.

12 If you say, "But we didn't know about this,"
won't He who weighs hearts consider it?
Won't He who protects your life know?
Won't He repay a person according to
his work?

13 Eat honey, my son, for it is good,
and the honeycomb is sweet to your palate;

14 realize that wisdom is the same for you.
If you find it, you will have a future,
and your hope will never fade.

15 Wicked man, don't set an ambush,
at the camp of the righteous man;
don't destroy his dwelling.

16 Though a righteous man falls seven times,
he will get up,
but the wicked will stumble into ruin.

17 Don't gloat when your enemy falls,
and don't let your heart rejoice
when he stumbles,

18 or the LORD will see, be displeased,
and turn His wrath away from him.

19 Don't be agitated by evildoers,
and don't envy the wicked.

20 For the evil have no future;
the lamp of the wicked will be put out.

21 My son, •fear the LORD, as well as the king,
and don't associate with rebels,

22 for destruction from them will come suddenly;
who knows what distress these two can bring?

23 These sayings also belong to the wise:
It is not good to show partiality in judgment.

24 Whoever says to the •guilty,
"You are innocent"—
people will curse him, and tribes
will denounce him;

25 but it will go well with those who convict
the guilty,
and a generous blessing will come to them.

26 He who gives an honest answer
gives a kiss on the lips.

27 Complete your outdoor work, and prepare
your field;
afterward, build your house.

28 Don't testify against your neighbor
without cause.
Don't deceive with your lips.

29 Don't say, "I'll do to him what he did to me;
I'll repay the man for what he has done."

30 I went by the field of a slacker
and by the vineyard of a man lacking sense.

31 Thistles had come up everywhere,
weeds covered the ground,
and the stone wall was ruined.

32 I saw, and took it to heart;
I looked, and received instruction:

33 a little sleep, a little slumber,
a little folding of the arms to rest,

34 and your poverty will come like a robber,
your need, like a bandit.

25 These too are proverbs of Solomon,
which the men of Hezekiah, king of Judah,
copied.

2 It is the glory of God to conceal a matter
and the glory of kings to investigate a matter.

3 As the heaven is high and the earth is deep,

so the hearts of kings cannot be investigated.
4 Remove impurities from silver,
and a vessel will be produced for a silversmith.
5 Remove the wicked from the king's presence,
and his throne will be established
in righteousness.
6 Don't brag about yourself before the king,
and don't stand in the place of the great;
7 for it is better for him to say to you,
"Come up here!"
than to demote you in plain view of a noble.
8 Don't take a matter to court hastily.
Otherwise, what will you do afterward
if your opponent humiliates you?
9 Make your case with your opponent
without revealing another's secret;
10 otherwise, the one who hears
will disgrace you,
and you'll never live it down.
11 A word spoken at the right time
is like gold apples on a silver tray.
12 A wise correction to a receptive ear
is like a gold ring or an ornament of gold.
13 To those who send him,
a trustworthy messenger
is like the coolness of snow on a harvest day;
he refreshes the life of his masters.
14 The man who boasts about a gift
that does not exist
is like clouds and wind without rain.
15 A ruler can be persuaded through patience,
and a gentle tongue can break a bone.
16 If you find honey, eat only what you need;
otherwise, you'll get sick from it and vomit.
17 Seldom set foot in your neighbor's house;
otherwise, he'll get sick of you and hate you.
18 A man giving false testimony
against his neighbor
is like a club, a sword, or a sharp arrow.
19 Trusting an unreliable person in a
difficult time
is like a rotten tooth or a faltering foot.
20 Singing songs to a troubled heart
is like taking off clothing on a cold day
or like pouring vinegar on soda.
21 If your enemy is hungry, give him food to eat,
and if he is thirsty, give him water to drink;
22 for you will heap burning coals on his head,
and the LORD will reward you.
23 The north wind produces rain,
and a backbiting tongue, angry looks.
24 Better to live on the corner of a roof
than to share a house with a nagging wife.
25 Good news from a distant land
is like cold water to a parched throat.
26 A righteous person who yields to the wicked
is like a muddied spring or a polluted well.
27 It is not good to eat too much honey
or to seek glory after glory.
28 A man who does not control his temper
is like a city whose wall is broken down.

26 Like snow in summer and rain at harvest,
honor is inappropriate for a fool.
2 Like a flitting sparrow or a fluttering swallow,
an undeserved curse goes nowhere.
3 A whip for the horse, a bridle for the donkey,
and a rod for the backs of fools.

4 Don't answer a fool according to
his foolishness
or you'll be like him yourself.
5 Answer a fool according to his foolishness
or he'll become wise in his own eyes.
6 The one who sends a message by a fool's hand
cuts off his own feet and drinks violence.
7 A proverb in the mouth of a fool
is like lame legs that hang limp.
8 Giving honor to a fool
is like binding a stone in a sling.
9 A proverb in the mouth of a fool
is like a stick with thorns,
brandished by the hand of a drunkard.
10 The one who hires a fool or who hires
those passing by
is like an archer who wounds everyone.
11 As a dog returns to its vomit,
so a fool repeats his foolishness.
12 Do you see a man who is wise in his own eyes?
There is more hope for a fool than for him.
13 The slacker says, "There's a lion in the road—
a lion in the public square!"
14 A door turns on its hinges,
and a slacker, on his bed.
15 The slacker buries his hand in the bowl;
he is too weary to bring it to his mouth.
16 In his own eyes, a slacker is wiser
than seven men who can answer sensibly.
17 A person who is passing by and meddles
in a quarrel that's not his
is like one who grabs a dog by the ears.
18 Like a madman who throws flaming darts
and deadly arrows,
19 so is the man who deceives his neighbor
and says, "I was only joking!"
20 Without wood, fire goes out;
without a gossip, conflict dies down.
21 As charcoal for embers and wood for fire,
so is a quarrelsome man for kindling strife.
22 A gossip's words are like choice food
that goes down to one's innermost being.
23 Smooth lips with an evil heart
are like glaze on an earthen vessel.
24 A hateful person disguises himself
with his speech
and harbors deceit within.
25 When he speaks graciously, don't believe him,
for there are seven abominations in his heart.
26 Though his hatred is concealed by deception,
his evil will be revealed in the assembly.
27 The one who digs a pit will fall into it,
and whoever rolls a stone—
it will come back on him.
28 A lying tongue hates those it crushes,
and a flattering mouth causes ruin.

27 Don't boast about tomorrow,
for you don't know what a day might bring.
2 Let another praise you, and not
your own mouth—
a stranger, and not your own lips.
3 A stone is heavy and sand, a burden,
but aggravation from a fool
outweighs them both.
4 Fury is cruel, and anger a flood,
but who can withstand jealousy?
5 Better an open reprimand

than concealed love.

6 The wounds of a friend are trustworthy,
but the kisses of an enemy are excessive.

7 A person who is full tramples
on a honeycomb,
but to a hungry person, any bitter thing
is sweet.

8 A man wandering from his home
is like a bird wandering from its nest.

9 Oil and incense bring joy to the heart,
and the sweetness of a friend is better
than self-counsel.

10 Don't abandon your friend
or your father's friend,
and don't go to your brother's house
in your time of calamity;
better a neighbor nearby than a brother
far away.

11 Be wise, my son, and bring my heart joy,
so that I can answer anyone who taunts me.

12 A sensible person sees danger and takes cover;
the inexperienced keep going
and are punished.

13 Take his garment,
for he has put up security for a stranger;
get collateral if it is for foreigners.

14 If one blesses his neighbor
with a loud voice early in the morning,
it will be counted as a curse to him.

15 An endless dripping on a rainy day
and a nagging wife are alike.

16 The one who controls her controls the wind
and grasps oil with his right hand.

17 Iron sharpens iron,
and one man sharpens another.

18 Whoever tends a fig tree will eat its fruit,
and whoever looks after his master
will be honored.

19 As water reflects the face,
so the heart reflects the person.

20 *Sheol and *Abaddon are never satisfied,
and people's eyes are never satisfied.

21 A crucible for silver, and a smelter for gold,
and a man for the words of his praise.

22 Though you grind a fool
in a mortar with a pestle along with grain,
you will not separate his foolishness
from him.

23 Know well the condition of your flock,
and pay attention to your herds,

24 for wealth is not forever;
not even a crown lasts for all time.

25 When hay is removed and new growth appears
and the grain from the hills is gathered in,

26 lambs will provide your clothing,
and goats, the price of a field;

27 there will be enough goat's milk
for your food—
food for your household
and nourishment for your female servants.

28 The wicked flee when no one
is pursuing them,
but the righteous are as bold as a lion.

2 When a land is in rebellion, it has
many rulers,
but with a discerning
and knowledgeable person, it endures.

3 A destitute leader who oppresses the poor
is like a driving rain that leaves no food.

4 Those who reject the law praise the wicked,
but those who keep the law battle
against them.

5 Evil men do not understand justice,
but those who seek the Lord
understand everything.

6 Better a poor man who lives with integrity
than a rich man who distorts right and wrong.

7 A discerning son keeps the law,
but a companion of gluttons humiliates
his father.

8 Whoever increases his wealth
through excessive interest
collects it for one who is kind to the poor.

9 Anyone who turns his ear away from hearing
the law—
even his prayer is detestable.

10 The one who leads the upright into an evil way
will fall into his own pit,
but the blameless will inherit what is good.

11 A rich man is wise in his own eyes,
but a poor man who has discernment
sees through him.

12 When the righteous triumph,
there is great rejoicing,
but when the wicked come to power,
people hide themselves.

13 The one who conceals his sins
will not prosper,
but whoever confesses and renounces them
will find mercy.

14 Happy is the one who is always reverent,
but one who hardens his heart falls
into trouble.

15 A wicked ruler over a helpless people
is like a roaring lion or a charging bear.

16 A leader who lacks understanding
is very oppressive,
but one who hates dishonest profit
prolongs his life.

17 A man burdened by bloodguilt
will be a fugitive until death.
Let no one help him.

18 The one who lives with integrity
will be helped,
but one who distorts right and wrong
will suddenly fall.

19 The one who works his land
will have plenty of food,
but whoever chases fantasies
will have his fill of poverty.

20 A faithful man will have many blessings,
but one in a hurry to get rich
will not go unpunished.

21 It is not good to show partiality—
yet a man may sin for a piece of bread.

22 A greedy man is in a hurry for wealth;
he doesn't know that poverty will come
to him.

23 One who rebukes a person will later find
more favor
than one who flatters with his tongue.

24 The one who robs his father or mother
and says, "That's no sin,"
is a companion to a man who destroys.

25 A greedy person provokes conflict,
but whoever trusts in the LORD will prosper.
26 The one who trusts in himself is a fool,
but one who walks in wisdom will be safe.
27 The one who gives to the poor
will not be in need,
but one who turns his eyes away
will receive many curses.
28 When the wicked come to power,
people hide,
but when they are destroyed,
the righteous flourish.

29 One who becomes stiff-necked,
after many reprimands
will be shattered instantly—
beyond recovery.
2 When the righteous flourish,
the people rejoice,
but when the wicked rule, people groan.
3 A man who loves wisdom brings joy
to his father,
but one who consorts with prostitutes
destroys his wealth.
4 By justice a king brings stability to a land,
but a man who demands "contributions"
demolishes it.
5 A man who flatters his neighbor
spreads a net for his feet.
6 An evil man is caught by sin,
but the righteous one sings and rejoices.
7 The righteous person knows the rights
of the poor,
but the wicked one does not understand
these concerns.
8 Mockers inflame a city,
but the wise turn away anger.
9 If a wise man goes to court with a fool,
there will be ranting and raving
but no resolution.
10 Bloodthirsty men hate an honest person,
but the upright care about him.
11 A fool gives full vent to his anger,
but a wise man holds it in check.
12 If a ruler listens to lies,
all his officials will be wicked.
13 The poor and the oppressor have this
in common:
the LORD gives light to the eyes of both.
14 A king who judges the poor with fairness—
his throne will be established forever.
15 A rod of correction imparts wisdom,
but a youth left to himself
is a disgrace to his mother.
16 When the wicked increase, rebellion increases,
but the righteous will see their downfall.
17 Discipline your son, and it will bring you
peace of mind
and give you delight.
18 Without revelation people run wild,
but one who listens to instruction
will be happy.
19 A slave cannot be disciplined by words;
though he understands, he doesn't respond.
20 Do you see a man who speaks too soon?
There is more hope for a fool than for him.
21 A slave pampered from his youth
will become arrogant later on.

22 An angry man stirs up conflict,
and a hot-tempered man increases rebellion.
23 A person's pride will humble him,
but a humble spirit will gain honor.
24 To be a thief's partner is to hate oneself;
he hears the curse but will not testify.
25 The fear of man is a snare,
but the one who trusts in the LORD
is protected.
26 Many seek a ruler's favor,
but a man receives justice from the LORD.
27 An unjust man is detestable to the righteous,
and one whose way is upright
is detestable to the wicked.

30 The words of Agur son of Jakeh. The oracle.
The man's oration to Ithiel, to Ithiel and Ucal:
2 I am more stupid than any other man,
and I lack man's ability to understand.
3 I have not gained wisdom,
and I have no knowledge of the Holy One.
4 Who has gone up to heaven and come down?
Who has gathered the wind in His hands?
Who has bound up the waters in a cloak?
Who has established all the ends of the earth?
What is His name,
and what is the name of His Son—
if you know?
5 Every word of God is pure;
He is a shield to those who take refuge
in Him.
6 Don't add to His words,
or He will rebuke you, and you will be proved
a liar.
7 Two things I ask of You;
don't deny them to me before I die:
8 Keep falsehood and deceitful words
far from me.
Give me neither poverty nor wealth;
feed me with the food I need.
9 Otherwise, I might have too much
and deny You, saying, "Who is the LORD?"
or I might have nothing and steal,
profaning the name of my God.
10 Don't slander a servant to his master
or he will curse you, and you will
become *guilty.
11 There is a generation that curses its father
and does not bless its mother.
12 There is a generation that is pure
in its own eyes,
yet is not washed from its filth.
13 There is a generation—how haughty its eyes
and pretentious its looks.
14 There is a generation whose teeth are swords,
whose fangs are knives,
devouring the oppressed from the land
and the needy from among mankind.
15 The leech has two daughters: "Give, Give!"
Three things are never satisfied;
four never say, "Enough!":
16 *Sheol; a childless womb;
earth, which is never satisfied with water;
and fire, which never says, "Enough!"
17 As for the eye that ridicules a father
and despises obedience to a mother,
may ravens of the valley pluck it out
and young vultures eat it.

18 Three things are beyond me;
   four I can't understand:
19 the way of an eagle in the sky,
   the way of a snake on a rock,
   the way of a ship at sea,
   and the way of a man with a young woman.
20 This is the way of an adulteress:
   she eats and wipes her mouth
   and says, "I've done nothing wrong."
21 The earth trembles under three things;
   it cannot bear up under four:
22 a servant when he becomes king,
   a fool when he is stuffed with food,
23 an unloved woman when she marries,
   and a servant girl when she ousts her queen.
24 Four things on earth are small,
   yet they are extremely wise:
25 the ants are not a strong people,
   yet they store up their food in the summer;
26 hyraxes are not a mighty people,
   yet they make their homes in the cliffs;
27 locusts have no king,
   yet all of them march in ranks;
28 a lizard can be caught in your hands,
   yet it lives in kings' palaces.
29 Three things are stately in their stride,
   even four are stately in their walk:
30 a lion, which is mightiest among beasts
   and doesn't retreat before anything,
31 a strutting rooster, a goat,
   and a king at the head of his army.
32 If you have been foolish by exalting yourself
   or if you've been scheming,
   put your hand over your mouth.
33 For the churning of milk produces butter,
   and twisting a nose draws blood,
   and stirring up anger produces strife.

31 The words of King Lemuel,
   an oracle that his mother taught him:
2 What should I say, my son?
   What, son of my womb?
   What, son of my vows?
3 Don't spend your energy on women
   or your efforts on those who destroy kings.
4 It is not for kings, Lemuel,
   it is not for kings to drink wine
   or for rulers to desire beer.
5 Otherwise, they will drink,
   forget what is decreed,
   and pervert justice for all the oppressed.
6 Give beer to one who is dying
   and wine to one whose life is bitter.
7 Let him drink so that he can forget his poverty
   and remember his trouble no more.

8 Speak up for those who have no voice,
   for the justice of all who are dispossessed.
9 Speak up, judge righteously,
   and defend the cause of the oppressed
      and needy.
10 Who can find a capable wife?
   She is far more precious than jewels.
11 The heart of her husband trusts in her,
   and he will not lack anything good.
12 She rewards him with good, not evil,
   all the days of her life.
13 She selects wool and flax
   and works with willing hands.
14 She is like the merchant ships,
   bringing her food from far away.
15 She rises while it is still night
   and provides food for her household
   and portions for her female servants.
16 She evaluates a field and buys it;
   she plants a vineyard with her earnings.
17 She draws on her strength
   and reveals that her arms are strong.
18 She sees that her profits are good,
   and her lamp never goes out at night.
19 She extends her hands to the spinning staff,
   and her hands hold the spindle.
20 Her hands reach out to the poor,
   and she extends her hands to the needy.
21 She is not afraid for her household
      when it snows,
   for all in her household are doubly clothed.
22 She makes her own bed coverings;
   her clothing is fine linen and purple.
23 Her husband is known at the city ·gates,
   where he sits among the elders of the land.
24 She makes and sells linen garments;
   she delivers belts to the merchants.
25 Strength and honor are her clothing,
   and she can laugh at the time to come.
26 She opens her mouth with wisdom
   and loving instruction is on her tongue.
27 She watches over the activities
      of her household
   and is never idle.
28 Her sons rise up and call her blessed.
   Her husband also praises her:
29 "Many women are capable,
   but you surpass them all!"
30 Charm is deceptive and beauty is fleeting,
   but a woman who ·fears the LORD
      will be praised.
31 Give her the reward of her labor,
   and let her works praise her
      at the city gates.

ECCLESIASTES

1 The words of the Teacher, son of David, king in Jerusalem.

2 "Absolute futility," says the Teacher.
"Absolute futility. Everything is futile."

3 What does a man gain for all his efforts
that he labors at under the sun?

4 A generation goes and a generation comes,
but the earth remains forever.

5 The sun rises and the sun sets;
panting, it returns to its place
where it rises.

6 Gusting to the south,
turning to the north,
turning, turning, goes the wind,
and the wind returns in its cycles.

7 All the streams flow to the sea,
yet the sea is never full.
The streams are flowing to the place,
and they flow there again.

8 All things are wearisome;
man is unable to speak.
The eye is not satisfied by seeing
or the ear filled with hearing.

9 What has been is what will be,
and what has been done is what will be done;
there is nothing new under the sun.

10 Can one say about anything,
"Look, this is new"?
It has already existed in the ages before us.

11 There is no remembrance of those
who came before;
and of those who will come after
there will also be no remembrance
by those who follow them.

12 I, the Teacher, have been king over Israel in Jerusalem. 13 I applied my mind to seek and explore through wisdom all that is done under heaven. God has given ‘people this miserable task to keep them occupied. 14 I have seen all the things that are done under the sun and have found everything to be futile, a pursuit of the wind.

15 What is crooked cannot be straightened;
what is lacking cannot be counted.

16 I said to myself, "Look, I have amassed wisdom far beyond all those who were over Jerusalem before me, and my mind has thoroughly grasped wisdom and knowledge." 17 I applied my mind to know wisdom and knowledge, madness and folly; I learned that this too is a pursuit of the wind.

18 For with much wisdom is much sorrow;
as knowledge increases, grief increases.

2 I said to myself, "Go ahead, I will test you with pleasure; enjoy what is good." But it turned out to be futile. 2 I said about laughter, "It is madness," and about pleasure, "What does this accomplish?" 3 I explored with my mind how to let my body enjoy life with wine and how to grasp folly—my mind still guiding me with wisdom—until I could see what is good for ‘people to do under heaven during the few days of their lives.

4 I increased my achievements. I built houses and planted vineyards for myself. 5 I made gardens and parks for myself and planted every kind of fruit tree in them. 6 I constructed reservoirs of water for myself from which to irrigate a grove of flourishing trees. 7 I acquired male and female servants and had slaves who were born in my house. I also owned many herds of cattle and flocks, more than all who were before me in Jerusalem. 8 I also amassed silver and gold for myself, and the treasure of kings and provinces. I gathered male and female singers for myself, and many concubines, the delights of men. 9 So I became great and surpassed all who were before me in Jerusalem; my wisdom also remained with me. 10 All that my eyes desired, I did not deny them. I did not refuse myself any pleasure, for I took pleasure in all my struggles. This was my reward for all my struggles. 11 When I considered all that I had accomplished and what I had labored to achieve, I found everything to be futile and a pursuit of the wind. There was nothing to be gained under the sun.

12 Then I turned to consider wisdom, madness, and folly, for what will the man be like who comes after the king? He will do what has already been done. 13 And I realized that there is an advantage to wisdom over folly, like the advantage of light over darkness.

14 The wise man has eyes in his head,
but the fool walks in darkness.

Yet I also knew that one fate comes to them both. 15 So I said to myself, "What happens to the fool will also happen to me. Why then have I been overly wise?" And I said to myself that this is also futile. 16 For, just like the fool, there is no lasting remembrance of the wise man, since in the days to come both will be forgotten. How is it that the wise man dies just like the fool? 17 Therefore, I hated life because the work that was done under the sun was distressing to me. For everything is futile and a pursuit of the wind.

18 I hated all my work that I labored at under the sun because I must leave it to the man who comes after me. 19 And who knows whether he will be a wise man or a fool? Yet he will take over all my work that I labored at skillfully under the sun. This too is futile. 20 So I began to give myself over to despair concerning all my work that I had labored at under the sun. 21 When there is a man whose work was done with wisdom, knowledge, and skill, and he must give his portion to a man who has not worked for it, this too is futile and a great wrong. 22 For what does a man get with all his work and all his efforts that he labors at under the sun? 23 For all his days are filled with grief, and his occupation is sorrowful; even at night, his mind does not rest. This too is futile.

24 There is nothing better for man than to eat, drink, and enjoy his work. I have seen that even this is from God's hand, 25 because who can eat and who can enjoy life apart from Him? 26 For to the man who is pleasing in His sight, He gives wisdom, knowledge, and joy, but to the sinner He gives the task of gathering and accumulating in order to give to the one who is pleasing in God's sight. This too is futile and a pursuit of the wind.

3 There is an occasion for everything,
and a time for every activity under heaven:

2 a time to give birth and a time to die;
a time to plant and a time to uproot;

3 a time to kill and a time to heal;

a time to tear down and a time to build;
4 a time to weep and a time to laugh;
   a time to mourn and a time to dance;
5 a time to throw stones and a time
     to gather stones;
   a time to embrace and a time
     to avoid embracing;
6 a time to search and a time to count as lost;
   a time to keep and a time to throw away;
7 a time to tear and a time to sew;
   a time to be silent and a time to speak;
8 a time to love and a time to hate;
   a time for war and a time for peace.

⁹What does the worker gain from his struggles? ¹⁰I have seen the task that God has given •people to keep them occupied. ¹¹He has made everything appropriate in its time. He has also put eternity in their hearts, but man cannot discover the work God has done from beginning to end. ¹²I know that there is nothing better for them than to rejoice and enjoy the good life. ¹³It is also the gift of God whenever anyone eats, drinks, and enjoys all his efforts. ¹⁴I know that all God does will last forever; there is no adding to it or taking from it. God works so that people will be in awe of Him. ¹⁵Whatever is, has already been, and whatever will be, already is. God repeats what has passed.

¹⁶I also observed under the sun: there is wickedness at the place of judgment and there is wickedness at the place of righteousness. ¹⁷I said to myself, "God will judge the righteous and the wicked, since there is a time for every activity and every work." ¹⁸I said to myself, "This happens concerning people, so that God may test them and they may see for themselves that they are like animals." ¹⁹For the fate of people and the fate of animals is the same. As one dies, so dies the other; they all have the same breath. People have no advantage over animals since everything is futile. ²⁰All are going to the same place; all come from dust, and all return to dust. ²¹Who knows if the spirit of people rises upward and the spirit of animals goes downward to the earth? ²²I have seen that there is nothing better than for a person to enjoy his activities because that is his reward. For who can enable him to see what will happen after he dies?

4 Again, I observed all the acts of oppression being done under the sun. Look at the tears of those who are oppressed; they have no one to comfort them. Power is with those who oppress them; they have no one to comfort them. ²So I admired the dead, who have already died, more than the living, who are still alive. ³But better than either of them is the one who has not yet existed, who has not seen the evil activity that is done under the sun.

⁴I saw that all labor and all skillful work is due to a man's jealousy of his friend. This too is futile and a pursuit of the wind.
5 The fool folds his arms
   and consumes his own flesh.
6 Better one handful with rest
   than two handfuls with effort and a pursuit
     of the wind.

⁷Again, I saw futility under the sun: ⁸There is a person without a companion, without even a son or brother, and though there is no end to all his struggles, his eyes are still not content with riches. "So for whom am I struggling," he asks, "and depriving myself from good?" This too is futile and a miserable task.

⁹Two are better than one because they have a good reward for their efforts. ¹⁰For if either falls, his companion can lift him up; but pity the one who falls without another to lift him up. ¹¹Also, if two lie down together, they can keep warm; but how can one person alone keep warm? ¹²And if someone overpowers one person, two can resist him. A cord of three strands is not easily broken.

¹³Better is a poor but wise youth than an old but foolish king who no longer pays attention to warnings. ¹⁴For he came from prison to be king, even though he was born poor in his kingdom. ¹⁵I saw all the living, who move about under the sun, follow a second youth who succeeds him. ¹⁶There is no limit to all the •people who were before them, yet those who come later will not rejoice in him. This too is futile and a pursuit of the wind.

5 Guard your steps when you go to the house of God. Better to draw near in obedience than to offer the sacrifice as fools do, for they ignorantly do wrong. ²Do not be hasty to speak, and do not be impulsive to make a speech before God. God is in heaven and you are on earth, so let your words be few. ³For dreams result from much work and a fool's voice from many words. ⁴When you make a vow to God, don't delay fulfilling it, because He does not delight in fools. Fulfill what you vow. ⁵Better that you do not vow than that you vow and not fulfill it. ⁶Do not let your mouth bring •guilt on you, and do not say in the presence of the messenger that it was a mistake. Why should God be angry with your words and destroy the work of your hands? ⁷For many dreams bring futility, so do many words. Therefore, •fear God.

⁸If you see oppression of the poor and perversion of justice and righteousness in the province, don't be astonished at the situation, because one official protects another official, and higher officials protect them. ⁹The profit from the land is taken by all; the king is served by the field.

¹⁰The one who loves money is never satisfied with money, and whoever loves wealth is never satisfied with income. This too is futile. ¹¹When good things increase, the ones who consume them multiply; what, then, is the profit to the owner, except to gaze at them with his eyes? ¹²The sleep of the worker is sweet, whether he eats little or much, but the abundance of the rich permits him no sleep.

¹³There is a sickening tragedy I have seen under the sun: wealth kept by its owner to his harm. ¹⁴That wealth was lost in a bad venture, so when he fathered a son, he was empty-handed. ¹⁵As he came from his mother's womb, so he will go again, naked as he came; he will take nothing for his efforts that he can carry in his hands. ¹⁶This too is a sickening tragedy: exactly as he comes, so he will go. What does the one gain who struggles for the wind? ¹⁷What is more, he eats in darkness all his days, with much sorrow, sickness, and anger.

¹⁸Here is what I have seen to be good: it is appropriate to eat, drink, and experience good in all the labor one does under the sun during the few days of his life God has given him, because that is his reward. ¹⁹Furthermore, every man to whom God has given riches and wealth, He has also allowed him to enjoy them, take his reward, and rejoice in his labor. This is a gift of God, ²⁰for he does not often consider the days of

his life because God keeps him occupied with the joy of his heart.

6 Here is a tragedy I have observed under the sun, and it weighs heavily on humanity: ²God gives a man riches, wealth, and honor so that he lacks nothing of all he desires for himself, but God does not allow him to enjoy them. Instead, a stranger will enjoy them. This is futile and a sickening tragedy. ³A man may father a hundred children and live many years. No matter how long he lives, if he is not satisfied by good things and does not even have a proper burial, I say that a stillborn child is better off than he. ⁴For he comes in futility and he goes in darkness, and his name is shrouded in darkness. ⁵Though a stillborn child does not see the sun and is not conscious, it has more rest than he. ⁶And if he lives a thousand years twice, but does not experience happiness, do not both go to the same place?

⁷ All man's labor is for his stomach,
   yet the appetite is never satisfied.

⁸What advantage then does the wise man have over the fool? What advantage is there for the poor person who knows how to conduct himself before others? ⁹Better what the eyes see than wandering desire. This too is futile and a pursuit of the wind.

¹⁰Whatever exists was given its name long ago, and it is known what man is. But he is not able to contend with the One stronger than he. ¹¹For when there are many words, they increase futility. What is the advantage for man? ¹²For who knows what is good for man in life, in the few days of his futile life that he spends like a shadow? Who can tell man what will happen after him under the sun?

7 A good name is better than fine perfume,
   and the day of one's death than the day
      of one's birth.
² It is better to go to a house of mourning
   than to go to a house of feasting,
   since that is the end of all mankind,
   and the living should take it to heart,
³ Grief is better than laughter,
   for when a face is sad, a heart may be glad.
⁴ The heart of the wise is in a house
      of mourning,
   but the heart of fools is in a house of pleasure.
⁵ It is better to listen to rebuke
      from a wise person
   than to listen to the song of fools,
⁶ for like the crackling of burning thorns
      under the pot,
   so is the laughter of the fool.
   This too is futile.
⁷ Surely, the practice of extortion turns
      a wise person into a fool,
   and a bribe destroys the mind.
⁸ The end of a matter is better
      than its beginning;
   a patient spirit is better than a proud spirit.
⁹ Don't let your spirit rush to be angry,
   for anger abides in the heart of fools.
¹⁰ Don't say, "Why were the former days better
      than these?"
   since it is not wise of you to ask this.
¹¹ Wisdom is as good as an inheritance
   and an advantage to those who see the sun,
¹² because wisdom is protection as money
      is protection,

and the advantage of knowledge
   is that wisdom preserves the life of its owner.
¹³ Consider the work of God,
   for who can straighten out
   what He has made crooked?

¹⁴In the day of prosperity be joyful, but in the day of adversity, consider: God has made the one as well as the other, so that man cannot discover anything that will come after him.

¹⁵In my futile life I have seen everything: there is a righteous man who perishes in spite of his righteousness, and there is a wicked man who lives long in spite of his evil. ¹⁶Don't be excessively righteous, and don't be overly wise. Why should you destroy yourself? ¹⁷Don't be excessively wicked, and don't be foolish. Why should you die before your time? ¹⁸It is good that you grasp the one and do not let the other slip from your hand. For the one ˙who fears God will end up with both of them.

¹⁹ Wisdom makes the wise man stronger
   than ten rulers of a city.
²⁰ There is certainly no righteous man
      on the earth
   who does good and never sins.

²¹Don't pay attention to everything ˙people say, or you may hear your servant cursing you, ²²for you know that many times you yourself have cursed others.

²³I have tested all this by wisdom. I resolved, "I will be wise," but it was beyond me. ²⁴What exists is beyond reach and very deep. Who can discover it? ²⁵I turned my thoughts to know, explore, and seek wisdom and an explanation for things, and to know that wickedness is stupidity and folly is madness. ²⁶And I find more bitter than death the woman who is a trap, her heart a net, and her hands chains. The one who pleases God will escape her, but the sinner will be captured by her. ²⁷"Look," says the Teacher, "I have discovered this by adding one thing to another to find out the explanation, ²⁸which my soul continually searches for but does not find: among a thousand people I have found one true man, but among all these I have not found a true woman. ²⁹Only see this: I have discovered that God made people upright, but they pursued many schemes."

8 Who is like the wise person, and who knows the interpretation of a matter? A man's wisdom brightens his face, and the sternness of his face is changed.

²Keep the king's command because of your oath made before God. ³Do not be in a hurry; leave his presence, and don't persist in a bad cause, since he will do whatever he wants. ⁴For the king's word is authoritative, and who can say to him, "What are you doing?" ⁵The one who keeps a command will not experience anything harmful, and a wise heart knows the right time and procedure. ⁶For every activity there is a right time and procedure, even though man's troubles are heavy on him. ⁷Yet no one knows what will happen because who can tell him what will happen? ⁸No one has authority over the wind to restrain it, and there is no authority over the day of death; there is no furlough in battle, and wickedness will not allow those who practice it to escape. ⁹All this I have seen, applying my mind to all the work that is done under the sun, at a time when one man has authority over another to his harm.

¹⁰In such circumstances, I saw the wicked buried. They came and went from the holy place, and they

were praised in the city where they did so. This too is futile. [11] Because the sentence against a criminal act is not carried out quickly, the heart of *people is filled with the desire to commit crime. [12] Although a sinner commits crime a hundred times and prolongs his life, yet I also know that it will go well with God-fearing people, for they are reverent before Him. [13] However, it will not go well with the wicked, and they will not lengthen their days like a shadow, for they are not reverent before God.

[14] There is a futility that is done on the earth: there are righteous people who get what the actions of the wicked deserve, and there are wicked people who get what the actions of the righteous deserve. I say that this too is futile. [15] So I commended enjoyment because there is nothing better for man under the sun than to eat, drink, and enjoy himself, for this will accompany him in his labor during the days of his life that God gives him under the sun.

[16] When I applied my mind to know wisdom and to observe the activity that is done on the earth (even though one's eyes do not close in sleep day or night), [17] I observed all the work of God and concluded that man is unable to discover the work that is done under the sun. Even though a man labors hard to explore it, he cannot find it; even if the wise man claims to know it, he is unable to discover it.

9 Indeed, I took all this to heart and explained it all: the righteous, the wise, and their works are in God's hands. *People don't know whether to expect love or hate. Everything lies ahead of them. [2] Everything is the same for everyone: there is one fate for the righteous and the wicked, for the good and the bad, for the *clean and the *unclean, for the one who sacrifices and the one who does not sacrifice. As it is for the good, so it is for the sinner; as for the one who takes an oath, so for the one who fears an oath. [3] This is an evil in all that is done under the sun: there is one fate for everyone. In addition, the hearts of people are full of evil, and madness is in their hearts while they live— after that they go to the dead. [4] But there is hope for whoever is joined with all the living, since a live dog is better than a dead lion. [5] For the living know that they will die, but the dead don't know anything. There is no longer a reward for them because the memory of them is forgotten. [6] Their love, their hate, and their envy have already disappeared, and there is no longer a portion for them in all that is done under the sun.

[7] Go, eat your bread with pleasure, and drink your wine with a cheerful heart, for God has already accepted your works. [8] Let your clothes be white all the time, and never let oil be lacking on your head. [9] Enjoy life with the wife you love all the days of your fleeting life, which has been given to you under the sun, all your fleeting days. For that is your portion in life and in your struggle under the sun. [10] Whatever your hands find to do, do with all your strength, because there is no work, planning, knowledge, or wisdom in *Sheol where you are going.

[11] Again I saw under the sun that the race is not to the swift, or the battle to the strong, or bread to the wise, or riches to the discerning, or favor to the skillful; rather, time and chance happen to all of them. [12] For man certainly does not know his time: like fish caught in a cruel net or like birds caught in a trap, so people are trapped in an evil time as it suddenly falls on them.

[13] I have observed that this also is wisdom under the sun, and it is significant to me: [14] There was a small city with few men in it. A great king came against it, surrounded it, and built large siege works against it. [15] Now a poor wise man was found in the city, and he delivered the city by his wisdom. Yet no one remembered that poor man. [16] And I said, "Wisdom is better than strength, but the wisdom of the poor man is despised, and his words are not heeded."

[17] The calm words of the wise are heeded
     more than the shouts of a ruler over fools.
[18] Wisdom is better than weapons of war,
     but one sinner can destroy much good.

10 Dead flies make a perfumer's oil ferment
     and stink;
   so a little folly outweighs wisdom and honor.
[2] A wise man's heart goes to the right,
     but a fool's heart to the left.
[3] Even when the fool walks along the road,
     his heart lacks sense,
     and he shows everyone he is a fool.
[4] If the ruler's anger rises against you,
     don't leave your place,
     for calmness puts great offenses to rest.

[5] There is an evil I have seen under the sun, an error proceeding from the presence of the ruler:
[6] The fool is appointed to great heights,
     but the rich remain in lowly positions.
[7] I have seen slaves on horses,
     but princes walking on the ground like slaves.
[8] The one who digs a pit may fall into it,
     and the one who breaks through a wall
     may be bitten by a snake.
[9] The one who quarries stones may be hurt
     by them;
     the one who splits trees may be endangered
     by them.
[10] If the ax is dull, and one does not sharpen
     its edge,
     then one must exert more strength;
     however, the advantage of wisdom is that
     it brings success.
[11] If the snake bites before it is charmed,
     then there is no advantage for the charmer.
[12] The words from the mouth of a wise man
     are gracious,
     but the lips of a fool consume him.
[13] The beginning of the words of his mouth
     is folly,
     but the end of his speaking is evil madness.
[14] Yet the fool multiplies words.
     No one knows what will happen,
     and who can tell anyone what will happen
     after him?
[15] The struggles of fools weary them,
     for they don't know how to go to the city.
[16] Woe to you, land, when your king is a youth
     and your princes feast in the morning.
[17] Blessed are you, land, when your king is a son
     of nobles
     and your princes feast at the proper time—
     for strength and not for drunkenness.
[18] Because of laziness the roof caves in,
     and because of negligent hands
     the house leaks.
[19] A feast is prepared for laughter,
     and wine makes life happy,

and money is the answer for everything.
20 Do not curse the king even in your thoughts,
  and do not curse a rich person
    even in your bedroom,
  for a bird of the sky may carry the message,
  and a winged creature may report the matter.

11

Send your bread on the surface
    of the waters,
  for after many days you may find it.
2 Give a portion to seven or even to eight,
  for you don't know what disaster may happen
    on earth.
3 If the clouds are full, they will pour out rain
    on the earth;
  whether a tree falls to the south or the north,
  the place where the tree falls, there it will lie.
4 One who watches the wind will not sow,
  and the one who looks at the clouds
    will not reap.
5 Just as you don't know the path of the wind,
  or how bones develop in the womb
    of a pregnant woman,
  so you don't know the work of God who makes
    everything.
6 In the morning sow your seed,
  and at evening do not let your hand rest,
  because you don't know which will succeed,
  whether one or the other,
  or if both of them will be equally good.
7 Light is sweet,
  and it is pleasing for the eyes to see the sun.
8 Indeed, if a man lives many years,
  let him rejoice in them all,
  and let him remember the days of darkness,
    since they will be many.
  All that comes is futile.
9 Rejoice, young man, while you are young,
  and let your heart be glad in the days
    of your youth.
  And walk in the ways of your heart
  and in the sight of your eyes;
  but know that for all of these things
    God will bring you to judgment.
10 Remove sorrow from your heart,
  and put away pain from your flesh,
  because youth and the prime of life
    are fleeting.

12

So remember your Creator in the days of your
youth:

Before the days of adversity come,
  and the years approach when you will say,
    "I have no delight in them";
2 before the sun and the light are darkened,
  and the moon and the stars,
  and the clouds return after the rain;
3 on the day when the guardians of the house
    tremble,
  and the strong men stoop,
  the women who grind cease because
    they are few,
  and the ones who watch through the windows
    see dimly,
4 the doors at the street are shut
  while the sound of the mill fades;
  when one rises at the sound of a bird,
  and all the daughters of song grow faint.
5 Also, they are afraid of heights and dangers
    on the road;
  the almond tree blossoms,
  the grasshopper loses its spring,
  and the caper berry has no effect;
  for man is headed to his eternal home,
  and mourners will walk around
    in the street;
6 before the silver cord is snapped,
  and the gold bowl is broken,
  and the jar is shattered at the spring,
  and the wheel is broken into the well;
7 and the dust returns to the earth
    as it once was,
  and the spirit returns to God who gave it.
8 "Absolute futility," says the Teacher. "Everything is futile."
9 In addition to the Teacher being a wise man, he constantly taught the •people knowledge; he weighed, explored, and arranged many proverbs. 10 The Teacher sought to find delightful sayings and write words of truth accurately. 11 The sayings of the wise are like goads, and those from masters of collections are like firmly embedded nails. The sayings are given by one Shepherd.
12 But beyond these, my son, be warned: there is no end to the making of many books, and much study wearies the body. 13 When all has been heard, the conclusion of the matter is: •fear God and keep His commands, because this is for all humanity. 14 For God will bring every act to judgment, including every hidden thing, whether good or evil.

SONG OF SONGS

1

Solomon's Finest Song.

W 2 Oh, that he would kiss me with the kisses
    of his mouth!
  For your love is more delightful
    than wine.
3 The fragrance of your perfume is intoxicating;
  your name is perfume poured out.
  No wonder young women adore you.
4 Take me with you—let us hurry.
  Oh, that the king would bring me
    to his chambers.

Y We will rejoice and be glad for you;
  we will praise your love more than wine.
W It is only right that they adore you.
5 Daughters of Jerusalem,
  I am dark like the tents of Kedar,
  yet lovely like the curtains of Solomon.
6 Do not stare at me because I am dark,
  for the sun has gazed on me.
  My mother's sons were angry with me;
  they made me a keeper of the vineyards.
  I have not kept my own vineyard.
7 Tell me, you, the one I love:

Where do you pasture your sheep?
Where do you let them rest at noon?
Why should I be like one who veils herself
beside the flocks of your companions?

M ⁸ If you do not know,
most beautiful of women,
follow the tracks of the flock,
and pasture your young goats
near the shepherds' tents.

⁹ I compare you, my darling,
to a mare among Pharaoh's chariots.

¹⁰ Your cheeks are beautiful with jewelry,
your neck with its necklace.

¹¹ We will make gold jewelry for you,
accented with silver.

W ¹² While the king is on his couch,
my perfume releases its fragrance.

¹³ My love is a sachet of myrrh to me,
spending the night between my breasts.

¹⁴ My love is a cluster of henna blossoms to me,
in the vineyards of En-gedi.

M ¹⁵ How beautiful you are, my darling.
How very beautiful!
Your eyes are doves.

W ¹⁶ How handsome you are, my love.
How delightful!
Our bed is lush with foliage;

¹⁷ the beams of our house are cedars,
and our rafters are cypresses.

2

I am a rose of Sharon,
a lily of the valleys.

M ² Like a lily among thorns,
so is my darling among the young women.

W ³ Like an apricot tree among the trees
of the forest,
so is my love among the young men.
I delight to sit in his shade,
and his fruit is sweet to my taste.

⁴ He brought me to the banquet hall,
and he looked on me with love.

⁵ Sustain me with raisins;
refresh me with apricots,
for I am lovesick.

⁶ His left hand is under my head,
and his right arm embraces me.

⁷ Young women of Jerusalem, I charge you
by the gazelles and the wild does of the field:
do not stir up or awaken love
until the appropriate time.

⁸ Listen! My love is approaching.
Look! Here he comes,
leaping over the mountains,
bounding over the hills.

⁹ My love is like a gazelle
or a young stag.
Look, he is standing behind our wall,
gazing through the windows,
peering through the lattice.

¹⁰ My love calls to me:

M Arise, my darling.
Come away, my beautiful one.

¹¹ For now the winter is past;
the rain has ended and gone away.

¹² The blossoms appear in the countryside.
The time of singing has come,
and the turtledove's cooing is heard
in our land.

¹³ The fig tree ripens its figs;
the blossoming vines give off their fragrance.
Arise, my darling.
Come away, my beautiful one.

¹⁴ My dove, in the clefts of the rock,
in the crevices of the cliff,
let me see your face,
let me hear your voice;
for your voice is sweet,
and your face is lovely.

(W) ¹⁵ Catch the foxes for us—
the little foxes that ruin the vineyards—
for our vineyards are in bloom.

W ¹⁶ My love is mine and I am his;
he feeds among the lilies.

¹⁷ Before the day breaks
and the shadows flee,
turn to me, my love, and be like a gazelle
or a young stag on the divided mountains.

3

In my bed at night
I sought the one I love;
I sought him, but did not find him.

² I will arise now and go about the city,
through the streets and the plazas.
I will seek the one I love.
I sought him, but did not find him.

³ The guards who go about the city found me.
I asked them, "Have you seen the one I love?"

⁴ I had just passed them
when I found the one I love.
I held on to him and would not let him go
until I brought him to my mother's house—
to the chamber of the one who conceived me.

⁵ Young women of Jerusalem, I charge you
by the gazelles and the wild does of the field:
do not stir up or awaken love
until the appropriate time.

N ⁶ What is this coming up from the wilderness
like columns of smoke,
scented with myrrh and frankincense
from every fragrant powder of the merchant?

⁷ It is Solomon's royal litter
surrounded by 60 warriors
from the mighty of Israel.

⁸ All of them are skilled with swords
and trained in warfare.
Each has his sword at his side
to guard against the terror of the night.

⁹ King Solomon made a sedan chair for himself
with wood from Lebanon.

¹⁰ He made its posts of silver,
its back of gold,
and its seat of purple.
Its interior is inlaid with love
by the young women of Jerusalem.

¹¹ Come out, young women of ⁎Zion,
and gaze at King Solomon,
wearing the crown his mother placed on him
the day of his wedding—
the day of his heart's rejoicing.

4

M How beautiful you are, my darling.
How very beautiful!
Behind your veil,
your eyes are doves.
Your hair is like a flock of goats
streaming down Mount Gilead.

² Your teeth are like a flock of newly shorn sheep

coming up from washing,
each one having a twin,
and not one missing.
3 Your lips are like a scarlet cord,
and your mouth is lovely.
Behind your veil,
your brow is like a slice of pomegranate.
4 Your neck is like the tower of David,
constructed in layers.
A thousand bucklers are hung on it—
all of them shields of warriors.
5 Your breasts are like two fawns,
twins of a gazelle, that feed among the lilies.
6 Before the day breaks
and the shadows flee,
I will make my way to the mountain of myrrh
and the hill of frankincense.
7 You are absolutely beautiful, my darling,
with no imperfection in you.
8 Come with me from Lebanon, my bride—
with me from Lebanon!
Descend from the peak of Amana,
from the summit of Senir and Hermon,
from the dens of the lions,
from the mountains of the leopards.
9 You have captured my heart, my sister,
my bride.
You have captured my heart with one glance
of your eyes,
with one jewel of your necklace.
10 How delightful your love is, my sister,
my bride.
Your love is much better than wine,
and the fragrance of your perfume
than any balsam.
11 Your lips drip sweetness like the honeycomb,
my bride.
Honey and milk are under your tongue.
The fragrance of your garments is like
the fragrance of Lebanon.
12 My sister, my bride, you are a locked garden—
a locked garden and a sealed spring.
13 Your branches are a paradise of pomegranates
with choicest fruits,
henna with nard—
14 nard and saffron, calamus and cinnamon,
with all the trees of frankincense,
myrrh and aloes,
with all the best spices.
15 You are a garden spring,
a well of flowing water
streaming from Lebanon.
W 16 Awaken, north wind—
come, south wind.
Blow on my garden,
and spread the fragrance of its spices.
Let my love come to his garden
and eat its choicest fruits.
5 M I have come to my garden—my sister,
my bride.
I gather my myrrh with my spices.
I eat my honeycomb with my honey.
I drink my wine with my milk.
N Eat, friends!
Drink, be intoxicated with love!
W 2 I sleep, but my heart is awake.
A sound! My love is knocking!

M Open to me, my sister, my darling,
my dove, my perfect one.
For my head is drenched with dew,
my hair with droplets of the night.
W 3 I have taken off my clothing.
How can I put it back on?
I have washed my feet.
How can I get them dirty?
4 My love thrust his hand through the opening,
and my feelings were stirred for him.
5 I rose to open for my love.
My hands dripped with myrrh,
my fingers with flowing myrrh
on the handles of the bolt.
6 I opened to my love,
but my love had turned and gone away.
I was crushed that he had left.
I sought him, but did not find him.
I called him, but he did not answer.
7 The guards who go about the city found me.
They beat and wounded me;
they took my cloak from me—
the guardians of the walls.
8 Young women of Jerusalem, I charge you:
if you find my love,
tell him that I am lovesick.
Y 9 What makes the one you love better
than another,
most beautiful of women?
What makes him better than another,
that you would give us this charge?
W 10 My love is fit and strong,
notable among ten thousand.
11 His head is purest gold.
His hair is wavy
and black as a raven.
12 His eyes are like doves
beside streams of water,
washed in milk
and set like jewels.
13 His cheeks are like beds of spice,
towers of perfume.
His lips are lilies,
dripping with flowing myrrh.
14 His arms are rods of gold
set with topaz.
His body is an ivory panel
covered with sapphires.
15 His legs are alabaster pillars
set on pedestals of pure gold.
His presence is like Lebanon,
as majestic as the cedars.
16 His mouth is sweetness.
He is absolutely desirable.
This is my love, and this is my friend,
young women of Jerusalem.
6 Y Where has your love gone,
most beautiful of women?
Which way has he turned?
We will seek him with you.
W 2 My love has gone down to his garden,
to beds of spice,
to feed in the gardens
and gather lilies.
3 I am my love's and my love is mine;
he feeds among the lilies.
M 4 You are as beautiful as Tirzah, my darling,

lovely as Jerusalem,
awe-inspiring as an army with banners.
⁵ Turn your eyes away from me,
for they captivate me.
Your hair is like a flock of goats
streaming down from Gilead.
⁶ Your teeth are like a flock of ewes
coming up from washing,
each one having a twin,
and not one missing.
⁷ Behind your veil,
your brow is like a slice of pomegranate.
⁸ There are 60 queens
and 80 concubines
and young women without number.
⁹ But my dove, my virtuous one, is unique;
she is the favorite of her mother,
perfect to the one who gave her birth.
Women see her and declare her fortunate;
queens and concubines also, and they sing
her praises:

Y ¹⁰ Who is this who shines like the dawn—
as beautiful as the moon,
bright as the sun,
awe-inspiring as an army with banners?

W ¹¹ I came down to the walnut grove
to see the blossoms of the valley,
to see if the vines were budding
and the pomegranates blooming.
¹² Before I knew it,
my desire put me
among the chariots of my noble people.

Y ¹³ Come back, come back, Shulammite!
Come back, come back, that we may look
at you!

M Why are you looking at the Shulammite,
as you look at the dance of the two camps?

7 How beautiful are your sandaled feet, princess!
The curves of your thighs are like jewelry,
the handiwork of a master.
² Your navel is a rounded bowl;
it never lacks mixed wine.
Your waist is a mound of wheat
surrounded by lilies.
³ Your breasts are like two fawns,
twins of a gazelle.
⁴ Your neck is like a tower of ivory,
your eyes like pools in Heshbon
by the gate of Bath-rabbim.
Your nose is like the tower of Lebanon
looking toward Damascus.
⁵ Your head crowns you like Mount Carmel,
the hair of your head like purple cloth—
a king could be held captive in your tresses.
⁶ How beautiful you are and how pleasant,
my love, with such delights!
⁷ Your stature is like a palm tree;
your breasts are clusters of fruit.
⁸ I said, "I will climb the palm tree
and take hold of its fruit."
May your breasts be like clusters of grapes,
and the fragrance of your breath like apricots.
⁹ Your mouth is like fine wine—

W flowing smoothly for my love,
gliding past my lips and teeth!
¹⁰ I belong to my love,
and his desire is for me.

¹¹ Come, my love,
let's go to the field;
let's spend the night
among the henna blossoms.
¹² Let's go early to the vineyards;
let's see if the vine has budded,
if the blossom has opened,
if the pomegranates are in bloom.
There I will give you my love.
¹³ The mandrakes give off a fragrance,
and at our doors is every delicacy—
new as well as old.
I have treasured them up for you, my love.

8 If only I could treat you like my brother,
one who nursed at my mother's breasts,
I would find you in public and kiss you,
and no one would scorn me.
² I would lead you, I would take you,
to the house of my mother who taught me.
I would give you spiced wine to drink
from my pomegranate juice.
³ His left hand is under my head,
and his right arm embraces me.
⁴ Young women of Jerusalem, I charge you:
do not stir up or awaken love
until the appropriate time.

Y ⁵ Who is this coming up from the wilderness,
leaning on the one she loves?

W I awakened you under the apricot tree.
There your mother conceived you;
there she conceived and gave you birth.
⁶ Set me as a seal on your heart,
as a seal on your arm.
For love is as strong as death;
ardent love is as unrelenting as ˙Sheol.
Love's flames are fiery flames—
the fiercest of all.
⁷ Mighty waters cannot extinguish love;
rivers cannot sweep it away.
If a man were to give all his wealth for love,
it would be utterly scorned.

B ⁸ Our sister is young;
she has no breasts.
What will we do for our sister
on the day she is spoken for?
⁹ If she is a wall,
we will build a silver parapet on it.
If she is a door,
we will enclose it with cedar planks.

W ¹⁰ I am a wall
and my breasts like towers.
So in his eyes I have become
like one who finds peace.
¹¹ Solomon owned a vineyard in Baal-hamon.
He leased the vineyard to tenants.
Each was to bring for his fruit
1,000 pieces of silver.
¹² I have my own vineyard.
The 1,000 are for you, Solomon,
but 200 for those who guard its fruits.

M ¹³ You who dwell in the gardens—
companions are listening for your voice—
let me hear you!

W ¹⁴ Hurry to me, my love,
and be like a gazelle
or a young stag
on the mountains of spices.

ISAIAH

1 The vision concerning Judah and Jerusalem that
Isaiah son of Amoz saw during the reigns of Uzziah,
Jotham, Ahaz, and Hezekiah, kings of Judah.

² Listen, heavens, and pay attention, earth,
for the LORD has spoken:
"I have raised children and brought them up,
but they have rebelled against Me.
³ The ox knows its owner,
and the donkey its master's feeding trough,
but Israel does not know;
My people do not understand."
⁴ Oh sinful nation,
people weighed down with iniquity,
brood of evildoers,
depraved children!
They have abandoned the LORD;
they have despised the Holy One of Israel;
they have turned their backs on Him.
⁵ Why do you want more beatings?
Why do you keep on rebelling?
The whole head is hurt,
and the whole heart is sick.
⁶ From the sole of the foot even to the head,
no spot is uninjured—
wounds, welts, and festering sores
not cleansed, bandaged,
or soothed with oil.
⁷ Your land is desolate,
your cities burned with fire;
foreigners devour your fields
before your very eyes—
a desolation demolished by foreigners.
⁸ Daughter ˙Zion is abandoned
like a shelter in a vineyard,
like a shack in a cucumber field,
like a besieged city.
⁹ If the LORD of ˙Hosts
had not left us a few survivors,
we would be like Sodom,
we would resemble Gomorrah.
¹⁰ Hear the word of the LORD,
you rulers of Sodom!
Listen to the instruction of our God,
you people of Gomorrah!
¹¹ "What are all your sacrifices to Me?"
asks the LORD.
"I have had enough of ˙burnt offerings
and rams
and the fat of well-fed cattle;
I have no desire for the blood of bulls,
lambs, or male goats.
¹² When you come to appear before Me,
who requires this from you—
this trampling of My courts?
¹³ Stop bringing useless offerings.
Your incense is detestable to Me.
New Moons and Sabbaths,
and the calling of solemn assemblies—
I cannot stand iniquity with a festival.
¹⁴ I hate your New Moons
and prescribed festivals.
They have become a burden to Me;
I am tired of putting up with them.

¹⁵ When you lift up your hands in prayer,
I will refuse to look at you;
even if you offer countless prayers,
I will not listen.
Your hands are covered with blood.
¹⁶ Wash yourselves. Cleanse yourselves.
Remove your evil deeds from My sight.
Stop doing evil.
¹⁷ Learn to do what is good.
Seek justice.
Correct the oppressor.
Defend the rights of the fatherless.
Plead the widow's cause.
¹⁸ Come, let us discuss this,"
says the LORD.
"Though your sins are like scarlet,
they will be as white as snow;
though they are as red as crimson,
they will be like wool.
¹⁹ If you are willing and obedient,
you will eat the good things of the land.
²⁰ But if you refuse and rebel,
you will be devoured by the sword."
For the mouth of the LORD has spoken.
²¹ The faithful city—
what an adulteress she has become!
She was once full of justice.
Righteousness once dwelt in her—
but now, murderers!
²² Your silver has become dross,
your beer is diluted with water.
²³ Your rulers are rebels,
friends of thieves.
They all love graft
and chase after bribes.
They do not defend the rights of the fatherless,
and the widow's case never comes
before them.
²⁴ Therefore the Lord GOD of Hosts,
the Mighty One of Israel, declares:
"Ah, I will gain satisfaction from My foes;
I will take revenge against My enemies.
²⁵ I will turn My hand against you
and will burn away your dross completely;
I will remove all your impurities.
²⁶ I will restore your judges to what
they once were,
and your advisers to their former state.
Afterward you will be called
the Righteous City,
a Faithful City."
²⁷ Zion will be redeemed by justice,
her repentant ones by righteousness.
²⁸ But both rebels and sinners will be destroyed,
and those who abandon the LORD will perish.
²⁹ Indeed, they will be ashamed
of the sacred trees
you desired,
and you will be embarrassed
because of the gardens
you have chosen.
³⁰ For you will become like an oak
whose leaves are withered,

and like a garden without water.
31 The strong one will become tinder,
and his work a spark;
both will burn together,
with no one to quench the flames.

2 The vision that Isaiah son of Amoz saw concerning
Judah and Jerusalem:
2 In the last days
the mountain of the Lord's house
will be established
at the top of the mountains
and will be raised above the hills.
All nations will stream to it,
3 and many peoples will come and say,
"Come, let us go up to the mountain
of the Lord,
to the house of the God of Jacob.
He will teach us about His ways
so that we may walk in His paths."
For instruction will go out of •Zion
and the word of the Lord from Jerusalem.
4 He will settle disputes among the nations
and provide arbitration for many peoples.
They will turn their swords into plows
and their spears into pruning knives.
Nations will not take up the sword
against other nations,
and they will never again train for war.
5 House of Jacob,
come and let us walk in the Lord's light.
6 For You have abandoned Your people,
the house of Jacob,
because they are full of •divination
from the East
and of fortune-tellers like the Philistines.
They are in league with foreigners.
7 Their land is full of silver and gold,
and there is no limit to their treasures;
their land is full of horses,
and there is no limit to their chariots.
8 Their land is full of idols;
they bow down to the work of their hands,
to what their fingers have made.
9 So humanity is brought low,
and man is humbled.
Do not forgive them!
10 Go into the rocks
and hide in the dust
from the terror of the Lord
and from His majestic splendor.
11 Human pride will be humbled,
and the loftiness of men will be brought low;
the Lord alone will be exalted on that day.
12 For a day belonging to the Lord of •Hosts
is coming
against all that is proud and lofty,
against all that is lifted up—it will
be humbled—
13 against all the cedars of Lebanon,
lofty and lifted up,
against all the oaks of Bashan,
14 against all the high mountains,
against all the lofty hills,
15 against every high tower,
against every fortified wall,
16 against every ship of Tarshish,
and against every splendid sea vessel.

17 So human pride will be brought low,
and the loftiness of men will be humbled;
the Lord alone will be exalted on that day.
18 The idols will vanish completely.
19 People will go into caves in the rocks
and holes in the ground,
away from the terror of the Lord
and from His majestic splendor,
when He rises to terrify the earth.
20 On that day people will throw
their silver and gold idols,
which they made to worship,
to the moles and the bats.
21 They will go into the caves of the rocks
and the crevices in the cliffs,
away from the terror of the Lord
and from His majestic splendor,
when He rises to terrify the earth.
22 Put no more trust in man,
who has only the breath in his nostrils.
What is he really worth?

3 Observe this: The Lord God of •Hosts
is about to remove from Jerusalem
and from Judah
every kind of security:
the entire supply of bread and water,
2 the hero and warrior,
the judge and prophet,
the fortune-teller and elder,
3 the commander of 50 and the dignitary,
the counselor, cunning magician,
and necromancer.
4 "I will make youths their leaders,
and the unstable will govern them."
5 The people will oppress one another,
man against man, neighbor against neighbor;
the youth will act arrogantly toward the elder,
and the worthless toward the honorable.
6 A man will even seize his brother
in his father's house, saying:
"You have a cloak—you be our leader!
This heap of rubble will be
under your control."
7 On that day he will cry out, saying:
"I'm not a healer.
I don't even have food or clothing
in my house.
Don't make me the leader of the people!"
8 For Jerusalem has stumbled
and Judah has fallen
because they have spoken and acted
against the Lord,
defying His glorious presence.
9 The look on their faces testifies against them,
and like Sodom, they flaunt their sin.
They do not conceal it.
Woe to them,
for they have brought evil on themselves.
10 Tell the righteous that it will go well for them,
for they will eat the fruit of their labor.
11 Woe to the wicked—it will go badly for them,
for what they have done will be done to them.
12 Youths oppress My people,
and women rule over them.
My people, your leaders mislead you;
they confuse the direction of your paths.
13 The Lord rises to argue the case

and stands to judge the people.
14 The LORD brings this charge
against the elders and leaders of His people:
"You have devastated the vineyard.
The plunder from the poor is in your houses.
15 Why do you crush My people
and grind the faces of the poor?"
This is the declaration
of the Lord GOD of Hosts.

16 The LORD also says:
Because the daughters of *Zion are haughty,
walking with heads held high
and seductive eyes,
going along with prancing steps,
jingling their ankle bracelets,
17 the Lord will put scabs on the heads
of the daughters of Zion,
and the LORD will shave their foreheads bare.

18 On that day the Lord will strip their finery: ankle bracelets, headbands, crescents, 19 pendants, bracelets, veils, 20 headdresses, ankle jewelry, sashes, perfume bottles, amulets, 21 signet rings, nose rings, 22 festive robes, capes, cloaks, purses, 23 garments, linen clothes, turbans, and veils.

24 Instead of perfume there will be a stench;
instead of a belt, a rope;
instead of beautifully styled hair, baldness;
instead of fine clothes, *sackcloth;
instead of beauty, branding.
25 Your men will fall by the sword,
your warriors in battle.
26 Then her gates will lament and mourn;
deserted, she will sit on the ground.

4 On that day seven women
will seize one man, saying,
"We will eat our own bread
and provide our own clothing.
Just let us be called by your name.
Take away our disgrace."

2 On that day the Branch of the LORD will be beautiful and glorious, and the fruit of the land will be the pride and glory of Israel's survivors. 3 Whoever remains in *Zion and whoever is left in Jerusalem will be called holy—all in Jerusalem who are destined to live— 4 when the Lord has washed away the filth of the daughters of Zion and cleansed the bloodguilt from the heart of Jerusalem by a spirit of judgment and a spirit of burning. 5 Then the LORD will create a cloud of smoke by day and a glowing flame of fire by night over the entire site of Mount Zion and over its assemblies. For there will be a canopy over all the glory, 6 and there will be a booth for shade from heat by day, and a refuge and shelter from storm and rain.

5 I will sing about the one I love,
a song about my loved one's vineyard:
The one I love had a vineyard
on a very fertile hill.
2 He broke up the soil, cleared it of stones,
and planted it with the finest vines.
He built a tower in the middle of it
and even dug out a winepress there.
He expected it to yield good grapes,
but it yielded worthless grapes.
3 So now, residents of Jerusalem
and men of Judah,
please judge between Me
and My vineyard.

4 What more could I have done for My vineyard
than I did?
Why, when I expected a yield of good grapes,
did it yield worthless grapes?
5 Now I will tell you
what I am about to do to My vineyard:
I will remove its hedge,
and it will be consumed;
I will tear down its wall,
and it will be trampled.
6 I will make it a wasteland.
It will not be pruned or weeded;
thorns and briers will grow up.
I will also give orders to the clouds
that rain should not fall on it.
7 For the vineyard of the LORD of *Hosts
is the house of Israel,
and the men of Judah,
the plant He delighted in.
He looked for justice
but saw injustice,
for righteousness,
but heard cries of wretchedness.
8 Woe to those who add house to house
and join field to field
until there is no more room
and you alone are left in the land.
9 I heard the LORD of Hosts say:
Indeed, many houses will become desolate,
grand and lovely ones without inhabitants.
10 For a ten-acre vineyard will yield
only six gallons,
and 10 bushels of seed will yield
only one bushel.
11 Woe to those who rise early in the morning
in pursuit of beer,
who linger into the evening,
inflamed by wine.
12 At their feasts they have lyre, harp,
tambourine, flute, and wine.
They do not perceive the LORD's actions,
and they do not see the work of His hands.
13 Therefore My people will go into exile
because they lack knowledge;
her dignitaries are starving,
and her masses are parched with thirst.
14 Therefore *Sheol enlarges its throat
and opens wide its enormous jaws,
and down go *Zion's dignitaries, her masses,
her crowds, and those who carouse in her!
15 Humanity is brought low, man is humbled,
and haughty eyes are humbled.
16 But the LORD of Hosts is exalted by His justice,
and the holy God is distinguished
by righteousness.
17 Lambs will graze
as if in their own pastures,
and strangers will eat
among the ruins of the rich.
18 Woe to those who drag wickedness
with cords of deceit
and pull sin along with cart ropes,
19 to those who say:
"Let Him hurry up and do His work quickly
so that we can see it!
Let the plan of the Holy One of Israel
take place

so that we can know it!"
20 Woe to those who call evil good
and good evil,
who substitute darkness for light
and light for darkness,
who substitute bitter for sweet
and sweet for bitter.
21 Woe to those who are wise
in their own opinion
and clever in their own sight.
22 Woe to those who are heroes at drinking wine,
who are fearless at mixing beer,
23 who acquit the *guilty for a bribe
and deprive the innocent of justice.
24 Therefore, as a tongue of fire consumes straw
and as dry grass shrivels in the flame,
so their roots will become
like something rotten
and their blossoms will blow away like dust,
for they have rejected
the instruction of the LORD of Hosts,
and they have despised
the word of the Holy One of Israel.
25 Therefore the LORD's anger burns
against His people.
He raised His hand against them
and struck them;
the mountains quaked,
and their corpses were like garbage
in the streets.
In all this, His anger is not removed,
and His hand is still raised to strike.
26 He raises a signal flag for the distant nations
and whistles for them from the ends
of the earth.
Look—how quickly and swiftly they come!
27 None of them grows weary or stumbles,
no one slumbers or sleeps.
No belt is loose
and no sandal strap broken.
28 Their arrows are sharpened,
and all their bows strung.
Their horses' hooves are like flint;
their chariot wheels are like a whirlwind.
29 Their roaring is like a lion's;
they roar like young lions;
they growl and seize their prey
and carry it off,
and no one can rescue it.
30 On that day they will roar over it,
like the roaring of the sea.
When one looks at the land,
there will be darkness and distress;
light will be obscured by clouds.

6 In the year that King Uzziah died, I saw the Lord seated on a high and lofty throne, and His robe filled the temple. ²Seraphim were standing above Him; each one had six wings: with two he covered his face, with two he covered his feet, and with two he flew. ³And one called to another:

Holy, holy, holy is the LORD of *Hosts;
His glory fills the whole earth.

⁴The foundations of the doorways shook at the sound of their voices, and the temple was filled with smoke. ⁵Then I said:

Woe is me for I am ruined
because I am a man of *unclean lips

and live among a people of unclean lips,
and because my eyes have seen the King,
the LORD of Hosts.

⁶Then one of the seraphim flew to me, and in his hand was a glowing coal that he had taken from the altar with tongs. ⁷He touched my mouth with it and said:

Now that this has touched your lips,
your wickedness is removed
and your sin is atoned for.

⁸Then I heard the voice of the Lord saying:

Who should I send?
Who will go for Us?

I said:

Here I am. Send me.

⁹And He replied:

Go! Say to these people:
Keep listening, but do not understand;
keep looking, but do not perceive.
10 Dull the minds of these people;
deafen their ears and blind their eyes;
otherwise they might see with their eyes
and hear with their ears,
understand with their minds,
turn back, and be healed.

11Then I said, "Until when, Lord?" And He replied:

Until cities lie in ruins without inhabitants,
houses are without people,
the land is ruined and desolate,
12 and the LORD drives the people far away,
leaving great emptiness in the land.
13 Though a tenth will remain in the land,
it will be burned again.
Like the terebinth or the oak
that leaves a stump when felled,
the holy *seed is the stump.

7 This took place during the reign of Ahaz, son of Jotham, son of Uzziah king of Judah: Rezin king of Aram, along with Pekah, son of Remaliah, king of Israel, waged war against Jerusalem, but he could not succeed. ²When it became known to the house of David that Aram had occupied Ephraim, the heart of Ahaz and the hearts of his people trembled like trees of a forest shaking in the wind.

³Then the LORD said to Isaiah, "Go out with your son Shear-jashub to meet Ahaz at the end of the conduit of the upper pool, by the road to the Fuller's Field. ⁴Say to him: Calm down and be quiet. Don't be afraid or cowardly because of these two smoldering stubs of firebrands, the fierce anger of Rezin and Aram, and the son of Remaliah. ⁵For Aram, along with Ephraim and the son of Remaliah, has plotted harm against you. They say, ⁶'Let us go up against Judah, terrorize it, and conquer it for ourselves. Then we can install Tabeel's son as king in it.'"

⁷This is what the Lord GOD says:

It will not happen; it will not occur.
8 The head of Aram is Damascus,
the head of Damascus is Rezin
(within 65 years
Ephraim will be too shattered to be a people),
9 the head of Ephraim is Samaria,
and the head of Samaria is the son
of Remaliah.
If you do not stand firm in your faith,
then you will not stand at all.

10Then the LORD spoke again to Ahaz: 11"Ask for

a sign from the Lᴏʀᴅ your God—from the depths of *Sheol to the heights of heaven."

¹²But Ahaz replied, "I will not ask. I will not test the Lᴏʀᴅ."

¹³Isaiah said, "Listen, house of David! Is it not enough for you to try the patience of men? Will you also try the patience of my God? ¹⁴Therefore, the Lord Himself will give you a sign: The virgin will conceive, have a son, and name him Immanuel. ¹⁵By the time he learns to reject what is bad and choose what is good, he will be eating butter and honey. ¹⁶For before the boy knows to reject what is bad and choose what is good, the land of the two kings you dread will be abandoned. ¹⁷The Lᴏʀᴅ will bring on you, your people, and the house of your father, such a time as has never been since Ephraim separated from Judah—the king of Assyria is coming."

¹⁸ On that day
the Lᴏʀᴅ will whistle to the fly
that is at the farthest streams of the Nile
and to the bee that is in the land of Assyria.
¹⁹ All of them will come and settle
in the steep ravines, in the clefts of the rocks,
in all the thornbushes, and in all the
water holes.

²⁰On that day the Lord will use a razor hired from beyond the Euphrates River—the king of Assyria—to shave the head, the hair on the legs, and to remove the beard as well.

²¹ On that day
a man will raise a young cow and two sheep,
²² and from the abundant milk they give
he will eat butter,
for every survivor in the land will eat butter
and honey.
²³ And on that day
every place where there were 1,000 vines,
worth 1,000 pieces of silver,
will become thorns and briers.
²⁴ A man will go there with bow and arrows
because the whole land will be thorns
and briers.
²⁵ You will not go to all the hills
that were once tilled with a hoe,
for fear of the thorns and briers.
Those hills will be places for oxen to graze
and for sheep to trample.

8 Then the Lᴏʀᴅ said to me, "Take a large piece of parchment and write on it with an ordinary pen: Maher-shalal-hash-baz. ²I have appointed trustworthy witnesses—Uriah the priest and Zechariah son of Jeberechiah."

³I was then intimate with the prophetess, and she conceived and gave birth to a son. The Lᴏʀᴅ said to me, "Name him Maher-shalal-hash-baz, ⁴for before the boy knows how to call out father or mother, the wealth of Damascus and the spoils of Samaria will be carried off to the king of Assyria."

⁵The Lᴏʀᴅ spoke to me again:

⁶ Because these people rejected
the slowly flowing waters of Shiloah
and rejoiced with Rezin
and the son of Remaliah,
⁷ the Lord will certainly bring against them
the mighty rushing waters
of the Euphrates River—
the king of Assyria and all his glory.

It will overflow its channels
and spill over all its banks.
⁸ It will pour into Judah,
flood over it, and sweep through,
reaching up to the neck;
and its spreading streams
will fill your entire land, Immanuel!
⁹ Band together, peoples, and be broken;
pay attention, all you distant lands;
prepare for war, and be broken;
prepare for war, and be broken.
¹⁰ Devise a plan; it will fail.
Make a prediction; it will not happen.
For God is with us.

¹¹For this is what the Lᴏʀᴅ said to me with great power, to keep me from going the way of this people:

¹² Do not call everything an alliance
these people say is an alliance.
Do not fear what they fear;
do not be terrified.
¹³ You are to regard only the Lᴏʀᴅ of *Hosts
as holy.
Only He should be *feared;
only He should be held in awe.
¹⁴ He will be a sanctuary;
but for the two houses of Israel,
He will be a stone to stumble over
and a rock to trip over,
and a trap and a snare to the inhabitants
of Jerusalem.
¹⁵ Many will stumble over these;
they will fall and be broken;
they will be snared and captured.
¹⁶ Bind up the *testimony.
Seal up the instruction among my disciples.
¹⁷ I will wait for the Lᴏʀᴅ,
who is hiding His face from the house
of Jacob.
I will wait for Him.

¹⁸Here I am with the children the Lᴏʀᴅ has given me to be signs and wonders in Israel from the Lᴏʀᴅ of Hosts who dwells on Mount *Zion. ¹⁹When they say to you, "Consult the spirits of the dead and the spiritists who chirp and mutter," shouldn't a people consult their God? Should they consult the dead on behalf of the living? ²⁰To the law and to the testimony! If they do not speak according to this word, there will be no dawn for them. ²¹They will wander through the land, dejected and hungry. When they are famished, they will become enraged, and, looking upward, will curse their king and their God. ²²They will look toward the earth and see only distress, darkness, and the gloom of affliction, and they will be driven into thick darkness.

9 Nevertheless, the gloom of the distressed land will not be like that of the former times when He humbled the land of Zebulun and the land of Naphtali. But in the future He will bring honor to the Way of the Sea, to the land east of the Jordan, and to Galilee of the nations.

² The people walking in darkness
have seen a great light;
a light has dawned
on those living in the land of darkness.
³ You have enlarged the nation
and increased its joy.
The people have rejoiced before You

as they rejoice at harvest time
and as they rejoice when dividing spoils.
⁴ For You have shattered their oppressive yoke
and the rod on their shoulders,
the staff of their oppressor,
just as You did on the day of Midian.
⁵ For the trampling boot of battle
and the bloodied garments of war
will be burned as fuel for the fire.
⁶ For a child will be born for us,
a son will be given to us,
and the government will be on His shoulders.
He will be named
Wonderful Counselor, Mighty God,
Eternal Father, Prince of Peace.
⁷ The dominion will be vast,
and its prosperity will never end.
He will reign on the throne of David
and over his kingdom,
to establish and sustain it
with justice and righteousness from now on
and forever.
The zeal of the Lᴏʀᴅ of *Hosts
will accomplish this.
⁸ The Lord sent a message against Jacob;
it came against Israel.
⁹ All the people—
Ephraim and the inhabitants of Samaria—
will know it.
They will say with pride and arrogance:
¹⁰ "The bricks have fallen,
but we will rebuild with cut stones;
the sycamores have been cut down,
but we will replace them with cedars."
¹¹ The Lᴏʀᴅ has raised up Rezin's adversaries
against him
and stirred up his enemies.
¹² Aram from the east and Philistia
from the west
have consumed Israel with open mouths.
In all this, His anger is not removed,
and His hand is still raised to strike.
¹³ The people did not turn to Him
who struck them;
they did not seek the Lᴏʀᴅ of Hosts.
¹⁴ So the Lᴏʀᴅ cut off Israel's head and tail,
palm branch and reed in a single day.
¹⁵ The head is the elder, the honored one;
the tail is the prophet, the lying teacher.
¹⁶ The leaders of the people mislead them,
and those they mislead are swallowed up.
¹⁷ Therefore the Lord does not rejoice
over Israel's young men
and has no compassion
on its fatherless and widows,
for everyone is a godless evildoer,
and every mouth speaks folly.
In all this, His anger is not removed,
and His hand is still raised to strike.
¹⁸ For wickedness burns like a fire
that consumes thorns and briers
and kindles the forest thickets
so that they go up in a column of smoke.
¹⁹ The land is scorched
by the wrath of the Lᴏʀᴅ of Hosts,
and the people are like fuel for the fire.
No one has compassion on his brother.

²⁰ They carve meat on the right,
but they are still hungry;
they have eaten on the left,
but they are still not satisfied.
Each one eats the flesh of his own arm.
²¹ Manasseh is with Ephraim,
and Ephraim with Manasseh;
together, both are against Judah.
In all this, His anger is not removed,
and His hand is still raised to strike.

10

Woe to those enacting crooked statutes
and writing oppressive laws
² to keep the poor from getting a fair trial
and to deprive the afflicted among my people
of justice,
so that widows can be their spoil
and they can plunder the fatherless.
³ What will you do on the day of punishment
when devastation comes from far away?
Who will you run to for help?
Where will you leave your wealth?
⁴ There will be nothing to do
except crouch among the prisoners
or fall among the slain.
In all this, His anger is not removed,
and His hand is still raised to strike.
⁵ Woe to Assyria, the rod of My anger—
the staff in their hands is My wrath.
⁶ I will send him against a godless nation;
I will command him to go
against a people destined for My rage,
to take spoils, to plunder,
and to trample them down like clay
in the streets.
⁷ But this is not what he intends;
this is not what he plans.
It is his intent to destroy
and to cut off many nations.
⁸ For he says,
"Aren't all my commanders kings?
⁹ Isn't Calno like Carchemish?
Isn't Hamath like Arpad?
Isn't Samaria like Damascus?
¹⁰ As my hand seized the idolatrous kingdoms,
whose idols exceeded those of Jerusalem
and Samaria,
¹¹ and as I did to Samaria and its idols
will I not also do to Jerusalem and its idols?"
¹²But when the Lord finishes all His work against
Mount *Zion and Jerusalem, He will say, "I will punish
the king of Assyria for his arrogant acts and the proud
look in his eyes." ¹³For he said:
I have done this by my own strength
and wisdom, for I am clever.
I abolished the borders of nations
and plundered their treasures;
like a mighty warrior, I subjugated
the inhabitants.
¹⁴ My hand has reached out, as if into a nest,
to seize the wealth of the nations.
Like one gathering abandoned eggs,
I gathered the whole earth.
No wing fluttered;
no beak opened or chirped.
¹⁵ Does an ax exalt itself
above the one who chops with it?
Does a saw magnify itself

above the one who saws with it?
It would be like a staff waving the one
who lifts it!
It would be like a rod lifting a man
who isn't wood!
16 Therefore the Lord GoD of *Hosts
will inflict an emaciating disease
on the well-fed of Assyria,
and He will kindle a burning fire
under its glory.
17 Israel's Light will become a fire,
and its Holy One, a flame.
In one day it will burn up Assyria's thorns
and thistles.
18 He will completely destroy
the glory of its forests and orchards
as a sickness consumes a person.
19 The remaining trees of its forest
will be so few in number
that a child could count them.

20 On that day the remnant of Israel and the survivors of the house of Jacob will no longer depend on the one who struck them, but they will faithfully depend on the LORD, the Holy One of Israel. 21 The remnant will return, the remnant of Jacob,
to the Mighty God.
22 Israel, even if your people were as numerous
as the sand of the sea,
only a remnant of them will return.
Destruction has been decreed;
justice overflows.
23 For throughout the land
the Lord GoD of Hosts
is carrying out a destruction that was decreed.

24 Therefore, the Lord GoD of Hosts says this: "My people who dwell in Zion, do not fear Assyria, though he strikes you with a rod and raises his staff over you as the Egyptians did. 25 In just a little while My wrath will be spent and My anger will turn to their destruction." 26 And the LORD of Hosts will brandish a whip against him as He did when He struck Midian at the rock of Oreb; and He will raise His staff over the sea as He did in Egypt.
27 On that day
his burden will fall from your shoulders,
and his yoke from your neck.
The yoke will be broken because of fatness.
28 Assyria has come to Aiath
and has gone through Migron,
storing his equipment at Michmash.
29 They crossed over at the ford, saying,
"We will spend the night at Geba."
The people of Ramah are trembling;
those at Gibeah of Saul have fled.
30 Cry aloud, daughter of Gallim!
Listen, Laishah!
Anathoth is miserable.
31 Madmenah has fled.
The inhabitants of Gebim have sought refuge.
32 Today he will stand at Nob,
shaking his fist at the mountain
of Daughter Zion,
the hill of Jerusalem.
33 Look, the Lord GoD of Hosts
will chop off the branches
with terrifying power,

and the tall trees will be cut down,
the high trees felled.
34 He is clearing the thickets of the forest
with an ax,
and Lebanon with its majesty will fall.

11 Then a shoot will grow from the stump
of Jesse,
and a branch from his roots will bear fruit.
2 The Spirit of the LORD will rest on Him—
a Spirit of wisdom and understanding,
a Spirit of counsel and strength,
a Spirit of knowledge and of the *fear
of the LORD.
3 His delight will be in the fear of the LORD.
He will not judge
by what He sees with His eyes,
He will not execute justice
by what He hears with His ears,
4 but He will judge the poor righteously
and execute justice for the oppressed
of the land.
He will strike the land
with discipline from His mouth,
and He will kill the wicked
with a command from His lips.
5 Righteousness will be a belt around His loins;
faithfulness will be a belt around His waist.
6 The wolf will live with the lamb,
and the leopard will lie down with the goat.
The calf, the young lion, and the fatling
will be together,
and a child will lead them.
7 The cow and the bear will graze,
their young ones will lie down together,
and the lion will eat straw like the ox.
8 An infant will play beside the cobra's pit,
and a toddler will put his hand
. into a snake's den.
9 None will harm or destroy another
on My entire holy mountain,
for the land will be as full
of the knowledge of the LORD
as the sea is filled with water.
10 On that day the root of Jesse
will stand as a banner for the peoples.
The nations will seek Him,
and His resting place will be glorious.
11 On that day the Lord will extend His hand a second time to recover—from Assyria, Egypt, Pathros, *Cush, Elam, *Shinar, Hamath, and the coasts and islands of the west—the remnant of His people who survive.
12 He will lift up a banner for the nations
and gather the dispersed of Israel;
He will collect the scattered of Judah
from the four corners of the earth.
13 Ephraim's envy will cease;
Judah's harassment will end.
Ephraim will no longer be envious of Judah,
and Judah will not harass Ephraim.
14 But they will swoop down
on the Philistine flank to the west.
Together they will plunder the people
of the east.
They will extend their power over Edom
and Moab,
and the Ammonites will be their subjects.
15 The LORD will divide the Gulf of Suez.

He will wave His hand over the Euphrates
with His mighty wind
and will split it into seven streams,
letting people walk through on foot.
16 There will be a highway for the remnant
of His people
who will survive from Assyria,
as there was for Israel
when they came up from the land of Egypt.

12 On that day you will say:
"I will praise You, Lord,
although You were angry with me.
Your anger has turned away,
and You have had compassion on me.
2 Indeed, God is my salvation;
I will trust Him and not be afraid,
for *Yah, the Lord,
is my strength and my song.
He has become my salvation."
3 You will joyfully draw water
from the springs of salvation,
4 and on that day you will say:
"Give thanks to Yahweh; proclaim His name!
Celebrate His works among the peoples.
Declare that His name is exalted.
5 Sing to Yahweh, for He has done
glorious things.
Let this be known throughout the earth.
6 Cry out and sing, citizen of *Zion,
for the Holy One of Israel is among you
in His greatness."

13 An *oracle against Babylon that Isaiah son of
Amoz saw:
2 Lift up a banner on a barren mountain.
Call out to them.
Wave your hand, and they will go
through the gates of the nobles.
3 I have commanded My chosen ones;   ·
I have also called My warriors,
who exult in My triumph,
to execute My wrath.
4 Listen, a tumult on the mountains,
like that of a mighty people!
Listen, an uproar among the kingdoms,
like nations being gathered together!
The Lord of *Hosts is mobilizing an army
for war.
5 They are coming from a far land,
from the distant horizon—
the Lord and the weapons of His wrath—
to destroy the whole country.
6 Wail! For the day of the Lord is near.
It will come like destruction
from the *Almighty.
7 Therefore everyone's hands will become weak,
and every man's heart will melt.
8 They will be horrified;
pain and agony will seize them;
they will be in anguish like a woman in labor.
They will look at each other,
their faces flushed with fear.
9 Look, the day of the Lord is coming—
cruel, with rage and burning anger—
to make the earth a desolation
and to destroy the sinners on it.
10 Indeed, the stars of the sky
and its constellations

will not give their light.
The sun will be dark when it rises,
and the moon will not shine.
11 I will bring disaster on the world,
and their own iniquity, on the wicked.
I will put an end to the pride of the arrogant
and humiliate the insolence of tyrants.
12 I will make man scarcer than gold,
and mankind more rare than the gold of Ophir.
13 Therefore I will make the heavens tremble,
and the earth will shake from its foundations
at the wrath of the Lord of Hosts,
on the day of His burning anger.
14 Like wandering gazelles
and like sheep without a shepherd,
each one will turn to his own people,
each one will flee to his own land.
15 Whoever is found will be stabbed,
and whoever is caught will die by the sword.
16 Their children will be smashed to death
before their eyes;
their houses will be looted,
and their wives raped.
17 Look! I am stirring up the Medes
against them,
who cannot be bought off with silver
and who have no desire for gold.
18 Their bows will cut young men to pieces.
They will have no compassion on little ones;
they will not look with pity on children.
19 And Babylon, the jewel of the kingdoms,
the glory of the pride of the Chaldeans,
will be like Sodom and Gomorrah
when God overthrew them.
20 It will never be inhabited
or lived in from generation to generation;
a nomad will not pitch his tent there,
and shepherds will not let their flocks
rest there.
21 But desert creatures will lie down there,
and owls will fill the houses.
Ostriches will dwell there,
and wild goats will leap about.
22 Hyenas will howl in the fortresses,
and jackals, in the luxurious palaces.
Babylon's time is almost up;
her days are almost over.

14 For the Lord will have compassion on Jacob
and will choose Israel again. He will settle them
on their own land. The foreigner will join them and
be united with the house of Jacob. 2 The nations will
escort Israel and bring it to its homeland. Then the
house of Israel will possess them as male and female
slaves in the Lord's land. They will make captives of
their captors and will rule over their oppressors.

3 When the Lord gives you rest from your pain, torment, and the hard labor you were forced to do, 4 you
will sing this song of contempt about the king of Babylon and say:
How the oppressor has quieted down,
and how the raging has become quiet!
5 The Lord has broken the staff of the wicked,
the scepter of the rulers.
6 It struck the peoples in anger
with unceasing blows.
It subdued the nations in rage
with relentless persecution.

7 All the earth is calm and at rest;
   people shout with a ringing cry.
8 Even the cypresses and the cedars of Lebanon
   rejoice over you:
   "Since you have been laid low,
   no woodcutter has come against us."
9 ˙Sheol below is eager to greet your coming.
   He stirs up the spirits of the departed
      for you—
   all the rulers of the earth.
   He makes all the kings of the nations
   rise from their thrones.
10 They all respond to you, saying:
   "You too have become as weak as we are;
   you have become like us!
11 Your splendor has been brought down
     to Sheol,
   along with the music of your harps.
   Maggots are spread out under you,
   and worms cover you."
12 Shining morning star,
   how you have fallen from the heavens!
   You destroyer of nations,
   you have been cut down to the ground.
13 You said to yourself:
   "I will ascend to the heavens;
   I will set up my throne
   above the stars of God.
   I will sit on the mount of the gods' assembly,
   in the remotest parts of the North.
14 I will ascend above the highest clouds;
   I will make myself like the ˙Most High."
15 But you will be brought down to Sheol
   into the deepest regions of the ˙Pit.
16 Those who see you will stare at you;
   they will look closely at you:
   "Is this the man who caused the earth
     to tremble,
   who shook the kingdoms,
17 who turned the world into a wilderness,
   who destroyed its cities
   and would not release the prisoners
     to return home?"
18 All the kings of the nations
   lie in splendor, each in his own tomb.
19 But you are thrown out without a grave,
   like a worthless branch,
   covered by those slain with the sword
   and dumped into a rocky pit
   like a trampled corpse.
20 You will not join them in burial,
   because you destroyed your land
   and slaughtered your own people.
   The offspring of evildoers
   will never be remembered.
21 Prepare a place of slaughter for his sons,
   because of the iniquity of their fathers.
   They will never rise up to possess a land
   or fill the surface of the earth with cities.

22 "I will rise up against them"—this is the declaration of the Lord of ˙Hosts—"and I will cut off from Babylon her reputation, remnant, offspring, and posterity"—this is the Lord's declaration. 23 "I will make her a swampland and a region for screech owls, and I will sweep her away with a broom of destruction."

               This is the declaration
               of the Lord of Hosts.

24 The Lord of Hosts has sworn:
   As I have purposed, so it will be;
   as I have planned it, so it will happen.
25 I will break Assyria in My land;
   I will tread him down on My mountain.
   Then his yoke will be taken from them,
   and his burden will be removed
     from their shoulders.
26 This is the plan prepared
   for the whole earth,
   and this is the hand stretched out
   against all the nations.
27 The Lord of Hosts Himself has planned it;
   therefore, who can stand in its way?
   It is His hand that is outstretched,
   so who can turn it back?
28 In the year that King Ahaz died, this ˙oracle came:
29 Don't rejoice, all of you in Philistia,
   because the rod of the one who struck you
     is broken.
   For a viper will come from the root of a snake,
   and from its egg comes a flying serpent.
30 Then the firstborn of the poor will be well fed,
   and the impoverished will lie down in safety,
   but I will kill your root with hunger,
   and your remnant will be slain.
31 Wail, you gates! Cry out, city!
   Tremble with fear, all Philistia!
   For a cloud of dust is coming from the north,
   and there is no one missing from
     the invader's ranks.
32 What answer will be given to the messengers
     from that nation?
   The Lord has founded ˙Zion,
   and His afflicted people find refuge in her.

15 An ˙oracle against Moab:
   Ar in Moab is devastated,
   destroyed in a night.
   Kir in Moab is devastated,
   destroyed in a night.
2 Dibon went up to its temple
   to weep at its ˙high places.
   Moab wails on Nebo and at Medeba.
   Every head is shaved;
   every beard is cut off.
3 In its streets they wear ˙sackcloth;
   on its rooftops and in its public squares
     everyone wails,
   falling down and weeping.
4 Heshbon and Elealeh cry out;
   their voices are heard as far away as Jahaz.
   Therefore the soldiers of Moab cry out,
   and they tremble.
5 My heart cries out over Moab,
   whose fugitives flee as far as Zoar,
   to Eglath-shelishiyah;
   they go up the slope of Luhith weeping;
   they raise a cry of destruction
   on the road to Horonaim.
6 The waters of Nimrim are desolate;
   the grass is withered, the foliage is gone,
   and the vegetation has vanished.
7 So they carry their wealth and belongings
   over the ˙Wadi of the Willows.
8 For their cry echoes
   throughout the territory of Moab.
   Their wailing reaches Eglaim;

their wailing reaches Beer-elim.
⁹ The waters of Dibon are full of blood,
but I will bring on Dibon even more
than this—
a lion for those who escape from Moab,
and for the survivors in the land.

16 Send lambs to the ruler of the land,
from Sela in the desert
to the mountain of Daughter •Zion.
² Like a bird fleeing,
forced from the nest,
the daughters of Moab
will be at the fords of the Arnon.
³ Give us counsel and make a decision.
Shelter us at noonday
with shade that is as dark as night.
Hide the refugees;
do not betray the one who flees.
⁴ Let my refugees stay with you;
be a refuge for Moab from the aggressor.
When the oppressor has gone,
destruction has ended,
and marauders have vanished from the land.
⁵ Then in the tent of David
a throne will be established by faithful love.
A judge who seeks what is right
and is quick to execute justice
will sit on the throne forever.
⁶ We have heard of Moab's pride—
how very proud he is—
his haughtiness, his pride, his arrogance,
and his empty boasting.
⁷ Therefore let Moab wail;
let every one of them wail for Moab.
Mourn, you who are completely devastated,
for the raisin cakes of Kir-hareseth.
⁸ For Heshbon's terraced vineyards
and the grapevines of Sibmah have withered.
The rulers of the nations
have trampled its choice vines
that reached as far as Jazer
and spread to the desert.
Their shoots spread out
and reached the Dead Sea.
⁹ So I join with Jazer
to weep for the vines of Sibmah;
I drench Heshbon and Elealeh with my tears.
Triumphant shouts have fallen silent
over your summer fruit and your harvest.
¹⁰ Joy and rejoicing have been removed
from the orchard;
no one is singing or shouting for joy
in the vineyards.
No one tramples grapes in the winepresses.
I have put an end to the shouting.
¹¹ Therefore I moan like the sound of a lyre
for Moab,
as does my innermost being for Kir-heres.
¹² When Moab appears on the •high place,
when he tires himself out
and comes to his sanctuary to pray,
it will do him no good.

¹³This is the message that the LORD previously announced about Moab. ¹⁴And now the LORD says, "In three years, as a hired worker counts years, Moab's splendor will become an object of contempt, in spite

of a very large population. And those who are left will be few and weak."

17 An •oracle against Damascus:
Look, Damascus is no longer a city.
It has become a ruined heap.
² The cities of Aroer are forsaken;
they will be places for flocks.
They will lie down without fear.
³ The fortress disappears from Ephraim,
and a kingdom from Damascus.
The remnant of Aram will be
like the splendor of the Israelites.
This is the declaration
of the LORD of •Hosts.
⁴ On that day
the splendor of Jacob will fade,
and his healthy body will become emaciated.
⁵ It will be as if a reaper had gathered
standing grain—
his arm harvesting the heads of grain—
and as if one had gleaned heads of grain
in the Valley of Rephaim.
⁶ Only gleanings will be left in Israel,
as if an olive tree had been beaten—
two or three berries at the very top of the tree,
four or five on its fruitful branches.
This is the declaration of the LORD,
the God of Israel.

⁷On that day people will look to their Maker and will turn their eyes to the Holy One of Israel. ⁸They will not look to the altars they made with their hands or to the •Asherahs and incense altars they made with their fingers.

⁹ On that day their strong cities will be
like the abandoned woods and mountaintops
that were abandoned because of the Israelites;
there will be desolation.
¹⁰ For you have forgotten the God
of your salvation,
and you have failed to remember
the rock of your strength;
therefore you will plant beautiful plants
and set out cuttings from exotic vines.
¹¹ On the day that you plant,
you will help them to grow,
and in the morning
you will help your seed to sprout,
but the harvest will vanish
on the day of disease and incurable pain.
¹² Ah! The roar of many peoples—
they roar like the roaring of the seas.
The raging of the nations—
they rage like the raging of mighty waters.
¹³ The nations rage like the raging
of many waters.
He rebukes them, and they flee far away,
driven before the wind like chaff on the hills
and like tumbleweeds before a gale.
¹⁴ In the evening—sudden terror!
Before morning—it is gone!
This is the fate of those who plunder us
and the lot of those who ravage us.

18 Ah! The land of buzzing insect wings
beyond the rivers of •Cush
² sends couriers by sea,
in reed vessels on the waters.
Go, swift messengers,

to a nation tall and smooth-skinned,
to a people feared far and near,
a powerful nation with a strange language,
whose land is divided by rivers.
³ All you inhabitants of the world
and you who live on the earth,
when a banner is raised on the mountains, look!
When a trumpet sounds, listen!
⁴ For, the Lᴏʀᴅ said to me:
I will quietly look out from My place,
like shimmering heat in sunshine,
like a rain cloud in harvest heat.
⁵ For before the harvest, when the blossoming
is over
and the blossom becomes a ripening grape,
He will cut off the shoots with a pruning knife,
and tear away and remove the branches.
⁶ They will all be left for the birds of prey
on the hills
and for the wild animals of the land.
The birds will spend the summer on them,
and all the animals, the winter on them.
⁷ At that time a gift will be brought to ˙Yahweh of
˙Hosts from a people tall and smooth-skinned, a people
feared far and near, a powerful nation with a strange
language, whose land is divided by rivers—to Mount
˙Zion, the place of the name of Yahweh of Hosts.

19 An ˙oracle against Egypt:
Look, the Lᴏʀᴅ rides on a swift cloud
and is coming to Egypt.
Egypt's idols will tremble before Him,
and Egypt's heart will melt within it.
² I will provoke Egypt against Egypt;
each will fight against his brother
and each against his friend,
city against city, kingdom against kingdom.
³ Egypt's spirit will be disturbed within it,
and I will frustrate its plans.
Then they will seek idols, ghosts,
spirits of the dead, and spiritists.
⁴ I will deliver Egypt into the hands
of harsh masters,
and a strong king will rule it.
This is the declaration
of the Lord Gᴏᴅ of ˙Hosts.
⁵ The waters of the sea will dry up,
and the river will be parched and dry.
⁶ The channels will stink;
they will dwindle, and Egypt's canals
will be parched.
Reed and rush will die.
⁷ The reeds by the Nile, by the mouth
of the river,
and all the cultivated areas of the Nile
will wither, blow away, and vanish.
⁸ Then the fishermen will mourn.
All those who cast hooks into the Nile
will lament,
and those who spread nets on the water
will shrivel up.
⁹ Those who work with flax will be dismayed;
the combers and weavers will turn pale.
¹⁰ Egypt's weavers will be dejected;
all her wage earners will be demoralized.
¹¹ The princes of Zoan are complete fools;
Pharaoh's wisest advisers give stupid advice!
How can you say to Pharaoh,

"I am one of the wise,
a student of eastern kings"?
¹² Where then are your wise men?
Let them tell you and reveal
what the Lᴏʀᴅ of Hosts has planned
against Egypt.
¹³ The princes of Zoan have been fools;
the princes of Memphis are deceived.
Her tribal chieftains have led Egypt astray.
¹⁴ The Lᴏʀᴅ has mixed within her a spirit
of confusion.
The leaders have made Egypt stagger
in all she does,
as a drunkard staggers in his vomit.
¹⁵ No head or tail, palm or reed,
will be able to do anything for Egypt.

¹⁶ On that day Egypt will be like women. She will
tremble with fear because of the threatening hand of
the Lᴏʀᴅ of Hosts when He raises it against her. ¹⁷ The
land of Judah will terrify Egypt; whenever Judah is
mentioned, Egypt will tremble because of what the
Lᴏʀᴅ of Hosts has planned against it.

¹⁸ On that day five cities in the land of Egypt will
speak the language of Canaan and swear loyalty to the
Lᴏʀᴅ of Hosts. One of the cities will be called the City
of the Sun.

¹⁹ On that day there will be an altar to the Lᴏʀᴅ in the
center of the land of Egypt and a pillar to the Lᴏʀᴅ near
her border. ²⁰ It will be a sign and witness to the Lᴏʀᴅ
of Hosts in the land of Egypt. When they cry out to the
Lᴏʀᴅ because of their oppressors, He will send them a
savior and leader, and he will rescue them. ²¹ The Lᴏʀᴅ
will make Himself known to Egypt, and Egypt will
know the Lᴏʀᴅ on that day. They will offer sacrifices
and offerings; they will make vows to the Lᴏʀᴅ and
fulfill them. ²² The Lᴏʀᴅ will strike Egypt, striking and
healing. Then they will return to the Lᴏʀᴅ and He will
hear their prayers and heal them.

²³ On that day there will be a highway from Egypt to
Assyria. Assyria will go to Egypt, Egypt to Assyria, and
Egypt will worship with Assyria.

²⁴ On that day Israel will form a triple alliance with
Egypt and Assyria—a blessing within the land. ²⁵ The
Lᴏʀᴅ of Hosts will bless them, saying, "Egypt My people, Assyria My handiwork, and Israel My inheritance
are blessed."

20 In the year that the chief commander, sent by
Sargon king of Assyria, came to Ashdod and attacked and captured it— ² during that time the Lᴏʀᴅ
had spoken through Isaiah son of Amoz, saying, "Go,
take off your ˙sackcloth and remove the sandals from
your feet," and he did so, going naked and barefoot—
³ the Lᴏʀᴅ said, "As My servant Isaiah has gone naked
and barefoot three years as a sign and omen against
Egypt and ˙Cush, ⁴ so the king of Assyria will lead the
captives of Egypt and the exiles of Cush, young and
old alike, naked and barefoot, with bared buttocks—to
Egypt's shame. ⁵ Those who made Cush their hope and
Egypt their boast will be dismayed and ashamed. ⁶ And
the inhabitants of this coastland will say on that day,
'Look, this is what has happened to those we relied on
and fled to for help to rescue us from the king of Assyria! Now, how will we escape?'"

21 An ˙oracle against the desert by the sea:
Like storms that pass over the ˙Negev,
it comes from the desert, from the land
of terror.

2 A troubling vision is declared to me:
"The treacherous one acts treacherously,
and the destroyer destroys.
Advance, Elam! Lay siege, you Medes!
I will put an end to all her groaning."
3 Therefore I am filled with anguish.
Pain grips me, like the pain of a woman
   in labor.
I am too perplexed to hear,
too dismayed to see.
4 My heart staggers;
horror terrifies me.
He has turned my last glimmer of hope
into sheer terror.
5 Prepare a table, and spread out a carpet!
Eat and drink!
Rise up, you princes, and oil the shields!
6 For the Lord has said to me,
"Go, post a lookout;
let him report what he sees.
7 When he sees riders—
pairs of horsemen,
riders on donkeys,
riders on camels—
he must pay close attention."
8 Then the lookout reported,
"Lord, I stand on the watchtower all day,
and I stay at my post all night.
9 Look, riders come—
horsemen in pairs."
And he answered, saying,
"Babylon has fallen, has fallen.
All the images of her gods
have been shattered on the ground."
10 My people who have been crushed
on the threshing floor,
I have declared to you
what I have heard from the Lord of ˙Hosts,
the God of Israel.
11 An oracle against Dumah:
One calls to me from Seir,
"Watchman, what is left of the night?
Watchman, what is left of the night?"
12 The watchman said,
"Morning has come, and also night.
If you want to ask, ask!
Come back again."
13 An oracle against Arabia:
In the desert brush
you will camp for the night,
you caravans of Dedanites.
14 Bring water for the thirsty.
The inhabitants of the land of Tema
meet the refugees with food.
15 For they have fled from swords,
from the drawn sword,
from the bow that is strung,
and from the stress of battle.
16 For the Lord said this to me: "Within one year,
as a hired worker counts years, all the glory of Kedar
will be gone. 17 The remaining Kedarite archers will be
few in number." For the Lord, the God of Israel, has
spoken.

22 An ˙oracle against the Valley of Vision:
What's the matter with you?
Why have all of you gone up to the rooftops?
2 The noisy city, the jubilant town,

is filled with revelry.
Your dead did not die by the sword;
they were not killed in battle.
3 All your rulers have fled together,
captured without a bow.
All your fugitives were captured together;
they had fled far away.
4 Therefore I said,
"Look away from me! Let me weep bitterly!
Do not try to comfort me
about the destruction of my dear people."
5 For the Lord God of ˙Hosts
had a day of tumult, trampling, and confusion
in the Valley of Vision—
people shouting and crying to the mountains;
6 Elam took up a quiver
with chariots and horsemen,
and Kir uncovered the shield.
7 Your best valleys were full of chariots,
and horsemen were positioned at the gates.
8 He removed the defenses of Judah.
On that day you looked to the weapons in the House
of the Forest. 9 You saw that there were many breaches
in the walls of the city of David. You collected water
from the lower pool. 10 You counted the houses of Jerusalem so that you could tear them down to fortify
the wall. 11 You made a reservoir between the walls for
the waters of the ancient pool, but you did not look to
the One who made it, or consider the One who created
it long ago.
12 On that day the Lord God of Hosts
called for weeping, for wailing,
   for shaven heads,
and for the wearing of ˙sackcloth.
13 But look: joy and gladness,
butchering of cattle, slaughtering of sheep,
eating of meat, and drinking of wine—
"Let us eat and drink, for tomorrow we die!"
14 The Lord of Hosts has directly revealed to me:
"This sin of yours will never be wiped out."
The Lord God of Hosts has spoken.

15 The Lord God of Hosts said: "Go to Shebna, that
steward who is in charge of the palace, and say to him:
16 What are you doing here? Who authorized you to
carve out a tomb for yourself here, carving your tomb
on the height and cutting a crypt for yourself out of
rock? 17 Look, you strong man! The Lord is about to
shake you violently. He will take hold of you, 18 wind
you up into a ball, and sling you into a wide land.
There you will die, and there your glorious chariots
will be—a disgrace to the house of your lord. 19 I will
remove you from your office; you will be ousted from
your position.
20 "On that day I will call for my servant, Eliakim son
of Hilkiah. 21 I will clothe him with your robe and tie
your sash around him. I will put your authority into
his hand, and he will be like a father to the inhabitants
of Jerusalem and to the House of Judah. 22 I will place
the key of the House of David on his shoulder; what he
opens, no one can close; what he closes, no one can
open. 23 I will drive him, like a peg, into a firm place.
He will be a throne of honor for his father's house.
24 They will hang on him the whole burden of his father's house: the descendants and the offshoots—all
the small vessels, from bowls to every kind of jar. 25 On
that day"—the declaration of the Lord of Hosts—"the
peg that was driven into a firm place will give way, be

cut off, and fall, and the load on it will be destroyed."
Indeed, the Lord has spoken.

23 An *oracle against Tyre:
Wail, ships of Tarshish,
for your haven has been destroyed.
Word has reached them from the land
of Cyprus.

² Mourn, inhabitants of the coastland,
you merchants of Sidon;
your agents have crossed the sea

³ on many waters.
Tyre's revenue was the grain from Shihor—
the harvest of the Nile.
She was the merchant among the nations.

⁴ Be ashamed Sidon, the stronghold of the sea,
for the sea has spoken:
"I have not been in labor or given birth.
I have not raised young men
or brought up young women."

⁵ When the news reaches Egypt,
they will be in anguish over the news
about Tyre.

⁶ Cross over to Tarshish;
wail, inhabitants of the coastland!

⁷ Is this your jubilant city,
whose origin was in ancient times,
whose feet have taken her
to settle far away?

⁸ Who planned this against Tyre,
the bestower of crowns,
whose traders are princes,
whose merchants are the honored ones
of the earth?

⁹ The Lord of *Hosts planned it,
to desecrate all its glorious beauty,
to disgrace all the honored ones of the earth.

¹⁰ Overflow your land like the Nile,
daughter of Tarshish;
there is no longer anything to restrain you.

¹¹ He stretched out His hand over the sea;
He made kingdoms tremble.
The Lord has commanded
that the Canaanite fortresses be destroyed.

¹² He said,
"You will not rejoice anymore,
ravished young woman, daughter of Sidon.
Get up and cross over to Cyprus—
even there you will have no rest!"

¹³ Look at the land of the Chaldeans—
a people who no longer exist.
Assyria destined it for desert creatures.
They set up their siege towers
and stripped its palaces.
They made it a ruin.

¹⁴ Wail, ships of Tarshish,
because your fortress is destroyed!

¹⁵ On that day Tyre will be forgotten for 70 years—
the life span of one king. At the end of 70 years, what
the song says about the prostitute will happen to Tyre:

¹⁶ Pick up your lyre,
stroll through the city,
prostitute forgotten by men.
Play skillfully,
sing many a song,
and you will be thought of again.

¹⁷ And at the end of the 70 years, the Lord will restore Tyre and she will go back into business, prostituting herself with all the kingdoms of the world on
the face of the earth. ¹⁸ But her profits and wages will
be dedicated to the Lord. They will not be stored or
saved, for her profit will go to those who live in the
Lord's presence, to provide them with ample food and
sacred clothing.

24 Look, the Lord is stripping the earth bare
and making it desolate.
He will twist its surface and scatter
its inhabitants:

² people and priest alike,
servant and master,
female servant and mistress,
buyer and seller,
lender and borrower,
creditor and debtor.

³ The earth will be stripped completely bare
and will be totally plundered,
for the Lord has spoken this message.

⁴ The earth mourns and withers;
the world wastes away and withers;
the exalted people of the earth waste away.

⁵ The earth is polluted by its inhabitants,
for they have transgressed teachings,
overstepped decrees,
and broken the everlasting covenant.

⁶ Therefore a curse has consumed the earth,
and its inhabitants have become *guilty;
the earth's inhabitants have been burned,
and only a few survive.

⁷ The new wine mourns;
the vine withers.
All the carousers now groan.

⁸ The joyful tambourines have ceased.
The noise of the jubilant has stopped.
The joyful lyre has ceased.

⁹ They no longer sing and drink wine;
beer is bitter to those who drink it.

¹⁰ The city of chaos is shattered;
every house is closed to entry.

¹¹ In the streets they cry for wine.
All joy grows dark;
earth's rejoicing goes into exile.

¹² Only desolation remains in the city;
its gate has collapsed in ruins.

¹³ For this is how it will be on earth
among the nations:
like a harvested olive tree,
like a gleaning after a grape harvest.

¹⁴ They raise their voices, they sing out;
they proclaim in the west
the majesty of the Lord.

¹⁵ Therefore, in the east honor the Lord!
In the islands of the west
honor the name of *Yahweh,
the God of Israel.

¹⁶ From the ends of the earth we hear songs:
The Splendor of the Righteous One.
But I said, "I waste away! I waste away!
Woe is me."
The treacherous act treacherously;
the treacherous deal very treacherously.

¹⁷ Panic, pit, and trap await you
who dwell on the earth.

¹⁸ Whoever flees at the sound of panic
will fall into a pit,
and whoever escapes from the pit

will be caught in a trap.
For the windows are opened from heaven,
and the foundations of the earth are shaken.
19 The earth is completely devastated;
the earth is split open;
the earth is violently shaken.
20 The earth staggers like a drunkard
and sways like a hut.
Earth's rebellion weighs it down,
and it falls, never to rise again.
21 On that day the LORD will punish
the host of heaven above
and kings of the earth below.
22 They will be gathered together
like prisoners in a pit.
They will be confined to a dungeon;
after many days they will be punished.
23 The moon will be put to shame
and the sun disgraced,
because the LORD of *Hosts will reign as king
on Mount *Zion in Jerusalem,
and He will display His glory
in the presence of His elders.

25 *Yahweh, You are my God;
I will exalt You. I will praise Your name,
for You have accomplished wonders,
plans formed long ago,
with perfect faithfulness.
2 For You have turned the city into a pile
of rocks,
a fortified city, into ruins;
the fortress of barbarians is no longer a city;
it will never be rebuilt.
3 Therefore, a strong people will honor You.
The cities of violent nations will *fear You.
4 For You have been a stronghold for the poor,
a stronghold for the needy person
in his distress,
a refuge from the rain, a shade from the heat.
When the breath of the violent
is like rain against a wall,
5 like heat in a dry land,
You subdue the uproar of barbarians.
As the shade of a cloud cools the heat
of the day,
so He silences the song of the violent.
6 The LORD of *Hosts will prepare a feast
for all the peoples on this mountain—
a feast of aged wine, choice meat,
finely aged wine.
7 On this mountain
He will destroy the burial shroud,
the shroud over all the peoples,
the sheet covering all the nations;
8 He will destroy death forever.
The Lord GOD will wipe away the tears
from every face
and remove His people's disgrace
from the whole earth,
for the LORD has spoken.
9 On that day it will be said,
"Look, this is our God;
we have waited for Him, and He has saved us.
This is the LORD; we have waited for Him.
Let us rejoice and be glad in His salvation."
10 For the LORD's power will rest
on this mountain.

But Moab will be trampled in his place
as straw is trampled in a dung pile.
11 He will spread out his arms in the middle of it,
as a swimmer spreads out his arms to swim.
His pride will be brought low,
along with the trickery of his hands.
12 The high-walled fortress
will be brought down,
thrown to the ground, to the dust.

26 On that day this song will be sung in the land
of Judah:
We have a strong city.
Salvation is established as walls and ramparts.
2 Open the gates
so a righteous nation can come in—
one that remains faithful.
3 You will keep the mind that is dependent
on You
in perfect peace,
for it is trusting in You.
4 Trust in the LORD forever,
because in *Yah, the LORD, is
an everlasting rock!
5 For He has humbled those who live
in lofty places—
an inaccessible city.
He brings it down; He brings it down
to the ground;
He throws it to the dust.
6 Feet trample it,
the feet of the humble,
the steps of the poor.
7 The path of the righteous is level;
You clear a straight path for the righteous.
8 Yes, Yahweh, we wait for You
in the path of Your judgments.
Our desire is for Your name and renown.
9 I long for You in the night;
yes, my spirit within me diligently seeks You,
for when Your judgments are in the land,
the inhabitants of the world
will learn righteousness.
10 But if the wicked man is shown favor,
he does not learn righteousness.
In a righteous land he acts unjustly
and does not see the majesty of the LORD.
11 LORD, Your hand is lifted up to take action,
but they do not see it.
They will see Your zeal for Your people,
and they will be put to shame.
The fire for Your adversaries
will consume them!
12 LORD, You will establish peace for us,
for You have also done all our work for us.
13 Yahweh our God, lords other than You
have ruled over us,
but we remember Your name alone.
14 The dead do not live;
departed spirits do not rise up.
Indeed, You have visited and destroyed them;
You have wiped out all memory of them.
15 You have added to the nation, LORD.
You have added to the nation;
You are honored.
You have expanded all the borders of the land.
16 LORD, they went to You in their distress;
they poured out whispered prayers

because Your discipline fell on them.

17 As a pregnant woman about to give birth
writhes and cries out in her pains,
so we were before You, Lord.

18 We became pregnant, we writhed in pain;
we gave birth to wind.
We have won no victories on earth,
and the earth's inhabitants have not fallen.

19 Your dead will live; their bodies will rise.
Awake and sing, you who dwell in the dust!
For you will be covered with the morning dew,
and the earth will bring out
the departed spirits.

20 Go, my people, enter your rooms
and close your doors behind you.
Hide for a little while until the wrath
has passed.

21 For look, the Lord is coming from His place
to punish the inhabitants of the earth
for their iniquity.
The earth will reveal the blood shed on it
and will no longer conceal her slain.

27 On that day the Lord with His harsh, great,
and strong sword, will bring judgment on Leviathan, the fleeing serpent—Leviathan, the twisting
serpent. He will slay the monster that is in the sea.

2 On that day
sing about a desirable vineyard:

3 I, *Yahweh, watch over it;
I water it regularly.
I guard it night and day
so that no one disturbs it.

4 I am not angry,
but if it produces thorns and briers for Me,
I will fight against it, trample it,
and burn it to the ground.

5 Or let it take hold of My strength;
let it make peace with Me—
make peace with Me.

6 In days to come, Jacob will take root.
Israel will blossom and bloom
and fill the whole world with fruit.

7 Did the Lord strike Israel
as He struck the one who struck Israel?
Was he killed like those killed by Him?

8 You disputed with her
by banishing and driving her away.
He removed her with His severe storm
on the day of the east wind.

9 Therefore Jacob's iniquity will be purged
in this way,
and the result of the removal of his sin
will be this:
when he makes all the altar stones
like crushed bits of chalk,
no *Asherah poles or incense altars
will remain standing.

10 For the fortified city will be deserted,
pastures abandoned and forsaken
like a wilderness.
Calves will graze there,
and there they will spread out and strip
its branches.

11 When its branches dry out, they will be
broken off.
Women will come and make fires with them,
for they are not a people with understanding.

Therefore their Maker will not
have compassion on them,
and their Creator will not be gracious
to them.

12 On that day
the Lord will thresh grain
from the Euphrates River
as far as the *Wadi of Egypt,
and you Israelites will be gathered one by one.

13 On that day
a great trumpet will be blown,
and those lost in the land of Assyria will come,
as well as those dispersed in the land of Egypt;
and they will worship the Lord
at Jerusalem on the holy mountain.

28 Woe to the majestic crown
of Ephraim's drunkards,
and to the fading flower
of its beautiful splendor,
which is on the summit above the rich valley.
Woe to those overcome with wine.

2 Look, the Lord has a strong and mighty one—
like a devastating hail storm,
like a storm with strong flooding waters.
He will bring it across the land with His hand.

3 The majestic crown of Ephraim's drunkards
will be trampled underfoot.

4 The fading flower of his beautiful splendor,
which is on the summit above the rich valley,
will be like a ripe fig
before the summer harvest.
Whoever sees it will swallow it
while it is still in his hand.

5 On that day
the Lord of *Hosts will become a crown
of beauty
and a diadem of splendor
to the remnant of His people,

6 a spirit of justice
to the one who sits in judgment,
and strength
to those who turn back the battle at the gate.

7 These also stagger because of wine
and stumble under the influence of beer:
priest and prophet stagger because of beer,
they are confused by wine.
They stumble because of beer,
they are muddled in their visions,
they stumble in their judgments.

8 Indeed, all their tables are covered with vomit;
there is no place without a stench.

9 Who is he trying to teach?
Who is he trying to instruct?
Infants just weaned from milk?
Babies removed from the breast?

10 For he says: "Law after law, law after law,
line after line, line after line,
a little here, a little there."

11 So He will speak to this people
with stammering speech
and in a foreign language.

12 He had said to them:
"This is the place of rest,
let the weary rest;
this is the place of repose."
But they would not listen.

13 Then the word of the Lord came to them:

"Law after law, law after law,
line after line, line after line,
a little here, a little there,"
so they go stumbling backward,
to be broken, trapped, and captured.
¹⁴ Therefore hear the word of the LORD,
      you mockers
who rule this people in Jerusalem.
¹⁵ For you said, "We have cut a deal with Death,
and we have made an agreement with *Sheol;
when the overwhelming scourge
      passes through,
it will not touch us,
because we have made falsehood our refuge
and have hidden behind treachery."
¹⁶ Therefore the Lord GOD said:
"Look, I have laid a stone in *Zion,
a tested stone,
a precious cornerstone, a sure foundation;
the one who believes will be unshakable.
¹⁷ And I will make justice the measuring line
and righteousness the mason's level."
Hail will sweep away the false refuge,
and water will flood your hiding place.
¹⁸ Your deal with Death will be dissolved,
and your agreement with Sheol will not last.
When the overwhelming scourge
      passes through,
you will be trampled.
¹⁹ Every time it passes through,
it will carry you away;
it will pass through every morning—
every day and every night.
Only terror will cause you
to understand the message.
²⁰ Indeed, the bed is too short to stretch out on,
and its cover too small to wrap up in.
²¹ For the LORD will rise up as He did
      at Mount Perazim.
He will rise in wrath, as at the Valley
      of Gibeon,
to do His work, His strange work,
and to perform His task, His disturbing task.
²² So now, do not mock,
or your shackles will become stronger.
Indeed, I have heard from the Lord GOD
      of Hosts
a decree of destruction for the whole land.
²³ Listen and hear my voice.
Pay attention and hear what I say.
²⁴ Does the plowman plow every day
      to plant seed?
Does he continuously break up and cultivate
      the soil?
²⁵ When he has leveled its surface,
does he not then scatter black cumin
      and sow cumin?
He plants wheat in rows and barley in plots,
with spelt as their border.
²⁶ His God teaches him order;
He instructs him.
²⁷ Certainly black cumin is not threshed
with a threshing board,
and a cart wheel is not rolled over the cumin.
But black cumin is beaten out with a stick,
and cumin with a rod.
²⁸ Bread grain is crushed,

but is not threshed endlessly.
Though the wheel
      of the farmer's cart rumbles,
his horses do not crush it.
²⁹ This also comes from the LORD of Hosts.
He gives wonderful advice;
He gives great wisdom.

29 Woe to Ariel, Ariel,
the city where David camped!
Continue year after year;
let the festivals recur.
² I will oppress Ariel,
and there will be mourning and crying,
and she will be to Me like an Ariel.
³ I will camp in a circle around you;
I will besiege you with earth ramps,
and I will set up my siege towers against you.
⁴ You will be brought down;
you will speak from the ground,
and your words will come from low
      in the dust.
Your voice will be like that of a spirit
      from the ground;
your speech will whisper from the dust.
⁵ Your many foes will be like fine dust,
and many of the ruthless, like blowing chaff.
Then suddenly, in an instant,
⁶ you will be visited by the LORD of *Hosts
with thunder, earthquake, and loud noise,
storm, tempest, and a flame
      of consuming fire.
⁷ All the many nations
going out to battle against Ariel—
all the attackers, the siege works against her,
and those who oppress her—
will then be like a dream, a vision in the night.
⁸ It will be like a hungry one who dreams
      he is eating,
then wakes and is still hungry;
and like a thirsty one who dreams
      he is drinking,
then wakes and is still thirsty,
      longing for water.
So it will be for all the many nations
who go to battle against Mount *Zion.
⁹ Stop and be astonished;
blind yourselves and be blind!
They are drunk, but not with wine;
they stagger, but not with beer.
¹⁰ For the LORD has poured out on you
an overwhelming urge to sleep;
He has shut your eyes—the prophets,
and covered your heads—the seers.
¹¹ For you the entire vision will be like the words of
a sealed document. If it is given to one who can read
and he is asked to read it, he will say, "I can't read it,
because it is sealed." ¹²And if the document is given to
one who cannot read and he is asked to read it, he will
say, "I can't read."
¹³The Lord said:
Because these people approach Me
      with their mouths
to honor Me with lip-service—
yet their hearts are far from Me,
and their worship consists of man-made rules
      learned by rote—
¹⁴ therefore I will again confound these people

with wonder after wonder.
The wisdom of their wise men will vanish,
and the understanding of the perceptive
will be hidden.

15 Woe to those who go to great lengths
to hide their plans from the LORD.
They do their works in darkness,
and say, "Who sees us? Who knows us?"

16 You have turned things around,
as if the potter were the same as the clay.
How can what is made say about its maker,
"He didn't make me"?
How can what is formed
say about the one who formed it,
"He doesn't understand what he's doing"?

17 Isn't it true that in just a little while
Lebanon will become an orchard,
and the orchard will seem like a forest?

18 On that day the deaf will hear
the words of a document,
and out of a deep darkness
the eyes of the blind will see.

19 The humble will have joy
after joy in the LORD,
and the poor people will rejoice
in the Holy One of Israel.

20 For the ruthless one will vanish,
the scorner will disappear,
and all those who lie in wait with evil intent
will be killed—

21 those who, with their speech,
accuse a person of wrongdoing,
who set a trap at the *gate for the mediator,
and without cause deprive the righteous
of justice.

22 Therefore, the LORD who redeemed Abraham says
this about the house of Jacob:
Jacob will no longer be ashamed
and his face will no longer be pale.

23 For when he sees his children,
the work of My hands within his nation,
they will honor My name,
they will honor the Holy One of Jacob
and stand in awe of the God of Israel.

24 Those who are confused
will gain understanding,
and those who grumble
will accept instruction.

30 Woe to the rebellious children!
This is the LORD's declaration.
They carry out a plan, but not Mine;
they make an alliance,
but against My will,
piling sin on top of sin.

2 They set out to go down to Egypt
without asking My advice,
in order to seek shelter
under Pharaoh's protection
and take refuge in Egypt's shadow.

3 But Pharaoh's protection will become
your shame,
and refuge in Egypt's shadow your disgrace.

4 For though his princes are at Zoan
and his messengers reach as far as Hanes,

5 everyone will be ashamed
because of a people who can't help.
They are of no benefit, they are no help;

they are good for nothing but shame
and reproach.

6 An *oracle about the animals of the *Negev:
Through a land of trouble and distress,
of lioness and lion,
of viper and flying serpent,
they carry their wealth on the backs
of donkeys
and their treasures on the humps of camels,
to a people who will not help them.

7 Egypt's help is completely worthless;
therefore, I call her:
*Rahab Who Just Sits.

8 Go now, write it on a tablet in their presence
and inscribe it on a scroll;
it will be for the future,
forever and ever.

9 They are a rebellious people,
deceptive children,
children who do not want to obey
the LORD's instruction.

10 They say to the seers, "Do not see,"
and to the prophets,
"Do not prophesy the truth to us.
Tell us flattering things.
Prophesy illusions.

11 Get out of the way!
Leave the pathway.
Rid us of the Holy One of Israel."

12 Therefore the Holy One of Israel says:
"Because you have rejected this message
and have trusted in oppression and deceit,
and have depended on them,

13 this iniquity of yours will be
like a spreading breach,
a bulge in a high wall
whose collapse will come in an instant—
suddenly!

14 Its collapse will be like the shattering
of a potter's jar, crushed to pieces,
so that not even a fragment of pottery
will be found among its shattered remains—
no fragment large enough to take fire
from a hearth
or scoop water from a cistern."

15 For the Lord GOD, the Holy One of Israel,
has said:
"You will be delivered by returning
and resting;
your strength will lie in quiet confidence.
But you are not willing."

16 You say, "No!
We will escape on horses"—
therefore you will escape!—
and, "We will ride on fast horses"—
but those who pursue you will be faster.

17 One thousand will flee at the threat of one,
at the threat of five you will flee,
until you alone remain
like a solitary pole on a mountaintop
or a banner on a hill.

18 Therefore the LORD is waiting
to show you mercy,
and is rising up to show you compassion,
for the LORD is a just God.
All who wait patiently for Him are happy.

19 For you people will live on *Zion in Jerusalem and

will never cry again. He will show favor to you at the sound of your cry; when He hears, He will answer you. ²⁰ The Lord will give you meager bread and water during oppression, but your Teacher will not hide Himself any longer. Your eyes will see your Teacher, ²¹ and whenever you turn to the right or to the left, your ears will hear this command behind you: "This is the way. Walk in it." ²² Then you will defile your silver-plated idols and your gold-plated images. You will throw them away like menstrual cloths, and call them filth.

²³ Then He will send rain for your seed that you have sown in the ground, and the food, the produce of the ground, will be rich and plentiful. On that day your cattle will graze in open pastures. ²⁴ The oxen and donkeys that work the ground will eat salted fodder scattered with winnowing shovel and fork. ²⁵ Streams flowing with water will be on every high mountain and every raised hill on the day of great slaughter when the towers fall. ²⁶ The moonlight will be as bright as the sunlight, and the sunlight will be seven times brighter—like the light of seven days—on the day that the Lord bandages His people's injuries and heals the wounds He inflicted.

27   Look, *Yahweh comes from far away,
      His anger burning and heavy with smoke.
      His lips are full of fury,
      and His tongue is like a consuming fire.
28   His breath is like an overflowing torrent
      that rises to the neck.
      He comes to sift the nations in a sieve
        of destruction
      and to put a bridle on the jaws of the peoples
      to lead them astray.
29   Your singing will be like that
      on the night of a holy festival,
      and your heart will rejoice
      like one who walks to the music of a flute,
      going up to the mountain of the Lord,
      to the Rock of Israel.
30   And the Lord will make the splendor
        of His voice heard
      and reveal His arm striking in angry wrath
      and a flame of consuming fire,
      in driving rain, a torrent, and hailstones.
31   Assyria will be shattered by the voice
        of the Lord.
      He will strike with a rod.
32   And every stroke of the appointed staff
      that the Lord brings down on him
      will be to the sound of tambourines and lyres;
      He will fight against him
        with brandished weapons.
33   Indeed! *Topheth has been ready
      for the king for a long time now.
      Its funeral pyre is deep and wide,
      with plenty of fire and wood.
      The breath of the Lord, like a torrent
        of brimstone,
      kindles it.

31   Woe to those who go down to Egypt for help
      and who depend on horses!
      They trust in the abundance of chariots
      and in the large number of horsemen.
      They do not look to the Holy One of Israel
      and they do not seek the Lord's help.
2   But He also is wise and brings disaster.
      He does not go back on what He says;

      He will rise up against the house
        of wicked men
      and against the allies of evildoers.
3   Egyptians are men, not God;
      their horses are flesh, not spirit.
      When the Lord raises His hand to strike,
      the helper will stumble
      and the one who is helped will fall;
      both will perish together.
4 For this is what the Lord said to me:
      As a lion or young lion growls over its prey
      when a band of shepherds is called out
        against it,
      and is not terrified by their shouting
      or subdued by their noise,
      so the Lord of *Hosts will come down
      to fight on Mount *Zion
      and on its hill.
5   Like hovering birds,
      so the Lord of Hosts will protect Jerusalem—
      by protecting it, He will rescue it,
      by sparing it, He will deliver it.

⁶ Return to the One the Israelites have greatly rebelled against. ⁷ For on that day, every one of you will reject the silver and gold idols that your own hands have sinfully made.

8   Then Assyria will fall,
      but not by human sword;
      a sword will devour him,
      but not one made by man.
      He will flee from the sword;
      his young men will be put to forced labor.
9   His rock will pass away because of fear,
      and his officers will be afraid because of
        the signal flag.

This is the Lord's declaration—whose fire is in Zion and whose furnace is in Jerusalem.

32   ¹ Indeed, a king will reign righteously,
      and rulers will rule justly.
2   Each will be like a shelter from the wind,
      a refuge from the rain,
      like streams of water in a dry land
      and the shade of a massive rock
        in an arid land.
3   Then the eyes of those who see will not
        be closed,
      and the ears of those who hear will listen.
4   The reckless mind will gain knowledge,
      and the stammering tongue will speak clearly
        and fluently.
5   A fool will no longer be called a noble,
      nor a scoundrel said to be important.
6   For a fool speaks foolishness
      and his mind plots iniquity.
      He lives in a godless way
      and speaks falsely about the Lord.
      He leaves the hungry empty
      and deprives the thirsty of drink.
7   The scoundrel's weapons are destructive;
      he hatches plots to destroy the needy with lies,
      even when the poor says what is right.
8   But a noble person plans noble things;
      he stands up for noble causes.
9   Stand up, you complacent women;
      listen to me.
      Pay attention to what I say,
      you overconfident daughters.

¹⁰ In a little more than a year
you overconfident ones will shudder,
for the vintage will fail
and the harvest will not come.

¹¹ Shudder, you complacent ones;
tremble, you overconfident ones!
Strip yourselves bare
and put *sackcloth around your waists.

¹² Beat your breasts in mourning
for the delightful fields and the fruitful vines,

¹³ for the ground of my people
growing thorns and briers,
indeed, for every joyous house
in the joyful city.

¹⁴ For the palace will be forsaken,
the busy city abandoned.
The hill and the watchtower will become
barren places forever,
the joy of wild donkeys,
and a pasture for flocks,

¹⁵ until the Spirit from heaven is poured out
on us.
Then the desert will become an orchard,
and the orchard will seem like a forest.

¹⁶ Then justice will inhabit the wilderness,
and righteousness will dwell in the orchard.

¹⁷ The result of righteousness will be peace;
the effect of righteousness
will be quiet confidence forever.

¹⁸ Then my people will dwell in a peaceful place,
in safe and secure dwellings.

¹⁹ But hail will level the forest,
and the city will sink into the depths.

²⁰ Those who sow seed are happy
beside abundant waters;
they let ox and donkey range freely.

33 Woe, you destroyer never destroyed,
you traitor never betrayed!
When you have finished destroying,
you will be destroyed.
When you have finished betraying,
they will betray you.

² Lord, be gracious to us! We wait for You.
Be our strength every morning
and our salvation in time of trouble.

³ The peoples flee at the thunderous noise;
the nations scatter when You rise
in Your majesty.

⁴ Your spoil will be gathered as locusts
are gathered;
people will swarm over it like an infestation
of locusts.

⁵ The Lord is exalted, for He dwells on high;
He has filled *Zion with justice
and righteousness.

⁶ There will be times of security for you—
a storehouse of salvation, wisdom,
and knowledge.
The *fear of the Lord is Zion's treasure.

⁷ Listen! Their warriors cry loudly in the streets;
the messengers of peace weep bitterly.

⁸ The highways are deserted;
travel has ceased.
An agreement has been broken,
cities despised,
and human life disregarded.

⁹ The land mourns and withers;

Lebanon is ashamed and decayed.
Sharon is like a desert;
Bashan and Carmel shake off their leaves.

¹⁰ "Now I will rise up," says the Lord.
"Now I will lift Myself up.
Now I will be exalted.

¹¹ You will conceive chaff;
you will give birth to stubble.
Your breath is fire that will consume you.

¹² The peoples will be burned to ashes,
like thorns cut down and burned in a fire.

¹³ You who are far off, hear what I have done;
you who are near, know My strength."

¹⁴ The sinners in Zion are afraid;
trembling seizes the ungodly:
"Who among us can dwell
with a consuming fire?
Who among us can dwell
with ever-burning flames?"

¹⁵ The one who lives righteously
and speaks rightly,
who refuses gain from extortion,
whose hand never takes a bribe,
who stops his ears from listening
to murderous plots
and shuts his eyes to avoid endorsing evil—

¹⁶ he will dwell on the heights;
his refuge will be the rocky fortresses,
his food provided, his water assured.

¹⁷ Your eyes will see the King in His beauty;
you will see a vast land.

¹⁸ Your mind will meditate on the past terror:
"Where is the accountant?
Where is the tribute collector?
Where is the one who spied out our defenses?"

¹⁹ You will no longer see the barbarians,
a people whose speech is difficult
to comprehend—
who stammer in a language that is
not understood.

²⁰ Look at Zion, the city of our festival times.
Your eyes will see Jerusalem,
a peaceful pasture, a tent
that does not wander;
its tent pegs will not be pulled up
nor will any of its cords be loosened.

²¹ For the majestic One, our Lord, will be there,
a place of rivers and broad streams
where ships that are rowed will not go,
and majestic vessels will not pass.

²² For the Lord is our Judge,
the Lord is our lawgiver,
the Lord is our King.
He will save us.

²³ Your ropes are slack;
they cannot hold the base of the mast
or spread out the flag.
Then abundant spoil will be divided,
the lame will plunder it,

²⁴ and none there will say, "I am sick."
The people who dwell there
will be forgiven their iniquity.

34 You nations, come here and listen;
you peoples, pay attention!
Let the earth hear, and all that fills it,
the world and all that comes from it.

² The Lord is angry with all the nations—

furious with all their armies.
He will set them apart for destruction,
   giving them over to slaughter.
³ Their slain will be thrown out,
   and the stench of their corpses will rise;
   the mountains will flow with their blood.
⁴ All the heavenly bodies will dissolve.
The skies will roll up like a scroll,
   and their stars will all wither
as leaves wither on the vine,
   and foliage on the fig tree.
⁵ When My sword has drunk its fill
   in the heavens,
it will then come down on Edom
and on the people I have *set apart
   for destruction.
⁶ The Lord's sword is covered with blood.
It drips with fat,
   with the blood of lambs and goats,
   with the fat of the kidneys of rams.
For the Lord has a sacrifice in Bozrah,
   a great slaughter in the land of Edom.
⁷ The wild oxen will be struck down with them,
   and young bulls with the mighty bulls.
Their land will be soaked with blood,
   and their soil will be saturated with fat.
⁸ For the Lord has a day of vengeance,
   a time of paying back Edom
   for its hostility against *Zion.
⁹ Edom's streams will be turned into pitch,
   her soil into sulfur;
   her land will become burning pitch.
¹⁰ It will never go out—day or night.
Its smoke will go up forever.
It will be desolate, from generation
   to generation;
no one will pass through it forever and ever.
¹¹ The desert owl and the screech owl
   will possess it,
and the great owl and the raven
   will dwell there.
The Lord will stretch out a measuring line
and a plumb line over her
   for her destruction and chaos.
¹² No nobles will be left to proclaim a king,
   and all her princes will come to nothing.
¹³ Her palaces will be overgrown with thorns;
   her fortified cities, with thistles and briers.
She will become a dwelling for jackals,
   an abode for ostriches.
¹⁴ The desert creatures will meet hyenas,
   and one wild goat will call to another.
Indeed, the screech owl will stay there
   and will find a resting place for herself.
¹⁵ The sand partridge will make her nest there;
   she will lay and hatch her eggs
and will gather her brood under her shadow.
Indeed, the birds of prey will gather there,
   each with its mate.
¹⁶ Search and read the scroll of the Lord:
Not one of them will be missing,
   none will be lacking its mate,
because He has ordered it by my mouth,
   and He will gather them by His Spirit.
¹⁷ He has ordained a lot for them;
His hand allotted their portion
   with a measuring line.

They will possess it forever;
they will dwell in it from generation
   to generation.

35 The wilderness and the dry land will be glad;
the desert will rejoice and blossom like a rose.
² It will blossom abundantly
and will also rejoice with joy and singing.
The glory of Lebanon will be given to it,
   the splendor of Carmel and Sharon.
They will see the glory of the Lord,
   the splendor of our God.
³ Strengthen the weak hands,
   steady the shaking knees!
⁴ Say to the cowardly:
   "Be strong; do not fear!
Here is your God; vengeance is coming.
God's retribution is coming; He will save you."
⁵ Then the eyes of the blind will be opened,
   and the ears of the deaf unstopped.
⁶ Then the lame will leap like a deer,
   and the tongue of the mute will sing for joy,
for water will gush in the wilderness,
   and streams in the desert;
⁷ the parched ground will become a pool
   of water,
and the thirsty land springs of water.
In the haunt of jackals, in their lairs,
   there will be grass, reeds, and papyrus.
⁸ A road will be there and a way;
   it will be called the Holy Way.
The *unclean will not travel on it,
but it will be for the one who walks the path.
   Even the fool will not go astray.
⁹ There will be no lion there,
   and no vicious beast will go up on it;
   they will not be found there.
But the redeemed will walk on it,
¹⁰ and the redeemed of the Lord will return
and come to *Zion with singing,
   crowned with unending joy.
Joy and gladness will overtake them,
   and sorrow and sighing will flee.

36 In the fourteenth year of King Hezekiah, Sennacherib king of Assyria attacked all the fortified cities of Judah and captured them. ²Then the king of Assyria sent the *Rabshakeh, along with a massive army, from Lachish to King Hezekiah at Jerusalem. The Assyrian stood near the conduit of the upper pool, by the road to the Fuller's Field. ³Eliakim son of Hilkiah, who was in charge of the palace, Shebna the court secretary, and Joah son of Asaph, the court historian, came out to him.

⁴The Rabshakeh said to them, "Tell Hezekiah: The great king, the king of Assyria, says this: What are you relying on? ⁵I say that your strategy and military preparedness are mere words. What are you now relying on that you have rebelled against me? ⁶Look, you are trusting in Egypt, that splintered reed of a staff that will enter and pierce the hand of anyone who leans on it. This is how Pharaoh king of Egypt is to all who trust in him. ⁷Suppose you say to me, 'We trust in the Lord our God.' Isn't He the One whose *high places and altars Hezekiah has removed, saying to Judah and Jerusalem, 'You are to worship at this altar'?
⁸Now make a deal with my master, the king of

Assyria. I'll give you 2,000 horses if you're able to supply riders for them! ⁹How then can you drive back a single officer among the weakest of my master's officers and trust in Egypt for chariots and horsemen? ¹⁰Have I attacked this land to destroy it without the Lord's approval? The Lord said to me, 'Attack this land and destroy it.'"

¹¹Then Eliakim, Shebna, and Joah said to the Rabshakeh, "Please speak to your servants in Aramaic, since we understand it. Don't speak to us in Hebrew within earshot of the people who are on the wall."

¹²But the Rabshakeh replied, "Has my master sent me to speak these words to your master and to you, and not to the men who are sitting on the wall, who are destined with you to eat their own excrement and drink their own urine?"

¹³Then the Rabshakeh stood and called out loudly in Hebrew:

Listen to the words of the great king, the king of Assyria! ¹⁴This is what the king says: "Don't let Hezekiah deceive you, for he cannot deliver you. ¹⁵Don't let Hezekiah persuade you to trust in the Lord, saying, 'The Lord will certainly deliver us! This city will not be handed over to the king of Assyria.'"

¹⁶Don't listen to Hezekiah, for this is what the king of Assyria says: "Make peace with me and surrender to me. Then every one of you may eat from his own vine and his own fig tree and drink water from his own cistern ¹⁷until I come and take you away to a land like your own land— a land of grain and new wine, a land of bread and vineyards. ¹⁸Beware that Hezekiah does not mislead you by saying, 'The Lord will deliver us.' Has any one of the gods of the nations delivered his land from the power of the king of Assyria? ¹⁹Where are the gods of Hamath and Arpad? Where are the gods of Sepharvaim? Have they delivered Samaria from my power? ²⁰Who among all the gods of these lands ever delivered his land from my power? So will the Lord deliver Jerusalem."

²¹But they kept silent; they didn't say anything, for the king's command was, "Don't answer him." ²²Then Eliakim son of Hilkiah, who was in charge of the palace, Shebna the court secretary, and Joah son of Asaph, the court historian, came to Hezekiah with their clothes torn and reported to him the words of the Rabshakeh.

37 When King Hezekiah heard their report, he tore his clothes, put on *sackcloth, and went to the Lord's temple. ²Then he sent Eliakim, who was in charge of the palace, Shebna the court secretary, and the leading priests, who were wearing sackcloth, to the prophet Isaiah son of Amoz. ³They said to him, "This is what Hezekiah says: 'Today is a day of distress, rebuke, and disgrace, for children have come to the point of birth, and there is no strength to deliver them. ⁴Perhaps *Yahweh your God will hear all the words of the *Rabshakeh, whom his master the king of Assyria sent to mock the living God, and will rebuke him for the words that Yahweh your God has heard. Therefore offer a prayer for the surviving remnant.'"

⁵So the servants of King Hezekiah went to Isaiah, ⁶who said to them, "Tell your master this, 'The Lord says: Don't be afraid because of the words you have heard, which the king of Assyria's attendants have

blasphemed Me with. ⁷I am about to put a spirit in him and he will hear a rumor and return to his own land, where I will cause him to fall by the sword.'"

⁸When the Rabshakeh heard that the king of Assyria had left Lachish, he returned and found him fighting against Libnah. ⁹The king had heard this about Tirhakah king of *Cush: "He has set out to fight against you." So when he heard this, he sent messengers to Hezekiah, saying, ¹⁰"Say this to Hezekiah king of Judah: 'Don't let your God, whom you trust, deceive you by promising that Jerusalem won't be handed over to the king of Assyria. ¹¹Look, you have heard what the kings of Assyria have done to all the countries: they *completely destroyed them. Will you be rescued? ¹²Did the gods of the nations that my predecessors destroyed rescue them—Gozan, Haran, Rezeph, and the Edenites in Telassar? ¹³Where is the king of Hamath, the king of Arpad, the king of the city of Sepharvaim, Hena, or Ivvah?'"

¹⁴Hezekiah took the letter from the messengers, read it, then went up to the Lord's temple and spread it out before the Lord. ¹⁵Then Hezekiah prayed to the Lord:

¹⁶Lord of *Hosts, God of Israel, who is enthroned above the *cherubim, You are God— You alone—of all the kingdoms of the earth. You made the heavens and the earth. ¹⁷Listen closely, Lord, and hear; open Your eyes, Lord, and see. Hear all the words that Sennacherib has sent to mock the living God. ¹⁸Lord, it is true that the kings of Assyria have devastated all these countries and their lands. ¹⁹They have thrown their gods into the fire, for they were not gods but made by human hands—wood and stone. So they have destroyed them. ²⁰Now, Lord our God, save us from his power so that all the kingdoms of the earth may know that You are the Lord—You alone.

²¹Then Isaiah son of Amoz sent a message to Hezekiah: "The Lord, the God of Israel, says: 'Because you prayed to Me about Sennacherib king of Assyria, ²²this is the word the Lord has spoken against him:

Virgin Daughter *Zion
despises you and scorns you;
Daughter Jerusalem shakes her head
behind your back.
²³ Who is it you have mocked and blasphemed?
Who have you raised your voice against
and lifted your eyes in pride?
Against the Holy One of Israel!
²⁴ You have mocked the Lord
through your servants.
You have said, "With my many chariots
I have gone up to the heights
of the mountains,
to the far recesses of Lebanon.
I cut down its tallest cedars,
its choice cypress trees.
I came to its distant heights,
its densest forest.
²⁵ I dug wells and drank water.
I dried up all the streams of Egypt
with the soles of my feet."
²⁶ Have you not heard?
I designed it long ago;
I planned it in days gone by.
I have now brought it to pass,

and you have crushed fortified cities
into piles of rubble.
²⁷ Their inhabitants have become powerless,
dismayed, and ashamed.
They are plants of the field,
tender grass,
grass on the rooftops,
blasted by the east wind.
²⁸ But I know your sitting down,
your going out and your coming in,
and your raging against Me.
²⁹ Because your raging against Me
and your arrogance have reached My ears,
I will put My hook in your nose
and My bit in your mouth;
I will make you go back
the way you came.

³⁰ "This will be the sign for you: This year you will
eat what grows on its own, and in the second year
what grows from that. But in the third year sow and
reap, plant vineyards and eat their fruit. ³¹The surviving remnant of the house of Judah will again take root
downward and bear fruit upward. ³²For a remnant will
go out from Jerusalem and survivors, from Mount
Zion. The zeal of the Lord of Hosts will accomplish
this.'

³³ "Therefore, this is what the Lord says about the
king of Assyria:
He will not enter this city
or shoot an arrow there
or come before it with a shield
or build up an assault ramp against it.
³⁴ He will go back
the way he came,
and he will not enter this city.
This is the Lord's declaration.
³⁵ I will defend this city and rescue it
because of Me
and because of My servant David."

³⁶Then the angel of the Lord went out and struck
down 185,000 in the camp of the Assyrians. When the
people got up the next morning—there were all the
dead bodies! ³⁷So Sennacherib king of Assyria broke
camp and left. He returned home and lived in Nineveh.
³⁸One day, while he was worshiping in the temple of
his god Nisroch, his sons Adrammelech and Sharezer
struck him down with the sword and escaped to the
land of Ararat. Then his son Esar-haddon became king
in his place.

38 In those days Hezekiah became terminally ill.
The prophet Isaiah son of Amoz came and said
to him, "This is what the Lord says: 'Put your affairs in
order, for you are about to die; you will not recover.'"

²Then Hezekiah turned his face to the wall and
prayed to the Lord. ³He said, "Please, Lord, remember
how I have walked before You faithfully and wholeheartedly, and have done what pleases You." And Hezekiah wept bitterly.

⁴Then the word of the Lord came to Isaiah: ⁵"Go
and tell Hezekiah that this is what the Lord God of
your ancestor David says: I have heard your prayer; I
have seen your tears. Look, I am going to add 15 years
to your life. ⁶And I will deliver you and this city from
the power of the king of Assyria; I will defend this city.
⁷This is the sign to you from the Lord that He will do
what He has promised: ⁸I am going to make the sun's
shadow that goes down on Ahaz's stairway go back by

10 steps." So the sun's shadow went back the 10 steps
it had descended.

⁹A poem by Hezekiah king of Judah after he had
been sick and had recovered from his illness:
¹⁰ I said: In the prime of my life
I must go to the gates of *Sheol;
I am deprived of the rest of my years.
¹¹ I said: I will never see the Lord,
the Lord in the land of the living;
I will not look on humanity any longer
with the inhabitants of what is passing away.
¹² My dwelling is plucked up and removed
from me
like a shepherd's tent.
I have rolled up my life like a weaver;
He cuts me off from the loom.
You make an end of me from day until night.
¹³ I thought until the morning:
He will break all my bones like a lion;
You make an end of me day and night.
¹⁴ I chirp like a swallow or a crane;
I moan like a dove.
My eyes grow weak looking upward.
Lord, I am oppressed; support me.
¹⁵ What can I say?
He has spoken to me,
and He Himself has done it.
I walk along slowly all my years
because of the bitterness of my soul,
¹⁶ Lord, because of these promises people live,
and in all of them is the life of my spirit
as well;
You have restored me to health
and let me live.
¹⁷ Indeed, it was for my own welfare
that I had such great bitterness;
but Your love has delivered me
from the *Pit of destruction,
for You have thrown all my sins
behind Your back.
¹⁸ For Sheol cannot thank You;
Death cannot praise You.
Those who go down to the Pit
cannot hope for Your faithfulness.
¹⁹ The living, only the living can thank You,
as I do today;
a father will make Your faithfulness known
to children.
²⁰ The Lord will save me;
we will play stringed instruments
all the days of our lives
at the house of the Lord.

²¹Now Isaiah had said, "Let them take a lump of
pressed figs and apply it to his infected skin, so that he
may recover." ²²And Hezekiah had asked, "What is the
sign that I will go up to the Lord's temple?"

39 At that time Merodach-baladan son of Baladan,
king of Babylon, sent letters and a gift to Hezekiah since he heard that he had been sick and had
recovered. ²Hezekiah was pleased with them, and
showed them his treasure house—the silver, the gold,
the spices, and the precious oil—and all his armory,
and everything that was found in his treasuries. There
was nothing in his palace and in all his realm that Hezekiah did not show them.

³Then the prophet Isaiah came to King Hezekiah

and asked him, "Where did these men come from and what did they say to you?"

Hezekiah replied, "They came to me from a distant country, from Babylon."

⁴ Isaiah asked, "What have they seen in your palace?"

Hezekiah answered, "They have seen everything in my palace. There isn't anything in my treasuries that I didn't show them."

⁵ Then Isaiah said to Hezekiah, "Hear the word of the LORD of ˙Hosts: ⁶ 'The time will certainly come when everything in your palace and all that your fathers have stored up until this day will be carried off to Babylon; nothing will be left,' says the LORD. ⁷ 'Some of your descendants who come from you will be taken away, and they will become eunuchs in the palace of the king of Babylon.'"

⁸ Then Hezekiah said to Isaiah, "The word of the LORD that you have spoken is good," for he thought: There will be peace and security during my lifetime.

40
"Comfort, comfort My people,"
     says your God.
² "Speak tenderly to Jerusalem,
     and announce to her
     that her time of forced labor is over,
     her iniquity has been pardoned,
     and she has received from the LORD's hand
     double for all her sins."
³ A voice of one crying out:
     Prepare the way of the LORD in the wilderness;
     make a straight highway for our God
     in the desert.
⁴   Every valley will be lifted up,
     and every mountain and hill will be leveled;
     the uneven ground will become smooth
     and the rough places, a plain.
⁵   And the glory of the LORD will appear,
     and all humanity together will see it,
     for the mouth of the LORD has spoken.
⁶   A voice was saying, "Cry out!"
     Another said, "What should I cry out?"
     "All humanity is grass,
     and all its goodness is like the flower
     of the field.
⁷   The grass withers, the flowers fade
     when the breath of the LORD blows on them;
     indeed, the people are grass.
⁸   The grass withers, the flowers fade,
     but the word of our God remains forever."
⁹   ˙Zion, herald of good news,
     go up on a high mountain.
     Jerusalem, herald of good news,
     raise your voice loudly.
     Raise it, do not be afraid!
     Say to the cities of Judah,
     "Here is your God!"
¹⁰   See, the Lord GOD comes with strength,
     and His power establishes His rule.
     His reward is with Him,
     and His gifts accompany Him.
¹¹   He protects His flock like a shepherd;
     He gathers the lambs in His arms
     and carries them in the fold of His garment.
     He gently leads those that are nursing.
¹²   Who has measured the waters in the hollow
     of his hand
     or marked off the heavens with the span
     of his hand?

Who has gathered the dust of the earth
     in a measure
     or weighed the mountains in a balance
     and the hills in the scales?
¹³   Who has directed the Spirit of the LORD,
     or who gave Him His counsel?
¹⁴   Who did He consult with?
     Who gave Him understanding
     and taught Him the paths of justice?
     Who taught Him knowledge
     and showed Him the way of understanding?
¹⁵   Look, the nations are like a drop in a bucket;
     they are considered as a speck of dust in
     the scales;
     He lifts up the islands like fine dust.
¹⁶   Lebanon is not enough for fuel,
     or its animals enough for a ˙burnt offering.
¹⁷   All the nations are as nothing before Him;
     they are considered by Him
     as nothingness and emptiness.
¹⁸   Who will you compare God with?
     What likeness will you compare Him to?
¹⁹   To an idol?—something that a smelter casts,
     and a metalworker plates with gold
     and makes silver welds for it?
²⁰   To one who shapes a pedestal,
     choosing wood that does not rot?
     He looks for a skilled craftsman
     to set up an idol that will not fall over.
²¹   Do you not know?
     Have you not heard?
     Has it not been declared to you
     from the beginning?
     Have you not considered
     the foundations of the earth?
²²   God is enthroned above the circle of the earth;
     its inhabitants are like grasshoppers.
     He stretches out the heavens like thin cloth
     and spreads them out like a tent to live in.
²³   He reduces princes to nothing
     and makes judges of the earth irrational.
²⁴   They are barely planted, barely sown,
     their stem hardly takes root in the ground
     when He blows on them and they wither,
     and a whirlwind carries them away
     like stubble.
²⁵   "Who will you compare Me to,
     or who is My equal?" asks the Holy One.
²⁶   Look up and see:
     who created these?
     He brings out the starry host by number;
     He calls all of them by name.
     Because of His great power and strength,
     not one of them is missing.
²⁷   Jacob, why do you say,
     and Israel, why do you assert:
     "My way is hidden from the LORD,
     and my claim is ignored by my God"?
²⁸   Do you not know?
     Have you not heard?
     ˙Yahweh is the everlasting God,
     the Creator of the whole earth.
     He never grows faint or weary;
     there is no limit to His understanding.
²⁹   He gives strength to the weary
     and strengthens the powerless.
³⁰   Youths may faint and grow weary,

and young men stumble and fall,
31 but those who trust in the Lord
will renew their strength;
they will soar on wings like eagles;
they will run and not grow weary;
they will walk and not faint.

41

"Be silent before Me, islands!
And let peoples renew their strength.
Let them approach, then let them testify;
let us come together for the trial.
2 Who has stirred him up from the east?
He calls righteousness to his feet.
The Lord hands nations over to him,
and he subdues kings.
He makes them like dust with his sword,
like wind-driven stubble with his bow.
3 He pursues them, going on safely,
hardly touching the path with his feet.
4 Who has performed and done this,
calling the generations from the beginning?
I, *Yahweh, am the first,
and with the last—I am He."
5 The islands see and are afraid,
the whole earth trembles.
They approach and arrive.
6 Each one helps the other,
and says to another, "Take courage!"
7 The craftsman encourages the metalworker;
the one who flattens with the hammer
supports the one who strikes the anvil,
saying of the soldering, "It is good."
He fastens it with nails so that it will not
fall over.
8 But you, Israel, My servant,
Jacob, whom I have chosen,
descendant of Abraham, My friend—
9 I brought you from the ends of the earth
and called you from its farthest corners.
I said to you: You are My servant;
I have chosen you and not rejected you.
10 Do not fear, for I am with you;
do not be afraid, for I am your God.
I will strengthen you; I will help you;
I will hold on to you with My righteous
right hand.
11 Be sure that all who are enraged against you
will be ashamed and disgraced;
those who contend with you
will become as nothing and will perish.
12 You will look for those who contend with you,
but you will not find them.
Those who war against you
will become absolutely nothing.
13 For I, Yahweh your God,
hold your right hand
and say to you: Do not fear,
I will help you.
14 Do not fear, you worm Jacob,
you men of Israel:
I will help you—
this is the Lord's declaration.
Your Redeemer is the Holy One of Israel.
15 See, I will make you
into a sharp threshing board,
new, with many teeth.
You will thresh mountains and pulverize them
and make hills into chaff.

16 You will winnow them
and a wind will carry them away,
a gale will scatter them.
But you will rejoice in the Lord;
you will boast in the Holy One of Israel.
17 The poor and the needy seek water,
but there is none;
their tongues are parched with thirst.
I, Yahweh, will answer them;
I, the God of Israel, will not forsake them.
18 I will open rivers on the barren heights,
and springs in the middle of the plains.
I will turn the desert into a pool of water
and dry land into springs of water.
19 I will plant cedars in the desert,
acacias, myrtles, and olive trees.
I will put juniper trees in the desert,
elms and cypress trees together,
20 so that all may see and know,
consider and understand,
that the hand of the Lord has done this,
the Holy One of Israel has created it.
21 "Submit your case," says the Lord.
"Present your arguments," says Jacob's King.
22 "Let them come and tell us
what will happen.
Tell us the past events,
so that we may reflect on them
and know the outcome,
or tell us the future.
23 Tell us the coming events,
then we will know that you are gods.
Indeed, do something good or bad,
then we will be in awe and perceive.
24 Look, you are nothing
and your work is worthless.
Anyone who chooses you is detestable.
25 I have raised up one from the north,
and he has come,
one from the east who invokes My name.
He will march over rulers as if they were mud,
like a potter who treads the clay.
26 Who told about this from the beginning,
so that we might know,
and from times past,
so that we might say: He is right?
No one announced it,
no one told it,
no one heard your words.
27 I was the first to say to *Zion:
Look! Here they are!
And I gave a herald of good news to Jerusalem.
28 When I look, there is no one;
there is no counselor among them;
when I ask them, they have nothing to say.
29 Look, all of them are a delusion;
their works are nonexistent;
their images are wind and emptiness.

42

"This is My Servant; I strengthen Him,
this is My Chosen One; I delight in Him.
I have put My Spirit on Him;
He will bring justice to the nations.
2 He will not cry out or shout
or make His voice heard in the streets.
3 He will not break a bruised reed,
and He will not put out a smoldering wick;
He will faithfully bring justice.

⁴ He will not grow weak or be discouraged
until He has established justice on earth.
The islands will wait for His instruction."
⁵ This is what God, •Yahweh, says—
who created the heavens and stretched
them out,
who spread out the earth and what comes
from it,
who gives breath to the people on it
and life to those who walk on it—
⁶ "I, Yahweh, have called You
for a righteous purpose,
and I will hold You by Your hand.
I will keep You and appoint You
to be a covenant for the people
and a light to the nations,
⁷ in order to open blind eyes,
to bring out prisoners from the dungeon,
and those sitting in darkness
from the prison house.
⁸ I am Yahweh, that is My name;
I will not give My glory to another
or My praise to idols.
⁹ The past events have indeed happened.
Now I declare new events;
I announce them to you before they occur."
¹⁰ Sing a new song to the LORD;
sing His praise from the ends of the earth,
you who go down to the sea with all
that fills it,
you islands with your inhabitants.
¹¹ Let the desert and its cities shout,
the settlements where Kedar dwells cry aloud.
Let the inhabitants of Sela sing for joy;
let them cry out from the mountaintops.
¹² Let them give glory to the LORD
and declare His praise in the islands.
¹³ The LORD advances like a warrior;
He stirs up His zeal like a soldier.
He shouts, He roars aloud,
He prevails over His enemies.
¹⁴ "I have kept silent from ages past;
I have been quiet and restrained Myself.
But now, I will groan like a woman in labor,
gasping breathlessly.
¹⁵ I will lay waste mountains and hills
and dry up all their vegetation.
I will turn rivers into islands
and dry up marshes.
¹⁶ I will lead the blind by a way
they did not know;
I will guide them on paths
they have not known.
I will turn darkness to light in front of them
and rough places into level ground.
This is what I will do for them,
and I will not forsake them.
¹⁷ They will be turned back
and utterly ashamed—
those who trust in idols
and say to metal-plated images:
You are our gods!
¹⁸ Listen, you deaf!
Look, you blind, so that you may see.
¹⁹ Who is blind but My servant,
or deaf like My messenger I am sending?
Who is blind like My dedicated one,

or blind like the servant of the LORD?
²⁰ Though seeing many things, you do not obey.
Though his ears are open, he does not listen."
²¹ The LORD was pleased, because of
His righteousness,
to magnify His instruction
and make it glorious.
²² But this is a people plundered and looted,
all of them trapped in holes
or imprisoned in dungeons.
They have become plunder
with no one to rescue them
and loot, with no one saying, "Give it back!"
²³ Who among you will pay attention to this?
Let him listen and obey in the future.
²⁴ Who gave Jacob to the robber,
and Israel to the plunderers?
Was it not the LORD?
Have we not sinned against Him?
They were not willing to walk in His ways,
and they would not listen to His instruction.
²⁵ So He poured out on Jacob His furious anger
and the power of war.
It surrounded him with fire, but he did not
know it;
it burned him, but he paid no attention.

43 Now this is what the LORD says—
the One who created you, Jacob,
and the One who formed you, Israel—
"Do not fear, for I have redeemed you;
I have called you by your name; you are Mine.
² I will be with you
when you pass through the waters,
and when you pass through the rivers,
they will not overwhelm you.
You will not be scorched
when you walk through the fire,
and the flame will not burn you.
³ For I •Yahweh your God,
the Holy One of Israel, and your Savior,
give Egypt as a ransom for you,
•Cush and Seba in your place.
⁴ Because you are precious in My sight
and honored, and I love you,
I will give people in exchange for you
and nations instead of your life.
⁵ Do not fear, for I am with you;
I will bring your descendants from the east,
and gather you from the west.
⁶ I will say to the north: Give them up!
and to the south: Do not hold them back!
Bring My sons from far away,
and My daughters from the ends
of the earth—
⁷ everyone called by My name
and created for My glory.
I have formed him; indeed, I have made him."
⁸ Bring out a people who are blind,
yet have eyes,
and are deaf, yet have ears.
⁹ All the nations are gathered together,
and the peoples are assembled.
Who among them can declare this,
and tell us the former things?
Let them present their witnesses
to vindicate themselves,
so that people may hear and say, "It is true."

¹⁰ "You are My witnesses"—
                    this is the LORD's declaration—
"and My servant whom I have chosen,
so that you may know and believe Me
and understand that I am He.
No god was formed before Me,
and there will be none after Me.
¹¹ I, I am Yahweh,
and there is no other Savior but Me.
¹² I alone declared, saved, and proclaimed—
and not some foreign god among you.
So you are My witnesses"—
                    this is the LORD's declaration—
"and I am God.
¹³ Also, from today on I am He alone,
and none can deliver from My hand.
I act, and who can reverse it?"

¹⁴This is what the LORD, your Redeemer, the Holy
One of Israel says:
Because of you, I will send to Babylon
and bring all of them as fugitives,
even the Chaldeans in the ships in which
they rejoice.
¹⁵ I am Yahweh, your Holy One,
the Creator of Israel, your King.
¹⁶ This is what the LORD says—
who makes a way in the sea,
and a path through surging waters,
¹⁷ who brings out the chariot and horse,
the army and the mighty one together
(they lie down, they do not rise again;
they are extinguished,
quenched like a wick)—
¹⁸ "Do not remember the past events,
pay no attention to things of old.
¹⁹ Look, I am about to do something new;
even now it is coming. Do you not see it?
Indeed, I will make a way in the wilderness,
rivers in the desert.
²⁰ The animals of the field will honor Me,
jackals and ostriches,
because I provide water in the wilderness,
and rivers in the desert,
to give drink to My chosen people.
²¹ The people I formed for Myself
will declare My praise.
²² "But Jacob, you have not called on Me,
because, Israel, you have become weary of Me.
²³ You have not brought Me your sheep
for •burnt offerings
or honored Me with your sacrifices.
I have not burdened you with offerings
or wearied you with incense.
²⁴ You have not bought Me aromatic cane
with silver,
or satisfied Me with the fat of your sacrifices.
But you have burdened Me with your sins;
you have wearied Me with your iniquities.
²⁵ "It is I who sweep away your transgressions
for My own sake
and remember your sins no more.
²⁶ Take Me to court; let us argue
our case together.
State your case, so that you may be vindicated.
²⁷ Your first father sinned,
and your mediators have rebelled against Me.
²⁸ So I defiled the officers of the sanctuary,

and •set Jacob apart for destruction
and Israel for abuse.

44 "And now listen, Jacob My servant,
Israel whom I have chosen.
² This is the word of the LORD
your Maker who formed you from the womb;
He will help you:
Do not fear; Jacob is My servant;
I have chosen Jeshurun.
³ For I will pour water on the thirsty land
and streams on the dry ground;
I will pour out My Spirit on your descendants
and My blessing on your offspring.
⁴ They will sprout among the grass
like poplars by flowing streams.
⁵ This one will say, 'I am the LORD's';
another will call himself by the name of Jacob;
still another will write on his hand,
'The LORD's,'
and name himself by the name of Israel."

⁶This is what the LORD, the King of Israel and its
Redeemer, the LORD of •Hosts, says:
I am the first and I am the last.
There is no God but Me.
⁷ Who, like Me, can announce the future?
Let him say so and make a case before Me,
since I have established an ancient people.
Let these gods declare the coming things,
and what will take place.
⁸ Do not be startled or afraid.
Have I not told you and declared it long ago?
You are my witnesses!
Is there any God but Me?
There is no other Rock; I do not know any.
⁹ All who make idols are nothing,
and what they treasure does not profit.
Their witnesses do not see or know anything,
so they will be put to shame.
¹⁰ Who makes a god or casts a metal image
for no profit?
¹¹ Look, all its worshipers will be put to shame,
and the craftsmen are humans.
They all will assemble and stand;
they all will be startled and put to shame.
¹² The ironworker labors over the coals,
shapes the idol with hammers,
and works it with his strong arm.
Also he grows hungry and his strength fails;
he doesn't drink water and is faint.
¹³ The woodworker stretches out
a measuring line,
he outlines it with a stylus;
he shapes it with chisels
and outlines it with a compass.
He makes it according to a human likeness,
like a beautiful person,
to dwell in a temple.
¹⁴ He cuts down cedars for his use,
or he takes a cypress or an oak.
He lets it grow strong among the trees
of the forest.
He plants a laurel, and the rain makes it grow.
¹⁵ It serves as fuel for man.
He takes some of it and warms himself;
also he kindles a fire and bakes bread;
he even makes it into a god and worships it;
he makes an idol from it and bows down to it.

16 He burns half of it in a fire,
and he roasts meat on that half.
He eats the roast and is satisfied.
He warms himself and says, "Ah!
I am warm, I see the blaze."

17 He makes a god or his idol with the rest of it.
He bows down to it and worships;
He prays to it, "Save me, for you are my god."

18 Such people do not comprehend
and cannot understand,
for He has shut their eyes so they cannot see,
and their minds so they cannot understand.

19 No one reflects,
no one has the perception or insight to say,
"I burned half of it in the fire,
I also baked bread on its coals,
I roasted meat and ate.
I will make something detestable with the rest
of it,
and I will bow down to a block of wood."

20 He feeds on ashes.
His deceived mind has led him astray,
and he cannot deliver himself,
or say, "Isn't there a lie in my right hand?"

21 Remember these things, Jacob,
and Israel, for you are My servant;
I formed you, you are My servant;
Israel, you will never be forgotten by Me.

22 I have swept away your transgressions
like a cloud,
and your sins like a mist.
Return to Me,
for I have redeemed you.

23 Rejoice, heavens, for the LORD has acted;
shout, depths of the earth.
Break out into singing, mountains,
forest, and every tree in it.
For the LORD has redeemed Jacob,
and glorifies Himself through Israel.

24 This is what the LORD, your Redeemer who formed
you from the womb, says:
I am •Yahweh, who made everything;
who stretched out the heavens by Myself;
who alone spread out the earth;

25 who destroys the omens of the false prophets
and makes fools of diviners;
who confounds the wise
and makes their knowledge foolishness;

26 who confirms the message of His servant
and fulfills the counsel of His messengers;
who says to Jerusalem, "She will
be inhabited,"
and to the cities of Judah, "They will
be rebuilt,"
and I will restore her ruins;

27 who says to the depths of the sea, "Be dry,"
and I will dry up your rivers;

28 who says to Cyrus, "My shepherd,
he will fulfill all My pleasure"
and says to Jerusalem, "She will be rebuilt,"
and of the temple, "Its foundation will be laid."

45 The LORD says this to Cyrus, His anointed,
whose right hand I have grasped
to subdue nations before him,
to disarm kings,
to open the doors before him
and the gates will not be shut:

2 "I will go before you
and level the uneven places;
I will shatter the bronze doors
and cut the iron bars in two.

3 I will give you the treasures of darkness
and riches from secret places,
so that you may know that I, •Yahweh,
the God of Israel call you by your name.

4 I call you by your name,
because of Jacob My servant
and Israel My chosen one.
I give a name to you,
though you do not know Me.

5 I am Yahweh, and there is no other;
there is no God but Me.
I will strengthen you,
though you do not know Me,

6 so that all may know from the rising
of the sun to its setting
that there is no one but Me.
I am Yahweh, and there is no other.

7 I form light and create darkness,
I make success and create disaster;
I, Yahweh, do all these things.

8 Heavens, sprinkle from above,
and let the skies shower righteousness.
Let the earth open up
so that salvation will sprout
and righteousness will spring up with it.
I, Yahweh, have created it.

9 Woe to the one who argues with his Maker—
one clay pot among many.
Does clay say to the one forming it,
'What are you making?'
Or does your work say,
'He has no hands'?

10 How absurd is the one who says to his father,
'What are you fathering?'
or to his mother,
'What are you giving birth to?'"

11 This is what the LORD,
the Holy One of Israel and its Maker, says:
"Ask Me what is to happen to My sons,
and instruct Me about the work of My hands.

12 I made the earth,
and created man on it.
It was My hands that stretched out
the heavens,
and I commanded all their host.

13 I have raised him up in righteousness,
and will level all roads for him.
He will rebuild My city,
and set My exiles free,
not for a price or a bribe,"
says the LORD of •Hosts.

14 This is what the LORD says:
The products of Egypt and the merchandise
of •Cush
and the Sabeans, men of stature,
will come over to you
and will be yours;
they will follow you,
they will come over in chains
and bow down to you.
They will confess to you:
God is indeed with you, and there is no other;
there is no other God.

15 Yes, You are a God who hides Himself,
God of Israel, Savior.
16 All of them are put to shame, even humiliated;
the makers of idols go in humiliation together.
17 Israel will be saved by the LORD
with an everlasting salvation;
you will not be put to shame or humiliated
for all eternity.
18 For this is what the LORD says—
God is the Creator of the heavens.
He formed the earth and made it.
He established it;
He did not create it to be empty,
but formed it to be inhabited—
"I am Yahweh,
and there is no other.
19 I have not spoken in secret,
somewhere in a land of darkness.
I did not say to the descendants of Jacob:
Seek Me in a wasteland.
I, Yahweh, speak truthfully;
I say what is right.
20 Come, gather together,
and draw near, you fugitives of the nations.
Those who carry their wooden idols,
and pray to a god who cannot save,
have no knowledge.
21 Speak up and present your case—
yes, let them take counsel together.
Who predicted this long ago?
Who announced it from ancient times?
Was it not I, Yahweh?
There is no other God but Me,
a righteous God and Savior;
there is no one except Me.
22 Turn to Me and be saved,
all the ends of the earth.
For I am God,
and there is no other.
23 By Myself I have sworn;
Truth has gone from My mouth,
a word that will not be revoked:
Every knee will bow to Me,
every tongue will swear allegiance.
24 It will be said to Me: Righteousness
and strength
is only in the LORD."
All who are enraged against Him
will come to Him and be put to shame.
25 All the descendants of Israel
will be justified and find glory through the LORD.

46 Bel crouches; Nebo cowers.
Their idols are consigned to beasts and cattle.
The images you carry are loaded,
as a burden for the weary animal.
2 The gods cower; they crouch together;
they are not able to rescue the burden,
but they themselves go into captivity.
3 "Listen to Me, house of Jacob,
all the remnant of the house of Israel,
who have been sustained from the womb,
carried along since birth.
4 I will be the same until your old age,
and I will bear you up when you turn gray.
I have made you, and I will carry you;
I will bear and save you.
5 Who will you compare Me or make Me equal to?

Who will you measure Me with,
so that we should be like each other?
6 Those who pour out their bags of gold
and weigh out silver on scales—
they hire a goldsmith and he makes it
into a god.
Then they kneel and bow down to it.
7 They lift it to their shoulder and bear it along;
they set it in its place, and there it stands;
it does not budge from its place.
They cry out to it but it doesn't answer;
it saves no one from his trouble.
8 Remember this and be brave;
take it to heart, you transgressors!
9 Remember what happened long ago,
for I am God, and there is no other;
I am God, and no one is like Me.
10 I declare the end from the beginning,
and from long ago what is not yet done,
saying: My plan will take place,
and I will do all My will.
11 I call a bird of prey from the east,
a man for My purpose from a far country.
Yes, I have spoken; so I will also bring it about.
I have planned it; I will also do it.
12 Listen to me, you hardhearted,
far removed from justice:
13 I am bringing My justice near;
it is not far away,
and My salvation will not delay.
I will put salvation in *Zion,
My splendor in Israel.

47 "Go down and sit in the dust,
Virgin Daughter Babylon.
Sit on the ground without a throne,
Daughter Chaldea!
For you will no longer be called pampered
and spoiled.
2 Take millstones and grind meal;
remove your veil,
strip off your skirt, bare your thigh,
wade through the streams.
3 Your nakedness will be uncovered,
and your shame will be exposed.
I will take vengeance;
I will spare no one.
4 The Holy One of Israel is our Redeemer;
*Yahweh of *Hosts is His name.
5 Daughter Chaldea,
sit in silence and go into darkness.
For you will no longer be called mistress
of kingdoms.
6 I was angry with My people;
I profaned My possession,
and I placed them under your control.
You showed them no mercy;
you made your yoke very heavy on the elderly.
7 You said, 'I will be the mistress forever.'
You did not take these things to heart
or think about their outcome.
8 So now hear this, lover of luxury,
who sits securely,
who says to herself,
'I exist, and there is no one else.
I will never be a widow
or know the loss of children.'
9 These two things will happen to you

suddenly, in one day:
loss of children and widowhood.
They will happen to you in their entirety,
in spite of your many sorceries
and the potency of your spells.
10 You were secure in your wickedness;
you said, 'No one sees me.'
Your wisdom and knowledge
led you astray.
You said to yourself,
'I exist, and there is no one else.'
11 But disaster will happen to you;
you will not know how to avert it.
And it will fall on you,
but you will be unable to ward it off.
Devastation will happen to you suddenly
and unexpectedly.
12 So take your stand with your spells
and your many sorceries,
which you have wearied yourself with
from your youth.
Perhaps you will be able to succeed;
perhaps you will inspire terror!
13 You are worn out with your many consultations.
So let them stand and save you—
the astrologers, who observe the stars,
who predict monthly
what will happen to you.
14 Look, they are like stubble;
fire burns them up.
They cannot deliver themselves
from the power of the flame.
This is not a coal for warming themselves,
or a fire to sit beside!
15 This is what they are to you—
those who have wearied you
and have traded with you from your youth—
each wanders on his own way;
no one can save you.

48 "Listen to this, house of Jacob—
those who are called by the name Israel
and have descended from Judah,
who swear by the name of *Yahweh
and declare the God of Israel,
but not in truth or righteousness.
2 For they are named after the Holy City,
and lean on the God of Israel;
His name is Yahweh of *Hosts.
3 I declared the past events long ago;
they came out of My mouth;
I proclaimed them.
Suddenly I acted, and they occurred.
4 Because I know that you are stubborn,
and your neck is iron
and your forehead bronze,
5 therefore I declared to you long ago.
I announced it to you before it occurred,
so you could not claim, 'My idol caused them;
my carved image and cast idol control them.'
6 You have heard it. Observe it all.
Will you not acknowledge it?
From now on I will announce new things
to you,
hidden things that you have not known.
7 They have been created now, and not long ago;
you have not heard of them before today,
so you could not claim, 'I already knew them!'

8 You have never heard; you have never known;
For a long time your ears have not been open.
For I knew that you were very treacherous,
and were known as a rebel from birth.
9 I will delay My anger for the honor
of My name,
and I will restrain Myself for your benefit
and for My praise,
so that you will not be destroyed.
10 Look, I have refined you, but not as silver;
I have tested you in the furnace of affliction.
11 I will act for My own sake, indeed, My own,
for how can I be defiled?
I will not give My glory to another.
12 Listen to Me, Jacob,
and Israel, the one called by Me:
I am He; I am the first,
I am also the last.
13 My own hand founded the earth,
and My right hand spread out the heavens;
when I summoned them,
they stood up together.
14 All of you, assemble and listen!
Who among the idols has declared
these things?
The Lord loves him;
he will accomplish His will against Babylon,
and His arm will be against the Chaldeans.
15 I—I have spoken;
yes, I have called him;
I have brought him,
and he will succeed in his mission.
16 Approach Me and listen to this.
From the beginning I have not spoken
in secret;
from the time anything existed, I was there."
And now the Lord God
has sent me and His Spirit.
17 This is what the Lord, your Redeemer, the Holy
One of Israel says:
I am Yahweh your God,
who teaches you for your benefit,
who leads you in the way you should go.
18 If only you had paid attention
to My commands.
Then your peace would have been like a river,
and your righteousness like the waves
of the sea.
19 Your descendants would have been
as countless as the sand,
and the offspring of your body like its grains;
their name would not be cut off
or eliminated from My presence.
20 Leave Babylon,
flee from the Chaldeans!
Declare with a shout of joy,
proclaim this,
let it go out to the end of the earth;
announce,
"The Lord has redeemed His servant Jacob!"
21 They did not thirst
when He led them through the deserts;
He made water flow for them from the rock;
He split the rock, and water gushed out.
22 "There is no peace for the wicked,"
says the Lord.

49

Coastlands, listen to me;
distant peoples, pay attention.
The LORD called me before I was born.
He named me while I was
    in my mother's womb.
2 He made my words like a sharp sword;
He hid me in the shadow of His hand.
He made me like a sharpened arrow;
He hid me in His quiver.
3 He said to me, "You are My Servant, Israel;
I will be glorified in him."
4 But I myself said: I have labored in vain,
I have spent my strength for nothing
    and futility;
yet my vindication is with the LORD,
and my reward is with my God.
5 And now, says the LORD,
who formed me from the womb to be
    His Servant,
to bring Jacob back to Him
so that Israel might be gathered to Him;
for I am honored in the sight of the LORD,
and my God is my strength—
6 He says,
"It is not enough for you to be My Servant
raising up the tribes of Jacob
and restoring the protected ones of Israel.
I will also make you a light for the nations,
to be My salvation to the ends of the earth."
7 This is what the LORD,
the Redeemer of Israel, his Holy One, says
to one who is despised,
to one abhorred by people,
to a servant of rulers:
"Kings will see and stand up,
and princes will bow down,
because of the LORD, who is faithful,
the Holy One of Israel—
    and He has chosen you."
8 This is what the LORD says:
I will answer you in a time of favor,
and I will help you in the day of salvation.
I will keep you, and I will appoint you
to be a covenant for the people,
to restore the land,
to make them possess
    the desolate inheritances,
9 saying to the prisoners: Come out,
and to those who are in darkness:
    Show yourselves.
They will feed along the pathways,
and their pastures will be on all
    the barren heights.
10 They will not hunger or thirst,
the scorching heat or sun will not strike them;
for their compassionate One will guide them,
and lead them to springs of water.
11 I will make all My mountains into a road,
and My highways will be raised up.
12 See, these will come from far away,
from the north and from the west,
and from the land of Sinim.
13 Shout for joy, you heavens!
Earth, rejoice!
Mountains break into joyful shouts!
For the LORD has comforted His people,
and will have compassion on His afflicted ones.

14 *Zion says, "The LORD has abandoned me;
The Lord has forgotten me!"
15 "Can a woman forget her nursing child,
or lack compassion for the child of her womb?
Even if these forget,
yet I will not forget you.
16 Look, I have inscribed you on the palms
    of My hands;
your walls are continually before Me.
17 Your builders hurry;
those who destroy and devastate you
    will leave you.
18 Look up, and look around.
They all gather together; they come to you.
As I live"—
                    this is the LORD's declaration—
"you will wear all your children as jewelry,
and put them on as a bride does.
19 For your waste and desolate places
and your land marked by ruins—
will now be indeed too small
    for the inhabitants,
and those who swallowed you up will be
    far away.
20 Yet as you listen, the children
that you have been deprived of will say,
'This place is too small for me;
make room for me so that I may settle.'
21 Then you will say within yourself,
'Who fathered these for me?
I was deprived of my children and unable
    to conceive,
exiled and wandering—
but who brought them up?
See, I was left by myself—
but these, where did they come from?'"
22 This is what the Lord GOD says:
Look, I will lift up My hand to the nations,
and raise My banner to the peoples.
They will bring your sons in their arms,
and your daughters will be carried
    on their shoulders.
23 Kings will be your foster fathers,
and their queens your nursing mothers.
They will bow down to you
with their faces to the ground,
and lick the dust at your feet.
Then you will know that I am *Yahweh;
those who put their hope in Me
will not be put to shame.
24 Can the prey be taken from the mighty,
or the captives of the righteous be delivered?
25 For this is what the LORD says:
"Even the captives of a mighty man
    will be taken,
and the prey of a tyrant will be delivered;
I will contend with the one who contends
    with you,
and I will save your children.
26 I will make your oppressors eat
    their own flesh,
and they will be drunk with their own blood
as with sweet wine.
Then all flesh will know
that I, Yahweh, am your Savior,
and your Redeemer, the Mighty One of Jacob."

50

This is what the Lord says:
Where is your mother's divorce certificate
that I used to send her away?
Or who were My creditors that I sold you to?
Look, you were sold for your iniquities,
and your mother was put away
because of your transgressions.

2 Why was no one there when I came?
Why was there no one to answer
when I called?
Is My hand too short to redeem?
Or do I have no power to deliver?
Look, I dry up the sea by My rebuke;
I turn the rivers into a wilderness;
their fish rot because of a lack of water
and die of thirst.

3 I dress the heavens in black
and make *sackcloth their clothing.

4 The Lord God has given Me
the tongue of those who are instructed
to know how to sustain the weary with a word.
He awakens Me each morning;
He awakens My ear to listen like those
being instructed.

5 The Lord God has opened My ear,
and I was not rebellious;
I did not turn back.

6 I gave My back to those who beat Me,
and My cheeks to those who tore out
My beard.
I did not hide My face from scorn and spitting.

7 The Lord God will help Me;
therefore I have not been humiliated;
therefore I have set My face like flint,
and I know I will not be put to shame.

8 The One who vindicates Me is near;
who will contend with Me?
Let us confront each other.
Who has a case against Me?
Let him come near Me!

9 In truth, the Lord God will help Me;
who will condemn Me?
Indeed, all of them will wear out
like a garment;
a moth will devour them.

10 Who among you *fears the Lord,
listening to the voice of His Servant?
Who among you walks in darkness,
and has no light?
Let him trust in the name of *Yahweh;
let him lean on his God.

11 Look, all you who kindle a fire,
who encircle yourselves with firebrands;
walk in the light of your fire
and in the firebrands you have lit!
This is what you'll get from My hand:
you will lie down in a place of torment.

51

Listen to Me, you who pursue righteousness,
you who seek the Lord:
Look to the rock from which you were cut,
and to the quarry from which you were dug.

2 Look to Abraham your father,
and to Sarah who gave birth to you in pain.
When I called him, he was only one;
I blessed him and made him many.

3 For the Lord will comfort *Zion;
He will comfort all her waste places,
and He will make her wilderness like Eden,
and her desert like the garden of the Lord.
Joy and gladness will be found in her,
thanksgiving and melodious song.

4 Pay attention to Me, My people,
and listen to Me, My nation;
for instruction will come from Me,
and My justice for a light to the nations.
I will bring it about quickly.

5 My righteousness is near,
My salvation appears,
and My arms will bring justice to the nations.
The coastlands will put their hope in Me,
and they will look to My strength.

6 Look up to the heavens,
and look at the earth beneath;
for the heavens will vanish like smoke,
the earth will wear out like a garment,
and its inhabitants will die like gnats.
But My salvation will last forever,
and My righteousness will never be shattered.

7 Listen to Me, you who know righteousness,
the people in whose heart is My instruction:
do not fear disgrace by men,
and do not be shattered by their taunts.

8 For the moth will devour them like a garment,
and the worm will eat them like wool.
But My righteousness will last forever,
and My salvation for all generations.

9 Wake up, wake up!
Put on the strength of the Lord's power.
Wake up as in days past,
as in generations of long ago.
Wasn't it You who hacked *Rahab to pieces,
who pierced the sea monster?

10 Wasn't it You who dried up the sea,
the waters of the great deep,
who made the sea-bed into a road
for the redeemed to pass over?

11 And the redeemed of the Lord will return
and come to Zion with singing,
crowned with unending joy.
Joy and gladness will overtake them,
and sorrow and sighing will flee.

12 I—I am the One who comforts you.
Who are you that you should fear man
who dies,
or a son of man who is given up like grass?

13 But you have forgotten the Lord, your Maker,
who stretched out the heavens
and laid the foundations of the earth.
You are in constant dread all day long
because of the fury of the oppressor,
who has set himself to destroy.
But where is the fury of the oppressor?

14 The prisoner is soon to be set free;
he will not die and go to the *Pit,
and his food will not be lacking.

15 For I am *Yahweh your God
who stirs up the sea so that its waves roar—
His name is Yahweh of *Hosts.

16 I have put My words in your mouth,
and covered you in the shadow of My hand,
in order to plant the heavens,
to found the earth,
and to say to Zion, "You are My people."

17 Wake yourself, wake yourself up!

Stand up, Jerusalem,
you who have drunk the cup of His fury
from the hand of the LORD;
you who have drunk the goblet to the dregs—
the cup that causes people to stagger.

18 There is no one to guide her
among all the children she has raised;
there is no one to take hold of her hand
among all the offspring she has brought up.

19 These two things have happened to you:
devastation and destruction,
famine and sword.
Who will grieve for you?
How can I comfort you?

20 Your children have fainted;
they lie at the head of every street
like an antelope in a net.
They are full of the LORD's fury,
the rebuke of your God.

21 So listen to this, afflicted
and drunken one—but not with wine.

22 This is what your Lord says—
Yahweh, even your God,
who defends His people—
"Look, I have removed
the cup of staggering from your hand;
that goblet, the cup of My fury.
You will never drink it again.

23 I will put it into the hands of your tormentors,
who said to you:
Lie down, so we can walk over you.
You made your back like the ground,
and like a street for those who walk on it.

52 "Wake up, wake up;
put on your strength, ˙Zion!
Put on your beautiful garments,
Jerusalem, the Holy City!
For the uncircumcised and the ˙unclean
will no longer enter you.

2 Stand up, shake the dust off yourself!
Take your seat, Jerusalem.
Remove the bonds from your neck,
captive Daughter Zion."

3 For this is what the LORD says:
"You were sold for nothing,
and you will be redeemed without silver."

4 For this is what the Lord GOD says:
"At first My people went down to Egypt
to live there,
then Assyria oppressed them without cause.

5 So now what have I here"—
this is the LORD's declaration—
"that My people are taken away for nothing?
Its rulers wail"—
this is the LORD's declaration—
"and My name is continually blasphemed
all day long.

6 Therefore My people will know My name;
therefore they will know on that day
that I am He who says:
Here I am."

7 How beautiful on the mountains
are the feet of the herald,
who proclaims peace,
who brings news of good things,
who proclaims salvation,
who says to Zion, "Your God reigns!"

8 The voices of your watchmen—
they lift up their voices,
shouting for joy together;
for every eye will see
when the LORD returns to Zion.

9 Be joyful, rejoice together,
you ruins of Jerusalem!
For the LORD has comforted
His people;
He has redeemed Jerusalem.

10 The LORD has displayed His holy arm
in the sight of all the nations;
all the ends of the earth will see
the salvation of our God.

11 Leave, leave, go out from there!
Do not touch anything unclean;
go out from her, purify yourselves,
you who carry the vessels of the LORD.

12 For you will not leave in a hurry,
and you will not have to take flight;
because the LORD is going before you,
and the God of Israel is your rear guard.

13 See, My Servant will act wisely;
He will be raised and lifted up
and greatly exalted.

14 Just as many were appalled at You—
His appearance was so disfigured
that He did not look like a man,
and His form did not resemble
a human being—

15 so He will sprinkle many nations.
Kings will shut their mouths because of Him,
For they will see what had not been told them,
and they will understand
what they had not heard.

53 Who has believed what we have heard?
And who has the arm of the LORD
been revealed to?

2 He grew up before Him like a young plant
and like a root out of dry ground.
He didn't have an impressive form
or majesty that we should look at Him,
no appearance that we should desire Him.

3 He was despised and rejected by men,
a man of suffering who knew
what sickness was.
He was like someone
people turned away from;
He was despised, and we didn't value Him.

4 Yet He Himself bore our sicknesses,
and He carried our pains;
but we in turn regarded Him stricken,
struck down by God, and afflicted.

5 But He was pierced because of
our transgressions,
crushed because of our iniquities;
punishment for our peace was on Him,
and we are healed by His wounds.

6 We all went astray like sheep;
we all have turned to our own way;
and the LORD has punished Him
for the iniquity of us all.

7 He was oppressed and afflicted,
yet He did not open His mouth.
Like a lamb led to the slaughter
and like a sheep silent before her shearers,
He did not open His mouth.

8 He was taken away because of oppression
 and judgment;
and who considered His fate?
For He was cut off from the land of the living;
He was struck because of
 my people's rebellion.
9 They made His grave with the wicked
and with a rich man at His death,
although He had done no violence
and had not spoken deceitfully.
10 Yet the Lord was pleased to crush Him
 severely.
When You make Him a 'restitution offering,
He will see His 'seed, He will prolong His days,
and by His hand, the Lord's pleasure
 will be accomplished.
11 He will see it out of His anguish,
and He will be satisfied with His knowledge.
My righteous Servant will justify many,
and He will carry their iniquities.
12 Therefore I will give Him the many
 as a portion,
and He will receive the mighty as spoil,
because He submitted Himself to death,
and was counted among the rebels;
yet He bore the sin of many
and interceded for the rebels.

54 "Rejoice, childless one, who did not
 give birth;
burst into song and shout,
you who have not been in labor!
For the children of the forsaken one
 will be more
than the children of the married woman,"
says the Lord.
2 "Enlarge the site of your tent,
and let your tent curtains be stretched out;
do not hold back;
lengthen your ropes,
and drive your pegs deep.
3 For you will spread out to the right
 and to the left,
and your descendants will dispossess nations
and inhabit the desolate cities.
4 Do not be afraid, for you will not
 be put to shame;
don't be humiliated, for you will not
 be disgraced.
For you will forget the shame of your youth,
and you will no longer remember
 the disgrace of your widowhood.
5 Indeed, your husband is your Maker—
His name is 'Yahweh of 'Hosts—
and the Holy One of Israel is your Redeemer;
He is called the God of all the earth.
6 For the Lord has called you,
like a wife deserted and wounded in spirit,
a wife of one's youth when she is rejected,"
says your God.
7 "I deserted you for a brief moment,
but I will take you back
 with great compassion.
8 In a surge of anger
I hid My face from you for a moment,
but I will have compassion on you
with everlasting love,"
says the Lord your Redeemer.

9 "For this is like the days of Noah to Me:
when I swore that the waters of Noah
would never flood the earth again,
so I have sworn that I will not be angry
 with you
or rebuke you.
10 Though the mountains move
and the hills shake,
My love will not be removed from you
and My covenant of peace will not be shaken,"
says your compassionate Lord.
11 "Poor Jerusalem, storm-tossed,
 and not comforted,
I will set your stones in black mortar,
and lay your foundations in sapphires.
12 I will make your fortifications out of rubies,
your gates out of sparkling stones,
and all your walls out of precious stones.
13 Then all your children will be taught
 by the Lord,
their prosperity will be great,
14 and you will be established
on a foundation of righteousness.
You will be far from oppression,
you will certainly not be afraid;
you will be far from terror,
it will certainly not come near you.
15 If anyone attacks you,
it is not from Me;
whoever attacks you
will fall before you.
16 Look, I have created the craftsman
who blows on the charcoal fire
and produces a weapon suitable for its task;
and I have created the destroyer
 to cause havoc.
17 No weapon formed against you will succeed,
and you will refute any accusation
raised against you in court.
This is the heritage of the Lord's servants,
and their righteousness is from Me."
 This is the Lord's declaration.

55 "Come, everyone who is thirsty,
come to the waters;
and you without money,
come, buy, and eat!
Come, buy wine and milk
without money and without cost!
2 Why do you spend money on what is not food,
and your wages on what does not satisfy?
Listen carefully to Me, and eat what is good,
and you will enjoy the choicest of foods.
3 Pay attention and come to Me;
listen, so that you will live.
I will make an everlasting covenant with you,
the promises assured to David.
4 Since I have made him a witness
 to the peoples,
a leader and commander for the peoples,
5 so you will summon a nation
 you do not know,
and nations who do not know you will run
 to you.
For the Lord your God,
even the Holy One of Israel,
has glorified you."
6 Seek the Lord while He may be found;

call to Him while He is near.
7 Let the wicked one abandon his way
 and the sinful one his thoughts;
 let him return to the Lord,
 so He may have compassion on him,
 and to our God, for He will freely forgive.
8 "For My thoughts are not your thoughts,
 and your ways are not My ways."
     This is the Lord's declaration.
9 "For as heaven is higher than earth,
 so My ways are higher than your ways,
 and My thoughts than your thoughts.
10 For just as rain and snow fall from heaven
 and do not return there
 without saturating the earth
 and making it germinate and sprout,
 and providing seed to sow
 and food to eat,
11 so My word that comes from My mouth
 will not return to Me empty,
 but it will accomplish what I please
 and will prosper in what I send it to do."
12 You will indeed go out with joy
 and be peacefully guided;
 the mountains and the hills will break
  into singing before you,
 and all the trees of the field will clap
  their hands.
13 Instead of the thornbush, a cypress
  will come up,
 and instead of the brier, a myrtle will come up;
 it will make a name for *Yahweh
 as an everlasting sign that will not
  be destroyed.

56 This is what the Lord says:
Preserve justice and do what is right,
 for My salvation is coming soon,
 and My righteousness will be revealed.
2 Happy is the man who does this,
 anyone who maintains this,
 who keeps the Sabbath without desecrating it,
 and keeps his hand from doing any evil.
3 No foreigner who has joined himself
  to the Lord
 should say,
 "The Lord will exclude me from His people";
 and the eunuch should not say,
 "Look, I am a dried-up tree."
4 For the Lord says this:
 "For the eunuchs who keep My Sabbaths,
 and choose what pleases Me,
 and hold firmly to My covenant,
5 I will give them, in My house and within
  My walls,
 a memorial and a name
 better than sons and daughters.
 I will give each of them an everlasting name
 that will never be cut off.
6 And the foreigners who join themselves
  to the Lord
 minister to Him, love the name of *Yahweh
 and become His servants,
 all who keep the Sabbath
  without desecrating it
 and who hold firmly to My covenant—
7 I will bring them to My holy mountain
 and let them rejoice in My house of prayer.

Their *burnt offerings and sacrifices
 will be acceptable on My altar,
 for My house will be called a house of prayer
 for all nations."
   8 This is the declaration of the Lord God,
    who gathers the dispersed of Israel:
 "I will gather to them still others
 besides those already gathered."
9 All you animals of the field and forest,
 come and eat!
10 Israel's watchmen are blind, all of them,
 they know nothing;
 all of them are mute dogs,
 they cannot bark;
 they dream, lie down,
 and love to sleep.
11 These dogs have fierce appetites;
 they never have enough.
 And they are shepherds
 who have no discernment;
 all of them turn to their own way,
 every last one for his own gain.
12 "Come, let me get some wine,
 let's guzzle some beer;
 and tomorrow will be like today,
 only far better!"

57 The righteous one perishes,
and no one takes it to heart;
 faithful men are swept away,
 with no one realizing
 that the righteous one is swept away
 from the presence of evil.
2 He will enter into peace—
 they will rest on their beds—
 everyone who lives uprightly.
3 But come here,
 you sons of a sorceress,
 offspring of an adulterer and a prostitute!
4 Who is it you are mocking?
 Who is it you are opening your mouth
 and sticking out your tongue at?
 Isn't it you, you rebellious children,
 you race of liars,
5 who burn with lust among the oaks,
 under every green tree,
 who slaughter children in the *wadis
 below the clefts of the rocks?
6 Your portion is among the smooth stones
  of the wadi;
 indeed, they are your lot.
 You have even poured out a *drink offering
  to them;
 you have offered a *grain offering;
 should I be satisfied with these?
7 You have placed your bed
 on a high and lofty mountain;
 you also went up there to offer sacrifice.
8 You have set up your memorial
 behind the door and doorpost.
 For away from Me, you stripped,
 went up, and made your bed wide,
 and you have made a bargain for yourself
  with them.
 You have loved their bed;
 you have gazed on their genitals.
9 You went to the king with oil
 and multiplied your perfumes;

you sent your couriers far away
and sent them down even to *Sheol.
10 You became weary on your many journeys,
but you did not say, "I give up!"
You found a renewal of your strength;
therefore you did not grow weak.
11 Who was it you dreaded and feared,
so that you lied and didn't remember Me
or take it to heart?
Have I not kept silent for such a long time
and you do not *fear Me?
12 I will expose your righteousness,
and your works—they will not profit you.
13 When you cry out,
let your collection of idols deliver you!
The wind will carry all of them off,
a breath will take them away.
But whoever takes refuge in Me
will inherit the land
and possess My holy mountain.
14 He said,
"Build it up, build it up, prepare the way,
remove every obstacle from My people's way."
15 For the High and Exalted One
who lives forever, whose name is Holy
says this:
"I live in a high and holy place,
and with the oppressed and lowly of spirit,
to revive the spirit of the lowly
and revive the heart of the oppressed.
16 For I will not accuse you forever,
and I will not always be angry;
for then the spirit would grow weak
before Me,
even the breath of man, which I have made.
17 Because of his sinful greed I was angry,
so I struck him; I was angry and hid;
but he went on turning back to the desires
of his heart.
18 I have seen his ways, but I will heal him;
I will lead him and restore comfort
to him and his mourners,
19 creating words of praise."
The LORD says,
"Peace, peace to the one who is far or near,
and I will heal him.
20 But the wicked are like the storm-tossed sea,
for it cannot be still,
and its waters churn up mire and muck.
21 There is no peace for the wicked,"
says my God.

58 "Cry out loudly, don't hold back!
Raise your voice like a trumpet.
Tell My people their transgression
and the house of Jacob their sins.
2 They seek Me day after day
and delight to know My ways,
like a nation that does what is right
and does not abandon the justice of their God.
They ask Me for righteous judgments;
they delight in the nearness of God."
3 "Why have we fasted, but You have not seen?
We have denied ourselves,
but You haven't noticed!"
"Look, you do as you please on the day
of your fast,
and oppress all your workers.

4 You fast with contention and strife
to strike viciously with your fist.
You cannot fast as you do today,
hoping to make your voice heard on high.
5 Will the fast I choose be like this:
A day for a person to deny himself,
to bow his head like a reed,
and to spread out *sackcloth and ashes?
Will you call this a fast
and a day acceptable to the LORD?
6 Isn't the fast I choose:
To break the chains of wickedness,
to untie the ropes of the yoke,
to set the oppressed free,
and to tear off every yoke?
7 Is it not to share your bread with the hungry,
to bring the poor and homeless
into your house,
to clothe the naked when you see him,
and not to ignore your own flesh and blood?
8 Then your light will appear like the dawn,
and your recovery will come quickly.
Your righteousness will go before you,
and the LORD's glory will be your rear guard.
9 At that time, when you call, the LORD
will answer;
when you cry out, He will say, 'Here I am.'
If you get rid of the yoke among you,
the finger-pointing and malicious speaking,
10 and if you offer yourself to the hungry,
and satisfy the afflicted one,
then your light will shine in the darkness,
and your night will be like noonday.
11 The LORD will always lead you,
satisfy you in a parched land,
and strengthen your bones.
You will be like a watered garden
and like a spring whose waters never run dry.
12 Some of you will rebuild the ancient ruins;
you will restore the foundations laid long ago;
you will be called the repairer of broken walls,
the restorer of streets where people live.
13 "If you keep from desecrating the Sabbath,
from doing whatever you want
on My holy day;
if you call the Sabbath a delight,
and the holy day of the LORD honorable;
if you honor it, not going your own ways,
seeking your own pleasure, or talking
too much;
14 then you will delight yourself in the LORD,
and I will make you ride over the heights
of the land,
and let you enjoy the heritage
of your father Jacob."
For the mouth of the LORD has spoken.

59 Indeed, the LORD's hand is not too short
to save,
and His ear is not too deaf to hear.
2 But your iniquities have built barriers
between you and your God,
and your sins have made Him hide His face
from you
so that He does not listen.
3 For your hands are defiled with blood
and your fingers, with iniquity;
your lips have spoken lies,

and your tongues mutter injustice.
⁴ No one makes claims justly;
no one pleads honestly.
They trust in empty and worthless words;
they conceive trouble and give birth
    to iniquity.
⁵ They hatch viper's eggs
and weave spider's webs.
Whoever eats their eggs will die;
crack one open, and a viper is hatched.
⁶ Their webs cannot become clothing,
and they cannot cover themselves
    with their works.
Their works are sinful works,
and violent acts are in their hands.
⁷ Their feet run after evil,
and they rush to shed innocent blood.
Their thoughts are sinful thoughts;
ruin and wretchedness are in their paths.
⁸ They have not known the path of peace,
and there is no justice in their ways.
They have made their roads crooked;
no one who walks on them will know peace.
⁹ Therefore justice is far from us,
and righteousness does not reach us.
We hope for light, but there is darkness;
for brightness, but we live in the night.
¹⁰ We grope along a wall like the blind;
we grope like those without eyes.
We stumble at noon as though
    it were twilight;
we are like the dead among those
    who are healthy.
¹¹ We all growl like bears
and moan like doves.
We hope for justice, but there is none;
for salvation, but it is far from us.
¹² For our transgressions have multiplied
    before You,
and our sins testify against us.
For our transgressions are with us,
and we know our iniquities:
¹³ transgression and deception against the Lord,
turning away from following our God,
speaking oppression and revolt,
conceiving and uttering lying words
    from the heart.
¹⁴ Justice is turned back,
and righteousness stands far off.
For truth has stumbled in the public square,
and honesty cannot enter.
¹⁵ Truth is missing,
and whoever turns from evil is plundered.
The Lord saw that there was no justice,
and He was offended.
¹⁶ He saw that there was no man—
He was amazed that there was
    no one interceding;
so His own arm brought salvation,
and His own righteousness supported Him.
¹⁷ He put on righteousness like a breastplate,
and a helmet of salvation on His head;
He put on garments of vengeance for clothing,
and He wrapped Himself in zeal as in a cloak.
¹⁸ So He will repay according to their deeds:
fury to His enemies,
retribution to His foes,

and He will repay the coastlands.
¹⁹ They will ˙fear the name of ˙Yahweh in the west
and His glory in the east;
for He will come like a rushing stream
driven by the wind of the Lord.
²⁰ "The Redeemer will come to ˙Zion,
and to those in Jacob who turn
    from transgression."
                   This is the Lord's declaration.
²¹ "As for Me, this is My covenant with them," says
the Lord: "My Spirit who is on you, and My words that
I have put in your mouth, will not depart from your
mouth, or from the mouth of your children, or from
the mouth of your children's children, from now on
and forever," says the Lord.

60 Arise, shine, for your light has come,
and the glory of the Lord shines over you.
² For look, darkness covers the earth,
and total darkness the peoples;
but the Lord will shine over you,
and His glory will appear over you.
³ Nations will come to your light,
and kings to the brightness of your radiance.
⁴ Raise your eyes and look around:
they all gather and come to you;
your sons will come from far away,
and your daughters will be carried on the hip.
⁵ Then you will see and be radiant,
and your heart will tremble and rejoice,
because the riches of the sea
    will become yours
and the wealth of the nations will come
    to you.
⁶ Caravans of camels will cover your land—
young camels of Midian and Ephah—
all of them will come from Sheba.
They will carry gold and frankincense
and proclaim the praises of the Lord.
⁷ All the flocks of Kedar will be gathered to you;
the rams of Nebaioth will serve you
and go up on My altar
    as an acceptable sacrifice.
I will glorify My beautiful house.
⁸ Who are these who fly like a cloud,
like doves to their shelters?
⁹ Yes, the islands will wait for Me
with the ships of Tarshish in the lead,
to bring your children from far away,
their silver and gold with them,
for the honor of the Lord your God,
the Holy One of Israel,
who has glorified you.
¹⁰ Foreigners will build up your walls,
and their kings will serve you.
Although I struck you in My wrath,
yet I will show mercy to you with My favor.
¹¹ Your gates will always be open;
they will never be shut day or night
so that the wealth of the nations
may be brought into you,
with their kings being led in procession.
¹² For the nation and the kingdom
that will not serve you will perish;
those nations will be annihilated.
¹³ The glory of Lebanon will come to you—
its pine, fir, and cypress together—
to beautify the place of My sanctuary,

and I will glorify My dwelling place.
14 The sons of your oppressors
will come and bow down to you;
all who reviled you
will fall facedown at your feet.
They will call you the City of the Lord,
*Zion of the Holy One of Israel.
15 Instead of your being deserted and hated,
with no one passing through,
I will make you an object of eternal pride,
a joy from age to age.
16 You will nurse on the milk of nations,
and nurse at the breast of kings;
you will know that I, *Yahweh, am your Savior
and Redeemer, the Mighty One of Jacob.
17 I will bring gold instead of bronze;
I will bring silver instead of iron,
bronze instead of wood,
and iron instead of stones.
I will appoint peace as your guard
and righteousness as your ruler.
18 Violence will never again be heard of
in your land;
devastation and destruction
will be gone from your borders.
But you will name your walls salvation
and your gates, praise.
19 The sun will no longer be your light by day,
and the brightness of the moon will not shine
on you;
but the Lord will be your everlasting light,
and your God will be your splendor.
20 Your sun will no longer set,
and your moon will not fade;
for the Lord will be your everlasting light,
and the days of your sorrow will be over.
21 Then all your people will be righteous;
they will possess the land forever;
they are the branch I planted,
the work of My hands,
so that I may be glorified.
22 The least will become a thousand,
the smallest a mighty nation.
I am Yahweh;
I will accomplish it quickly in its time.

61 The Spirit of the Lord God is on Me,
because the Lord has anointed Me
to bring good news to the poor.
He has sent Me to heal the brokenhearted,
to proclaim liberty to the captives
and freedom to the prisoners;
2 to proclaim the year of the Lord's favor,
and the day of our God's vengeance;
to comfort all who mourn,
3 to provide for those who mourn in *Zion;
to give them a crown of beauty
instead of ashes,
festive oil instead of mourning,
and splendid clothes instead of despair.
And they will be called righteous trees,
planted by the Lord
to glorify Him.
4 They will rebuild the ancient ruins;
they will restore the former devastations;
they will renew the ruined cities,
the devastations of many generations.
5 Strangers will stand and feed your flocks,

and foreigners will be your plowmen
and vinedressers.
6 But you will be called the Lord's priests;
they will speak of you as ministers of our God;
you will eat the wealth of the nations,
and you will boast in their riches.
7 Because your shame was double,
and they cried out, "Disgrace is their portion,"
therefore, they will possess double
in their land,
and eternal joy will be theirs.
8 For I *Yahweh love justice;
I hate robbery and injustice;
I will faithfully reward them
and make an everlasting covenant with them.
9 Their descendants will be known
among the nations,
and their posterity among the peoples.
All who see them will recognize
that they are a people the Lord has blessed.
10 I greatly rejoice in the Lord,
I exult in my God;
for He has clothed me with the garments
of salvation
and wrapped me in a robe of righteousness,
as a groom wears a turban
and as a bride adorns herself with her jewels.
11 For as the earth produces its growth,
and as a garden enables what is sown
to spring up,
so the Lord God will cause righteousness
and praise
to spring up before all the nations.

62 I will not keep silent because of *Zion,
and I will not keep still because of Jerusalem,
until her righteousness shines
like a bright light
and her salvation, like a flaming torch.
2 Nations will see your righteousness
and all kings, your glory.
You will be called by a new name
that the Lord's mouth will announce.
3 You will be a glorious crown
in the Lord's hand,
and a royal diadem in the palm of your God.
4 You will no longer be called Deserted,
and your land will not be called Desolate;
instead, you will be called My Delight
is in Her,
and your land Married;
for the Lord delights in you,
and your land will be married.
5 For as a young man marries a young woman,
so your sons will marry you;
and as a groom rejoices over his bride,
so your God will rejoice over you.
6 Jerusalem,
I have appointed watchmen on your walls;
they will never be silent, day or night.
There is no rest for you,
who remind the Lord.
7 Do not give Him rest
until He establishes and makes Jerusalem
the praise of the earth.
8 The Lord has sworn with His right hand
and His strong arm:
I will no longer give your grain

to your enemies for food,
and foreigners will not drink your new wine
you have labored for.
⁹ For those who gather grain will eat it
and praise the Lord,
and those who harvest the grapes will drink
the wine
in My holy courts.
¹⁰ Go out, go out through the gates;
prepare a way for the people!
Build it up, build up the highway;
clear away the stones!
Raise a banner for the peoples.
¹¹ Look, the Lord has proclaimed
to the ends of the earth,
"Say to Daughter Zion:
Look, your salvation is coming,
His reward is with Him,
and His gifts accompany Him."
¹² And they will be called the Holy People,
the Lord's Redeemed;
and you will be called Cared For,
A City Not Deserted.

63 Who is this coming from Edom
in crimson-stained garments from Bozrah—
this One who is splendid in His apparel,
rising up proudly in His great might?
It is I, proclaiming vindication,
powerful to save.
² Why are Your clothes red,
and Your garments like one who treads
a winepress?
³ I trampled the winepress alone,
and no one from the nations was with Me.
I trampled them in My anger
and ground them underfoot in My fury;
their blood spattered My garments,
and all My clothes were stained.
⁴ For I planned the day of vengeance,
and the year of My redemption came.
⁵ I looked, but there was no one to help,
and I was amazed that no one assisted;
so My arm accomplished victory for Me,
and My wrath assisted Me.
⁶ I crushed nations in My anger;
I made them drunk with My wrath
and poured out their blood on the ground.
⁷ I will make known the Lord's faithful love
and the Lord's praiseworthy acts,
because of all the Lord has done for us—
even the many good things
He has done for the house of Israel
and has done for them based on
His compassion
and the abundance of His faithful love.
⁸ He said, "They are indeed My people,
children who will not be disloyal,"
and He became their Savior.
⁹ In all their suffering, He suffered,
and the Angel of His Presence saved them.
He redeemed them
because of His love and compassion;
He lifted them up and carried them
all the days of the past.
¹⁰ But they rebelled
and grieved His Holy Spirit.
So He became their enemy

and fought against them.
¹¹ Then He remembered the days of the past,
the days of Moses and his people.
Where is He who brought them out of the sea
with the shepherds of His flock?
Where is He who put His Holy Spirit
among the flock?
¹² He sent His glorious arm
to be at Moses' right hand,
divided the waters before them
to obtain eternal fame for Himself,
¹³ and led them through the depths
like a horse in the wilderness,
so that they did not stumble.
¹⁴ Like cattle that go down into the valley,
the Spirit of the Lord gave them rest.
You led Your people this way
to make a glorious name for Yourself.
¹⁵ Look down from heaven and see
from Your lofty home—holy and beautiful.
Where is Your zeal and Your might?
Your yearning and Your compassion
are withheld from me.
¹⁶ Yet You are our Father,
even though Abraham does not know us
and Israel doesn't recognize us.
You, ˙Yahweh, are our Father;
from ancient times,
Your name is our Redeemer.
¹⁷ Why, Yahweh, do You make us stray
from Your ways?
You harden our hearts so we do not ˙fear You.
Return, because of Your servants,
the tribes of Your heritage.
¹⁸ Your holy people had a possession
for a little while,
but our enemies have trampled down
Your sanctuary.
¹⁹ We have become like those
You never ruled over,
like those not called by Your name.

64 If only You would tear the heavens open
and come down,
so that mountains would quake
at Your presence—
² as fire kindles the brushwood,
and fire causes water to boil—
to make Your name known to Your enemies,
so that nations will tremble at Your presence!
³ When You did awesome works
that we did not expect,
You came down,
and the mountains quaked at Your presence.
⁴ From ancient times no one has heard,
no one has listened,
no eye has seen any God except You,
who acts on behalf of the one who waits
for Him.
⁵ You welcome the one who joyfully does
what is right;
they remember You in Your ways.
But we have sinned, and You were angry.
How can we be saved if we remain
in our sins?
⁶ All of us have become like something ˙unclean,
and all our righteous acts are
like a polluted garment;

all of us wither like a leaf,
and our iniquities carry us away like the wind.
⁷ No one calls on Your name,
striving to take hold of You.
For You have hidden Your face from us
and made us melt because of our iniquity.
⁸ Yet LORD, You are our Father;
we are the clay, and You are our potter;
we all are the work of Your hands.
⁹ LORD, do not be terribly angry
or remember our iniquity forever.
Please look—all of us are Your people!
¹⁰ Your holy cities have become a wilderness;
•Zion has become a wilderness,
Jerusalem a desolation.
¹¹ Our holy and beautiful temple,
where our fathers praised You,
has been burned with fire,
and all that was dear to us lies in ruins.
¹² LORD, after all this, will You restrain Yourself?
Will You keep silent and afflict severely?

65 "I was sought by those who did not ask;
I was found by those who did not seek Me.
I said: Here I am, here I am,
to a nation that was not called by My name.
² I spread out My hands all day long
to a rebellious people
who walk in the wrong path,
following their own thoughts.
³ These people continually provoke Me
to My face,
sacrificing in gardens,
burning incense on bricks,
⁴ sitting among the graves,
spending nights in secret places,
eating the meat of pigs,
and putting polluted broth in their bowls.
⁵ They say, 'Keep to yourself,
don't come near me, for I am too holy
for you!'
These practices are smoke in My nostrils,
a fire that burns all day long.
⁶ It is written before Me:
I will not keep silent, but I will repay;
I will repay them fully
⁷ for your iniquities and the iniquities
of your fathers together,"
says the LORD.
"Because they burned incense
on the mountains
and reproached Me on the hills,
I will reward them fully
for their former deeds."
⁸ The LORD says this:
As the new wine is found in a bunch of grapes,
and one says, 'Don't destroy it,
for there's some good in it,'
so I will act because of My servants
and not destroy them all.
⁹ I will produce descendants from Jacob,
and heirs to My mountains from Judah;
My chosen ones will possess it,
and My servants will dwell there.
¹⁰ Sharon will be a pasture for flocks,
and the Valley of Achor a place for cattle
to lie down,
for My people who have sought Me.

¹¹ But you who abandon the LORD,
who forget My holy mountain,
who prepare a table for Fortune
and fill bowls of mixed wine for Destiny,
¹² I will destine you for the sword,
and all of you will kneel down
to be slaughtered,
because I called and you did not answer,
I spoke and you did not hear;
you did what was evil in My sight
and chose what I did not delight in.
¹³ Therefore, this is what the Lord GOD says:
My servants will eat,
but you will be hungry;
My servants will drink,
but you will be thirsty;
My servants will rejoice,
but you will be put to shame.
¹⁴ My servants will shout for joy
from a glad heart,
but you will cry out from an anguished heart,
and you will lament out of a broken spirit.
¹⁵ You will leave your name behind
as a curse for My chosen ones,
and the Lord GOD will kill you;
but He will give His servants another name.
¹⁶ Whoever is blessed in the land
will be blessed by the God of truth,
and whoever swears in the land
will swear by the God of truth.
For the former troubles will be forgotten
and hidden from My sight.
¹⁷ "For I will create a new heaven
and a new earth;
the past events will not be remembered
or come to mind.
¹⁸ Then be glad and rejoice forever
in what I am creating;
for I will create Jerusalem to be a joy
and its people to be a delight.
¹⁹ I will rejoice in Jerusalem
and be glad in My people.
The sound of weeping and crying
will no longer be heard in her.
²⁰ In her, a nursing infant will no longer live
only a few days,
or an old man not live out his days.
Indeed, the youth will die at a hundred years,
and the one who misses a hundred years
will be cursed.
²¹ People will build houses and live in them;
they will plant vineyards and eat their fruit.
²² They will not build and others live in them;
they will not plant and others eat.
For My people's lives will be
like the lifetime of a tree.
My chosen ones will fully enjoy
the work of their hands.
²³ They will not labor without success
or bear children destined for disaster,
for they will be a people blessed by the LORD
along with their descendants.
²⁴ Even before they call, I will answer;
while they are still speaking, I will hear.
²⁵ The wolf and the lamb will feed together,
and the lion will eat straw like the ox,
but the serpent's food will be dust!

They will not do what is evil or destroy
on My entire holy mountain,"
says the LORD.

66 This is what the LORD says:
Heaven is My throne,
and earth is My footstool.
What house could you possibly build for Me?
And what place could be My home?
² My hand made all these things,
and so they all came into being.
          This is the LORD's declaration.
I will look favorably on this kind of person:
one who is humble, submissive in spirit,
and trembles at My word.
³ One slaughters an ox, one kills a man;
one sacrifices a lamb, one breaks a dog's neck;
one offers a *grain offering, one offers
     pig's blood;
one offers incense, one praises an idol—
all these have chosen their ways
and delight in their detestable practices.
⁴ So I will choose their punishment,
and I will bring on them what they dread
because I called and no one answered;
I spoke and they didn't hear;
they did what was evil in My sight
and chose what I didn't delight in.
⁵ You who tremble at His word,
hear the word of the LORD:
"Your brothers who hate and exclude you
because of Me have said,
'Let the LORD be glorified
so that we can see your joy!'
But they will be put to shame."
⁶ A sound of uproar from the city!
A voice from the temple—
the voice of the LORD,
paying back His enemies what they deserve!
⁷ Before *Zion was in labor, she gave birth;
before she was in pain, she delivered a boy.
⁸ Who has heard of such a thing?
Who has seen such things?
Can a land be born in one day
or a nation be delivered in an instant?
Yet as soon as Zion was in labor,
she gave birth to her sons.
⁹ "Will I bring a baby to the point of birth
and not deliver it?"
says the LORD;
"or will I who deliver, close the womb?"
says your God.
¹⁰ Be glad for Jerusalem and rejoice over her,
all who love her.
Rejoice greatly with her,
all who mourn over her—
¹¹ so that you may nurse and be satisfied

from her comforting breast
and drink deeply and delight yourselves
from her glorious breasts.
¹² For this is what the LORD says:
I will make peace flow to her like a river,
and the wealth of nations like a flood;
you will nurse and be carried on her hip
and bounced on her lap.
¹³ As a mother comforts her son,
so I will comfort you,
and you will be comforted
in Jerusalem.
¹⁴ You will see, you will rejoice,
and you will flourish like grass;
then the LORD's power will be revealed
to His servants,
but He will show His wrath
against His enemies.
¹⁵ Look, the LORD will come with fire—
His chariots are like the whirlwind—
to execute His anger with fury
and His rebuke with flames of fire.
¹⁶ For the LORD will execute judgment
on all flesh with His fiery sword,
and many will be slain by the LORD.

¹⁷ "Those who dedicate and purify themselves to enter the groves following their leader, eating meat from pigs, vermin, and rats, will perish together."
          This is the LORD's declaration.

¹⁸ "Knowing their works and their thoughts, I have come to gather all nations and languages; they will come and see My glory. ¹⁹ I will establish a sign among them, and I will send survivors from them to the nations—to Tarshish, Put, Lud (who are archers), Tubal, Javan, and the islands far away—who have not heard of My fame or seen My glory. And they will proclaim My glory among the nations. ²⁰ They will bring all your brothers from all the nations as a gift to the LORD on horses and chariots, in litters, and on mules and camels, to My holy mountain Jerusalem," says the LORD, "just as the Israelites bring an offering in a *clean vessel to the house of the LORD. ²¹ I will also take some of them as priests and Levites," says the LORD.

²²   "For just as the new heavens
and the new earth,
which I will make,
will endure before Me"—
          this is the LORD's declaration—
"so your offspring and your name will endure.
²³ All mankind will come to worship Me
from one New Moon to another
and from one Sabbath to another,"
says the LORD.

²⁴ "As they leave, they will see the dead bodies of the men who have rebelled against Me; for their worm will never die, their fire will never go out, and they will be a horror to all mankind."

JEREMIAH

1 The words of Jeremiah, the son of Hilkiah, one of the priests living in Anathoth in the territory of Benjamin. ²The word of the LORD came to him in the thirteenth year of the reign of Josiah son of Amon, king of Judah. ³It also came throughout the days of Jehoiakim son of Josiah, king of Judah, until the fifth month of the eleventh year of Zedekiah son of Josiah, king of Judah, when the people of Jerusalem went into exile.

⁴The word of the LORD came to me:

5 I chose you before I formed you in the womb;
   I set you apart before you were born.
   I appointed you a prophet to the nations.

⁶But I protested, "Oh no, Lord GOD! Look, I don't know how to speak since I am only a youth."

⁷Then the LORD said to me:

   Do not say, "I am only a youth,"
   for you will go to everyone I send you to
   and speak whatever I tell you.
8 Do not be afraid of anyone,
   for I will be with you to deliver you.
              This is the LORD's declaration.

⁹Then the LORD reached out His hand, touched my mouth, and told me:

   I have now filled your mouth with My words.
10 See, I have appointed you today
    over nations and kingdoms
    to uproot and tear down,
    to destroy and demolish,
    to build and plant.

¹¹Then the word of the LORD came to me, asking, "What do you see, Jeremiah?"

I replied, "I see a branch of an almond tree."

¹²The LORD said to me, "You have seen correctly, for I watch over My word to accomplish it." ¹³Again the word of the LORD came to me inquiring, "What do you see?"

And I replied, "I see a boiling pot, its lip tilted from the north to the south."

¹⁴Then the LORD said to me, "Disaster will be poured out from the north on all who live in the land. ¹⁵Indeed, I am about to summon all the clans and kingdoms of the north."

              This is the LORD's declaration.

   They will come, and each king will set up
     his throne
   at the entrance to Jerusalem's gates.
   They will attack all her surrounding walls
   and all the other cities of Judah.

¹⁶"I will pronounce My judgments against them for all the evil they did when they abandoned Me to burn incense to other gods and to worship the works of their own hands.

¹⁷"Now, get ready. Stand up and tell them everything that I command you. Do not be intimidated by them or I will cause you to cower before them. ¹⁸Today, I am the One who has made you a fortified city, an iron pillar, and bronze walls against the whole land— against the kings of Judah, its officials, its priests, and the population. ¹⁹They will fight against you but never prevail over you, since I am with you to rescue you."

              This is the LORD's declaration.

2 The word of the LORD came to me: ²"Go and announce directly to Jerusalem that this is what the LORD says:

   I remember the loyalty of your youth,
   your love as a bride—
   how you followed Me in the wilderness,
   in a land not sown.
3 Israel was holy to the LORD,
   the ˙firstfruits of His harvest.
   All who ate of it found themselves ˙guilty;
   disaster came on them."
              This is the LORD's declaration.
4 Hear the word of the LORD, house of Jacob
   and all families of the house of Israel.
5 This is what the LORD says:
   What fault did your fathers find in Me
   that they went so far from Me,
   followed worthless idols,
   and became worthless themselves?
6 They stopped asking, "Where is the LORD
   who brought us from the land of Egypt,
   who led us through the wilderness,
   through a land of deserts and ravines,
   through a land of drought and darkness,
   a land no one traveled through
   and where no one lived?"
7 I brought you to a fertile land
   to eat its fruit and bounty,
   but after you entered, you defiled My land;
   you made My inheritance detestable.
8 The priests quit asking, "Where is the LORD?"
   The experts in the law no longer knew Me,
   and the rulers rebelled against Me.
   The prophets prophesied by ˙Baal
   and followed useless idols.
9 Therefore, I will bring a case
     against you again.
              This is the LORD's declaration.
   I will bring a case
     against your children's children.
10 Cross over to Cyprus and take a look.
    Send someone to Kedar
      and consider carefully;
    see if there has ever been anything like this:
11 Has a nation ever exchanged its gods?
    (But they were not gods!)
    Yet My people have exchanged their Glory
    for useless idols.
12 Be horrified at this, heavens;
    be shocked and utterly appalled.
              This is the LORD's declaration.
13 For My people have committed a double evil:
    They have abandoned Me,
    the fountain of living water,
    and dug cisterns for themselves,
    cracked cisterns that cannot hold water.
14 Is Israel a slave?
    Was he born into slavery?
    Why else has he become a prey?
15 The young lions have roared at him;
    they have roared loudly.
    They have laid waste his land.
    His cities are in ruins, without inhabitants.
16 The men of Memphis and Tahpanhes

have also broken your skull.

17 Have you not brought this on yourself
by abandoning the Lord your God
while He was leading you along the way?

18 Now what will you gain
by traveling along the way to Egypt
to drink the waters of the Nile?
What will you gain
by traveling along the way to Assyria
to drink the waters of the Euphrates?

19 Your own evil will discipline you;
your own apostasies will reprimand you.
Think it over and see how evil and bitter it is
for you to abandon the Lord your God
and to have no 'fear of Me.
　　　　　　This is the declaration
　　　　　　　of the Lord God of 'Hosts.

20 For long ago I broke your yoke;
I tore off your chains.
You insisted, "I will not serve!"
On every high hill
and under every green tree
you lie down like a prostitute.

21 I planted you, a choice vine
from the very best seed.
How then could you turn into
a degenerate, foreign vine?

22 Even if you wash with lye
and use a great amount of soap,
the stain of your sin is still in front of Me.
　　　　This is the Lord God's declaration.

23 How can you protest, "I am not defiled;
I have not followed the Baals"?
Look at your behavior in the valley;
acknowledge what you have done.
You are a swift young camel
twisting and turning on her way,

24 a wild donkey at home in the wilderness.
She sniffs the wind in the heat of her desire.
Who can control her passion?
All who look for her will not become tired;
they will find her in her mating season.

25 Keep your feet from going bare
and your throat from thirst.
But you say, "It's hopeless;
I love strangers,
and I will continue to follow them."

26 Like the shame of a thief when he is caught,
so the house of Israel has been put to shame.
They, their kings, their officials,
their priests, and their prophets

27 say to a tree, "You are my father,"
and to a stone, "You gave birth to me."
For they have turned their back to Me
and not their face,
yet in their time of disaster they beg,
"Rise up and save us!"

28 But where are your gods you made
for yourself?
Let them rise up and save you
in your time of disaster if they can,
for your gods are as numerous
as your cities, Judah.

29 Why do you bring a case against Me?
All of you have rebelled against Me.
　　　　　This is the Lord's declaration.

30 I have struck down your children in vain;
they would not accept discipline.
Your own sword has devoured
your prophets
like a ravaging lion.

31 Evil generation,
pay attention to the word of the Lord!
Have I been a wilderness to Israel
or a land of dense darkness?
Why do My people claim,
"We will go where we want;
we will no longer come to You"?

32 Can a young woman forget her jewelry
or a bride her wedding sash?
Yet My people have forgotten Me
for countless days.

33 How skillfully you pursue love;
you also teach evil women your ways.

34 Moreover, your skirts are stained
with the blood of the innocent poor.
You did not catch them breaking
and entering.
But in spite of all these things

35 you claim, "I am innocent.
His anger is sure to turn away from me."
But I will certainly judge you
because you have said, "I have not sinned."

36 How unstable you are,
constantly changing your ways!
You will be put to shame by Egypt
just as you were put to shame by Assyria.

37 Moreover, you will be led out from here
with your hands on your head
since the Lord has rejected those you trust;
you will not succeed even with their help.

3 If a man divorces his wife
and she leaves him to marry another,
can he ever return to her?
Wouldn't such a land become totally defiled?
But you!
You have played the prostitute
with many partners—
can you return to Me?
　　　　　This is the Lord's declaration.

2 Look to the barren heights and see.
Where have you not been immoral?
You sat waiting for them beside the highways
like a nomad in the desert.
You have defiled the land
with your prostitution and wickedness.

3 This is why the showers haven't come—
why there has been no spring rain.
You have the brazen look of a prostitute
and refuse to be ashamed.

4 Have you not lately called to Me, "My Father.
You were my friend in my youth.

5 Will He bear a grudge forever?
Will He be endlessly infuriated?"
This is what you have said,
but you have done the evil things
you are capable of.

6 In the days of King Josiah the Lord asked me, "Have you seen what unfaithful Israel has done? She has ascended every high hill and gone under every green tree to prostitute herself there. 7 I thought: After she has done all these things, she will return to Me. But she didn't return, and her treacherous sister Judah saw it. 8 I observed that it was because unfaithful

Israel had committed adultery that I had sent her away and had given her a certificate of divorce. Nevertheless, her treacherous sister Judah was not afraid but also went and prostituted herself. ⁹Indifferent to her prostitution, she defiled the land and committed adultery with stones and trees. ¹⁰Yet in spite of all this, her treacherous sister Judah didn't return to Me with all her heart—only in pretense."

> This is the Lord's declaration.

¹¹The Lord announced to me, "Unfaithful Israel has shown herself more righteous than treacherous Judah. ¹²Go, proclaim these words to the north, and say:

Return, unfaithful Israel.
> This is the Lord's declaration.
I will not look on you with anger,
for I am unfailing in My love.
> This is the Lord's declaration.
I will not be angry forever.
¹³ Only acknowledge your •guilt—
you have rebelled against the Lord your God.
You have scattered your favors to strangers
under every green tree
and have not obeyed My voice.
> This is the Lord's declaration.

¹⁴"Return, you faithless children"—this is the Lord's declaration—"for I am your master, and I will take you, one from a city and two from a family, and I will bring you to •Zion. ¹⁵I will give you shepherds who are loyal to Me, and they will shepherd you with knowledge and skill. ¹⁶When you multiply and increase in the land, in those days"—the Lord's declaration—"no one will say any longer, 'The ark of the Lord's covenant.' It will never come to mind, and no one will remember or miss it. It will never again be made. ¹⁷At that time Jerusalem will be called, •Yahweh's Throne, and all the nations will be gathered to it, to the name of Yahweh in Jerusalem. They will cease to follow the stubbornness of their evil hearts. ¹⁸In those days the house of Judah will join with the house of Israel, and they will come together from the land of the north to the land I have given your ancestors to inherit."

¹⁹ I thought: How I long to make you My sons
and give you a desirable land,
the most beautiful inheritance of all
the nations.
I thought: You will call Me, my Father,
and never turn away from Me.
²⁰ However, as a woman may betray her lover,
so you have betrayed Me, house of Israel.
> This is the Lord's declaration.
²¹ A sound is heard on the barren heights,
the children of Israel weeping and begging
for mercy,
for they have perverted their way;
they have forgotten the Lord their God.
²² Return, you faithless children.
I will heal your unfaithfulness.
"Here we are, coming to You,
for You are the Lord our God.
²³ Surely, falsehood comes from the hills,
commotion from the mountains,
but the salvation of Israel
is only in the Lord our God.
²⁴ From the time of our youth
the shameful one has consumed
what our fathers have worked for—
their flocks and their herds,

their sons and their daughters.
²⁵ Let us lie down in our shame;
let our disgrace cover us.
We have sinned against the Lord our God,
both we and our fathers,
from the time of our youth even to this day.
We have not obeyed the voice of the Lord
our God."

4 If you return, Israel—
        this is the Lord's declaration—
you will return to Me,
if you remove your detestable idols
from My presence
and do not waver,
² then you can swear, "As the Lord lives,"
in truth, in justice, and in righteousness,
then the nations will be blessed by Him
and will pride themselves in Him.

³For this is what the Lord says to the men of Judah and Jerusalem:

Break up the unplowed ground;
do not sow among the thorns.
⁴ Circumcise yourselves to the Lord;
remove the foreskin of your hearts,
men of Judah and residents of Jerusalem.
Otherwise, My wrath will break out like fire
and burn with no one to extinguish it
because of your evil deeds.

⁵Declare in Judah, proclaim in Jerusalem, and say:

Blow the ram's horn throughout the land.
Cry out loudly and say:
Assemble yourselves,
and let's flee to the fortified cities.
⁶ Lift up a signal flag toward •Zion.
Run for cover! Don't stand still!
For I am bringing disaster
from the north—
a great destruction.
⁷ A lion has gone up from his thicket;
a destroyer of nations has set out.
He has left his lair
to make your land a waste.
Your cities will be reduced
to uninhabited ruins.
⁸ Because of this, put on •sackcloth;
mourn and wail,
for the Lord's burning anger
has not turned away from us.

⁹"On that day"—this is the Lord's declaration—"the king and the officials will lose their courage. The priests will tremble in fear, and the prophets will be scared speechless."

¹⁰I said, "Oh no, Lord God, You have certainly deceived this people and Jerusalem, by announcing, 'You will have peace,' while a sword is at our throats."

¹¹"At that time it will be said to this people and to Jerusalem, 'A searing wind blows from the barren heights in the wilderness on the way to My dear people. It comes not to winnow or to sift; ¹²a wind too strong for this comes at My call. Now I will also pronounce judgments against them.'"

¹³ Look, he advances like clouds;
his chariots are like a storm.
His horses are swifter than eagles.
Woe to us, for we are ruined!
¹⁴ Wash the evil from your heart, Jerusalem,
so that you will be delivered.

How long will you harbor
malicious thoughts within you?
15 For a voice announces from Dan,
proclaiming malice from Mount Ephraim.
16 Warn the nations: Look!
Proclaim to Jerusalem:
Those who besiege are coming
from a distant land;
they raise their voices
against the cities of Judah.
17 They have her surrounded
like those who guard a field,
because she has rebelled against Me.
This is the LORD's declaration.
18 Your way of life and your actions
have brought this on you.
This is your punishment. It is very bitter,
because it has reached your heart!
19 My anguish, my anguish! I writhe in agony!
Oh, the pain in my heart!
My heart pounds;
I cannot be silent.
For you, my soul,
have heard the sound of the ram's horn—
the shout of battle.
20 Disaster after disaster is reported
because the whole land is destroyed.
Suddenly my tents are destroyed,
my tent curtains, in a moment.
21 How long must I see the signal flag
and hear the sound of the ram's horn?
22 "For My people are fools;
they do not know Me.
They are foolish children,
without understanding.
They are skilled in doing what is evil,
but they do not know how to do what is good."
23 I looked at the earth,
and it was formless and empty.
I looked to the heavens,
and their light was gone.
24 I looked at the mountains,
and they were quaking;
all the hills shook.
25 I looked, and no man was left;
all the birds of the sky had fled.
26 I looked, and the fertile field was a wilderness.
All its cities were torn down
because of the LORD
and His burning anger.
27 For this is what the LORD says:
The whole land will be a desolation,
but I will not finish it off.
28 Because of this, the earth will mourn;
the skies above will grow dark.
I have spoken; I have planned,
and I will not relent or turn back from it.
29 Every city flees
at the sound of the horseman and the archer.
They enter the thickets
and climb among the rocks.
Every city is abandoned;
no inhabitant is left.
30 And you, devastated one, what are you doing
that you dress yourself in scarlet,
that you adorn yourself with gold jewelry,
that you enlarge your eyes with paint?

You beautify yourself for nothing.
Your lovers reject you;
they want to take your life.
31 I hear a cry like a woman in labor,
a cry of anguish like one bearing
her first child.
The cry of Daughter Zion gasping for breath,
stretching out her hands:
Woe is me, for my life is weary
because of the murderers!

5 Roam through the streets of Jerusalem.
Look and take note;
search in her squares.
If you find one person,
any who acts justly,
who seeks to be faithful,
then I will forgive her.
2 When they say, "As the LORD lives,"
they are swearing falsely.
3 LORD, don't Your eyes look for faithfulness?
You have struck them, but they felt no pain.
You finished them off,
but they refused to accept discipline.
They made their faces harder than rock,
and they refused to return.
4 Then I thought:
They are just the poor;
they have played the fool.
For they don't understand the way of the LORD,
the justice of their God.
5 I will go to the powerful
and speak to them.
Surely they know the way of the LORD,
the justice of their God.
However, these also had broken the yoke
and torn off the chains.
6 Therefore, a lion from the forest
will strike them down.
A wolf from an arid plain will ravage them.
A leopard keeps watch over their cities.
Anyone who leaves them will be torn to pieces
because their rebellious acts are many,
their unfaithful deeds numerous.
7 Why should I forgive you?
Your children have abandoned Me
and sworn by those who are not gods.
I satisfied their needs, yet they
committed adultery;
they gashed themselves
at the prostitute's house.
8 They are well-fed, eager stallions,
each neighing after someone else's wife.
9 Should I not punish them for these things?
This is the LORD's declaration.
Should I not avenge Myself
on such a nation as this?
10 Go up among her vineyard terraces
and destroy them,
but do not finish them off.
Prune away her shoots,
for they do not belong to the LORD.
11 They, the house of Israel and the house
of Judah,
have dealt very treacherously with Me.
This is the LORD's declaration.
12 They have contradicted the LORD
and insisted, "It won't happen.

Harm won't come to us;
we won't see sword or famine."
¹³ The prophets become only wind,
for the Lord's word is not in them.
This will in fact happen to them.
¹⁴Therefore, this is what the Lord God of •Hosts says:
Because you have spoken this word,
I am going to make My words
become fire in your mouth.
These people are the wood,
and the fire will consume them.
¹⁵ I am about to bring a nation
from far away against you,
house of Israel.
                    This is the Lord's declaration.
It is an established nation,
an ancient nation,
a nation whose language you do not know
and whose speech you do not understand.
¹⁶ Their quiver is like an open grave;
they are all mighty warriors.
¹⁷ They will consume your harvest
and your food.
They will consume your sons
and your daughters.
They will consume your flocks and your herds.
They will consume your vines
and your fig trees.
They will destroy with the sword
your fortified cities
in which you trust.
¹⁸"But even in those days"—this is the Lord's declaration—"I will not finish you off. ¹⁹When people ask, 'For what offense has the Lord our God done all these things to us?' You will respond to them: Just as you abandoned Me and served foreign gods in your land, so will you serve strangers in a land that is not yours.

²⁰"Declare this in the house of Jacob; proclaim it in Judah, saying:
²¹ Hear this,
you foolish and senseless people.
They have eyes, but they don't see.
They have ears, but they don't hear.
²² Do you not •fear Me?
                    This is the Lord's declaration.
Do you not tremble before Me,
the One who set the sand as the boundary
of the sea,
an enduring barrier that it cannot cross?
The waves surge, but they cannot prevail.
They roar but cannot pass over it.
²³ But these people have stubborn
and rebellious hearts.
They have turned aside and have gone away.
²⁴ They have not said to themselves,
'Let's fear the Lord our God,
who gives the rain, both early and late,
in its season,
who guarantees to us the fixed weeks
of the harvest.'
²⁵ Your •guilty acts have diverted these things
from you.
Your sins have withheld My bounty from you,
²⁶ for wicked men live among My people.
They watch like fowlers lying in wait.
They set a trap;
they catch men.

²⁷ Like a cage full of birds,
so their houses are full of deceit.
Therefore they have grown powerful and rich.
²⁸ They have become fat and sleek.
They have also excelled in evil matters.
They have not taken up cases,
such as the case of the fatherless,
    so they might prosper,
and they have not defended the rights
of the needy.
²⁹ Should I not punish them for these things?
                    This is the Lord's declaration.
Should I not avenge Myself
on such a nation as this?
³⁰ A horrible, terrible thing
has taken place in the land.
³¹ The prophets prophesy falsely,
and the priests rule by their own authority.
My people love it like this.
But what will you do at the end of it?

6

"Run for cover, Benjaminites,
out of Jerusalem!
Sound the ram's horn in Tekoa;
raise a smoke signal over Beth-haccherem,
for disaster threatens from the north,
even great destruction.
² Though she is beautiful and delicate,
I will destroy Daughter •Zion.
³ Shepherds and their flocks will come
    against her;
they will pitch their tents all around her.
Each will pasture his own portion.
⁴ Set them apart for war against her;
rise up, let's attack at noon.
Woe to us, for the day is passing;
the evening shadows grow long.
⁵ Rise up, let's attack by night.
Let us destroy her fortresses."
⁶ For this is what the Lord of •Hosts says:
Cut down the trees;
raise a siege ramp against Jerusalem.
This city must be punished.
There is nothing but oppression within her.
⁷ As a well gushes out its water,
so she pours out her evil.
Violence and destruction resound in her.
Sickness and wounds keep coming
    to My attention.
⁸ Be warned, Jerusalem,
or I will turn away from you;
I will make you a desolation,
a land without inhabitants.
⁹ This is what the Lord of Hosts says:
Glean the remnant of Israel
as thoroughly as a vine.
Pass your hand once more
    like a grape gatherer
over the branches.
¹⁰ Who can I speak to and give such a warning
that they will listen?
Look, their ear is uncircumcised,
so they cannot pay attention.
See, the word of the Lord
    has become contemptible to them—
they find no pleasure in it.
¹¹ But I am full of the Lord's wrath;
I am tired of holding it back.

Pour it out on the children in the street,
on the gang of young men as well.
For both husband and wife will be captured,
the old with the very old.

12 Their houses will be turned over to others,
their fields and wives as well,
for I will stretch out My hand
against the inhabitants of the land.
This is the LORD's declaration.

13 For from the least to the greatest of them,
everyone is making profit dishonestly.
From prophet to priest,
everyone deals falsely.

14 They have treated
My people's brokenness superficially,
claiming, "Peace, peace,"
when there is no peace.

15 Were they ashamed when they acted
so abhorrently?
They weren't at all ashamed.
They can no longer feel humiliation.
Therefore, they will fall among the fallen.
When I punish them, they will collapse,
says the LORD.

16 This is what the LORD says:
Stand by the roadways and look.
Ask about the ancient paths:
Which is the way to what is good?
Then take it
and find rest for yourselves.
But they protested, "We won't!"

17 I appointed watchmen over you
and said: Listen for the sound
of the ram's horn.
But they protested, "We won't listen!"

18 Therefore listen, you nations
and you witnesses,
learn what the charge is against them.

19 Listen, earth!
I am about to bring disaster on these people,
the fruit of their own plotting,
for they have paid no attention to My word.
They have rejected My instruction.

20 What use to Me is frankincense from Sheba
or sweet cane from a distant land?
Your *burnt offerings are not acceptable;
your sacrifices do not please Me.

21 Therefore, this is what the LORD says:
I am going to place stumbling blocks
before these people;
fathers and sons together will stumble
over them;
friends and neighbors will also perish.

22 This is what the LORD says:
Look, an army is coming
from a northern land;
a great nation will be awakened
from the remote regions of the earth.

23 They grasp bow and javelin.
They are cruel and show no mercy.
Their voice roars like the sea,
and they ride on horses,
lined up like men in battle formation
against you, Daughter Zion.

24 We have heard about it,
and we are discouraged.
Distress has seized us—

pain like a woman in labor.

25 Don't go out to the fields;
don't walk on the road.
For the enemy has a sword;
terror is on every side.

26 My dear people, dress yourselves in *sackcloth
and roll in the dust.
Mourn as you would for an only son,
a bitter lament,
for suddenly the destroyer will come on us.

27 I have appointed you to be an assayer
among My people—
a refiner—
so you may know and assay their way of life.

28 All are stubborn rebels
spreading slander.
They are bronze and iron;
all of them are corrupt.

29 The bellows blow,
blasting the lead with fire.
The refining is completely in vain;
the evil ones are not separated out.

30 They are called rejected silver,
for the LORD has rejected them.

7 This is the word that came to Jeremiah from the LORD: [2]"Stand in the gate of the house of the LORD and there call out this word: Hear the word of the LORD, all you people of Judah who enter through these gates to worship the LORD.

[3]"This is what the LORD of *Hosts, the God of Israel, says: Correct your ways and your deeds, and I will allow you to live in this place. [4]Do not trust deceitful words, chanting: This is the temple of the LORD, the temple of the LORD, the temple of the LORD. [5]Instead, if you really change your ways and your actions, if you act justly toward one another, [6]if you no longer oppress the foreigner, the fatherless, and the widow and no longer shed innocent blood in this place or follow other gods, bringing harm on yourselves, [7]I will allow you to live in this place, the land I gave to your ancestors long ago and forever. [8]But look, you keep trusting in deceitful words that cannot help.

[9]"Do you steal, murder, commit adultery, swear falsely, burn incense to *Baal, and follow other gods that you have not known? [10]Then do you come and stand before Me in this house called by My name and say, 'We are delivered, so we can continue doing all these detestable acts'? [11]Has this house, which is called by My name, become a den of robbers in your view? Yes, I too have seen it.
This is the LORD's declaration.

[12]"But return to My place that was at Shiloh, where I made My name dwell at first. See what I did to it because of the evil of My people Israel. [13]Now, because you have done all these things"—this is the LORD's declaration—"and because I have spoken to you time and time again but you wouldn't listen, and I have called to you, but you wouldn't answer, [14]what I did to Shiloh I will do to the house that is called by My name—the house in which you trust—the place that I gave you and your ancestors. [15]I will drive you from My presence, just as I drove out all of your brothers, all the descendants of Ephraim.

[16]"As for you, do not pray for these people. Do not offer a cry or a prayer on their behalf, and do not beg Me, for I will not listen to you. [17]Don't you see how they behave in the cities of Judah and in the streets of

Jerusalem? [18]The sons gather wood, the fathers light the fire, and the women knead dough to make cakes for the queen of heaven, and they pour out •drink offerings to other gods so that they provoke Me to anger. [19]But are they really provoking Me?" This is the LORD's declaration. "Isn't it they themselves being provoked to disgrace?"

[20]Therefore, this is what the Lord GOD says: "Look, My anger—My burning wrath—is about to be poured out on this place, on man and beast, on the tree of the field, and on the produce of the land. My wrath will burn and not be quenched."

[21]This is what the LORD of Hosts, the God of Israel, says: "Add your •burnt offerings to your other sacrifices, and eat the meat yourselves, [22]for when I brought your ancestors out of the land of Egypt, I did not speak with them or command them concerning burnt offering and sacrifice. [23]However, I did give them this command: Obey Me, and then I will be your God, and you will be My people. You must follow every way I command you so that it may go well with you. [24]Yet they didn't listen or pay attention but followed their own advice and according to their own stubborn, evil heart. They went backward and not forward. [25]Since the day your ancestors came out of the land of Egypt until this day, I have sent all My servants the prophets to you time and time again. [26]However, they wouldn't listen to Me or pay attention but became obstinate; they did more evil than their ancestors.

[27]"When you speak all these things to them, they will not listen to you. When you call to them, they will not answer you. [28]You must therefore declare to them: This is the nation that would not listen to the voice of the LORD their God and would not accept discipline. Truth has perished—it has disappeared from their mouths. [29]Cut off the hair of your sacred vow and throw it away. Raise up a dirge on the barren heights, for the LORD has rejected and abandoned the generation under His wrath.

[30]"For the Judeans have done what is evil in My sight." This is the LORD's declaration. "They have set up their detestable things in the house that is called by My name and defiled it. [31]They have built the •high places of •Topheth in the Valley of Hinnom in order to burn their sons and daughters in the fire, a thing I did not command; I never entertained the thought.

[32]"Therefore, take note! Days are coming"—the LORD's declaration—"when this place will no longer be called Topheth and the Valley of Hinnom, but the Valley of Slaughter. Topheth will become a cemetery, because there will be no other burial place. [33]The corpses of these people will become food for the birds of the sky and for the wild animals of the land, with no one to scare them away. [34]I will remove from the cities of Judah and the streets of Jerusalem the sound of joy and gladness and the voices of the groom and the bride, for the land will become a desolate waste.

8 "At that time"—this is the LORD's declaration—"the bones of the kings of Judah, the bones of her officials, the bones of the priests, the bones of the prophets, and the bones of the residents of Jerusalem will be brought out of their graves. [2]They will be exposed to the sun, the moon, and the whole heavenly •host, which they have loved, served, followed, consulted, and worshiped. Their bones will not be collected and buried but will become like manure on the surface of the soil. [3]Death will be chosen over life by all the survivors of this evil family, those who remain wherever I have banished them." This is the declaration of the LORD of Hosts.

[4]"You are to say to them: This is what the LORD says:
Do people fall and not get up again?
    If they turn away, do they not return?
[5]   Why have these people turned away?
    Why is Jerusalem always turning away?
    They take hold of deceit;
    they refuse to return.
[6]   I have paid careful attention.
    They do not speak what is right.
    No one regrets his evil,
    asking, 'What have I done?'
    Everyone has stayed his course
    like a horse rushing into battle.
[7]   Even the stork in the sky
    knows her seasons.
    The turtledove, swallow, and crane
    are aware of their migration,
    but My people do not know
    the requirements of the LORD.
[8]   How can you claim, 'We are wise;
    the law of the LORD is with us'?
    In fact, the lying pen of scribes
    has produced falsehood.
[9]   The wise will be put to shame;
    they will be dismayed and snared.
    They have rejected the word of the LORD,
    so what wisdom do they really have?
[10]   Therefore, I will give their wives to other men,
    their fields to new occupants,
    for from the least to the greatest,
    everyone is making profit dishonestly.
    From prophet to priest,
    everyone deals falsely.
[11]   They have treated superficially the brokenness
    of My dear people,
    claiming, 'Peace, peace,'
    when there is no peace.
[12]   Were they ashamed when they acted
        so abhorrently?
    They weren't at all ashamed.
    They can no longer feel humiliation.
    Therefore, they will fall among the fallen.
    When I punish them, they will collapse,"
    says the LORD.
[13]   I will gather them and bring them to an end.
            This is the LORD's declaration.
    There will be no grapes on the vine,
    no figs on the fig tree,
    and even the leaf will wither.
    Whatever I have given them will be lost
        to them.
[14]   Why are we just sitting here?
    Gather together; let us enter
        the fortified cities
    and perish there,
    for the LORD our God has destroyed us.
    He has given us poisoned water to drink,
    because we have sinned against the LORD.
[15]   We hoped for peace, but there was
        nothing good;
    for a time of healing, but there was
        only terror.
[16]   From Dan the snorting of horses
        is heard.

At the sound of the neighing of mighty steeds,
the whole land quakes.
They come to devour the land and everything
in it,
the city and all its residents.

¹⁷ Indeed, I am about to send snakes among you,
poisonous vipers that cannot be charmed.
They will bite you.
This is the LORD's declaration.

¹⁸ My joy has flown away;
grief has settled on me.
My heart is sick.

¹⁹ Listen—the cry of my dear people
from a far away land,
"Is the LORD no longer in *Zion,
her King not within her?"
Why have they provoked me to anger
with their carved images,
with their worthless foreign idols?

²⁰ Harvest has passed, summer has ended,
but we have not been saved.

²¹ I am broken by the brokenness
of my dear people.
I mourn; horror has taken hold of me.

²² Is there no balm in Gilead?
Is there no physician there?
So why has the healing of my dear people
not come about?

9 If my head were a spring of water,
my eyes a fountain of tears,
I would weep day and night
over the slain of my dear people.

² If only I had a traveler's lodging place
in the wilderness,
I would abandon my people
and depart from them,
for they are all adulterers,
a solemn assembly of treacherous people.

³ They bent their tongues like their bows;
lies and not faithfulness prevail in the land,
for they proceed from one evil to another,
and they do not take Me into account.
This is the LORD's declaration.

⁴ Everyone has to be on guard
against his friend.
Don't trust any brother,
for every brother will certainly deceive,
and every friend spread slander.

⁵ Each one betrays his friend;
no one tells the truth.
They have taught their tongues to speak lies;
they wear themselves out doing wrong.

⁶ You live in a world of deception.
In their deception they refuse to know Me.
This is the LORD's declaration.

⁷ Therefore, this is what the LORD of *Hosts says:
I am about to refine them and test them,
for what else can I do
because of My dear people?

⁸ Their tongues are deadly arrows—
they speak deception.
With his mouth
a man speaks peaceably with his friend,
but inwardly he sets up an ambush.

⁹ Should I not punish them for these things?
This is the LORD's declaration.
Should I not avenge Myself

on such a nation as this?

¹⁰ I will raise weeping and a lament
over the mountains,
a dirge over the wilderness grazing land,
for they have been so scorched
that no one passes through.
The sound of cattle is no longer heard.
From the birds of the sky to the animals,
everything has fled—they have gone away.

¹¹ I will make Jerusalem a heap of rubble,
a jackals' den.
I will make the cities of Judah a desolation,
an uninhabited place.

¹² Who is the man wise enough to understand this? Who has the LORD spoken to, that he may explain it? Why is the land destroyed and scorched like a wilderness, so no one can pass through?

¹³ The LORD said, "It is because they abandoned My instruction that I set in front of them and did not obey My voice or walk according to it. ¹⁴ Instead, they followed the stubbornness of their hearts and followed after the *Baals as their fathers taught them." ¹⁵ Therefore, this is what the LORD of Hosts, the God of Israel, says: "I am about to feed this people *wormwood and give them poisonous water to drink. ¹⁶ I will scatter them among the nations that they and their fathers have not known. I will send a sword after them until I have finished them off."

¹⁷ This is what the LORD of Hosts says:
Consider, and summon the women
who mourn;
send for the skillful women.

¹⁸ Let them come quickly to raise a lament
over us
so that our eyes may overflow with tears,
our eyelids soaked with weeping.

¹⁹ For a sound of lamentation is heard
from *Zion:
How devastated we are.
We are greatly ashamed,
for we have abandoned the land;
our dwellings have been torn down.

²⁰ Now hear the word of the LORD, you women.
Pay attention to the word of His mouth.
Teach your daughters a lament
and one another a dirge,

²¹ for Death has climbed through our windows;
it has entered our fortresses,
cutting off children from the streets,
young men from the squares.

²² Speak as follows:
This is what the LORD says:
Human corpses will fall
like manure on the surface of the field,
like newly cut grain after the reaper
with no one to gather it.

²³ This is what the LORD says:
The wise man must not boast in his wisdom;
the strong man must not boast
in his strength;
the wealthy man must not boast in his wealth.

²⁴ But the one who boasts should boast in this,
that he understands and knows Me—
that I am *Yahweh, showing faithful love,
justice, and righteousness on the earth,
for I delight in these things.
This is the LORD's declaration.

²⁵ "The days are coming"—the Lord's declaration—"when I will punish all the circumcised yet uncircumcised: ²⁶ Egypt, Judah, Edom, the Ammonites, Moab, and all the inhabitants of the desert who clip the hair on their temples. All these nations are uncircumcised, and the whole house of Israel is uncircumcised in heart."

10 Hear the word that the Lord has spoken to you, house of Israel. ² This is what the Lord says:
Do not learn the way of the nations
or be terrified by signs in the heavens,
although the nations are terrified by them,
³   for the customs of the peoples are worthless.
Someone cuts down a tree from the forest;
it is worked by the hands of a craftsman
with a chisel.
⁴   He decorates it with silver and gold.
It is fastened with hammer and nails,
so it won't totter.
⁵   Like scarecrows in a cucumber patch,
their idols cannot speak.
They must be carried because
they cannot walk.
Do not fear them for they can do no harm—
and they cannot do any good.
⁶   •Yahweh, there is no one like You.
You are great;
Your name is great in power.
⁷   Who should not •fear You,
King of the nations?
It is what You deserve.
For among all the wise people of the nations
and among all their kingdoms,
there is no one like You.
⁸   They are both stupid and foolish,
instructed by worthless idols
made of wood!
⁹   Beaten silver is brought from Tarshish,
and gold from Uphaz
from the hands of a goldsmith,
the work of a craftsman.
Their clothing is blue and purple,
all the work of skilled artisans.
¹⁰   But Yahweh is the true God;
He is the living God and eternal King.
The earth quakes at His wrath,
and the nations cannot endure His rage.
¹¹ You are to say this to them, "The gods that did not make the heavens and the earth will perish from the earth and from under these heavens."
¹²   He made the earth by His power,
established the world by His wisdom,
and spread out the heavens
by His understanding.
¹³   When He thunders,
the waters in the heavens are in turmoil,
and He causes the clouds to rise
from the ends of the earth.
He makes lightning for the rain
and brings the wind from His storehouses.
¹⁴   Everyone is stupid and ignorant.
Every goldsmith is put to shame
by his carved image,
for his cast images are a lie;
there is no breath in them.
¹⁵   They are worthless, a work to be mocked.
At the time of their punishment

they will be destroyed.
¹⁶   Jacob's Portion is not like these
because He is the One who formed all things.
Israel is the tribe of His inheritance;
Yahweh of •Hosts is His name.
¹⁷   Gather up your belongings from the ground,
you who live under siege.
¹⁸ For this is what the Lord says:
Look, I am slinging out
the land's residents at this time
and bringing them such distress
that they will feel it.
¹⁹   Woe to me because of my brokenness—
I am severely wounded!
I exclaimed, "This is my intense suffering,
but I must bear it."
²⁰   My tent is destroyed;
all my tent cords are snapped.
My sons have departed from me and are
no more.
I have no one to pitch my tent again
or to hang up my curtains.
²¹   For the shepherds are stupid:
they don't seek the Lord.
Therefore they have not prospered,
and their whole flock is scattered.
²²   Listen! A noise—it is coming—
a great commotion from the land
to the north.
The cities of Judah will be made desolate,
a jackals' den.
²³   I know, Lord,
that a man's way of life is not his own;
no one who walks determines
his own steps.
²⁴   Discipline me, Lord, but with justice—
not in Your anger,
or You will reduce me to nothing.
²⁵   Pour out Your wrath on the nations
that don't recognize You
and on the families
that don't call on Your name,
for they have consumed Jacob;
they have consumed him and finished him off
and made his homeland desolate.

11 This is the word that came to Jeremiah from the Lord: ² "Listen to the words of this covenant and tell them to the men of Judah and the residents of Jerusalem. ³ You must tell them: This is what the Lord, the God of Israel, says: 'Let a curse be on the man who does not obey the words of this covenant, ⁴ which I commanded your ancestors when I brought them out of the land of Egypt, out of the iron furnace.' I declared: 'Obey Me, and do everything that I command you, and you will be My people, and I will be your God,' ⁵ in order to establish the oath I swore to your ancestors, to give them a land flowing with milk and honey, as it is today."

I answered, "'Amen, Lord.'"

⁶ The Lord said to me, "Proclaim all these words in the cities of Judah and in the streets of Jerusalem: Obey the words of this covenant and carry them out. ⁷ For I strongly warned your ancestors when I brought them out of the land of Egypt until today, warning them time and time again, 'Obey My voice.' ⁸ Yet they would not obey or pay attention; each one followed the stubbornness of his evil heart. So I brought on them

all the curses of this covenant, because they had not done what I commanded them to do."

⁹ The Lord said to me, "A conspiracy has been discovered among the men of Judah and the residents of Jerusalem. ¹⁰ They have returned to the sins of their ancestors who refused to obey My words and have followed other gods to worship them. The house of Israel and the house of Judah broke My covenant I made with their ancestors.

¹¹ "Therefore, this is what the Lord says: I am about to bring on them disaster that they cannot escape. They will cry out to Me, but I will not hear them. ¹² Then the cities of Judah and the residents of Jerusalem will go and cry out to the gods they have been burning incense to, but they certainly will not save them in their time of disaster. ¹³ Your gods are indeed as numerous as your cities, Judah, and the altars you have set up to Shame—altars to burn incense to •Baal—as numerous as the streets of Jerusalem.

¹⁴ "As for you, do not pray for these people. Do not raise up a cry or a prayer on their behalf, for I will not be listening when they call out to Me at the time of their disaster.

15 What right does My beloved have
    to be in My house,
    having carried out so many evil schemes?
    Can holy meat prevent your disaster
    so you can rejoice?
16 The Lord named you
    a flourishing olive tree,
    beautiful with well-formed fruit.
    He has set fire to it,
    and its branches are consumed
    with a great roaring sound.

¹⁷ "The Lord of •Hosts who planted you has decreed disaster against you, because of the harm the house of Israel and the house of Judah brought on themselves, provoking Me to anger by burning incense to Baal."

18 The Lord informed me, so I knew.
    Then You helped me to see their deeds,
19 for I was like a docile lamb led to slaughter.
    I didn't know that they had devised plots
        against me:
    "Let's destroy the tree with its fruit;
    let's cut him off from the land of the living
    so that his name will no longer
        be remembered."
20 But, Lord of Hosts, who judges righteously,
    who tests heart and mind,
    let me see Your vengeance on them,
    for I have presented my case to You.

²¹ Therefore, here is what the Lord says concerning the people of Anathoth who want to take your life. They warn, "You must not prophesy in the name of •Yahweh, or you will certainly die at our hand." ²² Therefore, this is what the Lord of Hosts says: "I am about to punish them. The young men will die by the sword; their sons and daughters will die by famine. ²³ They will have no remnant, for I will bring disaster on the people of Anathoth in the year of their punishment."

12 You will be righteous, Lord,
    even if I bring a case against You.
    Yet, I wish to contend with You:
    Why does the way of the wicked prosper?
    Why do all the treacherous live at ease?
2   You planted them, and they have taken root.
    They have grown and produced fruit.

    You are ever on their lips,
    but far from their conscience.
3   As for You, Lord, You know me; You see me.
    You test whether my heart is with You.
    Drag the wicked away like sheep to slaughter
    and set them apart for the day of killing.
4   How long will the land mourn
    and the grass of every field wither?
    Because of the evil of its residents,
    animals and birds have been swept away,
    for the people have said,
    "He cannot see what our end will be."
5   If you have raced with runners
    and they have worn you out,
    how can you compete with horses?
    If you stumble in a peaceful land,
    what will you do in the thickets of the Jordan?
6   Even your brothers—
    your own father's household—
    even they were treacherous to you;
    even they have cried out loudly after you.
    Do not have confidence in them,
    though they speak well of you.
7   I have abandoned My house;
    I have deserted My inheritance.
    I have given the love of My life
    into the hands of her enemies.
8   My inheritance has acted toward Me
    like a lion in the forest.
    She has roared against Me.
    Therefore, I hate her.
9   Is My inheritance like a hyena to Me?
    Are birds of prey circling her?
    Go, gather all the wild animals;
    bring them to devour her.
10 Many shepherds have destroyed My vineyard;
    they have trampled My plot of land.
    They have turned My desirable plot
    into a desolate wasteland.
11 They have made it a desolation.
    It mourns, desolate, before Me.
    All the land is desolate,
    but no one takes it to heart.
12 Over all the barren heights in the wilderness
    the destroyers have come,
    for the Lord has a sword that devours
    from one end of the earth to the other.
    No one has peace.
13 They have sown wheat but harvested thorns.
    They have exhausted themselves but have
        no profit.
    Be put to shame by your harvests
    because of the Lord's burning anger.

¹⁴ This is what the Lord says: "Concerning all My evil neighbors who attack the inheritance that I bequeathed to My people, Israel, I am about to uproot them from their land, and I will uproot the house of Judah from them. ¹⁵ After I have uprooted them, I will once again have compassion on them and return each one to his inheritance and to his land. ¹⁶ If they will diligently learn the ways of My people—to swear by My name, 'As •Yahweh lives,' just as they taught My people to swear by •Baal—they will be built up among My people. ¹⁷ However, if they will not obey, then I will uproot and destroy that nation."

                        This is the Lord's declaration.

13 This is what the Lord said to me: "Go and buy yourself a linen undergarment and put it on, but do not put it in water." ²So I bought underwear as the Lord instructed me and put it on.

³Then the word of the Lord came to me a second time: ⁴"Take the underwear that you bought and are wearing, and go at once to the Euphrates and hide it in a rocky crevice." ⁵So I went and hid it by the Euphrates, as the Lord commanded me.

⁶A long time later the Lord said to me, "Go at once to the Euphrates and get the underwear that I commanded you to hide there." ⁷So I went to the Euphrates and dug up the underwear and got it from the place where I had hidden it, but it was ruined—of no use at all.

⁸Then the word of the Lord came to me: ⁹"This is what the Lord says: Just like this I will ruin the great pride of both Judah and Jerusalem. ¹⁰These evil people, who refuse to listen to Me, who follow the stubbornness of their own hearts, and who have followed other gods to serve and worship—they will be like this underwear, of no use at all. ¹¹Just as underwear clings to one's waist, so I fastened the whole house of Israel and of Judah to Me"—this is the Lord's declaration—"so that they might be My people for My fame, praise, and glory, but they would not obey.

¹²"Say this to them: This is what the Lord, the God of Israel, says: Every jar should be filled with wine. Then they will respond to you, 'Don't we know that every jar should be filled with wine?' ¹³And you will say to them: This is what the Lord says: I am about to fill all who live in this land—the kings who reign for David on his throne, the priests, the prophets and all the residents of Jerusalem—with drunkenness. ¹⁴I will smash them against each other, fathers and sons alike"—this is the Lord's declaration. "I will allow no mercy, pity, or compassion to keep Me from destroying them."

¹⁵ Listen and pay attention. Do not be proud,
for the Lord has spoken.
¹⁶ Give glory to the Lord your God
before He brings darkness,
before your feet stumble
on the mountains at dusk.
You wait for light,
but He brings darkest gloom
and makes thick darkness.
¹⁷ But if you will not listen,
my innermost being will weep in secret
because of your pride.
My eyes will overflow with tears,
for the Lord's flock has been taken captive.
¹⁸ Say to the king and the queen mother:
Take a humble seat,
for your glorious crowns
have fallen from your heads.
¹⁹ The cities of the *Negev are under siege;
no one can help them.
All of Judah has been taken into exile,
taken completely into exile.
²⁰ Look up and see
those coming from the north.
Where is the flock entrusted to you,
the sheep that were your pride?
²¹ What will you say when He appoints
close friends as leaders over you,
ones you yourself trained?
Won't labor pains seize you,

as they do a woman in labor?
²² And when you ask yourself,
"Why have these things happened to me?"
It is because of your great *guilt
that your skirts have been stripped off,
your body exposed.
²³ Can the *Cushite change his skin,
or a leopard his spots?
If so, you might be able to do what is good,
you who are instructed in evil.
²⁴ I will scatter you like drifting chaff
before the desert wind.
²⁵ This is your lot,
what I have decreed for you—
this is the Lord's declaration—
because you have forgotten Me
and trusted in Falsehood.
²⁶ I will pull your skirts up over your face
so that your shame might be seen.
²⁷ Your adulteries and your lustful neighing,
your heinous prostitution
on the hills, in the fields—
I have seen your detestable acts.
Woe to you, Jerusalem!
You are *unclean—
for how long yet?

14 The word of the Lord that came to Jeremiah concerning the drought:
² Judah mourns;
her gates languish.
Her people are on the ground in mourning;
Jerusalem's cry rises up.
³ Their nobles send their servants for water.
They go to the cisterns;
they find no water;
their containers return empty.
They are ashamed and humiliated;
they cover their heads.
⁴ The ground is cracked
since no rain has fallen on the land.
The farmers are ashamed;
they cover their heads.
⁵ Even the doe in the field
gives birth and abandons her fawn
since there is no grass.
⁶ Wild donkeys stand on the barren heights
panting for air like jackals.
Their eyes fail
because there are no green plants.
⁷ Though our *guilt testifies against us,
*Yahweh, act for Your name's sake.
Indeed, our rebellions are many;
we have sinned against You.
⁸ Hope of Israel,
its Savior in time of distress,
why are You like a foreigner in the land,
like a traveler stopping only for the night?
⁹ Why are You like a helpless man,
like a warrior unable to save?
Yet You are among us, Yahweh,
and we are called by Your name.
Don't leave us!

¹⁰This is what the Lord says concerning these people:
Truly they love to wander;
they never rest their feet.
So the Lord does not accept them.

Now He will remember their guilt
and punish their sins.

¹¹ Then the Lord said to me, "Do not pray for the well-being of these people. ¹² If they fast, I will not hear their cry of despair. If they offer ˙burnt offering and ˙grain offering, I will not accept them. Rather, I will finish them off by sword, famine, and plague."

¹³ And I replied, "Oh no, Lord God! The prophets are telling them, 'You won't see sword or suffer famine. I will certainly give you true peace in this place.'"

¹⁴ But the Lord said to me, "These prophets are prophesying a lie in My name. I did not send them, nor did I command them or speak to them. They are prophesying to you a false vision, worthless ˙divination, the deceit of their own minds.

¹⁵ "Therefore, this is what the Lord says concerning the prophets who prophesy in My name, though I did not send them, and who say, 'There will never be sword or famine in this land.' By sword and famine these prophets will meet their end. ¹⁶ The people they are prophesying to will be thrown into the streets of Jerusalem because of the famine and the sword. There will be no one to bury them—they, their wives, their sons, and their daughters. I will pour out their own evil on them."

¹⁷   You are to speak this word to them:
Let my eyes overflow with tears;
day and night may they not stop,
for the virgin daughter of my people
has been destroyed by a great disaster,
an extremely severe wound.

¹⁸   If I go out to the field,
look—those slain by the sword!
If I enter the city,
look—those ill from famine!
For both prophet and priest
travel to a land they do not know.

¹⁹   Have You completely rejected Judah?
Do You detest ˙Zion?
Why do You strike us
with no hope of healing for us?
We hoped for peace,
but there was nothing good;
for a time of healing,
but there was only terror.

²⁰   We acknowledge our wickedness, Lord,
the guilt of our fathers;
indeed, we have sinned against You.

²¹   Because of Your name, don't despise us.
Don't disdain Your glorious throne.
Remember Your covenant with us;
do not break it.

²²   Can any of the worthless idols of the nations
bring rain?
Or can the skies alone give showers?
Are You not the Lord our God?
We therefore put our hope in You,
for You have done all these things.

15 Then the Lord said to me: "Even if Moses and Samuel should stand before Me, My compassions would not reach out to these people. Send them from My presence, and let them go. ² If they ask you, 'Where will we go?' you must tell them: This is what the Lord says:

Those destined for death, to death;
those destined for the sword, to the sword.
Those destined for famine, to famine;

those destined for captivity, to captivity.

³ "I will ordain four kinds of judgment for them"—this is the Lord's declaration—"the sword to kill, the dogs to drag away, and the birds of the sky and the wild animals of the land to devour and destroy. ⁴ I will make them a horror to all the kingdoms of the earth because of Manasseh son of Hezekiah, the king of Judah, for what he did in Jerusalem.

⁵   Who will have pity on you, Jerusalem?
Who will show sympathy toward you?
Who will turn aside
to ask about your welfare?

⁶   You have left Me.
                 This is the Lord's declaration.
You have turned your back,
so I have stretched out My hand against you
and destroyed you.
I am tired of showing compassion.

⁷   I scattered them with a winnowing fork
at the gates of the land.
I made them childless; I destroyed My people.
They would not turn from their ways.

⁸   I made their widows more numerous
than the sand of the seas.
I brought a destroyer at noon
against the mother of young men.
I suddenly released on her
agitation and terrors.

⁹   The mother of seven grew faint;
she breathed her last breath.
Her sun set while it was still day;
she was ashamed and humiliated.
The rest of them I will give over to the sword
in the presence of their enemies."
                 This is the Lord's declaration.

¹⁰   Woe is me, my mother,
that you gave birth to me,
a man who incites dispute and conflict
in all the land.
I did not lend or borrow,
yet everyone curses me.

¹¹ The Lord said:
I will certainly set you free and care for you.
I will certainly intercede for you
in a time of trouble,
in your time of distress, with the enemy.

¹²   Can anyone smash iron,
iron from the north, or bronze?

¹³   I will give up your wealth
and your treasures as plunder,
without cost, for all your sins
in all your borders.

¹⁴   Then I will make you serve your enemies
in a land you do not know,
for My anger will kindle a fire
that will burn against you.

¹⁵   You know, Lord;
remember me and take note of me.
Avenge me against my persecutors.
In Your patience, don't take me away.
Know that I suffer disgrace for Your honor.

¹⁶   Your words were found, and I ate them.
Your words became a delight to me
and the joy of my heart,
for I am called by Your name,
˙Yahweh God of ˙Hosts.

¹⁷   I never sat with the band of revelers,

and I did not celebrate with them.
Because Your hand was on me, I sat alone,
for You filled me with indignation.

18 Why has my pain become unending,
my wound incurable,
refusing to be healed?
You truly have become like a mirage to me—
water that is not reliable.

19 Therefore, this is what the Lord says:
If you return, I will restore you;
you will stand in My presence.
And if you speak noble words,
rather than worthless ones,
you will be My spokesman.
It is they who must return to you;
you must not return to them.

20 Then I will make you a fortified wall of bronze
to this people.
They will fight against you
but will not overcome you,
for I am with you
to save you and deliver you.
This is the Lord's declaration.

21 I will deliver you from the power of evil people
and redeem you from the control
of the ruthless.

16 The word of the Lord came to me: 2"You must not marry or have sons or daughters in this place. 3For this is what the Lord says concerning sons and daughters born in this place as well as concerning the mothers who bear them and the fathers who father them in this land: 4They will die from deadly diseases. They will not be mourned or buried but will be like manure on the face of the earth. They will be finished off by sword and famine. Their corpses will become food for the birds of the sky and for the wild animals of the land.

5"For this is what the Lord says: Don't enter a house where a mourning feast is taking place. Don't go to lament or sympathize with them, for I have removed My peace from these people"—this is the Lord's declaration—"as well as My faithful love and compassion. 6Both great and small will die in this land without burial. No lament will be made for them, nor will anyone cut himself or shave his head for them. 7Food won't be provided for the mourner to comfort him because of the dead. A cup of consolation won't be given him because of the loss of his father or mother. 8You must not enter the house where feasting is taking place to sit with them to eat and drink. 9For this is what the Lord of •Hosts, the God of Israel, says: I am about to eliminate from this place, before your very eyes and in your time, the sound of joy and gladness, the voice of the groom and the bride.

10"When you tell these people all these things, they will say to you, 'Why has the Lord declared all this great disaster against us? What is our •guilt? What is our sin that we have committed against the Lord our God?' 11Then you will answer them: Because your fathers abandoned Me"—this is the Lord's declaration—"and followed other gods, served them, and worshiped them. Indeed, they abandoned Me and did not keep My instruction. 12You did more evil than your fathers. Look, each one of you is following the stubbornness of his evil heart, not obeying Me. 13So I will hurl you from this land into a land that you and your fathers are

not familiar with. There you will worship other gods both day and night, for I will not grant you grace.

14"However, take note! The days are coming"—the Lord's declaration—"when it will no longer be said, 'As the Lord lives who brought the Israelites from the land of Egypt,' 15but rather, 'As the Lord lives who brought the Israelites from the land of the north and from all the other lands where He had banished them.' For I will return them to their land that I gave to their ancestors.

16"I am about to send for many fishermen"—this is the Lord's declaration—"and they will fish for them. Then I will send for many hunters, and they will hunt them down on every mountain and hill and out of the clefts of the rocks, 17for My gaze takes in all their ways. They are not concealed from Me, and their guilt is not hidden from My sight. 18I will first repay them double for their guilt and sin because they have polluted My land. They have filled My inheritance with the lifelessness of their detestable and abhorrent idols."

19 Lord, my strength and my stronghold,
my refuge in a time of distress,
the nations will come to You
from the ends of the earth, and they will say,
"Our fathers inherited only lies,
worthless idols of no benefit at all."

20 Can one make gods for himself?
But they are not gods.

21 "Therefore, I am about to inform them,
and this time I will make them know
My power and My might;
then they will know that My name is •Yahweh."

17 The sin of Judah is written
with an iron stylus.
With a diamond point
it is engraved on the tablet of their hearts
and on the horns of their altars,

2 while their children remember their altars
and their •Asherah poles, by the green trees
on the high hills—

3 My mountains in the countryside.
I will give up your wealth
and all your treasures as plunder
because of the sin of your •high places
in all your borders.

4 You will, on your own, relinquish
your inheritance
that I gave you.
I will make you serve your enemies
in a land you do not know,
for you have set My anger on fire;
it will burn forever.

5 This is what the Lord says:
The man who trusts in mankind,
who makes human flesh his strength
and turns his heart from the Lord is cursed.

6 He will be like a juniper in the •Arabah;
he cannot see when good comes
but dwells in the parched places
in the wilderness,
in a salt land where no one lives.

7 The man who trusts in the Lord,
whose confidence indeed is the Lord, is
blessed.

8 He will be like a tree planted by water:
it sends its roots out toward a stream,
it doesn't fear when heat comes,

and its foliage remains green.
It will not worry in a year of drought
or cease producing fruit.
⁹ The heart is more deceitful than anything else,
and incurable—who can understand it?
¹⁰ I, 'Yahweh, examine the mind,
I test the heart
to give to each according to his way,
according to what his actions deserve.
¹¹ He who makes a fortune unjustly
is like a partridge that hatches eggs
it didn't lay.
In the middle of his days
his riches will abandon him,
so in the end he will be a fool.
¹² A throne of glory
on high from the beginning
is the place of our sanctuary.
¹³ LORD, the hope of Israel,
all who abandon You
will be put to shame.
All who turn away from Me
will be written in the dirt,
for they have abandoned
the LORD, the fountain of living water.
¹⁴ Heal me, LORD, and I will be healed;
save me, and I will be saved,
for You are my praise.
¹⁵ Hear how they keep challenging me,
"Where is the word of the LORD?
Let it come!"
¹⁶ But I have not run away from being
Your shepherd,
and I have not longed for the fatal day.
You know my words were spoken
in Your presence.
¹⁷ Don't become a terror to me.
You are my refuge in the day of disaster.
¹⁸ Let my persecutors be put to shame,
but don't let me be put to shame.
Let them be terrified, but don't let me
be terrified.
Bring on them the day of disaster;
shatter them with total destruction.

¹⁹ This is what the LORD said to me, "Go and stand at the People's Gate, through which the kings of Judah enter and leave, as well as at all the gates of Jerusalem. ²⁰ Announce to them: Hear the word of the LORD, kings of Judah, all Judah, and all the residents of Jerusalem who enter through these gates. ²¹ This is what the LORD says: Watch yourselves; do not pick up a load and bring it in through the gates of Jerusalem on the Sabbath day. ²² You must not carry a load out of your houses on the Sabbath day or do any work, but you must consecrate the Sabbath day, just as I commanded your ancestors. ²³ They wouldn't listen or pay attention but became obstinate, not listening or accepting discipline.

²⁴ "However, if you listen to Me, says the LORD, and do not bring loads through the gates of this city on the Sabbath day and consecrate the Sabbath day and do no work on it, ²⁵ kings and princes will enter through the gates of this city. They will sit on the throne of David, riding in chariots and on horses with their officials, the men of Judah, and the residents of Jerusalem. This city will be inhabited forever. ²⁶ Then people will come from the cities of Judah and from the area around

Jerusalem, from the land of Benjamin and from the Judean foothills, from the hill country and from the 'Negev bringing 'burnt offerings and sacrifice, 'grain offerings and frankincense, and thank offerings to the house of the LORD. ²⁷ If you do not listen to Me to consecrate the Sabbath day by not carrying a load while entering the gates of Jerusalem on the Sabbath day, I will set fire to its gates, and it will consume the citadels of Jerusalem and not be extinguished."

18 This is the word that came to Jeremiah from the LORD: ² "Go down at once to the potter's house; there I will reveal My words to you." ³ So I went down to the potter's house, and there he was, working away at the wheel. ⁴ But the jar that he was making from the clay became flawed in the potter's hand, so he made it into another jar, as it seemed right for him to do.

⁵ The word of the LORD came to me: ⁶ "House of Israel, can I not treat you as this potter treats his clay?"—this is the LORD's declaration. "Just like clay in the potter's hand, so are you in My hand, house of Israel. ⁷ At one moment I might announce concerning a nation or a kingdom that I will uproot, tear down, and destroy it. ⁸ However, if that nation I have made an announcement about turns from its evil, I will relent concerning the disaster I had planned to do to it. ⁹ At another time I announce that I will build and plant a nation or a kingdom. ¹⁰ However, if it does what is evil in My sight by not listening to My voice, I will relent concerning the good I had said I would do to it. ¹¹ So now, say to the men of Judah and to the residents of Jerusalem: This is what the LORD says: I am about to bring harm to you and make plans against you. Turn now, each from your evil way, and correct your ways and your deeds. ¹² But they will say, 'It's hopeless. We will continue to follow our plans, and each of us will continue to act according to the stubbornness of his evil heart.'"

¹³ Therefore, this is what the LORD says:
Ask among the nations,
Who has heard things like these?
Virgin Israel has done a most terrible thing.
¹⁴ Does the snow of Lebanon ever leave
the highland crags?
Or does cold water flowing from a distance
ever fail?
¹⁵ Yet My people have forgotten Me.
They burn incense to false idols
that make them stumble in their ways
on the ancient roads
and walk on new paths, not the highway.
¹⁶ They have made their land a horror,
a perpetual object of scorn;
everyone who passes by it will be horrified
and shake his head.
¹⁷ I will scatter them before the enemy
like the east wind.
I will show them My back and not My face
on the day of their calamity.
¹⁸ Then certain ones said, "Come, let's make plans against Jeremiah, for instruction will never be lost from the priest, or counsel from the wise, or an 'oracle from the prophet. Come, let's denounce him and pay no attention to all his words."
¹⁹ Pay attention to me, LORD.
Hear what my opponents are saying!
²⁰ Should good be repaid with evil?
Yet they have dug a pit for me.

Remember how I stood before You
to speak good on their behalf,
to turn Your anger from them.
²¹ Therefore, hand their children over to famine,
and pour the sword's power on them.
Let their wives become childless and widowed,
their husbands slain by deadly disease,
their young men struck down by the sword
in battle.
²² Let a cry be heard from their houses
when You suddenly bring raiders
against them,
for they have dug a pit to capture me
and have hidden snares for my feet.
²³ But You, Lord, know
all their deadly plots against me.
Do not wipe out their *guilt;
do not blot out their sin before You.
Let them be forced to stumble before You;
deal with them in the time of Your anger.

19 This is what the Lord says: "Go, buy a potter's
clay jar. Take some of the elders of the people
and some of the leading priests ²and go out to the Valley of Hinnom near the entrance of the Potsherd Gate.
Proclaim there the words I speak to you. ³Say: Hear
the word of the Lord, kings of Judah and residents of
Jerusalem. This is what the Lord of *Hosts, the God
of Israel, says: I am going to bring such disaster on
this place that everyone who hears about it will shudder ⁴because they have abandoned Me and made this a
foreign place. They have burned incense in it to other
gods that they, their fathers, and the kings of Judah
have never known. They have filled this place with the
blood of the innocent. ⁵They have built *high places
to *Baal on which to burn their children in the fire
as burnt offerings to Baal, something I have never
commanded or mentioned; I never entertained the
thought.

⁶"Therefore, take note! The days are coming"—this
is the Lord's declaration—"when this place will no
longer be called Topheth and the Valley of Hinnom,
but the Valley of Slaughter. ⁷I will spoil the plans of
Judah and Jerusalem in this place. I will make them
fall by the sword before their enemies, by the hand of
those who want to take their life. I will provide their
corpses as food for the birds of the sky and for the wild
animals of the land. ⁸I will make this city desolate, an
object of scorn. Everyone who passes by it will be horrified and scoff because of all its wounds. ⁹I will make
them eat the flesh of their sons and their daughters,
and they will eat each other's flesh in the siege and distress that their enemies, those who want to take their
life, inflict on them.

¹⁰"Then you are to shatter the jar in the presence
of the people traveling with you, ¹¹and you are to proclaim to them: This is what the Lord of Hosts says: I
will shatter these people and this city, like one shatters
a potter's jar that can never again be mended. They
will bury the dead in Topheth because there is no other
place for burials. ¹²I will do so to this place"—this is
the declaration of the Lord—"and to its residents,
making this city like Topheth. ¹³The houses of Jerusalem and the houses of the kings of Judah will become impure like that place Topheth—all the houses
on whose rooftops they have burned incense to the
whole heavenly host and poured out *drink offerings
to other gods."

¹⁴Jeremiah came back from Topheth, where the
Lord had sent him to prophesy, stood in the courtyard of the Lord's temple, and proclaimed to all the
people, ¹⁵"This is what the Lord of Hosts, the God of
Israel, says: 'I am about to bring on this city—and on
all its dependent villages—all the disaster that I spoke
against it, for they have become obstinate, not obeying
My words.'"

20 Pashhur the priest, the son of Immer and
chief official in the temple of the Lord, heard
Jeremiah prophesying these things. ²So Pashhur had
Jeremiah the prophet beaten and put him in the stocks
at the Upper Benjamin Gate in the Lord's temple. ³The
next day, when Pashhur released Jeremiah from the
stocks, Jeremiah said to him, "The Lord does not call
you Pashhur, but Magor-missabib, ⁴for this is what the
Lord says, 'I am about to make you a terror to both
yourself and those you love. They will fall by the sword
of their enemies before your very eyes. I will hand Judah over to the king of Babylon, and he will deport
them to Babylon and put them to the sword. ⁵I will
give away all the wealth of this city, all its products and
valuables. Indeed, I will hand all the treasures of the
kings of Judah over to their enemies. They will plunder them, seize them, and carry them off to Babylon.
⁶As for you, Pashhur, and all who live in your house,
you will go into captivity. You will go to Babylon.
There you will die, and there you will be buried, you
and all your friends that you prophesied falsely to.'"

⁷ You deceived me, Lord, and I was deceived.
You seized me and prevailed.
I am a laughingstock all the time;
everyone ridicules me.
⁸ For whenever I speak, I cry out,
I proclaim, "Violence and destruction!"
because the word of the Lord has become
for me
constant disgrace and derision.
⁹ If I say, "I won't mention Him
or speak any longer in His name,"
His message becomes a fire burning
in my heart,
shut up in my bones.
I become tired of holding it in,
and I cannot prevail.
¹⁰ For I have heard the gossip of many people,
"Terror is on every side!
Report him; let's report him!"
Everyone I trusted watches for my fall.
"Perhaps he will be deceived
so that we might prevail against him
and take our vengeance on him."
¹¹ But the Lord is with me like a violent warrior.
Therefore, my persecutors will stumble
and not prevail.
Since they have not succeeded, they will be
utterly shamed,
an everlasting humiliation that will
never be forgotten.
¹² Lord of *Hosts, testing the righteous
and seeing the heart and mind,
let me see Your vengeance on them,
for I have presented my case to You.
¹³ Sing to the Lord!
Praise the Lord,
for He rescues the life of the needy
from the hand of evil people.

14 May the day I was born
    be cursed.
    May the day my mother bore me
    never be blessed.
15 May the man be cursed
    who brought the news to my father, saying,
    "A male child is born to you,"
    bringing him great joy.
16 Let that man be like the cities
    the LORD demolished without compassion.
    Let him hear an outcry in the morning
    and a war cry at noontime
17 because he didn't kill me in the womb
    so that my mother might have been my grave,
    her womb eternally pregnant.
18 Why did I come out of the womb
    to see only struggle and sorrow,
    to end my life in shame?

21 This is the word that came to Jeremiah from the LORD when King Zedekiah sent Pashhur son of Malchijah and the priest Zephaniah son of Maaseiah to Jeremiah, asking, ²"Ask the LORD on our behalf, since Nebuchadnezzar king of Babylon is making war against us. Perhaps the LORD will perform for us something like all His past wonderful works so that Nebuchadnezzar will withdraw from us."

³But Jeremiah answered, "This is what you are to say to Zedekiah: ⁴'This is what the LORD, the God of Israel, says: I will repel the weapons of war in your hands, those you are using to fight the king of Babylon and the Chaldeans who are besieging you outside the wall, and I will bring them into the center of this city. ⁵I will fight against you with an outstretched hand and a mighty arm, with anger, rage, and great wrath. ⁶I will strike the residents of this city, both man and beast. They will die in a great plague. ⁷Afterward'"—this is the LORD's declaration—"'King Zedekiah of Judah, his officers, and the people—those in this city who survive the plague, the sword, and the famine—I will hand over to King Nebuchadnezzar of Babylon, to their enemies, yes, to those who want to take their lives. He will put them to the sword; he won't spare them or show pity or compassion.'

⁸"But you must say to this people, 'This is what the LORD says: Look, I am presenting to you the way of life and the way of death. ⁹Whoever stays in this city will die by the sword, famine, and plague, but whoever goes out and surrenders to the Chaldeans who are besieging you will live and will retain his life like the spoils of war. ¹⁰For I have turned against this city to bring disaster and not good'"—this is the LORD's declaration. "'It will be handed over to the king of Babylon, who will burn it down.'

¹¹"And to the house of the king of Judah say this: 'Hear the word of the LORD! ¹²House of David, this is what the LORD says:

    Administer justice every morning,
    and rescue the victim of robbery
    from the hand of his oppressor,
    or My anger will flare up like fire
    and burn unquenchably
    because of their evil deeds.
13 Beware! I am against you,
    you who sit above the valley,
    you atop the rocky plateau—
              this is the LORD's declaration—
    you who say, "Who can come down against us?

Who can enter our hiding places?"
14 I will punish you according to
    what you have done—
              this is the LORD's declaration.
    I will kindle a fire in its forest
    that will consume everything around it.'"

22 This is what the LORD says: "Go down to the palace of the king of Judah and announce this word there. ²You are to say: Hear the word of the LORD, king of Judah, you who sit on the throne of David—you, your officers, and your people who enter these gates. ³This is what the LORD says: Administer justice and righteousness. Rescue the victim of robbery from the hand of his oppressor. Don't exploit or brutalize the foreigner, the fatherless, or the widow. Don't shed innocent blood in this place. ⁴For if you conscientiously carry out this word, then kings sitting on David's throne will enter through the gates of this palace riding on chariots and horses—they, their officers, and their people. ⁵But if you do not obey these words, then I swear by Myself"—this is the LORD's declaration—"that this house will become a ruin."

⁶For this is what the LORD says concerning the house of the king of Judah:

    You are like Gilead to Me,
    or the summit of Lebanon,
    but I will certainly turn you into a wilderness,
    uninhabited cities.
7   I will appoint destroyers against you,
    each with his weapons.
    They will cut down the choicest of your cedars
    and throw them into the fire.

⁸"Many nations will pass by this city and ask one another, 'Why did the LORD do such a thing to this great city?' ⁹They will answer, 'Because they abandoned the covenant of ·Yahweh their God and worshiped and served other gods.'"

10 Do not weep for the dead;
    do not mourn for him.
    Weep bitterly for the one who has gone away,
    for he will never return again
    and see his native land.

¹¹For this is what the LORD says concerning Shallum son of Josiah, king of Judah, who became king in place of his father Josiah: "He has left this place—he will never return here again, ¹²but he will die in the place where they deported him, never seeing this land again."

13 Woe for the one who builds his palace
    through unrighteousness,
    his upper rooms through injustice,
    who makes his fellow man serve without pay
    and will not give him his wages,
14 who says, "I will build myself a massive palace,
    with spacious upper rooms."
    He will cut windows in it,
    and it will be paneled with cedar
    and painted with vermilion.
15 Are you a king because you excel in cedar?
    Didn't your father eat and drink
    and administer justice and righteousness?
    Then it went well with him.
16 He took up the case of the poor and needy,
    then it went well.
    Is this not what it means to know Me?
              This is the LORD's declaration.
17 But you have eyes and a heart for nothing

except your own dishonest profit,
shedding innocent blood
and committing extortion and oppression.
[18] Therefore, this is what the Lord says concerning
Jehoiakim son of Josiah, king of Judah:
They will not mourn for him, saying,
"Woe, my brother!" or "Woe, my sister!"
They will not mourn for him, saying,
"Woe, lord! Woe, his majesty!"
[19] He will be buried like a donkey,
dragged off and thrown
outside the gates of Jerusalem.
[20] Go up to Lebanon and cry out;
raise your voice in Bashan;
cry out from Abarim,
for all your lovers have been crushed.
[21] I spoke to you when you were secure.
You said, "I will not listen."
This has been your way since youth;
indeed, you have never listened to Me.
[22] The wind will take charge of all
your shepherds,
and your lovers will go into captivity.
Then you will be ashamed and humiliated
because of all your evil.
[23] You residents of Lebanon,
nestled among the cedars,
how you will groan when labor pains
come on you,
agony like a woman in labor.
[24] "As I live," says the Lord, "though you, Coniah son
of Jehoiakim, the king of Judah, were a signet ring on
My right hand, I would tear you from it. [25] In fact, I
will hand you over to those you dread, who want to
take your life, to Nebuchadnezzar king of Babylon and
the Chaldeans. [26] I will hurl you and the mother who
gave birth to you into another land, where neither of
you were born, and there you will both die. [27] They will
never return to the land they long to return to."
[28] Is this man Coniah a despised, shattered pot,
a jar no one wants?
Why are he and his descendants hurled out
and cast into a land they have not known?
[29] Earth, earth, earth,
hear the word of the Lord!
[30] This is what the Lord says:
Record this man as childless,
a man who will not be successful
in his lifetime.
None of his descendants will succeed
in sitting on the throne of David
or ruling again in Judah.

23 "Woe to the shepherds who destroy and scatter
the sheep of My pasture!" This is the Lord's declaration. [2] "Therefore, this is what the Lord, the God
of Israel, says about the shepherds who shepherd My
people: You have scattered My flock, banished them,
and have not attended to them. I will attend to you
because of your evil acts"—this is the Lord's declaration. [3] "I will gather the remnant of My flock from
all the lands where I have banished them, and I will
return them to their grazing land. They will become
fruitful and numerous. [4] I will raise up shepherds over
them who will shepherd them. They will no longer be
afraid or dismayed, nor will any be missing." This is
the Lord's declaration.

[5] "The days are coming"—this is
the Lord's declaration—
"when I will raise up a Righteous
Branch of David.
He will reign wisely as king
and administer justice and righteousness
in the land.
[6] In His days Judah will be saved,
and Israel will dwell securely.
This is what He will be named:
·Yahweh Our Righteousness.
[7] "The days are coming"—the Lord's declaration—
"when it will no longer be said, 'As the Lord lives who
brought the Israelites from the land of Egypt,' [8] but, 'As
the Lord lives, who brought and led the descendants of
the house of Israel from the land of the north and from
all the other countries where I had banished them.'
They will dwell once more in their own land."
[9] Concerning the prophets:
My heart is broken within me,
and all my bones tremble.
I have become like a drunkard,
like a man overcome by wine,
because of the Lord,
because of His holy words.
[10] For the land is full of adulterers;
the land mourns because of the curse,
and the grazing lands in the wilderness
have dried up.
Their way of life has become evil,
and their power is not rightly used
[11] because both prophet and priest are ungodly,
even in My house I have found their evil.
This is the Lord's declaration.
[12] Therefore, their way will be to them
like slippery paths in the gloom.
They will be driven away and fall down there,
for I will bring disaster on them,
the year of their punishment.
This is the Lord's declaration.
[13] Among the prophets of Samaria
I saw something disgusting:
They prophesied by ·Baal
and led My people Israel astray.
[14] Among the prophets of Jerusalem also
I saw a horrible thing:
They commit adultery and walk in lies.
They strengthen the hands of evildoers,
and none turns his back on evil.
They are all like Sodom to Me;
Jerusalem's residents are like Gomorrah.
[15] Therefore, this is what the Lord of ·Hosts says concerning the prophets:
I am about to feed them ·wormwood
and give them poisoned water to drink,
for from the prophets of Jerusalem
ungodliness has spread throughout the land.
[16] This is what the Lord of Hosts says: "Do not listen to the words of the prophets who prophesy to you.
They are making you worthless. They speak visions
from their own minds, not from the Lord's mouth.
[17] They keep on saying to those who despise Me, 'The
Lord has said: You will have peace.' They have said to
everyone who follows the stubbornness of his heart,
'No harm will come to you.'"
[18] For who has stood in the council of the Lord
to see and hear His word?

Who has paid attention to His word
and obeyed?
19 Look, a storm from the LORD!
Wrath has gone out,
a whirling storm.
It will whirl about the heads of the wicked.
20 The LORD's anger will not turn back
until He has completely fulfilled the purposes
of His heart.
In time to come you will understand it clearly.
21 I did not send these prophets,
yet they ran with a message.
I did not speak to them,
yet they prophesied.
22 If they had really stood in My council,
they would have enabled My people to hear
My words
and would have turned them back
from their evil ways
and their evil deeds.

23 "Am I a God who is only near"—this is the LORD's
declaration—"and not a God who is far away? 24 Can a
man hide himself in secret places where I cannot see
him?"—the LORD's declaration. "Do I not fill the heavens and the earth?"—the LORD's declaration.
25 "I have heard what the prophets who prophesy
a lie in My name have said, 'I had a dream! I had a
dream!' 26 How long will this continue in the minds of
the prophets prophesying lies, prophets of the deceit
of their own minds? 27 Through their dreams that they
tell one another, they plan to cause My people to forget
My name as their fathers forgot My name through Baal
worship. 28 The prophet who has only a dream should
recount the dream, but the one who has My word
should speak My word truthfully, for what is straw
compared to grain?"—this is the LORD's declaration.
29 "Is not My word like fire"—this is the LORD's declaration—"and like a hammer that pulverizes rock?
30 Therefore, take note! I am against the prophets"—
the LORD's declaration—"who steal My words from
each other. 31 I am against the prophets"—the LORD's
declaration—"who use their own tongues to make a
declaration. 32 I am against those who prophesy false
dreams"—the LORD's declaration—"telling them and
leading My people astray with their falsehoods and
their boasting. It was not I who sent or commanded them, and they are of no benefit at all to these
people"—this is the LORD's declaration.
33 "Now when these people or a prophet or a priest
asks you, 'What is the burden of the LORD?' you will
respond to them: What is the burden? I will throw you
away"—this is the LORD's declaration. 34 "As for the
prophet, priest, or people who say, 'The burden of the
LORD,' I will punish that man and his household. 35 This
is what each man is to say to his friend and to his
brother, 'What has the LORD answered?' or 'What has
the LORD spoken?' 36 But no longer refer to the burden
of the LORD, for each man's word becomes his burden
and you pervert the words of the living God, the LORD
of Hosts, our God. 37 You must say to the prophet: What
has the LORD answered you? and What has the LORD
spoken? 38 But if you say, 'The burden of the LORD,' then
this is what the LORD says: Because you have said, 'The
burden of the LORD,' and I specifically told you not to
say, 'The burden of the LORD,' 39 I will surely forget you
and throw away from My presence both you and the
city that I gave you and your fathers. 40 I will bring on

you everlasting shame and humiliation that will never
be forgotten."

24 After Nebuchadnezzar king of Babylon had
deported Jeconiah son of Jehoiakim king of
Judah, the officials of Judah, and the craftsmen and
metalsmiths from Jerusalem and had brought them
to Babylon, the LORD showed me two baskets of figs
placed before the temple of the LORD. 2 One basket contained very good figs, like early figs, but the other basket contained very bad figs, so bad they were inedible.
3 The LORD said to me, "What do you see, Jeremiah?" I
said, "Figs! The good figs are very good, but the bad
figs are extremely bad, so bad they are inedible."
4 The word of the LORD came to me: 5 "This is what
the LORD, the God of Israel, says: Like these good figs,
so I regard as good the exiles from Judah I sent away
from this place to the land of the Chaldeans. 6 I will
keep My eyes on them for their good and will return
them to this land. I will build them up and not demolish them; I will plant them and not uproot them. 7 I
will give them a heart to know Me, that I am 'Yahweh.
They will be My people, and I will be their God because
they will return to Me with all their heart.
8 "But as for the bad figs, so bad they are inedible,
this is what the LORD says: in this way I will deal with
king Zedekiah of Judah, his officials, and the remnant of Jerusalem—those remaining in this land and
those living in the land of Egypt. 9 I will make them
an object of horror and disaster to all the kingdoms of
the earth, a disgrace, an object of scorn, ridicule, and
cursing, wherever I have banished them. 10 I will send
the sword, famine, and plague against them until they
have perished from the land I gave to them and their
ancestors."

25 This is the word that came to Jeremiah concerning all the people of Judah in the fourth
year of Jehoiakim son of Josiah, king of Judah (which
was the first year of Nebuchadnezzar king of Babylon). 2 The prophet Jeremiah spoke concerning all the
people of Judah and all the residents of Jerusalem as
follows: 3 "From the thirteenth year of Josiah son of
Amon, king of Judah, until this very day—23 years—
the word of the LORD has come to me, and I have
spoken to you time and time again, but you have not
obeyed. 4 The LORD sent all His servants the prophets
to you time and time again, but you have not obeyed
or even paid attention. 5 He announced, 'Turn, each
of you, from your evil way of life and from your evil
deeds. Live in the land the LORD gave to you and your
ancestors long ago and forever. 6 Do not follow other
gods to serve them and to worship them, and do not
provoke Me to anger by the work of your hands. Then
I will do you no harm.
7 "'But you would not obey Me'—this is the LORD's
declaration—'in order that you might provoke Me to
anger by the work of your hands and bring disaster on
yourselves.'
8 "Therefore, this is what the LORD of 'Hosts says:
'Because you have not obeyed My words, 9 I am going
to send for all the families of the north'—this is the
LORD's declaration—'and send for My servant Nebuchadnezzar king of Babylon, and I will bring them
against this land, against its residents, and against all
these surrounding nations, and I will 'completely destroy them and make them a desolation, a derision,
and ruins forever. 10 I will eliminate the sound of joy
and gladness from them—the voice of the groom and

the bride, the sound of the millstones and the light of the lamp. ¹¹This whole land will become a desolate ruin, and these nations will serve the king of Babylon for 70 years. ¹²When the 70 years are completed, I will punish the king of Babylon and that nation'—this is the LORD's declaration—'the land of the Chaldeans, for their *guilt, and I will make it a ruin forever. ¹³I will bring on that land all My words I have spoken against it, all that is written in this book that Jeremiah prophesied against all the nations. ¹⁴For many nations and great kings will enslave them, and I will repay them according to their deeds and the work of their hands.'"

¹⁵This is what the LORD, the God of Israel, said to me: "Take this cup of the wine of wrath from My hand and make all the nations I am sending you to, drink from it. ¹⁶They will drink, stagger, and go out of their minds because of the sword I am sending among them."

¹⁷So I took the cup from the LORD's hand and made all the nations drink from it, everyone the LORD sent me to. ¹⁸These included:

Jerusalem and the other cities of Judah, its kings and its officials, to make them a desolate ruin, an object of scorn and cursing—as it is today;

¹⁹Pharaoh king of Egypt, his officers, his leaders, all his people,

²⁰and all the mixed peoples;

all the kings of the land of Uz;

all the kings of the land of the Philistines— Ashkelon, Gaza, Ekron, and the remnant of Ashdod;

²¹Edom, Moab, and the Ammonites;

²²all the kings of Tyre,

all the kings of Sidon,

and the kings of the coastlands across the sea;

²³Dedan, Tema, Buz, and all those who shave their temples;

²⁴all the kings of Arabia,

and all the kings of the mixed peoples who have settled in the desert;

²⁵all the kings of Zimri,

all the kings of Elam,

and all the kings of Media;

²⁶all the kings of the north, both near and far from one another;

that is, all the kingdoms of the world which are on the face of the earth.

Finally, the king of Sheshach will drink after them.

²⁷"Then you are to say to them: This is what the LORD of Hosts, the God of Israel, says: Drink, get drunk, and vomit. Fall down and never get up again, as a result of the sword I am sending among you. ²⁸If they refuse to take the cup from you and drink, you are to say to them: This is what the LORD of Hosts says: You must drink! ²⁹For I am already bringing disaster on the city that bears My name, so how could you possibly go unpunished? You will not go unpunished, for I am summoning a sword against all the inhabitants of the earth"—this is the declaration of the LORD of Hosts.

³⁰"As for you, you are to prophesy all these things to them, and say to them:

The LORD roars from heaven;

He raises His voice from His holy dwelling.

He roars loudly over His grazing land;

He calls out with a shout, like those who tread grapes,

against all the inhabitants of the earth.

³¹ The tumult reaches to the ends of the earth

because the LORD brings a case

against the nations.

He enters into judgment with all flesh.

As for the wicked, He hands them over

to the sword—

this is the LORD's declaration.

³²"This is what the LORD of Hosts says:

Pay attention! Disaster spreads

from nation to nation.

A great storm is stirred up

from the ends of the earth."

³³Those slain by the LORD on that day will be spread from one end of the earth to the other. They will not be mourned, gathered, or buried. They will be like manure on the surface of the ground.

³⁴ Wail, you shepherds, and cry out.

Roll in the dust, you leaders of the flock.

Because the days of your slaughter have come,

you will fall and become shattered

like a precious vase.

³⁵ Flight will be impossible for the shepherds,

and escape, for the leaders of the flock.

³⁶ Hear the sound of the shepherds' cry,

the wail of the leaders of the flock,

for the LORD is destroying their pasture.

³⁷ Peaceful grazing land will become lifeless

because of the LORD's burning anger.

³⁸ He has left His den like a lion,

for their land has become a desolation

because of the sword of the oppressor,

because of His burning anger.

26 At the beginning of the reign of Jehoiakim son of Josiah, king of Judah, this word came from the LORD: ²"This is what the LORD says: Stand in the courtyard of the LORD's temple and speak all the words I have commanded you to speak to all Judah's cities that are coming to worship there. Do not hold back a word. ³Perhaps they will listen and return—each from his evil way of life—so that I might relent concerning the disaster that I plan to do to them because of the evil of their deeds. ⁴You are to say to them: This is what the LORD says: If you do not listen to Me by living according to My instruction that I set before you ⁵and by listening to the words of My servants the prophets I have been sending you time and time again, though you did not listen, ⁶I will make this temple like Shiloh. I will make this city an object of cursing for all the nations of the earth."

⁷The priests, the prophets, and all the people heard Jeremiah speaking these words in the temple of the LORD. ⁸He finished the address the LORD had commanded him to deliver to all the people. Then the priests, the prophets, and all the people took hold of him, yelling, "You must surely die! ⁹How dare you prophesy in the name of *Yahweh, 'This temple will become like Shiloh and this city will become an uninhabited ruin'!" Then all the people assembled against Jeremiah at the LORD's temple.

¹⁰When the officials of Judah heard these things, they went from the king's palace to the LORD's temple and sat at the entrance of the New Gate. ¹¹Then the priests and prophets said to the officials and all the people, "This man deserves the death sentence because he has prophesied against this city, as you have heard with your own ears."

[12] Then Jeremiah said to all the officials and the people, "The Lord sent me to prophesy all the words that you have heard against this temple and city. [13] So now, correct your ways and deeds and obey the voice of the Lord your God so that He might relent concerning the disaster that He warned about. [14] As for me, here I am in your hands; do to me what you think is good and right. [15] But know for certain that if you put me to death, you will bring innocent blood on yourselves, on this city, and on its residents, for it is certain the Lord has sent me to speak all these things directly to you."

[16] Then the officials and all the people told the priests and prophets, "This man doesn't deserve the death sentence, for he has spoken to us in the name of Yahweh our God!"

[17] Some of the elders of the land stood up and said to all the assembled people, [18] "Micah the Moreshite prophesied in the days of Hezekiah king of Judah and said to all the people of Judah, 'This is what the Lord of •Hosts says:

•Zion will be plowed like a field,
Jerusalem will become ruins,
and the temple mount a forested hill.'

[19] Did Hezekiah king of Judah and all the people of Judah put him to death? Did he not •fear the Lord and plead for the Lord's favor, and did not the Lord relent concerning the disaster He had pronounced against them? We are about to bring great harm on ourselves!"

[20] Another man was also prophesying in the name of Yahweh—Uriah son of Shemaiah from Kiriath-jearim. He prophesied against this city and against this land in words like all those of Jeremiah. [21] King Jehoiakim, all his warriors, and all the officials heard his words, and the king tried to put him to death. When Uriah heard, he fled in fear and went to Egypt. [22] But King Jehoiakim sent men to Egypt: Elnathan son of Achbor and certain other men with him went to Egypt. [23] They brought Uriah out of Egypt and took him to King Jehoiakim, who executed him with the sword and threw his corpse into the burial place of the common people. [24] But Ahikam son of Shaphan supported Jeremiah, so he was not handed over to the people to be put to death.

27 At the beginning of the reign of Zedekiah son of Josiah, king of Judah, this word came to Jeremiah from the Lord: [2] "This is what the Lord said to me: Make chains and yoke bars for yourself and put them on your neck. [3] Send word to the king of Edom, the king of Moab, the king of the Ammonites, the king of Tyre, and the king of Sidon through messengers who are coming to Zedekiah king of Judah in Jerusalem. [4] Command them to go to their masters, saying: This is what the Lord of •Hosts, the God of Israel, says: This is what you must say to your masters: [5] By My great strength and outstretched arm, I made the earth, and the people, and animals on the face of the earth. I give it to anyone I please. [6] So now I have placed all these lands under the authority of My servant Nebuchadnezzar, king of Babylon. I have even given him the wild animals to serve him. [7] All nations will serve him, his son, and his grandson until the time for his own land comes, and then many nations and great kings will enslave him.

[8] "As for the nation or kingdom that does not serve Nebuchadnezzar king of Babylon and does not place its neck under the yoke of the king of Babylon, that nation I will punish by sword, famine, and plague"—this is the Lord's declaration—"until through him I have destroyed it. [9] But as for you, do not listen to your prophets, diviners, dreamers, fortune-tellers, or sorcerers who say to you, 'Don't serve the king of Babylon!' [10] for they prophesy a lie to you so that you will be removed from your land. I will banish you, and you will perish. [11] But as for the nation that will put its neck under the yoke of the king of Babylon and serve him, I will leave it in its own land, and that nation will cultivate it and reside in it." This is the Lord's declaration.

[12] I spoke to Zedekiah king of Judah in the same way: "Put your necks under the yoke of the king of Babylon, serve him and his people, and live! [13] Why should you and your people die by the sword, famine, or plague as the Lord has threatened against any nation that does not serve the king of Babylon? [14] Do not listen to the words of the prophets who are telling you, 'You must not serve the king of Babylon,' for they are prophesying a lie to you. [15] 'I have not sent them'—this is the Lord's declaration—'and they are prophesying falsely in My name; therefore, I will banish you, and you will perish—you and the prophets who are prophesying to you.'"

[16] Then I spoke to the priests and all these people, saying, "This is what the Lord says: 'Do not listen to the words of your prophets. They are prophesying to you, claiming, "Look, very soon now the articles of the Lord's temple will be brought back from Babylon." They are prophesying a lie to you. [17] Do not listen to them. Serve the king of Babylon and live! Why should this city become a ruin? [18] If they are indeed prophets and if the word of the Lord is with them, let them intercede with the Lord of Hosts not to let the articles that remain in the Lord's temple, in the palace of the king of Judah, and in Jerusalem go to Babylon.' [19] For this is what the Lord of Hosts says about the pillars, the sea, the water carts, and the rest of the articles that still remain in this city, [20] those Nebuchadnezzar king of Babylon did not take when he deported Jeconiah son of Jehoiakim, king of Judah, from Jerusalem to Babylon along with all the nobles of Judah and Jerusalem. [21] Yes, this is what the Lord of Hosts, the God of Israel, says about the articles that remain in the temple of the Lord, in the palace of the king of Judah, and in Jerusalem: [22] 'They will be brought to Babylon and will remain there until I attend to them again.' This is the Lord's declaration. 'Then I will bring them up and restore them to this place.'"

28 In that same year, at the beginning of the reign of King Zedekiah of Judah, in the fifth month of the fourth year, the prophet Hananiah son of Azzur from Gibeon said to me in the temple of the Lord in the presence of the priests and all the people, [2] "This is what the Lord of •Hosts, the God of Israel, says: 'I have broken the yoke of the king of Babylon. [3] Within two years I will restore to this place all the articles of the Lord's temple that King Nebuchadnezzar of Babylon took from here and transported to Babylon. [4] And I will restore to this place Jeconiah son of Jehoiakim, king of Judah, and all the exiles from Judah who went to Babylon'—this is the Lord's declaration—'for I will break the yoke of the king of Babylon.'"

[5] The prophet Jeremiah replied to the prophet Hananiah in the presence of the priests and all the people who were standing in the temple of the Lord. [6] The prophet Jeremiah said, "'Amen! May the Lord do so. May the Lord make the words you have proph-

esied come true and may He restore the articles of the LORD's temple and all the exiles from Babylon to this place! [7] Only listen to this message I am speaking in your hearing and in the hearing of all the people. [8] The prophets who preceded you and me from ancient times prophesied war, disaster, and plague against many lands and great kingdoms. [9] As for the prophet who prophesies peace—only when the word of the prophet comes true will the prophet be recognized as one the LORD has truly sent."

[10] The prophet Hananiah then took the yoke bar from the neck of Jeremiah the prophet and broke it. [11] In the presence of all the people Hananiah proclaimed, "This is what the LORD says: 'In this way, within two years I will break the yoke of King Nebuchadnezzar of Babylon from the neck of all the nations.'" Jeremiah the prophet then went on his way.

[12] The word of the LORD came to Jeremiah after Hananiah the prophet had broken the yoke bar from the neck of Jeremiah the prophet: [13] "Go say to Hananiah: This is what the LORD says, 'You broke a wooden yoke bar, but in its place you will make an iron yoke bar.' [14] For this is what the LORD of Hosts, the God of Israel, says, 'I have put an iron yoke on the neck of all these nations that they might serve King Nebuchadnezzar of Babylon, and they will serve him. I have also put the wild animals under him.'"

[15] The prophet Jeremiah said to the prophet Hananiah, "Listen, Hananiah! The LORD did not send you, but you have led these people to trust in a lie. [16] Therefore, this is what the LORD says: 'I am about to send you off the face of the earth. You will die this year because you have spoken rebellion against the LORD.'" [17] And the prophet Hananiah died that year in the seventh month.

29 This is the text of the letter that Jeremiah the prophet sent from Jerusalem to the rest of the elders of the exiles, the priests, the prophets, and all the people Nebuchadnezzar had deported from Jerusalem to Babylon. [2] This was after King Jeconiah, the queen mother, the court officials, the officials of Judah and Jerusalem, the craftsmen, and the metalsmiths had left Jerusalem. [3] The letter was sent by Elasah son of Shaphan and Gemariah son of Hilkiah whom Zedekiah king of Judah had sent to Babylon to Nebuchadnezzar king of Babylon. The letter stated:

[4] This is what the LORD of ⋅Hosts, the God of Israel, says to all the exiles I deported from Jerusalem to Babylon: [5] "Build houses and live in them. Plant gardens and eat their produce. [6] Take wives and have sons and daughters. Take wives for your sons and give your daughters to men in marriage so that they may bear sons and daughters. Multiply there; do not decrease. [7] Seek the welfare of the city I have deported you to. Pray to the LORD on its behalf, for when it has prosperity, you will prosper."

[8] For this is what the LORD of Hosts, the God of Israel, says: "Don't let your prophets who are among you and your diviners deceive you, and don't listen to the dreams you elicit from them, [9] for they are prophesying falsely to you in My name. I have not sent them." This is the LORD's declaration.

[10] For this is what the LORD says: "When 70 years for Babylon are complete, I will attend to you and will confirm My promise concerning you to restore you to this place. [11] For I know the plans I have for you"—this is the LORD's declaration—"plans for your welfare, not for disaster, to give you a future and a hope. [12] You will call to Me and come and pray to Me, and I will listen to you. [13] You will seek Me and find Me when you search for Me with all your heart. [14] I will be found by you"—this is the LORD's declaration—"and I will restore your fortunes and gather you from all the nations and places where I banished you"— this is the LORD's declaration. "I will restore you to the place I deported you from."

[15] You have said, "The LORD has raised up prophets for us in Babylon!" [16] But this is what the LORD says concerning the king sitting on David's throne and concerning all the people living in this city—that is, concerning your brothers who did not go with you into exile. [17] This is what the LORD of Hosts says: "I am about to send against them sword, famine, and plague and will make them like rotten figs that are inedible because they are so bad. [18] I will pursue them with sword, famine, and plague. I will make them a horror to all the kingdoms of the earth—a curse and a desolation, an object of scorn and a disgrace among all the nations where I have banished them. [19] I will do this because they have not listened to My words"—this is the LORD's declaration—"that I sent to them with My servants the prophets time and time again. And you too have not listened." This is the LORD's declaration.

[20] Hear the word of the LORD, all you exiles I have sent from Jerusalem to Babylon. [21] This is what the LORD of Hosts, the God of Israel, says about Ahab son of Kolaiah and to Zedekiah son of Maaseiah, the ones prophesying a lie to you in My name: "I am about to hand them over to Nebuchadnezzar king of Babylon, and he will kill them before your very eyes. [22] Based on what happens to them, all the exiles of Judah who are in Babylon will create a curse that says, 'May the LORD make you like Zedekiah and Ahab, whom the king of Babylon roasted in the fire!' [23] because they have committed an outrage in Israel by committing adultery with their neighbors' wives and have spoken a lie in My name, which I did not command them. I am He who knows, and I am a witness." This is the LORD's declaration.

[24] To Shemaiah the Nehelamite you are to say, [25] "This is what the LORD of Hosts, the God of Israel, says: You in your own name have sent out letters to all the people of Jerusalem, to the priest Zephaniah son of Maaseiah, and to all the priests, saying: [26] 'The LORD has appointed you priest in place of Jehoiada the priest to be the chief officer in the temple of the LORD, responsible for every madman who acts like a prophet. You must confine him in the stocks and an iron collar. [27] So now, why have you not rebuked Jeremiah of Anathoth who has been acting like a prophet among you? [28] For he has sent word to us in Babylon, claiming, "The exile will be long. Build houses and settle down. Plant gardens and eat their produce."'"

[29] Zephaniah the priest read this letter in the hearing of Jeremiah the prophet. [30] Then the word of the LORD came to Jeremiah:

³¹ "Send a message to all the exiles, saying: This is what the Lord says concerning Shemaiah the Nehelamite. Because Shemaiah prophesied to you, though I did not send him, and made you trust a lie, ³² this is what the Lord says: I am about to punish Shemaiah the Nehelamite and his descendants. There will not be even one of his descendants living among these people, nor will any ever see the good that I will bring to My people"— this is the Lord's declaration—"for he has preached rebellion against the Lord."

30 This is the word that came to Jeremiah from the Lord. ² This is what the Lord, the God of Israel, says: "Write down on a scroll all the words that I have spoken to you, ³ for the days are certainly coming"—this is the Lord's declaration—"when I will restore the fortunes of My people Israel and Judah"— the Lord's declaration. "I will restore them to the land I gave to their ancestors and they will possess it."

⁴ These are the words the Lord spoke to Israel and Judah. ⁵ Yes, this is what the Lord says:

We have heard a cry of terror,
of dread—there is no peace.
⁶ Ask and see
whether a male can give birth.
Why then do I see every man
with his hands on his stomach like a woman
in labor
and every face turned pale?
⁷ How awful that day will be!
There will be none like it!
It will be a time of trouble for Jacob,
but he will be delivered out of it.

⁸ "On that day"—this is the declaration of the Lord of ⁕Hosts—"I will break his yoke from your neck and tear off your chains so strangers will never again enslave him. ⁹ They will serve the Lord their God and I will raise up David their king for them."

¹⁰ As for you, My servant Jacob,
do not be afraid—
this is the Lord's declaration—
and do not be dismayed, Israel,
for without fail I will save you from far away,
your descendants, from the land
of their captivity!
Jacob will return and have calm and quiet
with no one to frighten him.
¹¹ For I will be with you—
this is the Lord's declaration—
to save you!
I will bring destruction on all the nations
where I have scattered you;
however, I will not bring destruction on you.
I will discipline you justly,
and I will by no means leave you unpunished.
¹² For this is what the Lord says:
Your injury is incurable;
your wound most severe.
¹³ No one takes up the case for your sores.
There is no healing for you.
¹⁴ All your lovers have forgotten you;
they no longer look for you,
for I have struck you as an enemy would,
with the discipline of someone cruel,
because of your enormous ⁕guilt
and your innumerable sins.
¹⁵ Why do you cry out about your injury?
Your pain has no cure!

I have done these things to you
because of your enormous guilt
and your innumerable sins.
¹⁶ Nevertheless, all who devoured you
will be devoured,
and all your adversaries—all of them—
will go off into exile.
Those who plunder you will be plundered,
and all who raid you will be raided.
¹⁷ But I will bring you health
and will heal you of your wounds—
this is the Lord's declaration—
for they call you Outcast,
⁕Zion whom no one cares about.
¹⁸ This is what the Lord says:
I will certainly restore the fortunes
of Jacob's tents
and show compassion on his dwellings.
Every city will be rebuilt on its mound;
every citadel will stand on its proper site.
¹⁹ Thanksgiving will come out of them,
a sound of celebration.
I will multiply them,
and they will not decrease;
I will honor them, and they will not
be insignificant.
²⁰ His children will be as in past days;
his congregation will be established
in My presence.
I will punish all his oppressors.
²¹ Jacob's leader will be one of them;
his ruler will issue from him.
I will invite him to Me, and he will
approach Me,
for who would otherwise risk his life
to approach Me?
This is the Lord's declaration.
²² You will be My people,
and I will be your God.
²³ Look, a storm from the Lord!
Wrath has gone out,
a churning storm.
It will whirl about the heads of the wicked.
²⁴ The Lord's burning anger will not turn back
until He has completely fulfilled the purposes
of His heart.
In time to come you will understand it.

31 "At that time"—this is the Lord's declaration— "I will be the God of all the families of Israel, and they will be My people."

² This is what the Lord says:
They found favor in the wilderness—
the people who survived the sword.
When Israel went to find rest,
³ the Lord appeared to him from far away.
I have loved you with an everlasting love;
therefore, I have continued to extend
faithful love to you.
⁴ Again I will build you so that you will
be rebuilt,
Virgin Israel.
You will take up your tambourines again
and go out in joyful dancing.
⁵ You will plant vineyards again
on the mountains of Samaria;
the planters will plant and will enjoy the fruit.

⁶ For there will be a day when watchmen
     will call out
in the hill country of Ephraim,
"Get up, let's go up to •Zion,
to •Yahweh our God!"
⁷ For this is what the LORD says:
Sing with joy for Jacob;
shout for the chief of the nations!
Proclaim, praise, and say,
"LORD, save Your people,
the remnant of Israel!"
⁸ Watch! I am going to bring them
     from the northern land.
I will gather them from remote regions
     of the earth—
the blind and the lame will be with them,
along with those who are pregnant and those
     about to give birth.
They will return here as a great assembly!
⁹ They will come weeping,
but I will bring them back with consolation.
I will lead them to •wadis filled with water
by a smooth way where they will not stumble,
for I am Israel's Father,
and Ephraim is My firstborn.
¹⁰ Nations, hear the word of the LORD,
and tell it among the far off coastlands!
Say: The One who scattered Israel
     will gather him.
He will watch over him as a shepherd
     guards his flock,
¹¹ for the LORD has ransomed Jacob
and redeemed him from the power of one
     stronger than he.
¹² They will come and shout for joy
     on the heights of Zion;
they will be radiant with joy
because of the LORD's goodness,
because of the grain, the new wine,
     the fresh oil,
and because of the young of the flocks
     and herds.
Their life will be like an irrigated garden,
and they will no longer grow weak
     from hunger.
¹³ Then the young woman will rejoice
     with dancing,
while young and old men rejoice together.
I will turn their mourning into joy,
give them consolation,
and bring happiness out of grief.
¹⁴ I will refresh the priests with an abundance,
and My people will be satisfied
     with My goodness.
               This is the LORD's declaration.
¹⁵ This is what the LORD says:
A voice was heard in Ramah,
a lament with bitter weeping—
Rachel weeping for her children,
refusing to be comforted for her children
because they are no more.
¹⁶ This is what the LORD says:
Keep your voice from weeping
and your eyes from tears,
for the reward for your work will come—
               this is the LORD's declaration—

and your children will return
     from the enemy's land.
¹⁷ There is hope for your future—
               this is the LORD's declaration—
and your children will return
     to their own territory.
¹⁸ I have heard Ephraim moaning,
"You disciplined me,
     and I have been disciplined
like an untrained calf.
Restore me, and I will return,
for you, LORD, are my God.
¹⁹ After I returned, I repented;
After I was instructed, I struck my thigh
     in grief.
I was ashamed and humiliated
because I bore the disgrace of my youth."
²⁰ Isn't Ephraim a precious son to Me,
a delightful child?
Whenever I speak against him,
I certainly still think about him.
Therefore, My inner being yearns for him;
I will truly have compassion on him.
               This is the LORD's declaration.
²¹ Set up road markers for yourself;
establish signposts!
Keep the highway in mind,
the way you have traveled.
Return, Virgin Israel!
Return to these cities of yours.
²² How long will you turn here and there,
faithless daughter?
For the LORD creates something new
     in the land—
a female will shelter a man.

²³ This is what the LORD of •Hosts, the God of Israel,
says: "When I restore their fortunes, they will once
again speak this word in the land of Judah and in its
cities, 'May the LORD bless you, righteous settlement,
holy mountain.' ²⁴ Judah and all its cities will live in it
together—also farmers and those who move with the
flocks— ²⁵ for I satisfy the thirsty person and feed all
those who are weak."

²⁶ At this I awoke and looked around. My sleep had
been most pleasant to me.

²⁷ "The days are coming"—this is the LORD's declaration—"when I will sow the house of Israel and the
house of Judah with the seed of man and the seed of
beast. ²⁸ Just as I watched over them to uproot and
to tear them down, to demolish and to destroy, and
to cause disaster, so will I be attentive to build and to
plant them," says the LORD. ²⁹ "In those days, it will
never again be said:

The fathers have eaten sour grapes,
     and the children's teeth are set on edge.

³⁰ Rather, each will die for his own wrongdoing. Anyone who eats sour grapes—his own teeth will be set
on edge.

³¹ "Look, the days are coming"—this is the LORD's
declaration—"when I will make a new covenant with
the house of Israel and with the house of Judah.
³² This one will not be like the covenant I made with
their ancestors when I took them by the hand to bring
them out of the land of Egypt—a covenant they broke
even though I had married them"—the LORD's declaration. ³³ "Instead, this is the covenant I will make
with the house of Israel after those days"—the LORD's

declaration. "I will put My teaching within them and write it on their hearts. I will be their God, and they will be My people. ³⁴No longer will one teach his neighbor or his brother, saying, 'Know the Lord,' for they will all know Me, from the least to the greatest of them"— this is the Lord's declaration. "For I will forgive their wrongdoing and never again remember their sin."

³⁵This is what the Lord says:

The One who gives the sun for light by day,
the fixed order of moon and stars for light
by night,
who stirs up the sea and makes
its waves roar—
Yahweh of Hosts is His name:
³⁶   If this fixed order departs from My presence—
this is the Lord's declaration—
then also Israel's descendants will cease
to be a nation before Me forever.

³⁷This is what the Lord says:

If the heavens above can be measured
and the foundations
of the earth below explored,
I will reject all of Israel's descendants
because of all they have done—
this is the Lord's declaration.

³⁸"Look, the days are coming"—the Lord's declaration—"when the city from the Tower of Hananel to the Corner Gate will be rebuilt for the Lord. ³⁹A measuring line will once again stretch out straight to the hill of Gareb and then turn toward Goah. ⁴⁰The whole valley—the corpses, the ashes, and all the fields as far as the Kidron Valley to the corner of the Horse Gate to the east—will be holy to the Lord. It will never be uprooted or demolished again."

32 This is the word that came to Jeremiah from the Lord in the tenth year of Zedekiah king of Judah, which was the eighteenth year of Nebuchadnezzar. ²At that time, the army of the king of Babylon was besieging Jerusalem, and Jeremiah the prophet was imprisoned in the guard's courtyard in the palace of the king of Judah. ³Zedekiah king of Judah had imprisoned him, saying: "Why are you prophesying, 'This is what the Lord says: Look, I am about to hand this city over to Babylon's king, and he will capture it. ⁴Zedekiah king of Judah will not escape from the Chaldeans; indeed, he will certainly be handed over to Babylon's king. They will speak face to face and meet eye to eye. ⁵He will take Zedekiah to Babylon where he will stay until I attend to him'—this is the Lord's declaration. 'You will fight the Chaldeans, but you will not succeed'?"

⁶Jeremiah replied, "The word of the Lord came to me: ⁷Watch! Hanamel, the son of your uncle Shallum, is coming to you to say, 'Buy my field in Anathoth for yourself, for you own the right of redemption to buy it.'

⁸"Then my cousin Hanamel came to the guard's courtyard as the Lord had said and urged me, 'Please buy my field in Anathoth in the land of Benjamin, for you own the right of inheritance and redemption. Buy it for yourself.' Then I knew that this was the word of the Lord. ⁹So I bought the field in Anathoth from my cousin Hanamel, and I weighed out to him the money—17 ˙shekels of silver. ¹⁰I recorded it on a scroll, sealed it, called in witnesses, and weighed out the silver in the scales. ¹¹I took the purchase agreement—the sealed copy with its terms and conditions

and the open copy— ¹²and gave the purchase agreement to Baruch son of Neriah, son of Mahseiah. I did this in the sight of my cousin Hanamel, the witnesses who were signing the purchase agreement, and all the Judeans sitting in the guard's courtyard.

¹³"I instructed Baruch in their sight, ¹⁴"This is what the Lord of ˙Hosts, the God of Israel, says: Take these scrolls—this purchase agreement with the sealed copy and this open copy—and put them in an earthen storage jar so they will last a long time. ¹⁵For this is what the Lord of Hosts, the God of Israel, says: Houses, fields, and vineyards will again be bought in this land.'

¹⁶"After I had given the purchase agreement to Baruch, son of Neriah, I prayed to the Lord: ¹⁷Oh, Lord God! You Yourself made the heavens and earth by Your great power and with Your outstretched arm. Nothing is too difficult for You! ¹⁸You show faithful love to thousands but lay the fathers' sins on their sons' laps after them, great and mighty God whose name is ˙Yahweh of Hosts, ¹⁹the One great in counsel and mighty in deed, whose eyes are on all the ways of the sons of men in order to give to each person according to his ways and the result of his deeds. ²⁰You performed signs and wonders in the land of Egypt and do so to this very day both in Israel and among mankind. You made a name for Yourself, as is the case today. ²¹You brought Your people Israel out of Egypt with signs and wonders, with a strong hand and an outstretched arm, and with great terror. ²²You gave them this land You swore to give to their ancestors, a land flowing with milk and honey. ²³They entered and possessed it, but they did not obey Your voice or live according to Your instructions. They failed to perform all You commanded them to do, and so You have brought all this disaster on them. ²⁴Look! Siege ramps have come against the city to capture it, and the city, as a result of the sword, famine, and plague, has been handed over to the Chaldeans who are fighting against it. What You have spoken has happened. Look, You can see it! ²⁵Yet You, Lord God, have said to me: Buy the field with silver and call in witnesses—even though the city has been handed over to the Chaldeans!"

²⁶Then the word of the Lord came to Jeremiah: ²⁷"Look, I am Yahweh, the God of all flesh. Is anything too difficult for Me? ²⁸Therefore, this is what the Lord says: I am about to hand this city over to the Chaldeans, to Babylon's king Nebuchadnezzar, and he will capture it. ²⁹The Chaldeans who are going to fight against this city will come, set this city on fire, and burn it along with the houses where incense has been burned to ˙Baal on their rooftops and where ˙drink offerings have been poured out to other gods to provoke Me to anger. ³⁰From their youth, the Israelites and Judeans have done nothing but what is evil in My sight! They have done nothing but provoke Me to anger by the work of their hands"—this is the Lord's declaration— ³¹"for this city has caused My wrath and fury from the day it was built until now. I will therefore remove it from My presence, ³²because of all the evil the Israelites and Judeans have done to provoke Me to anger—they, their kings, their officials, their priests, and their prophets, the men of Judah, and the residents of Jerusalem. ³³They have turned their backs to Me and not their faces. Though I taught them time and time again, they do not listen and receive discipline. ³⁴They have placed their detestable things in the house that is called by My name and have defiled it. ³⁵They have

built the ˙high places of Baal in the Valley of Hinnom to make their sons and daughters pass through the fire to ˙Molech—something I had not commanded them. I had never entertained the thought that they do this detestable act causing Judah to sin! ³⁶"Now therefore, this is what the LORD, the God of Israel, says to this city about which you said, 'It has been handed over to Babylon's king through sword, famine, and plague': ³⁷I am about to gather them from all the lands where I have banished them in My anger, rage and great wrath, and I will return them to this place and make them live in safety. ³⁸They will be My people, and I will be their God. ³⁹I will give them one heart and one way so that for their good and for the good of their descendants after them, they will ˙fear Me always.

⁴⁰"I will make an everlasting covenant with them: I will never turn away from doing good to them, and I will put fear of Me in their hearts so they will never again turn away from Me. ⁴¹I will take delight in them to do what is good for them, and with all My heart and mind I will faithfully plant them in this land.

⁴²"For this is what the LORD says: Just as I have brought all this great disaster on these people, so am I about to bring on them all the good I am promising them. ⁴³Fields will be bought in this land about which you are saying, 'It's a desolation without man or beast; it has been handed over to the Chaldeans!' ⁴⁴Fields will be purchased with silver, the transaction written on a scroll and sealed, and witnesses will be called on in the land of Benjamin, in the areas surrounding Jerusalem, and in Judah's cities—the cities of the hill country, the cities of the Judean foothills, and the cities of the ˙Negev—because I will restore their fortunes."

This is the LORD's declaration.

33 While he was still confined in the guard's courtyard, the word of the LORD came to Jeremiah a second time: ²"The LORD who made the earth, the LORD who forms it to establish it, ˙Yahweh is His name, says this: ³Call to Me and I will answer you and tell you great and incomprehensible things you do not know. ⁴For this is what the LORD, the God of Israel, says concerning the houses of this city and the palaces of Judah's kings, the ones torn down for defense against the siege ramps and the sword: ⁵The people coming to fight the Chaldeans will fill the houses with the corpses of their own men that I strike down in My wrath and rage. I have hidden My face from this city because of all their evil. ⁶Yet I will certainly bring health and healing to it and will indeed heal them. I will let them experience the abundance of peace and truth. ⁷I will restore the fortunes of Judah and of Israel and will rebuild them as in former times. ⁸I will purify them from all the wrongs they have committed against Me, and I will forgive all the wrongs they have committed against Me, rebelling against Me. ⁹This city will bear on My behalf a name of joy, praise, and glory before all the nations of the earth, who will hear of all the good I will do for them. They will tremble with awe because of all the good and all the peace I will bring about for them.

¹⁰"This is what the LORD says: In this place, which you say is a ruin, without man or beast—that is, in Judah's cities and Jerusalem's streets that are a desolation without man, without inhabitant, and without beast—there will be heard again ¹¹a sound of joy and gladness, the voice of the groom and the bride, and the voice of those saying,

Praise the LORD of ˙Hosts,
for the LORD is good;
His faithful love endures forever

as they bring thank offerings to the temple of the LORD. For I will restore the fortunes of the land as in former times, says the LORD.

¹²"This is what the LORD of Hosts says: In this desolate place—without man or beast—and in all its cities there will once more be a grazing land where shepherds may rest flocks. ¹³The flocks will again pass under the hands of the one who counts them in the cities of the hill country, the cities of the Judean foothills, the cities of the ˙Negev, the land of Benjamin—the cities surrounding Jerusalem and Judah's cities, says the LORD.

¹⁴   "Look, the days are coming"—
    this is the LORD's declaration—
    "when I will fulfill the good promises
    that I have spoken
    concerning the house of Israel
    and the house of Judah.
¹⁵   In those days and at that time
    I will cause a Righteous Branch
    to sprout up for David,
    and He will administer justice
    and righteousness in the land.
¹⁶   In those days Judah will be saved,
    and Jerusalem will dwell securely,
    and this is what she will be named:
    Yahweh Our Righteousness.

¹⁷"For this is what the LORD says: David will never fail to have a man sitting on the throne of the house of Israel. ¹⁸The Levitical priests will never fail to have a man always before Me to offer ˙burnt offerings, to burn ˙grain offerings, and to make sacrifices."

¹⁹The word of the LORD came to Jeremiah: ²⁰"This is what the LORD says: If you can break My covenant with the day and My covenant with the night so that day and night cease to come at their regular time, ²¹then also My covenant with My servant David may be broken so that he will not have a son reigning on his throne, and the Levitical priests will not be My ministers. ²²The hosts of heaven cannot be counted; the sand of the sea cannot be measured. So, too, I will make the descendants of My servant David and the Levites who minister to Me innumerable."

²³The word of the LORD came to Jeremiah: ²⁴"Have you not noticed what these people have said? They say, 'The LORD has rejected the two families He had chosen.' My people are treated with contempt and no longer regarded as a nation among them. ²⁵This is what the LORD says: If I do not keep My covenant with the day and with the night and fail to establish the fixed order of heaven and earth, ²⁶then I might also reject the ˙seed of Jacob and of My servant David—not taking from his descendants rulers over the descendants of Abraham, Isaac, and Jacob. Instead, I will restore their fortunes and have compassion on them."

34 This is the word that came to Jeremiah from the LORD when Nebuchadnezzar, king of Babylon, all his army, all the earthly kingdoms under his control, and all other nations were fighting against Jerusalem and all its surrounding cities: ²"This is what the LORD, the God of Israel, says: Go, speak to Zedekiah, king of Judah, and tell him: This is what the LORD says: I am about to hand this city over to the king of Babylon, and he will burn it down. ³As for you, you

will not escape from his hand but are certain to be captured and handed over to him. You will meet the king of Babylon eye to eye and speak face to face; you will go to Babylon.

⁴"Yet hear the LORD's word, Zedekiah, king of Judah. This is what the LORD says concerning you: You will not die by the sword; ⁵you will die peacefully. There will be a burning ceremony for you just like the burning ceremonies for your fathers, the former kings who preceded you. 'Our king is dead!' will be the lament for you, for I have spoken this word." This is the LORD's declaration.

⁶So Jeremiah the prophet related all these words to Zedekiah king of Judah in Jerusalem ⁷while the king of Babylon's army was attacking Jerusalem and all of Judah's remaining cities—against Lachish and Azekah, for they were the only ones left of Judah's fortified cities.

⁸This is the word that came to Jeremiah from the LORD after King Zedekiah made a covenant with all the people who were in Jerusalem to proclaim freedom to them, ⁹so each man would free his male and female Hebrew slaves and no one would enslave his Judean brother. ¹⁰All the officials and people who entered into covenant to free their male and female slaves—in order not to enslave them any longer—obeyed and freed them. ¹¹Afterward, however, they changed their minds and took back their male and female slaves they had freed and forced them to become slaves again.

¹²Then the word of the LORD came to Jeremiah from the LORD: ¹³"This is what the LORD, the God of Israel, says: I made a covenant with your ancestors when I brought them out of the land of Egypt, out of the place of slavery, saying: ¹⁴At the end of seven years, each of you must free his Hebrew brother who sold himself to you. He may serve you six years, but then you must send him out free from you. But your ancestors did not obey Me or pay any attention. ¹⁵Today you repented and did what pleased Me, each of you proclaiming freedom for his neighbor. You made a covenant before Me at the temple called by My name. ¹⁶But you have changed your minds and profaned My name. Each has taken back his male and female slaves who had been freed to go wherever they wanted, and you have again subjugated them to be your slaves.

¹⁷"Therefore, this is what the LORD says: You have not obeyed Me by proclaiming freedom, each man for his brother and for his neighbor. I hereby proclaim freedom for you"—this is the LORD's declaration—"to the sword, to plague, and to famine! I will make you a horror to all the earth's kingdoms. ¹⁸As for those who disobeyed My covenant, not keeping the terms of the covenant they made before Me, I will treat them like the calf they cut in two in order to pass between its pieces. ¹⁹The officials of Judah and Jerusalem, the court officials, the priests, and all the people of the land who passed between the pieces of the calf ²⁰will be handed over to their enemies, to those who want to take their life. Their corpses will become food for the birds of the sky and for the wild animals of the land. ²¹I will hand Zedekiah king of Judah and his officials over to their enemies, to those who want to take their lives, to the king of Babylon's army that is withdrawing. ²²I am about to give the command"—this is the LORD's declaration—"and I will bring them back to this city. They will fight against it, capture it, and burn it

down. I will make Judah's cities a desolation, without inhabitant."

35 This is the word that came to Jeremiah from the LORD in the days of Jehoiakim son of Josiah, king of Judah: ²"Go to the house of the Rechabites, speak to them, and bring them to one of the chambers of the temple of the LORD to offer them a drink of wine."

³So I took Jaazaniah son of Jeremiah, son of Habazziniah, and his brothers and all his sons—the entire house of the Rechabites— ⁴and I brought them into the temple of the LORD to a chamber occupied by the sons of Hanan son of Igdaliah, a man of God, who had a chamber near the officials' chamber, which was above the chamber of Maaseiah son of Shallum the doorkeeper. ⁵I set jars filled with wine and some cups before the sons of the house of the Rechabites and said to them, "Drink wine!"

⁶But they replied, "We do not drink wine, for Jonadab, son of our ancestor Rechab, commanded: 'You and your sons must never drink wine. ⁷You must not build a house or sow seed or plant a vineyard. Those things are not for you. Rather, you must live in tents your whole life, so you may live a long time on the soil where you stay as a temporary resident.' ⁸We have obeyed the voice of Jonadab, son of our ancestor Rechab, in all he commanded us. So we haven't drunk wine our whole life—we, our wives, our sons, and our daughters. ⁹We also have not built houses to live in and do not have vineyard, field, or seed. ¹⁰But we have lived in tents and have obeyed and done as our ancestor Jonadab commanded us. ¹¹However, when Nebuchadnezzar king of Babylon marched into the land, we said: Come, let's go into Jerusalem to get away from the Chaldean and Aramean armies. So we have been living in Jerusalem."

¹²Then the word of the LORD came to Jeremiah: ¹³"This is what the LORD of 'Hosts, the God of Israel, says: Go, say to the men of Judah and the residents of Jerusalem: Will you not accept discipline by listening to My words?"—this is the LORD's declaration. ¹⁴"The words of Jonadab, son of Rechab, have been carried out. He commanded his sons not to drink wine, and they have not drunk to this very day because they have obeyed their ancestor's command. But I have spoken to you time and time again, and you have not obeyed Me! ¹⁵Time and time again I have sent you all My servants the prophets, proclaiming: Turn, each one from his evil way of life, and correct your actions. Stop following other gods to serve them. Live in the land that I gave you and your ancestors. But you would not pay attention or obey Me. ¹⁶Yes, the sons of Jonadab son of Rechab carried out their ancestor's command he gave them, but these people have not obeyed Me. ¹⁷Therefore, this is what the LORD, the God of Hosts, the God of Israel, says: I will certainly bring to Judah and to all the residents of Jerusalem all the disaster I have pronounced against them because I have spoken to them, but they have not obeyed, and I have called to them, but they would not answer."

¹⁸Jeremiah said to the house of the Rechabites: "This is what the LORD of Hosts, the God of Israel, says: 'Because you have obeyed the command of your ancestor Jonadab and have kept all his commands and have done all that he commanded you, ¹⁹this is what the LORD of Hosts, the God of Israel, says: Jonadab son of

Rechab will never fail to have a man to always stand before Me.'"

36 In the fourth year of Jehoiakim son of Josiah, king of Judah, this word came to Jeremiah from the LORD: ²"Take a scroll, and write on it all the words I have spoken to you concerning Israel, Judah, and all the nations from the time I first spoke to you during Josiah's reign until today. ³Perhaps when the house of Judah hears about all the disaster I am planning to bring on them, each one of them will turn from his evil way. Then I will forgive their wrongdoing and their sin."

⁴So Jeremiah summoned Baruch son of Neriah. At Jeremiah's dictation, Baruch wrote on a scroll all the words the LORD had spoken to Jeremiah. ⁵Then Jeremiah commanded Baruch, "I am restricted; I cannot enter the temple of the LORD, ⁶so you must go and read from the scroll—which you wrote at my dictation— the words of the LORD in the hearing of the people at the temple of the LORD on a day of fasting. You must also read them in the hearing of all the Judeans who are coming from their cities. ⁷Perhaps their petition will come before the LORD, and each one will turn from his evil way, for the anger and fury that the LORD has pronounced against this people are great." ⁸So Baruch son of Neriah did everything Jeremiah the prophet had commanded him. At the LORD's temple he read the LORD's words from the scroll.

⁹In the fifth year of Jehoiakim son of Josiah, king of Judah, in the ninth month, all the people of Jerusalem and all those coming in from Judah's cities into Jerusalem proclaimed a fast before the LORD. ¹⁰Then at the LORD's temple, in the chamber of Gemariah son of Shaphan the scribe, in the upper courtyard at the opening of the New Gate of the LORD's temple, in the hearing of all the people, Baruch read Jeremiah's words from the scroll.

¹¹When Micaiah son of Gemariah, son of Shaphan, heard all the words of the LORD from the scroll, ¹²he went down to the scribe's chamber in the king's palace. All the officials were sitting there—Elishama the scribe, Delaiah son of Shemaiah, Elnathan son of Achbor, Gemariah son of Shaphan, Zedekiah son of Hananiah, and all the other officials. ¹³Micaiah reported to them all the words he had heard when Baruch read from the scroll in the hearing of the people. ¹⁴Then all the officials sent word to Baruch through Jehudi son of Nethaniah, son of Shelemiah, son of Cushi, saying, "Bring the scroll that you read in the hearing of the people, and come." So Baruch son of Neriah took the scroll and went to them. ¹⁵They said to him, "Sit down and read it in our hearing." So Baruch read it in their hearing.

¹⁶When they had heard all the words, they turned to each other in fear and said to Baruch, "We must surely tell the king all these things." ¹⁷Then they asked Baruch, "Tell us—how did you write all these words? At his dictation?"

¹⁸Baruch said to them, "At his dictation. He recited all these words to me while I was writing on the scroll in ink." ¹⁹The officials said to Baruch, "You and Jeremiah must hide yourselves and tell no one where you are." ²⁰Then they came to the king at the courtyard, having deposited the scroll in the chamber of Elishama the scribe, and reported everything in the hearing of the king. ²¹The king sent Jehudi to get the scroll, and

he took it from the chamber of Elishama the scribe. Jehudi then read it in the hearing of the king and all the officials who were standing by the king. ²²Since it was the ninth month, the king was sitting in his winter quarters with a fire burning in front of him. ²³As soon as Jehudi would read three or four columns, Jehoiakim would cut the scroll with a scribe's knife and throw the columns into the blazing fire until the entire scroll was consumed by the fire in the brazier. ²⁴As they heard all these words, the king and all of his servants did not become terrified or tear their garments. ²⁵Even though Elnathan, Delaiah, and Gemariah had urged the king not to burn the scroll, he would not listen to them. ²⁶Then the king commanded Jerahmeel the king's son, Seraiah son of Azriel, and Shelemiah son of Abdeel to seize Baruch the scribe and Jeremiah the prophet, but the LORD had hidden them.

²⁷After the king had burned the scroll with the words Baruch had written at Jeremiah's dictation, the word of the LORD came to Jeremiah: ²⁸"Take another scroll, and once again write on it the very words that were on the original scroll that Jehoiakim king of Judah burned. ²⁹You are to proclaim concerning Jehoiakim king of Judah: This is what the LORD says: You have burned the scroll, saying, 'Why have you written on it: The king of Babylon will certainly come and destroy this land and cause it to be without man or beast?' ³⁰Therefore, this is what the LORD says concerning Jehoiakim king of Judah: He will have no one to sit on David's throne, and his corpse will be thrown out to be exposed to the heat of day and the frost of night. ³¹I will punish him, his descendants, and his officers for their wrongdoing. I will bring on them, on the residents of Jerusalem, and on the men of Judah all the disaster, which I warned them about but they did not listen."

³²Then Jeremiah took another scroll and gave it to Baruch son of Neriah, the scribe, and he wrote on it at Jeremiah's dictation all the words of the scroll that Jehoiakim, Judah's king, had burned in the fire. And many other words like them were added.

37 Zedekiah son of Josiah reigned as king in the land of Judah in place of Jehoiachin son of Jehoiakim, for Nebuchadnezzar king of Babylon made him king. ²He and his officers and the people of the land did not obey the words of the LORD that He spoke through Jeremiah the prophet.

³Nevertheless, King Zedekiah sent Jehucal son of Shelemiah and Zephaniah son of Maaseiah, the priest, to Jeremiah the prophet, requesting, "Please pray to the LORD our God for us!" ⁴Jeremiah was going about his daily tasks among the people, for they had not yet put him into the prison. ⁵Pharaoh's army had left Egypt, and when the Chaldeans, who were besieging Jerusalem, heard the report, they withdrew from Jerusalem.

⁶The word of the LORD came to Jeremiah the prophet: ⁷"This is what the LORD, the God of Israel, says: This is what you will say to Judah's king, who is sending you to inquire of Me: Watch: Pharaoh's army, which has come out to help you, is going to return to its own land of Egypt. ⁸The Chaldeans will then return and fight against this city. They will capture it and burn it down. ⁹This is what the LORD says: Don't deceive yourselves by saying, 'The Chaldeans will leave us for good,' for they will not leave. ¹⁰Indeed, if you were to strike down the entire Chaldean army that is fighting with

you, and there remained among them only the badly wounded men, each in his tent, they would get up and burn this city down."

¹¹When the Chaldean army withdrew from Jerusalem because of Pharaoh's army, ¹²Jeremiah started to leave Jerusalem to go to the land of Benjamin to claim his portion there among the people. ¹³But when he was at the Benjamin Gate, an officer of the guard was there, whose name was Irijah son of Shelemiah, son of Hananiah, and he apprehended Jeremiah the prophet, saying, "You are deserting to the Chaldeans."

¹⁴"That's a lie," Jeremiah replied. "I am not deserting to the Chaldeans!" Irijah would not listen to him but apprehended Jeremiah and took him to the officials. ¹⁵The officials were angry at Jeremiah and beat him and placed him in jail in the house of Jonathan the scribe, for it had been made into a prison. ¹⁶So Jeremiah went into a cell in the dungeon and stayed there many days.

¹⁷King Zedekiah later sent for him and received him, and in his house privately asked him, "Is there a word from the LORD?"

"There is," Jeremiah responded, and he continued, "You will be handed over to the king of Babylon." ¹⁸Then Jeremiah said to King Zedekiah, "How have I sinned against you or your servants or these people that you have put me in prison? ¹⁹Where are your prophets who prophesied to you, claiming, 'The king of Babylon will not come against you and this land'? ²⁰So now please listen, my lord the king. May my petition come before you. Don't send me back to the house of Jonathan the scribe, or I will die there."

²¹So King Zedekiah gave orders, and Jeremiah was placed in the guard's courtyard. He was given a loaf of bread each day from the baker's street until all the bread was gone from the city. So Jeremiah remained in the guard's courtyard.

38 Now Shephatiah son of Mattan, Gedaliah son of Pashhur, Jucal son of Shelemiah, and Pashhur son of Malchijah heard the words Jeremiah was speaking to all the people: ²"This is what the LORD says: 'Whoever stays in this city will die by the sword, famine, and plague, but whoever surrenders to the Chaldeans will live. He will keep his life like the spoils of war and will live.' ³This is what the LORD says: 'This city will most certainly be handed over to the king of Babylon's army, and he will capture it.'"

⁴The officials then said to the king, "This man ought to die, because he is weakening the morale of the warriors who remain in this city and of all the people by speaking to them in this way. This man is not seeking the well-being of this people, but disaster."

⁵King Zedekiah said, "Here he is; he's in your hands since the king can't do anything against you." ⁶So they took Jeremiah and dropped him into the cistern of Malchiah the king's son, which was in the guard's courtyard, lowering Jeremiah with ropes. There was no water in the cistern, only mud, and Jeremiah sank in the mud.

⁷But Ebed-melech, a ⋅Cushite court official employed in the king's palace, heard Jeremiah had been put into the cistern. While the king was sitting at the Benjamin Gate, ⁸Ebed-melech went from the king's palace and spoke to the king: ⁹"My lord the king, these men have been evil in all they have done to Jeremiah the prophet. They have dropped him into the cistern

where he will die from hunger, because there is no more bread in the city."

¹⁰So the king commanded Ebed-melech, the Cushite, "Take from here 30 men under your authority and pull Jeremiah the prophet up from the cistern before he dies."

¹¹So Ebed-melech took the men under his authority and went to the king's palace to a place below the storehouse. From there he took old rags and worn-out clothes and lowered them by ropes to Jeremiah in the cistern. ¹²Ebed-melech the Cushite cried out to Jeremiah, "Place these old rags and clothes between your armpits and the ropes." Jeremiah did so, ¹³and they pulled him up with the ropes and lifted him out of the cistern, but he continued to stay in the guard's courtyard.

¹⁴King Zedekiah sent for Jeremiah the prophet and received him at the third entrance of the LORD's temple. The king said to Jeremiah, "I am going to ask you something; don't hide anything from me."

¹⁵Jeremiah replied to Zedekiah, "If I tell you, you will kill me, won't you? Besides, if I give you advice, you won't listen to me anyway."

¹⁶King Zedekiah swore to Jeremiah in private, "As the LORD lives, who has given us this life, I will not kill you or hand you over to these men who want to take your life."

¹⁷Jeremiah therefore said to Zedekiah, "This is what the LORD, the God of ⋅Hosts, the God of Israel, says: 'If indeed you surrender to the officials of the king of Babylon, then you will live, this city will not be burned down, and you and your household will survive. ¹⁸But if you do not surrender to the officials of the king of Babylon, then this city will be handed over to the Chaldeans. They will burn it down, and you yourself will not escape from them.'"

¹⁹But King Zedekiah said to Jeremiah, "I am worried about the Judeans who have deserted to the Chaldeans. They may hand me over to the Judeans to abuse me."

²⁰"They will not hand you over," Jeremiah replied. "Obey the voice of the LORD in what I am telling you, so it may go well for you and you can live. ²¹But if you refuse to surrender, this is the verdict that the LORD has shown me: ²²All the women who remain in the palace of Judah's king will be brought out to the officials of the king of Babylon and will say:

Your trusted friends misled you
and overcame you.
Your feet sank into the mire,
and they deserted you.

²³All your wives and sons will be brought out to the Chaldeans. You yourself will not escape from them, for you will be seized by the king of Babylon and this city will burn down.'"

²⁴Then Zedekiah warned Jeremiah, "Don't let anyone know about these things or you will die. ²⁵If the officials hear that I have spoken with you and come and demand of you, 'Tell us what you said to the king; don't hide anything from us and we won't kill you. Also, what did the king say to you?' ²⁶then you will tell them, 'I was bringing before the king my petition that he not return me to the house of Jonathan to die there.'" ²⁷When all the officials came to Jeremiah and questioned him, he reported the exact words to them the king had commanded, and they quit speaking with him because nothing had been heard. ²⁸Jeremiah re-

mained in the guard's courtyard until the day Jerusalem was captured, and he was there when it happened.

39 In the ninth year of Zedekiah king of Judah, in the tenth month, King Nebuchadnezzar of Babylon advanced against Jerusalem with his entire army and laid siege to it. ²In the fourth month of Zedekiah's eleventh year, on the ninth day of the month, the city was broken into. ³All the officials of the king of Babylon entered and sat at the Middle Gate: Nergal-sharezer, Samgar, Nebusarsechim the Rab-saris, Nergal-sharezer the Rab-mag, and all the rest of the officials of Babylon's king.

⁴When he saw them, Zedekiah king of Judah and all the soldiers fled. They left the city at night by way of the king's garden through the gate between the two walls. They left along the route to the ˙Arabah. ⁵However, the Chaldean army pursued them and overtook Zedekiah in the plains of Jericho, arrested him, and brought him to Nebuchadnezzar, Babylon's king, at Riblah in the land of Hamath. The king passed sentence on him there.

⁶At Riblah the king of Babylon slaughtered Zedekiah's sons before his eyes, and he also slaughtered all Judah's nobles. ⁷Then he blinded Zedekiah and put him in bronze chains to take him to Babylon. ⁸The Chaldeans next burned down the king's palace and the people's houses and tore down the walls of Jerusalem. ⁹Nebuzaradan, the commander of the guards, deported the rest of the people to Babylon—those who had remained in the city and those deserters who had defected to him along with the rest of the people who had remained. ¹⁰However, Nebuzaradan, the commander of the guards, left in the land of Judah some of the poor people who owned nothing, and he gave them vineyards and fields at that time.

¹¹Speaking through Nebuzaradan, captain of the guard, King Nebuchadnezzar of Babylon gave orders concerning Jeremiah, saying: ¹²"Take him, look after him, and don't let any harm come to him; do for him whatever he says." ¹³Nebuzaradan, captain of the guard, Nebushazban the Rab-saris, Nergal-sharezer the Rab-mag, and all the captains of the king of Babylon ¹⁴had Jeremiah brought from the guard's courtyard and turned him over to Gedaliah son of Ahikam, son of Shaphan, to take him home. So he settled among his own people.

¹⁵Now the word of the LORD had come to Jeremiah when he was confined in the guard's courtyard: ¹⁶"Go tell Ebed-melech the ˙Cushite: This is what the LORD of ˙Hosts, the God of Israel, says: I am about to fulfill My words for harm and not for good against this city. They will take place before your eyes on that day. ¹⁷But I will rescue you on that day"—this is the LORD's declaration—"and you will not be handed over to the men you fear. ¹⁸Indeed, I will certainly deliver you so that you do not fall by the sword. Because you have trusted in Me, you will keep your life like the spoils of war." This is the LORD's declaration.

40 This is the word that came to Jeremiah from the LORD after Nebuzaradan, captain of the guard, released him at Ramah. When he found him, he was bound in chains with all the exiles of Jerusalem and Judah who were being exiled to Babylon. ²The captain of the guard took Jeremiah and said to him, "The LORD your God decreed this disaster on this place, ³and the LORD has fulfilled it. He has done just what He decreed. Because you people have sinned against

the LORD and have not obeyed Him, this thing has happened. ⁴Now pay attention: Today I am setting you free from the chains that were on your hands. If it pleases you to come with me to Babylon, come, and I will take care of you. But if it seems wrong to you to come with me to Babylon, go no farther. Look—the whole land is in front of you. Wherever it seems good and right for you to go, go there." ⁵When Jeremiah had not yet turned to go, Nebuzaradan said to him: "Return to Gedaliah son of Ahikam, son of Shaphan, whom the king of Babylon has appointed over the cities of Judah, and stay with him among the people or go wherever you want to go." So the captain of the guard gave him a ration and a gift and released him. ⁶Jeremiah therefore went to Gedaliah son of Ahikam at Mizpah, and he stayed with him among the people who remained in the land.

⁷When all the commanders of the armies in the field—they and their men—heard that the king of Babylon had appointed Gedaliah son of Ahikam over the land and that he had put him in charge of the men, women, and children from the poorest of the land who had not been deported to Babylon, ⁸they came to Gedaliah at Mizpah. The commanders included Ishmael son of Nethaniah, Johanan and Jonathan the sons of Kareah, Seraiah son of Tanhumeth, the sons of Ephai the Netophathite, and Jezaniah son of the Maacathite—they and their men.

⁹Gedaliah son of Ahikam, son of Shaphan, swore an oath to them and their men, assuring them, "Don't be afraid to serve the Chaldeans. Live in the land and serve the king of Babylon, and it will go well for you. ¹⁰As for me, I am going to live in Mizpah to represent you before the Chaldeans who come to us. As for you, gather wine, summer fruit, and oil, place them in your storage jars, and live in the cities you have captured."

¹¹When all the Judeans in Moab and among the Ammonites and in Edom and in all the other lands also heard that the king of Babylon had left a remnant in Judah and had appointed Gedaliah son of Ahikam, son of Shaphan, over them, ¹²they all returned from all the places where they had been banished and came to the land of Judah, to Gedaliah at Mizpah, and harvested a great amount of wine and summer fruit.

¹³Meanwhile, Johanan son of Kareah and all the commanders of the armies in the field came to Gedaliah at Mizpah ¹⁴and warned him, "Don't you realize that Baalis, king of the Ammonites, has sent Ishmael son of Nethaniah to kill you?" But Gedaliah son of Ahikam would not believe them. ¹⁵Then Johanan son of Kareah suggested to Gedaliah in private at Mizpah, "Let me go kill Ishmael son of Nethaniah. No one will know it. Why should he kill you and scatter all of Judah that has gathered to you so that the remnant of Judah would perish?"

¹⁶But Gedaliah son of Ahikam responded to Johanan son of Kareah, "Don't do that! What you're saying about Ishmael is a lie."

41 In the seventh month, Ishmael son of Nethaniah, son of Elishama, of the royal family and one of the king's chief officers, came with 10 men to Gedaliah son of Ahikam at Mizpah. They ate a meal together there in Mizpah, ²but then Ishmael son of Nethaniah and the 10 men who were with him got up and struck down Gedaliah son of Ahikam, son of Shaphan, with the sword; he killed the one the king of Babylon had appointed in the land. ³Ishmael also struck down all the Judeans who were with Gedaliah at Mizpah, as well as the Chaldean soldiers who were there.

⁴On the second day after he had killed Gedaliah, when no one knew yet, ⁵80 men came from Shechem, Shiloh, and Samaria who had shaved their beards, torn their garments, and gashed themselves, and who were carrying •grain and incense offerings to bring to the temple of the Lᴏʀᴅ. ⁶Ishmael son of Nethaniah came out of Mizpah to meet them, weeping as he came. When he encountered them, he said: "Come to Gedaliah son of Ahikam!" ⁷But when they came into the city, Ishmael son of Nethaniah and the men with him slaughtered them and threw them into a cistern.

⁸However, there were 10 men among them who said to Ishmael, "Don't kill us, for we have hidden treasure in the field—wheat, barley, oil, and honey!" So he stopped and did not kill them along with their companions. ⁹Now the cistern where Ishmael had thrown all the corpses of the men he had struck down was a large one that King Asa had made in the encounter with Baasha king of Israel. Ishmael son of Nethaniah filled it with the slain.

¹⁰Then Ishmael took captive all the remnant of the people of Mizpah including the daughters of the king—all those who remained in Mizpah over whom Nebuzaradan, captain of the guard, had appointed Gedaliah son of Ahikam. Ishmael son of Nethaniah took them captive and set off to cross over to the Ammonites.

¹¹When Johanan son of Kareah and all the commanders of the armies with him heard of all the evil that Ishmael son of Nethaniah had done, ¹²they took all their men and went to fight with Ishmael son of Nethaniah and found him by the great pool in Gibeon. ¹³When all the people with Ishmael saw Johanan son of Kareah and all the commanders of the army with him, they rejoiced, ¹⁴and all the people whom Ishmael had taken captive from Mizpah turned around and rejoined Johanan son of Kareah. ¹⁵But Ishmael son of Nethaniah escaped from Johanan with eight men and went to the Ammonites. ¹⁶Johanan son of Kareah and all the commanders of the armies with him then took from Mizpah all the remnant of the people whom he had recovered from Ishmael son of Nethaniah after Ishmael had killed Gedaliah son of Ahikam—men, soldiers, women, children, and court officials whom he brought back from Gibeon. ¹⁷They left, stopping in Geruth Chimham, which is near Bethlehem, in order to make their way into Egypt, ¹⁸away from the Chaldeans. For they feared them because Ishmael son of Nethaniah had struck down Gedaliah son of Ahikam, whom the king of Babylon had appointed in the land.

42 Then all the commanders of the armies, along with Johanan son of Kareah, Jezaniah son of Hoshaiah, and all the people from the least to the greatest, approached ²Jeremiah the prophet and said, "May our petition come before you; pray to the Lᴏʀᴅ your God on our behalf, on behalf of this entire remnant (for few of us remain out of the many, as you can see with your own eyes), ³that the Lᴏʀᴅ your God may tell us the way we should walk and the thing we should do."

⁴So Jeremiah the prophet said to them, "I have heard. I will now pray to the Lᴏʀᴅ your God according to your words, and every word that the Lᴏʀᴅ answers you I will tell you; I won't withhold a word from you."

⁵And they said to Jeremiah, "As for every word the Lᴏʀᴅ your God sends you to tell us, if we don't act accordingly, may the Lᴏʀᴅ be a true and faithful witness against us. ⁶Whether it is pleasant or unpleasant, we will obey the voice of the Lᴏʀᴅ our God to whom we are sending you so that it may go well with us. We will certainly obey the voice of the Lᴏʀᴅ our God!"

⁷Now at the end of 10 days, the word of the Lᴏʀᴅ came to Jeremiah, ⁸and he summoned Johanan son of Kareah, all the commanders of the armies who were with him, and all the people from the least to the greatest.

⁹He said to them, "This is what the Lᴏʀᴅ says, the God of Israel to whom you sent me to bring your petition before Him: ¹⁰'If you will indeed stay in this land, then I will rebuild and not demolish you, and I will plant and not uproot you, because I relent concerning the disaster that I have brought on you. ¹¹Don't be afraid of the king of Babylon whom you now fear; don't be afraid of him'—this is the Lᴏʀᴅ's declaration—'because I am with you to save you and deliver you from him. ¹²I will grant you compassion, and he will have compassion on you and allow you to return to your own soil. ¹³But if you say, 'We will not stay in this land,' so as not to obey the voice of the Lᴏʀᴅ your God, ¹⁴and if you say, 'No, instead we'll go to the land of Egypt where we will not see war or hear the sound of the ram's horn or hunger for food, and we'll live there,' ¹⁵then hear the word of the Lᴏʀᴅ, remnant of Judah! This is what the Lᴏʀᴅ of •Hosts, the God of Israel, says: If you are firmly resolved to go to Egypt and live there for a while, ¹⁶then the sword you fear will overtake you there in the land of Egypt, and the famine you are worried about will follow on your heels there to Egypt, and you will die there. ¹⁷All who resolve to go to Egypt to live there for a while will die by the sword, famine, and plague. They will have no one escape or survive from the disaster that I will bring on them.'

¹⁸"For this is what the Lᴏʀᴅ of Hosts, the God of Israel, says: 'Just as My anger and fury were poured out on Jerusalem's residents, so will My fury pour out on you if you go to Egypt. You will become an object of cursing, scorn, execration, and disgrace, and you will never see this place again.' ¹⁹The Lᴏʀᴅ has spoken concerning you, remnant of Judah: 'Don't go to Egypt.' Know for certain that I have warned you today! ²⁰You have led your own selves astray because you are the ones who sent me to the Lᴏʀᴅ your God, saying, 'Pray to the Lᴏʀᴅ our God on our behalf, and as for all that the Lᴏʀᴅ our God says, tell it to us, and we'll act accordingly.' ²¹For I have told you today, but you have not obeyed the voice of the Lᴏʀᴅ your God in everything He has sent me to tell you. ²²Now therefore, know for certain that by the sword, famine, and plague you will die in the place where you desired to go to live for a while."

43 When Jeremiah had finished speaking to all the people all the words of the Lᴏʀᴅ their God—all these words the Lᴏʀᴅ their God had sent him to give them— ²then Azariah son of Hoshaiah, Johanan son of Kareah, and all the other arrogant men responded to Jeremiah, "You are speaking a lie! The Lᴏʀᴅ our God has not sent you to say, 'You must not go to Egypt to live there for a while!' ³Rather, Baruch son of Neriah is inciting you against us to hand us over to the Chaldeans to put us to death or to deport us to Babylon!"

⁴So Johanan son of Kareah and all the commanders of the armies did not obey the voice of the Lᴏʀᴅ

to stay in the land of Judah. [5] Instead, Johanan son of Kareah and all the commanders of the armies took the whole remnant of Judah, those who had returned from all the nations where they had been banished to live in the land of Judah for a while— [6] the men, women, children, king's daughters, and everyone whom Nebuzaradan, captain of the guard, had allowed to remain with Gedaliah son of Ahikam son of Shaphan, along with Jeremiah the prophet and Baruch son of Neriah— [7] and they went to the land of Egypt because they did not obey the voice of the LORD. They went as far as Tahpanhes.

[8] Then the word of the LORD came to Jeremiah at Tahpanhes: [9] "Pick up some large stones and set them in the mortar of the brick pavement that is at the opening of Pharaoh's palace at Tahpanhes. Do this in the sight of the Judean men [10] and tell them: This is what the LORD of *Hosts, the God of Israel, says: I will send for My servant Nebuchadnezzar king of Babylon, and I will place his throne on these stones that I have embedded, and he will pitch his pavilion over them. [11] He will come and strike down the land of Egypt— those destined for death, to death; those destined for captivity, to captivity; and those destined for the sword, to the sword. [12] I will kindle a fire in the temples of Egypt's gods, and he will burn them and take them prisoner. He will *clean the land of Egypt as a shepherd picks lice off his garment, and he will leave there unscathed. [13] He will smash the sacred pillars of the sun temple in the land of Egypt and burn down the temples of the Egyptian gods."

44 This is the word that came to Jeremiah for all the Jews living in the land of Egypt—at Migdol, Tahpanhes, Memphis, and in the land of Pathros: [2] "This is what the LORD of *Hosts, the God of Israel, says: You have seen all the disaster I brought against Jerusalem and all Judah's cities; look, they are a ruin today without an inhabitant in them [3] because of their evil ways that provoked Me to anger, going and burning incense to serve other gods that they, you, and your fathers did not know. [4] So I sent you all My servants the prophets time and time again, saying: Don't do this detestable thing that I hate. [5] But they did not listen or pay attention; they did not turn from their evil or stop burning incense to other gods. [6] So My fierce wrath poured out and burned in Judah's cities and Jerusalem's streets so that they became the desolate ruin they are today.

[7] "So now, this is what the LORD, the God of Hosts, the God of Israel, says: Why are you doing such great harm to yourselves? You are cutting off man and woman, child and infant from Judah, leaving yourselves without a remnant. [8] You are provoking Me to anger by the work of your hands. You are burning incense to other gods in the land of Egypt where you have gone to live for a while. As a result, you will be cut off and become an object of cursing and insult among all the nations of earth. [9] Have you forgotten the evils of your fathers, the evils of Judah's kings, the evils of their wives, your own evils, and the evils of your wives that were committed in the land of Judah and in the streets of Jerusalem? [10] They have not become humble to this day, and they have not *feared or followed My instruction or My statutes that I set before you and your ancestors.

[11] "Therefore, this is what the LORD of Hosts, the God of Israel, says: I am about to turn against you to bring disaster, to cut off all Judah. [12] And I will take away the remnant of Judah, those who have resolved to go to the land of Egypt to live there for a while; they will meet their end. All of them in the land of Egypt will fall by the sword; they will meet their end by famine. From the least to the greatest, they will die by the sword and by famine. Then they will become an object of cursing, scorn, execration, and disgrace. [13] I will punish those living in the land of Egypt just as I punished Jerusalem by sword, famine, and plague. [14] Then the remnant of Judah—those going to live for a while there in the land of Egypt—will have no fugitive or survivor to return to the land of Judah where they are longing to return to live, for they will not return except for a few fugitives."

[15] However, all the men who knew that their wives were burning incense to other gods, all the women standing by—a great assembly—and all the people who were living in the land of Egypt at Pathros answered Jeremiah, [16] "As for the word you spoke to us in the name of *Yahweh, we are not going to listen to you! [17] Instead, we will do everything we said we would: burn incense to the queen of heaven and offer *drink offerings to her just as we, our fathers, our kings, and our officials did in Judah's cities and in Jerusalem's streets. Then we had enough food and good things and saw no disaster, [18] but from the time we ceased to burn incense to the queen of heaven and to offer her drink offerings, we have lacked everything, and through sword and famine we have met our end."

[19] And the women said, "When we burned incense to the queen of heaven and poured out drink offerings to her, was it apart from our husbands' knowledge that we made sacrificial cakes in her image and poured out drink offerings to her?"

[20] But Jeremiah responded to all the people—the men, women, and all the people who were answering him: [21] "As for the incense you burned in Judah's cities and in Jerusalem's streets—you, your fathers, your kings, your officials, and the people of the land—did the LORD not remember them? He brought this to mind. [22] The LORD can no longer bear your evil deeds and the detestable acts you have committed, so your land has become a waste, a desolation, and an object of cursing, without inhabitant, as you see today. [23] Because you burned incense and sinned against the LORD and didn't obey the LORD's voice and didn't follow His instruction, His statutes, and His testimonies, this disaster has come to you, as you see today."

[24] Then Jeremiah said to all the people, including all the women, "Hear the word of the LORD, all Judah who are in the land of Egypt. [25] This is what the LORD of Hosts, the God of Israel, says: 'As for you and your wives, you women have spoken with your mouths, and you men fulfilled it by your deeds, saying, "We will keep our vows that we have made to burn incense to the queen of heaven and to pour out drink offerings for her." Go ahead, confirm your vows! Pay your vows!'

[26] "Therefore, hear the word of the LORD, all you Judeans who live in the land of Egypt: 'I have sworn by My great name, says Yahweh, that My name will never again be invoked by anyone of Judah in all the land of Egypt, saying, "As the Lord GOD lives." [27] I am watching over them for disaster and not for good, and every man of Judah who is in the land of Egypt will meet his end by sword or famine until they are finished off. [28] Those who escape the sword will return

from the land of Egypt to the land of Judah only few in number, and the whole remnant of Judah, the ones going to the land of Egypt to live there for a while, will know whose word stands, Mine or theirs! ²⁹ This will be a sign to you'—this is the LORD's declaration—'that I am about to punish you in this place, so you may know that My words of disaster concerning you will certainly come to pass. ³⁰ This is what the LORD says: I am about to hand over Pharaoh Hophra, Egypt's king, to his enemies, to those who want to take his life, just as I handed over Judah's King Zedekiah to Babylon's King Nebuchadnezzar, who was his enemy, the one who wanted to take his life.'"

45 This is the word that Jeremiah the prophet spoke to Baruch son of Neriah when he wrote these words on a scroll at Jeremiah's dictation in the fourth year of Jehoiakim son of Josiah, king of Judah: ² "This is what the LORD, the God of Israel, says to you, Baruch: ³ 'You have said, "Woe is me, because the LORD has added misery to my pain! I am worn out with groaning and have found no rest."'

⁴ "This is what you are to say to him: 'This is what the LORD says: What I have built I am about to demolish, and what I have planted I am about to uproot—the whole land! ⁵ But as for you, do you seek great things for yourself? Stop seeking! For I am about to bring disaster on every living creature'—this is the LORD's declaration—'but I will grant you your life like the spoils of war wherever you go.'"

46 The word of the LORD that came to Jeremiah the prophet about the nations:
² About Egypt and the army of Pharaoh Neco, Egypt's king, which was defeated at Carchemish on the Euphrates River by Nebuchadnezzar king of Babylon in the fourth year of Judah's King Jehoiakim son of Josiah:

³   Deploy small shields and large;
       draw near for battle!
⁴   Harness the horses;
       mount the steeds;
       take your positions with helmets on!
       Polish the lances;
       put on armor!
⁵   Why have I seen this?
       They are terrified,
       they are retreating,
       their warriors are crushed,
       they flee headlong,
       they never look back,
       terror is on every side!
               This is the LORD's declaration.
⁶   The swift cannot flee,
       and the warrior cannot escape!
       In the north by the bank
          of the Euphrates River,
       they stumble and fall.
⁷   Who is this, rising like the Nile,
       like rivers whose waters churn?
⁸   Egypt rises like the Nile,
       and its waters churn like rivers.
       He boasts, "I will go up, I will cover the earth;
       I will destroy cities with their residents."
⁹   Rise up, you cavalry!
       Race furiously, you chariots!
       Let the warriors go out—
       •Cush and Put,
       who are able to handle shields,

       and the Ludim,
       who are able to handle and string the bow.
¹⁰   That day belongs to the Lord, the GOD
          of •Hosts,
       a day of vengeance to avenge Himself
       against His adversaries.
       The sword will devour and be satisfied;
       it will drink its fill of their blood,
       because it will be a sacrifice to the Lord,
          the GOD of Hosts,
       in the northern land by the Euphrates River.
¹¹   Go up to Gilead and get balm,
       Virgin Daughter Egypt!
       You have multiplied remedies in vain;
       there is no healing for you.
¹²   The nations have heard of your dishonor,
       and your outcry fills the earth,
       because warrior stumbles against warrior
       and together both of them have fallen.

¹³ This is the word the LORD spoke to Jeremiah the prophet about the coming of Nebuchadnezzar king of Babylon to defeat the land of Egypt:

¹⁴   Announce it in Egypt, and proclaim it
          in Migdol!
       Proclaim it in Memphis and in Tahpanhes!
       Say: Take positions! Prepare yourself,
       for the sword devours all around you.
¹⁵   Why have your strong ones been swept away?
       Each has not stood,
       for the LORD has thrust him down.
¹⁶   He continues to stumble.
       Indeed, each falls over the other.
       They say, "Get up! Let's return
          to our people
       and to the land of our birth,
       away from the sword that oppresses."
¹⁷   There they will cry out,
       "Pharaoh king of Egypt was all noise;
       he let the opportune moment pass."
¹⁸   As I live—
             this is the King's declaration;
             •Yahweh of Hosts is His name.
       He will come like Tabor among the mountains
       and like Carmel by the sea.
¹⁹   Get your bags ready for exile,
       inhabitant of Daughter Egypt!
       For Memphis will become a desolation,
       uninhabited ruins.
²⁰   Egypt is a beautiful young cow,
       but a horsefly from the north is coming
          against her.
²¹   Even her mercenaries among her
       are like stall-fed calves.
       They too will turn back;
       together they will flee;
       they will not take their stand,
       for the day of their calamity is coming
          on them,
       the time of their punishment.
²²   Egypt will hiss like a slithering snake,
       for the enemy will come with an army;
       with axes they will come against her
       like those who cut trees.
²³   They will cut down her forest—
            this is the LORD's declaration—
       though it is dense,
       for they are more numerous than locusts;

they cannot be counted.
²⁴ Daughter Egypt will be put to shame,
handed over to a northern people.

²⁵ The LORD of Hosts, the God of Israel, says: "I am about to punish Amon, god of Thebes, along with Pharaoh, Egypt, her gods, and her kings—Pharaoh and those trusting in him. ²⁶ I will hand them over to those who want to take their lives—to Nebuchadnezzar king of Babylon and his officers. But after this, it will be inhabited again as in ancient times."

This is the LORD's declaration.

²⁷ But you, My servant Jacob, do not be afraid,
and do not be discouraged, Israel,
for without fail I will save you from far away
and your descendants, from the land
of their captivity!
Jacob will return and have calm and quiet
with no one to frighten him.
²⁸ And you, My servant Jacob, do not be afraid—
this is the LORD's declaration—
for I will be with you.
I will bring destruction on all the nations
where I have banished you,
but I will not bring destruction on you.
I will discipline you with justice,
and I will by no means leave you unpunished.

47 This is the word of the LORD that came to Jeremiah the prophet about the Philistines before Pharaoh defeated Gaza. ² This is what the LORD says:

Look, waters are rising from the north
and becoming an overflowing ˙wadi.
They will overflow the land and everything
in it,
the cities and their inhabitants.
The people will cry out,
and every inhabitant of the land will wail.
³ At the sound of the stomping hooves
of his stallions,
the rumbling of his chariots,
and the clatter of their wheels,
fathers will not turn back for their sons,
because they will be utterly helpless
⁴ on account of the day that is coming
to destroy all the Philistines,
to cut off from Tyre and Sidon
every remaining ally.
Indeed, the LORD is about to destroy
the Philistines,
the remnant of the islands of Caphtor.
⁵ Baldness is coming to Gaza.
Ashkelon will become silent,
a remnant of their valley.
How long will you gash yourself?
⁶ Oh, sword of the LORD!
How long will you be restless?
Go back to your sheath;
be still; be silent!
⁷ How can it rest
when the LORD has given it a command?
He has assigned it
against Ashkelon and the shore of the sea.

48 About Moab, this is what the LORD of ˙Hosts, the God of Israel, says:

Woe to Nebo, because it is
about to be destroyed;
Kiriathaim will be put to shame; it will be
taken captive.

The fortress will be put to shame
and dismayed!
² There is no longer praise for Moab;
they plan harm against her in Heshbon:
Come, let's cut her off from nationhood.
Also, Madmen, you will be silenced;
the sword will pursue you.
³ A voice cries out from Horonaim,
"devastation and great disaster!"
⁴ Moab will be shattered;
her little ones will cry out.
⁵ For on the Ascent to Luhith
they will be weeping continually,
and on the descent to Horonaim
will be heard cries of distress
over the destruction:
⁶ Flee! Save your lives!
Be like a juniper bush in the wilderness.
⁷ Because you trust in your works
and treasures,
you will be captured also.
Chemosh will go into exile
with his priests and officials.
⁸ The destroyer will move against every town;
not one town will escape.
The valley will perish,
and the plain will be annihilated,
as the LORD has said.
⁹ Make Moab a salt marsh,
for she will run away;
her towns will become a desolation,
without inhabitant.
¹⁰ The one who does
the LORD's business deceitfully is cursed,
and the one who withholds
his sword from bloodshed is cursed.
¹¹ Moab has been left quiet since his youth,
settled like wine on its dregs.
He hasn't been poured from one container
to another
or gone into exile.
So his taste has remained the same,
and his aroma hasn't changed.
¹² Therefore look, the days are coming—
this is the LORD's declaration—
when I will send those to him,
who will pour him out.
They will empty his containers
and smash his jars.
¹³ Moab will be put to shame
because of Chemosh,
just as the house of Israel was put to shame
because of Bethel that they trusted in.
¹⁴ How can you say, "We are warriors—
mighty men ready for battle"?
¹⁵ The destroyer of Moab and its towns
has come up,
and the best of its young men
have gone down to slaughter.
This is the King's declaration;
˙Yahweh of Hosts is His name.
¹⁶ Moab's calamity is near at hand;
his disaster is rushing swiftly.
¹⁷ Mourn for him, all you surrounding nations,
everyone who knows his name.
Say: How the mighty scepter is shattered,
the glorious staff!

¹⁸ Come down from glory;
     sit on parched ground,
resident of the daughter of Dibon,
for the destroyer of Moab has come
     against you;
he has destroyed your fortresses.
¹⁹ Stand by the highway and look,
resident of Aroer!
Ask him who is fleeing or her who is escaping:
What happened?
²⁰ Moab is put to shame, indeed dismayed.
Wail and cry out!
Declare by the Arnon
that Moab is destroyed.

²¹ "Judgment has come to the land of the plateau—to Holon, Jahzah, Mephaath, ²² Dibon, Nebo, Beth-diblathaim, ²³ Kiriathaim, Beth-gamul, Beth-meon, ²⁴ Kerioth, Bozrah, and all the towns of the land of Moab, those far and near. ²⁵ Moab's •horn is chopped off; his arm is shattered."

                         This is the LORD's declaration.

²⁶ "Make him drunk, because he has exalted himself against the LORD. Moab will wallow in his own vomit, and he will also become a laughingstock. ²⁷ Wasn't Israel a laughingstock to you? Was he ever found among thieves? For whenever you speak of him you shake your head."

²⁸ Abandon the towns! Live in the cliffs,
residents of Moab!
Be like a dove
that nests inside the mouth of a cave.
²⁹ We have heard of Moab's pride,
great pride, indeed—
his insolence, arrogance, pride,
and haughty heart.
³⁰ I know his outburst.
                         This is the LORD's declaration.
It is empty.
His boast is empty.
³¹ Therefore, I will wail over Moab.
I will cry out for Moab, all of it;
he will moan for the men of Kir-heres.
³² I will weep for you, vine of Sibmah,
with more than the weeping for Jazer.
Your tendrils have extended to the sea;
they have reached to the sea and to Jazer.
The destroyer has fallen on your summer fruit
     and grape harvest.
³³ Joy and celebration are taken
     from the fertile field
and from the land of Moab.
I have stopped the flow of wine
     from the winepresses;
no one will tread with shouts of joy.
The shouting is not a shout of joy.

³⁴ "There is a cry from Heshbon to Elealeh; they raise their voices as far as Jahaz—from Zoar to Horonaim and Eglath-shelishiyah—because even the waters of Nimrim have become desolate. ³⁵ In Moab, I will stop"—this is the LORD's declaration—"the one who offers sacrifices on the •high place and burns incense to his gods. ³⁶ Therefore, My heart moans like flutes for Moab, and My heart moans like flutes for the people of Kir-heres. And therefore, the wealth he has gained has perished. ³⁷ Indeed, every head is bald and every beard clipped; on every hand is a gash and •sackcloth around the waist. ³⁸ On all the rooftops of Moab and in her public squares, everyone is mourning because I have shattered Moab like a jar no one wants." This is the LORD's declaration. ³⁹ "How broken it is! They wail! How Moab has turned his back! He is ashamed. Moab will become a laughingstock and a shock to all those around him."

⁴⁰ For this is what the LORD says:

He will swoop down like an eagle
and spread his wings against Moab.
⁴¹ The towns have been captured,
and the strongholds seized.
In that day the heart of Moab's warriors
will be like the heart of a woman
     with contractions.
⁴² Moab will be destroyed as a people
because he has exalted himself
     against the LORD.
⁴³ Panic, pit, and trap
await you, resident of Moab.
                         This is the LORD's declaration.
⁴⁴ He who flees from the panic will fall in the pit,
and he who climbs from the pit
will be captured in the trap,
for I will bring against Moab
the year of their punishment.
                         This is the LORD's declaration.
⁴⁵ Those who flee will stand exhausted
     in Heshbon's shadow
because fire has come out from Heshbon
and a flame from within Sihon.
It will devour Moab's forehead
and the skull of the noisemakers.
⁴⁶ Woe to you, Moab!
The people of Chemosh have perished
because your sons have been taken captive
and your daughters have gone into captivity.
⁴⁷ Yet, I will restore the fortunes of Moab
     in the last days.
                         This is the LORD's declaration.
The judgment on Moab ends here.

49 About the Ammonites, this is what the LORD says:

Does Israel have no sons?
Is he without an heir?
Why then has •Milcom dispossessed Gad
and his people settled in their cities?
² Therefore look, the days are coming—
              this is the LORD's declaration—
when I will make the shout of battle heard
against Rabbah of the Ammonites.
It will become a desolate mound,
and its villages will be burned down.
Israel will dispossess their dispossessors,
says the LORD.
³ Wail, Heshbon, for Ai is devastated;
cry out, daughters of Rabbah!
Clothe yourselves with •sackcloth, and lament;
run back and forth within your walls,
because Milcom will go into exile
together with his priests and officials.
⁴ Why do you brag about your valleys,
your flowing valley,
you faithless daughter?
You who trust in your treasures
and boast, "Who can attack me?"
⁵ Look, I am about to bring terror on you—
              this is the declaration of
              the Lord GOD of •Hosts—

from all those around you.
You will be banished, each man headlong,
with no one to gather up the fugitives.
⁶ But after that, I will restore the fortunes
of the Ammonites.
This is the LORD's declaration.

⁷ About Edom, this is what the LORD of Hosts says:
Is there no longer wisdom in Teman?
Has counsel perished from the prudent?
Has their wisdom rotted away?
⁸ Run! Turn back! Lie low,
residents of Dedan,
for I will bring Esau's calamity
on him
at the time I punish him.
⁹ If grape harvesters came to you,
wouldn't they leave some gleanings?
Were thieves to come in the night,
they would destroy only what they wanted.
¹⁰ But I will strip Esau bare;
I will uncover his secret places.
He will try to hide himself,
but he will be unable.
His descendants will be destroyed
along with his relatives and neighbors.
He will exist no longer.
¹¹ Abandon your fatherless; I will preserve them;
let your widows trust in Me.

¹² "For this is what the LORD says: If those who do not deserve to drink the cup must drink it, can you possibly remain unpunished? You will not remain unpunished, for you must drink it too. ¹³ For by Myself I have sworn"—this is the LORD's declaration—"Bozrah will become a desolation, a disgrace, a ruin, and a curse, and all her cities will become ruins forever."

¹⁴ I have heard a message from the LORD;
a messenger has been sent among the nations:
Assemble yourselves to come against her.
Rise up for war!
¹⁵ Look, I will certainly make you insignificant
among the nations,
despised among humanity.
¹⁶ As to the terror you cause,
your presumptuous heart has deceived you.
You who live in the clefts of the rock,
you who occupy the mountain summit,
though you elevate your nest like the eagle,
even from there I will bring you down.
This is the LORD's declaration.

¹⁷ "Edom will become a desolation. Everyone who passes by her will be horrified and scoff because of all her wounds. ¹⁸ As when Sodom and Gomorrah were overthrown along with their neighbors," says the LORD, "no one will live there; no human being will even stay in it as a temporary resident.

¹⁹ "Look, it will be like a lion coming from the thickets of the Jordan to the watered grazing land. Indeed, I will chase Edom away from her land in a flash. I will appoint whoever is chosen for her. For who is like Me? Who will summon Me? Who is the shepherd who can stand against Me?"

²⁰ Therefore, hear the plans that the LORD has drawn up against Edom and the strategies He has devised against the people of Teman: The flock's little lambs will certainly be dragged away, and their grazing land will be made desolate because of them. ²¹ At the sound of their fall the earth will quake; the sound of her cry will be heard at the ⁎Red Sea. ²² Look! It will be like an eagle soaring upward, then swooping down and spreading its wings over Bozrah. In that day the hearts of Edom's warriors will be like the heart of a woman with contractions.

²³ About Damascus:
Hamath and Arpad are put to shame,
for they have heard a bad report
and are agitated;
in the sea there is anxiety that cannot
be calmed.
²⁴ Damascus has become weak;
she has turned to run;
panic has gripped her.
Distress and labor pains have seized her
like a woman in labor.
²⁵ How can the city of praise not be abandoned,
the town that brings Me joy?
²⁶ Therefore, her young men will fall
in her public squares;
all the warriors will perish in that day.
This is the declaration of
the LORD of Hosts.
²⁷ I will set fire to the wall of Damascus;
it will consume Ben-hadad's citadels.

²⁸ About Kedar and the kingdoms of Hazor, which Nebuchadnezzar, Babylon's king, defeated, this is what the LORD says:
Rise up, go against Kedar,
and destroy the people of the east!
²⁹ They will take their tents and their flocks
along with their tent curtains
and all their equipment.
They will take their camels for themselves.
They will call out to them:
Terror is on every side!
³⁰ Run! Escape quickly! Lie low,
residents of Hazor—
this is the LORD's declaration—
for Nebuchadnezzar king of Babylon
has drawn up a plan against you;
he has devised a strategy against you.
³¹ Rise up, go up against a nation at ease,
one living in security.
This is the LORD's declaration.
They have no doors, not even a gate bar;
they live alone.
³² Their camels will become plunder,
and their massive herds of cattle will
become spoil.
I will scatter them to the wind
in every direction,
those who shave their temples;
I will bring calamity on them
across all their borders.
This is the LORD's declaration.
³³ Hazor will become a jackals' den,
a desolation forever.
No one will live there;
no human being will even stay in it as a
temporary resident.

³⁴ This is the word of the LORD that came to Jeremiah the prophet about Elam at the beginning of the reign of Zedekiah king of Judah. ³⁵ This is what the LORD of Hosts says:
I am about to shatter Elam's bow,
the source of their might.

³⁶ I will bring the four winds against Elam
from the four corners of the heavens,
and I will scatter them to all these winds.
There will not be a nation
to which Elam's banished ones will not go.
³⁷ I will devastate Elam before their enemies,
before those who want to take their lives.
I will bring disaster on them,
My burning anger.
                   This is the LORD's declaration.
I will send the sword after them
until I finish them off.
³⁸ I will set My throne in Elam,
and I will destroy the king and officials
    from there.
                   This is the LORD's declaration.
³⁹ In the last days,
I will restore the fortunes of Elam.
                   This is the LORD's declaration.

50

The word the LORD spoke about Babylon, the land of the Chaldeans, through Jeremiah the prophet:
² Announce to the nations;
proclaim and raise up a signal flag;
proclaim, and hide nothing.
Say: Babylon is captured;
Bel is put to shame;
Marduk is devastated;
her idols are put to shame;
her false gods, devastated.
³ For a nation from the north will come
    against her;
it will make her land desolate.
No one will be living in it—
both man and beast will escape.
⁴ In those days and at that time—
           this is the LORD's declaration—
the Israelites and Judeans will come together,
weeping as they come,
and will seek the LORD their God.
⁵ They will ask about ˙Zion,
turning their faces to this road.
They will come and join themselves
    to the LORD
in an everlasting covenant that will never
    be forgotten.
⁶ My people are lost sheep;
their shepherds have led them astray,
guiding them the wrong way
    in the mountains.
They have wandered from mountain
    to hill;
they have forgotten their resting place.
⁷ All who found them devoured them.
Their adversaries said, "We're not ˙guilty;
instead, they have sinned against the LORD,
their righteous grazing land,
the hope of their ancestors, the LORD."
⁸ Escape from Babylon;
depart from the Chaldeans' land.
Be like the rams that lead the flock.
⁹ For I will soon stir up and bring
    against Babylon
an assembly of great nations
    from the north country.
They will line up in battle formation
    against her;

from there she will be captured.
Their arrows will be like those
    of a skilled warrior
who does not return empty-handed.
¹⁰ The Chaldeans will become plunder;
all Babylon's plunderers will be fully satisfied.
                   This is the LORD's declaration.
¹¹ Because you rejoice,
because you sing in triumph—
you who plundered My inheritance—
because you frolic like a young cow
    treading grain
and neigh like stallions,
¹² your mother will be utterly humiliated;
she who bore you will be put to shame.
Look! She will lag behind all the nations—
a dry land, a wilderness, an ˙Arabah.
¹³ Because of the LORD's wrath,
she will not be inhabited;
she will become a desolation, every bit of her.
Everyone who passes through Babylon
will be horrified
and scoff because of all her wounds.
¹⁴ Line up in battle formation around Babylon,
all you archers!
Shoot at her! Do not spare an arrow,
for she has sinned against the LORD.
¹⁵ Raise a war cry against her on every side!
She has thrown up her hands in surrender;
her defense towers have fallen;
her walls are demolished.
Since this is the LORD's vengeance,
take out your vengeance on her;
as she has done, do the same to her.
¹⁶ Cut off the sower from Babylon
as well as him who wields the sickle
    at harvest time.
Because of the oppressor's sword,
each will turn to his own people,
each will flee to his own land.
¹⁷ Israel is a stray lamb, chased by lions.
The first who devoured him was the king
    of Assyria;
the last one who crushed his bones
was Nebuchadnezzar king of Babylon.
¹⁸ Therefore, this is what the LORD of ˙Hosts, the God of Israel, says: "I am about to punish the king of Babylon and his land just as I punished the king of Assyria.
¹⁹ I will return Israel to his grazing land,
and he will feed on Carmel and Bashan;
he will be satisfied
in the hill country of Ephraim and of Gilead.
²⁰ In those days and at that time—
           this is the LORD's declaration—
one will search for Israel's guilt,
but there will be none,
and for Judah's sins,
but they will not be found,
for I will forgive those I leave as a remnant.
²¹ "Go against the land of Merathaim,
and against those living in Pekod.
Put them to the sword;
˙completely destroy them—
           this is the LORD's declaration—
do everything I have commanded you.
²² The sound of war is in the land—
a great destruction.

²³ How the hammer of the whole earth
is cut down and smashed!
What a horror Babylon has become
among the nations!
²⁴ Babylon, I laid a trap for you, and you
were caught,
but you did not even know it.
You were found and captured
because you fought against the LORD.
²⁵ The LORD opened His armory
and brought out His weapons of wrath,
because it is a task of the Lord GOD of Hosts
in the land of the Chaldeans.
²⁶ Come against her
from the most distant places.
Open her granaries;
pile her up like mounds of grain
and completely destroy her.
Leave her no survivors.
²⁷ Put all her young bulls to the sword;
let them go down to the slaughter.
Woe to them, because their day has come,
the time of their punishment.
²⁸ There is a voice of fugitives
and those who escape
from the land of Babylon
announcing in Zion the vengeance of the LORD
our God,
the vengeance for His temple.
²⁹ Summon the archers to Babylon,
all who string the bow;
camp all around her; let none escape.
Repay her according to her deeds;
just as she has done, do the same to her,
for she has acted arrogantly against the LORD,
against the Holy One of Israel.
³⁰ Therefore, her young men will fall
in her public squares;
all the warriors will perish in that day.
This is the LORD's declaration.
³¹ Look, I am against you, you arrogant one—
this is the declaration of
the Lord GOD of Hosts—
because your day has come,
the time when I will punish you.
³² The arrogant will stumble and fall
with no one to pick him up.
I will set fire to his cities,
and it will consume everything around him."
³³ This is what the LORD of Hosts says:
Israelites and Judeans alike
have been oppressed.
All their captors hold them fast;
they refuse to release them.
³⁴ Their Redeemer is strong;
•Yahweh of Hosts is His name.
He will fervently plead their case
so that He might bring rest to the earth
but turmoil to those who live in Babylon.
³⁵ A sword is over the Chaldeans—
this is the LORD's declaration—
against those who live in Babylon,
against her officials, and against her sages.
³⁶ A sword is against the diviners,
and they will act foolishly.
A sword is against her heroic warriors,
and they will be terrified.

³⁷ A sword is against his horses and chariots
and against all the foreigners among them,
and they will be like women.
A sword is against her treasuries,
and they will be plundered.
³⁸ A drought will come on her waters,
and they will be dried up.
For it is a land of carved images,
and they go mad because of terrifying things.
³⁹ Therefore, desert creatures will live
with hyenas,
and ostriches will also live in her.
It will never again be inhabited
or lived in through all generations.
⁴⁰ Just as God demolished Sodom and Gomorrah
and their neighboring towns—
this is the LORD's declaration—
so no one will live there;
no human being will even stay in it
as a temporary resident.
⁴¹ Look! A people comes from the north.
A great nation and many kings will be
stirred up
from the remote regions of the earth.
⁴² They grasp bow and javelin.
They are cruel and show no mercy.
Their voice roars like the sea,
and they ride on horses,
lined up like men in battle formation
against you, Daughter Babylon.
⁴³ The king of Babylon has heard reports
about them,
and his hands fall helpless.
Distress has seized him—
pain, like a woman in labor.
⁴⁴ "Look, it will be like a lion coming from the thickets of the Jordan to the watered grazing land. Indeed, I will chase Babylon away from her land in a flash. I will appoint whoever is chosen for her. For who is like Me? Who will summon Me? Who is the shepherd who can stand against Me?"
⁴⁵ Therefore, hear the plans that the LORD has drawn up against Babylon and the strategies He has devised against the land of the Chaldeans: Certainly the flock's little lambs will be dragged away; certainly the grazing land will be made desolate because of them. ⁴⁶ At the sound of Babylon's conquest the earth will quake; a cry will be heard among the nations.

51 This is what the LORD says:
I am about to stir up a destructive wind
against Babylon
and against the population of Leb-qamai.
² I will send strangers to Babylon
who will scatter her and strip her land bare,
for they will come against her
from every side in the day of disaster.
³ Don't let the archer string his bow;
don't let him put on his armor.
Don't spare her young men;
•completely destroy her entire army!
⁴ Those who were slain will fall in the land
of the Chaldeans,
those who were pierced through,
in her streets.
⁵ For Israel and Judah are not left widowed
by their God, the LORD of •Hosts,
though their land is full of •guilt

against the Holy One of Israel.
⁶ Leave Babylon;
save your lives, each of you!
Don't perish because of her guilt.
For this is the time of the Lᴏʀᴅ's vengeance—
He will pay her what she deserves.
⁷ Babylon was a gold cup in the Lᴏʀᴅ's hand,
making the whole earth drunk.
The nations drank her wine;
therefore, the nations go mad.
⁸ Suddenly Babylon fell and was shattered.
Wail for her;
get balm for her wound—
perhaps she can be healed.
⁹ We tried to heal Babylon,
but she could not be healed.
Abandon her!
Let each of us go to his own land,
for her judgment extends to the sky
and reaches as far as the clouds.
¹⁰ The Lᴏʀᴅ has brought about our vindication;
come, let's tell in *Zion
what the Lᴏʀᴅ our God has accomplished.
¹¹ Sharpen the arrows!
Fill the quivers!
The Lᴏʀᴅ has put it into the mind
of the kings of the Medes
because His plan is aimed at Babylon
to destroy her,
for it is the Lᴏʀᴅ's vengeance,
vengeance for His temple.
¹² Raise up a signal flag
against the walls of Babylon;
fortify the watch post;
set the watchmen in place;
prepare the ambush.
For the Lᴏʀᴅ has both planned and accomplished
what He has threatened
against those who live in Babylon.
¹³ You who reside by many waters,
rich in treasures,
your end has come,
your life thread is cut.
¹⁴ The Lᴏʀᴅ of Hosts has sworn by Himself:
I will fill you up with men as with locusts,
and they will sing the victory song over you.
¹⁵ He made the earth by His power,
established the world by His wisdom,
and spread out the heavens
by His understanding.
¹⁶ When He thunders,
the waters in the heavens are
in turmoil,
and He causes the clouds
to rise from the ends of the earth.
He makes lightning for the rain
and brings the wind from His storehouses.
¹⁷ Everyone is stupid and ignorant.
Every goldsmith is put to shame
by his carved image,
for his cast images are a lie;
there is no breath in them.
¹⁸ They are worthless, a work to be mocked.
At the time of their punishment they will
be destroyed.
¹⁹ Jacob's Portion is not like these
because He is the One who formed all things.

Israel is the tribe of His inheritance;
*Yahweh of Hosts is His name.
²⁰ You are My battle club,
My weapons of war.
With you I will smash nations;
with you I will bring kingdoms to ruin.
²¹ With you I will smash the horse and its rider;
with you I will smash the chariot and its rider.
²² With you I will smash man and woman;
with you I will smash the old man
and the youth;
with you I will smash the young man
and the young woman.
²³ With you I will smash the shepherd
and his flock;
with you I will smash the farmer
and his ox-team.
With you I will smash governors and officials.
²⁴ "I will repay Babylon and all the residents of Chaldea for all their evil they have done in Zion before your very eyes."

This is the Lᴏʀᴅ's declaration.
²⁵ Look, I am against you,
devastating mountain—
this is the Lᴏʀᴅ's declaration—
you devastate the whole earth.
I will stretch out My hand against you,
roll you down from the cliffs,
and turn you into a charred mountain.
²⁶ No one will be able to retrieve a cornerstone
or a foundation stone from you,
because you will become desolate forever.
This is the Lᴏʀᴅ's declaration.
²⁷ Raise a signal flag in the land;
blow a ram's horn among the nations;
set apart the nations against her.
Summon kingdoms against her—
Ararat, Minni, and Ashkenaz.
Appoint a marshal against her;
bring up horses like a swarm of locusts.
²⁸ Set apart the nations for battle against her—
the kings of Media,
her governors and all her officials,
and all the lands they rule.
²⁹ The earth quakes and trembles
because the Lᴏʀᴅ's intentions against Babylon
stand:
to make the land of Babylon
an uninhabited desolation.
³⁰ Babylon's warriors have stopped fighting;
they sit in their strongholds.
Their might is exhausted;
they have become like women.
Babylon's homes have been set ablaze,
her gate bars are shattered.
³¹ Messenger races to meet messenger,
and herald to meet herald,
to announce to the king of Babylon
that his city has been captured
from end to end.
³² The fords have been seized,
the marshes set on fire,
and the soldiers are terrified.
³³ For this is what the Lᴏʀᴅ of Hosts, the God of Israel, says:
Daughter Babylon is like a threshing floor
at the time it is trampled.

In just a little while her harvest time
    will come.
34 "Nebuchadnezzar of Babylon
    has devoured me;
he has crushed me.
He has set me aside like an empty dish;
he has swallowed me like a sea monster;
he filled his belly with my delicacies;
he has vomited me out,"
35 says the inhabitant of Zion;
"Let the violence done to me and my family
    be done to Babylon.
Let my blood be on the inhabitants
    of Chaldea,"
says Jerusalem.
36 Therefore, this is what the LORD says:
I am about to plead your case
and take vengeance on your behalf;
I will dry up her sea
and make her fountain run dry.
37 Babylon will become a heap of rubble,
    a jackals' den,
a desolation and an object of scorn,
without inhabitant.
38 They will roar together like young lions;
they will growl like lion cubs.
39 While they are flushed with heat,
    I will serve them a feast,
and I will make them drunk so that they revel.
Then they will fall asleep forever
and never wake up.
                This is the LORD's declaration.
40 I will bring them down like lambs
    to the slaughter,
like rams together with male goats.
41 How Sheshach has been captured,
the praise of the whole earth seized.
What a horror Babylon has become
    among the nations!
42 The sea has risen over Babylon;
she is covered with its turbulent waves.
43 Her cities have become a desolation,
    a dry and arid land,
a land where no one lives,
where no human being passes through.
44 I will punish Bel in Babylon.
I will make him vomit what he swallowed.
The nations will no longer stream to him;
even Babylon's wall will fall.
45 Come out from among her, My people!
Save your lives, each of you,
from the LORD's burning anger.
46 May you not become cowardly and fearful
when the report is proclaimed in the land,
for the report will come one year,
and then another the next year.
There will be violence in the land
with ruler against ruler.
47 Therefore, look, the days are coming
when I will punish Babylon's carved images.
Her entire land will suffer shame,
and all her slain will lie fallen within her.
48 Heaven and earth and everything in them
will shout for joy over Babylon
because the destroyers from the north
will come against her.
                This is the LORD's declaration.

49 Babylon must fall because of the slain
    of Israel,
even as the slain of all the earth fell
because of Babylon.
50 You who have escaped the sword,
go and do not stand still!
Remember the LORD from far away,
and let Jerusalem come to your mind.
51 We are ashamed
because we have heard insults.
Humiliation covers our faces
because foreigners have entered
the holy places of the LORD's temple.
52 Therefore, look, the days are coming—
            this is the LORD's declaration—
when I will punish her carved images,
and the wounded will groan
throughout her land.
53 Even if Babylon should ascend to the heavens
and fortify her tall fortresses,
destroyers will come against her from Me.
            This is the LORD's declaration.
54 The sound of a cry from Babylon!
The sound of great destruction
from the land of the Chaldeans!
55 For the LORD is going to devastate Babylon;
He will silence her mighty voice.
Their waves roar like abundant waters;
the tumult of their voice resounds,
56 for a destroyer is coming against her,
    against Babylon.
Her warriors will be captured,
their bows shattered,
for the LORD is a God of retribution;
He will certainly repay.
57 I will make her princes and sages drunk,
along with her governors, officials,
    and warriors.
Then they will fall asleep forever
and never wake up.
            This is the King's declaration;
            Yahweh of Hosts is His name.
58 This is what Yahweh of Hosts says:
Babylon's thick walls will be
    totally demolished,
and her high gates consumed by fire.
The peoples will have labored for nothing;
the nations will exhaust themselves
    only to feed the fire.

59 This is what Jeremiah the prophet commanded Seraiah son of Neriah son of Mahseiah, the quarter-master, when he went to Babylon with King Zedekiah of Judah in the fourth year of Zedekiah's reign. 60 Jeremiah wrote on one scroll about all the disaster that would come to Babylon; all these words were written against Babylon.
61 Jeremiah told Seraiah, "When you get to Babylon, see that you read all these words aloud. 62 You must say, 'LORD, You have threatened to cut off this place so that no one will live in it—man or beast. Indeed, it will remain desolate forever.' 63 When you have finished reading this scroll, tie a stone to it and throw it into the middle of the Euphrates River. 64 Then say, 'In the same way, Babylon will sink and never rise again because of the disaster I am bringing on her. They will grow weary.'"
The words of Jeremiah end here.

52 Zedekiah was 21 years old when he became king and reigned 11 years in Jerusalem. His mother's name was Hamutal daughter of Jeremiah; she was from Libnah. ²Zedekiah did what was evil in the LORD's sight just as Jehoiakim had done. ³Because of the LORD's anger, it came to the point in Jerusalem and Judah that He finally banished them from His presence. Nevertheless, Zedekiah rebelled against the king of Babylon.

⁴In the ninth year of Zedekiah's reign, on the tenth day of the tenth month, King Nebuchadnezzar of Babylon advanced against Jerusalem with his entire army. They laid siege to the city and built a siege wall all around it. ⁵The city was under siege until King Zedekiah's eleventh year.

⁶By the ninth day of the fourth month the famine was so severe in the city that the people of the land had no food. ⁷Then the city was broken into, and all the warriors fled. They left the city by night by way of the gate between the two walls near the king's garden, though the Chaldeans surrounded the city. They made their way along the route to the ˙Arabah. ⁸The Chaldean army pursued the king and overtook Zedekiah in the plains of Jericho. Zedekiah's entire army was scattered from him. ⁹The Chaldeans seized the king and brought him to the king of Babylon at Riblah in the land of Hamath, and he passed sentence on him. ¹⁰At Riblah the king of Babylon slaughtered Zedekiah's sons before his eyes and also slaughtered the Judean commanders. ¹¹Then he blinded Zedekiah and bound him with bronze chains. The king of Babylon brought Zedekiah to Babylon, where he kept him in custody until his dying day.

¹²On the tenth day of the fifth month—which was the nineteenth year of King Nebuchadnezzar, king of Babylon—Nebuzaradan, the commander of the guards, entered Jerusalem as the representative of the king of Babylon. ¹³He burned the LORD's temple, the king's palace, all the houses of Jerusalem, and all the houses of the nobles. ¹⁴The whole Chaldean army with the commander of the guards tore down all the walls surrounding Jerusalem. ¹⁵Nebuzaradan, the commander of the guards, deported some of the poorest of the people, as well as the rest of the people who were left in the city, the deserters who had defected to the king of Babylon, and the rest of the craftsmen. ¹⁶But some of the poorest people of the land Nebuzaradan, the commander of the guards, left to be vinedressers and farmers.

¹⁷Now the Chaldeans broke into pieces the bronze pillars for the LORD's temple and the water carts and the bronze reservoir that were in the LORD's temple, and carried all the bronze to Babylon. ¹⁸They took the pots, shovels, wick trimmers, sprinkling basins, dishes, and all the bronze articles used in the temple service. ¹⁹The commander of the guards took away the bowls, firepans, sprinkling basins, pots, lampstands, pans, and ˙drink offering bowls—whatever was gold or silver.

²⁰As for the two pillars, the one reservoir, and the 12 bronze bulls under the water carts that King Solomon had made for the LORD's temple, the weight of the bronze of all these articles was beyond measure. ²¹One pillar was 27 feet tall, had a circumference of 18 feet, was hollow—four fingers thick— ²²and had a bronze capital on top of it. One capital, encircled by bronze latticework and pomegranates, stood 7¹/₂ feet high. The second pillar was the same, with pomegranates. ²³Each capital had 96 pomegranates all around it. All the pomegranates around the latticework numbered 100.

²⁴The commander of the guards also took away Seraiah the chief priest, Zephaniah the priest of the second rank, and the three doorkeepers. ²⁵From the city he took a court official who had been appointed over the warriors; seven trusted royal aides found in the city; the secretary of the commander of the army, who enlisted the people of the land for military duty; and 60 men from the common people who were found within the city. ²⁶Nebuzaradan, the commander of the guards, took them and brought them to the king of Babylon at Riblah. ²⁷The king of Babylon put them to death at Riblah in the land of Hamath. So Judah went into exile from its land.

²⁸These are the people Nebuchadnezzar deported: in the seventh year, 3,023 Jews; ²⁹in his eighteenth year, 832 people from Jerusalem; ³⁰in Nebuchadnezzar's twenty-third year, Nebuzaradan, the commander of the guards, deported 745 Jews. All together 4,600 people were deported.

³¹On the twenty-fifth day of the twelfth month of the thirty-seventh year of the exile of Judah's King Jehoiachin, Evil-merodach king of Babylon, in the first year of his reign, pardoned King Jehoiachin of Judah and released him from prison. ³²He spoke kindly to him and set his throne above the thrones of the kings who were with him in Babylon. ³³So Jehoiachin changed his prison clothes, and he dined regularly in the presence of the king of Babylon for the rest of his life. ³⁴As for his allowance, a regular allowance was given to him by the king of Babylon, a portion for each day until the day of his death, for the rest of his life.

LAMENTATIONS

א *Alef*

1 How she sits alone,
the city once crowded with people!
She who was great among the nations
has become like a widow.
The princess among the provinces
has been put to forced labor.

ב *Bet*

² She weeps aloud during the night,
with tears on her cheeks.
There is no one to offer her comfort,
not one from all her lovers.
All her friends have betrayed her;
they have become her enemies.

ג *Gimel*

³ Judah has gone into exile
following affliction and harsh slavery;
she lives among the nations
but finds no place to rest.
All her pursuers have overtaken her
in narrow places.

ד *Dalet*

4 The roads to ˙Zion mourn,
  for no one comes
     to the appointed festivals.
  All her gates are deserted;
  her priests groan,
  her young women grieve,
  and she herself is bitter.

ה *He*

5 Her adversaries have become her masters;
  her enemies are at ease,
  for the LORD has made her suffer
  because of her many transgressions.
  Her children have gone away
  as captives before the adversary.

ו *Vav*

6 All her splendor has vanished
  from Daughter Zion.
  Her leaders are like stags
  that find no pasture;
  they walk away exhausted
  before the hunter.

ז *Zayin*

7 During the days of her affliction
    and homelessness
  Jerusalem remembers all
    her precious belongings
  that were hers in days of old.
  When her people fell into the adversary's hand,
  she had no one to help.
  The adversaries looked at her,
  laughing over her downfall.

ח *Khet*

8 Jerusalem has sinned grievously;
  therefore, she has become an object of scorn.
  All who honored her now despise her,
  for they have seen her nakedness.
  She herself groans and turns away.

ט *Tet*

9 Her uncleanness stains her skirts.
  She never considered her end.
  Her downfall was astonishing;
  there was no one to comfort her.
  LORD, look on my affliction,
  for the enemy triumphs!

י *Yod*

10 The adversary has seized
  all her precious belongings.
  She has even seen the nations
  enter her sanctuary—
  those You had forbidden
  to enter Your assembly.

כ *Kaf*

11 All her people groan
  while they search for bread.
  They have traded their precious belongings
    for food
  in order to stay alive.
  LORD, look and see
  how I have become despised.

ל *Lamed*

12 Is this nothing to you, all you who pass by?

Look and see!
Is there any pain like mine,
which was dealt out to me,
which the LORD made me suffer
on the day of His burning anger?

מ *Mem*

13 He sent fire from heaven into my bones;
  He made it descend.
  He spread a net for my feet
  and turned me back.
  He made me desolate,
  sick all day long.

נ *Nun*

14 My transgressions have been formed
    into a yoke,
  fastened together by His hand;
  they have been placed on my neck,
  and the Lord has broken my strength.
  He has handed me over
  to those I cannot withstand.

ס *Samek*

15 The Lord has rejected
  all the mighty men within me.
  He has summoned an army against me
  to crush my young warriors.
  The Lord has trampled Virgin Daughter Judah
  like grapes in a winepress.

ע *Ayin*

16 I weep because of these things;
  my eyes flow with tears.
  For there is no one nearby to comfort me,
  no one to keep me alive.
  My children are desolate
  because the enemy has prevailed.

פ *Pe*

17 Zion stretches out her hands;
  there is no one to comfort her.
  The LORD has issued a decree against Jacob
  that his neighbors should be his adversaries.
  Jerusalem has become
  something impure among them.

צ *Tsade*

18 The LORD is just,
  for I have rebelled against His command.
  Listen, all you people;
  look at my pain.
  My young men and women
  have gone into captivity.

ק *Qof*

19 I called to my lovers,
  but they betrayed me.
  My priests and elders
  perished in the city
  while searching for food
  to keep themselves alive.

ר *Resh*

20 LORD, see how I am in distress.
  I am churning within;
  my heart is broken,
  for I have been very rebellious.
  Outside, the sword takes the children;
  inside, there is death.

שׁ Shin

21 People have heard me groaning,
but there is no one to comfort me.
All my enemies have heard of my misfortune;
they are glad that You have caused it.
Bring on the day You have announced,
so that they may become like me.

תּ Tav

22 Let all their wickedness come before You,
and deal with them
as You have dealt with me
because of all my transgressions.
For my groans are many,
and I am sick at heart.

א Alef

2 How the Lord has overshadowed
Daughter •Zion with His anger!
He has thrown down Israel's glory
from heaven to earth.
He has abandoned His footstool
in the day of His anger.

בּ Bet

2 Without compassion the Lord
has swallowed up
all the dwellings of Jacob.
In His wrath He has demolished
the fortified cities of Daughter Judah.
He brought them to the ground
and defiled the kingdom and its leaders.

גּ Gimel

3 He has cut off every •horn of Israel
in His burning anger
and withdrawn His right hand
in the presence of the enemy.
He has blazed against Jacob like a flaming fire
that consumes everything.

דּ Dalet

4 He has bent His bow like an enemy;
His right hand is positioned like an adversary.
He has killed everyone who was loved,
pouring out His wrath like fire
on the tent of Daughter Zion.

הּ He

5 The Lord is like an enemy;
He has swallowed up Israel.
He swallowed up all its palaces
and destroyed its fortified cities.
He has multiplied mourning and lamentation
within Daughter Judah.

ו Vav

6 He has done violence to His temple
as if it were a garden booth,
destroying His place of meeting.
The Lord has abolished
appointed festivals and Sabbaths in Zion.
He has despised king and priest
in His fierce anger.

ז Zayin

7 The Lord has rejected His altar,
repudiated His sanctuary;
He has handed the walls of her palaces
over to the enemy.
They have raised a shout in the house
of the Lord
as on the day of an appointed festival.

חּ Khet

8 The Lord determined to destroy
the wall of Daughter Zion.
He stretched out a measuring line
and did not restrain Himself from destroying.
He made the ramparts and walls grieve;
together they waste away.

טּ Tet

9 Zion's gates have fallen to the ground;
He has destroyed and shattered the bars
on her gates.
Her king and her leaders live
among the nations,
instruction is no more,
and even her prophets receive
no vision from the Lord.

י Yod

10 The elders of Daughter Zion
sit on the ground in silence.
They have thrown dust on their heads
and put on •sackcloth.
The young women of Jerusalem
have bowed their heads to the ground.

כּ Kaf

11 My eyes are worn out from weeping;
I am churning within.
My heart is poured out in grief
because of the destruction of my dear people,
because children and infants faint
in the streets of the city.

לּ Lamed

12 They cry out to their mothers:
Where is the grain and wine?
as they faint like the wounded
in the streets of the city,
as their lives fade away
in the arms of their mothers.

מ Mem

13 What can I say on your behalf?
What can I compare you to,
Daughter Jerusalem?
What can I liken you to,
so that I may console you,
Virgin Daughter Zion?
For your ruin is as vast as the sea.
Who can heal you?

נ Nun

14 Your prophets saw visions for you
that were empty and deceptive;
they did not reveal your •guilt
and so restore your fortunes.
They saw •oracles for you
that were empty and misleading.

ס Samek

15 All who pass by
scornfully clap their hands at you.
They mock and shake their heads
at Daughter Jerusalem:
Is this the city that was called

the perfection of beauty,
the joy of the whole earth?

פ Pe

16 All your enemies
open their mouths against you.
They hiss and gnash their teeth,
saying, "We have swallowed her up.
This is the day we have waited for!
We have lived to see it."

ע Ayin

17 The Lord has done what He planned;
He has accomplished His decree,
which He ordained in days of old.
He has demolished without compassion,
letting the enemy gloat over you
and exalting the horn of your adversaries.

צ Tsade

18 The hearts of the people cry out to the Lord.
Wall of Daughter Zion,
let your tears run down like a river
day and night.
Give yourself no relief
and your eyes no rest.

ק Qof

19 Arise, cry out in the night
from the first watch of the night.
Pour out your heart like water
before the Lord's presence.
Lift up your hands to Him
for the lives of your children
who are fainting from hunger
on the corner of every street.

ר Resh

20 Lord, look and consider
who You have done this to.
Should women eat their own children,
the infants they have nurtured?
Should priests and prophets
be killed in the Lord's sanctuary?

שׁ Shin

21 Both young and old
are lying on the ground in the streets.
My young men and women
have fallen by the sword.
You have killed them in the day of Your anger,
slaughtering without compassion.

ת Tav

22 You summoned my attackers on every side,
as if for an appointed festival day;
on the day of the Lord's anger
no one escaped or survived.
My enemy has destroyed
those I nurtured and reared.

א Alef

3

I am the man who has seen affliction
under the rod of God's wrath.
2 He has driven me away and forced me to walk
in darkness instead of light.
3 Yes, He repeatedly turns His hand
against me all day long.

ב Bet

4 He has worn away my flesh and skin;

He has shattered my bones.
5 He has laid siege against me,
encircling me with bitterness and hardship.
6 He has made me dwell in darkness
like those who have been dead for ages.

ג Gimel

7 He has walled me in so I cannot escape;
He has weighed me down with chains.
8 Even when I cry out and plead for help,
He rejects my prayer.
9 He has walled in my ways with cut stones;
He has made my paths crooked.

ד Dalet

10 He is a bear waiting in ambush,
a lion in hiding.
11 He forced me off my way and tore me
to pieces;
He left me desolate.
12 He strung His bow
and set me as the target for His arrow.

ה He

13 He pierced my kidneys
with His arrows.
14 I am a laughingstock to all my people,
mocked by their songs all day long.
15 He filled me with bitterness,
satiated me with ˙wormwood.

ו Vav

16 He ground my teeth on gravel
and made me cower in the dust.
17 My soul has been deprived of peace;
I have forgotten what happiness is.
18 Then I thought: My future is lost,
as well as my hope from the Lord.

ז Zayin

19 Remember my affliction
and my homelessness,
the wormwood and the poison.
20 I continually remember them
and have become depressed.
21 Yet I call this to mind,
and therefore I have hope:

ח Khet

22 Because of the Lord's faithful love
we do not perish,
for His mercies never end.
23 They are new every morning;
great is Your faithfulness!
24 I say: The Lord is my portion,
therefore I will put my hope in Him.

ט Tet

25 The Lord is good to those who wait for Him,
to the person who seeks Him.
26 It is good to wait quietly
for deliverance from the Lord.
27 It is good for a man to bear the yoke
while he is still young.

י Yod

28 Let him sit alone and be silent,
for God has disciplined him.
29 Let him put his mouth in the dust—
perhaps there is still hope.

30 Let him offer his cheek
to the one who would strike him;
let him be filled with shame.

‭כ‬ Kaf

31 For the Lord
will not reject us forever.
32 Even if He causes suffering,
He will show compassion
according to His abundant, faithful love.
33 For He does not enjoy bringing affliction
or suffering on ⋅mankind.

‭ל‬ Lamed

34 Crushing all the prisoners of the land
beneath one's feet,
35 denying justice to a man
in the presence of the ⋅Most High,
36 or suppressing a person's lawsuit—
the Lord does not approve of these things.

‭מ‬ Mem

37 Who is there who speaks and it happens,
unless the Lord has ordained it?
38 Do not both adversity and good
come from the mouth of the Most High?
39 Why should any living person complain,
any man, because of the punishment
for his sins?

‭נ‬ Nun

40 Let us search out and examine our ways,
and turn back to the Lord.
41 Let us lift up our hearts and our hands
to God in heaven:
42 We have sinned and rebelled;
You have not forgiven.

‭ס‬ Samek

43 You have covered Yourself in anger
and pursued us;
You have killed without compassion.
44 You have covered Yourself with a cloud
so that no prayer can pass through.
45 You have made us disgusting filth
among the peoples.

‭פ‬ Pe

46 All our enemies
open their mouths against us.
47 We have experienced panic and pitfall,
devastation and destruction.
48 My eyes flow with streams of tears
because of the destruction of my dear people.

‭ע‬ Ayin

49 My eyes overflow unceasingly,
without end,
50 until the Lord looks down
from heaven and sees.
51 My eyes bring me grief
because of the fate of all the women
in my city.

‭צ‬ Tsade

52 For no apparent reason, my enemies
hunted me like a bird.
53 They dropped me alive into a pit
and threw stones at me.

54 Water flooded over my head,
and I thought: I'm going to die!

‭ק‬ Qof

55 I called on Your name, ⋅Yahweh,
from the depths of the ⋅Pit.
56 You hear my plea:
Do not ignore my cry for relief.
57 You come near when I call on You;
You say: "Do not be afraid."

‭ר‬ Resh

58 You defend my cause, Lord;
You redeem my life.
59 Lord, You see the wrong done to me;
judge my case.
60 You see all their malice,
all their plots against me.

‭ש‬ Sin/‭ש‬ Shin

61 Lord, You hear their insults,
all their plots against me.
62 The slander and murmuring of my opponents
attack me all day long.
63 When they sit and when they rise, look,
I am mocked by their songs.

‭ת‬ Tav

64 You will pay them back
what they deserve, Lord,
according to the work of their hands.
65 You will give them a heart filled with anguish.
May Your curse be on them!
66 You will pursue them in anger and destroy them
under Your heavens.

‭א‬ Alef

4 How the gold has become tarnished,
the fine gold become dull!
The stones of the temple lie scattered
at the corner of every street.

‭ב‬ Bet

2 ⋅Zion's precious people—
once worth their weight in pure gold—
how they are regarded as clay jars,
the work of a potter's hands!

‭ג‬ Gimel

3 Even jackals offer their breasts
to nurse their young,
but my dear people have become cruel
like ostriches in the wilderness.

‭ד‬ Dalet

4 The nursing infant's tongue
clings to the roof of his mouth from thirst.
Little children beg for bread,
but no one gives them any.

‭ה‬ He

5 Those who used to eat delicacies
are destitute in the streets;
those who were reared in purple garments
huddle in garbage heaps.

‭ו‬ Vav

6 The punishment of my dear people
is greater than that of Sodom,
which was overthrown in an instant
without a hand laid on it.

ז *Zayin*

7 Her dignitaries were brighter than snow,
    whiter than milk;
  their bodies were more ruddy than coral,
    their appearance like sapphire.

ח *Khet*

8 Now they appear darker than soot;
    they are not recognized in the streets.
  Their skin has shriveled on their bones;
    it has become dry like wood.

ט *Tet*

9 Those slain by the sword are better off
    than those slain by hunger,
  who waste away, pierced with pain
    because the fields lack produce.

י *Yod*

10 The hands of compassionate women
    have cooked their own children;
  they became their food
    during the destruction of my dear people.

כ *Kaf*

11 The LORD has exhausted His wrath,
    poured out His burning anger;
  He has ignited a fire in Zion,
    and it has consumed her foundations.

ל *Lamed*

12 The kings of the earth
    and all the world's inhabitants did not believe
  that an enemy or adversary
    could enter Jerusalem's gates.

מ *Mem*

13 Yet it happened because of the sins
    of her prophets
  and the •guilt of her priests,
    who shed the blood of the righteous
      within her.

נ *Nun*

14 Blind, they stumbled in the streets,
    defiled by this blood,
  so that no one dared
    to touch their garments.

ס *Samek*

15 "Stay away! •Unclean!" people shouted
    at them.
  "Away, away! Don't touch us!"
  So they wandered aimlessly.
  It was said among the nations,
    "They can stay here no longer."

פ *Pe*

16 The LORD Himself has scattered them;
    He regards them no more.
  The priests are not respected;
    the elders find no favor.

ע *Ayin*

17 All the while our eyes were failing
    as we looked in vain for assistance;
  we watched from our towers
    for a nation that refused to help.

צ *Tsade*

18 Our steps were closely followed

so that we could not walk in our streets.
  Our end drew near; our time ran out.
  Our end had come!

ק *Qof*

19 Those who chased us were swifter
    than eagles in the sky;
  they relentlessly pursued us
    over the mountains
  and ambushed us in the wilderness.

ר *Resh*

20 The LORD's anointed, the breath of our life,
    was captured in their traps.
  We had said about him,
  "We will live under his protection
    among the nations."

ש *Sin*

21 So rejoice and be glad, Daughter Edom,
    you resident of the land of Uz!
  Yet the cup will pass to you as well;
    you will get drunk and expose yourself.

ת *Tav*

22 Daughter Zion, your punishment
    is complete;
  He will not lengthen your exile.
  But He will punish your iniquity,
    Daughter Edom,
  and will expose your sins.

5 •Yahweh, remember what has happened
    to us.
  Look, and see our disgrace!
2 Our inheritance has been turned over
    to strangers,
  our houses to foreigners.
3 We have become orphans, fatherless;
    our mothers are widows.
4 We must pay for the water we drink;
    our wood comes at a price.
5 We are closely pursued;
    we are tired, and no one offers us rest.
6 We made a treaty with Egypt
    and with Assyria, to get enough food.
7 Our fathers sinned; they no longer exist,
    but we bear their punishment.
8 Slaves rule over us;
    no one rescues us from their hands.
9 We secure our food at the risk of our lives
    because of the sword in the wilderness.
10 Our skin is as hot as an oven
    from the ravages of hunger.
11 Women are raped in •Zion,
    girls in the cities of Judah.
12 Princes are hung up by their hands;
    elders are shown no respect.
13 Young men labor at millstones;
    boys stumble under loads of wood.
14 The elders have left the city •gate,
    the young men, their music.
15 Joy has left our hearts;
    our dancing has turned to mourning.
16 The crown has fallen from our head.
    Woe to us, for we have sinned.
17 Because of this, our heart is sick;
    because of these, our eyes grow dim:
18 because of Mount Zion, which lies desolate

and has jackals prowling in it.
¹⁹ You, Lᴏʀᴅ, are enthroned forever;
Your throne endures from generation
to generation.
²⁰ Why have You forgotten us forever,

abandoned us for our entire lives?
²¹ Lᴏʀᴅ, restore us to Yourself, so we may return;
renew our days as in former times,
²² unless You have completely rejected us
and are intensely angry with us.

Ezekiel

1 In the thirtieth year, in the fourth month, on the fifth day of the month, while I was among the exiles by the Chebar Canal, the heavens opened and I saw visions of God. ²On the fifth day of the month—it was the fifth year of King Jehoiachin's exile— ³the word of the Lᴏʀᴅ came directly to Ezekiel the priest, the son of Buzi, in the land of the Chaldeans by the Chebar Canal. And the Lᴏʀᴅ's hand was on him there.

⁴I looked and there was a whirlwind coming from the north, a great cloud with fire flashing back and forth and brilliant light all around it. In the center of the fire, there was a gleam like amber. ⁵The form of four living creatures came from it. And this was their appearance: They had human form, ⁶but each of them had four faces and four wings. ⁷Their legs were straight, and the soles of their feet were like the hooves of a calf, sparkling like the gleam of polished bronze. ⁸They had human hands under their wings on their four sides. All four of them had faces and wings. ⁹Their wings were touching. The creatures did not turn as they moved; each one went straight ahead. ¹⁰The form of each of their faces was that of a man, and each of the four had the face of a lion on the right, the face of an ox on the left, and the face of an eagle. ¹¹That is what their faces were like. Their wings were spread upward; each had two wings touching that of another and two wings covering its body. ¹²Each creature went straight ahead. Wherever the Spirit wanted to go, they went without turning as they moved.

¹³The form of the living creatures was like the appearance of burning coals of fire and torches. Fire was moving back and forth between the living creatures; it was bright, with lightning coming out of it. ¹⁴The creatures were darting back and forth like flashes of lightning.

¹⁵When I looked at the living creatures, there was one wheel on the ground beside each creature that had four faces. ¹⁶The appearance of the wheels and their craftsmanship was like the gleam of beryl, and all four had the same form. Their appearance and craftsmanship was like a wheel within a wheel. ¹⁷When they moved, they went in any of the four directions, without pivoting as they moved. ¹⁸Their rims were large and frightening. Each of their four rims were full of eyes all around. ¹⁹So when the living creatures moved, the wheels moved beside them, and when the creatures rose from the earth, the wheels also rose. ²⁰Wherever the Spirit wanted to go, the creatures went in the direction the Spirit was moving. The wheels rose alongside them, for the spirit of the living creatures was in the wheels. ²¹When the creatures moved, the wheels moved; when the creatures stood still, the wheels stood still; and when the creatures rose from the earth, the wheels rose alongside them, for the spirit of the living creatures was in the wheels.

²²The shape of an expanse, with a gleam like awe-inspiring crystal, was spread out over the heads of the living creatures. ²³And under the expanse their wings extended one toward another. Each of them also had two wings covering their bodies. ²⁴When they moved, I heard the sound of their wings like the roar of mighty waters, like the voice of the *Almighty, and a sound of commotion like the noise of an army. When they stood still, they lowered their wings.

²⁵A voice came from above the expanse over their heads; when they stood still, they lowered their wings. ²⁶The shape of a throne with the appearance of sapphire stone was above the expanse. There was a form with the appearance of a human on the throne high above. ²⁷From what seemed to be His waist up, I saw a gleam like amber, with what looked like fire enclosing it all around. From what seemed to be His waist down, I also saw what looked like fire. There was a brilliant light all around Him. ²⁸The appearance of the brilliant light all around was like that of a rainbow in a cloud on a rainy day. This was the appearance of the form of the Lᴏʀᴅ's glory. When I saw it, I fell facedown and heard a voice speaking.

2 He said to me, "Son of man, stand up on your feet and I will speak with you." ²As He spoke to me, the Spirit entered me and set me on my feet, and I listened to the One who was speaking to me. ³He said to me: "Son of man, I am sending you to the Israelites, to the rebellious pagans who have rebelled against Me. The Israelites and their ancestors have transgressed against Me to this day. ⁴The children are obstinate and hardhearted. I am sending you to them, and you must say to them, 'This is what the Lord Gᴏᴅ says.' ⁵Whether they listen or refuse to listen—for they are a rebellious house—they will know that a prophet has been among them.

⁶"But you, son of man, do not be afraid of them or their words, though briers and thorns are beside you and you live among scorpions. Don't be afraid of their words or be discouraged by the look on their faces, for they are a rebellious house. ⁷But speak My words to them whether they listen or refuse to listen, for they are rebellious.

⁸"And you, son of man, listen to what I tell you: Do not be rebellious like that rebellious house. Open your mouth and eat what I am giving you." ⁹So I looked and saw a hand reaching out to me, and there was a written scroll in it. ¹⁰When He unrolled it before me, it was written on the front and back; words of lamentation, mourning, and woe were written on it.

3 He said to me: "Son of man, eat what you find here. Eat this scroll, then go and speak to the house of Israel." ²So I opened my mouth, and He fed me the scroll. ³"Son of man," He said to me, "eat and fill your stomach with this scroll I am giving you." So I ate it, and it was as sweet as honey in my mouth.

⁴Then He said to me: "Son of man, go to the house

of Israel and speak My words to them. ⁵For you are not being sent to a people of unintelligible speech or difficult language but to the house of Israel. ⁶You are not being sent to many peoples of unintelligible speech or difficult language, whose words you cannot understand. No doubt, if I sent you to them, they would listen to you. ⁷But the house of Israel will not want to listen to you because they do not want to listen to Me. For the whole house of Israel is hardheaded and hardhearted. ⁸Look, I have made your face as hard as their faces and your forehead as hard as their foreheads. ⁹I have made your forehead like a diamond, harder than flint. Don't be afraid of them or discouraged by the look on their faces, even though they are a rebellious house."

¹⁰Next He said to me: "Son of man, listen carefully to all My words that I speak to you and take them to heart. ¹¹Go to your people, the exiles, and speak to them. Tell them, 'This is what the Lord GOD says,' whether they listen or refuse to listen."

¹²The Spirit then lifted me up, and I heard a great rumbling sound behind me—praise the glory of the LORD in His place!— ¹³with the sound of the living creatures' wings brushing against each other and the sound of the wheels beside them, a great rumbling sound. ¹⁴So the Spirit lifted me up and took me away. I left in bitterness and in an angry spirit, and the LORD's hand was on me powerfully. ¹⁵I came to the exiles at Tel-abib, who were living by the Chebar Canal, and I sat there among them stunned for seven days.

¹⁶Now at the end of seven days the word of the LORD came to me: ¹⁷"Son of man, I have made you a watchman over the house of Israel. When you hear a word from My mouth, give them a warning from Me. ¹⁸If I say to the wicked person, 'You will surely die,' but you do not warn him—you don't speak out to warn him about his wicked way in order to save his life—that wicked person will die for his iniquity. Yet I will hold you responsible for his blood. ¹⁹But if you warn a wicked person and he does not turn from his wickedness or his wicked way, he will die for his iniquity, but you will have saved your life. ²⁰Now if a righteous person turns from his righteousness and practices iniquity, and I put a stumbling block in front of him, he will die. If you did not warn him, he will die because of his sin and the righteous acts he did will not be remembered. Yet I will hold you responsible for his blood. ²¹But if you warn the righteous person that he should not sin, and he does not sin, he will indeed live because he listened to your warning, and you will have saved your life."

²²Then the hand of the LORD was on me there, and He said to me, "Get up, go out to the plain, and I will speak with you there." ²³So I got up and went out to the plain. The LORD's glory was present there, like the glory I had seen by the Chebar Canal, and I fell facedown. He spoke with me and said: "Go, shut yourself inside your house. ²⁵And you, son of man, they will put ropes on you and bind you with them so you cannot go out among them. ²⁶I will make your tongue stick to the roof of your mouth, and you will be mute and unable to rebuke them, for they are a rebellious house. ²⁷But when I speak with you, I will open your mouth, and you will say to them, 'This is what the Lord GOD says.' Let the one who listens, listen, and let the one who refuses, refuse—for they are a rebellious house.

4 "Now you, son of man, take a brick, set it in front of you, and draw the city of Jerusalem on it. ²Then lay siege against it: construct a siege wall, build a ramp, pitch military camps, and place battering rams against it on all sides. ³Take an iron plate and set it up as an iron wall between yourself and the city. Turn your face toward it so that it is under siege, and besiege it. This will be a sign for the house of Israel.

⁴"Then lie down on your left side and place the iniquity of the house of Israel on it. You will bear their iniquity for the number of days you lie on your side. ⁵For I have assigned you the years of their iniquity according to the number of days you lie down, 390 days; so you will bear the iniquity of the house of Israel. ⁶When you have completed these days, lie down again, but on your right side, and bear the iniquity of the house of Judah. I have assigned you 40 days, a day for each year. ⁷You must turn your face toward the siege of Jerusalem with your arm bared, and prophesy against it. ⁸Be aware that I will put cords on you so you cannot turn from side to side until you have finished the days of your siege.

⁹"Also take wheat, barley, beans, lentils, millet, and spelt. Put them in a single container and make them into bread for yourself. You are to eat it during the number of days you lie on your side, 390 days. ¹⁰The food you eat each day will be eight ounces by weight; you will eat it from time to time. ¹¹You are also to drink water by measure, a sixth of a gallon, which you will drink from time to time. ¹²You will eat it as you would a barley cake and bake it over dried human excrement in their sight." ¹³The LORD said, "This is how the Israelites will eat their bread—ceremonially ˙unclean—among the nations where I will banish them."

¹⁴But I said, "Oh, Lord GOD, I have never been defiled. From my youth until now I have not eaten anything that died naturally or was mauled by wild beasts. And impure meat has never entered my mouth."

¹⁵He replied to me, "Look, I will let you use cow dung instead of human excrement, and you can make your bread over that." ¹⁶Then He said to me, "Son of man, I am going to cut off the supply of bread in Jerusalem. They will anxiously eat bread rationed by weight and in dread drink water by measure. ¹⁷So they will lack bread and water; everyone will be devastated and waste away because of their iniquity.

5 "Now you, son of man, take a sharp sword, use it as you would a barber's razor, and shave your head and beard. Then take a set of scales and divide the hair. ²You are to burn up a third of it in the city when the days of the siege have ended; you are to take a third and slash it with the sword all around the city; and you are to scatter a third to the wind, for I will draw a sword to chase after them. ³But you are to take a few strands from the hair and secure them in the folds of your robe. ⁴Take some more of them, throw them into the fire, and burn them in it. A fire will spread from it to the whole house of Israel.

⁵"This is what the Lord GOD says: I have set this Jerusalem in the center of the nations, with countries all around her. ⁶But she has rebelled against My ordinances with more wickedness than the nations, and against My statutes more than the countries that surround her. For her people have rejected My ordinances and have not walked in My statutes.

⁷"Therefore, this is what the Lord GOD says: Because you have been more insubordinate than the nations

around you—you have not walked in My statutes or kept My ordinances; you have not even kept the ordinances of the nations around you— ⁸therefore, this is what the Lord GOD says: See, I am against you, Jerusalem, and I will execute judgments within you in the sight of the nations: ⁹Because of all your detestable practices, I will do to you what I have never done before and what I will never do again. ¹⁰As a result, fathers will eat their sons within Jerusalem, and sons will eat their fathers. I will execute judgments against you and scatter all your survivors to every direction of the wind.

¹¹"Therefore, as I live"—this is the declaration of the Lord GOD—"I am going to cut you off and show you no pity, because you have defiled My sanctuary with all your detestable practices and abominations. Yes, I will not spare you. ¹²A third of your people will die by plague and be consumed by famine within you; a third will fall by the sword all around you; and I will scatter a third to every direction of the wind, and I will draw a sword to chase after them. ¹³When My anger is spent and I have vented My wrath on them, I will be appeased. Then after I have spent My wrath on them, they will know that I, ·Yahweh, have spoken in My jealousy.

¹⁴"I will make you a ruin and a disgrace among the nations around you, in the sight of everyone who passes by. ¹⁵So you will be a disgrace and a taunt, a warning and a horror, to the nations around you when I execute judgments against you in anger, wrath, and furious rebukes. I, Yahweh, have spoken. ¹⁶When I shoot deadly arrows of famine at them, arrows for destruction that I will send to destroy you, inhabitants of Jerusalem, I will intensify the famine against you and cut off your supply of bread. ¹⁷I will send famine and dangerous animals against you. They will leave you childless, Jerusalem. Plague and bloodshed will sweep through you, and I will bring a sword against you. I, Yahweh, have spoken."

6 The word of the LORD came to me: ²"Son of man, turn your face toward the mountains of Israel and prophesy against them. ³You are to say: Mountains of Israel, hear the word of the Lord GOD! This is what the Lord GOD says to the mountains and the hills, to the ravines and the valleys: I am about to bring a sword against you, and I will destroy your ·high places. ⁴Your altars will be desolated and your incense altars smashed. I will throw down your slain in front of your idols. ⁵I will lay the corpses of the Israelites in front of their idols and scatter your bones around your altars. ⁶Wherever you live the cities will be in ruins and the high places will be desolate, so that your altars will lie in ruins and be desecrated, your idols smashed and obliterated, your incense altars cut down, and your works wiped out. ⁷The slain will fall among you, and you will know that I am ·Yahweh.

⁸"Yet I will leave a remnant when you are scattered among the nations, for throughout the countries there will be some of you who will escape the sword. ⁹Then your survivors will remember Me among the nations where they are taken captive, how I was crushed by their promiscuous hearts that turned away from Me and by their eyes that lusted after their idols. They will loathe themselves because of the evil things they did, their detestable practices of every kind. ¹⁰And they will know that I am the LORD; I did not threaten to bring this disaster on them without a reason.

¹¹"This is what the Lord GOD says: Clap your hands, stamp your feet, and cry out over all the evil and detestable practices of the house of Israel, who will fall by the sword, famine, and plague. ¹²The one who is far off will die by plague; the one who is near will fall by the sword; and the one who remains and is spared will die of famine. In this way I will exhaust My wrath on them. ¹³You will all know that I am Yahweh when their slain lie among their idols around their altars, on every high hill, on all the mountaintops, and under every green tree and every leafy oak—the places where they offered pleasing aromas to all their idols. ¹⁴I will stretch out My hand against them, and wherever they live I will make the land a desolate waste, from the wilderness to Diblah. Then they will know that I am Yahweh."

7 And the word of the LORD came to me: ²"Son of man, this is what the Lord GOD says to the land of Israel:

An end! The end has come
on the four corners of the land.
³ The end is now upon you;
I will send My anger against you
and judge you according to your ways.
I will punish you for all
your detestable practices.
⁴ I will not look on you with pity or spare you,
but I will punish you for your ways
and for your detestable practices within you.
Then you will know that I am ·Yahweh."

⁵This is what the Lord GOD says:

Look, one disaster after another is coming!
⁶ An end has come; the end has come!
It has awakened against you.
Look, it is coming!
⁷ Doom has come on you,
inhabitants of the land.
The time has come; the day is near.
There will be panic on the mountains
and not celebration.
⁸ I will pour out My wrath on you very soon;
I will exhaust My anger against you
and judge you according to your ways.
I will punish you for all your
detestable practices.
⁹ I will not look on you with pity or spare you.
I will punish you for your ways
and for your detestable practices within you.
Then you will know
that it is I, Yahweh, who strikes.
¹⁰ Look, the day is coming!
Doom has gone out.
The rod has blossomed;
arrogance has bloomed.
¹¹ Violence has grown into a rod of wickedness.
None of them will remain:
none of their multitude,
none of their wealth,
and none of the eminent among them.
¹² The time has come; the day has arrived.
Let the buyer not rejoice
and the seller not mourn,
for wrath is on all her masses.
¹³ The seller will certainly not return
to what was sold
as long as he and the buyer remain alive.
For the vision concerning all its people
will not be revoked,

and none of them will preserve
his life because of his iniquity.
¹⁴ They have blown the trumpet
and prepared everything,
but no one goes to war,
for My wrath is on all her masses.
¹⁵ The sword is on the outside;
plague and famine are on the inside.
Whoever is in the field will die by the sword,
and famine and plague will devour
whoever is in the city.
¹⁶ The survivors among them will escape
and live on the mountains
like doves of the valley,
all of them moaning,
each over his own iniquity.
¹⁷ All their hands will become weak,
and all their knees will turn to water.
¹⁸ They will put on •sackcloth,
and horror will overwhelm them.
Shame will cover all their faces,
and all their heads will be bald.
¹⁹ They will throw their silver into the streets,
and their gold will seem like something filthy.
Their silver and gold will be unable
to save them
in the day of the Lord's wrath.
They will not satisfy their appetites
or fill their stomachs,
for these were the stumbling blocks
that brought about their iniquity.
²⁰ He appointed His beautiful ornaments
for majesty,
but they made their abhorrent images
from them,
their detestable things.
Therefore, I have made these
into something filthy for them.
²¹ I will hand these things over
to foreigners as plunder
and to the wicked of the earth as spoil,
and they will profane them.
²² I will turn My face from the wicked
as they profane My treasured place.
Violent men will enter it and profane it.
²³ Forge the chain,
for the land is filled with crimes of bloodshed,
and the city is filled with violence.
²⁴ So I will bring the most evil of nations
to take possession of their houses.
I will put an end to the pride of the strong,
and their sacred places will be profaned.
²⁵ Anguish is coming!
They will seek peace, but there will be none.
²⁶ Disaster after disaster will come,
and there will be rumor after rumor.
Then they will seek a vision from a prophet,
but instruction will perish from the priests
and counsel from the elders.
²⁷ The king will mourn;
the prince will be clothed in grief;
and the hands of the people of the land
will tremble.
I will deal with them according to
their own conduct,
and I will judge them by their own standards.
Then they will know that I am Yahweh.

8 In the sixth year, in the sixth month, on the fifth day of the month, I was sitting in my house and the elders of Judah were sitting in front of me, and there the hand of the Lord God came down on me. ²I looked, and there was a form that had the appearance of a man. From what seemed to be His waist down was fire, and from His waist up was something that looked bright, like the gleam of amber. ³He stretched out what appeared to be a hand and took me by the hair of my head. Then the Spirit lifted me up between earth and heaven and carried me in visions of God to Jerusalem, to the entrance of the inner gate that faces north, where the offensive statue that provokes jealousy was located. ⁴I saw the glory of the God of Israel there, like the vision I had seen in the plain.

⁵The Lord said to me, "Son of man, look toward the north." I looked to the north, and there was this offensive statue north of the altar gate, at the entrance. ⁶He said to me, "Son of man, do you see what they are doing here, more detestable things that the house of Israel is committing, so that I must depart from My sanctuary? You will see even more detestable things."

⁷Then He brought me to the entrance of the court, and when I looked there was a hole in the wall. ⁸He said to me, "Son of man, dig through the wall." So I dug through the wall, and there was a doorway. ⁹He said to me, "Go in and see the terrible and detestable things they are committing here." ¹⁰I went in and looked, and there engraved all around the wall was every form of detestable thing, crawling creatures and beasts, as well as all the idols of the house of Israel.

¹¹Seventy elders from the house of Israel were standing before them, with Jaazaniah son of Shaphan standing among them. Each had a firepan in his hand, and a fragrant cloud of incense was rising up. ¹²Then He said to me, "Son of man, do you see what the elders of the house of Israel are doing in the darkness, each at the shrine of his idol? For they are saying, 'The Lord does not see us. The Lord has abandoned the land.'" ¹³Again He said to me, "You will see even more detestable things, which they are committing."

¹⁴So He brought me to the entrance of the north gate of the Lord's house, and I saw women sitting there weeping for Tammuz. ¹⁵And He said to me, "Do you see this, son of man? You will see even more detestable things than these."

¹⁶So He brought me to the inner court of the Lord's house, and there were about 25 men at the entrance of the Lord's temple, between the portico and the altar, with their backs to the Lord's temple and their faces turned to the east. They were bowing to the east in worship of the sun. ¹⁷And He said to me, "Do you see this, son of man? Is it not enough for the house of Judah to commit the detestable things they are practicing here, that they must also fill the land with violence and repeatedly provoke Me to anger, even putting the branch to their nose? ¹⁸Therefore I will respond with wrath. I will not show pity or spare them. Though they cry out in My ears with a loud voice, I will not listen to them."

9 Then He called to me directly with a loud voice, "Come near, executioners of the city, each of you with a destructive weapon in his hand." ²And I saw six men coming from the direction of the Upper Gate, which faces north, each with a war club in his hand. There was another man among them, clothed in linen,

with writing equipment at his side. They came and stood beside the bronze altar.

³Then the glory of the God of Israel rose from above the ˙cherub where it had been, to the threshold of the temple. He called to the man clothed in linen with the writing equipment at his side. ⁴"Pass throughout the city of Jerusalem," the Lord said to him, "and put a mark on the foreheads of the men who sigh and groan over all the detestable practices committed in it."

⁵He spoke as I listened to the others, "Pass through the city after him and start killing; do not show pity or spare them! ⁶Slaughter the old men, the young men and women, as well as the older women and little children, but do not come near anyone who has the mark. Now begin at My sanctuary." So they began with the elders who were in front of the temple. ⁷Then He said to them, "Defile the temple and fill the courts with the slain. Go!" So they went out killing people in the city.

⁸While they were killing, I was left alone. And I fell facedown and cried out, "Oh, Lord God! Are You going to destroy the entire remnant of Israel when You pour out Your wrath on Jerusalem?"

⁹He answered me: "The iniquity of the house of Israel and Judah is extremely great; the land is full of bloodshed, and the city full of perversity. For they say, 'The Lord has abandoned the land; He does not see.' ¹⁰But as for Me, I will not show pity or spare them. I will bring their actions down on their own heads." ¹¹Then the man clothed in linen with the writing equipment at his side reported back, "I have done as You commanded me."

10 Then I looked, and there above the expanse over the heads of the ˙cherubim was something like sapphire stone resembling the shape of a throne that appeared above them. ²The Lord spoke to the man clothed in linen and said, "Go inside the wheelwork beneath the cherubim. Fill your hands with hot coals from among the cherubim and scatter them over the city." So he went in as I watched.

³Now the cherubim were standing to the south of the temple when the man went in, and the cloud filled the inner court. ⁴Then the glory of the Lord rose from above the cherub to the threshold of the temple. The temple was filled with the cloud, and the court was filled with the brightness of the Lord's glory. ⁵The sound of the cherubim's wings could be heard as far as the outer court; it was like the voice of ˙God Almighty when He speaks.

⁶After the Lord commanded the man clothed in linen, saying, "Take fire from inside the wheelwork, from among the cherubim," the man went in and stood beside a wheel. ⁷Then the cherub reached out his hand to the fire that was among them. He took some, and put it into the hands of the man clothed in linen, who took it and went out. ⁸The cherubim appeared to have the form of human hands under their wings.

⁹I looked, and there were four wheels beside the cherubim, one wheel beside each cherub. The luster of the wheels was like the gleam of beryl. ¹⁰In appearance, all four had the same form, like a wheel within a wheel. ¹¹When they moved, they would go in any of the four directions, without pivoting as they moved. But wherever the head faced, they would go in that direction, without pivoting as they went. ¹²Their entire bodies, including their backs, hands, wings, and the wheels that the four of them had, were full of eyes all around. ¹³As I listened the wheels were called "the

wheelwork." ¹⁴Each one had four faces: the first face was that of a cherub, the second that of a man, the third that of a lion, and the fourth that of an eagle.

¹⁵The cherubim ascended; these were the living creatures I had seen by the Chebar Canal. ¹⁶When the cherubim moved, the wheels moved beside them, and when they lifted their wings to rise from the earth, even then the wheels did not veer away from them. ¹⁷When the cherubim stood still, the wheels stood still, and when they ascended, the wheels ascended with them, for the spirit of the living creatures was in them.

¹⁸Then the glory of the Lord moved away from the threshold of the temple and stood above the cherubim. ¹⁹The cherubim lifted their wings and ascended from the earth right before my eyes; the wheels were beside them as they went. The glory of the God of Israel was above them, and it stood at the entrance to the eastern gate of the Lord's house.

²⁰These were the living creatures I had seen beneath the God of Israel by the Chebar Canal, and I recognized that they were cherubim. ²¹Each had four faces and each had four wings, with the form of human hands under their wings. ²²Their faces looked like the same faces I had seen by the Chebar Canal. Each creature went straight ahead.

11 The Spirit then lifted me up and brought me to the eastern gate of the Lord's house, which faces east, and at the gate's entrance were 25 men. Among them I saw Jaazaniah son of Azzur, and Pelatiah son of Benaiah, leaders of the people. ²The Lord said to me, "Son of man, these are the men who plan evil and give wicked advice in this city. ³They are saying, 'Isn't the time near to build houses? The city is the pot, and we are the meat.' ⁴Therefore, prophesy against them. Prophesy, son of man!"

⁵Then the Spirit of the Lord came on me, and He told me, "You are to say: This is what the Lord says: That is what you are thinking, house of Israel; and I know the thoughts that arise in your mind. ⁶You have multiplied your slain in this city, filling its streets with the dead.

⁷"Therefore, this is what the Lord God says: The slain you have put within it are the meat, and the city is the pot, but I will remove you from it. ⁸You fear the sword, so I will bring the sword against you." This is the declaration of the Lord God. ⁹"I will bring you out of the city and hand you over to foreigners; I will execute judgments against you. ¹⁰You will fall by the sword, and I will judge you at the border of Israel. Then you will know that I am ˙Yahweh. ¹¹The city will not be a pot for you, and you will not be the meat within it. I will judge you at the border of Israel, ¹²so you will know that I am Yahweh, whose statutes you have not followed and whose ordinances you have not practiced. Instead, you have acted according to the ordinances of the nations around you."

¹³Now while I was prophesying, Pelatiah son of Benaiah died. Then I fell facedown and cried out with a loud voice: "Oh, Lord God! Will You bring to an end the remnant of Israel?"

¹⁴The word of the Lord came to me again: ¹⁵"Son of man, your own relatives, those who have the right to redeem you, and the entire house of Israel, all of them, are those that the residents of Jerusalem have said this to, 'Stay away from the Lord; this land has been given to us as a possession.'

¹⁶"Therefore say: This is what the Lord God says:

Though I sent them far away among the nations and scattered them among the countries, yet for a little while I have been a sanctuary for them in the countries where they have gone.

¹⁷ "Therefore say: This is what the Lord God says: I will gather you from the peoples and assemble you from the countries where you have been scattered, and I will give you the land of Israel.

¹⁸ "When they arrive there, they will remove all its detestable things and practices from it. ¹⁹ And I will give them one heart and put a new spirit within them; I will remove their heart of stone from their bodies and give them a heart of flesh, ²⁰ so they may follow My statutes, keep My ordinances, and practice them. Then they will be My people, and I will be their God. ²¹ But as for those whose hearts pursue their desire for detestable things and practices, I will bring their actions down on their own heads." This is the declaration of the Lord God.

²² Then the ˚cherubim, with the wheels beside them, lifted their wings, and the glory of the God of Israel was above them. ²³ The glory of the Lord rose up from within the city and stood on the mountain east of the city. ²⁴ The Spirit lifted me up and brought me to Chaldea and to the exiles in a vision from the Spirit of God. After the vision I had seen left me, ²⁵ I spoke to the exiles about all the things the Lord had shown me.

12 The word of the Lord came to me: ² "Son of man, you are living among a rebellious house. They have eyes to see but do not see, and ears to hear but do not hear, for they are a rebellious house.

³ "Son of man, get your bags ready for exile and go into exile in their sight during the day. You will go into exile from your place to another place while they watch; perhaps they will understand, though they are a rebellious house. ⁴ During the day, bring out your bags like an exile's bags while they look on. Then in the evening go out in their sight like those going into exile. ⁵ As they watch, dig through the wall and take the bags out through it. ⁶ And while they look on, lift the bags to your shoulder and take them out in the dark; cover your face so that you cannot see the land. For I have made you a sign to the house of Israel."

⁷ So I did just as I was commanded. In the daytime I brought out my bags like an exile's bags. In the evening I dug through the wall by hand; I took them out in the dark, carrying them on my shoulder in their sight.

⁸ Then the word of the Lord came to me in the morning: ⁹ "Son of man, hasn't the house of Israel, that rebellious house, asked you, 'What are you doing?' ¹⁰ Say to them: This is what the Lord God says: This ˚oracle is about the prince in Jerusalem and all the house of Israel who are living there. ¹¹ You are to say, 'I am a sign for you. Just as I have done, so it will be done to them; they will go into exile, into captivity.' ¹² The prince who is among them will lift his bags to his shoulder in the dark and go out. They will dig through the wall to bring him out through it. He will cover his face so he cannot see the land with his eyes. ¹³ But I will spread My net over him, and he will be caught in My snare. I will bring him to Babylon, the land of the Chaldeans, yet he will not see it, and he will die there. ¹⁴ I will also scatter all the attendants who surround him and all his troops to every direction of the wind, and I will draw a sword to chase after them. ¹⁵ They will know that I am ˚Yahweh when I disperse them among the nations and

scatter them among the countries. ¹⁶ But I will spare a few of them from the sword, famine, and plague so they can tell about all their detestable practices among the nations where they go. Then they will know that I am Yahweh."

¹⁷ The word of the Lord came to me: ¹⁸ "Son of man, eat your bread with trembling and drink your water with shaking and anxiety. ¹⁹ Then say to the people of the land: This is what the Lord God says about the residents of Jerusalem in the land of Israel: They will eat their bread with anxiety and drink their water in dread, for their land will be stripped of everything in it because of the violence of all who live there. ²⁰ The inhabited cities will be destroyed, and the land will become a desolation. Then you will know that I am Yahweh."

²¹ Again the word of the Lord came to me: ²² "Son of man, what is this proverb you people have about the land of Israel, which goes:

The days keep passing by,
and every vision fails?

²³ Therefore say to them: This is what the Lord God says: I will put a stop to this proverb, and they will not use it again in Israel. But say to them: The days draw near, as well as the fulfillment of every vision. ²⁴ For there will no longer be any false vision or flattering ˚divination within the house of Israel. ²⁵ But I, Yahweh, will speak whatever message I will speak, and it will be done. It will no longer be delayed. For in your days, rebellious house, I will speak a message and bring it to pass." This is the declaration of the Lord God.

²⁶ The word of the Lord came to me: ²⁷ "Son of man, notice that the house of Israel is saying, 'The vision that he sees concerns many years from now; he prophesies about distant times.' ²⁸ Therefore say to them: This is what the Lord God says: None of My words will be delayed any longer. The message I speak will be fulfilled." This is the declaration of the Lord God.

13 The word of the Lord came to me: ² "Son of man, prophesy against the prophets of Israel who are prophesying. Say to those who prophesy out of their own imagination: Hear the word of the Lord! ³ This is what the Lord God says: Woe to the foolish prophets who follow their own spirit and have seen nothing. ⁴ Your prophets, Israel, are like jackals among ruins. ⁵ You did not go up to the gaps or restore the wall around the house of Israel so that it might stand in battle on the day of the Lord. ⁶ They see false visions and speak lying ˚divinations. They claim, 'This is the Lord's declaration,' when the Lord did not send them, yet they wait for the fulfillment of their message. ⁷ Didn't you see a false vision and speak a lying divination when you proclaimed, 'This is the Lord's declaration,' even though I had not spoken?

⁸ "Therefore, this is what the Lord God says: I am against you because you have spoken falsely and had lying visions." This is the declaration of the Lord God. ⁹ "My hand will be against the prophets who see false visions and speak lying divinations. They will not be present in the fellowship of My people or be recorded in the register of the house of Israel, and they will not enter the land of Israel. Then you will know that I am the Lord ˚Yahweh.

¹⁰ "Since they have led My people astray saying, 'Peace,' when there is no peace, for when someone builds a wall they plaster it with whitewash, ¹¹ therefore, tell those who plaster it that it will fall. Torrential

rain will come, and I will send hailstones plunging down, and a windstorm will be released. [12] Now when the wall has fallen, will you not be asked, 'Where is the coat of whitewash that you put on it?'

[13] "So this is what the Lord GOD says: I will release a windstorm in My wrath. Torrential rain will come in My anger, and hailstones will fall in destructive fury. [14] I will tear down the wall you plastered with whitewash and knock it to the ground so that its foundation is exposed. The city will fall, and you will be destroyed within it. Then you will know that I am Yahweh. [15] After I exhaust My wrath against the wall and against those who plaster it with whitewash, I will say to you: The wall is no more and neither are those who plastered it— [16] those prophets of Israel who prophesied to Jerusalem and saw a vision of peace for her when there was no peace." This is the declaration of the Lord GOD.

[17] "Now, son of man, turn toward the women of your people who prophesy out of their own imagination. Prophesy against them [18] and say: This is what the Lord GOD says: Woe to the women who sew magic bands on the wrist of every hand and who make veils for the heads of people of every height in order to ensnare lives. Will you ensnare the lives of My people but preserve your own? [19] You profane Me in front of My people for handfuls of barley and scraps of bread; you kill those who should not die and spare those who should not live, when you lie to My people, who listen to lies.

[20] "Therefore, this is what the Lord GOD says: I am against your magic bands that you ensnare people with like birds, and I will tear them from your arms. I will free the people you have ensnared like birds. [21] I will also tear off your veils and deliver My people from your hands, so that they will no longer be prey in your hands. Then you will know that I am Yahweh. [22] Because you have disheartened the righteous person with lies, even though I have not caused him grief, and because you have encouraged the wicked person not to turn from his evil way to save his life, [23] therefore you will no longer see false visions or practice divination. I will deliver My people from your hands. Then you will know that I am Yahweh."

14 Some of the elders of Israel came to me and sat down in front of me. [2] Then the word of the LORD came to me: [3] "Son of man, these men have set up idols in their hearts and have put sinful stumbling blocks before their faces. Should I be consulted by them at all?

[4] "Therefore, speak to them and tell them: This is what the Lord GOD says: When anyone from the house of Israel sets up idols in his heart, puts a sinful stumbling block before his face, and then comes to the prophet, I, *Yahweh, will answer him appropriately. I will answer him according to his many idols, [5] so that I may take hold of the house of Israel by their hearts. They are all estranged from Me because of their idols.

[6] "Therefore, say to the house of Israel: This is what the Lord GOD says: Repent and turn away from your idols; turn your faces away from all your detestable things. [7] For when anyone from the house of Israel or from the foreigners who reside in Israel separates himself from Me, setting up idols in his heart and putting a sinful stumbling block before his face, and then comes to the prophet to inquire of Me, I, Yahweh, will answer him Myself. [8] I will turn against that one and make him a sign and a proverb; I will cut him off from among My people. Then you will know that I am Yahweh.

[9] "But if the prophet is deceived and speaks a message, it was I, Yahweh, who deceived that prophet. I will stretch out My hand against him and destroy him from among My people Israel. [10] They will bear their punishment—the punishment of the one who inquires will be the same as that of the prophet— [11] in order that the house of Israel may no longer stray from following Me and no longer defile themselves with all their transgressions. Then they will be My people and I will be their God." This is the declaration of the Lord GOD.

[12] The word of the LORD came to me: [13] "Son of man, if a land sins against Me by acting faithlessly, and I stretch out My hand against it to cut off its supply of bread, to send famine through it, and to wipe out both man and animal from it, [14] even if these three men— Noah, Daniel, and Job—were in it, they would deliver only themselves by their righteousness." This is the declaration of the Lord GOD.

[15] "If I allow dangerous animals to pass through the land and depopulate it so that it becomes desolate, with no one passing through it for fear of the animals, [16] even if these three men were in it, as I live"—the declaration of the Lord GOD—"they could not deliver their sons or daughters. They alone would be delivered, but the land would be desolate.

[17] "Or if I bring a sword against that land and say: Let a sword pass through it, so that I wipe out both man and animal from it, [18] even if these three men were in it, as I live"—the declaration of the Lord GOD—"they could not deliver their sons or daughters, but they alone would be delivered.

[19] "Or if I send a plague into that land and pour out My wrath on it with bloodshed to wipe out both man and animal from it, [20] even if Noah, Daniel, and Job were in it, as I live"—the declaration of the Lord GOD—"they could not deliver their son or daughter. They would deliver only themselves by their righteousness.

[21] "For this is what the Lord GOD says: How much worse will it be when I send My four devastating judgments against Jerusalem—sword, famine, dangerous animals, and plague—in order to wipe out both man and animal from it! [22] Even so, there will be survivors left in it, sons and daughters who will be brought out. Indeed, they will come out to you, and you will observe their conduct and actions. Then you will be consoled about the devastation I have brought on Jerusalem, about all I have brought on it. [23] They will bring you consolation when you see their conduct and actions, and you will know that it was not without cause that I have done what I did to it." This is the declaration of the Lord GOD.

15 Then the word of the LORD came to me: [2] "Son of man, how does the wood of the vine, that branch among the trees of the forest, compare to any other wood? [3] Can wood be taken from it to make something useful? Or can anyone make a peg from it to hang things on? [4] In fact, it is put into the fire as fuel. The fire devours both of its ends, and the middle is charred. Can it be useful for anything? [5] Even when it was whole it could not be made into a useful object. How much less can it ever be made into anything useful when the fire has devoured it and it is charred!

[6] "Therefore, this is what the Lord GOD says: Like the wood of the vine among the trees of the forest, which I have given to the fire as fuel, so I will give up

the residents of Jerusalem. [7] I will turn against them. They may have escaped from the fire, but it will still consume them. And you will know that I am •Yahweh when I turn against them. [8] I will make the land desolate because they have acted unfaithfully." This is the declaration of the Lord GOD.

16 The word of the LORD came to me again: [2] "Son of man, explain Jerusalem's detestable practices to her. [3] You are to say: This is what the Lord GOD says to Jerusalem: Your origin and your birth were in the land of the Canaanites. Your father was an Amorite and your mother a Hittite. [4] As for your birth, your umbilical cord wasn't cut on the day you were born, and you weren't washed •clean with water. You were not rubbed with salt or wrapped in cloths. [5] No one cared enough about you to do even one of these things out of compassion for you. But you were thrown out into the open field because you were despised on the day you were born.

[6] "I passed by you and saw you lying in your blood, and I said to you as you lay in your blood: Live! Yes, I said to you as you lay in your blood: Live! [7] I made you thrive like plants of the field. You grew up and matured and became very beautiful. Your breasts were formed and your hair grew, but you were stark naked.

[8] "Then I passed by you and saw you, and you were indeed at the age for love. So I spread the edge of My garment over you and covered your nakedness. I pledged Myself to you, entered into a covenant with you, and you became Mine." This is the declaration of the Lord GOD. [9] "I washed you with water, rinsed off your blood, and anointed you with oil. [10] I clothed you in embroidered cloth and provided you with leather sandals. I also wrapped you in fine linen and covered you with silk. [11] I adorned you with jewelry, putting bracelets on your wrists and a chain around your neck. [12] I put a ring in your nose, earrings on your ears, and a beautiful tiara on your head. [13] So you were adorned with gold and silver, and your clothing was made of fine linen, silk, and embroidered cloth. You ate fine flour, honey, and oil. You became extremely beautiful and attained royalty. [14] Your fame spread among the nations because of your beauty, for it was perfect through My splendor, which I had bestowed on you." This is the declaration of the Lord GOD.

[15] "But you were confident in your beauty and acted like a prostitute because of your fame. You lavished your sexual favors on everyone who passed by. Your beauty became his. [16] You took some of your garments and made colorful •high places for yourself, and you engaged in prostitution on them. These places should not have been built, and this should never have happened! [17] You also took your beautiful jewelry made from the gold and silver I had given you, and you made male images so that you could engage in prostitution with them. [18] Then you took your embroidered garments to cover them, and set My oil and incense before them. [19] You also set before them as a pleasing aroma the food I gave you—the fine flour, oil, and honey that I fed you. That is what happened." This is the declaration of the Lord GOD.

[20] "You even took your sons and daughters you bore to Me and sacrificed them to these images as food. Wasn't your prostitution enough? [21] You slaughtered My children and gave them up when you passed them through the fire to the images. [22] In all your detestable practices and acts of prostitution, you did not remember the days of your youth when you were stark naked and lying in your blood.

[23] "Then after all your evil—Woe, woe to you!"—the declaration of the Lord GOD— [24] "you built yourself a mound and made yourself an elevated place in every square. [25] You built your elevated place at the head of every street and turned your beauty into a detestable thing. You spread your legs to everyone who passed by and increased your prostitution. [26] You engaged in promiscuous acts with Egyptian men, your well-endowed neighbors, and increased your prostitution to provoke Me to anger.

[27] "Therefore, I stretched out My hand against you and reduced your provisions. I gave you over to the desire of those who hate you, the Philistine women, who were embarrassed by your indecent behavior. [28] Then you engaged in prostitution with the Assyrian men because you were not satisfied. Even though you did this with them, you were still not satisfied. [29] So you extended your prostitution to Chaldea, the land of merchants, but you were not even satisfied with this!

[30] "How your heart was inflamed with lust"—the declaration of the Lord GOD—"when you did all these things, the acts of a brazen prostitute, [31] building your mound at the head of every street and making your elevated place in every square. But you were unlike a prostitute because you scorned payment. [32] You adulterous wife, who receives strangers instead of her husband! [33] Men give gifts to all prostitutes, but you gave gifts to all your lovers. You bribed them to come to you from all around for your sexual favors. [34] So you were the opposite of other women in your acts of prostitution; no one solicited you. When you paid a fee instead of one being paid to you, you were the opposite.

[35] "Therefore, you prostitute, hear the word of the LORD! [36] This is what the Lord GOD says: Because your lust was poured out and your nakedness exposed by your acts of prostitution with your lovers, and because of all your detestable idols and the blood of your children that you gave to them, [37] I am therefore going to gather all the lovers you pleased—all those you loved as well as all those you hated. I will gather them against you from all around and expose your nakedness to them so they see you completely naked. [38] I will judge you the way adulteresses and those who shed blood are judged. Then I will bring about your bloodshed in wrath and jealousy. [39] I will hand you over to them, and they will level your mounds and tear down your elevated places. They will strip off your clothes, take your beautiful jewelry, and leave you stark naked. [40] They will bring a mob against you to stone you and cut you to pieces with their swords. [41] Then they will burn down your houses and execute judgments against you in the sight of many women. I will stop you from being a prostitute, and you will never again pay fees for lovers. [42] So I will satisfy My wrath against you, and My jealousy will turn away from you. Then I will be silent and no longer angry. [43] Because you did not remember the days of your youth but enraged Me with all these things, I will also bring your actions down on your own head. This is the declaration of the Lord GOD. "Haven't you committed immoral acts in addition to all your detestable practices?

[44] "Look, everyone who uses proverbs will say this proverb about you:

Like mother, like daughter.

[45] You are the daughter of your mother, who despised

her husband and children. You are the sister of your sisters, who despised their husbands and children. Your mother was a Hittite and your father an Amorite. ⁴⁶ Your older sister was Samaria, who lived with her daughters to the north of you, and your younger sister was Sodom, who lived with her daughters to the south of you. ⁴⁷ Didn't you walk in their ways and do their detestable practices? It was only a short time before you behaved more corruptly than they did.

⁴⁸ "As I live"—the declaration of the Lord GOD— "your sister Sodom and her daughters have not behaved as you and your daughters have. ⁴⁹ Now this was the iniquity of your sister Sodom: she and her daughters had pride, plenty of food, and comfortable security, but didn't support the poor and needy. ⁵⁰ They were haughty and did detestable things before Me, so I removed them when I saw this. ⁵¹ But Samaria did not commit even half your sins. You have multiplied your detestable practices beyond theirs and made your sisters appear righteous by all the detestable things you have committed. ⁵² You must also bear your disgrace, since you have been an advocate for your sisters. For they appear more righteous than you because of your sins, which you committed more abhorrently than they did. So you also, be ashamed and bear your disgrace, since you have made your sisters appear righteous.

⁵³ "I will restore their fortunes, the fortunes of Sodom and her daughters and those of Samaria and her daughters. I will also restore your fortunes among them, ⁵⁴ so you will bear your disgrace and be ashamed of all you did when you comforted them. ⁵⁵ As for your sisters, Sodom and her daughters and Samaria and her daughters will return to their former state. You and your daughters will also return to your former state. ⁵⁶ Didn't you treat your sister Sodom as an object of scorn when you were proud, ⁵⁷ before your wickedness was exposed? It was like the time you were scorned by the daughters of Aram and all those around her, and by the daughters of the Philistines—those who treated you with contempt from every side. ⁵⁸ You yourself must bear the consequences of your indecency and detestable practices"—this is the LORD's declaration.

⁵⁹ "For this is what the Lord GOD says: I will deal with you according to what you have done, since you have despised the oath by breaking the covenant. ⁶⁰ But I will remember the covenant I made with you in the days of your youth, and I will establish an everlasting covenant with you. ⁶¹ Then you will remember your ways and be ashamed when you receive your older and younger sisters. I will give them to you as daughters, but not because of your covenant. ⁶² I will establish My covenant with you, and you will know that I am •Yahweh, ⁶³ so that when I make •atonement for all you have done, you will remember and be ashamed, and never open your mouth again because of your disgrace." This is the declaration of the Lord GOD.

17 The word of the LORD came to me: ² "Son of man, pose a riddle and speak a parable to the house of Israel. ³ You are to say: This is what the Lord GOD says:

A great eagle with great wings, long pinions,
and full plumage of many colors
came to Lebanon and took the top
of the cedar.
⁴   He plucked off its topmost shoot,
brought it to the land of merchants,
and set it in a city of traders.

⁵   Then he took some of the land's seed
and put it in a fertile field;
he set it like a willow,
a plant by abundant waters.
⁶   It sprouted and became a spreading vine,
low in height with its branches turned
toward him,
yet its roots stayed under it.
So it became a vine,
produced branches, and sent out shoots.
⁷   But there was another great eagle
with great wings and thick plumage.
And this vine bent its roots toward him!
It stretched out its branches to him
from its planting bed,
so that he might water it.
⁸   It had been planted
in a good field by abundant waters
in order to produce branches,
bear fruit, and become a splendid vine.
⁹ You are to say: This is what the Lord GOD says:
Will it flourish?
Will he not tear out its roots
and strip off its fruit
so that it shrivels?
All its fresh leaves will wither!
Great strength and many people
will not be needed to pull it from its roots.
¹⁰   Even though it is planted, will it flourish?
Won't it completely wither
when the east wind strikes it?
It will wither on the bed where it sprouted."

¹¹ The word of the LORD came to me: ¹² "Now say to that rebellious house: Don't you know what these things mean? Tell them: The king of Babylon came to Jerusalem, took its king and officials, and brought them back with him to Babylon. ¹³ He took one of the royal family and made a covenant with him, putting him under oath. Then he took away the leading men of the land, ¹⁴ so the kingdom might be humble and not exalt itself but might keep his covenant in order to endure. ¹⁵ However, this king revolted against him by sending his ambassadors to Egypt so they might give him horses and a large army. Will he flourish? Will the one who does such things escape? Can he break a covenant and still escape?

¹⁶ "As I live"—this is the declaration of the Lord GOD—"he will die in Babylon, in the land of the king who put him on the throne, whose oath he despised and whose covenant he broke. ¹⁷ Pharaoh will not help him with his great army and vast horde in battle, when ramps are built and siege walls constructed to destroy many lives. ¹⁸ He despised the oath by breaking the covenant. He did all these things even though he gave his hand in pledge. He will not escape!"

¹⁹ Therefore, this is what the Lord GOD says: "As I live, I will bring down on his head My oath that he despised and My covenant that he broke. ²⁰ I will spread My net over him, and he will be caught in My snare. I will bring him to Babylon and execute judgment on him there for the treachery he committed against Me. ²¹ All the fugitives among his troops will fall by the sword, and those who survive will be scattered to every direction of the wind. Then you will know that I, •Yahweh, have spoken."

²² This is what the Lord GOD says:
I will take a sprig

from the lofty top of the cedar and plant it.
I will pluck a tender sprig
    from its topmost shoots,
    and I will plant it
on a high towering mountain.
²³ I will plant it on Israel's high mountain
so that it may bear branches, produce fruit,
    and become a majestic cedar.
Birds of every kind will nest under it,
taking shelter in the shade of its branches.
²⁴ Then all the trees of the field will know
    that I am Yahweh.
I bring down the tall tree,
    and make the low tree tall.
I cause the green tree to wither
    and make the withered tree thrive.
I, Yahweh, have spoken
    and I will do it.

18 The word of the LORD came to me: ²"What do you mean by using this proverb concerning the land of Israel:

The fathers eat sour grapes,
    and the children's teeth are set on edge?

³As I live"—this is the declaration of the Lord GOD—"you will no longer use this proverb in Israel. ⁴Look, every life belongs to Me. The life of the father is like the life of the son—both belong to Me. The person who sins is the one who will die.

⁵"Now suppose a man is righteous and does what is just and right: ⁶He does not eat at the mountain shrines or raise his eyes to the idols of the house of Israel. He does not defile his neighbor's wife or come near a woman during her menstrual impurity. ⁷He doesn't oppress anyone but returns his collateral to the debtor. He does not commit robbery, but gives his bread to the hungry and covers the naked with clothing. ⁸He doesn't lend at interest or for profit but keeps his hand from wrongdoing and carries out true justice between men. ⁹He follows My statutes and keeps My ordinances, acting faithfully. Such a person is righteous; he will certainly live." This is the declaration of the Lord GOD.

¹⁰"Now suppose the man has a violent son, who sheds blood and does any of these things, ¹¹though the father has done none of them. Indeed, when the son eats at the mountain shrines and defiles his neighbor's wife, ¹²and when he oppresses the poor and needy, commits robbery, and does not return collateral, and when he raises his eyes to the idols, commits detestable acts, ¹³and lends at interest or for profit, will he live? He will not live! Since he has committed all these detestable acts, he will certainly die. His blood will be on him.

¹⁴"Now suppose he has a son who sees all the sins his father has committed, and though he sees them, he does not do likewise. ¹⁵He does not eat at the mountain shrines or raise his eyes to the idols of the house of Israel. He does not defile his neighbor's wife. ¹⁶He doesn't oppress anyone, hold collateral, or commit robbery. He gives his bread to the hungry and covers the naked with clothing. ¹⁷He keeps his hand from harming the poor, not taking interest or profit on a loan. He practices My ordinances and follows My statutes. Such a person will not die for his father's iniquity. He will certainly live. ¹⁸As for his father, he will die for his own iniquity because he practiced fraud, robbed his brother, and

did what was wrong among his people. ¹⁹But you may ask, 'Why doesn't the son suffer punishment for the father's iniquity?' Since the son has done what is just and right, carefully observing all My statutes, he will certainly live. ²⁰The person who sins is the one who will die. A son won't suffer punishment for the father's iniquity, and a father won't suffer punishment for the son's iniquity. The righteousness of the righteous person will be on him, and the wickedness of the wicked person will be on him.

²¹"Now if the wicked person turns from all the sins he has committed, keeps all My statutes, and does what is just and right, he will certainly live; he will not die. ²²None of the transgressions he has committed will be held against him. He will live because of the righteousness he has practiced. ²³Do I take any pleasure in the death of the wicked?" This is the declaration of the Lord GOD. "Instead, don't I take pleasure when he turns from his ways and lives? ²⁴But when a righteous person turns from his righteousness and practices iniquity, committing the same detestable acts that the wicked do, will he live? None of the righteous acts he did will be remembered. He will die because of the treachery he has engaged in and the sin he has committed.

²⁵"But you say, 'The Lord's way isn't fair.' Now listen, house of Israel: Is it My way that is unfair? Instead, isn't it your ways that are unfair? ²⁶When a righteous person turns from his righteousness and practices iniquity, he will die for this. He will die because of the iniquity he has practiced. ²⁷But if a wicked person turns from the wickedness he has committed and does what is just and right, he will preserve his life. ²⁸He will certainly live because he thought it over and turned from all the transgressions he had committed; he will not die. ²⁹But the house of Israel says, 'The Lord's way isn't fair.' Is it My ways that are unfair, house of Israel? Instead, isn't it your ways that are unfair?

³⁰"Therefore, house of Israel, I will judge each one of you according to his ways." This is the declaration of the Lord GOD. "Repent and turn from all your transgressions, so they will not be a stumbling block that causes your punishment. ³¹Throw off all the transgressions you have committed, and get yourselves a new heart and a new spirit. Why should you die, house of Israel? ³²For I take no pleasure in anyone's death." This is the declaration of the Lord GOD. "So repent and live!

19 "Now, lament for the princes of Israel ²and say:
    What was your mother? A lioness!
She lay down among the lions;
    she reared her cubs among the young lions.
³ She brought up one of her cubs,
    and he became a young lion.
After he learned to tear prey,
    he devoured people.
⁴ When the nations heard about him,
    he was caught in their pit.
Then they led him away with hooks
    to the land of Egypt.
⁵ When she saw that she waited in vain,
    that her hope was lost,
she took another of her cubs
    and made him a young lion.
⁶ He prowled among the lions,
    and he became a young lion.
After he learned to tear prey,
    he devoured people.

⁷ He devastated their strongholds
and destroyed their cities.
The land and everything in it shuddered
at the sound of his roaring.
⁸ Then the nations from
the surrounding provinces
set out against him.
They spread their net over him;
he was caught in their pit.
⁹ They put a wooden yoke on him with hooks
and led him away to the king of Babylon.
They brought him into the fortresses
so his roar could no longer be heard
on the mountains of Israel.
¹⁰ Your mother was like a vine in your vineyard,
planted by the water;
it was fruitful and full of branches
because of plentiful waters.
¹¹ It had strong branches, fit for the scepters
of rulers;
its height towered among the clouds.
So it was conspicuous for its height
as well as its many branches.
¹² But it was uprooted in fury,
thrown to the ground,
and the east wind dried up its fruit.
Its strong branches were torn off and dried up;
fire consumed them.
¹³ Now it is planted in the wilderness,
in a dry and thirsty land.
¹⁴ Fire has gone out from its main branch
and has devoured its fruit,
so that it no longer has a strong branch,
a scepter for ruling.
This is a lament and should be used as a lament."

20 In the seventh year, in the fifth month, on the tenth day of the month, some of Israel's elders came to consult the Lord, and they sat down in front of me. ² Then the word of the Lord came to me: ³ "Son of man, speak with the elders of Israel and tell them: This is what the Lord God says: Are you coming to consult Me? As I live, I will not be consulted by you." This is the declaration of the Lord God.

⁴ "Will you pass judgment against them, will you pass judgment, son of man? Explain the detestable practices of their fathers to them. ⁵ Say to them: This is what the Lord God says: On the day I chose Israel, I swore an oath to the descendants of Jacob's house and made Myself known to them in the land of Egypt. I swore to them, saying: I am ˙Yahweh your God. ⁶ On that day I swore to them that I would bring them out of the land of Egypt into a land I had searched out for them, a land flowing with milk and honey, the most beautiful of all lands. ⁷ I also said to them: Each of you must throw away the detestable things that are before your eyes and not defile yourselves with the idols of Egypt. I am Yahweh your God.

⁸ "But they rebelled against Me and were unwilling to listen to Me. None of them threw away the detestable things that were before their eyes, and they did not forsake the idols of Egypt. So I considered pouring out My wrath on them, exhausting My anger against them within the land of Egypt. ⁹ But I acted because of My name, so that it would not be profaned in the eyes of the nations they were living among, in whose sight I had made Myself known to Israel by bringing them out of Egypt.

¹⁰ "So I brought them out of the land of Egypt and led them into the wilderness. ¹¹ Then I gave them My statutes and explained My ordinances to them— the person who does them will live by them. ¹² I also gave them My Sabbaths to serve as a sign between Me and them, so they will know that I am Yahweh who sets them apart as holy.

¹³ "But the house of Israel rebelled against Me in the wilderness. They did not follow My statutes and they rejected My ordinances—the person who does them will live by them. They also completely profaned My Sabbaths. So I considered pouring out My wrath on them in the wilderness to put an end to them. ¹⁴ But I acted because of My name, so that it would not be profaned in the eyes of the nations in whose sight I had brought them out. ¹⁵ However, I swore to them in the wilderness that I would not bring them into the land I had given them—the most beautiful of all lands, flowing with milk and honey— ¹⁶ because they rejected My ordinances, profaned My Sabbaths, and did not follow My statutes. For their hearts went after their idols. ¹⁷ But I spared them from destruction and did not bring them to an end in the wilderness.

¹⁸ "Then I said to their children in the wilderness: Don't follow the statutes of your fathers, defile yourselves with their idols, or keep their ordinances. ¹⁹ I am Yahweh your God. Follow My statutes, keep My ordinances, and practice them. ²⁰ Keep My Sabbaths holy, and they will be a sign between Me and you, so you may know that I am Yahweh your God.

²¹ "But the children rebelled against Me. They did not follow My statutes or carefully keep My ordinances—the person who does them will live by them. They also profaned My Sabbaths. So I considered pouring out My wrath on them and exhausting My anger against them in the wilderness. ²² But I withheld My hand and acted because of My name, so that it would not be profaned in the eyes of the nations in whose sight I brought them out. ²³ However, I swore to them in the wilderness that I would disperse them among the nations and scatter them among the countries. ²⁴ For they did not practice My ordinances but rejected My statutes and profaned My Sabbaths, and their eyes were fixed on their fathers' idols. ²⁵ I also gave them statutes that were not good and ordinances they could not live by. ²⁶ When they made every firstborn pass through the fire, I defiled them through their gifts in order to devastate them so they would know that I am Yahweh.

²⁷ "Therefore, son of man, speak to the house of Israel, and tell them: This is what the Lord God says: In this way also your fathers blasphemed Me by committing treachery against Me: ²⁸ When I brought them into the land that I swore to give them and they saw any high hill or leafy tree, they offered their sacrifices and presented their offensive offerings there. They also sent up their pleasing aromas and poured out their ˙drink offerings there. ²⁹ So I asked them: What is this ˙high place you are going to? And it is called High Place to this day.

³⁰ "Therefore say to the house of Israel: This is what the Lord God says: Are you defiling yourselves the way your fathers did, and prostituting yourselves with their detestable things? ³¹ When you offer your gifts, making your children pass through the fire, you continue to defile yourselves with all your idols to this day. So should I be consulted by you, house of Israel? As I

live"—this is the declaration of the Lord God—"I will not be consulted by you!

³²"When you say, 'Let us be like the nations, like the peoples of other countries, worshiping wood and stone,' what you have in mind will never happen. ³³As I live"—the declaration of the Lord God—"I will rule over you with a strong hand, an outstretched arm, and outpoured wrath. ³⁴I will bring you from the peoples and gather you from the countries where you were scattered, with a strong hand, an outstretched arm, and outpoured wrath. ³⁵I will lead you into the wilderness of the peoples and enter into judgment with you there face to face. ³⁶Just as I entered into judgment with your fathers in the wilderness of the land of Egypt, so I will enter into judgment with you." This is the declaration of the Lord God. ³⁷"I will make you pass under the rod and will bring you into the bond of the covenant. ³⁸And I will also purge you of those who rebel and transgress against Me. I will bring them out of the land where they live as foreign residents, but they will not enter the land of Israel. Then you will know that I am Yahweh.

³⁹"As for you, house of Israel, this is what the Lord God says: Go and serve your idols, each of you. But afterward you will surely listen to Me, and you will no longer defile My holy name with your gifts and idols. ⁴⁰For on My holy mountain, Israel's high mountain"—the declaration of the Lord God—"there the entire house of Israel, all of them, will serve Me in the land. There I will accept them and will require your contributions and choicest gifts, all your holy offerings. ⁴¹When I bring you from the peoples and gather you from the countries where you have been scattered, I will accept you as a pleasing aroma. And I will demonstrate My holiness through you in the sight of the nations. ⁴²When I lead you into the land of Israel, the land I swore to give your fathers, you will know that I am Yahweh. ⁴³There you will remember your ways and all your deeds that you have defiled yourselves with, and you will loathe yourselves for all the evil things you have done. ⁴⁴You will know that I am Yahweh, house of Israel, when I have dealt with you because of My name rather than according to your evil ways and corrupt acts." This is the declaration of the Lord God.

⁴⁵The word of the Lord came to me: ⁴⁶"Son of man, face the south and preach against it. Prophesy against the forest land in the ʻNegev, ⁴⁷and say to the forest there: Hear the word of the Lord! This is what the Lord God says: I am about to ignite a fire in you, and it will devour every green tree and every dry tree in you. The blazing flame will not be extinguished, and every face from the south to the north will be scorched by it. ⁴⁸Then all people will see that I, Yahweh, have kindled it. It will not be extinguished."

⁴⁹Then I said, "Oh, Lord God, they are saying of me, 'Isn't he just posing riddles?'"

21 The word of the Lord came to me again: ²"Son of man, turn your face toward Jerusalem and preach against the sanctuaries. Prophesy against the land of Israel, ³and say to it: This is what the Lord says: I am against you. I will draw My sword from its sheath and cut off both the righteous and the wicked from you. ⁴Since I will cut off both the righteous and the wicked, My sword will therefore come out of its sheath against everyone from the south to the north. ⁵So all the people will know that I, ʻYahweh, have taken My sword from its sheath—it will not be sheathed again.

⁶"But you, son of man, groan! Groan bitterly with a broken heart right before their eyes. ⁷And when they ask you, 'Why are you groaning?' then say: Because of the news that is coming. Every heart will melt, and every hand will become weak. Every spirit will be discouraged, and every knee will turn to water. Yes, it is coming and it will happen." This is the declaration of the Lord God.

⁸The word of the Lord came to me: ⁹"Son of man, prophesy: This is what the Lord says! You are to proclaim:

A sword! A sword is sharpened
and also polished.
¹⁰ It is sharpened for slaughter,
polished to flash like lightning!
Should we rejoice?
The scepter of My son,
the sword despises every tree.
¹¹ The sword is given to be polished,
to be grasped in the hand.
It is sharpened, and it is polished,
to be put in the hand of the slayer.
¹² Cry out and wail, son of man,
for it is against My people.
It is against all the princes of Israel!
They are given over to the sword
with My people.
Therefore strike your thigh in grief.
¹³ Surely it will be a trial!
And what if the sword despises
even the scepter?
The scepter will not continue.
This is the declaration of the Lord God.
¹⁴ Therefore, son of man, prophesy
and clap your hands together.
Let the sword strike two times, even three.
It is a sword for massacre,
a sword for great massacre—
it surrounds them!
¹⁵ I have appointed a sword for slaughter
at all their gates,
so that their hearts may melt
and many may stumble.
Yes! It is ready to flash like lightning;
it is drawn for slaughter.
¹⁶ Slash to the right;
turn to the left—
wherever your blade is directed.
¹⁷ I also will clap My hands together,
and I will satisfy My wrath.
I, Yahweh, have spoken."

¹⁸Then the word of the Lord came to me: ¹⁹"Now you, son of man, mark out two roads that the sword of Babylon's king can take. Both of them should originate from the same land. And make a signpost at the fork in the road to each city. ²⁰Mark out a road that the sword can take to Rabbah of the Ammonites and to Judah into fortified Jerusalem. ²¹For the king of Babylon stands at the split in the road, at the fork of the two roads, to practice ·divination: he shakes the arrows, consults the idols, and observes the liver. ²²The answer marked Jerusalem appears in his right hand, indicating that he should set up battering rams, give the order to slaughter, raise a battle cry, set battering rams against the gates, build a ramp, and construct a siege wall. ²³It will seem like false divination in the eyes of those who have sworn an oath to the Babylonians, but

it will draw attention to their *guilt so that they will be captured.

²⁴"Therefore, this is what the Lord God says: Because you have drawn attention to your guilt, exposing your transgressions, so that your sins are revealed in all your actions, since you have done this, you will be captured by them.

²⁵   And you, profane and wicked prince of Israel,
    the day has come
    for your punishment."

²⁶This is what the Lord God says:

    Remove the turban, and take off the crown.
    Things will not remain as they are;
    exalt the lowly and bring down the exalted.

²⁷   A ruin, a ruin,
    I will make it a ruin!
    Yet this will not happen
    until He comes;
    I have given the judgment to Him.

²⁸"Now prophesy, son of man, and say: This is what the Lord God says concerning the Ammonites and their contempt. You are to proclaim:

    A sword! A sword
    is drawn for slaughter,
    polished to consume, to flash
    like lightning.

²⁹   While they offer false visions
    and lying divinations about you,
    the time has come to put you
    to the necks of the profane wicked ones;
    the day has come
    for your punishment.

³⁰   Return it to its sheath!
    I will judge you
    in the place where you were created,
    in the land of your origin.

³¹   I will pour out My indignation on you;
    I will blow the fire of My fury on you.
    I will hand you over to brutal men,
    skilled at destruction.

³²   You will be fuel for the fire.
    Your blood will be spilled in the land.
    You will not be remembered,
    for I, Yahweh, have spoken."

22 The word of the Lord came to me: ²"As for you, son of man, will you pass judgment? Will you pass judgment against the city of blood? Then explain all her detestable practices to her. ³You are to say: This is what the Lord God says: A city that sheds blood within her walls so that her time of judgment has come and who makes idols for herself so that she is defiled! ⁴You are *guilty of the blood you have shed, and you are defiled from the idols you have made. You have brought your judgment days near and have come to your years of punishment. Therefore, I have made you a disgrace to the nations and a mockery to all the lands. ⁵Those who are near and those far away from you will mock you, you infamous one full of turmoil.

⁶"Look, every prince of Israel within you has used his strength to shed blood. ⁷Father and mother are treated with contempt, and the foreign resident is exploited within you. The fatherless and widow are oppressed in you. ⁸You despise My holy things and profane My Sabbaths. ⁹There are men within you who slander in order to shed blood. People who live in you eat at the mountain shrines; they commit immoral acts within you. ¹⁰Men within you have sexual intercourse with their father's wife and violate women during their menstrual impurity. ¹¹One man within you commits a detestable act with his neighbor's wife; another wickedly defiles his daughter-in-law; and yet another violates his sister, his father's daughter. ¹²People who live in you accept bribes in order to shed blood. You take interest and profit on a loan and brutally extort your neighbors. You have forgotten Me." This is the declaration of the Lord God.

¹³"Now look, I clap My hands together against the dishonest profit you have made and against the blood shed among you. ¹⁴Will your courage endure or your hands be strong in the days when I deal with you? I, *Yahweh, have spoken, and I will act. ¹⁵I will disperse you among the nations and scatter you among the countries; I will purge your uncleanness. ¹⁶You will be profaned in the sight of the nations. Then you will know that I am Yahweh."

¹⁷The word of the Lord came to me: ¹⁸"Son of man, the house of Israel has become dross to Me. All of them are copper, tin, iron, and lead inside the furnace; they are the dross of silver. ¹⁹Therefore, this is what the Lord God says: Because all of you have become dross, I am about to gather you into Jerusalem. ²⁰Just as one gathers silver, copper, iron, lead, and tin into the furnace to blow fire on them and melt them, so I will gather you in My anger and wrath, put you inside, and melt you. ²¹Yes, I will gather you together and blow on you with the fire of My fury, and you will be melted within the city. ²²As silver is melted inside a furnace, so you will be melted inside the city. Then you will know that I, Yahweh, have poured out My wrath on you."

²³The word of the Lord came to me: ²⁴"Son of man, say to her: You are a land that has not been cleansed, that has not received rain in the day of indignation. ²⁵The conspiracy of her prophets within her is like a roaring lion tearing its prey: they devour people, seize wealth and valuables, and multiply the widows within her. ²⁶Her priests do violence to My instruction and profane My holy things. They make no distinction between the holy and the common, and they do not explain the difference between the *clean and the *unclean. They disregard My Sabbaths, and I am profaned among them.

²⁷"Her officials within her are like wolves tearing their prey, shedding blood, and destroying lives in order to make profit dishonestly. ²⁸Her prophets plaster with whitewash for them by seeing false visions and lying *divinations, and they say, 'This is what the Lord God says,' when the Lord has not spoken. ²⁹The people of the land have practiced extortion and committed robbery. They have oppressed the poor and needy and unlawfully exploited the foreign resident. ³⁰I searched for a man among them who would repair the wall and stand in the gap before Me on behalf of the land so that I might not destroy it, but I found no one. ³¹So I have poured out My indignation on them and consumed them with the fire of My fury. I have brought their actions down on their own heads." This is the declaration of the Lord God.

23 The word of the Lord came to me again: ²"Son of man, there were two women, daughters of the same mother, ³who acted like prostitutes in Egypt, behaving promiscuously in their youth. Their breasts were fondled there, and their virgin nipples caressed. ⁴The older one was named Oholah, and her sister was Oholibah. They became Mine and gave birth to sons and daughters. As for their names, Oholah represents Samaria and Oholibah represents Jerusalem.

⁵"Oholah acted like a prostitute even though she was Mine. She lusted after her lovers, the Assyrians: warriors ⁶dressed in blue, governors and prefects, all of them desirable young men, horsemen riding on steeds. ⁷She offered her sexual favors to them; all of them were the elite of Assyria. She defiled herself with all those she lusted after and with all their idols. ⁸She didn't give up her promiscuity that began in Egypt, when men slept with her in her youth, caressed her virgin nipples, and poured out their lust on her. ⁹Therefore, I handed her over to her lovers, the Assyrians she lusted for. ¹⁰They exposed her nakedness, seized her sons and daughters, and killed her with the sword. Since they executed judgment against her, she became notorious among women.

¹¹"Now her sister Oholibah saw this, but she was even more depraved in her lust than Oholah, and made her promiscuous acts worse than those of her sister. ¹²She lusted after the Assyrians: governors and prefects, warriors splendidly dressed, horsemen riding on steeds, all of them desirable young men. ¹³And I saw that she had defiled herself; both of them had taken the same path. ¹⁴But she increased her promiscuity when she saw male figures carved on the wall, images of the Chaldeans, engraved in vermilion, ¹⁵wearing belts on their waists and flowing turbans on their heads; all of them looked like officers, a depiction of the Babylonians in Chaldea, the land of their birth. ¹⁶At the sight of them she lusted after them and sent messengers to them in Chaldea. ¹⁷Then the Babylonians came to her, to the bed of love, and defiled her with their lust. But after she was defiled by them, she turned away from them in disgust. ¹⁸When she flaunted her promiscuity and exposed her nakedness, I turned away from her in disgust just as I turned away from her sister. ¹⁹Yet she multiplied her acts of promiscuity, remembering the days of her youth when she acted like a prostitute in the land of Egypt ²⁰and lusted after their lovers, whose sexual members were like those of donkeys and whose emission was like that of stallions. ²¹So you revisited the indecency of your youth, when the Egyptians caressed your nipples to enjoy your youthful breasts.

²²"Therefore Oholibah, this is what the Lord God says: I am going to incite your lovers against you, those you turned away from in disgust. I will bring them against you from every side: ²³the Babylonians and all the Chaldeans; Pekod, Shoa, and Koa; and all the Assyrians with them—desirable young men, all of them governors and prefects, officers and administrators, all of them riding on horses. ²⁴They will come against you with an alliance of nations and with weapons, chariots, and wagons. They will set themselves against you on every side with shields, bucklers, and helmets. I will delegate judgment to them, and they will judge you by their own standards. ²⁵When I vent My jealous rage on you, they will deal with you in wrath. They will cut off your nose and ears, and your descendants will fall by the sword. They will seize your sons and daughters, and your descendants will be consumed by fire. ²⁶They will strip off your clothes and take your beautiful jewelry. ²⁷So I will put an end to your indecency and sexual immorality, which began in the land of Egypt, and you will not look longingly at them or remember Egypt anymore.

²⁸"For this is what the Lord God says: I am going to hand you over to those you hate, to those you turned away from in disgust. ²⁹They will treat you with hatred, take all you have worked for, and leave you stark naked, so that the shame of your debauchery will be exposed, both your indecency and promiscuity. ³⁰These things will be done to you because you acted like a prostitute with the nations, defiling yourself with their idols. ³¹You have followed the path of your sister, so I will put her cup in your hand."

³²This is what the Lord God says:

You will drink your sister's cup,
which is deep and wide.
You will be an object of ridicule and scorn,
for it holds so much.
³³ You will be filled with drunkenness and grief,
with a cup of devastation and desolation,
the cup of your sister Samaria.
³⁴ You will drink it and drain it;
then you will gnaw its broken pieces,
and tear your breasts.
For I have spoken.

This is the declaration of the Lord God.
³⁵Therefore, this is what the Lord God says: "Because you have forgotten Me and cast Me behind your back, you must bear the consequences of your indecency and promiscuity."

³⁶Then the Lord said to me: "Son of man, will you pass judgment against Oholah and Oholibah? Then declare their detestable practices to them. ³⁷For they have committed adultery, and blood is on their hands; they have committed adultery with their idols. They have even made the children they bore to Me pass through the fire as food for the idols. ³⁸They also did this to Me: they defiled My sanctuary on that same day and profaned My Sabbaths. ³⁹On the same day they slaughtered their children for their idols, they entered My sanctuary to profane it. Yes, that is what they did inside My house.

⁴⁰"In addition, they sent for men who came from far away when a messenger was dispatched to them. And look how they came! You bathed, painted your eyes, and adorned yourself with jewelry for them. ⁴¹You sat on a luxurious couch with a table spread before it, on which you had set My incense and oil. ⁴²The sound of a carefree crowd was there. Drunkards from the desert were brought in, along with common men. They put bracelets on the women's hands and beautiful crowns on their heads. ⁴³Then I said concerning this woman worn out by adultery: Will they now have illicit sex with her, even her? ⁴⁴Yet they had sex with her as one does with a prostitute. This is how they had sex with Oholah and Oholibah, those obscene women. ⁴⁵But righteous men will judge them the way adulteresses and those who shed blood are judged, for they are adulteresses and blood is on their hands.

⁴⁶"This is what the Lord God says: Summon an assembly against them and consign them to terror and plunder. ⁴⁷The assembly will stone them and cut them down with their swords. They will kill their sons and daughters and burn their houses with fire. ⁴⁸So I will put an end to indecency in the land, and all the women will be admonished not to imitate your indecent behavior. ⁴⁹They will repay you for your indecency, and you will bear the consequences for your sins of idolatry. Then you will know that I am the Lord ·Yahweh."

24 The word of the LORD came to me in the ninth year, in the tenth month, on the tenth day of the month: ²"Son of man, write down today's date, this very day. The king of Babylon has laid siege to Jerusalem this very day. ³Now speak a parable to the rebellious house. Tell them: This is what the Lord GOD says:

Put the pot on the fire—
put it on,
and then pour water into it!
⁴ Place the pieces of meat in it,
every good piece—
thigh and shoulder.
Fill it with choice bones.
⁵ Take the choicest of the flock
and also pile up the fuel under it.
Bring it to a boil
and cook the bones in it."

⁶Therefore, this is what the Lord GOD says:

Woe to the city of bloodshed,
the pot that has rust inside it,
and whose rust will not come off!
Empty it piece by piece;
lots should not be cast for its contents.
⁷ For the blood she shed is still within her.
She put it out on the bare rock;
she didn't pour it on the ground
to cover it with dust.
⁸ In order to stir up wrath and take vengeance,
I have put her blood on the bare rock,
so that it would not be covered.

⁹Therefore, this is what the Lord GOD says:

Woe to the city of bloodshed!
I Myself will make the pile of kindling large.
¹⁰ Pile on the logs and kindle the fire!
Cook the meat well
and mix in the spices!
Let the bones be burned!
¹¹ Set the empty pot on its coals
so that it becomes hot
and its copper glows.
Then its impurity will melt inside it;
its rust will be consumed.
¹² It has frustrated every effort;
its thick rust will not come off.
Into the fire with its rust!
¹³ Because of the indecency
of your uncleanness—
since I tried to purify you,
but you would not be purified
from your uncleanness—
you will not be pure again
until I have satisfied My wrath on you.
¹⁴ I, ˚Yahweh, have spoken.
It is coming, and I will do it!
I will not refrain, I will not show pity,
and I will not relent.
I will judge you
according to your ways and deeds.
This is the declaration of the Lord GOD.

¹⁵Then the word of the LORD came to me: ¹⁶"Son of man, I am about to take the delight of your eyes away from you with a fatal blow. But you must not lament or weep or let your tears flow. ¹⁷Groan quietly; do not observe mourning rites for the dead. Put on your turban and strap your sandals on your feet; do not cover your mustache or eat the bread of mourners."

¹⁸I spoke to the people in the morning, and my wife died in the evening. The next morning I did just as I was commanded. ¹⁹Then the people asked me, "Won't you tell us what these things you are doing mean for us?"

²⁰So I answered them: "The word of the LORD came to me: ²¹'Say to the house of Israel: This is what the Lord GOD says: I am about to desecrate My sanctuary, the pride of your power, the delight of your eyes, and the desire of your heart. Also, the sons and daughters you left behind will fall by the sword. ²²Then you will do just as I have done: You will not cover your mustache or eat the bread of mourners. ²³Your turbans will remain on your heads and your sandals on your feet. You will not lament or weep but will waste away because of your sins and will groan to one another. ²⁴Now Ezekiel will be a sign for you. You will do everything that he has done. When this happens, you will know that I am the Lord Yahweh.

²⁵"'Son of man, know that on the day I take their stronghold from them, their pride and joy, the delight of their eyes and the longing of their hearts, as well as their sons and daughters, ²⁶on that day a fugitive will come to you and report the news. ²⁷On that day your mouth will be opened to talk with him; you will speak and no longer be mute. So you will be a sign for them, and they will know that I am Yahweh.'"

25 Then the word of the LORD came to me: ²"Son of man, turn your face toward the Ammonites and prophesy against them. ³Say to the Ammonites: Hear the word of the Lord GOD: This is what the Lord GOD says: Because you said, 'Good!' about My sanctuary when it was desecrated, about the land of Israel when it was laid waste, and about the house of Judah when they went into exile, ⁴therefore I am about to give you to the people of the east as a possession. They will set up their encampments and pitch their tents among you. They will eat your fruit and drink your milk. ⁵I will make Rabbah a pasture for camels and Ammon a sheepfold. Then you will know that I am ˚Yahweh.

⁶For this is what the Lord GOD says: "Because you clapped your hands, stamped your feet, and rejoiced over the land of Israel with wholehearted contempt, ⁷therefore I am about to stretch out My hand against you and give you as plunder to the nations. I will cut you off from the peoples and eliminate you from the countries. I will destroy you, and you will know that I am Yahweh."

⁸This is what the Lord GOD says: "Because Moab and Seir said, 'Look, the house of Judah is like all the other nations,' ⁹therefore I am about to expose Moab's flank beginning with its frontier cities, the pride of the land: Beth-jeshimoth, Baal-meon, and Kiriathaim. ¹⁰I will give it along with Ammon to the people of the east as a possession, so that Ammon will not be remembered among the nations. ¹¹So I will execute judgments against Moab, and they will know that I am Yahweh."

¹²This is what the Lord GOD says: "Because Edom acted vengefully against the house of Judah and incurred grievous ˚guilt by taking revenge on them, ¹³therefore this is what the Lord GOD says: I will stretch out My hand against Edom and cut off both man and animal from it. I will make it a wasteland; they will fall by the sword from Teman to Dedan. ¹⁴I will take My vengeance on Edom through My people Israel, and they will deal with Edom according to My anger and wrath. So they will know My vengeance." This is the declaration of the Lord GOD.

¹⁵This is what the Lord God says: "Because the Philistines acted in vengeance and took revenge with deep contempt, destroying because of their ancient hatred, ¹⁶therefore this is what the Lord God says: I am about to stretch out My hand against the Philistines, cutting off the Cherethites and wiping out what remains of the coastal peoples. ¹⁷I will execute great vengeance against them with furious rebukes. They will know that I am Yahweh when I take My vengeance on them."

26 In the eleventh year, on the first day of the month, the word of the Lord came to me: ²"Son of man, because Tyre said about Jerusalem, 'Good! The gateway to the peoples is shattered. She has been turned over to me. I will be filled now that she lies in ruins,' ³therefore this is what the Lord God says: See, I am against you, Tyre! I will raise up many nations against you, just as the sea raises its waves. ⁴They will destroy the walls of Tyre and demolish her towers. I will scrape the soil from her and turn her into a bare rock. ⁵She will become a place in the sea to spread nets, for I have spoken." This is the declaration of the Lord God. "She will become plunder for the nations, ⁶and her villages on the mainland will be slaughtered by the sword. Then they will know that I am 'Yahweh."

⁷For this is what the Lord God says: "See, I am about to bring King Nebuchadnezzar of Babylon, king of kings, against Tyre from the north with horses, chariots, cavalry, and a vast company of troops. ⁸He will slaughter your villages on the mainland with the sword. He will set up siege works against you, and will build a ramp and raise a wall of shields against you. ⁹He will direct the blows of his battering rams against your walls and tear down your towers with his iron tools. ¹⁰His horses will be so numerous that their dust will cover you. When he enters your gates as an army entering a breached city, your walls will shake from the noise of cavalry, wagons, and chariots. ¹¹He will trample all your streets with the hooves of his horses. He will slaughter your people with the sword, and your mighty pillars will fall to the ground. ¹²They will take your wealth as spoil and plunder your merchandise. They will also demolish your walls and tear down your beautiful homes. Then they will throw your stones, timber, and soil into the water. ¹³I will put an end to the noise of your songs, and the sound of your lyres will no longer be heard. ¹⁴I will turn you into a bare rock, and you will be a place to spread nets. You will never be rebuilt, for I, Yahweh, have spoken." This is the declaration of the Lord God.

¹⁵This is what the Lord God says to Tyre: "Won't the coasts and islands quake at the sound of your downfall, when the wounded groan and slaughter occurs within you? ¹⁶All the princes of the sea will descend from their thrones, remove their robes, and strip off their embroidered garments. They will clothe themselves with trembling; they will sit on the ground, tremble continually, and be appalled at you. ¹⁷Then they will lament for you and say of you:

How you have perished, city of renown,
  you who were populated from the seas!
She who was powerful on the sea,
  she and all of her inhabitants
  inflicted their terror.
¹⁸   Now the coastlands tremble
  on the day of your downfall;
  the islands in the sea
  are alarmed by your demise."

¹⁹For this is what the Lord God says: "When I make you a ruined city like other deserted cities, when I raise up the deep against you so that the mighty waters cover you, ²⁰then I will bring you down to be with those who descend to the ·Pit, to the people of antiquity. I will make you dwell in the underworld like ancient ruins, with those who descend to the Pit, so that you will no longer be inhabited or display your splendor in the land of the living. ²¹I will make you an object of horror, and you will no longer exist. You will be sought but will never be found again." This is the declaration of the Lord God.

27 The word of the Lord came to me: ²"Now, son of man, lament for Tyre. ³Say to Tyre, who is located at the entrance of the sea, merchant of the peoples to many coasts and islands: This is what the Lord God says:

Tyre, you declared,
  'I am perfect in beauty.'
⁴   Your realm was in the heart of the sea;
  your builders perfected your beauty.
⁵   They constructed all your planking
  with pine trees from Senir.
  They took a cedar from Lebanon
  to make a mast for you.
⁶   They made your oars of oaks from Bashan.
  They made your deck of cypress wood
  from the coasts of Cyprus,
  inlaid with ivory.
⁷   Your sail was made of
  fine embroidered linen from Egypt,
  and served as your banner.
  Your awning was of blue and purple fabric
  from the coasts of Elishah.
⁸   The inhabitants of Sidon and Arvad
  were your rowers.
  Your wise men were within you, Tyre;
  they were your captains.
⁹   The elders of Gebal and its wise men
  were within you, repairing your leaks.
  All the ships of the sea and their sailors
  came to you to barter for your goods.
¹⁰   Men of Persia, Lud, and Put
  were in your army, serving as your warriors.
  They hung shields and helmets in you;
  they gave you splendor.
¹¹   Men of Arvad and Helech
  were stationed on your walls all around,
  and Gammadites were in your towers.
  They hung their shields all around your walls;
  they perfected your beauty.

¹²"Tarshish was your trading partner because of your great wealth of every kind. They exchanged silver, iron, tin, and lead for your merchandise. ¹³Javan, Tubal, and Meshech were your merchants. They exchanged slaves and bronze utensils for your goods. ¹⁴Those from Beth-togarmah exchanged horses, war horses, and mules for your merchandise. ¹⁵Men of Dedan were also your merchants; many coasts and islands were your regular markets. They brought back ivory tusks and ebony as your payment. ¹⁶Aram was your trading partner because of your numerous products. They exchanged turquoise, purple and embroidered cloth, fine linen, coral, and rubies for your merchandise. ¹⁷Judah and the land of Israel were your merchants. They exchanged wheat from Minnith, meal, honey, oil, and balm, for your goods. ¹⁸Damascus was also your

trading partner because of your numerous products and your great wealth of every kind, trading in wine from Helbon and white wool. ¹⁹Vedan and Javan from Uzal dealt in your merchandise; wrought iron, cassia, and aromatic cane were exchanged for your goods. ²⁰Dedan was your merchant in saddlecloths for riding. ²¹Arabia and all the princes of Kedar were your business partners, trading with you in lambs, rams, and goats. ²²The merchants of Sheba and Raamah traded with you. They exchanged gold, the best of all spices, and all kinds of precious stones for your merchandise. ²³Haran, Canneh, Eden, the merchants of Sheba, Asshur, and Chilmad traded with you. ²⁴They were your merchants in choice garments, cloaks of blue and embroidered materials, and multicolored carpets, which were bound and secured with cords in your marketplace. ²⁵Ships of Tarshish were the carriers for your goods.

> So you became full and heavily loaded
>   in the heart of the sea.
> ²⁶ Your rowers have brought you
>   onto the high seas,
>   but the east wind has shattered you
>   in the heart of the sea.
> ²⁷ Your wealth, merchandise, and goods,
>   your sailors and captains,
>   those who repair your leaks,
>   those who barter for your goods,
>   and all the warriors within you,
>   with all the other people on board,
>   sink into the heart of the sea
>   on the day of your downfall.
> ²⁸ The countryside shakes
>   at the sound of your sailors' cries.
> ²⁹ All those who handle an oar
>   disembark from their ships.
>   The sailors and all the captains of the sea
>   stand on the shore.
> ³⁰ They raise their voices over you
>   and cry out bitterly.
>   They throw dust on their heads;
>   they roll in ashes.
> ³¹ They shave their heads because of you
>   and wrap themselves in *sackcloth.
>   They weep over you
>   with deep anguish and bitter mourning.
> ³² In their wailing they lament for you,
>   mourning over you:
>   Who was like Tyre,
>   silenced in the middle of the sea?
> ³³ When your merchandise was unloaded
>   from the seas,
>   you satisfied many peoples.
>   You enriched the kings of the earth
>   with your abundant wealth and goods.
> ³⁴ Now you are shattered by the sea
>   in the depths of the waters;
>   your goods and the people within you
>   have gone down.
> ³⁵ All the inhabitants of the coasts and islands
>   are appalled at you.
>   Their kings shudder with fear;
>   their faces are contorted.
> ³⁶ Those who trade among the peoples
>   mock you;
>   you have become an object of horror
>   and will never exist again."

28 The word of the LORD came to me: ²"Son of man, say to the ruler of Tyre: This is what the Lord GOD says:

> Your heart is proud,
>   and you have said, 'I am a god;
>   I sit in the seat of gods
>   in the heart of the sea.'
>   Yet you are a man and not a god,
>   though you have regarded your heart
>   as that of a god.
> ³ Yes, you are wiser than Daniel;
>   no secret is hidden from you!
> ⁴ By your wisdom and understanding
>   you have acquired wealth for yourself.
>   You have acquired gold and silver
>   for your treasuries.
> ⁵ By your great skill in trading
>   you have increased your wealth,
>   but your heart has become proud
>   because of your wealth."

⁶ Therefore this is what the Lord GOD says:

> Because you regard your heart as that
>   of a god,
> ⁷ I am about to bring strangers against you,
>   ruthless men from the nations.
>   They will draw their swords
>   against your magnificent wisdom
>   and will defile your splendor.
> ⁸ They will bring you down to the *Pit,
>   and you will die a violent death
>   in the heart of the sea.
> ⁹ Will you still say, 'I am a god,'
>   in the presence of those who kill you?
>   Yet you will be only a man, not a god,
>   in the hands of those who kill you.
> ¹⁰ You will die the death of the uncircumcised
>   at the hands of strangers.
>   For I have spoken.
>   This is the declaration of the Lord GOD.

¹¹The word of the LORD came to me: ¹²"Son of man, lament for the king of Tyre and say to him: This is what the Lord GOD says:

> You were the seal of perfection,
>   full of wisdom and perfect in beauty.
> ¹³ You were in Eden, the garden of God.
>   Every kind of precious stone covered you:
>   carnelian, topaz, and diamond,
>   beryl, onyx, and jasper,
>   sapphire, turquoise and emerald.
>   Your mountings and settings were crafted
>   in gold;
>   they were prepared on the day
>   you were created.
> ¹⁴ You were an anointed guardian cherub,
>   for I had appointed you.
>   You were on the holy mountain of God;
>   you walked among the fiery stones.
> ¹⁵ From the day you were created
>   you were blameless in your ways
>   until wickedness was found in you.
> ¹⁶ Through the abundance of your trade,
>   you were filled with violence, and you sinned.
>   So I expelled you in disgrace
>   from the mountain of God,
>   and banished you, guardian cherub,
>   from among the fiery stones.

¹⁷ Your heart became proud because of
     your beauty;
For the sake of your splendor
you corrupted your wisdom.
So I threw you down to the earth;
I made you a spectacle before kings.
¹⁸ You profaned your sanctuaries
by the magnitude of your iniquities
in your dishonest trade.
So I made fire come from within you,
and it consumed you.
I reduced you to ashes on the ground
in the sight of everyone watching you.
¹⁹ All those who know you among the nations
are appalled at you.
You have become an object of horror
and will never exist again."

²⁰The word of the LORD came to me: ²¹"Son of man, turn your face toward Sidon and prophesy against it. ²²You are to say: This is what the Lord GOD says:

Look! I am against you, Sidon,
and I will display My glory within you.
They will know that I am ʼYahweh
when I execute judgments against her
and demonstrate My holiness through her.
²³ I will send a plague against her
and bloodshed in her streets;
the slain will fall within her,
while the sword is against her on every side.
Then they will know that I am Yahweh.

²⁴"The house of Israel will no longer be hurt by prickly briers or painful thorns from all their neighbors who treat them with contempt. Then they will know that I am the Lord Yahweh.

²⁵"This is what the Lord GOD says: When I gather the house of Israel from the peoples where they are scattered and demonstrate My holiness through them in the sight of the nations, then they will live in their own land, which I gave to My servant Jacob. ²⁶They will live there securely, build houses, and plant vineyards. They will live securely when I execute judgments against all their neighbors who treat them with contempt. Then they will know that I am Yahweh their God."

29 In the tenth year, in the tenth month on the twelfth day of the month, the word of the LORD came to me: ²"Son of man, turn your face toward Pharaoh king of Egypt and prophesy against him and against all of Egypt. ³Speak to him and say: This is what the Lord GOD says:

Look, I am against you, Pharaoh
     king of Egypt,
the great monster lying in the middle
     of his Nile,
who says, 'My Nile is my own;
I made it for myself.'
⁴ I will put hooks in your jaws
and make the fish of your streams
cling to your scales.
I will haul you up
from the middle of your Nile,
and all the fish of your streams
will cling to your scales.
⁵ I will leave you in the desert,
you and all the fish of your streams.
You will fall on the open ground
and will not be taken away
or gathered for burial.

I have given you
to the beasts of the earth
and the birds of the sky as food.
⁶ Then all the inhabitants of Egypt
will know that I am ʼYahweh,
for they have been a staff made of reed
to the house of Israel.
⁷ When Israel grasped you by the hand,
you splintered, tearing all their shoulders;
when they leaned on you,
you shattered and made all
     their hips unsteady.

⁸"Therefore this is what the Lord GOD says: I am going to bring a sword against you and wipe out man and animal from you. ⁹The land of Egypt will be a desolate ruin. Then they will know that I am Yahweh. Because you said, 'The Nile is my own; I made it,' ¹⁰therefore, I am against you and your Nile. I will turn the land of Egypt into ruins, a desolate waste from Migdol to Syene, as far as the border of ʼCush. ¹¹No human foot will pass through it, and no animal foot will pass through it. It will be uninhabited for 40 years. ¹²I will make the land of Egypt a desolation among desolate lands, and its cities will be a desolation among ruined cities for 40 years. I will disperse the Egyptians among the nations and scatter them across the countries.

¹³"For this is what the Lord GOD says: At the end of 40 years I will gather the Egyptians from the nations where they were dispersed. ¹⁴I will restore the fortunes of Egypt and bring them back to the land of Pathros, the land of their origin. There they will be a lowly kingdom. ¹⁵Egypt will be the lowliest of kingdoms and will never again exalt itself over the nations. I will make them so small they cannot rule over the nations. ¹⁶It will never again be an object of trust for the house of Israel, drawing attention to their sin of turning to the Egyptians. Then they will know that I am the Lord Yahweh."

¹⁷In the twenty-seventh year in the first month, on the first day of the month, the word of the LORD came to me: ¹⁸"Son of man, Nebuchadnezzar king of Babylon made his army labor strenuously against Tyre. Every head was made bald and every shoulder chafed, but he and his army received no compensation from Tyre for the labor he expended against it. ¹⁹Therefore this is what the Lord GOD says: I am going to give the land of Egypt to Nebuchadnezzar king of Babylon, who will carry off its wealth, seizing its spoil and taking its plunder. This will be his army's compensation. ²⁰I have given him the land of Egypt as the pay he labored for, since they worked for Me." This is the declaration of the Lord GOD. ²¹"In that day I will cause a ʼhorn to sprout for the house of Israel, and I will enable you to speak out among them. Then they will know that I am Yahweh."

30 The word of the LORD came to me: ²"Son of man, prophesy and say: This is what the Lord GOD says:

Wail: Woe for the day!
³ For a day is near;
a day belonging to the LORD is near.
It will be a day of clouds,
a time of doom for the nations.
⁴ A sword will come against Egypt,
and there will be anguish in ʼCush
when the slain fall in Egypt,
and its wealth is taken away,

and its foundations are torn down.
⁵ Cush, Put, and Lud,
and all the various foreign troops,
plus Libya and the men of the covenant land
will fall by the sword along with them.
⁶ This is what the LORD says:
Those who support Egypt will fall,
and its proud strength will collapse.
From Migdol to Syene
they will fall within it by the sword.
     This is the declaration of the Lord GOD.
⁷ They will be desolate
among desolate lands,
and their cities will lie
among ruined cities.
⁸ They will know that I am *Yahweh
when I set fire to Egypt
and all its allies are shattered.
⁹ On that day, messengers will go out from Me in ships to terrify confident Cush. Anguish will come over them on the day of Egypt's doom. For indeed it is coming."

¹⁰ This is what the Lord GOD says:
I will put an end to the hordes of Egypt
by the hand of Nebuchadnezzar
king of Babylon.
¹¹ He along with his people,
ruthless men from the nations,
will be brought in to destroy the land.
They will draw their swords against Egypt
and fill the land with the slain.
¹² I will make the streams dry
and sell the land into the hands of evil men.
I will bring desolation
on the land and everything in it
by the hands of foreigners.
I, Yahweh, have spoken.
¹³ This is what the Lord GOD says:
I will destroy the idols and put an end
to the false gods in Memphis.
There will no longer be
a prince from the land of Egypt.
So I will instill fear in that land.
¹⁴ I will make Pathros desolate,
set fire to Zoan,
and execute judgments on Thebes.
¹⁵ I will pour out My wrath on Pelusium,
the stronghold of Egypt,
and will wipe out the crowds of Thebes.
¹⁶ I will set fire to Egypt;
Pelusium will writhe in anguish,
Thebes will be breached,
and Memphis will face foes in broad daylight.
¹⁷ The young men of On and Pi-beseth
will fall by the sword,
and those cities will go into captivity.
¹⁸ The day will be dark in Tehaphnehes,
when I break the yoke of Egypt there
and its proud strength
comes to an end in the city.
A cloud will cover Tehaphnehes,
and its villages will go into captivity.
¹⁹ So I will execute judgments against Egypt,
and they will know that I am Yahweh.

²⁰ In the eleventh year, in the first month, on the seventh day of the month, the word of the LORD came to me: ²¹ "Son of man, I have broken the arm of Pharaoh king of Egypt. Look, it has not been bandaged—no medicine has been applied and no splint put on to bandage it so that it can grow strong enough to handle a sword. ²² Therefore this is what the Lord GOD says: Look! I am against Pharaoh king of Egypt. I will break his arms, both the strong one and the one already broken, and will make the sword fall from his hand. ²³ I will disperse the Egyptians among the nations and scatter them among the countries. ²⁴ I will strengthen the arms of Babylon's king and place My sword in his hand. But I will break the arms of Pharaoh, and he will groan before him as a mortally wounded man. ²⁵ I will strengthen the arms of Babylon's king, but Pharaoh's arms will fall. They will know that I am Yahweh when I place My sword in the hand of Babylon's king and he wields it against the land of Egypt. ²⁶ When I disperse the Egyptians among the nations and scatter them among the countries, they will know that I am Yahweh."

31 In the eleventh year, in the third month, on the first day of the month, the word of the LORD came to me: ²"Son of man, say to Pharaoh king of Egypt and to his hordes:
Who are you like in your greatness?
³ Think of Assyria, a cedar in Lebanon,
with beautiful branches and shady foliage
and of lofty height.
Its top was among the clouds.
⁴ The waters caused it to grow;
the underground springs made it tall,
directing their rivers all around
the place where the tree was planted
and sending their channels
to all the trees of the field.
⁵ Therefore the cedar became greater in height
than all the trees of the field.
Its branches multiplied,
and its boughs grew long
as it spread them out
because of the plentiful water.
⁶ All the birds of the sky
nested in its branches,
and all the animals of the field
gave birth beneath its boughs;
all the great nations lived in its shade.
⁷ It was beautiful in its greatness,
in the length of its limbs,
for its roots extended to abundant water.
⁸ The cedars in God's garden could not rival it;
the pine trees couldn't compare
with its branches,
nor could the plane trees match its boughs.
No tree in the garden of God
could compare with it in beauty.
⁹ I made it beautiful with its many limbs,
and all the trees of Eden,
which were in God's garden, envied it.

¹⁰ "Therefore this is what the Lord GOD says: Since it became great in height and set its top among the clouds, and it grew proud on account of its height, ¹¹ I determined to hand it over to a ruler of nations; he would surely deal with it. I banished it because of its wickedness. ¹² Foreigners, ruthless men from the nations, cut it down and left it lying. Its limbs fell on the mountains and in every valley; its boughs lay broken in all the earth's ravines. All the peoples of the earth left its shade and abandoned it. ¹³ All the birds of the

sky nested on its fallen trunk, and all the animals of the field were among its boughs. ¹⁴This happened so that no trees planted beside water would become great in height and set their tops among the clouds, and so that no other well-watered trees would reach them in height. For they have all been consigned to death, to the underworld, among the •people who descend to the •Pit.

¹⁵"This is what the Lord GOD says: I caused grieving on the day the cedar went down to •Sheol. I closed off the underground deep because of it: I held back the rivers of the deep, and its abundant waters were restrained. I made Lebanon mourn on account of it, and all the trees of the field fainted because of it. ¹⁶I made the nations quake at the sound of its downfall, when I threw it down to Sheol to be with those who descend to the Pit. Then all the trees of Eden, all the well-watered trees, the choice and best of Lebanon, were comforted in the underworld. ¹⁷They too descended with it to Sheol, to those slain by the sword. As its allies they had lived in its shade among the nations.

¹⁸"Who then are you like in glory and greatness among Eden's trees? You also will be brought down to the underworld to be with the trees of Eden. You will lie among the uncircumcised with those slain by the sword. This is Pharaoh and all his hordes"—the declaration of the Lord GOD.

32 In the twelfth year, in the twelfth month, on the first day of the month, the word of the LORD came to me: ²"Son of man, lament for Pharaoh king of Egypt and say to him:

> You compare yourself to a lion of the nations,
> but you are like a monster in the seas.
> You thrash about in your rivers,
> churn up the waters with your feet,
> and muddy the rivers."

³This is what the Lord GOD says:

> I will spread My net over you
> with an assembly of many peoples,
> and they will haul you up in My net.
> ⁴ I will abandon you on the land
> and hurl you on the open field.
> I will cause all the birds of the sky
> to settle on you
> and let the beasts of the entire earth
> eat their fill of you.
> ⁵ I will put your flesh on the mountains
> and fill the valleys with your carcass.
> ⁶ I will drench the land
> with the flow of your blood,
> even to the mountains;
> the ravines will be filled with your gore.
> ⁷ When I snuff you out,
> I will cover the heavens
> and darken their stars.
> I will cover the sun with a cloud,
> and the moon will not give its light.
> ⁸ I will darken all the shining lights
> in the heavens over you,
> and will bring darkness on your land.
> This is the declaration of the Lord GOD.
> ⁹ I will trouble the hearts of many peoples,
> when I bring about your destruction
> among the nations,
> in countries you do not know.
> ¹⁰ I will cause many nations to be appalled
> at you,

> and their kings will shudder with fear
> because of you
> when I brandish My sword in front of them.
> On the day of your downfall
> each of them will tremble
> every moment for his life.

¹¹For this is what the Lord GOD says:

> The sword of Babylon's king
> will come against you!
> ¹² I will make your hordes fall
> by the swords of warriors,
> all of them ruthless men from the nations.
> They will ravage Egypt's pride,
> and all its hordes will be destroyed.
> ¹³ I will slaughter all its cattle
> that are beside many waters.
> No human foot will churn them again,
> and no cattle hooves will disturb them.
> ¹⁴ Then I will let their waters settle
> and will make their rivers flow like oil.
> This is the declaration of the Lord GOD.
> ¹⁵ When I make the land of Egypt a desolation,
> so that it is emptied of everything in it,
> when I strike down all who live there,
> then they will know that I am •Yahweh.

¹⁶"This is a lament that will be chanted; the women of the nations will chant it. They will chant it over Egypt and all its hordes." This is the declaration of the Lord GOD.

¹⁷In the twelfth year, on the fifteenth day of the month, the word of the LORD came to me: ¹⁸"Son of man, wail over the hordes of Egypt and bring Egypt and the daughters of mighty nations down to the underworld, to be with those who descend to the •Pit:

> ¹⁹ Who do you surpass in loveliness?
> Go down and be laid to rest
> with the uncircumcised!
> ²⁰ They will fall among those slain by the sword.
> A sword is appointed!
> They drag her and all her hordes away.
> ²¹ Warrior leaders will speak
> from the middle of •Sheol
> about him and his allies:
> They have come down;
> the uncircumcised lie
> slain by the sword.
> ²² Assyria is there with all her company;
> her graves are all around her.
> All of them are slain, fallen by the sword.
> ²³ Her graves are set in the deepest regions
> of the Pit,
> and her company is all around
> her burial place.
> All of them are slain, fallen by the sword—
> those who once spread terror
> in the land of the living.
> ²⁴ Elam is there
> with all her hordes around her grave.
> All of them are slain, fallen by the sword—
> those who went down
> to the underworld uncircumcised,
> who once spread their terror
> in the land of the living.
> They bear their disgrace
> with those who descend to the Pit.
> ²⁵ Among the slain
> they prepare a resting place for Elam

with all her hordes.
Her graves are all around her.
All of them are uncircumcised,
slain by the sword,
although their terror was once spread
in the land of the living.
They bear their disgrace
with those who descend to the Pit.
They are placed among the slain.
²⁶ Meshech and Tubal are there,
with all their hordes.
Their graves are all around them.
All of them are uncircumcised,
　slain by the sword,
although their terror was once spread
in the land of the living.
²⁷ They do not lie down
with the fallen warriors of the uncircumcised,
who went down to Sheol
with their weapons of war,
whose swords were placed under their heads.
The punishment for their sins
rested on their bones,
although the terror of these warriors
was once in the land of the living.
²⁸ But you will be shattered
and will lie down among the uncircumcised,
with those slain by the sword.
²⁹ Edom is there, her kings and all her princes,
who, despite their strength, have been placed
among those slain by the sword.
They lie down with the uncircumcised,
with those who descend to the Pit.
³⁰ All the leaders of the north
and all the Sidonians are there.
They went down in shame with the slain,
despite the terror their strength inspired.
They lie down uncircumcised
with those slain by the sword.
They bear their disgrace
with those who descend to the Pit.
³¹ Pharaoh will see them
and be comforted over all his hordes—
Pharaoh and all his army,
slain by the sword.
　　This is the declaration of the Lord GOD.
³² For I will spread My terror
in the land of the living,
so Pharaoh and all his hordes
will be laid to rest among the uncircumcised,
with those slain by the sword."
　　This is the declaration of the Lord GOD.

33 The word of the LORD came to me: ²"Son of man, speak to your people and tell them: Suppose I bring the sword against a land, and the people of that land select a man from among them, appointing him as their watchman, ³and he sees the sword coming against the land and blows his trumpet to warn the people. ⁴Then, if anyone hears the sound of the trumpet but ignores the warning, and the sword comes and takes him away, his blood will be on his own head. ⁵Since he heard the sound of the trumpet but ignored the warning, his blood is on his own hands. If he had taken warning, he would have saved his life. ⁶However, if the watchman sees the sword coming but doesn't blow the trumpet, so that the people aren't warned, and the sword comes and takes away their lives, then they have been taken away because of their iniquity, but I will hold the watchman accountable for their blood.

⁷"As for you, son of man, I have made you a watchman for the house of Israel. When you hear a word from My mouth, give them a warning from Me. ⁸If I say to the wicked, 'Wicked one, you will surely die,' but you do not speak out to warn him about his way, that wicked person will die for his iniquity, yet I will hold you responsible for his blood. ⁹But if you warn a wicked person to turn from his way and he doesn't turn from it, he will die for his iniquity, but you will have saved your life.

¹⁰"Now as for you, son of man, say to the house of Israel: You have said this, 'Our transgressions and our sins are heavy on us, and we are wasting away because of them! How then can we survive?' ¹¹Tell them: As I live"—the declaration of the Lord GOD—"I take no pleasure in the death of the wicked, but rather that the wicked person should turn from his way and live. Repent, repent of your evil ways! Why will you die, house of Israel?

¹²"Now, son of man, say to your people: The righteousness of the righteous person will not save him on the day of his transgression; neither will the wickedness of the wicked person cause him to stumble on the day he turns from his wickedness. The righteous person won't be able to survive by his righteousness on the day he sins. ¹³When I tell the righteous person that he will surely live, but he trusts in his righteousness and commits iniquity, then none of his righteousness will be remembered, and he will die because of the iniquity he has committed.

¹⁴"So when I tell the wicked person, 'You will surely die,' but he repents of his sin and does what is just and right— ¹⁵he returns collateral, makes restitution for what he has stolen, and walks in the statutes of life without practicing iniquity—he will certainly live; he will not die. ¹⁶None of the sins he committed will be held against him. He has done what is just and right; he will certainly live.

¹⁷"But your people say, 'The Lord's way isn't fair,' even though it is their own way that isn't fair. ¹⁸When a righteous person turns from his righteousness and commits iniquity, he will die on account of this. ¹⁹But if a wicked person turns from his wickedness and does what is just and right, he will live because of this. ²⁰Yet you say, 'The Lord's way isn't fair.' I will judge each of you according to his ways, house of Israel."

²¹ In the twelfth year of our exile, in the tenth month, on the fifth day of the month, a fugitive from Jerusalem came to me and reported, "The city has been taken!" ²²Now the hand of the LORD had been on me the evening before the fugitive arrived, and He opened my mouth before the man came to me in the morning. So my mouth was opened and I was no longer mute.

²³Then the word of the LORD came to me: ²⁴"Son of man, those who live in the ruins in the land of Israel are saying, 'Abraham was only one person, yet he received possession of the land. But we are many; the land has been given to us as a possession.' ²⁵Therefore say to them: This is what the Lord GOD says: You eat meat with blood in it, raise your eyes to your idols, and shed blood. Should you then receive possession of the land? ²⁶You have relied on your swords, you have committed detestable acts, and each of you has defiled

his neighbor's wife. Should you then receive possession of the land?

²⁷ "Tell them this: This is what the Lord God says: As surely as I live, those who are in the ruins will fall by the sword, those in the open field I have given to wild animals to be devoured, and those in the strongholds and caves will die by plague. ²⁸ I will make the land a desolate waste, and its proud strength will come to an end. The mountains of Israel will become desolate, with no one passing through. ²⁹ They will know that I am ·Yahweh when I make the land a desolate waste because of all the detestable acts they have committed.

³⁰ "Now, son of man, your people are talking about you near the city walls and in the doorways of their houses. One person speaks to another, each saying to his brother, 'Come and hear what the message is that comes from the Lord!' ³¹ So My people come to you in crowds, sit in front of you, and hear your words, but they don't obey them. Although they express love with their mouths, their hearts pursue dishonest profit. ³² Yes, to them you are like a singer of love songs who has a beautiful voice and plays skillfully on an instrument. They hear your words, but they don't obey them. ³³ Yet when it comes—and it will definitely come—then they will know that a prophet has been among them."

34 The word of the Lord came to me: ² "Son of man, prophesy against the shepherds of Israel. Prophesy, and say to them: This is what the Lord God says to the shepherds: Woe to the shepherds of Israel, who have been feeding themselves! Shouldn't the shepherds feed their flock? ³ You eat the fat, wear the wool, and butcher the fattened animals, but you do not tend the flock. ⁴ You have not strengthened the weak, healed the sick, bandaged the injured, brought back the strays, or sought the lost. Instead, you have ruled them with violence and cruelty. ⁵ They were scattered for lack of a shepherd; they became food for all the wild animals when they were scattered. ⁶ My flock went astray on all the mountains and every high hill. They were scattered over the whole face of the earth, and there was no one searching or seeking for them.

⁷ "Therefore, you shepherds, hear the word of the Lord. ⁸ As I live"—the declaration of the Lord God— "because My flock has become prey and food for every wild animal since they lack a shepherd, for My shepherds do not search for My flock, and because the shepherds feed themselves rather than My flock, ⁹ therefore, you shepherds, hear the word of the Lord!

¹⁰ "This is what the Lord God says: Look, I am against the shepherds. I will demand My flock from them and prevent them from shepherding the flock. The shepherds will no longer feed themselves, for I will rescue My flock from their mouths so that they will not be food for them.

¹¹ "For this is what the Lord God says: See, I Myself will search for My flock and look for them. ¹² As a shepherd looks for his sheep on the day he is among his scattered flock, so I will look for My flock. I will rescue them from all the places where they have been scattered on a cloudy and dark day. ¹³ I will bring them out from the peoples, gather them from the countries, and bring them into their own land. I will shepherd them on the mountains of Israel, in the ravines, and in all the inhabited places of the land. ¹⁴ I will tend them with good pasture, and their grazing place will be on Israel's lofty mountains. There they will lie down in a good grazing place; they will feed in rich pasture on the mountains of Israel. ¹⁵ I will tend My flock and let them lie down." This is the declaration of the Lord God. ¹⁶ "I will seek the lost, bring back the strays, bandage the injured, and strengthen the weak, but I will destroy the fat and the strong. I will shepherd them with justice.

¹⁷ "The Lord God says to you, My flock: I am going to judge between one sheep and another, between the rams and male goats. ¹⁸ Isn't it enough for you to feed on the good pasture? Must you also trample the rest of the pasture with your feet? Or isn't it enough that you drink the clear water? Must you also muddy the rest with your feet? ¹⁹ Yet My flock has to feed on what your feet have trampled, and drink what your feet have muddied.

²⁰ "Therefore, this is what the Lord God says to them: See, I Myself will judge between the fat sheep and the lean sheep. ²¹ Since you have pushed with flank and shoulder and butted all the weak ones with your horns until you scattered them all over, ²² I will save My flock, and they will no longer be prey for you. I will judge between one sheep and another. ²³ I will appoint over them a single shepherd, My servant David, and he will shepherd them. He will tend them himself and will be their shepherd. ²⁴ I, ·Yahweh, will be their God, and My servant David will be a prince among them. I, Yahweh, have spoken.

²⁵ "I will make a covenant of peace with them and eliminate dangerous animals in the land, so that they may live securely in the wilderness and sleep in the forest. ²⁶ I will make them and the area around My hill a blessing: I will send down showers in their season— showers of blessing. ²⁷ The trees of the field will give their fruit, and the land will yield its produce; My flock will be secure in their land. They will know that I am Yahweh when I break the bars of their yoke and rescue them from the hands of those who enslave them. ²⁸ They will no longer be prey for the nations, and the wild animals of the land will not consume them. They will live securely, and no one will frighten them. ²⁹ I will establish for them a place renowned for its agriculture, and they will no longer be victims of famine in the land. They will no longer endure the insults of the nations. ³⁰ Then they will know that I, Yahweh their God, am with them, and that they, the house of Israel, are My people." This is the declaration of the Lord God. ³¹ "You are My flock, the human flock of My pasture, and I am your God." This is the declaration of the Lord God.

35 The word of the Lord came to me: ² "Son of man, turn your face toward Mount Seir and prophesy against it. ³ Say to it: This is what the Lord God says:

> Look! I am against you, Mount Seir.
> I will stretch out My hand against you
> and make you a desolate waste.
> ⁴ I will turn your cities into ruins,
> and you will become a desolation.
> Then you will know that I am ·Yahweh.

⁵ "Because you maintained an ancient hatred and handed over the Israelites to the power of the sword in the time of their disaster, the time of final punishment, ⁶ therefore, as I live"—this is the declaration of the Lord God—"I will destine you for bloodshed, and it will pursue you. Since you did not hate bloodshed, it will pursue you. ⁷ I will make Mount Seir a desolate

waste and will cut off from it those who come and go. [8]I will fill its mountains with the slain; those slain by the sword will fall on your hills, in your valleys, and in all your ravines. [9]I will make you a perpetual desolation; your cities will not be inhabited. Then you will know that I am Yahweh.

[10]"Because you said, 'These two nations and two lands will be mine, and we will possess them'—though the LORD was there— [11]therefore, as I live"— the declaration of the Lord GOD—"I will treat you according to the anger and jealousy you showed in your hatred of them. I will make Myself known among them when I judge you. [12]Then you will know that I, Yahweh, have heard all the blasphemies you uttered against the mountains of Israel, saying, 'They are desolate. They have been given to us to devour!' [13]You boasted against Me with your mouth, and spoke many words against Me. I heard it Myself!

[14]"This is what the Lord GOD says: While the whole world rejoices, I will make you a desolation. [15]Just as you rejoiced over the inheritance of the house of Israel because it became a desolation, so I will deal with you: you will become a desolation, Mount Seir, and so will all Edom in its entirety. Then they will know that I am Yahweh.

36 "Son of man, prophesy to the mountains of Israel and say: Mountains of Israel, hear the word of the LORD. [2]This is what the Lord GOD says: Because the enemy has said about you, 'Good! The ancient heights have become our possession,' [3]therefore, prophesy and say: This is what the Lord GOD says: Because they have made you desolate and have trampled you from every side, so that you became a possession for the rest of the nations and an object of people's gossip and slander, [4]therefore, mountains of Israel, hear the word of the Lord GOD. This is what the Lord GOD says to the mountains and hills, to the ravines and valleys, to the desolate ruins and abandoned cities, which have become plunder and a mockery to the rest of the nations all around.

[5]"This is what the Lord GOD says: Certainly in My burning zeal I speak against the rest of the nations and all of Edom, who took My land as their own possession with wholehearted rejoicing and utter contempt so that its pastureland became plunder. [6]Therefore, prophesy concerning the land of Israel and say to the mountains and hills, to the ravines and valleys: This is what the Lord GOD says: Look, I speak in My burning zeal because you have endured the insults of the nations. [7]Therefore this is what the Lord GOD says: I swear that the nations all around you will endure their own insults.

[8]"You, mountains of Israel, will produce your branches and bear your fruit for My people Israel, since their arrival is near. [9]Look! I am on your side; I will turn toward you, and you will be tilled and sown. [10]I will fill you with people, with the whole house of Israel in its entirety. The cities will be inhabited and the ruins rebuilt. [11]I will fill you with people and animals, and they will increase and be fruitful. I will make you inhabited as you once were and make you better off than you were before. Then you will know that I am *Yahweh. [12]I will cause people, My people Israel, to walk on you; they will possess you, and you will be their inheritance. You will no longer deprive them of their children.

[13]"This is what the Lord GOD says: Because people

are saying to you, 'You devour men and deprive your nation of children,' [14]therefore, you will no longer devour men and deprive your nation of children." This is the declaration of the Lord GOD. [15]"I will no longer allow the insults of the nations to be heard against you, and you will not have to endure the reproach of the peoples anymore; you will no longer cause your nation to stumble." This is the declaration of the Lord GOD.

[16]The word of the LORD came to me: [17]"Son of man, while the house of Israel lived in their land, they defiled it with their conduct and actions. Their behavior before Me was like menstrual impurity. [18]So I poured out My wrath on them because of the blood they had shed on the land, and because they had defiled it with their idols. [19]I dispersed them among the nations, and they were scattered among the countries. I judged them according to their conduct and actions. [20]When they came to the nations where they went, they profaned My holy name, because it was said about them, 'These are the people of Yahweh, yet they had to leave His land in exile.' [21]Then I had concern for My holy name, which the house of Israel profaned among the nations where they went.

[22]"Therefore, say to the house of Israel: This is what the Lord GOD says: It is not for your sake that I will act, house of Israel, but for My holy name, which you profaned among the nations where you went. [23]I will honor the holiness of My great name, which has been profaned among the nations—the name you have profaned among them. The nations will know that I am Yahweh"—the declaration of the Lord GOD—"when I demonstrate My holiness through you in their sight.

[24]"For I will take you from the nations and gather you from all the countries, and will bring you into your own land. [25]I will also sprinkle clean water on you, and you will be *clean. I will cleanse you from all your impurities and all your idols. [26]I will give you a new heart and put a new spirit within you; I will remove your heart of stone and give you a heart of flesh. [27]I will place My Spirit within you and cause you to follow My statutes and carefully observe My ordinances. [28]Then you will live in the land that I gave your fathers; you will be My people, and I will be your God. [29]I will save you from all your uncleanness. I will summon the grain and make it plentiful, and will not bring famine on you. [30]I will also make the fruit of the trees and the produce of the field plentiful, so that you will no longer experience reproach among the nations on account of famine.

[31]"Then you will remember your evil ways and your deeds that were not good, and you will loathe yourselves for your iniquities and detestable practices. [32]It is not for your sake that I will act"—the declaration of the Lord GOD—"let this be known to you. Be ashamed and humiliated because of your ways, house of Israel!

[33]"This is what the Lord GOD says: On the day I cleanse you from all your iniquities, I will cause the cities to be inhabited, and the ruins will be rebuilt. [34]The desolate land will be cultivated instead of lying desolate in the sight of everyone who passes by. [35]Then they will say, 'This land that was desolate has become like the garden of Eden. The cities that were once ruined, desolate, and destroyed are now fortified and inhabited.' [36]Then the nations that remain around you will know that I, Yahweh, have rebuilt what was destroyed and have replanted what was desolate. I, Yahweh, have spoken and I will do it.

³⁷"This is what the Lord GOD says: I will respond to the house of Israel and do this for them: I will multiply them in number like a flock. ³⁸So the ruined cities will be filled with a flock of people, just as the flock of sheep for sacrifice is filled in Jerusalem during its appointed festivals. Then they will know that I am Yahweh."

37 The hand of the LORD was on me, and He brought me out by His Spirit and set me down in the middle of the valley; it was full of bones. ²He led me all around them. There were a great many of them on the surface of the valley, and they were very dry. ³Then He said to me, "Son of man, can these bones live?"

I replied, "Lord GOD, only You know."

⁴He said to me, "Prophesy concerning these bones and say to them: Dry bones, hear the word of the LORD! ⁵This is what the Lord GOD says to these bones: I will cause breath to enter you, and you will live. ⁶I will put tendons on you, make flesh grow on you, and cover you with skin. I will put breath in you so that you come to life. Then you will know that I am ᵃYahweh."

⁷So I prophesied as I had been commanded. While I was prophesying, there was a noise, a rattling sound, and the bones came together, bone to bone. ⁸As I looked, tendons appeared on them, flesh grew, and skin covered them, but there was no breath in them. ⁹He said to me, "Prophesy to the breath, prophesy, son of man. Say to it: This is what the Lord GOD says: Breath, come from the four winds and breathe into these slain so that they may live!" ¹⁰So I prophesied as He commanded me; the breath entered them, and they came to life and stood on their feet, a vast army.

¹¹Then He said to me, "Son of man, these bones are the whole house of Israel. Look how they say, 'Our bones are dried up, and our hope has perished; we are cut off.' ¹²Therefore, prophesy and say to them: This is what the Lord GOD says: I am going to open your graves and bring you up from them, My people, and lead you into the land of Israel. ¹³You will know that I am Yahweh, My people, when I open your graves and bring you up from them. ¹⁴I will put My Spirit in you, and you will live, and I will settle you in your own land. Then you will know that I am Yahweh. I have spoken, and I will do it." This is the declaration of the LORD.

¹⁵The word of the LORD came to me: ¹⁶"Son of man, take a single stick and write on it: Belonging to Judah and the Israelites associated with him. Then take another stick and write on it: Belonging to Joseph—the stick of Ephraim—and all the house of Israel associated with him. ¹⁷Then join them together into a single stick so that they become one in your hand. ¹⁸When your people ask you, 'Won't you explain to us what you mean by these things?'— ¹⁹tell them: This is what the Lord GOD says: I am going to take the stick of Joseph, which is in the hand of Ephraim, and the tribes of Israel associated with him, and put them together with the stick of Judah. I will make them into a single stick so that they become one in My hand.

²⁰"When the sticks you have written on are in your hand and in full view of the people, ²¹tell them: This is what the Lord GOD says: I am going to take the Israelites out of the nations where they have gone. I will gather them from all around and bring them into their own land. ²²I will make them one nation in the land, on the mountains of Israel, and one king will rule over all of them. They will no longer be two nations and will no longer be divided into two kingdoms. ²³They

will not defile themselves anymore with their idols, their detestable things, and all their transgressions. I will save them from all their apostasies by which they sinned, and I will cleanse them. Then they will be My people, and I will be their God. ²⁴My servant David will be king over them, and there will be one shepherd for all of them. They will follow My ordinances, and keep My statutes and obey them.

²⁵"They will live in the land that I gave to My servant Jacob, where your fathers lived. They will live in it forever with their children and grandchildren, and My servant David will be their prince forever. ²⁶I will make a covenant of peace with them; it will be an everlasting covenant with them. I will establish and multiply them and will set My sanctuary among them forever. ²⁷My dwelling place will be with them; I will be their God, and they will be My people. ²⁸When My sanctuary is among them forever, the nations will know that I, Yahweh, sanctify Israel."

38 The word of the LORD came to me: ²"Son of man, turn your face toward Gog, of the land of Magog, the chief prince of Meshech and Tubal. Prophesy against him ³and say: This is what the Lord GOD says: Look, I am against you, Gog, chief prince of Meshech and Tubal. ⁴I will turn you around, put hooks in your jaws, and bring you out with all your army, including horses and riders, who are all splendidly dressed, a huge company armed with shields and bucklers, all of them brandishing swords. ⁵Persia, ᵃCush, and Put are with them, all of them with shields and helmets; ⁶Gomer with all its troops; and Beth-togarmah from the remotest parts of the north along with all its troops—many peoples are with you.

⁷"Be prepared and get yourself ready, you and all your company who have been mobilized around you; you will be their guard. ⁸After a long time you will be summoned. In the last years you will enter a land that has been restored from war and regathered from many peoples to the mountains of Israel, which had long been a ruin. They were brought out from the peoples, and all of them now live securely. ⁹You, all of your troops, and many peoples with you will advance, coming like a thunderstorm; you will be like a cloud covering the land.

¹⁰"This is what the Lord GOD says: On that day, thoughts will arise in your mind, and you will devise an evil plan. ¹¹You will say, 'I will go up against a land of open villages; I will come against a tranquil people who are living securely, all of them living without walls and without bars or gates— ¹²in order to seize spoil and carry off plunder, to turn your hand against ruins now inhabited and against a people gathered from the nations, who have been acquiring cattle and possessions and who live at the center of the world.' ¹³Sheba and Dedan and the merchants of Tarshish with all its rulers will ask you, 'Have you come to seize spoil? Have you assembled your hordes to carry off plunder, to make off with silver and gold, to take cattle and possessions, to seize great spoil?'

¹⁴"Therefore prophesy, son of man, and say to Gog: This is what the Lord GOD says: On that day when My people Israel are dwelling securely, will you not know this ¹⁵and come from your place in the remotest parts of the north—you and many peoples with you, who are all riding horses—a mighty horde, a huge army? ¹⁶You will advance against My people Israel like a cloud covering the land. It will happen in the last days, Gog,

that I will bring you against My land so that the nations may know Me, when I show Myself holy through you in their sight.

¹⁷"This is what the Lord God says: Are you the one I spoke about in former times through My servants, the prophets of Israel, who for years prophesied in those times that I would bring you against them? ¹⁸Now on that day, the day when Gog comes against the land of Israel"—this is the declaration of the Lord God—"My wrath will flare up. ¹⁹I swear in My zeal and fiery rage: On that day there will be a great earthquake in the land of Israel. ²⁰The fish of the sea, the birds of the sky, the animals of the field, every creature that crawls on the ground, and every human being on the face of the earth will tremble before Me. The mountains will be thrown down, the cliffs will collapse, and every wall will fall to the ground. ²¹I will call for a sword against him on all My mountains"—the declaration of the Lord God—"and every man's sword will be against his brother. ²²I will execute judgment on him with plague and bloodshed. I will pour out torrential rain, hailstones, fire, and brimstone on him, as well as his troops and the many peoples who are with him. ²³I will display My greatness and holiness, and will reveal Myself in the sight of many nations. Then they will know that I am ⋅Yahweh.

39 "As for you, son of man, prophesy against Gog and say: This is what the Lord God says: Look, I am against you, Gog, chief prince of Meshech and Tubal. ²I will turn you around, drive you on, and lead you up from the remotest parts of the north. I will bring you against the mountains of Israel. ³Then I will knock your bow from your left hand and make your arrows drop from your right hand. ⁴You, all your troops, and the peoples who are with you will fall on the mountains of Israel. I will give you as food to every kind of predatory bird and to the wild animals. ⁵You will fall on the open field, for I have spoken." This is the declaration of the Lord God.

⁶"I will send fire against Magog and those who live securely on the coasts and islands. Then they will know that I am ⋅Yahweh. ⁷So I will make My holy name known among My people Israel and will no longer allow it to be profaned. Then the nations will know that I am Yahweh, the Holy One in Israel. ⁸Yes, it is coming, and it will happen." This is the declaration of the Lord God. "This is the day I have spoken about.

⁹"Then the inhabitants of Israel's cities will go out, kindle fires, and burn the weapons—the bucklers and shields, the bows and arrows, the clubs and spears. For seven years they will use them to make fires. ¹⁰They will not gather wood from the countryside or cut it down from the forests, for they will use the weapons to make fires. They will take the loot from those who looted them and plunder those who plundered them." This is the declaration of the Lord God.

¹¹"Now on that day I will give Gog a burial place there in Israel—the Valley of the Travelers east of the Sea. It will block those who travel through, for Gog and all his hordes will be buried there. So it will be called the Valley of Hamon-gog. ¹²The house of Israel will spend seven months burying them in order to cleanse the land. ¹³All the people of the land will bury them and their fame will spread on the day I display My glory." This is the declaration of the Lord God.

¹⁴"They will appoint men on a full-time basis to pass through the land and bury the invaders who remain on the surface of the ground, in order to cleanse it. They will make their search at the end of the seven months. ¹⁵When they pass through the land and one of them sees a human bone, he will set up a marker next to it until the buriers have buried it in the Valley of Hamon-gog. ¹⁶There will even be a city named Hamonah there. So they will cleanse the land.

¹⁷"Son of man, this is what the Lord God says: Tell every kind of bird and all the wild animals: Assemble and come! Gather from all around to My sacrificial feast that I am slaughtering for you, a great feast on the mountains of Israel; you will eat flesh and drink blood. ¹⁸You will eat the flesh of mighty men and drink the blood of the earth's princes: rams, lambs, male goats, and all the fattened bulls of Bashan. ¹⁹You will eat fat until you are satisfied and drink blood until you are drunk, at My sacrificial feast that I have prepared for you. ²⁰At My table you will eat your fill of horses and riders, of mighty men and all the warriors." This is the declaration of the Lord God.

²¹"I will display My glory among the nations, and all the nations will see the judgment I have executed and the hand I have laid on them. ²²From that day forward the house of Israel will know that I am Yahweh their God. ²³And the nations will know that the house of Israel went into exile on account of their iniquity, because they dealt unfaithfully with Me. Therefore, I hid My face from them and handed them over to their enemies, so that they all fell by the sword. ²⁴I dealt with them according to their uncleanness and transgressions, and I hid My face from them.

²⁵"So this is what the Lord God says: Now I will restore the fortunes of Jacob and have compassion on the whole house of Israel, and I will be jealous for My holy name. ²⁶They will feel remorse for their disgrace and all the unfaithfulness they committed against Me, when they live securely in their land with no one to frighten them. ²⁷When I bring them back from the peoples and gather them from the countries of their enemies, I will demonstrate My holiness through them in the sight of many nations. ²⁸They will know that I am Yahweh their God when I regather them to their own land after having exiled them among the nations. I will leave none of them behind. ²⁹I will no longer hide My face from them, for I will pour out My Spirit on the house of Israel." This is the declaration of the Lord God.

40 In the twenty-fifth year of our exile, at the beginning of the year, on the tenth day of the month in the fourteenth year after Jerusalem had been captured, on that very day the Lord's hand was on me, and He brought me there. ²In visions of God⋅He took me to the land of Israel and set me down on a very high mountain. On its southern slope was a structure resembling a city. ³He brought me there, and I saw a man whose appearance was like bronze, with a linen cord and a measuring rod in his hand. He was standing by the gate. ⁴He spoke to me: "Son of man, look with your eyes, listen with your ears, and pay attention to everything I am going to show you, for you have been brought here so that I might show it to you. Report everything you see to the house of Israel."

⁵Now there was a wall surrounding the outside of the temple. The measuring rod in the man's hand was six units of 21 inches; each unit was the standard length plus three inches. He measured the thickness of the wall structure; it was about 10 feet, and its height

was the same. ⁶Then he came to the gate that faced east and climbed its steps. He measured the threshold of the gate; it was 10 feet deep—the first threshold was 10 feet deep. ⁷Each recess was about 10 feet long and 10 feet deep, and there was a space of 8³/₄ feet between the recesses. The inner threshold of the gate on the temple side next to the gate's portico was about 10 feet. ⁸Next he measured the portico of the gate; ⁹it was 14 feet, and its pilasters were 3¹/₂ feet. The portico of the gate was on the temple side.

¹⁰There were three recesses on each side of the east gate, each with the same measurements, and the pilasters on either side also had the same measurements. ¹¹Then he measured the width of the gate's entrance; it was 17¹/₂ feet, while the width of the gateway was 22³/₄ feet. ¹²There was a barrier of 21 inches in front of the recesses on both sides, and the recesses on each side were 10¹/₂ feet square. ¹³Then he measured the gateway from the roof of one recess to the roof of the opposite one; the distance was 43³/₄ feet. The openings of the recesses faced each other. ¹⁴Next, he measured the pilasters—105 feet. The gate extended around to the pilaster of the court. ¹⁵The distance from the front of the gate at the entrance to the front of the gate's portico on the inside was 87¹/₂ feet. ¹⁶The recesses and their pilasters had beveled windows all around the inside of the gateway. The porticoes also had windows all around on the inside. Each pilaster was decorated with palm trees.

¹⁷Then he brought me into the outer court, and there were chambers and a paved surface laid out all around the court. Thirty chambers faced the pavement, ¹⁸which flanked the gates and corresponded to the length of the gates; this was the lower pavement. ¹⁹Then he measured the distance from the front of the lower gate to the exterior front of the inner court; it was 175 feet. This was the east; next the north is described.

²⁰He measured the gate of the outer court facing north, both its length and width. ²¹Its three recesses on each side, its pilasters, and its portico had the same measurements as the first gate: 87¹/₂ feet long and 43³/₄ feet wide. ²²Its windows, portico, and palm trees had the same measurements as those of the gate that faced east. Seven steps led up to the gate, and its portico was ahead of them. ²³The inner court had a gate facing the north gate, like the one on the east. He measured the distance from gate to gate; it was 175 feet.

²⁴He brought me to the south side, and there was also a gate on the south. He measured its pilasters and portico; they had the same measurements as the others. ²⁵Both the gate and its portico had windows all around, like the other windows. It was 87¹/₂ feet long and 43³/₄ feet wide. ²⁶Its stairway had seven steps, and its portico was ahead of them. It had palm trees on its pilasters, one on each side. ²⁷The inner court had a gate on the south. He measured from gate to gate on the south; it was 175 feet.

²⁸Then he brought me to the inner court through the south gate. When he measured the south gate, it had the same measurements as the others. ²⁹Its recesses, pilasters, and portico had the same measurements as the others. Both it and its portico had windows all around. It was 87¹/₂ feet long and 43³/₄ feet wide. ³⁰(There were porticoes all around, 43³/₄ feet long and 8³/₄ feet wide.) ³¹Its portico faced the outer court, and its pilasters were decorated with palm trees. Its stairway had eight steps.

³²Then he brought me to the inner court on the east side. When he measured the gate, it had the same measurements as the others. ³³Its recesses, pilasters, and portico had the same measurements as the others. Both it and its portico had windows all around. It was 87¹/₂ feet long and 43³/₄ feet wide. ³⁴Its portico faced the outer court, and its pilasters were decorated with palm trees on each side. Its stairway had eight steps.

³⁵Then he brought me to the north gate. When he measured it, it had the same measurements as the others, ³⁶as did its recesses, pilasters, and portico. It also had windows all around. It was 87¹/₂ feet long and 43³/₄ feet wide. ³⁷Its portico faced the outer court, and its pilasters were decorated with palm trees on each side. Its stairway had eight steps.

³⁸There was a chamber whose door opened into the portico of the gate. The *burnt offering was to be washed there. ³⁹Inside the portico of the gate there were two tables on each side, on which to slaughter the burnt offering, *sin offering, and *restitution offering. ⁴⁰Outside, as one approaches the entrance of the north gate, there were two tables on one side and two more tables on the other side of the gate's portico. ⁴¹So there were four tables inside the gate and four outside, eight tables in all on which the slaughtering was to be done. ⁴²There were also four tables of cut stone for the burnt offering, each 31¹/₂ inches long, 31¹/₂ inches wide, and 21 inches high. The utensils used to slaughter the burnt offerings and other sacrifices were placed on them. ⁴³There were three-inch hooks fastened all around the inside of the room, and the flesh of the offering was to be laid on the tables.

⁴⁴Outside the inner gate, within the inner court, there were chambers for the singers: one beside the north gate, facing south, and another beside the south gate, facing north. ⁴⁵Then the man said to me: "This chamber that faces south is for the priests who keep charge of the temple. ⁴⁶The chamber that faces north is for the priests who keep charge of the altar. These are the sons of Zadok, the ones from the sons of Levi who may approach the LORD to serve Him." ⁴⁷Next he measured the court. It was square, 175 feet long and 175 feet wide. The altar was in front of the temple.

⁴⁸Then he brought me to the portico of the temple and measured the pilasters of the portico; they were 8³/₄ feet thick on each side. The width of the gateway was 24¹/₂ feet, and the side walls of the gate were 5¹/₄ feet wide on each side. ⁴⁹The portico was 35 feet across and 21 feet deep, and 10 steps led up to it. There were pillars by the pilasters, one on each side.

41 Next he brought me into the great hall and measured the pilasters; on each side the width of the pilaster was 10¹/₂ feet. ²The width of the entrance was 17¹/₂ feet, and the side walls of the entrance were 8³/₄ feet wide on each side. He also measured the length of the great hall, 70 feet, and the width, 35 feet. ³He went inside the next room and measured the pilasters at the entrance; they were 3¹/₂ feet wide. The entrance was 10¹/₂ feet wide, and the width of the entrance's side walls on each side was 12¹/₄ feet. ⁴He then measured the length of the room adjacent to the great hall, 35 feet, and the width, 35 feet. And he said to me, "This is the most holy place."

⁵Then he measured the wall of the temple; it was 10¹/₂ feet thick. The width of the side rooms all around

the temple was seven feet. ⁶The side rooms were arranged one above another in three stories of 30 rooms each. There were ledges on the wall of the temple all around to serve as supports for the side rooms, so that the supports would not be in the temple wall itself. ⁷The side rooms surrounding the temple widened at each successive story, for the structure surrounding the temple went up by stages. This was the reason for the temple's broadness as it rose. And so, one would go up from the lowest story to the highest by means of the middle one.

⁸I saw that the temple had a raised platform surrounding it; this foundation for the side rooms was 10¹/₂ feet high. ⁹The thickness of the outer wall of the side rooms was 8³/₄ feet. The free space between the side rooms of the temple ¹⁰and the outer chambers was 35 feet wide all around the temple. ¹¹The side rooms opened into the free space, one entrance toward the north and another to the south. The area of free space was 8³/₄ feet wide all around.

¹²Now the building that faced the temple yard toward the west was 122¹/₂ feet wide. The wall of the building was 8³/₄ feet thick on all sides, and the building's length was 157¹/₂ feet.

¹³Then the man measured the temple; it was 175 feet long. In addition, the temple yard and the building, including its walls, were 175 feet long. ¹⁴The width of the front of the temple along with the temple yard to the east was 175 feet. ¹⁵Next he measured the length of the building facing the temple yard to the west, with its galleries on each side; it was 175 feet.

The interior of the great hall and the porticoes of the court— ¹⁶the thresholds, the beveled windows, and the balconies all around with their three levels opposite the threshold—were overlaid with wood on all sides. They were paneled from the ground to the windows (but the windows were covered), ¹⁷reaching to the top of the entrance, and as far as the inner temple and on the outside. On every wall all around, on the inside and outside, was a pattern ¹⁸carved with ˙cherubim and palm trees. There was a palm tree between each pair of cherubim. Each cherub had two faces: ¹⁹a human face turned toward the palm tree on one side, and a lion's face turned toward it on the other. They were carved throughout the temple on all sides. ²⁰Cherubim and palm trees were carved from the ground to the top of the entrance and on the wall of the great hall.

²¹The doorposts of the great hall were square, and the front of the sanctuary had the same appearance. ²²The altar was made of wood, 5¹/₄ feet high and 3¹/₂ feet long. It had corners, and its length and sides were of wood. The man told me, "This is the table that stands before the Lord."

²³The great hall and the sanctuary each had a double door, ²⁴and each of the doors had two swinging panels. There were two panels for one door and two for the other. ²⁵Cherubim and palm trees were carved on the doors of the great hall like those carved on the walls. There was a wooden canopy outside, in front of the portico. ²⁶There were beveled windows and palm trees on both sides, on the side walls of the portico, the side rooms of the temple, and the canopies.

42 Then the man led me out by way of the north gate into the outer court. He brought me to the group of chambers opposite the temple yard and opposite the building to the north. ²Along the length of the chambers, which was 175 feet, there was an entrance on the north; the width was 87¹/₂ feet. ³Opposite the 35 foot space belonging to the inner court and opposite the paved surface belonging to the outer court, the structure rose gallery by gallery in three tiers. ⁴In front of the chambers was a walkway toward the inside, 17¹/₂ feet wide and 175 feet long, and their entrances were on the north. ⁵The upper chambers were narrower because the galleries took away more space from them than from the lower and middle stories of the building. ⁶For they were arranged in three stories and had no pillars like the pillars of the courts; therefore the upper chambers were set back from the ground more than the lower and middle stories. ⁷A wall on the outside ran in front of the chambers, parallel to them, toward the outer court; it was 87¹/₂ feet long. ⁸For the chambers on the outer court were 87¹/₂ feet long, while those facing the great hall were 175 feet long. ⁹At the base of these chambers there was an entryway on the east side as one enters them from the outer court.

¹⁰In the thickness of the wall of the court toward the south, there were chambers facing the temple yard and the western building, ¹¹with a passageway in front of them, just like the chambers that faced north. Their length and width, as well as all their exits, measurements, and entrances, were identical. ¹²The entrance at the beginning of the passageway, the way in front of the corresponding wall as one enters on the east side, was similar to the entrances of the chambers that were on the south side.

¹³Then the man said to me, "The northern and southern chambers that face the temple yard are the holy chambers where the priests who approach the Lord will eat the most holy offerings. There they will deposit the most holy offerings—the ˙grain offerings, ˙sin offerings, and ˙restitution offerings—for the place is holy. ¹⁴Once the priests have entered, they must not go out from the holy area to the outer court until they have removed the clothes they minister in, for these are holy. They are to put on other clothes before they approach the public area."

¹⁵When he finished measuring inside the temple complex, he led me out by way of the gate that faced east and measured all around the complex.
> ¹⁶He measured the east side with a
> measuring rod;
> it was 875 feet by the measuring rod.
> ¹⁷He measured the north side;
> it was 875 feet by the measuring rod.
> ¹⁸He measured the south side;
> it was 875 feet by the measuring rod.
> ¹⁹Then he turned to the west side
> and measured 875 feet by the measuring rod.

²⁰He measured the temple complex on all four sides. It had a wall all around it, 875 feet long and 875 feet wide, to separate the holy from the common.

43 He led me to the gate, the one that faces east, ²and I saw the glory of the God of Israel coming from the east. His voice sounded like the roar of mighty waters, and the earth shone with His glory. ³The vision I saw was like the one I had seen when He came to destroy the city, and like the ones I had seen by the Chebar Canal. I fell facedown. ⁴The glory of the Lord entered the temple by way of the gate that faced east. ⁵Then the Spirit lifted me up and brought me to the inner court, and the glory of the Lord filled the temple.

[6] While the man was standing beside me, I heard someone speaking to me from the temple. [7] He said to me: "Son of man, this is the place of My throne and the place for the soles of My feet, where I will dwell among the Israelites forever. The house of Israel and their kings will no longer defile My holy name by their religious prostitution and by the corpses of their kings at their •high places. [8] Whenever they placed their threshold next to My threshold and their doorposts beside My doorposts, with only a wall between Me and them, they were defiling My holy name by the detestable acts they committed. So I destroyed them in My anger. [9] Now let them remove their prostitution and the corpses of their kings far from Me, and I will dwell among them forever.

[10] "As for you, son of man, describe the temple to the house of Israel, so that they may be ashamed of their iniquities. Let them measure its pattern, [11] and they will be ashamed of all that they have done. Reveal the design of the temple to them—its layout with its exits and entrances—its complete design along with all its statutes, design specifications, and laws. Write it down in their sight so that they may observe its complete design and all its statutes and may carry them out. [12] This is the law of the temple: all its surrounding territory on top of the mountain will be especially holy. Yes, this is the law of the temple.

[13] "These are the measurements of the altar in units of length (each unit being the standard length plus three inches): the gutter is 21 inches deep and 21 inches wide, with a rim of nine inches around its edge. This is the base of the altar. [14] The distance from the gutter on the ground to the lower ledge is $3\frac{1}{2}$ feet, and the width of the ledge is 21 inches. There are seven feet from the small ledge to the large ledge, whose width is also 21 inches. [15] The altar hearth is seven feet high, and four horns project upward from the hearth. [16] The hearth is square, 21 feet long by 21 feet wide. [17] The ledge is $24\frac{1}{2}$ feet long by $24\frac{1}{2}$ feet wide, with four equal sides. The rim all around it is $10\frac{1}{2}$ inches, and its gutter is 21 inches all around it. The altar's steps face east."

[18] Then He said to me: "Son of man, this is what the Lord GOD says: These are the statutes for the altar on the day it is constructed, so that •burnt offerings may be sacrificed on it and blood may be sprinkled on it: [19] You are to give a bull from the herd as a •sin offering to the Levitical priests who are from the offspring of Zadok, who approach Me in order to serve Me." This is the declaration of the Lord GOD. [20] "You must take some of its blood and apply it to the four horns of the altar, the four corners of the ledge, and all around the rim. In this way you will purify the altar and make •atonement for it. [21] Then you must take away the bull for the sin offering, and it must be burned outside the sanctuary in the place appointed for the temple.

[22] "On the second day you are to present an unblemished male goat as a sin offering. They will purify the altar just as they did with the bull. [23] When you have finished the purification, you are to present a young, unblemished bull and an unblemished ram from the flock. [24] You must present them before the LORD; the priests will throw salt on them and sacrifice them as a burnt offering to the LORD. [25] You will offer a goat for a sin offering each day for seven days. A young bull and a ram from the flock, both unblemished, must also be offered. [26] For seven days the priests are to make atone-ment for the altar and cleanse it. In this way they will consecrate it [27] and complete the days of purification. Then on the eighth day and afterward, the priests will offer your burnt offerings and •fellowship offerings on the altar, and I will accept you." This is the declaration of the Lord GOD.

44 The man then brought me back toward the sanctuary's outer gate that faced east, and it was closed. [2] The LORD said to me: "This gate will remain closed. It will not be opened, and no one will enter through it, because the LORD, the God of Israel, has entered through it. Therefore it will remain closed. [3] The prince himself will sit in the gateway to eat a meal before the LORD. He must enter by way of the portico of the gate and go out the same way."

[4] Then the man brought me by way of the north gate to the front of the temple. I looked, and the glory of the LORD filled His temple. And I fell facedown. [5] The LORD said to me: "Son of man, pay attention; look with your eyes and listen with your ears to everything I tell you about all the statutes and laws of the LORD's temple. Take careful note of the entrance of the temple along with all the exits of the sanctuary.

[6] "Say to the rebellious people, the house of Israel: This is what the Lord GOD says: I have had enough of all your detestable practices, house of Israel. [7] When you brought in foreigners, uncircumcised in both heart and flesh, to occupy My sanctuary, you defiled My temple while you offered My food—the fat and the blood. You broke My covenant by all your detestable practices. [8] You have not kept charge of My holy things but have appointed others to keep charge of My sanctuary for you.

[9] "This is what the Lord GOD says: No foreigner, uncircumcised in heart and flesh, may enter My sanctuary, not even a foreigner who is among the Israelites. [10] Surely the Levites who wandered away from Me when Israel went astray, and who strayed from Me after their idols, will bear the consequences of their sin. [11] Yet they will occupy My sanctuary, serving as guards at the temple gates and ministering at the temple. They will slaughter the •burnt offerings and other sacrifices for the people and will stand before them to serve them. [12] Because they ministered to the house of Israel before their idols and became a sinful stumbling block to them, therefore I swore an oath against them"—this is the declaration of the Lord GOD—"that they would bear the consequences of their sin. [13] They must not approach Me to serve Me as priests or come near any of My holy things or the most holy things. They will bear their disgrace and the consequences of the detestable acts they committed. [14] Yet I will make them responsible for the duties of the temple—for all its work and everything done in it.

[15] "But the Levitical priests descended from Zadok, who kept charge of My sanctuary when the Israelites went astray from Me, will approach Me to serve Me. They will stand before Me to offer Me fat and blood." This is the declaration of the Lord GOD. [16] "They are the ones who may enter My sanctuary and draw near to My table to serve Me. They will keep My mandate. [17] When they enter the gates of the inner court they must wear linen garments; they must not have on them anything made of wool when they minister at the gates of the inner court and within it. [18] They must wear linen turbans on their heads and linen undergarments around their waists. They are not to put on

anything that makes them sweat. ¹⁹Before they go out to the outer court, to the people, they must take off the clothes they have been ministering in, leave them in the holy chambers, and dress in other clothes so that they do not transmit holiness to the people through their clothes.

²⁰"They may not shave their heads or let their hair grow long, but must carefully trim their hair. ²¹No priest may drink wine before he enters the inner court. ²²He is not to marry a widow or a divorced woman, but must marry a virgin from the offspring of the house of Israel, or a widow who is the widow of a priest. ²³They must teach My people the difference between the holy and the common, and explain to them the difference between the ˙clean and the ˙unclean.

²⁴"In a dispute, they will officiate as judges and decide the case according to My ordinances. They must observe My laws and statutes regarding all My appointed festivals, and keep My Sabbaths holy. ²⁵A priest may not come near a dead person so that he becomes defiled. However, he may defile himself for a father, a mother, a son, a daughter, a brother, or an unmarried sister. ²⁶After he is cleansed, he is to count off seven days for himself. ²⁷On the day he goes into the sanctuary, into the inner court to minister in the sanctuary, he must present his ˙sin offering." This is the declaration of the Lord God.

²⁸"This will be their inheritance: I am their inheritance. You are to give them no possession in Israel: I am their possession. ²⁹They will eat the ˙grain offering, the sin offering, and the ˙restitution offering. Everything in Israel that is permanently dedicated to the Lord will belong to them. ³⁰The best of all the ˙firstfruits of every kind and contribution of every kind from all your gifts will belong to the priests. You are to give your first batch of dough to the priest so that a blessing may rest on your homes. ³¹The priests may not eat any bird or animal that died naturally or was mauled by wild beasts.

45 "When you divide the land by lot as an inheritance, you must set aside a donation to the Lord, a holy portion of the land, 8¹⁄₃ miles long and 6²⁄₃ miles wide. This entire tract of land will be holy. ²In this area there will be a square section for the sanctuary, 875 by 875 feet, with 87¹⁄₂ feet of open space all around it. ³From this holy portion, you will measure off an area 8¹⁄₃ miles long and 3¹⁄₃ miles wide, in which the sanctuary, the most holy place, will stand. ⁴It will be a holy area of the land to be used by the priests who minister in the sanctuary, who draw near to serve the Lord. It will be a place for their houses, as well as a holy area for the sanctuary. ⁵There will be another area 8¹⁄₃ miles long and 3¹⁄₃ miles wide for the Levites who minister in the temple; it will be their possession for towns to live in.

⁶"As the property of the city, you must set aside an area 1²⁄₃ of a mile wide and 8¹⁄₃ miles long, adjacent to the holy donation of land. It will be for the whole house of Israel. ⁷And the prince will have the area on each side of the holy donation of land and the city's property, adjacent to the holy donation and the city's property, stretching to the west on the west side and to the east on the east side. Its length will correspond to one of the tribal portions from the western boundary to the eastern boundary. ⁸This will be his land as a possession in Israel. My princes will no longer oppress My people but give the rest of the land to the house of Israel according to their tribes.

⁹"This is what the Lord God says: You have gone too far, princes of Israel! Put away violence and oppression and do what is just and right. Put an end to your evictions of My people." This is the declaration of the Lord God. ¹⁰"You must have honest scales, an honest dry measure, and an honest liquid measure. ¹¹The dry measure and the liquid measure will be uniform, with the liquid measure containing 5¹⁄₂ gallons and the dry measure holding half a bushel. Their measurement will be a tenth of the standard larger capacity measure. ¹²The ˙shekel will weigh 20 gerahs. Your mina will equal 60 shekels.

¹³"This is the contribution you are to offer: Three quarts from five bushels of wheat and three quarts from five bushels of barley. ¹⁴The quota of oil in liquid measures will be one percent of every cor. The cor equals 10 liquid measures or one standard larger capacity measure, since 10 liquid measures equal one standard larger capacity measure. ¹⁵And the quota from the flock is one animal out of every 200 from the well-watered pastures of Israel. These are for the ˙grain offerings, ˙burnt offerings, and ˙fellowship offerings, to make ˙atonement for the people." This is the declaration of the Lord God. ¹⁶"All the people of the land must take part in this contribution for the prince in Israel. ¹⁷Then the burnt offerings, grain offerings, and ˙drink offerings for the festivals, New Moons, and Sabbaths—for all the appointed times of the house of Israel—will be the prince's responsibility. He will provide the ˙sin offerings, grain offerings, burnt offerings, and fellowship offerings to make atonement on behalf of the house of Israel.

¹⁸"This is what the Lord God says: In the first month, on the first day of the month, you are to take a young, unblemished bull and purify the sanctuary. ¹⁹The priest must take some of the blood from the sin offering and apply it to the temple doorposts, the four corners of the altar's ledge, and the doorposts of the gate to the inner court. ²⁰You must do the same thing on the seventh day of the month for everyone who sins unintentionally or through ignorance. In this way you will make atonement for the temple.

²¹"In the first month, on the fourteenth day of the month, you are to celebrate the ˙Passover, a festival of seven days during which unleavened bread will be eaten. ²²On that day the prince will provide a bull as a sin offering on behalf of himself and all the people of the land. ²³During the seven days of the festival, he will provide seven bulls and seven rams without blemish as a burnt offering to the Lord on each of the seven days, along with a male goat each day for a sin offering. ²⁴He will also provide a grain offering of half a bushel per bull and half a bushel per ram, along with a gallon of oil for every half bushel. ²⁵At the festival that begins on the fifteenth day of the seventh month, he will provide the same things for seven days—the same sin offerings, burnt offerings, grain offerings, and oil.

46 "This is what the Lord God says: The gate of the inner court that faces east must be closed during the six days of work, but it will be opened on the Sabbath day and opened on the day of the New Moon. ²The prince should enter from the outside by way of the gate's portico and stand at the doorpost of the gate while the priests sacrifice his ˙burnt offerings and ˙fellowship offerings. He will bow in worship at

the threshold of the gate and then depart, but the gate must not be closed until evening. ³The people of the land will also bow in worship before the Lord at the entrance of that gate on the Sabbaths and New Moons.

⁴"The burnt offering that the prince presents to the Lord on the Sabbath day is to be six unblemished lambs and an unblemished ram. ⁵The ˙grain offering will be half a bushel with the ram, and the grain offering with the lambs will be whatever he wants to give, as well as a gallon of oil for every half bushel. ⁶On the day of the New Moon, the burnt offering is to be a young, unblemished bull, as well as six lambs and a ram without blemish. ⁷He will provide a grain offering of half a bushel with the bull, half a bushel with the ram, and whatever he can afford with the lambs, together with a gallon of oil for every half bushel. ⁸When the prince enters, he must go in by way of the gate's portico and go out the same way.

⁹"When the people of the land come before the Lord at the appointed times, whoever enters by way of the north gate to worship must go out by way of the south gate, and whoever enters by way of the south gate must go out by way of the north gate. No one must return through the gate by which he entered, but must go out by the opposite gate. ¹⁰When the people enter, the prince will enter with them, and when they leave, he will leave. ¹¹At the festivals and appointed times, the grain offering will be half a bushel with the bull, half a bushel with the ram, and whatever he wants to give with the lambs, along with a gallon of oil for every half bushel.

¹²"When the prince makes a freewill offering, whether a burnt offering or a fellowship offering as a freewill offering to the Lord, the gate that faces east must be opened for him. He is to offer his burnt offering or fellowship offering just as he does on the Sabbath day. Then he will go out, and the gate must be closed after he leaves.

¹³"You must offer an unblemished year-old male lamb as a daily burnt offering to the Lord; you will offer it every morning. ¹⁴You must also prepare a grain offering every morning along with it: three quarts, with one-third of a gallon of oil to moisten the fine flour—a grain offering to the Lord. This is a permanent statute to be observed regularly. ¹⁵They will offer the lamb, the grain offering, and the oil every morning as a regular burnt offering.

¹⁶"This is what the Lord God says: If the prince gives a gift to each of his sons as their inheritance, it will belong to his sons. It will become their property by inheritance. ¹⁷But if he gives a gift from his inheritance to one of his servants, it will belong to that servant until the year of freedom, when it will revert to the prince. His inheritance belongs only to his sons; it is theirs. ¹⁸The prince must not take any of the people's inheritance, evicting them from their property. He is to provide an inheritance for his sons from his own property, so that none of My people will be displaced from his own property."

¹⁹Then he brought me through the entrance that was at the side of the gate, into the priests' holy chambers, which faced north. I saw a place there at the far western end. ²⁰He said to me, "This is the place where the priests will boil the ˙restitution offering and the ˙sin offering, and where they will bake the grain offering, so that they do not bring them into the outer court and transmit holiness to the people." ²¹Next he

brought me into the outer court and led me past its four corners. There was a separate court in each of its corners. ²²In the four corners of the outer court there were enclosed courts, 70 feet long by 52¹⁄₂ feet wide. All four corner areas had the same dimensions. ²³There was a stone wall around the inside of them, around the four of them, with ovens built at the base of the walls on all sides. ²⁴He said to me: "These are the kitchens where those who minister at the temple will cook the people's sacrifices."

47 Then he brought me back to the entrance of the temple and there was water flowing from under the threshold of the temple toward the east, for the temple faced east. The water was coming down from under the south side of the threshold of the temple, south of the altar. ²Next he brought me out by way of the north gate and led me around the outside to the outer gate that faced east; there the water was trickling from the south side. ³As the man went out east with a measuring line in his hand, he measured off a third of a mile and led me through the water. It came up to my ankles. ⁴Then he measured off a third of a mile and led me through the water. It came up to my knees. He measured off another third of a mile and led me through the water. It came up to my waist. ⁵Again he measured off a third of a mile, and it was a river that I could not cross on foot. For the water had risen; it was deep enough to swim in, a river that could not be crossed on foot.

⁶He asked me, "Do you see this, son of man?" Then he led me back to the bank of the river. ⁷When I had returned, I saw a very large number of trees along both sides of the riverbank. ⁸He said to me, "This water flows out to the eastern region and goes down to the ˙Arabah. When it enters the sea, the sea of foul water, the water of the sea becomes fresh. ⁹Every kind of living creature that swarms will live wherever the river flows, and there will be a huge number of fish because this water goes there. Since the water will become fresh, there will be life everywhere the river goes. ¹⁰Fishermen will stand beside it from En-gedi to En-eglaim. These will become places where nets are spread out to dry. Their fish will consist of many different kinds, like the fish of the Mediterranean Sea. ¹¹Yet its swamps and marshes will not be healed; they will be left for salt. ¹²All kinds of trees providing food will grow along both banks of the river. Their leaves will not wither, and their fruit will not fail. Each month they will bear fresh fruit because the water comes from the sanctuary. Their fruit will be used for food and their leaves for medicine."

¹³This is what the Lord God says: "This is the border you will use to divide the land as an inheritance for the 12 tribes of Israel. Joseph will receive two shares. ¹⁴You will inherit it in equal portions, since I swore to give it to your ancestors. So this land will fall to you as an inheritance.

¹⁵"This is to be the border of the land:
On the north side it will extend from the Mediterranean Sea by way of Hethlon and Lebo-hamath to Zedad, ¹⁶Berothah, and Sibraim (which is between the border of Damascus and the border of Hamath), as far as Hazer-hatticon, which is on the border of Hauran. ¹⁷So the border will run from the sea to Hazar-enon at the border of Damascus, with the territory of Hamath to the north. This will be the northern side.

¹⁸On the east side it will run between Hauran and Damascus, along the Jordan between Gilead and the land of Israel; you will measure from the northern border to the eastern sea. This will be the eastern side.

¹⁹On the south side it will run from Tamar to the waters of Meribath-kadesh, and on to the Brook of Egypt as far as the Mediterranean Sea. This will be the southern side.

²⁰On the west side the Mediterranean Sea will be the border, from the southern border up to a point opposite Lebo-hamath. This will be the western side.

²¹"You are to divide this land among yourselves according to the tribes of Israel. ²²You will allot it as an inheritance for yourselves and for the foreigners living among you, who have fathered children among you. You will treat them like native-born Israelites; along with you, they will be allotted an inheritance among the tribes of Israel. ²³In whatever tribe the foreigner lives, you will assign his inheritance there." This is the declaration of the Lord God.

48 "Now these are the names of the tribes: From the northern end, along the road of Hethlon, to Lebo-hamath as far as Hazar-enon, at the northern border of Damascus, alongside Hamath and extending from the eastern side to the sea, will be Dan—one portion.

²Next to the territory of Dan, from the east side to the west, will be Asher—one portion.

³Next to the territory of Asher, from the east side to the west, will be Naphtali—one portion.

⁴Next to the territory of Naphtali, from the east side to the west, will be Manasseh—one portion.

⁵Next to the territory of Manasseh, from the east side to the west, will be Ephraim—one portion.

⁶Next to the territory of Ephraim, from the east side to the west, will be Reuben—one portion.

⁷Next to the territory of Reuben, from the east side to the west, will be Judah—one portion.

⁸"Next to the territory of Judah, from the east side to the west, will be the portion you donate to the Lord, 8¹/₃ miles wide, and as long as one of the tribal portions from the east side to the west. The sanctuary will be in the middle of it.

⁹"The special portion you donate to the Lord will be 8¹/₃ miles long and 3¹/₃ miles wide. ¹⁰This holy donation will be set apart for the priests alone. It will be 8¹/₃ miles long on the northern side, 3¹/₃ miles wide on the western side, 3¹/₃ miles wide on the eastern side, and 8¹/₃ miles long on the southern side. The Lord's sanctuary will be in the middle of it. ¹¹It is for the consecrated priests, the sons of Zadok, who kept My charge and did not go astray as the Levites did when the Israelites went astray. ¹²It will be a special donation for them out of the holy donation of the land, a most holy place adjacent to the territory of the Levites.

¹³"Next to the territory of the priests, the Levites will have an area 8¹/₃ miles long and 3¹/₃ miles wide. The total length will be 8¹/₃ miles and the width 3¹/₃ miles. ¹⁴They must not sell or exchange any of it, and

they must not transfer this choice part of the land, for it is holy to the Lord.

¹⁵"The remaining area, 1²/₃ of a mile wide and 8¹/₃ miles long, will be for common use by the city, for both residential and open space. The city will be in the middle of it. ¹⁶These are the city's measurements:

1¹/₂ miles on the north side;
1¹/₂ miles on the south side;
1¹/₂ miles on the east side;
and 1¹/₂ miles on the west side.

¹⁷The city's open space will extend:

425 feet to the north,
425 feet to the south,
425 feet to the east,
and 425 feet to the west.

¹⁸"The remainder of the length alongside the holy donation will be 3¹/₃ miles to the east and 3¹/₃ miles to the west. It will run alongside the holy donation. Its produce will be food for the workers of the city. ¹⁹The city's workers from all the tribes of Israel will cultivate it. ²⁰The entire donation will be 8¹/₃ miles by 8¹/₃ miles; you are to set apart the holy donation along with the city property as a square area.

²¹"The remaining area on both sides of the holy donation and the city property will belong to the prince. He will own the land adjacent to the tribal portions, next to the 8¹/₃ miles of the donation as far as the eastern border and next to the 8¹/₃ miles of the donation as far as the western border. The holy donation and the sanctuary of the temple will be in the middle of it. ²²Except for the Levitical property and the city property in the middle of the area belonging to the prince, the area between the territory of Judah and that of Benjamin will belong to the prince.

²³"As for the rest of the tribes:

From the east side to the west, will be Benjamin—one portion.

²⁴Next to the territory of Benjamin, from the east side to the west, will be Simeon—one portion.

²⁵Next to the territory of Simeon, from the east side to the west, will be Issachar—one portion.

²⁶Next to the territory of Issachar, from the east side to the west, will be Zebulun—one portion.

²⁷Next to the territory of Zebulun, from the east side to the west, will be Gad—one portion.

²⁸Next to the territory of Gad toward the south side, the border will run from Tamar to the waters of Meribath-kadesh, to the Brook of Egypt, and out to the Mediterranean Sea. ²⁹This is the land you are to allot as an inheritance to Israel's tribes, and these will be their portions." This is the declaration of the Lord God.

³⁰"These are the exits of the city:

On the north side, which measures 1¹/₂ miles, ³¹there will be three gates facing north, the gates of the city being named for the tribes of Israel: one, the gate of Reuben; one, the gate of Judah; and one, the gate of Levi.

³²On the east side, which is 1¹/₂ miles, there will be three gates: one, the gate of Joseph; one, the gate of Benjamin; and one, the gate of Dan.

³³On the south side, which measures 1¹/₂

miles, there will be three gates: one, the gate of Simeon; one, the gate of Issachar; and one, the gate of Zebulun.

³⁴ On the west side, which is 1½ miles, there will be three gates: one, the gate of Gad;

one, the gate of Asher; and one, the gate of Naphtali.

³⁵ The perimeter of the city will be six miles, and the name of the city from that day on will be: "Yahweh Is There."

DANIEL

1 In the third year of the reign of Jehoiakim king of Judah, Nebuchadnezzar king of Babylon came to Jerusalem and laid siege to it. ² The Lord handed Jehoiakim king of Judah over to him, along with some of the vessels from the house of God. Nebuchadnezzar carried them to the land of Babylon, to the house of his god, and put the vessels in the treasury of his god.

³ The king ordered Ashpenaz, the chief of his court officials, to bring some of the Israelites from the royal family and from the nobility— ⁴ young men without any physical defect, good-looking, suitable for instruction in all wisdom, knowledgeable, perceptive, and capable of serving in the king's palace—and to teach them the Chaldean language and literature. ⁵ The king assigned them daily provisions from the royal food and from the wine that he drank. They were to be trained for three years, and at the end of that time they were to serve in the king's court. ⁶ Among them, from the descendants of Judah, were Daniel, Hananiah, Mishael, and Azariah. ⁷ The chief official gave them other names: he gave the name Belteshazzar to Daniel, Shadrach to Hananiah, Meshach to Mishael, and Abednego to Azariah.

⁸ Daniel determined that he would not defile himself with the king's food or with the wine he drank. So he asked permission from the chief official not to defile himself. ⁹ God had granted Daniel favor and compassion from the chief official, ¹⁰ yet he said to Daniel, "My lord the king assigned your food and drink. I'm afraid of what would happen if he saw your faces looking thinner than those of the other young men your age. You would endanger my life with the king."

¹¹ So Daniel said to the guard whom the chief official had assigned to Daniel, Hananiah, Mishael, and Azariah, ¹² "Please test your servants for 10 days. Let us be given vegetables to eat and water to drink. ¹³ Then examine our appearance and the appearance of the young men who are eating the king's food, and deal with your servants based on what you see." ¹⁴ He agreed with them about this and tested them for 10 days. ¹⁵ At the end of 10 days they looked better and healthier than all the young men who were eating the king's food. ¹⁶ So the guard continued to remove their food and the wine they were to drink and gave them vegetables.

¹⁷ God gave these four young men knowledge and understanding in every kind of literature and wisdom. Daniel also understood visions and dreams of every kind. ¹⁸ At the end of the time that the king had said to present them, the chief official presented them to Nebuchadnezzar. ¹⁹ The king interviewed them, and among all of them, no one was found equal to Daniel, Hananiah, Mishael, and Azariah. So they began to serve in the king's court. ²⁰ In every matter of wisdom and understanding that the king consulted them about, he found them 10 times better than all the

diviner-priests and mediums in his entire kingdom. ²¹ Daniel remained there until the first year of King Cyrus.

2 In the second year of his reign, Nebuchadnezzar had dreams that troubled him, and sleep deserted him. ² So the king gave orders to summon the diviner-priests, mediums, sorcerers, and Chaldeans to tell the king his dreams. When they came and stood before the king, ³ he said to them, "I have had a dream and am anxious to understand it."

⁴ The Chaldeans spoke to the king (Aramaic begins here): "May the king live forever. Tell your servants the dream, and we will give the interpretation."

⁵ The king replied to the Chaldeans, "My word is final: If you don't tell me the dream and its interpretation, you will be torn limb from limb, and your houses will be made a garbage dump. ⁶ But if you make the dream and its interpretation known to me, you'll receive gifts, a reward, and great honor from me. So make the dream and its interpretation known to me."

⁷ They answered a second time, "May the king tell the dream to his servants, and we will give the interpretation."

⁸ The king replied, "I know for certain you are trying to gain some time, because you see that my word is final. ⁹ If you don't tell me the dream, there is one decree for you. You have conspired to tell me something false or fraudulent until the situation changes. So tell me the dream and I will know you can give me its interpretation."

¹⁰ The Chaldeans answered the king, "No one on earth can make known what the king requests. Consequently, no king, however great and powerful, has ever asked anything like this of any diviner-priest, medium, or Chaldean. ¹¹ What the king is asking is so difficult that no one can make it known to him except the gods, whose dwelling is not with mortals." ¹² Because of this, the king became violently angry and gave orders to destroy all the wise men of Babylon. ¹³ The decree was issued that the wise men were to be executed, and they searched for Daniel and his friends, to execute them.

¹⁴ Then Daniel responded with tact and discretion to Arioch, the commander of the king's guard, who had gone out to execute the wise men of Babylon. ¹⁵ He asked Arioch, the king's officer, "Why is the decree from the king so harsh?" Then Arioch explained the situation to Daniel. ¹⁶ So Daniel went and asked the king to give him some time, so that he could give the king the interpretation.

¹⁷ Then Daniel went to his house and told his friends Hananiah, Mishael, and Azariah about the matter, ¹⁸ urging them to ask the God of heaven for mercy concerning this mystery, so Daniel and his friends would not be killed with the rest of Babylon's wise men. ¹⁹ The mystery was then revealed to Daniel in a

vision at night, and Daniel praised the God of heaven [20] and declared:

> May the name of God
> be praised forever and ever,
> for wisdom and power belong to Him.
> [21] He changes the times and seasons;
> He removes kings and establishes kings.
> He gives wisdom to the wise
> and knowledge to those
> who have understanding.
> [22] He reveals the deep and hidden things;
> He knows what is in the darkness,
> and light dwells with Him.
> [23] I offer thanks and praise to You,
> God of my fathers,
> because You have given me
> wisdom and power.
> And now You have let me know
> what we asked of You,
> for You have let us know
> the king's mystery.

[24] Therefore Daniel went to Arioch, whom the king had assigned to destroy the wise men of Babylon. He came and said to him, "Don't kill the wise men of Babylon! Bring me before the king, and I will give him the interpretation."

[25] Then Arioch quickly brought Daniel before the king and said to him, "I have found a man among the Judean exiles who can let the king know the interpretation."

[26] The king said in reply to Daniel, whose name was Belteshazzar, "Are you able to tell me the dream I had and its interpretation?"

[27] Daniel answered the king: "No wise man, medium, diviner-priest, or astrologer is able to make known to the king the mystery he asked about. [28] But there is a God in heaven who reveals mysteries, and He has let King Nebuchadnezzar know what will happen in the last days. Your dream and the visions that came into your mind as you lay in bed were these: [29] Your Majesty, while you were in your bed, thoughts came to your mind about what will happen in the future. The revealer of mysteries has let you know what will happen. [30] As for me, this mystery has been revealed to me, not because I have more wisdom than anyone living, but in order that the interpretation might be made known to the king, and that you may understand the thoughts of your mind.

[31] "My king, as you were watching, a colossal statue appeared. That statue, tall and dazzling, was standing in front of you, and its appearance was terrifying. [32] The head of the statue was pure gold, its chest and arms were silver, its stomach and thighs were bronze, [33] its legs were iron, and its feet were partly iron and partly fired clay. [34] As you were watching, a stone broke off without a hand touching it, struck the statue on its feet of iron and fired clay, and crushed them. [35] Then the iron, the fired clay, the bronze, the silver, and the gold were shattered and became like chaff from the summer threshing floors. The wind carried them away, and not a trace of them could be found. But the stone that struck the statue became a great mountain and filled the whole earth.

[36] "This was the dream; now we will tell the king its interpretation. [37] Your Majesty, you are king of kings. The God of heaven has given you sovereignty, power, strength, and glory. [38] Wherever people live—or wild animals, or birds of the air—He has handed them over to you and made you ruler over them all. You are the head of gold.

[39] "After you, there will arise another kingdom, inferior to yours, and then another, a third kingdom, of bronze, which will rule the whole earth. [40] A fourth kingdom will be as strong as iron; for iron crushes and shatters everything, and like iron that smashes, it will crush and smash all the others. [41] You saw the feet and toes, partly of a potter's fired clay and partly of iron—it will be a divided kingdom, though some of the strength of iron will be in it. You saw the iron mixed with clay, [42] and that the toes of the feet were partly iron and partly fired clay—part of the kingdom will be strong, and part will be brittle. [43] You saw the iron mixed with clay—the peoples will mix with one another but will not hold together, just as iron does not mix with fired clay.

[44] "In the days of those kings, the God of heaven will set up a kingdom that will never be destroyed, and this kingdom will not be left to another people. It will crush all these kingdoms and bring them to an end, but will itself endure forever. [45] You saw a stone break off from the mountain without a hand touching it, and it crushed the iron, bronze, fired clay, silver, and gold. The great God has told the king what will happen in the future. The dream is true, and its interpretation certain."

[46] Then King Nebuchadnezzar fell down, paid homage to Daniel, and gave orders to present an offering and incense to him. [47] The king said to Daniel, "Your God is indeed God of gods, Lord of kings, and a revealer of mysteries, since you were able to reveal this mystery." [48] Then the king promoted Daniel and gave him many generous gifts. He made him ruler over the entire province of Babylon and chief governor over all the wise men of Babylon. [49] At Daniel's request, the king appointed Shadrach, Meshach, and Abednego to manage the province of Babylon. But Daniel remained at the king's court.

3 King Nebuchadnezzar made a gold statue, 90 feet high and nine feet wide. He set it up on the plain of Dura in the province of Babylon. [2] King Nebuchadnezzar sent word to assemble the satraps, prefects, governors, advisers, treasurers, judges, magistrates, and all the rulers of the provinces to attend the dedication of the statue King Nebuchadnezzar had set up. [3] So the satraps, prefects, governors, advisers, treasurers, judges, magistrates, and all the rulers of the provinces assembled for the dedication of the statue the king had set up. Then they stood before the statue Nebuchadnezzar had set up.

[4] A herald loudly proclaimed, "People of every nation and language, you are commanded: [5] When you hear the sound of the horn, flute, zither, lyre, harp, drum, and every kind of music, you are to fall down and worship the gold statue that King Nebuchadnezzar has set up. [6] But whoever does not fall down and worship will immediately be thrown into a furnace of blazing fire."

[7] Therefore, when all the people heard the sound of the horn, flute, zither, lyre, harp, and every kind of music, people of every nation and language fell down and worshiped the gold statue that King Nebuchadnezzar had set up.

[8] Some Chaldeans took this occasion to come forward and maliciously accuse the Jews. [9] They said to King Nebuchadnezzar, "May the king live forever.

[10] You as king have issued a decree that everyone who hears the sound of the horn, flute, zither, lyre, harp, drum, and every kind of music must fall down and worship the gold statue. [11] Whoever does not fall down and worship will be thrown into a furnace of blazing fire. [12] There are some Jews you have appointed to manage the province of Babylon: Shadrach, Meshach, and Abednego. These men have ignored you, the king; they do not serve your gods or worship the gold statue you have set up."

[13] Then in a furious rage Nebuchadnezzar gave orders to bring in Shadrach, Meshach, and Abednego. So these men were brought before the king. [14] Nebuchadnezzar asked them, "Shadrach, Meshach, and Abednego, is it true that you don't serve my gods or worship the gold statue I have set up? [15] Now if you're ready, when you hear the sound of the horn, flute, zither, lyre, harp, drum, and every kind of music, fall down and worship the statue I made. But if you don't worship it, you will immediately be thrown into a furnace of blazing fire—and who is the god who can rescue you from my power?"

[16] Shadrach, Meshach, and Abednego replied to the king, "Nebuchadnezzar, we don't need to give you an answer to this question. [17] If the God we serve exists, then He can rescue us from the furnace of blazing fire, and He can rescue us from the power of you, the king. [18] But even if He does not rescue us, we want you as king to know that we will not serve your gods or worship the gold statue you set up."

[19] Then Nebuchadnezzar was filled with rage, and the expression on his face changed toward Shadrach, Meshach, and Abednego. He gave orders to heat the furnace seven times more than was customary, [20] and he commanded some of the strongest soldiers in his army to tie up Shadrach, Meshach, and Abednego and throw them into the furnace of blazing fire. [21] So these men, in their trousers, robes, head coverings, and other clothes, were tied up and thrown into the furnace of blazing fire. [22] Since the king's command was so urgent and the furnace extremely hot, the raging flames killed those men who carried Shadrach, Meshach, and Abednego up. [23] And these three men, Shadrach, Meshach, and Abednego fell, bound, into the furnace of blazing fire.

[24] Then King Nebuchadnezzar jumped up in alarm. He said to his advisers, "Didn't we throw three men, bound, into the fire?"

"Yes, of course, Your Majesty," they replied to the king.

[25] He exclaimed, "Look! I see four men, not tied, walking around in the fire unharmed; and the fourth looks like a son of the gods."

[26] Nebuchadnezzar then approached the door of the furnace of blazing fire and called: "Shadrach, Meshach, and Abednego, you servants of the ˙Most High God—come out!" So Shadrach, Meshach, and Abednego came out of the fire. [27] When the satraps, prefects, governors, and the king's advisers gathered around, they saw that the fire had no effect on the bodies of these men: not a hair of their heads was singed, their robes were unaffected, and there was no smell of fire on them. [28] Nebuchadnezzar exclaimed, "Praise to the God of Shadrach, Meshach, and Abednego! He sent His angel and rescued His servants who trusted in Him. They violated the king's command and risked their lives rather than serve or worship any god except their own God. [29] Therefore I issue a decree that anyone of any people, nation, or language who says anything offensive against the God of Shadrach, Meshach, and Abednego will be torn limb from limb and his house made a garbage dump. For there is no other god who is able to deliver like this." [30] Then the king rewarded Shadrach, Meshach, and Abednego in the province of Babylon.

4 King Nebuchadnezzar,
To those of every people, nation, and language, who live in all the earth:

May your prosperity increase. [2] I am pleased to tell you about the miracles and wonders the ˙Most High God has done for me.

[3]   How great are His miracles,
     and how mighty His wonders!
     His kingdom is an eternal kingdom,
     and His dominion is from generation
         to generation.

[4] I, Nebuchadnezzar, was at ease in my house and flourishing in my palace. [5] I had a dream, and it frightened me; while in my bed, the images and visions in my mind alarmed me. [6] So I issued a decree to bring all the wise men of Babylon to me in order that they might make the dream's interpretation known to me. [7] When the diviner-priests, mediums, Chaldeans, and astrologers came in, I told them the dream, but they could not make its interpretation known to me.

[8] Finally Daniel, named Belteshazzar after the name of my god—and the spirit of the holy gods is in him—came before me. I told him the dream: [9] "Belteshazzar, head of the diviners, because I know that you have a spirit of the holy gods and that no mystery puzzles you, explain to me the visions of my dream that I saw, and its interpretation. [10] In the visions of my mind as I was lying in bed, I saw this:

There was a tree in the middle of the earth,
     and its height was great.
[11]   The tree grew large and strong;
     its top reached to the sky,
     and it was visible to the ends of the earth.
[12]   Its leaves were beautiful, its fruit
         was abundant,
     and on it was food for all.
     Wild animals found shelter under it,
     the birds of the air lived in its branches,
     and every creature was fed from it.

[13] "As I was lying in my bed, I also saw in the visions of my mind an observer, a holy one, coming down from heaven. [14] He called out loudly:

Cut down the tree and chop off its branches;
     strip off its leaves and scatter its fruit.
     Let the animals flee from under it,
     and the birds from its branches.
[15]   But leave the stump with its roots
         in the ground,
     and with a band of iron and bronze around it,
     in the tender grass of the field.
     Let him be drenched with dew from the sky
     and share the plants of the earth
     with the animals.
[16]   Let his mind be changed from that
         of a man,
     and let him be given the mind of an animal
     for seven periods of time.
[17]   This word is by decree of the observers;
     the matter is a command from the holy ones.

This is so the living will know
that the Most High is ruler
over the kingdom of men.
He gives it to anyone He wants
and sets the lowliest of men over it.

[18] This is the dream that I, King Nebuchadnezzar, had. Now, Belteshazzar, tell me the interpretation, because none of the wise men of my kingdom can make the interpretation known to me. But you can, because you have the spirit of the holy gods."

[19] Then Daniel, whose name is Belteshazzar, was stunned for a moment, and his thoughts alarmed him. The king said, "Belteshazzar, don't let the dream or its interpretation alarm you."

Belteshazzar answered, "My lord, may the dream apply to those who hate you, and its interpretation to your enemies! [20] The tree you saw, which grew large and strong, whose top reached to the sky and was visible to all the earth, [21] whose leaves were beautiful and its fruit abundant—and on it was food for all, under it the wild animals lived, and in its branches the birds of the air lived— [22] that tree is you, the king. For you have become great and strong: your greatness has grown and even reaches the sky, and your dominion extends to the ends of the earth.

[23] "The king saw an observer, a holy one, coming down from heaven and saying, 'Cut down the tree and destroy it, but leave the stump with its roots in the ground and with a band of iron and bronze around it, in the tender grass of the field. Let him be drenched with dew from the sky, and share food with the wild animals for seven periods of time.' [24] This is the interpretation, Your Majesty, and this is the sentence of the Most High that has been passed against my lord the king: [25] You will be driven away from people to live with the wild animals. You will feed on grass like cattle and be drenched with dew from the sky for seven periods of time, until you acknowledge that the Most High is ruler over the kingdom of men, and He gives it to anyone He wants. [26] As for the command to leave the tree's stump with its roots, your kingdom will be restored to you as soon as you acknowledge that Heaven rules. [27] Therefore, may my advice seem good to you my king. Separate yourself from your sins by doing what is right, and from your injustices by showing mercy to the needy. Perhaps there will be an extension of your prosperity."

[28] All this happened to King Nebuchadnezzar. [29] At the end of 12 months, as he was walking on the roof of the royal palace in Babylon, [30] the king exclaimed, "Is this not Babylon the Great that I have built by my vast power to be a royal residence and to display my majestic glory?"

[31] While the words were still in the king's mouth, a voice came from heaven: "King Nebuchadnezzar, to you it is declared that the kingdom has departed from you. [32] You will be driven away from people to live with the wild animals, and you will feed on grass like cattle for seven periods of time, until you acknowledge that the Most High is ruler over the kingdom of men, and He gives it to anyone He wants."

[33] At that moment the sentence against Nebuchadnezzar was executed. He was driven away from people. He ate grass like cattle, and his body was drenched with dew from the sky, until his hair grew like eagles' feathers and his nails like birds' claws.

[34] But at the end of those days, I, Nebuchadnezzar, looked up to heaven, and my sanity returned to me. Then I praised the Most High and honored and glorified Him who lives forever:

For His dominion is an everlasting dominion,
and His kingdom is from generation
to generation.
[35]   All the inhabitants of the earth are counted
as nothing,
and He does what He wants with the army
of heaven
and the inhabitants of the earth.
There is no one who can hold back His hand
or say to Him, "What have You done?"

[36] At that time my sanity returned to me, and my majesty and splendor returned to me for the glory of my kingdom. My advisers and my nobles sought me out, I was reestablished over my kingdom, and even more greatness came to me. [37] Now I, Nebuchadnezzar, praise, exalt, and glorify the King of heaven, because all His works are true and His ways are just. He is able to humble those who walk in pride.

5 King Belshazzar held a great feast for 1,000 of his nobles and drank wine in their presence. [2] Under the influence of the wine, Belshazzar gave orders to bring in the gold and silver vessels that his predecessor Nebuchadnezzar had taken from the temple in Jerusalem, so that the king and his nobles, wives, and concubines could drink from them. [3] So they brought in the gold vessels that had been taken from the temple, the house of God in Jerusalem, and the king and his nobles, wives, and concubines drank from them. [4] They drank the wine and praised their gods made of gold and silver, bronze, iron, wood, and stone.

[5] At that moment the fingers of a man's hand appeared and began writing on the plaster of the king's palace wall next to the lampstand. As the king watched the hand that was writing, [6] his face turned pale, and his thoughts so terrified him that his hip joints shook and his knees knocked together. [7] The king called out to bring in the mediums, Chaldeans, and astrologers. He said to these wise men of Babylon, "Whoever reads this inscription and gives me its interpretation will be clothed in purple, have a gold chain around his neck, and have the third highest position in the kingdom." [8] So all the king's wise men came in, but none could read the inscription or make its interpretation known to him. [9] Then King Belshazzar became even more terrified, his face turned pale, and his nobles were bewildered.

[10] Because of the outcry of the king and his nobles, the queen came to the banquet hall. "May the king live forever," she said. "Don't let your thoughts terrify you or your face be pale. [11] There is a man in your kingdom who has the spirit of the holy gods in him. In the days of your predecessor he was found to have insight, intelligence, and wisdom like the wisdom of the gods. Your predecessor, King Nebuchadnezzar, appointed him chief of the diviners, mediums, Chaldeans, and astrologers. Your own predecessor, the king, [12] did this because Daniel, the one the king named Belteshazzar, was found to have an extraordinary spirit, knowledge and perception, and the ability to interpret dreams, explain riddles, and solve problems. Therefore, summon Daniel, and he will give the interpretation."

[13] Then Daniel was brought before the king. The king said to him, "Are you Daniel, one of the Judean exiles that my predecessor the king brought from Ju-

dah? ¹⁴I've heard that you have the spirit of the gods in you, and that you have insight, intelligence, and extraordinary wisdom. ¹⁵Now the wise men and mediums were brought before me to read this inscription and make its interpretation known to me, but they could not give its interpretation. ¹⁶However, I have heard about you that you can give interpretations and solve problems. Therefore, if you can read this inscription and give me its interpretation, you will be clothed in purple, have a gold chain around your neck, and have the third highest position in the kingdom."

¹⁷Then Daniel answered the king, "You may keep your gifts, and give your rewards to someone else; however, I will read the inscription for the king and make the interpretation known to him. ¹⁸Your Majesty, the ˙Most High God gave sovereignty, greatness, glory, and majesty to your predecessor Nebuchadnezzar. ¹⁹Because of the greatness He gave him, all peoples, nations, and languages were terrified and fearful of him. He killed anyone he wanted and kept alive anyone he wanted; he exalted anyone he wanted and humbled anyone he wanted. ²⁰But when his heart was exalted and his spirit became arrogant, he was deposed from his royal throne and his glory was taken from him. ²¹He was driven away from people, his mind was like an animal's, he lived with the wild donkeys, he was fed grass like cattle, and his body was drenched with dew from the sky until he acknowledged that the Most High God is ruler over the kingdom of men and sets anyone He wants over it.

²²"But you his successor, Belshazzar, have not humbled your heart, even though you knew all this. ²³Instead, you have exalted yourself against the Lord of heaven. The vessels from His house were brought to you, and as you and your nobles, wives, and concubines drank wine from them, you praised the gods made of silver and gold, bronze, iron, wood, and stone, which do not see or hear or understand. But you have not glorified the God who holds your life-breath in His hand and who controls the whole course of your life. ²⁴Therefore, He sent the hand, and this writing was inscribed.

²⁵"This is the writing that was inscribed:

MENE, MENE, TEKEL, PARSIN.

²⁶This is the interpretation of the message:
    MENE means that God has numbered the
    days of your kingdom and brought it to an
    end.
²⁷TEKEL means that you have been weighed
    in the balance and found deficient.
²⁸PERES means that your kingdom has been
    divided and given to the Medes and Persians."

²⁹Then Belshazzar gave an order, and they clothed Daniel in purple, placed a gold chain around his neck, and issued a proclamation concerning him that he should be the third ruler in the kingdom. ³⁰That very night Belshazzar the king of the Chaldeans was killed, ³¹and Darius the Mede received the kingdom at the age of 62.

6 Darius decided to appoint 120 satraps over the kingdom, stationed throughout the realm, ²and over them three administrators, including Daniel. These satraps would be accountable to them so that the king would not be defrauded. ³Daniel distinguished himself above the administrators and satraps because he had an extraordinary spirit, so the king planned to set him over the whole realm. ⁴The administrators and

satraps, therefore, kept trying to find a charge against Daniel regarding the kingdom. But they could find no charge or corruption, for he was trustworthy, and no negligence or corruption was found in him. ⁵Then these men said, "We will never find any charge against this Daniel unless we find something against him concerning the law of his God."

⁶So the administrators and satraps went together to the king and said to him, "May King Darius live forever. ⁷All the administrators of the kingdom, the prefects, satraps, advisers, and governors have agreed that the king should establish an ordinance and enforce an edict that for 30 days, anyone who petitions any god or man except you, the king, will be thrown into the lions' den. ⁸Therefore, Your Majesty, establish the edict and sign the document so that, as a law of the Medes and Persians, it is irrevocable and cannot be changed." ⁹So King Darius signed the document.

¹⁰When Daniel learned that the document had been signed, he went into his house. The windows in its upper room opened toward Jerusalem, and three times a day he got down on his knees, prayed, and gave thanks to his God, just as he had done before. ¹¹Then these men went as a group and found Daniel petitioning and imploring his God. ¹²So they approached the king and asked about his edict: "Didn't you sign an edict that for 30 days any man who petitions any god or man except you, the king, will be thrown into the lions' den?"

The king answered, "As a law of the Medes and Persians, the order stands and is irrevocable."

¹³Then they replied to the king, "Daniel, one of the Judean exiles, has ignored you, the king, and the edict you signed, for he prays three times a day." ¹⁴As soon as the king heard this, he was very displeased; he set his mind on rescuing Daniel and made every effort until sundown to deliver him.

¹⁵Then these men went to the king and said to him, "You as king know it is a law of the Medes and Persians that no edict or ordinance the king establishes can be changed."

¹⁶So the king gave the order, and they brought Daniel and threw him into the lions' den. The king said to Daniel, "May your God, whom you serve continually, rescue you!" ¹⁷A stone was brought and placed over the mouth of the den. The king sealed it with his own signet ring and with the signet rings of his nobles, so that nothing in regard to Daniel could be changed. ¹⁸Then the king went to his palace and spent the night fasting. No diversions were brought to him, and he could not sleep.

¹⁹At the first light of dawn the king got up and hurried to the lions' den. ²⁰When he reached the den, he cried out in anguish to Daniel. "Daniel, servant of the living God," the king said, "has your God whom you serve continually been able to rescue you from the lions?"

²¹Then Daniel spoke with the king: "May the king live forever. ²²My God sent His angel and shut the lions' mouths. They haven't hurt me, for I was found innocent before Him. Also, I have not committed a crime against you my king."

²³The king was overjoyed and gave orders to take Daniel out of the den. So Daniel was taken out of the den, uninjured, for he trusted in his God. ²⁴The king then gave the command, and those men who had maliciously accused Daniel were brought and thrown into the lions' den—they, their children, and their wives.

They had not reached the bottom of the den before the lions overpowered them and crushed all their bones.

²⁵ Then King Darius wrote to those of every people, nation, and language who live in all the earth: "May your prosperity abound. ²⁶ I issue a decree that in all my royal dominion, people must tremble in fear before the God of Daniel:

> For He is the living God,
> and He endures forever;
> His kingdom will never be destroyed,
> and His dominion has no end.
> ²⁷ He rescues and delivers;
> He performs signs and wonders
> in the heavens and on the earth,
> for He has rescued Daniel
> from the power of the lions."

²⁸ So Daniel prospered during the reign of Darius and the reign of Cyrus the Persian.

7 In the first year of Belshazzar king of Babylon, Daniel had a dream with visions in his mind as he was lying in his bed. He wrote down the dream, and here is the summary of his account. ² Daniel said, "In my vision at night I was watching, and suddenly the four winds of heaven stirred up the great sea. ³ Four huge beasts came up from the sea, each different from the other.

⁴ "The first was like a lion but had eagle's wings. I continued watching until its wings were torn off. It was lifted up from the ground, set on its feet like a man, and given a human mind.

⁵ "Suddenly, another beast appeared, a second one, that looked like a bear. It was raised up on one side, with three ribs in its mouth between its teeth. It was told, 'Get up! Gorge yourself on flesh.'

⁶ "While I was watching, another beast appeared. It was like a leopard with four wings of a bird on its back. It had four heads and was given authority to rule.

⁷ "While I was watching in the night visions, a fourth beast appeared, frightening and dreadful, and incredibly strong, with large iron teeth. It devoured and crushed, and it trampled with its feet whatever was left. It was different from all the beasts before it, and it had 10 horns.

⁸ "While I was considering the horns, suddenly another horn, a little one, came up among them, and three of the first horns were uprooted before it. There were eyes in this horn like a man's, and it had a mouth that spoke arrogantly.

⁹ "As I kept watching,

> thrones were set in place,
> and the Ancient of Days took His seat.
> His clothing was white like snow,
> and the hair of His head like whitest wool.
> His throne was flaming fire;
> its wheels were blazing fire.
> ¹⁰ A river of fire was flowing,
> coming out from His presence.
> Thousands upon thousands served Him;
> ten thousand times ten thousand
> stood before Him.
> The court was convened,
> and the books were opened.

¹¹ "I watched, then, because of the sound of the arrogant words the horn was speaking. As I continued watching, the beast was killed and its body destroyed and given over to the burning fire. ¹² As for the rest of the beasts, their authority to rule was removed, but an extension of life was granted to them for a certain period of time. ¹³ I continued watching in the night visions,

> and I saw One like a son of man
> coming with the clouds of heaven.
> He approached the Ancient of Days
> and was escorted before Him.
> ¹⁴ He was given authority to rule,
> and glory, and a kingdom;
> so that those of every people,
> nation, and language
> should serve Him.
> His dominion is an everlasting dominion
> that will not pass away,
> and His kingdom is one
> that will not be destroyed.

¹⁵ "As for me, Daniel, my spirit was deeply distressed within me, and the visions in my mind terrified me. ¹⁶ I approached one of those who were standing by and asked him the true meaning of all this. So he let me know the interpretation of these things: ¹⁷ 'These huge beasts, four in number, are four kings who will rise from the earth. ¹⁸ But the holy ones of the 'Most High will receive the kingdom and possess it forever, yes, forever and ever.'

¹⁹ "Then I wanted to know the true meaning of the fourth beast, the one different from all the others, extremely terrifying, with iron teeth and bronze claws, devouring, crushing, and trampling with its feet whatever was left. ²⁰ I also wanted to know about the 10 horns on its head and about the other horn that came up, before which three fell—the horn that had eyes, and a mouth that spoke arrogantly, and that was more visible than the others. ²¹ As I was watching, this horn waged war against the holy ones and was prevailing over them ²² until the Ancient of Days arrived and a judgment was given in favor of the holy ones of the Most High, for the time had come, and the holy ones took possession of the kingdom.

²³ "This is what he said: 'The fourth beast will be a fourth kingdom on the earth, different from all the other kingdoms. It will devour the whole earth, trample it down, and crush it. ²⁴ The 10 horns are 10 kings who will rise from this kingdom. Another, different from the previous ones, will rise after them and subdue three kings. ²⁵ He will speak words against the Most High and oppress the holy ones of the Most High. He will intend to change religious festivals and laws, and the holy ones will be handed over to him for a time, times, and half a time. ²⁶ But the court will convene, and his dominion will be taken away, to be completely destroyed forever. ²⁷ The kingdom, dominion, and greatness of the kingdoms under all of heaven will be given to the people, the holy ones of the Most High. His kingdom will be an everlasting kingdom, and all rulers will serve and obey Him.'

²⁸ "This is the end of the interpretation. As for me, Daniel, my thoughts terrified me greatly, and my face turned pale, but I kept the matter to myself."

8 In the third year of King Belshazzar's reign, a vision appeared to me, Daniel, after the one that had appeared to me earlier. ² I saw the vision, and as I watched, I was in the fortress city of Susa, in the province of Elam. I saw in the vision that I was beside the Ulai Canal. ³ I looked up, and there was a ram standing beside the canal. He had two horns. The two horns were long, but one was longer than the other, and the longer one came up last. ⁴ I saw the ram charging to the west, the north, and the south. No animal could stand against him, and there was no rescue from his power. He did whatever he wanted and became great.

⁵As I was observing, a male goat appeared, coming from the west across the surface of the entire earth without touching the ground. The goat had a conspicuous horn between his eyes. ⁶He came toward the two-horned ram I had seen standing beside the canal and rushed at him with savage fury. ⁷I saw him approaching the ram, and infuriated with him, he struck the ram, shattering his two horns, and the ram was not strong enough to stand against him. The goat threw him to the ground and trampled him, and there was no one to rescue the ram from his power. ⁸Then the male goat became very great, but when he became powerful, the large horn was shattered. Four conspicuous horns came up in its place, pointing toward the four winds of heaven.

⁹From one of them a little horn emerged and grew extensively toward the south and the east and toward the beautiful land. ¹⁰It grew as high as the heavenly ˙host, made some of the stars and some of the host fall to the earth, and trampled them. ¹¹It made itself great, even up to the Prince of the host; it removed His daily sacrifice and overthrew the place of His sanctuary. ¹²Because of rebellion, a host, together with the daily sacrifice, will be given over. The horn will throw truth to the ground and will be successful in whatever it does.

¹³Then I heard a holy one speaking, and another holy one said to the speaker, "How long will the events of this vision last—the daily sacrifice, the rebellion that makes desolate, and the giving over of the sanctuary and of the host to be trampled?"

¹⁴He said to me, "For 2,300 evenings and mornings; then the sanctuary will be restored."

¹⁵While I, Daniel, was watching the vision and trying to understand it, there stood before me someone who appeared to be a man. ¹⁶I heard a human voice calling from the middle of the Ulai: "Gabriel, explain the vision to this man."

¹⁷So he approached where I was standing; when he came near, I was terrified and fell facedown. "Son of man," he said to me, "understand that the vision refers to the time of the end." ¹⁸While he was speaking to me, I fell into a deep sleep, with my face to the ground. Then he touched me, made me stand up, ¹⁹and said, "I am here to tell you what will happen at the conclusion of the time of wrath, because it refers to the appointed time of the end. ²⁰The two-horned ram that you saw represents the kings of Media and Persia. ²¹The shaggy goat represents the king of Greece, and the large horn between his eyes represents the first king. The four horns that took the place of the shattered horn represent four kingdoms. They will rise from that nation, but without its power.

²³ Near the end of their kingdoms,
when the rebels have reached
the full measure of their sin,
an insolent king, skilled in intrigue,
will come to the throne.

²⁴ His power will be great,
but it will not be his own.
He will cause terrible destruction
and succeed in whatever he does.
He will destroy the powerful
along with the holy people.

²⁵ He will cause deceit to prosper
through his cunning and by his influence,
and in his own mind he will
make himself great.
He will destroy many in a time of peace;
he will even stand against the Prince
of princes.
Yet he will be shattered—not by
human hands.

²⁶ The vision of the evenings and the mornings
that has been told is true.
Now you must seal up the vision
because it refers to many days in the future."

²⁷I, Daniel, was overcome and lay sick for days. Then I got up and went about the king's business. I was greatly disturbed by the vision and could not understand it.

9 In the first year of Darius, the son of Ahasuerus, a Mede by birth, who was ruler over the kingdom of the Chaldeans: ²In the first year of his reign, I, Daniel, understood from the books according to the word of the Lᴏʀᴅ to Jeremiah the prophet that the number of years for the desolation of Jerusalem would be 70. ³So I turned my attention to the Lord God to seek Him by prayer and petitions, with fasting, ˙sackcloth, and ashes.

⁴I prayed to the Lᴏʀᴅ my God and confessed:
Ah, Lord—the great and awe-inspiring God who keeps His gracious covenant with those who love Him and keep His commands— ⁵we have sinned, done wrong, acted wickedly, rebelled, and turned away from Your commands and ordinances. ⁶We have not listened to Your servants the prophets, who spoke in Your name to our kings, leaders, fathers, and all the people of the land.

⁷Lord, righteousness belongs to You, but this day public shame belongs to us: the men of Judah, the residents of Jerusalem, and all Israel—those who are near and those who are far, in all the countries where You have dispersed them because of the disloyalty they have shown toward You. ⁸Lᴏʀᴅ, public shame belongs to us, our kings, our leaders, and our fathers, because we have sinned against You. ⁹Compassion and forgiveness belong to the Lord our God, though we have rebelled against Him ¹⁰and have not obeyed the voice of the Lᴏʀᴅ our God by following His instructions that He set before us through His servants the prophets.

¹¹All Israel has broken Your law and turned away, refusing to obey You. The promised curse written in the law of Moses, the servant of God, has been poured out on us because we have sinned against Him. ¹²He has carried out His words that He spoke against us and against our rulers by bringing on us so great a disaster that nothing like what has been done to Jerusalem has ever been done under all of heaven. ¹³Just as it is written in the law of Moses, all this disaster has come on us, yet we have not appeased the Lᴏʀᴅ our God by turning from our iniquities and paying attention to Your truth. ¹⁴So the Lᴏʀᴅ kept the disaster in mind and brought it on us, for the Lᴏʀᴅ our God is righteous in all He has done. But we have not obeyed Him.

¹⁵Now, Lord our God, who brought Your people

out of the land of Egypt with a mighty hand and made Your name renowned as it is this day, we have sinned, we have acted wickedly. ¹⁶Lord, in keeping with all Your righteous acts, may Your anger and wrath turn away from Your city Jerusalem, Your holy mountain; for because of our sins and the iniquities of our fathers, Jerusalem and Your people have become an object of ridicule to all those around us.

¹⁷Therefore, our God, hear the prayer and the petitions of Your servant. Show Your favor to Your desolate sanctuary for the Lord's sake. ¹⁸Listen, my God, and hear. Open Your eyes and see our desolations and the city called by Your name. For we are not presenting our petitions before You based on our righteous acts, but based on Your abundant compassion. ¹⁹Lord, hear! Lord, forgive! Lord, listen and act! My God, for Your own sake, do not delay, because Your city and Your people are called by Your name.

²⁰While I was speaking, praying, confessing my sin and the sin of my people Israel, and presenting my petition before •Yahweh my God concerning the holy mountain of my God— ²¹while I was praying, Gabriel, the man I had seen in the first vision, came to me in my extreme weariness, about the time of the evening offering. ²²He gave me this explanation: "Daniel, I've come now to give you understanding. ²³At the beginning of your petitions an answer went out, and I have come to give it, for you are treasured by God. So consider the message and understand the vision:

²⁴   Seventy weeks are decreed
        about your people and your holy city—
    to bring the rebellion to an end,
    to put a stop to sin,
    to wipe away iniquity,
    to bring in everlasting righteousness,
    to seal up vision and prophecy,
    and to anoint the most holy place.
²⁵   Know and understand this:
    From the issuing of the decree
        to restore and rebuild Jerusalem
    until •Messiah the Prince
        will be seven weeks and 62 weeks.
    It will be rebuilt with a plaza and a moat,
    but in difficult times.
²⁶   After those 62 weeks
        the Messiah will be cut off
        and will have nothing.
    The people of the coming prince
        will destroy the city and the sanctuary.
    The end will come with a flood,
    and until the end there will be war;
        desolations are decreed.
²⁷   He will make a firm covenant
        with many for one week,
    but in the middle of the week
    he will put a stop to sacrifice and offering.
    And the abomination of desolation
        will be on a wing of the temple
    until the decreed destruction
    is poured out on the desolator."

10 In the third year of Cyrus king of Persia, a message was revealed to Daniel, who was named Belteshazzar. The message was true and was about a great conflict. He understood the message and had understanding of the vision.

²In those days I, Daniel, was mourning for three full weeks. ³I didn't eat any rich food, no meat or wine entered my mouth, and I didn't put any oil on my body until the three weeks were over. ⁴On the twenty-fourth day of the first month, as I was standing on the bank of the great river, the Tigris, ⁵I looked up, and there was a man dressed in linen, with a belt of gold from Uphaz around his waist. ⁶His body was like topaz, his face like the brilliance of lightning, his eyes like flaming torches, his arms and feet like the gleam of polished bronze, and the sound of his words like the sound of a multitude.

⁷Only I, Daniel, saw the vision. The men who were with me did not see it, but a great terror fell on them, and they ran and hid. ⁸I was left alone, looking at this great vision. No strength was left in me; my face grew deathly pale, and I was powerless. ⁹I heard the words he said, and when I heard them I fell into a deep sleep, with my face to the ground.

¹⁰Suddenly, a hand touched me and raised me to my hands and knees. ¹¹He said to me, "Daniel, you are a man treasured by God. Understand the words that I'm saying to you. Stand on your feet, for I have now been sent to you." After he said this to me, I stood trembling.

¹²"Don't be afraid, Daniel," he said to me, "for from the first day that you purposed to understand and to humble yourself before your God, your prayers were heard. I have come because of your prayers. ¹³But the prince of the kingdom of Persia opposed me for 21 days. Then Michael, one of the chief princes, came to help me after I had been left there with the kings of Persia. ¹⁴Now I have come to help you understand what will happen to your people in the last days, for the vision refers to those days."

¹⁵While he was saying these words to me, I turned my face toward the ground and was speechless. ¹⁶Suddenly one with human likeness touched my lips. I opened my mouth and said to the one standing in front of me, "My lord, because of the vision, anguish overwhelms me and I am powerless. ¹⁷How can someone like me, your servant, speak with someone like you, my lord? Now I have no strength, and there is no breath in me."

¹⁸Then the one with human likeness touched me again and strengthened me. ¹⁹He said, "Don't be afraid, you who are treasured by God. Peace to you; be very strong!"

As he spoke to me, I was strengthened and said, "Let my lord speak, for you have strengthened me."

²⁰He said, "Do you know why I've come to you? I must return at once to fight against the prince of Persia, and when I leave, the prince of Greece will come. ²¹No one has the courage to support me against them except Michael, your prince. However, I will tell you what is recorded in the book of truth.

11 ¹In the first year of Darius the Mede, I stood up to strengthen and protect him. ²Now I will tell you the truth.

"Three more kings will arise in Persia, and the fourth will be far richer than the others. By the power he gains through his riches, he will stir up everyone against the kingdom of Greece. ³Then a warrior king will arise; he will rule a vast realm and do whatever he wants. ⁴But as soon as he is established, his kingdom will be broken up and divided to the four winds of heaven, but not to his descendants; it will not be the same kingdom that he ruled, because his kingdom will be uprooted and will go to others besides them.

⁵ "The king of the South will grow powerful, but one of his commanders will grow more powerful and will rule a kingdom greater than his. ⁶ After some years they will form an alliance, and the daughter of the king of the South will go to the king of the North to seal the agreement. She will not retain power, and his strength will not endure. She will be given up, together with her entourage, her father, and the one who supported her during those times. ⁷ In the place of the king of the South, one from her family will rise up, come against the army, and enter the fortress of the king of the North. He will take action against them and triumph. ⁸ He will take even their gods captive to Egypt, with their metal images and their precious articles of silver and gold. For some years he will stay away from the king of the North, ⁹ who will enter the kingdom of the king of the South and then return to his own land.

¹⁰ "His sons will mobilize for war and assemble a large number of armed forces. They will advance, sweeping through like a flood, and will again wage war as far as his fortress. ¹¹ Infuriated, the king of the South will march out to fight with the king of the North who will raise a large army but they will be handed over to his enemy. ¹² When the army is carried off, he will become arrogant and cause tens of thousands to fall, but he will not triumph. ¹³ The king of the North will again raise a multitude larger than the first. After some years he will advance with a great army and many supplies.

¹⁴ "In those times many will rise up against the king of the South. Violent ones among your own people will assert themselves to fulfill a vision, but they will fail. ¹⁵ Then the king of the North will come, build up an assault ramp, and capture a well-fortified city. The forces of the South will not stand; even their select troops will not be able to resist. ¹⁶ The king of the North who comes against him will do whatever he wants, and no one can oppose him. He will establish himself in the beautiful land with total destruction in his hand. ¹⁷ He will resolve to come with the force of his whole kingdom and will reach an agreement with him. He will give him a daughter in marriage to destroy it, but she will not stand with him or support him. ¹⁸ Then he will turn his attention to the coasts and islands and capture many. But a commander will put an end to his taunting; instead, he will turn his taunts against him. ¹⁹ He will turn his attention back to the fortresses of his own land, but he will stumble, fall, and be no more.

²⁰ "In his place one will arise who will send out a tax collector for the glory of the kingdom; but within a few days he will be shattered, though not in anger or in battle.

²¹ "In his place a despised person will arise; royal honors will not be given to him, but he will come during a time of peace and seize the kingdom by intrigue. ²² A flood of forces will be swept away before him; they will be shattered, as well as the covenant prince. ²³ After an alliance is made with him, he will act deceitfully. He will rise to power with a small nation. ²⁴ During a time of peace, he will come into the richest parts of the province and do what his fathers and predecessors never did. He will lavish plunder, loot, and wealth on his followers, and he will make plans against fortified cities, but only for a time.

²⁵ "With a large army he will stir up his power and his courage against the king of the South. The king of the South will prepare for battle with an extremely large and powerful army, but he will not succeed, because plots will be made against him. ²⁶ Those who eat his provisions will destroy him; his army will be swept away, and many will fall slain. ²⁷ The two kings, whose hearts are bent on evil, will speak lies at the same table but to no avail, for still the end will come at the appointed time. ²⁸ The king of the North will return to his land with great wealth, but his heart will be set against the holy covenant; he will take action, then return to his own land.

²⁹ "At the appointed time he will come again to the South, but this time will not be like the first. ³⁰ Ships of Kittim will come against him, and being intimidated, he will withdraw. Then he will rage against the holy covenant and take action. On his return, he will favor those who abandon the holy covenant. ³¹ His forces will rise up and desecrate the temple fortress. They will abolish the daily sacrifice and set up the abomination of desolation. ³² With flattery he will corrupt those who act wickedly toward the covenant, but the people who know their God will be strong and take action. ³³ Those who are wise among the people will give understanding to many, yet they will die by sword and flame, and be captured and plundered for a time. ³⁴ When defeated, they will be helped by some, but many others will join them insincerely. ³⁵ Some of the wise will fall so that they may be refined, purified, and cleansed until the time of the end, for it will still come at the appointed time.

³⁶ "Then the king will do whatever he wants. He will exalt and magnify himself above every god, and he will say outrageous things against the God of gods. He will be successful until the time of wrath is completed, because what has been decreed will be accomplished. ³⁷ He will not show regard for the gods of his fathers, the god longed for by women, or for any other god, because he will magnify himself above all. ³⁸ Instead, he will honor a god of fortresses—a god his fathers did not know—with gold, silver, precious stones, and riches. ³⁹ He will deal with the strongest fortresses with the help of a foreign god. He will greatly honor those who acknowledge him, making them rulers over many and distributing land as a reward.

⁴⁰ "At the time of the end, the king of the South will engage him in battle, but the king of the North will storm against him with chariots, horsemen, and many ships. He will invade countries and sweep through them like a flood. ⁴¹ He will also invade the beautiful land, and many will fall. But these will escape from his power: Edom, Moab, and the prominent people of the Ammonites. ⁴² He will extend his power against the countries, and not even the land of Egypt will escape. ⁴³ He will get control over the hidden treasures of gold and silver and over all the riches of Egypt. The Libyans and •Cushites will also be in submission. ⁴⁴ But reports from the east and the north will terrify him, and he will go out with great fury to annihilate and •completely destroy many. ⁴⁵ He will pitch his royal tents between the sea and the beautiful holy mountain, but he will meet his end with no one to help him.

12 At that time
Michael the great prince
    who stands watch over your people
    will rise up.
There will be a time of distress
    such as never has occurred

since nations came into being until that time.
But at that time all your people
who are found written in the book will escape.
² Many of those who sleep in the dust
of the earth will awake,
some to eternal life,
and some to shame and eternal contempt.
³ Those who are wise will shine
like the bright expanse of the heavens,
and those who lead many to righteousness,
like the stars forever and ever.

⁴"But you, Daniel, keep these words secret and seal the book until the time of the end. Many will roam about, and knowledge will increase."

⁵ Then I, Daniel, looked, and two others were standing there, one on this bank of the river and one on the other. ⁶ One of them said to the man dressed in linen, who was above the waters of the river, "How long until the end of these extraordinary things?" ⁷ Then I heard the man dressed in linen, who was above the waters of the river. He raised both his hands toward heaven and swore by Him who lives eternally that it would be for a time, times, and half a time. When the power of the holy people is shattered, all these things will be completed.

⁸I heard but did not understand. So I asked, "My lord, what will be the outcome of these things?"

⁹He said, "Go on your way, Daniel, for the words are secret and sealed until the time of the end. ¹⁰Many will be purified, cleansed, and refined, but the wicked will act wickedly; none of the wicked will understand, but the wise will understand. ¹¹From the time the daily sacrifice is abolished and the abomination of desolation is set up, there will be 1,290 days. ¹²The one who waits for and reaches 1,335 days is blessed. ¹³But as for you, go on your way to the end; you will rest, then rise to your destiny at the end of the days."

HOSEA

1 The word of the LORD that came to Hosea son of Beeri during the reigns of Uzziah, Jotham, Ahaz, and Hezekiah, kings of Judah, and of Jeroboam son of Jehoash, king of Israel.

²When the LORD first spoke to Hosea, He said this to him:

Go and marry a promiscuous wife
and have children of promiscuity,
for the land is committing
blatant acts of promiscuity
by abandoning the LORD.

³So he went and married Gomer daughter of Diblaim, and she conceived and bore him a son. ⁴Then the LORD said to him:

Name him Jezreel, for in a little while
I will bring the bloodshed of Jezreel
on the house of Jehu
and put an end to the kingdom of the house
of Israel.

⁵ On that day I will break the bow of Israel
in the Valley of Jezreel.

⁶She conceived again and gave birth to a daughter, and the LORD said to him:

Name her No Compassion,
for I will no longer have compassion
on the house of Israel.
I will certainly take them away.

⁷ But I will have compassion on the house
of Judah,
and I will deliver them by the LORD their God.
I will not deliver them by bow, sword, or war,
or by horses and cavalry.

⁸After Gomer had weaned No Compassion, she conceived and gave birth to a son. ⁹Then the LORD said:

Name him Not My People,
for you are not My people,
and I will not be your God.

¹⁰ Yet the number of the Israelites
will be like the sand of the sea,
which cannot be measured or counted.
And in the place where they were told:
You are not My people,
they will be called: Sons of the living God.

¹¹ And the Judeans and the Israelites
will be gathered together.
They will appoint for themselves a single ruler
and go up from the land.
For the day of Jezreel will be great.

2 Call your brothers: My People
and your sisters: Compassion.

² Rebuke your mother; rebuke her.
For she is not My wife and I am not
her husband.
Let her remove the promiscuous look
from her face
and her adultery from between her breasts.

³ Otherwise, I will strip her naked
and expose her as she was on the day
of her birth.
I will make her like a desert
and like a parched land,
and I will let her die of thirst.

⁴ I will have no compassion on her children
because they are the children of promiscuity.

⁵ Yes, their mother is promiscuous;
she conceived them and acted shamefully.
For she thought, "I will go after my lovers,
the men who give me my food and water,
my wool and flax, my oil and drink."

⁶ Therefore, this is what I will do:
I will block her way with thorns;
I will enclose her with a wall,
so that she cannot find her paths.

⁷ She will pursue her lovers but not catch them;
she will seek them but not find them.
Then she will think,
"I will go back to my former husband,
for then it was better for me than now."

⁸ She does not recognize
that it is I who gave her the grain,
the new wine, and the oil.
I lavished silver and gold on her,
which they used for *Baal.

⁹ Therefore, I will take back My grain in its time

and My new wine in its season;
I will take away My wool and linen,
which were to cover her nakedness.
¹⁰ Now I will expose her shame
in the sight of her lovers,
and no one will rescue her from My hands.
¹¹ I will put an end to all her celebrations:
her feasts, New Moons, and Sabbaths—
all her festivals.
¹² I will devastate her vines and fig trees.
She thinks that these are her wages
that her lovers have given her.
I will turn them into a thicket,
and the wild animals will eat them.
¹³ And I will punish her for the days of the Baals
when she burned incense to them,
put on her rings and jewelry,
and went after her lovers,
but forgot Me.
This is the LORD's declaration.
¹⁴ Therefore, I am going to persuade her,
lead her to the wilderness,
and speak tenderly to her.
¹⁵ There I will give her vineyards back to her
and make the Valley of Achor
into a gateway of hope.
There she will respond as she did
in the days of her youth,
as in the day she came out of the land
of Egypt.
¹⁶ In that day—
this is the LORD's declaration—
you will call Me, "My husband,"
and no longer call Me, "My Baal."
¹⁷ For I will remove the names of the Baals
from her mouth;
they will no longer be remembered
by their names.
¹⁸ On that day I will make a covenant for them
with the wild animals, the birds of the sky,
and the creatures that crawl on the ground.
I will shatter bow, sword,
and weapons of war in the land
and will enable the people to rest securely.
¹⁹ I will take you to be My wife forever.
I will take you to be My wife in righteousness,
justice, love, and compassion.
²⁰ I will take you to be My wife in faithfulness,
and you will know •Yahweh.
²¹ On that day I will respond—
this is the LORD's declaration.
I will respond to the sky,
and it will respond to the earth.
²² The earth will respond to the grain,
the new wine, and the oil,
and they will respond to Jezreel.
²³ I will sow her in the land for Myself,
and I will have compassion
on No Compassion;
I will say to Not My People:
You are My people,
and he will say, "You are My God."

3 Then the LORD said to me, "Go again; show love to
a woman who is loved by another man and is an
adulteress, just as the LORD loves the Israelites though
they turn to other gods and love raisin cakes."
²So I bought her for 15 •shekels of silver and five
bushels of barley. ³I said to her, "You must live with
me many days. Don't be promiscuous or belong to any
man, and I will act the same way toward you."

⁴For the Israelites must live many days without king
or prince, without sacrifice or sacred pillar, and without •ephod or household idols. ⁵Afterward, the people
of Israel will return and seek the LORD their God and
David their king. They will come with awe to the LORD
and to His goodness in the last days.

4 Hear the word of the LORD, people of Israel,
for the LORD has a case
against the inhabitants of the land:
There is no truth, no faithful love,
and no knowledge of God in the land!
² Cursing, lying, murder, stealing,
and adultery are rampant;
one act of bloodshed follows another.
³ For this reason the land mourns,
and everyone who lives in it languishes,
along with the wild animals and the birds
of the sky;
even the fish of the sea disappear.
⁴ But let no one dispute; let no one argue,
for My case is against you priests.
⁵ You will stumble by day;
the prophet will also stumble with you
by night.
And I will destroy your mother.
⁶ My people are destroyed for lack of knowledge.
Because you have rejected knowledge,
I will reject you from serving as My priest.
Since you have forgotten the law of your God,
I will also forget your sons.
⁷ The more they multiplied,
the more they sinned against Me.
I will change their honor into disgrace.
⁸ They feed on the sin of My people;
they have an appetite for their transgressions.
⁹ The same judgment will happen
to both people and priests.
I will punish them for their ways
and repay them for their deeds.
¹⁰ They will eat but not be satisfied;
they will be promiscuous but not multiply.
For they have abandoned their devotion
to the LORD.
¹¹ Promiscuity, wine, and new wine
take away one's understanding.
¹² My people consult their wooden idols,
and their divining rods inform them.
For a spirit of promiscuity leads them astray;
they act promiscuously
in disobedience to their God.
¹³ They sacrifice on the mountaintops,
and they burn offerings on the hills,
and under oaks, poplars, and terebinths,
because their shade is pleasant.
And so your daughters act promiscuously
and your daughters-in-law commit adultery.
¹⁴ I will not punish your daughters
when they act promiscuously
or your daughters-in-law
when they commit adultery,
for the men themselves go off with prostitutes
and make sacrifices with cult prostitutes.
People without discernment are doomed.
¹⁵ Israel, if you act promiscuously,

don't let Judah become *guilty!
Do not go to Gilgal
or make a pilgrimage to Beth-aven,
and do not swear an oath: As the LORD lives!
16 For Israel is as obstinate as a stubborn cow.
Can the LORD now shepherd them
like a lamb in an open meadow?
17 Ephraim is attached to idols;
leave him alone!
18 When their drinking is over,
they turn to promiscuity.
Israel's leaders fervently love disgrace.
19 A wind with its wings will carry them off,
and they will be ashamed of their sacrifices.

5 Hear this, priests!
Pay attention, house of Israel!
Listen, royal house!
For the judgment applies to you
because you have been a snare at Mizpah
and a net spread out on Tabor.
2 Rebels are deeply involved in slaughter;
I will be a punishment for all of them.
3 I know Ephraim,
and Israel is not hidden from Me.
For now, Ephraim,
you have acted promiscuously;
Israel is defiled.
4 Their actions do not allow them
to return to their God,
for a spirit of promiscuity is among them,
and they do not know the LORD.
5 Israel's arrogance testifies against them.
Both Israel and Ephraim stumble
because of their wickedness;
even Judah will stumble with them.
6 They go with their flocks and herds
to seek the LORD
but do not find Him;
He has withdrawn from them.
7 They betrayed the LORD;
indeed, they gave birth
to illegitimate children.
Now the New Moon will devour them
along with their fields.
8 Blow the horn in Gibeah,
the trumpet in Ramah;
raise the war cry in Beth-aven:
After you, Benjamin!
9 Ephraim will become a desolation
on the day of punishment;
I announce what is certain
among the tribes of Israel.
10 The princes of Judah are like those
who move boundary markers;
I will pour out My fury on them like water.
11 Ephraim is oppressed,
crushed in judgment,
for he is determined to follow
what is worthless.
12 So I am like rot to Ephraim
and like decay to the house of Judah.
13 When Ephraim saw his sickness
and Judah his wound,
Ephraim went to Assyria
and sent a delegation to the great king.
But he cannot cure you or heal
your wound.

14 For I am like a lion to Ephraim
and like a young lion to the house of Judah.
Yes, I will tear them to pieces and depart.
I will carry them off,
and no one can rescue them.
15 I will depart and return to My place
until they recognize their *guilt and seek
My face;
they will search for Me in their distress.

6 Come, let us return to the LORD.
For He has torn us,
and He will heal us;
He has wounded us,
and He will bind up our wounds.
2 He will revive us after two days,
and on the third day He will raise us up
so we can live in His presence.
3 Let us strive to know the LORD.
His appearance is as sure as the dawn.
He will come to us like the rain,
like the spring showers that water the land.
4 What am I going to do with you, Ephraim?
What am I going to do with you, Judah?
Your loyalty is like the morning mist
and like the early dew that vanishes.
5 This is why I have used the prophets
to cut them down;
I have killed them with the words
of My mouth.
My judgment strikes like lightning.
6 For I desire loyalty and not sacrifice,
the knowledge of God rather than
*burnt offerings.
7 But they, like Adam, have violated
the covenant;
there they have betrayed Me.
8 Gilead is a city of evildoers,
tracked with bloody footprints.
9 Like raiders who wait in ambush for someone,
a band of priests murders on the road
to Shechem.
They commit atrocities.
10 I have seen something horrible in the house
of Israel:
Ephraim's promiscuity is there;
Israel is defiled.
11 A harvest is also appointed for you, Judah.
When I return My people from captivity,

7 ¹when I heal Israel,
the sins of Ephraim and the crimes of Samaria
will be exposed.
For they practice fraud;
a thief breaks in;
a raiding party pillages outside.
2 But they never consider that I remember
all their evil.
Now their sins are all around them;
they are right in front of My face.
3 They please the king with their evil,
the princes with their lies.
4 All of them commit adultery;
they are like an oven heated by a baker
who stops stirring the fire
from the kneading of the dough
until it is leavened.
5 On the day of our king,
the princes are sick with the heat of wine—

there is a conspiracy with traitors.

6 For they—their hearts like an oven—
draw him into their oven.
Their anger smolders all night;
in the morning it blazes like a flaming fire.

7 All of them are as hot as an oven,
and they consume their rulers.
All their kings fall;
not one of them calls on Me.

8 Ephraim has allowed himself to get mixed up
　with the nations.
Ephraim is unturned bread
　baked on a griddle.

9 Foreigners consume his strength,
but he does not notice.
Even his hair is streaked with gray,
but he does not notice.

10 Israel's arrogance testifies against them,
yet they do not return to *Yahweh their God,
and for all this, they do not seek Him.

11 So Ephraim has become like a silly,
　senseless dove;
they call to Egypt, and they go to Assyria.

12 As they are going, I will spread My net
　over them;
I will bring them down like birds of the sky.
I will discipline them in accordance
with the news that reaches their assembly.

13 Woe to them, for they fled from Me;
destruction to them, for they rebelled
　against Me!
Though I want to redeem them,
they speak lies against Me.

14 They do not cry to Me from their hearts;
rather, they wail on their beds.
They slash themselves for grain and new wine;
they turn away from Me.

15 I trained and strengthened their arms,
but they plot evil against Me.

16 They turn, but not to what is above;
they are like a faulty bow.
Their leaders will fall by the sword
because of the cursing of their tongue.
They will be ridiculed for this in the land
　of Egypt.

8 Put the horn to your mouth!
One like an eagle comes
against the house of the LORD,
because they transgress My covenant
and rebel against My law.

2 Israel cries out to Me,
"My God, we know You!"

3 Israel has rejected what is good;
an enemy will pursue him.

4 They have installed kings,
but not through Me.
They have appointed leaders,
but without My approval.
They make their silver and gold
into idols for themselves
for their own destruction.

5 Your calf-idol is rejected, Samaria.
My anger burns against them.
How long will they be incapable of innocence?

6 For this thing is from Israel—
a craftsman made it, and it is not God.
The calf of Samaria will be smashed to bits!

7 Indeed, they sow the wind
and reap the whirlwind.
There is no standing grain;
what sprouts fails to yield flour.
Even if they did,
foreigners would swallow it up.

8 Israel is swallowed up!
Now they are among the nations
like discarded pottery.

9 For they have gone up to Assyria
like a wild donkey going off on its own.
Ephraim has paid for love.

10 Even though they hire lovers
　among the nations,
I will now round them up,
and they will begin to decrease in number
under the burden of the king and leaders.

11 When Ephraim multiplied his altars for sin,
they became his altars for sinning.

12 Though I were to write out for him
ten thousand points of My instruction,
they would be regarded as something strange.

13 Though they offer sacrificial gifts
and eat the flesh,
the LORD does not accept them.
Now He will remember their *guilt
and punish their sins;
they will return to Egypt.

14 Israel has forgotten his Maker
　and built palaces;
Judah has also multiplied fortified cities.
I will send fire on their cities,
and it will consume their citadels.

9 Israel, do not rejoice jubilantly
　as the nations do,
for you have acted promiscuously,
　leaving your God.
You have loved the wages of a prostitute
on every grain-threshing floor.

2 Threshing floor and wine vat will not
　sustain them,
and the new wine will fail them.

3 They will not stay in the land of the LORD.
Instead, Ephraim will return to Egypt,
and they will eat *unclean food in Assyria.

4 They will not pour out
their wine offerings to the LORD,
and their sacrifices will not please Him.
Their food will be like the bread of mourners;
all who eat it become defiled.
For their bread will be
　for their appetites alone;
it will not enter the house of the LORD.

5 What will you do on a festival day,
on the day of the LORD's feast?

6 For even if they flee from devastation,
Egypt will gather them, and Memphis
　will bury them.
Thistles will take possession
　of their precious silver;
thorns will invade their tents.

7 The days of punishment have come;
the days of retribution have come.
Let Israel recognize it!
The prophet is a fool,
and the inspired man is insane,
because of the magnitude

of your *guilt and hostility.

8 Ephraim's watchman is with my God.
The prophet encounters a fowler's snare
on all his ways.
Hostility is in the house of his God!

9 They have deeply corrupted themselves
as in the days of Gibeah.
He will remember their guilt;
He will punish their sins.

10 I discovered Israel
like grapes in the wilderness.
I saw your fathers
like the first fruit of the fig tree
in its first season.
But they went to Baal-peor,
consecrated themselves to Shame,
and became detestable,
like the thing they loved.

11 Ephraim's glory will fly away like a bird:
no birth, no gestation, no conception.

12 Even if they raise children,
I will bereave them of each one.
Yes, woe to them when I depart from them!

13 I have seen Ephraim like Tyre,
planted in a meadow,
so Ephraim will bring out his children
to the executioner.

14 Give them, Lord—
What should You give?
Give them a womb that miscarries
and breasts that are dry!

15 All their evil appears at Gilgal,
for there I came to hate them.
I will drive them from My house
because of their evil, wicked actions.
I will no longer love them;
all their leaders are rebellious.

16 Ephraim is struck down;
their roots are withered;
they cannot bear fruit.
Even if they bear children,
I will kill the precious offspring
of their wombs.

17 My God will reject them
because they have not listened to Him;
they will become wanderers
among the nations.

10

Israel is a lush vine;
it yields fruit for itself.
The more his fruit increased,
the more he increased the altars.
The better his land produced,
the better they made the sacred pillars.

2 Their hearts are devious;
now they must bear their *guilt.
The Lord will break down their altars
and demolish their sacred pillars.

3 In fact, they are now saying,
"We have no king!
For we do not *fear the Lord.
What can a king do for us?"

4 They speak mere words,
taking false oaths while making covenants.
So lawsuits break out
like poisonous weeds in the furrows of a field.

5 The residents of Samaria will have anxiety
over the calf of Beth-aven.

Indeed, its idolatrous priests rejoiced over it;
the people will mourn over it,
over its glory.
It will certainly depart from them.

6 The calf itself will be taken to Assyria
as an offering to the great king.
Ephraim will experience shame;
Israel will be ashamed of its counsel.

7 Samaria's king will disappear
like foam on the surface of the water.

8 The *high places of Aven, the sin of Israel,
will be destroyed;
thorns and thistles will grow over their altars.
They will say to the mountains,
"Cover us!"
and to the hills, "Fall on us!"

9 Israel, you have sinned
since the days of Gibeah;
they have taken their stand there.
Will not war against the unjust
overtake them in Gibeah?

10 I will discipline them at My discretion;
nations will be gathered against them
to put them in bondage
for their two crimes.

11 Ephraim is a well-trained calf
that loves to thresh,
but I will place a yoke on her fine neck.
I will harness Ephraim;
Judah will plow;
Jacob will do the final plowing.

12 Sow righteousness for yourselves
and reap faithful love;
break up your unplowed ground.
It is time to seek the Lord
until He comes and sends righteousness
on you like the rain.

13 You have plowed wickedness
and reaped injustice;
you have eaten the fruit of lies.
Because you have trusted in your own way
and in your large number of soldiers,

14 the roar of battle will rise against your people,
and all your fortifications will be demolished
in a day of war,
like Shalman's destruction of Beth-arbel.
Mothers will be dashed to pieces
along with their children.

15 So it will be done to you, Bethel,
because of your extreme evil.
At dawn the king of Israel will be
totally destroyed.

11

When Israel was a child, I loved him,
and out of Egypt I called My son.

2 The more they called them,
the more they departed from Me.
They kept sacrificing to the *Baals
and burning offerings to idols.

3 It was I who taught Ephraim to walk,
taking them in My arms,
but they never knew that I healed them.

4 I led them with human cords,
with ropes of love.
To them I was like one
who eases the yoke from their jaws;
I bent down to give them food.

5 Israel will not return to the land of Egypt

and Assyria will be his king,
because they refused to repent.
⁶ A sword will whirl through his cities;
it will destroy and devour the bars of his gates,
because of their schemes.
⁷ My people are bent on turning from Me.
Though they call to Him on high,
He will not exalt them at all.
⁸ How can I give you up, Ephraim?
How can I surrender you, Israel?
How can I make you like Admah?
How can I treat you like Zeboiim?
I have had a change of heart;
My compassion is stirred!
⁹ I will not vent the full fury of My anger;
I will not turn back to destroy Ephraim.
For I am God and not man,
the Holy One among you;
I will not come in rage.
¹⁰ They will follow the LORD;
He will roar like a lion.
When He roars,
His children will come trembling
from the west.
¹¹ They will be roused like birds from Egypt
and like doves from the land of Assyria.
Then I will settle them in their homes.
                This is the LORD's declaration.
¹² Ephraim surrounds me with lies,
the house of Israel, with deceit.
Judah still wanders with God
and is faithful to the holy ones.

12

Ephraim chases the wind
and pursues the east wind.
He continually multiplies lies and violence.
He makes a covenant with Assyria,
and olive oil is carried to Egypt.
² The LORD also has a dispute with Judah.
He is about to punish Jacob
according to his ways;
He will repay him based on his actions.
³ In the womb he grasped his brother's heel,
and as an adult he wrestled with God.
⁴ Jacob struggled with the Angel and prevailed;
he wept and sought His favor.
He found him at Bethel,
and there He spoke with him.
⁵ *Yahweh is the God of *Hosts;
Yahweh is His name.
⁶ But you must return to your God.
Maintain love and justice,
and always put your hope in God.
⁷ A merchant loves to extort
with dishonest scales in his hands.
⁸ But Ephraim says:
"How rich I have become;
I made it all myself.
In all my earnings,
no one can find any crime in me
that I can be punished for!"
⁹ I have been Yahweh your God
ever since the land of Egypt.
I will make you live in tents again,
as in the festival days.
¹⁰ I spoke through the prophets
and granted many visions;
I gave parables through the prophets.

¹¹ Since Gilead is full of evil,
they will certainly come to nothing.
They sacrifice bulls in Gilgal;
even their altars will be like heaps of rocks
on the furrows of a field.
¹² Jacob fled to the land of Aram.
Israel worked to earn a wife;
he tended flocks for a wife.
¹³ The LORD brought Israel from Egypt
by a prophet,
and Israel was tended by a prophet.
¹⁴ Ephraim has provoked bitter anger,
so his Lord will leave his bloodguilt on him
and repay him for his contempt.

13

When Ephraim spoke, there was trembling;
he was exalted in Israel.
But he incurred *guilt through *Baal and died.
² Now they continue to sin
and make themselves a cast image,
idols skillfully made from their silver,
all of them the work of craftsmen.
People say about them,
"Let the men who sacrifice kiss the calves."
³ Therefore, they will be like the morning mist,
like the early dew that vanishes,
like chaff blown from a threshing floor,
or like smoke from a window.
⁴ I have been *Yahweh your God
ever since the land of Egypt;
you know no God but Me,
and no Savior exists besides Me.
⁵ I knew you in the wilderness,
in the land of drought.
⁶ When they had pasture,
they became satisfied;
they were satisfied,
and their hearts became proud.
Therefore they forgot Me.
⁷ So I will be like a lion to them;
I will lurk like a leopard on the path.
⁸ I will attack them
like a bear robbed of her cubs
and tear open the rib cage over their hearts.
I will devour them there like a lioness,
like a wild beast that would rip them open.
⁹ I will destroy you, Israel;
you have no help but Me.
¹⁰ Where now is your king,
that he may save you in all your cities,
and the rulers you demanded, saying,
"Give me a king and leaders"?
¹¹ I give you a king in My anger
and take away a king in My wrath.
¹² Ephraim's guilt is preserved;
his sin is stored up.
¹³ Labor pains come on him.
He is not a wise son;
when the time comes,
he will not be born.
¹⁴ I will ransom them from the power of *Sheol.
I will redeem them from death.
Death, where are your barbs?
Sheol, where is your sting?
Compassion is hidden from My eyes.
¹⁵ Although he flourishes among his brothers,
an east wind will come,

a wind from the LORD rising up
    from the desert.
His water source will fail,
    and his spring will run dry.
The wind will plunder the treasury
    of every precious item.
16 Samaria will bear her guilt
    because she has rebelled against her God.
They will fall by the sword;
    their little ones will be dashed to pieces,
    and their pregnant women ripped open.

14

Israel, return to •Yahweh your God,
    for you have stumbled in your sin.
2 Take words of repentance with you
    and return to the LORD.
Say to Him: "Forgive all our sin
    and accept what is good,
    so that we may repay You
    with praise from our lips.
3 Assyria will not save us,
    we will not ride on horses,
and we will no longer proclaim, 'Our gods!'
    to the work of our hands.
For the fatherless receives compassion
    in You."

4 I will heal their apostasy;
    I will freely love them,
    for My anger will have turned from him.
5 I will be like the dew to Israel;
    he will blossom like the lily
    and take root like the cedars of Lebanon.
6 His new branches will spread,
    and his splendor will be like the olive tree,
    his fragrance, like the forest of Lebanon.
7 The people will return and live
    beneath his shade.
They will grow grain
    and blossom like the vine.
His renown will be like the wine of Lebanon.
8 Ephraim, why should I have anything more
    to do with idols?
It is I who answer and watch over him.
I am like a flourishing pine tree;
    your fruit comes from Me.
9 Let whoever is wise understand these things,
    and whoever is insightful recognize them.
For the ways of the LORD are right,
    and the righteous walk in them,
    but the rebellious stumble in them.

JOEL

1

The word of the LORD that came to Joel son of
Pethuel:
2 Hear this, you elders;
    listen, all you inhabitants of the land.
Has anything like this ever happened
    in your days
    or in the days of your ancestors?
3 Tell your children about it,
    and let your children tell their children,
    and their children the next generation.
4 What the devouring locust has left,
    the swarming locust has eaten;
what the swarming locust has left,
    the young locust has eaten;
and what the young locust has left,
    the destroying locust has eaten.
5 Wake up, you drunkards, and weep;
    wail, all you wine drinkers,
because of the sweet wine,
    for it has been taken from your mouth.
6 For a nation has invaded My land,
    powerful and without number;
its teeth are the teeth of a lion,
    and it has the fangs of a lioness.
7 It has devastated My grapevine
    and splintered My fig tree.
It has stripped off its bark and thrown it away;
    its branches have turned white.
8 Grieve like a young woman dressed
    in •sackcloth,
    mourning for the husband of her youth.
9 •Grain and •drink offerings have been cut off
    from the house of the LORD;
the priests, who are ministers
    of the LORD, mourn.
10 The fields are destroyed;

the land grieves;
indeed, the grain is destroyed;
    the new wine is dried up;
    and the olive oil fails.
11 Be ashamed, you farmers,
    wail, you vinedressers,
    over the wheat and the barley,
because the harvest of the field has perished.
12 The grapevine is dried up,
    and the fig tree is withered;
the pomegranate, the date palm,
    and the apple—
all the trees of the orchard—have withered.
Indeed, human joy has dried up.
13 Dress in sackcloth and lament, you priests;
    wail, you ministers of the altar.
Come and spend the night in sackcloth,
    you ministers of my God,
because grain and drink offerings
    are withheld from the house of your God.
14 Announce a sacred fast;
    proclaim an assembly!
Gather the elders
    and all the residents of the land
at the house of the LORD your God,
    and cry out to the LORD.
15 Woe because of that day!
For the Day of the LORD is near
and will come as devastation
    from the •Almighty.
16 Hasn't the food been cut off
    before our eyes,
joy and gladness
    from the house of our God?
17 The seeds lie shriveled in their casings.
The storehouses are in ruin,

and the granaries are broken down,
because the grain has withered away.
18 How the animals groan!
The herds of cattle wander in confusion
since they have no pasture.
Even the flocks of sheep suffer punishment.
19 I call to You, LORD,
for fire has consumed
the pastures of the wilderness,
and flames have devoured
all the trees of the countryside.
20 Even the wild animals cry out to You,
for the river beds are dried up,
and fire has consumed
the pastures of the wilderness.

2 Blow the horn in *Zion;
sound the alarm on My holy mountain!
Let all the residents of the land tremble,
for the Day of the LORD is coming;
in fact, it is near—
2 a day of darkness and gloom,
a day of clouds and dense overcast,
like the dawn spreading over the mountains;
a great and strong people appears,
such as never existed in ages past
and never will again
in all the generations to come.
3 A fire destroys in front of them,
and behind them a flame devours.
The land in front of them
is like the Garden of Eden,
but behind them,
it is like a desert wasteland;
there is no escape from them.
4 Their appearance is like that of horses,
and they gallop like war horses.
5 They bound on the tops of the mountains.
Their sound is like the sound of chariots,
like the sound of fiery flames
consuming stubble,
like a mighty army deployed for war.
6 Nations writhe in horror before them;
all faces turn pale.
7 They attack as warriors attack;
they scale walls as men of war do.
Each goes on his own path,
and they do not change their course.
8 They do not push each other;
each man proceeds on his own path.
They dodge the arrows, never stopping.
9 They storm the city;
they run on the wall;
they climb into the houses;
they enter through the windows like thieves.
10 The earth quakes before them;
the sky shakes.
The sun and moon grow dark,
and the stars cease their shining.
11 The LORD raises His voice
in the presence of His army.
His camp is very large;
Those who carry out His command
are powerful.
Indeed, the Day of the LORD is terrible
and dreadful—
who can endure it?
12 Even now—
this is the LORD's declaration—

turn to Me with all your heart,
with fasting, weeping, and mourning.
13 Tear your hearts,
not just your clothes,
and return to the LORD your God.
For He is gracious and compassionate,
slow to anger, rich in faithful love,
and He relents from sending disaster.
14 Who knows? He may turn and relent
and leave a blessing behind Him,
so you can offer grain and wine
to the LORD your God.
15 Blow the horn in Zion!
Announce a sacred fast;
proclaim an assembly.
16 Gather the people;
sanctify the congregation;
assemble the aged;
gather the children,
even those nursing at the breast.
Let the groom leave his bedroom,
and the bride her honeymoon chamber.
17 Let the priests, the LORD's ministers,
weep between the portico and the altar.
Let them say:
"Have pity on Your people, LORD,
and do not make Your inheritance a disgrace,
an object of scorn among the nations.
Why should it be said among the peoples,
'Where is their God?'"

18 Then the LORD became jealous for His land and
spared His people. 19 The LORD answered His people:
Look, I am about to send you
grain, new wine, and olive oil.
You will be satiated with them,
and I will no longer make you
a disgrace among the nations.
20 I will drive the northerner far from you
and banish him to a dry and desolate land,
his front ranks into the Dead Sea,
and his rear guard into the Mediterranean Sea.
His stench will rise;
yes, his rotten smell will rise,
for he has done catastrophic things.
21 Don't be afraid, land;
rejoice and be glad,
for the LORD has done great things.
22 Don't be afraid, wild animals,
for the wilderness pastures
have turned green,
the trees bear their fruit,
and the fig tree and grapevine yield
their riches.
23 Children of Zion, rejoice and be glad
in the LORD your God,
because He gives you the autumn rain
for your vindication.
He sends showers for you,
both autumn and spring rain as before.
24 The threshing floors will be full of grain,
and the vats will overflow
with new wine and olive oil.
25 I will repay you for the years
that the swarming locust ate,
the young locust, the destroying locust,
and the devouring locust—
My great army that I sent against you.

26 You will have plenty to eat and be satisfied.
　　You will praise the name of •Yahweh your God,
　　who has dealt wondrously with you.
　　My people will never again be put to shame.
27 You will know that I am present in Israel
　　and that I am Yahweh your God,
　　and there is no other.
　　My people will never again be put to shame.
28 After this
　　I will pour out My Spirit on all humanity;
　　then your sons and your daughters
　　　　will prophesy,
　　your old men will have dreams,
　　and your young men will see visions.
29 I will even pour out My Spirit
　　on the male and female slaves in those days.
30 I will display wonders
　　in the heavens and on the earth:
　　blood, fire, and columns of smoke.
31 The sun will be turned to darkness
　　and the moon to blood
　　before the great and awe-inspiring Day
　　　　of the LORD comes.
32 Then everyone who calls
　　on the name of Yahweh will be saved,
　　for there will be an escape
　　for those on Mount Zion and in Jerusalem,
　　as the LORD promised,
　　among the survivors the LORD calls.

3 Yes, in those days and at that time,
　　when I restore the fortunes of Judah
　　　　and Jerusalem,
2 I will gather all the nations
　　and take them to the Valley of Jehoshaphat.
　　I will enter into judgment with them there
　　because of My people, My inheritance Israel.
　　The nations have scattered the Israelites
　　in foreign countries
　　and divided up My land.
3 They cast lots for My people;
　　they bartered a boy for a prostitute
　　and sold a girl for wine to drink.

4 And also: Tyre, Sidon, and all the territories of Philistia—what are you to Me? Are you paying Me back or trying to get even with Me? I will quickly bring retribution on your heads. 5 For you took My silver and gold and carried My finest treasures to your temples. 6 You sold the people of Judah and Jerusalem to the Greeks to remove them far from their own territory. 7 Look, I am about to rouse them up from the place where you sold them; I will bring retribution on your heads. 8 I will sell your sons and daughters into the hands of the people of Judah, and they will sell them to the Sabeans, to a distant nation, for the LORD has spoken.

9 Proclaim this among the nations:
　　Prepare for holy war;
　　rouse the warriors;
　　let all the men of war advance and attack!
10 Beat your plows into swords
　　and your pruning knives into spears.
　　Let even the weakling say, "I am a warrior."
11 Come quickly, all you surrounding nations;
　　gather yourselves.
　　Bring down Your warriors there, LORD.
12 Let the nations be roused
　　and come to the Valley of Jehoshaphat,
　　for there I will sit down
　　to judge all the surrounding nations.
13 Swing the sickle
　　because the harvest is ripe.
　　Come and trample the grapes
　　because the winepress is full;
　　the wine vats overflow
　　because the wickedness of the nations is great.
14 Multitudes, multitudes
　　in the valley of decision!
　　For the Day of the LORD is near
　　in the valley of decision..
15 The sun and moon will grow dark,
　　and the stars will cease their shining.
16 The LORD will roar from •Zion
　　and raise His voice from Jerusalem;
　　heaven and earth will shake.
　　But the LORD will be a refuge for His people,
　　a stronghold for the Israelites.
17 Then you will know
　　that I am •Yahweh your God,
　　who dwells in Zion, My holy mountain.
　　Jerusalem will be holy,
　　and foreigners will never overrun it again.
18 In that day
　　the mountains will drip with sweet wine,
　　and the hills will flow with milk.
　　All the streams of Judah will flow with water,
　　and a spring will issue from the LORD's house,
　　watering the Valley of Acacias.
19 Egypt will become desolate,
　　and Edom a desert wasteland,
　　because of the violence done to the people
　　　　of Judah
　　in whose land they shed innocent blood.
20 But Judah will be inhabited forever,
　　and Jerusalem from generation to generation.
21 I will pardon their bloodguilt,
　　which I have not pardoned,
　　for the LORD dwells in Zion.

AMOS

1 The words of Amos, who was one of the sheep breeders from Tekoa—what he saw regarding Israel in the days of Uzziah, king of Judah, and Jeroboam son of Jehoash, king of Israel, two years before the earthquake.
2 He said:
　　The LORD roars from •Zion

and raises His voice from Jerusalem;
　　the pastures of the shepherds mourn,
　　and the summit of Carmel withers.
3 The LORD says:
　　I will not relent
　　　　from punishing Damascus
　　for three crimes, even four,

because they threshed Gilead
with iron sledges.
4 Therefore, I will send fire
against Hazael's palace,
and it will consume Ben-hadad's citadels.
5 I will break down the gates of Damascus.
I will cut off the ruler from the Valley of Aven,
and the one who wields the scepter
from Beth-eden.
The people of Aram will be exiled to Kir.
The Lord has spoken.
6 The Lord says:
I will not relent from punishing Gaza
for three crimes, even four,
because they exiled a whole community,
handing them over to Edom.
7 Therefore, I will send fire against the walls
of Gaza,
and it will consume its citadels.
8 I will cut off the ruler from Ashdod,
and the one who wields the scepter
from Ashkelon.
I will also turn My hand against Ekron,
and the remainder of the Philistines
will perish.
The Lord God has spoken.
9 The Lord says:
I will not relent from punishing Tyre
for three crimes, even four,
because they handed over
a whole community of exiles to Edom
and broke a treaty of brotherhood.
10 Therefore, I will send fire against the walls
of Tyre,
and it will consume its citadels.
11 The Lord says:
I will not relent from punishing Edom
for three crimes, even four,
because he pursued his brother
with the sword.
He stifled his compassion,
his anger tore at them continually,
and he harbored his rage incessantly.
12 Therefore, I will send fire against Teman,
and it will consume the citadels of Bozrah.
13 The Lord says:
I will not relent from punishing
the Ammonites
for three crimes, even four,
because they ripped open
the pregnant women of Gilead
in order to enlarge their territory.
14 Therefore, I will set fire to the walls of Rabbah,
and it will consume its citadels.
There will be shouting on the day of battle
and a violent wind on the day of the storm.
15 Their king and his princes
will go into exile together.
The Lord has spoken.

2 The Lord says:
I will not relent from punishing Moab
for three crimes, even four,
because he burned the bones
of the king of Edom to lime.
2 Therefore, I will send fire against Moab,
and it will consume the citadels of Kerioth.
Moab will die with a tumult,

with shouting and the sound
of the ram's horn.
3 I will cut off the judge from the land
and kill all its officials with him.
The Lord has spoken.
4 The Lord says:
I will not relent from punishing Judah
for three crimes, even four,
because they have rejected the instruction
of the Lord
and have not kept His statutes.
The lies that their ancestors followed
have led them astray.
5 Therefore, I will send fire against Judah,
and it will consume the citadels of Jerusalem.
6 The Lord says:
I will not relent from punishing Israel
for three crimes, even four,
because they sell a righteous person for silver
and a needy person for a pair of sandals.
7 They trample the heads of the poor
on the dust of the ground
and block the path of the needy.
A man and his father have sexual relations
with the same girl,
profaning My holy name.
8 They stretch out beside every altar
on garments taken as collateral,
and in the house of their God,
they drink wine obtained through fines.
9 Yet I destroyed the Amorite as Israel advanced;
his height was like the cedars,
and he was as sturdy as the oaks;
I destroyed his fruit above
and his roots beneath.
10 And I brought you from the land of Egypt
and led you 40 years in the wilderness
in order to possess the land of the Amorite.
11 I raised up some of your sons as prophets
and some of your young men as Nazirites.
Is this not the case, Israelites?
This is the Lord's declaration.
12 But you made the Nazirites drink wine
and commanded the prophets,
"Do not prophesy."
13 Look, I am about to crush you in your place
as a wagon full of sheaves crushes grain.
14 Escape will fail the swift,
the strong one will not prevail by his strength,
and the brave will not save his life.
15 The archer will not stand his ground,
the one who is swift of foot
will not save himself,
and the one riding a horse will not save
his life.
16 Even the most courageous of the warriors
will flee naked on that day—
this is the Lord's declaration.

3 Listen to this message that the Lord has spoken
against you, Israelites, against the entire clan that
I brought from the land of Egypt:
2 I have known only you
out of all the clans of the earth;
therefore, I will punish you for all
your iniquities.
3 Can two walk together
without agreeing to meet?

⁴ Does a lion roar in the forest
when it has no prey?
Does a young lion growl from its lair
unless it has captured something?
⁵ Does a bird land in a trap on the ground
if there is no bait for it?
Does a trap spring from the ground
when it has caught nothing?
⁶ If a ram's horn is blown in a city,
aren't people afraid?
If a disaster occurs in a city,
hasn't the Lᴏʀᴅ done it?
⁷ Indeed, the Lord Gᴏᴅ does nothing
without revealing His counsel
to His servants the prophets.
⁸ A lion has roared;
who will not fear?
The Lord Gᴏᴅ has spoken;
who will not prophesy?
⁹ Proclaim on the citadels in Ashdod
and on the citadels in the land of Egypt:
Assemble on the mountains of Samaria
and see the great turmoil in the city
and the acts of oppression within it.
¹⁰ The people are incapable of doing right—
          this is the Lᴏʀᴅ's declaration—
those who store up violence and destruction
in their citadels.
¹¹ Therefore, the Lord Gᴏᴅ says:
An enemy will surround the land;
he will destroy your strongholds
and plunder your citadels.
¹² The Lᴏʀᴅ says:
As the shepherd snatches two legs
or a piece of an ear
from the lion's mouth,
so the Israelites who live in Samaria
will be rescued
with only the corner of a bed
or the cushion of a couch.
¹³ Listen and testify against the house of Jacob—
          this is the declaration of the Lord Gᴏᴅ,
                    the God of ·Hosts.
¹⁴ I will punish the altars of Bethel
on the day I punish Israel for its crimes;
the horns of the altar will be cut off
and fall to the ground.
¹⁵ I will demolish the winter house
and the summer house;
the houses inlaid with ivory will be destroyed,
and the great houses will come to an end.
          This is the Lᴏʀᴅ's declaration.

4 Listen to this message, you cows of Bashan
who are on the hill of Samaria,
women who oppress the poor
and crush the needy,
who say to their husbands,
"Bring us something to drink."
² The Lord Gᴏᴅ has sworn by His holiness:
Look, the days are coming
when you will be taken away with hooks,
every last one of you with fishhooks.
³ You will go through breaches in the wall,
each woman straight ahead,
and you will be driven along toward Harmon.
          This is the Lᴏʀᴅ's declaration.
⁴ Come to Bethel and rebel;

rebel even more at Gilgal!
Bring your sacrifices every morning,
your tenths every three days.
⁵ Offer leavened bread as a thank offering,
and loudly proclaim your freewill offerings,
for that is what you Israelites love to do!
          This is the Lᴏʀᴅ's declaration.
⁶ I gave you absolutely nothing to eat
in all your cities,
a shortage of food in all your communities,
yet you did not return to Me.
          This is the Lᴏʀᴅ's declaration.
⁷ I also withheld the rain from you
while there were still three months
          until harvest.
I sent rain on one city
but no rain on another.
One field received rain
while a field with no rain withered.
⁸ Two or three cities staggered
to another city to drink water
but were not satisfied,
yet you did not return to Me.
          This is the Lᴏʀᴅ's declaration.
⁹ I struck you with blight and mildew;
the locust devoured
your many gardens and vineyards,
your fig trees and olive trees,
yet you did not return to Me.
          This is the Lᴏʀᴅ's declaration.
¹⁰ I sent plagues like those of Egypt;
I killed your young men with the sword,
along with your captured horses.
I caused the stench of your camp
to fill your nostrils,
yet you did not return to Me.
          This is the Lᴏʀᴅ's declaration.
¹¹ I overthrew some of you
as I overthrew Sodom and Gomorrah,
and you were like a burning stick
snatched from a fire,
yet you did not return to Me—
          this is the Lᴏʀᴅ's declaration.
¹² Therefore, Israel, that is what I will do to you,
and since I will do that to you,
Israel, prepare to meet your God!
¹³ He is here:
the One who forms the mountains,
creates the wind,
and reveals His thoughts to man,
the One who makes the dawn out of darkness
and strides on the heights of the earth.
·Yahweh, the God of ·Hosts, is His name.

5 Listen to this message that I am singing for you, a
lament, house of Israel:
² She has fallen;
Virgin Israel will never rise again.
She lies abandoned on her land,
with no one to raise her up.
³ For the Lord Gᴏᴅ says:
The city that marches out a thousand strong
will have only a hundred left,
and the one that marches out
          a hundred strong
will have only ten left in the house of Israel.
⁴ For the Lᴏʀᴅ says to the house of Israel:
Seek Me and live!

⁵ Do not seek Bethel
  or go to Gilgal
  or journey to Beer-sheba,
  for Gilgal will certainly go into exile,
  and Bethel will come to nothing.
⁶ Seek *Yahweh and live,
  or He will spread like fire
  throughout the house of Joseph;
  it will consume everything,
  with no one at Bethel to extinguish it.
⁷ Those who turn justice into *wormwood
  throw righteousness to the ground.
⁸ The One who made the Pleiades and Orion,
  who turns darkness into dawn
  and darkens day into night,
  who summons the waters of the sea
  and pours them out over the face
    of the earth—
  Yahweh is His name.
⁹ He brings destruction on the strong,
  and it falls on the stronghold.
¹⁰ They hate the one who convicts the *guilty
  at the city *gate
  and despise the one who speaks with integrity.
¹¹ Therefore, because you trample on the poor
  and exact a grain tax from him,
  you will never live in the houses of cut stone
  you have built;
  you will never drink the wine
  from the lush vineyards
  you have planted.
¹² For I know your crimes are many
  and your sins innumerable.
  They oppress the righteous, take a bribe,
  and deprive the poor of justice at the gates.
¹³ Therefore, the wise person will keep silent
  at such a time,
  for the days are evil.
¹⁴ Seek good and not evil
  so that you may live,
  and the Lord, the God of *Hosts,
  will be with you,
  as you have claimed.
¹⁵ Hate evil and love good;
  establish justice in the gate.
  Perhaps the Lord, the God of Hosts,
    will be gracious
  to the remnant of Joseph.
¹⁶ Therefore Yahweh, the God of Hosts, the Lord,
says:
  There will be wailing in all the public squares;
  they will cry out in anguish in all the streets.
  The farmer will be called on to mourn,
  and professional mourners to wail.
¹⁷ There will be wailing in all the vineyards,
  for I will pass among you.
  The Lord has spoken.
¹⁸ Woe to you who long for the Day of the Lord!
  What will the Day of the Lord be for you?
  It will be darkness and not light.
¹⁹ It will be like a man who flees from a lion
  only to have a bear confront him.
  He goes home and rests his hand
    against the wall
  only to have a snake bite him.
²⁰ Won't the Day of the Lord
  be darkness rather than light,

even gloom without any brightness in it?
²¹ I hate, I despise your feasts!
  I can't stand the stench
  of your solemn assemblies.
²² Even if you offer Me
  your *burnt offerings and *grain offerings,
  I will not accept them;
  I will have no regard
  for your *fellowship offerings of fattened cattle.
²³ Take away from Me the noise of your songs!
  I will not listen to the music of your harps.
²⁴ But let justice flow like water,
  and righteousness, like an unfailing stream.

²⁵ "House of Israel, was it sacrifices and grain offerings that you presented to Me during the 40 years in the wilderness? ²⁶ But you have taken up Sakkuth your king and Kaiwan your star god, images you have made for yourselves. ²⁷ So I will send you into exile beyond Damascus." Yahweh, the God of Hosts, is His name. He has spoken.

6 Woe to those who are at ease in *Zion
  and to those who feel secure on the hill
    of Samaria—
  the notable people in this first of the nations,
  those the house of Israel comes to.
² Cross over to Calneh and see;
  go from there to great Hamath;
  then go down to Gath of the Philistines.
  Are you better than these kingdoms?
  Is their territory larger than yours?
³ You dismiss any thought of the evil day
  and bring in a reign of violence.
⁴ They lie on beds inlaid with ivory,
  sprawled out on their couches,
  and dine on lambs from the flock
  and calves from the stall.
⁵ They improvise songs to the sound of the harp
  and invent their own musical instruments
    like David.
⁶ They drink wine by the bowlful
  and anoint themselves with the finest oils
  but do not grieve over the ruin of Joseph.
⁷ Therefore, they will now go into exile
  as the first of the captives,
  and the feasting of those who sprawl out
  will come to an end.

⁸ The Lord God has sworn by Himself—this is the declaration of *Yahweh, the God of *Hosts:
  I loathe Jacob's pride
  and hate his citadels,
  so I will hand over the city and everything
    in it.

⁹ And if there are 10 men left in one house, they will die. ¹⁰ A close relative and burner will remove his corpse from the house. He will call to someone in the inner recesses of the house, "Any more with you?"
That person will reply, "None."
Then he will say, "Silence, because Yahweh's name must not be invoked."
¹¹ For the Lord commands:
  The large house will be smashed to pieces,
  and the small house to rubble.
¹² Do horses gallop on the cliffs;
  does anyone plow there with oxen?
  Yet you have turned justice into poison
  and the fruit of righteousness
    into *wormwood—

¹³   you who rejoice over Lo-debar
      and say, "Didn't we capture Karnaim
      for ourselves by our own strength?"
¹⁴   But look, I am raising up a nation
      against you, house of Israel—
                  this is the declaration of the Lord,
                        the God of Hosts—
      and they will oppress you
      from the entrance of Hamath
      to the Brook of the *Arabah.

7 The Lord God showed me this: He was forming a
swarm of locusts at the time the spring crop first
began to sprout—after the cutting of the king's hay.
²When the locusts finished eating the vegetation of the
land, I said, "Lord God, please forgive! How will Jacob
survive since he is so small?"
³The Lord relented concerning this. "It will not happen," He said.
⁴The Lord God showed me this: The Lord God was
calling for a judgment by fire. It consumed the great
deep and devoured the land. ⁵Then I said, "Lord God,
please stop! How will Jacob survive since he is so
small?"
⁶The Lord relented concerning this. "This will not
happen either," said the Lord God.
⁷He showed me this: The Lord was standing there
by a vertical wall with a plumb line in His hand. ⁸The
Lord asked me, "What do you see, Amos?"
    I replied, "A plumb line."
    Then the Lord said, "I am setting a plumb line
among My people Israel; I will no longer spare them:
⁹   Isaac's *high places will be deserted,
      and Israel's sanctuaries will be in ruins;
      I will rise up against the house of Jeroboam
      with a sword."
¹⁰Amaziah the priest of Bethel sent word to Jeroboam king of Israel, saying, "Amos has conspired
against you right here in the house of Israel. The land
cannot endure all his words, ¹¹for Amos has said this:
'Jeroboam will die by the sword, and Israel will certainly go into exile from its homeland.'"
¹²Then Amaziah said to Amos, "Go away, you seer!
Flee to the land of Judah. Earn your living and give
your prophecies there, ¹³but don't ever prophesy at
Bethel again, for it is the king's sanctuary and a royal
temple."
¹⁴So Amos answered Amaziah, "I was not a prophet
or the son of a prophet; rather, I was a herdsman, and
I took care of sycamore figs. ¹⁵But the Lord took me
from following the flock and said to me, 'Go, prophesy
to My people Israel.'"
¹⁶Now hear the word of the Lord. You say:
      Do not prophesy against Israel;
      do not preach against the house of Isaac.
¹⁷Therefore, this is what the Lord says:
      Your wife will be a prostitute in the city,
      your sons and daughters will fall by the sword,
      and your land will be divided up
      with a measuring line.
      You yourself will die on pagan soil,
      and Israel will certainly go into exile
      from its homeland.

8 The Lord God showed me this: A basket of summer
fruit. ²He asked me, "What do you see, Amos?"
    I replied, "A basket of summer fruit."
    The Lord said to me, "The end has come for My peo-
ple Israel; I will no longer spare them. ³In that day the
temple songs will become wailing"—this is the Lord
God's declaration. "Many dead bodies, thrown everywhere! Silence!"
⁴   Hear this, you who trample on the needy
      and do away with the poor of the land,
⁵   asking, "When will the New Moon be over
      so we may sell grain,
      and the Sabbath,
      so we may market wheat?
      We can reduce the measure
      while increasing the price
      and cheat with dishonest scales.
⁶   We can buy the poor with silver
      and the needy for a pair of sandals
      and even sell the chaff!"
⁷The Lord has sworn by the Pride of Jacob:
      I will never forget all their deeds.
⁸   Because of this, won't the land quake
      and all who dwell in it mourn?
      All of it will rise like the Nile;
      it will surge and then subside
      like the Nile in Egypt.
⁹   And in that day—
                  this is the declaration of the Lord God—
      I will make the sun go down at noon;
      I will darken the land in the daytime.
¹⁰   I will turn your feasts into mourning
      and all your songs into lamentation;
      I will cause everyone to wear *sackcloth
      and every head to be shaved.
      I will make that grief
      like mourning for an only son
      and its outcome like a bitter day.
¹¹   Hear this! The days are coming—
                  this is the declaration of the Lord God—
      when I will send a famine through the land:
      not a famine of bread or a thirst for water,
      but of hearing the words of the Lord.
¹²   People will stagger from sea to sea
      and roam from north to east,
      seeking the word of the Lord,
      but they will not find it.
¹³   In that day the beautiful young women,
      the young men also, will faint from thirst.
¹⁴   Those who swear by the *guilt of Samaria
      and say, "As your god lives, Dan,"
      or "As the way of Beer-sheba lives"—
      they will fall, never to rise again.

9 I saw the Lord standing beside the altar, and He
said:
      Strike the capitals of the pillars
      so that the thresholds shake;
      knock them down on the heads of all
          the people.
      Then I will kill the rest of them
          with the sword.
      None of those who flee will get away;
      none of the fugitives will escape.
²   If they dig down to *Sheol,
      from there My hand will take them;
      if they climb up to heaven,
      from there I will bring them down.
³   If they hide themselves
      on the top of Carmel,
      from there I will track them down
      and seize them;
      if they conceal themselves

from My sight on the sea floor,
from there I will command
the sea serpent to bite them.
⁴ And if they are driven
by their enemies into captivity,
from there I will command
the sword to kill them.
I will fix My eyes on them
for harm and not for good.
⁵ The Lord, the GOD of ˙Hosts—
He touches the earth;
it melts, and all who dwell in it mourn;
all of it rises like the Nile
and subsides like the Nile of Egypt.
⁶ He builds His upper chambers
in the heavens
and lays the foundation of His vault
on the earth.
He summons the waters of the sea
and pours them out on the face of the earth.
˙Yahweh is His name.
⁷ Israelites, are you not like the ˙Cushites to Me?
This is the LORD's declaration.
Didn't I bring Israel from the land of Egypt,
the Philistines from Caphtor,
and the Arameans from Kir?
⁸ Look, the eyes of the Lord GOD
are on the sinful kingdom,
and I will destroy it
from the face of the earth.
However, I will not totally destroy
the house of Jacob—
this is the LORD's declaration—
⁹ for I am about to give the command,
and I will shake the house of Israel

among all the nations,
as one shakes a sieve,
but not a pebble will fall to the ground.
¹⁰ All the sinners among My people
who say: "Disaster will never overtake
or confront us,"
will die by the sword.
¹¹ In that day
I will restore the fallen booth of David:
I will repair its gaps,
restore its ruins,
and rebuild it as in the days of old,
¹² so that they may possess
the remnant of Edom
and all the nations
that are called by My name—
this is the LORD's declaration—
He will do this.
¹³ Hear this! The days are coming—
this is the LORD's declaration—
when the plowman will overtake the reaper
and the one who treads grapes,
the sower of seed.
The mountains will drip with sweet wine,
and all the hills will flow with it.
¹⁴ I will restore the fortunes of My people Israel.
They will rebuild and occupy
ruined cities,
plant vineyards and drink their wine,
make gardens and eat their produce.
¹⁵ I will plant them on their land,
and they will never again be uprooted
from the land I have given them.
Yahweh your God has spoken.

OBADIAH

T he vision of Obadiah.
This is what the Lord GOD has said about Edom:
We have heard a message from the LORD;
a messenger has been sent among the nations:
"Rise up, and let us go to war against her."
² Look, I will make you insignificant
among the nations;
you will be deeply despised.
³ Your presumptuous heart has deceived you,
you who live in clefts of the rock
in your home on the heights,
who say to yourself,
"Who can bring me down to the ground?"
⁴ Though you seem to soar like an eagle
and make your nest among the stars,
even from there I will bring you down.
This is the LORD's declaration.
⁵ If thieves came to you,
if marauders by night—
how ravaged you would be!—
wouldn't they steal only what they wanted?
If grape pickers came to you,
wouldn't they leave some grapes?
⁶ How Esau will be pillaged,
his hidden treasures searched out!
⁷ Everyone who has a treaty with you

will drive you to the border;
everyone at peace with you
will deceive and conquer you.
Those who eat your bread
will set a trap for you.
He will be unaware of it.
⁸ In that day—
this is the LORD's declaration—
will I not eliminate the wise ones of Edom
and those who understand
from the hill country of Esau?
⁹ Teman, your warriors will be terrified
so that everyone from the hill country of Esau
will be destroyed by slaughter.
¹⁰ You will be covered with shame
and destroyed forever
because of violence done
to your brother Jacob.
¹¹ On the day you stood aloof,
on the day strangers captured his wealth,
while foreigners entered his ˙gate
and cast lots for Jerusalem,
you were just like one of them.
¹² Do not gloat over your brother
in the day of his calamity;
do not rejoice over the people of Judah

in the day of their destruction;
do not boastfully mock
in the day of distress.

13 Do not enter the gate of My people
in the day of their disaster.
Yes, you—do not gloat over their misery
in the day of their disaster
and do not appropriate their possessions
in the day of their disaster.

14 Do not stand at the crossroads
to cut off their fugitives,
and do not hand over their survivors
in the day of distress.

15 For the Day of the LORD is near,
against all the nations.
As you have done, so it will be done to you;
what you deserve will return
on your own head.

16 As you have drunk on My holy mountain,
so all the nations will drink continually.
They will drink and gulp down
and be as though they had never been.

17 But there will be a deliverance on Mount *Zion,
and it will be holy;
the house of Jacob will dispossess
those who dispossessed them.

18 Then the house of Jacob will be a blazing fire,
and the house of Joseph, a burning flame,
but the house of Esau will be stubble;
Jacob will set them on fire
and consume Edom.
Therefore no survivor will remain
of the house of Esau,
for the LORD has spoken.

19 People from the *Negev will possess
the hill country of Esau;
those from the Judean foothills
will possess
the land of the Philistines.
They will possess
the territories of Ephraim and Samaria,
while Benjamin will possess Gilead.

20 The exiles of the Israelites who are
in Halah
and who are among the Canaanites
as far as Zarephath
as well as the exiles of Jerusalem who are
in Sepharad
will possess the cities of the Negev.

21 Saviors will ascend Mount Zion
to rule over the hill country of Esau,
but the kingdom will be the LORD's.

JONAH

1 The word of the LORD came to Jonah son of Amittai: ²"Get up! Go to the great city of Nineveh and preach against it, because their wickedness has confronted Me." ³However, Jonah got up to flee to Tarshish from the LORD's presence. He went down to Joppa and found a ship going to Tarshish. He paid the fare and went down into it to go with them to Tarshish, from the LORD's presence.

⁴Then the LORD hurled a violent wind on the sea, and such a violent storm arose on the sea that the ship threatened to break apart. ⁵The sailors were afraid, and each cried out to his god. They threw the ship's cargo into the sea to lighten the load. Meanwhile, Jonah had gone down to the lowest part of the vessel and had stretched out and fallen into a deep sleep.

⁶The captain approached him and said, "What are you doing sound asleep? Get up! Call to your god. Maybe this god will consider us, and we won't perish."

⁷"Come on!" the sailors said to each other. "Let's cast lots. Then we'll know who is to blame for this trouble we're in." So they cast lots, and the lot singled out Jonah. ⁸Then they said to him, "Tell us who is to blame for this trouble we're in. What is your business and where are you from? What is your country and what people are you from?"

⁹He answered them, "I'm a Hebrew. I worship *Yahweh, the God of the heavens, who made the sea and the dry land."

¹⁰Then the men were even more afraid and said to him, "What is this you've done?" The men knew he was fleeing from the LORD's presence, because he had told them. ¹¹So they said to him, "What should we do to you to calm this sea that's against us?" For the sea was getting worse and worse.

¹²He answered them, "Pick me up and throw me into the sea so it may quiet down for you, for I know that I'm to blame for this violent storm that is against you." ¹³Nevertheless, the men rowed hard to get back to dry land, but they couldn't because the sea was raging against them more and more.

¹⁴So they called out to the LORD: "Please, Yahweh, don't let us perish because of this man's life, and don't charge us with innocent blood! For You, Yahweh, have done just as You pleased." ¹⁵Then they picked up Jonah and threw him into the sea, and the sea stopped its raging. ¹⁶The men *feared the LORD even more, and they offered a sacrifice to the LORD and made vows.

¹⁷Now the LORD had appointed a huge fish to swallow Jonah, and Jonah was in the fish three days and three nights.

2 Jonah prayed to the LORD his God from inside the fish:

2 I called to the LORD in my distress,
and He answered me.
I cried out for help in the belly of *Sheol;
You heard my voice.

3 You threw me into the depths,
into the heart of the seas,
and the current overcame me.
All Your breakers and Your billows
swept over me.

4 But I said: I have been banished
from Your sight,
yet I will look once more
toward Your holy temple.

5 The waters engulfed me up to the neck;
the watery depths overcame me;
seaweed was wrapped around my head.

6 I sank to the foundations of the mountains;

the earth with its prison bars closed
    behind me forever!
But You raised my life from the *Pit,
    Lᴏʀᴅ my God!
⁷ As my life was fading away,
    I remembered *Yahweh.
My prayer came to You,
    to Your holy temple.
⁸ Those who cling to worthless idols
    forsake faithful love,
⁹ but as for me, I will sacrifice to You
    with a voice of thanksgiving.
I will fulfill what I have vowed.
    Salvation is from the Lᴏʀᴅ!

¹⁰ Then the Lᴏʀᴅ commanded the fish, and it vomited Jonah onto dry land.

3 Then the word of the Lᴏʀᴅ came to Jonah a second time: ² "Get up! Go to the great city of Nineveh and preach the message that I tell you." ³ So Jonah got up and went to Nineveh according to the Lᴏʀᴅ's command.

Now Nineveh was an extremely large city, a three-day walk. ⁴ Jonah set out on the first day of his walk in the city and proclaimed, "In 40 days Nineveh will be demolished!" ⁵ The men of Nineveh believed in God. They proclaimed a fast and dressed in *sackcloth—from the greatest of them to the least.

⁶ When word reached the king of Nineveh, he got up from his throne, took off his royal robe, put on sackcloth, and sat in ashes. ⁷ Then he issued a decree in Nineveh:

By order of the king and his nobles: No man or beast, herd or flock, is to taste anything at all. They must not eat or drink water. ⁸ Furthermore, both man and beast must be covered with sackcloth, and everyone must call out earnestly to God. Each must turn from his evil ways and from the violence he is doing. ⁹ Who knows?

God may turn and relent; He may turn from His burning anger so that we will not perish.

¹⁰ Then God saw their actions—that they had turned from their evil ways—so God relented from the disaster He had threatened to do to them. And He did not do it.

4 But Jonah was greatly displeased and became furious. ² He prayed to the Lᴏʀᴅ: "Please, Lᴏʀᴅ, isn't this what I said while I was still in my own country? That's why I fled toward Tarshish in the first place. I knew that You are a merciful and compassionate God, slow to become angry, rich in faithful love, and One who relents from sending disaster. ³ And now, Lᴏʀᴅ, please take my life from me, for it is better for me to die than to live."

⁴ The Lᴏʀᴅ asked, "Is it right for you to be angry?"

⁵ Jonah left the city and sat down east of it. He made himself a shelter there and sat in its shade to see what would happen to the city. ⁶ Then the Lᴏʀᴅ God appointed a plant, and it grew up to provide shade over Jonah's head to ease his discomfort. Jonah was greatly pleased with the plant. ⁷ When dawn came the next day, God appointed a worm that attacked the plant, and it withered.

⁸ As the sun was rising, God appointed a scorching east wind. The sun beat down so much on Jonah's head that he almost fainted, and he wanted to die. He said, "It's better for me to die than to live."

⁹ Then God asked Jonah, "Is it right for you to be angry about the plant?"

"Yes," he replied. "It is right. I'm angry enough to die!"

¹⁰ So the Lᴏʀᴅ said, "You cared about the plant, which you did not labor over and did not grow. It appeared in a night and perished in a night. ¹¹ Should I not care about the great city of Nineveh, which has more than 120,000 people who cannot distinguish between their right and their left, as well as many animals?"

Mɪᴄᴀʜ

1 The word of the Lᴏʀᴅ that came to Micah the Moreshite—what he saw regarding Samaria and Jerusalem in the days of Jotham, Ahaz, and Hezekiah, kings of Judah.
² Listen, all you peoples;
    pay attention, earth and everyone in it!
The Lord Gᴏᴅ will be a witness against you,
    the Lord, from His holy temple.
³ Look, the Lᴏʀᴅ is leaving His place
    and coming down to trample
    the heights of the earth.
⁴ The mountains will melt beneath Him,
    and the valleys will split apart,
    like wax near a fire,
    like water cascading down a mountainside.
⁵ All this will happen because of
    Jacob's rebellion
    and the sins of the house of Israel.
What is the rebellion of Jacob?
    Isn't it Samaria?
And what is the *high place of Judah?
    Isn't it Jerusalem?
⁶ Therefore, I will make Samaria

    a heap of ruins in the countryside,
    a planting area for a vineyard.
I will roll her stones into the valley
    and expose her foundations.
⁷ All her carved images will be smashed
      to pieces;
all her wages will be burned in the fire,
    and I will destroy all her idols.
Since she collected the wages of a prostitute,
    they will be used again for a prostitute.
⁸ Because of this I will lament and wail;
    I will walk barefoot and naked.
I will howl like the jackals
    and mourn like ostriches.
⁹ For her wound is incurable
    and has reached even Judah;
it has approached the gate of my people,
    as far as Jerusalem.
¹⁰ Don't announce it in Gath,
    don't weep at all.
Roll in the dust in Beth-leaphrah.
¹¹ Depart in shameful nakedness,
    you residents of Shaphir;

the residents of Zaanan will not come out.
Beth-ezel is lamenting;
its support is taken from you.

12 Though the residents of Maroth
anxiously wait for something good,
disaster has come from the LORD
to the gate of Jerusalem.

13 Harness the horses to the chariot,
you residents of Lachish.
This was the beginning of sin
for Daughter •Zion,
because Israel's acts of rebellion can be traced
to you.

14 Therefore, send farewell gifts
to Moresheth-gath;
the houses of Achzib are a deception
to the kings of Israel.

15 I will again bring a conqueror
against you who live in Mareshah.
The nobility of Israel will come to Adullam.

16 Shave yourselves bald and cut off your hair
in sorrow for your precious children;
make yourselves as bald as an eagle,
for they have been taken from you into exile.

2 Woe to those who dream up wickedness
and prepare evil plans on their beds!
At morning light they accomplish it
because the power is in their hands.

2 They covet fields and seize them;
they also take houses.
They deprive a man of his home,
a person of his inheritance.

3 Therefore, the LORD says:
I am now planning a disaster
against this nation;
you cannot free your necks from it.
Then you will not walk so proudly
because it will be an evil time.

4 In that day one will take up a taunt
against you,
and lament mournfully, saying,
"We are totally ruined!
He measures out the allotted land
of my people.
How He removes it from me!
He allots our fields to traitors."

5 Therefore, there will be no one
in the assembly of the LORD
to divide the land by casting lots.

6 "Quit your preaching," they preach.
"They should not preach these things;
shame will not overtake us."

7 House of Jacob, should it be asked,
"Is the Spirit of the LORD impatient?
Are these the things He does?"
Don't My words bring good
to the one who walks uprightly?

8 But recently My people have risen up
like an enemy:
You strip off the splendid robe
from those who are
passing through confidently,
like those returning from war.

9 You force the women of My people
out of their comfortable homes,
and you take My blessing
from their children forever.

10 Get up and leave,
for this is not your place of rest,
because defilement brings destruction—
a grievous destruction!

11 If a man of wind comes
and invents lies:
"I will preach to you about wine and beer,"
he would be just the preacher for this people!

12 I will indeed gather all of you, Jacob;
I will collect the remnant of Israel.
I will bring them together like sheep in a pen,
like a flock in the middle of its fold.
It will be noisy with people.

13 One who breaks open the way
will advance before them;
they will break out, pass through the gate,
and leave by it.
Their King will pass through before them,
the LORD as their leader.

3 Then I said, "Now listen, leaders of Jacob,
you rulers of the house of Israel.
Aren't you supposed to know what is just?

2 You hate good and love evil.
You tear off people's skin
and strip their flesh from their bones.

3 You eat the flesh of my people
after you strip their skin from them
and break their bones.
You chop them up
like flesh for the cooking pot,
like meat in a cauldron."

4 Then they will cry out to the LORD,
but He will not answer them.
He will hide His face from them at that time
because of the crimes they have committed.

5 This is what the LORD says
concerning the prophets
who lead my people astray,
who proclaim peace
when they have food to sink their teeth into
but declare war against the one
who puts nothing in their mouths.

6 Therefore, it will be night for you—
without visions;
it will grow dark for you—
without •divination.
The sun will set on these prophets,
and the daylight will turn black over them.

7 Then the seers will be ashamed
and the diviners disappointed.
They will all cover their mouths
because there will be no answer from God.

8 As for me, however, I am filled with power
by the Spirit of the LORD,
with justice and courage,
to proclaim to Jacob his rebellion
and to Israel his sin.

9 Listen to this, leaders of the house of Jacob,
you rulers of the house of Israel,
who abhor justice
and pervert everything that is right,

10 who build •Zion with bloodshed
and Jerusalem with injustice.

11 Her leaders issue rulings for a bribe,
her priests teach for payment,
and her prophets practice divination
for money.

Yet they lean on the Lord, saying,
"Isn't the Lord among us?
No disaster will overtake us."
[12] Therefore, because of you,
Zion will be plowed like a field,
Jerusalem will become ruins,
and the hill of the temple mount
will be a thicket.

4 In the last days
the mountain of the Lord's house
will be established
at the top of the mountains
and will be raised above the hills.
Peoples will stream to it,
[2] and many nations will come and say,
"Come, let us go up to the mountain
of the Lord,
to the house of the God of Jacob.
He will teach us about His ways
so we may walk in His paths."
For instruction will go out of *Zion
and the word of the Lord from Jerusalem.
[3] He will settle disputes among many peoples
and provide arbitration for strong nations
that are far away.
They will beat their swords into plows,
and their spears into pruning knives.
Nation will not take up the sword
against nation,
and they will never again train for war.
[4] But each man will sit under his grapevine
and under his fig tree
with no one to frighten him.
For the mouth of the Lord of *Hosts
has promised this.
[5] Though all the peoples each walk
in the name of their gods,
we will walk in the name of *Yahweh our God
forever and ever.
[6] On that day—
this is the Lord's declaration—
I will assemble the lame
and gather the scattered,
those I have injured.
[7] I will make the lame into a remnant,
those far removed into a strong nation.
Then the Lord will rule over them
in Mount Zion
from this time on and forever.
[8] And you, watchtower for the flock,
fortified hill of Daughter Zion,
the former rule will come to you,
sovereignty will come to Daughter Jerusalem.
[9] Now, why are you shouting loudly?
Is there no king with you?
Has your counselor perished
so that anguish grips you like a woman
in labor?
[10] Writhe and cry out, Daughter Zion,
like a woman in labor,
for now you will leave the city
and camp in the open fields.
You will go to Babylon;
there you will be rescued;
there the Lord will redeem you
from the power of your enemies!

[11] Many nations have now assembled
against you;
they say, "Let her be defiled,
and let us feast our eyes on Zion."
[12] But they do not know the Lord's intentions
or understand His plan,
that He has gathered them
like sheaves to the threshing floor.
[13] Rise and thresh, Daughter Zion,
for I will make your horns iron
and your hooves bronze,
so you can crush many peoples.
Then you will *set apart their plunder
to the Lord for destruction,
their wealth to the Lord of all the earth.

5 Now, daughter who is under attack,
you slash yourself in grief;
a siege is set against us!
They are striking the judge of Israel
on the cheek with a rod.
[2] Bethlehem Ephrathah,
you are small among the clans of Judah;
One will come from you
to be ruler over Israel for Me.
His origin is from antiquity,
from eternity.
[3] Therefore, He will abandon them
until the time
when she who is in labor has given birth;
then the rest of His brothers will return
to the people of Israel.
[4] He will stand and shepherd them
in the strength of *Yahweh,
in the majestic name of Yahweh His God.
They will live securely,
for then His greatness will extend
to the ends of the earth.
[5] He will be their peace.
When Assyria invades our land,
when it marches against our fortresses,
we will raise against it seven shepherds,
even eight leaders of men.
[6] They will shepherd the land of Assyria
with the sword,
the land of Nimrod with a drawn blade.
So He will rescue us from Assyria
when it invades our land,
when it marches against our territory.
[7] Then the remnant of Jacob
will be among many peoples
like dew from the Lord,
like showers on the grass,
which do not wait for anyone
or linger for *mankind.
[8] Then the remnant of Jacob
will be among the nations,
among many peoples,
like a lion among animals of the forest,
like a young lion among flocks of sheep,
which tramples and tears as it passes through,
and there is no one to rescue them.
[9] Your hand will be lifted up
against your adversaries,
and all your enemies will be destroyed.
[10] In that day—
this is the Lord's declaration—
I will remove your horses from you

and wreck your chariots.
11 I will remove the cities of your land
and tear down all your fortresses.
12 I will remove sorceries from your hands,
and you will not have
any more fortune-tellers.
13 I will remove your carved images
and sacred pillars from you
so that you will not bow down again
to the work of your hands.
14 I will pull up the *Asherah poles
from among you
and demolish your cities.
15 I will take vengeance in anger and wrath
against the nations that have not obeyed Me.

6 Now listen to what the LORD is saying:
Rise, plead your case before the mountains,
and let the hills hear your voice.
2 Listen to the LORD's lawsuit,
you mountains and enduring foundations
of the earth,
because the LORD has a case
against His people,
and He will argue it against Israel.
3 My people, what have I done to you,
or how have I wearied you?
Testify against Me!
4 Indeed, I brought you up from the land
of Egypt
and redeemed you from that place of slavery.
I sent Moses, Aaron, and Miriam ahead of you.
5 My people,
remember what Balak king of Moab proposed,
what Balaam son of Beor answered him,
and what happened from the Acacia Grove
to Gilgal
so that you may acknowledge
the LORD's righteous acts.
6 What should I bring before the LORD
when I come to bow before God on high?
Should I come before Him
with *burnt offerings,
with year-old calves?
7 Would the LORD be pleased with thousands
of rams
or with ten thousand streams of oil?
Should I give my firstborn
for my transgression,
the child of my body for my own sin?
8 Mankind, He has told you what is good
and what it is the LORD requires of you:
to act justly,
to love faithfulness,
and to walk humbly with your God.
9 The voice of *Yahweh calls out to the city
(and it is wise to *fear Your name):
"Pay attention to the rod
and the One who ordained it.
10 Are there still the treasures of wickedness
and the accursed short measure
in the house of the wicked?
11 Can I excuse wicked scales
or bags of deceptive weights?
12 For the wealthy of the city are full of violence,
and its residents speak lies;
the tongues in their mouths are deceitful.
13 As a result, I have begun to strike you severely,

bringing desolation because of your sins.
14 You will eat but not be satisfied,
for there will be hunger within you.
What you acquire, you cannot save,
and what you do save,
I will give to the sword.
15 You will sow but not reap;
you will press olives
but not anoint yourself with oil;
and you will tread grapes
but not drink the wine.
16 The statutes of Omri
and all the practices of Ahab's house
have been observed;
you have followed their policies.
Therefore, I will make you a desolate place
and the city's residents an object of contempt;
you will bear the scorn of My people."

7 How sad for me!
For I am like one who—
when the summer fruit has been gathered
after the gleaning of the grape harvest—
finds no grape cluster to eat,
no early fig, which I crave.
2 Godly people have vanished from the land;
there is no one upright among the people.
All of them wait in ambush to shed blood;
they hunt each other with a net.
3 Both hands are good at accomplishing evil:
the official and the judge demand a bribe;
when the powerful man communicates
his evil desire,
they plot it together.
4 The best of them is like a brier;
the most upright is worse than a hedge
of thorns.
The day of your watchmen,
the day of your punishment, is coming;
at this time their panic is here.
5 Do not rely on a friend;
don't trust in a close companion.
Seal your mouth
from the woman who lies in your arms.
6 Surely a son considers his father a fool,
a daughter opposes her mother,
and a daughter-in-law is
against her mother-in-law;
a man's enemies are the men
of his own household.
7 But I will look to the LORD;
I will wait for the God of my salvation.
My God will hear me.
8 Do not rejoice over me, my enemy!
Though I have fallen, I will stand up;
though I sit in darkness,
the LORD will be my light.
9 Because I have sinned against Him,
I must endure the LORD's rage
until He argues my case
and establishes justice for me.
He will bring me into the light;
I will see His salvation.
10 Then my enemy will see,
and she will be covered with shame,
the one who said to me,
"Where is the LORD your God?"
My eyes will look at her in triumph;

at that time she will be trampled
like mud in the streets.
11 A day will come for rebuilding your walls;
on that day your boundary will be extended.
12 On that day people will come to you
from Assyria and the cities of Egypt,
even from Egypt to the Euphrates River
and from sea to sea
and mountain to mountain.
13 Then the earth will become a wasteland
because of its inhabitants
and as a result of their actions.
14 Shepherd Your people with Your staff,
the flock that is Your possession.
They live alone in a woodland
surrounded by pastures.
Let them graze in Bashan and Gilead
as in ancient times.
15 I will perform miracles for them
as in the days of your exodus
from the land of Egypt.
16 Nations will see and be ashamed
of all their power.

They will put their hands over their mouths,
and their ears will become deaf.
17 They will lick the dust like a snake;
they will come trembling out of
their hiding places
like reptiles slithering on the ground.
They will tremble in the presence of •Yahweh
our God;
they will stand in awe of You.
18 Who is a God like You,
removing iniquity and passing over rebellion
for the remnant of His inheritance?
He does not hold on to His anger forever,
because He delights in faithful love.
19 He will again have compassion on us;
He will vanquish our iniquities.
You will cast all our sins
into the depths of the sea.
20 You will show loyalty to Jacob
and faithful love to Abraham,
as You swore to our fathers
from days long ago.

NAHUM

1 The •oracle concerning Nineveh. The book of the
vision of Nahum the Elkoshite.
2 The Lord is a jealous and avenging God;
the Lord takes vengeance
and is fierce in wrath.
The Lord takes vengeance against His foes;
He is furious with His enemies.
3 The Lord is slow to anger but great in power;
the Lord will never leave
the •guilty unpunished.
His •path is in the whirlwind and storm,
and clouds are the dust beneath His feet.
4 He rebukes the sea so that it dries up,
and He makes all the rivers run dry.
Bashan and Carmel wither;
even the flower of Lebanon withers.
5 The mountains quake before Him,
and the hills melt;
the earth trembles at His presence—
the world and all who live in it.
6 Who can withstand His indignation?
Who can endure His burning anger?
His wrath is poured out like fire,
even rocks are shattered before Him.
7 The Lord is good,
a stronghold in a day of distress;
He cares for those who take refuge in Him.
8 But He will completely destroy Nineveh
with an overwhelming flood,
and He will chase His enemies into darkness.
9 Whatever you plot against the Lord,
He will bring it to complete destruction;
oppression will not rise up a second time.
10 For they will be consumed
like entangled thorns,
like the drink of a drunkard
and like straw that is fully dry.
11 One has gone out from you,

who plots evil against •Yahweh,
and is a wicked counselor.
12 This is what the Lord says:
Though they are strong and numerous,
they will still be mowed down,
and he will pass away.
Though I have afflicted you,
I will afflict you no longer.
13 For I will now break off his yoke from you
and tear off your shackles.
14 The Lord has issued an order concerning you:
There will be no offspring
to carry on your name.
I will eliminate the carved idol and cast image
from the house of your gods;
I will prepare your grave,
for you are contemptible.
15 Look to the mountains—
the feet of one bringing good news
and proclaiming peace!
Celebrate your festivals, Judah;
fulfill your vows.
For the wicked one will never again
march through you;
he will be entirely wiped out.

2 One who scatters is coming up
against you.
Man the fortifications!
Watch the road!
Brace yourself!
Summon all your strength!
2 For the Lord will restore the majesty of Jacob,
yes, the majesty of Israel,
though ravagers have ravaged them
and ruined their vine branches.
3 The shields of his warriors are dyed red;
the valiant men are dressed in scarlet.
The fittings of the chariot flash like fire

on the day of its battle preparations,
   and the spears are brandished.
⁴ The chariots dash madly through the streets;
   they rush around in the plazas.
   They look like torches;
   they dart back and forth like lightning.
⁵ He gives orders to his officers;
   they stumble as they advance.
   They race to its wall;
   the protective shield is set in place.
⁶ The river gates are opened,
   and the palace erodes away.
⁷ Beauty is stripped,
   she is carried away;
   her ladies-in-waiting moan
   like the sound of doves,
   and beat their breasts.
⁸ Nineveh has been like a pool of water
   from her first days,
   but they are fleeing.
   "Stop! Stop!" they cry,
   but no one turns back.
⁹ "Plunder the silver! Plunder the gold!"
   There is no end to the treasure,
   an abundance of every precious thing.
¹⁰ Desolation, decimation, devastation!
   Hearts melt,
   knees tremble,
   loins shake,
   every face grows pale!
¹¹ Where is the lions' lair,
   or the feeding ground of the young lions,
   where the lion and lioness prowled,
   and the lion's cub,
   with nothing to frighten them away?
¹² The lion mauled whatever its cubs needed
   and strangled prey for its lionesses.
   It filled up its dens with the kill,
   and its lairs with mauled prey.
¹³ Beware, I am against you.
                    This is the declaration
                    of the Lᴏʀᴅ of ˙Hosts.
   I will make your chariots go up in smoke
   and the sword will devour your young lions.
   I will cut off your prey from the earth,
   and the sound of your messengers
   will never be heard again.

3 Woe to the city of blood,
   totally deceitful,
   full of plunder,
   never without prey.
² The crack of the whip
   and rumble of the wheel,
   galloping horse
   and jolting chariot!
³ Charging horseman,
   flashing sword,
   shining spear;
   heaps of slain,
   mounds of corpses,
   dead bodies without end—
   they stumble over their dead.
⁴ Because of the continual prostitution
      of the prostitute,
   the attractive mistress of sorcery,
   who betrays nations by her prostitution
   and clans by her witchcraft,

⁵ I am against you.
                    This is the declaration
                    of the Lᴏʀᴅ of ˙Hosts.
   I will lift your skirts over your face
   and display your nakedness to nations,
   your shame to kingdoms.
⁶ I will throw filth on you
   and treat you with contempt;
   I will make a spectacle of you.
⁷ Then all who see you will recoil
      from you, saying,
   "Nineveh is devastated;
   who will show sympathy to her?"
   Where can I find anyone to comfort you?
⁸ Are you better than Thebes
   that sat along the Nile
   with water surrounding her,
   whose rampart was the sea,
   the river her wall?
⁹ ˙Cush and Egypt were her endless source
      of strength;
   Put and Libya were among her allies.
¹⁰ Yet she became an exile;
   she went into captivity.
   Her children were also dashed to pieces
   at the head of every street.
   They cast lots for her dignitaries,
   and all her nobles were bound in chains.
¹¹ You also will become drunk;
   you will hide yourself.
   You also will seek refuge from the enemy.
¹² All your fortresses are fig trees
   with figs that ripened first;
   when shaken, they fall—
   right into the mouth of the eater!
¹³ Look, your troops are like women among you;
   the gates of your land
   are wide open to your enemies.
   Fire will devour the bars of your gates.
¹⁴ Draw water for the siege;
   strengthen your fortresses.
   Step into the clay and tread the mortar;
   take hold of the brick-mold!
¹⁵ The fire will devour you there;
   the sword will cut you down.
   It will devour you like the young locust.
   Multiply yourselves like the young locust,
   multiply like the swarming locust!
¹⁶ You have made your merchants
   more numerous than the stars of the sky.
   The young locust strips the land
   and flies away.
¹⁷ Your court officials are like the swarming locust,
   and your scribes like clouds of locusts,
   which settle on the walls on a cold day;
   when the sun rises, they take off,
   and no one knows where they are.
¹⁸ King of Assyria, your shepherds slumber;
   your officers sleep.
   Your people are scattered across the mountains
   with no one to gather them together.
¹⁹ There is no remedy for your injury;
   your wound is severe.
   All who hear the news about you
   will clap their hands because of you,
   for who has not experienced
   your constant cruelty?

HABAKKUK

1 The °oracle that Habakkuk the prophet saw.
² How long, Lord, must I call for help
and You do not listen
or cry out to You about violence
and You do not save?
³ Why do You force me to look at injustice?
Why do You tolerate wrongdoing?
Oppression and violence are right in front of me.
Strife is ongoing, and conflict escalates.
⁴ This is why the law is ineffective
and justice never emerges.
For the wicked restrict the righteous;
therefore, justice comes out perverted.
⁵ Look at the nations and observe—
be utterly astounded!
For something is taking place in your days
that you will not believe
when you hear about it.
⁶ Look! I am raising up the Chaldeans,
that bitter, impetuous nation
that marches across the earth's open spaces
to seize territories not its own.
⁷ They are fierce and terrifying;
their views of justice and sovereignty
stem from themselves.
⁸ Their horses are swifter than leopards
and more fierce than wolves of the night.
Their horsemen charge ahead;
their horsemen come from distant lands.
They fly like an eagle, swooping to devour.
⁹ All of them come to do violence;
their faces are set in determination.
They gather prisoners like sand.
¹⁰ They mock kings,
and rulers are a joke to them.
They laugh at every fortress
and build siege ramps to capture it.
¹¹ Then they sweep by like the wind
and pass through.
They are °guilty; their strength is their god.
¹² Are You not from eternity, °Yahweh my God?
My Holy One, You will not die.
Lord, You appointed them
to execute judgment;
my Rock, You destined them to punish us.
¹³ Your eyes are too pure to look on evil,
and You cannot tolerate wrongdoing.
So why do You tolerate those
who are treacherous?
Why are You silent
while one who is wicked swallows up
one who is more righteous than himself?
¹⁴ You have made mankind
like the fish of the sea,
like marine creatures that have no ruler.
¹⁵ The Chaldeans pull them all up with a hook,
catch them in their dragnet,
and gather them in their fishing net;
that is why they are glad and rejoice.
¹⁶ That is why they sacrifice to their dragnet
and burn incense to their fishing net,
for by these things their portion is rich
and their food plentiful.
¹⁷ Will they therefore empty their net

and continually slaughter nations
without mercy?

2 I will stand at my guard post
and station myself on the lookout tower.
I will watch to see what He will say to me
and what I should reply about my complaint.
² The Lord answered me:
Write down this vision;
clearly inscribe it on tablets
so one may easily read it.
³ For the vision is yet for the appointed time;
it testifies about the end and will not lie.
Though it delays, wait for it,
since it will certainly come and not be late.
⁴ Look, his ego is inflated;
he is without integrity.
But the righteous one will live by his faith.
⁵ Moreover, wine betrays;
an arrogant man is never at rest.
He enlarges his appetite like °Sheol,
and like Death he is never satisfied.
He gathers all the nations to himself;
he collects all the peoples for himself.
⁶ Won't all of these take up a taunt against him,
with mockery and riddles about him?
They will say:
Woe to him who amasses what is not his—
how much longer?—
and loads himself with goods taken in pledge.
⁷ Won't your creditors suddenly arise,
and those who disturb you wake up?
Then you will become spoil for them.
⁸ Since you have plundered many nations,
all the peoples who remain will plunder you—
because of human bloodshed
and violence against lands, cities,
and all who live in them.
⁹ Woe to him who dishonestly makes
wealth for his house
to place his nest on high,
to escape from the reach of disaster!
¹⁰ You have planned shame for your house
by wiping out many peoples
and sinning against your own self.
¹¹ For the stones will cry out from the wall,
and the rafters will answer them
from the woodwork.
¹² Woe to him who builds a city
with bloodshed
and founds a town with injustice!
¹³ Is it not from the Lord of °Hosts
that the peoples labor only to fuel the fire
and countries exhaust themselves
for nothing?
¹⁴ For the earth will be filled
with the knowledge of the Lord's glory,
as the waters cover the sea.
¹⁵ Woe to him who gives his neighbors drink,
pouring out your wrath
and even making them drunk,
in order to look at their nakedness!
¹⁶ You will be filled with disgrace
instead of glory.

You also—drink,
and expose your uncircumcision!
The cup in the Lord's right hand
will come around to you,
and utter disgrace will cover your glory.

17 For your violence against Lebanon
will overwhelm you;
the destruction of animals will terrify you
because of your human bloodshed
and violence
against lands, cities, and all who live in them.

18 What use is a carved idol
after its craftsman carves it?
It is only a cast image, a teacher of lies.
For the one who crafts its shape trusts in it
and makes idols that cannot speak.

19 Woe to him who says to wood: Wake up!
or to mute stone: Come alive!
Can it teach?
Look! It may be plated with gold and silver,
yet there is no breath in it at all.

20 But the Lord is in His holy temple;
let everyone on earth
be silent in His presence.

3 A prayer of Habakkuk the prophet. According to
Shigionoth.

2 Lord, I have heard the report about You;
Lord, I stand in awe of Your deeds.
Revive Your work in these years;
make it known in these years.
In Your wrath remember mercy!

3 God comes from Teman,
the Holy One from Mount Paran.　·*Selah*
His splendor covers the heavens,
and the earth is full of His praise.

4 His brilliance is like light;
rays are flashing from His hand.
This is where His power is hidden.

5 Plague goes before Him,
and pestilence follows in His steps.

6 He stands and shakes the earth;
He looks and startles the nations.
The age-old mountains break apart;
the ancient hills sink down.
His pathways are ancient.

7 I see the tents of Cushan in distress;
the tent curtains of the land
of Midian tremble.

8 Are You angry at the rivers, Lord?
Is Your wrath against the rivers?
Or is Your rage against the sea
when You ride on Your horses,
Your victorious chariot?

9 You took the sheath from Your bow;
the arrows are ready to be used with an oath.
Selah
You split the earth with rivers.

10 The mountains see You and shudder;
a downpour of water sweeps by.
The deep roars with its voice
and lifts its waves high.

11 Sun and moon stand still
in their lofty residence,
at the flash of Your flying arrows,
at the brightness of Your shining spear.

12 You march across the earth with indignation;
You trample down the nations in wrath.

13 You come out to save Your people,
to save Your anointed.
You crush the leader of the house
of the wicked
and strip him from foot to neck.　*Selah*

14 You pierce his head
with his own spears;
his warriors storm out to scatter us,
gloating as if ready to secretly devour
the weak.

15 You tread the sea with Your horses,
stirring up the great waters.

16 I heard, and I trembled within;
my lips quivered at the sound.
Rottenness entered my bones;
I trembled where I stood.
Now I must quietly wait for the day of distress
to come against the people invading us.

17 Though the fig tree does not bud
and there is no fruit on the vines,
though the olive crop fails
and the fields produce no food,
though there are no sheep in the pen
and no cattle in the stalls,

18 yet I will triumph in ·Yahweh;
I will rejoice in the God of my salvation!

19 Yahweh my Lord is my strength;
He makes my feet like those of a deer
and enables me to walk on mountain heights!
For the choir director: on stringed instruments.

ZEPHANIAH

1 The word of the Lord that came to Zephaniah son
of Cushi, son of Gedaliah, son of Amariah, son of
Hezekiah, in the days of Josiah son of Amon, king of
Judah.

2 I will completely sweep away everything
from the face of the earth—
this is the Lord's declaration.

3 I will sweep away man and animal;
I will sweep away the birds of the sky
and the fish of the sea,
and the ruins along with the wicked.
I will cut off mankind

from the face of the earth.
This is the Lord's declaration.

4 I will stretch out My hand against Judah
and against all the residents of Jerusalem.
I will cut off every vestige of ·Baal
from this place,
the names of the pagan priests
along with the priests;

5 those who bow in worship on the rooftops
to the heavenly host;
those who bow and pledge loyalty to the Lord
but also pledge loyalty to ·Milcom;

⁶ and those who turn back from following
   the LORD,
 who do not seek the LORD or inquire of Him.
⁷ Be silent in the presence of the Lord GOD,
 for the Day of the LORD is near.
 Indeed, the LORD has prepared a sacrifice;
 He has consecrated His guests.
⁸ On the day of the LORD's sacrifice
 I will punish the officials, the king's sons,
 and all who are dressed in foreign clothing.
⁹ On that day I will punish
 all who skip over the threshold,
 who fill their master's house
 with violence and deceit.
¹⁰ On that day—
             this is the LORD's declaration—
 there will be an outcry from the Fish Gate,
 a wailing from the Second District,
 and a loud crashing from the hills.
¹¹ Wail, you residents of the Hollow,
 for all the merchants will be silenced;
 all those loaded with silver will be cut off.
¹² And at that time I will search Jerusalem
    with lamps
 and punish the men
    who settle down comfortably,
 who say to themselves:
 The LORD will not do good or evil.
¹³ Their wealth will become plunder
 and their houses a ruin.
 They will build houses but never live in them,
 plant vineyards but never drink their wine.
¹⁴ The great Day of the LORD is near,
 near and rapidly approaching.
 Listen, the Day of the LORD—
 then the warrior's cry is bitter.
¹⁵ That day is a day of wrath,
 a day of trouble and distress,
 a day of destruction and desolation,
 a day of darkness and gloom,
 a day of clouds and blackness,
¹⁶ a day of trumpet blast and battle cry
 against the fortified cities,
 and against the high corner towers.
¹⁷ I will bring distress on mankind,
 and they will walk like the blind
 because they have sinned against the LORD.
 Their blood will be poured out like dust
 and their flesh like dung.
¹⁸ Their silver and their gold
 will not be able to rescue them
 on the day of the LORD's wrath.
 The whole earth will be consumed
 by the fire of His jealousy.
 For He will make a complete,
 yes, a horrifying end
 of all the inhabitants of the earth.

2 Gather yourselves together;
 gather together, undesirable nation,
² before the decree takes effect
 and the day passes like chaff,
 before the burning of the LORD's anger
    overtakes you,
 before the day of the LORD's anger overtakes you.
³ Seek the LORD, all you humble of the earth,
 who carry out what He commands.
 Seek righteousness, seek humility;

perhaps you will be concealed
 on the day of the LORD's anger.
⁴ For Gaza will be abandoned,
 and Ashkelon will become a ruin.
 Ashdod will be driven out at noon,
 and Ekron will be uprooted.
⁵ Woe, inhabitants of the seacoast,
 nation of the Cherethites!
 The word of the LORD is against you,
 Canaan, land of the Philistines:
 I will destroy you until there is no one left.
⁶ The seacoast will become pasturelands
 with caves for shepherds and folds for sheep.
⁷ The coastland will belong
 to the remnant of the house of Judah;
 they will find pasture there.
 They will lie down in the evening
 among the houses of Ashkelon,
 for the LORD their God will return to them
 and restore their fortunes.
⁸ I have heard the taunting of Moab
 and the insults of the Ammonites,
 who have taunted My people
 and threatened their territory.
⁹ Therefore, as I live—
             this is the declaration of the LORD
                of •Hosts, the God of Israel—
 Moab will be like Sodom
 and the Ammonites like Gomorrah—
 a place overgrown with weeds,
 a salt pit, and a perpetual wasteland.
 The remnant of My people will plunder them;
 the remainder of My nation
    will dispossess them.
¹⁰ This is what they get for their pride,
 because they have taunted
    and acted arrogantly
 against the people of the LORD of Hosts.
¹¹ The LORD will be terrifying to them
 when He starves all the gods of the earth.
 Then all the distant coastlands of the nations
 will bow in worship to Him,
 each in its own place.
¹² You •Cushites will also be slain by My sword.
¹³ He will also stretch out His hand
    against the north
 and destroy Assyria;
 He will make Nineveh a desolate ruin,
 dry as the desert.
¹⁴ Herds will lie down in the middle of it,
 every kind of wild animal.
 Both the desert owl and the screech owl
 will roost in the capitals of its pillars.
 Their calls will sound from the window,
 but devastation will be on the threshold,
 for He will expose the cedar work.
¹⁵ This is the self-assured city
 that lives in security,
 that thinks to herself:
 I exist, and there is no one else.
 What a desolation she has become,
 a place for wild animals to lie down!
 Everyone who passes by her
 jeers and shakes his fist.

3 Woe to the city that is rebellious and defiled,
 the oppressive city!
² She has not obeyed;

she has not accepted discipline.
She has not trusted in *Yahweh;
she has not drawn near to her God.
³ The princes within her are roaring lions;
her judges are wolves of the night,
which leave nothing for the morning.
⁴ Her prophets are reckless—
treacherous men.
Her priests profane the sanctuary;
they do violence to instruction.
⁵ The righteous Lᴏʀᴅ is in her;
He does no wrong.
He applies His justice morning by morning;
He does not fail at dawn,
yet the one who does wrong knows no shame.
⁶ I have cut off nations;
their corner towers are destroyed.
I have laid waste their streets,
with no one to pass through.
Their cities lie devastated,
without a person, without an inhabitant.
⁷ I thought: You will certainly *fear Me
and accept correction.
Then her dwelling place
would not be cut off
based on all that I had allocated to her.
However, they became more corrupt
in all their actions.
⁸ Therefore, wait for Me—
this is the Lᴏʀᴅ's declaration—
until the day I rise up for plunder.
For My decision is to gather nations,
to assemble kingdoms,
in order to pour out My indignation on them,
all My burning anger;
for the whole earth will be consumed
by the fire of My jealousy.
⁹ For I will then restore
pure speech to the peoples
so that all of them may call
on the name of Yahweh
and serve Him with a single purpose.
¹⁰ From beyond the rivers of *Cush
My supplicants, My dispersed people,
will bring an offering to Me.
¹¹ On that day you will not be put to shame
because of everything you have done

in rebelling against Me.
For then I will remove
your proud, arrogant people from among you,
and you will never again be haughty
on My holy mountain.
¹² I will leave
a meek and humble people among you,
and they will take refuge in the name
of Yahweh.
¹³ The remnant of Israel will no longer
do wrong or tell lies;
a deceitful tongue will not be found
in their mouths.
But they will pasture and lie down,
with nothing to make them afraid.
¹⁴ Sing for joy, Daughter *Zion;
shout loudly, Israel!
Be glad and rejoice with all your heart,
Daughter Jerusalem!
¹⁵ The Lᴏʀᴅ has removed your punishment;
He has turned back your enemy.
The King of Israel, Yahweh, is among you;
you need no longer fear harm.
¹⁶ On that day it will be said to Jerusalem:
"Do not fear;
Zion, do not let your hands grow weak.
¹⁷ Yahweh your God is among you,
a warrior who saves.
He will rejoice over you with gladness.
He will bring you quietness with His love.
He will delight in you with shouts of joy."
¹⁸ I will gather those who have been driven
from the appointed festivals;
they will be a tribute from you
and a reproach on her.
¹⁹ Yes, at that time
I will deal with all who afflict you.
I will save the lame and gather the scattered;
I will make those who were disgraced
throughout the earth
receive praise and fame.
²⁰ At that time I will bring you back,
yes, at the time I will gather you.
I will give you fame and praise
among all the peoples of the earth,
when I restore your fortunes before your eyes.
Yahweh has spoken.

Hᴀɢɢᴀɪ

1 In the second year of King Darius, on the first day of the sixth month, the word of the Lᴏʀᴅ came through Haggai the prophet to Zerubbabel son of Shealtiel, the governor of Judah, and to Joshua son of Jehozadak, the high priest:

² "The Lᴏʀᴅ of *Hosts says this: These people say: The time has not come for the house of the Lᴏʀᴅ to be rebuilt."

³ The word of the Lᴏʀᴅ came through Haggai the prophet: ⁴ "Is it a time for you yourselves to live in your paneled houses, while this house lies in ruins?" ⁵ Now, the Lᴏʀᴅ of Hosts says this: "Think carefully about your ways:

⁶ You have planted much

but harvested little.
You eat
but never have enough to be satisfied.
You drink
but never have enough to become drunk.
You put on clothes
but never have enough to get warm.
The wage earner puts his wages
into a bag with a hole in it."

⁷ The Lᴏʀᴅ of Hosts says this: "Think carefully about your ways. ⁸ Go up into the hills, bring down lumber, and build the house. Then I will be pleased with it and be glorified," says the Lᴏʀᴅ. ⁹ "You expected much, but then it amounted to little. When you brought the

harvest to your house, I ruined it. Why?" This is the declaration of the LORD of Hosts. "Because My house still lies in ruins, while each of you is busy with his own house.

¹⁰ So on your account,
the skies have withheld the dew
and the land its crops.
¹¹ I have summoned a drought
on the fields and the hills,
on the grain, new wine, olive oil,
and whatever the ground yields,
on man and beast,
and on all that your hands produce."

¹²Then Zerubbabel son of Shealtiel, the high priest Joshua son of Jehozadak, and the entire remnant of the people obeyed the voice of the LORD their God and the words of the prophet Haggai, because the LORD their God had sent him. So the people ˙feared the LORD.

¹³Haggai, the LORD's messenger, delivered the LORD's message to the people, "I am with you"—this is the LORD's declaration.

¹⁴The LORD stirred up the spirit of Zerubbabel son of Shealtiel, governor of Judah, the spirit of the high priest Joshua son of Jehozadak, and the spirit of all the remnant of the people. They began work on the house of ˙Yahweh of Hosts, their God, ¹⁵on the twenty-fourth day of the sixth month, in the second year of King Darius.

2 On the twenty-first day of the seventh month, the word of the LORD came through Haggai the prophet: ²"Speak to Zerubbabel son of Shealtiel, governor of Judah, to the high priest Joshua son of Jehozadak, and to the remnant of the people: ³Who is left among you who saw this house in its former glory? How does it look to you now? Doesn't it seem like nothing to you? ⁴Even so, be strong, Zerubbabel"—this is the LORD's declaration. "Be strong, Joshua son of Jehozadak, high priest. Be strong, all you people of the land"—this is the LORD's declaration. "Work! For I am with you"— the declaration of the LORD of ˙Hosts. ⁵"This is the promise I made to you when you came out of Egypt, and My Spirit is present among you; don't be afraid."

⁶For the LORD of Hosts says this: "Once more, in a little while, I am going to shake the heavens and the earth, the sea and the dry land. ⁷I will shake all the nations so that the treasures of all the nations will come, and I will fill this house with glory," says the LORD of Hosts. ⁸"The silver and gold belong to Me"—this is the declaration of the LORD of Hosts. ⁹"The final glory of this house will be greater than the first," says the LORD of Hosts. "I will provide peace in this place"—this is the declaration of the LORD of Hosts.

¹⁰On the twenty-fourth day of the ninth month, in the second year of Darius, the word of the LORD came to Haggai the prophet: ¹¹"This is what the LORD of Hosts says: Ask the priests for a ruling. ¹²If a man is carrying consecrated meat in the fold of his garment, and it touches bread, stew, wine, oil, or any other food, does it become holy?"

The priests answered, "No."

¹³Then Haggai asked, "If someone defiled by contact with a corpse touches any of these, does it become defiled?"

The priests answered, "It becomes defiled."

¹⁴Then Haggai replied, "So is this people, and so is this nation before Me"—this is the LORD's declaration. "And so is every work of their hands; even what they offer there is defiled.

¹⁵"Now, reflect back from this day: Before one stone was placed on another in the LORD's temple, ¹⁶what state were you in? When someone came to a grain heap of 20 measures, it only amounted to 10; when one came to the winepress to dip 50 measures from the vat, it only amounted to 20. ¹⁷I struck you—all the work of your hands—with blight, mildew, and hail, but you didn't turn to Me"—this is the LORD's declaration. ¹⁸"Consider carefully from this day forward; from the twenty-fourth day of the ninth month, from the day the foundation of the LORD's temple was laid; consider it carefully. ¹⁹Is there still seed left in the granary? The vine, the fig, the pomegranate, and the olive tree have not yet produced. But from this day on I will bless you."

²⁰The word of the LORD came to Haggai a second time on the twenty-fourth day of the month: ²¹"Speak to Zerubbabel, governor of Judah: I am going to shake the heavens and the earth. ²²I will overturn royal thrones and destroy the power of the Gentile kingdoms. I will overturn chariots and their riders. Horses and their riders will fall, each by his brother's sword. ²³On that day"—this is the declaration of the LORD of Hosts—"I will take you, Zerubbabel son of Shealtiel, My servant"—this is the LORD's declaration—"and make you like My signet ring, for I have chosen you." This is the declaration of the LORD of Hosts.

ZECHARIAH

1 In the eighth month, in the second year of Darius, the word of the LORD came to the prophet Zechariah son of Berechiah, son of Iddo: ²"The LORD was extremely angry with your ancestors. ³So tell the people: This is what the LORD of ˙Hosts says: Return to Me"—this is the declaration of the LORD of Hosts— "and I will return to you, says the LORD of Hosts. ⁴Do not be like your ancestors; the earlier prophets proclaimed to them: This is what the LORD of Hosts says: Turn from your evil ways and your evil deeds. But they did not listen or pay attention to Me"—this is the LORD's declaration. ⁵"Where are your ancestors now? And do the prophets live forever? ⁶But didn't My words and My statutes that I commanded My servants the prophets overtake your ancestors? They repented and said: As the LORD of Hosts purposed to deal with us for our ways and deeds, so He has dealt with us."

⁷On the twenty-fourth day of the eleventh month, which is the month of Shebat, in the second year of Darius, the word of the LORD came to the prophet Zechariah son of Berechiah, son of Iddo:

⁸I looked out in the night and saw a man riding on a red horse. He was standing among the myrtle trees in the valley. Behind him were red, sorrel, and white horses. ⁹I asked, "What are these, my lord?"

The angel who was talking to me replied, "I will show you what they are."

¹⁰Then the man standing among the myrtle trees explained, "They are the ones the Lᴏʀᴅ has sent to patrol the earth."

¹¹They reported to the Angel of the Lᴏʀᴅ standing among the myrtle trees, "We have patrolled the earth, and right now the whole earth is calm and quiet."

¹²Then the Angel of the Lᴏʀᴅ responded, "How long, Lᴏʀᴅ of Hosts, will You withhold mercy from Jerusalem and the cities of Judah that You have been angry with these 70 years?" ¹³The Lᴏʀᴅ replied with kind and comforting words to the angel who was speaking with me.

¹⁴So the angel who was speaking with me said, "Proclaim: The Lᴏʀᴅ of Hosts says: I am extremely jealous for Jerusalem and •Zion. ¹⁵I am fiercely angry with the nations that are at ease, for I was a little angry, but they made it worse. ¹⁶Therefore, this is what the Lᴏʀᴅ says: In mercy, I have returned to Jerusalem; My house will be rebuilt within it"—this is the declaration of the Lᴏʀᴅ of Hosts—"and a measuring line will be stretched out over Jerusalem.

¹⁷"Proclaim further: This is what the Lᴏʀᴅ of Hosts says: My cities will again overflow with prosperity; the Lᴏʀᴅ will once more comfort Zion and again choose Jerusalem."

¹⁸Then I looked up and saw four •horns. ¹⁹So I asked the angel who was speaking with me, "What are these?"

And he said to me, "These are the horns that scattered Judah, Israel, and Jerusalem."

²⁰Then the Lᴏʀᴅ showed me four craftsmen. ²¹I asked, "What are they coming to do?"

He replied, "These are the horns that scattered Judah so no one could raise his head. These craftsmen have come to terrify them, to cut off the horns of the nations that raised their horns against the land of Judah to scatter it."

2 I looked up and saw a man with a measuring line in his hand. ²I asked, "Where are you going?"

He answered me, "To measure Jerusalem to determine its width and length."

³Then the angel who was speaking with me went out, and another angel went out to meet him. ⁴He said to him, "Run and tell this young man: Jerusalem will be inhabited without walls because of the number of people and livestock in it." ⁵The declaration of the Lᴏʀᴅ: "I will be a wall of fire around it, and I will be the glory within it."

⁶"Get up! Leave the land of the north"—this is the Lᴏʀᴅ's declaration—"for I have scattered you like the four winds of heaven"—this is the Lᴏʀᴅ's declaration. ⁷"Go, •Zion! Escape, you who are living with Daughter Babylon." ⁸For the Lᴏʀᴅ of •Hosts says this: "He has sent Me for His glory against the nations who are plundering you, for anyone who touches you touches the pupil of His eye. ⁹I will move against them with My power, and they will become plunder for their own servants. Then you will know that the Lᴏʀᴅ of Hosts has sent Me.

¹⁰"Daughter Zion, shout for joy and be glad, for I am coming to dwell among you"—this is the Lᴏʀᴅ's declaration. ¹¹"Many nations will join themselves to the Lᴏʀᴅ on that day and become My people. I will dwell among you, and you will know that the Lᴏʀᴅ of Hosts has sent Me to you. ¹²The Lᴏʀᴅ will take possession of

Judah as His portion in the Holy Land, and He will once again choose Jerusalem. ¹³Let all people be silent before the Lᴏʀᴅ, for He is coming from His holy dwelling."

3 Then he showed me Joshua the high priest standing before the Angel of the Lᴏʀᴅ, with Satan standing at his right side to accuse him. ²The Lᴏʀᴅ said to Satan: "The Lᴏʀᴅ rebuke you, Satan! May the Lᴏʀᴅ who has chosen Jerusalem rebuke you! Isn't this man a burning stick snatched from the fire?"

³Now Joshua was dressed with filthy clothes as he stood before the Angel. ⁴So the Angel of the Lᴏʀᴅ spoke to those standing before Him, "Take off his filthy clothes!" Then He said to him, "See, I have removed your •guilt from you, and I will clothe you with splendid robes."

⁵Then I said, "Let them put a •clean turban on his head." So a clean turban was placed on his head, and they clothed him in garments while the Angel of the Lᴏʀᴅ was standing nearby.

⁶Then the Angel of the Lᴏʀᴅ charged Joshua: ⁷"This is what the Lᴏʀᴅ of •Hosts says: If you walk in My ways and keep My instructions, you will both rule My house and take care of My courts; I will also grant you access among these who are standing here.

⁸"Listen, Joshua the high priest, you and your colleagues sitting before you; indeed, these men are a sign that I am about to bring My servant, the Branch. ⁹Notice the stone I have set before Joshua; on that one stone are seven eyes. I will engrave an inscription on it"—this is the declaration of the Lᴏʀᴅ of Hosts—"and I will take away the guilt of this land in a single day. ¹⁰On that day, each of you will invite his neighbor to sit under his vine and fig tree." This is the declaration of the Lᴏʀᴅ of Hosts.

4 The angel who was speaking with me then returned and roused me as one awakened out of sleep. ²He asked me, "What do you see?"

I replied, "I see a solid gold lampstand there with a bowl on its top. It has seven lamps on it and seven channels for each of the lamps on its top. ³There are also two olive trees beside it, one on the right of the bowl and the other on its left."

⁴Then I asked the angel who was speaking with me, "What are these, my lord?"

⁵"Don't you know what they are?" replied the angel who was speaking with me.

I said, "No, my lord."

⁶So he answered me, "This is the word of the Lᴏʀᴅ to Zerubbabel: 'Not by strength or by might, but by My Spirit,' says the Lᴏʀᴅ of •Hosts. ⁷What are you, great mountain? Before Zerubbabel you will become a plain. And he will bring out the capstone accompanied by shouts of: Grace, grace to it!'"

⁸Then the word of the Lᴏʀᴅ came to me: ⁹"Zerubbabel's hands have laid the foundation of this house, and his hands will complete it. Then you will know that the Lᴏʀᴅ of Hosts has sent me to you. ¹⁰For who scorns the day of small things? These seven eyes of the Lᴏʀᴅ, which scan throughout the whole earth, will rejoice when they see the plumb line in Zerubbabel's hand."

¹¹I asked him, "What are the two olive trees on the right and left of the lampstand?" ¹²And I questioned him further, "What are the two olive branches beside the two gold conduits, from which golden oil pours out?"

¹³Then he inquired of me, "Don't you know what these are?"

"No, my lord," I replied.

¹⁴"These are the two anointed ones," he said, "who stand by the Lord of the whole earth."

5 I looked up again and saw a flying scroll. ²"What do you see?" he asked me.

"I see a flying scroll," I replied, "30 feet long and 15 feet wide."

³Then he said to me, "This is the curse that is going out over the whole land, for every thief will be removed according to what is written on one side, and everyone who swears falsely will be removed according to what is written on the other side. ⁴I will send it out,"—this is the declaration of the Lord of ˙Hosts—"and it will enter the house of the thief and the house of the one who swears falsely by My name. It will stay inside his house and destroy it along with its timbers and stones."

⁵Then the angel who was speaking with me came forward and told me, "Look up and see what this is that is approaching."

⁶So I asked, "What is it?"

He responded, "It's a measuring basket that is approaching." And he continued, "This is their iniquity in all the land." ⁷Then a lead cover was lifted, and there was a woman sitting inside the basket. ⁸"This is Wickedness," he said. He shoved her down into the basket and pushed the lead weight over its opening. ⁹Then I looked up and saw two women approaching with the wind in their wings. Their wings were like those of a stork, and they lifted up the basket between earth and sky.

¹⁰So I asked the angel who was speaking with me, "Where are they taking the basket?"

¹¹"To build a shrine for it in the land of ˙Shinar," he told me. "When that is ready, the basket will be placed there on its pedestal."

6 Then I looked up again and saw four chariots coming from between two mountains. And the mountains were made of bronze. ²The first chariot had red horses, the second chariot black horses, ³the third chariot white horses, and the fourth chariot dappled horses—all strong horses. ⁴So I inquired of the angel who was speaking with me, "What are these, my lord?"

⁵The angel told me, "These are the four spirits of heaven going out after presenting themselves to the Lord of the whole earth. ⁶The one with the black horses is going to the land of the north, the white horses are going after them, but the dappled horses are going to the land of the south." ⁷As the strong horses went out, they wanted to go patrol the earth, and the Lord said, "Go, patrol the earth." So they patrolled the earth. ⁸Then He summoned me saying, "See, those going to the land of the north have pacified My Spirit in the northern land."

⁹The word of the Lord came to me: ¹⁰"Take an offering from the exiles, from Heldai, Tobijah, and Jedaiah, who have arrived from Babylon, and go that same day to the house of Josiah son of Zephaniah. ¹¹Take silver and gold, make crowns and place them on the head of Joshua son of Jehozadak, the high priest. ¹²You are to tell him: This is what the Lord of ˙Hosts says: Here is a man whose name is Branch; He will branch out from His place and build the Lord's temple. ¹³Yes, He will build the Lord's temple; He will be clothed in splendor and will sit on His throne and rule. There will also be a priest on His throne, and there will be peaceful coun-

sel between the two of them. ¹⁴The crown will reside in the Lord's temple as a memorial to Heldai, Tobijah, Jedaiah, and Hen son of Zephaniah. ¹⁵People who are far off will come and build the Lord's temple, and you will know that the Lord of Hosts has sent Me to you. This will happen when you fully obey the Lord your God."

7 In the fourth year of King Darius, the word of the Lord came to Zechariah on the fourth day of the ninth month, which is Chislev. ²Now the people of Bethel had sent Sharezer, Regem-melech, and their men to plead for the Lord's favor ³by asking the priests who were at the house of the Lord of ˙Hosts as well as the prophets, "Should we mourn and fast in the fifth month as we have done these many years?"

⁴Then the word of the Lord of Hosts came to me: ⁵"Ask all the people of the land and the priests: When you fasted and lamented in the fifth and in the seventh months for these 70 years, did you really fast for Me? ⁶When you eat and drink, don't you eat and drink simply for yourselves? ⁷Aren't these the words that the Lord proclaimed through the earlier prophets when Jerusalem was inhabited and secure, along with its surrounding cities, and when the southern region and the Judean foothills were inhabited?"

⁸The word of the Lord came to Zechariah: ⁹"The Lord of Hosts says this: Make fair decisions. Show faithful love and compassion to one another. ¹⁰Do not oppress the widow or the fatherless, the foreigner or the poor, and do not plot evil in your hearts against one another. ¹¹But they refused to pay attention and turned a stubborn shoulder; they closed their ears so they could not hear. ¹²They made their hearts like a rock so as not to obey the law or the words that the Lord of Hosts had sent by His Spirit through the earlier prophets. Therefore great anger came from the Lord of Hosts. ¹³Just as He had called, and they would not listen, so when they called, I would not listen," says the Lord of Hosts. ¹⁴"I scattered them with a windstorm over all the nations that had not known them, and the land was left desolate behind them, with no one coming or going. They turned a pleasant land into a desolation."

8 The word of the Lord of ˙Hosts came: ²"The Lord of Hosts says this: I am extremely jealous for ˙Zion; I am jealous for her with great wrath." ³The Lord says this: "I will return to Zion and live in Jerusalem. Then Jerusalem will be called the Faithful City, the mountain of the Lord of Hosts, and the Holy Mountain." ⁴The Lord of Hosts says this: "Old men and women will again sit along the streets of Jerusalem, each with a staff in hand because of advanced age. ⁵The streets of the city will be filled with boys and girls playing in them." ⁶The Lord of Hosts says this: "Though it may seem incredible to the remnant of this people in those days, should it also seem incredible to Me?"— this is the declaration of the Lord of Hosts. ⁷The Lord of Hosts says this: "I will save My people from the land of the east and the land of the west. ⁸I will bring them back to live in Jerusalem. They will be My people, and I will be their faithful and righteous God."

⁹The Lord of Hosts says this: "Let your hands be strong, you who now hear these words that the prophets spoke when the foundations were laid for the rebuilding of the temple, the house of the Lord of Hosts. ¹⁰For prior to those days neither man nor beast had wages. There was no safety from the enemy for anyone who came or went, for I turned everyone against

his neighbor. ¹¹But now, I will not treat the remnant of this people as in the former days"—this is the declaration of the LORD of Hosts. ¹²"For they will sow in peace: the vine will yield its fruit, the land will yield its produce, and the skies will yield their dew. I will give the remnant of this people all these things as an inheritance. ¹³As you have been a curse among the nations, house of Judah and house of Israel, so I will save you, and you will be a blessing. Don't be afraid; let your hands be strong." ¹⁴For the LORD of Hosts says this: "As I resolved to treat you badly when your fathers provoked Me to anger, and I did not relent," says the LORD of Hosts, ¹⁵"so I have resolved again in these days to do what is good to Jerusalem and the house of Judah. Don't be afraid. ¹⁶These are the things you must do: Speak truth to one another; make true and sound decisions within your ˙gates. ¹⁷Do not plot evil in your hearts against your neighbor, and do not love perjury, for I hate all this"—this is the LORD's declaration.

¹⁸Then the word of the LORD of Hosts came to me: ¹⁹"The LORD of Hosts says this: The fast of the fourth month, the fast of the fifth, the fast of the seventh, and the fast of the tenth will become times of joy, gladness, and cheerful festivals for the house of Judah. Therefore, love truth and peace." ²⁰The LORD of Hosts says this: "Peoples will yet come, the residents of many cities; ²¹the residents of one city will go to another, saying: Let's go at once to plead for the LORD's favor and to seek the LORD of Hosts. I am also going. ²²Many peoples and strong nations will come to seek the LORD of Hosts in Jerusalem and to plead for the LORD's favor." ²³The LORD of Hosts says this: "In those days, 10 men from nations of every language will grab the robe of a Jewish man tightly, urging: Let us go with you, for we have heard that God is with you."

9

An ˙Oracle

The word of the LORD
is against the land of Hadrach,
and Damascus is its resting place—
for the eyes of men
and all the tribes of Israel
are on the LORD—
² and also against Hamath, which borders it,
as well as Tyre and Sidon,
though they are very shrewd.
³ Tyre has built herself a fortress;
she has heaped up silver like dust
and gold like the dirt of the streets.
⁴ Listen! The Lord will impoverish her
and cast her wealth into the sea;
she herself will be consumed by fire.
⁵ Ashkelon will see it and be afraid;
Gaza too, and will writhe in great pain,
as will Ekron, for her hope will fail.
There will cease to be a king in Gaza,
and Ashkelon will become uninhabited.
⁶ A mongrel people will live in Ashdod,
and I will destroy the pride of the Philistines.
⁷ I will remove the blood from their mouths
and the detestable things
from between their teeth.
Then they too will become a remnant
for our God;
they will become like a clan in Judah
and Ekron like the Jebusites.
⁸ I will set up camp at My house
against an army,

against those who march back and forth,
and no oppressor will march
against them again,
for now I have seen with My own eyes.
⁹ Rejoice greatly, Daughter ˙Zion!
Shout in triumph, Daughter Jerusalem!
Look, your King is coming to you;
He is righteous and victorious,
humble and riding on a donkey,
on a colt, the foal of a donkey.
¹⁰ I will cut off the chariot from Ephraim
and the horse from Jerusalem.
The bow of war will be removed,
and He will proclaim peace to the nations.
His dominion will extend from sea to sea,
from the Euphrates River
to the ends of the earth.
¹¹ As for you,
because of the blood of your covenant,
I will release your prisoners
from the waterless cistern.
¹² Return to a stronghold,
you prisoners who have hope;
today I declare that I will restore double
to you.
¹³ For I will bend Judah as My bow;
I will fill that bow with Ephraim.
I will rouse your sons, Zion,
against your sons, Greece.
I will make you like a warrior's sword.
¹⁴ Then the LORD will appear over them,
and His arrow will fly like lightning.
The Lord GOD will sound the trumpet
and advance with the southern storms.
¹⁵ The LORD of ˙Hosts will defend them.
They will consume and conquer
with slingstones;
they will drink and be rowdy as if with wine.
They will be as full as the sprinkling basin,
like those at the corners of the altar.
¹⁶ The LORD their God will save them on that day
as the flock of His people;
for they are like jewels in a crown,
sparkling over His land.
¹⁷ How lovely and beautiful they will be!
Grain will make the young men flourish,
and new wine, the young women.

10

Ask the LORD for rain
in the season of spring rain.
The LORD makes the rain clouds,
and He will give them showers of rain
and crops in the field for everyone.
² For the idols speak falsehood,
and the diviners see illusions;
they relate empty dreams
and offer empty comfort.
Therefore the people wander like sheep;
they suffer affliction because there is
no shepherd.
³ My anger burns against the shepherds,
so I will punish the leaders.
For the LORD of ˙Hosts has tended His flock,
the house of Judah;
He will make them like His majestic steed
in battle.
⁴ The cornerstone will come from Judah.
The tent peg will come from them

and also the battle bow and every ruler.
Together ⁵they will be like warriors in battle
trampling down the mud of the streets.
They will fight because the LORD is with them,
and they will put horsemen to shame.
⁶ I will strengthen the house of Judah
and deliver the house of Joseph.
I will restore them
because I have compassion on them,
and they will be
as though I had never rejected them.
For I am •Yahweh their God,
and I will answer them.
⁷ Ephraim will be like a warrior,
and their hearts will be glad as if with wine.
Their children will see it and be glad;
their hearts will rejoice in Yahweh.
⁸ I will whistle and gather them
because I have redeemed them;
they will be as numerous as they once were.
⁹ Though I sow them among the nations,
they will remember Me in the distant lands;
they and their children will live and return.
¹⁰ I will bring them back from the land of Egypt
and gather them from Assyria.
I will bring them to the land of Gilead
and to Lebanon,
but it will not be enough for them.
¹¹ Yahweh will pass through the sea of distress
and strike the waves of the sea;
all the depths of the Nile will dry up.
The pride of Assyria will be brought down,
and the scepter of Egypt will come to an end.
¹² I will strengthen them in Yahweh,
and they will march in His name—
                this is Yahweh's declaration.

11 Open your gates, Lebanon,
and fire will consume your cedars.
² Wail, cypress, for the cedar has fallen;
the glorious trees are destroyed!
Wail, oaks of Bashan,
for the stately forest has fallen!
³ Listen to the wail of the shepherds,
for their glory is destroyed.
Listen to the roar of young lions,
for the thickets of the Jordan are destroyed.

⁴ •Yahweh my God says this: "Shepherd the flock intended for slaughter. ⁵Those who buy them slaughter
them but are not punished. Those who sell them say:
Praise the LORD because I have become rich! Even their
own shepherds have no compassion for them. ⁶Indeed,
I will no longer have compassion on the inhabitants
of the land"—this is the LORD's declaration. "Instead, I
will turn everyone over to his neighbor and his king.
They will devastate the land, and I will not deliver it
from them."

⁷So I shepherded the flock intended for slaughter,
the afflicted of the flock. I took two staffs, calling one
Favor and the other Union, and I shepherded the flock.
⁸In one month I got rid of three shepherds. I became
impatient with them, and they also detested me. ⁹Then
I said, "I will no longer shepherd you. Let what is dying
die, and let what is going astray go astray; let the rest
devour each other's flesh." ¹⁰Next I took my staff called
Favor and cut it in two, annulling the covenant I had
made with all the peoples. ¹¹It was annulled on that
day, and so the afflicted of the flock who were watching

me knew that it was the word of the LORD. ¹²Then I said
to them, "If it seems right to you, give me my wages;
but if not, keep them." So they weighed my wages, 30
pieces of silver.

¹³"Throw it to the potter," the LORD said to me—this
magnificent price I was valued by them. So I took the
30 pieces of silver and threw it into the house of the
LORD, to the potter. ¹⁴Then I cut in two my second staff,
Union, annulling the brotherhood between Judah and
Israel.

¹⁵The LORD also said to me: "Take the equipment of
a foolish shepherd. ¹⁶I am about to raise up a shepherd
in the land who will not care for those who are going
astray, and he will not seek the lost or heal the broken.
He will not sustain the healthy, but he will devour the
flesh of the fat sheep and tear off their hooves.
¹⁷ Woe to the worthless shepherd
who deserts the flock!
May a sword strike his arm
and his right eye!
May his arm wither away
and his right eye go completely blind!"

12 An •Oracle
The word of the LORD concerning Israel.
A declaration of the LORD,
who stretched out the heavens,
laid the foundation of the earth,
and formed the spirit of man within him.

²"Look, I will make Jerusalem a cup that causes
staggering for the peoples who surround the city. The
siege against Jerusalem will also involve Judah. ³On
that day I will make Jerusalem a heavy stone for all the
peoples; all who try to lift it will injure themselves severely when all the nations of the earth gather against
her. ⁴On that day"—this is the LORD's declaration—"I
will strike every horse with panic and its rider with
madness. I will keep a watchful eye on the house of Judah but strike all the horses of the nations with blindness. ⁵Then each of the leaders of Judah will think to
himself: The residents of Jerusalem are my strength
through the LORD of •Hosts, their God. ⁶On that day I
will make the leaders of Judah like a firepot in a wood-
pile, like a flaming torch among sheaves; they will
consume all the peoples around them on the right and
the left, while Jerusalem continues to be inhabited on
its site, in Jerusalem. ⁷The LORD will save the tents of
Judah first, so that the glory of David's house and the
glory of Jerusalem's residents may not be greater than
that of Judah. ⁸On that day the LORD will defend the
inhabitants of Jerusalem, so that on that day the one
who is weakest among them will be like David on that
day, and the house of David will be like God, like the
Angel of the LORD, before them. ⁹On that day I will set
out to destroy all the nations that come against Jerusalem.

¹⁰"Then I will pour out a spirit of grace and prayer
on the house of David and the residents of Jerusalem,
and they will look at Me whom they pierced. They will
mourn for Him as one mourns for an only child and
weep bitterly for Him as one weeps for a firstborn. ¹¹On
that day the mourning in Jerusalem will be as
great as the mourning of Hadad-rimmon in the plain
of Megiddo. ¹²The land will mourn, every family by
itself: the family of David's house by itself and their
women by themselves; the family of Nathan's house by
itself and their women by themselves; ¹³the family of
Levi's house by itself and their women by themselves;

the family of Shimei by itself and their women by themselves; [14] all the remaining families, every family by itself, and their women by themselves.

13 "On that day a fountain will be opened for the house of David and for the residents of Jerusalem, to wash away sin and impurity. [2] On that day"— this is the declaration of the Lord of ˙Hosts—"I will erase the names of the idols from the land, and they will no longer be remembered. I will remove the prophets and the ˙unclean spirit from the land. [3] If a man still prophesies, his father and his mother who bore him will say to him: You cannot remain alive because you have spoken falsely in the name of ˙Yahweh. When he prophesies, his father and his mother who bore him will pierce him through. [4] On that day every prophet will be ashamed of his vision when he prophesies; they will not put on a hairy cloak in order to deceive. [5] He will say: I am not a prophet; I work the land, for a man purchased me as a servant since my youth. [6] If someone asks him: What are these wounds on your chest?—then he will answer: I received the wounds in the house of my friends.

[7]   Sword, awake against My shepherd,
      against the man who is My associate—
                      this is the declaration
                       of the Lord of Hosts.
    Strike the shepherd, and the sheep
      will be scattered;
    I will also turn My hand against the little ones.
[8]   In the whole land—
               this is the Lord's declaration—
    two-thirds will be cut off and die,
    but a third will be left in it.
[9]   I will put this third through the fire;
    I will refine them as silver is refined
    and test them as gold is tested.
    They will call on My name,
    and I will answer them.
    I will say: They are My people,
    and they will say: Yahweh is our God."

14 A day of the Lord is coming when your plunder will be divided in your presence. [2] I will gather all the nations against Jerusalem for battle. The city will be captured, the houses looted, and the women raped. Half the city will go into exile, but the rest of the people will not be removed from the city. [3] Then the Lord will go out to fight against those nations as He fights on a day of battle. [4] On that day His feet will stand on the ˙Mount of Olives, which faces Jerusalem on the east. The Mount of Olives will be split in half from east to west, forming a huge valley, so that half the mountain will move to the north and half to the south. [5] You will flee by My mountain valley, for the valley of the mountains will extend to Azal. You

will flee as you fled from the earthquake in the days of Uzziah king of Judah. Then the Lord my God will come and all the holy ones with Him.

[6] On that day there will be no light; the sunlight and moonlight will diminish. [7] It will be a day known only to ˙Yahweh, without day or night, but there will be light at evening.

[8] On that day living water will flow out from Jerusalem, half of it toward the eastern sea and the other half toward the western sea, in summer and winter alike. [9] On that day Yahweh will become King over all the earth—Yahweh alone, and His name alone. [10] All the land from Geba to Rimmon south of Jerusalem will be changed into a plain. But Jerusalem will be raised up and will remain on its site from the Benjamin Gate to the place of the First Gate, to the Corner Gate, and from the Tower of Hananel to the royal winepresses. [11] People will live there, and never again will there be a curse of ˙complete destruction. So Jerusalem will dwell in security.

[12] This will be the plague the Lord strikes all the peoples with, who have warred against Jerusalem: their flesh will rot while they stand on their feet, their eyes will rot in their sockets, and their tongues will rot in their mouths. [13] On that day a great panic from the Lord will be among them, so that each will seize the hand of another, and the hand of one will rise against the other. [14] Judah will also fight at Jerusalem, and the wealth of all the surrounding nations will be collected: gold, silver, and clothing in great abundance. [15] The same plague as the previous one will strike the horses, mules, camels, donkeys, and all the animals that are in those camps.

[16] Then all the survivors from the nations that came against Jerusalem will go up year after year to worship the King, the Lord of ˙Hosts, and to celebrate the Festival of Booths. [17] Should any of the families of the earth not go up to Jerusalem to worship the King, the Lord of Hosts, rain will not fall on them. [18] And if the people of Egypt will not go up and enter, then rain will not fall on them; this will be the plague the Lord inflicts on the nations who do not go up to celebrate the Festival of Booths. [19] This will be the punishment of Egypt and all the nations that do not go up to celebrate the Festival of Booths.

[20] On that day, the words

HOLY TO THE LORD

will be on the bells of the horses. The pots in the house of the Lord will be like the sprinkling basins before the altar. [21] Every pot in Jerusalem and in Judah will be holy to the Lord of Hosts. Everyone who sacrifices will come and take some of the pots to cook in. And on that day there will no longer be a Canaanite in the house of the Lord of Hosts.

MALACHI

1 An *oracle: The word of the LORD to Israel through Malachi.

[2] "I have loved you," says the LORD.

But you ask: "How have You loved us?"

"Wasn't Esau Jacob's brother?" This is the LORD's declaration. "Even so, I loved Jacob, [3] but I hated Esau. I turned his mountains into a wasteland, and gave his inheritance to the desert jackals.'

[4] Though Edom says: "We have been devastated, but we will rebuild the ruins," the LORD of *Hosts says this: "They may build, but I will demolish. They will be called a wicked country and the people the LORD has cursed forever. [5] Your own eyes will see this, and you yourselves will say, 'The LORD is great, even beyond the borders of Israel.'

[6] "A son honors his father, and a servant his master. But if I am a father, where is My honor? And if I am a master, where is your *fear of Me? says *Yahweh of Hosts to you priests, who despise My name."

Yet you ask: "How have we despised Your name?"

[7] "By presenting defiled food on My altar."

You ask: "How have we defiled You?"

When you say: "The LORD's table is contemptible."

[8] "When you present a blind animal for sacrifice, is it not wrong? And when you present a lame or sick animal, is it not wrong? Bring it to your governor! Would he be pleased with you or show you favor?" asks the LORD of Hosts. [9] "And now ask for God's favor. Will He be gracious to us? Since this has come from your hands, will He show any of you favor?" asks the LORD of Hosts. [10] "I wish one of you would shut the temple doors, so you would no longer kindle a useless fire on My altar! I am not pleased with you," says the LORD of Hosts, "and I will accept no offering from your hands.

[11] "For My name will be great among the nations, from the rising of the sun to its setting. Incense and pure offerings will be presented in My name in every place because My name will be great among the nations," says Yahweh of Hosts.

[12] But you are profaning it when you say: "The Lord's table is defiled, and its product, its food, is contemptible." [13] You also say: "Look, what a nuisance!" "And you scorn it," says the LORD of Hosts. "You bring stolen, lame, or sick animals. You bring this as an offering! Am I to accept that from your hands?" asks the LORD.

[14] "The deceiver is cursed who has an acceptable male in his flock and makes a vow but sacrifices a defective animal to the Lord. For I am a great King," says Yahweh of Hosts, "and My name will be feared among the nations.

2 "Therefore, this decree is for you priests: [2] If you don't listen, and if you don't take it to heart to honor My name," says *Yahweh of *Hosts, "I will send a curse among you, and I will curse your blessings. In fact, I have already begun to curse them because you are not taking it to heart.

[3] "Look, I am going to rebuke your descendants, and I will spread animal waste over your faces, the waste from your festival sacrifices, and you will be taken away with it. [4] Then you will know that I sent you this decree so My covenant with Levi may continue," says the LORD of Hosts. [5] "My covenant with him was one of life and peace, and I gave these to him; it called for reverence, and he revered Me and stood in awe of My name. [6] True instruction was in his mouth, and nothing wrong was found on his lips. He walked with Me in peace and fairness and turned many from sin. [7] For the lips of a priest should guard knowledge, and people should seek instruction from his mouth, because he is the messenger of the LORD of Hosts.

[8] "You, on the other hand, have turned from the way. You have caused many to stumble by your instruction. You have violated the covenant of Levi," says the LORD of Hosts. [9] "So I in turn have made you despised and humiliated before all the people because you are not keeping My ways but are showing partiality in your instruction."

[10] Don't all of us have one Father? Didn't one God create us? Why then do we act treacherously against one another, profaning the covenant of our fathers? [11] Judah has acted treacherously, and a detestable thing has been done in Israel and in Jerusalem. For Judah has profaned the LORD's sanctuary, which He loves, and has married the daughter of a foreign god. [12] To the man who does this, may the LORD cut off any descendants from the tents of Jacob, even if they present an offering to the LORD of Hosts.

[13] And this is another thing you do: you cover the LORD's altar with tears, with weeping and groaning, because He no longer respects your offerings or receives them gladly from your hands.

[14] Yet you ask, "For what reason?" Because the LORD has been a witness between you and the wife of your youth. You have acted treacherously against her, though she was your marriage partner and your wife by covenant. [15] Didn't the one God make us with a remnant of His life-breath? And what does the One seek? A godly *offspring. So watch yourselves carefully, and do not act treacherously against the wife of your youth.

[16] "If he hates and divorces his wife," says the LORD God of Israel, "he covers his garment with injustice," says the LORD of Hosts. Therefore, watch yourselves carefully, and do not act treacherously.

[17] You have wearied the LORD with your words.

Yet you ask, "How have we wearied Him?"

When you say, "Everyone who does what is evil is good in the LORD's sight, and He is pleased with them," or "Where is the God of justice?"

3 "See, I am going to send My messenger, and he will clear the way before Me. Then the Lord you seek will suddenly come to His temple, the Messenger of the covenant you desire—see, He is coming," says the LORD of *Hosts. [2] But who can endure the day of His coming? And who will be able to stand when He appears? For He will be like a refiner's fire and like cleansing lye. [3] He will be like a refiner and purifier of silver; He will purify the sons of Levi and refine them like gold and silver. Then they will present offerings to the LORD in righteousness. [4] And the offerings of Judah and Jerusalem will please the LORD as in days of old and years gone by.

[5] "I will come to you in judgment, and I will be ready to witness against sorcerers and adulterers; against those who swear falsely; against those who oppress the widow and the fatherless, and cheat the wage earner; and against those who deny justice to the foreigner.

They do not *fear Me," says the Lord of Hosts. ⁶"Because I, *Yahweh, have not changed, you descendants of Jacob have not been destroyed.

⁷"Since the days of your fathers, you have turned from My statutes; you have not kept them. Return to Me, and I will return to you," says the Lord of Hosts.

But you ask: "How can we return?"

⁸"Will a man rob God? Yet you are robbing Me!"

You ask: "How do we rob You?"

"By not making the payments of the tenth and the contributions. ⁹You are suffering under a curse, yet you—the whole nation—are still robbing Me. ¹⁰Bring the full tenth into the storehouse so that there may be food in My house. Test Me in this way," says the Lord of Hosts. "See if I will not open the floodgates of heaven and pour out a blessing for you without measure. ¹¹I will rebuke the devourer for you, so that it will not ruin the produce of your land and your vine in your field will not fail to produce fruit," says the Lord of Hosts. ¹²"Then all the nations will consider you fortunate, for you will be a delightful land," says the Lord of Hosts.

¹³"Your words against Me are harsh," says the Lord. Yet you ask: "What have we spoken against You?"

¹⁴You have said: "It is useless to serve God. What have we gained by keeping His requirements and walking mournfully before the Lord of Hosts? ¹⁵So now we consider the arrogant to be fortunate. Not only do those who commit wickedness prosper, they even test God and escape."

¹⁶At that time those who feared the Lord spoke to one another. The Lord took notice and listened. So a book of remembrance was written before Him for those who feared Yahweh and had high regard for His name. ¹⁷"They will be Mine," says the Lord of Hosts, "a special possession on the day I am preparing. I will have compassion on them as a man has compassion on his son who serves him. ¹⁸So you will again see the difference between the righteous and the wicked, between one who serves God and one who does not serve Him.

4 "For indeed, the day is coming, burning like a furnace, when all the arrogant and everyone who commits wickedness will become stubble. The coming day will consume them," says the Lord of *Hosts, "not leaving them root or branches. ²But for you who *fear My name, the sun of righteousness will rise with healing in its wings, and you will go out and playfully jump like calves from the stall. ³You will trample the wicked, for they will be ashes under the soles of your feet on the day I am preparing," says the Lord of Hosts.

⁴"Remember the instruction of Moses My servant, the statutes and ordinances I commanded him at Horeb for all Israel. ⁵Look, I am going to send you Elijah the prophet before the great and awesome Day of the Lord comes. ⁶And he will turn the hearts of fathers to their children and the hearts of children to their fathers. Otherwise, I will come and strike the land with a curse."

THE
NEW TESTAMENT

MATTHEW

1 The historical record of Jesus Christ, the Son of David, the Son of Abraham:

2 Abraham fathered Isaac,
Isaac fathered Jacob,
Jacob fathered Judah and his brothers,

3 Judah fathered Perez and Zerah by Tamar,
Perez fathered Hezron,
Hezron fathered Aram,

4 Aram fathered Amminadab,
Amminadab fathered Nahshon,
Nahshon fathered Salmon,

5 Salmon fathered Boaz by Rahab,
Boaz fathered Obed by Ruth,
Obed fathered Jesse,

6 and Jesse fathered King David.
Then David fathered Solomon by Uriah's wife,

7 Solomon fathered Rehoboam,
Rehoboam fathered Abijah,
Abijah fathered Asa,

8 Asa fathered Jehoshaphat,
Jehoshaphat fathered Joram,
Joram fathered Uzziah,

9 Uzziah fathered Jotham,
Jotham fathered Ahaz,
Ahaz fathered Hezekiah,

10 Hezekiah fathered Manasseh,
Manasseh fathered Amon,
Amon fathered Josiah,

11 and Josiah fathered Jechoniah
and his brothers
at the time of the exile to Babylon.

12 Then after the exile to Babylon
Jechoniah fathered Shealtiel,
Shealtiel fathered Zerubbabel,

13 Zerubbabel fathered Abiud,
Abiud fathered Eliakim,
Eliakim fathered Azor,

14 Azor fathered Zadok,
Zadok fathered Achim,
Achim fathered Eliud,

15 Eliud fathered Eleazar,
Eleazar fathered Matthan,
Matthan fathered Jacob,

16 and Jacob fathered Joseph the husband
of Mary,
who gave birth to Jesus who is called
the •Messiah.

17 So all the generations from Abraham to David were 14 generations; and from David until the exile to Babylon, 14 generations; and from the exile to Babylon until the Messiah, 14 generations.

18 The birth of Jesus Christ came about this way: After His mother Mary had been •engaged to Joseph, it was discovered before they came together that she was pregnant by the Holy Spirit. 19 So her husband Joseph, being a righteous man, and not wanting to disgrace her publicly, decided to divorce her secretly.

20 But after he had considered these things, an angel of the Lord suddenly appeared to him in a dream, saying, "Joseph, son of David, don't be afraid to take Mary as your wife, because what has been conceived in her is by the Holy Spirit. 21 She will give birth to a son, and you are to name Him Jesus, because He will save His people from their sins."

22 Now all this took place to fulfill what was spoken by the Lord through the prophet:

23 **See, the virgin will become pregnant**
and give birth to a son,
and they will name Him Immanuel,

which is translated "God is with us." 24 When Joseph got up from sleeping, he did as the Lord's angel had commanded him. He married her 25 but did not know her intimately until she gave birth to a son. And he named Him Jesus.

2 After Jesus was born in Bethlehem of Judea in the days of King •Herod, •wise men from the east arrived unexpectedly in Jerusalem, 2 saying, "Where is He who has been born King of the Jews? For we saw His star in the east and have come to worship Him." 3 When King Herod heard this, he was deeply disturbed, and all Jerusalem with him. 4 So he assembled all the •chief priests and •scribes of the people and asked them where the •Messiah would be born.

5 "In Bethlehem of Judea," they told him, "because this is what was written by the prophet:

6 **And you, Bethlehem,** in the land of Judah,
are by no means **least among the leaders**
of Judah:
because out of you will come a leader
who will shepherd My people Israel."

7 Then Herod secretly summoned the wise men and asked them the exact time the star appeared. 8 He sent them to Bethlehem and said, "Go and search carefully for the child. When you find Him, report back to me so that I too can go and worship Him."

9 After hearing the king, they went on their way. And there it was—the star they had seen in the east! It led them until it came and stopped above the place where the child was. 10 When they saw the star, they were overjoyed beyond measure. 11 Entering the house, they saw the child with Mary His mother, and falling to their knees, they worshiped Him. Then they opened their treasures and presented Him with gifts: gold, frankincense, and myrrh. 12 And being warned in a dream not to go back to Herod, they returned to their own country by another route.

13 After they were gone, an angel of the Lord suddenly appeared to Joseph in a dream, saying, "Get up! Take the child and His mother, flee to Egypt, and stay there until I tell you. For Herod is about to search for the child to destroy Him." 14 So he got up, took the child and His mother during the night, and escaped to Egypt. 15 He stayed there until Herod's death, so that what was spoken by the Lord through the prophet might be fulfilled: **Out of Egypt I called My Son.**

16 Then Herod, when he saw that he had been outwitted by the wise men, flew into a rage. He gave orders to massacre all the male children in and around Bethlehem who were two years old and under, in keeping with the time he had learned from the wise men. 17 Then what was spoken through Jeremiah the prophet was fulfilled:

18 **A voice was heard in Ramah,**
weeping, and great mourning,
Rachel weeping for her children;
and she refused to be consoled,
because they were no more.

[19]After Herod died, an angel of the Lord suddenly appeared in a dream to Joseph in Egypt, [20]saying, "Get up! Take the child and His mother and go to the land of Israel, because those who sought the child's life are dead." [21]So he got up, took the child and His mother, and entered the land of Israel. [22]But when he heard that Archelaus was ruling over Judea in place of his father Herod, he was afraid to go there. And being warned in a dream, he withdrew to the region of Galilee. [23]Then he went and settled in a town called Nazareth to fulfill what was spoken through the prophets, that He will be called a ˙Nazarene.

3 In those days John the Baptist came, preaching in the Wilderness of Judea [2]and saying, "Repent, because the kingdom of heaven has come near!" [3]For he is the one spoken of through the prophet Isaiah, who said:

> A voice of one crying out in the wilderness:
> Prepare the way for the Lord;
> make His paths straight!

[4]John himself had a camel-hair garment with a leather belt around his waist, and his food was locusts and wild honey. [5]Then people from Jerusalem, all Judea, and all the vicinity of the Jordan were flocking to him, [6]and they were baptized by him in the Jordan River as they confessed their sins.

[7]When he saw many of the ˙Pharisees and ˙Sadducees coming to the place of his baptism, he said to them, "Brood of vipers! Who warned you to flee from the coming wrath? [8]Therefore produce fruit consistent with repentance. [9]And don't presume to say to yourselves, 'We have Abraham as our father.' For I tell you that God is able to raise up children for Abraham from these stones! [10]Even now the ax is ready to strike the root of the trees! Therefore, every tree that doesn't produce good fruit will be cut down and thrown into the fire.

[11]"I baptize you with water for repentance, but the One who is coming after me is more powerful than I. I am not worthy to remove His sandals. He Himself will baptize you with the Holy Spirit and fire. [12]His winnowing shovel is in His hand, and He will clear His threshing floor and gather His wheat into the barn. But the chaff He will burn up with fire that never goes out."

[13]Then Jesus came from Galilee to John at the Jordan, to be baptized by him. [14]But John tried to stop Him, saying, "I need to be baptized by You, and yet You come to me?"

[15]Jesus answered him, "Allow it for now, because this is the way for us to fulfill all righteousness." Then he allowed Him to be baptized.

[16]After Jesus was baptized, He went up immediately from the water. The heavens suddenly opened for Him, and He saw the Spirit of God descending like a dove and coming down on Him. [17]And there came a voice from heaven:

> This is My beloved Son.
> I take delight in Him!

4 Then Jesus was led up by the Spirit into the wilderness to be tempted by the Devil. [2]After He had fasted 40 days and 40 nights, He was hungry. [3]Then the tempter approached Him and said, "If You are the Son of God, tell these stones to become bread."

[4]But He answered, "It is written:

> Man must not live on bread alone
> but on every word that comes
> from the mouth of God."

[5]Then the Devil took Him to the holy city, had Him stand on the pinnacle of the temple, [6]and said to Him, "If You are the Son of God, throw Yourself down. For it is written:

> He will give His angels orders
> concerning you,
> and they will support you with their hands
> so that you will not strike
> your foot against a stone."

[7]Jesus told him, "It is also written: Do not test the Lord your God."

[8]Again, the Devil took Him to a very high mountain and showed Him all the kingdoms of the world and their splendor. [9]And he said to Him, "I will give You all these things if You will fall down and worship me."

[10]Then Jesus told him, "Go away, Satan! For it is written:

> Worship the Lord your God,
> and serve only Him."

[11]Then the Devil left Him, and immediately angels came and began to serve Him.

[12]When He heard that John had been arrested, He withdrew into Galilee. [13]He left Nazareth behind and went to live in Capernaum by the sea, in the region of Zebulun and Naphtali. [14]This was to fulfill what was spoken through the prophet Isaiah:

> [15]　Land of Zebulun and land of Naphtali,
> 　　along the sea road, beyond the Jordan,
> 　　Galilee of the Gentiles!
> [16]　The people who live in darkness
> 　　have seen a great light,
> 　　and for those living in the shadowland
> 　　　of death,
> 　　light has dawned.

[17]From then on Jesus began to preach, "Repent, because the kingdom of heaven has come near!"

[18]As He was walking along the Sea of Galilee, He saw two brothers, Simon, who was called Peter, and his brother Andrew. They were casting a net into the sea, since they were fishermen. [19]"Follow Me," He told them, "and I will make you fish for people!" [20]Immediately they left their nets and followed Him.

[21]Going on from there, He saw two other brothers, James the son of Zebedee, and his brother John. They were in a boat with Zebedee their father, mending their nets, and He called them. [22]Immediately they left the boat and their father and followed Him.

[23]Jesus was going all over Galilee, teaching in their ˙synagogues, preaching the good news of the kingdom, and healing every disease and sickness among the people. [24]Then the news about Him spread throughout Syria. So they brought to Him all those who were afflicted, those suffering from various diseases and intense pains, the demon-possessed, the epileptics, and the paralytics. And He healed them. [25]Large crowds followed Him from Galilee, ˙Decapolis, Jerusalem, Judea, and beyond the Jordan.

5 When He saw the crowds, He went up on the mountain, and after He sat down, His disciples came to Him. [2]Then He began to teach them, saying:

> [3]　"The poor in spirit are blessed,
> 　　for the kingdom of heaven is theirs.
> [4]　Those who mourn are blessed,
> 　　for they will be comforted.
> [5]　The gentle are blessed,
> 　　for they will inherit the earth.

6 Those who hunger and thirst
for righteousness are blessed,
for they will be filled.

7 The merciful are blessed,
for they will be shown mercy.

8 The pure in heart are blessed,
for they will see God.

9 The peacemakers are blessed,
for they will be called sons of God.

10 Those who are persecuted for righteousness
are blessed,
for the kingdom of heaven is theirs.

11 "You are blessed when they insult and persecute you and falsely say every kind of evil against you because of Me. 12 Be glad and rejoice, because your reward is great in heaven. For that is how they persecuted the prophets who were before you.

13 "You are the salt of the earth. But if the salt should lose its taste, how can it be made salty? It's no longer good for anything but to be thrown out and trampled on by men.

14 "You are the light of the world. A city situated on a hill cannot be hidden. 15 No one lights a lamp and puts it under a basket, but rather on a lampstand, and it gives light for all who are in the house. 16 In the same way, let your light shine before men, so that they may see your good works and give glory to your Father in heaven.

17 "Don't assume that I came to destroy the Law or the Prophets. I did not come to destroy but to fulfill. 18 For *I assure you: Until heaven and earth pass away, not the smallest letter or one stroke of a letter will pass from the law until all things are accomplished. 19 Therefore, whoever breaks one of the least of these commands and teaches people to do so will be called least in the kingdom of heaven. But whoever practices and teaches these commands will be called great in the kingdom of heaven. 20 For I tell you, unless your righteousness surpasses that of the *scribes and *Pharisees, you will never enter the kingdom of heaven.

21 "You have heard that it was said to our ancestors, **Do not murder**, and whoever murders will be subject to judgment. 22 But I tell you, everyone who is angry with his brother will be subject to judgment. And whoever says to his brother, 'Fool!' will be subject to the *Sanhedrin. But whoever says, 'You moron!' will be subject to *hellfire. 23 So if you are offering your gift on the altar, and there you remember that your brother has something against you, 24 leave your gift there in front of the altar. First go and be reconciled with your brother, and then come and offer your gift. 25 Reach a settlement quickly with your adversary while you're on the way with him, or your adversary will hand you over to the judge, the judge to the officer, and you will be thrown into prison. 26 I assure you: You will never get out of there until you have paid the last penny!

27 "You have heard that it was said, **Do not commit adultery.** 28 But I tell you, everyone who looks at a woman to lust for her has already committed adultery with her in his heart. 29 If your right eye *causes you to sin, gouge it out and throw it away. For it is better that you lose one of the parts of your body than for your whole body to be thrown into hell. 30 And if your right hand causes you to sin, cut it off and throw it away. For it is better that you lose one of the parts of your body than for your whole body to go into hell!

31 "It was also said, **Whoever divorces his wife must give her a written notice of divorce.** 32 But I tell you, everyone who divorces his wife, except in a case of sexual immorality, causes her to commit adultery. And whoever marries a divorced woman commits adultery.

33 "Again, you have heard that it was said to our ancestors, **You must not break your oath, but you must keep your oaths to the Lord.** 34 But I tell you, don't take an oath at all: either by heaven, because it is God's throne; 35 or by the earth, because it is His footstool; or by Jerusalem, because it is the city of the great King. 36 Neither should you swear by your head, because you cannot make a single hair white or black. 37 But let your word 'yes' be 'yes,' and your 'no' be 'no.' Anything more than this is from the evil one.

38 "You have heard that it was said, **An eye for an eye** and **a tooth for a tooth.** 39 But I tell you, don't resist an evildoer. On the contrary, if anyone slaps you on your right cheek, turn the other to him also. 40 As for the one who wants to sue you and take away your shirt, let him have your coat as well. 41 And if anyone forces you to go one mile, go with him two. 42 Give to the one who asks you, and don't turn away from the one who wants to borrow from you.

43 "You have heard that it was said, **Love your neighbor** and hate your enemy. 44 But I tell you, love your enemies and pray for those who persecute you, 45 so that you may be sons of your Father in heaven. For He causes His sun to rise on the evil and the good, and sends rain on the righteous and the unrighteous. 46 For if you love those who love you, what reward will you have? Don't even the tax collectors do the same? 47 And if you greet only your *brothers, what are you doing out of the ordinary? Don't even the Gentiles do the same? 48 Be perfect, therefore, as your heavenly Father is perfect.

6 "Be careful not to practice your righteousness in front of people, to be seen by them. Otherwise, you will have no reward from your Father in heaven. 2 So whenever you give to the poor, don't sound a trumpet before you, as the hypocrites do in the *synagogues and on the streets, to be applauded by people. *I assure you: They've got their reward! 3 But when you give to the poor, don't let your left hand know what your right hand is doing, 4 so that your giving may be in secret. And your Father who sees in secret will reward you.

5 "Whenever you pray, you must not be like the hypocrites, because they love to pray standing in the synagogues and on the street corners to be seen by people. I assure you: They've got their reward! 6 But when you pray, go into your private room, shut your door, and pray to your Father who is in secret. And your Father who sees in secret will reward you. 7 When you pray, don't babble like the idolaters, since they imagine they'll be heard for their many words. 8 Don't be like them, because your Father knows the things you need before you ask Him.

9 "Therefore, you should pray like this:

Our Father in heaven,
Your name be honored as holy.

10 Your kingdom come.
Your will be done
on earth as it is in heaven.

11 Give us today our daily bread.

12 And forgive us our debts,
as we also have forgiven our debtors.

13 And do not bring us
into temptation,

but deliver us from the evil one.
[For Yours is the kingdom
　and the power
　and the glory forever. *Amen.]

¹⁴ "For if you forgive people their wrongdoing, your heavenly Father will forgive you as well. ¹⁵ But if you don't forgive people, your Father will not forgive your wrongdoing.

¹⁶ "Whenever you fast, don't be sad-faced like the hypocrites. For they make their faces unattractive so their fasting is obvious to people. I assure you: They've got their reward! ¹⁷ But when you fast, put oil on your head, and wash your face, ¹⁸ so that you don't show your fasting to people but to your Father who is in secret. And your Father who sees in secret will reward you.

¹⁹ "Don't collect for yourselves treasures on earth, where moth and rust destroy and where thieves break in and steal. ²⁰ But collect for yourselves treasures in heaven, where neither moth nor rust destroys, and where thieves don't break in and steal. ²¹ For where your treasure is, there your heart will be also.

²² "The eye is the lamp of the body. If your eye is good, your whole body will be full of light. ²³ But if your eye is bad, your whole body will be full of darkness. So if the light within you is darkness—how deep is that darkness!

²⁴ "No one can be a *slave of two masters, since either he will hate one and love the other, or be devoted to one and despise the other. You cannot be slaves of God and of money.

²⁵ "This is why I tell you: Don't worry about your life, what you will eat or what you will drink; or about your body, what you will wear. Isn't life more than food and the body more than clothing? ²⁶ Look at the birds of the sky: They don't sow or reap or gather into barns, yet your heavenly Father feeds them. Aren't you worth more than they? ²⁷ Can any of you add a single *cubit to his height by worrying? ²⁸ And why do you worry about clothes? Learn how the wildflowers of the field grow: they don't labor or spin thread. ²⁹ Yet I tell you that not even Solomon in all his splendor was adorned like one of these! ³⁰ If that's how God clothes the grass of the field, which is here today and thrown into the furnace tomorrow, won't He do much more for you—you of little faith? ³¹ So don't worry, saying, 'What will we eat?' or 'What will we drink?' or 'What will we wear?' ³² For the idolaters eagerly seek all these things, and your heavenly Father knows that you need them. ³³ But seek first the kingdom of God and His righteousness, and all these things will be provided for you. ³⁴ Therefore don't worry about tomorrow, because tomorrow will worry about itself. Each day has enough trouble of its own.

7 "Do not judge, so that you won't be judged. ² For with the judgment you use, you will be judged, and with the measure you use, it will be measured to you. ³ Why do you look at the speck in your brother's eye but don't notice the log in your own eye? ⁴ Or how can you say to your brother, 'Let me take the speck out of your eye,' and look, there's a log in your eye? ⁵ Hypocrite! First take the log out of your eye, and then you will see clearly to take the speck out of your brother's eye. ⁶ Don't give what is holy to dogs or toss your pearls before pigs, or they will trample them with their feet, turn, and tear you to pieces.

⁷ "Keep asking, and it will be given to you. Keep searching, and you will find. Keep knocking, and the door will be opened to you. ⁸ For everyone who asks receives, and the one who searches finds, and to the one who knocks, the door will be opened. ⁹ What man among you, if his son asks him for bread, will give him a stone? ¹⁰ Or if he asks for a fish, will give him a snake? ¹¹ If you then, who are evil, know how to give good gifts to your children, how much more will your Father in heaven give good things to those who ask Him! ¹² Therefore, whatever you want others to do for you, do also the same for them—this is the Law and the Prophets.

¹³ "Enter through the narrow gate. For the gate is wide and the road is broad that leads to destruction, and there are many who go through it. ¹⁴ How narrow is the gate and difficult the road that leads to life, and few find it.

¹⁵ "Beware of false prophets who come to you in sheep's clothing but inwardly are ravaging wolves. ¹⁶ You'll recognize them by their fruit. Are grapes gathered from thornbushes or figs from thistles? ¹⁷ In the same way, every good tree produces good fruit, but a bad tree produces bad fruit. ¹⁸ A good tree can't produce bad fruit; neither can a bad tree produce good fruit. ¹⁹ Every tree that doesn't produce good fruit is cut down and thrown into the fire. ²⁰ So you'll recognize them by their fruit.

²¹ "Not everyone who says to Me, 'Lord, Lord!' will enter the kingdom of heaven, but only the one who does the will of My Father in heaven. ²² On that day many will say to Me, 'Lord, Lord, didn't we prophesy in Your name, drive out demons in Your name, and do many miracles in Your name?' ²³ Then I will announce to them, 'I never knew you! **Depart from Me, you lawbreakers!**'

²⁴ "Therefore, everyone who hears these words of Mine and acts on them will be like a sensible man who built his house on the rock. ²⁵ The rain fell, the rivers rose, and the winds blew and pounded that house. Yet it didn't collapse, because its foundation was on the rock. ²⁶ But everyone who hears these words of Mine and doesn't act on them will be like a foolish man who built his house on the sand. ²⁷ The rain fell, the rivers rose, the winds blew and pounded that house, and it collapsed. And its collapse was great!"

²⁸ When Jesus had finished this sermon, the crowds were astonished at His teaching, ²⁹ because He was teaching them like one who had authority, and not like their *scribes.

8 When He came down from the mountain, large crowds followed Him. ² Right away a man with a serious skin disease came up and knelt before Him, saying, "Lord, if You are willing, You can make me *clean."

³ Reaching out His hand He touched him, saying, "I am willing; be made clean." Immediately his disease was healed. ⁴ Then Jesus told him, "See that you don't tell anyone; but go, show yourself to the priest, and offer the gift that Moses prescribed, as a testimony to them."

⁵ When He entered Capernaum, a *centurion came to Him, pleading with Him, ⁶ "Lord, my servant is lying at home paralyzed, in terrible agony!"

⁷ "I will come and heal him," He told him.

⁸ "Lord," the centurion replied, "I am not worthy to have You come under my roof. But only say the word, and my servant will be cured. ⁹ For I too am a man

under authority, having soldiers under my command. I say to this one, 'Go!' and he goes; and to another, 'Come!' and he comes; and to my *slave, 'Do this!' and he does it."

[10] Hearing this, Jesus was amazed and said to those following Him, "I *assure you: I have not found anyone in Israel with so great a faith! [11] I tell you that many will come from east and west, and recline at the table with Abraham, Isaac, and Jacob in the kingdom of heaven. [12] But the sons of the kingdom will be thrown into the outer darkness. In that place there will be weeping and gnashing of teeth." [13] Then Jesus told the centurion, "Go. As you have believed, let it be done for you." And his servant was cured that very moment.

[14] When Jesus went into Peter's house, He saw his mother-in-law lying in bed with a fever. [15] So He touched her hand, and the fever left her. Then she got up and began to serve Him. [16] When evening came, they brought to Him many who were demon-possessed. He drove out the spirits with a word and healed all who were sick, [17] so that what was spoken through the prophet Isaiah might be fulfilled:

**He Himself took our weaknesses
and carried our diseases.**

[18] When Jesus saw large crowds around Him, He gave the order to go to the other side of the sea. [19] A *scribe approached Him and said, "Teacher, I will follow You wherever You go!"

[20] Jesus told him, "Foxes have dens and birds of the sky have nests, but the Son of Man has no place to lay His head."

[21] "Lord," another of His disciples said, "first let me go bury my father."

[22] But Jesus told him, "Follow Me, and let the dead bury their own dead."

[23] As He got into the boat, His disciples followed Him. [24] Suddenly, a violent storm arose on the sea, so that the boat was being swamped by the waves. But He was sleeping. [25] So the disciples came and woke Him up, saying, "Lord, save us! We're going to die!"

[26] But He said to them, "Why are you fearful, you of little faith?" Then He got up and rebuked the winds and the sea. And there was a great calm.

[27] The men were amazed and asked, "What kind of man is this?—even the winds and the sea obey Him!"

[28] When He had come to the other side, to the region of the Gadarenes, two demon-possessed men met Him as they came out of the tombs. They were so violent that no one could pass that way. [29] Suddenly they shouted, "What do You have to do with us, Son of God? Have You come here to torment us before the time?"

[30] Now a long way off from them, a large herd of pigs was feeding. [31] "If You drive us out," the demons begged Him, "send us into the herd of pigs."

[32] "Go!" He told them. So when they had come out, they entered the pigs. And suddenly the whole herd rushed down the steep bank into the sea and perished in the water. [33] Then the men who tended them fled. They went into the city and reported everything—especially what had happened to those who were demon-possessed. [34] At that, the whole town went out to meet Jesus. When they saw Him, they begged Him to leave their region.

9 So He got into a boat, crossed over, and came to His own town. [2] Just then some men brought to Him a paralytic lying on a mat. Seeing their faith, Jesus told the paralytic, "Have courage, son, your sins are forgiven."

[3] At this, some of the *scribes said among themselves, "He's blaspheming!"

[4] But perceiving their thoughts, Jesus said, "Why are you thinking evil things in your hearts? [5] For which is easier: to say, 'Your sins are forgiven,' or to say, 'Get up and walk'? [6] But so you may know that the *Son of Man has authority on earth to forgive sins"—then He told the paralytic, "Get up, pick up your mat, and go home." [7] And he got up and went home. [8] When the crowds saw this, they were awestruck and gave glory to God who had given such authority to men.

[9] As Jesus went on from there, He saw a man named Matthew sitting at the tax office, and He said to him, "Follow Me!" So he got up and followed Him.

[10] While He was reclining at the table in the house, many tax collectors and sinners came as guests to eat with Jesus and His disciples. [11] When the *Pharisees saw this, they asked His disciples, "Why does your Teacher eat with tax collectors and sinners?"

[12] But when He heard this, He said, "Those who are well don't need a doctor, but the sick do. [13] Go and learn what this means: **I desire mercy and not sacrifice.** For I didn't come to call the righteous, but sinners."

[14] Then John's disciples came to Him, saying, "Why do we and the Pharisees fast often, but Your disciples do not fast?"

[15] Jesus said to them, "Can the wedding guests be sad while the groom is with them? The time will come when the groom will be taken away from them, and then they will fast. [16] No one patches an old garment with unshrunk cloth, because the patch pulls away from the garment and makes the tear worse. [17] And no one puts new wine into old wineskins. Otherwise, the skins burst, the wine spills out, and the skins are ruined. But they put new wine into fresh wineskins, and both are preserved."

[18] As He was telling them these things, suddenly one of the leaders came and knelt down before Him, saying, "My daughter is near death, but come and lay Your hand on her, and she will live." [19] So Jesus and His disciples got up and followed him.

[20] Just then, a woman who had suffered from bleeding for 12 years approached from behind and touched the *tassel on His robe, [21] for she said to herself, "If I can just touch His robe, I'll be made well!"

[22] But Jesus turned and saw her. "Have courage, daughter," He said. "Your faith has made you well." And the woman was made well from that moment.

[23] When Jesus came to the leader's house, He saw the flute players and a crowd lamenting loudly. [24] "Leave," He said, "because the girl isn't dead, but sleeping." And they started laughing at Him. [25] But when the crowd had been put outside, He went in and took her by the hand, and the girl got up. [26] And this news spread throughout that whole area.

[27] As Jesus went on from there, two blind men followed Him, shouting, "Have mercy on us, Son of David!"

[28] When He entered the house, the blind men approached Him, and Jesus said to them, "Do you believe that I can do this?"

"Yes, Lord," they answered Him.

[29] Then He touched their eyes, saying, "Let it be done for you according to your faith!" [30] And their eyes were opened. Then Jesus warned them sternly, "Be sure that

no one finds out!" [31]But they went out and spread the news about Him throughout that whole area.

[32]Just as they were going out, a demon-possessed man who was unable to speak was brought to Him. [33]When the demon had been driven out, the man spoke. And the crowds were amazed, saying, "Nothing like this has ever been seen in Israel!"

[34]But the Pharisees said, "He drives out demons by the ruler of the demons!"

[35]Then Jesus went to all the towns and villages, teaching in their *synagogues, preaching the good news of the kingdom, and healing every disease and every sickness. [36]When He saw the crowds, He felt compassion for them, because they were weary and worn out, like sheep without a shepherd. [37]Then He said to His disciples, "The harvest is abundant, but the workers are few. [38]Therefore, pray to the Lord of the harvest to send out workers into His harvest."

10 Summoning His 12 disciples, He gave them authority over *unclean spirits, to drive them out and to heal every disease and sickness. [2]These are the names of the 12 apostles:

First, Simon, who is called Peter,
and Andrew his brother;
James the son of Zebedee,
and John his brother;

[3] Philip and Bartholomew;
Thomas and Matthew the tax collector;
James the son of Alphaeus, and Thaddaeus;

[4] Simon the Zealot, and Judas Iscariot,
who also betrayed Him.

[5]Jesus sent out these 12 after giving them instructions: "Don't take the road leading to other nations, and don't enter any *Samaritan town. [6]Instead, go to the lost sheep of the house of Israel. [7]As you go, announce this: 'The kingdom of heaven has come near.' [8]Heal the sick, raise the dead, cleanse those with skin diseases, drive out demons. You have received free of charge; give free of charge. [9]Don't take along gold, silver, or copper for your money-belts. [10]Don't take a traveling bag for the road, or an extra shirt, sandals, or a walking stick, for the worker is worthy of his food.

[11]"When you enter any town or village, find out who is worthy, and stay there until you leave. [12]Greet a household when you enter it, [13]and if the household is worthy, let your peace be on it. But if it is unworthy, let your peace return to you. [14]If anyone will not welcome you or listen to your words, shake the dust off your feet when you leave that house or town. [15]*I assure you: It will be more tolerable on the day of judgment for the land of Sodom and Gomorrah than for that town.

[16]"Look, I'm sending you out like sheep among wolves. Therefore be as shrewd as serpents and as harmless as doves. [17]Because people will hand you over to sanhedrins and flog you in their *synagogues, beware of them. [18]You will even be brought before governors and kings because of Me, to bear witness to them and to the nations. [19]But when they hand you over, don't worry about how or what you should speak. For you will be given what to say at that hour, [20]because you are not speaking, but the Spirit of your Father is speaking through you.

[21]"Brother will betray brother to death, and a father his child. Children will even rise up against their parents and have them put to death. [22]You will be hated by everyone because of My name. But the one who endures to the end will be delivered. [23]When they persecute you in one town, escape to another. For I assure you: You will not have covered the towns of Israel before the *Son of Man comes. [24]A disciple is not above his teacher, or a *slave above his master. [25]It is enough for a disciple to become like his teacher and a slave like his master. If they called the head of the house "*Beelzebul,' how much more the members of his household!

[26]"Therefore, don't be afraid of them, since there is nothing covered that won't be uncovered and nothing hidden that won't be made known. [27]What I tell you in the dark, speak in the light. What you hear in a whisper, proclaim on the housetops. [28]Don't fear those who kill the body but are not able to kill the soul; rather, fear Him who is able to destroy both soul and body in *hell. [29]Aren't two sparrows sold for a penny? Yet not one of them falls to the ground without your Father's consent. [30]But even the hairs of your head have all been counted. [31]So don't be afraid therefore; you are worth more than many sparrows.

[32]"Therefore, everyone who will acknowledge Me before men, I will also acknowledge him before My Father in heaven. [33]But whoever denies Me before men, I will also deny him before My Father in heaven. [34]Don't assume that I came to bring peace on the earth. I did not come to bring peace, but a sword. [35]For I came to turn

a man against his father,
a daughter against her mother,
a daughter-in-law against
    her mother-in-law;
[36] and a man's enemies will be
    the members of his household.

[37]The person who loves father or mother more than Me is not worthy of Me; the person who loves son or daughter more than Me is not worthy of Me. [38]And whoever doesn't take up his cross and follow Me is not worthy of Me. [39]Anyone finding his life will lose it, and anyone losing his life because of Me will find it.

[40]"The one who welcomes you welcomes Me, and the one who welcomes Me welcomes Him who sent Me. [41]Anyone who welcomes a prophet because he is a prophet will receive a prophet's reward. And anyone who welcomes a righteous person because he's righteous will receive a righteous person's reward. [42]And whoever gives just a cup of cold water to one of these little ones because he is a disciple—I assure you: He will never lose his reward!"

11 When Jesus had finished giving orders to His 12 disciples, He moved on from there to teach and preach in their towns. [2]When John heard in prison what the *Messiah was doing, he sent a message by his disciples [3]and asked Him, "Are You the One who is to come, or should we expect someone else?"

[4]Jesus replied to them, "Go and report to John what you hear and see: [5]the blind see, the lame walk, those with skin diseases are healed, the deaf hear, the dead are raised, and the poor are told the good news. [6]And if anyone is not *offended because of Me, he is blessed."

[7]As these men went away, Jesus began to speak to the crowds about John: "What did you go out into the wilderness to see? A reed swaying in the wind? [8]What then did you go out to see? A man dressed in soft clothes? Look, those who wear soft clothes are in kings' palaces. [9]But what did you go out to see? A prophet? Yes, I tell you, and far more than a prophet. [10]This is the one it is written about:

**Look, I am sending My messenger
ahead of You;
he will prepare Your way before You.**

¹¹"'I assure you: Among those born of women no one greater than John the Baptist has appeared, but the least in the kingdom of heaven is greater than he. ¹²From the days of John the Baptist until now, the kingdom of heaven has been suffering violence, and the violent have been seizing it by force. ¹³For all the prophets and the Law prophesied until John; ¹⁴if you're willing to accept it, he is the Elijah who is to come. ¹⁵Anyone who has ears should listen!

¹⁶"To what should I compare this generation? It's like children sitting in the marketplaces who call out to each other:

¹⁷ We played the flute for you,
    but you didn't dance;
  we sang a lament,
    but you didn't mourn!

¹⁸For John did not come eating or drinking, and they say, 'He has a demon!' ¹⁹The •Son of Man came eating and drinking, and they say, 'Look, a glutton and a drunkard, a friend of tax collectors and sinners!' Yet wisdom is vindicated by her deeds."

²⁰Then He proceeded to denounce the towns where most of His miracles were done, because they did not repent: ²¹"Woe to you, Chorazin! Woe to you, Bethsaida! For if the miracles that were done in you had been done in Tyre and Sidon, they would have repented in •sackcloth and ashes long ago! ²²But I tell you, it will be more tolerable for Tyre and Sidon on the day of judgment than for you. ²³And you, Capernaum, will you be exalted to heaven? You will go down to •Hades. For if the miracles that were done in you had been done in Sodom, it would have remained until today. ²⁴But I tell you, it will be more tolerable for the land of Sodom on the day of judgment than for you."

²⁵At that time Jesus said, "I praise You, Father, Lord of heaven and earth, because You have hidden these things from the wise and learned and revealed them to infants. ²⁶Yes, Father, because this was Your good pleasure. ²⁷All things have been entrusted to Me by My Father. No one knows the Son except the Father, and no one knows the Father except the Son and anyone to whom the Son desires to reveal Him.

²⁸"Come to Me, all of you who are weary and burdened, and I will give you rest. ²⁹All of you, take up My yoke and learn from Me, because I am gentle and humble in heart, and you will find rest for yourselves. ³⁰For My yoke is easy and My burden is light."

12 At that time Jesus passed through the grainfields on the Sabbath. His disciples were hungry and began to pick and eat some heads of grain. ²But when the •Pharisees saw it, they said to Him, "Look, Your disciples are doing what is not lawful to do on the Sabbath!"

³He said to them, "Haven't you read what David did when he and those who were with him were hungry— ⁴how he entered the house of God, and they ate the •sacred bread, which is not lawful for him or for those with him to eat, but only for the priests? ⁵Or haven't you read in the Law that on Sabbath days the priests in the temple violate the Sabbath and are innocent? ⁶But I tell you that something greater than the temple is here! ⁷If you had known what this means: **I desire mercy and not sacrifice**, you would not have con-

demned the innocent. ⁸For the •Son of Man is Lord of the Sabbath."

⁹Moving on from there, He entered their •synagogue. ¹⁰There He saw a man who had a paralyzed hand. And in order to accuse Him they asked Him, "Is it lawful to heal on the Sabbath?"

¹¹But He said to them, "What man among you, if he had a sheep that fell into a pit on the Sabbath, wouldn't take hold of it and lift it out? ¹²A man is worth far more than a sheep, so it is lawful to do what is good on the Sabbath."

¹³Then He told the man, "Stretch out your hand." So he stretched it out, and it was restored, as good as the other. ¹⁴But the Pharisees went out and plotted against Him, how they might destroy Him.

¹⁵When Jesus became aware of this, He withdrew from there. Huge crowds followed Him, and He healed them all. ¹⁶He warned them not to make Him known, ¹⁷so that what was spoken through the prophet Isaiah might be fulfilled:

¹⁸ **Here is My Servant whom I have chosen,
    My beloved in whom My soul delights;
    I will put My Spirit on Him,
    and He will proclaim justice to the nations.**
¹⁹ **He will not argue or shout,
    and no one will hear His voice in the streets.**
²⁰ **He will not break a bruised reed,
    and He will not put out a smoldering wick,
    until He has led justice to victory.**
²¹ **The nations will put their hope in His name.**

²²Then a demon-possessed man who was blind and unable to speak was brought to Him. He healed him, so that the man could both speak and see. ²³And all the crowds were astounded and said, "Perhaps this is the Son of David!"

²⁴When the Pharisees heard this, they said, "The man drives out demons only by •Beelzebul, the ruler of the demons."

²⁵Knowing their thoughts, He told them: "Every kingdom divided against itself is headed for destruction, and no city or house divided against itself will stand. ²⁶If Satan drives out Satan, he is divided against himself. How then will his kingdom stand? ²⁷And if I drive out demons by Beelzebul, who is it your sons drive them out by? For this reason they will be your judges. ²⁸If I drive out demons by the Spirit of God, then the kingdom of God has come to you. ²⁹How can someone enter a strong man's house and steal his possessions unless he first ties up the strong man? Then he can rob his house. ³⁰Anyone who is not with Me is against Me, and anyone who does not gather with Me scatters. ³¹Because of this, I tell you, people will be forgiven every sin and blasphemy, but the blasphemy against the Spirit will not be forgiven. ³²Whoever speaks a word against the Son of Man, it will be forgiven him. But whoever speaks against the Holy Spirit, it will not be forgiven him, either in this age or in the one to come.

³³"Either make the tree good and its fruit good, or make the tree bad and its fruit bad; for a tree is known by its fruit. ³⁴Brood of vipers! How can you speak good things when you are evil? For the mouth speaks from the overflow of the heart. ³⁵A good man produces good things from his storeroom of good, and an evil man produces evil things from his storeroom of evil. ³⁶I tell you that on the day of judgment people will have to account for every careless word they speak. ³⁷For by

your words you will be acquitted, and by your words you will be condemned."

³⁸Then some of the *scribes and Pharisees said to Him, "Teacher, we want to see a sign from You."

³⁹But He answered them, "An evil and adulterous generation demands a sign, but no sign will be given to it except the sign of the prophet Jonah. ⁴⁰For as Jonah was in the belly of the huge fish three days and three nights, so the Son of Man will be in the heart of the earth three days and three nights. ⁴¹The men of Nineveh will stand up at the judgment with this generation and condemn it, because they repented at Jonah's proclamation; and look—something greater than Jonah is here! ⁴²The queen of the south will rise up at the judgment with this generation and condemn it, because she came from the ends of the earth to hear the wisdom of Solomon; and look—something greater than Solomon is here!

⁴³"When an *unclean spirit comes out of a man, it roams through waterless places looking for rest but doesn't find any. ⁴⁴Then it says, 'I'll go back to my house that I came from.' And returning, it finds the house vacant, swept, and put in order. ⁴⁵Then off it goes and brings with it seven other spirits more evil than itself, and they enter and settle down there. As a result, that man's last condition is worse than the first. That's how it will also be with this evil generation."

⁴⁶He was still speaking to the crowds when suddenly His mother and brothers were standing outside wanting to speak to Him. ⁴⁷Someone told Him, "Look, Your mother and Your brothers are standing outside, wanting to speak to You."

⁴⁸But He replied to the one who told Him, "Who is My mother and who are My brothers?" ⁴⁹And stretching out His hand toward His disciples, He said, "Here are My mother and My brothers! ⁵⁰For whoever does the will of My Father in heaven, that person is My brother and sister and mother."

13 On that day Jesus went out of the house and was sitting by the sea. ²Such large crowds gathered around Him that He got into a boat and sat down, while the whole crowd stood on the shore.

³Then He told them many things in parables, saying: "Consider the sower who went out to sow. ⁴As he was sowing, some seed fell along the path, and the birds came and ate them up. ⁵Others fell on rocky ground, where there wasn't much soil, and they sprang up quickly since the soil wasn't deep. ⁶But when the sun came up they were scorched, and since they had no root, they withered. ⁷Others fell among thorns, and the thorns came up and choked them. ⁸Still others fell on good ground and produced a crop: some 100, some 60, and some 30 times what was sown. ⁹Anyone who has ears should listen!"

¹⁰Then the disciples came up and asked Him, "Why do You speak to them in parables?"

¹¹He answered them, "Because the *secrets of the kingdom of heaven have been given for you to know, but it has not been given to them. ¹²For whoever has, more will be given to him, and he will have more than enough. But whoever does not have, even what he has will be taken away from him. ¹³For this reason I speak to them in parables, because looking they do not see, and hearing they do not listen or understand. ¹⁴Isaiah's prophecy is fulfilled in them, which says:

**You will listen and listen,
yet never understand;**

**and you will look and look,
yet never perceive.**
¹⁵   **For this people's heart has grown callous;
their ears are hard of hearing,
and they have shut their eyes;
otherwise they might see with their eyes
and hear with their ears,
understand with their hearts
and turn back—
and I would cure them.**

¹⁶"But your eyes are blessed because they do see, and your ears because they do hear! ¹⁷For *I assure you: Many prophets and righteous people longed to see the things you see yet didn't see them; to hear the things you hear yet didn't hear them.

¹⁸"You, then, listen to the parable of the sower: ¹⁹When anyone hears the word about the kingdom and doesn't understand it, the evil one comes and snatches away what was sown in his heart. This is the one sown along the path. ²⁰And the one sown on rocky ground—this is one who hears the word and immediately receives it with joy. ²¹Yet he has no root in himself, but is short-lived. When pressure or persecution comes because of the word, immediately he stumbles. ²²Now the one sown among the thorns—this is one who hears the word, but the worries of this age and the seduction of wealth choke the word, and it becomes unfruitful. ²³But the one sown on the good ground—this is one who hears and understands the word, who does bear fruit and yields: some 100, some 60, some 30 times what was sown."

²⁴He presented another parable to them: "The kingdom of heaven may be compared to a man who sowed good seed in his field. ²⁵But while people were sleeping, his enemy came, sowed weeds among the wheat, and left. ²⁶When the plants sprouted and produced grain, then the weeds also appeared. ²⁷The landowner's *slaves came to him and said, 'Master, didn't you sow good seed in your field? Then where did the weeds come from?'

²⁸"'An enemy did this!' he told them.

"'So, do you want us to go and gather them up?' the slaves asked him.

²⁹"'No,' he said. 'When you gather up the weeds, you might also uproot the wheat with them. ³⁰Let both grow together until the harvest. At harvest time I'll tell the reapers: Gather the weeds first and tie them in bundles to burn them, but store the wheat in my barn.'"

³¹He presented another parable to them: "The kingdom of heaven is like a mustard seed that a man took and sowed in his field. ³²It's the smallest of all the seeds, but when grown, it's taller than the vegetables and becomes a tree, so that the birds of the sky come and nest in its branches."

³³He told them another parable: "The kingdom of heaven is like yeast that a woman took and mixed into 50 pounds of flour until it spread through all of it."

³⁴Jesus told the crowds all these things in parables, and He would not speak anything to them without a parable, ³⁵so that what was spoken through the prophet might be fulfilled:

**I will open My mouth in parables;
I will declare things kept secret
from the foundation of the world.**
³⁶Then He dismissed the crowds and went into the

house. His disciples approached Him and said, "Explain the parable of the weeds in the field to us."

³⁷ He replied: "The One who sows the good seed is the •Son of Man; ³⁸ the field is the world; and the good seed—these are the sons of the kingdom. The weeds are the sons of the evil one, ³⁹ and the enemy who sowed them is the Devil. The harvest is the end of the age, and the harvesters are angels. ⁴⁰ Therefore, just as the weeds are gathered and burned in the fire, so it will be at the end of the age. ⁴¹ The Son of Man will send out His angels, and they will gather from His kingdom everything that causes sin and those •guilty of lawlessness. ⁴² They will throw them into the blazing furnace where there will be weeping and gnashing of teeth. ⁴³ Then the righteous will shine like the sun in their Father's kingdom. Anyone who has ears should listen!

⁴⁴ "The kingdom of heaven is like treasure, buried in a field, that a man found and reburied. Then in his joy he goes and sells everything he has and buys that field.

⁴⁵ "Again, the kingdom of heaven is like a merchant in search of fine pearls. ⁴⁶ When he found one priceless pearl, he went and sold everything he had, and bought it.

⁴⁷ "Again, the kingdom of heaven is like a large net thrown into the sea. It collected every kind of fish, ⁴⁸ and when it was full, they dragged it ashore, sat down, and gathered the good fish into containers, but threw out the worthless ones. ⁴⁹ So it will be at the end of the age. The angels will go out, separate the evil people from the righteous, ⁵⁰ and throw them into the blazing furnace. In that place there will be weeping and gnashing of teeth.

⁵¹ "Have you understood all these things?"

"Yes," they told Him.

⁵² "Therefore," He said to them, "every student of Scripture instructed in the kingdom of heaven is like a landowner who brings out of his storeroom what is new and what is old." ⁵³ When Jesus had finished these parables, He left there.

⁵⁴ He went to His hometown and began to teach them in their •synagogue, so that they were astonished and said, "How did this wisdom and these miracles come to Him? ⁵⁵ Isn't this the carpenter's son? Isn't His mother called Mary, and His brothers James, Joseph, Simon, and Judas? ⁵⁶ And His sisters, aren't they all with us? So where does He get all these things?" ⁵⁷ And they were •offended by Him.

But Jesus said to them, "A prophet is not without honor except in his hometown and in his household." ⁵⁸ And He did not do many miracles there because of their unbelief.

14 At that time •Herod the tetrarch heard the report about Jesus. ² "This is John the Baptist!" he told his servants. "He has been raised from the dead, and that's why supernatural powers are at work in him."

³ For Herod had arrested John, chained him, and put him in prison on account of Herodias, his brother Philip's wife, ⁴ since John had been telling him, "It's not lawful for you to have her!" ⁵ Though he wanted to kill him, he feared the crowd, since they regarded him as a prophet.

⁶ But when Herod's birthday celebration came, Herodias's daughter danced before them and pleased Herod. ⁷ So he promised with an oath to give her whatever she might ask. ⁸ And prompted by her mother, she answered, "Give me John the Baptist's head here on

a platter!" ⁹ Although the king regretted it, he commanded that it be granted because of his oaths and his guests. ¹⁰ So he sent orders and had John beheaded in the prison. ¹¹ His head was brought on a platter and given to the girl, who carried it to her mother. ¹² Then his disciples came, removed the corpse, buried it, and went and reported to Jesus.

¹³ When Jesus heard about it, He withdrew from there by boat to a remote place to be alone. When the crowds heard this, they followed Him on foot from the towns. ¹⁴ As He stepped ashore, He saw a huge crowd, felt compassion for them, and healed their sick.

¹⁵ When evening came, the disciples approached Him and said, "This place is a wilderness, and it is already late. Send the crowds away so they can go into the villages and buy food for themselves."

¹⁶ "They don't need to go away," Jesus told them. "You give them something to eat."

¹⁷ "But we only have five loaves and two fish here," they said to Him.

¹⁸ "Bring them here to Me," He said. ¹⁹ Then He commanded the crowds to sit down on the grass. He took the five loaves and the two fish, and looking up to heaven, He blessed them. He broke the loaves and gave them to the disciples, and the disciples gave them to the crowds. ²⁰ Everyone ate and was filled. Then they picked up 12 baskets full of leftover pieces! ²¹ Now those who ate were about 5,000 men, besides women and children.

²² Immediately He made the disciples get into the boat and go ahead of Him to the other side, while He dismissed the crowds. ²³ After dismissing the crowds, He went up on the mountain by Himself to pray. When evening came, He was there alone. ²⁴ But the boat was already over a mile from land, battered by the waves, because the wind was against them. ²⁵ Around three in the morning, He came toward them walking on the sea. ²⁶ When the disciples saw Him walking on the sea, they were terrified. "It's a ghost!" they said, and cried out in fear.

²⁷ Immediately Jesus spoke to them. "Have courage! It is I. Don't be afraid."

²⁸ "Lord, if it's You," Peter answered Him, "command me to come to You on the water."

²⁹ "Come!" He said.

And climbing out of the boat, Peter started walking on the water and came toward Jesus. ³⁰ But when he saw the strength of the wind, he was afraid. And beginning to sink he cried out, "Lord, save me!"

³¹ Immediately Jesus reached out His hand, caught hold of him, and said to him, "You of little faith, why did you doubt?" ³² When they got into the boat, the wind ceased. ³³ Then those in the boat worshiped Him and said, "Truly You are the Son of God!"

³⁴ Once they crossed over, they came to land at Gennesaret. ³⁵ When the men of that place recognized Him, they alerted the whole vicinity and brought to Him all who were sick. ³⁶ They were begging Him that they might only touch the •tassel on His robe. And as many as touched it were made perfectly well.

15 Then •Pharisees and •scribes came from Jerusalem to Jesus and asked, ² "Why do Your disciples break the tradition of the elders? For they don't wash their hands when they eat!"

³ He answered them, "And why do you break God's commandment because of your tradition? ⁴ For God said:

Honor your father and your mother; and, **The one who speaks evil of father or mother must be put to death.**

[5] But you say, 'Whoever tells his father or mother, "Whatever benefit you might have received from me is a gift committed to the temple"— [6] he does not have to honor his father.' In this way, you have revoked God's word because of your tradition. [7] Hypocrites! Isaiah prophesied correctly about you when he said:

[8]   **These people honor Me with their lips,**
        but their heart is far from Me.
[9]   **They worship Me in vain,**
        teaching as doctrines the commands of men."

[10] Summoning the crowd, He told them, "Listen and understand: [11] It's not what goes into the mouth that defiles a man, but what comes out of the mouth, this defiles a man."

[12] Then the disciples came up and told Him, "Do You know that the Pharisees took offense when they heard this statement?"

[13] He replied, "Every plant that My heavenly Father didn't plant will be uprooted. [14] Leave them alone! They are blind guides. And if the blind guide the blind, both will fall into a pit."

[15] Then Peter replied to Him, "Explain this parable to us."

[16] "Are even you still lacking in understanding?" He asked. [17] "Don't you realize that whatever goes into the mouth passes into the stomach and is eliminated? [18] But what comes out of the mouth comes from the heart, and this defiles a man. [19] For from the heart come evil thoughts, murders, adulteries, sexual immoralities, thefts, false testimonies, blasphemies. [20] These are the things that defile a man, but eating with unwashed hands does not defile a man."

[21] When Jesus left there, He withdrew to the area of Tyre and Sidon. [22] Just then a Canaanite woman from that region came and kept crying out, "Have mercy on me, Lord, Son of David! My daughter is cruelly tormented by a demon."

[23] Yet He did not say a word to her. So His disciples approached Him and urged Him, "Send her away because she cries out after us."

[24] He replied, "I was sent only to the lost sheep of the house of Israel."

[25] But she came, knelt before Him, and said, "Lord, help me!"

[26] He answered, "It isn't right to take the children's bread and throw it to their dogs."

[27] "Yes, Lord," she said, "yet even the dogs eat the crumbs that fall from their masters' table!"

[28] Then Jesus replied to her, "Woman, your faith is great. Let it be done for you as you want." And from that moment her daughter was cured.

[29] Moving on from there, Jesus passed along the Sea of Galilee. He went up on a mountain and sat there, [30] and large crowds came to Him, having with them the lame, the blind, the deformed, those unable to speak, and many others. They put them at His feet, and He healed them. [31] So the crowd was amazed when they saw those unable to speak talking, the deformed restored, the lame walking, and the blind seeing. And they gave glory to the God of Israel.

[32] Now Jesus summoned His disciples and said, "I have compassion on the crowd, because they've already stayed with Me three days and have nothing to eat. I don't want to send them away hungry; otherwise they might collapse on the way."

[33] The disciples said to Him, "Where could we get enough bread in this desolate place to fill such a crowd?"

[34] "How many loaves do you have?" Jesus asked them.

"Seven," they said, "and a few small fish."

[35] After commanding the crowd to sit down on the ground, [36] He took the seven loaves and the fish, and He gave thanks, broke them, and kept on giving them to the disciples, and the disciples gave them to the crowds. [37] They all ate and were filled. Then they collected the leftover pieces—seven large baskets full. [38] Now those who ate were 4,000 men, besides women and children. [39] After dismissing the crowds, He got into the boat and went to the region of Magadan.

16 The *Pharisees and *Sadducees approached, and as a test, asked Him to show them a sign from heaven.

[2] He answered them: "When evening comes you say, 'It will be good weather because the sky is red.' [3] And in the morning, 'Today will be stormy because the sky is red and threatening.' You know how to read the appearance of the sky, but you can't read the signs of the times. [4] An evil and adulterous generation demands a sign, but no sign will be given to it except the sign of Jonah." Then He left them and went away.

[5] The disciples reached the other shore, and they had forgotten to take bread.

[6] Then Jesus told them, "Watch out and beware of the yeast of the Pharisees and Sadducees."

[7] And they discussed among themselves, "We didn't bring any bread."

[8] Aware of this, Jesus said, "You of little faith! Why are you discussing among yourselves that you do not have bread? [9] Don't you understand yet? Don't you remember the five loaves for the 5,000 and how many baskets you collected? [10] Or the seven loaves for the 4,000 and how many large baskets you collected? [11] Why is it you don't understand that when I told you, 'Beware of the yeast of the Pharisees and Sadducees,' it wasn't about bread?" [12] Then they understood that He did not tell them to beware of the yeast in bread, but of the teaching of the Pharisees and Sadducees.

[13] When Jesus came to the region of Caesarea Philippi, He asked His disciples, "Who do people say that the *Son of Man is?"

[14] And they said, "Some say John the Baptist; others, Elijah; still others, Jeremiah or one of the prophets."

[15] "But you," He asked them, "who do you say that I am?"

[16] Simon Peter answered, "You are the *Messiah, the Son of the living God!"

[17] And Jesus responded, "Simon son of Jonah, you are blessed because flesh and blood did not reveal this to you, but My Father in heaven. [18] And I also say to you that you are Peter, and on this rock I will build My church, and the forces of *Hades will not overpower it. [19] I will give you the keys of the kingdom of heaven, and whatever you bind on earth is already bound in heaven, and whatever you loose on earth is already loosed in heaven."

[20] And He gave the disciples orders to tell no one that He was the Messiah.

[21] From then on Jesus began to point out to His disciples that He must go to Jerusalem and suffer many things from the elders, *chief priests, and *scribes, be killed, and be raised the third day. [22] Then Peter took

Him aside and began to rebuke Him, "Oh no, Lord! This will never happen to You!"

[23] But He turned and told Peter, "Get behind Me, Satan! You are an offense to Me because you're not thinking about God's concerns, but man's."

[24] Then Jesus said to His disciples, "If anyone wants to come with Me, he must deny himself, take up his cross, and follow Me. [25] For whoever wants to save his *life will lose it, but whoever loses his life because of Me will find it. [26] What will it benefit a man if he gains the whole world yet loses his life? Or what will a man give in exchange for his life? [27] For the Son of Man is going to come with His angels in the glory of His Father, and then He will reward each according to what he has done. [28] *I assure you: There are some standing here who will not taste death until they see the Son of Man coming in His kingdom."

17 After six days Jesus took Peter, James, and his brother John and led them up on a high mountain by themselves. [2] He was transformed in front of them, and His face shone like the sun. Even His clothes became as white as the light. [3] Suddenly, Moses and Elijah appeared to them, talking with Him.

[4] Then Peter said to Jesus, "Lord, it's good for us to be here! If You want, I will make three *tabernacles here: one for You, one for Moses, and one for Elijah."

[5] While he was still speaking, suddenly a bright cloud covered them, and a voice from the cloud said:

This is My beloved Son.
I take delight in Him.
Listen to Him!

[6] When the disciples heard it, they fell facedown and were terrified.

[7] Then Jesus came up, touched them, and said, "Get up; don't be afraid." [8] When they looked up they saw no one except Him—Jesus alone. [9] As they were coming down from the mountain, Jesus commanded them, "Don't tell anyone about the vision until the *Son of Man is raised from the dead."

[10] So the disciples questioned Him, "Why then do the *scribes say that Elijah must come first?"

[11] "Elijah is coming and will restore everything," He replied. [12] "But I tell you: Elijah has already come, and they didn't recognize him. On the contrary, they did whatever they pleased to him. In the same way the Son of Man is going to suffer at their hands." [13] Then the disciples understood that He spoke to them about John the Baptist.

[14] When they reached the crowd, a man approached and knelt down before Him. [15] "Lord," he said, "have mercy on my son, because he has seizures and suffers severely. He often falls into the fire and often into the water. [16] I brought him to Your disciples, but they couldn't heal him."

[17] Jesus replied, "You unbelieving and rebellious generation! How long will I be with you? How long must I put up with you? Bring him here to Me." [18] Then Jesus rebuked the demon, and it came out of him, and from that moment the boy was healed.

[19] Then the disciples approached Jesus privately and said, "Why couldn't we drive it out?"

[20] "Because of your little faith," He told them. "For *I assure you: If you have faith the size of a mustard seed, you will tell this mountain, 'Move from here to there,' and it will move. Nothing will be impossible for you. [21] However, this kind does not come out except by prayer and fasting.]"

[22] As they were meeting in Galilee, Jesus told them, "The Son of Man is about to be betrayed into the hands of men. [23] They will kill Him, and on the third day He will be raised up." And they were deeply distressed.

[24] When they came to Capernaum, those who collected the double-drachma tax approached Peter and said, "Doesn't your Teacher pay the double-drachma tax?"

[25] "Yes," he said.

When he went into the house, Jesus spoke to him first, "What do you think, Simon? Who do earthly kings collect tariffs or taxes from? From their sons or from strangers?"

[26] "From strangers," he said.

"Then the sons are free," Jesus told him. [27] "But, so we won't *offend them, go to the sea, cast in a fishhook, and take the first fish that you catch. When you open its mouth you'll find a coin. Take it and give it to them for Me and you."

18 At that time the disciples came to Jesus and said, "Who is greatest in the kingdom of heaven?"

[2] Then He called a child to Him and had him stand among them. [3] "I assure you," He said, "unless you are converted and become like children, you will never enter the kingdom of heaven. [4] Therefore, whoever humbles himself like this child—this one is the greatest in the kingdom of heaven. [5] And whoever welcomes one child like this in My name welcomes Me.

[6] "But whoever *causes the downfall of one of these little ones who believe in Me—it would be better for him if a heavy millstone were hung around his neck and he were drowned in the depths of the sea! [7] Woe to the world because of offenses. For *offenses must come, but woe to that man by whom the offense comes. [8] If your hand or your foot causes your downfall, cut it off and throw it away. It is better for you to enter life maimed or lame, than to have two hands or two feet and be thrown into the eternal fire. [9] And if your eye causes your downfall, gouge it out and throw it away. It is better for you to enter life with one eye, rather than to have two eyes and be thrown into *hellfire!

[10] "See that you don't look down on one of these little ones, because I tell you that in heaven their angels continually view the face of My Father in heaven. [11] For the *Son of Man has come to save the lost.] [12] What do you think? If a man has 100 sheep, and one of them goes astray, won't he leave the 99 on the hillside and go and search for the stray? [13] And if he finds it, I assure you: He rejoices over that sheep more than over the 99 that did not go astray. [14] In the same way, it is not the will of your Father in heaven that one of these little ones perish.

[15] "If your brother sins against you, go and rebuke him in private. If he listens to you, you have won your brother. [16] But if he won't listen, take one or two more with you, so that **by the testimony of two or three witnesses every fact may be established.** [17] If he pays no attention to them, tell the church. But if he doesn't pay attention even to the church, let him be like an unbeliever and a tax collector to you. [18] I assure you: Whatever you bind on earth is already bound in heaven, and whatever you loose on earth is already loosed in heaven. [19] Again, I assure you: If two of you on earth agree about any matter that you pray for, it will be done for you by My Father in heaven. [20] For where two or three are gathered together in My name, I am there among them."

²¹Then Peter came to Him and said, "Lord, how many times could my brother sin against me and I forgive him? As many as seven times?"

²²"I tell you, not as many as seven," Jesus said to him, "but 70 times seven. ²³For this reason, the kingdom of heaven can be compared to a king who wanted to settle accounts with his •slaves. ²⁴When he began to settle accounts, one who owed 10,000 talents was brought before him. ²⁵Since he had no way to pay it back, his master commanded that he, his wife, his children, and everything he had be sold to pay the debt.

²⁶"At this, the slave fell facedown before him and said, 'Be patient with me, and I will pay you everything!' ²⁷Then the master of that slave had compassion, released him, and forgave him the loan.

²⁸"But that slave went out and found one of his fellow slaves who owed him 100 •denarii. He grabbed him, started choking him, and said, 'Pay what you owe!'

²⁹"At this, his fellow slave fell down and began begging him, 'Be patient with me, and I will pay you back.' ³⁰But he wasn't willing. On the contrary, he went and threw him into prison until he could pay what was owed. ³¹When the other slaves saw what had taken place, they were deeply distressed and went and reported to their master everything that had happened.

³²"Then, after he had summoned him, his master said to him, 'You wicked slave! I forgave you all that debt because you begged me. ³³Shouldn't you also have had mercy on your fellow slave, as I had mercy on you?' ³⁴And his master got angry and handed him over to the jailers to be tortured until he could pay everything that was owed. ³⁵So My heavenly Father will also do to you if each of you does not forgive his brother from his heart."

19 When Jesus had finished this instruction, He departed from Galilee and went to the region of Judea across the Jordan. ²Large crowds followed Him, and He healed them there. ³Some •Pharisees approached Him to test Him. They asked, "Is it lawful for a man to divorce his wife on any grounds?"

⁴"Haven't you read," He replied, "that He who created them in the beginning **made them male and female**," ⁵and He also said:

> "For this reason a man will leave
> his father and mother
> and be joined to his wife,
> and the two will become one flesh?

⁶So they are no longer two, but one flesh. Therefore, what God has joined together, man must not separate."

⁷"Why then," they asked Him, "did Moses command us to give divorce papers and to send her away?"

⁸He told them, "Moses permitted you to divorce your wives because of the hardness of your hearts. But it was not like that from the beginning. ⁹And I tell you, whoever divorces his wife, except for sexual immorality, and marries another, commits adultery."

¹⁰His disciples said to Him, "If the relationship of a man with his wife is like this, it's better not to marry!"

¹¹But He told them, "Not everyone can accept this saying, but only those it has been given to. ¹²For there are eunuchs who were born that way from their mother's womb, and there are eunuchs who were made by men, and there are eunuchs who have made themselves that way because of the kingdom of heaven. Let anyone accept this who can."

¹³Then children were brought to Him so He might put His hands on them and pray. But the disciples rebuked them. ¹⁴Then Jesus said, "Leave the children alone, and don't try to keep them from coming to Me, because the kingdom of heaven is made up of people like this." ¹⁵After putting His hands on them, He went on from there.

¹⁶Just then someone came up and asked Him, "Teacher, what good must I do to have eternal life?"

¹⁷"Why do you ask Me about what is good?" He said to him. "There is only One who is good. If you want to enter into life, keep the commandments."

¹⁸"Which ones?" he asked Him. Jesus answered:

> **Do not murder;**
> **do not commit adultery;**
> **do not steal;**
> **do not bear false witness;**
> ¹⁹ **honor your father and your mother;**
> **and love your neighbor as yourself.**

²⁰"I have kept all these," the young man told Him. "What do I still lack?"

²¹"If you want to be perfect," Jesus said to him, "go, sell your belongings and give to the poor, and you will have treasure in heaven. Then come, follow Me."

²²When the young man heard that command, he went away grieving, because he had many possessions.

²³Then Jesus said to His disciples, "'I assure you: It will be hard for a rich person to enter the kingdom of heaven! ²⁴Again I tell you, it is easier for a camel to go through the eye of a needle than for a rich person to enter the kingdom of God."

²⁵When the disciples heard this, they were utterly astonished and asked, "Then who can be saved?"

²⁶But Jesus looked at them and said, "With men this is impossible, but with God all things are possible."

²⁷Then Peter responded to Him, "Look, we have left everything and followed You. So what will there be for us?"

²⁸Jesus said to them, "I assure you: In the Messianic Age, when the •Son of Man sits on His glorious throne, you who have followed Me will also sit on 12 thrones, judging the 12 tribes of Israel. ²⁹And everyone who has left houses, brothers or sisters, father or mother, children, or fields because of My name will receive 100 times more and will inherit eternal life. ³⁰But many who are first will be last, and the last first.

20 "For the kingdom of heaven is like a landowner who went out early in the morning to hire workers for his vineyard. ²After agreeing with the workers on one •denarius for the day, he sent them into his vineyard. ³When he went out about nine in the morning, he saw others standing in the marketplace doing nothing. ⁴To those men he said, 'You also go to my vineyard, and I'll give you whatever is right.' So off they went. ⁵About noon and at three, he went out again and did the same thing. ⁶Then about five he went and found others standing around, and said to them, 'Why have you been standing here all day doing nothing?'

⁷"'Because no one hired us,' they said to him.

"'You also go to my vineyard,' he told them. ⁸When evening came, the owner of the vineyard told his foreman, 'Call the workers and give them their pay, starting with the last and ending with the first.'

⁹"When those who were hired about five came, they each received one denarius. ¹⁰So when the first ones came, they assumed they would get more, but they

also received a denarius each. ¹¹When they received it, they began to complain to the landowner: ¹²'These last men put in one hour, and you made them equal to us who bore the burden of the day and the burning heat!'

¹³"He replied to one of them, 'Friend, I'm doing you no wrong. Didn't you agree with me on a denarius? ¹⁴Take what's yours and go. I want to give this last man the same as I gave you. ¹⁵Don't I have the right to do what I want with my business? Are you jealous because I'm generous?'

¹⁶"So the last will be first, and the first last."

¹⁷While going up to Jerusalem, Jesus took the 12 disciples aside privately and said to them on the way: ¹⁸"Listen! We are going up to Jerusalem. The *Son of Man will be handed over to the *chief priests and *scribes, and they will condemn Him to death. ¹⁹Then they will hand Him over to the Gentiles to be mocked, flogged, and crucified, and He will be resurrected on the third day."

²⁰Then the mother of Zebedee's sons approached Him with her sons. She knelt down to ask Him for something. ²¹"What do you want?" He asked her.

"Promise," she said to Him, "that these two sons of mine may sit, one on Your right and the other on Your left, in Your kingdom."

²²But Jesus answered, "You don't know what you're asking. Are you able to drink the cup that I am about to drink?"

"We are able," they said to Him.

²³He told them, "You will indeed drink My cup. But to sit at My right and left is not Mine to give; instead, it belongs to those for whom it has been prepared by My Father." ²⁴When the 10 disciples heard this, they became indignant with the two brothers. ²⁵But Jesus called them over and said, "You know that the rulers of the Gentiles dominate them, and the men of high position exercise power over them. ²⁶It must not be like that among you. On the contrary, whoever wants to become great among you must be your servant, ²⁷and whoever wants to be first among you must be your *slave; ²⁸just as the Son of Man did not come to be served, but to serve, and to give His life—a ransom for many."

²⁹As they were leaving Jericho, a large crowd followed Him. ³⁰There were two blind men sitting by the road. When they heard that Jesus was passing by, they cried out, "Lord, have mercy on us, Son of David!" ³¹The crowd told them to keep quiet, but they cried out all the more, "Lord, have mercy on us, Son of David!"

³²Jesus stopped, called them, and said, "What do you want Me to do for you?"

³³"Lord," they said to Him, "open our eyes!" ³⁴Moved with compassion, Jesus touched their eyes. Immediately they could see, and they followed Him.

21 When they approached Jerusalem and came to Bethphage at the *Mount of Olives, Jesus then sent two disciples, ²telling them, "Go into the village ahead of you. At once you will find a donkey tied there, and a colt with her. Untie them and bring them to Me. ³If anyone says anything to you, you should say that the Lord needs them, and immediately he will send them."

⁴This took place so that what was spoken through the prophet might be fulfilled:

⁵ Tell Daughter *Zion,
   "Look, your King is coming to you,
   gentle, and mounted on a donkey,
   even on a colt,
   the foal of a beast of burden."

⁶The disciples went and did just as Jesus directed them. ⁷They brought the donkey and the colt; then they laid their robes on them, and He sat on them. ⁸A very large crowd spread their robes on the road; others were cutting branches from the trees and spreading them on the road. ⁹Then the crowds who went ahead of Him and those who followed kept shouting:

   Hosanna to the Son of David!
   He who comes in the name
   of the Lord is the blessed One!
   Hosanna in the highest heaven!

¹⁰When He entered Jerusalem, the whole city was shaken, saying, "Who is this?" ¹¹And the crowds kept saying, "This is the prophet Jesus from Nazareth in Galilee!"

¹²Jesus went into the *temple complex and drove out all those buying and selling in the temple. He overturned the money changers' tables and the chairs of those selling doves. ¹³And He said to them, "It is written, **My house will be called a house of prayer.** But you are making it **a den of thieves!**"

¹⁴The blind and the lame came to Him in the temple complex, and He healed them. ¹⁵When the *chief priests and the *scribes saw the wonders that He did and the children shouting in the temple complex, "*Hosanna* to the Son of David!" they were indignant ¹⁶and said to Him, "Do You hear what these children are saying?"

"Yes," Jesus told them. "Have you never read:

   **You have prepared praise
   from the mouths of children
   and nursing infants?**"

¹⁷Then He left them, went out of the city to Bethany, and spent the night there.

¹⁸Early in the morning, as He was returning to the city, He was hungry. ¹⁹Seeing a lone fig tree by the road, He went up to it and found nothing on it except leaves. And He said to it, "May no fruit ever come from you again!" At once the fig tree withered.

²⁰When the disciples saw it, they were amazed and said, "How did the fig tree wither so quickly?"

²¹Jesus answered them, "'I assure you: If you have faith and do not doubt, you will not only do what was done to the fig tree, but even if you tell this mountain, 'Be lifted up and thrown into the sea,' it will be done. ²²And if you believe, you will receive whatever you ask for in prayer."

²³When He entered the temple complex, the chief priests and the elders of the people came up to Him as He was teaching and said, "By what authority are You doing these things? Who gave You this authority?"

²⁴Jesus answered them, "I will also ask you one question, and if you answer it for Me, then I will tell you by what authority I do these things. ²⁵Where did John's baptism come from? From heaven or from men?"

They began to argue among themselves, "If we say, 'From heaven,' He will say to us, 'Then why didn't you believe him?' ²⁶But if we say, 'From men,' we're afraid of the crowd, because everyone thought John was a prophet." ²⁷So they answered Jesus, "We don't know."

And He said to them, "Neither will I tell you by what authority I do these things.

²⁸"But what do you think? A man had two sons. He

went to the first and said, 'My son, go, work in the vineyard today.'

²⁹"He answered, 'I don't want to!' Yet later he changed his mind and went. ³⁰Then the man went to the other and said the same thing.

"'I will, sir,' he answered. But he didn't go.

³¹"Which of the two did his father's will?"

"The first," they said.

Jesus said to them, "I assure you: Tax collectors and prostitutes are entering the kingdom of God before you! ³²For John came to you in the way of righteousness, and you didn't believe him. Tax collectors and prostitutes did believe him, but you, when you saw it, didn't even change your minds then and believe him.

³³"Listen to another parable: There was a man, a landowner, who planted a vineyard, put a fence around it, dug a winepress in it, and built a watchtower. He leased it to tenant farmers and went away. ³⁴When the grape harvest drew near, he sent his ˙slaves to the farmers to collect his fruit. ³⁵But the farmers took his slaves, beat one, killed another, and stoned a third. ³⁶Again, he sent other slaves, more than the first group, and they did the same to them. ³⁷Finally, he sent his son to them. 'They will respect my son,' he said.

³⁸"But when the tenant farmers saw the son, they said among themselves, 'This is the heir. Come, let's kill him and take his inheritance!' ³⁹So they seized him, threw him out of the vineyard, and killed him. ⁴⁰Therefore, when the owner of the vineyard comes, what will he do to those farmers?"

⁴¹"He will completely destroy those terrible men," they told Him, "and lease his vineyard to other farmers who will give him his produce at the harvest."

⁴²Jesus said to them, "Have you never read in the Scriptures:

> The stone that the builders rejected
> has become the cornerstone.
> This came from the Lord
> and is wonderful in our eyes?

⁴³Therefore I tell you, the kingdom of God will be taken away from you and given to a nation producing its fruit. [⁴⁴Whoever falls on this stone will be broken to pieces; but on whoever it falls, it will grind him to powder!]"

⁴⁵When the chief priests and the ˙Pharisees heard His parables, they knew He was speaking about them. ⁴⁶Although they were looking for a way to arrest Him, they feared the crowds, because they regarded Him as a prophet.

22 Once more Jesus spoke to them in parables: ²"The kingdom of heaven may be compared to a king who gave a wedding banquet for his son. ³He sent out his ˙slaves to summon those invited to the banquet, but they didn't want to come. ⁴Again, he sent out other slaves, and said, 'Tell those who are invited: Look, I've prepared my dinner; my oxen and fattened cattle have been slaughtered, and everything is ready. Come to the wedding banquet.'

⁵"But they paid no attention and went away, one to his own farm, another to his business. ⁶And the others seized his slaves, treated them outrageously and killed them. ⁷The king was enraged, so he sent out his troops, destroyed those murderers, and burned down their city.

⁸"Then he told his slaves, 'The banquet is ready, but those who were invited were not worthy. ⁹Therefore go to where the roads exit the city and invite everyone you find to the banquet.' ¹⁰So those slaves went out on the roads and gathered everyone they found, both evil and good. The wedding banquet was filled with guests. ¹¹But when the king came in to view the guests, he saw a man there who was not dressed for a wedding. ¹²So he said to him, 'Friend, how did you get in here without wedding clothes?' The man was speechless.

¹³"Then the king told the attendants, 'Tie him up hand and foot, and throw him into the outer darkness, where there will be weeping and gnashing of teeth.'

¹⁴"For many are invited, but few are chosen."

¹⁵Then the ˙Pharisees went and plotted how to trap Him by what He said. ¹⁶They sent their disciples to Him, with the ˙Herodians. "Teacher," they said, "we know that You are truthful and teach truthfully the way of God. You defer to no one, for You don't show partiality. ¹⁷Tell us, therefore, what You think. Is it lawful to pay taxes to Caesar or not?"

¹⁸But perceiving their malice, Jesus said, "Why are you testing Me, hypocrites? ¹⁹Show Me the coin used for the tax." So they brought Him a ˙denarius. ²⁰"Whose image and inscription is this?" He asked them.

²¹"Caesar's," they said to Him.

Then He said to them, "Therefore give back to Caesar the things that are Caesar's, and to God the things that are God's." ²²When they heard this, they were amazed. So they left Him and went away.

²³The same day some ˙Sadducees, who say there is no resurrection, came up to Him and questioned Him: ²⁴"Teacher, Moses said, **if a man dies, having no children, his brother is to marry his wife and raise up offspring for his brother.** ²⁵Now there were seven brothers among us. The first got married and died. Having no offspring, he left his wife to his brother. ²⁶The same happened to the second also, and the third, and so to all seven. ²⁷Then last of all the woman died. ²⁸In the resurrection, therefore, whose wife will she be of the seven? For they all had married her."

²⁹Jesus answered them, "You are deceived, because you don't know the Scriptures or the power of God. ³⁰For in the resurrection they neither marry nor are given in marriage but are like angels in heaven. ³¹Now concerning the resurrection of the dead, haven't you read what was spoken to you by God: ³²**I am the God of Abraham and the God of Isaac and the God of Jacob?** He is not the God of the dead, but of the living."

³³And when the crowds heard this, they were astonished at His teaching.

³⁴When the Pharisees heard that He had silenced the Sadducees, they came together. ³⁵And one of them, an expert in the law, asked a question to test Him: ³⁶"Teacher, which command in the law is the greatest?"

³⁷He said to him, "**Love the Lord your God with all your heart, with all your soul, and with all your mind.** ³⁸This is the greatest and most important command. ³⁹The second is like it: **Love your neighbor as yourself.** ⁴⁰All the Law and the Prophets depend on these two commands."

⁴¹While the Pharisees were together, Jesus questioned them, ⁴²"What do you think about the ˙Messiah? Whose Son is He?"

"David's," they told Him.

⁴³He asked them, "How is it then that David, inspired by the Spirit, calls Him 'Lord':

⁴⁴   **The Lord declared to my Lord,**

**'Sit at My right hand
until I put Your enemies under Your feet'**?

⁴⁵"If David calls Him 'Lord,' how then can the Messiah be his Son?" ⁴⁶No one was able to answer Him at all, and from that day no one dared to question Him anymore.

23 Then Jesus spoke to the crowds and to His disciples: ²"The *scribes and the *Pharisees are seated in the chair of Moses. ³Therefore do whatever they tell you, and observe it. But don't do what they do, because they don't practice what they teach. ⁴They tie up heavy loads that are hard to carry and put them on people's shoulders, but they themselves aren't willing to lift a finger to move them. ⁵They do everything to be observed by others: They enlarge their phylacteries and lengthen their *tassels. ⁶They love the place of honor at banquets, the front seats in the *synagogues, ⁷greetings in the marketplaces, and to be called "Rabbi' by people.

⁸"But as for you, do not be called 'Rabbi,' because you have one Teacher, and you are all *brothers. ⁹Do not call anyone on earth your father, because you have one Father, who is in heaven. ¹⁰And do not be called masters either, because you have one Master, the *Messiah. ¹¹The greatest among you will be your servant. ¹²Whoever exalts himself will be humbled, and whoever humbles himself will be exalted.

¹³"But woe to you, scribes and Pharisees, hypocrites! You lock up the kingdom of heaven from people. For you don't go in, and you don't allow those entering to go in.

[¹⁴"Woe to you, scribes and Pharisees, hypocrites! You devour widows' houses and make long prayers just for show. This is why you will receive a harsher punishment.]

¹⁵"Woe to you, scribes and Pharisees, hypocrites! You travel over land and sea to make one *proselyte, and when he becomes one, you make him twice as fit for *hell as you are!

¹⁶"Woe to you, blind guides, who say, 'Whoever takes an oath by the sanctuary, it means nothing. But whoever takes an oath by the gold of the sanctuary is bound by his oath.' ¹⁷Blind fools! For which is greater, the gold or the sanctuary that sanctified the gold? ¹⁸Also, 'Whoever takes an oath by the altar, it means nothing. But whoever takes an oath by the gift that is on it is bound by his oath.' ¹⁹Blind people! For which is greater, the gift or the altar that sanctifies the gift? ²⁰Therefore, the one who takes an oath by the altar takes an oath by it and by everything on it. ²¹The one who takes an oath by the sanctuary takes an oath by it and by Him who dwells in it. ²²And the one who takes an oath by heaven takes an oath by God's throne and by Him who sits on it.

²³"Woe to you, scribes and Pharisees, hypocrites! You pay a tenth of mint, dill, and cumin, yet you have neglected the more important matters of the law—justice, mercy, and faith. These things should have been done without neglecting the others. ²⁴Blind guides! You strain out a gnat, yet gulp down a camel!

²⁵"Woe to you, scribes and Pharisees, hypocrites! You *clean the outside of the cup and dish, but inside they are full of greed and self-indulgence! ²⁶Blind Pharisee! First clean the inside of the cup, so the outside of it may also become clean.

²⁷"Woe to you, scribes and Pharisees, hypocrites! You are like whitewashed tombs, which appear beautiful on the outside, but inside are full of dead men's bones and every impurity. ²⁸In the same way, on the outside you seem righteous to people, but inside you are full of hypocrisy and lawlessness.

²⁹"Woe to you, scribes and Pharisees, hypocrites! You build the tombs of the prophets and decorate the monuments of the righteous, ³⁰and you say, 'If we had lived in the days of our fathers, we wouldn't have taken part with them in shedding the prophets' blood.' ³¹You, therefore, testify against yourselves that you are sons of those who murdered the prophets. ³²Fill up, then, the measure of your fathers' sins!

³³"Snakes! Brood of vipers! How can you escape being condemned to hell? ³⁴This is why I am sending you prophets, sages, and scribes. Some of them you will kill and crucify, and some of them you will flog in your synagogues and hound from town to town. ³⁵So all the righteous blood shed on the earth will be charged to you, from the blood of righteous Abel to the blood of Zechariah, son of Berechiah, whom you murdered between the sanctuary and the altar. ³⁶I assure you: All these things will come on this generation!

³⁷"Jerusalem, Jerusalem! She who kills the prophets and stones those who are sent to her. How often I wanted to gather your children together, as a hen gathers her chicks under her wings, yet you were not willing! ³⁸See, your house is left to you desolate. ³⁹For I tell you, you will never see Me again until you say, **'He who comes in the name of the Lord is the blessed One'**!"

24 As Jesus left and was going out of the *temple complex, His disciples came up and called His attention to the temple buildings. ²Then He replied to them, "Don't you see all these things? *I assure you: Not one stone will be left here on another that will not be thrown down!"

³While He was sitting on the *Mount of Olives, the disciples approached Him privately and said, "Tell us, when will these things happen? And what is the sign of Your coming and of the end of the age?"

⁴Then Jesus replied to them: "Watch out that no one deceives you. ⁵For many will come in My name, saying, 'I am the *Messiah,' and they will deceive many. ⁶You are going to hear of wars and rumors of wars. See that you are not alarmed, because these things must take place, but the end is not yet. ⁷For nation will rise up against nation, and kingdom against kingdom. There will be famines and earthquakes in various places. ⁸All these events are the beginning of birth pains.

⁹"Then they will hand you over for persecution, and they will kill you. You will be hated by all nations because of My name. ¹⁰Then many will *take offense, betray one another and hate one another. ¹¹Many false prophets will rise up and deceive many. ¹²Because lawlessness will multiply, the love of many will grow cold. ¹³But the one who endures to the end will be delivered. ¹⁴This good news of the kingdom will be proclaimed in all the world as a testimony to all nations. And then the end will come.

¹⁵"So when you see **the abomination that causes desolation**, spoken of by the prophet Daniel, standing in the holy place" (let the reader understand), ¹⁶"then those in Judea must flee to the mountains! ¹⁷A man on the housetop must not come down to get things out of his house. ¹⁸And a man in the field must not go back to get his clothes. ¹⁹Woe to pregnant women and nursing mothers in those days! ²⁰Pray that your escape may

not be in winter or on a Sabbath. ²¹For at that time there will be great tribulation, the kind that hasn't taken place from the beginning of the world until now and never will again! ²²Unless those days were limited, no one would survive. But those days will be limited because of the elect.

²³"If anyone tells you then, 'Look, here is the Messiah!' or, 'Over here!' do not believe it! ²⁴False messiahs and false prophets will arise and perform great signs and wonders to lead astray, if possible, even the elect. ²⁵Take note: I have told you in advance. ²⁶So if they tell you, 'Look, He's in the wilderness!' don't go out; 'Look, He's in the inner rooms!' do not believe it. ²⁷For as the lightning comes from the east and flashes as far as the west, so will be the coming of the *Son of Man. ²⁸Wherever the carcass is, there the vultures will gather.

²⁹"Immediately after the tribulation of those days:

The sun will be darkened,
and the moon will not shed its light;
the stars will fall from the sky,
and the celestial powers will be shaken.

³⁰"Then the sign of the Son of Man will appear in the sky, and then all the peoples of the earth will mourn; and they will see the Son of Man coming on the clouds of heaven with power and great glory. ³¹He will send out His angels with a loud trumpet, and they will gather His elect from the four winds, from one end of the sky to the other.

³²"Now learn this parable from the fig tree: As soon as its branch becomes tender and sprouts leaves, you know that summer is near. ³³In the same way, when you see all these things, recognize that He is near—at the door! ³⁴I assure you: This generation will certainly not pass away until all these things take place. ³⁵Heaven and earth will pass away, but My words will never pass away.

³⁶"Now concerning that day and hour no one knows—neither the angels in heaven, nor the Son—except the Father only. ³⁷As the days of Noah were, so the coming of the Son of Man will be. ³⁸For in those days before the flood they were eating and drinking, marrying and giving in marriage, until the day Noah boarded the ark. ³⁹They didn't know until the flood came and swept them all away. So this is the way the coming of the Son of Man will be: ⁴⁰Then two men will be in the field: one will be taken and one left. ⁴¹Two women will be grinding at the mill: one will be taken and one left. ⁴²Therefore be alert, since you don't know what day your Lord is coming. ⁴³But know this: If the homeowner had known what time the thief was coming, he would have stayed alert and not let his house be broken into. ⁴⁴This is why you also must be ready, because the Son of Man is coming at an hour you do not expect.

⁴⁵"Who then is a faithful and sensible *slave, whom his master has put in charge of his household, to give them food at the proper time? ⁴⁶That slave whose master finds him working when he comes will be rewarded. ⁴⁷I assure you: He will put him in charge of all his possessions. ⁴⁸But if that wicked slave says in his heart, 'My master is delayed,' ⁴⁹and starts to beat his fellow slaves, and eats and drinks with drunkards, ⁵⁰that slave's master will come on a day he does not expect and at an hour he does not know. ⁵¹He will cut him to pieces and assign him a place with the hypocrites. In that place there will be weeping and gnashing of teeth.

25 "Then the kingdom of heaven will be like 10 virgins who took their lamps and went out to meet the groom. ²Five of them were foolish and five were sensible. ³When the foolish took their lamps, they didn't take olive oil with them. ⁴But the sensible ones took oil in their flasks with their lamps. ⁵Since the groom was delayed, they all became drowsy and fell asleep.

⁶"In the middle of the night there was a shout: 'Here's the groom! Come out to meet him.'

⁷"Then all those virgins got up and trimmed their lamps. ⁸But the foolish ones said to the sensible ones, 'Give us some of your oil, because our lamps are going out.'

⁹"The sensible ones answered, 'No, there won't be enough for us and for you. Go instead to those who sell, and buy oil for yourselves.'

¹⁰"When they had gone to buy some, the groom arrived. Then those who were ready went in with him to the wedding banquet, and the door was shut.

¹¹"Later the rest of the virgins also came and said, 'Master, master, open up for us!'

¹²"But he replied, 'I assure you: I do not know you!'

¹³"Therefore be alert, because you don't know either the day or the hour.

¹⁴"For it is just like a man going on a journey. He called his own *slaves and turned over his possessions to them. ¹⁵To one he gave five talents; to another, two; and to another, one—to each according to his own ability. Then he went on a journey. Immediately ¹⁶the man who had received five talents went, put them to work, and earned five more. ¹⁷In the same way the man with two earned two more. ¹⁸But the man who had received one talent went off, dug a hole in the ground, and hid his master's money.

¹⁹"After a long time the master of those slaves came and settled accounts with them. ²⁰The man who had received five talents approached, presented five more talents, and said, 'Master, you gave me five talents. Look, I've earned five more talents.'

²¹"His master said to him, 'Well done, good and faithful slave! You were faithful over a few things; I will put you in charge of many things. Share your master's joy!'

²²"Then the man with two talents also approached. He said, 'Master, you gave me two talents. Look, I've earned two more talents.'

²³"His master said to him, 'Well done, good and faithful slave! You were faithful over a few things; I will put you in charge of many things. Share your master's joy!'

²⁴"Then the man who had received one talent also approached and said, 'Master, I know you. You're a difficult man, reaping where you haven't sown and gathering where you haven't scattered seed. ²⁵So I was afraid and went off and hid your talent in the ground. Look, you have what is yours.'

²⁶"But his master replied to him, 'You evil, lazy slave! If you knew that I reap where I haven't sown and gather where I haven't scattered, ²⁷then you should have deposited my money with the bankers. And when I returned I would have received my money back with interest.

²⁸"'So take the talent from him and give it to the one who has 10 talents. ²⁹For to everyone who has, more will be given, and he will have more than enough. But from the one who does not have, even what he has will

be taken away from him. ³⁰And throw this good-for-nothing slave into the outer darkness. In that place there will be weeping and gnashing of teeth.'

³¹"When the •Son of Man comes in His glory, and all the angels with Him, then He will sit on the throne of His glory. ³²All the nations will be gathered before Him, and He will separate them one from another, just as a shepherd separates the sheep from the goats. ³³He will put the sheep on His right and the goats on the left. ³⁴Then the King will say to those on His right, 'Come, you who are blessed by My Father, inherit the kingdom prepared for you from the foundation of the world.

³⁵ For I was hungry
and you gave Me something to eat;
I was thirsty
and you gave Me something to drink;
I was a stranger and you took Me in;
³⁶ I was naked and you clothed Me;
I was sick and you took care of Me;
I was in prison and you visited Me.'

³⁷"Then the righteous will answer Him, 'Lord, when did we see You hungry and feed You, or thirsty and give You something to drink? ³⁸When did we see You a stranger and take You in, or without clothes and clothe You? ³⁹When did we see You sick, or in prison, and visit You?'

⁴⁰"And the King will answer them, 'I assure you: Whatever you did for one of the least of these •brothers of Mine, you did for Me.' ⁴¹Then He will also say to those on the left, 'Depart from Me, you who are cursed, into the eternal fire prepared for the Devil and his angels!

⁴² For I was hungry
and you gave Me nothing to eat;
I was thirsty
and you gave Me nothing to drink;
⁴³ I was a stranger
and you didn't take Me in;
I was naked
and you didn't clothe Me,
sick and in prison
and you didn't take care of Me.'

⁴⁴"Then they too will answer, 'Lord, when did we see You hungry, or thirsty, or a stranger, or without clothes, or sick, or in prison, and not help You?'

⁴⁵"Then He will answer them, 'I assure you: Whatever you did not do for one of the least of these, you did not do for Me either.'

⁴⁶"And they will go away into eternal punishment, but the righteous into eternal life."

26 When Jesus had finished saying all this, He told His disciples, ²"You know that the •Passover takes place after two days, and the •Son of Man will be handed over to be crucified."

³Then the •chief priests and the elders of the people assembled in the palace of the high priest, who was called Caiaphas, ⁴and they conspired to arrest Jesus in a treacherous way and kill Him. ⁵"Not during the festival," they said, "so there won't be rioting among the people."

⁶While Jesus was in Bethany at the house of Simon, a man who had a serious skin disease, ⁷a woman approached Him with an alabaster jar of very expensive fragrant oil. She poured it on His head as He was reclining at the table. ⁸When the disciples saw it, they were indignant. "Why this waste?" they asked. ⁹"This

might have been sold for a great deal and given to the poor."

¹⁰But Jesus, aware of this, said to them, "Why are you bothering this woman? She has done a noble thing for Me. ¹¹You always have the poor with you, but you do not always have Me. ¹²By pouring this fragrant oil on My body, she has prepared Me for burial. ¹³•I assure you: Wherever this gospel is proclaimed in the whole world, what this woman has done will also be told in memory of her."

¹⁴Then one of the Twelve—the man called Judas Iscariot—went to the chief priests ¹⁵and said, "What are you willing to give me if I hand Him over to you?" So they weighed out 30 pieces of silver for him. ¹⁶And from that time he started looking for a good opportunity to betray Him.

¹⁷On the first day of •Unleavened Bread the disciples came to Jesus and asked, "Where do You want us to prepare the Passover so You may eat it?"

¹⁸"Go into the city to a certain man," He said, "and tell him, 'The Teacher says: My time is near; I am celebrating the Passover at your place with My disciples.'" ¹⁹So the disciples did as Jesus had directed them and prepared the Passover. ²⁰When evening came, He was reclining at the table with the Twelve. ²¹While they were eating, He said, "I assure you: One of you will betray Me."

²²Deeply distressed, each one began to say to Him, "Surely not I, Lord?"

²³He replied, "The one who dipped his hand with Me in the bowl—he will betray Me. ²⁴The Son of Man will go just as it is written about Him, but woe to that man by whom the Son of Man is betrayed! It would have been better for that man if he had not been born."

²⁵Then Judas, His betrayer, replied, "Surely not I, •Rabbi?"

"You have said it," He told him.

²⁶As they were eating, Jesus took bread, blessed and broke it, gave it to the disciples, and said, "Take and eat it; this is My body." ²⁷Then He took a cup, and after giving thanks, He gave it to them and said, "Drink from it, all of you. ²⁸For this is My blood that establishes the covenant; it is shed for many for the forgiveness of sins. ²⁹But I tell you, from this moment I will not drink of this fruit of the vine until that day when I drink it in a new way in My Father's kingdom with you." ³⁰After singing psalms, they went out to the •Mount of Olives.

³¹Then Jesus said to them, "Tonight all of you will run away because of Me, for it is written:

**I will strike the shepherd,
and the sheep of the flock will be scattered.**

³²But after I have been resurrected, I will go ahead of you to Galilee."

³³Peter told Him, "Even if everyone runs away because of You, I will never run away!"

³⁴"I assure you," Jesus said to him, "tonight, before the rooster crows, you will deny Me three times!"

³⁵"Even if I have to die with You," Peter told Him, "I will never deny You!" And all the disciples said the same thing.

³⁶Then Jesus came with them to a place called Gethsemane, and He told the disciples, "Sit here while I go over there and pray." ³⁷Taking along Peter and the two sons of Zebedee, He began to be sorrowful and deeply distressed. ³⁸Then He said to them, "My soul is swallowed up in sorrow—to the point of death. Remain here and stay awake with Me." ³⁹Going a little farther,

He fell facedown and prayed, "My Father! If it is possible, let this cup pass from Me. Yet not as I will, but as You will."

⁴⁰Then He came to the disciples and found them sleeping. He asked Peter, "So, couldn't you stay awake with Me one hour? ⁴¹Stay awake and pray, so that you won't enter into temptation. The spirit is willing, but the flesh is weak."

⁴²Again, a second time, He went away and prayed, "My Father, if this cannot pass unless I drink it, Your will be done." ⁴³And He came again and found them sleeping, because they could not keep their eyes open. ⁴⁴After leaving them, He went away again and prayed a third time, saying the same thing once more. ⁴⁵Then He came to the disciples and said to them, "Are you still sleeping and resting? Look, the time is near. The Son of Man is being betrayed into the hands of sinners. ⁴⁶Get up; let's go! See, My betrayer is near."

⁴⁷While He was still speaking, Judas, one of the Twelve, suddenly arrived. A large mob, with swords and clubs, was with him from the chief priests and elders of the people. ⁴⁸His betrayer had given them a sign: "The One I kiss, He's the One; arrest Him!" ⁴⁹So he went right up to Jesus and said, "Greetings, Rabbi!" and kissed Him.

⁵⁰"Friend," Jesus asked him, "why have you come?"

Then they came up, took hold of Jesus, and arrested Him. ⁵¹At that moment one of those with Jesus reached out his hand and drew his sword. He struck the high priest's •slave and cut off his ear.

⁵²Then Jesus told him, "Put your sword back in its place because all who take up a sword will perish by a sword. ⁵³Or do you•think that I cannot call on My Father, and He will provide Me at once with more than 12 legions of angels? ⁵⁴How, then, would the Scriptures be fulfilled that say it must happen this way?"

⁵⁵At that time Jesus said to the crowds, "Have you come out with swords and clubs, as if I were a criminal, to capture Me? Every day I used to sit, teaching in the •temple complex, and you didn't arrest Me. ⁵⁶But all this has happened so that the prophetic Scriptures would be fulfilled." Then all the disciples deserted Him and ran away.

⁵⁷Those who had arrested Jesus led Him away to Caiaphas the high priest, where the •scribes and the elders had convened. ⁵⁸Meanwhile, Peter was following Him at a distance right to the high priest's courtyard. He went in and was sitting with the temple police to see the outcome.

⁵⁹The chief priests and the whole •Sanhedrin were looking for false testimony against Jesus so they could put Him to death. ⁶⁰But they could not find any, even though many false witnesses came forward. Finally, two who came forward ⁶¹stated, "This man said, 'I can demolish God's sanctuary and rebuild it in three days.'"

⁶²The high priest then stood up and said to Him, "Don't You have an answer to what these men are testifying against You?" ⁶³But Jesus kept silent. Then the high priest said to Him, "By the living God I place You under oath: tell us if You are the •Messiah, the Son of God!"

⁶⁴"You have said it," Jesus told him. "But I tell you, in the future you will see **the Son of Man seated at the right hand** of the Power and **coming on the clouds of heaven.**"

⁶⁵Then the high priest tore his robes and said, "He has blasphemed! Why do we still need witnesses? Look, now you've heard the blasphemy! ⁶⁶What is your decision?"

They answered, "He deserves death!" ⁶⁷Then they spit in His face and beat Him; others slapped Him ⁶⁸and said, "Prophesy to us, Messiah! Who hit You?"

⁶⁹Now Peter was sitting outside in the courtyard. A servant approached him and she said, "You were with Jesus the Galilean too."

⁷⁰But he denied it in front of everyone: "I don't know what you're talking about!"

⁷¹When he had gone out to the gateway, another woman saw him and told those who were there, "This man was with Jesus the •Nazarene!"

⁷²And again he denied it with an oath, "I don't know the man!"

⁷³After a little while those standing there approached and said to Peter, "You certainly are one of them, since even your accent gives you away."

⁷⁴Then he started to curse and to swear with an oath, "I do not know the man!" Immediately a rooster crowed, ⁷⁵and Peter remembered the words Jesus had spoken, "Before the rooster crows, you will deny Me three times." And he went outside and wept bitterly.

27 When daybreak came, all the •chief priests and the elders of the people plotted against Jesus to put Him to death. ²After tying Him up, they led Him away and handed Him over to •Pilate, the governor.

³Then Judas, His betrayer, seeing that He had been condemned, was full of remorse and returned the 30 pieces of silver to the chief priests and elders. ⁴"I have sinned by betraying innocent blood," he said.

"What's that to us?" they said. "See to it yourself!"

⁵So he threw the silver into the sanctuary and departed. Then he went and hanged himself.

⁶The chief priests took the silver and said, "It's not lawful to put it into the temple treasury, since it is blood money." ⁷So they conferred together and bought the potter's field with it as a burial place for foreigners. ⁸Therefore that field has been called "Blood Field" to this day. ⁹Then what was spoken through the prophet Jeremiah was fulfilled:

They took the 30 pieces of silver, the price of Him whose price was set by the Israelites, ¹⁰**and they gave them for the potter's field, as the Lord directed me.**

¹¹Now Jesus stood before the governor. "Are You the King of the Jews?" the governor asked Him.

Jesus answered, "You have said it." ¹²And while He was being accused by the chief priests and elders, He didn't answer.

¹³Then Pilate said to Him, "Don't You hear how much they are testifying against You?" ¹⁴But He didn't answer him on even one charge, so that the governor was greatly amazed.

¹⁵At the festival the governor's custom was to release to the crowd a prisoner they wanted. ¹⁶At that time they had a notorious prisoner called Barabbas. ¹⁷So when they had gathered together, Pilate said to them, "Who is it you want me to release for you—Barabbas, or Jesus who is called •Messiah?" ¹⁸For he knew they had handed Him over because of envy.

¹⁹While he was sitting on the judge's bench, his wife sent word to him, "Have nothing to do with that righteous man, for today I've suffered terribly in a dream because of Him!"

²⁰The chief priests and the elders, however, persuad-

ed the crowds to ask for Barabbas and to execute Jesus. ²¹The governor asked them, "Which of the two do you want me to release for you?"

"Barabbas!" they answered.

²²Pilate asked them, "What should I do then with Jesus, who is called Messiah?"

They all answered, "Crucify Him!"

²³Then he said, "Why? What has He done wrong?"

But they kept shouting, "Crucify Him!" all the more.

²⁴When Pilate saw that he was getting nowhere, but that a riot was starting instead, he took some water, washed his hands in front of the crowd, and said, "I am innocent of this man's blood. See to it yourselves!"

²⁵All the people answered, "His blood be on us and on our children!" ²⁶Then he released Barabbas to them. But after having Jesus flogged, he handed Him over to be crucified.

²⁷Then the governor's soldiers took Jesus into ˙headquarters and gathered the whole ˙company around Him. ²⁸They stripped Him and dressed Him in a scarlet military robe. ²⁹They twisted together a crown of thorns, put it on His head, and placed a reed in His right hand. And they knelt down before Him and mocked Him: "Hail, King of the Jews!" ³⁰Then they spit on Him, took the reed, and kept hitting Him on the head. ³¹When they had mocked Him, they stripped Him of the robe, put His clothes on Him, and led Him away to crucify Him.

³²As they were going out, they found a Cyrenian man named Simon. They forced this man to carry His cross. ³³When they came to a place called *Golgotha* (which means Skull Place), ³⁴they gave Him wine mixed with gall to drink. But when He tasted it, He would not drink it. ³⁵After crucifying Him they divided His clothes by casting lots. ³⁶Then they sat down and were guarding Him there. ³⁷Above His head they put up the charge against Him in writing:

THIS IS JESUS
THE KING OF THE JEWS.

³⁸Then two criminals were crucified with Him, one on the right and one on the left. ³⁹Those who passed by were yelling insults at Him, shaking their heads ⁴⁰and saying, "The One who would demolish the sanctuary and rebuild it in three days, save Yourself! If You are the Son of God, come down from the cross!" ⁴¹In the same way the chief priests, with the ˙scribes and elders, mocked Him and said, ⁴²"He saved others, but He cannot save Himself! He is the King of Israel! Let Him come down now from the cross, and we will believe in Him. ⁴³He has put His trust in God; let God rescue Him now—if He wants Him! For He said, 'I am God's Son.'" ⁴⁴In the same way even the criminals who were crucified with Him kept taunting Him.

⁴⁵From noon until three in the afternoon darkness came over the whole land. ⁴⁶About three in the afternoon Jesus cried out with a loud voice, *"Elí, Elí, lemá sabachtháni?"* that is, **"My God, My God, why have You forsaken Me?"**

⁴⁷When some of those standing there heard this, they said, "He's calling for Elijah!"

⁴⁸Immediately one of them ran and got a sponge, filled it with sour wine, fixed it on a reed, and offered Him a drink. ⁴⁹But the rest said, "Let's see if Elijah comes to save Him!"

⁵⁰Jesus shouted again with a loud voice and gave up His spirit. ⁵¹Suddenly, the curtain of the sanctuary was split in two from top to bottom; the earth quaked and

the rocks were split. ⁵²The tombs were also opened and many bodies of the ˙saints who had fallen ˙asleep were raised. ⁵³And they came out of the tombs after His resurrection, entered the holy city, and appeared to many.

⁵⁴When the ˙centurion and those with him, who were guarding Jesus, saw the earthquake and the things that had happened, they were terrified and said, "This man really was God's Son!"

⁵⁵Many women who had followed Jesus from Galilee and ministered to Him were there, looking on from a distance. ⁵⁶Among them were ˙Mary Magdalene, Mary the mother of James and Joseph, and the mother of Zebedee's sons.

⁵⁷When it was evening, a rich man from Arimathea named Joseph came, who himself had also become a disciple of Jesus. ⁵⁸He approached Pilate and asked for Jesus' body. Then Pilate ordered that it be released. ⁵⁹So Joseph took the body, wrapped it in ˙clean, fine linen, ⁶⁰and placed it in his new tomb, which he had cut into the rock. He left after rolling a great stone against the entrance of the tomb. ⁶¹Mary Magdalene and the other Mary were seated there, facing the tomb.

⁶²The next day, which followed the preparation day, the chief priests and the ˙Pharisees gathered before Pilate ⁶³and said, "Sir, we remember that while this deceiver was still alive He said, 'After three days I will rise again.' ⁶⁴Therefore give orders that the tomb be made secure until the third day. Otherwise, His disciples may come, steal Him, and tell the people, 'He has been raised from the dead.' Then the last deception will be worse than the first."

⁶⁵"You have a guard of soldiers," Pilate told them. "Go and make it as secure as you know how." ⁶⁶Then they went and made the tomb secure by sealing the stone and setting the guard.

28

After the Sabbath, as the first day of the week was dawning, ˙Mary Magdalene and the other Mary went to view the tomb. ²Suddenly there was a violent earthquake, because an angel of the Lord descended from heaven and approached the tomb. He rolled back the stone and was sitting on it. ³His appearance was like lightning, and his robe was as white as snow. ⁴The guards were so shaken from fear of him that they became like dead men.

⁵But the angel told the women, "Don't be afraid, because I know you are looking for Jesus who was crucified. ⁶He is not here! For He has been resurrected, just as He said. Come and see the place where He lay. ⁷Then go quickly and tell His disciples, 'He has been raised from the dead. In fact, He is going ahead of you to Galilee; you will see Him there.' Listen, I have told you."

⁸So, departing quickly from the tomb with fear and great joy, they ran to tell His disciples the news. ⁹Just then Jesus met them and said, "Good morning!" They came up, took hold of His feet, and worshiped Him. ¹⁰Then Jesus told them, "Do not be afraid. Go and tell My brothers to leave for Galilee, and they will see Me there."

¹¹As they were on their way, some of the guards came into the city and reported to the ˙chief priests everything that had happened. ¹²After the priests had assembled with the elders and agreed on a plan, they gave the soldiers a large sum of money ¹³and told them, "Say this, 'His disciples came during the night and stole Him while we were sleeping.' ¹⁴If

this reaches the governor's ears, we will deal with him and keep you out of trouble." [15] So they took the money and did as they were instructed. And this story has been spread among Jewish people to this day.

[16] The 11 disciples traveled to Galilee, to the mountain where Jesus had directed them. [17] When they saw Him, they worshiped, but some doubted. [18] Then Jesus came near and said to them, "All authority has been given to Me in heaven and on earth. [19] Go, therefore, and make disciples of all nations, baptizing them in the name of the Father and of the Son and of the Holy Spirit, [20] teaching them to observe everything I have commanded you. And remember, I am with you always, to the end of the age."

MARK

1 The beginning of the gospel of Jesus Christ, the Son of God. [2] As it is written in Isaiah the prophet:

**Look, I am sending My messenger ahead
　of You,
who will prepare Your way.**
[3]　**A voice of one crying out in the wilderness:
　Prepare the way for the Lord;
　make His paths straight!**

[4] John came baptizing in the wilderness and preaching a baptism of repentance for the forgiveness of sins. [5] The whole Judean countryside and all the people of Jerusalem were flocking to him, and they were baptized by him in the Jordan River as they confessed their sins. [6] John wore a camel-hair garment with a leather belt around his waist and ate locusts and wild honey. [7] He was preaching: "Someone more powerful than I will come after me. I am not worthy to stoop down and untie the strap of His sandals. [8] I have baptized you with water, but He will baptize you with the Holy Spirit."

[9] In those days Jesus came from Nazareth in Galilee and was baptized in the Jordan by John. [10] As soon as He came up out of the water, He saw the heavens being torn open and the Spirit descending to Him like a dove. [11] And a voice came from heaven:

You are My beloved Son;
I take delight in You!

[12] Immediately the Spirit drove Him into the wilderness. [13] He was in the wilderness 40 days, being tempted by Satan. He was with the wild animals, and the angels began to serve Him.

[14] After John was arrested, Jesus went to Galilee, preaching the good news of God: [15] "The time is fulfilled, and the kingdom of God has come near. Repent and believe in the good news!"

[16] As He was passing along by the Sea of Galilee, He saw Simon and Andrew, Simon's brother. They were casting a net into the sea, since they were fishermen. [17] "Follow Me," Jesus told them, "and I will make you fish for people!" [18] Immediately they left their nets and followed Him. [19] Going on a little farther, He saw James the son of Zebedee and his brother John. They were in their boat mending their nets. [20] Immediately He called them, and they left their father Zebedee in the boat with the hired men and followed Him.

[21] Then they went into Capernaum, and right away He entered the *synagogue on the Sabbath and began to teach. [22] They were astonished at His teaching because, unlike the *scribes, He was teaching them as one having authority.

[23] Just then a man with an *unclean spirit was in their synagogue. He cried out, [24] "What do You have to do with us, Jesus—Nazarene? Have You come to destroy us? I know who You are—the Holy One of God!"

[25] But Jesus rebuked him and said, "Be quiet, and come out of him!" [26] And the unclean spirit convulsed him, shouted with a loud voice, and came out of him.

[27] Then they were all amazed, so they began to argue with one another, saying, "What is this? A new teaching with authority! He commands even the unclean spirits, and they obey Him." [28] News about Him then spread throughout the entire vicinity of Galilee.

[29] As soon as they left the synagogue, they went into Simon and Andrew's house with James and John. [30] Simon's mother-in-law was lying in bed with a fever, and they told Him about her at once. [31] So He went to her, took her by the hand, and raised her up. The fever left her, and she began to serve them.

[32] When evening came, after the sun had set, they began bringing to Him all those who were sick and those who were demon-possessed. [33] The whole town was assembled at the door, [34] and He healed many who were sick with various diseases and drove out many demons. But He would not permit the demons to speak, because they knew Him.

[35] Very early in the morning, while it was still dark, He got up, went out, and made His way to a deserted place. And He was praying there. [36] Simon and his companions went searching for Him. [37] They found Him and said, "Everyone's looking for You!"

[38] And He said to them, "Let's go on to the neighboring villages so that I may preach there too. This is why I have come." [39] So He went into all of Galilee, preaching in their synagogues and driving out demons.

[40] Then a man with a serious skin disease came to Him and, on his knees, begged Him: "If You are willing, You can make me *clean."

[41] Moved with compassion, Jesus reached out His hand and touched him. "I am willing," He told him. "Be made clean." [42] Immediately the disease left him, and he was healed. [43] Then He sternly warned him and sent him away at once, [44] telling him, "See that you say nothing to anyone; but go and show yourself to the priest, and offer what Moses prescribed for your cleansing, as a testimony to them." [45] Yet he went out and began to proclaim it widely and to spread the news, with the result that Jesus could no longer enter a town openly. But He was out in deserted places, and they would come to Him from everywhere.

2 When He entered Capernaum again after some days, it was reported that He was at home. [2] So many people gathered together that there was no more room, not even in the doorway, and He was speaking the message to them. [3] Then they came to Him bringing a paralytic, carried by four men. [4] Since they were not able to bring him to Jesus because of the crowd, they removed the roof above where He was.

And when they had broken through, they lowered the mat on which the paralytic was lying.

[5] Seeing their faith, Jesus told the paralytic, "Son, your sins are forgiven."

[6] But some of the •scribes were sitting there, thinking to themselves: [7] "Why does He speak like this? He's blaspheming! Who can forgive sins but God alone?"

[8] Right away Jesus understood in His spirit that they were thinking like this within themselves and said to them, "Why are you thinking these things in your hearts? [9] Which is easier: to say to the paralytic, 'Your sins are forgiven,' or to say, 'Get up, pick up your mat, and walk'? [10] But so you may know that the •Son of Man has authority on earth to forgive sins," He told the paralytic, [11] "I tell you: get up, pick up your mat, and go home."

[12] Immediately he got up, picked up the mat, and went out in front of everyone. As a result, they were all astounded and gave glory to God, saying, "We have never seen anything like this!"

[13] Then Jesus went out again beside the sea. The whole crowd was coming to Him, and He taught them. [14] Then, moving on, He saw Levi the son of Alphaeus sitting at the tax office, and He said to him, "Follow Me!" So he got up and followed Him.

[15] While He was reclining at the table in Levi's house, many tax collectors and sinners were also guests with Jesus and His disciples, because there were many who were following Him. [16] When the scribes of the •Pharisees saw that He was eating with sinners and tax collectors, they asked His disciples, "Why does He eat with tax collectors and sinners?"

[17] When Jesus heard this, He told them, "Those who are well don't need a doctor, but the sick do need one. I didn't come to call the righteous, but sinners."

[18] Now John's disciples and the Pharisees were fasting. People came and asked Him, "Why do John's disciples and the Pharisees' disciples fast, but Your disciples do not fast?"

[19] Jesus said to them, "The wedding guests cannot fast while the groom is with them, can they? As long as they have the groom with them, they cannot fast. [20] But the time will come when the groom is taken away from them, and then they will fast in that day. [21] No one sews a patch of unshrunk cloth on an old garment. Otherwise, the new patch pulls away from the old cloth, and a worse tear is made. [22] And no one puts new wine into old wineskins. Otherwise, the wine will burst the skins, and the wine is lost as well as the skins. But new wine is for fresh wineskins."

[23] On the Sabbath He was going through the grainfields, and His disciples began to make their way picking some heads of grain. [24] The Pharisees said to Him, "Look, why are they doing what is not lawful on the Sabbath?"

[25] He said to them, "Have you never read what David and those who were with him did when he was in need and hungry— [26] how he entered the house of God in the time of Abiathar the high priest and ate the •sacred bread—which is not lawful for anyone to eat except the priests—and also gave some to his companions?" [27] Then He told them, "The Sabbath was made for man and not man for the Sabbath. [28] Therefore, the Son of Man is Lord even of the Sabbath."

3 Now He entered the •synagogue again, and a man was there who had a paralyzed hand. [2] In order to accuse Him, they were watching Him closely to see whether He would heal him on the Sabbath. [3] He told the man with the paralyzed hand, "Stand before us." [4] Then He said to them, "Is it lawful on the Sabbath to do what is good or to do what is evil, to save life or to kill?" But they were silent. [5] After looking around at them with anger and sorrow at the hardness of their hearts, He told the man, "Stretch out your hand." So he stretched it out, and his hand was restored. [6] Immediately the •Pharisees went out and started plotting with the •Herodians against Him, how they might destroy Him.

[7] Jesus departed with His disciples to the sea, and a large crowd followed from Galilee, Judea, [8] Jerusalem, Idumea, beyond the Jordan, and around Tyre and Sidon. The large crowd came to Him because they heard about everything He was doing. [9] Then He told His disciples to have a small boat ready for Him, so the crowd would not crush Him. [10] Since He had healed many, all who had diseases were pressing toward Him to touch Him. [11] Whenever the •unclean spirits saw Him, those possessed fell down before Him and cried out, "You are the Son of God!" [12] And He would strongly warn them not to make Him known.

[13] Then He went up the mountain and summoned those He wanted, and they came to Him. [14] He also appointed 12—He also named them apostles—to be with Him, to send them out to preach, [15] and to have authority to drive out demons.

[16] He appointed the Twelve:
> To Simon, He gave the name Peter;
[17] and to James the son of Zebedee,
> and to his brother John,
> He gave the name "Boanerges"
> (that is, "Sons of Thunder");
[18] Andrew;
> Philip and Bartholomew;
> Matthew and Thomas;
> James the son of Alphaeus,
> and Thaddaeus;
> Simon the Zealot,
[19] and Judas Iscariot,
> who also betrayed Him.

[20] Then He went home, and the crowd gathered again so that they were not even able to eat. [21] When His family heard this, they set out to restrain Him, because they said, "He's out of His mind."

[22] The •scribes who had come down from Jerusalem said, "He has •Beelzebul in Him!" and, "He drives out demons by the ruler of the demons!"

[23] So He summoned them and spoke to them in parables: "How can Satan drive out Satan? [24] If a kingdom is divided against itself, that kingdom cannot stand. [25] If a house is divided against itself, that house cannot stand. [26] And if Satan rebels against himself and is divided, he cannot stand but is finished!

[27] "On the other hand, no one can enter a strong man's house and rob his possessions unless he first ties up the strong man. Then he will rob his house. [28] I assure you: People will be forgiven for all sins and whatever blasphemies they may blaspheme. [29] But whoever blasphemes against the Holy Spirit never has forgiveness, but is •guilty of an eternal sin"— [30] because they were saying, "He has an unclean spirit."

[31] Then His mother and His brothers came, and standing outside, they sent word to Him and called Him. [32] A crowd was sitting around Him and told Him,

"Look, Your mother, Your brothers, and Your sisters are outside asking for You."

³³He replied to them, "Who are My mother and My brothers?" ³⁴And looking about at those who were sitting in a circle around Him, He said, "Here are My mother and My brothers! ³⁵Whoever does the will of God is My brother and sister and mother."

4 Again He began to teach by the sea, and a very large crowd gathered around Him. So He got into a boat on the sea and sat down, while the whole crowd was on the shore facing the sea. ²He taught them many things in parables, and in His teaching He said to them: ³"Listen! Consider the sower who went out to sow. ⁴As he sowed, this occurred: Some seed fell along the path, and the birds came and ate it up. ⁵Other seed fell on rocky ground where it didn't have much soil, and it sprang up right away, since it didn't have deep soil. ⁶When the sun came up, it was scorched, and since it didn't have a root, it withered. ⁷Other seed fell among thorns, and the thorns came up and choked it, and it didn't produce a crop. ⁸Still others fell on good ground and produced a crop that increased 30, 60, and 100 times what was sown." ⁹Then He said, "Anyone who has ears to hear should listen!"

¹⁰When He was alone with the Twelve, those who were around Him asked Him about the parables. ¹¹He answered them, "The ˙secret of the kingdom of God has been given to you, but to those outside, everything comes in parables ¹²so that

> they may look and look,
> yet not perceive;
> they may listen and listen,
> yet not understand;
> otherwise, they might turn back—
> and be forgiven."

¹³Then He said to them: "Don't you understand this parable? How then will you understand any of the parables? ¹⁴The sower sows the word. ¹⁵These are the ones along the path where the word is sown: when they hear, immediately Satan comes and takes away the word sown in them. ¹⁶And these are the ones sown on rocky ground: when they hear the word, immediately they receive it with joy. ¹⁷But they have no root in themselves; they are short-lived. When pressure or persecution comes because of the word, they immediately ˙stumble. ¹⁸Others are sown among thorns; these are the ones who hear the word, ¹⁹but the worries of this age, the seduction of wealth, and the desires for other things enter in and choke the word, and it becomes unfruitful. ²⁰But the ones sown on good ground are those who hear the word, welcome it, and produce a crop: 30, 60, and 100 times what was sown."

²¹He also said to them, "Is a lamp brought in to be put under a basket or under a bed? Isn't it to be put on a lampstand? ²²For nothing is concealed except to be revealed, and nothing hidden except to come to light. ²³If anyone has ears to hear, he should listen!" ²⁴Then He said to them, "Pay attention to what you hear. By the measure you use, it will be measured and added to you. ²⁵For to the one who has, it will be given, and from the one who does not have, even what he has will be taken away."

²⁶"The kingdom of God is like this," He said. "A man scatters seed on the ground; ²⁷he sleeps and rises—night and day, and the seed sprouts and grows—he doesn't know how. ²⁸The soil produces a crop by itself—first the blade, then the head, and then the ripe grain on the head. ²⁹But as soon as the crop is ready, he sends for the sickle, because the harvest has come."

³⁰And He said: "How can we illustrate the kingdom of God, or what parable can we use to describe it? ³¹It's like a mustard seed that, when sown in the soil, is smaller than all the seeds on the ground. ³²And when sown, it comes up and grows taller than all the vegetables, and produces large branches, so that the birds of the sky can nest in its shade."

³³He would speak the word to them with many parables like these, as they were able to understand. ³⁴And He did not speak to them without a parable. Privately, however, He would explain everything to His own disciples.

³⁵On that day, when evening had come, He told them, "Let's cross over to the other side of the sea." ³⁶So they left the crowd and took Him along since He was already in the boat. And other boats were with Him. ³⁷A fierce windstorm arose, and the waves were breaking over the boat, so that the boat was already being swamped. ³⁸But He was in the stern, sleeping on the cushion. So they woke Him up and said to Him, "Teacher! Don't You care that we're going to die?"

³⁹He got up, rebuked the wind, and said to the sea, "Silence! Be still!" The wind ceased, and there was a great calm. ⁴⁰Then He said to them, "Why are you fearful? Do you still have no faith?"

⁴¹And they were terrified and asked one another, "Who then is this? Even the wind and the sea obey Him!"

5 Then they came to the other side of the sea, to the region of the Gerasenes. ²As soon as He got out of the boat, a man with an ˙unclean spirit came out of the tombs and met Him. ³He lived in the tombs. No one was able to restrain him anymore—even with chains— ⁴because he often had been bound with shackles and chains, but had snapped off the chains and smashed the shackles. No one was strong enough to subdue him. ⁵And always, night and day, he was crying out among the tombs and in the mountains and cutting himself with stones.

⁶When he saw Jesus from a distance, he ran and knelt down before Him. ⁷And he cried out with a loud voice, "What do You have to do with me, Jesus, Son of the Most High God? I beg You before God, don't torment me!" ⁸For He had told him, "Come out of the man, you unclean spirit!"

⁹"What is your name?" He asked him.

"My name is Legion," he answered Him, "because we are many." ¹⁰And he kept begging Him not to send them out of the region.

¹¹Now a large herd of pigs was there, feeding on the hillside. ¹²The demons begged Him, "Send us to the pigs, so we may enter them." ¹³And He gave them permission. Then the unclean spirits came out and entered the pigs, and the herd of about 2,000 rushed down the steep bank into the sea and drowned there. ¹⁴The men who tended them ran off and reported it in the town and the countryside, and people went to see what had happened. ¹⁵They came to Jesus and saw the man who had been demon-possessed by the legion, sitting there, dressed and in his right mind; and they were afraid. ¹⁶The eyewitnesses described to them what had happened to the demon-possessed man and told about the pigs. ¹⁷Then they began to beg Him to leave their region.

¹⁸As He was getting into the boat, the man who had

been demon-possessed kept begging Him to be with Him. [19]But He would not let him; instead, He told him, "Go back home to your own people, and report to them how much the Lord has done for you and how He has had mercy on you." [20]So he went out and began to proclaim in the •Decapolis how much Jesus had done for him, and they were all amazed.

[21]When Jesus had crossed over again by boat to the other side, a large crowd gathered around Him while He was by the sea. [22]One of the •synagogue leaders, named Jairus, came, and when he saw Jesus, he fell at His feet [23]and kept begging Him, "My little daughter is at death's door. Come and lay Your hands on her so she can get well and live."

[24]So Jesus went with him, and a large crowd was following and pressing against Him. [25]A woman suffering from bleeding for 12 years [26]had endured much under many doctors. She had spent everything she had and was not helped at all. On the contrary, she became worse. [27]Having heard about Jesus, she came behind Him in the crowd and touched His robe. [28]For she said, "If I can just touch His robes, I'll be made well!" [29]Instantly her flow of blood ceased, and she sensed in her body that she was cured of her affliction.

[30]At once Jesus realized in Himself that power had gone out from Him. He turned around in the crowd and said, "Who touched My robes?"

[31]His disciples said to Him, "You see the crowd pressing against You, and You say, 'Who touched Me?'"

[32]So He was looking around to see who had done this. [33]Then the woman, knowing what had happened to her, came with fear and trembling, fell down before Him, and told Him the whole truth. [34]"Daughter," He said to her, "your faith has made you well. Go in peace and be free from your affliction."

[35]While He was still speaking, people came from the synagogue leader's house and said, "Your daughter is dead. Why bother the Teacher anymore?"

[36]But when Jesus overheard what was said, He told the synagogue leader, "Don't be afraid. Only believe." [37]He did not let anyone accompany Him except Peter, James, and John, James's brother. [38]They came to the leader's house, and He saw a commotion—people weeping and wailing loudly. [39]He went in and said to them, "Why are you making a commotion and weeping? The child is not dead but asleep."

[40]They started laughing at Him, but He put them all outside. He took the child's father, mother, and those who were with Him, and entered the place where the child was. [41]Then He took the child by the hand and said to her, *"Talitha koum!"* (which is translated, "Little girl, I say to you, get up!"). [42]Immediately the girl got up and began to walk. (She was 12 years old.) At this they were utterly astounded. [43]Then He gave them strict orders that no one should know about this and said that she should be given something to eat.

6 He went away from there and came to His hometown, and His disciples followed Him. [2]When the Sabbath came, He began to teach in the •synagogue, and many who heard Him were astonished. "Where did this man get these things?" they said. "What is this wisdom given to Him, and how are these miracles performed by His hands? [3]Isn't this the carpenter, the son of Mary, and the brother of James, Joses, Judas, and Simon? And aren't His sisters here with us?" So they were •offended by Him.

[4]Then Jesus said to them, "A prophet is not without honor except in his hometown, among his relatives, and in his household." [5]So He was not able to do any miracles there, except that He laid His hands on a few sick people and healed them. [6]And He was amazed at their unbelief.

Now He was going around the villages in a circuit, teaching. [7]He summoned the Twelve and began to send them out in pairs and gave them authority over •unclean spirits. [8]He instructed them to take nothing for the road except a walking stick: no bread, no traveling bag, no money in their belts. [9]They were to wear sandals, but not put on an extra shirt. [10]Then He said to them, "Whenever you enter a house, stay there until you leave that place. [11]If any place does not welcome you and people refuse to listen to you, when you leave there, shake the dust off your feet as a testimony against them."

[12]So they went out and preached that people should repent. [13]And they were driving out many demons, anointing many sick people with olive oil, and healing them.

[14]King •Herod heard of this, because Jesus' name had become well known. Some said, "John the Baptist has been raised from the dead, and that's why supernatural powers are at work in him." [15]But others said, "He's Elijah." Still others said, "He's a prophet—like one of the prophets."

[16]When Herod heard of it, he said, "John, the one I beheaded, has been raised!" [17]For Herod himself had given orders to arrest John and to chain him in prison on account of Herodias, his brother Philip's wife, whom he had married. [18]John had been telling Herod, "It is not lawful for you to have your brother's wife!" [19]So Herodias held a grudge against him and wanted to kill him. But she could not, [20]because Herod was in awe of John and was protecting him, knowing he was a righteous and holy man. When Herod heard him he would be very disturbed, yet would hear him gladly.

[21]Now an opportune time came on his birthday, when Herod gave a banquet for his nobles, military commanders, and the leading men of Galilee. [22]When Herodias's own daughter came in and danced, she pleased Herod and his guests. The king said to the girl, "Ask me whatever you want, and I'll give it to you." [23]So he swore oaths to her: "Whatever you ask me I will give you, up to half my kingdom."

[24]Then she went out and said to her mother, "What should I ask for?"

"John the Baptist's head!" she said.

[25]Immediately she hurried to the king and said, "I want you to give me John the Baptist's head on a platter—right now!"

[26]Though the king was deeply distressed, because of his oaths and the guests he did not want to refuse her. [27]The king immediately sent for an executioner and commanded him to bring John's head. So he went and beheaded him in prison, [28]brought his head on a platter, and gave it to the girl. Then the girl gave it to her mother. [29]When his disciples heard about it, they came and removed his corpse and placed it in a tomb.

[30]The apostles gathered around Jesus and reported to Him all that they had done and taught. [31]He said to them, "Come away by yourselves to a remote place and rest for a while." For many people were coming and going, and they did not even have time to eat. [32]So they went away in the boat by themselves to a remote place, [33]but many saw them leaving and recognized

them. People ran there by land from all the towns and arrived ahead of them. [34]So as He stepped ashore, He saw a huge crowd and had compassion on them, because they were like sheep without a shepherd. Then He began to teach them many things.

[35]When it was already late, His disciples approached Him and said, "This place is a wilderness, and it is already late! [36]Send them away, so they can go into the surrounding countryside and villages to buy themselves something to eat."

[37]"You give them something to eat," He responded.

They said to Him, "Should we go and buy 200 •denarii worth of bread and give them something to eat?"

[38]And He asked them, "How many loaves do you have? Go look."

When they found out they said, "Five, and two fish." [39]Then He instructed them to have all the people sit down in groups on the green grass. [40]So they sat down in ranks of hundreds and fifties. [41]Then He took the five loaves and the two fish, and looking up to heaven, He blessed and broke the loaves. He kept giving them to His disciples to set before the people. He also divided the two fish among them all. [42]Everyone ate and was filled. [43]Then they picked up 12 baskets full of pieces of bread and fish. [44]Now those who ate the loaves were 5,000 men.

[45]Immediately He made His disciples get into the boat and go ahead of Him to the other side, to Bethsaida, while He dismissed the crowd. [46]After He said good-bye to them, He went away to the mountain to pray. [47]When evening came, the boat was in the middle of the sea, and He was alone on the land. [48]He saw them being battered as they rowed, because the wind was against them. Around three in the morning He came toward them walking on the sea and wanted to pass by them. [49]When they saw Him walking on the sea, they thought it was a ghost and cried out; [50]for they all saw Him and were terrified. Immediately He spoke with them and said, "Have courage! It is I. Don't be afraid." [51]Then He got into the boat with them, and the wind ceased. They were completely astounded, [52]because they had not understood about the loaves. Instead, their hearts were hardened.

[53]When they had crossed over, they came to land at Gennesaret and beached the boat. [54]As they got out of the boat, people immediately recognized Him. [55]They hurried throughout that vicinity and began to carry the sick on mats to wherever they heard He was. [56]Wherever He would go, into villages, towns, or the country, they laid the sick in the marketplaces and begged Him that they might touch just the •tassel of His robe. And everyone who touched it was made well.

7 The •Pharisees and some of the •scribes who had come from Jerusalem gathered around Him. [2]They observed that some of His disciples were eating their bread with •unclean—that is, unwashed—hands. [3](For the Pharisees, in fact all the Jews, will not eat unless they wash their hands ritually, keeping the tradition of the elders. [4]When they come from the marketplace, they do not eat unless they have washed. And there are many other customs they have received and keep, like the washing of cups, jugs, copper utensils, and dining couches.) [5]Then the Pharisees and the scribes asked Him, "Why don't Your disciples live according to the tradition of the elders, instead of eating bread with ritually unclean hands?"

[6]He answered them, "Isaiah prophesied correctly about you hypocrites, as it is written:

**These people honor Me with their lips,
but their heart is far from Me.**
[7]   **They worship Me in vain,
teaching as doctrines the commands of men**.
[8]Disregarding the command of God, you keep the tradition of men." [9]He also said to them, "You completely invalidate God's command in order to maintain your tradition! [10]For Moses said:

Honor your father and your mother; and
**Whoever speaks evil of father or mother
must be put to death.**

[11]But you say, 'If a man tells his father or mother: Whatever benefit you might have received from me is Corban'" (that is, a gift committed to the temple), [12]"you no longer let him do anything for his father or mother. [13]You revoke God's word by your tradition that you have handed down. And you do many other similar things." [14]Summoning the crowd again, He told them, "Listen to Me, all of you, and understand: [15]Nothing that goes into a person from outside can defile him, but the things that come out of a person are what defile him. [[16]If anyone has ears to hear, he should listen!]"

[17]When He went into the house away from the crowd, the disciples asked Him about the parable. [18]And He said to them, "Are you also as lacking in understanding? Don't you realize that nothing going into a man from the outside can defile him? [19]For it doesn't go into his heart but into the stomach and is eliminated." (As a result, He made all foods •clean.) [20]Then He said, "What comes out of a person—that defiles him. [21]For from within, out of people's hearts, come evil thoughts, sexual immoralities, thefts, murders, [22]adulteries, greed, evil actions, deceit, promiscuity, stinginess, blasphemy, pride, and foolishness. [23]All these evil things come from within and defile a person."

[24]He got up and departed from there to the region of Tyre and Sidon. He entered a house and did not want anyone to know it, but He could not escape notice. [25]Instead, immediately after hearing about Him, a woman whose little daughter had an unclean spirit came and fell at His feet. [26]Now the woman was Greek, a Syrophoenician by birth, and she kept asking Him to drive the demon out of her daughter. [27]He said to her, "Allow the children to be satisfied first, because it isn't right to take the children's bread and throw it to the dogs."

[28]But she replied to Him, "Lord, even the dogs under the table eat the children's crumbs."

[29]Then He told her, "Because of this reply, you may go. The demon has gone out of your daughter." [30]When she went back to her home, she found her child lying on the bed, and the demon was gone.

[31]Again, leaving the region of Tyre, He went by way of Sidon to the Sea of Galilee, through the region of the •Decapolis. [32]They brought to Him a deaf man who also had a speech difficulty, and begged Jesus to lay His hand on him. [33]So He took him away from the crowd privately. After putting His fingers in the man's ears and spitting, He touched his tongue. [34]Then, looking up to heaven, He sighed deeply and said to him, *"Ephphatha!"* (that is, "Be opened!"). [35]Immediately his ears were opened, his speech difficulty was removed, and he began to speak clearly. [36]Then He ordered them

to tell no one, but the more He would order them, the more they would proclaim it. [37] They were extremely astonished and said, "He has done everything well! He even makes deaf people hear, and people unable to speak, talk!"

8 In those days there was again a large crowd, and they had nothing to eat. He summoned the disciples and said to them, [2] "I have compassion on the crowd, because they've already stayed with Me three days and have nothing to eat. [3] If I send them home hungry, they will collapse on the way, and some of them have come a long distance."

[4] His disciples answered Him, "Where can anyone get enough bread here in this desolate place to fill these people?"

[5] "How many loaves do you have?" He asked them.

"Seven," they said. [6] Then He commanded the crowd to sit down on the ground. Taking the seven loaves, He gave thanks, broke the loaves, and kept on giving them to His disciples to set before the people. So they served the loaves to the crowd. [7] They also had a few small fish, and when He had blessed them, He said these were to be served as well. [8] They ate and were filled. Then they collected seven large baskets of leftover pieces. [9] About 4,000 men were there. He dismissed them [10] and immediately got into the boat with His disciples and went to the district of Dalmanutha.

[11] The *Pharisees came out and began to argue with Him, demanding of Him a sign from heaven to test Him. [12] But sighing deeply in His Spirit, He said, "Why does this generation demand a sign? *I assure you: No sign will be given to this generation!" [13] Then He left them, got on board the boat again, and went to the other side.

[14] They had forgotten to take bread and had only one loaf with them in the boat. [15] Then He commanded them: "Watch out! Beware of the yeast of the Pharisees and the yeast of *Herod."

[16] They were discussing among themselves that they did not have any bread. [17] Aware of this, He said to them, "Why are you discussing that you do not have any bread? Don't you understand or comprehend? Is your heart hardened? [18] **Do you have eyes, and not see, and do you have ears, and not hear?** And do you not remember? [19] When I broke the five loaves for the 5,000, how many baskets full of pieces of bread did you collect?"

"Twelve," they told Him.

[20] "When I broke the seven loaves for the 4,000, how many large baskets full of pieces of bread did you collect?"

"Seven," they said.

[21] And He said to them, "Don't you understand yet?"

[22] Then they came to Bethsaida. They brought a blind man to Him and begged Him to touch him. [23] He took the blind man by the hand and brought him out of the village. Spitting on his eyes and laying His hands on him, He asked him, "Do you see anything?"

[24] He looked up and said, "I see people—they look to me like trees walking."

[25] Again Jesus placed His hands on the man's eyes, and he saw distinctly. He was cured and could see everything clearly. [26] Then He sent him home, saying, "Don't even go into the village."

[27] Jesus went out with His disciples to the villages of Caesarea Philippi. And on the road He asked His disciples, "Who do people say that I am?"

[28] They answered Him, "John the Baptist; others, Elijah; still others, one of the prophets."

[29] "But you," He asked them again, "who do you say that I am?"

Peter answered Him, "You are the *Messiah!"

[30] And He strictly warned them to tell no one about Him.

[31] Then He began to teach them that the *Son of Man must suffer many things and be rejected by the elders, the *chief priests, and the *scribes, be killed, and rise after three days. [32] He was openly talking about this. So Peter took Him aside and began to rebuke Him.

[33] But turning around and looking at His disciples, He rebuked Peter and said, "Get behind Me, Satan, because you're not thinking about God's concerns, but man's!"

[34] Summoning the crowd along with His disciples, He said to them, "If anyone wants to be My follower, he must deny himself, take up his cross, and follow Me. [35] For whoever wants to save his *life will lose it, but whoever loses his life because of Me and the gospel will save it. [36] For what does it benefit a man to gain the whole world yet lose his life? [37] What can a man give in exchange for his life? [38] For whoever is ashamed of Me and of My words in this adulterous and sinful generation, the Son of Man will also be ashamed of him when He comes in the glory of His Father with the holy angels."

9 Then He said to them, "'I assure you: There are some standing here who will not taste death until they see the kingdom of God come in power."

[2] After six days Jesus took Peter, James, and John and led them up on a high mountain by themselves to be alone. He was transformed in front of them, [3] and His clothes became dazzling—extremely white as no launderer on earth could whiten them. [4] Elijah appeared to them with Moses, and they were talking with Jesus.

[5] Then Peter said to Jesus, "'Rabbi, it's good for us to be here! Let us make three *tabernacles: one for You, one for Moses, and one for Elijah"— [6] because he did not know what he should say, since they were terrified.

[7] A cloud appeared, overshadowing them, and a voice came from the cloud:

This is My beloved Son;
listen to Him!

[8] Then suddenly, looking around, they no longer saw anyone with them except Jesus alone.

[9] As they were coming down from the mountain, He ordered them to tell no one what they had seen until the *Son of Man had risen from the dead. [10] They kept this word to themselves, discussing what "rising from the dead" meant.

[11] Then they began to question Him, "Why do the *scribes say that Elijah must come first?"

[12] "Elijah does come first and restores everything," He replied. "How then is it written about the Son of Man that He must suffer many things and be treated with contempt? [13] But I tell you that Elijah really has come, and they did whatever they pleased to him, just as it is written about him."

[14] When they came to the disciples, they saw a large crowd around them and scribes disputing with them. [15] All of a sudden, when the whole crowd saw Him, they were amazed and ran to greet Him. [16] Then He asked them, "What are you arguing with them about?"

[17] Out of the crowd, one man answered Him, "Teacher, I brought my son to You. He has a spirit that makes

him unable to speak. [18]Wherever it seizes him, it throws him down, and he foams at the mouth, grinds his teeth, and becomes rigid. So I asked Your disciples to drive it out, but they couldn't."

[19]He replied to them, "You unbelieving generation! How long will I be with you? How long must I put up with you? Bring him to Me." [20]So they brought him to Him. When the spirit saw Him, it immediately convulsed the boy. He fell to the ground and rolled around, foaming at the mouth. [21]"How long has this been happening to him?" Jesus asked his father.

"From childhood," he said. [22]"And many times it has thrown him into fire or water to destroy him. But if You can do anything, have compassion on us and help us."

[23]Then Jesus said to him, "'If You can'? Everything is possible to the one who believes."

[24]Immediately the father of the boy cried out, "I do believe! Help my unbelief."

[25]When Jesus saw that a crowd was rapidly coming together, He rebuked the *unclean spirit, saying to it, "You mute and deaf spirit, I command you: come out of him and never enter him again!"

[26]Then it came out, shrieking and convulsing him violently. The boy became like a corpse, so that many said, "He's dead." [27]But Jesus, taking him by the hand, raised him, and he stood up.

[28]After He went into a house, His disciples asked Him privately, "Why couldn't we drive it out?"

[29]And He told them, "This kind can come out by nothing but prayer [and fasting]."

[30]Then they left that place and made their way through Galilee, but He did not want anyone to know it. [31]For He was teaching His disciples and telling them, "The Son of Man is being betrayed into the hands of men. They will kill Him, and after He is killed, He will rise three days later." [32]But they did not understand this statement, and they were afraid to ask Him.

[33]Then they came to Capernaum. When He was in the house, He asked them, "What were you arguing about on the way?" [34]But they were silent, because on the way they had been arguing with one another about who was the greatest. [35]Sitting down, He called the Twelve and said to them, "If anyone wants to be first, he must be last of all and servant of all." [36]Then He took a child, had him stand among them, and taking him in His arms, He said to them, [37]"Whoever welcomes one little child such as this in My name welcomes Me. And whoever welcomes Me does not welcome Me, but Him who sent Me."

[38]John said to Him, "Teacher, we saw someone driving out demons in Your name, and we tried to stop him because he wasn't following us."

[39]"Don't stop him," said Jesus, "because there is no one who will perform a miracle in My name who can soon afterward speak evil of Me. [40]For whoever is not against us is for us. [41]And whoever gives you a cup of water to drink because of My name, since you belong to the *Messiah—I assure you: He will never lose his reward.

[42]"But whoever *causes the downfall of one of these little ones who believe in Me—it would be better for him if a heavy millstone were hung around his neck and he were thrown into the sea. [43]And if your hand causes your downfall, cut it off. It is better for you to enter life maimed than to have two hands and go to *hell—the unquenchable fire, [[44]where

Their worm does not die,
and the fire is not quenched.]

[45]And if your foot causes your downfall, cut it off. It is better for you to enter life lame than to have two feet and be thrown into hell— [the unquenchable fire, [46]where

Their worm does not die,
and the fire is not quenched.]

[47]And if your eye causes your downfall, gouge it out. It is better for you to enter the kingdom of God with one eye than to have two eyes and be thrown into hell, [48]where

Their worm does not die,
and the fire is not quenched.

[49]For everyone will be salted with fire. [50]Salt is good, but if the salt should lose its flavor, how can you make it salty? Have salt among yourselves and be at peace with one another."

10 He set out from there and went to the region of Judea and across the Jordan. Then crowds converged on Him again and, as He usually did, He began teaching them once more. [2]Some *Pharisees approached Him to test Him. They asked, "Is it lawful for a man to divorce his wife?"

[3]He replied to them, "What did Moses command you?"

[4]They said, "Moses permitted us to write divorce papers and send her away."

[5]But Jesus told them, "He wrote this command for you because of the hardness of your hearts. [6]But from the beginning of creation God **made them male and female.**

[7]　**For this reason a man will leave**
　　his father and mother
　　[**and be joined to his wife**],
[8]　**and the two will become one flesh.**

So they are no longer two, but one flesh. [9]Therefore what God has joined together, man must not separate."

[10]Now in the house the disciples questioned Him again about this matter. [11]And He said to them, "Whoever divorces his wife and marries another commits adultery against her. [12]Also, if she divorces her husband and marries another, she commits adultery."

[13]Some people were bringing little children to Him so He might touch them, but His disciples rebuked them. [14]When Jesus saw it, He was indignant and said to them, "Let the little children come to Me. Don't stop them, for the kingdom of God belongs to such as these. [15]*I assure you: Whoever does not welcome the kingdom of God like a little child will never enter it." [16]After taking them in His arms, He laid His hands on them and blessed them.

[17]As He was setting out on a journey, a man ran up, knelt down before Him, and asked Him, "Good Teacher, what must I do to inherit eternal life?"

[18]"Why do you call Me good?" Jesus asked him. "No one is good but One—God. [19]You know the commandments:

Do not murder;
do not commit adultery;
do not steal;
do not bear false witness;
do not defraud;
honor your father and mother."

[20]He said to Him, "Teacher, I have kept all these from my youth."

²¹Then, looking at him, Jesus loved him and said to him, "You lack one thing: Go, sell all you have and give to the poor, and you will have treasure in heaven. Then come, follow Me." ²²But he was stunned at this demand, and he went away grieving, because he had many possessions.

²³Jesus looked around and said to His disciples, "How hard it is for those who have wealth to enter the kingdom of God!" ²⁴But the disciples were astonished at His words. Again Jesus said to them, "Children, how hard it is to enter the kingdom of God! ²⁵It is easier for a camel to go through the eye of a needle than for a rich person to enter the kingdom of God."

²⁶So they were even more astonished, saying to one another, "Then who can be saved?"

²⁷Looking at them, Jesus said, "With men it is impossible, but not with God, because all things are possible with God."

²⁸Peter began to tell Him, "Look, we have left everything and followed You."

²⁹"I assure you," Jesus said, "there is no one who has left house, brothers or sisters, mother or father, children, or fields because of Me and the gospel, ³⁰who will not receive 100 times more, now at this time—houses, brothers and sisters, mothers and children, and fields, with persecutions—and eternal life in the age to come. ³¹But many who are first will be last, and the last first."

³²They were on the road, going up to Jerusalem, and Jesus was walking ahead of them. They were astonished, but those who followed Him were afraid. Taking the Twelve aside again, He began to tell them the things that would happen to Him.

³³"Listen! We are going up to Jerusalem. The •Son of Man will be handed over to the •chief priests and the •scribes, and they will condemn Him to death. Then they will hand Him over to the Gentiles, ³⁴and they will mock Him, spit on Him, flog Him, and kill Him, and He will rise after three days."

³⁵Then James and John, the sons of Zebedee, approached Him and said, "Teacher, we want You to do something for us if we ask You."

³⁶"What do you want Me to do for you?" He asked them.

³⁷They answered Him, "Allow us to sit at Your right and at Your left in Your glory."

³⁸But Jesus said to them, "You don't know what you're asking. Are you able to drink the cup I drink or to be baptized with the baptism I am baptized with?"

³⁹"We are able," they told Him.

Jesus said to them, "You will drink the cup I drink, and you will be baptized with the baptism I am baptized with. ⁴⁰But to sit at My right or left is not Mine to give; instead, it is for those it has been prepared for."

⁴¹When the other 10 disciples heard this, they began to be indignant with James and John.

⁴²Jesus called them over and said to them, "You know that those who are regarded as rulers of the Gentiles dominate them, and their men of high positions exercise power over them. ⁴³But it must not be like that among you. On the contrary, whoever wants to become great among you must be your servant, ⁴⁴and whoever wants to be first among you must be a •slave to all. ⁴⁵For even the Son of Man did not come to be served, but to serve, and to give His life—a ransom for many."

⁴⁶They came to Jericho. And as He was leaving Jericho with His disciples and a large crowd, Bartimaeus (the son of Timaeus), a blind beggar, was sitting by the road. ⁴⁷When he heard that it was Jesus the •Nazarene, he began to cry out, "Son of David, Jesus, have mercy on me!" ⁴⁸Many people told him to keep quiet, but he was crying out all the more, "Have mercy on me, Son of David!"

⁴⁹Jesus stopped and said, "Call him."

So they called the blind man and said to him, "Have courage! Get up; He's calling for you." ⁵⁰He threw off his coat, jumped up, and came to Jesus.

⁵¹Then Jesus answered him, "What do you want Me to do for you?"

"*Rabbouni,*" the blind man told Him, "I want to see!"

⁵²"Go your way," Jesus told him. "Your faith has healed you." Immediately he could see and began to follow Him on the road.

11 When they approached Jerusalem, at Bethphage and Bethany near the •Mount of Olives, He sent two of His disciples ²and told them, "Go into the village ahead of you. As soon as you enter it, you will find a young donkey tied there, on which no one has ever sat. Untie it and bring it here. ³If anyone says to you, 'Why are you doing this?' say, 'The Lord needs it and will send it back here right away.'"

⁴So they went and found a young donkey outside in the street, tied by a door. They untied it, ⁵and some of those standing there said to them, "What are you doing, untying the donkey?" ⁶They answered them just as Jesus had said, so they let them go. ⁷Then they brought the donkey to Jesus and threw their robes on it, and He sat on it.

⁸Many people spread their robes on the road, and others spread leafy branches cut from the fields. ⁹Then those who went ahead and those who followed kept shouting:

> •Hosanna!
> **He who comes in the name**
> **of the Lord is the blessed One!**
> ¹⁰ The coming kingdom
> of our father David is blessed!
> *Hosanna* in the highest heaven!

¹¹And He went into Jerusalem and into the •temple complex. After looking around at everything, since it was already late, He went out to Bethany with the Twelve.

¹²The next day when they came out from Bethany, He was hungry. ¹³After seeing in the distance a fig tree with leaves, He went to find out if there was anything on it. When He came to it, He found nothing but leaves, because it was not the season for figs. ¹⁴He said to it, "May no one ever eat fruit from you again!" And His disciples heard it.

¹⁵They came to Jerusalem, and He went into the temple complex and began to throw out those buying and selling in the temple. He overturned the money changers' tables and the chairs of those selling doves, ¹⁶and would not permit anyone to carry goods through the temple complex.

¹⁷Then He began to teach them: "Is it not written, **My house will be called a house of prayer for all nations**? But you have made it **a den of thieves**!" ¹⁸Then the •chief priests and the •scribes heard it and started looking for a way to destroy Him. For they were afraid of Him, because the whole crowd was astonished by His teaching.

¹⁹And whenever evening came, they would go out of the city.

²⁰Early in the morning, as they were passing by, they saw the fig tree withered from the roots up. ²¹Then Peter remembered and said to Him, "'Rabbi, look! The fig tree that You cursed is withered.'"

²²Jesus replied to them, "Have faith in God. ²³•I assure you: If anyone says to this mountain, 'Be lifted up and thrown into the sea,' and does not doubt in his heart, but believes that what he says will happen, it will be done for him. ²⁴Therefore I tell you, all the things you pray and ask for—believe that you have received them, and you will have them. ²⁵And whenever you stand praying, if you have anything against anyone, forgive him, so that your Father in heaven will also forgive you your wrongdoing. [²⁶But if you don't forgive, neither will your Father in heaven forgive your wrongdoing.]"

²⁷They came again to Jerusalem. As He was walking in the temple complex, the chief priests, the scribes, and the elders came ²⁸and asked Him, "By what authority are You doing these things? Who gave You this authority to do these things?"

²⁹Jesus said to them, "I will ask you one question; then answer Me, and I will tell you by what authority I am doing these things. ³⁰Was John's baptism from heaven or from men? Answer Me."

³¹They began to argue among themselves: "If we say, 'From heaven,' He will say, 'Then why didn't you believe him?' ³²But if we say, 'From men'"—they were afraid of the crowd, because everyone thought that John was a genuine prophet. ³³So they answered Jesus, "We don't know."

And Jesus said to them, "Neither will I tell you by what authority I do these things."

12 Then He began to speak to them in parables: "A man planted a vineyard, put a fence around it, dug out a pit for a winepress, and built a watchtower. Then he leased it to tenant farmers and went away. ²At harvest time he sent a •slave to the farmers to collect some of the fruit of the vineyard from the farmers. ³But they took him, beat him, and sent him away empty-handed. ⁴Again he sent another slave to them, and they hit him on the head and treated him shamefully. ⁵Then he sent another, and they killed that one. He also sent many others; they beat some and they killed some.

⁶"He still had one to send, a beloved son. Finally he sent him to them, saying, 'They will respect my son.' ⁷"But those tenant farmers said among themselves, 'This is the heir. Come, let's kill him, and the inheritance will be ours!' ⁸So they seized him, killed him, and threw him out of the vineyard.

⁹"Therefore, what will the owner of the vineyard do? He will come and destroy the farmers and give the vineyard to others. ¹⁰Haven't you read this Scripture:

The stone that the builders rejected
has become the cornerstone.
¹¹　This came from the Lord
　　and is wonderful in our eyes?"

¹²Because they knew He had said this parable against them, they were looking for a way to arrest Him, but they were afraid of the crowd. So they left Him and went away.

¹³Then they sent some of the •Pharisees and the •Herodians to Him to trap Him by what He said. ¹⁴When they came, they said to Him, "Teacher, we know You are truthful and defer to no one, for You don't show partiality but teach truthfully the way of God. Is it lawful to pay taxes to Caesar or not? ¹⁵Should we pay, or should we not pay?"

But knowing their hypocrisy, He said to them, "Why are you testing Me? Bring Me a •denarius to look at." ¹⁶So they brought one. "Whose image and inscription is this?" He asked them.

"Caesar's," they said.

¹⁷Then Jesus told them, "Give back to Caesar the things that are Caesar's, and to God the things that are God's." And they were amazed at Him.

¹⁸Some •Sadducees, who say there is no resurrection, came to Him and questioned Him: ¹⁹"Teacher, Moses wrote for us that **if a man's brother dies,** leaves his wife behind, and **leaves no child, his brother should take the wife and produce •offspring for his brother.** ²⁰There were seven brothers. The first took a wife, and dying, left no offspring. ²¹The second also took her, and he died, leaving no offspring. And the third likewise. ²²So the seven left no offspring. Last of all, the woman died too. ²³In the resurrection, when they rise, whose wife will she be, since the seven had married her?"

²⁴Jesus told them, "Are you not deceived because you don't know the Scriptures or the power of God? ²⁵For when they rise from the dead, they neither marry nor are given in marriage but are like angels in heaven. ²⁶Now concerning the dead being raised—haven't you read in the book of Moses, in the passage about the burning bush, how God spoke to him: **I am the God of Abraham and the God of Isaac and the God of Jacob**? ²⁷He is not God of the dead but of the living. You are badly deceived."

²⁸One of the •scribes approached. When he heard them debating and saw that Jesus answered them well, he asked Him, "Which command is the most important of all?"

²⁹"This is the most important," Jesus answered:

Listen, Israel! The Lord our God, the Lord is One. ³⁰**Love the Lord your God with all your heart, with all your soul, with all your mind, and with all your strength.**

³¹"The second is: **Love your neighbor as yourself.** There is no other command greater than these."

³²Then the scribe said to Him, "You are right, Teacher! You have correctly said that He is One, and there is no one else except Him. ³³And to love Him with all your heart, with all your understanding, and with all your strength, and to love your neighbor as yourself, is far more important than all the burnt offerings and sacrifices."

³⁴When Jesus saw that he answered intelligently, He said to him, "You are not far from the kingdom of God." And no one dared to question Him any longer.

³⁵So Jesus asked this question as He taught in the temple complex, "How can the scribes say that the •Messiah is the Son of David? ³⁶David himself says by the Holy Spirit:

The Lord declared to my Lord,
'Sit at My right hand
until I put Your enemies under Your feet.'

³⁷David himself calls Him 'Lord'; how then can the Messiah be his Son?" And the large crowd was listening to Him with delight.

³⁸He also said in His teaching, "Beware of the scribes, who want to go around in long robes, and who want greetings in the marketplaces, ³⁹the front seats in

the *synagogues, and the places of honor at banquets. [40] They devour widows' houses and say long prayers just for show. These will receive harsher punishment."

[41] Sitting across from the temple treasury, He watched how the crowd dropped money into the treasury. Many rich people were putting in large sums. [42] And a poor widow came and dropped in two tiny coins worth very little. [43] Summoning His disciples, He said to them, "'I assure you: This poor widow has put in more than all those giving to the temple treasury. [44] For they all gave out of their surplus, but she out of her poverty has put in everything she possessed—all she had to live on."

13 As He was going out of the *temple complex, one of His disciples said to Him, "Teacher, look! What massive stones! What impressive buildings!"

[2] Jesus said to him, "Do you see these great buildings? Not one stone will be left here on another that will not be thrown down!"

[3] While He was sitting on the *Mount of Olives across from the temple complex, Peter, James, John, and Andrew asked Him privately, [4] "Tell us, when will these things happen? And what will be the sign when all these things are about to take place?"

[5] Then Jesus began by telling them: "Watch out that no one deceives you. [6] Many will come in My name, saying, 'I am He,' and they will deceive many. [7] When you hear of wars and rumors of wars, don't be alarmed; these things must take place, but the end is not yet. [8] For nation will rise up against nation, and kingdom against kingdom. There will be earthquakes in various places, and famines. These are the beginning of birth pains.

[9] "But you, be on your guard! They will hand you over to sanhedrins, and you will be flogged in the *synagogues. You will stand before governors and kings because of Me, as a witness to them. [10] And the good news must first be proclaimed to all nations. [11] So when they arrest you and hand you over, don't worry beforehand what you will say. On the contrary, whatever is given to you in that hour—say it. For it isn't you speaking, but the Holy Spirit. [12] Then brother will betray brother to death, and a father his child. Children will rise up against parents and put them to death. [13] And you will be hated by everyone because of My name. But the one who endures to the end will be delivered.

[14] "When you see the **abomination that causes desolation** standing where it should not" (let the reader understand), "then those in Judea must flee to the mountains! [15] A man on the housetop must not come down or go in to get anything out of his house. [16] And a man in the field must not go back to get his clothes. [17] Woe to pregnant women and nursing mothers in those days! [18] Pray it won't happen in winter. [19] For those will be days of tribulation, the kind that hasn't been from the beginning of the world, which God created, until now and never will be again! [20] Unless the Lord limited those days, no one would survive. But He limited those days because of the elect, whom He chose.

[21] "Then if anyone tells you, 'Look, here is the *Messiah! Look—there!' do not believe it! [22] For false messiahs and false prophets will rise up and will perform signs and wonders to lead astray, if possible, the elect. [23] And you must watch! I have told you everything in advance.

[24] "But in those days, after that tribulation:

The sun will be darkened,
and the moon will not shed its light;
[25]　the stars will be falling from the sky,
and the celestial powers will be shaken.

[26] Then they will see the *Son of Man coming in clouds with great power and glory. [27] He will send out the angels and gather His elect from the four winds, from the end of the earth to the end of the sky.

[28] "Learn this parable from the fig tree: As soon as its branch becomes tender and sprouts leaves, you know that summer is near. [29] In the same way, when you see these things happening, know that He is near—at the door! [30] I assure you: This generation will certainly not pass away until all these things take place. [31] Heaven and earth will pass away, but My words will never pass away.

[32] "Now concerning that day or hour no one knows—neither the angels in heaven nor the Son—except the Father. [33] Watch! Be alert! For you don't know when the time is coming. [34] It is like a man on a journey, who left his house, gave authority to his *slaves, gave each one his work, and commanded the doorkeeper to be alert. [35] Therefore be alert, since you don't know when the master of the house is coming—whether in the evening or at midnight or at the crowing of the rooster or early in the morning. [36] Otherwise, he might come suddenly and find you sleeping. [37] And what I say to you, I say to everyone: Be alert!"

14 After two days it was the *Passover and the Festival of *Unleavened Bread. The *chief priests and the *scribes were looking for a treacherous way to arrest and kill Him. [2] "Not during the festival," they said, "or there may be a rioting among the people."

[3] While He was in Bethany at the house of Simon who had a serious skin disease, as He was reclining at the table, a woman came with an alabaster jar of pure and expensive fragrant oil of nard. She broke the jar and poured it on His head. [4] But some were expressing indignation to one another: "Why has this fragrant oil been wasted? [5] For this oil might have been sold for more than 300 *denarii and given to the poor." And they began to scold her.

[6] Then Jesus said, "Leave her alone. Why are you bothering her? She has done a noble thing for Me. [7] You always have the poor with you, and you can do what is good for them whenever you want, but you do not always have Me. [8] She has done what she could; she has anointed My body in advance for burial. [9] I assure you: Wherever the gospel is proclaimed in the whole world, what this woman has done will also be told in memory of her."

[10] Then Judas Iscariot, one of the Twelve, went to the chief priests to hand Him over to them. [11] And when they heard this, they were glad and promised to give him silver. So he started looking for a good opportunity to betray Him.

[12] On the first day of Unleavened Bread, when they sacrifice the Passover lamb, His disciples asked Him, "Where do You want us to go and prepare the Passover so You may eat it?"

[13] So He sent two of His disciples and told them, "Go into the city, and a man carrying a water jug will meet you. Follow him. [14] Wherever he enters, tell the owner of the house, 'The Teacher says, "Where is the guest room for Me to eat the Passover with My disciples?"' [15] He will show you a large room upstairs, furnished and ready. Make the preparations for us there." [16] So

the disciples went out, entered the city, and found it just as He had told them, and they prepared the Passover.

[17] When evening came, He arrived with the Twelve. [18] While they were reclining and eating, Jesus said, "I assure you: One of you will betray Me—one who is eating with Me!"

[19] They began to be distressed and to say to Him one by one, "Surely not I?"

[20] He said to them, "It is one of the Twelve—the one who is dipping bread with Me in the bowl. [21] For the *Son of Man will go just as it is written about Him, but woe to that man by whom the Son of Man is betrayed! It would have been better for that man if he had not been born."

[22] As they were eating, He took bread, blessed and broke it, gave it to them, and said, "Take it; this is My body."

[23] Then He took a cup, and after giving thanks, He gave it to them, and so they all drank from it. [24] He said to them, "This is My blood that establishes the covenant; it is shed for many. [25] I assure you: I will no longer drink of the fruit of the vine until that day when I drink it in a new way in the kingdom of God." [26] After singing psalms, they went out to the *Mount of Olives.

[27] Then Jesus said to them, "All of you will run away, because it is written:

**I will strike the shepherd,
and the sheep will be scattered.**

[28] But after I have been resurrected, I will go ahead of you to Galilee."

[29] Peter told Him, "Even if everyone runs away, I will certainly not!"

[30] "I assure you," Jesus said to him, "today, this very night, before the rooster crows twice, you will deny Me three times!"

[31] But he kept insisting, "If I have to die with You, I will never deny You!" And they all said the same thing.

[32] Then they came to a place named Gethsemane, and He told His disciples, "Sit here while I pray." [33] He took Peter, James, and John with Him, and He began to be deeply distressed and horrified. [34] Then He said to them, "My soul is swallowed up in sorrow—to the point of death. Remain here and stay awake." [35] Then He went a little farther, fell to the ground, and began to pray that if it were possible, the hour might pass from Him. [36] And He said, "*Abba, Father! All things are possible for You. Take this cup away from Me. Nevertheless, not what I will, but what You will."

[37] Then He came and found them sleeping. "Simon, are you sleeping?" He asked Peter. "Couldn't you stay awake one hour? [38] Stay awake and pray so that you won't enter into temptation. The spirit is willing, but the flesh is weak."

[39] Once again He went away and prayed, saying the same thing. [40] And He came again and found them sleeping, because they could not keep their eyes open. They did not know what to say to Him. [41] Then He came a third time and said to them, "Are you still sleeping and resting? Enough! The time has come. Look, the Son of Man is being betrayed into the hands of sinners. [42] Get up; let's go! See—My betrayer is near."

[43] While He was still speaking, Judas, one of the Twelve, suddenly arrived. With him was a mob, with swords and clubs, from the chief priests, the scribes, and the elders. [44] His betrayer had given them a signal. "The One I kiss," he said, "He's the One; arrest Him and take Him away under guard." [45] So when he came, he went right up to Him and said, "'Rabbi!'—and kissed Him. [46] Then they took hold of Him and arrested Him. [47] And one of those who stood by drew his sword, struck the high priest's *slave, and cut off his ear.

[48] But Jesus said to them, "Have you come out with swords and clubs, as though I were a criminal, to capture Me? [49] Every day I was among you, teaching in the *temple complex, and you didn't arrest Me. But the Scriptures must be fulfilled." [50] Then they all deserted Him and ran away.

[51] Now a certain young man, having a linen cloth wrapped around his naked body, was following Him. They caught hold of him, [52] but he left the linen cloth behind and ran away naked.

[53] They led Jesus away to the high priest, and all the chief priests, the elders, and the scribes convened. [54] Peter followed Him at a distance, right into the high priest's courtyard. He was sitting with the temple police, warming himself by the fire.

[55] The chief priests and the whole *Sanhedrin were looking for testimony against Jesus to put Him to death, but they could find none. [56] For many were giving false testimony against Him, but the testimonies did not agree. [57] Some stood up and were giving false testimony against Him, stating, [58] "We heard Him say, 'I will demolish this sanctuary made by human hands, and in three days I will build another not made by hands.'" [59] Yet their testimony did not agree even on this.

[60] Then the high priest stood up before them all and questioned Jesus, "Don't You have an answer to what these men are testifying against You?" [61] But He kept silent and did not answer anything. Again the high priest questioned Him, "Are You the *Messiah, the Son of the Blessed One?"

[62] "I am," said Jesus, "and all of you will see **the Son of Man seated at the right hand** of the Power and **coming with the clouds of heaven.**"

[63] Then the high priest tore his robes and said, "Why do we still need witnesses? [64] You have heard the blasphemy! What is your decision?"

And they all condemned Him to be deserving of death. [65] Then some began to spit on Him, to blindfold Him, and to beat Him, saying, "Prophesy!" The temple police also took Him and slapped Him.

[66] While Peter was in the courtyard below, one of the high priest's servants came. [67] When she saw Peter warming himself, she looked at him and said, "You also were with that *Nazarene, Jesus."

[68] But he denied it: "I don't know or understand what you're talking about!" Then he went out to the entryway, and a rooster crowed.

[69] When the servant saw him again she began to tell those standing nearby, "This man is one of them!"

[70] But again he denied it. After a little while those standing there said to Peter again, "You certainly are one of them, since you're also a Galilean!"

[71] Then he started to curse and to swear with an oath, "I don't know this man you're talking about!"

[72] Immediately a rooster crowed a second time, and Peter remembered when Jesus had spoken the word to him, "Before the rooster crows twice, you will deny Me three times." When he thought about it, he began to weep.

15 As soon as it was morning, the *chief priests had a meeting with the elders, *scribes, and the whole *Sanhedrin. After tying Jesus up, they led Him away and handed Him over to *Pilate.

² So Pilate asked Him, "Are You the King of the Jews?"

He answered him, "You have said it."

³ And the chief priests began to accuse Him of many things. ⁴ Then Pilate questioned Him again, "Are You not answering anything? Look how many things they are accusing You of!" ⁵ But Jesus still did not answer anything, so Pilate was amazed.

⁶ At the festival it was Pilate's custom to release for the people a prisoner they requested. ⁷ There was one named Barabbas, who was in prison with rebels who had committed murder during the rebellion. ⁸ The crowd came up and began to ask Pilate to do for them as was his custom. ⁹ So Pilate answered them, "Do you want me to release the King of the Jews for you?" ¹⁰ For he knew it was because of envy that the chief priests had handed Him over. ¹¹ But the chief priests stirred up the crowd so that he would release Barabbas to them instead.

¹² Pilate asked them again, "Then what do you want me to do with the One you call the King of the Jews?"

¹³ Again they shouted, "Crucify Him!"

¹⁴ Then Pilate said to them, "Why? What has He done wrong?"

But they shouted, "Crucify Him!" all the more.

¹⁵ Then, willing to gratify the crowd, Pilate released Barabbas to them. And after having Jesus flogged, he handed Him over to be crucified.

¹⁶ Then the soldiers led Him away into the courtyard (that is, *headquarters) and called the whole *company together. ¹⁷ They dressed Him in a purple robe, twisted together a crown of thorns, and put it on Him. ¹⁸ And they began to salute Him, "Hail, King of the Jews!" ¹⁹ They kept hitting Him on the head with a reed and spitting on Him. Getting down on their knees, they were paying Him homage. ²⁰ When they had mocked Him, they stripped Him of the purple robe, put His clothes on Him, and led Him out to crucify Him.

²¹ They forced a man coming in from the country, who was passing by, to carry Jesus' cross. He was Simon, a Cyrenian, the father of Alexander and Rufus. ²² And they brought Jesus to the place called *Golgotha* (which means Skull Place). ²³ They tried to give Him wine mixed with myrrh, but He did not take it. ²⁴ Then they crucified Him and divided His clothes, casting lots for them to decide what each would get. ²⁵ Now it was nine in the morning when they crucified Him. ²⁶ The inscription of the charge written against Him was:

THE KING OF THE JEWS.

²⁷ They crucified two criminals with Him, one on His right and one on His left. [²⁸ So the Scripture was fulfilled that says: **And He was counted among outlaws.**] ²⁹ Those who passed by were yelling insults at Him, shaking their heads, and saying, "Ha! The One who would demolish the sanctuary and build it in three days, ³⁰ save Yourself by coming down from the cross!" ³¹ In the same way, the chief priests with the scribes were mocking Him to one another and saying, "He saved others; He cannot save Himself! ³² Let the *Messiah, the King of Israel, come down now from the cross, so that we may see and believe." Even those who were crucified with Him were taunting Him.

³³ When it was noon, darkness came over the whole land until three in the afternoon. ³⁴ And at three Jesus cried out with a loud voice, *"Eloi, Eloi, lemá sabach-tháni?"* which is translated, "**My God, My God, why have You forsaken Me?**"

³⁵ When some of those standing there heard this, they said, "Look, He's calling for Elijah!" ³⁶ Someone ran and filled a sponge with sour wine, fixed it on a reed, offered Him a drink, and said, "Let's see if Elijah comes to take Him down!"

³⁷ But Jesus let out a loud cry and breathed His last. ³⁸ Then the curtain of the sanctuary was split in two from top to bottom. ³⁹ When the *centurion, who was standing opposite Him, saw the way He breathed His last, he said, "This man really was God's Son!"

⁴⁰ There were also women looking on from a distance. Among them were *Mary Magdalene, Mary the mother of James the younger and of Joses, and Salome. ⁴¹ When He was in Galilee, they would follow Him and help Him. Many other women had come up with Him to Jerusalem.

⁴² When it was already evening, because it was preparation day (that is, the day before the Sabbath), ⁴³ Joseph of Arimathea, a prominent member of the Sanhedrin who was himself looking forward to the kingdom of God, came and boldly went in to Pilate and asked for Jesus' body. ⁴⁴ Pilate was surprised that He was already dead. Summoning the centurion, he asked him whether He had already died. ⁴⁵ When he found out from the centurion, he gave the corpse to Joseph. ⁴⁶ After he bought some fine linen, he took Him down and wrapped Him in the linen. Then he placed Him in a tomb cut out of the rock, and rolled a stone against the entrance to the tomb. ⁴⁷ Now Mary Magdalene and Mary the mother of Joses were watching where He was placed.

16 When the Sabbath was over, *Mary Magdalene, Mary the mother of James, and Salome bought spices, so they could go and anoint Him. ² Very early in the morning, on the first day of the week, they went to the tomb at sunrise. ³ They were saying to one another, "Who will roll away the stone from the entrance to the tomb for us?" ⁴ Looking up, they observed that the stone—which was very large—had been rolled away. ⁵ When they entered the tomb, they saw a young man dressed in a long white robe sitting on the right side; they were amazed and alarmed.

⁶ "Don't be alarmed," he told them. "You are looking for Jesus the *Nazarene, who was crucified. He has been resurrected! He is not here! See the place where they put Him. ⁷ But go, tell His disciples and Peter, 'He is going ahead of you to Galilee; you will see Him there just as He told you.'"

⁸ So they went out and started running from the tomb, because trembling and astonishment overwhelmed them. And they said nothing to anyone, since they were afraid.

[⁹ Early on the first day of the week, after He had risen, He appeared first to Mary Magdalene, out of whom He had driven seven demons. ¹⁰ She went and reported to those who had been with Him, as they were mourning and weeping. ¹¹ Yet, when they heard that He was alive and had been seen by her, they did not believe it. ¹² Then after this, He appeared in a different form to two of them walking on their way into the country. ¹³ And they went and reported it to the rest, who did not believe them either.

[14] Later, He appeared to the Eleven themselves as they were reclining at the table. He rebuked their unbelief and hardness of heart, because they did not believe those who saw Him after He had been resurrected. [15] Then He said to them, "Go into all the world and preach the gospel to the whole creation. [16] Whoever believes and is baptized will be saved, but whoever does not believe will be condemned. [17] And these signs will accompany those who believe: In My name they will drive out demons; they will speak in new languages; [18] they will pick up snakes; if they should drink anything deadly, it will never harm them; they will lay hands on the sick, and they will get well."

[19] Then after speaking to them, the Lord Jesus was taken up into heaven and sat down at the right hand of God. [20] And they went out and preached everywhere, the Lord working with them and confirming the word by the accompanying signs.]

LUKE

1 Many have undertaken to compile a narrative about the events that have been fulfilled among us, [2] just as the original eyewitnesses and servants of the word handed them down to us. [3] It also seemed good to me, since I have carefully investigated everything from the very first, to write to you in an orderly sequence, most honorable Theophilus, [4] so that you may know the certainty of the things about which you have been instructed.

[5] In the days of King *Herod of Judea, there was a priest of Abijah's division named Zechariah. His wife was from the daughters of Aaron, and her name was Elizabeth. [6] Both were righteous in God's sight, living without blame according to all the commands and requirements of the Lord. [7] But they had no children because Elizabeth could not conceive, and both of them were well along in years.

[8] When his division was on duty and he was serving as priest before God, [9] it happened that he was chosen by lot, according to the custom of the priesthood, to enter the sanctuary of the Lord and burn incense. [10] At the hour of incense the whole assembly of the people was praying outside. [11] An angel of the Lord appeared to him, standing to the right of the altar of incense. [12] When Zechariah saw him, he was startled and overcome with fear. [13] But the angel said to him:

Do not be afraid, Zechariah,
because your prayer has been heard.
Your wife Elizabeth will bear you a son,
and you will name him John.
[14] There will be joy and delight for you,
and many will rejoice at his birth.
[15] For he will be great in the sight of the Lord
and will never drink wine or beer.
He will be filled with the Holy Spirit
while still in his mother's womb.
[16] He will turn many of the sons of Israel
to the Lord their God.
[17] And he will go before Him
in the spirit and power of Elijah,
to turn the hearts of fathers
to their children,
and the disobedient
to the understanding of the righteous,
to make ready for the Lord a prepared people.

[18] "How can I know this?" Zechariah asked the angel. "For I am an old man, and my wife is well along in years."

[19] The angel answered him, "I am Gabriel, who stands in the presence of God, and I was sent to speak to you and tell you this good news. [20] Now listen! You will become silent and unable to speak until the day these things take place, because you did not believe my words, which will be fulfilled in their proper time."

[21] Meanwhile, the people were waiting for Zechariah, amazed that he stayed so long in the sanctuary. [22] When he did come out, he could not speak to them. Then they realized that he had seen a vision in the sanctuary. He kept making signs to them and remained speechless. [23] When the days of his ministry were completed, he went back home.

[24] After these days his wife Elizabeth conceived and kept herself in seclusion for five months. She said, [25] "The Lord has done this for me. He has looked with favor in these days to take away my disgrace among the people."

[26] In the sixth month, the angel Gabriel was sent by God to a town in Galilee called Nazareth, [27] to a virgin *engaged to a man named Joseph, of the house of David. The virgin's name was Mary. [28] And the angel came to her and said, "Rejoice, favored woman! The Lord is with you." [29] But she was deeply troubled by this statement, wondering what kind of greeting this could be. [30] Then the angel told her:

Do not be afraid, Mary,
for you have found favor with God.
[31] Now listen:
You will conceive and give birth to a son,
and you will call His name Jesus.
[32] He will be great
and will be called the Son of the Most High,
and the Lord God will give Him
the throne of His father David.
[33] He will reign over the house of Jacob forever,
and His kingdom will have no end.

[34] Mary asked the angel, "How can this be, since I have not been intimate with a man?"

[35] The angel replied to her:

"The Holy Spirit will come upon you,
and the power of the Most High
will overshadow you.
Therefore, the holy One to be born
will be called the Son of God.

[36] And consider your relative Elizabeth—even she has conceived a son in her old age, and this is the sixth month for her who was called childless. [37] For nothing will be impossible with God."

[38] "I am the Lord's *slave," said Mary. "May it be done to me according to your word." Then the angel left her.

[39] In those days Mary set out and hurried to a town in the hill country of Judah [40] where she entered Zechariah's house and greeted Elizabeth. [41] When Elizabeth heard Mary's greeting, the baby leaped inside her, and

Elizabeth was filled with the Holy Spirit. [42] Then she exclaimed with a loud cry:

"You are the most blessed of women,
and your child will be blessed!

[43] How could this happen to me, that the mother of my Lord should come to me? [44] For you see, when the sound of your greeting reached my ears, the baby leaped for joy inside me! [45] She who has believed is blessed because what was spoken to her by the Lord will be fulfilled!"

[46] And Mary said:

My soul proclaims the greatness of the Lord,
[47] and my spirit has rejoiced in God
my Savior,
[48] because He has looked with favor
on the humble condition of His slave.
Surely, from now on all generations
will call me blessed,
[49] because the Mighty One
has done great things for me,
and His name is holy.
[50] His mercy is from generation
to generation
on those who fear Him.
[51] He has done a mighty deed with His arm;
He has scattered the proud
because of the thoughts of their hearts;
[52] He has toppled the mighty from their thrones
and exalted the lowly.
[53] He has satisfied the hungry
with good things
and sent the rich away empty.
[54] He has helped His servant Israel,
mindful of His mercy,
[55] just as He spoke to our ancestors,
to Abraham and his descendants forever.

[56] And Mary stayed with her about three months; then she returned to her home.

[57] Now the time had come for Elizabeth to give birth, and she had a son. [58] Then her neighbors and relatives heard that the Lord had shown her His great mercy, and they rejoiced with her.

[59] When they came to circumcise the child on the eighth day, they were going to name him Zechariah, after his father. [60] But his mother responded, "No! He will be called John."

[61] Then they said to her, "None of your relatives has that name." [62] So they motioned to his father to find out what he wanted him to be called. [63] He asked for a writing tablet and wrote:

HIS NAME IS JOHN.

And they were all amazed. [64] Immediately his mouth was opened and his tongue set free, and he began to speak, praising God. [65] Fear came on all those who lived around them, and all these things were being talked about throughout the hill country of Judea. [66] All who heard about him took it to heart, saying, "What then will this child become?" For, indeed, the Lord's hand was with him.

[67] Then his father Zechariah was filled with the Holy Spirit and prophesied:

[68] Praise the Lord, the God of Israel,
because He has visited
and provided *redemption for His people.
[69] He has raised up a *horn of salvation for us
in the house of His servant David,
[70] just as He spoke by the mouth

of His holy prophets in ancient times;
[71] salvation from our enemies
and from the clutches of those who hate us.
[72] He has dealt mercifully with our fathers
and remembered His holy covenant—
[73] the oath that He swore to our father Abraham.
He has given us the privilege,
[74] since we have been rescued
from our enemies' clutches,
to serve Him without fear
[75] in holiness and righteousness
in His presence all our days.
[76] And child, you will be called
a prophet of the Most High,
for you will go before the Lord
to prepare His ways,
[77] to give His people knowledge of salvation
through the forgiveness of their sins.
[78] Because of our God's merciful compassion,
the Dawn from on high will visit us
[79] to shine on those who live in darkness
and the shadow of death,
to guide our feet into the way of peace.

[80] The child grew up and became spiritually strong, and he was in the wilderness until the day of his public appearance to Israel.

2

In those days a decree went out from Caesar Augustus that the whole empire should be registered. [2] This first registration took place while Quirinius was governing Syria. [3] So everyone went to be registered, each to his own town.

[4] And Joseph also went up from the town of Nazareth in Galilee, to Judea, to the city of David, which is called Bethlehem, because he was of the house and family line of David, [5] to be registered along with Mary, who was *engaged to him and was pregnant. [6] While they were there, the time came for her to give birth. [7] Then she gave birth to her firstborn Son, and she wrapped Him snugly in cloth and laid Him in a feeding trough—because there was no room for them at the lodging place.

[8] In the same region, shepherds were staying out in the fields and keeping watch at night over their flock. [9] Then an angel of the Lord stood before them, and the glory of the Lord shone around them, and they were terrified. [10] But the angel said to them, "Don't be afraid, for look, I proclaim to you good news of great joy that will be for all the people: [11] Today a Savior, who is *Messiah the Lord, was born for you in the city of David. [12] This will be the sign for you: You will find a baby wrapped snugly in cloth and lying in a feeding trough."

[13] Suddenly there was a multitude of the heavenly host with the angel, praising God and saying:

[14] Glory to God in the highest heaven,
and peace on earth to people He favors!

[15] When the angels had left them and returned to heaven, the shepherds said to one another, "Let's go straight to Bethlehem and see what has happened, which the Lord has made known to us."

[16] They hurried off and found both Mary and Joseph, and the baby who was lying in the feeding trough. [17] After seeing them, they reported the message they were told about this child, [18] and all who heard it were amazed at what the shepherds said to them. [19] But Mary was treasuring up all these things in her heart and meditating on them. [20] The shepherds returned,

glorifying and praising God for all they had seen and heard, just as they had been told.

²¹When the eight days were completed for His circumcision, He was named Jesus—the name given by the angel before He was conceived. ²²And when the days of their purification according to the law of Moses were finished, they brought Him up to Jerusalem to present Him to the Lord ²³(just as it is written in the law of the Lord: **Every firstborn male will be dedicated to the Lord**) ²⁴and to offer a sacrifice (according to what is stated in the law of the Lord: **a pair of turtledoves or two young pigeons**).

²⁵There was a man in Jerusalem whose name was Simeon. This man was righteous and devout, looking forward to Israel's consolation, and the Holy Spirit was on him. ²⁶It had been revealed to him by the Holy Spirit that he would not see death before he saw the Lord's Messiah. ²⁷Guided by the Spirit, he entered the *temple complex. When the parents brought in the child Jesus to perform for Him what was customary under the law, ²⁸Simeon took Him up in his arms, praised God, and said:

²⁹   Now, Master,
     You can dismiss Your *slave in peace,
     as You promised.
³⁰   For my eyes have seen Your salvation.
³¹   You have prepared it
     in the presence of all peoples—
³²   a light for revelation to the Gentiles
     and glory to Your people Israel.

³³His father and mother were amazed at what was being said about Him. ³⁴Then Simeon blessed them and told His mother Mary: "Indeed, this child is destined to cause the fall and rise of many in Israel and to be a sign that will be opposed— ³⁵and a sword will pierce your own soul—that the thoughts of many hearts may be revealed."

³⁶There was also a prophetess, Anna, a daughter of Phanuel, of the tribe of Asher. She was well along in years, having lived with her husband seven years after her marriage, ³⁷and was a widow for 84 years. She did not leave the temple complex, serving God night and day with fasting and prayers. ³⁸At that very moment, she came up and began to thank God and to speak about Him to all who were looking forward to the *redemption of Jerusalem.

³⁹When they had completed everything according to the law of the Lord, they returned to Galilee, to their own town of Nazareth. ⁴⁰The boy grew up and became strong, filled with wisdom, and God's grace was on Him.

⁴¹Every year His parents traveled to Jerusalem for the *Passover Festival. ⁴²When He was 12 years old, they went up according to the custom of the festival. ⁴³After those days were over, as they were returning, the boy Jesus stayed behind in Jerusalem, but His parents did not know it. ⁴⁴Assuming He was in the traveling party, they went a day's journey. Then they began looking for Him among their relatives and friends. ⁴⁵When they did not find Him, they returned to Jerusalem to search for Him. ⁴⁶After three days, they found Him in the temple complex sitting among the teachers, listening to them and asking them questions. ⁴⁷And all those who heard Him were astounded at His understanding and His answers. ⁴⁸When His parents saw Him, they were astonished, and His mother said

to Him, "Son, why have You treated us like this? Your father and I have been anxiously searching for You."

⁴⁹"Why were you searching for Me?" He asked them. "Didn't you know that I had to be in My Father's house?" ⁵⁰But they did not understand what He said to them.

⁵¹Then He went down with them and came to Nazareth and was obedient to them. His mother kept all these things in her heart. ⁵²And Jesus increased in wisdom and stature, and in favor with God and with people.

3 In the fifteenth year of the reign of Tiberius Caesar, while Pontius *Pilate was governor of Judea, *Herod was tetrarch of Galilee, his brother Philip tetrarch of the region of Iturea and Trachonitis, and Lysanias tetrarch of Abilene, ²during the high priesthood of Annas and Caiaphas, God's word came to John the son of Zechariah in the wilderness. ³He went into all the vicinity of the Jordan, preaching a baptism of repentance for the forgiveness of sins, ⁴as it is written in the book of the words of the prophet Isaiah:

A voice of one crying out in the wilderness:
Prepare the way for the Lord;
make His paths straight!
⁵ **Every valley will be filled,**
and every mountain and hill will be made low;
the crooked will become straight,
the rough ways smooth,
⁶ **and everyone will see the salvation of God.**

⁷He then said to the crowds who came out to be baptized by him, "Brood of vipers! Who warned you to flee from the coming wrath? ⁸Therefore produce fruit consistent with repentance. And don't start saying to yourselves, 'We have Abraham as our father,' for I tell you that God is able to raise up children for Abraham from these stones! ⁹Even now the ax is ready to strike the root of the trees! Therefore, every tree that doesn't produce good fruit will be cut down and thrown into the fire."

¹⁰"What then should we do?" the crowds were asking him.

¹¹He replied to them, "The one who has two shirts must share with someone who has none, and the one who has food must do the same."

¹²Tax collectors also came to be baptized, and they asked him, "Teacher, what should we do?"

¹³He told them, "Don't collect any more than what you have been authorized."

¹⁴Some soldiers also questioned him: "What should we do?"

He said to them, "Don't take money from anyone by force or false accusation; be satisfied with your wages."

¹⁵Now the people were waiting expectantly, and all of them were debating in their minds whether John might be the *Messiah. ¹⁶John answered them all, "I baptize you with water, but One is coming who is more powerful than I. I am not worthy to untie the strap of His sandals. He will baptize you with the Holy Spirit and fire. ¹⁷His winnowing shovel is in His hand to clear His threshing floor and gather the wheat into His barn, but the chaff He will burn up with a fire that never goes out." ¹⁸Then, along with many other exhortations, he proclaimed good news to the people. ¹⁹But Herod the tetrarch, being rebuked by him about Herodias, his brother's wife, and about all the evil things Herod had done, ²⁰added this to everything else—he locked John up in prison.

²¹When all the people were baptized, Jesus also was baptized. As He was praying, heaven opened, ²²and the Holy Spirit descended on Him in a physical appearance like a dove. And a voice came from heaven:

You are My beloved Son.
I take delight in You!

²³As He began His ministry, Jesus was about 30 years old and was thought to be the

son of Joseph, son of Heli,
²⁴   son of Matthat, son of Levi,
son of Melchi, son of Jannai,
son of Joseph, ²⁵son of Mattathias,
son of Amos, son of Nahum,
son of Esli, son of Naggai,
²⁶   son of Maath, son of Mattathias,
son of Semein, son of Josech,
son of Joda, ²⁷son of Joanan,
son of Rhesa, son of Zerubbabel,
son of Shealtiel, son of Neri,
²⁸   son of Melchi, son of Addi,
son of Cosam, son of Elmadam,
son of Er, ²⁹son of Joshua,
son of Eliezer, son of Jorim,
son of Matthat, son of Levi,
³⁰   son of Simeon, son of Judah,
son of Joseph, son of Jonam,
son of Eliakim, ³¹son of Melea,
son of Menna, son of Mattatha,
son of Nathan, son of David,
³²   son of Jesse, son of Obed,
son of Boaz, son of Salmon,
son of Nahshon, ³³son of Amminadab,
son of Ram, son of Hezron,
son of Perez, son of Judah,
³⁴   son of Jacob, son of Isaac,
son of Abraham, son of Terah,
son of Nahor, ³⁵son of Serug,
son of Reu, son of Peleg,
son of Eber, son of Shelah,
³⁶   son of Cainan, son of Arphaxad,
son of Shem, son of Noah,
son of Lamech, ³⁷son of Methuselah,
son of Enoch, son of Jared,
son of Mahalaleel, son of Cainan,
³⁸   son of Enos, son of Seth,
son of Adam, son of God.

4 Then Jesus returned from the Jordan, full of the Holy Spirit, and was led by the Spirit in the wilderness ²for 40 days to be tempted by the Devil. He ate nothing during those days, and when they were over, He was hungry. ³The Devil said to Him, "If You are the Son of God, tell this stone to become bread."

⁴But Jesus answered him, "It is written: **Man must not live on bread alone.**"

⁵So he took Him up and showed Him all the kingdoms of the world in a moment of time. ⁶The Devil said to Him, "I will give You their splendor and all this authority, because it has been given over to me, and I can give it to anyone I want. ⁷If You, then, will worship me, all will be Yours."

⁸And Jesus answered him, "It is written:

Worship the Lord your God,
and serve Him only."

⁹So he took Him to Jerusalem, had Him stand on the pinnacle of the temple, and said to Him, "If You are the Son of God, throw Yourself down from here. ¹⁰For it is written:

He will give His angels orders concerning you,
to protect you, ¹¹and
they will support you with their hands,
so that you will not strike
your foot against a stone."

¹²And Jesus answered him, "It is said: **Do not test the Lord your God.**"

¹³After the Devil had finished every temptation, he departed from Him for a time.

¹⁴Then Jesus returned to Galilee in the power of the Spirit, and news about Him spread throughout the entire vicinity. ¹⁵He was teaching in their ˙synagogues, being acclaimed by everyone.

¹⁶He came to Nazareth, where He had been brought up. As usual, He entered the synagogue on the Sabbath day and stood up to read. ¹⁷The scroll of the prophet Isaiah was given to Him, and unrolling the scroll, He found the place where it was written:

¹⁸   **The Spirit of the Lord is on Me,**
because He has anointed Me
to preach good news to the poor.
He has sent Me
to proclaim freedom to the captives
and recovery of sight to the blind,
to set free the oppressed,
¹⁹   **to proclaim the year of the Lord's favor.**

²⁰He then rolled up the scroll, gave it back to the attendant, and sat down. And the eyes of everyone in the synagogue were fixed on Him. ²¹He began by saying to them, "Today as you listen, this Scripture has been fulfilled."

²²They were all speaking well of Him and were amazed by the gracious words that came from His mouth, yet they said, "Isn't this Joseph's son?"

²³Then He said to them, "No doubt you will quote this proverb to Me: 'Doctor, heal yourself. So all we've heard that took place in Capernaum, do here in Your hometown also.'"

²⁴He also said, "'I assure you: No prophet is accepted in his hometown. ²⁵But I say to you, there were certainly many widows in Israel in Elijah's days, when the sky was shut up for three years and six months while a great famine came over all the land. ²⁶Yet Elijah was not sent to any of them—but to a widow at Zarephath in Sidon. ²⁷And in the prophet Elisha's time, there were many in Israel who had serious skin diseases, yet not one of them was healed—only Naaman the Syrian."

²⁸When they heard this, everyone in the synagogue was enraged. ²⁹They got up, drove Him out of town, and brought Him to the edge of the hill that their town was built on, intending to hurl Him over the cliff. ³⁰But He passed right through the crowd and went on His way.

³¹Then He went down to Capernaum, a town in Galilee, and was teaching them on the Sabbath. ³²They were astonished at His teaching because His message had authority. ³³In the synagogue there was a man with an ˙unclean demonic spirit who cried out with a loud voice, ³⁴"Leave us alone! What do You have to do with us, Jesus—˙Nazarene? Have You come to destroy us? I know who You are—the Holy One of God!"

³⁵But Jesus rebuked him and said, "Be quiet and come out of him!"

And throwing him down before them, the demon came out of him without hurting him at all. ³⁶Amazement came over them all, and they kept saying to one another, "What is this message? For He commands the unclean spirits with authority and power, and they come out!" [37] And news about Him began to go out to every place in the vicinity.

[38] After He left the synagogue, He entered Simon's house. Simon's mother-in-law was suffering from a high fever, and they asked Him about her. [39] So He stood over her and rebuked the fever, and it left her. She got up immediately and began to serve them.

[40] When the sun was setting, all those who had anyone sick with various diseases brought them to Him. As He laid His hands on each one of them, He would heal them. [41] Also, demons were coming out of many, shouting and saying, "You are the Son of God!" But He rebuked them and would not allow them to speak, because they knew He was the •Messiah.

[42] When it was day, He went out and made His way to a deserted place. But the crowds were searching for Him. They came to Him and tried to keep Him from leaving them. [43] But He said to them, "I must proclaim the good news about the kingdom of God to the other towns also, because I was sent for this purpose." [44] And He was preaching in the synagogues of Galilee.

5 As the crowd was pressing in on Jesus to hear God's word, He was standing by Lake Gennesaret. [2] He saw two boats at the edge of the lake; the fishermen had left them and were washing their nets. [3] He got into one of the boats, which belonged to Simon, and asked him to put out a little from the land. Then He sat down and was teaching the crowds from the boat.

[4] When He had finished speaking, He said to Simon, "Put out into deep water and let down your nets for a catch."

[5] "Master," Simon replied, "we've worked hard all night long and caught nothing! But at Your word, I'll let down the nets."

[6] When they did this, they caught a great number of fish, and their nets began to tear. [7] So they signaled to their partners in the other boat to come and help them; they came and filled both boats so full that they began to sink.

[8] When Simon Peter saw this, he fell at Jesus' knees and said, "Go away from me, because I'm a sinful man, Lord!" [9] For he and all those with him were amazed at the catch of fish they took, [10] and so were James and John, Zebedee's sons, who were Simon's partners.

"Don't be afraid," Jesus told Simon. "From now on you will be catching people!" [11] Then they brought the boats to land, left everything, and followed Him.

[12] While He was in one of the towns, a man was there who had a serious skin disease all over him. He saw Jesus, fell facedown, and begged Him: "Lord, if You are willing, You can make me •clean."

[13] Reaching out His hand, He touched him, saying, "I am willing; be made clean," and immediately the disease left him. [14] Then He ordered him to tell no one: "But go and show yourself to the priest, and offer what Moses prescribed for your cleansing as a testimony to them."

[15] But the news about Him spread even more, and large crowds would come together to hear Him and to be healed of their sicknesses. [16] Yet He often withdrew to deserted places and prayed.

[17] On one of those days while He was teaching, •Pharisees and teachers of the law were sitting there who had come from every village of Galilee and Judea, and also from Jerusalem. And the Lord's power to heal was in Him. [18] Just then some men came, carrying on a mat a man who was paralyzed. They tried to bring him in and set him down before Him. [19] Since they could not find a way to bring him in because of the crowd, they went up on the roof and lowered him on the mat through the roof tiles into the middle of the crowd before Jesus.

[20] Seeing their faith He said, "Friend, your sins are forgiven you."

[21] Then the •scribes and the Pharisees began to think: "Who is this man who speaks blasphemies? Who can forgive sins but God alone?"

[22] But perceiving their thoughts, Jesus replied to them, "Why are you thinking this in your hearts? [23] Which is easier: to say, 'Your sins are forgiven you,' or to say, 'Get up and walk'? [24] But so you may know that the •Son of Man has authority on earth to forgive sins"—He told the paralyzed man, "I tell you: Get up, pick up your mat, and go home."

[25] Immediately he got up before them, picked up what he had been lying on, and went home glorifying God. [26] Then everyone was astounded, and they were giving glory to God. And they were filled with awe and said, "We have seen incredible things today!"

[27] After this, Jesus went out and saw a tax collector named Levi sitting at the tax office, and He said to him, "Follow Me!" [28] So, leaving everything behind, he got up and began to follow Him.

[29] Then Levi hosted a grand banquet for Him at his house. Now there was a large crowd of tax collectors and others who were guests with them. [30] But the Pharisees and their scribes were complaining to His disciples, "Why do you eat and drink with tax collectors and sinners?"

[31] Jesus replied to them, "The healthy don't need a doctor, but the sick do. [32] I have not come to call the righteous, but sinners to repentance."

[33] Then they said to Him, "John's disciples fast often and say prayers, and those of the Pharisees do the same, but Yours eat and drink."

[34] Jesus said to them, "You can't make the wedding guests fast while the groom is with them, can you? [35] But the time will come when the groom will be taken away from them—then they will fast in those days."

[36] He also told them a parable: "No one tears a patch from a new garment and puts it on an old garment. Otherwise, not only will he tear the new, but also the piece from the new garment will not match the old. [37] And no one puts new wine into old wineskins. Otherwise, the new wine will burst the skins, it will spill, and the skins will be ruined. [38] But new wine should be put into fresh wineskins. [39] And no one, after drinking old wine, wants new, because he says, 'The old is better.'"

6 On a Sabbath, He passed through the grainfields. His disciples were picking heads of grain, rubbing them in their hands, and eating them. [2] But some of the •Pharisees said, "Why are you doing what is not lawful on the Sabbath?"

[3] Jesus answered them, "Haven't you read what David and those who were with him did when he was hungry— [4] how he entered the house of God, and took and ate the •sacred bread, which is not lawful for any but the priests to eat? He even gave some to those who were with him." [5] Then He told them, "The •Son of Man is Lord of the Sabbath."

[6] On another Sabbath He entered the •synagogue and was teaching. A man was there whose right hand

was paralyzed. [7]The *scribes and Pharisees were watching Him closely, to see if He would heal on the Sabbath, so that they could find a charge against Him. [8]But He knew their thoughts and told the man with the paralyzed hand, "Get up and stand here." So he got up and stood there. [9]Then Jesus said to them, "I ask you: Is it lawful on the Sabbath to do what is good or to do what is evil, to save life or to destroy it?" [10]After looking around at them all, He told him, "Stretch out your hand." He did so, and his hand was restored. [11]They, however, were filled with rage and started discussing with one another what they might do to Jesus.

[12]During those days He went out to the mountain to pray and spent all night in prayer to God. [13]When daylight came, He summoned His disciples, and He chose 12 of them—He also named them apostles:

[14] Simon, whom He also named Peter,
and Andrew his brother;
James and John;
Philip and Bartholomew;

[15] Matthew and Thomas;
James the son of Alphaeus,
and Simon called the Zealot;

[16] Judas the son of James,
and Judas Iscariot, who became a traitor.

[17]After coming down with them, He stood on a level place with a large crowd of His disciples and a great number of people from all Judea and Jerusalem and from the seacoast of Tyre and Sidon. [18]They came to hear Him and to be healed of their diseases; and those tormented by *unclean spirits were made well. [19]The whole crowd was trying to touch Him, because power was coming out from Him and healing them all.

[20]Then looking up at His disciples, He said:
You who are poor are blessed,
because the kingdom of God is yours.

[21] You who are now hungry are blessed,
because you will be filled.
You who now weep are blessed,
because you will laugh.

[22] You are blessed when people hate you,
when they exclude you, insult you,
and slander your name as evil
because of the Son of Man.

[23]"Rejoice in that day and leap for joy! Take note—your reward is great in heaven, for this is the way their ancestors used to treat the prophets.

[24] But woe to you who are rich,
for you have received your comfort.

[25] Woe to you who are now full,
for you will be hungry.
Woe to you who are now laughing,
for you will mourn and weep.

[26] Woe to you
when all people speak well of you,
for this is the way their ancestors
used to treat the false prophets.

[27]"But I say to you who listen: Love your enemies, do what is good to those who hate you, [28]bless those who curse you, pray for those who mistreat you. [29]If anyone hits you on the cheek, offer the other also. And if anyone takes away your coat, don't hold back your shirt either. [30]Give to everyone who asks you, and from one who takes your things, don't ask for them back. [31]Just as you want others to do for you, do the same for them. [32]If you love those who love you, what credit is that to you? Even sinners love those who love them.

[33]If you do what is good to those who are good to you, what credit is that to you? Even sinners do that. [34]And if you lend to those from whom you expect to receive, what credit is that to you? Even sinners lend to sinners to be repaid in full. [35]But love your enemies, do what is good, and lend, expecting nothing in return. Then your reward will be great, and you will be sons of the Most High. For He is gracious to the ungrateful and evil. [36]Be merciful, just as your Father also is merciful.

[37]"Do not judge, and you will not be judged. Do not condemn, and you will not be condemned. Forgive, and you will be forgiven. [38]Give, and it will be given to you; a good measure—pressed down, shaken together, and running over—will be poured into your lap. For with the measure you use, it will be measured back to you."

[39]He also told them a parable: "Can the blind guide the blind? Won't they both fall into a pit? [40]A disciple is not above his teacher, but everyone who is fully trained will be like his teacher.

[41]"Why do you look at the speck in your brother's eye, but don't notice the log in your own eye? [42]Or how can you say to your brother, 'Brother, let me take out the speck that is in your eye,' when you yourself don't see the log in your eye? Hypocrite! First take the log out of your eye, and then you will see clearly to take out the speck in your brother's eye.

[43]"A good tree doesn't produce bad fruit; on the other hand, a bad tree doesn't produce good fruit. [44]For each tree is known by its own fruit. Figs aren't gathered from thornbushes, or grapes picked from a bramble bush. [45]A good man produces good out of the good storeroom of his heart. An evil man produces evil out of the evil storeroom, for his mouth speaks from the overflow of the heart.

[46]"Why do you call Me 'Lord, Lord,' and don't do the things I say? [47]I will show you what someone is like who comes to Me, hears My words, and acts on them: [48]He is like a man building a house, who dug deep and laid the foundation on the rock. When the flood came, the river crashed against that house and couldn't shake it, because it was well built. [49]But the one who hears and does not act is like a man who built a house on the ground without a foundation. The river crashed against it, and immediately it collapsed. And the destruction of that house was great!"

7 When He had concluded all His sayings in the hearing of the people, He entered Capernaum. [2]A *centurion's *slave, who was highly valued by him, was sick and about to die. [3]When the centurion heard about Jesus, he sent some Jewish elders to Him, requesting Him to come and save the life of his slave. [4]When they reached Jesus, they pleaded with Him earnestly, saying, "He is worthy for You to grant this, [5]because he loves our nation and has built us a *synagogue." [6]Jesus went with them, and when He was not far from the house, the centurion sent friends to tell Him, "Lord, don't trouble Yourself, since I am not worthy to have You come under my roof. [7]That is why I didn't even consider myself worthy to come to You. But say the word, and my servant will be cured. [8]For I too am a man placed under authority, having soldiers under my command. I say to this one, 'Go!' and he goes; and to another, 'Come!' and he comes; and to my slave, 'Do this!' and he does it."

[9]Jesus heard this and was amazed at him, and turning to the crowd following Him, He said, "I tell you, I

have not found so great a faith even in Israel!" [10]When those who had been sent returned to the house, they found the slave in good health.

[11]Soon afterward He was on His way to a town called Nain. His disciples and a large crowd were traveling with Him. [12]Just as He neared the gate of the town, a dead man was being carried out. He was his mother's only son, and she was a widow. A large crowd from the city was also with her. [13]When the Lord saw her, He had compassion on her and said, "Don't cry." [14]Then He came up and touched the open coffin, and the pall-bearers stopped. And He said, "Young man, I tell you, get up!"

[15]The dead man sat up and began to speak, and Jesus gave him to his mother. [16]Then fear came over everyone, and they glorified God, saying, "A great prophet has risen among us," and "God has visited His people." [17]This report about Him went throughout Judea and all the vicinity.

[18]Then John's disciples told him about all these things. So John summoned two of his disciples [19]and sent them to the Lord, asking, "Are You the One who is to come, or should we look for someone else?"

[20]When the men reached Him, they said, "John the Baptist sent us to ask You, 'Are You the One who is to come, or should we look for someone else?'"

[21]At that time Jesus healed many people of diseases, plagues, and evil spirits, and He granted sight to many blind people. [22]He replied to them, "Go and report to John the things you have seen and heard: The blind receive their sight, the lame walk, those with skin diseases are healed, the deaf hear, the dead are raised, and the poor are told the good news. [23]And anyone who is not •offended because of Me is blessed." [24]After John's messengers left, He began to speak to the crowds about John: "What did you go out into the wilderness to see? A reed swaying in the wind? [25]What then did you go out to see? A man dressed in soft robes? Look, those who are splendidly dressed and live in luxury are in royal palaces. [26]What then did you go out to see? A prophet? Yes, I tell you, and far more than a prophet. [27]This is the one it is written about:

Look, I am sending My messenger
ahead of You;
he will prepare Your way before You.

[28]I tell you, among those born of women no one is greater than John, but the least in the kingdom of God is greater than he."

[29](And when all the people, including the tax collectors, heard this, they acknowledged God's way of righteousness, because they had been baptized with John's baptism. [30]But since the •Pharisees and experts in the law had not been baptized by him, they rejected the plan of God for themselves.)

[31]"To what then should I compare the people of this generation, and what are they like? [32]They are like children sitting in the marketplace and calling to each other:

We played the flute for you,
but you didn't dance;
we sang a lament,
but you didn't weep!

[33]For John the Baptist did not come eating bread or drinking wine, and you say, 'He has a demon!' [34]The •Son of Man has come eating and drinking, and you say, 'Look, a glutton and a drunkard, a friend of tax collectors and sinners!' [35]Yet wisdom is vindicated by all her children."

[36]Then one of the Pharisees invited Him to eat with him. He entered the Pharisee's house and reclined at the table. [37]And a woman in the town who was a sinner found out that Jesus was reclining at the table in the Pharisee's house. She brought an alabaster jar of fragrant oil [38]and stood behind Him at His feet, weeping, and began to wash His feet with her tears. She wiped His feet with the hair of her head, kissing them and anointing them with the fragrant oil.

[39]When the Pharisee who had invited Him saw this, he said to himself, "This man, if He were a prophet, would know who and what kind of woman this is who is touching Him—she's a sinner!"

[40]Jesus replied to him, "Simon, I have something to say to you."

"Teacher," he said, "say it."

[41]"A creditor had two debtors. One owed 500 •denarii, and the other 50. [42]Since they could not pay it back, he graciously forgave them both. So, which of them will love him more?"

[43]Simon answered, "I suppose the one he forgave more."

"You have judged correctly," He told him. [44]Turning to the woman, He said to Simon, "Do you see this woman? I entered your house; you gave Me no water for My feet, but she, with her tears, has washed My feet and wiped them with her hair. [45]You gave Me no kiss, but she hasn't stopped kissing My feet since I came in. [46]You didn't anoint My head with olive oil, but she has anointed My feet with fragrant oil. [47]Therefore I tell you, her many sins are forgiven; that's why she loved much. But the one who is forgiven little, loves little." [48]Then He said to her, "Your sins are forgiven."

[49]Those who were at the table with Him began to say among themselves, "Who is this man who even forgives sins?"

[50]And He said to the woman, "Your faith has saved you. Go in peace."

8 Soon afterward He was traveling from one town and village to another, preaching and telling the good news of the kingdom of God. The Twelve were with Him, [2]and also some women who had been healed of evil spirits and sicknesses: Mary, called •Magdalene (seven demons had come out of her); [3]Joanna the wife of Chuza, •Herod's steward; Susanna; and many others who were supporting them from their possessions.

[4]As a large crowd was gathering, and people were flocking to Him from every town, He said in a parable: [5]"A sower went out to sow his seed. As he was sowing, some fell along the path; it was trampled on, and the birds of the sky ate it up. [6]Other seed fell on the rock; when it sprang up, it withered, since it lacked moisture. [7]Other seed fell among thorns; the thorns sprang up with it and choked it. [8]Still other seed fell on good ground; when it sprang up, it produced a crop: 100 times what was sown." As He said this, He called out, "Anyone who has ears to hear should listen!"

[9]Then His disciples asked Him, "What does this parable mean?" [10]So He said, "The •secrets of the kingdom of God have been given for you to know, but to the rest it is in parables, so that

Looking they may not see,
and hearing they may not understand.

[11]"This is the meaning of the parable: The seed is the word of God. [12]The seed along the path are those

who have heard and then the Devil comes and takes away the word from their hearts, so that they may not believe and be saved. [13]And the seed on the rock are those who, when they hear, welcome the word with joy. Having no root, these believe for a while and depart in a time of testing. [14]As for the seed that fell among thorns, these are the ones who, when they have heard, go on their way and are choked with worries, riches, and pleasures of life, and produce no mature fruit. [15]But the seed in the good ground—these are the ones who, having heard the word with an honest and good heart, hold on to it and by enduring, bear fruit.

[16]"No one, after lighting a lamp, covers it with a basket or puts it under a bed, but puts it on a lampstand so that those who come in may see its light. [17]For nothing is concealed that won't be revealed, and nothing hidden that won't be made known and come to light. [18]Therefore take care how you listen. For whoever has, more will be given to him; and whoever does not have, even what he thinks he has will be taken away from him."

[19]Then His mother and brothers came to Him, but they could not meet with Him because of the crowd. [20]He was told, "Your mother and Your brothers are standing outside, wanting to see You."

[21]But He replied to them, "My mother and My brothers are those who hear and do the word of God."

[22]One day He and His disciples got into a boat, and He told them, "Let's cross over to the other side of the lake." So they set out, [23]and as they were sailing He fell asleep. Then a fierce windstorm came down on the lake; they were being swamped and were in danger. [24]They came and woke Him up, saying, "Master, Master, we're going to die!" Then He got up and rebuked the wind and the raging waves. So they ceased, and there was a calm. [25]He said to them, "Where is your faith?"

They were fearful and amazed, asking one another, "Who can this be? He commands even the winds and the waves, and they obey Him!"

[26]Then they sailed to the region of the Gerasenes, which is opposite Galilee. [27]When He got out on land, a demon-possessed man from the town met Him. For a long time he had worn no clothes and did not stay in a house but in the tombs. [28]When he saw Jesus, he cried out, fell down before Him, and said in a loud voice, "What do You have to do with me, Jesus, You Son of the Most High God? I beg You, don't torment me!" [29]For He had commanded the *unclean spirit to come out of the man. Many times it had seized him, and though he was guarded, bound by chains and shackles, he would snap the restraints and be driven by the demon into deserted places.

[30]"What is your name?" Jesus asked him.

"Legion," he said—because many demons had entered him. [31]And they begged Him not to banish them to the *abyss.

[32]A large herd of pigs was there, feeding on the hillside. The demons begged Him to permit them to enter the pigs, and He gave them permission. [33]The demons came out of the man and entered the pigs, and the herd rushed down the steep bank into the lake and drowned. [34]When the men who tended them saw what had happened, they ran off and reported it in the town and in the countryside. [35]Then people went out to see what had happened. They came to Jesus and found the man the demons had departed from, sitting

at Jesus' feet, dressed and in his right mind. And they were afraid. [36]Meanwhile, the eyewitnesses reported to them how the demon-possessed man was delivered. [37]Then all the people of the Gerasene region asked Him to leave them, because they were gripped by great fear. So getting into the boat, He returned.

[38]The man from whom the demons had departed kept begging Him to be with Him. But He sent him away and said, [39]"Go back to your home, and tell all that God has done for you." And off he went, proclaiming throughout the town all that Jesus had done for him.

[40]When Jesus returned, the crowd welcomed Him, for they were all expecting Him. [41]Just then, a man named Jairus came. He was a leader of the *synagogue. He fell down at Jesus' feet and pleaded with Him to come to his house, [42]because he had an only daughter about 12 years old, and she was at death's door.

While He was going, the crowds were nearly crushing Him. [43]A woman suffering from bleeding for 12 years, who had spent all she had on doctors yet could not be healed by any, [44]approached from behind and touched the *tassel of His robe. Instantly her bleeding stopped.

[45]"Who touched Me?" Jesus asked.

When they all denied it, Peter said, "Master, the crowds are hemming You in and pressing against You."

[46]"Someone did touch Me," said Jesus. "I know that power has gone out from Me." [47]When the woman saw that she was discovered, she came trembling and fell down before Him. In the presence of all the people, she declared the reason she had touched Him and how she was instantly cured. [48]"Daughter," He said to her, "your faith has made you well. Go in peace."

[49]While He was still speaking, someone came from the synagogue leader's house, saying, "Your daughter is dead. Don't bother the Teacher anymore."

[50]When Jesus heard it, He answered him, "Don't be afraid. Only believe, and she will be made well." [51]After He came to the house, He let no one enter with Him except Peter, John, James, and the child's father and mother. [52]Everyone was crying and mourning for her. But He said, "Stop crying, for she is not dead but asleep."

[53]They started laughing at Him, because they knew she was dead. [54]So He took her by the hand and called out, "Child, get up!" [55]Her spirit returned, and she got up at once. Then He gave orders that she be given something to eat. [56]Her parents were astounded, but He instructed them to tell no one what had happened.

9 Summoning the Twelve, He gave them power and authority over all the demons, and power to heal diseases. [2]Then He sent them to proclaim the kingdom of God and to heal the sick.

[3]"Take nothing for the road," He told them, "no walking stick, no traveling bag, no bread, no money; and don't take an extra shirt. [4]Whatever house you enter, stay there and leave from there. [5]If they do not welcome you, when you leave that town, shake off the dust from your feet as a testimony against them." [6]So they went out and traveled from village to village, proclaiming the good news and healing everywhere.

[7]*Herod the tetrarch heard about everything that was going on. He was perplexed, because some said that John had been raised from the dead, [8]some that Elijah had appeared, and others that one of the ancient

prophets had risen. ⁹"I beheaded John," Herod said, "but who is this I hear such things about?" And he wanted to see Him.

¹⁰When the apostles returned, they reported to Jesus all that they had done. He took them along and withdrew privately to a town called Bethsaida. ¹¹When the crowds found out, they followed Him. He welcomed them, spoke to them about the kingdom of God, and cured those who needed healing.

¹²Late in the day, the Twelve approached and said to Him, "Send the crowd away, so they can go into the surrounding villages and countryside to find food and lodging, because we are in a deserted place here."

¹³"You give them something to eat," He told them.

"We have no more than five loaves and two fish," they said, "unless we go and buy food for all these people." ¹⁴(For about 5,000 men were there.)

Then He told His disciples, "Have them sit down in groups of about 50 each." ¹⁵They did so, and had them all sit down. ¹⁶Then He took the five loaves and the two fish, and looking up to heaven, He blessed and broke them. He kept giving them to the disciples to set before the crowd. ¹⁷Everyone ate and was filled. Then they picked up 12 baskets of leftover pieces.

¹⁸While He was praying in private and His disciples were with Him, He asked them, "Who do the crowds say that I am?"

¹⁹They answered, "John the Baptist; others, Elijah; still others, that one of the ancient prophets has come back."

²⁰"But you," He asked them, "who do you say that I am?"

Peter answered, "God's •Messiah!"

²¹But He strictly warned and instructed them to tell this to no one, ²²saying, "The •Son of Man must suffer many things and be rejected by the elders, •chief priests, and •scribes, be killed, and be raised the third day."

²³Then He said to them all, "If anyone wants to come with Me, he must deny himself, take up his cross daily, and follow Me. ²⁴For whoever wants to save his •life will lose it, but whoever loses his life because of Me will save it. ²⁵What is a man benefited if he gains the whole world, yet loses or forfeits himself? ²⁶For whoever is ashamed of Me and My words, the Son of Man will be ashamed of him when He comes in His glory and that of the Father and the holy angels. ²⁷I tell you the truth: There are some standing here who will not taste death until they see the kingdom of God."

²⁸About eight days after these words, He took along Peter, John, and James and went up on the mountain to pray. ²⁹As He was praying, the appearance of His face changed, and His clothes became dazzling white. ³⁰Suddenly, two men were talking with Him—Moses and Elijah. ³¹They appeared in glory and were speaking of His death, which He was about to accomplish in Jerusalem.

³²Peter and those with him were in a deep sleep, and when they became fully awake, they saw His glory and the two men who were standing with Him. ³³As the two men were departing from Him, Peter said to Jesus, "Master, it's good for us to be here! Let us make three •tabernacles: one for You, one for Moses, and one for Elijah"—not knowing what he said.

³⁴While he was saying this, a cloud appeared and overshadowed them. They became afraid as they entered the cloud. ³⁵Then a voice came from the cloud, saying:

This is My Son, the Chosen One;
listen to Him!

³⁶After the voice had spoken, only Jesus was found. They kept silent, and in those days told no one what they had seen.

³⁷The next day, when they came down from the mountain, a large crowd met Him. ³⁸Just then a man from the crowd cried out, "Teacher, I beg You to look at my son, because he's my only child. ³⁹Often a spirit seizes him; suddenly he shrieks, and it throws him into convulsions until he foams at the mouth; wounding him, it hardly ever leaves him. ⁴⁰I begged Your disciples to drive it out, but they couldn't."

⁴¹Jesus replied, "You unbelieving and rebellious generation! How long will I be with you and put up with you? Bring your son here."

⁴²As the boy was still approaching, the demon knocked him down and threw him into severe convulsions. But Jesus rebuked the •unclean spirit, cured the boy, and gave him back to his father. ⁴³And they were all astonished at the greatness of God.

While everyone was amazed at all the things He was doing, He told His disciples, ⁴⁴"Let these words sink in: The Son of Man is about to be betrayed into the hands of men."

⁴⁵But they did not understand this statement; it was concealed from them so that they could not grasp it, and they were afraid to ask Him about it.

⁴⁶Then an argument started among them about who would be the greatest of them. ⁴⁷But Jesus, knowing the thoughts of their hearts, took a little child and had him stand next to Him. ⁴⁸He told them, "Whoever welcomes this little child in My name welcomes Me. And whoever welcomes Me welcomes Him who sent Me. For whoever is least among you—this one is great."

⁴⁹John responded, "Master, we saw someone driving out demons in Your name, and we tried to stop him because he does not follow us."

⁵⁰"Don't stop him," Jesus told him, "because whoever is not against you is for you."

⁵¹When the days were coming to a close for Him to be taken up, He determined to journey to Jerusalem. ⁵²He sent messengers ahead of Him, and on the way they entered a village of the •Samaritans to make preparations for Him. ⁵³But they did not welcome Him, because He determined to journey to Jerusalem. ⁵⁴When the disciples James and John saw this, they said, "Lord, do You want us to call down fire from heaven to consume them?"

⁵⁵But He turned and rebuked them, ⁵⁶and they went to another village.

⁵⁷As they were traveling on the road someone said to Him, "I will follow You wherever You go!"

⁵⁸Jesus told him, "Foxes have dens, and birds of the sky have nests, but the Son of Man has no place to lay His head." ⁵⁹Then He said to another, "Follow Me."

"Lord," he said, "first let me go bury my father."

⁶⁰But He told him, "Let the dead bury their own dead, but you go and spread the news of the kingdom of God."

⁶¹Another also said, "I will follow You, Lord, but first let me go and say good-bye to those at my house."

⁶²But Jesus said to him, "No one who puts his hand to the plow and looks back is fit for the kingdom of God."

10 After this, the Lord appointed 70 others, and He sent them ahead of Him in pairs to every town and place where He Himself was about to go. ²He told them: "The harvest is abundant, but the workers are few. Therefore, pray to the Lord of the harvest to send out workers into His harvest. ³Now go; I'm sending you out like lambs among wolves. ⁴Don't carry a money-bag, traveling bag, or sandals; don't greet anyone along the road. ⁵Whatever house you enter, first say, 'Peace to this household.' ⁶If a son of peace is there, your peace will rest on him; but if not, it will return to you. ⁷Remain in the same house, eating and drinking what they offer, for the worker is worthy of his wages. Don't be moving from house to house. ⁸When you enter any town, and they welcome you, eat the things set before you. ⁹Heal the sick who are there, and tell them, 'The kingdom of God has come near you.' ¹⁰When you enter any town, and they don't welcome you, go out into its streets and say, ¹¹'We are wiping off as a witness against you even the dust of your town that clings to our feet. Know this for certain: The kingdom of God has come near.' ¹²I tell you, on that day it will be more tolerable for Sodom than for that town.

¹³"Woe to you, Chorazin! Woe to you, Bethsaida! For if the miracles that were done in you had been done in Tyre and Sidon, they would have repented long ago, sitting in ·sackcloth and ashes! ¹⁴But it will be more tolerable for Tyre and Sidon at the judgment than for you. ¹⁵And you, Capernaum, will you be exalted to heaven? No, you will go down to ·Hades! ¹⁶Whoever listens to you listens to Me. Whoever rejects you rejects Me. And whoever rejects Me rejects the One who sent Me."

¹⁷The Seventy returned with joy, saying, "Lord, even the demons submit to us in Your name."

¹⁸He said to them, "I watched Satan fall from heaven like a lightning flash. ¹⁹Look, I have given you the authority to trample on snakes and scorpions and over all the power of the enemy; nothing will ever harm you. ²⁰However, don't rejoice that the spirits submit to you, but rejoice that your names are written in heaven."

²¹In that same hour He rejoiced in the Holy Spirit and said, "I praise You, Father, Lord of heaven and earth, because You have hidden these things from the wise and the learned and have revealed them to infants. Yes, Father, because this was Your good pleasure. ²²All things have been entrusted to Me by My Father. No one knows who the Son is except the Father, and who the Father is except the Son, and anyone to whom the Son desires to reveal Him."

²³Then turning to His disciples He said privately, "The eyes that see the things you see are blessed! ²⁴For I tell you that many prophets and kings wanted to see the things you see yet didn't see them; to hear the things you hear yet didn't hear them."

²⁵Just then an expert in the law stood up to test Him, saying, "Teacher, what must I do to inherit eternal life?"

²⁶"What is written in the law?" He asked him. "How do you read it?"

²⁷He answered:

Love the Lord your God with all your heart, with all your soul, with all your strength, and with all your mind; and **your neighbor as yourself.**

²⁸"You've answered correctly," He told him. "Do this and you will live."

²⁹But wanting to justify himself, he asked Jesus, "And who is my neighbor?"

³⁰Jesus took up the question and said: "A man was going down from Jerusalem to Jericho and fell into the hands of robbers. They stripped him, beat him up, and fled, leaving him half dead. ³¹A priest happened to be going down that road. When he saw him, he passed by on the other side. ³²In the same way, a Levite, when he arrived at the place and saw him, passed by on the other side. ³³But a ·Samaritan on his journey came up to him, and when he saw the man, he had compassion. ³⁴He went over to him and bandaged his wounds, pouring on olive oil and wine. Then he put him on his own animal, brought him to an inn, and took care of him. ³⁵The next day he took out two ·denarii, gave them to the innkeeper, and said, 'Take care of him. When I come back I'll reimburse you for whatever extra you spend.'

³⁶"Which of these three do you think proved to be a neighbor to the man who fell into the hands of the robbers?"

³⁷"The one who showed mercy to him," he said.

Then Jesus told him, "Go and do the same."

³⁸While they were traveling, He entered a village, and a woman named Martha welcomed Him into her home. ³⁹She had a sister named Mary, who also sat at the Lord's feet and was listening to what He said. ⁴⁰But Martha was distracted by her many tasks, and she came up and asked, "Lord, don't You care that my sister has left me to serve alone? So tell her to give me a hand."

⁴¹The Lord answered her, "Martha, Martha, you are worried and upset about many things, ⁴²but one thing is necessary. Mary has made the right choice, and it will not be taken away from her."

11 He was praying in a certain place, and when He finished, one of His disciples said to Him, "Lord, teach us to pray, just as John also taught his disciples."

²He said to them, "Whenever you pray, say:

Father,
Your name be honored as holy.
Your kingdom come.
³ Give us each day our daily bread.
⁴ And forgive us our sins,
for we ourselves also forgive everyone
in debt to us.
And do not bring us into temptation."

⁵He also said to them: "Suppose one of you has a friend and goes to him at midnight and says to him, 'Friend, lend me three loaves of bread, ⁶because a friend of mine on a journey has come to me, and I don't have anything to offer him.' ⁷Then he will answer from inside and say, 'Don't bother me! The door is already locked, and my children and I have gone to bed. I can't get up to give you anything.' ⁸I tell you, even though he won't get up and give him anything because he is his friend, yet because of his friend's persistence, he will get up and give him as much as he needs.

⁹"So I say to you, keep asking, and it will be given to you. Keep searching, and you will find. Keep knocking, and the door will be opened to you. ¹⁰For everyone who asks receives, and the one who searches finds, and to the one who knocks, the door will be opened. ¹¹What father among you, if his son asks for a fish, will give him a snake instead of a fish? ¹²Or if he asks for an egg, will give him a scorpion? ¹³If you then, who are

evil, know how to give good gifts to your children, how much more will the heavenly Father give the Holy Spirit to those who ask Him?"

14 Now He was driving out a demon that was mute. When the demon came out, the man who had been mute, spoke, and the crowds were amazed. 15 But some of them said, "He drives out demons by *Beelzebul, the ruler of the demons!" 16 And others, as a test, were demanding of Him a sign from heaven.

17 Knowing their thoughts, He told them: "Every kingdom divided against itself is headed for destruction, and a house divided against itself falls. 18 If Satan also is divided against himself, how will his kingdom stand? For you say I drive out demons by Beelzebul. 19 And if I drive out demons by Beelzebul, who is it your sons drive them out by? For this reason they will be your judges. 20 If I drive out demons by the finger of God, then the kingdom of God has come to you. 21 When a strong man, fully armed, guards his estate, his possessions are secure. 22 But when one stronger than he attacks and overpowers him, he takes from him all his weapons he trusted in, and divides up his plunder. 23 Anyone who is not with Me is against Me, and anyone who does not gather with Me scatters.

24 "When an *unclean spirit comes out of a man, it roams through waterless places looking for rest, and not finding rest, it then says, 'I'll go back to my house where I came from.' 25 And returning, it finds the house swept and put in order. 26 Then it goes and brings seven other spirits more evil than itself, and they enter and settle down there. As a result, that man's last condition is worse than the first."

27 As He was saying these things, a woman from the crowd raised her voice and said to Him, "The womb that bore You and the one who nursed You are blessed!"

28 He said, "Even more, those who hear the word of God and keep it are blessed!"

29 As the crowds were increasing, He began saying: "This generation is an evil generation. It demands a sign, but no sign will be given to it except the sign of Jonah. 30 For just as Jonah became a sign to the people of Nineveh, so also the *Son of Man will be to this generation. 31 The queen of the south will rise up at the judgment with the men of this generation and condemn them, because she came from the ends of the earth to hear the wisdom of Solomon, and look— something greater than Solomon is here! 32 The men of Nineveh will rise up at the judgment with this generation and condemn it, because they repented at Jonah's proclamation, and look—something greater than Jonah is here!

33 "No one lights a lamp and puts it in the cellar or under a basket, but on a lampstand, so that those who come in may see its light. 34 Your eye is the lamp of the body. When your eye is good, your whole body is also full of light. But when it is bad, your body is also full of darkness. 35 Take care then, that the light in you is not darkness. 36 If, therefore, your whole body is full of light, with no part of it in darkness, it will be entirely illuminated, as when a lamp shines its light on you."

37 As He was speaking, a *Pharisee asked Him to dine with him. So He went in and reclined at the table. 38 When the Pharisee saw this, he was amazed that He did not first perform the ritual washing before dinner. 39 But the Lord said to him: "Now you Pharisees *clean the outside of the cup and dish, but inside you are full of greed and evil. 40 Fools! Didn't He who made the outside make the inside too? 41 But give from what is within to the poor, and then everything is clean for you.

42 "But woe to you Pharisees! You give a tenth of mint, rue, and every kind of herb, and you bypass justice and love for God. These things you should have done without neglecting the others.

43 "Woe to you Pharisees! You love the front seat in the *synagogues and greetings in the marketplaces. 44 "Woe to you! You are like unmarked graves; the people who walk over them don't know it."

45 One of the experts in the law answered Him, "Teacher, when You say these things You insult us too."

46 Then He said: "Woe also to you experts in the law! You load people with burdens that are hard to carry, yet you yourselves don't touch these burdens with one of your fingers.

47 "Woe to you! You build monuments to the prophets, and your fathers killed them. 48 Therefore, you are witnesses that you approve the deeds of your fathers, for they killed them, and you build their monuments. 49 Because of this, the wisdom of God said, 'I will send them prophets and apostles, and some of them they will kill and persecute,' 50 so that this generation may be held responsible for the blood of all the prophets shed since the foundation of the world— 51 from the blood of Abel to the blood of Zechariah, who perished between the altar and the sanctuary.

"Yes, I tell you, this generation will be held responsible.

52 "Woe to you experts in the law! You have taken away the key of knowledge! You didn't go in yourselves, and you hindered those who were going in."

53 When He left there, the *scribes and the Pharisees began to oppose Him fiercely and to cross-examine Him about many things; 54 they were lying in wait for Him to trap Him in something He said.

12 In these circumstances, a crowd of many thousands came together, so that they were trampling on one another. He began to say to His disciples first: "Be on your guard against the yeast of the *Pharisees, which is hypocrisy. 2 There is nothing covered that won't be uncovered, nothing hidden that won't be made known. 3 Therefore, whatever you have said in the dark will be heard in the light, and what you have whispered in an ear in private rooms will be proclaimed on the housetops.

4 "And I say to you, My friends, don't fear those who kill the body, and after that can do nothing more. 5 But I will show you the One to fear: Fear Him who has authority to throw people into *hell after death. Yes, I say to you, this is the One to fear! 6 Aren't five sparrows sold for two pennies? Yet not one of them is forgotten in God's sight. 7 Indeed, the hairs of your head are all counted. Don't be afraid; you are worth more than many sparrows!

8 "And I say to you, anyone who acknowledges Me before men, the *Son of Man will also acknowledge him before the angels of God, 9 but whoever denies Me before men will be denied before the angels of God. 10 Anyone who speaks a word against the Son of Man will be forgiven, but the one who blasphemes against the Holy Spirit will not be forgiven. 11 Whenever they bring you before *synagogues and rulers and authorities, don't worry about how you should defend your-

selves or what you should say. ¹²For the Holy Spirit will teach you at that very hour what must be said."

¹³Someone from the crowd said to Him, "Teacher, tell my brother to divide the inheritance with me."

¹⁴"Friend," He said to him, "who appointed Me a judge or arbitrator over you?" ¹⁵He then told them, "Watch out and be on guard against all greed because one's life is not in the abundance of his possessions."

¹⁶Then He told them a parable: "A rich man's land was very productive. ¹⁷He thought to himself, 'What should I do, since I don't have anywhere to store my crops? ¹⁸I will do this,' he said. 'I'll tear down my barns and build bigger ones and store all my grain and my goods there. ¹⁹Then I'll say to myself, "You have many goods stored up for many years. Take it easy; eat, drink, and enjoy yourself."'

²⁰"But God said to him, 'You fool! This very night your *life is demanded of you. And the things you have prepared—whose will they be?'

²¹"That's how it is with the one who stores up treasure for himself and is not rich toward God."

²²Then He said to His disciples: "Therefore I tell you, don't worry about your life, what you will eat; or about the body, what you will wear. ²³For life is more than food and the body more than clothing. ²⁴Consider the ravens: They don't sow or reap; they don't have a storeroom or a barn; yet God feeds them. Aren't you worth much more than the birds? ²⁵Can any of you add a *cubit to his height by worrying? ²⁶If then you're not able to do even a little thing, why worry about the rest?

²⁷"Consider how the wildflowers grow: They don't labor or spin thread. Yet I tell you, not even Solomon in all his splendor was adorned like one of these! ²⁸If that's how God clothes the grass, which is in the field today and is thrown into the furnace tomorrow, how much more will He do for you—you of little faith? ²⁹Don't keep striving for what you should eat and what you should drink, and don't be anxious. ³⁰For the Gentile world eagerly seeks all these things, and your Father knows that you need them.

³¹"But seek His kingdom, and these things will be provided for you. ³²Don't be afraid, little flock, because your Father delights to give you the kingdom. ³³Sell your possessions and give to the poor. Make moneybags for yourselves that won't grow old, an inexhaustible treasure in heaven, where no thief comes near and no moth destroys. ³⁴For where your treasure is, there your heart will be also.

³⁵"Be ready for service and have your lamps lit. ³⁶You must be like people waiting for their master to return from the wedding banquet so that when he comes and knocks, they can open the door for him at once. ³⁷Those *slaves the master will find alert when he comes will be blessed. *I assure you: He will get ready, have them recline at the table, then come and serve them. ³⁸If he comes in the middle of the night, or even near dawn, and finds them alert, those slaves are blessed. ³⁹But know this: If the homeowner had known at what hour the thief was coming, he would not have let his house be broken into. ⁴⁰You also be ready, because the Son of Man is coming at an hour that you do not expect."

⁴¹"Lord," Peter asked, "are You telling this parable to us or to everyone?"

⁴²The Lord said: "Who then is the faithful and sensible manager his master will put in charge of his household servants to give them their allotted food

at the proper time? ⁴³That slave whose master finds him working when he comes will be rewarded. ⁴⁴I tell you the truth: He will put him in charge of all his possessions. ⁴⁵But if that slave says in his heart, 'My master is delaying his coming,' and starts to beat the male and female slaves, and to eat and drink and get drunk, ⁴⁶that slave's master will come on a day he does not expect him and at an hour he does not know. He will cut him to pieces and assign him a place with the unbelievers. ⁴⁷And that slave who knew his master's will and didn't prepare himself or do it will be severely beaten. ⁴⁸But the one who did not know and did things deserving of blows will be beaten lightly. Much will be required of everyone who has been given much. And even more will be expected of the one who has been entrusted with more.

⁴⁹"I came to bring fire on the earth, and how I wish it were already set ablaze! ⁵⁰But I have a baptism to be baptized with, and how it consumes Me until it is finished! ⁵¹Do you think that I came here to give peace to the earth? No, I tell you, but rather division! ⁵²From now on, five in one household will be divided: three against two, and two against three.

⁵³ They will be divided, father against son,
    son against father,
    mother against daughter,
    daughter against mother,
    mother-in-law against her daughter-in-law,
    and daughter-in-law against mother-in-law."

⁵⁴He also said to the crowds: "When you see a cloud rising in the west, right away you say, 'A storm is coming,' and so it does. ⁵⁵And when the south wind is blowing, you say, 'It's going to be a scorcher!' and it is. ⁵⁶Hypocrites! You know how to interpret the appearance of the earth and the sky, but why don't you know how to interpret this time?

⁵⁷"Why don't you judge for yourselves what is right? ⁵⁸As you are going with your adversary to the ruler, make an effort to settle with him on the way. Then he won't drag you before the judge, the judge hand you over to the bailiff, and the bailiff throw you into prison. ⁵⁹I tell you, you will never get out of there until you have paid the last cent."

13 At that time, some people came and reported to Him about the Galileans whose blood *Pilate had mixed with their sacrifices. ²And He responded to them, "Do you think that these Galileans were more sinful than all Galileans because they suffered these things? ³No, I tell you; but unless you repent, you will all perish as well! ⁴Or those 18 that the tower in Siloam fell on and killed—do you think they were more sinful than all the people who live in Jerusalem? ⁵No, I tell you; but unless you repent, you will all perish as well!"

⁶And He told this parable: "A man had a fig tree that was planted in his vineyard. He came looking for fruit on it and found none. ⁷He told the vineyard worker, 'Listen, for three years I have come looking for fruit on this fig tree and haven't found any. Cut it down! Why should it even waste the soil?'

⁸"But he replied to him, 'Sir, leave it this year also, until I dig around it and fertilize it. ⁹Perhaps it will bear fruit next year, but if not, you can cut it down.'"

¹⁰As He was teaching in one of the *synagogues on the Sabbath, ¹¹a woman was there who had been disabled by a spirit for over 18 years. She was bent over and could not straighten up at all. ¹²When Jesus saw

her, He called out to her, "'Woman, you are free of your disability." [13] Then He laid His hands on her, and instantly she was restored and began to glorify God.

[14] But the leader of the synagogue, indignant because Jesus had healed on the Sabbath, responded by telling the crowd, "There are six days when work should be done; therefore come on those days and be healed and not on the Sabbath day."

[15] But the Lord answered him and said, "Hypocrites! Doesn't each one of you untie his ox or donkey from the feeding trough on the Sabbath and lead it to water? [16] Satan has bound this woman, a daughter of Abraham, for 18 years—shouldn't she be untied from this bondage on the Sabbath day?"

[17] When He had said these things, all His adversaries were humiliated, but the whole crowd was rejoicing over all the glorious things He was doing.

[18] He said, therefore, "What is the kingdom of God like, and what can I compare it to? [19] It's like a mustard seed that a man took and sowed in his garden. It grew and became a tree, and the birds of the sky nested in its branches."

[20] Again He said, "What can I compare the kingdom of God to? [21] It's like yeast that a woman took and mixed into 50 pounds of flour until it spread through the entire mixture."

[22] He went through one town and village after another, teaching and making His way to Jerusalem. [23] "Lord," someone asked Him, "are there few being saved?"

He said to them, [24] "Make every effort to enter through the narrow door, because I tell you, many will try to enter and won't be able [25] once the homeowner gets up and shuts the door. Then you will stand outside and knock on the door, saying, 'Lord, open up for us!' He will answer you, 'I don't know you or where you're from.' [26] Then you will say, 'We ate and drank in Your presence, and You taught in our streets!' [27] But He will say, 'I tell you, I don't know you or where you're from. Get away from Me, all you workers of unrighteousness!' [28] There will be weeping and gnashing of teeth in that place, when you see Abraham, Isaac, Jacob, and all the prophets in the kingdom of God but yourselves thrown out. [29] They will come from east and west, from north and south, and recline at the table in the kingdom of God. [30] Note this: Some are last who will be first, and some are first who will be last."

[31] At that time some 'Pharisees came and told Him, "Go, get out of here! 'Herod wants to kill You!"

[32] He said to them, "Go tell that fox, 'Look! I'm driving out demons and performing healings today and tomorrow, and on the third day I will complete My work.' [33] Yet I must travel today, tomorrow, and the next day, because it is not possible for a prophet to perish outside of Jerusalem!

[34] "Jerusalem, Jerusalem! She who kills the prophets and stones those who are sent to her. How often I wanted to gather your children together, as a hen gathers her chicks under her wings, but you were not willing! [35] See, your house is abandoned to you. And I tell you, you will not see Me until the time comes when you say, **'He who comes in the name of the Lord is the blessed One'!**"

14 One Sabbath, when He went to eat at the house of one of the leading 'Pharisees, they were watching Him closely. [2] There in front of Him was a man whose body was swollen with fluid. [3] In response,

Jesus asked the law experts and the Pharisees, "Is it lawful to heal on the Sabbath or not?" [4] But they kept silent. He took the man, healed him, and sent him away. [5] And to them, He said, "Which of you whose son or ox falls into a well, will not immediately pull him out on the Sabbath day?" [6] To this they could find no answer.

[7] He told a parable to those who were invited, when He noticed how they would choose the best places for themselves: [8] "When you are invited by someone to a wedding banquet, don't recline at the best place, because a more distinguished person than you may have been invited by your host. [9] The one who invited both of you may come and say to you, 'Give your place to this man,' and then in humiliation, you will proceed to take the lowest place.

[10] "But when you are invited, go and recline in the lowest place, so that when the one who invited you comes, he will say to you, 'Friend, move up higher.' You will then be honored in the presence of all the other guests. [11] For everyone who exalts himself will be humbled, and the one who humbles himself will be exalted."

[12] He also said to the one who had invited Him, "When you give a lunch or a dinner, don't invite your friends, your 'brothers, your relatives, or your rich neighbors, because they might invite you back, and you would be repaid. [13] On the contrary, when you host a banquet, invite those who are poor, maimed, lame, or blind. [14] And you will be blessed, because they cannot repay you; for you will be repaid at the resurrection of the righteous."

[15] When one of those who reclined at the table with Him heard these things, he said to Him, "The one who will eat bread in the kingdom of God is blessed!"

[16] Then He told him: "A man was giving a large banquet and invited many. [17] At the time of the banquet, he sent his 'slave to tell those who were invited, 'Come, because everything is now ready.'

[18] "But without exception they all began to make excuses. The first one said to him, 'I have bought a field, and I must go out and see it. I ask you to excuse me.'

[19] "Another said, 'I have bought five yoke of oxen, and I'm going to try them out. I ask you to excuse me.'

[20] "And another said, 'I just got married, and therefore I'm unable to come.'

[21] "So the slave came back and reported these things to his master. Then in anger, the master of the house told his slave, 'Go out quickly into the streets and alleys of the city, and bring in here the poor, maimed, blind, and lame!'

[22] "'Master,' the slave said, 'what you ordered has been done, and there's still room.'

[23] "Then the master told the slave, 'Go out into the highways and lanes and make them come in, so that my house may be filled. [24] For I tell you, not one of those men who were invited will enjoy my banquet!'"

[25] Now great crowds were traveling with Him. So He turned and said to them: [26] "If anyone comes to Me and does not hate his own father and mother, wife and children, brothers and sisters—yes, and even his own life—he cannot be My disciple. [27] Whoever does not bear his own cross and come after Me cannot be My disciple.

[28] "For which of you, wanting to build a tower, doesn't first sit down and calculate the cost to see if he has enough to complete it? [29] Otherwise, after he has

laid the foundation and cannot finish it, all the onlookers will begin to make fun of him, [30] saying, 'This man started to build and wasn't able to finish.'

[31] "Or what king, going to war against another king, will not first sit down and decide if he is able with 10,000 to oppose the one who comes against him with 20,000? [32] If not, while the other is still far off, he sends a delegation and asks for terms of peace. [33] In the same way, therefore, every one of you who does not say good-bye to all his possessions cannot be My disciple.

[34] "Now, salt is good, but if salt should lose its taste, how will it be made salty? [35] It isn't fit for the soil or for the manure pile; they throw it out. Anyone who has ears to hear should listen!"

15 All the tax collectors and sinners were approaching to listen to Him. [2] And the ·Pharisees and ·scribes were complaining, "This man welcomes sinners and eats with them!"

[3] So He told them this parable: [4] "What man among you, who has 100 sheep and loses one of them, does not leave the 99 in the open field and go after the lost one until he finds it? [5] When he has found it, he joyfully puts it on his shoulders, [6] and coming home, he calls his friends and neighbors together, saying to them, 'Rejoice with me, because I have found my lost sheep!' [7] I tell you, in the same way, there will be more joy in heaven over one sinner who repents than over 99 righteous people who don't need repentance.

[8] "Or what woman who has 10 silver coins, if she loses one coin, does not light a lamp, sweep the house, and search carefully until she finds it? [9] When she finds it, she calls her women friends and neighbors together, saying, 'Rejoice with me, because I have found the silver coin I lost!' [10] I tell you, in the same way, there is joy in the presence of God's angels over one sinner who repents."

[11] He also said: "A man had two sons. [12] The younger of them said to his father, 'Father, give me the share of the estate I have coming to me.' So he distributed the assets to them. [13] Not many days later, the younger son gathered together all he had and traveled to a distant country, where he squandered his estate in foolish living. [14] After he had spent everything, a severe famine struck that country, and he had nothing. [15] Then he went to work for one of the citizens of that country, who sent him into his fields to feed pigs. [16] He longed to eat his fill from the carob pods the pigs were eating, but no one would give him any. [17] When he came to his senses, he said, 'How many of my father's hired hands have more than enough food, and here I am dying of hunger! [18] I'll get up, go to my father, and say to him, Father, I have sinned against heaven and in your sight. [19] I'm no longer worthy to be called your son. Make me like one of your hired hands.' [20] So he got up and went to his father. But while the son was still a long way off, his father saw him and was filled with compassion. He ran, threw his arms around his neck, and kissed him. [21] The son said to him, 'Father, I have sinned against heaven and in your sight. I'm no longer worthy to be called your son.'

[22] "But the father told his ·slaves, 'Quick! Bring out the best robe and put it on him; put a ring on his finger and sandals on his feet. [23] Then bring the fattened calf and slaughter it, and let's celebrate with a feast, [24] because this son of mine was dead and is alive again; he was lost and is found!' So they began to celebrate.

[25] "Now his older son was in the field; as he came near the house, he heard music and dancing. [26] So he summoned one of the servants and asked what these things meant. [27] 'Your brother is here,' he told him, 'and your father has slaughtered the fattened calf because he has him back safe and sound.'

[28] "Then he became angry and didn't want to go in. So his father came out and pleaded with him. [29] But he replied to his father, 'Look, I have been slaving many years for you, and I have never disobeyed your orders, yet you never gave me a young goat so I could celebrate with my friends. [30] But when this son of yours came, who has devoured your assets with prostitutes, you slaughtered the fattened calf for him.'

[31] "'Son,' he said to him, 'you are always with me, and everything I have is yours. [32] But we had to celebrate and rejoice, because this brother of yours was dead and is alive again; he was lost and is found.'"

16 He also said to the disciples: "There was a rich man who received an accusation that his manager was squandering his possessions. [2] So he called the manager in and asked, 'What is this I hear about you? Give an account of your management, because you can no longer be my manager.'

[3] "Then the manager said to himself, 'What should I do, since my master is taking the management away from me? I'm not strong enough to dig; I'm ashamed to beg. [4] I know what I'll do so that when I'm removed from management, people will welcome me into their homes.'

[5] "So he summoned each one of his master's debtors. 'How much do you owe my master?' he asked the first one.

[6] "'A hundred measures of olive oil,' he said.

"'Take your invoice,' he told him, 'sit down quickly, and write 50.'

[7] "Next he asked another, 'How much do you owe?'

"'A hundred measures of wheat,' he said.

"'Take your invoice,' he told him, 'and write 80.'

[8] "The master praised the unrighteous manager because he had acted astutely. For the sons of this age are more astute than the sons of light in dealing with their own people. [9] And I tell you, make friends for yourselves by means of the unrighteous money so that when it fails, they may welcome you into eternal dwellings. [10] Whoever is faithful in very little is also faithful in much, and whoever is unrighteous in very little is also unrighteous in much. [11] So if you have not been faithful with the unrighteous money, who will trust you with what is genuine? [12] And if you have not been faithful with what belongs to someone else, who will give you what is your own? [13] No household slave can be the ·slave of two masters, since either he will hate one and love the other, or he will be devoted to one and despise the other. You can't be slaves to both God and money."

[14] The ·Pharisees, who were lovers of money, were listening to all these things and scoffing at Him. [15] And He told them: "You are the ones who justify yourselves in the sight of others, but God knows your hearts. For what is highly admired by people is revolting in God's sight.

[16] "The Law and the Prophets were until John; since then, the good news of the kingdom of God has been proclaimed, and everyone is strongly urged to enter it. [17] But it is easier for heaven and earth to pass away than for one stroke of a letter in the law to drop out.

[18] "Everyone who divorces his wife and marries

another woman commits adultery, and everyone who marries a woman divorced from her husband commits adultery.

¹⁹ "There was a rich man who would dress in purple and fine linen, feasting lavishly every day. ²⁰ But a poor man named Lazarus, covered with sores, was left at his gate. ²¹ He longed to be filled with what fell from the rich man's table, but instead the dogs would come and lick his sores. ²² One day the poor man died and was carried away by the angels to Abraham's side. The rich man also died and was buried. ²³ And being in torment in ˙Hades, he looked up and saw Abraham a long way off, with Lazarus at his side. ²⁴ 'Father Abraham!' he called out, 'Have mercy on me and send Lazarus to dip the tip of his finger in water and cool my tongue, because I am in agony in this flame!'

²⁵ "'Son,' Abraham said, 'remember that during your life you received your good things, just as Lazarus received bad things, but now he is comforted here, while you are in agony. ²⁶ Besides all this, a great chasm has been fixed between us and you, so that those who want to pass over from here to you cannot; neither can those from there cross over to us.'

²⁷ "'Father,' he said, 'then I beg you to send him to my father's house— ²⁸ because I have five brothers—to warn them, so they won't also come to this place of torment.'

²⁹ "But Abraham said, 'They have Moses and the prophets; they should listen to them.'

³⁰ "'No, father Abraham,' he said. 'But if someone from the dead goes to them, they will repent.'

³¹ "But he told him, 'If they don't listen to Moses and the prophets, they will not be persuaded if someone rises from the dead.'"

17 He said to His disciples, "Offenses will certainly come, but woe to the one they come through! ² It would be better for him if a millstone were hung around his neck and he were thrown into the sea than for him to cause one of these little ones to ˙stumble. ³ Be on your guard. If your brother sins, rebuke him, and if he repents, forgive him. ⁴ And if he sins against you seven times in a day, and comes back to you seven times, saying, 'I repent,' you must forgive him."

⁵ The apostles said to the Lord, "Increase our faith."

⁶ "If you have faith the size of a mustard seed," the Lord said, "you can say to this mulberry tree, 'Be uprooted and planted in the sea,' and it will obey you.

⁷ "Which one of you having a ˙slave tending sheep or plowing will say to him when he comes in from the field, 'Come at once and sit down to eat'? ⁸ Instead, will he not tell him, 'Prepare something for me to eat, get ready, and serve me while I eat and drink; later you can eat and drink'? ⁹ Does he thank that slave because he did what was commanded? ¹⁰ In the same way, when you have done all that you were commanded, you should say, 'We are good-for-nothing slaves; we've only done our duty.'"

¹¹ While traveling to Jerusalem, He passed between Samaria and Galilee. ¹² As He entered a village, 10 men with serious skin diseases met Him. They stood at a distance ¹³ and raised their voices, saying, "Jesus, Master, have mercy on us!"

¹⁴ When He saw them, He told them, "Go and show yourselves to the priests." And while they were going, they were healed.

¹⁵ But one of them, seeing that he was healed, returned and, with a loud voice, gave glory to God. ¹⁶ He

fell facedown at His feet, thanking Him. And he was a ˙Samaritan.

¹⁷ Then Jesus said, "Were not 10 cleansed? Where are the nine? ¹⁸ Didn't any return to give glory to God except this foreigner?" ¹⁹ And He told him, "Get up and go on your way. Your faith has made you well."

²⁰ Being asked by the ˙Pharisees when the kingdom of God will come, He answered them, "The kingdom of God is not coming with something observable; ²¹ no one will say, 'Look here!' or 'There!' For you see, the kingdom of God is among you."

²² Then He told the disciples: "The days are coming when you will long to see one of the days of the ˙Son of Man, but you won't see it. ²³ They will say to you, 'Look there!' or 'Look here!' Don't follow or run after them. ²⁴ For as the lightning flashes from horizon to horizon and lights up the sky, so the Son of Man will be in His day. ²⁵ But first He must suffer many things and be rejected by this generation.

²⁶ "Just as it was in the days of Noah, so it will be in the days of the Son of Man: ²⁷ People went on eating, drinking, marrying and giving in marriage until the day Noah boarded the ark, and the flood came and destroyed them all. ²⁸ It will be the same as it was in the days of Lot: People went on eating, drinking, buying, selling, planting, building. ²⁹ But on the day Lot left Sodom, fire and sulfur rained from heaven and destroyed them all. ³⁰ It will be like that on the day the Son of Man is revealed. ³¹ On that day, a man on the housetop, whose belongings are in the house, must not come down to get them. Likewise the man who is in the field must not turn back. ³² Remember Lot's wife! ³³ Whoever tries to make his ˙life secure will lose it, and whoever loses his life will preserve it. ³⁴ I tell you, on that night two will be in one bed: One will be taken and the other will be left. ³⁵ Two women will be grinding grain together: One will be taken and the other left. [³⁶ Two will be in a field: One will be taken, and the other will be left.]"

³⁷ "Where, Lord?" they asked Him.

He said to them, "Where the corpse is, there also the vultures will be gathered."

18 He then told them a parable on the need for them to pray always and not become discouraged: ² "There was a judge in a certain town who didn't fear God or respect man. ³ And a widow in that town kept coming to him, saying, 'Give me justice against my adversary.'

⁴ "For a while he was unwilling, but later he said to himself, 'Even though I don't fear God or respect man, ⁵ yet because this widow keeps pestering me, I will give her justice, so she doesn't wear me out by her persistent coming.'"

⁶ Then the Lord said, "Listen to what the unjust judge says. ⁷ Will not God grant justice to His elect who cry out to Him day and night? Will He delay to help them? ⁸ I tell you that He will swiftly grant them justice. Nevertheless, when the ˙Son of Man comes, will He find that faith on earth?"

⁹ He also told this parable to some who trusted in themselves that they were righteous and looked down on everyone else: ¹⁰ "Two men went up to the ˙temple complex to pray, one a ˙Pharisee and the other a tax collector. ¹¹ The Pharisee took his stand and was praying like this: 'God, I thank You that I'm not like other people—greedy, unrighteous, adulterers, or even like

this tax collector. [12] I fast twice a week; I give a tenth of everything I get.'

[13] "But the tax collector, standing far off, would not even raise his eyes to heaven but kept striking his chest and saying, 'God, turn Your wrath from me—a sinner!' [14] I tell you, this one went down to his house *justified rather than the other; because everyone who exalts himself will be humbled, but the one who humbles himself will be exalted."

[15] Some people were even bringing infants to Him so He might touch them, but when the disciples saw it, they rebuked them. [16] Jesus, however, invited them: "Let the little children come to Me, and don't stop them, because the kingdom of God belongs to such as these. [17] *I assure you: Whoever does not welcome the kingdom of God like a little child will never enter it."

[18] A ruler asked Him, "Good Teacher, what must I do to inherit eternal life?"

[19] "Why do you call Me good?" Jesus asked him. "No one is good but One—God. [20] You know the commandments:

> **Do not commit adultery;**
> **do not murder;**
> **do not steal;**
> **do not bear false witness;**
> **honor your father and mother."**

[21] "I have kept all these from my youth," he said.

[22] When Jesus heard this, He told him, "You still lack one thing: Sell all that you have and distribute it to the poor, and you will have treasure in heaven. Then come, follow Me."

[23] After he heard this, he became extremely sad, because he was very rich.

[24] Seeing that he became sad, Jesus said, "How hard it is for those who have wealth to enter the kingdom of God! [25] For it is easier for a camel to go through the eye of a needle than for a rich person to enter the kingdom of God."

[26] Those who heard this asked, "Then who can be saved?"

[27] He replied, "What is impossible with men is possible with God."

[28] Then Peter said, "Look, we have left what we had and followed You."

[29] So He said to them, "I assure you: There is no one who has left a house, wife or *brothers, parents or children because of the kingdom of God, [30] who will not receive many times more at this time, and eternal life in the age to come."

[31] Then He took the Twelve aside and told them, "Listen! We are going up to Jerusalem. Everything that is written through the prophets about the Son of Man will be accomplished. [32] For He will be handed over to the Gentiles, and He will be mocked, insulted, spit on; [33] and after they flog Him, they will kill Him, and He will rise on the third day."

[34] They understood none of these things. This saying was hidden from them, and they did not grasp what was said.

[35] As He drew near Jericho, a blind man was sitting by the road begging. [36] Hearing a crowd passing by, he inquired what this meant. [37] "Jesus the *Nazarene is passing by," they told him.

[38] So he called out, "Jesus, Son of David, have mercy on me!" [39] Then those in front told him to keep quiet, but he kept crying out all the more, "Son of David, have mercy on me!"

[40] Jesus stopped and commanded that he be brought to Him. When he drew near, He asked him, [41] "What do you want Me to do for you?"

"Lord," he said, "I want to see!"

[42] "Receive your sight!" Jesus told him. "Your faith has healed you." [43] Instantly he could see, and he began to follow Him, glorifying God. All the people, when they saw it, gave praise to God.

19 He entered Jericho and was passing through. [2] There was a man named Zacchaeus who was a chief tax collector, and he was rich. [3] He was trying to see who Jesus was, but he was not able because of the crowd, since he was a short man. [4] So running ahead, he climbed up a sycamore tree to see Jesus, since He was about to pass that way. [5] When Jesus came to the place, He looked up and said to him, "Zacchaeus, hurry and come down because today I must stay at your house."

[6] So he quickly came down and welcomed Him joyfully. [7] All who saw it began to complain, "He's gone to lodge with a sinful man!"

[8] But Zacchaeus stood there and said to the Lord, "Look, I'll give half of my possessions to the poor, Lord! And if I have extorted anything from anyone, I'll pay back four times as much!"

[9] "Today salvation has come to this house," Jesus told him, "because he too is a son of Abraham. [10] For the *Son of Man has come to seek and to save the lost."

[11] As they were listening to this, He went on to tell a parable because He was near Jerusalem, and they thought the kingdom of God was going to appear right away.

[12] Therefore He said: "A nobleman traveled to a far country to receive for himself authority to be king and then return. [13] He called 10 of his *slaves, gave them 10 minas, and told them, 'Engage in business until I come back.'

[14] "But his subjects hated him and sent a delegation after him, saying, 'We don't want this man to rule over us!'

[15] "At his return, having received the authority to be king, he summoned those slaves he had given the money to, so he could find out how much they had made in business. [16] The first came forward and said, 'Master, your mina has earned 10 more minas.'

[17] "'Well done, good slave!' he told him. 'Because you have been faithful in a very small matter, have authority over 10 towns.'

[18] "The second came and said, 'Master, your mina has made five minas.'

[19] "So he said to him, 'You will be over five towns.'

[20] "And another came and said, 'Master, here is your mina. I have kept it hidden away in a cloth [21] because I was afraid of you, for you're a tough man: you collect what you didn't deposit and reap what you didn't sow.'

[22] "He told him, 'I will judge you by what you have said, you evil slave! If you knew I was a tough man, collecting what I didn't deposit and reaping what I didn't sow, [23] why didn't you put my money in the bank? And when I returned, I would have collected it with interest!' [24] So he said to those standing there, 'Take the mina away from him and give it to the one who has 10 minas.'

[25] "But they said to him, 'Master, he has 10 minas.'

[26] "I tell you, that to everyone who has, more will be given; and from the one who does not have, even what he does have will be taken away. [27] But bring here these

enemies of mine, who did not want me to rule over them, and slaughter them in my presence.'"

²⁸When He had said these things, He went on ahead, going up to Jerusalem. ²⁹As He approached Bethphage and Bethany, at the place called the *Mount of Olives, He sent two of the disciples ³⁰and said, "Go into the village ahead of you. As you enter it, you will find a young donkey tied there, on which no one has ever sat. Untie it and bring it here. ³¹If anyone asks you, 'Why are you untying it?' say this: 'The Lord needs it.'"

³²So those who were sent left and found it just as He had told them. ³³As they were untying the young donkey, its owners said to them, "Why are you untying the donkey?"

³⁴"The Lord needs it," they said. ³⁵Then they brought it to Jesus, and after throwing their robes on the donkey, they helped Jesus get on it. ³⁶As He was going along, they were spreading their robes on the road. ³⁷Now He came near the path down the Mount of Olives, and the whole crowd of the disciples began to praise God joyfully with a loud voice for all the miracles they had seen:

³⁸ **The King who comes**
in the name of the Lord
is the blessed One.
Peace in heaven
and glory in the highest heaven!

³⁹Some of the *Pharisees from the crowd told Him, "Teacher, rebuke Your disciples."

⁴⁰He answered, "I tell you, if they were to keep silent, the stones would cry out!"

⁴¹As He approached and saw the city, He wept over it, ⁴²saying, "If you knew this day what would bring peace—but now it is hidden from your eyes. ⁴³For the days will come on you when your enemies will build an embankment against you, surround you, and hem you in on every side. ⁴⁴They will crush you and your children within you to the ground, and they will not leave one stone on another in you, because you did not recognize the time of your visitation."

⁴⁵He went into the *temple complex and began to throw out those who were selling, ⁴⁶and He said, "It is written, **My house will be a house of prayer,** but you have made it **a den of thieves!**"

⁴⁷Every day He was teaching in the temple complex. The *chief priests, the *scribes, and the leaders of the people were looking for a way to destroy Him, ⁴⁸but they could not find a way to do it, because all the people were captivated by what they heard.

20 One day as He was teaching the people in the *temple complex and proclaiming the good news, the *chief priests and the scribes, with the elders, came up ²and said to Him: "Tell us, by what authority are You doing these things? Who is it who gave You this authority?"

³He answered them, "I will also ask you a question. Tell Me, ⁴was the baptism of John from heaven or from men?"

⁵They discussed it among themselves: "If we say, 'From heaven,' He will say, 'Why didn't you believe him?' ⁶But if we say, 'From men,' all the people will stone us, because they are convinced that John was a prophet."

⁷So they answered that they did not know its origin.

⁸And Jesus said to them, "Neither will I tell you by what authority I do these things."

⁹Then He began to tell the people this parable: "A man planted a vineyard, leased it to tenant farmers, and went away for a long time. ¹⁰At harvest time he sent a *slave to the farmers so that they might give him some fruit from the vineyard. But the farmers beat him and sent him away empty-handed. ¹¹He sent yet another slave, but they beat that one too, treated him shamefully, and sent him away empty-handed. ¹²And he sent yet a third, but they wounded this one too and threw him out.

¹³"Then the owner of the vineyard said, 'What should I do? I will send my beloved son. Perhaps they will respect him.'

¹⁴"But when the tenant farmers saw him, they discussed it among themselves and said, 'This is the heir. Let's kill him, so the inheritance will be ours!' ¹⁵So they threw him out of the vineyard and killed him.

"Therefore, what will the owner of the vineyard do to them? ¹⁶He will come and destroy those farmers and give the vineyard to others."

But when they heard this they said, "No—never!"

¹⁷But He looked at them and said, "Then what is the meaning of this Scripture:

The stone that the builders rejected—
this has become the cornerstone?

¹⁸Everyone who falls on that stone will be broken to pieces, and if it falls on anyone, it will grind him to powder!"

¹⁹Then the scribes and the chief priests looked for a way to get their hands on Him that very hour, because they knew He had told this parable against them, but they feared the people.

²⁰They watched closely and sent spies who pretended to be righteous, so they could catch Him in what He said, to hand Him over to the governor's rule and authority. ²¹They questioned Him, "Teacher, we know that You speak and teach correctly, and You don't show partiality, but teach truthfully the way of God. ²²Is it lawful for us to pay taxes to Caesar or not?"

²³But detecting their craftiness, He said to them, ²⁴"Show Me a *denarius. Whose image and inscription does it have?"

"Caesar's," they said.

²⁵"Well then," He told them, "give back to Caesar the things that are Caesar's and to God the things that are God's."

²⁶They were not able to catch Him in what He said in public, and being amazed at His answer, they became silent.

²⁷Some of the *Sadducees, who say there is no resurrection, came up and questioned Him: ²⁸"Teacher, Moses wrote for us that **if a man's brother** has a wife, and **dies childless, his brother should take the wife and produce *offspring for his brother.** ²⁹Now there were seven brothers. The first took a wife and died without children. ³⁰Also the second ³¹and the third took her. In the same way, all seven died and left no children. ³²Finally, the woman died too. ³³In the resurrection, therefore, whose wife will the woman be? For all seven had married her."

³⁴Jesus told them, "The sons of this age marry and are given in marriage. ³⁵But those who are counted worthy to take part in that age and in the resurrection from the dead neither marry nor are given in marriage. ³⁶For they cannot die anymore, because they are like angels and are sons of God, since they are sons of the resurrection. ³⁷Moses even indicated in the passage about the burning bush that the dead are raised,

where he calls the Lord **the God of Abraham and the God of Isaac and the God of Jacob.** [38]He is not God of the dead but of the living, because all are living to Him."

[39]Some of the scribes answered, "Teacher, You have spoken well." [40]And they no longer dared to ask Him anything.

[41]Then He said to them, "How can they say that the *Messiah is the Son of David? [42]For David himself says in the Book of Psalms:

> **The Lord declared to my Lord,**
> **'Sit at My right hand**
> [43]   **until I make Your enemies Your footstool.'**

[44]David calls Him 'Lord'; how then can the Messiah be his Son?"

[45]While all the people were listening, He said to His disciples, [46]"Beware of the scribes, who want to go around in long robes and who love greetings in the marketplaces, the front seats in the *synagogues, and the places of honor at banquets. [47]They devour widows' houses and say long prayers just for show. These will receive greater punishment."

21 He looked up and saw the rich dropping their offerings into the temple treasury. [2]He also saw a poor widow dropping in two tiny coins. [3]"I tell you the truth," He said. "This poor widow has put in more than all of them. [4]For all these people have put in gifts out of their surplus, but she out of her poverty has put in all she had to live on."

[5]As some were talking about the *temple complex, how it was adorned with beautiful stones and gifts dedicated to God, He said, [6]"These things that you see— the days will come when not one stone will be left on another that will not be thrown down!"

[7]"Teacher," they asked Him, "so when will these things be? And what will be the sign when these things are about to take place?"

[8]Then He said, "Watch out that you are not deceived. For many will come in My name, saying, 'I am He,' and, 'The time is near.' Don't follow them. [9]When you hear of wars and rebellions, don't be alarmed. Indeed, these things must take place first, but the end won't come right away."

[10]Then He told them: "Nation will be raised up against nation, and kingdom against kingdom. [11]There will be violent earthquakes, and famines and plagues in various places, and there will be terrifying sights and great signs from heaven. [12]But before all these things, they will lay their hands on you and persecute you. They will hand you over to the *synagogues and prisons, and you will be brought before kings and governors because of My name. [13]It will lead to an opportunity for you to witness. [14]Therefore make up your minds not to prepare your defense ahead of time, [15]for I will give you such words and a wisdom that none of your adversaries will be able to resist or contradict. [16]You will even be betrayed by parents, brothers, relatives, and friends. They will kill some of you. [17]You will be hated by everyone because of My name, [18]but not a hair of your head will be lost. [19]By your endurance gain your *lives.

[20]"When you see Jerusalem surrounded by armies, then recognize that its desolation has come near. [21]Then those in Judea must flee to the mountains! Those inside the city must leave it, and those who are in the country must not enter it, [22]because these are days of vengeance to fulfill all the things that are written. [23]Woe to pregnant women and nursing mothers in those days, for there will be great distress in the land and wrath against this people. [24]They will fall by the edge of the sword and be led captive into all the nations, and Jerusalem will be trampled by the Gentiles until the times of the Gentiles are fulfilled.

[25]"Then there will be signs in the sun, moon, and stars; and there will be anguish on the earth among nations bewildered by the roaring sea and waves. [26]People will faint from fear and expectation of the things that are coming on the world, because the celestial powers will be shaken. [27]Then they will see the *Son of Man coming in a cloud with power and great glory. [28]But when these things begin to take place, stand up and lift up your heads, because your *redemption is near!"

[29]Then He told them a parable: "Look at the fig tree, and all the trees. [30]As soon as they put out leaves you can see for yourselves and recognize that summer is already near. [31]In the same way, when you see these things happening, recognize that the kingdom of God is near. [32]*I assure you: This generation will certainly not pass away until all things take place. [33]Heaven and earth will pass away, but My words will never pass away.

[34]"Be on your guard, so that your minds are not dulled from carousing, drunkenness, and worries of life, or that day will come on you unexpectedly [35]like a trap. For it will come on all who live on the face of the whole earth. [36]But be alert at all times, praying that you may have strength to escape all these things that are going to take place and to stand before the Son of Man."

[37]During the day, He was teaching in the temple complex, but in the evening He would go out and spend the night on what is called the *Mount of Olives. [38]Then all the people would come early in the morning to hear Him in the temple complex.

22 The Festival of *Unleavened Bread, which is called *Passover, was drawing near. [2]The *chief priests and the *scribes were looking for a way to put Him to death, because they were afraid of the people.

[3]Then Satan entered Judas, called Iscariot, who was numbered among the Twelve. [4]He went away and discussed with the chief priests and temple police how he could hand Him over to them. [5]They were glad and agreed to give him silver. [6]So he accepted the offer and started looking for a good opportunity to betray Him to them when the crowd was not present.

[7]Then the Day of Unleavened Bread came when the Passover lamb had to be sacrificed. [8]Jesus sent Peter and John, saying, "Go and prepare the Passover meal for us, so we can eat it."

[9]"Where do You want us to prepare it?" they asked Him.

[10]"Listen," He said to them, "when you've entered the city, a man carrying a water jug will meet you. Follow him into the house he enters. [11]Tell the owner of the house, 'The Teacher asks you, "Where is the guest room where I can eat the Passover with My disciples?"' [12]Then he will show you a large, furnished room upstairs. Make the preparations there."

[13]So they went and found it just as He had told them, and they prepared the Passover.

[14]When the hour came, He reclined at the table, and the apostles with Him. [15]Then He said to them, "I have fervently desired to eat this Passover with you before I

suffer. ¹⁶For I tell you, I will not eat it again until it is fulfilled in the kingdom of God." ¹⁷Then He took a cup, and after giving thanks, He said, "Take this and share it among yourselves. ¹⁸For I tell you, from now on I will not drink of the fruit of the vine until the kingdom of God comes."

¹⁹And He took bread, gave thanks, broke it, gave it to them, and said, "This is My body, which is given for you. Do this in remembrance of Me."

²⁰In the same way He also took the cup after supper and said, "This cup is the new covenant established by My blood; it is shed for you. ²¹But look, the hand of the one betraying Me is at the table with Me! ²²For the ˙Son of Man will go away as it has been determined, but woe to that man by whom He is betrayed!"

²³So they began to argue among themselves which of them it could be who was going to do this thing.

²⁴Then a dispute also arose among them about who should be considered the greatest. ²⁵But He said to them, "The kings of the Gentiles dominate them, and those who have authority over them are called 'Benefactors.' ²⁶But it must not be like that among you. On the contrary, whoever is greatest among you must become like the youngest, and whoever leads, like the one serving. ²⁷For who is greater, the one at the table or the one serving? Isn't it the one at the table? But I am among you as the One who serves. ²⁸You are the ones who stood by Me in My trials. ²⁹I bestow on you a kingdom, just as My Father bestowed one on Me, ³⁰so that you may eat and drink at My table in My kingdom. And you will sit on thrones judging the 12 tribes of Israel.

³¹"Simon, Simon, look out! Satan has asked to sift you like wheat. ³²But I have prayed for you that your faith may not fail. And you, when you have turned back, strengthen your brothers."

³³"Lord," he told Him, "I'm ready to go with You both to prison and to death!"

³⁴"I tell you, Peter," He said, "the rooster will not crow today until you deny three times that you know Me!"

³⁵He also said to them, "When I sent you out without money-bag, traveling bag, or sandals, did you lack anything?"

"Not a thing," they said.

³⁶Then He said to them, "But now, whoever has a money-bag should take it, and also a traveling bag. And whoever doesn't have a sword should sell his robe and buy one. ³⁷For I tell you, what is written must be fulfilled in Me: **And He was counted among the outlaws.** Yes, what is written about Me is coming to its fulfillment."

³⁸"Lord," they said, "look, here are two swords."

"Enough of that!" He told them.

³⁹He went out and made His way as usual to the ˙Mount of Olives, and the disciples followed Him. ⁴⁰When He reached the place, He told them, "Pray that you may not enter into temptation." ⁴¹Then He withdrew from them about a stone's throw, knelt down, and began to pray, ⁴²"Father, if You are willing, take this cup away from Me—nevertheless, not My will, but Yours, be done."

[⁴³Then an angel from heaven appeared to Him, strengthening Him. ⁴⁴Being in anguish, He prayed more fervently, and His sweat became like drops of blood falling to the ground.] ⁴⁵When He got up from prayer and came to the disciples, He found them sleeping, exhausted from their grief. ⁴⁶"Why are you sleeping?" He asked them. "Get up and pray, so that you won't enter into temptation."

⁴⁷While He was still speaking, suddenly a mob was there, and one of the Twelve named Judas was leading them. He came near Jesus to kiss Him, ⁴⁸but Jesus said to him, "Judas, are you betraying the Son of Man with a kiss?"

⁴⁹When those around Him saw what was going to happen, they asked, "Lord, should we strike with the sword?" ⁵⁰Then one of them struck the high priest's ˙slave and cut off his right ear.

⁵¹But Jesus responded, "No more of this!" And touching his ear, He healed him. ⁵²Then Jesus said to the chief priests, temple police, and the elders who had come for Him, "Have you come out with swords and clubs as if I were a criminal? ⁵³Every day while I was with you in the ˙temple complex, you never laid a hand on Me. But this is your hour—and the dominion of darkness."

⁵⁴They seized Him, led Him away, and brought Him into the high priest's house. Meanwhile Peter was following at a distance. ⁵⁵They lit a fire in the middle of the courtyard and sat down together, and Peter sat among them. ⁵⁶When a servant saw him sitting in the firelight, and looked closely at him, she said, "This man was with Him too."

⁵⁷But he denied it: "Woman, I don't know Him!"

⁵⁸After a little while, someone else saw him and said, "You're one of them too!"

"Man, I am not!" Peter said.

⁵⁹About an hour later, another kept insisting, "This man was certainly with Him, since he's also a Galilean."

⁶⁰But Peter said, "Man, I don't know what you're talking about!" Immediately, while he was still speaking, a rooster crowed. ⁶¹Then the Lord turned and looked at Peter. So Peter remembered the word of the Lord, how He had said to him, "Before the rooster crows today, you will deny Me three times." ⁶²And he went outside and wept bitterly.

⁶³The men who were holding Jesus started mocking and beating Him. ⁶⁴After blindfolding Him, they kept asking, "Prophesy! Who hit You?" ⁶⁵And they were saying many other blasphemous things against Him.

⁶⁶When daylight came, the elders of the people, both the chief priests and the scribes, convened and brought Him before their ˙Sanhedrin. ⁶⁷They said, "If You are the ˙Messiah, tell us."

But He said to them, "If I do tell you, you will not believe. ⁶⁸And if I ask you, you will not answer. ⁶⁹But from now on, the Son of Man will be seated at the right hand of the Power of God."

⁷⁰They all asked, "Are You, then, the Son of God?"

And He said to them, "You say that I am."

⁷¹"Why do we need any more testimony," they said, "since we've heard it ourselves from His mouth?"

23 Then their whole assembly rose up and brought Him before ˙Pilate. ²They began to accuse Him, saying, "We found this man subverting our nation, opposing payment of taxes to Caesar, and saying that He Himself is the ˙Messiah, a King."

³So Pilate asked Him, "Are You the King of the Jews?"

He answered him, "You have said it."

⁴Pilate then told the ˙chief priests and the crowds, "I find no grounds for charging this man."

⁵But they kept insisting, "He stirs up the people, teaching throughout all Judea, from Galilee where He started even to here."

⁶When Pilate heard this, he asked if the man was a Galilean. ⁷Finding that He was under ˙Herod's jurisdiction, he sent Him to Herod, who was also in Jerusalem during those days. ⁸Herod was very glad to see Jesus; for a long time he had wanted to see Him because he had heard about Him and was hoping to see some miracle performed by Him. ⁹So he kept asking Him questions, but Jesus did not answer him. ¹⁰The chief priests and the ˙scribes stood by, vehemently accusing Him. ¹¹Then Herod, with his soldiers, treated Him with contempt, mocked Him, dressed Him in a brilliant robe, and sent Him back to Pilate. ¹²That very day Herod and Pilate became friends. Previously, they had been hostile toward each other.

¹³Pilate called together the chief priests, the leaders, and the people, ¹⁴and said to them, "You have brought me this man as one who subverts the people. But in fact, after examining Him in your presence, I have found no grounds to charge this man with those things you accuse Him of. ¹⁵Neither has Herod, because he sent Him back to us. Clearly, He has done nothing to deserve death. ¹⁶Therefore, I will have Him whipped and then release Him." [¹⁷For according to the festival he had to release someone to them.]

¹⁸Then they all cried out together, "Take this man away! Release Barabbas to us!" ¹⁹(He had been thrown into prison for a rebellion that had taken place in the city, and for murder.)

²⁰Pilate, wanting to release Jesus, addressed them again, ²¹but they kept shouting, "Crucify! Crucify Him!"

²²A third time he said to them, "Why? What has this man done wrong? I have found in Him no grounds for the death penalty. Therefore, I will have Him whipped and then release Him."

²³But they kept up the pressure, demanding with loud voices that He be crucified. And their voices won out. ²⁴So Pilate decided to grant their demand ²⁵and released the one they were asking for, who had been thrown into prison for rebellion and murder. But he handed Jesus over to their will.

²⁶As they led Him away, they seized Simon, a Cyrenian, who was coming in from the country, and laid the cross on him to carry behind Jesus. ²⁷A large crowd of people followed Him, including women who were mourning and lamenting Him. ²⁸But turning to them, Jesus said, "Daughters of Jerusalem, do not weep for Me, but weep for yourselves and your children. ²⁹Look, the days are coming when they will say, 'The women without children, the wombs that never bore and the breasts that never nursed, are fortunate!' ³⁰Then they will begin **to say to the mountains, 'Fall on us!' and to the hills, 'Cover us!'** ³¹For if they do these things when the wood is green, what will happen when it is dry?"

³²Two others—criminals—were also led away to be executed with Him. ³³When they arrived at the place called The Skull, they crucified Him there, along with the criminals, one on the right and one on the left. [³⁴Then Jesus said, "Father, forgive them, because they do not know what they are doing."] And they divided His clothes and cast lots.

³⁵The people stood watching, and even the leaders kept scoffing: "He saved others; let Him save Himself if this is God's Messiah, the Chosen One!" ³⁶The sol-diers also mocked Him. They came offering Him sour wine ³⁷and said, "If You are the King of the Jews, save Yourself!"

³⁸An inscription was above Him:

THIS IS THE KING OF THE JEWS.

³⁹Then one of the criminals hanging there began to yell insults at Him: "Aren't You the Messiah? Save Yourself and us!"

⁴⁰But the other answered, rebuking him: "Don't you even fear God, since you are undergoing the same punishment? ⁴¹We are punished justly, because we're getting back what we deserve for the things we did, but this man has done nothing wrong." ⁴²Then he said, "Jesus, remember me when You come into Your kingdom!"

⁴³And He said to him, "'I assure you: Today you will be with Me in paradise."

⁴⁴It was now about noon, and darkness came over the whole land until three, ⁴⁵because the sun's light failed. The curtain of the sanctuary was split down the middle. ⁴⁶And Jesus called out with a loud voice, "Father, **into Your hands I entrust My spirit.**" Saying this, He breathed His last.

⁴⁷When the ˙centurion saw what happened, he began to glorify God, saying, "This man really was righteous!" ⁴⁸All the crowds that had gathered for this spectacle, when they saw what had taken place, went home, striking their chests. ⁴⁹But all who knew Him, including the women who had followed Him from Galilee, stood at a distance, watching these things.

⁵⁰There was a good and righteous man named Joseph, a member of the ˙Sanhedrin, ⁵¹who had not agreed with their plan and action. He was from Arimathea, a Judean town, and was looking forward to the kingdom of God. ⁵²He approached Pilate and asked for Jesus' body. ⁵³Taking it down, he wrapped it in fine linen and placed it in a tomb cut into the rock, where no one had ever been placed. ⁵⁴It was preparation day, and the Sabbath was about to begin. ⁵⁵The women who had come with Him from Galilee followed along and observed the tomb and how His body was placed. ⁵⁶Then they returned and prepared spices and perfumes. And they rested on the Sabbath according to the commandment.

24 On the first day of the week, very early in the morning, they came to the tomb, bringing the spices they had prepared. ²They found the stone rolled away from the tomb. ³They went in but did not find the body of the Lord Jesus. ⁴While they were perplexed about this, suddenly two men stood by them in dazzling clothes. ⁵So the women were terrified and bowed down to the ground.

"Why are you looking for the living among the dead?" asked the men. ⁶"He is not here, but He has been resurrected! Remember how He spoke to you when He was still in Galilee, ⁷saying, 'The ˙Son of Man must be betrayed into the hands of sinful men, be crucified, and rise on the third day'?" ⁸And they remembered His words.

⁹Returning from the tomb, they reported all these things to the Eleven and to all the rest. ¹⁰˙Mary Magdalene, Joanna, Mary the mother of James, and the other women with them were telling the apostles these things. ¹¹But these words seemed like nonsense to them, and they did not believe the women. ¹²Peter, however, got up and ran to the tomb. When he stooped

to look in, he saw only the linen cloths. So he went home, amazed at what had happened.

¹³Now that same day two of them were on their way to a village called Emmaus, which was about seven miles from Jerusalem. ¹⁴Together they were discussing everything that had taken place. ¹⁵And while they were discussing and arguing, Jesus Himself came near and began to walk along with them. ¹⁶But they were prevented from recognizing Him. ¹⁷Then He asked them, "What is this dispute that you're having with each other as you are walking?" And they stopped walking and looked discouraged.

¹⁸The one named Cleopas answered Him, "Are You the only visitor in Jerusalem who doesn't know the things that happened there in these days?"

¹⁹"What things?" He asked them.

So they said to Him, "The things concerning Jesus the •Nazarene, who was a Prophet powerful in action and speech before God and all the people, ²⁰and how our •chief priests and leaders handed Him over to be sentenced to death, and they crucified Him. ²¹But we were hoping that He was the One who was about to •redeem Israel. Besides all this, it's the third day since these things happened. ²²Moreover, some women from our group astounded us. They arrived early at the tomb, ²³and when they didn't find His body, they came and reported that they had seen a vision of angels who said He was alive. ²⁴Some of those who were with us went to the tomb and found it just as the women had said, but they didn't see Hím."

²⁵He said to them, "How unwise and slow you are to believe in your hearts all that the prophets have spoken! ²⁶Didn't the •Messiah have to suffer these things and enter into His glory?" ²⁷Then beginning with Moses and all the Prophets, He interpreted for them the things concerning Himself in all the Scriptures.

²⁸They came near the village where they were going, and He gave the impression that He was going farther. ²⁹But they urged Him: "Stay with us, because it's almost evening, and now the day is almost over." So He went in to stay with them.

³⁰It was as He reclined at the table with them that He took the bread, blessed and broke it, and gave it to them. ³¹Then their eyes were opened, and they recognized Him, but He disappeared from their sight. ³²So they said to each other, "Weren't our hearts ablaze within us while He was talking with us on the road and explaining the Scriptures to us?" ³³That very hour they got up and returned to Jerusalem. They found the Eleven and those with them gathered together, ³⁴who said, "The Lord has certainly been raised, and has appeared to Simon!" ³⁵Then they began to describe what had happened on the road and how He was made known to them in the breaking of the bread.

³⁶And as they were saying these things, He Himself stood among them. He said to them, "Peace to you!" ³⁷But they were startled and terrified and thought they were seeing a ghost. ³⁸"Why are you troubled?" He asked them. "And why do doubts arise in your hearts? ³⁹Look at My hands and My feet, that it is I Myself! Touch Me and see, because a ghost does not have flesh and bones as you can see I have." ⁴⁰Having said this, He showed them His hands and feet. ⁴¹But while they still were amazed and unbelieving because of their joy, He asked them, "Do you have anything here to eat?" ⁴²So they gave Him a piece of a broiled fish, ⁴³and He took it and ate in their presence.

⁴⁴Then He told them, "These are My words that I spoke to you while I was still with you—that everything written about Me in the Law of Moses, the Prophets, and the Psalms must be fulfilled." ⁴⁵Then He opened their minds to understand the Scriptures. ⁴⁶He also said to them, "This is what is written: The Messiah would suffer and rise from the dead the third day, ⁴⁷and repentance for forgiveness of sins would be proclaimed in His name to all the nations, beginning at Jerusalem. ⁴⁸You are witnesses of these things. ⁴⁹And look, I am sending you what My Father promised. As for you, stay in the city until you are empowered from on high."

⁵⁰Then He led them out as far as Bethany, and lifting up His hands He blessed them. ⁵¹And while He was blessing them, He left them and was carried up into heaven. ⁵²After worshiping Him, they returned to Jerusalem with great joy. ⁵³And they were continually in the •temple complex praising God.

JOHN

1 In the beginning was the Word,
and the Word was with God,
and the Word was God.
² He was with God in the beginning.
³ All things were created through Him,
and apart from Him not one thing was created
that has been created.
⁴ Life was in Him,
and that life was the light of men.
⁵ That light shines in the darkness,
yet the darkness did not overcome it.
⁶ There was a man named John
who was sent from God.
⁷ He came as a witness
to testify about the light,
so that all might believe through him.
⁸ He was not the light,
but he came to testify about the light.

⁹ The true light, who gives light to everyone,
was coming into the world.
¹⁰ He was in the world,
and the world was created through Him,
yet the •world did not recognize Him.
¹¹ He came to His own,
and His own people did not receive Him.
¹² But to all who did receive Him,
He gave them the right to be children of God,
to those who believe in His name,
¹³ who were born,
not of blood,
or of the will of the flesh,
or of the will of man,
but of God.
¹⁴ The Word became flesh
and took up residence among us.
We observed His glory,

the glory as the •One and Only Son
from the Father,
full of grace and truth.
15 (John testified concerning Him
and exclaimed,
"This was the One of whom I said,
'The One coming after me has surpassed me,
because He existed before me.'")
16 Indeed, we have all received grace after grace
from His fullness,
17 for the law was given through Moses,
grace and truth came through Jesus Christ.
18 No one has ever seen God.
The One and Only Son—
the One who is at the Father's side—
He has revealed Him.

19 This is John's testimony when the •Jews from Jerusalem sent priests and Levites to ask him, "Who are you?"
20 He did not refuse to answer, but he declared: "I am not the •Messiah."
21 "What then?" they asked him. "Are you Elijah?"
"I am not," he said.
"Are you the Prophet?"
"No," he answered.
22 "Who are you, then?" they asked. "We need to give an answer to those who sent us. What can you tell us about yourself?"
23 He said, "I am a **voice of one crying out in the wilderness: Make straight the way of the Lord**—just as Isaiah the prophet said."
24 Now they had been sent from the •Pharisees. 25 So they asked him, "Why then do you baptize if you aren't the Messiah, or Elijah, or the Prophet?"
26 "I baptize with water," John answered them. "Someone stands among you, but you don't know Him. 27 He is the One coming after me, whose sandal strap I'm not worthy to untie."
28 All this happened in Bethany across the Jordan, where John was baptizing.
29 The next day John saw Jesus coming toward him and said, "Here is the Lamb of God, who takes away the sin of the world! 30 This is the One I told you about: 'After me comes a man who has surpassed me, because He existed before me.' 31 I didn't know Him, but I came baptizing with water so He might be revealed to Israel."
32 And John testified, "I watched the Spirit descending from heaven like a dove, and He rested on Him. 33 I didn't know Him, but He who sent me to baptize with water told me, 'The One you see the Spirit descending and resting on—He is the One who baptizes with the Holy Spirit.' 34 I have seen and testified that He is the Son of God!"
35 Again the next day, John was standing with two of his disciples. 36 When he saw Jesus passing by, he said, "Look! The Lamb of God!"
37 The two disciples heard him say this and followed Jesus. 38 When Jesus turned and noticed them following Him, He asked them, "What are you looking for?"
They said to Him, "'Rabbi' (which means "Teacher"), "where are You staying?"
39 "Come and you'll see," He replied. So they went and saw where He was staying, and they stayed with Him that day. It was about 10 in the morning.
40 Andrew, Simon Peter's brother, was one of the two who heard John and followed Him. 41 He first found

his own brother Simon and told him, "We have found the Messiah!" (which means "Anointed One"), 42 and he brought Simon to Jesus.
When Jesus saw him, He said, "You are Simon, son of John. You will be called •Cephas" (which means "Rock").
43 The next day He decided to leave for Galilee. Jesus found Philip and told him, "Follow Me!"
44 Now Philip was from Bethsaida, the hometown of Andrew and Peter. 45 Philip found Nathanael and told him, "We have found the One Moses wrote about in the Law (and so did the prophets): Jesus the son of Joseph, from Nazareth!"
46 "Can anything good come out of Nazareth?" Nathanael asked him.
"Come and see," Philip answered.
47 Then Jesus saw Nathanael coming toward Him and said about him, "Here is a true Israelite; no deceit is in him."
48 "How do you know me?" Nathanael asked.
"Before Philip called you, when you were under the fig tree, I saw you," Jesus answered.
49 "Rabbi," Nathanael replied, "You are the Son of God! You are the King of Israel!"
50 Jesus responded to him, "Do you believe only because I told you I saw you under the fig tree? You will see greater things than this." 51 Then He said, "I assure you: You will see heaven opened and the angels of God ascending and descending on the •Son of Man."

2 On the third day a wedding took place in Cana of Galilee. Jesus' mother was there, and 2 Jesus and His disciples were invited to the wedding as well. 3 When the wine ran out, Jesus' mother told Him, "They don't have any wine."
4 "What has this concern of yours to do with Me, •woman?" Jesus asked. "My hour has not yet come."
5 "Do whatever He tells you," His mother told the servants.
6 Now six stone water jars had been set there for Jewish purification. Each contained 20 or 30 gallons.
7 "Fill the jars with water," Jesus told them. So they filled them to the brim. 8 Then He said to them, "Now draw some out and take it to the chief servant." And they did.
9 When the chief servant tasted the water (after it had become wine), he did not know where it came from—though the servants who had drawn the water knew. He called the groom 10 and told him, "Everyone sets out the fine wine first, then, after people have drunk freely, the inferior. But you have kept the fine wine until now."
11 Jesus performed this first sign in Cana of Galilee. He displayed His glory, and His disciples believed in Him.
12 After this, He went down to Capernaum, together with His mother, His brothers, and His disciples, and they stayed there only a few days.
13 The Jewish •Passover was near, so Jesus went up to Jerusalem. 14 In the •temple complex He found people selling oxen, sheep, and doves, and He also found the money changers sitting there. 15 After making a whip out of cords, He drove everyone out of the temple complex with their sheep and oxen. He also poured out the money changers' coins and overturned the tables. 16 He told those who were selling doves, "Get these things out of here! Stop turning My Father's house into a marketplace!"

[17] And His disciples remembered that it is written:
Zeal for Your house will consume Me.

[18] So the *Jews replied to Him, "What sign of authority will You show us for doing these things?"

[19] Jesus answered, "Destroy this sanctuary, and I will raise it up in three days."

[20] Therefore the Jews said, "This sanctuary took 46 years to build, and will You raise it up in three days?" [21] But He was speaking about the sanctuary of His body. [22] So when He was raised from the dead, His disciples remembered that He had said this. And they believed the Scripture and the statement Jesus had made.

[23] While He was in Jerusalem at the Passover Festival, many trusted in His name when they saw the signs He was doing. [24] Jesus, however, would not entrust Himself to them, since He knew them all [25] and because He did not need anyone to testify about man; for He Himself knew what was in man.

3 There was a man from the *Pharisees named Nicodemus, a ruler of the *Jews. [2] This man came to Him at night and said, "*Rabbi, we know that You have come from God as a teacher, for no one could perform these signs You do unless God were with him."

[3] Jesus replied, "*I assure you: Unless someone is born again, he cannot see the kingdom of God."

[4] "But how can anyone be born when he is old?" Nicodemus asked Him. "Can he enter his mother's womb a second time and be born?"

[5] Jesus answered, "I assure you: Unless someone is born of water and the Spirit, he cannot enter the kingdom of God. [6] Whatever is born of the flesh is flesh, and whatever is born of the Spirit is spirit. [7] Do not be amazed that I told you that you must be born again. [8] The wind blows where it pleases, and you hear its sound, but you don't know where it comes from or where it is going. So it is with everyone born of the Spirit."

[9] "How can these things be?" asked Nicodemus.

[10] "Are you a teacher of Israel and don't know these things?" Jesus replied. [11] "I assure you: We speak what We know and We testify to what We have seen, but you do not accept Our testimony. [12] If I have told you about things that happen on earth and you don't believe, how will you believe if I tell you about things of heaven? [13] No one has ascended into heaven except the One who descended from heaven—the *Son of Man. [14] Just as Moses lifted up the snake in the wilderness, so the Son of Man must be lifted up, [15] so that everyone who believes in Him will have eternal life.

[16] "For God loved the world *in this way: He gave His *One and Only Son, so that everyone who believes in Him will not perish but have eternal life. [17] For God did not send His Son into the world that He might condemn the world, but that the world might be saved through Him. [18] Anyone who believes in Him is not condemned, but anyone who does not believe is already condemned, because he has not believed in the name of the One and Only Son of God.

[19] "This, then, is the judgment: The light has come into the world, and people loved darkness rather than the light because their deeds were evil. [20] For everyone who practices wicked things hates the light and avoids it, so that his deeds may not be exposed. [21] But anyone who lives by the truth comes to the light, so that his works may be shown to be accomplished by God."

[22] After this, Jesus and His disciples went to the Judean countryside, where He spent time with them and baptized. [23] John also was baptizing in Aenon near Salim, because there was plenty of water there. People were coming and being baptized, [24] since John had not yet been thrown into prison.

[25] Then a dispute arose between John's disciples and a Jew about purification. [26] So they came to John and told him, "Rabbi, the One you testified about, and who was with you across the Jordan, is baptizing—and everyone is flocking to Him."

[27] John responded, "No one can receive a single thing unless it's given to him from heaven. [28] You yourselves can testify that I said, 'I am not the *Messiah, but I've been sent ahead of Him.' [29] He who has the bride is the groom. But the groom's friend, who stands by and listens for him, rejoices greatly at the groom's voice. So this joy of mine is complete. [30] He must increase, but I must decrease."

[31] The One who comes from above is above all. The one who is from the earth is earthly and speaks in earthly terms. The One who comes from heaven is above all. [32] He testifies to what He has seen and heard, yet no one accepts His testimony. [33] The one who has accepted His testimony has affirmed that God is true. [34] For God sent Him, and He speaks God's words, since He gives the Spirit without measure. [35] The Father loves the Son and has given all things into His hands. [36] The one who believes in the Son has eternal life, but the one who refuses to believe in the Son will not see life; instead, the wrath of God remains on him.

4 When Jesus knew that the *Pharisees heard He was making and baptizing more disciples than John [2] (though Jesus Himself was not baptizing, but His disciples were), [3] He left Judea and went again to Galilee. [4] He had to travel through Samaria, [5] so He came to a town of Samaria called Sychar near the property that Jacob had given his son Joseph. [6] Jacob's well was there, and Jesus, worn out from His journey, sat down at the well. It was about six in the evening.

[7] A woman of Samaria came to draw water.

"Give Me a drink," Jesus said to her, [8] for His disciples had gone into town to buy food.

[9] "How is it that You, a Jew, ask for a drink from me, a *Samaritan woman?" she asked Him. For Jews do not associate with Samaritans.

[10] Jesus answered, "If you knew the gift of God, and who is saying to you, 'Give Me a drink,' you would ask Him, and He would give you living water."

[11] "Sir," said the woman, "You don't even have a bucket, and the well is deep. So where do You get this 'living water'? [12] You aren't greater than our father Jacob, are You? He gave us the well and drank from it himself, as did his sons and livestock."

[13] Jesus said, "Everyone who drinks from this water will get thirsty again. [14] But whoever drinks from the water that I will give him will never get thirsty again—ever! In fact, the water I will give him will become a well of water springing up within him for eternal life."

[15] "Sir," the woman said to Him, "give me this water so I won't get thirsty and come here to draw water."

[16] "Go call your husband," He told her, "and come back here."

[17] "I don't have a husband," she answered.

"You have correctly said, 'I don't have a husband,'" Jesus said. [18] "For you've had five husbands, and the man you now have is not your husband. What you have said is true."

[19] "Sir," the woman replied, "I see that You are a prophet. [20] Our fathers worshiped on this mountain, yet you Jews say that the place to worship is in Jerusalem."

[21] Jesus told her, "Believe Me, ʻwoman, an hour is coming when you will worship the Father neither on this mountain nor in Jerusalem. [22] You Samaritans worship what you do not know. We worship what we do know, because salvation is from the Jews. [23] But an hour is coming, and is now here, when the true worshipers will worship the Father in spirit and truth. Yes, the Father wants such people to worship Him. [24] God is spirit, and those who worship Him must worship in spirit and truth."

[25] The woman said to Him, "I know that ʻMessiah is coming" (who is called Christ). "When He comes, He will explain everything to us."

[26] "I am He," Jesus told her, "the One speaking to you."

[27] Just then His disciples arrived, and they were amazed that He was talking with a woman. Yet no one said, "What do You want?" or "Why are You talking with her?"

[28] Then the woman left her water jar, went into town, and told the men, [29] "Come, see a man who told me everything I ever did! Could this be the Messiah?" [30] They left the town and made their way to Him.

[31] In the meantime the disciples kept urging Him, "ʻRabbi, eat something."

[32] But He said, "I have food to eat that you don't know about."

[33] The disciples said to one another, "Could someone have brought Him something to eat?"

[34] "My food is to do the will of Him who sent Me and to finish His work," Jesus told them. [35] "Don't you say, 'There are still four more months, then comes the harvest'? Listen to what I'm telling you: Open your eyes and look at the fields, for they are ready for harvest. [36] The reaper is already receiving pay and gathering fruit for eternal life, so the sower and reaper can rejoice together. [37] For in this case the saying is true: 'One sows and another reaps.' [38] I sent you to reap what you didn't labor for; others have labored, and you have benefited from their labor."

[39] Now many Samaritans from that town believed in Him because of what the woman said when she testified, "He told me everything I ever did." [40] Therefore, when the Samaritans came to Him, they asked Him to stay with them, and He stayed there two days. [41] Many more believed because of what He said. [42] And they told the woman, "We no longer believe because of what you said, for we have heard for ourselves and know that this really is the Savior of the world."

[43] After two days He left there for Galilee. [44] Jesus Himself testified that a prophet has no honor in his own country. [45] When they entered Galilee, the Galileans welcomed Him because they had seen everything He did in Jerusalem during the festival. For they also had gone to the festival.

[46] Then He went again to Cana of Galilee, where He had turned the water into wine. There was a certain royal official whose son was ill at Capernaum. [47] When this man heard that Jesus had come from Judea into Galilee, he went to Him and pleaded with Him to come down and heal his son, for he was about to die.

[48] Jesus told him, "Unless you people see signs and wonders, you will not believe."

[49] "Sir," the official said to Him, "come down before my boy dies!"

[50] "Go," Jesus told him, "your son will live." The man believed what Jesus said to him and departed.

[51] While he was still going down, his ʻslaves met him saying that his boy was alive. [52] He asked them at what time he got better. "Yesterday at seven in the morning the fever left him," they answered. [53] The father realized this was the very hour at which Jesus had told him, "Your son will live." Then he himself believed, along with his whole household.

[54] This, therefore, was the second sign Jesus performed after He came from Judea to Galilee.

5 After this, a Jewish festival took place, and Jesus went up to Jerusalem. [2] By the Sheep Gate in Jerusalem there is a pool, called Bethesda in ʻHebrew, which has five colonnades. [3] Within these lay a large number of the sick—blind, lame, and paralyzed [—waiting for the moving of the water, [4] because an angel would go down into the pool from time to time and stir up the water. Then the first one who got in after the water was stirred up recovered from whatever ailment he had].

[5] One man was there who had been sick for 38 years. [6] When Jesus saw him lying there and knew he had already been there a long time, He said to him, "Do you want to get well?"

[7] "Sir," the sick man answered, "I don't have a man to put me into the pool when the water is stirred up, but while I'm coming, someone goes down ahead of me."

[8] "Get up," Jesus told him, "pick up your mat and walk!" [9] Instantly the man got well, picked up his mat, and started to walk.

Now that day was the Sabbath, [10] so the ʻJews said to the man who had been healed, "This is the Sabbath! It's illegal for you to pick up your mat."

[11] He replied, "The man who made me well told me, 'Pick up your mat and walk.'"

[12] "Who is this man who told you, 'Pick up your mat and walk'?" they asked. [13] But the man who was cured did not know who it was, because Jesus had slipped away into the crowd that was there.

[14] After this, Jesus found him in the ʻtemple complex and said to him, "See, you are well. Do not sin anymore, so that something worse doesn't happen to you." [15] The man went and reported to the Jews that it was Jesus who had made him well.

[16] Therefore, the Jews began persecuting Jesus because He was doing these things on the Sabbath. [17] But Jesus responded to them, "My Father is still working, and I am working also." [18] This is why the Jews began trying all the more to kill Him: Not only was He breaking the Sabbath, but He was even calling God His own Father, making Himself equal with God.

[19] Then Jesus replied, "ʻI assure you: The Son is not able to do anything on His own, but only what He sees the Father doing. For whatever the Father does, the Son also does these things in the same way. [20] For the Father loves the Son and shows Him everything He is doing, and He will show Him greater works than these so that you will be amazed. [21] And just as the Father raises the dead and gives them life, so the Son also gives life to anyone He wants to. [22] The Father, in fact, judges no one but has given all judgment to the Son, [23] so that all people will honor the Son just as they honor the Father. Anyone who does not honor the Son does not honor the Father who sent Him.

²⁴"I assure you: Anyone who hears My word and believes Him who sent Me has eternal life and will not come under judgment but has passed from death to life.

²⁵"I assure you: An hour is coming, and is now here, when the dead will hear the voice of the Son of God, and those who hear will live. ²⁶For just as the Father has life in Himself, so also He has granted to the Son to have life in Himself. ²⁷And He has granted Him the right to pass judgment, because He is the ˙Son of Man. ²⁸Do not be amazed at this, because a time is coming when all who are in the graves will hear His voice ²⁹and come out—those who have done good things, to the resurrection of life, but those who have done wicked things, to the resurrection of judgment.

³⁰"I can do nothing on My own. I judge only as I hear, and My judgment is righteous, because I do not seek My own will, but the will of Him who sent Me.

³¹"If I testify about Myself, My testimony is not valid. ³²There is Another who testifies about Me, and I know that the testimony He gives about Me is valid. ³³You have sent messengers to John, and he has testified to the truth. ³⁴I don't receive man's testimony, but I say these things so that you may be saved. ³⁵John was a burning and shining lamp, and for a time you were willing to enjoy his light.

³⁶"But I have a greater testimony than John's because of the works that the Father has given Me to accomplish. These very works I am doing testify about Me that the Father has sent Me. ³⁷The Father who sent Me has Himself testified about Me. You have not heard His voice at any time, and you haven't seen His form. ³⁸You don't have His word living in you, because you don't believe the One He sent. ³⁹You pore over the Scriptures because you think you have eternal life in them, yet they testify about Me. ⁴⁰And you are not willing to come to Me so that you may have life.

⁴¹"I do not accept glory from men, ⁴²but I know you—that you have no love for God within you. ⁴³I have come in My Father's name, yet you don't accept Me. If someone else comes in his own name, you will accept him. ⁴⁴How can you believe? While accepting glory from one another, you don't seek the glory that comes from the only God. ⁴⁵Do not think that I will accuse you to the Father. Your accuser is Moses, on whom you have set your hope. ⁴⁶For if you believed Moses, you would believe Me, because he wrote about Me. ⁴⁷But if you don't believe his writings, how will you believe My words?"

6 After this, Jesus crossed the Sea of Galilee (or Tiberias). ²And a huge crowd was following Him because they saw the signs that He was performing by healing the sick. ³So Jesus went up a mountain and sat down there with His disciples.

⁴Now the ˙Passover, a Jewish festival, was near. ⁵Therefore, when Jesus looked up and noticed a huge crowd coming toward Him, He asked Philip, "Where will we buy bread so these people can eat?" ⁶He asked this to test him, for He Himself knew what He was going to do.

⁷Philip answered, "Two hundred ˙denarii worth of bread wouldn't be enough for each of them to have a little."

⁸One of His disciples, Andrew, Simon Peter's brother, said to Him, ⁹"There's a boy here who has five barley loaves and two fish—but what are they for so many?"

¹⁰Then Jesus said, "Have the people sit down."

There was plenty of grass in that place, so they sat down. The men numbered about 5,000. ¹¹Then Jesus took the loaves, and after giving thanks He distributed them to those who were seated—so also with the fish, as much as they wanted.

¹²When they were full, He told His disciples, "Collect the leftovers so that nothing is wasted." ¹³So they collected them and filled 12 baskets with the pieces from the five barley loaves that were left over by those who had eaten.

¹⁴When the people saw the sign He had done, they said, "This really is the Prophet who was to come into the world!" ¹⁵Therefore, when Jesus knew that they were about to come and take Him by force to make Him king, He withdrew again to the mountain by Himself.

¹⁶When evening came, His disciples went down to the sea, ¹⁷got into a boat, and started across the sea to Capernaum. Darkness had already set in, but Jesus had not yet come to them. ¹⁸Then a high wind arose, and the sea began to churn. ¹⁹After they had rowed about three or four miles, they saw Jesus walking on the sea. He was coming near the boat, and they were afraid.

²⁰But He said to them, "It is I. Don't be afraid!" ²¹Then they were willing to take Him on board, and at once the boat was at the shore where they were heading.

²²The next day, the crowd that had stayed on the other side of the sea knew there had been only one boat. They also knew that Jesus had not boarded the boat with His disciples, but that His disciples had gone off alone. ²³Some boats from Tiberias came near the place where they ate the bread after the Lord gave thanks. ²⁴When the crowd saw that neither Jesus nor His disciples were there, they got into the boats and went to Capernaum looking for Jesus.

²⁵When they found Him on the other side of the sea, they said to Him, "˙Rabbi, when did You get here?"

²⁶Jesus answered, "˙I assure you: You are looking for Me, not because you saw the signs, but because you ate the loaves and were filled. ²⁷Don't work for the food that perishes but for the food that lasts for eternal life, which the ˙Son of Man will give you, because God the Father has set His seal of approval on Him."

²⁸"What can we do to perform the works of God?" they asked.

²⁹Jesus replied, "This is the work of God—that you believe in the One He has sent."

³⁰"What sign then are You going to do so we may see and believe You?" they asked. "What are You going to perform? ³¹Our fathers ate the manna in the wilderness, just as it is written: **He gave them bread from heaven to eat.**"

³²Jesus said to them, "I assure you: Moses didn't give you the bread from heaven, but My Father gives you the real bread from heaven. ³³For the bread of God is the One who comes down from heaven and gives life to the world."

³⁴Then they said, "Sir, give us this bread always!"

³⁵"I am the bread of life," Jesus told them. "No one who comes to Me will ever be hungry, and no one who believes in Me will ever be thirsty again. ³⁶But as I told you, you've seen Me, and yet you do not believe. ³⁷Everyone the Father gives Me will come to Me, and the one who comes to Me I will never cast out. ³⁸For I have come down from heaven, not to do My will, but the

will of Him who sent Me. [39] This is the will of Him who sent Me: that I should lose none of those He has given Me but should raise them up on the last day. [40] For this is the will of My Father: that everyone who sees the Son and believes in Him may have eternal life, and I will raise him up on the last day."

[41] Therefore the ˈJews started complaining about Him because He said, "I am the bread that came down from heaven." [42] They were saying, "Isn't this Jesus the son of Joseph, whose father and mother we know? How can He now say, 'I have come down from heaven'?"

[43] Jesus answered them, "Stop complaining among yourselves. [44] No one can come to Me unless the Father who sent Me draws him, and I will raise him up on the last day. [45] It is written in the Prophets: **And they will all be taught by God.** Everyone who has listened to and learned from the Father comes to Me— [46] not that anyone has seen the Father except the One who is from God. He has seen the Father.

[47] "I assure you: Anyone who believes has eternal life. [48] I am the bread of life. [49] Your fathers ate the manna in the wilderness, and they died. [50] This is the bread that comes down from heaven so that anyone may eat of it and not die. [51] I am the living bread that came down from heaven. If anyone eats of this bread he will live forever. The bread that I will give for the life of the world is My flesh."

[52] At that, the Jews argued among themselves, "How can this man give us His flesh to eat?"

[53] So Jesus said to them, "I assure you: Unless you eat the flesh of the Son of Man and drink His blood, you do not have life in yourselves. [54] Anyone who eats My flesh and drinks My blood has eternal life, and I will raise him up on the last day, [55] because My flesh is real food and My blood is real drink. [56] The one who eats My flesh and drinks My blood lives in Me, and I in him. [57] Just as the living Father sent Me and I live because of the Father, so the one who feeds on Me will live because of Me. [58] This is the bread that came down from heaven; it is not like the manna your fathers ate—and they died. The one who eats this bread will live forever."

[59] He said these things while teaching in the ˈsynagogue in Capernaum.

[60] Therefore, when many of His disciples heard this, they said, "This teaching is hard! Who can accept it?"

[61] Jesus, knowing in Himself that His disciples were complaining about this, asked them, "Does this ˈoffend you? [62] Then what if you were to observe the Son of Man ascending to where He was before? [63] The Spirit is the One who gives life. The flesh doesn't help at all. The words that I have spoken to you are spirit and are life. [64] But there are some among you who don't believe." (For Jesus knew from the beginning those who would not believe and the one who would betray Him.) [65] He said, "This is why I told you that no one can come to Me unless it is granted to him by the Father."

[66] From that moment many of His disciples turned back and no longer accompanied Him. [67] Therefore Jesus said to the Twelve, "You don't want to go away too, do you?"

[68] Simon Peter answered, "Lord, who will we go to? You have the words of eternal life. [69] We have come to believe and know that You are the Holy One of God!"

[70] Jesus replied to them, "Didn't I choose you, the Twelve? Yet one of you is the Devil!" [71] He was referring to Judas, Simon Iscariot's son, one of the Twelve, because he was going to betray Him.

7 After this, Jesus traveled in Galilee, since He did not want to travel in Judea because the ˈJews were trying to kill Him. [2] The Jewish Festival of Tabernacles was near, [3] so His brothers said to Him, "Leave here and go to Judea so Your disciples can see Your works that You are doing. [4] For no one does anything in secret while he's seeking public recognition. If You do these things, show Yourself to the world." [5] (For not even His brothers believed in Him.)

[6] Jesus told them, "My time has not yet arrived, but your time is always at hand. [7] The world cannot hate you, but it does hate Me because I testify about it—that its deeds are evil. [8] Go up to the festival yourselves. I'm not going up to the festival yet, because My time has not yet fully come." [9] After He had said these things, He stayed in Galilee.

[10] After His brothers had gone up to the festival, then He also went up, not openly but secretly. [11] The Jews were looking for Him at the festival and saying, "Where is He?" [12] And there was a lot of discussion about Him among the crowds. Some were saying, "He's a good man." Others were saying, "No, on the contrary, He's deceiving the people." [13] Still, nobody was talking publicly about Him because they feared the Jews.

[14] When the festival was already half over, Jesus went up into the ˈtemple complex and began to teach. [15] Then the Jews were amazed and said, "How does He know the Scriptures, since He hasn't been trained?"

[16] Jesus answered them, "My teaching isn't Mine but is from the One who sent Me. [17] If anyone wants to do His will, he will understand whether the teaching is from God or if I am speaking on My own. [18] The one who speaks for himself seeks his own glory. But He who seeks the glory of the One who sent Him is true, and there is no unrighteousness in Him. [19] Didn't Moses give you the law? Yet none of you keeps the law! Why do you want to kill Me?"

[20] "You have a demon!" the crowd responded. "Who wants to kill You?"

[21] "I did one work, and you are all amazed," Jesus answered. [22] "Consider this: Moses has given you circumcision—not that it comes from Moses but from the fathers—and you circumcise a man on the Sabbath. [23] If a man receives circumcision on the Sabbath so that the law of Moses won't be broken, are you angry at Me because I made a man entirely well on the Sabbath? [24] Stop judging according to outward appearances; rather judge according to righteous judgment."

[25] Some of the people of Jerusalem were saying, "Isn't this the man they want to kill? [26] Yet, look! He's speaking publicly and they're saying nothing to Him. Can it be true that the authorities know He is the ˈMessiah? [27] But we know where this man is from. When the Messiah comes, nobody will know where He is from."

[28] As He was teaching in the temple complex, Jesus cried out, "You know Me and you know where I am from. Yet I have not come on My own, but the One who sent Me is true. You don't know Him; [29] I know Him because I am from Him, and He sent Me."

[30] Then they tried to seize Him. Yet no one laid a hand on Him because His hour had not yet come. [31] However, many from the crowd believed in Him and said, "When the Messiah comes, He won't perform more signs than this man has done, will He?"

[32] The ˈPharisees heard the crowd muttering these

things about Him, so the •chief priests and the Pharisees sent temple police to arrest Him.

³³ Then Jesus said, "I am only with you for a short time. Then I'm going to the One who sent Me. ³⁴ You will look for Me, but you will not find Me; and where I am, you cannot come."

³⁵ Then the Jews said to one another, "Where does He intend to go so we won't find Him? He doesn't intend to go to the Dispersion among the Greeks and teach the Greeks, does He? ³⁶ What is this remark He made: 'You will look for Me, and you will not find Me; and where I am, you cannot come'?"

³⁷ On the last and most important day of the festival, Jesus stood up and cried out, "If anyone is thirsty, he should come to Me and drink! ³⁸ The one who believes in Me, as the Scripture has said, will have streams of living water flow from deep within him." ³⁹ He said this about the Spirit. Those who believed in Jesus were going to receive the Spirit, for the Spirit had not yet been received because Jesus had not yet been glorified.

⁴⁰ When some from the crowd heard these words, they said, "This really is the Prophet!" ⁴¹ Others said, "This is the Messiah!" But some said, "Surely the Messiah doesn't come from Galilee, does He? ⁴² Doesn't the Scripture say that the Messiah comes from David's offspring and from the town of Bethlehem, where David once lived?" ⁴³ So a division occurred among the crowd because of Him. ⁴⁴ Some of them wanted to seize Him, but no one laid hands on Him.

⁴⁵ Then the temple police came to the chief priests and Pharisees, who asked them, "Why haven't you brought Him?"

⁴⁶ The police answered, "No man ever spoke like this!"

⁴⁷ Then the Pharisees responded to them: "Are you fooled too? ⁴⁸ Have any of the rulers or Pharisees believed in Him? ⁴⁹ But this crowd, which doesn't know the law, is accursed!"

⁵⁰ Nicodemus—the one who came to Him previously, being one of them—said to them, ⁵¹ "Our law doesn't judge a man before it hears from him and knows what he's doing, does it?"

⁵² "You aren't from Galilee too, are you?" they replied. "Investigate and you will see that no prophet arises from Galilee."

8 [⁵³ So each one went to his house. ¹ But Jesus went to the •Mount of Olives.

² At dawn He went to the •temple complex again, and all the people were coming to Him. He sat down and began to teach them.

³ Then the •scribes and the •Pharisees brought a woman caught in adultery, making her stand in the center. ⁴ "Teacher," they said to Him, "this woman was caught in the act of committing adultery. ⁵ In the law Moses commanded us to stone such women. So what do You say?" ⁶ They asked this to trap Him, in order that they might have evidence to accuse Him.

Jesus stooped down and started writing on the ground with His finger. ⁷ When they persisted in questioning Him, He stood up and said to them, "The one without sin among you should be the first to throw a stone at her."

⁸ Then He stooped down again and continued writing on the ground. ⁹ When they heard this, they left one by one, starting with the older men. Only He was left, with the woman in the center. ¹⁰ When Jesus stood

up, He said to her, "'Woman, where are they? Has no one condemned you?"

¹¹ "No one, Lord," she answered.

"Neither do I condemn you," said Jesus. "Go, and from now on do not sin anymore."]

¹² Then Jesus spoke to them again: "I am the light of the world. Anyone who follows Me will never walk in the darkness but will have the light of life."

¹³ So the Pharisees said to Him, "You are testifying about Yourself. Your testimony is not valid."

¹⁴ "Even if I testify about Myself," Jesus replied, "My testimony is valid, because I know where I came from and where I'm going. But you don't know where I come from or where I'm going. ¹⁵ You judge by human standards. I judge no one. ¹⁶ And if I do judge, My judgment is true, because I am not alone, but I and the Father who sent Me judge together. ¹⁷ Even in your law it is written that the witness of two men is valid. ¹⁸ I am the One who testifies about Myself, and the Father who sent Me testifies about Me."

¹⁹ Then they asked Him, "Where is Your Father?"

"You know neither Me nor My Father," Jesus answered. "If you knew Me, you would also know My Father." ²⁰ He spoke these words by the treasury, while teaching in the temple complex. But no one seized Him, because His hour had not come.

²¹ Then He said to them again, "I'm going away; you will look for Me, and you will die in your sin. Where I'm going, you cannot come."

²² So the •Jews said again, "He won't kill Himself, will He, since He says, 'Where I'm going, you cannot come'?"

²³ "You are from below," He told them, "I am from above. You are of this world; I am not of this •world. ²⁴ Therefore I told you that you will die in your sins. For if you do not believe that I am He, you will die in your sins."

²⁵ "Who are You?" they questioned.

"Precisely what I've been telling you from the very beginning," Jesus told them. ²⁶ "I have many things to say and to judge about you, but the One who sent Me is true, and what I have heard from Him—these things I tell the world."

²⁷ They did not know He was speaking to them about the Father. ²⁸ So Jesus said to them, "When you lift up the •Son of Man, then you will know that I am He, and that I do nothing on My own. But just as the Father taught Me, I say these things. ²⁹ The One who sent Me is with Me. He has not left Me alone, because I always do what pleases Him."

³⁰ As He was saying these things, many believed in Him. ³¹ So Jesus said to the Jews who had believed Him, "If you continue in My word, you really are My disciples. ³² You will know the truth, and the truth will set you free."

³³ "We are descendants of Abraham," they answered Him, "and we have never been enslaved to anyone. How can You say, 'You will become free'?"

³⁴ Jesus responded, "'I assure you: Everyone who commits sin is a •slave of sin. ³⁵ A slave does not remain in the household forever, but a son does remain forever. ³⁶ Therefore, if the Son sets you free, you really will be free. ³⁷ I know you are descendants of Abraham, but you are trying to kill Me because My word is not welcome among you. ³⁸ I speak what I have seen in the presence of the Father; therefore, you do what you have heard from your father."

³⁹"Our father is Abraham!" they replied.

"If you were Abraham's children," Jesus told them, "you would do what Abraham did. ⁴⁰But now you are trying to kill Me, a man who has told you the truth that I heard from God. Abraham did not do this! ⁴¹You're doing what your father does."

"We weren't born of sexual immorality," they said. "We have one Father—God."

⁴²Jesus said to them, "If God were your Father, you would love Me, because I came from God and I am here. For I didn't come on My own, but He sent Me. ⁴³Why don't you understand what I say? Because you cannot listen to My word. ⁴⁴You are of your father the Devil, and you want to carry out your father's desires. He was a murderer from the beginning and has not stood in the truth, because there is no truth in him. When he tells a lie, he speaks from his own nature, because he is a liar and the father of liars. ⁴⁵Yet because I tell the truth, you do not believe Me. ⁴⁶Who among you can convict Me of sin? If I tell the truth, why don't you believe Me? ⁴⁷The one who is from God listens to God's words. This is why you don't listen, because you are not from God."

⁴⁸The Jews responded to Him, "Aren't we right in saying that You're a •Samaritan and have a demon?"

⁴⁹"I do not have a demon," Jesus answered. "On the contrary, I honor My Father and you dishonor Me. ⁵⁰I do not seek My glory; the One who seeks it also judges. ⁵¹I assure you: If anyone keeps My word, he will never see death—ever!"

⁵²Then the Jews said, "Now we know You have a demon. Abraham died and so did the prophets. You say, 'If anyone keeps My word, he will never taste death—ever!' ⁵³Are You greater than our father Abraham who died? Even the prophets died. Who do You pretend to be?"

⁵⁴"If I glorify Myself," Jesus answered, "My glory is nothing. My Father—you say about Him, 'He is our God'—He is the One who glorifies Me. ⁵⁵You've never known Him, but I know Him. If I were to say I don't know Him, I would be a liar like you. But I do know Him, and I keep His word. ⁵⁶Your father Abraham was overjoyed that he would see My day; he saw it and rejoiced."

⁵⁷The Jews replied, "You aren't 50 years old yet, and You've seen Abraham?"

⁵⁸Jesus said to them, "I assure you: Before Abraham was, I am."

⁵⁹At that, they picked up stones to throw at Him. But Jesus was hidden and went out of the temple complex.

9 As He was passing by, He saw a man blind from birth. ²His disciples questioned Him: "'Rabbi, who sinned, this man or his parents, that he was born blind?"

³"Neither this man nor his parents sinned," Jesus answered. "This came about so that God's works might be displayed in him. ⁴We must do the works of Him who sent Me while it is day. Night is coming when no one can work. ⁵As long as I am in the world, I am the light of the world."

⁶After He said these things He spit on the ground, made some mud from the saliva, and spread the mud on his eyes. ⁷"Go," He told him, "wash in the pool of Siloam" (which means "Sent"). So he left, washed, and came back seeing.

⁸His neighbors and those who formerly had seen him as a beggar said, "Isn't this the man who sat begging?" ⁹Some said, "He's the one." "No," others were saying, "but he looks like him."

He kept saying, "I'm the one!"

¹⁰Therefore they asked him, "Then how were your eyes opened?"

¹¹He answered, "The man called Jesus made mud, spread it on my eyes, and told me, 'Go to Siloam and wash.' So when I went and washed I received my sight."

¹²"Where is He?" they asked.

"I don't know," he said.

¹³They brought the man who used to be blind to the •Pharisees. ¹⁴The day that Jesus made the mud and opened his eyes was a Sabbath. ¹⁵So again the Pharisees asked him how he received his sight.

"He put mud on my eyes," he told them. "I washed and I can see."

¹⁶Therefore some of the Pharisees said, "This man is not from God, for He doesn't keep the Sabbath!" But others were saying, "How can a sinful man perform such signs?" And there was a division among them.

¹⁷Again they asked the blind man, "What do you say about Him, since He opened your eyes?"

"He's a prophet," he said.

¹⁸The •Jews did not believe this about him—that he was blind and received sight—until they summoned the parents of the one who had received his sight. ¹⁹They asked them, "Is this your son, the one you say was born blind? How then does he now see?"

²⁰"We know this is our son and that he was born blind," his parents answered. ²¹"But we don't know how he now sees, and we don't know who opened his eyes. Ask him; he's of age. He will speak for himself." ²²His parents said these things because they were afraid of the Jews, since the Jews had already agreed that if anyone confessed Him as •Messiah, he would be banned from the •synagogue. ²³This is why his parents said, "He's of age; ask him."

²⁴So a second time they summoned the man who had been blind and told him, "Give glory to God. We know that this man is a sinner!"

²⁵He answered, "Whether or not He's a sinner, I don't know. One thing I do know: I was blind, and now I can see!"

²⁶Then they asked him, "What did He do to you? How did He open your eyes?"

²⁷"I already told you," he said, "and you didn't listen. Why do you want to hear it again? You don't want to become His disciples too, do you?"

²⁸They ridiculed him: "You're that man's disciple, but we're Moses' disciples. ²⁹We know that God has spoken to Moses. But this man—we don't know where He's from!"

³⁰"This is an amazing thing," the man told them. "You don't know where He is from, yet He opened my eyes! ³¹We know that God doesn't listen to sinners, but if anyone is God-fearing and does His will, He listens to him. ³²Throughout history no one has ever heard of someone opening the eyes of a person born blind. ³³If this man were not from God, He wouldn't be able to do anything."

³⁴"You were born entirely in sin," they replied, "and are you trying to teach us?" Then they threw him out.

³⁵When Jesus heard that they had thrown the man out, He found him and asked, "Do you believe in the •Son of Man?"

[36] "Who is He, Sir, that I may believe in Him?" he asked.

[37] Jesus answered, "You have seen Him; in fact, He is the One speaking with you."

[38] "I believe, Lord!" he said, and he worshiped Him.

[39] Jesus said, "I came into this world for judgment, in order that those who do not see will see and those who do see will become blind."

[40] Some of the Pharisees who were with Him heard these things and asked Him, "We aren't blind too, are we?"

[41] "If you were blind," Jesus told them, "you wouldn't have sin. But now that you say, 'We see'—your sin remains.

10

[1] "'I assure you: Anyone who doesn't enter the sheep pen by the door but climbs in some other way, is a thief and a robber. [2] The one who enters by the door is the shepherd of the sheep. [3] The doorkeeper opens it for him, and the sheep hear his voice. He calls his own sheep by name and leads them out. [4] When he has brought all his own outside, he goes ahead of them. The sheep follow him because they recognize his voice. [5] They will never follow a stranger; instead they will run away from him, because they don't recognize the voice of strangers."

[6] Jesus gave them this illustration, but they did not understand what He was telling them.

[7] So Jesus said again, "I assure you: I am the door of the sheep. [8] All who came before Me are thieves and robbers, but the sheep didn't listen to them. [9] I am the door. If anyone enters by Me, he will be saved and will come in and go out and find pasture. [10] A thief comes only to steal and to kill and to destroy. I have come so that they may have life and have it in abundance.

[11] "I am the good shepherd. The good shepherd lays down his life for the sheep. [12] The hired man, since he is not the shepherd and doesn't own the sheep, leaves them and runs away when he sees a wolf coming. The wolf then snatches and scatters them. [13] This happens because he is a hired man and doesn't care about the sheep.

[14] "I am the good shepherd. I know My own sheep, and they know Me, [15] as the Father knows Me, and I know the Father. I lay down My life for the sheep. [16] But I have other sheep that are not of this fold; I must bring them also, and they will listen to My voice. Then there will be one flock, one shepherd. [17] This is why the Father loves Me, because I am laying down My life so I may take it up again. [18] No one takes it from Me, but I lay it down on My own. I have the right to lay it down, and I have the right to take it up again. I have received this command from My Father."

[19] Again a division took place among the •Jews because of these words. [20] Many of them were saying, "He has a demon and He's crazy! Why do you listen to Him?" [21] Others were saying, "These aren't the words of someone demon-possessed. Can a demon open the eyes of the blind?"

[22] Then the Festival of Dedication took place in Jerusalem, and it was winter. [23] Jesus was walking in the •temple complex in Solomon's Colonnade. [24] Then the Jews surrounded Him and asked, "How long are You going to keep us in suspense? If You are the •Messiah, tell us plainly."

[25] "I did tell you and you don't believe," Jesus answered them. "The works that I do in My Father's name testify about Me. [26] But you don't believe because you are not My sheep. [27] My sheep hear My voice, I know them, and they follow Me. [28] I give them eternal life, and they will never perish—ever! No one will snatch them out of My hand. [29] My Father, who has given them to Me, is greater than all. No one is able to snatch them out of the Father's hand. [30] The Father and I are one."

[31] Again the Jews picked up rocks to stone Him.

[32] Jesus replied, "I have shown you many good works from the Father. Which of these works are you stoning Me for?"

[33] "We aren't stoning You for a good work," the Jews answered, "but for blasphemy, because You—being a man—make Yourself God."

[34] Jesus answered them, "Isn't it written in your scripture, **I said, you are gods**? [35] If He called those whom the word of God came to 'gods'—and the Scripture cannot be broken— [36] do you say, 'You are blaspheming' to the One the Father set apart and sent into the world, because I said: I am the Son of God? [37] If I am not doing My Father's works, don't believe Me. [38] But if I am doing them and you don't believe Me, believe the works. This way you will know and understand that the Father is in Me and I in the Father." [39] Then they were trying again to seize Him, yet He eluded their grasp.

[40] So He departed again across the Jordan to the place where John had been baptizing earlier, and He remained there. [41] Many came to Him and said, "John never did a sign, but everything John said about this man was true." [42] And many believed in Him there.

11

Now a man was sick, Lazarus, from Bethany, the village of Mary and her sister Martha. [2] Mary was the one who anointed the Lord with fragrant oil and wiped His feet with her hair, and it was· her brother Lazarus who was sick. [3] So the sisters sent a message to Him: "Lord, the one You love is sick."

[4] When Jesus heard it, He said, "This sickness will not end in death but is for the glory of God, so that the Son of God may be glorified through it." [5] Now Jesus loved Martha, her sister, and Lazarus. [6] So when He heard that he was sick, He stayed two more days in the place where He was. [7] Then after that, He said to the disciples, "Let's go to Judea again."

[8] "Rabbi," the disciples told Him, "just now the •Jews tried to stone You, and You're going there again?"

[9] "Aren't there 12 hours in a day?" Jesus answered. "If anyone walks during the day, he doesn't stumble, because he sees the light of this world. [10] If anyone walks during the night, he does stumble, because the light is not in him." [11] He said this, and then He told them, "Our friend Lazarus has fallen •asleep, but I'm on My way to wake him up."

[12] Then the disciples said to Him, "Lord, if he has fallen asleep, he will get well."

[13] Jesus, however, was speaking about his death, but they thought He was speaking about natural sleep. [14] So Jesus then told them plainly, "Lazarus has died. [15] I'm glad for you that I wasn't there so that you may believe. But let's go to him."

[16] Then Thomas (called "Twin") said to his fellow disciples, "Let's go so that we may die with Him."

[17] When Jesus arrived, He found that Lazarus had already been in the tomb four days. [18] Bethany was near Jerusalem (about two miles away). [19] Many of the Jews had come to Martha and Mary to comfort them about their brother. [20] As soon as Martha heard that Jesus was

coming, she went to meet Him. But Mary remained seated in the house.

²¹Then Martha said to Jesus, "Lord, if You had been here, my brother wouldn't have died. ²²Yet even now I know that whatever You ask from God, God will give You."

²³"Your brother will rise again," Jesus told her.

²⁴Martha said, "I know that he will rise again in the resurrection at the last day."

²⁵Jesus said to her, "I am the resurrection and the life. The one who believes in Me, even if he dies, will live. ²⁶Everyone who lives and believes in Me will never die—ever. Do you believe this?"

²⁷"Yes, Lord," she told Him, "I believe You are the •Messiah, the Son of God, who comes into the world."

²⁸Having said this, she went back and called her sister Mary, saying in private, "The Teacher is here and is calling for you."

²⁹As soon as she heard this, she got up quickly and went to Him. ³⁰Jesus had not yet come into the village but was still in the place where Martha had met Him. ³¹The Jews who were with her in the house consoling her saw that Mary got up quickly and went out. So they followed her, supposing that she was going to the tomb to cry there.

³²When Mary came to where Jesus was and saw Him, she fell at His feet and told Him, "Lord, if You had been here, my brother would not have died!"

³³When Jesus saw her crying, and the Jews who had come with her crying, He was angry in His spirit and deeply moved. ³⁴"Where have you put him?" He asked.

"Lord," they told Him, "come and see."

³⁵Jesus wept.

³⁶So the Jews said, "See how He loved him!" ³⁷But some of them said, "Couldn't He who opened the blind man's eyes also have kept this man from dying?"

³⁸Then Jesus, angry in Himself again, came to the tomb. It was a cave, and a stone was lying against it. ³⁹"Remove the stone," Jesus said.

Martha, the dead man's sister, told Him, "Lord, he's already decaying. It's been four days."

⁴⁰Jesus said to her, "Didn't I tell you that if you believed you would see the glory of God?"

⁴¹So they removed the stone. Then Jesus raised His eyes and said, "Father, I thank You that You heard Me. ⁴²I know that You always hear Me, but because of the crowd standing here I said this, so they may believe You sent Me." ⁴³After He said this, He shouted with a loud voice, "Lazarus, come out!" ⁴⁴The dead man came out bound hand and foot with linen strips and with his face wrapped in a cloth. Jesus said to them, "Loose him and let him go."

⁴⁵Therefore, many of the Jews who came to Mary and saw what He did believed in Him. ⁴⁶But some of them went to the •Pharisees and told them what Jesus had done.

⁴⁷So the •chief priests and the Pharisees convened the •Sanhedrin and said, "What are we going to do since this man does many signs? ⁴⁸If we let Him continue in this way, everyone will believe in Him! Then the Romans will come and remove both our place and our nation."

⁴⁹One of them, Caiaphas, who was high priest that year, said to them, "You know nothing at all! ⁵⁰You're not considering that it is to your advantage that one man should die for the people rather than the whole nation perish." ⁵¹He did not say this on his own, but

being high priest that year he prophesied that Jesus was going to die for the nation, ⁵²and not for the nation only, but also to unite the scattered children of God. ⁵³So from that day on they plotted to kill Him. ⁵⁴Therefore Jesus no longer walked openly among the Jews but departed from there to the countryside near the wilderness, to a town called Ephraim. And He stayed there with the disciples.

⁵⁵The Jewish •Passover was near, and many went up to Jerusalem from the country to purify themselves before the Passover. ⁵⁶They were looking for Jesus and asking one another as they stood in the •temple complex: "What do you think? He won't come to the festival, will He?" ⁵⁷The chief priests and the Pharisees had given orders that if anyone knew where He was, he should report it so they could arrest Him.

12 Six days before the •Passover, Jesus came to Bethany where Lazarus was, the one Jesus had raised from the dead. ²So they gave a dinner for Him there; Martha was serving them, and Lazarus was one of those reclining at the table with Him. ³Then Mary took a pound of fragrant oil—pure and expensive nard—anointed Jesus' feet, and wiped His feet with her hair. So the house was filled with the fragrance of the oil.

⁴Then one of His disciples, Judas Iscariot (who was about to betray Him), said, ⁵"Why wasn't this fragrant oil sold for 300 •denarii and given to the poor?" ⁶He didn't say this because he cared about the poor but because he was a thief. He was in charge of the moneybag and would steal part of what was put in it.

⁷Jesus answered, "Leave her alone; she has kept it for the day of My burial. ⁸For you always have the poor with you, but you do not always have Me."

⁹Then a large crowd of the Jews learned He was there. They came not only because of Jesus, but also to see Lazarus the one He had raised from the dead. ¹⁰Therefore the •chief priests decided to kill Lazarus also ¹¹because he was the reason many of the Jews were deserting them and believing in Jesus.

¹²The next day, when the large crowd that had come to the festival heard that Jesus was coming to Jerusalem, ¹³they took palm branches and went out to meet Him. They kept shouting: "'***Hosanna!*** He who comes in the name of the Lord is the blessed One**—the King of Israel!"

¹⁴Jesus found a young donkey and sat on it, just as it is written: ¹⁵**Fear no more, Daughter •Zion. Look, your King is coming, sitting on a donkey's colt.**

¹⁶His disciples did not understand these things at first. However, when Jesus was glorified, then they remembered that these things had been written about Him and that they had done these things to Him. ¹⁷Meanwhile, the crowd, which had been with Him when He called Lazarus out of the tomb and raised him from the dead, continued to testify. ¹⁸This is also why the crowd met Him, because they heard He had done this sign.

¹⁹Then the •Pharisees said to one another, "You see? You've accomplished nothing. Look—the world has gone after Him!"

²⁰Now some Greeks were among those who went up to worship at the festival. ²¹So they came to Philip, who was from Bethsaida in Galilee, and requested of him, "Sir, we want to see Jesus."

²²Philip went and told Andrew; then Andrew and

Philip went and told Jesus. ²³ Jesus replied to them, "The hour has come for the *Son of Man to be glorified.

²⁴ "*I assure you: Unless a grain of wheat falls to the ground and dies, it remains by itself. But if it dies, it produces a large crop. ²⁵ The one who loves his life will lose it, and the one who hates his life in this world will keep it for eternal life. ²⁶ If anyone serves Me, he must follow Me. Where I am, there My servant also will be. If anyone serves Me, the Father will honor him.

²⁷ "Now My soul is troubled. What should I say— Father, save Me from this hour? But that is why I came to this hour. ²⁸ Father, glorify Your name!"

Then a voice came from heaven: "I have glorified it, and I will glorify it again!"

²⁹ The crowd standing there heard it and said it was thunder. Others said that an angel had spoken to Him. ³⁰ Jesus responded, "This voice came, not for Me, but for you. ³¹ Now is the judgment of this world. Now the ruler of this *world will be cast out. ³² As for Me, if I am lifted up from the earth I will draw all people to Myself." ³³ He said this to signify what kind of death He was about to die.

³⁴ Then the crowd replied to Him, "We have heard from the scripture that the *Messiah will remain forever. So how can You say, 'The Son of Man must be lifted up'? Who is this Son of Man?"

³⁵ Jesus answered, "The light will be with you only a little longer. Walk while you have the light so that darkness doesn't overtake you. The one who walks in darkness doesn't know where he's going. ³⁶ While you have the light, believe in the light so that you may become sons of light." Jesus said this, then went away and hid from them.

³⁷ Even though He had performed so many signs in their presence, they did not believe in Him. ³⁸ But this was to fulfill the word of Isaiah the prophet, who said:

> Lord, who has believed our message?
> And who has the arm of the Lord
> been revealed to?

³⁹ This is why they were unable to believe, because Isaiah also said:

⁴⁰
> He has blinded their eyes
> and hardened their hearts,
> so that they would not see with their eyes
> or understand with their hearts,
> and be converted,
> and I would heal them.

⁴¹ Isaiah said these things because he saw His glory and spoke about Him.

⁴² Nevertheless, many did believe in Him even among the rulers, but because of the Pharisees they did not confess Him, so they would not be banned from the *synagogue. ⁴³ For they loved praise from men more than praise from God.

⁴⁴ Then Jesus cried out, "The one who believes in Me believes not in Me, but in Him who sent Me. ⁴⁵ And the one who sees Me sees Him who sent Me. ⁴⁶ I have come as a light into the world, so that everyone who believes in Me would not remain in darkness. ⁴⁷ If anyone hears My words and doesn't keep them, I do not judge him; for I did not come to judge the world but to save the world. ⁴⁸ The one who rejects Me and doesn't accept My sayings has this as his judge: The word I have spoken will judge him on the last day. ⁴⁹ For I have not spoken on My own, but the Father Himself who sent Me has given Me a command as to what I should say and what I should speak. ⁵⁰ I know that His command is eternal

life. So the things that I speak, I speak just as the Father has told Me."

13 Before the *Passover Festival, Jesus knew that His hour had come to depart from this world to the Father. Having loved His own who were in the world, He loved them to the end.

² Now by the time of supper, the Devil had already put it into the heart of Judas, Simon Iscariot's son, to betray Him. ³ Jesus knew that the Father had given everything into His hands, that He had come from God, and that He was going back to God. ⁴ So He got up from supper, laid aside His robe, took a towel, and tied it around Himself. ⁵ Next, He poured water into a basin and began to wash His disciples' feet and to dry them with the towel tied around Him.

⁶ He came to Simon Peter, who asked Him, "Lord, are You going to wash my feet?"

⁷ Jesus answered him, "What I'm doing you don't understand now, but afterward you will know."

⁸ "You will never wash my feet—ever!" Peter said.

Jesus replied, "If I don't wash you, you have no part with Me."

⁹ Simon Peter said to Him, "Lord, not only my feet, but also my hands and my head."

¹⁰ "One who has bathed," Jesus told him, "doesn't need to wash anything except his feet, but he is completely *clean. You are clean, but not all of you." ¹¹ For He knew who would betray Him. This is why He said, "You are not all clean."

¹² When Jesus had washed their feet and put on His robe, He reclined again and said to them, "Do you know what I have done for you? ¹³ You call Me Teacher and Lord. This is well said, for I am. ¹⁴ So if I, your Lord and Teacher, have washed your feet, you also ought to wash one another's feet. ¹⁵ For I have given you an example that you also should do just as I have done for you.

¹⁶ "*I assure you: A *slave is not greater than his master, and a messenger is not greater than the one who sent him. ¹⁷ If you know these things, you are blessed if you do them. ¹⁸ I'm not speaking about all of you; I know those I have chosen. But the Scripture must be fulfilled: **The one who eats My bread has raised his heel against Me.**

¹⁹ "I am telling you now before it happens, so that when it does happen you will believe that I am He. ²⁰ I assure you: Whoever receives anyone I send receives Me, and the one who receives Me receives Him who sent Me."

²¹ When Jesus had said this, He was troubled in His spirit and testified, "I assure you: One of you will betray Me!"

²² The disciples started looking at one another— uncertain which one He was speaking about. ²³ One of His disciples, the one Jesus loved, was reclining close beside Jesus. ²⁴ Simon Peter motioned to him to find out who it was He was talking about. ²⁵ So he leaned back against Jesus and asked Him, "Lord, who is it?"

²⁶ Jesus replied, "He's the one I give the piece of bread to after I have dipped it." When He had dipped the bread, He gave it to Judas, Simon Iscariot's son. ²⁷ After Judas ate the piece of bread, Satan entered him. Therefore Jesus told him, "What you're doing, do quickly."

²⁸ None of those reclining at the table knew why He told him this. ²⁹ Since Judas kept the money-bag, some thought that Jesus was telling him, "Buy what we need

for the festival," or that he should give something to the poor. ³⁰After receiving the piece of bread, he went out immediately. And it was night.

³¹When he had gone out, Jesus said, "Now the •Son of Man is glorified, and God is glorified in Him. ³²If God is glorified in Him, God will also glorify Him in Himself and will glorify Him at once.

³³"Children, I am with you a little while longer. You will look for Me, and just as I told the •Jews, 'Where I am going you cannot come,' so now I tell you.

³⁴"I give you a new command: Love one another. Just as I have loved you, you must also love one another. ³⁵By this all people will know that you are My disciples, if you have love for one another."

³⁶"Lord," Simon Peter said to Him, "where are You going?"

Jesus answered, "Where I am going you cannot follow Me now, but you will follow later."

³⁷"Lord," Peter asked, "why can't I follow You now? I will lay down my life for You!"

³⁸Jesus replied, "Will you lay down your life for Me? I assure you: A rooster will not crow until you have denied Me three times.

14 "Your heart must not be troubled. Believe in God; believe also in Me. ²In My Father's house are many dwelling places; if not, I would have told you. I am going away to prepare a place for you. ³If I go away and prepare a place for you, I will come back and receive you to Myself, so that where I am you may be also. ⁴You know the way to where I am going."

⁵"Lord," Thomas said, "we don't know where You're going. How can we know the way?"

⁶Jesus told him, "I am the way, the truth, and the life. No one comes to the Father except through Me.

⁷"If you know Me, you will also know My Father. From now on you do know Him and have seen Him."

⁸"Lord," said Philip, "show us the Father, and that's enough for us."

⁹Jesus said to him, "Have I been among you all this time without your knowing Me, Philip? The one who has seen Me has seen the Father. How can you say, 'Show us the Father'? ¹⁰Don't you believe that I am in the Father and the Father is in Me? The words I speak to you I do not speak on My own. The Father who lives in Me does His works. ¹¹Believe Me that I am in the Father and the Father is in Me. Otherwise, believe because of the works themselves.

¹²"I assure you: The one who believes in Me will also do the works that I do. And he will do even greater works than these, because I am going to the Father. ¹³Whatever you ask in My name, I will do it so that the Father may be glorified in the Son. ¹⁴If you ask Me anything in My name, I will do it.

¹⁵"If you love Me, you will keep My commands. ¹⁶And I will ask the Father, and He will give you another •Counselor to be with you forever. ¹⁷He is the Spirit of truth. The •world is unable to receive Him because it doesn't see Him or know Him. But you do know Him, because He remains with you and will be in you. ¹⁸I will not leave you as orphans; I am coming to you.

¹⁹"In a little while the world will see Me no longer, but you will see Me. Because I live, you will live too. ²⁰In that day you will know that I am in My Father, you are in Me, and I am in you. ²¹The one who has My commands and keeps them is the one who loves Me. And the one who loves Me will be loved by My Father. I also will love him and will reveal Myself to him."

²²Judas (not Iscariot) said to Him, "Lord, how is it You're going to reveal Yourself to us and not to the world?"

²³Jesus answered, "If anyone loves Me, he will keep My word. My Father will love him, and We will come to him and make Our home with him. ²⁴The one who doesn't love Me will not keep My words. The word that you hear is not Mine but is from the Father who sent Me.

²⁵"I have spoken these things to you while I remain with you. ²⁶But the Counselor, the Holy Spirit—the Father will send Him in My name—will teach you all things and remind you of everything I have told you. ²⁷Peace I leave with you. My peace I give to you. I do not give to you as the world gives. Your heart must not be troubled or fearful. ²⁸You have heard Me tell you, 'I am going away and I am coming to you.' If you loved Me, you would have rejoiced that I am going to the Father, because the Father is greater than I. ²⁹I have told you now before it happens so that when it does happen you may believe. ³⁰I will not talk with you much longer, because the ruler of the world is coming. He has no power over Me. ³¹On the contrary, I am going away so that the world may know that I love the Father. Just as the Father commanded Me, so I do.

"Get up; let's leave this place.

15 "I am the true vine, and My Father is the vineyard keeper. ²Every branch in Me that does not produce fruit He removes, and He prunes every branch that produces fruit so that it will produce more fruit. ³You are already •clean because of the word I have spoken to you. ⁴Remain in Me, and I in you. Just as a branch is unable to produce fruit by itself unless it remains on the vine, so neither can you unless you remain in Me.

⁵"I am the vine; you are the branches. The one who remains in Me and I in him produces much fruit, because you can do nothing without Me. ⁶If anyone does not remain in Me, he is thrown aside like a branch and he withers. They gather them, throw them into the fire, and they are burned. ⁷If you remain in Me and My words remain in you, ask whatever you want and it will be done for you. ⁸My Father is glorified by this: that you produce much fruit and prove to be My disciples.

⁹"As the Father has loved Me, I have also loved you. Remain in My love. ¹⁰If you keep My commands you will remain in My love, just as I have kept My Father's commands and remain in His love.

¹¹"I have spoken these things to you so that My joy may be in you and your joy may be complete. ¹²This is My command: Love one another as I have loved you. ¹³No one has greater love than this, that someone would lay down his life for his friends. ¹⁴You are My friends if you do what I command you. ¹⁵I do not call you •slaves anymore, because a slave doesn't know what his master is doing. I have called you friends, because I have made known to you everything I have heard from My Father. ¹⁶You did not choose Me, but I chose you. I appointed you that you should go out and produce fruit and that your fruit should remain, so that whatever you ask the Father in My name, He will give you. ¹⁷This is what I command you: Love one another.

¹⁸"If the •world hates you, understand that it hated Me before it hated you. ¹⁹If you were of the world, the world would love you as its own. However, because you are not of the world, but I have chosen you out

of it, the world hates you. ²⁰Remember the word I spoke to you: 'A slave is not greater than his master.' If they persecuted Me, they will also persecute you. If they kept My word, they will also keep yours. ²¹But they will do all these things to you on account of My name, because they don't know the One who sent Me. ²²If I had not come and spoken to them, they would not have sin. Now they have no excuse for their sin. ²³The one who hates Me also hates My Father. ²⁴If I had not done the works among them that no one else has done, they would not have sin. Now they have seen and hated both Me and My Father. ²⁵But this happened so that the statement written in their scripture might be fulfilled: They hated Me for no reason.

²⁶"When the *Counselor comes, the One I will send to you from the Father—the Spirit of truth who proceeds from the Father—He will testify about Me. ²⁷You also will testify, because you have been with Me from the beginning.

16 "I have told you these things to keep you from *stumbling. ²They will ban you from the *synagogues. In fact, a time is coming when anyone who kills you will think he is offering service to God. ³They will do these things because they haven't known the Father or Me. ⁴But I have told you these things so that when their time comes you may remember I told them to you. I didn't tell you these things from the beginning, because I was with you.

⁵"But now I am going away to Him who sent Me, and not one of you asks Me, 'Where are You going?' ⁶Yet, because I have spoken these things to you, sorrow has filled your heart. ⁷Nevertheless, I am telling you the truth. It is for your benefit that I go away, because if I don't go away the *Counselor will not come to you. If I go, I will send Him to you. ⁸When He comes, He will convict the world about sin, righteousness, and judgment: ⁹About sin, because they do not believe in Me; ¹⁰about righteousness, because I am going to the Father and you will no longer see Me; ¹¹and about judgment, because the ruler of this *world has been judged.

¹²"I still have many things to tell you, but you can't bear them now. ¹³When the Spirit of truth comes, He will guide you into all the truth. For He will not speak on His own, but He will speak whatever He hears. He will also declare to you what is to come. ¹⁴He will glorify Me, because He will take from what is Mine and declare it to you. ¹⁵Everything the Father has is Mine. This is why I told you that He takes from what is Mine and will declare it to you.

¹⁶"A little while and you will no longer see Me; again a little while and you will see Me."

¹⁷Therefore some of His disciples said to one another, "What is this He tells us: 'A little while and you will not see Me; again a little while and you will see Me'; and, 'because I am going to the Father'?" ¹⁸They said, "What is this He is saying, 'A little while'? We don't know what He's talking about!"

¹⁹Jesus knew they wanted to question Him, so He said to them, "Are you asking one another about what I said, 'A little while and you will not see Me; again a little while and you will see Me'?

²⁰"I assure you: You will weep and wail, but the world will rejoice. You will become sorrowful, but your sorrow will turn to joy. ²¹When a woman is in labor she has pain because her time has come. But when she has given birth to a child, she no longer remembers

the suffering because of the joy that a person has been born into the world. ²²So you also have sorrow now. But I will see you again. Your hearts will rejoice, and no one will rob you of your joy. ²³In that day you will not ask Me anything.

"I assure you: Anything you ask the Father in My name, He will give you. ²⁴Until now you have asked for nothing in My name. Ask and you will receive, so that your joy may be complete.

²⁵"I have spoken these things to you in figures of speech. A time is coming when I will no longer speak to you in figures, but I will tell you plainly about the Father. ²⁶In that day you will ask in My name. I am not telling you that I will make requests to the Father on your behalf. ²⁷For the Father Himself loves you, because you have loved Me and have believed that I came from God. ²⁸I came from the Father and have come into the world. Again, I am leaving the world and going to the Father."

²⁹"Ah!" His disciples said. "Now You're speaking plainly and not using any figurative language. ³⁰Now we know that You know everything and don't need anyone to question You. By this we believe that You came from God."

³¹Jesus responded to them, "Do you now believe? ³²Look: An hour is coming, and has come, when each of you will be scattered to his own home, and you will leave Me alone. Yet I am not alone, because the Father is with Me. ³³I have told you these things so that in Me you may have peace. You will have suffering in this world. Be courageous! I have conquered the world."

17 Jesus spoke these things, looked up to heaven, and said:

Father,
the hour has come.
Glorify Your Son
so that the Son may glorify You,
² for You gave Him authority
over all flesh;
so He may give eternal life
to all You have given Him.
³ This is eternal life:
that they may know You, the only true God,
and the One You have sent—Jesus Christ.
⁴ I have glorified You on the earth
by completing the work You gave Me to do.
⁵ Now, Father, glorify Me in Your presence
with that glory I had with You
before the world existed.
⁶ I have revealed Your name
to the men You gave Me from the world.
They were Yours, You gave them to Me,
and they have kept Your word.
⁷ Now they know that all things
You have given to Me are from You,
⁸ because the words that You gave Me,
I have given them.
They have received them
and have known for certain
that I came from You.
They have believed that You sent Me.
⁹ I pray for them.
I am not praying for the *world
but for those You have given Me,
because they are Yours.
¹⁰ Everything I have is Yours,
and everything You have is Mine,

and I have been glorified in them.
11 I am no longer in the world,
but they are in the world,
and I am coming to You.
Holy Father,
protect them by Your name
that You have given Me,
so that they may be one as We are one.
12 While I was with them,
I was protecting them by Your name
that You have given Me.
I guarded them and not one of them is lost,
except the son of destruction,
so that the Scripture may be fulfilled.
13 Now I am coming to You,
and I speak these things in the world
so that they may have My joy completed
in them.
14 I have given them Your word.
The world hated them
because they are not of the world,
as I am not of the world.
15 I am not praying
that You take them out of the world
but that You protect them from the evil one.
16 They are not of the world,
as I am not of the world.
17 "Sanctify them by the truth;
Your word is truth.
18 As You sent Me into the world,
I also have sent them into the world.
19 I sanctify Myself for them,
so they also may be sanctified by the truth.
20 I pray not only for these,
but also for those who believe in Me
through their message.
21 May they all be one,
as You, Father, are in Me and I am in You.
May they also be one in Us,
so the world may believe You sent Me.
22 I have given them the glory
You have given Me.
May they be one as We are one.
23 I am in them and You are in Me.
May they be made completely one,
so the world may know You have sent Me
and have loved them as You have loved Me.
24 Father,
I desire those You have given Me
to be with Me where I am.
Then they will see My glory,
which You have given Me
because You loved Me
before the world's foundation.
25 Righteous Father!
The world has not known You.
However, I have known You,
and these have known that You sent Me.
26 I made Your name known to them
and will make it known,
so the love You have loved Me with
may be in them and I may be in them.

18 After Jesus had said these things, He went out with His disciples across the Kidron Valley, where there was a garden, and He and His disciples went into it. ²Judas, who betrayed Him, also knew the place, because Jesus often met there with His disciples.

³So Judas took a *company of soldiers and some temple police from the *chief priests and the *Pharisees and came there with lanterns, torches, and weapons.
⁴Then Jesus, knowing everything that was about to happen to Him, went out and said to them, "Who is it you're looking for?"
⁵"Jesus the *Nazarene," they answered.
"I am He," Jesus told them.
Judas, who betrayed Him, was also standing with them. ⁶When He told them, "I am He," they stepped back and fell to the ground.
⁷Then He asked them again, "Who is it you're looking for?"
"Jesus the Nazarene," they said.
⁸"I told you I am He," Jesus replied. "So if you're looking for Me, let these men go." ⁹This was to fulfill the words He had said: "I have not lost one of those You have given Me."
¹⁰Then Simon Peter, who had a sword, drew it, struck the high priest's *slave, and cut off his right ear. (The slave's name was Malchus.)
¹¹At that, Jesus said to Peter, "Sheathe your sword! Am I not to drink the cup the Father has given Me?"
¹²Then the company of soldiers, the commander, and the Jewish temple police arrested Jesus and tied Him up. ¹³First they led Him to Annas, for he was the father-in-law of Caiaphas, who was high priest that year. ¹⁴Caiaphas was the one who had advised the *Jews that it was advantageous that one man should die for the people.
¹⁵Meanwhile, Simon Peter was following Jesus, as was another disciple. That disciple was an acquaintance of the high priest; so he went with Jesus into the high priest's courtyard. ¹⁶But Peter remained standing outside by the door. So the other disciple, the one known to the high priest, went out and spoke to the girl who was the doorkeeper and brought Peter in.
¹⁷Then the slave girl who was the doorkeeper said to Peter, "You aren't one of this man's disciples too, are you?"
"I am not!" he said. ¹⁸Now the slaves and the temple police had made a charcoal fire, because it was cold. They were standing there warming themselves, and Peter was standing with them, warming himself.
¹⁹The high priest questioned Jesus about His disciples and about His teaching.
²⁰"I have spoken openly to the world," Jesus answered him. "I have always taught in the *synagogue and in the *temple complex, where all the Jews congregate, and I haven't spoken anything in secret. ²¹Why do you question Me? Question those who heard what I told them. Look, they know what I said."
²²When He had said these things, one of the temple police standing by slapped Jesus, saying, "Is this the way you answer the high priest?"
²³"If I have spoken wrongly," Jesus answered him, "give evidence about the wrong; but if rightly, why do you hit Me?"
²⁴Then Annas sent Him bound to Caiaphas the high priest.
²⁵Now Simon Peter was standing and warming himself. They said to him, "You aren't one of His disciples too, are you?"
He denied it and said, "I am not!"
²⁶One of the high priest's slaves, a relative of the man whose ear Peter had cut off, said, "Didn't I see you with Him in the garden?"

²⁷Peter then denied it again. Immediately a rooster crowed.

²⁸Then they took Jesus from Caiaphas to the governor's ˙headquarters. It was early morning. They did not enter the headquarters themselves; otherwise they would be defiled and unable to eat the ˙Passover.

²⁹Then ˙Pilate came out to them and said, "What charge do you bring against this man?"

³⁰They answered him, "If this man weren't a criminal, we wouldn't have handed Him over to you."

³¹So Pilate told them, "Take Him yourselves and judge Him according to your law."

"It's not legal for us to put anyone to death," the Jews declared. ³²They said this so that Jesus' words might be fulfilled signifying what kind of death He was going to die.

³³Then Pilate went back into the headquarters, summoned Jesus, and said to Him, "Are You the King of the Jews?"

³⁴Jesus answered, "Are you asking this on your own, or have others told you about Me?"

³⁵"I'm not a Jew, am I?" Pilate replied. "Your own nation and the chief priests handed You over to me. What have You done?"

³⁶"My kingdom is not of this ˙world," said Jesus. "If My kingdom were of this world, My servants would fight, so that I wouldn't be handed over to the Jews. As it is, My kingdom does not have its origin here."

³⁷"You are a king then?" Pilate asked.

"You say that I'm a king," Jesus replied. "I was born for this, and I have come into the world for this: to testify to the truth. Everyone who is of the truth listens to My voice."

³⁸"What is truth?" said Pilate.

After he had said this, he went out to the Jews again and told them, "I find no grounds for charging Him. ³⁹You have a custom that I release one prisoner to you at the Passover. So, do you want me to release to you the King of the Jews?"

⁴⁰They shouted back, "Not this man, but Barabbas!" Now Barabbas was a revolutionary.

19 Then ˙Pilate took Jesus and had Him flogged. ²The soldiers also twisted together a crown of thorns, put it on His head, and threw a purple robe around Him. ³And they repeatedly came up to Him and said, "Hail, King of the Jews!" and were slapping His face.

⁴Pilate went outside again and said to them, "Look, I'm bringing Him outside to you to let you know I find no grounds for charging Him."

⁵Then Jesus came out wearing the crown of thorns and the purple robe. Pilate said to them, "Here is the man!"

⁶When the ˙chief priests and the temple police saw Him, they shouted, "Crucify! Crucify!"

Pilate responded, "Take Him and crucify Him yourselves, for I find no grounds for charging Him."

⁷"We have a law," the ˙Jews replied to him, "and according to that law He must die, because He made Himself the Son of God."

⁸When Pilate heard this statement, he was more afraid than ever. ⁹He went back into the ˙headquarters and asked Jesus, "Where are You from?" But Jesus did not give him an answer. ¹⁰So Pilate said to Him, "You're not talking to me? Don't You know that I have the authority to release You and the authority to crucify You?"

¹¹"You would have no authority over Me at all," Jesus answered him, "if it hadn't been given you from above. This is why the one who handed Me over to you has the greater sin."

¹²From that moment Pilate made every effort to release Him. But the Jews shouted, "If you release this man, you are not Caesar's friend. Anyone who makes himself a king opposes Caesar!"

¹³When Pilate heard these words, he brought Jesus outside. He sat down on the judge's bench in a place called the Stone Pavement (but in ˙Hebrew *Gabbatha*). ¹⁴It was the preparation day for the ˙Passover, and it was about six in the morning. Then he told the Jews, "Here is your king!"

¹⁵But they shouted, "Take Him away! Take Him away! Crucify Him!"

Pilate said to them, "Should I crucify your king?"

"We have no king but Caesar!" the chief priests answered.

¹⁶So then, because of them, he handed Him over to be crucified.

Therefore they took Jesus away. ¹⁷Carrying His own cross, He went out to what is called Skull Place, which in Hebrew is called *Golgotha*. ¹⁸There they crucified Him and two others with Him, one on either side, with Jesus in the middle. ¹⁹Pilate also had a sign lettered and put on the cross. The inscription was:

JESUS THE NAZARENE
THE KING OF THE JEWS.

²⁰Many of the Jews read this sign, because the place where Jesus was crucified was near the city, and it was written in Hebrew, Latin, and Greek. ²¹So the chief priests of the Jews said to Pilate, "Don't write, 'The King of the Jews,' but that He said, 'I am the King of the Jews.'"

²²Pilate replied, "What I have written, I have written."

²³When the soldiers crucified Jesus, they took His clothes and divided them into four parts, a part for each soldier. They also took the tunic, which was seamless, woven in one piece from the top. ²⁴So they said to one another, "Let's not tear it, but cast lots for it, to see who gets it." They did this to fulfill the Scripture that says: **They divided My clothes among themselves, and they cast lots for My clothing.** And this is what the soldiers did.

²⁵Standing by the cross of Jesus were His mother, His mother's sister, Mary the wife of Clopas, and ˙Mary Magdalene. ²⁶When Jesus saw His mother and the disciple He loved standing there, He said to His mother, "˙Woman, here is your son." ²⁷Then He said to the disciple, "Here is your mother." And from that hour the disciple took her into his home.

²⁸After this, when Jesus knew that everything was now accomplished that the Scripture might be fulfilled, He said, "I'm thirsty!" ²⁹A jar full of sour wine was sitting there; so they fixed a sponge full of sour wine on hyssop and held it up to His mouth. ³⁰When Jesus had received the sour wine, He said, "It is finished!" Then bowing His head, He gave up His spirit.

³¹Since it was the preparation day, the Jews did not want the bodies to remain on the cross on the Sabbath (for that Sabbath was a special day). They requested that Pilate have the men's legs broken and that their bodies be taken away. ³²So the soldiers came and broke the legs of the first man and of the other one who had

been crucified with Him. ³³When they came to Jesus, they did not break His legs since they saw that He was already dead. ³⁴But one of the soldiers pierced His side with a spear, and at once blood and water came out. ³⁵He who saw this has testified so that you also may believe. His testimony is true, and he knows he is telling the truth. ³⁶For these things happened so that the Scripture would be fulfilled: **Not one of His bones will be broken.** ³⁷Also, another Scripture says: **They will look at the One they pierced.**

³⁸After this, Joseph of Arimathea, who was a disciple of Jesus—but secretly because of his fear of the Jews—asked Pilate that he might remove Jesus' body. Pilate gave him permission, so he came and took His body away. ³⁹Nicodemus (who had previously come to Him at night) also came, bringing a mixture of about 75 pounds of myrrh and aloes. ⁴⁰Then they took Jesus' body and wrapped it in linen cloths with the aromatic spices, according to the burial custom of the Jews. ⁴¹There was a garden in the place where He was crucified. A new tomb was in the garden; no one had yet been placed in it. ⁴²They placed Jesus there because of the Jewish preparation and since the tomb was nearby.

20 On the first day of the week ·Mary Magdalene came to the tomb early, while it was still dark. She saw that the stone had been removed from the tomb. ²So she ran to Simon Peter and to the other disciple, the one Jesus loved, and said to them, "They have taken the Lord out of the tomb, and we don't know where they have put Him!"

³At that, Peter and the other disciple went out, heading for the tomb. ⁴The two were running together, but the other disciple outran Peter and got to the tomb first. ⁵Stooping down, he saw the linen cloths lying there, yet he did not go in. ⁶Then, following him, Simon Peter came also. He entered the tomb and saw the linen cloths lying there. ⁷The wrapping that had been on His head was not lying with the linen cloths but was folded up in a separate place by itself. ⁸The other disciple, who had reached the tomb first, then entered the tomb, saw, and believed. ⁹For they still did not understand the Scripture that He must rise from the dead. ¹⁰Then the disciples went home again.

¹¹But Mary stood outside facing the tomb, crying. As she was crying, she stooped to look into the tomb. ¹²She saw two angels in white sitting there, one at the head and one at the feet, where Jesus' body had been lying. ¹³They said to her, "·Woman, why are you crying?"

"Because they've taken away my Lord," she told them, "and I don't know where they've put Him." ¹⁴Having said this, she turned around and saw Jesus standing there, though she did not know it was Jesus.

¹⁵"Woman," Jesus said to her, "why are you crying? Who is it you are looking for?"

Supposing He was the gardener, she replied, "Sir, if you've removed Him, tell me where you've put Him, and I will take Him away."

¹⁶Jesus said, "Mary."

Turning around, she said to Him in ·Hebrew, "*Rabbouni!*"—which means "Teacher."

¹⁷"Don't cling to Me," Jesus told her, "for I have not yet ascended to the Father. But go to My brothers and tell them that I am ascending to My Father and your Father—to My God and your God."

¹⁸Mary Magdalene went and announced to the disciples, "I have seen the Lord!" And she told them what He had said to her.

¹⁹In the evening of that first day of the week, the disciples were gathered together with the doors locked because of their fear of the ·Jews. Then Jesus came, stood among them, and said to them, "Peace to you!" ²⁰Having said this, He showed them His hands and His side. So the disciples rejoiced when they saw the Lord.

²¹Jesus said to them again, "Peace to you! As the Father has sent Me, I also send you." ²²After saying this, He breathed on them and said, "Receive the Holy Spirit. ²³If you forgive the sins of any, they are forgiven them; if you retain the sins of any, they are retained."

²⁴But one of the Twelve, Thomas (called "Twin"), was not with them when Jesus came. ²⁵So the other disciples kept telling him, "We have seen the Lord!"

But he said to them, "If I don't see the mark of the nails in His hands, put my finger into the mark of the nails, and put my hand into His side, I will never believe!"

²⁶After eight days His disciples were indoors again, and Thomas was with them. Even though the doors were locked, Jesus came and stood among them. He said, "Peace to you!" ²⁷Then He said to Thomas, "Put your finger here and observe My hands. Reach out your hand and put it into My side. Don't be an unbeliever, but a believer."

²⁸Thomas responded to Him, "My Lord and my God!"

²⁹Jesus said, "Because you have seen Me, you have believed. Those who believe without seeing are blessed."

³⁰Jesus performed many other signs in the presence of His disciples that are not written in this book. ³¹But these are written so that you may believe Jesus is the ·Messiah, the Son of God, and by believing you may have life in His name.

21 After this, Jesus revealed Himself again to His disciples by the Sea of Tiberias. He revealed Himself in this way: ²Simon Peter, Thomas (called "Twin"), Nathanael from Cana of Galilee, Zebedee's sons, and two others of His disciples were together.

³"I'm going fishing," Simon Peter said to them.

"We're coming with you," they told him. They went out and got into the boat, but that night they caught nothing.

⁴When daybreak came, Jesus stood on the shore. However, the disciples did not know it was Jesus.

⁵"Men," Jesus called to them, "you don't have any fish, do you?"

"No," they answered.

⁶"Cast the net on the right side of the boat," He told them, "and you'll find some." So they did, and they were unable to haul it in because of the large number of fish. ⁷Therefore the disciple, the one Jesus loved, said to Peter, "It is the Lord!"

When Simon Peter heard that it was the Lord, he tied his outer garment around him (for he was stripped) and plunged into the sea. ⁸But since they were not far from land (about 100 yards away), the other disciples came in the boat, dragging the net full of fish. ⁹When they got out on land, they saw a charcoal fire there, with fish lying on it, and bread.

¹⁰"Bring some of the fish you've just caught," Jesus told them. ¹¹So Simon Peter got up and hauled the net

ashore, full of large fish—153 of them. Even though there were so many, the net was not torn.

[12]"Come and have breakfast," Jesus told them. None of the disciples dared ask Him, "Who are You?" because they knew it was the Lord. [13]Jesus came, took the bread, and gave it to them. He did the same with the fish.

[14]This was now the third time Jesus appeared to the disciples after He was raised from the dead.

[15]When they had eaten breakfast, Jesus asked Simon Peter, "Simon, son of John, do you love Me more than these?"

"Yes, Lord," he said to Him, "You know that I love You."

"Feed My lambs," He told him.

[16]A second time He asked him, "Simon, son of John, do you love Me?"

"Yes, Lord," he said to Him, "You know that I love You."

"Shepherd My sheep," He told him.

[17]He asked him the third time, "Simon, son of John, do you love Me?"

Peter was grieved that He asked him the third time, "Do you love Me?" He said, "Lord, You know everything! You know that I love You."

"Feed My sheep," Jesus said. [18]"I assure you: When you were young, you would tie your belt and walk wherever you wanted. But when you grow old, you will stretch out your hands and someone else will tie you and carry you where you don't want to go." [19]He said this to signify by what kind of death he would glorify God. After saying this, He told him, "Follow Me!"

[20]So Peter turned around and saw the disciple Jesus loved following them. That disciple was the one who had leaned back against Jesus at the supper and asked, "Lord, who is the one that's going to betray You?" [21]When Peter saw him, he said to Jesus, "Lord—what about him?"

[22]"If I want him to remain until I come," Jesus answered, "what is that to you? As for you, follow Me."

[23]So this report spread to the *brothers that this disciple would not die. Yet Jesus did not tell him that he would not die, but, "If I want him to remain until I come, what is that to you?"

[24]This is the disciple who testifies to these things and who wrote them down. We know that his testimony is true.

[25]And there are also many other things that Jesus did, which, if they were written one by one, I suppose not even the world itself could contain the books that would be written.

ACTS

1 I wrote the first narrative, Theophilus, about all that Jesus began to do and teach [2]until the day He was taken up, after He had given orders through the Holy Spirit to the apostles He had chosen. [3]After He had suffered, He also presented Himself alive to them by many convincing proofs, appearing to them during 40 days and speaking about the kingdom of God.

[4]While He was together with them, He commanded them not to leave Jerusalem, but to wait for the Father's promise. "This," He said, "is what you heard from Me; [5]for John baptized with water, but you will be baptized with the Holy Spirit not many days from now."

[6]So when they had come together, they asked Him, "Lord, are You restoring the kingdom to Israel at this time?"

[7]He said to them, "It is not for you to know times or periods that the Father has set by His own authority. [8]But you will receive power when the Holy Spirit has come on you, and you will be My witnesses in Jerusalem, in all Judea and Samaria, and to the ends of the earth."

[9]After He had said this, He was taken up as they were watching, and a cloud took Him out of their sight. [10]While He was going, they were gazing into heaven, and suddenly two men in white clothes stood by them. [11]They said, "Men of Galilee, why do you stand looking up into heaven? This Jesus, who has been taken from you into heaven, will come in the same way that you have seen Him going into heaven."

[12]Then they returned to Jerusalem from the mount called the Mount of Olives, which is near Jerusalem—a Sabbath day's journey away. [13]When they arrived, they went to the room upstairs where they were staying:

Peter, John,
James, Andrew,
Philip, Thomas,
Bartholomew, Matthew,
James the son of Alphaeus,
Simon the Zealot,
and Judas the son of James.

[14]All these were continually united in prayer, along with the women, including Mary the mother of Jesus, and His brothers.

[15]During these days Peter stood up among the *brothers—the number of people who were together was about 120—and said: [16]"Brothers, the Scripture had to be fulfilled that the Holy Spirit through the mouth of David spoke in advance about Judas, who became a guide to those who arrested Jesus. [17]For he was one of our number and was allotted a share in this ministry." [18]Now this man acquired a field with his unrighteous wages. He fell headfirst and burst open in the middle, and all his insides spilled out. [19]This became known to all the residents of Jerusalem, so that in their own language that field is called *Hakeldama* (that is, Field of Blood). [20]"For it is written in the Book of Psalms:

**Let his dwelling become desolate;
let no one live in it;** and
Let someone else take his position.

[21]"Therefore, from among the men who have accompanied us during the whole time the Lord Jesus went in and out among us— [22]beginning from the baptism of John until the day He was taken up from us—from among these, it is necessary that one become a witness with us of His resurrection."

[23]So they proposed two: Joseph, called Barsabbas, who was also known as Justus, and Matthias. [24]Then they prayed, "You, Lord, know the hearts of all; show

which of these two You have chosen ²⁵to take the place in this apostolic service that Judas left to go to his own place." ²⁶Then they cast lots for them, and the lot fell to Matthias. So he was numbered with the 11 apostles.

2 When the day of Pentecost had arrived, they were all together in one place. ²Suddenly a sound like that of a violent rushing wind came from heaven, and it filled the whole house where they were staying. ³And tongues, like flames of fire that were divided, appeared to them and rested on each one of them. ⁴Then they were all filled with the Holy Spirit and began to speak in different *languages, as the Spirit gave them ability for speech.

⁵There were Jews living in Jerusalem, devout men from every nation under heaven. ⁶When this sound occurred, a crowd came together and was confused because each one heard them speaking in his own language. ⁷And they were astounded and amazed, saying, "Look, aren't all these who are speaking Galileans? ⁸How is it that each of us can hear in our own native language? ⁹Parthians, Medes, Elamites; those who live in Mesopotamia, in Judea and Cappadocia, Pontus and *Asia, ¹⁰Phrygia and Pamphylia, Egypt and the parts of Libya near Cyrene; visitors from Rome, both Jews and *proselytes, ¹¹Cretans and Arabs—we hear them speaking the magnificent acts of God in our own languages." ¹²They were all astounded and perplexed, saying to one another, "What could this be?" ¹³But some sneered and said, "They're full of new wine!"

¹⁴But Peter stood up with the Eleven, raised his voice, and proclaimed to them: "Men of Judah and all you residents of Jerusalem, let me explain this to you and pay attention to my words. ¹⁵For these people are not drunk, as you suppose, since it's only nine in the morning. ¹⁶On the contrary, this is what was spoken through the prophet Joel:

¹⁷ **And it will be** in the last days, says God,
that **I will pour out My Spirit**
on all humanity;
then your sons and your daughters
will prophesy,
your young men will see visions,
and your old men will dream dreams.
¹⁸ **I will even pour out My Spirit**
on My male and female *slaves in those days,
and they will prophesy.
¹⁹ **I will display wonders in the heaven** above
and signs on the earth below:
blood and fire and a cloud of smoke.
²⁰ **The sun will be turned to darkness**
and the moon to blood
before the great and remarkable Day of the
Lord comes.
²¹ **Then everyone who calls**
on the name of the Lord will be saved.

²²"Men of Israel, listen to these words: This Jesus the *Nazarene was a man pointed out to you by God with miracles, wonders, and signs that God did among you through Him, just as you yourselves know. ²³Though He was delivered up according to God's determined plan and foreknowledge, you used lawless people to nail Him to a cross and kill Him. ²⁴God raised Him up, ending the pains of death, because it was not possible for Him to be held by it. ²⁵For David says of Him:

I saw the Lord ever before me;
because He is at my right hand,
I will not be shaken.

²⁶ **Therefore my heart was glad,**
and my tongue rejoiced.
Moreover, my flesh will rest in hope,
²⁷ **because You will not leave me in *Hades**
or allow Your Holy One to see decay.
²⁸ **You have revealed the paths of life to me;**
You will fill me with gladness
in Your presence.

²⁹"Brothers, I can confidently speak to you about the patriarch David: He is both dead and buried, and his tomb is with us to this day. ³⁰Since he was a prophet, he knew that God had sworn an oath to him to seat one of his descendants on his throne. ³¹Seeing this in advance, he spoke concerning the resurrection of the *Messiah:

He was not left in Hades,
and His flesh did not experience decay.

³²"God has resurrected this Jesus. We are all witnesses of this. ³³Therefore, since He has been exalted to the right hand of God and has received from the Father the promised Holy Spirit, He has poured out what you both see and hear. ³⁴For it was not David who ascended into the heavens, but he himself says:

The Lord declared to my Lord,
'Sit at My right hand
³⁵ **until I make Your enemies Your footstool.'**

³⁶"Therefore let all the house of Israel know with certainty that God has made this Jesus, whom you crucified, both Lord and Messiah!"

³⁷When they heard this, they came under deep conviction and said to Peter and the rest of the apostles: "Brothers, what must we do?"

³⁸"Repent," Peter said to them, "and be baptized, each of you, in the name of Jesus Christ for the forgiveness of your sins, and you will receive the gift of the Holy Spirit. ³⁹For the promise is for you and for your children, and for all who are far off, as many as the Lord our God will call." ⁴⁰And with many other words he testified and strongly urged them, saying, "Be saved from this corrupt generation!"

⁴¹So those who accepted his message were baptized, and that day about 3,000 people were added to them. ⁴²And they devoted themselves to the apostles' teaching, to the fellowship, to the breaking of bread, and to the prayers.

⁴³Then fear came over everyone, and many wonders and signs were being performed through the apostles. ⁴⁴Now all the believers were together and held all things in common. ⁴⁵They sold their possessions and property and distributed the proceeds to all, as anyone had a need. ⁴⁶Every day they devoted themselves to meeting together in the *temple complex, and broke bread from house to house. They ate their food with a joyful and humble attitude, ⁴⁷praising God and having favor with all the people. And every day the Lord added to them those who were being saved.

3 Now Peter and John were going up together to the *temple complex at the hour of prayer at three in the afternoon. ²And a man who was lame from birth was carried there and placed every day at the temple gate called Beautiful, so he could beg from those entering the temple complex. ³When he saw Peter and John about to enter the temple complex, he asked for help. ⁴Peter, along with John, looked at him intently and said, "Look at us." ⁵So he turned to them, expecting to get something from them. ⁶But Peter said, "I don't have silver or gold, but what I have, I give you:

In the name of Jesus Christ the ᵛNazarene, get up and walk!" ⁷Then, taking him by the right hand he raised him up, and at once his feet and ankles became strong. ⁸So he jumped up, stood, and started to walk, and he entered the temple complex with them—walking, leaping, and praising God. ⁹All the people saw him walking and praising God, ¹⁰and they recognized that he was the one who used to sit and beg at the Beautiful Gate of the temple complex. So they were filled with awe and astonishment at what had happened to him.

¹¹ While he was holding on to Peter and John, all the people, greatly amazed, ran toward them in what is called Solomon's Colonnade. ¹²When Peter saw this, he addressed the people: "Men of Israel, why are you amazed at this? Or why do you stare at us, as though we had made him walk by our own power or godliness? ¹³The God of Abraham, Isaac, and Jacob, the God of our fathers, has glorified His Servant Jesus, whom you handed over and denied in the presence of ᵛPilate, when he had decided to release Him. ¹⁴But you denied the Holy and Righteous One and asked to have a murderer given to you. ¹⁵You killed the source of life, whom God raised from the dead; we are witnesses of this. ¹⁶By faith in His name, His name has made this man strong, whom you see and know. So the faith that comes through Him has given him this perfect health in front of all of you.

¹⁷"And now, ᵛbrothers, I know that you did it in ignorance, just as your leaders also did. ¹⁸But what God predicted through the mouth of all the prophets—that His ᵛMessiah would suffer—He has fulfilled in this way. ¹⁹Therefore repent and turn back, so that your sins may be wiped out, that seasons of refreshing may come from the presence of the Lord, ²⁰and that He may send Jesus, who has been appointed for you as the Messiah. ²¹Heaven must welcome Him until the times of the restoration of all things, which God spoke about by the mouth of His holy prophets from the beginning. ²²Moses said:

> **The Lord your God will raise up for you a Prophet like me from among your brothers. You must listen to Him in everything He will say to you.** ²³**And everyone who will not listen to that Prophet will be completely cut off from the people.**

²⁴"In addition, all the prophets who have spoken, from Samuel and those after him, have also announced these days. ²⁵You are the sons of the prophets and of the covenant that God made with your ancestors, saying to Abraham, **And all the families of the earth will be blessed through your offspring.** ²⁶God raised up His Servant and sent Him first to you to bless you by turning each of you from your evil ways."

4 Now as they were speaking to the people, the priests, the commander of the temple police, and the ᵛSadducees confronted them, ²because they were provoked that they were teaching the people and proclaiming the resurrection from the dead, using Jesus as the example. ³So they seized them and put them in custody until the next day, since it was already evening. ⁴But many of those who heard the message believed, and the number of the men came to about 5,000.

⁵The next day, their rulers, elders, and ᵛscribes assembled in Jerusalem ⁶with Annas the high ᵛpriest, Caiaphas, John and Alexander, and all the members of the high-priestly family. ⁷After they had Peter and John stand before them, they asked the question: "By what power or in what name have you done this?"

⁸Then Peter was filled with the Holy Spirit and said to them, "Rulers of the people and elders: ⁹If we are being examined today about a good deed done to a disabled man—by what means he was healed— ¹⁰let it be known to all of you and to all the people of Israel, that by the name of Jesus Christ the ᵛNazarene—whom you crucified and whom God raised from the dead— by Him this man is standing here before you healthy. ¹¹This Jesus is

> **the stone rejected by you builders, which has become the cornerstone.**

¹²There is salvation in no one else, for there is no other name under heaven given to people, and we must be saved by it."

¹³When they observed the boldness of Peter and John and realized that they were uneducated and untrained men, they were amazed and recognized that they had been with Jesus. ¹⁴And since they saw the man who had been healed standing with them, they had nothing to say in response. ¹⁵After they had ordered them to leave the ᵛSanhedrin, they conferred among themselves, ¹⁶saying, "What should we do with these men? For an obvious sign, evident to all who live in Jerusalem, has been done through them, and we cannot deny it! ¹⁷However, so this does not spread any further among the people, let's threaten them against speaking to anyone in this name again." ¹⁸So they called for them and ordered them not to preach or teach at all in the name of Jesus.

¹⁹But Peter and John answered them, "Whether it's right in the sight of God for us to listen to you rather than to God, you decide; ²⁰for we are unable to stop speaking about what we have seen and heard."

²¹After threatening them further, they released them. They found no way to punish them, because the people were all giving glory to God over what had been done; ²²for this sign of healing had been performed on a man over 40 years old.

²³After they were released, they went to their own people and reported everything the ᵛchief priests and the elders had said to them. ²⁴When they heard this, they all raised their voices to God and said, "Master, You are the One who made the heaven, the earth, and the sea, and everything in them. ²⁵You said through the Holy Spirit, by the mouth of our father David Your servant:

> **Why did the Gentiles rage**
> **and the peoples plot futile things?**
> ²⁶ **The kings of the earth took their stand**
> **and the rulers assembled together**
> **against the Lord and against His ᵛMessiah.**

²⁷"For, in fact, in this city both ᵛHerod and Pontius ᵛPilate, with the Gentiles and the people of Israel, assembled together against Your holy Servant Jesus, whom You anointed, ²⁸to do whatever Your hand and Your plan had predestined to take place. ²⁹And now, Lord, consider their threats, and grant that Your ᵛslaves may speak Your message with complete boldness, ³⁰while You stretch out Your hand for healing, signs, and wonders to be performed through the name of Your holy Servant Jesus." ³¹When they had prayed, the place where they were assembled was shaken, and they were all filled with the Holy Spirit and began to speak God's message with boldness.

³²Now the large group of those who believed were

of one heart and mind, and no one said that any of his possessions was his own, but instead they held everything in common. ³³And the apostles were giving testimony with great power to the resurrection of the Lord Jesus, and great grace was on all of them. ³⁴For there was not a needy person among them, because all those who owned lands or houses sold them, brought the proceeds of the things that were sold, ³⁵and laid them at the apostles' feet. This was then distributed for each person's basic needs.

³⁶Joseph, a Levite and a Cypriot by birth, the one the apostles called Barnabas, which is translated Son of Encouragement, ³⁷sold a field he owned, brought the money, and laid it at the apostles' feet.

5 But a man named Ananias, with his wife Sapphira, sold a piece of property. ²However, he kept back part of the proceeds with his wife's knowledge, and brought a portion of it and laid it at the apostles' feet. ³Then Peter said, "Ananias, why has Satan filled your heart to lie to the Holy Spirit and keep back part of the proceeds from the field? ⁴Wasn't it yours while you possessed it? And after it was sold, wasn't it at your disposal? Why is it that you planned this thing in your heart? You have not lied to men but to God!" ⁵When he heard these words, Ananias dropped dead, and a great fear came on all who heard. ⁶The young men got up, wrapped his body, carried him out, and buried him.

⁷There was an interval of about three hours; then his wife came in, not knowing what had happened. ⁸"Tell me," Peter asked her, "did you sell the field for this price?"

"Yes," she said, "for that price."

⁹Then Peter said to her, "Why did you agree to test the Spirit of the Lord? Look! The feet of those who have buried your husband are at the door, and they will carry you out!"

¹⁰Instantly she dropped dead at his feet. When the young men came in, they found her dead, carried her out, and buried her beside her husband. ¹¹Then great fear came on the whole church and on all who heard these things.

¹²Many signs and wonders were being done among the people through the hands of the apostles. By common consent they would all meet in Solomon's Colonnade. ¹³None of the rest dared to join them, but the people praised them highly. ¹⁴Believers were added to the Lord in increasing numbers—crowds of both men and women. ¹⁵As a result, they would carry the sick out into the streets and lay them on cots and mats so that when Peter came by, at least his shadow might fall on some of them. ¹⁶In addition, a large group came together from the towns surrounding Jerusalem, bringing sick people and those who were tormented by •unclean spirits, and they were all healed.

¹⁷Then the high priest took action. He and all his colleagues, those who belonged to the party of the •Sadducees, were filled with jealousy. ¹⁸So they arrested the apostles and put them in the city jail. ¹⁹But an angel of the Lord opened the doors of the jail during the night, brought them out, and said, ²⁰"Go and stand in the •temple complex, and tell the people all about this life." ²¹In obedience to this, they entered the temple complex at daybreak and began to teach.

When the high priest and those who were with him arrived, they convened the •Sanhedrin—the full Senate of the sons of Israel—and sent orders to the jail to have them brought. ²²But when the temple police

got there, they did not find them in the jail, so they returned and reported, ²³"We found the jail securely locked, with the guards standing in front of the doors, but when we opened them, we found no one inside!" ²⁴As the commander of the temple police and the •chief priests heard these things, they were baffled about them, as to what could come of this.

²⁵Someone came and reported to them, "Look! The men you put in jail are standing in the temple complex and teaching the people." ²⁶Then the commander went with the temple police and brought them in without force, because they were afraid the people might stone them. ²⁷After they brought them in, they had them stand before the Sanhedrin, and the high priest asked, ²⁸"Didn't we strictly order you not to teach in this name? And look, you have filled Jerusalem with your teaching and are determined to bring this man's blood on us!"

²⁹But Peter and the apostles replied, "We must obey God rather than men. ³⁰The God of our fathers raised up Jesus, whom you had murdered by hanging Him on a tree. ³¹God exalted this man to His right hand as ruler and Savior, to grant repentance to Israel, and forgiveness of sins. ³²We are witnesses of these things, and so is the Holy Spirit whom God has given to those who obey Him."

³³When they heard this, they were enraged and wanted to kill them. ³⁴A •Pharisee named Gamaliel, a teacher of the law who was respected by all the people, stood up in the Sanhedrin and ordered the men to be taken outside for a little while. ³⁵He said to them, "Men of Israel, be careful about what you're going to do to these men. ³⁶Not long ago Theudas rose up, claiming to be somebody, and a group of about 400 men rallied to him. He was killed, and all his partisans were dispersed and came to nothing. ³⁷After this man, Judas the Galilean rose up in the days of the census and attracted a following. That man also perished, and all his partisans were scattered. ³⁸And now, I tell you, stay away from these men and leave them alone. For if this plan or this work is of men, it will be overthrown; ³⁹but if it is of God, you will not be able to overthrow them. You may even be found fighting against God." So they were persuaded by him. ⁴⁰After they called in the apostles and had them flogged, they ordered them not to speak in the name of Jesus and released them. ⁴¹Then they went out from the presence of the Sanhedrin, rejoicing that they were counted worthy to be dishonored on behalf of the Name. ⁴²Every day in the temple complex, and in various homes, they continued teaching and proclaiming the good news that Jesus is the •Messiah.

6 In those days, as the number of the disciples was multiplying, there arose a complaint by the Hellenistic Jews against the Hebraic Jews that their widows were being overlooked in the daily distribution. ²Then the Twelve summoned the whole company of the disciples and said, "It would not be right for us to give up preaching about God to handle financial matters. ³Therefore, •brothers, select from among you seven men of good reputation, full of the Spirit and wisdom, whom we can appoint to this duty. ⁴But we will devote ourselves to prayer and to the preaching ministry." ⁵The proposal pleased the whole company. So they chose Stephen, a man full of faith and the Holy Spirit, and Philip, Prochorus, Nicanor, Timon, Parmenas, and Nicolaus, a •proselyte from Antioch. ⁶They had them

stand before the apostles, who prayed and laid their hands on them.

⁷So the preaching about God flourished, the number of the disciples in Jerusalem multiplied greatly, and a large group of priests became obedient to the faith.

⁸Stephen, full of grace and power, was performing great wonders and signs among the people. ⁹Then some from what is called the Freedmen's •Synagogue, composed of both Cyrenians and Alexandrians, and some from Cilicia and •Asia, came forward and disputed with Stephen. ¹⁰But they were unable to stand up against his wisdom and the Spirit by whom he was speaking.

¹¹Then they persuaded some men to say, "We heard him speaking blasphemous words against Moses and God!" ¹²They stirred up the people, the elders, and the •scribes; so they came, dragged him off, and took him to the •Sanhedrin. ¹³They also presented false witnesses who said, "This man does not stop speaking blasphemous words against this holy place and the law. ¹⁴For we heard him say that Jesus, this •Nazarene, will destroy this place and change the customs that Moses handed down to us." ¹⁵And all who were sitting in the Sanhedrin looked intently at him and saw that his face was like the face of an angel.

7 ¹"Is this true?" the high priest asked.
²"Brothers and fathers," he said, "listen: The God of glory appeared to our father Abraham when he was in Mesopotamia, before he settled in Haran, ³and said to him:

> Get out of your country
> and away from your relatives,
> and come to the land
> that I will show you.

⁴"Then he came out of the land of the Chaldeans and settled in Haran. From there, after his father died, God had him move to this land you now live in. ⁵He didn't give him an inheritance in it, not even a foot of ground, but He promised to give it to him as a possession, and to his descendants after him, even though he was childless. ⁶God spoke in this way:

> His descendants would be strangers
> in a foreign country,
> and they would enslave
> and oppress them 400 years.
> ⁷ I will judge the nation
> that they will serve as •slaves, God said.
> After this, they will come out
> and worship Me in this place.

⁸Then He gave him the covenant of circumcision. After this, he fathered Isaac and circumcised him on the eighth day; Isaac did the same with Jacob, and Jacob with the 12 patriarchs.

⁹"The patriarchs became jealous of Joseph and sold him into Egypt, but God was with him ¹⁰and rescued him out of all his troubles. He gave him favor and wisdom in the sight of Pharaoh, king of Egypt, who appointed him ruler over Egypt and over his whole household. ¹¹Then a famine and great suffering came over all of Egypt and Canaan, and our ancestors could find no food. ¹²When Jacob heard there was grain in Egypt, he sent our ancestors the first time. ¹³The second time, Joseph was revealed to his brothers, and Joseph's family became known to Pharaoh. ¹⁴Joseph then invited his father Jacob and all his relatives, 75 people in all, ¹⁵and Jacob went down to Egypt. He

and our ancestors died there, ¹⁶were carried back to Shechem, and were placed in the tomb that Abraham had bought for a sum of silver from the sons of Hamor in Shechem.

¹⁷"As the time was drawing near to fulfill the promise that God had made to Abraham, the people flourished and multiplied in Egypt ¹⁸until a different king who did not know Joseph ruled over Egypt. ¹⁹He dealt deceitfully with our race and oppressed our ancestors by making them leave their infants outside, so they wouldn't survive. ²⁰At this time Moses was born, and he was beautiful in God's sight. He was cared for in his father's home three months, ²¹and when he was left outside, Pharaoh's daughter adopted and raised him as her own son. ²²So Moses was educated in all the wisdom of the Egyptians and was powerful in his speech and actions.

²³"As he was approaching the age of 40, he decided to visit his brothers, the Israelites. ²⁴When he saw one of them being mistreated, he came to his rescue and avenged the oppressed man by striking down the Egyptian. ²⁵He assumed his brothers would understand that God would give them deliverance through him, but they did not understand. ²⁶The next day he showed up while they were fighting and tried to reconcile them peacefully, saying, 'Men, you are brothers. Why are you mistreating each other?'

²⁷"But the one who was mistreating his neighbor pushed him away, saying:

> Who appointed you a ruler and a judge over us?
> ²⁸Do you want to kill me, the same way you
> killed the Egyptian yesterday?

²⁹"At this disclosure, Moses fled and became an exile in the land of Midian, where he fathered two sons. ³⁰After 40 years had passed, an angel appeared to him in the wilderness of Mount Sinai, in the flame of a burning bush. ³¹When Moses saw it, he was amazed at the sight. As he was approaching to look at it, the voice of the Lord came: ³²I am the God of your fathers—the God of Abraham, of Isaac, and of Jacob. So Moses began to tremble and did not dare to look.

³³"Then the Lord said to him:

> Remove the sandals from your feet, for the
> place where you are standing is holy ground.
> ³⁴I have observed the oppression of My people
> in Egypt; I have heard their groaning and have
> come down to rescue them. And now, come, I
> will send you to Egypt.

³⁵"This Moses, whom they rejected when they said, Who appointed you a ruler and a judge?—this one God sent as a ruler and a redeemer by means of the angel who appeared to him in the bush. ³⁶This man led them out and performed wonders and signs in the land of Egypt, at the Red Sea, and in the wilderness 40 years.

³⁷"This is the Moses who said to the Israelites, God will raise up for you a Prophet like me from among your brothers. ³⁸He is the one who was in the congregation in the wilderness together with the angel who spoke to him on Mount Sinai, and with our ancestors. He received living oracles to give to us. ³⁹Our ancestors were unwilling to obey him, but pushed him away, and in their hearts turned back to Egypt. ⁴⁰They told Aaron:

> Make us gods who will go before us. As for this
> Moses who brought us out of the land of Egypt,
> we don't know what's happened to him.

⁴¹They even made a calf in those days, offered sacrifice

to the idol, and were celebrating what their hands had made. [42] Then God turned away and gave them up to worship the host of heaven, as it is written in the book of the prophets:

> **House of Israel, did you bring Me offerings**
> **and sacrifices**
> **40 years in the wilderness?**
> [43] **No, you took up the tent of Moloch**
> **and the star of your god Rephan,**
> **the images that you made to worship.**
> **So I will deport you beyond Babylon!**

[44] "Our ancestors had the tabernacle of the testimony in the wilderness, just as He who spoke to Moses commanded him to make it according to the pattern he had seen. [45] Our ancestors in turn received it and with Joshua brought it in when they dispossessed the nations that God drove out before our fathers, until the days of David. [46] He found favor in God's sight and asked that he might provide a dwelling place for the God of Jacob. [47] But it was Solomon who built Him a house. [48] However, the Most High does not dwell in sanctuaries made with hands, as the prophet says:

> [49] **Heaven is My throne,**
> **and earth My footstool.**
> **What sort of house will you build for Me?**
> **says the Lord,**
> **or what is My resting place?**
> [50] **Did not My hand make all these things?**

[51] "You stiff-necked people with uncircumcised hearts and ears! You are always resisting the Holy Spirit; as your ancestors did, so do you. [52] Which of the prophets did your fathers not persecute? They even killed those who announced beforehand the coming of the Righteous One, whose betrayers and murderers you have now become. [53] You received the law under the direction of angels and yet have not kept it."

[54] When they heard these things, they were enraged in their hearts and gnashed their teeth at him. [55] But Stephen, filled by the Holy Spirit, gazed into heaven. He saw God's glory, with Jesus standing at the right hand of God, and he said, [56] "Look! I see the heavens opened and the ˙Son of Man standing at the right hand of God!"

[57] Then they screamed at the top of their voices, covered their ears, and together rushed against him. [58] They threw him out of the city and began to stone him. And the witnesses laid their robes at the feet of a young man named Saul. [59] They were stoning Stephen as he called out: "Lord Jesus, receive my spirit!" [60] Then he knelt down and cried out with a loud voice, "Lord, do not charge them with this sin!" And saying this, he fell ˙asleep.

8 Saul agreed with putting him to death.
On that day a severe persecution broke out against the church in Jerusalem, and all except the apostles were scattered throughout the land of Judea and Samaria. [2] Devout men buried Stephen and mourned deeply over him. [3] Saul, however, was ravaging the church. He would enter house after house, drag off men and women, and put them in prison.

[4] So those who were scattered went on their way preaching the message of good news. [5] Philip went down to a city in Samaria and proclaimed the ˙Messiah to them. [6] The crowds paid attention with one mind to what Philip said, as they heard and saw the signs he was performing. [7] For ˙unclean spirits, crying out with a loud voice, came out of many who were possessed,

and many who were paralyzed and lame were healed. [8] So there was great joy in that city.

[9] A man named Simon had previously practiced sorcery in that city and astounded the ˙Samaritan people, while claiming to be somebody great. [10] They all paid attention to him, from the least of them to the greatest, and they said, "This man is called the Great Power of God!" [11] They were attentive to him because he had astounded them with his sorceries for a long time. [12] But when they believed Philip, as he preached the good news about the kingdom of God and the name of Jesus Christ, both men and women were baptized. [13] Then even Simon himself believed. And after he was baptized, he went around constantly with Philip and was astounded as he observed the signs and great miracles that were being performed.

[14] When the apostles who were at Jerusalem heard that Samaria had welcomed God's message, they sent Peter and John to them. [15] After they went down there, they prayed for them, so the Samaritans might receive the Holy Spirit. [16] For He had not yet come down on any of them; they had only been baptized in the name of the Lord Jesus. [17] Then Peter and John laid their hands on them, and they received the Holy Spirit.

[18] When Simon saw that the Holy Spirit was given through the laying on of the apostles' hands, he offered them money, [19] saying, "Give me this power too, so that anyone I lay hands on may receive the Holy Spirit."

[20] But Peter told him, "May your silver be destroyed with you, because you thought the gift of God could be obtained with money! [21] You have no part or share in this matter, because your heart is not right before God. [22] Therefore repent of this wickedness of yours, and pray to the Lord that the intent of your heart may be forgiven you. [23] For I see you are poisoned by bitterness and bound by iniquity."

[24] "Please pray to the Lord for me," Simon replied, "so that nothing you have said may happen to me."

[25] Then, after they had testified and spoken the message of the Lord, they traveled back to Jerusalem, evangelizing many villages of the Samaritans.

[26] An angel of the Lord spoke to Philip: "Get up and go south to the road that goes down from Jerusalem to Gaza." (This is the desert road.) [27] So he got up and went. There was an Ethiopian man, a eunuch and high official of Candace, queen of the Ethiopians, who was in charge of her entire treasury. He had come to worship in Jerusalem [28] and was sitting in his chariot on his way home, reading the prophet Isaiah aloud.

[29] The Spirit told Philip, "Go and join that chariot."

[30] When Philip ran up to it, he heard him reading the prophet Isaiah, and said, "Do you understand what you're reading?"

[31] "How can I," he said, "unless someone guides me?" So he invited Philip to come up and sit with him. [32] Now the Scripture passage he was reading was this:

> **He was led like a sheep to the slaughter,**
> **and as a lamb is silent before its shearer,**
> **so He does not open His mouth.**
> [33] **In His humiliation justice was denied Him.**
> **Who will describe His generation?**
> **For His life is taken from the earth.**

[34] The eunuch replied to Philip, "I ask you, who is the prophet saying this about—himself or another person?" [35] So Philip proceeded to tell him the good news about Jesus, beginning from that Scripture.

[36] As they were traveling down the road, they came to some water. The eunuch said, "Look, there's water! What would keep me from being baptized?" [[37] And Philip said, "If you believe with all your heart you may." And he replied, "I believe that Jesus Christ is the Son of God."] [38] Then he ordered the chariot to stop, and both Philip and the eunuch went down into the water, and he baptized him. [39] When they came up out of the water, the Spirit of the Lord carried Philip away, and the eunuch did not see him any longer. But he went on his way rejoicing. [40] Philip appeared in Azotus, and he was traveling and evangelizing all the towns until he came to Caesarea.

9 Meanwhile, Saul was still breathing threats and murder against the disciples of the Lord. He went to the high priest [2] and requested letters from him to the *synagogues in Damascus, so that if he found any men or women who belonged to the Way, he might bring them as prisoners to Jerusalem. [3] As he traveled and was nearing Damascus, a light from heaven suddenly flashed around him. [4] Falling to the ground, he heard a voice saying to him, "Saul, Saul, why are you persecuting Me?"

[5] "Who are You, Lord?" he said.

"I am Jesus, the One you are persecuting," He replied. [6] "But get up and go into the city, and you will be told what you must do."

[7] The men who were traveling with him stood speechless, hearing the sound but seeing no one. [8] Then Saul got up from the ground, and though his eyes were open, he could see nothing. So they took him by the hand and led him into Damascus. [9] He was unable to see for three days and did not eat or drink.

[10] There was a disciple in Damascus named Ananias. And the Lord said to him in a vision, "Ananias!"

"Here I am, Lord!" he said.

[11] "Get up and go to the street called Straight," the Lord said to him, "to the house of Judas, and ask for a man from Tarsus named Saul, since he is praying there. [12] In a vision he has seen a man named Ananias coming in and placing his hands on him so he can regain his sight."

[13] "Lord," Ananias answered, "I have heard from many people about this man, how much harm he has done to Your *saints in Jerusalem. [14] And he has authority here from the *chief priests to arrest all who call on Your name."

[15] But the Lord said to him, "Go! For this man is My chosen instrument to take My name to Gentiles, kings, and the Israelites. [16] I will show him how much he must suffer for My name!"

[17] So Ananias left and entered the house. Then he placed his hands on him and said, "Brother Saul, the Lord Jesus, who appeared to you on the road you were traveling, has sent me so that you can regain your sight and be filled with the Holy Spirit."

[18] At once something like scales fell from his eyes, and he regained his sight. Then he got up and was baptized. [19] And after taking some food, he regained his strength.

Saul was with the disciples in Damascus for some days. [20] Immediately he began proclaiming Jesus in the synagogues: "He is the Son of God."

[21] But all who heard him were astounded and said, "Isn't this the man who, in Jerusalem, was destroying those who called on this name and then came here for the purpose of taking them as prisoners to the chief priests?"

[22] But Saul grew more capable and kept confounding the Jews who lived in Damascus by proving that this One is the *Messiah.

[23] After many *days had passed, the Jews conspired to kill him, [24] but their plot became known to Saul. So they were watching the gates day and night intending to kill him, [25] but his disciples took him by night and lowered him in a large basket through an opening in the wall.

[26] When he arrived in Jerusalem, he tried to associate with the disciples, but they were all afraid of him, since they did not believe he was a disciple. [27] Barnabas, however, took him and brought him to the apostles and explained to them how Saul had seen the Lord on the road and that He had talked to him, and how in Damascus he had spoken boldly in the name of Jesus. [28] Saul was coming and going with them in Jerusalem, speaking boldly in the name of the Lord. [29] He conversed and debated with the Hellenistic Jews, but they attempted to kill him. [30] When the *brothers found out, they took him down to Caesarea and sent him off to Tarsus.

[31] So the church throughout all Judea, Galilee, and Samaria had peace, being built up and walking in the *fear of the Lord and in the encouragement of the Holy Spirit, and it increased in numbers.

[32] As Peter was traveling from place to place, he also came down to the saints who lived in Lydda. [33] There he found a man named Aeneas, who was paralyzed and had been bedridden for eight years. [34] Peter said to him, "Aeneas, Jesus Christ heals you. Get up and make your bed," and immediately he got up. [35] So all who lived in Lydda and Sharon saw him and turned to the Lord.

[36] In Joppa there was a disciple named Tabitha, which is translated Dorcas. She was always doing good works and acts of charity. [37] In those days she became sick and died. After washing her, they placed her in a room upstairs. [38] Since Lydda was near Joppa, the disciples heard that Peter was there and sent two men to him who begged him, "Don't delay in coming with us." [39] So Peter got up and went with them. When he arrived, they led him to the room upstairs. And all the widows approached him, weeping and showing him the robes and clothes that Dorcas had made while she was with them. [40] Then Peter sent them all out of the room. He knelt down, prayed, and turning toward the body said, "Tabitha, get up!" She opened her eyes, saw Peter, and sat up. [41] He gave her his hand and helped her stand up. Then he called the saints and widows and presented her alive. [42] This became known throughout Joppa, and many believed in the Lord. [43] And Peter stayed on many days in Joppa with Simon, a leather tanner.

10 There was a man in Caesarea named Cornelius, a *centurion of what was called the Italian *Regiment. [2] He was a devout man and feared God along with his whole household. He did many charitable deeds for the Jewish people and always prayed to God. [3] About three in the afternoon he distinctly saw in a vision an angel of God who came in and said to him, "Cornelius!"

[4] Looking intently at him, he became afraid and said, "What is it, lord?"

The angel told him, "Your prayers and your acts of

charity have come up as a memorial offering before God. ⁵Now send men to Joppa and call for Simon, who is also named Peter. ⁶He is lodging with Simon, a tanner, whose house is by the sea."

⁷When the angel who spoke to him had gone, he called two of his household slaves and a devout soldier, who was one of those who attended him. ⁸After explaining everything to them, he sent them to Joppa. ⁹The next day, as they were traveling and nearing the city, Peter went up to pray on the housetop about noon. ¹⁰Then he became hungry and wanted to eat, but while they were preparing something, he went into a visionary state. ¹¹He saw heaven opened and an object that resembled a large sheet coming down, being lowered by its four corners to the earth. ¹²In it were all the four-footed animals and reptiles of the earth, and the birds of the sky. ¹³Then a voice said to him, "Get up, Peter; kill and eat!"

¹⁴"No, Lord!" Peter said. "For I have never eaten anything common and ritually ˙unclean!"

¹⁵Again, a second time, a voice said to him, "What God has made ˙clean, you must not call common." ¹⁶This happened three times, and then the object was taken up into heaven.

¹⁷While Peter was deeply perplexed about what the vision he had seen might mean, the men who had been sent by Cornelius, having asked directions to Simon's house, stood at the gate. ¹⁸They called out, asking if Simon, who was also named Peter, was lodging there.

¹⁹While Peter was thinking about the vision, the Spirit told him, "Three men are here looking for you. ²⁰Get up, go downstairs, and accompany them with no doubts at all, because I have sent them."

²¹Then Peter went down to the men and said, "Here I am, the one you're looking for. What is the reason you're here?"

²²They said, "Cornelius, a centurion, an upright and God-fearing man, who has a good reputation with the whole Jewish nation, was divinely directed by a holy angel to call you to his house and to hear a message from you." ²³Peter then invited them in and gave them lodging.

The next day he got up and set out with them, and some of the brothers from Joppa went with him. ²⁴The following day he entered Caesarea. Now Cornelius was expecting them and had called together his relatives and close friends. ²⁵When Peter entered, Cornelius met him, fell at his feet, and worshiped him. ²⁶But Peter helped him up and said, "Stand up! I myself am also a man." ²⁷While talking with him, he went on in and found that many had come together there. ²⁸Peter said to them, "You know it's forbidden for a Jewish man to associate with or visit a foreigner. But God has shown me that I must not call any person common or unclean. ²⁹That's why I came without any objection when I was sent for. So I ask: Why did you send for me?"

³⁰Cornelius replied, "Four days ago at this hour, at three in the afternoon, I was praying in my house. Just then a man in a dazzling robe stood before me ³¹and said, 'Cornelius, your prayer has been heard, and your acts of charity have been remembered in God's sight. ³²Therefore send someone to Joppa and invite Simon here, who is also named Peter. He is lodging in Simon the tanner's house by the sea.' ³³Therefore I immediately sent for you, and you did the right thing

in coming. So we are all present before God, to hear everything you have been commanded by the Lord."

³⁴Then Peter began to speak: "Now I really understand that God doesn't show favoritism, ³⁵but in every nation the person who fears Him and does righteousness is acceptable to Him. ³⁶He sent the message to the Israelites, proclaiming the good news of peace through Jesus Christ—He is Lord of all. ³⁷You know the events that took place throughout Judea, beginning from Galilee after the baptism that John preached: ³⁸how God anointed Jesus of Nazareth with the Holy Spirit and with power, and how He went about doing good and healing all who were under the tyranny of the Devil, because God was with Him. ³⁹We ourselves are witnesses of everything He did in both the Judean country and in Jerusalem, yet they killed Him by hanging Him on a tree. ⁴⁰God raised up this man on the third day and permitted Him to be seen, ⁴¹not by all the people, but by us, witnesses appointed beforehand by God, who ate and drank with Him after He rose from the dead. ⁴²He commanded us to preach to the people and to solemnly testify that He is the One appointed by God to be the Judge of the living and the dead. ⁴³All the prophets testify about Him that through His name everyone who believes in Him will receive forgiveness of sins."

⁴⁴While Peter was still speaking these words, the Holy Spirit came down on all those who heard the message. ⁴⁵The circumcised believers who had come with Peter were astounded because the gift of the Holy Spirit had been poured out on the Gentiles also. ⁴⁶For they heard them speaking in other ˙languages and declaring the greatness of God.

Then Peter responded, ⁴⁷"Can anyone withhold water and prevent these people from being baptized, who have received the Holy Spirit just as we have?" ⁴⁸And he commanded them to be baptized in the name of Jesus Christ. Then they asked him to stay for a few days.

11 The apostles and the ˙brothers who were throughout Judea heard that the Gentiles had welcomed God's message also. ²When Peter went up to Jerusalem, those who stressed circumcision argued with him, ³saying, "You visited uncircumcised men and ate with them!"

⁴Peter began to explain to them in an orderly sequence, saying: ⁵"I was in the town of Joppa praying, and I saw, in a visionary state, an object that resembled a large sheet coming down, being lowered by its four corners from heaven, and it came to me. ⁶When I looked closely and considered it, I saw the four-footed animals of the earth, the wild beasts, the reptiles, and the birds of the sky. ⁷Then I also heard a voice telling me, 'Get up, Peter; kill and eat!'

⁸"No, Lord!' I said. 'For nothing common or ritually ˙unclean has ever entered my mouth!' ⁹But a voice answered from heaven a second time, 'What God has made ˙clean, you must not call common.' ¹⁰"Now this happened three times, and then everything was drawn up again into heaven. ¹¹At that very moment, three men who had been sent to me from Caesarea arrived at the house where we were. ¹²Then the Spirit told me to accompany them with no doubts at all. These six brothers accompanied me, and we went into the man's house. ¹³He reported to us how he had seen the angel standing in his house and saying, 'Send to Joppa, and call for Simon, who is also

named Peter. [14] He will speak a message to you that you and all your household will be saved by.'

[15] "As I began to speak, the Holy Spirit came down on them, just as on us at the beginning. [16] Then I remembered the word of the Lord, how He said, 'John baptized with water, but you will be baptized with the Holy Spirit.' [17] Therefore, if God gave them the same gift that He also gave to us when we believed on the Lord Jesus Christ, how could I possibly hinder God?"

[18] When they heard this they became silent. Then they glorified God, saying, "So God has granted repentance resulting in life even to the Gentiles!"

[19] Those who had been scattered as a result of the persecution that started because of Stephen made their way as far as Phoenicia, Cyprus, and Antioch, speaking the message to no one except Jews. [20] But there were some of them, Cypriot and Cyrenian men, who came to Antioch and began speaking to the Hellenists, proclaiming the good news about the Lord Jesus. [21] The Lord's hand was with them, and a large number who believed turned to the Lord. [22] Then the report about them was heard by the church that was at Jerusalem, and they sent out Barnabas to travel as far as Antioch. [23] When he arrived and saw the grace of God, he was glad and encouraged all of them to remain true to the Lord with a firm resolve of the heart, [24] for he was a good man, full of the Holy Spirit and of faith. And large numbers of people were added to the Lord. [25] Then he went to Tarsus to search for Saul, [26] and when he found him he brought him to Antioch. For a whole year they met with the church and taught large numbers. The disciples were first called Christians at Antioch.

[27] In those days some prophets came down from Jerusalem to Antioch. [28] Then one of them, named Agabus, stood up and predicted by the Spirit that there would be a severe famine throughout the Roman world. This took place during the time of Claudius. [29] So each of the disciples, according to his ability, determined to send relief to the brothers who lived in Judea. [30] They did this, sending it to the elders by means of Barnabas and Saul.

12 About that time King •Herod cruelly attacked some who belonged to the church, [2] and he killed James, John's brother, with the sword. [3] When he saw that it pleased the Jews, he proceeded to arrest Peter too, during the days of •Unleavened Bread. [4] After the arrest, he put him in prison and assigned four squads of four soldiers each to guard him, intending to bring him out to the people after the •Passover. [5] So Peter was kept in prison, but prayer was being made earnestly to God for him by the church.

[6] On the night before Herod was to bring him out for execution, Peter, bound with two chains, was sleeping between two soldiers, while the sentries in front of the door guarded the prison. [7] Suddenly an angel of the Lord appeared, and a light shone in the cell. Striking Peter on the side, he woke him up and said, "Quick, get up!" Then the chains fell off his wrists. [8] "Get dressed," the angel told him, "and put on your sandals." And he did so. "Wrap your cloak around you," he told him, "and follow me." [9] So he went out and followed, and he did not know that what took place through the angel was real, but thought he was seeing a vision. [10] After they passed the first and second guard posts, they came to the iron gate that leads into the city, which

opened to them by itself. They went outside and passed one street, and immediately the angel left him.

[11] Then Peter came to himself and said, "Now I know for certain that the Lord has sent His angel and rescued me from Herod's grasp and from all that the Jewish people expected." [12] When he realized this, he went to the house of Mary, the mother of John Mark, where many had assembled and were praying. [13] He knocked at the door in the gateway, and a servant named Rhoda came to answer. [14] She recognized Peter's voice, and because of her joy, she did not open the gate but ran in and announced that Peter was standing at the gateway.

[15] "You're crazy!" they told her. But she kept insisting that it was true. Then they said, "It's his angel!" [16] Peter, however, kept on knocking, and when they opened the door and saw him, they were astounded.

[17] Motioning to them with his hand to be silent, he explained to them how the Lord had brought him out of the prison. "Report these things to James and the •brothers," he said. Then he departed and went to a different place.

[18] At daylight, there was a great commotion among the soldiers as to what could have become of Peter. [19] After Herod had searched and did not find him, he interrogated the guards and ordered their execution. Then Herod went down from Judea to Caesarea and stayed there.

[20] He had been very angry with the Tyrians and Sidonians. Together they presented themselves before him. They won over Blastus, who was in charge of the king's bedroom, and through him they asked for peace, because their country was supplied with food from the king's country. [21] So on an appointed day, dressed in royal robes and seated on the throne, Herod delivered a public address to them. [22] The assembled people began to shout, "It's the voice of a god and not of a man!" [23] At once an angel of the Lord struck him because he did not give the glory to God, and he became infected with worms and died. [24] Then God's message flourished and multiplied. [25] After they had completed their relief mission, Barnabas and Saul returned to Jerusalem, taking along John who is called Mark.

13 In the church that was at Antioch there were prophets and teachers: Barnabas, Simeon who was called Niger, Lucius the Cyrenian, Manaen, a close friend of •Herod the tetrarch, and Saul.

[2] As they were ministering to the Lord and fasting, the Holy Spirit said, "Set apart for Me Barnabas and Saul for the work I have called them to." [3] Then after they had fasted, prayed, and laid hands on them, they sent them off.

[4] Being sent out by the Holy Spirit, they came down to Seleucia, and from there they sailed to Cyprus. [5] Arriving in Salamis, they proclaimed God's message in the Jewish •synagogues. They also had John as their assistant. [6] When they had gone through the whole island as far as Paphos, they came across a sorcerer, a Jewish false prophet named Bar-Jesus. [7] He was with the •proconsul, Sergius Paulus, an intelligent man. This man summoned Barnabas and Saul and desired to hear God's message. [8] But Elymas the sorcerer (this is the meaning of his name) opposed them and tried to turn the proconsul away from the faith.

[9] Then Saul—also called Paul—filled with the Holy Spirit, stared straight at the sorcerer [10] and said, "You son of the Devil, full of all deceit and all fraud, enemy of all righteousness! Won't you ever stop perverting

the straight paths of the Lord? [11] Now, look! The Lord's hand is against you. You are going to be blind, and will not see the sun for a time." Suddenly a mist and darkness fell on him, and he went around seeking someone to lead him by the hand.

[12] Then the proconsul, seeing what happened, believed and was astonished at the teaching about the Lord.

[13] Paul and his companions set sail from Paphos and came to Perga in Pamphylia. John, however, left them and went back to Jerusalem. [14] They continued their journey from Perga and reached Antioch in Pisidia. On the Sabbath day they went into the synagogue and sat down. [15] After the reading of the Law and the Prophets, the leaders of the synagogue sent word to them, saying, "Brothers, if you have any message of encouragement for the people, you can speak."

[16] Then Paul stood up and motioned with his hand and said: "Men of Israel, and you who fear God, listen! [17] The God of this people Israel chose our ancestors, exalted the people during their stay in the land of Egypt, and led them out of it with a mighty arm. [18] And for about 40 years He put up with them in the wilderness; [19] then after destroying seven nations in the land of Canaan, He gave their land to them as an inheritance. [20] This all took about 450 years. After this, He gave them judges until Samuel the prophet. [21] Then they asked for a king, so God gave them Saul the son of Kish, a man of the tribe of Benjamin, for 40 years. [22] After removing him, He raised up David as their king and testified about him: '**I have found David** the son of Jesse, **a man loyal to Me,** who will carry out all My will.'

[23] "From this man's descendants, according to the promise, God brought the Savior, Jesus, to Israel. [24] Before He came to public attention, John had previously proclaimed a baptism of repentance to all the people of Israel. [25] Then as John was completing his life's work, he said, 'Who do you think I am? I am not the One. But look! Someone is coming after me, and I am not worthy to untie the sandals on His feet.'

[26] "Brothers, sons of Abraham's race, and those among you who fear God, the message of this salvation has been sent to us. [27] For the residents of Jerusalem and their rulers, since they did not recognize Him or the voices of the prophets that are read every Sabbath, have fulfilled their words by condemning Him. [28] Though they found no grounds for the death penalty, they asked *Pilate to have Him killed. [29] When they had fulfilled all that had been written about Him, they took Him down from the tree and put Him in a tomb. [30] But God raised Him from the dead, [31] and He appeared for many days to those who came with Him from Galilee to Jerusalem, who are now His witnesses to the people. [32] And we ourselves proclaim to you the good news of the promise that was made to our ancestors. [33] God has fulfilled this for us, their children, by raising up Jesus, as it is written in the second Psalm:

You are My Son;
today I have become Your Father.

[34] Since He raised Him from the dead, never to return to decay, He has spoken in this way, **I will grant you the faithful covenant blessings made to David.** [35] Therefore He also says in another passage, **You will not allow Your Holy One to see decay.** [36] For David, after serving his own generation in God's plan, fell *asleep, was buried with his fathers, and decayed. [37] But the One God raised up did not decay. [38] Therefore, let

it be known to you, brothers, that through this man forgiveness of sins is being proclaimed to you, [39] and everyone who believes in Him is *justified from everything that you could not be justified from through the law of Moses. [40] So beware that what is said in the prophets does not happen to you:

[41]   **Look, you scoffers,**
       marvel and vanish away,
       because I am doing a work in your days,
       a work that you will never believe,
       even if someone were to explain it to you."

[42] As they were leaving, the people begged that these matters be presented to them the following Sabbath. [43] After the synagogue had been dismissed, many of the Jews and devout *proselytes followed Paul and Barnabas, who were speaking with them and persuading them to continue in the grace of God.

[44] The following Sabbath almost the whole town assembled to hear the message of the Lord. [45] But when the Jews saw the crowds, they were filled with jealousy and began to oppose what Paul was saying by insulting him.

[46] Then Paul and Barnabas boldly said: "It was necessary that God's message be spoken to you first. But since you reject it and consider yourselves unworthy of eternal life, we now turn to the Gentiles! [47] For this is what the Lord has commanded us:

I have made you
a light for the Gentiles
to bring salvation
to the ends of the earth."

[48] When the Gentiles heard this, they rejoiced and glorified the message of the Lord, and all who had been appointed to eternal life believed. [49] So the message of the Lord spread through the whole region. [50] But the Jews incited the prominent women, who worshiped God, and the leading men of the city. They stirred up persecution against Paul and Barnabas and expelled them from their district. [51] But they shook the dust off their feet against them and went to Iconium. [52] And the disciples were filled with joy and the Holy Spirit.

14 The same thing happened in Iconium; they entered the Jewish *synagogue and spoke in such a way that a great number of both Jews and Greeks believed. [2] But the Jews who refused to believe stirred up and poisoned the minds of the Gentiles against the brothers. [3] So they stayed there for some time and spoke boldly in reliance on the Lord, who testified to the message of His grace by granting that signs and wonders be performed through them. [4] But the people of the city were divided, some siding with the Jews and some with the apostles. [5] When an attempt was made by both the Gentiles and Jews, with their rulers, to assault and stone them, [6] they found out about it and fled to the Lycaonian towns called Lystra and Derbe, and to the surrounding countryside. [7] And there they kept evangelizing.

[8] In Lystra a man without strength in his feet, lame from birth, and who had never walked, sat [9] and heard Paul speaking. After observing him closely and seeing that he had faith to be healed, [10] Paul said in a loud voice, "Stand upright on your feet!" And he jumped up and started to walk around.

[11] When the crowds saw what Paul had done, they raised their voices, saying in the Lycaonian language, "The gods have come down to us in the form of men!" [12] And they started to call Barnabas, Zeus, and Paul,

Hermes, because he was the main speaker. [13] Then the priest of Zeus, whose temple was just outside the town, brought oxen and garlands to the gates. He, with the crowds, intended to offer sacrifice.

[14] The apostles Barnabas and Paul tore their robes when they heard this and rushed into the crowd, shouting: [15] "Men! Why are you doing these things? We are men also, with the same nature as you, and we are proclaiming good news to you, that you should turn from these worthless things to the living God, **who made the heaven, the earth, the sea, and everything in them.** [16] In past generations He allowed all the nations to go their own way, [17] although He did not leave Himself without a witness, since He did what is good by giving you rain from heaven and fruitful seasons and satisfying your hearts with food and happiness." [18] Even though they said these things, they barely stopped the crowds from sacrificing to them.

[19] Then some Jews came from Antioch and Iconium, and when they had won over the crowds and stoned Paul, they dragged him out of the city, thinking he was dead. [20] After the disciples surrounded him, he got up and went into the town. The next day he left with Barnabas for Derbe.

[21] After they had evangelized that town and made many disciples, they returned to Lystra, to Iconium, and to Antioch, [22] strengthening the disciples by encouraging them to continue in the faith and by telling them, "It is necessary to pass through many troubles on our way into the kingdom of God."

[23] When they had appointed elders in every church and prayed with fasting, they committed them to the Lord in whom they had believed. [24] Then they passed through Pisidia and came to Pamphylia. [25] After they spoke the message in Perga, they went down to Attalia. [26] From there they sailed back to Antioch where they had been entrusted to the grace of God for the work they had now completed. [27] After they arrived and gathered the church together, they reported everything God had done with them and that He had opened the door of faith to the Gentiles. [28] And they spent a considerable time with the disciples.

15 Some men came down from Judea and began to teach the brothers: "Unless you are circumcised according to the custom prescribed by Moses, you cannot be saved!" [2] But after Paul and Barnabas had engaged them in serious argument and debate, the church arranged for Paul and Barnabas and some others of them to go up to the apostles and elders in Jerusalem concerning this controversy. [3] When they had been sent on their way by the church, they passed through both Phoenicia and Samaria, explaining in detail the conversion of the Gentiles, and they created great joy among all the brothers.

[4] When they arrived at Jerusalem, they were welcomed by the church, the apostles, and the elders, and they reported all that God had done with them. [5] But some of the believers from the party of the *Pharisees stood up and said, "It is necessary to circumcise them and to command them to keep the law of Moses!"

[6] Then the apostles and the elders assembled to consider this matter. [7] After there had been much debate, Peter stood up and said to them: "Brothers, you are aware that in the early days God made a choice among you, that by my mouth the Gentiles would hear the gospel message and believe. [8] And God, who knows the heart, testified to them by giving the Holy Spirit, just

as He also did to us. [9] He made no distinction between us and them, cleansing their hearts by faith. [10] Now then, why are you testing God by putting a yoke on the disciples' necks that neither our ancestors nor we have been able to bear? [11] On the contrary, we believe we are saved through the grace of the Lord Jesus in the same way they are."

[12] Then the whole assembly fell silent and listened to Barnabas and Paul describing all the signs and wonders God had done through them among the Gentiles. [13] After they stopped speaking, James responded: "Brothers, listen to me! [14] Simeon has reported how God first intervened to take from the Gentiles a people for His name. [15] And the words of the prophets agree with this, as it is written:

[16] **After these things I will return**
   and rebuild David's fallen tent.
   I will rebuild its ruins
   and set it up again,
[17] **so the rest of humanity**
   may seek the Lord—
   even all the Gentiles
   who are called by My name,
   declares the Lord who does these things,
[18] **known from long ago.**

[19] Therefore, in my judgment, we should not cause difficulties for those among the Gentiles who turn to God, [20] but instead we should write to them to abstain from things polluted by idols, from sexual immorality, from eating anything that has been strangled, and from blood. [21] For since ancient times, Moses has had those who proclaim him in every city, and every Sabbath day he is read aloud in the *synagogues."

[22] Then the apostles and the elders, with the whole church, decided to select men who were among them and to send them to Antioch with Paul and Barnabas: Judas, called Barsabbas, and Silas, both leading men among the brothers. [23] They wrote this letter to be delivered by them:

From the apostles and the elders, your brothers,
To the brothers among the Gentiles in Antioch,
Syria, and Cilicia:
Greetings:
[24] Because we have heard that some without our authorization went out from us and troubled you with their words and unsettled your hearts, [25] we have unanimously decided to select men and send them to you along with our dearly loved Barnabas and Paul, [26] who have risked their lives for the name of our Lord Jesus Christ. [27] Therefore we have sent Judas and Silas, who will personally report the same things by word of mouth. [28] For it was the Holy Spirit's decision—and ours—to put no greater burden on you than these necessary things: [29] that you abstain from food offered to idols, from blood, from eating anything that has been strangled, and from sexual immorality. You will do well if you keep yourselves from these things.
Farewell.

[30] Then, being sent off, they went down to Antioch, and after gathering the assembly, they delivered the letter. [31] When they read it, they rejoiced because of its encouragement. [32] Both Judas and Silas, who were also prophets themselves, encouraged the brothers and strengthened them with a long message. [33] After spending some time there, they were sent back in

peace by the •brothers to those who had sent them. ³⁵But Paul and Barnabas, along with many others, remained in Antioch teaching and proclaiming the message of the Lord.

³⁶After some time had passed, Paul said to Barnabas, "Let's go back and visit the brothers in every town where we have preached the message of the Lord and see how they're doing." ³⁷Barnabas wanted to take along John Mark. ³⁸But Paul did not think it appropriate to take along this man who had deserted them in Pamphylia and had not gone on with them to the work. ³⁹There was such a sharp disagreement that they parted company, and Barnabas took Mark with him and sailed off to Cyprus. ⁴⁰Then Paul chose Silas and departed, after being commended to the grace of the Lord by the brothers. ⁴¹He traveled through Syria and Cilicia, strengthening the churches.

16 Then he went on to Derbe and Lystra, where there was a disciple named Timothy, the son of a believing Jewish woman, but his father was a Greek. ²The •brothers at Lystra and Iconium spoke highly of him. ³Paul wanted Timothy to go with him, so he took him and circumcised him because of the Jews who were in those places, since they all knew that his father was a Greek. ⁴As they traveled through the towns, they delivered the decisions reached by the apostles and elders at Jerusalem for them to observe. ⁵So the churches were strengthened in the faith and increased in number daily.

⁶They went through the region of Phrygia and Galatia and were prevented by the Holy Spirit from speaking the message in •Asia. ⁷When they came to Mysia, they tried to go into Bithynia, but the Spirit of Jesus did not allow them. ⁸So, bypassing Mysia, they came down to Troas. ⁹During the night a vision appeared to Paul: A Macedonian man was standing and pleading with him, "Cross over to Macedonia and help us!" ¹⁰After he had seen the vision, we immediately made efforts to set out for Macedonia, concluding that God had called us to evangelize them.

¹¹Then, setting sail from Troas, we ran a straight course to Samothrace, the next day to Neapolis, ¹²and from there to Philippi, a Roman colony, which is a leading city of that district of Macedonia. We stayed in that city for a number of days. ¹³On the Sabbath day we went outside the city gate by the river, where we thought there was a place of prayer. We sat down and spoke to the women gathered there. ¹⁴A woman named Lydia, a dealer in purple cloth from the city of Thyatira, who worshiped God, was listening. The Lord opened her heart to pay attention to what was spoken by Paul. ¹⁵After she and her household were baptized, she urged us, "If you consider me a believer in the Lord, come and stay at my house." And she persuaded us.

¹⁶Once, as we were on our way to prayer, a •slave girl met us who had a spirit of prediction. She made a large profit for her owners by fortune-telling. ¹⁷As she followed Paul and us she cried out, "These men, who are proclaiming to you the way of salvation, are the slaves of the Most High God." ¹⁸And she did this for many days.

But Paul was greatly aggravated and turning to the spirit, said, "I command you in the name of Jesus Christ to come out of her!" And it came out right away.

¹⁹When her owners saw that their hope of profit was gone, they seized Paul and Silas and dragged them into the marketplace to the authorities. ²⁰Bringing them before the chief magistrates, they said, "These men are seriously disturbing our city. They are Jews ²¹and are promoting customs that are not legal for us as Romans to adopt or practice."

²²Then the mob joined in the attack against them, and the chief magistrates stripped off their clothes and ordered them to be beaten with rods. ²³After they had inflicted many blows on them, they threw them in jail, ordering the jailer to keep them securely guarded. ²⁴Receiving such an order, he put them into the inner prison and secured their feet in the stocks.

²⁵About midnight Paul and Silas were praying and singing hymns to God, and the prisoners were listening to them. ²⁶Suddenly there was such a violent earthquake that the foundations of the jail were shaken, and immediately all the doors were opened, and everyone's chains came loose. ²⁷When the jailer woke up and saw the doors of the prison open, he drew his sword and was going to kill himself, since he thought the prisoners had escaped.

²⁸But Paul called out in a loud voice, "Don't harm yourself, because all of us are here!"

²⁹Then the jailer called for lights, rushed in, and fell down trembling before Paul and Silas. ³⁰Then he escorted them out and said, "Sirs, what must I do to be saved?"

³¹So they said, "Believe on the Lord Jesus, and you will be saved—you and your household." ³²Then they spoke the message of the Lord to him along with everyone in his house. ³³He took them the same hour of the night and washed their wounds. Right away he and all his family were baptized. ³⁴He brought them into his house, set a meal before them, and rejoiced because he had believed God with his entire household.

³⁵When daylight came, the chief magistrates sent the police to say, "Release those men!"

³⁶The jailer reported these words to Paul: "The magistrates have sent orders for you to be released. So come out now and go in peace."

³⁷But Paul said to them, "They beat us in public without a trial, although we are Roman citizens, and threw us in jail. And now are they going to smuggle us out secretly? Certainly not! On the contrary, let them come themselves and escort us out!"

³⁸Then the police reported these words to the magistrates. They were afraid when they heard that Paul and Silas were Roman citizens. ³⁹So they came and apologized to them, and escorting them out, they urged them to leave town. ⁴⁰After leaving the jail, they came to Lydia's house where they saw and encouraged the brothers, and departed.

17 Then they traveled through Amphipolis and Apollonia and came to Thessalonica, where there was a Jewish •synagogue. ²As usual, Paul went to the synagogue, and on three Sabbath days reasoned with them from the Scriptures, ³explaining and showing that the •Messiah had to suffer and rise from the dead: "This Jesus I am proclaiming to you is the Messiah." ⁴Then some of them were persuaded and joined Paul and Silas, including a great number of God-fearing Greeks, as well as a number of the leading women.

⁵But the Jews became jealous, and they brought together some scoundrels from the marketplace, formed a mob, and started a riot in the city. Attacking Jason's house, they searched for them to bring them out to the public assembly. ⁶When they did not find them,

they dragged Jason and some of the •brothers before the city officials, shouting, "These men who have turned the world upside down have come here too, [7]and Jason has received them as guests! They are all acting contrary to Caesar's decrees, saying that there is another king—Jesus!" [8]The Jews stirred up the crowd and the city officials who heard these things. [9]So taking a security bond from Jason and the others, they released them.

[10]As soon as it was night, the brothers sent Paul and Silas off to Berea. On arrival, they went into the synagogue of the Jews. [11]The people here were more open-minded than those in Thessalonica, since they welcomed the message with eagerness and examined the Scriptures daily to see if these things were so. [12]Consequently, many of them believed, including a number of the prominent Greek women as well as men. [13]But when the Jews from Thessalonica found out that God's message had been proclaimed by Paul at Berea, they came there too, agitating and disturbing the crowds. [14]Then the brothers immediately sent Paul away to go to the sea, but Silas and Timothy stayed on there. [15]Those who escorted Paul brought him as far as Athens, and after receiving instructions for Silas and Timothy to come to him as quickly as possible, they departed.

[16]While Paul was waiting for them in Athens, his spirit was troubled within him when he saw that the city was full of idols. [17]So he reasoned in the synagogue with the Jews and with those who worshiped God and in the marketplace every day with those who happened to be there. [18]Then also, some of the Epicurean and Stoic philosophers argued with him. Some said, "What is this pseudo-intellectual trying to say?" Others replied, "He seems to be a preacher of foreign deities"—because he was telling the good news about Jesus and the Resurrection.

[19]They took him and brought him to the Areopagus, and said, "May we learn about this new teaching you're speaking of? [20]For what you say sounds strange to us, and we want to know what these ideas mean." [21]Now all the Athenians and the foreigners residing there spent their time on nothing else but telling or hearing something new.

[22]Then Paul stood in the middle of the Areopagus and said: "Men of Athens! I see that you are extremely religious in every respect. [23]For as I was passing through and observing the objects of your worship, I even found an altar on which was inscribed:

TO AN UNKNOWN GOD.

Therefore, what you worship in ignorance, this I proclaim to you. [24]The God who made the world and everything in it—He is Lord of heaven and earth and does not live in shrines made by hands. [25]Neither is He served by human hands, as though He needed anything, since He Himself gives everyone life and breath and all things. [26]From one man He has made every nationality to live over the whole earth and has determined their appointed times and the boundaries of where they live. [27]He did this so they might seek God, and perhaps they might reach out and find Him, though He is not far from each one of us. [28]For in Him we live and move and exist, as even some of your own poets have said, 'For we are also His offspring.' [29]Being God's offspring then, we shouldn't think that the divine nature is like gold or silver or stone, an image fashioned by human art and imagination.

[30]"Therefore, having overlooked the times of ignorance, God now commands all people everywhere to repent, [31]because He has set a day when He is going to judge the world in righteousness by the Man He has appointed. He has provided proof of this to everyone by raising Him from the dead."

[32]When they heard about resurrection of the dead, some began to ridicule him. But others said, "We'd like to hear from you again about this." [33]Then Paul left their presence. [34]However, some men joined him and believed, including Dionysius the Areopagite, a woman named Damaris, and others with them.

18

After this, he left Athens and went to Corinth, [2]where he found a Jewish man named Aquila, a native of Pontus, who had recently come from Italy with his wife Priscilla because Claudius had ordered all the Jews to leave Rome. Paul came to them, [3]and being of the same occupation, stayed with them and worked, for they were tentmakers by trade. [4]He reasoned in the •synagogue every Sabbath and tried to persuade both Jews and Greeks.

[5]When Silas and Timothy came down from Macedonia, Paul was occupied with preaching the message and solemnly testified to the Jews that Jesus is the •Messiah. [6]But when they resisted and blasphemed, he shook his robe and told them, "Your blood is on your own heads! I am innocent. From now on I will go to the Gentiles." [7]So he left there and went to the house of a man named Titius Justus, a worshiper of God, whose house was next door to the synagogue. [8]Crispus, the leader of the synagogue, believed the Lord, along with his whole household. Many of the Corinthians, when they heard, believed and were baptized.

[9]Then the Lord said to Paul in a night vision, "Don't be afraid, but keep on speaking and don't be silent. [10]For I am with you, and no one will lay a hand on you to hurt you, because I have many people in this city." [11]And he stayed there a year and six months, teaching the word of God among them.

[12]While Gallio was •proconsul of Achaia, the Jews made a united attack against Paul and brought him to the judge's bench. [13]"This man," they said, "persuades people to worship God contrary to the law!"

[14]As Paul was about to open his mouth, Gallio said to the Jews, "If it were a matter of a crime or of moral evil, it would be reasonable for me to put up with you Jews. [15]But if these are questions about words, names, and your own law, see to it yourselves. I don't want to be a judge of such things." [16]So he drove them from the judge's bench. [17]Then they all seized Sosthenes, the leader of the synagogue, and beat him in front of the judge's bench. But none of these things concerned Gallio.

[18]So Paul, having stayed on for many days, said good-bye to the •brothers and sailed away to Syria. Priscilla and Aquila were with him. He shaved his head at Cenchreae because he had taken a vow. [19]When they reached Ephesus he left them there, but he himself entered the synagogue and engaged in discussion with the Jews. [20]And though they asked him to stay for a longer time, he declined, [21]but he said good-bye and stated, "I'll come back to you again, if God wills." Then he set sail from Ephesus.

[22]On landing at Caesarea, he went up and greeted the church and went down to Antioch. [23]And after spending some time there, he set out, traveling

through one place after another in the Galatian territory and Phrygia, strengthening all the disciples.

²⁴A Jew named Apollos, a native Alexandrian, an eloquent man who was powerful in the use of the Scriptures, arrived in Ephesus. ²⁵This man had been instructed in the way of the Lord; and being fervent in spirit, he spoke and taught the things about Jesus accurately, although he knew only John's baptism. ²⁶He began to speak boldly in the synagogue. After Priscilla and Aquila heard him, they took him home and explained the way of God to him more accurately. ²⁷When he wanted to cross over to Achaia, the brothers wrote to the disciples urging them to welcome him. After he arrived, he greatly helped those who had believed through grace. ²⁸For he vigorously refuted the Jews in public, demonstrating through the Scriptures that Jesus is the Messiah.

19 While Apollos was in Corinth, Paul traveled through the interior regions and came to Ephesus. He found some disciples ²and asked them, "Did you receive the Holy Spirit when you believed?"

"No," they told him, "we haven't even heard that there is a Holy Spirit."

³"Then what baptism were you baptized with?" he asked them.

"With John's baptism," they replied.

⁴Paul said, "John baptized with a baptism of repentance, telling the people that they should believe in the One who would come after him, that is, in Jesus."

⁵When they heard this, they were baptized in the name of the Lord Jesus. ⁶And when Paul laid his hands on them, the Holy Spirit came on them, and they began to speak in other ⁎languages and to prophesy. ⁷Now there were about 12 men in all.

⁸Then he entered the ⁎synagogue and spoke boldly over a period of three months, engaging in discussion and trying to persuade them about the things of the kingdom of God. ⁹But when some became hardened and would not believe, slandering the Way in front of the crowd, he withdrew from them and met separately with the disciples, conducting discussions every day in the lecture hall of Tyrannus. ¹⁰And this went on for two years, so that all the inhabitants of ⁎Asia, both Jews and Greeks, heard the message about the Lord.

¹¹God was performing extraordinary miracles by Paul's hands, ¹²so that even facecloths or work aprons that had touched his skin were brought to the sick, and the diseases left them, and the evil spirits came out of them.

¹³Then some of the itinerant Jewish exorcists attempted to pronounce the name of the Lord Jesus over those who had evil spirits, saying, "I command you by the Jesus that Paul preaches!" ¹⁴Seven sons of Sceva, a Jewish ⁎chief priest, were doing this. ¹⁵The evil spirit answered them, "I know Jesus, and I recognize Paul—but who are you?" ¹⁶Then the man who had the evil spirit leaped on them, overpowered them all, and prevailed against them, so that they ran out of that house naked and wounded. ¹⁷This became known to everyone who lived in Ephesus, both Jews and Greeks. Then fear fell on all of them, and the name of the Lord Jesus was magnified. ¹⁸And many who had become believers came confessing and disclosing their practices, ¹⁹while many of those who had practiced magic collected their books and burned them in front of everyone. So they calculated their value and found it to be 50,000 pieces

of silver. ²⁰In this way the Lord's message flourished and prevailed.

²¹When these events were over, Paul resolved in the Spirit to pass through Macedonia and Achaia and go to Jerusalem. "After I've been there," he said, "I must see Rome as well!" ²²So after sending two of those who assisted him, Timothy and Erastus, to Macedonia, he himself stayed in Asia for a while.

²³During that time there was a major disturbance about the Way. ²⁴For a person named Demetrius, a silversmith who made silver shrines of Artemis, provided a great deal of business for the craftsmen. ²⁵When he had assembled them, as well as the workers engaged in this type of business, he said: "Men, you know that our prosperity is derived from this business. ²⁶You both see and hear that not only in Ephesus, but in almost all of Asia, this man Paul has persuaded and misled a considerable number of people by saying that gods made by hand are not gods! ²⁷So not only do we run a risk that our business may be discredited, but also that the temple of the great goddess Artemis may be despised and her magnificence come to the verge of ruin—the very one all of Asia and the world adore."

²⁸When they had heard this, they were filled with rage and began to cry out, "Great is Artemis of the Ephesians!" ²⁹So the city was filled with confusion, and they rushed all together into the amphitheater, dragging along Gaius and Aristarchus, Macedonians who were Paul's traveling companions. ³⁰Though Paul wanted to go in before the people, the disciples did not let him. ³¹Even some of the provincial officials of Asia, who were his friends, sent word to him, pleading with him not to take a chance by going into the amphitheater. ³²Meanwhile, some were shouting one thing and some another, because the assembly was in confusion, and most of them did not know why they had come together. ³³Then some of the crowd gave Alexander advice when the Jews pushed him to the front. So motioning with his hand, Alexander wanted to make his defense to the people. ³⁴But when they recognized that he was a Jew, a united cry went up from all of them for about two hours: "Great is Artemis of the Ephesians!"

³⁵However, when the city clerk had calmed the crowd down, he said, "Men of Ephesus! What man is there who doesn't know that the city of the Ephesians is the temple guardian of the great Artemis, and of the image that fell from heaven? ³⁶Therefore, since these things are undeniable, you must keep calm and not do anything rash. ³⁷For you have brought these men here who are not temple robbers or blasphemers of our goddess. ³⁸So if Demetrius and the craftsmen who are with him have a case against anyone, the courts are in session, and there are ⁎proconsuls. Let them bring charges against one another. ³⁹But if you want something else, it must be decided in a legal assembly. ⁴⁰In fact, we run a risk of being charged with rioting for what happened today, since there is no ⁎justification that we can give as a reason for this disorderly gathering." ⁴¹After saying this, he dismissed the assembly.

20 After the uproar was over, Paul sent for the disciples, encouraged them, and after saying good-bye, departed to go to Macedonia. ²And when he had passed through those areas and exhorted them at length, he came to Greece ³and stayed three months. When he was about to set sail for Syria, a plot was devised against him by the Jews, so a decision was made to go back through Macedonia. ⁴He was accompanied

by Sopater son of Pyrrhus from Berea, Aristarchus and Secundus from Thessalonica, Gaius from Derbe, Timothy, and Tychicus and Trophimus from •Asia. [5] These men went on ahead and waited for us in Troas, [6] but we sailed away from Philippi after the days of •Unleavened Bread. In five days we reached them at Troas, where we spent seven days.

[7] On the first day of the week, we assembled to break bread. Paul spoke to them, and since he was about to depart the next day, he extended his message until midnight. [8] There were many lamps in the room upstairs where we were assembled, [9] and a young man named Eutychus was sitting on a window sill and sank into a deep sleep as Paul kept on speaking. When he was overcome by sleep, he fell down from the third story and was picked up dead. [10] But Paul went down, fell on him, embraced him, and said, "Don't be alarmed, for his •life is in him!" [11] After going upstairs, breaking the bread, and eating, Paul conversed a considerable time until dawn. Then he left. [12] They brought the boy home alive and were greatly comforted.

[13] Then we went on ahead to the ship and sailed for Assos, intending to take Paul on board there. For these were his instructions, since he himself was going by land. [14] When he met us at Assos, we took him on board and came to Mitylene. [15] Sailing from there, the next day we arrived off Chios. The following day we crossed over to Samos, and the day after, we came to Miletus. [16] For Paul had decided to sail past Ephesus so he would not have to spend time in Asia, because he was hurrying to be in Jerusalem, if possible, for the day of Pentecost.

[17] Now from Miletus, he sent to Ephesus and called for the elders of the church. [18] And when they came to him, he said to them: "You know, from the first day I set foot in Asia, how I was with you the whole time— [19] serving the Lord with all humility, with tears, and with the trials that came to me through the plots of the Jews— [20] and that I did not shrink back from proclaiming to you anything that was profitable or from teaching it to you in public and from house to house. [21] I testified to both Jews and Greeks about repentance toward God and faith in our Lord Jesus.

[22] "And now I am on my way to Jerusalem, bound in my spirit, not knowing what I will encounter there, [23] except that in town after town the Holy Spirit testifies to me that chains and afflictions are waiting for me. [24] But I count my life of no value to myself, so that I may finish my course and the ministry I received from the Lord Jesus, to testify to the gospel of God's grace. [25] "And now I know that none of you will ever see my face again—everyone I went about preaching the kingdom to. [26] Therefore I testify to you this day that I am innocent of everyone's blood, [27] for I did not shrink back from declaring to you the whole plan of God. [28] Be on guard for yourselves and for all the flock that the Holy Spirit has appointed you to as •overseers, to shepherd the church of God, which He purchased with His own blood. [29] I know that after my departure savage wolves will come in among you, not sparing the flock. [30] And men will rise up from your own number with deviant doctrines to lure the disciples into following them. [31] Therefore be on the alert, remembering that night and day for three years I did not stop warning each one of you with tears.

[32] "And now I commit you to God and to the message of His grace, which is able to build you up and to give you an inheritance among all who are •sanctified. [33] I have not coveted anyone's silver or gold or clothing. [34] You yourselves know that these hands have provided for my needs and for those who were with me. [35] In every way I've shown you that by laboring like this, it is necessary to help the weak and to keep in mind the words of the Lord Jesus, for He said, 'It is more blessed to give than to receive.'"

[36] After he said this, he knelt down and prayed with all of them. [37] There was a great deal of weeping by everyone. They embraced Paul and kissed him, [38] grieving most of all over his statement that they would never see his face again. Then they escorted him to the ship.

21 After we tore ourselves away from them and set sail, we came by a direct route to Cos, the next day to Rhodes, and from there to Patara. [2] Finding a ship crossing over to Phoenicia, we boarded and set sail. [3] After we sighted Cyprus, leaving it on the left, we sailed on to Syria and arrived at Tyre, because the ship was to unload its cargo there. [4] So we found some disciples and stayed there seven days. Through the Spirit they told Paul not to go to Jerusalem. [5] When our days there were over, we left to continue our journey, while all of them, with their wives and children, escorted us out of the city. After kneeling down on the beach to pray, [6] we said good-bye to one another. Then we boarded the ship, and they returned home.

[7] When we completed our voyage from Tyre, we reached Ptolemais, where we greeted the •brothers and stayed with them one day. [8] The next day we left and came to Caesarea, where we entered the house of Philip the evangelist, who was one of the Seven, and stayed with him. [9] This man had four virgin daughters who prophesied. [10] While we were staying there many days, a prophet named Agabus came down from Judea. [11] He came to us, took Paul's belt, tied his own feet and hands, and said, "This is what the Holy Spirit says: 'In this way the Jews in Jerusalem will bind the man who owns this belt and deliver him into Gentile hands.'" [12] When we heard this, both we and the local people begged him not to go up to Jerusalem.

[13] Then Paul replied, "What are you doing, weeping and breaking my heart? For I am ready not only to be bound but also to die in Jerusalem for the name of the Lord Jesus." [14] Since he would not be persuaded, we stopped talking and simply said, "The Lord's will be done!"

[15] After these days we got ready and went up to Jerusalem. [16] Some of the disciples from Caesarea also went with us and brought us to Mnason, a Cypriot and an early disciple, with whom we were to stay.

[17] When we reached Jerusalem, the brothers welcomed us gladly. [18] The following day Paul went in with us to James, and all the elders were present. [19] After greeting them, he related in detail what God did among the Gentiles through his ministry.

[20] When they heard it, they glorified God and said, "You see, brother, how many thousands of Jews there are who have believed, and they are all zealous for the law. [21] But they have been told about you that you teach all the Jews who are among the Gentiles to abandon Moses, by telling them not to circumcise their children or to walk in our customs. [22] So what is to be done? They will certainly hear that you've

come. ²³Therefore do what we tell you: We have four men who have obligated themselves with a vow. ²⁴Take these men, purify yourself along with them, and pay for them to get their heads shaved. Then everyone will know that what they were told about you amounts to nothing, but that you yourself are also careful about observing the law. ²⁵With regard to the Gentiles who have believed, we have written a letter containing our decision that they should keep themselves from food sacrificed to idols, from blood, from what is strangled, and from sexual immorality."

²⁶Then the next day, Paul took the men, having purified himself along with them, and entered the temple, announcing the completion of the purification days when the offering for each of them would be made. ²⁷As the seven days were about to end, the Jews from *Asia saw him in the *temple complex, stirred up the whole crowd, and seized him, ²⁸shouting, "Men of Israel, help! This is the man who teaches everyone everywhere against our people, our law, and this place. What's more, he also brought Greeks into the temple and has profaned this holy place." ²⁹For they had previously seen Trophimus the Ephesian in the city with him, and they supposed that Paul had brought him into the temple complex.

³⁰The whole city was stirred up, and the people rushed together. They seized Paul, dragged him out of the temple complex, and at once the gates were shut. ³¹As they were trying to kill him, word went up to the commander of the *regiment that all Jerusalem was in chaos. ³²Taking along soldiers and *centurions, he immediately ran down to them. Seeing the commander and the soldiers, they stopped beating Paul. ³³Then the commander came up, took him into custody, and ordered him to be bound with two chains. He asked who he was and what he had done. ³⁴Some in the mob were shouting one thing and some another. Since he was not able to get reliable information because of the uproar, he ordered him to be taken into the barracks. ³⁵When Paul got to the steps, he had to be carried by the soldiers because of the mob's violence, ³⁶for the mass of people followed, yelling, "Take him away!"

³⁷As he was about to be brought into the barracks, Paul said to the commander, "Am I allowed to say something to you?"

He replied, "Do you know Greek? ³⁸Aren't you the Egyptian who raised a rebellion some time ago and led 4,000 Assassins into the wilderness?"

³⁹Paul said, "I am a Jewish man from Tarsus of Cilicia, a citizen of an important city. Now I ask you, let me speak to the people."

⁴⁰After he had given permission, Paul stood on the steps and motioned with his hand to the people. When there was a great hush, he addressed them in the *Hebrew language: ¹"Brothers and fathers, listen now to my defense before you." ²When they heard that he was addressing them in the Hebrew language, they became even quieter. ³He continued, "I am a Jewish man, born in Tarsus of Cilicia but brought up in this city at the feet of Gamaliel and educated according to the strict view of our patriarchal law. Being zealous for God, just as all of you are today, ⁴I persecuted this Way to the death, binding and putting both men and women in jail, ⁵as both the high priest and the whole council of elders can testify about me. After I received letters from them to the brothers, I traveled

22

to Damascus to bring those who were prisoners there to be punished in Jerusalem.

⁶"As I was traveling and near Damascus, about noon an intense light from heaven suddenly flashed around me. ⁷I fell to the ground and heard a voice saying to me, 'Saul, Saul, why are you persecuting Me?'

⁸"I answered, 'Who are You, Lord?'

"He said to me, 'I am Jesus the *Nazarene, the One you are persecuting!' ⁹Now those who were with me saw the light, but they did not hear the voice of the One who was speaking to me.

¹⁰"Then I said, 'What should I do, Lord?'

"And the Lord told me, 'Get up and go into Damascus, and there you will be told about everything that is assigned for you to do.'

¹¹"Since I couldn't see because of the brightness of that light, I was led by the hand by those who were with me, and came into Damascus. ¹²Someone named Ananias, a devout man according to the law, having a good reputation with all the Jews residing there, ¹³came and stood by me and said, 'Brother Saul, regain your sight.' And in that very hour I looked up and saw him. ¹⁴Then he said, 'The God of our fathers has appointed you to know His will, to see the Righteous One, and to hear the sound of His voice. ¹⁵For you will be a witness for Him to all people of what you have seen and heard. ¹⁶And now, why delay? Get up and be baptized, and wash away your sins by calling on His name.'

¹⁷"After I came back to Jerusalem and was praying in the *temple complex, I went into a visionary state ¹⁸and saw Him telling me, 'Hurry and get out of Jerusalem quickly, because they will not accept your testimony about Me!'

¹⁹"But I said, 'Lord, they know that in *synagogue after synagogue I had those who believed in You imprisoned and beaten. ²⁰And when the blood of Your witness Stephen was being shed, I was standing by and approving, and I guarded the clothes of those who killed him.'

²¹"Then He said to me, 'Go, because I will send you far away to the Gentiles.'"

²²They listened to him up to this word. Then they raised their voices, shouting, "Wipe this person off the earth—it's a disgrace for him to live!"

²³As they were yelling and flinging aside their robes and throwing dust into the air, ²⁴the commander ordered him to be brought into the barracks, directing that he be examined with the scourge, so he could discover the reason they were shouting against him like this. ²⁵As they stretched him out for the lash, Paul said to the *centurion standing by, "Is it legal for you to scourge a man who is a Roman citizen and is uncondemned?"

²⁶When the centurion heard this, he went and reported to the commander, saying, "What are you going to do? For this man is a Roman citizen."

²⁷The commander came and said to him, "Tell me—are you a Roman citizen?"

"Yes," he said.

²⁸The commander replied, "I bought this citizenship for a large amount of money."

"But I was born a citizen," Paul said.

²⁹Therefore, those who were about to examine him withdrew from him at once. The commander too was alarmed when he realized Paul was a Roman citizen and he had bound him.

[30] The next day, since he wanted to find out exactly why Paul was being accused by the Jews, he released him and instructed the •chief priests and all the •Sanhedrin to convene. Then he brought Paul

23 down and placed him before them. [1] Paul looked intently at the •Sanhedrin and said, "Brothers, I have lived my life before God in all good conscience until this day." [2] But the high priest Ananias ordered those who were standing next to him to strike him on the mouth. [3] Then Paul said to him, "God is going to strike you, you whitewashed wall! You are sitting there judging me according to the law, and in violation of the law are you ordering me to be struck?"

[4] And those standing nearby said, "Do you dare revile God's high priest?"

[5] "I did not know, brothers, that he was the high priest," replied Paul. "For it is written, **You must not speak evil of a ruler of your people.**" [6] When Paul realized that one part of them were •Sadducees and the other part were •Pharisees, he cried out in the Sanhedrin, "Brothers, I am a Pharisee, a son of Pharisees! I am being judged because of the hope of the resurrection of the dead!" [7] When he said this, a dispute broke out between the Pharisees and the Sadducees, and the assembly was divided. [8] For the Sadducees say there is no resurrection, and no angel or spirit, but the Pharisees affirm them all.

[9] The shouting grew loud, and some of the •scribes of the Pharisees' party got up and argued vehemently: "We find nothing evil in this man. What if a spirit or an angel has spoken to him?" [10] When the dispute became violent, the commander feared that Paul might be torn apart by them and ordered the troops to go down, rescue him from them, and bring him into the barracks.

[11] The following night, the Lord stood by him and said, "Have courage! For as you have testified about Me in Jerusalem, so you must also testify in Rome."

[12] When it was day, the Jews formed a conspiracy and bound themselves under a curse: neither to eat nor to drink until they had killed Paul. [13] There were more than 40 who had formed this plot. [14] These men went to the •chief priests and elders and said, "We have bound ourselves under a solemn curse that we won't eat anything until we have killed Paul. [15] So now you, along with the Sanhedrin, make a request to the commander that he bring him down to you as if you were going to investigate his case more thoroughly. However, before he gets near, we are ready to kill him."

[16] But the son of Paul's sister, hearing about their ambush, came and entered the barracks and reported it to Paul. [17] Then Paul called one of the •centurions and said, "Take this young man to the commander, because he has something to report to him."

[18] So he took him, brought him to the commander, and said, "The prisoner Paul called me and asked me to bring this young man to you, because he has something to tell you."

[19] Then the commander took him by the hand, led him aside, and inquired privately, "What is it you have to report to me?"

[20] "The Jews," he said, "have agreed to ask you to bring Paul down to the Sanhedrin tomorrow, as though they are going to hold a somewhat more careful inquiry about him. [21] Don't let them persuade you, because there are more than 40 of them arranging to ambush him, men who have bound themselves under

a curse not to eat or drink until they kill him. Now they are ready, waiting for a commitment from you."

[22] So the commander dismissed the young man and instructed him, "Don't tell anyone that you have informed me about this."

[23] He summoned two of his centurions and said, "Get 200 soldiers ready with 70 cavalry and 200 spearmen to go to Caesarea at nine tonight. [24] Also provide mounts so they can put Paul on them and bring him safely to Felix the governor."

[25] He wrote a letter of this kind:

[26] Claudius Lysias,

To the most excellent governor Felix:

Greetings.

[27] When this man had been seized by the Jews and was about to be killed by them, I arrived with my troops and rescued him because I learned that he is a Roman citizen. [28] Wanting to know the charge they were accusing him of, I brought him down before their Sanhedrin. [29] I found out that the accusations were about disputed matters in their law, and that there was no charge that merited death or chains. [30] When I was informed that there was a plot against the man, I sent him to you right away. I also ordered his accusers to state their case against him in your presence.

[31] Therefore, the soldiers took Paul during the night and brought him to Antipatris as they were ordered. [32] The next day, they returned to the barracks, allowing the cavalry to go on with him. [33] When these men entered Caesarea and delivered the letter to the governor, they also presented Paul to him. [34] After he read it, he asked what province he was from. So when he learned he was from Cilicia, [35] he said, "I will give you a hearing whenever your accusers get here too." And he ordered that he be kept under guard in •Herod's •palace.

24 After five days Ananias the high priest came down with some elders and a lawyer named Tertullus. These men presented their case against Paul to the governor. [2] When he was called in, Tertullus began to accuse him and said: "Since we enjoy great peace because of you, and reforms are taking place for the benefit of this nation by your foresight, [3] we acknowledge this in every way and everywhere, most excellent Felix, with utmost gratitude. [4] However, so that I will not burden you any further, I beg you in your graciousness to give us a brief hearing. [5] For we have found this man to be a plague, an agitator among all the Jews throughout the Roman world, and a ringleader of the sect of the •Nazarenes! [6] He even tried to desecrate the temple, so we apprehended him [and wanted to judge him according to our law. [7] But Lysias the commander came and took him from our hands with great force, [8] commanding his accusers to come to you.] By examining him yourself you will be able to discern all these things we are accusing him of." [9] The Jews also joined in the attack, alleging that these things were so.

[10] When the governor motioned to him to speak, Paul replied: "Because I know you have been a judge of this nation for many years, I am glad to offer my defense in what concerns me. [11] You are able to determine that it is no more than 12 days since I went up to worship in Jerusalem. [12] They didn't find me disputing with anyone or causing a disturbance among the crowd, either in the •temple complex or in the •syna-

gogues or anywhere in the city. ¹³Neither can they provide evidence to you of what they now bring against me. ¹⁴But I confess this to you: I worship my fathers' God according to the Way, which they call a sect, believing all the things that are written in the Law and in the Prophets. ¹⁵And I have a hope in God, which these men themselves also accept, that there is going to be a resurrection, both of the righteous and the unrighteous. ¹⁶I always do my best to have a clear conscience toward God and men. ¹⁷After many years, I came to bring charitable gifts and offerings to my nation, ¹⁸and while I was doing this, some Jews from *Asia found me ritually purified in the temple, without a crowd and without any uproar. ¹⁹It is they who ought to be here before you to bring charges, if they have anything against me. ²⁰Either let these men here state what wrongdoing they found in me when I stood before the *Sanhedrin, ²¹or about this one statement I cried out while standing among them, 'Today I am being judged before you concerning the resurrection of the dead.'"

²²Since Felix was accurately informed about the Way, he adjourned the hearing, saying, "When Lysias the commander comes down, I will decide your case." ²³He ordered that the *centurion keep Paul under guard, though he could have some freedom, and that he should not prevent any of his friends from serving him.

²⁴After some days, when Felix came with his wife Drusilla, who was Jewish, he sent for Paul and listened to him on the subject of faith in Christ Jesus. ²⁵Now as he spoke about righteousness, self-control, and the judgment to come, Felix became afraid and said, "Leave for now, but when I find time I'll call for you." ²⁶At the same time he was also hoping that money would be given to him by Paul. For this reason he sent for him quite often and conversed with him.

²⁷After two years had passed, Felix received a successor, Porcius Festus, and because he wished to do a favor for the Jews, Felix left Paul in prison.

25 Three days after Festus arrived in the province, he went up to Jerusalem from Caesarea. ²Then the *chief priests and the leaders of the Jews presented their case against Paul to him; and they appealed, ³asking him to do them a favor against Paul, that he might summon him to Jerusalem. They were preparing an ambush along the road to kill him. ⁴However, Festus answered that Paul should be kept at Caesarea, and that he himself was about to go there shortly. ⁵"Therefore," he said, "let the men of authority among you go down with me and accuse him, if there is any wrong in this man."

⁶When he had spent not more than eight or 10 days among them, he went down to Caesarea. The next day, seated at the judge's bench, he commanded Paul to be brought in. ⁷When he arrived, the Jews who had come down from Jerusalem stood around him and brought many serious charges that they were not able to prove, ⁸while Paul made the defense that, "Neither against the Jewish law, nor against the temple, nor against Caesar have I sinned at all."

⁹Then Festus, wanting to do a favor for the Jews, replied to Paul, "Are you willing to go up to Jerusalem, there to be tried before me on these charges?"

¹⁰But Paul said: "I am standing at Caesar's tribunal, where I ought to be tried. I have done no wrong to the Jews, as even you can see very well. ¹¹If then I am doing wrong, or have done anything deserving of death,

I do not refuse to die, but if there is nothing to what these men accuse me of, no one can give me up to them. I appeal to Caesar!"

¹²After Festus conferred with his council, he replied, "You have appealed to Caesar; to Caesar you will go!"

¹³After some days had passed, King Agrippa and Bernice arrived in Caesarea and paid a courtesy call on Festus. ¹⁴Since they stayed there many days, Festus presented Paul's case to the king, saying, "There's a man who was left as a prisoner by Felix. ¹⁵When I was in Jerusalem, the chief priests and the elders of the Jews presented their case and asked for a judgment against him. ¹⁶I answered them that it's not the Romans' custom to give any man up before the accused confronts the accusers face to face and has an opportunity to give a defense concerning the charges. ¹⁷Therefore, when they had assembled here, I did not delay. The next day I sat at the judge's bench and ordered the man to be brought in. ¹⁸Concerning him, the accusers stood up and brought no charge of the sort I was expecting. ¹⁹Instead they had some disagreements with him about their own religion and about a certain Jesus, a dead man Paul claimed to be alive. ²⁰Since I was at a loss in a dispute over such things, I asked him if he wished to go to Jerusalem and be tried there concerning these matters. ²¹But when Paul appealed to be held for trial by the Emperor, I ordered him to be kept in custody until I could send him to Caesar."

²²Then Agrippa said to Festus, "I would like to hear the man myself."

"Tomorrow you will hear him," he replied.

²³So the next day, Agrippa and Bernice came with great pomp and entered the auditorium with the commanders and prominent men of the city. When Festus gave the command, Paul was brought in. ²⁴Then Festus said: "King Agrippa and all men present with us, you see this man about whom the whole Jewish community has appealed to me, both in Jerusalem and here, shouting that he should not live any longer. ²⁵Now I realized that he had not done anything deserving of death, but when he himself appealed to the Emperor, I decided to send him. ²⁶I have nothing definite to write to my lord about him. Therefore, I have brought him before all of you, and especially before you, King Agrippa, so that after this examination is over, I may have something to write. ²⁷For it seems unreasonable to me to send a prisoner and not to indicate the charges against him."

26 Agrippa said to Paul, "It is permitted for you to speak for yourself."

Then Paul stretched out his hand and began his defense: ²"I consider myself fortunate, King Agrippa, that today I am going to make a defense before you about everything I am accused of by the Jews, ³especially since you are an expert in all the Jewish customs and controversies. Therefore I beg you to listen to me patiently.

⁴"All the Jews know my way of life from my youth, which was spent from the beginning among my own nation and in Jerusalem. ⁵They had previously known me for quite some time, if they were willing to testify, that according to the strictest party of our religion I lived as a *Pharisee. ⁶And now I stand on trial for the hope of the promise made by God to our fathers, ⁷the promise our 12 tribes hope to attain as they earnestly serve Him night and day. King Agrippa, I am being accused by the Jews because of this hope. ⁸Why is it

considered incredible by any of you that God raises the dead? ⁹In fact, I myself supposed it was necessary to do many things in opposition to the name of Jesus the ˙Nazarene. ¹⁰I actually did this in Jerusalem, and I locked up many of the ˙saints in prison, since I had received authority for that from the ˙chief priests. When they were put to death, I cast my vote against them. ¹¹In all the ˙synagogues I often tried to make them blaspheme by punishing them. I even pursued them to foreign cities since I was greatly enraged at them.

¹²"I was traveling to Damascus under these circumstances with authority and a commission from the chief priests. ¹³King Agrippa, while on the road at midday, I saw a light from heaven brighter than the sun, shining around me and those traveling with me. ¹⁴We all fell to the ground, and I heard a voice speaking to me in the ˙Hebrew language, 'Saul, Saul, why are you persecuting Me? It is hard for you to kick against the goads.'

¹⁵"Then I said, 'Who are You, Lord?'

"And the Lord replied: 'I am Jesus, the One you are persecuting. ¹⁶But get up and stand on your feet. For I have appeared to you for this purpose, to appoint you as a servant and a witness of what you have seen and of what I will reveal to you. ¹⁷I will rescue you from the people and from the Gentiles. I now send you to them ¹⁸to open their eyes so they may turn from darkness to light and from the power of Satan to God, that by faith in Me they may receive forgiveness of sins and a share among those who are ˙sanctified.'

¹⁹"Therefore, King Agrippa, I was not disobedient to the heavenly vision. ²⁰Instead, I preached to those in Damascus first, and to those in Jerusalem and in all the region of Judea, and to the Gentiles, that they should repent and turn to God, and do works worthy of repentance. ²¹For this reason the Jews seized me in the ˙temple complex and were trying to kill me. ²²To this very day, I have obtained help that comes from God, and I stand and testify to both small and great, saying nothing else than what the prophets and Moses said would take place— ²³that the ˙Messiah must suffer, and that as the first to rise from the dead, He would proclaim light to our people and to the Gentiles."

²⁴As he was making his defense this way, Festus exclaimed in a loud voice, "You're out of your mind, Paul! Too much study is driving you mad!"

²⁵But Paul replied, "I'm not out of my mind, most excellent Festus. On the contrary, I'm speaking words of truth and good judgment. ²⁶For the king knows about these matters. It is to him I am actually speaking boldly. For I am convinced that none of these things escapes his notice, since this was not done in a corner. ²⁷King Agrippa, do you believe the prophets? I know you believe."

²⁸Then Agrippa said to Paul, "Are you going to persuade me to become a Christian so easily?"

²⁹"I wish before God," replied Paul, "that whether easily or with difficulty, not only you but all who listen to me today might become as I am—except for these chains."

³⁰So the king, the governor, Bernice, and those sitting with them got up, ³¹and when they had left they talked with each other and said, "This man is doing nothing that deserves death or chains."

³²Then Agrippa said to Festus, "This man could have been released if he had not appealed to Caesar."

27 When it was decided that we were to sail to Italy, they handed over Paul and some other prisoners to a ˙centurion named Julius, of the Imperial ˙Regiment. ²So when we had boarded a ship of Adramyttium, we put to sea, intending to sail to ports along the coast of ˙Asia. Aristarchus, a Macedonian of Thessalonica, was with us. ³The next day we put in at Sidon, and Julius treated Paul kindly and allowed him to go to his friends to receive their care. ⁴When we had put out to sea from there, we sailed along the northern coast of Cyprus because the winds were against us. ⁵After sailing through the open sea off Cilicia and Pamphylia, we reached Myra in Lycia. ⁶There the centurion found an Alexandrian ship sailing for Italy and put us on board. ⁷Sailing slowly for many days, we came with difficulty as far as Cnidus. Since the wind did not allow us to approach it, we sailed along the south side of Crete off Salmone. ⁸With yet more difficulty we sailed along the coast and came to a place called Fair Havens near the city of Lasea.

⁹By now much time had passed, and the voyage was already dangerous. Since the Fast was already over, Paul gave his advice ¹⁰and told them, "Men, I can see that this voyage is headed toward damage and heavy loss, not only of the cargo and the ship but also of our lives." ¹¹But the centurion paid attention to the captain and the owner of the ship rather than to what Paul said. ¹²Since the harbor was unsuitable to winter in, the majority decided to set sail from there, hoping somehow to reach Phoenix, a harbor on Crete open to the southwest and northwest, and to winter there.

¹³When a gentle south wind sprang up, they thought they had achieved their purpose. They weighed anchor and sailed along the shore of Crete. ¹⁴But not long afterward, a fierce wind called the "northeaster" rushed down from the island. ¹⁵Since the ship was caught and was unable to head into the wind, we gave way to it and were driven along. ¹⁶After running under the shelter of a little island called Cauda, we were barely able to get control of the skiff. ¹⁷After hoisting it up, they used ropes and tackle and girded the ship. Then, fearing they would run aground on the Syrtis, they lowered the drift-anchor, and in this way they were driven along. ¹⁸Because we were being severely battered by the storm, they began to jettison the cargo the next day. ¹⁹On the third day, they threw the ship's gear overboard with their own hands.

²⁰For many days neither sun nor stars appeared, and the severe storm kept raging. Finally all hope that we would be saved was disappearing. ²¹Since many were going without food, Paul stood up among them and said, "You men should have followed my advice not to sail from Crete and sustain this damage and loss. ²²Now I urge you to take courage, because there will be no loss of any of your lives, but only of the ship. ²³For this night an angel of the God I belong to and serve stood by me, ²⁴and said, 'Don't be afraid, Paul. You must stand before Caesar. And, look! God has graciously given you all those who are sailing with you.' ²⁵Therefore, take courage, men, because I believe God that it will be just the way it was told to me. ²⁶However, we must run aground on a certain island."

²⁷When the fourteenth night came, we were drifting in the Adriatic Sea, and in the middle of the night the sailors thought they were approaching land. ²⁸They took a sounding and found it to be 120 feet deep; when they had sailed a little farther and sounded again, they

found it to be 90 feet deep. [29]Then, fearing we might run aground in some rocky place, they dropped four anchors from the stern and prayed for daylight to come.

[30]Some sailors tried to escape from the ship; they had let down the skiff into the sea, pretending that they were going to put out anchors from the bow. [31]Paul said to the centurion and the soldiers, "Unless these men stay in the ship, you cannot be saved." [32]Then the soldiers cut the ropes holding the skiff and let it drop away.

[33]When it was about daylight, Paul urged them all to take food, saying, "Today is the fourteenth day that you have been waiting and going without food, having eaten nothing. [34]Therefore I urge you to take some food. For this has to do with your survival, since none of you will lose a hair from your head." [35]After he said these things and had taken some bread, he gave thanks to God in the presence of all of them, and when he broke it, he began to eat. [36]They all became encouraged and took food themselves. [37]In all there were 276 of us on the ship. [38]When they had eaten enough, they began to lighten the ship by throwing the grain overboard into the sea.

[39]When daylight came, they did not recognize the land but sighted a bay with a beach. They planned to run the ship ashore if they could. [40]After casting off the anchors, they left them in the sea, at the same time loosening the ropes that held the rudders. Then they hoisted the foresail to the wind and headed for the beach. [41]But they struck a sandbar and ran the ship aground. The bow jammed fast and remained immovable, while the stern began to break up by the pounding of the waves.

[42]The soldiers' plan was to kill the prisoners so that no one could swim away and escape. [43]But the centurion kept them from carrying out their plan because he wanted to save Paul, so he ordered those who could swim to jump overboard first and get to land. [44]The rest were to follow, some on planks and some on debris from the ship. In this way, everyone safely reached the shore.

28 Once ashore, we then learned that the island was called Malta. [2]The local people showed us extraordinary kindness, for they lit a fire and took us all in, since it was raining and cold. [3]As Paul gathered a bundle of brushwood and put it on the fire, a viper came out because of the heat and fastened itself to his hand. [4]When the local people saw the creature hanging from his hand, they said to one another, "This man is probably a murderer, and though he has escaped the sea, Justice does not allow him to live!" [5]However, he shook the creature off into the fire and suffered no harm. [6]They expected that he would swell up or suddenly drop dead. But after they waited a long time and saw nothing unusual happen to him, they changed their minds and said he was a god.

[7]Now in the area around that place was an estate belonging to the leading man of the island, named Publius, who welcomed us and entertained us hospitably for three days. [8]Publius's father was in bed suffering from fever and dysentery. Paul went to him, and praying and laying his hands on him, he healed him. [9]After this, the rest of those on the island who had diseases also came and were cured. [10]So they heaped many honors on us, and when we sailed, they gave us what we needed.

[11]After three months we set sail in an Alexandrian ship that had wintered at the island, with the Twin Brothers as its figurehead. [12]Putting in at Syracuse, we stayed three days. [13]From there, after making a circuit along the coast, we reached Rhegium. After one day a south wind sprang up, and the second day we came to Puteoli. [14]There we found believers and were invited to stay with them for seven days.

And so we came to Rome. [15]Now the believers from there had heard the news about us and had come to meet us as far as the Forum of Appius and the Three Taverns. When Paul saw them, he thanked God and took courage. [16]When we entered Rome, Paul was permitted to stay by himself with the soldier who guarded him.

[17]After three days he called together the leaders of the Jews. When they had gathered he said to them: "Brothers, although I have done nothing against our people or the customs of our ancestors, I was delivered as a prisoner from Jerusalem into the hands of the Romans. [18]After they examined me, they wanted to release me, since I had not committed a capital offense. [19]Because the Jews objected, I was compelled to appeal to Caesar; it was not as though I had any accusation against my nation. [20]For this reason I've asked to see you and speak to you. In fact, it is for the hope of Israel that I'm wearing this chain."

[21]Then they said to him, "We haven't received any letters about you from Judea. None of the brothers has come and reported or spoken anything evil about you. [22]But we would like to hear from you what you think. For concerning this sect, we are aware that it is spoken against everywhere."

[23]After arranging a day with him, many came to him at his lodging. From dawn to dusk he expounded and witnessed about the kingdom of God. He tried to persuade them concerning Jesus from both the Law of Moses and the Prophets. [24]Some were persuaded by what he said, but others did not believe.

[25]Disagreeing among themselves, they began to leave after Paul made one statement: "The Holy Spirit correctly spoke through the prophet Isaiah to your ancestors [26]when He said,

Go to these people and say:
You will listen and listen,
yet never understand;
and you will look and look,
yet never perceive.
[27]   For the hearts of these people
have grown callous,
their ears are hard of hearing,
and they have shut their eyes;
otherwise they might see with their eyes
and hear with their ears,
understand with their heart,
and be converted,
and I would heal them.

[28]Therefore, let it be known to you that this saving work of God has been sent to the Gentiles; they will listen!" [[29]After he said these things, the Jews departed, while engaging in a prolonged debate among themselves.]

[30]Then he stayed two whole years in his own rented house. And he welcomed all who visited him, [31]proclaiming the kingdom of God and teaching the things concerning the Lord Jesus Christ with full boldness and without hindrance.

ROMANS

1 Paul, a *slave of Christ Jesus, called as an apostle and singled out for God's good news— ²which He promised long ago through His prophets in the Holy Scriptures— ³concerning His Son, Jesus Christ our Lord, who was a descendant of David according to the flesh ⁴and who has been declared to be the powerful Son of God by the resurrection from the dead according to the Spirit of holiness. ⁵We have received grace and apostleship through Him to bring about the obedience of faith among all the nations, on behalf of His name, ⁶including yourselves who also belong to Jesus Christ by calling:

⁷To all who are in Rome, loved by God, called as *saints.

Grace to you and peace from God our Father and the Lord Jesus Christ.

⁸First, I thank my God through Jesus Christ for all of you because the news of your faith is being reported in all the world. ⁹For God, whom I serve with my spirit in telling the good news about His Son, is my witness that I constantly mention you, ¹⁰always asking in my prayers that if it is somehow in God's will, I may now at last succeed in coming to you. ¹¹For I want very much to see you, so I may impart to you some spiritual gift to strengthen you, ¹²that is, to be mutually encouraged by each other's faith, both yours and mine.

¹³Now I want you to know, *brothers, that I often planned to come to you (but was prevented until now) in order that I might have a fruitful ministry among you, just as among the rest of the Gentiles. ¹⁴I am obligated both to Greeks and barbarians, both to the wise and the foolish. ¹⁵So I am eager to preach the good news to you also who are in Rome.

¹⁶For I am not ashamed of the gospel, because it is God's power for salvation to everyone who believes, first to the Jew, and also to the Greek. ¹⁷For in it God's righteousness is revealed from faith to faith, just as it is written: **The righteous will live by faith.**

¹⁸For God's wrath is revealed from heaven against all godlessness and unrighteousness of people who by their unrighteousness suppress the truth, ¹⁹since what can be known about God is evident among them, because God has shown it to them. ²⁰For His invisible attributes, that is, His eternal power and divine nature, have been clearly seen since the creation of the world, being understood through what He has made. As a result, people are without excuse. ²¹For though they knew God, they did not glorify Him as God or show gratitude. Instead, their thinking became nonsense, and their senseless minds were darkened. ²²Claiming to be wise, they became fools ²³and exchanged the glory of the immortal God for images resembling mortal man, birds, four-footed animals, and reptiles.

²⁴Therefore God delivered them over in the cravings of their hearts to sexual impurity, so that their bodies were degraded among themselves. ²⁵They exchanged the truth of God for a lie, and worshiped and served something created instead of the Creator, who is praised forever. *Amen.

²⁶This is why God delivered them over to degrading passions. For even their females exchanged natural sexual relations for unnatural ones. ²⁷The males in the same way also left natural relations with females and were inflamed in their lust for one another. Males committed shameless acts with males and received in their own persons the appropriate penalty of their error.

²⁸And because they did not think it worthwhile to acknowledge God, God delivered them over to a worthless mind to do what is morally wrong. ²⁹They are filled with all unrighteousness, evil, greed, and wickedness. They are full of envy, murder, quarrels, deceit, and malice. They are gossips, ³⁰slanderers, God-haters, arrogant, proud, boastful, inventors of evil, disobedient to parents, ³¹undiscerning, untrustworthy, unloving, and unmerciful. ³²Although they know full well God's just sentence—that those who practice such things deserve to die—they not only do them, but even applaud others who practice them.

2 Therefore, any one of you who judges is without excuse. For when you judge another, you condemn yourself, since you, the judge, do the same things. ²We know that God's judgment on those who do such things is based on the truth. ³Do you really think—anyone of you who judges those who do such things yet do the same—that you will escape God's judgment? ⁴Or do you despise the riches of His kindness, restraint, and patience, not recognizing that God's kindness is intended to lead you to repentance? ⁵But because of your hardness and unrepentant heart you are storing up wrath for yourself in the day of wrath, when God's righteous judgment is revealed. ⁶**He will repay each one according to his works:** ⁷eternal life to those who by persistence in doing good seek glory, honor, and immortality; ⁸but wrath and indignation to those who are self-seeking and disobey the truth but are obeying unrighteousness; ⁹affliction and distress for every human being who does evil, first to the Jew, and also to the Greek; ¹⁰but glory, honor, and peace for everyone who does what is good, first to the Jew, and also to the Greek. ¹¹There is no favoritism with God.

¹²All those who sinned without the law will also perish without the law, and all those who sinned under the law will be judged by the law. ¹³For the hearers of the law are not righteous before God, but the doers of the law will be declared righteous. ¹⁴So, when Gentiles, who do not have the law, instinctively do what the law demands, they are a law to themselves even though they do not have the law. ¹⁵They show that the work of the law is written on their hearts. Their consciences confirm this. Their competing thoughts will either accuse or excuse them ¹⁶on the day when God judges what people have kept secret, according to my gospel through Christ Jesus.

¹⁷Now if you call yourself a Jew, and rest in the law, boast in God, ¹⁸know His will, and approve the things that are superior, being instructed from the law, ¹⁹and if you are convinced that you are a guide for the blind, a light to those in darkness, ²⁰an instructor of the ignorant, a teacher of the immature, having the full expression of knowledge and truth in the law— ²¹you then, who teach another, don't you teach yourself? You who preach, "You must not steal"—do you steal? ²²You who say, "You must not commit adultery"—do you commit adultery? You who detest idols, do you rob their temples? ²³You who boast in the law, do you dishonor God by breaking the law? ²⁴For, as it is written:

The name of God is blasphemed among the Gentiles because of you.

²⁵ For circumcision benefits you if you observe the law, but if you are a lawbreaker, your circumcision has become uncircumcision. ²⁶ Therefore if an uncircumcised man keeps the law's requirements, will his uncircumcision not be counted as circumcision? ²⁷ A man who is physically uncircumcised, but who fulfills the law, will judge you who are a lawbreaker in spite of having the letter of the law and circumcision. ²⁸ For a person is not a Jew who is one outwardly, and true circumcision is not something visible in the flesh. ²⁹ On the contrary, a person is a Jew who is one inwardly, and circumcision is of the heart—by the Spirit, not the letter. That man's praise is not from men but from God.

3 So what advantage does the Jew have? Or what is the benefit of circumcision? ² Considerable in every way. First, they were entrusted with the spoken words of God. ³ What then? If some did not believe, will their unbelief cancel God's faithfulness? ⁴ Absolutely not! God must be true, even if everyone is a liar, as it is written:

> **That You may be justified in Your words**
> **and triumph when You judge.**

⁵ But if our unrighteousness highlights God's righteousness, what are we to say? I use a human argument: Is God unrighteous to inflict wrath? ⁶ Absolutely not! Otherwise, how will God judge the world? ⁷ But if by my lie God's truth is amplified to His glory, why am I also still judged as a sinner? ⁸ And why not say, just as some people slanderously claim we say, "Let us do what is evil so that good may come"? Their condemnation is deserved!

⁹ What then? Are we any better? Not at all! For we have previously charged that both Jews and Gentiles are all under sin, ¹⁰ as it is written:

> **There is no one righteous, not even one.**
> ¹¹ **There is no one who understands;**
> **there is no one who seeks God.**
> ¹² **All have turned away;**
> **all alike have become useless.**
> **There is no one who does what is good,**
> **not even one.**
> ¹³ **Their throat is an open grave;**
> **they deceive with their tongues.**
> **Vipers' venom is under their lips.**
> ¹⁴ **Their mouth is full of cursing and bitterness.**
> ¹⁵ **Their feet are swift to shed blood;**
> ¹⁶ **ruin and wretchedness are in their paths,**
> ¹⁷ **and the path of peace they have not known.**
> ¹⁸ **There is no fear of God before their eyes.**

¹⁹ Now we know that whatever the law says speaks to those who are subject to the law, so that every mouth may be shut and the whole world may become subject to God's judgment. ²⁰ For no one will be •justified in His sight by the works of the law, because the knowledge of sin comes through the law.

²¹ But now, apart from the law, God's righteousness has been revealed—attested by the Law and the Prophets ²²—that is, God's righteousness through faith in Jesus Christ, to all who believe, since there is no distinction. ²³ For all have sinned and fall short of the glory of God. ²⁴ They are justified freely by His grace through the •redemption that is in Christ Jesus. ²⁵ God presented Him as a •propitiation through faith in His blood, to demonstrate His righteousness, because in His restraint God passed over the sins previously committed. ²⁶ God presented Him to demonstrate His righteousness at the present time, so that He would be righteous and declare righteous the one who has faith in Jesus.

²⁷ Where then is boasting? It is excluded. By what kind of law? By one of works? No, on the contrary, by a law of faith. ²⁸ For we conclude that a man is justified by faith apart from the works of the law. ²⁹ Or is God for Jews only? Is He not also for Gentiles? Yes, for Gentiles too, ³⁰ since there is one God who will justify the circumcised by faith and the uncircumcised through faith. ³¹ Do we then cancel the law through faith? Absolutely not! On the contrary, we uphold the law.

4 What then can we say that Abraham, our physical ancestor, has found? ² If Abraham was •justified by works, he has something to brag about—but not before God. ³ For what does the Scripture say?

> **Abraham believed God,**
> **and it was credited to him for righteousness.**

⁴ Now to the one who works, pay is not considered as a gift, but as something owed. ⁵ But to the one who does not work, but believes on Him who declares the ungodly to be righteous, his faith is credited for righteousness.

⁶ Likewise, David also speaks of the blessing of the man God credits righteousness to apart from works:

> ⁷ **How joyful are those whose lawless acts**
> **are forgiven**
> **and whose sins are covered!**
> ⁸ **How joyful is the man**
> **the Lord will never charge with sin!**

⁹ Is this blessing only for the circumcised, then? Or is it also for the uncircumcised? For we say, **Faith was credited to Abraham for righteousness.** ¹⁰ In what way then was it credited—while he was circumcised, or uncircumcised? Not while he was circumcised, but uncircumcised. ¹¹ And he received the sign of circumcision as a seal of the righteousness that he had by faith while still uncircumcised. This was to make him the father of all who believe but are not circumcised, so that righteousness may be credited to them also. ¹² And he became the father of the circumcised, who are not only circumcised but who also follow in the footsteps of the faith our father Abraham had while he was still uncircumcised.

¹³ For the promise to Abraham or to his descendants that he would inherit the world was not through the law, but through the righteousness that comes by faith. ¹⁴ If those who are of the law are heirs, faith is made empty and the promise is canceled. ¹⁵ For the law produces wrath. And where there is no law, there is no transgression.

¹⁶ This is why the promise is by faith, so that it may be according to grace, to guarantee it to all the descendants—not only to those who are of the law but also to those who are of Abraham's faith. He is the father of us all ¹⁷ in God's sight. As it is written: **I have made you the father of many nations.** He believed in God, who gives life to the dead and calls things into existence that do not exist. ¹⁸ He believed, hoping against hope, so that he became **the father of many nations** according to what had been spoken: **So will your descendants be.** ¹⁹ He considered his own body to be already dead (since he was about 100 years old) and also considered the deadness of Sarah's womb, without weakening in the faith. ²⁰ He did not waver in unbelief at God's promise but was strengthened in his faith and gave glory to

God, [21] because he was fully convinced that what He had promised He was also able to perform. [22] Therefore, **it was credited to him for righteousness.** [23] Now **it was credited to him** was not written for Abraham alone, [24] but also for us. It will be credited to us who believe in Him who raised Jesus our Lord from the dead. [25] He was delivered up for our trespasses and raised for our justification.

5 Therefore, since we have been declared righteous by faith, we have peace with God through our Lord Jesus Christ. [2] We have also obtained access through Him by faith into this grace in which we stand, and we rejoice in the hope of the glory of God. [3] And not only that, but we also rejoice in our afflictions, because we know that affliction produces endurance, [4] endurance produces proven character, and proven character produces hope. [5] This hope will not disappoint us, because God's love has been poured out in our hearts through the Holy Spirit who was given to us.

[6] For while we were still helpless, at the appointed moment, Christ died for the ungodly. [7] For rarely will someone die for a just person—though for a good person perhaps someone might even dare to die. [8] But God proves His own love for us in that while we were still sinners, Christ died for us! [9] Much more then, since we have now been declared righteous by His blood, we will be saved through Him from wrath. [10] For if, while we were enemies, we were reconciled to God through the death of His Son, then how much more, having been reconciled, will we be saved by His life! [11] And not only that, but we also rejoice in God through our Lord Jesus Christ. We have now received this reconciliation through Him.

[12] Therefore, just as sin entered the world through one man, and death through sin, in this way death spread to all men, because all sinned. [13] In fact, sin was in the world before the law, but sin is not charged to a person's account when there is no law. [14] Nevertheless, death reigned from Adam to Moses, even over those who did not sin in the likeness of Adam's transgression. He is a prototype of the Coming One.

[15] But the gift is not like the trespass. For if by the one man's trespass the many died, how much more have the grace of God and the gift overflowed to the many by the grace of the one man, Jesus Christ. [16] And the gift is not like the one man's sin, because from one sin came the judgment, resulting in condemnation, but from many trespasses came the gift, resulting in *justification. [17] Since by the one man's trespass, death reigned through that one man, how much more will those who receive the overflow of grace and the gift of righteousness reign in life through the one man, Jesus Christ.

[18] So then, as through one trespass there is condemnation for everyone, so also through one righteous act there is life-giving justification for everyone. [19] For just as through one man's disobedience the many were made sinners, so also through the one man's obedience the many will be made righteous. [20] The law came along to multiply the trespass. But where sin multiplied, grace multiplied even more [21] so that, just as sin reigned in death, so also grace will reign through righteousness, resulting in eternal life through Jesus Christ our Lord.

6 What should we say then? Should we continue in sin so that grace may multiply? [2] Absolutely not! How can we who died to sin still live in it? [3] Or are you unaware that all of us who were baptized into Christ Jesus were baptized into His death? [4] Therefore we were buried with Him by baptism into death, in order that, just as Christ was raised from the dead by the glory of the Father, so we too may *walk in a new way of life. [5] For if we have been joined with Him in the likeness of His death, we will certainly also be in the likeness of His resurrection. [6] For we know that our old self was crucified with Him in order that sin's dominion over the body may be abolished, so that we may no longer be enslaved to sin, [7] since a person who has died is freed from sin's claims. [8] Now if we died with Christ, we believe that we will also live with Him, [9] because we know that Christ, having been raised from the dead, will not die again. Death no longer rules over Him. [10] For in light of the fact that He died, He died to sin once for all; but in light of the fact that He lives, He lives to God. [11] So, you too consider yourselves dead to sin but alive to God in Christ Jesus.

[12] Therefore do not let sin reign in your mortal body, so that you obey its desires. [13] And do not offer any parts of it to sin as weapons for unrighteousness. But as those who are alive from the dead, offer yourselves to God, and all the parts of yourselves to God as weapons for righteousness. [14] For sin will not rule over you, because you are not under law but under grace.

[15] What then? Should we sin because we are not under law but under grace? Absolutely not! [16] Don't you know that if you offer yourselves to someone as obedient *slaves, you are slaves of that one you obey—either of sin leading to death or of obedience leading to righteousness? [17] But thank God that, although you used to be slaves of sin, you obeyed from the heart that pattern of teaching you were transferred to, [18] and having been liberated from sin, you became enslaved to righteousness. [19] I am using a human analogy because of the weakness of your flesh. For just as you offered the parts of yourselves as slaves to moral impurity, and to greater and greater lawlessness, so now offer them as slaves to righteousness, which results in *sanctification. [20] For when you were slaves of sin, you were free from allegiance to righteousness. [21] So what fruit was produced then from the things you are now ashamed of? For the end of those things is death. [22] But now, since you have been liberated from sin and have become enslaved to God, you have your fruit, which results in sanctification—and the end is eternal life! [23] For the wages of sin is death, but the gift of God is eternal life in Christ Jesus our Lord.

7 Since I am speaking to those who understand law, *brothers, are you unaware that the law has authority over someone as long as he lives? [2] For example, a married woman is legally bound to her husband while he lives. But if her husband dies, she is released from the law regarding the husband. [3] So then, if she gives herself to another man while her husband is living, she will be called an adulteress. But if her husband dies, she is free from that law. Then, if she gives herself to another man, she is not an adulteress.

[4] Therefore, my brothers, you also were put to death in relation to the law through the crucified body of the *Messiah, so that you may belong to another—to Him who was raised from the dead—that we may bear fruit for God. [5] For when we were in the flesh, the sinful passions operated through the law in every part of us and bore fruit for death. [6] But now we have been released from the law, since we have died to what held us, so

that we may serve in the new way of the Spirit and not in the old letter of the law.

⁷What should we say then? Is the law sin? Absolutely not! On the contrary, I would not have known sin if it were not for the law. For example, I would not have known what it is to covet if the law had not said, **Do not covet.** ⁸And sin, seizing an opportunity through the commandment, produced in me coveting of every kind. For apart from the law sin is dead. ⁹Once I was alive apart from the law, but when the commandment came, sin sprang to life ¹⁰and I died. The commandment that was meant for life resulted in death for me. ¹¹For sin, seizing an opportunity through the commandment, deceived me, and through it killed me. ¹²So then, the law is holy, and the commandment is holy and just and good.

¹³Therefore, did what is good cause my death? Absolutely not! On the contrary, sin, in order to be recognized as sin, was producing death in me through what is good, so that through the commandment, sin might become sinful beyond measure. ¹⁴For we know that the law is spiritual, but I am made out of flesh, sold into sin's power. ¹⁵For I do not understand what I am doing, because I do not practice what I want to do, but I do what I hate. ¹⁶And if I do what I do not want to do, I agree with the law that it is good. ¹⁷So now I am no longer the one doing it, but it is sin living in me. ¹⁸For I know that nothing good lives in me, that is, in my flesh. For the desire to do what is good is with me, but there is no ability to do it. ¹⁹For I do not do the good that I want to do, but I practice the evil that I do not want to do. ²⁰Now if I do what I do not want, I am no longer the one doing it, but it is the sin that lives in me. ²¹So I discover this principle: When I want to do what is good, evil is with me. ²²For in my inner self I joyfully agree with God's law. ²³But I see a different law in the parts of my body, waging war against the law of my mind and taking me prisoner to the law of sin in the parts of my body. ²⁴What a wretched man I am! Who will rescue me from this dying body? ²⁵I thank God through Jesus Christ our Lord! So then, with my mind I myself am a slave to the law of God, but with my flesh, to the law of sin.

8 Therefore, no condemnation now exists for those in Christ Jesus, ²because the Spirit's law of life in Christ Jesus has set you free from the law of sin and of death. ³What the law could not do since it was limited by the flesh, God did. He condemned sin in the flesh by sending His own Son in flesh like ours under sin's domain, and as a sin offering, ⁴in order that the law's requirement would be accomplished in us who do not •walk according to the flesh but according to the Spirit. ⁵For those who live according to the flesh think about the things of the flesh, but those who live according to the Spirit, about the things of the Spirit. ⁶For the mind-set of the flesh is death, but the mind-set of the Spirit is life and peace. ⁷For the mind-set of the flesh is hostile to God because it does not submit itself to God's law, for it is unable to do so. ⁸Those who are in the flesh cannot please God. ⁹You, however, are not in the flesh, but in the Spirit, since the Spirit of God lives in you. But if anyone does not have the Spirit of Christ, he does not belong to Him. ¹⁰Now if Christ is in you, the body is dead because of sin, but the Spirit is life because of righteousness. ¹¹And if the Spirit of Him who raised Jesus from the dead lives in you, then He who raised Christ from the dead will also bring your mortal bodies to life through His Spirit who lives in you.

¹²So then, •brothers, we are not obligated to the flesh to live according to the flesh, ¹³for if you live according to the flesh, you are going to die. But if by the Spirit you put to death the deeds of the body, you will live. ¹⁴All those led by God's Spirit are God's sons. ¹⁵For you did not receive a spirit of slavery to fall back into fear, but you received the Spirit of adoption, by whom we cry out, "•*Abba*, Father!" ¹⁶The Spirit Himself testifies together with our spirit that we are God's children, ¹⁷and if children, also heirs—heirs of God and coheirs with Christ—seeing that we suffer with Him so that we may also be glorified with Him.

¹⁸For I consider that the sufferings of this present time are not worth comparing with the glory that is going to be revealed to us. ¹⁹For the creation eagerly waits with anticipation for God's sons to be revealed. ²⁰For the creation was subjected to futility—not willingly, but because of Him who subjected it—in the hope ²¹that the creation itself will also be set free from the bondage of corruption into the glorious freedom of God's children. ²²For we know that the whole creation has been groaning together with labor pains until now. ²³And not only that, but we ourselves who have the Spirit as the •firstfruits—we also groan within ourselves, eagerly waiting for adoption, the •redemption of our bodies. ²⁴Now in this hope we were saved, yet hope that is seen is not hope, because who hopes for what he sees? ²⁵But if we hope for what we do not see, we eagerly wait for it with patience.

²⁶In the same way the Spirit also joins to help in our weakness, because we do not know what to pray for as we should, but the Spirit Himself intercedes for us with unspoken groanings. ²⁷And He who searches the hearts knows the Spirit's mind-set, because He intercedes for the •saints according to the will of God.

²⁸We know that all things work together for the good of those who love God: those who are called according to His purpose. ²⁹For those He foreknew He also predestined to be conformed to the image of His Son, so that He would be the firstborn among many brothers. ³⁰And those He predestined, He also called; and those He called, He also •justified; and those He justified, He also glorified.

³¹ What then are we to say about these things?
　　If God is for us, who is against us?
³² He did not even spare His own Son
　　but offered Him up for us all;
　　how will He not also with Him grant
　　　us everything?
³³ Who can bring an accusation
　　　against God's elect?
　　God is the One who justifies.
³⁴ Who is the one who condemns?
　　Christ Jesus is the One who died,
　　but even more, has been raised;
　　He also is at the right hand of God
　　and intercedes for us.
³⁵ Who can separate us from the love of Christ?
　　Can affliction or anguish or persecution
　　or famine or nakedness or danger or sword?
³⁶ As it is written:
　　Because of You
　　we are being put to death all day long;
　　we are counted as sheep to be slaughtered.

³⁷ No, in all these things we are
more than victorious
through Him who loved us.
³⁸ For I am persuaded that not even death or life,
angels or rulers,
things present or things to come,
hostile powers,
³⁹ height or depth, or any other created thing
will have the power to separate us
from the love of God that is in Christ Jesus
our Lord!

9 I speak the truth in Christ—I am not lying; my conscience is testifying to me with the Holy Spirit— ² that I have intense sorrow and continual anguish in my heart. ³ For I could almost wish to be cursed and cut off from the •Messiah for the benefit of my •brothers, my own flesh and blood. ⁴ They are Israelites, and to them belong the adoption, the glory, the covenants, the giving of the law, the temple service, and the promises. ⁵ The ancestors are theirs, and from them, by physical descent, came the Messiah, who is God over all, praised forever. •Amen.

⁶ But it is not as though the word of God has failed. For not all who are descended from Israel are Israel. ⁷ Neither are they all children because they are Abraham's descendants. On the contrary, **your •offspring will be traced through Isaac.** ⁸ That is, it is not the children by physical descent who are God's children, but the children of the promise are considered to be the offspring. ⁹ For this is the statement of the promise: **At this time I will come, and Sarah will have a son.** ¹⁰ And not only that, but also Rebekah received a promise when she became pregnant by one man, our ancestor Isaac. ¹¹ For though her sons had not been born yet or done anything good or bad, so that God's purpose according to election might stand— ¹² not from works but from the One who calls—she was told: **The older will serve the younger.** ¹³ As it is written: **I have loved Jacob, but I have hated Esau.**

¹⁴ What should we say then? Is there injustice with God? Absolutely not! ¹⁵ For He tells Moses:

**I will show mercy
to whom I will show mercy,
and I will have compassion
on whom I will have compassion.**

¹⁶ So then it does not depend on human will or effort but on God who shows mercy. ¹⁷ For the Scripture tells Pharaoh:

**I raised you up for this reason
so that I may display My power in you
and that My name may be proclaimed in all
the earth.**

¹⁸ So then, He shows mercy to those He wants to, and He hardens those He wants to harden.

¹⁹ You will say to me, therefore, "Why then does He still find fault? For who can resist His will?" ²⁰ But who are you, a mere man, to talk back to God? Will what is formed say to the one who formed it, "Why did you make me like this?" ²¹ Or has the potter no right over the clay, to make from the same lump one piece of pottery for honor and another for dishonor? ²² And what if God, desiring to display His wrath and to make His power known, endured with much patience objects of wrath ready for destruction? ²³ And what if He did this to make known the riches of His glory on objects of mercy that He prepared beforehand for glory— ²⁴ on us, the ones He also called, not only from the Jews but also from the Gentiles? ²⁵ As He also says in Hosea:

**I will call Not My People, My People,
and she who is Unloved, Beloved.**
²⁶ **And it will be in the place where
they were told,
you are not My people,
there they will be called sons of the living God.**
²⁷ But Isaiah cries out concerning Israel:

**Though the number of Israel's sons
is like the sand of the sea,
only the remnant will be saved;**
²⁸ **for the Lord will execute His sentence
completely and decisively on the earth.**

²⁹ And just as Isaiah predicted:

**If the Lord of •Hosts had not left us offspring,
we would have become like Sodom,
and we would have been made like Gomorrah.**

³⁰ What should we say then? Gentiles, who did not pursue righteousness, have obtained righteousness—namely the righteousness that comes from faith. ³¹ But Israel, pursuing the law for righteousness, has not achieved the righteousness of the law. ³² Why is that? Because they did not pursue it by faith, but as if it were by works. They stumbled over the stumbling stone. ³³ As it is written:

**Look! I am putting a stone in •Zion
to stumble over
and a rock to trip over,
yet the one who believes on Him
will not be put to shame.**

10 •Brothers, my heart's desire and prayer to God concerning them is for their salvation! ²I can testify about them that they have zeal for God, but not according to knowledge. ³ Because they disregarded the righteousness from God and attempted to establish their own righteousness, they have not submitted themselves to God's righteousness. ⁴ For Christ is the end of the law for righteousness to everyone who believes. ⁵ For Moses writes about the righteousness that is from the law: **The one who does these things will live by them.** ⁶ But the righteousness that comes from faith speaks like this: **Do not say in your heart, "Who will go up to heaven?"** that is, to bring Christ down ⁷ or, **"Who will go down into the •abyss?"** that is, to bring Christ up from the dead. ⁸ On the contrary, what does it say? **The message is near you, in your mouth and in your heart.** This is the message of faith that we proclaim: ⁹ If you confess with your mouth, "Jesus is Lord," and believe in your heart that God raised Him from the dead, you will be saved. ¹⁰ One believes with the heart, resulting in righteousness, and one confesses with the mouth, resulting in salvation. ¹¹ Now the Scripture says, **Everyone who believes on Him will not be put to shame,** ¹² for there is no distinction between Jew and Greek, since the same Lord of all is rich to all who call on Him. ¹³ For **everyone who calls on the name of the Lord will be saved.**

¹⁴ But how can they call on Him they have not believed in? And how can they believe without hearing about Him? And how can they hear without a preacher? ¹⁵ And how can they preach unless they are sent? As it is written: **How beautiful are the feet of those who announce the gospel of good things!** ¹⁶ But all did not obey the gospel. For Isaiah says, **Lord, who has believed our message?** ¹⁷ So faith comes from what is heard, and what is heard comes through the message

about Christ. [18]But I ask, "Did they not hear?" Yes, they did:

> Their voice has gone out to all the earth,
> and their words to the ends
> of the inhabited world.

[19]But I ask, "Did Israel not understand?" First, Moses said:

> I will make you jealous
> of those who are not a nation;
> I will make you angry by a nation
> that lacks understanding.

[20]And Isaiah says boldly:

> I was found
> by those who were not looking for Me;
> I revealed Myself
> to those who were not asking for Me.

[21]But to Israel he says: **All day long I have spread out My hands to a disobedient and defiant people.**

11 I ask, then, has God rejected His people? Absolutely not! For I too am an Israelite, a descendant of Abraham, from the tribe of Benjamin. [2]God has not rejected His people whom He foreknew. Or don't you know what the Scripture says in the passage about Elijah—how he pleads with God against Israel?

[3] > **Lord, they have killed Your prophets**
> **and torn down Your altars.**
> **I am the only one left,**
> **and they are trying to take my life!**

[4]But what was God's reply to him? **I have left 7,000 men for Myself who have not bowed down to ·Baal.** [5]In the same way, then, there is also at the present time a remnant chosen by grace. [6]Now if by grace, then it is not by works; otherwise grace ceases to be grace.

[7]What then? Israel did not find what it was looking for, but the elect did find it. The rest were hardened, [8]as it is written:

> God gave them a spirit of insensitivity,
> eyes that cannot see
> and ears that cannot hear,
> to this day.

[9]And David says:

> Let their feasting become a snare and a trap,
> a pitfall and a retribution to them.
[10] > Let their eyes be darkened so they cannot see,
> and their backs be bent continually.

[11]I ask, then, have they stumbled in order to fall? Absolutely not! On the contrary, by their stumbling, salvation has come to the Gentiles to make Israel jealous. [12]Now if their stumbling brings riches for the world, and their failure riches for the Gentiles, how much more will their full number bring!

[13]Now I am speaking to you Gentiles. In view of the fact that I am an apostle to the Gentiles, I magnify my ministry, [14]if I can somehow make my own people jealous and save some of them. [15]For if their rejection brings reconciliation to the world, what will their acceptance mean but life from the dead? [16]Now if the ·firstfruits offered up are holy, so is the whole batch. And if the root is holy, so are the branches.

[17]Now if some of the branches were broken off, and you, though a wild olive branch, were grafted in among them and have come to share in the rich root of the cultivated olive tree, [18]do not brag that you are better than those branches. But if you do brag—you do not sustain the root, but the root sustains you. [19]Then you will say, "Branches were broken off so that I might be grafted in." [20]True enough; they were

broken off by unbelief, but you stand by faith. Do not be arrogant, but be afraid. [21]For if God did not spare the natural branches, He will not spare you either. [22]Therefore, consider God's kindness and severity: severity toward those who have fallen but God's kindness toward you—if you remain in His kindness. Otherwise you too will be cut off. [23]And even they, if they do not remain in unbelief, will be grafted in, because God has the power to graft them in again. [24]For if you were cut off from your native wild olive and against nature were grafted into a cultivated olive tree, how much more will these—the natural branches—be grafted into their own olive tree?

[25]So that you will not be conceited, ·brothers, I do not want you to be unaware of this ·mystery: A partial hardening has come to Israel until the full number of the Gentiles has come in. [26]And in this way all Israel will be saved, as it is written:

> The Liberator will come from ·Zion;
> He will turn away godlessness from Jacob.
[27] > And this will be My covenant with them
> when I take away their sins.

[28]Regarding the gospel, they are enemies for your advantage, but regarding election, they are loved because of the patriarchs, [29]since God's gracious gifts and calling are irrevocable. [30]As you once disobeyed God, but now have received mercy through their disobedience, [31]so they too have now disobeyed, resulting in mercy to you, so that they also now may receive mercy. [32]For God has imprisoned all in disobedience, so that He may have mercy on all.

[33] > Oh, the depth of the riches
> both of the wisdom and the knowledge of God!
> How unsearchable His judgments
> and untraceable His ways!
[34] > For who has known the mind of the Lord?
> Or who has been His counselor?
[35] > Or who has ever first given to Him,
> and has to be repaid?
[36] > For from Him and through Him
> and to Him are all things.
> To Him be the glory forever. ·Amen.

12 Therefore, ·brothers, by the mercies of God, I urge you to present your bodies as a living sacrifice, holy and pleasing to God; this is your spiritual worship. [2]Do not be conformed to this age, but be transformed by the renewing of your mind, so that you may discern what is the good, pleasing, and perfect will of God.

[3]For by the grace given to me, I tell everyone among you not to think of himself more highly than he should think. Instead, think sensibly, as God has distributed a measure of faith to each one. [4]Now as we have many parts in one body, and all the parts do not have the same function, [5]in the same way we who are many are one body in Christ and individually members of one another. [6]According to the grace given to us, we have different gifts:

> If prophecy,
> use it according to the standard of one's faith;
[7] > if service, in service;
> if teaching, in teaching;
[8] > if exhorting, in exhortation;
> giving, with generosity;
> leading, with diligence;
> showing mercy, with cheerfulness.

[9]Love must be without hypocrisy. Detest evil; cling

to what is good. ¹⁰Show family affection to one another with brotherly love. Outdo one another in showing honor. ¹¹Do not lack diligence; be fervent in spirit; serve the Lord. ¹²Rejoice in hope; be patient in affliction; be persistent in prayer. ¹³Share with the •saints in their needs; pursue hospitality. ¹⁴Bless those who persecute you; bless and do not curse. ¹⁵Rejoice with those who rejoice; weep with those who weep. ¹⁶Be in agreement with one another. Do not be proud; instead, associate with the humble. Do not be wise in your own estimation. ¹⁷Do not repay anyone evil for evil. Try to do what is honorable in everyone's eyes. ¹⁸If possible, on your part, live at peace with everyone. ¹⁹Friends, do not avenge yourselves; instead, leave room for His wrath. For it is written: **Vengeance belongs to Me; I will repay,** says the Lord. ²⁰But

> **If your enemy is hungry, feed him.**
> **If he is thirsty, give him something to drink.**
> **For in so doing**
> **you will be heaping fiery coals on his head.**

²¹Do not be conquered by evil, but conquer evil with good.

13 Everyone must submit to the governing authorities, for there is no authority except from God, and those that exist are instituted by God. ²So then, the one who resists the authority is opposing God's command, and those who oppose it will bring judgment on themselves. ³For rulers are not a terror to good conduct, but to bad. Do you want to be unafraid of the authority? Do what is good, and you will have its approval. ⁴For government is God's servant for your good. But if you do wrong, be afraid, because it does not carry the sword for no reason. For government is God's servant, an avenger that brings wrath on the one who does wrong. ⁵Therefore, you must submit, not only because of wrath, but also because of your conscience. ⁶And for this reason you pay taxes, since the authorities are God's public servants, continually attending to these tasks. ⁷Pay your obligations to everyone: taxes to those you owe taxes, tolls to those you owe tolls, respect to those you owe respect, and honor to those you owe honor.

⁸Do not owe anyone anything, except to love one another, for the one who loves another has fulfilled the law. ⁹The commandments:

> **Do not commit adultery;**
> **do not murder;**
> **do not steal;**
> **do not covet;**

and whatever other commandment—all are summed up by this: **Love your neighbor as yourself.** ¹⁰Love does no wrong to a neighbor. Love, therefore, is the fulfillment of the law.

¹¹Besides this, knowing the time, it is already the hour for you to wake up from sleep, for now our salvation is nearer than when we first believed. ¹²The night is nearly over, and the daylight is near, so let us discard the deeds of darkness and put on the armor of light. ¹³Let us •walk with decency, as in the daylight: not in carousing and drunkenness; not in sexual impurity and promiscuity; not in quarreling and jealousy. ¹⁴But put on the Lord Jesus Christ, and make no plans to satisfy the fleshly desires.

14 Accept anyone who is weak in faith, but don't argue about doubtful issues. ²One person believes he may eat anything, but one who is weak eats only vegetables. ³One who eats must not look down on one who does not eat, and one who does not eat must not criticize one who does, because God has accepted him. ⁴Who are you to criticize another's household slave? Before his own Lord he stands or falls. And he will stand. For the Lord is able to make him stand.

⁵One person considers one day to be above another day. Someone else considers every day to be the same. Each one must be fully convinced in his own mind. ⁶Whoever observes the day, observes it for the honor of the Lord. Whoever eats, eats for the Lord, since he gives thanks to God; and whoever does not eat, it is for the Lord that he does not eat it, yet he thanks God. ⁷For none of us lives to himself, and no one dies to himself. ⁸If we live, we live for the Lord; and if we die, we die for the Lord. Therefore, whether we live or die, we belong to the Lord. ⁹Christ died and came to life for this: that He might rule over both the dead and the living. ¹⁰But you, why do you criticize your brother? Or you, why do you look down on your brother? For we will all stand before the tribunal of God. ¹¹For it is written:

> **As I live, says the Lord,**
> **every knee will bow to Me,**
> **and every tongue will give praise to God.**

¹²So then, each of us will give an account of himself to God.

¹³Therefore, let us no longer criticize one another. Instead decide never to put a stumbling block or pitfall in your brother's way. ¹⁴(I know and am persuaded by the Lord Jesus that nothing is •unclean in itself. Still, to someone who considers a thing to be unclean, to that one it is unclean.) ¹⁵For if your brother is hurt by what you eat, you are no longer •walking according to love. Do not destroy that one Christ died for by what you eat. ¹⁶Therefore, do not let your good be slandered, ¹⁷for the kingdom of God is not eating and drinking, but righteousness, peace, and joy in the Holy Spirit. ¹⁸Whoever serves Christ in this way is acceptable to God and approved by men.

¹⁹So then, we must pursue what promotes peace and what builds up one another. ²⁰Do not tear down God's work because of food. Everything is •clean, but it is wrong for a man to cause stumbling by what he eats. ²¹It is a noble thing not to eat meat, or drink wine, or do anything that makes your brother stumble. ²²Do you have a conviction? Keep it to yourself before God. The man who does not condemn himself by what he approves is blessed. ²³But whoever doubts stands condemned if he eats, because his eating is not from a conviction, and everything that is not from a conviction is sin.

15 Now we who are strong have an obligation to bear the weaknesses of those without strength, and not to please ourselves. ²Each one of us must please his neighbor for his good, to build him up. ³For even the •Messiah did not please Himself. On the contrary, as it is written, **The insults of those who insult You have fallen on Me.** ⁴For whatever was written in the past was written for our instruction, so that we may have hope through endurance and through the encouragement from the Scriptures. ⁵Now may the God who gives endurance and encouragement allow you to live in harmony with one another, according to the command of Christ Jesus, ⁶so that you may glorify the God and Father of our Lord Jesus Christ with a united mind and voice.

⁷Therefore accept one another, just as the Messiah also accepted you, to the glory of God. ⁸For I say that the Messiah became a servant of the circumcised on

behalf of God's truth, to confirm the promises to the fathers, [9] and so that Gentiles may glorify God for His mercy. As it is written:

Therefore I will praise You
 among the Gentiles,
and I will sing psalms to Your name.

[10] Again it says: Rejoice, you Gentiles, with His people! [11] And again:

Praise the Lord, all you Gentiles;
all the peoples should praise Him!

[12] And again, Isaiah says:

The root of Jesse will appear,
the One who rises to rule the Gentiles;
the Gentiles will hope in Him.

[13] Now may the God of hope fill you with all joy and peace as you believe in Him so that you may overflow with hope by the power of the Holy Spirit.

[14] My *brothers, I myself am convinced about you that you also are full of goodness, filled with all knowledge, and able to instruct one another. [15] Nevertheless, I have written to remind you more boldly on some points because of the grace given me by God [16] to be a minister of Christ Jesus to the Gentiles, serving as a priest of God's good news. My purpose is that the offering of the Gentiles may be acceptable, *sanctified by the Holy Spirit. [17] Therefore I have reason to boast in Christ Jesus regarding what pertains to God. [18] For I would not dare say anything except what Christ has accomplished through me to make the Gentiles obedient by word and deed, [19] by the power of miraculous signs and wonders, and by the power of God's Spirit. As a result, I have fully proclaimed the good news about the Messiah from Jerusalem all the way around to Illyricum. [20] My aim is to evangelize where Christ has not been named, so that I will not build on someone else's foundation, [21] but, as it is written:

Those who were not told about Him will see,
and those who have not heard
 will understand.

[22] That is why I have been prevented many times from coming to you. [23] But now I no longer have any work to do in these provinces, and I have strongly desired for many years to come to you [24] whenever I travel to Spain. For I hope to see you when I pass through, and to be assisted by you for my journey there, once I have first enjoyed your company for a while. [25] Right now I am traveling to Jerusalem to serve the *saints, [26] for Macedonia and Achaia were pleased to make a contribution for the poor among the saints in Jerusalem. [27] Yes, they were pleased, and indeed are indebted to them. For if the Gentiles have shared in their spiritual benefits, then they are obligated to minister to Jews in material needs. [28] So when I have finished this and safely delivered the funds to them, I will visit you on the way to Spain. [29] I know that when I come to you, I will come in the fullness of the blessing of Christ.

[30] Now I appeal to you, brothers, through our Lord Jesus Christ and through the love of the Spirit, to join with me in fervent prayers to God on my behalf. [31] Pray that I may be rescued from the unbelievers in Judea, that the gift I am bringing to Jerusalem may be acceptable to the saints, [32] and that, by God's will, I may come to you with joy and be refreshed together with you. [33] The God of peace be with all of you. *Amen.

16 I commend to you our sister Phoebe, who is a servant of the church in Cenchreae. [2] So you should welcome her in the Lord in a manner worthy of the *saints and assist her in whatever matter she may require your help. For indeed she has been a benefactor of many—and of me also.

[3] Give my greetings to Prisca and Aquila, my coworkers in Christ Jesus, [4] who risked their own necks for my life. Not only do I thank them, but so do all the Gentile churches. [5] Greet also the church that meets in their home.
Greet my dear friend Epaenetus, who is the first convert to Christ from *Asia.
[6] Greet Mary, who has worked very hard for you.
[7] Greet Andronicus and Junia, my fellow countrymen and fellow prisoners. They are noteworthy in the eyes of the apostles, and they were also in Christ before me.
[8] Greet Ampliatus, my dear friend in the Lord.
[9] Greet Urbanus, our coworker in Christ, and my dear friend Stachys.
[10] Greet Apelles, who is approved in Christ.
Greet those who belong to the household of Aristobulus.
[11] Greet Herodion, my fellow countryman.
Greet those who belong to the household of Narcissus who are in the Lord.
[12] Greet Tryphaena and Tryphosa, who have worked hard in the Lord.
Greet my dear friend Persis, who has worked very hard in the Lord.
[13] Greet Rufus, chosen in the Lord; also his mother—and mine.
[14] Greet Asyncritus, Phlegon, Hermes, Patrobas, Hermas, and the *brothers who are with them.
[15] Greet Philologus and Julia, Nereus and his sister, and Olympas, and all the saints who are with them.
[16] Greet one another with a holy kiss.
All the churches of Christ send you greetings.

[17] Now I urge you, brothers, to watch out for those who cause dissensions and obstacles contrary to the doctrine you have learned. Avoid them, [18] for such people do not serve our Lord Christ but their own appetites. They deceive the hearts of the unsuspecting with smooth talk and flattering words.

[19] The report of your obedience has reached everyone. Therefore I rejoice over you. But I want you to be wise about what is good, yet innocent about what is evil. [20] The God of peace will soon crush Satan under your feet. The grace of our Lord Jesus be with you.

[21] Timothy, my coworker, and Lucius, Jason, and Sosipater, my fellow countrymen, greet you.

[22] I Tertius, who wrote this letter, greet you in the Lord.

[23] Gaius, who is host to me and to the whole church, greets you. Erastus, the city treasurer, and our brother Quartus greet you.

[[24] The grace of our Lord Jesus Christ be with you all.]

[25] Now to Him who has power to strengthen you according to my gospel and the proclamation about Jesus Christ, according to the revelation of the *mystery kept silent for long ages [26] but now revealed and made known through the prophetic Scriptures, according to the command of the eternal God to advance the obedience of faith among all nations— [27] to the only wise God, through Jesus Christ—to Him be the glory forever! *Amen.

1 CORINTHIANS

1 Paul, called as an apostle of Christ Jesus by God's will, and Sosthenes our brother:

²To God's church at Corinth, to those who are ˙sanctified in Christ Jesus and called as ˙saints, with all those in every place who call on the name of Jesus Christ our Lord—both their Lord and ours.

³Grace to you and peace from God our Father and the Lord Jesus Christ.

⁴I always thank my God for you because of God's grace given to you in Christ Jesus, ⁵that by Him you were enriched in everything—in all speech and all knowledge. ⁶In this way, the testimony about Christ was confirmed among you, ⁷so that you do not lack any spiritual gift as you eagerly wait for the revelation of our Lord Jesus Christ. ⁸He will also strengthen you to the end, so that you will be blameless in the day of our Lord Jesus Christ. ⁹God is faithful; you were called by Him into fellowship with His Son, Jesus Christ our Lord.

¹⁰Now I urge you, ˙brothers, in the name of our Lord Jesus Christ, that all of you agree in what you say, that there be no divisions among you, and that you be united with the same understanding and the same conviction. ¹¹For it has been reported to me about you, my brothers, by members of Chloe's household, that there is rivalry among you. ¹²What I am saying is this: Each of you says, "I'm with Paul," or "I'm with Apollos," or "I'm with ˙Cephas," or "I'm with Christ." ¹³Is Christ divided? Was it Paul who was crucified for you? Or were you baptized in Paul's name? ¹⁴I thank God that I baptized none of you except Crispus and Gaius, ¹⁵so that no one can say you were baptized in my name. ¹⁶I did, in fact, baptize the household of Stephanas; beyond that, I don't know if I baptized anyone else. ¹⁷For Christ did not send me to baptize, but to evangelize—not with clever words, so that the cross of Christ will not be emptied of its effect.

¹⁸For the message of the cross is foolishness to those who are perishing, but it is God's power to us who are being saved. ¹⁹For it is written:

> **I will destroy the wisdom of the wise,**
> **and I will set aside the understanding**
> **of the experts.**

²⁰Where is the philosopher? Where is the scholar? Where is the debater of this age? Hasn't God made the world's wisdom foolish? ²¹For since, in God's wisdom, the ˙world did not know God through wisdom, God was pleased to save those who believe through the foolishness of the message preached. ²²For the Jews ask for signs and the Greeks seek wisdom, ²³but we preach Christ crucified, a stumbling block to the Jews and foolishness to the Gentiles. ²⁴Yet to those who are called, both Jews and Greeks, Christ is God's power and God's wisdom, ²⁵because God's foolishness is wiser than human wisdom, and God's weakness is stronger than human strength.

²⁶Brothers, consider your calling: Not many are wise from a human perspective, not many powerful, not many of noble birth. ²⁷Instead, God has chosen what is foolish in the world to shame the wise, and God has chosen what is weak in the world to shame the strong. ²⁸God has chosen what is insignificant and despised in the world—what is viewed as nothing—to bring to nothing what is viewed as something, ²⁹so that no one can boast in His presence. ³⁰But it is from

Him that you are in Christ Jesus, who became God-given wisdom for us—our righteousness, sanctification, and ˙redemption, ³¹in order that, as it is written: **The one who boasts must boast in the Lord.**

2 When I came to you, ˙brothers, announcing the testimony of God to you, I did not come with brilliance of speech or wisdom. ²For I didn't think it was a good idea to know anything among you except Jesus Christ and Him crucified. ³I came to you in weakness, in fear, and in much trembling. ⁴My speech and my proclamation were not with persuasive words of wisdom but with a powerful demonstration by the Spirit, ⁵so that your faith might not be based on men's wisdom but on God's power.

⁶However, we do speak a wisdom among the mature, but not a wisdom of this age, or of the rulers of this age, who are coming to nothing. ⁷On the contrary, we speak God's hidden wisdom in a ˙mystery, a wisdom God predestined before the ages for our glory. ⁸None of the rulers of this age knew this wisdom, for if they had known it, they would not have crucified the Lord of glory. ⁹But as it is written:

> **What eye did not see and ear did not hear,**
> **and what never entered the human mind—**
> **God prepared this for those who love Him.**

¹⁰Now God has revealed these things to us by the Spirit, for the Spirit searches everything, even the depths of God. ¹¹For who among men knows the thoughts of a man except the spirit of the man that is in him? In the same way, no one knows the thoughts of God except the Spirit of God. ¹²Now we have not received the spirit of the ˙world, but the Spirit who comes from God, so that we may understand what has been freely given to us by God. ¹³We also speak these things, not in words taught by human wisdom, but in those taught by the Spirit, explaining spiritual things to spiritual people. ¹⁴But the unbeliever does not welcome what comes from God's Spirit, because it is foolishness to him; he is not able to understand it since it is evaluated spiritually. ¹⁵The spiritual person, however, can evaluate everything, yet he himself cannot be evaluated by anyone. ¹⁶For

> **who has known the Lord's mind,**
> **that he may instruct Him?**

But we have the mind of Christ.

3 ˙Brothers, I was not able to speak to you as spiritual people but as people of the flesh, as babies in Christ. ²I gave you milk to drink, not solid food, because you were not yet ready for it. In fact, you are still not ready, ³because you are still fleshly. For since there is envy and strife among you, are you not fleshly and living like unbelievers? ⁴For whenever someone says, "I'm with Paul," and another, "I'm with Apollos," are you not unspiritual people?

⁵What then is Apollos? And what is Paul? They are servants through whom you believed, and each has the role the Lord has given. ⁶I planted, Apollos watered, but God gave the growth. ⁷So then neither the one who plants nor the one who waters is anything, but only God who gives the growth. ⁸Now the one planting and the one watering are one in purpose, and each will receive his own reward according to his own labor. ⁹For we are God's coworkers. You are God's field, God's

building. [10]According to God's grace that was given to me, I have laid a foundation as a skilled master builder, and another builds on it. But each one must be careful how he builds on it. [11]For no one can lay any other foundation than what has been laid down. That foundation is Jesus Christ. [12]If anyone builds on that foundation with gold, silver, costly stones, wood, hay, or straw, [13]each one's work will become obvious, for the day will disclose it, because it will be revealed by fire; the fire will test the quality of each one's work. [14]If anyone's work that he has built survives, he will receive a reward. [15]If anyone's work is burned up, it will be lost, but he will be saved; yet it will be like an escape through fire.

[16]Don't you yourselves know that you are God's sanctuary and that the Spirit of God lives in you? [17]If anyone destroys God's sanctuary, God will destroy him; for God's sanctuary is holy, and that is what you are.

[18]No one should deceive himself. If anyone among you thinks he is wise in this age, he must become foolish so that he can become wise. [19]For the wisdom of this *world is foolishness with God, since it is written: **He catches the wise in their craftiness;** [20]and again, **The Lord knows that the reasonings of the wise are meaningless.** [21]So no one should boast in human leaders, for everything is yours— [22]whether Paul or Apollos or *Cephas or the world or life or death or things present or things to come—everything is yours, [23]and you belong to Christ, and Christ belongs to God.

4 A person should consider us in this way: as servants of Christ and managers of God's *mysteries. [2]In this regard, it is expected of managers that each one of them be found faithful. [3]It is of little importance to me that I should be evaluated by you or by any human court. In fact, I don't even evaluate myself. [4]For I am not conscious of anything against myself, but I am not justified by this. The One who evaluates me is the Lord. [5]Therefore don't judge anything prematurely, before the Lord comes, who will both bring to light what is hidden in darkness and reveal the intentions of the hearts. And then praise will come to each one from God.

[6]Now, *brothers, I have applied these things to myself and Apollos for your benefit, so that you may learn from us the saying: "Nothing beyond what is written." The purpose is that none of you will be inflated with pride in favor of one person over another. [7]For who makes you so superior? What do you have that you didn't receive? If, in fact, you did receive it, why do you boast as if you hadn't received it? [8]You are already full! You are already rich! You have begun to reign as kings without us—and I wish you did reign, so that we could also reign with you! [9]For I think God has displayed us, the apostles, in last place, like men condemned to die: We have become a spectacle to the world and to angels and to men. [10]We are fools for Christ, but you are wise in Christ! We are weak, but you are strong! You are distinguished, but we are dishonored! [11]Up to the present hour we are both hungry and thirsty; we are poorly clothed, roughly treated, homeless; [12]we labor, working with our own hands. When we are reviled, we bless; when we are persecuted, we endure it; [13]when we are slandered, we respond graciously. Even now, we are like the world's garbage, like the dirt everyone scrapes off their sandals.

[14]I'm not writing this to shame you, but to warn you as my dear children. [15]For you can have 10,000 instructors in Christ, but you can't have many fathers. For I became your father in Christ Jesus through the gospel. [16]Therefore I urge you to imitate me. [17]This is why I have sent Timothy to you. He is my dearly loved and faithful son in the Lord. He will remind you about my ways in Christ Jesus, just as I teach everywhere in every church. [18]Now some are inflated with pride, as though I were not coming to you. [19]But I will come to you soon, if the Lord wills, and I will know not the talk but the power of those who are inflated with pride. [20]For the kingdom of God is not a matter of talk but of power. [21]What do you want? Should I come to you with a rod, or in love and a spirit of gentleness?

5 It is widely reported that there is sexual immorality among you, and the kind of sexual immorality that is not even tolerated among the Gentiles—a man is living with his father's wife. [2]And you are inflated with pride, instead of filled with grief so that he who has committed this act might be removed from your congregation. [3]For though I am absent in body but present in spirit, I have already decided about the one who has done this thing as though I were present. [4]When you are assembled in the name of our Lord Jesus with my spirit and with the power of our Lord Jesus, [5]turn that one over to Satan for the destruction of the flesh, so that his spirit may be saved in the Day of the Lord.

[6]Your boasting is not good. Don't you know that a little yeast permeates the whole batch of dough? [7]*Clean out the old yeast so that you may be a new batch. You are indeed unleavened, for Christ our *Passover has been sacrificed. [8]Therefore, let us observe the feast, not with old yeast or with the yeast of malice and evil but with the unleavened bread of sincerity and truth.

[9]I wrote to you in a letter not to associate with sexually immoral people. [10]I did not mean the immoral people of this *world or the greedy and swindlers or idolaters; otherwise you would have to leave the world. [11]But now I am writing you not to associate with anyone who claims to be a believer who is sexually immoral or greedy, an idolater or verbally abusive, a drunkard or a swindler. Do not even eat with such a person. [12]For what business is it of mine to judge outsiders? Don't you judge those who are inside? [13]But God judges outsiders. **Put away the evil person from among yourselves.**

6 If any of you has a legal dispute against another, do you dare go to court before the unrighteous, and not before the *saints? [2]Or don't you know that the saints will judge the *world? And if the world is judged by you, are you unworthy to judge the smallest cases? [3]Don't you know that we will judge angels—not to mention ordinary matters? [4]So if you have cases pertaining to this life, do you select those who have no standing in the church to judge? [5]I say this to your shame! Can it be that there is not one wise person among you who is able to arbitrate between his *brothers? [6]Instead, believer goes to court against believer, and that before unbelievers!

[7]Therefore, to have legal disputes against one another is already a moral failure for you. Why not rather put up with injustice? Why not rather be cheated? [8]Instead, you act unjustly and cheat—and you do this to believers! [9]Don't you know that the unrighteous will not inherit God's kingdom? Do not be deceived:

No sexually immoral people, idolaters, adulterers, or anyone practicing homosexuality, [10]no thieves, greedy people, drunkards, verbally abusive people, or swindlers will inherit God's kingdom. [11]And some of you used to be like this. But you were washed, you were •sanctified, you were •justified in the name of the Lord Jesus Christ and by the Spirit of our God.

[12]"Everything is permissible for me," but not everything is helpful. "Everything is permissible for me," but I will not be brought under the control of anything. [13]"Food for the stomach and the stomach for food," but God will do away with both of them. The body is not for sexual immorality but for the Lord, and the Lord for the body. [14]God raised up the Lord and will also raise us up by His power. [15]Don't you know that your bodies are a part of Christ's body? So should I take a part of Christ's body and make it part of a prostitute? Absolutely not! [16]Don't you know that anyone joined to a prostitute is one body with her? For Scripture says, **The two will become one flesh.** [17]But anyone joined to the Lord is one spirit with Him.

[18]Run from sexual immorality! "Every sin a person can commit is outside the body." On the contrary, the person who is sexually immoral sins against his own body. [19]Don't you know that your body is a sanctuary of the Holy Spirit who is in you, whom you have from God? You are not your own, [20]for you were bought at a price. Therefore glorify God in your body.

7 Now in response to the matters you wrote about: "It is good for a man not to have relations with a woman." [2]But because sexual immorality is so common, each man should have his own wife, and each woman should have her own husband. [3]A husband should fulfill his marital responsibility to his wife, and likewise a wife to her husband. [4]A wife does not have the right over her own body, but her husband does. In the same way, a husband does not have the right over his own body, but his wife does. [5]Do not deprive one another sexually—except when you agree for a time, to devote yourselves to prayer. Then come together again; otherwise, Satan may tempt you because of your lack of self-control. [6]I say the following as a concession, not as a command. [7]I wish that all people were just like me. But each has his own gift from God, one person in this way and another in that way.

[8]I say to the unmarried and to widows: It is good for them if they remain as I am. [9]But if they do not have self-control, they should marry, for it is better to marry than to burn with desire.

[10]I command the married—not I, but the Lord— a wife is not to leave her husband. [11]But if she does leave, she must remain unmarried or be reconciled to her husband—and a husband is not to leave his wife. [12]But I (not the Lord) say to the rest: If any brother has an unbelieving wife and she is willing to live with him, he must not leave her. [13]Also, if any woman has an unbelieving husband and he is willing to live with her, she must not leave her husband. [14]For the unbelieving husband is set apart for God by the wife, and the unbelieving wife is set apart for God by the husband. Otherwise your children would be corrupt, but now they are set apart for God. [15]But if the unbeliever leaves, let him leave. A brother or a sister is not bound in such cases. God has called you to live in peace. [16]For you, wife, how do you know whether you will save your husband? Or you, husband, how do you know whether you will save your wife?

[17]However, each one must live his life in the situation the Lord assigned when God called him. This is what I command in all the churches. [18]Was anyone already circumcised when he was called? He should not undo his circumcision. Was anyone called while uncircumcised? He should not get circumcised. [19]Circumcision does not matter and uncircumcision does not matter, but keeping God's commands does. [20]Each person should remain in the life situation in which he was called. [21]Were you called while a •slave? It should not be a concern to you. But if you can become free, by all means take the opportunity. [22]For he who is called by the Lord as a slave is the Lord's freedman. Likewise he who is called as a free man is Christ's slave. [23]You were bought at a price; do not become slaves of men. [24]•Brothers, each person should remain with God in whatever situation he was called.

[25]About virgins: I have no command from the Lord, but I do give an opinion as one who by the Lord's mercy is trustworthy. [26]Therefore I consider this to be good because of the present distress: It is fine for a man to remain as he is. [27]Are you bound to a wife? Do not seek to be loosed. Are you loosed from a wife? Do not seek a wife. [28]However, if you do get married, you have not sinned, and if a virgin marries, she has not sinned. But such people will have trouble in this life, and I am trying to spare you. [29]And I say this, brothers: The time is limited, so from now on those who have wives should be as though they had none, [30]those who weep as though they did not weep, those who rejoice as though they did not rejoice, those who buy as though they did not possess, [31]and those who use the world as though they did not make full use of it. For this world in its current form is passing away.

[32]I want you to be without concerns. An unmarried man is concerned about the things of the Lord—how he may please the Lord. [33]But a married man is concerned about the things of the world—how he may please his wife— [34]and his interests are divided. An unmarried woman or a virgin is concerned about the things of the Lord, so that she may be holy both in body and in spirit. But a married woman is concerned about the things of the world—how she may please her husband. [35]Now I am saying this for your own benefit, not to put a restraint on you, but because of what is proper and so that you may be devoted to the Lord without distraction.

[36]But if any man thinks he is acting improperly toward his virgin, if she is past marriageable age, and so it must be, he can do what he wants. He is not sinning; they can get married. [37]But he who stands firm in his heart (who is under no compulsion, but has control over his own will) and has decided in his heart to keep his own virgin, will do well. [38]So then he who marries his virgin does well, but he who does not marry will do better.

[39]A wife is bound as long as her husband is living. But if her husband dies, she is free to be married to anyone she wants—only in the Lord. [40]But she is happier if she remains as she is, in my opinion. And I think that I also have the Spirit of God.

8 About food offered to idols: We know that "we all have knowledge." Knowledge inflates with pride, but love builds up. [2]If anyone thinks he knows anything, he does not yet know it as he ought to know it. [3]But if anyone loves God, he is known by Him.

[4]About eating food offered to idols, then, we know

that "an idol is nothing in the world," and that "there is no God but one." [5]For even if there are so-called gods, whether in heaven or on earth—as there are many "gods" and many "lords"—

[6] yet for us there is one God, the Father.
All things are from Him,
and we exist for Him.
And there is one Lord, Jesus Christ.
All things are through Him,
and we exist through Him.

[7]However, not everyone has this knowledge. In fact, some have been so used to idolatry up until now that when they eat food offered to an idol, their conscience, being weak, is defiled. [8]Food will not make us acceptable to God. We are not inferior if we don't eat, and we are not better if we do eat. [9]But be careful that this right of yours in no way becomes a stumbling block to the weak. [10]For if someone sees you, the one who has this knowledge, dining in an idol's temple, won't his weak conscience be encouraged to eat food offered to idols? [11]Then the weak person, the brother for whom Christ died, is ruined by your knowledge. [12]Now when you sin like this against the *brothers and wound their weak conscience, you are sinning against Christ. [13]Therefore, if food causes my brother to fall, I will never again eat meat, so that I won't cause my brother to fall.

9 Am I not free? Am I not an apostle? Have I not seen Jesus our Lord? Are you not my work in the Lord? [2]If I am not an apostle to others, at least I am to you, for you are the seal of my apostleship in the Lord. [3]My defense to those who examine me is this: [4]Don't we have the right to eat and drink? [5]Don't we have the right to be accompanied by a Christian wife like the other apostles, the Lord's brothers, and *Cephas? [6]Or do Barnabas and I alone have no right to refrain from working? [7]Who ever goes to war at his own expense? Who plants a vineyard and does not eat its fruit? Or who shepherds a flock and does not drink the milk from the flock? [8]Am I saying this from a human perspective? Doesn't the law also say the same thing? [9]For it is written in the law of Moses, **Do not muzzle an ox while it treads out grain.** Is God really concerned with oxen? [10]Or isn't He really saying it for us? Yes, this is written for us, because he who plows ought to plow in hope, and he who threshes should do so in hope of sharing the crop. [11]If we have sown spiritual things for you, is it too much if we reap material benefits from you? [12]If others have this right to receive benefits from you, don't we even more?

However, we have not made use of this right; instead we endure everything so that we will not hinder the gospel of Christ. [13]Don't you know that those who perform the temple services eat the food from the temple, and those who serve at the altar share in the offerings of the altar? [14]In the same way, the Lord has commanded that those who preach the gospel should earn their living by the gospel.

[15]But I have used none of these rights, and I have not written this to make it happen that way for me. For it would be better for me to die than for anyone to deprive me of my boast! [16]For if I preach the gospel, I have no reason to boast, because an obligation is placed on me. And woe to me if I do not preach the gospel! [17]For if I do this willingly, I have a reward, but if unwillingly, I am entrusted with a stewardship. [18]What then is my reward? To preach the gospel and offer it free of charge and not make full use of my authority in the gospel.

[19]Although I am a free man and not anyone's slave, I have made myself a *slave to everyone, in order to win more people. [20]To the Jews I became like a Jew, to win Jews; to those under the law, like one under the law—though I myself am not under the law—to win those under the law. [21]To those who are without that law, like one without the law—not being without God's law but within Christ's law—to win those without the law. [22]To the weak I became weak, in order to win the weak. I have become all things to all people, so that I may by every possible means save some. [23]Now I do all this because of the gospel, so I may become a partner in its benefits.

[24]Don't you know that the runners in a stadium all race, but only one receives the prize? Run in such a way to win the prize. [25]Now everyone who competes exercises self-control in everything. However, they do it to receive a crown that will fade away, but we a crown that will never fade away. [26]Therefore I do not run like one who runs aimlessly or box like one beating the air. [27]Instead, I discipline my body and bring it under strict control, so that after preaching to others, I myself will not be disqualified.

10 Now I want you to know, *brothers, that our fathers were all under the cloud, all passed through the sea, [2]and all were baptized into Moses in the cloud and in the sea. [3]They all ate the same spiritual food, [4]and all drank the same spiritual drink. For they drank from a spiritual rock that followed them, and that rock was Christ. [5]But God was not pleased with most of them, for they were struck down in the wilderness.

[6]Now these things became examples for us, so that we will not desire evil things as they did. [7]Don't become idolaters as some of them were; as it is written, **The people sat down to eat and drink, and got up to play.** [8]Let us not commit sexual immorality as some of them did, and in a single day 23,000 people fell dead. [9]Let us not test Christ as some of them did and were destroyed by snakes. [10]Nor should we complain as some of them did, and were killed by the destroyer. [11]Now these things happened to them as examples, and they were written as a warning to us, on whom the ends of the ages have come. [12]So, whoever thinks he stands must be careful not to fall. [13]No temptation has overtaken you except what is common to humanity. God is faithful, and He will not allow you to be tempted beyond what you are able, but with the temptation He will also provide a way of escape so that you are able to bear it.

[14]Therefore, my dear friends, flee from idolatry. [15]I am speaking as to wise people. Judge for yourselves what I say. [16]The cup of blessing that we give thanks for, is it not a sharing in the blood of Christ? The bread that we break, is it not a sharing in the body of Christ? [17]Because there is one bread, we who are many are one body, for all of us share that one bread. [18]Look at the people of Israel. Do not those who eat the sacrifices participate in what is offered on the altar? [19]What am I saying then? That food offered to idols is anything, or that an idol is anything? [20]No, but I do say that what they sacrifice, they sacrifice to demons and not to God. I do not want you to participate with demons! [21]You cannot drink the cup of the Lord and the cup of demons. You cannot share in the Lord's table and the

table of demons. [22] Or are we provoking the Lord to jealousy? Are we stronger than He?

[23] "Everything is permissible," but not everything is helpful. "Everything is permissible," but not everything builds up. [24] No one should seek his own good, but the good of the other person.

[25] Eat everything that is sold in the meat market, asking no questions for conscience' sake, [26] for **the earth is the Lord's, and all that is in it.** [27] If one of the unbelievers invites you over and you want to go, eat everything that is set before you, without raising questions of conscience. [28] But if someone says to you, "This is food offered to an idol," do not eat it, out of consideration for the one who told you, and for conscience' sake. [29] I do not mean your own conscience, but the other person's. For why is my freedom judged by another person's conscience? [30] If I partake with thanks, why am I slandered because of something I give thanks for?

[31] Therefore, whether you eat or drink, or whatever you do, do everything for God's glory. [32] Give no offense to the Jews or the Greeks or the church of God, [33] just as I also try to please all people in all things, not seeking my own profit, but the profit of many, so that they may be saved. [1] Imitate me, as I also imitate Christ.

11

[2] Now I praise you because you always remember me and keep the traditions just as I delivered them to you. [3] But I want you to know that Christ is the head of every man, and the man is the head of the woman, and God is the head of Christ. [4] Every man who prays or prophesies with something on his head dishonors his head. [5] But every woman who prays or prophesies with her head uncovered dishonors her head, since that is one and the same as having her head shaved. [6] So if a woman's head is not covered, her hair should be cut off. But if it is disgraceful for a woman to have her hair cut off or her head shaved, she should be covered. [7] A man, in fact, should not cover his head, because he is God's image and glory, but woman is man's glory. [8] For man did not come from woman, but woman came from man. [9] And man was not created for woman, but woman for man. [10] This is why a woman should have a symbol of authority on her head, because of the angels. [11] In the Lord, however, woman is not independent of man, and man is not independent of woman. [12] For just as woman came from man, so man comes through woman, and all things come from God.

[13] Judge for yourselves: Is it proper for a woman to pray to God with her head uncovered? [14] Does not even nature itself teach you that if a man has long hair it is a disgrace to him, [15] but that if a woman has long hair, it is her glory? For her hair is given to her as a covering. [16] But if anyone wants to argue about this, we have no other custom, nor do the churches of God.

[17] Now in giving the following instruction I do not praise you, since you come together not for the better but for the worse. [18] For to begin with, I hear that when you come together as a church there are divisions among you, and in part I believe it. [19] There must, indeed, be factions among you, so that those who are approved may be recognized among you. [20] Therefore, when you come together, it is not really to eat the Lord's Supper. [21] For at the meal, each one eats his own supper ahead of others. So one person is hungry while another gets drunk! [22] Don't you have houses to eat and drink in? Or do you look down on the church

of God and embarrass those who have nothing? What should I say to you? Should I praise you? I do not praise you for this!

[23] For I received from the Lord what I also passed on to you: On the night when He was betrayed, the Lord Jesus took bread, [24] gave thanks, broke it, and said, "This is My body, which is for you. Do this in remembrance of Me."

[25] In the same way, after supper He also took the cup and said, "This cup is the new covenant established by My blood. Do this, as often as you drink it, in remembrance of Me." [26] For as often as you eat this bread and drink the cup, you proclaim the Lord's death until He comes.

[27] Therefore, whoever eats the bread or drinks the cup of the Lord in an unworthy way will be *guilty of sin against the body and blood of the Lord. [28] So a man should examine himself; in this way he should eat the bread and drink from the cup. [29] For whoever eats and drinks without recognizing the body, eats and drinks judgment on himself. [30] This is why many are sick and ill among you, and many have fallen *asleep. [31] If we were properly evaluating ourselves, we would not be judged, [32] but when we are judged, we are disciplined by the Lord, so that we may not be condemned with the *world.

[33] Therefore, my *brothers, when you come together to eat, wait for one another. [34] If anyone is hungry, he should eat at home, so that when you gather together you will not come under judgment. And I will give instructions about the other matters whenever I come.

12

Now concerning what comes from the Spirit: *brothers, I do not want you to be unaware. [2] You know that when you were pagans, you used to be led off to the idols that could not speak. [3] Therefore I am informing you that no one speaking by the Spirit of God says, "Jesus is cursed," and no one can say, "Jesus is Lord," except by the Holy Spirit.

[4] Now there are different gifts, but the same Spirit. [5] There are different ministries, but the same Lord. [6] And there are different activities, but the same God activates each gift in each person. [7] A demonstration of the Spirit is given to each person to produce what is beneficial:

[8] to one is given a message of wisdom
      through the Spirit,
      to another, a message of knowledge
      by the same Spirit,
[9] to another, faith by the same Spirit,
      to another, gifts of healing by the one Spirit,
[10] to another, the performing of miracles,
      to another, prophecy,
      to another, distinguishing between spirits,
      to another, different kinds of languages,
      to another, interpretation of *languages.

[11] But one and the same Spirit is active in all these, distributing to each person as He wills.

[12] For as the body is one and has many parts, and all the parts of that body, though many, are one body—so also is Christ. [13] For we were all baptized by one Spirit into one body—whether Jews or Greeks, whether *slaves or free—and we were all made to drink of one Spirit. [14] So the body is not one part but many. [15] If the foot should say, "Because I'm not a hand, I don't belong to the body," in spite of this it still belongs to the body. [16] And if the ear should say, "Because I'm not an eye, I don't belong to the body," in spite of this it still

belongs to the body. [17] If the whole body were an eye, where would the hearing be? If the whole body were an ear, where would the sense of smell be? [18] But now God has placed each one of the parts in one body just as He wanted. [19] And if they were all the same part, where would the body be? [20] Now there are many parts, yet one body.

[21] So the eye cannot say to the hand, "I don't need you!" Or again, the head can't say to the feet, "I don't need you!" [22] But even more, those parts of the body that seem to be weaker are necessary. [23] And those parts of the body that we think to be less honorable, we clothe these with greater honor, and our unpresentable parts have a better presentation. [24] But our presentable parts have no need of clothing. Instead, God has put the body together, giving greater honor to the less honorable, [25] so that there would be no division in the body, but that the members would have the same concern for each other. [26] So if one member suffers, all the members suffer with it; if one member is honored, all the members rejoice with it.

[27] Now you are the body of Christ, and individual members of it. [28] And God has placed these in the church:

first apostles, second prophets,
third teachers, next miracles,
then gifts of healing, helping,
managing, various kinds of languages.
[29] Are all apostles? Are all prophets?
Are all teachers? Do all do miracles?
[30] Do all have gifts of healing?
Do all speak in other languages?
Do all interpret?

[31] But desire the greater gifts. And I will show you an even better way.

13 If I speak human or angelic *languages
but do not have love,
I am a sounding gong or a clanging cymbal.
[2] If I have the gift of prophecy
and understand all *mysteries
and all knowledge,
and if I have all faith
so that I can move mountains
but do not have love, I am nothing.
[3] And if I donate all my goods to feed the poor,
and if I give my body in order to boast
but do not have love, I gain nothing.
[4] Love is patient, love is kind.
Love does not envy,
is not boastful, is not conceited,
[5] does not act improperly,
is not selfish, is not provoked,
and does not keep a record of wrongs.
[6] Love finds no joy in unrighteousness
but rejoices in the truth.
[7] It bears all things, believes all things,
hopes all things, endures all things.
[8] Love never ends.
But as for prophecies,
they will come to an end;
as for languages, they will cease;
as for knowledge, it will come to an end.
[9] For we know in part,
and we prophesy in part.
[10] But when the perfect comes,
the partial will come to an end.
[11] When I was a child,

I spoke like a child,
I thought like a child,
I reasoned like a child.
When I became a man,
I put aside childish things.
[12] For now we see indistinctly,
as in a mirror,
but then face to face.
Now I know in part,
but then I will know fully,
as I am fully known.
[13] Now these three remain:
faith, hope, and love.
But the greatest of these is love.

14 Pursue love and desire spiritual gifts, and above all that you may prophesy. [2] For the person who speaks in another *language is not speaking to men but to God, since no one understands him; however, he speaks *mysteries in the Spirit. [3] But the person who prophesies speaks to people for edification, encouragement, and consolation. [4] The person who speaks in another language builds himself up, but he who prophesies builds up the church. [5] I wish all of you spoke in other languages, but even more that you prophesied. The person who prophesies is greater than the person who speaks in languages, unless he interprets so that the church may be built up.

[6] But now, *brothers, if I come to you speaking in other languages, how will I benefit you unless I speak to you with a revelation or knowledge or prophecy or teaching? [7] Even inanimate things that produce sounds—whether flute or harp—if they don't make a distinction in the notes, how will what is played on the flute or harp be recognized? [8] In fact, if the trumpet makes an unclear sound, who will prepare for battle? [9] In the same way, unless you use your tongue for intelligible speech, how will what is spoken be known? For you will be speaking into the air. [10] There are doubtless many different kinds of languages in the world, and all have meaning. [11] Therefore, if I do not know the meaning of the language, I will be a foreigner to the speaker, and the speaker will be a foreigner to me. [12] So also you—since you are zealous for spiritual gifts, seek to excel in building up the church.

[13] Therefore the person who speaks in another language should pray that he can interpret. [14] For if I pray in another language, my spirit prays, but my understanding is unfruitful. [15] What then? I will pray with the spirit, and I will also pray with my understanding. I will sing with the spirit, and I will also sing with my understanding. [16] Otherwise, if you praise with the spirit, how will the uninformed person say "'Amen" at your giving of thanks, since he does not know what you are saying? [17] For you may very well be giving thanks, but the other person is not being built up. [18] I thank God that I speak in other languages more than all of you; [19] yet in the church I would rather speak five words with my understanding, in order to teach others also, than 10,000 words in another language.

[20] Brothers, don't be childish in your thinking, but be infants in regard to evil and adult in your thinking. [21] It is written in the law:

**I will speak to these people
by people of other languages
and by the lips of foreigners,
and even then, they will not listen to Me,**

says the Lord. [22] It follows that speaking in other

languages is intended as a sign, not for believers but for unbelievers. But prophecy is not for unbelievers but for believers. ²³Therefore, if the whole church assembles together and all are speaking in other languages and people who are uninformed or unbelievers come in, will they not say that you are out of your minds? ²⁴But if all are prophesying and some unbeliever or uninformed person comes in, he is convicted by all and is judged by all. ²⁵The secrets of his heart will be revealed, and as a result he will fall facedown and worship God, proclaiming, "God is really among you."

²⁶What then is the conclusion, brothers? Whenever you come together, each one has a psalm, a teaching, a revelation, another language, or an interpretation. All things must be done for edification. ²⁷If any person speaks in another language, there should be only two, or at the most three, each in turn, and someone must interpret. ²⁸But if there is no interpreter, that person should keep silent in the church and speak to himself and to God. ²⁹Two or three prophets should speak, and the others should evaluate. ³⁰But if something has been revealed to another person sitting there, the first prophet should be silent. ³¹For you can all prophesy one by one, so that everyone may learn and everyone may be encouraged. ³²And the prophets' spirits are under the control of the prophets, ³³since God is not a God of disorder but of peace.

As in all the churches of the •saints, ³⁴the women should be silent in the churches, for they are not permitted to speak, but should be submissive, as the law also says. ³⁵And if they want to learn something, they should ask their own husbands at home, for it is disgraceful for a woman to speak in the church meeting. ³⁶Did the word of God originate from you, or did it come to you only?

³⁷If anyone thinks he is a prophet or spiritual, he should recognize that what I write to you is the Lord's command. ³⁸But if anyone ignores this, he will be ignored. ³⁹Therefore, my brothers, be eager to prophesy, and do not forbid speaking in other languages. ⁴⁰But everything must be done decently and in order.

15 Now •brothers, I want to clarify for you the gospel I proclaimed to you; you received it and have taken your stand on it. ²You are also saved by it, if you hold to the message I proclaimed to you—unless you believed for no purpose. ³For I passed on to you as most important what I also received:

that Christ died for our sins
according to the Scriptures,
⁴   that He was buried,
that He was raised on the third day
according to the Scriptures,
⁵   and that He appeared to •Cephas,
then to the Twelve.
⁶   Then He appeared to over 500 brothers
at one time;
most of them are still alive,
but some have fallen •asleep.
⁷   Then He appeared to James,
then to all the apostles.
⁸   Last of all, as to one abnormally born,
He also appeared to me.

⁹For I am the least of the apostles, unworthy to be called an apostle, because I persecuted the church of God. ¹⁰But by God's grace I am what I am, and His grace toward me was not ineffective. However, I worked more than any of them, yet not I, but God's

grace that was with me. ¹¹Therefore, whether it is I or they, so we proclaim and so you have believed.

¹²Now if Christ is proclaimed as raised from the dead, how can some of you say, "There is no resurrection of the dead"? ¹³But if there is no resurrection of the dead, then Christ has not been raised; ¹⁴and if Christ has not been raised, then our proclamation is without foundation, and so is your faith. ¹⁵In addition, we are found to be false witnesses about God, because we have testified about God that He raised up Christ—whom He did not raise up if in fact the dead are not raised. ¹⁶For if the dead are not raised, Christ has not been raised. ¹⁷And if Christ has not been raised, your faith is worthless; you are still in your sins. ¹⁸Therefore, those who have fallen asleep in Christ have also perished. ¹⁹If we have put our hope in Christ for this life only, we should be pitied more than anyone.

²⁰But now Christ has been raised from the dead, the •firstfruits of those who have fallen asleep. ²¹For since death came through a man, the resurrection of the dead also comes through a man. ²²For as in Adam all die, so also in Christ all will be made alive. ²³But each in his own order: Christ, the firstfruits; afterward, at His coming, those who belong to Christ. ²⁴Then comes the end, when He hands over the kingdom to God the Father, when He abolishes all rule and all authority and power. ²⁵For He must reign until He puts all His enemies under His feet. ²⁶The last enemy to be abolished is death. ²⁷For **God has put everything under His feet.** But when it says "everything" is put under Him, it is obvious that He who puts everything under Him is the exception. ²⁸And when everything is subject to Christ, then the Son Himself will also be subject to the One who subjected everything to Him, so that God may be all in all.

²⁹Otherwise what will they do who are being baptized for the dead? If the dead are not raised at all, then why are people baptized for them? ³⁰Why are we in danger every hour? ³¹I affirm by the pride in you that I have in Christ Jesus our Lord: I die every day! ³²If I fought wild animals in Ephesus with only human hope, what good did that do me? If the dead are not raised, **Let us eat and drink, for tomorrow we die.** ³³Do not be deceived: "Bad company corrupts good morals." ³⁴Come to your senses and stop sinning, for some people are ignorant about God. I say this to your shame.

³⁵But someone will say, "How are the dead raised? What kind of body will they have when they come?" ³⁶Foolish one! What you sow does not come to life unless it dies. ³⁷And as for what you sow—you are not sowing the future body, but only a seed, perhaps of wheat or another grain. ³⁸But God gives it a body as He wants, and to each of the seeds its own body. ³⁹Not all flesh is the same flesh; there is one flesh for humans, another for animals, another for birds, and another for fish. ⁴⁰There are heavenly bodies and earthly bodies, but the splendor of the heavenly bodies is different from that of the earthly ones. ⁴¹There is a splendor of the sun, another of the moon, and another of the stars; for one star differs from another star in splendor. ⁴²So it is with the resurrection of the dead:

Sown in corruption, raised in incorruption;
⁴³   sown in dishonor, raised in glory;
sown in weakness, raised in power;
⁴⁴   sown a natural body, raised a spiritual body.
If there is a natural body, there is also a spiritual body.
⁴⁵So it is written: **The first man Adam became a liv-**

ing being; the last Adam became a life-giving Spirit. ⁴⁶However, the spiritual is not first, but the natural, then the spiritual.

⁴⁷ The first man was from the earth
and made of dust;
the second man is from heaven.

⁴⁸ Like the man made of dust,
so are those who are made of dust;
like the heavenly man,
so are those who are heavenly.

⁴⁹ And just as we have borne
the image of the man made of dust,
we will also bear
the image of the heavenly man.

⁵⁰Brothers, I tell you this: Flesh and blood cannot inherit the kingdom of God, and corruption cannot inherit incorruption. ⁵¹Listen! I am telling you a *mystery:

We will not all fall asleep,
but we will all be changed,

⁵² in a moment, in the blink of an eye,
at the last trumpet.
For the trumpet will sound,
and the dead will be raised incorruptible,
and we will be changed.

⁵³ For this corruptible must be clothed
with incorruptibility,
and this mortal must be clothed
with immortality.

⁵⁴ When this corruptible is clothed
with incorruptibility,
and this mortal is clothed
with immortality,
then the saying that is written will take place:
Death has been swallowed up in victory.

⁵⁵ **Death, where is your victory?**
Death, where is your sting?

⁵⁶ Now the sting of death is sin,
and the power of sin is the law.

⁵⁷ But thanks be to God, who gives us the victory
through our Lord Jesus Christ!

⁵⁸Therefore, my dear brothers, be steadfast, immovable, always excelling in the Lord's work, knowing that your labor in the Lord is not in vain.

16 Now about the collection for the *saints: You should do the same as I instructed the Galatian churches. ²On the first day of the week, each of you is to set something aside and save in keeping with how he prospers, so that no collections will need to be made when I come. ³When I arrive, I will send with letters those you recommend to carry your gracious gift to Jerusalem. ⁴If it is suitable for me to go as well, they can travel with me.

⁵I will come to you after I pass through Macedonia—for I will be traveling through Macedonia— ⁶and perhaps I will remain with you or even spend the winter, so that you may send me on my way wherever I go. ⁷I don't want to see you now just in passing, for I hope to spend some time with you, if the Lord allows. ⁸But I will stay in Ephesus until Pentecost, ⁹because a wide door for effective ministry has opened for me— yet many oppose me. ¹⁰If Timothy comes, see that he has nothing to fear from you, because he is doing the Lord's work, just as I am. ¹¹Therefore, no one should look down on him. Send him on his way in peace so he can come to me, for I am expecting him with the brothers.

¹²About our brother Apollos: I strongly urged him to come to you with the brothers, but he was not at all willing to come now. However, he will come when he has an opportunity.

¹³Be alert, stand firm in the faith, act like a man, be strong. ¹⁴Your every action must be done with love.

¹⁵*Brothers, you know the household of Stephanas: They are the *firstfruits of Achaia and have devoted themselves to serving the saints. I urge you ¹⁶also to submit to such people, and to everyone who works and labors with them. ¹⁷I am pleased to have Stephanas, Fortunatus, and Achaicus present, because these men have made up for your absence. ¹⁸For they have refreshed my spirit and yours. Therefore recognize such people.

¹⁹The churches of *Asia greet you. Aquila and Priscilla greet you warmly in the Lord, along with the church that meets in their home. ²⁰All the brothers greet you. Greet one another with a holy kiss.

²¹This greeting is in my own hand—Paul. ²²If anyone does not love the Lord, a curse be on him. *Marana tha* that is, Lord, come! ²³The grace of the Lord Jesus be with you. ²⁴My love be with all of you in Christ Jesus.

2 CORINTHIANS

1 Paul, an apostle of Christ Jesus by God's will, and Timothy our brother:

To God's church at Corinth, with all the *saints who are throughout Achaia.

²Grace to you and peace from God our Father and the Lord Jesus Christ.

³Praise the God and Father of our Lord Jesus Christ, the Father of mercies and the God of all comfort. ⁴He comforts us in all our affliction, so that we may be able to comfort those who are in any kind of affliction, through the comfort we ourselves receive from God. ⁵For as the sufferings of Christ overflow to us, so through Christ our comfort also overflows. ⁶If we are afflicted, it is for your comfort and salvation. If we are

comforted, it is for your comfort, which is experienced in your endurance of the same sufferings that we suffer. ⁷And our hope for you is firm, because we know that as you share in the sufferings, so you will share in the comfort.

⁸For we don't want you to be unaware, *brothers, of our affliction that took place in *Asia: we were completely overwhelmed—beyond our strength—so that we even despaired of life. ⁹Indeed, we personally had a death sentence within ourselves, so that we would not trust in ourselves but in God who raises the dead. ¹⁰He has delivered us from such a terrible death, and He will deliver us. We have put our hope in Him that He will deliver us again ¹¹while you join in helping us by your

prayers. Then many will give thanks on our behalf for the gift that came to us through the prayers of many.

¹²For this is our confidence: The testimony of our conscience is that we have conducted ourselves in the world, and especially toward you, with God-given sincerity and purity, not by fleshly wisdom but by God's grace. ¹³Now we are writing nothing to you other than what you can read and also understand. I hope you will understand completely— ¹⁴as you have partially understood us—that we are your reason for pride, as you are ours, in the day of our Lord Jesus.

¹⁵I planned with this confidence to come to you first, so you could have a double benefit, ¹⁶and to go on to Macedonia with your help, then come to you again from Macedonia and be given a start by you on my journey to Judea. ¹⁷So when I planned this, was I irresponsible? Or what I plan, do I plan in a purely human way so that I say "Yes, yes" and "No, no" simultaneously? ¹⁸As God is faithful, our message to you is not "Yes and no." ¹⁹For the Son of God, Jesus Christ, who was preached among you by us—by me and Silvanus and Timothy—did not become "Yes and no"; on the contrary, a final "Yes" has come in Him. ²⁰For every one of God's promises is "Yes" in Him. Therefore, the "Amen" is also spoken through Him by us for God's glory. ²¹Now it is God who strengthens us, with you, in Christ and has anointed us. ²²He has also sealed us and given us the Spirit as a down payment in our hearts.

²³I call on God as a witness, on my life, that it was to spare you that I did not come to Corinth. ²⁴I do not mean that we have control of your faith, but we are workers with you for your joy, because you stand 2 by faith. ¹In fact, I made up my mind about this: I would not come to you on another painful visit. ²For if I cause you pain, then who will cheer me other than the one being hurt by me? ³I wrote this very thing so that when I came I wouldn't have pain from those who ought to give me joy, because I am confident about all of you that my joy will also be yours. ⁴For I wrote to you with many tears out of an extremely troubled and anguished heart—not that you should be hurt, but that you should know the abundant love I have for you.

⁵If anyone has caused pain, he has caused pain not so much to me but to some degree—not to exaggerate—to all of you. ⁶The punishment inflicted by the majority is sufficient for that person. ⁷As a result, you should instead forgive and comfort him. Otherwise, this one may be overwhelmed by excessive grief. ⁸Therefore I urge you to reaffirm your love to him. ⁹I wrote for this purpose: to test your character to see if you are obedient in everything. ¹⁰If you forgive anyone, I do too. For what I have forgiven—if I have forgiven anything—it is for you in the presence of Christ. ¹¹I have done this so that we may not be taken advantage of by Satan. For we are not ignorant of his schemes.

¹²When I came to Troas to preach the gospel of Christ, the Lord opened a door for me. ¹³I had no rest in my spirit because I did not find my brother Titus, but I said good-bye to them and left for Macedonia.

¹⁴But thanks be to God, who always puts us on display in Christ and through us spreads the aroma of the knowledge of Him in every place. ¹⁵For to God we are the fragrance of Christ among those who are being saved and among those who are perishing. ¹⁶To some we are an aroma of death leading to death, but to others, an aroma of life leading to life. And who is competent for this? ¹⁷For we are not like the many who market God's message for profit. On the contrary, we speak with sincerity in Christ, as from God and before God.

3 Are we beginning to commend ourselves again? Or do we need, like some, letters of recommendation to you or from you? ²You yourselves are our letter, written on our hearts, recognized and read by everyone. ³It is clear that you are Christ's letter, produced by us, not written with ink but with the Spirit of the living God—not on stone tablets but on tablets that are hearts of flesh.

⁴We have this kind of confidence toward God through Christ. ⁵It is not that we are competent in ourselves to consider anything as coming from ourselves, but our competence is from God. ⁶He has made us competent to be ministers of a new covenant, not of the letter, but of the Spirit. For the letter kills, but the Spirit produces life.

⁷Now if the ministry of death, chiseled in letters on stones, came with glory, so that the Israelites were not able to look directly at Moses' face because of the glory from his face—a fading glory— ⁸how will the ministry of the Spirit not be more glorious? ⁹For if the ministry of condemnation had glory, the ministry of righteousness overflows with even more glory. ¹⁰In fact, what had been glorious is not glorious now by comparison because of the glory that surpasses it. ¹¹For if what was fading away was glorious, what endures will be even more glorious.

¹²Therefore, having such a hope, we use great boldness. ¹³We are not like Moses, who used to put a veil over his face so that the Israelites could not stare at the end of what was fading away, ¹⁴but their minds were closed. For to this day, at the reading of the old covenant, the same veil remains; it is not lifted, because it is set aside only in Christ. ¹⁵Even to this day, whenever Moses is read, a veil lies over their hearts, ¹⁶but whenever a person turns to the Lord, the veil is removed. ¹⁷Now the Lord is the Spirit, and where the Spirit of the Lord is, there is freedom. ¹⁸We all, with unveiled faces, are looking as in a mirror at the glory of the Lord and are being transformed into the same image from glory to glory; this is from the Lord who is the Spirit.

4 Therefore, since we have this ministry because we were shown mercy, we do not give up. ²Instead, we have renounced shameful secret things, not 'walking in deceit or distorting God's message, but commending ourselves to every person's conscience in God's sight by an open display of the truth. ³But if our gospel is veiled, it is veiled to those who are perishing. ⁴In their case, the god of this age has blinded the minds of the unbelievers so they cannot see the light of the gospel of the glory of Christ, who is the image of God. ⁵For we are not proclaiming ourselves but Jesus Christ as Lord, and ourselves as your 'slaves because of Jesus. ⁶For God who said, "Let light shine out of darkness," has shone in our hearts to give the light of the knowledge of God's glory in the face of Jesus Christ.

⁷Now we have this treasure in clay jars, so that this extraordinary power may be from God and not from us. ⁸We are pressured in every way but not crushed; we are perplexed but not in despair; ⁹we are persecuted but not abandoned; we are struck down but not destroyed. ¹⁰We always carry the death of Jesus in our body, so that the life of Jesus may also be revealed in our body. ¹¹For we who live are always given over to

death because of Jesus, so that Jesus' life may also be revealed in our mortal flesh. [12]So death works in us, but life in you. [13]And since we have the same spirit of faith in keeping with what is written, **I believed, therefore I spoke,** we also believe, and therefore speak. [14]We know that the One who raised the Lord Jesus will raise us also with Jesus and present us with you. [15]Indeed, everything is for your benefit, so that grace, extended through more and more people, may cause thanksgiving to increase to God's glory.

[16]Therefore we do not give up. Even though our outer person is being destroyed, our inner person is being renewed day by day. [17]For our momentary light affliction is producing for us an absolutely incomparable eternal weight of glory. [18]So we do not focus on what is seen, but on what is unseen. For what is seen is temporary, but what is unseen is eternal.

5 For we know that if our temporary, earthly dwelling is destroyed, we have a building from God, an eternal dwelling in the heavens, not made with hands. [2]Indeed, we groan in this body, desiring to put on our dwelling from heaven, [3]since, when we are clothed, we will not be found naked. [4]Indeed, we groan while we are in this tent, burdened as we are, because we do not want to be unclothed but clothed, so that mortality may be swallowed up by life. [5]And the One who prepared us for this very purpose is God, who gave us the Spirit as a down payment.

[6]So, we are always confident and know that while we are at home in the body we are away from the Lord. [7]For we 'walk by faith, not by sight, [8]and we are confident and satisfied to be out of the body and at home with the Lord. [9]Therefore, whether we are at home or away, we make it our aim to be pleasing to Him. [10]For we must all appear before the tribunal of Christ, so that each may be repaid for what he has done in the body, whether good or worthless.

[11]Therefore, because we know the 'fear of the Lord, we seek to persuade people. We are completely open before God, and I hope we are completely open to your consciences as well. [12]We are not commending ourselves to you again, but giving you an opportunity to be proud of us, so that you may have a reply for those who take pride in the outward appearance rather than in the heart. [13]For if we are out of our mind, it is for God; if we have a sound mind, it is for you. [14]For Christ's love compels us, since we have reached this conclusion: If One died for all, then all died. [15]And He died for all so that those who live should no longer live for themselves, but for the One who died for them and was raised.

[16]From now on, then, we do not know anyone in a purely human way. Even if we have known Christ in a purely human way, yet now we no longer know Him in this way. [17]Therefore, if anyone is in Christ, he is a new creation; old things have passed away, and look, new things have come. [18]Everything is from God, who reconciled us to Himself through Christ and gave us the ministry of reconciliation: [19]That is, in Christ, God was reconciling the world to Himself, not counting their trespasses against them, and He has committed the message of reconciliation to us. [20]Therefore, we are ambassadors for Christ, certain that God is appealing through us. We plead on Christ's behalf, "Be reconciled to God." [21]He made the One who did not know sin to be sin for us, so that we might become the righteousness of God in Him.

6 Working together with Him, we also appeal to you, "Don't receive God's grace in vain." [2]For He says:

> **I heard you in an acceptable time,**
> **and I helped you in the day of salvation.**

Look, now is the acceptable time; now is the day of salvation.

[3]We give no opportunity for stumbling to anyone, so that the ministry will not be blamed. [4]But as God's ministers, we commend ourselves in everything:

> by great endurance, by afflictions,
> by hardship, by difficulties,
> [5] by beatings, by imprisonments,
> by riots, by labors,
> by sleepless nights, by times of hunger,
> [6] by purity, by knowledge,
> by patience, by kindness,
> by the Holy Spirit, by sincere love,
> [7] by the message of truth,
> by the power of God;
> through weapons of righteousness
> on the right hand and the left,
> [8] through glory and dishonor,
> through slander and good report;
> as deceivers yet true;
> [9] as unknown yet recognized;
> as dying and look—we live;
> as being disciplined yet not killed;
> [10] as grieving yet always rejoicing;
> as poor yet enriching many;
> as having nothing yet possessing everything.

[11]We have spoken openly to you, Corinthians; our heart has been opened wide. [12]You are not limited by us, but you are limited by your own affections. [13]I speak as to my children. As a proper response, you should also be open to us.

[14]Do not be mismatched with unbelievers. For what partnership is there between righteousness and lawlessness? Or what fellowship does light have with darkness? [15]What agreement does Christ have with Belial? Or what does a believer have in common with an unbeliever? [16]And what agreement does God's sanctuary have with idols? For we are the sanctuary of the living God, as God said:

> **I will dwell among them**
> **and walk among them,**
> **and I will be their God,**
> **and they will be My people.**
> [17] **Therefore, come out from among them**
> **and be separate, says the Lord;**
> **do not touch any unclean thing,**
> **and I will welcome you.**
> [18] **I will be a Father to you,**
> **and you will be sons and daughters to Me,**
> **says the Lord Almighty.**

7 Therefore, dear friends, since we have such promises, let us 'cleanse ourselves from every impurity of the flesh and spirit, completing our 'sanctification in the 'fear of God.

[2]Accept us. We have wronged no one, corrupted no one, defrauded no one. [3]I don't say this to condemn you, for I have already said that you are in our hearts, to live together and to die together. [4]I have great confidence in you; I have great pride in you. I am filled with encouragement; I am overcome with joy in all our afflictions.

[5]In fact, when we came into Macedonia, we had no rest. Instead, we were troubled in every way: conflicts

on the outside, fears inside. [6]But God, who comforts the humble, comforted us by the arrival of Titus, [7]and not only by his arrival, but also by the comfort he received from you. He told us about your deep longing, your sorrow, and your zeal for me, so that I rejoiced even more. [8]For even if I grieved you with my letter, I do not regret it—even though I did regret it since I saw that the letter grieved you, yet only for a little while. [9]Now I rejoice, not because you were grieved, but because your grief led to repentance. For you were grieved as God willed, so that you didn't experience any loss from us. [10]For godly grief produces a repentance not to be regretted and leading to salvation, but worldly grief produces death. [11]For consider how much diligence this very thing—this grieving as God wills—has produced in you: what a desire to clear yourselves, what indignation, what fear, what deep longing, what zeal, what justice! In every way you showed yourselves to be pure in this matter. [12]So even though I wrote to you, it was not because of the one who did wrong, or because of the one who was wronged, but in order that your diligence for us might be made plain to you in the sight of God. [13]For this reason we have been comforted.

In addition to our comfort, we rejoiced even more over the joy Titus had, because his spirit was refreshed by all of you. [14]For if I have made any boast to him about you, I have not been embarrassed; but as I have spoken everything to you in truth, so our boasting to Titus has also turned out to be the truth. [15]And his affection toward you is even greater as he remembers the obedience of all of you, and how you received him with fear and trembling. [16]I rejoice that I have complete confidence in you.

8 We want you to know, *brothers, about the grace of God granted to the churches of Macedonia: [2]During a severe testing by affliction, their abundance of joy and their deep poverty overflowed into the wealth of their generosity. [3]I testify that, on their own, according to their ability and beyond their ability, [4]they begged us insistently for the privilege of sharing in the ministry to the *saints, [5]and not just as we had hoped. Instead, they gave themselves especially to the Lord, then to us by God's will. [6]So we urged Titus that just as he had begun, so he should also complete this grace to you. [7]Now as you excel in everything—faith, speech, knowledge, and in all diligence, and in your love for us—excel also in this grace.

[8]I am not saying this as a command. Rather, by means of the diligence of others, I am testing the genuineness of your love. [9]For you know the grace of our Lord Jesus Christ: Though He was rich, for your sake He became poor, so that by His poverty you might become rich. [10]Now I am giving an opinion on this because it is profitable for you, who a year ago began not only to do something but also to desire it. [11]But now finish the task as well, that just as there was eagerness to desire it, so there may also be a completion from what you have. [12]For if the eagerness is there, it is acceptable according to what one has, not according to what he does not have. [13]It is not that there may be relief for others and hardship for you, but it is a question of equality— [14]at the present time your surplus is available for their need, so their abundance may also become available for our need, so there may be equality. [15]As it has been written:

The person who gathered much

did not have too much,
and the person who gathered little
did not have too little.

[16]Thanks be to God who put the same concern for you into the heart of Titus. [17]For he accepted our urging and, being very diligent, went out to you by his own choice. [18]We have sent with him the brother who is praised throughout the churches for his gospel ministry. [19]And not only that, but he was also appointed by the churches to accompany us with this gift that is being administered by us for the glory of the Lord Himself and to show our eagerness to help. [20]We are taking this precaution so no one can criticize us about this large sum administered by us. [21]For we are making provision for what is right, not only before the Lord but also before men. [22]We have also sent with them our brother. We have often tested him in many circumstances and found him to be diligent—and now even more diligent because of his great confidence in you. [23]As for Titus, he is my partner and coworker serving you; as for our brothers, they are the messengers of the churches, the glory of Christ. [24]Therefore, show them proof before the churches of your love and of our boasting about you.

9 Now concerning the ministry to the *saints, it is unnecessary for me to write to you. [2]For I know your eagerness, and I brag about you to the Macedonians: "Achaia has been prepared since last year," and your zeal has stirred up most of them. [3]But I sent the brothers so our boasting about you in the matter would not prove empty, and so you would be prepared just as I said. [4]For if any Macedonians come with me and find you unprepared, we, not to mention you, would be embarrassed in that situation. [5]Therefore I considered it necessary to urge the brothers to go on ahead to you and arrange in advance the generous gift you promised, so that it will be ready as a gift and not as an extortion.

[6]Remember this: The person who sows sparingly will also reap sparingly, and the person who sows generously will also reap generously. [7]Each person should do as he has decided in his heart—not reluctantly or out of necessity, for God loves a cheerful giver. [8]And God is able to make every grace overflow to you, so that in every way, always having everything you need, you may excel in every good work. [9]As it is written:

He scattered;
He gave to the poor;
His righteousness endures forever.

[10]Now the One who provides seed for the sower and bread for food will provide and multiply your seed and increase the harvest of your righteousness. [11]You will be enriched in every way for all generosity, which produces thanksgiving to God through us. [12]For the ministry of this service is not only supplying the needs of the saints, but is also overflowing in many acts of thanksgiving to God. [13]They will glorify God for your obedience to the confession of the gospel of Christ, and for your generosity in sharing with them and with others through the proof provided by this service. [14]And they will have deep affection for you in their prayers on your behalf because of the surpassing grace of God in you. [15]Thanks be to God for His indescribable gift.

10 Now I, Paul, make a personal appeal to you by the gentleness and graciousness of Christ—I who am humble among you in person but bold toward you when absent. [2]I beg you that when I am present I

will not need to be bold with the confidence by which I plan to challenge certain people who think we are behaving in an unspiritual way. ³For though we live in the body, we do not wage war in an unspiritual way, ⁴since the weapons of our warfare are not worldly, but are powerful through God for the demolition of strongholds. We demolish arguments ⁵and every high-minded thing that is raised up against the knowledge of God, taking every thought captive to obey Christ. ⁶And we are ready to punish any disobedience, once your obedience has been confirmed.

⁷Look at what is obvious. If anyone is confident that he belongs to Christ, he should remind himself of this: Just as he belongs to Christ, so do we. ⁸For if I boast some more about our authority, which the Lord gave for building you up and not for tearing you down, I am not ashamed. ⁹I don't want to seem as though I am trying to terrify you with my letters. ¹⁰For it is said, "His letters are weighty and powerful, but his physical presence is weak, and his public speaking is despicable." ¹¹Such a person should consider this: What we are in the words of our letters when absent, we will be in actions when present.

¹²For we don't dare classify or compare ourselves with some who commend themselves. But in measuring themselves by themselves and comparing themselves to themselves, they lack understanding. ¹³We, however, will not boast beyond measure but according to the measure of the area of ministry that God has assigned to us, which reaches even to you. ¹⁴For we are not overextending ourselves, as if we had not reached you, since we have come to you with the gospel of Christ. ¹⁵We are not bragging beyond measure about other people's labors. But we have the hope that as your faith increases, our area of ministry will be greatly enlarged, ¹⁶so that we may proclaim the good news to the regions beyond you, not boasting about what has already been done in someone else's area of ministry. ¹⁷So **the one who boasts must boast in the Lord.** ¹⁸For it is not the one commending himself who is approved, but the one the Lord commends.

11 I wish you would put up with a little foolishness from me. Yes, do put up with me. ²For I am jealous over you with a godly jealousy, because I have promised you in marriage to one husband—to present a pure virgin to Christ. ³But I fear that, as the serpent deceived Eve by his cunning, your minds may be seduced from a complete and pure devotion to Christ. ⁴For if a person comes and preaches another Jesus, whom we did not preach, or you receive a different spirit, which you had not received, or a different gospel, which you had not accepted, you put up with it splendidly!

⁵Now I consider myself in no way inferior to the "super-apostles." ⁶Though untrained in public speaking, I am certainly not untrained in knowledge. Indeed, we have always made that clear to you in everything. ⁷Or did I commit a sin by humbling myself so that you might be exalted, because I preached the gospel of God to you free of charge? ⁸I robbed other churches by taking pay from them to minister to you. ⁹When I was present with you and in need, I did not burden anyone, for the brothers who came from Macedonia supplied my needs. I have kept myself, and will keep myself, from burdening you in any way. ¹⁰As the truth of Christ is in me, this boasting of mine will

not be stopped in the regions of Achaia. ¹¹Why? Because I don't love you? God knows I do!

¹²But I will continue to do what I am doing, in order to deny the opportunity of those who want an opportunity to be regarded just as our equals in what they boast about. ¹³For such people are false apostles, deceitful workers, disguising themselves as apostles of Christ. ¹⁴And no wonder! For Satan disguises himself as an angel of light. ¹⁵So it is no great thing if his servants also disguise themselves as servants of righteousness. Their destiny will be according to their works.

¹⁶I repeat: No one should consider me a fool. But if you do, at least accept me as a fool, so I too may boast a little. ¹⁷What I say in this matter of boasting, I don't speak as the Lord would, but foolishly. ¹⁸Since many boast in an unspiritual way, I will also boast. ¹⁹For you, being so wise, gladly put up with fools! ²⁰In fact, you put up with it if someone enslaves you, if someone devours you, if someone captures you, if someone dominates you, or if someone hits you in the face. ²¹I say this to our shame: We have been weak.

But in whatever anyone dares to boast—I am talking foolishly—I also dare:

²²   Are they Hebrews? So am I.
Are they Israelites? So am I.
Are they the •seed of Abraham?
   So am I.
²³   Are they servants of Christ?
I'm talking like a madman—I'm a better one:
with far more labors,
many more imprisonments,
far worse beatings, near death
   many times.
²⁴   Five times I received 39 lashes from Jews.
²⁵   Three times I was beaten with rods
   by the Romans.
Once I was stoned by my enemies.
Three times I was shipwrecked.
I have spent a night and a day
in the open sea.
²⁶   On frequent journeys, I faced
dangers from rivers,
dangers from robbers,
dangers from my own people,
dangers from the Gentiles,
dangers in the city,
dangers in the open country,
dangers on the sea,
and dangers among false •brothers;
²⁷   labor and hardship,
many sleepless nights, hunger and thirst,
often without food, cold, and lacking clothing.

²⁸Not to mention other things, there is the daily pressure on me: my care for all the churches. ²⁹Who is weak, and I am not weak? Who is made to •stumble, and I do not burn with indignation? ³⁰If boasting is necessary, I will boast about my weaknesses. ³¹The God and Father of the Lord Jesus, who is praised forever, knows I am not lying. ³²In Damascus, the governor under King Aretas guarded the city of the Damascenes in order to arrest me, ³³so I was let down in a basket through a window in the wall and escaped his hands.

12 Boasting is necessary. It is not profitable, but I will move on to visions and revelations of the Lord. ²I know a man in Christ who was caught up into the third heaven 14 years ago. Whether he was in the

body or out of the body, I don't know, God knows. ³I know that this man—whether in the body or out of the body I don't know, God knows— ⁴was caught up into paradise. He heard inexpressible words, which a man is not allowed to speak. ⁵I will boast about this person, but not about myself, except of my weaknesses. ⁶For if I want to boast, I will not be a fool, because I will be telling the truth. But I will spare you, so that no one can credit me with something beyond what he sees in me or hears from me, ⁷especially because of the extraordinary revelations. Therefore, so that I would not exalt myself, a thorn in the flesh was given to me, a messenger of Satan to torment me so I would not exalt myself. ⁸Concerning this, I pleaded with the Lord three times to take it away from me. ⁹But He said to me, "My grace is sufficient for you, for power is perfected in weakness." Therefore, I will most gladly boast all the more about my weaknesses, so that Christ's power may reside in me. ¹⁰So I take pleasure in weaknesses, insults, catastrophes, persecutions, and in pressures, because of Christ. For when I am weak, then I am strong.

¹¹I have become a fool; you forced it on me. I should have been endorsed by you, since I am not in any way inferior to the "super-apostles," even though I am nothing. ¹²The signs of an apostle were performed with great endurance among you—not only signs but also wonders and miracles. ¹³So in what way were you treated worse than the other churches, except that I personally did not burden you? Forgive me this wrong!

¹⁴Now I am ready to come to you this third time. I will not burden you, for I am not seeking what is yours, but you. For children are not obligated to save up for their parents, but parents for their children. ¹⁵I will most gladly spend and be spent for you. If I love you more, am I to be loved less? ¹⁶Now granted, I have not burdened you; yet sly as I am, I took you in by deceit! ¹⁷Did I take advantage of you by anyone I sent you? ¹⁸I urged Titus to come, and I sent the brother with him. Did Titus take advantage of you? Didn't we •walk in the same spirit and in the same footsteps?

¹⁹You have thought all along that we were defending ourselves to you. No, in the sight of God we are speaking in Christ, and everything, dear friends, is for building you up. ²⁰For I fear that perhaps when I come I will not find you to be what I want, and I may not be found by you to be what you want; there may be quarreling, jealousy, outbursts of anger, selfish ambitions, slander, gossip, arrogance, and disorder. ²¹I fear that when I come my God will again humiliate me in your presence, and I will grieve for many who sinned before and have not repented of the moral impurity, sexual immorality, and promiscuity they practiced.

13 This is the third time I am coming to you. **Every fact must be established by the testimony of two or three witnesses.** ²I gave a warning when I was present the second time, and now I give a warning while I am absent to those who sinned before and to all the rest: If I come again, I will not be lenient, ³since you seek proof of Christ speaking in me. He is not weak toward you, but powerful among you. ⁴In fact, He was crucified in weakness, but He lives by God's power. For we also are weak in Him, yet toward you we will live with Him by God's power.

⁵Test yourselves to see if you are in the faith. Examine yourselves. Or do you yourselves not recognize that Jesus Christ is in you?—unless you fail the test. ⁶And I hope you will recognize that we do not fail the test. ⁷Now we pray to God that you do nothing wrong—not that we may appear to pass the test, but that you may do what is right, even though we may appear to fail. ⁸For we are not able to do anything against the truth, but only for the truth. ⁹In fact, we rejoice when we are weak and you are strong. We also pray that you become fully mature. ¹⁰This is why I am writing these things while absent, that when I am there I will not use severity, in keeping with the authority the Lord gave me for building up and not for tearing down.

¹¹Finally, •brothers, rejoice. Become mature, be encouraged, be of the same mind, be at peace, and the God of love and peace will be with you. ¹²Greet one another with a holy kiss. All the •saints greet you.

¹³The grace of the Lord Jesus Christ, and the love of God, and the fellowship of the Holy Spirit be with all of you.

GALATIANS

1 Paul, an apostle—not from men or by man, but by Jesus Christ and God the Father who raised Him from the dead— ²and all the •brothers who are with me:

To the churches of Galatia.

³Grace to you and peace from God the Father and our Lord Jesus Christ, ⁴who gave Himself for our sins to rescue us from this present evil age, according to the will of our God and Father. ⁵To whom be the glory forever and ever. •Amen.

⁶I am amazed that you are so quickly turning away from Him who called you by the grace of Christ and are turning to a different gospel— ⁷not that there is another gospel, but there are some who are troubling you and want to change the good news about the •Messiah. ⁸But even if we or an angel from heaven should preach to you a gospel other than what we have preached to you, a curse be on him! ⁹As we have said before, I now say again: If anyone preaches to you a gospel contrary to what you received, a curse be on him!

¹⁰For am I now trying to win the favor of people, or God? Or am I striving to please people? If I were still trying to please people, I would not be a •slave of Christ.

¹¹Now I want you to know, brothers, that the gospel preached by me is not based on human thought. ¹²For I did not receive it from a human source and I was not taught it, but it came by a revelation from Jesus Christ.

¹³For you have heard about my former way of life in Judaism: I persecuted God's church to an extreme degree and tried to destroy it. ¹⁴I advanced in Judaism beyond many contemporaries among my people, because I was extremely zealous for the traditions of my ancestors. ¹⁵But when God, who from my birth set me apart and called me by His grace, was pleased ¹⁶to re-

veal His Son in me, so that I could preach Him among the Gentiles, I did not immediately consult with anyone. [17] I did not go up to Jerusalem to those who had become apostles before me; instead I went to Arabia and came back to Damascus.

[18] Then after three years I did go up to Jerusalem to get to know ˙Cephas, and I stayed with him 15 days. [19] But I didn't see any of the other apostles except James, the Lord's brother. [20] Now I am not lying in what I write to you. God is my witness.

[21] Afterward, I went to the regions of Syria and Cilicia. [22] I remained personally unknown to the Judean churches in Christ; [23] they simply kept hearing: "He who formerly persecuted us now preaches the faith he once tried to destroy." [24] And they glorified God because of me.

2 Then after 14 years I went up again to Jerusalem with Barnabas, taking Titus along also. [2] I went up according to a revelation and presented to them the gospel I preach among the Gentiles—but privately to those recognized as leaders—so that I might not be running, or have run the race, in vain. [3] But not even Titus who was with me, though he was a Greek, was compelled to be circumcised. [4] This issue arose because of false brothers smuggled in, who came in secretly to spy on the freedom that we have in Christ Jesus, in order to enslave us. [5] But we did not give up and submit to these people for even an hour, so that the truth of the gospel might be preserved for you.

[6] Now from those recognized as important (what they really were makes no difference to me; God does not show favoritism)—they added nothing to me. [7] On the contrary, they saw that I had been entrusted with the gospel for the uncircumcised, just as Peter was for the circumcised, [8] since the One at work in Peter for an apostleship to the circumcised was also at work in me for the Gentiles. [9] When James, ˙Cephas, and John, recognized as pillars, acknowledged the grace that had been given to me, they gave the right hand of fellowship to me and Barnabas, agreeing that we should go to the Gentiles and they to the circumcised. [10] They asked only that we would remember the poor, which I made every effort to do.

[11] But when Cephas came to Antioch, I opposed him to his face because he stood condemned. [12] For he regularly ate with the Gentiles before certain men came from James. However, when they came, he withdrew and separated himself, because he feared those from the circumcision party. [13] Then the rest of the Jews joined his hypocrisy, so that even Barnabas was carried away by their hypocrisy. [14] But when I saw that they were deviating from the truth of the gospel, I told Cephas in front of everyone, "If you, who are a Jew, live like a Gentile and not like a Jew, how can you compel Gentiles to live like Jews?"

[15] We who are Jews by birth and not "Gentile sinners" [16] know that no one is ˙justified by the works of the law but by faith in Jesus Christ. And we have believed in Christ Jesus so that we might be justified by faith in Christ and not by the works of the law, because by the works of the law no human being will be justified. [17] But if we ourselves are also found to be "sinners" while seeking to be justified by Christ, is Christ then a promoter of sin? Absolutely not! [18] If I rebuild the system I tore down, I show myself to be a lawbreaker. [19] For through the law I have died to the law, so that I might live for God. I have been crucified

with Christ [20] and I no longer live, but Christ lives in me. The life I now live in the body, I live by faith in the Son of God, who loved me and gave Himself for me. [21] I do not set aside the grace of God, for if righteousness comes through the law, then Christ died for nothing.

3 You foolish Galatians! Who has hypnotized you, before whose eyes Jesus Christ was vividly portrayed as crucified? [2] I only want to learn this from you: Did you receive the Spirit by the works of the law or by hearing with faith? [3] Are you so foolish? After beginning with the Spirit, are you now going to be made complete by the flesh? [4] Did you suffer so much for nothing—if in fact it was for nothing? [5] So then, does God supply you with the Spirit and work miracles among you by the works of the law or by hearing with faith?

[6] Just as Abraham **believed God, and it was credited to him for righteousness,** [7] then understand that those who have faith are Abraham's sons. [8] Now the Scripture saw in advance that God would ˙justify the Gentiles by faith and told the good news ahead of time to Abraham, saying, **All the nations will be blessed through you.** [9] So those who have faith are blessed with Abraham, who had faith.

[10] For all who rely on the works of the law are under a curse, because it is written: **Everyone who does not continue doing everything written in the book of the law is cursed.** [11] Now it is clear that no one is justified before God by the law, because **the righteous will live by faith.** [12] But the law is not based on faith; instead, **the one who does these things will live by them.** [13] Christ has ˙redeemed us from the curse of the law by becoming a curse for us, because it is written: **Everyone who is hung on a tree is cursed.** [14] The purpose was that the blessing of Abraham would come to the Gentiles by Christ Jesus, so that we could receive the promised Spirit through faith.

[15] ˙Brothers, I'm using a human illustration. No one sets aside or makes additions to even a human covenant that has been ratified. [16] Now the promises were spoken to Abraham and to his ˙seed. He does not say "and to seeds," as though referring to many, but referring to one, **and to your seed,** who is Christ. [17] And I say this: The law, which came 430 years later, does not revoke a covenant that was previously ratified by God and cancel the promise. [18] For if the inheritance is from the law, it is no longer from the promise; but God granted it to Abraham through the promise.

[19] Why then was the law given? It was added because of transgressions until the Seed to whom the promise was made would come. The law was put into effect through angels by means of a mediator. [20] Now a mediator is not for just one person, but God is one. [21] Is the law therefore contrary to God's promises? Absolutely not! For if a law had been given that was able to give life, then righteousness would certainly be by the law. [22] But the Scripture has imprisoned everything under sin's power, so that the promise by faith in Jesus Christ might be given to those who believe. [23] Before this faith came, we were confined under the law, imprisoned until the coming faith was revealed. [24] The law, then, was our guardian until Christ, so that we could be justified by faith. [25] But since that faith has come, we are no longer under a guardian, [26] for you are all sons of God through faith in Christ Jesus.

[27] For as many of you as have been baptized into Christ have put on Christ like a garment. [28] There is

no Jew or Greek, *slave or free, male or female; for you are all one in Christ Jesus. [29] And if you belong to Christ, then you are Abraham's seed, heirs according

4 to the promise. [1] Now I say that as long as the heir is a child, he differs in no way from a *slave, though he is the owner of everything. [2] Instead, he is under guardians and stewards until the time set by his father. [3] In the same way we also, when we were children, were in slavery under the elemental forces of the world. [4] When the time came to completion, God sent His Son, born of a woman, born under the law, [5] to *redeem those under the law, so that we might receive adoption as sons. [6] And because you are sons, God has sent the Spirit of His Son into our hearts, crying, "'*Abba*, Father!" [7] So you are no longer a slave but a son, and if a son, then an heir through God.

[8] But in the past, when you didn't know God, you were enslaved to things that by nature are not gods. [9] But now, since you know God, or rather have become known by God, how can you turn back again to the weak and bankrupt elemental forces? Do you want to be enslaved to them all over again? [10] You observe special days, months, seasons, and years. [11] I am fearful for you, that perhaps my labor for you has been wasted.

[12] I beg you, *brothers: Become like me, for I also became like you. You have not wronged me; [13] you know that previously I preached the gospel to you because of a physical illness. [14] You did not despise or reject me though my physical condition was a trial for you. On the contrary, you received me as an angel of God, as Christ Jesus Himself.

[15] What happened to this sense of being blessed you had? For I testify to you that, if possible, you would have torn out your eyes and given them to me. [16] Have I now become your enemy by telling you the truth? [17] They are enthusiastic about you, but not for any good. Instead, they want to isolate you so you will be enthusiastic about them. [18] Now it is always good to be enthusiastic about good—and not just when I am with you. [19] My children, I am again suffering labor pains for you until Christ is formed in you. [20] I would like to be with you right now and change my tone of voice, because I don't know what to do about you.

[21] Tell me, those of you who want to be under the law, don't you hear the law? [22] For it is written that Abraham had two sons, one by a slave and the other by a free woman. [23] But the one by the slave was born according to the impulse of the flesh, while the one by the free woman was born as the result of a promise. [24] These things are illustrations, for the women represent the two covenants. One is from Mount Sinai and bears children into slavery—this is Hagar. [25] Now Hagar is Mount Sinai in Arabia and corresponds to the present Jerusalem, for she is in slavery with her children. [26] But the Jerusalem above is free, and she is our mother. [27] For it is written:

Rejoice, childless woman,
who does not give birth.
Burst into song and shout,
you who are not in labor,
for the children of the desolate are many,
more numerous than those
of the woman who has a husband.

[28] Now you, brothers, like Isaac, are children of promise. [29] But just as then the child born according to the flesh persecuted the one born according to the Spirit, so also now. [30] But what does the Scripture say?

Drive out the slave and her son, for the son of the slave will never be a coheir with the son of the free woman.

[31] Therefore, brothers, we are not children of the slave but of the free woman.

5 Christ has liberated us to be free. Stand firm then and don't submit again to a yoke of slavery. [2] Take note! I, Paul, tell you that if you get yourselves circumcised, Christ will not benefit you at all. [3] Again I testify to every man who gets himself circumcised that he is obligated to keep the entire law. [4] You who are trying to be *justified by the law are alienated from Christ; you have fallen from grace. [5] For through the Spirit, by faith, we eagerly wait for the hope of righteousness. [6] For in Christ Jesus neither circumcision nor uncircumcision accomplishes anything; what matters is faith working through love.

[7] You were running well. Who prevented you from obeying the truth? [8] This persuasion did not come from the One who called you. [9] A little yeast leavens the whole lump of dough. [10] I have confidence in the Lord you will not accept any other view. But whoever it is that is confusing you will pay the penalty. [11] Now *brothers, if I still preach circumcision, why am I still persecuted? In that case the offense of the cross has been abolished. [12] I wish those who are disturbing you might also get themselves castrated!

[13] For you were called to be free, brothers; only don't use this freedom as an opportunity for the flesh, but serve one another through love. [14] For the entire law is fulfilled in one statement: **Love your neighbor as yourself.** [15] But if you bite and devour one another, watch out, or you will be consumed by one another.

[16] I say then, *walk by the Spirit and you will not carry out the desire of the flesh. [17] For the flesh desires what is against the Spirit, and the Spirit desires what is against the flesh; these are opposed to each other, so that you don't do what you want. [18] But if you are led by the Spirit, you are not under the law.

[19] Now the works of the flesh are obvious: sexual immorality, moral impurity, promiscuity, [20] idolatry, sorcery, hatreds, strife, jealousy, outbursts of anger, selfish ambitions, dissensions, factions, [21] envy, drunkenness, carousing, and anything similar. I tell you about these things in advance—as I told you before—that those who practice such things will not inherit the kingdom of God.

[22] But the fruit of the Spirit is love, joy, peace, patience, kindness, goodness, faith, [23] gentleness, self-control. Against such things there is no law. [24] Now those who belong to Christ Jesus have crucified the flesh with its passions and desires. [25] Since we live by the Spirit, we must also follow the Spirit. [26] We must not become conceited, provoking one another, envying one another.

6 *Brothers, if someone is caught in any wrongdoing, you who are spiritual should restore such a person with a gentle spirit, watching out for yourselves so you also won't be tempted. [2] Carry one another's burdens; in this way you will fulfill the law of Christ. [3] For if anyone considers himself to be something when he is nothing, he deceives himself. [4] But each person should examine his own work, and then he will have a reason for boasting in himself alone, and not in respect to someone else. [5] For each person will have to carry his own load.

[6] The one who is taught the message must share

all his good things with the teacher. ⁷Don't be deceived: God is not mocked. For whatever a man sows he will also reap, ⁸because the one who sows to his flesh will reap corruption from the flesh, but the one who sows to the Spirit will reap eternal life from the Spirit. ⁹So we must not get tired of doing good, for we will reap at the proper time if we don't give up. ¹⁰Therefore, as we have opportunity, we must work for the good of all, especially for those who belong to the household of faith.

¹¹Look at what large letters I use as I write to you in my own handwriting. ¹²Those who want to make a good impression in the flesh are the ones who would compel you to be circumcised—but only to avoid being persecuted for the cross of Christ. ¹³For even the circumcised don't keep the law themselves; however, they want you to be circumcised in order to boast about your flesh. ¹⁴But as for me, I will never boast about anything except the cross of our Lord Jesus Christ. The *world has been crucified to me through the cross, and I to the world. ¹⁵For both circumcision and uncircumcision mean nothing; what matters instead is a new creation. ¹⁶May peace come to all those who follow this standard, and mercy to the Israel of God!

¹⁷From now on, let no one cause me trouble, because I bear on my body scars for the cause of Jesus. ¹⁸Brothers, the grace of our Lord Jesus Christ be with your spirit. *Amen.

EPHESIANS

1 Paul, an apostle of Christ Jesus by God's will:
To the faithful *saints in Christ Jesus at Ephesus. ²Grace to you and peace from God our Father and the Lord Jesus Christ.

³Praise the God and Father of our Lord Jesus Christ, who has blessed us in Christ with every spiritual blessing in the heavens. ⁴For He chose us in Him, before the foundation of the world, to be holy and blameless in His sight. In love ⁵He predestined us to be adopted through Jesus Christ for Himself, according to His favor and will, ⁶to the praise of His glorious grace that He favored us with in the Beloved.

⁷We have *redemption in Him through His blood, the forgiveness of our trespasses, according to the riches of His grace ⁸that He lavished on us with all wisdom and understanding. ⁹He made known to us the *mystery of His will, according to His good pleasure that He planned in Him ¹⁰for the administration of the days of fulfillment—to bring everything together in the *Messiah, both things in heaven and things on earth in Him.

¹¹We have also received an inheritance in Him, predestined according to the purpose of the One who works out everything in agreement with the decision of His will, ¹²so that we who had already put our hope in the Messiah might bring praise to His glory.

¹³When you heard the message of truth, the gospel of your salvation, and when you believed in Him, you were also sealed with the promised Holy Spirit. ¹⁴He is the down payment of our inheritance, for the redemption of the possession, to the praise of His glory.

¹⁵This is why, since I heard about your faith in the Lord Jesus and your love for all the saints, ¹⁶I never stop giving thanks for you as I remember you in my prayers. ¹⁷I pray that the God of our Lord Jesus Christ, the glorious Father, would give you a spirit of wisdom and revelation in the knowledge of Him. ¹⁸I pray that the perception of your mind may be enlightened so you may know what is the hope of His calling, what are the glorious riches of His inheritance among the saints, ¹⁹and what is the immeasurable greatness of His power to us who believe, according to the working of His vast strength.

²⁰He demonstrated this power in the Messiah by raising Him from the dead and seating Him at His right hand in the heavens— ²¹far above every ruler and authority, power and dominion, and every title given, not only in this age but also in the one to come. ²²And **He put everything under His feet** and appointed Him as head over everything for the church, ²³which is His body, the fullness of the One who fills all things in every way.

2 And you were dead in your trespasses and sins ²in which you previously *walked according to the ways of this world, according to the ruler who exercises authority over the lower heavens, the spirit now working in the disobedient. ³We too all previously lived among them in our fleshly desires, carrying out the inclinations of our flesh and thoughts, and we were by nature children under wrath as the others were also. ⁴But God, who is rich in mercy, because of His great love that He had for us, ⁵made us alive with the *Messiah even though we were dead in trespasses. You are saved by grace! ⁶Together with Christ Jesus He also raised us up and seated us in the heavens, ⁷so that in the coming ages He might display the immeasurable riches of His grace through His kindness to us in Christ Jesus. ⁸For you are saved by grace through faith, and this is not from yourselves; it is God's gift— ⁹not from works, so that no one can boast. ¹⁰For we are His creation, created in Christ Jesus for good works, which God prepared ahead of time so that we should walk in them.

¹¹So then, remember that at one time you were Gentiles in the flesh—called "the uncircumcised" by those called "the circumcised," which is done in the flesh by human hands. ¹²At that time you were without the Messiah, excluded from the citizenship of Israel, and foreigners to the covenants of the promise, without hope and without God in the world. ¹³But now in Christ Jesus, you who were far away have been brought near by the blood of the Messiah. ¹⁴For He is our peace, who made both groups one and tore down the dividing wall of hostility. In His flesh, ¹⁵He made of no effect the law consisting of commands and expressed in regulations, so that He might create in Himself one new man from the two, resulting in peace. ¹⁶He did this so that He might reconcile both to God in one body through the cross and put the hostility to death by it. ¹⁷When the Messiah came, He proclaimed the good news of peace to you who were far away and peace to those who were near. ¹⁸For through Him we both have access by one Spirit to the Father. ¹⁹So then you are no

longer foreigners and strangers, but fellow citizens with the *saints, and members of God's household, [20]built on the foundation of the apostles and prophets, with Christ Jesus Himself as the cornerstone. [21]The whole building, being put together by Him, grows into a holy sanctuary in the Lord. [22]You also are being built together for God's dwelling in the Spirit.

3 For this reason, I, Paul, the prisoner of Christ Jesus on behalf of you Gentiles— [2]you have heard, haven't you, about the administration of God's grace that He gave to me for you? [3]The *mystery was made known to me by revelation, as I have briefly written above. [4]By reading this you are able to understand my insight about the mystery of the *Messiah. [5]This was not made known to people in other generations as it is now revealed to His holy apostles and prophets by the Spirit: [6]The Gentiles are coheirs, members of the same body, and partners of the promise in Christ Jesus through the gospel. [7]I was made a servant of this gospel by the gift of God's grace that was given to me by the working of His power.

[8]This grace was given to me—the least of all the *saints—to proclaim to the Gentiles the incalculable riches of the Messiah, [9]and to shed light for all about the administration of the mystery hidden for ages in God who created all things. [10]This is so God's multifaceted wisdom may now be made known through the church to the rulers and authorities in the heavens. [11]This is according to His eternal purpose accomplished in the Messiah, Jesus our Lord. [12]In Him we have boldness and confident access through faith in Him. [13]So then I ask you not to be discouraged over my afflictions on your behalf, for they are your glory.

[14]For this reason I kneel before the Father [15]from whom every family in heaven and on earth is named. [16]I pray that He may grant you, according to the riches of His glory, to be strengthened with power in the inner man through His Spirit, [17]and that the Messiah may dwell in your hearts through faith. I pray that you, being rooted and firmly established in love, [18]may be able to comprehend with all the saints what is the length and width, height and depth of God's love, [19]and to know the Messiah's love that surpasses knowledge, so you may be filled with all the fullness of God.

[20]Now to Him who is able to do above and beyond all that we ask or think according to the power that works in us— [21]to Him be glory in the church and in Christ Jesus to all generations, forever and ever. *Amen.

4 Therefore I, the prisoner for the Lord, urge you to *walk worthy of the calling you have received, [2]with all humility and gentleness, with patience, accepting one another in love, [3]diligently keeping the unity of the Spirit with the peace that binds us. [4]There is one body and one Spirit—just as you were called to one hope at your calling— [5]one Lord, one faith, one baptism, [6]one God and Father of all, who is above all and through all and in all.

[7]Now grace was given to each one of us according to the measure of the *Messiah's gift. [8]For it says:

When He ascended on high,
He took prisoners into captivity;
He gave gifts to people.

[9]But what does "He ascended" mean except that He descended to the lower parts of the earth? [10]The One who descended is also the One who ascended far above all the heavens, that He might fill all things. [11]And He personally gave some to be apostles, some prophets,

some evangelists, some pastors and teachers, [12]for the training of the *saints in the work of ministry, to build up the body of Christ, [13]until we all reach unity in the faith and in the knowledge of God's Son, growing into a mature man with a stature measured by Christ's fullness. [14]Then we will no longer be little children, tossed by the waves and blown around by every wind of teaching, by human cunning with cleverness in the techniques of deceit. [15]But speaking the truth in love, let us grow in every way into Him who is the head— Christ. [16]From Him the whole body, fitted and knit together by every supporting ligament, promotes the growth of the body for building up itself in love by the proper working of each individual part.

[17]Therefore, I say this and testify in the Lord: You should no longer walk as the Gentiles walk, in the futility of their thoughts. [18]They are darkened in their understanding, excluded from the life of God, because of the ignorance that is in them and because of the hardness of their hearts. [19]They became callous and gave themselves over to promiscuity for the practice of every kind of impurity with a desire for more and more.

[20]But that is not how you learned about the Messiah, [21]assuming you heard about Him and were taught by Him, because the truth is in Jesus. [22]You took off your former way of life, the old self that is corrupted by deceitful desires; [23]you are being renewed in the spirit of your minds; [24]you put on the new self, the one created according to God's likeness in righteousness and purity of the truth.

[25]Since you put away lying, **Speak the truth, each one to his neighbor,** because we are members of one another. [26]**Be angry and do not sin.** Don't let the sun go down on your anger, [27]and don't give the Devil an opportunity. [28]The thief must no longer steal. Instead, he must do honest work with his own hands, so that he has something to share with anyone in need. [29]No foul language is to come from your mouth, but only what is good for building up someone in need, so that it gives grace to those who hear. [30]And don't grieve God's Holy Spirit. You were sealed by Him for the day of *redemption. [31]All bitterness, anger and wrath, shouting and slander must be removed from you, along with all malice. [32]And be kind and compassionate to one another, forgiving one another, just as God also forgave you in Christ.

5 Therefore, be imitators of God, as dearly loved children. [2]And *walk in love, as the *Messiah also loved us and gave Himself for us, a sacrificial and fragrant offering to God. [3]But sexual immorality and any impurity or greed should not even be heard of among you, as is proper for *saints. [4]Coarse and foolish talking or crude joking are not suitable, but rather giving thanks. [5]For know and recognize this: Every sexually immoral or impure or greedy person, who is an idolater, does not have an inheritance in the kingdom of the Messiah and of God.

[6]Let no one deceive you with empty arguments, for God's wrath is coming on the disobedient because of these things. [7]Therefore, do not become their partners. [8]For you were once darkness, but now you are light in the Lord. Walk as children of light— [9]for the fruit of the light results in all goodness, righteousness, and truth— [10]discerning what is pleasing to the Lord. [11]Don't participate in the fruitless works of darkness, but instead expose them. [12]For it is shameful even to

mention what is done by them in secret. [13] Everything exposed by the light is made clear, [14] for what makes everything clear is light. Therefore it is said:

Get up, sleeper, and rise up from the dead,
and the Messiah will shine on you.

[15] Pay careful attention, then, to how you walk—not as unwise people but as wise— [16] making the most of the time, because the days are evil. [17] So don't be foolish, but understand what the Lord's will is. [18] And don't get drunk with wine, which leads to reckless actions, but be filled by the Spirit:

[19]   speaking to one another
in psalms, hymns, and spiritual songs,
singing and making music
from your heart to the Lord,
[20]   giving thanks always for everything
to God the Father
in the name of our Lord Jesus Christ,
[21]   submitting to one another
in the fear of Christ.

[22] Wives, submit to your own husbands as to the Lord, [23] for the husband is the head of the wife as Christ is the head of the church. He is the Savior of the body. [24] Now as the church submits to Christ, so wives are to submit to their husbands in everything. [25] Husbands, love your wives, just as Christ loved the church and gave Himself for her [26] to make her holy, cleansing her with the washing of water by the word. [27] He did this to present the church to Himself in splendor, without spot or wrinkle or anything like that, but holy and blameless. [28] In the same way, husbands are to love their wives as their own bodies. He who loves his wife loves himself. [29] For no one ever hates his own flesh but provides and cares for it, just as Christ does for the church, [30] since we are members of His body.

[31]   **For this reason a man will leave**
his father and mother
and be joined to his wife,
and the two will become one flesh.

[32] This *mystery is profound, but I am talking about Christ and the church. [33] To sum up, each one of you is to love his wife as himself, and the wife is to respect her husband.

6 Children, obey your parents as you would the Lord, because this is right. [2] **Honor your father and mother,** which is the first commandment with a promise, [3] **so that it may go well with you and that you may have a long life in the land.** [4] Fathers, don't stir up anger in your children, but bring them up in the training and instruction of the Lord.

[5] *Slaves, obey your human masters with fear and trembling, in the sincerity of your heart, as to Christ. [6] Don't work only while being watched, in order to please men, but as slaves of Christ, do God's will from your heart. [7] Serve with a good attitude, as to the Lord and not to men, [8] knowing that whatever good each one does, slave or free, he will receive this back from the Lord. [9] And masters, treat your slaves the same way, without threatening them, because you know that both their Master and yours is in heaven, and there is no favoritism with Him.

[10] Finally, be strengthened by the Lord and by His vast strength. [11] Put on the full armor of God so that you can stand against the tactics of the Devil. [12] For our battle is not against flesh and blood, but against the rulers, against the authorities, against the world powers of this darkness, against the spiritual forces of evil in the heavens. [13] This is why you must take up the full armor of God, so that you may be able to resist in the evil day, and having prepared everything, to take your stand. [14] Stand, therefore,

with truth like a belt around your waist,
righteousness like armor on your chest,
[15]   and your feet sandaled with readiness
for the gospel of peace.
[16]   In every situation take the shield
of faith,
and with it you will be able
to extinguish
all the flaming arrows of the evil one.
[17]   Take the helmet of salvation,
and the sword of the Spirit,
which is God's word.

[18] Pray at all times in the Spirit with every prayer and request, and stay alert in this with all perseverance and intercession for all the *saints. [19] Pray also for me, that the message may be given to me when I open my mouth to make known with boldness the mystery of the gospel. [20] For this I am an ambassador in chains. Pray that I might be bold enough in Him to speak as I should.

[21] Tychicus, our dearly loved brother and faithful servant in the Lord, will tell you all the news about me so that you may be informed. [22] I am sending him to you for this very reason, to let you know how we are and to encourage your hearts.

[23] Peace to the *brothers, and love with faith, from God the Father and the Lord Jesus Christ. [24] Grace be with all who have undying love for our Lord Jesus Christ.

PHILIPPIANS

1 Paul and Timothy, slaves of Christ Jesus:
To all the *saints in Christ Jesus who are in Philippi, including the *overseers and deacons.
[2] Grace to you and peace from God our Father and the Lord Jesus Christ.

[3] I give thanks to my God for every remembrance of you, [4] always praying with joy for all of you in my every prayer, [5] because of your partnership in the gospel from the first day until now. [6] I am sure of this, that He who started a good work in you will carry it on to completion until the day of Christ Jesus. [7] It is right for me to think this way about all of you, because I have you in my heart, and you are all partners with me in grace, both in my imprisonment and in the defense and establishment of the gospel. [8] For God is my witness, how deeply I miss all of you with the affection of Christ Jesus. [9] And I pray this: that your love will keep on growing in knowledge and every kind of discernment, [10] so that you can approve the things that are superior and can be pure and blameless in the day of Christ, [11] filled with the fruit of righteousness that comes through Jesus Christ to the glory and praise of God.

[12] Now I want you to know, *brothers, that what has happened to me has actually resulted in the advance of the gospel, [13] so that it has become known throughout the whole imperial guard, and to everyone else, that my imprisonment is in the cause of Christ. [14] Most of the brothers in the Lord have gained confidence from my imprisonment and dare even more to speak the message fearlessly. [15] To be sure, some preach Christ out of envy and strife, but others out of good will. [16] These do so out of love, knowing that I am appointed for the defense of the gospel; [17] the others proclaim Christ out of rivalry, not sincerely, seeking to cause me anxiety in my imprisonment. [18] What does it matter? Just that in every way, whether out of false motives or true, Christ is proclaimed. And in this I rejoice. Yes, and I will rejoice [19] because I know this will lead to my deliverance through your prayers and help from the Spirit of Jesus Christ. [20] My eager expectation and hope is that I will not be ashamed about anything, but that now as always, with all boldness, Christ will be highly honored in my body, whether by life or by death.

[21] For me, living is Christ and dying is gain. [22] Now if I live on in the flesh, this means fruitful work for me; and I don't know which one I should choose. [23] I am pressured by both. I have the desire to depart and be with Christ—which is far better— [24] but to remain in the flesh is more necessary for you. [25] Since I am persuaded of this, I know that I will remain and continue with all of you for your progress and joy in the faith, [26] so that, because of me, your confidence may grow in Christ Jesus when I come to you again.

[27] Just one thing: Live your life in a manner worthy of the gospel of Christ. Then, whether I come and see you or am absent, I will hear about you that you are standing firm in one spirit, with one mind, working side by side for the faith that comes from the gospel, [28] not being frightened in any way by your opponents. This is a sign of destruction for them, but of your deliverance—and this is from God. [29] For it has been given to you on Christ's behalf not only to believe in Him, but also to suffer for Him, [30] having the same struggle that you saw I had and now hear that I have.

2 If then there is any encouragement in Christ, if any consolation of love, if any fellowship with the Spirit, if any affection and mercy, [2] fulfill my joy by thinking the same way, having the same love, sharing the same feelings, focusing on one goal. [3] Do nothing out of rivalry or conceit, but in humility consider others as more important than yourselves. [4] Everyone should look out not only for his own interests, but also for the interests of others.

[5] Make your own attitude that of Christ Jesus,
[6]   who, existing in the form of God,
    did not consider equality with God
    as something to be used
      for His own advantage.
[7]   Instead He emptied Himself
    by assuming the form of a *slave,
    taking on the likeness of men.
    And when He had come as a man
    in His external form,
[8]   He humbled Himself by becoming obedient
    to the point of death—
    even to death on a cross.
[9]   For this reason God highly exalted Him
    and gave Him the name
    that is above every name,

[10]   so that at the name of Jesus
    every knee will bow—
    of those who are in heaven and on earth
    and under the earth—
[11]   and every tongue should confess
    that Jesus Christ is Lord,
    to the glory of God the Father.

[12] So then, my dear friends, just as you have always obeyed, not only in my presence, but now even more in my absence, work out your own salvation with fear and trembling. [13] For it is God who is working in you, enabling you both to desire and to work out His good purpose. [14] Do everything without grumbling and arguing, [15] so that you may be blameless and pure, children of God who are faultless in a crooked and perverted generation, among whom you shine like stars in the world. [16] Hold firmly to the message of life. Then I can boast in the day of Christ that I didn't run or labor for nothing. [17] But even if I am poured out as a *drink offering on the sacrifice and service of your faith, I am glad and rejoice with all of you. [18] In the same way you should also be glad and rejoice with me.

[19] Now I hope in the Lord Jesus to send Timothy to you soon so that I also may be encouraged when I hear news about you. [20] For I have no one else like-minded who will genuinely care about your interests; [21] all seek their own interests, not those of Jesus Christ. [22] But you know his proven character, because he has served with me in the gospel ministry like a son with a father. [23] Therefore, I hope to send him as soon as I see how things go with me. [24] I am convinced in the Lord that I myself will also come quickly.

[25] But I considered it necessary to send you Epaphroditus—my brother, coworker, and fellow soldier, as well as your messenger and minister to my need— [26] since he has been longing for all of you and was distressed because you heard that he was sick. [27] Indeed, he was so sick that he nearly died. However, God had mercy on him, and not only on him but also on me, so that I would not have one grief on top of another. [28] For this reason, I am very eager to send him so that you may rejoice when you see him again and I may be less anxious. [29] Therefore, welcome him in the Lord with all joy and hold men like him in honor, [30] because he came close to death for the work of Christ, risking his life to make up what was lacking in your ministry to me.

3 Finally, my *brothers, rejoice in the Lord. To write to you again about this is no trouble for me and is a protection for you.

[2] Watch out for "dogs," watch out for evil workers, watch out for those who mutilate the flesh. [3] For we are the circumcision, the ones who serve by the Spirit of God, boast in Christ Jesus, and do not put confidence in the flesh— [4] although I once also had confidence in the flesh. If anyone else thinks he has grounds for confidence in the flesh, I have more: [5] circumcised the eighth day; of the nation of Israel, of the tribe of Benjamin, a Hebrew born of Hebrews; regarding the law, a *Pharisee; [6] regarding zeal, persecuting the church; regarding the righteousness that is in the law, blameless.

[7] But everything that was a gain to me, I have considered to be a loss because of Christ. [8] More than that, I also consider everything to be a loss in view of the surpassing value of knowing Christ Jesus my Lord. Because of Him I have suffered the loss of all things and consider them filth, so that I may gain Christ [9] and be

found in Him, not having a righteousness of my own from the law, but one that is through faith in Christ— the righteousness from God based on faith. [10]My goal is to know Him and the power of His resurrection and the fellowship of His sufferings, being conformed to His death, [11]assuming that I will somehow reach the resurrection from among the dead.

[12]Not that I have already reached the goal or am already fully mature, but I make every effort to take hold of it because I also have been taken hold of by Christ Jesus. [13]Brothers, I do not consider myself to have taken hold of it. But one thing I do: Forgetting what is behind and reaching forward to what is ahead, [14]I pursue as my goal the prize promised by God's heavenly call in Christ Jesus. [15]Therefore, all who are mature should think this way. And if you think differently about anything, God will reveal this also to you. [16]In any case, we should live up to whatever truth we have attained. [17]Join in imitating me, brothers, and observe those who live according to the example you have in us. [18]For I have often told you, and now say again with tears, that many live as enemies of the cross of Christ. [19]Their end is destruction; their god is their stomach; their glory is in their shame. They are focused on earthly things, [20]but our citizenship is in heaven, from which we also eagerly wait for a Savior, the Lord Jesus Christ. [21]He will transform the body of our humble condition into the likeness of His glorious body, by the power that enables Him to subject everything to Himself.

4 So then, my •brothers, you are dearly loved and longed for—my joy and crown. In this manner stand firm in the Lord, dear friends. [2]I urge Euodia and I urge Syntyche to agree in the Lord. [3]Yes, I also ask you, true partner, to help these women who have contended for the gospel at my side, along with Clement and the rest of my coworkers whose names are in the book of life. [4]Rejoice in the Lord always. I will say it again: Rejoice! [5]Let your graciousness be known to everyone. The Lord is near. [6]Don't worry about anything, but in everything, through prayer and petition with thanksgiving, let your requests be made known to God. [7]And the peace of God, which surpasses every thought, will guard your hearts and minds in Christ Jesus.

[8]Finally brothers, whatever is true, whatever is honorable, whatever is just, whatever is pure, whatever is lovely, whatever is commendable—if there is any moral excellence and if there is any praise—dwell on these things. [9]Do what you have learned and received and heard and seen in me, and the God of peace will be with you.

[10]I rejoiced in the Lord greatly that once again you renewed your care for me. You were, in fact, concerned about me but lacked the opportunity to show it. [11]I don't say this out of need, for I have learned to be content in whatever circumstances I am. [12]I know both how to have a little, and I know how to have a lot. In any and all circumstances I have learned the secret of being content—whether well fed or hungry, whether in abundance or in need. [13]I am able to do all things through Him who strengthens me. [14]Still, you did well by sharing with me in my hardship.

[15]And you Philippians know that in the early days of the gospel, when I left Macedonia, no church shared with me in the matter of giving and receiving except you alone. [16]For even in Thessalonica you sent gifts for my need several times. [17]Not that I seek the gift, but I seek the profit that is increasing to your account. [18]But I have received everything in full, and I have an abundance. I am fully supplied, having received from Epaphroditus what you provided—a fragrant offering, an acceptable sacrifice, pleasing to God. [19]And my God will supply all your needs according to His riches in glory in Christ Jesus. [20]Now to our God and Father be glory forever and ever. •Amen.

[21]Greet every •saint in Christ Jesus. Those brothers who are with me greet you. [22]All the saints greet you, but especially those from Caesar's household. [23]The grace of the Lord Jesus Christ be with your spirit.

COLOSSIANS

1 Paul, an apostle of Christ Jesus by God's will, and Timothy our brother:

[2]To the •saints in Christ at Colossae, who are faithful •brothers.

Grace to you and peace from God our Father.

[3]We always thank God, the Father of our Lord Jesus Christ, when we pray for you, [4]for we have heard of your faith in Christ Jesus and of the love you have for all the saints [5]because of the hope reserved for you in heaven. You have already heard about this hope in the message of truth, the gospel [6]that has come to you. It is bearing fruit and growing all over the world, just as it has among you since the day you heard it and recognized God's grace in the truth. [7]You learned this from Epaphras, our dearly loved fellow •slave. He is a faithful servant of the •Messiah on your behalf, [8]and he has told us about your love in the Spirit.

[9]For this reason also, since the day we heard this, we haven't stopped praying for you. We are asking that you may be filled with the knowledge of His will in all wisdom and spiritual understanding, [10]so that you may •walk worthy of the Lord, fully pleasing to Him, bearing fruit in every good work and growing in the knowledge of God. [11]May you be strengthened with all power, according to His glorious might, for all endurance and patience, with joy [12]giving thanks to the Father, who has enabled you to share in the saints' inheritance in the light. [13]He has rescued us from the domain of darkness and transferred us into the kingdom of the Son He loves. [14]We have •redemption, the forgiveness of sins, in Him.

[15]   He is the image of the invisible God,
      the firstborn over all creation.
[16]   For everything was created by Him,
      in heaven and on earth,
      the visible and the invisible,
      whether thrones or dominions
      or rulers or authorities—
      all things have been created through Him
       and for Him.
[17]   He is before all things,
      and by Him all things hold together.

¹⁸ He is also the head of the body, the church;
He is the beginning,
the firstborn from the dead,
so that He might come to have
first place in everything.

¹⁹ For God was pleased to have
all His fullness dwell in Him,

²⁰ and through Him to reconcile
everything to Himself
by making peace
through the blood of His cross—
whether things on earth or things in heaven.

²¹ Once you were alienated and hostile in your minds because of your evil actions. ²² But now He has reconciled you by His physical body through His death, to present you holy, faultless, and blameless before Him— ²³ if indeed you remain grounded and steadfast in the faith and are not shifted away from the hope of the gospel that you heard. This gospel has been proclaimed in all creation under heaven, and I, Paul, have become a servant of it.

²⁴ Now I rejoice in my sufferings for you, and I am completing in my flesh what is lacking in Christ's afflictions for His body, that is, the church. ²⁵ I have become its servant, according to God's administration that was given to me for you, to make God's message fully known, ²⁶ the ˙mystery hidden for ages and generations but now revealed to His saints. ²⁷ God wanted to make known among the Gentiles the glorious wealth of this mystery, which is Christ in you, the hope of glory. ²⁸ We proclaim Him, warning and teaching everyone with all wisdom, so that we may present everyone mature in Christ. ²⁹ I labor for this, striving with His strength that works powerfully in me.

2 For I want you to know how great a struggle I have for you, for those in Laodicea, and for all who have not seen me in person. ² I want their hearts to be encouraged and joined together in love, so that they may have all the riches of assured understanding and have the knowledge of God's ˙mystery—Christ. ³ All the treasures of wisdom and knowledge are hidden in Him.

⁴ I am saying this so that no one will deceive you with persuasive arguments. ⁵ For I may be absent in body, but I am with you in spirit, rejoicing to see how well ordered you are and the strength of your faith in Christ.

⁶ Therefore, as you have received Christ Jesus the Lord, ˙walk in Him, ⁷ rooted and built up in Him and established in the faith, just as you were taught, overflowing with gratitude.

⁸ Be careful that no one takes you captive through philosophy and empty deceit based on human tradition, based on the elemental forces of the world, and not based on Christ. ⁹ For the entire fullness of God's nature dwells bodily in Christ, ¹⁰ and you have been filled by Him, who is the head over every ruler and authority. ¹¹ You were also circumcised in Him with a circumcision not done with hands, by putting off the body of flesh, in the circumcision of the ˙Messiah. ¹² Having been buried with Him in baptism, you were also raised with Him through faith in the working of God, who raised Him from the dead. ¹³ And when you were dead in trespasses and in the uncircumcision of your flesh, He made you alive with Him and forgave us all our trespasses. ¹⁴ He erased the certificate of debt, with its obligations, that was against us and opposed to us, and has taken it out of the way by nailing it to the cross. ¹⁵ He disarmed the rulers and authorities and disgraced them publicly; He triumphed over them by Him.

¹⁶ Therefore, don't let anyone judge you in regard to food and drink or in the matter of a festival or a new moon or a Sabbath day. ¹⁷ These are a shadow of what was to come; the substance is the Messiah. ¹⁸ Let no one disqualify you, insisting on ascetic practices and the worship of angels, claiming access to a visionary realm and inflated without cause by his unspiritual mind. ¹⁹ He doesn't hold on to the head, from whom the whole body, nourished and held together by its ligaments and tendons, develops with growth from God.

²⁰ If you died with the Messiah to the elemental forces of this world, why do you live as if you still belonged to the world? Why do you submit to regulations: ²¹ "Don't handle, don't taste, don't touch"? ²² All these regulations refer to what is destroyed by being used up; they are commands and doctrines of men. ²³ Although these have a reputation of wisdom by promoting ascetic practices, humility, and severe treatment of the body, they are not of any value in curbing self-indulgence.

3 So if you have been raised with the ˙Messiah, seek what is above, where the Messiah is, seated at the right hand of God. ² Set your minds on what is above, not on what is on the earth. ³ For you have died, and your life is hidden with the Messiah in God. ⁴ When the Messiah, who is your life, is revealed, then you also will be revealed with Him in glory.

⁵ Therefore, put to death what belongs to your worldly nature: sexual immorality, impurity, lust, evil desire, and greed, which is idolatry. ⁶ Because of these, God's wrath comes on the disobedient, ⁷ and you once ˙walked in these things when you were living in them. ⁸ But now you must also put away all the following: anger, wrath, malice, slander, and filthy language from your mouth. ⁹ Do not lie to one another, since you have put off the old self with its practices ¹⁰ and have put on the new self. You are being renewed in knowledge according to the image of your Creator. ¹¹ In Christ there is not Greek and Jew, circumcision and uncircumcision, barbarian, Scythian, ˙slave and free; but Christ is all and in all.

¹² Therefore, God's chosen ones, holy and loved, put on heartfelt compassion, kindness, humility, gentleness, and patience, ¹³ accepting one another and forgiving one another if anyone has a complaint against another. Just as the Lord has forgiven you, so you must also forgive. ¹⁴ Above all, put on love—the perfect bond of unity. ¹⁵ And let the peace of the Messiah, to which you were also called in one body, control your hearts. Be thankful. ¹⁶ Let the message about the Messiah dwell richly among you, teaching and admonishing one another in all wisdom, and singing psalms, hymns, and spiritual songs, with gratitude in your hearts to God. ¹⁷ And whatever you do, in word or in deed, do everything in the name of the Lord Jesus, giving thanks to God the Father through Him.

¹⁸ Wives, be submissive to your husbands, as is fitting in the Lord.

¹⁹ Husbands, love your wives and don't be bitter toward them.

²⁰ Children, obey your parents in everything, for this pleases the Lord.

²¹ Fathers, do not exasperate your children, so they won't become discouraged.

²²Slaves, obey your human masters in everything. Don't work only while being watched, in order to please men, but work wholeheartedly, fearing the Lord. ²³Whatever you do, do it enthusiastically, as something done for the Lord and not for men, ²⁴knowing that you will receive the reward of an inheritance from the Lord. You serve the Lord Christ. ²⁵For the wrongdoer will be paid back for whatever wrong he has done, and there is no favoritism.

4 Masters, supply your ˙slaves with what is right and fair, since you know that you too have a Master in heaven.

²Devote yourselves to prayer; stay alert in it with thanksgiving. ³At the same time, pray also for us that God may open a door to us for the message, to speak the ˙mystery of the ˙Messiah, for which I am in prison, ⁴so that I may reveal it as I am required to speak. ⁵Act wisely toward outsiders, making the most of the time. ⁶Your speech should always be gracious, seasoned with salt, so that you may know how you should answer each person.

⁷Tychicus, our dearly loved brother, faithful servant, and fellow slave in the Lord, will tell you all the news about me. ⁸I have sent him to you for this very purpose, so that you may know how we are and so that he may encourage your hearts. ⁹He is with Onesimus, a faithful and dearly loved brother, who is one of you. They will tell you about everything here.

¹⁰Aristarchus, my fellow prisoner, greets you, as does Mark, Barnabas's cousin (concerning whom you have received instructions: if he comes to you, welcome him), ¹¹and so does Jesus who is called Justus. These alone of the circumcision are my coworkers for the kingdom of God, and they have been a comfort to me. ¹²Epaphras, who is one of you, a slave of Christ Jesus, greets you. He is always contending for you in his prayers, so that you can stand mature and fully assured in everything God wills. ¹³For I testify about him that he works hard for you, for those in Laodicea, and for those in Hierapolis. ¹⁴Luke, the dearly loved physician, and Demas greet you. ¹⁵Give my greetings to the ˙brothers in Laodicea, and to Nympha and the church in her home. ¹⁶When this letter has been read among you, have it read also in the church of the Laodiceans; and see that you also read the letter from Laodicea. ¹⁷And tell Archippus, "Pay attention to the ministry you have received in the Lord, so that you can accomplish it."

¹⁸This greeting is in my own hand—Paul. Remember my imprisonment. Grace be with you.

1 THESSALONIANS

1 Paul, Silvanus, and Timothy:
To the church of the Thessalonians in God the Father and the Lord Jesus Christ.
Grace to you and peace.
²We always thank God for all of you, remembering you constantly in our prayers. ³We recall, in the presence of our God and Father, your work of faith, labor of love, and endurance of hope in our Lord Jesus Christ, ⁴knowing your election, ˙brothers loved by God. ⁵For our gospel did not come to you in word only, but also in power, in the Holy Spirit, and with much assurance. You know what kind of men we were among you for your benefit, ⁶and you became imitators of us and of the Lord when, in spite of severe persecution, you welcomed the message with joy from the Holy Spirit. ⁷As a result, you became an example to all the believers in Macedonia and Achaia. ⁸For the Lord's message rang out from you, not only in Macedonia and Achaia, but in every place that your faith in God has gone out. Therefore, we don't need to say anything, ⁹for they themselves report what kind of reception we had from you: how you turned to God from idols to serve the living and true God ¹⁰and to wait for His Son from heaven, whom He raised from the dead—Jesus, who rescues us from the coming wrath.

2 For you yourselves know, ˙brothers, that our visit with you was not without result. ²On the contrary, after we had previously suffered, and we were treated outrageously in Philippi, as you know, we were emboldened by our God to speak the gospel of God to you in spite of great opposition. ³For our exhortation didn't come from error or impurity or an intent to deceive. ⁴Instead, just as we have been approved by God to be entrusted with the gospel, so we speak, not to please men, but rather God, who examines our hearts.

⁵For we never used flattering speech, as you know, or had greedy motives—God is our witness— ⁶and we didn't seek glory from people, either from you or from others. ⁷Although we could have been a burden as Christ's apostles, instead we were gentle among you, as a nursing mother nurtures her own children. ⁸We cared so much for you that we were pleased to share with you not only the gospel of God but also our own lives, because you had become dear to us. ⁹For you remember our labor and hardship, brothers. Working night and day so that we would not burden any of you, we preached God's gospel to you. ¹⁰You are witnesses, and so is God, of how devoutly, righteously, and blamelessly we conducted ourselves with you believers. ¹¹As you know, like a father with his own children, ¹²we encouraged, comforted, and implored each one of you to ˙walk worthy of God, who calls you into His own kingdom and glory.

¹³This is why we constantly thank God, because when you received the message about God that you heard from us, you welcomed it not as a human message, but as it truly is, the message of God, which also works effectively in you believers. ¹⁴For you, brothers, became imitators of God's churches in Christ Jesus that are in Judea, since you have also suffered the same things from people of your own country, just as they did from the Jews ¹⁵who killed both the Lord Jesus and the prophets and persecuted us; they displease God and are hostile to everyone, ¹⁶hindering us from speaking to the Gentiles so that they may be saved. As a result, they are always completing the number of their sins, and wrath has overtaken them at last.

¹⁷But as for us, brothers, after we were forced to leave you for a short time (in person, not in heart), we greatly desired and made every effort to return and

see you face to face. [18]So we wanted to come to you— even I, Paul, time and again—but Satan hindered us. [19]For who is our hope or joy or crown of boasting in the presence of our Lord Jesus at His coming? Is it not you? [20]For you are our glory and joy!

3 Therefore, when we could no longer stand it, we thought it was better to be left alone in Athens. [2]And we sent Timothy, our brother and God's coworker in the gospel of Christ, to strengthen and encourage you concerning your faith, [3]so that no one will be shaken by these persecutions. For you yourselves know that we are appointed to this. [4]In fact, when we were with you, we told you previously that we were going to suffer persecution, and as you know, it happened. [5]For this reason, when I could no longer stand it, I also sent him to find out about your faith, fearing that the tempter had tempted you and that our labor might be for nothing.

[6]But now Timothy has come to us from you and brought us good news about your faith and love and reported that you always have good memories of us, wanting to see us, as we also want to see you. [7]Therefore, brothers, in all our distress and persecution, we were encouraged about you through your faith. [8]For now we live, if you stand firm in the Lord. [9]How can we thank God for you in return for all the joy we experience before our God because of you, [10]as we pray very earnestly night and day to see you face to face and to complete what is lacking in your faith?

[11]Now may our God and Father Himself, and our Lord Jesus, direct our way to you. [12]And may the Lord cause you to increase and overflow with love for one another and for everyone, just as we also do for you. [13]May He make your hearts blameless in holiness before our God and Father at the coming of our Lord Jesus with all His saints. Amen.

4 Finally then, brothers, we ask and encourage you in the Lord Jesus, that as you have received from us how you must walk and please God—as you are doing—do so even more. [2]For you know what commands we gave you through the Lord Jesus.

[3]For this is God's will, your sanctification: that you abstain from sexual immorality, [4]so that each of you knows how to control his own body in sanctification and honor, [5]not with lustful desires, like the Gentiles who don't know God. [6]This means one must not transgress against and defraud his brother in this matter, because the Lord is an avenger of all these offenses, as we also previously told and warned you. [7]For God has not called us to impurity but to sanctification. [8]Therefore, the person who rejects this does not reject man, but God, who also gives you His Holy Spirit.

[9]About brotherly love: You don't need me to write you because you yourselves are taught by God to love one another. [10]In fact, you are doing this toward all the brothers in the entire region of Macedonia. But we encourage you, brothers, to do so even more, [11]to seek to lead a quiet life, to mind your own business, and to work with your own hands, as we commanded you, [12]so that you may walk properly in the presence of outsiders and not be dependent on anyone.

[13]We do not want you to be uninformed, brothers, concerning those who are asleep, so that you will not grieve like the rest, who have no hope. [14]Since we believe that Jesus died and rose again, in the same way God will bring with Him those who have fallen asleep through Jesus. [15]For we say this to you by a revelation from the Lord: We who are still alive at the Lord's coming will certainly have no advantage over those who have fallen asleep. [16]For the Lord Himself will descend from heaven with a shout, with the archangel's voice, and with the trumpet of God, and the dead in Christ will rise first. [17]Then we who are still alive will be caught up together with them in the clouds to meet the Lord in the air and so we will always be with the Lord. [18]Therefore encourage one another with these words.

5 About the times and the seasons: Brothers, you do not need anything to be written to you. [2]For you yourselves know very well that the Day of the Lord will come just like a thief in the night. [3]When they say, "Peace and security," then sudden destruction comes on them, like labor pains come on a pregnant woman, and they will not escape. [4]But you, brothers, are not in the dark, for this day to overtake you like a thief. [5]For you are all sons of light and sons of the day. We do not belong to the night or the darkness. [6]So then, we must not sleep, like the rest, but we must stay awake and be serious. [7]For those who sleep, sleep at night, and those who get drunk are drunk at night. [8]But since we belong to the day, we must be serious and put the armor of faith and love on our chests, and put on a helmet of the hope of salvation. [9]For God did not appoint us to wrath, but to obtain salvation through our Lord Jesus Christ, [10]who died for us, so that whether we are awake or asleep, we will live together with Him. [11]Therefore encourage one another and build each other up as you are already doing.

[12]Now we ask you, brothers, to give recognition to those who labor among you and lead you in the Lord and admonish you, [13]and to regard them very highly in love because of their work. Be at peace among yourselves. [14]And we exhort you, brothers: warn those who are irresponsible, comfort the discouraged, help the weak, be patient with everyone. [15]See to it that no one repays evil for evil to anyone, but always pursue what is good for one another and for all.

[16]   Rejoice always!
[17]   Pray constantly.
[18]   Give thanks in everything,
        for this is God's will for you
            in Christ Jesus.
[19]   Don't stifle the Spirit.
[20]   Don't despise prophecies,
[21]   but test all things.
        Hold on to what is good.
[22]   Stay away from every kind of evil.

[23]Now may the God of peace Himself sanctify you completely. And may your spirit, soul, and body be kept sound and blameless for the coming of our Lord Jesus Christ. [24]He who calls you is faithful, who also will do it. [25]Brothers, pray for us also. [26]Greet all the brothers with a holy kiss. [27]I charge you by the Lord that this letter be read to all the brothers. [28]The grace of our Lord Jesus Christ be with you.

2 THESSALONIANS

1 Paul, Silvanus, and Timothy:
To the church of the Thessalonians in God our Father and the Lord Jesus Christ.

²Grace to you and peace from God our Father and the Lord Jesus Christ.

³We must always thank God for you, *brothers. This is right, since your faith is flourishing and the love each one of you has for one another is increasing. ⁴Therefore, we ourselves boast about you among God's churches—about your endurance and faith in all the persecutions and afflictions you endure. ⁵It is a clear evidence of God's righteous judgment that you will be counted worthy of God's kingdom, for which you also are suffering, ⁶since it is righteous for God to repay with affliction those who afflict you ⁷and to reward with rest you who are afflicted, along with us. This will take place at the revelation of the Lord Jesus from heaven with His powerful angels, ⁸taking vengeance with flaming fire on those who don't know God and on those who don't obey the gospel of our Lord Jesus. ⁹These will pay the penalty of eternal destruction from the Lord's presence and from His glorious strength ¹⁰in that day when He comes to be glorified by His *saints and to be admired by all those who have believed, because our testimony among you was believed. ¹¹And in view of this, we always pray for you that our God will consider you worthy of His calling, and will, by His power, fulfill every desire for goodness and the work of faith, ¹²so that the name of our Lord Jesus will be glorified by you, and you by Him, according to the grace of our God and the Lord Jesus Christ.

2 Now concerning the coming of our Lord Jesus Christ and our being gathered to Him: We ask you, *brothers, ²not to be easily upset in mind or troubled, either by a spirit or by a message or by a letter as if from us, alleging that the Day of the Lord has come. ³Don't let anyone deceive you in any way. For that day will not come unless the apostasy comes first and the man of lawlessness is revealed, the son of destruction. ⁴He opposes and exalts himself above every so-called god or object of worship, so that he sits in God's sanctuary, publicizing that he himself is God.

⁵Don't you remember that when I was still with you I told you about this? ⁶And you know what currently restrains him, so that he will be revealed in his time. ⁷For the *mystery of lawlessness is already at work, but the one now restraining will do so until he is out of the way, ⁸and then the lawless one will be revealed. The Lord Jesus will destroy him with the breath of His mouth and will bring him to nothing with the brightness of His coming. ⁹The coming of the lawless one is based on Satan's working, with all kinds of false miracles, signs, and wonders, ¹⁰and with every unrighteous deception among those who are perishing. They perish because they did not accept the love of the truth in order to be saved. ¹¹For this reason God sends them a strong delusion so that they will believe what is false, ¹²so that all will be condemned—those who did not believe the truth but enjoyed unrighteousness.

¹³But we must always thank God for you, brothers loved by the Lord, because from the beginning God has chosen you for salvation through *sanctification by the Spirit and through belief in the truth. ¹⁴He called you to this through our gospel, so that you might obtain the glory of our Lord Jesus Christ. ¹⁵Therefore, brothers, stand firm and hold to the traditions you were taught, either by our message or by our letter.

¹⁶May our Lord Jesus Christ Himself and God our Father, who has loved us and given us eternal encouragement and good hope by grace, ¹⁷encourage your hearts and strengthen you in every good work and word.

3 Finally, *brothers, pray for us that the Lord's message may spread rapidly and be honored, just as it was with you, ²and that we may be delivered from wicked and evil men, for not all have faith. ³But the Lord is faithful; He will strengthen and guard you from the evil one. ⁴We have confidence in the Lord about you, that you are doing and will do what we command. ⁵May the Lord direct your hearts to God's love and Christ's endurance.

⁶Now we command you, brothers, in the name of our Lord Jesus Christ, to keep away from every brother who *walks irresponsibly and not according to the tradition received from us. ⁷For you yourselves know how you must imitate us: We were not irresponsible among you; ⁸we did not eat anyone's food free of charge; instead, we labored and struggled, working night and day, so that we would not be a burden to any of you. ⁹It is not that we don't have the right to support, but we did it to make ourselves an example to you so that you would imitate us. ¹⁰In fact, when we were with you, this is what we commanded you: "If anyone isn't willing to work, he should not eat." ¹¹For we hear that there are some among you who walk irresponsibly, not working at all, but interfering with the work of others. ¹²Now we command and exhort such people by the Lord Jesus Christ that quietly working, they may eat their own food. ¹³Brothers, do not grow weary in doing good.

¹⁴And if anyone does not obey our instruction in this letter, take note of that person; don't associate with him, so that he may be ashamed. ¹⁵Yet don't treat him as an enemy, but warn him as a brother.

¹⁶May the Lord of peace Himself give you peace always in every way. The Lord be with all of you. ¹⁷This greeting is in my own hand—Paul. This is a sign in every letter; this is how I write. ¹⁸The grace of our Lord Jesus Christ be with all of you.

1 TIMOTHY

1 Paul, an apostle of Christ Jesus by the command of God our Savior and of Christ Jesus our hope:

² To Timothy, my true son in the faith.

Grace, mercy, and peace from God the Father and Christ Jesus our Lord.

³ As I urged you when I went to Macedonia, remain in Ephesus so that you may instruct certain people not to teach different doctrine ⁴ or to pay attention to myths and endless genealogies. These promote empty speculations rather than God's plan, which operates by faith. ⁵ Now the goal of our instruction is love that comes from a pure heart, a good conscience, and a sincere faith. ⁶ Some have deviated from these and turned aside to fruitless discussion. ⁷ They want to be teachers of the law, although they don't understand what they are saying or what they are insisting on. ⁸ But we know that the law is good, provided one uses it legitimately. ⁹ We know that the law is not meant for a righteous person, but for the lawless and rebellious, for the ungodly and sinful, for the unholy and irreverent, for those who kill their fathers and mothers, for murderers, ¹⁰ for the sexually immoral and homosexuals, for kidnappers, liars, perjurers, and for whatever else is contrary to the sound teaching ¹¹ based on the glorious gospel of the blessed God, which was entrusted to me.

¹² I give thanks to Christ Jesus our Lord who has strengthened me, because He considered me faithful, appointing me to the ministry— ¹³ one who was formerly a blasphemer, a persecutor, and an arrogant man. But I received mercy because I acted out of ignorance in unbelief. ¹⁴ And the grace of our Lord overflowed, along with the faith and love that are in Christ Jesus. ¹⁵ This saying is trustworthy and deserving of full acceptance: "Christ Jesus came into the world to save sinners"—and I am the worst of them. ¹⁶ But I received mercy for this reason, so that in me, the worst of them, Christ Jesus might demonstrate His extraordinary patience as an example to those who would believe in Him for eternal life. ¹⁷ Now to the King eternal, immortal, invisible, the only God, be honor and glory forever and ever. ·Amen.

¹⁸ Timothy, my son, I am giving you this instruction in keeping with the prophecies previously made about you, so that by them you may strongly engage in battle, ¹⁹ having faith and a good conscience. Some have rejected these and have suffered the shipwreck of their faith. ²⁰ Hymenaeus and Alexander are among them, and I have delivered them to Satan, so that they may be taught not to blaspheme.

2 First of all, then, I urge that petitions, prayers, intercessions, and thanksgivings be made for everyone, ² for kings and all those who are in authority, so that we may lead a tranquil and quiet life in all godliness and dignity. ³ This is good, and it pleases God our Savior, ⁴ who wants everyone to be saved and to come to the knowledge of the truth.

⁵ For there is one God
    and one mediator between God and humanity,
    Christ Jesus, Himself human,
⁶ who gave Himself—a ransom for all,
    a testimony at the proper time.

⁷ For this I was appointed a herald, an apostle (I am telling the truth; I am not lying), and a teacher of the Gentiles in faith and truth.

⁸ Therefore, I want the men in every place to pray, lifting up holy hands without anger or argument. ⁹ Also, the women are to dress themselves in modest clothing, with decency and good sense, not with elaborate hairstyles, gold, pearls, or expensive apparel, ¹⁰ but with good works, as is proper for women who affirm that they worship God. ¹¹ A woman should learn in silence with full submission. ¹² I do not allow a woman to teach or to have authority over a man; instead, she is to be silent. ¹³ For Adam was created first, then Eve. ¹⁴ And Adam was not deceived, but the woman was deceived and transgressed. ¹⁵ But she will be saved through childbearing, if she continues in faith, love, and holiness, with good judgment.

3 This saying is trustworthy: "If anyone aspires to be an ·overseer, he desires a noble work." ² An overseer, therefore, must be above reproach, the husband of one wife, self-controlled, sensible, respectable, hospitable, an able teacher, ³ not addicted to wine, not a bully but gentle, not quarrelsome, not greedy— ⁴ one who manages his own household competently, having his children under control with all dignity. ⁵ (If anyone does not know how to manage his own household, how will he take care of God's church?) ⁶ He must not be a new convert, or he might become conceited and fall into the condemnation of the Devil. ⁷ Furthermore, he must have a good reputation among outsiders, so that he does not fall into disgrace and the Devil's trap.

⁸ Deacons, likewise, should be worthy of respect, not hypocritical, not drinking a lot of wine, not greedy for money, ⁹ holding the ·mystery of the faith with a clear conscience. ¹⁰ And they must also be tested first; if they prove blameless, then they can serve as deacons. ¹¹ Wives, too, must be worthy of respect, not slanderers, self-controlled, faithful in everything. ¹² Deacons must be husbands of one wife, managing their children and their own households competently. ¹³ For those who have served well as deacons acquire a good standing for themselves, and great boldness in the faith that is in Christ Jesus.

¹⁴ I write these things to you, hoping to come to you soon. ¹⁵ But if I should be delayed, I have written so that you will know how people ought to act in God's household, which is the church of the living God, the pillar and foundation of the truth. ¹⁶ And most certainly, the mystery of godliness is great:

    He was manifested in the flesh,
    vindicated in the Spirit,
    seen by angels,
    preached among the nations,
    believed on in the world,
    taken up in glory.

4 Now the Spirit explicitly says that in later times some will depart from the faith, paying attention to deceitful spirits and the teachings of demons, ² through the hypocrisy of liars whose consciences are seared. ³ They forbid marriage and demand abstinence from foods that God created to be received with gratitude by those who believe and know the truth. ⁴ For everything created by God is good, and nothing should

be rejected if it is received with thanksgiving, ⁵since it is sanctified by the word of God and by prayer.

⁶If you point these things out to the •brothers, you will be a good servant of Christ Jesus, nourished by the words of the faith and the good teaching that you have followed. ⁷But have nothing to do with irreverent and silly myths. Rather, train yourself in godliness, ⁸for

the training of the body has a limited benefit,
but godliness is beneficial in every way,
since it holds promise for the present life
and also for the life to come.

⁹This saying is trustworthy and deserves full acceptance. ¹⁰In fact, we labor and strive for this, because we have put our hope in the living God, who is the Savior of everyone, especially of those who believe.

¹¹Command and teach these things. ¹²Let no one despise your youth; instead, you should be an example to the believers in speech, in conduct, in love, in faith, in purity. ¹³Until I come, give your attention to public reading, exhortation, and teaching. ¹⁴Do not neglect the gift that is in you; it was given to you through prophecy, with the laying on of hands by the council of elders. ¹⁵Practice these things; be committed to them, so that your progress may be evident to all. ¹⁶Pay close attention to your life and your teaching; persevere in these things, for by doing this you will save both yourself and your hearers.

5 Do not rebuke an older man, but exhort him as a father, younger men as brothers, ²older women as mothers, and with all propriety, the younger women as sisters.

³Support widows who are genuinely widows. ⁴But if any widow has children or grandchildren, they must learn to practice godliness toward their own family first and to repay their parents, for this pleases God. ⁵The real widow, left all alone, has put her hope in God and continues night and day in her petitions and prayers; ⁶however, she who is self-indulgent is dead even while she lives. ⁷Command this also, so they won't be blamed. ⁸But if anyone does not provide for his own, that is his own household, he has denied the faith and is worse than an unbeliever.

⁹No widow should be placed on the official support list unless she is at least 60 years old, has been the wife of one husband, ¹⁰and is well known for good works—that is, if she has brought up children, shown hospitality, washed the •saints' feet, helped the afflicted, and devoted herself to every good work. ¹¹But refuse to enroll younger widows, for when they are drawn away from Christ by desire, they want to marry ¹²and will therefore receive condemnation because they have renounced their original pledge. ¹³At the same time, they also learn to be idle, going from house to house; they are not only idle, but are also gossips and busybodies, saying things they shouldn't say. ¹⁴Therefore, I want younger women to marry, have children, manage their households, and give the adversary no opportunity to accuse us. ¹⁵For some have already turned away to follow Satan. ¹⁶If any believing woman has widows in her family, she should help them, and the church should not be burdened, so that it can help those who are genuinely widows.

¹⁷The elders who are good leaders should be considered worthy of an ample honorarium, especially those who work hard at preaching and teaching. ¹⁸For the Scripture says:

Do not muzzle an ox
while it is treading out the grain, and,
the worker is worthy of his wages.

¹⁹Don't accept an accusation against an elder unless it is supported by two or three witnesses. ²⁰Publicly rebuke those who sin, so that the rest will also be afraid. ²¹I solemnly charge you before God and Christ Jesus and the elect angels to observe these things without prejudice, doing nothing out of favoritism. ²²Don't be too quick to appoint anyone as an elder, and don't share in the sins of others. Keep yourself pure. ²³Don't continue drinking only water, but use a little wine because of your stomach and your frequent illnesses. ²⁴Some people's sins are obvious, going before them to judgment, but the sins of others surface later. ²⁵Likewise, good works are obvious, and those that are not obvious cannot remain hidden.

6 All who are under the yoke as •slaves must regard their own masters to be worthy of all respect, so that God's name and His teaching will not be blasphemed. ²Those who have believing masters should not be disrespectful to them because they are •brothers, but should serve them better, since those who benefit from their service are believers and dearly loved.

Teach and encourage these things. ³If anyone teaches other doctrine and does not agree with the sound teaching of our Lord Jesus Christ and with the teaching that promotes godliness, ⁴he is conceited, understanding nothing, but has a sick interest in disputes and arguments over words. From these come envy, quarreling, slander, evil suspicions, ⁵and constant disagreement among people whose minds are depraved and deprived of the truth, who imagine that godliness is a way to material gain. ⁶But godliness with contentment is a great gain.

⁷ For we brought nothing into the world,
and we can take nothing out.
⁸ But if we have food and clothing,
we will be content with these.

⁹But those who want to be rich fall into temptation, a trap, and many foolish and harmful desires, which plunge people into ruin and destruction. ¹⁰For the love of money is a root of all kinds of evil, and by craving it, some have wandered away from the faith and pierced themselves with many pains.

¹¹ But you, man of God, run from these things,
and pursue righteousness, godliness, faith,
love, endurance, and gentleness.
¹² Fight the good fight for the faith;
take hold of eternal life
that you were called to
and have made a good confession about
in the presence of many witnesses.

¹³In the presence of God, who gives life to all, and of Christ Jesus, who gave a good confession before Pontius •Pilate, I charge you ¹⁴to keep the command without fault or failure until the appearing of our Lord Jesus Christ. ¹⁵God will bring this about in His own time. He is

the blessed and only Sovereign,
the King of kings,
and the Lord of lords,
¹⁶ the only One who has immortality,
dwelling in unapproachable light;
no one has seen or can see Him,
to Him be honor and eternal might.
•Amen.

¹⁷Instruct those who are rich in the present age not

to be arrogant or to set their hope on the uncertainty of wealth, but on God, who richly provides us with all things to enjoy. [18]Instruct them to do what is good, to be rich in good works, to be generous, willing to share, [19]storing up for themselves a good reserve for the age to come, so that they may take hold of life that is real.

[20]Timothy, guard what has been entrusted to you, avoiding irreverent, empty speech and contradictions from the "knowledge" that falsely bears that name. [21]By professing it, some people have deviated from the faith.

Grace be with all of you.

2 TIMOTHY

1 Paul, an apostle of Christ Jesus by God's will, for the promise of life in Christ Jesus:

[2]To Timothy, my dearly loved son.

Grace, mercy, and peace from God the Father and Christ Jesus our Lord.

[3]I thank God, whom I serve with a clear conscience as my ancestors did, when I constantly remember you in my prayers night and day. [4]Remembering your tears, I long to see you so that I may be filled with joy, [5]clearly recalling your sincere faith that first lived in your grandmother Lois, then in your mother Eunice, and that I am convinced is in you also.

[6]Therefore, I remind you to keep ablaze the gift of God that is in you through the laying on of my hands. [7]For God has not given us a spirit of fearfulness, but one of power, love, and sound judgment.

[8]So don't be ashamed of the testimony about our Lord, or of me His prisoner. Instead, share in suffering for the gospel, relying on the power of God.

[9]   He has saved us and called us
     with a holy calling,
     not according to our works,
     but according to His own purpose and grace,
     which was given to us in Christ Jesus
     before time began.
[10] This has now been made evident
     through the appearing of our Savior
       Christ Jesus,
     who has abolished death
     and has brought life and immortality to light
     through the gospel.

[11]For this gospel I was appointed a herald, apostle, and teacher, [12]and that is why I suffer these things. But I am not ashamed, because I know the One I have believed in and am persuaded that He is able to guard what has been entrusted to me until that day.

[13]Hold on to the pattern of sound teaching that you have heard from me, in the faith and love that are in Christ Jesus. [14]Guard, through the Holy Spirit who lives in us, that good thing entrusted to you. [15]This you know: All those in *Asia have turned away from me, including Phygelus and Hermogenes. [16]May the Lord grant mercy to the household of Onesiphorus, because he often refreshed me and was not ashamed of my chains. [17]On the contrary, when he was in Rome, he diligently searched for me and found me. [18]May the Lord grant that he obtain mercy from Him on that day. And you know very well how much he ministered at Ephesus.

2 You, therefore, my son, be strong in the grace that is in Christ Jesus. [2]And what you have heard from me in the presence of many witnesses, commit to faithful men who will be able to teach others also.

[3]Share in suffering as a good soldier of Christ Jesus. [4]No one serving as a soldier gets entangled in the concerns of civilian life; he seeks to please the recruiter. [5]Also, if anyone competes as an athlete, he is not crowned unless he competes according to the rules. [6]The hardworking farmer ought to be the first to get a share of the crops. [7]Consider what I say, for the Lord will give you understanding in everything.

[8]Keep your attention on Jesus Christ as risen from the dead and descended from David. This is according to my gospel. [9]I suffer for it to the point of being bound like a criminal, but God's message is not bound. [10]This is why I endure all things for the elect: so that they also may obtain salvation, which is in Christ Jesus, with eternal glory. [11]This saying is trustworthy:

   For if we have died with Him,
     we will also live with Him;
[12] if we endure, we will also reign with Him;
     if we deny Him, He will also deny us;
[13] if we are faithless, He remains faithful,
     for He cannot deny Himself.

[14]Remind them of these things, charging them before God not to fight about words; this is in no way profitable and leads to the ruin of the hearers. [15]Be diligent to present yourself approved to God, a worker who doesn't need to be ashamed, correctly teaching the word of truth. [16]But avoid irreverent, empty speech, for this will produce an even greater measure of godlessness. [17]And their word will spread like gangrene; Hymenaeus and Philetus are among them. [18]They have deviated from the truth, saying that the resurrection has already taken place, and are overturning the faith of some. [19]Nevertheless, God's solid foundation stands firm, having this inscription:

The Lord knows those who are His, and
Everyone who names the name of the Lord
must turn away from unrighteousness.

[20]Now in a large house there are not only gold and silver bowls, but also those of wood and clay, some for honorable use, some for dishonorable. [21]So if anyone purifies himself from anything dishonorable, he will be a special instrument, set apart, useful to the Master, prepared for every good work.

[22]Flee from youthful passions, and pursue righteousness, faith, love, and peace, along with those who call on the Lord from a pure heart. [23]But reject foolish and ignorant disputes, knowing that they breed quarrels. [24]The Lord's *slave must not quarrel, but must be gentle to everyone, able to teach, and patient, [25]instructing his opponents with gentleness. Perhaps God will grant them repentance leading them to the knowledge of the truth. [26]Then they may come to their senses and escape the Devil's trap, having been captured by him to do his will.

3 But know this: Difficult times will come in the last days. [2]For people will be lovers of self, lovers of money, boastful, proud, blasphemers, disobedient to

parents, ungrateful, unholy, [3]unloving, irreconcilable, slanderers, without self-control, brutal, without love for what is good, [4]traitors, reckless, conceited, lovers of pleasure rather than lovers of God, [5]holding to the form of godliness but denying its power. Avoid these people!

[6]For among them are those who worm their way into households and capture idle women burdened down with sins, led along by a variety of passions, [7]always learning and never able to come to a knowledge of the truth. [8]Just as Jannes and Jambres resisted Moses, so these also resist the truth, men who are corrupt in mind, worthless in regard to the faith. [9]But they will not make further progress, for their lack of understanding will be clear to all, as theirs was also.

[10]But you have followed my teaching, conduct, purpose, faith, patience, love, and endurance, [11]along with the persecutions and sufferings that came to me in Antioch, Iconium, and Lystra. What persecutions I endured! Yet the Lord rescued me from them all. [12]In fact, all those who want to live a godly life in Christ Jesus will be persecuted. [13]Evil people and impostors will become worse, deceiving and being deceived. [14]But as for you, continue in what you have learned and firmly believed. You know those who taught you, [15]and you know that from childhood you have known the sacred Scriptures, which are able to give you wisdom for salvation through faith in Christ Jesus. [16]All Scripture is inspired by God and is profitable for teaching, for rebuking, for correcting, for training in righteousness, [17]so that the man of God may be complete, equipped for every good work.

4 I solemnly charge you before God and Christ Jesus, who is going to judge the living and the dead, and because of His appearing and His kingdom: [2]Proclaim the message; persist in it whether convenient or not; rebuke, correct, and encourage with great patience and teaching. [3]For the time will come when they will not tolerate sound doctrine, but according to their own desires, will multiply teachers for themselves because they have an itch to hear something new. [4]They will turn away from hearing the truth and will turn aside to myths. [5]But as for you, be serious about everything, endure hardship, do the work of an evangelist, fulfill your ministry.

[6]For I am already being poured out as a ˙drink offering, and the time for my departure is close. [7]I have fought the good fight, I have finished the race, I have kept the faith. [8]There is reserved for me in the future the crown of righteousness, which the Lord, the righteous Judge, will give me on that day, and not only to me, but to all those who have loved His appearing.

[9]Make every effort to come to me soon, [10]for Demas has deserted me, because he loved this present world, and has gone to Thessalonica. Crescens has gone to Galatia, Titus to Dalmatia. [11]Only Luke is with me. Bring Mark with you, for he is useful to me in the ministry. [12]I have sent Tychicus to Ephesus. [13]When you come, bring the cloak I left in Troas with Carpus, as well as the scrolls, especially the parchments. [14]Alexander the coppersmith did great harm to me. The Lord will repay him according to his works. [15]Watch out for him yourself because he strongly opposed our words.

[16]At my first defense, no one stood by me, but everyone deserted me. May it not be counted against them. [17]But the Lord stood with me and strengthened me, so that the proclamation might be fully made through me and all the Gentiles might hear. So I was rescued from the lion's mouth. [18]The Lord will rescue me from every evil work and will bring me safely into His heavenly kingdom. To Him be the glory forever and ever! ˙Amen.

[19]Greet Prisca and Aquila, and the household of Onesiphorus. [20]Erastus has remained at Corinth; I left Trophimus sick at Miletus. [21]Make every effort to come before winter. Eubulus greets you, as do Pudens, Linus, Claudia, and all the ˙brothers.

[22]The Lord be with your spirit. Grace be with you.

TITUS

1 Paul, a ˙slave of God and an apostle of Jesus Christ, to build up the faith of God's elect and their knowledge of the truth that leads to godliness, [2]in the hope of eternal life that God, who cannot lie, promised before time began. [3]In His own time He has revealed His message in the proclamation that I was entrusted with by the command of God our Savior:

[4]To Titus, my true son in our common faith.

Grace and peace from God the Father and Christ Jesus our Savior.

[5]The reason I left you in Crete was to set right what was left undone and, as I directed you, to appoint elders in every town: [6]one who is blameless, the husband of one wife, having faithful children not accused of wildness or rebellion. [7]For an ˙overseer, as God's administrator, must be blameless, not arrogant, not hot-tempered, not addicted to wine, not a bully, not greedy for money, [8]but hospitable, loving what is good, sensible, righteous, holy, self-controlled, [9]holding to the faithful message as taught, so that he will be able both to encourage with sound teaching and to refute those who contradict it.

[10]For there are also many rebellious people, full of empty talk and deception, especially those from Judaism. [11]It is necessary to silence them; they overthrow whole households by teaching what they shouldn't in order to get money dishonestly. [12]One of their very own prophets said,

Cretans are always liars, evil beasts,
lazy gluttons.

[13]This testimony is true. So, rebuke them sharply, that they may be sound in the faith [14]and may not pay attention to Jewish myths and the commands of men who reject the truth.

[15]To the pure, everything is pure, but to those who are defiled and unbelieving nothing is pure; in fact, both their mind and conscience are defiled. [16]They profess to know God, but they deny Him by their works. They are detestable, disobedient, and disqualified for any good work.

2 But you must say the things that are consistent with sound teaching. [2]Older men are to be level headed, worthy of respect, sensible, and sound in faith, love, and endurance. [3]In the same way, older women

are to be reverent in behavior, not slanderers, not addicted to much wine. They are to teach what is good, [4]so they may encourage the young women to love their husbands and to love their children, [5]to be self-controlled, pure, homemakers, kind, and submissive to their husbands, so that God's message will not be slandered.

[6]In the same way, encourage the young men to be self-controlled [7]in everything. Make yourself an example of good works with integrity and dignity in your teaching. [8]Your message is to be sound beyond reproach, so that the opponent will be ashamed, having nothing bad to say about us.

[9]·Slaves are to be submissive to their masters in everything, and to be well-pleasing, not talking back [10]or stealing, but demonstrating utter faithfulness, so that they may adorn the teaching of God our Savior in everything.

[11]For the grace of God has appeared with salvation for all people, [12]instructing us to deny godlessness and worldly lusts and to live in a sensible, righteous, and godly way in the present age, [13]while we wait for the blessed hope and appearing of the glory of our great God and Savior, Jesus Christ. [14]He gave Himself for us to ·redeem us from all lawlessness and to cleanse for Himself a people for His own possession, eager to do good works.

[15]Say these things, and encourage and rebuke with all authority. Let no one disregard you.

3 Remind them to be submissive to rulers and authorities, to obey, to be ready for every good work, [2]to slander no one, to avoid fighting, and to be kind, always showing gentleness to all people. [3]For we too were once foolish, disobedient, deceived, enslaved by various passions and pleasures, living in malice and envy, hateful, detesting one another.

[4] But when the kindness of God our Savior
and His love
for mankind appeared,
[5] He saved us—
not by works of righteousness
that we had done,
but according to His mercy—
through the washing of regeneration
and renewal by the Holy Spirit.
[6] He poured out this Spirit on us abundantly
through Jesus Christ our Savior
[7] so that, having been ·justified by His grace,
we may become heirs with the hope
of eternal life.

[8]This saying is trustworthy. I want you to insist on these things, so that those who have believed God might be careful to devote themselves to good works. These are good and profitable for everyone. [9]But avoid foolish debates, genealogies, quarrels, and disputes about the law, for they are unprofitable and worthless. [10]Reject a divisive person after a first and second warning, [11]knowing that such a person is perverted and sins, being self-condemned.

[12]When I send Artemas or Tychicus to you, make every effort to come to me in Nicopolis, for I have decided to spend the winter there. [13]Diligently help Zenas the lawyer and Apollos on their journey, so that they will lack nothing.

[14]And our people must also learn to devote themselves to good works for cases of urgent need, so that they will not be unfruitful. [15]All those who are with me greet you. Greet those who love us in the faith. Grace be with all of you.

PHILEMON

Paul, a prisoner of Christ Jesus, and Timothy our brother:

To Philemon our dear friend and coworker, [2]to Apphia our sister, to Archippus our fellow soldier, and to the church that meets in your home.

[3]Grace to you and peace from God our Father and the Lord Jesus Christ.

[4]I always thank my God when I mention you in my prayers, [5]because I hear of your love and faith toward the Lord Jesus and for all the ·saints. [6]I pray that your participation in the faith may become effective through knowing every good thing that is in us for the glory of Christ. [7]For I have great joy and encouragement from your love, because the hearts of the saints have been refreshed through you, brother.

[8]For this reason, although I have great boldness in Christ to command you to do what is right, [9]I appeal to you, instead, on the basis of love. I, Paul, as an elderly man and now also as a prisoner of Christ Jesus, [10]appeal to you for my son, Onesimus. I fathered him while I was in chains. [11]Once he was useless to you, but now he is useful both to you and to me. [12]I am sending him back to you as a part of myself. [13]I wanted to keep him with me, so that in my imprisonment for the gospel he might serve me in your place. [14]But I didn't want to do anything without your consent, so that your good deed might not be out of obligation, but of your own free will. [15]For perhaps this is why he was separated from you for a brief time, so that you might get him back permanently, [16]no longer as a ·slave, but more than a slave—as a dearly loved brother. He is especially so to me, but even more to you, both in the flesh and in the Lord.

[17]So if you consider me a partner, accept him as you would me. [18]And if he has wronged you in any way, or owes you anything, charge that to my account. [19]I, Paul, write this with my own hand: I will repay it—not to mention to you that you owe me even your own self. [20]Yes, brother, may I have joy from you in the Lord; refresh my heart in Christ. [21]Since I am confident of your obedience, I am writing to you, knowing that you will do even more than I say. [22]But meanwhile, also prepare a guest room for me, for I hope that through your prayers I will be restored to you.

[23]Epaphras, my fellow prisoner in Christ Jesus, greets you, and so do [24]Mark, Aristarchus, Demas, and Luke, my coworkers.

[25]The grace of the Lord Jesus Christ be with your spirit.

Hebrews

1 Long ago God spoke to the fathers by the prophets at different times and in different ways. ²In these last days, He has spoken to us by His Son. God has appointed Him heir of all things and made the universe through Him. ³The Son is the radiance of God's glory and the exact expression of His nature, sustaining all things by His powerful word. After making purification for sins, He sat down at the right hand of the Majesty on high. ⁴So He became higher in rank than the angels, just as the name He inherited is superior to theirs.

⁵For to which of the angels did He ever say, **You are My Son; today I have become Your Father,** or again, **I will be His Father, and He will be My Son?** ⁶When He again brings His firstborn into the world, He says, **And all God's angels must worship Him.** ⁷And about the angels He says:

> **He makes His angels winds,**
> **and His servants a fiery flame,**

⁸but to the Son:

> **Your throne, God,**
> **is forever and ever,**
> **and the scepter of Your kingdom**
> **is a scepter of justice.**
> ⁹ **You have loved righteousness**
> **and hated lawlessness;**
> **this is why God, Your God,**
> **has anointed You**
> **with the oil of joy**
> **rather than Your companions.**

¹⁰And:

> **In the beginning, Lord,**
> **You established the earth,**
> **and the heavens are the works of Your hands;**
> ¹¹ **they will perish, but You remain.**
> **They will all wear out like clothing;**
> ¹² **You will roll them up like a cloak,**
> **and they will be changed like a robe.**
> **But You are the same,**
> **and Your years will never end.**

¹³Now to which of the angels has He ever said:

> **Sit at My right hand**
> **until I make Your enemies Your footstool?**

¹⁴Are they not all ministering spirits sent out to serve those who are going to inherit salvation?

2 We must, therefore, pay even more attention to what we have heard, so that we will not drift away. ²For if the message spoken through angels was legally binding and every transgression and disobedience received a just punishment, ³how will we escape if we neglect such a great salvation? It was first spoken by the Lord and was confirmed to us by those who heard Him. ⁴At the same time, God also testified by signs and wonders, various miracles, and distributions of gifts from the Holy Spirit according to His will.

⁵For He has not subjected to angels the world to come that we are talking about. ⁶But one has somewhere testified:

> **What is man that You remember him,**
> **or the son of man that You care for him?**
> ⁷ **You made him lower than the angels**
> **for a short time;**
> **You crowned him with glory and honor**

> ⁸ **and subjected everything under his feet.**

For in **subjecting everything** to him, He left nothing that is not subject to him. As it is, we do not yet see **everything subjected** to him. ⁹But we do see Jesus—**made lower than the angels for a short time** so that by God's grace He might taste death for everyone—crowned with glory and honor because of His suffering in death.

¹⁰For in bringing many sons to glory, it was entirely appropriate that God—all things exist for Him and through Him—should make the source of their salvation perfect through sufferings. ¹¹For the One who •sanctifies and those who are sanctified all have one Father. That is why Jesus is not ashamed to call them •brothers, ¹²saying:

> **I will proclaim Your name to My brothers;**
> **I will sing hymns to You in the congregation.**

¹³Again, **I will trust in Him.** And again, **Here I am with the children God gave Me.**

¹⁴Now since the children have flesh and blood in common, Jesus also shared in these, so that through His death He might destroy the one holding the power of death—that is, the Devil— ¹⁵and free those who were held in slavery all their lives by the fear of death. ¹⁶For it is clear that He does not reach out to help angels, but to help Abraham's offspring. ¹⁷Therefore, He had to be like His brothers in every way, so that He could become a merciful and faithful high priest in service to God, to make •propitiation for the sins of the people. ¹⁸For since He Himself was tested and has suffered, He is able to help those who are tested.

3 Therefore, holy •brothers and companions in a heavenly calling, consider Jesus, the apostle and high priest of our confession; ²He was faithful to the One who appointed Him, just as Moses was in all God's household. ³For Jesus is considered worthy of more glory than Moses, just as the builder has more honor than the house. ⁴Now every house is built by someone, but the One who built everything is God. ⁵Moses was faithful as a servant in all God's household, as a testimony to what would be said in the future. ⁶But Christ was faithful as a Son over His household. And we are that household if we hold on to the courage and the confidence of our hope.

⁷Therefore, as the Holy Spirit says:

> **Today, if you hear His voice,**
> ⁸ **do not harden your hearts as in the rebellion,**
> **on the day of testing in the wilderness,**
> ⁹ **where your fathers tested Me, tried Me,**
> **and saw My works** ¹⁰**for 40 years.**
> **Therefore I was provoked with that generation**
> **and said, "They always go astray**
> **in their hearts,**
> **and they have not known My ways."**
> ¹¹ **So I swore in My anger,**
> **"They will not enter My rest."**

¹²Watch out, brothers, so that there won't be in any of you an evil, unbelieving heart that departs from the living God. ¹³But encourage each other daily, while it is still called **today,** so that none of you is hardened by sin's deception. ¹⁴For we have become companions of the •Messiah if we hold firmly until the end the reality that we had at the start. ¹⁵As it is said:

Today, if you hear His voice,
do not harden your hearts as in the rebellion.
[16]For who heard and rebelled? Wasn't it really all who came out of Egypt under Moses? [17]And who was He provoked with for 40 years? Was it not with those who sinned, whose bodies fell in the wilderness? [18]And who did He swear to that they would not enter His rest, if not those who disobeyed? [19]So we see that they were unable to enter because of unbelief.

4 Therefore, while the promise to enter His rest remains, let us fear that none of you should miss it. [2]For we also have received the good news just as they did; but the message they heard did not benefit them, since they were not united with those who heard it in faith [3](for we who have believed enter the rest), in keeping with what He has said:

So I swore in My anger,
they will not enter My rest.
And yet His works have been finished since the foundation of the world, [4]for somewhere He has spoken about the seventh day in this way:

And on the seventh day
God rested from all His works.
[5]Again, in that passage He says, **They will never enter My rest.** [6]Since it remains for some to enter it, and those who formerly received the good news did not enter because of disobedience, [7]again, He specifies a certain day—**today**—speaking through David after such a long time, as previously stated:

Today, if you hear His voice,
do not harden your hearts.
[8]For if Joshua had given them rest, God would not have spoken later about another day. [9]Therefore, a Sabbath rest remains for God's people. [10]For the person who has entered His rest has rested from his own works, just as God did from His. [11]Let us then make every effort to enter that rest, so that no one will fall into the same pattern of disobedience.

[12]For the word of God is living and effective and sharper than any double-edged sword, penetrating as far as the separation of soul and spirit, joints and marrow. It is able to judge the ideas and thoughts of the heart. [13]No creature is hidden from Him, but all things are naked and exposed to the eyes of Him to whom we must give an account.

[14]Therefore, since we have a great high priest who has passed through the heavens—Jesus the Son of God—let us hold fast to the confession. [15]For we do not have a high priest who is unable to sympathize with our weaknesses, but One who has been tested in every way as we are, yet without sin. [16]Therefore let us approach the throne of grace with boldness, so that we may receive mercy and find grace to help us at the proper time.

5 For every high priest taken from men is appointed in service to God for the people, to offer both gifts and sacrifices for sins. [2]He is able to deal gently with those who are ignorant and are going astray, since he is also subject to weakness. [3]Because of this, he must make a sin offering for himself as well as for the people. [4]No one takes this honor on himself; instead, a person is called by God, just as Aaron was. [5]In the same way, the *Messiah did not exalt Himself to become a high priest, but the One who said to Him, **You are My Son; today I have become Your Father,** [6]also said in another passage, **You are a priest forever in the order of Melchizedek.**

[7]During His earthly life, He offered prayers and appeals with loud cries and tears to the One who was able to save Him from death, and He was heard because of His reverence. [8]Though He was God's Son, He learned obedience through what He suffered. [9]After He was perfected, He became the source of eternal salvation for all who obey Him, [10]and He was declared by God a high priest in the order of Melchizedek.

[11]We have a great deal to say about this, and it's difficult to explain, since you have become too lazy to understand. [12]Although by this time you ought to be teachers, you need someone to teach you the basic principles of God's revelation again. You need milk, not solid food. [13]Now everyone who lives on milk is inexperienced with the message about righteousness, because he is an infant. [14]But solid food is for the mature—for those whose senses have been trained to distinguish between good and evil.

6 Therefore, leaving the elementary message about the *Messiah, let us go on to maturity, not laying again the foundation of repentance from dead works, faith in God, [2]teaching about ritual washings, laying on of hands, the resurrection of the dead, and eternal judgment. [3]And we will do this if God permits.

[4]For it is impossible to renew to repentance those who were once enlightened, who tasted the heavenly gift, became companions with the Holy Spirit, [5]tasted God's good word and the powers of the coming age, [6]and who have fallen away, because, to their own harm, they are recrucifying the Son of God and holding Him up to contempt. [7]For ground that has drunk the rain that has often fallen on it and that produces vegetation useful to those it is cultivated for receives a blessing from God. [8]But if it produces thorns and thistles, it is worthless and about to be cursed, and will be burned at the end.

[9]Even though we are speaking this way, dear friends, in your case we are confident of the better things connected with salvation. [10]For God is not unjust; He will not forget your work and the love you showed for His name when you served the *saints—and you continue to serve them. [11]Now we want each of you to demonstrate the same diligence for the final realization of your hope, [12]so that you won't become lazy but will be imitators of those who inherit the promises through faith and perseverance.

[13]For when God made a promise to Abraham, since He had no one greater to swear by, He swore by Himself:
[14]   **I will indeed bless you,**
     and I will greatly multiply you.
[15]And so, after waiting patiently, Abraham obtained the promise. [16]For men swear by something greater than themselves, and for them a confirming oath ends every dispute. [17]Because God wanted to show His unchangeable purpose even more clearly to the heirs of the promise, He guaranteed it with an oath, [18]so that through two unchangeable things, in which it is impossible for God to lie, we who have fled for refuge might have strong encouragement to seize the hope set before us. [19]We have this hope as an anchor for our lives, safe and secure. It enters the inner sanctuary behind the curtain. [20]Jesus has entered there on our behalf as a forerunner, because He has become a high priest forever in the order of Melchizedek.

7 For this Melchizedek—
     King of Salem, priest of the Most High God,
     who met Abraham and blessed him

as he returned from defeating the kings,

2   and Abraham gave him a tenth of everything;
    first, his name means king of righteousness,
    then also, king of Salem,
    meaning king of peace;

3   without father, mother, or genealogy,
    having neither beginning of days nor end
    of life,
    but resembling the Son of God—

remains a priest forever.

⁴Now consider how great this man was—even Abraham the patriarch gave a tenth of the plunder to him! ⁵The sons of Levi who receive the priestly office have a command according to the law to collect a tenth from the people—that is, from their ˙brothers—though they have also descended from Abraham. ⁶But one without this lineage collected tenths from Abraham and blessed the one who had the promises. ⁷Without a doubt, the inferior is blessed by the superior. ⁸In the one case, men who will die receive tenths, but in the other case, Scripture testifies that he lives. ⁹And in a sense Levi himself, who receives tenths, has paid tenths through Abraham, ¹⁰for he was still within his ancestor when Melchizedek met him.

¹¹If then, perfection came through the Levitical priesthood (for under it the people received the law), what further need was there for another priest to appear, said to be in the order of Melchizedek and not in the order of Aaron? ¹²For when there is a change of the priesthood, there must be a change of law as well. ¹³For the One these things are spoken about belonged to a different tribe. No one from it has served at the altar. ¹⁴Now it is evident that our Lord came from Judah, and Moses said nothing about that tribe concerning priests.

¹⁵And this becomes clearer if another priest like Melchizedek appears, ¹⁶who did not become a priest based on a legal command concerning physical descent but based on the power of an indestructible life. ¹⁷For it has been testified:

> You are a priest forever
> in the order of Melchizedek.

¹⁸So the previous command is annulled because it was weak ˙and unprofitable ¹⁹(for the law perfected nothing), but a better hope is introduced, through which we draw near to God. ²⁰None of this happened without an oath. For others became priests without an oath, ²¹but He became a priest with an oath made by the One who said to Him:

> The Lord has sworn,
> and He will not change His mind,
> You are a priest forever.

²²So Jesus has also become the guarantee of a better covenant.

²³Now many have become Levitical priests, since they are prevented by death from remaining in office. ²⁴But because He remains forever, He holds His priesthood permanently. ²⁵Therefore, He is always able to save those who come to God through Him, since He always lives to intercede for them.

²⁶For this is the kind of high priest we need: holy, innocent, undefiled, separated from sinners, and exalted above the heavens. ²⁷He doesn't need to offer sacrifices every day, as high priests do—first for their own sins, then for those of the people. He did this once for all when He offered Himself. ²⁸For the law appoints as high priests men who are weak, but the promise of the

oath, which came after the law, appoints a Son, who has been perfected forever.

8 Now the main point of what is being said is this: We have this kind of high priest, who sat down at the right hand of the throne of the Majesty in the heavens, ²a minister of the sanctuary and the true tabernacle that was set up by the Lord and not man. ³For every high priest is appointed to offer gifts and sacrifices; therefore it was necessary for this priest also to have something to offer. ⁴Now if He were on earth, He wouldn't be a priest, since there are those offering the gifts prescribed by the law. ⁵These serve as a copy and shadow of the heavenly things, as Moses was warned when he was about to complete the tabernacle. For God said, **Be careful that you make everything according to the pattern that was shown to you on the mountain.** ⁶But Jesus has now obtained a superior ministry, and to that degree He is the mediator of a better covenant, which has been legally enacted on better promises.

⁷For if that first covenant had been faultless, there would have been no occasion for a second one. ⁸But finding fault with His people, He says:

> Look, the days are coming, says the Lord,
> when I will make a new covenant
> with the house of Israel
> and with the house of Judah—
> 9   not like the covenant
> that I made with their ancestors
> on the day I took them by their hands
> to lead them out of the land of Egypt.
> I disregarded them, says the Lord,
> because they did not continue in My covenant.
> 10   But this is the covenant
> that I will make with the house of Israel
> after those days, says the Lord:
> I will put My laws into their minds
> and write them on their hearts.
> I will be their God,
> and they will be My people.
> 11   And each person will not teach
> his fellow citizen,
> and each his brother, saying, "Know the Lord,"
> because they will all know Me,
> from the least to the greatest of them.
> 12   For I will be merciful to their wrongdoing,
> and I will never again remember their sins.

¹³By saying, **a new covenant,** He has declared that the first is old. And what is old and aging is about to disappear.

9 Now the first covenant also had regulations for ministry and an earthly sanctuary. ²For a tabernacle was set up, and in the first room, which is called the holy place, were the lampstand, the table, and the presentation loaves. ³Behind the second curtain, the tabernacle was called the most holy place. ⁴It contained the gold altar of incense and the ark of the covenant, covered with gold on all sides, in which there was a gold jar containing the manna, Aaron's staff that budded, and the tablets of the covenant. ⁵The ˙cherubim of glory were above it overshadowing the ˙mercy seat. It is not possible to speak about these things in detail right now.

⁶With these things set up this way, the priests enter the first room repeatedly, performing their ministry. ⁷But the high priest alone enters the second room, and he does that only once a year, and never without

blood, which he offers for himself and for the sins of the people committed in ignorance. [8]The Holy Spirit was making it clear that the way into the most holy place had not yet been disclosed while the first tabernacle was still standing. [9]This is a symbol for the present time, during which gifts and sacrifices are offered that cannot perfect the worshiper's conscience. [10]They are physical regulations and only deal with food, drink, and various washings imposed until the time of restoration.

[11]But the •Messiah has appeared, high priest of the good things that have come. In the greater and more perfect tabernacle not made with hands (that is, not of this creation), [12]He entered the most holy place once for all, not by the blood of goats and calves, but by His own blood, having obtained eternal •redemption. [13]For if the blood of goats and bulls and the ashes of a young cow, sprinkling those who are defiled, sanctify for the purification of the flesh, [14]how much more will the blood of the Messiah, who through the eternal Spirit offered Himself without blemish to God, cleanse our consciences from dead works to serve the living God?

[15]Therefore, He is the mediator of a new covenant, so that those who are called might receive the promise of the eternal inheritance, because a death has taken place for redemption from the transgressions committed under the first covenant. [16]Where a will exists, the death of the one who made it must be established. [17]For a will is valid only when people die, since it is never in force while the one who made it is living. [18]That is why even the first covenant was inaugurated with blood. [19]For when every command had been proclaimed by Moses to all the people according to the law, he took the blood of calves and goats, along with water, scarlet wool, and hyssop, and sprinkled the scroll itself and all the people, [20]saying, **This is the blood of the covenant that God has commanded for you.** [21]In the same way, he sprinkled the tabernacle and all the articles of worship with blood. [22]According to the law almost everything is purified with blood, and without the shedding of blood there is no forgiveness.

[23]Therefore it was necessary for the copies of the things in the heavens to be purified with these sacrifices, but the heavenly things themselves to be purified with better sacrifices than these. [24]For the Messiah did not enter a sanctuary made with hands (only a model of the true one) but into heaven itself, so that He might now appear in the presence of God for us. [25]He did not do this to offer Himself many times, as the high priest enters the sanctuary yearly with the blood of another. [26]Otherwise, He would have had to suffer many times since the foundation of the world. But now He has appeared one time, at the end of the ages, for the removal of sin by the sacrifice of Himself. [27]And just as it is appointed for people to die once—and after this, judgment— [28]so also the Messiah, having been offered once to bear the sins of many, will appear a second time, not to bear sin, but to bring salvation to those who are waiting for Him.

10 Since the law has only a shadow of the good things to come, and not the actual form of those realities, it can never perfect the worshipers by the same sacrifices they continually offer year after year. [2]Otherwise, wouldn't they have stopped being offered, since the worshipers, once purified, would no longer have any consciousness of sins? [3]But in the sacrifices there is a reminder of sins every year. [4]For it

is impossible for the blood of bulls and goats to take away sins.

[5]Therefore, as He was coming into the world, He said:

> **You did not want sacrifice and offering,**
> **but You prepared a body for Me.**
> [6] **You did not delight**
> **in whole burnt offerings and sin offerings.**
> [7] **Then I said, "See—**
> **it is written about Me**
> **in the volume of the scroll—**
> **I have come to do Your will, God!"**

[8]After He says above, **You did not want or delight in sacrifices and offerings, whole burnt offerings and sin offerings** (which are offered according to the law), [9]He then says, **See, I have come to do Your will.** He takes away the first to establish the second. [10]By this will of God, we have been •sanctified through the offering of the body of Jesus Christ once and for all.

[11]Every priest stands day after day ministering and offering the same sacrifices time after time, which can never take away sins. [12]But this man, after offering one sacrifice for sins forever, sat down at the right hand of God. [13]He is now waiting until His enemies are made His footstool. [14]For by one offering He has perfected forever those who are sanctified. [15]The Holy Spirit also testifies to us about this. For after He says:

> [16] **This is the covenant I will make with them**
> **after those days, says the Lord:**
> **I will put My laws on their hearts**
> **and write them on their minds,**

[17]He adds:

> **I will never again remember**
> **their sins and their lawless acts.**

[18]Now where there is forgiveness of these, there is no longer an offering for sin.

[19]Therefore, •brothers, since we have boldness to enter the sanctuary through the blood of Jesus, [20]by a new and living way He has opened for us through the curtain (that is, His flesh), [21]and since we have a great high priest over the house of God, [22]let us draw near with a true heart in full assurance of faith, our hearts sprinkled •clean from an evil conscience and our bodies washed in pure water. [23]Let us hold on to the confession of our hope without wavering, for He who promised is faithful. [24]And let us be concerned about one another in order to promote love and good works, [25]not staying away from our worship meetings, as some habitually do, but encouraging each other, and all the more as you see the day drawing near.

[26]For if we deliberately sin after receiving the knowledge of the truth, there no longer remains a sacrifice for sins, [27]but a terrifying expectation of judgment and the fury of a fire about to consume the adversaries. [28]If anyone disregards Moses' law, he dies without mercy, based on the testimony of two or three witnesses. [29]How much worse punishment do you think one will deserve who has trampled on the Son of God, regarded as profane the blood of the covenant by which he was sanctified, and insulted the Spirit of grace? [30]For we know the One who has said, **Vengeance belongs to Me, I will repay,** and again, **The Lord will judge His people.** [31]It is a terrifying thing to fall into the hands of the living God!

[32]Remember the earlier days when, after you had been enlightened, you endured a hard struggle with sufferings. [33]Sometimes you were publicly exposed

to taunts and afflictions, and at other times you were companions of those who were treated that way. [34]For you sympathized with the prisoners and accepted with joy the confiscation of your possessions, knowing that you yourselves have a better and enduring possession. [35]So don't throw away your confidence, which has a great reward. [36]For you need endurance, so that after you have done God's will, you may receive what was promised.

[37] For yet in **a very little while,**
       the Coming One will come and not delay.
[38] **But My righteous one will live by faith;**
       and if he draws back,
       I have no pleasure in him.

[39]But we are not those who draw back and are destroyed, but those who have faith and obtain life.

11 Now faith is the reality of what is hoped for, the proof of what is not seen. [2]For our ancestors won God's approval by it.

[3]By faith we understand that the universe was created by God's command, so that what is seen has been made from things that are not visible.

[4]By faith Abel offered to God a better sacrifice than Cain did. By faith he was approved as a righteous man, because God approved his gifts, and even though he is dead, he still speaks through his faith.

[5]By faith Enoch was taken away so he did not experience death, and **he was not to be found because God took him away.** For prior to his removal he was approved, since he had pleased God. [6]Now without faith it is impossible to please God, for the one who draws near to Him must believe that He exists and rewards those who seek Him.

[7]By faith Noah, after he was warned about what was not yet seen and motivated by godly fear, built an ark to deliver his family. By faith he condemned the world and became an heir of the righteousness that comes by faith.

[8]By faith Abraham, when he was called, obeyed and went out to a place he was going to receive as an inheritance. He went out, not knowing where he was going. [9]By faith he stayed as a foreigner in the land of promise, living in tents with Isaac and Jacob, coheirs of the same promise. [10]For he was looking forward to the city that has foundations, whose architect and builder is God.

[11]By faith even Sarah herself, when she was unable to have children, received power to conceive offspring, even though she was past the age, since she considered that the One who had promised was faithful. [12]Therefore from one man—in fact, from one as good as dead—came offspring as numerous as the stars of heaven and as innumerable as the grains of sand by the seashore.

[13]These all died in faith without having received the promises, but they saw them from a distance, greeted them, and confessed that they were foreigners and temporary residents on the earth. [14]Now those who say such things make it clear that they are seeking a homeland. [15]If they were thinking about where they came from, they would have had an opportunity to return. [16]But they now desire a better place—a heavenly one. Therefore God is not ashamed to be called their God, for He has prepared a city for them.

[17]By faith Abraham, when he was tested, offered up Isaac. He received the promises and he was offering his unique son, [18]the one it had been said about, **Your** **'seed will be traced through Isaac.** [19]He considered God to be able even to raise someone from the dead, and as an illustration, he received him back.

[20]By faith Isaac blessed Jacob and Esau concerning things to come. [21]By faith Jacob, when he was dying, blessed each of the sons of Joseph, and **he worshiped,** **leaning on the top of his staff.** [22]By faith Joseph, as he was nearing the end of his life, mentioned the exodus of the Israelites and gave instructions concerning his bones.

[23]By faith, after Moses was born, he was hidden by his parents for three months, because they saw that the child was beautiful, and they didn't fear the king's edict. [24]By faith Moses, when he had grown up, refused to be called the son of Pharaoh's daughter [25]and chose to suffer with the people of God rather than to enjoy the short-lived pleasure of sin. [26]For he considered the reproach because of the 'Messiah to be greater wealth than the treasures of Egypt, since his attention was on the reward.

[27]By faith he left Egypt behind, not being afraid of the king's anger, for Moses persevered as one who sees Him who is invisible. [28]By faith he instituted the 'Passover and the sprinkling of the blood, so that the destroyer of the firstborn might not touch the Israelites. [29]By faith they crossed the Red Sea as though they were on dry land. When the Egyptians attempted to do this, they were drowned.

[30]By faith the walls of Jericho fell down after being encircled by the Israelites for seven days. [31]By faith Rahab the prostitute received the spies in peace and didn't perish with those who disobeyed.

[32]And what more can I say? Time is too short for me to tell about Gideon, Barak, Samson, Jephthah, David, Samuel, and the prophets, [33]who by faith conquered kingdoms, administered justice, obtained promises, shut the mouths of lions, [34]quenched the raging of fire, escaped the edge of the sword, gained strength after being weak, became mighty in battle, and put foreign armies to flight. [35]Women received their dead—they were raised to life again. Some men were tortured, not accepting release, so that they might gain a better resurrection, [36]and others experienced mockings and scourgings, as well as bonds and imprisonment. [37]They were stoned, they were sawed in two, they died by the sword, they wandered about in sheepskins, in goatskins, destitute, afflicted, and mistreated. [38]The 'world was not worthy of them. They wandered in deserts and on mountains, hiding in caves and holes in the ground.

[39]All these were approved through their faith, but they did not receive what was promised, [40]since God had provided something better for us, so that they would not be made perfect without us.

12 Therefore, since we also have such a large cloud of witnesses surrounding us, let us lay aside every weight and the sin that so easily ensnares us. Let us run with endurance the race that lies before us, [2]keeping our eyes on Jesus, the source and perfecter of our faith, who for the joy that lay before Him endured a cross and despised the shame and has sat down at the right hand of God's throne.

[3]For consider Him who endured such hostility from sinners against Himself, so that you won't grow weary and lose heart. [4]In struggling against sin, you have not yet resisted to the point of shedding your blood. [5]And

you have forgotten the exhortation that addresses you as sons:

> **My son, do not take the Lord's**
> **discipline lightly**
> **or faint when you are reproved by Him,**
> ⁶ **for the Lord disciplines the one He loves**
> **and punishes every son He receives.**

⁷Endure suffering as discipline: God is dealing with you as sons. For what son is there that a father does not discipline? ⁸But if you are without discipline—which all receive—then you are illegitimate children and not sons. ⁹Furthermore, we had natural fathers discipline us, and we respected them. Shouldn't we submit even more to the Father of spirits and live? ¹⁰For they disciplined us for a short time based on what seemed good to them, but He does it for our benefit, so that we can share His holiness. ¹¹No discipline seems enjoyable at the time, but painful. Later on, however, it yields the fruit of peace and righteousness to those who have been trained by it.

¹²Therefore strengthen your tired hands and weakened knees, ¹³and make straight paths for your feet, so that what is lame may not be dislocated but healed instead.

¹⁴Pursue peace with everyone, and holiness—without it no one will see the Lord. ¹⁵Make sure that no one falls short of the grace of God and that no root of bitterness springs up, causing trouble and by it, defiling many. ¹⁶And make sure that there isn't any immoral or irreverent person like Esau, who sold his birthright in exchange for one meal. ¹⁷For you know that later, when he wanted to inherit the blessing, he was rejected because he didn't find any opportunity for repentance, though he sought it with tears.

¹⁸For you have not come to what could be touched, to a blazing fire, to darkness, gloom, and storm, ¹⁹to the blast of a trumpet, and the sound of words. (Those who heard it begged that not another word be spoken to them, ²⁰for they could not bear what was commanded: **And if even an animal touches the mountain, it must be stoned!** ²¹The appearance was so terrifying that Moses said, **I am terrified and trembling.**) ²²Instead, you have come to Mount ˙Zion, to the city of the living God (the heavenly Jerusalem), to myriads of angels in festive gathering, ²³to the assembly of the firstborn whose names have been written in heaven, to God who is the Judge of all, to the spirits of righteous people made perfect, ²⁴to Jesus (mediator of a new covenant), and to the sprinkled blood, which says better things than the blood of Abel.

²⁵Make sure that you do not reject the One who speaks. For if they did not escape when they rejected Him who warned them on earth, even less will we if we turn away from Him who warns us from heaven. ²⁶His voice shook the earth at that time, but now He has promised, **Yet once more I will shake not only the earth but also heaven.** ²⁷This expression, "Yet once more," indicates the removal of what can be shaken— that is, created things—so that what is not shaken might remain. ²⁸Therefore, since we are receiving

a kingdom that cannot be shaken, let us hold on to grace. By it, we may serve God acceptably, with reverence and awe, ²⁹for our God is a consuming fire.

13 Let brotherly love continue. ²Don't neglect to show hospitality, for by doing this some have welcomed angels as guests without knowing it. ³Remember the prisoners, as though you were in prison with them, and the mistreated, as though you yourselves were suffering bodily. ⁴Marriage must be respected by all, and the marriage bed kept undefiled, because God will judge immoral people and adulterers. ⁵Your life should be free from the love of money. Be satisfied with what you have, for He Himself has said, **I will never leave you or forsake you.** ⁶Therefore, we may boldly say:

> **The Lord is my helper;**
> **I will not be afraid.**
> **What can man do to me?**

⁷Remember your leaders who have spoken God's word to you. As you carefully observe the outcome of their lives, imitate their faith. ⁸Jesus Christ is the same yesterday, today, and forever. ⁹Don't be led astray by various kinds of strange teachings; for it is good for the heart to be established by grace and not by foods, since those involved in them have not benefited. ¹⁰We have an altar from which those who serve the tabernacle do not have a right to eat. ¹¹For the bodies of those animals whose blood is brought into the most holy place by the high priest as a sin offering are burned outside the camp. ¹²Therefore Jesus also suffered outside the gate, so that He might ˙sanctify the people by His own blood. ¹³Let us then go to Him outside the camp, bearing His disgrace. ¹⁴For we do not have an enduring city here; instead, we seek the one to come. ¹⁵Therefore, through Him let us continually offer up to God a sacrifice of praise, that is, the fruit of our lips that confess His name. ¹⁶Don't neglect to do what is good and to share, for God is pleased with such sacrifices. ¹⁷Obey your leaders and submit to them, for they keep watch over your souls as those who will give an account, so that they can do this with joy and not with grief, for that would be unprofitable for you. ¹⁸Pray for us; for we are convinced that we have a clear conscience, wanting to conduct ourselves honorably in everything. ¹⁹And I especially urge you to pray that I may be restored to you very soon.

²⁰Now may the God of peace, who brought up from the dead our Lord Jesus—the great Shepherd of the sheep—with the blood of the everlasting covenant, ²¹equip you with all that is good to do His will, working in us what is pleasing in His sight, through Jesus Christ. Glory belongs to Him forever and ever. ˙Amen.

²²˙Brothers, I urge you to receive this message of exhortation, for I have written to you briefly. ²³Be aware that our brother Timothy has been released. If he comes soon enough, he will be with me when I see you. ²⁴Greet all your leaders and all the ˙saints. Those who are from Italy greet you. ²⁵Grace be with all of you.

JAMES

1 James, a *slave of God and of the Lord Jesus Christ:
To the 12 tribes in the Dispersion.

Greetings.

² Consider it a great joy, my *brothers, whenever you experience various trials, ³ knowing that the testing of your faith produces endurance. ⁴ But endurance must do its complete work, so that you may be mature and complete, lacking nothing.

⁵ Now if any of you lacks wisdom, he should ask God, who gives to all generously and without criticizing, and it will be given to him. ⁶ But let him ask in faith without doubting. For the doubter is like the surging sea, driven and tossed by the wind. ⁷ That person should not expect to receive anything from the Lord. ⁸ An indecisive man is unstable in all his ways.

⁹ The brother of humble circumstances should boast in his exaltation, ¹⁰ but the one who is rich should boast in his humiliation because he will pass away like a flower of the field. ¹¹ For the sun rises with its scorching heat and dries up the grass; its flower falls off, and its beautiful appearance is destroyed. In the same way, the rich man will wither away while pursuing his activities.

¹² A man who endures trials is blessed, because when he passes the test he will receive the crown of life that God has promised to those who love Him.

¹³ No one undergoing a trial should say, "I am being tempted by God." For God is not tempted by evil, and He Himself doesn't tempt anyone. ¹⁴ But each person is tempted when he is drawn away and enticed by his own evil desires. ¹⁵ Then after desire has conceived, it gives birth to sin, and when sin is fully grown, it gives birth to death.

¹⁶ Don't be deceived, my dearly loved brothers. ¹⁷ Every generous act and every perfect gift is from above, coming down from the Father of lights; with Him there is no variation or shadow cast by turning. ¹⁸ By His own choice, He gave us a new birth by the message of truth so that we would be the *firstfruits of His creatures.

¹⁹ My dearly loved brothers, understand this: Everyone must be quick to hear, slow to speak, and slow to anger, ²⁰ for man's anger does not accomplish God's righteousness. ²¹ Therefore, ridding yourselves of all moral filth and evil, humbly receive the implanted word, which is able to save you.

²² But be doers of the word and not hearers only, deceiving yourselves. ²³ Because if anyone is a hearer of the word and not a doer, he is like a man looking at his own face in a mirror. ²⁴ For he looks at himself, goes away, and immediately forgets what kind of man he was. ²⁵ But the one who looks intently into the perfect law of freedom and perseveres in it, and is not a forgetful hearer but one who does good works—this person will be blessed in what he does.

²⁶ If anyone thinks he is religious without controlling his tongue, then his religion is useless and he deceives himself. ²⁷ Pure and undefiled religion before our God and Father is this: to look after orphans and widows in their distress and to keep oneself unstained by the *world.

2 My *brothers, do not show favoritism as you hold on to the faith in our glorious Lord Jesus Christ. ² For example, a man comes into your meeting wearing a gold ring and dressed in fine clothes, and a poor man dressed in dirty clothes also comes in. ³ If you look with favor on the man wearing the fine clothes and say, "Sit here in a good place," and yet you say to the poor man, "Stand over there," or, "Sit here on the floor by my footstool," ⁴ haven't you discriminated among yourselves and become judges with evil thoughts?

⁵ Listen, my dear brothers: Didn't God choose the poor in this world to be rich in faith and heirs of the kingdom that He has promised to those who love Him? ⁶ Yet you dishonored that poor man. Don't the rich oppress you and drag you into the courts? ⁷ Don't they blaspheme the noble name that was pronounced over you at your baptism?

⁸ Indeed, if you keep the royal law prescribed in the Scripture, **Love your neighbor as yourself**, you are doing well. ⁹ But if you show favoritism, you commit sin and are convicted by the law as transgressors. ¹⁰ For whoever keeps the entire law, yet fails in one point, is *guilty of breaking it all. ¹¹ For He who said, **Do not commit adultery**, also said, **Do not murder**. So if you do not commit adultery, but you do murder, you are a lawbreaker.

¹² Speak and act as those who will be judged by the law of freedom. ¹³ For judgment is without mercy to the one who hasn't shown mercy. Mercy triumphs over judgment.

¹⁴ What good is it, my brothers, if someone says he has faith but does not have works? Can his faith save him?

¹⁵ If a brother or sister is without clothes and lacks daily food ¹⁶ and one of you says to them, "Go in peace, keep warm, and eat well," but you don't give them what the body needs, what good is it? ¹⁷ In the same way faith, if it doesn't have works, is dead by itself.

¹⁸ But someone will say, "You have faith, and I have works." Show me your faith without works, and I will show you faith from my works. ¹⁹ You believe that God is one; you do well. The demons also believe—and they shudder.

²⁰ Foolish man! Are you willing to learn that faith without works is useless? ²¹ Wasn't Abraham our father justified by works when he offered Isaac his son on the altar? ²² You see that faith was active together with his works, and by works, faith was perfected. ²³ So the Scripture was fulfilled that says, **Abraham believed God, and it was credited to him for righteousness**, and he was called God's friend. ²⁴ You see that a man is *justified by works and not by faith alone. ²⁵ And in the same way, wasn't Rahab the prostitute also justified by works when she received the messengers and sent them out by a different route? ²⁶ For just as the body without the spirit is dead, so also faith without works is dead.

3 Not many should become teachers, my *brothers, knowing that we will receive a stricter judgment, ² for we all stumble in many ways. If anyone does not stumble in what he says, he is a mature man who is also able to control his whole body. ³ Now when we put bits into the mouths of horses to

make them obey us, we also guide the whole animal. ⁴And consider ships: Though very large and driven by fierce winds, they are guided by a very small rudder wherever the will of the pilot directs. ⁵So too, though the tongue is a small part of the body, it boasts great things. Consider how large a forest a small fire ignites. ⁶And the tongue is a fire. The tongue, a world of unrighteousness, is placed among the parts of our bodies. It pollutes the whole body, sets the course of life on fire, and is set on fire by *hell.

⁷Every sea creature, reptile, bird, or animal is tamed and has been tamed by man, ⁸but no man can tame the tongue. It is a restless evil, full of deadly poison. ⁹We praise our Lord and Father with it, and we curse men who are made in God's likeness with it. ¹⁰Praising and cursing come out of the same mouth. My brothers, these things should not be this way. ¹¹Does a spring pour out sweet and bitter water from the same opening? ¹²Can a fig tree produce olives, my brothers, or a grapevine produce figs? Neither can a saltwater spring yield fresh water.

¹³Who is wise and has understanding among you? He should show his works by good conduct with wisdom's gentleness. ¹⁴But if you have bitter envy and selfish ambition in your heart, don't brag and deny the truth. ¹⁵Such wisdom does not come from above but is earthly, unspiritual, demonic. ¹⁶For where envy and selfish ambition exist, there is disorder and every kind of evil. ¹⁷But the wisdom from above is first pure, then peace-loving, gentle, compliant, full of mercy and good fruits, without favoritism and hypocrisy. ¹⁸And the fruit of righteousness is sown in peace by those who cultivate peace.

4 What is the source of wars and fights among you? Don't they come from the cravings that are at war within you? ²You desire and do not have. You murder and covet and cannot obtain. You fight and war. You do not have because you do not ask. ³You ask and don't receive because you ask with wrong motives, so that you may spend it on your evil desires.

⁴Adulteresses! Don't you know that friendship with the *world is hostility toward God? So whoever wants to be the world's friend becomes God's enemy. ⁵Or do you think it's without reason the Scripture says that the Spirit who lives in us yearns jealously?

⁶But He gives greater grace. Therefore He says:

God resists the proud,
but gives grace to the humble.

⁷Therefore, submit to God. But resist the Devil, and he will flee from you. ⁸Draw near to God, and He will draw near to you. Cleanse your hands, sinners, and purify your hearts, double-minded people! ⁹Be miserable and mourn and weep. Your laughter must change to mourning and your joy to sorrow. ¹⁰Humble yourselves before the Lord, and He will exalt you.

¹¹Don't criticize one another, *brothers. He who criticizes a brother or judges his brother criticizes the law and judges the law. But if you judge the law, you are not a doer of the law but a judge. ¹²There is one lawgiver and judge who is able to save and to destroy. But who are you to judge your neighbor?

¹³Come now, you who say, "Today or tomorrow we will travel to such and such a city and spend a year there and do business and make a profit." ¹⁴You don't even know what tomorrow will bring—what your life will be! For you are like smoke that appears for a little while, then vanishes.

¹⁵Instead, you should say, "If the Lord wills, we will live and do this or that." ¹⁶But as it is, you boast in your arrogance. All such boasting is evil. ¹⁷So it is a sin for the person who knows to do what is good and doesn't do it.

5 Come now, you rich people! Weep and wail over the miseries that are coming on you. ²Your wealth is ruined and your clothes are moth-eaten. ³Your silver and gold are corroded, and their corrosion will be a witness against you and will eat your flesh like fire. You stored up treasure in the last days! ⁴Look! The pay that you withheld from the workers who reaped your fields cries out, and the outcry of the harvesters has reached the ears of the Lord of *Hosts. ⁵You have lived luxuriously on the land and have indulged yourselves. You have fattened your hearts for the day of slaughter. ⁶You have condemned—you have murdered—the righteous man; he does not resist you.

⁷Therefore, *brothers, be patient until the Lord's coming. See how the farmer waits for the precious fruit of the earth and is patient with it until it receives the early and the late rains. ⁸You also must be patient. Strengthen your hearts, because the Lord's coming is near.

⁹Brothers, do not complain about one another, so that you will not be judged. Look, the judge stands at the door!

¹⁰Brothers, take the prophets who spoke in the Lord's name as an example of suffering and patience. ¹¹See, we count as blessed those who have endured. You have heard of Job's endurance and have seen the outcome from the Lord. The Lord is very compassionate and merciful.

¹²Now above all, my brothers, do not swear, either by heaven or by earth or with any other oath. Your "yes" must be "yes," and your "no" must be "no," so that you won't fall under judgment.

¹³Is anyone among you suffering? He should pray. Is anyone cheerful? He should sing praises. ¹⁴Is anyone among you sick? He should call for the elders of the church, and they should pray over him after anointing him with olive oil in the name of the Lord. ¹⁵The prayer of faith will save the sick person, and the Lord will restore him to health; if he has committed sins, he will be forgiven. ¹⁶Therefore, confess your sins to one another and pray for one another, so that you may be healed. The urgent request of a righteous person is very powerful in its effect. ¹⁷Elijah was a man with a nature like ours; yet he prayed earnestly that it would not rain, and for three years and six months it did not rain on the land. ¹⁸Then he prayed again, and the sky gave rain and the land produced its fruit.

¹⁹My brothers, if any among you strays from the truth, and someone turns him back, ²⁰let him know that whoever turns a sinner from the error of his way will save his *life from death and cover a multitude of sins.

1 PETER

1 Peter, an apostle of Jesus Christ:
To the temporary residents dispersed in Pontus, Galatia, Cappadocia, ·Asia, and Bithynia, chosen ²according to the foreknowledge of God the Father and set apart by the Spirit for obedience and for sprinkling with the blood of Jesus Christ.

May grace and peace be multiplied to you.

³Praise the God and Father of our Lord Jesus Christ. According to His great mercy, He has given us a new birth into a living hope through the resurrection of Jesus Christ from the dead ⁴and into an inheritance that is imperishable, uncorrupted, and unfading, kept in heaven for you. ⁵You are being protected by God's power through faith for a salvation that is ready to be revealed in the last time. ⁶You rejoice in this, though now for a short time you have had to struggle in various trials ⁷so that the genuineness of your faith—more valuable than gold, which perishes though refined by fire—may result in praise, glory, and honor at the revelation of Jesus Christ. ⁸You love Him, though you have not seen Him. And though not seeing Him now, you believe in Him and rejoice with inexpressible and glorious joy, ⁹because you are receiving the goal of your faith, the salvation of your souls.

¹⁰Concerning this salvation, the prophets who prophesied about the grace that would come to you searched and carefully investigated. ·¹¹They inquired into what time or what circumstances the Spirit of Christ within them was indicating when He testified in advance to the messianic sufferings and the glories that would follow. ¹²It was revealed to them that they were not serving themselves but you. These things have now been announced to you through those who preached the gospel to you by the Holy Spirit sent from heaven. Angels desire to look into these things.

¹³Therefore, with your minds ready for action, be serious and set your hope completely on the grace to be brought to you at the revelation of Jesus Christ. ¹⁴As obedient children, do not be conformed to the desires of your former ignorance. ¹⁵But as the One who called you is holy, you also are to be holy in all your conduct; ¹⁶for it is written, **Be holy, because I am holy.**

¹⁷And if you address as Father the One who judges impartially based on each one's work, you are to conduct yourselves in fear during the time of your temporary residence. ¹⁸For you know that you were ·redeemed from your empty way of life inherited from the fathers, not with perishable things like silver or gold, ¹⁹but with the precious blood of Christ, like that of a lamb without defect or blemish. ²⁰He was chosen before the foundation of the world but was revealed at the end of the times for you ²¹who through Him are believers in God, who raised Him from the dead and gave Him glory, so that your faith and hope are in God.

²²By obedience to the truth, having purified yourselves for sincere love of the ·brothers, love one another earnestly from a pure heart, ²³since you have been born again—not of perishable seed but of imperishable—through the living and enduring word of God. ²⁴For

> All flesh is like grass,
> and all its glory like a flower of the grass.
> The grass withers, and the flower falls,
> ²⁵ but the word of the Lord endures forever.

And this is the word that was preached as the gospel to you.

2 So rid yourselves of all malice, all deceit, hypocrisy, envy, and all slander. ²Like newborn infants, desire the pure spiritual milk, so that you may grow by it for your salvation, ³since **you have tasted that the Lord is good.** ⁴Coming to Him, a living stone—rejected by men but chosen and valuable to God—⁵you yourselves, as living stones, are being built into a spiritual house for a holy priesthood to offer spiritual sacrifices acceptable to God through Jesus Christ. ⁶For it is contained in Scripture:

> **Look! I lay a stone in ·Zion,**
> **a chosen and honored cornerstone,**
> **and the one who believes in Him**
> **will never be put to shame!**

⁷So honor will come to you who believe, but for the unbelieving,

> **The stone that the builders rejected—**
> **this One has become the cornerstone,**

⁸and

> **A stone to stumble over,**
> **and a rock to trip over.**

They stumble because they disobey the message; they were destined for this.

> ⁹ But you are **a chosen race, a royal priesthood,**
> **a holy nation, a people for His possession,**
> **so that you may proclaim the praises**
> of the One who called you out of darkness
> into His marvelous light.
> ¹⁰ Once you were not a people,
> but now you are God's people;
> you had not received mercy,
> but now you have received mercy.

¹¹Dear friends, I urge you as strangers and temporary residents to abstain from fleshly desires that war against you. ¹²Conduct yourselves honorably among the Gentiles, so that in a case where they speak against you as those who do what is evil, they will, by observing your good works, glorify God on the day of visitation.

¹³Submit to every human authority because of the Lord, whether to the Emperor as the supreme authority ¹⁴or to governors as those sent out by him to punish those who do what is evil and to praise those who do what is good. ¹⁵For it is God's will that you silence the ignorance of foolish people by doing good. ¹⁶As God's ·slaves, live as free people, but don't use your freedom as a way to conceal evil. ¹⁷Honor everyone. Love the brotherhood. Fear God. Honor the Emperor.

¹⁸Household slaves, submit with all fear to your masters, not only to the good and gentle but also to the cruel. ¹⁹For it brings favor if, mindful of God's will, someone endures grief from suffering unjustly. ²⁰For what credit is there if you sin and are punished, and you endure it? But when you do what is good and suffer, if you endure it, this brings favor with God.

> ²¹ For you were called to this,
> because Christ also suffered for you,
> leaving you an example,
> so that you should follow in His steps.
> ²² He **did not commit sin,**
> **and no deceit was found in His mouth;**

²³ when He was reviled,
    He did not revile in return;
    when He was suffering,
    He did not threaten
    but entrusted Himself to the One
      who judges justly.
²⁴ He Himself bore our sins
    in His body on the tree,
    so that, having died to sins,
    we might live for righteousness;
    you have been healed by **His wounds.**
²⁵ For you **were like sheep going astray,**
    but you have now returned
    to the Shepherd and Guardian of your souls.

3 In the same way, wives, submit yourselves to your own husbands so that, even if some disobey the Christian message, they may be won over without a message by the way their wives live ² when they observe your pure, reverent lives. ³ Your beauty should not consist of outward things like elaborate hairstyles and the wearing of gold ornaments or fine clothes. ⁴ Instead, it should consist of what is inside the heart with the imperishable quality of a gentle and quiet spirit, which is very valuable in God's eyes. ⁵ For in the past, the holy women who put their hope in God also beautified themselves in this way, submitting to their own husbands, ⁶ just as Sarah obeyed Abraham, calling him lord. You have become her children when you do what is good and are not frightened by anything alarming.

⁷ Husbands, in the same way, live with your wives with an understanding of their weaker nature yet showing them honor as coheirs of the grace of life, so that your prayers will not be hindered.

⁸ Now finally, all of you should be like-minded and sympathetic, should love believers, and be compassionate and humble, ⁹ not paying back evil for evil or insult for insult but, on the contrary, giving a blessing, since you were called for this, so that you can inherit a blessing.

¹⁰   For **the one who wants to love life**
    and to see good days
    must keep his tongue from evil
    and his lips from speaking deceit,
¹¹   **and he must turn away from evil**
    and do what is good.
    He must seek peace and pursue it,
¹²   **because the eyes of the Lord are**
    on the righteous
    and His ears are open
    to their request.
    But the face of the Lord is against
    · those who do what is evil.

¹³ And who will harm you if you are deeply committed to what is good? ¹⁴ But even if you should suffer for righteousness, you are blessed. **Do not fear what they fear or be disturbed,** ¹⁵ but honor the ·Messiah as Lord in your hearts. Always be ready to give a defense to anyone who asks you for a reason for the hope that is in you. ¹⁶ However, do this with gentleness and respect, keeping your conscience clear, so that when you are accused, those who denounce your Christian life will be put to shame. ¹⁷ For it is better to suffer for doing good, if that should be God's will, than for doing evil.

¹⁸   For Christ also suffered for sins once for all,
    the righteous for the unrighteous,
    that He might bring you to God,
after being put to death in the fleshly realm
    but made alive in the spiritual realm.

¹⁹ In that state He also went and made a proclamation to the spirits in prison ²⁰ who in the past were disobedient, when God patiently waited in the days of Noah while an ark was being prepared. In it a few—that is, eight people—were saved through water. ²¹ Baptism, which corresponds to this, now saves you (not the removal of the filth of the flesh, but the pledge of a good conscience toward God) through the resurrection of Jesus Christ. ²² Now that He has gone into heaven, He is at God's right hand with angels, authorities, and powers subject to Him.

4 Therefore, since Christ suffered in the flesh, equip yourselves also with the same resolve—because the one who suffered in the flesh has finished with sin— ² in order to live the remaining time in the flesh, no longer for human desires, but for God's will. ³ For there has already been enough time spent in doing what the pagans choose to do: carrying on in unrestrained behavior, evil desires, drunkenness, orgies, carousing, and lawless idolatry. ⁴ So they are surprised that you don't plunge with them into the same flood of wild living—and they slander you. ⁵ They will give an account to the One who stands ready to judge the living and the dead. ⁶ For this reason the gospel was also preached to those who are now dead, so that, although they might be judged by men in the fleshly realm, they might live by God in the spiritual realm.

⁷ Now the end of all things is near; therefore, be serious and disciplined for prayer. ⁸ Above all, maintain an intense love for each other, since **love covers a multitude of sins.** ⁹ Be hospitable to one another without complaining. ¹⁰ Based on the gift each one has received, use it to serve others, as good managers of the varied grace of God. ¹¹ If anyone speaks, it should be as one who speaks God's words; if anyone serves, it should be from the strength God provides, so that God may be glorified through Jesus Christ in everything. To Him belong the glory and the power forever and ever. ·Amen.

¹² Dear friends, don't be surprised when the fiery ordeal comes among you to test you as if something unusual were happening to you. ¹³ Instead, rejoice as you share in the sufferings of the ·Messiah, so that you may also rejoice with great joy at the revelation of His glory. ¹⁴ If you are ridiculed for the name of Christ, you are blessed, because the Spirit of glory and of God rests on you. ¹⁵ None of you, however, should suffer as a murderer, a thief, an evildoer, or a meddler. ¹⁶ But if anyone suffers as a "Christian," he should not be ashamed but should glorify God in having that name. ¹⁷ For the time has come for judgment to begin with God's household, and if it begins with us, what will the outcome be for those who disobey the gospel of God?

¹⁸   And **if a righteous person is saved**
    with difficulty,
    what will become of the ungodly
    and the sinner?

¹⁹ So those who suffer according to God's will should, while doing what is good, entrust themselves to a faithful Creator.

5 Therefore, as a fellow elder and witness to the sufferings of the ·Messiah and also a participant in the glory about to be revealed, I exhort the elders among you: ² Shepherd God's flock among you, not overseeing out of compulsion but freely, according to God's will; not for the money but eagerly; ³not lording it over those entrusted to you, but being examples to the flock. ⁴And when the chief Shepherd appears, you will receive the unfading crown of glory.

⁵In the same way, you younger men, be subject to the elders. And all of you clothe yourselves with humility toward one another, because

> **God resists the proud**
> **but gives grace to the humble.**

⁶Humble yourselves, therefore, under the mighty hand of God, so that He may exalt you at the proper time, ⁷casting all your care on Him, because He cares about you.

⁸Be serious! Be alert! Your adversary the Devil is prowling around like a roaring lion, looking for any-one he can devour. ⁹Resist him and be firm in the faith, knowing that the same sufferings are being experienced by your fellow believers throughout the world.

¹⁰Now the God of all grace, who called you to His eternal glory in Christ Jesus, will personally restore, establish, strengthen, and support you after you have suffered a little. ¹¹The dominion belongs to Him forever. ˙Amen.

¹²I have written you this brief letter through Silvanus (I know him to be a faithful brother) to encourage you and to testify that this is the true grace of God. Take your stand in it! ¹³The church in Babylon, also chosen, sends you greetings, as does Mark, my son. ¹⁴Greet one another with a kiss of love. Peace to all of you who are in Christ.

2 PETER

1 Simeon Peter, a ˙slave and an apostle of Jesus Christ:

To those who have obtained a faith of equal privilege with ours through the righteousness of our God and Savior Jesus Christ.

²May grace and peace be multiplied to you through the knowledge of God and of Jesus our Lord.

³His divine power has given us everything required for life and godliness through the knowledge of Him who called us by His own glory and goodness. ⁴By these He has given us very great and precious promises, so that through them you may share in the divine nature, escaping the corruption that is in the world because of evil desires. ⁵For this very reason, make every effort to supplement your faith with goodness, goodness with knowledge, ⁶knowledge with self-control, self-control with endurance, endurance with godliness, ⁷godliness with brotherly affection, and brotherly affection with love. ⁸For if these qualities are yours and are increasing, they will keep you from being useless or unfruitful in the knowledge of our Lord Jesus Christ. ⁹The person who lacks these things is blind and shortsighted and has forgotten the cleansing from his past sins. ¹⁰Therefore, ˙brothers, make every effort to confirm your calling and election, because if you do these things you will never stumble. ¹¹For in this way, entry into the eternal kingdom of our Lord and Savior Jesus Christ will be richly supplied to you.

¹²Therefore I will always remind you about these things, even though you know them and are established in the truth you have. ¹³I consider it right, as long as I am in this bodily tent, to wake you up with a reminder, ¹⁴knowing that I will soon lay aside my tent, as our Lord Jesus Christ has also shown me. ¹⁵And I will also make every effort that you may be able to recall these things at any time after my departure.

¹⁶For we did not follow cleverly contrived myths when we made known to you the power and coming of our Lord Jesus Christ; instead, we were eyewitnesses of His majesty. ¹⁷For when He received honor and glory from God the Father, a voice came to Him from the Majestic Glory:

> This is My beloved Son.
> I take delight in Him!

¹⁸And we heard this voice when it came from heaven while we were with Him on the holy mountain. ¹⁹So we have the prophetic word strongly confirmed. You will do well to pay attention to it, as to a lamp shining in a dismal place, until the day dawns and the morning star rises in your hearts. ²⁰First of all, you should know this: No prophecy of Scripture comes from one's own interpretation, ²¹because no prophecy ever came by the will of man; instead, men spoke from God as they were moved by the Holy Spirit.

2 But there were also false prophets among the people, just as there will be false teachers among you. They will secretly bring in destructive heresies, even denying the Master who bought them, and will bring swift destruction on themselves. ²Many will follow their unrestrained ways, and the way of truth will be blasphemed because of them. ³They will exploit you in their greed with deceptive words. Their condemnation, pronounced long ago, is not idle, and their destruction does not sleep.

⁴For if God didn't spare the angels who sinned but threw them down into Tartarus and delivered them to be kept in chains of darkness until judgment; ⁵and if He didn't spare the ancient world, but protected Noah, a preacher of righteousness, and seven others, when He brought a flood on the world of the ungodly; ⁶and if He reduced the cities of Sodom and Gomorrah to ashes and condemned them to ruin, making them an example to those who were going to be ungodly; ⁷and if He rescued righteous Lot, distressed by the unrestrained behavior of the immoral ⁸(for as he lived among them, that righteous man tormented himself day by day with the lawless deeds he saw and heard)— ⁹then the Lord knows how to rescue the godly from trials and to keep the unrighteous under punishment until the day of judgment, ¹⁰especially those who follow the polluting desires of the flesh and despise authority.

Bold, arrogant people! They do not tremble when they blaspheme the glorious ones; ¹¹however, angels, who are greater in might and power, do not bring a slanderous charge against them before the Lord. ¹²But these people, like irrational animals—creatures of instinct born to be caught and destroyed—speak blasphemies about things they don't understand, and in their destruction they too will be destroyed, ¹³suffering harm as the payment for unrighteousness. They consider it a pleasure to carouse in the daytime. They are spots and blemishes, delighting in their deceptions as they feast with you. ¹⁴They have eyes full of adultery and are always looking for sin. They seduce unstable people and have hearts trained in greed. Children under a curse! ¹⁵They have gone astray by abandoning the straight path and have followed the path of Balaam, the son of Bosor, who loved the wages of unrighteousness ¹⁶but received a rebuke for his transgression: A donkey that could not talk spoke with a human voice and restrained the prophet's irrationality.

¹⁷These people are springs without water, mists driven by a whirlwind. The gloom of darkness has been reserved for them. ¹⁸For by uttering boastful, empty words, they seduce, with fleshly desires and debauchery, people who have barely escaped from those who live in error. ¹⁹They promise them freedom, but they themselves are ˙slaves of corruption, since people are enslaved to whatever defeats them. ²⁰For if, having escaped the world's impurity through the knowledge of our Lord and Savior Jesus Christ, they are again entangled in these things and defeated, the last state is worse for them than the first. ²¹For it would have been better for them not to have known the way of righteousness than, after knowing it, to turn back from the holy command delivered to them. ²²It has happened to them according to the true proverb: **A dog returns to its own vomit,** and, "a sow, after washing itself, wallows in the mud."

3 Dear friends, this is now the second letter I have written to you; in both letters, I want to develop a genuine understanding with a reminder, ²so that you can remember the words previously spoken by the holy prophets and the command of our Lord and Savior given through your apostles. ³First, be aware of this: Scoffers will come in the last days to scoff, living according to their own desires, ⁴saying, "Where is the promise of His coming? Ever since the fathers fell ˙asleep, all things continue as they have been since the beginning of creation." ⁵They willfully ignore this: Long ago the heavens and the earth were brought about from water and through water by the word of God. ⁶Through these waters the world of that time perished when it was flooded. ⁷But by the same word, the present heavens and earth are stored up for fire, being kept until the day of judgment and destruction of ungodly men.

⁸Dear friends, don't let this one thing escape you: With the Lord one day is like a thousand years, and a thousand years like one day. ⁹The Lord does not delay His promise, as some understand delay, but is patient with you, not wanting any to perish but all to come to repentance.

¹⁰But the Day of the Lord will come like a thief; on that day the heavens will pass away with a loud noise, the elements will burn and be dissolved, and the earth and the works on it will be disclosed. ¹¹Since all these things are to be destroyed in this way, it is clear what sort of people you should be in holy conduct and godliness ¹²as you wait for and earnestly desire the coming of the day of God. The heavens will be on fire and be dissolved because of it, and the elements will melt with the heat. ¹³But based on His promise, we wait for the new heavens and a new earth, where righteousness will dwell.

¹⁴Therefore, dear friends, while you wait for these things, make every effort to be found at peace with Him without spot or blemish. ¹⁵Also, regard the patience of our Lord as an opportunity for salvation, just as our dear brother Paul has written to you according to the wisdom given to him. ¹⁶He speaks about these things in all his letters in which there are some matters that are hard to understand. The untaught and unstable twist them to their own destruction, as they also do with the rest of the Scriptures.

¹⁷Therefore, dear friends, since you know this in advance, be on your guard, so that you are not led away by the error of lawless people and fall from your own stability. ¹⁸But grow in the grace and knowledge of our Lord and Savior Jesus Christ. To Him be the glory both now and to the day of eternity. ˙Amen.

1 JOHN

1 What was from the beginning,
 what we have heard,
 what we have seen with our eyes,
 what we have observed
 and have touched with our hands,
 concerning the Word of life—
² that life was revealed,
 and we have seen it
 and we testify and declare to you
 the eternal life that was with the Father
 and was revealed to us—
³ what we have seen and heard
 we also declare to you,
 so that you may have fellowship
 along with us;
 and indeed our fellowship is with the Father
 and with His Son Jesus Christ.
⁴ We are writing these things
 so that our joy may be complete.

⁵Now this is the message we have heard from Him and declare to you: God is light, and there is absolutely no darkness in Him. ⁶If we say, "We have fellowship with Him," yet we ˙walk in darkness, we are lying and are not practicing the truth. ⁷But if we walk in the light as He Himself is in the light, we have fellowship with one another, and the blood of Jesus His Son cleanses us from all sin. ⁸If we say, "We have no sin," we are deceiving ourselves, and the truth is not in us. ⁹If we confess our sins, He is faithful and righteous to forgive us our sins and to cleanse us from all unrighteousness. ¹⁰If we say, "We don't have any sin," we make Him a liar, and His word is not in us.

2 My little children, I am writing you these things so that you may not sin. But if anyone does sin, we have an ˙advocate with the Father—Jesus Christ the Righteous One. ²He Himself is the ˙propitiation for our sins, and not only for ours, but also for those of the whole world.

³This is how we are sure that we have come to know Him: by keeping His commands. ⁴The one who says, "I have come to know Him," yet doesn't keep His commands, is a liar, and the truth is not in him. ⁵But whoever keeps His word, truly in him the love of God is perfected. This is how we know we are in Him: ⁶The

one who says he remains in Him should ˙walk just as He walked.

⁷Dear friends, I am not writing you a new command but an old command that you have had from the beginning. The old command is the message you have heard. ⁸Yet I am writing you a new command, which is true in Him and in you, because the darkness is passing away and the true light is already shining.

⁹The one who says he is in the light but hates his brother is in the darkness until now. ¹⁰The one who loves his brother remains in the light, and there is no cause for stumbling in him. ¹¹But the one who hates his brother is in the darkness, walks in the darkness, and doesn't know where he's going, because the darkness has blinded his eyes.

¹² I am writing to you, little children,
      because your sins have been forgiven
      because of Jesus' name.
¹³ I am writing to you, fathers,
      because you have come to know
      the One who is from the beginning.
      I am writing to you, young men,
      because you have had victory
         over the evil one.
¹⁴ I have written to you, children,
      because you have come to know the Father.
      I have written to you, fathers,
      because you have come to know
      the One who is from the beginning.
      I have written to you, young men,
      because you are strong,
      God's word remains in you,
      and you have had victory over the evil one.

¹⁵Do not love the ˙world or the things that belong to the world. If anyone loves the world, love for the Father is not in him. ¹⁶For everything that belongs to the world—the lust of the flesh, the lust of the eyes, and the pride in one's lifestyle—is not from the Father, but is from the world. ¹⁷And the world with its lust is passing away, but the one who does God's will remains forever.

¹⁸Children, it is the last hour. And as you have heard, "Antichrist is coming," even now many antichrists have come. We know from this that it is the last hour. ¹⁹They went out from us, but they did not belong to us; for if they had belonged to us, they would have remained with us. However, they went out so that it might be made clear that none of them belongs to us.

²⁰But you have an anointing from the Holy One, and all of you have knowledge. ²¹I have not written to you because you don't know the truth, but because you do know it, and because no lie comes from the truth. ²²Who is the liar, if not the one who denies that Jesus is the ˙Messiah? This one is the antichrist: the one who denies the Father and the Son. ²³No one who denies the Son can have the Father; he who confesses the Son has the Father as well.

²⁴What you have heard from the beginning must remain in you. If what you have heard from the beginning remains in you, then you will remain in the Son and in the Father. ²⁵And this is the promise that He Himself made to us: eternal life. ²⁶I have written these things to you about those who are trying to deceive you.

²⁷The anointing you received from Him remains in you, and you don't need anyone to teach you. Instead, His anointing teaches you about all things and is true and is not a lie; just as He has taught you, remain in Him.

²⁸So now, little children, remain in Him, so that when He appears we may have boldness and not be ashamed before Him at His coming. ²⁹If you know that He is righteous, you know this as well: Everyone who does what is right has been born of Him.

3 ¹Look at how great a love the Father has given us that we should be called God's children. And we are! The reason the ˙world does not know us is that it didn't know Him. ²Dear friends, we are God's children now, and what we will be has not yet been revealed. We know that when He appears, we will be like Him because we will see Him as He is. ³And everyone who has this hope in Him purifies himself just as He is pure.

⁴Everyone who commits sin also breaks the law; sin is the breaking of law. ⁵You know that He was revealed so that He might take away sins, and there is no sin in Him. ⁶Everyone who remains in Him does not sin; everyone who sins has not seen Him or known Him.

⁷Little children, let no one deceive you! The one who does what is right is righteous, just as He is righteous. ⁸The one who commits sin is of the Devil, for the Devil has sinned from the beginning. The Son of God was revealed for this purpose: to destroy the Devil's works. ⁹Everyone who has been born of God does not sin, because His seed remains in him; he is not able to sin, because he has been born of God. ¹⁰This is how God's children—and the Devil's children—are made evident.

Whoever does not do what is right is not of God, especially the one who does not love his brother. ¹¹For this is the message you have heard from the beginning: We should love one another, ¹²unlike Cain, who was of the evil one and murdered his brother. And why did he murder him? Because his works were evil, and his brother's were righteous. ¹³Do not be surprised, ˙brothers, if the world hates you. ¹⁴We know that we have passed from death to life because we love our brothers. The one who does not love remains in death. ¹⁵Everyone who hates his brother is a murderer, and you know that no murderer has eternal life residing in him.

¹⁶This is how we have come to know love: He laid down His life for us. We should also lay down our lives for our brothers. ¹⁷If anyone has this world's goods and sees his brother in need but closes his eyes to his need—how can God's love reside in him?

¹⁸Little children, we must not love with word or speech, but with truth and action. ¹⁹This is how we will know we belong to the truth and will convince our conscience in His presence, ²⁰even if our conscience condemns us, that God is greater than our conscience, and He knows all things.

²¹Dear friends, if our conscience doesn't condemn us, we have confidence before God ²²and can receive whatever we ask from Him because we keep His commands and do what is pleasing in His sight. ²³Now this is His command: that we believe in the name of His Son Jesus Christ, and love one another as He commanded us. ²⁴The one who keeps His commands remains in Him, and He in him. And the way we know that He remains in us is from the Spirit He has given us.

4 Dear friends, do not believe every spirit, but test the spirits to determine if they are from God, because many false prophets have gone out into the world. ²This is how you know the Spirit of God: Every spirit who confesses that Jesus Christ has come in the flesh is from God. ³But every spirit who does not confess Jesus is not from God. This is the spirit of the antichrist; you have heard that he is coming, and he is already in the world now.

⁴You are from God, little children, and you have conquered them, because the One who is in you is greater than the one who is in the world. ⁵They are from the *world. Therefore what they say is from the world, and the world listens to them. ⁶We are from God. Anyone who knows God listens to us; anyone who is not from God does not listen to us. From this we know the Spirit of truth and the spirit of deception.

⁷Dear friends, let us love one another, because love is from God, and everyone who loves has been born of God and knows God. ⁸The one who does not love does not know God, because God is love. ⁹God's love was revealed among us in this way: God sent His *One and Only Son into the world so that we might live through Him. ¹⁰Love consists in this: not that we loved God, but that He loved us and sent His Son to be the *propitiation for our sins. ¹¹Dear friends, if God loved us in this way, we also must love one another. ¹²No one has ever seen God. If we love one another, God remains in us and His love is perfected in us.

¹³This is how we know that we remain in Him and He in us: He has given assurance to us from His Spirit. ¹⁴And we have seen and we testify that the Father has sent His Son as the world's Savior. ¹⁵Whoever confesses that Jesus is the Son of God—God remains in him and he in God. ¹⁶And we have come to know and to believe the love that God has for us. God is love, and the one who remains in love remains in God, and God remains in him.

¹⁷In this, love is perfected with us so that we may have confidence in the day of judgment, for we are as He is in this world. ¹⁸There is no fear in love; instead, perfect love drives out fear, because fear involves punishment. So the one who fears has not reached perfection in love. ¹⁹We love because He first loved us.

²⁰If anyone says, "I love God," yet hates his brother, he is a liar. For the person who does not love his brother he has seen cannot love the God he has not seen. ²¹And we have this command from Him: The one who loves God must also love his brother.

5 Everyone who believes that Jesus is the *Messiah has been born of God, and everyone who loves the Father also loves the one born of Him. ²This is how we know that we love God's children when we love God and obey His commands. ³For this is what love for God is: to keep His commands. Now His commands are not a burden, ⁴because whatever has been born of God conquers the *world. This is the victory that has conquered the world: our faith. ⁵And who is the one who conquers the world but the one who believes that Jesus is the Son of God?

⁶Jesus Christ—He is the One who came by water and blood, not by water only, but by water and by blood. And the Spirit is the One who testifies, because the Spirit is the truth. ⁷For there are three that testify: ⁸the Spirit, the water, and the blood—and these three are in agreement. ⁹If we accept the testimony of men, God's testimony is greater, because it is God's testimony that He has given about His Son. ¹⁰(The one who believes in the Son of God has this testimony within him. The one who does not believe God has made Him a liar, because he has not believed in the testimony God has given about His Son.) ¹¹And this is the testimony: God has given us eternal life, and this life is in His Son.

¹²The one who has the Son has life. The one who doesn't have the Son of God does not have life. ¹³I have written these things to you who believe in the name of the Son of God, so that you may know that you have eternal life.

¹⁴Now this is the confidence we have before Him: Whenever we ask anything according to His will, He hears us. ¹⁵And if we know that He hears whatever we ask, we know that we have what we have asked Him for.

¹⁶If anyone sees his brother committing a sin that does not bring death, he should ask, and God will give life to him—to those who commit sin that doesn't bring death. There is sin that brings death. I am not saying he should pray about that. ¹⁷All unrighteousness is sin, and there is sin that does not bring death.

¹⁸We know that everyone who has been born of God does not sin, but the One who is born of God keeps him, and the evil one does not touch him.

¹⁹We know that we are of God, and the whole world is under the sway of the evil one.

²⁰And we know that the Son of God has come and has given us understanding so that we may know the true One. We are in the true One—that is, in His Son Jesus Christ. He is the true God and eternal life.

²¹Little children, guard yourselves from idols.

2 JOHN

The Elder:
 To the elect lady and her children: I love all of you in the truth—and not only I, but also all who have come to know the truth— ²because of the truth that remains in us and will be with us forever.

³Grace, mercy, and peace will be with us from God the Father and from Jesus Christ, the Son of the Father, in truth and love.

⁴I was very glad to find some of your children *walking in the truth, in keeping with a command we have received from the Father. ⁵So now I urge you, dear lady—not as if I were writing you a new command, but one we have had from the beginning— that we love one another. ⁶And this is love: that we walk according to His commands. This is the command as you have heard it from the beginning: you must walk in love.

⁷Many deceivers have gone out into the world; they do not confess the coming of Jesus Christ in the flesh. This is the deceiver and the antichrist. ⁸Watch

yourselves so you don't lose what we have worked for, but that you may receive a full reward. [9] Anyone who does not remain in Christ's teaching but goes beyond it, does not have God. The one who remains in that teaching, this one has both the Father and the Son. [10] If anyone comes to you and does not bring this teaching, do not receive him into your home, and don't say, "Welcome," to him; [11] for the one who says, "Welcome," to him shares in his evil works.

[12] Though I have many things to write to you, I don't want to do so with paper and ink. Instead, I hope to be with you and talk face to face so that our joy may be complete. [13] The children of your elect sister send you greetings.

3 JOHN

T he Elder:
To my dear friend Gaius: I love you in the truth. [2] Dear friend, I pray that you may prosper in every way and be in good health physically just as you are spiritually. [3] For I was very glad when some *brothers came and testified to your faithfulness to the truth—how you are *walking in the truth. [4] I have no greater joy than this: to hear that my children are walking in the truth.

[5] Dear friend, you are showing faithfulness by whatever you do for the brothers, especially when they are strangers. [6] They have testified to your love in front of the church. You will do well to send them on their journey in a manner worthy of God, [7] since they set out for the sake of the Name, accepting nothing from pagans. [8] Therefore, we ought to support such men so that we can be coworkers with the truth.

[9] I wrote something to the church, but Diotrephes, who loves to have first place among them, does not receive us. [10] This is why, if I come, I will remind him of the works he is doing, slandering us with malicious words. And he is not satisfied with that! He not only refuses to welcome the brothers himself, but he even stops those who want to do so and expels them from the church.

[11] Dear friend, do not imitate what is evil, but what is good. The one who does good is of God; the one who does evil has not seen God. [12] Demetrius has a good testimony from everyone, and from the truth itself. And we also testify for him, and you know that our testimony is true.

[13] I have many things to write you, but I don't want to write to you with pen and ink. [14] I hope to see you soon, and we will talk face to face.

Peace be with you. The friends send you greetings. Greet the friends by name.

JUDE

J ude, a *slave of Jesus Christ and a brother of James: To those who are the called, loved by God the Father and kept by Jesus Christ.

[2] May mercy, peace, and love be multiplied to you.

[3] Dear friends, although I was eager to write you about the salvation we share, I found it necessary to write and exhort you to contend for the faith that was delivered to the *saints once for all. [4] For some men, who were designated for this judgment long ago, have come in by stealth; they are ungodly, turning the grace of our God into promiscuity and denying Jesus Christ, our only Master and Lord.

[5] Now I want to remind you, though you know all these things: The Lord first saved a people out of Egypt and later destroyed those who did not believe; [6] and He has kept, with eternal chains in darkness for the judgment of the great day, the angels who did not keep their own position but deserted their proper dwelling. [7] In the same way, Sodom and Gomorrah and the cities around them committed sexual immorality and practiced perversions, just as angels did, and serve as an example by undergoing the punishment of eternal fire.

[8] Nevertheless, these dreamers likewise defile their flesh, reject authority, and blaspheme glorious ones. [9] Yet Michael the archangel, when he was disputing with the Devil in a debate about Moses' body, did not dare bring an abusive condemnation against him but said, "The Lord rebuke you!" [10] But these people blaspheme anything they don't understand. What they know by instinct like unreasoning animals—they destroy themselves with these things. [11] Woe to them! For they have traveled in the way of Cain, have abandoned themselves to the error of Balaam for profit, and have perished in Korah's rebellion.

[12] These are the ones who are like dangerous reefs at your love feasts. They feast with you, nurturing only themselves without fear. They are waterless clouds carried along by winds; trees in late autumn—fruitless, twice dead, pulled out by the roots; [13] wild waves of the sea, foaming up their shameful deeds; wandering stars for whom the blackness of darkness is reserved forever!

[14] And Enoch, in the seventh generation from Adam, prophesied about them:

> Look! The Lord comes
> with thousands of His holy ones
> [15] to execute judgment on all
> and to convict them
> of all their ungodly acts
> that they have done in an ungodly way,
> and of all the harsh things ungodly sinners
> have said against Him.

[16] These people are discontented grumblers, *walking according to their desires; their mouths utter arrogant words, flattering people for their own advantage.

[17] But you, dear friends, remember what was predicted by the apostles of our Lord Jesus Christ; [18] they told you, "In the end time there will be scoffers walking according to their own ungodly desires." [19] These people create divisions and are unbelievers, not having the Spirit.

[20] But you, dear friends, as you build yourselves up in your most holy faith and pray in the Holy Spirit,

²¹ keep yourselves in the love of God, expecting the mercy of our Lord Jesus Christ for eternal life. ²² Have mercy on those who doubt; ²³ save others by snatching them from the fire; have mercy on others but with fear, hating even the garment defiled by the flesh.

²⁴ Now to Him who is able to protect you from stumbling and to make you stand in the presence of His glory, blameless and with great joy, ²⁵ to the only God our Savior, through Jesus Christ our Lord, be glory, majesty, power, and authority before all time, now and forever. ˙Amen.

REVELATION

1 The revelation of Jesus Christ that God gave Him to show His ˙slaves what must quickly take place. He sent it and signified it through His angel to His slave John, ² who testified to God's word and to the testimony about Jesus Christ, in all he saw. ³ The one who reads this is blessed, and those who hear the words of this prophecy and keep what is written in it are blessed, because the time is near!

⁴ John:

To the seven churches in ˙Asia.

Grace and peace to you from the One who is, who was, and who is coming; from the seven spirits before His throne; ⁵ and from Jesus Christ, the faithful witness, the firstborn from the dead and the ruler of the kings of the earth.

To Him who loves us and has set us free from our sins by His blood, ⁶ and made us a kingdom, priests to His God and Father—the glory and dominion are His forever and ever. ˙Amen.

⁷   **Look! He is coming with the clouds,**
    and every eye will see Him,
  including those who pierced Him.
  And all the families of the earth
  will mourn over Him.
    This is certain. Amen.

⁸ "I am the ˙Alpha and the Omega," says the Lord God, "the One who is, who was, and who is coming, the Almighty."

⁹ I, John, your brother and partner in the tribulation, kingdom, and endurance that are in Jesus, was on the island called Patmos because of God's word and the testimony about Jesus. ¹⁰ I was in the Spirit on the Lord's day, and I heard a loud voice behind me like a trumpet ¹¹ saying, "Write on a scroll what you see and send it to the seven churches: Ephesus, Smyrna, Pergamum, Thyatira, Sardis, Philadelphia, and Laodicea."

¹² I turned to see whose voice it was that spoke to me. When I turned I saw seven gold lampstands, ¹³ and among the lampstands was One like the ˙Son of Man, dressed in a long robe and with a gold sash wrapped around His chest. ¹⁴ His head and hair were white like wool—white as snow—and His eyes like a fiery flame. ¹⁵ His feet were like fine bronze as it is fired in a furnace, and His voice like the sound of cascading waters. ¹⁶ He had seven stars in His right hand; a sharp double-edged sword came from His mouth, and His face was shining like the sun at midday.

¹⁷ When I saw Him, I fell at His feet like a dead man. He laid His right hand on me and said, "Don't be afraid! I am the First and the Last, ¹⁸ and the Living One. I was dead, but look—I am alive forever and ever, and I hold the keys of death and ˙Hades. ¹⁹ Therefore write what you have seen, what is, and what will take place after this. ²⁰ The ˙secret of the seven stars you saw in My right hand and of the seven gold lampstands is this:

The seven stars are the angels of the seven churches, and the seven lampstands are the seven churches.

2 "Write to the angel of the church in Ephesus:
"The One who holds the seven stars in His right hand and who walks among the seven gold lampstands says: ² I know your works, your labor, and your endurance, and that you cannot tolerate evil. You have tested those who call themselves apostles and are not, and you have found them to be liars. ³ You also possess endurance and have tolerated many things because of My name and have not grown weary. ⁴ But I have this against you: You have abandoned the love you had at first. ⁵ Remember then how far you have fallen; repent, and do the works you did at first. Otherwise, I will come to you and remove your lampstand from its place—unless you repent. ⁶ Yet you do have this: You hate the practices of the Nicolaitans, which I also hate.

⁷ "Anyone who has an ear should listen to what the Spirit says to the churches. I will give the victor the right to eat from the tree of life, which is in God's paradise.

⁸ "Write to the angel of the church in Smyrna:
"The First and the Last, the One who was dead and came to life, says: ⁹ I know your affliction and poverty, yet you are rich. I know the slander of those who say they are Jews and are not, but are a ˙synagogue of Satan. ¹⁰ Don't be afraid of what you are about to suffer. Look, the Devil is about to throw some of you into prison to test you, and you will have affliction for 10 days. Be faithful until death, and I will give you the crown of life.

¹¹ "Anyone who has an ear should listen to what the Spirit says to the churches. The victor will never be harmed by the second death.

¹² "Write to the angel of the church in Pergamum:
"The One who has the sharp, double-edged sword says: ¹³ I know where you live—where Satan's throne is! And you are holding on to My name and did not deny your faith in Me, even in the days of Antipas, My faithful witness who was killed among you, where Satan lives. ¹⁴ But I have a few things against you. You have some there who hold to the teaching of Balaam, who taught Balak to place a stumbling block in front of the Israelites: to eat meat sacrificed to idols and to commit sexual immorality. ¹⁵ In the same way, you also have those who hold to the teaching of the Nicolaitans. ¹⁶ Therefore repent! Otherwise, I will come to you quickly and fight against them with the sword of My mouth.

¹⁷ "Anyone who has an ear should listen to what the Spirit says to the churches. I will give the victor some of the hidden manna. I will also give him a white stone, and on the stone a new name is inscribed that no one knows except the one who receives it.

¹⁸ "Write to the angel of the church in Thyatira:

"The Son of God, the One whose eyes are like a fiery flame and whose feet are like fine bronze, says: [19] I know your works—your love, faithfulness, service, and endurance. Your last works are greater than the first. [20] But I have this against you: You tolerate the woman Jezebel, who calls herself a prophetess and teaches and deceives My *slaves to commit sexual immorality and to eat meat sacrificed to idols. [21] I gave her time to repent, but she does not want to repent of her sexual immorality. [22] Look! I will throw her into a sickbed and those who commit adultery with her into great tribulation, unless they repent of her practices. [23] I will kill her children with the plague. Then all the churches will know that I am the One who examines minds and hearts, and I will give to each of you according to your works. [24] I say to the rest of you in Thyatira, who do not hold this teaching, who haven't known the deep things of Satan—as they say—I do not put any other burden on you. [25] But hold on to what you have until I come. [26] The one who is victorious and keeps My works to the end: I will give him authority over the nations—

[27]   and he will shepherd them
       with an iron scepter;
     he will shatter them like pottery—

just as I have received this from My Father. [28] I will also give him the morning star.

[29] "Anyone who has an ear should listen to what the Spirit says to the churches.

3 "Write to the angel of the church in Sardis:
    "The One who has the seven spirits of God and the seven stars says: I know your works; you have a reputation for being alive, but you are dead. [2] Be alert and strengthen what remains, which is about to die, for I have not found your works complete before My God. [3] Remember, therefore, what you have received and heard; keep it, and repent. But if you are not alert, I will come like a thief, and you have no idea at what hour I will come against you. [4] But you have a few people in Sardis who have not defiled their clothes, and they will walk with Me in white, because they are worthy. [5] In the same way, the victor will be dressed in white clothes, and I will never erase his name from the book of life but will acknowledge his name before My Father and before His angels.

[6] "Anyone who has an ear should listen to what the Spirit says to the churches.

[7] "Write to the angel of the church in Philadelphia:
    "The Holy One, the True One, the One who has the key of David, who opens and no one will close, and closes and no one opens says: [8] I know your works. Because you have limited strength, have kept My word, and have not denied My name, look, I have placed before you an open door that no one is able to close. [9] Take note! I will make those from the *synagogue of Satan, who claim to be Jews and are not, but are lying—note this—I will make them come and bow down at your feet, and they will know that I have loved you. [10] Because you have kept My command to endure, I will also keep you from the hour of testing that is going to come over the whole world to test those who live on the earth. [11] I am coming quickly. Hold on to what you have, so that no one takes your crown. [12] The victor: I will make him a pillar in the sanctuary of My God, and he will never go out again. I will write on him the name of My God and the name of the city of My God—the new Jerusalem, which comes down out of heaven from My God—and My new name.

[13] "Anyone who has an ear should listen to what the Spirit says to the churches.

[14] "Write to the angel of the church in Laodicea:
    "The *Amen, the faithful and true Witness, the Originator of God's creation says: [15] I know your works, that you are neither cold nor hot. I wish that you were cold or hot. [16] So, because you are lukewarm, and neither hot nor cold, I am going to vomit you out of My mouth. [17] Because you say, 'I'm rich; I have become wealthy and need nothing,' and you don't know that you are wretched, pitiful, poor, blind, and naked, [18] I advise you to buy from Me gold refined in the fire so that you may be rich, white clothes so that you may be dressed and your shameful nakedness not be exposed, and ointment to spread on your eyes so that you may see. [19] As many as I love, I rebuke and discipline. So be committed and repent. [20] Listen! I stand at the door and knock. If anyone hears My voice and opens the door, I will come in to him and have dinner with him, and he with Me. [21] The victor: I will give him the right to sit with Me on My throne, just as I also won the victory and sat down with My Father on His throne.

[22] "Anyone who has an ear should listen to what the Spirit says to the churches."

4 After this I looked, and there in heaven was an open door. The first voice that I had heard speaking to me like a trumpet said, "Come up here, and I will show you what must take place after this."

[2] Immediately I was in the Spirit, and a throne was set there in heaven. One was seated on the throne, [3] and the One seated looked like jasper and carnelian stone. A rainbow that looked like an emerald surrounded the throne. [4] Around that throne were 24 thrones, and on the thrones sat 24 elders dressed in white clothes, with gold crowns on their heads. [5] Flashes of lightning and rumblings of thunder came from the throne. Seven fiery torches were burning before the throne, which are the seven spirits of God. [6] Something like a sea of glass, similar to crystal, was also before the throne. Four living creatures covered with eyes in front and in back were in the middle and around the throne. [7] The first living creature was like a lion; the second living creature was like a calf; the third living creature had a face like a man; and the fourth living creature was like a flying eagle. [8] Each of the four living creatures had six wings; they were covered with eyes around and inside. Day and night they never stop, saying:

       Holy, holy, holy,
       Lord God, the Almighty,
       who was, who is, and who is coming.

[9] Whenever the living creatures give glory, honor, and thanks to the One seated on the throne, the One who lives forever and ever, [10] the 24 elders fall down before the One seated on the throne, worship the One who lives forever and ever, cast their crowns before the throne, and say:

[11]   Our Lord and God,
       You are worthy to receive
       glory and honor and power,
       because You have created all things,
       and because of Your will
       they exist and were created.

5 Then I saw in the right hand of the One seated on the throne a scroll with writing on the inside and on the back, sealed with seven seals. [2] I also saw a mighty angel proclaiming in a loud voice, "Who is worthy to open the scroll and break its seals?" [3] But no

one in heaven or on earth or under the earth was able to open the scroll or even to look in it. [4]And I cried and cried because no one was found worthy to open the scroll or even to look in it.

[5]Then one of the elders said to me, "Stop crying. Look! The Lion from the tribe of Judah, the Root of David, has been victorious so that He may open the scroll and its seven seals." [6]Then I saw One like a slaughtered lamb standing between the throne and the four living creatures and among the elders. He had seven horns and seven eyes, which are the seven spirits of God sent into all the earth. [7]He came and took the scroll out of the right hand of the One seated on the throne.

[8]When He took the scroll, the four living creatures and the 24 elders fell down before the Lamb. Each one had a harp and gold bowls filled with incense, which are the prayers of the *saints. [9]And they sang a new song:

> You are worthy to take the scroll
> and to open its seals,
> because You were slaughtered,
> and You *redeemed people
> for God by Your blood
> from every tribe and language
> and people and nation.
> [10] You made them a kingdom
> and priests to our God,
> and they will reign on the earth.

[11]Then I looked and heard the voice of many angels around the throne, and also of the living creatures and of the elders. Their number was countless thousands, plus thousands of thousands. [12]They said with a loud voice:

> The Lamb who was slaughtered is worthy
> to receive power and riches
> and wisdom and strength
> and honor and glory and blessing!

[13]I heard every creature in heaven, on earth, under the earth, on the sea, and everything in them say:

> Blessing and honor and glory and dominion
> to the One seated on the throne,
> and to the Lamb, forever and ever!

[14]The four living creatures said, "'Amen," and the elders fell down and worshiped.

6 Then I saw the Lamb open one of the seven seals, and I heard one of the four living creatures say with a voice like thunder, "Come!" [2]I looked, and there was a white horse. The horseman on it had a bow; a crown was given to him, and he went out as a victor to conquer.

[3]When He opened the second seal, I heard the second living creature say, "Come!" [4]Then another horse went out, a fiery red one, and its horseman was empowered to take peace from the earth, so that people would slaughter one another. And a large sword was given to him.

[5]When He opened the third seal, I heard the third living creature say, "Come!" And I looked, and there was a black horse. The horseman on it had a set of scales in his hand. [6]Then I heard something like a voice among the four living creatures say, "A quart of wheat for a *denarius, and three quarts of barley for a denarius—but do not harm the olive oil and the wine."

[7]When He opened the fourth seal, I heard the voice of the fourth living creature say, "Come!" [8]And I looked, and there was a pale green horse. The horse-

man on it was named Death, and *Hades was following after him. Authority was given to them over a fourth of the earth, to kill by the sword, by famine, by plague, and by the wild animals of the earth.

[9]When He opened the fifth seal, I saw under the altar the people slaughtered because of God's word and the testimony they had. [10]They cried out with a loud voice: "Lord, the One who is holy and true, how long until You judge and avenge our blood from those who live on the earth?" [11]So a white robe was given to each of them, and they were told to rest a little while longer until the number would be completed of their fellow slaves and their *brothers, who were going to be killed just as they had been.

[12]Then I saw Him open the sixth seal. A violent earthquake occurred; the sun turned black like *sackcloth made of goat hair; the entire moon became like blood; [13]the stars of heaven fell to the earth as a fig tree drops its unripe figs when shaken by a high wind; [14]the sky separated like a scroll being rolled up; and every mountain and island was moved from its place.

[15]Then the kings of the earth, the nobles, the military commanders, the rich, the powerful, and every *slave and free person hid in the caves and among the rocks of the mountains. [16]And they said to the mountains and to the rocks, "Fall on us and hide us from the face of the One seated on the throne and from the wrath of the Lamb, [17]because the great day of Their wrath has come! And who is able to stand?"

7 After this I saw four angels standing at the four corners of the earth, restraining the four winds of the earth so that no wind could blow on the earth or on the sea or on any tree. [2]Then I saw another angel, who had the seal of the living God rise up from the east. He cried out in a loud voice to the four angels who were empowered to harm the earth and the sea: [3]"Don't harm the earth or the sea or the trees until we seal the *slaves of our God on their foreheads." [4]And I heard the number of those who were sealed:

> 144,000 sealed from every tribe
> of the Israelites:
> [5] 12,000 sealed from the tribe of Judah,
> 12,000 from the tribe of Reuben,
> 12,000 from the tribe of Gad,
> [6] 12,000 from the tribe of Asher,
> 12,000 from the tribe of Naphtali,
> 12,000 from the tribe of Manasseh,
> [7] 12,000 from the tribe of Simeon,
> 12,000 from the tribe of Levi,
> 12,000 from the tribe of Issachar,
> [8] 12,000 from the tribe of Zebulun,
> 12,000 from the tribe of Joseph,
> 12,000 sealed from the tribe of Benjamin.

[9]After this I looked, and there was a vast multitude from every nation, tribe, people, and language, which no one could number, standing before the throne and before the Lamb. They were robed in white with palm branches in their hands. [10]And they cried out in a loud voice:

> Salvation belongs to our God,
> who is seated on the throne,
> and to the Lamb!

[11]All the angels stood around the throne, the elders, and the four living creatures, and they fell facedown before the throne and worshiped God, [12]saying:

> *Amen! Blessing and glory and wisdom
> and thanksgiving and honor

and power and strength
be to our God forever and ever. Amen.

¹³Then one of the elders asked me, "Who are these people robed in white, and where did they come from?"

¹⁴I said to him, "Sir, you know."

Then he told me:

These are the ones coming out
of the great tribulation.
They washed their robes and made them white
in the blood of the Lamb.

¹⁵ For this reason they are before the throne
of God,
and they serve Him day and night
in His sanctuary.
The One seated on the throne
will shelter them:

¹⁶ They will no longer hunger;
they will no longer thirst;
the sun will no longer strike them,
nor will any heat.

¹⁷ For the Lamb who is at the center
of the throne
will shepherd them;
He will guide them to springs of living waters,
and God will wipe away every tear
from their eyes.

8 When He opened the seventh seal, there was silence in heaven for about half an hour. ²Then I saw the seven angels who stand in the presence of God; seven trumpets were given to them. ³Another angel, with a gold incense burner, came and stood at the altar. He was given a large amount of incense to offer with the prayers of all the •saints on the gold altar in front of the throne. ⁴The smoke of the incense, with the prayers of the saints, went up in the presence of God from the angel's hand. ⁵The angel took the incense burner, filled it with fire from the altar, and hurled it to the earth; there were rumblings of thunder, flashes of lightning, and an earthquake. ⁶And the seven angels who had the seven trumpets prepared to blow them.

⁷The first angel blew his trumpet, and hail and fire, mixed with blood, were hurled to the earth. So a third of the earth was burned up, a third of the trees were burned up, and all the green grass was burned up.

⁸The second angel blew his trumpet, and something like a great mountain ablaze with fire was hurled into the sea. So a third of the sea became blood, ⁹a third of the living creatures in the sea died, and a third of the ships were destroyed.

¹⁰The third angel blew his trumpet, and a great star, blazing like a torch, fell from heaven. It fell on a third of the rivers and springs of water. ¹¹The name of the star is Wormwood. So, many of the people died from the waters, because they had been made bitter.

¹²The fourth angel blew his trumpet, and a third of the sun was struck, a third of the moon, and a third of the stars, so that a third of them were darkened. A third of the day was without light, and the night as well.

¹³I looked again and heard an eagle flying high overhead, crying out in a loud voice, "Woe! Woe! Woe to those who live on the earth, because of the remaining trumpet blasts that the three angels are about to sound!"

9 The fifth angel blew his trumpet, and I saw a star that had fallen from heaven to earth. The key to the shaft of the •abyss was given to him. ²He opened the shaft of the abyss, and smoke came up out of the shaft like smoke from a great furnace so that the sun and the air were darkened by the smoke from the shaft. ³Then locusts came out of the smoke on to the earth, and power was given to them like the power that scorpions have on the earth. ⁴They were told not to harm the grass of the earth, or any green plant, or any tree, but only people who do not have God's seal on their foreheads. ⁵They were not permitted to kill them but were to torment them for five months; their torment is like the torment caused by a scorpion when it strikes a man. ⁶In those days people will seek death and will not find it; they will long to die, but death will flee from them.

⁷The appearance of the locusts was like horses equipped for battle. Something like gold crowns was on their heads; their faces were like men's faces; ⁸they had hair like women's hair; their teeth were like lions' teeth; ⁹they had chests like iron breastplates; the sound of their wings was like the sound of chariots with many horses rushing into battle; ¹⁰and they had tails with stingers like scorpions, so that with their tails they had the power to harm people for five months. ¹¹They had as their king the angel of the abyss; his name in Hebrew is •Abaddon, and in Greek he has the name Apollyon. ¹²The first woe has passed. There are still two more woes to come after this.

¹³The sixth angel blew his trumpet. From the four horns of the gold altar that is before God, I heard a voice ¹⁴say to the sixth angel who had the trumpet, "Release the four angels bound at the great river Euphrates." ¹⁵So the four angels who were prepared for the hour, day, month, and year were released to kill a third of the human race. ¹⁶The number of mounted troops was 200 million; I heard their number. ¹⁷This is how I saw the horses in my vision: The horsemen had breastplates that were fiery red, hyacinth blue, and sulfur yellow. The heads of the horses were like lions' heads, and from their mouths came fire, smoke, and sulfur. ¹⁸A third of the human race was killed by these three plagues—by the fire, the smoke, and the sulfur that came from their mouths. ¹⁹For the power of the horses is in their mouths and in their tails, for their tails, which resemble snakes, have heads, and they inflict injury with them.

²⁰The rest of the people, who were not killed by these plagues, did not repent of the works of their hands to stop worshiping demons and idols of gold, silver, bronze, stone, and wood, which are not able to see, hear, or walk. ²¹And they did not repent of their murders, their sorceries, their sexual immorality, or their thefts.

10 Then I saw another mighty angel coming down from heaven, surrounded by a cloud, with a rainbow over his head. His face was like the sun, his legs were like fiery pillars, ²and he had a little scroll opened in his hand. He put his right foot on the sea, his left on the land, ³and he cried out with a loud voice like a roaring lion. When he cried out, the seven thunders spoke with their voices. ⁴And when the seven thunders spoke, I was about to write. Then I heard a voice from heaven, saying, "Seal up what the seven thunders said, and do not write it down!"

⁵Then the angel that I had seen standing on the sea

and on the land raised his right hand to heaven. ⁶He swore an oath by the One who lives forever and ever, who created heaven and what is in it, the earth and what is in it, and the sea and what is in it: "There will no longer be an interval of time, ⁷but in the days of the sound of the seventh angel, when he will blow his trumpet, then God's •hidden plan will be completed, as He announced to His servants the prophets."

⁸Now the voice that I heard from heaven spoke to me again and said, "Go, take the scroll that lies open in the hand of the angel who is standing on the sea and on the land."

⁹So I went to the angel and asked him to give me the little scroll. He said to me, "Take and eat it; it will be bitter in your stomach, but it will be as sweet as honey in your mouth."

¹⁰Then I took the little scroll from the angel's hand and ate it. It was as sweet as honey in my mouth, but when I ate it, my stomach became bitter. ¹¹And I was told, "You must prophesy again about many peoples, nations, languages, and kings."

11 Then I was given a measuring reed like a rod, with these words: "Go and measure God's sanctuary and the altar, and count those who worship there. ²But exclude the courtyard outside the sanctuary. Don't measure it, because it is given to the nations, and they will trample the holy city for 42 months. ³I will empower my two witnesses, and they will prophesy for 1,260 days, dressed in •sackcloth." ⁴These are the two olive trees and the two lampstands that stand before the Lord of the earth. ⁵If anyone wants to harm them, fire comes from their mouths and consumes their enemies; if anyone wants to harm them, he must be killed in this way. ⁶These men have the power to close up the sky so that it does not rain during the days of their prophecy. They also have power over the waters to turn them into blood and to strike the earth with every plague whenever they want.

⁷When they finish their testimony, the beast that comes up out of the •abyss will make war with them, conquer them, and kill them. ⁸Their dead bodies will lie in the public square of the great city, which prophetically is called Sodom and Egypt, where also their Lord was crucified. ⁹And representatives from the peoples, tribes, languages, and nations will view their bodies for three and a half days and not permit their bodies to be put into a tomb. ¹⁰Those who live on the earth will gloat over them and celebrate and send gifts to one another because these two prophets brought judgment to those who live on the earth.

¹¹But after 3½ days, the breath of life from God entered them, and they stood on their feet. So great fear fell on those who saw them. ¹²Then they heard a loud voice from heaven saying to them, "Come up here." They went up to heaven in a cloud, while their enemies watched them. ¹³At that moment a violent earthquake took place, a tenth of the city fell, and 7,000 people were killed in the earthquake. The survivors were terrified and gave glory to the God of heaven. ¹⁴The second woe has passed. Take note: The third woe is coming quickly!

¹⁵The seventh angel blew his trumpet, and there were loud voices in heaven saying:

The kingdom of the •world has become
  the kingdom
of our Lord and of His •Messiah,
and He will reign forever and ever!

¹⁶The 24 elders, who were seated before God on their thrones, fell facedown and worshiped God, ¹⁷saying:

We thank You, Lord God, the Almighty,
  who is and who was,
because You have taken Your great power
  and have begun to reign.
¹⁸ The nations were angry,
  but Your wrath has come.
The time has come
  for the dead to be judged
and to give the reward
  to Your servants the prophets,
  to the •saints, and to those who fear
    Your name,
  both small and great,
and the time has come to destroy
  those who destroy the earth.

¹⁹God's sanctuary in heaven was opened, and the ark of His covenant appeared in His sanctuary. There were flashes of lightning, rumblings of thunder, an earthquake, and severe hail.

12 A great sign appeared in heaven: a woman clothed with the sun, with the moon under her feet and a crown of 12 stars on her head. ²She was pregnant and cried out in labor and agony as she was about to give birth. ³Then another sign appeared in heaven: There was a great fiery red dragon having seven heads and 10 horns, and on his heads were seven diadems. ⁴His tail swept away a third of the stars in heaven and hurled them to the earth. And the dragon stood in front of the woman who was about to give birth, so that when she did give birth he might devour her child. ⁵But she gave birth to a Son—a male who is going to shepherd all nations with an iron scepter—and her child was caught up to God and to His throne. ⁶The woman fled into the wilderness, where she had a place prepared by God, to be fed there for 1,260 days.

⁷Then war broke out in heaven: Michael and his angels fought against the dragon. The dragon and his angels also fought, ⁸but he could not prevail, and there was no place for them in heaven any longer. ⁹So the great dragon was thrown out—the ancient serpent, who is called the Devil and Satan, the one who deceives the whole world. He was thrown to earth, and his angels with him.

¹⁰Then I heard a loud voice in heaven say:

The salvation and the power
  and the kingdom of our God
  and the authority of His •Messiah
have now come,
  because the accuser of our •brothers
  has been thrown out:
the one who accuses them
  before our God day and night.
¹¹ They conquered him
  by the blood of the Lamb
  and by the word of their testimony,
  for they did not love their lives
    in the face of death.
¹² Therefore rejoice, you heavens,
  and you who dwell in them!
Woe to the earth and the sea,
  for the Devil has come down to you
    with great fury,
  because he knows he has a short time.

¹³When the dragon saw that he had been thrown to earth, he persecuted the woman who gave birth to

the male child. [14] The woman was given two wings of a great eagle, so that she could fly from the serpent's presence to her place in the wilderness, where she was fed for a time, times, and half a time. [15] From his mouth the serpent spewed water like a river flowing after the woman, to sweep her away in a torrent. [16] But the earth helped the woman. The earth opened its mouth and swallowed up the river that the dragon had spewed from his mouth. [17] So the dragon was furious with the woman and left to wage war against the rest of her offspring—those who keep God's commands and have the testimony about Jesus. [18] He stood on the sand of the sea.

13 And I saw a beast coming up out of the sea. He had 10 horns and seven heads. On his horns were 10 diadems, and on his heads were blasphemous names. [2] The beast I saw was like a leopard, his feet were like a bear's, and his mouth was like a lion's mouth. The dragon gave him his power, his throne, and great authority. [3] One of his heads appeared to be fatally wounded, but his fatal wound was healed. The whole earth was amazed and followed the beast. [4] They worshiped the dragon because he gave authority to the beast. And they worshiped the beast, saying, "Who is like the beast? Who is able to wage war against him?"

[5] A mouth was given to him to speak boasts and blasphemies. He was also given authority to act for 42 months. [6] He began to speak blasphemies against God: to blaspheme His name and His dwelling—those who dwell in heaven. [7] And he was permitted to wage war against the *saints and to conquer them. He was also given authority over every tribe, people, language, and nation. [8] All those who live on the earth will worship him, everyone whose name was not written from the foundation of the world in the book of life of the Lamb who was slaughtered.

[9] If anyone has an ear, he should listen:
[10]   If anyone is destined for captivity,
         into captivity he goes.
       If anyone is to be killed with a sword,
         with a sword he will be killed.
This demands the perseverance and faith of the saints.

[11] Then I saw another beast coming up out of the earth; he had two horns like a lamb, but he sounded like a dragon. [12] He exercises all the authority of the first beast on his behalf and compels the earth and those who live on it to worship the first beast, whose fatal wound was healed. [13] He also performs great signs, even causing fire to come down from heaven to earth in front of people. [14] He deceives those who live on the earth because of the signs that he is permitted to perform on behalf of the beast, telling those who live on the earth to make an image of the beast who had the sword wound and yet lived. [15] He was permitted to give a spirit to the image of the beast, so that the image of the beast could both speak and cause whoever would not worship the image of the beast to be killed. [16] And he requires everyone—small and great, rich and poor, free and *slave—to be given a mark on his right hand or on his forehead, [17] so that no one can buy or sell unless he has the mark: the beast's name or the number of his name.

[18] Here is wisdom: The one who has understanding must calculate the number of the beast, because it is the number of a man. His number is 666.

14 Then I looked, and there on Mount *Zion stood the Lamb, and with Him were 144,000 who had His name and His Father's name written on their fore-

heads. [2] I heard a sound from heaven like the sound of cascading waters and like the rumbling of loud thunder. The sound I heard was also like harpists playing on their harps. [3] They sang a new song before the throne and before the four living creatures and the elders, but no one could learn the song except the 144,000 who had been *redeemed from the earth. [4] These are the ones not defiled with women, for they have kept their virginity. These are the ones who follow the Lamb wherever He goes. They were redeemed from the human race as the *firstfruits for God and the Lamb. [5] No lie was found in their mouths; they are blameless.

[6] Then I saw another angel flying high overhead, having the eternal gospel to announce to the inhabitants of the earth—to every nation, tribe, language, and people. [7] He spoke with a loud voice: "Fear God and give Him glory, because the hour of His judgment has come. Worship the Maker of heaven and earth, the sea and springs of water."

[8] A second angel followed, saying: "It has fallen, Babylon the Great has fallen, who made all nations drink the wine of her sexual immorality, which brings wrath."

[9] And a third angel followed them and spoke with a loud voice: "If anyone worships the beast and his image and receives a mark on his forehead or on his hand, [10] he will also drink the wine of God's wrath, which is mixed full strength in the cup of His anger. He will be tormented with fire and sulfur in the sight of the holy angels and in the sight of the Lamb, [11] and the smoke of their torment will go up forever and ever. There is no rest day or night for those who worship the beast and his image, or anyone who receives the mark of his name. [12] This demands the perseverance of the *saints, who keep God's commands and their faith in Jesus."

[13] Then I heard a voice from heaven saying, "Write: The dead who die in the Lord from now on are blessed."

"Yes," says the Spirit, "let them rest from their labors, for their works follow them!"

[14] When I looked, and there was a white cloud, and One like the Son of Man was seated on the cloud, with a gold crown on His head and a sharp sickle in His hand. [15] Another angel came out of the sanctuary, crying out in a loud voice to the One who was seated on the cloud, "Use your sickle and reap, for the time to reap has come, since the harvest of the earth is ripe." [16] So the One seated on the cloud swung His sickle over the earth, and the earth was harvested.

[17] Then another angel who also had a sharp sickle came out of the sanctuary in heaven. [18] Yet another angel, who had authority over fire, came from the altar, and he called with a loud voice to the one who had the sharp sickle, "Use your sharp sickle and gather the clusters of grapes from earth's vineyard, because its grapes have ripened." [19] So the angel swung his sickle toward earth and gathered the grapes from earth's vineyard, and he threw them into the great winepress of God's wrath. [20] Then the press was trampled outside the city, and blood flowed out of the press up to the horses' bridles for about 180 miles.

15 Then I saw another great and awe-inspiring sign in heaven: seven angels with the seven last plagues, for with them, God's wrath will be completed. [2] I also saw something like a sea of glass mixed with fire, and those who had won the victory over the beast, his image, and the number of his name, were standing on the sea of glass with harps from God. [3] They sang

the song of God's servant Moses and the song of the Lamb:

> Great and awe-inspiring are Your works,
> Lord God, the Almighty;
> righteous and true are Your ways,
> King of the Nations.
> ⁴ Lord, who will not fear
> and glorify Your name?
> Because You alone are holy,
> for all the nations will come
> and worship before You
> because Your righteous acts
> have been revealed.

⁵ After this I looked, and the heavenly sanctuary—the tabernacle of testimony—was opened. ⁶ Out of the sanctuary came the seven angels with the seven plagues, dressed in *clean, bright linen, with gold sashes wrapped around their chests. ⁷ One of the four living creatures gave the seven angels seven gold bowls filled with the wrath of God who lives forever and ever. ⁸ Then the sanctuary was filled with smoke from God's glory and from His power, and no one could enter the sanctuary until the seven plagues of the seven angels were completed.

16 Then I heard a loud voice from the sanctuary saying to the seven angels, "Go and pour out the seven bowls of God's wrath on the earth." ² The first went and poured out his bowl on the earth, and severely painful sores broke out on the people who had the mark of the beast and who worshiped his image.

³ The second poured out his bowl into the sea. It turned to blood like a dead man's, and all life in the sea died.

⁴ The third poured out his bowl into the rivers and the springs of water, and they became blood. ⁵ I heard the angel of the waters say:

> You are righteous,
> who is and who was, the Holy One,
> for You have decided these things.
> ⁶ Because they poured out
> the blood of the *saints and the prophets,
> You also gave them blood to drink;
> they deserve it!

⁷ Then I heard someone from the altar say:

> Yes, Lord God, the Almighty,
> true and righteous are Your judgments.

⁸ The fourth poured out his bowl on the sun. He was given the power to burn people with fire, ⁹ and people were burned by the intense heat. So they blasphemed the name of God, who had the power over these plagues, and they did not repent and give Him glory.

¹⁰ The fifth poured out his bowl on the throne of the beast, and his kingdom was plunged into darkness. People gnawed their tongues because of their pain ¹¹ and blasphemed the God of heaven because of their pains and their sores, yet they did not repent of their actions.

¹² The sixth poured out his bowl on the great river Euphrates, and its water was dried up to prepare the way for the kings from the east. ¹³ Then I saw three unclean spirits like frogs coming from the dragon's mouth, from the beast's mouth, and from the mouth of the false prophet. ¹⁴ For they are spirits of demons performing signs, who travel to the kings of the whole world to assemble them for the battle of the great day of God, the Almighty.

¹⁵ "Look, I am coming like a thief. The one who is alert and remains clothed so that he may not go around naked and people see his shame is blessed."

¹⁶ So they assembled them at the place called in Hebrew, Armagedon.

¹⁷ Then the seventh poured out his bowl into the air, and a loud voice came out of the sanctuary from the throne, saying, "It is done!" ¹⁸ There were flashes of lightning and rumblings of thunder. And a severe earthquake occurred like no other since man has been on the earth—so great was the quake. ¹⁹ The great city split into three parts, and the cities of the nations fell. Babylon the Great was remembered in God's presence; He gave her the cup filled with the wine of His fierce anger. ²⁰ Every island fled, and the mountains disappeared. ²¹ Enormous hailstones, each weighing about 100 pounds, fell from the sky on people, and they blasphemed God for the plague of hail because that plague was extremely severe.

17 Then one of the seven angels who had the seven bowls came and spoke with me: "Come, I will show you the judgment of the notorious prostitute who sits on many waters. ² The kings of the earth committed sexual immorality with her, and those who live on the earth became drunk on the wine of her sexual immorality." ³ So he carried me away in the Spirit to a desert. I saw a woman sitting on a scarlet beast that was covered with blasphemous names and had seven heads and 10 horns. ⁴ The woman was dressed in purple and scarlet, adorned with gold, precious stones, and pearls. She had a gold cup in her hand filled with everything vile and with the impurities of her prostitution. ⁵ On her forehead a cryptic name was written:

BABYLON THE GREAT
THE MOTHER OF PROSTITUTES
AND OF THE VILE THINGS OF THE EARTH.

⁶ Then I saw that the woman was drunk on the blood of the *saints and on the blood of the witnesses to Jesus. When I saw her, I was greatly astonished.

⁷ Then the angel said to me, "Why are you astonished? I will tell you the *secret meaning of the woman and of the beast, with the seven heads and the 10 horns, that carries her. ⁸ The beast that you saw was, and is not, and is about to come up from the *abyss and go to destruction. Those who live on the earth whose names have not been written in the book of life from the foundation of the world will be astonished when they see the beast that was, and is not, and will be present again.

⁹ "Here is the mind with wisdom: The seven heads are seven mountains on which the woman is seated. ¹⁰ They are also seven kings: Five have fallen, one is, the other has not yet come, and when he comes, he must remain for a little while. ¹¹ The beast that was and is not, is himself an eighth king, yet he belongs to the seven and is going to destruction. ¹² The 10 horns you saw are 10 kings who have not yet received a kingdom, but they will receive authority as kings with the beast for one hour. ¹³ These have one purpose, and they give their power and authority to the beast. ¹⁴ These will make war against the Lamb, but the Lamb will conquer them because He is Lord of lords and King of kings. Those with Him are called, chosen, and faithful."

¹⁵ He also said to me, "The waters you saw, where the prostitute was seated, are peoples, multitudes, nations, and languages. ¹⁶ The 10 horns you saw, and the beast, will hate the prostitute. They will make her desolate and naked, devour her flesh, and burn her up with fire. ¹⁷ For God has put it into their hearts to carry out His

plan by having one purpose and to give their kingdom to the beast until God's words are accomplished. [18] And the woman you saw is the great city that has an empire over the kings of the earth."

18 After this I saw another angel with great authority coming down from heaven, and the earth was illuminated by his splendor. [2] He cried in a mighty voice:

It has fallen,
Babylon the Great has fallen!
She has become a dwelling for demons,
a haunt for every *unclean spirit,
a haunt for every unclean bird,
and a haunt for every unclean
　　and despicable beast.
[3]　For all the nations have drunk
the wine of her sexual immorality,
which brings wrath.
The kings of the earth
have committed sexual immorality with her,
and the merchants of the earth
have grown wealthy from her excessive luxury.

[4] Then I heard another voice from heaven:

Come out of her, My people,
so that you will not share in her sins
or receive any of her plagues.
[5]　For her sins are piled up to heaven,
and God has remembered her crimes.
[6]　Pay her back the way she also paid,
and double it according to her works.
In the cup in which she mixed,
mix a double portion for her.
[7]　As much as she glorified herself
　　and lived luxuriously,
give her that much torment and grief,
for she says in her heart,
"I sit as a queen;
I am not a widow,
and I will never see grief."
[8]　For this reason her plagues will come
　　in one day—
death and grief and famine.
She will be burned up with fire,
because the Lord God who judges her
is mighty.

[9] The kings of the earth who have committed sexual immorality and lived luxuriously with her will weep and mourn over her when they see the smoke of her burning. [10] They will stand far off in fear of her torment, saying:

Woe, woe, the great city,
Babylon, the mighty city!
For in a single hour
your judgment has come.

[11] The merchants of the earth will also weep and mourn over her, because no one buys their merchandise any longer— [12] merchandise of gold, silver, precious stones, and pearls; fine fabrics of linen, purple, silk, and scarlet; all kinds of fragrant wood products; objects of ivory; objects of expensive wood, brass, iron, and marble; [13] cinnamon, spice, incense, myrrh, and frankincense; wine, olive oil, fine wheat flour, and grain; cattle and sheep; horses and carriages; and slaves and human lives.

[14]　The fruit you craved has left you.
All your splendid and glamorous things
　　are gone;
they will never find them again.

[15] The merchants of these things, who became rich from her, will stand far off in fear of her torment, weeping and mourning, [16] saying:

Woe, woe, the great city,
dressed in fine linen, purple, and scarlet,
adorned with gold, precious stones,
　　and pearls,
[17]　for in a single hour
such fabulous wealth was destroyed!

And every shipmaster, seafarer, the sailors, and all who do business by sea, stood far off [18] as they watched the smoke from her burning and kept crying out: "Who is like the great city?" [19] They threw dust on their heads and kept crying out, weeping, and mourning:

Woe, woe, the great city,
where all those who have ships
　　on the sea
became rich from her wealth,
for in a single hour she was destroyed.
[20]　Rejoice over her, heaven,
and you *saints, apostles, and prophets,
because God has executed your judgment
　　on her!

[21] Then a mighty angel picked up a stone like a large millstone and threw it into the sea, saying:

In this way, Babylon the great city
will be thrown down violently
and never be found again.
[22]　The sound of harpists, musicians,
flutists, and trumpeters
will never be heard
　　in you again;
no craftsman of any trade
will ever be found in you again;
the sound of a mill
will never be heard in you again;
[23]　the light of a lamp
will never shine in you again;
and the voice of a groom and bride
will never be heard in you again.
All this will happen
because your merchants
were the nobility of the earth,
because all the nations were deceived
by your sorcery,
[24]　and the blood of prophets and saints,
and of all those slaughtered on earth,
was found in you.

19 After this I heard something like the loud voice of a vast multitude in heaven, saying:

*Hallelujah!
Salvation, glory, and power belong
　　to our God,
[2]　because His judgments are true and righteous,
because He has judged
　　the notorious prostitute
who corrupted the earth
　　with her sexual immorality;
and He has avenged the blood of His *slaves
that was on her hands.

[3] A second time they said:

Hallelujah!
Her smoke ascends forever and ever!

[4] Then the 24 elders and the four living creatures fell down and worshiped God, who is seated on the throne, saying:

*Amen! Hallelujah!

⁵A voice came from the throne, saying:

Praise our God,
all His slaves, who fear Him,
both small and great!

⁶Then I heard something like the voice of a vast multitude, like the sound of cascading waters, and like the rumbling of loud thunder, saying:

Hallelujah, because our Lord God,
the Almighty,
has begun to reign!

⁷   Let us be glad, rejoice, and give Him glory,
because the marriage of the Lamb has come,
and His wife has prepared herself.

⁸   She was given fine linen to wear, bright
and pure.

For the fine linen represents the righteous acts of the ˙saints.

⁹Then he said to me, "Write: Those invited to the marriage feast of the Lamb are fortunate!" He also said to me, "These words of God are true." ¹⁰Then I fell at his feet to worship him, but he said to me, "Don't do that! I am a fellow slave with you and your ˙brothers who have the testimony about Jesus. Worship God, because the testimony about Jesus is the spirit of prophecy."

¹¹Then I saw heaven opened, and there was a white horse. Its rider is called Faithful and True, and He judges and makes war in righteousness. ¹²His eyes were like a fiery flame, and many crowns were on His head. He had a name written that no one knows except Himself. ¹³He wore a robe stained with blood, and His name is the Word of God. ¹⁴The armies that were in heaven followed Him on white horses, wearing pure white linen. ¹⁵A sharp sword came from His mouth, so that He might strike the nations with it. He will shepherd them with an iron scepter. He will also trample the winepress of the fierce anger of God, the Almighty. ¹⁶And He has a name written on His robe and on His thigh:

KING OF KINGS AND LORD OF LORDS.

¹⁷Then I saw an angel standing on the sun, and he cried out in a loud voice, saying to all the birds flying high overhead, "Come, gather together for the great supper of God, ¹⁸so that you may eat the flesh of kings, the flesh of commanders, the flesh of mighty men, the flesh of horses and of their riders, and the flesh of everyone, both free and slave, small and great."

¹⁹Then I saw the beast, the kings of the earth, and their armies gathered together to wage war against the rider on the horse and against His army. ²⁰But the beast was taken prisoner, and along with him the false prophet, who had performed the signs in his presence. He deceived those who accepted the mark of the beast and those who worshiped his image with these signs. Both of them were thrown alive into the lake of fire that burns with sulfur. ²¹The rest were killed with the sword that came from the mouth of the rider on the horse, and all the birds were filled with their flesh.

20 Then I saw an angel coming down from heaven with the key to the ˙abyss and a great chain in his hand. ²He seized the dragon, that ancient serpent who is the Devil and Satan, and bound him for 1,000 years. ³He threw him into the abyss, closed it, and put a seal on it so that he would no longer deceive the nations until the 1,000 years were completed. After that, he must be released for a short time.

⁴Then I saw thrones, and people seated on them who were given authority to judge. I also saw the people who had been beheaded because of their testimony about Jesus and because of God's word, who had not worshiped the beast or his image, and who had not accepted the mark on their foreheads or their hands. They came to life and reigned with the ˙Messiah for 1,000 years. ⁵The rest of the dead did not come to life until the 1,000 years were completed. This is the first resurrection. ⁶Blessed and holy is the one who shares in the first resurrection! The second death has no power over them, but they will be priests of God and of the Messiah, and they will reign with Him for 1,000 years.

⁷When the 1,000 years are completed, Satan will be released from his prison ⁸and will go out to deceive the nations at the four corners of the earth, Gog and Magog, to gather them for battle. Their number is like the sand of the sea. ⁹They came up over the surface of the earth and surrounded the encampment of the ˙saints, the beloved city. Then fire came down from heaven and consumed them. ¹⁰The Devil who deceived them was thrown into the lake of fire and sulfur where the beast and the false prophet are, and they will be tormented day and night forever and ever.

¹¹Then I saw a great white throne and One seated on it. Earth and heaven fled from His presence, and no place was found for them. ¹²I also saw the dead, the great and the small, standing before the throne, and books were opened. Another book was opened, which is the book of life, and the dead were judged according to their works by what was written in the books. ¹³Then the sea gave up its dead, and Death and ˙Hades gave up their dead; all were judged according to their works. ¹⁴Death and Hades were thrown into the lake of fire. This is the second death, the lake of fire. ¹⁵And anyone not found written in the book of life was thrown into the lake of fire.

21 Then I saw a new heaven and a new earth, for the first heaven and the first earth had passed away, and the sea no longer existed. ²I also saw the Holy City, new Jerusalem, coming down out of heaven from God, prepared like a bride adorned for her husband.

³Then I heard a loud voice from the throne:

Look! God's dwelling is with humanity,
and He will live with them.
They will be His people,
and God Himself will be with them
and be their God.

⁴   He will wipe away every tear from their eyes.
Death will no longer exist;
grief, crying, and pain will exist no longer,
because the previous things have passed away.

⁵Then the One seated on the throne said, "Look! I am making everything new." He also said, "Write, because these words are faithful and true." ⁶And He said to me, "It is done! I am the ˙Alpha and the Omega, the Beginning and the End. I will give water as a gift to the thirsty from the spring of life. ⁷The victor will inherit these things, and I will be his God, and he will be My son. ⁸But the cowards, unbelievers, vile, murderers, sexually immoral, sorcerers, idolaters, and all liars—their share will be in the lake that burns with fire and sulfur, which is the second death."

⁹Then one of the seven angels, who had held the seven bowls filled with the seven last plagues, came and spoke with me: "Come, I will show you the bride, the wife of the Lamb." ¹⁰He then carried me away in the Spirit to a great and high mountain and showed me the holy city, Jerusalem, coming down out of heaven from God, ¹¹arrayed with God's glory. Her radi-

ance was like a very precious stone, like a jasper stone, bright as crystal. [12] The city had a massive high wall, with 12 gates. Twelve angels were at the gates; the names of the 12 tribes of Israel's sons were inscribed on the gates. [13] There were three gates on the east, three gates on the north, three gates on the south, and three gates on the west. [14] The city wall had 12 foundations, and the 12 names of the Lamb's 12 apostles were on the foundations.

[15] The one who spoke with me had a gold measuring rod to measure the city, its gates, and its wall. [16] The city is laid out in a square; its length and width are the same. He measured the city with the rod at 12,000 *stadia.* Its length, width, and height are equal. [17] Then he measured its wall, 144 *cubits according to human measurement, which the angel used. [18] The building material of its wall was jasper, and the city was pure gold like clear glass.

[19] The foundations of the city wall were adorned with every kind of precious stone:

> the first foundation jasper,
> the second sapphire,
> the third chalcedony,
> the fourth emerald,
> [20] the fifth sardonyx,
> the sixth carnelian,
> the seventh chrysolite,
> the eighth beryl,
> the ninth topaz,
> the tenth chrysoprase,
> the eleventh jacinth,
> the twelfth amethyst.

[21] The 12 gates are 12 pearls; each individual gate was made of a single pearl. The broad street of the city was pure gold, like transparent glass.

[22] I did not see a sanctuary in it, because the Lord God the Almighty and the Lamb are its sanctuary. [23] The city does not need the sun or the moon to shine on it, because God's glory illuminates it, and its lamp is the Lamb. [24] The nations will walk in its light, and the kings of the earth will bring their glory into it. [25] Each day its gates will never close because it will never be night there. [26] They will bring the glory and honor of the nations into it. [27] Nothing profane will ever enter it: no one who does what is vile or false, but only those written in the Lamb's book of life.

22 Then he showed me the river of living water, sparkling like crystal, flowing from the throne of God and of the Lamb [2] down the middle of the broad street of the city. The tree of life was on both sides of the river, bearing 12 kinds of fruit, producing its fruit every month. The leaves of the tree are for healing the nations, [3] and there will no longer be any curse. The throne of God and of the Lamb will be in the city, and His *slaves will serve Him. [4] They will see His face, and His name will be on their foreheads. [5] Night will no longer exist, and people will not need lamplight or sunlight, because the Lord God will give them light. And they will reign forever and ever.

[6] Then he said to me, "These words are faithful and true. And the Lord, the God of the spirits of the prophets, has sent His angel to show His slaves what must quickly take place."

[7] "Look, I am coming quickly! The one who keeps the prophetic words of this book is blessed."

[8] I, John, am the one who heard and saw these things. When I heard and saw them, I fell down to worship at the feet of the angel who had shown them to me. [9] But he said to me, "Don't do that! I am a fellow slave with you, your *brothers the prophets, and those who keep the words of this book. Worship God." [10] He also said to me, "Don't seal the prophetic words of this book, because the time is near. [11] Let the unrighteous go on in unrighteousness; let the filthy go on being made filthy; let the righteous go on in righteousness; and let the holy go on being made holy."

[12] "Look! I am coming quickly, and My reward is with Me to repay each person according to what he has done. [13] I am the *Alpha and the Omega, the First and the Last, the Beginning and the End.

[14] "Blessed are those who wash their robes, so that they may have the right to the tree of life and may enter the city by the gates. [15] Outside are the dogs, the sorcerers, the sexually immoral, the murderers, the idolaters, and everyone who loves and practices lying.

[16] "I, Jesus, have sent My angel to attest these things to you for the churches. I am the Root and the Offspring of David, the Bright Morning Star."

[17] Both the Spirit and the bride say, "Come!" Anyone who hears should say, "Come!" And the one who is thirsty should come. Whoever desires should take the living water as a gift.

[18] I testify to everyone who hears the prophetic words of this book: If anyone adds to them, God will add to him the plagues that are written in this book. [19] And if anyone takes away from the words of this prophetic book, God will take away his share of the tree of life and the holy city, written in this book.

[20] He who testifies about these things says, "Yes, I am coming quickly."

*Amen! Come, Lord Jesus!

[21] The grace of the Lord Jesus be with all the *saints. Amen.

HCSB BULLET NOTES

The HCSB Bullet Notes are one of the unique features of the Holman Christian Standard Bible®. These notes explain frequently used biblical words or terms. These "bullet" words (for example: •abyss) are marked with a bullet only on their first occurrence in a chapter of the biblical text. Other frequently used words, like •gate, are marked with bullets only where the use of the word fits the definitions given below.

Abaddon	A Hebrew word for either the grave or the realm of the dead	asleep	A term used in reference to believers who have died
Abba	The Aramaic word for father	atone/	A theological term for God's
abyss	The bottomless pit or the depths (of the sea); it is the prison for Satan and the demons.	atonement	provision to deal with human sin; in the OT, it primarily means purification. In some contexts forgiveness, pardon, expiation, propitiation, or reconciliation is included. The basis of atonement is substitutionary sacrifice offered in faith. The OT sacrifices were types and shadows of the great and final sacrifice of Jesus on the cross.
acrostic	A device in Hebrew poetry in which each verse begins with a successive letter of the Hebrew alphabet		
advocate	The Greek word *parakletos* means one called alongside to help, counsel, or protect; it is used of the Holy Spirit in Jn and 1Jn.		
Almighty	The Hebrew word is *El Shaddai*; *El* means God, but the meaning of *Shaddai* is disputed; traditionally it is translated "Almighty."	Baal	A fertility god who was the main god of the Canaanite religion and the god of rain and thunderstorms; it is also the Hebrew word meaning "lord," "master," "owner," or "husband."
Alpha and Omega	The first and last letters of the Greek alphabet; it is used to refer to God the Father in Rv 1:8 and 21:6 and to Jesus, God the Son, in Rv 22:13.	Beelzebul	A term of slander, which was variously interpreted "lord of flies," "lord of dung," or "ruler of demons"
Amen	The transliteration of a Hebrew word signifying that something is certain, valid, truthful, or faithful; it is often used at the end of biblical songs, hymns, and prayers.	Bread of the Presence	Bread that was offered in Yahweh's presence, that is, inside His house, not out on the altar (Lv 24:5-9)
annihilate(d)	During periods of war in Canaan and its neighboring countries, this was the destruction of a city, its inhabitants, and their possessions, including livestock.	brother(s)	The Greek word *adelphoi* can be used as a reference to males only or to groups that include both males and females. It is the context of each usage that determines the proper meaning.
Arabah	The section of the Great Rift in Palestine, extending from the Jordan Valley and the Dead Sea to the Gulf of Aqabah; the Hebrew word can also be translated as "plain," referring to any plain or to any part of the Arabah.	burnt offering(s)	Or *holocaust*; an offering completely burned to ashes; it was used in connection with worship, seeking God's favor, expiating sin, or averting judgment.
Asaph	A musician appointed by David to oversee the music used in worship at the Temple; 12 psalms are attributed to Asaph.	cause(s) the downfall of/ cause(s) to sin	The Greek word *skandalizo* has a root meaning of snare or trap but has no real English counterpart.
Asherah(s)/ Asherah pole(s)	A Canaanite fertility goddess who was the mother of the god Baal; also the wooden poles associated with the worship of her	centurion	A Roman officer who commanded about 100 soldiers
Ashtoreth(s)	A Canaanite goddess of fertility, love, and war, who was the daughter of Asherah and consort of Baal; the plural form of her name in Hebrew is *Ashtaroth*.	Cephas	The Aramaic word for rock; it is parallel to the Greek word *petros* from which the English name Peter is derived.
		cherub(im)	A class of winged angels, associated with the throne of God, who function as guardians and who prevented Adam and Eve from returning to the garden of Eden
Asia	A Roman province that is now part of modern Turkey; it did not refer to the modern continent of Asia.	chief priest(s)	A group of Jewish temple officers that included the high priest, captain of the temple, temple overseers, and treasurers

clean	When something is clean, it is holy or acceptable to God. When it is unclean, it is unholy (such as an unclean spirit). The term can be used in a ritual sense to apply to moral standards for living.
company	Or *cohort*; a Roman military unit that numbered as many as 600 men
completely destroy	During periods of war in Canaan and its neighboring countries, this was the destruction of a city, its inhabitants, and their possessions, including livestock.
Counselor	The Greek word *parakletos* means one called alongside to help, counsel, or protect; it is used of the Holy Spirit in Jn and 1Jn.
cubit(s)	An OT measurement of distance that equaled about 18 inches
Cush/Cushite	The lands of the Nile in southern Egypt, including Nubia and Northern Sudan; also the people who lived in that region
Decapolis	Originally, it referred to a federation of 10 Gentile towns east of the Jordan River.
denarius/ denarii	A small silver Roman coin, which was equal to a day's wage for a common laborer
divination	An attempt to foresee future events or discover hidden knowledge by means of physical objects such as water, arrows, flying birds, or animal livers
drink offering(s)	An offering of a specified amount of wine or beer given along with animal sacrifices; it was poured over the sacrifice before it was burned.
engaged	Jewish engagement was a binding agreement that could only be broken by divorce.
ephod	A vest-like garment, extending below the waist and worn under the breastpiece; it was used by both the priests and the high priest.
everyone	Literally *sons of man* or *sons of Adam*
family redeemer	A family member who had certain obligations of marriage, redeeming an estate, and punishment of a wrongdoer
fear(s) God or the Lord/ fear of the Lord/fear Yahweh	No single English word conveys every aspect of the word *fear* in this phrase. The meaning includes worshipful submission, reverential awe, and obedient respect to the covenant-keeping God of Israel.

fellowship sacrifice(s) or offering(s)	An animal offering was given to maintain and strengthen a person's relationship with God. It was not required as a remedy for impurity or sin but was an expression of thanksgiving for various blessings. An important function of this sacrifice was to provide meat for the priests and the participants in the sacrifice; also called the peace offering or the sacrifice of well-being.
firstfruits	The agricultural products harvested first and given to God as an offering with more products to come in later harvests; it is also used as a metaphor for the first people to come to faith or for Jesus, the first person to rise from the dead, or for the Spirit who is given to believers as the first portion (or down payment) of our salvation with more to come in eternity.
gate(s)	The center for community discussions, political meetings, and trying of court cases
Gittith	Perhaps an instrument, musical term, tune from Gath, or song for the grape harvest
God Almighty	The Hebrew word is *El Shaddai*; *El* means God, but the meaning of *Shaddai* is disputed; traditionally it is translated "Almighty."
grain offering(s)	An offering given along with animal sacrifices or given by itself; a portion was burnt and the priests and participant ate the remainder.
guilt/guilty	The liability to be punished for a fault, a sin, an act, or an omission unless there is forgiveness or atonement; the term normally concerns an objective fact, not a subjective feeling.
Hades	The Greek word for the place of the dead; it corresponds to the Hebrew word *Sheol*.
Hallelujah!	Or *Praise the Lord!*; it literally means *Praise Yah!* (a shortened form of *Yahweh*).
headquarters	The Latin word *Praetorium* was used by Greek writers for the residence of the Roman governor; it may also refer to military headquarters, the imperial court, or the emperor's guard.
Hebrew	Or *Aramaic*; the translation of this word is debated since some claim Aramaic was commonly spoken in Palestine during NT times. More recently others claim that Hebrew was the spoken language.

hell/hellfire	The Greek word is *gehenna*; it is the Aramaic term for the Valley of Hinnom on the south side of Jerusalem; formerly, it was a place of human sacrifice, and in NT times, a place for the burning of garbage; it is the place of final judgment for those rejecting Christ.
Herod	Name of the Idumean family ruling Palestine from 37 B.C. to ca A.D. 95; the main rulers from this family mentioned in the NT are:
Herod I	(37 B.C.–4 B.C.) He was also known as Herod the Great; he built the great temple in Jerusalem and massacred the male babies in Bethlehem.
Herod Antipas	(4 B.C.–A.D. 39) The son of Herod the Great; he ruled one-fourth of his father's kingdom (Galilee and Perea); he killed John the Baptist and mocked Jesus.
Herod Agrippa I	(A.D. 37–44) The grandson of Herod the Great; he beheaded James the apostle and imprisoned Peter.
Herod Agrippa II	(A.D. 52–ca 95) The great-grandson of Herod the Great; he heard Paul's defense.
Herodians	They were the political supporters of Herod the Great and his family.
hidden plan	Translation of the Greek word *musterion*; it is a secret hidden in the past but now revealed.
Higgaion	Term used for a musical notation, for a device denoting a pause in an instrumental interlude, or for a murmuring harp tone
high place(s)	An ancient place of worship most often associated with pagan religions; it was usually built on an elevated location.
horn	A symbol of power based on the strength of animal horns
Hosanna	A term of praise derived from the Hebrew word for save
Host(s)	Military forces consisting of God's angels, sometimes including the sun, moon, and stars, and occasionally Israel
human race	Literally *sons of man* or *sons of Adam*
I assure you	This is a phrase used only by Jesus to testify to the certainty and importance of His words; in Mt, Mk, and Lk it is literally *Amen, I say to you*; in Jn it is literally *Amen, amen, I say to you*.

in this way	The Greek word *houtos,* commonly translated in Jn 3:16 as "so" or "so much," occurs over 200 times in the NT. Almost without exception it is an adverb of manner, not degree (for example, see Mt. 1:18). It only means "so much" when modifying an adjective (see Gl 3:3; Rv 16:18). Manner seems primarily in view in Jn 3:16, which explains the HCSB's rendering.
Jews	In Jn, the term Jews usually indicates those in Israel who were opposed to Jesus, particularly the Jewish authorities in Jerusalem who led the nation.
justification/ justify/ justified	The act of God as judge that declares sinners (who were in the wrong) to be right or righteous in His sight. God is just in doing this because Jesus died on the cross to take away their sins and to give them His own righteousness (2Co 5:21). The sinner receives this justification by faith and by grace when he trusts Christ's work.
language(s)	The Greek word *glossa* can refer to the tongue as the organ of speech (see Mk 7:33) or to the language the tongue produces. In certain NT passages, scholars differ on whether the term refers to human languages or to ecstatic speech capable only of divine interpretation ("speaking in tongues").
Leviathan	Or *twisting one*; a mythological sea serpent or dragon associated with the chaos at creation; sometimes it is applied to an animal such as a crocodile.
life/lives	The same Greek word *(psyche)* can be translated life or soul.
mankind	Literally *sons of man* or *sons of Adam*
Mary Magdalene	Or *Mary of Magdala*; Magdala was probably a town on the western shore of the Sea of Galilee, north of Tiberias.
Maskil	It is from a Hebrew word meaning *to be prudent* or *to have insight*; it could also mean a contemplative, instructive, or wisdom psalm.
men	Literally *sons of man* or *sons of Adam*
mercy seat	Or *place of atonement*; it was the gold lid on the ark of the covenant that was first used in the tabernacle and later in the temple.

Messiah	Or *the Christ*; the Greek word is *Christos* and means *the anointed one*. Where the NT emphasizes *Christos* as a name of our Lord or has a Gentile context, "Christ" is used. Where the NT *Christos* has a Jewish context, the title "Messiah" is used.
Miktam	A musical term of uncertain meaning; it possibly denotes a plaintive style.
Milcom	An Ammonite god who was the equivalent of Baal, the Canaanite storm god
Molech	A Canaanite god associated with death and the underworld; the worship ritual of passing someone through the fire is connected with him. This ritual could have been either fire-walking or child sacrifice.
Most High	The Hebrew word is *Elyon*; it is often used with other names of God, such as Hebrew *El (God)* or *Yahweh (Lord)*; it is used to refer to God as the supreme being.
Mount of Olives	A mountain east of Jerusalem across the Kidron Valley
mystery	Translation of the Greek word *musterion*; it is a secret hidden in the past but now revealed.
Nazarene	A person from Nazareth; growing up in Nazareth was an aspect of the Messiah's humble beginnings.
Negev	An arid region in the southern part of Israel; the Hebrew word means south.
offend(ed)	The Greek word *skandalizo* has a root meaning of snare or trap but has no real English counterpart.
offspring	This term is used literally or metaphorically to refer to plants or grain, sowing or harvest, male reproductive seed, human children or physical descendants, and also to spiritual children or to Christ (see seed).
One and Only	Or *one of a kind*, or *incomparable*, or *only begotten*; the Greek word can refer to someone's only child as in Lk 7:12; 8:42; 9:38. It can also refer to someone's special child as in Heb 11:17.
oracle	A prophetic speech of a threatening or menacing character; it was often against the nations.
overseer(s)	Or *elder(s)*, or *bishop(s)*
palace	The Latin word *Praetorium* was used by Greek writers for the residence of the Roman governor; it may also refer to military headquarters, the imperial court, or the emperor's guard.
Passover	The Israelite festival celebrated on the fourteenth day of the first month, in the early spring; it was a celebration of the deliverance of the Israelites from Egypt, commemorating the final plague on Egypt when the firstborn were killed.
people	Literally *sons of man*, or *sons of Adam*
perverted men	Literally *sons of Belial*; in Hebrew, the basic meaning of Belial is worthless.
Pharisee(s)	A religious sect of Judaism that followed the whole written and oral law
Pilate	Pontius Pilate was governor of the province of Judea A.D. 26–36.
Pit	A term for either the grave or the realm of the dead
proconsul	The chief Roman government official in a senatorial province who presided over Roman court hearings
propitiation	The removal of divine wrath; Jesus' death is the means that turns God's wrath from the sinner.
proselyte(s)	A person from another race or religion who went through a prescribed ritual to become a Jew
Rabbi	The Hebrew word means *my great one*; it is used for a recognized teacher of the Scriptures.
Rabshakeh	The title of a high-ranking Assyrian official who was the chief cupbearer to the king
Rahab	Or *boisterous one*; it is the name of a mythological sea serpent or dragon defeated at the time of creation. Scripture sometimes uses the name metaphorically to describe Egypt.
redemption/ redeemed	The deliverance from bondage by a payment or ransom (Mk 10:45; 1Pt 1:18-19)
Red Sea	Literally *Sea of Reeds*
regiment	Or *cohort*; a Roman military unit that numbered as many as 600 men
restitution offering(s)	An offering that was a penalty for unintentional sins, primarily committed in relation to the tabernacle or temple; it is traditionally translated *trespass* or *guilt offering*.
sackcloth	A garment made of poor quality material and worn as a sign of grief and mourning

sacred bread	Literally *bread of presentation*; these were 12 loaves of bread, representing the 12 tribes of Israel and put on the table in the holy place in the tabernacle and later in the temple. The priests ate the previous week's loaves.	**Sheol**	A Hebrew word for either the grave or the realm of the dead
Sadducee(s)	A religious sect of Judaism that mainly followed the first 5 books of the OT (the Torah or Pentateuch)	**Shinar**	A land in Mesopotamia, including ancient Sumer and Babylon; it is modern Iraq.
saint(s)/ sanctification/ sanctify/ sanctified	The work of the Holy Spirit that separates believers in Jesus from the world; at the time of saving faith in Jesus, the believer is made a saint; therefore, all believers are saints. The believer participates with the Spirit in a process of transformation that continues until glorification. The goal of sanctification is progressive conformity to the image of Jesus Christ.	**sin offering(s)**	Or *purification offering*; it was the most important OT sacrifice for cleansing from impurities. It provided purification from sin and certain forms of ceremonial uncleanness.
		slave(s)	The strong Greek word *doulos* cannot be accurately translated in English as servant or bond servant; the HCSB translates this word as slave, not out of insensitivity to the legitimate concerns of modern English speakers, but out of a commitment to accurately convey the brutal reality of the Roman Empire's inhumane institution as well as the ownership called for by Christ.
Samaritan(s)	A people of mixed, Gentile/Jewish ancestry who lived between Galilee and Judea and were hated by the Jews	**Son of Man**	Most frequent title Jesus used for Himself (Mt 8:20; see also Dn 7:13)
Sanhedrin	The supreme council of Judaism; it had 70 members and was patterned after Moses' 70 elders.	**song of ascents**	A term that probably refers to the songs pilgrims sang as they traveled the roads going up to worship in Jerusalem (Pss 120–134)
scribe(s)	A professional group in Judaism that copied the law of Moses and interpreted it, especially in legal cases	**soul**	The same Greek word (*psyche*) can be translated life or soul.
secret	Translation of the Greek word *musterion*; it is a secret hidden in the past but now revealed.	**stumble**	The Greek word *skandalizo* has a root meaning of snare or trap but has no real English counterpart.
seed	This term is used literally or metaphorically to refer to plants or grain, sowing or harvest, male reproductive seed, human children or physical descendants, and also to spiritual children or to Christ (Gl 3:16).	**synagogue**	A place where the Jewish people met for prayer, worship, and teaching of the Scriptures
		tabernacle	Or *tent*, or *shelter*; a term used for temporary housing
Selah	A Hebrew word whose meaning is uncertain; various interpretations include: (1) a musical notation, (2) a pause for silence, (3) a signal for worshipers to fall prostrate on the ground, (4) a term for the worshipers to call out, and (5) a word meaning forever.	**take offense**	The Greek word *skandalizo* has a root meaning of snare or trap but has no real English counterpart.
		tassel	Fringe put on the clothing of devout Jews to remind them to keep the law
set apart for destruction	During periods of war in Canaan and its neighboring countries, this was the destruction of a city, its inhabitants, and their possessions, including livestock.	**temple complex**	In the Jerusalem temple, the complex included the sanctuary (the holy place and the holy of holies), at least 4 courtyards (for priests, Jews, women, and Gentiles), numerous gates, and several covered walkways.
shekel(s)	In the OT the *shekel* is a measurement of weight that came to be used as money, either gold or silver.	**testimony**	A reference to either the Mosaic law in general or to a specific section of the law, the Ten Commandments, which were written on stone tablets and placed in the ark of the covenant (also called the ark of the testimony)
Sheminith	A musical term meaning *instruments* or *on the instrument of eight strings*	**Topheth**	A place of human sacrifice that was located outside Jerusalem in the Hinnom Valley (Jr 7:31-32)

unclean	When something is clean, it is holy or acceptable to God. When it is unclean, it is unholy (such as an unclean spirit). The term can be used in a ritual sense to apply to moral standards for living.
Unleavened Bread	A seven-day festival celebrated in conjunction with the Passover (Ex 12:1-20)
Urim & Thummim	Two objects used by Israelite priests to determine God's will
wadi	A valley, ravine, or stream that is dry except in the rainy season
walk(ed)/ walking	A term often used in a figurative way to mean "way of life" or "behavior"
wicked men	Literally *sons of Belial*; in Hebrew, the basic meaning of Belial is worthless.
wise men	The Greek word is *magoi*; the English word "magi" is based on a Persian word. They were eastern sages who observed the heavens for signs and omens.
woman	When used in direct address, "Woman" was not a term of disrespect but of honor.
world	The organized Satanic system that is opposed to God and hostile to Jesus and His followers; it also refers to the non-Christian culture including governments, educational systems, and businesses.
wormwood	A small shrub that was used as a medicinal herb and noted for its bitter taste
Yah/Yahweh	Or *The Lord*; it is the personal name of God in Hebrew; "Yah" is the shortened form. Yahweh is used in places where the personal name of God is discussed (Ps 68:4) or in places of His self-identification (Is 42:8).
Zion	Originally a term for the fortified section of Jerusalem and then, by extension, used for the temple and the city of Jerusalem both in the present time and in the future

WHERE TO TURN

Frequently Asked Questions

If God exists, why isn't His exact identity more obvious?

That God exists is a fact most people have agreed on throughout history. It is the exact identity of God that causes disagreement. Why is the exact identity of God not more obvious? Perhaps God's identity is more obvious than you think. Jesus told a parable about a man who died and went to Hades, a place of permanent suffering. The condemned man insinuated to Father Abraham that God's identity was not as obvious as it should have been, otherwise he wouldn't have ended up in Hades. He begged Father Abraham to send someone from the dead to warn his brothers about Hades so they would avoid it by repenting. Father Abraham responded: "If they don't listen to Moses and the prophets, they will not be persuaded if someone rises from the dead" (Lk 16:31). God has made His identity clear. Our problem is that we are like children who cover their ears and shout, "I can't hear you!" In our sinfulness we are not so eager to learn truth about God after all because it costs us some of the things we love best: our independence, our opinions, and our sinful ways. The Christian poet T. S. Eliot once said, "Humankind cannot bear very much reality." Similarly, we could say that sinful humanity cannot bear very much reality about God.

Has science proven there is no God?

The existence of an immaterial and eternal God is beyond the purview of science, which studies material reality and the laws and forces that help explain the structure and function of the universe. But science has its roots in biblical teachings. First, the Bible says God created humanity in His image. One implication is that our minds are ready-made for understanding the world if we will bother to investigate it. Second, God commanded Adam to "be fruitful, multiply, fill the earth, and subdue it." This is a call to stewardship of the earth. Such stewardship requires us to observe the law-like regularities and exquisite complexities in nature, not to exploit the creation but to take care of it. It is no accident that many of the pioneers of science held a biblical worldview that expects the orderly, law-like phenomena that enable life to flourish.

Has science proven miracles are impossible?

The idea that science has proven the impossibility of miracles stems from a faulty understanding of the relationship between God and science. This mistaken view, held by Christians and agnostics alike, gives the laws of nature a status that they don't have in reality. The biblical understanding is that phenomena that function in a law-like manner, as well as those for which we have yet to identify regularities, all owe their being to God moment by moment. A meteorologist might well have given a thorough scientific explanation of the parting of the Red Sea during the exodus. The Bible hints at that possibility when it says, "The Lord drove the sea back with a powerful east wind all that night and turned the sea into dry land" (Ex 14:21). In this case the miracle was not that a scientific explanation was lacking. It was the timing of the Israelites being at the edge of the Red Sea when the strong east wind dried up the Sea. God is not beholden to scientific law. Scientific law is our attempt to make sense of what God is doing all the time.

If God is good, why does He allow evil to exist?

Scripture affirms God's unlimited power (Mt 19:26), His perfect goodness (Hab 1:13), and the reality of evil (Gn 6:5–6). God doesn't give a comprehensive account of why He allows evil. For those who will follow and read the evidence carefully, God sets forth a pattern that shows His purposes are perfectly good. Where He allows evil, He turns that evil to a greater good (Gn 50:15–21). The greatest example of this pattern is the death of Jesus, through whom God's enemies are made His children (Rm 5:6–11).

How important is it that we believe the right things about God?

When you board a jet, you do so because you believe the jet is air-worthy and it will get you to your destination safely. If you did not believe that, you would not board. If your belief in the jet's safety were mistaken, you would want someone to tell you so. Our beliefs about the jet and the reality about the jet are not necessarily lined up in agreement. Clearly it is important that our beliefs about the jet line up with realities about the jet. How much more is at stake when it comes to beliefs about God! God is our maker and judge. If what you believe about God turns out to be false, you have staked everything on a faulty foundation. "What does it benefit a man to gain the whole world yet lose his life? What can a man give in exchange for his life?" (Mk 8:36–37)

Am I personally at odds with God? What is sin?

Human beings are naturally at odds with God (Rm 3:10–18). This aversion to God may be hidden by a veneer of respectability, but given the right circumstances it becomes evident in each of us. As a school boy, Jean-Paul Sartre, one of the leading atheist thinkers of the 20th century, was playing with matches and burned a small rug. As he tried to cover up his misdeed he felt the gaze of God. Young Sartre fell into a rage against God. By Sartre's account, "He never looked at me again." In reality, it is Sartre who never looked at God again. Sin is a refusal to live humbly under God's reign and acknowledge our obligations to Him; we are all guilty of this and thus need forgiveness.

What is the reason anyone is sent to hell?

Sin violates God's law, which expresses His righteous character. Sin thus involves rebellion against the Creator-King whose throne is founded on righteousness and justice (Ps 97:2). Sin incurs a debt of guilt and punishment (Col 2:14). The crucifixion of the innocent and eternal God-Man, Jesus Christ, is the only possible satisfaction of divine justice, but it is only for those who "attach" themselves to Christ by faith. Others must endure their own punishment for their offenses against the infinite and holy God.

How can God send devout Buddhists, Muslims, etc. to hell?

Only one God is the Creator and Ruler of all. Sin violates His laws, summarized as "Love the LORD your God with all your heart, . . . soul, and . . . strength" (Dt 6:4). Such love has no room for other gods (Dt 5:7). Worship of false gods, no matter how devout your worship, involves rebellion against the true God who provided salvation only through His Son, Jesus Christ (Ac 4:12). Imagine the pain and offense your parents would feel if you identified someone else as father and mother. In a similar way, it is painful and offensive to God when we misidentify Him, saying things of Him that are not true and which conflict with His eternal nature.

Why cannot God just annihilate those who die in unbelief?

Scripture says that God is both perfectly just and loving, and that the penalty for living in rebellion against God is eternal punishment (Mt 25:46; Lk 12:4–5; Jn 5:28–29; Rv 9:5–6; 16:10–11). Annihilation would not satisfy God's perfect justice because the offense of our sins is infinite. Just as the reward for faith-righteousness through Christ is eternal fellowship with God, the penalty for rebellion against Him is eternal ruin and separation from God.

If there is one God, why are there so many religions?

God has made Himself known to everyone through creation and the conscience (Rm 1:18–19). This knowledge of God has not been well received by human beings. Rather than acknowledging who God is and being grateful to Him, we have suppressed this original knowledge. The result is a darkening of the mind. People create gods they prefer rather than worshiping God as He is (Rm 1:23). Given the diversity of people and cultures, it is no surprise that there are a variety of religions.

What makes Jesus different from other religious teachers?

If a man told you that he is both God and a humble human, you would recommend a psychiatric evaluation. Jesus, in effect, made those very claims simultaneously. "All things have been entrusted to Me by My Father. No one knows the Son except the Father, and no one knows the Father except the Son and anyone to whom the Son desires to reveal Him" (Mt 11:27). "I am gentle and humble in heart" (Mt 11:29). Jesus differs from other religious teachers in being able to make both paradoxical claims truthfully. His words are vindicated in His well-documented bodily resurrection from the dead (1Co 15:1–19).

How did Jesus make it possible for us to go to heaven?

That sense of justice that arises in you when you are wronged or when you see others treated unjustly may be one of the most important clues to understanding yourself and your relationship to God. Wrongs cry out to be righted. But who can right them? When we are honest, we realized that in thought, word, and deed we have wronged God and others. We have failed to love God with every fiber of our being and have not come close to caring for our neighbors as for ourselves. The good news is that God's Son, Jesus the Messiah, has taken the consequences of our sins on Himself in His death on the cross. He calls us simply to trust Him. A criminal who died next to Jesus asked Jesus to remember him when He came into His kingdom. This man realized he could not make right the wrongs he had done. But his faith in Jesus brought this response from Jesus: "I assure you: Today you will be with Me in paradise" (Lk 23:43).

How do I become a Christian?

It's simple, but not easy. First you must confess that you are sinful and have failed to honor God as you should. Next you must repent—turn away from sin and selfishness—and trust God. Then you must believe Jesus' sacrifice is sufficient to save you and invite Him to be your Lord and Savior (Ac 20:21; Rm 10:9). That's it. Reading the Bible, praying, and going to church naturally follow from your decision to follow Christ.

Isn't the Bible full of mistakes?

Jesus trusted the Old Testament Scriptures (Mt 26:54; Jn 10:35). His endorsement is important, especially given His miracles and resurrection from the dead. In Matthew 22:29, Jesus told the Sadducees, "You are deceived, because you don't know the Scriptures or the power of God." The Bible is the standard of what is correct and what is mistaken. And before Jesus was crucified, He promised His disciples they would have the Spirit's guidance in preaching and writing the New Testament revelation (Jn 14:26; 16:13).

Hasn't the Bible been altered a lot since it was written?

The New Testament is by far the best attested text from the ancient world. Thousands of manuscripts produced between the second and fourteenth centuries provide strong evidence for the reliability of the New Testament. There are some 20,000 handwritten manuscripts of the New Testaments written in a variety of languages, 5,500 of which are ancient Greek manuscripts. A dozen of the Greek manuscripts date from the second century, 64 from the third century, and 48 from the fourth century. Being able to compare manuscripts enables scholars to achieve a high level of confidence in what the original text said. Scholars have found 200,000 errors or variants in 10,000 different places in the New Testament. Not one of these variants affects an essential doctrine of Christian faith. Between 97 and 99 percent of the New Testament text can be recovered with certainty.

If Christianity is true, why do Christians disagree about so much?

True Christians agree on the essentials: sinful humanity needs a Savior; Jesus died and rose again to redeem people (1Co 15:3–4). Naturally, those who claim to be Christians but really aren't will disagree with true Christians on many points (Rm 16:17–18). But even genuine Christians tend to quarrel about nonessential matters because we are imperfect, fallen human beings beset by temptation (Jms 4:1–4) and prone to read Scripture with bias and closed hearts. Further, on some topics the Bible does not present enough evidence to ensure a unified conclusion is reached among believers. About these topics there should be mutual tolerance for differing opinions.

Does the Bible reflect bias against women?

Scripture honors single women, widows, wives, mothers, homemakers, businesswomen, and spiritual leaders like Deborah, Anna, Phoebe, Priscilla, Lois, and Eunice. The Bible granted women greater rights and dignity than did other contemporary cultures (Jos 17:3–4). Jesus valued and affirmed women so much that He shocked His disciples (Jn 4:7–27). Women are co-image-bearers (Gn 1:27), key persons in the Messiah's genealogy (Mt 1:5), and coheirs of eternal life (Gl 3:28–29).

Is the God of the Bible hateful and self-centered?

It is only reasonable to conclude that God is the most valuable of all beings. After all, His power, knowledge, and virtue eclipse those of all other beings. If God were to set His highest love on anything other than Himself, He would be guilty of idolatry. So it is fitting that God insists on being honored as the greatest value in the universe. And yet He loves us and offers us forgiveness through faith in His Son, Jesus Christ. Those who reject God and His offered mercy in Christ justly encounter divine wrath.

Why does God allow Satan to tempt us?

Mankind gave Satan authority to continue tempting us when Adam and Eve took the serpent's bait in the garden (see Nm 33:55). Satan's aim is to convince us that God is not trustworthy, not worthy of worship, and that we should praise God only when He is blessing us (Jb 1:9–11). In the same way that God allowed Satan to tempt Job, He allows us to be tempted in order to demonstrate that He deserves our worship for who He is, no matter what our life circumstances are.

What church should I attend?

In individualistic North America, church affiliation has come to be seen as a matter of "take it or leave it." But the idea of "just Jesus and me" is foreign to the Bible. Those who trust Jesus as Savior and Lord are incorporated into the fellowship of the church. Deciding on a particular church is not a matter to be taken lightly. Seek a church that worships God in spirit and in truth, that takes the Bible seriously and teaches its whole counsel, that seeks and welcomes those who need to be reconciled to God, and that helps all members of the body identify and use their unique spiritual gifts.

Suggested Resources
for Further Study

If you wish to learn more about the basics of the Bible and Christianity, the following study tools may assist you.

The *HCSB Study Bible* (Hard Cover Edition: 978-1-58640-506-9) provides book introductions that explain the historical context and main themes of all 66 books of the Bible, plus it includes many helpful features such as maps, charts, study notes, and topical essays. You can also access some of the features of the HCSB Study Bible at www.mystudybible.com.

The *Holman Illustrated Bible Dictionary* (978-0-8054-2836-0). Of all the Bible study tools available, a Bible dictionary is at the top of the list of recommended resources for those who want to study the Bible. The *Holman Illustrated Bible Dictionary* is a vast storehouse of easy-to-find, easy-to-grasp, useful information that will enrich your study of the Bible.

One Minute Bible for Starters: A 90 Day Journey for New Christians by Lawrence Kimbrough (978-0-8054-9386-3) takes you on a 90-day journey through the Scriptures, stopping at a key verse every day. Don't be surprised if you are tempted to read more than one day's reading at a time! This resource is recommended and purchased by churches to give to new believers.